DRAMA

OF THE

English Renaissance

II

THE STUART PERIOD

EDITED BY

RUSSELL A. FRASER
UNIVERSITY OF MICHIGAN

AND

NORMAN RABKIN
UNIVERSITY OF CALIFORNIA, BERKELEY

MACMILLAN PUBLISHING CO., INC.
NEW YORK
COLLIER MACMILLAN PUBLISHERS
LONDON

MACMILLAN PUBLISHING CO., INC.
866 Third Avenue, New York, New York 10022

COLLIER MACMILLAN CANADA, LTD.

Library of Congress Cataloging in Publication Data

Main entry under title:

Drama of the English Renaissance.

Includes bibliographical references.
CONTENTS: 1. The Tudor period.—2. The Stuart period.
1. English drama—Early modern and Elizabethan, 1500–1600. 2. English drama—17th century. I. Fraser, Russell A. II. Rabkin, Norman.
PR1263.D75   822'.009   74-7709
ISBN 0-02-339570-2 (v. 1)
ISBN 0-02-339581-8 (v. 2)

Printing   10 11   Year   8 9 0

ISBN   0-02-339580-X

Drama of the English Renaissance

II

THE STUART PERIOD

Preface

THE forty-one plays gathered in these volumes constitute the most extensive new survey of Renaissance drama in over forty years, and reflect both changes in taste and advances in scholarship since earlier collections. The editors have attempted to provide the materials for a truer view of the theater in which Shakespeare worked than has hitherto been possible in anthologies. Marlowe, Jonson, and Webster, by most accounts the best of Shakespeare's contemporaries, are represented by their major plays; the reader will not have to settle for half of TAMBURLAINE or for Jonson without BARTHOLOMEW FAIR. For such playwrights the choices were relatively easy to make. For others they were not so easy, largely because of the extraordinary number of plays worthy of attention that they left us.

In making selections, the editors have been guided by several principles. We have taken pains not to omit plays of unique quality that have, albeit for different reasons, held their interest through many generations—BUSSY D'AMBOIS, for example, and A WOMAN KILLED WITH KINDNESS. We have been concerned to include plays of major intrinsic and historical interest that have not previously been included in anthologies and in some cases are not readily available to the modern reader—THE ROARING GIRL and A CHASTE MAID IN CHEAPSIDE, SUMMER'S LAST WILL AND TESTAMENT and A LOOKING GLASS FOR LONDON AND ENGLAND, for example. We have tried where possible to substitute for plays repeatedly presented more for their typicality than for their unique value other plays equally characteristic but rather less shopworn—GALLATHEA, THE DUTCH COURTESAN, and A KING AND NO KING, for example. And we have attempted to represent some of the best playwrights by excellent plays too often overlooked (some of them, in fact, never previously anthologized)—THE WIDOW'S TEARS, for example, and HYDE PARK, PERKIN WARBECK, and DAVID AND BETHSABE. On the whole, *Drama of the English Renaissance* includes those plays that have inspired the warmest admiration and the most acute criticism in recent decades. No one will find here every play that he would like to; each of the editors, in fact, has had regretfully to accept the decision to omit several plays close to his heart. Given the generous limits we have been allowed, however, and the principles we have had to consider in making our selections, we are satisfied that the contents of these volumes come as close as we could hope to the just representation of a great corpus of drama.

In the decades since the last major anthologies of Renaissance drama, much has occurred in scholarship that has helped the editors and will work to the reader's advantage. In many instances, new methods of textual study that make it possible to distinguish between an author's words and later accretions have revealed the copytext most closely reflecting what the playwright originally wrote. Many of the plays included have been subjected to textual study that has solved problems and swept away the dust of earlier and sometimes rather casual editing. Lexicographical research, critical studies, and individual editions of the plays have made the glossing of difficulties a surer business than it once was. The texts here presented have been produced by collating the earliest reliable editions of each play with modern scholarly recensions where they exist. Like most recent texts, ours are conservative, admitting emendation only when we are certain that it is justified. Although we have not attempted to record all variants, or to give the history of speculation about particular cruces, we have flagged the important differences among early editions where relevant, and we have always indicated emendations and supplied the original readings in footnotes. Because of the nature and purposes of this collection, we have not thought it appropriate to assign individual credit to the countless editors over the past four centuries who have solved particular puzzles, but we can assure the reader that the texts have been fortified by consultation of a vast body of work.

Spelling and punctuation have been made to accord throughout with modern American usage. We have retained old spellings only in certain instances: where modernization would affect scansion, where pronunciation would be obviously and radically different, where the meaning of the word has changed as much as its spelling, and in a few special cases, such as the retention of *Bethsabe* for *Bathsheba*.We have not attempted, like some editors, to retain old spellings (e.g., *murther* for *murder*, *vild* for *vile*, *wrack* for *wreck*, *bankrout* for *bankrupt*) that merely indicate slight differences in the pronunciation of words that have remained current. Editors who retain old spellings such as these inadvertently obscure the fact that the entire pronunciation of our language has changed considerably since Shakespeare's time, even when no archaic spelling signals the differences. The commendatory verses, epistles dedicatory, and other prefatory material reproduced with each play have been included only when they contribute to the appreciation of the selected authoritative text. We omit less pertinent prefatory matter and that derived from editions subsequent to the ones followed in this collection. Stage directions are those of the original editions unless they are printed between brackets, in which case they are editorial additions; we have added directions only when they are necessary to prevent confusion or obscurity, for Renaissance dramatists tend to make the action clear through their dialogue. In a few instances, for special reasons, the lists of dramatis personae are reproduced directly from the original texts; more often they have been rearranged and modernized.

Where act and scene divisions are missing or incomplete in the original texts they have been added, generally in accordance with the conventions of five-act structure and always in brackets; in a few cases—e.g., ARDEN OF FEVERSHAM, A WOMAN KILLED WITH KINDNESS, and MUCEDORUS—where the five-act structure is not so clear, scenes have been numbered serially. Jonson poses a unique problem in this respect. Scrupulously faithful to neoclassical convention, he indicates a new scene each time a new character enters. Not to follow his system is to misrepresent the appearance he wanted his texts to have, but to imitate it is to imply a lack of flow that in fact characterizes only the printed text and not the stage performance. For pedagogical purposes we have therefore settled on a compromise: two of the plays are divided according to Jonson's principles, the other two according to modern usage. In early editions, final *-ed* is often rendered *-'d*, sometimes though not always to indicate that the final *e* is not to be pronounced. We have consistently restored the missing *e*; to make the scansion clear, we have marked with an accent all final *-ed* syllables that are to be pronounced. Lineation is sometimes problematic in dramatic texts of the period, sometimes because the playwright did not give adequate signals to the compositor, sometimes because the compositor changed verse to prose to make an excessive text fit in the space left on his page or changed prose to verse when he needed to fill space. We have generally followed the division into verse and prose of the copytext, except where it is clear that the division was not the author's. We have chosen not to add scene locations at the heads of scenes. Contemporary editions generally did not have them, and in the absence of elaborate scenery playwrights trained their audiences to recognize all that needed to be known about the locale from the dialogue and action. More often than not, therefore, the heading is gratuitous, and it frequently clutters the text with such useless rubrics as "A Street" and "Another Part of the Forest."

Footnotes gloss words and phrases that are beyond the resources of standard modern desk dictionaries, foreign words, *doubles entendres* not immediately evident to the modern reader, and historical, geographical, and mythological allusions. In deciding how much to gloss, we have opted for too much rather than too little. Our own experience as teachers of the drama has warned us that students often come to the reading of Renaissance plays unequipped with the literary knowledge that editors of half a century ago could take for granted. Except where a playwright's borrowing of details of language from particular sources constitutes a significant allusion or a fact important to an adequate response to the play, we have not footnoted sources. The introductions to individual plays discuss such matters as date, authorship, sources, and theatrical history, and offer brief and modest critical guidelines in no way intended to usurp the teacher's role or to impose on the student's creative response.

The initials at the end of the introduction to each play indicate which of the editors has had primary responsibility for the text and apparatus of that play.

The editors wish to express warm gratitude to D. Anthony English of Macmillan for his generous help and his sharp eye. We should also like to record our gratitude to Frances Long, production supervisor, and Charles Farrell, designer, for their skill, care, and devoted commitment to a complex and exacting project.

R. A. F.
N. R.

Contents

Introduction

THE ENGLISH DRAMA FROM ITS BEGINNINGS
TO THE CLOSING OF THE THEATERS

ENGLISH Renaissance drama is primarily an exfoliating, perhaps a grand perversion, of the religious drama of the Middle Ages. The medieval playwright who gives the lead to his successors in the Renaissance differs from them significantly. He is an anonymous maker—compare for the difference the self-proclaiming Ben Jonson—and he is not consciously artistic—compare Webster repudiating popular taste in his high and mighty preface to THE WHITE DEVIL, Chapman getting up the classics for BUSSY D'AMBOIS, the *oeuvre* of Christopher Marlowe. Medieval plays are written, more or less laconically, to inculcate piety—the writer is heuristic or intentional—at the same time to communicate pleasure—the writer, paradoxically, has no fixed intention.

Sometimes the first or didactic impulse submerges the second and so obliterates the play. One rises benumbed from *The Castle of Perseverance*, sodden with the weight of the Seven Deadly Virtues. Sometimes the relation between teaching and delighting is reversed. The didactic element in the waning Middle Ages is often perfunctory, not so engrossing as theatrical "business." What is apt to be engrossing in the religious drama, not less than in the secular drama of the twentieth century, is visceral excitement without reference to meaning or cause.

When, in a fifteenth-century enacting of the conversion of Mary Magdalene, Christ utters the injunction *Vade in pace*, the stage direction requires to the satisfaction of the crowd, not sacred but profane satisfaction, that "seven devils devoid from the woman." The art is not disclosed with which the exorcizing of these devils is managed. In the Croxton Play of the Sacrament attention to theatrical "realism" is paramount, attention to morality is reflexive, like genuflecting before the altar. The subject is the enlightenment of Sir Jonathus the Jew. Having struck at the Host and caused it to bleed, the impious hero discovers that he cannot take his hand away. He is not persuaded of his folly. The Host is nailed to a pillar, the Jew's servants begin to pull, the arm of Sir Jonathus comes loose from his body. The vulgar hilarity adumbrates faithfully the Horse-Courser scene in DOCTOR FAUSTUS. And still the Jew remains obdurate. The Host and hand are unnailed and immersed in a burning cauldron that turns to blood and bursts asunder in full view of the crowd. Blood flows perceptibly over the stage. From the shattered fragments an image with bleeding wounds appears and disappears as it changes again into bread. It is the moment of epiphany. Sir Jonathus, as his eyes are opened, lapses from the tepid faith of his fathers.

Perhaps, in this fifteenth-century miracle play, there is more of designing than achieving. Verisimilar representations that really carry the impress of physical fact must wait on the more inventive techniques of the new theater of the Renaissance. In Andrea Palladio's Teatro Olimpico at Vicenza (1580–84), that theater is realized. But Palladio's reconstruction looks backward (not backward to the Middle Ages but to the Roman architect Vitruvius, the contemporary of Caesar Augustus). It is an academic exercise and as such without issue. But the spirit that animates the Renaissance architect really to represent the physical world, what Chapman calls the "superficies of the green center," quickens elsewhere and with notable issue. Inigo Jones is responsive to it in his engineering of scenes and machines for the masques and barriers of the Jacobean and Caroline stage. It is implicit in the zeal of painters like Mantegna and Michelangelo and Leonardo to impart perspective to what one sees on that stage. "Oh, what a delightful thing is this perspective!" says the fifteenth-century painter Paolo Uccello. To this expression of delight in realistic representation, the medieval maker turns a deaf ear.

Medieval man is incurious of the realistic art of classical Greece, which the Renaissance rediscovers and renews. He prefers the flat surfaces of ancient Assyria. His figures do not recede in the middle distance but are piled one on top of the other. His representation of life is not naturalistic. But that is not as he is ignorant or artless.

An ardor for the truth that inheres in superficies leads to the recovery, as by the designers Furtenbach (1632) and Sabbattini (1638), of the revolving prisms or *periaktoi* of the classical stage, which facilitate a more rapid changing of the set; or the elaborating of the *scena ductilis*, which permits a veritable Seacoast of Bohemia, arranged to produce the effect of perspective, to be run on in grooves from the flies.

The intent is to make superfluous the naive appeal to the inner eye. The result is an invading and diminishing of the playwright's domain. "Today," says Sabbattini, "no good show can be presented without complete or partial change of scenery." As each stipulated place is conceded physical integrity, the *intermezzi* or musical diversions that allow the *régisseur* to work his magic come to rival the play itself. To Jonson's disciple Thomas Nabbes, place is not poetry. It is a shifting and palpable scene,

> Which is translated as the music plays
> Betwixt the acts.

In this heightening of realism but not of the real, all the cunning of the *régisseur* is required to mask the slow passage of time. Sebastiano Serlio, the most famous designer of the sixteenth century, is sufficiently cunning. "For these times," he advises, "when the actors are not on the scene"—it is, in its implication, an extraordinary phrase—"the architect will have ready some processions of small figures . . . cut of heavy cardboard and painted. . . . [or] a troop of people passing over, some on foot, some on horseback, with the muffled sound of voices and drums and trumpets." Behind the scenes the *régisseur*, whose labors are concealed by this press of cardboard figures and this bruit of sound, makes ready the new bit of business that is to come, in deference to a cinematic conception of reality.

As Hamlet's injunction to hold up the mirror to nature is modified to mean a canonizing of the art of *trompe l'oeil*, the immense apron stage of the Elizabethans and their predecessors, which had been the common ground of serious and farcical matter and on which, with no shifting of scene, the drunken porter in *Macbeth* had uttered his whimsical scurrilities and the children of Lady Macduff had been murdered, is attenuated to a boxlike and representational chamber. Simultaneous action is a thing of the past. Settings are made exclusive and are genuinely rendered, but not in words. Serlio's drawings initiate the process. Palaces denote the tragic scene, and humble shops and city dwellings the comic. The satyric scene, as it is proper to country persons, must "be composed of trees, rocks, hills," and so forth. In this distinguishing among kinds, decorum is observed; and the art of Shakespeare, which depends for its habitation on a muse of fire, gives place to the art of William Cartwright, in whose tragicomedy *The Royal Slave* (1636) words are made nugatory by the specifying and featuring of seven distinct scenes, devised appropriately by Inigo Jones, the real contriver of the whole, up there in the flies above the proscenium, manipulating his *scena ductilis* like the god from the machine.

Jones, a good man of the theater, is committed primarily to entertain. Modern readers or auditors are not likely to grudge the commitment. But the greatest of English playwrights, though no slouch as an entertainer, is also profoundly moral. The moral vision that animates Shakespeare's plays is not dictated, however, by an abstract notion of the shape the world ought to take. It derives from hard scrutiny of the world as it is and a devoted recording of what the playwright has seen there.

Shakespeare is mostly himself alone. The art of his predecessors tends increasingly to produce two discrete dramas, each the same in origin (as the medieval drama is Christian through and through) but different in motivation. On the one hand there is the expressionist art of the morality play in which the dramatis personae are essentially cartoons who function to drive home the truth that sets us free, on the other the imitative drama of the man-god Jesus Christ and his friends and foes, whose poignant or fearful laboring in a real world is often aloof from doctrinal considerations.

When these two kinds or impulses (by whatever name one calls them) are conjunctive, the drama flourishes. When the two move apart, it verges on decay. This is to summarize in a few words a great and complicated story.

Imitative drama is nascent already in the performances of wandering minstrels or *mimi*, who were popular before the Middle Ages began and who, in more sophisticated avatars—for example, the French mime Marcel Marceau, whose mimetic art is wholly nonverbal—remain popular today. The minstrel is making rudimentary drama as his repertory includes lyric and narrative dialogue—the *aube* or lovers' parting, like the parting of Romeo and Juliet; pastoral dialogue—like that in Yeats's poem *Shepherd and Goatherd*, or the eclogues of Spenser and Sidney; most significantly the enacting of a debate or *estrif* between protagonists—the essence of the dramatic situation and illustrated by John Heywood in his sixteenth-century interlude, THE FOUR PP.

The drama is an argument in which important differences are composed. It is also a celebration. The festive roots of the drama are discovered in the morris dance, an ancient and partly mysterious entertainment. The morris dance is associated in the Middle Ages with the descent of the pentecostal dove on Whitsunday. The occasion is happy, also august, and across it falls a shadow. On this shadow the Middle Ages are insistent. The light needs the dark. Enter to the dance the hobbyhorse, capering grotesquely, even obscenely, in his wicker frame. The miming of the half-human creature —who can say from what recesses he derives—evokes laughter but tinged with dismay. In SUMMER'S LAST WILL AND TESTAMENT, Thomas Nashe brings the hobbyhorse on stage. The archetypal drama in which he figures is a comedy, like life itself. So rejoicing comes first: "Spring, the sweet spring, is the year's pleasant king." But Nashe knows that the description is meagre. Already summer's testament is drawn:

> Beauty is but a flower,
> Which wrinkles will devour;
> Brightness falls from the air;
> Queens have died young and fair.
> Dust hath closed Helen's eye.
> I am sick, I must die.
>   Lord have mercy on us!

The drama, not least in its origins, is a particolored thing in which joy and sadness intermingle. Such entertainment as it affords us is complex, therefore lifelike. That is not what the poet means in resembling earth to a player's stage. Perhaps in this context it is fair to wrest his meaning.

The street pageant or *tableau vivant* plays its part in the development of the drama, as it emphasizes what the eye can see. So does the tournament, in its origins a debate for mortal stakes. Another strand or source is the primitive folk ceremony, which becomes the folk play and begets, far later, the sacrificial epiphany of EDWARD II. In the Revesby Sword Dance, symbolic of the return of spring after the deadness of winter, a character is slain and given life again, as in the medieval Easter plays—or in *The Winter's Tale*. From the masking and mumming of the Feast of Fools, a burlesquing of the divine service, and secular burlesques like the *sotie* or fools' comedy, the road is a long one that leads to the *danse macabre* of THE DUCHESS OF MALFI. But the road is perceptible.

Literary history is prone to take the road at a gallop. Sometimes a more leisurely transit is indicated. What happens along the way is worth affectionate curiosity: because our ancestors were there before us and we will honor them as we are pious, but also because the end or hypothetical goal to which the historian tends is nascent in the beginning and often more clear as it is nascent.

The Feast of Fools is a beginning, the origin of dramatic art in France. It is also contributory to the drama in England. So far, that is only to offer a footnote. But how are we to understand this Christianized survival of the Roman Saturnalia, during which the conducting of all business is suspended and slaves displace their masters as rulers of the roast? The workaday world is turned upside down, the Golden Age returns. In the Middle Ages, during the "Liberty of December" or the Festival of the Ass, hell breaks loose—or say that the chains are struck. The priest puts away his clerical garb and puts on woman's clothing or the paraphernalia of the stage. He drinks on the high altar: the holy of holies is profaned. He dances in the choir and parodies the service, he chants ribald songs and burns rubbish in the censer. An ass, draped in a chasuble, is led down the nave while the congregation brays in chorus. "This is the day of gladness." So runs the proclamation. "Let those who are of doleful countenance get away from here. Those who celebrate the Feast of the Ass desire to be joyful."

They desire also to poke fun in farcical representations at the establishment under which they groan—or of which they form a part! That is a kind of joy. When the great man is pulled down, or when he is exorcized, we are sad—and glad. This ambiguous feeling is at the heart of our response to tragic drama.

Comic and serious scenes, set to rhyme or presented in dumb show, characterize the Feast of Buffoons, which the hierarchy succeeds at last in driving from the church—only to find itself confronted in the less docile world outside by the Kingdom of Sots, the irreverent creation of the lawyers. Like their Roman antecedents in the time of the Kalends, the lawyers want to be free of their station, and free for a little while of themselves. Aristotle's word is catharsis.

As speeches and dialogue begin to inform these crude entertainments—Philostrate in *A Midsummer Night's Dream* is charged with the auditioning, presumably with the censoring of the entertainers—the creating of an Office of Revels is indicated (1545) to guard against *lèse majesté*. The person of the sovereign is sacrosanct and so it is spared. But, as Hamlet remarks idly, the king is a thing. In terms of what really matters, nothing is spared. Censorship can hardly be efficacious, unless the drama is stifled altogether as by the Commonwealth of Saints in the mid-seventeenth century or by the Licensing Act in the time of Henry Fielding. For the rude handling of sacred totems is what the drama is all about.

The roots of the drama are many. Its chief source is one and is to be found in the ecclesiastical liturgy of the Roman Catholic Church. After all, the drama is a rite. What this means is suggested vividly in the Mass, "an extramundane and extratemporal act in which Christ is sacrificed and then resurrected in the transformed substances." The ritual of Christ's sacrificial death is not, Jung thinks, "a repetition of the historical event but the original, unique, and eternal act. The experience of the Mass is therefore a participation in the transcendence of life, which overcomes all bounds of space and time. It is a moment of eternity in time."

These are good words and true—except that the Mass, like the drama emerging from it, is not wholly extratemporal or extramundane. The varieties of religious experience resemble the multiform experience of art in that each is not for an age but for all time; and also as each is insistently provincial. God is actualized, not symbolized, in the bread and wine, the ordinary stuff on which the drama feeds.

As early as the ninth century, parts of the Mass are being amplified by mimetic action, soon to entail costume, and antiphonal chanting, in which the two halves of the Choir engage in a musical dialogue, to produce what is known as the trope. To the Introit or opening chant for the Easter service, which commemorates the most dramatic of all the Christian stories, a short and simple passage is added. Here are the words of the so-called *Quem quaeritis* trope, which presents the three Marys at the tomb of Jesus and the angel who watches there:

Whom seek ye in the sepulchre, O Christians?
Jesus of Nazareth, who was crucified, O angel.
He is not here, He has arisen as He foretold:
Go, announce that He has arisen from the grave.

Subsequently this musical colloquy is enriched by stage properties: the grave cloth in which Christ had been laid and which must be spread out "before the eyes of the clergy"; dynamic business that serves to move forward the "plot": women coming with spices to anoint their dead Lord, the angel showing the empty tomb; audience participation: the monks who look on but not tacitly, who crystallize for us the meaning of that communion which is the dramatic experience as they join in the singing that acknowledges the Resurrection. They are not spectators, or not wholly. They collaborate in the play in which their own vindication and renewal are accomplished. Quoting St. Paul: "If Christ be not risen, then is our preaching vain, and your faith also is vain." In nuclear form, here are all the elements of theater.

With the passion for literal representation goes a passion for complete representation. Death is always prolegomenary. Resurrection must follow as the day the night. It is complemented—necessarily, to an intelligence or psychology that sees our life as a mingled yarn—by the vulgar comedy of an oil merchant or *unguentarius* from whom ointment for the dead body is purchased, not without haggling over the cost. One trope introduces the Race to the Tomb of the apostles

Peter and John, another the appearance of the risen Christ to Mary Magdalene. "In the meantime let one come, prepared beforehand in the likeness of a gardener, and standing at the head of the sepulchre let him say. . . . 'Mary!' And falling prostrate at his feet, let Mary say: 'Rabboni!'" Anyone with a feeling for the stage will hold his breath at this intimation of the great recognition scenes in Renaissance drama.

The rudimentary play, transferred now to the Monday of Passion Week, continues to grow, incorporates the Journey to Emmaus or *Peregrini*, and the story of the Doubting Apostle, Didymus called Thomas, who, as he has got to thrust his fingers in the wounds to verify the Resurrection and the Life, is the perfect emblem of the impulse to dramatic representation.

A Christmas play, the *Officium Pastorum* or Office of the Shepherds, imitates the success of the Easter trope. *Obstetrices* or midwives assist at the divine birth, the Magi are presented as they follow the star (a chandelier carrying candles and suspended from the roof of the church), and heed the angelic warning to take another way home. Herod rages as his wicked purpose is balked, and resolves on and consummates the Massacre of the Innocents. Old Testament prophets like Daniel and Moses announce the coming of Christ (the so-called *Ordo Prophetarum*) and are corroborated by profane witnesses like Virgil and the Sibyl (more mingling of the yarn in deference to a catholic view of history). Daniel leads on the Babylonian king Nebuchadnezzar, who claps him in the fiery furnace, there "on stage," emitting flames.

By the twelfth century, the Christmas play has reached for its materials as far back as the Fall of the Angels. If the "whole" story is at issue, why not? The Easter play is dramatizing Christ's Harrowing of Hell, in its earliest version an *estrif* or *débat* declaimed by the Anglo-Saxon minstrel called the *scop*—the pagan past informing the Christian present—and the comic and sorry fortunes of Mary Magdalene, the archetype of the fallen woman.

With regard to these stories, the Bible is mute. And so non-Scriptural sources begin to be levied on—the Apocryphal Gospels, pseudo-histories like *The Golden Legend*—to appease the thirst for completeness. The son of Pontius Pilate, for whom we must consult our imaginary forces, is represented, flourishing his poleax. The conversion of Mary Magdalene conducts naturally to the conversion of St. Paul, thence to the metamorphosis of that fictitious hero-villain, Sir Jonathus the Jew.

In time and given its encyclopedic bias, the religious drama trenches on the integrity of the Mass. Stage directions, as they are increasingly complex, tell us what has happened: "Let a manger be prepared at the back of the altar." "Let there be many boys as if they were angels in the roof of the church." St. Paul, who puts on the new man to the ire of his contemporaries, is described as escaping "from some high place" and being "let down in a basket to the ground." By the eleventh century the Office of the Shepherds undergoes an obligatory transfer to the Matins or Morning Service. The Passion Play passes from the clergy, is presented now by laymen, as at Siena in 1200. In the theatrical pageantry, in the art and architecture of this Tuscan city, which may stand as the apotheosis of the medieval spirit, the Kingdom of God appears to be realized on earth. The effective agency is, however, the devoted cunning of man.

Secular performers make for secular plays. The flamboyant Duke Moraud, who seduces his daughter and achieves the murder of his wife and incest-begotten child in a fourteenth-century chronicle drama, is brought at last to repentance. Ostensibly his story is a moral story. In fact it is as sensational as the lurid novels of Robert Greene or the crude pandering of Thomas Preston or the sickly phosphorescence of Marston and Ford. Something is gained in the new freedom conceded the playwright, and something is lost.

What is gained, as the drama moves from the choir to the nave, thence to the church porch, thence to the public square is the creating of a truly democratic or people's art, a phenomenon often willed by sentimentalists and legislated by cynics in our time—Berthold Brecht; Stalin and his congeners—but actualized only rarely. By the beginning of the fourteenth century this phenomenon is matter of fact. The lay guilds with which all townsmen were affiliated have assumed the creating and managing and performing of the play. The dramatizing of the Flight into Egypt is the business of the stable keepers, the Last Supper of the bakers. The audience for whom they perform is the total community. The great occasion of performance is the Feast of Corpus Christi, occurring in late May or early June. The sacrifice and resurrection of Christ are commemorated, and in the rites of spring the pagan past is resumed. The dead god is buried in the flower garden (*nell'orto del fiore*), and like the sleeping flower is biding his time. If the medieval Franciscan Jacopone da Todi sounds like T. S. Eliot in *The Waste Land*, that is because the same truths, or memories rather, are common to the present and the past.

An Elizabethan poet, who has seen St. Christopher "wade and pass with Christ amid the brook," recalls the miracles and mummings on the day of the feast:

> Sebastian full of feathered shafts the dint of dart
>   doth feel,
> There walketh Catherine with her sword in hand,
>   and cruel wheel,
> The chalice and the singing cake with Barbara is
>   led,
> And sundry other Pageants played in worship of
>   this bread.

The play remains at least formally worshipful. It is a *representatio miraculi*, a miracle play, or else its cousin german a mystery. To distinguish between the two kinds is ticklish. Each incorporates material not founded necessarily on biblical stories. With these stories the mystery play begins; then the net is widened. The miracle play deals more generally with the wonder-working and martyrdom of the saints. The greatest of the mystery plays, and a work of perennial authenticity, is *The Second Shepherds' Play* by the anonymous Wakefield Master, who lived and wrote in the earlier fifteenth century and whose genius illuminated the theatrical cycle associated with his native city.

Humor is not scanted in the mysteries, nor pathos nor homely detail. The first murderer Cain is as villainous as Hell, he is a blasphemer, he is obscene; he is also a figure of fun. So are Herod and Pontius Pilate. And so is the Devil, "in his feathers all ragged and rent." Evil is incongruous, therefore comic.

Noah's wife Gib is comic, a real termagant made of flesh and blood; she is more than comic as she declines to take refuge in the Ark, leaving her "gossips" behind her. Mary and Joseph are not saccharine persons as in our popular iconography, nor are they cut from alabaster. We do not so much worship as salute them, a medieval couple beset with such problems as are the lot of the rest of us. Joseph, as the York *Birth of Jesus* presents him, is a man getting older and verging on petulance:

Ah, Lord, what! the weather is cold!
The fellest freeze that ever I feld!

We indulge him ironically and acknowledge his right to complain. In the Brome Manor *Abraham and Isaac*, the protagonists speak and act from their nature, hence tug at the heart. When Isaac, who has piled the faggots for his own immolation, discovers that he is about to die, when—as the sword is lifted to strike—he can say to his father: "I pray you bless me with your hand," the audience is moved exactly as it is persuaded of horror and pity, self-abasement, gain-giving, human love.

Specificity is the *métier* of the medieval playwright. The cubits or dimensions of the Ark are not less important to him than the moral of the piece: the unnatural behavior that makes for the Flood. In the Wakefield version of the Deluge, Noah lowers a plummet to sound the depth of the waters. We wait on the issue; he cares and so do we. As the soldiers of Herod begin the slaughter of the Innocents, a woman rushes on stage and strikes them with her pot ladle. The Coventry Manuscript is insistent on that ladle. It is worth a thousand words. In the enacting at York of the Crucifixion story, the soldiers who carry the Cross find it a heavy burden. They have got to set it down to catch their breath, they have got to drive wedges to make it stand upright: trivial business but stabbing the life into the scene.

To convey the touch of nature that "makes the whole world kin" is within the province of any writer in any time or tongue. The gradual displacing of Latin by vernacular speech—language, as Ben Jonson will put it many years later, "such as men do use"—seems, however, crucial to the illusion of reality as fabricated by the medieval playwright. The school plays of the Renaissance, in which Latin is resuscitated from blind fealty to the classical past, are dead. The native drama of the Middle Ages is living still. The Tailors and Shearmen in the N. Towne play sing all the better, they come home to us more nearly, as they sing in native accents:

As I rode out this enderes night,
Of three jolly shepherds I saw a sight,
And all about their fold a star shone bright.
They sang terli, terlow—
So merrily the shepherds their pipes can blow.

The music of Shakespeare, in *Love's Labor's Lost*, in *As You Like It*, is not so far in the future.

As the drama is naturalized, the impulse to panoramic representation grows more insistent. The common tongue, evidently, runs on without let. More than fifty plays or "pageants," which begin with the beginning or Creation of the World and end only with the Day of Doom, comprise the cycle at York. The vast panorama that unfolds before our eyes is sometimes naive, it is never less than palpable. If a hailstorm is required, starch rattles on stage; if thunder, hogsheads are beaten. An earthquake is not beyond the realm of possibility: the Drapers have fashioned an apparatus for suggesting it. On Judgment Day the dead are seen to rise in their shrouds. The creation of Eve is witnessed to as God lifts from Adam's side "a rib colored red." The carrying off of the student in Greene's FRIAR BACON AND FRIAR BUNGAY is anticipated in the presence on stage of devils incarnate who depart this middle earth with their prey through a fiery Hell Mouth with a "nether chap" made to open and close. Into that Hell Mouth Doctor Faustus will disappear.

The winding up of Marlowe's play is spectacular and quintessentially human. It riddles us with light, but it does not surprise us. We are inclined to say easily that Marlowe is of the Renaissance, "which is characterized by the discovery of the world and by the discovery of man." (The historian Jacob Burckhardt is echoing and predicting all those tiresome panegyrists of modern times for whom man is the measure and earth the kingdom into which he has entered at last.) Medieval man is customarily presented as indifferent to the pull of the physical world: this time and this place. If one thinks, however, of the substantial repertory of plays—always localized, temporalized—that constitute the Wakefield or Towneley Cycle and the N. Towne or Ludus Coventriae Cycle, and that survive from York and Chester, a different picture begins to come clear. The mind of the Middle Ages, whatever its formal obeisance, was not always beating on God.

To do well what one is doing is of course a form of prayer, though not as the churches conceive it. The medieval maker is prayerful as he devotes himself to the exigencies of his craft. Because the play must be available to the entire community, he utilizes a pageant wagon in which the play is reenacted, presumably from first to last light, to accommodate the crowds as they arrive from other stations. Alternatively, less probably, a single presentation suffices, and thereafter the total audience moves on. At each station the play is advertised by banner bearers or *vexillatores* who go before crying the Banns. The pageant itself, gay with vanes, a crest, and streamers, sided with wainscoting, looks forward perhaps to the multilevel structure that is the Elizabethan stage.

Conjecture is necessary, for the latter not less than the former. It is tenable, however, to see in the mind's eye an upper level or stage, strewn with rushes and sometimes employing a curtain to "discover" the actors, and a lower level, also curtained, which functioned concurrently as a "green room" or tiring house and as another area for playing. "I am Alpha et Omega," God announces from the upper level in a play presented by the Grocers of Norwich. (God is recognizable as he wears a girdle and a white leather garment, for the making of which six skins are required.) Below him, in his view, the sacrifice of Isaac is readied, the humbling of Balaam is accomplished, as the hero manqué of the *Ordo Prophetarum* falls on his knees and addresses the deity "*in supremo loco.*"

Action is vertical, a possibility exploited eagerly by the Elizabethan playwright—Shakespeare, for instance. "Down, down, I come, like glistering Phaëton," cries Richard II to Bolingbroke in the "base court" below. The medieval playwright has it both ways. An angel, like King Richard, descends to Jesus in the Garden of Gethsemane, proffers him a chalice, then —says the N. Towne Manuscript—"ascendeth again suddenly." To make manifest her creation, "Eve rises from below": from the wainscotted section of the wagon where, as in a Cappers' Pageant, three men with windlasses are hidden.

What these men are up to is the glory and the tribulation of the stage to the present. It is their job—undertaken then as now with the abandon of the wholly sincere, hence blinkered man—to contrive a burning bush for Moses, to part the Red Sea and insure that it overwhelm the Egyptians, to make a mechanical serpent (*artificiose compositus*) crawl toward the tree of good and evil, somehow to manage the Conception of the Virgin: a stage direction from the N. Towne cycle envisages the three persons of the Trinity "entering all three to her bosom." Judas, in the N. Towne *Trial of Christ*, is required to hang himself. He fulfills the requirement with such fidelity to fact that he almost chokes to death, suffers a heart attack, and must be cut down and carried off by his fellows. A Passion Play of the fourteenth century is knocked to pieces by the discharging of a cannon in Hell. Flames and a tempest signalize the conversion of St. Paul, on whom the Holy Spirit is made to descend. Calm after storm.

As the art of the technician in the cellerage is perfected, the action of the play, more and more given over to hijinks, spills from the pageant, as generations before it had abandoned the narrow confines of the Mass. Now Herod, at Coventry, rages "in the street also," in the unencumbered area called the *platea*. He is availing himself of what space he can find. He needs it. He is "wode" or mad. So, in absurd and splendid ways, is his "designer" or "director," whose enthusiasm for sheer effect is already anticipating the art of Inigo Jones in Jonson's time or Jo Mielziner in our own.

The *platea* in which Herod's passion is vented recalls the nave of the church, in which action had oscillated about permanent stations: cross, manger, sepulchre, and Hell Mouth. These stations survive in the drama of the later Middle Ages, which is always conventionalized, however frantic the action, and always incremental, incorporating faithfully whatever has gone before. (This faithfulness to the art of the past will be decisive for the art of the future.) No drop curtain obscures the *locus* or place, the *sedes* or seat, the *domus* or house that break the *platea* and serve to define it. On that otherwise unbroken area no factitious props obtrude. If the playwright desires that it represent the road to Calvary or the Den of Irksomeness or a city street between the houses of Damon and Erostrato, as later in Gascoigne's comedy SUPPOSES, he has only to say so. In Marlowe's EDWARD II, Queen Isabella, who was just now in Flanders, is discovered abruptly greeting friends at home. Marlowe makes her say: "Welcome to England all with prosperous winds." And we are there. An impoverished stage is paradoxically the richer for its impoverishment. To delineate place is the function of language. The gory tableaux in TAMBURLAINE are represented only sketchily but conveyed all the same— and are the better for want of representation.

The fixed stations, though palpable, can never be indigenous. They do not denote, or not in perpetuity. They are always confronting us and they are always one. This means that they must obliterate time and betoken different places, as by an act of will—and what potential for symbolic theater is embryonic in that merely physical imperative. The *domus* perhaps is the manger in which Jesus is born, and the sepulchre in which he is laid. *Respice finem.* Where Mosby and Alice (to look forward in time) dramatize their adulterous passion, "honeying and making love over the nasty sty," there Arden of Feversham is murdered—and there the conspirators are apprehended and condemned. The *sedes* or seat, in "real" fact a step or two from the *domus* or *locus*, in symbolic fact (which transcends and clarifies common-garden reality) many miles distant, will represent the throne of Herod and the throne of God. "We mind true things by what their mockeries be."

When Kent in *King Lear* is trussed up in the stocks, he is occupying the *sedes*; Edgar the Bedlam is seen simultaneously—failing the proscenium arch and the curtain depending from it, we have no recourse but to see him—on the heath or *locus*, supposedly far away: as eighteenth-century editors like to put it, in "another part of the forest." The modern theater knows better than to show us simultaneously, in the teeth of what is possible, two good men at the lowest point of Fortune's wheel. In fact their juxtaposition goes far to encapsulate the theme of the play. Simultaneous action, in which theme is embodied, is one legacy of the medieval drama to the drama of the Renaissance.

The more ample frame the play requires as it leaves the pageant wagon is provided by the building of scaffolds, sufficiently flexible to open and shut, sufficiently versatile to represent on demand the Interior of Hell, Damascus, the House of Wantonness.

Etymologically, a scaffold is a stage. In Andrew

Marvell's Horatian Ode to Oliver Cromwell, a great poem of the seventeenth century, the soldiers who are the auditors encompass this stage, clapping their bloody hands in token of the death of King Charles. The soldiers are applauding a performance. It is as often a sanguinary performance. For a stage is also a scaffold on which felons are executed. The Passion of Christ, as an Elizabethan chronicler remembers, is played "upon a scaffold." Black Will the murderer—quoting from the epilogue to ARDEN OF FEVERSHAM—was burned in Flushing "on a stage." The dramatist who works this ambiguous ground is like the public hangman. In his hands he carries life and death.

The medieval scaffold is more hospitable than the modern box set, is able to accommodate a house or *domus* for the high priests, a "mansion" for the devils, a pulpit for St. Paul. Around it is the old *platea*, then—another concentric circle—"the assembly that here sitteth or stands." No rigid demarcation separates this assembly from the actors beyond the "footlights" as in our more fastidious theater, where the actor keeps the wind between himself and the audience. Fluidity, inter-penetrating, are of the essence in the staging of the medieval drama. The Apostle "rideth forth with his servants"—to quote from a Conversion play of the late fifteenth century—"about the place [*platea*], and out of the place." Sticklers—"stytelerys" or marshals—sweep his way through the crowd.

If the play is presented in the open fields or suburbs, like *The Pride of Life* or *The Castle of Perseverance*, the crowd is confined within a ditch or line of ramparts that defines the outer limits of this primitive theater. Or the hall of a great house is utilized, or an innyard, open only to the sky. The fixed periphery suggests the emergent character of the drama as a professional enterprise. *Mankind*, which is played in an atrium or innyard—like that of the George Inn below the Thames in Southwark—interrupts the action *in medias res*. New-guise and Now-a-Days pass among the crowd. They are speaking of Titivillus, the stock name for the devil in the medieval drama whose function is precisely to titillate:

He loveth no groats, no pence, or tuppence:
Give us red royals if ye will see his abominable presence!

The crowd gets its money's worth. A stage direction from *The Castle of Perseverance* enjoins on the fiend a volatile performance: "And he that shall play Belial, look that he have gunpowder burning in pipes in his hands and in his ears and in his arse when he goeth to battle."

But the battle is the thing. What the crowd is watch-ing is the confrontation of characters who are in-creasingly tenuous even as the action in which they participate is rendered increasingly with an eye to verisimilar detail. That is not true in essentials of the mystery play. Though it has its fair share of exiguous characters like 1st and 2nd *Puer* and 1st and 2nd *Miles*, it is still its palpable self in the Age of Elizabeth, still commingling delight with instruction, until in Shake-speare's boyhood a reformed religion conspires to drive it from the boards. It is emphatically true of the final flowering of the medieval drama which is the morality play, a didactic dramatizing of life in allegorical terms. The watchword of the morality is *universalia ante rem*, the general before the particular exemplification.

Conrad says, in his preface to *The Nigger of the Narcissus*: "All art appeals primarily to the senses, and the artistic aim when expressing itself in the written word must also make its appeal through the senses, if its high desire is to reach the secret spring of responsive emotions." The morality play repudiates this judgment. Like Plato it contemns the senses and seeks a better way to truth.

The dramatis personae who populate the morality are recognized—but to speak of recognition is in-apposite now—as the Devil and his colleagues, Envy and Wrath; or Caro the Flesh, and Sloth, Gluttony, and Lechery; or the World, and Covetousness and Pride: three abstractions or allegorical figures in the company of the Seven Deadly Sins. When, in *The Summoning of Everyman*, the greatest of the moralities, the hero is abandoned by Kindred and Cousin, the latter offers as excuse a cramp in his toe. That saving and indispensable gratuity is the exception that proves the rule.

From the morality play, toes and cramps and real persons are pretty much excluded. The author sees them as impertinent or as subversive of the thesis he wants to convey. This thesis is not objectified. If the hero of the play is duplicitous, like Volpone, he does not get his requital at the hands of the parasite Mosca. He is given, by Confession, a scourge called Penance, and by Knowledge a black garment in token of contri-tion. Rarely is he given a habitation and a name. We do not meet in these plays particular or parochial figures—like the fraudulent Socialist whom O'Casey in *The Plough and the Stars* calls the Covey. What the drama-tist is bidding for is the type or essence of the fraudu-lent Socialist—such a one as Georg Kaiser's Gentleman in Gray. The difference between the two is the dif-ference between the definite and the indefinite article. Truth, on one reading, inheres in the latter. To the Jacobean or Caroline playwright—Tourneur in THE REVENGER'S TRAGEDY, Ford in *The Broken Heart*—this reading remains powerfully seductive. Massinger in A NEW WAY TO PAY OLD DEBTS, Middleton in A CHASTE MAID IN CHEAPSIDE, as they fashion char-acters called Wellborn, Yellowhammer a goldsmith, Sir Walter Whorehound who needs no definition, are appealing from flesh and blood not less than their fifteenth-century forebears.

In comedy of the conventional (mathematical) kind, as the eye is on plot and the persons are counters, the appeal from their integrity is potentially successful. In tragedy it is foredoomed to fail. Tourneur at least is writing a kind of comedy. So by turns is Marlowe. The aesthetic of the morality play is a viable aesthetic so long as the governing intention is, in the broadest sense, comic. One can say that this intention is fulfilled as the pallid notation that is the hero is "safely stowed." The ending of *Everyman* is a happy ending. If we do not laugh we assuredly rejoice, the sense of a divine comedy. In the surviving drama of the fifteenth century —in *The Castle of Perseverance*, the most distended of the moralities, in *Mankind*, in *Wisdom, or Mind, Will, and Understanding*—this sense is pervasive. The first extant morality play, *The Pride of Life*, lacks its conclusion. No matter for that. It is *ipso facto* that the unregenerate king who is the protagonist should finally turn to repentance.

The putative repentance of the hero, if it makes for satisfaction, fails to get at us where we live. The hero is a cipher. He does not really impinge on the fortunes of his contemporaries, whose plight we do not take seriously so long as we can greet them as *Mulier* or *Senex* or those neighborly nonentities *Proximus* and *Vicinus*. By such reservations the playwright is, however, unperturbed. He is not out to wring our hearts but to dramatize for us the naked contention of attitudes and ideas. The latter are embodied only as far as they must be.

Generally in this contention we are not trusted by the playwright to look and listen, then to draw our conclusions. A Nuntius or Expositor gives the burden of the whole. In *Everyman* he fixes us with a bony finger:

> Here shall you see how Fellowship and Jollity,
> Both Strength, Pleasure, and Beauty,
> Will fade from thee as flower in May.

The hero, expiring, has strength enough to exclaim: "Take example, all ye that this do hear or see." If, one feels, the play has predeceased him, that is possibly the reaction of a frivolous modern person who does not impute to the theater the power to save his soul. One should give the morality its due.

Belaboring of the moral, as by the homiletic "Doctor" to whom *Everyman* assigns the last word, distinguishes or vitiates the mystery play also. Crudity of exposition we have always with us. Even Shakespeare nods. The Nuntius survives, with a leg up from Senecan tragedy, in the plays of Chapman and Kyd. This is to say that the morality, in its failings, is hardly peculiar. But it is possible to represent the vices of style that denote it as speaking obliquely to a different view of theater from that one associates with Ibsen and Strindberg and O'Neill, a view of theater the Middle Ages transmit to the Renaissance. If there are no surprises in store for the audience, which is in possession of the ending of the play in the beginning, attention and interest are likely to shift from questions of vulgar curiosity—who did what: the province of melodrama— to questions of etiology or cause.

Edmund Wilson, in an irritable attack on the popularity of the mystery novel, inquires rhetorically: "Who gives a damn who murdered Roger Ackroyd?" The makers of the morality have put this question to themselves and resolved it: their indifference is patent. So is that of their greater successors in the Renaissance. *Macbeth* is sufficiently violent but not conventionally mysterious or suspenseful. Neither is THE DUCHESS OF MALFI. Shakespeare and Webster have their mind on other business.

As the medieval dramatist tips his hand in beginning the work, he overplays his hand in the ending. Everyman is not relinquished at the moment of climax. The body of the hero descends into the grave but the soul goes marching on. A didactic epilogue recapitulates his story. The plough is simply turned round in the furrow. The epilogue is redundant. But it functions to rationalize the event. We are not left mesmerized, as in the conclusion of Ibsen's *Ghosts* or Strindberg's *The Father* or O'Neill's *Long Day's Journey into Night*. The dramatist is unwilling to focus disproportionate attention—as he might put it if he were an analytical critic, the index of a more self-conscious age—on the great drop scene. What he wants is a frame. He blunders in fulfilling this desideratum, he fatigues us; but it is important to grasp the psychology that underlies his intention, for that psychology, again, is quick or vital in the succeeding age. "Cut is the branch that might have grown full straight." Marlowe is not appending a homily to DOCTOR FAUSTUS. He is willing us to avert our eyes from the sensational fact, to estimate the whole, to see it in perspective. That is the function of the chorus with which *Don Giovanni* concludes. It is the function of the epilogue Horatio delivers over the body of Hamlet.

Hamlet wins our allegiance partly as he figures in a consequential story, partly as we shall not see his like again. The story as moral fable or Psychomachia, a war to the death between vice and virtue, descends to the Renaissance from the morality play, the indigenous hero and his particularized milieu from the mystery. Mediating between these two kinds, taking from either, is a third, which is the interlude. With the vogue of the interlude in the earlier sixteenth century, the drama of the Renaissance begins.

Henry Medwall, the first dramatist writing in English with whose name we are familiar, defines the interlude on one side in *Fulgens and Lucrece*. The play is broken in two parts. We take collation, inter-ludus, and then the play resumes. But the definition is merely formal. More to the point is the playwright's attention to vulgar comedy and homely detail. The pietistic impulse is evidently on the wane. The impulse succeeding to it is often disingenuous and not the province of the interlude alone. A play like *Hickscorner* appears to dramatize the folly of sniping at religion, a play like *Youth* the sad declension of the Prodigal Son. Each of these plays is superficially moral, and in each—as showing is better than telling—juicy possibilities inhere. One says to oneself in the movies, How disgusting is the dalliance of David and Bethsabe.

Early sixteenth-century drama is not always so complacent. John Rastell's *Nature of the Four Elements* is what it purports to be, a dramatic lecture on geography. The plays of the early Tudor poet John Skelton are not so much plays as political tractates. Gascoigne's *Glass of Government*, a half century further on, instructs us in the right way to handle recalcitrant children. When Bishop John Bale, a theatrical champion of the Protestant cause, dramatizes the adventures of King John, he surrounds his eponymous hero with tenebrous characters like Private Wealth, Dissimulation, Widow England and her blind son Commonalty. Maybe we are instructed.

The interlude as such has little to do with instruction. First of all it is mundane. Medwall, harking back to the morality play, denominates as A and B the servants who attend on his pair of rival lovers. But he fleshes them out. Medwall is a priest but in the world and of it. This same affiliation to thingness is manifest in Sir David Lindsay's *Satire of the Three Estates*, technically a morality play in its ethical bias and in its predilection for capital-letter abstractions, technically an interlude as it is divided in halves for collation, more significantly a portent of the renascent age or a throwing back to the age of cycle drama in that it stoops to comedy, stoops to examine the ground on which we stand. A veritable protagonist, John the Commonweal, appears—never mind the offputting name—to utter the immortal line: "Christ Jesus had no property but the gallows." In Nicholas Udall's propaganda play *Respublica*, we recognize in the speech of a real country fellow the dialect of the Cotswolds and are made aware instinctively—whatever the professed intention of the author—that more than polemicizing is in the cards. What does language "such as men do use"—like the southwestern dialect of GAMMER GURTON'S NEEDLE —have to do with the kingdom of God? There is an answer to the question but the makers of the morality would not have entertained it.

The interlude does not throw down a gauntlet to the past. At least the pretense of piety remains, as in the hortatory close of THE FOUR PP. But the warp and woof of Heywood's play—that of most of his plays— is farcical altercation. The shrewish heroine of *Johan-Johan*, a woman no better than she should be, would soon be dead, says her cuckolded husband, if the priest did not "now and then . . . give her absolution upon a bed."

Farce is not amenable to extended treatment and so the interlude is likely to be brief. Brevity, if the soul of wit, is not always productive of it. Characters in Heywood, who is pedantically faithful to the tradition of the medieval *débat*, are unrelievedly disputatious. Their talk is, however, not the talk of the homilies but of the *fabliaux*. Heywood's mentor is the Chaucer of *The Miller's Tale*. The consolations of philosophy are proffered but are not really to his purpose. That is true of John Redford's *Wit and Science*, a farce tricked out in the habiliments of the morality play, as also of Rastell's *Calisto and Melebea*. For each of these writers the Latin tag is applicable: *Cucullus non facit monachum*. "The cowl does not make the monk." Neither does moral garnishing make the play.

What makes the play and communicates to us the sense of an ending and beginning is suggested by Rastell, in his "New Comedy in English in manner of an Interlude." The Spanish source from which he is working is neither Scriptural nor hagiographical. It approximates the modern novel, especially in content, and that is more than inert information. Now for the first time, wholly secular material begins to infiltrate the drama. Mostly this material is made available to the Renaissance by the revival of interest, from the late fifteenth century forward, in the drama of classical Rome.

Pope's famous lines are simplistic; still they offer us a pointer to what is new or renascent in the Renaissance:

> At length Erasmus, that great injured name,
> (The glory of the priesthood and the shame!)
> Stemmed the wild torrent of a barbarous age,
> And drove those holy Vandals off the stage.

The Vandals are the monks, without whose assiduous cultivating of the drama Shakespeare & Co. would not be thinkable. Erasmus is only one of the fellowship of Humanists—More and Colet, Vives in Spain, Linacre, Grocyn, William Lilly—whose office was to stem or redivert the torrent descending from the medieval past. It is, however, true that monkish drama is provisional —its concern is with eschatology: last things; also true that the phenomenon called Humanism introduced to the practicing playwright the comedies of Plautus, and Terence in his original dress, and the tragedies of Seneca. Roman comedy is more carefully articulated than the medieval play. Senecan tragedy is less hopeful —not just by definition: sometimes tragedy cheers us up—also more sanguinary, and mannerist in language, exemplifying in every line the self-conscious artist, a classical personage out of favor in the Middle Ages and regenerate as the modern age begins.

The prayer Erasmus formulates, wittily but earnestly, in the early decades of the sixteenth century: "*Sancta Socrate, ora pro nobis*"—a prayer that elevates man to a position of primacy and disuses the anthropomorphic God who had dominated in the medieval drama— reverberates in the new drama as well as in the church.

The new drama is egocentric. Overreach, who writes *nil ultra* to his proudest hopes, is the typical protagonist. That is a nice setoff to the new or heliocentric universe hypothesized by Copernicus. Earth is diminished to a speck in the infinity of space, concurrently, perhaps defiantly, man is aggrandized. In rueful knowledge even more than in ignorance, man desires to know that the universe revolves around him. To this desire, the new drama addresses itself.

The new drama is also preoccupied with form. In all art, content is circumscribed by form. Of some art it is possible to speak more radically than this. Say: "*pièce bien faite*" and we know what is coming. Content is form in the comedies of Plautus, rediscovered by the Renaissance, as also in the comedies of Terence, the only classical playwright known to the Middle Ages but sicklied over or Christianized in the tenth century by a well-meaning nun of Gandersheim.

Form means the five-act structure, the division of the acts into scenes, the honoring of the Unities, as in Gascoigne's Roman comedy SUPPOSES: a single set, basically a single story, and unfolding in a few hours' space. Most of all, form is defined in the sense the play communicates of an integer or coherence.

Construction, the architect's province, is not to be scoffed at as mere carpentry. Many writers of quality— Marlowe, for example—are innocent of it. The Eliza-

bethan playwright who masters this finicking art—
Dekker in THE SHOEMAKER'S HOLIDAY, Jonson in
EPICOENE, Chapman in THE WIDOW'S TEARS, the
early Shakespeare—goes to school to Roman comedy,
sometimes redacted and brought up to date by the
theater of the Italian Renaissance. Performance of
Latin plays was common in Italy from the mid-
fifteenth century, in England a century later. As the
playwright is unwilling simply to translate, he will seek
to revivify the material at which he is laboring, to give
it a new and independent lease on life. That is how it is
with Nicholas Udall's Plautine comedy *Ralph Roister
Doister*, or GAMMER GURTON'S NEEDLE, each English to the core but exotic or Italianate English in the
feeling each manifests for classical form. "An Italianate
Englishman," says the humanist Roger Ascham, "is a
devil incarnate." But that is a half truth.

Sometimes in medieval art the Old Testament
prophets are seen to carry on their shoulders the
Apostles or Evangelists who promulgate the new dispensation. This figure describes the hybrid that is
Renaissance comedy. Gascoigne is supported partly by
his English antecedents and also by Ariosto, the great
Italian. But Ariosto takes strength from Plautus and
Terence. His classical comedies of the early sixteenth
century, as they are refreshed in spirit by the self-
conscious artistry of the past, "stem the wild torrent"
of the panoramic play. The result, given time, is the
comelier artifact or supremely crafted machine that
Jonson patents and hands on to his successors.

In Italianate comedy as a kind, the intricate workings
of the machine take precedence. Character is of ancillary importance and is assimilated by and large in the
type. We encounter the Braggart, usually a Spaniard
(like Don Armado in *Love's Labor's Lost*), or the
Pedant (like Lugier in Fletcher's THE WILD-GOOSE
CHASE), or the grumbling Servant (Grumio in *The
Taming of the Shrew*). The Friar, crooked, bumbling,
or omnicompetent as the plot requires, is the last resort
of every Renaissance playwright. An intriguing lady's
maid, designated the Soubrette, is familiar as Sybil in
THE SHOEMAKER'S HOLIDAY or Margaret in *Much
Ado About Nothing* or Pero in BUSSY D'AMBOIS. The
Professional Man, predictably the butt of ridicule, is
the doctor or lawyer in a hundred plays from Gascoigne
to the theater of the twentieth century: Cleander in
SUPPOSES, Voltore the advocate in Jonson's VOL-
PONE, Dr. Percy Paramour in *The Philanderer* by
Bernard Shaw. The Mage or Sorcerer recurs as
Faustus or Friar Bacon, the Parasite as Dodger or
Marall or Mosca (who is more than the type: always
the hallmark of greatness), the Nurse as Juliet's Nurse
or Putana in 'TIS PITY SHE'S A WHORE.

These enduring stereotypes lie ready to hand in
Roman comedy, in the *Commedia erudita* of Ariosto, in
the popular Italian drama known as the *Commedia
dell'arte*. But one finds them elsewhere and closer to
home. The psychology that prefers the type to the
indigenous thing is that of the morality play. It is often
said of Falstaff that he descends from the *Miles
Gloriosus* of Plautus, the story of a blustering soldier.

His more obvious antecedent is the medieval Vice. The
capital-letter characters who participate in the comical
farrago that is SUMMER'S LAST WILL AND TESTA-
MENT are classical only on their face. Their essential
provenance is the allegorical theater of the fifteenth
century; the business to which Nashe commits them—
the logomachy or word-war—is a resuming of the
medieval debate. In so many ways the cask, which is
Renaissance drama, still smells of the wine that steeped
it first.

The rediscovery of Vitruvius enforces the point. To
this classical architect the new drama is indebted for an
illusory backdrop made of canvas, which is stretched on
wooden frames, cut with doors and decorated by
"prospects" in perspective—like the "painted cloth"
of the City of Rome that the theatrical manager Philip
Henslowe records as among his properties. But what
the audience is looking at is still the monoscenic stage of
the mysteries and moralities. The medieval playwright
is banking on our good will as when his surrogate in-
forms us: "Here is the town of Emmaus in which Jesus
Christ was entertained." Two and three centuries later
the Elizabethan playwright is still put to asserting that
this is the Forest of Arden. The old *sedes* or *domus* is
still there, metamorphosed to the players' houses,
which give on the old *platea* through the openings in
the permanent structure across the back of the stage.
One corner of this structure will represent—you must
take the playwright's word—the palace of Alexander
the Great (as in Lyly's *Campaspe*, a play of the 1580s),
another the studio of Apelles the painter. Between the
doors that admit to these houses-by-courtesy is the
playing area, still much as it was when Termagant, the
ranting deity of the Moslems, tore a passion to tatters.
In logistical terms, radical innovation is still to seek.
God's "Alpha et Omega," the voice from the pageant
wagon, is proleptic.

In the conventional English comedy of the sixteenth
century, action is confined to the street before two
adjacent houses—as in *The Comedy of Errors* or
GAMMER GURTON'S NEEDLE. Perhaps this generic
street or playing area was encircled with galleries,
mostly for the spectators, partly for the use of the
players themselves, like the medieval innyard or
the "theater of cruelty"—Paris Garden, south of the
Thames—where bears and bulls were baited. Perhaps,
taking a hint from the mounting of street pageants on
scaffolding or trestles, it was raised aloft, like the
elevated stage of the pageant wagon, and closed at the
rear with a "tiring house" and a curtain or arras.
Behind the arras Falstaff is detected, fast asleep and
snorting like a horse. Through the arras Polonius is
stabbed. Perhaps the refectories of the London law
schools and the sister universities of Oxford and Cambridge commended themselves to the players as they
were able to utilize for their entrances and exists the
paneled screen or reredos, pierced with two doors, that
gave access to the hall. Orsino enters through the
reredos, at the Middle Temple in 1602, to speak the
opening lines of *Twelfth Night*. The point to take hold
of, from this mingling of guesswork and ascertainable

fact, is that the Elizabethan theater is not so much new as reminiscent.

When the carpenter James Burbage constructs the first permanent playhouse in England—the Theater of 1576, rebuilt two decades later as the Globe—he combines the seating plan of the inn or bear garden—an octagon (or square or circle) of galleries surrounding an open yard—with the "stage" arrangement of the great hall. His theater, like the Rose and Swan and Fortune for which it serves as a model, is able to accommodate as many as three thousand people. But the old rapport between the auditor and actor remains undiminished. The Citizen and his Wife, in THE KNIGHT OF THE BURNING PESTLE, are amusing as they take the play to heart; their naive response is also instructive. It suggests the sense of verity, of the play as an intimate and personal experience, that radiates from the apron stage and communicates itself to the groundlings who stand in the pit and their hypothetical betters ensconced in the galleries above them.

As it happens, THE KNIGHT OF THE BURNING PESTLE is aggressively indifferent to the taste of the groundlings. The Citizen-Grocer has blundered into the performance, or so Francis Beaumont wants us to believe. Neither is he standing, unless to stretch his legs. Partly, Beaumont's play is interesting to us as it documents the increasing segregation of the audience along the lines of money and class. The author of an old-fashioned comedy like MUCEDORUS, as he is writing in the Age of Elizabeth, an ecumenical age and hence in terms of the theater more nearly democratic, can appeal simultaneously to the "boisterous butchers, cutting cobblers, hardhanded masons" and "the best of the nobility and gentry." Subsequently the chaff is winnowed from the wheat. The old refectory of the Blackfriars, equipped with seats and artificial lighting, is converted to a private theater whose more select patrons are no longer exposed to the vagaries of the weather or the stinking breath of the plebs whom the price of admission effectively excludes. The talents of boy actors are successfully exploited, like the Children of the Chapel whose habit is to "berattle" or abuse the public stage. "Do the boys carry it away?" Hamlet inquires; and is answered: "Ay, that they do, my lord, Hercules and his load, too"—a dispirited reference to the sign that hung before the Globe, a public theater, and exhibited Hercules bearing the world on his shoulders.

The medieval audience is heterogeneous and that is better for the commonweal, hence better for the play. Exclusivity breeds narrowness of vision. But Nashe in SUMMER'S LAST WILL AND TESTAMENT is writing evidently for private performance, and in this case—as the author is opening himself to his friends—the play is more assured for the exclusive *mise-en-scène*. Though Webster is very sore at the want of "a full and understanding auditory," it is in a public theater that THE WHITE DEVIL is first performed. "The breath that comes from the uncapable multitude"—living perforce on herring and onions—is not sufficiently noxious to poison the play. The split between private and public

is consequential for the future—it is worth our asking: Who goes to the theater today?—but it does not serve, or not yet, to obliterate the character of dramatic representation as a living thing felt on the pulses.

The new theater, like the old, and whether public or private, is a multilevel structure. At Paul's or Blackfriars the audience is thankful in that it has a roof above its head. The audience at the Globe is not so lucky. The stage butts on a gallery ascending to the rear—from which Bel-Imperia in THE SPANISH TRAGEDY can look down on Hieronimo emoting in the arbor. The "heavens" or "shadow" that overtop the stage admit, as in *Cymbeline*, of the majestic descent of Jove, lowered like St. Paul in his basket. From the topmost tier of the galleries the pennant flies, announcing the afternoon's performance; the modern equivalent of the *vexillator* blows his trumpet: and Prospero "on the top" appears, like the God of the mysteries, accompanied by "solemn and strange music." Far below, in the floor of the stage, trap doors open on a subterranean area whence fog billows up, as in ARDEN OF FEVERSHAM, and the distillations of Subtle in THE ALCHEMIST are exploded.

Properties remain metonymic. The scene is suggested in one spectacular detail, like the golden cage in which Bajazeth is trundled or the tree with golden apples that emblematizes the contest between Vandermast and Friars Bacon and Bungay. Costumes are resplendent, as on the medieval stage—Gaveston in EDWARD II "wears a lord's revènue on his back"—and as careless as before of historical decorum—the imperial characters of Massinger's THE ROMAN ACTOR are well-attired gentlefolk, not of antiquity but of the London of Massinger's time. The memorable scenes of Renaissance drama still preserve their independence of technical gimmickry. Even after the triumph of "mountebank" Jones, they turn almost wholly on the intelligent use of an uncluttered stage.

Jonson, in the middle scenes of VOLPONE, illustrates superbly. The ambiguous hero, feigning deathly illness, lies on his bed in the alcove or inner stage. The curtains or traverse conceal him from sight on the unlucky entrance of the ingenuous Bonario. How to get Bonario out of the way? The task falls to Mosca, who hides the young man behind one of the pillars that hold up the "heavens" or thrusts him in at a door, left or right rear. Enter at this point the legacy hunter Corvino with his young and desirable wife. Mosca converses with them momentarily on the center apron, then man and wife "retire to one side" and talk together. Corvino departs. The parasite instructs Bonario to "walk the while Into that gallery at the upper end"—the balcony or second level above the inner stage, accessible through the doors that lead to the green room. Now the peak moment is at hand. Volpone, throwing aside the curtains, throwing off his pretended sickness, attempts the rape of Celia. In the nick of time, Jonson makes Bonario "leap out from where Mosca had placed him."

It is a great *coup de théatre*. Lustful purpose is foiled, and the proposition reaffirmed that the meat and drink of living theater is not verisimilar representation but simultaneous action and the concurrent exploiting of different levels and parts of the stage. These resources are available already to the medieval playwright. He does not have at command the skills of the new professional companies like the King's Men or the Admiral's Men, but he has what he needs to have for the making of sufficient drama.

This is not to gainsay the importance to the theater of the Renaissance of humanistic scholarship or Italian comedy or the classical matrix from which it derives. Only it is to claim priority for the medieval matrix. Not until the erecting of the proscenium arch in the early years of the seventeenth century does the scene begin to alter.

John Lyly is a harbinger of the changing scene but not so much in stagecraft as in language. The Euphuistic movement Lyly inaugurates or makes notorious with the publication in 1579 of the cloying novel called *Euphues* or *The Anatomy of Wit* is signalized by the elaborate use of parallelism, analogy, antithesis. The style affected by Lyly and his epigones—Shakespeare among them in *Love's Labor's Lost*—is a highfalutin style and easy to ridicule—but only as one considers it with the eye of hindsight. The manage of that style—the metaphor from horsemanship seems congruous—needs a sinewy arm and a mind turning over. Lyly's comedies of the 1580s, written mostly for the popular companies of boy actors, constitute the forging house of Elizabethan rhetoric. Already in GALLATHEA there begins to emerge the disciplined and graceful utterance, the exactitude of phrasing that one associates with the greater dramatists of the seventeenth century. Lyly's language seems a parody made after the fact: Falstaff imitating King Henry. But that is because the palace of language is not entered through niggarding but first of all through the gates of excess.

Lyly's contemporary George Peele, his younger colleague Thomas Dekker, show us how this is so. In plays like DAVID AND BETHSABE, Peele is trying his hand at the fashioning of a new linguistic instrument for the purposes of theatrical declamation. He is the type of the opportunist—by no means a pejorative word when used of language—absorbed in the process of manipulating words. The entail of this process is the creating, even before Marlowe, of that blank verse line that is the vehicle now, not only for the poet in his closet, but also for dramatic give and take.

When Dekker in THE SHOEMAKER'S HOLIDAY wants to approximate the language of cultivated persons —or possibly to make a parade of words—he resorts to the formal bantering called *stichomythia*. Two characters—let them be Hic and Ille—engage in verbal altercation. One speaks a line of verse; the other answers, capping the rhyme:

H. Why do you stay, and not pursue your game?
I. I'll hold my life, their hunting-nags be lame.
H. A deer more dear is found within this place.
I. But not the deer, sir, which you had in chase.
H. I chased the deer, but this dear chaseth me.
I. The strangest hunting that ever I see.

The performance is anguishing. Dekker is applying the screws. But the violence he does to language has an unexpected issue. The more the writer is committed to artificiality in the beginning, the more spontaneous or natural-seeming will be the utterance he engenders, and even if, like Moses, he is only prophetic of it. Nashe is more than prophetic, but the same comment holds of his willful torturing of language. Shakespeare stands on the shoulders of Lyly and Nashe. Being natural, as Oscar Wilde makes a character observe, is so difficult a pose to keep up. The point is that the pose requires practice.

There is this further point: when language is highly stylized, virtuosity is everywhere to the fore. The playwright is pulling the strings and desires our witnessing and applause. When on the other hand he is seeking to rouse our emotions, he takes pains to conceal himself and his expertise. In tragic drama, he is invisible like the god of the creation. In comic drama, he is all brazenly the "god from the machine." Plot is conspicuous and turns on contrivance, characters are submerged in their extravagant function, attention to rhetoric is overt.

The cartoons Dekker sponsors take part in a romantic action that relates to life only incidentally. What Dekker is casting for is "fine tickling sport." The ultimate sport is the resolving of the riddle, a mathematical exercise and independent of volition. We need a *deus ex machina* to do the business for us. Dekker in the last act of the play suggests how this need will be met: "Enter the King and his train over the stage."

Though THE SHOEMAKER'S HOLIDAY smells of the East End of London and cheers us with its inoffensive smut: "she shall be laid at one side like an old pair of shoes"—where "she" is a wife bereft of her husband—"and be occupied for no use," though the play is interstitially a real and homely thing, it is essentially a well-turned machine.

The machine is still running four hundred years later. Its arbitrariness is, however, apparent when we compare it with the work of a more "organic" maker, like Greene in FRIAR BACON AND FRIAR BUNGAY. Greene looks to be writing the standard slick romance. And in fact, he is a great caterer to the prevailing fashion: see his essay, with Thomas Lodge, at exemplary drama, A LOOKING GLASS FOR LONDON AND ENGLAND. Like Dekker, he takes us from the cottage to the court. That is the indicated progress and is guaranteed to please. But his plot, or double plot, is a red herring. Though the major persons in each comedy undergo a radical change, the change in Dekker is exterior, a matter of clothing; in Greene it is intrinsic, a matter of character.

Beaumont in THE KNIGHT OF THE BURNING PESTLE is also exploiting disguise. Rafe, the grocer's apprentice, lives a lie. In this, he is potentially tragic. But the delusion of the hero is productive of laughter alone. We do not learn from his quixotic behavior that "there is no darkness but ignorance." Incongruity in Beaumont's play is not the means to an end but the end in itself. Beaumont thinks the middle class is amusing as it is so little *au courant*. In Dekker, the middle class is exalted. Better a poor man's wife than a king's whore! Each playwright is more keen on riding his hobby horse than on depicting the foibles appurtenant to us all.

The astute maker of formulaic comedy will insure that all friends taste the wages of their virtue. MUCE-DORUS, a naive parable of the testing and rewarding of virtue, is the most popular of Renaissance comedies—it goes on, in its own time, like *East Lynne*—as it sticks so closely to convention. This implies, perhaps requires, that the testing is adventitious, the rewards are parceled out, the protagonists on whom they drop are not deserving but only lucky. Desert argues recognition.

First-class comedy begins with the delighted discovery of inapposite conduct but that is not where it ends. Already in the 1580s, Greene knows where it ends. He is not a comic dramatist of the first class. His humor is not so sophisticated as Beaumont's, his style is the old-fashioned aureate style—anybody's possession—not indelibly personal like the style of Thomas Nashe. If we laugh at the testing of his heroine, that is not as he would wish us to laugh. But Greene aspires to the seriousness that is the line of division between genuine comedy and farce. His deluded persons find out at last who they are. Friar Bacon, the white magician who assumes the role of God, breaks his wand as the depth of his opacity is borne in upon him. The resolution of the plot coincides with the doffing of disguise—not spectacles and wigs but mistaken identity. Iago will say, also Viola in *Twelfth Night*: "I am not what I am." Disguise in Robert Greene is more than skin deep. The romantic comedies of Shakespeare are predicted.

Greene is vastly inferior to Shakespeare. But the leap from Greene to Shakespeare is conceivable. The greater issues perceptibly from the lesser. This means that Renaissance comedy flowers quickly and makes a continuum. That is not true of Renaissance tragedy.

Early essays in this kind seek to take strength from the classical past and are enervated by it—GORBODUC, for instance, by intention a reprise of Senecan tragedy but surviving today largely for "historical" reasons. Sackville and Norton, the authors of this first attempt in English at the writing of dramatic blank verse, initiate the error that learned partisans of the theater have been compounding ever since. Essential Seneca is the tragic vision and lies outside their ken. Inessential Seneca is the unpropitious form—we call it closet drama as the closet is its proper preserve—and on this they rivet their attention. The form of Senecan tragedy is inimical to theater, unless in the hands of a great poet like Racine. Stasis describes it. Action is recapitulated after the fact—huddled up unnecessarily, Kyd and Marlowe will decide. The Chorus or Ghost or Nuntius does duty for ocular proof. That is partly because Seneca is a fastidious playwright, partly as he is emulating Greek drama. Horrifying incident is pervasive in what he writes. Possibly, he thinks, telling is better than showing?

Thomas Preston in the 1560s, a meretricious entertainer whom one sees as always counting the house, does not think so. For the wrong reasons, Preston turns out to be right. CAMBYSES, his bastardizing of Senecan tragedy, is a revolting play and a portent of great things to come. Preston's achievement is to enact on stage the violence which Seneca consigns to report. The wicked king Cambyses is accused by his advisor Praxaspes of drinking to excess. To disprove the accusation Cambyses orders that the little son of the advisor be stood before him as a target. If the king is drunk, he will fail of his aim. The king is sober, if just sufficiently.

> I have dispatched him! Down he doth fall!
> As right as a line his heart I have hit.

But Cambyses—or Preston—has another card to play. "My knight," he says, "with speed his heart cut out and give it unto me." The knight, complying, hands over the heart, presumably a bladder filled with animal's blood. The audience is stupefied. This is revolution.

Two decades later Thomas Kyd, whose invention is dedicated to going Preston one better, concludes the greatest theatrical success in the whole repertory of Renaissance drama with a quarry of the slain that, for vulgar ferocity, is more like truth than fiction. Kyd takes the honors among writers of his time in accommodating Roman Seneca to the Elizabethan stage. He creates, in the process, the tragedy of blood. It is not possible to overestimate the impact of THE SPANISH TRAGEDY. Of its numerous progeny, *Hamlet* is only the most famous.

Both Kyd and Shakespeare are writing Senecan tragedy. Each of them, in the beginning, elects to focus on revenge and the horrors attendant on it—the sinister mumming of the Play-within-the-play, the Dumb Show in which murder is emblematized, the Ghost who, like Lazarus, has "come back to tell you all," the madness of the hero, real or feigned.

Here Kyd and Shakespeare go their different ways. Hamlet is mad as he falters beneath the burden of the mystery. Hieronimo is mad in fulfillment of the exigencies of the plot. Hamlet is a veritable protagonist who harrows us with fear and wonder, Hieronimo a stick figure whose antics are intended solely to tease our nerve endings.

But *Hamlet* and THE SPANISH TRAGEDY have this in common: each, building on Seneca, repudiates his static form in favor of vigorous action on stage. We do not gather from hearsay that Hieronimo has stabbed the Duke of Castille or Hamlet the King of Denmark. We see the business—and so we avouch it. In Kyd it is factitious business. But the pointless hurly burly of THE SPANISH TRAGEDY, as it is not simply reported but represented, is decisive for the greater art of the seventeenth century.

In the years just before and after the new century begins, nostalgic writers like Fulke Greville, Samuel Daniel, Jonson in two plays invoking "the reader extraordinary," seek to exhume the pure Senecan model. Luckily for the future, it is Kyd's impure amalgam that carries the day. If we, to whom Renaissance drama has come down, are the beneficiaries of

Kyd, how are we lucky? The answer is that living theater is not language alone. The heroes and heroines who dominate in the theater of the seventeenth century are apt to strike us in cold print as so many ephemerids. But the vengeful or splenetic man, the glosing courtesan, the honest whore, the roistering young woman with a heart of gold are more than the words that denote them not simply because Tourneur and Marston and Dekker and Middleton are more talented than Kyd but because these writers have gone to school to the author of THE SPANISH TRAGEDY.

Sometimes what they learn is flummery, as when Shirley in HYDE PARK parades real horses over the apron. We are on the way to *Fanciulla del West*. Jonson is more tactful in BARTHOLOMEW FAIR as his art is less realistic than mimetic. But Jonson, when he has got down from his high classical horse, also craves the witnessing of our eyes and ears. As to the story Heywood wants us to swallow in A WOMAN KILLED WITH KINDNESS, we would not take it from report. It is a groatsworth of vice with a million of repentance. Beaumont and Fletcher, assuaging easy tears with raucous laughter, are more practiced in legerdemain, and that is what A KING AND NO KING comes down to. Credibility goes to either play as adulterous passion is bodied forth on stage. The bodying forth is Kyd's signal contribution. Failing it, we should leave the theater, like the skeptical Didymus, shaking our heads in disbelief.

To say that the play's the thing is to say that a chemical transformation occurs when the words on the page are handed over to the players. Shakespeare is not better when we read him in our study, but wanting a dimension. Charles Lamb, contending for that passive view of drama, is wrong. It takes two to make a quarrel, more than two to make a play. The drama is public communion and the playwright one of many who participate in its creation. The lyric poet works alone. His achievement is not necessarily less considerable than that of the dramatic poet. But it is a different kind of achievement.

The Renaissance playwright who learns from Kyd to appeal to our senses tends in his solicitude to confound them. Like his medieval antecedents, he is mostly a panoramic playwright. The representation he wants to set before us is a total representation. John Ford does not chronicle the fall of Perkin Warbeck but first the rise and then the fall of that unlucky pretender. The risk he runs is of dispersing our attention. Senecan tragedy declines the gambit.

The *Hercules Furens* focuses narrowly on the consummating of a single and compendious design. As the play begins, the labors of Hercules are already behind him. The austerity that is willing to ignore such spectacular material just because it is impertinent material comes hard to the Elizabethans. Their eye is not so often on the whole as the parts. How relevant is the encounter of Theridamas and Olympia to the central action of TAMBURLAINE? Marlowe, whose play is a tissue of interpolated scenes, might answer that it makes a good story.

But another and more cogent answer is possible. The proliferating of incident, the refracting of the single plot are productive, at last and at best, not of confusion but complementary action. The subplot of the lustful idiot or Changeling in the tragedy by Middleton and Rowley illuminates the lustful business that deranges the major persons of the play. The comic anarchs or clowns whom Ford admits to PERKIN WARBECK comment in their folly on that greater anarch who is the equivocal hero and who, in a play that pays homage to the Unities, would hold the stage alone. Panoramic drama in the hands of its greatest practitioners confesses a unity that is more than formal, the unity of similar cause.

The forging of this unity makes an absorbing story. Marlowe in his brief and dazzling career struggles with the intractable data of history in the attempt to discover from the ebb and flow of things a pattern that is not imposed but organic. The two parts of TAMBURLAINE, the tragedies of Dido and the Guise, THE JEW OF MALTA, DOCTOR FAUSTUS, record his partial failure.

Failure is relative. Better to fail with Shakespeare in *Cymbeline* than to succeed with Dryden in *All for Love*. Earlier attempts at locating form in historical material —which is by definition formless—plays like the *Famous Victories of Henry V*, *The Troublesome Reign of King John*, Thomas Legge's Latin chronicle of *Richardus Tertius*—merit speedy interment in a footnote. Marlowe's failure is heroic. The great scene exerts its fatal fascination. It is something to be tempted. Marlowe's predecessors are secure as their stature is so much less than his. What they make is humdrum. Marlowe makes the mighty line and it reverberates forever. But in his work the sense of ineluctable progression, in which the ending is predicable of the beginning, goes by the boards.

The tragic history of EDWARD II is Marlowe's closest and most successful approximation of dramatic coherence, as opposed to the stringing together of a series of incandescent speeches. From the welter of miscellaneous detail that is his primary source— Holinshed's *Chronicles of England, Scotland, and Ireland* —he is canny enough to pick and choose, to aggrandize and depress. The result is tragedy that makes a total configuration. It is an inestimable achievement. Shakespeare is greater. But Marlowe comes first.

Marlowe and Kyd are close contemporaries whose paths cross sensationally in the year of Marlowe's violent death. It is Kyd who brings the charge of heresy against his fellow dramatist. But the connection between those two is only chronological, hence a fortuitous connection. Marlowe as a writer of tragedy is the genuine article. Kyd differs from Marlowe not in degree but in kind. Only a few years separate THE SPANISH TRAGEDY from DOCTOR FAUSTUS and EDWARD II. But in these years a quantum jump occurs. One can describe what happens. To account for what happens is harder.

Abraham and Isaac is a better piece of work than much of the brummagem stuff that survives from the sixteenth and seventeenth centuries. In this play, however—in every medieval play—God is always present, on stage or in the wings, to redress the balance. The makers of tragedy in the Renaissance, even when they have got to their wit's end, do not rely on the interposition of God. Their religious persuasion does not matter. In last things, they are agnostic or Manichean. Massinger was perhaps a Catholic, Jonson and Shirley both Protestant and Catholic, Marston subsequently an Anglican priest, Chapman a Stoic, Marlowe an atheist, and Shakespeare everything and nothing. When they enter the theater, they leave the church behind. In Renaissance tragedy, no one follows Everyman into the grave. No one ventures to say what lies over yonder.

The source of this bleak taciturnity is moot. To invoke the classics is conventional. *Vide* the fall of Constantinople in 1453: "the second death of Homer and of Plato," Greek scholars trekking westward and bringing with them these sacred relics, Humanism edified and rising, the tragic afflatus rising with it. The vulgarity of this sequence, as it offers to explain, is apparent. There is a chain and also a missing link. Shakespeare did not know Sophocles and is closer to Sophocles in spirit than is Euripides, his fellow Greek.

But Shakespeare knew Seneca, so did everyone else (the publishing in 1581 of the so-called "Ten Tragedies" is like a shot heard round the world), and though this fact is not strictly causal it is elucidatory. For Seneca is a mirror in which Renaissance tragedy reveals its essential features, and like a mirror or concave lens he does more than reflect: he gathers the light and transmits it. The Elizabethans discover their own lineaments in him, but this discovery not only corroborates: it is itself a creative act, as when we say that images fresh images beget.

What Seneca sees, and the Elizabethans have glimpsed already, is the death of a countervailing goodness. *Deus absconditus.* Seneca says to the Roman poet Lucretius: "we have made everything into darkness for ourselves" (*omnia nobis fecimus tenebras*). Like the medieval playwright he stresses human culpability. But in medieval drama the darkness, though self-imposed, always lifts at the end. The characteristic movement, as in Dante's *Commedia*, is upward from darkness to light. In Seneca's *Phaedra*, in his *Thyestes*, good meets evil and is borne under by it. Why is that?

In the *Hercules Oetaeus*, a woman maddened by jealousy tells of the wild beasts she harbors within her. Chapman in BUSSY D'AMBOIS, remembering this passage, sees it as definitive of our natural condition. Men are not "in human state Till they embrace within their wife's two breasts All Pelion and Cythaeron with their beasts." We want to remember that it was on Mount Cythaeron that Oedipus confronted the Sphinx.

Medieval man is sufficiently cognizant of the beast who journeys with us. The story of Tristan and Ysolt says it all. We are yoked to a roaring lion: the judgment of St. James the Apostle. When Seneca's Thyestes attests to our vagrant nature—"Out of experience I speak: one may choose ill fortune in preference to good"—he might be echoing St. Paul.

But the Christian Middle Ages are sustained in the conviction of grace abounding. It is precisely this conviction that is wanting to Seneca as to the tragic dramatists of the Renaissance. Simply as we are men we put on the shirt of Nessus, commend the poison to ourselves. That has always been true. But now abruptly there is no succor. Chapman's heroine Tamyra, aware that even the sun cannot shine at pleasure, asks a question to which the answer is foreordained:

Oh, how can we, that are but motes to him . . .
Disperse our passions' fumes with our weak labors?

Out of this awareness, the rhetoric of high tragedy is made:

Man is a torch borne in the wind: a dream
But of a shadow, summed with all his substance.

Tragedy is daunting as it leaves us naked to our enemies. But tragedy is inspiriting as it presents the naked man against the sky. We are deflected but inviolate. In Seneca's *Medea* the tragic heroine is utterly lost. "Of all your great resources nothing remains." But the Nurse, who proffers this bitter truth, is answered: "Medea remains!" Integrity in the final toils is the possession of Webster's heroine, henceforward our possession, as when she cries: "I am Duchess of Malfi still!"

Shakespeare seems to suggest that we are caught in the toils as we make our will lord of our reason. Perhaps an alternative is available to us? But the difference between Shakespeare and the others who are his satellites is only ostensible. Always, the vicious mole of nature is triumphant. The pales and forts of reason go down. "But oh, vain boast! Who can control his fate?" The fate Othello hypothesizes is not dispensed from Olympus, as in the melodramatic fiction of Thomas Hardy. It is an emanation of ourselves. "Man's character is his daimon," Heraclitus observes, and from this daimon there is evidently no escape.

In one particular, Shakespeare does really stand apart. Though the tragic denouement with which he confronts us is sufficiently dour, what happens in preface to it is felt as illustrative or contingent. In the tragedies of his contempories, meaning is elusive. Fact is exhausted in its own spectacular being. THE WHITE DEVIL, THE DUCHESS OF MALFI are replete with incongruous figures. Oxymoron describes them: the forcible associating of immiscible things. "You speak as if a man should know what kind of fowl is coffined in a baked meat before you cut it open." "Could I be one of their flattering panders, I would hang on their ears like a horse leech till I were full, and then drop off." In Shakespeare, language is bizarre to light up the disjunction between the norm and the perverting of the norm. Macbeth calls his lady and accomplice "dearest chuck." In Webster there is no disjunction because there is no sense of declension or falling off. Horror is the norm. Hence the language is unexpectedly congruous. The Psychomachia or war of vice and virtue is given away. Webster disbelieves it and so it is unavailable to him. Life is independent of moral agency or choice. The Duchess of Malfi is destroyed not as she is moral or immoral but as she ventures to move in the world. The world, a bad dog, turns and rends her. The wilderness into which she is going is life itself.

If moral choice is irrelevant, the possibility of conflict is aborted. It is idle to speak of results. There are only events. No motive impels the hero or hero-villain. He is. The tragedy in which he figures is sound and fury. This is not to depreciate the art of John Webster, who is preeminent, also characteristic in his time—except that preeminence argues idiosyncrasy. To define is to delimit, also—as the definition is truly catholic—to praise. What is lost has been spoken to, what is left—by no means dregs and lees—is the untrammeled personality: megalopsychia or greatness of soul.

What claims and reservations are enjoined on us, who are the auditors, by this residual greatness? A sufficient answer will acknowledge that in Renaissance tragedy—always waiving Shakespeare, who is a vagrant star—we do not levy on moral judgment to censure or approve. Worth in the protagonist is a dependency of his caloric quotient. That is true for Marlowe and Chapman and Ford. Like Webster they put their money on one tremendous effect. They can do no other.

> The glory of my deed
> Darkened the midday sun, made noon as night.

But Giovanni in the final scene of 'TIS PITY SHE'S A WHORE is communing only with himself.

Kyd is a clumsy playwright who cannot manage without resort to cheap contrivance. Arbitrariness is at the heart of Websterian tragedy but not because Webster is clumsy, rather as he has no answers. We are here as on a darkling plain. Coincidence in Webster is not an expedient but a principle.

It is possible to see Kyd as an amiable man with a living to make, the shopkeeper type or *genus Britannicus*, who is shrewd enough to estimate the utility of trading in horror. Webster is not amiable nor does he dramatize horror because he thinks it will cash. His despairing vision is alien to Cyril Tourneur, whose name is always linked with Webster's but whose fundamental bias is radically different. Tourneur delights in horror for its own sake. He is the poet laureate of the Grand Guignol. One does not say of him, as perhaps of Kyd or Preston, that he wouldn't hurt a fly. Tourneur is nasty in the grain and that is the source of his continuing vitality.

Of the two plays attributed to him, *The Atheist's Tragedy* is the less successful—necessarily, for the whole bag of tricks had already been opened. What Tourneur does can be done only once. The Turkish caliph who puts his siblings to death is unattractive, and stands alone. To have no successors is a measure of Tourneur's greatness, also his limitation.

In THE REVENGER'S TRAGEDY, the most macabre of the tragedies of blood, this jejune and talented writer reaches for immortality and achieves it. The achievement is narrow and correspondingly intense. Palpable virtue eludes him. The chaste sister of the revengers is a chess figure whose maneuvering or testing is meant to entertain. Evil is Tourneur's forte as it pierces to the quick. What he spreads before us, like a self-conscious craftsman delighting in his wares, almost hugging himself as he displays them, is a disinterested panoply of evil. Were we to recoil, as from the blinding of old Gloucester or Oedipus the King, we should frustrate his purpose. He wants us to attest to the harmony of the design. In this harmony he creates, murderous egoism is the common chord. It does not make for trepidation but applause.

The misogyny of *Hamlet* is corrosive. In Tourneur it is a flattering unction. Wives are made to go to bed and feed. Never tell a woman a secret overnight: your doctor may find it in the urinal in the morning. Any kindred, next to the rim of the sister, is men's meat in these days. Ford will make the reservation obsolete.

From the tragedy of blood, as opposed to the tragedy of terror like THE DUCHESS OF MALFI and *King Lear*, real flesh and blood are resolutely excluded. What Vendice calls "sweet occasions" take precedence. Their contriving, as in comedy, is an intellectual exercise. The Revenger, exclaiming pleasantly, "sa, sa, thump" as he stabs the old Duke, is committing violence on a mannequin. Comparison is proper to the machinations of Barabas and Ithamore in THE JEW OF MALTA. In either case, the right response is jocularity. Summing up his villainy for the benefit of those who are still left alive, Vendice observes complacently, "'Twas somewhat witty carried." The auditors are supposed to agree. Of course this agreement is perverse. People are not to be treated as things. But that is how Tourneur treats them and so long as he holds us in the grip of his monstrous and dispassionate *jeu d'esprit*, it is hard to complain.

There is this endemic difficulty in founding one's art on sensation. With each electrifying triumph it is necessary to step up the voltage, as the sensibilities of the audience grow progressively more jaded. Ford in *The Broken Heart* mines sexual frustration to make a powerful if overheated play. Perhaps in the carnal love of a brother and sister a richer lode is potential? Colonel Bob Ingersoll, that whimsical agnostic, stands on the stump before a crowd of true believers and dares God to strike him dead. Consternation reigns. But where does the blasphemer go from there? What is horrifying to Preston and Kyd is already old hat to Marlowe and Tourneur and embarrassing to James Shirley, to whom the obsequies of the drama are entrusted. The tragedy of blood, like an insatiable cormorant, preys on itself.

Well before the mid-seventeenth century, the distinction has begun to blur between the burgeoning horrors enacted on the London stage, which still claims title to be the custodian of form, and the haphazard carnage of the bear pit and the cock pit and the bull ring, all of them contiguous to the old Globe Theater in Southwark. Tragedy originates in these squalid places, down there on the bestial floor, and is always in danger of reverting to its origins. As the saving gulf is obliterated between art and life, dumb animals do not suffice any longer to slake the taste for blood. Men and women are gored and baited and tossed on the horns.

The Unnatural Combat, the title Massinger chooses in dramatizing the hideous tale of the Cenci, is the right generic title for the drama in the years of its decline. The Great Rebellion of the seventeenth century, which culminates in the beheading of the King—life imitating art—is generally represented as putting period to Renaissance tragedy. It only administers the *coup de grâce*.

Comedy dies harder and is still flourishing in England long after the Protector and his Presbyterian killjoys have compelled the closing of all theaters. That is partly because comedy, even at its highest pitch in Shakespeare and Jonson, does not require the participation of human beings in the round, who seem to act out their story independent of the god from the machine. In Renaissance comedy, as in the morality plays whence it derives, the protagonists are "all frail." It is up to the playwright to conduct them to salvation. To a degree he also is treating people as things.

Sometimes Shakespeare belies the proposition. Falstaff is comic, and autonomous. Pistol, Nym, and Bardolph are, however, "humorous" characters, not more voluntaristic than Jonson's Bobadil or Beaumont's Merrythought or Touchwood Senior in Middleton's A CHASTE MAID IN CHEAPSIDE. Mostly, Shakespeare is assimilated to his contemporaries in the making of comedy. Like the rest, he is Augustinian or Calvinistic in his psychology. By fiat he arranges that "tempests are kind and salt waves fresh in love!" The denouement to which he treats us—saying, in effect, "what you will"—is almost always a little cursory, it is even faintly contemptuous. "The man shall have his mare again, and all shall be well." But this negligent saying is instinct with affection—here he takes leave of Augustine and Calvin—for the aberrant characters who are in the playwright's charge, for the world these characters inhabit.

The Comedy of Humors is the agreed-on domicile for characters whose innate bias or want of sufficiency incline them to "run all one way." Over this domicile, Ben Jonson is supposed to preside. But Renaissance comedy from the beginning, and once more on its recrudescence in the late seventeenth century, is essentially the comedy of psychological determinism—or say, to be less emphatic: the capacity of characters envisaged by Marston and Chapman and Massinger is likely to be exhausted in the names these playwrights assign them. The substantiality of Allworth or George Downright in Jonson's *Everyman in His Humor* or Mr. Haircut in Shirley's comedy *The Lady of Pleasure* is not more in question than that of Abstinence or Chastity in *The Castle of Perseverance*. This suggests that the play as a total congeries is more than the cartoons it assembles and stakes out its claim to be real in ways independent of conventional reality.

Jonson, after Shakespeare, is the premier comic playwright of the Renaissance. But he is not *sui generis*, except in point of talent. This is not to blink the surpassing greatness of plays like VOLPONE, THE ALCHEMIST, EPICOENE, BARTHOLOMEW FAIR. Only it is to locate them.

Jonson's comedies are normative as character is fined down, normative also as they give their allegiance less to life than art. Mosca the fly is artistic as he fashions "the foxtrap," Jonson as he is the rhetorician par excellence. The hyperbolic speeches of Volpone and Sir Epicure Mammon are not accessible to traditional criticism, which is always talking about truth to life. In Jonson's plays, we are proffered a golden alternative. Villainy is transmogrified by language, and so moral judgment is effaced. Lovewit in THE ALCHEMIST speaks for us all: "I love a teeming wit as I love my nourishment."

Bitter business is pervasive in Jonson, and denotative of Jacobean comedy as a kind. Compare Chapman in THE WIDOW'S TEARS. But as the play is a convention that abides by its own set of rules, the acrimony does not infect, at least it does not cancel the humor. The given in VOLPONE is the ancient game of legacy-hunting. Already the Romans have a name for it: *captatio*. The beauty of the game is that it engages the intellect alone.

The dramatis personae who figure in this game are incapable of suffering. If we prick them, they do not bleed. It is a source of relief to us and insures that aroused emotion does not distort the cold brilliance of the playwright's design.

In Elizabethan refurbishings of the old biblical drama, like Lodge and Greene's A LOOKING GLASS FOR LONDON AND ENGLAND, design means *parti pris*. The authors are jealous of our salvation. Anyway, that is what they want us to think. Design in Jonson, as mostly in the comic dramatists of the Jacobean and Caroline periods, is consummated in the enacting of an amoral conflict between knaves and fools. By custom, Jonson is designated a satirist who scourges our vices with a view to correcting them. It is more nearly just to present him as a savage ironist who sees and dramatizes social intercourse as "little more than the crimes, follies, and misfortunes of mankind." Perhaps in the ending of his plays vice is punished. If virtue is not often triumphant, that is because it is in scanty supply. More impressive and more pertinent is the hoisting of the engineer with his own petard. Like the villainous Subtle—but who dwells on the villainy?—Jonson aims to "blow up gamester after gamester, As they do [fire]crackers in a puppet-play."

Because Jonson is writing comedy, we laugh. Because a moral is incumbent upon him, he provides it. But the moral is *pro forma*. Are we edified by the conclusion of THE ALCHEMIST? The "moral" of VOLPONE is not that money is the root of all evil—a prescriptive saying, in its implication—but that "Money is the world's soul." Jonson, seeing so much, is satisfied to report. The fun is in the verifying of the observation. No sequitur follows.

In the illegitimate form known as tragicomedy, prescriptive sayings abound. So do salacity, melancholy posturing (always mixed judiciously with mirth), horror (but always nipped in the bud). The playwright is not reporting, like Jonson, but confecting. His confection is various, it is also bland. The idea is to insure that everyone is satisfied, concurrently that no one is offended. Tragicomedy, says Fletcher, who is its most adroit exponent, "is not so called in respect of mirth and killing but in respect it wants deaths, which is enough to make it no tragedy, yet brings some near it, which is enough to make it no comedy." The definition, as it is translated to fact, enables the audience to have its cake and eat it.

The greatest writers of the Renaissance, and not only in England, seem to be paying homage to this dubious aesthetic. Characteristically, their art is a hybrid art as it yokes together genres or kinds that by convention are disparate. (It is the same in the art of their medieval forebears.) The result is a repertory of tragic and comic drama that is still sustaining us, four hundred years later. The result is not really surprising if, like Shakespeare in *The Two Noble Kinsmen*, one is taking for his pattern the crazy quilt that is our common experience. Truth to life, read prosaically, read myopically, is just as inapposite here as in the enameled verses of Ben Jonson. If "God's own truth is life"—what the poet Patrick Kavanagh asks us to accept—the equivalence will include "even the grotesque shapes of its foulest fire."

In *The Two Noble Kinsmen*, perhaps in *Henry VIII*, Fletcher collaborates with Shakespeare. (That is the conventional view, although it has been questioned.) When he goes it alone, as in the tragicomic *Philaster*, he sets himself to give us all the gloom of *Hamlet* but titivated with a happy ending. He also is making a hybrid but not as he is looking at life. His eye is on the box office.

The waning of dramatic integrity—as the drama of the Renaissance, like any other phenomenon in fee to time, moves downward to entropy—is not, however, to be read in terms of cupidity. The drama is in straits—so is the novel, so is pictorial art—as it eschews mimetic representation in favor of verisimilitude, which is truth to life conceived simplistically. With respect to the tragedy of blood, the point need not be labored. But the same point is unexpectedly tenable of elegant diversions like the pastoral and the masque. Bric-a-brac is "real" and so are gouts of blood. For each, the formula goes: the more real, the less lifelike.

Lyly, who expunges as he can every vestige of corporality from his plays, is verging—sequentially—on the writing of pastoral; so is Peele in *The Arraignment of Paris*, a rarefied composition and hence contrasting nicely with the horrors Peele indulges in his *Battle of Alcazar*. Daniel, taking as a model Guarini's *Pastor Fido*, than which no play was ever less in debt to reality, disposes mock shepherds in an artificial landscape. He is making good our flight to Arcadia or Eden's garden before the fall. Fletcher, in *The Faithful Shepherdess*, as he senses our growing ennui (for once that old chestnut, the "Jacobean temper," has its uses), so attenuates flesh and blood and probability that we need never advert to the vexatious business which is life outside the playhouse.

But exactly as real business is attenuated, the simulacrum of real business is enlarged. What we see is

nonsense, Fletcher's chastely erotic heroine who lives beside her lover's tomb, but this nonsense is presented with meticulous attention to detail. That is how the bucolic Peele and the sanguinary Peele come together. The common denominator is adherence to the truth that abides in superficies.

The fascination with this truth explains the vogue of the masque, a courtly entertainment excelling in novel and spectacular representation and relegating the drama, which one wants to distinguish from "theater," to the role of a picture frame. Jonson, who is preeminent as a writer of masques, dislikes the relegating and says so. His collaborator, the designer and architect Inigo Jones, dismisses the protest. As he is constant to the bent of his genius, Jones is right. But the vindicating of that genius is the death of the play, which dwindles to a production. Jonson, composing masques for the court of King James, is still primarily a playwright. A generation later, Milton writes *Comus* and calls it a masque. But Milton is wholecloth a poet.

The contention of genuine drama with other and inimical forms of entertainment is resolved or stifled in the closing of the theaters. The resolution is on one side untimely. For the drama, even in the years of its decadence, is not wholly petrified and has in fact begun to quicken just as the ax is laid to the root. This quickening is manifest in the growth of social comedy. Shirley in HYDE PARK and in *The Lady of Pleasure* is writing social comedy as his attention is more to manners than to plot. The accenting or attending is auspicious for the future. In the history of the drama, nothing wholly dies. The present is renewed as it looks to the past; at the same time it makes ready its own supercession.

In the new kind of play, which Fletcher executes triumphantly in THE WILD-GOOSE CHASE, ancillary characters still approximate to straw men. The footboy who enters grumbling as the play begins is only the truculent servant of the *Commedia dell'arte*. The mechanical exercise that is the snaring of the wild goose is more on Fletcher's mind, as he is what he is, than the moral situation in which his feckless hero is involved.

But after all what we remember in the comedy of manners, in Fletcher as later in Congreve, is not the mathematics of plot. It is the dramatizing of the war of the sexes. The grace note in this warfare is verbal felicity. The play is a witful altercation between well-bred men and women. The arrogant bachelor who is the hero of the play is confirmed in his misogyny. English women are distasteful to him as their buttocks are narrow as pins. But the heroine who pursues him is not to be rejected altogether. Were he half tippled and in want of a woman, he might turn and peruse her.

On the confounding of the impudent Don Juan, Fletcher hangs his story. This story is engrossing as it delineates, not the artificial courtship and the inevitable, hence inconsequential, marriage of a *papier-maché* female and a little man on a wedding cake but the sexual and psychological relationship of a real man and woman. The heroine, like Shakespeare's Rosalind, is not crushed by her presumptive failure. "I shall live after it," she thinks. "Whilst I have meat and drink, love cannot starve me."

For the last time in the history of Renaissance drama, we participate in the miracle of transubstantiation. The word is made flesh. In the beginning, almost eight hundred years before, is the ending. Once more, the Real Presence is vouchsafed us.

To the iconoclastic temperament, whose hegemony is confirmed in the reign of King Charles, this Presence betokens perdition. Substantiality is a fiction. The proposition is urged with increasing virulence by the religious reformer as also by the scientist or new philosopher, who appeals from the world of phenomenal fact to the abstract Forms that lie behind it. "What man," the Puritan preacher inquires, "could bear to have either his beauty likened to a misshapen picture or himself called the idol of a man?" It is the question Plato raises and, from the side of science, Galileo and Descartes.

The drama is idolatrous as it prefers the mendacious or trivial thing—the misshapen picture that is the man in his habit as he lived—to the universal representation. For that reason, the drama is reprehended. Already in the reign of King James, a puritanical poet is admonishing its patrons for their willingness to "affect vain shadows and let slide The true substance as a thing unspied." But shadow and substance are turned upside down, as in the play by Paul Vincent Carroll.

Words in their ordinary acceptance are no help to us here. Shadows, like those that flit across the stage, are to be read as denoting corporality, which is not substantial but ephemeral. That is what is meant by representing the playgoer as abandoning himself to "vainglorious show." The language to which he listens is "wrapped up . . . in dark riddles," but not as it is difficult, rather as it deals in the lower case. To the connoisseur of generic resemblances, truth is better

perceived and more nearly itself as we thrust it forth "nakedly . . . without a covering."

The "player-like fashionist" who fills "the benches in taverns or theaters" is indifferent to truth or unable to perceive it. Like the owl at midday, he closes his eyes to the "light of the gospel which owls cannot see," preferring the refracted light of the playhouse. (We remember Plato's strictures on the Idols of the Cave.) His "partial love," says a covenanting minister, is "to a carnal liberty." The delimiting word is important.

By use and wont, we identify carnality with looseness. The seventeenth century decides that this identifying is misapprehension. Carnality means solidity. Etymologically, there is precedent for that. The real thing is ideal, what was never in nature. Carnality does not argue moral corruption, or not critically. It argues intellectual corruption. We have come to the heart of the matter in assessing the rising protest against the stage.

The playwright puts us out of the way of truth. But the "duty of a legislator," as Plato instructs the new draconians who inaugurate the kingdom of heaven on earth, "is and always will be to teach you the truth." In fulfillment of this duty, the drama is disfranchised. "Whereas," runs the pitiless and benevolent edict of September 2, 1642,

> the distracted state of England, threatened with a cloud of blood by a civil war, calls for all possible means to appease and avert the wrath of God, it is therefore thought fit and ordained by the Lords and Commons in this parliament assembled that, while these set causes and set times of humiliation continue, public stage plays shall cease and be forborne.

So there comes to an end the greatest period in the history of the English drama, perhaps in the history of the world. R. A. F.

Cyril Tourneur

[c. 1580–1626]

THE REVENGER'S TRAGEDY

WHAT little is known of the life of Cyril Tourneur is recapitulated, perhaps at greater length than ascertainable fact allows, in Allardyce Nicoll's edition of the collected work (1929). The first notice of Tourneur is the publication in 1600 of a satirical poem entitled *The Transformed Metamorphosis*. THE REVENGER'S TRAGEDY appeared in 1607. A year later, the printer George Eld, using the same sheets but a different title page, brought out another issue, which advertises the play as having been "sundry times acted by the King's Majesty's Servants." Lineating the text of the play poses a problem, for the compositor was evidently indifferent to distinctions between prose and verse. Either medium seems tenable in passages like I.ii, 133–42—Spurio's speech—or in the dialogue between Lussorioso and Hippolito on the entrance of the disguised Vindice in II. ii.

THE REVENGER'S TRAGEDY is in straitened compass a great play, among the major successes of Renaissance drama and still powerful in performance today. The hard and macabre jocosity, the cruel fleering comedy—more cruel as it is wittily incongruous—secure Tourneur's position as one of the most gifted of the sons of Ben Jonson, in spirit if not in fact, and as the legitimate heir of Marlowe in his character of deliberate and self-delighted assaulter of our sensibilities. Perhaps THE REVENGER'S TRAGEDY wears a little, given this unremitting assault. Though Tourneur echoes and imitates Shakespeare, it is the surface of Shakespeare's plays rather than the humanity pervasive in them that engages his fascinated attention. But he is not committed to high tragedy, despite the promise of the title. His metier is the horror play, and in this kind he is unexcelled.

Tourneur's second well-known play, *The Atheist's Tragedy*, an inferior composition, was entered under his name in the Stationers' Register for 1611 and published in that year. Evidently a third play followed.

This was *The Nobleman* (designated as by Tourneur in Stationers' Register, 15 February 1611–12), which no longer is extant. It is known that Tourneur was employed by the powerful Cecil family (one of whose members he delineated in a "Character" sketch) and by Sir Francis Vere (whose death he lamented in banal couplets). He saw military service in the Netherlands and was a participant in the famous Cadiz voyage against the Spaniards. Falling sick aboard ship, he was put off at Kinsale, where he died in February 1626.

Possible influences on THE REVENGER'S TRAGEDY include the plays of John Marston, Middleton's comedies of intrigue, perhaps a tragedy by the hack writer Henry Chettle, surely Marlowe's violent farce THE JEW OF MALTA, and more surely still the plays of Shakespeare, especially *Hamlet*. Analogous stories (from William Painter's *Palace of Pleasure*, 1566–67; and the *Ethiopian History* of Heliodorus, translated by Thomas Underdown in 1587) are reprinted as appendixes by R. A. Foakes in his edition (1966) of the play.

In the late nineteenth century various scholars began to deny Tourneur's authorship of THE REVENGER'S TRAGEDY and, largely on the basis of style, to put forward Webster or Marston or Middleton as author. It is true that Tourneur's name was not linked to the play until the second half of the seventeenth century, true also that the play was entered in the Stationers' Register (7 October 1607) with Middleton's comedy *A Trick to Catch the Old One*. The case for Middleton has been supported by his statement that he had satisfied a debt to the manager of the Queen's Revels Company at Blackfriars, Robert Keysar, by turning over to Keysar in 1606 a tragedy called *The Viper and Her Brood*. This play is said to be THE REVENGER'S TRAGEDY. But even the most persuasive modern proponent of Middleton acknowledges that the THE REVENGER'S TRAGEDY has "not been proved beyond question" to be his work. As that is so, best to leave it to Cyril Tourneur. R. A. F.

The Revenger's Tragedy

DRAMATIS PERSONÆ

THE DUKE
LUSSURIOSO,[1] the Duke's son and heir
SPURIO,[2] a bastard son of the Duke
AMBITIOSO,[3] the Duchess' eldest son
SUPERVACUO,[4] the Duchess' second son
YOUNGER SON of the Duchess
VINDICE,[5] a revenger, also called
   PIATO[6] in disguise } brothers of Castiza
HIPPOLITO, also called CARLO

ANTONIO } Nobles
PIERO
DONDOLO,[7] a servant of Gratiana
Nobles, Judges, Gentlemen, Officers, Prison Keeper,
   Servants
THE DUCHESS
CASTIZA[8]
GRATIANA,[9] mother of Castiza

ACT ONE

SCENE ONE

Enter VINDICE, *the* DUKE, DUCHESS,
LUSSURIOSO, *her son,* SPURIO, *the bastard,*
with a train, pass over the stage with torchlight.

Vin. Duke: royal lecher: go, gray-haired adultery,
And thou his son, as impious steeped as he:
And thou his bastard true-begot in evil:
And thou his duchess that will do[1] with devil:
Four excellent characters![2]—oh, that marrowless age
Would stuff the hollow bones with damned desires,
And 'stead of heat kindle infernal fires
Within the spendthrift veins of a dry[3] duke,
A parched and juiceless luxur.[4] O God! one
That has scarce blood enough to live upon,   10
And he to riot it like a son and heir?[5]
Oh, the thought of that
Turns my abusèd heart-strings into fret.[6]
Thou sallow picture[7] of my poisoned love,
My study's ornament, thou shell of death,
Once the bright face of my betrothèd lady,
When life and beauty naturally filled out
These ragged imperfections;
When two heaven-pointed diamonds were set
In those unsightly[8] rings—then 'twas a face   20
So far beyond the artificial shine
Of any woman's bought[9] complexion
That the uprightest man—if such there be,
That sin but seven times a day—broke custom
And made up eight with looking after her.
Oh, she was able to ha' made a usurer's son
Melt all his patrimony[10] in a kiss,
And what his father fifty years told[11]
To have consumed, and yet his suit been cold.
But oh accursèd palace!   30
Thee when thou wert appareled in thy flesh,
The old duke poisoned,

Because thy purer part would not consent
Unto his palsy-lust: for old men lustful
Do show like young men angry—eager, violent,
Outbid like their limited performances[12]—
Oh, 'ware an old man hot and vicious:
Age as in gold, in lust is covetous.
Vengeance, thou murder's quit-rent,[13] and whereby
Thou showest thyself tenant to tragedy,   40
Oh, keep thy day, hour, minute, I beseech,
For those thou hast determined.[14] Hum, who e'er
   knew
Murder unpaid, faith give revenge her due
She's kept touch hitherto—be merry, merry,
Advance thee, o thou terror[15] to fat folks
To have their costly three-piled[16] flesh worn off

DRAMATIS PERSONÆ
[1] *Lussurioso:* Luxurious, i.e., lecherous.
[2] *Spurio:* Bastard.   [3] *Ambitioso:* Ambitious.
[4] *Supervacuo:* Vain, foolish.
[5] *Vindice:* Revenger of wrongs and abuses.
[6] *Piato:* Dish served at a feast; a covered or "plated"
thing.   [7] *Dondolo:* Fool.
[8] *Castiza:* Chastity.   [9] *Gratiana:* Grace.

I.i.
[1] *do:* copulate.
[2] *characters:* not "persons" but alluding to the moral
character or nature they bear.
[3] *dry:* impotent through age and disease.
[4] *luxur:* lecher.
[5] *son and heir:* given proverbially to riotous behavior.
[6] *fret:* a ring of gut on a stringed musical instrument to
control the fingering.   [7] *picture:* the skull he is holding.
[8] *unsightly:* unseeing; also in our sense.
[9] *bought:* as with cosmetics.
[10] *patrimony:* inherited property.
[11] *told:* counted (in coin).
[12] *Outbid . . . performances:* The angry youth is "limited"
as he is immature; the old man as he is impotent.
[13] *quit-rent:* requital; literally, rent paid by a tenant to a
landlord instead of services.   [14] *determined:* judged.
[15] *terror:* again addressing the skull.
[16] *three-piled:* like costly, hence thick velvet.

As bare as this—for banquets, ease and laughter
Can make great [17] men, as greatness goes by clay,
But wise men, little, are more great than they.

Enter [his] brother HIPPOLITO.

Hip. Still sighing o'er death's vizard? [18]
Vin.   Brother,
   welcome,   50
What comfort bringest thou? How go things at court?
Hip. In silk and silver, brother: never braver. [19]
Vin.   Puh,
Thou playest upon my meaning, prithee say
Has that bald madam, Opportunity, [20]
Yet thought upon's, speak, are we happy yet?
Thy wrongs and mine are for one scabbard fit.
Hip. It may prove happiness?
Vin.   What is't may prove?
Give me to taste.
Hip.   Give me your hearing then.
You know my place at court.
Vin.   Ay, the duke's chamber.
But 'tis a marvel thou'rt not turned out yet!   60
Hip. Faith, I have been shoved at, but 'twas still my
   hap [21]
To hold by the duchess' skirt, you guess at that,
Whom such a coat keeps up can ne'er fall flat—
But to the purpose.
Last evening predecessor unto this,
The duke's son warily inquired for me,
Whose pleasure I attended: he began
By policy [22] to open and unhusk me
About the time and common rumor:
But I had so much wit to keep my thoughts   70
Up in their built houses, yet afforded him
An idle satisfaction without danger,
But the whole aim and scope of his intent
Ended in this: conjuring me in private
To seek some strange-digested [23] fellow forth
Of ill-contented nature, either disgraced

---

[17] *great:* punning ironically on physical size.
[18] *vizard:* face, mask.   [19] *braver:* more splendid.
[20] *Opportunity:* or "occasion," depicted as bald behind;
hence, one had better take her by the forelock—instantly.
[21] *hap:* chance.   [22] *policy:* craft.
[23] *strange-digested:* oddly made: ill sorting.
[24] *grooms:* servants.   [25] *blood:* mettlesome fellow.
[26] *base-coined:* counterfeit; perhaps, by analogy, "illegitimate."   [27] *reach:* understand.
[28] *should:* would have to.   [29] *spoke:* described.
[30] *put on:* disguise myself as.
[31] *right:* proper (for the times).
[32] *prefer:* seek to advance.   [33] *foretop:* forelock.
[34] *mole:* which destroys a lawn by working beneath it, as
the "French disease" or syphilis causes one's hair to fall out.
[35] *habit:* costume.   [36] *quaintly:* cleverly.
[37] *coin:* counterfeit.
[38] *But . . . belief:* Vindice believes completely in the integrity of his mother and sister, with one exception—that,
as they are women, they are gullible.
[39] *Carlo:* known otherwise in the play as Hippolito.
[40] *Italy:* trisyllabic.
[41] *law's a woman:* as in the familiar image of Justice,
blindfolded, and holding scales and sword.
[42] *compelled:* forced (to live).

In former times, or by new grooms [24] displaced
Since his stepmother's nuptials: such a blood, [25]
A man that were for evil only good;
To give you the true word some base-coined [26] pander.
Vin. I reach [27] you, for I know his heat is such,   81
Were there as many concubines as ladies
He would not be contained, he must fly out.
I wonder how ill-featured, vile proportioned
That one should [28] be, if she were made for woman,
Whom at the insurrection of his lust
He would refuse for once: heart, I think none;
Next to a skull, though more unsound than one,
Each face he meets he strongly dotes upon.
Hip. Brother y'ave truly spoke [29] him!   90
He knows not you, but I'll swear you know him.
Vin. And therefore I'll put on [30] that knave for once,
And be a right [31] man then, a man o' the time,
For to be honest is not to be i'the world.
Brother, I'll be that strange composèd fellow.
Hip. And I'll prefer [32] you, brother.
Vin.   Go to, then,
The smallest advantage fattens wrongèd men.
It may point out occasion; if I meet her
I'll hold her by the foretop [33] fast enough
Or like the French mole [34] heave up hair and all.   100
I have a habit [35] that will fit it quaintly [36]—
Here comes our mother.

[Enter GRATIANA *and* CASTIZA.*]*

Hip.   And sister.
Vin.   We must coin. [37]
Women are apt you know to take false money,
But I dare stake my soul for these two creatures,
Only excuse excepted, that they'll swallow
Because their sex is easy in belief. [38]
Grat. What news from court, son Carlo? [39]
Hip.   Faith,
   mother,
'Tis whispered there the duchess' youngest son
Has played a rape on lord Antonio's wife.
Grat. On that religious lady!   110
Cas. Royal blood: monster! he deserves to die,
If Italy [40] had no more hopes but he.
Vin. Sister y'ave sentenced most direct, and true,
The law's a woman, [41] and would she were you.
Mother, I must take leave of you.
Grat. Leave for what?
Vin.   I intend speedy travel.
Hip. That he does, madam.
Grat.   Speedy indeed!
Vin. For since my worthy father's funeral,
My life's unnatural to me, e'en compelled, [42]
As if I lived now when I should be dead.   120
Grat. Indeed he was a worthy gentleman,
Had his estate been fellow to his mind.
Vin. The duke did much deject him.
Grat.   Much?
Vin.   Too much.
And through disgrace oft smothered in his spirit
When it would mount, surely I think he died
Of discontent, the nobleman's consumption.

Grat. Most sure he did.

Vin.   Did he? 'Lack,—you know all,
You were his midnight secretary.[43]

Grat.   No,
He was too wise to trust me with his thoughts.

Vin. [*Aside*] I' faith, then, father, thou wast wise
    indeed,   130
"Wives are but made to go to bed and feed."
Come mother, sister: you'll bring me onward, brother?

Hip. I will.

Vin. [*Aside*] I'll quickly turn into another.
                            Exeunt.

[I.ii]

Enter the old DUKE, LUSSURIOSO, *his son, the*
DUCHESS, [SPURIO], *the bastard, the Duchess'*
two sons AMBITIOSO *and* SUPERVACUO, *the third,*
her youngest, brought out with Officers *for the rape,*
[*and*] *two* Judges.

Duke. Duchess, it is your youngest son, we're sorry,
His violent act has e'en drawn blood of honor
And stained our honors,
Thrown ink upon the forehead of our state
Which envious spirits will dip their pens into
After our death, and blot us in our tombs.
For that which would seem treason in our lives
Is laughter when we're dead. Who dares now whisper
That dares not then speak out, and e'en proclaim
With loud words and broad pens[1] our closest[2] shame.

1 Judge. Your Grace hath spoke like to your silver[3]
    years,   11
Full of confirmed gravity; for what is it to have
A flattering false insculption[4] on a tomb
And in men's hearts reproach? The 'boweled[5] corpse
May be seared[6] in, but, with free tongue I speak:
The faults of great men through their sear clothes
    break.

Duke. They do, we're sorry for't, it is our fate,
To live in fear and die to live in hate.
I leave him to your sentence: doom[7] him, lords,
The fact[8] is great—whilst I sit by and sigh.   20

Duch. My gracious lord, I pray be merciful,
Although his trespass far exceed his years;
Think him to be your own as I am yours,
Call him not son-in-law:[9] the law I fear
Will fall too soon upon his name and him.
Temper his fault with pity.

Lus.   Good my lord,
Then 'twill not taste so bitter and unpleasant
Upon the judge's palate; for offenses
Gilt o'er with mercy show like fairest women,
Good only for their beauties, which washed off,   30
No sin is uglier.

Amb.   I beseech your grace,
Be soft and mild, let not relentless Law
Look with an iron forehead on our brother.

Spur. He yields small comfort yet [*Aside*]—hope he
    shall die;
And if a bastard's wish might stand force,

Would all the court were turned into a corse.

Duch. No pity yet? Must I rise fruitless then—.
A wonder[10] in a woman—are my knees
Of such low metal[11] that without respect—

1 Judge. Let the offender stand forth,   40
'Tis the duke's pleasure that impartial doom[12]
Shall take first hold of his unclean attempt.[13]
A rape! why 'tis the very core of lust,
Double adultery.

Young. Son. So, sir.

2 Judge.   And which was worse,
Committed on the lord Antonio's wife,
That general honest[14] lady. Confess my lord:
What moved you to't?

Young. Son.   Why, flesh and blood, my lord:
What should move men unto a woman else?

Lus. Oh, do not jest[15] thy doom, trust not an ax
Or sword too far; the law is a wise serpent   50
And quickly can beguile thee of thy life.
Though marriage only has made thee my brother,
I love thee so far: play not with thy death.

Young. Son. I thank you, troth,[16] good admonitions,
    faith,
If I'd the grace now to make use of them.

1 Judge. That lady's name has spread such a fair
    wing
Over all Italy that if our tongues
Were sparing toward the fact, judgment itself
Would be condemned and suffer in men's thoughts.

Young. Son. Well then, 'tis done, and it would please
    me well   60
Were it to do again. Sure she's a goddess,
For I'd no power to see her and to live;[17]
It falls out true in this for I must die.
Her beauty was ordained to be my scaffold,
And yet methinks I might be easier ceased;
My fault being sport, let me but die in jest.

1 Judge. This be the sentence—

Duch. Oh, keep't upon your tongue, let it not slip,
Death too soon steals out of a lawyer's lip,
Be not so cruel-wise.

1 Judge.   Your grace must pardon us,   70
'Tis but the justice of the law.

Duch.   The law
Is grown more subtle than a woman should be.

---

43 *secretary:* keeper of secrets.

I.ii.

1 *broad pens:* open and explicit reports.

2 *closest:* most secret.

3 *silver:* alluding to his white hair.

4 *insculption:* carved tribute.

5 *'boweled:* disemboweled (to preserve from decay).

6 *seared:* sealed, wrapped in waterproof cerements or graveclothes (as in the next line).   7 *doom:* judge.

8 *fact:* crime.   9 *son-in-law:* stepson.

10 *wonder:* that a woman should rise (swell as with child) and yet remain fruitless (childless).

11 *metal:* mettle, worth.   12 *doom:* judgment.

13 *attempt:* assault.   14 *general honest:* always chaste.

15 *jest:* joke about.   16 *troth:* believe it.

17 *live:* go on living; with "die" (have sexual intercourse) as implicit.

Spur. [*Aside*] Now, now he dies, rid 'em away.
Duch. [*Aside*] Oh, what it is to have an old-cool duke
To be as slack in tongue as in performance.[18]
1 Judge. Confirmed, this be the doom irrevocable.
Duch. Oh!
1 Judge.   Tomorrow early—
Duch.   Pray be abed, my lord.
1 Judge. Your grace much wrongs[19] yourself.
Amb.   No,
    'tis that tongue,
Your too much right does do us too much wrong.
1 Judge. Let that offender—
Duch.   Live, and be in health.
1 Judge. Be on a scaffold—
Duke.   Hold, hold, my lord.
Spur. [*Aside*]   Pox
    on't,   81
What makes my dad speak now?
Duke. We will defer the judgment till next sitting,
In the meantime let him be kept close prisoner:
Guard, bear him hence.
Amb. [*Aside*]   Brother, this makes for[20] thee,
Fear not, we'll have a trick to set thee free.
Young. Son. [*Aside*] Brother, I will expect it from
    you both,
And in that hope I rest.
Sup.   Farewell, be merry.
                    Exit [YOUNGER SON] *with a guard.*
Spur. Delayed, deferred, nay then, if judgment have
Cold blood, flattery and bribes will kill it.   90
Duke. About it then, my lords, with your best
    powers,
More serious business calls upon our hours.
                        Exeunt; manet[21] DUCHESS.
Duch. Was't ever known step-duchess was so mild
And calm as I? Some now would plot his death
With easy doctors, those loose-living men,
And make his withered grace fall to his grave
And keep church better.[22]
Some second wife would do this, and dispatch
Her double loathèd lord at meat or sleep.
Indeed 'tis true, an old man's twice a child.   100
Mine cannot speak! one of his single words
Would quite have freed my youngest dearest son

---

[18] *performance*: sexual performance.
[19] *wrongs*: dishonors.   [20] *makes for*: sustains.
[21] *L*: remains.
[22] *keep church better*: as by being buried in it.
[23] *kill . . . forehead*: as by giving him horns.
[24] *hatted*: lower class (because women in that station were compelled by statute to wear hats to support their manufacture).   [25] *respects*: considerations.
[26] *hard question*: difficult to answer.
[27] *he . . . windows*: he was tall enough when on horseback to look over the tops of windows into houses, half shuttered as for a holiday.   [28] *'light*: alight.
[29] *penthouse*: upper part of an Elizabethan house, which hung over the street.
[30] *check the signs*: knock against the sign boards (including "barbers' basins"—shaving dishes, below) that tradesmen hung before their shops.
[31] *set . . . off*: once you get started (like a beggar on horseback), you'll never stop.   [32] *bid fair*: make a good try.

From death or durance, and have made him walk
With a bold foot upon the thorny law,
Whose prickles should bow under him; but 'tis not:
And therefore wedlock faith shall be forgot.
I'll kill him in his forehead,[23] hate there feed—
That wound is deepest though it never bleed;
And here comes he whom my heart points unto,
His bastard son, but my love's true-begot;   110
Many a wealthy letter have I sent him
Swelled up with jewels, and the timorous man
Is yet but coldly kind;

                        [*Enter* SPURIO.]

That jewel's mine that quivers in his ear,
Mocking his master's chillness and vain fear—
H'as spied me now.
Spur.   Madam? Your grace so private?
My duty on your hand.
Duch. Upon my hand, sir Troth, I think you'd fear?
To kiss my hand, too, if my lip stood there.
Spur. Witness I would not, madam.

                            [*He kisses her.*]

Duch.   'Tis a wonder,
For ceremony has made many fools.   121
It is as easy way unto a duchess
As to a hatted[24] dame, if her love answer,
But that by timorous honors, pale respects,[25]
Idle degrees of fear, men make their ways
Hard of themselves. What have you thought of me?
Spur. Madam, I ever think of you, in duty,
Regard and—
Duch.   Puh, upon my love I mean.
Spur. I would 'twere love, but 't 'as a fouler name
Than lust; you are my father's wife, your grace may
    guess now   130
What I could call it.
Duch.   Why th'art his son but falsely,
'Tis a hard question[26] whether he begot thee.
Spur. I' faith, 'tis true, too; I'm an uncertain man
Of more uncertain woman; may be his groom
O' the stable begot me—you know I know not.
He could ride a horse well, a shrewd suspicion—marry!
He was wondrous tall, he had his length, i' faith,
For peeping over half-shut holiday windows:[27]
Men would desire him 'light.[28] When he was afoot
He made a goodly show under a penthouse,[29]   140
And when he rid his hat would check the signs[30]
And clatter barbers' basins.
Duch.   Nay, set you a-horseback
    once
You'll ne'er 'light off.[31]
Spur.   Indeed, I am a beggar.
Duch. That's more the sign th' art great—but to our
    love.
Let it stand firm both in thought and mind
That the duke was thy father: as no doubt then
He bid fair[32] for't, thy injury is the more;
For had he cut thee a right diamond,
Thou had'st been next set in the dukedom's ring,
When his worn self like age's easy slave   150

Had dropped out of the collet [33] into the grave.
What wrong can equal this? Canst thou be tame
And think upon't?
    Spur.   No, mad and think upon't.
    Duch. Who would not be revenged of [34] such a father,
E'en in the worst way? I would thank that sin
That could most injury [35] him, and be in league with it.
Oh, what a grief 'tis that a man should live
But once i' the world, and then to live a bastard,
The curse o' the womb, the thief of nature,
Begot against the seventh commandment,   160
Half damned in the conception by the justice
Of that unbribed everlasting law.
    Spur. Oh, I'd a hot-backed devil to [36] my father.
    Duch. Would not this mad e'en patience, make blood
      rough? [37]
Who but an eunuch would not sin, his bed
By one false minute disinherited?
    Spur. Ay, there's the vengeance that my birth was
      wrapped in,
I'll be revenged for all: now hate begin,
I'll call foul incest but a venial sin.
    Duch. Cold still: in vain then must a duchess woo?
    Spur. Madam, I blush to say what I will do.   171
    Duch. Thence flew sweet comfort, earnest [38] and
      farewell.

                    [She kisses him.]

    Spur. Oh, one incestuous kiss picks open hell.
    Duch. Faith, now, old duke, my vengeance shall
      reach high,
I'll arm thy brow with woman's heraldry. [39]

                            Exit.

    Spur. Duke, thou did'st do me wrong and by thy act
Adultery is my nature;
Faith, if the truth were known I was begot
After some gluttonous dinner—some stirring [40] dish
Was my first father; when deep healths went round
And ladies' cheeks were painted red with wine,   181
Their tongues as short [41] and nimble as their heels,
Uttering words sweet and thick; and when they rose
Were merrily disposed to fall again. [42]
In such a whispering and withdrawing hour,
When base male bawds kept sentinel at stair-head
Was I stolen [43] softly—oh, damnation met
The sin of feasts, drunken adultery.
I feel it swell me; my revenge is just,
I was begot in impudent wine and lust.   190
Stepmother, I consent to thy desires,
I love thy mischief well but I hate thee,
And those three cubs, thy sons, wishing confusion,
Death, and disgrace may be their epitaphs;
As for my brother, the duke's only son, [44]
Whose birth is more beholding to report
Than mine, and yet perhaps as falsely sown
—Women must not be trusted with their own—
I'll loose [45] my days upon him, hate all I!
Duke, on thy brow I'll draw my bastardy: 200
For indeed a bastard by nature should make cuckolds
Because he is the son of a cuckold maker.

                            Exit.

[I.iii]

    Enter VINDICE *and* HIPPOLITO, VINDICE *in*
    disguise to attend LUSSURIOSO, *the* Duke's *son.*

    Vin. What, brother, am I far enough from myself? [1]
    Hip. As if another man had been sent whole
Into the world and none wist [2] how he came.
    Vin. It will confirm me bold—the child o' the court;
Let blushes dwell i' the country. Impudence,
Thou goddess of the palace, mistress of mistresses,
To whom the costly-perfumed people pray,
Strike thou my forehead into dauntless marble,
Mine eyes to steady sapphires; turn my visage
And if I must needs glow let me blush inward   10
That this immodest season may not spy
That scholar in my cheeks, fool bashfulness,
That maid in the old time whose flush of grace
Would never suffer her to get good clothes. [3]
Our maids are wiser and are less ashamed—
Save Grace the bawd I seldom hear grace named!
    Hip. Nay, brother, you reach out o' the verge [4] now—

      [Enter LUSSURIOSO *attended by* Servants.]

'Sfoot, the duke's son! settle your looks.
    Vin. Pray let me not be doubted.
    Hip. My lord—
    Lus.   Hippolito?—Be absent, leave us.
                      [Exeunt Servants.]
    Hip. My lord, after long search, wary inquiries   21
And politic siftings [5] I made choice of yon fellow
Whom I guess rare [6] for many deep employments:
This our age swims within him; and if time [7]
Had so much hair I should take him for time,
He is so near kin to this present minute.
    Lus. 'Tis enough,
We thank thee: yet words are but great men's blanks; [8]
Gold though it be dumb does utter the best thanks.

                      [Gives him money.]

    Hip. Your plenteous honor—an excellent fellow, my
      lord.   30

---

[33] *collet:* setting for a precious stone.   [34] *of:* on.
[35] *injury:* injure.   [36] *to:* for.
[37] *make . . . rough:* rouse the blood to anger.
[38] *earnest:* of more to come.   [39] *woman's heraldry:* horns.
[40] *stirring:* stimulating.
[41] *short:* like "thick" (inarticulate from drink), below.
[42] *when . . . again:* they were ready to lie with one man after
another. Q "rise."   [43] *stolen:* counterfeited.
[44] *only son:* Lussurioso, the only legitimate son.
[45] *loose:* let loose (for mischief).

I.iii.
[1] *far . . . myself:* sufficiently disguised.
[2] *wist:* knew.
[3] *clothes:* inappropriate to Truth, which was depicted in
emblem literature as a naked woman.
[4] *out o' the verge:* beyond acceptable limits.
[5] *siftings:* assayings, close scrutiny.   [6] *rare:* excellent.
[7] *Time:* personified as bald except for the forelock and
hence to be seized without delay, like opportunity or occasion.
[8] *blanks:* documents not yet validated by a signature, and
so without value.

Lus. So, give us leave [9]—

                   [*Exit* HIPPOLITO.]

            Welcome, be not far off,

We must be better acquainted. Push,[10] be bold

With us, thy hand.

Vin.   With all my heart, i' faith!

How dost, sweet musk-cat?[11] When shall we lie

     together?

Lus. [*Aside*] Wondrous knave!

Gather him into boldness:[12] 'sfoot, the slave's

Already as familiar as an ague

And shakes me at his pleasure—Friend, I can

Forget myself in private, but elsewhere

I pray do you remember me.[13]   40

    Vin. Oh, very well, sir—I conster[14] myself saucy!

Lus. What hast been—of what profession?

Vin. A bone setter.

Lus.   A bone setter!

Vin.   A bawd, my lord,

One that sets bones together.

Lus.   Notable bluntness!

Fit, fit for me, e'en trained up to my hand.—

Thou hast been scrivener[15] to much knavery then?

    Vin. Fool[16] to abundance, sir; I have been witness

To the surrenders of a thousand virgins

And not so little;

I have seen patrimonies washed a-pieces,[17]   50

Fruit fields turned into bastards,[18]

And in a world of acres

Not so much dust due to the heir 'twas left to

As would well gravel[19] a petition.

    Lus. [*Aside*] Fine villain! troth, I like him

     wondrously,

He's e'en shaped for my purpose.—Then thou knowest

In the world strange lust?

Vin.   Oh, Dutch[20] lust! fulsome

     lust!

Drunken procreation, which begets so many drunkards;

Some father dreads not, gone to bed in wine,

To slide from the mother and cling the daughter-in-

     law;   60

Some uncles are adulterous with their nieces,

Brother with brothers' wives—oh, hour of incest!

Any kin now next to the rim[21] o' the sister

Is man's meat in these days, and in the morning,

When they are up and dressed and their mask on,

Who can perceive this, save that eternal eye

That sees through flesh and all? Well—if anything be

     damned

It will be twelve o'clock at night: that twelve

Will never 'scape;

It is the Judas of the hours, wherein   70

Honest salvation is betrayed to sin.

    Lus. In troth it is too; but let this talk glide.

It is our blood to err though hell gaped[22] loud:

Ladies know Lucifer fell, yet still are proud!

Now, sir, wert thou as secret as thou'rt subtle

And deeply fathomed into all estates,[23]

I would embrace thee for a near[24] employment,

And thou should'st swell in money and be able

To make lame beggars crouch to thee.

Vin.   My lord?

Secret? I ne'er had that disease o' the mother,[25]   80

I praise my father! why are men made close

But to keep thoughts in best? I grant you this:

Tell but some woman a secret over night,

Your doctor may find it in the urinal i' the morning;

But, my lord—

    Lus.   So, thou'rt confirmed in me[26]

And thus I enter[27] thee.

                              [*Gives him money.*]

Vin.   This Indian[28] devil

Will quickly enter any man: but a usurer,

He prevents[29] that by entering the devil first!

    Lus. Attend me, I am past my depth in lust

And I must swim or drown. All my desires   90

Are leveled at a virgin not far from court,

To whom I have conveyed by messenger

Many waxed lines[30] full of my neatest[31] spirit,

And jewels that were able to ravish her

Without the help of man: all which and more

She, foolish-chaste, sent back, the messengers

Receiving frowns for answers.

Vin.   Possible?

'Tis a rare phoenix whoe'er she be,

If your desires be such, she so repugnant:[32]

In troth, my lord, I'd be revenged and marry her.

    Lus. Push; the dowry of her blood[33] and of her

     fortunes   101

Are both too mean—good enough to be bad withal.

I'm one of that number can defend

Marriage is good; yet rather keep a friend.[34]

Give me my bed by stealth—there's true delight;

What breeds a loathing in't but night by night?

    Vin. A very fine religion!

    Lus.   Therefore thus:

I'll trust thee in the business of my heart

Because I see thee well experienced

In this luxurious[35] day wherein we breathe: 110

---

[9] *give us leave:* leave us.

[10] *Push:* Pish! (don't stand on ceremony).

[11] *musk-cat:* courtesan (because perfumed).

[12] *Gather . . . boldness:* There's no need to inspirit him.

[13] *remember me:* know me for the dignified person I am.

[14] *conster:* construe.   [15] *scrivener:* clerk, agent.

[16] *Fool:* Lackey, tool.

[17] *patrimonies . . . a-pieces:* inheritances dissipated.

[18] *Fruit . . . bastards:* (1) Sold for the maintaining of bastards; (2) True stock debased by being grafted or converted to fake.   [19] *gravel:* sand (to dry the ink).

[20] *Dutch:* The Dutch were proverbially "fulsome" or excessive in drinking, the prelude to lust.   [21] *rim:* womb.

[22] *gaped:* yawned.   [23] *estates:* kinds of people.

[24] *near:* closely concerning me.

[25] *disease . . . mother:* hysteria; hence, "talking too much."

[26] *confirmed in me:* made secure in my confidence.

[27] *enter:* write down; admit.

[28] *Indian:* silver and gold, mined in the Indies.

[29] *prevents:* anticipates.

[30] *waxed lines:* sealed lines; alternatively, hyperbolic messages, waxing of love.

[31] *neatest:* purest, as of wine ("spirit").

[32] *repugnant:* recalcitrant.   [33] *blood:* family.

[34] *friend:* mistress.   [35] *luxurious:* lecherous.

Go thou and with a smooth enchanting tongue
Bewitch her ears and cozen her of all grace;
Enter upon the portion of her soul,
Her honor, which she calls her chastity,
And bring it into expense,³⁶ for honesty
Is like a stock of money laid to sleep
Which, ne'er so little broke, does never keep.
  Vin. You have given it the tang,³⁷ i' faith, my lord;
Make known the lady to me and my brain
Shall swell with strange invention: I will move³⁸ it   120
Till I expire with speaking and drop down
Without a word to save me—but I'll work—
  Lus. We thank thee and will raise³⁹ thee; receive her
name.
It is the only daughter to Madam Gratiana,
The late widow.
  Vin. [*Aside*] Oh, my sister, my sister!
  Lus. Why dost walk aside?
  Vin. My lord, I was thinking how I might begin,
As thus—"oh, lady"—or twenty hundred devices:
Her very bodkin⁴⁰ will put a man in.⁴¹
  Lus. Ay, or the wagging⁴² of her hair.   130
  Vin. No, that shall put you in, my lord.
  Lus. Shall't? Why, content: dost know the daughter
then?
  Vin. Oh, excellent well by sight.
  Lus.   That was her brother
That did prefer thee to us.
  Vin.   My lord, I think so,
I knew I had seen him somewhere.
  Lus. And therefore prithee let thy heart to him
Be as a virgin, close.
  Vin.   Oh, my good lord.
  Lus. We may laugh at that simple⁴³ age within him—
  Vin. Ha! ha! ha!
  Lus. Himself being made the subtle instrument   140
To wind up⁴⁴ a good fellow.
  Vin.   That's I, my lord.
  Lus. That's thou.
To entice and work⁴⁵ his sister.
  Vin. A pure novice!
  Lus.   'Twas finely managed.
  Vin. Gallantly carried: a pretty-perfumed villain!
  Lus. I've bethought me.
If she prove chaste still and immoveable,
Venture upon the mother, and with gifts
As I will furnish thee, begin with her.
  Vin. Oh, fie, fie, that's the wrong end, my lord.   150
'Tis mere impossible that a mother by any gifts
Should become a bawd to her own daughter!
  Lus. Nay, then, I see thou'rt but a puny⁴⁶
In the subtle mystery of a woman:
Why, 'tis held now no dainty dish: the name⁴⁷
Is so in league with age⁴⁸ that nowadays
It does eclipse three quarters of a mother.
  Vin. Does it so, my lord?
Let me alone,⁴⁹ then, to eclipse the fourth.
  Lus. Why, well said; come, I'll furnish thee: but
first   160
Swear to be true in all.
  Vin.   True?

  Lus.   Nay, but swear!
  Vin. Swear? I hope your honor little doubts my
faith.
  Lus. Yet, for my humors' sake, 'cause I love
swearing—
  Vin. 'Cause you love swearing, 'slud,⁵⁰ I will,
  Lus. Why, enough:
Ere long look to be made of better stuff.
  Vin. That will do well indeed, my lord.
  Lus. Attend⁵¹ me.

                                              [*Exit.*]

  Vin. Oh,
Now let me burst, I've eaten noble poison!   170
We are made strange fellows, brother, innocent
villains:
Wilt not be angry when thou hear'st on't, think'st thou?
I' faith, thou shalt. Swear me to foul my sister!
Sword, I durst make a promise of him to thee,
Thou shalt dis-heir him, it shall be thine honor;
And yet, now angry froth is down in me,
It would not prove the meanest policy
In this disguise to try the faith of both;
Another might have had the self-same office,
Some slave that would have wrought effectually,   180
Ay and perhaps o'erwrought 'em: therefore I,
Being thought traveled, will apply myself
Unto the self-same form, forget my nature,
As if no part about me were kin to 'em,
So touch⁵² 'em—though I durst almost for good⁵³
Venture my lands in heaven upon their good.⁵⁴

                                              Exit.

[I.iv]

*Enter the discontented Lord ANTONIO, whose wife
the Duchess' youngest son ravished; he discovering the
body of her dead to certain lords and [to PIERO and]*
HIPPOLITO.

  Ant. Draw nearer, lords, and be sad witnesses
Of a fair comely building newly fallen,
Being falsely undermined. Violent rape
Has played a glorious act: behold, my lords,
A sight that strikes man out of me.
  Pier. That virtuous lady!
  Ant.   Precedent for wives!
  Hip. The blush of many women, whose chaste
presence

---

³⁶ *bring . . . expense:* see what it costs.
³⁷ *given . . . tang:* caught the flavor of it precisely.
³⁸ *move:* urge.   ³⁹ *raise:* i.e., in fortune.
⁴⁰ *bodkin:* hairpin.
⁴¹ *put . . . in:* serve to get a man started.
⁴² *wagging:* movement (with implications of indiscretion.)
⁴³ *simple:* innocent, foolish.
⁴⁴ *wind up.:* incite; Nicoll makes the entire phrase proverbial—"serve a thief."   ⁴⁵ *work:* manipulate.
⁴⁶ *puny:* mere beginner.   ⁴⁷ *name:* bawd (above).
⁴⁸ *age:* middle age.   ⁴⁹ *Let me alone:* Leave it to me.
⁵⁰ *'slud:* God's blood.   ⁵¹ *Attend:* Wait on.
⁵² *touch:* test, as by applying a touchstone.
⁵³ *for good:* absolutely.
⁵⁴ *good:* Most editors emend to "blood."

Would e'en call shame up to their cheeks
And make pale wanton sinners have good colors—
   Ant. Dead!   10
Her honor first drunk poison, and her life,
Being fellows in one house, did pledge her honor.
   Pier. Oh, grief of many!
   Ant.   I marked not this before:
A prayer book the pillow to her cheek;
This was her rich confection,[1] and another
Placed in her right hand with a leaf tucked up,
Pointed to these words:
Melius virtute mori, quam per dedecus vivere.[2]
True and effectual[3] it is indeed.
   Hip. My lord, since you invite us to your sorrows,
Let's truly taste 'em, that with equal comfort   21
As to ourselves we may relieve your wrongs:
We have grief too that yet walks without tongue:
Curae leves loquuntur, majores stupent.[4]
   Ant. You deal with truth, my lord.
Lend me but your attentions and I'll cut
Long grief into short words: last reveling night,
When torchlight made an artificial noon
About the court, some courtiers in the mask,
Putting on better faces than their own,   30
Being full of fraud and flattery, amongst whom
The Duchess' youngest son—that moth[5] to honor—
Filled up a room;[6] and with long lust to eat
Into my wearing,[7] amongst all the ladies
Singled out that dear form, who ever lived
As cold in lust as she is now in death—
Which that step-duchess' monster knew too well—
And therefore in the height of all the revels,
When music was heard loudest, courtiers busiest,
And ladies great with laughter—oh, vicious minute!   40
Unfit, but for relation,[8] to be spoke of—
Then with a face more impudent than his vizard
He harried her amidst a throng of panders
That live upon damnation of both kinds
And fed the ravenous vulture of his lust.
Oh, death to think on't! she, her honor forced,
Deemed it a nobler dowry for her name
To die with poison than to live with shame.
   Hip. A wondrous lady of rare fire compact,
She's made her name an empress[9] by that act.   50

I.iv.
  [1] *confection:* medicinal preservative.
  [2] *L.:* Better to die in virtue than to live dishonored.
  [3] *effectual:* answering the purpose.
  [4] *L.:* misquoting Seneca, *Hippolytus,* 1. 607: "Small cares
speak out, greater ones do not."
  [5] *moth:* whose function was to eat, hence destroy.
  [6] *room:* place.
  [7] *wearing:* clothing; metaphorically, Antonio's honor and
happiness.   [8] *for relation:* the need to inform you.
  [9] *empress:* Editors suggest a pun on "impresa" or emblem.
  [10] *court it:* be revealed in the court.

II.i.
  [1] *child's-part:* legacy.
  [2] *Dondolo:* A character with the same name and signifying "bald fool" appears in Marston's play *The Fawn*
(1606), whence Tourneur's immediate inspiration—though
the circuitous manner of speaking obviously recalls Osric in
Hamlet.   [3] *cut . . . way:* don't be so prolix.

   Pier. My lord, what judgment follows the
    offender?
   Ant. Faith, none, my lord, it cools and is deferred.
   Pier. Delay the doom for rape?
   Ant. Oh, you must note who 'tis should die—
The Duchess' son. She'll look to be a saver:
"Judgment in this age is near kin to favor."
   Hip. Nay then, step forth, thou bribeless officer;

                         [*Draws sword:*]

I bind you all in steel to bind you surely,
Here let your oaths meet, to be kept and paid
Which else will stick like rust and shame the blade;   60
Strengthen my vow, that if at the next sitting
Judgment speak all in gold and spare the blood
Of such a serpent, e'en before their seats
To let his soul out, which long since was found
Guilty in heaven.
   All.   We swear it and will act it.
   Ant. Kind gentlemen, I thank you in mine ire.
   Hip. 'Twere pity
The ruins of so fair a monument
Should not be dipped in the defacer's blood.
   Pier. Her funeral shall be wealthy, for her name   70
Merits a tomb of pearl. My lord Antonio,
For this time wipe your lady from your eyes;
No doubt our grief and yours may one day court it[10]
When we are more familiar with revenge.
   Ant. That is my comfort, gentlemen, and I joy
In this one happiness above the rest,
Which will be called a miracle at last,
That being an old man I'd a wife so chaste.

                            Exeunt.

ACT TWO

SCENE ONE

Enter CASTIZA, *the sister.*

   Cas. How hardly shall that maiden be beset
Whose only fortunes are her constant thoughts,
That has no other child's-part[1] but her honor
That keeps her low and empty in estate.
Maids and their honors are like poor beginners:
Were not sin rich there would be fewer sinners:
Why had not virtue a revènue? Well,
I know the cause: 'twould have impoverished hell.

[*Enter* DONDOLO.[2]]

How now, Dondolo.   9
   Don. Madonna, there is one as they say a thing of
flesh and blood, a man I take him, by his beard, that
would very desirously mouth to mouth with you.
   Cas. What's that?
   Don. Show his teeth in your company.
   Cas. I understand thee not.
   Don. Why, speak with you, Madonna.
   Cas. Why, say so madman and cut off a great deal of
dirty way.[3] Had it not been better spoke, in ordinary
words, that one would speak with me?   19

Don. Ha, ha, that's as ordinary as two shillings; I would strive a little to show myself in my place.[4] A gentleman-usher [5] scorns to use the phrase and fancy of a servingman.

Cas. Yours be your own, sir; go direct him hither.

                               [*Exit* DONDOLO.]

I hope some happy tidings from my brother
That lately traveled, whom my soul affects.[6]
Here he comes.

      Enter VINDICE, *her brother, disguised.*

Vin. Lady, the best of wishes to your sex:
Fair skins and new gowns.

                        [*Gives her a letter.*]

Cas.   Oh, they shall thank you,
    sir—
Whence this?
Vin.   Oh, from a dear and worthy friend,   30
Mighty!
Cas. From whom?
Vin.   The duke's son.
Cas.   Receive that!

      A box o' the ear to her brother.

I swore I'd put anger in my hand
And pass the virgin limits of myself
To him that next appeared in that base office,
To be his sin's attorney. Bear to him
That figure of my hate upon thy cheek
Whilst 'tis yet hot, and I'll reward thee for't;
Tell him my honor shall have a rich name
When several harlots shall share his with shame:
Farewell, commend me to him in my hate!   40
                               Exit.

Vin. It is the sweetest box [7] that e'er my nose came
    nigh:
The finest drawn-work cuff [8] that e'er was worn:
I'll love this blow forever, and this cheek
Shall still henceforward take the wall of this.[9]
Oh, I'm above my tongue! most constant sister,
In this thou hast right honorable shown;
Many are called by their honor that have none,
Thou art approved forever in my thoughts.
It is not in the power of words to taint thee,
And yet for the salvation of my oath,   50
As my resolve in that point, I will lay
Hard siege unto my mother, though I know
A siren's tongue could not bewitch her so.

          [*Enter* GRATIANA.]

Mass,[10] fitly, here she comes: thanks my disguise:
Madam, good afternoon.
Grat.   Y'are welcome, sir.
Vin. The next of Italy [11] commends him to you:
Our mighty expectation, the duke's son.
Grat. I think myself much honored that he pleases
To rank me in his thoughts.
Vin.   So may you lady:
One that is like to be our sudden [12] duke—   60
The crown gapes for him every tide [13]—and then

Commander o'er us all; do but think on him,
How blest were they now that could pleasure him,
E'en with anything almost.
Grat.   Ay, save their honor.
Vin. Tut, one would let a little of that go too
And ne'er be seen in't: [14] ne'er be seen in't, mark you.
I'd wink and let it go—
Grat.   Marry, but I would not.
Vin. Marry, but I would, I hope; I know you would
    too
If you'd that blood now which you gave your daughter;
To her indeed 'tis, this wheel [15] comes about;   70
That man that must be all this perhaps ere morning
—For his white [16] father does but mold away—
Has long desired your daughter.
Grat.   Desired?
Vin. Nay, but hear me:
He desires now that will command hereafter,
Therefore be wise; I speak as more a friend
To you than him. Madam, I know y'are poor,
And 'lack the day,
There are too many poor ladies already;
Why should you vex [17] the number? 'Tis despised.   80
Live wealthy, rightly understand the world
And chide away that foolish country girl
Keeps company with your daughter, chastity.
Grat. Oh, fie, fie, the riches of the world cannot hire
A mother to such a most unnatural task.
Vin. No, but a thousand angels [18] can.
Men have no power, angels must work you to it,
The world descends into such base-born evils
That forty angels can make four score devils.
There will be fools still, I perceive, still fools.   90
Would I be poor, dejected,[19] scorned of greatness,
Swept from the palace, and see other daughters
Spring with the dew o' the court, having mine own
So much desired and loved—by the duke's son!
No, I would raise my state [20] upon her breast
And call her eyes my tenants; I would count
My yearly maintenance upon her cheeks,
Take coach upon her lip, and all her parts
Should keep men after men [21] and I would ride
In pleasure upon pleasure.   100
You took great pains for her, once when it was,
Let her requite it now, though it be but some.[22]
You brought her forth, she may well bring you home.[23]

---

    [4] *place:* function.
    [5] *gentleman-usher:* an attendant, himself a gentleman, on one of higher rank.   [6] *affects:* love.
    [7] *box:* punning on box of sweetmeats or perfumes.
    [8] *drawn-work cuff:* (1) the print (cuff, blow) of her hand on his cheek; (2) a cuff made of patterned threads.
    [9] *take . . . this:* enjoy precedence of the other cheek.
    [10] *Mass:* By the Mass.
    [11] *next of Italy:* heir to the duke.
    [12] *our sudden:* imminently our.   [13] *tide:* "hour."
    [14] *ne'er . . . in't:* not be observed (in forfeiting one's honor).   [15] *wheel:* of fortune.
    [16] *white:* white-haired.   [17] *vex:* aggravate; make more.
    [18] *angels:* gold coins.   [19] *dejected:* lowly.
    [20] *state:* rank.   [21] *men after men:* retainers(?).
    [22] *but some:* only in part.
    [23] *bring you home:* make you rich.

Grat. Oh, heavens, this overcomes me!

Vin. [*Aside*] Not, I hope, already?

Grat. [*Aside*] It is too strong for me. Men know, that know us,
We are so weak their words can overthrow us.
He touched me nearly, made my virtues bate [24]
When his tongue struck upon my poor estate.

Vin. [*Aside*] I e'en quake to proceed, my spirit turns
      edge, [25]   110
I fear me she's unmothered, yet I'll venture [26]—
That woman is all male whom none can enter!
What think you now, lady, speak, are you wiser?
What said advancement to you? Thus it said:
The daughter's fall lifts up the mother's head:
Did it not, madam? But I'll swear it does
In many places. Tut, this age fears no man—
"'Tis no shame to be bad, because 'tis common."

Grat. Ay, that's the comfort on't.

Vin.   The comfort on't!
I keep the best for last; can these persuade you   120
To forget heaven—and—

                              [*Gives her gold.*]

Grat.   Ay, these are they—

Vin.   Oh!

Grat. That enchant our sex; these are the means.
That govern our affections. That woman will
Not be troubled with the mother [27] long
That sees the comfortable shine of you;
I blush to think what for your sakes I'll do.

Vin. [*Aside*] O suffering heaven with thy invisible
      finger
E'en at this instant turn the precious side
Of both mine eyeballs inward, not to see myself.

Grat. Look you, sir.

Vin.   Holla.

Grat.   Let this thank your pains.

Vin. Oh, you're a kind madam. [28]   131

Grat. I'll see how I can move.

Vin.   Your words will sting.

Grat. If she be still chaste I'll ne'er call her mine.

Vin. [*Aside*] Spoke truer than you meant it.

Grat. Daughter Castiza.

                [*Enter* CASTIZA.]

---

[24] *bate:* dwindle.

[25] *turns edge:* is blunted: Vindice fears to go on.

[26] *venture:* pronounced "venter" so as to rhyme with "enter," following.

[27] *the mother:* hysteria, associated with a displacing of the womb; and punning obviously on maternal propriety.

[28] *madam:* sardonically, as of a whorehouse. Q "madman."

[29] *honest:* chaste.   [30] *square out:* measure.

[31] *clip:* embrace.

[32] *You . . . fee:* Women cannot know themselves without giving of themselves.   [33] *coy:* disdainful.

[34] *'haviors:* behavior.

[35] *ashore:* from their station on the shore.

[36] *rich:* abundant (because no merchant would strive to possess it).

[37] *keep less charge:* pay less heed; also, "incur less expense."   [38] *intends:* determines.

[39] *petitionary people:* suitors at court.

Cas.   Madam.

Vin.   Oh, she's yonder.
Meet her. Troops of celestial soldiers guard her heart:
Yon dam has devils enough to take her part.

Cas. Madam, what makes yon evil-officed man
In presence of you?

Grat.   Why?

Cas.   He lately brought
Immodest writing sent from the duke's son   140
To tempt me to dishonorable act.

Grat. Dishonorable act? Good honorable fool,
That wouldst be honest [29] 'cause thou wouldst be so,
Producing no one reason but thy will;
And 't'as a good report, prettily commended—
But pray by whom? Mean people, ignorant people!
The better sort I'm sure cannot abide it,
And by what rule should we square out [30] our lives
But by our betters' actions? Oh, if thou knew'st
What 'twere to lose it, thou would never keep it: 150
But there's a cold curse laid upon all maids,
Whilst others clip [31] the sun they clasp the shades!
Virgnity is paradise, locked up.
You cannot come by yourselves without fee, [32]
And 'twas decreed that man should keep the key:
Deny advancement, treasure, the duke's son!

Cas. I cry you mercy; lady, I mistook you,
Pray, did you see my mother? Which way went you?
Pray God I have not lost her.

Vin. [*Aside*]   Prettily put by.

Grat. Are you as proud to me as coy [33] to him?   160
Do you not know me now?

Cas.   Why, are you she?
The worlds' so changed, one shape into another.
It is a wise child now that knows her mother.

Vin. [*Aside*] Most right, i' faith.

Grat.   I owe your cheek my hand
For that presumption now, but I'll forget it;
Come, you shall leave those childish 'haviors [34]
And understand your time; fortunes flow to you
—What, will you be a girl?
If all feared drowning that spy waves ashore, [35]   170
Gold would grow rich [36] and all the merchants poor.

Cas. It is a pretty saying of a wicked one,
But methinks now it does not show so well
Out of your mouth—better in his.

Vin. [*Aside*] Faith bad enough in both
Were I in earnest—as I'll seem no less.—
I wonder, lady, your own mothers' words
Cannot be taken, nor stand in full force.
'Tis honesty you urge: what's honesty?
'Tis but heaven's beggar; and what woman is   180
So foolish to keep honesty
And be not able to keep herself? No,
Times are grown wiser and will keep less charge. [37]
A maid that has small portion now intends [38]
To break up house and live upon her friends;
How blest are you: you have happiness alone;
Others must fall to thousands, you to one
Sufficient in himself to make your forehead
Dazzle the world with jewels, and petitionary people [39]
Start at your presence.

Grat.   Oh, if I were young   190
I should be ravished!⁴⁰

Cas.   Ay, to lose your honor.

Vin. 'Slid,⁴¹ how can you lose your honor
To deal⁴² with my lord's grace?
He'll add more honor to it by his title;
Your mother will tell you how.

Grat.   That I will

Vin. Oh, think upon the pleasure of the palace,
Securèd ease and state; the stirring⁴³ meats
Ready to move out of the dishes
That e'en now quicken⁴⁴ when they're eaten;
Banquets abroad⁴⁵ by torchlight, music, sports,   200
Bare-headed vassals⁴⁶ that had ne'er the fortune
To keep on their own hats, but let horns⁴⁷ wear 'em;
Nine coaches waiting—hurry, hurry, hurry—

Cas. Ay, to the devil!

Vin. [*Aside*] Ay, to the devil.—To the duke, by my
     faith!

Grat. Ay, to the duke. Daughter, you'd scorn to think
O' the devil an⁴⁸ you were there once.

Vin. [*Aside*] True, for most there are as proud as he
For his heart,⁴⁹ i' faith.—
Who'd sit at home in a neglected room   210
Dealing⁵⁰ her short-lived beauty to the pictures
That are useless⁵¹ as old men, when those
Poorer in face and fortune than herself
Walk with a hundred acres on their backs—
Fair meadows cut into green foreparts⁵²—oh,
It was the greatest blessing ever happened to women
When farmers' sons agreed, and met again,⁵³
To wash their hands and come up gentlemen;⁵⁴
The commonwealth has flourished ever since.
Lands that were meat by the rod⁵⁵—that labor's
     spared—   220
Tailors ride down and measure 'em by the yard.⁵⁶
Fair trees, those comely foretops⁵⁷ of the field,
Are cut to maintain head-tires—⁵⁸ much untold.⁵⁹
All thrives but chastity, she lies a-cold.
Nay, shall I come nearer to you: mark but this:
Why are there so few honest women but
Because 'tis the poorer profession?
That's accounted best that's best followed,
Least in trade, least in fashion,
And that's not honesty, believe it; and do   230
But note the low and dejected price of it:
"Lose but a pearl, we search and cannot brook it;⁶⁰
But that⁶¹ once gone, who is so mad to look⁶² it?"

Grat. Troth, he says true.

Cas.   False! I defy you both:
I have endured you with an ear of fire,
Your tongues have struck hot irons on my face;
Mother, come from that poisonous woman there.

Grat. Where?

Cas. Do you not see her? She's too inward then:
Slave, perish in thy office; you heavens please   240
Henceforth to make the mother a disease
Which first begins with me; yet I've outgone⁶³ you.
                                            Exit.

Vin. [*Aside*] Oh, angels, clap your wings upon the
     skies

And give this virgin crystal plaudities!⁶⁴

Grat. Peevish,⁶⁵ coy, foolish! but return this answer:
My lord shall be most welcome when his pleasure
Conducts him this way; I will sway mine own:
Women with women can work best alone.
                                            Exit.

Vin. Indeed, I'll tell him so.
Oh, more uncivil,⁶⁶ more unnatural   250
Than those base-titled creatures that look downward,⁶⁷
Why does not heaven turn black or with a frown
Undo the world? Why does not earth start up
And strike the sins that tread upon it? Oh,
Were't not for gold and women there would be no
     damnation,
Hell would look like a lord's great kitchen without fire
     in't;
But 'twas decreed before the world began
That they should be the hooks to catch at man.
                                            Exit.

[II.ii]

Enter LUSSURIOSO *with* HIPPOLITO, VINDICE'S
                    brother.

Lus. I much applaud
Thy judgment, thou art well read in a fellow,
And 'tis the deepest art to study man.
I know this which I never learned in schools,
The world's divided into knaves and fools.

Hip. [*Aside*] Knave in your face, my lord—behind
     your back!

---

⁴⁰ *ravished:* delighted. Castiza in what follows puns on
"raped."   ⁴¹ *'Slid:* God's eyelid.
⁴² *deal:* sexually.   ⁴³ *stirring:* sexually stimulating.
⁴⁴ *quicken:* make you quicken or grow lively.
⁴⁵ *abroad:* out of doors.
⁴⁶ *Bare-headed vassals:* Liegemen who have to doff their
hats (also, by innuendo, lay down their wives) in the presence of royalty.
⁴⁷ *horns:* not only the cuckold's horns but also antlers
serving as hatracks.   ⁴⁸ *an:* if.
⁴⁹ *For his heart:* an intensive—"To the life."
⁵⁰ *Dealing:* Communicating, showing off.
⁵¹ *useless:* in a sexual sense.
⁵² *foreparts:* ornamental stomachers that covered the
breasts; park before a manor house.
⁵³ *met again:* agreed(?).
⁵⁴ *come up gentlemen:* rise in rank, as by coming to court.
⁵⁵ *meat by the rod:* measured, meted out by length and
total area.
⁵⁶ *yard:* The tailor's cloth-yard is also cant for "penis."
⁵⁷ *foretops:* locks of hair.   ⁵⁸ *head-tires:* head-dresses.
⁵⁹ *much untold:* the cost not reckoned; much more could
be said(?).   ⁶⁰ *brook it:* endure its loss.
⁶¹ *that:* chastity.   ⁶² *look:* trouble himself about.
⁶³ *outgone:* been too much for(?).
⁶⁴ *crystal plaudities:* applause from the Heaven Crystalline
where the angels dwelt.   ⁶⁵ *Peevish:* Perverse.
⁶⁶ *uncivil:* stronger sense than now—"lacking in civiliza-
tion."
⁶⁷ *those . . . downward:* perhaps a reminiscence of Sir Walter Raleigh's report (in his description of Guiana) of "a
nation of people whose heads appear not above their
shoulders . . . [who] have their eyes in their shoulders, and
their mouths in the middle of their breasts." See also *Othello,*
I. iii. 144–45; and *The Tempest,* III. iii. 46–7.

Lus. And I much thank thee that thou hast preferred[1]
A fellow of discourse,[2] well mingled,
And whose brain time hath seasoned.
 Hip.   True, my lord,
We shall find season[3] once, I hope.—[*Aside*] O villain,
To make such an unnatural slave of me!—But—   11

      [*Enter* VINDICE *disguised.*]

 Lus. Mass, here he comes.
 Hip.[*Aside*]   And now shall I
Have free leave to depart.
 Lus.   Your absence—leave us.
 Hip. [*Aside*] Are not my thoughts true? I must re-
  move;
But, brother, you may stay.
Heart, we are both made bawds a new found way!
              Exit.
 Lus. Now, we're an even number: a third man's
Dangerous, especially her brother.
Say, be free, have I a pleasure toward?
 Vin.   Oh, my lord.
 Lus. Ravish me in thine answer: art thou rare,   20
Hast thou beguiled her of salvation
And rubbed hell o'er with honey? Is she a woman?
 Vin. In all but in desire.
 Lus.   Then she's in nothing—
I bate in courage[4] now.
 Vin.   The word I brought
Might well have made indifferent honest naught;[5]
A right good woman in these days is changed
Into white[6] money with less labor far—
Many a maid has turned to Mahomet[7]
With easier working. I durst undertake,
Upon the pawn and forfeit of my life,   30
With half those words to flat[8] a Puritan's wife,
But she is close[9] and good; yet 'tis a doubt
By this time—oh, the mother, the mother!
 Lus. I never thought their sex had been a wonder
Until this minute: what fruit from the mother?

 Vin.[*Aside*] Now must I blister my soul, be
  forsworn,
Or shame the woman that received[10] me first.
I will be true; thou[11] livest not to proclaim;[12]
Spoke to a dying man shame has no shame.
My lord.
 Lus. Who's that?
 Vin.   Here's none but I, my lord.   40
 Lus. What would thy haste utter?
 Vin.   Comfort.
 Lus.   Welcome.
 Vin. The maid being dull, having no mind to travel
Into unknown lands, what did me I straight
But set spurs to the mother; golden spurs
Will put her to a false gallop in a trice.
 Lus. Is't possible that in this
The mother should be damned before the daughter?
 Vin. Oh, that's good manners, my lord: the mother
  for
Her age must go foremost, you know.
 Lus. Thou'st spoke that true! but where comes in
  this comfort?   50
 Vin. In a fine place, my lord. The unnatural
  mother
Did with her tongue so hard beset her honor
That the poor fool was struck to silent wonder;
Yet still the maid like an unlighted taper
Was cold and chaste, save that her mother's breath
Did blow fire on her cheeks. The girl departed
But the good ancient madam, half mad, threw me
These promising words which I took deeply note of:
"My lord shall be most welcome,"—
 Lus.   Faith, I thank her!
 Vin. "When his pleasure conducts him this way"—
 Lus. That shall be soon, i' faith!
 Vin.   "I will sway mine
  own"—   61
 Lus. She does the wiser, I commend her for't.
 Vin. "Women with women can work best alone."
 Lus. By this light[13] and so they can; give 'em
Their due, men are not comparable to 'em.
 Vin. No, that's true, for you shall have one woman
Knit more in a hour than any man
Can ravel[14] again in seven and twenty year.
 Lus. Now my desires are happy, I'll make 'em
  freemen[15] now.
Thou art a precious fellow, faith I love thee,   70
Be wise and make it thy revènue: beg, leg![16]
What office couldst thou be ambitious for?
 Vin. Office, my lord? Marry, if I might
Have my wish I would have one that was never begged
  yet.
 Lus. Nay, then thou canst have none.
 Vin.   Yes, my lord,
I could pick out another office yet,
Nay, and keep a horse and drab[17] upon it.
 Lus. Prithee, good bluntness, tell me—
 Vin. Why, I would desire but this, my lord:
To have all the fees behind the arras,[18] and all   80
The farthingales that fall plump about
Twelve o'clock at night upon the rushes.[19]

II.ii.
 [1] *preferred:* recommended.
 [2] *of discourse:* capable in speaking.
 [3] *season:* opportunity (for revenge).
 [4] *courage:* hope (with sexual connotation).
 [5] *indifferent ... naught:* women who are reasonably chaste wicked.   [6] *white:* silver.
 [7] *turned to Mahomet:* abandoned her Christian faith for an alien religion.   [8] *flat:* make lie down.
 [9] *is close:* keeps herself to herself.
 [10] *received:* greeted (as at his conception or birth).
 [11] *thou:* Lussurioso.   [12] *proclaim:* repeat any words.
 [13] *By this light:* True!   [14] *ravel:* unravel.
 [15] *make 'em freemen:* enfranchise (from their former condition of servitude).   [16] *beg, leg:* bow, like a suppliant.
 [17] *drab:* whore.
 [18] *fees ... arras:* money accruing from all the lewd assignations made behind the tapestry hangings that stood out from the wall and allowed those who would not be observed (like Polonius) to hide behind them. Vindice sees himself, in company with many favored courtiers in the reign of James I, as a monopolist.
 [19] *farthingales ... rushes:* hooped petticoats that are dropped straightaway at midnight on the straw mattings (that covered the floor).

Lus. Thou'rt a mad apprehensive[20] knave:
Dost think to make any great purchase[21] of that?
  Vin. Oh, 'tis an unknown thing, my lord; I wonder
'T'as been missed so long!
  Lus. Well, this night I'll visit her, and 'tis till then
A year in my desires. Farewell, attend,
Trust me with thy preferment.

                                                         Exit.

  Vin.   My loved lord.—
Oh, shall I kill him o' the wrong-side now? No,   90
Sword thou wast never a back-biter yet.
I'll pierce him to his face, he shall die looking upon
    me;
Thy veins are swelled with lust, this shall unfill 'em:
Great men were gods if beggars could not kill 'em.
Forgive me, heaven, to call my mother wicked,
Oh, lessen not my days upon the earth!
I cannot honor her;[22] by this I fear me
Her tongue has turned my sister into use.[23]
I was a villain not to be forsworn
To this our lecherous hope, the duke's son;   100
For lawyers, merchants, some divines and all,[24]
Count beneficial perjury[25] a sin small.
It shall go hard yet but I'll guard her honor
And keep the ports[26] sure.

                 Enter HIPPOLITO.

  Hip. Brother, how goes the world? I would know
    news
Of you, but[27] I have news to tell you.
  Vin. What, in the name of knavery?
  Hip.   Knavery, faith:
This vicious old duke's worthily abused,
The pen[28] of his bastard writes him cuckold!
  Vin. His bastard?
  Hip.   Pray believe it; he and the duchess
By night meet in their linen, they have been seen   111
By stair-foot panders.
  Vin.   Oh, sin foul and deep,
Great faults are winked at when the duke's asleep.
See, see, here comes the Spurio—

             Enter [SPURIO *with two men.*]

  Hip.   Monstrous luxur![29]
  Vin. Unbraced:[30] two of his valiant bawds with him.
Oh, there's a wicked whisper; hell is in his ear.
Stay, let's observe his passage.[31]—
  Spur. Oh, but are you sure on't?
  Serv. My lord, most sure on't, for 'twas spoke by one
That is most inward with the duke's son's lust.   120
That he intends within this hour to steal
Unto Hippolito's sister, whose chaste life
The mother has corrupted for his use.
  Spur. Sweet word, sweet occasion, faith, then,
    brother,
I'll disinherit you in as short time
As I was when I was begot in haste,
I'll damn you at your pleasure: precious deed!
After your lust, oh, 'twill be fine to bleed!
Come, let our passing out be soft and wary.

                                                       Exeunt.

  Vin. Mark, there, there, that step! now to the
    duchess;   130
This their second meeting writes the duke cuckold
With new additions,[32] his horns newly revived;
Night, thou that lookest like funeral herald's fees[33]
Torn down betimes[34] i' the morning, thou hangest fitly
To grace those sins that have no grace at all.
Now 'tis full sea[35] abed over the world,
There's juggling[36] of all sides. Some that were maids
E'en at sunset are now perhaps i' the toll-book;[37]
This woman in immodest thin apparel
Lets in her friend by water,[38] here a dame   140
Cunning nails leather hinges to a door
To avoid proclamation.
Now cuckolds are a-coining, apace, apace, apace, apace!
And careful sisters[39] spin that thread i' the night
That does maintain them and their bawds i' the day.
  Hip. You flow well, brother.
  Vin.   Puh, I'm shallow yet,
Too sparing and too modest; shall I tell thee,
If every trick were told that's dealt by night
There are few here that would not blush outright.
  Hip. I am of that belief, too.
  Vin.   Who's this comes?   150

               [*Enter* LUSSURIOSO.]

The duke's son up so late! brother, fall back
And you shall learn some mischief.—My good lord.
  Lus. Piato, why, the man I wished for, come,
I do embrace this season for the fittest
To taste of that young lady.
  Vin. [*Aside*]   Heart and hell!
  Hip. [*Aside*] Damned villain!
  Vin. [*Aside*] I ha' no way now to cross it,[40] but to kill
    him.
  Lus. Come, only thou and I.
  Vin.   My lord, my lord.
  Lus. Why dost thou start us?[41]

---

[20] *apprehensive:* quick to understand.
[21] *purchase:* profit.
[22] *lessen . . . her:* following Exodus 20:12: "Honor thy father and thy mother, that thy days may be long upon the land."
[23] *use:* usury; the selling of her virginity is seen as making for interest or profit.   *some . . . and all:* not a few.
[25] *beneficial perjury:* perhaps alluding to the "Jesuitical" doctrine that equivocation in a good cause was justifiable.
[26] *ports:* gates (with sexual entendre).
[27] *but:* except that(?).
[28] *pen:* with obvious pun on "penis."   [29] *luxur:* lecher.
[30] *Unbraced:* With his doublet unfastened.
[31] *Stay . . . passage:* Presumably they hide behind one of the pillars supporting the "heavens."
[32] *additions:* "honors."
[33] *fees:* by transference, the black pennons, etc., with which the professional and highly paid attenders on funerals memorialized the virtues of the deceased.
[34] *betimes:* early.   [35] *full sea:* high tide (sexually).
[36] *juggling:* deceiving.
[37] *toll-book:* which registered animals for sale at a market (hence "prostitutes"), for the purpose of taxing the proceeds.
[38] *by water:* who comes to her in a boat as from the Thames.   [39] *sisters:* whores.
[40] *cross it:* avert his purpose.   [41] *start us:* startle me.

Vin. I'd almost forgot—the bastard!
Lus.   What of him?
Vin. This night, this hour—this minute, now— 161
Lus. What? What?
Vin.   Shadows⁴² the duchess—
Lus.   Horrible word.
Vin. And like strong poison eats
Into the duke your father's forehead.
Lus.   Oh!
Vin. He makes horn royal.
Lus.   Most ignoble slave!
Vin. This is the fruit of two beds.⁴³
Lus.   I am mad.
Vin. That passage he trod warily.
Lus.   He did!
Vin. And hushed his villains every step he took.
Lus. His villains! I'll confound them.
Vin. Take 'em finely, finely now.   170
Lus. The duchess' chamber door shall not control
   me.
              Exeunt [LUSSURIOSO *and* VINDICE].
Hip. Good, happy, swift, there's gunpowder i' the
   court,
Wildfire at midnight! in this heedless fury
He may show violence to cross⁴⁴ himself:
I'll follow the event.⁴⁵
                                     Exit.

[II.iii]
   [*The* DUKE *and* DUCHESS *in bed.*] *Enter again*
        [LUSSURIOSO *and* VINDICE].

Lus. Where is that villain?¹
Vin. Softly, my lord, and you may take 'em twisted.
Lus. I care not how!
Vin.   Oh, 'twill be glorious,
To kill 'em doubled, when they're heaped—be soft, my
   lord.
Lus. Away! my spleen² is not so lazy—thus, and
   thus,

---

⁴² *Shadows:* Covers, "tups."
⁴³ *fruit . . . beds:* results of the Duke's begetting the bastard in a bed other than his own.   ⁴⁴ *cross:* frustrate.
⁴⁵ *event:* outcome.
II.iii.
   ¹ *Where . . . villain:* This half line, which completes the
iambic pentameter line begun by Hippolito at the end of
scene ii, illustrates the arbitrariness of scene divisions. Action does begin anew and so a new scene is indicated, but
greater emphasis ought to attend on the fact that the total
action is a seamless whole, unbroken by the fall of a front
curtain.   ² *spleen:* the seat of anger.
   ³ *upper:* farthest from the door; hence, nearest to the
bedchamber and perhaps including the meaning "heavenly."
   ⁴ *heaves:* signs.   ⁵ *unclear:* not freed of sin.
   ⁶ *nerves:* sinews.   ⁷ *be myself:* reign as duke.
   ⁸ *'file:* defile.   ⁹ *abused:* deceived.
   ¹⁰ *our thought:* what we could have hoped.
   ¹¹ *frightful:* making for fright (as by noisy action); or
descriptive of the deed of killing the father and ruler.
   ¹² *dissemble a flight:* steal off.
   ¹³ *Out . . . Guilty:* Begone, you who are the cause.
   ¹⁴ *harlots':* generic term of abuse, not necessarily suggesting women.   ¹⁵ *out o' the socket:* topsy turvy.

I'll shake their eyelids ope and with my sword
Shut 'em again for ever: villain! strumpet!

                              [*They stand over the bed.*]

Duke. You, upper³ guard, defend us!
Duch.   Treason, treason!
Duke. Oh, take me not in sleep, I have great sins,
I must have days, nay, months, dear son, with   10
Penitential heaves,⁴
To lift 'em out and not to die unclear;⁵
Oh, thou wilt kill me both in heaven and here.
   Lus. I am amazed to death.
Duke.   Nay, villain, traitor,
Worse than the foulest epithet, now I'll grip thee
E'en with the nerves⁶ of wrath, and throw thy head
Amongst the lawyers. Guard!

   Enter Nobles *and* Sons [AMBITIOSO *and* SUPER-
              VACUO, *with* HIPPOLITO].

   1 Nob. How comes the quiet of your grace dis-
      turbed?
Duke. This boy that should be myself⁷ after me
Would be myself before me, and in heat   20
Of that ambition bloodily rushed in
Intending to depose me in my bed.
   2 Nob. Duty and natural loyalty forfend!
   Duch. He called his father villain and me strumpet,
A word that I abhor to 'file⁸ my lips with.
   Amb. That was not so well done, brother!
   Lus.   I am
      abused:⁹
I know there's no excuse can do me good.
   Vin. [*Aside to* HIPPOLITO] 'Tis now good policy to
      be from sight;
His vicious purpose to our sister's honor
Is crossed beyond our thought.¹⁰   30
   Hip. You little dreamed his father slept here?
   Vin. Oh, 'twas far beyond me.
But since it fell so—without frightful¹¹ word—
Would he had killed him, 'twould have eased our
      swords.

   [VINDICE *and* HIPPOLITO] *dissemble a flight.*¹²

Duke. Be comforted, our duchess, he shall die.
   Lus. Where's this slave-pander now? Out of mine
      eye,
Guilty¹³ of this abuse.

              Enter SPURIO *with his villains.*

   Spur. Y'are villains, fablers,
You have knaves' chins and harlots'¹⁴ tongues, you lie,
And I will damn you with one meal a day!   40
   1 Serv. Oh, good my lord!
   Spur.   'Sblood you shall never sup.
   2 Serv. Oh, I beseech you, sir!
   Spur.   To let my sword
Catch cold so long and miss him!
   1 Serv.   Troth, my lord,
'Twas his intent to meet there.
   Spur.   Heart, he's yonder!
Ha? What news here? Is the day out o' the socket,¹⁵

That it is noon at midnight, the court up?
How comes the guard so saucy with his[16] elbows?
   Lus. The bastard here?
Nay, then, the truth of my intent shall out—
My lord and father, hear me.
   Duke.   Bear him hence.   50
   Lus. I can with loyalty excuse—
   Duke. Excuse? To prison with the villain:
Death shall not long lag after him.
   Spur. [*Aside*] Good, i' faith 'tis not much amiss.
   Lus. Brothers, my best release lies on your tongues,
I pray persuade for me.
   Amb.   It is our duties:
Make yourself sure of us.
   Sup.   We'll sweat in pleading.
   Lus. And I may live to thank you.
                  Exit [*with* Guards].
   Amb. [*Aside*]   No, thy death
Shall thank me better.
   Spur. [*Aside*]   He's gone—I'll after him,
And know his trespass, seem to bear a part   60
In all his ills—but with a Puritan[17] heart.
                      Exit.
   Amb. Now, brother, let our hate and love be
     woven
So subtly together that in speaking
One word for his life, we may make three for his
     death;
The craftiest pleader gets most gold for breath.
   Sup. Set on, I'll not be far behind you, brother.
   Duke. Is't possible a son should
Be disobedient as far as the sword?
It is the highest, he can go no farther.
   Amb. My gracious lord, take pity.
   Duke.   Pity, boys?   70
   Amb. Nay, we'd be loath to move your grace too
     much:
We know the trespass is unpardonable,
Black, wicked and unnatural.
   Sup. In a son, oh, monstrous!
   Amb.   Yet, my lord,
A duke's soft hand strokes the rough head of law
And makes it lie smooth.
   Duke.   But my hand shall ne'er do't.
   Amb. That as you please, my lord.
   Sup.   We must needs
     confess
Some[18] father would have entered into hate
So deadly pointed, that before his eyes
He would ha' seen the execution sound[19]   80
Without corrupted favor.
   Amb.   But, my lord,
Your Grace may live the wonder of all times
In pardoning that offense which never yet
Had face to beg a pardon.
   Duke.   Honey,[20] how's this?
   Amb. Forgive him, good my lord, he's your own
     son,
And—I must needs say—'twas the vilelier done.
   Sup. He's the next heir; yet this true reason
     gathers;

None can possess that dispossess their fathers.
Be merciful—
   Duke. [*Aside*] Here's no stepmother's wit:[21]
I'll try 'em both upon their love and hate.   90
   Amb. Be merciful—although—
   Duke.   You have prevailed,
My wrath like flaming wax hath spent itself,
I know 'twas but some peevish moon[22] in him:
Go, let him be released.
   Sup. [*Aside*]   'Sfoot, how now, brother?
   Amb. Your grace doth please to speak beside your
     spleen;[23]
I would it[24] were so happy.
   Duke.   Why, go release him.
   Sup. Oh, my good lord, I know the fault's too
     weighty
And full of general loathing, too inhuman,
Rather by all men's voices worthy death.
   Duke. 'Tis true, too. Here, then, receive this signet;
Doom shall pass. Direct it to the judges.   101
He shall die ere many days;—make haste.
   Amb. All speed that may be.
We could have wished his burden not so sore,
We knew your grace did but delay before.
          Exeunt [AMBITIOSO *and* SUPERVACUO].
   Duke. Here's envy with a poor thin cover o'er it,
Like scarlet hid in lawn,[25] easily spied through;
This their ambition by the mother's side
Is dangerous and for safety must be purged.
I will prevent[26] their envies, sure it was   110
But some mistaken fury in our son
Which these aspiring boys would climb upon;
He shall be released suddenly.[27]

            Enter Nobles.

   1 Nob. Good morning to your grace.
   Duke.   Welcome, my
     lords.
   2 Nob. Our knees[28] shall take away the office of our
     feet for ever,
Unless your grace bestow a father's eye
Upon the clouded fortunes of your son,
And in compassionate virtue[29] grant him that
Which makes e'en mean men happy: liberty.
   Duke. [*Aside*] How seriously their loves and honors
     woo   120
For that which I am about to pray them do.—
Which— rise, my lords, your knees sign his release:
We freely pardon him.

---

16 *his:* Lussurioso's.
17 *Puritan:* Hypocritical.
18 *Some:* Another.
19 *sound:* carried out soundly.
20 *Honey:* Honied words.
21 *Here's . . . wit:* They're not so bright as their stepmother (I see what they are up to).
22 *peevish moon:* perverse fit of lunacy.
23 *beside your spleen:* putting your anger to one side.
24 *it:* the outcome.
25 *scarlet . . . lawn:* rich red cloth showing through transparent linen.
26 *prevent:* anticipate; also, "frustrate."
27 *suddenly:* immediately.
28 *knees:* The nobles kneel at this point.
29 *virtue:* power.

1 Nob. We owe your grace much thanks, and he
　much duty.
　　　　　　　　　　　　　　　Exeunt [Nobles].
　Duke. It well becomes that judge to nod at crimes
That does commit greater himself and lives.
I may forgive a disobedient error
That expect pardon for adultery,
And in my old days am a youth in lust.
Many a beauty have I turned to poison　　　　　130
In the denial,[30] covetous of all;
Age hot, is like a monster to be seen:
My hairs are white and yet my sins are green.

　　　　　　　　　　　　　　　　　　[*Exit.*]

ACT THREE

Scene One

Enter Ambitioso *and* Supervacuo.

　Sup. Brother, let my opinion sway you once;
I speak it for the best to have him die
Surest and soonest; if the signet come
Unto the judge's hands, why then his doom
Will be deferred till sittings and court-days,
Juries and further; faiths are bought and sold,
Oaths in these days are but the skin of gold.[1]
　Amb. In troth, 'tis true too.
　Sup.　　　　　　　　Then let's set by[2] the
　judges
And fall[3] to the officers; tis' but mistaking
The duke our father's meaning, and where he named
"Ere many days" 'tis but forgetting that　　　11
And have him die i' the morning.
　Amb.　　　　　　　　Excellent!
Then am I heir—duke in a minute!
　Sup. [*Aside*]　　　　　　　Nay,
And he[4] were once puffed out,[5] here is a pin
Should quickly prick your bladder.
　Amb.　　　　　　　Blest occasion!
He being packed[6] we'll have some trick and wile
To wind our youngest brother out of prison
That lies in for the rape; the lady's dead
And people's thoughts will soon be buri**è**d.
　Sup. We may with safety do't and live and feed:　20
The duchess' sons are too proud to bleed.

------

　[30] *turned . . . denial:* poisoned when she refused me, who
am. . . .

III.i.
　[1] *but . . . gold:* only valuable as they serve to mock-
solemnize a business deal.　　　[2] *set by:* ignore.
　[3] *fall:* appeal.　　　[4] *he:* Lussurioso.
　[5] *puffed out:* extinguished, like a candle.
　[6] *packed:* sent on his way.
　[7] *set . . . executioner:* sharpen his ax; and so, by transference, whet on the man himself.　　　[8] *Meet:* Appropriate.

III.ii.
　[1] *But:* Only.　　　　　　　[2] *myself:* the duke.

III.iii.
　[1] *that:* he that.　　　[2] *black:* in sin.　　　[3] *to be:* duke.

　Amb. We are, i' faith, to say true. Come, let's not
　linger—
I'll to the officers, go you before
And set an edge upon the executioner.[7]
　Sup. Let me alone to grind him.
　　　　　　　　　　　　　　　　　Exit.
　Amb.　　　　　　　　Meet;[8] farewell.
I am next now, I rise just in that place
Where thou'rt cut off—upon thy neck, kind brother;
The falling of one head lifts up another.
　　　　　　　　　　　　　　　　　Exit.

[III.ii.]

Enter, with the Nobles, Lussurioso, *from prison.*

　Lus. My lords, I am so much indebted to your loves
For this, oh, this delivery.
　1 Nob.　　　　　　　But[1] our duties,
My lord, unto the hopes that grow in you.
　Lus. If e'er I live to be myself,[2] I'll thank you.
Oh liberty, thou sweet and heavenly dame!
But hell, for prison, is too mild a name!
　　　　　　　　　　　　　　　　　Exeunt.

[III.iii]

Enter Ambitioso *and* Supervacuo *with* Officers.

　Amb. Officers, here's the duke's signet, your firm
　warrant,
Brings the command of present death along with it
Unto our brother, the duke's son; we are sorry
That we are so unnaturally employed
In such an unkind office, fitter far
For enemies than brothers.
　Sup.　　　　　　　　But you know
The duke's command must be obeyed.
　1 Off. It must and shall, my lord—this morning
　then,
So suddenly?
　Amb.　　　Ay, alas, poor good soul,
He must breakfast betimes, the executioner　　　10
Stands ready to put forth his cowardly valor.
　2 Off. Already?
　Sup. Already, i' faith; oh, sir, destruction hies,
And that[1] is least impudent, soonest dies.
　1 Off. Troth, you say true, my lord; we take our
　leaves.
Our office shall be sound, we'll not delay
The third part of a minute.
　Amb.　　　　　　　Therein you show
Yourselves good men and upright officers;
Pray let him die as private as he may,
Do him that favor, for the gaping people　　　20
Will but trouble him at his prayers
And make him curse and swear and so die black.[2]
Will you be so far kind?
　1 Off.　　　　　　　It shall be done, my lord.
　Amb. Why, we do thank you; if we live to be,[3]
You shall have a better office.
　2 Off.　　　　　　Your good lordship.
　Sup. Commend us to the scaffold in our tears.

1 Off. We'll weep and do your commendations.

                     Exeunt [Officers].

Amb. Fine fools in office!

Sup.   Things fall out so fit!

Amb. So happily! come, brother, ere next clock

His head will be made serve a bigger block.[4]   30

                          Exeunt.

[III.iv]

        Enter [*in prison*] YOUNGER SON.[1]

Young. Son. Keeper.[2]

Keep.   My lord.

Young. Son.   No news lately from

our brothers?

Are they unmindful of us?

Keep. My lord, a messenger came newly in

And brought this from 'em.

             [*He gives him a letter.*]

Young. Son.   Nothing but paper

comforts?

I looked for my delivery before this;

Had they been worth their oaths—prithee, be from us;

                   [*Exit* Keeper.]

Now, what say you, forsooth? Speak out, I pray:

                [*He reads the*] *letter.*

"Brother, be of good cheer"—

'Slud[3] it begins like a whore with good cheer!

"Thou shalt not be long a prisoner"—   10

Not five and thirty year like a bankrupt, I think so!

"We have thought upon a device to get thee out by a

trick"—

By a trick! Pox o' your trick and it be so long a playing.

"And so rest comforted, be merry and expect it

suddenly"—

Be merry, hang merry, draw and quarter merry, I'll be

mad!

Is't not strange that a man

Should lie in[4] a whole month for a woman?

Well, we shall see how sudden our brothers

Will be in their promise, I must expect still a trick:

I shall not be long a prisoner. How now, what news?

           [*Enter* Keeper.]

Keep. Bad news, my lord, I am discharged of you.

Young. Son. Slave, call'st thou that bad news! I

thank you, brothers.   22

Keep. My lord, 'twill prove so; here come the

officers

Into whose hands I must commit you.

                   [*Exit* Keeper.]

Young. Son. Ha, officers? What, why?

           [*Enter* Officers.]

1 Off. You must pardon us, my lord,

Our office must be sound, here is our warrant,

The signet from the duke; you must straight suffer.

Young. Son. Suffer? I'll suffer you to be gone, I'll

suffer you

To come no more—what would you have me suffer?

2 Off. My lord, those words were better changed to

prayers,   31

The time's but brief with you; prepare to die.

Young. Son. Sure, 'tis not so.

3 Off.   It is too true, my lord.

Young. Son. I tell you 'tis not, for the duke my

father

Deferred me till next sitting,[5] and I look

E'en every minute, threescore times an hour,

For a release, a trick, wrought by my brothers.

1 Off. A trick, my lord? If you expect such comfort

Your hope's as fruitless as a barren woman:

Your brothers were the unhappy messengers   40

That brought this powerful token for your death.

Young. Son. My brothers! no, no!

2 Off.   'Tis most true, my

lord.

Young. Son. My brothers to bring a warrant for my

death:

How strange this shows!

3 Off.   There's no delaying time.

Young. Son. Desire 'em hither, call 'em up, my

brothers—

They shall deny it to your faces!

1 Off.   My lord,

They're far enough by this, at least at court,

And this most strict command they left behind 'em.

When grief swum in their eyes: they showed like

brothers,

Brim-full of heavy sorrow; but the duke   50

Must have his pleasure.

Young. Son.   His pleasure?

1 Off. These were their last words which my memory

bears:

"Commend us to the scaffold in our tears."

Young. Son. Pox dry their tears: what should I do

with tears?

I hate 'em worse than any citizen's son[6]

Can hate salt water. Here came a letter now,

New bleeding from their pens, scarce stinted[7] yet—

Would I'd been torn in pieces when I tore it—

Look you officious whoresons, words of comfort:

"Not long a prisoner."   60

1 Off. It says true in that, sir, for you must suffer

presently.

Young. Son. A villainous Duns[8] upon the letter:

knavish exposition!

---

    [4] *block:* on which he will be executed, as opposed to the
smaller block or dummy for hatmaking

III.iv.

    [1] *Younger Son:* Q "Junior Brother."

    [2] *Keeper:* Who has been awaiting his cue at the rear of the
stage.   [3] *'Slud:* God's blood.

    [4] *lie in:* punning on confinement in preparation for child-
birth.   [5] *sitting:* of the court.

    [6] *citizen's son:* who does not wish to go to sea.

    [7] *stinted:* stopped (alluding to the "blood"—ink).

    [8] *Duns:* Dunce (from the medieval Scholastic philosopher
Duns Scotus, whose hairsplitting made him a type of foolishness in the Renaissance).

Look you then here, sir: "We'll get thee out by a trick,"
    says he.
  2 Off. That may hold too, sir, for you know
A trick[9] is commonly four cards, which was meant
By us four officers.
    Young. Son.   Worse and worse dealing.[10]
  1 Off. The hour beckons us,
The headsman waits: lift up your eyes to heaven.
    Young. Son. I thank you, faith, good pretty
      wholesome counsel!
I should look up to heaven, as you said,   70
Whilst he behind me cozens me of my head!
Ay, that's the trick.
  3 Off.   You delay too long, my lord.
    Young. Son. Stay, good authority's bastards:[11] since
    I must
Through brothers' perjury die, oh, let me venom
Their souls with curses.
  1 Off.   Come, 'tis no time to curse.
    Young. Son. Must I bleed then without respect of
    sign?[12] Well—
My fault was sweet sport which the world approves;
I die for that which every woman loves.
                        Exeunt.

[III.v]

Enter VINDICE *[disguised] with* HIPPOLITO,
his brother.

  Vin. Oh, sweet, delectable, rare, happy, ravishing!
  Hip. Why, what's the matter, brother?
  Vin.   Oh, 'tis able
To make a man spring up and knock his forehead
Against yon silver ceiling.[1]
  Hip.   Prithee, tell me
Why may not I partake with you? You vowed once
To give me share to[2] every tragic thought.

---

   [9] *trick:* denoting also a hand of cards.
  [10] *dealing:* grim punning on card play.
  [11] *bastards:* illegitimate officers (because employed in a
perjured or false action).
  [12] *without . . . sign:* with no proper signalizing of the event;
or perhaps, technically, "without astrological concurrence."
III.v.
   [1] *silver ceiling:* the painted "heavens" covering the stage.
   [2] *to:* in.   [3] *divide:* share; impart the news.
   [4] *angle:* corner.   [5] *shape:* disguise as villain.
   [6] *most dreadfully digested:* concocted to occasion fear.
   [7] *missed me:* left me out.   [8] *find:* catch up with.
   [9] *apprehensions:* anticipations.
  [10] *stoops unto:* lowers himself to the level of.
  [11] *And . . . prices:* If "vices" is used as a personification
like the Vice character in the earlier drama, the phrase means
"There are more secretly wicked persons abroad, whose
wickedness is both prevalent and undisclosed, than there
are open and manifest prostitutes, who advertise and sell
themselves."
  [12] *tires:* a headdress, necessarily completed with a wig and
veil.   [13] *respect:* care about.
  [14] *shell:* of no consequence.
  [15] *beguiled:* entertained; with sense of "fooled" in the
next line.   [16] *such:* a business.
  [17] *quaint:* curious, ingenious.

  Vin. By th' Mass, I think I did, too:
Then I'll divide[3] it to thee. The old duke,
Thinking my outward shape and inward heart
Are cut out of one piece—for he that prates his
    secrets,
His heart stands o' the outside—hires me by price 11
To greet him with a lady
In some place veiled from the eyes o' the court,
Some darkened blushless angle[4] that is guilty
Of his forefathers' lusts, and great folks' riots;
To which I easily, to maintain my shape,[5]
Consented, and did wish his impudent grace
To meet her here in this unsunnèd lodge
Wherein 'tis night at noon, and here the rather
Because unto the torturing of his soul   20
The bastard and the duchess have appointed
Their meeting too in this luxurious circle—
Which most afflicting sight will kill his eyes
Before we kill the rest of him.
  Hip. 'Twill, i' faith, most dreadfully digested.[6]
I see not how you could have missed me,[7] brother.
  Vin. True, but the violence of my joy forgot it.
  Hip. Ay; but where's that lady now?
  Vin.   Oh, at that word
I'm lost again, you cannot find[8] me yet,
I'm in a throng of happy apprehensions![9]   30
He's suited for a lady: I have took care
For a delicious lip, a sparkling eye:
You shall be witness, brother,
Be ready, stand with your hat off.
                        Exit.
  Hip. Troth, I wonder what lady it should be.
Yet 'tis no wonder, now I think again,
To have a lady stoop to a duke, that stoops unto[10] his
    men:
'Tis common to be common, through the world,
And there's more private common shadowing vices
Than those who are known both by their names and
    prices.[11]   40
'Tis part of my allegiance to stand bare
To the duke's concubine—and here she comes.

Enter VINDICE *with the skull of his love dressed up
in tires.*[12]

  Vin. Madam, his grace will not be absent long.
Secret? Ne'er doubt us, madam. 'Twill be worth
Three velvet gowns to your ladyship. Known?
Few ladies respect[13] that; disgrace? A poor thin shell![14]
'Tis the best grace you have to do it well;
I'll save your hand that labor, I'll unmask you.

        [VINDICE *unmasks the skull.*]

  Hip. Why, brother, brother.
  Vin. Art thou beguiled[15] now? Tut, a lady can 50
At such,[16] all hid, beguile a wiser man.
Have I not fitted the old surfeiter
With a quaint[17] piece of beauty? Age and bare bone
Are e'er allied in action. Here's an eye
Able to tempt a great man—to serve God;
A pretty hanging lip, that has forgot now to dissemble.
Methinks this mouth should make a swearer tremble,

A drunkard clasp his teeth, and not undo 'em
To suffer wet damnation to run through 'em.
Here's a cheek keeps her color, let the wind [18] go
    whistle: 60
Spout rain, we fear thee not, be hot or cold
All's one with us. And is not he absurd
Whose fortunes are upon their faces set,
That fear no other God but wind and wet?
   Hip. Brother, y'ave spoke that right.
Is this the form that, living, shone so bright?
   Vin. The very same.
And now methinks I could e'en chide myself
For doting on her beauty, though her death
Shall be revenged after no common action.   70
Does the silkworm [19] expand her yellow labors
For thee? For thee does she undo herself?
Are lordships sold to maintain ladyships
For the poor benefit of a bewitching minute?
Why does yon fellow falsify highways [20]
And put his life between the judge's lips
To refine [21] such a thing, keeps horse and men
To beat their valors [22] for her?
Surely we're all mad people and they,
Whom we think are, are not: we mistake those. 80
'Tis we are mad in sense, they but in clothes.
   Hip. Faith, and in clothes too we, give us our due.
   Vin. Does every proud and self-affecting [23] dame
Camphor [24] her face for this, and grieve her maker
In sinful baths of milk, when many an infant starves
For her superfluous outside—all for this?
Who now bids twenty pound a night, prepares
Music, perfumes and sweetmeats? All are hushed,
Thou may'st lie chaste now! It were fine, methinks,
To have thee seen at revels, forgetful feasts   90
And unclean brothels; sure 'twould fright the sinner
And make him a good coward, put a reveler
Out of his antic amble, [25]
And cloy an epicure with empty dishes.
Here might a scornful and ambitious woman
Look though and through herself; see, ladies, with false
    forms
You deceive men but cannot deceive worms.
Now to my tragic business. Look you, brother,
I have not fashioned this only for show
And useless property, [26] no—it shall bear a part 100
E'en in it [27] own revenge. This very skull,
Whose mistress the duke poisoned with this drug,
The mortal curse of the earth, shall be revenged
In the like strain [28] and kiss his lips to death.
As much as the dumb thing can, he shall feel;
What fails in poison we'll supply in steel.
   Hip. Brother, I do applaud thy constant vengeance,
The quaintness of thy malice, above thought.
   Vin. So, 'tis laid on; now come and welcome, Duke,
I have her for thee. I protest it, brother,   110
Methinks she makes almost as fair a sign [29]
As some old gentlewoman in a periwig.
Hide thy face now for shame, thou hadst need have a
    mask now.
'Tis vain when beauty flows, but when it fleets
This [30] would become graves better than the streets.

   Hip. You have my voice in that. Hark, the duke's
    come.
   Vin. Peace—let's observe what company he brings
And how he does absent [31] 'em, for you know
He'll wish all private. Brother, fall you back a little
With the bony lady.
   Hip.   That I will.
   Vin.   So, so—   120
Now nine years' vengeance crowd into a minute.
                                [They retire.]

[Enter the DUKE *and* Gentlemen.]

   Duke. You shall have leave to leave us, with this
    charge:
Upon our lives, if we be missed by the duchess
Or any of the nobles, to give out
We're privately rid forth.
   Vin.   Oh, happiness!
   Duke. With some few honorable gentlemen, you may
    say:
You may name those that are away from court.
   Gent. Your will and pleasure shall be done, my lord.
                    [Exeunt Gentlemen.]
   Vin. Privately rid forth?   129
He strives to make sure work on't.

                              [He advances.]

                     Your good grace.
   Duke. Piato! well done. Hast brought her? What
    lady is't?
   Vin. Faith, my lord, a country lady, a little
Bashful at first as most of them are, but after
The first kiss, my lord, the worst is past with them.
Your grace knows now what you have to do. She's [32]
    somewhat
A grave look with her, but—
   Duke.   I love that best, conduct
    her.
   Vin. [*Aside*] Have at all! [33]
   Duke. In gravest looks the greatest faults seem less:
Give me that sin that's robed in holiness.
   Vin. [*Aside*] Back with the torch; brother, raise the
    perfumes.   140
   Duke. How sweet can a duke breathe? Age has no
    fault. [34]

---

[18] *wind:* which is powerless to remove *this* "natural" complexion.

[19] *silkworm:* who spins a yellowish cocoon, the fruit of which is also costly, like yellow gold.

[20] *falsify highways:* as by acting the highwayman or thief.

[21] *refine:* make more elegant, as by lavishing money on.

[22] *beat their valors:* expend their courage.

[23] *self-affecting:* self-loving.

[24] *Camphor:* Cream (with cosmetics made partly of camphor).   [25] *antic amble:* grotesque dance.

[26] *property:* appurtenance to stage business.

[27] *it:* its (acceptable early form of the genitive).

[28] *strain:* way.   [29] *sign:* show(?).

[30] *'Tis . . . This:* A mask is to no purpose when beauty is present, but when it disappears (as in death), the skull that is disclosed. . . .   [31] *absent:* get rid of.   [32] *She's:* She has.

[33] *Have at all!:* A summons to battle—"Now for it!"

[34] *fault:* flaw (that my dukedom cannot make good).

Pleasure should meet in a perfumèd mist.
Lady, sweetly encountered: I came from court,
I must be bold with you—oh! what's this? Oh!

[He kisses the skull.]

Vin. Royal villain, white[35] devil!
Duke.   Oh!
Vin. Brother—place the torch here that his
affrighted eyeballs
May start into those hollows. Duke, dost know
Yon dreadful vizard? View it well; 'tis the skull
Of Gloriana, whom thou poisonedst last.[36]
Duke. Oh, 't as poisoned me!   150
Vin. Didst not know that till now?
Duke.   What are you
two?
Vin. Villains all three! the very ragged[37] bone
Has been sufficiently revenged.
Duke. Oh, Hippolito—call treason!
Hip. Yes, my good lord. Treason, treason, treason!

Stamping on him.

Duke. Then I'm betrayed.
Vin. Alas, poor lecher: in the hands of knaves
A slavish duke is baser than his slaves.
Duke. My teeth are eaten out.
Vin.   Hadst any left?
Hip.   I think
but few.
Vin. Then those that did eat are eaten.
Duke.   Oh, my
tongue!   160
Vin. Your tongue? 'Twill teach you to kiss closer,
Not like a slobbering Dutchman.[38] You have eyes
still:
Look, monster, what a lady hast thou made[39] me
My once betrothed wife.
Duke.   Is it thou, villain? Nay then—
Vin. 'Tis I, 'tis Vindice, 'tis I!
Hip. And let this comfort thee. Our lord and father
Fell sick upon the infection of thy frowns
And died in sadness. Be that thy hope of life.
Duke.   Oh!
Vin. He had his tongue, yet grief made him die
speechless.

---

35 *white:* fair-appearing (the devil being black).
36 *last:* as the most recent of his victims.
37 *ragged:* rough.
38 *slobbering Dutchman:* proverbial for drunkenness and
lust; hence the adjective. Q "Flobbering" (befouling),
which may be correct.   39 *made:* made for.
40 *pestilent:* plague-stricken.
41 *rides . . . brow:* the inevitable allusion to the cuckold's
horns, with "rides" signifying sexual intercourse.
42 *clips:* embraces.   43 *hires:* rewards.
44 *Once . . . quitted:* Sooner or later before they die, adulterers are punished (by being cuckolded) for their adultery.
45 *quittance:* quit; revenge.
46 *not . . . object:* being unable to endure what he sees.
47 *Whist:* Hush.
48 *doubtful:* alluding to his uncertain parentage.
49 *rubs:* puts thoughts of.   50 *waxen fire:* candles.
51 *hasped:* clasped (with her).

Puh, 'tis but early yet; now I'll begin   170
To stick thy soul with ulcers; I will make
Thy spirit grievous sore, it shall not rest
But like some pestilent[40] man, toss in thy breast.
Mark me, duke,
Thou'rt a renowned, high, and mighty cuckold!
Duke.   Oh!
Vin. Thy bastard, thy bastard rides a-hunting in thy
brow.[41]
Duke. Millions of deaths!
Vin.   Nay, to afflict thee more,
Here in this lodge they meet for damnèd clips:[42]
Those eyes shall see the incest of their lips.   179
Duke. Is there a hell besides this, villains?
Vin.   Villain?
Nay, heaven is just, scorns are the hires[43] of scorns,
I ne'er knew yet adulterer without horns.
Hip. Once ere they die 'tis quitted.[44]
Vin.   Hark the music,
Their banquet is prepared, they're coming—
Duke. Oh, kill me not with that sight.
Vin. Thou shalt not lose that sight for all thy
dukedom.
Duke. Traitors, murderers!
Vin. What, is not thy tongue eaten out yet?
Then we'll invent a silence. Brother, stifle the torch.
Duke. Treason! murder!   190
Vin. Nay, faith, we'll have you hushed. Now with thy
dagger
Nail down his tongue, and mine shall keep possession
About his heart; if he but gasp he dies.
We dread not death to quittance[45] injuries. Brother,
If he but wink, not brooking the foul object,
Let our two other hands tear up his lids
And make his eyes, like comets, shine through blood.
When the bad bleeds, then is the tragedy good.   198
Hip. Whist,[47] brother, music's at our ear: they come.

Enter [SPURIO] *the bastard, meeting the* DUCHESS.
[They kiss.]

Spur. Had not that kiss a taste of sin 'twere sweet.
Duch. Why, there's no pleasure sweet but it is sinful.
Spur. True, such a bitter sweetness fate hath given;
Best side to us, is the worst side to heaven.
Duch. Push, come, 'tis the old duke thy doubtful[48]
father—
The thought of him rubs[49] heaven in thy way;
But I protest by yonder waxen fire,[50]
Forget him or I'll poison him.
Spur. Madam, you urge a thought which ne'er had
life,
So deadly do I loathe him for my birth
That, if he took me hasped[51] within his bed,   210
I would add murder to adultery
And with my sword give up his years to death.
Duch. Why, now thou'rt sociable: let's in and feast.
Loudest music, sound: pleasure is banquet's guests.
                    Exeunt [SPURIO *and* DUCHESS].
Duke. I cannot brook—
                              [Dies.]
Vin.   The brook is turned to blood.

Hip. Thanks to loud music.

Vin.   'Twas our friend indeed;
'Tis state,⁵² in music for a duke to bleed.
The dukedom wants a head, though yet unknown;⁵³
As fast as they peep up let's cut 'em down.

                                        Exeunt.

[III.vi]

Enter the Duchess' two sons, AMBITIOSO *and*
SUPERVACUO.

Amb. Was not his execution rarely plotted?
We are the duke's sons now.

Sup. Ay, you may thank my policy¹ for that.

Amb. Your policy for what?

Sup. Why, was't not my invention, brother,
To slip² the judges, and, in lesser compass,³
Did not I draw the model⁴ of his death,
Advising you to sudden officers
And e'en extemporal⁵ execution?

Amb. Heart, 'twas a thing I thought on, too.   10

Sup. You thought on't, too! 'sfoot,⁶ slander not
your thoughts
With glorious untruth: I know 'twas from you.⁷

Amb. Sir, I say 'twas in my head.

[*Sup.*]   Ay, like your brains,
then:
Ne'er to come out as long as you lived.

Amb. You'd have the honor on't, forsooth, that your
wit
Led him to the scaffold.

Sup.   Since it is my due
I'll publish't—but⁸ I'll ha't, in spite of you.

Amb. Methinks y'are much too bold, you should a
little
Remember us, brother, next to be honest⁹ duke.

Sup. [*Aside*] Ay, it shall be as easy for you to be
duke   20
As to be honest, and that's never, i' faith.

Amb. Well, cold he is by this time, and because
We're both ambitious be it our amity,
And let the glory be shared equally.

Sup. I am content to that.

Amb. This night our younger brother shall out of
prison:
I have a trick.

Sup.   A trick? Prithee, what is't?

Amb. We'll get him out by a wile.

Sup.   Prithee, what
wile?

Amb. No, sir, you shall not know it till it be done,
For then you'd swear 'twere yours.

[*Enter an* Officer *with a head in his hand.*]

Sup.   How now, what's
he?   30

Amb. One of the officers.

Sup.   Desired news.

Amb.   How now,
my friend?

Off. My lords, under your pardon, I am allotted
To that desertless¹⁰ office to present you
With the yet bleeding head—

Sup. [*Aside*]   Ha! ha! excellent!

Amb. [*Aside*] All's sure our own—brother, canst
weep, thinkst thou?
'Twould grace our flattery much; think of some dame,
'Twill teach thee to dissemble.

Sup. [*Aside*] I have thought—now for yourself.

Amb. Our sorrows are so fluent
Our eyes o'erflow our tongues; words spoke in tears   40
Are like the murmurs of the waters, the sound
Is loudly heard but cannot be distinguished.¹¹

Sup. How died he pray?

Off.   Oh, full of rage and spleen.

Sup. He died most valiantly, then: we're glad to
hear it.

Off. We could not woo him once to pray.

Amb. He showed himself a gentleman in that,
Give him his due.

Off.   But in the stead of prayer
He drew forth oaths.

Sup.   Then did he pray, dear heart,
Although you understood him not.

Off.   My lords,
E'en at his last—with pardon be it spoke—   50
He cursed you both.

Sup.   He cursed us? 'Las, good soul.

Amb. It was not in our powers, but the duke's
pleasure.
[*Aside*] Finely dissembled o' both sides! sweet fate,
Oh, happy opportunity!

Enter LUSSURIOSO.

Lus.   Now, my lords—

Amb. and Sup.   Oh!

Lus. Why do you shun me, brothers? You may come
nearer now,
The savor¹² of the prison has forsook me,
I thank such kind lords as yourselves I'm free.

Amb. Alive!

Sup.   In health!

Amb.   Released!
We were both e'en amazed with joy to see it.

Lus. I am much to thank you.   60

Sup. Faith, we spared no tongue unto my lord the
duke.

Amb. I know your delivery, brother,
Had not been half so sudden but for us.

---

⁵² *state:* proper to his lofty rank.
⁵³ *yet unknown:* nobody knows it yet.

III.vi.
  ¹ *policy:* craft.   ² *slip:* bypass.
  ³ *compass:* degree.   ⁴ *model:* plan.
  ⁵ *sudden . . . extemporal:* employ swift officers and also
hasty (i.e., without resorting to normal legal procedures).
  ⁶ *'sfoot:* God's foot.   ⁷ *from you:* no part of your idea.
  ⁸ *but:* only.   ⁹ *honest:* honorable.
  ¹⁰ *desertless:* unrewarding.
  ¹¹ *distinguished:* understood, interpreted.
  ¹² *savor:* stench.

Sup. Oh, how we pleaded.

Lus.   Most deserving brothers;
In my best studies I will think of it.

                                        Exit.

Amb. Oh, death and vengeance!

Sup.   Hell and torments!

Amb.   Slave!
Camest thou to delude us?

Off.   Delude you, my lords?

Sup. Ay villain: where's this head now?

Off.   Why here,
    my lord;
Just after his delivery you both came
With warrant from the duke to behead your brother.

Amb. Ay, our brother, the duke's son.   71

Off. The duke's son, my lord, had his release
    before you came.

Amb. Whose head's that, then?

Off.   His, whom you left
    command for—
Your own brother's.

Amb.   Our brother's? Oh, furies!

Sup. Plagues!

Amb.   Confusions!

Sup.   Darkness!

Amb.   Devils!

Sup. Fell it out so accursedly?

Amb.   So damnedly?

Sup. Villain, I'll brain thee with it!

Off.   Oh, my good
    lord!

Sup. The devil overtake thee!

Amb.   Oh, fatal—

Sup. Oh, prodigious [13] to our bloods!

Amb.   Did we
    dissemble?

Sup. Did we make our tears women [14] for thee?   80

Amb. Laugh and rejoice for thee?

Sup.   Bring warrant for
    thy death?

Amb. Mock off thy head?

Sup.   You had a trick,
You had a wile, forsooth.

Amb.   A murrain [15] meet 'em!
There's none of these wiles that ever come to good;
I see now there is nothing sure in mortality but
    mortality. [16]
Well no more words—shalt be revenged, i' faith.
Come throw off clouds now, brother; think of
    vengeance

---

[13] *prodigious:* portentous of evil.
[14] *our tears women:* ourselves weep hypocritically like
women.   [15] *murrain:* plague.
[16] *mortality . . . mortality:* life . . . death.
[17] *Sirrah:* Lussurioso (the mode of address is contemptuous).
IV.i.
[1] *wittily elected:* intelligently chosen.   [2] *will:* deliberate.
[3] *in . . . forehead:* to prevent his being cuckolded.
[4] *razed:* grazed.   [5] *Jars:* Comes (discordantly).
[6] *iron age:* sword; shackles; bitter time, the last and
worst of the mythical four ages of antiquity.

And deeper settled hate. Sirrah, [17] sit fast:
We'll put down all, but thou shalt down at last.

                                        Exeunt.

ACT FOUR

Scene One

Enter LUSSURIOSO *with* HIPPOLITO.

Lus. Hippolito.

Hip.   My lord: has your good lordship
Aught to command me in?

Lus.   I prithee leave us.

Hip. How's this? Come, and leave us?

Lus.   Hippolito.

Hip. Your honor, I stand ready for any duteous
    employment.

Lus. Heart, what makest thou here?

Hip. [*Aside*]   A pretty lordly
    humor:
He bids me to be present; to depart;
Something has stung his honor.

Lus.   Be nearer, draw nearer;
You're not so good, methinks, I'm angry with you.

Hip. With me, my lord? I'm angry with myself
    for't.

Lus. You did prefer a goodly fellow to me: 10
'Twas wittily elected, [1] 'twas—I thought
He'd been a villain, and he proves a knave!
To me a knave!

Hip.   I chose him for the best, my lord:
'Tis much my sorrow if neglect in him
Breed discontent in you.

Lus.   Neglect? 'Twas will: [2] judge of
    it:
Firmly to tell of an incredible act
Not to be thought, less to be spoken of,
'Twixt my stepmother and the bastard—oh,
Incestuous sweets between 'em!

Hip.   Fie, my lord.

Lus. I, in kind loyalty to my father's forehead, [3]   20
Made this a desperate arm, and in that fury
Committed treason on the lawful bed
And with my sword e'en razed [4] my father's bosom,
For which I was within a stroke of death.

Hip. Alack, I'm sorry. [*Aside*] 'Sfoot, just upon the
    stroke
Jars [5] in my brother: 'twill be villainous music!

Enter VINDICE.

Vin. My honored lord.

Lus. Away, prithee, forsake us: hereafter we'll not
    know thee.

Vin. Not know me, my lord? Your lordship cannot
    choose.

Lus. Begone I say, thou art a false knave.   30

Vin. Why, the easier to be known, my lord.

Lus. Push, I shall prove too bitter with a word,
Make thee a perpetual prisoner
And lay this iron age [6] upon thee.

Vin. [*Aside*]   Mum,

For there's a doom would make a woman dumb.
Missing the bastard next him, the wind's come about;[7]
Now 'tis my brother's turn to stay, mine to go out.

                                  Exit.

  Lus. Has greatly moved me.
  Hip.   Much to blame, i' faith.
  Lus. But I'll recover, to his ruin. 'Twas told me
    lately,
I know not whether falsely, that you'd a brother.   40
  Hip. Who I? Yes, my good lord, I have a brother.
  Lus. How chance the court ne'er saw him? Of what
    nature?
How does he apply[8] his hours?
  Hip.   Faith, to curse Fates
Who, as he thinks, ordained him to be poor;
Keeps at home full of want and discontent.
  Lus. There's hope in him, for discontent and want
Is the best clay to mold a villain of;
Hippolito, wish him repair to us;
If there be aught in him to please our blood[9]
For thy sake we'll advance him, and build fair   50
His meanest fortunes; for it is in us
To rear up towers from cottages.
  Hip. It is so, my lord; he will attend your honor,
But he's a man in whom much melancholy dwells.
  Lus. Why, the better: bring him to court.
  Hip. With willingness and speed. [*Aside*] Whom he
    cast off
E'en now, must now succeed.[10] Brother, disguise must
    off;
In thine own shape now I'll prefer thee to him:
How strangely does himself work to undo him.

                                    Exit.

  Lus. This fellow will come fitly; he shall kill   60
That other slave that did abuse my spleen
And made it swell to treason. I have put
Much of my heart into him; he must die.
He that knows great men's secrets, and proves slight,[11]
That man ne'er lives to see his beard turn white.
Ay, he shall speed[12] him: I'll employ the[13] brother,
Slaves are but nails to drive out one another.
He being of black[14] condition, suitable
To want and ill content, hope of preferment
Will grind him to an edge.   70

          The Nobles *enter.*[15]

  1 Nob. Good days unto your honor.
  Lus.   My kind lords,
I do return the like.
  2 Nob.   Saw you my lord the duke?
  Lus. My lord and father: is he from court?
  1 Nob. He's sure from court, but where, which way
    his pleasure
Took, we know not nor can we hear on't.

        [*Enter more* Nobles.]

  Lus. Here come those should tell—saw you my lord
    and father?
  3 Nob. Not since two hours before noon, my lord,
And then he privately rid forth.
  Lus. Oh, he's rode forth.

  1 Nob.   'Twas wondrous privately.
  2 Nob. There's none i' the court had any knowledge
    on't.   80
  Lus. His grace is old, and sudden,[16] 'tis no treason
To say the duke my father has a humor,
Or such a toy,[17] about him; what in us
Would appear light,[18] in him seems virtuous.
  3 Nob. 'Tis oracle,[19] my lord.

                                    Exeunt.

        [IV.ii]

    Enter VINDICE *and* HIPPOLITO, VINDICE *out*
               of his disguise.

  Hip. So, so, all's as it should be, y'are yourself.
  Vin. How that great villain puts me to my shifts![1]
  Hip. He that did lately in disguise reject thee
Shall, now thou art thyself, as much respect thee.
  Vin. 'Twill be the quainter fallacy; but brother,
'Sfoot, what use will he put me to now, thinks't thou?
  Hip. Nay, you must pardon me in that, I know not;
H'as some employment for you, but what 'tis
He and his secretary the devil knows best.
  Vin. Well, I must suit my tongue to his desires   10
What color soe'er they be, hoping at last
To pile up all my wishes on his breast.[2]
  Hip. Faith, brother, he himself shows the way.
  Vin. Now the duke is dead the realm is clad in clay;[3]
His death being not yet known, under his name
The people still are governed; well, thou his son
Art not long-lived, thou shalt not 'joy his death:
To kill thee then I should most honor thee,
For 'twould stand firm in every man's belief
Thou'st[4] a kind child, and only diedst with grief.   20
  Hip. You fetch about well; but let's talk in present.[5]
How will you appear in fashion[6] different,
As well as in apparel, to make all things possible?
If you be but once tripped we fall for ever.
It is not the least policy to be doubtful;[7]
You must change tongue—familiar was your first.
  Vin. Why, I'll bear me in some strain of melancholy
And string myself with heavy sounding wire
Like such an instrument that speaks merry things
    sadly.

---

    [7] *Missing . . . about:* Editorial insertion of a comma after
"bastard" makes the line mean "Having missed killing
Spurio, and then Lussurioso, I find that my fortunes have
fallen."   [8] *apply:* spend.
   [9] *blood:* inclination.   [10] *succeed:* himself.
  [11] *slight:* untrustworthy.   [12] *speed:* kill.
  [13] *the:* Q "thee."   [14] *black:* melancholic.
  [15] *The . . . enter:* Q has Lussurioso speak these words.
  [16] *sudden:* capricious, "humorous."   [17] *toy:* whim.
  [18] *light:* frivolous.   [19] *oracle:* truth.

IV.ii.
  [1] *shifts:* cunning.   [2] *To . . . breast:* as by killing him.
  [3] *clad in clay:* dead; enfeebled.   [4] *Thou'st:* Thou wast.
  [5] *You . . . present:* You talk cleverly in circles, but let's get
down to business.   [6] *fashion:* manner, breeding.
  [7] *It . . . doubtful:* It's wise to anticipate trouble.

Hip. Then 'tis as I meant, I gave you out   30
At first in discontent.
    Vin.   I'll turn[8] myself, and then—
    Hip. 'Sfoot, here he comes—hast thought upon't?
    Vin. Salute him, fear not me.

          [*Enter* LUSSURIOSO.]

    Lus.   Hippolito.
    Hip. Your lordship.
    Lus.   What's he yonder?
    Hip. 'Tis Vindice, my discontented brother,
Whom, 'cording to your will I've brought to court.
    Lus. Is that thy brother? Beshrew me,[9] a good
presence;
I wonder h'as been from the court so long.
Come nearer.
    Hip. Brother: lord Lussurioso, the duke's son.   40
    Lus. Be more near to us: welcome, nearer yet.
    Vin. How don you? God you god den.[10]

        [VINDICE] *snatches off his hat and makes*
                        legs[11] *to him.*

    Lus.   We thank thee.
How strangely such a coarse, homely salute
Shows in the place, where we greet in fire—
Nimble and desperate[12] tongues! should we name
God in a salutation 'twould ne'er be 'stood on't—
    heaven!
Tell me, what has made thee so melancholy?
    Vin. Why, going to law.
    Lus. Why, will that make a man melancholy?   49
    Vin. Yes, to look long upon ink and black buckram.[13]
I went me to law in *anno quadragesimo secundo*, and I
waded out of it in *anno sextagesimo tertio.*[14]
    Lus. What, three and twenty years[15] in law?

---

    [8] *turn:* change.   [9] *Beshrew me:* The devil take me!
    [10] *don . . . den:* Vindice in his greeting is affecting rustic
speech, appropriate to one who has been absent from court.
    [11] *makes legs:* bows.
    [12] *desperate:* abandoned, appropriate to courtiers who
decline to invoke God as Vindice has done.
    [13] *black buckram:* of which the lawyer's bag or "brief-
case" was made.
    [14] *L.:* forty-second year . . . sixty-third year.
    [15] *three and twenty years:* Lussurio's computation is awry.
    [16] *pullen:* poultry.   [17] *terms:* when the law was sitting.
    [18] *canvassed:* brought to question.
    [19] *Barbary:* Barbarous.
    [20] *writ of error:* which sought to overturn a legal judgment.
    [21] *sasarara:* writ of certiorari issued by a superior court to
overturn the judgment of a lower court.
    [22] *bent:* disposition; curve.
    [23] *how . . . him:* The sense is that the rich landlord, when
on his deathbed, is still thinking of documents regarding
dispossession of property and promissory notes ("forfeitures
and obligations"), which are locked up where he can keep
his eye on them.   [24] *gossips:* the women attending on him.
    [25] *whurls:* makes the death rattle.   [26] *conceit:* witty idea.
    [27] *in picture:* not literally drawn or painted but moralized
in words.   [28] *published:* known to be.
    [29] *pared . . . quick:* got at him where he lives.
    [30] *And . . . out:* You've missed my point.
    [31] *in colors:* by being represented or given out for what
they are.   [32] *parlous:* perilous.

    Vin. I have known those that have been five and
fifty, and all about pullen[16] and pigs.
    Lus. May it be possible such men should breathe to
vex the terms[17] so much?
    Vin. 'Tis food to some, my lord. There are old men
at the present that are so poisoned with the affectation
of law words, having had many suits canvassed,[18]   60
that their common talk is nothing but Barbary[19] Latin;
they cannot so much as pray, but in law, that their sins
may be removed with a writ of error,[20] and their souls
fetched up to heaven with a sasarara.[21]
    [*Lus.*] It seems most strange to me;
Yet all the world meets round in the same bent:[22]
Where the heart's set, there goes the tongue's consent.
How dost apply thy studies, fellow?
    Vin. Study? Why, to think how a great rich man lies
a-dying, and a poor cobbler tolls the bell for him;   70
how he cannot depart the world, and see the great chest
stand before him;[23] when he lies speechless, how he will
point you readily to all the boxes, and when he is past all
memory, as the gossips[24] guess, then thinks he of forfeitures and obligations. Nay, when to all men's hearings he whurls[25] and rattles in the throat, he's busy
threatening his poor tenants; and this would last me
now some seven years thinking, or thereabouts! but I
have a conceit[26] a-coming in picture[27] upon this, I
draw it myself, which, i' faith, la, I'll present to   80
your honor; you shall not choose but like it, for your
lordship shall give me nothing for it.
    Lus. Nay, you mistake me then,
For I am published[28] bountiful enough;
Let's taste of your conceit.
    Vin. In picture, my lord?
    Lus.   Ay, in picture.
    Vin.   Marry, this
      it is:
"A usuring father to be boiling in hell, and his son and
heir with a whore dancing over him."
    Hip. [*Aside*] Ha's pared him to the quick.[29]
    Lus. The conceit's pretty, i' faith—   90
But tak't upon my life 'twill ne'er be liked.
    Vin. No? Why, I'm sure the whore will be liked well
      enough!
    Hip. [*Aside*] Ay, if she were out o' the picture he'd
like her then himself.
    Vin. And as for the son and heir, he shall be an eye-
sore to no young revelers, for he shall be drawn in cloth
of gold breeches.
    Lus. And thou hast put my meaning in the pockets
And canst not draw that out.[30] My thought was this:
To see the picture of a usuring father   100
Boiling in hell—our rich men would ne'er like it.
    Vin. Oh, true, I cry you heartily mercy; I know the
reason: for some of 'em had rather be damned indeed
than damned in colors.[31]
    Lus. [*Aside*] A parlous[32] melancholy! h'as wit enough
To murder any man, and I'll give him means.—
I think thou art ill-moneyed?
    Vin.   Money! ho, ho.
'T'as been my want so long 'tis now my scoff;
I've e'en forgot what color silver's of!

Lus. [*Aside*] It hits as I could wish.

Vin.   I get good clothes
Of those that dread my humor, and for table room   111
I feed on those that cannot be rid of me.

Lus. [*Gives* VINDICE *money.*] Somewhat to set thee
   up withal.

Vin. Oh, mine eyes!

Lus.   How now, man?

Vin.   Almost struck
   blind!
This bright unusual shine to me seems proud:
I dare not look till the sun be in a cloud.

Lus. [*Aside*] I think I shall affect[33] his melancholy;—
How are they[34] now?

Vin.   The better for your asking.

Lus. You shall be better yet if you but fasten
Truly on my intent. Now y'are both present   120
I will unbrace[35] such a close private villain
Unto your vengeful swords, the like ne'er heard of,
Who hath disgraced you much and injured us.

Hip. Disgraced us, my lord?

Lus.   Ay, Hippolito.
I kept it here till now that both your angers
Might meet him at once.

Vin.   I'm covetous
To know the villain.

Lus.   You know him—that slave-pander
Piato, whom we threatened last
With irons in perpetual prisonment.

Vin. [*Aside*] All this is I!

Hip.   Is't he, my lord?   130

Lus. I'll tell you—you first preferred him to me.

Vin. Did you, brother?

Hip.   I did indeed.

Lus. And the ungrateful villain
To quit[36] that kindness, strongly wrought with me,
Being as you see a likely man for pleasure,
With jewels to corrupt your virgin sister.

Hip. Oh, villain!

Vin.   He shall surely die that did it.

Lus. I, far from thinking any virgin harm,
Especially knowing her to be as chaste
As that part which scarce suffers to be touched,   140
The eye, would not endure him,—

Vin.   Would you not, my
   lord?
'Twas wondrous honorably done.

Lus. But with some fine frowns kept him out.

Vin.   Out,
   slave!

Lus. What did me he but in revenge of that
Went of his own free will to make infirm
Your sister's honor, whom I honor with my soul
For chaste respect; and, not prevailing there
—As 'twas but desperate folly to attempt it—
In mere spleen, by the way, waylays your mother,
Whose honor being a coward, as it seems,   150
Yielded by little force.

Vin.   Coward, indeed.

Lus. He, proud of their advantage, as he thought,
Brought me these news for[37] happy; but I

—Heaven forgive me for't—

Vin.   What did your honor?

Lus. In rage pushed him from me,
Trampled beneath his throat,[38] spurned him and
   bruised:
Indeed I was too cruel, to say truth.

Hip. Most nobly managed.

Vin. [*Aside*] Has not heaven an ear? Is all the
   lightning wasted?

Lus. If I now were so impatient in a modest[39] cause,
What should you be?

Vin.   Full mad: he shall not live   161
To see the moon change.

Lus.   He's about the palace.
Hippolito, entice him this way, that thy brother
May take full mark of him.

Hip. Heart! that shall not need, my lord,
I can direct him so far.

Lus.   Yet for my hate's sake
Go, wind[40] him this way; I'll see him bleed myself.

Hip. [*Aside*] What now, brother?

Vin. [*Aside*] Nay, e'en what you will; y'are put to't,
   brother?

Hip. [*Aside*] An impossible task, I'll swear,   170
To bring him hither that's already here.

                              Exit HIPPOLITO.

Lus. Thy name? I have forgot it.

Vin.   Vindice, my lord.

Lus. 'Tis a good name, that.

Vin.   Ay, a revenger.

Lus. It does betoken courage, thou shouldst be
   valiant
And kill thine enemies.

Vin.   That's my hope, my lord.

Lus. This slave is one.

Vin.   I'll doom him.

Lus.   Then I'll praise
   thee.
Do thou observe[41] me best and I'll best raise thee.

                      Enter HIPPOLITO.

Vin. Indeed, I thank you.

Lus. Now, Hippolito, where's the slave-pander?

Hip. Your good lordship   180
Would have a loathsome sight of him, much offensive?
He's not in case[42] now to be seen, my lord,
The worst of all that deadly sins is in him:
That beggarly damnation, drunkeness.

Lus. Then he's a double slave.

Vin. [*Aside*] 'Twas well conveyed, upon a sudden
   wit.[43]

Lus. What, are you both firmly resolved? I'll see him
Dead myself!

Vin.   Or else let not us live.

---

[33] *affect:* like.   [34] *they:* Vindice's eyes.
[35] *unbrace:* lay open.   [36] *quit:* requite.
[37] *for:* as being.   [38] *beneath his throat:* on his body.
[39] *modest:* his grievance being nothing to theirs.
[40] *wind:* entice (metaphor from hunting).
[41] *observe:* minister to.   [42] *case:* a state.
[43] *conveyed . . . wit:* done with extemporaneous cleverness.

Lus. You may direct your brother to take note of him.
Hip. I shall.   190
Lus. Rise but in this and you shall never fall.
Vin. Your honor's vassals.
Lus. [*Aside*]   This was wisely carried;
Deep policy in us makes fools of such:
Then must a slave die, when he knows too much.
                                          Exit LUSSURIOSO.

Vin. O thou almighty patience, 'tis my wonder
That such a fellow, impudent and wicked,
Should not be cloven as he stood
Or with a secret wind burst open!
Is there no thunder left, or is't kept up
In stock for heavier vengeance?

                              [*Thunder*]

                    There it goes!   200
Hip. Brother, we lose ourselves.[44]
Vin.   But I have found it,
'Twill hold, 'tis sure, thanks to any spirit
That mingled it 'mongst my inventions.
Hip.   What is't?
Vin. 'Tis sound and good, thou shalt partake it,
I'm hired to kill myself.
Hip.   True.
Vin. Prithee, mark it;
And the old duke being dead but not conveyed[45]
—For he's already missed too—and you know
Murder will peep out of the closest husk—
Hip. Most true!
Vin.   What say you then to this device:
If we dressed up the body of the duke—   211
Hip. In that disguise of yours!
Vin.   Y'are quick, y'ave
    reached it.
Hip. I like it wondrously.
Vin. And being in drink, as you have published[46]
    him,
To lean him on his elbow as if sleep had caught him
—Which claims most interest in such sluggy[47] men.
Hip. Good yet; but here's a doubt.
We, thought by th' duke's son to kill that pander,
Shall, when he is known, be thought to kill the duke.
Vin. Neither, oh, thanks! it is substantial;[48]   220
For that disguise being on him, which I wore,
It will be thought I, which he calls the pander,
Did kill the duke and fled away in his
Apparel, leaving him so disguised

To avoid swift pursuit.
Hip.   Firmer and firmer.
Vin. Nay, doubt not, 'tis in grain,[49] I warrant
It hold color.
Hip.   Let's about it.
Vin. But by the way too, now I think on't, brother,
Let's conjure[50] that base devil out of our mother.
                                          Exeunt.

[IV.iii]

Enter the DUCHESS *arm in arm with the bastard*
[SPURIO]: *he seemeth lasciviously to*[1] *her ; after*
them enter SUPERVACUO, *running with a rapier:*
his brother [AMBITIOSO] *stops him.*

Spur. Madam, unlock yourself; should it be seen,
Your arm would be suspected.
Duch. Who is't that dares suspect or[2] this, or these?[3]
May not we deal our favors where we please?
Spur. I'm confident you may.
                              Exeunt [SPURIO *and* DUCHESS].
Amb. 'Sfoot, brother, hold!
Sup.   Would let the bastard
    shame us?
Amb. Hold, hold, brother! there's fitter time than
    now.
Sup. Now, when I see it!
Amb.   'Tis too much seen already.
Sup. Seen and known:
The nobler she is, the baser is she grown.   10
Amb. If she were bent lasciviously—the fault
Of mighty women that sleep soft—oh, death,
Must she needs choose such an unequal[4] sinner
To make all worse?
Sup. A bastard! the duke's bastard! shame heaped
    on shame!
Amb. Oh, our disgrace!
Most women have small waist the world throughout,
But their desires are thousand miles about.
Sup. Come, stay not here: let's after and prevent:
Or else they'll sin faster than we'll repent.   20
                                          Exeunt.

[IV.iv]

Enter VINDICE *and* HIPPOLITO *bringing out their*
mother [GRATIANA], *one by one shoulder, and the*
other by the other, with daggers in their hands.

Vin. O thou for whom no name is bad enough!
Grat. What mean my sons? What, will you murder
    me?
Vin. Wicked, unnatural parent!
Hip.   Fiend of women!
Grat. Oh! are sons turned monsters? Help!
Vin.   In vain.
Grat. Are you so barbarous, to set iron nipples[1]
Upon the breast that gave you suck?
Vin.   That breast
Is turned to quarlèd[2] poison.
Grat. Cut[3] not your days for't: am not I your mother
Vin. Thou dost usurp that title now by fraud,

---

[44] *lose ourselves:* forget what we are about.
[45] *conveyed:* disposed of.   [46] *published:* advertised.
[47] *sluggy:* sluggish.   [48] *substantial:* solid; it will hold.
[49] *in grain:* fast; not to be washed away.
[50] *conjure:* as by exorcising.
IV.iii.
    [1] *to:* i.e., look at.   [2] *or:* either.
    [3] *this . . . these:* kisses, embraces.
    [4] *unequal:* to her in station.
IV.iv.
    [1] *iron nipples:* presumably their daggers.
    [2] *quarlèd:* curdled.
    [3] *Cut:* Shorten, as by being subject to law (a reminiscence
of the earlier invoking, at II. ii. 96, of Exodus 20:12).

For in that shell of mother breeds a bawd.   10

Grat. A bawd! oh, name far loathsomer than hell!

Hip. It should be so, knewest thou thy office[4] well.

Grat. I hate it.

Vin. Ah, is't possible. Thou[5] only? You powers on high,

That women should dissemble when they die?

Grat. Dissemble?

Vin.   Did not the duke's son direct

A fellow of the world's condition[6] hither

That did corrupt all that was good in thee,

Made thee uncivilly forget thyself

And work our sister to his lust?

Grat.   Who, I?   20

That had been monstrous? I defy that man

For any such intent. None lives so pure

But shall be soiled with slander—

Good son, believe it not.

Vin.   Oh, I'm in doubt

Whether I'm myself or no!

Stay—let me look again upon this face:

Who shall be saved when mothers have no grace?

Hip. 'Twould make one half despair.

Vin.   I was the man:

Defy me now! let's see: do't modestly.

Grat. Oh, hell unto my soul.   30

Vin. In that disguise, I, sent from the duke's son,

Tried you, and found you base metal,

As any villain might have done.

Grat. Oh, no: no tongue but yours could have bewitched me so.

Vin. Oh, nimble in damnation, quick in tune:[7]

There is no devil could strike fire so soon!

I am confuted in a word.

Grat. O sons, forgive me, to myself I'll prove more true;

You that should honor me—I kneel to you.

[She kneels and weeps.]

Vin. A mother to give aim[8] to her own daughter!   40

Hip. True, brother: how far beyond nature 'tis,

Though many mothers do't!

Vin. Nay, and you draw tears once, go you to bed;[9]

Wet will make iron blush and change to red:[10]

Brother, it rains, 'twill spoil your dagger, house it.

Hip. 'Tis done.

Vin. I' faith, 'tis a sweet shower, it does much good;

The fruitful grounds and meadows of her soul

Has been long dry. Pour down, thou blessèd dew.

Rise, mother; troth, this shower has made you higher.

Grat. O you heavens, take this infectious[11] spot out of my soul!   51

I'll rinse it in seven waters of mine eyes;

Make my tears salt enough to taste of grace;[12]

To weep is to our sex naturally given,

But to weep truly—that's a gift from heaven!

Vin. Nay, I'll kiss you now; kiss her, brother,

Let's marry her to our souls, wherein's no lust,

And honorably love her.

Hip.   Let it be.

Vin. For honest women are so seld[13] and rare,

'Tis good to cherish those poor few that are.   60

O you of easy wax, do but imagine,

Now the disease has left you, how leprously

That office would have clinged unto your forehead.

All mothers that had any graceful hue

Would have worn masks to hide their face at you.

It would have grown to this, at your foul name

Green-colored[14] maids would have turned red with shame.

Hip. And then, our sister full of hire[15] and baseness—

Vin. There had been boiling lead again![16]

The duke's son's great concubine!   70

A drab of state, a cloth o' silver slut,

To have her train borne up and her soul

Trail i' the dirt: great!

Hip.   To be miserably great:

Rich, to be eternally wretched.

Vin. O common madness:

Ask but the thriving'st harlot in cold blood,[17]

She'd give the world to make her honor good.

Perhaps you'll say, but only to the duke's son

In private—why, she first begins with one

Who afterward to thousand proves a whore: 80

"Break ice in one place it will crack in more."

Grat. Most certainly applied!

Hip. O brother, you forget our business.

Vin. And well remembered; joy's a subtle elf,[18]

I think man's happiest when he forgets himself.

Farewell once dried, now holy-watered mead:[19]

Our hearts wear feathers that before wore lead.

Grat. I'll give you this: that one I never knew

Plead better for, and 'gainst the devil, than you.

Vin. You make me proud on't.   90

Hip. Commend us in all virtue to our sister.

Vin. Ay, for the love of heaven, to that true maid.

Grat. With my best words.

Vin.   Why, that was motherly said.

Exeunt [VINDICE *and* HIPPOLITO].

Grat. I wonder now what fury did transport me;

I feel good thoughts begin to settle in me.

Oh, with what forehead[20] can I look on her

---

[4] *office:* as mother.

[5] *Thou:* Presumably Vindice addresses God, whose name may have been replaced by the censor or printer with "powers," in deference to the Jacobean abhorrence of invoking the deity.   [6] *of . . . condition:* corrupted.

[7] *in tune:* with wickedness.

[8] *aim:* instruction in shooting (i.e., being seductive).

[9] *go . . . bed:* Vindice sheathes his dagger, which he has been apostrophizing.   [10] *red:* rust.

[11] *infectious:* infected.

[12] *grace:* identified evidently with salt or "savor."

[13] *seld:* seldom found.   [14] *Green-colored:* Callow, young.

[15] *hire:* money (the wages of sin).

[16] *There . . . again:* Perhaps Vindice is alluding to his own agitation at the thought, perhaps to the requital of the deed.

[17] *in cold blood:* soberly; or: when she is sober.

[18] *joy's . . . elf:* Joy's particular kind of cunning is explicated by the next line.

[19] *Farewell . . . mead:* Gratiana is the "mead" or meadow who is addressed.

[20] *forehead:* countenance ("how can I look on her").

Whose honor I've so impiously beset
—And here she comes.

[*Enter* CASTIZA.]

Cas. Now, mother, you have wrought with me so
    strongly
That what[21] for my advancement, as to calm   100
The trouble of your tongue, I am content—
  Grat. Content to what?
  Cas.   To do as you have wished me,
To prostitute my breast to the duke's son
And put myself to common usury.
  Grat. I hope you will not so.
  Cas.   Hope you I will not?
That's not the hope you look to be saved in.
  Grat. Truth, but it is.
  Cas.   Do not deceive yourself:
I am, as you, e'en out of marble wrought:[22]
What would you now, are ye not pleased yet with me?
You shall not wish me to be more lascivious   110
Than I intend to be.
  Grat.   Strike not me cold.
  Cas. How often have you charged me on your
    blessing
To be a cursèd woman! When you knew
Your blessing had no force to make me lewd
You laid your curse upon me. That did more
—The mother's curse is heavy; where that fights,
Sons set in storm and daughters lose their lights.[23]
  Grat. Good child, dear maid, if there be any spark
Of heavenly intellectual[24] fire within thee,
Oh, let my breath revive it to a flame: 120
Put not all out with woman's willful follies.
I am recovered of that foul disease[25]
That haunts too many mothers: kind[26] forgive me,
Make me not sick in health. If then
My words prevailed when they were wickedness,
How much more now when they are just and good!
  Cas. I wonder what you mean: are not you she
For those whose infect[27] persuasions I could scarce

Kneel out my prayers, and had much ado
In three hours' reading to untwist so much   130
Of the black serpent as you wound about me?
  Grat. 'Tis unfruitful, held[28] tedious, to repeat what's
    past:
I'm now your present[29] mother.
  Cas.   Push, now 'tis too late.
  Grat. Bethink again, thou knowest not what thou
    sayest.
  Cas. No—deny advancement, treasure, the Duke's
    son?
  Grat. Oh, see, I spoke those words, and now they
    poison me:
What will the deed do then?
Advancement? True: as high as shame can pitch;[30]
For treasure? Who e'er knew a harlot rich
Or could build by the purchase[31] of her sin   140
An hospital[32] to keep their bastards in?
The duke's son! oh, when women are young courtiers
They are sure to be old beggars;
To know the miseries most harlots taste
Thou'd'st wish thyself unborn when thou art unchaste.
  Cas. O mother, let me twine about your neck
And kiss you till my soul melt on your lips:
I did but this to try you.
  Grat.   Oh, speak truth!
  Cas. Indeed I did not;[33] for no tongue has force
To alter me from honest.   150
If maidens would,[34] men's words could have no power;
A virgin honor is a crystal tower
Which being weak is guarded with good spirits:
Until she basely yields, no ill inherits.[35]
  Grat. O happy child! faith and thy birth hath saved
    me.
'Mongst thousand daughters happiest of all others!
Be thou a glass[36] for maids, and I for mothers.

                              Exeunt.

---

[21] *what:* as much.
[22] *e'en . . . wrought:* constant to my purpose.
[23] *Sons . . . lights:* punning on celestial imagery—"suns."
[24] *intellectual:* as opposed to physical, of the senses.
[25] *disease:* punning, as the next line makes clear, on "mother"—hysteria.   [26] *kind:* nature.
[27] *infect:* infected.
[28] *held:* emended by some editors to "child."
[29] *present:* in my present character.
[30] *pitch:* ascend (denoting the highest point to which the falcon soars before it "stoops" or falls on its prey).
[31] *purchase:* accrual.   [32] *hospital:* orphanage.
[33] *not:* speak truth.
[34] *would:* persevere in honesty (chastity).
[35] *inherits:* resides there.   [36] *glass:* mirror.

V.i.
[1] *lay:* wager.   [2] *that's I:* the duke's body.
[3] *Michaelmas Term:* This lasted eight weeks and hence provided eight weekly reporting days for the sheriff to rejoin or "return" to an injunction of the court. The sense is to the multiple number of ways of saying the same thing.
[4] *enow:* enough.
[5] *flesh-flies:* his scavenger-like retainers.

ACT FIVE

SCENE ONE

Enter VINDICE *and* HIPPOLITO [*with the
Duke's body*].

  Vin. So, so, he leans well; take heed you wake him
    not, brother.
  Hip. I warrant you, my life for yours.
  Vin. That's a good lay,[1] for I must kill myself!
Brother, that's I:[2] that sits for me: do you mark it. And
I must stand ready here to make away myself yonder; I
must sit to be killed, and stand to kill myself—I could
vary it not so little as thrice over again, 't'as some eight
returns like Michaelmas Term.[3]
  Hip. That's enow,[4] o' conscience.   9
  Vin. But, sirrah, does the duke's son come single?
  Hip. No, there's the hell on't, his faith's too feeble to
go alone. He brings flesh-flies[5] after him that will buzz
against supper time, and hum for his coming out.
  Vin. Ah, the fly-flop of vengeance beat 'em to pieces!
Here was the sweetest occasion, the fittest hour to have
made my revenge familiar with him—show him the body

of the duke his father, and how quaintly he died like
a politician[6] in hugger-mugger[7]—made no man acquainted with it, and in catastrophe[8] slain him over his
father's breast! And, oh, I'm mad to lose such a sweet
opportunity.   21

Hip. Nay push, prithee be content! There's no remedy present; may not hereafter times open in as fair
faces as this?

Vin. They may if they can paint so well.

Hip. Come now, to avoid all suspicion let's forsake
this room and be going to meet the duke's son.

Vin. Content, I'm for any weather. Heart, step
close,[9] here he comes!

Enter LUSSURIOSO.

Hip. My honored lord.   30

Lus. Oh, me—you both present.

Vin. E'en newly, my lord, just as your lordship
entered now. About this place we had notice given he
should be, but in some loathsome plight or other.

Hip. Came your honor private?

Lus. Private enough for this: only a few attend my
  coming out.

Hip. [*Aside*] Death rot those few!

Lus. Stay—yonder's the slave.

Vin. Mass, there's the slave indeed, my lord;
[*Aside*] 'Tis a good child, he calls his father slave!   40

Lus. Ay, that's the villain, the damned villain!
  softly,
Tread easy.

Vin.   Puh, I warrant you, my lord,
We'll stifle in our breaths.

Lus. [*Aside*]   That will do well.
Base rogue, thou sleepest thy last! 'Tis policy
To have him killed in's sleep, for if he waked
He would betray all to them.

Vin.   But, my lord—

Lus.   Ha? What
  say'st?

Vin. Shall we kill him now he's drunk?

Lus.   Ay, best of all.

Vin. Why, then he will ne'er live to be sober.

Lus. No matter: let him reel to hell.

Vin. But being so full of liquor I fear he will put out
  all the fire!   50

Lus. Thou art a mad breast![10]

Vin. [*Aside*] And leave none to warm your lordship's gols[11] withal.—For he that dies drunk falls into
hell fire like a bucket o' water: qush, qush.

Lus. Come, be ready, nake[12] your swords, think of
your wrongs: this slave has injured you.

Vin. Troth, so he has, and he has paid well for't.

Lus. Meet with him now.

Vin.   You'll bear us out,[13] my
  lord?

Lus. Puh, am I a lord for nothing, think you?
Quickly now!

Vin.   Sa, sa, sa, thump!

                          [*He stabs the body.*]

                          There he lies!   60

Lus. Nimbly done. Ha! O villains, murderers,
'Tis the old duke my father!

Vin. [*Aside*]   That's a jest.

Lus. What, stiff and cold already?
Oh, pardon me to call you from your names,[14]
'Tis none of your deed; that villain Piato
Whom you thought now to kill has murdered him
And left him thus disguised.

Hip.   And not unlikely.

Vin. Oh, rascal, was he not ashamed
To put the duke into a greasy doublet?

Lus. He has been cold and stiff—who knows how
  long?   70

Vin. [*Aside*] Marry, that do I!

Lus. No words, I pray, of anything intended!

Vin. Oh, my lord.

Hip. I would fain have your lordship think that we
Have small reason to prate.

Lus. Faith, thou sayest true, I'll forthwith send to
  court
For all the nobles, bastard, duchess, all—
How here by miracle we found him dead
And, in his raiment,[15] that foul villain fled.

Vin. That will be the best way, my lord, to
  clear   80
Us all; let's cast about to be clear.

Lus. Ho! Nencio, Sordido, and the rest!

Enter all [*his* Followers].

1 [*Sor.*] My lord.

2 [*Nen.*]   My lord.

Lus. Be witness of a strange spectacle.
Choosing for private conference that sad room
We found the duke my father 'gealed[16] in blood.

1 [*Sor.*] My lord the duke! run, hie thee, Nencio,
Startle the court by signifying so much.

                          [*Exit* NENCIO.]

Vin. [*Aside*] This much by wit a deep revenger
  can:
When murder's known, to be the clearest[17] man.   90
We're farthest off, and with as bold an eye
Survey his body as the standers-by.

Lus. My royal father, too basely let blood
By a malevolent slave!

Hip. [*Aside*]   Hark! he calls thee
Slave again.

Vin. [*Aside*] H'as lost, he may!

Lus.   O sight,
Look hither, see, his lips are gnawn with poison!

Vin. How? His lips? By the Mass, they be!

---

  6 *politician:* in the pejorative sense of "devious man."
  7 *hugger-mugger:* secret.
  8 *catastrophe:* conclusion (a theatrical term).
  9 *step close:* hide (though Vindice ignores the injunction).
  10 *breast:* heart (though uncorrected copies of Q read
"beast").   11 *gols:* hands.
  12 *nake:* unsheathe.   13 *bear us out:* make our excuses.
  14 *from your names:* villains—which you are not.
  15 *his raiment:* the duke's clothing.
  16 *'gealed:* congealed.
  17 *clearest:* most free from suspicion.

Lus. O villain—O rogue—O slave—O rascal!
Hip. [*Aside*] Oh, good deceit!—He quits him with
   like terms.[18]
1 [*Voice Within*]. Where?
2 [*Voice Within*].   Which way?   100

[*Enter* AMBITIOSO *and* SUPERVACUO, *with*
   Nobles.]

Amb. Over what roof hangs this prodigious
   comet[19]
In deadly fire?
Lus.   Behold, behold, my lords:
The duke my father's murdered by a vassal
That owes[20] this habit, and here left disguised.

[*Enter the* DUCHESS *and* SPURIO.]

Duch. My lord and husband!
2 [*Nob.*]   Reverend majesty.
1 [*Nob.*] I have seen these clothes often attending on
   him.
Vin. [*Aside*] That nobleman has been in the
   country,[21] for he does not lie.
Sup. [*Aside*] Learn of our mother—let's dissemble
   too!
I am glad he's vanished: so I hope are you?   110
Amb. [*Aside*] Ay, you may take my word for't.
Spur. [*Aside*]   Old
   dad dead?
I, one of his cast sins, will send the fates
Most hearty commendations by his own son;
I'll tug in the new stream[22] till strength be done.
Lus. Where be those two that did affirm to us
My lord the duke was privately rid forth?
1 [*Nob.*] Oh, pardon us, my lords, he gave that
   charge
Upon our lives, if he were missed at court,
To answer so. He rode not anywhere,
We left him private with that fellow, here.   120
Vin. [*Aside*] Confirmed.[23]
Lus. Oh, heavens, that false charge was his death.
Impudent beggars! durst you to our face
Maintain such a false answer? Bear him straight
To execution.
1 [*Nob.*]   My lord!
Lus.   Urge me no more.
In this, the excuse may be called half the murder.

---

[18] *quits . . . terms:* repays his father with the same language
the father had addressed to him.
[19] *prodigious comet:* understood to be ominous of doom.
[20] *owes:* owns.   [21] *in the country:* proverbial for honesty.
[22] *tug . . . stream:* swim with the current.
[23] *Confirmed:* True—and hence my innocence is established.   [24] *stick:* stand fast(?); keep quiet(?).
[25] *indifferent wits:* mediocre intellects.
[26] *post horse:* swift messengers.
[27] *foreign:* explicable perhaps as a bitter joke addressed to
the audience—"This is how it is in foreign countries, not in
England!"
[28] *Courtiers . . . twelves:* Their voluble tongues are three
sizes bigger than their shoes.   [29] *mean season:* meantime.
[30] *bethink the latest:* consider the last.   [31] *falls:* changes.
[32] *firm:* safe.   [33] *mark:* target—Lussurioso.

Vin. [*Aside*] You've sentenced well.
Lus.   Away, see it be
   done.

          [*Exit 1* Noble *under guard.*]
Vin. [*Aside*] Could you not stick?[24] See what
   confession doth.
Who would not lie when men are hanged for truth?
Hip. [*Aside*] Brother, how happy is our vengeance!
Vin. [*Aside*]   Why, it hits
Past the apprehension of indifferent wits.[25]   131
Lus. My lord, let post horse[26] be sent
Into all places to entrap the villain.
Vin. [*Aside*] Post horse! ha, ha.
2 [*Nob.*] My lord, we're something bold to know
   our duty,
Your father's accidentally departed,
The titles that were due to him meet you.
Lus. Meet me? I'm not at leisure, my good lord,
I've many griefs to dispatch out o' the way.—
[*Aside*] Welcome sweet titles!—Talk to me, my lords,
Of sepulchers and mighty emperors' bones,   141
That's thought for me.
Vin. [*Aside*] So, one may see by this how foreign[27]
   markets go:
Courtiers have feet o' the nine and tongues o' the
   twelves:[28]
They flatter dukes, and dukes flatter themselves.
2 [*Nob.*] My lord, it is your shine must comfort us.
Lus. Alas, I shine in tears like the sun in April.
3 [*Nob.*] You're now my lord's grace.
Lus. My lord's grace? I perceive you'll have it so.
2 [*Nob.*] 'Tis but your own.
Lus.   Then heavens give me
   grace to be so.   150
Vin. [*Aside*] He prays well for himself!
3 [*Nob.*]   Madam, all
   sorrow
Must run their circles into joys; no doubt but time
Will make the murderer bring forth himself.
Vin. [*Aside*] He were an ass then, i' faith!
3 [*Nob.*]   In the mean
   season[29]
Let us bethink the latest[30] funeral honors
Due to the duke's cold body; and, withal,
Calling to memory our new happiness
Spread in his royal son,—lords, gentlemen,
Prepare for revels!
Vin. [*Aside*]   Revels!
3 [*Nob.*]   Time hath several falls:[31]
Griefs lift up joys, feasts put down funerals.   160
Lus. Come, then, my lords, my favors to you all.
[*Aside*] The duchess is suspected foully bent;
I'll begin dukedom with her banishment.
          Exeunt DUKE [LUSSURIOSO], Nobles,
                    and DUCHESS.
Hip. [*Aside*] Revels.
Vin. [*Aside*] Ay, that's the word. We are firm[32] yet:
Strike one strain more and then we crown our wit.
          Exeunt [VINDICE *and* HIPPOLITO].
Spur. Well, have [at] the fairest mark[33]—
So said the duke when he begot me—

And if I miss his heart or near about
Then have at any—a bastard scorns to be out.   170
                             [Exit.]

    Sup. Notest thou that Spurio, brother?
    Amb. Yes, I note him, to our shame.
    Sup.   He shall not
Live: his hair shall not grow much longer.
In this time of revels tricks may be set afoot.
Seest thou yon new moon? It shall outlive
The new duke by much: this hand shall dispossess
Him: then we're mighty.
A mask[34] is treason's license: that build upon—
'Tis murder's best face, when a vizard's on!
                 Exit [SUPERVACUO].
    Amb. Is't so? 'Tis very good: 180
And do you think to be duke then, kind brother?
I'll see fair play: drop one, and there lies t'other.
                 Exit [AMBITIOSO].

[V.ii]

    Enter VINDICE *and* HIPPOLITO *with* PIERO
              and other Lords.

    Vin. My lord, be all of music! strike[1] old griefs into
      other countries
That flow in too much milk and have faint livers,[2]
Not daring to stab home their discontents.
Let our hid flames break out as fire, as lightning,
To blast this villainous dukedom vexed with sin:
Wind up your souls to their full height again.[3]
    Pier. How?
    1 Lord.   Which way?
    3 Lord.   Any way! our wrongs are
      such,
We cannot justly be revenged too much.
    Vin. You shall have all enough. Revels are toward,
And those few nobles that have long suppressed you
Are busied to the furnishing of a mask   11
And do affect[4] to make a pleasant tale on't.
The masking suits are fashioning; now comes in
That which must glad us all: we to take pattern
Of all those suits, the color, trimming, fashion,
E'en to an undistinguished hair[5] almost.
Then entering first, observing the true form,[6]
Within a strain[7] or two we shall find leisure
To steal our swords out handsomely,
And when they think their pleasure sweet and good,   20
In midst of all their joys they shall sigh blood!
    Pier. Weightily, effectually!
    3 Lord.   Before the t'other
      maskers come—
    Vin. We're gone, all done and past.
    Pier. But how for the duke's guard?
    Vin.   Let that alone:
By one and one their strength shall be drunk down.
    Hip. There are five hundred gentlemen in the action
That will apply themselves and not stand idle.
    Pier. Oh, let us hug your bosoms!
    Vin.   Come, my lords,
Prepare for deeds, let other times have words.
                     Exeunt.

[V.iii]

    In a dumb show: the possessing[1] of the young Duke
    [LUSSURIOSO] *with all his* Nobles; *then sounding*
    music; a furnished table is brought forth; then enters
    the Duke [LUSSURIOSO] *and his* Nobles *to the*
      banquet. A blazing star[2] appeareth.

    1 Nob. Many harmonious hours and choicest
      pleasures
Fill up the royal numbers of your years.
    Lus. My lords, we're pleased to thank you—though
      we know
'Tis but your duty now to wish it so.
    [1] Nob. That shine makes us all happy.
    3 Nob. His grace frowns?
    2 Nob.   Yet we must say he
      smiles.
    1 Nob. I think we must.
    Lus. [*Aside*] That foul incontinent[3] duchess we have
      banished:
The bastard shall not live. After these revels
I'll begin strange ones: he and the stepsons
Shall pay their lives for the first subsidies;[4]   10
We must not frown so soon, else 't'ad been now.
    1 Nob. My gracious lord, please you prepare for
      pleasure;
The mask is not far off.
    Lus.   We are for pleasure:
Beshrew thee, what art thou?[5] Madest me start!
Thou has committed treason!—A blazing star!
    1 Nob. A blazing star! oh, where, my lord?
    Lus.   Spy out.
    2 Nob. See, see, my lords, a wondrous dreadful one!
    Lus. I am not pleased at that ill-knotted fire,
That bushing[6]-flaring star. Am not I duke?
It should not quake[7] me now. Had it appeared   20
Before it,[8] I might then have justly feared:
But yet they say, whom art[9] and learning weds,
When stars wear locks[10] they threaten great men's
      heads.
Is it so? You are read,[11] my lords.

---

   [34] *mask:* disguise ("vizard," below); masque, appropriate
to revels.

V.ii.
   [1] *strike:* throw (with associated sense of "strike up the
music").   [2] *flow . . . livers:* are faint-hearted.
   [3] *Wind . . . again:* Play the man (with a metaphorical
reminiscence of music—"Tighten the strings of the instrument").   [4] *affect:* desire; feign.
   [5] *an undistinguished hair:* the smallest detail (an observer
being unable to find a hair or particle not tallying precisely).
   [6] *form:* of the dance.   [7] *strain:* of music.

V.iii.
   [1] *possessing:* coronation.
   [2] *blazing star:* a theatrical flare or burst of light in token
of the festivities; also ominous of death.
   [3] *incontinent:* unchaste.
   [4] *subsidies:* taxes levied by the sovereign.
   [5] *thou:* the star.   [6] *bushing:* as of a comet's tail.
   [7] *quake:* affright.   [8] *it:* his installation as duke.
   [9] *art:* practical skill.   [10] *locks:* trails of "hair" or fire.
   [11] *read:* well read.

1 Nob.   May it please your
grace,
It shows great anger.
      Lus.   That does not please our grace.
2 Nob. Yet here's the comfort, my lord: many
      times
When it seems most,[12] it threatens farthest off.
      Lus. Faith, and I think so too.
1 Nob.   Beside, my lord,
You're gracefully established with the loves
Of all your subjects; and for natural death,   30
I hope it will be threescore years a-coming.
      Lus. True—no more but threescore years?
1 Nob. Fourscore I hope, my lord.
2 Nob.   And fivescore I.
3 Nob. But 'tis my hope, my lord, you shall ne'er
      die.
      Lus. Give me thy hand: these others I rebuke:
He that hopes so, is fittest for a duke.
Thou shalt sit next me. Take your places, lords,
We're ready now for sports, let 'em set on.
You thing![13] we shall forget you quite anon.
3 Nob. I hear 'em coming, my lord.

      Enter the Mask of Revengers, *the two brothers*
      [VINDICE *and* HIPPOLITO], *and two* Lords *more*.

      Lus.   Ah, 'tis well!   40
[*Aside*] Brothers, and bastard, you dance next in hell!

      The Revengers *dance. At the end* [*they*] *steal out
      their swords and these four kill the four at the table,
      in their chairs. It thunders.*

Vin. Mark: thunder! dost know thy cue, thou
      big-voiced crier?
Duke's groans are thunder's watchwords.
      Hip. So, my lords, you have enough.
      Vin. Come, let's away—no lingering.
      Hip.   Follow—go!
                    Exeunt [*all but* VINDICE].
Vin. No power is angry when the lustful die:
When thunder claps,[14] heaven likes the tragedy.
                                   Exit.
Lus. Oh, oh.

      Enter the other Mask of Intended Murderers,
      stepsons [AMBITIOSO *and* SUPERVACUO], *bastard*
      [SPURIO], *and a fourth* Man *coming in dancing.
      The* DUKE [LUSSURIOSO] *recovers a little in voice,
      and groans, calls "A guard! Treason!" at which
      they all start out of their measure,[15] and turning
      towards the table they find them all to be murdered.*

Spur. Whose groan was that?
Lus.   Treason. A guard.

─────────────────────────

[12] *most:* to threaten near at hand.   [13] *thing:* the star.
[14] *claps:* with secondary meaning of "applauds."
[15] *measure:* dance.   [16] *sped:* dispatched.
[17] SUP.: Q gives this line to Spurio.
[18] *Law you:* La you; what say you.
[19] *marrow:* food to chew on.
[20] *be expressed:* speak my thought.

Amb. How now! all murdered!
Sup.   Murdered!   50
4 [*Nob.*] And those his nobles?
Amb. [*Aside*]   Here's a labor saved:
I thought to have sped[16] him. 'Sblood—how came this?
Sup.[17] Then I proclaim myself. Now I am duke.
Amb. Thou duke! brother thou liest.

                    [*Stabs* SUPERVACUO.]

Spur.   Slave! So dost
      thou.

                    [*Stabs* AMBITIOSO.]

4 [*Nob.*] Base villain, hast thou slain my lord and
      master?

                    [*Stabs* SPURIO.]

      Enter the first men [*and* VINDICE, HIPPOLITO].

Vin. Pistols, treason, murder! Help, guard my lord
      the duke!

                    [*Enter* ANTONIO *and guard*.]

Hip. Lay hold upon this traitor!

                    [*Guard seizes* 4 Noble.]

Lus.   Oh.
Vin. Alas, the duke is murdered.
Hip.   And the nobles.
Vin. Surgeons, surgeons!—[*Aside*] Heart, does he
      breathe so long?
Ant. A piteous tragedy, able to make   60
An old man's eyes bloodshot.
Lus.   Oh.
Vin. Look to my lord the duke. [*Aside*] A
      vengeance throttle him!—
Confess, thou murderous and unhallowed man,
Didst thou kill all these?
4 [*Nob.*]   None but the bastard, I.
Vin. How came the duke slain, then?
4 [*Nob.*]   We found him
      so.
Lus. O villain.
Vin. Hark.
Lus.   Those in the mask did murder us.
Vin. Law you[18] now, sir:
O marble impudence—will you confess now?
4 [*Nob.*] 'Sblood, 'tis all false!   70
Ant. Away with that foul monster
Dipped in a prince's blood.
4 [*Nob.*]   Heart, 'tis a lie.
Ant. Let him have bitter execution.
                    [*Exit* 4 Noble *guarded*.]
Vin. [*Aside*] New marrow![19] no, I cannot be
      expressed.[20]—
How fares my lord the duke?
Lus.   Farewell to all:
He that climbs highest has the greatest fall.
My tongue is out of office.
Vin.   Air, gentlemen, air.—
[*Whispers*] Now thou'lt not prate on't, 'twas Vindice
      murdered thee!

Lus. Oh.

Vin. [*Whispers*] Murdered thy father!

Lus.   Oh.

Vin. [*Whispers*]   And I am
he!
Tell nobody.—

[LUSSURIOSO *dies.*]

    So, so. The duke's departed.   80

Ant. It was a deadly hand that wounded him;
The rest, ambitious who should rule and sway
After his death, were so made all away.

Vin. My lord was unlikely. [21]

Hip.   Now the hope
Of Italy lies in your reverend years.

Vin. Your hair will make the silver age again,
When there was fewer, but more honest men.

Ant. The burden's weighty and will press age down:
May I so rule that heaven may keep [22] the crown.

Vin. The rape of your good lady has been
    'quited   90
With death on death.

Ant.   Just is the law above.
But of all things it puts me most to wonder
How the old duke came murdered.

Vin.   Oh, my lord.

Ant. It was the strangeliest carried: I not heard of
    the like.

Hip. 'Twas all done for the best, my lord.

Vin. All for your grace's good. We may be bold
To speak it now: 'twas somewhat witty [23] carried,—
Though we say it. 'Twas we two murdered him!

Ant. You two?

Vin. None else, i' faith, my lord. Nay, 'twas well
    managed.   100

Ant. Lay hands upon those villains.

Vin.   How? On us?

Ant. Bear 'em to speedy execution.

Vin. Heart! was't not for your good, my lord?

Ant. My good! away with 'em! such an old man as
    he!
You that would murder him would murder me!

Vin. Is't come about? [24]

Hip.   'Sfoot, brother you begun.

Vin. May not we set as well as the duke's son? [25]
Thou hast no conscience: [26] are we not revenged?
Is there one enemy left alive amongst those?
'Tis time to die when we are ourselves our foes.   110
When murderers shut deeds close, this curse does seal
    'em:
If none disclose 'em, they themselves reveal 'em!
This murder might have slept in tongueless brass [27]
But for ourselves, and the world died an ass.
Now I remember too, here was Piato
Brought forth a knavish sentence once:
No doubt—said he—but time
Will make the murderer bring forth himself.
'Tis well he died, he was a witch! [28]
And now, my lord, since we are in for ever,   120
This work was ours, which else might have been
    slipped; [29]
And if we list we could have nobles clipped [30]
And go for less than beggars. But we hate
To bleed so cowardly: we have enough—
I' faith, we're well—our mother turned, [31] our sister
    true,
We die after a nest of dukes! adieu.

        Exeunt [VINDICE *and* HIPPOLITO *guarded.*]

Ant. How subtly was that murder closed! [32] Bear up
Those tragic bodies; 'tis a heavy season.
Pray heaven their blood may wash away all treason.

                                                Exit.

F I N I S

---

[21] *unlikely:* a poor choice as duke.   [22] *keep:* watch over.

[23] *witty:* cleverly.

[24] *come about:* fallen out so (with allied sense of "turned around").   [25] *son:* with pun on "sun," following "set."

[26] *conscience:* sense.   [27] *brass:* as in a church monument.

[28] *witch:* being able to prophesy.

[29] *been slipped:* gone undetected.

[30] *nobles clipped:* our collaborators in the masking executed, with pun on trimming (clipping) the edges of precious coins (nobles).   [31] *turned:* converted.

[32] *closed:* concealed.

Ben Jonson

[1572-1637]

VOLPONE; OR, THE FOX

BEN JONSON was born probably in London, in the royal demesne of Westminster. He studied at the Westminster School under the famous antiquary and historian William Camden, but was forced to leave school, presumably for economic reasons, and to go to work for his stepfather as a bricklayer. In the 1590s he saw military service in Flanders and killed his own man in single combat between the armies. Later in the same decade, while in the employ of Philip Henslowe, he landed in prison as the result of a similar if more equivocal episode. Having killed a fellow actor in a duel, Jonson escaped death himself only by pleading benefit of clergy.

Jonson's career in the theater begins for the record in 1597, in which year he is noted in Henslowe's diary as the recipient of a loan. In 1598 his first great success, *Every Man in His Humor*, was performed by the Lord Chamberlain's Men, with Shakespeare as one of the cast. The companion comedy, *Every Man Out of His Humor*, followed a year later. Thereafter and for more than three decades, a great spate of theatrical work in different genres appeared at regular intervals. Jonson's proficiency in satirical comedy is illustrated by *Cynthia's Revels* (1600) and *The Poetaster* (1601), the latter attacking Marston and Dekker. With Marston and Chapman he collaborated in the ill-starred comedy *Eastward Ho!* (1605), which, because of a passage offensive to the Scots, whose sovereign James VI had now become James I of England, occasioned the temporary imprisonment of the authors. Hack work—the amplifying and refurbishing for Henslowe of the endlessly popular SPANISH TRAGEDY—alternated with ambitious essays in classical tragedy. But though Jonson set high store by *Sejanus* (1603) and *Catiline* (1611), neither play was successful in its time and neither has been well received since. That is not for want of merit. Jonson's versifying of Cicero's indictment of Catiline is worthy of its great model. But the protagonists of the two plays lack complexity, hence humanity, as they are unrelievedly villainous. The hero-villain Brutus is Shakespeare's version of Catiline.

Though Jonson did not create the masque, he was the preeminent and most prolific maker of this aristocratically fashionable entertainment. *The Masque of Blackness*, produced at Whitehall Palace in 1605, inaugurated his association with the architect Inigo Jones as designer. Recurrent quarreling between the two men led ultimately to Jonson's loss of favor at court, an event coincident with the decline of his health and his dramatic vitality. The end of Jonson's story in the reign of King Charles makes disconsolate reading.

Among the plays Jonson wrote in the last twenty years of his life, perhaps *The Devil Is an Ass* (1616) and *The Staple of News* (1625) are best remembered. They pale, however, before his great comedies of the earlier Jacobean period, VOLPONE (1606), EPICOENE (1609), THE ALCHEMIST (1610), and BARTHOLOMEW FAIR (1614).

Jonson is also a great lyric poet, among the greatest in English. He is a trail-blazing if essentially commonplace critic. In fact, the history of English criticism may be said to begin with him. As a personality, he was powerfully influential on the younger wits who formed the Tribe of Ben and who eulogized him in a tributary volume on his death in 1637. Jonson's epitaph in Westminster Abbey reads: "O rare Ben Jonson." It is spare praise but sufficient.

Jonson wrote VOLPONE in five weeks' time, early in 1606. In that year the comedy was acted by Shakespeare's company, now designated the King's Men, at the Globe, and subsequently before the universities of Oxford and Cambridge. To these "noble sisters" the quarto of 1607, published by Thomas Thorpe, is dedicated. A copy of the quarto, carefully corrected but essentially unrevised, furnished the text for the Folio version of 1616, on which this edition is based. Still another version, less accurately printed, appeared in the folio of 1640.

Though no specific source of the play is known, Jonson is obviously drawing on the Roman tradition of *captatio* or legacy-hunting, familiar to him from the writings of the late Greek rhetorician and satirist Lucian and the Roman satirist Juvenal. Other hints derive from Petronius, the author of the *Satyricon*, the epigrammatist Martial, Erasmus in *The Praise of Folly*, and Henry Cornelius Agrippa, a sixteenth-century German magus and political writer.

VOLPONE is notable for its plethora of scene divisions. Such divisions as merely denote the entrance of a new character have been ignored here as pedantic, hence unnecessary. In other plays of Jonson included in this volume, practice has been dictated by the editor's sense of pedagogical propriety. The governing rule has been to make for maximum clarity in presentation. Jonson's often excessive punctuation, which it is possible to read as attesting to his costive temperament more than to considerations of grammar or syntax, has been slightly modified.

Some of the stage directions that appeared in the original play are nonetheless bracketed in this edition because they were originally printed in somewhat different form—as cut-in marginal directions in the body of the play, with the place or places of their intended use indicated within the speeches by dashes.

Jonson in this play, as sometimes in the poetry (for example, the scatological verses "On the Famous Voyage"), verges on the disgusting. But to locate the key to the immense achievement in his supposed morbidity, as some critics have done, is malapropos. The key to VOLPONE, also its greatness, is titanic energy. Jonson exemplifies as well as any artist of the English Renaissance, Shakespeare not excluded, the validity on its own narrow ground of Plato's criticism of art. In a phrase, power in execution bears everything before it and with the result that questions of morality are felt as impertinent. Jonson's dramatic writing is molten,

therefore convincing. We are grateful, as when we bear witness to a miracle, for the famous song to Celia (III. iii), though the villain who sings it is up to no good. By the same token, we applaud the final unmasking not because it vindicates poetic justice, rather as it is the last and wittiest *jeu d'esprit* in a play that never ceases to surprise us. If we assent to the pious ejaculations of Bonario and Celia in the concluding scene, our assent—and Jonson's—is only formal. Certainly we do not assent to the ostensible moral of the piece, as supplied unhelpfully by the homiletic Advocate. The playwright anticipates our amused and scornful demur, in fact is bidding for it. He is the antithesis of the preacher and his natural antagonist. His purpose is not to edify but to entertain. In fulfilling this purpose, he has no peer in the history of our drama but one.   R. A. F.

Volpone; or, The Fox

[DEDICATION]

TO THE
MOST NOBLE AND MOST EQUAL SISTERS
THE TWO FAMOUS UNIVERSITIES
FOR THEIR
LOVE AND ACCEPTANCE SHOWN TO HIS POEM
IN THE PRESENTATION
BEN JONSON
THE GRATEFUL ACKNOWLEDGER
DEDICATES BOTH IT AND HIMSELF.

DRAMATIS PERSONÆ

VOLPONE, *a magnifico*
MOSCA, *his parasite*
VOLTORE, *an advocate*
CORBACCIO, *an old gentleman*
CORVINO, *a merchant*
BONARIO, *a young gentleman,* [*son to Corbaccio*]
[SIR] POLITIC WOULD-BE, *a Knight*
PEREGRINE, *a gentleman traveler*
NANO, *a dwarf*
CASTRONE, *a eunuch*
ANDROGYNO, *a hermaphrodite*

Grege [*i.e., mob*]
Commandadori, *officers* [*of justice*]
Mercatori, *three merchants*
Avocatori, *four magistrates*
Notario, *the register*

FINE MADAM WOULD-BE, *The Knight's wife*
CELIA, *The Merchant's wife*

Servitori, *servants*
[Two Waiting-]women

THE SCENE: VENICE

THE ARGUMENT

V olpone, childless, rich, feigns sick, despairs,
O ffers his state to hopes of several heirs,
L ies languishing; his parasite receives
P resents of all, assures, deludes; then weaves
O ther cross plots, which ope themselves, are told.
N ew tricks for safety are sought; they thrive: when bold,
E ach tempts the other again, and all are sold.

PROLOGUE

Now, luck yet send us, and a little wit
   Will serve to make our play hit;
According to the palates[1] of the season
   Here is rhyme, not empty of reason.
This we were bid to credit from our poet,
   Whose true scope, if you would know it,
In all his poems still[2] hath been his measure,
   To mix profit with your pleasure;
And not as some, whose throats their envy failing,
   Cry hoarsely, All he writes is railing;   10
And when his plays come forth, think they can flout
   them,
   With saying, He was a year about them.
To this there needs no lie, but this his creature,
   Which was two months since no feature:

PROLOGUE
¹ *palates:* taste.   ² *still:* continually.

And though he dares give them five lives to mend it,
'Tis known, five weeks fully penned it,
From his own hand, without a coadjutor,[3]
  Novice, journeyman, or tutor.
Yet thus much I can give you as a token
  Of his play's worth, no eggs are broken,   20
Nor quaking custards[4] with fierce teeth affrighted,
  Wherewith your rout[5] are so delighted;
Nor hales he in a gull[6] old ends[7] reciting,
  To stop gaps in his loose writing;
With such a deal of monstrous and forced action,

As might make Bethlem a faction:[8]
Nor made he his play for jests stolen from each table,[9]
  But makes jests to fit his fable;
And so presents quick[10] comedy refined,
  As best critics have designed.   30
The laws of time, place, persons[11] he observeth,
  From no needful rule he swerveth.
All gall and copperas[12] from his ink he draineth,
  Only a little salt remaineth;
Wherewith he'll rub your cheeks, till red with laughter,
  They shall look fresh a week after.

ACT ONE

SCENE ONE

[*Enter* VOLPONE *and* MOSCA.[1]]

Volp. Good morning to the day; and next, my gold!
Open the shrine, that I may see my saint.

[MOSCA *draws the curtain and discovers piles of gold,*
plate, jewels, etc.]

Hail the world's soul, and mine! more glad than is
The teeming earth to see the longed-for sun
Peep through the horns of the celestial Ram,[2]
Am I, to view thy splendor darkening his;
That lying here, amongst my other hoards,
Show'st like a flame by night, or like the day
Struck out of chaos, when all darkness fled
Unto the center. O thou son of Sol,[3]   10
But brighter than thy father, let me kiss,
With adoration, thee, and every relic
Of sacred treasure in this blessèd room.
Well did wise poets, by thy glorious name,
Title that age[4] which they would have the best;
Thou being the best of things, and far transcending
All style of joy, in children, parents, friends,
Or any other waking dream on earth:
Thy looks when they to Venus[5] did ascribe,
They should have given her twenty thousand Cupids;
Such are thy beauties and our loves! Dear saint,   21
Riches, the dumb god, that giv'st all men tongues,
That canst do naught, and yet mak'st men do all things;
The price of souls; even hell, with thee to boot,
Is made worth heaven. Thou art virtue, fame,
Honor, and all things else. Who can get thee,
He shall be noble, valiant, honest, wise—
  Mos. And what he will, sir. Riches are in fortune
A greater good than wisdom is in nature.
  Volp. True, my beloved Mosca. Yet I glory   30
More in the cunning purchase[6] of my wealth
Than in the glad possession, since I gain
No common way. I use no trade, no venture;[7]
I wound no earth with ploughshares, fat no beasts
To feed the shambles; have no mills for iron,[8]
Oil, corn, or men, to grind 'hem into powder;
I blow no subtle glass,[9] expose no ships
To threat'nings of the furrow-facèd sea;

I turn no monies in the public bank,
Nor usure private.
  Mos.   No sir, nor devour   40
Soft prodigals. You shall ha' some will swallow
A melting heir as glibly as your Dutch[10]
Will pills of butter, and ne'er purge for it;
Tear forth the fathers of poor families
Out of their beds, and coffin them alive
In some kind clasping prison, where their bones
May be forthcoming, when the flesh is rotten.
But your sweet nature doth abhor these courses;
You loathe the widow's or the orphan's tears
Should wash your pavements, or their piteous cries   50
Ring in your roofs, and beat the air for vengeance.
  Volp. Right, Mosca; I do loathe it.
  Mos.   And, besides, sir,
You are not like the thresher that doth stand
With a huge flail, watching a heap of corn,
And, hungry, dares not taste the smallest grain,
But feeds on mallows, and such bitter herbs;
Nor like the merchant, who hath filled his vaults
With Romagnia,[11] and rich Candian[12] wines,

---

   [3] *coadjutor:* collaborator.
   [4] *custards:* like those set on the lord mayor's table at city feasts for the fool to jump into.
   [5] *rout:* mob.   [6] *gull:* fool.
   [7] *old ends:* stale saws and sayings.
   [8] *make . . . faction:* turn the inhabitants of Bedlam, the London madhouse, into supporters.
   [9] *jests . . . table:* plagiarized from other authors.
   [10] *quick:* lively.
   [11] *laws . . . persons:* unities, prescribing a single day for the entire action, which must occur in a single setting, and which must feature characters who are decorous: faithful to the type they embody.
   [12] *copperas:* vitriol, i.e., bitterness.

I.i.
   [1] *Mosca:* the fly.   [2] *Ram:* zodiacal sign of Aries.
   [3] *Sol:* the sun.   [4] *age:* Golden Age.
   [5] *Venus:* described as "golden" by classical poets.
   [6] *cunning purchase:* ingenious acquisition.
   [7] *venture:* speculation.
   [8] *no . . . iron:* Volpone does not waste timber.
   [9] *glass:* for which Venice and its environs were famous.
   [10] *Dutch:* supposed to be fond of butter.
   [11] *Romagnia:* sweet Greek wine; accent on next-to-last syllable.
   [12] *Candian:* Malmsey wine from Greece and Crete (Candy).

Yet drinks the lees of Lombard's vinegar:
You will not lie in straw, whilst moths and worms   60
Feed on your sumptuous hangings and soft beds;
You know the use of riches, and dare give now
From that bright heap, to me, your poor observer,[13]
Or to your dwarf, or your hermaphrodite,
Your eunuch, or what other household trifle[14]
Your pleasure allows maintenance—
   Volp.   Hold thee, Mosca,
Take of my hand; thou strik'st on truth in all,
And they are envious[15] term thee parasite.
Call forth my dwarf, my eunuch, and my fool,
And let 'hem make me sport.

                         [*Exit* MOSCA.]
            What should I do,   70
But cocker up my genius,[16] and live free
To all delights my fortune calls me to?
I have no wife, no parent, child, ally,
To give my substance to: but whom I make
Must be my heir; and this makes men observe[17] me:
This draws new clients daily to my house,
Women and men of every sex and age,
That bring me presents, send me plate, coin, jewels
With hope that when I die (which they expect
Each greedy minute) it shall then return   80
Tenfold upon them; whilst some, covetous
Above the rest, seek to engross[18] me whole,
And counter-work the one unto the other,
Contend in gifts, as they would seem in love.
All which I suffer,[19] playing with their hopes,
And am content to coin 'hem into profit,

---

[13] *observer*: follower.   [14] *trifle*: hanger-on.
[15] *envious*: "who" is understood to follow.
[16] *cocker . . . genius*: indulge my disposition.
[17] *observe*: dote on.   [18] *engross*: appropriate.
[19] *suffer*: endure.   [20] *bearing . . . hand*: beguiling them.
[21] *Letting . . . lips*: as in the game of bob-cherry, in which one tries to bite the suspended fruit.
[22] *false . . . verse*: loose four-stressed verse, familiar from the medieval moralities.   [23] *here*: pointing to Androgyno.
[24] *Aethalides*: herald of the Argonauts, who inherited perfect memory from his father Mercury.
[25] *Euphorbus*: Trojan hero, slain by Menelaus, "the cuckold of Sparta."
[26] *Hermotimus*: mentioned with Pyrrhus of Delos in Diogenes Laertius. (What Jonson is after in this catalogue of those who harbor the soul of Pythagoras is sonority more than sense.)   [27] *sophist of Greece*: Pythagoras.
[28] *Hight Aspasia*: Called Aspasia, the mistress of Pericles.
[29] *meretrix*: whore, as in *Cambyses*.
[30] *Crates the cynic*: philosopher of Thebes.
[31] *itself*: Gallus, the "cobbler's cock" in Lucian's dialogue, is host to the soul of Pythagoras, who relates his transmigrations to his master.   [32] *brock*: badger.
[33] *one . . . three*: Number is the principle of harmony and morality in the Pythagorean system.
[34] *Quater*: The *quaternio* represented the number ten or decade as a four-tiered triangle (Trigon) of dots.
[35] *golden thigh*: this ancient tradition is glanced at in *The Alchemist*, and remembered by Yeats in "Among School Children."
[36] *reformation*: i.e., the Protestant Reformation.
[37] *old doctrine*: Roman Catholic.
[38] *Carthusian*: This severe order prescribed fish instead of meat; the Pythagoreans disallowed even fish, as also speaking for a five-year period.
[39] *beans*: forbidden by Pythagoras.

And look upon their kindness, and take more,
And look on that; still bearing them in hand,[20]
Letting the cherry knock against their lips,[21]
And draw it by their mouths, and back again.—   90
How now!

   [*Re-enter* MOSCA *with* NANO, ANDROGYNO, *and*
                CASTRONE.]

   Nano. Now, room for fresh gamesters, who do will
      you to know,
They do bring you neither play nor university show;
And therefore do intreat you that whatsoever they
      rehearse,
May not fare a whit the worse, for the false pace of the
      verse.[22]
If you wonder at this, you will wonder more ere we pass,
For know, here[23] is enclosed the soul of Pythagoras,
That juggler divine, as hereafter shall follow;
Which soul, fast and loose, sir, came first from Apollo,
And was breathed into Aethalides,[24] Mercurius his son,
Where it had the gift to remember all that ever was
      done.   101
From thence it fled forth, and made quick trans-
      migration
To goldy-locked Euphorbus,[25] who was killed in good
      fashion,
At the siege of old Troy by the cuckold of Sparta.
Hermotimus[26] was next (I find it in my charta),
To whom it did pass, where no sooner it was missing,
But with one Pyrrhus of Delos it learned to go a-fishing;
And thence did it enter the sophist of Greece.[27]
From Pythagore, she went into a beautiful piece,
Hight Aspasia,[28] the meretrix;[29] and the next toss of
      her   110
Was again of a whore, she became a philosopher,
Crates the cynic,[30] as itself[31] doth relate it:
Since kings, knights, and beggars, knaves, lords and
      fools gat it,
Besides ox and ass, camel, mule, goat, and brock;[32]
In all which it hath spoke, as in the cobbler's cock.
But I come not here to discourse of that matter,
Or his one, two, or three,[33] or his great oath, "By
      Quater!"[34]
His musics, his trigon, his golden thigh,[35]
Or his telling how elements shift; but I
Would ask, how of late thou hast suffered translation,
And shifted thy coat in these days of reformation.[36] 121
   Andr. Like one of the reformed, a fool, as you see,
Counting all old doctrine[37] heresy.
   Nano. But not on thine own forbid meats hast thou
      ventured?
   Andr. On fish, when first a Carthusian[38] I entered.
   Nano. Why, then thy dogmatical silence hath left
      thee?
   Andr. Of that an obstreperous lawyer bereft me.
   Nano. O wonderful change, when sir lawyer forsook
      thee!
For Pythagore's sake, what body then took thee?   129
   Andr. A good dull mule.
   Nano.   And how! by that means
Thou wert brought to allow of the eating of beans?[39]

Andr. Yes.

Nano.   But from the mule into whom didst thou
   pass?

Andr. Into a very strange beast, by some writers
   called an ass;
By others a precise, pure, illuminate brother [40]
Of those devour flesh, and sometimes one another;
And will drop you forth a libel, or a sanctified lie,
Betwixt every spoonful of a nativity-pie. [41]

Nano. Now quit thee, for heaven, of that profane
   nation,
And gently [42] report thy next transmigration.

Andr. To the same that I am.

Nano   A creature of delight,
And, what is more than a fool, a hermaphrodite!   141
Now, pray thee, sweet soul, in all thy variation,
Which body wouldst thou choose to take up thy
   station?

Andr. Troth, this I am in: even here would I tarry.

Nano. 'Cause here the delight of each sex thou canst
   vary!

Andr. Alas, those pleasures be stale and forsaken.
No, 'tis your fool wherewith I am so taken,
The only one creature that I can call blessèd;
For all other forms I have proved most distressèd.

Nano. Spoke true, as thou wert in Pythagoras still,
This learnèd opinion we celebrate will,   151
Fellow eunuch, as behoves us, with our wit and art,
To dignify that whereof ourselves are so great and
   special a part.

Volp. Now, very, very pretty. Mosca, this
Was thy invention?

Mos.   If it please my patron,
Not else.

Volp. It doth, good Mosca.

Mos.   Then it was, sir.

SONG

Fools, they are the only nation
Worth men's envy or admiration;
Free from care or sorrow-taking,
Selves and others merry making: 160
All they speak or do is sterling.
Your fool he is your great man's darling,
And your ladies' sport and pleasure;
Tongue and babble are his treasure.
E'en his face begetteth laughter,
And he speaks truth free from slaughter. [43]
He's the grace of every feast,
And sometimes the chiefest guest;
Hath his trencher [44] *and his stool,*
When wit waits upon the fool.   170
   Oh, who would not be
   He, he, he?

One knocks without.

Volp. Who's that? Away! Look, Mosca.

Mos.   Fool, begone!

[*Exeunt* NANO, CASTRONE, *and* ANDROGYNO.]
'Tis Signior Voltore, the advocate.
I know him by his knock.

Volp.   Fetch me my gown,
My furs, and night-caps; say my couch is changing.
And let him entertain himself awhile
Without i' the gallery.

[*Exit* MOSCA.]
                Now, now my clients
Begin their visitation! Vulture, kite, [45]
Raven, and gorcrow, [46] all my birds of prey,   180
That think me turning carcass, now they come:
I am not for 'hem yet.

[*Re-enter* MOSCA.]

                How now! the news?

Mos. A piece of plate, sir.

Volp.   Of what bigness?

Mos.   Huge,
Massy, and antique, with your name inscribed,
And arms engraven.

Volp.   Good! and not a fox
Stretched on the earth, with fine delusive sleights,
Mocking a gaping crow? ha, Mosca!

Mos.   Sharp, sir.

Volp. Give me my furs. Why dost thou laugh so,
   man?

Mos. I cannot choose, sir, when I apprehend
What thoughts he has without now, as he walks: 190
That this might be the last gift he should give;
That this would fetch you; if you died today,
And gave him all, what he should be tomorrow;
What large return would come of all his ventures
How he should worshipped be, and reverenced;
Ride with his furs, and foot-cloths, waited on
By herds of fools and clients, have clear way
Made for his mule, [47] as lettered as himself,
Be called the great and learnèd advocate;
And then concludes, there's nought impossible.   200

Volp. Yes, to be learnèd, Mosca.

Mos.   Oh, no: rich
Implies it. Hood an ass with reverend purple,
So you can hide his two ambitious [48] ears,
And he shall pass for a cathedral doctor. [49]

Volp. My caps, my caps, good Mosca. Fetch him in.

Mos. Stay, sir; your ointment for your eyes.

Volp.   That's true;
Dispatch, dispatch: I long to have possession
Of my new present.

Mos.   That, and thousands more,
I hope to see you lord of.

Volp.   Thanks, kind Mosca.

Mos. And that, when I am lost in blended dust,   210
And hundreds such as I am, in succession—

[40] *illuminate brother:* "inspired" Puritan.
[41] *nativity-pie:* Christmas-pie (the "precise" Puritans were averse to the suffix "mass").   [42] *gently:* civilly.
[43] *free from slaughter:* with impunity ("slaughter" and "laughter" are understood to rhyme).
[44] *trencher:* wooden plate.
[45] *kite:* Lady Would-be, who is called subsequently a she-wolf.   [46] *gorcrow:* carrion crow.
[47] *mule:* appropriate to an advocate.
[48] *ambitious:* prominent.
[49] *cathedral doctor:* one who holds a professorial chair.

Volp. Nay, that were too much, Mosca.

Mos.   You shall live

Still to delude these harpies.

Volp.   Loving Mosca!

'Tis well: my pillow now, and let him enter.

                                [*Exit* MOSCA.]

Now, my feignèd cough, my phthisic,[50] and my gout,

My apoplexy, palsy, and catarrhs,

Help, with your forcèd functions, this my posture,

Wherein, this three year, I have milked their hopes.

He comes; I hear him—Uh[*Coughing*] uh, uh! uh!

Oh—

[*Re-enter* MOSCA *with* VOLTORE.]

Mos. You still are what you were, sir. Only you,

Of all the rest, are he commands his love,   221

And you do wisely to preserve it thus,

With early visitation, and kind notes[51]

Of your good meaning to him, which, I know,

Cannot but come most grateful. Patron! sir!

Here's Signior Voltore is come—

Volp. [*Faintly*]   What say you?

Mos. Sir, Signior Voltore is come this morning

To visit you.

Volp.   I thank him.

Mos.   And hath brought

A piece of antique plate, bought of St. Mark,[52]

With which he here presents you.

Volp.   He is welcome.   230

Pray him to come more often.

Mos.   Yes.

Volt.   What says he?

Mos. He thanks you, and desires you see him often.

Volp. Mosca.

Mos.   My patron!

Volp.   Bring him near, where is he?

I long to feel his hand.

Mos.   The plate is here, sir.

Volt. How fare you, sir?

Volp.   I thank you, Signior Voltore;

Where is the plate? Mine eyes are bad.

Volt.   I'm sorry

To see you still thus weak.

Mos. [*Aside*]   That he is not weaker.

Volp. You are too munificent.

Volt.   No, sir; would to heaven,

I could as well give health to you, as that plate!

Volp. You give, sir, what you can; I thank you. Your

    love   240

Hath taste in this, and shall not be unanswered.

---

[50] *phthisic:* consumption.

[51] *notes:* tokens, i.e., the piece of plate.

[52] *of St. Mark:* from a goldsmith in the Piazza San Marco.

[53] *still:* continually.

[54] *write . . . family:* make me a member of your household.

[55] *large: generous.*   [56] *mere:* absolute.

[57] *And . . . them:* The voice pause after "return" counts as a syllable in the making of the iambic pentameter line.

[58] *provoking:* engendering; money that works to a purpose, as by bribery.   [59] *put . . . up:* pocket it.

[60] *perplexed:* ambiguous.

[61] *cecchine:* chequin, Venetian gold coin.

I pray you see me often.

Volt.   Yes, I shall, sir.

Volp. Be not far from me.

Mos.   Do you observe that, sir?

Volp. Hearken unto me still;[53] it will concern you.

Mos. You are a happy man, sir; know your good.

Volp. I cannot now last long—

Mos.   You are his heir, sir.

Volt. Am I?

Volp.   I feel me going, Uh! uh! uh! uh!

I'm sailing to my port, uh! uh! uh! uh!

And I am glad I am so near my haven.   249

Mos. Alas, kind gentleman! well, we must all go—

Volt. But, Mosca—

Mos.   Age will conquer.

Volt.   Pray thee, hear me.

Am I inscribed his heir for certain?

Mos.   Are you!

I do beseech you, sir, you will vouchsafe

To write me i' your family.[54] All my hopes

Depend upon your worship. I am lost

Except the rising sun do shine on me.

Volt. It shall both shine, and warm thee, Mosca.

Mos.   Sir,

I am a man that have not done your love

All the worst offices: here I wear your keys,

See all your coffers and your caskets locked,   260

Keep the poor inventory of your jewels,

Your plate, and monies; am your steward, sir,

Husband your goods here.

Volt.   But am I sole heir?

Mos. Without a partner, sir: confirmed this morning.

The wax is warm yet, and the ink scarce dry

Upon the parchment.

Volt.   Happy, happy me!

By what good chance, sweet Mosca?

Mos.   Your desert, sir;

I know no second cause.

Volt.   Thy modesty

Is loath to know it; well, we shall requite it.

Mos. He ever liked your course, sir; that first took

    him.   270

I oft have heard him say how he admired

Men of your large[55] profession, that could speak

To every cause, and things mere[56] contraries,

Till they were hoarse again, yet all be law;

That, with most quick agility, could turn,

And return; make knots, and undo them;[57]

Give forked counsel; take provoking[58] gold

On either hand, and put it up;[59] these men,

He knew, would thrive with their humility.

And, for his part, he thought he should be blest   280

To have his heir of such a suffering spirit,

So wise, so grave, of so perplexed[60] a tongue,

And loud withal, that would not wag, nor scarce

Lie still without a fee; when every word

Your worship but lets fall is a cecchine![61]

                        Another knocks.

Who's that? One knocks. I would not have you seen sir.

And yet—pretend you came, and went in haste;

I'll fashion an excuse—and, gentle sir,
When you do come to swim in golden lard,
Up to the arms in honey, that your chin   290
Is borne up stiff with fatness of the flood,
Think on your vassal, but remember me:
I ha' not been your worst of clients.
   Volt.   Mosca!—
   Mos. When will you have your inventory brought,
     sir?
Or see a copy of the will?—Anon![62]
I'll bring 'hem to you, sir. Away, begone,
Put business i' your face.

                   [*Exit* VOLTORE.]
   Volp.   Excellent Mosca!
Come hither, let me kiss thee.
   Mos.   Keep you still, sir.
Here is Corbaccio.
   Volp.   Set the plate away.
The vulture's gone, and the old raven's come.[63]   300
   Mos. Betake you to your silence, and your sleep.
Stand there and multiply.[64]

     [*Putting the plate with the rest of the treasure*.]
                 Now we shall see
A wretch who is indeed more impotent
Than this can feign to be; yet hopes to hop
Over his grave.

          [*Enter* CORBACCIO.]

         Signior Corbaccio!
You're very welcome, sir.
   Corb.   How does your patron?
   Mos. Troth, as he did, sir; no amends.
   Corb.   What! mends he?
   Mos. No, sir, he is rather worse.
   Corb.   That's well. Where is he?
   Mos. Upon his couch, sir, newly fall'n asleep.   309
   Corb. Does he sleep well?
   Mos.   No wink, sir, all this night,
Nor yesterday; but slumbers.[65]
   Corb.   Good! he should take
Some counsel of physicians. I have brought him
An opiate here, from mine own doctor.
   Mos. He will not hear of drugs.
   Corb.   Why? I myself
Stood by while it was made, saw all the ingredients,
And know it cannot but most gently work.
My life for his, 'tis but to make him sleep.
   Volp. [*Aside*] Ay, his last sleep, if he would take it.
   Mos.   Sir,
He has no faith in physic.[66]
   Corb.   Say you, say you?
   Mos. He has no faith in physic. He does think   320
Most of your doctors are the greater danger,
And worse disease, to escape. I often have
Heard him protest that your physician
Should never be his heir.
   Corb.   Not I his heir?
   Mos. Not your physician, sir.
   Corb.   Oh, no, no, no.
I do not mean it.

   Mos.   No, sir, nor their fees
He cannot brook. He says they flay a man
Before they kill him.
   Corb.   Right, I do conceive[67] you.
   Mos. And then they do it by experiment,[68]
For which the law not only doth absolve 'hem   330
But gives them great reward: and he is loath
To hire his death so.
   Corb.   It is true, they kill
With as much license as a judge.
   Mos.   Nay, more;
For he but kills, sir, where the law condemns,
And these can kill him too.
   Corb.   Ay, or me,
Or any man. How does his apoplex?
Is that strong on him still?
   Mos.   Most violent.
His speech is broken, and his eyes are set,
His face drawn longer than 'twas wont—
   Corb.   How! how!
Stronger than he was wont?
   Mos.   No, sir, his face   340
Drawn longer than 'twas wont.
   Corb.   Oh, good!
   Mos.   His mouth
Is ever gaping, and his eyelids hang.
   Corb.   Good.
   Mos. A freezing numbness stiffens all his joints,
And make the color of his flesh like lead.
   Corb.   'Tis good.
   Mos. His pulse beats slow, and dull.
   Corb.   Good symptoms still.
   Mos. And from his brain—
   Corb.   Ha! how! not from his brain?
   Mos. Yes, sir, and from his brain.
   Corb.   I conceive you; good.
   Mos. Flows a cold sweat, with a continual rheum,[69]
Forth the resolvèd[70] corners of his eyes.
   Corb. Is't possible? Yet I am better, ha!   350
How does he with the swimming of his head?
   Mos. Oh, sir, 'tis past the scotomy;[71] he now
Hath lost his feeling, and hath left[72] to snort.
You hardly can perceive him, that he breathes.
   Corb. Excellent, excellent! sure I shall outlast him.
This makes me young again, a score of years.
   Mos. I was a-coming for you, sir.
   Corb.   Has he made his will?
What has he given me?
   Mos.   No, sir.
   Corb.   Nothing! ha?
   Mos. He has not made his will, sir.
   Corb.   Oh, oh, oh!
What then did Voltore, the lawyer, here?   360

---

[62] *Anon:* Right away (to Corbaccio).
[63] *vulture, raven:* Voltore and Corbaccio.
[64] *Stand . . . multiply:* to the plate.
[65] *slumbers:* dozes.   [66] *physic:* medicine.
[67] *conceive:* understand.
[68] *by experiment:* as an experiment.   [69] *rheum:* flowing.
[70] *Forth . . . resolvèd:* From the dissolving.
[71] *scotomy:* dizziness.   [72] *left:* left off; stopped snoring.

Mos. He smelt a carcass, sir, when he but heard
My master was about his testament;
As I did urge him to it for your good—
  Corb. He came unto him, did he? I thought so.
  Mos. Yes, and presented him this piece of plate.
  Corb. To be his heir?
  Mos.   I do not know, sir.
  Corb.   True:
I know it too.
  Mos.   By your own scale, sir.
  Corb. [*Aside*]   Well,
I shall prevent[73] him yet.—See, Mosca, look,
Here I have brought a bag of bright cecchines,
Will quite weigh down his plate.
  Mos.   Yea, marry,[74] sir. 370
This is true physic, this your sacred medicine;[75]
No talk of opiates to this great elixir!
  Corb. 'Tis *aurum palpabile*, if not *potabile*.[76]
  Mos. It shall be ministered to him in his bowl.
  Corb. Ay, do, do, do.
  Mos.   Most blessèd cordial!
This will recover him.
  Corb.   Yes, do, do, do.
  Mos. I think it were not best, sir.
  Corb.   What?
  Mos.   To recover him.
  Corb. Oh, no, no, no; by no means.
  Mos.   Why, sir, this
Will work some strange effect, if he but feel it.
  Corb. 'Tis true, therefore forbear; I'll take my
    venture:[77]   380
Give me it again.
  Mos.   At no hand;[78] pardon me.
You shall not do yourself that wrong, sir. I
Will so advise you, you shall have it all.
  Corb. How?
  Mos.   All, sir; 'tis your right, your own; no man
Can claim a part: 'tis yours without a rival,
Decreed by destiny.
  Corb.   How, how, good Mosca?
  Mos. I'll tell you sir. This fit he shall recover.
  Corb. I do conceive you.
  Mos.   And on first advantage
Of his gained[79] sense, will I re-importune him
Unto the making of his testament: 390
And show him this.
                          [*Pointing to the money.*]
  Corb.   Good, good.
  Mos.   'Tis better yet,

If you will hear, sir,
  Corb.   Yes, with all my heart.
  Mos. Now would I counsel you, make home with
    speed.
There, frame a will, whereto you shall inscribe
My master your sole heir.
  Corb.   And disinherit
My son!
  Mos. Oh, sir, the better: for that color[80]
Shall make it much more taking.[81]
  Corb.   Oh, but[82] color?
  Mos. This will, sir, you shall send it unto me.
Now, when I come to enforce,[83] as I will do,   399
Your cares, your watchings, and your many prayers,
Your more than many gifts, your this day's present,
And last, produce your will; where, without thought,
Or least regard, unto your proper issue,[84]
A son so brave,[85] and highly meriting,
The stream of your diverted[86] love hath thrown you
Upon my master, and made him your heir:
He cannot be so stupid, or stone-dead,
But out of conscience and mere gratitude—
  Corb. He must pronounce me his?
  Mos.   'Tis true.
  Corb.   This plot
Did I think on before.
  Mos.   I do believe it.   410
  Corb. Do you not believe it?
  Mos.   Yes, sir.
  Corb.   Mine own project.
  Mos. Which, when he hath done, sir—
  Corb.   Published me
    his heir?
  Mos. And you so certain to survive him—
  Corb.   Ay.
  Mos. Being so lusty[87] a man—
  Corb.   'Tis true.
  Mos.   Yes, sir—
  Corb. I thought on that too. See, how he should be
The very organ to express my thoughts!
  Mos. You have not only done yourself a good—
  Corb. But multiplied it on my son.
  Mos.   'Tis right, sir.
  Corb. Still, my invention.
  Mos.   'Las, sir! heaven knows,
It hath been all my study, all my care   420
(I e'en grow gray withal), how to work things—
  Corb. I do conceive, sweet Mosca.
  Mos.   You are he
For whom I labor here.
  Corb.   Ay, do, do, do:
I'll straight about it.
  Mos. [*Aside*]   Rook go with you,[88] raven!
  Corb. I know thee honest.
  Mos. [*Aside*]   You do lie, sir!
  Corb.   And—
  Mos. [*Aside*] Your knowledge is no better than your
    ears, sir.
  Corb. I do not doubt to be a father to thee.
  Mos. [*Aside*] Nor I to gull[89] my brother of his
    blessing.

[73] *prevent:* forestall.
[74] *marry:* an interjection—"indeed!"
[75] *medicine:* disyllabic.
[76] *'Tis . . . potabile:* The sovereign remedy is gold that can be felt if not drunk.   [77] *venture:* gift.
[78] *at . . . hand:* by no means.   [79] *gained:* regained.
[80] *color:* appearance.   [81] *taking:* persuasive.
[82] *but:* only.   [83] *enforce:* urge.
[84] *proper issue:* own child.   [85] *brave:* fine.
[86] *diverted:* turned (from your son).   [87] *lusty:* vigorous.
[88] *Rook . . . you:* May you be rooked, cheated; with a pun on "rook" = "crow," Latin *corvus* ("raven").
[89] *gull:* cheat.

Corb. I may ha' my youth restored to me, why not?
Mos. [*Aside*] Your worship is a precious ass!
Corb.   What
          sayest thou?   430
Mos. I do desire your worship to make haste, sir.
Corb. 'Tis done, 'tis done; I go.
                              [*Exit;* VOLPONE *leaps from his couch.*]
Volp.   Oh, I shall burst!
Let out my sides, let out my sides—
Mos.   Contain
Your flux[90] of laughter, sir: you know this hope
Is such a bait, it covers any hook.
Volp. Oh, but thy working, and thy placing it!
I cannot hold; good rascal, let me kiss thee:
I never knew thee in so rare a humor.
Mos. Alas, sir, I but do as I am taught;
Follow your grave instructions; give 'hem words;   440
Pour oil into their ears, and send them hence.
Volp. 'Tis true, 'tis true. What a rare punishment
Is avarice to itself!
Mos.   Ay, with our help, sir.
Volp. So many cares, so many maladies,
So many fears attending on old age.
Yea, death so often called on, as no wish
Can be more frequent with 'hem, their limbs faint,
Their senses dull, their seeing, hearing, going,[91]
All dead before them; yea, their very teeth,
Their instruments of eating, failing them: 450
Yet this is reckoned life! Nay, here was one,
Is now gone home, that wishes to live longer!
Feels not his gout, nor palsy; feigns himself
Younger by scores of years, flatters his age
With confident belying it, hopes he may
With charms like Aeson,[92] have his youth restored;
And with these thoughts so battens, as if fate
Would be as easily cheated on[93] as he,
And all turns air!

                                        [*Another knocks.*]
                              Who's that there, now? A third!
Mos. Close, to your couch again; I hear his voice.
It is Corvino,[94] our spruce merchant.

                    [VOLPONE *lies down as before.*]

Volp.   Dead.   461
Mos. Another bout, sir, with your eyes.[95] Who's
          there?

                    [*Enter* CORVINO.]

Signior Corvino! Come most wished for! Oh,
How happy were you, if you knew it, now!
Corv. Why? What? Wherein?
Mos.   The tardy hour is
          come, sir.
Corv. He is not dead?
Mos.   Not dead, sir, but as good;
He knows no man.
Corv.   How shall I do then?
Mos.   Why, sir?
Corv. I have brought him here a pearl.
Mos.   Perhaps he has

So much remembrance left as to know you, sir.
He still calls on you: nothing but your name   470
Is in his mouth. Is your pearl orient,[96] sir?
Corv. Venice was never owner of the like.
Volp. [*Faintly*] Signior Corvino!
Mos.   Hark.
Volp.   Signior Corvino.
Mos. He calls you; step and give it him. He's here,
          sir.
And he has brought you a rich pearl.
Corv.   How do you, sir?
Tell him it doubles the twelve caract.[97]
Mos.   Sir,
He cannot understand, his hearing's gone;
And yet it comforts him to see you—
Corv.   Say
I have a diamond for him, too.
Mos.   Best show it, sir:
Put it into his hand; 'tis only there   480
He apprehends. He has his feeling yet.
See how he grasps it!
Corv.   'Las, good gentleman!
How pitiful the sight is!
Mos.   Tut, forget, sir.
The weeping of an heir should still be laughter
Under a visor.[98]
Corv.   Why, am I his heir?
Mos. Sir, I am sworn, I may not show the will
Till he be dead; but here has been Corbaccio,
Here has been Voltore, here were others too,
I cannot number 'hem, they were so many;
All gaping here for legacies. But I,   490
Taking the vantage of his naming you,
"Signior Corvino, Signior Corvino," took
Paper, and pen, and ink, and there I asked him
Whom he would have his heir! "Corvino." Who
Should be executor? "Corvino." And
To any question he was silent to,
I still interpreted the nods he made,
Through weakness, for consent: and sent home th'
          others,
Nothing bequeathed them, but to cry and curse.   499
Corv. Oh, my dear Mosca.

                                        [*They embrace*]
                              Does he not perceive us?
Mos. No more than a blind harper. He knows no
          man,
No face of friend, nor name of any servant,
Who 'twas that fed him last, or gave him drink:
Not those he had begotten, or brought up,
Can he remember.
Corv.   Has he children?
Mos.   Bastards,
Some dozen, or more, that he begot on beggars,

---

[90] *flux:* outburst.   [91] *going:* ability to walk.
[92] *Aeson:* whom Medea restored to youth.
[93] *cheated on:* cheated.   [94] *Corvino:* crow.
[95] *Another . . . eyes:* Mosca anoints Volpone's eyes, to
make them clear.   [96] *orient:* especially lustrous.
[97] *caract:* carat.   [98] *visor:* mask (of pretended grief).

Gypsies, and Jews, and black-moors, when he was
   drunk.
Knew you not that, sir? 'Tis the common fable.
The dwarf, the fool, the eunuch, are all his.
He's the true father of his family,[99]   510
In all save[100] me:—but he has given 'hem nothing.
   Corv. That's well, that's well! Art sure he does not
   hear us?
   Mos. Sure, sir! why, look you, credit your own sense.
[*Shouts in* VOLPONE'*s ear.*] The pox[101] approach, and
   add to your diseases,
If it would send you hence the sooner, sir,
For your incontinence, it hath deserved it
Throughly and throughly, and the plague to boot!—
You may come near, sir.—Would you would once close
Those filthy eyes of yours, that flow with slime, 519
Like two frog-pits; and those same hanging cheeks,
Covered with hide instead of skin—Nay, help,[102] sir—
That look like frozen dish-clouts set on end!
   Corv. Or like an old smoked wall, on which the rain
Ran down in streaks!
   Mos.   Excellent, sir! Speak out:
You may be louder yet; a culverin[103]
Dischargèd in his ear would hardly bore it.
   Corv. His nose is like a common sewer, still running.
   Mos. 'Tis good! and what his mouth!
   Corv.   A very draught.
   Mos. Oh, stop it up—
   Corv.   By no means.
   Mos.   Pray you, let me.
Faith I could stifle him rarely with a pillow   530
As well as any woman that should keep[104] him.
   Corv. Do as you will; but I'll begone.
   Mos.   Be so;
It is your presence makes him last so long.
   Corv. I pray you use no violence.
   Mos.   No, sir! why?
Why should you be thus scrupulous, pray you, sir?
   Corv. Nay, at your discretion.
   Mos.   Well, good sir, be gone.
   Corv. I will not trouble him now to take my pearl.[105]
   Mos. Puh! nor your diamond. What a needless care.
Is this afflicts you? Is not all here yours?
Am not I here, whom you have made your creature?
That owe my being to you?
   Corv.   Grateful Mosca!   541
Thou art my friend, my fellow, my companion,
My partner, and shalt share in all my fortunes.
   Mos. Excepting one.
   Corv.   What's that?

---

[99] *family:* household of servants.   [100] *save:* except.
[101] *pox:* venereal disease.   [102] *help:* i.e., to abuse Volpone.
[103] *culverin:* small cannon.
[104] *keep:* care for (sardonically).
[105] *pearl:* which Volpone is holding.   [106] *purchase:* loot.
[107] *fat:* grow fat.   [108] *Politic:* Crafty.
[109] *squire:* gentleman, with the scornful implication of
"pander."   [110] *face:* (1) beauty, (2) impudence.
[111] *dishonest:* unchaste.
[112] *o' . . . year:* Without blemish.   [113] *blood:* passion.
[114] *window:* here and hereafter, for "windore" in original.
[115] *near:* closely.

   Mos.   Your gallant wife, sir.
                 [*Exit* CORVINO.]
Now is he gone. We had no other means
To shoot him hence but this.
   Volp.   My divine Mosca!
Thou hast today outgone thyself.

                 Another knocks.

               Who's there?
I will be troubled with no more. Prepare
Me music, dances, banquets, all delights.
The Turk is not more sensual in his pleasures   550
Than will Volpone. Let me see; a pearl!
A diamond! plate! cecchines! good morning's
   purchase.[106]
Why, this is better than rob churches, yet;
Or fat,[107] by eating, once a month, a man—
Who is 't?
   Mos. The beauteous Lady Would-be, sir,
Wife to the English knight, Sir Politic[108] Would-be,
(This is the style, sir, is directed me,)
Hath sent to know how you have slept tonight,
And if you would be visited?
   Volp.   Not now: 559
Some three hours hence.
   Mos.   I told the squire[109] so much.
   Volp. When I am high with mirth and wine; then,
   then.
'Fore heaven, I wonder at the desperate valor
Of the bold English, that they dare let loose
Their wives to all encounters!
   Mos.   Sir, this knight
Had not his name for nothing, he is politic,
And knows, howe'er his wife affect strange airs,
She hath not yet the face[110] to be dishonest.[111]
But had she Signior Corvino's wife's face—
   Volp. Has she so rare a face?
   Mos.   Oh, sir, the wonder,
The blazing star of Italy! a wench   570
O' the first year,[112] a beauty ripe as harvest!
Whose skin is whiter than a swan all over,
Than silver, snow, or lilies; a soft lip,
Would tempt you to eternity of kissing!
And flesh that melteth in the touch to blood![113]
Bright as your gold, and lovely as your gold!
   Volp. Why had not I known this before?
   Mos.   Alas, sir,
Myself but yesterday discovered it.
   Volp. How might I see her?
   Mos.   Oh, not possible;
She's kept as warily as is your gold;   580
Never does come abroad, never takes air
But at a window.[114] All her looks are sweet,
As the first grapes or cherries, and are watched
As near[115] as they are.
   Volp.   I must see her.
   Mos.   Sir,
There is a guard of ten spies thick upon her,
All his whole household; each of which is set
Upon his fellow, and have all their charge,
When he goes out, when he comes in, examined.

Volp. I will go see her, though but at her
  window.   589
Mos. In some disguise then.
Volp.   That is true; I must
Maintain mine own shape still the same. We'll think.
                                                    [*Exeunt.*]

ACT TWO

SCENE ONE

[*Enter* SIR POLITIC WOULD-BE *and* PEREGRINE.[1]]

S. Pol. Sir, to a wise man, all the world's his soil.[2]
It is not Italy, nor France, nor Europe,
That must bound me, if my fates call me forth.
Yet I protest, it is no salt[3] desire
Of seeing countries, shifting a religion,
Nor any disaffection to the state
Where I was bred, and unto which I owe
My dearest plots, hath brought me out; much less
That idle, antique, stale, gray-headed project
Of knowing men's minds and manners, with Ulysses!
But a peculiar humor of my wife's   11
Laid for this height[4] of Venice, to observe,
To quote,[5] to learn the language, and so forth—
I hope you travel, sir, with license?[6]
Per.   Yes.
S. Pol. I dare the safelier converse—How long, sir,
Since you left England?
Per.   Seven weeks.
S. Pol.   So lately![7]
You ha' not been with my lord ambassador?
Per. Not yet sir.
S. Pol.   Pray you, what news, sir, vents[8] our
  climate?
I heard last night a most strange thing reported
By some of my lord's followers, and I long   20
To hear how 'twill be seconded.[9]
Per.   What was 't, sir?
S. Pol. Marry, sir, of a raven[10] that should build[11]
In a ship royal of the King's
Per. [*Aside*]   This fellow,
Does he gull me,[12] trow?[13] Or is gulled? Your name sir?
S. Pol. My name is Politic Would-be.
Per. [*Aside*]   Oh, that speaks him.
A knight, sir?
S. Pol. A poor knight, sir.
Per.   Your lady
Lies[14] here in Venice, for intelligence[15]
Of tires,[16] and fashions, and behavior,
Among the courtesans? The fine Lady Would-be?
S. Pol. Yes, sir; the spider and the bee oftimes   30
Suck from one flower.
Per.   Good Sir Politic,
I cry you mercy;[17] I have heard much of you,
'Tis true, sir, of your raven.
S. Pol.   On your knowledge?
Per. Yes, and your lion's whelping in the Tower.[18]
S. Pol. Another whelp?
Per.   Another, sir.
S. Pol.   Now heaven!

What prodigies be these? The fires at Berwick![19]
And the new star![20] these things concurring, strange,
And full of omen! Saw you those meteors?
Per. I did, sir.
S. Pol.   Fearful! Pray you, sir, confirm me,
Were there three porpoises[21] seen above the bridge   40
As they give out?
Per.   Six, and a sturgeon, sir.
S. Pol. I am astonished.
Per.   Nay, sir, be not so;
I'll tell you a greater prodigy than these.
S. Pol. What should these things portend?
Per.   The very day
(Let me be sure) that I put forth from London,
There was a whale discovered in the river,
As high as Woolwich, that had waited there,
Few know how many months, for the subversion
Of the Stode[22] fleet.
S. Pol.   Is't possible? Believe it,
'Twas either sent from Spain, or the archduke's:[23]   50
Spinola's whale,[24] upon my life, my credit!
Will they not leave these projects? Worthy sir,
Some other news.
Per.   Faith, Stone the fool is dead,
And they do lack a tavern fool extremely.
S. Pol. Is Mass'[25] Stone dead?
Per.   He's dead, sir; why, I hope
You thought him not immortal? [*Aside*] Oh, this
  knight,
Were he well known, would be a precious thing
To fit our English stage. He that should write
But such a fellow, should be thought to feign
Extremely, if not maliciously.
S. Pol.   Stone dead!   60
Per. Dead.—Lord! how deeply, sir, you apprehend
  it![26]
He was no kinsman to you?

II.i.
  [1] *Peregrine:* Traveler.   [2] *soil:* native country.
  [3] *salt:* wanton.
  [4] *Laid . . . height:* Directed toward this latitude.
  [5] *quote:* take note of.
  [6] *license:* permission from the King.
  [7] *lately:* recently.   [8] *vents:* publishes.
  [9] *seconded:* confirmed.   [10] *raven:* bird of ill omen.
  [11] *should build:* is said to have built.
  [12] *gull me:* make a fool of me.
  [13] *trow:* expletive—"in faith."   [14] *Lies:* Sojourns.
  [15] *intelligence:* information.   [16] *tires:* attire.
  [17] *I . . . mercy:* I beg your pardon.
  [18] *Tower:* Tower of London, where lion cubs were born
just before the play was written.
  [19] *Berwick:* on the Scottish border, where ghostly armies
were reported in 1605.
  [20] *new star:* discovered by Kepler in 1604.
  [21] *porpoises:* The annalist Stow mentions the appearance
near London of a porpoise and whale in 1606.
  [22] *Stode:* Stade, port city near Hamburg, Germany.
  [23] *archduke's:* governor of the Spanish Netherlands.
  [24] *Spinola's whale:* The Marquis of Spinola, who commanded the Spanish army in the Netherlands, was credited
with having sent a whale to drown London by spouting
water on the city.
  [25] *Mass':* a vulgar shortening of Master.
  [26] *apprehend it:* take it to heart.

S. Pol.   That[27] I know of.
Well! that same fellow was an unknown[28] fool.
   Per. And yet you knew him, it seems?
S. Pol.   I did so, Sir.
I knew him one of the most dangerous heads
Living within the state, and so I held him.
   Per. Indeed, sir?
S. Pol.   While he lived, in action.
He has received weekly intelligence,
Upon my knowledge, out of the Low Countries,
For all parts of the world, in cabbages;[29]   70
And those dispensed again to ambassadors,
In oranges, musk-melons, apricots,
Lemons, pome-citrons, and such like; sometimes
In Colchester oysters, and your Selsey cockles.
   Per. You make me wonder.
S. Pol.   Sir, upon my knowledge.
Nay, I've observed him, at your public ordinary,[30]
Take his advertisement[31] from a traveler,
A concealed[32] statesman, in a trencher of meat;
And instantly, before the meal was done,
Convey an answer in a tooth-pick.
   Per.   Strange!   80
How could this be, sir?
S. Pol.   Why, the meat was cut
So like his character,[33] and so laid as he
Must easily read the cipher.
   Per.   I have heard
He could not read, sir.
S. Pol.   So 'twas given out,
In polity,[34] by those that did employ him.
But he could read, and had your languages.[35]
And to 't, as sound a noddle[36]—
   Per.   I have heard, sir,
That your baboons were spies, and that they were
A kind of subtle nation near to China.
   S. Pol. Ay, ay, your Mamuluchi.[37] Faith, they had
Their hand in a French plot or two; but they   91
Were so extremely given to women, as[38]
They made discovery of all. Yet I
Had my advices[39] here, on Wednesday last,
From one of their own coat,[40] they were returned,
Made their relations,[41] as the fashion is,
And now stand fair for fresh employment.

---

  [27] *That:* i.e., Not that.
  [28] *unknown:* inexpressible, without bottom.
  [29] *cabbages:* imported from Holland.
  [30] *ordinary:* tavern.
  [31] *advertisement:* "intelligence" (information).
  [32] *concealed:* disguised.
  [33] *character:* cipher or code, which the shape of the meat spelled out.   [34] *in polity:* for political reasons.
  [35] *had . . . languages:* knew languages.   [36] *noddle:* head.
  [37] *Mamuluchi:* Mamelukes.   [38] *as:* that.
  [39] *advices:* dispatches (as from a diplomatic pouch).
  [40] *coat:* kind.   [41] *relations:* reports.   [42] *tie:* debt.
  [43] *vulgar:* common.   [44] *cried:* taught (an affectation).
  [45] *brave bloods:* gallant youth.   [46] *ingenuous:* noble.
  [47] *I . . . it:* I do not boast about it.
  [48] *high kind:* important matter.
  [49] *dear tongues:* valued languages.
  [50] *quacksalvers:* charlatans.   [51] *venting:* selling.
  [52] *lewd:* ignorant.   [53] *terms and shreds:* technical jargon.
  [54] *utter:* sell, vend.

   Per. [*Aside*]   Heart!
This Sir Pol will be ignorant of nothing.—
It seems, sir, you know all.
S. Pol.   Not all, sir; but
I have some general notions, I do love   100
To note and to observe: though I live out,
Free from the active torrent, yet I'd mark
The currents and the passages of things.
For mine own private use; and know the ebbs
And flows of state.
   Per.   Believe it, sir, I hold
Myself in no small tie[42] unto my fortunes,
For casting me thus luckily upon you,
Whose knowledge, if your bounty equal it,
May do me great assistance, in instruction
For my behavior, and my bearing, which   110
Is yet so rude and raw.
   S. Pol.   Why? Came you forth
Empty of rules for travel?
   Per.   Faith, I had
Some common ones, from out that vulgar[43] grammar,
Which he that cried[44] Italian to me taught me.
   S. Pol. Why, this it is that spoils all our brave
     bloods,[45]
Trusting our hopeful gentry unto pedants,
Fellows of outside, and mere bark. You seem
To be a gentleman of ingenuous[46] race—
I not profess it,[47] but my fate hath been
To be, where I have been consulted with,   120
In this high kind,[48] touching some great men's sons,
Persons of blood and honor—

   [*Enter* MOSCA *and* NANO *disguised, followed by*
          workmen.]

   Per.   Who be these, sir?
   Mos. Under that window, there 't must be. The
     same.
   S. Pol. Fellows, to mount a bank. Did your
     instructor
In the dear tongues[49] never discourse to you
Of the Italian mountebanks?
   Per.   Yes, sir.
   S. Pol.   Why,
Here shall you see one.
   Per.   They are quacksalvers,[50]
Fellows that live by venting[51] oils and drugs.
   S. Pol. Was that the character he gave you of them?
   Per. As I remember.
   S. Pol.   Pity his ignorance.   130
They are the only knowing men of Europe!
Great scholars, excellent physicians,
Most admired statesmen, professed favorites,
And cabinet counselors to the greatest princes;
The only languaged men of all the world!
   Per. And, I have heard, they are most lewd[52]
     impostors;
Made all of terms and shreds;[53] no less beliers
Of great men's favors, than their own vile med'cines;
Which they will utter[54] upon monstrous oaths;
Selling the drug for twopence, ere they part,   140
Which they have valued at twelve crowns before.

S. Pol. Sir, calumnies are answered best with silence.
Yourself shall judge.—Who is it mounts, my friends?
Mos. Scoto of Mantua,[55] sir.
S. Pol.   Is't he? Nay, then
I'll proudly promise, sir, you shall behold
Another man than has been phant'sied[56] to you.
I wonder yet, that he should mount his bank
Here in this nook, that has been wont t' appear
In face of the Piazza!—here he comes.   149

[*Enter* VOLPONE, *disguised as a mountebank doctor,
and followed by a crowd (i.e.* Grege) *of people.*]

Volp. [*To Nano.*] Mount, Zany.[57]
Grege. Follow, follow, follow, follow, follow!
S. Pol. See how the people follow him! he's a man
May write ten thousand crowns in bank here. Note,
Mark but his gesture:—I do use[58] to observe
The state[59] he keeps in getting up.
Per.   'Tis worth it, sir.
Volp. Most noble gentlemen, and my worthy pat-
rons! It may seem strange that I, your Scoto Man-
tuano, who was ever wont to fix my bank in face of the
public Piazza, near the shelter of the Portico to the
Procuratia,[60] should now, after eight months' ab-   160
sence from this illustrious city of Venice, humbly retire
myself into an obscure nook of the Piazza.
S. Pol. Did not I now object the same?[61]
Per.   Peace, sir.
Volp. Let me tell you: I am not, as your Lombard
proverb saith, cold on my feet;[62] or content to part with
my commodities at a cheaper rate than I accustomed;
look not for it. Nor that the calumnious reports of that
impudent detractor, and shame to our profession
(Alessandro Buttone,[63] I mean), who gave out, in
public, I was condemned *a'sforzato*[64] to the   170
galleys, for poisoning the Cardinal Bembo's—cook,[65]
hath at all attached,[66] much less dejected me. No, no,
worthy gentlemen; to tell you true, I cannot endure to
see the rabble of these ground *ciarlitani*[67] that spread
their cloaks on the pavement, as if they meant to do
feats of activity[68] and then come in lamely, with their
moldy tales out of Boccacio, like stale Tabarine[69] the
fabulist:[70] some of them discoursing their travels, and
of their tedious captivity in the Turk's galleys, when
indeed, were the truth known, they were the Chris-   180
tian's galleys, where very temperately they eat[71] bread,
and drunk water, as a wholesome penance enjoined
them by their confessors, for base pilferies.
S. Pol. Note but his bearing, and contempt of these.
Volp. These turdy-facy-nasty-paty-lousy-fartical
rogues, with one poor groat's-worth of unprepared
antimony, finely wrapped up in several *scartoccios*,[72]
are able, very well, to kill their twenty a week, and play;
yet these meager, starved spirits, who have half
stopped the organs of their minds with earthly   190
appilations,[73] want not their favorers among your
shriveled salad-eating artisans, who are overjoyed that
they may have their half-per'th[74] of physic; though it
purge 'hem into another world, it makes no matter.
S. Pol. Excellent! ha' you heard better language, sir?
Volp. Well, let 'hem go. And, gentlemen, honorable

gentlemen, know, that for this time, our bank, being
thus removed from the clamors of the *canaglia*,[75] shall
be the scene of pleasure and delight; for I have nothing
to sell, little or nothing to sell.   200
S. Pol. I told you, sir, his end.
Per.   You did so, sir.
Volp. I protest, I, and my six servants, are not able
to make of this precious liquor, so fast as it is fetched
away from my lodging by gentlemen of your city;
strangers of the *Terra-firma;*[76] worshipful merchants;
ay, and senators too, who, ever since my arrival, have
detained me to their uses, by their splendidous liberali-
ties. And worthily; for, what avails your rich man to
have his magazines[77] stuffed with *moscadelli*,[78] or of
the purest grape, when his physicians prescribe   210
him, on pain of death, to drink nothing but water
cocted[79] with aniseeds? O health, health! the blessing
of the rich! the riches of the poor! who can buy thee at
too dear a rate, since there is no enjoying this world
without thee? Be not so sparing of your purses, honorable gentlemen, as to abridge the natural course of
life—
Per. You see his end.
S. Pol.   Ay, is't not good?   218
Volp. For when a humid flux, or catarrh, by the
mutability of air, falls from your head into an arm or
shoulder, or any other part, take you a ducat, or your
cecchine of gold, and apply to the place affected: see
what good effect it can work. No, no, 'tis this blessed
unguento,[80] this rare extraction, that hath only power to
disperse all malignant humors, that proceed either of
hot, cold, moist, or windy causes—
Per. I would he had put in dry too.
S. Pol.   Pray you observe.
Volp. "To fortify the most indigest and crude[81]
stomach, ay, were it of one that, through extreme weakness, vomited blood, applying only a warm napkin   230
to the place, after the unction and fricace;[82]—for the

---

[55] *Scoto of Mantua:* Italian juggler who visited England.
[56] *phant'sied:* fancied, falsely described.
[57] *Zany:* Clown.   [58] *I . . . use:* It is my custom.
[59] *state:* ceremony.
[60] *Procuratia:* residence of the procurators (leading
officials) of San Marco.
[61] *object . . . same:* make the same point.
[62] *cold . . . feet:* i.e., poor.
[63] *Buttone:* apparently a fellow mountebank.
[64] *It.:* to forced labor.
[65] *cook:* The dash preceding suggests that the audience
is being prepared for a less prosaic word, like "mistress"
(the Cardinal being a notorious voluptuary).
[66] *attached:* arrested.
[67] ground *ciarlitani* (*It.*): common imposters.
[68] *feats . . . activity:* acrobatics, juggling tricks.
[69] *Tabarine:* Italian comedian prominent in Jonson's
lifetime.   [70] *fabulist:* teller of tall stories.   [71] *eat:* ate.
[72] *It.:* paper containers as used by apothecaries.
[73] *appilations:* obstructions.
[74] *half-per'th:* half pennyworth.
[75] *It.:* "canaille," rabble.
[76] *L.:* Venetian possessions on the mainland.
[77] *magazines:* storehouses.   [78] *It.:* muscatel wines.
[79] *cocted:* boiled.   [80] *It.:* ointment.
[81] *crude:* lacking power to digest.
[82] *fricace:* chafing.

vertigine[83] in the head, putting but a drop into your nostrils, likewise behind the ears; a most sovereign and approved remedy; the *mal caduco*,[84] cramps, convulsions, paralysies, epilepsies, *tremor cordis*,[85] retired nerves,[86] ill vapors of the spleen, stoppings of the liver, the stone, the strangury,[87] *hernia ventosa*,[88] *iliaca passio*;[89] stops a *dysenteria* immediately; easeth the torsion[90] of the small guts; and cures *melancholia hypondriaca*, being taken and applied, according to   240 my printed receipt.

[*Pointing to his bill and his glass.*]

For this is the physician, this the medicine; this counsels, this cures; this gives the direction, this works the effect; and in sum, both together may be termed an abstract of the theoric and practice in the Aesculapian[91] art. 'Twill cost you eight crowns. And,—Zan Fritada,[92] pray thee sing a verse extempore in honor of it.

S. Pol. How do you like him, sir?
Per.   Most strangely, I!
S. Pol. Is not his language rare?
Per.   But[93] alchemy,
I never heard the like; or Broughton's[94] books.   250

[NANO *sings.*]

SONG

Had old Hippocrates, or Galen,[95]
That to their books put med'cines all in,
But known this secret, they had never
(Of which they will be guilty ever)
Been murderers of so much paper,
Or wasted many a hurtless taper;
No Indian drug had e'er been famed,
Tobacco, sassafras[96] not named;
Ne[97] yet of guacum[98] one small stick, sir,
Nor Raymund Lully's[99] great elixir.   260

---

[83] *L.:* vertigo.   [84] *L.:* epilepsy.
[85] *L.:* palpitation of the heart.
[86] *retired nerves:* shrunken sinews.
[87] *strangury:* condition of painful urination.
[88] *L.:* gaseous tumor.   [89] *L.:* colic.
[90] *torsion:* cramps.   [91] *Aesculapian:* i.e., medical.
[92] *Zan Fritada:* a real zany of the time; here, the name given to Nano.   [93] *But:* Except for.
[94] *Broughton's:* Hugh Broughton, a contemporary and highly abstruse Puritan, whom Jonson lampoons in *The Alchemist.*
[95] *Hippocrates . . . Galen:* the most celebrated medical names of antiquity.
[96] *Tobacco, sassafras:* to which medicinal properties were attributed.   [97] *Ne:* Nor.
[98] *guacum:* drug obtained from the bark of a tree.
[99] *Raymond Lully:* fourteenth-century Majorcan mystic and "scientist," reputed to have discovered the elixir of life.
[100] *Danish Gonswart:* perhaps a certain Berthold Schwarz (= "swart"), identified as a Dane said to have invented guns.
[101] *Paracelsus:* sixteenth-century German physician who kept his wonderworking devil in the pommel of his sword.
[102] *signiory . . . Sanità:* directors of the Venetian hospital.
[103] *divers:* many.
[104] *experimented receipts:* tested remedies.
[105] *assayed:* attempted.   [106] *alembics:* retorts.
[107] *simples:* herbs.   [108] *It.:* smoke.
[109] *Balloo:* Ballon (Venetian ball game).
[110] *withal:* in addition.   [111] *gossip:* familiar friend.

Ne had been known the Danish Gonswart,[100]
Or Paracelsus,[101] *with his long sword.*

Per. All this, yet, will not do; eight crowns is high.
Volp. No more.—Gentlemen, if I had but time to discourse to you the miraculous effects of this my oil, surnamed *oglio del Scoto;* with the countless catalogue of those I have cured of the aforesaid, and many more diseases; the patents and privileges of all the princes and commonwealths of Christendom; or but the depositions of those that appeared on my part,   270 before the signiory of the Sanità[102] and most learned College of Physicians; where I was authorized, upon notice taken of the admirable virtues of my medicaments, and mine own excellency in matter of rare and unknown secrets, not only to disperse them publicly in this famous city, but in all the territories that happily joy under the government of the most pious and magnificent states of Italy. But may some other gallant fellow say, oh, there be divers[103] that make profession to have as good, and as experimented receipts[104] as   280 yours: indeed, very many have assayed,[105] like apes, in imitation of that, which is really and essentially in me, to make of this oil; bestowed great cost in furnaces, stills, alembics,[106] continual fires, and preparation of the ingredients (as indeed there goes to it six hundred several simples,[107] besides some quantity of human fat, for the conglutination, which we buy of the anatomists), but when these practitioners come to the last decoction, blow, blow, puff, puff, and all flies in *fumo.*[108] Ha, ha, ha! Poor wretches! I rather pity   290 their folly and indiscretion than their loss of time and money; for those may be recovered by industry, but to be a fool born is a disease incurable.

For myself, I always from my youth have endeavored to get the rarest secrets, and book them, either in exchange or for money. I spared nor cost nor labor where anything was worthy to be learned. And, gentlemen, honorable gentlemen, I will undertake, by virtue of chemical art, out of the honorable hat that covers your head, to extract the four elements; that is   300 to say, the fire, air, water, and earth, and return you your felt without burn or stain. For, whilst others have been at the Balloo,[109] I have been at my book; and am now past the craggy paths of study, and come to the flowery plains of honor and reputation.

S. Pol. I do assure you, sir, that is his aim.
Volp. But to our price—
Per.   And that withal,[110] Sir Pol.
Volp. You all know, honorable gentlemen, I never valued this *ampulla*, or vial, at less than eight crowns; but for this time, I am content to be deprived of   310 it for six; six crowns is the price, and less in courtesy I know you cannot offer me; take it or leave it, howsoever, both it and I am at your service. I ask you not as the value of the thing, for then I should demand of you a thousand crowns, so the Cardinals Montalto, Fernese, the great Duke of Tuscany, my gossip,[111] with divers other princes, have given me; but I despise money. Only to show my affection to you, honorable gentlemen, and your illustrious state here, I have neglected the

messages of these princes, mine own offices, 320
framed my journey hither, only to present you with the
fruits of my travels. Tune your voices once more to
the touch of your instruments, and give the honorable
assembly some delightful recreation."

Per. What monstrous and most painful circumstance
Is here, to get some three or four gazets,[112]
Some threepence i' the whole! for that 'twill come to.

[NANO *sings.*]

SONG

You that would last long, list to my song,
Make no more coil,[113] but buy of this oil.
Would you be ever fair and young?   330
Stout of teeth, and strong of tongue?
Tart of palate? Quick of ear?
Sharp of sight? Of nostril clear?
Moist of hand?[114] And light of foot?
Or, I will come nearer to't,
Would you live free from all diseases?
Do the act your mistress pleases,
Yet fright all aches[115] from your bones?
Here's a med'cine for the nones."[116]   339

Volp. Well, I am in a humor at this time to make a
present of the small quantity my coffer contains, to the
rich in courtesy, and to the poor for God's sake. Wherefore now mark: I asked you six crowns, and six crowns,
at other times, you have paid me; you shall not give me
six crowns, nor five, nor four, nor three, nor two, nor
one; nor half a ducat; no, nor a *moccinigo*.[117] Sixpence
it will cost you, or six hundred pound—expect no lower
price, for, by the banner of my front,[118] I will not bate
a *bagatine*,[119]—that I will have, only, a pledge of your
loves, to carry something from amongst you, to   350
show I am not contemned[120] by you. Therefore, now,
toss your handkerchiefs, cheerfully, cheerfully; and
be advertised that the first heroic spirit that deigns
to grace me with a handkerchief, I will give it a little
remembrance of something, beside, shall please it
better than if I had presented it with a double pistolet.[121]

Per. Will you be that heroic spark, Sir Pol?

CELIA, *at the window, throws down her handkerchief.*

Oh, see! the window has prevented[122] you.   359
Volp. Lady, I kiss your bounty; and for this timely
grace you have done your poor Scoto of Mantua, I will
return you, over and above my oil, a secret of that
high and inestimable nature, shall make you for ever
enamored on that minute, wherein your eye first descended on so mean, yet not altogether to be despised,
an object. Here is a powder concealed in this paper,
of which, if I should speak to the worth, nine thousand volumes were but as one page, that page as a line,
that line as a word; so short is this pilgrimage of man
(which some call life) to the expressing of it.   370
Would I reflect on the price? Why, the whole world
were but as an empire, that empire as a province, that
province as a bank, that bank as a private purse to the
purchase of it. I will only tell you it is the powder

that, made Venus a goddess (given her by Apollo),
that kept her perpetually young, cleared her wrinkles
firmed her gums, filled her skin, colored her hair; from
her derived[123] to Helen, and at the sack of Troy unfortunately lost—till now, in this our age, it was as
happily recovered, by a studious antiquary, out of   380
some ruins of Asia, who sent a moiety[124] of it to the
court of France (but much sophisticated[125]), wherewith the ladies there now color their hair. The rest,
at this present, remains with me, extracted to a
quintessence, so that, wherever it but touches, in youth
it perpetually preserves, in age restores the complexion,
seats your teeth, did they dance like virginal jacks,[126]
firm as a wall: makes them white as ivory, that were
black as—   390

[*Enter* CORVINO.]

Corv. Spite o' the devil, and my shame! come down
    here;
Come down—No house but mine to make your
    scene?[127]
Signior Flaminio,[128] will you down, sir? Down?
What, is my wife your Franciscina,[129] sir?
No windows on the whole Piazza, here,
To make your properties, but mine? But mine?

He beats away the mountebank, &c.

Heart! ere tomorrow I shall be new christened,
And called the *Pantalone di Besogniosi*,[130]
About the town.
Per.   What should this mean, Sir Pol?
S. Pol. Some trick of state, believe it. I will home.
Per. It may be some design on you.
S. Pol.   I know not.   400
I'll stand upon my guard.
Per.   It is your best, sir.
S. Pol. This three weeks, all my advices, all my
    letters,
They have been intercepted.
Per.   Indeed, sir!
Best have a care.
S. Pol.   Nay, so I will.
Per.   This knight,
I may not lose him, for my mirth, till night.

[*Exeunt.*]

---

[112] *gazets:* small Venetian coins.   [113] *coil:* fuss.
[114] *Moist . . . hand:* denoting fruitfulness.
[115] *aches:* pronounced "aitches."
[116] *nones:* nonce, occasion.   [117] *It.:* small Venetian coin.
[118] *the . . . front:* the flag that advertises his act.
[119] *It.:* another trivial coin.   [120] *contemned:* rejected.
[121] *pistolet:* Spanish gold coin.
[122] *prevented:* forestalled.   [123] *derived:* imparted.
[124] *moiety:* part.   [125] *sophisticated:* adulterated.
[126] *virginal jacks:* pieces of wood fitted with quills that
plucked the strings of the virginal. In fact, the reference is,
erroneously, to the keys.
[127] *scene:* the stage Volpone has erected.
[128] *Flaminio:* Italian actor; here used generically.
[129] *Franciscina:* the serving-maid or Columbine of the
Commedia dell' Arte.
[130] *Pantalone di Besogniosi:* the jealous old gull, another
stock character in the *Commedia.*

[*Enter* VOLPONE *and* MOSCA.]

Volp. Oh, I am wounded!
Mos.   Where, sir?
Volp.   Not without;
Those blows were nothing. I could bear them ever.
But angry Cupid, bolting[1] from her eyes,
Hath shot himself into me like a flame;
Where now he flings about his burning heat,
As in a furnace an ambitious[2] fire,
Whose vent is stopped. The fight is all within me.
I cannot live, except thou help me, Mosca;
My liver[3] melts, and I, without the hope
Of some soft air, from her refreshing breath,   10
Am but a heap of cinders.
Mos.   'Las, good sir,
Would you had never seen her!
Volp.   Nay, would thou
Hadst never told me of her!
Mos.   Sir, 'tis true;
I do confess I was unfortunate,
And you unhappy; but I'm bound in conscience,
No less than duty, to effect my best
To your release of torment, and I will, sir.
Volp. Dear Mosca, shall I hope?
Mos.   Sir, more than dear,
I will not bid you to despair of aught
Within a human compass.
Volp.   Oh, there spoke   20
My better angel. Mosca, take my keys,
Gold, plate, and jewels, all's at thy devotion.[4]
Employ them how thou wilt, nay, coin me too,
So thou in this but crown my longings, Mosca.
Mos. Use but your patience.
Volp.   So I have.
Mos.   I doubt not
To bring success to your desires.
Volp.   Nay, then,
I not repent me of my late disguise.
Mos. If you can horn him,[5] sir, you need not.
Volp.   True:
Besides, I never meant him for my heir.

---

[1] *bolting:* shooting.   [2] *ambitious:* swelling.
[3] *liver:* seat of violent passions, such as love.
[4] *devotion:* disposing.
[5] *horn him:* make him a cuckold.
[6] *epilogue:* the beating; or perhaps Mosca is speaking aside and meditating already his plot against Volpone.

[1] *dole . . . faces:* lot (range) of grimaces.
[2] *rings:* appropriate to jugglers.
[3] *toad-stone:* supposed jewel with fabulous properties found in the head of a toad.   [4] *cope-stitch:* embroidery.
[5] *tilt-feathers:* worn at a tournament or tilting.
[6] *starched:* contemporary fashion.
[7] *fricace . . . mother:* massage for hysteria.
[8] *cittern:* zither.
[9] *Lady Vanity:* Assume that stock role in the old morality plays, and join Volpone's troupe.
[10] *dealer:* suggestion of "prostitute."

Is not the color o' my beard and eyebrows   30
To make me known?
Mos.   No jot.
Volp.   I did it well.
Mos. So well, would I could follow you in mine,
With half the happiness! and yet I would
Escape your epilogue.[6]
Volp.   But were they gulled
With a belief that I was Scoto?
Mos.   Sir,
Scoto himself could hardly have distinguished!
I have not time to flatter you now, we'll part;
And as I prosper, so applaud my art.

                                        [*Exeunt.*]

[*Enter* CORVINO, *dragging in* CELIA.]

Corv. Death of mine honor, with the city's fool!
A juggling, tooth-drawing, prating mountebank!
And at a public window! Where, whilst he,
With his strained action, and his dole of faces,[1]
To his drug-lecture, draws your itching ears,
A crew of old, unmarried, noted lechers,
Stood leering up like satyrs, and you smile
Most graciously, and fan your favors forth,
To give your hot spectators satisfaction!
What, was your mountebank their call? Their
  whistle?   10
Or were you enamored on his copper rings,[2]
His saffron jewel, with the toad-stone[3] in't,
Or his embroidered suit, with the cope-stitch,[4]
Made of a hearse cloth? Or his old tilt-feather?[5]
Or his starched[6] beard! Well you shall have him, yes!
He shall come home, and minister unto you
The fricace for the mother.[7] Or, let me see,
I think you'd rather mount; would you not mount?
Why, if you'll mount, you may; yes, truly, you may!
And so you may be seen, down to the foot.   20
Get you a cittern,[8] Lady Vanity,[9]
And be a dealer[10] with the virtuous man.
Make one. I'll but protest myself a cuckold,
And save your dowry. I am a Dutchman, I!
For if you thought me an Italian,
You would be damned ere you did this, you whore!
Thou'dst tremble, to imagine, that the murder
Of father, mother, brother, all thy race,
Should follow, as the subject of my justice.   29
Cel. Good sir, have patience.
Corv.   What couldst thou propose
Less to thyself, than in this heat of wrath,
And stung with my dishonor, I should strike
This steel into thee, with as many stabs
As thou wert gazed upon with goatish eyes?
Cel. Alas, sir, be appeased! I could not think
My being at the window should more now
Move your impatience than at other times.
Corv. No! not to seek and entertain a parley
With a known knave, before a multitude!
You were an actor with your handkerchief,   40

Which he most sweetly kissed in the receipt,
And might, no doubt, return it with a letter,
And point the place where you might meet; your
    sister's,
Your mother's, or your aunt's might serve the turn.
    Cel. Why, dear sir, when do I make these excuses
Or ever stir abroad, but to the church?
And that so seldom—
    Corv.   Well, it shall be less;
And thy restraint before was liberty
To what I now decree. And therefore mark me.
First, I will have this bawdy light dammed up;   50
And till't be done, some two or three yards off,
I'll chalk a line, o'er which if thou but chance
To set thy desperate foot, more hell, more horror,
More wild remorseless rage shall seize on thee,
Than on a conjurer that had heedless left
His circle's safety ere his devil was laid.
Then here's a lock[11] which I will hang upon thee,
And, now I think on't, I will keep thee backwards;
Thy lodging shall be backwards; thy walks backwards;
Thy prospect, all be backwards; and no pleasure,   60
That thou shalt know but backwards. Nay, since you
    force
My honest nature, know, it is your own,
Being too open, makes me use you thus:
Since you will not contain your subtle nostrils
In a sweet room, but they must snuff the air
Of rank and sweaty passengers.[12]

                                    Knock within.

                    One knocks.
Away, and be not seen, pain of thy life;
Not look toward the window; if thou dost—
Nay, stay, hear this—let me not prosper, whore,
But I will make thee an anatomy,[13]   70
Dissect thee mine own self, and read a lecture
Upon thee to the city, and in public.
Away!—

                                    [*Exit* CELIA.]

            [*Enter* Servitore.]

        Who's there?
    Serv.   'Tis Signior Mosca, sir.
    Corv. Let him come in.

                                    [*Exit Servitore.*]
                    His master's dead; there's yet
Some good to help the bad.—

            [*Enter* MOSCA.]

                    My Mosca, welcome!
I guess your news.
    Mos.   I fear you cannot, sir.
    Corv. Is't not his death?
    Mos.   Rather the contrary.
    Corv. Not his recovery?
    Mos.   Yes, sir.
    Corv.   I am cursed,
I am bewitched, my crosses meet to vex me.   79
How? How? How? How?
    Mos.   Why, sir, with Scoto's oil.

Corbaccio and Voltore brought of it,
Whilst I was busy in an inner room—
    Corv. Death! that damned mountebank! But for the
    law
Now, I could kill the rascal; it cannot be
His oil should have that virtue.[14] Ha' not I
Known him a common rogue, come fiddling in
To the *osteria*,[15] with a tumbling[16] whore,
And, when he has done all his forced tricks, been glad
Of a poor spoonful of dead wine, with flies in't?
It cannot be. All his ingredients   90
Are a sheep's gall, a roasted bitch's marrow,
Some few sod[17] earwigs, pounded caterpillars,
A little capon's grease, and fasting spittle.[18]
I know 'hem to a dram.
    Mos.   I know not, sir.
But some on't, there, they poured into his ears,
Some in his nostrils, and recovered him;
Applying but the fricace.
    Corv.   Pox o' that fricace!
    Mos. And since, to seem the more officious[19]
And flatt'ring of his health, there, they have had,
At extreme fees, the college of physicians   100
Consulting on him, how they might restore him;
Where one would have a cataplasm[20] of spices,
Another a flayed ape clapped to his breast,
A third would ha' it a dog, a fourth an oil,
With wild cats' skins: at last, they all resolved
That to preserve him, was no other means
But some young woman must be straight sought out,
Lusty, and full of juice, to sleep by him;
And to this service most unhappily,
And most unwillingly, am I now employed,   110
Which here I thought to pre-acquaint you with,
For your advice, since it concerns you most;
Because I would not do that thing might cross
Your ends, on whom I have my sole dependence, sir.
Yet, if I do it not, they may delate[21]
My slackness to my patron, work me out
Of his opinion; and there all your hopes,
Ventures, or whatsoever, are all frustrate!
I do but tell you, sir. Besides, they are all   119
Now striving who shall first present him; therefore—
I could entreat you, briefly conclude somewhat;
Prevent 'hem if you can.
    Corv.   Death to my hopes,
This is my villainous fortunes! Best to hire
Some common courtesan.
    Mos.   Ay, I thought on that, sir;
But they are all so subtle, full of art—
And age again doting and flexible,[22]

---

[11] *lock:* chastity girdle.   [12] *passengers:* passers-by.
[13] *anatomy:* cadaver for a surgeon to demonstrate on.
[14] *virtue:* sovereign power.
[15] *osteria:* hostelry, inn.   [16] *tumbling:* acrobatic.
[17] *sod:* seethed, boiled.
[18] *fasting spittle:* saliva taken from one who has been
fasting.   [19] *officious:* dutiful.
[20] *cataplasm:* poultice.
[21] *delate:* relate, in the manner of an informer.
[22] *flexible:* easily manipulated.

So as—I cannot tell—we may, perchance,
Light on a quean²³ may cheat us all.
    Corv.   'Tis true.
    Mos. No, no: it must be one that has no tricks, sir,
Some simple thing, a creature made unto it;   130
Some wench you may command. Ha' you no
        kinswoman?
Godso—Think, think, think, think, think, think, think,
        sir.
One o' the doctors offered there his daughter.
    Corv. How!
    Mos.   Yes, Signior Lupo,²⁴ the physician.
    Corv. His daughter!
    Mos.   And a virgin, sir, Why, alas,
He knows the state of's body, what it is;
That naught can warm his blood, sir, but a fever;
Nor any incantation raise his spirit.
A long forgetfulness hath seized that part.
Besides, sir, who shall know it? Some one or two—
    Corv. I pray thee give me leave. If any man   141
But I had had this luck—The thing in't self,
I know, is nothing—Wherefore should not I
As well command my blood and my affections
As this dull doctor? In the point of honor,
The cases are all one of wife and daughter.
    Mos. [*Aside*] I hear him coming.²⁵
    Corv.   She shall do't: 'tis
        done.
Slight!²⁶ if this doctor, who is not engaged,
Unless 't be for his counsel, which is nothing,
Offer his daughter, what should I, that am   150
So deeply in? I will prevent²⁷ him: Wretch!
Covetous wretch!—Mosca, I have determined.
    Mos. How, sir?
    Corv.   We'll make all sure. The party you
        wot²⁸ of
Shall be mine own wife, Mosca.
    Mos.   Sir, the thing,
But that I would not seem to counsel you,
I should have motioned²⁹ to you, at the first.
And make your count, you have cut all their throats.
Why, 'tis directly taking a possession!
And in his next fit, we may let him go.
'Tis but to pull the pillow from his head,   160
And he is throttled. It had been done before
But for your scrupulous doubts.
    Corv.   Ay, a plague on't,
My conscience fools my wit! Well, I'll be brief,
And so be thou, lest they should be before us.
Go home, prepare him, tell him with what zeal
And willingness I do it. Swear it was

On the first hearing, as thou mayst do, truly,
Mine own free motion.
    Mos.   Sir, I warrant you,
I'll so possess him with it, that the rest
Of his starved clients shall be banished all,   170
And only you received. But come not, sir,
Until I send, for I have something else
To ripen for your good, you must not know't.
    Corv. But do not you forget to send now.
    Mos.   Fear not.
                                                    [*Exit.*]
    Corv. Where are you, wife? My Celia! wife!

                    [*Re-enter* CELIA.]

                                                —What,
        blubbering?
Come, dry those tears. I think thou thought'st me in
        earnest.
Ha! by this light I talked so but to try thee.
Methinks, the lightness of the occasion
Should ha' confirmed thee. Come, I am not jealous.
    Cel. No!
    Corv.   Faith I am not, I, nor never was;   180
It is a poor unprofitable humor.
Do not I know, if women have a will,
They'll do³⁰ 'gainst all the watches o' the world,
And that the fiercest spies are tamed with gold?
Tut, I am confident in thee, thou shalt see't;
And see I'll give thee cause too, to believe it.
Come kiss me. Go, and make thee ready straight,
In all thy best attire, thy choicest jewels,
Put 'hem all on, and, with 'hem, thy best looks.
We are invited to a solemn feast,   190
At old Volpone's, where it shall appear
How far I am free from jealousy or fear.
                                                [*Exeunt.*]

                    ACT THREE

                    SCENE ONE

                [*Enter* MOSCA.]

    Mos. I fear I shall begin to grow in love
With my dear self, and my most prosperous parts,
They do so spring and burgeon. I can feel
A whimsy¹ i' my blood: I know not how,
Success hath made me wanton. I could skip
Out of my skin now, like a subtle snake,
I am so limber. Oh! your parasite
Is a most precious thing, dropped from above,
Not bred 'mongst clods and clotpoles, here on earth.
I muse, the mystery² was not made a science,   10
It is so liberally³ professed! Almost
All the wise world is little else, in nature,
But parasites or sub-parasites. And yet
I mean not those that have your bare town-art,
To know who's fit to feed 'hem; have no house,
No family, no care, and therefore mold
Tales for men's ears, to bait that sense; or get
Kitchen-invention,⁴ and some stale receipts⁵

---

²³ *quean:* harlot.   ²⁴ *Lupo:* Wolf.   ²⁵ *coming:* yielding.
²⁶ *Slight!:* interjection—"God's light!"
²⁷ *prevent:* forestall.   ²⁸ *wot:* know.
²⁹ *motioned:* proposed.   ³⁰ *do:* commit adultery.
III.i.
    ¹ *whimsy:* whim.
    ² *mystery:* profession of parasite.   ³ *liberally:* widely.
    ⁴ *Kitchen-invention:* Skill in cookery.
    ⁵ *receipts:* recipes.

To please the belly, and the groin; nor those,
With their court dog-tricks, that can fawn and fleer,   20
Make their revenue[6] out of legs[7] and faces,
Echo my lord, and lick away a moth.
But your fine elegant rascal, that can rise
And stoop, almost together, like an arrow;
Shoot through the air as nimbly as a star;
Turn short as doth a swallow; and be here,
And there, and here, and yonder, all at once;
Present to any humor, all occasion;
And change a visor[8] swifter than a thought!
This is the creature had the art born with him;   30
Toils not to learn it, but doth practice it
Out of most excellent nature: and such sparks
Are the true parasites, others but their zanies.[9]

[*Enter* BONARIO.]

Who's this? Bonario, old Corbaccio's son?
The person I was bound to seek. Fair sir,
You are happily met.
    Bon.   That cannot be by thee.
    Mos. Why, sir?
    Bon.   Nay, pray thee know thy way, and
        leave me.
I would be loath to interchange discourse
With such a mate[10] as thou art.
    Mos.   Courteous sir,
Scorn not my poverty.
    Bon.   Not I, by heaven;   40
But thou shalt give me leave to hate thy baseness.
    Mos. Baseness!
    Bon.   Ay; answer me, is not thy sloth
Sufficient argument? Thy flattery?
Thy means of feeding?
    Mos.   Heaven be good to me!
These imputations are too common, sir,
And easily stuck on virtue when she's poor.
You are unequal[11] to me, and however
Your sentence may be righteous, yet you are not,
That, ere you know me, thus proceed in censure.
St. Mark bear witness 'gainst you, 'tis inhuman.   50

[*Weeps.*]

    Bon. [*Aside*] What! does he weep? The sign is soft
        and good:
I do repent me that I was so harsh.
    Mos. 'Tis true, that, swayed by strong necessity,
I am enforced to eat my careful[12] bread
With too much obsequy;[13] 'tis true, beside,
That I am fain to spin mine own poor raiment
Out of my mere observance,[14] being not born
To a free fortune. But that I have done
Base offices, in rending friends asunder,
Dividing families, betraying counsels,   60
Whispering false lies, or mining[15] men with praises,
Trained[16] their credulity with perjuries,
Corrupted chastity, or am in love
With mine own tender ease, but would not rather
Prove[17] the most rugged and laborious course,
That might redeem my present estimation,[18]
Let me here perish, in all hope of goodness.

    Bon. [*Aside*] This cannot be a personated[19] passion.
I was to blame so to mistake thy nature;
Pray thee forgive me and speak out thy business.   70
    Mos. Sir, it concerns you; and though I may seem
At first to make a main[20] offense in manners,
And in my gratitude unto my master;
Yet for the pure love which I bear[21] all right,
And hatred of the wrong, I must reveal it.
This very hour your father is in purpose
To disinherit you—
    Bon.   How!
    Mos.   And thrust you forth
As a mere stranger to his blood. 'Tis true, sir.
The work no way engageth me, but, as
I claim an interest in the general state   80
Of goodness and true virtue, which I hear
To abound in you; and for which mere respect,[22]
Without a second aim, sir, I have done it.
    Bon. This tale hath lost thee much of the late trust
Thou hadst with me; it is impossible.
I know not how to lend it any thought,
My father should be so unnatural.
    Mos. It is a confidence that well becomes
Your piety;[23] and formed, no doubt, it is
From your own simple innocence, which makes   90
Your wrong[24] more monstrous and abhorred. But, sir,
I now will tell you more. This very minute,
It is, or will be doing; and if you
Shall be but pleased to go with me, I'll bring you,
I dare not say where you shall see, but where
Your ear shall be a witness of the deed;
Hear yourself written bastard, and professed
The common issue of the earth.[25]
    Bon.   I'm mazed!
    Mos. Sir, if I do it not, draw your just sword,
And score your vengeance on my front and face;   100
Mark me your villain: you have too much wrong,
And I do suffer for you, sir. My heart
Weeps blood in anguish—
    Bon.   Lead; I follow thee.

[*Exeunt.*]

[III.ii]

[*Enter* VOLPONE.]

    Volp. Mosca stays long, methinks.—Bring forth
        your sports,
And help to make the wretched time more sweet.

[*Enter* NANO, ANDROGYNO, *and* CASTRONE.]

---

  6 *revenue:* accent on second syllable.   7 *legs:* bows.
  8 *visor:* expression.   9 *zanies:* imitators.
  10 *mate:* base fellow,   11 *unequal:* unjust.
  12 *careful:* earned in sorrow.
  13 *obsequy:* obsequiousness.   14 *observance:* service.
  15 *mining:* undermining.   16 *Trained:* Deceived.
  17 *Prove:* Attempt.   18 *estimation:* reputation.
  19 *personated:* put on.   20 *main:* great.
  21 *bear:* i.e., bear to.
  22 *for . . . respect:* on this consideration alone.
  23 *piety:* filial piety.   24 *wrong:* injury.
  25 *professed . . . earth:* proclaimed a nobody.

Nano. Dwarf, fool, and eunuch, well met here
    we be.
A question it were now, whether [1] of us three,
Being all the known delicates [2] of a rich man,
In pleasing him, claim the precedency can?
  Cast. I claim for myself.
  Andr.   And so doth the fool.
  Nano. 'Tis foolish indeed. Let me set you both to
    school.
First for your dwarf, he's little and witty,
And everything, as it is little, is pretty;   10
Else why do men say to a creature of my shape,
So soon as they see him, It's a pretty little ape?
And why a pretty ape, but for pleasing imitation
Of greater men's actions, in a ridiculous fashion?
Beside, this feat [3] body of mine doth not crave
Half the meat, drink, and cloth, one of your bulks will
    have.
Admit your fool's face be the mother of laughter,
Yet, for his brain, it must always come after;
And though that do feed him, it's a pitiful case,
His body is beholding to such a bad face.   20

                      One knocks.

Volp. Who's there? My couch; away! look! Nano,
  see
        [Exeunt ANDROGYNO *and* CASTRONE.]
Give me my caps first—go, inquire.
                    [Exit NANO.]
              Now, Cupid
Send [4] it be Mosca, and with fair return!
  Nano [*Within*] It is the beauteous madam—
  Volp.   Would-be—is it?
  Nano. The same.
  Volp.   Now torment on me! Squire her in;
For she will enter, or dwell here for ever.
Nay, quickly. I fear that my fit were past!
A second hell too, that my loathing this
Will quite expel my appetite to the other. [5]
Would she were taking now her tedious leave.   30
Lord, how it threats me what I am to suffer!

[*Re-enter* NANO *with* LADY POLITIC WOULD-BE.]

  L. Pol. I thank you, good sir. Pray you signify
Unto your patron I am here.—This band [6]
Shows not my neck enough.—I trouble you, sir;
Let me request you bid one of my women
Come hither to me. In good faith, I am dressed
Most favorably today! It is no matter:
'Tis well enough.

[*Enter* First Waiting-woman.]
           Look, see these petulant things,
How they have done this!
  Volp. [*Aside*]   I do feel the fever
Entering in at mine ears. Oh, for a charm,   40
To fright it hence!
  L. Pol.   Come nearer. Is this curl
In his [7] right place, or this? Why is this higher
Than all the rest? You ha' not washed [8] your eyes yet!
Or do they not stand even i' your head?
Where is your fellow? Call her.
                  [Exit Woman.]
  Nano.   Now, St. Mark
Deliver us! anon she'll beat her women,
Because her nose is red.

[*Re-enter* First *with* Second Woman.]

  L. Pol.   I pray you view
This tire, [9] forsooth: are all things apt, or no?
  1 Wom. One hair a little here sticks out, forsooth.
  L. Pol. Does't so, forsooth, and where was your
    dear [10] sight,   50
When it did so, forsooth! What now! bird-eyed? [11]
And you, too? Pray you, both approach and mend it.
Now, by that light I muse [12] you are not ashamed!
I, that have preached these things so oft unto you,
Read you the principles, argued all the grounds,
Disputed every fitness, every grace,
Called you to counsel of so frequent dressings.
  Nano. [*Aside*] More carefully than of your fame or
    honor.
  L. Pol. Made you acquainted what an ample dowry
The knowledge of these things would be unto you, 60
Able alone to get you noble husbands
At your return: and you thus to neglect it!
Besides, you seeing what a curious [13] nation
The Italians are, what will they say of me?
"The English lady cannot dress herself."
Here's a fine imputation to our country!
Well, go your ways, and stay i' the next room.
This fucus [14] was too coarse too; it's no matter.—
Good sir, you'll give 'hem entertainment? [15] 69
          [Exeunt NANO *and* Waiting-women.]
  Volp. The storm comes toward me.
  L. Pol.   How does my
    Volpone?
  Volp. Troubled with noise, I cannot sleep. I dreamt
That a strange fury entered now my house,
And, with the dreadful tempest of her breath,
Did cleave my roof asunder.
  L. Pol.   Believe me, and I
Had the most fearful dream, could I remember't—
  Volp. [*Aside*] Out on my fate! I ha' given her the
    occasion
How to torment me: she will tell me hers.
  L. Pol. Methought the golden mediocrity, [16]
Polite, and delicate—
  Volp.   Oh, if you do love me,
No more: I sweat and suffer at the mention   80
Of any dream; feel how I tremble yet.

III.ii.
[1] *whether:* which.
[2] *known delicates:* established delights.
[3] *feat:* delicate.   [4] *Send:* Grant.   [5] *other:* Celia.
[6] *band:* ruff.   [7] *his:* its.   [8] *washed:* i.e., opened.
[9] *tire:* headdress.   [10] *dear:* precious (sarcastically).
[11] *bird-eyed:* eagle-eyed (sarcastically).
[12] *muse:* wonder.   [13] *curious:* fastidious.
[14] *fucus:* cosmetic.
[15] *give . . . entertainment:* take care of them.
[16] *golden mediocrity:* golden mean (*auream mediocritam*).

L. Pol. Alas, good soul! the passion of the heart.[17]
Seed-pearl[18] were good now, boiled with syrup of
    apples,
Tincture of gold, and coral, citron-pills,
Your elicampane root, myrobalanes—
    Volp. [*Aside*] Ah, me, I have ta'en a grasshopper[19]
    by the wing!
    L. Pol. Burnt silk and amber. You have muscadel
Good i' the house—
    Volp.   You will not drink, and part?
    L. Pol. No, fear not that. I doubt we shall not get
Some English saffron, half a dram would serve;   90
Your sixteen cloves, a little musk, dried mints;
Bugloss, and barley-meal—
    Volp. [*Aside*]   She's in again!
Before I feigned disease, now I have one.
    L. Pol. And these applied with a right scarlet cloth.
    Volp. [*Aside*] Another flood of words! a very torrent!
    L. Pol. Shall I, sir, make you a poultice?
    Volp.   No, no, no.
I'm very well, you need prescribe no more.
    L. Pol. I have a little studied physic; but now
I'm all for music, save, i' the forenoons,
An hour or two for painting. I would have   100
A lady, indeed, to have all letters and arts,
Be able to discourse, to write, to paint,
But principal, as Plato holds, your music,
And so does wise Pythagoras. I take it,
Is your true rapture; when there is concent[20]
In face, in voice, and clothes: and is, indeed,
Our sex's chiefest ornament.
    Volp.   The poet
As old in time as Plato, and as knowing,
Says that your highest female grace is silence.
    L. Pol. Which o' your poets? Petrarch,[21] or Tasso,
    or Dante?   110
Guarini? Ariosto? Aretine?
Cieco di Hadria? I have read them all.
    Volp. [*Aside*] Is everything a cause to my
    destruction?
    L. Pol. I think I ha' two or three of 'hem about me.
    Volp. [*Aside*] The sun, the sea, will sooner both stand
    still
Than her eternal tongue! nothing can'scape it.
    L. Pol. Here's *Pastor Fido*[22]—
    Volp. [*Aside*]   Profess obstinate
    silence;
That's now my safest.[23]
    L. Pol.   All our English writers,
I mean such as are happy[24] in the Italian,
Will deign to steal out of this author, mainly;   120
Almost as much as from Montagnie:[25]
He has so modern and facile a vein,
Fitting the time, and catching the court-ear!
Your Petrarch is more passionate, yet he,
In days of sonnetting, trusted 'hem with much;[26]
Dante is hard, and few can understand him.
But for a desperate wit, there's Aretine;
Only his pictures[27] are a little obscene—
You mark me not.
    Volp.   Alas, my mind's perturbed.

    L. Pol. Why, in such cases, we must cure ourselves.
Make use of our philosophy—
    Volp.   Oy, me!   131
    L. Pol. And as we find our passions do rebel,
Encounter 'hem with treason, or divert 'hem,
By giving scope unto some other humor
Of lesser danger: as, in politic bodies,
There's nothing more doth overwhelm the judgment
And cloud the understanding, than too much
Settling and fixing, and, as 'twere, subsiding
Upon one object. For the incorporating
Of these same outward things, into that part,   140
Which we call mental, leaves some certain fæces
That stop the organs, and, as Plato says,
Assassinate our knowledge.
    Volp. [*Aside*]   Now, the spirit
Of patience help me!
    L. Pol.   Come, in faith, I must
Visit you more a days, and make you well:
Laugh and be lusty.
    Volp. [*Aside*]   My good angel save me!
    L. Pol. There was but one sole man in all the world
With whom I e'er could sympathize; and he
Would lie you, often, three, four hours together
To hear me speak; and be sometime so rapt,   150
As he would answer me quite from the purpose,
Like you, and you are like him, just. I'll discourse,
An't be but only, sir, to bring you asleep,
How we did spend our time and loves together,
For some six years.
    Volp.   Oh, oh, oh, oh, oh, oh!
    L. Pol. For we were *coætanei*,[28] and brought up—
    Volp. Some power, some fate, some fortune rescue
    me!

[*Enter* MOSCA.]

    Mos. God save you, madam!
    L. Pol.   Good sir.
    Volp.   Mosca! welcome,
Welcome to my redemption.
    Mos.   Why, sir?
    Volp.   Oh,
Rid me of this my torture, quickly, there.   160
My madam with the everlasting voice:
The bells[29] in time of pestilence ne'er made
Like noise, or were in that perpetual motion!

---

[17] *passion . . . heart:* heartburn.
[18] *Seed-pearl:* Here Lady Would-be begins a list of
popular remedies.
[19] *grasshopper:* alluding to the noise it makes.
[20] *concent:* harmony.
[21] *Petrarch:* Except for Cieco (literally, the blind one of
Adria, whose real name is Luigi Groto), these are all famous
Renaissance writers.
[22] *Pastor Fido: The Faithful Shepherd* by Guarini.
[23] *safest:* safest way.   [24] *happy:* fluent.
[25] *Montagnie:* Montaigne, the French essayist (pronounced as four syllables).
[26] *trusted . . . much:* i.e., English poets borrowed widely
from Petrarch's love sonnets.
[27] *pictures:* Aretino's lascivious sonnets were written to
illustrate obscene engravings.   [28] *coaetanei:* of equal age.
[29] *bells:* which tolled constantly in time of plague.

The cock-pit comes not near it. All my house,
But now, steamed like a bath with her thick breath,
A lawyer could not have been heard; nor scarce
Another woman, such a hail of words
She has let fall. For hell's sake, rid her hence.

   Mos. Has she presented?[30]
Volp.   Oh, I do not care!
I'll take her absence upon any price,   170
With any loss.
   Mos.   Madam—
   L. Pol.   I ha' brought your patron
A toy, a cap here, of mine own work.
   Mos.   'Tis well.
I had forgot to tell you I saw your knight,
Where you would little think it.—
   L. Pol.   Where?
   Mos.   Marry,
Where yet, if you make haste, you may apprehend him,
Rowing upon the water in a *gondole*,
With the most cunning courtesan of Venice.
   L. Pol. Is't true?
   Mos.   Pursue 'hem, and believe your eyes:
Leave me to make your gift.

                    [Exit LADY POLITIC.]
               I knew 'twould take:
For, lightly,[31] they that use themselves most license,
Are still most jealous.
   Volp.   Mosca, hearty thanks,   181
For thy quick fiction, and delivery of me.
Now to my hopes, what sayst thou?

      [Re-enter LADY POLITIC WOULD-BE.]

   L. Pol.   But do you hear, sir?—
   Volp. Again! I fear a paroxysm.
   L. Pol.   Which way
Rowed they together?
   Mos.   Toward the Rialto.[32]
   L. Pol. I pray you lend me your dwarf.
   Mos.   I pray you
take him.

                  [Exit LADY POLITIC.]
Your hopes, sir, are like happy blossoms, fair,
And promise timely fruit, if you will stay
But the maturing; keep you at your couch,
Corbaccio will arrive straight, with the will.   190
When he is gone, I'll tell you more.

                          [Exit.]

---

[30] *presented:* made you a present.   [31] *lightly:* often.
[32] *Rialto:* bridge over the Grand Canal.
[33] *wanton:* lively.   [34] *primero:* card game.   [35] *go:* bid.
[36] *encounter:* like "go" and "draw," a term from the card game. Volpone, punning, draws the curtains of the inner stage, and looks forward to his encounter with Celia.

III.iii.
[1] *concealed:* Bonario hides, perhaps behind a pillar supporting the "heavens" over the stage.
[2] *they:* the supposed panders who are rivals to Corvino.
[3] *presently:* at once.
[4] *hither:* Corvino and Celia presumably move away from center stage.
[5] *off:* Mosca presumably opens the curtains on the inner stage and confers with Volpone. Now Corvino and Celia come forward again.   [6] *move't:* suggest it.

   Volp.   My blood,
My spirits are returned; I am alive;
And, like your wanton[33] gamester at primero,[34]
Whose thought had whispered to him, not go[35] less,
Methinks I lie, and draw—for an encounter.[36]

       [III.iii]

      [Enter MOSCA *and* BONARIO.]

   Mos. Sir, here concealed[1] you may hear all. But,
   pray you,
Have patience, sir.

                       One knocks.

           The same's your father knocks.
I am compelled to leave you.

                         [Exit.]
   Bon.   Do so.—Yet.
Cannot my thought imagine this a truth.

  [Re-enter MOSCA *and* CORVINO, CELIA *following.]*

   Mos. Death on me! you are come too soon, what
   meant you?
Did not I say I would send?
   Corv.   Yes, but I feared
You might forget it, and then they[2] prevent us.
   Mos. [Aside] Prevent! Did e'er man haste so for his
   horns?
A courtier would not ply it so for a place.—
Well, now there's no helping it, stay here;   10
I'll presently[3] return.

                         [Exit.]
   Corv.   Where are you, Celia?
You know not wherefore I have brought you hither?
   Cel. Not well, except you told me.
   Corv.   Now I will:
Hark hither.[4]

         [Re-enter MOSCA.]

                    To Bonario.
   Mos.   Sir, your father hath sent word,
It will be half an hour ere he come;
And therefore, if you please to walk the while
Into that gallery—at the upper end,
There are some books to entertain the time.
And I'll take care no man shall come unto you, sir.
   Bon. Yes, I will stay there.— *[Aside]* I do doubt
   this fellow.   20

                         [Exit.]
   Mos. There; he is far enough; he can hear nothing:
And for his father, I can keep him off.[5]
   Corv. Nay, now, there is no starting back, and
   therefore,
Resolve upon it: I have so decreed.
It must be done. Nor would I move't[6] afore,
Because I would avoid all shifts and tricks,
That might deny me.
   Cel.   Sir, let me beseech you,
Affect not these strange trials; if you doubt
My chastity, why, lock me up for ever;

Make me the heir of darkness. Let me live   30
Where I may please your fears, if not your trust.
   Corv. Believe it, I have no such humor, I.
All that I speak I mean; yet I'm not mad;
Not horn-mad,[7] see you? Go to, show yourself
Obedient, and a wife.
   Cel.   O heaven!
   Corv.   I say it,
Do so.
   Cel. Was this the train?[8]
   Corv.   I've told you reasons;
What the physicians have set down; how much
It may concern me; what my engagements are;
My means, and the necessity of those means
For my recovery. Wherefore, if you be   40
Loyal, and mine, be won, respect my venture.
   Cel. Before your honor?
   Corv.   Honor! tut, a breath.
There's no such thing in nature; a mere term
Invented to awe fools. What is my gold
The worse for touching, clothes for being looked on?
Why, this 's no more. An old decrepit wretch,
That has no sense, no sinew; takes his meat
With other's fingers: only knows to gape
When you do scald his gums; a voice, a shadow;
And what can this man hurt you?
   Cel. [*Aside*]   Lord! what spirit   50
Is this hath entered him?
   Corv.   And for your fame,
That's such a jig;[9] as if I would go tell it,
Cry it on the Piazza! Who shall know it
But he that cannot speak it, and this fellow,
Whose lips are i' my pocket? Save yourself.
If you'll proclaim't, you may; I know no other
Should come to know it.
   Cel.   Are heaven and saints then
    nothing?
Will they be blind or stupid?
   Corv.   How!
   Cel.   Good sir,
Be jealous still, emulate them; and think
What hate they burn with toward every sin.   60
   Corv. I grant you: if I thought it were a sin
I would not urge you. Should I offer this
To some young Frenchman, or hot Tuscan blood
That had read Aretine, conned all his prints,
Knew every quirk[10] within lust's labyrinth,
And were professed critic[11] in lechery;
And I would look upon him, and applaud him,
This were a sin: but here, 'tis contrary,
A pious work, mere charity for physic,
And honest polity, to assure mine own.   70
   Cel. O heaven! canst thou suffer such a change?
   Volp. Thou art mine honor, Mosca, and my pride
My joy, my tickling, my delight! Go bring 'hem.
   Mos. Please you draw near, sir.
   Corv.   Come on, what—
You will not be rebellious? By that light—
   Mos.   Sir,
Signior Corvino, here, is come to see you.
   Volp.   Oh!

   Mos. And hearing of the consultation had,
So lately, for your health, is come to offer,
Or rather, sir, to prostitute—
   Corv.   Thanks, sweet Mosca.
   Mos. Freely, unasked, or unintreated—
   Corv.   Well.   80
   Mos. As the true fervent instance of his love,
His own most fair and proper wife; the beauty
Only of price[12] in Venice—
   Corv.   'Tis well urged.
   Mos. To be your comfortress, and to preserve you.
   Volp. Alas, I am past, already! pray you, thank him
For his good care and promptness; but for that,
'Tis a vain labor e'en to fight 'gainst heaven;
Applying fire to stone—[*Coughing*] uh, uh, uh, uh!
Making a dead leaf grow again. I take
His wishes gently, though; and you may tell him   90
What I have done for him. Marry, my state is hopeless.
Will him to pray for me, and to use his fortune
With reverence when he comes to 't.
   Mos.   Do you hear, sir?
Go to him with your wife.
   Corv.   Heart of my father!
Wilt thou persist thus? Come, I pray thee, come.
Thou seest 'tis nothing, Celia. By this hand
I shall grow violent. Come, do't, I say.
   Cel. Sir, kill me, rather. I will take down poison,
Eat burning coals, do anything—
   Corv.   Be damned!
Heart, I will drag thee hence home by the hair;   100
Cry thee a strumpet through the streets; rip up
Thy mouth unto thine ears; and slit thy nose,
Like a raw rochet![13]—Do not tempt me: come,
Yield, I am loath—Death! I will buy some slave
Whom I will kill, and bind thee to him alive!
And at my window hang you forth, devising
Some monstrous crime, which I, in capital letters,
Will eat into thy flesh with *aquafortis*,[14]
And burning corsives,[15] on this stubborn breast.
Now, by the blood thou hast incensed, I'll do it!   110
   Cel. Sir, what you please, you may, I am your
    martyr.
   Corv. Be not thus obstinate, I ha' not deserved it.
Think who it is intreats you. Pray thee, sweet—
Good faith, thou shalt have jewels, gowns, attires,
What thou wilt think, and ask. Do but go kiss him.
Or touch him but. For my sake. At my suit—
This once. No! not! I shall remember this.
Will you disgrace me thus? Do you thirst[16] my
    undoing?
   Mos. Nay, gentle lady, be advised.
   Corv.   No, no.   119
She has watched her time. God's precious, this is scurvy,
'Tis very scurvy; and you are—
   Mos.   Nay, good sir.

---

7 *horn-mad:* (1) like a beast, (2) cuckold.
8 *train:* stratagem.   9 *jig:* farce.
10 *quirk:* twist.   11 *critic:* expert.
12 *Only . . . price:* Most precious.
13 *rochet:* red-colored fish.   14 *aquafortis:* acid.
15 *corsives:* corrosives.   16 *thirst:* thirst after.

Corv. An arrant locust[17]—by heaven, a locust!—
Whore, crocodile, that hast thy tears prepared,
Expecting how thou'lt bid 'hem flow—
 Mos.   Nay, pray you,
 sir!
She will consider.
 Cel.   Would my life would serve
To satisfy—
 Corv. 'Sdeath! if she would but speak to him,
And save my reputation, 'twere somewhat;
But spitefully to affect my utter ruin!
 Mos. Ay, now you have put your fortune in her
 hands.
Why i'faith, it is her modesty, I must quit[18] her. 130
If you were absent, she would be more coming;[19]
I know it: and dare undertake for her.
What woman can before her husband? Pray you,
Let us depart, and leave her here.
 Corv.   Sweet Celia,
Thou mayst redeem all yet. I'll say no more:
If not, esteem yourself as lost. Nay, stay there.
          [*Exit with* MOSCA.]
 Cel. O God, and his good angels! whither, whither,
Is shame fled human breasts? That with such ease,
Men dare put off your honors, and their own?
Is that, which ever was a cause of life, 140
Now placed beneath the basest circumstance,
And modesty an exile made, for money?
 Volp. Ay, in Corvino, and such earth-fed minds,

    He leaps off from his couch.

That never tasted the true heaven of love.
Assure thee, Celia, he that would sell thee,
Only for hope of gain, and that uncertain,
He would have sold his part of paradise
For ready money, had he met a cope-man.[20]
Why art thou mazed to see me thus revived?
Rather applaud thy beauty's miracle; 150
Tis thy great work that hath, not now alone,
But sundry times raised me, in several shapes,
And, but this morning, like a mountebank,
To see thee at thy window, ay, before
I would have left my practice,[21] for thy love,
In varying figures,[22] I would have contended
With the blue Proteus,[23] or the hornèd flood.[24]
Now art thou welcome.

 Cel.   Sir!
 Volp.   Nay, fly me not.
Nor let thy false imagination
That I was bed-rid, make thee think I am so. 160
Thou shalt not find it. I am now as fresh,
As hot, as high, and in as jovial plight
As, when, in that so celebrated scene,
At recitation of our comedy,
For entertainment of the great Valois,[25]
I acted young Antinous[26] and attracted
The eyes and ears of all the ladies present,
To admire each graceful gesture, note, and
 footing.
           [*Sings.*]

SONG[27]

Come, my Celia, let us prove
While we can, the sports of love, 170
Time will not be ours for ever,
He, at length, our good will sever;
Spend not then his gifts in vain:
Suns that set may rise again;
But if once we lose this light,
'Tis with us perpetual night.
Why should we defer our joys?
Fame and rumor are but toys.[28]
Cannot we delude the eyes
Of a few poor household spies? 180
Or his easier ears beguile,
Thus removèd by our wile?
'Tis no sin love's fruits to steal;
But the sweet thefts to reveal:
To be taken, to be seen,
These have crimes accounted been.

 Cel. Some serene[29] blast me, or dire lightning strike
This my offending face.
 Volp.   Why droops my Celia?
Thou hast, in the place of a base husband, found
A worthy lover: use thy fortune well, 190
With secrecy and pleasure. See, behold,
What thou art queen of; not in expectation,
As I feed others: but possessed and crowned.
See, here, a rope of pearl; and each more orient[30]
Than that the brave Egyptian queen caroused.[31]
Dissolve and drink them. See, a carbuncle,
May put out both the eyes of our St. Mark;
A diamond would have bought Lollia Paulina,[32]
When she came in like star-light, hid with jewels,
That were the spoils of provinces. Take these 200
And wear, and lose 'hem; yet remains an earring
To purchase them again, and this whole state.
A gem but worth a private patrimony.
Is nothing; we will eat such at a meal.
The heads of parrots, tongues of nightingales,
The brains of peacocks, and of estriches,
Shall be our food, and, could we get the phoenix,[33]
Though nature lost her kind, she were our dish.
 Cel. Good sir, these things might move a mind
 affected
With such delights; but I, whose innocence 210

---

[17] *locust:* i.e., plague.   [18] *quit:* acquit.
[19] *coming:* forthcoming, forward. [20] *cope-man:* pedlar.
[21] *practice:* trick.   [22] *figures:* shapes.
[23] *blue Proteus:* sea-colored god who could transform
himself at will.
[24] *hornèd flood:* river god whose shapes included that of a
bull.
[25] *Valois:* King Henry III of France, entertained in
Venice in the later sixteenth century.
[26] *Antinous:* beautiful favorite of the Roman Emperor
Hadrian.   [27] *Song:* adapted from Catullus.
[28] *toys:* trifles.   [29] *serene:* noxious dew or mist.
[30] *orient:* lustrous, like the sun rising in the east.
[31] *queen caroused:* Cleopatra, who drank dissolved pearls.
[32] *Lollia Paulina:* extravagant wife of the Roman Emperor
Caligula. [33] *phoenix:* unique bird that lived forever.

Is all I can think wealthy, or worth th' enjoying,
And which, once lost, I have nought to lose beyond it,
Cannot be taken with these sensual baits.
If you have conscience—
　　Volp.　　　　　　　　'Tis the beggar's virtue;
If thou hast wisdom, hear me, Celia.
Thy baths shall be the juice of July-flowers,
Spirit of roses, and of violets,
The milk of unicorns, and panthers' breath
Gathered in bags, and mixed with Cretan wines.
Our drink shall be preparèd gold and amber;　　　220
Which we will take until my roof whirl round
With the vertigo: and my dwarf shall dance,
My eunuch sing, my fool make up the antic,[34]
Whilst we, in changèd shapes, act Ovid's tales,[35]
Thou, like Europa now, and I like Jove,[36]
Then I like Mars, and thou like Erycine.[37]
So of the rest, till we have quite run through,
And wearied all the fables of the gods.
Then will I have thee in more modern forms,
Attirèd like some sprightly dame of France,　　　230
Brave Tuscan lady, or proud Spanish beauty;
Sometimes unto the Persian sophy's[38] wife;
Or the grand signior's[39] mistress; and for change,
To one of our most artful courtesans,
Or some quick[40] Negro, or cold Russian;
And I will meet thee in as many shapes:
Where we may so transfuse our wandering souls
Out at our lips, and score up sums of pleasures,
　　　　　　　　　　　　　　　　　　　　[*Sings.*]
　　That the curious shall not know
　　How to tell[41] them as they flow;　　　240
　　And the envious, when they find
　　What their number is, be pined.

　Cel.　If you have ears that will be pierced—or eyes
That can be opened—a heart that may be touched—
Or any part that yet sounds man about you—
If you have touch of holy saints—or heaven—
Do me the grace to let me 'scape—if not,
Be bountiful and kill me. You do know,
I am a creature, hither ill betrayed,
By one whose shame I would forget it were.　　　250
If you will deign me neither of these graces,
Yet feed your wrath, sir, rather than your lust
(It is a vice comes nearer manliness),
And punish that unhappy crime of nature,
Which you miscall my beauty. Flay my face,
Or poison it with ointment for seducing
Your blood to this rebellion. Rub these hands
With what may cause an eating leprosy,
E'en to my bones and marrow: anything
That may disfavor[42] me, save in my honor—　　　260
And I will kneel to you, pray for you, pay down
A thousand hourly vows, sir, for your health;
Report, and think you virtuous—
　　Volp.　　　　　　　　　Think me cold,
Frozen, and impotent, and so report me?
That I had Nestor's hernia,[43] thou wouldst think.
I do degenerate, and abuse my nation,
To play with opportunity thus long;

I should have done the act, and then have parleyed.
Yield, or I'll force thee.
　Cel.　　　　　　　　Oh, just God!
　Volp.　　　　　　　　　　　In vain—
　Bon.　Forbear, foul ravisher! libidinous swine!　　　270

　　　He leaps out from where MOSCA *had placed him.*

Free the forcèd lady, or thou diest, impostor.
But that I am loath to snatch thy punishment
Out of the hand of justice, thou shouldst yet
Be made the timely sacrifice of vengeance,
Before this altar and this dross, thy idol.—
Lady, let's quit the place, it is the den
Of villainy; fear nought, you have a guard:
And he ere long shall meet his just reward.
　　　　　　　　　　　[*Exeunt* BONARIO *and* CELIA.]
　Volp.　Fall on me, roof, and bury me in ruin!
Become my grave, that wert my shelter! oh!　　　280
I am unmasked, unspirited,[44] undone,
Betrayed to beggary, to infamy—

　　　　　　　　　　[*Enter* MOSCA.]

　Mos.　Where shall I run, most wretched shame of
　　men,
To beat out my unlucky brains?
　Volp.　　　　　　　　　Here, here.
What! dost thou bleed?
　Mos.　　　　　　　Oh, that his well-driven sword
Had been so courteous to have cleft me down
Unto the navel, ere I lived to see
My life, my hopes, my spirits, my patron, all
Thus desperately engagèd[45] by my error!
　Volp.　Woe on thy fortune!
　Mos.　　　　　　　　And my follies, sir.　　　290
　Volp.　Thou hast made me miserable.
　Mos.　　　　　　　　　　And myself, sir,
Who would have thought he would have hearkened
　　so?
　Volp.　What shall we do?
　Mos.　　　　　　　I know not; if my heart
Could expiate the mischance, I'd pluck it out.
Will you be pleased to hang me, or cut my throat?
And I'll requite you,[46] sir. Let's die like Romans,[47]
Since we have lived like Grecians.[48]

　　　　　　　　　　　　They knock without.

　Volp.　　　　　　　　Hark! who's there?
I hear some footing; officers, the Saffi,[49]
Come to apprehend us! I do feel the brand
Hissing already at my forehead; now　　　300

---

[34] *antic:* dance.　　[35] *Ovid's tales: Metamorphoses.*
[36] *Jove:* who in the shape of a bull made love to Europa.
[37] *Erycine:* Venus.　　[38] *sophy's:* shah's.
[39] *grand signior's:* Turkish sultan's.　　[40] *quick:* lively.
[41] *tell:* count.　　[42] *disfavor:* disfigure.
[43] *Nestor's hernia:* impotence, appropriate to the aged
Greek counselor.　　[44] *unspirited:* dispirited.
[45] *engagèd:* entrapped.　　[46] *requite you:* do the same.
[47] *die . . . Romans:* commit suicide.
[48] *Grecians:* proverbially merry.
[49] *Saffi:* Venetian police.

Mine ears are boring.[50]

Mos.   To your couch, sir, you.
Make that place good, however.[51]

[VOLPONE *lies down as before.*]

Guilty men
Suspect what they deserve still.

[*Enter* CORBACCIO.]

Signior Corbaccio!

Corb. Why, how now, Mosca?
Mos.   Oh, undone, amazed, sir.
Your son, I know not by what accident,
Acquainted with your purpose to my patron,
Touching your will, and making him your heir,
Entered our house with violence, his sword drawn,
Sought for you, called you wretch, unnatural,
Vowed he would kill you.
Corb.   Me!
Mos.   Yes, and my patron. 310
Corb. This act shall disinherit him indeed.
Here is the will.
Mos.   'Tis well sir.
Corb.   Right and well.
Be you as careful[52] now for me.

[*Enter* VOLTORE *behind.*]

Mos.   My life, sir,
Is not more tendered.[53] I am only yours.
Corb. How does he? Will he die shortly, think'st
   thou?
Mos. I fear
He'll outlast May.
Corb.   Today?
Mos.   No, last out May, sir.
Corb. Couldst thou not give a dram?
Mos.   Oh, by no means,
   sir.
Corb. Nay, I'll not bid you.

[VOLTORE *comes forward.*]

Volt.   This is a knave, I see.
Mos. [*Aside*] How! Signior Voltore! did he hear
   me?
Volt. Parasite!
Mos. Who's that?—Oh, sir, most timely
   welcome—
Volt.   Scarce,   320
To the discovery of your tricks, I fear.
You are his, only? And mine also, are you not?
Mos. Who? I, sir!
Volt.   You sir. What device is this
About a will?

Mos.   A plot for you, sir.
Volt.   Come,
Put not your foists[54] upon me; I shall scent 'hem.
Mos. Did you not hear it?
Volt.   Yes, I hear Corbaccio
Hath made your patron there his heir.
Mos.   'Tis true,
By my device, drawn to it by my plot,
With hope—
Volt.   Your patron should reciprocate?
And you have promised?
Mos.   For your good I did, sir. 330
Nay more, I told his son, brought, hid him here,
Where he might hear his father pass the deed;
Being persuaded to it by this thought, sir,
That the unnaturalness, first, of the act,
And then his father's oft disclaiming[55] in him
(Which I did mean t' help on), would sure enrage him
To do some violence upon his parent,
On which the law should take sufficient hold,
And you be stated[56] in a double hope.
Truth be my comfort, and my conscience,   340
My only aim was to dig you a fortune
Out of these two old rotten sepulchers—
Volt. I cry thee mercy, Mosca.
Mos.   Worth your patience,
And your great merit, sir. And see the change!
Volt. Why, what success?[57]
Mos.   Most hapless! you must
   help, sir.
Whilst we expected the old raven, in comes
Corvino's wife, sent hither by her husband—
Volt. What, with a present?
Mos.   No, sir, on visitation
(I'll tell you how anon); and staying long,
The youth he grows impatient, rushes forth,   350
Seizeth the lady, wounds me, makes her swear
(Or he would murder her, that was his vow)
To affirm my patron to have done her rape:
Which how unlike it is, you see! And hence,
With that pretext he's gone, to accuse his father,
Defame my patron, defeat you—
Volt.   Where is her husband?
Let him be sent for straight.
Mos.   Sir, I'll go fetch him.
Volt. Bring him to the *Scrutineo.*[58]
Mos.   Sir, I will.
Volt. This must be stopped.
Mos.   Oh, you do nobly, sir.
Alas, 'twas labored all, sir, for your good;   360
Nor was there want of counsel in the plot.
But fortune can, at any time, o'erthrow
The project of a hundred learnèd clerks,[59] sir.
Corb. What's that?
Volt.   Wilt please you, sir, to go
   along?

[*Exit* VOLTORE *and* CORBACCIO.]

Mos. Patron, go in, and pray for our success.
Volp. Need makes devotion.[60] Heaven your labor
   bless!

[*Exeunt.*]

---

[50] *boring:* being pierced, in token of his crime.
[51] *however:* in any case.   [52] *careful:* provident.
[53] *tendered:* carefully provided for.
[54] *foists:* tricks.
[55] *disclaiming:* repudiating paternity.
[56] *stated:* placed.   [57] *success:* result.
[58] *Scrutineo:* Senate-house.   [59] *clerks:* scholars.
[60] *Need ... devotion:* Necessity makes us pious.

ACT FOUR

SCENE ONE

[*Enter* SIR POLITIC WOULD-BE *and*
PEREGRINE.]

S. Pol. I told you sir, it[1] was a plot. You see
What observation is! You mentioned[2] me
For some instructions. I will tell you, sir
(Since we are met here in this height of Venice),
Some few particulars I have set down,
Only for this meridian, fit to be known
Of your crude traveler; and they are these.
I will not touch, sir, at your phrase, or clothes,
For they are old.
    Per.   Sir, I have better.
    S. Pol.   Pardon,
I meant, as they are themes.[3]
    Per.   Oh, sir, proceed: 10
I'll slander you no more of wit, good sir.
    S. Pol. First, for your garb,[4] it must be grave and
    serious,
Very reserved and locked; not tell a secret
On any terms, not to your father: scarce
A fable, but with caution: make sure choice
Both of your company and discourse; beware
You never speak a truth—
    Per.   How!
    S. Pol.   Not to strangers,
For those be they you must converse with most;
Others I would not know,[5] sir, but at distance.
So as I still might be a saver in 'hem:[6]   20
You shall have tricks else passed upon you hourly.
And then, for your religion, profess none,
But wonder at the diversity of all;
And, for your part, protest, were there no other
But simply the laws o' the land, you could content you.
Nic. Machiavel and Monsieur Bodin,[7] both
Were of this mind. Then must you learn the use
And handling of your silver fork[8] at meals,
The metal[9] of your glass (these are main matters
With your Italian), and to know the hour   30
When you must eat your melons and your figs.
    Per. Is that a point of state too?
    S. Pol.   Here it is.
For your Venetian, if he see a man
Preposterous[10] in the least, he has him straight;
He has; he strips him. I'll acquaint you, sir,
I now have lived here 'tis some fourteen months.
Within the first week of my landing here,
All took me for a citizen of Venice,
I knew the forms so well—
    Per. [*Aside*]   And nothing else.
    S. Pol. I had read Contarene,[11] took me a house,   40
Dealt with my Jews to furnish it with movables.[12]
Well, if I could but find one man, one man
To mine own heart, whom I durst trust, I would—
    Per. What, what, sir?
    S. Pol.   Make him rich; make him a
    fortune.
He should not think again. I would command it.

    Per. As how?
    S. Pol.   With certain projects that I have,
Which I may not discover.[13]
    Per. [*Aside*]   If I had
But one to wager with, I would lay odds now,
He tells me instantly.
    S. Pol.   One is, and that
I care not greatly who knows, to serve the state   50
Of Venice with red herrings for three years,
And at a certain rate, from Rotterdam,
Where I have correspondence. There's a letter,
Sent me from one o' the States,[14] and to that purpose.
He cannot write his name, but that's his mark.
    Per. He is a chandler?[15]
    S. Pol.   No, a cheesemonger.
There are some others too with whom I treat
About the same negotiation,
And I will undertake it: for 'tis thus.
I'll do't with ease, I have cast[16] it all. Your hoy[17]   60
Carries but three men in her, and a boy;
And she shall make me three returns a year:
So if there come but one of three, I save;
If two, I can defalk.[18] But this is now,
If my main project fail.
    Per.   Then you have others?
    S. Pol. I should be loath to draw the subtle air
Of such a place, without my thousand aims.
I'll not dissemble, sir; where'er I come,
I love to be considerative;[19] and 'tis true,
I have at my free hours thought upon   70
Some certain goods unto the state of Venice,
Which I do call my cautions;[20] and, sir, which
I mean, in hope of pension, to propound
To the Great Council, then unto the Forty,
So to the Ten. My means are made already—
    Per. By whom?
    S. Pol.   Sir, one that though his place be
    obscure,
Yet he can sway, and they will hear him. He's
A *commandadore.*
    Per.   What! a common sergeant?

IV.i.

    [1] *it:* presumably the driving out of Volpone by Corvino.
    [2] *mentioned:* applied to.
    [3] *themes:* It is not Peregrine's language or clothing that is old, but the subject—"we have already discussed it."
    [4] *garb:* demeanor.   [5] *know:* great.
    [6] *as . . . them:* that I might keep up acquaintance with them.
    [7] *Machiavel . . . Bodin:* Machiavelli is cited because of his reputation for godlessness and hypocrisy; Jean Bodin, the sixteenth-century French political writer, for his purely expedient advocacy of religious toleration.
    [8] *fork:* not much used in the early seventeenth century.
    [9] *metal:* material.   [10] *Preposterous:* Unconventional.
    [11] *Contarene:* Cardinal Gasparo Contarini, late sixteenth-century political writer.
    [12] *movables:* furniture.   [13] *discover:* reveal.
    [14] *one . . . States:* someone in the States-General of Holland.
    [15] *chandler:* candle maker (evidently the letter is greasy).
    [16] *cast:* calculated.   [17] *hoy:* small boat.
    [18] *defalk:* defalcate, reduce the expense.
    [19] *considerative:* thoughtful.   [20] *cautions:* precautions.

S. Pol. Sir, such as they are, put it in their mouths,
What they should say, sometimes; as well as greater.
I think I have my notes to show you—
    Per.   Good sir.   81
S. Pol. But you shall swear unto me, on your gentry,
Not to anticipate—
    Per.   I, sir!
    S. Pol.   Nor reveal
A circumstance—My paper is not with me.
    Per. Oh, but you remember, sir.
    S. Pol.   My first is
Concerning tinder-boxes. You must know,
No family is here without its box.
Now, sir, it being so portable a thing,
Put case,[21] that you or I were ill affected
Unto the state, sir; with it in our pockets,   90
Might not I go into the Arsenal,
Or you come out again, and none the wiser?
    Per. Except yourself, sir.
    S. Pol.   Go to, then. I therefore
Advertise to the state, how fit it were
That none but such as were known patriots,
Sound lovers of their country, should be suffered
To enjoy them in their houses; and even those
Sealed at some office, and at such a bigness
As might not lurk in pockets.
    Per.   Admirable!
    S. Pol. My next is, how to inquire, and be resolved,
By present demonstration, whether a ship,   101
Newly arrived from Soria,[22] or from
Any suspected part of all the Levant,
Be guilty of the plague: and where they use
To lie out forty, fifty days, sometimes,
About the Lazaretto,[23] for their trial;
I'll save that charge and loss unto the merchant,
And in an hour clear the doubt.
    Per.   Indeed, sir!
    S. Pol. Or—I will lose my labor.
    Per.   My faith, that's much.
    S. Pol. Nay, sir, conceive me. 'T will cost me in
        onions,[24]   110
Some thirty livres—
    Per.   Which is one pound sterling.
    S. Pol. Beside my waterworks: for this I do, sir.
First, I bring in your ship 'twixt two brick walls;
But those the state shall venture. On the one
I strain[25] me a fair tarpaulin, and in that
I stick my onions, cut in halves; the other
Is full of loopholes, out of which I thrust
The noses of my bellows; and those bellows

I keep, with waterworks, in perpetual motion,
Which is the easiest matter of a hundred.   120
Now, sir, your onion, which doth naturally
Attract the infection, and your bellows blowing
The air upon him,[26] will show instantly,
By his changed color, if there be contagion;
Or else remain as fair as at the first.
Now 'tis known, 'tis nothing.
    Per.   You are right, sir.
    S. Pol. I would I had my note.
    Per.   Faith, so would I.
But you ha' done well for once, sir.
    S. Pol.   Were I false,
Or would be made so, I could show you reasons
How I could sell this state now to the Turk,   130
Spite of their galleys, or their—
    Per.   Pray you, Sir Pol.
    S. Pol. I have 'hem not about me.
    Per.   That I feared.
They are there, sir.
    S. Pol.   No, this is my diary,
Wherein I note my actions of the day.
    Per. Pray you let's see, sir. What is here?
        "*Notandum,*
A rat had gnawn my spur-leathers: notwithstanding,
I put on new, and did go forth; but first
I threw three beans over the threshold. Item,
I went and bought two toothpicks, whereof one
I burst immediately, in a discourse   140
With a Dutch merchant, 'bout *ragion' del stato*.[27]
From him I went and paid a *moccinigo*
For piecing[28] my silk stockings; by the way
I cheapened sprats;[29] and at St. Mark's I urined."
Faith, these are politic notes!
    S. Pol.   Sir, I do slip[30]
No action of my life, thus I quote[31] it.
    Per. Believe me, it is wise!
    S. Pol.   Nay, sir, read forth.

[*Enter* LADY POLITIC WOULD-BE, NANO, *and
        two* Waiting-women.]

    L. Pol. Where should this loose knight be, trow?
        Sure he's housed.
    Nano. Why, then, he's fast.[32]
    L. Pol.   Ay, he plays both[33]
        with me.   150
I pray you stay. This heat will do more harm
To my complexion than his heart is worth.
(I do not care to hinder, but to take him.)
How it[34] comes off!
    1 Wom.   My master's yonder.
    L. Pol.   Where?
    2 Wom. With a young gentleman.
    L. Pol.   That same's the party,
In man's apparel! Pray you, sir, jog my knight.[35]
I will be tender to his reputation,
However he demerit.[36]
    S. Pol.   My lady!
    Per.   Where?
    S. Pol. 'Tis she indeed, sir; you shall know her.
        She is,   160

---

[21] *Put case:* Suppose.   [22] *Soria:* Syria.
[23] *Lazaretto:* pest-house, where victims of the plague
were quarantined.
[24] *onions:* supposedly a remedy for the plague.
[25] *strain:* stretch.   [26] *him:* it.
[27] *It.:* affairs of state.   [28] *piecing:* mending.
[29] *cheapened sprats:* bargained for fish.   [30] *slip:* omit.
[31] *quote:* record.   [32] *fast:* secure.
[33] *both:* i.e., fast and loose.   [34] *it:* i.e., her cosmetics.
[35] *jog . . . knight:* get his attention.
[36] *demerit:* is at fault.

Were she not mine, a lady of that merit,
For fashion and behavior; and for beauty
I durst compare—
    Per.   It seems you are not jealous,
That dare commend her.
    S. Pol.   Nay, and for discourse—
    Per. Being your wife, she cannot miss that.
    S. Pol.   Madam,
Here is a gentleman, pray you, use him fairly;
He seems a youth, but he is—
    L. Pol.   None.
    S. Pol.   Yes, one
Has put his face as soon into the world—
    L. Pol. You mean, as early? But today?
    S. Pol.   How's this?
    L. Pol. Why, in this habit, sir; you apprehend me.
Well, Master Would-be, this doth not become you;
I had thought the odor, sir, of your good name   172
Had been more precious to you; that you would not
Have done this dire massàcre on your honor;
One of your gravity, and rank besides!
But knights, I see, care little for the oath
They make to ladies; chiefly their own ladies.
    S. Pol. Now, by my spurs, the symbol of my
        knighthood—
    Per. [*Aside*] Lord, how his brain is humbled for
        an oath!
    S. Pol. I reach [37] you not.
    L. Pol.   Right, sir, your polity   180
May bear it through thus. [*To* PEREGRINE] Sir, a
    word with you.
I would be loath to contest publicly
With any gentlewoman, or to seem
Froward, or violent, as the courtier [38] says;
It comes too near rusticity in a lady,
Which I would shun by all means: and however
I may deserve from Master Would-be, yet
T' have one fair gentlewoman thus be made
The unkind instrument to wrong another,
And one she knows not, ay, and to perséver: 190
In my poor judgment, it not warranted [39]
From being a solecism [40] in our sex,
If not in manners.
    Per.   How is this!
    S. Pol.   Sweet madam,
Come nearer to your aim.
    L. Pol.   Marry, and will, sir.
Since you provoke me with your impudence,
And laughter of your light land-siren here,
Your Sporus, [41] your hermaphrodite—
    Per.   What's here?
Poetic fury and historic storms!
    S. Pol. The gentleman, believe it, is of worth
And of our nation.
    L. Pol.   Ay, your Whitefriars nation. [42]   200
Come, I blush for you, Master Would-be, I;
And am ashamed you should ha' no more forehead, [43]
Than thus to be the patron, or St. George,
To a lewd harlot, a base fricatrice, [44]
A female devil, in a male outside.
    S. Pol.   Nay,

And [45] you be such a one, I must bid adieu
To your delights. The case appears too liquid. [46]
                       [*Exit.*]
    L. Pol. Ay, you may carry't clear, with your
        state-face! [47]
But for your carnival concupiscence, [48]
Who here is fled for liberty of conscience,   210
From furious persecution of the marshal,
Her will I disc'ple. [49]
    Per.   This is fine, i' faith!
And do you use this often? Is this part
Of your wit's exercise, 'gainst you have occasion?
Madam—
    L. Pol. Go to, sir,
    Per.   Do you hear me, lady?
Why, if your knight have set you to beg shirts,
Or to invite me home, you might have done it
A nearer way by far.
    L. Pol.   This cannot work you
Out of my snare.
    Per.   Why, am I in it, then?
Indeed your husband told me you were fair,   220
And so you are; only your nose inclines,
That side that's next the sun, to the queen-apple. [50]
    L. Pol. This cannot be endured by any patience.

[*Enter* MOSCA.]

    Mos. What's the matter, madam?
    L. Pol.   If the senate
Right not my quest in this, I will protest 'hem
To all the world no aristocracy.
    Mos. What is the injury, lady?
    L. Pol.   Why, the callet [51]
You told me of, here I have ta'en disguised.
    Mos. Who? This! What means your ladyship?
        The creature
I mentioned to you is apprehended now,   230
Before the senate; you shall see her—
    L. Pol.   Where?
    Mos. I'll bring you to her. This young gentleman,
I saw him land this morning at the port.
    L. Pol. Is't possible! How has my judgment
        wandered?
Sir, I must, blushing, say to you, I have erred;
And plead your pardon.
    Per.   What, more changes yet!
    L. Pol. I hope you ha' not the malice to remember

---

[37] *reach:* understand.
[38] *courtier:* perhaps Castiglione's celebrated treatise on
manners.   [39] *warranted:* immune.
[40] *solecism:* impropriety.
[41] *Sporus:* eunuch whom the Emperor Nero dressed as a
woman and married.
[42] *Whitefriars nation:* unsavory London district where
criminals enjoyed the immunity once accorded to the church
of the Carmelites or Whitefriars.   [43] *forehead:* shame.
[44] *fricatrice:* prostitute.   [45] *And:* If.
[46] *liquid:* clear.   [47] *state-face:* as of a grave counselor.
[48] *carnival concupiscence:* wench for whom you lust.
[49] *disc'ple:* discipline.
[50] *your . . . queen-apple:* you have a red nose, like a cider
apple.   [51] *callet:* whore.

A gentlewoman's passion. If you stay
In Venice here, please you to use me, sir—
   Mos. Will you go, madam?
   L. Pol.   Pray you, sir, use me; in faith,
The more you see me the more I shall conceive   241
You have forgot our quarrel.
       [*Exeunt* LADY WOULD-BE, MOSCA, NANO, *and*
                          Waiting-women.]
   Per.   This is rare!
Sir Politic Would-be? No, Sir Politic Bawd,[52]
To bring me thus acquainted with his wife!
Well, wise Sir Pol, since you have practiced thus
Upon my freshman-ship, I'll try your salt-head,[53]
What proof it is against a counter-plot.
                            [*Exit.*]

[IV.ii]

   [*Enter* VOLTORE, CORBACCIO, CORVINO, *and*
               MOSCA.]

   Volt. Well, now you know the carriage of the
     business,
Your constancy is all that is required
Unto the safety of it.
   Mos.   Is the lie
Safely conveyed amongst us? Is that sure?
Knows every man his burden?
   Corv.   Yes.
   Mos.   Then shrink not.
   Corv. But knows the advocate the truth?
   Mos.   Oh, sir,
By no means. I devised a formal tale,
That salved your reputation. But be valiant, sir.
   Corv. I fear no one but him that this his pleading
Should make him stand for a co-heir—
   Mos.   Co-halter!   10
Hang him; we will but use his tongue, his noise,
As we do croaker's[1] here.
   Corv.   Ay, what shall he do?
   Mos. When we ha' done, you mean?
   Corv.   Yes.
   Mos.   Why, we'll
     think:
Sell him for mummia.[2] He's half dust already.
                      To VOLTORE.
Do you not smile, to see this buffalo,[3]
How he doth sport it with his head? I should,
If all were well and past.—Sir, only you
                    To CORBACCIO.
Are he that shall enjoy the crop of all,
And these not know for whom they toil.

   Corb.   Ay, peace.
   Mos. But you shall eat it. [*Aside*] Much!—
   Worshipful sir,   20
       To CORVINO, *then to* VOLTORE *again.*
Mercury[4] sit upon your thundering tongue,
Or the French Hercules,[5] and make your language
As conquering as his club, to beat along,
As with a tempest, flat, our adversaries;
But much more yours, sir.
   Volt.   Here they come, ha' done.
   Mos. I have another witness, if you need, sir,
I can produce.
   Volt.   Who is it?
   Mos.   Sir, I have her.

   [*Enter* Avocatori, *and take their seats,* BONARIO,
     CELIA, Notario, Commandadori, Saffi, etc.]

   1 Avoc. The like of this the senate never heard of.
   2 Avoc. 'Twill come most strange to them when
     we report it.
   4 Avoc. The gentlewoman has been ever held   30
Of unreprovèd name.
   3 Avoc.   So the young man.
   4 Avoc. The more unnatural part that of his father.
   2 Avoc. More of the husband.
   1 Avoc.   I not know to give
His act a name, it is so monstrous![6]
   4 Avoc. But the impostor, he's a thing created
To exceed example!
   1 Avoc.   And all after-times!
   2 Avoc. I never heard a true voluptuary
Described but him.
   3 Avoc.   Appear yet those were cited?
   Not. All but the old magnifico, Volpone.   39
   1 Avoc. Why is not he here?
   Mos.   Please your fatherhoods,
Here is his advocate: himself's so weak,
So feeble—
   4 Avoc. What are you?
   Bon.   His parasite,
His knave, his pander. I beseech the court
He may be forced to come, that your grave eyes
May bear strong witness of his strange impostures.
   Volt. Upon my faith and credit with your virtues,
He is not able to endure the air.
   2 Avoc. Bring him, however.
   3 Avoc.   We will see him.
   4 Avoc.   Fetch him.
                   [*Exeunt* Officers.]
   Volt. Your fatherhoods' fit pleasures be obeyed;
But sure, the sight will rather move your pities   50
Than indignation. May it please the court,
In the meantime, he may be heard in me.
I know this place most void of prejudice,
And therefore crave it, since we have no reason
To fear our truth should hurt our cause.
   3 Avoc.   Speak free.
   Volt. Then know, most honored fathers, I must now
Discover to your strangely abusèd ears,
The most prodigious and most frontless[7] piece
Of solid impudence, and treachery,

That ever vicious nature yet brought forth   60
To shame the state of Venice. This lewd woman,
That wants no artificial looks or tears
To help the visor[8] she has now put on,
Hath long been known a close[9] adulteress
To that lascivious youth there; not suspected,
I say, but known, and taken in the act
With him; and by this man, the easy husband,
Pardoned; whose timeless[10] bounty makes him now
Stand here, the most unhappy, innocent person,
That ever man's own goodness made accused.   70
For these not knowing how to owe[11] a gift
Of that dear grace, but with their shame; being placed
So above all powers of their gratitude,
Began to hate the benefit; and in place
Of thanks, devise t' extirpe[12] the memory
Of such an act: wherein I pray your fatherhoods
To observe the malice, yea, the rage of creatures.
Discovered in their evils: and what heart
Such take, even from their crimes—but that anon
Will more appear.—This gentleman, the father,   80
Hearing of this foul fact, with many others,
Which daily struck at his too tender ears,
And grieved in nothing more than that he could not
Preserve himself a parent (his son's ills
Growing to that strange flood), at last decreed
To disinherit him.
    1 Avoc.   These be strange turns!
    2 Avoc. The young man's fame was ever fair and
        honest.
    Volt. So much more full of danger is his vice,
That can beguile so under shade of virtue.
But, as I said, my honored sires, his father   90
Having this settled purpose, by what means
To him betrayed, we know not, and this day
Appointed for the deed; that parricide,
I cannot style him better, by confederacy
Preparing this his paramour to be there,
Entered Volpone's house (who was the man,
Your fatherhoods must understand, designed
For the inheritance), there sought his father—
But with what purpose sought he him, my lords?
I tremble to pronounce it, that a son   100
Unto a father, and to such a father,
Should have so foul, felonious intent!
It was to murder him: when being prevented
By his more happy absence, what then did he?
Not check his wicked thoughts; no, now new deeds
(Mischief doth ever end where it begins)—
An act of horror, fathers! he dragged forth
The agèd gentleman that had there lain bed-rid
Three years and more, out of his innocent couch,
Naked upon the floor, there left him; wounded   110
His servant in the face; and with this strumpet,
The stale[13] to his forged practice, who was glad
To be so active—(I shall here desire
Your fatherhoods to note but my collections,[14]
As most remarkable—) thought at once to stop
His father's ends, discredit his free choice
In the old gentleman, redeem themselves,
By laying infamy upon this man,

To whom, with blushing, they should owe their lives.
    1 Avoc. What proofs have you of this?
    Bon.   Most honored
        fathers,   120
I humbly crave there be no credit given
To this man's mercenary tongue.
    2 Avoc.   Forbear.
    Bon. His soul moves in his fee.
    3 Avoc.   Oh, sir.
    Bon.   This fellow,
For six sols[15] more would plead against his Maker.
    1 Avoc. You do forget yourself.
    Volt.   Nay, nay, grave fathers,
Let him have scope. Can any man imagine
That he will spare his accuser, that would not
Have spared his parent?
    1 Avoc.   Well, produce your proofs.
    Cel. I would I could forget I were a creature.   129
    Volt. Signior Corbaccio!
    4 Avoc.   What is he?
    Volt.   The father.
    2 Avoc. Has he had an oath?
    Not.   Yes.
    Corb.   What must I do now?
    Not. Your testimony's craved.
    Corb.   Speak to the knave?
I'll ha' my mouth first stopped with earth; my heart
Abhors his knowledge. I disclaim in him.
    1 Avoc. But for what cause?
    Corb.   The mere portent[16] of
        nature!
He is an utter stranger to my loins.
    Bon. Have they made[17] you to this?
    Corb.   I will not hear thee,
Monster of men, swine, goat, wolf, parricide!
Speak not, thou viper.
    Bon.   Sir, I will sit down,
And rather wish my innocence should suffer   140
Than I resist the authority of a father.
    Volt. Signior Corvino!
    2 Avoc.   This is strange.
    1 Avoc.   Who's this?
    Not. The husband.
    4 Avoc.   Is he sworn?
    Not.   He is.
    3 Avoc.   Speak then.
    Corv. This woman, please your fatherhoods, is a
        whore,
Of most hot exercise, more than a partrich,[18]
Upon record—
    1 Avoc.   No more.
    Corv.   Neighs like a jennet.[19]
    Not. Preserve the honor of the court.
    Corv.   I shall,

---

[8] *visor:* mask.   [9] *close:* secret.   [10] *timeless:* ill-timed.
[11] *owe:* acknowledge.   [12] *extirpe:* extirpate.
[13] *stale:* decoy.   [14] *collections:* deductions.
[15] *sols:* halfpennies.   [16] *portent:* prodigy, monster.
[17] *made:* worked, manipulated.
[18] *partrich:* partridge, proverbially libidinous.
[19] *jennet:* horse.

And modesty of your most reverend ears.
And yet I hope that I may say these eyes
Have seen her glued unto that piece of cedar,   150
That fine well timbered gallant: and that here [20]
The letters may be read, thorough the horn, [21]
That makes the story perfect. [22]

Mos.   Excellent! Sir.

Corv. [*Aside to* MOSCA] There is no shame in this
 now, is there?

Mos.   None.

Corv. Or if I said, I hope that she were onward
To her damnation, if there be a hell
Greater than whore and woman; a good Catholic
May make the doubt.

3 Avoc.   His grief hath made him frantic.

1 Avoc. Remove him hence.

2 Avoc.   Look to the woman.

She swoons.

Corv.   Rare!
Prettily feigned again!

4 Avoc.   Stand from about her.   160

1 Avoc. Give her the air.

3 Avoc.   What can you say?

Mos.   My wound,
May it please your wisdom, speaks for me, received
In aid of my good patron, when he missed
His sought-for father, when that well-taught dame
Had her cue given her to cry out a rape.

Bon. O most laid [23] impudence! fathers—

3 Avoc.   Sir, be silent.
You had your hearing free, so must they theirs.

2 Avoc. I do begin to doubt [24] the imposture here.

4 Avoc. This woman has too many moods.

Volt.   Grave fathers,
She is a creature of a most professed   170
And prostituted lewdness.

Corv.   Most impetuous,
Unsatisfied, grave fathers!

Volt.   May her feignings
Not take your wisdoms. But this day she baited
A stranger, a grave knight, with her loose eyes,
And more lascivious kisses. This man saw 'hem
Together on the water, in a gondola.

Mos. Here is the lady herself, that saw 'hem too,
Without; who then had in the open streets
Pursued them, but for saving her knight's honor.   179

1 Avoc. Produce that lady.

2 Avoc.   Let her come.

[*Exit* MOSCA.]

4 Avoc.   These things,
They strike with wonder.

3 Avoc.   I am turned a stone.

---

[20] *here:* i.e., on my forehead, where the horns of the
cuckold are evident.
[21] *horn:* The alphabet ("letters") studied in school was
covered by transparent horn.
[22] *perfect:* complete.   [23] *laid:* plotted.
[24] *doubt:* suspect.   [25] *chameleon:* changeable.
[26] *hyena:* proverbially treacherous.
[27] *pertinancy:* pertinacity.   [28] *strappado:* torture.

[*Re-enter* MOSCA *with* LADY WOULD-BE.]

Mos. Be resolute, madam.

L. Pol.   Ay, this same is she.

[*Pointing to* CELIA.]

Out, thou chameleon [25] harlot! now thine eyes
Vie tears with the hyena. [26] Dar'st thou look
Upon my wrongèd face? I cry your pardons,
I fear I have forgettingly transgressed
Against the dignity of the court—

2 Avoc.   No, madam.

L. Pol. And been exorbitant—

2 Avoc.   You have not, lady.

4 Avoc. These proofs are strong.

L. Pol.   Surely, I had no
 purpose   189
To scandalize your honors, or my sex's.

3 Avoc.   We do believe it.

L. Pol. Surely you may believe it.

2 Avoc.   Madam, we do.

L. Pol. Indeed you may; my breeding
Is not so coarse—

4 Avoc. We know it.

L. Pol.   To offend
With pertinancy [27]—

3 Avoc.   Lady—

L. Pol.   Such a presence!
No surely.

1 Avoc. We well think it.

L. Pol.   You may think it.

1 Avoc. Let her o'er come. What witnesses have you,
To make good your report?

Bon.   Our consciences.

Cel. And heaven, that never fails the innocent.

4 Avoc. These are no testimonies.

Bon.   Not in your courts,
Where multitude and clamor overcomes.   200

1 Avoc. Nay, then you do wax insolent.

VOLPONE *is brought in, as impotent.*

Volt.   Here, here,
The testimony comes that will convince,
And put to utter dumbness their bold tongues!
See here, grave fathers, here's the ravisher,
The rider on men's wives, the great impostor,
The grand voluptuary! Do you not think
These limbs should affect venery? Or these eyes
Covet a concubine? Pray you mark these hands;
Are they not fit to stroke a lady's breasts?
Perhaps he doth dissemble!

Bon.   So he does.   210

Volt. Would you ha' him tortured?

Bon.   I would have
 him proved.

Volt. Best try him then with goads, or burning irons;
Put him to the strappado. [28] I have heard
The rack hath cured the gout. Faith, give it him,
And help him of a malady; be courteous.
I'll undertake, before these honored fathers,
He shall have yet as many left diseases,

As she has known adulterers, or thou strumpets.
Oh, my most equal[29] hearers, if these deeds,
Acts of this bold and most exorbitant strain,   220
May pass with sufferance, what one citizen
But owes the forfeit of his life, yea, fame,
To him that dares traduce him? Which of you
Are safe, my honored fathers? I would ask,
With leave of your grave fatherhoods, if their plot
Have any face or color like to truth?
Or if, unto the dullest nostril here,
It smell not rank, and most abhorrèd slander?
I crave your care of this good gentleman,
Whose life is much endangered by their fable.   230
And as for them, I will conclude with this,
That vicious persons, when they are hot, and fleshed[30]
In impious acts, their constancy abounds.
Damned deeds are done with greatest confidence.

1 Avoc. Take 'hem to custody, and sever them.
2 Avoc. 'Tis pity two such prodigies should live.
1 Avoc. Let the old gentleman be returned with care.
                    [*Exeunt* Officers *with* VOLPONE.]
I'm sorry our credulity wronged him.
4 Avoc. These are two creatures!
3 Avoc.   I have an earthquake
    in me.
2 Avoc. Their shame, even in their cradles, fled
    their faces.   240
4 Avoc. You have done a worthy service to the
    state, sir,
In their discovery.
1 Avoc. [*To* VOLTORE] You shall hear, ere night,
What punishment the court decrees upon 'hem.
            [*Exeunt* Avocatori, Notario, *and* Officers *with*
                    BONARIO *and* CELIA.]
Volt. We thank your fatherhoods. How like you it?
Mos.   Rare.
I'd ha' your tongue, sir, tipped with gold for this.
I'd ha' you be the heir to the whole city.
The earth I'd have want[31] men ere you want living.
They're bound to erect your statue in St. Mark's.
Signior Corvino, I would have you go
And show yourself that you have conquered.
Corv.   Yes.   250
Mos. It was much better that you should profess
Yourself a cuckold thus, than that the other
Should have been proved.
Corv.   Nay, I considered that.
Now it is her fault.
Mos.   Then it had been yours.
Corv. True; I do doubt this advocate still.
Mos.   I' faith,
You need not, I dare ease you of that care.
Corv. I trust thee, Mosca.
                                    [*Exit.*]
Mos.   As your own soul, sir.
Corb.   Mosca!
Mos. Now for your business, sir.
Corb.   How! hav' you
    business?
Mos. Yes, yours, sir.
Corb.   Oh, none else.

Mos.   None else, not I.
Corb. Be careful then.
Mos.   Rest you with both your
    eyes, sir.   260
Corb. Dispatch it.
Mos.   Instantly.
Corb.   And look that all,
Whatever, be put in, jewels, plate, moneys,
Household stuff, bedding, curtains.
Mos.   Curtain-rings, sir—
Only, the advocate's fee must be deducted.
Corb. I'll pay him now; you'll be too prodigal.
Mos. Sir, I must tender it.
Corb.   Two cecchines is well?
Mos. No, six, sir.
Corb. 'Tis too much.
Mos.   He talked a great while.
You must consider that, sir.
Corb.   Well, there's three—
Mos. I'll give it him.
Corb.   Do so, and there's for thee.   269
                                                    [*Exit.*]
Mos. Bountiful bones! What horrid strange offense
Did he commit 'gainst nature, in his youth,
Worthy this age?—[*To* VOLTORE] You see, sir, how I
    work
Unto your ends. Take you no notice.
Volt.   No,
I'll leave you.
                                                    [*Exit.*]
Mos. All is yours, the devil and all.
Good advocate!—Madam, I'll bring you home.
L. Pol. No, I'll go see your patron.
Mos.   That you shall not.
I'll tell you why. My purpose is to urge
My patron to reform his will, and for
The zeal you have shown today, whereas before
You were but third or fourth, you shall be now   280
Put in the first—which would appear as begged
If you were present. Therefore—
L. Pol.   You shall sway me.
                                                    [*Exeunt.*]

ACT FIVE

SCENE ONE

[*Enter* VOLPONE.]

Volp. Well, I am here, and all this brunt is past.
I ne'er was in dislike with my disguise
Till this fled moment. Here 'twas good, in private;
But in your public,—*Cavè*[1] whilst I breathe.
'Fore God, my left leg, 'gan to have the cramp,
And I apprehended straight some power had struck me
With a dead palsy. Well! I must be merry,
And shake it off. A many of these fears

---

[29] *equal:* just.   [30] *fleshed:* hardened.   [31] *want:* lack.
V.i.
   [1] *Cavè:* Beware.

Would out me into some villainous disease,
Should they come thick upon me. I'll prevent 'hem.   10
Give me a bowl of lusty wine, to fright
This humor from my heart.

He drinks.

                    Hum, hum, hum!
'Tis almost gone already. I shall conquer.
Any device now of rare ingenious knavery,
That would possess me with a violent laughter,
Would make me up again. So, so, so, so!

Drinks again.

This heat is life; 'tis blood by this time—Mosca!

[*Enter* MOSCA.]

  Mos. How now, sir? Does the day look clear again?
Are we recovered, and wrought out of error,
Into our way, to see our path before us?   20
Is our trade free once more?
  Volp.   Exquisite Mosca!
  Mos. Was it not carried learnedly?
  Volp.   And stoutly.
Good wits are greatest in extremities.
  Mos. It were folly beyond thought to trust
Any grand act unto a cowardly spirit.
You are not taken with it enough, methinks.
  Volp. Oh, more than if I had enjoyed the wench.
The pleasure of all woman-kind's not like it.
  Mos. Why, now you speak, sir. We must here be
    fixed;
Here we must rest; this is our masterpiece;   30
We cannot think to go beyond this.
  Volp.   True,
Thou hast played thy prize, my precious Mosca.
  Mos.   Nay, sir,
To gull the court—
  Volp.   And quite divert the torrent
Upon the innocent.
  Mos.   Yes, and to make
So rare a music out of discords—
  Volp.   Right.
That yet to me's the strangest, how th' hast borne it!
That these, being so divided 'mongst themselves,
Should not scent somewhat, or in me or thee,
Or doubt their own side.
  Mos.   True, they will not see't,
Too much light blinds 'hem, I think. Each of 'hem   40
Is so possessed and stuffed with his own hopes
That anything unto the contrary,
Never so true, or never so apparent,
Never so palpable, they will resist it—
  Volp. Like a temptation of the devil.
  Mos.   Right, sir.
Merchants may talk of trade, and your great signiors

Of land that yields well; but if Italy
Have any glebe[2] more fruitful than these fellows,
I am deceived. Did not your advocate rare?[3]
  Volp. Oh—"My most honored fathers, my grave
    fathers,   50
Under correction of your fatherhoods,
What face of truth is here? If these strange deeds
May pass, most honored fathers"—I had much ado
To forbear laughing.
  Mos.   It seemed to me, you sweat, sir.
  Volp. In troth, I did a little.
  Mos.   But confess, sir,
Were you not daunted?
  Volp.   In good faith, I was
A little in a mist, but not dejected;
Never but still myself.
  Mos.   I think it, sir.
Now, so truth help me, I must needs say this, sir,
And out of conscience for your advocate,   60
He has taken pains, in faith, sir, and deserved,
In my poor judgement, I speak it under favor,
Not to contrary you, sir, very richly—
Well—to be cozened.[4]
  Volp.   Troth and I think so too,
By that I heard him in the latter end.
  Mos. Oh, but before, sir: had you heard him first
Draw it to certain heads, then aggravate,[5]
Then use his vehement figures[6]—I looked still
When he would shift a shirt;[7] and doing this
Out of pure love, no hope of gain—
  Volp.   'Tis right.   70
I cannot answer him Mosca, as I would,
Not yet; but for thy sake, at thy entreaty,
I will begin, even now—to vex 'hem all,
This very instant.
  Mos.   Good sir.
  Volp.   Call the dwarf
And eunuch forth.
  Mos.   Castrone, Nano!

[*Enter* CASTRONE *and* NANO.]

  Nano.   Here.
  Volp. Shall we have a jig now?
  Mos.   What you please, sir.
  Volp.   Go,
Straight give out about the streets, you two,
That I am dead. Do it with constancy,
Sadly,[8] do you hear? Impute it to the grief
Of this late slander.

          [*Exeunt* CASTRONE *and* NANO.]

  Mos.   What do you mean, sir?
  Volp.   Oh,   80
I shall have instantly my Vulture, Crow,
Raven, come flying hither, on the news,
To peck for carrion, my she-wolf, and all,
Greedy, and full of expectation—
  Mos. And then to have it ravished from their
    mouths!
  Volp. 'Tis true. I will ha' thee put on a gown,
And take upon thee, as thou wert mine heir;
Show 'hem a will. Open that chest, and reach

---

  [2] *glebe:* soil.   [3] *rare:* rarely.   [4] *cozened:* cheated.
  [5] *Draw . . . aggravate:* Order his argument and then make
it more emphatic.   [6] *figures:* rhetorical figures, to persuade.
  [7] *shift . . . shirt:* change his clothing, given the violence
of his address. Presumably Voltore has worked himself into
a sweat.   [8] *Sadly:* Seriously.

Forth one of those that has the blanks; I'll straight
Put in thy name.
    Mos.   It will be rare, sir.
    Volp.   Ay,   90
When they ev'n gape, and find themselves deluded—
    Mos. Yes.
    Volp.   And thou use them scurvily! Dispatch,
Get on thy gown.
    Mos.   But what, sir, if they ask
After the body?
    Volp.   Say, it was corrupted.
    Mos. I'll say it stunk, sir; and was fain to have it
Coffined up instantly, and sent away.
    Volp. Anything; what thou wilt. Hold, here's my
    will.
Get thee a cap, a count-book,[9] pen and ink,
Papers afore thee; sit as thou wert taking
An inventory of parcels. I'll get up   100
Behind the curtain, on a stool, and hearken:
Sometime peep over, see how they do look,
With what degrees their blood doth leave their faces.
Oh, 'twill afford me a rare meal of laughter!
    Mos. Your advocate will turn stark dull upon it.
    Volp. It will take off his oratory's edge.
    Mos. But your clarissimo,[10] old roundback, he
Will crump[11] you like a hog-louse, with the touch.
    Volp. And what Corvino?
    Mos.   Oh, sir, look for him,
Tomorrow morning, with a rope and dagger,   110
To visit all the streets. He must run mad,
My lady too, that came into the court,
To bear false witness for your worship—
    Volp.   Yes,
And kissed me 'fore the fathers, when my face
Flowed all with oils—
    Mos.   And sweat, sir. Why, your gold
Is such another med'cine, it dries up
All those offensive savors: it transforms
The most deformed, and restores 'hem lovely,
As 'twere the strange poetical girdle.[12] Jove
Could not invent t' himself a shroud more subtle   120
To pass Acrisius' guards.[13] It is the thing
Makes all the world her grace, her youth, her beauty.
    Volp. I think she loves me.
    Mos.   Who? The lady, sir?
She's jealous of you.
    Volp.   Dost thou say so?

                        [Knocking within.]

    Mos.   Hark,
There's some already.
    Volp.   Look.
    Mos.   It is the Vulture;
He has the quickest scent.
    Volp.   I'll to my place,
Thou to thy posture.
    Mos.   I am set.
    Volp.   But, Mosca,
Play the artificer[14] now, torture 'hem rarely.

              [Enter VOLTORE.*]*

    Volt. How now, my Mosca?
    Mos. [*Writing*]   "Turkey carpets,
    nine—"
    Volt. Taking an inventory! that is well.   130
    Mos. "Two suits of bedding, tissue—"
    Volt.   Where's the
    will?
Let me read that, the while.

    [Enter Servants *with* CORBACCIO *in a chair.]*

    Corb.   So, set me down,
And get you home.
                      [Exeunt Servants.]
    Volt.   Is he come now, to trouble us!
    Mos. "Of cloth of gold, two more—"
    Corb.   Is it done, Mosca?
    Mos. "Of several vellets,[15] eight—"
    Volt.   I like his care.
    Corb. Dost thou not hear?

              [Enter CORVINO.*]*

    Corv.   Ha! is the hour come, Mosca?
    Volp. Ay, now they muster.

    VOLPONE *peeps from behind a traverse.*[16]

    Corv.   What does the advocate
    here,
Or this Corbaccio?
    Corb.   What do these here?

    [Enter LADY POLITIC WOULD-BE.*]*

    L. Pol.   Mosca!
Is his thread spun?
    Mos.   "Eight chests of linen—"
    Volp.   Oh,
My fine Dame Would-be, too!
    Corv.   Mosca, the will,   140
That I may show it these, and rid 'hem hence.
    Mos. "Six chests of diaper,[17] four of damask,"—
    There

    [Gives them the will carelessly, over his shoulder.]

    Corb. Is that the will?
    Mos.   "Down-beds, and bolsters—"
    Volp.   Rare!
Be busy still. Now they begin to flutter.
They never think of me. Look, see, see, see!
How their swift eyes run over the long deed,
Unto the name, and to the legacies,
What is bequeathed them there—
    Mos.   "Ten suits of hangings—"

---

   9 *count-book:* account book.
   10 *clarissimo:* Venetian grandee.
   11 *crump:* curl up (himself; "you" is an ethical dative,
not objective).   12 *girdle:* worn by Venus.
   13 *Jove . . . guards:* By changing himself to a shower of
gold, Jove got access to the chamber of Danaë, the daughter
of Acrisius.   14 *artificer:* craftsman in trickery.
   15 *vellets:* velvets.
   16 *traverse:* perhaps a curtain closing off the inner stage;
or a movable screen.   17 *diaper:* linen.

Volp. Ay i' their garters,[18] Mosca. Now their hopes
Are at the gasp.
Volt.   Mosca the heir!
Corb.   What's that?   150
Volp. My advocate is dumb. Look to my merchant,
He has heard of some strange storm, a ship is lost,
He faints. My lady will swoon. Old glazen-eyes,
He hath not reached his despair yet.
Corb.   All these
Are out of hope. I am, sure, the man.
Corv. But, Mosca—
Mos.   "Two cabinets—"
Corv.   Is this in
earnest?
Mos.   "One
Of ebony—"
Corv.   Or do you but delude me?
Mos. "The other, mother of pearl!"—I am very busy.
Good faith, it is a fortune thrown upon me—
"Item, one salt [19] of agate"—not my seeking.   160
L. Pol. Do you hear, sir?
Mos.   "A perfumed box"—Pray
you forbear,
You see I am troubled—"made of an onyx—"
L. Pol.   How!
Mos. Tomorrow or next day, I shall be at leisure
To talk with you all.
Corv.   Is this my large hope's issue?
L. Pol. Sir, I must have a fairer answer.
Mos.   Madam!
Marry, and shall. Pray you, fairly quit my house.
Nay, raise no tempest with your looks; but hark you
Remember what your ladyship offered [20] me
To put you in an heir. Go to, think on it:
And what you said e'en your best madams did   170
For maintenance; and why not you? Enough.
Go home, and use the poor Sir Pol, your knight, well,
For fear I tell some riddles; go, be melancholy.
            [*Exit* LADY WOULD-BE.]
Volp. Oh, my fine devil!
Corv.   Mosca, pray you a word.
Mos. Lord! Will not you take your dispatch hence
yet?
Methinks, of all, you should have been the example.
Why should you stay here? With what thought, what
promise?
Hear you; do you not know, I know you an ass,
And that you would most fain have been a wittol [21]
If fortune would have let you? That you are   180
A declared cuckold, on good terms? This pearl,
You'll say, was yours? Right: this diamond?
I'll not deny't, but thank you. Much here else?

It may be so. Why, think that these good works
May help to hide your bad. I'll not betray you;
Although you be but extraordinary,
And have it [22] only in title, it sufficeth.
Go home, be melancholic too, or mad.
                [*Exit* CORVINO.]
Volp. Rare Mosca! how his villainy becomes him!
Volt. Certain he doth delude all these for me.   190
Corb. Mosca the heir!
Volp.   Oh, his four eyes [23] have
found it.
Corb. I am cozened, cheated, by a parasite slave.
Harlot,[24] thou hast gulled me.
Mos.   Yes, sir. Stop your mouth
Or I shall draw the only tooth is left.
Are not you he, that filthy covetous wretch,
With the three legs,[25] that here, in hope of prey,
Have, any time this three years, snuffed about,
With your most groveling nose, and would have hired
Me to the poisoning of my patron, sir.
Are not you he that have today in court   200
Professed the disinheriting of your son?
Perjured yourself? Go home, and die, and stink.
If you but croak a syllable, all comes out.
Away, and call your porters!
             [*Exit* CORBACCIO.]
         Go, go, stink.
Volp. Excellent varlet!
Volt.   Now, my faithful Mosca,
I find thy constancy—
Mos.   Sir!
Volt.   Sincere.
Mos. [*Writing*]   "A table
Of porphyry"—I mar'le [26] you'll be thus troublesome.
Volt. Nay, leave off now, they are gone.
Mos.   Why, who are
you?
What! who did send for you? Oh, cry you mercy,
Reverend sir! good faith, I am grieved for you,   210
That any chance of mine should thus defeat
Your (I must needs say) most deserving travails. [27]
But I protest, sir, it was cast upon me,
And I could almost wish to be without it,
But that the will o' the dead must be observed.
Marry, my joy is that you need it not.
You have a gift, sir (thank your education),
Will never let you want, while there are men,
And malice, to breed causes.[28] Would I had
But half the like, for all my fortune, sir!   220
If I have any suits, as I do hope,
Things being so easy and direct, I shall not,
I will make bold with your obstreperous aid,
Conceive me—for your fee, sir. In mean time,
You that have so much law, I know ha' the conscience
Not to be covetous of what is mine.
Good sir, I thank you for my plate; 'twill help
To set up a young man. Good faith, you look
As you were costive.[29] Best go home and purge, sir.
              [*Exit* VOLTORE.]

[VOLPONE *comes from behind the traverse.*]

---

18 *garters:* with which they may hang themselves.
19 *salt:* saltcellar.   20 *offered:* i.e., herself.
21 *wittol:* deliberate cuckold.   22 *it:* name of cuckold.
23 *four eyes:* Corbaccio wears glasses.
24 *Harlot:* used originally of men and women indifferently—scoundrel.
25 *three legs:* his own and the cane that supports him.
26 *mar'le:* marvel.   27 *travails:* labors, sufferings.
28 *causes:* lawsuits.   29 *costive:* constipated.

Volp. Bid him eat lettuce [30] well. My witty mischief,
Let me embrace thee. O that I could now   231
Transform thee to a Venus—Mosca, go,
Straight take my habit of clarissimo, [31]
And walk the streets. Be seen, torment 'hem more.
We must pursue, as well as plot. Who would
Have lost this feast?
   Mos.   I doubt it will lose them.
   Volp. Oh, my recovery shall recover all.
That I could now but think on some disguise
To meet 'hem in, and ask 'hem questions.
How I would vex 'hem still at every turn!   240
   Mos. Sir, I can fit you.
   Volp.   Canst thou?
   Mos.   Yes, I know
One o' the commandadori, sir, so like you; [32]
Him will I straight make drunk, and bring you his
    habit.
   Volp. A rare disguise, and answering thy brain!
Oh, I will be a sharp disease unto 'hem.
   Mos. Sir, you must look for curses—
   Volp.   Till they burst.
The Fox fares ever best when he is curst. [33]
                      [*Exeunt.*]

[V.ii]

[*Enter* PEREGRINE *disguised, and three* Merchants.]

Per. Am I enough disguised?
1 Merch.   I warrant you.
Per. All my ambition is to fright him only.
2 Merch. If you could ship him away, 'twere
    excellent.
3 Merch. To Zant, or to Aleppo!
Per.   Yes, and ha' his
Adventures put i' the Book of Voyages, [1]
And his gulled story [2] registered for truth.
Well, gentlemen, when I am in a while,
And that you think us warm in our discourse,
Know your approaches.
   1 Merch.   Trust it to our care.
                    [*Exeunt* Merchants.]

[*Enter* Waiting-woman.]

Per. Save you, fair lady! Is Sir Pol within?   10
Wom. I do not know, sir.
Per.   Pray you say unto him
Here is a merchant, upon urgent business,
Desires to speak with him.
   Wom.   I will see, sir.
                    [*Exit.*]
   Per.   Pray you.
I see the family is all female here.

[*Re-enter* Waiting-woman.]

Wom. He says, sir, he has weighty affairs of state,
That now require him whole. Some other time
You may possess him.
   Per.   Pray you say again,
If those require him whole, these will exact him, [3]

Whereof I bring him tidings.
                    [*Exit* Woman.]
          What might be
His grave affair of state now! how to make   20
Bolognian sausages here in Venice, sparing
One o' the ingredients?

[*Re-enter* Waiting-woman.]

Wom.   Sir, he says, he knows
By your word "tidings" [4] that you are no statesman,
And therefore wills you stay.
   Per.   Sweet, pray you return him.
I have not read so many proclamations,
And studied them for words, as he has done—
But—here he deigns to come.
                    [*Exit* Woman.]

[*Enter* SIR POLITIC.]

S. Pol.   Sir, I must crave
Your courteous pardon. There hath chanced today
Unkind disaster 'twixt my lady and me;
And I was penning my apology,   30
To give her satisfaction, as you came now.
   Per. Sir, I am grieved I bring you worse disaster.
The gentleman you met at the port today,
That told you he was newly arrived—
   S. Pol.   Ay, was
A fugitive punk? [5]
   Per.   No, sir, a spy set on you.
And he has made relation to the Senate,
That you professed to him to have a plot
To sell the State of Venice to the Turk.
   S. Pol.   Oh, me!
   Per. For which warrants are signed by this time,
To apprehend you, and to search your study   40
For papers—
   S. Pol.   Alas, sir, I have none, but notes
Drawn out of play-books—
   Per.   All the better, sir.
   S. Pol. And some essays. What shall I do?
   Per.   Sir, best
Convey yourself into a sugar-chest:
Or, if you could lie round, a frail [6] were rare.
And I could send you aboard.
   S. Pol.   Sir, I but talked so,
For discourse sake merely.
   Per.   Hark! they are there.

                    They knock without.

---

30 *lettuce:* remedy for constipation.
31 *habit . . . clarissimo:* costume of a grandee.
32 *so . . . you:* if it please you.
33 *curst:* for escaping—proverbial.

V.ii.
  1 *Book of Voyages:* like Hakluyt's great collections of English and foreign voyages and travels.
  2 *gulled story:* story of his gulling.
  3 *exact him:* insist on his presence.
  4 *tidings:* A statesman would have said, more pretentiously, "intelligence."
  5 *punk:* prostitute. Sir Pol has evidently accepted his wife's erroneous impression.
  6 *frail:* rush basket for packing fruit.

S. Pol. I am a wretch, a wretch!
Per.   What will you do, sir?
Ha' you ne'er a currant-butt[7] to leap into?
They'll put you to the rack; you must be sudden.   50
S. Pol. Sir, I have an ingine[8]—
3 Merch.   Sir Politic Would-be!
2 Merch. Where is he?
S. Pol.   That I have thought upon
    before time.
Per. What is it?
S. Pol.   I shall ne'er endure the torture.
Marry, it is, sir, of a tortoise-shell,
Fitted for these extremities. Pray you sir, help me.
Here I've a place, sir, to put back my legs,
Please you to lay it on, sir, with this cap,
And my black gloves. I'll lie, sir, like a tortoise,
Till they are gone.
Per.   And call you this an ingine?
S. Pol. Mine own device—Good sir, bid my wife's
    women   60
To burn my papers.

They [the three Merchants] rush in.

1 Merch.   Where is he hid?
3 Merch.   We must,
And will sure find him.
2 Merch.   Which is his study?
1 Merch.   What
Are you, sir?
Per.   I am a merchant, that came here
To look upon this tortoise.
3 Merch.   How!
1 Merch.   St. Mark!
What beast is this?
Per.   It is a fish.
2 Merch.   Come out here!
Per. Nay, you may strike him, sir, and tread upon
    him.
He'll bear a cart.
1 Merch.   What, to run over him?
Per.   Yes.
3 Merch. Let's jump upon him.
2 Merch.   Can he not go?
Per.   He
    creeps, sir.
1 Merch. Let's see him creep.
Per.   No, good sir, you will
    hurt him.   69

2 Merch. Heart, I will see him creep, or prick his guts.
3 Merch. Come out here!
Per.   Pray you, sir. [Aside to SIR
    POLITIC] Creep a little.
1 Merch.   Forth.
2 Merch. Yet farther.
Per.   Good sir! [Aside] Creep.
2 Merch.   We'll
    see his legs.

They pull off the shell and discover him.

3 Merch. Ods so, he has garters!
1 Merch.   Ay, and gloves!
2 Merch.   Is this
Your fearful tortoise?
Per.   Now, Sir Pol, we are even.
For your next project I shall be prepared.
I am sorry for the funeral of your notes, sir.
1 Merch. 'Twere a rare motion[9] to be seen in Fleet
    street.
2 Merch. Ay i' the Term.
1 Merch.   Or Smithfield, in the fair.[10]
3 Merch. Methinks 'tis but a melancholic sight.   79
Per. Farewell, most politic tortoise!
                    [Exeunt PEREGRINE and Merchants.]

[Re-enter Waiting-woman.]

S. Pol.   Where's my lady?
Knows she of this?
Wom.   I know not, sir.
S. Pol.   Inquire—
                                    [Exit Woman.]
Oh, I shall be the fable of all feasts,
The freight of the gazetti,[11] ship-boys' tale;
And, which is worst, even talk for ordinaries.[12]

[Re-enter Waiting-woman.]

Wom. My lady's come most melancholic home,
And says, sir, she will straight to sea, for physic.
S. Pol. And I, to shun this place and clime for ever,
Creeping with house on back, and think it well
To shrink my poor head in my politic shell.
                                    [Exeunt.]

[V.iii]

[Enter VOLPONE in the habit of a commandadore,
    and MOSCA in that of a clarissimo.]

Volp. Am I then like him?
Mos.   Oh, sir, you are he:
No man can sever[1] you.
Volp.   Good.
Mos.   But what am I?
Volp. 'Fore heaven, a brave clarissimo; thou
    becom'st it!
Pity thou wert not born one.
Mos. [Aside]   If I hold
My made one,[2] 'twill be well.
Volp.   I'll go and see
What news first at the court.
                                    [Exit.]

---

7 *currant-butt:* cask for storing currants.
8 *ingine:* contrivance.   9 *motion:* puppet show.
10 *Fleet-street . . . fair:* Variously, places and occasions proper to sideshows: freaks were shown in Fleet Street and at Bartholomew Fair, and were especially popular during the academic term of the law courts, when London was full of visitors.
11 *freight . . . gazetti:* subject of the newspapers.
12 *ordinaries:* taverns.

V.iii.
1 *sever:* distinguish.
2 *made one:* as opposed to "born one"—assumed character.

Mos.   Do so. My Fox
Is out on[3] his hole, and ere he shall re-enter,
I'll make him languish in his borrowed case,[4]
Except[5] he come to composition[6] with me.
Androgyno, Castrone, Nano!

[*Enter* Androgyno, Castrone, *and* Nano.]

All.   Here   10
Mos Go, recreate yourselves abroad; go, sport —
                                   [*Exeunt.*]
So, now I have the keys, and am possessed.
Since he will needs be dead afore his time,
I'll bury him, or gain by him: I am his heir,
And so will keep me, till he share at least.
To cozen him of all, were but a cheat
Well placed. No man would construe it a sin.
Let his sport pay for 't. This is called the Fox-trap.
                                   [*Exit.*]

[V.iv]

[*Enter* Corbaccio *and* Corvino.]

Corb. They say the court is set.
Corv.   We must maintain
Our first tale good, for both our reputations.
Corb. Why, mine's no tale. My son would there have
     killed me.
Corv. That's true, I had forgot.[*Aside*] Mine is,
     I am sure.
But for your will, sir.
Corb.   Ay, I'll come upon him
For that hereafter, now his patron's dead.

[*Enter* Volpone.]

Volp. Signior Corvino! and Corbaccio! sir,
Much joy unto you.
Corv.   Of what?
Volp.   The sudden good
Dropped down upon you—
Corb.   Where?
Volp.   And none knows how,
From old Volpone, sir.
Corb.   Out, arrant knave!   10
Volp. Let not your too much wealth, sir, make you
     furious.
Corb. Away, thou varlet.
Volp.   Why, sir?
Corb.   Dost thou mock me?
Volp. You mock the world, sir. Did you not change
     wills?
Corb. Out, harlot!
Volp.   Oh, belike[1] you are the man,
Signior Corvino? Faith, you carry it well;
You grow not mad withal; I love your spirit;
You are not over-leavened[2] with your fortune.
You should ha' some would swell now, like a wine-fat,[3]
With such an autumn—Did he give you all, sir?
Corv. Avoid,[4] you rascal!
Volp.   Troth, your wife has shown
Herself, a very[5] woman; but you are well,   21
You need not care, you have a good estate,

To bear it out, sir, better by this chance:
Except Corbaccio have a share.
Corb.   Hence, varlet.
Volp. You will not be a'known,[6] sir; why, 'tis wise.
Thus do all gamesters, at all games, dissemble.
No man will seem to win.
                    [*Exeunt* Corvino *and* Corbaccio.]
                         Here comes my vulture,
Heaving his beak up i' the air, and snuffing.

[*Enter* Voltore.]

Volt. Outstripped thus, by a parasite! a slave,
Would run on errands, and make legs for crumbs.   30
Well, what I'll do—
Volp.   The court stays for your worship.
I e'en rejoice, sir, at your worship's happiness,
And that it fell into so learnèd hands,
That understand the fingering—
Volt.   What do you mean?
Volp. I mean to be a suitor to your worship,
For the small tenement, out of reparations,[7]
That, at the end of your long row of houses,
By the Piscaria.[8] It was, in Volpone's time,
Your predecessor, ere he grew diseased,
A handsome, pretty, customed[9] bawdy-house   40
As any was in Venice, none dispraised:
But fell with him: his body and that house
Decayed together.
Volt.   Come, sir, leave your prating.
Volp. Why, if your worship give me but your
     hand,[10]
That I may ha' the refusal, I have done.
'Tis a mere toy to you, sir; candle-rents;[11]
As your learned worship knows—
Volt.   What do I know?
Volp. Marry, no end of your wealth, sir; God
     decrease it!
Volt. Mistaking knave! what, mock'st thou my
     misfortune?
                                   [*Exit.*]
Volp. His blessing on your heart, sir; would
     'twere more!—   50
Now to my first again, at the next corner.
                                   [*Exit.*]

[*Enter* Corbaccio *and* Corvino; Mosca
     passing over the stage.]

Corb. See, in our habit! see the impudent varlet!
Corv. That I could shoot mine eyes at him, like
     gun-stones![12]

[*Enter* Volpone.]

---

³ *on:* of.   ⁴ *case:* disguise.   ⁵ *Except:* Unless.
⁶ *composition:* agreement.
V.iv.
   ¹ *belike:* perhaps.   ² *over-leavened:* swelled up.
   ³ *fat:* vat.   ⁴ *Avoid:* Be gone.   ⁵ *very:* true.
   ⁶ *a'known:* recognized.   ⁷ *reparations:* repair.
   ⁸ *Piscaria:* fish market.   ⁹ *customed:* well-patronized.
   ¹⁰ *hand:* agreement.
   ¹¹ *candle-rents:* income from deteriorating property.
   ¹² *gun-stones:* cannonballs.

Volp. But is this true, sir, of the parasite?

Corb. Again, to afflict us! monster!

Volp.   In good faith, sir,
I'm heartily grieved, a beard of your grave length
Should be so over-reached,[13] I never brooked[14]
That parasite's hair; methought his nose should cozen.
There still was somewhat in his look, did promise
The bane of a clarissimo.

Corb.   Knave—

Volp.   Methinks   60
Yet you, that are so traded[15] i' the world,
A witty merchant, the fine bird, Corvino,
That have such moral emblems on your name,[16]
Should not have sung your shame, and dropped your
       cheese,[17]
To let the Fox laugh at your emptiness.

Corv. Sirrah, you think the privilege of the place,
And your red saucy cap, that seems to me
Nailed to your jolt-head[18] with those two cecchines,[19]
Can warrant your abuses. Come you hither:
You shall perceive, sir, I dare beat you; approach.   70

Volp. No haste, sir, I do know your valor well,
Since you durst publish what you are, sir.

Corv.   Tarry,
I'd speak with you.

Volp.   Sir, sir, another time—

Corv. Nay, now.

Volp.   O God, sir! I were a wise man,
Would stand the fury of a distracted cuckold.

                    MOSCA *walks by them.*

Corb. What, come again!

Volp.   Upon 'em, Mosca; save me.

Corb. The air's infected where he breathes.

Corv.   Let's fly him.
                    [*Exeunt* CORVINO *and* CORBACCIO.]

Volp. Excellent basilisk![20] Turn upon the vulture.

                    [*Enter* VOLTORE.]

Volt. Well, flesh-fly, it is summer with you now;
Your winter will come on.

Mos.   Good advocate,   80
Pray thee not rail, nor threaten out of place thus;
Thou'lt make a solecism, as madam says.
Get you a biggen[21] more; your brain breaks loose.
                    [*Exit.*]

Volt. Well, sir.

Volp.   Would you ha' me beat the insolent
       slave,

---

[13] *over-reached:* outwitted.
[14] *brooked:* could endure.   [15] *traded:* experienced.
[16] *name:* of "crow," to which contemporary emblem
books assigned particular qualities.
[17] *sung . . . cheese:* In Aesop's fable, the crow opens its
mouth to reply to the crafty fox and lets fall the cheese.
[18] *jolt-head:* blockhead.   [19] *cecchines:* gilt buttons.
[20] *basilisk:* fabled serpent, to look on which was fatal.
[21] *biggen:* cap.   [22] *familiar:* spirit, devil.
[23] *Justinian:* Roman emperor famous for his codifying of
the law.
V.v.
[1] *possessed:* as by a devil.

Throw dirt upon his first good clothes?

Volt.   This same
Is doubtless some familiar.[22]

Volp.   Sir, the court,
In troth, stays for you. I am mad, a mule
That never read Justinian,[23] should get up,
And ride an advocate. Had you no quirk
To avoid gullage, sir, by such a creature?   90
I hope you do but jest; he has not done it.
This 's but confederacy to blind the rest.
You are the heir?

Volt.   A strange, officious,
Troublesome knave! Thou dost torment me.

Volp.   I know—
It cannot be, sir, that you should be cozened;
'Tis not within the wit of man to do it.
You are so wise, so prudent; and 'tis fit
That wealth and wisdom still should go together.
                    [*Exeunt.*]

[V.v]

[*Enter four* Avocatori, Notario, BONARIO, CELIA,
CORBACCIO, CORVINO, Commandadori, Saffi, etc.]

1 Avoc. Are all the parties here?

Not.   All but the advocate.

2 Avoc. And here he comes.

                    [*Enter* VOLTORE *and* VOLPONE.]

1 Avoc.   Then bring 'hem forth
       to sentence.

Volt. O my most honored fathers, let your mercy
Once win upon your justice, to forgive—
I am distracted—

Volp. [*Aside*] What will he do now?

Volt.   Oh,
I know not which to address myself to first;
Whether your fatherhoods, or these innocents—

Corv. [*Aside*] Will he betray himself?

Volt.   Whom equally
I have abused, out of most covetous ends—   9

Corv. The man is mad!

Corb.   What's that?

Corv.   He is possessed.[1]

Volt. For which, now struck in conscience, here I
       prostrate
Myself at your offended feet, for pardon.

1, 2 Avoc. Arise.

Celia.   O heaven, how just thou art!

Volp. [*Aside*]   I am
       caught
I' mine own noose—

Corv. [*To* CORBACCIO] Be constant, sir; naught
       now
Can help but impudence.

1 Avoc.   Speak forward.

Comm.   Silence!

Volt. It is not passion in me, reverend fathers,
But only conscience, conscience, my good sires,
That makes me now tell truth. That parasite,

That knave, hath been the instrument of all.
  1 Avoc. Where is that knave? Fetch him.
  Volp.   I go.
                                  [Exit.]
  Corv.   Grave
    fathers,   20
This man's distracted; he confessed it now:
For, hoping to be old Volpone's heir,
Who now is dead—
  3 Avoc.   How!
  2 Avoc.   Is Volpone dead?
  Corv. Dead since, grave fathers.
  Bon.   O sure vengeance!
  1 Avoc.   Stay,
Then he was no deceiver.
  Volt.   Oh, no, none:
This parasite, grave fathers.
  Corv.   He does speak
Out of mere envy 'cause the servant's made
The thing he gaped for. Please your fatherhoods,
This is the truth, though I'll not justify
The other, but he may be some-deal[2] faulty.   30
  Volt. Ay, to your hopes, as well as mine, Corvino.
But I'll use modesty. Pleaseth your wisdoms,
To view these certain[3] notes, and but confer[4] them;
And as I hope favor, they shall speak clear truth.
  Corv. The devil has entered him!
  Bon.   Or bides in you.
  4 Avoc. We have done ill, by a public officer
To send for him, if he be heir.
  2 Avoc.   For whom?
  4 Avoc. Him that they call the parasite.
  3 Avoc.   'Tis true,
He is a man of great estate, now left.
  4 Avoc. Go you, and learn his name, and say the
    court   40
Entreats his presence here, but to the clearing
Of some few doubts.
                          [Exit Notario.]
  2 Avoc.   This same's a labyrinth!
  1 Avoc. Stand you unto your first report?
  Corv.   My state,
My life, my fame—
  Bon.   Where is it?
  Corv.   Are at the stake.
  1 Avoc. Is yours so too?
  Corb.   The advocate's a knave,
And has a forkèd tongue—
  2 Avoc.   Speak to the point.
  Corb. So is the parasite too.
  1 Avoc.   This is confusion.
  Volt. I do beseech your fatherhoods, read but those—
  Corv. And credit nothing the false spirit hath writ.
It cannot be but he's possessed, grave fathers. 50
                            [Exeunt.]

[V.vi]

[Enter VOLPONE.]

  Volp. To make a snare for mine own neck! and run
My head into it, willfully! with laughter!

When I had newly 'scaped, was free and clear!
Out of mere wantonness! Oh, the dull devil
Was in this brain of mine when I devised it,
And Mosca gave it second; he must now
Help to sear up[1] this vein, or we bleed dead.

[Enter NANO, ANDROGYNO, *and* CASTRONE.]

How now! who let you loose? Whither go you now?
What, to buy gingerbread, or to drown kitlings?[2]
  Nano. Sir, Master Mosca called us out of doors, 10
And bid us all go play, and took the keys.
  Andr.   Yes.
  Volp. Did Master Mosca take the keys? Why, so!
I'm farther in. These are my fine conceits![3]
I must be merry, with a mischief to me!
What a vile wretch was I, that could not bear
My fortune soberly? I must ha' my crochets,
And my conundrums! Well, go you, and seek him.
His meaning may be truer than my fear.
Bid him, he straight come to me to the court;
Thither will I, and, if 't be possible,   20
Unscrew my advocate, upon new hopes.
When I provoked him, then I lost myself.
                          [Exeunt.]

[V.vii]

[Four Avocatori, BONARIO, CELIA, CORBACCIO,
CORVINO, Commandadori, Saffi, etc., *as before.]*

  1 Avoc. These things can ne'er be reconciled. He
    here
Professeth that the gentleman was wronged,
And that the gentlewoman was brought thither,
Forced by her husband, and there left.
  Volt.   Most true.
  Cel. How ready is heaven to those that pray!
  1 Avoc.   But that
Volpone would have ravished her, he holds
Utterly false, knowing his impotence.
  Corv. Grave fathers, he is possessed; again, I say,
Possessed. Nay, if there be possession and
Obsession[1] he has both.
  3 Avoc.   Here comes our officer. 10

[Enter VOLPONE.]

  Volp. The parasite will straight be here, grave
    fathers.
  4 Avoc. You might invent some other name, sir
    varlet.
  3 Avoc. Did not the notary meet him?
  Volp.   Not that I know.
  4 Avoc. His coming will clear all.
  2 Avoc.   Yet it is misty.

---

    [2] *some-deal:* somewhat.   [3] *certain:* particular.
    [4] *confer:* compare.
V.vi.
    [1] *sear up:* cauterize.   [2] *kitlings:* kittens.
    [3] *conceits:* imaginings, stratagems.
V.vii.
    [1] *possession . . . Obsession:* the evil spirit controlling from
within; and attacking from without.

Volt. May't please your fatherhoods—

VOLPONE *whispers the Advocate.*

Volp.   Sir, the parasite
Willed me to tell you that his master lives;
That you are still the man; your hopes the same;
And this was only a jest—
    Volt.   How?
    Volp.   Sir, to try
If you were firm, and how you stood affected.
    Volt. Art sure he lives?
    Volp.   Do I live, sir?
    Volt.   Oh, me!   20
I was too violent.
    Volp.   Sir, you may redeem it.
They said you were possessed. Fall down, and seem
    so.
I'll help to make it good.

VOLTORE *falls.*

God bless the man
Stop your wind hard, and swell—See, see, see, see!
He vomits crooked pins! [2] His eyes are set,
Like a dead hare's hung in a poulter's shop!
His mouth's running away! [3] Do you see, signior?
Now it is in his belly.
    Corb.   Ay, the devil!
    Volp. Now in his throat.
    Corv.   Ay, I perceive it plain.
    Volt. 'Twill out, 'twill out! stand clear. See where it
    flies,   30
In shape of a blue toad, with a bat's wings!
Do you not see it, sir?
    Corb.   What? I think I do.
    Corv. 'Tis too manifest.
    Volp.   Look! He comes to himself!
    Volt. Where am I?
    Volp.   Take good heart, the worst is past, sir.
You are possessed.
    1 Avoc.   What accident is this!
    2 Avoc. Sudden, and full of wonder!
    3 Avoc.   If he were
Possessed, as it appears, all this is nothing.
    Corv. He has been often subject to these fits.
    1 Avoc. Show him that writing:—do you know it,
    sir?
    Volp. [*Whispers* VOLTORE.] Deny it, sir, forswear
    it; know it not.   40
    Volt. Yes, I do know it well, it is my hand;
But all that it contains is false.
    Bon.   O practice!
    2 Avoc. What maze is this!
    1 Avoc.   Is he not guilty then,
Whom you there name the parasite?
    Volt.   Grave fathers,
No more than his good patron, old Volpone.
    4 Avoc. Why, he is dead.
    Volt.   Oh, no, my honored fathers,

He lives—
    1 Avoc. How! lives?
    Volt.   Lives.
    2 Avoc.   This is subtler yet!
    3 Avoc. You said he was dead.
    Volt.   Never.
    3 Avoc.   You said so.
    Corv.   I
    heard so.
    4 Avoc. Here comes the gentleman; make him way.

[*Enter* MOSCA.]

    3 Avoc.   A
    stool.
    4 Avoc. [*Aside*] A proper [4] man; and were Volpone
    dead,   50
A fit match for my daughter.
    3 Avoc.   Give him way.
    Volp. [*Aside to* MOSCA] Mosca, I was almost lost;
    the advocate
Had betrayed all; but now it is recovered.
All's on the hinge again—Say I am living.
    Mos. What busy knave is this!—Most reverend
    fathers,
I sooner had attended your grave pleasures,
But that my order for the funeral
Of my dear patron did require me—
    Volp. [*Aside*]   Mosca!
    Mos. Whom I intend to bury like a gentleman.
    Volp. [*Aside*] Ay, quick, [5] and cozen me of all.
    2 Avoc.   Still
    stranger!   60
More intricate!
    1 Avoc.   And come about again!
    4 Avoc. [*Aside*] It is a match, my daughter is
    bestowed.
    Mos. [*Aside to* VOLPONE] Will you give me half?
    Volp.   First
    I'll be hanged.
    Mos.   I know
Your voice is good, cry not so loud.
    1 Avoc.   Demand [6]
The advocate.—Sir, did not you affirm
Volpone was alive?
    Volp.   Yes, and he is;
This gentleman told me so. [*Aside to* MOSCA] Thou
    shalt have half.
    Mos. Whose drunkard is this same? Speak, some
    that know him.
I never saw his face. [*Aside to* VOLPONE] I cannot now
Afford it you so cheap.
    Volp.   No!
    1 Avoc.   What say you?   70
    Volt. The officer told me.
    Volp.   I did, grave fathers,
And will maintain he lives, with mine own life,
And that this creature told me. [*Aside*] I was born
With all good stars my enemies.
    Mos.   Most grave fathers,
If such an insolence as this must pass
Upon me, I am silent; 'twas not this

---

[2] *He . . . pins:* as bewitched persons were supposed to do.
[3] *running away:* contorted.   [4] *proper:* handsome.
[5] *quick:* alive.   [6] *Demand:* Question.

For which you sent, I hope.

2 Avoc.   Take him away.

Volp. Mosca!

3 Avoc.   Let him be whipped.

Volp.   Wilt thou betray me?
Cozen me?

3 Avoc. And taught to bear himself
Toward a person of his rank.

4 Avoc.   Away   80

[The Officers *seize* Volpone.]

Mos. I humbly thank your fatherhoods.

Volp. [*Aside*]   Soft, soft:
    whipped!
And lose all that I have! If I confess,
It cannot be much more.

4 Avoc.   Sir, are you married?

Volp. They'll be allied anon: I must be resolute.

He puts off his disguise.

The Fox shall here uncase.

Mos.   Patron!

Volp.   Nay, now
My ruin shall not come alone; your match
I'll hinder sure. My substance shall not glue you,
Nor screw you into a family.

Mos.   Why, patron!

Volp. I am Volpone, and this is my knave;
This [*Pointing to* Voltore], his own knave; this
    [*To* Corbaccio], avarice's fool;   90
This [*To* Corvino], a chimera[7] of wittol, fool, and
    knave.
And, reverend fathers, since we all can hope
Nought but a sentence, let's not now despair it.
You hear me brief.

Corv.   May it please your fatherhoods—

Comm. Silence.

1 Avoc.   The knot is now undone by miracle.

2 Avoc. Nothing can be more clear.

3 Avoc.   Or can more prove
These innocent.

1 Avoc.   Give 'hem their liberty.

Bon. Heaven could not long let such gross crimes be
    hid.

2 Avoc. If this be held the highway to get riches,
May I be poor!

3 Avoc.   This is not the gain, but torment.   100

1 Avoc. These possess wealth, as sick men possess
    fevers,
Which trulier may be said to possess them.

2 Avoc. Disrobe that parasite.

Corv., Mos.   Most honored fathers—

1 Avoc. Can you plead aught to stay the course of
    justice?
If you can, speak.

Corv., Volt.   We beg favor.

Cel.   And mercy.

1 Avoc. You hurt your innocence, suing for the
    guilty.
Stand forth; and first the parasite. You appear
T'have been the chiefest minister, if not plotter,

In all these lewd impostures, and now, lastly,
Have with your impudence abused the court,   110
And habit of a gentleman of Venice,
Being a fellow of no birth or blood.
For which our sentence is, first, thou be whipped;
Then live a perpetual prisoner in our galleys.

Volp. I thank you for him.

Mos.   Bane to thy wolfish nature!

1 Avoc. Deliver him to the Saffi.

[Mosca *is carried out.*]
           Thou, Volpone,
By blood and rank a gentleman, canst not fall
Under like censure; but our judgment on thee
Is, that thy substance[8] all be straight confiscate
To the hospital of the Incurabili.   120
And since the most was gotten by imposture,
By feigning lame, gout, palsy, and such diseases,
Thou art to lie in prison, cramped with irons,
Till thou be'st sick and lame indeed. Remove him.

Volp. This is called mortifying[9] of a Fox.

[Volpone *is taken away.*]

1 Avoc. Thou, Voltore, to take away the scandal,
Thou hast given all worthy men of thy profession,
Art banished from their fellowship, and our state.
Corbaccio!—bring him near. We here possess
Thy son of all thy state, and confine thee   130
To the monastery of San Spirito;
Where, since thou knew'st not how to live well here,
Thou shalt be learned to die well.

Corb.   Ha! what said he?

Comm. You shall know anon, sir.

1 Avoc.   Thou, Corvino,
    shalt
Be straight embarked from thine own house, and
    rowed
Round about Venice, through the Grand Canal,
Wearing a cap, with fair long ass's ears,
Instead of horns! and so to mount, a paper
Pinned on thy breast, to the berlina.[10]

Corv.   Yes,
And have mine eyes beat out with stinking fish,   140
Bruised fruit, and rotten eggs—'tis well. I am glad
I shall not see my shame yet.

1 Avoc.   And to expiate
Thy wrongs done to thy wife, thou art to send her
Home to her father, with her dowry trebled.
And these are all your judgments.

All.   Honored fathers—

1 Avoc. Which may not be revoked. Now you
    begin,
When crimes are done, and past, and to be punished,
To think what your crimes are. Away with them.
Let all that see these vices thus rewarded,
Take heart, and love to study 'hem. Mischiefs feed
Like beasts, till they be fat, and then they bleed.   151

[*Exeunt.*]

---

[7] *chimera:* fabled monster.   [8] *substance:* goods.
[9] *mortifying:* pun; fowl are "mortified" or made tender
by hanging them up for some time after they have been
killed.   [10] *berlina:* pillory.

VOLPONE [*comes forward*].

The seasoning of a play is the applause.
Now, though the Fox be punished by the laws,
He yet doth hope, there is no suffering due,
For any fact [11] which he hath done 'gainst you.
If there be, censure him; here he doubtful stands.
If not, fare jovially, and clap your hands.

[*Exit.*]

F I N I S

---

[11] *fact:* crime.

Ben Jonson

EPICOENE; OR, THE SILENT WOMAN

JONSON'S EPICOENE; OR, THE SILENT WOMAN was written probably in 1609. The play was first performed at the Whitefriars theater by the Children of Her Majesty's Revels in that year, and not apparently to unreserved applause. As Jonson suggests in a subsequent prologue, he had been taken—falsely, he claims—as libeling contemporary persons under the guise of his dramatis personae. (See, in this connection, II.iii, n. 35.) EPICOENE was entered for publication in the Stationers' Register on September 20, 1610. The text on which this edition is based is that of the Folio of 1616—necessarily, for the supposed quarto editions of 1609 and 1612 are no longer extant. Jonson says, however, in his dedication to the Folio version, that not a line or syllable in it differs "from the simplicity of the first copy." As in our edition of VOLPONE, the excessively meticulous division into scenes has been scanted. Only when the place shifts is the scene understood to change. Jonson's own stage directions were positioned in the Folio in the outside margin opposite the relevant speeches. This is a style we cannot preserve in our format; since it is necessary to confine all stage directions to the text area, Jonson's directions have usually been placed after the speeches to which they refer.

The plot is reminiscent of VOLPONE and looks forward to THE ALCHEMIST in its strict adherence to the unities of place and time. A single day suffices for the story Jonson presents. His London settings, though various, are generically one. EPICOENE is unlike Jonson's earlier comedies in that, except for the songs, it is written throughout in prose.

Borrowings, as before, are manifold. Shakespeare's enacting in *Twelfth Night* of the mock combat between Viola and Sir Andrew Aguecheek provides the basis for the duel between La Foole and Sir John Daw. The comic story of the morose protagonist who is tricked into marrying a garrulous wife is old and familiar. Jonson came to it by way of the Greek sophist Libanius, a writer of the early Christian centuries. Other sources include Ovid, in his love poetry, the Roman comic dramatists Plautus and Terence, and the Roman satirists Juvenal and Martial.

With the reopening of the theaters at the Restoration, EPICOENE was recognized widely for the great stage success it is, exciting particularly the admiration of John Dryden. It ought to excite the admiration of audiences in the twentieth century, for it is a highly contemporary play (signifying partly that it is not for an age but for all time) that addresses itself with uncommon frankness and a vigorous and sophisticated sensibility to the mores of the early seventeenth century. This cankered period, in its curious mixture of brutal candor and hypocrisy, bears uncanny comparison with our own. Jonson is always an unillusioned writer, whatever the material that engages his attention. Here his cold and penetrating eye is turned on the amatory encounters of men and women who pretend to gentility. These encounters are the obverse of romantic and suggest little of the gentle heart. The hallmark of EPICOENE, which distinguishes it from the great comedies it precedes and follows, is its sexual toughness. The witty dialogue manifests an indurated character that is at a remove from the exuberant cynicism of VOLPONE or THE ALCHEMIST. Compare, for example, Truewit's long discourse on the technique of seducing a woman, in IV.i; or, in the following scene, the unsentimental treatment by the ladies of the College of contraception and extramarital affairs. Sheridan, who creates his own College or School for Scandal two centuries later, is simply not in it. Reading this play, we look forward irresistibly to certain Restoration comedies, like *The Country Wife*, *The Plain Dealer*, *The Man of Mode*, Dryden's *Marriage à la Mode*. Wycherley, Etherege, and Dryden bring their own true fire, in Jonson's phrase, to the comedy of sexual and fiscal intrigue. Their obvious antecedent is, however, the mordant psychologist of THE SILENT WOMAN. Jonson, who on his own ground has no equal among Jacobean playwrights, is also unique in impressing his peculiar temper on the drama of the age that is to come.

R. A. F.

Epicoene; or, The Silent Woman

[THE DEDICATION]

To the truly Noble, by all Titles.

Sir FRANCIS STUART[1]

Sir,

My hope is not so nourished by example, as it will conclude this dumb piece should please you, by cause[2] it hath pleased others before; but by trust, that when you have read it, you will find it worthy to have displeased none. This makes[3] that I now number you, not only in the names of favor, but the names of justice, to what I write; and do, presently, call you to the exercise of that noblest, and, manliest virtue: as coveting rather to be freed in my fame by the authority of a judge, than the credit of an undertaker.[4] Read therefore, I pray you, and censure.[5] There is not a line, or syllable in it changed from the simplicity of the first copy. And, when you shall consider, through the certain hatred of some, how much a man's innocency may be endangered by an uncertain accusation, you will, I doubt not, so begin to hate the iniquity of such natures, as I shall love the contumely[6] done me, whose end was so honorable, as to be wiped off by your sentence.

Your unprofitable, but true lover,[7]

Ben Jonson.

DRAMATIS PERSONÆ[1]

Morose, *a gentleman that loves no noise*
Sir Dauphine Eugenie, *a knight, his nephew*
Ned Clerimont, *a gentleman, his friend*
Truewit, *another friend*
Epicoene, *supposed the Silent Woman, a young gentleman*
Sir John Daw, *a knight*
Sir Amorous La Foole, *a knight also*
Thomas Otter, *a land and sea captain*
Cutbeard, *a barber*

Mute, *one of Morose's servants*
Page to Clerimont
Madame Haughty,
Madame Centaure, } *Ladies Collegiates*[2]
Mistress Dol Mavis,
Mistress Trusty, *the Lady Haughty's woman,* } *Pretenders*[3]
Mistress Otter, *the Captain's wife,*
Parson, Pages, Servants

The Scene: London

THE PROLOGUE

Truth says, of old the art of making plays
  Was to content the people; and their praise
  Was to the poet money, wine, and bays.[1]
But in this age a sect of writers are
  That only for particular likings care,
  And will taste nothing that is popular.
With such we mingle neither brains nor breasts;[2]
  Our wishes, like to those[3] make public feasts,
  Are not to please the cook's taste but the guests.
Yet if those cunning palates hither come,   10
  They shall find guests' entreaty,[4] and good room;
  And though all relish not, sure there will be some,
That when they leave their seats shall make 'hem say,
  Who wrote that piece, could so have wrote a play,
  But that he knew this was the better way.

DEDICATION
  [1] *Sir Francis Stuart:* Sea captain and drinking companion of Jonson's at the Mermaid Tavern.   [2] *by cause:* because.
  [3] *makes:* is the reason.   [4] *undertaker:* guarantor.
  [5] *censure:* judge.   [6] *contumely:* insult.
  [7] *lover:* i.e., friend (no erotic suggestion).

DRAMATIS PERSONÆ
  [1] *Dramatis Personæ:* Amplified from Folio listing.
  [2] *Ladies Collegiates:* Members of a particular set or society.   [3] *Pretenders:* Aspirants, candidates.

THE PROLOGUE
  [1] *bays:* laurels, sacred to poetry.
  [2] *With . . . breasts:* We do not consult the exotic taste of such writers.   [3] *those:* i.e., those who.
  [4] *entreaty:* entertainment.

For, to present all custard or all tart,
  And have no other meats to bear a part,
  Or to want bread and salt, were but coarse art.
The poet prays you then, with better thought
  To sit; and when his cates[5] are all in brought, 20
  Though there be none far-fet,[6] there will dear-
     bought,[7]

Be fit for ladies: some for lords, knights, squires;
  Some for your waiting-wench, and city-wires;[8]
  Some for your men, and daughters of Whitefriars.[9]
Nor is it only while you keep your seat
  Here that his feast will last; but you shall eat
  A week at ord'naries[10] on his broken meat:
      If his muse be true,
      Who commends her to you.

ANOTHER

OCCASIONED BY SOME PERSONS' IMPERTINENT EXCEPTION

The ends of all, who for the scene do write,
Are, or should be, to profit and delight.
And still 't hath been the praise of all best times,
So persons were not touched[1] to tax[2] the crimes.
Then in this play, which we present tonight,
And make the object of your ear and sight,
On forfeit of yourselves,[3] think nothing true:
Lest so you make the maker to judge you.
For he knows, poet never credit gained
By writing truths, but things, like truths, well feigned,
If any yet will, with particular sleight   11
Of application, wrest[4] what he doth write;
And that he meant, or him, or her, will say:
They make a libel, which he made a play.

ACT ONE

SCENE ONE

[Enter] CLERIMONT, Boy.

Cler. Ha' you got the song yet perfect I gave you, boy?

He comes out making himself ready.

Boy. Yes, sir.
Cler. Let me hear it.
Boy. You shall, sir; but i' faith let nobody else.

Cler. Why, I pray?
Boy. It will get you the dangerous name of a poet in town, sir; besides me a perfect deal of ill-will at the mansion you wot[1] of, whose lady is the argument[2] of it; where now I am the welcomest thing under a man that comes there.   11
Cler. I think;[3] and above a man too, if the truth were racked[4] out of you.
Boy. No, faith, I'll confess before, sir. The gentlewomen play with me, and throw me o' the bed, and carry me in to my lady; and she kisses me with her oiled face, and puts a peruke[5] o' my head; and asks me an[6] I will wear her gown? And I say no; and then she hits me a blow o' the ear, and calls me innocent, and lets me go.   20
Cler. No marvel if the door be kept shut against your master, when the entrance is so easy to you—Well, sir, you shall go there no more, lest I be fain to seek your voice in my lady's rushes[7] a fortnight hence. Sing, sir.

                           Boy *sings.*

[*Still to be neat, still to be dressed*]—

[*Enter* TRUEWIT.]

Tru. Why, here's the man that can melt away his time, and never feels it! what between his mistress abroad and his ingle[8] at home, high fare, soft lodging, fine clothes, and his fiddle; he thinks the hours ha' no wings, or the day no post-horse. Well, sir gallant, were   30

---

  [5] *cates*: delicacies.   [6] *far-fet*: fetched from afar.
  [7] *dear-bought*: costly.
  [8] *city-wires*: pretentious citizens' wives, who supported with wire the fashionable ruffs they wore about their necks.
  [9] *daughters of Whitefriars*: presumably whores, who enjoyed in this unsavory district the immunity once accorded to the church of the Carmelites or Whitefriars. So *Volpone*, IV.i, n. 42, p. 84.   [10] *ord'naries*: taverns.

ALTERNATE PROLOGUE
  [1] *Touched*: Singled out.   [2] *tax*: reprehend.
  [3] *On . . . yourselves*: At the risk of penalty to yourselves.
  [4] *wrest*: twist, as by sleight of hand, to personal satire.

I.i.
  [1] *wot*: know.   [2] *argument*: subject.
  [3] *I think*: So I think.   [4] *racked*: tortured.
  [5] *peruke*: wig.   [6] *an*: if.
  [7] *rushes*: which covered the floor.
  [8] *ingle*: catamite (homosexual lover).

you struck with the plague this minute, or condemned to any capital punishment tomorrow, you would begin then to think, and value every article o' your time, esteem it at the true rate, and give all for it.

Cler. Why, what should a man do?

Tru. Why, nothing; or that which, when 'tis done, is as idle. Hearken after the next horse-race, or hunting-match, lay wagers, praise Puppy, or Pepper-corn, Whitefoot, Franklin; swear upon White-mane's[9] party; spend aloud, that my lords may hear you; visit   40 my ladies at night, and be able to give 'hem the character of every bowler or better o' the green. These be the things wherein your fashionable men exercise themselves, and I for company.[10]

Cler. Nay, if I have thy authority, I'll not leave[11] yet. Come, the other are considerations,[12] when we come to have gray heads and weak hams, moist eyes and shrunk members.[13] We'll think on 'hem then; then we'll pray and fast.   49

Tru. Ay, and destine only that time of age to goodness, which our want of ability will not let us employ in evil!

Cler. Why, then 'tis time enough.

Tru. Yes; as if a man should sleep all the term,[14] and think to effect his business the last day. O Clerimont, this time, because it is an incorporeal thing, and not subject to sense, we mock ourselves the fineliest[15] out of it, with vanity and misery indeed, not seeking an end of wretchedness, but only changing the matter still.

Cler. Nay, thou'lt not leave now—   60

Tru. See but our common disease![16] with what justice can we complain, that great men will not look upon us, nor be at leisure to give our affairs such dispatch as we expect, when we will never do it to ourselves? Nor hear, nor regard ourselves?

Cler. Foh! thou hast read Plutarch's *Morals*,[17] now, or some such tedious fellow; and it shows so vilely with thee, 'fore God, 'twill spoil thy wit utterly. Talk to me of pins, and feathers, and ladies, and rushes,[18] and such things; and leave this stoicity[19] alone till thou makest sermons.   71

Tru. Well, sir; if it will not take, I have learned to lose as little of my kindness as I can. I'll do good to no man against his will, certainly. When were you at the college?

Cler. What college?

Tru. As if you knew not!

Cler. No, faith, I came but from court yesterday.

Tru. Why, is it not arrived there yet, the news? A new foundation, sir, here i' the town, of ladies, that   80 call themselves the collegiates, an order between courtiers and country-madams, that live from[20] their husbands; and give entertainment to all the wits, and braveries[21] o' the time, as they call 'hem: cry down, or up, what they like or dislike in a brain or a fashion, with most masculine, or rather hermaphroditical[22] authority; and every day gain to their college some new probationer.[23]

Cler. Who is the president?

Tru. The grave and youthful matron, the Lady Haughty.   90

Cler. A pox of her autumnal face, her pieced[24]

beauty! there's no man can be admitted till she be ready now-a-days, till she has painted, and perfumed, and washed, and scoured, but the boy here; and him she wipes her oiled lips upon, like a sponge. I have made a song. I pray thee hear it, o' the subject.

SONG.[25]

Still to be neat, still to be dressed,
As you were going to a feast;
Still to be powdered, still perfumed:
Lady, is it to be presumed,   100
Though art's hid causes are not found,
All is not sweet, all is not sound.

Give me a look, give me a face,
That makes simplicity a grace;
Robes loosely flowing, hair as free:
Such sweet neglect more taketh me,
Than all the adulteries[26] of art.
They strike mine eyes, but not my heart.

Tru. And I am clearly o' the other side: I love a good dressing before any beauty o' the world. Oh, a   110 woman is then like a delicate garden; nor is there one kind of it. She may vary every hour; take often counsel of her glass, and choose the best. If she have good ears, show 'em; good hair, lay it out; good legs, wear short clothes; a good hand, discover[27] it often; practice any art to mend breath, cleanse teeth, repair eyebrows; paint and profess[28] it.

Cler. How! publicly?

Tru. The doing of it, not the manner: that must be private. Many things that seem foul i' the doing,   120 do please done.[29] A lady should, indeed, study her face, when we think she sleeps; nor, when the doors are shut, should men be inquiring; all is sacred within then. Is it for us to see their perukes put on, their false teeth, their complexion, their eyebrows, their nails? You see gilders[30] will not work, but enclosed.[31] They must not

---

[9] *Puppy . . . White-mane's:* Jonson notes in margin: "Horses o' the time."

[10] *for company:* i.e., distraction, amusement.

[11] *leave:* leave off.

[12] *considerations:* worth considering.

[13] *members:* genitals.

[14] *term:* when the law courts were sitting.

[15] *fineliest:* in the finest manner.

[16] *disease:* infirmity, vice.

[17] *Morals:* Philemon Holland's translation of this homiletic treatise had been published in 1603.

[18] *rushes:* here, things of no account.

[19] *stoicity:* stoicism.   [20] *from:* apart from.

[21] *braveries:* gallants.

[22] *hermaphroditical:* both masculine and feminine.

[23] *probationer:* novice, newly initiated.

[24] *pieced:* pieced out, as by cosmetics.

[25] *Song:* When in the opening lines of this scene, Clerimont commands his page to sing and the boy complies, it is plausible to suppose that he utters a few lines from what follows here.   [26] *adulteries:* tricks, like face painting.

[27] *discover:* show.   [28] *profess:* acknowledge.

[29] *done:* when done.

[30] *gilders:* those who paint or adorn.

[31] *but enclosed:* unless they are in private.

discover how little serves, with the help of art, to adorn a great deal. How long did the canvas hang afore Aldgate? Were the people suffered to see the city's Love and Charity,[32] while they were rude stone, before 130 they were painted and burnished? No; no more should servants approach their mistresses, but when they are complete and finished.

Cler. Well said, my Truewit.

Tru. And a wise lady will keep a guard always upon the place, that she may do things securely. I once followed a rude fellow into a chamber, where the poor madam, for haste, and troubled, snatched at her peruke to cover her baldness, and put it on the wrong way.

Cler. O prodigy![33]   140

Tru. And the unconscionable knave held her in compliment an hour with that reversed face, when I still[34] looked when she should talk from the other side.

Cler. Why, thou shouldst ha' relieved her.

Tru. No, faith, I let her alone, as we'll let this argument, if you please, and pass to another. When saw you Dauphine Eugenie?

Cler. Not these three days. Shall we go to him this morning? He is very melancholic, I hear.   149

Tru. Sick o' the uncle,[35] is he? I met that stiff piece of formality, his uncle, yesterday, with a huge turban of nightcaps on his head, buckled over his ears.

Cler. Oh, that's his custom when he walks abroad. He can endure no noise, man.

Tru. So I have heard. But is the disease so ridiculous in him as it is made?[36] They say he has been upon divers treaties[37] with the fish-wives and orange-women; and articles propounded between them: marry, the chimney-sweepers will not be drawn in.   159

Cler. No, nor the broom-men; they stand out stiffly. He cannot endure a costard-monger,[38] he swoons if he hear one.

Tru. Methinks a smith should be ominous.

Cler. Or any hammer man.[39] A brazier[40] is not suffered to dwell in the parish, nor an armorer. He would have hanged a pewterer's 'prentice once upon a Shrove-Tuesday's riot,[41] for being o' that trade, when the rest were quit.[42]

Tru. A trumpet should fright him terribly, or the hautboys.[43]   170

Cler. Out of his senses. The waits[44] of the city have a pension of him not to come near that ward. This youth practised on[45] him one night like the bellman;[46] and never left till he had brought him down to the door with a long sword; and there left him flourishing with the air.

Boy. Why, sir, he hath chosen a street to lie in so narrow at both ends that it will receive no coaches, nor carts, nor any of these common noises: and therefore we that love him devise to bring him in such as we 180 may, now and then, for his exercise, to breathe him. He would grow resty[47] else in his ease. His virtue would rust without action. I entreated a bearward[48] one day to come down with the dogs of some four parishes that way, and I thank him he did; and cried his games under Master Morose's window:[49] till he was sent crying away with his head made a most bleeding spectacle to the multitude. And another time, a fencer marching to his prize[50] had his drum most tragically run through, for taking that street in his way at my request.   190

Tru. A good wag! how does he for the bells?[51]

Cler. Oh, i' the Queen's time, he was wont to go out of town every Saturday at ten o'clock, or on holyday eves. But now, by reason of the sickness, the perpetuity of ringing[52] has made him devise a room, with double walls and treble ceilings; the windows close shut and caulked; and there he lives by candlelight. He turned away a man last week, for having a pair of new shoes that creaked. And this fellow waits on him now in tennis-court socks,[53] or slippers soled with wool: 200 and they talk each to other in a trunk.[54] See, who comes here?

[*Enter* Sir Dauphine Eugenie.]

Dauph. How now! what ail you, sirs? Dumb?

Tru. Struck into stone, almost, I am here, with tales o' thine uncle. There was never such a prodigy heard of.

Dauph. I would you would once lose this subject, my masters, for my sake. They are such as you are, that have brought me into that predicament I am with him.

Tru. How is that?   209

Dauph. Marry, that he will disinherit me; no more. He thinks I and my company are authors of all the ridiculous Acts and Monuments[55] are told of him.

Tru. 'Slid,[56] I would be the author of more to vex him; that purpose deserves it: it gives thee law[57] of plaguing him. I'll tell thee what I would do. I would make a false almanack, get it printed; and then have him drawn out on a coronation day to the Tower-wharf, and kill him with the noise of the ordnance.[58] Disinherit thee! he cannot, man. Art thou next of blood, and his sister's son?   220

Dauph. Ay, but he will thrust me out of it, he vows, and marry.

---

[32] *canvas . . . Charity:* Jonson refers to the construction of a pair of statues adorning one of the gates in the old London wall and concealed from the public until finished.

[33] *prodigy:* miracle.   [34] *still:* continually.

[35] *sick . . . uncle:* hysterical (Jonson's private joke by analogy to the familiar malady known as "the mother"); also the literal uncle, Morose.   [36] *made:* made out to be.

[37] *treaties:* Morose has sought to persuade the street vendors not to cry their wares.

[38] *costard-monger:* seller of apples.

[39] *hammer man:* metal worker.   [40] *brazier:* brass worker.

[41] *riot:* On Shrove Tuesday, in preface to the abstinence of Lent, merry making was common.   [42] *quit:* acquitted.

[43] *hautboys:* "oboes"—by extension, "oboe player," here "street musicians."   [44] *waits:* street musicians.

[45] *practised on:* deluded.   [46] *bellman:* night watchman.

[47] *resty:* lazy.   [48] *bearward:* keeper of tame bears.

[49] *window: here and hereafter for "windore" in original.*

[50] *prize:* fencing match.   [51] *bells:* church bells.

[52] *sickness . . . ringing:* deaths from the protracted plague cause the church bells to ring constantly.

[53] *tennis-court socks:* woolen slippers, and hence silent.

[54] *trunk:* speaking tube.

[55] *Acts and Monuments:* The title of John Foxe's famous Protestant hagiographical *Book of Martyrs,* first published 1554.   [56] *'Slid:* i.e., God's lid.

[57] *gives thee law:* authorizes you.

[58] *ordnance:* shooting of guns.

Tru. How! that's a more[59] portent. Can he endure no noise, and will venture on a wife?

Cler. Yes: why, thou art a stranger, it seems, to his best trick yet. He has employed a fellow this half-year all over England to hearken him out a dumb[60] woman; be she of any form, or any quality, so she be able to bear children: her silence is dowry enough, he says.

Tru. But I trust to God he has found none.   230

Cler. No: but he has heard of one that's lodged i' the next street to him, who is exceedingly soft-spoken; thrifty of her speech; that spends but six words a day. And her he's about now, and shall have her.

Tru. Is't possible! who is his agent i' the business?

Cler. Marry, a barber, one Cutbeard; an honest fellow, one that tells Dauphine all here.

Tru. Why, you oppress me with wonder; a woman, and a barber, and love no noise!   239

Cler. Yes, faith. The fellow trims him[61] silently, and has not the knack with his shears or his fingers;[62] and that continence in a barber he thinks so eminent a virtue, as it has made him chief of his counsel.

Tru. Is the barber to be seen, or the wench?

Cler. Yes, that they are.

Tru. I pray thee, Dauphine, let's go thither.

Dauph. I have some business now, I cannot, i' faith.

Tru. You shall have no business shall make you neglect this, sir; we'll make her talk, believe it; or, if she will not, we can give out at least so much as shall   250 interrupt the treaty; we will break it. Thou art bound in conscience, when he suspects thee without cause, to torment him.

Dauph. Not I, by any means. I'll give no suffrage to't. He shall never ha' that plea against me, that I opposed the least fant'sy of his. Let it lie upon my stars to be guilty,[63] I'll be innocent.

Tru. Yes, and be poor, and beg; do, innocent: when some groom of his has got him an heir, or this barber, if he himself cannot. Innocent! I prithee, Ned, where lies she? Let him be innocent still.   261

Cler. Why, right over against the barber's; in the house where Sir John Daw lies.

Tru. You do not mean to confound me!

Cler. Why?

Tru. Does he that would marry her know so much?

Cler. I cannot tell.

Tru. 'Twere enough of imputation to[64] her with him.

Cler. Why?   270

Tru. The only talking sir i' th' town! Jack Daw! and he teach her not to speak! God b' wi' you. I have some business too.

Cler. Will you not go thither, then?

Tru. Not with the danger to meet Daw, for mine ears.

Cler. Why, I thought you two had been upon very good terms.

Tru. Yes, of keeping distance.

Cler. They say he is a very good scholar.   280

Tru. Ay, and he says it first. A pox on him, a fellow that pretends only to learning, buys titles,[65] and nothing else of books in him!

Cler. The world reports him to be very learned.

Tru. I am sorry the world should so conspire to belie him.

Cler. Good faith, I have heard very good things come from him.

Tru. You may; there's none so desperately ignorant to deny that; would they were his own! God b' wi' you, gentlemen.   291

[*Exit.*]

Cler. This is very abrupt!

Dauph. Come, you are a strange open man, to tell everything thus.

Cler. Why, believe it, Dauphine, Truewit's a very honest fellow.

Dauph. I think no other; but this frank nature of his is not for secrets.

Cler. Nay then, you are mistaken, Dauphine: I know where he has been well trusted, and discharged the trust very truly, and heartily.   301

Dauph. I contend not, Ned; but with the fewer a business is carried, it is ever the safer. Now we are alone, if you'll go thither, I am for[66] you.

Cler. When were you there?

Dauph. Last night: and such a Decameron of sport[67] fallen out! Boccace never thought of the like. Daw does nothing but court her; and the wrong way. He would lie with her, and praises her modesty; desires that she would talk and be free, and commends her   310 silence in verses; which he reads, and swears are the best that ever man made. Then rails at his fortunes, stamps, and mutines,[68] why he is not made a counselor, and called to affairs of state.

Cler. I pray thee, let's go. I would fain partake this. —Some water, boy.

[*Exit* Boy.]

Dauph. We are invited to dinner together, he and I, by one that came thither to him, Sir La Foole.

Cler. Oh, that's a precious mannikin![69]

Dauph. Do you know him?   320

Cler. Ay, and he will know you too, if e'er he saw you but once, though you should meet him at church in the midst of prayers. He is one of the braveries, though he be none o' the wits. He will salute a judge upon the bench, and a bishop in the pulpit, a lawyer when he is pleading at the bar, and a lady when she is dancing in a masque, and put her out.[70] He does give plays and suppers, and invites his guests to 'hem, aloud,

---

[59] *more:* more serious.   [60] *dumb:* silent.

[61] *trims him:* ethical dative: "him" means the manner of working.

[62] *knack . . . fingers:* Unlike other barbers, he does not snap his fingers: he is silent.

[63] *Let . . . guilty:* Even though my fate—as written in the stars—predestines my guilt.

[64] *imputation to:* an accusation against.

[65] *buys titles:* is a patron of authors, or perhaps only a name dropper, who does not read beyond the title page.

[66] *for:* with.

[67] *Decameron of sport:* like Boccaccio's amusing masterpiece.   [68] *mutines:* mutinies; rebels.

[69] *mannikin:* literally, "dummy."

[70] *out:* i.e., of countenance.

out of his window, as they ride by in coaches. He has a lodging in the Strand[71] for the purpose. Or to 330 watch when ladies are gone to the China-houses,[72] or the Exchange,[73] that he may meet 'hem by chance, and give 'hem presents, some two or three hundred pounds' worth of toys, to be laughed at. He is never without a spare banquet, or sweetmeats in his chamber, for there women to alight at, and come up to for a bait.[74]

Dauph. Excellent! he was a fine youth last night; but now he is much finer! what is his Christian name? I ha' forgot.

[*Re-enter* Boy.]

Cler. Sir Amorous La Foole.   340

Boy. The gentleman is here below that owns that name.

Cler. 'Heart, he's come to invite me to dinner, I hold[75] my life.

Dauph. Like enough: pray thee, let's ha' him up.

Cler. Boy, marshal him.

Boy. With a truncheon,[76] sir?

Cler. Away, I beseech you. [*Exit* Boy.]—I'll make him tell us his pedigree now; and what meat he has to dinner; and who are his guests; and the whole course of his fortunes, with a breath.   351

[*Enter* SIR AMOROUS LA FOOLE.]

La F. 'Save, dear Sir Dauphine, honored Master Clerimont!

Cler. Sir Amorous! you have very much honested[77] my lodging with your presence.

La F. Good faith, it is a fine lodging—almost as delicate a lodging as mine.

Cler. Not so, sir.

La. F. Excuse me, sir, if it were i' the Strand, I assure you. I am come, Master Clerimont, to entreat you wait upon[78] two or three ladies, to dinner, today.   361

Cler. How, sir! wait upon 'hem? Did you ever see me carry dishes!

---

71 *Strand:* where the gentry lived.
72 *China-houses:* places of fashionable resort, where artifacts from the East were sold.
73 *Exchange:* the New (Stock) Exchange in the Strand, built in the period when the play was being written.
74 *bait:* light repast.   75 *I hold:* On.
76 *truncheon:* marshal's staff.   77 *honested:* honored.
78 *wait upon:* "attend"; but also with suggestion of performing menial service.   79 *dispense with:* excuse.
80 *terrible boys:* bullies, always looking for a public quarrel.
81 *amphibium:* defining the previous phrase: "by sea and by land."   82 *China-woman:* dealer in china wear.
83 *coat:* of arms.
84 *or . . . azure . . . gules:* heraldic colors—gold, blue, red.
85 *brace:* pair.   86 *godwits:* marsh birds.
87 *knighted in Ireland:* not, presumably, for service but sycophancy: knighthoods conferred by Essex in the Irish campaign of 1599 were notoriously cheapened.
88 *jerkin:* short coat, usually of leather.
89 *Island voyage:* attack on the Azores, 1597.
90 *Cadiz:* "Caliz" in the original; attacked and burned by the English, 1596.
91 *take up:* any one of various meanings, all tending to aggrandize La Foole's position—"purchase" or 'borrow" or "lend" or "play the patron."
92 *your half:* half as successful as you.

La F. No, sir, dispense with[79] me; I meant, to bear 'hem company.

Cler. Oh, that I will, sir: the doubtfulness o' your phrase, believe it, sir, would breed you a quarrel once an hour with the terrible boys,[80] if you should but keep 'hem fellowship a day.   369

La F. It should be extremely against my will, sir, if I contested with any man.

Cler. I believe it, sir. Where hold you your feast?

La F. At Tom Otter's, sir.

Dauph. Tom Otter! what's he?

La F. Captain Otter, sir; he is a kind of gamester, but he has had command both by sea and by land.

Dauph. Oh, then he is *animal amphibium?*[81]

La F. Ay, sir: his wife was the rich China-woman,[82] that the courtiers visited so often; that gave the rare entertainment. She commands all at home.

Cler. Then she is Captain Otter.   381

La F. You say very well, sir; she is my kinswoman, a La Foole by the mother side, and will invite any great ladies for my sake.

Dauph. Not of the La Fooles of Essex?

La F. No, sir; the La Fooles of London.

Cler. [*Aside*] Now he's in.

La F. They all come out of our house, the La Fooles o' the north, the La Fooles of the west, the La Fooles of the east and south—we are as ancient a family 390 as any is in Europe—but I myself am descended lineally of the French La Fooles—and, we do bear for our coat[83] yellow, or *or*, checkered *azure*, and *gules*,[84] and some three or four colors more, which is a very noted coat, and has sometimes been solemnly worn by divers nobility of our house—but let that go, antiquity is not respected now.—I had a brace[85] of fat does sent me, gentlemen, and half a dozen of pheasants, a dozen or two of godwits,[86] and some other fowl, which I would have eaten, while they are good, and in 400 good company—there will be a great lady or two, my Lady Haughty, my Lady Centaure, Mistress Dol Mavis—and they come o' purpose to see the silent gentlewoman, Mistress Epicoene, that honest Sir John Daw has promised to bring thither—and then, Mistress Trusty, my lady's woman, will be there too, and this honorable knight, Sir Dauphine, with yourself, Master Clerimont —and we'll be very merry, and have fiddlers, and dance—I have been a mad wag in my time, and have spent some crowns since I was a page in 410 court, to my Lord Lofty, and after, my lady's gentleman-usher, who got me knighted in Ireland,[87] since it pleased my elder brother to die.—I had as fair a gold jerkin[88] on that day as any was worn in the Island voyage,[89] or at Cadiz,[90] none dispraised; and I came over in it hither, showed myself to my friends in court, and after went down to my tenants in the country, and surveyed my lands, let new leases, took their money, spent it in the eye o' the land here, upon ladies—and now I can take up[91] at my pleasure.   420

Dauph. Can you take up ladies, sir?

Cler. Oh, let him breathe, he has not recovered.

Dauph. Would I were your half[92] in that commodity!

La F. No, sir, excuse me: I meant money, which can

take up anything. I have another guest or two to invite, and say as much to, gentlemen. I'll take my leave abruptly, in hope you will not fail—Your servant.

[Exit.]

Dauph. We will not fail you, sir precious La Foole; but she shall, that your ladies come to see, if I have credit afore[93] Sir Daw.   430

Cler. Did you ever hear such a wind-fucker[94] as this?

Dauph. Or such a rook[95] as the other, that will betray his mistress to be seen! come, 'tis time we prevented it.

Cler. Go.

[Exeunt.]

ACT TWO

SCENE ONE

[Enter MOROSE *with a speaking tube in his hand, followed by* MUTE.]

Mor. Cannot I yet find out a more compendious[1] method, than by this trunk, to save my servants the labor of speech, and mine ears the discord of sound? Let me see: all discourses but mine own afflict me; they seem harsh, impertinent, and irksome. Is it not possible that thou shouldst answer me by signs, and I apprehend[2] thee, fellow? Speak not, though I question you. You have taken the ring off from the street door, as I bade you? Answer me not by speech, but by silence; unless it be otherwise—   10

At the breaches, still the fellow makes legs or signs.[3]

[MUTE *makes a leg.*] very good. And you have fastened on a thick quilt, or flock-bed,[4] on the outside of the door; that if they knock with their daggers, or with brickbats, they can make no noise?—But[5] with your leg, your answer, unless it be otherwise. [*Makes a leg.*]—Very good. This is not only fit modesty in a servant, but good state and discretion in a master. And you have been with Cutbeard the barber, to have him come to me? [*Makes a leg.*]—Good. And he will come presently?[6] Answer me not but with your leg,   20 unless it be otherwise: if it be otherwise, shake your head, or shrug. [*Makes a leg.*]—So!Your Italian and Spaniard[7] are wise in these: and it is a frugal and comely gravity. How long will it be ere Cutbeard come? Stay; if an hour, hold up your whole hand; if half an hour, two fingers; if a quarter, one. [*Holds up a finger bent.*]— Good: half a quarter? 'Tis well. And have you given him a key, to come in without knocking? [*Makes a leg.*] —Good. And is the lock oiled, and the hinges, today? [*Makes a leg.*]—Good. And the quilting of the stairs   30 nowhere worn out and bare? [*Makes a leg.*]—Very good. I see, by much doctrine and impulsion[8] it may be effected; stand by. The Turk, in this divine discipline, is admirable, exceeding all the potentates of the earth; still waited on by mutes; and all his commands so executed; yea, even in the war, as I have heard, and in his marches, most of his charges and directions given by signs, and with silence: an exquisite art! and I am heartily ashamed, and angry oftentimes, that the princes of Christendom should suffer a barbarian to   40

transcend 'hem in so high a point of felicity. I will practise it hereafter.

One winds a horn without.

—How now? Oh! oh! what villain, what prodigy of mankind is that? Look.

[Exit MUTE. *Horn] Again.*

Oh, cut his throat, cut his throat! what murderer, hellbound, devil can this be?

[Re-enter MUTE.]

Mute. It is a post[9] from the court—

Mor. Out, rogue! and must thou blow thy horn too?

Mute. Alas, it is a post from the court, sir, that says he must speak with you, pain of death—   50

Mor. Pain of thy life, be silent!

[Enter TRUEWIT.]

Tru. By your leave, sir;—I am a stranger here—Is your name Master Morose? Is your name Master Morose? Fishes? Pythagoreans[10] all! this is strange. What say you, sir? Nothing! Has Harpocrates been here with his club,[11] among you? Well, sir, I will believe you to be the man at this time: I will venture upon you, sir. Your friends at court commend 'hem to you, sir—

Mor. O men! O manners! Was there ever such an impudence?   60

Tru. And are extremely solicitous for you, sir.

Mor. Whose knave[12] are you?

Tru. Mine own knave, and your compeer,[13] sir.

Mor. Fetch me my sword—

Tru. You shall taste the one half of my dagger, if you do, groom; and you the other, if you stir, sir. Be patient, I charge you, in the King's name, and hear me without insurrection. They say you are to marry; to marry! Do you mark, sir?

Mor. How then, rude companion![14]   70

Tru. Marry, your friends do wonder, sir, the Thames being so near, wherein you may drown so handsomely; or London Bridge, at a low fall,[15] with a fine leap, to hurry you down the stream; or, such a delicate

---

93   *credit afore:* i.e., precedence in rank.
94   *wind-fucker:* windhover (hawk), whose wings constantly beat the air.
95   *rook:* raucous bird; figuratively, "gull" or "simpleton."

II.i.
1   *more compendious:* i.e., less elaborate.
2   *apprehend:* understand.
3   *breaches . . . legs or signs:* bows or signs, during the pauses (breaches), marked by the dashes, in Morose's speech. In the original folio this stage direction was printed as a marginal note, and the additional editorial stage directions added here were taken to be implied by the dashes.
4   *flock-bed:* stuffed with wool or cotton.
5   *But:* Only.   6   *presently:* right away.
7   *Italian and Spaniard:* Noted for taciturnity.
8   *doctrine and impulsion:* teaching and compulsion.
9   *post:* messenger.
10   *Fishes? Pythagoreans:* Proverbially dumb.
11   *Harpocrates . . . club:* God of silence, represented in antiquity with a club.   12   *knave:* servant.
13   *compeer:* i.e., as good as you.
14   *companion:* base fellow.   15   *low fall:* ebb tide.

steeple i' the town, as Bow,[16] to vault from; or, a braver height, as Paul's.[17] Or, if you affected to do it nearer home, and a shorter way, an excellent garret-window into the street; or, a beam in the said garret, with this halter[18]

He shows him a halter.

which they have sent, and desire, that you would   80 sooner commit your grave head to this knot, than to the wedlock noose; or, take a little sublimate,[19] and go out of the world like a rat; or, a fly, as one said, with a straw[20] i' your arse; any way rather than follow this goblin matrimony. Alas, sir, do you ever think to find a chaste wife in these times? Now? When there are so many masques, plays, Puritan preachings, mad folks, and other strange sights to be seen daily, private and public? If you had lived in King Etheldred's time, sir, or Edward the Confessor,[21] you might, perhaps,   90 have found one in some cold country hamlet, then, a dull frosty wench, would have been contented with one man: now, they will as soon be pleased with one leg or one eye. I'll tell you, sir, the monstrous hazards you shall run with a wife.

Mor. Good sir, have I ever cozened[22] any friends of yours of their land? Bought their possessions? Taken forfeit of their mortgage? Begged a reversion[23] from 'hem? Bastarded their issue? What have I done that may deserve this?   100

Tru. Nothing, sir, that I know, but your itch of marriage.

Mor. Why, if I had made an assassinate[24] upon your father, vitiated[25] your mother, ravished your sisters—

Tru. I would kill you, sir, I would kill you, if you had.

Mor. Why, you do more in this, sir. It were a vengeance centuple,[26] for all facinorous[27] acts that could be named, to do that[28] you do.

Tru. Alas, sir, I am but a messenger: I but tell you, what you must hear. It seems, your friends are careful[29] after your soul's health, sir, and would have you   110 know the danger (but you may do your pleasure for all them, I persuade not, sir). If, after you are married, your wife do run away with a vaulter,[30] or the Frenchman that walks upon ropes,[31] or him that dances the jig, or a fencer for his skill at his weapon; why, it is not their fault, they have discharged their consciences, when you know what may happen. Nay, suffer valiantly, sir, for I must tell you all the perils that you are obnoxious[32] to. If she be fair, young and vegetous,[33] no sweet- 120 meats ever drew more flies; all the yellow doublets and great roses[34] i' the town will be there. If foul and crooked, she'll be with them, and buy those doublets and roses, sir. If rich, and that you marry her dowry, not her, she'll reign in your house as imperious as a widow. If noble, all her kindred will be your tyrants. If fruitful, as proud as May and humorous[35] as April; she must have her doctors, her midwives, her nurses, her longings every hour; though it be for the dearest morsel of man. If learned, there was never such a parrot; all   130 your patrimony will be too little for the guests that must be invited, to hear her speak Latin and Greek: and you must lie with[36] her in those languages too, if you will please her. If precise,[37] you must feast all the silenced[38] brethren, once in three days; salute the sisters; entertain the whole family, or wood[39] of 'hem and hear long-winded exercises, singings and catechizings, which you are not given to, and yet must give for, to please the zealous matron your wife, who, for the holy cause, will cozen you over and above.   140 You begin to sweat, sir?—but this is not half, i' faith: you may do your pleasure, notwithstanding, as I said before; I come not to persuade you.

[*The* MUTE *is stealing away.*]

Upon my faith, master servingman, if you do stir, I will beat you.

Mor. Oh, what is my sin! what is my sin!

Tru. Then, if you love your wife, or rather dote on her, sir, oh, how she'll torture you, and take pleasure i' your torments! you shall lie with her but when she lists;[40] she will not hurt her beauty, her complex-   150 ion; or it must be for that jewel or that pearl when she does; every half-hour's pleasure must be bought anew, and with the same pain and charge you[41] wooed her at first. Then you must keep what servants she please; what company she will; that friend must not visit you without her license; and him she loves most, she will seem to hate eagerliest, to decline[42] your jealousy; or, feign to be jealous of you first; and for that cause go live with her she-friend, or cousin at the college, that can instruct her in all the mysteries of writing   160 letters, corrupting servants, taming spies; where she must have that rich gown for such a great day; a new one for the next; a richer for the third; be served in silver;[43] have the chamber filled with a succession of grooms, footmen, ushers, and other messengers; besides embroiderers, jewelers, tire-women,[44] sempsters, feathermen,[45] perfumers; whilst she feels not how the land drops away, nor the acres melt; nor foresees the

---

[16] *Bow:* St. Mary-le-Bow, destroyed in the great fire of 1666.   [17] *Paul's:* the roof of St. Paul's cathedral.

[18] *halter:* for hanging himself with.

[19] *sublimate:* poison.

[20] *fly . . . straw:* fly and spider fights, the contestants being prodded on with a straw, were popular amusements.

[21] *King . . . Confessor:* in the good old days.

[22] *cozened:* cheated.   [23] *reversion:* right of succession.

[24] *assassinate:* assassination.

[25] *vitiated:* corrupted (in morals).

[26] *centuple:* hundredfold.   [27] *facinorous:* criminal.

[28] *that:* what.   [29] *careful:* literally, "full of care."

[30] *vaulter:* acrobat.

[31] *Frenchman . . . ropes:* Jonson is perhaps remembering an acrobatic performance of this nature recorded in 1600.

[32] *obnoxious:* liable.   [33] *vegetous:* vigorous.

[34] *yellow . . . roses:* gallants (who affected the wearing of knotted ribbons or "shoe-roses").

[35] *humorous:* changeable.   [36] *lie with:* make love to.

[37] *precise:* puritanical.

[38] *silenced:* driven from the Church in 1604 for their various heresies.

[39] *wood:* crowd—Latin *silva* is a wood or forest; hence generically a collection.   [40] *lists:* wishes.

[41] *you:* with which you.   [42] *decline:* turn away.

[43] *silver:* dishes.   [44] *tire-women:* dressmakers.

[45] *feathermen:* dealers in feathers.

change, when the mercer⁴⁶ has your woods for her velvets; never weighs what her pride costs, sir; so 170 she may kiss a page, or a smooth chin, that has the despair of a beard; be a stateswoman, know all the news, what was done at Salisbury, what at the Bath,⁴⁷ what at court, what in progress;⁴⁸ or so she may censure⁴⁹ poets, and authors, and styles, and compare 'hem; Daniel with Spenser, Jonson with the t'other youth,⁵⁰ and so forth: or be thought cunning in controversies, or the very knots of divinity; and have often in her mouth the state of the question;⁵¹ and then skip to the mathematics and demonstration; and answer, in religion to one, in state to another, in bawdry to a third.

Mor. Oh, oh!   182

Tru. All this is very true, sir. And then her going in disguise to that conjurer, and this cunning woman:⁵² where the first question is, how soon you shall die? Next, if her present servant⁵³ love her? Next, that if she shall have a new servant? And how many? Which of her family would make the best bawd, male or female? What precedence she shall have by her next match? And sets down the answers, and believes 'hem above the scriptures. Nay, perhaps she'll study the art.⁵⁴   191

Mor. Gentle sir, ha' you done? Ha' you had your pleasure o' me? I'll think of these things.

Tru. Yes, sir; and then comes reeking home of vapor and sweat, with going a foot, and lies in⁵⁵ a month of a new face, all oil and birdlime; and rises in asses' milk, and is cleansed with a new fucus.⁵⁶ God b' wi' you, sir. One thing more, which I had almost forgot. This too, with whom you are to marry, may have made a conveyance of her virginity aforehand, as your wise 200 widows do of their states, before they marry, in trust to some friend, sir. Who can tell? Or if she have not done it yet, she may do, upon the wedding day, or the night before, and antedate you cuckold. The like has been heard of in nature. 'Tis no devised,⁵⁷ impossible thing, sir. God b' wi' you: I'll be bold to leave this rope with you, sir, for a remembrance.—Farewell, Mute.

                       [*Exit.*]

Mor. Come, ha' me to my chamber; but first shut the door.   210

            The horn again.

Oh, shut the door, shut the door! is he come again?

            [*Enter* CUTBEARD.]

Cut. 'Tis I, sir, your barber.

Mor. O Cutbeard, Cutbeard, Cutbeard! here has been a cut-throat with me: help me into my bed, and give me physic with thy counsel.

                     [*Exeunt.*]

[II.ii]

Enter DAW, CLERIMONT, DAUPHINE, EPICOENE.

Daw. Nay, and¹ she will, let her refuse at her own charges;² 'tis nothing to me, gentlemen. But she will not be invited to the like feasts or guests every day.

Cler. Oh, by no means, she may not refuse—to stay at home, if you love your reputation. 'Slight,³ you are invited thither o' purpose to be seen, and laughed at by the lady of the college, and her shadows.⁴ This trumpeter hath proclaimed you.

           They dissuade her privately.

Dauph. You shall not go; let him be laughed at in your stead, for not bringing you: and put him to 10 his extemporal⁵ faculty of fooling and talking aloud, to satisfy the company.

Cler. [*Aside to* EPICOENE] He will suspect us; talk aloud. Pray, Mistress Epicoene, let's see your verses; we will have Sir John Daw's leave; do not conceal your servants' merit, and your own glories.

Epi. They'll prove my servant's glories, if you have his leave so soon.

Dauph. His vainglories, lady!

Daw. Show 'hem, show 'hem, mistress! I dare own⁶ 'hem.   21

Epi. Judge you, what glories.

Daw. Nay, I'll read 'hem myself, too: an author must recite his own works. It is a madrigal of modesty.

     "*Modest and fair, for fair and good are near*
            Neighbors, howe'er."—

Dauph. Very good.

Cler. Ay, is't not?

Daw. "*No noble virtue ever was alone,*
            But two in one."   30

Dauph. Excellent!

Cler. That again, I pray, Sir John.

Dauph. It has something in't like rare wit and sense.

Cler. Peace.

Daw. "*No noble virtue ever was alone,*
            But two in one.
    Then, when I praise sweet modesty, I praise
            Bright beauty's rays:
    And having praised both beauty and modesty,
            I have praised thee."   40

Dauph. Admirable!

Cler. How it chimes, and cries tink⁷ i' the close, divinely!

Dauph. Ay, 'tis Seneca.

---

⁴⁶ *mercer:* dealer in fabrics.
⁴⁷ *Salisbury . . . Bath:* Reference is perhaps to racing in the former city, bathing in the medicinal springs in the latter.
⁴⁸ *progress:* royal journey through the country.
⁴⁹ *censure:* offer to judge.
⁵⁰ *t'other youth:* Some editors suggest Shakespeare, a tempting suggestion; though perhaps Daniel, first named, is more plausible.
⁵¹ *state . . . question:* a cant phrase: she affects to know all the facts and circumstances of a particular affair.
⁵² *conjurer . . . woman:* male and female fortune tellers.
⁵³ *servant:* lover.   ⁵⁴ *art:* astrology.
⁵⁵ *lies in:* is brought to bed (analogy to childbirth).
⁵⁶ *fucus:* cosmetic.
⁵⁷ *devised:* invented; hence "made up."
II.ii.
¹ *and:* if.   ² *charges:* expense.
³ *'Slight:* God's light (conventional oath).
⁴ *shadows:* parasites.
⁵ *extemporal:* impromptu; what he does by nature.
⁶ *own:* acknowledge.   ⁷ *cries tink:* tinkles.

Cler. No, I think 'tis Plutarch.

Daw. The dor on[8] Plutarch and Seneca! I hate it: they are mine own imaginations,[9] by that light. I wonder those fellows have such credit with gentlemen.

Cler. They are very grave authors.   49

Daw. Grave asses! mere essayists! a few loose sentences, and that's all. A man would talk so his whole age. I do utter as good things every hour, if they were collected and observed, as either of 'hem.

Dauph. Indeed, Sir John!

Cler. He must needs, living among the wits and braveries too.

Dauph. Ay, and being president of 'hem, as he is.

Daw. There's Aristotle, a mere commonplace fellow; Plato, a discourser; Thucydides and Livy, tedious and dry; Tacitus, an entire knot: sometimes worth the untying, very seldom.   61

Cler. What do you think of the poets, Sir John?

Daw. Not worthy to be named for authors. Homer, an old tedious, prolix ass, talks of curriers,[10] and chines[11] of beef. Virgil, of dunging of land and bees.[12] Horace, of I know not what.

Cler. I think so.

Daw. And so Pindarus, Lycophron, Anacreon, Catullus, Seneca the tragedian, Lucan, Propertius, Tibullus, Martial, Juvenal, Ausonius, Statius, Politian, Valerius Flaccus, and the rest—   71

Cler. What a sack full of their names he has got!

Dauph. And how he pours 'hem out! Politian with Valerius Flaccus!

Cler. Was not the character[13] right of him?

Dauph. As could be made, i' faith.

Daw. And Persius, a crabbed coxcomb, not to be endured.

Dauph. Why, whom do you account for authors, Sir John Daw?   80

Daw. *Syntagma juris civilis, Corpus juris civilis, Corpus juris canonici,*[14] the King of Spain's bible[15]—

Dauph. Is the King of Spain's bible an author?

Cler. Yes, and *Syntagma.*

Dauph. What was that *Syntagma,* sir?

Daw. A civil lawyer, a Spaniard.

Dauph. Sure, *Corpus* was a Dutchman.

Cler. Ay, both the *Corpuses,* I knew 'hem: they were very corpulent authors.   89

Daw. And then there's Vatablus, Pomponatius, Symancha;[16] the other are not to be received within the thought of a scholar.

Dauph. 'Fore God, you have a simple learned servant, lady, in titles.

Cler. I wonder that he is not called to the helm, and made a counselor.

Dauph. He is one extraordinary.

Cler. Nay, but in ordinary! to say truth, the state wants such.

Dauph. Why, that will follow.   100

Cler. I muse a mistress can be so silent to the dotes[17] of such a servant.

Daw. 'Tis her virtue, sir. I have written somewhat of her silence too.

Dauph. In verse, Sir John?

Cler. What else?

Dauph. Why, how can you justify your own being of a poet, that so slight all the old poets?

Daw. Why, every man that writes in verse is not a poet; you have[18] of the wits that write verses, 110 and yet are no poets: they are poets that live by it, the poor fellows that live by it.

Dauph. Why, would not you live by your verses, Sir John?

Cler. No, 'twere pity he should. A knight live by his verses? He did not make 'hem to that end, I hope.

Dauph. And yet the noble Sidney lives by his, and the noble family not ashamed.

Cler. Ay, he professed himself; but Sir John Daw has more caution: he'll not hinder his own rising 120 i' the state so much. Do you think he will? Your verses, good Sir John, and no "poems."

Daw. *"Silence in woman, is like speech in man,*
　　　　Deny 't who can."

Dauph. Not I, believe it: your reason, sir.

Daw.　　　　*"Nor is't a tale,*
　　　That female vice should be a virtue male,
　　　Or masculice vice a female virtue be:
　　　　You shall it see
　　　　Proved with increase,   130
　　I know to speak, and she to hold her peace."

Do you conceive[19] me, gentlemen?

Dauph. No, faith; how mean you "with increase," Sir John?

Daw. Why, with increase is, when I court her for the common cause of mankind, and she says nothing, but *consentire videtur;*[20] and in time is *gravida.*[21]

Dauph. Then this is a ballad of procreation?

Cler. A madrigal of procreation; you mistake.

Epi. Pray give me verses again, servant.   140

Daw. If you'll ask 'hem aloud, you shall.

[*Enter* TRUEWIT.]

Cler. See, here's Truewit again! where hast thou been, in the name of madness, thus accoutred with[22] thy horn?

---

[8] *dor on:* "dor" is a beetle (hence obnoxious), also a mockery. The general sense is clearly a contemptuous dismissing of the two authors.

[9] *mine own imaginations:* presumably glossed by what follows—"I do utter as good things every hour"(?).

[10] *curriers:* men who rub down or "dress" horses; or, by transference, leather.

[11] *chines:* backbone of an animal, with the adjoining flesh. See *Iliad.* VII. 321.

[12] *dunging . . . bees:* as in the *Georgics.*

[13] *character:* description.

[14] *L.:* Compilations of civil and canon law.

[15] *King of Spain's bible:* The *Biblia Regia,* printed by Christopher Plantin at Antwerp in 1569–72. Philip II of Spain was the nominal patron of this venture but found it inconvenient ever to pay for it.

[16] *Vatablus . . . Symancha:* scholars of the late fifteenth and sixteenth centuries.   [17] *dotes:* endowments.

[18] *have:* know.   [19] *conceive:* understand.

[20] *L.:* appears to consent.   [21] *L.:* pregnant.

[22] *accoutred with:* i.e., "carrying."

Tru. Where the sound of it might have pierced your senses with gladness, had you been in ear-reach of it. Dauphine, fall down and worship me; I have forbid the bans, lad. I have been with thy virtuous uncle, and have broke the match.

Dauph. You ha' not, I hope. 150

Tru. Yes, faith; and thou shouldst hope otherwise, I should repent me: this horn got me entrance; kiss it. I had no other way to get in, but by feigning to be a post; but when I got in once, I proved none, but rather the contrary, turned him into a post, or a stone, or what is stiffer, with thundering into him the incommodities of a wife, and the miseries of marriage. If ever Gorgon²³ were seen in the shape of a woman, he hath seen her in my description. I have put him off o' that scent forever. Why do you not applaud and adore me, sirs? 160 Why stand you mute? Are you stupid? You are not worthy o' the benefit.

Dauph. Did not I tell you? Mischief!

Cler. I would you had placed this benefit somewhere else.

Tru. Why so?

Cler. 'Slight, you have done the most inconsiderate, rash, weak thing, that ever man did to his friend.

Dauph. Friend! if the most malicious enemy I have had studied to inflict an injury upon me, it could not be greater. 171

Tru. Wherein, for God's sake? Gentlemen, come to yourselves again.

Dauph. But I presaged²⁴ thus much afore to you.

Cler. Would my lips had been soldered when I spake on't! 'slight, what moved you to be thus impertinent?²⁵

Tru. My masters, do not put on this strange face to pay my courtesy; off with this visor. Have good turns done you, and thank 'hem this way! 179

Dauph. 'Fore heaven, you have undone me. That which I have plotted for, and been maturing now these four months, you have blasted in a minute. Now I am lost, I may speak. This gentlewoman was lodged here by me o' purpose, and, to be put upon my uncle, hath professed this obstinate silence for my sake, being my entire friend, and one that for the requital of such a fortune as to marry him, would have made me very ample conditions; where now all my hopes are utterly miscarried by this unlucky accident. 189

Cler. Thus 'tis when a man will be ignorantly officious, do services, and not know his why. I wonder what courteous itch possessed you. You never did absurder part i' your life, nor a greater trespass to friendship, to humanity.

Dauph. Faith, you may forgive it best; 'twas your cause principally.

Cler. I know it; would it had not.

[*Enter* CUTBEARD.]

Dauph. How now, Cutbeard! what news? 198

Cut. The best, the happiest that ever was, sir. There has been a mad gentleman with your uncle this morning.—I think this be the gentleman—that has almost talked him out of his wits, with threatening him from marriage—

Dauph. On, I pray thee.

Cut. And your uncle, sir, he thinks 'twas done by your procurement; therefore he will see the party you wot²⁶ of presently; and if he like her, he says, and that she be so inclining to dumb²⁷ as I have told him, he swears he will marry her today, instantly, and not defer it a minute longer. 210

Dauph. Excellent! beyond our expectation!

Tru. Beyond your expectation? By this light, I knew it would be thus.

Dauph. Nay, sweet Truewit, forgive me.

Tru. No, I was "ignorantly officious, impertinent"; this was the "absurd, weak part."

Cler. Wilt thou ascribe that to merit now, was mere fortune? 218

Tru. Fortune! mere providence. Fortune had not a finger in't. I saw it must necessarily in nature fall out so: my genius is never false to me in these things. Show me how it could be otherwise.

Dauph. Nay, gentlemen, contend not; 'tis well now.

Tru. Alas, I let him go on with "inconsiderate," and "rash," and what he pleased.

Cler. Away, thou strange justifier of thyself, to be wiser than thou wert, by the event.²⁸

Tru. Event! by this light, thou shalt never persuade me but²⁹ I foresaw it as well as the stars themselves.

Dauph. Nay, gentlemen, 'tis well now. Do you 230 two entertain Sir John Daw with discourse, while I send her away with instructions.

Tru. I'll be acquainted with her first, by your favor.

Cler. Master Truewit, lady, a friend of ours.

Tru. I am sorry I have not known you sooner, lady, to celebrate this rare virtue of your silence.

[*Exeunt* DAUPHINE, EPICOENE, *and* CUTBEARD.]

Cler. Faith, and you had come sooner, you should ha' seen and heard her well celebrated in Sir John Daw's madrigals. 239

Tru. Jack Daw, God save you. When saw you La Foole?

Daw. Not since last night, Master Truewit.

Tru. That's a miracle! I thought you two had been inseparable.

Daw. He's gone to invite his guests.

Tru. Gods so! 'tis true! what a false memory have I towards that man! I am one. I met him even now, upon that he calls his delicate fine black horse, rid into foam, with posting from place to place, and person to person, to give 'hem the cue— 250

Cler. Lest they should forget?

Tru. Yes: there was never poor captain took more pains at a muster to show³⁰ men, than he at this meal to show friends.

Daw. It is his quarter-feast, sir.

Cler. What! do you say so, Sir John?

---

²³ *Gorgon:* Mythical creature whose glance turned the beholder to stone. ²⁴ *presaged:* predicted.
²⁵ *impertinent:* out of the way; not to the purpose.
²⁶ *wot:* know. ²⁷ *dumb:* dumbness.
²⁸ *event:* result. ²⁹ *but:* but that.
³⁰ *show:* show off, as on parade.

Tru. Nay, Jack Daw will not be out, at the best friends he has, to the talent of his wit. Where's his mistress, to hear and applaud him? Is she gone? 261

Daw. Is Mistress Epicoene gone?

Cler. Gone afore, with Sir Dauphine, I warrant, to the place.

Tru. Gone afore! that were a manifest injury, a disgrace and a half; to refuse him at such a festival time as this, being a bravery, and a wit too!

Cler. Tut, he'll swallow it like cream: he's better read in *Jure civili*,[31] than to esteem anything a disgrace is offered him from a mistress.

Daw. Nay, let her e'en go; she shall sit alone, and be dumb in her chamber a week together, for John Daw, I warrant her. Does she refuse me? 271

Cler. No, sir, do not take it so to heart; she does not refuse you, but a little neglect you. Good faith, Truewit, you were to blame, to put it into his head, that she does refuse him.

Tru. Sir, she does refuse him palpably,[32] however you mince it. An' I were as he, I would swear to speak ne'er a word to her today for't.

Daw. By this light, no more I will not.

Tru. Nor to anybody else, sir. 280

Daw. Nay, I will not say so, gentlemen.

Cler. It had been an excellent happy condition for the company, if you could have drawn him to it.

Daw. I'll be very melancholic, i' faith.

Cler. As a dog, if I were as you, Sir John.

Tru. Or a snail, or a hog-louse. I would roll myself up for this day; in troth, they should not unwind me.

Daw. By this picktooth,[33] so I will.

Cler. 'Tis well done: he begins already to be angry with his teeth. 290

Daw. Will you go, gentlemen?

Cler. Nay, you must walk alone if you be right melancholic, Sir John.

Tru. Yes, sir, we'll dog you, we'll follow you afar off.
[*Exit* DAW.]

Cler. Was there ever such a two yards of knighthood measured out by time, to be sold to laughter?

Tru. A mere talking mole, hang him! no mushroom was ever so fresh.[34] A fellow so utterly nothing, as he knows not what he would be. 300

Cler. Let's follow him: but first let's go to Dauphine, he's hovering about the house to hear what news.

Tru. Content.
[*Exeunt.*]

---

[31] *L.*: Common law (as it affected citizens).
[32] *palpably*: obviously. [33] *picktooth*: toothpick.
[34] *fresh*: ironic—"rotten."
II.iii.
[1] *Mute . . . leg*: Jonson's marginal stage direction II. i. 10 has indicated that "breaches" or dashes in the text require "making a leg" or gesturing by the character he is addressing. So here. [2] *prefer*: put forward. [3] *Give*: Stand.
[4] *favor*: appearance.
[5] *her . . . blood*: i.e., we are a match.
[6] *has . . . of*: is exactly attuned to.
[7] *courtless*: uncourtly.
[8] *audacious*: confident, self-possessed.
[9] *plausible*: pleasing. [10] *jump right*: agree.

II.iii

Enter MOROSE, EPICOENE, CUTBEARD, MUTE.

Mor. Welcome, Cutbeard! draw near with your fair charge and in her ear softly entreat her to unmask.

[EPICOENE *takes off her mask.*]

So! is the door shut? [MUTE *makes a leg.*[1]]—Enough! Now, Cutbeard, with the same discipline I use to my family, I will question you. As I conceive, Cutbeard, this gentlewoman is she you have provided, and brought, in hope she will fit me in the place and person of a wife? Answer me not but with your leg, unless it be otherwise. [CUTBEARD *makes a leg.*]—Very well done, Cutbeard. I conceive besides, Cutbeard, 10 you have been pre-acquainted with her birth, education, and qualities, or else you would not prefer[2] her to my acceptance, in the weighty consequence of marriage. [*Makes a leg.*]—This I conceive, Cutbeard. Answer me not but with your leg, unless it be otherwise. [*Makes a leg.*]—Very well done, Cutbeard. Give[3] aside now a little, and leave me to examine her condition and aptitude to my affection.

He goes about her and views her.

—She is exceeding fair, and of a special good favor;[4] a sweet composition or harmony of limbs; her 20 temper of beauty has the true height of my blood.[5] The knave hath exceedingly well fitted me without: I will now try her within.—Come near, fair gentlewoman; let not my behavior seem rude, though unto you, being rare, it may haply appear strange. *She curtsies.*—Nay, lady, you may speak, though Cutbeard and my man might not; for of all sounds, only the sweet voice of a fair lady has the just length of[6] mine ears. I beseech you, say, lady; out of the first fire of meeting eyes, they say, love is stricken: do you feel any 30 such motion suddenly shot into you, from any part you see in me? Ha, lady? *Curtsy.*—Alas, lady, these answers by silent curtsies from you are too courtless[7] and simple. I have ever had my breeding in court; and she that shall be my wife must be accomplished with courtly and audacious[8] ornaments. Can you speak, lady?

She speaks softly.

Epi. Judge you, forsooth.

Mor. What say you, lady? Speak out, I beseech you.

Epi. Judge you, forsooth. 40

Mor. O' my judgment, a divine softness! but can you naturally, lady, as I enjoin these by doctrine and industry, refer yourself to the search of my judgment, and, not taking pleasure in your tongue, which is a woman's chiefest pleasure, think it plausible[9] to answer me by silent gestures, so long as my speeches jump right[10] with what you conceive? *Curtsy.*— Excellent! divine! if it were possible she should hold out thus! peace, Cutbeard, thou art made for ever, as thou hast made me, if this felicity have lasting; but I 50 will try her further. Dear lady, I am courtly, I tell you, and I must have mine ears banqueted with pleasant and

witty conferences, pretty girds,[11] scoffs, and dalliance
in her that I mean to choose for my bedfere.[12] The
ladies in court think it a most desperate impair[13] to
their quickness of wit, and good carriage, if they cannot
give occasion for a man to court 'hem; and when an
amorous discourse is set on foot, minister as good matter
to continue it as himself. And do you alone so much
differ from all them, that what they, with so much   60
circumstance,[14] affect and toil for, to seem learned, to
seem judicious, to seem sharp and conceited,[15] you can
bury in yourself with silence, and rather trust your
graces to the fair conscience of virtue, than to the
world's, or your own proclamation?

Epi. [*Softly.*] I should be sorry else.

Mor. What say you, lady? Good lady, speak out.

Epi. I should be sorry else.

Mor. That sorrow doth fill me with gladness! O
Morose! thou art happy above mankind! pray that   70
thou mayst contain thyself. I will only put her to it once
more, and it shall be with the utmost touch[16] and test
of their sex. But hear me, fair lady; I do also love to see
her whom I shall choose for my heicfar,[17] to be the first
and principal in all fashions, precede all the dames at
court by a fortnight, have her council of tailors, lineners,
lace-women, embroiderers; and sit with 'hem sometimes twice a day upon French intelligences,[18] and
then come forth varied like nature, or oftener than she,
and better by the help of art, her emulous[19] ser-   80
vant. This do I affect: and how will you be able, lady,
with this frugality of speech, to give the manifold but
necessary instructions, for that bodies,[20] these sleeves,
those skirts, this cut,[21] that stitch, this embroidery, that
lace, this wire,[22] those knots, that ruff, those roses, this
girdle, that fan, the t'other scarf, these gloves? Ha!
what say you, lady?

Epi. [*Softly.*] I'll leave it to you, sir.

Mor. How lady? Pray you rise a note.

Epi. I leave it to wisdom and you, sir.   90

Mor. Admirable creature! I will trouble you no more.
I will not sin against so sweet a simplicity. Let me now
be bold to print on those divine lips the seal of being
mine. Cutbeard, I give thee the lease of thy house free;
thank me not but with thy leg. [CUTBEARD *makes a
leg.*]—I know what thou wouldst say, she's poor and her
friends deceased. She has brought a wealthy dowry in
her silence, Cutbeard; and in respect of her poverty,
Cutbeard, I shall have her more loving and obedient,
Cutbeard. Go thy ways, and get me a minister   100
presently, with a soft low voice, to marry us: and pray
him he will not be impertinent, but brief as he can;
away: softly, Cutbeard.

                 [*Exit* CUTBEARD.]

Sirrah, conduct your mistress into the dining room,
your now mistress.

         [*Exit* MUTE, *followed by* EPICOENE.]

O, my felicity! how I shall be revenged on mine insolent
kinsman, and his plots to fright me from marrying! this
night I will get[23] an heir, and thrust him out of my
blood like a stranger. He would be knighted, forsooth,
and thought by that means to reign over me; his   110
title must do it. No, kinsman, I will now make you bring

me the tenth lord's and the sixteenth[24] lady's letter,
kinsman; and it shall do you no good, kinsman. Your
knighthood itself shall come on its knees, and it shall
be rejected; it shall be sued for its fees to execution,[25]
and not be redeemed; it shall cheat at the twelve-penny
ordinary,[26] it[27] knighthood, for its diet, all the term
time, and tell tales for it in the vacation to the hostess;
or it knighthood shall do worse, take sanctuary in Coleharbor,[28] and fast. It shall fright all it friends   120
with borrowing letters; and when one of the fourscore
hath brought it knighthood ten shillings, it knighthood
shall go to the Cranes,[29] or the Bear at the Bridge-foot,[30]
and be drunk in fear; it shall not have money to discharge one tavern-reckoning, to invite the old creditors
to forbear it knighthood, or the new, that should be,
to trust it knighthood. It shall be the tenth name in
the bond to take up the commodity of pipkins[31] and
stone-jugs: and the part thereof shall not furnish it
knighthood forth for the attempting of[32] a baker's   130
widow, a brown baker's[33] widow. It shall give it knighthood's name for a stallion,[34] to all gamesome citizens'
wives, and be refused, when the master of a dancing
school, or how[35] do you call him the worst reveller in
the town, is taken: it shall want clothes, and by reason
of that, wit, to fool to[36] lawyers. It shall not have hope
to repair itself by Constantinople, Ireland, or Virginia;[37]
but the best and last fortune to it knighthood, shall be
to make Dol Tear-sheet or Kate Common[38] a lady, and
so it knighthood may eat.   140

                       [*Exit.*]

---

[11] *girds:* mocks.

[12] *bedfere:* bedfellow; "fere" is "companion."

[13] *impair:* impairment.   [14] *circumstance:* ado.

[15] *conceited:* imaginative.

[16] *touch:* from the process of testing the quality of precious
metals by rubbing them against a "touchstone."

[17] *heicfar:* heifer (the word denotes Morose's estimation
of women).   [18] *intelligences:* news, gossip from abroad.

[19] *emulous:* imitating—"Art imitates Nature."

[20] *bodies:* bodice.   [21] *cut:* open work; slash in the garment.

[22] *wire:* see Prologue, n. 8.   [23] *get:* beget.

[24] *tenth . . . sixteenth:* i.e., Morose will make his kinsman
execute the most demeaning services.

[25] *to execution:* up to the moment when the sheriff enforces the judgment of the court (and hence renders the
erstwhile knight a beggar).

[26] *twelve-penny ordinary:* cheapest kind of restaurant.

[27] *it:* its (the archaic form is used here and in what follows
contemptuously, as if Morose were addressing a child).

[28] *Coleharbor:* disreputable London district where debtors
and vagrants took sanctuary.

[29] *Cranes:* Tavern—the Three Cranes in the Vintry,
located in the same disreputable part of town as Coleharbor.

[30] *Bear at the Bridge-foot:* another tavern, this one on the
Surrey side of the Thames at the foot of London Bridge.

[31] *pipkins:* Moneylenders, to get around the statute against
usury, forced borrowers to buy worthless goods in addition
to the money advanced them.

[32] *attempting of:* seeking to marry.

[33] *brown baker's:* baker of cheap bread (Morose adds insult
to injury).   [34] *stallion:* male whore.

[35] *how:* Editors conjecture a personal reference here, perhaps to the chronicler Edmund Howes.

[36] *fool to:* dupe; play the fool to(?).

[37] *Constantinople, Ireland, or Virginia:* places where
Dauphine might hope to recover his fortunes by trade or
colonization.   [38] *Dol . . . Common:* generically, a whore.

[II.iv]

Enter Truewit, Dauphine, Clerimont.

Tru. Are you sure he is not gone by?

Dauph. No, I stayed in the shop ever since.

Cler. But he may take the other end of the lane.

Dauph. No, I told him I would be here at this end; I appointed him hither.

Tru. What a barbarian it is to stay then!

Dauph. Yonder he comes.

Cler. And his charge left behind him, which is a very good sign, Dauphine.

[*Enter* Cutbeard.]

Dauph. How now, Cutbeard; succeeds it or no?　10

Cut. Past imagination, sir, *omnia secunda;* you could not have prayed to have had it so well. *Saltat senex,*[1] as it is i' the proverb; he does triumph in his felicity, admires the party! he has given me the lease of my house too! and I am now going for a silent minister to marry 'hem, and away.

Tru. 'Slight! get one o' the silenced ministers; a zealous brother[2] would torment him purely.[3]

Cut. Cum privilegio,[4] sir.　19

Dauph. Oh, by no means; let's do nothing to hinder it now: when 'tis done and finished, I am for you, for any device of vexation.

Cut. And that shall be within this half hour, upon my dexterity,[5] gentlemen. Contrive what you can; in the mean time, *bonis avibus.*[6]

[*Exit.*]

Cler. How the slave doth Latin it!

Tru. It would be made a jest to posterity, sirs, this day's mirth, if ye will.

Cler. Beshrew his heart that will not, I pronounce.

Dauph. And for my part. What is 't?　30

Tru. To translate[7] all La Foole's company and his feast hither today, to celebrate this bride-ale.[8]

Dauph. Ay, marry; but how will 't be done?

Tru. I'll undertake the directing of all the lady-guests thither, and then the meat must follow.

Cler. For God's sake, let's effect it; it will be an excellent comedy of affliction, so many several[9] noises.

Dauph. But are they not at the other place already, think you?　39

Tru. I'll warrant you for the college-honors: one o' their faces has not the priming color laid on yet, nor the other her smock sleeked.[10]

Cler. Oh, but they'll rise earlier than ordinary to a feast.

Tru. Best go see, and assure ourselves.

Cler. Who knows the house?

Tru. I'll lead you. Were you never there yet?

Dauph. Not I.

Cler. Nor I.　49

Tru. Where ha' you lived then? Not know Tom Otter!

Cler. No: for God's sake, what is he?

Tru. An excellent animal, equal with your Daw or La Foole, if not transcendent;[11] and does Latin it as much as your barber. He is his wife's subject; he calls her princess, and at such times as these follows her up and down the house like a page, with his hat off, partly for heat, partly for reverence. At this instant he is marshalling of[12] his bull, bear, and horse.

Dauph. What be those, in the name of Sphinx?　60

Tru. Why, sir, he has been a great man at the Bear-garden[13] in his time; and from that subtle sport has ta'en the witty denomination[14] of his chief carousing cups. One he calls his bull, another his bear, another his horse. And then he has his lesser glasses, that he calls his deer and his ape; and several degrees of 'hem too; and never is well, nor thinks any entertainment perfect, till these be brought out, and set o' the cupboard.

Cler. For God's love!—we should miss this if we should not go.　70

Tru. Nay, he has a thousand things as good, that will speak[15] him all day. He will rail on his wife, with certain commonplaces,[16] behind her back, and to her face—

Dauph. No more of him. Let's go see him, I petition you.

[*Exeunt.*]

ACT THREE

Scene One

Enter Captain Otter *and Mistress* Otter.

Ot. Nay, good princess, hear me *pauca verba.*[1]

Mrs. Ot. By that light, I'll ha' you chained up, with your bull-dogs and bear-dogs, if you be not civil the sooner. I'll send you to kennel, i' faith. You were best bait me with your bull, bear, and horse. Never a time that the courtiers or collegiates come to the house, but you make it a Shrove Tuesday! I would have you get your Whitsuntide velvet cap, and your staff i' your hand, to entertain 'hem; yes, in troth, do.　9

Ot. Not so, princess, neither; but under correction,[2] sweet princess, gi' me leave. These things I am known to the courtiers by. It is reported to them for my humor;[3] and they receive it so, and do expect it. Tom Otter's bull, bear, and horse is known all over England, *in rerum natura.*[4]

II.iv.

[1] *omnia . . . senex:* The sense of the proverb is that "All's well"; the second phrase means "The old man jumps (for joy)."　　[2] *zealous brother:* Puritan.　　[3] *purely:* absolutely.

[4] *L.:* With authority. Presumably Cutbeard is delighted to comply.　　[5] *dexterity:* befitting a barber.

[6] *L.:* i.e., "It looks good"; or "May it go well." Reference is to the augury divined from the entrails of birds.

[7] *translate:* transport.　　[8] *bride-ale:* wedding feast.

[9] *several:* separate.　　[10] *sleeked:* smoothed; ironed.

[11] *transcendent:* i.e., overgoing them.

[12] *marshalling of:* obsolete verbal substantive; the preposition is gratuitous.

[13] *Bear-garden:* Paris Garden, on the Surrey side of the Thames, where bears were baited.

[14] *denomination:* naming.　　[15] *speak:* expose.

[16] *commonplaces:* proverbs; saws and sayings.

III.i.

[1] *L.:* few words.

[2] *under correction:* polite phrase, like "begging your pardon," or "I may be wrong, but," etc.

[3] *humor:* whim.　　[4] *L.:* in the nature of things.

Mrs. Ot. 'Fore me, I will *na-ture* 'hem over to Paris-garden, and *na-ture* you thither too if you pronounce 'hem again. Is a bear a fit beast, or a bull, to mix in society with great ladies? Think i' your discretion, in any good polity.[5]   20

Ot. The horse then, good princess.

Mrs. Ot. Well, I am contented for the horse; they love to be well horsed, I know: I love it myself.

Ot. And it is a delicate fine horse this: *Poetarum Pegasus.*[6] Under correction, princess, Jupiter did turn himself into a—*taurus*, or bull, under correction, good princess.

[*Enter* TRUEWIT, CLERIMONT, *and* DAUPHINE, *behind.*]

Mrs. Ot. By my integrity, I'll send you over to the Bankside; I'll commit you to the master of the Garden if I hear but a syllable more. Must my house or   30 my roof be polluted with the scent of bears and bulls, when it is perfumed for great ladies? Is this according to the instrument[7] when I married you? That I would be princess, and reign in mine own house; and you would be my subject, and obey me? What did you bring me, should make you thus peremptory? Do I allow you your half-crown a day, to spend where you will, among your gamesters, to vex and torment me at such times as these? Who gives you your maintenance, I pray you? Who allows you your horse-meat and   40 man's-meat? Your three suits[8] of apparel a year? Your four pair of stockings, one silk,[9] three worsted? Your clean linen, your bands and cuffs, when I can get you to wear 'hem?—'tis mar'l[10] you ha' 'hem on now. Who graces you with courtiers or great personages, to speak to you out of their coaches, and come home to your house? Were you ever so much as looked upon by a lord or a lady before I married you, but on the Easter or Whitsun holidays? And then out at the banqueting-house[11] window when Ned Whiting or George Stone[12] were at the stake?   51

Tru. For God's sake, let's go stave her off him.

Mrs. Ot. Answer me to that. And did not I take you up from thence, in an old greasy buff doublet, with points,[13] and green velvet sleeves, out at the elbows? You forget this.

Tru. She'll worry[14] him, if we help not in time.

[*They come forward.*]

Mrs. Ot. Oh, here are some o' the gallants. Go to, behave yourself distinctly,[15] and with good morality; or, I protest, I'll take away your exhibition.[16]   60

Tru. By your leave, fair Mistress Otter, I'll be bold to enter these gentlemen in your acquaintance.

Mrs. Ot. It shall not be obnoxious, or difficil,[17] sir.

Tru. How does my noble captain? Is the bull, bear, and horse in *rerum natura* still?

Ot. Sir, *sic visum superis.*[18]

Mrs. Ot. I would you would but intimate[19] 'hem, do. Go your ways in, and get toasts and butter made for the woodcocks.[20] That's a fit province for you.

Cler. Alas, what a tyranny is this poor fellow married to.   71

Tru. Oh, but the sport will be anon, when we get him loose.

Dauph. Dares he ever speak?

Tru. No Anabaptist[21] ever railed with the like license: but mark her language in the meantime, I beseech you.

Mrs. Ot. Gentlemen, you are very aptly come. My cousin, Sir Amorous, will be here briefly.[22]

Tru. In good time, lady. Was not Sir John Daw here, to ask for him, and the company?   81

Mrs. Ot. I cannot assure you, Master Truewit. Here was a very melancholy knight in a ruff, that demanded my subject[23] for somebody, a gentleman, I think.

Cler. Ay, that was he, lady.

Mrs. Ot. But he departed straight,[24] I can resolve[25] you.

Dauph. What an excellent choice phrase this lady expresses in!

Tru. Oh, sir, she is the only authentical courtier, that is not naturally bred one, in the city.   91

Mrs. Ot. You have taken that report upon trust, gentlemen.

Tru. No, I assure you, the court governs[26] it so, lady, in your behalf.

Mrs. Ot. I am the servant of the court and courtiers, sir.

Tru. They are rather your idolaters.

Mrs. Ot. Not so, sir.

[*Enter* CUTBEARD.]

Dauph. How now, Cutbeard! any cross?[27]   100

Cut. Oh, no, sir, *Omnia bene.*[28] 'Twas never better o' the hinges;[29] all's sure. I have so pleased him with a curate, that he's gone to't almost with the delight he hopes for soon.

Dauph. What is he for a vicar?

Cut. One that has catched a cold, sir, and can scarce be heard six inches off; as if he spoke out of a bulrush that were not picked, or his throat were full of pith: a fine quick fellow, and an excellent barber of prayers.[30]

---

5 *polity:* society.   6 *L.:* the winged horse of poetry.
7 *instrument: legal agreement.*
8 *three suits:* proper to a servant, like worsted stockings, below.   9 *silk:* for holidays, like Whitsuntide, above.
10 *mar'l:* marvel.
11 *banqueting-house:* at Whitehall palace, where bears and bulls were baited before the King on holidays.
12 *Ned Whiting . . . George Stone:* famous bears of the time.   13 *points:* laces.
14 *worry:* stronger sense than now: as a dog worries or shakes a rat.   15 *distinctly:* properly.
16 *exhibition:* allowance.
17 *difficil:* difficult (the lady's speech is understood to be affected).   18 *L.:* so it appears to those above.
19 *intimate:* announce.   20 *woodcocks:* fools.
21 *Anabaptist:* generically, "Puritan," "dissenter," and hence synonymous to Jonson's mind with intemperate speech.   22 *briefly:* soon.
23 *subject:* Mrs. Otter, in her character of "princess," is speaking of her husband.   24 *straight:* immediately.
25 *resolve:* assure.   26 *governs:* determines.
27 *cross:* impediment.   28 *L.:* All's well.
29 *o'the hinges:* i.e., "on the rails"—a smooth operation.
30 *barber of prayers:* as he clips them short.

I came to tell you, sir, that you might *omnem movere lapidem*,[31] as they say, be ready with your vexation. 111

Dauph. Gramercy,[32] honest Cutbeard! be thereabouts with thy key to let us in.

Cut. I will not fail you, sir; *Ad manum.*[33]

                                  [*Exit.*]

Tru. Well, I'll go watch my coaches.

Cler. Do; and we'll send Daw to you, if you meet him not.

                    [*Exit* TRUEWIT.]

Mrs. Ot. Is Master Truewit gone?

Dauph. Yes, lady, there is some unfortunate business fallen out. 120

Mrs. Ot. So I judged by the physiognomy of the fellow that came in; and I had a dream last night too of the new pageant,[34] and my lady mayoress, which is always very ominous to me. I told it my Lady Haughty t'other day, when her honor came hither to see some China stuffs; and she expounded it out of Artemidorus,[35] and I have found it since very true. It has done me many affronts.

Cler. Your dream, lady? 129

Mrs. Ot. Yes, sir, anything I do but dream o' the city. It stained me a damask tablecloth, cost me eighteen pound at one time; and burnt me a black satin gown, as I stood by the fire at my Lady Centaure's chamber in the college, another time. A third time, at the lord's masque, it dropped all my wire and my ruff with wax candle, that I could not go up to the banquet. A fourth time, as I was taking coach to go to Ware, to meet a friend, it dashed me a new suit all over (a crimson satin doublet and black velvet skirts) with a brewer's horse, that I was fain to go in and 140 shift[36] me, and kept my chamber a leash[37] of days for the anguish of it.

Dauph. These were dire mischances, lady.

Cler. I would not dwell in the city an 't were so fatal to me.

Mrs. Ot. Yes, sir: but I do take advice of my doctor to dream of it as little as I can.

Dauph. You do well, Mistress Otter.

[*Enter Sir* JOHN DAW,
and is taken aside by CLERIMONT.]

Mrs. Ot. Will it please you to enter the house farther, gentlemen? 150

Dauph. And your favor,[38] lady: but we stay to speak with a knight, Sir John Daw, who is here come. We shall follow you, lady.

Mrs. Ot. At your own time, sir. It is my cousin, Sir Amorous his[39] feast—

Dauph. I know it, lady.

Mrs. Ot. And mine together. But it is for his honor, and therefore I take no name of it, more than of the place.

Dauph. You are a bounteous kinswoman. 160

Mrs. Ot. Your servant, sir.

                                  [*Exit.*]

[CLERIMONT *comes forward with* DAW.]

Cler. Why, do not you know it, Sir John Daw?

Daw. No, I am a rook if I do.

Cler. I'll tell you then; she's married by this time! And whereas you were put i' the head,[40] that she was gone with Sir Dauphine, I assure you Sir Dauphine has been the noblest, honestest friend to you, that ever gentleman of your quality could boast of. He has discovered the whole plot, and made your mistress so acknowledging, and indeed so ashamed of her 170 injury to you, that she desires you to forgive her, and but grace her wedding with your presence today. She is to be married to a very good fortune, she says, his uncle, old Morose; and she willed me in private to tell you, that she shall be able to do you more favors, and with more security now than before.

Daw. Did she say so, i' faith?

Cler. Why, what do you think of me, Sir John! ask Sir Dauphine!

Daw. Nay, I believe you. Good Sir Dauphine, did she desire me to forgive her? 181

Dauph. I assure you, Sir John, she did.

Daw. Nay, then, I do with all my heart, and I'll be jovial.

Cler. Yes, for look you, sir, this was the injury to you. La Foole intended this feast to honor her bridal day, and made you the property[41] to invite the college ladies, and promise to bring her; and then at the time she would have appeared, as his friend, to have given you the dor.[42] Whereas now, Sir Dauphine has brought 190 her to a feeling of it, with this kind of satisfaction, that you shall bring all the ladies to the place where she is, and be very jovial; and there she will have a dinner, which shall be in your name; and so disappoint La Foole, to make you good again, and, as it were, a saver i' the main.[43]

Daw. As I am a knight, I honor her; and forgive her heartily.

Cler. About it then presently. Truewit is gone before to confront the coaches, and to acquaint you 200 with so much, if he meet you. Join with him, and 'tis well.—

[*Enter Sir* AMOROUS LA FOOLE.]

See; here comes your antagonist; but take you no notice, but be very jovial.

La. F. Are the ladies come, Sir John Daw, and your mistress?

                                  [*Exit* DAW.]

---

[31] *L.:* move every stone.

[32] *Gramercy:* Thanks (though *OED* does not cite until after Jonson's time).   [33] *L.:* At hand—"I'll be there."

[34] *pageant:* prepared for the inaugural of the Lord Mayor.

[35] *Artemidorus:* Greek physician who wrote on the interpretation of dreams.   [36] *shift:* change.

[37] *leash:* a trio of hounds, hawks, hares; hence, generically, "three."   [38] *And your favor:* By your leave.

[39] *his:* Modern usage would drop the adjectival pronoun and make the subject possessive—"Amorous's."

[40] *you . . . head:* it was put in your head.

[41] *property:* instrument.   [42] *dor:* mock.

[43] *saver . . . main:* successful gambler. "Throwing the main" is, having rolled the dice, to call any number from five through nine.

Sir Dauphine! you are exceeding welcome, and honest
Master Clerimont. Where's my cousin? Did you see
no collegiates, gentlemen?

Dauph. Collegiates! Do you not hear, Sir Amorous,
how you are abused?   211

La F. How, sir!

Cler. Will you speak so kindly to Sir John Daw, that
has done you such an affront?

La F. Wherein, gentlemen? Let me be a suitor to
you to know, I beseech you.

Cler. Why, sir, his mistress is married today to Sir
Dauphine's uncle, your cousin's neighbor, and he has
diverted all the ladies, and all your company thither, to
frustrate your provision,[44] and stick a disgrace   220
upon you. He was here to have enticed us away from
you too: but we told him his own,[45] I think.

La F. Has Sir John Daw wronged me so inhumanly?

Dauph. He has done it, Sir Amorous, most maliciously and treacherously: but if you'll be ruled by us, you
shall quit him, i' faith.

La F. Good gentlemen, I'll make one,[46] believe it.
How, I pray?

Dauph. Marry, sir, get me your pheasants, and your
godwits, and your best meat, and dish it in silver   230
dishes of your cousin's presently: and say nothing, but
clap me a clean towel about you, like a sewer;[47] and,
bareheaded, march afore it with a good confidence ('tis
but over the way, hard by) and we'll second you, where
you shall set it o' the board, and bid 'hem welcome to
't, which shall show 'tis yours, and disgrace his preparation utterly: and, for your cousin, whereas she should
be troubled here at home with care of making and giving
welcome, she shall transfer all that labor thither, and be a
principal guest herself; sit ranked with the college   240
honors, and be honored, and have her health drunk as
often, as bare,[48] and as loud as the best of 'hem.

La F. I'll go tell her presently. It shall be done, that's
resolved.

                                                              [*Exit.*]

Cler. I thought he would not hear it out but 'twould
take him.

Dauph. Well, there be guests and meat now; how
shall we do for music?

Cler. The smell of the venison, going through the
street, will invite one noise[49] of fiddlers or other.   250

Dauph. I would it would call the trumpeters thither.

Cler. Faith, there is hope, they have intelligence of all
feasts. There's good correspondence betwixt them and
the London cooks. 'Tis twenty to one but we have 'hem.

Dauph. 'Twill be a most solemn day for my uncle,
and an excellent fit of mirth for us.

Cler. Ay, if we can hold up the emulation[50] betwixt
Foole and Daw, and never bring them to expostulate.[51]

Dauph. Tut, flatter 'hem both, as Truewit says, and
you may take their understandings in a purse-   260
net.[52] They'll believe themselves to be just such men as
we make 'hem, neither more nor less. They have nothing, not the use of their senses, but by tradition.

Cler. See! Sir Amorous has his towel on already.

He [LA FOOLE] *enters like a sewer.*

Have you persuaded your cousin?

La F. Yes, 'tis very feasible: she'll do anything, she
says, rather than the La Fooles should be disgraced.

Dauph. She is a noble kinswoman. It will be such a
pest'ling[53] device, Sir Amorous; it will pound all your
enemy's practices to powder, and blow him up with his
own mine, his own train.[54]   271

La F. Nay, we'll give fire, I warrant you.

Cler. But you must carry[55] it privately, without any
noise, and take no notice by any means—

[*Re-enter* Captain OTTER.]

Ot. Gentlemen, my princess says you shall have all
her silver dishes, *festinate:*[56] and she's gone to alter
her tire a little, and go with you—

Cler. And yourself too, Captain Otter?

Dauph. By any means, sir.   279

Ot. Yes, sir, I do mean it: but I would entreat my
cousin Sir Amorous, and you, gentlemen, to be suitors
to my princess, that I may carry my bull and my bear,
as well as my horse.

Cler. That you shall do, Captain Otter.

La F. My cousin will never consent, gentlemen.

Dauph. She must consent, Sir Amorous, to reason.

La F. Why, she says they are no decorum among
ladies.

Ot. But they are *decora,*[57] and that's better, sir.   289

Cler. Ay, she must hear argument. Did not Pasiphaë,
who was a queen, love a bull?[58] And was not Calisto,
the mother of Arcas, turned into a bear, and made a star,
Mistress Ursula,[59] i' the heavens?

Ot. O Lord; that I could ha' said as much! I will
have these stories painted i' the Bear-garden, *ex Ovidii
Metamorphosi.*[60]

Dauph. Where is your princess, Captain? Pray be
our leader.

Ot. That I shall, sir.

Cler. Make haste, good Sir Amorous.   300

                                                              [*Exeunt.*]

[III.ii]

[*Enter* MOROSE, EPICOENE, Parson, CUTBEARD.]

Mor. Sir, there's an angel[1] for yourself, and a brace[2]
of angels for your cold. Muse not at this manage[3] of my

---

[44] *provision:* preparations.
[45] *told . . . own:* let him know the truth about himself.
[46] *make one:* join with you.   [47] *sewer:* waiter.
[48] *bare:* bare-headed: the proposer of the toast takes off
his hat to the lady.   [49] *noise:* band.
[50] *emulation:* contention, ill will (though not so glossed by
OED until later in the century).
[51] *expostulate:* reason; "talk things out."
[52] *purse-net:* purse drawn together at the mouth with a
string.   [53] *pest'ling:* crushing (as with a pestle).
[54] *train:* the line of gunpowder which ignites the mine.
[55] *carry:* manage.   [56] *L.:* in haste.
[57] *L.:* beautiful.   [58] *bull:* one of Jupiter's disguises.
[59] *Ursula:* the constellation Ursa Minor or Lesser Bear.
[60] *L.:* out of Ovid's *Metamorphoses,* whence the story of
Calisto (but not Pasiphaë).

III.ii.
[1] *angel:* gold coin.   [2] *brace:* pair.   [3] *manage:* exercise.

bounty. It is fit we should thank fortune, double to[4] nature, for any benefit she confers upon us; besides, it is your imperfection,[5] but my solace.

Par. I thank your worship; so is it mine now.

The Parson *speaks as having a cold.*

Mor. What says he, Cutbeard?

Cut. He says *Praesto*,[6] sir, whensoever your worship needs him, he can be ready with the like. He got this cold with sitting up late, and singing catches[7] with cloth-workers.   11

Mor. No more. I thank him.

Par. God keep your worship, and give you much joy with your fair spouse!—Umh, umh.   *He coughs.*

Mor. Oh, oh! stay, Cutbeard! let him give me five shillings of my money back. As it is bounty to reward benefits, so is it equity to mulct[8] injuries. I will have it. What says he?

Cut. He cannot change it, sir.

Mor. It must be changed.   20

Cut. [*Aside to* Parson] Cough again.

Mor. What says he?

Cut. He will cough out the rest, sir.

Par. Umh, umh, umh.   *Again.*

Mor. Away, away with him! stop his mouth! away! I forgive it.—

      [*Exit* Cutbeard *thrusting out the* Parson.]

Epi. Fie, Master Morose, that you will use this violence to a man of the church.

Mor. How!   29

Epi. It does not become your gravity or breeding, as you pretend[9] in court, to have offered this outrage on a waterman,[10] or any more boisterous creature, much less on a man of his civil[11] coat.

Mor. You can speak then!

Epi. Yes sir.

Mor. Speak out, I mean.

Epi. Ay, sir. Why, do you think you had married a

statue, or a motion[12] only? One of the French puppets, with the eyes turned with a wire? Or some innocent[13] out of the hospital, that would stand with her   40 hands thus,[14] and a plaise[15] mouth, and look upon you?

Mor. O immodesty! a manifest woman! What, Cutbeard!

Epi. Nay, never quarrel with Cutbeard, sir; it is too late now. I confess it doth bate[16] somewhat of the modesty I had, when I writ simply maid: but hope I shall make it a stock still competent[17] to the estate and dignity of your wife.

Mor. She can talk!   50

Epi. Yes, indeed, sir.

[*Enter* Mute.]

Mor. What, sirrah! none of my knaves there? Where is this impostor Cutbeard?

[Mute *makes signs.*]

Epi. Speak to him, fellow speak to him! I'll have none of this coacted,[18] unnatural dumbness in my house, in a family where I govern.

[*Exit* Mute.]

Mor. She is my regent already! I have married a Penthesilea,[19] a Semiramis;[20] sold my liberty to a distaff![21]

[*Enter* Truewit.]

Tru. Where's Master Morose?   60

Mor. Is he come again! Lord have mercy upon me!

Tru. I wish you all joy, Mistress Epicoene, with your grave and honorable match.

Epi. I return you the thanks, Master Truewit, so friendly a wish deserves.

Mor. She has acquaintance too!

Tru. God save you, sir, and give you all contentment in your fair choice, here! before, I was the bird of night to you, the owl;[22] but now I am the messenger of peace, a dove, and bring you the glad wishes of many friends to the celebration of this good hour.   71

Mor. What hour, sir?

Tru. Your marriage hour, sir. I commend your resolution, that, notwithstanding all the dangers I laid afore you, in the voice of a night-crow,[23] would yet go on, and be yourself. It shows you are a man constant to your own ends, and upright to your purposes, that would not be put off with left-handed[24] cries.

Mor. How should you arrive at the knowledge of so much?   80

Tru. Why, did you ever hope, sir, committing the secrecy of it to a barber, that less than the whole town should know it? You might as well ha' told it the conduit[25] or the bakehouse,[26] or the infantry[27] that follow the court, and with more security. Could your gravity forget so old and noted a remnant[28] as, *Lippis et tonsoribus notum?*[29] Well, sir, forgive it yourself now, the fault, and be communicable with your friends. Here will be three or four fashionable ladies from the college to visit you presently, and their train of minions and followers.   91

---

  [4] *double to:* twice as much as.

  [5] *imperfection:* i.e., the Parson's cold, which keeps him quiet.   [6] *Praesto:* I stand ready.

  [7] *catches:* rounds (songs).   [8] *mulct:* punish, as by fine.

  [9] *pretend:* aspire to.

  [10] *waterman:* Thames boatman: low fellow, and proverbially noisy.

  [11] *civil:* sober (though *OED* does not so gloss until later).

  [12] *motion:* puppet.   [13] *innocent:* witless creature.

  [14] *thus:* palms up, in the attitude of a suppliant(?).

  [15] *plaise:* puckered, wry; hence "silent."

  [16] *bate:* diminish.

  [17] *stock . . . competent:* supply (of modesty) sufficing.

  [18] *coacted:* compulsory.

  [19] *Penthesilea:* Amazonian queen.

  [20] *Semiramis:* Babylonian warrior queen.

  [21] *distaff:* on which wool or flax was wound; woman's business, and hence generically a woman.

  [22] *owl:* ill-omened bird.

  [23] *night-crow:* "aboding luckless time," as in Shakespeare's 3 *Henry VI,* V. vi. 45.   [24] *left-handed:* sinister.

  [25] *conduit:* water pipe (which echoes).

  [26] *bakehouse:* presumably where crowds foregather.

  [27] *infantry:* mean servants (given to gossiping).

  [28] *remnant:* proverbial scrap or tag.

  [29] *L.:* Known (even) to half-blind barbers.

Mor. Bar my doors! bar my doors! where are all my eaters? My mouths,[30] now?—

[*Enter* Servants.]

Bar up my doors, you varlets!

Epi. He is a varlet that stirs to such an office. Let 'hem stand open. I would see him that dares move his eyes toward it. Shall I have a barricado made against my friends, to be barred of any pleasure they can bring in to me with honorable visitation?

[*Exeunt* Servants.]

Mor. O Amazonian impudence!   100

Tru. Nay, faith, in this, sir, she speaks but reason. And, methinks, is more continent[31] than you. Would you go to bed so presently, sir, afore noon? A man of your head and hair[32] should owe more to that reverend ceremony, and not mount the marriage-bed like a town-bull, or a mountain-goat; but stay the due season; and ascend it then with religion and fear. Those delights are to be steeped in the humor and silence of the night; and give the day to other open pleasures, and jollities of feasting, of music, of revels, of discourse: we'll   110 have all, sir, that may make your Hymen[33] high and happy.

Mor. O my torment, my torment!

Tru. Nay, if you endure the first half hour, sir, so tediously, and with this irksomeness, what comfort or hope can this fair gentlewoman make to herself here-after, in the consideration of so many years as are to come—

Mor. Of my affliction. Good sir, depart, and let her do it alone.   120

Tru. I have done, sir.

Mor. That cursed barber!

Tru. Yes, faith, a cursed wretch indeed, sir.

Mor. I have married his cittern,[34] that's common to all men. Some plague above the plague—

Tru. All Egypt's ten plagues.

Mor. Revenge me on him!

Tru. 'Tis very well, sir. If you had laid on a curse or two more, I'll assure you he'll bear 'hem. As, that he may get the pox with seeking to cure it, sir; or,   130 that while he is curling another man's hair, his own may drop off; or, for burning some male bawd's lock,[35] he may have his brain beat out with the curling-iron.

Mor. No, let the wretch live wretched. May he get the itch[36] and his shop so lousy, as no man dare come at him, nor he come at no man!

Tru. Ay, and if he would swallow all his balls[37] for pills, let not them purge him.

Mor. Let his warming-pan be ever cold.

Tru. A perpetual frost underneath it, sir.   140

Mor. Let him never hope to see fire again.

Tru. But in hell, sir.

Mor. His chairs be always empty, his scissors rust, and his combs mold in their cases.

Tru. Very dreadful that! and may he lose the inven-tion, sir, of carving lanterns in paper.[38]

Mor. Let there be no bawd carted that year, to employ a basin[39] of his: but let him be glad to eat his sponge for bread.

Tru. And drink lotium[40] to it, and much good do him.   151

Mor. Or, for want of bread—

Tru. Eat ear-wax, sir. I'll help you. Or draw his own teeth, and add them to the lute-string.[41]

Mor. No, beat the old ones to powder, and make bread of them.

Tru. Yes, make meal o' the millstones.

Mor. May all the botches and burns that he has cured on others break out upon him.   159

Tru. And he now forget the cure of 'hem in himself, sir; or, if he do remember it, let him ha' scraped all his linen into lint for't, and have not a rag left him to set up with.

Mor. Let him never set up again, but have the gout in his hands for ever. Now, no more, sir.

Tru. Oh, that last was too high set! you might go less with him, i' faith, and be revenged enough: as, that he be never able to new-paint his pole—

Mor. Good sir, no more, I forgot myself.

Tru. Or, want credit to take up with a combmaker—

Mor. No more, sir.   171

Tru. Or, having broken his glass in a former despair, fall now into a much greater, of ever getting another—

Mor. I beseech you, no more.

Tru. Or that he never be trusted with trimming of any but chimney-sweepers[42]—

Mor. Sir—

Tru. Or, may he cut a collier's[43] throat with his razor, by chance-medley[44] and yet hang for 't.   179

Mor. I will forgive him rather than hear any more. I beseech you, sir.

[*Enter* DAW, Lady HAUGHTY, CENTAURE, MAVIS, *and* TRUSTY.]

Daw. This way, madam.

Mor. Oh, the sea breaks in upon me! another flood!

---

[30] *eaters . . . mouths:* servants (viewed as parasites, like Gobbo in *The Merchant of Venice*).

[31] *continent:* temperate.

[32] *head and hair:* intellect and quality.

[33] *Hymen:* Nupitals.

[34] *cittern:* a variety of lute, on which customers played while waiting to be barbered.

[35] *burning . . . lock:* curling a pander's hair.

[36] *itch:* at worst, "venereal disease."

[37] *balls:* soap (laxative).

[38] *carving . . . paper:* perhaps a sneering allusion to Jonson's great antagonist, "mountebank" and "tireman" Inigo Jones, the most celebrated theatrical designer of the age. Elsewhere in Jonson (*Tale of a Tub*, V), the covering of vessels with oiled lantern-paper is associated with barbers and cutlers. The designer is perhaps likened inferentially to such low persons as he is mocked (in "An Expostulation with Inigo Jones") for producing spectacular lighting effects in the same way.

[39] *bawd . . . basin:* Pimps and prostitutes were exposed in carts to public contempt, evinced by ringing on basins borrowed from the barbers.

[40] *lotium:* stale urine, used to set hair.

[41] *draw . . . string:* Barbers acted also as dentists and hung up extracted teeth on a string in their shops.

[42] *chimney-sweepers:* necessarily filthy.

[43] *collier's:* charcoal maker, or coal miner.

[44] *chance-medley:* accidental homicide.

an inundation! I shall be overwhelmed with noise. It
beats already at my shores. I feel an earthquake in
myself for 't.

Daw. 'Give you joy, mistress.

Mor. Has she servants too!

Daw. I have brought some ladies here to see and
know you.　　　　　190

[*She kisses them severally,*[45] *as he presents them.*]

—My Lady Haughty—this my Lady Centaure—
Mistress Dol Mavis—Mistress Trusty, my Lady
Haughty's woman. Where's your husband? Let's see
him: can he endure no noise? Let me come to him.

Mor. What nomenclator[46] is this!

Tru. Sir John Daw, sir, your wife's servant, this.

Mor. A Daw, and her servant! Oh, 'tis decreed, 'tis
decreed of me, and[47] she have such servants.

[*Going.*]

Tru. Nay, sir, you must kiss the ladies; you must
not go away now; they come toward you to seek you
out.　　　　　201

Hau. I' faith, Master Morose, would you steal a
marriage thus, in the midst of so many friends, and not
acquaint us? Well, I'll kiss you, notwithstanding the
justice of my quarrel: you shall give me leave, mistress,
to use a becoming familiarity with your husband.

Epi. Your ladyship does me an honor in it, to let
me know he is so worthy your favor: as you have done
both him and me grace to visit so unprepared a pair
to entertain you.　　　　　210

Mor. Compliment! compliment!

Epi. But I must lay the burden of that upon my
servant here.

Hau. It shall not need, Mistress Morose; we will all
bear rather than one shall be oppressed.

Mor. I know it: and you will teach her the faculty, if
she be[48] to learn it.

[*Walks aside.*]

Hau. Is this the Silent Woman?

Cen. Nay, she has found her tongue since she was
married, Master Truewit says.　　　　　220

Hau. Oh, Master Truewit! 'Save you. What kind of
creature is your bride here? She speaks, methinks!

Tru. Yes, madam, believe it, she is a gentlewoman of
very absolute[49] behavior, and of a good race.

Hau. And Jack Daw told us she could not speak!

Tru. So it was carried in plot, madam, to put her
upon this old fellow, by Sir Dauphine, his nephew, and
one or two more of us: but she is a woman of an excellent assurance, and an extraordinary happy wit and
tongue. You shall see her make rare sport with Daw ere
night.　　　　　231

Hau. And he brought us to laugh at her!

Tru. That falls out often, madam, that he that thinks
himself the master-wit, is the master-fool. I assure your
ladyship, ye cannot laugh at her.

Hau. No, we'll have her to the college. And she have
wit, she shall be one of us, shall she not, Centaure?
We'll make her a collegiate.

Cen. Yes, faith, madam, and Mavis and she will set
up a side.[50]　　　　　240

Tru. Believe it, madam, and Mistress Mavis, she will
sustain her part.

Mav. I'll tell you that when I have talked with her,
and tried her.

Hau. Use her very civilly, Mavis.

Mav. So I will, madam.

[*Whispers to her.*]

Mor. [*Aside*] Blessed minute, that they would whisper thus ever!

Tru. In the mean time, madam, would but your
ladyship help to vex him a little: you know his　250
disease; talk to him about the wedding ceremonies, or
call for your gloves,[51] or—

Hau. Let me alone.[52] Centaure, help me.—Master
bridegroom, where are you?

Mor. [*Aside*] Oh, it was too miraculously good to
last!

Hau. We see no ensigns[53] of a wedding here; no
character of a bride-ale: where be our scarves and our
gloves? I pray you, give 'hem us. Let's know your
bride's colors,[54] and yours at least.　　　　　260

Cen. Alas, madam, he has provided none.

Mor. Had I known your ladyship's painter, I would.

Hau. He has given it you, Centaure, i' faith. But do
you hear, Master Morose! a jest will not absolve you in
this manner. You that have sucked the milk of the
court, and from thence have been brought up to the very
strong meats and wine of it; been a courtier from the
biggen to the nightcap,[55] as we may say, and you to
offend in such a high point of ceremony as this, and let
your nupitals want all marks of solemnity! How　270
much plate have you lost[56] today (if you had but regarded your profit), what gifts, what friends, through
your mere rusticity![57]

Mor. Madam—

Hau. Pardon me, sir, I must insinuate[58] your errors
to you. No gloves? No garters? No scarves? No epithalamium?[59] No masque?

Daw. Yes, madam, I'll make an epithalamium, I
promised my mistress; I have begun it already: will
your ladyship hear it?　　　　　280

Hau. Ay, good Jack Daw.

Mor. Will it please your ladyship command a chamber, and be private with your friend? You shall have
your choice of rooms to retire to after: my whole house

---

[45] *severally:* one by one.　　[46] *nomenclator:* presenter.
[47] *'tis . . . and:* judgment is passed on me that.
[48] *be:* be apt.
[49] *absolute:* perfect; alternatively, arbitrary.
[50] *set . . . side:* act as partners (as in a card game).
[51] *gloves:* which ladies were made a present of at weddings.
[52] *Let me alone:* Leave it to me.
[53] *ensigns:* signs, tokens.
[54] *colors:* In elaborate nuptials, opposing parties of tilters
or mock combatants, each party dressed in a color designating the bride or groom, might be introduced.
[55] *the biggen . . . nightcap:* infancy to old age (a "biggen"
is a baby's bonnet).
[56] *plate have you lost:* silver or gold wedding presents have
you forfeited.　　　　　　　　[57] *rusticity:* boorishness.
[58] *insinuate:* hint at.　　[59] *epithalamium:* marriage ode.

is yours. I know it hath been your ladyship's errand
into the city at other times; however, now you have been
unhappily diverted upon me; but I shall be loath to
break any honorable custom of your ladyship's. And
therefore, good madam—   289

Epi. Come, you are a rude bridegroom, to entertain
ladies of honor in this fashion.

Cen. He is a rude groom, indeed.

Tru. By that light, you deserve to be grafted,[60] and
have your horns reach from one side of the island to the
other. Do not mistake me, sir; I but speak this to give
the ladies some heart again, not for any malice to you.

Mor. Is this your bravo,[61] ladies?

Tru. As God help me, if you utter such another
word, I'll take mistress bride in, and begin to[62] you
in a very sad cup, do you see? Go to, know your
friends, and such as love you.   301

[*Enter* CLERIMONT *followed by a number of*
Musicians.]

Cler. By your leave, ladies. Do you want any music?
I have brought you variety of noises. Play, sirs, all of
you.

Music of all sorts.

Mor. Oh, a plot, a plot, a plot upon me! this day I
shall be their anvil to work on, they will grate me
asunder. 'Tis worse than the noise of a saw.

Cler. No, they are hair, rosin, and guts. I can give
you the receipt.

Tru. Peace, boys!   310

Cler. Play! I say.

Tru. Peace, rascals! you see who's your friend now,
sir? Take courage, put on a martyr's resolution. Mock
down all their attemptings with patience. 'Tis but a
day, and I would suffer heroically. Should an ass exceed
me in fortitude? No. You betray your infirmity with
your hanging dull ears, and make them insult: bear up
bravely, and constantly.

LA FOOLE *passes over, sewing*[63] *the meat.*

Look you here, sir, what honor is done you unexpected,
by your nephew; a wedding dinner come, and a   320
knight-sewer before it, for the more reputation. And
fine Mistress Otter, your neighbor, in the rump or tail
of it.

Mor. Is that Gorgon, that Medusa come! hide me!
hide me.

Tru. I warrant you, sir, she will not transform you.[64]
Look upon her with a good courage. Pray you entertain
her, and conduct your guests in. No? Mistress bride,
will you entreat in the ladies? Your bridegroom is so
shamefaced here.   330

Epi. Will it please your ladyship, madam?

Hau. With the benefit of your company, mistress.

Epi. Servant, pray you perform your duties.

Daw. And glad to be commanded, mistress.

Cen. How like you her wit, Mavis?

Mav. Very prettily, absolutely well.

Mrs. Ot. 'Tis my place.

Mav. You shall pardon me, Mistress Otter.

Mrs. Ot. Why, I am a collegiate.

Mav. But not in ordinary.[65]   340

Mrs. Ot. But I am.

Mav. We'll dispute that within.

[*Exeunt* Ladies.]

Cler. Would this had lasted a little longer.

Tru. And that they had sent for the heralds.[66]

[*Enter* Captain OTTER.]

—Captain Otter! what news?

Ot. I have brought my bull, bear, and horse, in
private, and yonder are the trumpeters without, and
the drum, gentlemen.

The drum and trumpets sound.

Mor. Oh, oh, oh!   349

Ot. And we will have a rouse[67] in each of 'hem,
anon, for bold Britons, i' faith.

[*They sound again.*]

Mor. Oh, oh, oh!

[*Exit hastily.*]

All. Follow, follow, follow!

[*Exeunt.*]

ACT FOUR

SCENE ONE

[*Enter* TRUEWIT *and* CLERIMONT.]

Tru. Was there ever poor bridegroom so tormented?
Or man, indeed?

Cler. I have not read of the like in the chronicles of
the land.

Tru. Sure, he cannot but go to a place of rest, after
all this purgatory.

Cler. He may presume it, I think.

Tru. The spitting, the coughing, the laughter, the
neezing,[1] the farting, dancing, noise of the music, and
her masculine and loud commanding, and urging   10
the whole family,[2] makes him think he has married a
fury.

Cler. And she carries it up bravely.

Tru. Ay, she takes any occasion to speak: that's the
height on't.[3]

Cler. And how soberly Dauphine labors to satisfy
him, that it was none of his plot!

Tru. And has almost brought him to the faith, i' the
article. Here he comes.—

[*Enter* SIR DAUPHINE.]

---

[60] *grafted:* with horns (cuckolded).
[61] *bravo:* hired bully.   [62] *begin to:* pledge.
[63] *sewing:* serving.
[64] *transform you:* into stone (as the Gorgon did).
[65] *in ordinary:* belonging to the regular staff or class.
[66] *heralds:* to settle the question of rank; "in ordinary" or
not.
[67] *rouse:* carouse (as substantive); deep draught of liquor.
IV.i.
[1] *neezing:* sneezing.   [2] *family:* household.
[3] *height on't:* best of it.

Where is he now? What's become of him, Dauphine?   21

Dauph. Oh, hold me up a little, I shall go away i' the jest [4] else. He has got on his whole nest of night caps, and locked himself up i' the top o' the house, as high as ever he can climb from the noise. I peeped in at a cranny, and saw him sitting over a cross-beam o' the roof, like him o' the saddler's horse in Fleet Street,[5] upright: and he will sleep there.

Cler. But where are your collegiates?

Dauph. Withdrawn with the bride in private.   30

Tru. Oh, they are instructing her i' the college-grammar. If she have grace with them, she knows all their secrets instantly.

Cler. Methinks the Lady Haughty looks well today, for all my dispraise of her i' the morning. I think I shall come about to thee again, Truewit.

Tru. Believe it, I told you right. Women ought to repair the losses time and years have made i' their features, with dressings. And an intelligent woman, if she know by herself the least defect, will be most   40 curious [6] to hide it: and it becomes her. If she be short, let her sit much, lest, when she stands, she be thought to sit. If she have an ill foot, let her wear her gown the longer, and her shoe the thinner. If a fat hand and scald [7] nails, let her carve [8] the less, and act in gloves. If a sour breath, let her never discourse fasting, and always talk at her distance. If she have black and rugged [9] teeth, let her offer the less at laughter, especially if she laugh wide and open.   49

Cler. Oh, you shall have some women, when they laugh you would think they brayed, it is so rude and—

Tru. Ay, and others, that will stalk i' their gait like an estrich,[10] and take huge strides. I cannot endure such a sight. I love measure [11] 'n the feet, and number [12] i' the voice: they are gentlenesses that oftentimes draw no less than the face.

Dauph. How camest thou to study these creatures so exactly? I would thou wouldst make me a proficient.

Tru. Yes, but you must leave to live i' your   60 chamber, then, a month together upon *Amadis de Gaul*,[13] or *Don Quixote*, as you are wont; and come abroad where the matter is frequent, to court, to tiltings,

public shows and feasts, to plays, and church sometimes; thither they come to show their new tires too, to see, and to be seen. In these places a man shall find whom to love, whom to play with, whom to touch once, whom to hold ever. The variety arrests his judgment. A wench to please a man comes not down dropping from the ceiling, as he lies on his back droning [14] a tobacco pipe. He must go where she is.   71

Dauph. Yes, and be never the near.[15]

Tru. Out, heretic! that diffidence makes thee worthy it should be so.

Cler. He says true to you, Dauphine.

Dauph. Why?

Tru. A man should not doubt to overcome any woman. Think he can vanquish 'hem, and he shall: for though they deny, their desire is to be tempted. Penelope [16] herself cannot hold out long. Ostend,[17] you   80 saw, was taken at last. You must persèver and hold to your purpose. They would solicit us, but that they are afraid. Howsoever, they wish in their hearts we should solicit them. Praise 'hem, flatter 'hem, you shall never want eloquence or trust: even the chastest delight to feel themselves that way rubbed. With praises you must mix kisses too. If they take them they'll take more—though they strive, they would be overcome.

Cler. Oh, but a man must beware of force.   89

Tru. It is to them an acceptable violence, and has oft-times the place of the greatest courtesy. She that might have been forced, and you let her go free without touching, though she then seem to thank you, will ever hate you after; and glad i' the face, is assuredly sad at the heart.

Cler. But all women are not to be taken all ways.

Tru. 'Tis true; no more than all birds, or all fishes. If you appear learned to an ignorant wench, or jocund to a sad, or witty to a foolish, why, she presently begins to mistrust herself. You must approach them i'   100 their own height, their own line; for the contrary makes many that fear to commit themselves to noble and worthy fellows, run into the embraces of a rascal. If she love wit, give verses, though you borrow 'hem of a friend, or buy 'hem, to have good. If valor, talk of your sword, and be frequent in the mention of quarrels, though you be staunch [18] in fighting. If activity, be seen o' your barbary [19] often, or leaping over stools, for the credit of your back. If she love good clothes or dressing, have your learned council about you every   110 morning, French tailor, barber, linener, etc. Let your powder, your glass, and your comb be your dearest acquaintance. Take more care for the ornament of your head, than the safety; and wish the commonwealth rather troubled, than a hair about you. That will take her. Then, if she be covetous and craving, do you promise anything, and perform sparingly; so shall you keep her in appetite still. Seem as you would give, but be like a barren field that yields little, or unlucky dice to foolish and hoping gamesters. Let your gifts be   120 slight and dainty, rather than precious. Let cunning be above cost. Give cherries at time of year, or apricots; and say, they were sent you out o' the country, though you bought 'hem in Cheapside. Admire her tires; like

---

[4] *go . . . jest:* die laughing.

[5] *saddler's . . . Street:* perhaps a painted figure hanging before a tavern; or a now-vanished statue like that of Charles I "at Charing Cross, where sits a black man on a black horse."   [6] *curious:* painstaking.   [7] *scald:* scabbed.

[8] *carve:* gesture.   [9] *rugged:* broken, uneven.

[10] *estrich:* ostrich.   [11] *measure:* measured gait.

[12] *number:* periodicity; even speech.

[13] *Amadis de Gaul:* Famous chivalric romance, much execrated by sober writers of the period, including Jonson (who was contemptuous also of Cervantes' novel).

[14] *droning:* smoking.   [15] *near:* nearer.

[16] *Penelope:* Ulysses' long-suffering wife, the type of constancy.

[17] *Ostend:* which fell to the Spaniards in 1604 after a siege of three years.

[18] *staunch:* not inclined to boast. The sense seems to be "Though you are not much inclined to fight."

[19] *barbary:* horse.

her in all fashions; compare her in every habit to some
deity; invent excellent dreams to flatter her, and riddles;
or, if she be a great one, perform always the second
parts[20] to her: like what she likes, praise whom she
praises, and fail not to make the household and servants
yours, yea, the whole family, and salute 'hem by   130
their names ('tis but light cost, if you can purchase
'hem so), and make her physician your pensioner,[21]
and her chief woman. Nor will it be out of your gain
to make love to her too, so she follow, not usher her
lady's pleasure. All blabbing is taken away when she
comes to be a part of the crime.

Dauph. On what courtly lap hast thou late[22] slept,
to come forth so sudden and absolute a courtling?[23]

Tru. Good faith, I should rather question you, that
are so hearkening after these mysteries. I begin to   140
suspect your diligence, Dauphine. Speak, art thou in
love in earnest?

Dauph. Yes, by my troth, am I! 'twere ill dissembling
before thee.

Tru. With which of 'hem, I pray thee?

Dauph. With all the collegiates.

Cler. Out on thee! we'll keep you at home, believe it,
i' the stable, and you be such a stallion.

Tru. No. I like him well. Men should love wisely,
and all women: some one for the face, and let her   150
please the eye; another for the skin, and let her please
the touch; a third for the voice, and let her please the
ear; and where the objects mix, let the senses so too.
Thou wouldst think it strange if I should make 'hem
all in love with thee afore night!

Dauph. I would say, thou hadst the best philtre[24] i'
the world, and couldst do more than Madam Medea,[25]
or Doctor Foreman.[26]

Tru. If I do not, let me play the mountebank for my
meat while I live, and the bawd for my drink.   160

Dauph. So be it, I say.

[*Enter* OTTER, DAW, *and* LA FOOLE.]

Ot. O Lord, gentlemen, how my knights and I have
missed you here!

Cler. Why, Captain, what service, what service?

Ot. To see me bring up my bull, bear, and horse to
fight.

Daw. Yes, faith, the captain says we shall be his
dogs to bait 'hem.

Dauph. A good employment.

Tru. Come on, let's see a course[27] then.   170

La F. I am afraid my cousin will be offended, if she
come.

Ot. Be afraid of nothing. Gentlemen, I have placed
the drum and the trumpets, and one to give 'hem the
sign when you are ready. Here's my bull for myself, and
my bear for Sir John Daw, and my horse for Sir
Amorous. Now set your foot to mine,[28] and yours to
his, and—

La F. Pray God my cousin come not.   179

Ot. St. George and St. Andrew, fear no cousins.
Come, sound, sound!

[*Drum and trumpets sound.*]

Et rauco strepuerunt cornua cantu.[29]

[*They drink.*]

Tru. Well said, Captain, i' faith; well fought at the
bull.[30]

Cler. Well held at the bear.

Tru. Low, low! Captain.

Dauph. Oh, the horse has kicked off his dog already.

La F. I cannot drink it, as I am a knight.

Tru. Gods so! off with his spurs, somebody.

La F. It goes against my conscience. My cousin will
be angry with it.   191

Daw. I ha' done mine.

Tru. You fought high and fair, Sir John.

Cler. At the head.

Dauph. Like an excellent bear-dog.

Cler. You take no notice of the business, I hope?

Daw. Not a word, sir; you see we are jovial.

Ot. Sir Amorous, you must not equivocate. It must
be pulled down,[31] for all my cousin.   199

Cler. 'Sfoot, if you take not your drink, they'll think
you are discontented with something; you'll betray all,
if you take the least notice.

La F. Not I; I'll both drink and talk then.

Ot. You must pull the horse on his knees, Sir
Amorous; fear no cousins. *Jacta est alea.*[32]

Tru. Oh, now he's in his vein, and bold. The least
hint given him of his wife now will make him rail
desperately.

Cler. Speak to him of her.   209

Tru. Do you, and I'll fetch her to the hearing of it.
[*Exit.*]

Dauph. Captain He-Otter, your She-Otter is coming,
your wife.

Ot. Wife! Buz![33] *Titivilitium!*[34] There's no such
thing in nature. I confess, gentlemen, I have a cook, a
laundress, a house-drudge, that serves my necessary
turns, and goes under that title; but he's an ass that will
be so uxorious[35] to tie his affection to one circle. Come,
the name dulls appetite. Here, replenish again; another
bout.

[*Fills the cups again.*]

Wives are nasty, sluttish animals.   220

Dauph. Oh, Captain.

---

[20] *second parts:* inferior; i.e., play second fiddle.
[21] *pensioner:* i.e., get him in your pocket, as by bribing
him.   [22] *late:* recently.   [23] *courtling:* courtier.
[24] *philtre:* love potion.
[25] *Medea:* celebrated for her skill in magic, as when she
assisted Jason in stealing the golden fleece.
[26] *Doctor Foreman:* astrologer and quack doctor of the
time, and sought after as maker of love potions.
[27] *course:* bear baiting.   [28] *set . . . mine:* back me up.
[29] *L.:* Quoting Virgil, *Aeneid,* viii. 2: "And the horns
blared with raucous sound."
[30] *well . . . bull:* The metaphors that follow, almost to the
exit of Truewit, are drawn from the cant of bear baiting and
bull baiting.   [31] *pulled down:* drunk off.
[32] *L.:* The die is cast: Caesar, on crossing the Rubicon.
[33] *Buz:* exclamation of impatience or contempt.
[34] *L.:* a trifle.   [35] *uxorious:* dominated by his wife.

Ot. As ever the earth bare, *tribus verbis.*[36] Where's Master Truewit?

Daw. He's slipped aside, sir.

Cler. But you must drink and be jovial.

Daw. Yes, give it me.

La F. And me too.

Daw. Let's be jovial.

La F. As jovial as you will.   229

Ot. Agreed. Now you shall ha' the bear, cousin, and Sir John Daw the horse, and I'll ha' the bull still. Sound, Tritons[37] o' the Thames!

[Drums and trumpets sound again.]

Nunc est bibendum, nunc pede libero[38]—

MOROSE *speaks from above: the trumpets sounding.*

Mor. Villains, murderers, sons of the earth,[39] and traitors, what do you there?

Cler. Oh, now the trumpets have waked him, we shall have his company.

Ot. A wife is a scurvy clogdogdo,[40] an unlucky thing, a very foresaid[41] bear-whelp, without any good fashion or breeding, *mala bestia.*[42]   240

His wife is brought out [by TRUEWIT] *to hear him.*

Dauph. Why did you marry one then, Captain?

Ot. A pox! I married with six thousand pound, I. I was in love with that. I ha' not kissed my fury these forty weeks.

Cler. The more to blame you, Captain.

Tru. Nay, Mistress Otter, hear him a little first.

Ot. She has a breath worse than my grandmother's, *profecto.*[43]

Mrs. Ot. O treacherous liar! kiss me, sweet Master Truewit, and prove him a slandering knave.   250

Tru. I'll rather believe you, lady.

Ot. And she has a peruke[44] that's like a pound of hemp, made up in shoe-threads.

Mrs. Ot. O viper, mandrake!

Ot. A most vile face! and yet she spends me[45] forty pound a year in mercury and hog's-bones.[46] All her teeth were made i' the Blackfriars, both her eyebrows i' the Strand, and her hair in Silver-street.[47] Every part o' the town owns a piece of her.

Mrs. Ot. I cannot hold.   260

Ot. She takes herself asunder still when she goes to bed, into some twenty boxes; and about next day noon is put together again, like a great German clock;[48] and so comes forth, and rings a tedious larum to the whole house, and then is quiet again for an hour, but for her quarters.[49]—Ha' you done me right, gentlemen?

Mrs. Ot. No, sir, I'll do you right with my quarters, with my quarters![50]

She falls upon him and beats him.

Ot. Oh, hold, good princess.

Tru. Sound, sound!   270

[Drum and trumpets sound.]

Cler. A battle, a battle!

Mrs. Ot. You notorious stinkardly bearward,[51] does my breath smell?

Ot. Under correction,[52] dear princess. Look to my bear and my horse, gentlemen.

Mrs. Ot. Do I want teeth and eyebrows, thou bull-dog?

Tru. Sound, sound still.

[They sound again.]

Ot. No, I protest, under correction—   279

Mrs. Ot. Ay, now you are under correction, you protest; but you did not protest before correction, sir. Thou Judas, to offer to betray thy princess! I'll make thee an example—

MOROSE *descends with a long sword.*

Mor. I will have no such examples in my house, Lady Otter.

Mrs. Ot. Ah—

[Mrs. OTTER, DAW, *and* LA FOOLE *run off.]*

Mor. Mistress Mary Ambree,[53] your examples are dangerous. Rogues, hell hounds, Stentors![54] out of my doors, you sons of noise and tumult, begot on an ill May-day,[55] or when the Galley-foist[56] is afloat to   290 Westminster! A trumpeter could not be conceived but then.

[Drives out the Musicians.]

Dauph. What ails you, sir?

Mor. They have rent my roof, walls, and all my windows asunder with their brazen throats.

[Exit.]

Tru. Best follow him, Dauphine.

Dauph. So I will.

Cler. Where's Daw and La Foole?   298

Ot. They are both run away, sir. Good gentlemen,

---

[36] *L.:* i.e., in a word.

[37] *Tritons:* Trumpeters of Neptune, the sea-god.

[38] *L.:* Quoting Horace, *Odes,* I. xxxvii. 1: "Now is the time for drinking, now with free foot."

[39] *sons of the earth:* bastards.

[40] *clogdogdo:* clog(?) (precise meaning unknown).

[41] *foresaid:* giving to the word the superlative sense: "absolute," "extreme."   [42] *L.:* evil animal.

[43] *L.:* really and truly.   [44] *peruke:* head of hair.

[45] *spends me:* ethical dative.

[46] *mercury and hogs'-bones:* used in making cosmetics.

[47] *Blackfriars . . . Silver-street:* The street names pun on Mistress Otter's ugly appearance ("strand" means filament of hair; here, presumably, a good deal of hair).

[48] *German clock:* proverbially always in need of repair.

[49] *but . . . quarters:* except that she rings her alarm to sound each quarter-hour.

[50] *quarters:* here, the parts of the body, hands and feet, with which Mistress Otter pummels her husband.

[51] *bearward:* bear keeper.

[52] *Under correction:* a polite disclaimer: "Begging your pardon."

[53] *Mary Ambree:* heroine of a ballad celebrating her supposed exploits as a soldier at the siege of Ghent, 1584.

[54] *Stentors:* Noise makers (after the loud-voiced or "stentorian" herald of the Greeks at the siege of Troy).

[55] *ill May-day:* alluding to the London rioting against foreign tradesmen on May-day 1517.

[56] *Galley-foist:* state barge on which the new Lord Mayor traveled to Westminster for his inaugural; hence an occasion of celebration and tumult.

help to pacify my princess, and speak to the great ladies for me. Now must I go lie with the bears this fortnight, and keep out o' the way, till my peace be made, for[57] this scandal[58] she has taken. Did you not see my bull-head, gentlemen?

Cler. Is't not on,[59] Captain?

Tru. No; but he may make a new one, by that[60] is on.

Ot. Oh, here 'tis. And you come over, gentlemen, and ask for Tom Otter, we'll go down to Ratcliff,[61] and have a course i' faith, for[62] all these disasters. There's *bona spes*[63] left. 310

Tru. Away, Captain, get off while you are well.

[*Exit* OTTER.]

Cler. I am glad we are rid of him.

Tru. You had never been unless we had put his wife upon him. His humor is as tedious at last as it was ridiculous at first.

[*Exeunt.*]

[IV.ii]

[*Enter*] HAUGHTY, Mistress OTTER, MAVIS, DAW, LA FOOLE, CENTAURE, EPICOENE, TRUEWIT, CLERIMONT.

Hau. We wondered why you shrieked so, Mistress Otter.

Mrs. Ot. O God, madam, he came down with a huge long naked weapon in both his hands, and looked so dreadfully! sure he's beside himself.

Mav. Why, what made you there, Mistress Otter?

Mrs. Ot. Alas, Mistress Mavis, I was chastising my subject, and thought nothing of him.

Daw. Faith, mistress, you must do so too. Learn to chastise. Mistress Otter corrects her husband so he dares not speak, but under correction. 11

La F. And with his hat off to her: 'twould do you good to see.

Hau. In sadness,[1] 'tis good and mature counsel; practise it, Morose. I'll call you Morose still now, as I call Centaure and Mavis; we four will be all one.

Cen. And you'll come to the college, and live with us?

Hau. Make him give you milk and honey.

Mav. Look how you manage him at first, you shall have him ever after. 21

Cen. Let him allow you your coach and four horses, your woman, your chamber-maid, your page, your gentleman-usher, your French cook, and four grooms.

Hau. And go with us to Bedlam, to the china houses, and to the Exchange.

Cen. It will open the gate to your fame.

Hau. Here's Centaure has immortalized herself with taming of her wild male. 29

Mav. Ay, she has done the miracle of the kingdom.

Epi. But, ladies, do you count it lawful to have such plurality of servants, and do 'hem all graces?

Hau. Why not? And why should women deny their favors to men? Are they the poorer or the worse?

Daw. Is the Thames the less for the dyers' water,[2] mistress?

La F. Or a torch for lighting many torches?

Tru. Well said, La Foole; what a new one he has got! 39

Cen. They are empty losses women fear in this kind.

Hau. Besides, ladies should be mindful of the approach of age, and let no time want his due use. The best of our days pass first.

Mav. We are rivers that cannot be called back, madam: she that now excludes her lovers may live to lie a forsaken beldam[3] in a frozen bed.

Cen. 'Tis true, Mavis; and who will wait on us to coach then? Or write, or tell us the news then? Make anagrams of our names, and invite us to the Cockpit,[4] and kiss our hands all the play-time, and draw their weapons for our honors? 51

Hau. Not one.

Daw. Nay, my mistress is not altogether unintelligent of these things; here be in presence have tasted of her favors.

Cler. What a neighing hobby-horse is this!

Epi. But not with intent to boast 'hem again, servant. And have you those excellent receipts, madam, to keep yourselves from bearing of children? 59

Hau. Oh, yes, Morose. How should we maintain our youth and beauty else? Many births of a woman make her old, as many crops make the earth barren.

[*Enter* MOROSE *and* DAUPHINE.]

Mor. O my cursed angel, that instructed me to this fate!

Dauph. Why, sir?

Mor. That I should be seduced by so foolish a devil as a barber will make!

Dauph. I would I had been worthy, sir, to have partaken your counsel; you should never have trusted it to such a minister. 70

Mor. Would I could redeem it with the loss of an eye, nephew, a hand, or any other member.

Dauph. Marry, God forbid, sir, that you should geld yourself, to anger your wife.

Mor. So it would rid me of her! and that I did supererogatory penance in a belfry, at Westminster-hall, i' the Cockpit, at the fall of a stag, the Tower-wharf—what place is there else?—London-bridge, Paris-garden, Billingsgate,[5] when the noises are at their height, and loudest. Nay, I would sit out a play that 80 were nothing but fights at sea, drum, trumpet, and target![6]

Dauph. I hope there shall be no such need, sir. Take patience, good uncle. This is but a day, and 'tis well worn too now.

---

[57] *for:* because of.   [58] *scandal:* offense.
[59] *on:* i.e., your own head.   [60] *that:* Otter's head.
[61] *Ratcliff:* in Limehouse, a rough district on the London docks.   [62] *for:* despite.   [63] *L.:* good hope.
IV.ii.
[1] *In sadness:* Seriously.
[2] *Is . . . water:* Is a woman poorer or depleted for giving of herself sexually?   [3] *beldam:* old crone, witch.
[4] *Cockpit:* theater where cocks were fought.
[5] *Billingsgate:* where fish and produce were sold; a place of tumult like all the others cited.   [6] *target:* shield.

Mor. Oh, 'twill be so for ever, nephew, I foresee it, for ever. Strife and tumult are the dowry that comes with a wife.

Tru. I told you so, sir, and you would not believe me.

Mor. Alas, do not rub those wounds, Master 90 Truewit, to blood again; 'twas my negligence. Add not affliction to affliction. I have perceived the effect of it too late in Madame Otter.

Epi. How do you, sir?

Mor. Did you ever hear a more unnecessary question? As if she did not see! why, I do as you see, empress, empress.

Epi. You are not well, sir; you look very ill! something has distempered you. 99

Mor. O horrible, monstrous impertinencies! would not one of these have served, do you think, sir? Would not one of these have served?

Tru. Yes, sir, but these are but notes of female kindness, sir; certain tokens that she has a voice, sir.

Mor. Oh, is it so! come, an't be no otherwise— What say you?

Epi. How do you feel yourself, sir?

Mor. Again that!

Tru. Nay, look you, sir, you would be friends with your wife upon unconscionable terms; her silence. 110

Epi. They say you are run mad, sir.

Mor. Not for love, I assure you, of you; do you see?

Epi. O lord, gentlemen! lay hold on him, for God's sake. What shall I do? Who's his physician, can you tell, that knows the state of his body best, that I might send for him? Good sir, speak. I'll send for one of my doctors else.

Mor. What, to poison me, that I might die intestate,[7] and leave you possessed of all? 119

Epi. Lord, how idly he talks, and how his eyes sparkle! he looks green about the temples! do you see what blue spots he has!

Cler. Ay, 'tis melancholy.[8]

Epi. Gentlemen, for heaven's sake, counsel me. Ladies—servant, you have read Pliny and Paracelsus.[9] Ne'er a word now to comfort a poor gentlewoman? Ah me, what fortune had I to marry a distracted man!

Daw. I'll tell you, mistress—

Tru. How rarely she holds it up!

Mor. What mean you, gentlemen? 130

Epi. What will you tell me, servant?

Daw. The disease in Greek is called μανια,[10] in Latin

insania, furor, vel ecstasis melancholica, that is, egressio, when a man ex melancholico evadit fanaticus.[11]

Mor. Shall I have a lecture read upon me alive?

Daw. But he may be but phreneticus yet, mistress; and phrenetis [12] is only delirium, or so.

Epi. Ay, that is for the disease, servant; but what is this to the cure? We are sure enough of the disease.

Mor. Let me go. 140

Tru. Why, we'll entreat her to hold her peace, sir.

Mor. Oh, no, labor not to stop her. She is like a conduit-pipe, that will gush out with more force when she opens again.

Hau. I'll tell you, Morose, you must talk divinity to him altogether, or moral philosophy.

La F. Ay, and there's an excellent book of moral philosophy, madam, of Reynard the Fox, and all the beasts, called *Doni's Philosophy.*[13]

Cen. There is indeed, Sir Amorous La Foole. 150

Mor. O misery!

La F. I have read it, my Lady Centaure, all over, to my cousin here.

Mrs. Ot. Ay, and 'tis a very good book as any is, of the moderns.

Daw. Tut, he must have Seneca read to him, and Plutarch, and the ancients; the moderns are not for this disease.

Cler. Why, you discommended them too today, Sir John. 160

Daw. Ay, in some cases; but in these they are best, and Aristotle's *Ethics.*

Mav. Say you so, Sir John? I think you are deceived: you took it upon trust.

Hau. Where's Trusty, my woman? I'll end this difference. I prithee, Otter, call her. Her father and mother were both mad, when they put her to me.

Mor. I think so. Nay, gentlemen, I am tame. This is but an exercise, I know, a marriage ceremony, which I must endure. 170

Hau. And one of 'hem, I know not which, was cured with the *Sick Man's Salve,* and the other with Greene's *Groats-worth of Wit.*[14]

Tru. A very cheap cure, madam.

[Enter TRUSTY.*]*

Hau. Ay, it's very feasible.

Mrs. Ot. My lady called for you, Mistress Trusty; you must decide a controversy.

Hau. Oh, Trusty, which was it you said, your father, or your mother, that was cured with the *Sick Man's Salve?* 180

Tr. My mother, madam, with the *Salve.*

Tru. Then it was the *Sick Woman's* salve?

Tr. And my father with the *Groat's-worth of Wit.* But there was other means used: we had a preacher that would preach folk asleep still; and so they were prescribed to go to church by an old woman that was their physician, thrice a week—

Epi. To sleep!

Tr. Yes, forsooth: and every night they read themselves asleep on those books. 190

---

[7] *intestate:* without having made a will.

[8] *melancholy:* in the old (medical) sense of frenzied.

[9] *Pliny and Paracelsus:* Writers on natural history and medicine.					[10] *Gr.:* mania.

[11] *L.:* insanity, madness, the ecstasy (frenzy) of melancholy, when melancholia results in madness.

[12] *L.:* delirious, delirium.

[13] *Doni's Philosophy:* Originally an ancient Indian volume of fables translated from the Italian by Sir Thomas North in 1601, and here confused by La Foole with the popular tale of Reynard the Fox.

[14] *Sick . . . Wit:* The first, a devotional tract by the Puritan preacher Thomas Becon, was published in 1562; the second, supposedly the deathbed repentance of the popular romancer Robert Greene, in 1592.

Epi. Good faith, it stands with great reason. I would I knew where to procure those books.

Mor. Oh!

La F. I can help you with one of 'hem. Mistress Morose, the *Groat's-worth of Wit.*

Epi. But I shall disfurnish you, Sir Amorous: can you spare it?

La F. Oh, yes, for a week or so; I'll read it myself to him.   199

Epi. No, I must do that, sir; that must be my office.

Mor. Oh, oh.

Epi. Sure he would do well enough if he could sleep.

Mor. No, I should do well enough if you could sleep. Have I no friend that will make her drunk, or give her a little laudanum, or opium?

Tru. Why, sir, she talks ten times worse in her sleep.

Mor. How!

Cler. Do you not know that, sir? Never ceases all night.

Tru. And snores like a porpoise.[15]   210

Mor. Oh, redeem me, fate; redeem me, fate! for how many causes may a man de divorced, nephew?

Dauph. I know not, truly, sir.

Tru. Some divine[16] must resolve you in that, sir, or canon[17] lawyer.

Mor. I will not rest, I will not think of any other hope or comfort, till I know.

                                        [*Exit with* DAUPHINE.]

Cler. Alas, poor man!

Tru. You'll make him mad, indeed, ladies, if you pursue this.   220

Hau. No, we'll let him breathe now, a quarter of an hour, or so.

Cler. By my faith, a large truce!

Hau. Is that his keeper, that is gone with him?

Daw. It is his nephew, madam.

La F. Sir Dauphine Eugenie.

Cen. He looks like a very pitiful knight—

Daw. As can be. This marriage has put him out of all.

La F. He has not a penny in his purse, madam.

Daw. He is ready to cry all this day.   230

La F. A very shark;[18] he set me i' the nick t'other night at primero.[19]

Tru. How these swabbers[20] talk!

Cler. Ay, Otter's wine has swelled their humors above a spring-tide.

Hau. Good Morose, let's go in again. I like your couches exceeding well; we'll go lie and talk there.

[*Exeunt* HAUGHTY, CENTAURE, MAVIS, TRUSTY, LA FOOLE, *and* DAW; EPICOENE *following them is stopped by* TRUEWIT.]

Epi. I wait on you, madam.

Tru. 'Slight, I will have 'hem as silent as signs, and their post too, ere I ha' done. Do you hear, lady-   240 bride? I pray thee now, as thou art a noble wench continue this discourse of Dauphine within; but praise him exceedingly. Magnify him with all the height of affection thou canst—I have some purpose in't—and but beat off these two rooks, Jack Daw and his fellow, with any discontentment, hither, and I'll honor thee for ever.

Epi. I was about it here. It angered me to the soul, to hear 'hem begin to talk so malepert.[21]

Tru. Pray thee perform it, and thou winn'st me an idolater to thee everlasting.   251

Epi. Will you go in and hear me do't?

Tru. No, I'll stay here. Drive 'hem out of your company, 'tis all I ask; which cannot be any way better done than by extolling Dauphine, whom they have so slighted.

Epi. I warrant you; you shall expect one of 'hem presently.

                                                          [*Exit.*]

Cler. What a cast of kastrils[22] are these, to hawk after ladies, thus!   260

Tru. Ay, and strike at such an eagle as Dauphine.

Cler. He will be mad when we tell him. Here he comes.

                        [*Re-enter* DAUPHINE.]

Cler. Oh, sir, you are welcome.

Tru. Where's thine uncle?

Dauph. Run out o' doors in his nightcaps, to talk with a casuist[23] about his divorce. It works admirably.

Tru. Thou wouldst ha' said so, and thou hadst been here! the ladies have laughed at thee most comically, since thou went'st, Dauphine.   270

Cler. And asked if thou wert thine uncle's keeper.

Tru. And the brace of baboons answered, Yes; and said thou wert a pitiful poor fellow, and didst live upon posts,[24] and hadst nothing but three suits of apparel, and some few benevolences that the lords gave thee to fool[25] to 'hem, and swagger.

Dauph. Let me not live, I'll beat 'hem. I'll bind 'hem both to grand-madam's bed-posts, and have 'hem baited[26] with monkeys.   279

Tru. Thou shalt not need, they shall be beaten to thy hand, Dauphine. I have an execution[27] to serve upon 'hem, I warrant thee, shall serve; trust my plot.

Dauph. Ay, you have many plots! so you had one to make all the wenches in love with me.

Tru. Why, if I do it not yet afore night, as near as 'tis, and that they do not every one invite thee, and be ready to scratch[28] for thee, take the mortgage of my wit.

Cler. 'Fore God, I'll be his witness, thou shalt have it, Dauphine: thou shalt be his fool for ever, if thou dost not.   290

Tru. Agreed. Perhaps 'twill be his better estate. Do you observe this gallery, or rather lobby indeed? Here

---

[15] *porpoise:* F "porcpisce"
[16] *divine:* clergyman.
[17] *canon:* church.
[18] *shark:* card sharp.
[19] *set . . . primero:* beat me at a card game, perhaps with a suggestion of dishonesty.
[20] *swabbers:* contemptuous—from common sailors who "swab" the decks.
[21] *malepert:* impudently.
[22] *cast of kastrils:* pair of falcons (used contemptuously here: "windfuckers").
[23] *casuist:* churchman who adjudicated cases of conscience.
[24] *live upon posts:* run errands like a post-boy.
[25] *fool:* play the fool.
[26] *baited:* attacked.
[27] *execution:* writ.
[28] *scratch:* fight.

are a couple of studies,[29] at each end one: here will
I act such a tragi-comedy between the Guelphs and
Ghibellines,[30] Daw and La Foole—which of 'hem
comes out first, will I seize on—you two shall be the
chorus behind the arras,[31] and whip out between the
acts and speak. If I do not make 'hem keep the peace for
this remnant of the day, if not of the year, I have failed
once—I hear Daw coming: hide, and do not laugh, for
God's sake.   301

[*They withdraw.*]

[*Re-enter* DAW.]

Daw. Which is the way into the garden, trow?[32]
Tru. Oh, Jack Daw! I am glad I have met with you.
In good faith, I must have this matter go no further be-
tween you. I must ha' it taken up.[33]
Daw. What matter, sir? Between whom?
Tru. Come, you disguise it—Sir Amorous and you.
If you love me, Jack, you shall make use of your philos-
ophy now, for this once, and deliver me your sword.
This is not the wedding the Centaurs were at,[34]   310
though there be a she one here.

[*Takes his sword.*]

The bride has entreated me I will see no blood shed at
her bridal; you saw her whisper me erewhile.
Daw. As I hope to finish Tacitus,[35] I intend no mur-
der.
Tru. Do you not wait for Sir Amorous?
Daw. Not I, by my knighthood.
Tru. And your scholarship too?
Daw. And my scholarship too.   319
Tru. Go to, then I return you your sword, and ask
you mercy; but put it not up, for you will be assaulted.
I understood that you had apprehended[36] it, and walked
here to brave him; and that you had held your life con-
temptible in regard of your honor.

---

[29] *studies:* represented presumably by the side doors
opening on each end of the stage.
[30] *Guelphs and Ghibellines:* warring Italian factions in
thirteenth-century Italy.
[31] *arras:* tapestry, probably hanging from the back of the
stage and so a convenient place for eavesdroppers to hide.
[32] *trow:* expletive—"truly."   [33] *taken up:* made up.
[34] *wedding . . . at:* A drunken Centaur provoked a famous
quarrel at the marriage of the King of the Lapithae, by
carrying off the bride.   [35] *Tacitus:* Roman historian.
[36] *apprehended:* understood.   [37] *visor:* mask.
[38] *wight:* person.   [39] *errand'st:* arrantest; veriest.
[40] *protested:* notorious.
[41] *possession:* of property forfeited by the owner; taking
possession was likely, therefore, to be a dangerous business
to the new owner (hence "Armed!").
[42] *principal:* the genuine article: La Foole.
[43] *furnished him strangely:* as with the two-hand sword and
other accouterments, below.
[44] *halberds:* shafts with an axlike blade.
[45] *peitronels, calivers:* pistols, light muskets.
[46] *justice . . . hall:* characteristically bedecked with weapons and armor.
[47] *sessed:* assessed—the richer the man, the greater was his
military obligation to the state.   [48] *foils:* fencing matches.
[49] *St. Pulchre's:* St. Sepulchre's, well-known London
church.

Daw. No, no; no such thing, I assure you. He and I
parted now as good friends as could be.
Tru. Trust not you to that visor.[37] I saw him since
dinner with another face: I have known many men in
my time vexed with losses, with deaths, and with abuses;
but so offended a wight[38] as Sir Amorous did I   330
never see or read of. For taking away his guests, sir,
today, that's the cause; and he declares it behind your
back with such threatenings and contempts—He said to
Dauphine you were the errand'st[39] ass—
Daw. Ay, he may say his pleasure.
Tru. And swears you are so protested[40] a coward,
that he knows you will never do him any manly or single
right; and therefore he will take his course.   338
Daw. I'll give him any satisfaction, sir—but fighting.
Tru. Ay, sir: but who knows what satisfaction he'll
take? Blood he thirsts for, and blood he will have; and
whereabouts on you he will have it, who knows but
himself?
Daw. I pray you, Master Truewit, be you a mediator.
Tru. Well, sir, conceal yourself then in this study till
I return.

[*He puts him up.*]

Nay, you must be content to be locked in; for, for mine
own reputation, I would not have you seen to receive a
public disgrace, while I have the matter in managing.
Gods so, here he comes; keep your breath close,   350
that he do not hear you sigh—In good faith, Sir
Amorous, he is not this way; I pray you be merciful,
do not murder him; he is a Christian, as good as you:
you are armed as if you sought a revenge on all his race.
Good Dauphine, get him away from this place. I never
knew a man's choler so high, but he would speak to his
friends, he would hear reason.—Jack Daw, Jack Daw!
asleep!
Daw. [*Within*] Is he gone, Master Truewit?
Tru. Ay; did you hear him?   360
Daw. O God, yes.
Tru. What a quick ear fear has!

[DAW *comes out of the closet.*]

Daw. But is he so armed as you say?
Tru. Armed! did you ever see a fellow set out to
take possession?[41]
Daw. Ay, sir.
Tru. That may give you some light to conceive of
him; but 'tis nothing to the principal.[42] Some false
brother i' the house has furnished him strangely.[43] Or,
if it were out o' the house, it was Tom Otter.   370
Daw. Indeed he's a captain; and his wife is his kinswoman.
Tru. He has got somebody's old two-hand sword, to
mow you off at the knees. And that sword hath spawned
such a dagger!—But then he is so hung with pikes,
halberds,[44] peitronels, calivers,[45] and muskets, that
he looks like a justice-of-peace's hall:[46] a man of two
thousand a year is not sessed[47] at so many weapons as
he has on. There was never fencer challenged at so many
several foils.[48] You would think he meant to   380
murder all St. Pulchre's[49] parish. If he could but vic-

tual himself[50] for half a year, in his breeches,[51] he is sufficiently armed to over-run a country.

Daw. Good lord! what means he, sir! I pray you, Master Truewit, be you a mediator.

Tru. Well, I'll try if he will be appeased with a leg or an arm; if not—you must die once.

Daw. I would be loath to lose my right arm, for writing madrigals.   389

Tru. Why, if he will be satisfied with a thumb or a little finger, all's one to me. You must think, I'll do my best.

He puts him up again, and then comes forth.

Daw. Good sir, do.

Cler. What hast thou done?

Tru. He will let me do nothing, man, he does all afore me; he offers his left arm.

Cler. His left wing, for a Jack Daw.

Dauph. Take it, by all means.

Tru. How! maim a man for ever, for a jest? What a conscience hast thou!   400

Dauph. 'Tis no loss to him: he has no employment for his arms but to eat spoon-meat.[52] Beside, as good maim his body as his reputation.

Tru. He is a scholar and a wit, and yet he does not think so. But he loses no reputation with us, for we all resolved him an ass before. To your places again.

Cler. I pray thee, let me be in at the other a little.

Tru. Look, you'll spoil all; these be ever your tricks.

Cler. No, but I could hit of some things that thou wilt miss, and thou wilt say are good ones.   410

Tru. I warrant you.[53] I pray, forbear, I'll leave it off else.

Dauph. Come away, Clerimont.

[DAUPHINE *and* CLERIMONT *withdrew as before.*]

[*Enter* LA FOOLE.]

Tru. Sir Amorous!

La F. Master Truewit.

Tru. Whither were you going?

La F. Down into the court to make water.[54]

Tru. By no means, sir; you shall rather tempt your breeches.[55]

La F. Why, sir?   420

Tru. Enter here, if you love your life.

[*Opening the door of the other study.*]

La F. Why! why!

Tru. Question till your throat be cut, do: dally till the enraged soul find you.

La F. Who's that?

Tru. Daw it is: will you in?

La F. Ay, ay, I'll in: what's the matter?

Tru. Nay, if he had been cool enough to tell us that, there had been some hope to atone[56] you; but he seems so implacably enraged!   430

La F. 'Slight, let him rage. I'll hide myself.

Tru. Do, good sir. But what have you done to him within that should provoke him thus? You have broke some jest upon him afore the ladies.

La F. Not I, never in my life, broke jest upon any

man. The bride was praising Sir Dauphine, and he went away in snuff,[57] and I followed him; unless he took offense at me in his drink erewhile, that I would not pledge all the horse[58] full.   439

Tru. By my faith, and that may be; you remember well. But he walks the round[59] up and down, through every room o' the house, with a towel in his hand, crying, "Where's La Foole? Who saw La Foole?" And when Dauphine and I demanded the cause, we can force no answer from him, but—"O revenge, how sweet art thou! I will strangle him in this towel"—which leads us to conjecture that the main cause of his fury is for bringing your meat today with a towel about you, to his discredit.

La F. Like enough. Why, and he be angry for that I'll stay here till his anger be blown over.   451

Tru. A good becoming resolution, sir. If you can put it on o' the sudden.

La F. Yes, I can put it on. Or, I'll away into the country presently.

Tru. How will you go out o' the house, sir? He knows you are i' the house, and he'll watch this se'n-night[60] but he'll have you. He'll outwait a sergeant[61] for you.

La F. Why, then I'll stay here.

Tru. You must think how to victual yourself in time then.   461

La F. Why, sweet Master Truewit, will you entreat my cousin Otter to send me a cold venison pasty,[62] a bottle or two of wine, and a chamber pot.

Tru. A stool were better, sir, of Sir A-jax[63] his invention.

La F. Ay, that will be better indeed; and a pallet to lie on.

Tru. Oh, I would not advise you to sleep by any means.   470

La F. Would you not, sir? Why, then I will not.

Tru. Yet there's another fear—

La F. Is there! what is't?

Tru. No, he cannot break open this door with his boot, sure.

La F. I'll set my back against it, sir. I have a good back.

Tru. But then if he should batter.

La F. Batter! if he dare, I'll have an action of battery against him.   480

---

[50] *victual himself:* keep himself supplied with provisions.

[51] *breeches:* which current fashion dictated should be worn enormously stuffed out; the point is to La Foole's ferocious appearance.

[52] *spoon-meat:* soft or liquid food, appropriate to infants or invalids.   [53] *I warrant you:* No doubt!

[54] *make water:* urinate.

[55] *tempt your breeches:* i.e., restrain yourself (whatever the danger of wetting your pants).   [56] *atone:* reconcile.

[57] *in snuff:* in a huff.

[58] *horse:* used contemptuously of a man.

[59] *walk the round:* like a sentry on patrol.

[60] *se'n-night:* week.   [61] *sergeant:* sheriff's officer.

[62] *pasty:* pie.

[63] *A-jax:* A "jakes" is a stool or privy; the pun was given currency by Sir John Harington's *Metamorphosis of Ajax,* 1596, advocating the use of water closets.

Tru. Cast you [64] the worst. He has sent for powder already, and what he will do with it no man knows: perhaps blow up the corner o' the house where he suspects you are. Here he comes; in quickly.

He feigns as if one were present, to fright the other, who is run in to hide himself.

I protest, Sir John Daw, he is not this way: what will you do? Before God, you shall hang no petard [65] here. I'll die rather. Will you not take my word! I never knew one but would be satisfied.—Sir Amorous [*Speaks through the keyhole*] there's no standing out. He has made a petard of an old brass pot, to force your   490 door. Think upon some satisfaction, or terms, to offer him.

La F. [*Within*] Sir, I'll give him any satisfaction. I dare give any terms.

Tru. You'll leave it to me then?

La F. Ay, sir: I'll stand to any conditions.

He calls forth CLERIMONT *and* DAUPHINE.

Tru. How now—what think you, sirs? Were't not a difficult thing to determine which of these two feared most?   499

Cler. Yes, but this fears the bravest: [66] the other a whiniling [67] dastard, Jack Daw! But La Foole, a brave heroic coward! and is afraid in a great look and a stout accent. I like him rarely.

Tru. Had it not been pity these two should ha' been concealed?

Cler. Shall I make a motion?

Tru. Briefly. For I must strike while 'tis hot.

Cler. Shall I go fetch the ladies to the catastrophe? [68]

Tru. Umh? Ay, by my troth.   509

Dauph. By no mortal [69] means. Let them continue in the state of ignorance, and err still; think 'hem wits and fine fellows, as they have done. 'Twere sin to reform them.

Tru. Well, I will have 'hem fetched, now I think on't, for a private purpose of mine: do, Clerimont, fetch 'hem, and discourse to 'hem all that's past, and bring 'hem into the gallery here.

Dauph. This is thy extreme vanity, now! thou think'st thou wert undone if every jest thou mak'st were not published.   520

Tru. Thou shalt see how unjust thou art presently. Clerimont, say it was Dauphine's plot.

[*Exit* CLERIMONT.]

Trust me not if the whole drift be not for thy good. There's a carpet [70] i' the next room, put it on, with this scarf over thy face, and a cushion o' thy head, and be ready when I call Amorous. Away!

[*Exit* DAUPHINE.]

—John Daw!

[*Goes to* DAW'S *closet and brings him out.*]

Daw. What good news, sir?

Tru. Faith, I have followed and argued with him hard for you. I told him you were a knight, and a   530 scholar, and that you knew fortitude did consist *magis patiendo quam faciendo, magis ferendo quam feriendo.*[71]

Daw. It doth so indeed, sir.

Tru. And that you would suffer, I told him: so at first he demanded, by my troth, in my conceit, too much.

Daw. What was it, sir?

Tru. Your upper lip and six o' your fore-teeth.

Daw. 'Twas unreasonable.

Tru. Nay, I told him plainly, you could not spare 'hem all. So after long argument *pro et con*, as you   540 know, I brought him down to your two butter-teeth,[72] and them he would have.

Daw. Oh, did you so? Why, he shall have 'hem.

Tru. But he shall not, sir, by your leave. The conclusion is this, sir: because you shall be very good friends hereafter, and this never to be remembered or up-braided; besides, that he may not boast he has done any such thing to you in his own person: he is to come here in disguise, give you five kicks in private, sir, take your sword from you, and lock you up in that study   550 during pleasure: which will be but a little while, we'll get it released presently.

Daw. Five kicks! he shall have six, sir, to be friends.

Tru. Believe me, you shall not overshoot yourself, to send him that word by me.

Daw. Deliver it, sir. He shall have it with all my heart, to be friends.

Tru. Friends! Nay, and he should not be so, and heartily too, upon these terms, he shall have me to enemy while I live. Come, sir, bear it bravely.   560

Daw. O God, sir, 'tis nothing.

Tru. True! What's six kicks to a man that reads Seneca? [73]

Daw. I have had a hundred, sir.

Tru. Sir Amorous!—No speaking one to another, or rehearsing old matters.

DAUPHINE *comes forth, and kicks him.*

Daw. One, two, three, four, five. I protest, Sir Amorous, you shall have six.   568

Tru. Nay, I told you you should not talk. Come, give him six, and he will needs.—Your sword. Now return to your safe custody; you shall presently meet afore the ladies, and be the dearest friends one to another.—Give me the scarf now, thou shalt beat the other barefaced. Stand by.

[*Following* TRUEWIT'S *instructions,* DAUPHINE *has kicked* DAW *once again, taken his sword, and put him back into the study; he now retires, and* TRUEWIT *goes to the other closet and releases* LA FOOLE.]

Sir Amorous!

---

[64] *Cast you:* Ready yourself for.

[65] *petard:* explosive.

[66] *bravest:* best; with an obvious pun on the contradiction in terms.   [67] *whiniling:* whining.

[68] *catastrophe:* denouement.

[69] *mortal:* emphatic expletive.

[70] *carpet:* tapestry table cover.

[71] *L.:* more in suffering than doing, more in bearing than beating.   [72] *butter-teeth:* front teeth.

[73] *Seneca:* in his character of Stoic philosopher.

La F. What's here! a sword?

Tru. I cannot help it, without[74] I should take the quarrel upon myself. Here he has sent you his sword—

La F. I'll receive none on't.   579

Tru. And he wills you to fasten it against a wall, and break your head in some few several places against the hilts.

La F. I will not: tell him roundly. I cannot endure to shed my own blood.

Tru. Will you not?

La F. No. I'll beat it against a fair flat wall, if that will satisfy him: if not, he shall beat it himself, for Amorous.

Tru. Why, this is strange starting off, when a man undertakes for you! I offend him another condition; will you stand to that?   591

La F. Ay, what is't?

Tru. That you will be beaten in private.

La F. Yes, I am content, at the blunt.[75]

[*Enter, above,* HAUGHTY, CENTAURE, MAVIS,
Mistress OTTER, EPICOENE, *and* TRUSTY.]

Tru. Then you must submit yourself to be hood-winked in this scarf, and be led to him, where he will take your sword from you, and make you bear a blow over the mouth *gules*,[76] and tweaks by the nose *sans nombre*.   599

La F. I am content. But why must I be blinded?[77]

Tru. That's for your good, sir; because if he should grow insolent upon this, and publish it hereafter to your disgrace (which I hope he will not do), you might swear safely, and protest he never beat you to your knowledge.

La F. Oh, I conceive.

Tru. I do not doubt but you'll be perfect good friends upon't, and not dare to utter an ill thought one of another in future.

La F. Not I, as God help me, of him.   610

Tru. Nor he of you, sir. If he should—

[*Binds his eyes, then leads him forward.*]

—Come, sir. All hid,[78] Sir John!

DAUPHINE *enters to tweak him.*

La F. Oh, Sir John, Sir John! Oh, o-o-o-o-o-Oh—

Tru. Good Sir John, leave tweaking, you'll blow his nose off.[79] 'Tis Sir John's pleasure you should retire into the study.

[*Puts him up again.*]

—Why, now you are friends. All bitterness between you I hope is buried; you shall come forth by and by Damon and Pythias[80] upon't, and embrace with all the rankness[81] of friendship that can be. I   620 trust we shall have 'hem tamer i' their language hereafter. Dauphine, I worship thee. God's will, the ladies have surprised us!

[*Enter*] HAUGHTY, CENTAURE, MAVIS,
Mistress OTTER, EPICOENE, *and* TRUSTY,
having discovered[82] *part of the past scene above.*

Hau. Centaure, how our judgments were imposed on by these adulterate knights!

Cen. Nay, madam, Mavis was more deceived than we; 'twas her commendation uttered[83] 'hem in the college.

Mav. I commended but their wits, madam, and their braveries.[84] I never looked toward their valors.   630

Hau. Sir Dauphine is valiant, and a wit, too, it seems.

Mav. And a bravery[85] too.

Hau. Was this his project?

Mrs. Ot. So Master Clerimont intimates, madam.

Hau. Good Morose, when you come to the college, will you bring him with you? He seems a very perfect gentleman.

Epi. He is so, madam, believe it.

Cen. But when will you come, Morose?   640

Epi. Three or four days hence, madam, when I have got me a coach and horses.

Hau. No, tomorrow, good Morose; Centaure shall send you her coach.

Mav. Yes, faith, do, and bring Sir Dauphine with you.

Hau. She has promised that, Mavis.

Mav. He is a very worthy gentleman in his exteriors, madam.

Hau. Ay, he shows he is judicial in his clothes.   650

Cen. And yet not so superlatively neat as some, madam, that have their faces set in a brake![86]

Hau. Ay, and have every hair in form.

Mav. That wear purer linen than ourselves, and profess more neatness than the French hermaphrodite.[87]

Epi. Ay, ladies, they, what they tell one of us, have told a thousand, and are the only thieves of our fame, that think to take us with that perfume, or with that lace, and laugh at us unconscionably when they have done.

Hau. But Sir Dauphine's carelessness becomes him.

Cen. I could love a man for such a nose.   661

Mav. Or such a leg.

Cen. He has an exceeding good eye, madam.

Mav. And a very good lock![88]

Cen. Good Morose, bring him to my chamber first.

Mrs. Ot. Please your honors to meet at my house, madam.

Tru. See how they eye thee, man! they are taken, I warrant thee.

[HAUGHTY *comes forward.*]

---

[74] *without:* unless.
[75] *at the blunt:* with a weapon whose point is capped.
[76] *gules:* heraldic term—"red"; hence "bloody."
[77] *blinded:* blindfolded—"hoodwinked."
[78] *All hid:* the cry in hide-and-seek.
[79] *blow . . . off:* destroy his nose.
[80] *Damon and Pythias:* proverbial types of fast friends.
[81] *rankness:* corruption: ironic contradiction in terms.
[82] *discovered:* witnessed.   [83] *uttered:* introduced.
[84] *braveries:* fineries.   [85] *bravery:* gallant.
[86] *brake:* frame in which unruly colts were held fast when shod; faces so "set" would be frozen—too perfect.
[87] *French hermaphrodite:* Presumably a contemporary "freak" in whom the parts or characteristics of both sexes were combined.
[88] *lock:* hair twisted and often tied to form a love lock.

Hau. You have unbraced[89] our brace of knights here, Master Truewit. 671

Tru. Not I, madam; it was Sir Dauphine's ingine:[90] who, if he have disfurnished your ladyship of any guard or service by it, is able to make the place good again in himself.

Hau. There's no suspicion of that, sir.

Cen. God so, Mavis, Haughty is kissing.

Mav. Let us go too, and take part.

[*They come forward.*]

Hau. But I am glad of the fortune (beside the discovery of two such empty caskets) to gain the knowledge of so rich a mine of virtue as Sir Dauphine. 681

Cen. We would be all glad to style him of our friendship, and see him at the college.

Mav. He cannot mix with a sweeter society, I'll prophesy, and I hope he himself will think so.

Dauph. I should be rude to imagine otherwise, lady.

Tru. Did not I tell thee, Dauphine! Why, all their actions are governed by crude opinion, without reason or cause; they know not why they do anything; but as they are informed, believe, judge, praise, con- 690 demn, love, hate, and in emulation one of another, do all these things alike. Only they have a natural inclination sways 'hem generally to the worst, when they are left to themselves. But pursue it, now thou hast 'hem.

Hau. Shall we go in again, Morose?

Epi. Yes, madam.

Cen. We'll entreat Sir Dauphine's company.

Tru. Stay,[91] good madam, the interview of the two friends, Pylades and Orestes:[92] I'll fetch 'hem out to you straight. 700

Hau. Will you, Master Truewit?

Dauph. Ay; but, noble ladies, do not confess in your countenance, or outward bearing to 'hem, any discovery of their follies, that we may see how they will bear up again, with what assurance and erection.[93]

Hau. We will not, Sir Dauphine.

Cen., Mav. Upon our honors, Sir Dauphine.

[TRUEWIT *goes to the first closet.*]

Tru. Sir Amorous, Sir Amorous! the ladies are here.

La F. [*Within*] Are they? 710

Tru. Yes; but slip out by and by, as their backs are turned, and meet Sir John here, as by chance when I call you.—Jack Daw!

[*He goes to the other closet.*]

Daw. [*Within*] What say you, sir?

Tru. Whip out behind me suddenly, and no anger i' your looks to your adversary. Now, now!

---

[89] *unbraced:* exposed (with a pun on "brace" or pair, following). [90] *ingine:* scheme.

[91] *Stay:* Stay on; don't go until.

[92] *Pylades and Orestes:* like Damon and Pythias above.

[93] *erection:* exaltation (perhaps with a pun on tumescence).

[94] *prevent:* anticipate.

[95] *begged:* forfeited to a courtier as a result of the supposed manslaughter (below). [96] *intergatories:* interrogatories.

[97] *proctors:* church lawyers.

[LA FOOLE *and* DAW *slip out of their respective closets, and salute each other.*]

La F. Noble Sir John Daw! where ha' you been?

Daw. To seek you, Sir Amorous.

La F. Me! I honor you.

Daw. I prevent[94] you, sir. 720

Cler. They have forgot their rapiers.

Tru. Oh, they meet in peace, man.

Dauph. Where's your sword, Sir John?

Cler. And yours, Sir Amorous?

Daw. Mine! my boy had it forth to mend the handle, e'en now.

La F. And my gold handle was broke too, and my boy had it forth.

Dauph. Indeed, sir!—how their excuses meet!

Cler. What a consent there is i' the handles! 730

Tru. Nay, there is so i' the points too, I warrant you.

Mrs. Ot. O me! madam, he comes again, the madman! away!

[Ladies, DAW, *and* LA FOOLE *run off.*]

[*Enter*] MOROSE.

Mor. What make these naked weapons here, gentlemen?

He had found the two swords drawn within.

Tru. O sir! Here hath like to been murder since you went; a couple of knights fallen out about the bride's favors! we were fain to take away their weapons; your house had been begged[95] by this time else.

Mor. For what? 740

Cler. For manslaughter, sir, as being accessory.

Mor. And for her favors?

Tru. Ay, sir, heretofore, not present.—Clerimont, carry 'hem their swords now. They have done all the hurt they will do.

[*Exit* CLERIMONT *with the two swords.*]

Dauph. Ha' you spoke with a lawyer, sir?

Mor. Oh, no! there is such a noise i' the court, that they have frighted me home with more violence than I went! such speaking and counter-speaking, with their several voices of citations, appellations, allega- 750 tions, certificates, attachments, intergatories,[96] references, convictions, and afflictions indeed, among the doctors and proctors,[97] that the noise here is silence to't, a kind of calm midnight!

Tru. Why, sir, if you would be resolved indeed, I can bring you hither a very sufficient lawyer, and a learned divine, that shall enquire into every least scruple for you.

Mor. Can you, Master Truewit?

Tru. Yes, and are very sober, grave persons, that will dispatch it in a chamber, with a whisper or two. 761

Mor. Good sir, shall I hope this benefit from you, and trust myself into your hands?

Tru. Alas, sir! your nephew and I have been ashamed and oft-times mad, since you went, to think how you are abused. Go in, good sir, and lock yourself up till we call you; we'll tell you more anon, sir.

Mor. Do your pleasure with me, gentlemen. I believe in you, and that deserves no delusion.

[*Exit.*]

Tru. You shall find none, sir;—but heaped, heaped plenty of vexation.   771

Dauph. What wilt thou do now, Wit?

Tru. Recover⁹⁸ me hither Otter and the barber, if you can, by any means, presently.

Dauph. Why? To what purpose?

Tru. Oh, I'll make the deepest divine and gravest lawyer out o' them two, for him—

Dauph. Thou canst not, man; these are waking dreams.   779

Tru. Do not fear me. Clap but a civil gown with a welt⁹⁹ o' the one, and a canonical cloak with sleeves o' the other, and give 'hem a few terms i' their mouths, if there come not forth as able a doctor and complete a parson, for this turn, as may be wished, trust not my election. And I hope, without wronging the dignity of either profession, since they are but persons put on, and for mirth's sake, to torment him. The barber smatters Latin, I remember.

Dauph. Yes, and Otter too.   789

Tru. Well then, if I make 'hem not wrangle out this case to his no comfort, let me be thought a Jack Daw or La Foole, or anything worse. Go you to your ladies, but first send for them.

Dauph. I will.

[*Exeunt.*]

ACT FIVE

SCENE ONE

[*Enter* LA FOOLE, CLERIMONT, *and* DAW.]

La F. Where had you our swords, Master Clerimont?

Cler. Why, Dauphine took 'hem from the madman.

La F. And he took 'hem from our boys, I warrant you.

Cler. Very like, sir.

La F. Thank you, good Master Clerimont. Sir John Daw and I are both beholden to you.

Cler. Would I knew how to make you so, gentlemen!

Daw. Sir Amorous and I are your servants, sir.   10

[*Enter* MAVIS.]

Mav. Gentlemen, have any of you a pen and ink? I would fain write out a riddle in Italian, for Sir Dauphine to translate.

Cler. Not I, in troth, lady; I am no scrivener.¹

Daw. I can furnish you, I think, lady.

[*Exeunt* DAW *and* MAVIS.]

Cler. He has it in the haft of a knife, I believe.

La F. No, he has his box of instruments.

Cler. Like a surgeon!

La F. For the mathematics: his squire,² his compasses, his brass pens, and blacklead, to draw maps of every place and person where he comes.   21

Cler. How, maps of persons!

La F. Yes, sir, of Nomentack,³ when he was here, and of the Prince of Moldavia,⁴ and of his⁵ mistress, Mistress Epicoene.

[*Re-enter* DAW.]

Cler. Away! he ha' not found out her latitude, I hope.

La F. You are a pleasant gentleman, sir.

Cler. Faith, now we are in private, let's wanton it a little, and talk waggishly.—Sir John, I am telling Sir Amorous here that you two govern the ladies wherever you come; you carry the feminine gender afore you.   31

Daw. They shall rather carry us afore them, if they will, sir.

Cler. Nay, I believe that they do withal—but that you are the prime men in their affections, and direct all their actions—

Daw. Not I; Sir Amorous is.

La F. I protest Sir John is.

Daw. As I hope to rise i' the state, Sir Amorous, you ha' the person.   40

La F. Sir John, you ha' the person, and the discourse too.

Daw. Not I, sir. I have no discourse—and then you have activity beside.

La F. I protest, Sir John, you come as high from Tripoly as I do, every whit: and lift as many joined stools, and leap over 'hem, if you would use it.⁶

Cler. Well, agree on't together, knights; for between you, you divide the kingdom or commonwealth of ladies' affections. I see it, and can perceive a little   50 how they observe you, and fear you indeed. You could tell strange stories, my masters, if you would, I know.

Daw. Faith, we have seen somewhat, sir.

La F. That we have—velvet petticoats, and wrought smocks,⁷ or so.

Daw. Ay, and—

Cler. Nay, out with it, Sir John; do not envy your friend the pleasure of hearing, when you have had the delight of tasting.

Daw. Why—a— Do you speak, Sir Amorous.   60

La F. No, do you, Sir John Daw.

Daw. I' faith, you shall.

La F. I' faith, you shall.

Daw. Why, we have been—

---

⁹⁸ *Recover:* Bring back to.

⁹⁹ *civil . . . welt:* generically, lawyer's bordered gown ("civil" is opposed to "ecclesiastical" or "canonical," below).

V.i.

¹ *scrivener:* professional copyist.   ² *squire:* square.

³ *Nomentack:* Indian chief and follower of Powhattan, brought to England in 1605.

⁴ *Prince of Moldavia:* Stephano Janiculo, who sought to marry the King's cousin, Lady Arabella Stuart.

⁵ *his:* i.e., Daw's.

⁶ *I . . . it:* La Foole's speech is obscure in detail, clear enough in sense. To "come from Tripoli" is to excel in acrobatics, here sexual. "Joined stools" (as opposed to stools of rough make) are suggestive of women (cf. the fool to Lear in *King Lear:* "I took you for a joint stool"); as "leap" is cant for sexual intercourse.

⁷ *velvet . . . smocks:* as worn by courtesans.

La F. In the great bed at Ware[8] together in our time.
On, Sir John.

Daw. Nay, do you, Sir Amorous.

Cler. And these ladies with you, knights?

La F. No, excuse us, sir.

Daw. We must not wound reputation.   70

La F. No matter—they were these, or others. Our
bath cost us fifteen pound when we came home.

Cler. Do you hear, Sir John? You shall tell me but
one thing truly, as you love me.

Daw. If I can, I will, sir.

Cler. You lay in the same house with the bride here?

Daw. Yes, and conversed[9] with her hourly, sir.

Cler. And what humor is she of? Is she coming[10]
and open, free?

Daw. Oh, exceedingly open, sir. I was her servant,[11]
and Sir Amorous was to be.   81

Cler. Come, you have both had favors from her? I
know, and have heard so much.

Daw. Oh, no, sir.

La F. You shall excuse us, sir; we must not wound
reputation.

Cler. Tut, she is married now, and you cannot hurt
her with any report; and therefore speak plainly: how
many times, i' faith? Which of you led first? ha!

La F. Sir John had her maidenhaid, indeed.   90

Daw. Oh, it pleases him to say so, sir; but Sir Amorous knows what's what as well.

Cler. Dost thou, i' faith, Amorous?

La F. In a manner, sir.

Cler. Why, I commend you, lads. Little knows Don
Bridegroom of this; nor shall he for me.

Daw. Hang him, mad ox![12]

Cler. Speak softly; here comes his nephew, with the
Lady Haughty. He'll get the ladies from you, sirs, if
you look not to him in time.   100

La F. Why, if he do, we'll fetch 'hem home again, I
warrant you.

[*Exit with* DAW. CLERIMONT *walks aside.*]

[*Enter* DAUPHINE *and* HAUGHTY.]

Hau. I assure you, Sir Dauphine, it is the price and
estimation of your virtue only that hath embarked me to
this adventure; and I could not but make out[13] to tell
you so: nor can I repent me of the act, since it is always
an argument of some virtue in ourselves, that we love
and affect it so in others.

Dauph. Your ladyship sets too high a price on my
weakness.   110

Hau. Sir, I can distinguish gems from pebbles—

Dauph. [*Aside.*] Are you so skillful in stones?[14]

Hau. And howsoever I may suffer in such a judgment as yours, by admitting equality of rank or society
with Centaure or Mavis—

Dauph. You do not, madam; I perceive they are your
mere foils.

Hau. Then are you a friend to truth, sir. It makes
me love you the more. It is not the outward but the inward man that I affect. They are not apprehensive of an
eminent perfection, but love flat and dully.   121

Cen. [*Within*] Where are you, my Lady Haughty?

Hau. I come presently, Centaure.—My chamber, sir,
my page shall show you; and Trusty, my woman,
shall be ever awake for you: you need not fear to communicate anything with her, for she is a Fidelia.[15] I
pray you wear this jewel for my sake, Sir Dauphine.—

[*Enter* CENTAURE.]

Where's Mavis, Centaure?

Cen. Within, madam, a-writing. I'll follow you presently.   130

[*Exit* HAUGHTY.]

I'll but speak a word with Sir Dauphine.

Dauph. With me, madam?

Cen. Good Sir Dauphine, do not trust Haughty, nor
make any credit to her[16] whatever you do besides, Sir
Dauphine, I give you this caution, she is a perfect
courtier, and loves nobody but for her uses; and for her
uses she loves all. Besides, her physicians give her out
to be none o' the clearest,[17] whether she pay 'hem or no,
heaven knows; and she's about fifty too, and pargets![18]
See her in a forenoon. Here comes Mavis, a worse   140
face than she! you would not like this by[19] candle-light.

[*Enter* MAVIS.]

If you'll come to my chamber one o' these mornings
early, or late in an evening, I'll tell you more. Where's
Haughty, Mavis?

Mav. Within, Centaure.

Cen. What ha' you there?

Mav. An Italian riddle for Sir Dauphine,—you shall
not see it, i' faith, Centaure.

[*Exit* CENTAURE.]

—Good Sir Dauphine, solve it for me: I'll call for it
anon.   150

[*Exit.*]

[CLERIMONT *comes forward*]

Cler. How now, Dauphine! how dost thou quit thy
self of these females?

Dauph. 'Slight, they haunt me like fairies, and give
me jewels here; I cannot be rid of 'hem.

Cler. Oh, you must not tell, though.[20]

Dauph. Mass,[21] I forgot that: I was never so assaulted. One loves for virtue, and bribes me with this

[*Shows the jewel.*]

—another loves me with caution, and so would possess

---

[8] *great bed at Ware:* famous and enormous bed, now in
the Victoria and Albert Museum, and able to accommodate
twelve people.   [9] *conversed:* had sexual intercourse.
[10] *coming:* forthcoming; but continuing also the sexual
innuendo, as with "open," below.   [11] *servant:* lover.
[12] *ox:* with the inevitable suggestion of horns.
[13] *make out:* manage.   [14] *stones:* testicles.
[15] *Fidelia:* Trusty one.
[16] *make . . . her:* give her any credit (belief).
[17] *clearest:* i.e., she has the pox.
[18] *pargets:* plasters herself with cosmetics.
[19] *by:* even by.
[20] *you . . . though:* Gifts made by fairies were not to be
revealed without incurring misfortune.
[21] *Mass:* By the Mass.

me; a third brings me a riddle here: and all are jealous, and rail each at other.   160

Cler. A riddle! pray let me see it.

He reads the paper.

"Sir Dauphine, I chose this way of intimation for privacy. The ladies here, I know, have both hope and purpose to make a collegiate and servant of you. If I might be so honored as to appear at any end of so noble a work, I would enter into a fame[22] of taking physic tomorrow, and continue it four or five days, or longer, for your visitation.

Mavis."

By my faith, a subtle one! Call you this a riddle? What's their plain dealing, trow?   171

Dauph. We lack Truewit to tell us that.

Cler. We lack him for somewhat else too: his knights reformadoes[23] are wound up as high and insolent as ever they were.

Dauph. You jest.

Cler. No drunkards, either with wine or vanity, ever confessed such stories of themselves. I would not give a fly's leg in balance against all the women's reputations here, if they could be but thought to speak truth;   180 and for the bride, they have made their affidavit against her directly—

Dauph. What, that they have lain with her?

Cler. Yes; and tell times and circumstances, with the cause why, and the place where. I had almost brought 'hem to affirm that they had done it today.

Dauph. Not both of 'hem?

Cler. Yes, faith; with a sooth[24] or two more I had effected it. They would ha' set it down under their hands.   190

Dauph. Why, they will be our sport, I see, still, whether we will or no.

Enter TRUEWIT.

Tru. Oh, are you here? Come, Dauphine. Go call your uncle presently. I have fitted my divine and my canonist, dyed their beards and all. The knaves do not know themselves, they are so exalted and altered. Preferment[25] changes any man. Thou shalt keep one door and I another, and then Clerimont in the midst, that he may have no means of escape from their caviling, when they grow hot once again. And then the women   200 (as I have given the bride her instructions) to break in upon him i' the l'envoy.[26] Oh, 'twill be full and twanging![27] away! fetch him.

[Exit DAUPHINE.]

[Enter OTTER, *disguised as a divine, and* CUTBEARD *as a canon lawyer.]*

Come, master doctor, and master parson, look to your parts now, and discharge 'hem bravely; you are well set forth, perform it as well. If you chance to be out,[28]do not confess it with standing still, or humming, or gaping one at another; but go on, and talk aloud and eagerly;

use vehement action, and only remember your terms, and you are safe. Let the matter go where it will: 210 you have many will do so. But at first be very solemn and grave, like your garments, though you loose yourselves after, and skip out like a brace of jugglers on a table. Here he comes! set your faces, and look superciliously while I present you.

[Enter DAUPHINE *with* MOROSE.]

Mor. Are these the two learned men?

Tru. Yes, sir; please you salute 'hem?

Mor. Salute 'hem! I had rather do anything than wear out time so unfruitfully, sir. I wonder how these common forms, as *God save you*, and *You are wel-*   220 *come*, are come to be a habit in our lives! or, *I am glad to see you!* When I cannot see what the profit can be of these words, so long as it is no whit better with him whose affairs are sad and grievous, that he hears this saluation.

Tru. 'Tis true, sir; we'll go to the matter then.— Gentlemen, master doctor, and master parson, I have acquainted you sufficiently with the business for which you are come hither; and you are not now to inform yourselves in the state of the question, I know.   230 This is the gentleman who expects your resolution, and therefore, when you please, begin.

Ot. Please you, master doctor.

Cut. Please you, good master parson.

Ot. I would hear the canon law speak first.

Cut. It must give place to positive divinity, sir.

Mor. Nay, good gentlemen, do not throw me into circumstances.[29] Let your comforts arrive quickly at me, those that are. Be swift in affording me my peace, if so I shall hope any. I love not your disputations,   240 or your court tumults. And that it be not strange to you, I will tell you. My father, in my education, was wont to advise me, that I should always collect and contain my mind, not suffering it to flow loosely; that I should look to what things were necessary to the carriage of my life, and what not; embracing the one and eschewing the other. In short, that I should endear myself to rest, and avoid turmoil; which now is grown to be another nature to me. So that I come not to your public pleadings, or your places of noise; not that   250 I neglect those things that make for the dignity of the commonwealth; but for the mere avoiding of clamors and impertinencies[30] of orators, that know not how to be silent. And for the cause of noise, am I now a suitor to you. You do not know in what a misery I have been exercised this day, what a torrent of evil! my very house turns round with the tumult! I dwell in a windmill! the perpetual motion is here, and not at Eltham.[31]

---

[22] *fame*: rumor.   [23] *reformadoes*: freed.
[24] *sooth*: smooth word.
[25] *Preferment*: Advancement (in rank).
[26] *l'envoy*: conclusion.   [27] *twanging*: stunning.
[28] *out*: i.e., of your parts.
[29] *circumstances*: niggling details.
[30] *impertinencies*: irrelevancies.
[31] *Eltham*: where lived the Dutch inventor Cornelis Drebbel, famous for his perpetual motion machine.

Tru. Well, good master doctor, will you break the ice? master parson will wade after.   260

Cut. Sir, though unworthy, and the weaker, I will presume.

Ot. 'Tis no presumption, *domine* doctor.

Mor. Yet again!

Cut. Your question is, for how many causes a man may have *divortium legitimum*, a lawful divorce. First you must understand the nature of the word, divorce, *a divertendo* [32]—

Mor. No excursions [33] upon words, good doctor; to the question briefly.   270

Cut. I answer then, the canon law affords [34] divorce but in a few cases; and the principal is in the common case, the adulterous case. But there are *duodecim impedimenta*, twelve impediments, as we call 'hem, all which do not *dirimere contractum*, but *irritum reddere matrimonium*, as we say in the canon law, *not take away the bond, but cause a nullity therein.*

Mor. I understood you before: good sir, avoid your impertinency of translation.

Ot. He cannot open [35] this too much, sir, by your favor.   281

Mor. Yet more!

Tru. Oh, you must give the learned men leave, sir.— To your impediments, master doctor.

Cut. The first is *impedimentum erroris.*

Ot. Of which there are several *species.*

Cut. Ay, as *error personæ.*

Ot. If you contract yourself to one person, thinking her another.

Cut. Then, *error fortunæ.*   290

Ot. If she be a beggar, and you thought her rich.

Cut. Then, *error qualitatis.*

Ot. If she prove stubborn or headstrong, that you thought obedient.

Mor. How! is that, sir, a lawful impediment? One at once, I pray you, gentlemen.

Ot. Ay, *ante copulam*, but not *post copulam*, sir.

Cut. Master parson says right. *Nec post nuptiarum benedictionem.* [36] It doth indeed but *irrita reddere sponsalia*, annul the contract; after marriage it is of no obstancy. [37]   301

Tru. Alas, sir, what a hope are we fallen from by this time!

Cut. The next is *conditio :* if you thought her free

born and she prove a bond-woman, there is impediment of estate and condition.

Ot. Ay, but, master doctor, those servitudes are *sublatæ* [38] now, among us Christians.

Cut. By your favor, master parson—

Ot. You shall give me leave, master doctor.   310

Mor. Nay, gentlemen, quarrel not in that question; it concerns not my case: pass to the third.

Cut. Well, then, the third is *votum.* If either party have made a vow of chastity. But that practice, as master parson said of the other, is taken away among us, thanks be to discipline. [39] The fourth is *cognatio :* if the persons be of kin within the degrees.

Ot. Ay: do you know what the degrees are, sir?

Mor. No, nor I care not, sir; they offer me no comfort in the question, I am sure.   320

Cut. But there is a branch of this impediment may, which is *cognatio spiritualis.* If you were her godfather, sir, then the marriage is incestuous.

Ot. That comment is absurd and superstitious, master doctor. I cannot endure it. Are we not all brothers and sisters, and as much akin in that as godfathers and goddaughters?

Mor. O me! to end the controversy, I never was a godfather, I never was a godfather in my life, sir. Pass to the next.   330

Cut. The fifth is *crimen adulterii:* the known case. The sixth, *cultus disparitas*, difference of religion. Have you ever examined her, what religion she is of?

Mor. No I would rather she were of none than be put to the trouble of it!

Ot. You may have it done for you, sir.

Mor. By no means, good sir; on to the rest. Shall you ever come to an end, think you?

Tru. Yes, he has done half, sir. On to the rest.—Be patient, and expect, sir.   340

Cut. The seventh is, *vis:* if it were upon compulsion or force.

Mor. Oh, no, it was too voluntary, mine; too voluntary.

Cut. The eighth is, *ordo:* if ever she have taken holy orders.

Ot. That's superstitious, too.

Mor. No matter, master parson; would she would go into a nunnery yet.

Cut. The ninth is, *ligamen:* if you were bound, sir, to any other before,   351

Mor. I thrust myself too soon into these fetters.

Cut. The tenth is, *publica honestas:* which is *inchoata quaedam affinitas.* [40]

Ot. Ay, or *affinitas orta ex sponsalibus;* and is but *leve impedimentum.* [41]

Mor. I feel no air of comfort blowing to me in all this.

Cut. The eleventh is, *affinitas ex fornicatione.* [42]

Ot. Which is no less *vera affinitas* [43] than the other, master doctor.   360

Cut. True, *quæ oritur ex legitimo matrimonio.* [44]

Ot. You say right, venerable doctor. And, *nascitur ex eo, quod per conjugium duae personae efficiuntur una caro* [45]—

Tru. Hey-day, now they begin!

Cut. I conceive you, master parson. *Ita per fornicationem æque est verus pater, qui sic generat* [46]—

Ot. *Et vere filius qui sic generatur* [47]—

Mor. What's all this to me?

Cler. Now it grows warm.   370

Cut. The twelfth and last is, *si forte coire nequibis.* [48]

Ot. Ay, that is *impedimentum gravissimum.* [49] It doth utterly annul and annihilate that. If you have *manifestam frigiditatem,* [50] you are well, sir.

Tru. Why, there is comfort come at length, sir. Confess yourself but a man unable, and she will sue to be divorced first.

Ot. Ay, or if there be *morbus perpetuus, et insanabilis;* [51] as *paralysis, elephantiasis,* or so—

Dauph. Oh, but *frigiditas* is the fairer way, gentlemen.   381

Ot. You say troth, sir, and as it is in the canon, master doctor—

Cut. I conceive you, sir.

Cler. Before he speaks!

Ot. That boy, or child, under years, is not fit for marriage, because he cannot *reddere debitum.* [52] So your *omnipotentes*—

Tru. [*Aside to* OTTER] Your *impotentes,* you whoreson lobster!   390

Ot. Your *impotentes,* I should say, are *minime apti ad contrahenda matrimonium.* [53]

Tru. *Matrimonium!* we shall have most unmatrimonial Latin with you: *matrimonia,* and be hanged.

Dauph. You put 'hem out, man.

Cut. But then there will arise a doubt, master parson, in our case, *post matrimonium:* that *frigiditate praeditus* [54] —do you conceive me, sir?

Ot. Very well, sir.

Cut. Who cannot *uti uxore pro uxora,* may *habere eam pro sorore.* [55]   401

Ot. Absurd, absurd, absurd, and merely apostatical! [56]

Cut. You shall pardon me, master parson, I can prove it.

Ot. You can prove a will, master doctor, you can prove nothing else. Does not the verse of your own canon say: *Haec socianda vetant conubia, facta retractant?* [57]

Cut. I grant you; but how do they *retractare,* master parson?   410

Mor. Oh, this was it I feared.

Ot. *In aeternum,* [58] sir.

Cut. That's false in divinity, by your favor.

Ot. 'Tis false in humanity to say so. Is he not *prorsus inutilis ad thorum?* Can he *praestare fidem datam?* [59] I would fain know.

Cut. Yes; how if he do *convalere?* [60]

Ot. He cannot *convalere,* it is impossible.

Tru. Nay, good sir, attend the learned men; they'll think you neglect them 'lse.   420

Cut. Or if he do *simulare* himself *frigidum, odio uxoris,* [61] or so?

Ot. I say he is *adulter manifestus,* [62] then.

Dauph. They dispute it very learnedly, i' faith.

Ot. And *prostitutor uxoris,* [63] and this is positive.

Mor. Good sir, let me escape.

Tru. You will not do me that wrong, sir?

Ot. And, therefore, if he be *manifeste frigidus,* sir—

Cut. Ay, if he be *manifeste frigidus,* I grant you—

Ot. Why, that was my conclusion.   430

Cut. And mine too.

Tru. Nay, hear the conclusion, sir.

Ot. Then, *frigiditatis causa*—

Cut. Yes, *causa frigiditatis*—

Mor. Oh, mine ears!

Ot. She may have *libellum divortii* [64] against you.

Cut. Ay, *divortii libellum* she will sure have.

Mor. Good echoes, forbear.

Ot. If you confess it.—

Cut. Which I would do, sir—   440

Mor. I will do anything.

Ot. And clear myself in *foro conscientiae* [65]—

Cut. Because you want indeed—

Mor. Yet more!

Ot. *Exercendi potestate.* [66]

[EPICOENE *rushes in, followed by* HAUGHTY, CENTAURE, MAVIS, Mistress OTTER, DAW, *and* LA FOOLE.]

Epi. I will not endure it any longer. Ladies, I beseech you help me. This is such a wrong as never was offered to poor bride before. Upon her marriage day to have her husband conspire against her, and a couple of mercenary companions to be brought in for   450 form's sake, to persuade a separation! If you had blood or virtue in you, gentlemen, you would not suffer such earwigs [67] about a husband, or scorpions to creep between man and wife.

Mor. O the variety and changes of my torment!

Hau. Let 'hem be cudgeled out of doors by our grooms.

Cen. I'll lend you my footman.

---

[46] *L.:* Thus through fornication is he equally a true father, who thus begets.

[47] *L.:* And he truly a son who is thus begotten.

[48] *L.:* if by chance you should be unable to copulate.

[49] *L.:* the heaviest impediment.

[50] *L.:* manifest frigidity.

[51] *L.:* perpetual disease, and incurable.

[52] *L.:* pay his debt.

[53] *L.:* impotent persons are least fit for contracting matrimony.

[54] *L.:* after the marriage: that the frigid man.

[55] *L.:* use a wife as a wife, may have her as a sister.

[56] *apostatical:* retrograde; not to the purpose. But sonority is more than sense here.

[57] *L.:* quoting Aquinas, who concludes his list of impediments to marriage: "These things forbid marriages to be contracted, and when done revoke the contract."

[58] *L.:* Forever.

[59] *L.:* absolutely useless in bed? Can he carry out the oath he has given?   [60] *L.:* recover (his virility).

[61] *L.:* pretend to be frigid, from hatred of his wife.

[62] *L.:* an open adulterer.

[63] *L.:* prostitutor of his wife.   [64] *L.:* bill of divorce.

[65] *L.:* legal proverb—"at the bar of conscience."

[66] *L.:* Power of doing.

[67] *earwigs:* insects (insinuating creatures).

Mav. We'll have our men blanket[68] 'hem i' the hall.

Mrs. Ot. As there was one at our house, madam, for peeping in at the door.   461

Daw. Content, i' faith.

Tru. Stay, ladies and gentlemen; you'll hear before you proceed?

Mav. I'ld ha' the bridegroom blanketed too.

Cen. Begin with him first.

Hau. Yes, by my troth.

Mor. O mankind[69] generation!

Dauph. Ladies, for my sake forbear.

Hau. Yes, for Sir Dauphine's sake.   470

Cen. He shall command us.

La F. He is as fine a gentleman of his inches, madam, as any is about the town, and wears as good colors when he list.

Tru. Be brief, sir, and confess your infirmity; she'll be a-fire to be quit of you, if she but hear that named once, you shall not entreat her to stay; she'll fly you like one that had the marks[70] upon him.

Mor. Ladies, I must crave all your pardons—

Tru. Silence, ladies.   480

Mor. For a wrong I have done to your whole sex, in marrying this fair and virtuous gentlewoman—

Cler. Hear him, good ladies.

Mor. Being guilty of an infirmity which, before I conferred with these learned man, I thought I might have concealed—

Tru. But now being better informed in his conscience by them, he is to declare it, and give satisfaction by asking your public forgiveness.

Mor. I am no man, ladies.   490

All. How!

Mor. Utterly unable in nature, by reason of frigidity, to perform the duties or any the least office of a husband.

Mav. Now out upon him, prodigious creature![71]

Cen. Bridegroom uncarnate![72]

Hau. And would you offer it to a young gentlewoman!

Mrs. Ot. A lady of her longings?

Epi. Tut, a device, a device, this! it smells rankly, ladies. A mere comment[73] of his own.   500

Tru. Why, if you suspect that, ladies, you may have him searched—

Daw. As the custom is, by a jury of physicians.

La F. Yes, faith, 'twill be brave.

Mor. O me, must I undergo that?

Mrs. Ot. No, let women search him, madam: we can do it ourselves.

Mor. Out on me! worse.

Epi. No, ladies, you shall not need, I'll take him with all his faults.   510

---

[68] *blanket:* toss in a blanket.
[69] *mankind:* mad.
[70] *marks:* i.e., of the plague.
[71] *prodigious creature:* monster.
[72] *uncarnate:* unincarnate; not flesh and blood.
[73] *comment:* fiction.   [74] *L.:* up to the wife.
[75] *L.:* break the contract and render it void.
[76] *L.:* carnally.

Mor. Worst of all!

Cler. Why then, 'tis no divorce, doctor, if she consent not?

Cut. No, if the man be *frigidus*, it is *de parte uxoris*,[74] that we grant *libellum divortii*, in the law.

Ot. Ay, it is the same in theology.

Mor. Worse, worse than worst!

Tru. Nay, sir, be not utterly disheartened; we have yet a small relic of hope left, as near as our comfort is blown out. Clerimont, produce your brace of   520 knights. What was that, master parson, you told me *in errore qualitatis*, e'en now? [*Aside*] Dauphine, whisper the bride, that she carry it as if she were guilty and ashamed.

Ot. Marry, sir, *in errore qualitatis* (which master doctor did forbear to urge), if she be found *corrupta*, that is, vitiated or broken up, that was *pro virgine desponsa*, espoused for a maid—

Mor. What then, sir?   529

Ot. It doth *dirimere contractum*, and *irritum reddere*[75] too.

Tru. If this be true, we are happy again, sir, once more. Here are an honorable brace of knights that shall affirm so much.

Daw. Pardon us, good Master Clerimont.

La F. You shall excuse us, Master Clerimont.

Cler. Nay, you must make it good now, knights, there is no remedy; I'll eat no words for you, nor no men: you know you spoke it to me.

Daw. Is this gentlemanlike, sir?   540

Tru. [*Aside to* DAW] Jack Daw, he's worse than Sir Amorous; fiercer a great deal—[*Aside to* LA FOOLE] Sir Amorous, beware, there be ten Daws in this Clerimont.

La F. I'll confess it, sir.

Daw. Will you, Sir Amorous, will you wound reputation?

La F. I am resolved.

Tru. So should you be too, Jack Daw: what should keep you off? She is but a woman, and in disgrace. He'll be glad on't.   551

Daw. Will he? I thought he would ha' been angry.

Cler. You will dispatch, knights; it must be done, i'faith.

Tru. Why, an' it must, it shall, sir, they say. They'll ne'er go back. [*Aside to them*] Do not tempt his patience.

Daw. It is true indeed, sir.

La F. Yes, I assure you, sir.

Mor. What is true, gentlemen? What do you assure me?   560

Daw. That we have known your bride, sir—

La F. In good fashion. She was our mistress, or so—

Cler. Nay, you must be plain, knights, as you were to me.

Ot. Ay, the question is, if you have *carnaliter*,[76] or no?

La F. *Carnaliter!* what else, sir?

Ot. It is enough; a plain nullity.

Epi. I am undone, I am undone!

Mor. O let me worship and adore you, gentlemen!

Epi. I am undone!   571

Mor. Yes, to my hand,[77] I thank these knights. Master parson, let me thank you otherwise.

[Gives him money.]

Cen. And ha' they confessed?

Mav. Now, out upon 'hem, informers!

Tru. You see what creatures you may bestow your favors on, madams.

Hau. I would except against 'hem as beaten knights, wench, and not good witnesses in law.

Mrs. Ot. Poor gentlewoman, how she takes it!   580

Hau. Be comforted, Morose, I love you the better for't.

Cen. So do I, I protest.

Cut. But, gentlemen, you have not known her since *matrimonium?*

Daw. Not today, master doctor.

La F. No, sir, not today.

Cut. Why, then I say, for any act before, the *matrimonium* is good and perfect; unless the worshipful bridegroom did precisely, before witness, demand, if she were *virgo ante nuptias.*[78]   591

Epi. No, that he did not, I assure you, master doctor.

Cut. If he cannot prove that, it is *ratum conjugium,*[79] notwithstanding the premisses; and they do no way *impedire.* And this is my sentence, this I pronounce.

Ot. I am of master doctor's resolution too, sir; if you made not that demand *ante nuptias.*

Mor. O my heart! wilt thou break? Wilt thou break? This is worst of all worst worsts that hell could have devised! Marry a whore, and so much noise!   600

Dauph. Come, I see now plain confederacy in this doctor and this parson, to abuse a gentleman. You study his affliction. I pray be gone, companions.[80]—And, gentlemen, I begin to suspect you for having parts with 'hem.—Sir, will it please you hear me?

Mor. Oh, do not talk to me; take not from me the pleasure of dying in silence, nephew.

Dauph. Sir, I must speak to you. I have been long your poor despised kinsman, and many a hard thought has strengthened you against me: but now it shall   610 appear if either I love you or your peace, and prefer them to all the world beside. I will not be long or grievous to you, sir. If I free you of this unhappy match absolutely and instantly, after all this trouble, and almost in your despair, now—

Mor. It cannot be.

Dauph. Sir, that you be never troubled with a murmur of it more, what shall I hope for, or deserve of you?

Mor. Oh, what thou wilt, nephew! thou shalt deserve me, and have me.   620

Dauph. Shall I have your favor perfect to me, and love hereafter?

Mor. That, and anything beside. Make thine own conditions. My whole estate is thine. Manage it, I will become thy ward.

Dauph. Nay, sir, I will not be so unreasonable.

Epi. Will Sir Dauphine be mine enemy too?

Dauph. You know I have been long a suitor to you, uncle, that out of your estate, which is fifteen hundred a year, you would allow me but five hundred dur-   630

ing life, and assure the rest upon me after; to which I have often, by myself and friends, tendered you a writing to sign, which you would never consent or incline to. If you please but to effect it now—

Mor. Thou shalt have it, nephew. I will do it, and more.

Dauph. If I quit you not presently, and for ever, of this cumber,[81] you shall have power instantly, afore all these, to revoke your act, and I will become whose slave you will give me to forever.   640

Mor. Where is the writing? I will seal to it, that, or to a blank, and write thine own conditions.

Epi. O me, most unfortunate, wretched gentlewoman!

Hau. Will Sir Dauphine do this?

Epi. Good sir, have some compassion on me.

Mor. Oh, my nephew knows you, belike; away, crocodile![82]

Cen. He does it not sure without good ground.

Dauph. Here, sir.   650

[Gives him the parchments.]

Mor. Come, nephew, give me the pen. I will subscribe to anything, and seal to what thou wilt for my deliverance. Thou art my restorer. Here I deliver it thee as my deed. If there be a word in it lacking, or writ with false orthography, I protest before—I will not take the advantage.

[Returns the writings.]

Dauph. Then here is your release, sir.

He takes off EPICOENE'S *peruke.*

You have married a boy, a gentleman's son that I have brought up this half year at my great charges, and for this composition which I have now made with   660 you. What say you, master doctor? This is *justum im pedimentum,* I hope, *error personae?*

Ot. Yes, sir, *in primo gradu.*

Cut. In *primo gradu.*

Dauph. I thank you, good doctor Cutbeard, and parson Otter.

He pulls off their beards and disguises.

You are beholden to 'hem, sir, that have taken this pains for you; and my friend, Master Truewit, who enabled 'hem for the business. Now you may go in and rest; be as private as you will, sir.   670

[Exit MOROSE.]

I'll not trouble you till you trouble me with your funeral, which I care not how soon it come.—Cutbeard, I'll make your lease good. Thank me not, but with your leg, Cutbeard. And Tom Otter, your princess shall be reconciled to you.—How now, gentlemen, do you look at me?

---

[77] *to my hand:* i.e., the marriage is annulled.
[78] *L.:* a virgin before the marriage.
[79] *L.:* a valid marriage.
[80] *companions:* base fellows.   [81] *cumber:* encumbrance.
[82] *crocodile:* Epicoene is weeping.

Cler. A boy!

Dauph. Yes, Mistress Epicoene.

Tru. Well, Dauphine, you have lurched your friends of the better half of the garland,[83] by concealing 680 this part of the plot! But much good do it thee, thou deserv'st it, lad. And, Clerimont, for thy unexpected bringing in these two to confession, wear my part of it freely. Nay, Sir Daw and Sir La Foole, you see the gentlewoman that has done you the favors! we are all thankful to you, and so should the womankind here, specially for lying on her, though not with her! you meant so, I am sure? But that we have stuck it upon you today, in your own imagined persons, and so lately, this Amazon, the champion of the sex, should 690 beat you now thriftily, for the common slanders which ladies receive from such cuckoos as you are. You are they that, when no merit or fortune can make you hope to enjoy their bodies, will yet lie with their reputations, and make their fame suffer. Away, you common moths of these, and all ladies' honors. Go, travail[84] to make legs and faces, and come home with some new matter to be laughed at. You deserve to live in an air as corrupted as that wherewith you feed rumor.

[*Exeunt* DAW *and* LA FOOLE.]

—Madams, you are mute upon this new meta- 700 morphosis! But here stands she that has vindicated your fames. Take heed of such insectae[85] hereafter. And let it not trouble you, that you have discovered any mysteries to this young gentleman. He is almost of years, and will make a good visitant within this twelve-month. In the mean time, we'll all undertake for his secrecy, that can speak so well of his silence.

[*Comes forward.*]

—Spectators, if you like this comedy, rise cheerfully, and now Morose is gone in, clap your hands. It may be that noise will cure him, at least please him. 711

[*Exeunt.*]

THE   END

---

[83] *lurched . . . garland:* cheated of the glory. Jonson is evidently remembering, perhaps mocking, a very similar line by Shakespeare in *Coriolanus* (II.ii. 102), written probably between 1607 and 1609.

[84] *travail:* original spelling of "travel," which emphasizes its arduous nature.

[85] *insectae:* insects.

Ben Jonson

THE ALCHEMIST

THE ALCHEMIST was first performed by the King's Men in their recently reacquired indoor theater, the Blackfriars, in 1610. Not surprisingly, it remained popular during the thirty-two years before the closing of the theaters and was frequently revived after the Restoration; it has been played successfully ever since. Its text appeared first in the quarto of 1612, but Jonson's careful revision for the folio edition of his *Works* in 1616 is the authoritative text and the basis for the present edition. In accordance with his neoclassical principles, Jonson marked a new scene each time a character enters, and his scene divisions are retained, though unemphatically; they do not necessarily indicate a clearing of the stage, and indeed there may be no such clearing between the third and fourth acts.

No play of the period can be said to be freer of debt to a previous model. The idea of the deserted house taken over owes its inspiration to Plautus' *Mostellaria*, and some incidents in the action (e.g., the trick played on Dapper) may draw on contemporary records of actual events; but the conception and the plot are powerfully original inventions. On the other hand, Jonson studied a multitude of works, in composing his comedy, with a care unmatched among his contemporaries, and the dense alchemical lore of the play is carefully derived from a number of technical works on the subject. Similarly, the satire on Puritans is worked out by allusion to the works of his victims, particularly those of his chief victim, Hugh Broughton. Much of the play's effectiveness can be credited to Jonson's ear, his ability to ape the voice as well as the words of the canting Puritan, the would-be braggart looking for instruction in the art of pretended anger, the effete sensualist, the lowlife of London, and above all the alchemist, whose occupation, part conscious fraud and part wishful science, inflamed the imaginations of Englishmen and Europeans who coveted gold and believed that God had created the world to serve them with its riches.

It is tempting to apply to Jonson's masterpiece his own words about Shakespeare: it is not of an age but for all time. THE ALCHEMIST owes some of its transcendence of its own day to the eccentricities of its author's genius. Jonson was virtually unique among his contemporaries in refusing to take romantic love seriously. He was entirely so in his neoclassical insistence on the unities of place and time, which would have inconvenienced the majority of contemporary dramatists; for unlike him they believed that character could change, suddenly or over a period of time, and that one of the things plays did was to provide plots allowing for the portrayal of such changes. He was alone in his hardheaded assumption that freedom is the goal of human life and that it consists entirely in the sheer intelligence required to dodge one's own irrationalities and the snares of others. These quirks make Jonson more an antique Roman than an Elizabethan. But it is as wrong to see him therefore as not of an age as it is misleading of him to have suggested that Shakespeare did not epitomize the age he transcended. In significant respects THE ALCHEMIST is an apotheosis of the comedy of its period. To be sure, Jonson's use of a fixed set, in which the same stage entrance always represents the same fictive door, is contrary to the practice of the stagecraft of his day, but the choreographed movement of a large group of characters through the intricacies of an ever-moving plot only brings to a climax what audiences had come to expect. The comedy of gulling and the satiric distortion of a London whose topography and sociology are minutely observed owe much to earlier comedies by Middleton, Marston, Chapman, and others, and to the pamphlets of Greene, Nashe, Lodge, and the like. The subject of THE ALCHEMIST is Jonson's world, and his treatment presents the psyche of a particular society, obsessed with gold and power, language, and solipsistic triumph by wit. If we rightly find alchemy turning into a metaphor for the creative power of the imagination, for the abilities to make art and to prey on others, to dream and to deceive oneself, and hence a figure for the drives that make us human for better and for worse, we do Jonson an injustice in forgetting that his comedy of the human condition is founded, just as much as Molière's, on the peculiar form that man's madness took at a unique moment in history that would be irrecoverable but for the legacy of Jonson.   N. R.

The Alchemist

TO THE READER[1]

IF THOU beest more, thou art an understander,[2] and then I trust thee. If thou art one that tak'st up, and but a pretender, beware at what hands thou receiv'st thy commodity; for thou wert never more fair in the way to be coz'ned than in this age in poetry, especially in plays, wherein now the concupiscence[3] of jigs and antics[4] so reigneth, as to run away from nature and be afraid of her is the only point of art that tickles the spectators. But how out of purpose and place do I name art, when the professors[5] are grown so obstinate 10 contemners of it, and presumers on their own naturals,[6] as they are deriders of all diligence that way, and, by simple mocking at the terms when they understand not the things, think to get off wittily with their ignorance! Nay, they are esteemed the more learned and sufficient for this by the multitude, through their excellent vice[7] of judgment. For they commend writers as they do fencers or wrestlers; who, if they come in robustiously[8] and put[9] for it with a great deal of violence, are received for the braver fellows; when many times their own 20 rudeness[10] is the cause of their disgrace, and a little touch of their adversary gives all that boisterous force the foil.[11] I deny not but that these men who always seek to do more than enough may some time happen on some thing that is good and great; but very seldom, and when it comes, it doth not recompense the rest of their ill. It sticks out, perhaps, and is more eminent, because all is sordid and vile about it; as lights are more discerned in a thick darkness than a faint shadow. I speak not this out of a hope to do good on any man 30 against his will; for I know, if it were put to the question[12] of theirs and mine, the worse would find more suffrages, because the most favor common errors. But I give thee this warning, that there is a great difference between those that (to gain the opinion of[13] copy[14]) utter all they can, however unfitly, and those that use election[15] and a mean.[16] For it is only the disease of the unskillful to think rude things greater than polished, or scattered more numerous than composed.

DRAMATIS PERSONÆ

SUBTLE, the Alchemist
FACE, the Housekeeper, [servant to Lovewit, assistant to Subtle]
DOL COMMON, their colleague, [a prostitute]
DAPPER, a clerk
[ABEL] DRUGGER, a tobacco-man[1]
LOVEWIT, master of the house
[Sir] EPICURE MAMMON, a Knight

[PERTINAX] SURLY, a gamester
TRIBULATION [WHOLESOME], a Pastor of Amsterdam[2]
ANANIAS, a Deacon there
KASTRIL, the angry boy
DAME PLIANT, his sister, a widow
Neighbors, Officers [a Parson]

THE SCENE: LONDON

TO THE READER
    [1] This preface is taken from the quarto; it was not reprinted in the folio.
    [2] *understander:* with pun—auditor, one who stands in the theater pit.   [3] *concupiscence:* desire.
    [4] *antics:* grotesque people.
    [5] *professors:* those who profess, i.e., playwrights.
    [6] *naturals:* mental endowments.   [7] *vice:* depravity.
    [8] *robustiously:* boisterously.   [9] *put:* try.
    [10] *rudeness:* lack of skill.   [11] *foil:* throw.
    [12] *question:* vote.   [13] *opinion of:* reputation for.
    [14] *copy:* copiousness.   [15] *election:* discrimination.
    [16] *use . . . mean:* exercise moderation.

DRAMATIS PERSONÆ
    [1] *Tobacco-man:* tobacconist.
    [2] *Amsterdam:* a center for zealous Puritans, many of them English.

144

THE ARGUMENT

T he sickness[1] hot, a master quit, for fear,
H is house in town, and left one servant there.
E ase him corrupted, and gave means to know
A Cheater and his punk,[2] who, now brought low,
L eaving their narrow practice, were become
C oz'ners[3] at large; and, only wanting[4] some
H ouse to set up, with him they here contract,
E ach for a share, and all begin to act.
M uch company they draw, and much abuse,
I n casting figures,[5] telling fortunes, news,   10
S elling of flies,[6] flat bawdry, with the stone;[7]
T ill it, and they, and all in fume[8] are gone.

PROLOGUE

Fortune, that favors fools, these two short hours
  We wish away, both for your sakes and ours,
Judging spectators; and desire in place,
  To th' author justice, to ourselves but grace.
Our scene is London, 'cause we would make known,
  No country's mirth is better than our own.
No clime breeds better matter for your whore,
Bawd, squire,[1] imposter, many persons more,
Whose manners, now called humors,[2] feed the stage;
  And which have still[3] been subject for the rage   10
Or spleen of comic writers. Though this pen
  Did never aim to grieve, but better[4] men,

Howe'er the age he lives in doth endure
  The vices that she breeds, above their cure.
But when the wholesome remedies are sweet,
  And, in their working, gain and profit meet,
He hopes to find no spirit so much diseased,
  But will with such fair correctives[5] be pleased.
For here he doth not fear who can apply.[6]
  If there be any that will sit so nigh   20
Unto the stream, to look what it doth run,
  They shall find things, they'd think, or wish, were
They are so natural follies, but so shown,   [done;
  As even the doers may see, and yet not own.

ACT ONE

SCENE ONE

[*Enter*] FACE, SUBTLE, [*and, behind them*] DOL
COMMON.

Face. Believe 't, I will.
Sub.   Thy worst. I fart at thee.
Dol Com. Ha' you your wits? Why, gentlemen! for
  love—

Face. Sirrah, I'll strip you—
Sub.   What to do? Lick figs[1]
Out at my—
Face.   Rogue, rogue, out of all your sleights.
Dol Com. Nay, look ye. Sovereign, general, are you
  madmen?
Sub. Oh, let the wild sheep loose. I'll gum your silks
With good strong water,[2] an you come.
Dol Com.   Will you have
The neighbors hear you? Will you betray all?
Hark! I hear somebody.
Face.   Sirrah—
Sub.   I shall mar
All that the tailor has made, if you approach.   10
Face. You most notorious whelp, you insolent slave,
Dare you do this?
Sub.   Yes faith, yes faith.
Face.   Why, who
Am I, my mongrel? Who am I?
Sub.   I'll tell you,
Since you know not yourself—
Face.   Speak lower, rogue.
Sub. Yes. You were once (time's not long past) the
  good,
Honest, plain, livery-three-pound-thrum,[3] that kept

THE ARGUMENT
  [1] *sickness:* plague.   [2] *punk:* whore.
  [3] *Coz'ners:* Cheaters.   [4] *wanting:* lacking.
  [5] *figures:* horoscopes.   [6] *flies:* familiar spirits.
  [7] *stone:* philosopher's stone.   [8] *fume:* smoke.

PROLOGUE
  [1] *squire:* pimp.
  [2] *humors:* fluids (blood, bile, phlegm, black bile) which in
various combinations govern physiology and personality.
  [3] *still:* always.   [4] *better:* improve.
  [5] *correctives:* medicines.
  [6] *apply:* make application to particular people.

I.i.
  [1] *figs:* piles.   [2] *strong water:* acid.
  [3] *livery . . . thrum:* shabbily dressed, poorly paid depen-
dant.

Your master's worship's house here in the Friars,[4]
For the vacations—[5]
   Face.   Will you be so loud?
   Sub. Since, by my means, translated suburb-
     captain.[6]
   Face. By your means, doctor dog!
   Sub.   Within man's
memory,   20
All this I speak of.
   Face.   Why, I pray you, have I
Been countenanced by you, or you by me?
Do but collect,[7] sir, where I met you first.
   Sub. I do not hear well.
   Face.   Not of this, I think it.
But I shall put you in mind, sir: at Pie-corner,[8]
Taking your meal of steam in, from cooks' stalls,
Where, like the father of hunger, you did walk
Piteously costive,[9] with your pinched-horn-nose,
And your complexion of the Roman wash,[10]
Stuck full of black and melancholic worms,   30
Like powder-corns[11] shot at th' artillery-yard.
   Sub. I wish you could advance your voice a little.
   Face. When you went pinned up in the several rags
Y' had raked and picked from dunghills, before day,
Your feet in moldy slippers, for your kibes,[12]
A felt of rug,[13] and a thin threaden cloak,
That scarce would cover your no-buttocks—
   Sub.   So, sir!
   Face. When all your alchemy, and your algebra,
Your minerals, vegetals, and animals,   39
Your conjuring, coz'ning, and your dozen of trades,
Could not relieve your corpse with so much linen
Would make you tinder, but to see a fire;
I ga' you count'nance, credit for your coals,
Your stills, your glasses, your materials;
Built you a furnace, drew you customers,
Advanced all your black arts; lent you, beside,
A house to practice in—
   Sub.   Your master's house!
   Face. Where you have studied the more thriving
     skill
Of bawdry since.
   Sub.   Yes, in your master's house.
You and the rats here kept possession.   50
Make it not strange. I know you were one could keep
The buttery-hatch still locked, and save the chippings,[14]
Sell the dole beer to aqua-vitae men,[15]
The which, together with your Christmas vails[16]
At post-and-pair,[17] your letting out of counters,[18]
Made you a pretty stock, some twenty marks,[19]
And gave you credit to converse with cobwebs
Here, since your mistress' death hath broke up house.
   Face. You might talk softlier, rascal.
   Sub.   No, you scarab,[20]
I'll thunder you in pieces. I will teach you   60
How to beware to tempt a Fury again
That carries tempest in his hand and voice.
   Face. The place has made you valiant.
   Sub.   No, your
     clothes.
Thou vermin, have I ta'en thee out of dung,

So poor, so wretched, when no living thing
Would keep thee company, but a spider or worse?
Raised thee from brooms and dust and wat'ring-pots?
Sublimed[21] thee, and exalted[22] thee, and fixed[23]
     thee
I' the third region, called our state of grace?[24]   69
Wrought thee to spirit, to quintessence, with pains
Would twice have won me the philosopher's work?[25]
Put thee in words and fashion? made thee fit
For more than ordinary[26] fellowships?
Giv'n thee thy oaths, thy quarreling dimensions?[27]
Thy rules to cheat at horse-race, cock-pit, cards,
Dice, or whatever gallant tincture[28] else?
Made thee a second in mine own great art?
And have I this for thanks! Do you rebel?
Do you fly out[29] the projection?[30]   79
Would you be gone now?
   Dol Com.   Gentlemen, what mean you?
Will you mar all?
   Sub.   Slave, thou hadst had no name—
   Dol. Com. Will you undo yourselves with civil war?
   Sub. Never been known, past *equi clibanum,*[31]
The heat of horse-dung, under ground, in cellars,
Or an ale-house, darker than deaf John's;[32] been lost
To all mankind, but laundresses and tapsters,[33]
Had not I been.
   Dol. Com.   Do you know who hears you, sovereign!
   Face. Sirrah—
   Dol Com.   Nay, general, I thought you were
     civil.
   Face. I shall turn desperate, if you grow thus loud.
   Sub. And hang thyself, I care not.
   Face.   Hang thee, collier,
And all thy pots and pans, in picture[34] I will,   91
Since thou hast moved me—
   Dol Com. [*Aside*]   Oh, this 'll o'erthrow all.

---

[4] *Friars:* Blackfriars, London district where Jonson lived and *The Alchemist* was performed.
[5] *vacations:* recesses between court sessions.
[6] *translated suburb-captain:* elevated to "captain" of a disreputable district.   [7] *collect:* recollect.
[8] *Pie-corner:* district in Smithfield where cooked food was sold.   [9] *costive:* constipated.   [10] *Roman wash:* sallow(?).
[11] *corns:* grains.   [12] *kibes:* chilblains.
[13] *felt . . . rug:* hat of coarse material.
[14] *chippings:* dole-bread, given to the poor at buttery-hatch door.   [15] *aqua-vitae men:* distillers or sellers of spirits.
[16] *vails:* tips.   [17] *post-and-pair:* card game.
[18] *letting . . . counters:* renting tokens to players.
[19] *marks:* the mark was 13s.4d.   [20] *scarab:* dung beetle.
[21] *sublimed:* (alch.) purified by distillation.
[22] *exalted:* (alch.) raised to a higher "degree," concentrated.   [23] *fixed:* deprived of volatility or fluidity.
[24] *state of grace:* i.e., purest of the three layers of the air.
[25] *work:* stone.   [26] *ordinary:* tavern.
[27] *dimensions:* quarrelling rules.
[28] *tincture:* (alch.) quintessence of a substance.
[29] *fly out:* explode.
[30] *projection:* transmutation of metals to gold by casting powdered philosopher's stone on it in a crucible.
[31] *L.:* heat of rotting horse-dung, used in alchemy.
[32] *deaf John's:* unknown alehouse.
[33] *tapsters:* alehouse keepers.
[34] *in picture:* advertising his dishonesty (colliers were proverbially untrustworthy.)

Face. Write thee up bawd in Paul's,[35] have all thy
    tricks
Of coz'ning with a hollow coal,[36] dust, scrapings,
Searching for things lost, with a sieve and shears,[37]
Erecting figures in your rows of houses,[38]
And taking in of shadows with a glass,[39]
Told in red letters;[40] and a face cut for thee,
Worse than Gamaliel Ratsey's.[41]
    Dol Com.   Are you sound?
Ha' you your senses, masters?
    Face.   I will have   100
A book, but barely reckoning thy impostures,
Shall prove a true philosopher's stone to printers.
    Sub. Away, you trencher-rascal![42]
    Face.   Out, you dog-
    leech,[43]
The vomit of all prisons—
    Dol Com.   Will you be
Your own destructions, gentlemen?
    Face.   Still spewed out
For lying too heavy o' the basket.[44]
    Sub.   Cheater.
    Face. Bawd.
    Sub.   Cow-herd.
    Face.   Conjurer.
    Sub.   Cutpurse.
    Face.   Witch.
    Dol Com.   Oh, me.
We are ruined! lost! Ha' you no more regard
To your reputations? Where's your judgment?
    'Slight,

---

[35] *Paul's:* St. Paul's Cathedral, where citizens met for business and notices were posted.

[36] *coz'ning . . . coal:* an alchemist's trick, secreting silver in a coal which burns away to reveal it.

[37] *Searching . . . shears:* a kind of divination to catch a thief.

[38] *Erecting . . . houses:* diagramming planet positions in the zodiac.

[39] *taking . . . glass:* reading a crystal ball, to be performed by a virgin.

[40] *red letters:* rubricated headings of books and broadsides.

[41] *Gamaliel Ratsey:* famous highwayman who robbed in a mask and was executed in 1605.

[42] *trencher-rascal:* scoundrelly parasite, glutton.

[43] *dog-leech:* low-class veterinarian.

[44] *lying . . . basket:* eating more than his share of prison food.   [45] *republic:* commonwealth, fraternity.

[46] *brach:* bitch.

[47] *tricesimo* (L.) *. . . Eight:* first statute against sorcery, 33 Henry VIII (1541).   [48] *laund'ring:* washing gold in acid.

[49] *barbing:* clipping off the edges.

[50] *coxcomb:* fool's hat.   [51] *menstrue:* solvent.

[52] *marshal:* provost-marshal.   [53] *dog-bolt:* scoundrel.

[54] *apocryphal:* phony.

[55] *Puritan in Blackfriars:* Puritans sold feathers as clothing ornaments in the district.

[56] *powder:* ground philosopher's stone.

[57] *Fall . . . couples:* work, like hunting dogs, in a pair.

[58] *term:* one of the four annual court sessions.

[59] *fermentation:* sixth process in the conversion of metal to gold.

[60] *cibation:* the seventh process, feeding fresh substance to replace that lost by earlier processes.

[61] *Sol:* (sun) gold.   [62] *Luna:* (moon) silver.

Have yet some care of me, o' your republic[45]—   110
    Face. Away this brach.[46] I'll bring thee, rogue,
    within
The statute of sorcery, *tricesimo tertio*
Of Harry the Eight,[47] ay, and perhaps thy neck
Within a noose, for laund'ring[48] gold and barbing[49] it.
    Dol Com. You'll bring your head within a coxcomb,[50]
    will you?

                She catcheth out FACE *his sword,*
                and breaks SUBTLE'S *glass.*

And you, sir, with your menstrue,[51] gather it up.
'Sdeath, you abominable pair of stinkards,
Leave off your barking, and grow one again,
Or, by the light that shines, I'll cut your throats.
I'll not be made a prey unto the marshal[52]   120
For ne'er a snarling dog-bolt[53] o' you both.
Ha' you together cozened all this while,
And all the world, and shall it now be said,
You've made most courteous shift to cozen yourselves?
[*To* FACE] You will accuse him! you will bring him in
Within the statute? Who shall take your word?
A whoreson, upstart, apocryphal[54] captain,
Whom not a Puritan in Blackfriars[55] will trust
So much as for a feather! [*To* SUBTLE] And you, too,
Will give the cause, forsooth? You will insult,   130
And claim a primacy in the divisions?
You must be chief? As if you only had
The powder[56] to project with, and the work
Were not begun out of equality!
The venture tripartite? All things in common?
Without priority? 'Sdeath, you perpetual curs,
Fall to your couples[57] again, and cozen kindly,
And heartily, and lovingly, as you should,
And lose not the beginning of a term,[58]
Or, by this hand, I shall grow factious too,   140
And take my part, and quit you.
    Face.   'T is his fault;
He ever murmurs, and objects his pains,
And says the weight of all lies upon him.
    Sub. Why, so it does.
    Dol Com.   How does it? Do not we
Sustain our parts?
    Sub.   Yes, but they are not equal.
    Dol Com. Why, if your part exceed today, I hope
Ours may tomorrow match it.
    Sub.   Ay, they may.
    Dol Com. May, murmuring mastiff? Ay, and do.
    Death on me!
[*To* FACE] Help me to throttle him.

               [*Seizes* SUBTLE *by the throat.*]

    Sub.   Dorothy! Mistress
    Dorothy!
'Ods precious, I'll do anything. What do you mean?
    Dol Com. Because o' your fermentation,[59] and
    cibation?[60]   151
    Sub. Not I, by heaven—
    Dol Com.   Your Sol[61] and Luna[62]—
    [*To* FACE] Help me.
    Sub. Would I were hanged then! I'll conform myself.

Dol Com. Will you, sir? Do so then, and quickly:
  swear.
  Sub. What should I swear?
  Dol Com.   To leave your faction,[63] sir,
And labor kindly in the common work.
  Sub. Let me not breathe if I meant aught beside.
I only used those speeches as a spur
To him.
  Dol Com. I hope we need no spurs, sir. Do we?   159
  Face. 'Slid,[64] prove today who shall shark[65] best.
  Sub.   Agreed.
  Dol Com. Yes, and work close and friendly.
  Sub.   'Slight,[66] the knot
Shall grow the stronger for this breach, with me.

                [They shake hands.]

  Dol Com. Why, so, my good baboons! Shall we go
  make
A sort[67] of sober, precise[68] neighbors,
That scarce have smiled twice sin' the king came in,[69]
A feast of laughter at our follies? Rascals,
Would run themselves from[70] breath, to see me ride,[71]
Or you t' have but a hole to thrust your heads in,
For which you should pay ear-rent?[72] No, agree.
And may Don Provost[73] ride a-feasting long,   170
In his old velvet jerkin and stained scarfs,
My noble sovereign, and worthy general,
Ere we contribute a new crewel[74] garter
To his most worsted worship.
  Sub.   Royal Dol!
Spoken like Claridiana,[75] and thyself.
  Face. For which at supper, thou shalt sit in triumph,
And not be styled Dol Common, but Dol Proper,
Dol Singular; the longest cut[76] at night
Shall draw thee for his Dol Particular.

                 [Bell rings.]

  Sub. Who's that? One rings. To the window, Dol!—
  Pray heav'n   180
The master do not trouble us this quarter.[77]
  Face. Oh, fear not him. While there dies one a week
O' the plague, he's safe from thinking toward London.
Beside, he's busy at his hop-yards now;
I had a letter from him. If he do,
He'll send such word, for airing o' the house,
As you shall have sufficient time to quit it.
Though we break up a fortnight, 't is no matter.
  Sub. Who is it, Dol?
  Dol. Com.   A fine young quodling.[78]
  Face.   Oh,
My lawyer's clerk, I lighted on last night,   190
In Holborn,[79] at the Dagger.[80] He would have
—I told you of him—a familiar,[81]
To rifle[82] with at horses, and win cups.
  Dol Com. Oh, let him in.
  Sub.   Stay. Who shall do 't?
  Face.   Get you
Your robes on; I will meet him, as going out.
  Dol Com. And what shall I do?
  Face.   Not be seen; away!

             [Exit DOL COMMON.*]*

Seem you very reserved.
  Sub.   Enough.

                   [Exit.]
  Face.   God be wi' you, sir.
I pray you, let him know that I was here: 198
His name is Dapper. I would gladly have stayed, but—

I.ii

  [Dap.] [Within] Captain, I am here.
  Face.   Who's that?—
  He's come, I think, doctor.

            [Enter DAPPER.*]*

Good faith, sir, I was going away.
  Dap.   In truth,
I'm very sorry, captain.
  Face.   But I thought
Sure I should meet you.
  Dap.   Ay, I'm very glad.
I had a scurvy writ or two to make,
And I had lent my watch last night to one
That dines to-day at the shrieve's, and so was robbed
Of my pass-time.

  [Re-enter SUBTLE *in his velvet cap and gown.]*

           Is this the cunning-man?
  Face. This is his worship.
  Dap.   Is he a doctor?
  Face.   Yes.
  Dap. And ha' you broke[1] with him, captain?
  Face.   Ay.
  Dap.   And
  how?   10
  Face. Faith, he does make the matter, sir, so dainty,
I know not what to say.
  Dap.   Not so, good captain.
  Face. Would I were fairly rid on 't, believe me.
  Dap. Nay, now you grieve me, sir. Why should you
  wish so?
I dare assure you, I'll not be ungrateful.
  Face. I cannot think you will, sir. But the law
Is such a thing—and then, he says, Read's matter[2]
Falling so lately—
  Dap.   Read? he was an ass,

---

[63] *faction:* quarreling.   [64] *'Slid:* by God's eyelid.
[65] *shark:* cheat.   [66] *'Slight:* by God's light.
[67] *sort:* group.   [68] *precise:* puritanical.
[69] *sin' . . . in:* i.e., since 1603.   [70] *from:* out of.
[71] *ride:* be carted as a whore.
[72] *pay . . . rent:* have your ears cut off in the pillory.
[73] *Don Provost:* the hangman.   [74] *crewel:* worsted.
[75] *Claridiana:* romance heroine.
[76] *longest cut:* winning draw.   [77] *quarter:* of the year.
[78] *quodling:* green apple, raw youth.
[79] *Holborn:* London district.
[80] *Dagger:* tavern famous for pies.
[81] *familiar:* familiar spirit.   [82] *rifle:* gamble.

I.ii.
[1] *broke:* broached the matter.
[2] *Read's matter:* case of a magician indicted and pardoned
in 1607–8 for invoking spirits.

And dealt, sir, with a fool.
    Face.   It was a clerk, sir.
    Dap. A clerk!
    Face.   Nay, hear me, sir. You know the law
Better, I think—
    Dap.   I should, sir, and the danger;   21
You know, I showed the statute to you.
    Face.   You did so.
    Dap. And will I tell then! By this hand of flesh,
Would it might never write good court-hand[3] more,
If I discover. What do you think of me,
That I am a chiaus?[4]
    Face.   What's that?
    Dap.   The Turk was here—
As one would say, do you think I am a Turk?
    Face. I'll tell the doctor so.
    Dap.   Do, good sweet captain.
    Face. Come, noble doctor, pray thee, let's prevail;
This is the gentleman, and he is no chiaus.   30
    Sub. Captain, I have returned you all my answer.
I would do much, sir, for your love—but this
I neither may, nor can.
    Face.   Tut, do not say so.
You deal now with a noble fellow, doctor,
One that will thank you richly; and he's no chiaus.
Let that, sir, move you.
    Sub.   Pray you, forbear—
    Face.   He has
Four angels[5] here.
    Sub.   You do me wrong, good sir.
    Face. Doctor, wherein? To tempt you with these
    spirits?
    Sub. To tempt my art and love, sir, to my peril.
'Fore heav'n, I scarce can think you are my friend,   40
That so would draw me to apparent danger.
    Face. I draw you? A horse draw you, and a halter,
You, and your flies together—
    Dap.   Nay, good captain.
    Face. That know no difference of men.
    Sub.   Good words, sir.
    Face. Good deeds, sir, Doctor Dogs'-meat. 'Slight,
    I bring you
No cheating Clim o' the Cloughs or Claribels,[6]
That look as big as five-and-fifty and flush,[7]
And spit out secrets like hot custard—
    Dap.   Captain!
    Face. Nor any melancholic underscribe,

Shall tell the vicar;[8] but a special gentle,   50
That is the heir to forty marks a year,
Consorts with the small poets of the time,
Is the sole hope of his old grandmother,
That knows the law, and writes you six fair hands,[9]
Is a fine clerk, and has his ciph'ring[10] perfect;
Will take his oath o' the Greek Xenophon,[11]
If need be, in his pocket, and can court
His mistress out of Ovid.[12]
    Dap.   Nay, dear captain—
    Face. Did you not tell me so?
    Dap.   Yes; but I'd ha' you
Use master doctor with some more respect.   60
    Face. Hang him, proud stag, with his broad velvet
    head.[13]
But for your sake, I'd choke ere I would change
An article of breath with such a puck-fist[14]
Come, let's be gone.
    Sub.   Pray you, le' me speak with you.
    Dap. His worship calls you, captain.
    Face.   I am sorry
I e'er embarked myself in such a business.
    Dap. Nay, good sir; he did call you.
    Face.   Will he take then?
    Sub. First, hear me—
    Face.   Not a syllable, 'less you take.
    Sub. Pray ye, sir—
    Face.   Upon no terms but an *assumpsit.*[15]
    Sub. Your humor must be law.

                         He takes the money.

    Face.   Why now, sir, talk.
Now I dare hear you with mine honor. Speak.   71
So may this gentleman too.
    Sub.   Why, sir—

                [Offering to whisper to FACE.]

    Face.   No whisp'ring.
    Sub. 'Fore heav'n, you do not apprehend the loss
You do yourself in this.
    Face.   Wherein? For what?
    Sub. Marry, to be so importunate for one
That, when he has it, will undo you all;
He'll win up all the money i' the town.
    Face. How!
    Sub.   Yes, and blow up gamester after
    gamester,
As they do crackers[16] in a puppet-play.
If I do give him a familiar,   80
Give you him all you play for; never set[17] him,
For he will have it.
    Face.   You're mistaken, doctor.
Why, he does ask one but for cups and horses,
A rifling fly; none o' your great familiars.
    Dap. Yes, captain, I would have it for all games.
    Sub. I told you so.

                *[*FACE *takes* DAPPER *aside.]*

    Face.   'Slight, that's a new business!
I understood you, a tame bird, to fly
Twice in a term, or so, on Friday nights,

---

    [3] *court-hand:* script used in courts.
    [4] *chiaus:* from Turkish for messenger, alluding to recent incident involving a Turkish impostor.
    [5] *angels:* gold coins, worth approximately 10s.
    [6] *Clim . . . Claribels:* ballad and romance characters.
    [7] *five . . . flush:* winning hands in the card game of primero.   [8] *vicar:* official in ecclesiastical courts.
    [9] *six . . . hands:* the scripts appropriate to various documents.   [10] *ciph'ring:* account-keeping.
    [11] *Xenophon:* nonsense or lost allusion, replacing Q "Testament" because of censorship rules.
    [12] *Ovid:* the Roman poet's *Art of Love.*
    [13] *velvet head:* pun on deer's horn-skin and doctor's velvet cap.   [14] *puck-fist:* puff-ball, braggart.
    [15] *assumpsit:* (law) voluntary verbal promise.
    [16] *crackers:* fireworks.   [17] *set:* bet against.

When you had left the office, for a nag
Of forty or fifty shillings.
   Dap.   Ay, 'tis true, sir;   90
But I do think, now, I shall leave the law,
And therefore—
   Face.   Why, this changes quite the case!
D' you think that I dare move him?
   Dap.   If you please, sir;
All's one to him, I see.
   Face.   What! for that money?
I cannot with my conscience; nor should you
Make the request, methinks.
   Dap.   No, sir, I mean
To add consideration.[18]
   Face.   Why, then, sir,
I'll try. [*To* SUBTLE] Say that it were for all games,
    doctor?
   Sub. I say then, not a mouth shall eat for him[19]
At any ordinary, but o' the score,   100
That is a gaming mouth, conceive me.
   Face.   Indeed!
   Sub. He'll draw you all the treasure of the realm,
If it be set him.
   Face.   Speak you this from art?
   Sub. Ay, sir, and reason too, the ground of art
He's o' the only best complexion,
The Queen of Faery loves.
   Face.   What! Is he?
   Sub.   Peace.
He'll overhear you. Sir, should she but see him—
   Face. What?
   Sub.   Do not you tell him.
   Face.   Will he win at cards too?
   Sub. The spirits of dead Holland, living Isaac,[20]
You'd swear were in him; such a vigorous luck   110
As cannot be resisted. 'Slight, he'll put
Six o' your gallants to a cloak,[21] indeed.
   Face. A strange success, that some man shall be born
    to!
   Sub. He hears you, man—
   Dap.   Sir, I'll not be ingrateful.
   Face. Faith, I have a confidence in his good nature:
You hear, he says he will not be ingrateful.
   Sub. Why, as you please; my venture follows yours.
   Face. Troth, do it, doctor; think him trusty, and
    make him.
He may make us both happy in an hour;   119
Win some five thousand pound, and send us two on't.[22]
   Dap. Believe it, and I will, sir.
   Face.   And you shall, sir.
You have heard all?

                    FACE *takes him aside.*

   Dap.   No, what was't? Nothing, I, sir.
   Face. Nothing?
   Dap.   A little, sir.
   Face.   Well, a rare star
Reigned at your birth.
   Dap.   At mine, sir! No.
   Face.   The doctor
Swears that you are—

   Sub.   Nay, captain, you'll tell all now.
   Face. Allied to the Queen of Faery.
   Dap.   Who? That I am?
Believe it, no such matter—
   Face.   Yes, and that
You were born with a caul[23] o' your head.
   Dap.   Who says so?
   Face.   Come,
You know it well enough, though you dissemble it.
   Dap. I' fac,[24] I do not; you are mistaken.
   Face.   How!   130
Swear by your fac? And in a thing so known
Unto the doctor? How shall we, sir, trust you
I' the other matter? Can we ever think,
When you have won five or six thousand pound,
You'll send us shares in 't, by this rate?
   Dap.   By Jove, sir,
I'll win ten thousand pound, and send you half.
I' fac's no oath.
   Sub.   No, no, he did but jest.
   Face. Go to. Go thank the doctor. He's your friend,
To take it so.
   Dap.   I thank his worship.
   Face.   So?
Another angel.
   Dap.   Must I?
   Face.   Must you! 'slight,   140
What else is thanks? Will you be trivial?[25]—

               [DAPPER *gives him the money.*]

                       Doctor,
When must he come for his familiar?
   Dap. Shall I not ha' it with me?
   Sub.   Oh, good sir!
There must a world of ceremonies pass;
You must be bathed and fumigated first;
Besides, the Queen of Faery does not rise
Till it be noon.
   Face.   Not if she danced tonight.[26]
   Sub. And she must bless it.
   Face.   Did you never see
Her royal grace yet?
   Dap.   Whom?
   Face.   Your aunt of Faery?
   Sub. Not since she kissed him in the cradle, captain,
I can resolve you that.[27]
   Face.   Well, see her grace,   151
Whate'er it cost you, for a thing that I know.
It will be somewhat hard to compass; but
However, see her. You are made, believe it,
If you can see her. Her grace is a lone woman,
And very rich, and if she take a fancy,
She will do strange things. See her, at any hand.

---

  [18] *consideration:* recompense.
  [19] *not . . . him:* i.e., gamblers won't have enough left to
buy food.
  [20] *dead . . . Isaac:* obscure allusion to fifteenth-century
Dutch alchemists.   [21] *to a cloak:* i.e., stop them.
  [22] *on't:* of it.   [23] *caul:* membrane, a favorable omen.
  [24] *I'fac:* In faith.   [25] *trivial:* petty, mean.
  [26] *tonight:* last night.   [27] *resolve . . . that:* answer that.

'Slid, she may hap to leave you all she has!
It is the doctor's fear.
 Dap.   How will 't be done, then?
 Face. Let me alone,[28] take you no thought. Do you
But say to me, "Captain, I'll see her grace." 161
 Dap. Captain, I'll see her grace.
 Face.   Enough.

       One knocks without.

 Sub.   Who's there?
Anon!—[*Aside to* FACE.] Conduct him forth by the
 back way.—
Sir, against one o'clock prepare yourself;
Till when, you must be fasting; only, take
Three drops of vinegar in at your nose,
Two at your mouth, and one at either ear;
Then bathe your fingers' ends and wash your eyes,
To sharpen your five senses, and cry "hum"
Thrice, and then "buz" as often; and then come. 170
 Face. Can you remember this?
 Dap.   I warrant you.
 Face. Well then, away. 'Tis but your bestowing
Some twenty nobles[29] 'mong her grace's servants,
And put on a clean shirt. You do not know
What grace her grace may do you in clean linen.
     [*Exeunt* FACE *and* DAPPER.]

I.iii

[*Sub.*] Come in! good wives, I pray you, forbear me
 now;
Troth, I can do you no good till afternoon.—

     [*Enter* DRUGGER.]

What is your name, say you? Abel Drugger?
 Drug. Yes, sir.
 Sub.   A seller of tobacco?
 Drug.   Yes, sir.
 Sub.   Umh!
Free of the Grocers?[1]
 Drug.   Ay, an't please you.
 Sub.   Well—
Your business, Abel?
 Drug.   This, an't[2] please your worship:
I am a young beginner, and am building
Of a new shop, an't like your worship, just

At corner of a street.—Here's the plot on 't.—
And I would know by art, sir, of your worship, 10
Which way I should make my door, by necromancy,
And where my shelves; and which should be for boxes,
And which for pots. I would be glad to thrive, sir;
And I was wished[3] to your worship by a gentleman,
One captain Face, that says you know men's planets,
And their good angels, and their bad.
 Sub.   I do,
If I do see 'em—

     [*Enter* FACE.]

 Face. What! my honest Abel?
Thou art well met here.
 Drug.   Troth, sir, I was speaking,
Just as your worship came here, of your worship.
I pray you, speak for me to master doctor. 20
 Face. He shall do anything. Doctor, do you hear?
This is my friend Abel, an honest fellow;
He lets me have good tobacco, and he does not
Sophisticate it with sack-lees or oil,
Nor washes it in muscadel and grains,
Nor buries it in gravel, under ground,
Wrapped up in greasy leather or pissed clouts,[4]
But keeps it in fine lily pots that, opened,
Smell like conserve of roses, or French beans.[5]
He has his maple block, his silver tongs, 30
Winchester pipes, and fire of juniper:[6]
A neat, spruce, honest fellow, and no goldsmith.[7]
 Sub. He's a fortunate fellow, that I am sure on.
 Face. Already, sir, ha' you found it? Lo thee, Abel!
 Sub. And in right way toward riches—
 Face.   Sir.
 Sub.   This
 summer
He will be of the clothing[8] of his company,
And next spring called to the scarlet.[9] Spend what he
 can.
 Face. What, and so little beard?
 Sub.   Sir, you must think,
He may have a receipt to make hair come.
But he'll be wise, preserve his youth, and fine[10] for 't;
His fortune looks for him another way. 41
 Face. 'Slid, doctor, how canst thou know this so
 soon?
I am amused[11] at that.
 Sub.   By a rule, captain,
In metoposcopy,[12] which I do work by;
A certain star i' the forehead, which you see not.
Your chestnut or your olive-colored face
Does never fail, and your long ear doth promise.
I knew 't by certain spots, too, in his teeth,
And on the nail of his mercurial[13] finger. 49
 Face. Which finger's that?
 Sub.   His little finger. Look.
You were born upon a Wednesday?
 Drug.   Yes, indeed, sir.
 Sub. The thumb, in chiromancy,[14] we give Venus;
The forefinger to Jove; the midst to Saturn;
The ring to Sol; the least to Mercury,
Who was the lord, sir, of his horoscope,

---

28 *Let me alone:* Leave it to me.
29 *nobles:* coins worth 6s.8d.

I.iii.
 1 *Free . . . Grocers:* member of the Grocers' Company.
 2 *an't:* if it.   3 *wished:* recommended.
 4 *clouts:* rags. 5 *French beans:* with fragrant flowers.
 6 *maple . . . juniper:* facilities for preparing and smoking
in tobacco shops.   7 *goldsmith:* usurer.
 8 *of the clothing:* wearing the livery.
 9 *called . . . scarlet:* made sheriff.
 10 *fine:* pay the fine for refusing to serve as sheriff.
 11 *amused:* puzzled.
 12 *metoposcopy:* character-reading by physiognomy.
 13 *mercurial:* Mercury was patron of businessmen and
thieves.   14 *chiromancy:* divination by hand analysis.

His house of life being Libra, which foreshowed
He should be a merchant, and should trade with
   balance.
   Face. Why, this is strange! Is't not, honest Nab?
   Sub. There is a ship now coming from Ormus,[15]
That shall yield him such a commodity   60
Of drugs—This is the west, and this the south?

[Pointing to the plan.]

   Drug. Yes, sir.
   Sub.   And those are your two sides?
   Drug.   Ay, sir.
   Sub. Make me your door then, south; your broad
   side, west;
And on the east side of your shop, aloft,
Write Mathlai, Tarmiel, and Baraborat;
Upon the north part, Rael, Velel, Thiel.[16]
They are the names of those mercurial spirits
That do fright flies from boxes.
   Drug.   Yes, sir.
   Sub.   And
Beneath your threshold, bury me a loadstone
To draw in gallants that wear spurs; the rest,   70
They'll seem[17] to follow.
   Face.   That's a secret, Nab!
   Sub. And, on your stall, a puppet, with a vice,[18]
And a court-fucus,[19] to call city-dames.
You shall deal much with minerals.
   Drug.   Sir, I have,
At home, already—
   Sub.   Ay, I know, you've arsenic,
Vitriol,[20] sal-tartar,[21] argaile,[22] alkali,[23]
Cinoper;[24] I know all.—This fellow, captain,
Will come, in time, to be a great distiller,
And give a say[25]—I will not say directly,
But very fair[26]—at the philosopher's stone.   80
   Face. Why, how now, Abel! is this true?
   Drug. [*Aside to* FACE]   Good
   captain,
What must I give?
   Face.   Nay, I'll not counsel thee.
Thou hear'st what wealth (he says, spend what thou
   canst)
Th' art like to come to.
   Drug.   I would gi' him a crown.
   Face. A crown! and toward such a fortune? Heart,
Thou shalt rather gi' him thy shop. No gold about thee?
   Drug. Yes, I have a portague,[27] I ha' kept this half-
   year.
   Face. Out on thee, Nab! 'Slight, there was such an
   offer—
Shalt keep 't no longer, I'll gi' it him for thee.
Doctor, Nab prays your worship to drink this, and
   swears   90
He will appear more grateful, as your skill
Does raise him in the world.
   Drug.   I would entreat
Another favor of his worship.
   Face.   What is't, Nab?
   Drug. But to look over, sir, my almanac,
And cross out my ill-days, that I may neither

Bargain nor trust upon them.
   Face.   That he shall, Nab.
Leave it, it shall be done, 'gainst afternoon.
   Sub. And a direction for his shelves.
   Face.   Now, Nab,
Art thou well pleased, Nab?
   Drug.   'Thank, sir, both your
   worships.
   Face. Away.

[Exit DRUGGER.]

Why, now, you smoky persecutor of nature!   100
Now do you see, that something's to be done,
Beside your beech-coal,[28] and your cor'sive[29] waters,
Your crosslets,[30] crucibles, and cucurbites?[31]
You must have stuff brought home to you, to work on!
And yet you think I am at no expense
In searching out these veins, then following 'em,
Then trying 'em out. 'Fore God, my intelligence[32]
Costs me more money than my share oft comes to,
In these rare works.
   Sub.   You're pleasant, sir.—How now?

I.iv

[Enter DOL COMMON.]

[*Sub.*] What says my dainty Dolkin?
   Dol Com.   Yonder fish-wife
Will not away. And there's your giantess,
The bawd of Lambeth.[1]
   Sub.   Heart, I cannot speak with 'em.
   Dol Com. Not afore night, I have told 'em, in a voice
Thorough the trunk, like one of your familiars.
But I have spied Sir Epicure Mammon—
   Sub.   Where?
   Dol Com. Coming along, at far end of the lane,
Slow of his feet, but earnest of his tongue
To one that's with him.
   Sub.   Face, go you and shift.[2]
Dol, you must presently[3] make ready too.   10

[Exit FACE.]

   Dol Com. Why, what's the matter?
   Sub.   Oh, I did look for
   him
With the sun's rising; marvel he could sleep!
This is the day I am to perfect for him

---

15 *Ormus:* Hormuz, on Persian Gulf.
16 *Mathlai . . . Thiel:* spirits, named in a work of occult
philosophy.   17 *seem:* be seen.
18 *puppet . . . vice:* doll operated by a mechanism.
19 *fucus:* cosmetic.   20 *Vitriol:* Sulfuric acid.
21 *sal-tartar:* carbonate of potash.
22 *argaile:* cream of tartar.   23 *alkali:* soda-ash.
24 *Cinoper:* Cinnabar, red mercuric sulfide.
25 *give a say:* make a try.
26 *very fair:* i.e., he has a good chance.
27 *portague:* gold coin, worth from £3.5s. to £4.10s.
28 *beech-coal:* the best charcoal.   29 *cor'sive:* corrosive.
30 *crosslets:* melting pots.   31 *cucurbites:* retorts.
32 *intelligence:* information.

I.iv.
1 *Lambeth:* disreputable quarter.
2 *shift:* change clothes.   3 *presently:* immediately.

The magisterium,[4] our great work, the stone;
And yield it, made, into his hands; of which
He has, this month, talked as he were possessed.
And now he's dealing pieces on 't away.
Methinks I see him ent'ring ordinaries,
Dispensing for the pox, and plaguy houses,[5]
Reaching his dose, walking Moorfields[6] for lepers,   20
And off'ring citizens' wives pomander[7]-bracelets
As his preservative, made of the elixir;
Searching the 'spital,[8] to make old bawds young;
And the highways, for beggars to make rich.
I see no end of his labors. He will make
Nature ashamed of her long sleep; when art,
Who's but a step-dame, shall do more than she,
In her best love to mankind, ever could.
If his dream last, he'll turn the age to gold.

                                        [*Exeunt.*]

ACT TWO

SCENE ONE

[*Enter* SIR EPICURE MAMMON *and* SURLY.]

[*Mam.*] Come on, sir. Now you set your foot on
    shore
In *Novo Orbe;*[1] here's the rich Peru,
And there within, sir, are the golden mines,
Great Solomon's Ophir![2] He was sailing to 't
Three years, but we have reached it in ten months.
This is the day wherein, to all my friends,
I will pronounce the happy word, "Be rich;
This day you shall be spectatissimi."[3]
You shall no more deal with the hollow die,
Or the frail card. No more be at charge of keeping   10
The livery-punk[4] for the young heir, that must
Seal,[5] at all hours, in his shirt. No more,
If he deny, ha' him beaten to 't, as he is

That brings him the commodity. No more
Shall thirst of satin, or the covetous hunger
Of velvet entrails for a rude-spun cloak,
To be displayed at Madam Augusta's,[6] make
The sons of sword and hazard fall before
The golden calf, and on their knees, whole nights,
Commit idolatry with wine and trumpets,   20
Or go a-feasting after drum and ensign.
No more of this. You shall start up young viceroys,
And have your punks and punkettees,[7] my Surly.
And unto thee I speak it first, "be rich."
Where is my Subtle there? Within, ho!
    [*Face.*] *Within*   Sir,
He'll come to you by and by.
    Mam.   That's his fire-drake,[8]
His Lungs,[9] his Zephyrus,[10] he that puffs his coals,
Till he firk[11] nature up, in her own center.
You are not faithful, sir. This night I'll change
All that is metal in my house to gold,   30
And, early in the morning, will I send
To all the plumbers and the pewterers
And buy their tin and lead up; and to Lothbury[12]
For all the copper.
    Sur.   What, and turn that, too?
    Mam. Yes, and I'll purchase Devonshire and
        Cornwall,[13]
And make them perfect Indies! You admire[14] now?
    Sur. No, faith.
    Mam.   But when you see th' effects of the
        Great Med'cine,
Of which one part projected on a hundred
Of Mercury, or Venus,[15] or the Moon,
Shall turn it to as many of the Sun;   40
Nay, to a thousand, so *ad infinitum:*
You will believe me.
    Sur.   Yes, when I see 't, I will.
But if my eyes do cozen me so, and I
Giving 'em no occasion, sure I'll have
A whore, shall piss 'em out next day.
    Mam.   Ha! why?
Do you think I fable with you? I assure you,
He that has once the flower of the sun,
The perfect ruby, which we call elixir,
Not only can do that, but by its virtue,
Can confer honor, love, respect, long life;   50
Give safety, valor, yea, and victory,
To whom he will. In eight-and-twenty days,
I'll make an old man of fourscore a child.
    Sur. No doubt; he's that already.
    Mam.   Nay, I mean,
Restore his years, renew him, like an eagle,
To the fifth age;[16] make him get sons and daughters,
Young giants; as our philosophers have done,
The ancient patriarchs, afore the flood,
But taking, once a week, on a knife's point,
The quantity of a grain of mustard of it;   60
Become stout Marses, and beget young Cupids.
    Sur. The decayed vestals of Pict-hatch[17] would
        thank you,
That keep the fire alive there.
    Mam.   'Tis the secret

---

[4] *magisterium:* master work.
[5] *plaguy houses:* quarantined pest houses for the plague-ridden.
[6] *Moorfields:* area north of London where lepers were allowed to beg.
[7] *pomander:* perfume ball to protect against plague.
[8] *'spital:* hospital.

II.i.
[1] *L.:* the New World.
[2] *Great . . . Ophir:* Solomon was said to have used the philosopher's stone to make gold in Ophir, at a safe distance of three years' voyage.
[3] *spectatissimi:* especially looked up to.
[4] *livery-punk:* prostitute-accomplice.
[5] *Seal:* Assign his wealth to the cheaters.
[6] *Madam Augusta:* brothel keeper.
[7] *punkettees:* little punks.
[8] *fire-drake:* fiery dragon; worker with fire.
[9] *Lungs:* alchemist's assistant who blows the fire.
[10] *Zephyrus:* West Wind.   [11] *firk:* stir.
[12] *Lothbury:* London street, in Coleman Street Ward.
[13] *Devonshire and Cornwall:* where copper and tin were mined.   [14] *admire:* wonder.
[15] *Venus:* planet of copper.
[16] *fifth age:* i.e., of the seven; mature manhood.
[17] *Pict-hatch:* notorious haunt of prostitutes, opposite the Charterhouse at Rotten Row.

Of nature naturized[18] 'gainst all infestions,
Cures all diseases coming of all causes;
A month's grief in a day, a year's in twelve;
And, of what age soever, in a month,
Past all the doses of your drugging doctors.
I'll undertake, withal, to fright the plague
Out o' the kingdom in three months.
 Sur.   And I'll   70
Be bound, the players shall sing your praises then,[19]
Without their poets.
 Mam.   Sir, I'll do 't. Meantime,
I'll give away so much unto my man,
Shall serve th' whole city with preservative
Weekly; each house his dose, and at the rate—
 Sur. As he that built the water-work[20] does with
  water?
 Mam. You are incredulous.
 Sur.   Faith, I have a humor,
I would not willingly be gulled. Your stone
Cannot transmute me.
 Mam.   Pertinax Surly,
Will you believe antiquity? Records?   80
I'll show you a book where Moses, and his sister,
And Solomon have written of the art;
Ay, and a treatise penned by Adam—
 Sur.   How!
 Mam. O' the philosopher's stone, and in High
  Dutch.[21]
 Sur. Did Adam write, sir, in High Dutch?
 Mam.   He did;
Which proves it was the primitive tongue.
 Sur.   What paper?
 Mam. On cedar board.
 Sur.   Oh, that, indeed, they say,
Will last 'gainst worms.
 Mam.   'Tis like your Irish wood,
'Gainst cobwebs. I have a piece of Jason's fleece[22] too,
Which was no other than a book of alchemy, 90
Writ in large sheepskin, a good fat ram-vellum.
Such was Pythagoras' thigh,[23] Pandora's tub,[24]
And all that fable of Medea's charms,
The manner of our work; the bulls, our furnace,
Still breathing fire; our *argent-vive*,[25] the dragon;
The dragon's teeth,[26] mercury sublimate,
That keeps the whiteness, hardness, and the biting;
And they are gathered into Jason's helm,
Th' alembic,[27] and then sowed in Mars[28] his field,
And thence sublimed so often, till they are fixed. 100
Both this, th' Hesperian garden,[29] Cadmus' story,
Jove's shower,[30] the boon of Midas,[31] Argus' eyes,[32]
Boccace his Demogorgon,[33] thousands more,
All abstract riddles[34] of our stone.—How now!

II.ii

 [*Enter* FACE, *disguised as a laboratory assistant*.]

 [*Mam.*] Do we succeed? Is our day come? And holds
  it?
 Face. The evening will set red upon you, sir;
You have color for it, crimson: the red ferment
Has done his office; three hours hence prepare you

To see projection.
 Mam.   Pertinax, my Surly,
Again I say to thee, aloud, "be rich."
This day thou shalt have ingots; and tomorrow
Give lords th' affront.[1]—Is it, my Zephyrus, right?
Blushes the bolt's-head?[2]
 Face.   Like a wench with child, sir,
That were but now discovered to her master. 10
 Mam. Excellent witty Lungs!—My only care is
Where to get stuff enough now, to project on;
This town will not half serve me.
 Face.   No, sir? Buy
The covering off o' churches.
 Mam.   That's true.
 Face.   Yes.
Let 'em stand bare, as do their auditory;
Or cap 'em new with shingles.
 Mam.   No, good thatch:
Thatch will lie light upo' the rafters, Lungs.
Lungs, I will manumit[3] thee from the furnace;
I will restore thee thy complexion, Puff,
Lost in the embers; and repair this brain, 20
Hurt wi' the fume o' the metals.
 Face.   I have blown, sir,
Hard, for your worship; thrown by many a coal,
When 't was not beech; weighed those I put in, just,[4]
To keep your heat still even. These bleared eyes
Have waked to read your several colors, sir,
Of the pale citron, the green lion, the crow,
The peacock's tail, the plumed swan.
 Mam.   And lastly,

---

 [18] *naturized:* created, as opposed to creating.
 [19] *players . . . then:* because theaters were closed during plague outbreaks.
 [20] *water-work:* pumping station, built 1594 near London Bridge, supplying Thames water to houses.
 [21] *High Dutch:* High German, claimed by some contemporary crackpots to be the original language.
 [22] *Jason's fleece:* the golden fleece which Jason and Medea acquired on the Argonautic expedition.
 [23] *Pythagoras' thigh:* the Greek philosopher was said to have a golden thigh.
 [24] *Pandora's tub:* the box of human troubles given the first mortal woman by Zeus, which out of curiosity she opened.
 [25] *L.:* quicksilver.
 [26] *dragon's teeth:* (Greek myth) sown by the Phoenician prince Cadmus, from which grew soldiers, some of whom founded Thebes with him.
 [27] *alembic:* retort, in this case Jason's helmet.
 [28] *Mars:* planet of iron.
 [29] *Hesperian garden:* (Greek mythology) where the golden apples of youth grew.
 [30] *Jove's shower:* Jupiter wooed the maiden Danäe disguised as a shower of gold.
 [31] *boon of Midas:* the gift that enabled the king to turn what he touched to gold.
 [32] *Argus' eyes:* the hundred eyes of the giant Juno assigned to guard Io from her husband Jupiter's advances, later transferred to the peacock's tail.
 [33] *Boccace his Demogorgon:* ancestor of the gods, according to Boccaccio's *Genealogia Deorum.*
 [34] *abstract riddles:* hieroglyphs, secret writings.
II.ii.
 [1] *give . . . affront:* look them boldly in the face.
 [2] *bolt's-head:* globular flask with long cylindrical neck.
 [3] *manumit:* free.   [4] *just:* accurately.

Thou hast descried the flower, the *sanguis agni?*[5]
Face.　Yes, sir.
Mam.　　　　　Where's master?
Face.　　　　　　　　　At's prayers, sir, he;
Good man, he's doing his devotions　　　　　　　　30
For the success.
Mam.　　　　Lungs, I will set a period
To all thy labors; thou shalt be the master
Of my seraglio.
Face.　　　　Good, sir.
Mam.　　　　　　　But do you hear?
I'll geld you, Lungs.
Face.　　　　　　　Yes, sir.
Mam.　　　　　　　For I do mean
To have a list of wives and concubines
Equal with Solomon, who had the stone
Alike with me; and I will make me a back
With the elixir, that shall be as tough
As Hercules, to encounter fifty a night.[6]—
Th'art sure thou saw'st it blood?
Face.　　　　　　　Both blood and spirit,
sir.　　　　　　　　　　　　　　　　　　　40
Mam. I will have all my beds blown up, not stuffed;
Down is too hard. And then, mine oval room
Filled with such pictures as Tiberius[7] took
From Elephantis, and dull Aretine[8]
But coldly imitated. Then, my glasses
Cut in more subtle angles, to disperse
And multiply the figures, as I walk
Naked between my succubae.[9] My mists
I'll have of perfume, vapored 'bout the room,
To lose our selves in; and my baths, like pits　　　50
To fall into; from whence we will come forth,
And roll us dry in gossamer and roses.—
Is it arrived at ruby?—Where I spy
A wealthy citizen, or rich lawyer,
Have a sublimed pure wife, unto that fellow
I'll send a thousand pound to be my cuckold.
Face. And I shall carry it?
Mam.　　　　　　No, I'll ha' no bawds
But fathers and mothers; they will do it best,
Best of all others. And my flatterers
Shall be the pure, and gravest of divines　　　　60
That I can get for money. My mere fools,

Eloquent burgesses, and then my poets
The same that writ so subtly of the fart,
Whom I will entertain still for that subject.
The few that would give out themselves to be
Court-and town-stallions, and, each where, belie
Ladies who are known most innocent, for them,
These will I beg, to make me eunuchs of,
And they shall fan me with ten estrich[10] tails
Apiece, made in a plume to gather wind.　　　　70
We will be brave, Puff, now we ha' the med'cine.
My meat shall all come in, in Indian shells,
Dishes of agate set in gold, and studded
With emeralds, sapphires, hyacinths,[11] and rubies.
The tongues of carps, dormice, and camels' heels,
Boiled i' the spirit of Sol, and dissolved pearl
(Apicius'[12] diet, 'gainst the epilepsy):
And I will eat these broths with spoons of amber,
Headed with diamond and carbuncle.
My foot-boy shall eat pheasants, calvered[13] salmons,
Knots,[14] godwits,[15] lampreys.[16] I myself will have　81
The beards of barbels[17] served instead of salads;
Oiled mushrooms; and the swelling unctuous paps
Of a fat pregnant sow, newly cut off,
Dressed with an exquisite and poignant sauce;
For which, I'll say unto my cook, "There's gold;
Go forth, and be a knight."
Face.　　　　　　Sir, I'll go look
A little, how it heightens.
　　　　　　　　　　　　　　　　　　[*Exit.*]
Mam.　　　　　　Do.—My shirts
I'll have of taffeta-sarsnet,[18] soft and light
As cobwebs; and for all my other raiment,　　　　90
It shall be such as might provoke the Persian,[19]
Were he to teach the world riot anew.
My gloves of fishes and birds' skins, perfumed
With gums of paradise,[20] and eastern air—
Sur. And do you think to have the stone with this?
Mam. No, I do think t' have all this with the stone.
Sur. Why, I have heard he must be *homo frugi,*[21]
A pious, holy, and religious man,
One free from mortal sin, a very virgin.
Mam. That makes it, sir; he is so. But I buy it;　100
My venture brings it me. He, honest wretch,
A notable, superstitious, good soul,
Has worn his knees bare and his slippers bald
With prayer and fasting for it. And, sir, let him
Do it alone, for me, still. Here he comes.
Not a profane word afore him; 't is poison.

---

[5] *L.:* blood of the lamb.
[6] *Hercules . . . night:* the hero made Thestius' fifty daughters pregnant in one night.
[7] *Tiberius:* Roman emperor 14 B.C. to A.D. 37.
[8] *Elephantis . . . Aretine:* erotic writers, the former a lost poet of classical antiquity, and the latter an Italian, 1492–1556, who illustrated bawdy pictures with their verses.
[9] *succubae:* female demons who have intercourse with men.　　　　[10] *estrich:* ostrich.
[11] *hyacinths:* ancient gems.
[12] *Apicius:* gourmand of early Roman empire, reputed as author of a cook book.　　　[13] *calvered:* sliced alive.
[14] *Knots:* Wildfowl.　　　[15] *godwits:* marsh birds.
[16] *lampreys:* eels.　　　[17] *barbels:* carplike fish.
[18] *taffeta-sarsnet:* fine silk.
[19] *Persian:* proverbial for luxury.
[20] *gums of paradise:* from the east, where the Garden of Eden had been.
[21] *L.:* temperate man.

II.iii

[*Enter* SUBTLE.]

[*Mam.*] Good morrow, father.
Sub.　　　　　　　Gentle son, good
morrow,
And to your friend there. What is he is with you?
Mam. An heretic, that I did bring along,
In hope, sir, to convert him.
Sub.　　　　　Son, I doubt
You're covetous, that thus you meet your time

I' the just point,[1] prevent[2] your day at morning.
This argues something worthy of a fear
Of importune and carnal appetite.
Take heed you do not cause the blessing leave you,
With your ungoverned haste. I should be sorry   10
To see my labors, now e'en at perfection,
Got by long watching[3] and large patience,
Not prosper where my love and zeal hath placed 'em:
Which (heaven I call to witness, with your self,
To whom I have poured my thoughts) in all my ends,
Have looked no way, but unto public good,
To pious uses, and dear charity,
Now grown a prodigy with men. Wherein
If you, my son, should now prevaricate,[4]
And to your own particular lusts employ   20
So great and catholic[5] a bliss, be sure
A curse will follow, yea, and overtake
Your subtle and most secret ways.
    Mam.   I know, sir;
You shall not need to fear me; I but come
To ha' you confute this gentleman.
    Sur.   Who is,
Indeed, sir, somewhat costive of belief
Toward your stone; would not be gulled.
    Sub.   Well, son,
All that I can convince him in, is this,
The work is done; bright Sol is in his robe.
We have a med'cine of the triple soul,[6]   30
The glorified spirit. Thanks be to heaven,
And make us worthy of it!—[*To* FACE.] Ulen
    Ꚋpiegel![7]
    Face. [*Within*] Anon, sir.
    Sub.   Look well to the register,
And let your heat still lessen by degrees,
To the aludels.[8]
    Face. [*Within*] Yes, sir.
    Sub.   Did you look
O' the bolt's-head yet?
    Face. [*Within*]   Which? On D, sir?
    Sub.   Ay;
What's the complexion?
    Face. [*Within*]   Whitish.
    Sub.   Infuse vinegar,
To draw his volatile substance and his tincture,
And let the water in glass E be filtered,
And put into the gripe's egg.[9] Lute[10] him well;   40
And leave him closed *in balneo.*[11]
    Face. [*Within*]   I will, sir.
    Sur. [*Aside*] What a brave language here is! next to
    canting![12]
    Sub. I have another work you never saw, son,
That three days since passed the philosopher's wheel,
In the lent[13] heat of Athanor;[14] and 's become
Sulfur o' nature.
    Mam.   But 'tis for me?
    Sub.   What need you?
You have enough in that is perfect.
    Mam.   Oh, but—
    Sub. Why, this is covetise!
    Mam.   No, I assure you,
I shall employ it all in pious uses,

Founding of colleges and grammar schools,   50
Marrying young virgins, building hospitals,
And, now and then, a church.

            [*Enter* FACE.]

    Sub.   How now!
    Face.   Sir, please you,
Shall I not change the filter?
    Sub.   Marry, yes;
And bring me the complexion of glass B.
            [*Exit* FACE.]
    Mam. Ha' you another?
    Sub.   Yes, son; were I assured
Your piety were firm, we would not want
The means to glorify it: but I hope the best.
I mean to tinct C in sand-heat to-morrow,
And give him imbibition.[15]
    Mam.   Of white oil?
    Sub. No, sir, of red. F is come over the helm too,
I thank my maker, in St. Mary's bath,   61
And shows *lac virginis.*[16] Blessèd be heaven!
I sent you of his faeces[17] there calcined;
Out of the calx,[18] I ha' won the salt of mercury.
    Mam. By pouring on your rectified[19] water?
    Sub. Yes, and reverberating in Athanor.

            [*Re-enter* FACE.]

How now! what color says it?
    Face.   The ground black, sir.
    Mam. That's your crow's head?
    Sur. [*Aside*]   Your cock's comb's,
    is it not?
    Sub. No, 'tis not perfect. Would it were the crow!
That work wants something.
    Sur. [*Aside*]   Oh, I looked for this,   70
The hay is a-pitching.[20]
    Sub.   Are you sure you loosed 'em
I' their own menstrue?
    Face.   Yes, sir, and then married 'em,
And put 'em in a bolt's-head nipped to digestion,[21]

---

   [1] *I' . . . point:* exactly.   [2] *prevent:* anticipate.
   [3] *watching:* staying up.   [4] *prevaricate:* act dishonestly.
   [5] *catholic:* general.
   [6] *triple soul:* the human soul was held to consist of three parts.
   [7] *Ulen Spiegel:* Til Owlglass, rascally hero of German tales.
   [8] *aludels:* pear-shaped earthenware pots that could be fitted together for sublimation.
   [9] *gripe's egg:* vessel shaped like egg of the huge mythical griffin.   [10] *Lute:* enclose in clay to protect from heat.
   [11] *L.:* in a bath of water or sand, as in a *bain-marie* (l. 61 below).   [12] *canting:* thieves' slang.
   [13] *lent:* slow.
   [14] *Athanor:* digesting furnace in which constant heat was supplied by self-feeding charcoal.
   [15] *imbibition:* steeping in liquid.
   [16] *L.:* virgin's milk, i.e., mercury.   [17] *faeces:* sediment.
   [18] *calx:* powder produced by thoroughly roasting or burning ("calcining") a metal or mineral.
   [19] *rectified:* distilled.
   [20] *hay . . . a-pitching:* snare is being set.
   [21] *digestion:* slow change.

According as you bade me, when I set
The liquor of Mars[22] to circulation
In the same heat.
    Sub.   The process then was right.
    Face. Yes, by the token, sir, the retort brake,
And what was saved was put into the pelican,[23]
And signed with Hermes' seal.[24]
    Sub.   I think 't was so.
We should have a new amalgama.[25]
    Sur. [*Aside*]   Oh, this ferret   80
Is rank as any polecat.
    Sub.   But I care not;
Let him e'en die; we have enough beside,
In embrion.[26] H has his white shirt on?
    Face.   Yes, sir,
He's ripe for inceration;[27] he stands warm,
In his ash-fire. I would not you should let
Any die now, if I might counsel, sir,
For luck's sake to the rest. It is not good.
    Mam. He says right.
    Sur. [*Aside*]   Ay, are you bolted?
    Face.   Nay, I know
't, sir,
I've seen th' ill fortune. What is some three ounces
Of fresh materials?
    Mam.   Is 't no more?
    Face.   No more, sir,   90
Of gold, t' amalgam with some six of mercury.
    Mam. Away, here's money. What will serve?
    Face.   Ask
him, sir.
    Mam. How much?
    Sub.   Give him nine pound; you may
gi' him ten.
    Sur. [*Aside*] Yes, twenty, and be cozened; do.
    Mam.   There
't is.

                [*Gives* FACE *the money.*]

    Sub. This needs not; but that you will have it, so,
To see conclusions of all. For two
Of our inferior works are at fixation;
A third is in ascension.[28] Go your ways.
Ha' you set the oil of Luna in kemia?[29]   99
    Face. Yes, sir.
    Sub.   And the philosopher's vinegar?
    Face.   Ay.
                    [*Exit.*]
    Sur. [*Aside*] We shall have a salad!
    Mam.   When do you make
projection?

    Sub. Son, be not hasty, I exalt our med'cine,
By hanging him *in balneo vaporoso*,
And giving him solution; then congeal him;
And then dissolve him; then again congeal him;
For look, how oft I iterate the work,
So many times I add unto his virtue.
As, at first one ounce convert a hundred,
After his second loose,[31] he'll turn a thousand;
His third solution, ten; his fourth, a hundred;   110
After his fifth, a thousand thousand ounces
Of any imperfect metal, into pure
Silver or gold, in all examinations
As good as any of the natural mine.
Get you your stuff here against afternoon,
Your brass, your pewter, and your andirons.
    Mam. Not those of iron?
    Sub.   Yes, you may bring them
too;
We'll change all metals.
    Sur. [*Aside*]   I believe you in that.
    Mam. Then I may send my spits?
    Sub.   Yes, and your
racks.
    Sur. And dripping-pans, and pot-hangers, and
hooks?   120
Shall he not?
    Sub.   If he please.
    Sur.   —To be an ass.
    Sub. How, sir!
    Mam.   This gent'man you must bear withal.
I told you he had no faith.
    Sur.   And little hope, sir;
But much less charity, should I gull myself.
    Sub. Why, what have you observed, sir, in our art,
Seems so impossible?
    Sur.   But your whole work, no more.
That you should hatch gold in a furnace, sir,
As they do eggs in Egypt!
    Sub.   Sir, do you
Believe that eggs are hatched so?
    Sur.   If I should?
    Sub. Why, I think that the greater miracle.   130
No egg but differs from a chicken more
Than metals in themselves.
    Sur.   That cannot be.
The egg's ordained by nature to that end,
And is a chicken *in potentia*.[32]
    Sub. The same we say of lead and other metals,
Which would be gold if they had time.
    Mam.   And that
Our art doth further.
    Sub.   Ay, for 't were absurd
To think that nature in the earth bred gold
Perfect i' the instant: something went before.
There must be remote matter.
    Sur.   Ay, what is that?   140
    Sub. Marry, we say—
    Mam.   Ay, now it heats: stand, father,
Pound him to dust.
    Sub.   It is, of the one part,
A humid exhalation, which we call

---

[22] *liquor of Mars:* molten iron.
[23] *pelican:* subliming vessel with long neck.
[24] *Hermes' seal:* sealed neck of a flask.
[25] *amalgama:* mixture of metal with mercury.
[26] *embrion:* beginning stage.
[27] *inceration:* mixing of solid and fluid to produce waxlike substance.   [28] *ascension:* distillation.
[29] *kemia:* chemical analysis.
[30] *philosopher's vinegar:* acid or mercury used to dissolve metals.   [31] *loose:* solution.   [32] *L.:* potentially.

Materia liquida,[33] or the unctuous water;
On th' other part, a certain crass and viscous
Portion of earth; both which, concorporate,
Do make the elementary matter of gold;
Which is not yet *propria materia*,[34]
But common to all metals and all stones.
For, where it is forsaken of that moisture,   150
And hath more dryness, it becomes a stone;
Where it retains more of the humid fatness,
It turns to sulfur, or to quicksilver,
Who are the parents of all other metals.
Nor can this remote matter suddenly
Progress so from extreme unto extreme,
As to grow gold, and leap o'er all the means.[35]
Nature doth first beget th' imperfect, then
Proceeds she to the perfect. Of that airy
And oily water, mercury is engendered;   160
Sulfur o' the fat and earthy part; the one,
Which is the last, supplying the place of male,
The other of the female, in all metals.
Some do believe hermaphrodeity,
That both do act and suffer. But these two
Make the rest ductile, malleable, extensive.[36]
And even in gold they are; for we do find
Seeds of them by our fire, and gold in them;
And can produce the species of each metal
More perfect thence, than nature doth in earth.   170
Beside, who doth not see in daily practice
Art can beget bees, hornets, beetles, wasps,
Out of the carcasses and dung of creatures;
Yea, scorpions of an herb, being rightly placed.
And these are living creatures, far more perfect
And excellent than metals.
    Mam.   Well said, father!
Nay, if he take you in hand, sir, with an argument,
He'll bray[37] you in a mortar.
    Sur.   Pray you, sir, stay.
Rather than I'll be brayed, sir, I'll believe
That alchemy is a pretty kind of game,   180
Somewhat like tricks o' the cards, to cheat a man
With charming.
    Sub.   Sir?
    Sur.   What else are all your terms,
Whereon no one o' your writers 'grees with other?
Of your elixir, your *lac virginis*,
Your stone, your med'cine, and your chrysosperm[38]
Your sal, your sulfur, and your mercury,
Your oil of height,[39] your tree of life,[40] your blood,
Your marchesite,[41] your tutty,[42] your magnesia,[43]
Your toad, your crow, your dragon, and your panther,[44]
Your sun, your moon, your firmament, your adrop,[45]
Your lato, azoch, zernich, chibrit, heautarit,[46]   191
And then your red man, and your white woman[47]
With all your broths, your menstrues, and materials
Of piss and egg-shells, women's terms, man's blood,
Hair o' the head, burnt clouts, chalk, merds,[48] and clay,
Powder of bones, scalings of iron, glass,
And worlds of other strange ingredients,
Would burst a man to name?
    Sub.   And all these, named,
Intending but one thing; which art our writers

Used to obscure their art.
    Mam.   Sir, so I told him,   200
Because the simple idiot should not learn it,
And make it vulgar.
    Sub.   Was not all the knowledge
Of the Egyptians writ in mystic symbols?
Speak not the Scriptures oft in parables?
Are not the choicest fables of the poets,
That were the fountains and first springs of wisdom,
Wrapped in perplexèd allegories?
    Mam.   I urged that
And cleared to him, that Sisyphus[49] was damned
To roll the ceaseless stone, only because
He would have made ours common.

                          DOL *is seen.*

              Who is this?   210
    Sub. God's precious!—what do you mean? Go in,
    good lady,
Let me entreat you.
                     [DOL *retires.*]
    —Where's this varlet?

           [*Re-enter* FACE.]

    Face.   Sir?
    Sub. You very knave! do you use me thus?
    Face.   Wherein, sir?
    Sub. Go in and see, you traitor. Go!
                     [*Exit* FACE.]
    Mam.   Who is it, sir?
    Sub. Nothing, sir; nothing.
    Mam.   What's the matter, good sir?
I have not seen you thus distempered: who is 't?
    Sub. All arts have still had, sir, their adversaries;
But ours the most ignorant.—

                 FACE *returns.*

                What now?
    Face. 'T was not my fault, sir; she would speak with
    you.
    Sub. Would she, sir? Follow me.
        [*Exit* SUBTLE; FACE *is stopped by* MAMMON.]
    Mam.   Stay, Lungs.
    Face.   I dare
    not, sir.   220
    Mam. Stay, man; what is she?
    Face.   A lord's sister, sir.

---

[33] *L.*: liquid matter.   [34] *L.*: specific substance.
[35] *means*: intermediate stages.
[36] *extensive*: capable of being extended.
[37] *bray*: pound small.   [38] *chrysosperm*: seed of gold.
[39] *oil of height*: prime salt, basis of other salts.
[40] *tree of life*: philosopher's stone.
[41] *marchesite*: white iron pyrites.   [42] *tutty*: zinc oxide.
[43] *magnesia*: an alchemical substance.
[44] *toad . . . panther*: colors indicating stages in the process.
[45] *adrop*: lead.
[46] *lato . . . heautarit*: metals and chemical substances.
[47] *red . . . woman*: sulfur and mercury.
[48] *merds*: faeces.
[49] *Sisyphus*: in Greek mythology, punished for revealing divine secrets by having perpetually to roll a stone to the top of a slope.

Mam. How! pray thee, stay.

Face.   She's mad, sir, and sent
hither—
He'll be mad too—

Mam.   I warrant thee.—Why sent hither?

Face. Sir, to be cured.

Sub. [*Within*]   Why, rascal!

Face.   Lo, you!—here, sir!

                                        He goes out.

Mam. 'Fore God, a Bradamante,[50] a brave piece.

Sur. Heart, this is a bawdy-house! I'll be burnt else.

Mam. Oh, by this light, no! Do not wrong him. He's
Too scrupulous that way; it is his vice.
No, he's a rare physician, do him right,
An excellent Paracelsian,[51] and has done   230
Strange cures with mineral physic. He deals all
With spirits, he; he will not hear a word
Of Galen,[52] or his tedious recipes.—

                    FACE *again.*

How now, Lungs!

Face.   Softly, sir; speak softly. I meant
To ha' told your worship all. This must not hear.

Mam. No, he will not be gulled; let him alone.

Face. Y'are very right, sir; she is a most rare scholar,
And is gone mad with studying Broughton's[53] works.
If you but name a word touching the Hebrew,
She falls into her fit, and will discourse   240
So learnedly of genealogies,
As you would run mad too, to hear her, sir.

Mam. How might one do t' have conference with
her, Lungs?

Face. Oh, divers have run mad upon the conference.
I do not know, sir: I am sent in haste
To fetch a vial.

Sur.   Be not gulled, Sir Mammon.

Mam. Wherein? Pray ye, be patient.

Sur.   Yes, as you are,
And trust confederate knaves and bawds and whores.

Mam. You are too foul, believe it.—Come here,
Ulen,
One word.

Face.   I dare not, in good faith.

                                        [*Going*]

Mam.   Stay, knave.   250

Face. He's extreme angry that you saw her, sir.

Mam. Drink that.

                          [*Gives him money.*]

---

[50] *Bradamante:* Amazon in Ariosto's *Orlando Furioso.*
[51] *Paracelsian:* follower of Paracelsus (1493–1541), who first combined medicine and chemistry, and earned reputation as a quack.
[52] *Galen:* more traditional medical authority (130–210), who used vegetable rather than mineral remedies.
[53] *Broughton:* rabbinical scholar, 1549–1612.
[54] *vegetal:* lively person.   [55] *original:* cause.
[56] *L.:* philosopher's stone.
[57] *lunary:* moonwort, a fern; mercury.
[58] *gleek:* card game.   [59] *L.:* paste for sealing vessels.
[60] *L.:* plain solvent.
[61] *quicksilver . . . sulfur:* cures for venereal disease.
[62] *Temple church:* where lawyers and clients often met by appointment.

What is she when she's out of her fit?

Face. Oh, the most affablest creature, sir! so merry!
So pleasant! she'll mount you up, like quicksilver,
Over the helm; and circulate like oil,
A very vegetal:[54] discourse of state,
Of mathematics, bawdry, anything—

Mam. Is she no way accessible? No means,
No trick to give a man a taste of her—wit—
Or so?—Ulen?

Face.   I'll come to you again, sir.   260

                                        [*Exit.*]

Mam. Surly, I did not think one o' your breeding
Would traduce personages of worth.

Sur.   Sir Epicure,
Your friend to use; yet still loath to be gulled:
I do not like your philosophical bawds.
Their stone is lechery enough to pay for,
Without this bait.

Mam.   Heart, you abuse yourself.
I know the lady, and her friends, and means,
The original[55] of this disaster. Her brother
Has told me all.

Sur.   And yet you ne'er saw her
Till now!

Mam. Oh, yes, but I forgot. I have, believe it,   270
One o' the treacherous'st memories, I do think,
Of all mankind.

Sur.   What call you her brother?

Mam.   My lord—
He wi' not have his name known, now I think on 't.

Sur. A very treacherous memory!

Mam.   O' my faith—

Sur. Tut, if you ha' it not about you, pass it
Till we meet next.

Mam.   Nay, by this hand, 'tis true.
He's one I honor, and my noble friend;
And I respect his house.

Sur.   Heart! can it be
That a grave sir, a rich, that has no need,
A wise sir, too, at other times, should thus,   280
With his own oaths and arguments make hard means
To gull himself? An this be your elixir,
Your *lapis mineralis*,[56] and your lunary,[57]
Give me your honest trick yet at primero
Or gleek,[58] and take your *lutum sapientis*,[59]
Your *menstruum simplex!*[60] I'll have gold before you,
And with less danger of the quicksilver,
Or the hot sulfur.[61]

                    [*Re-enter* FACE.]

Face.   Here's one from Captain Face, sir,

                                        To SURLY

Desires you meet him i' the Temple church,[62]
Some half-hour hence, and upon earnest business.—

                    He whispers MAMMON.

Sir, if you please to quit us now, and come   291
Again within two hours, you shall have
My master busy examining o' the works;
And I will steal you in unto the party,

That you may see her converse.—[*To* SURLY] Sir,
    shall I say
You'll meet the captain's worship?
    Sur.   Sir, I will.—
[*Aside*] But, by attorney,[63] and to a second purpose.
Now I am sure it is a bawdy-house;
I'll swear it, were the marshal here to thank me:
The naming this commander doth confirm it.   300
Don Face! why he's the most authentic dealer
I' these commodities, the superintendent
To all the quainter[64] traffickers in town!
He is the visitor,[65] and does appoint
Who lies with whom, and at what hour; what price;
Which gown, and in what smock; what fall;[66] what
    tire.
Him will I prove,[67] by a third person, to find
The subtleties of this dark labyrinth:
Which if I do discover, dear Sir Mammon,
You'll give your poor friend leave, though no
    philosopher,   310
To laugh; for you that are, 't is thought, shall weep.
    Face. Sir, he does pray you'll not forget.
    Sur.   I will not, sir.
Sir Epicure, I shall leave you?
                               [*Exit.*]
    Mam.   I follow you straight.
    Face. But do so, good sir, to avoid suspicion.
This gent'man has a parlous[68] head.
    Mam.   But wilt thou, Ulen,
Be constant to thy promise?
    Face.   As my life, sir.
    Mam. And wilt thou insinuate what I am, and praise
    me,
And say I am a noble fellow?
    Face.   Oh, what else, sir?
And that you'll make her royal with the stone,
An empress; you yourself king of Bantam.[69]   320
    Mam. Wilt thou do this?
    Face.   Will I, sir!
    Mam.   Lungs, my Lungs!
I love thee.
    Face. Send your stuff, sir, that my master
May busy himself about projection.
    Mam. Thou'st witched me, rogue: take, go.

                      [*Gives him money*]

    Face.   Your
    jack,[70] and all, sir.
    Mam. Thou art a villain—I will send my jack,
And the weights too. Slave, I could bite thine ear.
Away, thou dost not care for me.
    Face.   Not I, sir?
    Mam. Come, I was born to make thee, my good
    weasel,
Set thee on a bench, and ha' thee twirl a chain[71]
With the best lord's vermin of 'em all.
    Face.   Away, sir.   330
    Mam. A count, nay, a count palatine[72]—
    Face.   Good sir, go.
    Mam. Shall not advance thee better: no, nor faster.
                                 [*Exit.*]

II.iv

                [*Enter* SUBTLE *and* DOL.]

    [*Sub.*] Has he bit? Has he bit?
    Face.   And swallowed, too,
    my Subtle.
I ha' given him line, and now he plays, i' faith.
    Sub. And shall we twitch him?
    Face.   Thorough both the
    gills.
A wench is a rare bait, with which a man
No sooner's taken, but he straight firks[1] mad.
    Sub. Dol, my Lord Whatchum's sister, you must
    now
Bear yourself Statelich.[2]
    Dol Com.   Oh, let me alone,
I'll not forget my race, I warrant you.
I'll keep my distance, laugh and talk aloud;
Have all the tricks of a proud scurvy lady,   10
And be as rude's her women.
    Face.   Well said, sanguine![3]
    Sub. But will he send his andirons?
    Face.   His jack too,
And 's iron shoeing-horn; I ha' spoke to him. Well,
I must not lose my wary gamester yonder.
    Sub. Oh, Monsieur Caution, that will not be gulled?
    Face. Ay, If I can strike a fine hook into him, now!—
The Temple church, there I have cast mine angle.
Well, pray for me. I'll about it.

                      One knocks.

    Sub.   What, more gudgeons!
Dol, scout, scout!

                [DOL *goes to the window.*]

            Stay, Face, you must go to the door;
'Pray God it be my Anabaptist[5]—Who is 't, Dol?   20
    Dol Com. I know him not: he looks like a gold-end-
    man.[6]
    Sub. Gods so! 'tis he, he said he would send. What
    call you him?
The sanctified elder, that should deal
For Mammon's jack and andirons! Let him in.
Stay, help me off, first, with my gown.
                [*Exit* FACE *with the gown.*]
                       Away,

---

   [63] *by attorney:* in disguise.
   [64] *quainter:* with pun on "cunt."
   [65] *visitor:* inspector.
   [66] *fall:* flat collar, as opposed to ruff.   [67] *prove:* test.
   [68] *parlous:* perilous.
   [69] *Bantam:* in Java, where Drake was elaborately entertained in 1580.   [70] *jack:* mechanical spit turner.
   [71] *chain:* steward's badge.
   [72] *count palatine:* holding power over his county equal to
that of the king.
II.iv.
   [1] *firks:* goes.   [2] *Ger.:* in a stately manner.
   [3] *sanguine:* one with a humor that includes amorousness
among its qualities.   [4] *gudgeons:* baitfish, fools.
   [5] *Anabaptist:* member of a radical Protestant sect.
   [6] *gold-end-man:* buyer of odd bits of gold and silver.

Madam, to your withdrawing chamber.[7]

                          [*Exit* DOL.]
                     Now,
In a new tune, new gesture, but old language.
This fellow is sent from one negotiates with me
About the stone too, for the holy brethren
Of Amsterdam, the exiled saints, that hope   30
To raise their discipline by it. I must use him
In some strange fashion now, to make him admire me.

II.v

           [*Enter* ANANIAS.]

[*Sub.*] Where is my drudge?

            [*Enter* FACE.]

Face.   Sir!
Sub.   Take away the recipient,[1]
And rectify your menstrue from the phlegma.[2]
Then pour it o' the Sol, in the cucurbite,
And let 'em macerate[3] together.
Face.   Yes, sir.
And save the ground?
Sub.   No: *terra damnata*[4]
Must not have entrance in the work.—Who are you?
Anan. A faithful brother, if it please you.
Sub.   What's that?
A Lullianist?[5] a Ripley?[6] *Filius artis?*[7]
Can you sublime and dulcify?[8] Calcine?
Know you the sapor pontic? Sapor stiptic?[9]   10
Or what is homogene, or heterogene?
Anan. I understand no heathen language, truly.
Sub. Heathen! you Knipperdoling![10] Is *ars sacra*,[11]

---

[7] *withdrawing chamber:* private room.
II.v.
[1] *recipient:* vessel for condensing product of distillation.
[2] *phlegma:* watery, inodorous, tasteless substance obtained by distilling.   [3] *macerate:* soften by steeping.
[4] *L.:* "ground," dregs.
[5] *Lullianist:* follower of Raymond Lully, thirteenth-century Spanish courtier reputed to be alchemist.
[6] *Ripley:* fifteenth-century English follower of Lully.
[7] *L.:* Son of the art.
[8] *dulcify:* dissolve salts out of a substance.
[9] *sapor pontic . . . Sapor stiptic:* two of the classified tastes.
[10] *Knipperdoling:* a leader of the Anabaptist rising in Münster, 1534–6.   [11] *ars sacra:* sacred art, alchemy.
[12] *chrysopoeia:* making of gold.
[13] *spagyrica:* Paracelsian word for alchemical process.
[14] *pamphysic:* knowledge of all nature.
[15] *panarchic:* all-ruling.
[16] *vexations and martyrizations:* alchemical process in the treatment of metals.
[17] *putrefaction:* chemical decomposition.
[18] *ablution:* washing away impurities.
[19] *Cohobation:* repeated distillation.
[20] *vivification:* restoration of a metal to its natural state.
[21] *mortification:* alteration of the nature of a metal.
[22] *L.:* mixture of acids, solvent for gold.
[23] *trine . . . spheres:* planets at 120-degree intervals through the order of the spheres.
[24] *Malleation:* hammering.
[25] *L.:* extreme punishment for gold.
[26] *oleosity:* oiliness.   [27] *suscitability:* excitability.

Or chrysopoeia,[12] or spagyrica,[13]
Or the pamphysic,[14] or panarchic[15] knowledge,
A heathen language?
Anan.   Heathen Greek, I take it.
Sub. How! heathen Greek?
Anan.   All's heathen but the
   Hebrew.
Sub. Sirrah my varlet, stand you forth and speak to
   him
Like a philosopher; answer i' the language.
Name the vexations and the martyrizations[16]   20
Of metals in the work.
Face.   Sir, putrefaction,[17]
Solution, ablution,[18] sublimation,
Cohobation,[19] calcination, ceration, and
Fixation.
Sub. This is heathen Greek, to you, now?—
And when comes vivification?[20]
Face.   After mortification.[21]
Sub. What's cohobation?
Face.   'Tis the pouring on
Your *aqua regis*,[22] and then drawing him off,
To the trine circle of the seven spheres.[23]
Sub. What's the proper passion of metals?
Face.   Malleation.[24]
Sub. What's your *ultimum supplicium auri?*[25]
Face.   Antimonium.
Sub. This's heathen Greek to you?—And what's
   your mercury?   31
Face. A very fugitive, he will be gone, sir.
Sub. How know you him?
Face.   By his viscosity,
His oleosity,[26] and his suscitability.[27]
Sub. How do you sublime him?
Face.   With the calce of
   egg-shells,
White marble, talc.
Sub.   Your magisterium now,
What's that?
Face. Shifting, sir, your elements,
Dry into cold, cold into moist, moist into hot,
Hot into dry.
Sub.   This's heathen Greek to you still?—
Your *lapis philosophicus?*
Face.   'Tis a stone, and not   40
A stone; a spirit, a soul, and a body,
Which if you do dissolve, it is dissolved;
If you coagulate, it is coagulated;
If you make it to fly, it flieth.
Sub.   Enough.
                         [*Exit* FACE.]
This's heathen Greek to you? What are you, sir?
Anan. Please you, a servant of the exiled brethren,
That deal with widows' and with orphans' goods,
And make a just account unto the saints:
A deacon.
Sub. Oh, you are sent from Master Wholesome,
Your teacher?
Anan.   From Tribulation Wholesome,   50
Our very zealous pastor.
Sub.   Good. I have

Some orphans' goods to come here.
 Anan.   Of what kind, sir?
 Sub. Pewter and brass, andirons and kitchen-ware;
Metals, that we must use our med'cine on:
Wherein the brethren may have a penn'orth
For ready money.
 Anan.   Were the orphans' parents
Sincere professors?
 Sub.   Why do you ask?
 Anan.   Because
We then are to deal justly, and give, in truth,
Their utmost value.
 Sub.   'Slid, you'd cozen else,
An if their parents were not of the faithful?—   60
I will not trust you, now I think on't,
Till I ha' talked with your pastor. Ha' you brought
 money
To buy more coals?
 Anan.   No, surely.
 Sub.   No? How so?
 Anan. The brethren bid me say unto you, sir,
Surely, they will not venture any more
Till they may see projection.
 Sub.   How!
 Anan.   You've had
For the instruments, as bricks, and loam, and glasses,
Already thirty pound; and for materials,
They say, some ninety more. And they have heard since,
That one at Heidelberg made it of an egg,   70
And a small paper of pin-dust.[28]
 Sub.   What's your name?
 Anan. My name is Ananias.
 Sub.   Out, the varlet
That cozened the apostles! Hence, away!
Flee, mischief! had your holy consistory[29]
No name to send me, of another sound
Than wicked Ananias? Send your elders
Hither to make atonement for you, quickly,
And gi' me satisfaction; or out goes
The fire; and down th' alembics, and the furnace,
Piger Henricus,[30] or what not. Thou wretch! 80
Both *sericon*[31] and *bufo*[32] shall be lost,
Tell 'em. All hope of rooting out the bishops,
Or th' anti-Christian hierarchy shall perish,
If they stay threescore minutes; the aqueity,[33]
Terreity,[34] and sulfureity
Shall run together again, and all be annulled,
Thou wicked Ananias!
        [*Exit* ANANIAS.]
     This will fetch 'em,
And make 'em haste towards their gulling more.
A man must deal like a rough nurse, and fright
Those that are froward to an appetite.   90

II.vi

[*Enter* FACE, *in his Captain's uniform, followed by*
     DRUGGER.]

[*Face.*] He's busy with his spirits, but we'll upon him.
 Sub. How now! What mates,[1] what Bayards[2] ha' we
 here?

 Face. I told you he would be furious.—Sir, here's
 Nab
Has brought you another piece of gold to look on;
[*Aside to* DRUGGER] We must appease him. Give it
 me,—and prays you,
You would devise—what is it, Nab?
 Drug.   A sign, sir.
 Face. Ay, a good lucky one, a thriving sign, doctor.
 Sub. I was devising now.
 Face.[*Aside to* SUBTLE] 'Slight, do not say so,
He will repent he ga' you any more.—
What say you to his constellation, doctor, 10
The Balance?
 Sub.   No, that way is stale and common.
A townsman born in Taurus gives the bull,
Or the bull's head; in Aries, the ram.
A poor device. No, I will have his name
Formed in some mystic character, whose radii,[3]
Striking the senses of the passersby,
Shall, by a virtual[4] influence, breed affections
That may result upon the party owns it:
As thus—
 Face. Nab!
 Sub.   He first shall have a bell, that's Abel;
And by it standing one whose name is Dee,[5] 20
In a rug gown, there's D, and Rug, that's drug;
And right anenst[6] him a dog snarling er;
There's Drugger, Abel Drugger. That's his sign.
And here's now mystery and hieroglyphic![7]
 Face. Abel, thou art made.
 Drug.   Sir, I do thank his
 worship.
 Face. Six o' thy legs[8] more will not do it, Nab.
He has brought you a pipe of tobacco, doctor.
 Drug.   Yes, sir.
I have another thing I would impart—
 Face. Out with it, Nab.
 Drug.   Sir, there is lodged, hard by
 me,
A rich young widow—
 Face.   Good! a *bona roba?*[9] 30
 Drug. But nineteen at the most.
 Face.   Very good, Abel.
 Drug. Marry, she's not in fashion yet; she wears
A hood, but 't stands a cop.[10]
 Face.   No matter, Abel.

---

[28] *pin-dust:* metal filings.
[29] *consistory:* puritan assembly.
[30] *Piger Henricus:* a kind of furnace.
[31] *sericon:* red tincture. [32] *bufo:* black tincture.
[33] *aqueity:* watery quality.
[34] *Terreity:* Earthy quality.

II.vi.
[1] *mates:* lowlife.
[2] *Bayards:* horses, from Charlemagne's magic horse;
fools.   [3] *radii:* rays.
[4] *virtual:* from its virtues.
[5] *Dee:* John Dee, 1527–1608, mathematician, philosopher,
astrologer, etc.   [6] *anenst:* opposite.
[7] *hieroglyphic:* figure concealing a sacred truth.
[8] *legs:* bows.   [9] *L.:* prostitute.
[10] *a cop:* high on the head.

Drug. And I do now and then give her a fucus—
Face. What! dost thou deal, Nab?
Sub.   I did tell you,
   captain,
Drug. And physic too, sometime, sir; for which she
   trusts me
With all her mind. She's come up here of purpose
To learn the fashion.
Face.   Good.—[*Aside.*] His match too!—
   On, Nab.
Drug. And she does strangely long to know her
   fortune.   39
Face. God's lid, Nab, send her to the doctor, hither.
Drug. Yes, I have spoke to her of his worship already;
But she's afraid it will be blown abroad,
And hurt her marriage.
Face.   Hurt it! 'tis the way
To heal it, if 'twere hurt; to make it more
Followed and sought. Nab, thou shalt tell her this.
She'll be more known, more talked of; and your widows
Are ne'er of any price till they be famous;
Their honor is their multitude of suitors.
Send her. It may be thy good fortune. What?
Thou dost not know?
Drug.   No, sir, she'll never marry   50
Under a knight; her brother has made a vow.
Face. What! and dost thou despair, my little Nab,
Knowing what the doctor has set down for thee,
And seeing so many o' the city dubbed?[11]
One glass o' thy water,[12] with a madam I know,
Will have it done, Nab. What's her brother? A knight?
Drug. No, sir, a gentleman newly warm in's land, sir,
Scarce cold in his one-and-twenty, that does govern
His sister here; and is a man himself
Of some three thousand a year, and is come up   60
To learn to quarrel, and to live by his wits,
And will go down again, and die i' the country.
Face. How! to quarrel?
Drug.   Yes, sir, to carry quarrels,
As gallants do; to manage 'em by line.[13]
Face. 'Slid, Nab! the doctor is the only man
In Christendom for him. He has made a table,
With mathematical demonstrations,
Touching the art of quarrels. He will give him
An instrument to quarrel by. Go, bring 'em both,
Him and his sister. And, for thee, with her   70
The doctor happ'ly[14] may persuade. Go to.
'Shalt give his worship a new damask suit
Upon the premises.
Sub.   Oh, good captain!
Face.   He shall;

---

[11] *dubbed:* knighted.   [12] *water:* love potion(?), urine(?).
[13] *by line:* methodically.   [14] *happ'ly:* perhaps.
[15] *in tail:* entail (tied up so that it cannot be bequeathed at
pleasure), with sexual pun.   [16] *grains:* weight.
III.i.
   [1] *saints:* Puritan brethren.
   [2] *separation:* Amsterdam exile of the Anabaptists.
   [3] *language of Canaan:* see Isaiah xix: 18.
   [4] *mark . . . beast:* mark of the damned (Revelation xvi: 2).
   [5] *bend unto:* submit to.

He is the honestest fellow, doctor. Stay not,
No offers; bring the damask, and the parties.
Drug. I'll try my power, sir.
Face.   And thy will too, Nab.
Sub. 'Tis good tobacco, this! What is't an ounce?
Face. He'll send you a pound, doctor.
Sub.   Oh, no.
Face.   He will do't.
It is the goodest soul!—Abel, about it.
Thou shalt know more anon. Away, be gone.   80
                                   [*Exit* DRUGGER.]
A miserable rogue, and lives with cheese,
And has the worms. That was the cause, indeed,
Why he came now. He dealt with me in private,
To get a med'cine for 'em.
Sub.   And shall, sir. This works.
Face. A wife, a wife for one on's, my dear Subtle!
We'll e'en draw lots, and he that fails shall have
The more in goods the other has in tail.[15]
Sub. Rather the less; for she may be so light
She may want grains.[16]
Face.   Ay, or be such a burden
A man would scarce endure her for the whole.   90
Sub. Faith, best let's see her first, and then
   determine.
Face. Content. But Dol must ha' no breath on't.
Sub.   Mum.
Away you, to your Surly yonder, catch him.
Face. Pray God I ha' not stayed too long.
Sub.   I fear it.
                                        [*Exeunt.*]

ACT THREE

SCENE ONE

[*Enter* TRIBULATION WHOLESOME *and* ANANIAS.]

[*Trib.*] These chastisements are common to the
   saints,[1]
And such rebukes we of the separation[2]
Must bear with willing shoulders, as the trials
Sent forth to tempt our frailties.
Anan.   In pure zeal,
I do not like the man; he is a heathen,
And speaks the language of Canaan,[3] truly.
Trib. I think him a profane person indeed.
Anan.   He bears
The visible mark of the beast[4] in his forehead.
And for his stone, it is a work of darkness,
And with philosophy blinds the eyes of man.   10
Trib. Good brother, we must bend unto[5] all means
That may give furtherance to the holy cause.
Anan. Which his cannot: the sanctified cause
Should have a sanctified course.
Trib.   Not always necessary.
The children of perdition are oft times
Made instruments even of the greatest works.
Besides, we should give somewhat to man's nature,
The place he lives in, still about the fire,
And fume of metals, that intoxicate

The brain of man, and make him prone to passion.   20
Where have you greater atheists than your cooks?
Or more profane, or choleric, than your glass-men?[6]
More anti-Christian than your bell-founders?
What makes the devil so devilish, I would ask you,
Satan, our common enemy, but his being
Perpetually about the fire, and boiling
Brimstone and arsenic? We must give, I say,
Unto the motives, and the stirrers up
Of humors in the blood. It may be so,
Whenas the work is done, the stone is made,   30
This heat of his may turn into a zeal,
And stand up for the beauteous discipline
Against the menstruous[7] cloth and rag of Rome.[8]
We must await his calling and the coming
Of the good spirit. You did fault t' upbraid him
With the brethren's blessing of Heidelberg, weighing
What need we have to hasten on the work,
For the restoring of the silenced saints,[9]
Which ne'er will be but by the philosopher's stone.
And so a learned elder, one of Scotland,[10]   40
Assured me; *aurum potabile*[11] being
The only med'cine for the civil magistrate,
T' incline him to a feeling of the cause;
And must be daily used in the disease.
    Anan. I have not edified more, truly, by man,
Not since the beautiful light first shone on me,
And I am sad my zeal hath so offended.
    Trib. Let us call on him then.
    Anan.   The motion's[12] good,
And of the spirit; I will knock first.

                                        [*Knocks.*]

                        Peace be within!

III.ii

[SUBTLE *admits* TRIBULATION *and* ANANIAS.]

[*Sub.*] Oh, are you come? 'Twas time. Your
    threescore minutes
Were at the last thread, you see; and down had gone
Furnus acediae,[1] *turris circulatorius:*[2]
Limbec, bolt's-head, retort, and pelican
Had all been cinders. Wicked Ananias!
Art thou returned? Nay, then, it goes down yet.
    Trib. Sir, be appeasèd; he is come to humble
Himself in spirit, and to ask your patience,
If too much zeal hath carried him aside
From the due path.
    Sub.   Why, this doth qualify![3]   10
    Trib. The brethren had no purpose, verily,
To give you the least grievance; but are ready
To lend their willing hands to any project
The spirit and you direct.
    Sub.   This qualifies more!
    Trib. And for the orphans' goods, let them be valued,
Or what is needful else to the holy work,
It shall be numbered; here, by me, the saints
Throw down their purse before you.
    Sub.   This qualifies most!
Why, thus it should be, now you understand.

Have I discoursed so unto you of our stone,   20
And of the good that it shall bring your cause?
Showed you (beside the main of hiring forces
Abroad, drawing the Hollanders, your friends,
From th' Indies, to serve you, with all their fleet)
That even the med'cinal use shall make you a faction
And party in the realm? As, put the case,
That some great man in state, he have the gout,
Why, you but send three drops of your elixir,
You help him straight: there you have made a friend.
Another has the palsy or the dropsy,   30
He takes of your incombustible[4] stuff,
He's young again: there you have made a friend.
A lady that is past the feat of body,[5]
Though not of mind, and hath her face decayed
Beyond all cure of paintings, you restore
With the oil of talc: there you have made a friend;
And all her friends. A lord that is a leper,
A knight that has the bone-ache,[6] or a squire
That hath both these, you make 'em smooth and sound
With a bare fricace[7] of your med'cine; still   40
You increase your friends.
    Trib.   Ay, 'tis very pregnant.
    Sub. And then the turning of this lawyer's pewter
To plate at Christmas—
    Anan.   Christ-tide,[8] I pray you.
    Sub. Yet, Ananias?
    Anan.   I have done.
    Sub.   Or changing
His parcel gilt[9] to massy[10] gold. You cannot
But raise you friends. With all, to be of power
To pay an army in the field, to buy
The King of France out of his realms, or Spain
Out of his Indies. What can you not do
Against lords spiritual or temporal,   50
That shall oppone[11] you?
    Trib.   Verily, 'tis true.
We may be temporal lords ourselves, I take it.
    Sub. You may be anything, and leave off to make
Long-winded exercises; or suck up
Your ha and hum in a tune. I not deny,
But such as are not gracèd in a state,
May, for their ends, be adverse in religion,
And get a tune to call the flock together.

---

    [6] *glass-men:* glass-blowers.
    [7] *menstruous:* polluted with menstrual blood.
    [8] *Rome:* the Catholic Church in a familiar Puritan image
as the whore of Babylon "drunk with the blood of the saints
. . . and the martyrs" (Revelation, xvii:6).
    [9] *silenced saints:* Puritan clergy prevented from preaching
in England.
    [10] *Scotland:* where the Puritans had considerable power.
    [11] *L.:* drinkable gold, i.e., bribery.   [12] *motion:* proposal.
III.ii.
    [1] *L.:* Furnace of sloth.   [2] *L.:* circulation tower, still.
    [3] *qualify:* modify.
    [4] *incombustible:* the power to withstand fire was prized in
certain materials, and held in contrast with susceptibility to
putrefactions.   [5] *feat of body:* sexual intercourse.
    [6] *bone-ache:* syphilis.   [7] *fricace:* liniment.
    [8] *Christ-tide:* Zealous Puritans shunned the Catholic
"mass".   [9] *parcel gilt:* partly gilded silverware.
    [10] *massy:* solid.   [11] *oppone:* oppose.

For, to say sooth, a tune does much with women
And other phlegmatic people; it is your bell.   60
   Anan. Bells are profane; a tune may be religious.
   Sub. No warning with you? Then farewell my
     patience.
'Slight, it shall down; I will not be thus tortured.
   Trib. I pray you, sir.
   Sub.   All shall perish. I have spoke it.
   Trib. Le me find grace, sir, in your eyes; the man,
He stands corrected: neither did his zeal,
But as yourself, allow a tune somewhere,
Which now, being to'ard[12] the stone, we shall not need.
   Sub. No, nor your holy vizard, to win widows
To give you legacies; or make zealous wives   70
To rob their husbands for the common cause;
Nor take the start[13] of bonds broke but one day,
And say they were forfeited by providence.
Nor shall you need o'er night to eat huge meals,
To celebrate your next day's fast the better;
The whilst the brethren and the sisters, humbled,
Abate the stiffness of the flesh. Nor cast
Before your hungry hearers scrupulous bones;[14]
As whether a Christian may hawk or hunt,
Or whether matrons of the holy assembly   80
May lay their hair out, or wear doublets,
Or have that idol, starch, about their linen.
   Anan. It is indeed an idol.
   Trib.   Mind him not, sir.
I do command thee, spirit (of zeal, but trouble),
To peace within him. Pray you, sir, go on.
   Sub. Nor shall you need to libel 'gainst the prelates,
And shorten so your ears[15] against the hearing
Of the next wire-drawn[16] grace. Nor of necessity
Rail against plays, to please the alderman
Whose daily custard[17] you devour; nor lie   90
With zealous rage till you are hoarse. Not one
Of these so singular arts. Nor call yourselves
By names of Tribulation, Persecution,
Restraint, Long-patience, and such like affected
By the whole family or wood[18] of you,
Only for glory, and to catch the ear
Of the disciple.
   Trib.   Truly, sir, they are
Ways that the godly brethren have invented,
For propagation of the glorious cause,
As very notable means, and whereby also   100
Themselves grow soon, and profitably, famous.
   Sub. Oh, but the stone, all's idle to 't! nothing!
The art of angels, nature's miracle,
The divine secret that doth fly in clouds

From east to west, and whose tradition
Is not from men, but spirits.
   Anan.   I hate traditions;
I do not trust them—
   Trib.   Peace!
   Anan.   They are popish all.
I will not peace! I will not—
   Trib.   Ananias!
   Anan. Please the profane, to grieve the godly!
I may not.
   Sub. Well, Ananias, thou shalt overcome.   110
   Trib. It is an ignorant zeal that haunts him, sir,
But truly else a very faithful brother,
A botcher,[19] and a man, by revelation,
That hath a competent knowledge of the truth.
   Sub. Has he a competent sum there i' the bag
To buy the goods within? I am made guardian,
And must, for charity and conscience' sake,
Now see the most be made for my poor orphan,
Though I desire the brethren, too, good gainers;
There they are within. When you have viewed and
     bought 'em,   120
And ta'en the inventory of what they are,
They are ready for projection; there's no more
To do: cast on the med'cine, so much silver
As there is tin there, so much gold as brass,
I'll gi' it you in by weight.
   Trib.   But how long time,
Sir, must the saints expect yet?
   Sub.   Let me see,
How's the moon now? Eight, nine, ten days hence,
He will be silver potate;[20] then three days
Before he citronize.[21] Some fifteen days,
The magisterium will be perfected.   130
   Anan. About the second day of the third week,
In the ninth month?[22]
   Sub.   Yes, my good Ananias.
   Trib. What will the orphans' goods arise to, think
     you?
   Sub. Some hundred marks, as much as filled three
     cars,
Unladed now: you'll make six millions of 'em—
But I must ha' more coals laid in.
   Trib.   How?
   Sub.   Another load,
And then we ha' finished. We must now increase
Our fire to *ignis ardens*[23]; we are past
Fimus equinus, balnei, cineris,[24]
And all those lenter heats. If the holy purse   140
Should with this draught fall low, and that the saints
Do need a present sum, I have a trick
To melt the pewter, you shall buy now instantly,
And with a tincture make you as good Dutch dollars[25]
As any are in Holland.
   Trib.   Can you so?
   Sub. Ay, and shall bide the third examination.
   Anan. It will be joyful tidings to the brethren.
   Sub. But you must carry it secret.
   Trib.   Ay; but stay;
This act of coining, is it lawful?
   Anan.   Lawful!

---

[12] *to'ard*: near possessing.
[13] *take the start*: claim as forfeit.
[14] *scrupulous bones*: arguments about trivial scruples.
[15] *shorten . . . ears*: have them cut off as punishment.
[16] *wire-drawn*: long drawn out.   [17] *custard*: pie.
[18] *wood*: group.   [19] *botcher*: tailor who did repairs.
[20] *potate*: liquified.   [21] *citronize*: turn yellow.
[22] *second . . . month*: Puritans rejected pagan names of
days and months.   [23] *L.*: hottest degree of fire.
[24] *L.*: The other three degrees of heat produced by horse-
dung, bath, and ashes.
[25] *dollars*: thaler, silver coins worth 5s.

We know no magistrate; or, if we did,   150
This's foreign coin.
   Sub.   It is no coining, sir.
It is but casting.
   Trib.   Ha! you distinguish well;
Casting of money may be lawful.
   Anan.   'Tis, sir.
   Trib. Truly, I take it so.
   Sub.   There is no scruple,
Sir, to be made of it; believe Ananias;
This case of conscience he is studied in.
   Trib. I'll make a question of it to the brethren.
   Anan. The brethren shall approve it lawful, doubt
   not.
Where shall't be done?
   Sub.   For that we'll talk anon.

                     Knock without.

There's some to speak with me. Go in, I pray you,   160
And view the parcels. That's the inventory.
I'll come to you straight.
            [*Exeunt* TRIBULATION *and* ANANIAS.]
            Who is it?—Face! appear.

III.iii

         [*Enter* FACE *in his uniform.*]

   [*Sub.*] How now! good prize?
   Face.   Good pox! yond'
   costive cheater
Never came on.[1]
   Sub.   How then?
   Face.   I ha' walked the round[2]
Till now, and no such thing.
   Sub.   And ha' you quit him?
   Face. Quit him! An hell would quit him too, he were
   happy.
'Slight! would you have me stalk like a mill-jade,
All day, for one that will not yield us grains?[3]
I know him of old.
   Sub.   Oh, but to ha' gulled him,
Had been a mastery.
   Face.   Let him go, black boy!
And turn thee, that some fresh news may possess thee.
A noble count, a don of Spain (my dear   10
Delicious compeer, and my party[4]-bawd),
Who is come hither private for his conscience
And brought munition with him, six great slops,[5]
Bigger than three Dutch hoys,[6] beside round trunks,[7]
Furnish'd with pistolets[8] and pieces of eight,[9]
Will straight be here, my rogue, to have thy bath,
(That is the color)[10] and to make his batt'ry
Upon our Dol, our castle, our cinqueport,[11]
Our Dover pier, our what thou wilt. Where is she?
She must prepare perfumes, delicate linen,   20
The bath in chief, a banquet, and her wit,
For she must milk his epididymis.[12]
Where is the doxy?[13]
   Sub.   I'll send her to thee;
And but dispatch my brace of little John Leydens[14]

And come again myself.
   Face.   Are they within then?
   Sub. Numb'ring the sum.
   Face.   How much?
   Sub.   A hundred
   marks, boy.
                      [*Exit.*]
   Face. Why, this's a lucky day. Ten pounds of
   Mammon!
Three o' my clerk! a portague o' my grocer!
This o' the brethren! Beside reversions[15]
And states[16] to come, i' the widow, and my count!   30
My share today will not be bought for forty—

             [*Enter* DOL.]

   Dol Com.   What?
   Face. Pounds, dainty Dorothy! Art thou so near?
   Dol Com. Yes. Say, lord general, how fares our
   camp?[17]
   Face. As with the few that had entrenched themselves
Safe, by their discipline, against a world, Dol,
And laughed within those trenches, and grew fat
With thinking on the booties, Dol, brought in
Daily by their small parties. This dear hour,
A doughty don is taken with my Dol;
And thou mayst make his ransom what thou wilt,   40
My Dowsabel;[18] he shall be brought here, fettered
With thy fair looks, before he sees thee; and thrown
In a down-bed, as dark as any dungeon;
Where thou shalt keep him waking with thy drum;
Thy drum,[19] my Dol, thy drum; till he be tame
As the poor blackbirds were i' the great frost,
Or bees are with a basin; and so hive him
I' the swan-skin coverlid and cambric sheets,
Till he work honey and wax, my little God's-gift.[20]
   Dol Com. What is he, general?
   Face.   An *adalantado*,[21]   50
A grandee, girl. Was not my Dapper here yet?
   Dol Com. No.
   Face.   Nor my Drugger?
   Dol Com.   Neither.
   Face.   A pox on 'em,

III.iii.
[1] *came on:* showed up.
[2] *walked the round:* kept a lookout, with play on "round,"
i.e., Temple-church.   [3] *grains:* money.
[4] *party:* fellow.   [5] *slops:* breeches.
[6] *hoys:* ships.   [7] *trunks:* padded breeches.
[8] *pistolets:* Spanish gold coins worth 17s.
[9] *pieces of eight:* Spanish silver pesos worth eight reales.
[10] *color:* pretense.
[11] *cinqueport:* like Dover, one of five ports in southeast
England.
[12] *epididymis:* a long narrow tube attached to the posterior
border of the adjoining outer surface of the testicle and
connected to the vas deferens.
[13] *doxy:* whore, beggar's mistress.
[14] *John Leyden:* Anabaptist leader in Münster rising.
[15] *reversions:* benefits to come.   [16] *states:* estates.
[17] *Say . . . camp: The Spanish Tragedy*, I. ii. 1.
[18] *Dowsabel:* pastoral name, meaning "sweet and pretty."
[19] *drum:* belly(?).
[20] *God's-gift:* Greek meaning of Dorothea.
[21] *Sp.:* provincial governor.

They are so long a-furnishing![22] such stinkards
Would[23] not be seen upon these festival days.—

[Re-enter SUBTLE.*]*

How now! ha' you done?
   Sub.   Done. They are gone; the sum
Is here in bank, my Face. I would we knew
Another chapman[24] now would buy 'em outright.
   Face. 'Slid, Nab shall do't against he ha' the widow,
To furnish household.
   Sub.   Excellent, well thought on.
Pray God he come.
   Face.   I pray he keep away   60
Till our new business be o'erpast.
   Sub.   But, Face,
How cam'st thou by this secret don?
   Face.   A spirit
Brought me th' intelligence in a paper here,
As I was conjuring yonder in my circle
For Surly; I ha' my flies abroad. Your bath
Is famous, Subtle, by my means. Sweet Dol,
You must go tune your virginal,[25] no losing
O' the least time. And—do you hear?—good action!
Firk[26] like a flounder; kiss like a scallop, close;
And tickle him with thy mother-tongue. His great   70
Verdugoship[27] has not a jot of language;[28]
So much the easier to be cozened, my Dolly.
He will come here in a hired coach, obscure,
And our own coachman, whom I have sent as guide,
No creature else.—Who's that?

One knocks. [DOL *looks out the window.*]

   Sub.   It i' not he?
   Face. Oh, no, not yet this hour.
   Sub.   Who is't?
   Dol Com.   Dapper,
Your clerk.
   Face.   God's will then, Queen of Faery,
On with your tire;

                            [Exit DOL.*]*
          and, doctor, with your robes.
Let's dispatch him, for God's sake.
   Sub.   'Twill be long.
   Face. I warrant you, take but the cues I give you,
It shall be brief enough.

                 *[*FACE *looks out.*]*
             'Slight, here are more!   81
Abel, and, I think, the angry boy, the heir,
That fain would quarrel.
   Sub.   And the widow?
   Face.   No,
Not that I see. Away!

                     [Exit SUBTLE.*]*

---

[22] *a-furnishing:* making their contribution.
[23] *Would:* Should.   [24] *chapman:* merchant.
[25] *virginal:* spinet, with pun.   [26] *Firk:* Move briskly.
[27] *Verdugoship: verdugo,* Spanish for hangman.
[28] *language:* English.
III.iv.
  [1] *ordinarily:* with pun on ordinary, tavern.

III.iv

[Enter DAPPER.*]*

  [Face.]   Oh, sir, you are welcome.
The doctor is within, a-moving for you.
(I have had the most ado to win him to it.)
He swears you'll be the darling o' the dice;
He never heard her highness dote till now, he says.
Your aunt has giv'n you the most gracious words
That can be thought on.
   Dap.   Shall I see her grace?
   Face. See her, and kiss her too.

[Enter DRUGGER, *followed by* KASTRIL.*]*

                      What, honest Nab!
Hast brought the damask?
   Drug.   No, sir; here's tobacco.
   Face. 'Tis well done, Nab; thou'lt bring the damask
   too.
   Drug. Yes. Here's the gentleman, captain, master
   Kastril,   10
I have brought to see the doctor.
   Face.   Where's the widow?
   Drug. Sir, as he likes, his sister, he says, shall come.
   Face. Oh, is it so? Good time. Is your name Kastril,
   sir?
   Kast. Ay, and the best o' the Kastrils, I'd be sorry
   else,
By fifteen hundred a year. Where is this doctor?
My mad tobacco-boy here tells me of one
That can do things. Has he any skill?
   Face.   Wherein, sir?
   Kast. To carry a business, manage a quarrel fairly,
Upon fit terms.
   Face.   It seems, sir, y' are but young
About the town that can make that a question.   20
   Kast. Sir, not so young but I have heard some
   speech
Of the angry boys, and seen 'em take tobacco;
And in his shop; and I can take it too.
And I would fain be one of 'em, and go down
And practice i' the country.
   Face.   Sir, for the duello,
The doctor, I assure you, shall inform you,
To the least shadow of a hair; and show you
An instrument he has of his own making,
Wherewith, no sooner shall you make report
Of any quarrel, but he will take the height on't   30
Most instantly, and tell in what degree
Of safety it lies in, or mortality.
And how it may be borne, whether in a right line,
Or a half circle; or may else be cast
Into an angle blunt, if not acute:
All this he will demonstrate. And then, rules
To give and take the lie by.
   Kast.   How! to take it?
   Face. Yes, in oblique he'll show you, or in circle;
But never in diameter. The whole town
Study his theorems, and dispute them ordinarily[1]   40
At the eating academies.
   Kast.   But does he teach

Living by the wits too?
   Face.   Anything whatever.
You cannot think that subtlety but he reads it.
He made me a captain. I was a stark pimp,
Just o' your standing, 'fore I met with him;
It's not two months since. I'll tell you his method.
First, he will enter you at some ordinary.
   Kast. No, I'll not come there; you shall pardon me.
   Face.   For
    why, sir?
   Kast. There's gaming there, and tricks.
   Face.   Why, would
    you be
A gallant, and not game?
   Kast.   Ay, 'twill spend a man.   50
   Face. Spend you! It will repair you when you are
    spent.
How do they live by their wits there, that have vented[2]
Six times your fortunes?
   Kast.   What, three thousand a year!
   Face. Ay, forty thousand.
   Kast.   Are there such?
   Face.   Ay, sir,
And gallants yet. Here's a young gentleman
Is born to nothing, forty marks a year,
Which I count nothing. He's to be initiated,
And have a fly o' the doctor. He will win you,
By unresistible luck, within this fortnight,
Enough to buy a barony. They will set him   60
Upmost, at the groom-porter's,[3] all the Christmas;
And for the whole year through, at every place
Where there is play, present him with the chair,
The best attendance, the best drink, sometimes
Two glasses of canary,[4] and pay nothing;
The purest linen and the sharpest knife,
The partridge next his trencher, and somewhere
The dainty bed, in private, with the dainty.
You shall ha' your ordinaries bid for him,
As playhouses for a poet; and the master   70
Pray him aloud to name what dish he affects,[5]
Which must be buttered shrimps; and those that drink
To no mouth else will drink to his, as being
The goodly president mouth of all the board.
   Kast. Do you not gull one?
   Face.   'Ods my life! do you
    think it?
You shall have a cast[6] commander, (can but get
In credit with a glover, or a spurrier,
For some two pair of either's ware aforehand)
Will, by most swift posts,[7] dealing with him,
Arrive at competent means to keep himself,   80
His punk, and naked boy, in excellent fashion,
And be admired for 't.
   Kast.   Will the doctor teach this?
   Face. He will do more, sir. When your land is gone,
(As men of spirit hate to keep earth long),
In a vacation, when small money is stirring,
And ordinaries suspended till the term,
He'll show a perspective,[8] where on one side
You shall behold the faces and the persons
Of all sufficient young heirs in town,

Whose bonds are current for commodity;   90
On th' other side, the merchants' forms, and others,
That without help of any second broker,
Who would expect a share, will trust such parcels;
In the third square, the very street and sign
Where the commodity dwells, and does but wait
To be delivered, be it pepper, soap.
Hops, or tobacco, oatmeal, woad,[9] or cheeses.
All which you may so handle, to enjoy
To your own use, and never stand obliged.
   Kast. I' faith! is he such a fellow?
   Face.   Why, Nab here
    knows him.   100
And then for making matches, for rich widows,
Young gentlewomen, heirs, the fortunat'st man!
He's sent to, far and near, all over England,
To have his counsel, and to know their fortunes.
   Kast. God's will, my suster shall see him.
   Face.   I'll tell you, sir,
What he did tell me of Nab. It's a strange thing!
(By the way, you must eat no cheese, Nab, it breeds
    melancholy,
And that same melancholy breeds worms) but pass
    it[10]—
He told me honest Nab here was ne'er at tavern
But once in's life.
   Drug.   Truth, and no more I was not.   110
   Face. And then he was so sick—
   Drug.   Could he tell you
    that too?
   Face. How should I know it?
   Drug.   In troth, we had been
    a-shooting,
And had a piece of fat ram-mutton to supper,
That lay so heavy o' my stomach—
   Face.   And he has no head
To bear any wine; for what with the noise o' the
    fiddlers,
And care of his shop, for he dares keep no servants—
   Drug. My head did so ache—
   Face.   As he was fain to be
    brought home,
The doctor told me. And then a good old woman—
   Drug. Yes, faith, she dwells in Seacoal Lane,[11] did
    cure me.
With sodden[12] ale, and pellitory o' the wall;[13]   120
Cost me but twopence. I had another sickness
Was worse than that.
   Face.   Ay, that was with the grief
Thou took'st for being 'sess'd at eighteenpence
For the waterwork.
   Drug.   In truth, and it was like
T' have cost me almost my life.

---

   [2] *vented:* spent.
   [3] *groom-porter:* officer in charge of royal gaming tables.
   [4] *canary:* sweet light wine from Canary Islands.
   [5] *affects:* likes.   [6] *cast:* fired.
   [7] *by . . . posts:* swiftly.   [8] *perspective:* magic glass.
   [9] *woad:* dye.   [10] *pass it:* let it pass.
   [11] *Seacoal Lane:* London street in poor district.
   [12] *sodden:* boiled.   [13] *pellitory . . . wall:* medicinal herb.

Face.   Thy hair went off?
Drug. Yes, sir; 'twas done for spite.
Face.   Nay, so says the
  doctor.
Kast. Pray thee, tobacco-boy, go fetch my suster;
I'll see this learnèd boy before I go;
And so shall she.
Face.   Sir, he is busy now,
But if you have a sister to fetch hither,   130
Perhaps your own pains may command her sooner;
And he by that time will be free.
Kast.   I go.
                                    [*Exit.*]
Face. Drugger, she's thine. The damask.
                          [*Exit* DRUGGER.]
                          [*Aside*] Subtle and I
Must wrestle for her.—Come on, Master Dapper,
You see how I turn clients here away,
To give your cause dispatch. Ha' you performed
The ceremonies were enjoined you?
Dap.   Yes, o' the vinegar,
And the clean shirt.
Face.   'Tis well; that shirt may do you
More worship than you think. Your aunt's afire,
But that she will not show it, t' have a sight on you.
Ha' you provided for her grace's servants?   141
Dap. Yes, here are six score Edward shillings.
Face. Good!
Dap.   And an old Harry's sovereign.
Face.   Very good!
Dap. And three James shillings, and an Elizabeth
  groat,
Just twenty nobles.
Face.   Oh, you are too just.
I would you had had the other noble in Maries.
Dap. I have some Philip and Maries.
Face.   Ay, those same
Are best of all; where are they? Hark, the doctor.

III.v

[*Enter*] SUBTLE, *disguised like a priest of Faery.*

[*Sub.*] Is yet her grace's cousin come?
Face.   He is come.
Sub. And is he fasting?
Face.   Yes.
Sub.   And hath cried "hum"?
Face. Thrice, you must answer.
Dap.   Thrice.
Sub.   And as oft "buz"?
Face. If you have, say.
Dap.   I have.
Sub.   Then, to her cuz,
Hoping that he hath vinegared his senses,
As he was bid, the Faery Queen dispenses,

By me, this robe, the petticoat of fortune;
Which that he straight put on, she doth importune.
And though to fortune near be her petticoat,
Yet nearer is her smock, the Queen doth note,   10
And therefore, even of that a piece she hath sent,
Which, being a child, to wrap him in was rent;
And prays him for a scarf he now will wear it,
With as much love as then her grace did tear it,
About his eyes, to show he is fortunate;

                  They blind him with a rag.

And, trusting unto her to make his state,[1]
He'll throw away all worldly pelf[2] about him;
Which that he will perform, she doth not doubt him.
Face. She need not doubt him, sir. Alas, he has
  nothing
But what he will part withal as willingly,   20
Upon her grace's word—throw away your purse—
As she would ask it—handkerchiefs and all—
She cannot bid that thing but he'll obey.—
If you have a ring about you, cast it off,
Or a silver seal at your wrist; her grace will send

                  He throws away, as they bid him.

Her fairies here to search you, therefore deal
Directly with her highness. If they find
That you conceal a mite, you are undone.
Dap. Truly, there's all.
Face.   All what?
Dap.   My money; truly.
Face. Keep nothing that is transitory about you.
[*Aside to* SUBTLE] Bid Dol play music.—Look, the
  elves are come   31

              DOL *enters with a cittern.*[3]

To pinch you, if you tell not truth. Advise you.

                        They pinch him.

Dap. Oh! I have a paper with a spur-royal[4] in't.
Face.   Ti, ti.
They knew't, they say.
Sub.   Ti, ti, ti, ti. He has more yet.
Face. Ti, ti-ti-ti. I' the tother pocket?
Sub.   Titi, titi, titi, titi.
They must pinch him or he will never confess, they say.

                  [*They pinch him again.*]

Dap. Oh, oh!
Face.   Nay, pray you, hold; he is her grace's
  nephew!
Ti, ti, ti? What care you? Good faith, you shall care.—
Deal plainly, sir, and shame the fairies. Show   39
You are an innocent.[5]
Dap.   By this good light, I ha' nothing.
Sub. Ti ti, ti ti to ta. He does equivocate,[6] she says:
Ti, ti do ti, ti ti do, ti da; and swears by the light when
  he is blinded.
Dap. By this good dark, I ha' nothing but a half-
  crown
Of gold about my wrist that my love gave me,
And a leaden heart I wore sin' she forsook me.

III.v.
  [1] *state:* fortune.   [2] *pelf:* goods, riches.
  [3] *cittern:* guitar-like instrument.
  [4] *spur-royal:* gold coin worth 16s.
  [5] *innocent:* guiltless person; fool.
  [6] *equivocate:* use language deceptively.

Face. I thought 'twas something. And would you incur
Your aunt's displeasure for these trifles? Come,
I had rather you had thrown away twenty half-crowns.

         [Takes it off.]

You may wear your leaden heart still.—How now!

     [Enter DOL.*]*

Sub. What news, Dol?
Dol Com.   Yonder's your knight, Sir
 Mammon.   50
Face. God's lid, we never thought of him till now!
Where is he?
Dol Com. Here, hard by. He's at the door.
Sub. And you are not ready now! Dol, get his suit.
          [Exit DOL.*]*
He must not be sent back.
 Face.   Oh, by no means.
What shall we do with this same puffin [7] here,
Now he's o' the spit?
 Sub.   Why, lay him back awhile,
With some device.

   [Re-enter DOL *with* FACE'S *clothes.]*

   —*Ti, ti ti, ti ti ti.* Would her grace
 speak with me?
I come.—Help, Dol!

   He [FACE] *speaks through the keyhole, the*
      other [MAMMON] *knocking.*

 Face.   Who's there? Sir Epicure,
My master's i' the way. Please you to walk
Three or four turns, but till his back be turned,   60
And I am for you.—Quickly, Dol!
 Sub.   Her grace
Commends her kindly to you, Master Dapper.
 Dap. I long to see her grace.
 Sub.   She now is set
At dinner in her bed, and she has sent you,
From her own private trencher, a dead mouse
And a piece of gingerbread, to be merry withal
And stay your stomach, lest you faint with fasting.
Yet if you could hold out till she saw you, she says,
It would be better for you.
 Face.   Sir, he shall
Hold out, an't were this two hours, for her highness;
I can assure you that. We will not lose   71
All we ha' done.—
 Sub.   He must nor see, nor speak
To anybody, till then.
 Face.   For that we'll put, sir,
A stay [8] in's mouth.
 Sub.   Of what?
 Face.   Of gingerbread.
Make you it fit. He that hath pleased her grace
Thus far, shall not now crinkle [9] for a little.—
Gape, sir, and let him fit you.

    [They gag him with gingerbread.]

 Sub.   Where shall we now

Bestow him?
 Dol Com. I' the privy.
 Sub.   Come along, sir,
I now must show you Fortune's privy lodgings.
 Face. Are they perfumed, and his bath ready?
 Sub.   All;
Only the fumigation's somewhat strong.   81

   *[*FACE *speaks through the keyhole.]*

 Face. Sir Epicure, I am yours, sir, by and by.
       [Exeunt with DAPPER.*]*

ACT FOUR

SCENE ONE

[FACE *admits* MAMMON.]

[Face.] Oh, sir, y' are come i' the only finest time—
Mam. Where's master?
Face.   Now preparing for
 projection, sir.
Your stuff will be all changed shortly.
 Mam.   Into gold?
 Face. To gold and silver, sir.
 Mam.   Silver I care not for.
 Face. Yes, sir, a little to give beggars.
 Mam.   Where's the lady?
 Face. At hand here. I ha' told her such brave things
 o' you,
Touching your bounty and your noble spirit—
 Mam.   Hast thou?
 Face. As she is almost in her fit to see you.
But, good sir, no divinity i' your conference,
For fear of putting her in rage.
 Mam.   I warrant thee.   10
 Face. Six men will not hold her down. And then,
If the old man should hear or see you—
 Mam.   Fear not.
 Face. The very house, sir, would run mad. You
 know it,
How scrupulous he is, and violent,
'Gainst the least act of sin. Physic or mathematics,
Poetry, state, or bawdry, as I told you,
She will endure, and never startle; but
No word of controversy.
 Mam.   I am schooled, good Ulen.
 Face. And you must praise her house, remember that
And her nobility.
 Mam.   Let me alone: 20
No herald, no, nor antiquary, Lungs,
Shall do it better. Go.
 Face. [*Aside*]   Why, this is yet
A kind of modern [1] happiness, to have
Dol Common for a great lady.

           [Exit.]

---

[7] *puffin:* sea-bird, puffed-up person.   [8] *stay:* gag.
[9] *crinkle:* shrink back.
IV.i.
 [1] *modern:* commonplace.

Mam.   Now, Epicure,
Heighten thyself, talk to her all in gold;
Rain her as many showers as Jove did drops
Unto his Danaë;[2] show the god a miser,
Compared with Mammon. What! the stone will do't.
She shall feel gold, taste gold, hear gold, sleep gold;
Nay, we will *concumbere*[3] gold. I will be puissant   30
And mighty in my talk to her.—

[*Re-enter* FACE *with* DOL *richly dressed.*]

                                        Here she comes.
Face. [*Aside to* DOL] To him, Dol, suckle him.—
          This is the noble knight
I told your ladyship—
Mam.   Madam, with your pardon,
I kiss your vesture.
Dol Com.   Sir, I were uncivil
If I would suffer that; my lip to you, sir.
   Mam. I hope my lord your brother be in health, lady.
   Dol Com. My lord my brother is, though I no lady,
          sir.
   Face. [*To* DOL] Well said, my Guinea bird.[4]
   Mam.   Right
          noble madam—
   Face. [*Aside*] Oh, we shall have most fierce idolatry.
   Mam. 'Tis your prerogative.
   Dol Com.   Rather your courtesy.
   Mam. Were there nought else t' enlarge your virtues
          to me,   41
These answers speak your breeding and your blood.
   Dol Com. Blood we boast none, sir; a poor baron's
          daughter.
   Mam. Poor! and gat you? Profane not. Had your
          father
Slept all the happy remnant of his life
After the act, lien but there still, and panted,
H'had done enough to make himself, his issue,
And his posterity noble.
   Dol Com.   Sir, although
We may be said to want the gilt and trappings,
The dress of honor, yet we strive to keep   50
The seeds and the materials.
   Mam.   I do see
The old ingredient, virtue, was not lost,
Nor the drug, money, used to make your compound.
There is a strange nobility i' your eye,
This lip, that chin! Methinks you do resemble
One o' the Austriac[5] princes.

Face. [*Aside*]   Very like,
Her father was an Irish costermonger.[6]
   Mam. The house of Valois, just, had such a nose,[7]
And such a forehead yet the Medici
Of Florence boast.
   Dol Com.   Troth, and I have been likened   60
To all these princes.
   Face. [*Aside*]   I'll be sworn, I heard it.
   Mam. I know not how! it is not any one,
But e'en the very choice of all their features.
   Face. [*Aside*] I'll in, and laugh.
                                        [*Exit.*]
   Mam.   A certain touch, or air,
That sparkles a divinity beyond
An earthly beauty!
   Dol Com.   Oh, you play the courtier.
   Mam. Good lady, gi' me leave—
   Dol Com.   In faith, I may not,
To mock me, sir.
   Mam.   To burn i' this sweet flame;
The phoenix never knew a nobler death.
   Dol Com. Nay, now you court the courtier, and
          destroy   70
What you would build. This art, sir, i' your words,
Calls your whole faith in question.
   Mam.   By my soul—
   Dol Com. Nay, oaths are made o' the same air, sir.
   Mam.   Nature
Never bestowed upon mortality
A more unblamed, a more harmonious feature,[8]
She played the step-dame in all faces else.
Sweet madam, le' me be particular—
   Dol Com. Particular, sir? I pray you, know your
          distance.
   Mam. In no ill sense, sweet lady, but to ask
How your fair graces pass the hours? I see   80
Y' are lodged here, i' the house of a rare man,
An excellent artist; but what's that to you?
   Dol Com. Yes, sir. I study here the mathematics,[9]
And distillation.[10]
   Mam.   Oh, I cry your pardon.
He's a divine instructor! can extract
The souls of all things by his art; call all
The virtues and the miracles of the sun
Into a temperate furnace; teach dull nature
What her own forces are. A man the emp'ror
Has courted above Kelley;[11] sent his medals   90
And chains t' invite him.
   Dol Com.   Ay, and for his physic,[12] sir—
   Mam. Above the art of Aesculapius,[13]
That drew the envy of the thunderer!
I know all this, and more.
   Dol Com.   Troth, I am taken, sir,
Whole with these studies that contemplate nature.
   Mam. It is a noble humor; but this form
Was not intended to so dark a use.
Had you been crooked, foul, of some coarse mould,
A cloister had done well; but such a feature,
That might stand up the glory of a kingdom,   100
To live recluse is a mere solecism,[14]
Though in a nunnery. It must not be.

---

[2] *Jove . . . Danaë:* Zeus took the form of a shower of gold
to visit the imprisoned daughter of the King of Argos, and
she became the mother of Perseus.   [3] *L.:* fornicate.
   [4] *Guinea bird:* prostitute.
   [5] *Austriac:* Habsburg, with large lower lips.
   [6] *costermonger:* appleseller.   [7] *nose:* i.e., Roman.
   [8] *feature:* composition.
   [9] *mathematics:* including astrology.
   [10] *distillation:* chemistry.
   [11] *Kelley:* Edward Kelley (1555–95), alchemist imprisoned
by Emperor Rudolph II after his failure to produce the
promised philosopher's stone.   [12] *physic:* medicine.
   [13] *Aesculapius:* in Greek mythology, killed by Zeus's
thunder for restoring the dead to life.
   [14] *solecism:* impropriety.

I muse my lord your brother will permit it!
You should spend half my land first, were I he.
Does not this diamond better on my finger
Than i' the quarry?
   Dol Com.   Yes.
   Mam.   Why, you are like it.
You were created, lady, for the light.
Here, you shall wear it; take it, the first pledge
Of what I speak, to bind you to believe me.
   Dol Com.   In chains of adamant?
   Mam.   Yes, the strongest
   bands.   110
And take a secret too.—Here, by your side,
Doth stand this hour the happiest man in Europe.
   Dol Com.   You are contented, sir?
   Mam.   Nay, in true being,
The envy of princes and the fear of states.
   Dol Com.   Say you so, Sir Epicure?
   Mam.   Yes, and thou
   shalt prove it,
Daughter of honor. I have cast mine eye
Upon thy form, and I will rear this beauty
Above all styles.
   Dol Com.   You mean no treason, sir?
   Mam. No, I will take away that jealousy.¹⁵
I am the lord of the philosopher's stone,   120
And thou the lady.
   Dol Com.   How, sir! ha' you that?
   Mam. I am the master of the mastery.
This day the good old wretch here o' the house
Has made it for us. Now he's at projection.
Think therefore thy first wish now, let me hear it;
And it shall rain into thy lap, no shower,
But floods of gold, whole cataracts, a deluge,
To get a nation on thee.
   Dol Com.   You are pleased, sir,
To work on the ambition of our sex.
   Mam. I'm pleased the glory of her sex should know,
This nook here of the Friars is no climate   131
For her to live obscurely in, to learn
Physic and surgery, for the constable's wife
Of some odd hundred¹⁶ in Essex; but come forth,
And taste the air of palaces; eat, drink
The toils of emp'rics,¹⁷ and their boasted practice;
Tincture of pearl, and coral, gold, and amber;
Be seen at feasts and triumphs; have it asked,
What miracle she is; set all the eyes
Of court a-fire, like a burning-glass,   140
And work 'em into cinders, when the jewels
Of twenty states adorn thee, and the light
Strikes out the stars; that, when they name is
   mentioned,
Queens may look pale; and, we but showing our love,
Nero's Poppaea¹⁸ may be lost in story!
Thus will we have it.
   ·*Dol Com.*   I could well consent, sir.
But in a monarchy, how will this be?
The prince will soon take notice, and both seize
You and your stone, it being a wealth unfit
For any private subject.
   Mam.   If he knew it.   150

   Dol Com. Yourself do boast it, sir.
   Mam.   To thee, my life.
   Dol Com. Oh, but beware, sir! you may come to end
The remnant of your days in a loathed prison
By speaking of it.
   Mam.   'Tis no idle fear!
We'll therefore go with all, my girl, and live
In a free state, where we will eat our mullets,
Soused in high-country wines, sup pheasants' eggs,
And have our cockles boiled in silver shells;
Our shrimps to swim again, as when they lived,
In a rare butter made of dolphins' milk,   160
Whose cream does look like opals; and with these
Delicate meats set ourselves high for pleasure,
And take us down again, and then renew
Our youth and strength with drinking the elixir,
And so enjoy a perpetuity
Of life and lust. And thou shalt ha' thy wardrobe
Richer than Nature's, still to change thyself,
And vary oft'ner for thy pride than she,
Or Art, her wise and almost-equal servant.

               [*Re-enter* FACE.]

   Face. Sir, you are too loud. I hear you every word
Into the laboratory. Some fitter place;   171
The garden, or great chamber. [*Aside*] How like you
   her?
   Mam. Excellent, Lungs! there's for thee.

               [*Gives him money.*]

   Face.   But do you
   hear?
Good sir, beware, no mention of the rabbins.¹⁹
   Mam. We think not on 'em.
   Face.   Oh, it is well, sir.
           [*Exeunt* MAMMON *and* DOL.]
               —Subtle!

IV.ii

              [*Enter* SUBTLE.]

[*Face.*] Dost thou not laugh?
   Sub.   Yes; are they gone?
   Face.   All's clear.
   Sub. The widow is come.
   Face.   And your quarreling
   disciple?
   Sub. Ay.
   Face. I must to my captainship again then.
   Sub. Stay, bring 'em in first.
   Face.   So I meant. What is she?
A bonnibel?¹

---

¹⁵ *jealousy:* suspicion.
¹⁶ *hundred:* subdivision of a county.
¹⁷ *emp'rics:* applied scientists.
¹⁸ *Poppaea:* to marry her, Nero murdered his own wife
and mother; he later killed her too.
¹⁹ *rabbins:* Jewish biblical scholars.
IV.ii.
  ¹ *bonnibel:* pretty girl.

Sub. I know not.

Face. We'll draw lots;
You'll stand to that?

Sub. What else?

Face. Oh, for a suit,[2]
To fall now like a curtain flap!

Sub. To th' door, man.

Face. You'll ha' the first kiss, 'cause I am not ready.
                                                    [*Exit.*]

Sub. Yes, and perhaps hit you through the nostrils.[3]

Face. [*Within*] Who would you speak with?

Kast. [*Within*]   Where's
    the captain?

Face. [*Within*] Gone, sir,   10
About some business.

Kast. [*Within*]   Gone?

Face. [*Within*]   He'll return straight.
But master doctor, his lieutenant, is here.

[*Enter* KASTRIL, *followed by* DAME PLIANT.]

Sub. Come near, my worshipful boy, my *terrae fili*,[4]
That is, my boy of land; make thy approaches.
Welcome; I know thy lusts[5] and thy desires,
And I will serve and satisfy 'em. Begin,
Charge me from thence, or thence, or in this line;
Here is my center; ground thy quarrel.

Kas.   You lie.

Sub. How, child of wrath and anger! the loud lie?
For what, my sudden boy?

Kas.   Nay, that look you to,   20
I am aforehand.

Sub.   Oh, this's no true grammar,
And as ill logic! You must render causes, child,
Your first and second intentions, know your canons
And your divisions, moods, degrees, and differences,
Your predicaments, substance, and accident,
Series extern and intern, with their causes
Efficient, material, formal, final,
And ha' your elements perfect—[6]

Kast.   What is this?
The angry tongue he talks in?

Sub.   That false precept,
Of being aforehand, has deceived a number,   30
And made 'em enter quarrels oftentimes
Before they were aware; and afterward,
Against their wills.

Kast.   How must I do then, sir?

Sub. I cry this lady mercy; she should first
Have been saluted. I do call you lady,

Because you are to be one ere't be long,
My soft and buxom widow.

                                    He kisses her.

Kast.   Is she, i' faith?

Sub. Yes, or my art is an egregious liar.

Kast. How know you?

Sub.   By inspection on her forehead,
And subtlety[7] of her lip, which must be tasted   40
Often to make a judgment.

                                He kisses her again.

                        'Slight, she melts
Like a myrobolane.[8] Here is yet a line,
In *rivo frontis*,[9] tells me he is no knight.

Dame Pli. What is he then, sir?

Sub.   Let me see your hand.
Oh, your *linea fortunae*[10] makes it plain;
And *stella* here *in monte veneris*.[11]
But, most of all, *junctura annularis*.[12]
He is a soldier, or a man of art, lady,
But shall have some great honor shortly.

Dame Pli.   Brother,
He's a rare man, believe me!

[*Re-enter* FACE, *in his uniform.*]

Kast.   Hold your peace.   50
Here comes the tother rare man.—'Save you, captain.

Face. Good Master Kastril! is this your sister?

Kast.   Ay, sir.
Please you to kuss her, and be proud to know her.

Face. I shall be proud to know you, lady.

                                    [*Kisses her.*]

Dame Pli.   Brother,
He calls me lady, too.

Kast.   Ay, peace; I heard it.

                                    [*Takes her aside.*]

Face. The count is come.

Sub.   Where is he?

Face.   At the door.

Sub. Why, you must entertain him.

Face.   What'll you do
With these the while?

Sub.   Why, have 'em up, and show 'em
Some fustian[13] book, or the dark glass.[14]

Face.   'Fore God,
She is a delicate dabchick! I must have her.   60
                                    [*Exit.*]

Sub. [*Aside*] Must you! Ay, if your fortune will,
    you must.—
Come, sir, the captain will come to us presently.
I'll ha' you to my chamber of demonstrations,
Where I'll show you both the grammar and logic
And rhetoric of quarreling; my whole method
Drawn out in tables; and my instrument,
That hath the several scale upon't, shall make you
Able to quarrel at a straw's breadth by moonlight.
And, lady, I'll have you look in a glass,
Some half an hour, but to clear your eyesight,   70

---

[2] *suit:* i.e., his captain's uniform.
[3] *hit . . . nostrils:* put your nose out of joint.
[4] *L.:* son of earth; low-born person; spirit in alchemy.
[5] *lusts:* desires.
[6] *you . . . perfect:* Subtle teaches Kastril in the jargon of
Scholastic logic.
[7] *subtlety:* pun—an elaborate confectionery.
[8] *myrobolane:* sugar plum.   [9] *L.:* frontal vein.
[10] *L.:* line of fortune.
[11] *L.:* "star on the hill of Venus," at the base of the thumb.
[12] *L.:* joint of the ring-finger.
[13] *fustian:* worthless, pretentious.
[14] *dark glass:* fortune-teller's crystal.

Against [15] you see your fortune; which is greater
Than I may judge upon the sudden, trust me.

                 [Exeunt.]

IV.iii

        [Enter FACE.*]*

[Face.] Where are you, doctor?
Sub. *[Within]*   I'll come to you
  presently.
   Face. I will ha' this same widow, now I ha' seen her,
On any composition.[1]

        [Enter SUBTLE.*]*

   Sub.   What do you say?
   Face. Ha' you disposed of them?
   Sub.   I ha' sent 'em up.
   Face. Subtle, in troth, I needs must have this widow.
   Sub. Is that the matter?
   Face.   Nay, but hear me.
   Sub.   Go to.
If you rebel once, Dol shall know it all.
Therefore be quiet, and obey your chance.
   Face. Nay, thou art so violent now. Do but conceive,
Thou art old, and canst not serve[2]—
   Sub.   Who cannot? I?
'Slight, I will serve her with thee, for a—
   Face.   Nay,   11
But understand; I'll gi' you composition.
   Sub. I will not treat with thee. What! sell my
  fortune?
'Tis better than my birthright. Do not murmur.
Win her, and carry her. If you grumble, Dol
Knows it directly.
   Face.   Well, sir, I am silent.
Will you go help to fetch in Don in state?

                 [Exit.]

   Sub. I follow you, sir. We must keep Face in awe,
Or he will overlook[3] us like a tyrant.

   [Re-enter FACE, *introducing* SURLY *disguised as a
            Spanish nobleman.]*

Brain of a tailor! who comes here? Don John![4]   20
   Sur. Señores, beso las manos à vuestras mercedes.[5]
   Sub. Would you had stooped a little, and kissed our
  anos.
   Face. Peace, Subtle!
   Sub.   Stab me; I shall never hold,
  man.
He looks in that deep ruff like a head in a platter,
Served in by a short cloak upon two trestles.
   Face. Or what do you say to a collar of brawn,[6] cut
  down
Beneath the souse,[7] and wriggled with a knife?
   Sub. 'Slud, he does look too fat to be a Spaniard.
   Face. Perhaps some Fleming or some Hollander got
  him   29
In d'Alva's[8] time; Count Egmont's[9] bastard.
   Sub.   Don,
Your scurvy, yellow, Madrid face is welcome.
   Sur. Gratia.[10]

   Sub.   He speaks out of a fortification.
Pray God he ha' no squibs[11] in those deep sets.[12]
   Sur. Por dios, señores, muy linda casa![13]
   Sub. What says he?
   Face.   Praises the house, I think;
I know no more but's action.
   Sub.   Yes, the *casa*,
My precious Diego,[14] will prove fair enough
To cozen you in. Do you mark? You shall
Be cozened, Diego.
   Face.   Cozened, do you see,
My worthy Donzel,[15] cozened.
   Sur.   Entiendo.[16]   40
   Sub. Do you intend it? So do we, dear Don.
Have you brought pistolets or portagues,
My solemn Don? *[To* FACE*]* Dost thou feel any?

             He feels his pockets.

   Face.   Full.
   Sub. You shall be emptied, Don, pumped and drawn
Dry, as they say.
   Face.   Milked, in troth, sweet Don.
   Sub. See all the monsters; the great lion[17] of all,
  Don.
   Sur. Con licencia, se puede ver à esta señora?[18]
   Sub. What talks he now?
   Face.   O' the señora.
   Sub.   Oh, Don,
That is the lioness, which you shall see
Also, my Don.
   Face.   'Slid, Subtle, how shall we do?   50
   Sub. For what?
   Face.   Why, Dol's employed, you know.
   Sub.   That's true.
'Fore heav'n I know not: he must stay,[19] that's all.
   Face. Stay? that he must not by no means.
   Sub.   No! why?
   Face. Unless you'll mar all. 'Slight, he'll suspect it;
And then he will not pay, not half so well.
This is a travelled punk-master, and does know
All the delays; a notable hot rascal,
And looks already rampant.
   Sub.   'Sdeath, and Mammon
Must not be troubled.
   Face.   Mammon! in no case.

---

[15] *Against:* until.
IV.iii.
[1] *composition:* terms.   [2] *serve:* i.e., sexually.
[3] *overlook:* dominate.
[4] *Don John:* Spaniard (contemptuous).
[5] *Sp.:* Gentlemen, I kiss your hands.
[6] *collar of brawn:* pig's-neck meat.   [7] *souse:* ear.
[8] *d'Alva:* governor of Netherlands, 1567–73.
[9] *Egmont:* Flemish patriot executed by D'Alva in 1568.
[10] *Sp.:* Gracias, thank you.   [11] *squibs:* explosives.
[12] *sets:* pleats.
[13] *Sp.:* By God, sirs, a very pretty house.
[14] *Diego:* Spaniard.   [15] *Donzel:* little Don.
[16] *Sp.:* I understand.
[17] *lion:* one of those shown to tourists in the Tower of
London.
[18] *Sp.:* If you please, may I see this lady?
[19] *stay:* wait.

Sub. What shall we do then?

Face.   Think: you must be
sudden.   60

*Sur. Entiendo que la señora es tan hermosa, que
codìcio tan à verla como la bien aventuranza de mi vida.*[20]

Face. Mi vida! 'Slid, Subtle, he puts me in mind o'
the widow.

What dost thou say to draw her to 't, ha!
And tell her it is her fortune? All our venture
Now lies upon't. It is but one man more,
Which on's[21] chance to have her: and beside,
There is no maidenhead to be feared or lost.
What dost thou think on't, Subtle?

Sub.   Who, I? Why—

Face. The credit of our house, too, is engaged.   70

Sub. You made me an offer for my share erewhile.
What wilt thou gi' me, i'faith?

Face.   Oh, by that light,
I'll not buy now. You know your doom to me.
E'en take your lot, obey your chance, sir; win her,
And wear her out for me.

Sub.   'Slight, I'll not work[22] her
then.

Face. It is the common cause; therefore bethink
you.

Dol else must know it, as you said.

Sub.   I care not.

Sur. Señores, porque se tarda tanto?[23]

Sub. Faith, I am not fit, I am old.

Face.   That's now no
reason, sir.

Sur. Puede ser de hazer burla de mi amor?[24]   80

Face. You hear the Don too? By this air, I call,
And loose the hinges.[25] Dol!

Sub.   A plague of hell—

Face. Will you then do?

Sub.   Y'are a terrible rogue!
I'll think of[26] this. Will you, sir, call the widow?

Face. Yes, and I'll take her, too, with all her faults,
Now I do think on't better.

Sub.   With all my heart, sir;
Am I discharged o' the lot?

Face.   As you please.

Sub.   Hands.

[They shake hands.]

---

[20] *Sp.:* I understand that the lady is so beautiful that I am anxious to see her as the high fortune of my life.
[21] *Which on's:* Whichever of us.   [22] *work:* work on.
[23] *Sp.:* Gentlemen, why so much delay?
[24] *Sp.:* Perhaps you make fun of my love?
[25] *loose . . . hinges:* i.e., of our fellowship.
[26] *think of:* remember.
[27] *Sp.:* By this honored beard.
[28] *Sp.:* I fear, gentlemen, that you're playing some trick on me.   [29] *Sp.:* right away, sir.
[30] *fubbed:* cheated.   [31] *flawed:* flayed.
[32] *tawed:* soaked.

IV.iv.
[1] *nick:* critical point.   [2] *Stoop:* Bow.
[3] *garb:* fashion.   [4] *pavane:* stately Spanish dance.
[5] *titillation:* perfume.   [6] *scheme:* horoscope.

Face. Remember now, that upon any change
You never claim her.

Sub.   Much good joy and health to you,
sir.

Marry a whore! Fate, let me wed a witch first.   90

Sur. Por estas honradas barbas—[27]

Sub.   He swears by his
beard.

Dispatch, and call the brother, too.

[Exit FACE.]

Sur.   *Tengo dúda, señores,
Que no me hágan alguna traycion.*[28]

Sub. How, issue on? Yes, *presto, señor.*[29] Please you
Enthratha the *chambratha,* worthy Don,
Where if you please the fates, in your *bathada,*
You shall be soaked, and stroked, and tubbed, and
rubbed,
And scrubbed, and fubbed,[30] dear Don, before you go.
You shall in faith, my scurvy baboon Don,
Be curried, clawed, and flawed,[31] and tawed,[32] indeed.
I will the heartilier go about it now,   101
And make the widow a punk so much the sooner,
To be revenged on this impetuous Face:
The quickly doing of it is the grace.

[Exeunt SUBTLE and SURLY.]

IV.iv

[Enter FACE, KASTRIL and DAME PLIANT.]

[Face.] Come, lady. *[To KASTRIL]* I knew the
doctor would not leave
Till he had found the very nick[1] of her fortune.

Kast. To be a countess, say you?

Face.   A Spanish countess, sir.

Dame Pli. Why, is that better than an English
countess?

Face. Better! 'Slight, make you that a question, lady?

Kast. Nay, she is a fool, captain, you must pardon
her.

Face. Ask him from your courtier to your inns-of-
courtman,
To your mere milliner; they will tell you all,
Your Spanish jennet is the best horse; your Spanish
Stoop[2] is the best garb;[3] your Spanish beard   10
Is the best cut; your Spanish ruffs are the best
Wear; your Spanish pavane[4] the best dance;
Your Spanish titillation[5] in a glove
The best perfume; and for your Spanish pike
And Spanish blade, let your poor captain speak.
Here comes the doctor.

[Enter SUBTLE with a paper.]

Sub.   My most honored lady,
For so I am now to style you, having found
By this my scheme,[6] you are to undergo
An honorable fortune very shortly,   19
What will you say now, if some—

Face.   I ha' told her all, sir,
And her right worshipful brother here, that she shall be
A countess; do not delay 'em, sir; a Spanish countess

Sub. Still, my scarce-worshipful captain, you can keep
No secret. Well, since he has told you, madam,
Do you forgive him, and I do.
Kast. She shall do that, sir;
I'll look to't; 'tis my charge.
Sub. Well, then, nought rests
But that she fit her love now to her fortune.
Dame Pli. Truly I shall never brook a Spaniard.
Sub. No?
Dame Pli. Never, sin' eighty-eight,[7] could I abide 'em,   29
And that was some three year afore I was born, in truth.
Sub. Come, you must love him, or be miserable;
Choose which you will.
Face. By this good rush,[8] persuade her.
She will cry strawberries[9] else within this twelvemonth.
Sub. Nay, shads and mackerel, which is worse.
Face. Indeed, sir!
Kast. God's lid, you shall love him, or I'll kick you.
Dame Pli. Why, I'll do as you will ha' me, brother.
Kast. Do, Or by this hand I'll maul you.
Face. Nay, good sir, Be not so fierce.
Sub. No, my enragèd child;
She will be ruled. What, when she comes to taste
The pleasure of a countess! to be courted—   40
Face. And kissed and ruffled![10]
Sub. Ay, behind the hangings.
Face. And then come forth in pomp!
Sub. And know her state!
Face. Of keeping all th' idolators o' the chamber
Barer to her[11] than at their prayers!
Sub. Is served Upon the knee!
Face. And has her pages, ushers, Footmen, and coaches—
Sub. Her six mares—
Face. Nay, eight!
Sub. To hurry her through London, to th' Exchange,[12]
Bet'lem,[13] the China-houses[14]—
Face. Yes, and have
The citizens gape at her, and praise her tires,[15]
And my lord's goose-turd bands,[16] that rides with her!
Kast. Most brave! By this hand, you are not my suster   51
If you refuse.
Dame Pli. I will not refuse, brother.

[*Enter* SURLY.]

Sur. Que es esto, señores, que non se venga?
Esta tardanza me mata![17]
Face. It is the count come!
The doctor knew he would be here, by his art.

Sub. En gallanta madama, Don! gallantissima![18]
Sur. Por todos los dioses, la mas acabada
Hermosura, que he visto en mi vida![19]
Face. Is't not a gallant language that they speak?
Kast. An admirable language! Is't not French?   60
Face. No, Spanish, sir.
Kast. It goes like law-French?
And that, they say, is the courtliest language.
Face. List, sir.
Sur. El sol ha perdido su lumbre, con el
Resplandor que tràe esta dama! Válgame dios![21]
Face. H'admires your sister.
Kast. Must not she make curt'sy?
Sub. 'Ods will, she must go to him, man, and kiss him!
It is the Spanish fashion for the women
To make first court.
Face. 'Tis true he tells you, sir;
His art knows all.
Sur. Porqué no se acùde?[22]   69
Kast. He speaks to her, I think.
Face. That he does, sir.
Sur. Por el amor de díos, qué es esto que se tarda?[23]
Kast. Nay, see: she will not understand him! gull, Noddy!
Dame Pli. What say you, brother?
Kast. Ass, my suster,
Go kuss him, as the cunning man would ha' you;
I'll thrust a pin i' your buttocks else.
Face. Oh, no, sir.
Sur. Señora mia, mi persona muy indigna esta
Allegar à tanta hermosura.[24]
Face. Does he not use her bravely?
Kast. Bravely, i' faith!
Face. Nay, he will use her better.
Kast. Do you think so?
Sur. Señora, si sera servida, entremos.[25]   80
[*Exit with* DAME PLIANT.]
Kast. Where does he carry her?
Face. Into the garden, sir;
Take you no thought. I must interpret for her.

---

[7] *eighty-eight:* year of the Armada.
[8] *rush:* bit of floor covering.
[9] *cry strawberries:* be a fruit-seller.   [10] *ruffled:* tousled.
[11] *Barer to her:* hats off in sign of respect.
[12] *Exchange:* the New Exchange in the Strand, market area.   [13] *Bet'lem:* Bethlehem Hospital for the insane.
[14] *China-houses:* shops purveying oriental luxuries.
[15] *tires:* clothes.
[16] *goose-turd bands:* greenish-yellow collars.
[17] *Sp.:* Why doesn't she come, gentlemen? The delay is killing me.   [18] *Sp.:* A fine madam, Don! Very fine.
[19] *Sp.:* By all the gods, the most perfect beauty I have seen in my life.
[20] *law-French:* degenerate Norman French still used then in the courts.
[21] *Sp.:* The sun has lost his light with the splendor the lady brings, God bless me!
[22] *Sp.:* Why doesn't she come to me?
[23] *Sp.:* For the love of God, why does she delay?
[24] *Sp.:* Lady, my person is quite unworthy to approach such beauty.
[25] *Sp.:* Lady, if it is convenient to you, let us go in.

Sub. [*Aside to* FACE] Give Dol the word.[26]

[*Exit* FACE.]

—Come,
my fierce child, advance,
We'll to our quarreling lesson again.
  Kast.   Agreed.
I love a Spanish boy with all my heart.
  Sub. Nay, and by this means, sir, you shall be
    brother
To a great count.
  Kast.   Ay, I knew that at first.
This match will advance the house of the Kastrils.
  Sub. 'Pray God your sister prove but pliant.
  Kast.   Why,
Her name is so, by her other husband.
  Sub.   How!   90
  Kast. The Widow Pliant. Knew you not that?
  Sub.   No,
    faith, sir;
Yet, by the erection of her figure,[27] I guessed it.
Come, let's go practice.
  Kast.   Yes, but do you think, doctor,
I e'er shall quarrel well?
  Sub.   I warrant you.

[*Exeunt.*]

IV.v

[*Enter* DOL *followed by* MAMMON.]

In her fit of talking.

[*Dol Com.*] For, after Alexander's death—
  Mam.   Good lady—
  Dol Com. That Perdiccas and Antigonus were slain,
The two that stood, Seleuc' and Ptolemy[1]—
  Mam.   Madam—
  Dol Com. Made up the two legs, and the fourth beast,
That was Gog-north and Egypt-south: which after
Was called Gog-iron-leg and South-iron-leg—
  Mam.   Lady—
  Dol Com. And then Gog-hornèd. So was Egypt, too
Then Egypt-clay-leg, and Gog-clay-leg—
  Mam.   Sweet madam—
  Dol Com. And last Gog-dust, and Egypt-dust, which
    fall

---

[26] *word:* i.e., the cue to go mad.
[27] *figure:* horoscope, with pun.

IV.v.
  [1] *Perdiccas . . . Ptolemy:* the four generals of Alexander the Great, interpreted by scholars as the four kingdoms in Daniel's interpretation of Nebuchadnezzar's dream (ll. 4–10).
  [2] *chain:* historical period in Broughton's scheme.
  [3] *Salem:* Jerusalem.   [4] *Eber:* originator of Hebrew.
  [5] *Javan:* in the family line of those who first spoke the gentile languages.
  [6] *lay:* quiet, with pun.
  [7] *Talmud:* repository of Jewish law and scriptural interpretation.
  [8] *Helen's . . . Cittim:* pedantry garbled from Broughton.
  [9] *Kimchi:* twelfth-century Jewish biblical scholar.
  [10] *Onkelos:* first-century Old Testament scholar.
  [11] *Aben Ezra:* Rabbi Ben Ezra, eleventh-century scholar of biblical materials in Arabic.

In the last link of the fourth chain.[2] And these   10
Be stars in story, which none see, or look at—
  Mam. What shall I do?
  Dol Com.   For, as he says, except
We call the rabbins, and the heathen Greeks—
  Mam. Dear lady—
  Dol Com.   To come from Salem,[3] and from
    Athens,
And teach the people of Great Britain—

[*Enter* FACE, *in his laboratory assistant's dress.*]

  Face.   What's the
    matter, sir?
  Dol Com. To speak the tongue of Eber[4] and
    Javan—[5]
  Mam.   Oh,
She's in her fit.
  Dol Com.   We shall know nothing—
  Face.   Death, sir,
We are undone!
  Dol Com.   Where then a learnèd linguist
Shall see the ancient used communion
Of vowels and consonants—
  Face.   My master will hear! 20
  Dol Com. A wisdom, which Pythagoras held most
    high—
  Mam. Sweet honorable lady!
  Dol Com.   To comprise
All sounds of voices in few marks of letters.
  Face. Nay, you must never hope to lay[6] her now.

They speak together.

Dol Com. And so we may arrive by Talmud[7] skill,	*Face.* How did you put her onto 't?
	Mam. Alas, I talked
And profane Greek, to raise the building up	Of a fifth monarchy I would erect
Of Helen's house against the Ismaelite	With the philosopher's stone, by chance, and she
King of Thogarma, and his habergions	Falls on the other four straight.
	Face. Out of Broughton!
Brimstony, blue, and fiery; and the force	I told you so. 'Slid, stop her mouth.
	Mam. Is't best?
Of king Abaddon, and the beast of Cittim:[8] 30	*Face.* She'll never leave else. If the old man hear her, 30
Which rabbi David Kimchi,[9] Onkelos,[10]	We are but faeces, ashes.
	Sub. [*Within*] What's to do there?
And Aben Ezra[11] do interpret Rome.	*Face.* Oh, we are lost! now she hears him, she is quiet.

Upon SUBTLE's *entry they disperse.* [*Exeunt* FACE *and* DOL.]

  Mam. Where shall I hide me!
  Sub.   How! what sight is
    here?
Close deeds of darkness, and that shun the light!
Bring him again. Who is he? What, my son!
Oh, I have lived too long.
  Mam.   Nay, good, dear father,
There was no unchaste purpose.
  Sub.   Not? And flee me

When I come in?
Mam.   That was my error.
Sub.   Error?
Guilt, guilt, my son; give it the right name. No marvel
If I found check in our great work within,   40
When such affairs as these were managing!
  Mam. Why, have you so?
  Sub.   It has stood still this half
    hour,
And all the rest of our less works gone back.
Where is the instrument of wickedness,
My lewd false drudge?
  Mam.   Nay, good sir, blame not him;
Believe me, 'twas against his will or knowledge.
I saw her by chance.
  Sub.   Will you commit more sin,
T'excuse a varlet?
  Mam.   By my hope, 'tis true, sir.
  Sub. Nay, then I wonder less, if you, for whom
The blessing was prepared, would so tempt heaven,
And lose your fortunes.
  Mam.   Why, sir?
  Sub.   This'll retard   51
The work a month at least.
  Mam.   Why, if it do,
What remedy? But think it not, good father;
Our purposes were honest.
  Sub.   As they were,
So the reward will prove.

                A great crack and noise within.

                          How now! ay me!
God and all saints be good to us.—

                    [*Re-enter* FACE.]

                              What's that?
  Face. Oh, sir, we are defeated! All the works
Are flown *in fumo*,[12] every glass is burst!
Furnace and all rent down, as if a bolt
Of thunder had been driven through the house.   60
Retorts, receivers, pelicans, bolt-heads,
All struck in shivers! Help, good sir! alas,

            SUBTLE *falls down, as in a swoon.*

Coldness and death invades him. Nay, Sir Mammon,
Do the fair offices of a man! you stand
As you were readier to depart than he.

                          One knocks.

Who's there? My lord her brother is come.
  Mam.   Ha, Lungs!
  Face. His coach is at the door. Avoid his sight,
For he's as furious as his sister is mad.
  Mam. Alas!
  Face.   My brain is quite undone with the fume,
    sir,
I ne'er must hope to be mine own man again.   70
  Mam. Is all lost, Lungs? Will nothing be preserved
Of all our cost?
  Face.   Faith, very little, sir;
A peck of coals or so, which is cold comfort, sir.

  Mam. Oh, my voluptuous mind! I am justly
    punished.
  Face. And so am I, sir.
  Mam.   Cast from all my hopes—
  Face. Nay, certainties, sir.
  Mam.   By mine own base affections.

          SUBTLE *seems come to himself.*

  Sub. Oh, the curst fruits of vice and lust!
  Mam.   Good father,
It was my sin. Forgive it.
  Sub.   Hangs my roof
Over us still, and will not fall, O justice,
Upon us, for this wicked man!
  Face.   Nay, look, sir,   80
You grieve him now with staying in his sight.
Good sir, the nobleman will come too, and take you,
And that may breed a tragedy.
  Mam.   I'll go.
  Face. Ay, and repent at home, sir. It may be,
For some good penance you may ha' it yet;
A hundred pound to the box at Bet'lem—
  Mam.   Yes.
  Face. For the restoring such as ha' their wits.
  Mam.   I'll do't.
  Face. I'll send one to you to receive it.
  Mam.   Do.
Is no projection left?
  Face.   All flown, or stinks, sir.
  Mam. Will nought be saved that's good for med'cine,
    think'st thou?   90
  Face. I cannot tell, sir. There will be perhaps
Something about the scraping of the shards,
Will cure the itch,—though not your itch of mind, sir.
It shall be saved for you, and sent home. Good sir,
This way, for fear the lord should meet you.
                              [*Exit* MAMMON.]
  Sub.   Face!
  Face. Ay.
  Sub.   Is he gone?
  Face.   Yes, and as heavily
As all the gold he hoped for were in his blood.
Let us be light though.
  Sub.   Ay, as balls, and bound
And hit our heads against the roof for joy:
There's so much of our care now cast away.   100
  Face. Now to our Don.
  Sub. Yes, your young widow by this time
Is made a countess, Face; she's been in travail
Of a young heir for you.
  Face.   Good, sir.
  Sub.   Off with your case,[13]
And greet her kindly, as a bridegroom should,
After these common hazards.
  Face.   Very well, sir.
Will you go fetch Don Diego off the while?
  Sub. And fetch him over[14] too, if you'll be pleased,
    sir.

---

[12] *L.:* in smoke.   [13] *case:* disguise.
[14] *fetch . . . over:* get the better of him.

Would Dol were in her place, to pick his pockets now!
    Face. Why, you can do it as well, if you would set
       to't.   110
I pray you prove your virtue.
    Sub.   For your sake, sir.
                                  [Exeunt.]

IV.vi

[Enter SURLY *as a Spaniard and* DAME PLIANT.*]*

    [Sur.] Lady, you see into what hands you are fall'n;
'Mongst what a nest of villains! and how near
Your honor was t'have catched a certain clap,[1]
Through your credulity, had I but been
So punctually forward, as place, time,
And other circumstance would ha' made a man;
For y'are a handsome woman; would you were wise too.
I am a gentleman come here disguised,
Only to find the knaveries of this citadel;
And where I might have wronged your honor, and have
    not,   10
I claim some interest in your love. You are,
They say, a widow, rich; and I'm a bachelor,
Worth nought. Your fortunes may make me a man,
As mine ha' preserved you a woman. Think upon it,
And whether I have deserved you or no.
    Dame Pli.   I will, sir.
    Sur. And for these household-rogues, let me alone
To treat with them.

                    [Enter SUBTLE.*]*

    Sub.   How doth my noble Diego,
And my dear madam countess? Hath the count
Been courteous, lady? Liberal and open?
Donzel, methinks you look melancholic,   20
After your *coitum*, and scurvy! truly,
I do not like the dullness of your eye;
It hath a heavy cast, 'tis upsee Dutch,[2]
And says you are a lumpish[3] whore-master.
Be lighter, I will make your pockets so.

               He falls to picking of them.

    Sur. Will you, Don Bawd and Pick-purse?

               [Knocks him down.]

                    How now!
    reel you?
Stand up, sir, you shall find, since I am so heavy,
I'll gi' you equal weight.
    Sub.   Help! murder!
    Sur.   No, sir,
There's no such thing intended. A good cart

IV.vi.
  [1] *clap:* gonorrhea; i.e., trouble.
  [2] *upsee Dutch:* in the manner of the Dutch.
  [3] *lumpish:* dull.
  [4] *cart . . . whip:* punishment for bawds.
  [5] *parcel-broker:* part-broker.
  [6] *touch:* touchstone, used to test gold.
  [7] *ephemerides:* astronomical almanacs.
  [8] *green sickness:* anemia.

And a clean whip[4] shall ease you of that fear.   30
I am the Spanish Don that should be cozened,
Do you see? Cozened? Where's your Captain Face,
That parcel-broker,[5] and whole-bawd, all rascal?

        [Enter FACE *in his uniform.]*

    Face. How, Surly!
    Sur.   Oh, make your approach, good
       captain.
I've found from whence your copper rings and spoons
Come now, wherewith you cheat abroad in taverns.
'Twas here you learned t'anoint your boot with
    brimstone,
Then rub men's gold on't for a kind of touch,[6]
And say 'twas naught, when you had changed the
    color,
That you might ha't for nothing. And this doctor,   40
Your sooty, smoky-bearded compeer, he
Will close you so much gold in a bolt's-head
And, on a turn, convey i' the stead another
With sublimed mercury, that shall burst i' the heat,
And fly out all *in fumo!* then weeps Mammon;
Then swoons his worship. Or, he is the Faustus,
                  *[FACE *slips out.]*
That casteth figures and can conjure, cures
Plagues, piles, and pox, by the ephemerides,[7]
And holds intelligence with all the bawds
And midwives of three shires; while you send in—   50
Captain!—What! is he gone?—damsels with child,
Wives that are barren, or the waiting-maid
With the green sickness.[8]

        [Seizes SUBTLE *as he is escaping.]*

      —Nay, sir, you must tarry,
Though he be scaped; and answer by the ears, sir.

IV.vii

       [Re-enter FACE *with* KASTRIL.*]*

    [Face.] Why, now's the time, if ever you will quarrel
Well, as they say, and be a true-born child.
The doctor and your sister both are abused.
    Kast. Where is he? Which is he? He is a slave,
Whate'er he is, and the son of a whore.—Are you
The man, sir, I would know?
    Sur.   I should be loath, sir,
To confess so much.
    Kast.   Then you lie i' your throat.
    Sur.   How!
    Face. *[To* KASTRIL] A very arrant rogue, sir,
      and a cheater,
Employed here by another conjurer
That does not love the doctor, and would cross him,
If he knew how.
    Sur.   Sir, you are abused.
    Kast.   You lie: 11
And 'tis no matter.
    Face.   Well said, sir! He is
The impudent'st rascal—
    Sur.   You are indeed. Will you hear
    me, sir?

Face. By no means. Bid him be gone.

Kast.   Begone, sir,
quickly.

Sur. This's strange! Lady, do you inform your
brother.

Face. There is not such a foist¹ in all the town.
The doctor had² him presently; and finds yet
The Spanish count will come here. [*Aside to* SUBTLE]
Bear up,³ Subtle.

Sub. Yes, sir, he must appear within this hour.

Face. And yet this rogue would come in a disguise,   21
By the temptation of another spirit,
To trouble our art, though he could not hurt it.

Kast.   Ay,
I know—[*To his sister*] Away, you talk like a foolish
mauther.⁴

Sur. Sir, all is truth she says.

Face.   Do not believe him, sir.
He is the lying'st swabber!⁵ Come your ways, sir.

Sur. You are valiant out of⁶ company!

Kast.   Yes, how
then, sir?

[*Enter* DRUGGER *with a piece of damask.*]

Face. Nay, here's an honest fellow too that knows
him,
And all his tricks. [*Aside to* DRUGGER] Make good
what I say, Abel;
This cheater would ha' cozened thee o' the widow.—
He owes this honest Drugger here seven pound,   30
He has had on him in twopenny'orths of tobacco.

Drug. Yes, sir. And's damned himself three terms
to pay me.

Face. And what does he owe for lotium⁷?

Drug.   Thirty
shillings, sir;
And for six syringes.

Sur.   Hydra⁸ of villainy!

Face. Nay, sir, you must quarrel him out o' the
house.

Kast. I will.
—Sir, if you get not out o' doors, you lie;
And you are a pimp.

Sur.   Why, this is madness, sir,
Not valor in you. I must laugh at this.

Kast. It is my humor; you are a pimp, and a trig,⁹
And an Amadis de Gaul, or a Don Quixote.¹⁰   40

Drug. Or a Knight o' the Curious Coxcomb, do you
see?

[*Enter* ANANIAS.]

Anan. Peace to the household!

Kast.   I'll keep peace for no man.

Anan. Casting of dollars is concluded lawful.

Kast. Is he the constable?

Sub.   Peace, Ananias.

Face.   No, sir.

Kast. Then you are an otter, and a shad, a whit,¹¹
A very tim.¹²

Sur. You'll hear me, sir?

Kast.   I will not.

Anan. What is the motive?

Sub.   Zeal in the young
gentleman,
Against his Spanish slops.

Anan.   They are profane,
Lewd, superstitious, and idolatrous breeches.

Sur. New rascals!

Kast.   Will you be gone, sir?

Anan.   Avoid,
Satan!   50
Thou art not of the light! That ruff of pride
About thy neck betrays thee, and is the same
With that which the unclean birds, in seventy-seven,¹³
Were seen to prank it¹⁴ with on divers coasts:
Thou look'st like Antichrist, in that lewd hat.

Sur. I must give way.

Kast.   Be gone, sir.

Sur.   But I'll take
A course with you—

Anan.   Depart, proud Spanish fiend!

Sur. Captain and doctor—

Anan.   Child of perdition!

Kast.   Hence, sir!—
[*Exit* SURLY.]
Did I not quarrel bravely?

Face.   Yes, indeed, sir.

Kast. Nay, an I give my mind to't, I shall do't.   60

Face. Oh, you must follow, sir, and threaten him
tame.
He'll turn again else.

Kast.   I'll re-turn him then.
[*Exit.*]

Face. Drugger, this rogue prevented us, for thee.
We had determined that thou should'st ha' come
In a Spanish suit, and ha' carried her so; and he,
A brokerly slave, goes, puts it on himself.
Hast brought the damask?

Drug.   Yes, sir.

Face.   Thou must borrow
A Spanish suit. Hast thou no credit with the players?

Drug. Yes, sir; did you never see me play the fool?

Face. I know not, Nab. [*Aside*] Thou shalt, if I can
help it.   70
Hieronimo's¹⁵ old cloak, ruff, and hat will serve;
I'll tell thee more when thou bring'st 'em.
[*Exit* DRUGGER.]

IV.vii.
¹ *foist:* crook.   ² *had:* found him out.
³ *Bear up:* Help me.
⁴ *mauther:* young woman (country dialect).
⁵ *swabber:* ordinary sailor.
⁶ *out of:* when you are away from.
⁷ *lotium:* stale urine, a hair dressing.
⁸ *Hydra:* many-headed monster killed by Hercules.
⁹ *trig:* coxcomb.
¹⁰ *Amadis . . . Quixote:* romance heroes.
¹¹ *whit:* bawd(?).   ¹² *tim:* unknown term of contempt.
¹³ *seventy-seven:* unexplained allusion.
¹⁴ *prank it:* dress up.
¹⁵ *Hieronimo:* protagonist of *The Spanish Tragedy,* perhaps
played by Jonson himself in a revival for which he may have
written some scenes.

SUBTLE *hath whispered with him this while.*

Anan.   Sir, I know
The Spaniard hates the Brethren, and hath spies
Upon their actions; and that this was one
I make no scruple.—But the Holy Synod[16]
Have been in prayer and meditation for it;
And 'tis revealed no less to them than me,
That casting of money is most lawful.
Sub.   True.
But here I cannot do it; if the house
Should chance to be suspected, all would out,   80
And we be locked up in the Tower for ever,
To make gold there for th' state, never come out.
And then are you defeated.
Anan.   I will tell
This to the elders and the weaker Brethren,
That the whole company of the Separation
May join in humble prayer again.
Sub.   And fasting.
Anan. Yea, for some fitter place. The peace of mind
Rest with these walls.
Sub.   Thanks, courteous Ananias.
                              [*Exit* ANANIAS.]
Face. What did he come for?
Sub.   About casting dollars,
Presently, out of hand. And so I told him,   90
A Spanish minister came here to spy
Against the faithful—
Face.   I conceive. Come, Subtle,
Thou art so down upon the least disaster!
How wouldst thou ha' done, if I had not helped thee
       out?
Sub. I thank thee, Face, for the angry boy, i' faith.
Face. Who would ha' looked it should ha' been that
       rascal
Surly? He had dyed his beard and all. Well, sir,
Here's damask come to make you a suit.
Sub.   Where's
       Drugger?
Face. He is gone to borrow me a Spanish habit;
I'll be the count now.
Sub.   But where's the widow?   100
Face. Within, with my lord's sister; Madam Dol
Is entertaining her.
Sub.   By your favor, Face,
Now she is honest, I will stand again.
Face. You will not offer it!
Sub.   Why?
Face.   Stand to your word,
Or—here comes Dol. She knows—
Sub.   Y'are tyrannous
       still.
                    [*Enter* DOL *hastily.*]

Face. Strict for my right.—How now, Dol? Hast
       told her

The Spanish count will come?
Dol Com.   Yes, but another is
       come
You little looked for!
Face.   Who's that?
Dol Com.   Your master—
The master of the house.
Sub.   How, Dol!
Face.   She lies,
This is some trick. Come, leave your quiblins,[17]
       Dorothy.   110
Dol Com. Look out and see.

                    [FACE *goes to the window.*]

Sub.   Art thou in earnest?
Dol Com.   'Slight,
Forty o' the neighbors are about him, talking.
Face. 'Tis he, by this good day.
Dol Com.   'Twill prove ill day
For some on us.
Face.   We are undone, and taken.
Dol Com. Lost, I'm afraid.
Sub.   You said he would not
       come,
While there died one a week within the liberties.[18]
Face. No: 'twas within the walls.
Sub.   Was't so? Cry you
       mercy;
I thought the liberties. What shall we do now, Face?
Face. Be silent; not a word, if he call or knock.
I'll into mine old shape again and meet him,   120
Of Jeremy, the butler. I' the meantime,
Do you two pack up all the goods and purchase[19]
That we can carry i' the two trunks. I'll keep him
Off for today, if I cannot longer, and then
At night I'll ship you both away to Ratcliff,[20]
Where we will meet tomorrow, and there we'll share.
Let Mammon's brass and pewter keep[21] the cellar;
We'll have another time for that. But, Dol,
'Pray thee go heat a little water quickly;
Subtle must shave me. All my captain's beard   130
Must off, to make me appear smooth Jeremy.
You'll do't?
Sub.   Yes, I'll shave you as well as I can.
Face. And not cut my throat, but trim me?
Sub.   You
       shall see, sir.
                              [*Exeunt.*]

ACT FIVE

SCENE ONE

[*Enter* LOVEWIT *with a crowd of* Neighbors.]

[*Love.*] Has there been such resort, say you?
1 Neigh.   Daily, sir.
2 Neigh. And nightly, too.
3 Neigh.   Ay, some as brave as lords.
4 Neigh. Ladies and gentlewomen.
5 Neigh.   Citizens' wives.

---

[16] *Holy Synod:* Puritan assembly.   [17] *quiblins:* quibbles.
[18] *liberties:* district outside the walls but under city
authority.   [19] *purchase:* winnings.
[20] *Ratcliff:* seafaring area, downriver.   [21] *keep:* stay in.

1 Neigh. And knights.

6 Neigh.   In coaches.

2 Neigh.   Yes, and oyster-
women.

1 Neigh. Beside other gallants.

3 Neigh.   Sailors' wives.

4 Neigh.   Tobacco
men.

5 Neigh. Another Pimlico.[1]

Love.   What should my knave
advance,

To draw this company? He hung out no banners
Of a strange calf with five legs to be seen,
Or a huge lobster with six claws?

6 Neigh.   No, sir,

3 Neigh. We had gone in then, sir.

Love.   He has no gift   10
Of teaching i' the nose that e'er I knew of.
You saw no bills set up that promised cure
Of agues or the tooth-ache?

2 Neigh.   No such thing, sir!

Love. Nor heard a drum struck[2] for baboons or
puppets?

5 Neigh. Neither, sir.

Love.   What device should he bring
forth now?

I love a teeming wit as I love my nourishment.
'Pray God he ha' not kept such open house
That he hath sold my hangings and my bedding!
I left him nothing else. If he have eat 'em,
A plague o' the moth, say I! Sure he has got   20
Some bawdy pictures to call all this ging:[3]
The Friar and the Nun; or the new motion[4]
Of the knight's courser covering the parson's mare;
The boy of six year old, with the great thing;
Or 't may be, he has the fleas that run at tilt
Upon a table, or some dog to dance.
When saw you him?

1 Neigh.   Who, sir, Jeremy?

2 Neigh.   Jeremy butler?
We saw him not this month.

Love.   How!

4 Neigh.   Not these five weeks,
sir.

6 Neigh. These six weeks, at the least.

Love.   You amaze me,
neighbors!

5 Neigh. Sure, if your worship know not where he is,
He's slipped away.

6 Neigh.   Pray God he be not made away.   31

Love. Ha! it's no time to question, then.

                            He knocks.

6 Neigh.   About
Some three weeks since I heard a doleful cry,
As I sat up a-mending my wife's stockings.

Love. This's strange, that none will answer! did'st
thou hear
A cry, sayst thou?

6 Neigh.   Yes, sir, like unto a man
That had been strangled an hour, and could not speak.

2 Neigh. I heard it, too, just this day three weeks, at
two o'clock
Next morning.

Love.   These be miracles, or you make 'em so!
A man an hour strangled, and could not speak,   40
And both you heard him cry?

3 Neigh.   Yes, downward, sir.

Love. Thou art a wise fellow. Give me thy hand, I
pray thee.
What trade art thou on?

3 Neigh.   A smith, an't please your
worship.

Love. A smith! then lend me thy help to get this
door open.

3 Neigh. That I will presently, sir, but fetch my
tools—

                            [Exit.]

1 Neigh. Sir, best to knock again afore you break it.

V.ii

Love. I will.

                  [LOVEWIT knocks again.]

            [Enter FACE in his butler's livery.]

Face.   What mean you, sir?

1, 2, 4 Neigh.   Oh, here's Jeremy!

Face. Good sir, come from the door.

Love.   Why, what's the
matter?

Face. Yet farther, you are too near yet.

Love.   I' the name of
wonder,
What means the fellow!

Face.   The house, sir, has been
visited.

Love. What, with the plague? Stand thou then
farther.

Face.   No, sir,
I had it not.

Love.   Who had it then? I left
None else but thee i' the house.

Face.   Yes, sir, my fellow,
The cat that kept the buttery had it on her
A week before I spied it; but I got her
Conveyed away i' the night; and so I shut   10
The house up for a month—

Love.   How!

Face.   Purposing then, sir,
T'have burnt rose-vinegar, treacle, and tar,
And ha' made it sweet, that you should ne'er ha' known
it;
Because I knew the news would but afflict you, sir.

Love. Breathe less, and farther off! Why this is
stranger!

V.i.

[1] *Pimlico:* popular resort at Hogsden.

[2] *drum struck:* as an advertisement.   [3] *ging:* gang.

[4] *motion:* puppet show.

The neighbors tell me all here that the doors
Have still been open—
 Face.   How, sir!
 Love.   Gallants, men and
  women,
And of all sorts, tag-rag, been seen to flock here
In threaves,[1] these ten weeks, as to a second Hogsden,
In days of Pimlico and Eye-bright.[2]
 Face.   Sir,   20
Their wisdoms will not say so.
 Love.   Today they speak
Of coaches and gallants; one in a French hood
Went in, they tell me; and another was seen
In a velvet gown at the window; divers more
Pass in and out.
 Face.   They did pass through the doors then,
Or walls, I assure their eye-sights, and their spectacles;
For here, sir, are the keys, and here have been,
In this my pocket, now above twenty days!
And for before, I kept the fort alone there.
But that 'tis yet not deep i' the afternoon, 30
I should believe my neighbors had seen double
Through the black pot,[3] and made these apparitions!
For, on my faith to your worship, for these three weeks
And upwards, the door has not been opened.
 Love.   Strange!
 1 Neigh. Good faith, I think I saw a coach.
 2 Neigh.   And I too,
I'd ha' been sworn.
 Love. Do you but think it now?
And but one coach?
 4 Neigh. We cannot tell, sir; Jeremy
Is a very honest fellow.
 Face.   Did you see me at all?
 1 Neigh. No; that we are sure on.
 2 Neigh.   I'll be sworn o' that.
 Love. Fine rogues to have your testimonies built on!

 [*Re-enter* Third Neighbor, *with his tools.*]

 3 Neigh. Is Jeremy come!
 1 Neigh.   Oh, yes; you may leave
  your tools;   41
We were deceived, he says.
 2 Neigh.   He's had the keys,
And the door has been shut these three weeks.
 3 Neigh.   Like
  enough.
 Love. Peace, and get hence, you changelings.[4]

 [*Enter* SURLY *and* MAMMON.]

 Face. [*Aside*]   Surly come!
And Mammon made acquainted! they'll tell all.
How shall I beat them off? What shall I do?
Nothing's more wretched than a guilty conscience.

V.ii.
 [1] *threaves:* droves. [2] *Eye-bright:* tavern or resort.
 [3] *black pot:* mug. [4] *changelings:* idiots.
V.iii.
 [1] *mere chancel:* in fact, part of a church.
 [2] *lights:* animals' lungs when sold as butcher's meat.

 [*Sur.*] No, sir, he was a great physician. This,
It was no bawdy-house, but a mere chancel![1]
You knew the lord and his sister.
 Mam.   Nay, good Surly.
 Sur. The happy word, "be rich"—
 Mam.   Play not the
  tyrant.
 Sur. Should be today pronounced to all your friends.
And where be your andirons now? And your brass
  pots,
That should ha' been golden flagons, and great wedges?
 Mam. Let me but breathe. What, they ha' shut their
  doors,
Methinks!

   MAMMON *and* SURLY *knock.*

 Sur. Ay, now 'tis holiday with them.
 Mam.   Rogues,
Cozeners, imposors, bawds!
 Face.   What mean you, sir? 10
 Mam. To enter if we can.
 Face.   Another man's house?
Here is the owner, sir; turn you to him,
And speak your business.
 Mam.   Are you, sir, the owner?
 Love. Yes, sir.
 Mam. And are those knaves, within, your
  cheaters?
 Love. What knaves, what cheaters?
 Mam.   Subtle and his
  Lungs.
 Face. The gentleman is distracted, sir. No lungs
Nor lights[2] ha' been seen here these three weeks, sir,
Within these doors, upon my word.
 Sur.   Your word,
Groom arrogant!
 Face. Yes, sir. I am the housekeeper,
And know the keys ha' not been out o' my hands. 20
 Sur. This's a new Face.
 Face.   You do mistake the house, sir.
What sign was't at?
 Sur. You rascal! this is one
O' the confederacy. Come, let's get officers,
And force the door.
 Love. Pray you stay, gentlemen.
 Sur. No, sir, we'll come with warrant.
 Mam.   Ay, and then
We shall ha' your doors open.
    [*Exeunt* MAMMON *and* SURLY.]
 Love.   What means this?
 Face. I cannot tell, sir.
 1 Neigh. These are two o' the gallants
That we do think we saw.
 Face. Two o' the fools!
You talk as idly as they. Good faith, sir,
I think the moon has crazed 'em all.

   [*Enter* KASTRIL.]

    [*Aside*] Oh, me,

The angry boy come too! he'll make a noise,   31
And ne'er away till he have betrayed us all.

KASTRIL knocks.

Kast. What, rogues, bawds, slaves, you'll open the
    door anon!
Punk, cockatrice,[3] my suster! By this light,
I'll fetch the marshal to you. You are a whore
To keep your castle—
    Face.   Who would you speak with, sir?
Kast. The bawdy doctor, and the cozening captain,
And puss my suster.
    Love.   This is something, sure.
Face. Upon my trust, the doors were never open,
    sir.
Kast. I have heard all their tricks, told me twice
    over,   40
By the fat knight and the lean gentleman.
Love. Here comes another.

[Enter ANANIAS and TRIBULATION.]

Face.   Ananias too!
And his pastor!
    Trib.   The doors are shut against us.

They beat, too, at the door.

Anan. Come forth, you seed of sulfur, sons of fire!
Your stench, it is broke forth; abomination
Is in the house.
    Kast.   Ay, my suster's there.
    Anan.   The place,
It is become a cage of unclean birds.
Kast. Yes, I will fetch the scavenger, and the
    constable.
Trib. You shall do well.
Anan.   We'll join to weed them out.
Kast. You will not come then, punk device,[4] my
    suster!   50
Anan. Call her not sister; she is a harlot verily.
Kast. I'll raise the street.
Love.   Good gentlemen, a word.
Anan. Satan, avoid, and hinder not our zeal!

[Exeunt ANANIAS, TRIBULATION, and
                                        KASTRIL.]

Love. The world's turned Bet'lem.
Face.   These are all
    broke loose,
Out of St. Kather'ne's,[5] where they use to keep
The better sort of mad-folks.
    1 Neigh.   All these persons
We saw go in and out here.
    2 Neigh.   Yes, indeed, sir.
3 Neigh. These were the parties.
    Face.   Peace, you
    drunkards. Sir,
I wonder at it. Please you to give me leave
To touch the door; I'll try an the lock be changed.   60
    Love. It mazes me!

[FACE goes to the door]

Good faith, sir, I believe

There's no such thing; 'tis all *deceptio visus*—[6]
[*Aside*] Would I could get him away.

DAPPER cries out within.

Dap.   Master captain!
    Master doctor!
Love. Who's that?
Face. [*Aside*]   Our clerk within, that I forgot!—
    I know not, sir.
Dap. [*Within*] For God's sake, when will her grace
    be at leisure?
Face.   Ha!
Illusions, some spirit o' the air! [*Aside*] His gag is
    melted,
And now he sets out the throat.[7]
    Dap. [*Within*]   I am almost stifled—
Face. [*Aside*] Would you were altogether.
Love.   'Tis i' the
    house.
Ha! list.
    Face. Believe it, sir, i' the air.
    Love.   Peace, you.
Dap. [*Within*] Mine aunt's grace does not use me
    well.
Sub. [*Within*] You fool,   70
Peace, you'll mar all.

[FACE speaks through the keyhole, while
            LOVEWIT <i>advances and overhears.</i>]</div>

Face.   Or you will else, you rogue.
Love. Oh, is it so? Then you converse with
    spirits!—
Come, sir. No more o' your tricks, good Jeremy.
The truth, the shortest way.
    Face.   Dismiss this rabble, sir.—
[*Aside*] What shall I do? I am catched.
    Love.   Good
    neighbors,
I thank you all. You may depart.

[Exeunt Neighbors.]
                                —Come, sir,

You know that I am an indulgent master;
And therefore conceal nothing. What's your med'cine,
To draw so many several sorts of wild fowl?
    Face. Sir, you were wont to affect mirth and wit—
But here's no place to talk on't i' the street.   81
Give me but leave to make the best of my fortune,
And only pardon me th' abuse of your house;
It's all I beg. I'll help you to a widow,
In recompense, that you shall gi' me thanks for,
Will make you seven years younger, and a rich one.
'Tis but your putting on a Spanish cloak;
I have her within. You need not fear the house;
It was not visited.[8]
    Love.   But by me, who came
Sooner than you expected.

---

[3] *cockatrice:* fabulous serpent with a deadly glance,
hatched from a cock's egg.   [4] *punk device:* arrant whore.
    [5] *St. Katherine's:* an old hospital.   [6] *L.:* illusion.
    [7] *sets . . . throat:* raises his voice.
    [8] *visited:* i.e., by plague.

Face.   It is true, sir.   90
'Pray you forgive me.
Love.   Well, let's see your widow.
                                            [*Exeunt.*]

V.iv

[*Enter* SUBTLE, *leading in* DAPPER, *with his eyes bound
      as before.*]

   [*Sub.*] How! ha' you eaten your gag?
   Dap.   Yes, faith, it
      crumbled
Away i' my mouth.
   Sub.   You ha' spoiled all then.
   Dap.   No,
I hope my aunt of Faery will forgive me.
   Sub. Your aunt's a gracious lady; but in troth
You were to blame.
   Dap.   The fume did overcome me,
And I did do't to stay my stomach. 'Pray you
So satisfy her grace.

            [*Enter* FACE *in his uniform.*]

                Here comes the captain.
   Face. How now! Is his mouth down?¹
   Sub.   Ay, he has
      spoken!
   Face. [*Aside*] A pox, I heard him, and you too.
      [*Aloud*] He's undone then.—
[*Aside to* SUBTLE] I have been fain to say, the house is
      haunted   10
With spirits, to keep churl² back.
   Sub.   And hast thou done it?
   Face. Sure, for this night.
   Sub.   Why, then triumph and sing
Of Face so famous, the precious king
Of present wits.
   Face.   Did you not hear the coil³
About the door?
   Sub.   Yes, and I dwindled with it.
   Face. [*Aside*] Show him his aunt, and let him be
      dispatched;
I'll send her to you.

                                    [*Exit* FACE.]
   Sub.   Well, sir, your aunt her grace
Will give you audience presently, on my suit,
And the captain's word that you did not eat your gag
In any contempt of her highness.

                              [*Unbinds his eyes.*]

   Dap.   Not I, in troth, sir.

V.iv.
   ¹ *mouth down:* gag gone.
   ² *churl:* countryman (because of his hopyards).
   ³ *coil:* disturbance.   ⁴ *kind:* natural.
   ⁵ *bird:* fly, familiar spirit.   ⁶ *come on:* descend from.
   ⁷ *Woolsack:* tavern in Farringdon Ward, London.
   ⁸ *Dagger furmety:* cooked cereal; the Dagger is the inn of
I. i. 192.
   ⁹ *Heaven and Hell:* taverns in Westminster, on site of
present House of Commons.
   ¹⁰ *mumchance . . . rich:* games.   ¹¹ *learn:* teach.

[*Enter*] DOL *like the Queen of Faery.*

   Sub. Here she is come. Down o' your knees and
      wriggle: 21
She has a stately presence.

         [DAPPER *kneels and shuffles toward her.*]

                Good. Yet nearer,
And bid, God save you!
   Dap.   Madam!
   Sub.   And your aunt.
   Dap. And my most gracious aunt, God save your
      grace.
   Dol Com. Nephew, we thought to have been angry
      with you;
But that sweet face of yours hath turned the tide,
And made it flow with joy, that ebbed of love.
Arise, and touch our velvet gown.
   Sub.   The skirts,
And kiss 'em. So.
   Dol Com.   Let me now stroke that head.   29
*Much, nephew, shalt thou win, much shalt thou spend;
Much shalt thou give away; much shalt thou lend.*
   Sub. [*Aside*] Ay, much indeed!—why do you not
      thank her grace?
   Dap. I cannot speak for joy.
   Sub.   See, the kind⁴ wretch!
Your grace's kinsman right.
   Dol Com.   Give me the bird.—⁵
Here is your fly in a purse, about your neck, cousin;
Wear it, and feed it about this day sev'n-night,
On your right wrist—
   Sub.   Open a vein with a pin
And let it suck but once a week; till then,
You must not look on't.
   Dol Com.   No. And, kinsman,
Bear yourself worthy of the blood you come on.⁶   40
   Sub. Her grace would ha' you eat no more
         Woolsack⁷ pies,
Nor Dagger furmety.⁸
   Dol Com.   Nor break his fast
In Heaven and Hell.⁹
   Sub.   She's with you everywhere!
Nor play with costermongers, at mumchance, traytrip,
God-make-you-rich¹⁰ (when as your aunt has done it);
      but keep
The gallant'st company, and the best games—
   Dap.   Yes, sir.
   Sub. Gleek and primero; and what you get, be true
      to us.
   Dap. By this hand, I will.
   Sub.   You may bring's a thousand
      pound
Before tomorrow night, if but three thousand
Be stirring, an you will.
   Dap.   I swear I will then.   50
   Sub. Your fly will learn¹¹ you all games.
   Face. [*Within*]   Ha' you
      done there?
   Sub. Your grace will command him no more duties?
   Dol Com.   No;

But come and see me often. I may chance
To leave him three or four hundred chests of treasure,
And some twelve thousand acres of fairy land,
If he game well and comely with good gamesters.

   Sub. There's a kind aunt; kiss her departing part.—
But you must sell your forty mark a year now.

   Dap. Ay, sir, I mean.

   Sub.   Or, gi't away; pox on't!

   Dap. I'll gi't mine aunt. I'll go and fetch the writings.

   Sub. 'Tis well; away.

                      [Exit DAPPER.]

[Re-enter FACE.]

   Face.   Where's Subtle?

   Sub.   Here. What
   news?   61

   Face. Drugger is at the door; go take his suit,
And bid him fetch a parson presently
Say he shall marry the widow. Thou shalt spend
A hundred pound by the service!

                    [Exit SUBTLE.]
                Now, Queen Dol,
Have you packed up all?

   Dol Com.   Yes.

   Face.   And how do you like
The Lady Pliant?

   Dol Com.   A good dull innocent.

[Re-enter SUBTLE.]

   Sub. Here's your Hieronimo's cloak and hat.

   Face.   Give
   me 'em.

   Sub. And the ruff too?

   Face.   Yes; I'll come to you presently.
                           [Exit.]

   Sub. Now he is gone about his project, Dol,   70
I told you of, for the widow.

   Dol Com.   'Tis direct
Against our articles.

   Sub.   Well, we'll fit him, wench.
Hast thou gulled her of her jewels or her bracelets?

   Dol Com. No, but I will do't.

   Sub.   Soon at night, my
   Dolly,
When we are shipped, and all our goods aboard,
Eastward for Ratcliff, we will turn our course
To Brainford,[12] westward, if thou sayst the word,
And take our leaves of this o'erweening rascal,
This peremptory Face.

   Dol Com.   Content; I'm weary of him.

   Sub. Thou'st cause, when the slave will run a-
   wiving, Dol,   80
Against the instrument that was drawn between us.

   Dol Com. I'll pluck his bird as bare as I can.

   Sub.   Yes, tell
   her
She must by any means address some present
To th' cunning man, make him amends for wronging
His art with her suspicion; send a ring
Or chain of pearl; she will be tortured else
Extremely in her sleep, say, and ha' strange things

Come to her. Wilt thou?

   Dol Com.   Yes.

   Sub.   My fine flitter-mouse,[13]
My bird o' the night! We'll tickle it[14] at the Pigeons,[15]
When we have all, and may unlock the trunks,   90
And say, this's mine, and thine; and thine, and mine.

                           They kiss.

[Re-enter FACE.]

   Face. What now! a-billing?

   Sub.   Yes, a little exalted
In the good passage of our stock-affairs.[16]

   Face. Drugger has brought his parson; take him in,
   Subtle,
And send Nab back again to wash his face.

   Sub. I will. And shave himself?

   Face.   If you can get him.
                        [Exit SUBTLE.]

   Dol Com. You are hot upon it, Face, whate'er it is!

   Face. A trick that Dol shall spend ten pound a
   month by.

[Re-enter SUBTLE.]

Is he gone?

   Sub.   The chaplain waits you i' the hall, sir.

   Face. I'll go bestow him.

                           [Exit.]

   Dol Com.   He'll now marry her
   instantly.   100

   Sub. He cannot yet, he is not ready. Dear Dol,
Cozen her of all thou canst. To deceive him
Is no deceit, but justice, that would break
Such an inextricable tie as ours was.

   Dol Com. Let me alone to fit him.

[Re-enter FACE.]

   Face.   Come, my
   venturers,
You ha' packed up all? Where be the trunks? Bring
   forth.

   Sub. Here.

   Face.   Let's see 'em. Where's the money?

   Sub.   Here,
In this.

   Face. Mammon's ten pound; eight score before.
The Brethren's money this. Drugger's and Dapper's?
What paper's that?

   Dol Com.   The jewel of the waiting maid's,
That stole it from her lady, to know certain—   111

   Face. If she should have precedence of her
   mistress?

   Dol Com. Yes.

   Face. What box is that?

   Sub.   The fish-wives' rings,
   I think,

---

12 *Brainford:* Brentford, upriver.   13 *flitter-mouse:* bat.
14 *tickle it:* enjoy ourselves.
15 *Pigeons:* Brentford tavern.
16 *stock-affairs:* business.

And th'ale-wives' single money.[17] Is't not, Dol?
   Dol Com. Yes, and the whistle that the sailor's wife
Brought you to know an her husband were with
    Ward.[18]
   Face. We'll wet it[19] tomorrow; and our silver
    beakers
And tavern cups. Where be the French petticoats
And girdles and hangers?[20]
   Sub.   Here, i' the trunk,
And the bolts of lawn.
   Face.   Is Drugger's damask there,   120
And the tobacco?
   Sub.   Yes.
   Face.   Give me the keys.
   Dol Com. Why you the keys?
   Sub.   No matter, Dol;
    because
We shall not open 'em before he comes.
   Face. 'Tis true, you shall not open them, indeed;
Nor have 'em forth, do you see? Not forth, Dol.
   Dol Com.   No?
   Face. No, my smock-rampant. The right is, my
    master
Knows all, has pardoned me, and he will keep 'em.
Doctor, 'tis true—you look—for all your figures!
I sent for him, indeed. Wherefore, good partners,
Both he and she, be satisfied; for here   130
Determines the indenture tripartite
'Twixt Subtle, Dol, and Face. All I can do
Is to help you over the wall, o' the back-side,[21]
Or lend you a sheet to save your velvet gown, Dol.
Here will be officers presently; bethink you
Of some course suddenly to scape the dock;[22]
For thither you'll come else.

                    Some knock.

              Hark you, thunder.
   Sub. You are a precious fiend!
   Officers. [*Without*]   Open the door.
   Face. Dol, I am sorry for thee, i' faith; but hear'st
    thou?
It shall go hard but I will place thee somewhere.   140
Thou shalt ha' my letter to Mistress Amo—
   Dol Com.   Hang you!
   Face. Or Madam Caesarean.[23]
   Dol Com.   Pox upon you, rogue,
Would I had but time to beat thee!
   Face.   Subtle,
Let's know where you set up next; I'll send you

A customer now and then, for old acquaintance.
What new course ha' you?
   Sub.   Rogue, I'll hang myself,
That I may walk a greater devil than thou,
And haunt thee i' the flock-bed and the buttery.[24]
                       [*Exeunt.*]

V.v

[*Enter* LOVEWIT *in the Spanish costume, with the* Parson.
          Knocking at the door.]

   [*Love.*] What do you mean, my masters?
   Mam. [*Without*]   Open your
    door,
Cheaters, bawds, conjurers.
   Officer. [*Without*]   Or we'll break it open.
   Love. What warrant have you?
   Officer. [*Without*]   Warrant enough, sir,
    doubt not,
If you'll not open it.
   Love.   Is there an officer there?
   Officer. [*Without*] Yes, two or three for[1] failing.
   Love.   Have
    but patience,
And I will open it straight.

        [*Enter* FACE *in his butler's livery.*]

   Face.   Sir, ha' you done?
Is it a marriage? Perfect?
   Love.   Yes, my brain.
   Face. Off with your ruff and cloak then; be yourself,
    sir.
   Sur. [*Without*] Down with the door.
   Kast. [*Without*]   'Slight, ding[2] it
    open.

            [LOVEWIT *opens the door*]

   Love. Hold,
Hold, gentlemen, what means this violence?   10

   [MAMMON, SURLY, KASTRIL, ANANIAS,
    TRIBULATION, *and* Officers *rush in.*]

   Mam. Where is this collier?
   Sur.   And my Captain Face?
   Mam. These day-owls.
   Sur.   That are birding in men's
    purses.
   Mam. Madam Suppository.[3]
   Kast.   Doxy, my suster.
   Anan.   Locusts
Of the foul pit.
   Trib.   Profane as Bel and the Dragon.[4]
   Anan. Worse than the grasshoppers, or the lice of
    Egypt.[5]
   Love. Good gentlemen, hear me. Are you officers,
And cannot stay this violence?
   Officer.   Keep the peace.
   Love. Gentlemen, what is the matter? Whom do
    you seek?
   Mam. The chemical cozener.

---

[17] *single money:* small change.
[18] *Ward:* famous pirate.   [19] *wet it:* drink.
[20] *hangers:* sword-loops on belts.
[21] *back-side:* rear of property.   [22] *dock:* prisoner's pen.
[23] *Mistress Amo, Madam Caesarean:* brothel-keepers.
[24] *flock-bed . . . buttery:* at bed and board.

V.v.
[1] *for:* against.   [2] *ding:* strike down.
[3] *Suppository:* punning on the medicinal device and
impostor.   [4] *Bel . . . Dragon:* apocryphal book of Bible.
[5] *grasshoppers . . . Egypt:* plagues visited by the Lord to
aid Moses.

Sur.   And the captain
    pandar.
Kast. The nun[6] my suster.
Mam.   Madam Rabbi,
Anan.   Scorpions,
And caterpillars.
Love.   Fewer at once, I pray you.   21
Officer. One after another, gentlemen, I charge you,
By virtue of my staff—
Anan.   They are the vessels
Of pride, lust, and the cart.
Love.   Good zeal, lie still
A little while.
Trib.   Peace, Deacon Ananias.
Love. The house is mine here, and the doors are
    open;
If there be any such persons as you seek for,
Use your authority, search on o' God's name.
I am but newly come to town, and finding
This tumult 'bout my door, to tell you true,   30
It somewhat mazed me; till my man here, fearing
My more displeasure, told me he had done
Somewhat an insolent part, let out my house
(Belike presuming on my known aversion
From any air o' the town while there was sickness),
To a doctor and a captain; who, what they are
Or where they be, he knows not.
Mam.   Are they gone?
Love. You may go in and search, sir.

    They [MAMMON, ANANIAS, TRIBULATION]
                                    enter [*the house*].

                                    Here, I find
The empty walls worse than I left 'em, smoked,
A few cracked pots, and glasses, and a furnace;   40
The ceiling filled with poesies of the candle,[7]
And "Madam with a dildo"[8] writ o' the walls.
Only one gentlewoman I met here,
That is within, that said she was a widow—
Kast. Ay, that's my suster; I'll go thump her. Who
    is she?

                                    [*Goes in.*]

Love. And should ha' married a Spanish count, but
    he,
When he came to't, neglected her so grossly
That I, a widower, am gone through with[9] her.
Sur. How? Have I lost her, then?
Love.   Were you the Don,
    sir?
Good faith, now, she does blame you extremely, and
    says   50
You swore, and told her you had ta'en the pains
To dye your beard, and umber o'er your face,
Borrowed a suit and ruff, all for her love;
And then did nothing. What an oversight
And want of putting forward, sir, was this!
Well fare an old harquebuzier,[10] yet
Could prime his powder, and give fire, and hit,
All in a twinkling.

                    MAMMON *comes forth.*

Mam.   The whole nest are fled!
Love. What sort of birds were they?
Mam.   A kind of
    choughs,[11]
Or thievish daws, sir, that have picked my purse   60
Of eight score and ten pounds within these five
    weeks,
Beside my first materials; and my goods,
That lie i' the cellar, which I am glad they ha' left,
I may have home yet.
Love.   Think you so, sir?
Mam.   Ay.
Love. By order of law, sir, but not otherwise.
Mam. Not mine own stuff?
Love.   Sir, I can take no
    knowledge
That they are yours but by public means.
If you can bring certificate that you were gulled of
    'em,
Or any formal writ out of a court,
That you did cozen yourself, I will not hold them.   70
Mam. I'll rather lose 'em.
Love.   That you shall not, sir,
By me, in troth. Upon these terms, they're yours.
What, should they ha' been, sir, turned into
    gold, all?
Mam.   No.
I cannot tell. It may be they should. What then?
Love. What a great loss in hope have you sustained!
Mam. Not I; the commonwealth has.
Face.   Ay, he would
    ha' built
The city new, and made a ditch about it
Of silver, should have run with cream from Hogsden,
That every Sunday in Moorfields the younkers[12]   79
And tits and tom-boys[13] should have fed on, gratis.
Mam. I will go mount a turnip-cart,[14] and preach
The end o' the world within these two months.—
    Surly,
What! in a dream?
Sur.   Must I needs cheat myself
With that same foolish vice of honesty!
Come, let us go and harken out[15] the rogues.
That Face I'll mark for mine, if e'er I meet him.
Face. If I can hear of him, sir, I'll bring you word
Unto your lodging; for in troth, they were strangers
To me; I thought 'em honest as myself, sir.

                    [*Exeunt* SURLY *and* MAMMON.]

    They [ANANIAS *and* TRIBULATION] *come forth.*

Trib. 'Tis well, the saints shall not lose all yet. Go
And get some carts—
Love.   For what, my zealous friends?   91
Anan. To bear away the portion of the righteous

---

    6 *nun:* whore.
    7 *poesies . . . candle:* graffiti written with smoke.
    8 *dildo:* phallus.   9 *am . . . with:* have got married to.
    10 *harquebuzier:* musketeer.   11 *choughs:* crowlike birds.
    12 *younkers:* young men.
    13 *tits and tom-boys:* young girls.
    14 *turnip-cart:* farm-cart.   15 *harken out:* search out.

Out of this den of thieves.

Love.   What is that portion?

Anan. The goods, sometimes the orphans', that the
Brethren bought with their silver pence.

Love.   What, those i'
        the cellar,
The knight Sir Mammon claims?

Anan.   I do defy
The wicked Mammon, so do all the Brethren.
Thou profane man! I ask thee with what conscience
Thou canst advance that idol against us   99
That have the seal?[16] Were not the shillings numbered
That made the pounds? Were not the pounds told out,
Upon the second day of the fourth week,
In the eight month, upon the table dormant,[17]
The year of the last patience of the saints,[18]
Six hundred and ten?

Love.   Mine earnest vehement botcher,
And deacon also, I cannot dispute with you;
But if you get you not away the sooner,
I shall confute you with a cudgel.

Anan.   Sir!

Trib. Be patient, Ananias.

Anan.   I am strong,
And will stand up, well girt, against an host   110
That threaten Gad in exile.

Love.   I shall send you
To Amsterdam, to your cellar.

Anan.   I will pray there,
Against thy house. May dogs defile thy walls,
And wasps and hornets breed beneath thy roof,
This seat of falsehood, and this cave of coz'nage!

        [*Exeunt* ANANIAS *and* TRIBULATION.]

        DRUGGER *enters and he beats him away.*

Love. Another too?

Drug.   Not I, sir, I am no Brother.

Love. Away, you Harry Nicholas![19] do you talk?
                              [*Exit* DRUGGER.]

Face. No, this was Abel Drugger.

                              To the Parson.

                    Good sir, go,
And satisy him; tell him all is done.
He stayed too long a-washing of his face.   120
The doctor, he shall hear of him at Westchester;

---

[16] *seal:* mark of God's favor.
[17] *table dormant:* permanent side-table.
[18] *last . . . saints:* last years of earth, which millenarian divines expected to end in A.D. 2000.
[19] *Harry Nicholas:* Henrick Niclaes, Anabaptist leader of sect of The Family of Love.
[20] *tupped:* mated, covered (used of sheep).
[21] *mammet:* doll.   [22] *touse:* abuse roughly.
[23] *mun:* must.   [24] *feize:* beat.
[25] *buckle . . . tools:* take up your weapons.
[26] *copy:* "tune."
[27] *stoop:* swoop, falcony term applied to a kestril (small hawk).   [28] *jovy:* jovial.
[29] *candor:* honor.   [30] *canon:* rule.
[31] *decorum:* appropriateness of action to genre and character-type.

And of the captain, tell him, at Yarmouth, or
Some good port-town else, lying for a wind.
                              [*Exit* Parson.]
If you get off the angry child now, sir—

        [*Enter* KASTRIL, *dragging in his sister*
                DAME PLIANT.]

Kast. Come on, you ewe, you have matched most
        sweetly, ha' you not?
Did not I say, I would never ha' you tupped[20]
But by a dubbed boy, to make you a lady-tom?
'Slight, you are a mammet![21] Oh, I could touse[22] you
        now.
Death, mun[23] you marry with a pox!

Love.   You lie, boy;
As sound as you; and I am aforehand with you.

Kast.   Anon?

Love. Come, will you quarrel? I will feize[24] you,
        sirrah;   131
Why do you not buckle to your tools?[25]

Kast.   God's light,
This is a fine old boy as e'er I saw!

Love. What, do you change your copy[26] now?
        Proceed;
Here stands my dove: stoop[27] at her if you dare.

Kast. 'Slight, I must love him! I cannot choose, i'
        faith,
An I should be hanged for't. Suster, I protest,
I honor thee for this match.

Love.   Oh, do you so, sir?

Kast. Yes, an thou canst take tobacco and drink, old
        boy,
I'll give her five hundred pound more to her marriage,
Than her own state.

Love.   Fill a pipe-full, Jeremy.   141

Face. Yes, but go in and take it, sir.

Love.   We will.
I will be ruled by thee in anything, Jeremy.

Kast. 'Slight, thou art not hide-bound, thou art a
        jovy[28] boy!
Come, let's in, I pray thee, and take our whiffs.

Love. Whiff in with your sister, brother boy.
        [*Exeunt* KASTRIL *and* DAME PLIANT.]
                                        That
        master
That had received such happiness by a servant,
In such a widow, and with so much wealth,
Were very ungrateful, if he would not be
A little indulgent to that servant's wit,   150
And help his fortune, though with some small strain
Of his own candor.[29] [*To the audience*] Therefore,
        gentlemen,
And kind spectators, if I have outstripped
An old man's gravity, or strict canon,[30] think
What a young wife and a good brain may do:
Stretch age's truth sometimes, and crack it too.—
Speak for thyself, knave.

Face.   So I will, sir. [*To the audience*]
        —Gentlemen,
My part a little fell in this last scene,
Yet 'twas decorum.[31] And though I am clean   160

Got off from Subtle, Surly, Mammon, Dol,
Hot Ananias, Dapper, Drugger, all
With whom I traded; yet I put myself

On you, that are my country; [32] and this pelf
Which I have got, if you do quit [33] me, rests,
To feast you often, and invite new guests.

[*Exeunt.*]

F I N I S

---

[32] *country:* reference to legal constitution of a jury, which
tries "by God and country."   [33] *quit:* acquit.

Ben Jonson

BARTHOLOMEW FAIR

THE LAST of Jonson's great plays, BARTHOLO-MEW FAIR was first performed by Lady Elizabeth's Men at the Hope Theater on October 31, 1614, and repeated before the King the next day, earning great success each time. It does not seem to have been offered again, however, and some have speculated that outraged Puritan sensibilities such as were ultimately to close the theaters prevailed against the comedy. Both staging and printing have unusual aspects. In a persuasive account of the staging offered in his edition of the play in the Yale Ben Jonson, Eugene M. Waith argues that the five locales recurrent at the fair are represented, in a late version of the simultaneous staging of medieval drama, by booths, bowers, and the like that remain on the stage throughout the fair episode and that, in contrast to normal Elizabethan practice, always represent the same locales. Although such may well have been the case, it need not have been so, and the conservative directions printed here permit a more conventional use of the stage. The text unfortunately did not enjoy the careful shepherding of earlier plays. The play was performed two years before the publication of the folio *Works*, but Jonson did not include it in the volume. Instead he made plans to make it part of a second volume, and in fact had it printed in folio in 1631 along with his next two plays. For some reason he decided not to go ahead with publication, and only in 1640 was it collected, along with the other two plays printed in 1631 and with some additional work, in the second volume of the *Works*. By then Jonson was dead, and in any case the 1631 printing job had been so poor that we cannot assume that the play expresses its author's intentions in every respect. The modern editor is lucky to be able to begin with the standard old-spelling text of Jonson by Herford and Simpson, and he is aided by a number of excellent editions of more recent vintage that have collated many extant copies of the first edition and left little in doubt.

Bartholomew (pronounced "Bartlemy") fair began every August twenty-fourth in the district of Smithfield. Its history stretched back into the twelfth century, and it was by Jonson's time very much what he presented: a coming together of citizens of every class, gulls, pickpockets, avaricious tradesmen, conmen, gawkers, whores: a cross-section of the city on holiday. It provided for Jonson what the setting of each of his best plays had given him before, a real world in the projection of which he could make a microcosm. As Venice allowed him to focus on the madness endemic in a world that promises limitless power and wealth to the most enterprising, as alchemy gave him a central metaphor for the desire of the imagination to transform the world to its own desires, so the fair gave him a new lens through which to project the follies of the metropolis. Something seems to have happened to Jonson in the years after the bitter defeat of his unloved tragedy *Catiline* in 1611, and for a short moment in his career he emerges amused rather than outraged, as ready to accept the spirit of holiday as are his characters. This is not to say that he is no longer satirical. In fact, the new comedy presents new versions of the familiar butts: hypocritical and pedantic Puritans, scoundrels pretending sober virtue, gulls asking to be gulled, angry men too wrathful to see the proper objects of their disapproval, stumbling authority figures, women feeble of mind and spirit, and the like. But for the moment of BARTHOLOMEW FAIR Jonson was no longer the scourge of human vice but the humorously detached, if not quite warmhearted, observer of a universal folly that no one, he implies, entirely escapes. Not that the spirit of the Smithfield fair is that of the shoemaker's holiday Dekker had imagined some years before, for, as Joel H. Kaplan points out in a fine essay ("Dramatic and Moral Energy in Ben Jonson's *Bartholomew Fair*," *Renaissance Drama*, New Series III, 1970), Dekker's simpler strategy is to reconcile the stridently opposed claims of humanity by idealizing and sentimentalizing, while Jonson insists that we see our unity in our universal participation in folly.

On the stage BARTHOLOMEW FAIR is immediately accessible and delightful; in the reading, at least the first time through, it is rather difficult. In part the difficulty stems from the sheer multitude of characters, each of whom turns out to have a voice as characteristic as his own eccentricity; in greater part perhaps from the play's advance beyond anything Jonson had done before. Still observing the unity of time, he has buried his clock more deeply beneath the play's surface than he had done in THE ALCHEMIST, and one is no longer drawn inexorably toward a single showdown. Situating the action as much as ever within one locale, he has made the fair the center of such busy activity that the swirling never stops. Above all, concerned as much as before with the most classical of the unities, he has daringly founded the oneness of the action rather on the harmony of innumerable interacting elements than on a plot dominated by a single character operating a comprehensive scheme. Ursula the pig-woman can well be taken as the presiding genius of the fair, and she has been so interpreted by critics as different from one another as Herford and Simpson on the one hand, who saw her as the spirit of the fair and its sordid fleshliness, and Jackson I. Cope on the other, who argues that Jonson identifies her with the iconographic figure *Discordia* misruling in a symbolic realm. But one can argue that the play consists of a number of overlays in each of which its whole world can be seen from a different character's viewpoint: Cokes, Jonson's finest gull, for example, can be seen as the victim whose eagerness to be gulled organizes all the fair's activities; the puppet show can be taken as the central image and Leatherhead, its presenter, as lord of a world of debased art; Justice Overdo, in his feckless search for "enormities," can stand for the fair as image of a world in which justice is overcome by folly; Knockem's obsession with "vapors" suggests a psychology not unlike Jonson's own humors; Trouble-All's pathetic madness epitomizes the solipsistic helplessness of everyone else. The fact is that all of these centers function simultaneously; only the fair itself, presented with a complexity of attitude that defies simple description, serves as the magnetic core of the play and its final meaning. If the relative plotlessness of a play thus concerned with a holiday fair as the instrument for anatomizing a city and a world makes for initial arduousness in reading, it compensates ultimately by rewards such as even Jonson does not yield elsewhere.

N. R.

Bartholomew Fair

THE PROLOGUE[1] TO THE KING'S MAJESTY

Your majesty is welcome to a Fair;
Such place, such men, such language and such ware,
You must expect; with these, the zealous noise
Of your land's faction,[2] scandalized at toys,[3]
As babies,[4] hobbyhorses,[5] puppet-plays,
And such like rage, whereof the petulant ways
Yourself have known, and have been vexed with long.
These for your sport, without particular wrong[6]
Or just complaint of any private man
Who of himself or shall think well or can,   10
The maker doth present, and hopes tonight
To give you for a fairing,[7] true delight.

DRAMATIS PERSONÆ

JOHN LITTLEWIT, *a proctor*[1]
SOLOMON, *his man*
WIN LITTLEWIT, *his wife*
DAME PURECRAFT, *her mother and a widow*
ZEAL-OF-THE-LAND BUSY, *her suitor, a Banbury*[2]
WINWIFE, *his rival, a gentleman*   [man
QUARLOUS, *his companion, a gamester*[3]
BARTHOLOMEW COKES,[4] *an esquire of Harrow*
HUMPHREY WASP, *his man*
ADAM OVERDO, *a justice of peace*
DAME OVERDO, *his wife*
GRACE WELLBORN, *his ward*
LANTERN LEATHERHEAD, *a hobbyhorse-seller*
JOAN TRASH, *a gingerbread-woman*
EZEKIEL EDGWORTH, *a cutpurse*
NIGHTINGALE, *a ballad-singer*
URSULA, *a pig-woman*
MOONCALF,[5] *her tapster*

JORDAN KNOCKEM, *a horse courser,*[6] *and ranger*[7] *o'*
VAL CUTTING,[9] *a roarer*[10]   [*Turnbull*[8]
CAPTAIN WHIT, *a bawd*
PUNK[11] ALICE, *mistress o' the game*[12]
TROUBLE-ALL, *a madman*
HAGGIS }
BRISTLE } *watchmen*
POACHER, *a beadle*[13]
FILCHER }
SHARKWELL[14] } *doorkeepers*[15]
PUPPY, *a wrestler*
NORTHERN, *a clothier*
TINDERBOX-MAN[16]
Costermonger
Corncutter
Passengers[17]
Puppets

PROLOGUE
[1] *Prologue:* to court performance, November 1, 1614.
[2] *faction:* i.e., the Puritans.   [3] *toys:* trifles.
[4] *babies:* dolls.
[5] *hobbyhorses:* of wicker, used in morris-dances, festive dances performed in costume.
[6] *particular wrong:* satire aimed at individuals.
[7] *fairing:* present brought from a fair.

DRAMATIS PERSONÆ
[1] *proctor:* legal agent.
[2] *Banbury:* Oxfordshire, Puritan center.
[3] *gamester:* rake.   [4] *Cokes:* Fool.
[5] *Mooncalf:* Congenital monster.
[6] *horse-courser:* dealer in horses already broken in.
[7] *ranger:* keeper of a park; rake.
[8] *Turnbull:* Turnmill Street, prostitutes' haunt.
[9] *Cutting:* Bullying.   [10] *roarer:* bully, rowdy brawler.
[11] *Punk:* Prostitute.   [12] *mistress . . . game:* prostitute.
[13] *beadle:* official messenger.
[14] *Sharkwell:* "Shark," cheat.
[15] *doorkeepers:* theater ticket-sellers.
[16] *Tinderbox-man:* F "Mousetrap-man."
[17] *Passengers:* Passers-by.

THE INDUCTION ON THE STAGE

[*Enter*] STAGE-KEEPER.[1]

Stage. Gentlemen, have a little patience, they are e'en upon coming, instantly. He that should begin the play, Master Littlewit, the proctor, has a stitch new fallen in his black silk stocking; 'twill be drawn up ere you can tell[2] twenty. He plays one o' the Arches,[3] that dwells about the Hospital,[4] and he has a very pretty part. But for the whole play, will you ha' the truth on't? (I am looking, lest the poet hear me, or his man, Master Brome,[5] behind the arras[6].) It is like to be a very conceited[7] scurvy one, in plain English. When't   10 comes to the Fair once, you were e'en as good go to Virginia for anything there is of Smithfield.[8] He has not hit the humors,[9] he does not know 'em; he has not conversed with the Barthol'mew-birds,[10] as they say; he has ne'er a sword-and-buckler man[11] in his Fair, nor a little Davy[12] to take toll o' the bawds there, as in my time, nor a Kindheart,[13] if anybody's teeth should chance to ache in his play. Nor a juggler with a well-educated ape to come over the chain for the King of England and back again for the Prince, and sit still   20 on his arse for the Pope and the King of Spain! None o' these fine sights! Nor has he the canvas-cut i' the night for a hobbyhorse-man to creep in to his she-neighbor and take his leap there! Nothing! No, and some writer (that I know) had had but the penning o' this matter, he would ha' made you such a jig-a-jog i' the booths, you should ha' thought an earthquake had been i' the Fair! But these master-poets, they will ha' their own absurd courses; they will be informed of nothing! He has, sir-reverence,[14] kicked me three or four   30 times about the tiring-house,[15] I thank him, for but offering to put in, with my experience. I'll be judged by you, gentlemen, now, but for one conceit of mine. Would not a fine pump upon the stage ha' done well for a property now? And a punk set under upon her head, with her stern upward, and ha' been soused by my witty young masters o' the Inns o' Court? What think you o' this for a show, now? He will not hear o' this! I am an ass! I! and yet I kept the stage in Master Tarlton's[16] time, I thank my stars. Ho! and that   40 man had lived to have played in *Bartholomew Fair*, you should ha' seen him ha' come in, and ha' been cozened i' the cloth-quarter,[17] so finely! And Adams,[18] the rogue, ha' leaped and capered upon him and ha' dealt his vermin[19] about as though they had cost him nothing. And then a substantial watch to ha' stol'n in upon 'em and taken 'em away with mistaking words,[20] as the fashion is in the stage-practice.

[*Enter*] BOOK-HOLDER,[21] SCRIVENER.

Book. How now? What rare discourse are you fall'n upon? Ha! ha' you found any familiars here, that you are so free? What's the business?   51
Stage. Nothing, but the understanding gentlemen o' the ground[22] here asked my judgment.
Book. Your judgment, rascal? For what? Sweeping the stage? Or gathering up the broken apples for the bears[23] within? Away, rogue, it's come to a fine degree in these spectacles when such a youth as you pretend to a judgement.

[*Exit* STAGE-KEEPER.]

And yet he may, i' the most o' this matter i' faith: for the author hath writ it just to his meridian,[24] and   60 the scale of the grounded judgments here, his play-fellows in wit. Gentlemen, not for want of a prologue, but by way of a new one, I am sent out to you here with a scrivener and certain articles drawn out in haste between our author and you; which if you please to hear, and as they appear reasonable, to approve of, the play will follow presently. Read, scribe, gi' me the counterpane.[25]
Scriv. Articles of Agreement indented between the spectators or hearers at the Hope on the Bankside[26]   70 in the County of Surrey, on the one party; and the author of *Bartholomew Fair* in the said place and county, on the other party: the one and thirtieth day of October, 1614, and in the twelfth year of the reign of our Sovereign Lord, James, by the grace of God King of England, France, and Ireland; Defender of the Faith; and of Scotland the seven and fortieth.

INDUCTION
[1] *Stage-keeper:* Theater handyman and janitor.
[2] *tell:* count.
[3] *Arches:* proctor in the Court of Arches held in Bow Church.
[4] *Hospital:* the venerable medical institution of St. Bartholomew's in Smithfield.
[5] *Brome:* Richard Brome, d. 1652, Jonson's servant, to be a playwright in later years.
[6] *arras:* cloth hanging on tiring-house facade at stage rear.
[7] *conceited:* fantastic.
[8] *Smithfield:* site of the Fair, near Moorfields, a recreation area immediately north of the city.
[9] *humors:* characteristic (and usually odd) personality traits.
[10] *Barthol'mew-birds:* odd types frequenting the Fair.
[11] *sword . . . man:* ruffian.
[12] *little Davy:* well-known ruffian.
[13] *Kindheart:* itinerant tooth-drawer.
[14] *sir-reverence:* with all respect.
[15] *tiring-house:* booth at back of stage where actors dressed.
[16] *Tarlton's:* referring to principal comedian of the Queen's Men, d. 1588.
[17] *cloth-quarter:* booths along a wall of St. Bartholomew's Church where cloth was sold and where one of *Tarlton's Jests*, a popular collection of anecdotes, told how the clown was cozened of his clothes by a "cony-catcher."
[18] *Adams:* John Adams, another actor in the Queen's Men.
[19] *vermin:* fleas.
[20] *mistaking words:* like the malapropisms of Dogberry and company in *Much Ado about Nothing.*
[21] *Book-holder:* Prompter.
[22] *understanding . . . ground:* standees in the theater pit, below stage level.
[23] *bears:* the Hope Theatre, successor to the Globe, was used both for plays and for bear-baiting.
[24] *meridian:* highest level of his understanding.
[25] *counterpane:* counterpart of the indenture.
[26] *Bankside:* area on south side of Thames where the Hope, like the Globe before it, was located.

INPRIMIS, It is covenanted and agreed by and between the parties above-said and the said spectators and hearers, as well the curious[27] and envious as 80 the favoring and judicious, as also the grounded judgments and understandings, do for themselves severally covenant and agree, to remain in the places their money or friends have put them in, with patience, for the space of two hours and an half, and somewhat more. In which time the author promiseth to present them, by us, with a new sufficient play called *Bartholomew Fair*, merry, and as full of noise as sport, made to delight all, and to offend none; provided they have either the wit or the honesty to think well of themselves.   90

It is further agreed that every person here have his or their free-will of censure,[28] to like or dislike at their own charge, the author having now departed with his right: it shall be lawful for any man to judge his six pen'orth,[29] his twelve pen'orth, so to his eighteen-pence, two shillings, half a crown to the value of his place: provided always his place get not above his wit. And if he pay for half a dozen, he may censure for all them too, so that he will undertake that they shall be silent. He shall put in for censures here, as they 100 do for lots at the lottery;[30] marry, if he drop but six-pence at the door, and will censure a crown's worth, it is thought there is no conscience or justice in that.

It is also agreed that every man here exercise his own judgment, and not censure by contagion,[31] or upon trust, from another's voice or face that sits by him, be he never so first in the commission of wit;[32] as also, that he be fixed and settled in his censure, that what he approves, or not approves today, he will do the same tomorrow, and if tomorrow the next day, and 110 so the next week (if need be), and not to be brought about by any that sits on the bench[33] with him, though they indict and arraign plays daily. He that will swear *Jeronimo*[34] or *Andronicus*[35] are the best plays yet shall pass unexcepted at here as a man whose judgment shows it is constant, and hath stood still these five and

twenty or thirty years. Though it be an ignorance, it is a virtuous and staid ignorance; and next to truth, a confirmed error does well; such a one the author knows where to find him.   120

It is further covenanted, concluded and agreed, that how great soever the expectation be, no person here is to expect more than he knows or better ware than a Fair will afford; neither to look back to the sword-and-buckler age of Smithfield, but content himself with the present. Instead of a little Davy to take toll o' the bawds, the author doth promise a strutting horse-courser with a leer[36] drunkard, two or three to attend him in as good equipage as you would wish. And then for Kindheart the tooth-drawer, a fine oily pig- 130 woman with her tapster to bid you welcome, and a consort of roarers for music. A wise Justice of Peace *meditant*, instead of a juggler with an ape. A civil cut-purse *searchant*. A sweet singer of new ballads *allurant*; and as fresh an hypocrite as ever was broached *rampant*. If there be never a servant-monster[37] i' the Fair, who can help it? he says; nor a nest of antics?[38] He is loth to make nature afraid in his plays, like those that beget *Tales*,[39] *Tempests*,[40] and such like drolleries,[41] to mix his head with other men's heels, let the 140 concupiscence of jigs and dances reign as strong as it will amongst you; yet if the puppets will please anybody, they shall be entreated to come in.

In consideration of which, it is finally agreed by the foresaid hearers and spectators that they neither in themselves conceal, nor suffer by them to be concealed, any state-decipherer or politic[42] picklock of the scene so solemnly ridiculous as to search out who was meant by the gingerbread-woman, who by the hobbyhorse-man, who by the costermonger, nay, who by their 150 wares; or that will pretend to affirm, on his own inspired ignorance, what Mirror of Magistrates[43] is meant by the justice, what great lady by the pig-woman, what concealed statesman by the seller of mousetraps, and so of the rest. But that such person or persons so found be left discovered[44] to the mercy of the author as a forfeiture to the stage and your laughter aforesaid; as also, such as shall so desperately or ambitiously play the fool by his place aforesaid, to challenge[45] the author of scurrility because the 160 language somewhere savors of Smithfield, the booth, and the pig-broth, or of profaneness because a madman cries, "God quit[46] you," or "bless you." In witness whereof, as you have preposterously[47] put to your seals already (which is your money), you will now add the other part of suffrage,[48] your hands. The play shall presently[49] begin. And though the Fair be not kept in the same region that some here perhaps would have it, yet think that therein the author hath observed a special decorum,[50] the place being as dirty as 170 Smithfield, and as stinking every whit.

Howsoever, he prays you to believe his ware is still[51] the same, else you will make him justly suspect that he that is so loth to look on a baby or an hobbyhorse here would be glad to take up a commodity[52] of them, at any laughter, or loss, in another place.

[*Exeunt.*]

---

[27] *curious*: particular, demanding.   [28] *censure*: judgment.
[29] *six pen'orth*: price of cheapest place in the theater; all these prices are higher than normal.
[30] *lottery*: royally sponsored to further the Virginia voyage and plantation.   [31] *contagion*: infection.
[32] *commission of wit*: appointed board of critics.
[33] *bench*: in court; on stage.
[34] *Jeronimo*: The Spanish Tragedy.
[35] *Andronicus*: Titus Andronicus, Shakespeare's gory first tragedy, 1594.   [36] *leer*: sly.
[37] *servant-monster*: Caliban, in *The Tempest*, 1611.
[38] *antics*: dancers in grotesque costumes.
[39] *Tales*: The Winter's Tale, 1611.
[40] *Tempests*: The Tempest.
[41] *drolleries*: comical entertainments.
[42] *politic*: politically adroit.
[43] *mirror of magistrates*: exemplar for governors: title of several collections of cautionary tales, in one of which, Whetstone's *Mirror for Magistrates of Cities* (1584), governors are advised to frequent places of entertainment disguised in order to discover their true nature.
[44] *discovered*: revealed.   [45] *challenge*: accuse.
[46] *quit*: requite.   [47] *preposterously*: in reverse order.
[48] *suffrage*: approval.   [49] *presently*: at once.
[50] *decorum*: aesthetic appropriateness.
[51] *still*: always.   [52] *commodity*: quantity.

ACT ONE

SCENE ONE

[Enter] LITTLEWIT.

Lit. A pretty conceit, and worth the finding! I ha' such luck to spin out these fine things still, and like a silkworm, out of myself. Here's Master Barthol'mew Cokes, of Harrow o' th' Hill, i' th' county of Middlesex, Esquire, takes forth his license to marry Mistress Grace Wellborn of the said place and county. And when does he take it forth? Today! the four and twentieth of August! Barthol'mew day! Barthol'mew upon Barthol'mew! there's the device![1] who would have marked such a leap-frog[2] chance now? A very less than ames- 10 ace[3] on two dice! Well, go thy ways, John Littlewit, Proctor John Littlewit, one o' the pretty wits o' Paul's, the Littlewit of London (so thou art called) and something beside. When a quirk[4] or a quiblin[5] does 'scape thee, and thou dost not watch, and apprehend it, and bring it afore the constable of conceit—there now, I speak quib[6] too—let 'em carry thee out o' the arch-deacon's court[7] into his kitchen and make a Jack[8] of thee instead of a John. (There I am again, la!) 19

[Enter WIN.*]*

Win, good morrow, Win. Ay marry, Win! Now you look finely indeed, Win! This cap does convince![9] You'd not ha' worn it, Win, nor ha' had it velvet, but a rough country beaver, with a copper band, like the cony[10] skin woman of Budge Row?[11] Sweet Win, let me kiss it! And her fine high shoes, like the Spanish lady![12] Good Win, go[13] a little; I would fain see thee pace, pretty Win! By this fine cap, I could never leave kissing on't.

Win. Come, indeed la, you are such a fool, still! 29

Lit. No, but half a one, Win; you are the tother half: man and wife make one fool, Win. (Good!) Is there the proctor, or doctor indeed, i' the diocese, that ever had the fortune to win him such a Win! (There I am again!) I do feel conceits coming upon me, more than I am able to turn tongue to. A pox o' these pretenders to wit, your Three Cranes, Mitre and Mermaid men![14] Not a corn[15] of true salt nor a grain of right mustard amongst them all. They may stand for places or so, again[16] the next witfall, and pay twopence in a quart more for their canary[17] than other men. But gi' me the man can 40 start up a justice of wit out of six-shillings beer,[18] and give the law to all the poets, and poet-suckers,[19] i' town, because they are the players' gossips![20] 'Slid,[21] other men have wives as fine as the players, and as well dressed. Come hither, Win.

[Kisses her.]

I.ii

[Enter] WINWIFE.

Winw. Why, how now, Master Littlewit! Measuring of lips or molding of kisses? Which is it?

Lit. Troth, I am a little taken with my Win's dressing here! Does't not fine, Master Winwife? How do you apprehend,[1] sir? She would not ha' worn this habit. I challenge all Cheapside[2] to show such another—Moorfields,[3] Pimlico[4] Path, or the Exchange,[5] in a summer evening—with a lace to boot, as this has. Dear Win, let Master Winwife kiss you. He comes a-wooing to our mother, Win, and may be our father perhaps, Win. There's no harm in him, Win. 11

Winw. None i' the earth, Master Littlewit.

[Kisses her.]

Lit. I envy no man my delicates,[6] sir.

Winw. Alas, you ha' the garden where they grow still! A wife here with a strawberry breath, cherry lips, apricot cheeks, and a soft velvet head, like a melicotton.[7]

Lit. Good i' faith! Now dullness upon me, that I had not that before him, that I should not light on't as well as he! Velvet head! 19

Winw. But my taste, Master Littlewit, tends to fruit of a later kind; the sober matron, your wife's mother.

Lit. Ay! We know you are a suitor, sir. Win and I both wish you well; by this licence here, would you had her, that your two names were as fast in it, as here are a couple. Win would fain have a fine young father i' law with a feather, that her mother might hood it and chain it[8] with Mistress Overdo. But you do not take the right course, Master Winwife.

Winw. No, Master Littlewit? Why?

Lit. You are not mad enough. 30

Winw. How? Is madness a right course?

Lit. I say nothing, but I wink upon Win. You have a friend, one Master Quarlous, comes here sometimes?

Winw. Why? He makes no love to her, does he?

Lit. Not a tokenworth[9] that ever I saw, I assure you, but—

---

[1] *device:* gimmick.   [2] *leap-frog:* unusual.
[3] *ames-ace:* two aces, lowest throw possible with two dice.
[4] *quirk:* quip.   [5] *quiblin:* quibble, pun.
[6] *quib:* quibbling.   [7] *archdeacon's court:* the Arches.
[8] *Jack:* Knave.
[9] *convince:* overpower, i.e., look stunning.
[10] *cony:* rabbit.
[11] *Budge Row:* skinners' and furriers' street.
[12] *Spanish lady:* Englishwomen affected the shoes with high cork heels worn by Spanish women.   [13] *go:* walk.
[14] *Three . . . men:* frequenters of popular London taverns (the Mermaid was Jonson's favorite).
[15] *corn:* grain.   [16] *again:* against, in anticipation of.
[17] *canary:* sweet wine.
[18] *six . . . beer:* beer sold at six shillings a barrel.
[19] *poet-suckers:* young poets.   [20] *gossips:* friends.
[21] *'Slid:* by God's eyelid.

[1] *apprehend:* think.
[2] *Cheapside:* district of cloth merchants.
[3] *Moorfields:* park north of the city reclaimed from marshes.
[4] *Pimlico:* tavern in Hogsden, near the city, noted for cakes and ale.
[5] *Exchange:* the New Exchange, fashionable shopping district in the Strand.   [6] *delicates:* delicacies.
[7] *melicotton:* hybrid peach-quince.
[8] *hood . . . it:* dress up like a city matron.
[9] *tokenworth:* farthing's worth.

Winw. What?

Lit. He is the more madcap o' the two. You do not apprehend me.

Win. You have a hot coal i' your mouth now, you cannot hold. 41

Lit. Let me out with it, dear Win.

Win. I'll tell him myself.

Lit. Do, and take all the thanks, and much good do thy pretty heart, Win.

Win. Sir, my mother has had her nativity-water cast[10] lately by the cunning men in Cow Lane, and they ha' told her her fortune, and do ensure her she shall never have happy hour unless she marry within this sen'night, and when it is, it must be a madman, they say. 51

Lit. Ay, but it must be a gentleman madman.

Win. Yes, so the tother man of Moorfields says.

Winw. But does she believe 'em?

Lit. Yes, and has been at Bedlam[11] twice since, every day, to inquire if any gentleman be there, or to come there, mad!

Winw. Why, this is a confederacy,[12] a mere piece of practice upon her, by these imposters! 59

Lit. I tell her so; or else say I that they mean some young madcap-gentleman (for the devil can equivocate, as well as a shopkeeper), and therefore would I advise you to be a little madder than Master Quarlous hereafter.

Winw. Where is she? Stirring yet?

Lit. Stirring! Yes, and studying an old elder, come from Banbury, a suitor that puts in here at meal-tide, to praise the painful[13] brethren or pray that the sweet singers[14] may be restored; says a grace as long as his breath lasts him! Sometime the spirit is so strong 70 with him, it gets quite out of him, and then my mother, or Win, are fain to fetch it again with malmsey,[15] or *aqua coelestis.*[16]

Win. Yes indeed, we have such a tedious life with him for his diet, and his clothes too; he breaks his buttons, and cracks seams at every saying he sobs out.

Lit. He cannot abide my vocation, he says.

Win. No, he told my mother a proctor was a claw of the Beast, and that she had little less than committed abomination in marrying me so as she has done. 80

Lit. Every line, he says, that a proctor writes, when it comes to be read in the bishop's court, is a long black hair, kembed[17] out of the tail of Antichrist.

Winw. When came this proselyte?

Lit. Some three days since.

[*Enter*] QUARLOUS.

Quar. O sir, ha' you ta'en soil[1] here? It's well a man may reach you after three hours running yet! What an unmerciful companion art thou to quit thy lodging at such ungentlemanly hours! None but a scattered covey of fiddlers, or one of these rag-rakers in dunghills, or some marrowbone man[2] at most, would have been up when thou wert gone abroad, by all description. I pray thee what ailest thou, thou canst not sleep? Hast thou thorns i' thy eye-lids or thistles i' thy bed?

Winw. I cannot tell: it seems you had neither i' your feet, that took this pain to find me. 11

Quar. No, and I had, all the lyam-hounds[3] o' the City should have drawn after you by the scent rather. Master John Littlewit! God save you, sir. 'Twas a hot night with some of us, last night, John. Shall we pluck a hair o' the same wolf today, Proctor John?

Lit. Do you remember, Master Quarlous, what we discoursed on last night?

Quar. Not I, John: nothing that I either discourse or do; at those times I forfeit all to forgetfulness. 20

Lit. No? Not concerning Win? Look you: there she is, and dressed as I told you she should be. Hark you, sir, had you forgot?

Quar. By this head, I'll beware how I keep you company, John, when I am drunk, and you have this dangerous memory! That's certain.

Winw. Why sir?

Quar. Why? [*To* WINWIFE] We were all a little stained last night, sprinkled with a cup or two, and I agreed with Proctor John here to come and do some- 30 what with Win (I know not what 'twas) today; and he puts me in mind on't now; he says he was coming to fetch me. Before truth, if you have that fearful quality, John, to remember, when you are sober, John, what you promise drunk, John, I shall take heed of you, John. For this once, I am content to wink[4] at you. Where's your wife?—Come hither, Win.

He kisseth her.

Win. Why, John! do you see this, John? Look you! help me, John. 39

Lit. O Win, fie, what do you mean, Win? Be womanly, Win; make an outcry to your mother, Win? Master Quarlous is an honest gentleman, and our worshipful good friend, Win, and he is Master Winwife's friend too; and Master Winwife comes a suitor to your mother, Win, as I told you before, Win, and may perhaps be our father, Win. They'll do you no harm, Win, they are both our worshipful good friends. Master Quarlous! You must know Master Quarlous, Win; you must not quarrel with Master Quarlous, Win.

Quar. No, we'll kiss again and fall in.[5] 50

[*Kisses her again.*]

Lit. Yes, do, good Win.

Win. I' faith you are a fool, John.

Lit. A fool-John she calls me; do you mark that, gentlemen? Pretty littlewit of velvet! a fool-John!

---

[10] *nativity . . . cast:* urine diagnosed for a horoscope.
[11] *Bedlam:* Bethlehem Hospital, London insane asylum.
[12] *confederacy:* conspiracy.   [13] *painful:* assiduous.
[14] *sweet singers:* Puritans.   [15] *malmsey:* rich sweet wine.
[16] *L.:* cordial made from wine.
[17] *kembed:* combed.

[1] *soil:* refuge (hunting).
[2] *marrowbone man:* one gone out to pray, down on his shins.   [3] *lyam-hounds:* bloodhounds.
[4] *wink:* close my eyes and not see.   [5] *fall in:* make up.

Quar. She may call you an apple-John,[6] if you use this.

Winw. Pray thee forbear, for my respect somewhat.

Quar. Hoy-day! how respective[7] you are become o' the sudden! I fear this family will turn you reformed too; pray you come about again. Because she is in   60 possibility to be your daughter-in-law and may ask you blessing hereafter when she courts it to Tottenham[8] to eat cream—well, I will forbear, sir; but i' faith, would thou wouldst leave thy exercise of widow-hunting once, this drawing after[9] an old reverend smock by the splay-foot![10] There cannot be an ancient tripe or trillibub[11] i' the town but thou art straight nosing it; and 'tis a fine occupation thou'lt confine thyself to when thou has got one—scrubbing a piece of buff, as if thou hadst the perpetuity of Pannyer Alley[12] to stink in, or per-   70 haps, worse, currying a carcass that thou hast bound thyself to alive. I'll be sworn, some of them that thou art or hast been a suitor to are so old as no chaste or married pleasure can ever become 'em; the honest instrument of procreation has forty years since left to belong to 'em; thou must visit 'em, as thou wouldst do a tomb, with a torch, or three handfuls of link,[13] flaming hot, and so thou mayst hap to make 'em feel thee, and after, come to inherit according to thy inches. A sweet course for a man to waste the brand of life   80 for, to be still raking himself a fortune in an old woman's embers; we shall ha' thee, after thou hast been but a month married to one of 'em, look like the quartan ague[14] and the black jaundice met in a face, and walk as if thou hadst borrowed legs of a spinner[15] and voice of a cricket. I would endure to hear fifteen sermons a week for[16] her, and such coarse and loud ones as some of 'em must be; I would e'en desire of fate I might dwell in a drum and take in my sustenance with an old broken tobacco-pipe and a straw. Dost thou ever   90 think to bring thine ears or stomach to the patience of a dry grace, as long as thy tablecloth and droned out by thy son here, that might be thy father, till all the meat o' thy board has forgot it was that day i' the kitchen? Or to brook the noise made, in a question of predestination, by the good laborers and painful eaters assembled together, put to 'em by the matron, your spouse, who moderates with a cup of wine, ever and anon, and a sentence out of Knox[17] between? Or   100 the perpetual spitting, before and after a sober drawn[18] exhortation of six hours, whose better part was the hum-ha-hum? Or to hear prayers groaned out over thy iron-chests as if they were charms to break 'em? And all this, for the hope of two apostle-spoons,[19] to suffer! And a cup to eat a caudle[20] in! For that will be thy legacy. She'll ha' conveyed her state,[21] safe enough from thee, an she be a right widow.

Winw. Alas, I am quite off that scent now.

Quar. How so?   109

Winw. Put off by a brother of Banbury, one that, they say, is come here and governs all already.

Quar. What do you call him? I knew divers of those Banburians when I was in Oxford.

Winw. Master Littlewit can tell us.

Lit. Sir! good Win, go in, and if Master Barthol'-mew Cokes his man come for the license (the little old fellow), let him speak with me. What say you, gentlemen?

                          [*Exit* WIN.]

Winw. What call you the reverend elder you told me of, your Banbury man?   120

Lit. Rabbi[22] Busy, sir; he is more than an elder, he is a prophet, sir.

Quar. Oh, I know him! a baker, is he not?

Lit. He was a baker sir, but he does dream now, and see visions; he has given over his trade.

Quar. I remember that too: out of a scruple he took, that (in spiced[23] conscience) those cakes he made were served to bridals, maypoles, morrises,[24] and such profane feasts and meetings; his Christian name is Zeal-of-the-Land.   130

Lit. Yes, sir, Zeal-of-the-Land Busy.

Winw. How, what a name's there!

Lit. Oh, they have all such names, sir. He was witness for Win here (they will not be called godfathers), and named her Win-the-Fight; you thought her name had been Winifred, did you not?

Winw. I did indeed.

Lit. He would ha' thought himself a stark reprobate, if it had.   139

Quar. Ay, for there was a blue-starch-woman[25] o' the name, at the same time. A notable hypocritical vermin it is; I know him. One that stands[26] upon his face more than his faith at all times; ever in seditious motion, and reproving for vainglory; of a most lunatic conscience and spleen, and affects the violence of singularity[27] in all he does (he has undone a grocer here, in Newgate-market, that broke with him, trusted[28] him with currants, as arrant a zeal as he, that's by the way). By his profession,[29] he will ever be i' the state of innocence, though, and childhood; derides all   150 antiquity; defies any other learning than inspiration; and what discretion soever years should afford him, it is all prevented[30] in his original ignorance. Ha' not to

---

[6] *apple-John:* apple kept until shriveled; pimp.

[7] *respective:* considerate, deferential.

[8] *Tottenham:* Tottenham Court, where cakes, ale and cream were sold.

[9] *drawing after:* tracking by scent (hunting).

[10] *splay-foot:* clumsy flatfoot, a term of abuse.

[11] *tripe or trillibub:* entrails; contemptuous name for a fat person.

[12] *Pannyer Alley:* leather makers' or dealers' haunt.

[13] *link:* tow and pitch for torches.

[14] *quartan ague:* fever with recurrent paroxysm every fourth day.   [15] *spinner:* spider.   [16] *for:* rather than.

[17] *Knox:* 1505–72, leader of Scottish Reformation.

[18] *drawn:* drawn out.

[19] *apostle-spoons:* common baptismal gift, silver spoons with figures of the apostles on their handles.

[20] *caudle:* gruel for the sick.

[21] *conveyed . . . state:* willed her estate to another.

[22] *Rabbi:* Puritans modeled much of their ceremony on the Old Testament.   [23] *spiced:* overscrupulous.

[24] *morrises:* morris-dances.

[25] *blue . . . woman:* Because starch was used on fancy clothes, Puritans disapproved of it.   [26] *stands:* relies.

[27] *singularity:* dissent.   [28] *trusted:* supplied on credit.

[29] *By . . . profession:* According to what he says.

[30] *prevented:* forestalled.

do with him, for he is a fellow of a most arrogant and invincible dullness, I assure you. Who is this?

I.iv

[Enter WASP, WIN.]

Wasp. By your leave, gentlemen, with all my heart to you, and God you[1] good morrow. Master Littlewit, my business is to you. Is this license ready?

Lit. Here, I ha' it for you in my hand, Master Humphrey.

Wasp. That's well; nay, never open or read it to me; it's labor in vain, you know. I am no clerk, I scorn to be saved by my book;[2] i' faith I'll hang first. Fold it up o' your word and gi' it me. What must you ha' for't?

Lit. We'll talk of that anon, Master Humphrey.   10

Wasp. Now, or not at all, good master proctor; I am for no anons, I assure you.

Lit. Sweet Win, bid Solomon send me the little black box within, in my study.

Wasp. Ay, quickly, good mistress, I pray you; for I have both eggs o' the spit and iron i' the fire. Say what you must have, good Master Littlewit.

                              [*Exit* WIN.]

Lit. Why, you know the price, Master Numps.[3]

Wasp. I know? I know nothing. Ay, what tell you me of knowing? Now I am in haste. Sir, I do not   20 know, and I will not know, and I scorn to know, and yet (now I think on't) I will and do know as well as another; you must have a mark[4] for your thing here, and eightpence for the box. I could ha' saved twopence i' that an[5] I had brought it myself, but here's fourteen shillings for you. Good Lord! how long your little wife stays! pray God, Solomon, your clerk, be not looking i' the wrong box, master proctor.

Lit. Good i' faith! No, I warrant you, Solomon is wiser than so, sir.   30

Wasp. Fie, fie, fie, by your leave, Master Littlewit, this is scurvy, idle, foolish and abominable; with all my heart, I do not like it.

Winw. Do you hear? Jack Littlewit, what business does thy pretty head think this fellow may have, that he keeps such a coil[6] with?

Quar. More than buying of gingerbread i' the

Cloister[7] here (for that we allow him), or a gilt pouch i' the Fair?

Lit. Master Quarlous, do not mistake him; he is his master's both-hands, I assure you.   41

Quar. What? To pull on his boots, a-mornings, or his stockings, does he?

Lit. Sir, if you have a mind to mock him, mock him softly, and look t'other way, for if he apprehend you flout him once, he will fly at you presently. A terrible testy old fellow, and his name is Wasp too.

Quar. Pretty insect! make much on him.

Wasp. A plague o' this box, and the pox too, and on him that made it, and her that went for't, and all   50 that should ha' sought it, sent it, or brought it! Do you see, sir?

Lit. Nay, good Master Wasp.

Wasp. Good Master Hornet, turd i' your teeth, hold you your tongue. Do not I know you? Your father was a 'pothecary, and sold glisters,[8] more than he gave, I wusse.[9] And turd i' your little wife's teeth too; here she comes; 'twill make her spit, as fine as she is, for all her velvet-custard[10] on her head, sir.

[*Re-enter* WIN.]

Lit. Oh, be civil, Master Numps.   60

Wasp. Why, say I have a humor[11] not to be civil; how then? Who shall compel me? You?

Lit. Here is the box, now.

Wasp. Why a pox o' your box, once again; let your little wife stale[12] in it, and she will. Sir, I would have you to understand, and these gentlemen too, if they please—

Winw. With all our hearts, sir.

Wasp. That I have a charge, gentlemen.

Lit. They do apprehend, sir.   70

Wasp. Pardon me, sir, neither they nor you can apprehend me yet. (You are an ass.) I have a young master; he is now upon his making and marring; the whole care of his well-doing is now mine. His foolish schoolmasters have done nothing but run up and down the country with him to beg puddings[13] and cake-bread of his tenants, and almost spoiled him; he has learned nothing, but to sing catches and repeat "*Rattle bladder rattle*," and "*O Madge.*" I dare not let him walk alone for fear of learning of vile tunes which   80 he will sing at supper and in the sermon-times! If he meet but a carman[14] i' the street, and I find him not talk to keep him off on[15] him, he will whistle him and all his tunes over at night in his sleep! He has a head full of bees![16] I am fain[17] now, for this little time I am absent, to leave him in charge with a gentlewoman; 'tis true, she is a justice of peace his wife, and a gentle-woman o' the hood,[18] and his natural sister; but what may happen under a woman's government, there's the doubt. Gentlemen, you do not know him. He is   90 another manner of piece than you think for! but nineteen year old, and yet he is taller than either of you by the head, God bless him.

Quar. [*Aside*] Well, methinks this is a fine fellow!

Winw. He has made his master a finer by this description, I should think.

---

[1] *God you:* God give you.
[2] *clerk . . . book:* One sentenced for a capital crime could plead benefit of clergy by proving that he could read, and escape the penalty.   [3] *Numps:* nickname for Humphrey.
[4] *mark:* 13s. 4d.   [5] *an:* = "and"; if.
[6] *keeps . . . coil:* bustles about.
[7] *Cloister:* Christ Church Cloisters, near Smithfield, where "fairings" were sold during Bartholomew Fair.
[8] *glisters:* enemas.   [9] *I wusse:* = "iwis"; indeed.
[10] *custard:* fruit or meat pie, suggested by her velvet hat.
[11] *humor:* physiologically induced disposition; tempera-mental bent.   [12] *stale:* urinate.
[13] *puddings:* sausages.
[14] *carman:* carrier; proverbial for his whistling.
[15] *on:* of.   [16] *has . . . bees:* is crazy and excitable.
[17] *fain:* obliged.
[18] *o' the hood:* entitled to wear a hood.

Quar. [*Aside*] 'Faith, much about one; it's cross and pile[19] whether,[20] for a new farthing.

Wasp. I'll tell you, gentlemen—

Lit. Will't please you drink, Master Wasp?   100

Wasp. Why, I ha' not talked so long to be dry, sir, you see no dust or cobwebs come out o' my mouth, do you? You'd ha' me gone, would you?

Lit. No, but you were in haste e'en now, Master Numps.

Wasp. What an' I were? So I am still, and yet I will stay, too; meddle you with your match, your Win, there; she has as little wit as her husband, it seems. I have others to talk to.   109

Lit. She's my match indeed, and as little wit as I, good!

Wasp. We ha' been but a day and a half in town, gentlemen, 'tis true; and yesterday i' the afternoon, we walked London, to show the city to the gentlewoman he shall marry, Mistress Grace; but, afore I will endure such another half day, with him, I'll be drawn with a good gib-cat[21] through the great pond at home, as his uncle Hodge was! Why, we could not meet that heathen thing, all day, but stayed[22] him. He would name you all the signs over, as he went, aloud; and where he   120 spied a parrot or a monkey, there he was pitched, with all the little-long-coats[23] about him, male and female; no getting him away! I thought he would ha' run mad o' the black boy in Bucklersbury[24] that takes the scurvy, roguy tobacco there.

Lit. You say true, Master Numps; there's such a one indeed.

Wasp. It's no matter whether there be or no; what's that to you?   129

Quar. [*Aside*] He will not allow of John's reading[25] at any hand.

I.v

[*Enter* COKES, MISTRESS OVERDO, GRACE.]

Cokes. O Numps! are you here, Numps? Look where I am, Numps! and Mistress Grace, too! Nay, do not look angerly, Numps; my sister is here, and all. I do not come without her.

Wasp. What the mischief, do you come with her? Or she with you?

Cokes. We came all to seek you, Numps.

Wasp. To seek me? Why, did you all think I was lost? Or run away with your fourteen shillings worth of small ware here? Or that I had changed it i' the   10 Fair, for hobbyhorses? 'Sprecious[1]—to seek me!

Mrs. O. Nay, good Master Numps, do you show discretion, though he be exorbitant, as Master Overdo says, and't be but for conservation of the peace.

Wasp. Marry gip,[2] goody[3] she-justice, Mistress French-hood![4] Turd i' your teeth; and turd i' your French-hood's teeth, too, to do you service, do you see? Must you quote your Adam to me? You think you are madam regent still, Mistress Overdo, when I am in place? No such matter, I assure you; your reign is out when I am in, dame.   21

Mrs. O. I am content to be in abeyance, sir, and be governed by you; so should he too, if he did well; but 'twill be expected you should also govern your passions.

Wasp. Will't so, forsooth? Good Lord! how sharp you are! With being at Bedlam yesterday? Whetstone[5] has set an edge upon you, has he?

Mrs. O. Nay, if you know not what belongs to your dignity, I do, yet, to mine.

Wasp. Very well, then.   30

Cokes. Is this the license, Numps? For love's sake, let me see't. I never saw a license.

Wasp. Did you not so? Why, you shall not see't, then.

Cokes. An you love me, good Numps.

Wasp. Sir, I love you, and yet I do not love you, i' these fooleries. Set your heart at rest; there's nothing in't but hard words; and what would you see't for?

Cokes. I would see the length and the breadth on't, that's all; and I will see't now, so I will.   40

Wasp. You sha' not see it here.

Cokes. Then I'll see't at home, and I'll look upo' the case here.

Wasp. Why, do so; a man must give way to him a little in trifles, gentlemen. These are errors, diseases of youth, which he will mend when he comes to judgment and knowledge of matters. I pray you conceive so, and I thank you. And I pray you pardon him, and I thank you again.

Quar. Well, this dry nurse, I say still, is a delicate man.[6]   51

Winw. And I am for the cosset,[7] his charge! Did you ever see a fellow's face more accuse him for an ass?

Quar. Accuse him? It confesses him one without accusing. What pity 'tis yonder wench should marry such a cokes!

Winw. 'Tis true.

Quar. She seems to be discreet, and as sober as she is handsome.   59

Winw. Ay, and if you mark her, what a restrained scorn she casts upon all his behavior and speeches!

Cokes. Well, Numps, I am now for another piece of business more, the Fair, Numps, and then—

---

[19] *cross and pile:* heads or tails.   [20] *whether:* which.
[21] *gib-cat:* tomcat; the allusion is to a practical joke in which a bet is made against a rustic that a cat can pull him through a pond; one end of a rope is tied to him, the other thrown across a pond and tied to a cat, which is then hauled by the accomplices in the trick so that the victim is dragged through the water.   [22] *stayed:* waited for.
[23] *little ... coats:* children.
[24] *Bucklersbury:* street of grocers and apothecaries (who sold tobacco).   [25] *reading:* comment.

I.v.

[1] *'Sprecious:* By God's precious blood.
[2] *Marry gip:* originally "by Mary Gipsy," "by St. Mary of Egypt," confused with "gip" (= "gee-up") spoken to a horse—get out, get along with you.
[3] *goody:* polite title applied to married woman of humble station.
[4] *French-hood:* garment affected by citizen's wives.
[5] *Whetstone:* probably name of a keeper at the Hospital, with pun.   [6] *delicate man:* nice fellow.
[7] *cosset:* spoiled child.

Wasp. Bless me! deliver me, help, hold me! the Fair!

Cokes. Nay, never fidge[8] up and down, Numps, and vex itself. I am resolute Barthol'mew, in this; I'll make no suit on't to you. 'Twas all the end of my journey, indeed, to show Mistress Grace my Fair. I call't my Fair, because of Barthol'mew; you know my name is Barthol'mew, and Barthol'mew Fair.   70

Lit. That was mine afore, gentlemen, this morning. I had that i' faith, upon his license; believe me, there he comes after me.

Quar. Come, John, this ambitious wit of yours, I am afraid, will do you no good i' the end.

Lit. No, why, sir?

Quar. You grow so insolent with it, and overdoing, John, that if you look not to it and tie it up, it will bring you to some obscure place in time, and there 'twill leave you.   80

Winw. Do not trust it too much, John; be more sparing, and use it but now and then. A wit is a dangerous thing, in this age; do not overbuy[9] it.

Lit. Think you so, gentlemen? I'll take heed on't, hereafter.

Win. Yes, do, John.

Cokes. A pretty little soul, this same Mistress Littlewit! would I might marry her.

Grace. [*Aside*] So would I, or anybody else, so I might 'scape you.   90

Cokes. Numps, I will see it, Numps, 'tis decreed: never be melancholy for the matter.

Wasp. Why, see it, sir, see it, do see it! Who hinders you? Why do you not go see it? 'Slid, see it.

Cokes. The Fair, Numps, the Fair.

Wasp. Would the Fair and all the drums and rattles in't were i' your belly for me; they are already i' your brain. He that had the means to travel your head now should meet finer sights than any are i' the Fair and make a finer voyage on't, to see it all hung with   100 cockleshells, pebbles, fine wheat-straws, and here and there a chicken's feather and a cobweb.

Quar. [*Aside*] Good faith, he looks, methinks, an' you mark him, like one that were made to catch flies, with his Sir Cranion[10] legs.

Winw. [*Aside*] And his Numps, to flap 'em away.

Wasp. God be wi' you, sir, there's your bee in a box, and much good do't you.

Cokes. Why, your friend, and Barthol'mew, an' you be so contumacious.   110

Quar. What mean you, Numps?

Wasp. I'll not be guilty, I, gentlemen.

Mrs. O. You will not let him go, brother, and lose him?

Cokes. Who can hold that will away? I had rather lose him than the Fair, I wusse.

Wasp. You do not know the inconvenience, gentlemen, you persuade to, nor what trouble I have with him in these humors. If he go to the Fair, he will buy of everything to a baby there, and household-stuff   120 for that too. If a leg or an arm on him did not grow on, he would lose it i' the press. Pray heaven I bring him off with one stone![11] and then he is such a ravener after fruit! You will not believe what a coil[12] I had, t'other day, to compound a business between a Catherine-pear[13]-woman and him, about snatching! 'Tis intolerable, gentlemen!

Winw. Oh! but you must not leave him, now, to these hazards, Numps.   129

Wasp. Nay, he knows too well I will not leave him, and that makes him presume. Well, sir, will you go now? If you have such an itch i' your feet to foot it to the Fair, why do you stop? Am I your tarriers?[14] Go, will you go? Sir, why do you not go?

Cokes. O Numps! have I brought you about? Come, Mistress Grace, and sister, I am resolute Bat,[15] i' faith, still.

Grace. Truly, I have no such fancy to the Fair, nor ambition to see it; there's none goes thither of any quality[16] or fashion.   140

Cokes. O Lord, sir! You shall pardon me, Mistress Grace, we are enow of ourselves to make it a fashion; and for qualities,[17] let Numps alone, he'll find qualities.

[*Exeunt* COKES, WASP, GRACE, MISTRESS OVERDO.]

Quar. What a rogue in apprehension[18] is this! to understand her language no better.

Winw. Ay, and offer to marry to her? Well, I will leave the chase of my widow for today, and directly to the Fair. These flies cannot, this hot season, but engender us excellent creeping sport.   149

Quar. A man that has but a spoonful of brain would think so. Farewell, John.

[*Exeunt* QUARLOUS, WINWIFE.]

Lit. Win, you see, 'tis in fashion to go to the Fair, Win; we must to the Fair too, you and I, Win. I have an affair i' the Fair, Win, a puppet-play of mine own making—say nothing—that I writ for the motion-man,[19] which you must see, Win.

Win. I would I might, John, but my mother will never consent to such a "profane motion," she will call it.   159

Lit. Tut, we'll have a device, a dainty one—now, Wit, help at a pinch, good Wit come, come, good Wit, and't be thy will—I have it, Win, I have it i' faith, and 'tis a fine one. Win, long to eat of a pig, sweet Win, i' the Fair, do you see? I' the heart o' the Fair, not at Pie Corner.[20] Your mother will do anything, Win, to satisfy your longing, you know. Pray thee long, presently, and be sick o' the sudden, good Win. I'll go in and tell her. Cut thy lace i' the meantime, and play the hypocrite, sweet Win.   169

Win. No, I'll not make me unready[21] for it. I can be

---

   [8] *fidge:* move about restlessly.
   [9] *overbuy:* pay too much for.
   [10] *Sir Cranion:* a crane-fly.   [11] *stone:* testicle.
   [12] *coil:* trouble.   [13] *Catherine-pear:* a small early variety.
   [14] *tarriers:* hinderers.
   [15] *Bat:* diminutive of Bartholomew.
   [16] *quality:* high social status.
   [17] *qualities:* characteristics.
   [18] *apprehension:* understanding.
   [19] *motion-man:* puppet-master.
   [20] *Pie Corner:* where cookshops were.
   [21] *make ... unready:* undress.

hypocrite enough, though I were never so strait-laced.

Lit. You say true; you have been bred i' the family and brought up to't. Our mother is a most elect hypocrite, and has maintained us all this seven year with it, like gentlefolks.

Win. Ay, let her alone, John; she is not a wise willful widow for nothing, nor a sanctified sister for a song. And let me alone too; I ha' somewhat o' the mother²² in me, you shall see. Fetch her, fetch her. Ah, ah.   180

[*Exit* LITTLEWIT.]

I.vi

[*Enter* PURECRAFT, LITTLEWIT.]

Pure. Now, the blaze of the beauteous discipline¹ fright away this evil from our house! How now, Win-the-Fight, child, how do you? Sweet child, speak to me.

Win. Yes, forsooth.

Pure. Look up, sweet Win-the-Fight, and suffer not the enemy to enter you at this door. Remember that your education has been with the purest. What polluted one was it that named first the unclean beast, pig, to you, child?

Win. Uh, uh.   10

Lit. Not I, o' my sincerity, mother; she longed above three hours, ere she would let me know it. Who was it, Win?

Win. A profane black thing with a beard, John.

Pure. Oh, resist it, Win-the-Fight; it is the tempter, the wicked tempter; you may know it by the fleshly motion² of pig. Be strong against it and its foul temptations in these assaults, whereby it broacheth³ flesh and blood, as it were, on the weaker side, and pray against its carnal provocations, good child, sweet child, pray.   21

Lit. Good mother, I pray you that she may eat some pig, and her belly full, too; and do not you cast away your own child, and perhaps one of mine, with your tale of the tempter.—How do you, Win? Are you not sick?

Win. Yes, a great deal, John. Uh, uh.

Pure. What shall we do? Call our zealous brother Busy hither, for his faithful fortification in this charge of the adversary. Child, my dear child, you shall eat pig, be comforted, my sweet child.   31

[*Exit* LITTLEWIT.]

Win. Ay, but i' the Fair, mother.

Pure. I mean i' the Fair, if it can be anyway made or found lawful.—Where is our brother Busy? Will he not come?—Look up, child.

[*Re-enter* LITTLEWIT.]

Lit. Presently, mother, as soon as he has cleansed his beard. I found him, fast by the teeth i' the cold turkey-pie i' the cupboard, with a great white loaf on his left hand and a glass of malmsey on his right.

Pure. Slander not the brethren, wicked one.   40

Lit. Here he is now, purified, mother.

[*Enter*] BUSY.

Pure. O brother Busy! your help here to edify and raise us up in a scruple.⁴ My daughter Win-the-Fight is visited with a natural disease⁵ of women called "A longing to eat pig."

Lit. Ay sir, a Barthol'mew pig, and in the Fair.

Pure. And I would be satisfied from you, religiously-wise, whether a widow of the sanctified assembly or a widow's daughter may commit the act, without offense to the weaker sisters.   50

Busy. Verily, for the disease of longing, it is a disease, a carnal disease, or appetite, incident to women; and as it is carnal, and incident, it is natural, very natural. Now pig, it is a meat, and a meat that is nourishing, and may be longed for, and so consequently eaten; it may be eaten; very, exceeding well eaten; but in the Fair, and as a Barthol'mew-pig, it cannot be eaten, for the very calling it a Barthol'mew-pig, and to eat it so, is a spice⁶ of idolatry, and you make the Fair no better than one of the high places.⁷ This, I take it, is the state of the question. A high place.   61

Lit. Ay, but in state of necessity, place should give place, Master Busy. (I have a conceit left, yet.)

Pure. Good brother Zeal-of-the-Land, think to make it as lawful as you can.

Lit. Yes, sir, and as soon as you can; for it must be sir; you see the danger my little wife is in, sir.

Pure. Truly, I do love my child dearly, and I would not have her miscarry or hazard her first fruits if it might be otherwise.   70

Busy. Surely, it may be otherwise, but it is subject to construction, subject, and hath a face of offense with the weak, a great face, a foul face, but that face may have a veil put over it, and be shadowed, as it were. It may be eaten, and in the Fair, I take it, in a booth, the tents of the wicked. The place is not much, not very much; we may be religious in midst of the profane, so it be eaten with a reformed mouth, with sobriety, and humbleness; not gorged in with gluttony or greediness. There's the fear; for, should she go there, as taking   80 pride in the place or delight in the unclean dressing, to feed the vanity of the eye or the lust of the palate, it were not well, it were not fit, it were abominable, and not good.

Lit. Nay, I knew that afore, and told her on't; but courage, Win, we'll be humble enough; we'll seek out the homeliest booth i' the Fair, that's certain; rather than fail, we'll eat it o' the ground.

Pure. Ay, and I'll go with you myself, Win-the-Fight, and my brother, Zeal-of-the-Land, shall go with us too, for our better consolation.   91

Win. Uh, uh.

Lit. Ay, and Solomon too, Win; the more the

---

²² *mother:* hysteria, held to originate in the womb; with puns on her mother and her pregnancy.

I.vi.
¹ *beauteous discipline:* Puritan faith.   ² *motion:* urging.
³ *broacheth:* breaks into.
⁴ *scruple:* question of conscience.
⁵ *disease:* discomfort.   ⁶ *spice:* kind.
⁷ *high places:* where Israelites worshiped idols.

merrier, Win; [*Aside to* WIN] we'll leave Rabbi Busy in a booth.—Solomon, my cloak.

[Enter] SOLOMON.

Sol. Here, sir.

Busy. In the way of comfort to the weak, I will go, and eat. I will eat exceedingly, and prophesy. There may be a good use made of it, too, now I think on't: by the public eating of swine's flesh, to profess our   100 hate and loathing of Judaism, whereof the brethren stand taxed.[8] I will therefore eat; yea, I will eat exceedingly.

Lit. Good, i' faith, I will eat heartily too, because I will be no Jew; I could never away[9] with that stiff-necked generation. And truly, I hope my little one will be like me, that cries for pig so, i' the mother's belly.

Busy. Very likely, exceeding likely, very exceeding likely.

[Exeunt.]

ACT TWO

SCENE ONE

[Enter JUSTICE OVERDO.*]*

Just. Well, in justice' name, and the King's, and for the Commonwealth![1] defy all the world, Adam Overdo, for a disguise, and all story; for thou hast fitted thyself, I swear. Fain would I meet the Lynceus[2] now, that eagle's eye, that piercing Epidaurian serpent[3] (as my Quintus Horace calls him), that could discover a justice of peace (and lately of the quorum[4]) under this covering. They may have seen many a fool in the habit of a justice; but never till now, a justice in the habit of a fool. Thus must we do, though, that wake[5] for the   10 public good; and thus hath the wise magistrate done in all ages. There is a doing of right out of wrong, if the way be found. Never shall I enough commend a worthy worshipful man, sometime a capital member of this city, for his high wisdom in this point, who would take you now the habit of a porter, now of a carman, now of the dog-killer, in this month of August; and in the winter of a seller of tinder-boxes. And what would he do in all these shapes? Marry, go you into every ale-house, and down into every cellar; measure the   20 length of puddings, take the gauge of black pots and cans, ay, and custards, with a stick; and their circumference, with a thread; weigh the loaves of bread on his middle-finger; then would he sent for 'em, home; give the puddings to the poor, the bread to the hungry, the custards to his children; break the pots, and burn the cans, himself; he would not trust his corrupt officers; he would do't himself. Would all men in authority would follow this worthy precedent! For, alas, as we are public persons, what do we know? Nay, what   30 can we know? We hear with other men's ears; we see with other men's eyes; a foolish constable or a sleepy watchman is all our information: he slanders a gentleman by the virtue of his place, as he calls it, and we, by the vice of ours, must believe him; as, a while agone, they made me, yea me, to mistake an honest zealous pursuivant[6] for a seminary,[7] and a proper young Bachelor of Music for a bawd. This we are subject to, that live in high place. All our intelligence[8] is idle, and most of our intelligencers knaves; and,   40 by your leave, ourselves though little better, if not arrant fools, for believing 'em. I, Adam Overdo, am resolved therefore to spare spy-money hereafter, and make mine own discoveries. Many are the yearly enormities of this Fair, in whose courts of Pie-powders[9] I have had the honor during the three days sometimes to sit as judge. But this is the special day for detection of those foresaid enormities. Here is my black book for the purpose, this the cloud that hides me; under this covert I shall see and not be seen. On Junius   50 Brutus.[10] And as I began, so I'll end: in justice' name and the King's, and for the Commonwealth!

II.ii

[Enter LEATHERHEAD, TRASH, Passengers.*]*

Lea. The Fair's pestilence[1] dead, methinks; people come not abroad today, whatever the matter is. Do you hear, Sister Trash, lady o' the basket? Sit farther with your ginger-bread-progeny there, and hinder not the prospect of my shop, or I'll ha' it proclaimed i' the Fair what stuff they are made on.

Trash. Why, what stuff are they made on, Brother Leatherhead? Nothing but what's wholesome, I assure you.

Lea. Yes, stale bread, rotten eggs, musty ginger, and dead honey, you know.   11

Just. [*Aside*] Ay! have I met with enormity so soon?

Lea. I shall mar your market, old Joan.

Trash. Mar my market, thou too-proud pedlar? Do thy worst; I defy thee, ay, and thy stable of hobby-horses. I pay for my ground as well as thou dost; and thou wrong'st me, for all thou art parcel[2]-poet, and an inginer,[3] I'll find a friend shall right me and make a

---

ballad of thee and thy cattel⁴ all over. Are you puffed
up with the pride of your wares? Your arsedine?⁵   20

Lea. Go to, old Joan, I'll talk with you anon; and
take you down⁶ too afore Justice Overdo; he is the man
must charm you. I'll ha' you i' the Pie-powders.

Trash. Charm me? I'll meet thee face to face afore
his worship, when thou dar'st; and though I be a little
crooked o' my body, I'll be found as upright in my
dealing as any woman in Smithfield, I. Charm me?

Just. [*Aside*] I am glad to hear my name in their
terror, yet; this is doing of justice.   29

Lea. What do you lack?⁷ What is't you buy? What
do you lack? Rattles, drums, halberts, horses, babies o'
the best? Fiddles o' the' finest?

        Enter COSTERMONGER, NIGHTINGALE.

Cost. Buy any pears, pears, fine, very fine pears!
Trash. Buy any gingerbread, gilt gingerbread!

Night. *Hey, now the Fair's a-filling!*
        Oh, for a tune to startle
        The birds o' the booths here billing
        Yearly with old Saint Bartle!
        The drunkards they are wading,
        *The punks and chapmen*⁸ *trading;*   40
        *Who'd see the Fair without his lading?*⁹

Buy any ballads; new ballads?

            [*Enter*] URSULA.

Urs. Fie upon't! Who would wear out their youth
and prime thus in roasting of pigs that had any cooler
vocation? Hell's a kind of cold cellar to¹⁰ 't, a very fine
vault, o' my conscience! What, Mooncalf!

Moon. [*Within*] Here, mistress.
Night. How now, Urs'la? In a heat, in a heat?
Urs. My chair, you false faucet¹¹ you; and my
morning's draught, quickly, a bottle of ale to   50
quench me, rascal. I am all fire and fat, Nightingale; I
shall e'en melt away to the first woman, a rib again, I
am afraid. I do water the ground in knots¹² as I go,
like a great garden-pot; you may follow me by the S's I
make.

Night. Alas, good Urs; was 'Zekiel here this morning?
Urs. 'Zekiel? What 'Zekiel?
Night. 'Zekiel Edgworth, the civil cutpurse, you
know him well enough; he that talks bawdy to you still;
I call him my secretary.¹³   60

Urs. He promised to be here this morning, I remember.

Night. When he comes, bid him stay; I'll be back
again presently.

Urs. Best take your morning's dew in your belly,
Nightingale.

        MOONCALF *brings in the chair.*

Come, sir, set it here; did not I bid you should get this
chair let out o' the sides for me, that my hips might
play? You'll never think of anything till your dame be
rump-galled. 'Tis well, changeling;¹⁴ because it   70
can take in your grasshopper's thighs, you care for no
more. Now, you look as you had been i' the corner o'

the booth, fleaing¹⁵ your breech with a candle's end,
and set fire o' the Fair. Fill, stoat,¹⁶ fill.

Just. [*Aside*] This pig-woman do I know, and I will
put her in for my second enormity. She hath been
before me, punk, pinnace,¹⁷ and bawd, any time these
two and twenty years, upon record i' the Pie-powders.

Urs. Fill again, you unlucky vermin.
Moon. 'Pray you be not angry, mistress; I'll ha' it
widened anon.   81

Urs. No, no, I shall e'en dwindle away to't ere the
Fair be done, you think, now you ha' heated me? A poor
vexed thing I am; I feel myself dropping¹⁸ already,
as fast as I can. Two stone o' suet a day is my proportion. I can but hold life and soul together, with this
—here's to you, Nightingale—and a whiff of tobacco, at
most. Where's my pipe now? Not filled? Thou arrant
incubee.¹⁹   89

Night. Nay, Urs'la, thou'lt gall between the tongue
and the teeth with fretting²⁰ now.

Urs. How can I hope that ever he'll discharge his
place of trust—tapster, a man of reckoning²¹ under
me—that remembers nothing I say to him?

                [*Exit* NIGHTINGALE.]

But look to't, sirrah, you were best; threepence a pipe-
full, I will ha' made of all my whole half-pound of
tobacco, and a quarter of a pound of coltsfoot²² mixed
with it too, to itch²³ it out. I that have dealt so long in
the fire will not be to seek²⁴ in smoke now. Then, six
and twenty shillings a barrel I will advance²⁵   100
o' my beer, and fifty shillings a hundred o' my bottle-
ale; I ha' told you the ways how to raise it. Froth your
cans well i' the filling, at length, rogue, and jog your
bottles o' the buttock, sirrah, then skink²⁶ out the first
glass, ever, and drink with all companies, though you
be sure to be drunk; you'll misreckon the better and be
less ashamed on't. But your true trick, rascal, must be
to be ever busy, and mis-take away the bottles and cans
in haste before they be half drunk off, and never hear
anybody call (if they should chance to mark you), 110
till you ha' brought fresh, and be able to forswear 'em.
Give me a drink of ale.

Just. [*Aside*] This is the very womb and bed of

---

    ⁴ *cattel:* stock in trade.
    ⁵ *arsedine:* imitation gold leaf for decorating toys.
    ⁶ *take down:* humble.
    ⁷ *what . . . lack:* the merchant's cry.
    ⁸ *chapmen:* customers.   ⁹ *lading:* load of purchases.
    ¹⁰ *to:* compared to.   ¹¹ *faucet:* barrel tap.
    ¹² *knots:* crisscross lines.
    ¹³ *secretary:* confidant, accomplice.
    ¹⁴ *changeling:* idiot; ugly or stupid child left by fairies in
the crib of another.   ¹⁵ *fleaing:* ridding of fleas.
    ¹⁶ *stoat:* weasel, a lean creature.
    ¹⁷ *pinnace:* go-between, prostitute; literally, a boat that
goes between ship and shore.
    ¹⁸ *dropping:* losing weight and perspiring, which in
Ursula's argument amount to the same thing. The stage
direction "dropping" at her entrance in II.iii presumably
indicates that she is visibly perspiring.
    ¹⁹ *incubee:* demon.   ²⁰ *fretting:* gnawing.
    ²¹ *reckoning:* distinction; account-keeping.
    ²² *coltsfoot:* kind of grass used as an adulterant in tobacco.
    ²³ *itch:* eke.   ²⁴ *to seek:* wanting.
    ²⁵ *advance:* raise the price. ²⁶ *skink:* draw out.

enormity! gross as herself! This must all down for enormity, all, every whit on't.

One knocks.

Urs. Look who's there, sirrah! Five shillings a pig is my price, at least; if it be a sow-pig, sixpence more; if she be a great-bellied wife, and long for't, sixpence more for that.   119

Just. [*Aside*] *O tempora! O mores!*[27] I would not ha' lost my discovery of this one grievance for my place and worship[28] o' the bench. How is the poor subject abused here! Well, I will fall in with her, and with her Mooncalf, and win out wonders of enormity.—By thy leave, goodly woman, and the fatness of the Fair, oily as the King's constable's lamp, and shining as his shoeing-horn! hath thy ale virtue, or thy beer strength? that the tongue of man may be tickled? and his palate pleased in the morning? Let thy pretty nephew here go search and see.   130

Urs. What new roarer is this?

Moon. O Lord! do you not know him, mistress, 'tis mad Arthur of Bradley[29] that makes the orations. Brave master, old Arthur of Bradley, how do you? Welcome to the Fair. When shall we hear you again, to handle your matters? With your back again a booth, ha? I ha' been one o' your little disciples, i' my days!

Just. Let me drink, boy, with my love, thy aunt, here, that I may be eloquent; but of thy best, lest it be bitter in my mouth, and my words fall foul on the Fair.   141

Urs. Why dost thou not fetch him drink? And offer him to sit?

Moon. Is't ale, or beer, Master Arthur?

Just. Thy best, pretty stripling, thy best; the same thy dove drinketh and thou drawest on holy days.

Urs. Bring him a sixpenny bottle of ale; they say, a fool's handsel[30] is lucky.

Just. Bring both, child. Ale for Arthur, and beer for Bradley. Ale for thine aunt, boy.   150

[*Exit* MOONCALF.]

[*Aside*] My disguise takes to the very wish and reach of it. I shall, by the benefit of this, discover enough and more, and yet get off with the reputation of what I

would be; a certain middling thing, between a fool and a madman.

[II.iii]

[*Enter* KNOCKEM.]

Kno. What! my little lean Urs'la! my she-bear! art thou alive yet? With thy litter of pigs, to grunt out another Barthol'mew Fair? Ha!

Urs. Yes, and to amble afoot, when the Fair is done, to hear you groan out of a cart, up the heavy hill.[1]

Kno. Of Holborn, Urs'la, meanst thou so? For what? For what, pretty Urs?

Urs. For cutting halfpenny purses, or stealing little penny dogs out o' the Fair.

Kno. Oh good words, good words, Urs.   10

Just. [*Aside*] Another special enormity. A cutpurse of the sword! the boot, and the feather! Those are his marks.

[*Re-enter* MOONCALF.]

Urs. You are one of those horse-leeches[2] that gave out I was dead in Turnbull-street of a surfeit of bottle-ale and tripes?

Kno. No, 'twas better meat, Urs: cow's udders, cow's udders!

Urs. Well, I shall be meet[3] with your mumbling mouth one day.   20

Kno. What? Thou'lt poison me with a newt in a bottle of ale, wilt thou? Or a spider in a tobacco-pipe, Urs? Come, there's no malice in these fat folks; I never fear thee, and I can 'scape thy lean Mooncalf here. Let's drink it out, good Urs, and no vapors![4]

[*Exit* URSULA.]

Just. Dost thou hear, boy? (There's for thy ale, and the remnant for thee.) Speak in thy faith of a faucet, now; is this goodly person before us here, this vapors, a knight of the knife?

Moon. What mean you by that, Master Arthur?   30

Just. I mean a child of the horn-thumb,[5] a babe of booty, boy; a cutpurse.

Moon. Oh, Lord, sir! far from it. This is Master Dan Knockem; Jordan,[6] the ranger of Turnbull. He is a horse-courser, sir.

Just. Thy dainty dame, though, called him cutpurse.

Moon. Like enough, sir; she'll do forty such things in an hour (an you listen to her) for her recreation, if the toy[7] take her i' the greasy kerchief. It makes her fat, you see. She battens[8] with it.   40

Just. [*Aside*] Here might I ha' been deceived now, and ha' put a fool's blot upon myself, if I had not played an after-game o' discretion.

URSULA *comes in again dropping.*[9]

Kno. Alas, poor Urs, this's an ill season for thee.

Urs. Hang yourself, hackney-man.[10]

Kno. How? How? Urs, vapors! motion breed vapors?

Urs. Vapors? Never tusk[11] nor twirl your dibble,[12] good Jordan; I know what you'll take to a very drop. Though you be captain o' the roarers, and fight well at

---

[27] *L.:* "O age! O manners!" Cicero's first oration *v.* Catiline.   [28] *worship:* honor.

[29] *mad . . . Bradley:* ballad hero.

[30] *handsel:* first money taken by a merchant in the morning, kept for good luck.

II.iii.

[1] *hill:* Holborn Hill, as he is carted to his execution at Tyburn.

[2] *horse-leeches:* veterinarians; aquatic sucking worm; rapacious, insatiable fellow.   [3] *meet:* even.

[4] *vapors:* Knockem's all-purpose word refers most often to causeless quarreling and to the capricious, often affected personality and behavior that Jonson himself called humors.

[5] *horn-thumb:* thimble worn by cutpurse to help in the use of his knife.   [6] *Jordan:* The name means chamberpot.

[7] *toy:* whim.   [8] *battens:* grows fat.

[9] See n. 18 to II.ii. above.

[10] *hackney-man:* one who keeps horses for hire.

[11] *tusk:* tuft.   [12] *dibble:* spade-beard.

the case[13] of piss-pots, you shall not fright me with   50
your lion-chap,[14] sir, nor your tusks.[15] You angry? You
are hungry. Come, a pig's head will stop your mouth
and stay your stomach at all times.

Kno. Thou art such another mad merry Urs still!
Troth, I do make conscience of vexing thee now i' the
dog-days,[16] this hot weather, for fear of foundering[17]
thee i' the body, and melting down a pillar of the Fair.
Pray thee take thy chair again, and keep state,[18] and
let's have a fresh bottle of ale, and a pipe of tobacco,
and no vapors. I'll ha' this belly o' thine taken up[19]   60
and thy grass scoured,[20] wench. Look! here's Ezekiel
Edgworth; a fine boy of his inches as any is i' the Fair!
has still money in his purse, and will pay all with a kind
heart; and good vapors.

II.iv

[*Enter*] EDGWORTH, NIGHTINGALE, CORNCUTTER,
TINDERBOX-MAN, Passengers.

Edg. That I will, indeed, willingly, Master Knockem.
Fetch some ale, and tobacco.

[*Exit* MOONCALF.]

Lea. What do you lack, gentlemen? Maid: see a fine
hobbyhorse for your young master; cost you but a token
a week his provender.[1]

Corn. Ha' you any corns i' your feet and toes?

Tind. Buy a mousetrap, a mousetrap, or a tormentor[2]
for a flea.

Trash. Buy some gingerbread.

Night. Ballads, ballads! fine new ballads: 10
Hear for your love, and buy for your money!
A delicate ballad o' "The Ferret and the Coney!"
"A Preservative again' the Punks' Evil!"
Another of "Goose-green[3] Starch and the Devil!"
"A Dozen of Divine Points," and "The Godly
      Garters!"
"The Fairing of Good Counsel," of an ell[4] and three
      quarters!
What is't you buy?
"The Windmill Blown Down by the Witch's Fart!"
Or "Saint George, That Oh! did Break the Dragon's
      Heart!"

[*Re-enter* MOONCALF.]

Edg. Master Nightingale, come hither, leave your
mart[5] a little.   21

Night. Oh, my secretary! What says my secretary?

Just. Child o' the bottles, what's he? What's he?

Moon. A civil young gentleman, Master Arthur, that
keeps company with the roarers and disburses all still.[6]
He has ever money in his purse; he pays for them, and
they roar for him; one does good offices for another.
They call him the secretary, but he serves nobody. A
great friend of the ballad-man's, they are never
asunder.   30

Just. What pity 'tis so civil a young man should
haunt this debauched company! Here's the bane of the
youth of our time apparent. A proper penman, I see't

in his countenance; he has a good clerk's look with
him, and I warrant him a quick hand.

Moon. A very quick hand, sir.

[*Exit.*]

Edg. All the purses and purchase[7] I give you today
by conveyance,[8] bring hither to Urs'la's presently.
Here we will meet at night in her lodge, and share.
Look you choose good places for your standing i' the
Fair when you sing, Nightingale.   41

This they whisper, that OVERDO *hears it not.*

Urs. Ay, near the fullest passages; and shift[9] 'em
often.

Edg. And i' your singing you must use your hawk's
eye nimbly, and fly the purse to a mark[10] still, where 'tis
worn and o' which side, that you may gi' me the sign
with your beak, or hang your head that way i' the tune.

Urs. Enough, talk no more on't, your friendship,
masters, is not now to begin. Drink your draught of
indenture,[11] your sup of covenant, and away; the   50
Fair fills apace, company begins to come in, and I ha'
ne'er a pig ready, yet.

Kno. Well said! Fill the cups, and light the tobacco.
Let's give fire i' th' works and noble vapors.

Edg. And shall we ha' smocks,[12] Urs'la, and good
whimsies,[13] ha?

Urs. Come, you are i' your bawdy vein! the best the
Fair will afford, 'Zekiel, if bawdy Whit keep his word.

[*Re-enter* MOONCALF.]

How do the pigs, Mooncalf?

Moon. Very passionate,[14] mistress, one on 'em has
wept out an eye. Master Arthur o' Bradley is   61
melancholy, here; nobody talks to him. Will you any
tobacco, Master Arthur?

Just. No, boy, let my meditations alone.

Moon. He's studying for an oration, now.

Just. [*Aside*] If I can, with this day's travail and all my
policy[15] but rescue this youth here out of the hands of
the lewd man and the strange woman, I will sit down
at night and say with my friend Ovid, *Iamque opus
exegi, quod nec Jovis ira, nec ignis, etc.*[16]   70

---

[13] *case:* pair.   [14] *chap:* jaw.   [15] *tusks:* mustache.
[16] *dog-days:* hot days of August under the supposed influence of Sirius, the dog star.
[17] *foundering:* afflicting a horse with a characteristic illness.
[18] *state:* ceremonious posture.
[19] *taken up:* reduced (veterinary).   [20] *scoured:* purged.

II.iv.
[1] *provender:* feed.   [2] *tormentor:* trap.
[3] *Goose-green:* yellowish green.
[4] *ell:* 45-inch measure.   [5] *mart:* selling.
[6] *still:* always.   [7] *purchase:* booty.
[8] *conveyance:* transference, light-fingered carrying off or
stealing.   [9] *shift:* change your location.
[10] *fly . . . mark:* hawking—the hunting bird shows where
the prey is.   [11] *draught of indenture:* a traditional pun.
[12] *smocks:* whores.   [13] *whimsies:* wenches.
[14] *passionate:* sorrowful.   [15] *policy:* scheming.
[16] *L.:* "And now I have finished my work, which neither
the wrath of Jove nor fire," etc. ["shall be able to undo"],
Ovid, *Metamorphoses,* xv. 871–72.

Kno. Here, 'Zekiel; here's a health to Urs'la, and a kind vapor. Thou hast money i' thy purse still; and store![17] How dost thou come by it? Pray thee vapor thy friends some in a courteous vapor.

Edg. Half I have, Master Dan Knockem, is always at your service.

Just. [*Aside*] Ha, sweet nature! What goshawk would prey upon such a lamb?

Kno. Let's see what 'tis, 'Zekiel! Count it, come, fill him to pledge me.   80

II.v

[*Enter*] WINWIFE, QUARLOUS.

Winw. We are here before 'em, methinks.

Quar. All the better, we shall see 'em come in now.

Lea. What do you lack, gentlemen, what is't you lack? A fine horse? A lion? A bull? A bear? A dog, or a cat? An excellent fine Barthol'mew-bird? Or an instrument? What is't you lack?

Quar. 'Slid! here's Orpheus among the beasts, with his fiddle and all!

Trash. Will you buy any comfortable[1] bread, gentlemen?   10

Quar. And Ceres[2] selling her daughter's picture in gingerwork!

Winw. That these people should be so ignorant to think us chapmen[3] for 'em! Do we look as if we would buy gingerbread? Or hobbyhorses?

Quar. Why, they know no better ware than they have nor better customers than come. And our very being here makes us fit to be demanded, as well as others. Would Cokes would come! there were a true customer for 'em.   20

Kno. How much is't? Thirty shillings? Who's yonder! Ned Winwife? And Tom Quarlous, I think! Yes. (Gi' me it all, gi' me it all.) Master Winwife! Master Quarlous! will you take a pipe of tobacco with us? (Do not discredit me now, 'Zekiel.)

Winw. Do not see him! He is the roaring horse-courser; pray thee, let's avoid him: turn down this way.

Quar. 'Slud,[4] I'll see him, and roar with him too, and he roared as loud as Neptune; pray thee go with me.

Winw. You may draw me to as likely an inconvenience, when you please, as this.   31

Quar. Go to then, come along; we ha' nothing to do, man, but to see sights now.

Kno. Welcome, Master Quarlous and Master Winwife! will you take any froth and smoke with us?

Quar. Yes, sir, but you'll pardon us if we knew not of so much familiarity between us afore.

Kno. As what, sir?

Quar. To be so lightly invited to smoke and froth.

Kno. A good vapor! Will you sit down, sir? This is old Urs'la's mansion; how like you her bower?   41 Here you may ha' your punk and your pig in state, sir, both piping hot.

Quar. I had rather ha' my punk cold, sir.

Just. [*Aside*] There's for me: punk! and pig!

Urs. What, Mooncalf? You rogue.

She calls within.

Moon. By and by; the bottle is almost off,[5] mistress. Here, Master Arthur.

Urs. I'll part you and your play-fellow there i' the guarded[6] coat, an you sunder not the sooner.   50
[*Exit.*]

Kno. Master Winwife, you are proud, methinks; you do not talk nor drink; are you proud?

Winw. Not of the company I am in, sir, nor the place, I assure you.

Kno. You do not except[7] at the company! Do you? Are you in vapors, sir?

Moon. Nay, good Master Dan Knockem, respect my mistress' bower, as you call it; for the honor of our booth, none o' your vapors here.   59

She comes out with a firebrand.

Urs. Why, you thin lean polecat you, and they have a mind to be i' their vapors, must you hinder 'em? What did you know, vermin, if they would ha' lost a cloak, or such a trifle? Must you be drawing the air of pacification here, while I am tormented within i' the fire, you weasel?

Moon. Good mistress, 'twas in the behalf of your booth's credit that I spoke.

Urs. Why? Would my booth ha' broke[8] if they had fallen out in't, sir? Or would their heat ha' fired it? In, you rogue, and wipe the pigs, and mend the fire,   70 that they fall not, or I'll both baste and roast you till your eyes drop out like 'em. (Leave the bottle behind you, and be curst a while.)

[*Exit* MOONCALF.]

Quar. Body o' the Fair! what's this? Mother o' the bawds?

Kno. No, she's mother o' the pigs, sir, mother o' the pigs!

Winw. Mother o' the Furies, I think, by her firebrand.

Quar. Nay, she is too fat to be a Fury, sure some walking sow of tallow!   81

Winw. An inspired[9] vessel[10] of kitchen-stuff!

She drinks this while.

Quar. She'll make excellent gear[11] for the coach-makers here in Smithfield to anoint wheels and axle-trees with.

Urs. Ay, ay, gamesters, mock a plain plump soft wench o' the suburbs,[12] do, because she's juicy and wholesome. You must ha' your thin pinched ware, pent

---

[17] *store:* plenty.

II.v.
[1] *comfortable:* strengthening, refreshing.
[2] *Ceres:* goddess of agriculture, mother of Proserpina.
[3] *chapmen:* customers.   [4] *'Slud:* by God's blood.
[5] *off:* empty.   [6] *guarded:* trimmed with braid.
[7] *except:* take exception to.   [8] *broke:* gone bankrupt.
[9] *inspired:* divinely influenced.
[10] *vessel:* Puritan term for person.   [11] *gear:* stuff.
[12] *suburbs:* prostitutes' haunt.

up i' the compass of a dog-collar (or 'twill not do), that looks like a long laced[13] conger,[14] set upright, and a green feather, like fennel, i' the jowl[15] on't.   91

Kno. Well said, Urs, my good Urs; to 'em, Urs.

Quar. Is she your quagmire, Dan Knockem? Is this your bog?[16]

Night. We shall have a quarrel presently.

Kno. How? Bog? Quagmire? Foul vapors! Hum'h!

Quar. Yes, he that would venture for't, I assure him, might sink into her and be drowned a week ere any friend he had could find where he were.

Winw. And then he would be a fortnight weighing[17] up again.   101

Quar. 'Twere like falling into a whole shire of butter; they had need be a team of Dutchmen[18] should draw him out.

Kno. Answer 'em, Urs; where's thy Barthol'mew-wit now, Urs, thy Barthol'mew-wit?

Urs. Hang 'em, rotten, roguy cheaters, I hope to see 'em plagued one day (poxed[19] they are already, I am sure) with lean playhouse poultry,[20] that has the bony rump sticking out like the ace of spades or the   110 point of a partizan,[21] that every rib of 'em is like the tooth of a saw; and will so grate 'em with their hips and shoulders, as (take 'em altogether) they were as good lie with a hurdle.[22]

Quar. Out upon her, how she drips! She's able to give a man the sweating sickness[23] with looking on her.

Urs. Marry[24] look off, with a patch[25] o' your face; and a dozen i' your breech, though they be o' scarlet, sir. I ha' seen as fine outsides as either o' yours bring lousy linings to the brokers[26] ere now twice a week!   120

Quar. Do you think there may be a fine cucking-stool[27] i' the Fair to be purchased? One large enough, I mean. I know there is a pond of capacity for her.

Urs. For your mother, you rascal; out, you rogue, you hedgebird,[28] you pimp, you pannier-man's[29] bastard, you!

Quar. Ha, ha, ha.

Urs. Do you sneer, you dog's-head, you trendle-tail![30] You look as you were begotten atop of a cart in harvest-time, when the whelp was hot and   130 eager. Go, snuff after your brother's bitch, Mistress Commodity.[31] That's the livery you wear; 'twill be out at the elbows shortly. It's time you went to't, for the tother remnant.

Kno. Peace, Urs, peace, Urs; they'll kill the poor whale and make oil of her. Pray thee go in.

Urs. I'll see 'em poxed first, and piled,[32] and double piled.

Winw. Let's away; her language grows greasier than her pigs.   140

Urs. Does't so, snotty nose? Good Lord! are you sniveling? You were engendered on a she-beggar in a barn when the bald thrasher, your sire, was scarce warm.

Winw. Pray thee, let's go.

Quar. No, 'faith; I'll stay the end of her now; I know she cannot last long; I find by her similes she wanes apace.

Urs. Does she so? I'll set you gone. Gi' me my pig-pan hither a little. I'll scald you hence, and you will not go.   151

                    [*Exit.*]

Kno. Gentlemen, these are very strange vapors! And very idle vapors! I assure you.

Quar. You are a very serious ass, we assure you.

Kno. Hum'h! ass? And serious? Nay, then pardon me my vapor. I have a foolish vapor, gentlemen: any man that does vapor me the ass, Master Quarlous—

Quar. What then, Master Jordan?

Kno. I do vapor him the lie.

Quar. Faith, and to any man that vapors me the lie, I do vapor that.   161

                    [*Strikes him.*]

Kno. Nay, then, vapors upon vapors.

Edg., Night. 'Ware the pan, the pan, the pan; she comes with the pan, gentlemen. God bless the woman.

URSULA *comes in with the scalding-pan. They fight. She falls with it.*

Urs. Oh!

                    [*Exeunt* QUARLOUS, WINWIFE.]

Trash. What's the matter?

Just. Goodly woman!

Moon. Mistress!

Urs. Curse of hell, that ever I saw these fiends, Oh! I ha' scalded my leg, my leg, my leg, my leg. I ha'   170 lost a limb in the service! Run for some cream and salad oil, quickly! Are you under-peering,[33] you baboon? Rip off my hose, an' you be men, men, men!

Moon. Run you for some cream, good mother Joan. I'll look to your basket.

                    [*Exit* TRASH.]

Lea. Best sit up i' your chair, Urs'la. Help, gentle-men.

Kno. Be of good cheer, Urs; thou hast hindered me the currying[34] of a couple of stallions here that abused the good race[35] bawd o' Smithfield; 'twas time for 'em to go.   181

Night. I' faith, when the pan came they had made

---

[13] *laced:* striped.   [14] *conger:* eel.   [15] *jowl:* fish-head.

[16] *quagmire . . . bog:* corner of horsedealer's yard where unsound horses could stand up to their knees in wet clay.

[17] *weighing:* raising (nautical).

[18] *Dutchmen:* known as eaters of butter.

[19] *poxed:* syphilitic.   [20] *poultry:* whores.

[21] *partizan:* long-handled spear.

[22] *hurdle:* portable barrier.

[23] *sweating sickness:* a febrile disease marked by heavy sweating, frequently fatal in the sixteenth and seventeenth centuries.   [24] *Marry:* by Saint Mary.

[25] *patch:* mark of venereal disease.

[26] *brokers:* secondhand dealers.

[27] *cucking-stool:* chair in which scolds were ducked in ponds.   [28] *hedgebird:* robber.

[29] *pannier-man's:* referring to the man in charge of pedlars, fish hawkers, etc.   [30] *trendle-tail:* mongrel.

[31] *Commodity:* Something dealt in; i.e., a whore.

[32] *piled:* made bald by venereal disease.

[33] *under-peering:* peering under my dress.

[34] *currying:* beating.   [35] *race:* breed.

you run else.—This had been a fine time for purchase,[36] if you had ventured.

Edg. Not a whit, these fellows were too fine to carry money.

Kno. Nightingale, get some help to carry her leg out o' the air; take off her shoes; body o' me, she has the mallanders, the scratches, the crown scab, and the quitter bone [37] i' the tother leg.   190

Urs. Oh! the pox, why do you put me in mind o' my leg, thus to make it prick and shoot? Would you ha' me i' the Hospital afore my time?

Kno. Patience, Urs. Take a good heart, 'tis but a blister, as big as a windgall;[38] I'll take it away with the white of an egg, a little honey, and hog's grease; ha' thy pasterns[39] well rolled,[40] and thou shalt pace again by tomorrow. I'll tend thy booth and look to thy affairs the while; thou shalt sit i' thy chair, and give directions, and shine Ursa major.   200

[*Exeunt* KNOCKEM, MOONCALF, URSULA.]

II.vi

[*Enter* COKES, WASP, MISTRESS OVERDO, GRACE.]

Just. These are the fruits of bottle-ale and tobacco! the foam of the one and the fumes of the other! Stay, young man, and despise not the wisdom of these few hairs that are grown gray in care of thee.

Edg. Nightingale, stay a little. Indeed I'll hear some o' this!

Cokes. Come, Numps, come, where are you? Welcome into the Fair, Mistress Grace.

Edg. 'Slight, he will call company, you shall see, and put us into doings presently.   10

Just. Thirst not after that frothy liquor, ale; for who knows, when he openeth the stopple, what may be in the bottle? Hath not a snail, a spider, yea, a newt been found there? Thirst not after it, youth; thirst not after it.

Cokes. This is a brave fellow, Numps; let's hear him.

Wasp. 'Sblood, how brave [1] is he? In a guarded coat? You were best truck[2] with him; e'en strip, and truck presently; it will become you. Why will you hear him? Because he is an ass, and may be akin to the Cokeses?

Cokes. Oh, good Numps!   21

Just. Neither do thou lust after that tawny weed tobacco.

Cokes. Brave words!

Just. Whose complexion is like the Indian's that vents it!

Cokes. Are they not brave words, sister?

Just. And who can tell if, before the gathering and making up thereof, the alligarta[3] hath not pissed thereon?   30

Wasp. 'Heart, let 'em be brave words, as brave as they will! and they were all the brave words in a country, how then? Will you away yet? Ha' you enough on him? Mistress Grace, come you away, I pray you, be not you accessory. If you do lose your license, or somewhat else, sir, with list'ning to his fables, say Numps is a witch, with all my heart, do, say so.

Cokes. Avoid,[4] i' your satin doublet, Numps.   39

Just. The creeping venom of which subtle serpent, as some late writers affirm, neither the cutting of the perilous plant, nor the drying of it, nor the lighting, or burning, can any way persway[5] or assuage.

Cokes. Good, i' faith! is't not, sister?

Just. Hence it is, that the lungs of the tobacconist[6] are rotted, the liver spotted, the brain smoked like the backside of the pig-woman's booth here, and the whole body within black as her pan you saw e'en now without.

Cokes. A fine similitude, that, sir! did you see the pan?   50

Edg. Yes, sir.

Just. Nay, the hole in the nose here, of some tobacco-takers, or the third nostril (if I may so call it), which makes that they can vent the tobacco out like the ace of clubs, or rather the flower-de-lys,[7] is caused from the tobacco, the mere tobacco! when the poor innocent pox, having nothing to do there, is miserably and most unconscionably slandered.

Cokes. Who would ha' missed this, sister?

Mrs. O. Not anybody but Numps.   60

Cokes. He does not understand.

Edg. Nor you feel.

He picketh his purse.

Cokes. What would you have, sister, of a fellow that knows nothing but a basket-hilt[8] and an old fox[9] in't? The best music i' the Fair will not move a log.

Edg. In, to Urs'la, Nightingale, and carry her comfort; see it told. This fellow was sent to us by fortune for our first fairing.

[*Exit* NIGHTINGALE.]

Just. But what speak I of the diseases of the body, children of the Fair?   70

Cokes. That's to us, sister. Brave i' faith!

Just. Hark, O you sons and daughters of Smithfield! and hear what malady it doth the mind; it causeth swearing, it causeth swaggering, it causeth snuffling, and snarling, and now and then a hurt.

Mrs. O. He hath something of Master Overdo, methinks, brother.

Cokes. So methought, sister, very much of my brother Overdo; and 'tis when he speaks.   79

Just. Look into any angle o' the town—the Straits, or the Bermudas[10]—where the quarreling lesson is read, and how do they entertain the time but with bottle-ale and tobacco? The lecturer is o' one side, and his pupils o' the other; but the seconds[11] are still

---

[36] *purchase:* robbery.
[37] *mallanders . . . bone:* diseases of horse legs and feet.
[38] *windgall:* tumor on horses' leg.
[39] *pasterns:* horse's ankles.   [40] *rolled:* bandaged.

II.vi.
[1] *brave:* resplendent.   [2] *truck:* deal.
[3] *alligarta:* alligator.   [4] *Avoid:* Get away.
[5] *persway:* mitigate.   [6] *tobacconist:* smoker.
[7] *flower-de-lys:* fleur-de-lis.
[8] *basket-hilt:* hilt shaped like a basket.   [9] *fox:* sword.
[10] *straits . . . Bermudas:* London district populated by thieves and prostitutes.   [11] *seconds:* props.

bottle-ale and tobacco, for which the lecturer reads and the novices pay. Thirty pound a week in bottle-ale! forty in tobacco! and ten more in ale again. Then for a suit to drink in, so much, and (that being slavered) so much for another suit, and then a third suit, and a fourth suit! and still the bottle-ale slavereth, and the tobacco stinketh!   91

Wasp. Heart of a madman! are you rooted here? Will you never away? What can any man find out in this bawling fellow, to grow here for? He is a full handful higher sin' he heard him. Will you fix here? And set up a booth, sir?

Just. I will conclude briefly—

Wasp. Hold your peace, you roaring rascal; I'll run my head i' your chaps else. You were best build a booth, and entertain him, make your will, and you say   100 the word, and him your heir! Heart, I never knew one taken with a mouth of a peck,[12] afore. By this light, I'll carry you away o' my back, and you will not come.

He gets him up on pick-pack.

Cokes. Stay, Numps, stay, set me down. I ha' lost my purse, Numps, oh, my purse! one o' my fine purses is gone.

Mrs. O. Is't indeed, brother?

Cokes. Ay, as I am an honest man, would I were an arrant rogue else! a plague of all roguy, damned cut-purses for me.   110

Wasp. Bless 'em with all my heart, with all my heart, do you see! now, as I am no infidel, that I know of, I am glad on't. Ay, I am; here's my witness! do you see, sir! I did not tell you of his fables, I? No, no, I am a dull malt-horse,[13] I, I know nothing. Are you not justly served i' your conscience now? Speak i' your conscience. Much good do you with all my heart, and his good heart that has it, with all my heart again.

Edg. [*Aside*] This fellow is very charitable; would he had a purse too! But I must not be too bold all at a time.   121

Cokes. Nay, Numps, it is not my best purse.

Wasp. Not your best! Death! why should it be your worst? Why should it be any, indeed, at all? Answer me to that, gi' me a reason from you, why it should be any?

Cokes. Nor my gold, Numps; I ha' that yet; look here else, sister.

Wasp. Why so, there's all the feeling he has!

Mrs. O. I pray you, have a better care of that, brother.   131

Cokes. Nay, so I will, I warrant you; let him catch this that catch can. I would fain see him get this, look you here.

Wasp. So, so, so, so, so, so, so, so! Very good.

Cokes. I would ha' him come again, now, and but offer at it. Sister, will you take notice of a good jest? I will put it just where th' other was, and if we ha' good luck, you shall see a delicate fine trap to catch the cut-purse nibbling.   140

Edg. [*Aside*] Faith, and he'll try ere you be out o' the Fair.

Cokes. Come, Mistress Grace, prithee be not melan-choly for my mischance; sorrow wi' not keep it sweetheart.

Grace. I do not think on't, sir.

Cokes. 'Twas but a little scurvy white money,[14] hang it: it may hang the cutpurse, one day. I ha' gold left to gi' thee a fairing, yet, as hard as the world goes. Nothing angers me but that nobody here looked like a cutpurse, unless 'twere Numps.   151

Wasp. How? I? I look like a cutpurse? Death! your sister's a cutpurse! and your mother and father and all your kin were cutpurses! And here is a rogue is the bawd o' the cutpurses, whom I will beat to begin with.

They speak all together; and WASP *beats the* JUSTICE.

Just. Hold thy hand, child of wrath, and heir of anger, make it not Childermass[15] day in thy fury, or the feast of the French Barthol'mew, parent of the Massacre.[16]

Cokes. Numps, Numps!   160

Mrs. O. Good Master Humphrey.

Wasp. You are the Patrico![17] are you? The patri-arch of the cutpurses? You share, sir, they say, let them share this with you. Are you i' your hot fit of preaching again? I'll cool you.

Just. Murder, murder, murder!

[*Exeunt.*]

ACT THREE

SCENE ONE

[*Enter*] WHIT, HAGGIS, BRISTLE, LEATHERHEAD, TRASH.

Whit. Nay, 'tish all gone, now![1] dish 'tish phen tou vilt not be phitin call, Mas[h]ter Offisher! phat ish a man te better to lishen out noishes for tee and tou art in an oder 'orld—being very shuffishient noishes and gallantsh too, one o' their brabblesh[2] would have fed ush all dish fortnight; but tou art so bushy about beg-gersh still, tou hast no leishure to intend[3] shentlemen, and't be.

Hag. Why, I told you, Davy Bristle.   9

Bris. Come, come, you told me a pudding, Toby Haggis;[4] a matter of nothing; I am sure it came to nothing! you said, "Let's go to Urs'la's," indeed; but then you met the man with the monsters, and I could not get you from him. An old fool, not leave seeing yet?

Hag. Why, who would ha' thought anybody would

---

[12] *peck*: eight quarts.   [13] *malt-horse*: dray-horse.
[14] *white money*: silver.
[15] *Childermass*: Feast of Innocents, commemorating the slaughter of the innocent children.
[16] *French . . . massacre*: On St. Bartholomew's day 1572, Huguenots were massacred in Paris.
[17] *Patrico*: hedge-priest, illiterate parson (slang).

III.i.
[1] *Nay . . . now*: Whit speaks Elizabethan stage-Irish.
[2] *brabblesh*: brabbles, noisy quarrels.
[3] *intend*: attend to.
[4] *Haggis*: Haggis is a pudding made of innards; Bristle puns on the name.

ha' quarreled so early? Or that the ale o' the Fair would ha' been up so soon?

Whit. Phy, phat a clock tost tou tink it ish, man?

Hag. I cannot tell.   19

Whit. Tou art a vishe vatchman, i' te mean teeme.[5]

Hag. Why, should the watch go by the clock, or the clock by the watch, I pray?

Bris. One should go by another, if they did well.

Whit. Tou art right now! phen didst tou ever know or hear of a shufficient vatchman but he did tell the clock, phat bushiness soever he had?

Bris. Nay, that's most true, a sufficient watchman knows what o'clock it is.

Whit. Shleeping, or vaking! ash well as te clock him-shelf, or te jack[6] dat shtrikes him!   30

Bris. Let's inquire of Master Leatherhead, or Joan Trash here. Master Leatherhead, do you hear, Master Leatherhead?

Whit. If it be a Ledderhead, tish a very tick Ledderhead, tat sho mush noish vill not piersh him.

Lea. I have a little business now; good friends, do not trouble me.

Whit. Phat? Because o' ty wrought neet-cap, and ty phelvet sherkin, man? Phy? I have sheen tee in ty ledder sherkin ere now, mashter o' de hobbyhorses, as bushy and as stately as tou sheem'st to be.   41

Trash. Why, what an' you have, Captain Whit? He has his choice of jerkins, you may see by that, and his caps, too, I assure you, when he pleases to be either sick or employed.

Lea. God-a-mercy, Joan, answer for me.

Whit. Away, be not sheen i' my company; here be shentlemen and men of vorship.

            [*Exeunt* HAGGIS, BRISTLE.]

III.ii

[*Enter*] QUARLOUS, WINWIFE.

Quar. We had wonderful ill luck to miss this prologue o' the purse, but the best is we shall have five acts of him ere night; he'll be spectacle enough! I'll answer for't.

Whit. Oh, Creesh! Duke Quarlous, how dosht tou? Tou dosht not know me, I fear? I am te vishesht man but Justish Overdo in all Barthol'mew Fair, now. Gi' me twelvepence from tee, I vill help tee to a vife vorth forty marks for't, an't be.

Quar. Away, rogue, pimp, away.   10

Whit. And she shall show tee as fine cut 'ork[1] for't in her shmock too, as tou cansht vish i' faith; vilt tou have her, vorshipful Vinvife? I vill help tee to her, here, be an't be, in te pig-quarter, gi' me ty twel'pence from tee.

Winw. Why, there's twel'pence; pray thee, wilt thou be gone?

Whit. Tou art a vorthy man, and a vorshipful man still.

Quar. Get you gone, rascal.   20

Whit. I do mean it, man. Prinsh Quarlous, if tou hasht need on me, tou shalt find me here, at Urs'la's; I vill see phat ale and punk ish i' te pigshty for tee, bless ty good vorship.

            [*Exit.*]

[*Enter*] BUSY, PURECRAFT, LITTLEWIT, WIN.

Quar. Look! who comes here! John Littlewit!

Winw. And his wife, and my widow, her mother—the whole family.

Quar. 'Slight,[2] you must gi' em all fairings, now!

Winw. Not I, I'll not see 'em.   29

Quar. They are going a-feasting. What schoolmaster's that is with 'em?

Winw. That's my rival, I believe, the baker!

Busy. So, walk on in the middle way, fore-right,[3] turn neither to the right hand nor to the left; let not your eyes be drawn aside with vanity, nor your ear with noises.

Quar. [*Aside*] Oh, I know him by that start!

Lea. What do you lack? What do you buy, pretty mistress! a fine hobbyhorse, to make your son a tilter?[4] A drum to make him a soldier? A fiddle, to make 40 him a reveler? What is't you lack? Little dogs for your daughter? or babies, male, or female?

Busy. Look not toward them, hearken not. The place is Smithfield, or the field of smiths, the grove of hobbyhorses and trinkets; the wares are the wares of devils. And the whole Fair is the shop of Satan! They are hooks, and baits, very baits, that are hung out on every side, to catch you and to hold you, as it were, by the gills, and by the nostrils, as the fisher doth; therefore, you must not look, nor turn toward them. The 50 heathen man[5] could stop his ears with wax, against the harlot o' the sea; do you the like, with your fingers, against the bells of the Beast.

Winw. What flashes comes from him!

Quar. Oh, he has those of his oven! A notable hot baker 'twas, when he plied the peel.[6] He is leading his flock into the Fair, now.

Winw. Rather driving 'em to the pens, for he will let 'em look upon nothing.   59

[*Enter*] KNOCKEM, WHIT.

Kno. Gentlewomen, the weather's hot! whither walk you? Have a care o' your fine velvet caps; the Fair is dusty. Take a sweet delicate[7] booth, with boughs, here, i' the way, and cool yourselves i' the shade, you and your friends. The best pig and bottle-ale i' the Fair, sir. Old Urs'la is cook, there you may read: the pig's head speaks it.

---

[5] *te ... teeme:* the meantime.

[6] *jack:* figure that strikes the clock.

III.ii.

[1] *cut 'ork:* cutwork, lace, badge of high-class whores.

[2] *'Slight:* God's light.   [3] *fore-right:* straight ahead.

[4] *tilter:* jouster.

[5] *heathen man:* Ulysses; in fact, it was his crew's ears he stopped with wax while, lashed to the mast, he listened to the sirens' song.

[6] *peel:* long-handled shovel for handling loaves.

[7] *delicate:* delightful.

LITTLEWIT *is gazing at the sign; which is the pig's head with a large writing under it.*

Poor soul, she has had a stringhalt, the maryhinchco:[8] but she's prettily amended.

Whit. A delicate show-pig, little mistress, with shweet sauce, and crackling, like de bay leaf i' de 70 fire, la! tou shalt ha' de clean side o' de table-clot and dy glass vashed with phatersh of Dame Annessh Cleare.[9]

[*Exit.*]

Lit. This's fine, verily; "Here be the best pigs, and she does roast 'em as well as ever she did," the pig's head says.

Kno. Excellent, excellent, mistress, with fire o' juniper[10] and rosemary branches! the oracle of the pig's head, that, sir.   79

Pure. Son, were you not warned of the vanity of the eye? Have you forgot the wholesome admonition so soon?

Lit. Good mother, how shall we find a pig if we do not look about for't? Will it run off o' the spit into our mouths, think you? As in Lubberland?[11] And cry, 'We, we'?

Busy. No, but your mother, religiously wise, conceiveth it may offer itself by other means to the sense, as by way of steam, which I think it doth, here in this place.—Huh, huh.—Yes, it doth.   90

BUSY *scents after it like a hound.*

And it were a sin of obstinacy, great obstinacy, high and horrible obstinacy, to decline, or resist the good titillation of the famelic[12] sense, which is the smell. Therefore be bold (huh, huh, huh); follow the scent. Enter the tents of the unclean for once and satisfy your wife's frailty. Let your frail wife be satisfied; your zealous mother and my suffering self will also be satisfied.

Lit. Come, Win, as good winny[13] here as go farther and see nothing.

Busy. We 'scape so much of the other vanities by our early entering.   101

Pure. It is an edifying consideration.

Win. This is scurvy, that we must come into the Fair and not look on't.

Lit. Win, have patience, Win, I'll tell you more anon.

Kno. Mooncalf, entertain within there; the best pig i' the booth, a pork-like pig. These are Banbury-bloods, o' the sincere[14] stud,[15] come a-pig-hunting. Whit, wait, Whit, look to your charge.   109

Busy. A pig prepare, presently, let a pig be prepared to us.

[*Exeunt* BUSY, LITTLEWIT, WIN, PURECRAFT.]

[*Enter*] MOONCALF, URSULA.

Moon. 'Slight, who be these?

Urs. Is this the good service, Jordan, you'd do me?

Kno. Why, Urs? Why, Urs? Thou'lt ha' vapors i' thy leg again presently; pray thee go in, 't may turn to the scratches else.

Urs. Hang your vapors, they are stale, and stink like you; are these the guests o' the game you promised to fill my pit withal today?

Kno. Ay, what ail they, Urs?   120

Urs. Ail they? They are all sippers, sippers o' the city; they look as they would not drink off two penn'orth of bottle-ale amongst 'em.

Moon. A body may read that i' their small printed[16] ruffs.

Kno. Away, thou art a fool, Urs, and thy Mooncalf too, i' your ignorant vapors, now! hence! good guests, I say right hypocrites, good gluttons. In, and set a couple o' pigs o' the board, and half a dozen of the biggest bottles a-fore 'em and call Whit. I do not 130 love to hear innocents abused—fine ambling hypocrites! and a stone[17] puritan, with a sorrel[18] head, and beard, good mouthed gluttons—two to a pig, away.

[*Exit* MOONCALF.]

Urs. Are you sure they are such?

Kno. O' the right breed; thou shalt try 'em by the teeth,[19] Urs. Where's this Whit?

[*Re-enter* WHIT.]

Whit.

Behold, man, and see, what a worthy man am ee!
With the fury of my sword, and the shaking of my beard,
I will make ten thousand men afeared.   139

Kno. Well said, brave Whit; in, and fear the ale out o' the bottles into the bellies of the brethren, and the sisters; drink to the cause, and pure vapors.

[*Exeunt* KNOCKEM, WHIT, URSULA.]

Quar. My roarer is turned tapster, methinks. Now were a fine time for thee, Winwife, to lay aboard[20] thy widow; thou'lt never be master of a better season or place; she that will venture herself into the Fair and a pig-box will admit any assault, be assured of that.

Winw. I love not enterprises of that suddenness, though.   149

Quar. I'll warrant thee, then, no wife out o' the widow's hundred.[21] If I had but as much title to her as to have breathed once on that strait stomacher[22] of hers, I would now assure myself to carry[23] her yet ere she went out of Smithfield. Or she should carry me, which were the fitter sight, I confess. But you are a modest undertaker,[24] by circumstances and degrees;

---

[8] *stringhalt . . . maryhinchco:* disease of horse's legs.
[9] *Dame . . . Cleare:* spring named for the rich London widow Annis Clare, who drowned herself in it.
[10] *juniper:* burned to purify the air.
[11] *Lubberland:* never-never land where roast pigs were fancied to run about asking to be eaten.
[12] *famelic:* of hunger.   [13] *winny:* stay.
[14] *sincere:* genuine.   [15] *stud:* breed.
[16] *small printed:* neatly folded, a Puritan fashion.
[17] *stone:* male (cf. "stone-horse," stallion).
[18] *sorrel:* chestnut-colored (used to describe horses).
[19] *by . . . teeth:* as horses are judged for age.
[20] *lay aboard:* place one's ship alongside another for attack.
[21] *hundred:* county subdivision, used metaphorically here of the class of widows.
[22] *stomacher:* stiff ornamental covering for chest and abdomen.   [23] *carry:* win.
[24] *undertaker:* one who undertakes something.

come, 'tis disease in thee, not judgment; I should offer
at²⁵ all together. Look, here's the poor fool again that
was stung by the wasp erewhile.   159

III.iii

[Enter] JUSTICE.

Just. I will make no more orations shall¹ draw on
these tragical conclusions. And I begin now to think
that, by a spice of collateral² justice, Adam Overdo
deserved this beating; for I, the said Adam, was one
cause (a by-cause³) why the purse was lost—and my
wife's brother's purse too, which they know not of yet.
But I shall make very good mirth with it, at supper
(that will be the sport), and put my little friend Master
Humphrey Wasp's choler quite out of countenance.
When, sitting at the upper end o' my table, as I use, 10
and drinking to my brother Cokes and Mistress Alice
Overdo, as I will, my wife, for their good affection to
old Bradley, I deliver to 'em it was I that was cudgeled,
and show 'em the marks. To see what bad events may
peep out o' the tail of good purposes! The care I had of
that civil young man I took fancy to this morning, (and
have not left it yet) drew me to that exhortation, which
drew the company, indeed, which drew the cutpurse;
which drew the money; which drew my brother Cokes
his loss; which drew on Wasps' anger; which drew 20
on my beating—a pretty gradation! And they shall ha'
it i' their dish, i' faith, at night for fruit; I love to be
merry at my table. I had thought once, at one special
blow he ga' me, to have revealed myself. But then (I
thank thee, fortitude) I remembered that a wise man
(and who is ever so great a part o' the commonwealth
in himself) for no particular disaster ought to abandon
a public good design. The husbandman ought not, for
one unthankful year, to forsake the plow; the shepherd
ought not, for one scabbed sheep, to throw by his 30
tar⁴-box; the pilot ought not, for one leak i' the poop,
to quit the helm; nor the alderman ought not, for one
custard more, at a meal, to give up his cloak; the
constable ought not to break his staff and forswear the
watch for one roaring night; nor the piper o' the parish
(*ut parvis componere magna solebam*⁵) to put up his pipes
for one rainy Sunday. These are certain knocking conclusions, out of which I am resolved, come what come
can; come beating, come imprisonment, come infamy,
come banishment, nay, come the rack, come the 40
hurdle, welcome all; I will not discover who I am till

---

²⁵ *offer at:* make a try at.
III.iii.
¹ *shall:* that shall.   ² *collateral:* concomitant.
³ *by-cause:* incidental cause.   ⁴ *tar:* sheep-sore salve.
⁵ *L.:* as I used to compare great things with small (with
"*ut*" substituted for "*sic*"), Virgil, *Eclogues*, I. 23.

III.iv.
¹ *pair o' smiths:* toys(?), alarm clock bell mechanism(?).
² *scourse:* deal.
³ *Michaelmas term:* law-court session beginning September 29.   ⁴ *caroche:* fine carriage.
⁵ *cheaping of:* bargaining for.

my due time; and yet still all shall be, as I said ever, in
Justice' name, and the King's, and for the Commonwealth!
Winw. What does he talk to himself and act so
seriously? Poor fool!

                               [Exit] JUSTICE.
Quar. No matter what. Here's fresher argument, intend that.

III.iv

Enter COKES, MISTRESS OVERDO, GRACE, WASP.

Cokes. Come, Mistress Grace, come sister, here's
more fine sights yet, i' faith. God's lid, where's
Numps?
Lea. What do you lack, gentlemen? What is't you
buy? Fine rattles? Drums? Babies? Little dogs? And
birds for ladies? What do you lack?
Cokes. Good honest Numps, keep afore, I am so
afraid thou'lt lose somewhat; my heart was at my
mouth when I missed thee.
Wasp. You were best buy a whip i' your hand to
drive me.   11
Cokes. Nay, do not mistake, Numps, thou art so apt
to mistake; I would but watch the goods. Look you
now, the treble fiddle was e'en almost like to be lost.
Wasp. Pray you take heed you lose not yourself.
Your best way were e'en get up and ride for more
surety. Buy a token's worth of great pins to fasten
yourself to my shoulder.
Lea. What do you lack, gentlemen? Fine purses,
pouches, pin-cases, pipes? What is't you lack? A 20
pair o' smiths¹ to wake you i' the morning? Or a fine
whistling bird?
Cokes. Numps, here be finer things than any we ha'
bought, by odds! and more delicate horses, a great deal!
good Numps, stay, and come hither.
Wasp. Will you scourse² with him? You are in
Smithfield; you may fit yourself with a fine easy-going
street-nag for your saddle again' Michaelmas term,³do;
has he ne'er a little odd cart for you to make a caroche⁴
on i' the country with four pied hobbyhorses? 30
Why the measles should you stand here, with your
train, cheaping of⁵ dogs, birds, and babies? You ha'
no children to bestow 'em on? Ha' you?
Cokes. No, but again' I ha' children, Numps, that's
all one.
Wasp. Do, do, do, do; how many shall you have,
think you? An I were as you, I'd buy for all my tenants,
too. They are a kind o' civil savages that will part with
their children for rattles, pipes, and knives. You were
best buy a hatchet or two and truck with 'em.   40
Cokes. Good Numps, hold that little tongue o' thine,
and save it a labor. I am resolute Bat, thou know'st.
Wasp. A resolute fool you are, I know, and a very
sufficient coxcomb, with all my heart; nay, you have
it, sir, and you be angry, turd i' your teeth, twice (if I
said not once afore); and much good do you.
Winw. [*Aside*] Was there ever such a self-affliction?
And so impertinent?

Quar. [*Aside*] Alas! his care will go near to crack[6] him; let's in, and comfort him.   50

Wasp. Would I have been set i' the ground, all but the head on me, and had my brains bowled at, or threshed out, when first I underwent this plague of a charge!

Quar. How now, Numps! Almost tired i' your protectorship? Overparted?[7] Overparted?

Wasp. Why, I cannot tell, sir; it may be I am; does't grieve you?

Quar. No, I swear does't not, Numps, to satisfy you.   60

Wasp. Numps? 'Sblood, you are fine and familiar! How long ha' we been acquainted, I pray you?

Quar. I think it may be remembered, Numps, that? 'Twas since morning sure.

Wasp. Why, I hope I know't well enough, sir; I did not ask to be told.

Quar. No? Why then?

Wasp. It's no matter why; you see with your eyes, now, what I said to you today? You'll believe me another time?   70

Quar. Are you removing the Fair, Numps?

Wasp. A pretty question! and a very civil one! Yes, faith, I ha' my lading you see, or shall have anon; you may know whose beast I am by my burden. If the pannier-man's[8] jack[9] were ever better known by his loins of mutton, I'll be flayed and feed dogs for him when his time comes.

Winw. How melancholy Mistress Grace is yonder! Pray thee let's go enter ourselves in grace, with her.

Cokes. Those six horses, friend, I'll have—   80

Wasp. How!

Cokes. And the three Jew's trumps;[10] and half a dozen o' birds, and that drum (I have one drum already) and your smiths (I like that device o' your smiths, very pretty well) and four halberts—and (le' me see) that fine painted great lady, and her three women for state,[11] I'll have.

Wasp. No, the shop; buy the whole shop, it will be best, the shop, the shop!

Lea. If his worship please.   90

Wasp. Yes, and keep it during the Fair, bobchin.[12]

Cokes. Peace, Numps. Friend, do not meddle with him, an you be wise and would show your head above board; he will sting through your wrought nightcap, believe me. A set of these violins I would buy too, for a delicate young noise[13] I have i' the country, that are every one a size less than another, just like your fiddles. I would fain have a fine young masque[14] at my marriage, now I think on't; but I do want such a number o' things. And Numps will not help me now, and I dare not speak to him.   101

Trash. Will your worship buy any gingerbread, very good bread, comfortable bread?

Cokes. Gingerbread! Yes, let's see.

He runs to her shop.

Wasp. There's the tother springe![15]

Lea. Is this well, goody Joan? To interrupt my market? In the midst? And call away my customers? Can you answer this, at the Pie-powders?

Trash. Why? If his mastership have a mind to buy, I hope my ware lies as open as another's; I may show my ware as well as you yours.   111

Cokes. Hold your peace; I'll content you both: I'll buy up his shop, and thy basket.

Wasp. Will you i' faith?

Lea. Why should you put him from it, friend?

Wasp. Cry you mercy! you'd be sold too, would you? What's the price on you? Jerkin, and all as you stand? Ha' you any qualities?[16]

Trash. Yes. Goodman Angry-man, you shall find he has qualities, if you cheapen[17] him.   120

Wasp. Godso,[18] you ha' the selling of him! what are they? Will they be bought for love or money?

Trash. No indeed, sir.

Wasp. For what then? Victuals?

Trash. He scorns victuals, sir; he has bread and butter at home, thanks be to God! And yet he will do more for a good meal, if the toy take him i' the belly; marry then they must not set him at lower end; if they do, he'll go away, though he fast. But put him atop o' the table, where his place is, and he'll do you forty   130 fine things. He has not been sent for and sought out for nothing, at your great city-suppers, to put down Coriat[19] and Cokely,[20] and been laughed at for his labor; he'll play you all the puppets i' the town over, and the players, every company, and his own company too; he spares nobody!

Cokes. I' faith?

Trash. He was the first, sir, that ever baited the fellow i' the bear's skin,[21] an't like your worship; no dog ever came near him since. And for fine motions![22]

Cokes. Is he good at those too? Can he set out a   141 masque, trow?[23]

Trash. O Lord, master! sought to far and near, for his inventions; and he engrosses all:[24] he makes all the puppets i' the Fair.

Cokes. Dost thou, in troth, old velvet jerkin? Give me thy hand.

Trash. Nay, sir, you shall see him in his velvet jerkin, and a scarf[25] too, at night, when you hear him interpret Master Littlewit's motion.   150

Cokes. Speak no more, but shut up shop presently, friend. I'll buy both it and thee too, to carry down with

---

[6] *crack:* craze.   [7] *Overparted:* Given too hard a part.
[8] *pannier-man's:* referring to a servant in Inns of Court.
[9] *jack:* servant.   [10] *trumps:* harps.
[11] *state:* appearance of greatness.   [12] *bobchin:* fool.
[13] *noise:* band of musicians.
[14] *masque:* company of masquers.
[15] *springe:* bird-snare.   [16] *qualities:* accomplishments.
[17] *cheapen:* bargain for.
[18] *Godso:* a meaningless exclamation; but the same word is a domesticated variant, in the period, of *cazzo*, Italian for penis.
[19] *Coriat:* Thomas Coryat, jester in Prince Henry's household and traveler, author of *Coryat's Crudities* (1611), to which Jonson contributed mock-commendatory verses.
[20] *Cokely:* a jester.
[21] *He . . . skin:* An actor at the Fortune, dressed as a bear, was baited by men dressed as dogs.
[22] *motions:* puppet-shows.   [23] *trow:* do you suppose.
[24] *engrosses all:* has a monopoly.   [25] *scarf:* sash.

me, and her hamper, beside. Thy shop shall furnish out
the masque, and hers the banquet;[26] I cannot go less,
to set out anything with credit. What's the price, at a
word, o' thy whole shop, case and all as it stands?

Lea. Sir, it stands me in[27] six and twenty shillings
sevenpence halfpenny, besides three shillings for my
ground.

Cokes. Well, thirty shillings will do all, then! And
what comes yours to?   161

Trash. Four shillings and elevenpence, sir, ground
and all, an't like your worship.

Cokes. Yes, it does like my worship very well, poor
woman; that's five shillings more. What a masque shall I
furnish out for forty shillings! (twenty pound Scotch[28])
And a banquet of gingerbread! There's a stately thing!
Numps! Sister! And my wedding gloves too! (That I
never thought on afore.) All my wedding gloves,
gingerbread! Oh, me! what a device will there be,   170
to make 'em eat their fingers' ends! And delicate
brooches for the bridemen! And all! And then I'll ha'
this posy put to 'em: "For the best grace," meaning
Mistress Grace, my wedding posy.[29]

Grace. I am beholden to you, sir, and to your Barthol'mew-wit.

Wasp. You do not mean this, do you? Is this your
first purchase?

Cokes. Yes, faith, and I do not think, Numps, but
thou'lt say it was the wisest act that ever I did in my
wardship.   181

Wasp. Like enough! I shall say anything, I!

III.v

[*Enter*] JUSTICE, EDGWORTH, NIGHTINGALE.

Just. [*Aside*] I cannot beget a project, with all my
political[1] brain, yet; my project is how to fetch off this
proper young man from his debauched company. I
have followed him all the Fair over, and still I find him
with this songster; and I begin shrewdly to suspect their
familiarity; and the young man of a terrible taint,
poetry! with which idle disease if he be infected, there's
no hope of him in a state-course.[2] *Actum est*[3] of him
for a commonwealths-man[4] if he go to't in rhyme
once.   10

Edg. [*To* NIGHTINGALE] Yonder he is buying o'
gingerbread. Set in quickly, before he part with too
much on his money.

Night. [*Sings*] *My masters and friends, and good
people, draw near, etc.*

---

[26] *banquet:* dessert.   [27] *stands . . . in:* costs.
[28] *twenty . . . Scotch:* one twelfth of a pound sterling in
1603.   [29] *posy:* motto.
III.v.
    [1] *political:* shrewd.
    [2] *state-course:* life devoted to public affairs(?).
    [3] *L.:* He's "all through".
    [4] *commonwealths-man:* good citizen.
    [5] *lime-bush:* bush smeared with birdlime as a snare.
    [6] *mess:* banqueting group.
    [7] *pictures:* coins (with portraits on them).
    [8] *"Paggington's Pound":* a dance tune.

Cokes. Ballads! hark, hark! pray thee, fellow, stay a
little; good Numps, look to the goods. What ballads
hast thou? Let me see, let me see myself.

He runs to the Ballad-man.

Wasp. Why, so! he's flown to another lime-bush;[5]
there he will flutter as long more, till he ha' n'er a   20
feather left. Is there a vexation like this, gentlemen?
Will you believe me now, hereafter? Shall I have credit
with you?

Quar. Yes, faith, shalt thou, Numps, and thou art
worthy on't, for thou sweatest for't. I never saw a
young pimp errant and his squire better matched.

Winw. Faith, the sister comes after 'em well, too.

Grace. Nay, if you saw the justice her husband, my
guardian, you were fitted for the mess;[6] he is such a
wise one his way—   30

Winw. I wonder we see him not here.

Grace. Oh! he is too serious for this place, and yet
better sport than the other three, I assure you, gentlemen; where'er he is, though't be o' the bench.

Cokes. How dost thou call it? A "Caveat Against
Cutpurses"! a good jest, i' faith. I would fain see that
demon, your cutpurse, you talk of, that delicate-handed
devil; they say he walks hereabout: I would see him
walk, now. Look you, sister, here, here, let him come,
sister, and welcome.   40

He shows his purse boastingly.

Ballad-man, does any cutpurses haunt hereabout? Pray
thee, raise me one or two: begin and show me one.

Night. Sir, this is a spell against 'em, spick and span
new; and 'tis made as 'twere in mine own person, and
I sing it in mine own defense. But 'twill cost a penny
alone if you buy it.

Cokes. No matter for the price; thou dost not know
me, I see; I am an odd Barthol'mew.

Mrs. O. Has't a fine picture, brother?   49

Cokes. Oh, sister, do you remember the ballads over
the nursery-chimney at home o' my own pasting up?
There be brave pictures. Other manner of pictures
than these, friend.

Wasp. Yet these will serve to pick the pictures[7] out
o' your pockets, you shall see.

Cokes. So I heard 'em say. Pray thee mind him not,
fellow: he'll have an oar in everything.

Night. It was intended, sir, as if a purse should
chance to be cut in my presence; now, I may be blameless, though, as by the sequel, will more plainly
appear.   61

Cokes. We shall find that i' the matter. Pray thee,
begin.

Night. To the tune of "Paggington's Pound,"[8] sir.

Cokes. Fa, la la la, la la la, fa la la la. Nay, I'll put thee
in tune, and all! Mine own country dance! Pray thee
begin.

Night. It is a gentle admonition, you must know, sir,
both to the purse-cutter and the purse-bearer.

Cokes. Not a word more, out o' the tune, and   70
thou lov'st me: Fa, la la la, la la la, fa la la la. Come,
when?

    Night.   *Cokes.*
My masters and friends and good people
   draw near,
And look to your purses, for that I do say; Ha, ha, this
And though little money in theæ you do chimes! Good
   bear, counsel at first
It cost more to get, than to lose in a day. dash.
   You oft have been told,
   Both the young and the old, Good!
And bidden beware of the cut-purse so bold; Well said! He
Then if you take heed not, free me from were to blame
   the curse, that would not,
Who both give you warning for and[9] *the* i' faith.
   cut-purse.   81
Youth, youth, thou hadst better been
   starved by thy nurse
Than live to be hanged for cutting a purse.

   Cokes. Good i' faith, how say you, Numps? Is there
any harm i' this?
   Night.   *Cokes.*
It hath been upbraided to men of my trade
That oftentimes we are the cause of this The more cox-
   crime. combs they that
Alack and for pity, why should it be said? did it, I wusse.
As if they regarded or places, or time.
   Examples have been   90
   Of some that were seen
In Westminster Hall,[10] *yea the pleaders*
   between;
Then why should the judges be free
   from this curse;
More than my poor self, for cutting the God a mercy
   purse; for that! Why
Youth, youth, thou hadst better been should they be
   starved by thy nurse, more free
Than live to be hanged for cutting a purse. indeed?

   Cokes. That again, good ballad-man, that again.

       He sings the burden with him.

Oh, rare! I would fain rub mine elbow[11] now, but I
dare not pull out my hand. On, I pray thee; he that
made this ballad shall be poet to my masque.   100
   Night.   *Cokes.*
At Worcester, 'tis known well, and even i'
   the jail,
A knight of good worship did there show his
   face,
Against the foul sinners, in zeal for to rail,
And lost (ipso facto) *his purse in the place.* Is it possible?
   Nay, once from the seat
   Of judgment so great
A judge there did lose a fair pouch of velvet I' faith?
O Lord for thy mercy, how wicked or worse
Are those that so venture their necks for a purse!
Youth, youth, thou hadst better been starved by
   thy nurse,   110
Than live to be hanged for cutting a purse.

   Cokes. [Sings] *Youth, youth, etc.*

Pray thee, stay a little, friend; yet o' thy conscience,
Numps, speak, is there any harm i' this?
   Wasp. To tell you true, 'tis too good for you, 'less
you had grace to follow it.
   Just. [Aside] It doth discover enormity, I'll mark it
more: I ha' not liked a paltry piece of poetry so well a
good while.
   Cokes. [Sings] *Youth, youth, etc.*   120
Where's this youth, now? A man must call upon him,
for his own good, and yet he will not appear. Look here,
here's for him; handy-dandy,[12] which hand will he
have?

       He shows his purse.

On, I pray thee, with the rest. I do hear of him, but I
cannot see him, this Master Youth, the cutpurse.
   Night.   *Cokes.*
At plays and at sermons, and at the sessions,
'Tis daily their practice such booty to make:
Yea, under the gallows, at executions,
They stick not the stare-abouts'[13] *purses to*
   take.   130
   Nay, one without grace,
   At a far better place,
At court, and in Christmas, before the That was a fine
   King's face. fellow! I would
Alack then for pity, must I bear the curse have him now.
That only belongs to the cunning cutpurse?
   Cokes. But where's their cunning, now, when they
should use it? They are all chained now, I warrant you.
                   [*Sings.*
Youth, youth, thou hadst better been starved by
   thy nurse,
Than live to be hanged for cutting a purse.   139

The rat-catcher's charm[14] are all fools and asses to this?
A pox on 'em, that they will not come! that a man
should have such a desire to a thing, and want it.
   Quar. 'For God, I'd give half the Fair, and 'twere
mine, for a cutpurse for him, to save his longing.
   Cokes. Look you, sister, here, here, where is't now?
Which pocket is't in, for a wager?

       He shows his purse again.

   Wasp. I beseech you leave your wagers, and let him
end his matter, an't may be.
   Cokes. Oh, are you edified, Numps?
   Just. [Aside] Indeed he does interrupt him too
much; there Numps spoke to purpose.   151
   Cokes. Sister, I am an ass, I cannot keep my purse.

       [*He shows it*] *again.*

On, on; I pray thee, friend.

---

[9] *for and:* and also.
[10] *Westminster Hall:* where courts of Common Law and Chancery were held.   [11] *rub . . . elbow:* show pleasure.
[12] *handy-dandy:* children's game in which the object is to guess which hand conceals an object.
[13] *stare-abouts:* rubberneckers.
[14] *ratcatcher's charm:* rats were said to be charmed away in Ireland.

[*During the song*] EDGWORTH *gets up to him and tickles him in the ear with a straw twice to draw his hand out of his pocket.*

Night.

But, oh, you vile nation of cutpurses all,
Relent and repent, and amend and be
sound,
And know that you ought not, by honest
men's fall,
Advance your own fortunes, to die above
ground,
 And though you go gay,
 In silks as you may,
It is not the high way to heaven (as they
say).
Repent then, repent you, for better, for
worse,
And kiss not the gallows for cutting a purse.
Youth, youth, thou hadst better been
starved by thy nurse,
Than live to be hanged for cutting a purse.

Winw. Will you see sport? Look, there's a fellow gathers up[15] to him, mark.

Quar. Good, i' faith! Oh, he has lighted on the wrong pocket. 160

Winw. He has it, 'fore God he is a brave fellow; pity he should be detected.

All. An excellent ballad! an excellent ballad!

Edg. Friend, let me ha' the first, let me ha' the first, I pray you.

Cokes. Pardon me, sir. First come, first served, and I'll buy the whole bundle too. 169

Winw. [*Aside*] That conveyance was better than all, did you see't? He has given the purse to the ballad-singer.

Quar. [*Aside*] Has he?

Edg. Sir, I cry you mercy; I'll not hinder the poor man's profit; pray you, mistake me not.

Cokes. Sir, I take you for an honest gentleman, if that be mistaking; I met you today afore: ha! hum'h! O God! my purse is gone, my purse, my purse, etc.

Wasp. Come, do not make a stir, and cry yourself an ass through the Fair afore your time. 180

Cokes. Why, hast thou it, Numps? Good Numps, how came you by it? I mar'l![16]

Wasp. I pray you seek some other gamester to play the fool with; you may lose it time enough, for all your Fair-wit.

Cokes. By this good hand, glove and all, I ha' lost it already, if thou hast it not; feel else, and Mistress Grace's handkercher,[17] too, out o' the tother pocket.

Wasp. Why, 'tis well; very well, exceeding pretty, and well. 190

Edg. Are you sure you ha' lost it, sir?

Cokes. O God! yes; as I am an honest man, I had it but e'en now, at "Youth, youth."

Night. I hope you suspect not me, sir.

Edg. Thee? that were a jest indeed! Dost thou think the gentleman is foolish? Where hadst thou hands, I pray thee? Away, ass, away.

        [*Exit* NIGHTINGALE.]

Just. [*Aside*] I shall be beaten again if I be spied.

Edg. Sir, I suspect an odd fellow yonder is stealing away. 200

Mrs. O. Brother, it is the preaching fellow! You shall suspect[18] him. He was at your tother purse, you know! Nay, stay, sir, and view the work you ha' done; an you be beneficed[19] at the gallows and preach there, thank your own handiwork.

Cokes. Sir, you shall take no pride in your preferment: you shall be silenced quickly.

Just. What do you mean, sweet buds of gentility?

Cokes. To ha' my pennyworths out on you, bud. No less than two purses a day serve you? I thought you a simple fellow when my man Numps beat you i' the morning, and pitied you— 212

Mrs. O. So did I, I'll be sworn, brother; but now I see he is a lewd and pernicious enormity, as Master Overdo calls him.

Just. [*Aside*] Mine own words turned upon me like swords.

Cokes. Cannot a man's purse be at quiet for you i' the master's pocket, but you must entice it forth and debauch it?[20] 220

      [OVERDO *is carried off.*]

Wasp. Sir, sir, keep your debauch and your fine Barthol'mew-terms to yourself, and make as much on 'em as you please. But gi' me this from you, i' the meantime; I beseech you, see if I can look to this.

Cokes. Why, Numps?

Wasp. Why? Because you are an ass, sir, there's a reason the shortest way, and you will needs ha' it; now you ha' got the trick of losing, you'd lose your breech, an't 'twere loose. I know you, sir; come, deliver. 229

   WASP *takes the license from him.*

You'll go and crack the vermin you breed now, will you? 'Tis very fine, will you ha' the truth on't? They are such retchless[21] flies as you are, that blow cutpurses abroad in every corner; your foolish having of money makes 'em. An there were no wiser than I, sir, the trade should lie open for you, sir, it should i' faith, sir. I would teach your wit to come to your head, sir, as well as your land to come into your hand, I assure you, sir.

Winw. Alack, good Numps.

Wasp. Nay, gentlemen, never pity me, I am not worth it. Lord send me at home once, to Harrow 240 o' the Hill again; if I travel any more, call me Coriat; with all my heart.

   [*Exeunt* WASP, COKES, *and* MISTRESS OVERDO.]

Quar. Stay, sir, I must have a word with you in private. Do you hear?

Edg. With me, sir? What's your pleasure, good sir?

Quar. Do not deny it. You are a cutpurse, sir; this gentleman here and I saw you, nor do we mean to detect you, though we can sufficiently inform ourselves, toward the danger of concealing you; but you must do us a piece of service. 251

Edg. Good gentlemen, do not undo me; I am a civil young man, and but a beginner indeed.

---

[15] *gathers up:* draws close.
[16] *mar'l:* marvel.
[17] *handkercher:* vulgar form.
[18] *suspect:* take notice of.
[19] *beneficed:* have a church living.
[20] *entice, debauch:* synonyms, justifying Wasp's criticism of his language.
[21] *retchless:* careless.

Quar. Sir, your beginning shall bring on your ending, for us. We are no catchpoles[22] nor constables. That
you are to undertake is this: you saw the old fellow
with the black box here?

Edg. The little old governor,[23] sir?

Quar. That same. I see you have flown him to a
mark already. I would ha' you get away that box from
him and bring it us.   261

Edg. Would you ha' the box and all, sir? Or only
that that is in't? I'll get you that, and leave him the box
to play with still, which will be the harder o' the two,
because I would gain your worship's good opinion
of me.

Winw. He says well; 'tis the greater mast'ry, and
'twill make the more sport when 'tis missed.

Edg. Ay, and 'twill be the longer a-missing, to draw
on the sport.   270

Quar. But look you do it now, sirrah, and keep your
word, or—

Edg. Sir, if ever I break my word, with a gentleman,
may I never read word[24] at my need. Where shall I
find you?

Quar. Somewhere i' the Fair, hereabouts. Dispatch
it quickly.

                                    [*Exit* EDGWORTH.]
—I would fain see the careful fool deluded! Of all
beasts, I love the serious ass, he that takes pains to be
one and plays the fool with the greatest diligence that
can be.   281

Grace. Then you would not choose, sir, but love my
guardian, Justice Overdo, who is answerable to that
description, in every hair of him.

Quar. So I have heard. But how came you, Mistress
Wellborn, to be his ward or have relation to him at
first?

Grace. 'Faith, through a common calamity; he
bought me,[25] sir, and now he will marry me to his wife's
brother, this wise gentleman that you see, or else I must
pay value o' my land.   291

Quar. 'Slid, is there no device of disparagement,[26]
or so? Talk with some crafty fellow, some picklock o'
the law! Would I had studied a year longer i' the Inns
of Court, and't had been but i' your case.

Winw. [*Aside*] Ay, Master Quarlous, are you proffer-
ing?

Grace. You'd bring but little aid, sir.

Winw. [*Aside*] I'll look to you i' faith, gamester.—
An unfortunate foolish tribe you are fall'n into, lady;
I wonder you can endure 'em.   301

Grace. Sir, they that cannot work their fetters off
must wear 'em.

Winw. You see what care they have on you, to leave
you thus.

Grace. Faith, the same they have of themselves, sir. I
cannot greatly complain if this were all the plea I had
against 'em.

Winw. 'Tis true! but will you please to withdraw
with us a little, and make them think they have   310
lost you. I hope our manners ha' been such hitherto,
and our language as will give you no cause to doubt
yourself[27] in our company.

Grace. Sir, I will give myself no cause; I am so
secure of mine own manners as I suspect not yours.

Quar. Look where John Littlewit comes.

Winw. Away, I'll not be seen by him.

Quar. No, you were not best; he'd tell his mother,
the widow.

Winw. Heart, what do you mean?   320

Quar. Cry you mercy, is the wind there? Must not
the widow be named?

            [*Exeunt* GRACE, WINWIFE, QUARLOUS.]

III.vi

[*Enter*] LITTLEWIT, WIN.

Lit. Do you hear, Win, Win?

Win. What say you, John?

Lit. While they are paying the reckoning, Win, I'll
tell you a thing, Win: we shall never see any sights i'
the Fair, Win, except you long still, Win; good Win,
sweet Win, long to see some hobbyhorses and some
drums and rattles and dogs and fine devices, Win. The
bull with the five legs, Win, and the great hog. Now
you ha' begun with pig, you may long for anything,
Win, and so for my motion, Win.   10

Win. But we sha' not eat o' the bull and the hog,
John; how shall I long then?

Lit. Oh, yes! Win; you may long to see, as well as to
taste, Win. How did the 'pothecary's wife, Win, that
longed to see the anatomy,[1] Win? Or the lady, Win,
that desired to spit i' the great lawyer's mouth after an
eloquent pleading? I assure you they longed, Win;
good Win, go in, and long.

                        [*Exeunt* LITTLEWIT, WIN.]

Trash. I think we are rid of our new customer,
brother Leatherhead, we shall hear no more of him.   20

                                    They plot to be gone.

Lea. All the better. Let's pack up all and be gone
before he find us.

Trash. Stay a little; yonder comes a company. It
may be we may take some more money.

[*Enter*] KNOCKEM, BUSY.

Kno. Sir, I will take your counsel and cut my hair
and leave vapors. I see that tobacco and bottle-ale and
pig and Whit and very Urs'la herself is all vanity.

Busy. Only pig was not comprehended in my admonition; the rest were. For long hair, it is an ensign of
pride, a banner, and the world is full of those   30
banners, very full of banners. And bottle-ale is a drink
of Satan's, a diet-drink[2] of Satan's, devised to puff us

---

[22] *catchpoles:* sheriff's officers.   [23] *governor:* tutor.

[24] *read word:* cf. I. iv. 6–7.

[25] *bought me:* from the King, who sold the guardianship
of minor wards (minors heir to tenants holding royal land).

[26] *disparagement:* marriage to someone of inferior rank,
which a guardian could not enforce.

[27] *doubt yourself:* fear.

III.vi.

[1] *anatomy:* skeleton.   [2] *diet-drink:* medicine.

up and make us swell in this latter age of vanity, as the smoke of tobacco to keep us in mist and error; but the fleshly woman (which you call Urs'la) is above all to be avoided, having the marks upon her of the three enemies of man: the world, as being in the Fair; the devil, as being in the fire; and the flesh, as being herself.

[*Enter*] PURECRAFT.

Pure. Brother Zeal-of-the-Land! what shall we do? My daughter, Win-the-Fight, is fall'n into her fit of longing again.   41

Busy. For more pig? There is no more, is there?

Pure. To see some sights i' the Fair.

Busy. Sister, let her fly the impurity of the place swiftly, lest she partake of the pitch thereof. Thou art the seat of the Beast, O Smithfield, and I will leave thee. Idolatry peepeth out on every side of thee.

Kno. An excellent right hypocrite! now his belly is full, he falls a-railing and kicking, the jade. A very good vapor! I'll in, and joy Urs'la with telling how her   50 pig works; two and a half he eat to his share. And he has drunk a pailful. He eats with his eyes as well as his teeth.

                               [*Exit.*]

Lea. What do you lack, gentlemen? What is't you buy? Rattles, drums, babies—

Busy. Peace with thy apocryphal[3] wares, thou profane publican,[4] thy bells, thy dragons, and thy Toby's dogs.[5] Thy hobbyhorse is an idol, a very idol, a fierce and rank idol; and thou the Nebuchadnezzar, the proud Nebuchadnezzar of the Fair, that sett'st it   60 up, for children to fall down to and worship.

Lea. Cry you mercy, sir, will you buy a fiddle to fill up your noise?

[*Re-enter* LITTLEWIT, WIN.]

Lit. Look, Win. Do, look o' God's name, and save your longing. Here be fine sights.

Pure. Ay child, so you hate 'em, as our Brother Zeal does, you may look on 'em.

Lea. Or what do you say to a drum, sir?

Busy. It is the broken belly of the Beast, and thy bellows there are his lungs, and these pipes are his   70 throat, those feathers are of his tail, and thy rattles the gnashing of his teeth.

Trash. And what's my gingerbread, I pray you?

Busy. The provender that pricks him up.[6] Hence with thy basket of popery, thy nest of images,[7] and whole legend[8] of ginger-work.

Lea. Sir, if you be not quiet the quicklier, I'll ha' you clapped fairly by the heels for disturbing the Fair.

Busy. The sin of the Fair provokes me; I cannot be silent.   80

Pure. Good brother Zeal!

Lea. Sir, I'll make you silent, believe it.

---

[3] *apocryphal:* phony (the Puritans rejected the Apocrypha).   [4] *publican:* excommunicated person.
[5] *bells . . . dogs:* Bel, the Dragon, and Tobias' dog figure in stories in the Apocrypha.   [6] *pricks . . . up:* stimulates.
[7] *images:* gingerbread figures of St. Bartholomew.
[8] *legend:* saint's life.   [9] *flasket:* long shallow basket.

Lit. [*Aside to* LEATHERHEAD] I'd give a shilling you could, i' faith, friend.

Lea. Sir, give me your shilling; I'll give you my shop if I do not, and I'll leave it in pawn with you i' the meantime.

Lit. A match i' faith, but do it quickly then.   89
                     [*Exit* LEATHERHEAD.]

Busy. Hinder me not, woman.

               He speaks to the Widow.

I was moved in spirit to be here this day in this Fair, this wicked and foul Fair (and fitter may it be called a foul than a Fair) to protest against the abuses of it, the foul abuses of it, in regard of the afflicted saints, that are troubled, very much troubled, exceedingly troubled, with the opening of the merchandise of Babylon again, and the peeping of popery upon the stalls, here, here in the high places. See you not Goldylocks, the purple strumpet, there, in her yellow gown and green sleeves? The profane pipes, the tinkling timbrels? A shop of relics.   100

Lit. Pray you forbear, I am put in trust with 'em.

Busy. And this idolatrous grove of images, this flasket[9] of idols! which I will pull down—

              Overthrows the gingerbread.

Trash. Oh, my ware, my ware, God bless it.

Busy. —In my zeal, and glory to be thus exercised.

       LEATHERHEAD *enters with* Officers.

Lea. Here he is; pray you lay hold on his zeal; we cannot sell a whistle, for him, in tune. Stop his noise first!

Busy. Thou canst not; 'tis sanctified noise. I will make a loud and most strong noise, till I have daunted the profane enemy. And for this cause—   111

Lea. Sir, here's no man afraid of you, or your cause. You shall swear it i' the stocks sir.

Busy. I will thrust myself into the stocks upon the pikes of the land.

Lea. Carry him away.

Pure. What do you mean, wicked men?

Busy. Let them alone; I fear them not.

       [*Exeunt* Officers *with* BUSY, *followed by*
                           PURECRAFT.]

Lit. Was not this shilling well ventured, Win, for our liberty? Now we may go play, and see over   120 the Fair, where we list, ourselves; my mother is gone after him, and let her e'en go and loose us.

Win. Yes, John, but I know not what to do.

Lit. For what, Win?

Win. For a thing, I am ashamed to tell you, i' faith, and 'tis too far to go home.

Lit. I pray thee be not ashamed, Win. Come, i' faith thou shall not be ashamed; is it anything about the hobbyhorse-man? An't be, speak freely.

Win. Hang him, base bobchin, I scorn him; no, I have very great what sha' call 'em, John.   131

Lit. Oh! is that all, Win? We'll go back to Captain Jordan; to the pig-woman's, Win: he'll help us, or she with a dripping pan, or an old kettle, or something. The poor greasy soul loves you, Win, and after we'll visit the Fair all over, Win, and see my puppet-play, Win; you know it's a fine matter, Win.

[*Exeunt* LITTLEWIT, WIN.]

Lea. Let's away; I counseled you to pack up afore, Joan.   139

Trash. A pox of his Bedlam purity. He has spoiled half my ware; but the best is, we lose nothing if we miss our first merchant.[10]

Lea. It shall be hard for him to find or know us when we are translated[11], Joan.

[*Exeunt.*]

ACT FOUR

SCENE ONE

[*Enter*] TROUBLE-ALL, BRISTLE, HAGGIS, COKES, JUSTICE.

Tro. My masters, I do make no doubt but you are officers.

Bris. What then, sir?

Tro. And the King's loving and obedient subjects.

Bris. Obedient, friend? Take heed what you speak, I advise you; Oliver[1] Bristle advises you. His loving subjects, we grant you; but not his obedient, at this time, by your leave; we know ourselves a little better than so; we are to command, sir, and such as you are to be obedient. Here's one of his obedient subjects   10 going to the stocks, and we'll make you such another, if you talk.

Tro. You are all wise enough i' your places, I know.

Bris. If you know it, sir, why do you bring it in question?

Tro. I question nothing, pardon me. I do only hope you have warrant for what you do, and so, quit you, and so, multiply you.

He goes away again.

Hag. What's he? Bring him up to the stocks there. Why bring you him not up?   20

[TROUBLE-ALL] comes again.

Tro. If you have Justice Overdo's warrant, 'tis well; you are safe; that is the warrant of warrants. I'll not give this button for any man's warrant else.

Bris. Like enough, sir; but let me tell you, an you play away your buttons thus you will want 'em ere night, for any store[2] I see about you: you might keep 'em, and save pins, I wusse.

[TROUBLE-ALL] goes away.

Just. [*Aside*] What should he be, that doth so esteem and advance my warrant? He seems a sober and discreet person! It is a comfort to a good conscience   30 to be followed with a good fame in his sufferings. The world will have a pretty taste by this how I can bear adversity; and it will beget a kind of reverence toward me hereafter, even from mine enemies, when they shall see I carry my calamity nobly, and that it doth neither break me nor bend me.

Hag. Come, sir, here's a place for you to preach in. Will you put in your leg?

They put him in the stocks.

Just. That I will, cheerfully.

Bris. O' my conscience, a seminary! He kisses the stocks.   41

Cokes. Well, my masters, I'll leave him with you; now I see him bestowed, I'll go look for my goods and Numps.

Hag. You may, sir, I warrant you; where's the tother bawler? Fetch him too, you shall find 'em both fast enough.

[*Exit* COKES.]

Just. [*Aside*] In the midst of this tumult, I will yet be the author of mine own rest, and, not minding their fury, sit in the stocks in that calm as shall be able to trouble a triumph.   51

[TROUBLE-ALL] comes again.

Tro. Do you assure me upon your words? May I undertake for you, if I be asked the question, that you have this warrant?

Hag. What's this fellow, for God's sake?

Tro. Do but show me Adam Overdo, and I am satisfied.

Goes out.

Bris. He is a fellow that is distracted, they say, one Trouble-All; he was an officer in the court of Pie-powders here last year, and put out on his place by Justice Overdo.   61

Just. Ha!

Bris. Upon which he took an idle[3] conceit, and's run mad upon't. So that, ever since, he will do nothing but by Justice Overdo's warrant; he will not eat a crust, nor drink a little, nor make him in his apparel ready. His wife, sir-reverence, cannot get him make his water, or shift his shirt, without his warrant.

Just. [*Aside*] If this be true, this is my greatest disaster! how am I bound to satisfy this poor man,   70 that is of so good a nature to me, out of his wits, where there is no room left for dissembling!

[TROUBLE-ALL] comes in.

Tro. If you cannot show me Adam Overdo, I am in doubt of you; I am afraid you cannot answer[4] it.

Goes again.

Hag. Before me, neighbor Bristle, (and now I think on't better) Justice Overdo is a very peremptory[5] person.

Bris. Oh! are you advised[6] of that? And a severe justicer, by your leave.

Just. [*Aside*] Do I hear ill o' that side, too?   80

Bris. He will sit as upright o' the bench, an you

---

[10] *merchant:* customer.   [11] *translated:* transformed.

IV.i.

[1] *Oliver:* called Davy at III. i. 8.   [2] *store:* supply.

[3] *idle:* foolish.

[4] *answer:* answer to, make defense against.

[5] *peremptory:* F "parantory," perhaps a malapropism.

[6] *advised:* aware.

mark him, as a candle i' the socket, and give light to the whole court in every business.

Hag. But he will burn blue and swell like a boil (God bless us) an' he be angry.

Bris. Ay, and he will be angry too, when him list,[7] that's more; and when he is angry, be it right or wrong, he has the law on's side ever. I mark that too.

Just. [*Aside*] I will be more tender hereafter. I see compassion may become a justice, though it be a weakness, I confess, and nearer a vice than a virtue.　　91

Hag. Well, take him out o' the stocks again. We'll go a sure way to work; we'll ha' the ace of hearts of our side, if we can.

　　　　　　　　　　　They take the JUSTICE *out.*

[*Enter*] POACHER, BUSY, PURECRAFT.

Poacher. Come, bring him away to his fellow, there. Master Busy, we shall rule your legs, I hope, though we cannot rule your tongue.

Busy. No, minister of darkness, no, thou canst not rule my tongue; my tongue it is mine own, and with it I will both knock, and mock down your Barthol'mew-abominations, till you be made a hissing to the　101 neighbor parishes round about.

Hag. Let him alone; we have devised better upon't.

Pure. And shall he not into the stocks then?

Bris. No, mistress, we'll have 'em both to Justice Overdo, and let him do over 'em as is fitting. Then I and my gossip Haggis and my beadle Poacher are discharged.[8]

Pure. Oh, I thank you, blessed, honest men!

Bris. Nay, never thank us, but thank this madman that comes here, he put it in our heads.　　　111

[TROUBLE-ALL] *comes again.*

Pure. Is he mad? Now heaven increase his madness, and bless it, and thank it; sir, your poor handmaid thanks you.

Tro. Have you a warrant? An you have a warrant, show it.

Pure. Yes, I have a warrant out of the Word,[9] to give thanks for removing any scorn intended to the brethren.

Tro. It is Justice Overdo's warrant that I look for: if you have not that, keep your word, I'll keep mine. Quit ye, and multiply ye.　　　121

　　　　　　　　　　　[*Exeunt all but* TROUBLE-ALL.]

IV.ii

[*Enter*] EDGWORTH, NIGHTINGALE.

Edg. Come away, Nightingale, I pray thee.

Tro. Whither go you? Where's your warrant?

Edg. Warrant, for what, sir?

Tro. For what you go about; you know how fit it is;

an you have no warrant, bless you, I'll pray for you, that's all I can do.

　　　　　　　　　　　　　　　　　Goes out.

Edg. What means he?

Night. A madman that haunts the Fair; do you not know him? It's marvel he has not more followers after his ragged heels.　　　10

Edg. Beshrew him, he startled me; I thought he had known of our plot. Guilt's a terrible thing! Ha' you prepared the costermonger?

Night. Yes, and agreed for his basket of pears; he is at the corner here, ready. And your prize, he comes down, sailing, that way, all alone without his protector; he is rid of him, it seems.

Edg. Ay, I know; I should ha' followed his protectorship for a feat I am to do upon him, but this offered itself so i' the way, I could not let it 'scape: here　20 he comes; whistle. Be this sport called "Dorring the Dottrell."[1]

Night. Wh, wh, wh, wh, etc.

　　　　　　　　　　　　NIGHTINGALE *whistles.*

[*Enter* COKES.]

Cokes. By this light, I cannot find my gingerbread-wife, nor my hobbyhorse-man, in all the Fair now to ha' my money again. And I do not know the way out on't, to go home for more, do you hear, friend, you that whistle? What tune is that you whistle?

Night. A new tune I am practicing, sir.　　　29

Cokes. Dost thou know where I dwell, I pray thee? Nay, on with thy tune, I ha' no such haste for an answer: I'll practice with thee.

[*Enter* COSTERMONGER.]

Cost. Buy any pears, very fine pears, pears fine.

　　　　NIGHTINGALE *sets his foot afore him, and he falls*
　　　　　　　　　　　　　　　　　with his basket.

Cokes. Godso! a muss,[2] a muss, a muss, a muss.

Cost. Good gentleman, my ware, my ware; I am a poor man. Good sir, my ware.

Night. Let me hold your sword, sir; it troubles you.

Cokes. Do, and my cloak, an thou wilt; and my hat, too.　　　39

　　　COKES *falls a-scrambling whilst they run away with*
　　　　　　　　　　　　　　　　　his things.

Edg. A delicate boy! methinks he out-scrambles 'em all. I cannot persuade myself but he goes to grammar school yet, and plays the truant today.

Night. Would he had another purse to cut, 'Zekiel.

Edg. Purse? A man might cut out his kidneys, I think, and he never feel 'em, he is so earnest at the sport.

Night. His soul is halfway out on's body at the game.

Edg. Away, Nightingale; that way.

　　　[NIGHTINGALE *runs off with his sword, cloak,*
　　　　　　　　　　　　　　　　　and hat.]

Cokes. I think I am furnished for Catherine pears for one undermeal.[3] Gi' me my cloak.　　　50

7　*him list:* he likes (F "his list").
8　*discharged:* freed from responsibility.
9　*Word:* the Bible.
IV.ii.
　1　*"Dorring the Dottrell":* tricking the simpleton (*dottrell* = plover, a bird easily taken).　　　2　*muss:* scramble.
　3　*undermeal:* afternoon meal.

Cost. Good gentleman, give me my ware.

Cokes. Where's the fellow I ga' my cloak to? My cloak? And my hat? Ha! God's lid, is he gone? Thieves, thieves; help me to cry;[4] gentlemen.

He runs out.

Edg. Away, costermonger, come to us to Urs'la's.

[Exit COSTERMONGER.*]*

Talk of him to have a soul? 'Heart,[5] if he have any more than a thing given him instead of salt, only to keep him from stinking, I'll be hanged afore my time, presently. Where should it be, trow? In his blood? He has not so much to'ard it in his whole body as will 60 maintain a good flea; and if he take this course, he will not ha' so much land left as to rear a calf within this twelvemonth. Was there ever green plover so pulled! That his little overseer had been here now, and been but tall enough to see him steal pears in exchange for his beaver hat and his cloak thus! I must go find him out next for his black box and his patent[6] (it seems) he has of his place; which I think the gentleman would have a reversion[7] of, that spoke to me for it so earnestly.

[Exit.]

*He [*COKES*] comes again.*

Cokes. Would I might lose my doublet, and hose 70 too, as I am an honest man, and never stir, if I think there be anything but thieving and coz'ning i' this whole Fair. Barthol'mew-Fair, quoth he; an ever any Barthol'mew had that luck in't that I have had, I'll be martyred for him, and in Smithfield, too.

Throws away his pears.

I ha' paid for my pears, a rot on 'em, I'll keep 'em no longer. You were choke-pears[8] to me; I had been better ha' gone to mum-chance[9] for you, I wusse. Methinks the Fair should not have used me thus, and 'twere but for my name's sake; I would not ha' used a dog o' the name so. Oh, Numps will triumph now! 81

TROUBLE-ALL *comes again.*

Friend, do you know who I am? Or where I lie? I do not myself, I'll be sworn. Do but carry[10] me home, and I'll please thee; I ha' money enough there. I ha' lost myself and my cloak and my hat, and my fine sword, and my sister, and Numps, and Mistress Grace (a gentlewoman that I should ha' married), and a cutwork handkercher she ga' me, and two purses today. And my bargain o' hobbyhorses and gingerbread, which grieves me worst of all. 90

Tro. By whose warrant, sir, have you done all this?

Cokes. Warrant? Thou art a wise fellow, indeed; as if a man need a warrant to lose anything with.

Tro. Yes, Justice Overdo's warrant, a man may get and lose with; I'll stand to't.

Cokes. Justice Overdo? Dost thou know him? I lie[11] there, he is my brother-in-law, he married my sister. Pray thee, show me the way; dost thou know the house?

Tro. Sir, show me your warrant; I know nothing without a warrant, pardon me. 101

Cokes. Why, I warrant thee, come along; thou shalt

see I have wrought pillows there, and cambric sheets, and sweet bags[12] too. Pray thee guide me to the house.

Tro. Sir, I'll tell you; go you thither yourself, first, alone; tell your worshipful brother your mind; and but bring me three lines of his hand, or his clerk's, with "Adam Overdo" underneath. Here I'll stay you; I'll obey you, and I'll guide you presently. 109

Cokes. [Aside] 'Slid, this is an ass, I ha' found him; pox upon me, what do I talking to such a dull fool?— Farewell; you are a very coxcomb, do you hear?

Tro. I think I am; if Justice Overdo sign to it, I am, and so we are all; he'll quit us all, multiply us all.

[Exeunt.]

IV.iii

[Enter] GRACE; QUARLOUS *[and]* WINWIFE *with their swords drawn.*

Grace. Gentlemen, this is no way that you take; you do but breed one another trouble and offense, and give me no contentment at all. I am no she that affects[1] to be quarreled for, or have my name or fortune made the question of men's swords.

Quar. 'Slood, we love you.

Grace. If you both love me, as you pretend, your own reason will tell you but one can enjoy me; and to that point there leads a directer line than by my infamy, which must follow if you fight. 'Tis true, 10 I have professed it to you ingenuously that, rather than to be yoked with this bridegroom is appointed me, I would take up any husband, almost upon any trust. Though subtlety[2] would say to me, I know, he is a fool and has an estate, and I might govern him and enjoy a friend beside. But these are not my aims; I must have a husband I must love, or I cannot live with him. I shall ill make one of these politic[3] wives!

Winw. Why, if you can like either of us, lady, say which is he, and the other shall swear instantly to desist. 21

Quar. Content, I accord to that willingly.

Grace. Sure you think me a woman of an extreme levity, gentlemen, or a strange fancy, that, meeting you by chance in such a place as this, both at one instant, and not yet of two hours' acquaintance, neither of you deserving afore the other of me, I should so forsake my modesty, though I might affect one more particularly, as to say, "This is he," and name him. 29

Quar. Why, wherefore should you not? What should hinder you?

Grace. If you would not give it to my modesty, allow it yet to my wit; give me so much of woman, and cunning as not to betray myself impertinently. How can I judge of you, so far as to a choice, without know-

---

[4] *cry:* raise a hue and cry.   [5] *'Heart:* God's heart.
[6] *patent:* document conferring an office.
[7] *reversion:* right of succession.
[8] *choke-pears:* coarse pears.   [9] *mum-chance:* a dice game.
[10] *carry:* lead.   [11] *lie:* lodge.   [12] *sweet bags:* sachets.

IV.iii.
[1] *affects:* likes.   [2] *subtlety:* cunning.
[3] *politic:* scheming.

ing you more? You are both equal and alike to me yet; and so indifferently affected by me as each of you might be the man if the other were away. For[4] you are reasonable creatures; you have understanding and discourse.[5] And if fate send me an understanding 40 husband, I have no fear at all but mine own manners shall make him a good one.

Quar. Would I were put forth to making[6] for you, then.

Grace. It may be you are, you know not what's toward[7] you. Will you consent to a motion of mine, gentlemen?

Winw. Whatever it be, we'll presume reasonableness, coming from you.

Quar. And fitness, too.   50

Grace. I saw one of you buy a pair of tables,[8] e'en now.

Winw. Yes, here they be, and maiden ones too, unwritten in.

Grace. The fitter for what they may be employed in. You shall write, either of you, here, a word or a name, what you like best; but of two or three syllables at most; and the next person that comes this way—because destiny has a high hand in business of this nature—I'll demand, which of the two words he 60 or she doth approve; and according to that sentence, fix my resolution and affection without change.

Quar. Agreed, my word is conceived already.

Winw. And mine shall not be long creating after.

Grace. But you shall promise, gentlemen, not to be curious to know which of you it is, [is][9] taken; but give me leave to conceal that till you have brought me either home or where I may safely tender[10] myself.

Winw. Why, that's but equal.[11]

Quar. We are pleased.   70

Grace. Because I will bind both your endeavors to work together, friendly and jointly, each to the other's fortune, and have myself fitted with some means to make him that is forsaken a part of amends.

Quar. These conditions are very courteous. Well, my word is out of the *Arcadia*, then: "Argalus."[12]

Winw. And mine out of the play:[13] "Palamon."

TROUBLE-ALL *comes again.*

Tro. Have you any warrant for this, gentlemen?

Quar., Winw. Ha!

Tro. There must be a warrant had, believe it.   80

Winw. For what?

Tro. For whatsoever it is, anything indeed, no matter what.

Quar. 'Slight, here's a fine ragged prophet, dropped down i' the nick!

Tro. Heaven quit you, gentlemen.

Quar. Nay, stay a little. Good lady, put him to the question.

Grace. You are content, then?

Quar., Winw. Yes, yes.   90

Grace. Sir, here are two names written—

Tro. Is Justice Overdo one?

Grace. How, sir? I pray you read 'em to yourself—it is for a wager between these gentlemen—and, with a stroke or any difference[14] mark which you approve best.

Tro. They may be both worshipful names for aught I know, mistress, but Adam Overdo had been worth three of 'em, I assure you, in this place; that's in plain English.

Grace. This man amazes me! I pray you, like one of 'em, sir.   101

Tro. I do like him there, that has the best warrant. Mistress, to save your longing (and multiply him), it may be this. [*Marks the book.*] But I am ay still for Justice Overdo, that's my conscience. And quit you.
                    [*Exit.*]

Winw. Is't done, lady?

Grace. Ay, and strangely as ever I saw! What fellow is this, trow?

Quar. No matter what, a fortuneteller we ha' made him. Which is't, which is't?   110

Grace. Nay, did you not promise not to inquire?

[*Enter*] EDGWORTH.

Quar. 'Slid, I forgot that; pray you pardon me. Look, here's our Mercury come. The license arrives i' the finest time, too! 'Tis but scraping out Cokes his name, and 'tis done.

Winw. How now, lime-twig?[15] Hast thou touched?

Edg. Not yet, sir; except you would go with me, and see't, it's not worth speaking on. The act is nothing without a witness. Yonder he is, your man with the box, fall'n into the finest company, and so transported 120 with vapors; they ha' got in a northern clothier and one Puppy, a western man, that's come to wrestle before my Lord Mayor[16] anon, and Captain Whit, and one Val Cutting, that helps Captain Jordan to roar, a circling boy;[17] with whom your Numps is so taken that you may strip him of his clothes if you will. I'll undertake to geld him for you, if you had but a surgeon ready to sear him. And Mistress Justice there is the goodest woman! She does so love 'em all over, in terms of justice, and the style of authority, with her 130 hood upright—that I beseech you come away, gentlemen, and see't.

Quar. 'Slight, I would not lose it for the Fair. What'll you do, Ned?

Winw. Why, stay here about for you; Mistress Wellborn must not be seen.

Quar. Do so, and find out a priest i' the meantime; I'll bring the license. Lead; which way is't?

Edg. Here, sir, you are o' the backside o' the booth already, you may hear the noise.   140
                    [*Exeunt.*]

---

[4] *For:* Because.   [5] *discourse:* rationality.
[6] *to making:* for training.   [7] *toward:* in store for.
[8] *tables:* pads of paper.   [9] *is:* not in F.
[10] *tender:* look after.   [11] *equal:* fair.
[12] "*Argalus*": character in Sidney's pastoral romantic epic.
[13] *play:* probably Shakespeare's *The Two Noble Kinsmen,* 1613, based on Chaucer's *Knight's Tale* about Palamon and Arcite.   [14] *difference:* distinguishing mark.
[15] *lime-twig:* twig smeared with birdlime; thief.
[16] *wrestle . . . Mayor:* a regular Fair activity.
[17] *circling boy:* see IV. iv. 143–46; no other known meaning for this nonce phrase.

IV.iv

[*Enter*] KNOCKEM, NORTHERN, PUPPY,
CUTTING, WHIT, WASP, MISTRESS
OVERDO.

Kno. Whit, bid Val Cutting continue the vapors for
a lift, Whit, for a lift.[1]

Nor. I'll ne mare, I'll ne mare, the eale's too meeghty.

Kno. How now! my Galloway Nag,[2] the staggers?[3]
Ha! Whit, gi' him a slit i' the forehead. Cheer up, man;
a needle and thread to stitch his ears. I'd cure him now
an I had it, with a little butter and garlic, long-pepper
and grains. Where's my horn?[4] I'll gi' him a mash[5]
presently shall take away this dizziness.

Pup. Why, where are you, zurs? Do you vlinch and
leave us i' the zuds now?   11

Nor. I'll ne mare, I is e'en as vull as a paiper's[6] bag,
by my troth, I.

Pup. Do my northern cloth zhrink i' the wetting, ha?

Kno. Why, well said, old flea-bitten, thou'lt never
tire, I see.

They fall to their vapors again.

Cut. No, sir, but he may tire, if it please him.

Whit. Who told dee sho? That he vuld never teer,
man?   19

Cut. No matter who told him so, so long as he knows.

Kno. Nay, I know nothing, sir, pardon me there.

[*Enter*] EDGWORTH, QUARLOUS.

Edg. They are at it still, sir, this they call vapors.

Whit. He shall not pardon dee, captain; dou shalt
not be pardoned. Pre'dee, shweetheart, do not pardon
him.

Cut. 'Slight, I'll pardon him, an I list, whosoever
says nay to't.

Quar. Where's Numps? I miss him.

Wasp. Why, I say nay to't.

Quar. Oh, there he is!   30

Kno. To what do you say nay, sir?

*Here they continue their game of vapors, which is
nonsense: every man to oppose the last man
that spoke, whether it concerned
him or no.*

Wasp. To anything, whatsoever it is, so long as I do
not like it.

Whit. Pardon me, little man, dou musht like it a
little.

Cut. No, he must not like it at all, sir; there you are i'
the wrong.

Whit. I tink I be, he musht not like it, indeed.

Cut. Nay, then he both must and will like it, sir, for
all you.   40

Kno. If he have reason, he may like it, sir.

Whit. By no meansh, captain, upon reason; he may
like nothing upon reason.

Wasp. I have no reason, nor I will hear of no reason,
nor I will look for no reason, and he is an ass that either
knows any, or looks for't from me.

Cut. Yes, in some sense you may have reason, sir.

Wasp. Ay, in some sense, I care not if I grant you.

Whit. Pardon me, thou ougsht to grant him nothing,
in no shensh, if dou do love dyself, angry man.   50

Wasp. Why then, I do grant him nothing, and I have
no sense.

Cut. 'Tis true, thou hast no sense indeed.

Wasp. 'Slid, but I have sense, now I think on't
better, and I will grant him anything, do you see?

Kno. He is i' the right, and does utter a sufficient
vapor.

Cut. Nay, it is no sufficient vapor, neither; I deny
that.

Kno. Then it is a sweet vapor.   60

Cut. It may be a sweet vapor.

Wasp. Nay, it is no sweet vapor, neither, sir; it
stinks, and I'll stand to't.

Whit. Yes, I tink it dosh shtink, captain. All vapor
dosh shtink.

Wasp. Nay, then it does not stink, sir, and it shall
not stink.

Cut. By your leave, it may sir.

Wasp. Ay, by my leave, it may stink; I know that.

Whit. Pardon me, thou knowesht nothing; it cannot
by thy leave, angry man.   71

Wasp. How can it not?

Kno. Nay, never question him, for he is i' the right.

Whit. Yesh, I am i' de right, I confesh it; so ish de
little man too.

Wasp. I'll have nothing confessed that concerns me.
I am not i' the right, nor never was i' the right, nor never
will be i' the right, while I am in my right mind.

Cut. Mind? Why, here's no man minds you, sir, nor
anything else.   80

They drink again.

Pup. Vriend, will you mind[7] this that we do?

Quar. Call you this vapors? This is such belching of
quarrel as I never heard. Will you mind your business,
sir?

Edg. You shall see, sir.

Nor. I'll ne mair, my waimb[8] warks too mickle with
this aureadly.

Edg. Will you take that, Master Wasp, that nobody
should mind you?   89

Wasp. Why? What ha' you to do? Is't any matter to
you?

Edg. No, but methinks you should not be unminded,
though.

Wasp. Nor I wu' not be, now I think on't; do you
hear, new acquaintance, does no man mind me, say
you?

Cut. Yes, sir, every man here minds you, but how?

IV.iv.
  [1] *lift:* theft, trick.   [2] *Galloway Nag:* small Scots horse.
  [3] *staggers:* brain disease in horses, treated as Knockem
suggests.
  [4] *horn:* instrument for giving medicine to a horse.
  [5] *mash:* mixture of boiled grains fed warm to horses.
  [6] *paiper's:* bagpiper's.   [7] *mind:* watch.
  [8] *waimb:* womb, stomach.

Wasp. Nay, I care as little how, as you do; that was
not my question. 99
Whit. No, noting was ty question; tou art a learned
man, and I am a valiant man; i' faith la, tou shalt speak
for me, and I vill fight for tee.
Kno. Fight for him, Whit? A gross vapor; he can
fight for himself.
Wasp. It may be I can, but it may be I wu' not; how
then?
Cut. Why, then you may choose.
Wasp. Why, and I'll choose whether I'll choose or
no.
Kno. I think you may, and 'tis true; and I allow it
for a resolute vapor. 111
Wasp. Nay, then, I do think you do not think and it
is no resolute vapor.
Cut. Yes, in some sort he may allow you.
Kno. In no sort, sir, pardon me, I can allow him
nothing. You mistake the vapor.
Wasp. He mistakes nothing, sir, in no sort.
Whit. Yes, I pre dee now, let him mistake.
Wasp. A turd i' your teeth, never pre dee me, for I
will have nothing mistaken. 120
Kno. Turd, ha, turd? A noisome vapor; strike,
Whit.

They fall by the ears.
[EDGWORTH *steals the license out of the box, and exit.*]

Mrs. O. Why, gentlemen, why, gentlemen, I charge
you upon my authority, conserve the peace. In the
King's name and my husband's, put up your weapons;
I shall be driven to commit[9] you myself, else.
Quar. Ha, ha, ha.
Wasp. Why do you laugh, sir?
Quar. Sir, you'll allow me my Christian liberty; I
may laugh, I hope. 130
Cut. In some sort[10] you may, and in some sort you
may not, sir.
Kno. Nay, in some sort,[11] sir, he may neither laugh
nor hope in this company.
Wasp. Yes, then he may both laugh and hope in any
sort, an't please him.
Quar. Faith, and I will then, for it doth please me
exceedingly.
Wasp. No exceedingly neither, sir.
Kno. No, that vapor is too lofty. 140
Quar. Gentlemen, I do not play well at your game of
vapors; I am not very good at it, but—
Cut. Do you hear, sir? I would speak with you in
circle!

He draws a circle on the ground.

Quar. In circle, sir? What would you with me in
circle?
Cut. Can you lend me a piece, a jacobus,[12] in circle?
Quar. 'Slid, your circle will prove more costly than
your vapors, then. Sir, no, I lend you none.
Cut. Your beard's not well turned up, sir. 150

[*Touches* QUARLOUS' *beard.*]

Quar. How, rascal? Are you playing with my beard?
I'll break circle with you.

They draw all, and fight.

Pup., Nor. Gentlemen, gentlemen!
Kno. [*Aside*] Gather up, Whit, gather up, Whit,
good vapors.

[*Exit.*]

Mrs. O. What mean you? Are you rebels? Gentlemen! Shall I send out a sergeant-at-arms or a writ o'
rebellion against you? I'll commit you, upon my
womanhood, for a riot, upon my justice-hood, if you
persist. 160

[*Exeunt* QUARLOUS, CUTTING.]

Wasp. Upon your justice-hood? Marry shit o' your
hood; you'll commit?[13] Spoke like a true justice of
peace's wife, indeed, and a fine female lawyer! Turd i'
your teeth for a fee, now.
Mrs. O. Why, Numps, in Master Overdo's name, I
charge you.
Wasp. Good Mistress Underdo, hold your tongue.
Mrs. O. Alas! poor Numps.
Wasp. Alas! And why alas from you, I beseech you?
Or why poor Numps, Goody Rich?[14] Am I come 170
to be pitied by your tuft taffeta[15] now? Why, mistress,
I knew Adam, the clerk, your husband, when he was
Adam scrivener and writ for twopence a sheet, as high
as he bears his head now, or you your hood, dame.
What are you, sir?

The Watch *comes in.*

Bris. We be men and no infidels. What is the matter
here and the noises? Can you tell?
Wasp. Heart, what ha' you to do? Cannot a man
quarrel in quietness, but he must be put out on't by
you? What are you? 180
Bris. Why, we be his majesty's watch, sir.
Wasp. Watch? 'Sblood, you are a sweet watch, indeed. A body would think, and you watched well o'
nights, you should be contented to sleep at this time o'
day. Get you to your fleas and your flock-beds,[16] you
rogues, your kennels, and lie down close.
Bris. Down? Yes, we will down, I warrant you;
down with him in his majesty's name, down, down
with him, and carry him away to the pigeon-holes.[17]
Mrs. O. I thank you honest friends, in the behalf o'
the crown and the peace, and in Master Overdo's name
for suppressing enormities. 192

[WHIT *points to* NORTHERN *and*
PUPPY.]

Whit. Stay, Bristle, here ish a noder brash o' drunkards, but very quiet, special drunkards, will pay dee five

---

[9] *commit:* send to prison. [10] *sort:* kind.
[11] *sort:* group. [12] *jacobus:* gold sovereign of James I.
[13] *commit:* with pun, "fornicate."
[14] *Rich:* The Rich family owned the site and buildings of
the former monastery of St. Bartholomew and thus of the
present Cloth Fair.
[15] *tuft taffeta:* fine silk made more luxurious by raised
designs. [16] *flock-beds:* beds stuffed with wool.
[17] *pigeon-holes:* stocks.

shillings very well. Take 'em to dee, in de graish o' God. One of 'em does change cloth for ale in the Fair here, te oder ish a strong man, a mighty man, my lord mayor's man and a wrestler. He has wreshled so long with the bottle here that the man with the beard[18] hash almosht streek up hish heelsh.   200

Bris. 'Slid, the clerk o' the market[19] has been to cry him all the Fair over here for my lord's service.

Whit. Tere he ish, pre dee taik him hensh, and make ty best on him.

            [*Exit* Watch *with* WASP, NORTHERN, PUPPY.]

How now, woman o' shilk, vat ailsh ty shweet faish? Art tou melancholy?

Mrs. O. A little distempered with these enormities. Shall I entreat a courtesy of you, captain?

Whit. Entreat a hundred, velvet voman, I vill do it; shpeak out.   210

Mrs. O. I cannot with modesty speak it out, but—

Whit. I vill do it, and more, and more, for dee. What Urs'la, and't be bitch, and't be bawd, and't be!

[*Enter*] URSULA.

Urs. How now, rascal? What roar you for? Old pimp.

Whit. Here, put up de cloaks, Ursh; de purchase; pre dee now, shweet Ursh, help dis good brave voman to a jordan,[20] and't be.

Urs. 'Slid call your Captain Jordan to her, can you not?   220

Whit. Nay, pre dee leave dy consheits, and bring the velvet woman to de—

Urs. I bring her! Hang her; heart, must I find a common pot for every punk i' your purlieus?[21]

Whit. Oh, good voordsh, Ursh; it ish a guest o' velvet, i' fait la.

Urs. Let her sell her hood, and buy a sponge, with a pox to her; my vessel is employed, sir. I have but one, and 'tis the bottom of an old bottle. An honest proctor and his wife are at it, within; if she'll stay her time, so.   231

Whit. As soon ash tou cansht, shweet Ursh. Of a valiant man I tink I am the patientsh man i' the world, or in all Smithfield.

[*Re-enter* KNOCKEM.]

Kno. How now, Whit? Close vapors, stealing your leaps? Covering[22] in corners, ha?

Whit. No, fait, captain, dough tou beesht a vishe man, dy vit is a mile hence now. I vas procuring a shmall courtesy for a woman of fashion here.   239

Mrs. O. Yes, captain, though I am justice of peace's wife, I do love men of war and the sons of the sword when they come before my husband.

Kno. Say'st thou so, filly? Thou shalt have a leap presently; I'll horse thee myself else.

Urs. Come, will you bring her in now? And let her take her turn?

Whit. Gramercy, good Ursh, I tank dee.

Mrs. O. Master Overdo shall thank her.

                             [*Exit.*]

IV.v

[*Enter*] LITTLEWIT, WIN.

Lit. Good Gammer[1] Urs; Win and I are exceedingly beholden to you and to Captain Jordan and Captain Whit. Win, I'll be bold to leave you i' this good company, Win, for half an hour or so, Win, while I go and see how my matter goes forward and if the puppets be perfect; and then I'll come and fetch you, Win.

Win. Will you leave me alone with two men, John?

Lit. Ay, they are honest gentlemen, Win, Captain Jordan and Captain Whit; they'll use you very civilly, Win. God b' w' you, Win.   10

                             [*Exit.*]

Urs. What's[2] her husband gone?

Kno. On his false gallop,[3] Urs, away.

Urs. An' you be right Barthol'mew-birds, now show yourselves so; we are undone for want of fowl i' the Fair here. Here will be 'Zekiel Edgworth and three or four gallants with him at night, and I ha' neither plover nor quail[4] for 'em; persuade this between you two, to become a bird o' the game, while I work the velvet woman within, as you call her.

Kno. I conceive thee, Urs! go thy ways.   20

                         [*Exit* URSULA.]

Dost thou hear, Whit? Is't not pity my delicate dark chestnut here—with the fine lean head, large forehead, round eyes, even mouth, sharp ears, long neck, thin crest, close withers, plain back, deep sides, short fillets, and full flanks; with a round belly, a plump buttock, large thighs, knit knees, straight legs, short pasterns, smooth hoofs, and short heels—should lead a dull honest woman's life, that might live the life of a lady?

Whit. Yes, by my fait and trot it is, captain; de honesht woman's life is a scurvy dull life, indeed la.   30

Win. How, sir? Is an honest woman's life a scurvy life?

Whit. Yes, fait, shweetheart, believe him, de leef of a bond-woman! But if dou vilt harken to me, I vill make tee a free-woman, and a lady: dou shalt live like a lady, as te captain saish.

Kno. Ay, and be honest, too, sometimes; have her wires[5] and her tires,[6] her green gowns[7] and velvet petticoats.   39

Whit. Ay, and ride to Ware and Rumford[8] i' dy coash, shee de players, be in love vit 'em; sup vit gallantsh, be drunk, and cost dee noting.

Kno. Brave vapors!

Whit. And lie by twenty on 'em if dou pleash, sweetheart.

---

[18] *man . . . beard:* jug shaped like a head.
[19] *clerk . . . market:* Fair official.   [20] *jordan:* privy.
[21] *purlieus:* suburbs.
[22] *Covering:* Copulating (of horses).

IV.v.
[1] *Gammer:* rustic title for old woman, corruption of grandmother.   [2] *What's:* For what has.
[3] *false gallop:* canter.   [4] *plover, quail:* loose women.
[5] *wires:* to support the ruff.   [6] *tires:* dresses.
[7] *green gowns:* proverbial—dresses stained by the grass in pastoral seductions.
[8] *Ware and Rumford:* popular places for assignations.

Win. What, and be honest still? That were fine sport.

Whit. Tish common, shweetheart, tou may'st do it, by my hand. It shall be justified to ty husband's faish, now; tou shalt be as honesht as the skin between his hornsh, la!   51

Kno. Yes, and wear a dressing, top and topgallant,[9] to compare with e'er a husband on 'em all, for a fore-top.[10] It is the vapor of spirit in the wife to cuckold nowadays, as it is the vapor of fashion in the husband not to suspect. Your prying cat-eyed-citizen is an abominable vapor.

Win. Lord, what a fool have I been!

Whit. Mend then, and do everything like a lady, hereafter; never know ty husband, from another man.

Kno. Nor any one man from another, but i' the   61 dark.

Whit. Ay, and then it ish no dishgrace to know any man.

[*Re-enter* URSULA.]

Urs. Help, help here!

Kno. How now? What vapor's there?

Urs. Oh, you are a sweet ranger! and look well to your walks. Yonder is your punk of Turnbull, Ramping Alice, has fall'n upon the poor gentlewoman within, and pulled her hood over her ears and her hair through it.   71

ALICE *enters, beating the* Justice's wife.

Mrs. O. Help, help, i' the King's name!

Alice. A mischief on you, they are such as you are that undo us and take our trade from us, with your tuft taffeta haunches.

Kno. How now, Alice!

Alice. The poor common whores can ha' no traffic for the privy rich ones; your caps and hoods of velvet call away our customers and lick the fat from us.

Urs. Peace, you foul-ramping jade, you—   80

Alice. 'Od's foot, you bawd in grease,[11] are you talking?

Kno. Why, Alice, I say.

Alice. Thou sow of Smithfield, thou.

Urs. Thou tripe of Turnbull.

Kno. Cat-a-mountain[12]-vapors! ha!

Urs. You know where you were tawed[13] lately, both lashed and slashed you were in Bridewell.[14]

Alice. Ay, by the same token, you rid[15] that week, and broke out the bottom o' the cart, night-tub.[16]   90

---

[9] *top and topgallant:* sails.
[10] *foretop:* top of a foremast or of the head.
[11] *in grease:* fat, ready for slaughter (of animals).
[12] *Cat-a-mountain:* Wildcat.
[13] *tawed:* softened by beating.
[14] *Bridewell:* prison for prostitutes.
[15] *rid:* whores were taken to prison in carts.
[16] *night-tub:* container for night soil (excrement).
[17] *waistcoat:* a feminine undergarment, when worn so that it shows the badge of a whore.
IV.vi.
  [1] *stale:* urinate.   [2] *presently:* immediately.
  [3] *take part of:* partake of.   [4] *moiety:* share.

Kno. Why, lion face! ha! do you know who I am? Shall I tear ruff, slit waistcoat,[17] make rags of petticoat! Ha! go to, vanish, for fear of vapors. Whit, a kick, Whit, in the parting vapor.

              [*They kick out* ALICE.]

Come, brave woman, take a good heart; thou shalt be a lady, too.

Whit. Yes, fait, dey shall all both be ladies and write Madam. I vill do't myself for dem. Do, is the vord, and D is the middle letter of Madam; DD, put 'em together and make deeds, without which all words are   100 alike, la.

Kno. 'Tis true, Urs'la, take 'em in, open thy ward-robe and fit 'em to their calling. Green gowns, crimson petticoats, green women! my Lord Mayor's green women! guests o' the game, true bred. I'll provide you a coach to take the air in.

Win. But do you think you can get one?

Kno. Oh, they are as common as wheelbarrows where there are great dunghills. Every pettifogger's wife has 'em; for first he buys a coach that he   110 may marry, and then he marries that he may be made cuckold in't; for if their wives ride not to their cuckold-ing, they do 'em no credit. Hide and be hidden, ride and be ridden, says the vapor of experience.

    [*Exeunt* URSULA, WIN, MISTRESS OVERDO.]

IV.vi

[*Enter*] TROUBLE-ALL.

Tro. By what warrant does it say so?

Kno. Ha! mad child o' the Pie-powders, art thou there? Fill us a fresh can, Urs; we may drink together.

Tro. I may not drink without a warrant, captain.

Kno. 'Slood, thou'll not stale[1] without a warrant, shortly. Whit, give me pen, ink, and paper. I'll draw him a warrant presently.[2]

Tro. It must be Justice Overdo's!

Kno. I know, man. Fetch the drink, Whit.   9

Whit. I pre dee now, be very brief, captain, for de new ladies stay for dee.

Kno. Oh, as brief as can be; here 'tis already. *Adam Overdo.*

Tro. Why, now, I'll pledge you, captain.

Kno. Drink it off. I'll come to thee, anon, again.

                     [*Exeunt.*]

[*Enter*] QUARLOUS, EDGWORTH.

Quar. Well, sir. You are now discharged. Beware of being spied, hereafter.

             QUARLOUS *to the* Cutpurse.

Edg. Sir, will it please you, enter in here at Urs'la's and take part of[3] a silken gown, a velvet petticoat, or a wrought smock? I am promised such, and I can spare any gentleman a moiety.[4]   21

Quar. Keep it for your companions in beastliness, I am none of 'em, sir. If I had not already forgiven you a greater trespass or thought you yet worth my beating, I would instruct your manners, to whom you made your offers. But go your ways, talk not to me; the hangman is only fit to discourse with you; the hand of beadle is too merciful a punishment for your trade of life.

[*Exit* EDGWORTH.]

I am sorry I employed this fellow; for he thinks me such: *Facinus quos inquinat, aequat.*[5] But it was for sport. And would I make it serious, the getting of this license is nothing to me, without other circumstances concur. I do think how impertinently[6] I labor, if the word be not mine that the ragged fellow marked; and what advantage I have given Ned Winwife in this time now, of working her, though it be mine. He'll go near to form[7] to her what a debauched rascal I am, and fright her out of all good conceit of me. I should do so by him, I am sure, if I had the opportunity. But my hope is in her temper yet; and it must needs be next to despair that is grounded on any part of a woman's discretion. I would give, by my troth, now, all I could spare (to my clothes and my sword) to meet my tattered soothsayer again, who was my judge i' the question, to know certainly whose word he has damned or saved. For till then I live but under a reprieve. I must seek him. Who be these?

Enter WASP *with the* Officers, [BRISTLE *and* POACHER].

Wasp. Sir, you are a Welsh cuckold, and a prating runt,[8] and no constable.   49
Bris. You say very well. Come put in his leg in the middle roundel, and let him hole there.
Wasp. You stink of leeks, metheglin,[9] and cheese. You rogue.
Bris. Why, what is that to you, if you sit sweetly in the stocks in the meantime? If you have a mind to stink too, your breeches sit close enough to your bum. Sit you merry, sir.
Quar. How now, Numps?
Wasp. It is no matter how; pray you look off.
Quar. Nay, I'll not offend you, Numps. I thought you had sat there to be seen.   61
Wasp. And to be sold, did you not? Pray you mind your business, an you have any.
Quar. Cry you mercy, Numps. Does your leg lie high enough?

[*Enter* HAGGIS.]

Bris. How now, neighbor Haggis, what says Justice Overdo's worship to the other offenders?
Hag. Why, he says just nothing, what should he say? Or where should he say? He is not to be found, man. He ha' not been seen i' the Fair here all this live-long day, never since seven o'clock i' the morning. His clerks know not what to think on't. There is no court of Pie-powders yet. Here they be returned.

[*Enter others of the watch with* JUSTICE *and* BUSY.]

Bris. What shall be done with 'em, then, in your discretion?[10]
Hag. I think we were best put 'em in the stocks, in discretion[11] (there they will be safe in discretion[12]) for the valor[13] of an hour or such a thing, till his worship come.

Bris. It is but a hole matter if we do, neighbor   80 Haggis.—Come, sir, here is company for you; heave up the stocks.
Wasp. [*Aside*] I shall put a trick upon your Welsh diligence, perhaps.

As they open the stocks, WASP *puts his shoe on his hand and slips it in for his leg.*

Bris. Put in your leg, sir.
Quar. What, Rabbi Busy! Is he come?

They bring BUSY *and put him in.*

Busy. I do obey thee; the lion may roar, but he cannot bite. I am glad to be thus separated from the heathen of the land and put apart in the stocks for the holy cause.   90
Wasp. What are you, sir?
Busy. One that rejoiceth in his affliction, and sitteth here to prophesy the destruction of fairs and May-games, wakes and Whitsun-ales, and doth sigh and groan for the reformation of these abuses.

They put JUSTICE *in the stocks.*

Wasp. And do you sigh and groan too, or rejoice in your affliction.
Just. I do not feel it, I do not think of it, it is a thing without[14] me. Adam, thou art above these batt'ries, these contumelies. *In te manca ruit fortuna,* as thy   100 friend Horace says; thou art one, *Quem neque pauperies, neque mors, neque vincula terrent.*[15] And therefore, as another friend of thine says (I think it be thy friend Persius), *Non te quaesiveris extra.*[16]
Quar. What's here! a stoic i' the stocks? The fool is turned philosopher.
Busy. Friend, I will leave[17] to communicate my spirit with you, if I hear any more of those superstitious relics, those lists[18] of Latin, the very rags of Rome and patches of popery.   110
Wasp. Nay, an' you begin to quarrel, gentlemen, I'll leave you. I ha' paid for quarreling too lately. Look you, a device, but shifting in a hand for a foot. God b' w' you.

He gets out.

Busy. Wilt thou then leave thy brethren in tribulation?
Wasp. For this once, sir.

[*Exit.*]

Busy. Thou art a halting neutral—stay him there, stop him—that will not endure the heat of persecution.

---

[5] *L.:* "Crime eliminates distinctions among those it stains," Lucan, *Pharsalia,* v. 290.
[6] *impertinently:* to no purpose.   [7] *form:* formulate.
[8] *runt:* ignorant, uncouth person.
[9] *metheglin:* Welsh mead.   [10] *discretion:* judgment.
[11] *discretion:* prudence.   [12] *discretion:* separation.
[13] *valor:* amount.
[14] *without:* outside; the justice speaks stoical cant here.
[15] *L.:* "Against you fortune is crippled . . . Whom neither poverty nor death nor chains can frighten," adapted from Horace, *Satires,* II. vii. 83–88.
[16] *L.:* "Look to no one outside yourself," Persius, *Satires,* I. 7.   [17] *leave:* cease.   [18] *lists:* strips of cloth.

Bris. How now, what's the matter?   119

Busy. He is fled, he is fled, and dares not sit it out.

Bris. What, has he made an escape? Which way?
Follow, neighbor Haggis.

[Exeunt BRISTLE and HAGGIS.]

[Enter] PURECRAFT.

Pure. Oh, me! in the stocks! Have the wicked prevailed?

Busy. Peace, religious sister, it is my calling; comfort
yourself, an extraordinary calling, and done for my
better standing, my surer standing, hereafter.

The Madman [TROUBLE-ALL] enters.

Tro. By whose warrant, by whose warrant, this?

Quar. Oh, here's my man dropped in, I looked for.

Just. Ha!   130

Pure. O good sir, they have set the faithful here to
be wondered at, and provided holes for the holy of the
land.

Tro. Had they warrant for it? Showed they Justice
Overdo's hand? If they had no warrant, they shall
answer it.

[Re-enter BRISTLE and HAGGIS.]

Bris. Sure you did not lock the stocks sufficiently,
neighbor Toby!

Hag. No! see if you can lock 'em better.

Bris. They are very sufficiently locked, and truly,
yet something is in the matter.   141

Tro. True, your warrant is the matter that is in
question; by what warrant?

Bris. Madman, hold your peace; I will put you in
his room else, in the very same hole, do you see?

Quar. How! Is he a madman?

Tro. Show me Justice Overdo's warrant; I obey you.

Hag. You are a mad fool; hold your tongue.

[Exeunt BRISTLE and HAGGIS.]

Tro. In Justice Overdo's name I drink to you, and
here's my warrant.   150

Shows his can.

Just. [*Aside*] Alas, poor wretch! How it earns[19] my
heart for him!

Quar. [*Aside*] If he be mad, it is in vain to question
him. I'll try, though.—Friend, there was a gentlewoman showed you two names some hour since.
Argalus and Palamon, to mark in a book; which of 'em
was it you marked?

Tro. I mark no name but Adam Overdo; that is the

name of names. He only is the sufficient magistrate;
and that name I reverence; show it me.   160

Quar. [*Aside*] This fellows' mad indeed; I am further
off now than a-fore.

Just. [*Aside*] I shall not breathe in peace till I have
made him some amends.

Quar. [*Aside*] Well, I will make another use of him,
is come in my head; I have a nest of beards in my
trunk,[20] one something like his.

The Watchmen come back again.

Bris. This mad fool has made me that I know not
whether I have locked the stocks or no; I think I
locked 'em.   170

Tro. Take Adam Overdo in your mind and fear
nothing.

Bris. 'Slid, madness itself, hold thy peace and take
that.

[Strikes him.]

Tro. Strikest thou without a warrant? Take thou
that.

The Madman fights with 'em, and they leave open the
stocks.

Busy. We are delivered by miracle; fellow in fetters,
let us not refuse the means; this madness was of the
spirit; the malice of the enemy hath mocked itself.   179

[Exeunt BUSY and JUSTICE.]

Pure. Mad, do they call him! The world is mad
in error, but he is mad in truth. I love him o' the
sudden (the cunning man said all true), and shall love
him, more and more. How well it becomes a man to be
mad in truth! Oh, that I might be his yoke-fellow and
be mad with him; what a many should we draw to
madness in truth with us.

[Exit.]

The Watch, missing them, are affrighted.

Bris. How now! All 'scaped? Where's the woman?
It is witchcraft! Her velvet hat is a witch, o' my conscience, or my key, t' one![21] the madman was a devil,
and I am an ass; so bless me, my place, and mine   190
office.

[Exeunt.]

ACT FIVE

SCENE ONE

[Enter] LEATHERHEAD, FILCHER, SHARKWELL.

Lea. Well, Luck and Saint Barthol'mew! Out with
the sign[1] of our invention, in the name of Wit, and do
you beat the drum the while; all the foul i' the Fair, I
mean all the dirt in Smithfield (that's one of Master
Littlewit's carwhitchets[2] now), will be thrown at our
banner today if the matter does not please the people.
Oh, the motions that I, Lantern Leatherhead, have
given light to, i' my time, since my Master Pod[3] died!

---

[19] *earns:* grieves.

[20] *trunk:* trunk-hose, stuffed baggy breeches covering the
hips and upper thighs.

[21] *t'one:* the one or the other.

V.i.

[1] *sign:* a cloth painted with a picture, the banner of *l.* 6.

[2] *carwhitchets:* puns.

[3] *Pod:* "Pod was a Master of motions before him,"
Jonson's marginal note; presumably Pod was a real puppet-
master.

"Jerusalem" was a stately thing; and so was "Ninive," and "The City of Norwich"; and "Sodom and Gomorrah," with the rising o' the prentices and pulling down the bawdy houses there upon Shrove Tuesday.[4] But "The Gunpowder Plot,"[5] there was a get-penny! I have presented that to an eighteen or twentypence audience nine times in an afternoon. Your home-born projects[6] prove ever the best, they are so easy, and familiar; they put too much learning i' their things nowadays, and that I fear will be the spoil o' this. Littlewit? I say, Micklewit! if not too mickle![7] Look to your gathering there, Goodman Filcher.   20

Fil. I warrant you, sir.

Lea. And there come any gentlefolks, take twopence a piece, Sharkwell.

Shark. I warrant you, sir, threepence an we can.
                              [*Exeunt.*]

V.ii

The JUSTICE *comes in like a porter.*

Just. This later disguise I have borrowed of a porter shall carry me out of all my great and good ends; which however interrupted, were never destroyed in me. Neither is the hour of my severity yet come, to reveal myself, wherein, cloud-like, I will break out in rain and hail, lightning and thunder, upon the head of enormity. Two main works I have to prosecute: first, one is to invent some satisfaction for the poor kind wretch who is out of his wits for my sake; and yonder I see him coming; I will walk aside, and project for it.   10

[*Enter*] WINWIFE, GRACE.

Winw. I wonder where Tom Quarlous is, that he returns not; it may be he is struck[1] in here to seek us.

Grace. See, here's our madman again.

[*Enter*] QUARLOUS, PURECRAFT. QUARLOUS *in the habit of the madman is mistaken by* MISTRESS PURECRAFT.

Quar. [*Aside*] I have made myself as like him as his gown and cap will give me leave.

Pure. Sir, I love you, and would be glad to be mad with you in truth.

Winw. How! my widow in love with a madman?

Pure. Verily, I can be as mad in spirit as you.   19

Quar. By whose warrant? Leave your canting.[2]— Gentlewoman, have I found you? (Save ye, quit ye, and multiply ye.) Where's your book? 'Twas a sufficient name I marked; let me see't, be not afraid to show't me.

He desires to see the book of MISTRESS GRACE.

Grace. What would you with it, sir?

Quar. Mark it again and again at your service.

Grace. Here it is, sir, this was it you marked.

Quar. Palamon? Fare you well, fare you well.

Winw. How, Palamon!

Grace. Yes, faith, he has discovered it to you now, and therefore 'twere vain to disguise it longer; I am yours, sir, by the benefit of your fortune.   31

Winw. And you have him, mistress, believe it, that shall never give you cause to repent her benefit, but make you rather to think that, in this choice, she had both her eyes.[3]

Grace. I desire to put it to no danger of protestation.
                        [*Exeunt* GRACE *and* WINWIFE.]

Quar. Palamon the word and Winwife the man?

Pure. Good sir, vouchsafe a yoke-fellow in your madness; shun not one of the sanctified sisters that would draw with you, in truth.   40

Quar. Away, you are a herd of hypocritical proud ignorants, rather wild than mad. Fitter for woods and the society of beasts than houses and the congregation of men. You are the second part of the society of canters, outlaws to order and discipline, and the only privileged church-robbers of Christendom. Let me alone. Palamon the word and Winwife the man?

Pure. [*Aside*] I must uncover myself unto him or I shall never enjoy him, for all the cunning men's promises.—Good sir, hear me: I am worth six   50 thousand pound; my love to you is become my rack; I'll tell you all and the truth, since you hate the hypocrisy of the parti-colored brotherhood. These seven years, I have been a willful holy widow only to draw feasts and gifts from my entangled suitors: I am also by office an assisting sister of the deacons and a devourer instead of a distributor of the alms. I am a special maker of marriages for our decayed brethren with our rich widows, for a third part of their wealth, when they are married, for the relief of the poor elect; as   60 also our poor handsome young virgins with our wealthy bachelors or widowers; to make them steal from their husbands when I have confirmed them in the faith and got all put into their custodies. And if I ha' not my bargain, they may sooner turn a scolding drab into a silent minister[4] than make me leave pronouncing reprobation, and damnation unto them. Our elder, Zeal-of-the-Land, would have had me, but I know him to be the capital knave of the land, making himself rich by being made feoffee in trust[5] to deceased brethren,   70 and coz'ning their heirs by swearing the absolute gift of their inheritance. And thus, having eased my conscience and uttered my heart with the tongue of my love, enjoy all my deceits together, I beseech you. I should not have revealed this to you, but that in time[6] I think you are mad; and I hope you'll think me so too, sir?

Quar. Stand aside; I'll answer you presently.

He considers with himself of it.

---

[4] *Shrove Tuesday:* on Mardi Gras, their festival day, prentices traditionally attacked the brothels.
[5] *"The Gunpowder Plot":* on November 5, 1605, Guy Fawkes led a Catholic conspiracy in an attempt to blow up Parliament.   [6] *projects:* schemes.   [7] *mickle:* great.
V.ii.
[1] *struck:* gone.   [2] *canting:* pious jargon.
[3] *she . . . eyes:* Fortune was held to be blind.
[4] *silent minister:* Puritan excommunicated for noncompliance with canons adopted by Hampton Court Conference of 1604.
[5] *feoffee in trust:* trustee invested with a freehold estate.
[6] *in time:* at a suitable time(?).

Why should not I marry this six thousand pound, now I think on't? And a good trade too that she has beside, ha? The tother wench Winwife is sure of; there's no expectation for me there! Here I may make myself some saver;[7] yet, if she continue mad, there's the question. It is money that I want; why should I not marry the money when 'tis offered me? I have a license and all, it is but razing out one name and putting in another. There's no playing with a man's fortune. I am resolved! I were truly mad, an I would not!—Well, come your ways, follow me; an you will be mad, I'll show you a warrant!

He takes her along with him.

Pure. Most zealously; it is that I zealously desire.   90

The JUSTICE *calls him.*

Just. Sir, let me speak with you.
Quar. By whose warrant?
Just. The warrant that you tender and respect so: Justice Overdo's! I am the man, friend Trouble-All, though thus disguised, as the careful magistrate ought for the good of the republic, in the Fair, and the weeding out of enormity. Do you want a house or meat or drink or clothes? Speak whatsoever it is, it shall be supplied you; what want you?
Quar. Nothing but your warrant.   100
Just. My warrant? For what?
Quar. To be gone, sir.
Just. Nay, I pray thee, stay; I am serious and have not many words nor much time to exchange with thee; think what may do thee good.
Quar. Your hand and seal will do me a great deal of good; nothing else in the whole Fair that I know.
Just. If it were to an end, thou should'st have it willingly.
Quar. Why, it will satisfy me; that's end enough to look on; an you will not gi' it me, let me go.   111
Just. Alas! thou shalt ha' it presently. I'll but step into the scrivener's hereby and bring it. Do not go away.

The JUSTICE *goes out.*

Quar. [*Aside*] Why, this madman's shape will prove a very fortunate one, I think! Can a ragged robe produce these effects? If this be the wise justice, and he bring me his hand, I shall go near to make some use on't.

[JUSTICE] *returns.*

He is come already!   120
Just. Look thee! here is my hand and seal, *Adam*

---

make . . . saver: compensate for loss (gambler's term).
conscience: good judgment.
reducing: leading back.
V.iii.
master . . . monuments: guide to the tombs and sights of Westminster Abbey.   *fantastical:* capricious.
interlude: play.
voluntary: volunteer, obligating them by serving them without pay.

Overdo; if there be anything to be written above in the paper that thou want'st now or at any time hereafter, think on't. It is my deed; I deliver it so. Can your friend write?
Quar. Her hand for a witness, and all is well.
Just. With all my heart.

He urgeth MISTRESS PURECRAFT.

Quar. [*Aside*] Why should not I ha' the conscience[8] to make this a bond of a thousand pound now? Or what I would else?   130
Just. Look you, there it is; and I deliver it as my deed again.
Quar. Let us now proceed in madness.

He takes her in with him.

Just. Well, my conscience is much eased; I ha' done my part; though it doth him no good, yet Adam hath offered satisfaction! The sting is removed from hence. Poor man, he is much altered with his affliction; it has brought him low! Now, for my other work, reducing[9] the young man I have followed so long in love from the brink of his bane to the center of safety. Here or in some such like vain place I shall be sure to find him.   140
I will wait the good time.

V.iii

[*Enter*] COKES, [*followed by boys,*] SHARKWELL, FILCHER.

Cokes. How now? What's here to do? Friend, art thou the master of the monuments?[1]
Shark. 'Tis a motion, an't please your worship.
Just. [*Aside*] My fantastical[2] brother-in-law, Master Barthol'mew Cokes!
Cokes. A motion, what's that?

He reads the bill.

"The ancient modern history of *Hero and Leander,* otherwise called *The Touchstone of True Love,* with as true a trial of friendship between Damon and Pythias, two faithful friends o' the Bankside." Pretty, i' faith; what's the meaning on't? Is't an interlude?[3] Or what is't?   10
Fil. Yes, sir; please you come near, we'll take your money within.
Cokes. Back with these children; they do so follow me up and down.

The boys o' the Fair follow him.

[*Enter*] LITTLEWIT.

Lit. By your leave, friend.
Fil. You must pay, sir, an you go in.
Lit. Who, I? I perceive thou know'st not me. Call the master o' the motion.   20
Shark. What, do you not know the author, fellow Filcher? You must take no money of him; he must come in *gratis.* Master Littlewit is a voluntary;[4] he is the author.
Lit. Peace, speak not too loud; I would not have any

notice taken that I am the author till we see how it passes.

Cokes. Master Littlewit, how dost thou?

Lit. Master Cokes! you are exceeding well met: what, in your doublet and hose, without a cloak or a hat?   31

Cokes. I would I might never stir, as I am an honest man, and by that fire;[5] I have lost all i' the Fair, and all my acquaintance too. Didst thou meet anybody that I know, Master Littlewit? My man Numps, or my sister Overdo, or Mistress Grace? Pray thee, Master Littlewit, lend me some money to see the interlude here; I'll pay thee again, as I am a gentleman. If thou'lt but carry me home, I have money enough there.   39

Lit. O sir, you shall command it; what, will a crown serve you?

Cokes. I think it will. What do we pay for coming in, fellows?

Fil. Twopence, sir.

Cokes. Twopence? There's twelvepence, friend; nay, I am a gallant as simple as I look now if you see me with my man about me and my artillery[6] again.

Lit. Your man was i' the stocks e'en now, sir.

Cokes. Who, Numps?

Lit. Yes, faith.   50

Cokes. For what, i' faith? I am glad o' that; remember to tell me on't anon; I have enough now! What manner of matter is this, Master Littlewit? What kind of actors ha' you? Are they good actors?

Lit. Pretty youths, sir, all children, both old and young; here's the master of 'em—

[*Enter*] LEATHERHEAD.

Lea. Call me not Leatherhead, but Lantern.[7]

LEATHERHEAD *whispers to* LITTLEWIT.

Lit. Master Lantern, that gives light to the business.

Cokes. In good time, sir, I would fain see 'em. I would be glad to drink with the young company. Which is the tiring house?   61

Lea. Troth sir, our tiring-house is somewhat little; we are but beginners, yet, pray pardon us; you cannot go upright in't.

Cokes. No? Not now my hat is off? What would you have done with me if you had had me, feather and all, as I was once today? Ha' you none of your pretty impudence boys now to bring stools, fill tobacco, fetch ale, and beg money, as they have at other houses? Let me see some o' your actors.   70

Lit. Show him 'em, show him 'em. Master Lantern, this is a gentleman that is a favorer of the quality.[8]

Just. [*Aside*] Ay, the favoring of this licentious quality is the consumption of many a young gentleman; a pernicious enormity.

Cokes. What, do they live in baskets?

Lea. They do lie in a basket, sir; they are o' the small players.

He [LEATHERHEAD] *brings them out in a basket.*

Cokes. These be players minors indeed. Do you call these players?   80

Lea. They are actors, sir, and as good as any, none dispraised, for dumb shows; indeed, I am the mouth[9] of 'em all!

Cokes. Thy mouth will hold 'em all. I think one Taylor[10] would go near to beat all this company with a hand bound behind him.

Lit. Ay, and eat 'em[11] all, too, an they were in cakebread.

Cokes. I thank you for that, Master Littlewit, a good jest! Which is your Burbage[12] now?   90

Lea. What mean you by that, sir?

Cokes. Your best actor. Your Field?[13]

Lit. Good, i' faith! You are even with me, sir.

Lea. This is he that acts young Leander, sir. He is extremely beloved of the womenkind, they do so affect[14] his action, the green gamesters[15] that come here; and this is lovely Hero; this with the beard, Damon; and this, pretty Pythias: this is the ghost of King Dionysius in the habit of a scrivener, as you shall see anon, at large.[16]   100

Cokes. Well they are a civil company; I like 'em for that. They offer not to fleer nor jeer nor break jests, as the great players do; and then there goes not so much charge to the feasting of 'em or making 'em drunk as to the other, by reason of their littleness. Do they use to play perfect? Are they never flustered?

Lea. No, sir, I thank my industry and policy for it; they are as well-governed a company, though I say it— and here is young Leander, is as proper an actor of his inches, and shakes his head like an ostler.[17]   110

Cokes. But do you play it according to the printed book?[18] I have read that.

Lea. By no means, sir.

Cokes. No? How then?

Lea. A better way, sir; that is too learned and poetical for our audience. What do they know what Hellespont is? "Guilty of true love's blood?" Or what Abydos is? Or "the other Sestos hight?"   118

Cokes. Th' art i' the right; I do not know myself.

Lea. No, I have entreated Master Littlewit to take a little pains to reduce it to a more familiar strain for our people.

Cokes. How, I pray thee, good Master Littlewit?

Lit. It pleases him to make a matter of it, sir. But

---

[5] *fire:* in Ursula's booth.   [6] *artillery:* sword.

[7] *Call . . . Lantern:* i.e., to prevent recognition.

[8] *quality:* (acting) profession.   [9] *mouth:* interpreter.

[10] *Taylor:* proverbially timid tailor; John Taylor the Water Poet, who had recently won by default a wit combat at the Hope Theater and amused the audience; Joseph Taylor, actor in Lady Elizabeth's company, probably in the cast of *Bartholomew Fair.*

[11] *eat 'em:* Tailors proverbially ate a great deal.

[12] *Burbage:* famous tragic actor, 1573–1619.

[13] *Field:* Nathan Field, 1587–1619, actor, playwright, disciple of Jonson, also probably in the cast.

[14] *affect:* like.   [15] *green gamesters:* loose women.

[16] *at large:* fully.

[17] *ostler:* perhaps an allusion to the actor William Ostler (d. shortly after the performance of the play), who had acted in some of Jonson's earlier plays.

[18] *printed book:* Marlowe's *Hero and Leander,* published 1598, from which Leatherhead is about to quote.

there is no such matter, I assure you. I have only made
it a little easy and modern [19] for the times, sir, that's all;
as, for the Hellespont, I imagine our Thames here; and
then Leander I make a dyer's son, about Puddle
Wharf; [20] and Hero a wench o' the Bankside, [21] who
going over one morning, to old Fish Street, [22] 130
Leander spies her land at Trig Stairs, [23] and falls in love
with her. Now do I introduce Cupid, having metamorphosed himself into a drawer, and he strikes Hero
in love with a pint of sherry; and other pretty passages
there are, o' the friendship, that will delight you sir,
and please you of judgment.

Cokes. I'll be sworn they shall; I am in love with the
actors already, and I'll be allied to [24] them presently.
(They respect gentlemen, these fellows.) Hero shall be
my fairing; but, which of my fairings? [25] Le' me 140
see—i' faith, my fiddle! and Leander my fiddlestick;
then Damon my drum; and Pythias my pipe, and the
ghost of Dionysius my hobbyhorse. All fitted.

V.iv

[*Enter*] WINWIFE, GRACE.

Winw. Look, yonder's your Cokes gotten in among
his play-fellows; I thought we could not miss him at
such a spectacle.

Grace. Let him alone; he is so busy, he will never
spy us.

Lea. Nay, good sir.

COKES *is handling the puppets.*

Cokes. I warrant thee, I will not hurt her, fellow;
what, dost think me uncivil? I pray be not jealous. I
am toward [1] a wife.   9

Lit. Well, good Master Lantern, make ready to
begin, that I may fetch my wife, and look you be perfect; you undo me else i' my reputation.

Lea. I warrant you, sir, do not you breed too great
an expectation of it among your friends; that's the only
hurter of these things.

Lit. No, no, no.

                                                    [*Exit.*]

Cokes. I'll stay here, and see; pray thee let me see.

Winw. How diligent and troublesome [2] he is!

Grace. The place becomes him, methinks.   19

Just. [*Aside*] My ward Mistress Grace in the com-

---

[19] *modern:* commonplace.
[20] *Puddle Wharf:* water gate to the Thames near Blackfriars.
[21] *Bankside:* south bank of the Thames, site of theaters.
[22] *Fish Street:* center of fish trade.
[23] *Trig Stairs:* stairs down to the landing near Puddle
Wharf.
[24] *allied to:* joined with.
[25] *fairings:* i.e., what he takes away from the fair.
V.iv.
[1] *toward:* about to get.   [2] *troublesome:* painstaking.
[3] *tall:* fine.   [4] *aqua vitae:* ardent spirits.
[5] *By:* With reference to. [6] *private house:* private theater.
[7] *all-to-be-madam:* call me madam.
[8] *eder-oder:* one or the other.
[9] *Delia:* lady of Samuel Daniel's Sonnets, 1592.

pany of a stranger? I doubt I shall be compelled to
discover myself before my time!

[*Enter*] KNOCKEM, EDGWORTH, WIN, WHIT, MISTRESS OVERDO.

The Door-keepers *speak.*

Fil. Twopence apiece, gentlemen, an excellent
motion.

Kno. Shall we have fine fireworks and good vapors?

Shark. Yes, captain, and waterworks too.

Whit. I pre dee, take a care o' dy shmall lady, there,
Edgworth; I will look to dish tall [3] lady myself.

Lea. Welcome, gentlemen; welcome, gentlemen.

Whit. Pre dee, mashter o' de monshtersh, help a very
sick lady, here, to a chair, to shit in.   31

Lea. Presently, sir.

They bring MISTRESS OVERDO *a chair.*

Whit. Good fait now, Urs'la's ale and *aqua vitae* [4]
ish to blame for't; shit down, shweetheart, shit down,
and shleep a little.

Edg. Madam, you are very welcome hither.

Kno. Yes, and you shall see very good vapors.

Just. [*Aside*] Here is my care come! I like to see him
in so good company; and yet I wonder that persons of
such fashion, should resort hither!   40

By [5] EDGWORTH.

Edg. This is a very private house, [6] madam.

Lea. Will it please your ladyship sit, madam?

The Cutpurse *courts* MISTRESS LITTLEWIT.

Win. Yes, good man. They do so all-to-be-madam [7]
me, I think they think me a very lady!

Edg. What else, madam?

Win. Must I put off my mask to him?

Edg. Oh, by no means.

Win. How should my husband know me, then?

Kno. Husband? An idle vapor; he must not know
you, nor you him; there's the true vapor.   50

Just. [*Aside*] Yea, I will observe more of this.—Is
this a lady, friend?

Whit. Ay, and dat is anoder lady, shweetheart; if dou
hasht a mind to 'em give me twelvepence from tee, and
dou shalt have eder-oder [8] on 'em!

Just. [*Aside*] Ay? This will prove my chiefest enormity; I will follow this.

Edg. Is not this a finer life, lady, than to be clogged
with a husband?

Win. Yes, a great deal. When will they begin, trow,
in the name o' the motion?   61

Edg. By and by, madam; they stay but for company.

Kno. Do you hear, puppet-master, these are tedious
vapors; when begin you?

Lea. We stay but for Master Littlewit, the author
who is gone for his wife; and we begin presently.

Win. That's I, that's I.

Edg. That was you, lady; but now you are no such
poor thing.   69

Kno. Hang the author's wife, a running vapor! Here
be ladies will stay for ne'er a Delia [9] o' 'em all.

Whit. But hear me now, here ish one o' de ladish, ashleep; stay till she but vake, man.

[*Enter*] WASP. *The* Door-keepers *again.*

Wasp. How now, friends? What's here to do?

Fil. Twopence a piece, sir, the best motion in the Fair.

Wasp. I believe you lie; if you do, I'll have my money again and beat you.

Winw. Numps is come!   79

Wasp. Did you see a master of mine come in here, a tall young squire of Harrow o' the Hill, Master Barthol'mew Cokes?

Fil. I think there be such a one within.

Wasp. Look he be, you were best; but it is very likely. I wonder I found him not at all the rest. I ha' been at the Eagle, and the Black Wolf, and the Bull with the five legs and two pizzles (he was a calf at Uxbridge Fair, two years agone), and at the Dogs that dance the morris, and the Hare o' the tabor, and missed him at all these! Sure this must needs be some fine sight that holds him so, if it have him.   91

Cokes. Come, come, are you ready now?

Lea. Presently, sir.

Wasp. Hoyday, he's at work in his doublet and hose. Do you hear, sir? Are you employed, that you are bareheaded and so busy?

Cokes. Hold your peace, Numps; you ha' been i' the stocks, I hear.

Wasp. Does he know that? Nay, then the date of my authority is out; I must think no longer to reign;   100 my government is at an end. He that will correct another must want fault in himself.

Winw. Sententious Numps! I never heard so much from him before.

Lea. Sure, Master Littlewit will not come; please you take your place, sir; we'll begin.

Cokes. I pray thee do, mine ears long to be at it, and my eyes too. O Numps, i' the stocks, Numps? Where's your sword, Numps?

Wasp. I pray you intend your game, sir; let me alone.   111

Cokes. Well then, we are quit for all. Come, sit down, Numps; I'll interpret to thee. Did you see Mistress Grace? It's no matter, neither, now I think on't; tell me anon.

Winw. A great deal of love and care he expresses.

Grace. Alas! would you have him to express more than he has? That were tyranny.

Cokes. Peace ho; now, now.   119

Lea. Gentles,[10] *that no longer your expectations may wander,*
Behold our chief actor, amorous Leander,
With a great deal of cloth lapped about him like a scarf,
For he yet serves his father, a dyer at Puddle Wharf,
Which place we'll make bold with, to call it our Abydos;
As the Bankside is our Sestos, and let it not be denied us.
Now, as he is beating, to make the dye take the fuller,[11]
Who chances to come by but fair Hero in a sculler?
And, seeing Leander's naked leg and goodly calf,
Cast at him, from the boat, a sheep's eye and a half.

Now she is landed, and the sculler come back;   130
By and by you shall see what Leander doth lack.

Pup. Lean. Cole,[12] Cole, old Cole.

Lea.   *That is the sculler's name without control.*[13]

Pup. Lean. Cole, Cole, I say, Cole.

Lea.   *We do hear you.*

Pup. Lean.   Old Cole.

Lea. Old Cole? Is the dyer turned collier?[14] *How do you sell?*

Pup. Lean. A pox o' your manners, kiss my hole here, and smell.

Lea. Kiss your hole, and smell? There's manners indeed.

Pup. Lean. Why, Cole, I say, Cole.

Lea.   *It's sculler you need!*

Pup. Lean. Ay, and be hanged.

Lea.   *Be hanged; look your yonder,*
Old Cole, you must go hang with Master Leander.   139

Pup. Cole. Where is he?

Pup. Lean.   *Here, Cole, what fairest of fairs*
Was that fare that thou landest but now at Trig Stairs?

Cokes. What was that, fellow? Pray thee tell me, I scarce understand 'em.

Lea. Leander does ask, sir, what fairest of fairs
Was the fare that he landed but now at Trig Stairs?

Pup. Cole. It is lovely Hero.

Pup. Lean. Nero?

Pup. Cole. No, Hero.

Lea. It is Hero   149
Of the Bankside, he saith, to tell you truth without erring,
Is come over into Fish Street to eat some fresh herring.
Leander says no more, but as fast as he can
Gets on all his best clothes, and will after to the Swan.[15]

Cokes. Most admirable good, is't not?

Lea. Stay, sculler.

Pup. Cole.   *What say you?*

Lea.   *You must stay for Leander,*
And carry him to the wench.

Pup. Cole.   *You rogue, I am no pander.*

Cokes. He says he is no pander. 'Tis a fine language; I understand it now.

Lea. Are you no pander, Goodman Cole? Here's no man says you are,
You'll grow a hot Cole, it seems; pray you stay for your fare.   160

Pup. Cole. Will he come away?

Lea.   *What do you say?*

Pup. Cole.   *I'd ha' him come away.*

Lea. Would you ha' Leander come away? Why 'pray, sir, stay.

---

[10] *Gentles:* the puppet play recalls *Hero and Leander* and, in its style as well as its action, Richard Edwardes' *Damon and Pythias,* 1565.

[11] *fuller:* more thoroughly.

[12] *Cole:* name for a pander.

[13] *without control:* said freely.

[14] *collier:* term of abuse; colliers were proverbially dishonest.

[15] *Swan:* an inn.

You are angry, Goodman Cole; I believe the fair maid
Came over wi' you o' trust. Tell us, sculler, are you paid?

 Pup. Cole. Yes, Goodman Hogrubber[16] o' Pickt-
hatch.[17]

 Lea. How, Hogrubber o' Pickt-hatch?

 Pup. Cole. Ay, Hogrubber o' Pickt-hatch. Take you
that.

The Puppet *strikes him over the pate.*

 Lea. Oh, my head!

 Pup. Cole. Harm watch, harm catch.   169

 Cokes. Harm watch, harm catch, he says: very good
i' faith, the sculler had like to ha' knocked you, sirrah.

 Lea. Yes, but that his fare called him away.

 Pup. Lean. Row apace, row apace, row, row, row, row,
row.

 Lea. You are knavishly loaden, sculler; take heed where
you go.

 Pup. Cole. Knave i' your face, Goodman Rogue.

 Pup. Lean.   Row,
row, row, row, row, row.

 Cokes. He said "knave i' your face," friend.

 Lea. Ay, sir, I heard him. But there's no talking to
these watermen, they will ha' the last word.

 Cokes. God's my life! I am not allied to the sculler
yet; he shall be Dauphin my boy.[18] But my 180
Fiddlestick[19] does fiddle in and out too much; I pray
thee speak to him on't; tell him I would have him tarry
in my sight more.

 Lea. I pray you be content; you'll have enough on
him, sir.

Now, gentles, I take it, here is none of you so stupid,
But that you have heard of a little god of love, called
 Cupid;
Who out of kindness to Leander, hearing he but saw her,
This present day and hour doth turn himself to a drawer.
And because he would have their first meeting to be merry,
He strikes Hero in love to him with a pint of sherry, 191
Which he tells her from amorous Leander is sent her,
Who after him into the room of Hero doth venter.

 Pup. Jon. A pint of sack, score a pint of sack i' the
Coney.[20]

PUPPET LEANDER *goes into* MISTRESS
HERO'S *room.*

 Cokes. Sack?[21] You said but e'en now it should be
sherry.

 Pup. Jon. Why so it is; sherry, sherry, sherry.

 Cokes. "Sherry, sherry, sherry." By my troth he
makes me merry. I must have a name for Cupid, too.

---

[16] *Hogrubber:* Swineherd.
[17] *Pickt-hatch:* haunt of prostitutes.
[18] *Dauphin . . . boy:* alluding to a lost ballad quoted by
Edgar in *Lear*, III. iv. 101–2. [19] *Fiddlestick:* Leander.
[20] *Coney:* name of a room in the tavern.
[21] *Sack:* generic name for white wines including sherry;
Cokes betrays his ignorance.
[22] *dead lift:* desperate situation.
[23] *nine days' wonder:* temporary novelty.
[24] *condition:* on condition that.
[25] *hobbyhorse . . . forgotten:* reference to another popular
ballad. [26] *scab:* scoundrel. [27] *Pink:* Stab.

Let me see; thou mightst help me now, an thou 200
wouldest, Numps, at a dead lift,[22] but thou art dreaming o' the stocks still! Do not think on't, I have forgot
it; 'tis but a nine days' wonder[23] man; let it not trouble
thee.

 Wasp. I would the stocks were about your neck, sir;
condition[24] I hung by the heels in them, till the wonder
were off from you, with all my heart.

 Cokes. Well said, resolute Numps. But hark you,
friend, where is the friendship all this while between
my drum, Damon, and my pipe, Pythias? 210

 Lea. You shall see by and by, sir!

 Cokes. You think my hobbyhorse is forgotten,[25] too;
no, I'll see 'em all enact before I go; I shall not know
which to love best else.

 Kno. This gallant has interrupting vapors, troublesome vapors, Whit; puff with him.

 Whit. No, I pre dee, captain, let him alone. He is a
child i' faith, la.

 Lea. Now, gentles, to the friends, who in number are
two,
And lodged in that ale-house in which fair Hero does do.
Damon (for some kindness done him the last week) 221
Is come fair Hero in Fish Street this morning to seek;
Pythias does smell the knavery of the meeting,
And now you shall see their true friendly greeting.

 Pup. Pyth. You whoremasterly slave, you.

 Cokes. Whoremasterly slave you? Very friendly and
familiar, that.

 Pup. Dam. Whoremaster i' thy face.
Thou hast lien with her thyself, I'll prove't i' this place.

 Cokes. Damon says Pythias has lien with her himself;
he'll prove't in this place. 231

 Lea. They are whoremasters both, sir, that's a plain
case.

 Pup. Pyth. You lie, like a rogue.

 Lea. Do I lie, like a rogue?

 Pup. Pyth. A pimp, and a scab.[26]

 Lea. A pimp, and a scab?
I say between you, you have both but one drab.

 Pup. Dam. You lie again.

 Lea. Do I lie again?

 Pup. Dam. Like a rogue again. 240

 Lea. Like a rogue again?

 Pup. Pyth. And you are a pimp, again.

 Cokes. And you are a pimp again, he says.

 Pup. Dam. And a scab again.

 Cokes. And a scab again, he says.

 Lea. And I say again, you are both whoremasters again,
and you have both but one drab again.

They fight.

 Pup. Dam., Pyth. Dost thou, dost thou, dost thou?

 Lea. What, both at once?

 Pup. Pyth. Down with him, Damon. 250

 Pup. Dam. Pink[27] his guts, Pythias.

 Lea. What, so malicious?
Will ye murder me, masters both, i' mine own house?

 Cokes. Ho! well acted, my drum; well acted, my
pipe; well acted still.

 Wasp. Well acted, with all my heart.

Lea. Hold, hold your hands.

Cokes. Ay, both your hands, for my sake! for you ha'
both done well.

Pup. Dam. Gramercy, pure Pythias.   260

Pup. Pyth. Gramercy, dear Damon.

Cokes. Gramercy to you both, my pipe and my drum.

Pup. Dam., Pyth. Come now, we'll together to breakfast
to Hero.

Lea. 'Tis well, you can go to breakfast to Hero;
You have given me my breakfast, with a 'hone and
'honero.[28]

Cokes. How is't, friend; ha' they hurt thee?

Lea. Oh, no!

Between you and I, sir, we do but make show.
Thus, gentles, you perceive, without any denial,   269
'Twixt Damon and Pythias here, friendship's true trial.
Though hourly they quarrel thus, and roar each with other,
They fight you no more than does brother with brother,
But friendly together, at the next man they meet
They let fly their anger, as here you might see't.

Cokes. Well, we have seen't, and thou hast felt it,
whatsoever thou sayest. What's next? What's next?

Lea. This while young Leander with fair Hero is
drinking,
And Hero grown drunk, to any man's thinking!
Yet was it not three pints of sherry could flaw[29] *her,*
Till Cupid, distinguished like Jonas the drawer,   280
From under his apron, where his lechery lurks,
Put love in her sack. Now mark how it works.

Pup. Hero. O Leander, Leander, my dear, my dear
Leander,
I'll for ever be thy goose, so thou'lt be my gander.

Cokes. Excellently well said, fiddle; she'll ever be his
goose, so he'll be her gander: was't not so?

Lea. Yes, sir, but mark his answer, now.

Pup. Lean. And, sweetest of geese, before I go to bed,
I'll swim o'er the Thames, my goose, thee to tread.[30]

Cokes. Brave! he will swim o'er the Thames, and
tread his goose tonight, he says.   291

Lea. Ay, peace, sir, they'll be angry if they hear you
eaves-dropping, now they are setting their match.

Pup. Lean. But lest the Thames should be dark, my
goose, my dear friend,
Let thy window be provided of a candle's end.

Pup. Hero. Fear not, my gander, I protest I should
handle
My matters very ill, if I had not a whole candle.

Pup. Lean. Well, then, look to't, and kiss me to boot.

Lea. Now, here come the friends again, Pythias and
Damon,   299
And under their cloaks they have of bacon a gammon.

DAMON and PYTHIAS enter.

Pup. Pyth. Drawer, fill some wine here.

Lea.   How, some wine there?
There's company already, sir; pray, forbear!

Pup. Dam. 'Tis Hero.

Lea.   Yes, but she will not be taken,
After sack, and fresh herring, with your Dunmow-bacon.[31]

Pup. Pyth. You lie, it's Westfabian.

Lea.   Westphalian you should say.

Pup. Damon. If you hold not your peace, you are a
coxcomb, I would say.

LEANDER *and* HERO *are kissing.*

Pup. Pyth. What's here? What's here? Kiss, kiss upon
kiss.

Lea. Ay, wherefore should they not? What harm is in
this?
'Tis Mistress Hero.

Pup. Dam.   Mistress Hero's a whore.

Lea. Is she a whore? Keep you quiet, or sir knave out of
door.   310

Pup. Dam. Knave out of door?

Pup. Hero.   Yes, knave, out of door.

Pup. Damon. Whore out of door.

Here the Puppets *quarrel and fall together*
by the ears.

Pup. Hero.   I say, knave, out of
door.

Pup. Dam. I say, whore, out of door.

Pup. Pyth.   Yea, so say I too.

Pup. Hero. Kiss the whore o' the arse.

Lea.   Now you ha'
something to do.
You must kiss her o' the arse, she says.

Pup. Dam., Pyth. So we will, so we will.

[*They kick her.*]

Pup. Hero. Oh, my haunches, oh, my haunches, hold,
hold.

Lea. Stand'st thou still?
Leander, where art thou? Stand'st thou still like a sot,
And not offer'st to break both their heads with a pot?
See who's at thine elbow there! Puppet Jonas and Cupid.

Pup. Jon. Upon 'em, Leander, be not so stupid.   322

They fight.

Pup. Lean. You goat-bearded slave!

Pup. Dam.   You whoremaster knave.

Pup. Lean. Thou art a whoremaster.

Pup. Jon.   Whoremaster all.

Lea. See, Cupid with a word has ta'en up the brawl.

Kno. These be fine vapors!

Cokes. By this good day they fight bravely! Do they
not, Numps?

Wasp. Yes, they lacked but you to be their second all
this while.   330

Lea. This tragical encounter, falling out thus to busy us,
It raises up the ghost of their friend Dionysius:[32]
Not like a monarch, but the master of a school,
In a scrivener's furred gown, which shows he is no fool;

---

[28] *'hone and 'honero:* alas (Scots).

[29] *flaw:* make drunk.   [30] *tread:* copulate.

[31] *Dunmow-bacon:* the "flitch" given to a couple who could
convince a jury of maids and bachelors in Little Dunmow,
Essex, that they had never quarreled or regretted marrying
once during the first year of their marriage.

[32] *Dionysius:* Dionysius the Younger, tyrant of Syracuse
367–343 B.C., was said by Cicero and others to have taught
school after his expulsion.

For therein he hath wit enough to keep himself warm.
"O Damon," he cries, "and Pythias; what harm
Hath poor Dionysius done you in his grave,
That after his death, you should fall out thus and rave,
And call amorous Leander whoremaster knave?"

Pup. Dion.[33] *I cannot, I will not, I promise you,*
    endure it.   340

V.v

[*Enter*] BUSY.

Busy. Down with Dagon,[1] down with Dagon; 'tis I
will no longer endure your profanations.

Lea. What mean you, sir?

Busy. I will remove Dagon there, I say, that idol,
that heathenish idol, that remains, as I may say, a beam,
a very beam, not a beam of the sun, nor a beam of the
moon, nor a beam of a balance, neither a house-beam,
nor a weaver's beam, but a beam in the eye, in the eye
of the brethren; a very great beam, an exceeding great
beam; such as are your stage-players, rhymers,   10
and morris-dancers, who have walked hand in hand in
contempt of the brethren and the cause, and been borne
out by instruments[2] of no mean countenance.[3]

Lea. Sir, I present nothing but what is licensed by
authority.

Busy. Thou art all license, even licentiousness itself,
Shimei![4]

Lea. I have the Master of the Revels'[5] hand for't, sir.

Busy. The master of rebels' hand, thou hast:
Satan's! hold thy peace, thy scurrility, shut up thy   20
mouth. Thy profession is damnable, and in pleading
for it thou dost plead for Baal.[6] I have long opened my
mouth wide and gaped; I have gaped as the oyster for
the tide after thy destruction, but cannot compass it by
suit or dispute, so that I look for a bickering ere long
and then a battle.

Kno. Good Banbury-vapors.

Cokes. Friend, you'd have an ill match on't if you
bicker with him here; though he be no man o' the fist,
he has friends that will go to cuffs for him. Numps, will
not you take our side?   31

Edg. Sir, it shall not need; in my mind, he offers him
a fairer course, to end it by disputation! Hast thou
nothing to say for thyself, in defense of thy quality?

Lea. Faith, sir, I am not well studied in these controversies, between the hypocrites and us. But here's

one of my motion, Puppet Dionysius, shall undertake
him, and I'll venture the cause on't.

Cokes. Who? My hobbyhorse? Will he dispute with
him?   40

Lea. Yes, sir, and make a hobby-ass of him, I hope.

Cokes. That's excellent! indeed he looks like the best
scholar of 'em all. Come, sir, you must be as good as
your word now.

Busy. I will not fear to make my spirit and gifts
known! Assist me, zeal; fill me, fill me; that is, make
me full.

Winw. What a desperate, profane wretch is this! is
there any ignorance or impudence like his? To call his
zeal to fill him against a puppet?   50

Grace.[7] I know no fitter match than a puppet to
commit[8] with an hypocrite!

Busy. First, I say unto thee, idol, thou hast no calling.

Pup. Dion. You lie, I am called Dionysius.

Lea. The motion says you lie, he is called Dionysius
i' the matter, and to that calling he answers.

Busy. I mean no vocation, idol, no present lawful
calling.

Pup. Dion. Is yours a lawful calling?   59

Lea. The motion asketh if yours be a lawful calling?

Busy. Yes, mine is of the spirit.

Pup. Dion. Then idol is a lawful calling.

Lea. He says, then idol is a lawful calling! For you
called him idol, and your calling is of the spirit.

Cokes. Well disputed, hobbyhorse!

Busy. Take not part with the wicked, young gallant.
He neigheth and hinnyeth;[9] all is but hinnying
sophistry. I call him idol again. Yet I say his calling, his
profession is profane, it is profane, idol.

Pup. Dion. It is not profane!   70

Lea. It is not profane, he says.

Busy. It is profane.

Pup. Dion. It is not profane.

Busy. It is profane.

Pup. Dion. It is not profane.

Lea. Well said, confute him with "not," still. You
cannot bear him down with your base noise, sir.

Busy. Nor he me, with his treble creaking, though
he creak like the chariot wheels of Satan; I am zealous
for the cause—   80

Lea. As a dog for a bone.

Busy. And I say it is profane, as being the page of
pride, and the waiting-woman of vanity.

Pup. Dion. Yea? What say you to your tire-women,[10]
then?

Lea. Good.

Pup. Dion. Or feather-makers i' the Friars, that are
o' your faction of faith? Are not they, with their perukes
and their puffs, their fans and their huffs, as much pages
of pride, and waiters upon vanity? What say you?
What say you? What say you?   91

Busy. I will not answer for them.

Pup. Dion. Because you cannot, because you cannot.
Is a bugle-[11]maker a lawful calling? Or the confect-[12]
maker's; such you have there? Or your French
fashioner?[13] You'd have all the sin within yourselves,
would you not? Would you not?

---

[33] *Dion.:* F "Pup.D."; some editors implausibly assign to
Damon.

V.v.
  [1] *Dagon:* Philistine god.   [2] *instruments:* agents.
  [3] *countenance:* reputation.
  [4] *Shimei:* enemy of David, 2 Samuel xvi: 5–13.
  [5] *Master of the Revels:* royal licenser of plays.
  [6] *Baal:* pagan deity.
  [7] *Grace:* F "Qua."
                            [8] *commit:* fight.
  [9] *hinnyeth:* whinnies.   [10] *tire-women:* dressmakers.
  [11] *bugle:* glass bead.   [12] *confect:* candy.
  [13] *fashioner:* tailor.

Busy. No, Dagon.

Pup. Dion. What then, Dagonet?[14] Is a puppet worse than these?   100

Busy. Yes, and my main argument against you is that you are an abomination, for the male among you putteth on the apparel of the female, and the female of the male.[15]

Pup. Dion. You lie, you lie, you lie abominably.

Cokes. Good, by my troth, he has given him the lie thrice.

Pup. Dion. It is your old stale argument against the players, but it will not hold against the puppets, for we have neither male nor female amongst us. And   110 that thou may'st see, if thou wilt, like a malicious purblind zeal as thou art!

The PUPPET *takes up his garment.*

Edg. By my faith, there he has answered you, friend; by plain demonstration.

Pup. Dion. Nay, I'll prove, against e'er a rabbin[16] of 'em all that my standing is as lawful as his, that I speak by inspiration as well as he, that I have as little to do with learning as he, and do scorn her helps as much as he.

Busy. I am confuted; the cause hath failed me.   120

Pup. Dion. Then be converted, be converted.

Lea. Be converted, I pray you, and let the play go on!

Busy. Let it go on. For I am changed and will become a beholder with you!

Cokes. That's brave i' faith. Thou hast carried it away, hobbyhorse; on with the play!

The JUSTICE *discovers himself.*

Just. Stay, now do I forbid, I Adam Overdo! Sit still, I charge you.

Cokes. What, my brother-i'-law!

Grace. My wise guardian!   130

Edg. Justice Overdo!

Just. It is time to take enormity by the forehead and brand it; for I have discovered enough.

V.vi

[*Enter*] QUARLOUS (*like the* Madman) [*and*] PURECRAFT (*a while after*).

Quar. Nay, come, mistress bride. You must do as I do now. You must be mad with me, in truth. I have here Justice Overdo for it.

Just. Peace, good Trouble-All; come hither, and you shall trouble none. I will take the charge of you and your friend too. You also, young man, shall be my care; stand there.

To the Cutpurse *and* MISTRESS LITTLEWIT.

Edg. Now, mercy upon me.

The rest are stealing away.

Kno. Would we were away, Whit; these are dangerous vapors; best fall off with our birds, for fear o' the cage.[1]   11

Just. Stay, is not my name your terror?

Whit. Yesh, faith, man, and it ish for tat we would be gone, man.

[*Enter*] LITTLEWIT.

Lit. O gentlemen! did you not see a wife of mine? I ha' lost my little wife, as I shall be trusted, my little pretty Win; I left her at the great woman's house in trust yonder, the pig-woman's with Captain Jordan, and Captain Whit, very good men, and I cannot hear of her. Poor fool, I fear she's stepped aside. Mother, did you not see Win?   21

Just. If this grave matron be your mother, sir, stand by her, *et digito compesce labellum;*[2] I may perhaps spring a wife for you anon. Brother Barthol'mew, I am sadly sorry to see you so lightly given and such a disciple of enormity, with your grave governor Humphrey; but stand you both there, in the middle place; I will reprehend you in your course. Mistress Grace, let me rescue you out of the hands of the stranger.

Winw. Pardon me, sir, I am a kinsman of hers.   30

Just. Are you so? Of what name, sir?

Winw. Winwife, sir.

Just. Master Winwife? I hope you have won no wife of her, sir. If you have, I will examine the possibility of it at fit leisure. Now, to my enormities. Look upon me, O London! and see me, O Smithfield! the example of justice, and Mirror of Magistrates; the true top of formality and scourge of enormity. Hearken unto my labors and but observe my discoveries, and compare Hercules with me, if thou dar'st, of old; or Colum-   40 bus; Magellan; or our countryman Drake of later times. Stand forth, you weeds of enormity, and spread. [*To* BUSY] First, Rabbi Busy, thou super-lunatical hypocrite. [*To* LEATHERHEAD] Next, thou other extremity, thou profane professor of puppetry, little better than poetry. [*To the* Horse-courser, *and* Cutpurse] Then thou strong debaucher and seducer of youth, witness this easy and honest young man. [*Then* CAPTAIN WHIT *and* MISTRESS LITTLEWIT] Now thou, esquire of dames, madams, and twelvepenny ladies. Now my green   50 madam herself, of the price. Let me unmask your Ladyship.

Lit. Oh, my wife, my wife, my wife!

Just. Is she your wife? *Redde te Harpocratem!*[3]

Enter TROUBLE-ALL, URSULA, NIGHTINGALE.

Tro. By your leave, stand by, my masters; be uncovered.

Urs. Oh, stay him, stay him; help to cry, Nightingale; my pan, my pan.

Just. What's the matter?

Night. He has stol'n Gammer Urs'la's pan.   60

---

[14] *Dagonet:* King Arthur's fool.
[15] *my . . . male:* recurrent Puritan argument against plays.
[16] *rabbin:* rabbi.

V.vi.
[1] *cage:* prison.
[2] *L.:* "and hold a finger to your lips" (lest you be an informer), Juvenal, *Satires,* I. 160.
[3] *L.:* Make yourself a Harpocrates (god of silence).

Tro. Yes, and I fear no man but Justice Overdo.

Just. Urs'la? Where is she? Oh, the sow of enormity, this! [*To* URSULA *and* NIGHTINGALE] Welcome, stand you there; you, songster, there.

Urs. An please your worship, I am in no fault: a gentleman stripped him in my booth and borrowed his gown and his hat, and he ran away with my goods here for it.

Just. [*To* QUARLOUS] Then this is the true madman, and you are the enormity!   70

Quar. You are i' the right, I am mad, but from the gown outward.

Just. Stand you there.

Quar. Where you please, sir.

MISTRESS OVERDO [*waking*] *is sick: and her husband is silenced.*

Mrs. O. Oh, lend me a basin, I am sick, I am sick. Where's Master Overdo? Bridget,[4] call hither my Adam.

Just. How?

Whit. Dy very own wife, i' fait, worshipful Adam.

Mrs. O. Will not my Adam come at me? Shall I see him no more, then?   81

Quar. Sir, why do you not go on with the enormity? Are you oppressed with it? I'll help you. Hark you, sir, i' your ear: your "innocent young man" you have ta'en such care of all this day is a cutpurse that hath got all your brother Cokes his things and helped you to your beating and the stocks; if you have a mind to hang him now, and show him your magistrate's wit, you may; but I should think it were better, recovering the goods, and to save your estimation[5] in him. I thank you,   90 sir, for the gift of your ward, Mistress Grace; look you, here is your hand and seal, by the way. Master Winwife, give you joy, you are Palamon, you are possessed o' the gentlewoman, but she must pay me value; here's warrant for it. And honest madman, there's thy gown and cap again; I thank thee for my wife. [*To the* Widow] Nay, I can be mad, sweetheart, when I please still; never fear me. And careful Numps, where's he? I thank him for my license.

WASP *misseth the license.*

Wasp. How!   100

Quar. 'Tis true, Numps.

Wasp. I'll be hanged then.

Quar. Look i' your box, Numps. [*To* JUSTICE] Nay, sir, stand not you fixed here, like a stake in Finsbury[6] to be shot at, or the whipping post i' the Fair, but get your wife out o' the air; it will make her worse else; and remember you are but Adam, flesh and blood! You have your frailty; forget your other name of Overdo and invite us all to supper. There you and I will compare our discoveries, and drown the memory of all enormity in your bigg'st bowl at home.   111

Cokes. How now, Numps, ha' you lost it? I warrant, 'twas when thou wert i' the stocks. Why dost not speak?

Wasp. I will never speak while I live again, for aught I know.

Just. Nay, Humphrey, if I be patient, you must be so too; this pleasant conceited gentleman hath wrought upon my judgment and prevailed. I pray you take care of your sick friend, Mistress Alice, and my good friends all—   121

Quar. And no enormities.

Just. I invite you home with me to my house, to supper. I will have none fear to go along, for my intents are *ad correctionem, non ad destructionem; ad aedificandum, non ad diruendum;*[7] so lead on.

Cokes. Yes, and bring the actors along; we'll ha' the rest o' the play at home.   [*Exeunt.*]

THE EPILOGUE

Your majesty hath seen the play, and you
  Can best allow it from your ear and view.
You know the scope of writers, and what store
  Of leave is given them, if they take not more
And turn it into license. You can tell
  If we have used that leave you gave us well;
Or whether we to rage or license break,
  Or be profane, or make profane men speak.
This is your power to judge, great sir, and not
  The envy of a few. Which if we have got,   10
We value less what their dislike can bring,
  If it so happy be, t' have pleased the King.

T H E   E N D

---

[4] *Bridget:* Jonson's mistake for "Grace"(?); absent-minded call to a servant not present(?).

[5] *estimation:* repute.

[6] *Finsbury:* field north of London used for archery.

[7] *L.:* for correction, not for destruction; for building, not for tearing down.

John Marston

[c. 1575–1634]

THE DUTCH COURTESAN

MARSTON'S father was a prominent and wealthy lawyer who spent most of his life at the Middle Temple. The poet joined his father's guild after earning his B.A. at Brasenose College, Oxford, in 1594, but his heart was not in the law: when John Marston, Senior, died in 1599 he left "to second son John my furniture &c. in my chambers in the Middle Temple, my law books &c. to my second son whom I hoped would have profited by them in the study of the law but man proposeth and God disposeth &c." It was the life of letters that attracted the young man's attention, and by the end of the 1590s he was publishing verse satires, directed more often than not against the kinds of young men with whom he associated in the legal world. His early works include *The Scourge of Villainy* and the Ovidian *Metamorphosis of Pygmalion's Image* (both 1598), which earned him an immediate reputation and a swift silencing when in 1599 the Archbishop of Canterbury and the Bishop of London ordered Marston's two books burned, along with the satirical work of two lesser writers, and banned the publication of further satires or epigrams; the cause of the bookburning was probably the obscenity of some of the writing. Philip J. Finkelpearl, in his invaluable *John Marston of the Middle Temple: An Elizabethan Dramatist in His Social Setting*, points out that Marston had in any case already given indications that he was finished with verse satire, and by 1599 he was embarked on the series of some eight plays to which he would devote his talents for the next decade.

Those plays, all of which were published separately in quarto and most of which were to be collected in folio in 1633, constitute a unique body of work. Marston was unusual among his fellow dramatists in writing exclusively for the companies of children who performed at the private theaters; only one play, *The Malcontent*, was performed by the King's Men, and that in a version somewhat refurbished from the original and with an induction by Webster. Perhaps what Marston could assume about the literacy of his audience had as much to do with the hubristic grandiloquence of his rhetoric as did his life in the legal world; he reached wildly for striking images and exotic words, which Ben Jonson parodied in the figure of Crispinus in his *Poetaster*, the last blow in a scurrilous exchange of hot-tempered personal attacks that came to be known as the War of the Theaters. The satirist in Marston found full expression in his plays alongside another part of his personality, the sentimental idealist, and most of his serious drama is so skewed by his personality as never quite to fit the standard generic categories. Thus *Antonio and Mellida* and its sequel *Antonio's Revenge* are a tragicomedy and a tragedy, respectively, which hover constantly on the brink of black comedy, and the brilliant *Malcontent* engineers a clever plot to enable its villains as well as its virtuous characters to pour out an endless stream of righteous and sardonic fury. The scurrility of Marston's literary temperament makes for plays that seem even more peculiar when one remembers that they are played by boys. His idiosyncrasies make his work a fascinating legacy, but the plays are marred by an unusual amateurism that is apparent in the frequent awkwardness of structure and exposition and in a thematic murkiness often oddly paired with its homiletic intensity. Marston's play writing turned out to be only an episode in his life: in 1608 his satire aimed too close to the King, and he was arrested; sometime thereafter he took orders in the Church of England and spent the rest of his life away from London. He died in 1634.

Although no performances are recorded before 1613, THE DUTCH COURTESAN was probably written between 1603 and 1605; in the former year Florio's translation of Montaigne appeared, providing a direct source for many passages, and in the latter the Stationers' Register lists it as having recently been performed by the Children of Queen Anne's Revels. The source of the main plot is a story in Nicolas de Montreux's *Les Bergeries de Juliette*; as the notes indicate, Marston quotes freely from a number of literary works, and Montaigne seems to have influenced the moral focus of the main plot as well as supplying language. For the subplot there is no single source, but episodes are borrowed from a number of places; thus the goblet scene is based on a story in Painter's *Palace of Pleasure* and the cloak scene on Jonson's *Every Man in His Humor*. The play was published in quarto (Q) in 1605, and that edition is the basis of the present text. Not revived until 1613, Marston's tragicomedy was the foundation of several Restoration and eighteenth-century plays.

The play has interesting similarities to the kind of city comedy that Middleton was just beginning to write for the same kind of audience and to the generic experiments Beaumont and Fletcher, not yet together, were composing during the same time. Marston's hallmarks are all here: not only the flamboyant style, but also the intense confusion of his intellectuality, insisting on a misogyny that is implicitly undercut by the characters of Beatrice and Crispinella, devoting speech after speech to a passionate argument about the place of lust in human psychology that the play never resolves, drawing one's attention to ingenious parallels of imagery, language, and incident among the three plots while making it difficult to perceive the point of the parallelism. But in other respects THE DUTCH COURTESAN speaks as much for its time as for its author: the relationship between Tysefew and Crispinella is a significant skirmish in the war between the sexes that shifted ground from *Much Ado about Nothing* to THE WILD-GOOSE CHASE, later to HYDE PARK, and ultimately to *The Way of the World*; the tragicomic structure, the juxtaposition of cynicism and sentimentality, the obsessive concern with and fear of sexuality, and the antiplebeian bias of the play are signs of a changing climate in the theater of the new century.   N. R.

The Dutch Courtesan

DRAMATIS PERSONÆ

FRANCISCHINA, *a Dutch courtesan*
MARY FAUGH,[1] *an old woman*
SIR LIONEL FREEVILL ⎱ *two old knights*
SIR HUBERT SUBBOYS ⎰
YOUNG FREEVILL, *Sir Lionel's son*
BEATRICE ⎱ *Sir Hubert's daughters*
CRISPINELLA ⎰
PUTIFER,[2] *their nurse*
TYSEFEW,[3] *a blunt gallant*
CAQUETEUR,[4] *a prattling gull*

MALHEUREUX,[5] *young Freevill's unhappy friend*
COCLEDEMOY,[6] *a knavishly witty City companion*
MASTER MULLIGRUB,[7] *a vintner*
MISTRESS MULLIGRUB, *his wife*
MASTER BURNISH, *a goldsmith*
LIONEL, *his man*
HOLIFERNES REINSCURE,[8] *a barber's boy*
Three Watchmen
[Pages
Gentlemen]

PROLOGUE

Slight hasty labors in this easy[1] play
Present not what you would, but what we may:
For this vouchsafe to know, the only end
Of our now study is not to offend.
Yet think not but, like others, rail we could
(Best art presents, not what it can, but should):
And if our pen in this seem over-slight,
We strive not to instruct, but to delight.
As for some few we know of purpose here
To tax and scout,[2] know, firm art cannot fear   10
Vain rage; only the highest grace we pray
Is, you'll not tax until you judge our play.
Think and then speak: 'tis rashness, and not wit,
To speak what is in passion, and not judgment, fit.
Sit, then, with fair expectance, and survey
Nothing but passionate man in his slight play,
Who hath this only ill—to some deemed worst—
A modest diffidence and self-mistrust.

FABULAE ARGUMENTUM[3]

The difference betwixt the love of a courtesan and a wife is the full scope of the play, which, intermixed with the deceits of a witty city jester, fills up the comedy.

ACT ONE

SCENE ONE

Turpe est difficiles habere nugas.[1]

Enter three Pages *with lights.* MULLIGRUB, FREEVILL, MALHEUREUX, TYSEFEW, *and* CAQUETEUR.

Free. Nay, comfort, my good host Shark,[2] my good Mulligrub.

Mal. Advance thy snout; do not suffer thy sorrowful nose to drop on thy Spanish leather jerkin, most hardly-honest Mulligrub.

Free. What, cogging[3] Cocledemoy is run away with a nest of goblets?[4] True, what then? They will be hammered out[5] well enough, I warrant you.

Mul. Sure, some wise man would find them out presently.[6]   10

243

Free. Yes, sure, if we could find out some wise man presently.

Mal. How was the plate lost? How did it vanish?

Free. In most sincere prose, thus: that man of much money, some wit, but less honesty, cogging Cocledemoy, comes this night late into mine host's Mulligrub's tavern here, calls for a room. The house being full, Cocledemoy, consorted with[7] his movable chattel, his instrument of fornication, the bawd Mistress Mary Faugh, are imparlored next the street. Good poul- 20 try was their food—blackbird, lark, woodcock; and mine host here comes in, cries "God bless you!" and departs. A blind harper enters, craves audience, uncaseth,[8] plays, The drawer,[9] for female privateness' sake, is nodded out, who, knowing that whosoever will hit the mark of profit must, like those that shoot in stone-bows,[10] wink with one eye, grows blind o' the right side and departs.

Caq. He shall answer for that winking with one eye at the last day.   30

Mal. Let him have day[11] till then, and he will wink with both his eyes.

Free. Cocledemoy, perceiving none in the room but the blind harper, whose eyes heaven had shut up from beholding wickedness, unclasps a casement to the street very patiently, pockets up three bowls unnaturally, thrusts his wench forth the window, and himself most preposterously,[12] with his heels forward, follows. The unseeing harper plays on, bids the empty dishes and the treacherous candles much good do them. The   40 drawer returns; but out, alas, not only the birds, but also the nest of goblets were flown away. Laments are raised—

Ty. Which did not pierce the heavens.

Free. The drawers moan, mine host doth cry, the bowls are gone.

Mul. *His finis Priami!*[13]

Mal. Nay, be not jaw-fallen,[14] my most sharking Mulligrub.

Free. 'Tis your just affliction; remember the sins of the cellar,[15] and repent, repent.   51

Mul. I am not jaw-fallen but I will hang the conycatching[16] Cocledemoy, and there's an end of 't.

[*Exit.*]

Caq. [*To* TYSEFEW] Is it a right stone? It shows well by candlelight.

Ty.[17] So do many things that are counterfeit, but I assure you this is a right diamond.

Caq. Might I borrow it of you? It will not a little grace my finger in visitation[18] of my mistress.

Ty. Why, use it, most sweet Caqueteur, use it.   60

Caq. Thanks, good sir. [*To the others*] 'Tis grown high night. Gentles, rest to you.

[*Exit with a* Page.]

Ty. A torch!—sound wench, soft sleep, and sanguine dreams to you both.—On, boy!

[*Exit with a* Page.]

Free. Let me bid you good rest.

Mal. Not so; trust me, I must bring my friend home. I dare not give you up to your own company; I fear the warmth of wine and youth will draw you to some common house of lascivious entertainment.   69

Free. Most necessary buildings, Malheureux; ever since my intention of marriage, I do pray for their continuance.

Mal. Loved sir, your reason?

Free. Marry, lest my house should be made one. I would have married men love the stews as Englishmen loved the Low Countries:[19] wish war should be maintained there lest it should come home to their own doors. What, suffer a man to have a hole to put his head in though he go to the pillory for it. Youth and appetite are above[20] the club of Hercules.[21]   80

Mal. This lust is a most deadly sin, sure.

Free. Nay, 'tis a most lively sin, sure.

Mal. Well, I am sure, 'tis one of the head[22] sins.

Free. Nay, I am sure it is one of the middle sins.

Mal. Pity, 'tis grown a most daily vice.

Free. But a more nightly vice, I assure you.

Mal. Well, 'tis a sin.

Free. Ay, or else few men would wish to go to heaven; and, not to disguise with my friend, I am now going the way of all flesh.   90

Mal. Not to a courtesan?

Free.   A courteous one.

Mal. What, to a sinner?

Free.   A very publican.

Mal. Dear my loved friend, let me be full[23] with you.

Know, sir, the strongest argument that speaks
Against the soul's eternity is lust,
That wise man's folly and the fool's wisdom:
But to grow wild in loose lasciviousness,
Given up to heat and sensual appetite,
Nay, to expose your health and strength and name,
Your precious time, and with that time the hope   100
Of due preferment, advantageous means
Of any worthy end, to the stale[24] use,
The common bosom, of a money-creature,
One that sells human flesh, a mangonist.[25]

Free. Alas, good creatures, what would you have them do? Would you have them get their living by the curse of man, the sweat of their brows? So they do. Every man must follow his trade, and every woman

---

[7] *consorted with:* accompanied by, perhaps with sexual second meaning.   [8] *uncaseth:* removes harp from case.

[9] *drawer:* tapster.

[10] *stone-bows:* crossbows using stones as missiles.

[11] *day:* time to defer his payment.

[12] *preposterously:* literally, rear end first.

[13] *L.:* "This was Priam's end" (misquoted from *Aeneid,* II. 554).   [14] *jaw-fallen:* crestfallen.

[15] *cellar:* wine-cellar.   [16] *cony-catching:* cheating.

[17] *Tysefew:* Here and at *l.* 60, Q reads "Free."

[18] *visitation:* visiting.

[19] *Low Countries:* Netherlands, where England preferred to fight the Spanish.   [20] *above:* stronger than.

[21] *club of Hercules:* traditional icon of physical strength.

[22] *head:* chief, capital.   [23] *full:* frank.

[24] *stale:* made worthless by time.

[25] *mangonist:* furbisher of inferior goods for sale.

her occupation. A poor, decayed mechanical man's[26] wife, her husband is laid up; may not she lawfully   110 be laid down when her husband's only rising is by his wife's falling? A captain's wife wants means, her commander lies in open field abroad; may not she lie in civil arms at home? A waiting gentlewoman that had wont to take say[27] to her lady miscarries[28] or so; the court misfortune throws her down; may not the city courtesy take her up? Do you know no alderman would pity such a woman's case? Why, is charity grown a sin? Or relieving the poor and impotent an offense? You will say beasts take no money for their fleshly   120 entertainment. True, because they are beasts, therefore beastly; only men give to loose[29] because they are men, therefore manly; and, indeed, wherein should they bestow their money better? In land, the title may be cracked;[30] in houses, they may be burnt; in apparel, 'twill wear; in wine, alas for pity, our throat is but short. But employ your money upon women, and, a thousand to nothing, some one of them will bestow that on you which shall stick by you as long as you live. They are no ingrateful persons; they will give *quid*[31] for   130 *quo*.[32] Do ye protest, they'll swear; do you rise, they'll fall; do you fall, they'll rise; do you give them the French crown,[33] they'll give you the French——[34] *O justus justa justum!*[35] They sell their bodies; do not better persons sell their souls? Nay, since all things have been sold—honor, justice, faith, nay, even God Himself—
Ay me, what base ignobleness is it
To sell the pleasure of a wanton bed?
Why do men scrape, why heap to full heaps join?   140
But for his mistress, who would care for coin?
For this I hold to be denied of no man:
All things are made for man, and man for woman.
Give me my fee.[36]
   Mal. Of ill you merit well. My heart's good friend,

---

[26] *mechanical man's:* artisan's.
[27] *say:* delicate serge material; test (i.e., she tries out her mistress's lovers).   [28] *miscarries:* becomes pregnant.
[29] *loose:* loose living.   [30] *cracked:* faulty.
[31] *quid:* Q "quite."   [32] *quid for quo:* tit for tat.
[33] *French crown:* coin; baldness caused by venereal disease.
[34] *French ——:* pox, venereal disease.
[35] *L.:* nominative singular forms for "just."
[36] *fee:* for a lawyer's advocacy.   [37] *curious:* careful.
[38] *L.:* The more common a good is, the better.
[39] *Family of Love:* millenarian Dutch sect associated by English opponents with free love; brothel.
[40] *Tanakin:* Dutch diminutive of Ann.
[41] *impropriation:* property held by a religious house.
[42] *froe:* Dutch woman.   [43] *perdy:* by God.
I.ii.
[1] *aunt:* bawd.
[2] *restitution is Catholic:* i.e., Catholics demanded return of property expropriated under Henry VIII.
[3] *L.:* the time is past.
[4] *glister-pipe:* tube for administering enemas (clysters).
[5] *Diana:* goddess of virginity.
[6] *toasts:* spiced toast dipped in wine.
[7] *pox:* venereal disease.
[8] *supportress . . . surgeons:* the bawd supplies the health professions with patients.
[9] *enhanceress:* one who raises prices.

Leave yet at length, at length; for know this ever,
'Tis no such sin to err, but to persever.
   Free. Beauty is woman's virtue, love the life's music, and woman the daintiness or second course of heaven's curious[37] workmanship. Since, then, beauty, love,   150 and woman are good, how can the love of woman's beauty be bad? And *Bonum, quo communius, eo melius;*[38] wilt then go with me.
   Mal. Whither?
   Free. To a house of salvation.
   Mal. Salvation?
   Free. Yes, 'twill make thee repent. Wilt go to the Family of Love![39] I will show thee my creature: a pretty, nimble-eyed Dutch Tanakin;[40] an honest, soft-hearted impropriation;[41] a soft, plump, round-   160 cheeked froe,[42] that has beauty enough for her virtue, virtue enough for a woman, and woman enough for any reasonable man in my knowledge. Wilt pass along with me?
   Mal. What, to a brothel? To behold an impudent prostitution? Fie on't! I shall hate the whole sex to see her; the most odious spectacle the earth can present is an immodest, vulgar woman.
   Free. Good, still; my brain shall keep't. You must go as you love me.   170
   Mal. Well, I'll go to make her loathe the shame she's in.
The sight of vice augments the hate of sin.
   Free. The sight of vice augments the hate of sin. Very fine, perdy![43]

                                              Exeunt.

[I.ii]

             Enter COCLEDEMOY *and* MARY FAUGH.

   Coc. Mary! Mary Faugh!
   Mary. Hem!
   Coc. Come, my worshipful, rotten, rough-bellied bawd. Ha! my blue-toothed patroness of natural wickedness, give me the goblets.
   Mary. By yea and by nay, Master Cocledemoy, I fear you'll play the knave and restore them.
   Coc. No, by the Lord, aunt,[1] restitution is Catholic,[2] and thou know'st we love—
   Mary. What?   10
   Coc. Oracles are ceased; *tempus praeteritum.*[3] Dost hear, my worshipful glister-pipe,[4] thou ungodly fire that burnt Diana's[5] temple? Dost hear, bawd?
   Mary. In very good truthness, you are the foulest-mouthed, profane, railing brother! Call a woman the most ungodly names! I must confess we all eat of the forbidden fruit; and, for mine own part, though I am one of the Family of Love and, as they say, a bawd that covers the multitude of sins, yet I trust I am none of the wicked that eat fish o' Fridays.   20
   Coc. Hang toasts![6] I rail at thee, my worshipful organ-bellows that fills the pipes, my fine rattling, phlegmy cough o' the lungs and cold with a pox?[7] I rail at thee? What, my right precious pandress, supportress of barber-surgeons[8] and enhanceress[9] of

lotium[10] and diet-drink![11] I rail at thee, necessary damnation? I'll make an oration, I, in praise of thy most courtly-in-fashion and most pleasurable function, I.

Mary. I prithee do; I love to hear myself praised, as well as any old lady, I.   30

Coc. List, then: a bawd, first for her profession or vocation, it is most worshipful of all the twelve companies;[12] for as that trade is most honorable that sells the best commodities—as the draper[13] is more worshipful than the pointmaker,[14] the silkman more worshipful than the draper, and the goldsmith more honorable than both, little Mary—so the bawd above all. Her shop has the best ware; for where these sell but cloth, satins, and jewels, she sells divine virtues as virginity, modesty, and such rare gems, and those not like   40 a petty[15] chapman,[16] by retail, but like a great merchant, by wholesale. Wa, ha, ho![17] And who are her customers? Not base corncutters[18] or sowgelders but most rare wealthy knights and most rare bountiful lords are her customers. Again, whereas no trade or vocation profiteth but by the loss and displeasure of another—as the merchant thrives not but by the licentiousness of giddy and unsettled youth, the lawyer but by the vexation of his client, the physician but by the maladies of his patient—only my smooth-   50 gummed bawd lives by others' pleasure and only grows rich by others' rising.[19] O merciful gain! O righteous income! So much for her vocation, trade, and life. As for their death, how can it be bad, since their wickedness is always before their eyes and a death's head[20] most commonly on their middle finger? To conclude 'tis most certain they must needs both live well and die well since most commonly they live in Clerkenwell[21] and die in Bridewell.[22] *Dixi*,[23] Mary.   59

Enter FREEVILL *and* MALHEUREUX [*preceded by a Page with a light*].

Free. Come along; yonder's the preface or exordium to my wench, the bawd.—Fetch, fetch!

[*Exit* MARY.]
What, Master Cocledemoy! is your knaveship yet stirring? Look to it, Mulligrub lies for you.

Coc. The more fool he; I can lie for myself, worshipful friend. Hang toasts! I vanish? Ha, my fine boy, thou art a scholar and hast read Tully's *Offices*,[24] my fine knave. Hang toasts!

Free. The vintner will toast you and[25] he catch you.

Coc. I will draw[26] the vintner to the stoop,[27] and when he runs low tilt[28] him. Ha, my fine knave, art going to thy recreation?   71

Free. Yes, my capricious rascal.

Coc. Thou wilt look like a fool, then, by and by.

Free. Look like a fool? Why?

Coc. Why, according to the old saying: a beggar when he is lousing of himself looks like a philosopher, a hard-bound[29] philosopher when he is on the stool looks like a tyrant, and a wise man when he is in his belly-act[30] looks like a fool. God give your worship good rest; grace and mercy keep your syringe straight and your lotium[31] unspilt!   81

[*Exit* COCLEDEMOY.]

Enter FRANCISCHINA.

Free. See, sir, this is she.

Mal. This?

Free. This.

Mal. A courtesan? [*Aside*] Now cold blood defend me; what a proportion[32] afflicts me!

Fran. O mine aderliver[33] love, vat sall me do to requit dis your mush affection?

Free. Marry, salute my friend, clip[34] his neck, and kiss him welcome.   90

Fran. O' mine art, sir, you bin very velcome.

Free. Kiss her, man, with a more familiar affection. So!

[FREEVILL *kisses* FRANCISCHINA.]

Come, what entertainment? Go to your lute.

Exit FRANCISCHINA.
—And how dost approve my sometimes elected? She's none of your ramping[35] cannibals that devour man's flesh, nor any of your Curtian gulfs[36] that will never be satisfied until the best thing a man has be thrown into them. I loved her with my heart until my soul showed me the imperfection of my body and placed my   100 affection on a lawful love, my modest Beatrice, which if this short-heels[37] knew, there were no being for me with eyes before her face. But, faith, dost thou not somewhat excuse my sometimes[38] incontinency with her enforcive beauties? Speak!

Mal. Hah! she is a whore, is she not?

Free. Whore? Fie, whore! You may call her a courtesan, a cockatrice,[39] or (as that worthy spirit of an eternal happiness[40] said) a suppository. But whore! Fie! 'tis not in fashion to call things by their right   110 names. Is a great merchant a cuckold, you must say he

---

[10] *lotium:* stale urine used by barbers as "lye" for the hair.
[11] *diet-drink:* medicine.
[12] *companies:* trade associations.
[13] *draper:* maker of or dealer in woolen cloth.
[14] *pointmaker:* maker of laces for fastening garments.
[15] *petty:* small.   [16] *chapman:* merchant.
[17] *Wa, ha, ho:* falconer's call.
[18] *corncutters:* chiropodists.   [19] *rising:* with a bawdy pun.
[20] *death's head:* skull on the ring worn by Elizabethan bawds.   [21] *Clerkenwell:* rough London district.
[22] *Bridewell:* house of correction for prostitutes and vagrants.
[23] *L.:* I have spoken, indicating end of an oration.
[24] Tully's *Offices:* Cicero's *De Officiis*, which prescribes a moral code.   [25] *and:* if.
[26] *draw:* lure (falconry); with pun, "cause ale to flow."
[27] *stoop:* swoop (falconry); with pun, "stoup," "tankard."
[28] *tilt:* thrust at (falconry); with pun, "knock him over."
[29] *hard-bound:* constipated.
[30] *belly-act:* sexual intercourse.   [31] *lotium:* semen.
[32] *proportion:* disproportion of humors, access of passion (hot blood).   [33] *aderliver:* alderliefest, dearest (Dutch).
[34] *clip:* embrace.   [35] *ramping:* wild.
[36] *Curtian gulfs:* Marcus Curtius saved Rome by leaping, armed and mounted, into a chasm that had opened in the Forum so that it closed.   [37] *short-heels:* prostitute.
[38] *sometimes:* former.   [39] *cockatrice:* prostitute.
[40] *worthy . . . happiness:* Ariosto, who punned in the title of his play *I Suppositi* (the supposed ones). Gascoigne's *Supposes* is a translation.

is one of the livery;[41] is a great lord a fool, you must say
he is weak; is a gallant pocky,[42] you must say he has the
court scab. Come, she's your mistress, or so.

[Re-]enter FRANCISCHINA *with her lute.*

[*To* FRANCISCHINA]—Come, siren, your voice!
  Fran. Vill not you stay in mine bosom tonight, love?
  Free. By no means, sweet breast; this gentleman has
vowed to see me chastely laid.
  Fran. He shall have a bed, too, if dat it please him.
  Free. Peace! you tender him offense; he is one of a
professed abstinence. Siren, your voice, and away!   121
  Fran. [*She sings to her lute.*]

THE SONG

    The dark is my delight,
      So 'tis the nightingale's.
    My music's in the night,
      So is the nightingale's.
    My body is but little,
      So is the nightingale's.
    I love to sleep 'gainst prickle,[43]
      So doth the nightingale.

  Free. Thanks. Buss!   130
                [*Kisses her*]
So! The night grows old; good rest.
  Fran. Rest to mine dear love; rest, and no long ab-
sence.
  Free. Believe me, not long.
  Fran. Sall ick not believe you long?
              Exit FRANCISCHINA.
  Free. Oh yes. [*To* Page] Come, *via!* away, boy! On!
          Exit, his Page *lighting him.*

[Re-]enter FREEVILL *and seems to overhear*
MALHEUREUX.

  Mal. Is she unchaste? Can such a one be damned?
O love and beauty, ye two eldest seeds
Of the vast chaos, what strong right you have
Even in things divine, our very souls!   140
  Free. [*Aside*] Wha, ha, ho! Come, bird, come! Stand,
    peace!
  Mal. Are strumpets, then, such things so delicate?
Can custom spoil what nature made so good?
Or is their custom bad? Beauty's for use!
I never saw a sweet face vicious:
It might be proud, inconstant, wanton, nice,[44]
But never tainted with unnatural vice.
Their worst is, their best art is love to win.
Oh, that to love should be or[45] shame or sin.

---

  [41] *livery:* livery companies, trade guilds.
  [42] *pocky:* syphilitic.
  [43] *I . . . prickle:* The nightingale was represented em-
blematically as sleeping with its breast against a thorn, which
accounted for its nocturnal song.   [44] *nice:* lascivious.
  [45] *or:* either.   [46] *To:* Against, compared to.
  [47] *eld:* age.   [48] *L.:* apostate.   [49] *cast:* cast off.
II.i.
  [1] *gaged:* pledged.   [2] *Cantat:* He sings.
  [3] *nice:* delicate.   [4] *shamefastness:* modesty.
  [5] *protested:* declared.

  Free. [*Aside*] By the Lord, he's caught! laughter
    eternal!   150
  Mal. Soul, I must love her. Destiny is weak
To[46] my affection. A common love!
Blush not, faint breast!
That which is ever loved of most is best.
Let colder eld[47] the strong'st objections move!
No love's without some lust, no life without some love.
  Free. [*To* MALHEUREUX] Nay, come on, good sir;
what, though the most odious spectacle the world can
present be an immodest, vulgar woman! yet, sir, for my
sake—   160
  Mal. Well, sir, for your sake I'll think better of them.
  Free. Do, good sir, and pardon me that have brought
    you in.
You know the sight of vice augments the hate of sin.
  Mal. Hah! will you go home, sir? 'Tis high bedtime.
  Free. With all my heart, sir; only do not chide me.
I must confess—
  Mal.   A wanton lover you have been.
  Free. Oh, that to love should be or shame or sin.
  Mal. Say ye?
  Free. Let colder eld the strong'st objections move!
  Mal. How's this?   170
  Free. No love's without some lust, no life without
some love! go your ways for an *apostata!*[48] I be-
lieve my cast[49] garment must be let out in the seams
for you when all is done:
Of all the fools that would all man out-thrust,
He that 'gainst nature would seem wise is worst.
                 Exeunt.

ACT TWO

SCENE ONE

Enter FREEVILL, *Pages with torches, and* Gentlemen
with music.

  Free. The morn is yet but young. Here, gentlemen,
This is my Beatrice' window, this the chamber
Of my betrothèd dearest, whose chaste eyes,
Full of loved sweetness and clear cheerfulness,
Have gaged[1] my soul to her enjoyings,
Shredding away all those weak under-branches
Of base affections and unfruitful heats.
Here bestow your music to my voice.
    Cantat.[2] [*Exeunt* Gentlemen *with* Pages.]

Enter BEATRICE *above.*

Always a virtuous name to my chaste love!
  Bea. Loved sir,   10
The honor of your wish return to you.
I cannot with a mistress' compliment,
Forcèd discourses, or nice[3] art of wit
Give entertain to your dear wishèd presence;
But safely thus, what hearty gratefulness,
Unsullen silence, unaffected modesty,
And an unignorant shamefastness[4] can express,
Receive as your protested[5] due. Faith, my heart,
I am your servant.

Oh, let not my secure[6] simplicity   20
Breed your mislike, as one quite void of skill;
'Tis grace enough in us not to be ill.[7]
I can some good, and, faith, I mean no hurt;
Do not, then, sweet, wrong sober ignorance.
I judge you all of virtue, and our vows
Should kill all fears that base distrust can move.
My soul, what say you: still you love?
    Free.   Still!
My vow is up above me and, like time,
Irrevocable. I am sworn all yours.
No beauty shall untwine our arms, no face   30
In my eyes can or shall seem fair;
And would to God only to me you might
Seem only fair; let others disesteem
Your matchless graces, so might I safer seem.
Envy I covet not; far, far be all ostent,[8]
Vain boasts of beauties, soft joys, and the rest;
He that is wise pants on a private beast.
So could I live in desert most unknown,
Yourself to me enough were populous.
Your eyes shall be my joys, my wine that still[9]   40
Shall drown my often cares. Your only[10] voice
Shall cast a slumber on my list'ning sense.
You with soft lip shall only ope mine eyes
And suck their lids asunder. Only you
Shall make me wish to live, and not fear death,
So on your cheeks I might yield latest breath.
Oh, he that thus may live and thus shall die
May well be envied of a deity.
    Bea. Dear my loved heart, be not so passionate;
Nothing extreme lives long.
    Free.   But not to be   50
Extreme; nothing in love's extreme; my love
Receives no mean.
    Bea.   I give you faith; and, prithee,
Since, poor soul, I am so easy to believe thee,
Make it much more pity to deceive me.
Wear this slight favor in my remembrance.

                Throweth down a ring to him.

    Free. Which when I part from, hope, the best of life,
Ever part from me.
    Bea. I take you and your word, which may ever live
your servant. See, day is quite broke up—the best of
hours.   60
    Free. Good morrow, graceful mistress. Our nuptial
day holds.
    Bea. With happy constancy, a wishèd day.
                           Exit.
    Free. Myself and all content rest with you.

        Enter MALHEUREUX.

    Mal. The studious[11] morn with paler cheek draws
      on
The day's bold light. Hark, how the freeborn birds
Carol their unaffected passions!

                The nightingales sing.

Now sing they sonnets; thus they cry, "We love!"
O breath of heaven! thus they, harmless souls,

Give entertain to mutual affects.[12]   70
They have no bawds, no mercenary beds,
No politic restraints, no artificial heats,
No faint dissemblings; no custom makes them blush,
No shame afflicts their name. O you happy beasts,
In whom an inborn heat is not held sin,
How far transcend you wretched, wretched man,
Whom national custom, tyrannous respects
Of slavish order, fetters, lames his power,
Calling that sin in us which in all things else
Is Nature's highest virtue!   80
O miseri quorum gaudia crimen habent![13]
Sure nature against virtue cross doth fall,
Or virtue's self is oft unnatural.
That I should love a strumpet! I, a man of snow!
Now, shame forsake me, whither am I fallen!
A creature of a public use! my friend's love, too!
To live to be a talk to men, a shame
To my professèd virtue! O accursèd reason,
How many eyes hast thou to see thy shame,
And yet how blind once to prevent defame!   90
    Free. Diaboli virtus in lumbis est![14] Morrow, my
friend. Come, I could make a tedious scene of this now,
but what—pah! thou art in love with a courtesan! why,
sir, should we loathe all strumpets, some men should
hate their own mothers or sisters; a sin against kind,[15]
I can tell you.
    Mal. May it beseem a wise man to be in love?
    Free. Let wise men alone; 'twill beseem thee and me
well enough.
    Mal. Shall I not offend the vow-band of our friend-
ship?   101
    Free. What, to affect[16] that which thy friend affec-
ted? By heaven, I resign her freely; the creature and I
must grow off.[17] By this time she has assuredly heard
of my resolved marriage, and no question swears,
"God's sacrament, ten tousand divils!" I'll resign, i'
faith.
    Mal. I would but embrace her, hear her speak, and
at the most but kiss her.
    Free. Oh, friend, he that could live with the smoke of
roast meat might live at a cheap rate.   111
    Mal. I shall ne'er prove heartily received;
A kind of flat ungracious modesty,
An insufficient dullness, stains my 'havior.
    Free. No matter, sir. Insufficiency and sottishness
are much commendable in a most discommendable
action. Now could I swallow thee. Thou hadst wont to
be so harsh and cold, I'll tell thee. Hell and the prodigies
of angry Jove are not so fearful to a thinking mind as a
man without affection. Why, friend, philosophy   120

---

6 *secure:* overconfident.   7 *ill:* blameworthy.
8 *ostent:* show.   9 *still:* always.   10 *only:* peerless.
11 *studious:* diligent.   12 *affects:* affections.
13 *L.:* "O miserable they whose joys in fault we lay!" An
obscure Latin writer quoted by Montaigne; in the translation
by Florio in which Marston read Montaigne.
14 *L.:* "The devil's masterpiece lies in our loins, saith St.
Jerome"; Florio's translation of the Montaigne quotation.
15 *kind:* nature.   16 *affect:* love.
17 *grow off:* separate.

and nature are all one; love is the center in which all
lines close the common bond of being.

Mal. Oh, but a chaste, reservèd privateness,
A modest continence!

Free. I'll tell thee what, take this as firmest sense:
Incontinence will force a continence;
Heat wasteth heat, light defaceth light;
Nothing is spoiled but by his proper [18] might.
This is something too weighty for thy floor. [19]

Mal. But howsoe'er you shade it, the world's eye
Shines hot and open on't.   131
Lying, malice, envy are held but slidings, [20]
Errors of rage, when custom and the world
Calls lust a crime spotted with blackest terrors.

Free. Where errors are held crimes, crimes are but
errors.

Along, sir, to her. She's an arrant strumpet; and a
strumpet is a serpigo, [21] venomed gonorrhy to man—
things actually possessed. Yet since thou art in love—

Offers to go out and suddenly draws back.

and again, as good make use of a statue, a body without
a soul, a carcass three months dead; yet since thou art
in love—   141

Mal. Death, man, my destiny I cannot choose.

Free. Nay, I hope so. Again, they sell but only flesh,
no jot affection; so that even in the enjoying, *Absentem
marmoreamque putes.* [22] Yet since you needs must love—

Mal. Unavoidable, though folly worse than madness!

Free. It's true;
But since you needs must love, you must know this:
He that must love, a fool and he must kiss!—

Enter COCLEDEMOY.

Master Cocledemoy, *ut vales, domine!* [23]   150

Coc. *Ago tibi gratias,* [24] my worshipful friend.
How does your friend?

Free. Out, you rascal.

Coc. Hang toasts, you are an ass. Much o' your
worship's brain lies in your calves. Bread o' God, boy,
I was at supper last night with a new-weaned bulchin [25]
—bread o' God!—drunk, horribly drunk, horribly
drunk. There was a wench, one Frank Frailty, a punk, [26]
an honest polecat, [27] of a clean [28] instep, sound leg,
smooth thigh, and the nimble devil in her buttock.   160
Ah, fist [29] o' grace! when saw you Tysefew or Master
Caqueteur, that prattling gallant of a good draught,

common customs, fortunate impudence, and sound
fart?

Free. Away, rogue.

Coc. Hang toasts, my fine boy, my companions are
worshipful.

Mal. Yes, I hear you are taken up with scholars and
churchmen.   169

Enter HOLIFERNES *the Barber.*

Coc. *Quanquam te Marce fili,* [30] my fine boy. [*To*
FREEVILL] Does your worship want a barber-
surgeon?

Free. Farewell, knave, beware the Mulligrubs.

Exeunt FREEVILL *and* MALHEUREUX.

Coc. Let the Mulligrubs beware the knave.—What,
a barber-surgeon, my delicate boy?

Hol. Yes, sir, an apprentice to surgery.

Coc. 'Tis my fine boy. To what bawdy house doth
your master belong? What's thy name?

Hol. Holifernes Reinscure.   179

Coc. Reinscure? Good Master Holifernes, I desire
your further acquaintance—nay, pray ye be covered,
my fine boy; kill thy itch and heal thy scabs. Is thy
master rotten?

Hol. My father forsooth is dead—

Coc.   And laid in his grave.
       Alas, what comfort shall Peggy then have!

Hol. None but me, sir, that's my mother's son, I
assure you.

Coc. Mother's son? A good witty boy; would live to
read an homily well. And to whom are you going now?

Hol. Marry, forsooth, to trim [31] Master Mulligrub
the vintner.   192

Coc. Do you know Master Mulligrub?

Hol. My godfather, sir.

Coc. Good boy! hold up thy chops. [32] I pray thee do
one thing for me. My name is Gudgeon. [33]

Hol. Good Master Gudgeon.

Coc. Lend me thy basin, razor, and apron.

Hol. O Lord, sir.

Coc. Well spoken; good English. But what's thy furniture [34] worth?   201

Hol. O Lord, sir, I know not.

Coc. Well spoken; a boy of a good wit. Hold this
pawn. [35] Where dost dwell?

Hol. At the sign of the Three Razors, sir.

Coc. A sign of good shaving, my catastrophonical [36]
fine boy. I have an odd jest to trim Master Mulligrub
for a wager. A jest, boy, a humor, I'll return thy things
presently. Hold.

Hol. What mean you, good Master Gudgeon?   210

Coc. Nothing, faith, but a jest, boy. Drink that.
                                                  [*Gives money.*]
I'll recoil [37] presently.

Hol. You'll not stay long?

Coc. As I am an honest man. The Three Razors?

Hol. Ay, sir.

Exit HOLIFERNES.

Coc. Good; and if I shave not Master Mulligrub, my
wit has no edge, and I may go cack [38] in my pewter. Let

---

[18] *proper:* own.   [19] This is more than you can bear.
[20] *slidings:* backslidings.   [21] *serpigo:* skin disease.
[22] *L.:* "Of marble you would think she were, or that she
were not present there"; Martial as quoted by Montaigne
and translated by Florio.   [23] *L.:* good day, sir.
[24] *L.:* I thank you.   [25] *bulchin:* bull-calf, gallant.
[26] *punk:* whore.   [27] *polecat:* whore.
[28] *clean:* well-shaped.   [29] *fist:* breaking of wind.
[30] *L.:* "Although, Marcus, my son"; beginning of Cicero's *De Officiis.*   [31] *trim:* shave; cheat.
[32] *chops:* jaws.   [33] *Gudgeon:* a bait-fish; fool.
[34] *furniture:* gear.   [35] *pawn:* pledge.
[36] *catastrophonical:* Q "catastraphomicall."
[37] *recoil:* return.   [38] *cack:* defecate.

me see: a barber. My scurvy tongue will discover [39] me; must dissemble, must disguise. For my beard, my false hair; for my tongue, Spanish, Dutch, or Welsh;   220 no, a Northern barber. Very good. Widow Reinscure's man, well; newly entertained,[40] right. So! hang toasts! all cards have white backs, and all knaves would seem to have white breasts. So proceed now, worshipful Cocledemoy.

Exit COCLEDEMOY *in his barber's furniture.*

[II.ii]

Enter MARY FAUGH *and* FRANCISCHINA, *with her hair loose, chafing.*

Mary. Nay, good sweet daughter, do not swagger[1] so. You hear your love is to be married, true; he does cast you off, right; he will leave you to the world. What then? Though blue and white, black and green leave you, may not red and yellow entertain you? Is there but one color in the rainbow?

Fran. Grand grincome[2] on your sentences.[3] God's sacrament, ten tousand devils take you. You ha' brought mine love, mine honor, mine body, all to noting!   9

Mary. To nothing! I'll be sworn I have brought them to all the things I could. I ha' made as much o' your maidenhead: and you had been mine own daughter, I could not ha' sold your maidenhead oft'ner than I ha' done. I ha' sworn for you, God forgive me! I have made you acquainted with the Spaniard, Don Skirtoll; with the Italian, Master Beieroane; with the Irish lord, Sir Patrick; with the Dutch merchant, Haunce Herkin Glukin Skellam Flapdragon; and specially with the greatest French, and now lastly with this English (yet, in my conscience), an honest gentleman. And am I   20 now grown one of the accursed with you for my labor? Is this my reward? Am I called bawd? Well, Mary Faugh, go thy ways, Mary Faugh; thy kind heart will bring thee to the hospital.[4]

Fran. Nay, good naunt,[5] you'll help me to anoder love, vill you not?

Mary. Out, thou naughty belly; wouldst thou make me thy bawd? Thou'st best make me thy bawd; I ha' kept counsel for thee. Who paid the apothecary? Was't not honest Mary Faugh? Who redeemed thy petti-   30 coat and mantle? Was't not honest Mary Faugh? Who helped thee to thy custom, not of swaggering Ireland captains nor of two-shilling Inns o' Court men,[6] but with honest flat-caps,[7] wealthy flat-caps that pay for their pleasure the best of any men in Europe, nay, which is more, in London? And dost thou defy me, vile creature?

Fran. Foutra[8] 'pon you, vitch, bawd, polecat. Paugh! did you not praise Freevill to mine love?   39

Mary. I did praise, I confess, I did praise him; I said he was a fool, an unthrift, a true whoremaster, I confess; a constant drab-keeper,[9] I confess. But what, the wind is turned.

Fran. It is, it is, vile woman, reprobate woman, naughty woman, it is! Vat sall become of mine poor flesh now? Mine body must turn Turk for twopence. O Divila, life o' mine art! Ick sall be revenged. Do ten tousand hell damn me, ick sall have the rogue troat cut;

and his love, and his friend, and all his affinity sall smart, sall die, sall hang. Now legion of devil seize   50 him. De gran' pest, St. Anthony's fire,[10] and de hot Neapolitan poc rot him.

Enter FREEVILL *and* MALHEUREUX.

Free. Francischina!

Fran. O mine seet,[11] dear'st, kindest, mine loving! O mine tousand, ten tousand, delicated, petty seetart! ah, mine aderlievest affection!

Free. Why, monkey, no fashion in you? Give entertain to my friend.

Fran. Ick sall make de most of you dat courtesy may. —Aunt Mary! Mettre[12] Faugh! stools, stools for dese gallants!   61

Cantat Gallice.[13]

> *Mine mettre sing non oder song—*
> *Frolic, frolic, sir!—*
> *But still complain me do her wrong:—*
> *Lighten your heart, sir!*
> *For me did but kiss her,*
> *For me did but kiss her,*
> *And so let go.*

[*To* FREEVILL] Your friend is very heavy; ick sall ne'er like such sad[14] company.   70

Free. No, thou delightest only in light company.

Fran. By mine trot, he been very sad.—Vat ail you, sir?

Mal. A toothache, lady, a paltry rheum.[15]

Fran. De diet is very goot for de rheum.

Free. How far off dwells the house-surgeon, Mary Faugh?

Mary. You are a profane fellow, i' faith, I little thought to hear such ungodly terms come from your lips.   80

Fran. Pridee now, 'tis but a toy,[16] a very trifle.

Free. I care not for the value, Frank, but, i' faith—

Fran. I' fait, me must needs have it. [*Aside*] Dis is Beatrice' ring; oh, could I get it! [*To* FREEVILL] Seet, pridee, now, as ever you have embraced me with a hearty arm, a warm thought, or a pleasing touch, as ever you will profess to love me, as ever you do wish me life, give me dis ring, dis little ring.

Free. Prithee be not uncivilly importunate; sha' not ha't. Faith, I care not for thee nor thy jealousy. Sha' not ha't, i' faith.   91

Fran. You do not love me. I hear of Sir Hubert Sub-

---

[39] *discover:* reveal.   [40] *entertained:* employed.

II.ii.

[1] *swagger:* bluster.   [2] *grincome:* venereal disease.
[3] *sentences:* sententious sayings.
[4] *hospital:* poorhouse.   [5] *naunt:* aunt.
[6] *Inns o' Court men:* lawyers and law students.
[7] *flat-caps:* tradesmen, from their woolen caps.
[8] *Foutra:* obscene oath (French *foutre*).
[9] *drab-keeper:* whoremaster.
[10] *St. Anthony's fire:* erisypelas.   [11] *seet:* sweet.
[12] *Mettre:* mistress.   [13] *Gallice:* in French.
[14] *sad:* serious.   [15] *rheum:* cold.
[16] *toy:* worthless thing.

boys' daughter, Mistress Beatrice. God's sacrament, ick
could scratch out her eyes and suck the holes.

Free. Go! y'are grown a punk rampant.

Fran. So? Get thee gone; ne'er more behold min
eyes, by thee made wretched.

Free. Mary Faugh, farewell. Farewell, Frank!

[*Exit* MARY FAUGH.]

Fran. Sall I not ha' de ring?

Free. No, by the Lord.   100

Fran. By te Lord?

Free. By the Lord.

Fran. Go to your new blowze,[17] your unproved
sluttery, your modest mettre, forsooth!

Free. Marry, will I, forsooth.

Fran. Will you marry, forsooth?

Free. Do not turn witch before thy time.
[*To* MALHEUREUX]With all my heart, sir, you will
    stay.

Mal. I am no whit myself. *Video meliora proboque*,[18]
But raging lust my fate all strong doth move: 110
The gods themselves cannot be wise and love.

Free. Your wishes to you.

Exit FREEVILL.

Mal. Beauty entirely choice—

Fran. Pray ye, prove a man of fashion and neglect
the neglected.

Mal. Can such a rarity be neglected? Can there be
measure or sin in loving such a creature?

Fran. Oh, min poor forsaken heart!

Mal. I cannot contain; he saw thee not that left thee.
If there be wisdom, reason, honor, grace,   120
Or any foolishly esteemèd virtue
In giving o'er possession of such beauty,
Let me be vicious, so I may be loved.
Passion, I am thy slave. Sweet, it shall be my grace
That I account thy love my only virtue.
Shall I swear I am thy most vowèd servant?

Fran. Mine vowed? Go, go, go, I can no more of
love. No, no, no, you bin all unconstant. O unfaithful
men, tyrants, betrayers. De very enjoying us loseth us;
and, when you only ha' made us hateful, you only hate
us. O mine forsaken heart!   131

Mal. [*Aside*] I must not rave. Silence and modesty,
two customary virtues. [*To* FRANCISCHINA] Will you
be my mistress?

Fran. Mettress? Ha, ha, ha!

Mal. Will you lie with me?

Fran. Lie with you? Oh, no! You men will out-lie
any woman. Fait, me no more can love.

Mal. No matter; let me enjoy your bed.   139

Fran. O vile man, vat do you tink on me? Do you
take me to be a beast, a creature that for sense only will
entertain love, and not only for love, love? O brutish
abomination!

Mal. Why, then, I pray thee love, and with thy love
enjoy me.

Fran. Give me reason to affect you. Will you swear
you love me?

Mal. So seriously that I protest no office so dangerous, no deed so unreasonable, no cost so heavy, but
I vow to the utmost tentation[19] of my best being to effect it.   151

Fran. Sall I, or can I, trust again? O fool,
How natural 'tis for us to be abused!
Sall ick be sure that no satiety,
No enjoying, not time, shall languish your affection?

Mal. If there be aught in brain, heart, or hand
Can make you doubtless, I am your vowed servant.

Fran. Will you do one ting for me?

Mal. Can I do it?   159

Fran. Yes, yes, but ick do not love dis same Freevill.

Mal. Well?

Fran. Nay, I do hate him.

Mal. So?

Fran. By this kiss, I hate him.

Mal. I love to feel such oaths; swear again.

Fran. No, no. Did you ever hear of any that loved at
the first sight?

Mal. A thing most proper.

Fran. Now, fait, I judge it all incredible until this
hour I saw you, pretty fair-eyed yout. Would you enjoy
me?   171

Mal. Rather than my breath, even as my being.

Fran. Vell, had ick not made a vow—

Mal. What vow?

Fran. Oh, let me forget it; it makes us both despair.

Mal. Dear soul, what vow?

Fran. Hah! good morrow, gentle sir; endeavor to
forget me as I must be enforced to forget all men.
Sweet mind, rest in you.   179

Mal. Stay, let not my desire burst me. Oh, my impatient heat endures no resistance, no protraction;
there is no being for me but your[20] sudden enjoying.

Fran. I do not love Freevill.

Mal. But what vow? What vow?

Fran. So long as Freevill lives, I must not love.

Mal. Then he—

Fran. Must—

Mal. Die.

Fran. Ay. No, there is no such vehemence in your
affects. Would I were anything, so he were not!   190

Mal. Will you be mine when he is not?

Fran. Will I? Dear, dear breast, by this most zealous
kiss—but I will not persuade you; but if you hate him
that I loathe most deadly—yet, as you please, I'll persuade noting.

Mal. Will you be only mine?

Fran. Vill I? How hard 'tis for true love to dissemble! I am only yours.

Mal. 'Tis as irrevocable as breath: he dies.
Your love?

Fran.   My vow, not until he be dead,   200
Which that I may be sure not to infringe,
Dis token of his death sall satisfy.
He has a ring, as dear as the air to him,
His new love's gift: tat got and brought to me,
I shall assurèd your possessèd rest.

---

[17] *blowze:* wench.
[18] *L.:* "I see and approve the better," Ovid, *Metamorphoses*,
VII. 20 (followed there by *deteriora sequor*, "I follow the
worse").   [19] *tentation:* trial.   [20] *your:* of you.

Mal. To kill a man!

Fran. Oh, done safely; a quarrel sudden picked, with an advantage strike; then bribe; a little coin, all's safe, dear soul. But I'll not set you on.   209

Mal. Nay, he is gone. The ring? Well, come, little more liberal of thy love.

Fran. Not yet; my vow.

Mal.   O heaven, there is no hell But love's prolongings. Dear, farewell.

Fran.   Farewell.
[*Aside*] Now does my heart swell high, for my revenge Has birth and form. First, friend sall kill his friend; He dat survives, I'll hang; besides, de chaste Beatrice I'll vex. Only de ring— Dat got, the world sall know the worst of evils: Woman corrupted is the worst of devils.

Ex[eunt] FRANCISCHINA [*and* MARY FAUGH].

Mal. To kill my friend! oh, 'tis to kill myself!   220 Yet man's but man's excrement, man breeding man As he does worms, or this.

                          To spoil this nothing! The body of a man is of the selfsame soil As ox or horse; no murder to kill these. As for that only part which makes us man, Murder wants power to touch't. O wit,[21] how vile, How hellish art thou when thou raisest nature 'Gainst sacred faith! Think more to kill a friend To gain a woman, to lose a virtuous self For appetite and sensual end, whose very having   230 Loseth all appetite and gives satiety— That corporal end, remorse and inward blushings Forcing us loathe the steam of our own heats, Whilst friendship closed in virtue, being spiritual, Tastes no such languishings and moments' pleasure With much repentance, but like rivers flow, And further that they run, they bigger grow. Lord, how was I misgone![22] How easy 'tis to err When passion will not give us leave to think! A learned, that is an honest, man may fear,   240 And lust, and rage, and malice, and anything When he is taken uncollected[23] suddenly: 'Tis sin of cold blood, mischief with waked eyes, That is the damnèd and the truly vice; Not he that's passionless, but he 'bove passion's wise. My friend shall know it all.

                                         Exit.

[II.iii]

Enter MASTER MULLIGRUB *and* MISTRESS MULLIGRUB, *she with bag of money.*

Mist. Mul. It is right, I assure you, just fifteen pounds.

Mul. Well, Cocledemoy, 'tis thou putt'st me to this charge; but, and I catch thee, I'll charge thee with as many irons. Well, is the barber come? I'll be trimmed and then to Cheapside[1] to buy a fair piece of plate to furnish the loss. Is the barber come?

Mist. Mul. Truth, husband, surely heaven is not pleased with our vocation. We do wink at the sins of our people, our wines are Protestants,[2] and—I   10 speak it to my grief and to the burden of my conscience —we fry our fish with salt butter.

                                         Exit.

Mul. Go, look to your business; mend the matter, and score false[3] with a vengeance.

Enter COCLEDEMOY *like a barber.*

Welcome, friend. Whose man?

Coc. Widow Reinscure's man; and shall please your good worship, my name's Andrew Shark.

Mul. How does my godson, good Andrew?

Coc. Very well. He's gone to trim Master Quicquid, our parson. Hold up your head.   20

Mul. How long have you been a barber, Andrew?

Coc. Not long, sir; this two year.

Mul. What, and a good workman already! I dare scarce trust my head to thee.

Coc. Oh, fear not; we ha' polled[4] better men than you. We learn the trade very quickly. Will your good worship be shaven or cut?

Mul. As you will. What trade didst live by before thou turnedst barber, Andrew?   29

Coc. I was a pedlar in Germany, but my countrymen thrive better by this trade.

Mul. What's the news, barber? Thou art sometimes at Court.

Coc. Sometimes poll a page or so, sir.

Mul. And what's the news? How do all my good lords and all my good ladies, and all the rest of my acquaintance?

Coc. [*Aside*] What an arrogant knave's this! I'll acquaintance ye!

He spieth the bag.

'Tis cash! [*To* MULLIGRUB] Say ye, sir?   40

Mul. And what news? What news, good Andrew?

Coc. Marry, sir, you know the conduit at Greenwich and the under-holes that spouts up water?

Mul. Very well; I was washed there one day, and so was my wife; you might have wrung her smock, i' faith. But what o' those holes?

Coc. Thus, sir, out of those little holes, in the midst of the night, crawled out twenty-four huge, horrible, monstrous, fearful, devouring—

Mul. Bless us!   50

Coc. Serpents, which no sooner were beheld but they turned to mastiffs, which howled; those mastiffs instantly turned to cocks, which crowed; those cocks in a moment were changed to bears, which roared; which bears are at this hour to be yet seen in Paris Garden,[5] living upon nothing but toasted cheese and green onions.

---

21 *wit:* mind.   22 *misgone:* gone astray.
23 *uncollected:* distracted, un-self-controlled.

II.iii.
   1 *Cheapside:* London market district.
   2 *Protestants:* i.e., Anglican, too Catholic for Puritans.
   3 *score false:* cheat in charging.   4 *polled:* clipped.
   5 *Paris Garden:* bear-baiting arena on south bank of Thames.

Mul. By the Lord, and this may be. My wife and I will go see them; this portends something.

Coc. [*Aside*] Yes, worshipful fist, thou'st feel what portends by and by.   60

Mul. And what more news? You shave the world, especially you barber-surgeons; you know the ground of many things; you are cunning privy[6] searchers. By the mass, you scour all. What more news?

Coc. They say, sir, that twenty-five couple of Spanish jennets are to be seen hand in hand dance the old measures, whilst six goodly Flanders mares play to them on a noise[7] of flutes.

Mul. O monstrous! This is a lie, o' my word. Nay, and this be not a lie—I am no fool, I warrant!—nay, make an ass of me once—   71

Coc. Shut your eyes close; wink! sure, sir, this ball[8] will make you smart.

Mul. I do wink.

Coc. Your head will take cold. I will put on your good worship's nightcap whilst I shave you.

COCLEDEMOY *puts on a coxcomb*[9] *on*
MULLIGRUB's *head.*

[*Aside*] So, mum! hang toasts! faugh! *via!* Sparrows must peck and Cocledemoy munch.

[*Exit* COCLEDEMOY.]

Mul. Ha, ha, ha! twenty-five couple of Spanish jennets to dance the old measures! Andrew makes   80 my worship laugh, i' faith. Dost take me for an ass, Andrew? Dost know one Cocledemoy in town? He made me an ass last night, but I'll ass him. Art thou free, Andrew? Shave me well; I shall be one of the Common Council[10] shortly, and, then, Andrew—why Andrew, Andrew, dost leave me in the suds?

Cantat.

Why, Andrew, I shall be blind with winking. Ha Andrew! wife! Andrew! What means this? Wife! my money! wife!   89

Enter MISTRESS MULLIGRUB.

Mist. Mul. What's the noise with you? What ail you?

Mul. Where's the barber?

Mist. Mul. Gone. I saw him depart long since. Why, are not you trimmed?

Mul. Trimmed! O wife, I am shaved. Did you take hence the money?

Mist. Mul. I touched it not, as I am religious.

Mul. O Lord, I have winked fair!

Enter HOLIFERNES.

Hol. I pray, godfather, give me your blessing.

Mul. O Holifernes! O where's thy mother's Andrew?

Hol. Blessing, godfather.   100

Mul. The devil choke thee! where's Andrew, thy mother's man?

Hol. My mother hath none such, forsooth.

Mul. My money, fifteen pounds; plague of all Andrews! who was't trimmed me?

Hol. I know not, godfather; only one met me, as I was coming to you, and borrowed my furniture, as he said, for a jest sake.

Mul. What kind of fellow?

Hol. A thick, elderly, stub-bearded fellow.   110

Mul. Cocledemoy, Cocledemoy! raise all the wise men in the street; I'll hang him with mine own hands. O wife, some *rosa solis!*[11]

Mist. Mul. Good husband, take comfort in the Lord. I'll play the devil, but I'll recover it. Have a good conscience; 'tis but a week's cutting[12] in the term.[13]

Mul. O wife! O wife! O Jack! how does thy mother? Is there any fiddlers in the house?

Mist. Mul. Yes, Master Creak's noise.   119

Mul. Bid 'em play, laugh, make merry. Cast up my accounts, for I'll go hang myself presently. I will not curse, but a pox on Cocledemoy! He has polled and shaved me; he has trimmed me!

Exeunt.

ACT THREE

SCENE ONE

Enter BEATRICE, CRISPINELLA, *and* NURSE
PUTIFER.

Put. Nay, good child o' love, once more Master Freevill's sonnet[1] o' the kiss you gave him!

Bea. Sh'a't,[2] good nurse. [*Reads.*]
> *Purest lips, soft banks of blisses,*
> *Self alone, deserving kisses,*
> *Oh, give me leave to,* etc.

Crisp. Pish, sister Beatrice! prithee read no more; my stomach o' late stands against kissing extremely.

Bea. Why, good Crispinella?   9

Crisp. By the faith and trust I bear to my face, 'tis grown one of the most unsavory ceremonies. Body o' beauty, 'tis one of the most unpleasing, injurious customs to ladies. Any fellow that has but one nose on his face, and standing[3] collar and skirts also lined with taffety sarcenet,[4] must salute us on the lips as familiarly —Soft skins save us! there was a stub-bearded John-a-Stile[5] with a ployden's[6] face saluted me last day and struck his bristles through my lips; I ha' spent ten shillings in pomatum since to skin them again. Marry, if a nobleman or a knight with one lock[7] visit us,   20 though his unclean goose-turd-green[8] teeth ha' the palsy, his nostrils smell worse than a putrified

---
6 *privy:* secret; toilet; private parts.
7 *noise:* band.   8 *ball:* of soap.
9 *coxcomb:* fool's cap.   10 *Common Council:* aldermen.
11 *rosa solis:* a liqueur.   12 *cutting:* cheating.
13 *term:* period when law-courts are in session.

III.i.
1 *sonnet:* short poem.   2 *Sh'a't:* Thou shalt have it.
3 *standing:* embroidered, high, stiff, and fashionable.
4 *taffety sarcenet:* fine silk.
5 *John-a-Stile:* fictitious name for party in a legal action; cf. John Doe.
6 *ployden:* probably lawyer, after the lawyer Edmund Plowden (Ployden), 1515–1585.   7 *one lock:* of hair left.
8 *goose-turd-green:* yellowish green.

maribone, and his loose beard drops into our bosom, yet we must kiss him with a cur'sy. A curse! for my part, I had as lief they would break wind in my lips.

Bea. Fie, Crispinella, you speak too broad.

Crisp. No jot, sister. Let's ne'er be ashamed to speak what we be not ashamed to think; I dare as boldly speak venery[9] as think venery.   29

Bea. Faith, sister, I'll be gone if you speak so broad.

Crisp. Will you so? Now bashfulness seize you! we pronounce boldly robbery, murder, treason, which deeds must needs be far more loathsome than an act which is so natural, just, and necessary as that of procreation. You shall have an hypocritical vestal virgin speak that with close teeth publicly which she will receive with open mouth privately. For my own part, I consider nature without apparel, without disguising of custom or compliment. I give thoughts words, and words truth, and truth boldness. She whose honest   40 freeness makes it her virtue to speak what she thinks will make it her necessity to think what is good. I love no prohibited things, and yet I would have nothing prohibited by policy but by virtue; for, as in the fashion of time, those books that are called in[10] are most in sale and request, so in nature those actions that are most prohibited are most desired.

Bea. Good quick sister, stay your pace. We are private, but the world would censure you, for truly severe modesty is women's virtue.   50

Crisp. Fie, fie! virtue is a free, pleasant, buxom quality. I love a constant countenance well; but this froward, ignorant coyness, sour, austere, lumpish, uncivil privateness, that promises nothing but rough skins and hard stools, ha! fie on't! good for nothing but for nothing.—Well, nurse, and what do you conceive of all this?

Put. Nay, faith, my conceiving days be done. Marry, for kissing, I'll defend that; that's within my compass. But for my own part, here's Mistress Beatrice is to   60 be married, with the grace of God. A fine gentleman he is shall have her, and I warrant a strong; he has a leg like a post, a nose like a lion, a brow like a bull, and a beard of most fair expectation. This week you must marry him, and I now will read a lecture to you both, how you shall behave yourselves to your husbands the first month of your nuptial. I ha' broke my skull about it, I can tell you, and there is much brain in it.

Crisp. Read it to my sister, good nurse, for I assure you I'll ne'er marry.   70

Put. Marry, God forfend! what will you do then?

Crisp. Faith, strive against the flesh. Marry? No, faith; husbands are like lots in the lottery: you may draw forty blanks before you find one that has any prize in him. A husband generally is a careless, domineering thing that grows like coral, which as long as it is under water is soft and tender, but as soon as it has got his branch above the waves is presently hard, stiff, not to be bowed but burst; so when your husband is a suitor and under your choice, Lord, how supple he is,   80 how obsequious, how at your service, sweet lady! Once married, got up his head above, a stiff, crooked, knobby, inflexible, tyrannous creature he grows; then

they turn like water: more you would embrace, the less you hold. I'll live my own woman, and if the worst come to the worst, I had rather prove a wag than a fool.

Bea. O, but a virtuous marriage—

Crisp. Virtuous marriage? There is no more affinity betwixt virtue and marriage than betwixt a man and his horse. Indeed, virtue gets up upon marriage some-   90 times and manageth it in the right way, but marriage is of another piece; for as a horse may be without a man, and a man without a horse, so marriage, you know, is often without virtue, and virtue, I am sure, more oft without marriage. But thy match, sister, by my troth, I think 'twill do well. He's a well-shaped, clean-lipped gentleman, of a handsome but not affected fineness,[11] a good faithful eye, and a well-humored cheek. Would he did not stoop in the shoulders, for thy sake. See, here he is.   100

Enter FREEVILL *and* TYSEFEW.

Free. Good day, sweet.

Crisp. Good morrow, brother. Nay, you shall have my lip.—Good morrow, servant.

Ty. Good morrow, sweet life.

Crisp. Life? Dost call thy mistress life?

Ty. Life, yes, why not life?

Crisp. How many mistresses hast thou?

Ty. Some nine.

Crisp. Why, then, thou hast nine lives, like a cat.

Ty. Mew! You would be taken up[12] for that.   110

Crisp. Nay, good, let me still sit; we low statures love still to sit, lest when we stand we may be supposed to sit.

Ty. Dost not wear high cork shoes, chopines?[13]

Crisp. Monstrous ones. I am, as many other are, pieced[14] above and pieced beneath.

Ty. Still the best part in the—

Crisp. And yet all will scarce make me so high as one of the giants' stilts that stalks before my lord mayor's pageant.   120

Ty. By the Lord, so I thought 'twas for something Mistress Joyce jested at thy high insteps.

Crisp. She might well enough, and long enough, before I would be ashamed of my shortness. What I made or can mend myself I may blush at; but what nature put upon me, let her be ashamed for me; I ha' nothing to do with it. I forget my beauty.

Ty. Faith, Joyce is a foolish, bitter creature.

Crisp. A pretty, mildewed wench she is.

Ty. And fair—   130

Crisp. As myself.

Ty. Oh, you forget your beauty now.

Crisp. Troth, I never remember my beauty but as some men do religion, for controversy's sake.

Bea. A motion,[15] sister—

---

[9] *venery:* sex.   [10] *called in:* withdrawn from circulation.
[11] *fineness:* of appearance.   [12] *taken up:* scolded.
[13] *chopines:* these shoes were worn by fashionable women.
[14] *pieced:* added to (by a high hairdo).
[15] *motion:* proposal; puppet show (in her response, Crispinella names some popular shows).

Crisp. Ninevy, *Julius Caesar, Jonas*, or *The Destruction of Jerusalem?*

Bea. My love here—

Crisp. Prithee, call him not love: 'tis the drab's phrase; nor sweet honey, nor my cony,[16] nor dear duckling: 'tis the citizen terms; but call him—   141

Bea. What?

Crisp. Anything. What's the motion?

Bea. You know this night our parents have intended solemnly to contract us; and my love, to grace the feast, hath promised a masque.

Free. You'll make one, Tysefew, and Caqueteur shall fill up a room.

Ty. 'Fore heaven, well remembered! he borrowed a diamond of me last night to grace his finger in   150 your visitation. The lying creature will swear some strange thing on it now.

Enter CAQUETEUR.

Crisp. Peace, he's here. Stand close, lurk.

Caq. Good morrow, most dear and worthy to be most wise. How does my mistress?

Crisp. Morrow, sweet servant; you glister. Prithee, let's see that stone.

Caq. A toy, lady, I bought to please my finger.

Crisp. Why, I am more precious to you than your finger.   160

Caq. Yes, or than all my body, I swear.

Crisp. Why, then, let it be bought to please me. Come, I am no professed beggar.

Caq. Troth, mistress! zoons! forsooth, I protest!

Crisp. Nay, if you turn Protestant for such a toy—

Caq. In good deed, la! Another time I'll give you a—

Crisp. Is this yours to give?

Caq. O God! Forsooth, mine, quoth you? Nay, as for that—   169

Crisp. Now I remember, I ha' seen this on my servant Tysefew's finger.

Caq. Such another.

Crisp. Nay, I am sure this is it.

Caq. Troth, 'tis, forsooth. The poor fellow wanted money to pay for supper last night, and so pawned it to me. 'Tis a pawn, i' faith, or else you should have it.

Ty. [*Aside to* CAQUETEUR] Hark ye, thou base lying —How dares thy impudence hope to prosper? Were't not for the privilege of this respected company, I would so bang thee.   180

Crisp. Come hither, servant. What's the matter betwixt you two?

Caq. Nothing. [*Aside to* CRISPINELLA] But, hark you, he did me some uncivil discourtesies last night, for which, because I should not call him to account, he

desires to make me any satisfaction. The coward trembles at my very presence, but I ha' him on the hip;[17] I'll take the forfeit on his ring.

Ty. What's that you whisper to her?   189

Caq. Nothing, sir, but satisfy her that the ring was not pawned but only lent by you to grace my finger; and so told her I craved your pardon for being too familiar or, indeed, overbold with your reputation.

Crisp. Yes, indeed, he did. He said you desired to . make him any satisfaction for an uncivil discourtesy you did him last night, but he said he had you o' the hip and would take the forfeit of your ring.

Ty. How now, ye base poltroon?

Caq. Hold, hold! My mistress speaks by contraries.

Ty. Contraries?   200

Caq. She jests, faith, only jests.

Crisp. Sir, I'll no more o' your service. You are a child; I'll give you to my nurse.

Put. And he come to me, I can tell you, as old as I am, what to do with him.

Caq. I offer my service, forsooth.

Ty. Why, so; now every dog has his bone to gnaw on.

Free. The masque holds, Master Caqueteur.

Caq. I am ready, sir. [*To* PUTIFER] Mistress, I'll dance with you. Ne'er fear, I'll grace you.   210

Put. I tell you, I can my singles and my doubles and my trick o' twenty, my carantapace, my traverse forward, and my falling back[18] yet, i' faith.

Bea. Mine! The provision for the night is ours. Much must be our care; till night we leave you. I am your servant; be not tyrannous. Your virtue won me; faith, my love's not lust. Good, wrong me not; my most fault is much trust.

Free. Until night only; my heart be with you.—Farewell, sister.   220

Crisp. Adieu, brother. Come on, sister, for these sweetmeats.

Free. Let's meet and practice presently.

Ty. Content. We'll but fit our pumps.[19]—Come, ye pernicious vermin!

Exeunt [*all but* FREEVILL].

Enter MALHEUREUX.

Free. My friend; wished hours! what news from Babylon? How does the woman of sin and natural concupiscence?

Mal. The eldest child of nature ne'er beheld so damned a creature.   230

Free. What! *In nova fert animus mutatas dicere formas.*[20] Which way bears the tide?

Mal. Dear loved sir, I find a mind courageously vicious may put on a desperate security, but can never be blessed with a firm enjoying and self-satisfaction.

Free. What passion is this, my dear Lindabrides?[21]

Mal. 'Tis well, we both may jest. I ha' been tempted to your death.

Free. What, is the rampant cockatrice grown mad for the loss of her men?   240

Mal. Devilishly mad.

Free. As most assured of my second love?

Mal. Right.

---

[16] *cony:* rabbit.

[17] *on the hip:* at a disadvantage (wrestling).

[18] *singles . . . back:* dance steps, with sexual pun on the last.   [19] *pumps:* dancing shoes.

[20] *L.:* "My mind is bent to tell of bodies changed into new forms," Ovid, *Metamorphoses,* I. i.

[21] *Lindabrides:* character in a sixteenth-century Spanish romance.

Free. She would have had this ring.

Mal. Ay, and this heart; and in true proof you were slain, I should bring her this ring, from which she was assured you would not part until from life you parted. For which deed, and only for which deed, I should possess her sweetness.   249

Free. O bloody villainess! Nothing is defamed but by his proper self. Physicians abuse remedies, lawyers spoil the law, and women only shame women. You ha' vowed my death?

Mal. My lust, not I, before my reason would; yet I must use her. That I, a man of sense, should conceive endless pleasure in a body whose soul I know to be so hideously black!

Free. That a man at twenty-three should cry, "O sweet pleasure!" and at forty-three should sigh, "O sharp pox!" But consider man furnished with   260 omnipotency, and you overthrow him; thou must cool thy impatient appetite. 'Tis fate, 'tis fate.

Mal. I do malign my creation that I am subject to passion. I must enjoy her.

Free. I have it; mark. I give a masque tonight
To my love's kindred. In that thou shalt go;
In that we two make show of falling out,
Give seeming challenge, instantly depart
With some suspicion to present²² fight.
We will be seen as going to our swords;   270
And after meeting, this ring only lent,
I'll lurk in some obscure place till rumor
(The common bawd to loose suspicions)
Have feigned me slain, which, in respect myself
Will not be found, and our late seeming quarrel,
Will quickly sound to all as earnest truth.
Then to thy wench; protest me surely dead,
Show her this ring, enjoy her, and, blood cold,
We'll laugh at folly.

Mal.   Oh, but think of it.

Free. Think of it! come, away Virtue, let sleep thy
  passions;   280
What old times held as crimes are now but fashions.

                                               Exeunt.

[III.ii]

Enter MASTER BURNISH *and* LIONEL : MASTER
  MULLIGRUB, *with a standing cup in his hand,*¹
and an obligation in the other. COCLEDEMOY *stands
  at the other door, disguised like a French pedlar,
            and overhears them.*

Mul. I am not at this time furnished, but there's my bond for your plate.

Bur. Your bill had been sufficient; y'are a good man. A standing cup parcel-gilt,² of thirty-two ounces, eleven pound, seven shillings, the first of July. Good plate, good man, good day, good all.

Mul. 'Tis my hard fortune; I will hang the knave. No, first he shall half rot in fetters in the dungeon, his conscience made despairful. I'll hire a knave o' purpose shall assure him he is damned, and after see him   10

with mine own eyes hanged without singing any psalm. Lord, that he has but one neck!

Bur. You are too tyrannous. You'll use me no further?

Mul. No, sir; lend me your servant, only to carry the plate home. I have occasion of an hour's absence.

Bur. With easy consent, sir. [*To* LIONEL] Haste, and be careful.

                                        Exit BURNISH.

Mul. Be very careful, I pray thee; to my wife's own hands.   20

Li. Secure yourself, sir.

Mul. To her own hand.

Li. Fear not; I have delivered greater things than this to a woman's own hand.

                                        [*Exit* LIONEL.]

Coc. Mounsier, please you to buy a fine delicate ball, sweet ball, a camphor ball?

Mul. Prithee, away!

Coc. Or³ a ball to scour, a scouring ball, a ball to be shaved?   29

Mul. For the love of God, talk not of shaving! I have been shaved; mischief and a thousand devils seize him! I have been shaved.

                                      Exit MULLIGRUB.

Coc. The fox grows fat when he is cursed. I'll shave ye smoother yet. Turd on a tile-stone! my lips have a kind of rheum⁴ at this bowl; I'll hav't! I'll gargalize⁵ my throat with this vintner, and when I have done with him, spit him out. I'll shark. Conscience does not repine. Were I to bite an honest gentleman, a poor grogaran⁶ poet, or a penurious parson that had but ten pigs' tails in a twelvemonth⁷ and for want of   40 learning had but one good stool in a fortnight, I were damned beyond the works of supererogation.⁸ But to wring the withers of my gouty, barmed,⁹ spigot-frigging¹⁰ jumbler of elements, Mulligrub, I hold it as lawful as sheep-shearing, taking eggs from hens, caudles¹¹ from asses, or buttered shrimps from horses; they make no use of them, were not provided for them. And therefore, worshipful Cocledemoy, hang toasts! on, in grace and virtue to proceed. Only beware, beware degrees.¹² There be rounds in a ladder and knots in   50 a halter; 'ware carts.¹³ Hang toasts! the Common Council has decreed it. I must draw a lot for the great goblet.

                                                 Exit.

----

²² *present*: immediate.

III.ii.
  ¹ *standing cup*: cup with a foot or base.
  ² *parcel-gilt*: gilt on the inner surface.   ³ *Or*: Q "One".
  ⁴ *rheum*: watering.   ⁵ *gargalize*: gargle.
  ⁶ *grogaran*: cheap cloth.
  ⁷ *penurious . . . twelvemonth*: the parson's poor position brings him little in the way of food.
  ⁸ *beyond . . . supererogation*: beyond the salvation afforded by the deeds of others on one's behalf.
  ⁹ *barmed*: fermented.
  ¹⁰ *frigging*: tampering; the phrase alludes to Mulligrub's adulteration of what he serves.
  ¹¹ *caudles*: warm porridge for the sick.
  ¹² *degrees*: steps, rungs on the ladder to the gallows.
  ¹³ *carts*: in which criminals were taken to be executed.

[III.iii]

Enter MISTRESS MULLIGRUB *and* LIONEL,
with a goblet.

Mist. Mul. Nay, I pray you, stay and drink. And how does your mistress? I know her very well; I have been inward[1] with her, and so has many more. She was ever a good, patient creature, i' faith. With all my heart, I'll remember your master, an honest man; he knew me before I was married. An honest man he is, and a crafty. He comes forward in the world well, I warrant him, and his wife is a proper woman, that she is. Well, she has been as proper a woman as any in Cheap;[2] she paints[3] now, and yet she keeps her   10 husband's old customers to him still. In troth, a fine-faced wife in a wainscot carved seat is a worthy ornament to a tradesman's shop, and an attractive, I warrant; her husband shall find it in the custom of his ware, I'll assure him. God be with you, good youth. I acknowledge the receipt.

Exit LIONEL.

I acknowledge all the receipt—sure, 'tis very well spoken. I acknowledge the receipt. Thus 'tis to have good education and to be brought up in a tavern. I do keep as gallant and as good company, though I say   20 it, as any she in London. Squires, gentlemen, and knights diet at my table, and I do lend some of them money; and full many fine men go upon my score,[4] as simple as I stand here, and I trust them; and truly they very knightly and courtly promise fair, give me very good words and a piece of flesh when time of year serves.[5] Nay, though my husband be a citizen and's cap's made of wool, yet I ha' wit and can see my good as soon as another; for I have all the thanks. My silly[6] husband, alas, he knows nothing of it; 'tis I that bear; 'tis I that must bear a brain for all.   31

[*Enter* COCLEDEMOY.]

Coc. Fair hour to you, mistress!

Mist. Mul. [*Aside*] Fair hour! Fine term; faith, I'll score it up anon. [*To* COCLEDEMOY] A beautiful thought to you, sir.

Coc. Your husband, and my master, Master Burnish, has sent you a jowl[7] of fresh salmon; and they both will come to dinner to season your new cup with the best wine; which cup your husband entreats you to send back by me that his arms may be graved o' the side, which he forgot before it was sent.   41

Mist. Mul. By what token are you sent? By no token? Nay, I have wit.

Coc. He sent me by the same token that he was dry-shaved[8] this morning.

Mist. Mul. A sad token, but true. Here, sir.

[*Gives the cup.*]

I pray you commend me to your master, but especially to your mistress. Tell them they shall be most sincerely welcome.   49

Exit.

Coc. Shall be most sincerely welcome! Worshipful Cocledemoy, lurk close. Hang toasts! Be not ashamed of thy quality. Every man's turd smells well in's own nose. Vanish, foist.[9]

Exit.

[*Re-*]*enter* MISTRESS MULLIGRUB, *with* Servants *and furniture for the table.*

Mist. Mul. Come, spread these table diaper[10] napkins and—do you hear?—perfume. This parlor does so smell of profane tobacco. I could never endure this ungodly tobacco since one of our elders assured me, upon his knowledge, tobacco was not used in the congregation of the Family of Love. Spread, spread handsomely. Lord, these boys do things arsy-varsy![11] you show   60 your bringing up! I was a gentlewoman by my sister's side; I can tell ye so methodically. Methodically—I wonder where I got that word. O, Sir Aminadab Ruth bade me kiss him methodically. I had it somewhere, and I had it indeed.

Enter MASTER MULLIGRUB.

Mul. Mind, be not desperate; I'll recover all. All things with me shall seem honest that can be profitable.
He must ne'er wince, that would or thrive or save,
To be called niggard, cuckold, cutthroat, knave.

Mist. Mul. Are they come, husband?   70

Mul. Who? What? How now? What feast towards in my private parlor?

Mist. Mul. Pray leave your foolery. What, are they come?

Mul. Come? Who come?

Mist. Mul. You need not make't so strange.

Mul. Strange?

Mist. Mul. Ay, strange. You know no man that sent me word that he and his wife would come to dinner to me, and sent this jowl of fresh salmon beforehand?   80

Mul. Peace, not I! peace! The messenger hath mistaken the house; let's eat it up quickly before it be inquired for. Sit to it. Some vinegar, quick. Some good luck yet. Faith, I never tasted salmon relished better. Oh, when a man feeds at other men's cost!

Mist. Mul. Other men's cost! Why, did not you send this jowl of salmon?

Mul. No.

Mist. Mul. By Master Burnish' man?

Mul. No.   90

Mist. Mul. Sending me word that he and his wife would come to dinner to me?

Mul. No, no.

Mist. Mul. To season my new bowl?

Mul. Bowl?

Mist. Mul. And withal willed me to send the bowl back?

Mul. Back?

III.iii.
   [1] *inward:* intimate; like other words that follow, it has sexual connotations.   [2] *Cheap:* Cheapside.
   [3] *paints:* i.e., her face.   [4] *score:* accounts.
   [5] *piece . . . serves:* game in season, with sexual innuendo.
   [6] *silly:* foolish.   [7] *jowl:* head and shoulders.
   [8] *dry-shaved:* cheated.   [9] *foist:* cheat, smell.
   [10] *diaper:* patterned linen.   [11] *arsy-varsy:* backside first.

Mist. Mul. That you might have your arms graved on
the side?   100

Mul. Ha?

Mist. Mul. By the same token you were dry-shaven
this morning before you went forth?

Mul. Pah! how this salmon stinks!

Mist. Mul. And thereupon sent the bowl back, prepared dinner—nay, and I bear not a brain!

Mul. Wife, do not vex me! Is the bowl gone? Is it
delivered?

Mist. Mul. Delivered? Yes, sure, 'tis delivered.   109

Mul. I will never more say my prayers; do not make
me mad. 'Tis common. Let me not cry like a woman!
Is it gone?

Mist. Mul. Gone! God is my witness, I delivered it
with no more intention to be cozened[12] on't than the
child new born; and yet—

Mul. Look to my house! I am haunted with evil
spirits. Hear me; do hear me. If I have not my goblet
again, heaven, I'll to the devil; I'll to a conjuror. Look
to my house! I'll raise all the wise men i' the street.
                                                                 [*Exit.*]

Mist. Mul. Deliver us? What words are these? I
trust in God he is but drunk, sure.   121

[*Re-*]*enter* COCLEDEMOY.

Coc. [*Aside*] I must have the salmon to worship.
Cocledemoy, now for the masterpiece. God bless thy
neck-piece,[13] and foutra![*To* MISTRESS MULLIGRUB]
Fair mistress, my master—

Mist. Mul. Have I caught you?—What, Roger!

Coc. Peace, good mistress. I'll tell you all. A jest, a
very mere jest. Your husband only took sport to fright
you. The bowl's at my master's; and there is your husband, who sent me in all haste, lest you should be   130
over-frighted with his feigning, to come to dinner to
him—

Mist. Mul. Praise heaven it is no worse.

Coc. And desired me to desire you to send the jowl
of salmon before, and yourself to come after to them;
my mistress would be right glad to see you.

Mist. Mul. I pray carry it. Now thank them entirely.
Bless me, I was never so out of my skin in my life. Pray
thank your mistress most entirely.   139

Coc. [*Aside*] So now, figo![14] worshipful Moll Faugh
and I will munch. Cheaters and bawds go together like
washing and wringing.
                                                                 Exit.

Mist. Mul. Beshrew[15] his heart for his labor! How
everything about me quivers! [*To* Servant.] What,
Christian! my hat and apron. Here, take my sleeves.[16]
And how I tremble! So, I'll gossip it[17] now for't, that's
certain. Here has been revolutions and false fires indeed.

[*Re-*]*enter* MULLIGRUB.

Mul. Whither now? What's the matter with you
now? Whither are you a-gadding?   149

Mist. Mul. Come, come, play the fool no more: will
you go?

Mul. Whither, in the rank name of madness, whither?

Mist. Mul. Whither? Why, to Master Burnish, to

eat the jowl of salmon. Lord, how strange you make it!

Mul. Why so? Why so?

Mist. Mul. Why so! why, did not you send the self-
same fellow for the jowl of salmon that had the cup?

Mul. 'Tis well, 'tis very well.

Mist. Mul. And willed me to come and eat it with
you at the goldsmith's?   160

Mul. Oh, ay, ay, ay. Art in thy right wits?

Mist. Mul. Do you hear? Make a fool of somebody
else. And you make an ass of me, I'll make an ox[18] of
you—do ye see?

Mul. Nay, wife, be patient; for, look you, I may be
mad, or drunk, or so; for my own part, though you can
bear more than I, yet I can do well: I will not curse nor
cry,[19] but heaven knows what I think. Come, let's go
hear some music. I will never more say my prayers.
Let's go hear some doleful music. Nay, if heaven   170
forget to prosper knaves, I'll go no more to the synagogue.[20] Now I am discontented, I'll turn sectary;[21]
that is fashion.

                                                                 Exeunt.

ACT FOUR

SCENE ONE

Enter SIR HUBERT SUBBOYS, SIR LIONEL
FREEVILL, CRISPINELLA, [Ladies *and*
Gentlemen], Servants *with lights.*

Sir Hub. More lights! Welcome, Sir Lionel Freevill,
brother Freevill, shortly. Look to your lights!

Serv. The masquers are at hand.

Sir Hub. Call down our daughter. Hark, they are at
hand. Rank handsomely.[1]

Enter the Masquers; *they dance.*
Enter MALHEUREUX *and take* BEATRICE
from FREEVILL. *They draw.*

Free. Know, sir, I have the advantage of the place;
You are not safe. I would deal even[2] with you.

Mal. So.
                               They exchange gloves as pledges.

Free. So.

Bea. I do beseech you, sweet, do not for me   10
Provoke your fortune.

Sir Lion. What sudden flaw is risen?

Sir Hub.   From whence
    comes this?

Free. An ulcer long time lurking now is burst.

Sir Hub. Good sir, the time and your designs are
    soft.[3]

---

[12] *cozened:* cheated.   [13] *neck-piece:* the jowl.
[14] *figo:* name of a contemptuous gesture.
[15] *Beshrew:* Curse.   [16] *sleeves:* separate garments.
[17] *gossip it:* join in.   [18] *ox:* cuckold, by giving horns.
[19] *cry:* Q "cary."
[20] *synagogue:* Puritan word for church.
[21] *sectary:* dissenter.

IV.i.
[1] *Rank handsomely:* Take places appropriately for dance.
[2] *even:* fairly.   [3] *soft:* agreeable, peaceful.

Bea. Ay, dear, sir, counsel him, advise him; 'twill relish well from your carving.—Good, my sweet, rest safe.

Free. All's well, all's well. This shall be ended straight.

Sir Hub. The banquet stays;[4] there we'll discourse more large.

Free. Marriage must not make men cowards.

Sir Lion.   Nor rage fools.   20

Sir Hub. 'Tis valor not where heat but reason rules.

[*Exeunt.*] *Only* TYSEFEW *and* CRISPINELLA *stay.*

Ty. But do you hear, lady, you proud ape, you; What was the jest you brake[5] of me even now?

Crisp. Nothing. I only said you were all mettle,[6] that you had a brazen face, a leaden brain, and a copper beard.

Ty. Quicksilver! thou little more than a dwarf, and something less than a woman.

Crisp. A wisp,[7] a wisp, a wisp! Will you go to the banquet?   30

Ty. By the Lord, I think thou wilt marry shortly, too; thou growest somewhat foolish already.

Crisp. Oh, i' faith, 'tis a fair thing to be married, and a necessary. To hear this word *must.* If our husbands be proud, we must bear his contempt; if noisome, we must bear with the goat under his armholes; if a fool, we must bear his babble;[8] and, which is worse, if a loose liver, we must live upon unwholesome reversions. Where, on the contrary side, our husbands, because they may, and we must, care not for us. Things   40 hoped with fear and got with strugglings are men's high pleasures when duty pales and flats their appetite.

Ty. What a tart monkey is this! By heaven, if thou hadst not so much wit I could find in my heart to marry thee. Faith, bear with me for all this.

Crisp. Bear with thee? I wonder how thy mother could bear thee ten months in her belly when I cannot endure thee two hours in mine eye.

Ty. Alas for you, sweet soul! by the Lord, you are grown a proud, scurvy, apish, idle, disdainful,   50 scoffing—God's foot, because you have read *Euphues and His England,*[9] *Palmerin de Oliva,*[10] and the *Legend of Lies!*[11]

Crisp. Why, i' faith, yet, servant, you of all others should bear with my known unmalicious humors; I have always in my heart given you your due respect: and, heaven may be sworn, I have privately given fair speech of you, and protested—

Ty. Nay, look you, for my own part, if I have not as religiously vowed my heart to you, been drunk to   60 your health, swallowed flapdragons,[12] eat glasses, drunk urine, stabbed arms,[13] and done all the offices of protested gallantry for your sake; and yet you tell me I have a brazen face, a leaden brain, and a copper beard. Come, yet, and it please you.

Crisp. No, no, you do not love me.

Ty. By ——,[14] but I do now; and whosoever dares say that I do not love you, nay, honor you, and if you would vouchsafe to marry—   69

Crisp. Nay, as for that, think on't as you will, but God's my record, and my sister knows I have taken drink and slept upon't, that if ever I marry it shall be you; and I will marry, and yet I hope I do not say it shall be you neither.

Ty. By heaven, I shall be as soon weary of health as of your enjoying. Will you cast a smooth cheek upon me?

Crisp. I cannot tell. I have no crumped[15] shoulders, my back needs no mantle,[16] and yet marriage is honorable. Do you think ye shall prove a cuckold?

Ty. No, by the Lord, not I.   80

Crisp. Why, I thank you, i' faith. Heigh-ho! I slept on my back this morning and dreamt the strangest dreams. Good Lord, how things will come to pass! Will you go to the banquet?

Ty. If you will be mine, you shall be your own. My purse, my body, my heart is yours; only be silent in my house, modest at my table, and wanton in my bed, and the Empress of Europe cannot content and shall not be contented better.   89

Crisp. Can any kind heart speak more discreetly affectionately? My father's consent, and as for mine—

Ty. Then thus, and thus, so Hymen[17] should begin;

[*He kisses her.*]

Sometimes a falling out proves falling in.

[*Exeunt.*]

[IV.ii]

Enter FREEVILL, *speaking to some within;* MALHEUREUX *at the other door.*

Free. As you respect my virtue, give me leave
To satisfy my reason, though not blood.
So, all runs right; our feignèd rage hath ta'en
To fullest life;[1] they[2] are much possessed
Of force[3] most, most all quarrel. Now, my right friend,
Resolve me with open breast, free and true heart,
Cannot thy virtue, having space to think
And fortify her weakened powers with reason,
Discourses, meditations,[4] discipline,
Divine ejaculatories,[5] and all those aids against devils—
Cannot all these curb thy low appetite   11
And sensual fury?

Mal. There is no God in blood, no reason in desire.

---

  [4] *stays:* awaits.   [5] *brake:* broke.
  [6] *mettle:* with a common pun on metal, spelled the same way.   [7] *wisp:* figure of straw for a scold to rail at.
  [8] *babble:* chatter; bauble.
  [9] *Euphues . . . England:* 1580 sequel to Lyly's famous romance *Euphues,* 1578.
  [10] *Palmerin de Oliva:* romance translated by Anthony Munday.   [11] *Legend of Lies:* fictitious.
  [12] *flapdragons:* burning raisins snatched from flaming brandy and swallowed.
  [13] *stabbed arms:* dropped blood into a glass and drank it with wine.   [14] ——: *so* Q.   [15] *crumped:* bent.
  [16] *back . . . mantle:* i.e., to cover a hunchback.
  [17] *Hymen:* Marriage.

IV.ii.
  [1] *ta'en . . . life:* been fully effective.
  [2] *they:* they who.   [3] *force:* mental power.
  [4] *meditations:* formal exercises in thinking.
  [5] *ejaculatories:* short prayers.

Shall I but live? Shall I not be forced to act
Some deed whose very name is hideous?
  Free. No.
  Mal.   Then I must enjoy Francischina.
  Free.   You shall:
I'll lend this ring; show it to that fair devil.
It will resolve me dead;
Which rumor, with my artificial absence,
Will make most firm. Enjoy her suddenly.   20
  Mal. But if report go strong that you are slain,
And that by me, whereon I may be seized,
Where shall I find your being?
  Free. At Master Shatewe's the jeweler's, to whose
    breast
I'll trust our secret purpose.
  Mal.   Ay, rest yourself;
Each man hath follies.
  Free.   But those worst of all,
Who with a willing eye do, seeing, fall.
  Mal. 'Tis true, but truth seems folly in madness'
    spectacles.
I am not now myself, no man. Farewell.
  Free.   Farewell.   29
  Mal. When woman's in the heart, in the soul hell.
                     Exit MALHEUREUX.
  Free. Now repentance, the fool's whip, seize thee.
Nay, if there be no means I'll be thy friend,
But not thy vice's; and with greatest sense
I'll force thee feel thy errors to the worst.
The vilest of dangers thou shalt sink into.
No jeweler shall see me; I will lurk
Where none shall know or think; close I'll withdraw
And leave thee with two friends—a whore and knave.[6]
But is this virtue in me? No, not pure;
Nothing extremely best with us endures.   40
No use in simple purities; the elements
Are mixed for use. Silver without alloy
Is all too eager [7] to be wrought for use:
Nor precise [8] virtues ever purely good
Holds useful size with temper of weak blood.
Then let my course be borne, though with side wind,[9]
The end being good, the means are well assigned.
                          Exit.

[IV.iii]

Enter FRANCISCHINA *melancholy,*
    COCLEDEMOY *leading her.*

  Coc. Come, catafugo,[1] Frank[2] o' Frank Hall! who,
who, ho! excellent! ha, here's a plump-rumped wench,
with a breast softer than a courtier's tongue, an old
lady's gums, or an old man's *mentula*.[3] My fine rogue—
  Fran. Pah, you poltroon!
  Coc. Goody fist, flumpum pumpum! ah, my fine
wagtail,[4] thou art as false, as prostituted and adulterate,
as some translated manuscript. Buss, fair whore, buss!
  Fran. God's sacrament, pox!   9
  Coc. Hadamoy key,[5] dost thou frown, *medianthon
teukey*? Nay, look here. *Numeron key*, silver *blithefor
cany, os cany* goblet: *us key ne moy blegefoy oteeston* pox
on you, gosling!

  Fran. By me fait, dis bin very fine langage. Ick sall
bush ye now! Ha, be garzon,[6] vare had you dat plate?
  Coc. Hedemoy key, get you gone, punk rampant, *key*,
common up-tail!

Enter MARY FAUGH *in haste.*

  Mary. Oh, daughter, cousin, niece, servant, mistress!
  Coc. Humpum, plumpum squat, I am gone.   19
                        Exit COCLEDEMOY.
  Mary. There is one Master Malheureux at the door
desires to see you. He says he must not be denied, for
he hath sent you this ring, and withal says 'tis done.
  Fran. Vat sall me do now, God's sacrament? Tell
him two hours hence he sall be most affectionately velcome. Tell him—vat sall me do?—tell him ick am bin
in my bate,[7] and ick sall perfume my seets, mak-a mine
body so delicate [8] for his arm, two hours hence.
  Mary. I shall satisfy him; two hours hence, well.
                        Exit MARY FAUGH.
  Fran. Now ick sall revange! Hay, begar[9]! me sall
tartar [10] de whole generation! mine brain vork it.   30
Freevill is dead; Malheureux sall hang; and mine rival,
Beatrice, ick sall make run mad.

[Re-]enter MARY FAUGH.

  Mary. He's gone, forsooth, to eat a caudle of cockstones,[11] and will return within this two hours.
  Fran. Very vell. Give monies to some fellow to squire
me; ick sall go abroad.
  Mary. There's a lusty [12] bravo [13] beneath, a stranger,
but a good stale rascal. He swears valiantly, kicks a
bawd right virtuously, and protests with an empty
pocket right desperately. He'll squire you.   40
  Fran. Very velcome. Mine fan! Ick sall retorn
presantly.

                    [Exit MARY FAUGH.]
Now sall me be revange. Ten tousant devla! dere sall be
no Got in me but passion, no tought but rage, no mercy
but blood, no spirit but divla in me. Dere sall noting
tought good for me, but dat is mischievous for others.
                            Exit.

[IV.iv]

Enter SIR HUBERT, SIR LIONEL, BEATRICE,
  CRISPINELLA, *and* Nurse, TYSEFEW *following.*

  Sir Lion. Did no one see him since? Pray God—nay,
all is well. A little heat, what? He is but withdrawn.
And yet I would to God—but fear you nothing.

---

6 *knave:* either himself disguised or Cocledemoy.
7 *eager:* brittle.   8 *precise:* rigorous.
9 *side wind:* indirect means.

IV.iii.
1 *catafugo:* spitfire (Spanish).
2 *Frank:* abbreviation of Francischina; free, licentious.
3 *L.:* penis.   4 *wagtail:* courtesan.
5 *Hadamoy key:* Cocledemoy's nonsense is untranslatable.
6 *be garzon:* by God's son.   7 *bate:* bath.
8 *delicate:* delightful.   9 *begar:* by God.
10 *tartar:* torture.
11 *cockstones:* kidney beans, an aphrodisiac.
12 *lusty:* vigorous.   13 *bravo:* bold villain.

Bea. Pray God that all be well, or would I were not.

Ty. He's not to be found, sir, anywhere.

Sir Lion. You must not make a heavy face presage an ill event. I like your sister well; she's quick and lively. Would she would marry, faith.

Crisp. Marry? Nay, and I would marry, methinks an old man's a quiet thing.   10

Sir Lion. Ha, mass; and so he is.

Crisp. You are a widower?

Sir Lion. That I am, i' faith, fair Crispinella; and I can tell you, would you affect me, I have it in me yet, i' faith.

Crisp. Troth, I am in love. Let me see your hand. Would you cast yourself away upon me willingly?

Sir Lion. Will I? Ay, by the—

Crisp. Would you be a cuckold willingly? By my troth, 'tis a comely, fine, and handsome sight for   20 one of my years to marry an old man; truth, 'tis restorative. What a comfortable thing it is to think of her husband, to hear his venerable cough o' the everlastings,[1] to feel his rough skin, his summer hands and winter legs, his almost no eyes, and assuredly no teeth; and then to think what she must dream of when she considers others' happiness and her own want—'tis a worthy and notorious comfortable match.

Sir Lion. Pish, pish! will you have me?

Crisp. Will you assure me—   30

Sir Lion. Five-hundred pound jointure?

Crisp. That you will die within this fortnight?

Sir Lion. No, by my faith, Crispinella.

Crisp. Then Crispinella, by her faith, assures you she'll have none of you.

Enter FREEVILL, *disguised like a pander, and* FRANCISCHINA.

Free. By'r leave, gentles and men of nightcaps,[2] I would speak, but that here stands one is able to express her own tale best.

Fran. Sir, mine speech is to you. You had a son, Matre Freevill?   40

Sir Lion. Had, ha, and have!

Fran. No point;[3] me am come to assure you dat one Mestre Malheureux hath killed him.

Bea. Oh, me! wretched, wretched!

Sir Hub. Look to our daughter.

Sir Lion. How art thou informed?

Fran. If dat it please you to go vid me, ick sall bring you where you sall hear Malheureux vid his own lips confess it; and dere ye may apprehend him, and revenge your and mine love's blood.   50

Sir Hub. Your love's blood, mistress! Was he your love?

Fran. He was so, sir; let your daughter hear it. Do not veep, lady. De yong man dat be slain did not love you, for he still lovit me ten tousant tousant times more dearly.

Bea. O my heart! I will love you the better; I cannot hate what he affected. O passion! O my grief! which way wilt break, think, and consume?

Crisp. Peace.

Bea. Dear woes cannot speak.   60

Fran. For look you, lady, dis your ring he gave me, vid most bitter jests at your scorned kindness.

Bea. He did not ill not to love me, but sure he did not well to mock me: gentle minds will pity though they cannot love. Yet peace and my love sleep with him!— unlace, good nurse.—Alas, I was not so ambitious of so supreme an happiness that he should only love me; 'twas joy enough for me, poor soul, that I only might only love him.   69

Fran. Oh, but to be abused, scorned, scoffed at! Oh, ten tousand divla, by such a one, and unto such a one!

Bea. I think you say not true.—Sister, shall we know one another in the other world?

Crisp. What means my sister?

Bea. I would fain see him again. O my tortured mind!

Freevill is more than dead; he is unkind.

[Exeunt] BEATRICE *and* CRISPINELLA *and* Nurse.

Sir Hub. Convey her in, and so, sir, as you said, Set a strong watch.

Sir Lion.   Ay, sir, and so pass along With this same common woman. [*To* FRANCISCHINA] —You must make it good.

Fran. Ick sall, or let me pay for his, mine blood.   80

Sir Hub. Come, then, along all, with quiet speed.

Sir Lion.   O fate!

Ty. Oh, sir, be wisely sorry, but not passionate.

[Exeunt ;] manet FREEVILL.

Free. I will go and reveal myself. Stay! no, no! Grief endears love. Heaven; to have such a wife Is happiness to breed pale envy in the saints. Thou worthy, dove-like virgin without gall, Cannot (that woman's evil) jealousy, Despite disgrace, nay, which is worst, contempt, Once stir thy faith? O truth, how few sisters hast thou! Dear memory!   90 With what a suff'ring sweetness, quiet modesty, Yet deep affection, she received my death! And then with what a patient, yet oppressèd kindness She took my lewdly[4] intimated wrongs. Oh, the dearest of heaven! Were there but three such women in the world, Two might be saved. Well, I am great With expectation to what devilish end This woman of foul soul will drive her plots; But Providence all wicked art o'ertops,   100 And impudence must know, though stiff as ice, That fortune doth not alway dote on vice.

Exit.

[IV.v]

Enter SIR HUBERT, SIR LIONEL, TYSEFEW, FRANCISCHINA, *and three* [Constables] *with halberds.*[1]

Sir Hub. Plant a watch there. Be very careful, sirs. The rest with us.

IV.iv.
[1] *cough . . . everlastings:* eternal or fatal cough.
[2] *men . . . nightcaps:* nocturnal bullies, or men of law.
[3] *No point:* Not at all.   [4] *lewdly:* ignorantly.
IV.v.
[1] *halberds:* combination spears and battle-axes.

Ty. The heavy night grows to her depth of quiet;
'Tis about mid-darkness.

Fran. Mine shambre is hard by; ick sall bring you to
it presantment.[2]

Sir Lion. Deep silence. On.

Exeunt. [The Watch *remains.]*

Coc. [Within] Wa, ha, ho!

Enter MULLIGRUB.

Mul. It was his voice; 'tis he. He sups with his
cupping-glasses.[3] 'Tis late; he must pass this way.   10
I'll ha' him; I'll ha' my fine boy, my worshipful
Cocledemoy. I'll moy[4] him. He shall be hanged in
lousy linen; I'll hire some sectary to make him an
heretic before he die, and when he is dead, I'll piss on
his grave.

Enter COCLEDEMOY.

Coc. Ah, my fine punks, good night, Frank Frailty,
Frail o' Frail Hall! *Bonus noches,*[5] my *ubiquitari!*[6]

Mul. 'Ware polling and shaving, sir!

Coc. A wolf, a wolf, a wolf!   19

Exit COCLEDEMOY, *leaving his cloak behind him.*

Mul. Here's something yet! a cloak, a cloak. Yet I'll
after; he cannot 'scape the watch. I'll hang him if I have
any mercy.[7] I'll slice him.

Exit.

[Re-]enter COCLEDEMOY. [The Watch advances.]

1 Con. Who goes there? Come before the constable.

Coc. Bread o' God, constable, you are a watch for the
devil. Honest men are robbed under your nose. There's
a false knave in the habit of a vintner set upon me; he
would have had my purse, but I took me to my heels.
Yet he got my cloak: a plain stuff[8] cloak, poor, yet
'twill serve to hang him. 'Tis my loss, poor man that I
am.   30

[Exit.]

2 Con. Masters, we must watch better. Is't not
strange that knaves, drunkards, and thieves should be
abroad, and yet we of the watch, scriveners, smiths, and
tailors, never stir?

[Re-]enter MULLIGRUB, running with COCLEDEMOY's cloak.

1 Con. Hark! who goes there?

Mul. An honest man and a citizen.

2 Con. Appear, appear! what are you?

Mul. A simple vintner.

1 Con. A vintner, ha? And simple? Draw nearer,
nearer. Here's the cloak!   40

2 Con. Ay, master vintner, we know you. A plain
stuff cloak: 'tis it.

1 Con. Right, come! Oh, thou varlet, does not thou
know that the wicked cannot 'scape the eyes of the
constable?

Mul. What means this violence? As I am an honest
man, I took the cloak—

1 Con. As you are a knave, you took the cloak; we
are your witnesses for that.

Mul. But hear me, hear me. I'll tell you what I am.

2 Con. A thief you are.   51

Mul. I tell you my name is Mulligrub.

1 Con. I will grub[9] you. In with him to the stocks.
There let him sit till tomorrow morning, that Justice
Quodlibet may examine him.

Mul. Why, but I tell thee—

2 Con. Why, but I tell thee. We'll tell thee now.

[The Constables *put* MULLIGRUB *in the stocks.]*

Mul. Am I not mad? Am I not an ass? Why, scabs—
God's foot, let me out!   59

2 Con. Ay, ay, let him prate; he shall find matter[10]
in us scabs,[11] I warrant. God's-so, what good members
of the commonwealth do we prove!

1 Con. Prithee, peace! let's remember our duties,
and let go sleep in the fear of God.

[Exeunt, having left MULLIGRUB *in the stocks.*

Mul. Who goes there? Illo, ho, ho![12] zounds, shall I
run mad, lose my wits? Shall I be hanged?—Hark,
who goes there? Do not fear to be poor, Mulligrub;
thou hast a sure stock[13] now.

[Re-]enter COCLEDEMOY like a bellman.[14]

Coc.   The night grows old,
              And many a cuckold   70
              Is now—Wha, ha, ha, ho!
              Maids on their backs
              Dream of sweet smacks
              And warm—Wo, ho, ho, ho!

I must go comfort my venerable Mulligrub; I must
fiddle[15] him till he fist. Fough!—

              Maids in your night-rails,[16]
              Look well to your light—.
              Keep close your locks,
              And down your smocks;   80
              Keep a broad eye,
              And a close thigh—

Excellent, excellent!—who's there? Now, Lord, Lord—
Master Mulligrub!—deliver us! What does your worship in the stocks? I pray come out, sir.

Mul. Zounds, man, I tell thee I am locked!

Coc. Locked! O world! O men! O time! O night!
that canst not discern virtue and wisdom and one of the
Common Council! What is your worship in for?

Mul. For—a plague on't!—suspicion of felony.   90

Coc. Nay, and it be such a trifle, Lord, I could weep
to see your good worship in this taking.[17] Your worship

---

[2] *presantment:* right away.

[3] *cupping-glasses:* used for letting blood; here, wine
glasses.   [4] *moy:* ruin(?) not in OED.

[5] *Bonus noches:* good night (corrupt Spanish).

[6] *L.:* ubiquitous people.

[7] *mercy:* i.e., power to exercise mercy.

[8] *stuff:* woolen.   [9] *grub:* dig out.

[10] *matter:* sense; pus.   [11] *scabs:* scoundrels; sores.

[12] *Illo . . . ho:* falconer's cry.   [13] *stock:* supply.

[14] *bellman:* night watchman.   [15] *fiddle:* cheat.

[16] *night-rails:* night dress.

[17] *taking:* arrested condition; upset state.

has been a good friend to me; and, though you have forgot me, yet I knew your wife before she was married; and, since, I have found your worship's door open, and I have knocked, and God knows what I have saved. And do I live to see your worship stocked!

Mul. Honest bellman, I perceive thou know'st me; I prithee call the watch.
Inform the constable of my reputation,   100
That I may no longer abide in this shameful habitation.
And hold thee all I have about me.

                      Gives him his purse.

Coc. 'Tis more than I deserve, sir. Let me alone for your delivery.
Mul. Do, and then let me alone with Cocledemoy. I'll moy him!
Coc.   *Maids in your—*

              [*Re-enter the* Constables.]

Master Constable, who's that i'th' stocks?
1 Con. One for a robbery; one Mulligrub he calls himself. Mulligrub? Bellman, know'st thou him?   110
Coc. Know him! Oh, Master Constable, what good service have you done! know him? He's a strong[18] thief; his house has been suspected for a bawdy tavern a great while, and a receipt[19] for cutpurses, 'tis most certain. He has been long in the black book,[20] and is he ta'en now?
2 Con. By'r Lady, my masters, we'll not trust the stocks with him; we'll have him to the justice's, get a *mittimus*[21] to Newgate[22] presently.—Come, sir, come on, sir!   120
Mul. Ha! does your rascalship yet know my worship in the end?
1 Con. Ay, the end of your worship we know.
Mul. Ha, goodman constable, here's an honest fellow can tell you what I am.
2 Con. 'Tis true, sir; y'are a strong thief, he says, on his own knowledge. Bind fast, bind fast! We know you: we'll trust no stocks with you. Away with him to the jail instantly.
Mul. Why, but dost hear—Bellman! rogue! rascal! God's—why, but—   131
        The Constable *drags away* MULLIGRUB.
Coc. Why, but! wha, ha, ha! excellent, excellent! ha, my fine Cocledemoy, my vintner fists! I'll make him fart crackers[23] before I ha' done with him. Tomorrow is the day of judgment. Afore the Lord God, my knavery grows unperegal![24] 'Tis time to take a nap,

until half an hour hence; God give your worship music content, and rest.

                        Exeunt.

ACT FIVE

SCENE ONE

Enter FRANCISCHINA, SIR LIONEL, TYSEFEW,
   [FREEVILL *disguised as before*], *with* Officers.

Fran. You bin very velcome to mine shambra.
Sir Lion. But how know ye, how are ye assured Both of the deed and of his sure return?
Fran. Oh, mynheer, ick sall tell you. Mettre Malheureux came all breatless running a[1] my shambra, his sword all bloody: he tell-a me he had kill Freevill and prayed-a me to conceal him. Ick flatter him, bid bring monies, he should live and lie vid me. He went whilst ick—me hope vidout sins—out of mine mush love to Freevill betray him.   10
Sir Lion. Fear not, 'tis well; good works get grace for sin.

           She conceals them behind the curtain.

Fran. Dere, peace, rest dere; so, softly, all go in.
[*Aside*] De net is lay; now sall ick be revenge.
If dat me knew a dog dat Freevill love,
Me would puisson him; for know de deepest hell
As a revenging woman's naught so fell.[2]

              Enter MARY FAUGH.

Mary. Ho, Cousin Frank, the party you wot[3] of, Master Malheureux.
Fran.   Bid him come up, I pride.

           Cantat saltatque cum cithera.[4]

              Enter MALHEUREUX.

Fran. O mynheer man, aderliver love,
Mine ten tousant times velcome love.   20
Ha, by mine trat,[5] you bin de just—vat sall me say?
Vat seet honey name sall I call you?
Mal.   Any from you
Is pleasure. Come, my loving prettiness,
Where's thy chamber? I long to touch your sheets.
Fran. No, no, not yet, mine seetest, soft-lipped love;
You sall not gulp down all delights at once.
Be min trat, dis all-fles-lovers, dis ravenous wenches
Dat sallow all down whole, vill have all at one bit.
Fie, fie, fie! Be min fait, dey do eat comfits[6] vid spoons.
No, no, I'll make you chew your pleasure vit love;   30
De more degrees and steps, de more delight,
De more endearèd is de pleasure height.
Mal. What, you're a learnèd wanton, and proceed
By art.
Fran. Go, little vag. Pleasure should have
A crane's long neck, to relish de ambrosia
Of delight. And ick pride tell me, for me loves
To hear of manhood very mush, i' fait.
Ick pride—vat vas me a-saying?—oh, ick pride
Tell-a me, how did you kill-a Mettre Freevill?

---

[18] *strong:* formidable.
[19] *receipt:* place for receiving stolen goods.
[20] *black book:* record of those liable to censure or punishment.   [21] *mittimus:* warrant to imprison.
[22] *Newgate:* London prison.   [23] *crackers:* firecrackers.
[24] *unperegal:* peerless.

V.i.
 [1] *Fr.:* to.   [2] *fell:* terrible.   [3] *wot:* know.
 [4] *Cantat . . . cithera:* She sings and dances to the cithern (a kind of lute).   [5] *trat:* troth.
 [6] *comfits:* sweets made of preserved fruit.

Mal. Why, quarreled o' set purpose, drew him out,
Singled[7] him, and having th' advantage   41
Of my sword and might, ran him through and through.

Fran. Vat did you vid him van he was sticken?

Mal. I dragged him by the heels to the next wharf
And spurned[8] him in the river.

Those in ambush rusheth forth and take him.

Sir Lion. Seize, seize him. O monstrous! O ruthless
   villain!

Mal. What mean you, gentlemen? By heaven—

Ty. Speak not of anything that's good.

Mal. Your errors gives you passion; Freevill lives.

Sir Lion. Thy own lips say thou liest.

Mal.   Let me die   50
If at Shatewe's the jeweler he lives not safe untouched.

Ty. Meantime to strictest guard, to sharpest prison.

Mal. No rudeness gentlemen: I'll go undragged.
O wicked, wicked devil!

Exit [*with* Officers].

Sir Lion.   Sir, the day
Of trial is this morn. Let's prosecute
The sharpest rigor and severest end;
Good men are cruel when they're vice's friend.

Sir Hub. Woman, we thank thee with no empty
   hand;

[*Gives money.*]

Strumpets are fit, fit for something. Farewell.

All save FREEVILL *depart.*

Free. Ay, for hell!   60
O thou unreprievable, beyond all
Measure of grace damned immediately!
That things of beauty created for sweet use,
Soft comfort, and as the very music of life,
Custom should make so unutterably hellish.
O heaven,
What difference is in women and their life!
What man, but worthy name of man, would leave
The modest pleasures of a lawful bed,
The holy union of two equal hearts,   70
Mutually holding either dear as health,
The undoubted issues, joys of chaste sheets,
The unfeignèd embrace of sober ignorance,
To twine th'unhealthful loins of common loves,
The prostituted impudence of things
Senseless like those by cataracts of Nile,
Their use so vile takes away sense. How vile
To love a creature made of blood and hell,
Whose use makes weak, whose company doth shame,
Whose bed doth beggar, issue doth defame.   80

[*Re-*]*enter* FRANCISCHINA.

Fran. Mettre Freevill live! Ha, ha! Live at Mestre
Shatewe's! Mush[9] at Mettre Shatewe's! Freevill is
dead; Malheureux sall hang; and, sweet divil! dat
Beatrice would but run mad, dat she would but run
mad, den me would dance and sing. [*To* FREEVILL]
Mettre Don Dubon, me pray ye now go to Mestress
Beatrice; tell her Freevill is sure dead, and dat he curse
herself especially, for dat he was sticked in her quarrel,
swearing in his last gasp dat if it had bin in mine quarrels 'twould never have grieved him.   90

Free. I will.

Fran. Pridee do, and say anyting dat vill vex her.

Free. Let me alone to vex her.

Fran. Vill you? Vill you mak-a her run mad? Here,
take dis ring; say me scorn to wear anyting dat was hers
or his. I pridee torment her. Ick cannot love her; she
honest and virtuous, forsooth!

Free. Is she so? O vile creature! then let me alone
with her.   99

Fran. Vat, will you mak-a her mad? Seet, by min
trat, be pretta servan! Bush! Ick sall go to bet now.

[*Exit.*]

Free. Mischief, whither wilt thou?
O thou tearless woman, how monstrous is thy devil!
The end of hell as[10] thee! how miserable
Were it to be virtuous, if thou couldst prosper!
I'll to my love, the faithful Beatrice;
She has wept enough, and, faith, dear soul, too much.
But yet how sweet it is to think how dear
One's life was to his love: how mourned his death!
'Tis joy not to be expressed with breath.   110
But, oh, let him that would such passion drink
Be quiet of his speech, and only think.

Exit.

[V.ii]

Enter BEATRICE *and* CRISPINELLA.

Bea. Sister, cannot a woman kill herself? Is it not
lawful to die when we should not live?

Crisp. O sister, 'tis a question not for us; we must do
what God will.

Bea. What God will! Alas, can torment be His glory?
Or our grief His pleasure? Does not the nurse's nipple,
juiced over with wormwood, bid the child it should not
suck? And does not heaven, when it hath made our
breath bitter unto us, say we should not live? O my
best sister,   10
To suffer wounds when one may 'scape this rod
Is against nature, that is, against God!

Crisp. Good sister, do not make me weep. Sure Free-
vill was not false;
I'll gage my life that strumpet, out of craft
And some close[1] second end, hath maliced[2] him.

Bea. O sister, if he were not false, whom have I lost!
If he were, what grief to such unkindness!
From head to foot I am all misery;
Only in this, some justice I have found: 20
My grief is like my love, beyond all bound.

Enter Nurse [PUTIFER].

Put. My servant, Master Caqueteur, desires to visit
you.

---

7 *Singled:* Took him alone.   8 *spurned:* kicked.
9 *Mush:* Much, of course.   10 *as:* is as.
V.ii.
1 *close:* secret.   2 *maliced:* maligned.

Crisp. For grief's sake, keep him out! his discourse is like the long word *Honorificabilitudinitatibus*,[3] a great deal of sound and no sense. His company is like a parenthesis to a discourse: you may admit it, or leave it out, it makes no matter.

[*Exit* Nurse.]

Enter FREEVILL *in his* [*disguise*].

Free. By your leave, sweet creatures.

Crisp. Sir, all I can yet say of you is, you are uncivil.

Free. You must deny it. [*To* BEATRICE] By your
    sorrow's leave,   31
I bring some music to make sweet your grief.

Bea. Whate'er you please. Oh, break my heart! Canst thou yet pant? Oh, dost thou yet survive? Thou didst not love him if thou now canst live!

Free. [*Sings*]

> O Love, how strangely sweet
>   Are thy weak[4] passions,
> That love and joy should meet
>   In selfsame fashions!
> Oh, who can tell   40
>   The cause why this should move?
> But only this,
>   No reason ask of Love!

BEATRICE *swoons.*

Crisp. Hold, peace! The gentlest soul is swooned. O my best sister!

Free. Ha! get you gone, close the doors. My Beatrice!

Discovers himself.

Cursed be my indiscreet trials! O my immeasurably
    loving!

Crisp. She stirs; give air, she breathes.

Bea. Where am I, ha? How have I slipped off life? Am I in heaven? O my Lord, though not loving, 50 By our eternal being, yet give me leave To rest by thy dear side. Am I not in heaven?

Free. O eternally much loved, recollect your
    spirits!

Bea. Ha, you do speak! I do see you; I do live! I would not die now: let me not burst with wonder!

Free. Call up your blood; I live to honor you As the admirèd glory of your sex. Nor ever hath my love been false to you; Only I presumed to try your faith too much, For which I most am grievèd.   60

Crisp. Brother, I must be plain with you; you have
    wronged us.

Free. I am not so covetous to deny it; But yet, when my discourse hath stayed your quaking, You will be smoother-lipped; and the delight And satisfaction which we all have got

Under these strange disguisings, when you know, You will be mild and quiet, forget at last. It is much joy to think on sorrows past.

Bea. Do you, then, live? And are you not untrue? Let me not die with joy! pleasure's more extreme 70 Than grief; there's nothing sweet to man but mean.[5]

Free. Heaven cannot be too gracious to such
    goodness.
I shall discourse to you the several chances,[6] but, hark, I must yet rest disguised. The sudden close of many drifts now meet; Where pleasure hath some profit, art is sweet.

Enter TYSEFEW.

Ty. News, news, news, news.

Crisp. Oysters, oysters, oysters, oysters.

Ty. Why, is not this well now? Is not this better than louring and pouting and puling, which is hateful to 80 the living and vain to the dead? Come, come, you must live by the quick,[7] when all is done. And for my own part, let my wife laugh at me when I am dead, so she'll smile upon me whilst I live. But to see a woman whine, and yet keep her eyes dry; mourn, and yet keep her cheeks fat; nay, to see a woman claw her husband by the feet when he is dead, that would have scratched him by the face when he was living—this now is somewhat ridiculous.

Crisp. Lord, how you prate.   90

Ty. And yet I was afraid, i' faith, that I should ha' seen a garland on this beauty's hearse; but time, truth, experience, and variety are great doers with women.

Crisp. But what's the news? The news, I pray you?

Ty. I pray you? Ne'er pray me, for by your leave you may command me. This 'tis: The public sessions, which this day is past, Hath doomed to death ill-fortuned Malheureux.

Crisp. But, sir, we heard he offered to make good That Freevill lived at Shatewe's the jeweler's— 100

Bea. And that 'twas but a plot betwixt them two.

Ty. Oh, ay, ay, he gaged his life with it; but know, When all approached the test, Shatewe denied He saw or heard of any such complot,[8] Or of Freevill; so that his own defense Appeared so false that, like a madman's sword, He struck his own heart. He hath the course of law And instantly must suffer. But the jest— If hanging be a jest, as many make it— Is to take notice of one Mulligrub,   110 A sharking vintner.

Free. What of him, sir?

Ty. Nothing but hanging. The whoreson slave is mad before he hath lost his senses.

Free. Was his fact[9] clear and made apparent, sir?

Ty. No, faith, suspicious; for 'twas thus protested: A cloak was stolen; that cloak he had; he had it, Himself confessed, by force. The rest of his defense The choler of a justice wronged in wine, Joined with malignance of some hasty jurors, 120 Whose wit was lighted by the justice' nose; The knave was cast.[10] But, Lord, to hear his moan, His prayers, his wishes, his zeal ill-timed, and his words

---

  [3] *L.:* dative/ablative plural for "honorableness," famous as longest of words.   [4] *weak:* debilitating.
  [5] *mean:* moderation.   [6] *chances:* events.
  [7] *quick:* living.   [8] *complot:* plot.
  [9] *fact:* deed.   [10] *cast:* condemned.

Unpitied, would make a dead man rise and smile,
Whilst he observed how fear can make men vile.
    Crisp. Shall we go meet the execution?
    Bea. I shall be ruled by you.
    Ty. By my troth, a rare motion. You must haste,
For malefactors goes like the world, upon wheels.[11]
    Bea. Will you man[12] us? [*To* FREEVILL] You shall
    be our guide.   130
    Free. I am your servant.
    Ty. Ha, servant! Zounds, I am no companion for
    panders.
You're best make him your love.
    Bea. So will I, sir; we must live by the quick, you
    say.
    Ty. 'Sdeath o' virtue! What a damned thing's this!
Who'll trust fair faces, tears, and vows? 'Sdeath, not I!
She is a woman—that is, she can lie.
    Crisp. Come, come, turn not a man of time,[13] to
    make all ill
Whose goodness you conceive not, since the worst of
    chance
Is to crave grace for heedless ignorance.   140
                            Exeunt.

[V.iii]

        Enter COCLEDEMOY *like a Sergeant.*

    Coc. So, I ha' lost my sergeant in an ecliptic[1] mist.
Drunk, horrible drunk; he is fine. So now will I fit[2]
myself; I hope this habit will do me no harm. I am an
honest man already, fit, fit, fit as a punk's tail, that
serves everybody. By this time my vintner thinks of
nothing but hell and sulfur; he farts fire and brimstone
already. Hang toasts! the execution approacheth.

    Enter SIR LIONEL, SIR HUBERT, MALHEUREUX
    pinioned, TYSEFEW, BEATRICE, FREEVILL,
      CRISPINELLA, FRANCISCHINA, *and*
        [Officers *with*] *halberds.*

    Mal. I do not blush, although condemned by laws;
No kind of death is shameful but the cause,
Which I do know is none; and yet my lust   10
Hath made the one, although not cause, most just.
May I not be reprieved? Freevill is but mislodged;
Some lethargy hath seized him—no, much malice.
Do not lay blood upon your souls with good intents;
Men may do ill, and law sometime repents.

    COCLEDEMOY *picks* MALHEUREUX'
        pocket of his purse.

    Sir Lion. Sir, sir, prepare; vain is all lewd[3] defense.
    Mal. Conscience was law, but now law's conscience.
My endless peace is made, and to the poor—
My purse, my purse!   19
    Coc. Ay, sir, and it shall please you, the poor has your
purse already.
    Mal. You are a wily man. [*To* FRANCISCHINA]
But now, thou source of devils, O, how I loathe
The very memory of that I adored!

He that's of fair blood, well-miened, of good breeding,
Best famed, of sweet acquaintance and true friends,
And would with desperate impudence lose all these,
And hazard landing at this fatal shore,
Let him ne'er kill nor steal, but love a whore.
    Fran. De man does rave. Tink o' Got, tink o' Got,
and bid de flesh, de world, and the dibil farewell.   31
    Mal. Farewell.
    Free. Farewell.

        FREEVILL *discovers himself.*

    Fran. Vat is't you see? Ha!
    Free. Sir, your pardon; with my this defense,
Do not forget protested violence
Of your low affections; no requests,
No arguments of reason, no known danger,
No assurèd wicked bloodiness,
Could draw your heart from this damnation.   40
    Mal. Why, stay.
    Fran. Unprosperous divil, vat sall me do now?
    Free. Therefore, to force you from the truer danger,
I wrought the feignèd,[4] suffering this fair devil
In shape of woman to make good her plot;
And, knowing that the hook was deeply fast,
I gave her line at will till, with her own vain strivings,
See here she's tired.[5] O thou comely damnation,
Dost think that vice is not to be withstood?
Oh, what is woman merely[6] made of blood?   50
    Sir Lion. You 'maze us all; let us not be lost in
    darkness.
    Free. All shall be lighted, but this time and place
Forbids longer speech; only what you can think
Has been extremely ill is only hers.
    Sir Lion. To severest prison with her.
With what heart canst live? What eyes behold a face?
    Fran. Ick vill not speak. Torture, torture your fill,
For me am worse than hanged; me ha' lost my will.

      Exit FRANCISCHINA *with the guard.*

    Sir Lion. To the extremest whip and jail.
    Free. Frolic, how is it, sir?[7]   60
    Mal. I am myself. How long was't ere I could
Persuade my passion to grow calm to you.
Rich sense makes good bad language, and a friend
Should weigh no action but the action's end.
I am now worthy yours, when, before,
The beast of man, loose blood, distempered us.
He that lust rules cannot be virtuous.

    Enter MULLIGRUB, MISTRESS MULLIGRUB,
        and Officers.

    Off. On afore there; room for the prisoners.

---

[11] *upon wheels:* i.e., in carts.   [12] *man:* attend.
[13] *man of time:* timeserver.

V.iii.
  [1] *ecliptic:* of an eclipse.   [2] *fit:* furnish.
  [3] *lewd:* unskilled.   [4] *feignèd:* deception.
  [5] *tired:* like a played-out fish. [6] *merely:* completely.
  [7] *sir:* Q "sirs."

Mul. I pray you, do not lead me to execution through Cheapside; I owe Master Burnish, the goldsmith, 70 money, and I fear he'll set a sergeant on my back for it.

Coc. Trouble not your sconce,[8] my Christian brother,[9] but have an eye unto the main chance. I will warrant your shoulders; as for your neck, Plinius Secundus, or Marcus Tullius Cicero, or somebody it is, says that a threefold cord[10] is hardly broken.

Mul. Well, I am not the first honest man that hath been cast away, and I hope shall not be the last.

Coc. O sir, have a good stomach and maws:[11] you shall have a joyful supper.   80

Mul. In troth, I have no stomach to it. And it please you, take my trencher;[12] I use to fast at nights.

Mist. Mul. O husband, I little thought you should have come to think on God thus soon. Nay, and you had been hanged deservedly, it would never have grieved me. I have known of many honest, innocent men have been hanged deservedly, but to be cast away for nothing.

Coc. Good woman, hold your peace, your prittles and your prattles, your bibbles and your babbles; 90 for I pray you hear me in private. I am a widower, and you are almost a widow; shall I be welcome to your houses, to your tables, and your other things?

Mist. Mul. I have a piece of mutton[13] and a feather-bed for you at all times. I pray, make haste.

Mul. I do here make my confession. If I owe any man anything, I do heartily forgive him; if any man owe me anything, let him pay my wife.

Coc. I will look to your wife's payment, I warrant you.   100

Mul. And now, good yoke-fellow, leave thy poor Mulligrub.

Mist. Mul. Nay, then I were unkind;[14] i' faith, I will not leave you until I have seen you hang.

Coc. But brother, brother,[15] you must think of your sins and iniquities. You have been a broacher of profane vessels; you have made us drink of the juice of the whore of Babylon.[16] For whereas good ale, perrys,[17] braggets,[18] ciders, and metheglins[19] was the true an-

cient British and Troyan[20] drinks, you ha' brought 110 in Popish wines, Spanish wines, French wines, *tam Marti quam Mercurio*,[21] both muscadine and malmsey,[22] to the subversion, staggering, and sometimes overthrow of many a good Christian. You ha' been a great jumbler.[23] Oh, remember the sins of your nights; for your night works ha' been unsavory in the taste of your customers.

Mul. I confess, I confess, and I forgive as I would be forgiven. Do you know one Cocledemoy?   119

Coc. Oh, very well. Know him! An honest man he is, and a comely, an upright dealer with his neighbors, and their wives speak good things of him.

Mul. Well, wheresoe'er he is, or whatsoe'er he is, I'll take it on my death he's the cause of my hanging. I heartily forgive him; and if he would come forth he might save me, for he only knows the why and the wherefore.

Coc. You do, from your hearts and midriffs and entrails, forgive him, then? You will not let him rot in rusty irons, procure him to be hanged in lousy linen without a song, and, after he is dead, piss on his grave?

Mul. That hard heart of mine has procured all this, but I forgive as I would be forgiven.   133

Coc. Hang toasts, my worshipful Mulligrub! behold thy Cocledemoy, my fine vintner, my castrophonical[24] fine boy! behold and see.

[Discovers himself.]

Ty. Bliss o' the blessed, who would but look for two knaves here!

Coc. No knave, worshipful friend, no knave; for, observe, honest Cocledemoy restores whatsoever 140 he has got, to make you know that whatsoe'er he has done has been only *euphoniae gratia*[25]—for wit's sake: I acquit this vintner as he has acquitted me. All has been done for emphasis of wit, my fine boy, my worshipful friends.

Ty. Go, you are a flattering knave.

Coc. I am so; 'tis a good thriving trade. It comes forward better than the seven liberal sciences[26] or the nine cardinal virtues,[27] which may well appear in this: you shall never have flattering knave turn cour- 150 tier, and yet I have read of many courtiers that have turned flattering knaves.

Sir Hub. Was't even but so? Why, then, all's well.

Mul. I could even weep for joy.

Mist. Mul. I could weep, too, but God knows for what.

Ty. Here's another tack[28] to be given: your son and daughter.

Sir Hub. Is't possible? Heart, ay, all my heart! will you be joined here?   160

Ty. Yes, faith, father; marriage and hanging are spun both in one hour.

Coc. Why, then, my worshipful good friends, I bid myself most heartily welcome to your merry nuptials and wanton jigga-joggies.

[Coming forward and addressing the audience.]

---

8 *sconce:* head.   9 *brother:* Q "brothers."
10 *threefold cord:* see Ecclesiastes 4:12.   11 *maws:* jaws.
12 *trencher:* dinner plate.
13 *piece of mutton:* prostitute.   14 *unkind:* unnatural.
15 *brother, brother:* Q "brothers, brothers."
16 *whore of Babylon:* Roman church.
17 *perrys:* pear cider.
18 *braggets:* drink made of honey and ale fermented together.   19 *metheglins:* strong version of mead.
20 *Troyan:* Brute, great-grandson of Trojan Aeneas, was held to have founded London.
21 *L.:* as much for Mars (war) as for Mercury (commerce).
22 *muscadine and malmsey:* strong sweet wines.
23 *jumbler:* one who adulterates wine with water; cf. III. ii, 38.   24 *castrophonical:* Q "catastraphomical."
25 *L.:* for the sake of pleasant sound.
26 *sciences:* grammar, logic, rhetoric (*trivium*), arithmetic, geometry, music, astronomy (*quadrivium*).
27 *virtues:* actually seven: justice, prudence, temperance, fortitude (natural), faith, hope, and charity (theological).
28 *tack:* match, joining.

And now, my very fine Heliconian[29] gallants, and you,
my worshipful friends in the middle region:[30]
If with content our hurtless mirth hath been,
Let your pleased minds at our much care be seen;

For he shall find, that slights such trivial wit,   170
'Tis easier to reprove than better it.
We scorn to fear, and yet we fear to swell;
We do not hope 'tis best: 'tis all, if well.

Exeunt.

F I N I S

---

[29] *Heliconian:* devoted to the muses, inhabitants of Mt.
Helicon.
[30] *middle region:* the audience, or perhaps a part of it.

George Chapman
[c. 1559-1634]

BUSSY D'AMBOIS

GEORGE CHAPMAN, a native of Hertfordshire, is best known as the translator of Homer's *Iliad* and *Odyssey*. Keats's famous sonnet, "On First Looking into Chapman's Homer," is no doubt responsible for this instantaneous if somewhat equivocal identification. The great translation of Homer, which began to appear in 1598, was completed in 1616. Other Homeric poems were published about 1624. The *Iliad*, finished in 1611, was dedicated to the King's son and heir presumptive, Prince Henry, whose patronage Chapman enjoyed until the untimely death of the Prince in 1612, an event that put an end to further favor from the Court and resulted in the continuing impoverishment of the author until his own death in 1634.

But Chapman's unquestioned eminence among the writers of this time—there are not many who take precedence of him—does not rest, entirely or even chiefly, on his work in translation. He is himself a gifted and original poet, as witness *The Shadow of Night* (the publication of which in 1594 represents our first uncontested record of his activity), and the continuation and completing of Marlowe's *Hero and Leander* (1598). He is also a vigorous and idiosyncratic personality who comes through to us more vividly than the majority of his colleagues who wrote for the Elizabethan stage. It is likely that, anterior to his literary career, he served as a soldier in the Netherlands, perhaps in the period 1582–91. In this service Chapman resembles Jonson and Gascoigne.

His earliest successes as a playwright were achieved in the writing of comedy. Philip Henslowe, the theatrical entrepreneur, records in his diary (February 1596) a performance of *The Blind Beggar of Alexandria* for the Admiral's Men. This initial venture was followed by *A Humorous Day's Mirth* (1597), also for Henslowe, and indebted as the title suggests to the new fashion of presenting "humor" characters, whose bias inclines them to run all one way. Such characters are dominant in *All Fools* (1598–99), which takes for its model two plays of Terence. Other comedies by Chapman include *The Gentleman Usher* (1601–2), *May Day* (1601–2), *Monsieur D'Olive* (1604–5), and THE WIDOW'S TEARS (1612), perhaps the best of them all. An additional play, *Sir Giles Goosecap* (1606), has often been ascribed to him.

Early in the seventeenth century Chapman was writing for the Children of the Chapel—called Children of the Queen's Revels after 1604—at the Blackfriars Theater. In collaboration with Marston and Jonson, he composed for this group the comedy called *Eastward Ho* (1605), which, because of its satire on the Scots, gave offense to the Scottish-born sovereign James I and occasioned the imprisonment of the authors. Chapman's career seems marked by contentiousness. The tragedy of *Byron*, written later in the same decade and for the same company, stirred fresh trouble for its portrayal of French royalty on stage and its imprudent glancing at contemporary political business.

Before the beginning of the seventeenth century, Chapman had already earned a considerable reputation in the theater. The literary clergyman Francis Meres designates him, in a famous commonplace book of 1598, as among the best writers in comedy and tragedy. It is in the latter kind that he most excels. The tragedies for which he is chiefly remembered are worked up from French history, not remote but of his own time: plays like BUSSY D'AMBOIS (1607), his greatest achievement in theater, the two parts of the *Conspiracy and the Tragedy of Charles, Duke of Byron* (1607–8), and *The Revenge of Bussy D'Ambois* (1610–11). With *The Tragedy of Chabot* (1612–13), written in collaboration with James Shirley, and *Caesar and Pompey*, dating from the same period but not published until 1631, Chapman's career as a dramatist apparently comes to an end.

In everything he wrote, Chapman's learning and his dedication to scholarship are reflected. At Oxford, where he is supposed to have studied, he is represented as proficient in Latin and Greek. The influence of Italian comedies and *novelle* are apparent in the plays, as also that of classical writers like Seneca, Virgil, Plutarch (the *Moralia*), and Epictetus (in Latin). For the *Byron* plays and *The Revenge of Bussy D'Ambois* he consults Jean de Serres' history of France, as translated and updated by his kinsman and friend Edward Grimestone in 1607. For BUSSY D'AMBOIS, he probably went back in mind to Marlowe's *Massacre at Paris*, a tragedy of the Guise. It is interesting that, like Marlowe in most of his work, he should disvalue rank in favor of native capacity: the historical Bussy was not, what Chapman makes him, a man of inferior station. The career, this dramatist seems to be saying, is to the talents.

BUSSY D'AMBOIS is generally held to have been written about 1604, though some scholars contend for an earlier date. Publication in quarto by William Aspley followed the entry of the play in the Stationers' Register for 3 June 1607. The 1607 quarto was reissued without alteration in 1608. A third quarto, printed by A. N. for Robert Lunne, appeared in 1641.

Revision by Chapman is postulated about 1610,

perhaps to make the play mesh more effectively with its sequel, written at that time. The 1641 quarto is in fact radically different from its predecessors, and is advertised on the title page as "much corrected and amended by the author before his death." Until recently, scholars have tended to take this advertisement—which is perhaps little more than the conventional puffing of his wares by the publisher—at face value. Accepting it, they have offered as text a version of BUSSY D'AMBOIS in which the stage directions of the original are expanded (in the main, usefully), passages of dialogue are emended and amplified or even transposed (the powerful ending is unaccountably moved forward in the play), comic material is introduced, as well as a prologue and epilogue, scenes are reordered. For example, what is printed as V.ii in 1607 becomes V.iii in 1641. Maffé's lines in I.i are broken by the interpolated stage direction (which anticipates the next scene): "Table, chessboard, and tapers behind the arras." Here and elsewhere it looks as if the reviser is working from a prompt copy. Some few emendations in 1641 are dictated obviously by the need to conform with the edict of 1606 that forbade the abuse (i.e., the use) of the name of God in stage plays.

By and large, the reviser of the 1607 quarto was seeking to make the play more clear in utterance and line—and with reason, for Chapman is an extremely difficult writer. But was the reviser Chapman himself?

There is no certain reason to think so, despite the claims of the title page. On the other hand, it is virtually certain that he did rework his first version in some particulars, though not on anything like the scale represented by the recension that is the 1641 quarto. The job of an editor is to decide, in comparing the two quartos, what "must" be of Chapman's composition in the latter. The present text gives primacy to the quarto of 1607 and (except for stage directions) admits only infrequently additions from 1641. In each case, such additions are noted.

Chapman's style is peculiar to himself; eccentric in syntax, fuliginous in thought, he mingles much smoke with his fire. From BUSSY D'AMBOIS alone a cento of eloquent passages might be compiled, but often, as we return to them soberly, we see that eloquence is the garb for sentiments or ideas that are, if unexceptionable, also sufficiently commonplace. Often these unexceptionable sentiments are attached to characters who ought not, in propriety, to bespeak them. Bussy himself is not only a man for all seasons, he is a roughneck whose philosophy is exhausted in fighting at the drop of a hat. Sometimes Chapman seems oblivious of the ambiguous nature of his hero. In this again he reminds us of Marlowe. If, however, the comparison suggests his limitation, it functions also to point up his greatness. Among the makers of tragic declamation in the Renaissance, he ranks with Marlowe and Webster. It is an exalted station.

R. A. F.

Bussy D'Ambois

DRAMATIS PERSONÆ

HENRY III, *King of France*
MONSIEUR, *his brother*
The Duke of GUISE
The Count of MONTSURRY
BUSSY D'AMBOIS
BARRISOR⎫
L'ANOU ⎬ *courtiers; enemies of Bussy D'Ambois*
PYRHOT ⎭
BRISAC ⎫ *courtiers; friends of Bussy D'Ambois*
MELYNELL⎭
BEAUMOND, *an attendant of the King*
COMOLET, *a friar*
MAFFÉ, *steward to Monsieur*

NUNTIUS, *a messenger*
Murderers
BEHEMOTH ⎫ *spirits*
CARTOPHYLAX⎭
Ghost *of the friar*
ELENOR, *Duchess of Guise*
TAMYRA, *Countess of Montsurry*
BEAUPRÉ, *niece to Elenor*
ANNABLE, *maid to Elenor*
PERO, *maid to Tamyra*
CHARLOTTE, *maid to Beaupré*
PYRHA, *a court lady*
Lords, Ladies, Pages, Servants, Spirits, etc.

THE PROLOGUE

Not out of confidence that none but we [1]
Are able to present this tragedy,
Nor out of envy at the grace of late
It did receive, nor yet to derogate
From their [2] deserts, who give out boldly that
They move with equal feet on the same flat; [3]
Neither for all, nor any of such ends,
We offer it, gracious and noble friends,
To your review; we, far from emulation
(And, charitably judge, from imitation)   10
With this work entertain you, a piece known,
And still believed in court to be our own.
To quit our claim, doubting our right or merit,
Would argue in us poverty of spirit

Which we must not subscribe to: Field [4] is gone,
Whose action first did give it name, and one [5]
Who came the nearest to him, is denied
By his gray beard to show the height and pride
Of D'Ambois' youth and bravery; [6] yet to hold
Our title still afoot, and not grow cold   20
By giving it o'er, a third man [7] with his best
Of care and pains defends our interest;
As Richard he was liked, nor do we fear
In personating D'Ambois he'll appear
To faint, or go less, so [8] your free consent,
As heretofore, give him encouragement.

PROLOGUE
   [1] *we:* the King's Men.
   [2] *their:* alluding to another company of actors.
   [3] *move . . . flat:* tread the boards with as much skill.
   [4] *Field:* Nathaniel Field, who first played the title part for the King's Men and to whom Chapman addressed laudatory verses in 1612.
   [5] *one:* possibly Richard Burbage, the famous tragic "lead" of the King's Men (b. about 1567 and hence no longer young).
   [6] *bravery:* splendor, "dash."
   [7] *third man:* identified generally as Elliard Swanston.
   [8] *so:* so long as.

I.i.
   [1] *on his head:* upside down.   [2] *need:* necessity; penury.
   [3] *statuaries:* statue makers.
   [4] *tympanous:* swollen (as with pride), tumorous.
   [5] *statists:* politicians (in pejorative sense).

ACT ONE

SCENE ONE

Enter BUSSY D'AMBOIS, *poor.*

Bus. Fortune, not reason, rules the state of things,
Reward goes backwards, honor on his head; [1]
Who is not poor, is monstrous; only need [2]
Gives form and worth to every human seed.
As cedars beaten with incessant storms,
So great men flourish; and do imitate
Unskillful statuaries, [3] who suppose,
In forging a Colossus, if they make him
Straddle enough, strut, and look big, and gape,
Their work is goodly: so our tympanous [4] statists [5]   10
In their affected gravity of voice,

Sourness of countenance, manners' cruelty,
Authority, wealth, and all the spawn of fortune,
Think they bear all the kingdom's worth before them;
Yet differ not from those colossic statues
Which, with heroic forms without o'er-spread,
Within are nought but mortar, flint, and lead.
Man is a torch borne in the wind; a dream
But of a shadow, summed with all his substance;[6]
And as great seamen, using all their powers　　　　　20
And skills in Neptune's deep invisible paths,
In tall ships richly built and ribbed with brass,
To put a girdle round about the world,
When they have done it, coming near their haven,
Are glad to give a warning-piece,[7] and call
A poor staid[8] fisherman, that never passed
His country's sight, to waft and guide them in;
So when we wander furthest through the waves
Of glassy glory and the gulfs of state,
Topped with all titles, spreading all our reaches,[9]　　30
As if each private arm would sphere the world,
We must to virtue for her guide resort.
Or we shall shipwreck in our safest port.

　　　　　　　　　　　　　　　　　　He lies down.

　　　　　[*Enter*] MONSIEUR *with two* Pages.

Mons. There is no second place in numerous state[10]
That holds more than a cipher;[11] in a king
All places are contained. His words and looks
Are like the flashes and the bolts of Jove;
His deeds inimitable, like the sea
That shuts still as it opes, and leaves no tracts
Nor prints of precedent for poor men's facts.　　　40
There's but a thread betwixt me and a crown;
I would not wish it cut, unless by nature;
Yet to prepare me for that likely fortune,
'Tis fit I get resolvèd[12] spirits about me.
I followèd D'Ambois to this green retreat,
A man of spirit beyond the reach of fear,
Who, discontent with his neglected worth,
Neglects the light, and loves obscure abodes;
But he is young and haughty, apt to take
Fire at advancement, to bear state[13] and flourish;　50
In his rise therefore shall my bounties shine:
None loathes the world so much, nor loves to scoff it,
But gold and grace will make him surfeit of[14] it.
What, D'Ambois?
　　Bus.　　　　　He, sir.
　　Mons.　　　　　　　　　Turned to earth, alive?
Up, man, the sun shines on thee.
　　Bus.　　　　　　　　　Let it shine.
I am no mote to play in't, as great men are.
　　Mons. Thinkest thou men great in state, motes in the
　　　sun?
They say so that would have thee freeze in shades,
That, like the gross Sicilian gourmandist,[15]
Empty their noses in the cates[16] they love,　　　60
That none may eat but they. Do thou but bring
Light to the banquet fortune sets before thee,
And thou wilt loathe lean darkness like thy death.
Who would believe thy mettle could let sloth
Rust and consume it? If Themistocles[17]

Had lived obscured thus in th'Athenian state,
Xerxes[18] had made both him and it his slaves.
If brave Camillus[19] had lurked so in Rome,
He had not five times been dictator there,
Nor four times triumphed. If Epaminondas,[20]　　70
Who lived twice twenty years obscured in Thebes,
Had lived so still, he had been still unnamed,
And paid his country nor himself their right;
But, putting forth his strength, he rescued both
From imminent ruin, and like burnished steel,
After long use he shined; for as the light
Not only serves to show, but render us
Mutually profitable, so our lives
In acts exemplary not only win
Ourselves good names, but do to others give　　　80
Matter for virtuous deeds, by which we live.[21]
　　Bus. What would you wish me do?
　　Mons.　　　　　　　　　Leave the
　　　troubled streams,
And live as thrivers do at the wellhead.
　　Bus. At the wellhead? Alas, what should I do
With that enchanted glass? See devils there?
Or, like a strumpet, learn to set my looks
In an eternal brake,[22] or practice juggling,
To keep my face still fast, my heart still loose;
Or bear, like dames' schoolmistresses[23] their riddles,
Two tongues, and be good only for a shift;[24]　　90
Flatter great lords, to put them still in mind
Why they were made lords; or please portly ladies
With a good carriage, tell them idle tales
To make their physic[25] work; spend a man's life
In sights and visitations that will make
His eyes as hollow as his mistress' heart;
To do none good, but those that have no need;
To gain being forward, though you break for haste
All the commandments ere you break your fast,
But believe backwards,[26] make your period　　100
And creed's last article, "I believe in God,"

---

[6] *summed . . . substance:* when what he's done and has are
added up.
[7] *give a warning-piece:* fire a signal gun.
[8] *staid:* sober; lacking their glamorous credentials.
[9] *spreading . . . reaches:* putting out all our sail.
[10] *numerous state:* a populous kingdom.
[11] *holds . . . cipher:* is more than nothing.
[12] *resolvèd:* resolute.
[13] *bear state:* fill a great place greatly.
[14] *surfeit of:* gourmandize on.
[15] *Sicilian gourmandist:* Gnatho the glutton, in the
Eunuchus of Terence.　　　　　　　　[16] *cates:* delicacies.
[17] *Themistocles:* Athenian democratic statesman (c. 528–
462 B.C.) and, like Bussy, a "new man," self-made.
[18] *Xerxes:* King of Persia 486–465 B.C., defeated by
Themistocles at the naval battle of Salamis.
[19] *Camillus:* the savior of Rome after the Gallic invasion
of 387–386 B.C.
[20] *Epaminondas:* soldier and statesman of the fourth century B.C. who engineered the restoration of Theban power.
[21] *live:* are remembered after our death; also, "truly live,"
an inactive life being not to live at all.　　[22] *brake:* vise.
[23] *dames' schoolmistresses:* teachers of young women; hence,
given the tenor of the passage, "bawds."
[24] *a shift:* crooked business; also, "smock."
[25] *physic:* medicine, laxative.
[26] *believe backwards:* do not do as you profess.

And, hearing villainies preached, t'unfold their art
Learn to commit them? 'Tis a great man's part.
Shall I learn this there?
　　Mons.　　　　　　　No, thou need'st not learn,
Thou hast the theory, now go there and practice.
　　Bus.　Ay, in a threadbare suit; when men come there,
They must have high naps,[27] and go from thence bare.
A man may drown the parts of ten rich men
In one poor suit; brave barks[28] and outward gloss
Attract court eyes, be in-parts ne'er so gross.　　　　110
　　Mons.　Thou shalt have gloss enough, and all things
　　　fit
T'enchase[29] in all show thy long-smothered spirit.
Be ruled by me then. The rude[30] Scythians
Painted blind Fortune's powerful hands with wings
To show her gifts come swift and suddenly,
Which if her favorite be not swift to take,
He loses them forever. Then be ruled;
Stay but awhile here and I'll send to thee.
　　　Exit MONSIEUR [*with the* Pages]. BUSSY *remains.*
　　Bus.　What will he send? Some crowns? It is to sow
　　　them
Upon my spirit, and make them spring a crown　　120
Worth millions of the seed-crowns he will send.
Like to disparking[31] noble husbandmen,
He'll put his plow into me, plow me up;
But his unsweating thrift is policy,[32]
And learning-hating policy is ignorant
To fit his seed-land soil;[33] a smooth plain ground
Will never nourish any politic seed;
I am for honest actions, not for great:
If I may bring up a new fashion,
And rise in court with virtue, speed[34] his plow.　　130
The King hath known me long as well as he,
Yet could my fortune never fit the length
Of both their understandings till this hour.
There is a deep nick[35] in Time's restless wheel
For each man's good, when which nick comes, it strikes;
As rhetoric yet works not persuasion,
But only is a mean to make it work,
So no man riseth by his real merit,
But when it cries "clink"[36] in his raiser's spirit.
Many will say, that cannot rise at all,　　　　140
Man's first hour's rise is first step to his fall.
I'll venture that; men that fall low[37] must die,
As well as men cast headlong from the sky.

---

[27] *high naps:* costly clothing.
[28] *brave barks:* fine coverings.　　　[29] *enchase:* set in gold.
[30] *rude:* barbarous, a conventional epithet for Scythians.
[31] *disparking:* who from need of money convert parks to
fields for planting.
[32] *policy:* craft (pejorative, as with "politic" below).
[33] *Like . . . soil:* Though this passage is first printed in
Q1641, it is retained here for its consonance with Chapman's
style and metaphorical turn. Q1607 reads simply "But he's
no husband here. A smooth plain ground," etc.
[34] *speed:* success attend.
[35] *nick:* mechanism for striking the hour.
[36] *it . . . "clink":* the hour strikes.
[37] *low:* only a little distance.
[38] *Humor:* Disposition (physiologically determined).
[39] *Cry you mercy:* I beg your pardon (ironically).
[40] *that:* that which.　　　　　　　[41] *tall:* brave.

　　　　　　　　Enter MAFFÉ.

　　Maf.　—Humor[38] of princes! Is this man indued
With any merit worth a thousand crowns?
Will my lord have me be so ill a steward
Of his revènue, to dispose a sum
So great with so small cause as shows in him?
I must examine this.—Is your name D'Ambois?
　　Bus.　Sir?
　　Maf.　　Is your name D'Ambois?
　　Bus.　　　　　　　Who have we
　　　here?　　　　　　　　　　　　　　150
Serve you the Monsieur?
　　Maf.　　　　　　How?
　　Bus.　　　　　　　Serve you the
　　　Monsieur?
　　Maf.　Sir, y'are very hot. I serve the Monsieur,
But in such place as gives me the command
Of all his other servants. And because
His grace's pleasure is to give your good
A pass through my command, methinks you might
Use me with more good fashion.
　　Bus.　　　　　　　Cry you mercy.[39]
Now you have opened my dull eyes, I see you,
And would be glad to see the good you speak of.
What might I call your name?
　　Maf.　　　　　　Monsieur Maffé.　　160
　　Bus.　Monsieur Maffé? Then, good Monsieur Maffé,
Pray, let me know you better.
　　Maf.　　　　　　Pray do so,
That you may use me better. For yourself,
By your no better outside, I would judge you
To be a poet; have you given my lord
Some pamphlet?
　　Bus.　　　Pamphlet?
　　Maf.　　　　　　Pamphlet, sir, I say.
　　Bus.　Did his wise excellency leave the good
That is to pass your charge to my poor use
To your discretion?
　　Maf.　　　　Though he did not, sir,
I hope 'tis no bad office to ask reason　　　　170
How that[40] his grace gives me in charge, goes from me?
　　Bus.　That's very perfect, sir.
　　Maf.　　　　　Why, very good, sir;
I pray, then, give me leave; if for no pamphlet,
May I not know what other merit in you
Makes his compunction willing to relieve you?
　　Bus.　No merit in the world, sir.
　　Maf.　　　　　　That is strange.
Y'are a poor soldier, are you?
　　Bus.　　　　　That I am, sir.
　　Maf.　And have commanded?
　　Bus.　　　　　　Ay, and gone without,
　　　sir.
　　Maf.　[*Aside*] I see the man; a hundred crowns will
　　　make him
Swagger, and drink healths to his highness' bounty,
And swear he could not be more bountiful.　　181
So there's nine hundred crowns saved.—Here, tall[41]
　　　soldier,
His grace hath sent you a whole hundred crowns.

Bus. A hundred, sir? Nay, do his highness right;
I know his hand is larger, and perhaps
I may deserve more than my outside shows;
I am a scholar, as I am a soldier,
And I can poetize, and, being well encouraged,
May sing his fame for giving, yours for delivering
Like a most faithful steward what he gives.   190
    Maf. What shall your subject be?
    Bus.   I care not much,
If to his excellence I sing the praise
Of fair great noses,[42] and to your deserts
The reverend virtues of a faithful steward.
What qualities have you, sir, beside your chain
And velvet jacket?[43] Can your worship dance?
    Maf. [*Aside*] A merry fellow, 'faith; it seems my lord
Will have him for his jester; and, believe it,
Such men are now no fools; 'tis a knight's place.
If I, to save my lord some crowns, should urge him
T'abate his bounty, I should not be heard;   201
I would to heaven I were an arrant ass,
For then I should be sure to have the ears[44]
Of these great men, where now their jesters have them.
'Tis good to please him, yet I'll take no notice
Of his preferment, but in policy
Will still be grave and serious, lest he think
I fear his wooden dagger.[45]—Here, Sir Ambo,
A thousand crowns I bring you from my lord;
Serve God, play the good husband;[46] you may make
This a good standing[47] living: 'tis a bounty   211
His highness might perhaps have bestowed better.
    Bus. Go, y'are a rascal; hence, away, you rogue!
    Maf. What mean you, sir?
    Bus.   Hence! Prate no more,
Or, by thy villain's blood, thou pratest thy last.
A barbarous groom grudge at his master's bounty!
But since I know he would as much abhor
His hind[48] should argue what he gives his friend,
Take that, sir, for your aptness to dispute.
                      [*Strikes him.*] *Exit.*
    Maf. These crowns are sown in blood; blood be
      their fruit.   220
                             Exit.

[I.ii]

HENRY, GUISE, MONTSURRY, ELENOR,
TAMYRA, BEAUPRÉ, PERO, CHARLOTTE,
PYRHA, ANNABEL. [HENRY *and* GUISE *are
playing chess.*]

    Hen. Duchess of Guise, your grace is much enriched
In the attendance of this English virgin[1]
That will initiate her prime of youth,
Disposed to court conditions, under hand
Of your preferred instructions and command,
Rather than any in the English court,
Whose ladies are not matched in Christendom
For graceful and confirmed[2] behaviors,
More than the court, where they are bred, is equaled.
    Guise. I like not their court form; it is too
      crestfallen[3]   10

In all observance,[4] making semi-gods
Of their great nobles, and of their old Queen[5]
An ever-young and most immortal goddess.
    Hen. Assure you, cousin Guise, so great a courtier,
So full of majesty and royal parts,
No queen in Christendom may boast herself.
Her court approves[6] it, that's a court indeed,
Not mixed with rudeness used in common houses,
But, as courts should be th'abstracts[7] of their kingdoms
In all the beauty, state, and worth they hold,   20
So is hers, amply, and by her informed.[8]
The world is not contracted in a man[9]
With more proportion and expression
Than in her court, her kingdom. Our French court
Is a mere mirror of confusion to it.
The king and subject, lord and every slave,
Dance a continual hay;[10] our rooms of state
Kept like our stables; no place more observed
Than a rude market-place: and though our custom
Keep this assured deformity from our sight,   30
'Tis ne'er the less essentially unsightly,
Which they would soon see, would they change their
      form
To this of ours, and then compare them both;
Which we must not affect,[11] because in kingdoms
Where the king's change doth breed the subject's
      terror,
Pure innovation is more gross than error.
    Mont. No question we shall see them imitate,
Though a-far off, the fashions of our courts,
As they have ever aped us in attire;
Never were men so weary of their skins,   40
And apt to leap out of themselves as they,
Who, when they travel[12] to bring forth rare men,
Come home delivered of a fine French suit;
Their brains lie with their tailors, and get[13] babies
For their most complete issue; he's first born
To all the moral virtues that first greets

---

[42] *great noses:* alluding to Anjou's large nose, a subject of contemporary mirth.
    [43] *chain . . . jacket:* emblematic of a steward.
    [44] *ears:* attention (but punning unconsciously on an ass's ears, proper to Maffé).
    [45] *wooden dagger:* emblematic of a jester, and recalling the conventional accouterment of the Vice who accompanied the Devil in the morality plays and interludes.
    [46] *husband:* husbandman; provident man.
    [47] *standing:* continuing; and perhaps with a pun on tumescence, suggested by "husband" in the preceding line.
    [48] *hind:* peasant; slave.

I.ii.
    [1] *English virgin:* Annable.
    [2] *confirmed:* long established.
    [3] *crestfallen;* slavishly dutiful.
    [4] *observance:* respect it pays to rank.
    [5] *old Queen:* Elizabeth, whose death in 1603 almost surely preceded the writing of this unflattering comment.
    [6] *approves:* attests to.   [7] *abstracts:* epitomes.
    [8] *informed:* pervaded.
    [9] *man:* seen here as the epitome or microcosm of the greater world or macrocosm.   [10] *hay:* country dance.
    [11] *affect:* desire.   [12] *travel:* with a pun on "travail."
    [13] *get:* beget.

The light with a new fashion, which becomes them
Like apes, disfigured with the attires of men.

Hen. No question they much wrong their real worth
In affectation of outlandish scum;   50
But they have faults, and we; they foolish proud
To jet[14] in others' plumes so haughtily,
We proud that they are proud of foolery,
Holding our worths more còmplete for their vaunts.[15]

Enter MONSIEUR, D'AMBOIS.

Mons. Come, mine own sweetheart,[16] I will enter[17]
thee.
Sir, I have brought this gentleman t'attend you,
And pray you would vouchsafe to do him grace.

Hen. D'Ambois, I think.

Bus.   That's still my name, my
lord,
Though I be something altered[18] in attire.

Hen. I like your alteration, and must tell you   60
I have expected th'offer of your service;
For we, in fear to make mild virtue proud,
Use not to seek her out in any man.

Bus. Nor doth she use to seek out any man:
He that will win, must woo her; she's not shameless.

Mons. I urged her modesty in him, my lord,
And gave her those rites that he says she merits.

Hen. If you have wooed and won, then, brother,
wear him.

Mons. Th'art mine, my love. See, here's the Guise's
duchess, the Countess of Montsurry, Beaupré.   70

Come, I'll enseam[19] thee. Ladies, y'are too many to be
in council;[20] I have here a friend that I would gladly
enter in your graces.

Duch. If you enter him in our graces, methinks by
his blunt behavior he should come out of himself.

Tam. Has he never been courtier, my lord?

Mons. Never, my lady.

Beau. And why did the toy[21] take him in th' head
now?

Bus. 'Tis leap-year, lady, and therefore very good
to enter[22] a courtier.   81

Tam. The man's a courtier at first sight.

Bus. I can sing prick-song,[23] lady, at first sight; and
why not be a courtier as suddenly?

Beau. Here's a courtier rotten before he be ripe.[24]

Bus. Think me not impudent, lady; I am yet no
courtier: I desire to be one, and would gladly take entrance, madam, [*To the* DUCHESS] under your princely
colors.

Enter BARRISOR, L'ANOU, PYRHOT.

Guise. Sir, know you me?   90

Bus. My lord?

Guise. I know not you; whom do you serve?

Bus. Serve,[25] my lord!

Guise. Go to, companion,[26] your courtship's too
saucy.

Bus. [*Aside*] Saucy! Companion! 'Tis the Guise, but
yet those terms might have been spared of the Guiserd.[27] Companion! He's jealous, by this light. Are you
blind of that side, sir. I'll to her again for that. Forth,
madam, for the honor of courtship.   100

Guise. Cease your courtship, or by heaven I'll cut
your throat.

Bus. Cut my throat? Cut a whetstone![28] Good
Accius Naevius, do as much with your tongue, as he
did with a razor: cut my throat!

Guise. I'll do't, by this hand.

Bus. That hand dares not do't; y'ave cut too many
throats already, Guise, and robbed the realm of many
thousand souls more precious than thine own. Come,
madam, talk on; 'sfoot,[29] can you not talk? Talk on, I
say; more courtship, as you love it.   III

Bar. What new-come gallant have we here that dares
mate[30] the Guise thus?

L'An. 'Sfoot, 'tis D'Ambois. The duke mistakes
him, on my life, for some knight of the new edition.[31]

Bus. Cut my throat! I would the King feared thy
cutting of his throat no more than I fear thy cutting of
mine.

Guise. So, sir, so.

Pyr. Here's some strange distemper.   120

Bar. Here's a sudden transmigration with D'Ambois
—out of the knights' ward[32] into the duchess' bed.

L'An. See what a metamorphosis a brave suit can
work.

Pyr. 'Slight,[33] step to the Guise and discover[34] him.

Bar. By no means; let the new suit work; we'll see
the issue.

Guise. Leave your courtship.

Bus. I will not. I say, mistress, and I will stand[35]

---

[14] *jet:* strut.

[15] *To . . . vaunts:* Following Q1641; Q1607 reads "To be
the pictures of our vanity, We . . . foolery."

[16] *sweetheart:* with no erotic suggestion, as now.

[17] *enter:* prefer; sponsor.

[18] *altered:* Bussy enters in his new clothes, making an ironic
comment on Montsurry's indictment of fashion.

[19] *enseam:* introduce; but also "stitch together" or
"grease" (each implying sexual coupling).

[20] *too . . . council:* and, hence, "to keep a secret"(?).

[21] *toy:* trifling fancy.

[22] *enter:* with sexual implication, picking up "leap-year"
and "prick-song" in what follows.

[23] *prick-song:* music written down in notes or "pricked,"
as opposed to extemporaneous music.

[24] *rotten . . . ripe:* like the fruit of the medlar tree, which
resembles a small apple and is eaten when decayed. The
sexual *entendre* turns on the supposed resemblance of the
rotten (open) fruit to the pudendum or anus, "rotten"
suggesting also venereal disease. The primary point is to
Bussy's forwardness.

[25] *Serve:* perhaps taken by Bussy as suggesting one who
waits on table.

[26] *companion:* fellow (contemptuously).

[27] *Guiserd:* followers of the Guise.

[28] *Cut a whetstone:* as did the Roman augurer Accius
Naevius, making use of a razor.   [29] *'sfoot:* God's foot.

[30] *mate:* checkmate, defy.

[31] *of . . . edition:* as created by James I, whose wholesale
disposing of titles was a contemporary scandal.

[32] *ward:* posture of defense (metaphor from fencing); that
part of the debtors' prison called the Counter where persons
of station were imprisoned.   [33] *'Slight:* God's light.

[34] *discover:* identify.

[35] *stand:* again with a pun on tumescence.

unto it, that if a woman may have three servants,[36] a
man may have threescore mistresses.   131

Guise. Sirrah, I'll have you whipped out of the court
for this insolence.

Bus. Whipped? Such another syllable out o' th'
presence,[37] if thou darest for thy dukedom.

Guise. Remember, poltroon.

Mons. Pray thee, forbear.

Bus. Passion of death! Were not the King here, he
should strow the chamber like a rush.[38]

Mons. But leave courting his wife, then.   140

Bus. I will not. I'll court her in despite of him. Not
court her! Come, madam, talk on, fear me nothing.
[*To* GUISE] Well may'st thou drive thy master from the
court, but never D'Ambois.

Mons. His great heart will not down, 'tis like the sea,
That partly by his own internal heat,
Partly the stars' daily and nightly motion,
Ardor and light, and partly of the place
The divers[39] frames, and chiefly by the moon,
Bristled with surges, never will be won—   150
No, not when th' hearts of all those powers are burst—
To make retreat into his settled home,
Till he be crowned with his own quiet foam.

Hen. You have the mate.[40] Another?

Guise. No more.

> *Exit* GUISE; *after him the* KING, MONSIEUR
> *whispering.*

Bar. Why, here's the lion, scared with the throat of
a dunghill cock,[41] a fellow that has newly shaked off his
shackles; now does he crow for that victory.

L'An. 'Tis one of the best jigs[42] that ever was acted.

Pyr. Whom does the Guise suppose him to be,
trow?[43]   161

L'An. Out of doubt, some new denizened[44] lord,
and thinks that suit come new out o' th' mercer's[45]
books.

Bar. I have heard of a fellow, that by a fixed imagination looking upon a bull-baiting, had a visible pair of
horns grew out of his forehead, and I believe this
gallant, overjoyed with the conceit[46] of Monsieur's cast
suit, imagines himself to be the Monsieur.

L'An. And why not? As well as the ass, stalking in
the lion's case,[47] bare himself like a lion roaring all the
huger beasts out of the forest?   172

Pyr. Peace, he looks this way.

Bar. Marry, let him look, sir; what will you say now
if the Guise be gone to fetch a blanket[48] for him?

L'An. 'Faith, I believe it for his honor.

Pyr. But, if D'Ambois carry it clean?[49]

> *Exeunt* Ladies.

Bar. True, when he curvets[50] in the blanket.

Pyr. Ay, marry, sir.

L'An. 'Sfoot, see how he stares on's.   180

Bar. Lord bless us, let's away.

Bus. Now, sir, take your full view; how does the
object please ye?

Bar. If you ask my opinion, sir, I think your suit fits
as well as if't had been made for you.

Bus. So, sir, and was that the subject of your ridiculous jollity?

L'An. What's that to you, sir?   188

Bus. Sir, I have observed all your fleerings,[51] and
resolve yourselves ye shall give a strict account for't.

> *Enter* BRISAC *and* MELYNELL.

Pyr. Oh, strange credulity! Do you think yourself
such a singular subject for laughter that none can fall
into our merriment but you?

Bar. This jealousy[52] of yours, sir, confesses some
close[53] defect in yourself that we never dreamed of.

L'An. We held discourse of a perfumed ass, that,
being disguised with a lion's case, imagined himself a
lion. I hope that touched not you.

Bus. So, sir; your descants do marvelous well fit this
ground;[54] we shall meet where your buffoonly laughters
will cost ye the best blood in your bodies.   201

Bar. For life's sake, let's be gone; he'll kill's outright.

Bus. Go at your pleasures, I'll be your ghost to haunt
you; and[55] ye sleep on't, hang me.

L'An. Go, go, sir; court your mistress.

Pyr. And be advised; we shall have odds against you.

Bus. Tush, valor stands not in number! I'll maintain
it that one man may beat three boys.

Bris. Nay, you shall have no odds of him in number,
sir; he's a gentleman as good as the proudest of you,
and ye shall not wrong him.   211

Bar. Not, sir?

Mel. Not, sir: though he be not so rich, he's a better
man than the best of you; and I will not endure it.

L'An. Not you, sir?

Bris. No, sir, nor I.

Bus. I should thank you for this kindness, if I thought
these perfumed musk-cats,[56] being out of this privilege,[57] durst but once mew at us.

---

[36] *servants:* lovers.
[37] *presence:* of royalty, fighting being forbidden at Court.
[38] *rush:* matting for the floor (in lieu of the modern carpeting).
[39] *divers:* as substantive—the seabed and the environing shores.
[40] *mate:* alluding to the game of chess going forward, and to the Guise's discomfiture.
[41] *cock:* of whom the lion was proverbially afraid.
[42] *jigs:* not simply dances but farcical skits employing song and dance and concluding a play or presented in the interval.
[43] *trow:* think you.
[44] *denizened:* naturalized—another jibe at the King's creation of an instant nobility.   [45] *mercer's:* silk dealer's.
[46] *conceit:* "fixed imagination."
[47] *case:* habit, skin—alluding to Aesop's fable of the ass who dressed himself as a lion.
[48] *blanket:* in which Bussy will be tossed.
[49] *carry it clean:* get the better of him.
[50] *curvets:* leaps (metaphor from horsemanship).
[51] *fleerings:* mocks and grimaces.
[52] *jealousy:* suspiciousness.   [53] *close:* secret.
[54] *descants . . . ground:* comments . . . matter (Bussy's
clothing; also the presence chamber, which inhibits him from
punishing his mockers). Metaphor derives from music, the
"ground" signifying the melodic theme and the "descant"
the variations that embroider or accompany it.
[55] *and:* if.
[56] *musk-cats:* whose sexual organs were the source of
perfume.   [57] *this privilege:* the Court.

Bar. Does your confident spirit doubt that, sir?
Come follow us and try.   221
  L'An. Come, sir, we'll lead you a dance.

                                          Exeunt.

ACT TWO

SCENE ONE

HENRY, GUISE, BEAUMOND, NUNTIUS.[1]

Hen. This desperate quarrel sprung out of their
    envies
To D'Ambois' sudden bravery,[2] and great spirit.
  Guise. Neither is worth their envy.
  Hen.   Less than either
Will make the gall of Envy overflow;
She feeds on outcast entrails like a kite;[3]
In which foul heap, if any ill lies hid,
She sticks her beak into it, shakes it up,
And hurls it all abroad, that all may view it.
Corruption is her nutriment; but touch her
With any precious ointment, and you kill her: 10
When she finds any filth in men, she feasts,
And with her black throat bruits[4] it through the world,
Being[5] sound and healthful; but if she but taste
The slenderest pittance of commended virtue,
She surfeits of it, and is like a fly
That passes all the body's soundest parts,
And dwells upon the sores; or if her squint eye
Have power to find none there, she forges some.
She makes that crooked ever which is straight;
Calls valor giddiness, justice tyranny;   20
A wise man may shun her, she not herself:
Whithersoever she flies from her harms,
She bears her foe still clasped in her own arms;
And therefore, cousin Guise, let us avoid her.

NUNTIUS [*comes forward*].

Nunt. What Atlas or Olympus lifts his head
So far past covert,[6] that with air enough
My words may be informed,[7] and from his height

II.i.
  [1] *Nuntius:* Messenger, whose function is to relate what is
not shown and who was familiar from medieval drama and
from the tragedies of Seneca. Since the Nuntius does not
speak until later in the scene, one may imagine him as
occupying at first a retired position on stage.
  [2] *bravery:* of dress more than conduct.
  [3] *kite:* scavenger bird.   [4] *bruits:* noises.
  [5] *Being:* As being (i.e., the filth).   [6] *covert:* hiding.
  [7] *informed:* given form.   [8] *event:* the issue.
  [9] *bonfires . . . wood:* i.e., serving to inflame one another.
  [10] *Pyrrho's:* alluding to the Greek philosopher whose name
has become proverbial for skepticism.
  [11] *Spartan King:* Menelaus, with whom Paris proposed to
settle the Trojan War in single combat. Homer (and Chapman in his *Iliads*, III. 83) relates the story.
  [12] *advised:* having taken thought.
  [13] *Ripped up:* Brought to discussion (but, as the metaphor
is pursued, by interposing his rapier).
  [14] *conclude:* finish, by taking the quarrel on themselves.
  [15] *Approve:* Prove.   [16] *spritely:* spiritedly.

I may been seen and heard through all the world?
A tale so worthy, and so fraught with wonder
Sticks in my jaws, and labors with event.[8]   30
  Hen. Comest thou from D'Ambois?
  Nunt.   From him, and
    the rest,
His friends and enemies, whose stern fight I saw,
And heard their words before and in the fray.
  Hen. Relate at large what thou has seen and heard.
  Nunt. I saw fierce D'Ambois and his two brave
    friends
Enter the field, and at their heels their foes,
Which were the famous soldiers, Barrisor,
L'Anou, and Pyrhot, great in deeds of arms.
All which arrived at the evenest piece of earth
The field afforded, the three challengers   40
Turned head, drew all their rapiers, and stood ranked,
When face to face the three defendants met them,
Alike prepared, and resolute alike,
Like bonfires of contributory wood.[9]
Every man's look showed, fed with either's spirit,
As one had been a mirror to another,
Like forms of life and death; each took from other;
And so were life and death mixed at their heights,
That you could see no fear of death, for life,
Nor love of life, for death; but in their brows   50
Pyrrho's[10] opinion in great letters shone,
That life and death in all respects are one.
  Hen. Passed there no sort of words at their
    encounter?
  Nunt. As Hector, 'twixt the hosts of Greece and
    Troy,
When Paris and the Spartan King[11] should end
The nine years' war, held up his brazen lance
For signal that both hosts should cease from arms
And hear him speak; so Barrisor, advised,[12]
Advanced his naked rapier 'twixt both sides,
Ripped up[13] the quarrel, and compared six lives   60
Then laid in balance with six idle words;
Offered remission and contrition too;
Or else that he and D'Ambois might conclude[14]
The others' dangers. D'Ambois liked the last;
But Barrisor's friends, being equally engaged
In the main quarrel, never would expose
His life alone to that they all deserved.
And—for the other offer of remission—
D'Ambois, that like a laurel put in fire
Sparkled and spit, did much much more than scorn   70
That his wrong should incense him so like chaff
To go so soon out, and like lighted paper
Approve[15] his spirit at once both fire and ashes;
So drew they lots, and in them Fates appointed
That Barrisor should fight with fiery D'Ambois,
Pyrhot with Melynell, with Brisac, L'Anou.
And then like flame and powder they commixed
So spritely[16] that I wished they had been spirits,
That the ne'er-shutting wounds they needs must open
Might, as they opened, shut and never kill.   80
But D'Ambois' sword, that lightened as it flew,
Shot like a pointed comet at the face
Of manly Barrisor, and there it stuck.

Thrice plucked he at it, and thrice drew on thrusts
From him that of himself was free as fire;
Who thrust still as he plucked, yet (past belief!)
He with his subtle eye, hand, body, scaped;
At last, the deadly-bitten point tugged off,
On fell his yet undaunted foe so fiercely
That,[17] only made more horrid with his wound,   90
Great D'Ambois shrunk, and gave a little ground;
But soon returned, redoubled[18] in his danger,
And at the heart of Barrisor sealed[19] his anger.
Then, as in Arden I have seen an oak
Long shook with tempests, and his lofty top
Bent to his root, which being at length made loose,
Even groaning with his weight, he 'gan to nod
This way and that, as loath his curlèd brows,
Which he had oft wrapped in the sky with storms,
Should stoop; and yet, his radical[20] fibers burst,   100
Stormlike he fell, and hid the fear-cold earth:
So fell stout Barrisor, that had stood the shocks
Of ten set battles in your highness' war
'Gainst the sole soldier of the world, Navarre.[21]
   Guise. Oh, piteous and horrid murder!
   Beau.   Such a life
Methinks had metal in it to survive
An age of men.
   Hen.   Such often soonest end.
—Thy felt[22] report calls on;[23] we long to know
On what events the other have arrived.
   Nun. Sorrow and fury, like two opposite fumes[24]
Met in the upper region of a cloud,   111
At the report made by this worthy's fall
Brake from the earth, and with them rose revenge,
Entering with fresh powers his two noble friends;
And under that odds fell surcharged[25] Brisac,
The friend of D'Ambois, before fierce L'Anou;
Which D'Ambois seeing, as I once did see,
In my young travels through Armenia,
An angry unicorn in his full career
Charge with too quick an eye a jeweler,   120
That watched him for the treasure of his brow,[26]
And ere he could get shelter of a tree,[27]
Nail him with his rich antler to the earth:
So D'Ambois ran upon revenged L'Anou,
Who, eyeing th' eager point borne in his face,
And giving back, fell back, and in his fall
His foe's uncurbèd sword stopped in his heart:
By which time all the life-strings of the tw'other
Were cut, and both fell as their spirits flew
Upwards, and still hunt honor at the view.[28]   130
And now, of all the six, sole D'Ambois stood.
Untouched, save only with the others' blood.
   Hen. All slain outright?
   Nun.   All slain outright but he,
Who, kneeling in the warm life of his friends,
All feebled with the blood his rapier rained,
He kissed their pale cheeks, and bade both farewell—
And see the bravest man the French earth bears.

   Enter MONSIUER, D'AMBOIS *bare.*[29]

   Bus. Now is the time; y'are princely vowed, my
   friend;

Perform it princely, and obtain my pardon.
   Mons. Else heaven forgive not me; come on, brave
   friend.

           [They kneel before HENRY.]

If ever Nature held herself her own,   141
When the great trial of a king and subject
Met in one blood, both from one belly springing,
Now prove her virtue and her greatness one,
Or make the t'one the greater with the t'other,
As true kings should, and for your brother's love,
Which is a special species of true virtue,
Do that[30] you could not do, not being a king.
   Hen. Brother, I know your suit; these willful
   murders
Are ever past our pardon.
   Mons.   Manly slaughter   150
Should never bear th'account of willful murder;
It being a spice[31] of justice, where with life
Offending past law equal life is laid
In equal balance, to scourge that offense
By law of reputation, which to men
Exceeds all positive law, and what that leaves
To true men's valors, not prefixing[32] rights
Of satisfaction suited to their wrongs,
A free man's eminence may supply and take.
   Hen. This would make every man that thinks him
   wronged   160
Or is offended, or in wrong or right,
Lay on this violence; and all vaunt themselves
Law-menders and suppliers, though mere butchers;
Should this fact, though of justice, be forgiven?
   Mons. Oh, no, my lord; it would make cowards fear
To touch the reputations of full[33] men;
When only they are left to imp[34] the law,
Justice will soon distinguish murderous minds
From just revengers: had my friend been slain,
His enemy surviving, he should die,   170
Since he had added to a murdered fame,
Which was in his intent, a murdered man;
And this had worthily been willful murder;
But my friend only saved his fame's dear life,
Which is above life, taking th'under value,[35]

---

  [17] *That:* That he (Barrisor).
  [18] *redoubled:* repeating a blow.
  [19] *sealed:* consummated (as when wax is affixed to the
finished document).   [20] *radical:* root.
  [21] *Navarre:* the Protestant champion, subsequently (on his
conversion to Catholicism) King Henry IV of France.
  [22] *felt:* moving.   [23] *on:* for more.
  [24] *fumes:* exhalations from the earth that, on escaping from
a cloud, were understood to cause thunder.
  [25] *surcharged:* overloaded; hence, "beaten down."
  [26] *treasure . . . brow:* the fabled unicorn's horn, which,
powdered, was understood to possess magical qualities.
  [27] *tree:* into which, as contemporary emblem literature
attested, the unicorn drove his horn and was impaled.
  [28] *hunt . . . view:* pursue the sighted quarry (honor), like
hunting dogs.
  [29] *bare:* uncovered, in token of the royal presence.
  [30] *that:* i.e., grant pardon.   [31] *spice:* sort, species.
  [32] *prefixing:* establishing beforehand.
  [33] *full:* complete, as opposed to "cowards."
  [34] *imp:* piece out.   [35] *under value:* mere physical life.

Which, in the wrong it did, was forfeit to him;
And in this fact only preserves a man
In his uprightness, worthy to survive
Millions of such as murder men alive.[36]

Hen. Well, brother, rise, and raise your friend
    withal[37]   180
From death to life; and, D'Ambois, let your life,
Refined by passing through this merited death,
Be purged from more such foul pollution;
Nor on your scape,[38] nor valor, more presuming
To be again so violent.

Bus.   My lord,
I loathe as much a deed of unjust death,
As law itself doth; and to tyrannize,
Because I have a little spirit to dare
And power to do, as to be tyrannized.
This is a grace that, on my knees redoubled,[39]   190
I crave to double this my short life's gift,
And shall your royal bounty centuple,[40]
That I may so make good what God and Nature
Have given me for my good: since I am free,
Offending no just law, let no law make
By any wrong it does, my life her slave:
When I am wronged, and that law fails to right me,
Let me be king myself, as man was made,
And do a justice that exceeds the law;
If my wrong pass the power of single valor   200
To right and expiate, then be you my king,
And do a right, exceeding Law and Nature.
Who to himself is law, no law doth need,
Offends no king, and is a king indeed.

Hen. Enjoy what thou entreatest; we give but ours.

Bus. What you have given, my lord, is ever yours.
        Exit KING, BEAUMOND, *and* Attendants.

Guise. Mort Dieu, who would have pardoned such a
    murder?
                                              Exit.

Mons. Now vanish horrors into court attractions,
For which let this balm make thee fresh and fair.

Bus. How shall I quite[41] your love?

Mons.   Be true to the end:
I have obtained a kingdom[42] with my friend.   211
                                         Exeunt.

---

[36] *murder . . . alive:* kill men's reputations while leaving
their bodies intact.   [37] *withal:* also.
   [38] *scape:* escape.   [39] *redoubled:* rekneeling.
   [40] *centuple:* increase a hundredfold.   [41] *quite:* repay.
   [42] *kingdom:* Henry's, which Monsieur intends to seize.
II.ii.
   [1] *still borne:* always tolerated (with pun on "stillborn,"
dead at birth).   [2] *sudden:* impetuous.
   [3] *his . . . conceit:* in him no proper opinion.
   [4] *welcome:* i.e., from him—he should have given admittance in himself to better manners.   [5] *sleight:* tricks.
   [6] *project:* variously glossed; "impudent" or like an alchemical (hence fraudulent) projector who affects to transmute base metals into gold (picking up "test") in the next
line and referring to Bussy's new garments.
   [7] *late exceptions:* recent objections.   [8] *stand:* endure.
   [9] *manly:* after the fashion of men.   [10] *it:* the law.
   [11] *as:* as if.   [12] *her superficies:* the surface of the earth.
   [13] *his:* the fume's.   [14] *bars:* hindrances.
   [15] *engines:* instruments.

[II.ii]

[*Enter*] MONTSURRY, TAMYRA, BEAUPRÉ,
    PERO[*with a book*], CHARLOTTE, PYRHA.

Mont. He will have pardon sure.

Tam.   'Twere pity else;
For though his great spirit something overflow,
All faults are still borne[1] that from greatness grow.
But such a sudden[2] courtier saw I never.

Beau. He was too sudden, which indeed was
    rudeness.

Tam. True, for it argued his no due conceit[3]
Both of the place and greatness of the persons,
Nor of our sex; all which—we all being strangers
To his encounter—should have made more manners
Deserve more welcome.[4]

Mont.   All this fault is found   10
Because he loved the duchess and left you.

Tam. Alas, love give her joy. I am so far
From envy of her honor that I swear,
Had he encountered me with such proud sleight,[5]
I would have put that project[6] face of his
To a more test than did her duchess-ship.

Beau. Why, by your leave, my lord, I'll speak it here,
Although she be my aunt, she scarce was modest,
When she perceived the duke her husband take
Those late exceptions[7] to her servant's courtship,   20
To entertain him.

Tam.   Ay, and stand[8] him still,
Letting her husband give her servant place.
Though he did manly,[9] she should be a woman.

                     Enter GUISE.

Guise. D'Ambois is pardoned! Where's a king?
    Where law?
See how it[10] runs, much like a turbulent sea;
Here high and glorious, as[11] it did contend
To wash the heavens and make the stars more pure;
And here so low, it leaves the mud of hell
To every common view. Come, Count Montsurry,
We must consult of this.

Tam.   Stay not, sweet lord.   30

Mont. Be pleased, I'll straight return.
                               Exit with GUISE.

Tam.   Would that
    would please me.

Beau. I'll leave you, madam, to your passions.
I see there's change of weather in your looks.
   [*Exit with* CHARLOTTE *and* PYRHA. PERO *remains*
                                 reading her book.]

Tam. I cannot cloak it; but as when a fume,
Hot, dry and gross, within the womb of earth
Or in her superficies[12] begot,
When extreme cold hath struck it to her heart,
The more it is compressed, the more it rageth,
Exceeds his[13] prison's strength that should contain it,
And then it tosseth temples in the air,   40
All bars[14] made engines[15] to his insolent fury;
So, of a sudden, my licentious fancy
Riots within me. Not my name and house
Nor my religion to this hour observed

Can stand above it; I must utter that
That will in parting break more strings in me
Than death when life parts; and that holy man
That, from my cradle, counseled for my soul,
I now must make an agent for my blood.   49

Enter MONSIEUR.

  Mons. Yet is my mistress gracious?
  Tam.   Yet unanswered?
  Mons. Pray thee regard thine own good, if not mine,
And cheer my love for that; you do not know
What you may be by me, nor what without me;
I may have power t'advance and pull down any.
  Tam. That's not my study; one way I am sure
You shall not pull down [16] me; my husband's height
Is crown to all my hopes; and his retiring
To any mean state shall be my aspiring.
Mine honor's in mine own hands, spite of kings.
  Mons. Honor, what's that? Your second maidenhead.
And what is that? A word; the word is gone,   61
The thing remains; the rose is plucked, the stalk
Abides; an easy loss where no lack's found.
Believe it, there's as small lack in the loss
As there is pain i'th' losing. Archers ever
Have two strings to a bow; and shall great Cupid,
Archer of archers both in men and women,
Be worse provided than a common archer?
A husband and a friend [17] all wise wives have.
  Tam. Wise wives they are that on such strings
          depend,   70
With a firm [18] husband weighing a dissolute friend.
  Mons. Still you stand on your husband; so do all
The common sex of you, when y'are encountered
With one ye cannot fancy: all men know
You live in court here by your own election,
Frequenting all our solemn sports and triumphs,
All the most youthful company of men.
And wherefore do you this? To please your husband?
'Tis gross and fulsome; [19] if your husband's pleasure
Be all your object, and you aim at honor   80
In living close to him, get you from court;
You may have him at home; these common put-offs
For common women serve. "My honor! Husband!"
Dames maritorious [20] ne'er were meritorious: [21]
Speak plain, and say "I do not like you, sir;
Y'are an ill-favored fellow in my eye,"
And I am answered.
  Tam.   Then, I pray, be answered.
For, in good faith, my lord, I do not like you
In that sort you like.
  Mons.   Then have at you here!
Take with a politic hand this rope of pearl,   90
And, though you be not amorous, yet be wise.
Take me for wisdom; he that you can love
Is ne'er the further from you.
  Tam.   Now it [22] comes
So ill prepared, that I may take a poison
Under a medicine as good cheap as it;
I will not have it were it worth the world.
  Mons. Horror of death! Could I but please your
     eye,

You would give me the like, ere you loose me.
"Honor and husband!"
  Tam.   By this light, my lord,
Y'are a vile fellow, and I'll tell the King   100
Your occupation of dishonoring ladies,
And of his court: a lady cannot live
As she was born, and with that sort of pleasure
That fits her state, but she must be defamed
With an infamous lord's detraction.
Who would endure the court if these attempts
Of open and professed lust must be borne?—
Who's there? [*To* PERO] Come on, dame, you are at
     your book
When men are at your mistress; have I taught you
Any such waiting-woman's quality?   110
  Mons. Farewell, "good husband!"
                          Exit MONSIEUR.
  Tam.   Farewell, wicked
     lord!

Enter MONTSURRY.

  Mont. Was not the Monsieur here?
  Tam.   Yes, to good
     purpose;
And your cause is as good to seek him too,
And haunt his company.
  Mont.   Why, what's the matter?
  Tam. Matter of death, were I some husband's
     wife. [23]
I cannot live at quiet in my chamber
For opportunities [24] almost to rapes
Offered me by him.
  Mont.   Pray thee bear with him:
Thou know'st he is a bachelor and a courtier,
Ay, and a prince; and their prerogatives   120
Are to [25] their laws, as to [26] their pardons are
Their reservations, after parliaments—
One quits another: [27] form [28] gives all their essence.
That prince doth high in virtue's reckoning stand
That will entreat a vice, and not command.
So far bear with him; should another man
Trust to his privilege, he should trust to death.
Take comfort, then, my comfort, nay, triumph
And crown thyself; thou partest with victory.
My presence is so clearly dear to thee   130
That other men's appear worse than they be.
For this night yet, bear with my forced absence;

---

[16] *pull down:* with sexual innuendo.   [17] *friend:* lover.
[18] *firm:* perhaps with suggestion of sexual capacity.
[19] *fulsome:* disgusting.
[20] *maritorious:* doting on one's husband.
[21] *meritorious:* in conventional sense; also designating a
prostitute's ability to earn money.
[22] *it:* presumably the rope of pearls, which, dissolved, were
used medicinally: here, a fatal medicine.
[23] *Matter . . . wife:* If I were married to a different husband, he would seek to kill Monsieur.
[24] *opportunities:* importunities.   [25] *Are to:* Are(?).
[26] *as to:* as(?).
[27] *Their . . . another:* They issue pardons with reservation
aforethought, revoking them when Parliament is no longer
sitting(?). One action cancels the other.
[28] *form:* what they are on the surface.

Thou knowest my business, and with how much weight
My vow hath charged [29] it.
    Tam.   True, my lord, and never
My fruitless love shall let [30] your serious profit;
Yet, sweet lord, do not stay; [31] you know my soul
Is so long time without me, [32] and I dead
As you are absent.
    Mont.   By this kiss, receive
My soul for hostage, till I see my love.
    Tam. The morn shall let me see you?
    Mont.   With the sun
I'll visit thy more comfortable beauties.   141
    Tam. This is my comfort, that the sun hath left
The whole world's beauty ere my sun leaves me.
    Mont. 'Tis late night now, indeed; farewell, my
    light.
                               Exit.

    Tam. Farewell, my light and life. But not in him,
In mine own dark love and light bent to another. [33]
Alas, that in the wave [34] of our affections
We should supply it with a full dissembling,
In which each youngest maid is grown a mother. [35]
Frailty is fruitful, one sin gets [36] another: 150
Our loves like sparkles are, that brightest shine
When they go out; most vice shows most divine.
—Go, maid, to bed; lend me your book, I pray—
Not, like yourself, for form; [37] I'll this night trouble
None of your services: make sure the doors,
And call your other fellows to their rest.
    Pero. I will. [*Aside*] Yet I will watch to know why
    you watch.
                               Exit.

    Tam. Now all the peaceful regents of the night,
Silently gliding exhalations,
Languishing winds, and murmuring falls of waters,
Sadness of heart and ominous secureness, [38]   161
Enchantments, dead sleeps, all the friends of rest
That ever wrought upon the life of man,
Extend your utmost strengths, and this charmed hour
Fix like the center! [39] Make the violent wheels
Of Time and Fortune stand, and great existence,
The Maker's treasury, now not seem to be,
To all but my approaching friends and me!
They come, alas, they come! fear, fear and hope
Of one thing, at one instant, fight in me.   170

---

[29] *charged:* loaded.   [30] *let:* hinder.
[31] *stay:* i.e., away.
[32] *so . . . me:* absent from my body for so long as you are
away.   [33] *In . . . another:* from Q1641.
[34] *wave:* wavering (though emendation to "wane" is perhaps indicated).
[35] *grown a mother:* already fully accomplished or matured.
[36] *gets:* begets.
[37] *form:* outward pretense of reading.
[38] *secureness:* false security.   [39] *center:* of the earth.
[40] *color:* pretense.
[41] *first orb: primum mobile,* which, in the Ptolemaic system,
enclosed and gave motion to the other spheres encircling the
earth.   [42] *set:* fixed.
[43] *dispersed:* rumored abroad.   [44] *resolve:* explain to.
[45] *presumèd:* presumptuous.
[46] *confirmation:* letter written.
[47] *circumstantial:* roundabout.

I love what most I loathe, and cannot live
Unless I compass that that holds my death.
For love is hateful without love again,
And he I love will loathe me, when he sees
I fly my sex, my virtue, my renown,
To run so madly on a man unknown.

                            The vault opens.

See, see, the gulf is opening that will swallow
Me and my fame for ever; I will in,
And cast myself off, as I ne'er had been.
                               Exit.

FRIAR *and* D'AMBOIS *ascend.*

    Fri. Come, worthiest son, I am past measure glad
That you, whose worth I have approved so long,   181
Should be the object of her fearful love;
Since both your wit and spirit can adapt
Their full force to supply her utmost weakness.
You know her worths and virtues, for report
Of all that know is to a man a knowledge.
You know, besides, that our affections' storm,
Raised in our blood, no reason can reform.
Though she seek then their satisfaction,
Which she must needs, or rest unsatisfied,   190
Your judgment will esteem her peace thus wrought
Nothing less dear than if yourself had sought;
And with another color, [40] which my art
Shall teach you to lay on, yourself must seem
The only agent, and the first orb [41] move
In this our set [42] and cunning world of love.
    Bus. Give me the color, my most honored father,
And trust my cunning then to lay it on.
    Fri. 'Tis this, good son; Lord Barrisor, whom you
    slew,
Did love her dearly, and with all fit means   200
Hath urged his acceptation, of all which
She keeps one letter written in his blood.
You must say thus, then, that you heard from me
How much herself was touched in conscience
With a report—which is, in truth, dispersed [43]—
That your main quarrel grew about her love,
Lord Barrisor imagining your courtship
Of the great Guise's duchess, in the presence,
Was by you made to his elected mistress;
And so made me your mean now to resolve [44] her,   210
Choosing by my direction this night's depth
For the more clear avoiding of all note
Of your presumèd [45] presence; and with this,
To clear her hands of such a lover's blood,
She will so kindly thank and entertain you,
Methinks I see how—ay, and ten to one,
Show you the confirmation [46] in his blood,
Lest you should think report and she did feign,
That you shall so have circumstantial [47] means
To come to the direct, which must be used;   220
For the direct is crooked; love comes flying;
The height of love is still won with denying.
    Bus. Thanks, honored father.
    Fri.   She must never know
That you know anything of any love

Sustained on her part; for, learn this of me,
In anything a woman does alone,
If she dissemble, she thinks 'tis not done;
If not[48] dissemble, nor a little chide,
Give her her wish, she is not satisfied;
To have a man think that she never seeks   230
Does her more good than to have all she likes;
This frailty sticks in them beyond their sex,
Which to reform, reason is too perplex.[49]
Urge reason to them, it will do no good;
Humor,[50] that is the chariot of our food
In everybody, must in them be fed,
To carry their affections by it bred.
Stand close!

Enter TAMYRA *with a book.*

  Tam. Alas, I fear my strangeness[51] will retire him.
If he go back, I die; I must prevent it,   240
And cheer his onset with my sight at least,
And that's the most; though every step he takes
Goes to my heart, I'll rather die than seem
Not to be strange to that I most esteem.
  Fri. Madam!
  Tam.   Ah!
  Fri.   You will pardon me, I hope,
That so beyond your expectation
And at a time for visitants so unfit
I, with my noble friend here, visit you.
You know that my access at any time
Hath ever been admitted; and that friend   250
That my care will presume to bring with me
Shall have all circumstance of worth in him
To merit as free welcome as myself.
  Tam. Oh, father, but at this suspicious hour
You know how apt best men are to suspect us
In any cause that makes suspicious shadow
No greater than the shadow of a hair;
And y'are to blame. What though my lord and husband
Lie forth tonight, and since I cannot sleep
When he is absent I sit up tonight;   260
Though all the doors are sure, and all our servants
As sure bound with their sleeps; yet there is One
That sits above, whose eye no sleep can bind;
He sees through doors, and darkness, and our thoughts;
And therefore as we should avoid with fear
To think amiss ourselves before his search,
So should we be as curious[52] to shun
All cause that other think not ill of us.
  Bus. Madam, 'tis far from that; I only heard
By this my honored father that your conscience   270
Was something troubled with a false report
That Barrisor's blood should something touch your
     hand,
Since he imagined I was courting you,
When I was bold to change words with the duchess,
And therefore made his quarrel, which my presence,
Presumed on with[53] my father at this season
For the more care of so curious honor,
Can well resolve your conscience is most false.
  Tam. And is it therefore that you come, good sir?
Then crave I now your pardon and my father's,   280

And swear your presence does me so much comfort,
That all I have it binds to your requital.
Indeed, sir, 'tis most true that a report
Is spread, alleging that his love to me
Was reason of your quarrel; and because
You shall not think I feign it for my glory
That he importuned me for his court service,[54]
I'll show you his hand, set down in blood,
To that vain purpose. Good sir, then come in.
Father, I thank you now a thousandfold.   290
               Exit TAMYRA *and* D'AMBOIS.
  Fri. May it be worth it to you, honored daughter.
                    The FRIAR *descends.*

ACT THREE

SCENE ONE

Enter D'AMBOIS, TAMYRA.

  Tam. Oh, my dear servant, in thy close embraces
I have set open all the doors of danger
To my encompassed[1] honor, and my life.
Before, I was secure against death and hell,
But now am subject to the heartless[2] fear
Of every shadow, and of every breath,
And would change firmness with an aspen leaf.
So confident a spotless conscience is,
So weak a guilty: oh, the dangerous siege
Sin lays about us, and the tyranny   10
He exercises when he hath expunged![3]
Like to the horror of a winter's thunder,
Mixed with a gushing storm, that suffer nothing
To stir abroad on earth but their own rages,
Is Sin, when it hath gathered head[4] above us:
No roof, no shelter can secure us so,
But he will drown our cheeks in fear or woe.
  Bus. Sin is a coward, madam, and insults[5]
But[6] on our weakness, in his truest valor,
And so our ignorance tames us, that we let   20
His shadows fright us; and like empty clouds,
In which our faulty apprehensions[7] forge
The forms of dragons, lions, elephants,
When they hold no proportion,[8] the sly charms
Of the witch Policy makes him like a monster
Kept only to show men for servile[9] money.
That false hag often paints him in her cloth[10]

---

  [48] *If not:* If she does not.   [49] *perplex:* involved.
  [50] *Humor:* The four bodily fluids that, according to the
dominant medical tradition, determine one's nature or disposition are here seen as governing absolutely.
  [51] *strangeness:* coolness.   [52] *curious:* careful.
  [53] *with:* in concert with.
  [54] *for . . . service:* to fulfill his role as courtly lover.

III.i.
  [1] *encompassed:* beleaguered.   [2] *heartless:* craven.
  [3] *expunged:* conquered.   [4] *head:* power.
  [5] *insults:* triumphs.   [6] *But:* Only.
  [7] *apprehensions:* understandings.
  [8] *proportion:* resemblance.
  [9] *servile:* from Q1641; Q1607 reads "goddess."
  [10] *cloth:* painted cloth with which rooms were hung.

Ten times more monstrous than he is in troth.
In three of us the secret of our meeting
Is only guarded, and three friends as one   30
Have ever been esteemed, as our three powers
That in our one soul are as one united.[11]
Why should we fear, then? For my truth, I swear,
Sooner shall torture be the sire to pleasure,
And health be grievous to men long time sick,
Than the dear jewel of your fame in me
Be made an outcast to your infamy;
Nor shall my value, sacred to your virtues,
Only give free course to it from myself,[12]
But make it fly out of the mouths of kings   40
In golden vapors and with awful[13] wings.
    Tam. It rests as[14] all kings' seals were set in thee.

       Exit D'AMBOIS. TAMYRA *remains.*

It is not I but urgent destiny,
That—as great statesmen for their general end
In politic justice, make poor men offend—
Enforceth my offense to make it just.
What shall weak dames do, when th' whole work of
    nature
Hath a strong finger in each one of us?
Needs must that[15] sweep away the silly cobweb
Of our still-undone labors;[16] that lays still   50
Our powers to it,[17] as to the line the stone,
Not to the stone the line should be opposed.[18]
We cannot keep our constant course in virtue.
What is alike at all parts? Every day
Differs from other, every hour and minute;
Ay, every thought in our false clock of life
Oftimes inverts the whole circumference.[19]
We must be sometimes one, sometimes another.
Our bodies are but thick clouds to our souls,
Through which they cannot shine when they desire.
When all the stars, and even the sun himself,   61
Must stay[20] the vapors' times that he exhales[21]
Before he can make good his beams to us,
Oh, how can we, that are but motes to him,
Wandering at random in his ordered rays,

---

  [11] *three . . . united:* alluding to the rational (human), sensible (animal), and vegetable (plant) souls that unite in man.
  [12] *Only . . . myself:* Give free course to it from myself alone.   [13] *awful:* inspiring awe.
  [14] *It rests as:* The secret remains as inviolable as if.
  [15] *that:* the "strong finger." A vigorous sexual innuendo is almost necessarily indicated.
  [16] *labors:* i.e., our efforts to be virtuous.
  [17] *that . . . it:* natural inclination is omnipotent and bids us "go to it."
  [18] *the . . . opposed:* i.e., in a building, it is the plumb line (analogous to natural inclination) that governs the laying of the stones, rather than the stones the position of the line.
  [19] *inverts . . . circumference:* turns the hands of the clock counterclockwise, thus belying the face or "circumference" that should tell the time aright.   [20] *stay:* wait on.
  [21] *exhales:* sucks up (from the earth).
  [22] *ready:* dressed.   [23] *fantasy:* whimsy.
  [24] *liberally:* freely.
  [25] *Atlas:* who, for supporting the Titans in their war against Jove, was compelled to bear the heavens on his shoulders.
III.ii.
  [1] *truss:* seize.

Disperse our passions' fumes with our weak labors,
That are more thick and black than all earth's vapors?

       Enter MONTSURRY.

    Mont. Good day, my love! What, up and ready,[22]
    too!
    Tam. Both, my dear lord; not all this night made I
Myself unready, or could sleep a wink.   70
    Mont. Alas, what troubled my true love, my peace,
From being at peace within her better self?
Or how could sleep forbear to seize thy beauties
When he might challenge them as his just prize?
    Tam. I am in no power earthly, but in yours;
To what end should I go to bed, my lord,
That wholly missed the comfort of my bed?
Or how should sleep possess my faculties,
Wanting the proper closer of mine eyes?
    Mont. Then will I never more sleep night from thee.
All mine own business, all the King's affairs,   81
Shall take the day to serve them; every night
I'll ever dedicate to thy delight.
    Tam. Nay, good my lord, esteem not my desires
Such doters on their humors that my judgment
Cannot subdue them to your worthier pleasure.
A wife's pleased husband must her object be
In all her acts, not her soothed fantasy.[23]
    Mont. Then come, my love, now pay those rites to
    sleep
Thy fair eyes owe him; shall we now to bed?   90
    Tam. Oh, no, my lord; your holy friar says
All couplings in the day that touch the bed
Adulterous are, even in the married;
Whose grave and worthy doctrine, well I know,
Your faith in him will liberally[24] allow.
    Mont. He's a most learned and religious man;
Come to the presence then, and see great D'Ambois,
Fortune's proud mushroom shot up in a night,
Stand like an Atlas[25] underneath the King;
Which greatness with him Monsieur now envies   100
As bitterly and deadly as the Guise.
    Tam. What! He that was but yesterday his maker,
His raiser, and preserver?
    Mont.   Even the same.
Each natural agent works but to this end,
To render that it works on like itself;
Which since the Monsieur in his act on D'Ambois
Cannot to his ambitious end effect,
But that, quite opposite, the King hath power,
In his love borne to D'Ambois, to convert
The point of Monsieur's aim on his own breast,   110
He turns his outward love to inward hate.
A prince's love is like the lightning's fume,
Which no man can embrace but must consume.

                       Exeunt.

[III.ii]

HENRY, D'AMBOIS, MONSIEUR, GUISE,
DUCHESS, ANNABEL, Attendants.

    Hen. Speak home, my Bussy! Thy impartial words
Are like brave falcons that dare truss[1] a fowl

Much greater than themselves; flatterers are kites
That check at nothing; [2] thou shalt be my eagle,
And bear my thunder underneath thy wings;
Truth's words, like jewels, hang in th' ears of kings.

   Bus. Would I might live to see no Jews hang there
Instead of jewels—sycophants, I mean,
Who use truth like the Devil, his true foe,
Cast by the angel to the pit of fears,   10
And bound in chains; truth seldom decks kings' ears.
Slave Flattery, like a rippier's [3] legs rolled up
In boots of hay-ropes, [4] with kings' soothèd [5] guts
Swaddled and strappled, [6] now lives only free.
Oh, 'tis a subtle knave; how like the plague
Unfelt he strikes into the brain of truth,
And rageth in his entrails when he can,
Worse than the poison of a red-haired [7] man.

   Hen. Fly at him and his brood! I cast thee off, [8]
And once more give thee surname of mine eagle.   20

   Bus. I'll make you sport enough, then. Let me have
My lucerns [9] too, or dogs inured [10] to hunt
Beasts of most rapine, but to put them up, [11]
And if I truss not, let me not be trusted.
Show me a great man by the people's voice,
Which is the voice of God, that by his greatness
Bombasts [12] his private roofs with public riches;
That affects [13] royalty, rising from a clapdish; [14]
That rules so much more than his suffering [15] king,
That he makes kings of his subordinate slaves: 30
Himself and them graduate [16]—like woodmongers,
Piling a stack of billets [17]—from the earth,
Raising each other into steeples' heights;
Let him convey [18] this on the turning props [19]
Of Protean [20] law, and, his own counsel keeping, [21]
Keep all upright [22]—let me but hawk at him,
I'll play the vulture, and so thump his liver, [23]
That, like a huge unlading argosy, [24]
He shall confess all, and you then may hang him.
Show me a clergyman, that is in voice   40
A lark of heaven, in heart a mole of earth;
That hath good living, and a wicked life;
A temperate look, and a luxurious gut;
Turning the rents of his superfluous cures [25]
Into your pheasants and your partridges,
Venting their quintessence as men read Hebrew [26]—
Let me but hawk at him, and, like the other,
He shall confess all, and you then may hang him.
Show me a lawyer that turns sacred law—
The equal [27] renderer of each man his own,   50
The scourge of rapine and extortion,
The sanctuary and impregnable defense
Of retired learning and oppressèd virtue—
Into a harpy, [28] that eats all but's own,
Into the damned sins it punisheth,
Into the synagogue of thieves and atheists,
Blood into gold, and justice into lust—
Let me but hawk at him, as at the t'other,
He shall confess all, and you then may hang him.

   Enter MONTSURRY, TAMYRA, *and* PERO.

   Guise. Where will you find such game as you would
    hawk at?   60

   Bus. I'll hawk about your house for one of them.

   Guise. Come, y'are a glorious [29] ruffian, and run
    proud [30]
Of [31] the King's headlong [32] graces; hold your breath,
Or, by that poisoned vapor, not the King
Shall back your murderous valor against me.

   Bus. I would the King would make his presence free
But for one charge [33] betwixt us: by the reverence
Due to the sacred space 'twixt kings and subjects,
Here would I make thee cast that popular purple, [34]
In which thy proud soul sits and braves [35] thy
    Sovereign.   70

   Mons. Peace, peace, I pray thee peace.

   Bus.   Let him peace
    first
That made the first war.

   Mons.   He's the better man.

   Bus. And, therefore, may do worst?

   Mons.   He has more
    titles.

   Bus. So Hydra [36] had more heads.

   Mons.   He's greater
    known.

   Bus. His greatness is the people's; mine's mine own.

   Mons. He's nobly born.

   Bus.   He is not; I am noble.

---

   [2] *check at nothing:* for no reason turn from their quarry to pursue less dangerous prey (metaphor from hawking).
   [3] *rippier's:* fishmonger's.
   [4] *hay-ropes:* in lieu of more substantial boots.
   [5] *soothèd:* flattered.   [6] *strappled:* covered.
   [7] *red-haired:* emblematic of a traitor: like the archtraitor Judas.   [8] *cast thee off:* release thee for flight.
   [9] *lucerns:* lynxes, or perhaps hunting dogs.
   [10] *inured:* accustomed.
   [11] *but . . . up:* only to start them from cover.
   [12] *Bombasts:* Stuffs out.   [13] *affects:* pretends to.
   [14] *clapdish:* beggar's dish.
   [15] *suffering:* in the primary sense of one who suffers; but also one who gives license to the behavior described.
   [16] *graduate:* rising by degrees, making a hierarchy.
   [17] *billets:* timber.
   [18] *convey:* carry; with secondary sense of "steal."
   [19] *props:* wheels (as of the woodmonger's cart, but also suggesting fortune's wheel).
   [20] *Protean:* endlessly mutable, after Proteus, the old man of the sea, who could change his shape at will.
   [21] *his . . . keeping:* maintaining a discreet silence.
   [22] *upright:* i.e., the stack of billets and hence, metaphorically, the specious hierarchy he has constructed; but suggesting also the maintaining of a good face on things.
   [23] *liver:* recalling Prometheus, whose liver was eaten by a vulture sent in punishment from Jove.
   [24] *unlading argosy:* unloading merchant vessel.
   [25] *cures:* parishes or benefices from which he collected income but which he did not himself serve.
   [26] *as . . . Hebrew:* i.e., backward.
   [27] *equal:* impartial.
   [28] *harpy:* fabulous winged monster with a woman's face and body, and cited here for its rapacity and filth—like a kite.
   [29] *glorious:* boastful.
   [30] *run proud:* are proud; and with secondary meaning of "are in heat."   [31] *Of:* On account of.
   [32] *headlong:* rash.   [33] *charge:* encounter.
   [34] *popular purple:* regal dress worn by the Guise to impress the populace.   [35] *braves:* defies.
   [36] *Hydra:* the many-headed monster slain by Hercules.

And noblesse in his [37] blood hath no gradation, [38]
But in his merit. [39]
   Guise.   Th'art not nobly born,
But bastard to the Cardinal of Ambois.
   Bus. Thou liest, proud Guiserd; let me fly, my lord.
   Hen. Not in my face, my eagle; violence flies   81
The sanctuaries of a prince's eyes.
   Bus. Still shall we chide and foam upon this bit? [40]
Is the Guise only great in faction? [41]
Stands he not by himself? Proves he th'opinion
That men's souls are without them? [42] Be a duke,
And lead me to the field.
   Guise.   Come, follow me.
   Hen. Stay them! Stay, D'Ambois! Cousin Guise, I
     wonder
Your equal [43] disposition brooks so ill
A man so good, that only would uphold   90
Man in his native noblesse, from whose fall
All our dissensions rise; that in himself,
Without the outward patches of our frailty,
Riches and honor, knows he comprehends [44]
Worth with the greatest: kings had never borne
Such boundless eminence over other men
Had all maintained the spirit and state of D'Ambois;
Nor had the full impartial hand of Nature
That all things gave in her original, [45]
Without these definite terms of mine and thine,   100
Been turned [46] unjustly to the hand of fortune,
Had all preserved her in her prime, like D'Ambois;
No envy, no disjunction had dissolved,
Or plucked out one stick of the golden faggot [47]

---

[37] *his:* its.   [38] *gradation:* hierarchical ranking.
[39] *But . . . merit:* Only intrinsic worth confers noblesse—
a popular topos or proverbial formulation.   [40] *bit:* curb.
[41] *in faction:* by virtue of his supporters; also, equating
"faction" and "treason."
[42] *without them:* only appurtenances, like the Guise's regal
dress.   [43] *equal:* equable.
[44] *comprehends:* contains within himself.
[45] *her original:* the beginning.   [46] *turned:* converted.
[47] *faggot: fasces,* or bundle of sticks indissolubly bound
and so suggesting concord.
[48] *world of Saturn:* the Golden Age.
[49] *ingenuous:* naturally noble.
[50] *Hermean rod:* Caduceus, the wing-topped staff with
two snakes curled around it, symbolic of peace, carried by
Hermes, messenger of the gods.
[51] *motion:* proposal.   [52] *deprave:* vilify.
[53] *rack:* torture.
[54] *Juno:* who engendered the giant Typhon.
[55] *ordnance:* thunderbolt, with which Typhon was struck
down by Jove and buried subsequently under Mt. Etna.
[56] *implied:* employed.   [57] *cast:* calculate.
[58] *gadding:* rambling.
[59] *rising:* with a pun on tumescence, suggested by "falls"
in the preceding line.
[60] *make . . . advantage:* commit follies and so play into
their enemies' hands.
[61] *women . . . candles:* Though women are inferior, they
give direction to men (with an implicit identification of
"candles" and "penises").
[62] *women:* servants, like Tamyra's maid, Pero.
[63] *charmed:* i.e., with bribes.   [64] *close:* secret.
[65] *most . . . chase:* the hart.   [66] *piece:* gun.
[67] *beat his vault:* clear away rivals from his rutting-place or
thicket.   [68] *venery:* rutting, sexual sport.

In which the world of Saturn [48] was comprised,
Had all been held together with the nerves,
The genius, and th' ingenuous [49] soul of D'Ambois.
Let my hand therefore be the Hermean rod [50]
To part and reconcile, and so conserve you,
As my combined embracers and supporters.   110
   Bus. 'Tis our King's motion, [51] and we shall not
     seem
To worst eyes womanish, though we change thus soon
Never so great grudge for his greater pleasure.
   Guise. I seal to that, and so the manly freedom
That you so much profess, hereafter prove not
A bold and glorious license to deprave, [52]
To me his hand shall prove the Hermean rod
His grace affects, in which submissive sign
On this his sacred right hand I lay mine.
   Bus. 'Tis well, my lord, and so your worthy
     greatness   120
Engender not the greater insolence,
Nor make you think it a prerogative
To rack [53] men's freedoms with the ruder wrongs,
My hand, stuck full of laurel, in true sign
'Tis wholly dedicate to righteous peace,
In all submission kisseth th' other side.
   Hen. Thanks to ye both; and kindly I invite ye
Both to a banquet, where we'll sacrifice
Full cups to confirmation of your loves;
At which, fair ladies, I entreat your presence.   130
          Exeunt HENRY, D'AMBOIS, Ladies.
   Mons. What had my bounty drunk when it raised
     him?
   Guise. Y'ave stuck us up a very proper flag,
That takes more wind than we with all our sails.
   Mons. Oh, so he spreads and flourishes.
   Guise.   He must
     down,
Upstarts should never perch too near a crown.
   Mons. 'Tis true, my lord; and as this doting hand,
Even out of earth, like Juno, [54] struck this giant,
So Jove's great ordnance [55] shall be here implied [56]
To strike him under th' Etna of his pride:
To which work lend your hands, and let us cast [57]   140
Where we may set snares for his gadding [58] greatness.
I think it best, amongst our greatest women;
For there is no such trap to catch an upstart
As a loose downfall; and indeed their falls
Are th' ends of all men's rising: [59] if great men
And wise make scapes to please advantage [60]
'Tis with a woman: women, that worst may,
Still hold men's candles: [61] they direct and know
All things amiss in all men, and their women [62]
All things amiss in them; through whose charmed [63]
     mouths   150
We may see all the close [64] scapes of the court.
When the most royal beast of chase, [65] being old
And cunning in his choice of lairs and haunts,
Can never be discovered to the bow,
The piece [66] or hound, yet where his custom is
To beat his vault, [67] and he ruts with his hind,
The place is marked, and by his venery [68]
He still is taken. Shall we then attempt

The chiefest mean to that discovery here,
And court our greatest ladies' greatest women   160
With shows of love and liberal promises?
'Tis but our breath. If something given in hand
Sharpen their hopes of more, 'twill be well ventured.
    Guise. No doubt of that; and 'tis an excellent point
Of our devised investigation.
    Mons. I have already broke the ice, my lord,
With the most trusted woman of your countess,
And hope I shall wade through to our discovery.
    Mont. Take say[69] of her, my lord, she comes most
        fitly,
And we will to the other.

        Enter CHARLOTTE, ANNABEL, PERO.

    Guise.   Y'are engaged.[70]   170
    Ann. Nay, pray, my lord, forbear.
    Mont. What, skittish, servant?
    Ann. No, my lord, I am not so fit for your service.
    Char. Pray pardon me now, my lord; my lady expects
me.
    Guise. I'll satisfy her expectation, as far as an uncle
may.
    Mons. Well said, a spirit of courtship of[71] all hands!
now, mine own Pero, hast thou remembered me for the
discovery I entreated thee to make concerning thy   180
mistress? Speak boldly, and be sure of all things I have
promised.
    Pero. Building on that you have sworn, my lord, I
may speak; and much the rather, because my lady
hath not trusted me with that I can tell you; for now I
cannot be said to betray her.
    Mons. That's all one, so it be not to one that will
betray thee; forth, I beseech thee.
    Pero. To tell you truth, my lord, I have made a
strange discovery.   190
    Mons. Excellent Pero, thou revivest me; may I sink
quick[72] into earth here if my tongue discover it.
    Pero. 'Tis thus, then: this last night, my lord lay
forth, and I, wondering my lady's sitting up, stole at
midnight from my pallet, and, having before made a
hole both through the wall and arras to her inmost
chamber, I saw D'Ambois and she set close at a banquet.
    Mons. D'Ambois?
    Pero. Even he, my lord.
    Mons. Dost thou not dream, wench?   200
    Pero. No, my lord, he is the man.
    Mons. The devil he is, and thy lady his dam:[73]
infinite regions betwixt a woman's tongue and her
heart! Is this our goddess of chastity? I thought I could
not be so slighted, if she had not her freight[74] besides,
and therefore plotted this with her woman. Dear Pero,
I will advance thee forever; but tell me now—God's
precious, it transforms me with admiration[75]—sweet
Pero, whom should she trust with his conveyance?[76]
Or, all the doors being made sure, how could his conveyance be performed?   211
    Pero. Nay, my lord, that amazes me; I cannot by
any study so much as guess at it.
    Mons. Well, let's favor our apprehensions[77] with for-
bearing that a little; for, if my heart were not hooped

with adamant, the conceit[78] of this would have burst it.
But hark thee.

                                    Whispers [*to* PERO].

    Char. I swear to your grace, all that I can conjecture
touching my Lady your niece is a strong affection she
bears to the English Milor.   220
    Guise. All, quod you?[79] 'Tis enough, I assure you,
but tell me.

                                            [*Whispers.*]

    Mont. I pray thee, resolve me: the duke will never
imagine that I am busy about's wife. Hath D'Ambois
any privy access to her?
    Ann. No, my lord; D'Ambois neglects her, as she
takes it, and is therefore suspicious that either your
countess, or the Lady Beaupré,[80] hath closely entertained him.   229
    Mont. By'r lady, a likely suspicion, and very near the
life, if she marks it—especially of my wife.
    Mons. [*aside to* PERO] Come, we'll put off[81] all with
seeming only to have courted.—Away, dry palm![82]
Sh'as a liver[83] as hard as a biscuit; a man may go a
whole voyage with her, and get nothing but tempests at
her windpipe.
    Guise. Here's one, I think, has swallowed a porcu-
pine, she casts pricks from her tongue so.
    Mont. And here's a peacock seems to have devoured
one of the Alps, she has so swelling a spirit, and is so
cold of her kindness.   241
    Char. We be no windfalls, my lord; ye must gather
us with the ladder of matrimony, or we'll hang till we
be rotten.
    Mons. Indeed, that's the way to make ye right open-
arses.[84] But, alas, ye have no portions fit for such
husbands as we wish you.
    Pero. Portions, my lord? Yes, and such portions as
your principality cannot purchase.
    Mons. What, woman, what are those portions?   250
    Pero. Riddle my riddle, my lord.
    Mons. Ay, marry, wench, I think thy portion is a
right riddle; a man shall never find it out. But let's hear
it.
    Pero. You shall, my lord.

    What's that, that being most rare's most cheap?
    That if you sow, you never reap?
    That when it grows most, most you in it;
    And still you lose it when you win it?

---

  ⁶⁹ *Take say:* Make assay (trial).
  ⁷⁰ *engaged:* caught.   ⁷¹ *of:* on.
  ⁷² *quick:* alive.   ⁷³ *his dam:* the devil's wife.
  ⁷⁴ *freight:* cargo (with obscene innuendo).
  ⁷⁵ *admiration:* wonder.
  ⁷⁶ *his conveyance:* bringing him to her.
  ⁷⁷ *favor our apprehensions:* give our thinking a rest.
  ⁷⁸ *conceit:* thought.   ⁷⁹ *quod you:* do you say.
  ⁸⁰ *countess ... Beaupré:* Q1607 transposes the titles,
making Beaupré a countess.   ⁸¹ *put off:* disguise.
  ⁸² *dry palm:* emblematic of chastity.
  ⁸³ *liver:* the seat of passion.
  ⁸⁴ *open-arses:* medlars. See I. ii. n.24.

That when 'tis commonest, 'tis dearest,   260
And when 'tis farthest off, 'tis nearest?

Mons. Is this your portion?

Pero. Even this, my lord.

Mons. Believe me, I cannot riddle it.

Pero. No, my lord: 'tis my chastity, which you shall
neither riddle[85] nor fiddle.

Mons. Your chastity? Let me begin with the end of
you; how is a woman's chastity nearest a man 'tis
farthest off?   269

Pero. Why, my lord, when you cannot get it, it goes
to th' heart on you; and that, I think, comes most near
you; and I am sure it shall be far enough off; and so I
leave you to my mercy.

                                                    Exeunt Women.

Mons. Farewell, riddle!

Guise. Farewell, medlar!

Mont. Farewell, winter plum![86]

Mons. Now, my lords, what fruit of our inquisition?
Feel you nothing budding yet? Speak, good my Lord
Montsurry.   279

Mont. Nothing but this: D'Ambois is negligent in
observing the duchess, and therefore she is suspicious
that your niece or my wife closely entertains him.

Mons. Your wife, my lord? Think you that
possible?

Mont. Alas, I know she flies him like her last hour.

Mons. Her last hour? Why, that comes upon her the
more she flies it. Does D'Ambois so,[87] think you?

Mont. That's not worth the answering. 'Tis horrible
to think with what monsters women's imaginations
engross[88] them when they are once enamored,   290
and what wonders they will work for their satisfaction
They will make a sheep valiant, a lion fearful.

---

[85] *riddle:* i.e., violate.

[86] *winter plum:* cold and late ripening; hence, opposed to
"medlar."   [87] *Does . . . so:* Come upon her.

[88] *engross:* preoccupy; coarsen; swell.

[89] *unsounded:* deeper than plummet sounds or fathoms.

[90] *Scylla and Charybdis:* the rock and whirlpool between
which Ulysses had to sail.

[91] *monster-formèd clouds:* The image is of imposture. Perhaps Chapman is thinking of the cloud made to resemble
Hera, whose rape Ixion attempted, begetting on the cloud
the monstrous Centaur.

[92] *no statesman:* not even a statesman or corrupt politician.

[93] *Cerberus:* the three-headed dog who guarded the por-
tals of Hades.

[94] *Sybilla's cave:* proverbial for a den of prophecy.

[95] *resemble:* liken.

[96] *circle:* which the conjuror drew about him and within
which he stood to protect himself from the devil he had
raised.

[97] *what leapest thou at?:* The answer is implicit in what
follows: Bussy, imagining a crown in the air, seeks to pluck
it down.

[98] *Titan:* Hyperion, the last of the Titans, who occupied
the "chair" or chariot of the sun until displaced by Apollo.

[99] *Impale:* Surround.

[100] *retired:* private, self-communing.

[101] *still:* continually.   [102] *will not:* i.e., doubt.

[103] *if . . . wise:* they do not think themselves wise men
unless they are told flattering lies (made fools of).

[104] *this:* i.e., bargain in addition.

[105] *prove we:* though we prove.   [106] *live:* let us live.

Mons. And an ass confident, my lord, 'tis true, and
more will come forth shortly; get you to the banquet.

                                      Exit GUISE *and* MONTSURRY.

Oh, the unsounded[89] sea of women's bloods,
That when 'tis calmest, is most dangerous!
Not any wrinkle creaming in their faces,
When in their hearts are Scylla and Charybdis,[90]
Which still are hid in monster-formèd clouds,[91]
Where never day shines, nothing ever grows   300
But weeds and poisons that no statesman[92] knows.
Not Cerberus[93] ever saw the damnèd nooks
Hid with the veil of women's virtuous looks.
I will conceal all yet, and give more time
To D'Ambois' trial, now upon my hook;
He awes my throat, else like Sybilla's cave[94]
It should breathe oracles; I fear him strangely,
And may resemble[95] his advancèd valor
Unto a spirit raised without a circle,[96]
Endangering him that ignorantly raised him,   310
And for whose fury he hath learned no limit.

                                      Enter D'AMBOIS.

How now, what leapest thou at?[97]

Bus.   O royal object!

Mons. Thou dreamest awake; object in th'empty
    air?

Bus. Worthy the head of Titan,[98] worth his chair.

Mons. Pray thee, what meanest thou?

Bus.   See you not a
    crown
Impale[99] the forehead of the great King Monsieur?

Mons. Oh, fie upon thee!

Bus.   Sir, that is the subject
Of all these your retired[100] and sole discourses.

Mons. Wilt thou not leave that wrongful supposition?
This still[101] hath made me doubt thou dost not love me.
Wilt thou do one thing for me then sincerely?   321

Bus. Ay, anything, but killing of the King.

Mons. Still in that discord, and ill-taken note?

Bus. Come, do not doubt me, and command me all
    things.

Mons. I will not,[102] then; and now by all my love
Shown to thy virtues, and by all fruits else
Already sprung from that affection,
I charge thee utter, even with all the freedom
Both of thy noble nature and thy friendship,
The full and plain state of me in thy thoughts.   330

Bus. What, utter plainly what I think of you?
Why, this swims quite against the stream of greatness;
Great men would rather hear their flatteries,
And, if they be not made fools, are not wise.[103]

Mons. I am no such great fool, and therefore charge
    thee
Even from the root of thy free heart, display me.

Bus. Since you affect it in such serious terms,
If yourself first will tell me what you think
As freely and as heartily of me,
I'll be as open in my thoughts of you.   340

Mons. A bargain, of mine honor! And make this,[104]
That prove we[105] in our full dissection
Never so foul, live[106] still the sounder friends.

Bus. What else, sir? Come, begin, and speak me
　　simply.[107]
　Mons. I will, I swear. I think thee then a man
That dares as much as a wild horse or tiger,
As headstrong and as bloody; and to feed
The ravenous wolf of thy most cannibal valor,
Rather than not employ it, thou wouldst turn
Hackster[108] to any whore, slave to a Jew,　　　　　350
Or English usurer, to force possessions,
And cut men's throats of[109] mortgagèd estates;
Or thou wouldst tire[110] thee like a tinker's wife
And murder market-folks; quarrel with sheep,[111]
And run as mad as Ajax; serve a butcher;
Do anything but killing of the King:
That in thy valor th'art like other naturals[112]
That have strange gifts in nature, but no soul
Diffused quite through, to make them of a piece,
But stop at humors,[113] that are more absurd,　　　360
Childish, and villainous than that hackster, whore,
Slave, cutthroat, tinker's bitch, compared before;
And in those humors wouldst envy, betray,
Slander, blaspheme, change each hour a religion,
Do anything, but killing of the King:
That in that valor—which is still my dunghill
To which I carry all filth in thy house—
Th'art more ridiculous and vainglorious
Than any mountebank, and impudent
Than any painted bawd; which not to soothe,　　370
And glorify thee like a Jupiter Hammon,[114]
Thou eatest thy heart in vinegar, and thy gall
Turns all thy blood to poison, which is cause
Of that toad pool[115] that stands in thy complexion,
And makes thee, with a cold and earthy moisture,
Which is the dam of putrefaction,
As plague to thy damned pride, rot as thou livest,
To study calumnies and treacheries,
To thy friends' slaughters like a screech-owl[116] sing,
And to all mischiefs, but to kill the King.　　　　380
　Bus. So! have you said?
　Mons.　　　　　　　How thinkest thou? Do I
flatter?
Speak I not like a trusty friend to thee?
　Bus. That ever any man was blessed withal;
So here's for me! I think you are at worst
No devil, since y'are like to be no king;
Of which, with any friend of yours I'll lay
This poor stillado[117] here, 'gainst all the stars,
Ay, and 'gainst all your treacheries, which are more,
That you did never good, but to do ill;
But ill of all sorts, free and for itself;　　　　　390
That—like a murdering piece,[118] making lanes in
　armies,
The first man of a rank, the whole rank falling—
If you have wronged one man, y'are so far
From making him amends, that all his race,
Friends, and associates fall into your chase:
That y'are for perjuries the very prince
Of all intelligencers;[119] and your voice
Is like an eastern wind, that, where it flies,
Knits nets of caterpillars, with which you catch
The prime of all the fruits the kingdom yields;　　400

That your political[120] head is the cursèd fount
Of all the violence, rapine, cruelty,
Tyranny, and atheism flowing through the realm:
That y'ave a tongue so scandalous, 'twill cut
A perfect crystal; and a breath that will
Kill to[121] that wall a spider; you will jest
With God, and your soul to the devil tender
For lust; kiss horror, and with death engender;
That your foul body is a Lernean fen[122]
Of all the maladies breeding in all men;　　　　410
That you are utterly without a soul;
And, for your life, the thread of that was spun
When Clotho slept, and let her breathing rock
Fall in the dirt; and Lachesis[123] still draws it,
Dipping her twisting fingers in a bowl
Defiled, and crowned with virtue's forcèd soul;
And lastly, which I must for gratitude
Ever remember, that of all my height[124]
And dearest life are the only spring,
Only in royal hope to kill the King.　　　　　420
　Mons. Why, now I see thou lovest me; come to the
　banquet.

　　　　　　　　　　　　　　　　　Exeunt.

ACT FOUR

SCENE ONE

HENRY, MONSIEUR *with a letter*, GUISE,
MONTSURRY, BUSSY, ELENOR, TAMYRA,
BEAUPRÉ, PERO, CHARLOTTE, ANNABEL,
PYRHA, *with four* Pages.

Hen. Ladies, ye have not done our banquet right,
Nor looked upon it with those cheerful rays
That lately turned your breaths to floods of gold;
Your looks, methinks, are not drawn out with thoughts
So clear and free as heretofore, but fare

---

[107] *simply:* truly.
[108] *Hackster:* Cutthroat serving as bodyguard.
[109] *of:* over.　　　　　　　　　　　[110] *tire:* dress.
[111] *quarrel with sheep:* like the maddened Ajax, who
thought himself attacking the Greeks.
[112] *naturals:* idiots.
[113] *stop at humors:* The idiot is freakish as the four humors
are not nicely or precisely mixed in him and as each expresses
itself independently or radically.
[114] *Jupiter Hammon:* or "Ammon," an oracle, whose testimony would presumably comfort the listener.
[115] *toad pool:* stagnant pond.
[116] *screech-owl:* portending death.
[117] *stillado:* stiletto(?) (*OED* cites only this one usage, and
queries it).　　　　　　　　　　[118] *piece:* cannon.
[119] *intelligencers:* spies.
[120] *political:* polite (pejorative).　　[121] *to:* as far as.
[122] *Lernean fen:* the swamp where the Hydra lived.
[123] *Clotho . . . Lachesis:* who, with Atropos, comprised the
three Fates or Furies who governed the span of life. Here,
Clotho drops her life-giving ("breathing") distaff ("rock"),
and Lachesis, whose office is to draw out the thread, makes
it even dirtier by steeping it in a bowl brimming ("crowned")
with vice (virtue violated or "forcèd").
[124] *height:* advancement.

As if the thick[1] complexions of men
Governed within them.
    Bus.   'Tis not like, my lord,
That men in women rule, but contrary;
For as the moon of all things God created
Not only is the most appropriate image   10
Or glass to show them how they wax and wane,
But in her light and motion likewise bears
Imperial influences that command
In all their powers, and make them[2] wax and wane;
So women, that of all things made of nothing
Are the most perfect images of the moon,
Or still-unweaned[3] sweet mooncalves[4] with white faces,
Not only are patterns of change to men,
But, as the tender moonshine of their beauties
Clears or is cloudy, make men glad or sad.   20
    Mons. But here the moons are changed, as the King
      notes,
And either men rule in them, or some power
Beyond their voluntary motions,
For nothing can recover their lost faces.
    Bus. None can be always one. Our griefs and joys
Hold several[5] scepters in us, and have times
For their predominance, which grief now in them
Doth claim as proper to his diadem.
And grief's a natural sickness of the blood,
That time to part asks, as his coming had;   30
Only slight fools, grieved, suddenly are glad;
A man may say t' a dead man, "Be revived,"
As well as to one sorrowful, "Be not grieved."
[*To the* Duchess] And therefore, princely mistress, in
    all wars
Against these base foes that insult on weakness,
And still fight housed behind the shield of nature,
Of tyrannous law, treachery, or beastly need,
Your servant cannot help; authority here
Goes with corruption, something like some states
That back worst men: valor to them must creep   40
That, to themselves left, would fear him asleep.
    Duch. Ye all take that for granted that doth rest[6]
Yet to be proved; we all are as we were,
As merry and as free in thought as ever.

IV.i.
    [1] *thick:* cloudy.
    [2] *them:* women (who are governed by the moon as well as being an epitome of it).
    [3] *unweaned:* immature; still sucking at the teat.
    [4] *mooncalves:* children of the moon—"lunatics."
    [5] *several:* separate.   [6] *rest:* remain.
    [7] *Additions:* Titles.   [8] *learns:* teaches.
    [9] *high forms:* dunces' chairs.
    [10] *liver:* the seat of love; but also with a suggestion of Prometheus, whose liver was preyed on by an "eagle's (vulture's) beak" (III. ii, n. 23).   [11] *nice:* finicking.
    [12] *Horns:* signalizing his cuckolding.
    [13] *armed:* with horns.
    [14] *enchanted . . . cockscombs:* occult sacrifices in which fowls whose heads have been uncovered were burned; also, literally, the combs of cocks, which figured in the ceremonials of witchcraft.
    [15] *crooked hams:* bent knees, denoting the sycophant (who is also denoted by the doffing of the hat—"bare").
    [16] *box-tree:* low and tough.   [17] *stilled:* distilled.

    Guise. And why then can ye not disclose your
      thoughts?
    Tam. Methinks the man hath answered for us well.
    Mons. The man? Why, madam, d'ye not know his
      name?
    Tam. Man is a name of honor for a king:
Additions[7] take away from each chief thing.
The school of modesty not to learn learns[8] dames.   50
They sit in high forms[9] there, that know men's names.
    Mons. Hark, sweetheart, here's a bound set to your
      valor!
It cannot enter here, no, not to notice
Of what your name is; your great eagle's beak,
Should you fly at her, had as good encounter
An Albion cliff, as her more craggy liver.[10]
    Bus. I'll not attempt her, sir; her sight and name,
By which I only know her, doth deter me.
    Hen. So they do all men else.
    Mons.   You would say so
If you knew all.
    Tam.   Knew all, my lord? What mean you?
    Mons. All that I know, madam.
    Tam.   That you know?
    Speak it.   61
    Mons. No, 'tis enough I feel it.
    Hen.   But, methinks
Her courtship is more than heretofore;
True courtiers should be modest, but not nice,[11]
Bold, but not impudent, pleasure love, not vice.
    Mons. Sweetheart, come hither! what if one should
      make
Horns[12] at Montsurry? Would it strike him jealous
Through all the proofs of his chaste lady's virtues?
    Bus. No, I think not.
    Mons.   Not if I named the man   70
With whom I would make him suspicious
His wife hath armed[13] his forehead?
    Bus.   So you might
Have your great nose made less indeed, and slit,
Your eyes thrust out.
    Mons.   Peace, peace, I pray thee, peace.
Who dares do that? The brother of his king?
    Bus. Were your king brother in you; all your
      powers,
Stretched in the arms of great men and their bawds,
Set close down by you; all your stormy laws
Spouted with lawyers' mouths, and gushing blood,
Like to so many torrents; all your glories,
Making you terrible, like enchanted flames   80
Fed with bare cockscombs[14] and with crooked hams;[15]
All your prerogatives, your shames and tortures;
All daring heaven, and opening hell about you—
Were I the man ye wronged so and provoked,
Though ne'er so much beneath you, like a box-tree[16]
I would, out of the toughness of my root,
Ram hardness in my lowness and, like death
Mounted on earthquakes, I would trot through all
Honors and horrors; through foul and fair,
And from your whole strength toss you into air.   90
    Mons. Go, th'art a devil! Such another spirit
Could not be stilled[17] from all th' Armenian dragons.

O my love's glory, heir to all I have,
—That's all I can say, and that all I swear—
If thou outlive me, as I know thou must,
Or else hath Nature no proportioned end [18]
To her great labors; she hath breathed a spirit
Into thy entrails, of effect to swell
Into another great Augustus Caesar,
Organs and faculties fitted to her greatness;   100
And should that perish like a common spirit,
Nature's a courtier and regards no merit.

   Hen. Here's nought but whispering with us; like a
    calm
Before a tempest, when the silent air
Lays her soft ear close to the earth to hearken
For that she fears is coming to afflict her;
Some fate doth join [19] our ears to hear it coming.
Come, my brave eagle, let's to covert fly;
I see almighty Aether [20] in the smoke   110
Of all his clouds descending, and the sky
Hid in the dim ostents [21] of tragedy.

          Exit HENRY *with* D'AMBOIS *and* Ladies.
   Guise. [*Aside to* MONSIEUR] Now stir the humor,
    and begin the brawl. [22]
   Mont. The King and D'Ambois now are grown all
    one.

        [MONSIEUR *makes horns at* MONTSURRY]

   Mons. Nay, they are two, my lord.
   Mont.   How's that?
   Mons.   No more.
   Mont. I must have more, my lord.
   Mons.   What, more than
    two?
   Mont. How monstrous is this!
   Mons.   Why?
   Mont.   You make me
    horns!
   Mons. Not I, it is a work without my power;
Married men's ensigns [23] are not made with fingers;
Of divine fabric they are, not men's hands;
Your wife, you know, is a mere [24] Cynthia; [25]   120
And she must fashion horns out of her nature.
   Mont. But doth she? Dare you charge her? Speak,
    false prince.
   Mons. I must not speak, my lord; but if you'll use
The learning of a nobleman, and read,
Here's something to [26] those points; soft, you must
    pawn
Your honor, having read it, to return it.

          Enter TAMYRA, PERO.

   Mont. Not I! I pawn mine honor for a paper?
   Mons. You must not buy it under.
          Exeunt GUISE *and* MONSIEUR.
   Mont.   Keep it then,
And keep fire in your bosom.
   Tam.   What says he?
   Mont. You must make good the rest.
   Tam.   How fares my
    lord?   130
Takes my love anything to heart he says?

   Mont. Come, y'are a—
   Tam.   What, my lord?
   Mont.   The plague
    of Herod [27]
Feast in his rotten entrails.
   Tam.   Will you wreak
Your anger's just cause given by him, on me?
   Mont. By him?
   Tam.   By him, my lord; I have admired [28]
You could all this time be at concord with him,
That still hath played such discords on your honor.
   Mont. Perhaps 'tis with some proud [29] string of my
    wife's.
   Tam. How's that, my lord?
   Mont.   Your tongue will still
    admire,
Till my head be the miracle of the world.   140
   Tam. Oh, woe is me!

               She seems to swound. [30]

   Pero.   What does your lordship
    mean?
Madam, be comforted; my lord but tries [31] you.
Madam! Help, good my lord, are you not moved?
Do your set [32] looks print in your words your thoughts?
Sweet lord, clear up those eyes, for shame of noblesse;
Merciless creature! But it is enough,
You have shot home, your words are in her heart;
She has not lived to bear a trial now.
   Mont. Look up, my love, and by this kiss receive
My soul amongst thy spirits, [33] for supply
To thine chased with my fury.
   Tam.   Oh, my lord,   151
I have too long lived to hear this from you.
   Mont. 'Twas from my troubled blood, and not from
    me.
—I know not how I fare; a sudden night
Flows through my entrails, aud a headlong chaos
Murmurs within me, which I must digest,
And not drown her in my confusions,
That was my life's joy, being best informed. [34]—
Sweet, you must needs forgive me, that my love,
Like to a fire disdaining his suppression,   160
Raged being discouraged; my whole heart is wounded
When any least thought in you is but touched,
And shall be till I know your former merits,

---

  [18] *proportioned end:* end proportionate.
  [19] *join:* enjoin.   [20] *Aether:* Jove.   [21] *ostents:* shows.
  [22] *brawl:* with secondary sense of "dance."
  [23] *ensigns:* emblems.   [24] *mere:* absolute.
  [25] *Cynthia:* Goddess of chastity and of the moon; hence
(below) her natural ability to "fashion horns."
  [26] *to:* appertaining to.   [27] *plague of Herod:* worms.
  [28] *admired:* wondered.
  [29] *proud:* signifying "in heat."   [30] *swound:* swoon.
  [31] *tries:* tests.
  [32] *set:* as by a compositor who sets type (anticipating
"print" in what follows).
  [33] *spirits:* vegetable, vital, and animal, which connected
body to soul and which could be transferred from one person
to another (like the debilitated Tamyra), as by a kiss.
  [34] *informed:* pervaded with form or harmony (when she
was his joy).

Your name and memory, altogether crave
In loathed oblivion their eternal grave;
And then, you must hear from me, there's no mean[35]
In any passion I shall feel for you;
Love is a razor cleansing, being well used,
But fetcheth blood still, being the least abused;
To tell you briefly all—the man that left me   170
When you appeared, did turn me worse than woman,
And stabbed me to the heart thus with his hand.

                    [*Makes horns*]

Tam. O happy woman! Comes my stain from him?
It[36] is my beauty, and that innocence proves
That slew Chimaera, rescued Peleus
From all the savage beasts in Pelion,
And raised the chaste Athenian prince from hell:[37]
All suffering with me, they for women's lusts,
I for a man's, that[38] the Augean stable[39]
Of his foul sin would empty in my lap.   180
How this guilt shunned me! Sacred Innocence,[40]
That where thou fearest art dreadful, and his face
Turned in flight from thee, that had thee in chase;
Come, bring me to him; I will tell the serpent
Even to his teeth[41] whence, in mine honor's soil,[42]
A pitched field starts up 'twixt my Lord and me,
That his throat lies, and he shall curse his fingers,[43]
For being so governed by his filthy soul.

Mont. I know not if himself will vaunt t'have been
The princely author of the slavish sin,
Or any other; he would have resolved me,   191
Had you not come, not by his word, but writing,
Would I have sworn to give it him again,
And pawned mine honor to him for a paper.

Tam. See how he flies me still! 'Tis a foul heart
That fears his own hand.[44] Good my lord, make haste
To see the dangerous paper; be not nice
For any trifle, jeweled with your honor,
To pawn your honor;[45] and with it confer[46]
My nearest woman here in all she knows,   200
Who, if the sun or Cerberus[47] could have seen
Any stain in me, might as much as they;
And, Pero, here I charge thee by my love,
And all proofs of it, which I might call bounties,
By all that thou hast seen seem good in me,
And all the ill which thou shouldst spit from thee,
By pity of the wound my lord hath given me,
Not as thy mistress now, but a poor woman,
To death given over, rid me of my pains;
Pour on thy powder;[48] clear thy breast of me.[49]   210
My lord is only here; here speak thy worst,
Thy best will do me mischief; if thou sparest me,
Never shine good thought on thy memory!
Resolve my lord, and leave me desperate.

Pero. My lord!—my lord hath played a prodigal's
        part,
To break his stock[50] for nothing; and an insolent,
To cut a Gordian[51] when he could not loose it:
What violence is this, to put true fire
To a false train,[52] to blow up long-crowned peace
With sudden outrage, and believe a man   220
Sworn to the shame of women, 'gainst a woman
Born to their honors!

                    [MONTSURRY *offers to go.*]

                    I'll attend your lordship.
Tam. No, I will write[53]—for I shall never more
Speak with the fugitive—where I will defy him,
Were he ten times the brother of my King.

                                        Exeunt.

[IV.ii]

Music. TAMYRA *enters with* PERO, *her maid,
        bearing a letter.*

Tam. Away, deliver it.
                                    Exit PERO.
                    Oh, may my lines,
Filled with the poison of a woman's hate,
When he shall open them, shrink up his eyes
With torturous darkness, such as stands in hell,
Stuck full of inward horrors, never lighted,
With which are all things to be feared, affrighted[1]

            BUSSY *ascends with the* FRIAR.

Father!
Bus. How is it with my honored mistress?

Tam. O servant, help, and save me from the gripes
Of shame and infamy.
    Bus.   What insensate stock[2]
Or rude[3] inanimate vapor without fashion,[4]   10
Durst take into his Epimethean[5] breast
A box of such plagues as the danger yields
Incurred in this discovery? He had better
Ventured his breast in the consuming reach
Of the hot surfeits[6] cast out of the clouds
Or stood the bullets that, to wreak[7] the sky,
The Cyclops[8] ram in Jove's artillery.
    Fri. We soon will take the darkness from his face
That did that deed of darkness; we will know
What now the Monsieur and your husband do,   20
What is contained in the secret paper
Offered by Monsieur, and your love's events.[9]
To which ends, honored daughter, at your motion,[10]
I have put on these exorcising rites,
And, by my power of learned holiness
Vouchsafed me from above, I will command
Our resolution of[11] a raisèd spirit.
    Tam. Good father, raise him in some beauteous form,
That with least terror I may brook his sight.
    Fri. Stand sure together, then, whate'er ye see,   30
And stir not, as ye tender[12] all our lives.

             He puts on his robes.

*Occidentalium legionum spiritualium imperator (magnus
ille Behemoth) veni, veni, comitatus cum Astaroth loco-
tenente invicto. Adjuro te per Stygis inscrutabilia arcana,
per ipsos irremeabiles anfractus Averni: adesto o Behemoth,
tu cui pervia sunt Magnatum scrinia; veni, per Noctis et
tenebrarum abdita profundissima; per labentia sidera; per
ipsos motus horarum furtivos, Hecatesque altum silentium!
Appare in forma spiritali, lucente, splendida et amabili.[13]*

         Thunder. [BEHEMOTH *rises. Enter*
     CARTOPHYLAX[14] *and other* Spirits.]

    Beh. What would the holy Friar?
    Fri.   I would see   40
What now the Monsieur and Montsurry do,
And see the secret paper that the Monsieur
Offered to Count Montsurry, longing much
To know on[15] what events the secret loves
Of these two honored persons shall arrive.
    Beh. Why calledst thou me to this accursèd light,
To these light purposes? I am Emperor
Of that inscrutable darkness where are hid
All deepest truths, and secrets never seen,
All which I know, and command legions   50
Of knowing spirits that can do more than these.
Any of this my guard that circle me
In these blue fires and out of whose dim fumes
Vast murmurs use[16] to break, and from their sounds
Articulate voices, can do ten parts more
Than open such slight truths as you require.
    Fri. From the last night's black depth I called up one
Of the inferior ablest ministers,
And he could not resolve me; send one then
Out of thine own command, to fetch the paper   60
That Monsieur hath to show to Count Montsurry.

    Beh. I will. Cartophylax, thou that properly
Hast in thy power all papers so inscribed,
Glide through all bars to it and fetch that paper.
    Cart. I will.

             A torch removes.[17]

    Fri.   Till he returns, great Prince of Darkness,
Tell me if Monsieur and the Count Montsurry
Are yet encountered.
    Beh.   Both them and the Guise
Are now together.
    Fri.   Show us all their persons,
And represent the place, with all their actions.
    Beh. The spirit will straight[18] return, and then I'll
     show thee.   70

             [*The torch returns.*]

See, he is come. Why broughtest thou not the paper?
    Cart. He hath prevented[19] me, and got a spirit
Raised by another great in our command,
To take the guard of it before I came.
    Beh. This is your slackness, not t' invoke our powers
When first your acts set forth to their effects;[20]
Yet shall you see it and themselves: behold
They come here, and the earl now holds the paper.

        Enter MONSIEUR, GUISE, MONTSURRY,
                with a paper.

    Bus. May we not hear them?
    Beh.[21]   No, be still and see.
    Bus. I will go fetch the paper.
    Fri.   Do not stir;   80
There's too much distance and too many locks
'Twixt you and them, how near soe'er they seem,
For any man to interrupt their secrets.
    Tam. O honored spirit, fly into the fancy[22]

---

    [2] *insensate stock:* unfeeling block.
    [3] *rude:* amorphous.   [4] *fashion:* form.
    [5] *Epimethean:* alluding to Epimetheus, the brother of
Prometheus, who opened Pandora's box of plagues.
    [6] *hot surfeits:* lightning.   [7] *wreak:* avenge.
    [8] *Cyclops:* one-eyed giants, who supplied Jove's artillery
with thunderbolts in his war against the Titans and his father
Chronos, who had previously overthrown his own father
Uranus, "the sky," who begot the Titans.
    [9] *events:* issue.   [10] *motion:* instance.
    [11] *resolution of:* answer from.   [12] *tender:* value.
    [13] *L.:* Emperor of the legions of western spirits (that great
Behemoth), come, come, accompanied by Astaroth, uncon-
quered lieutenant. I adjure you by the hidden mysteries of
Styx, by those untraceable windings of Avernus: be present,
O Behemoth, you to whom the cabinets of the Mighty are
open; come, by the deepest caves of Night and the shades;
by the wandering stars; by those stealthy motions of the
hours, and the deep silence of Hecate! Appear in spiritual
form, full of light, splendid and lovely.
    [14] *Cartophylax:* One who carries papers.   [15] *on:* to.
    [16] *use:* are wont.
    [17] *removes:* is taken away (denoting the departure of
Cartophylax and his "blue fires").
    [18] *straight:* immediately.   [19] *prevented:* anticipated.
    [20] *their effects:* achieve their purpose.
    [21] *Behemoth:* Early editions assign to Monsieur.
    [22] *fancy:* "fantasy"; intermediate in human beings be-
tween raw sensory perception and rational understanding.

Of my offended lord, and do not let him
Believe what there the wicked man hath written.
 Beh. Persuasion hath already entered him
Beyond reflection;[23] peace till their departure.
 Mons. There is a glass of ink[24] wherein you see
How to make ready black-faced tragedy.   90
You now discern, I hope, through all her paintings,
Her gasping wrinkles and fame's sepulchers.[25]
 Guise. Think you he feigns, my lord? What hold[26]
  you now?
Do we malign your wife, or honor you?
 Mons. What, stricken dumb! Nay, fie, lord, be not
  daunted;
Your case is common; were it ne'er so rare,
Bear it as rarely! Now to laugh were manly;
A worthy man should imitate the weather
That sings in tempests, and, being clear, is silent.
 Guise. Go home, my lord, and force your wife to
  write   100
Such loving stuff to D'Ambois as she used
When she desired his presence.
 Mons.   Do, my lord,
And make her name her concealed messenger,
That close and most inenarrable[27] pander,
That passeth all our studies to exquire;[28]
By whom convey the letter to her love;
And so you shall be sure to have him come
Within the thirsty reach of your revenge;
Before which, lodge an ambush in her chamber
Behind the arras, of your stoutest men   110
All close and soundly armed; and let them share
A spirit amongst them that would serve a thousand.

    Enter PERO *with a letter.*

 Guise. Yet stay a little; see, she sends for you.
 Mons. Poor, loving lady; she'll make all good yet,
Think you not so, my lord?

   MONTSURRY *stabs* PERO *and exit.*

 Guise.   Alas, poor soul!
 Mons. This was ill done, i' faith.
 Pero.   'Twas nobly done,
And I forgive his lordship from my soul.

---

 [23] *reflection:* turning back.
 [24] *glass of ink:* mirror—which is the writing.
 [25] *sepulchers:* tombs, in which her reputation ("fame") is
buried. [26] *hold:* believe. [27] *inenarrable:* indescribable.
 [28] *passeth . . . exquire:* surpasseth . . . discover.
 [29] *I . . . volume:* Q1641 clarifies the meaning: "I hope it
rather be a bitter volume," etc.   [30] *presently:* at once.
 [31] *clap:* blow; venereal disease. [32] *darkly:* obliquely.
 [33] *stay:* withhold; emended variously to "stain" or
"dye"): See V.ii.32. [34] *yourself:* i.e., remain untouched.
 [35] *but:* unless.
 [36] *And . . . policy:* Q1641 clarifies: "And curb his valor
with your policies."   [37] *revoke:* call back.
 [38] *abuse:* being abused by them.
 [39] *strow:* strew, cover over.
 [40] *at full date:* when time is ripe. [41] *kennel:* gutter.
 [42] *flanked:* outflanked (picking up the military metaphor
suggested by "close mines").
 [43] *feeling center:* conscious earth, seen as the "center" of
the Ptolemaic universe.

 Mons. Then much good do't thee, Pero! Hast a
  letter?
 Pero. I hope it be, at least, if not a volume[29]
Of worthy curses for your perjury.   120
 Mons. Now, out upon her.
 Guise.   Let me see, my lord,
 Mons. You shall presently.[30] How fares my
  Pero?
Who's there?

    Enter Servant.

    Take in this maid, sh'as caught a
  clap,[31]
And fetch my surgeon to her; come, my lord,
We'll now peruse our letter.
       Exeunt MONSIEUR, GUISE.
 Pero.   Furies rise
Out of the black lines, and torment his soul.
           Lead her out.
 Tam. Hath my lord slain my woman?
 Beh.   No, she lives.
 Fri. What shall become of us?
 Beh.   All I can say,
Being called thus late, is brief, and darkly,[32] this:
If D'Ambois' mistress stay[33] not her white hand 130
With his forced blood, he shall remain untouched;
So, father, shall yourself,[34] but[35] by yourself.
To make this augury plainer, when the voice
Of D'Ambois shall invoke me, I will rise,
Shining in greater light, and show him all
That will betide ye all; meantime, be wise,
And let him curb his rage with policy.[36]
       [*He descends with his spirits.*]
 Bus. Will he appear to me when I invoke him?
 Fri. He will, be sure.
 Bus.   It must be shortly then;
For his dark words have tied my thoughts on knots
Till he dissolve, and free them.
 Tam.   In meantime, 141
Dear servant, till your powerful voice revoke[37] him,
Be sure to use the policy he advised;
Lest fury in your too quick knowledge taken
Of our abuse,[38] and your defense of me,
Accuse me more than any enemy;
And, father, you must on my lord impose
Your holiest charges, and the Church's power
To temper his hot spirit and disperse
The cruelty and the blood I know his hand 150
Will shower upon our heads, if you put not
Your finger to the storm, and hold it up,
As my dear servant here must do with Monsieur.
 Bus. I'll soothe his plots, and strow[39] my hate with
  smiles,
Till all at once the close mines of my heart
Rise at full date,[40] and rush into his blood.
I'll bind his arm in silk, and rub his flesh
To make the vein swell, that his soul may gush
Into some kennel[41] where it longs to lie,
And policy shall be flanked[42] with policy. 160
Yet shall the feeling center[43] where we meet
Groan with the weight of my approaching feet;

I'll make th' inspired [44] threshals [45] of his court
Sweat with the weather of my horrid steps,
Before I enter; yet will I appear
Like calm security before a ruin;
A politician must like lightning melt
The very marrow, and not print the skin.
His ways must not be seen; the superficies [46]
Of the green center must not taste his feet,   170
When hell is plowed up with his wounding tracts,[47]
And all his harvest reaped from hellish facts.[48]

Exeunt.

ACT FIVE

SCENE ONE

MONTSURRY, *bare, unbraced,*[1] *pulling* TAMYRA
in by the hair; FRIAR. *One bearing light, a standish*[2]
and paper, which[3] *sets a table.*

Fri. My lord, remember that your soul must seek
Her peace, as well as your revengeful blood;
You ever to this hour have proved yourself
A noble, zealous, and obedient son
T'our holy mother; be not an apostate.
Your wife's offense serves not, were it the worst
You can imagine, without greater proofs
To sever your eternal bonds and hearts;
Much less to touch her with a bloody hand.
Nor is it manly, much less husbandly,   10
To expiate any frailty in your wife
With churlish strokes or beastly odds of strength.
The stony birth of clouds [4] will touch no laurel,
Nor any sleeper;[5] your wife is your laurel,
And sweetest sleeper; do not touch her, then;
Be not more rude than the wild seed of vapor
To her that is more gentle than it [6] rude;
In whom kind nature suffered one offense
But to set off her other excellence.
Mont. Good father, leave us; interrupt no more   20
The course I must run for mine honor sake.
Rely on my love to her, which her fault
Cannot extinguish; will she but disclose
Who was the hateful minister of her love,
And through what maze he served it, we are friends.
Fri. It is a damned work to pursue those secrets,
That would ope more sin, and prove springs of
slaughter;
Nor is't a path for Christian feet to touch,
But out of all way to the health of souls,
A sin impossible to be forgiven;   30
Which he that dares commit—
Mont.   Good father, cease;
Tempt not a man distracted; I am apt
To outrages that I shall ever rue!
I will not pass the verge that bounds a Christian,
Nor break the limits of a man nor husband.
Fri. Then God inspire ye both with thoughts and
deeds
Worthy his high respect, and your own souls.

Exit FRIAR.

Mont. Who shall remove the mountain from my
heart,
Ope the seven times-heat [7] furnace of my thoughts,
And set [8] fit outcries for a soul in hell?   40

MONTSURRY *turns a key.*

Oh, now it nothing fits my cares to speak
But thunder,[9] or to take into my throat
The trump of heaven,[10] with whose determinate [11]
blasts
The winds shall burst, and the enragèd seas
Be drunk up in his sounds; that my hot woes,
Vented enough, I might convert to vapor,
Ascending from my infamy unseen,
Shorten the world, preventing [12] the last breath
That kills the living, and regenerates death.
Tam. My lord, my fault, as you may censure [13] it
With too strong arguments, is past your pardon.   51
But how the circumstances may excuse me
God knows, and your more temperate mind hereafter
May let my penitent miseries make you know.
Mont. Hereafter? 'Tis is a supposed infinite,
That from this point will rise eternally.[14]
Fame grows in going;[15] in the scapes of virtue,
Excuses damn her:[16] they be fires in cities
Enraged with those winds that less lights extinguish.
Come, siren, sing, and dash against my rocks   60
Thy ruffian galley,[17] laden for thy lust.
Sing, and put all the nets into thy voice
With which thou drewest into thy strumpet's lap
The spawn [18] of Venus, and in which ye danced;[19]

---

[44] *inspired:* blown on (as by the bad weather coming);
also, conscious prophetically and so fearful of what is coming.
[45] *threshals:* thresholds; also (possibly): "weapons" and,
by metonymy, those who carry them, his soldiers.
[46] *superficies:* surface.   [47] *tracts:* tracks.   [48] *facts:* deeds.
V.i.
[1] *bare, unbraced:* bare-headed and with his doublet not
fastened to his hose.
[2] *standish:* receptacle for pen and ink.
[3] *which:* who (the table-setter presumably exits).
[4] *stony . . . clouds:* thunderbolt.
[5] *laurel . . . sleeper:* supposed to be safe from the thunderbolt.   [6] *it:* it is.   [7] *heat:* heated.
[8] *set:* compose (metaphor, incongruously, from music).
[9] *it . . . thunder:* only thunder is adequate to express my
cares.
[10] *trump of heaven:* which will sound for the Last
Judgment.
[11] *determinate:* final; bringing all things to an end.
[12] *preventing:* anticipating.   [13] *censure:* judge; reprove.
[14] *Hereafter . . . eternally:* i.e., Montsurry will hardly become temperate in future but anguished forever.
[15] *Fame . . . going:* Reputation—presumably hers for ill
doing—will increase as the story is circulated.
[16] *in . . . her:* When virtue falls from itself (as opposed to
vice), any attempt to extenuate the fall would only blacken
her more.
[17] *ruffian galley:* Bussy, loaded with that which will satisfy
the lust of Tamyra, who will lure him to his destruction like
the siren who sought to entice Ulysses.
[18] *spawn:* semen; the imagery from fishing suggests whor-
ing in Elizabethan argot.
[19] *danced:* proverbially, to dance in a net is to think oneself unobserved. The image of the net, following reference
to Venus, perhaps calls up the entrapment of her lover Mars
by her cuckolded husband, Vulcan.

That, in thy lap's stead, I may dig his tomb,
And quit his manhood [20] with a woman's sleight, [21]
Who [22] never is deceived in her deceit.
Sing (that is, write), and then take from mine eyes
The mists that hide the most inscrutable pander
That ever lapped up an adulterous vomit;   70
That I may see the devil, and survive
To be a devil, and then [23] learn to wive;
That I may hang him, and then cut him down,
Then cut him up, [24] and with my soul's beams search
The cranks [25] and caverns of his brain, and study
The errant [26] wilderness of a woman's face,
Where men cannot get out, for [27] all the comets
That have been lighted at it, though they know
That adders lie a-sunning in their smiles,
That basilisks [28] drink their poison from their eyes,   80
And no way there to coast out to their hearts; [29]
Yet still they wander there, and are not stayed
Till they be fettered, nor secure before
All cares distract them, nor in human state
Till they embrace within their wife's two breasts
All Pelion and Cythaeron [30] with their beasts.
Why write you not?
        Tam.   O good my lord, forbear
In wreak of great sins to engender greater,
And make my love's corruption generate murder.
        Mont. It follows needfully as child and parent;   90
The chain-shot [31] of thy lust is yet aloft,
And it must murder; 'tis thine own dear twin.
No man can add height to a woman's sin.
Vice never doth her just hate so provoke,
As when she rageth under virtue's cloak.

---

[20] *quit his manhood:* requite his virility.   [21] *sleight:* trick.
[22] *Who:* Bussy, who (if the ambiguous syntax makes any
sense) is going to be tricked by Tamyra this time, though he
is not customarily deceived by her devices.
[23] *then:* i.e., only when I have become adept in all devilry.
[24] *That . . . up:* alluding to the protracted execution of
hanging, drawing, and quartering.   [25] *cranks:* windings.
[26] *errant:* in the conventional sense, but also anticipating
"comets"—vagrant, wandering from their appointed course
and so betokening disaster—in the following line.
[27] *for:* despite.
[28] *basilisks:* fabulous creatures whose breath and look were
mortal.
[29] *hearts:* seen as denying haven to the voyager who cannot
get free of the woman's face.
[30] *Pelion and Cythaeron:* mountains in Greece associated
with wild beasts.
[31] *chain-shot:* cannonballs linked by chains.
[32] *ashes:* i.e., his own; though he is shriveled almost to
nothing, the torture she has invented for him still sustains
him in life.   [33] *withal:* with.
[34] *there:* i.e., on her person, where they were broken first.
[35] *characters:* letters.
[36] *Thy:* i.e., My (legal right to make you suffer).
[37] *Gorgon:* which, to look on, turned one to stone.
[38] *Dissolve:* Renew; soften (as opposed to his stoniness).
[39] *I express Thee:* i.e., Montsurry in his own monstrousness
is expressing or delineating faithfully the monstrous picture
she has held up to him.
[40] *thy monstrous idol:* i.e., the petrified monster she has
made him.   [41] *other engine:* the rack.
[42] *habituate:* naturalized, as by use and wont.
[43] *Thy . . . through:* Permeated (used transitively) thy
poisons (apostrophizing the rack)(?).
[44] *wrongs:* i.e., those she has committed.

Write! for it must be; by this ruthless steel,
By this impartial torture, and the death
Thy tyrannies have invented in my entrails,
To quicken life in dying, and hold up
The spirits in fainting, teaching to preserve   100
Torments in ashes, [32] that will ever last.
Speak! Will you write?
        Tam.   Sweet lord, enjoin my sin
Some other penance than what makes it worse.
Hide in some gloomy dungeon my loathed face,
And let condemnèd murderers let me down,
Stopping their noses, my abhorrèd food.
Hang me in chains, and let me eat these arms
That have offended: bind me face to face
To some dead woman, taken from the cart
Of execution, till death and time   110
In grains of dust dissolve me; I'll endure:
Or any torture that your wrath's invention
Can fright all pity from the world withal. [33]
But to betray a friend with show of friendship,
That is too common for the rare revenge
Your rage affecteth; here then are my breasts,
Last night your pillows; here my wretched arms,
As late the wishèd confines of your life.
Now break them as you please, and all the bounds
Of manhood, noblesse, and religion.   120
        Mont. Where all these have been broken, they are
                kept
In doing their justice there; [34] thine arms have lost
Their privilege in lust, and in their torture
Thus they must pay it.

                                        Stabs her.

        Tam.   O Lord!
        Mont.   Till thou writest,
I'll write in wounds, my wrong's fit characters, [35]
Thy [36] right of sufferance. Write!
        Tam.   Oh, kill me, kill me!
Dear husband, be not crueler than death;
You have beheld some Gorgon; [37] feel, oh, feel
How you are turned to stone; with my heart-blood
Dissolve [38] yourself again, or you will grow   130
Into the image of all tyranny.
        Mont. As thou art of adultery; I will still
Prove thee my like in ill, being most a monster;
Thus I express thee [39] yet.

                                        Stabs her again.

        Tam.   And yet I live.
        Mont. Ay, for thy monstrous idol [40] is not done yet.
This tool hath wrought enough; now, torture, use
This other engine [41] on th' habituate [42] powers
Of her thrice-damned and whorish fortitude.

                        Enter Servants.

Use the most madding pains in her that ever
Thy venoms soaked through, [43] making most of death,
That she weigh her wrongs [44] with them, and then   141
Stand, Vengeance, on thy steepest rock, a victor!
        Tam. Oh, who is turned into my lord and husband?
Husband! my lord! None but my lord and husband!

Heaven, I ask thee remission of my sins,
Not of my pains; husband, oh, help me, husband!

The FRIAR *ascends with a sword drawn.*

Fri. What rape of honor and religion!
Oh, wrack [45] of nature!

Falls and dies. [46]

Tam.   Poor man! Oh, my father!
Father, look up! Oh, let me down, my lord,
And I will write.
Mont.   Author of prodigies! [47]   150
What new flame breaks out of the firmament,
That turns up counsels never known before?
Now is it [48] true, earth moves, and heaven stands still;
Even heaven itself must see and suffer ill.
The too huge bias [49] of the world hath swayed
Her back-part upwards, and with that she braves
This hemisphere, that long her mouth hath mocked!
The gravity of her religious face,
Now grown too weighty with her sacrilege
And here discerned sophisticate [50] enough,   160
Turns to th' Antipodes; [51] and all the forms
That her illusions [52] have impressed in her,
Have eaten through her back; and now all see
How she is riveted with hypocrisy.
Was this the way? Was he the mean [53] betwixt you?
Tam. He was, he was, kind innocent man, he was.
Mont. Write, write a word or two.
Tam.   I will, I will.
I'll write, but in my blood, that he may see
These lines come from my wounds, and not from me.

Writes.

Mont. Well might he [54] die for thought: methinks
   the frame   170
And shaken joints of the whole world should crack
To see her [55] parts so disproportionate;
And that his general beauty cannot stand
Without these stains in the particular man. [56]
Why wander I so far? Here, here was she
That was a whole world without spot to me,
Though now a world of spots; oh, what a lightning
Is man's delight in women! what a bubble
He builds his state, fame, life on, when he marries!
Since all earth's pleasures are so short and small,   180
The way t'enjoy it, is t'abjure it all.
Enough! I must be messenger myself,
Disguised like this [57] strange creature: in, I'll after,
To see what guilty light gives this cave [58] eyes,
And to the world sing new impieties.
          Exeunt [Servants]. *He puts the* FRIAR *in the vault*
          and follows. She wraps herself in the arras.

[V.ii]

   [*Enter*] BUSSY D'AMBOIS *with two* Pages.

Bus. Sit up tonight, and watch; I'll speak with none
But the old friar, who bring to me.
Pages.   We will, sir.

Exeunt.

Bus. What violent heat is this? Methinks the fire
Of twenty lives doth on a sudden flash
Through all my faculties; the air goes high [1]
In this close chamber, and the frighted earth

Thunder.

Trembles, and shrinks beneath me; the whole house
Cracks with his shaken burden.

Enter the FRIAR'S *ghost.*

                    Bless me, heaven!
Ghost. Note what I want, [2] my son, and be
   forewarned.
Oh, there are bloody deeds past and to come.   10
I cannot stay; a fate doth ravish me;
I'll meet thee in the chamber of thy love.

Exit.

Bus. What dismal change is here! The good old
   Friar
Is murdered, being made known to serve my love;
Note what he wants? He wants his utmost weed, [3]
He wants his life and body: which of these
Should be the want he means, and may supply me
With any fit forewarning? This strange vision,
Together with the dark prediction
Used by the Prince of Darkness that was raised   20
By this embodied shadow, [4] stir my thoughts
With reminiscion [5] of the Spirit's promise,
Who told me that by any invocation
I should have power to raise him, though it wanted
The powerful words and decent [6] rites of art.
Never had my set [7] brain such need of spirit
T'instruct and cheer it; now then I will claim
Performance of his free and gentle vow
T'appear in greater light, and make more plain
His rugged [8] oracle? I long to know   30

---

[45] *wrack:* wreck, destruction; remnant or fragment; and
punning on "rack."
[46] *dies:* not killed by another but, as Behemoth had prophesied, by himself—of shock.
[47] *prodigies:* monsters; untoward events as predicted by a
comet or "new flame."
[48] *it:* the Copernican version of a heliocentric universe.
[49] *bias:* the flattened or protuberant construction of a
bowlingball, inclining it to run in a certain direction. But
"bias" is used in a pejorative sense, suggesting evil inclination that has turned the world topsyturvy. What Montsurry
sees is the hitherto concealed evil of the world now apparent
and flaunting the light, where previously grave and hypocritical professions of sanctity had been uttered.
[50] *sophisticate:* alloyed with vice.
[51] *Antipodes:* the "Bottom."   [52] *illusions:* deceits.
[53] *mean:* middleman.   [54] *he:* presumably Bussy.
[55] *her:* Tamyra's, torn by the rack.
[56] *And . . . man:* An interjected reflection—"And to think
that in Man's sum of beauty there must be comprised the
wickedness of individual men"—the latter being felt as the
condition of the former.   [57] *this:* i.e., the Friar.
[58] *cave:* vault.

V.ii.
[1] *goes high:* becomes noisome(?); alternatively, "agitated."
[2] *want:* lack.   [3] *utmost weed:* outer garment.
[4] *embodied shadow:* ghost (given material form).
[5] *reminiscion:* remembrance.   [6] *decent:* appropriate.
[7] *set:* resolute.   [8] *rugged:* as yet confused.

How my dear mistress fares, and be informed
What hand she now holds on the troubled blood
Of her incensèd lord: methought the Spirit,
When he had uttered his perplexed presage,
Threw his changed countenance headlong into clouds;
His forehead bent, as it would hide his face,
He knocked his chin against his darkened breast,
And struck a churlish silence through his powers.
Terror of darkness! O thou king of flames![9]
That with thy music-footed[10] horse dost strike   40
The clear light out of crystal[11] on dark earth,
And hurlest instructive fire[12] about the world,
Wake, wake the drowsy and enchanted night,
That sleeps with dead eyes in this heavy riddle!
Or[13] thou great prince of shades where never sun
Sticks his far-darted beams, whose eyes are made
To see in darkness, and see ever best
Where sense is blindest, open now the heart
Of thy abashèd[14] oracle, that, for fear
Of some ill it includes, would fain lie hid,   50
And rise thou with it in thy greater light.

Thunders. BEHEMOTH *rises up with his* Spirits.

Beh. Thus, to observe my vow of apparition[15]
In greater light, and explicate thy fate,
I come; and tell thee that, if thou obey
The summons that thy mistress next will send thee,
Her hand shall be thy death.
Bus.   When will she send?
Beh. Soon as I set again, where late I rose.
Bus. Is the old Friar slain?
Beh.   No, and yet lives not.
Bus. Died he a natural death?
Beh.   He did.
Bus.   Who then
Will my dear mistress send?
Beh.   I must not tell thee.   60

Bus. Who lets[16] thee?
Beh.   Fate.
Bus.   Who are Fate's ministers?
Beh. The Guise and Monsieur.
Bus.   A fit pair of shears[17]
To cut the threads of kings and kingly spirits,
And consorts[18] fit to sound forth harmony
Set to the falls of kingdoms! Shall the hand
Of my kind mistress kill me?
Beh.   If thou yield
To her next summons. Y'are fair-warned; farewell!
                              Thunders. Exit.
Bus. I must fare well, however, though I die,
My death consenting[19] with his augury.
Should not my powers obey when she commands,   70
My motion must be rebel to my will,
My will to life. If, when I have obeyed,
Her hand should so reward me, they must arm it,
Bind me and force it; or, I lay[20] my soul,
She rather would convert it many times
On her own bosom, even to many deaths.[21]
But were there danger of such violence,
I know 'tis far from her intent to send.
And who she should send is as far from thought,
Since he is dead, whose only mean she used.   80

                              [*One*] *knocks.*

Who's there? Look to the door, and let him in,
Though politic Monsieur or the violent Guise.

Enter MONTSURRY *like the* FRIAR, *with a letter
written in blood.*

Mont. Hail to my worthy son.
Bus. O lying spirit![22] Welcome, loved father;
How fares my dearest mistress?
Mont.   Well, as ever,
Being well as ever thought on by her lord;
Whereof she sends this witness in her hand
And prays, for urgent cause, your speediest presence.
Bus. What! writ in blood?
Mont.   Ay, 'tis the ink of lovers.
Bus. Oh, 'tis a sacred witness of her love.   90
So much elixir[23] of her blood as this,
Dropped in the lightest[24] dame, would make her firm[25]
As heat to[26] fire; and, like to all the signs,[27]
Commands[28] the life confined in all my veins;
Oh, how it multiplies my blood with spirit,[29]
And makes me apt t'encounter death and hell.
But come, kind father, you fetch me to heaven,
And to that end your holy weed was given.

                              Exeunt.

[V.iii]

Enter MONSIEUR *and* GUISE *above.*

Mons. Now shall we see that Nature hath no end
In her great works reponsive[1] to their worths,
That she, who makes so many eyes and souls
To see and foresee, is stark blind herself;
And as illiterate men say Latin prayers

---

[9] *Terror . . . flames:* Apollo, as god of light, is invoked first to illuminate the dark riddle.
[10] *music-footed:* appropriate to Apollo's role as god of music.
[11] *crystal:* the crystalline sphere that, in the Ptolemaic universe, contained the sun.
[12] *instructive fire:* light that reveals the truth.
[13] *Or:* If Apollo is unavailing, the Prince of Darkness, who can see in the dark, will be invoked.
[14] *abashèd:* reticent; communicating too little.
[15] *apparition:* appearance (with pun on "ghost").
[16] *lets:* prevents.
[17] *shears:* wielded by Atropos, the third of the Fates.
[18] *consorts:* confederates; musical instruments or the musicians themselves.   [19] *consenting:* agreeing.
[20] *lay:* wager.
[21] *deaths:* with conventional suggestion of sexual intercourse.   [22] *spirit:* Behemoth.
[23] *elixir:* quintessence and so able to effect anything.
[24] *lightest:* most lascivious.
[25] *firm:* chaste, "essentially."   [26] *to:* is the essence of.
[27] *signs:* zodiacal constellations, seen as determining man's life.
[28] *Commands:* It commands.
[29] *spirit:* i.e., the animal spirits engendered in the heart which, rising to the brain, make one "apt to encounter."
V.iii.
[1] *responsive:* proportionate.

By rote of heart and daily iteration,[2]
In whose hot zeal a man would think they knew
What they ran so away with, and were sure
To have rewards proportioned to their labors,
Yet may implore their own confusions   10
For anything they know—which often times
It falls out they incur; so Nature lays
A mass of stuff together, and by use,[3]
Or by the mere necessity of matter,[4]
Ends such a work, fills it, or leaves it empty
Of strength or virtue, error or clear truth,
Not knowing what she does; but usually
Gives that which we call merit to a man,
And believe should arrive him on[5] huge riches,
Honor, and happiness, that effects his ruin;   20
Right as in ships of war whole lasts[6] of powder
Are laid, men think, to make them last, and guard them,
When a disordered spark that powder taking,
Blows up with sudden violence and horror
Ships that, kept empty, had sailed long with terror.[7]
   Guise. He that observes but like a worldly man
That which doth oft succeed, and by th' events
Values the worth of things, will think it true
That Nature works at random, just with you.
But with as much decorum she may make   30
A thing that from the feet up to the throat
Hath all the wondrous fabric man should have,
And leave it headless, for an absolute[8] man,
As give a whole man valor, virtue, learning,
Without an end more excellent than those
On whom she no such worthy part bestows.
   Mons. Why, you shall see it here; here will be one
Young, learnèd, valiant, virtuous, and full-manned;[9]
One on whom Nature spent so rich a hand
That on an ominous eye she wept to see   40
So much consumed her virtuous treasury.[10]
Yet as the winds sing through a hollow tree
And, since it lets them pass through, let it stand;
But a tree solid, since it gives no way
To their wild rages, they rend up by th' root:
So this full creature now shall reel and fall
Before the frantic puffs of purblind[11] chance,
That pipes through empty men, and makes them dance.
Not so the sea raves on the Lybian sands,
Tumbling her billows in each others' neck;   50
Not so the surges of the Euxine[12] sea
Near to the frosty pole, where free Boötes[13]
From those dark deep waves turns his radiant team,
Swell, being enraged, even from their inmost drop,
As fortune swings about the restless state
Of virtue, now thrown into all man's hate.[14]

   Thunder. The FRIAR'S *Ghost enters and discovers*
     TAMYRA *wrapped in a canopy.*[15]

   Ghost. Revive those stupid thoughts,[16] and sit not
    thus
Gathering[17] the horrors of your servant's slaughter,
So urged by your hand and so imminent,
Into an idle fancy, but devise   60
How to prevent it; watch when he shall rise,
And with a sudden outcry of his murder,

Blow[18] his retreat before he be engaged.
   Tam. O father, have my dumb woes waked your
    death?
When will our human griefs be at their height?
Man is a tree that hath no top in cares,
No root in comforts; all his power to live
Is given to no end, but t'have power to grieve.
   Ghost. 'Tis the just curse of our abused creation
Which we must suffer here, and scape hereafter.   70
He hath the great mind that submits to all
He sees inevitable; he the small
That carps at earth and her foundation shaker,[19]
And rather than himself will mend his maker.

     D'AMBOIS [*appears*] *at the gulf.*[20]

   Tam. Away, my love, away! Thou wilt be murdered.
   Bus. Murdered? I know not what that Hebrew[21]
    means;
That word had ne'er been named had all been
    D'Ambois.
Murdered? By heaven, he is my murderer
That shows me not a murderer; what such bug[22]
Abhorreth[23] not the very sleep of D'Ambois?   80
Murdered? Who dares give all the room I see
To D'Ambois' reach, or look with any odds
His fight i'th' face, upon whose hand sits death,
Whose sword hath wings, and every feather pierceth?
Let in my politic visitants, let them in,
Though entering like so many moving armors.
Fate is more strong than arms, and sly than treason,
And I at all parts buckled[24] in my fate.
Dare they not come?

   Enter Murderers [*at one door*] *with* FRIAR
     at the other door.

   Tam.   They come.
   1 Mur.   Come all at once.
   Ghost. Back, coward murderers, back!
   All.   Defend us,
    heaven!   90
               Exeunt all but the first.

---

  [2] *By . . . iteration:* Mechanically.
  [3] *use:* habitual practice.
  [4] *mere . . . matter:* i.e., the properties inhering in it.
  [5] *arrive him on:* bring him to.   [6] *lasts:* measures.
  [7] *with terror:* i.e., even though fearful of the enemies from
whom the powder was supposed to protect them.
  [8] *absolute:* perfect.
  [9] *full-manned:* perfect in virtue—but also continuing the
nautical image.   [10] *virtuous treasury:* treasury of virtues.
  [11] *purblind:* here, wholly blind.   [12] *Euxine:* Black.
  [13] *Boötes:* The northern constellation known as the Wagon
and drawn by a team of oxen.
  [14] *Not . . . hate:* These eight lines are adapted from
Seneca's *Agamemnon,* ll. 64–72.
  [15] *Thunder . . . canopy:* Stage direction conflates Q1607
and Q1641. "Canopy" is the "arras" (from which Tamyra
is now unwrapped).
  [16] *Revive . . . thoughts:* Awake from your lethargy.
  [17] *Gathering:* i.e., in imagination.
  [18] *Blow:* Sound, signal.   [19] *foundation shaker:* God.
  [20] *gulf:* vault.   [21] *Hebrew:* i.e., incomprehensible word.
  [22] *bug:* bogey.   [23] *Abhorreth:* Feareth.
  [24] *buckled:* armored.

1 Mur. Come ye not on?

Bus.   No, slave, nor goest thou
off.

Stand you so firm?—Will it²⁵ not enter here?
You have a face yet. So! In thy life's flame

[Kills him.]

I burn the first rites to my mistress' fame.

Ghost. Breathe²⁶ thee, brave son, against the other
charge.

Bus. Oh, is it true then that my sense first told me?
Is my kind father dead?

Tam.   He is, my love.

'Twas the earl, my husband, in his weed, that brought
thee.

Bus. That was a speeding sleight,²⁷ and well
resembled.

Where is that angry Earl? My lord, come forth   100
And show your own face in your own affair;
Take not into your noble veins the blood
Of these base villains, nor the light reports
Of blistered²⁸ tongues for clear and weighty truth,
But me against the world, in pure defense
Of your rare lady, to whose spotless name
I stand here as a bulwark, and project²⁹
A life to her renown, that ever yet
Hath been untainted, even in envy's eye,
And, where it³⁰ would protect, a sanctuary.   110
Brave earl, come forth, and keep your scandal in.
'Tis not our fault if you enforce the spot,³¹
Nor the wreak³² yours, if you perform it not.

Enter MONTSURRY, *with all the*
Murderers.

Mont. Cowards, a fiend or spirit beat ye off?
They are your own faint spirits that have forged

---

²⁵ *it:* his sword.
²⁶ *Breathe:* Rest.
²⁷ *speeding sleight:* successful trick.
²⁸ *blistered:* lying.
²⁹ *project:* offer.
³⁰ *it:* i.e., her renown.
³¹ *enforce the spot:* emphasize the dishonor.
³² *wreak:* vengeance.
³³ *divines:* divine parts; clergymen, who hold out promise of immortality.
³⁴ *Vespasian:* Roman Emperor, A.D. 69–79.
³⁵ *splinted:* supported.
³⁶ *And . . . grooms:* These four lines are preserved from Q1641 because the reference to Vespasian occurs in Grimestone's *General Inventory* (see introduction).
³⁷ *equal:* impartial.
³⁸ *where:* i.e., the East; Saba, famous for its spices.
³⁹ *Iberian:* Western; the Iberian peninsula.
⁴⁰ *Hecate:* Goddess of the Underworld.
⁴¹ *burning axletree:* the equatorial line about which the spheres revolved.
⁴² *chariot:* i.e., the polar star in the constellation Ursa Minor; hence the Arctic (both Great and Little Bear are close to the Wagon, Boötes, explaining the reference to "chariot").
⁴³ *And . . . Bear:* These seven lines are modeled on Seneca's *Hercules Oetaeus*, ll. 1518–26.
⁴⁴ *worthless:* unavailing; devoid of the worth appropriate to the end of such a man.
⁴⁵ *fautor:* accomplice.
⁴⁶ *stilled:* instilled; distilled.
⁴⁷ *spirit:* The "quintessence" sought by the alchemists, whom Bussy, as distiller, is imitating; also, the animal spirits (as before) that engender action.

The fearful shadows that your eyes deluded.
The fiend was in you; cast him out then, thus.

[*They fight.*] D'AMBOIS *hath* MONTSURRY *down.*

Tam. Favor my lord, my love, oh, favor him!

Bus. I will not touch him: take your life, my lord,
And be appeased.

Pistols shot within. [BUSSY *is wounded.*]

Oh, then the coward Fates   120
Have maimed themselves, and ever lost their honor.

Ghost. What have ye done, slaves? Irreligious
lord!

Bus. Forbear them, father; 'tis enough for me
That Guise and Monsieur, death and destiny,
Come behind D'Ambois. Is my body, then,
But penetrable flesh? And must my mind
Follow my blood? Can my divine part add
No aid to th' earthly in extremity?
Then these divines³³ are but for form, not fact.
Man is of two sweet courtly friends compact,   130
A mistress and a servant: let my death
Define life nothing but a courtier's breath.
Nothing is made of naught, of all things made,
Their abstract being a dream but of a shade.
I'll not complain to earth yet, but to heaven,
And, like a man, look upwards even in death.
And if Vespasian³⁴ thought in majesty
An emperor might die standing, why not I?

She offers to help him.

Nay, without help, in which I will exceed him;
For he died splinted³⁵ with his chamber grooms.³⁶
Prop me, true sword, as thou hast ever done!   141
The equal³⁷ thought I bear of life and death
Shall make me faint on no side; I am up;
Here like a Roman statue I will stand
Till death hath made me marble. Oh, my fame,
Live in despite of murder! Take thy wings
And haste thee where³⁸ the gray-eyed Morn perfumes
Her rosy chariot with Sabaean spices!
Fly, where the Evening from th' Iberian³⁹ vales
Takes on her swarthy shoulders Hecate,⁴⁰   150
Crowned with a grove of oaks: fly where men feel
The burning axletree,⁴¹ and those that suffer
Beneath the chariot⁴² of the snowy Bear:⁴³
And tell them all that D'Ambois now is hasting
To the eternal dwellers; that a thunder
Of all their sighs together, for their frailties
Beheld in me, may quit my worthless⁴⁴ fall
With a fit volley for my funeral.

Ghost. Forgive thy murderers.

Bus.   I forgive them all;
[*To* MONTSURRY] And you, my lord, their fautor;⁴⁵
for true sign   160
Of which unfeigned remission take my sword;
Take it, and only give it motion,
And it shall find the way to victory
By his own brightness, and th' inherent valor
My fight hath stilled⁴⁶ into't with charms of spirit.⁴⁷
And let me pray you that my weighty blood,

Laid in one scale of your impartial spleen,[48]
May sway the forfeit of my worthy love [49]
Weighed in the other; and be reconciled
With all forgiveness to your matchless wife.   170
 Tam. Forgive thou me, dear servant, and this hand
That led thy life to this unworthy end;
Forgive it, for the blood with which 'tis stained,
In which I writ the summons of thy death—
The forcèd summons—by this bleeding wound,
By this here in my bosom, and by this
That makes me hold up both my hands imbrued [50]
For thy dear pardon.
 Bus.   Oh, my heart is broken!
Fate nor these murderers, Monsieur nor the Guise,
Have any glory in my death, but this,   180
This killing spectacle, this prodigy.[51]
My sun [52] is turned to blood 'gainst whose red beams
Pindus and Ossa,[53] hid in endless snow,
Laid on my heart and liver,[54] from their veins
Melt like two hungry torrents, eating rocks,
Into the ocean of all human life,
And make it bitter,[55] only with my blood.
Oh, frail condition of strength, valor, virtue,
In me, like warning fire upon the top
Of some steep beacon,[56] on a steeper hill,   190
Made to express [57] it; like a falling star
Silently glanced,[58] that like a thunderbolt
Looked to have stuck [59] and shook the firmament.
            Dies.

 Ghost. [*To* MONTSURRY] Son of the earth,[60] whom
  my unrested [61] soul
Rues [62] t'have begotten in the faith of heaven,
Since thy revengeful spirit hath rejected
The charity it commands, and the remission,
To serve and worship the blind rage of blood,
Assay to gratulate [63] and pacify
The soul fled from this worthy [64] by performing   200
The Christian reconcilement he besought
Betwixt thee and thy lady; let her wounds,
Manlessly [65] digged in her, be eased and cured
With balm of thine own tears; or be assured
Never to rest free from my haunt and horror.
 Mont. See how she merits this; still sitting by,
And mourning his fall more than her own fault!
 Ghost. Remove, dear daughter, and content thy
  husband;
So piety wills thee, and thy servant's [66] peace.
 Tam. O wretched piety, that art so distract   210
In thine own constancy, and in thy right
Must be unrighteous: if I right my friend
I wrong my husband; if his wrong I shun,
The duty of my friend I leave undone:
Ill plays on both sides; here and there, it riseth;
No place, no good, so good, but ill compriseth;
My soul more scruple breeds than my blood, sin;
Virtue imposeth more than any stepdame.
Oh, had I never married but for form,
Never vowed faith but purposed to deceive,   220
Never made conscience of[67] any sin,
But cloaked it privately and made it common;
Nor never honored [68] been in blood or mind;

Happy had I been then, as others are
Of the like license; I had then been honored;
Lived without envy; custom had benumbed
All sense of scruple and all note of frailty;
My fame had been untouched, my heart unbroken:
But, shunning all, I strike on all offense;
O husband! dear friend! O my conscience!   230
 Mont. I must not yield to pity nor to love
So servile and so traitorous: cease, my blood,
To wrestle with my honor, fame, and judgment:
Away, forsake my house, forbear complaints
Where thou hast bred them: here all things full [69]
Of their own shame and sorrow; leave my house.
 Tam. Sweet lord, forgive me, and I will be gone,
And till these wounds, that never balm shall close
Till death hath entered at them—so I love them,
Being opened by your hands—by death be cured,   240
I never more will grieve you with my sight,
Never endure that any roof shall part
Mine eyes and heaven; but to the open deserts,
Like to hunted tigers I will fly,
Eating my heart, shunning the steps of men,
And look on no side till I be arrived.[70]
 Mont. I do forgive thee, and upon my knees,
With hands held up to heaven, wish that mine honor
Would suffer reconcilement to my love;
But since it will not, honor, never serve   250
My love with flourishing object, till it sterve![71]
And as this taper, though it upwards look,

---

 [48] *impartial spleen:* impersonal anger(?); or, more logically, "judgment."
 [49] *forfeit . . . love:* loss—by Montsurry of Tamyra(?)—which Bussy's spilt blood is to oversway.
 [50] *imbrued:* bloodstained.
 [51] *this prodigy:* presumably the monstrous sight of the bleeding Tamyra, the only "glory" accruing to Monsieur and the Guise.
 [52] *My sun:* Either Bussy himself or Tamyra, or both.
 [53] *Pindus and Ossa:* beneath which the vanquished Titans were imprisoned.
 [54] *heart and liver:* the source of the burning passion that consumes him.
 [55] *bitter:* The adjective suggests a reminiscence of Revelation VIII: 8–11, in which the end of the world is signalized by the casting of a mountain and star into the sea, thereby made "bitter" to men. But the passage is clear enough without the allusion.
 [56] *beacon:* like those lit throughout England to warn of the coming of the Spanish Armada in 1588.
 [57] *express:* make (the fire) more conspicuous.
 [58] *glanced:* glimpsed; or "glancing." The star, like the warning fire, is ephemeral. [59] *stuck:* pierced.
 [60] *Son . . . earth:* hence, "base."
 [61] *unrested:* because confined to Purgatory.
 [62] *Rues:* Repents. (The sense seems to be that the Friar regrets having offered religious instruction to Montsurry.)
 [63] *Assay to gratulate:* Seek to repay.
 [64] *worthy:* i.e., Bussy.
 [65] *Manlessly:* In a cowardly or inhuman way.
 [66] *servant's:* i.e., Bussy's.
 [67] *made conscience of:* let my conscience be troubled by.
 [68] *honored:* honorable, as opposed to the sense of "been honored," below.
 [69] *Where . . . full:* The line is metrically imperfect; perhaps a verb—"are," "be,"—has dropped out between "here" and "all." [70] *arrived:* i.e., at death.
 [71] *sterve:* die.

Downwards must needs consume, so let our love![72]
As, having lost his honey,[73] the sweet taste
Runs into savor,[74] and will needs retain
A spice of his first parents,[75] till, like life,
It sees[76] and dies; so let our love! And lastly,
As when the flame is suffered to look up,
It keeps its luster, but, being thus turned down,
His natural course of useful light inverted,   260
His own stuff[77] puts it out, so let our love!
Now turn from me, as here I turn from thee,
And may both points of heaven's straight axletree
Conjoin in one, before thyself and me.

Exeunt severally.[78]

Ghost. My terrors are struck inward, and no more
My penance will allow they shall enforce
Earthly afflictions but upon myself.
Farewell, brave relics[79] of a complete man;
Look up and see thy spirit made a star;
Join flames with Hercules,[80] and when thou settest   270
Thy radiant forehead in the firmament,[81]
Make the vast continent crack with thy receipt.[82]
Spread to a world of fire,[83] and th'agèd sky
Cheer with new sparks of old humanity.

Exit.

EPILOGUE

WITH many hands you have seen D'Ambois slain,
Yet by your grace he may revive again,
And every day grow stronger in his skill
To please, as we presume he is in will.
The best deserving actors of the time
Had their ascents; and by degrees did climb
To their full height, a place to study due.
To make him tread in their path lies in you;
He'll not forget his makers, but still prove
His thankfulness, as you increase your love.   10

FINIS

---

[72] *so let our love:* i.e., look up to heaven (implying forgiveness of what's past) but perish even so (because Montsurry's "honor" cannot be reconciled), as the candle wastes away while its light rises.   [73] *honey:* wax (from bees).

[74] *savor:* perfume.   [75] *first parents:* the bees.

[76] *sees:* What the expiring candle—like the dying man or the love that is ending—"sees" is moot. Perhaps its final vision is of nothingness.

[77] *stuff:* the wax dripping downward into the flame.

[78] *severally:* separately.   [79] *relics:* remains.

[80] *Hercules:* who is made a star on his death, and whose story, as retold by Seneca, is much in Chapman's mind in this scene.

[81] *firmament:* all the spheres enclosing earth. "Continent," in what follows, must be synonymous.

[82] *thy receipt:* receiving thee.

[83] *fire:* Bussy is seen as piercing the circle of fire that enclosed the earth in the Ptolemaic system and, simultaneously, as setting the firmament afire, "cheering" it thereby because reinvesting it with what he carries in himself: fiery vestiges of that "old" and better humanity that lived in the Golden Age, now to be restored.

George Chapman

THE WIDOW'S TEARS

THE LAST of Chapman's comedies appeared in
quarto (Q) in 1612, its only authoritative edition, which may have been printed not from
Chapman's final version of the play but rather from a
carefully prepared draft that, though it does not represent its author's final thoughts, had nevertheless been
marked by the playhouse personnel (hence so much
detail in the stage directions). There is no record of the
play's first performance; the title page claims it was
played both at the Blackfriars and at the Whitefriars;
in any case, it is a private theater play and was acted by
a boys' company. The frequent allusions to James I's
indiscriminate distribution of knighthoods date it
clearly after 1603, and 1605 is the commonly accepted
best guess as to date. Though readers will doubtless be
tempted to compare THE WIDOW'S TEARS with Cervantes' "Tale of Foolish Curiosity" in *Don Quixote*,
the story of a man who mistakenly tests the fidelity of
his exemplary wife against the temptations of his own
prolonged absence and his best friend's charms, and
with the direct heir of that tale, the anonymous *Second
Maiden's Tragedy* (perhaps Middleton's), the source of
the Cynthia–Lysander plot is clearly the *Satyricon* of
Petronius Arbiter, cxii.

THE WIDOW'S TEARS is as remarkable for its
apparent slightness as BUSSY D'AMBOIS for its den-
sity. The reader, in fact, may at first see little in the
comedy to reassure him that it is by the author of the
tragedy. But closer scrutiny will find significant links
between Bussy and Tharsalio and between the unique
combination of cynicism and idealism in both plays;
they are linked by an underlying misogyny as well, but
that is as much a feature of the private theaters in the
early seventeenth century as it is a revelation of the
character of any writer for them. The connections

between the two plays may run deeper. In a brilliant
essay in his *The Theater and the Dream: From Metaphor
to Form in Renaissance Drama*, Jackson I. Cope argues
that THE WIDOW'S TEARS uses mythological
materials to which it alludes to become a veiled allegory
in Chapman's learned manner, playing on ideas about
life as drama and about sexuality that the poet derived
from his immersion in Continental philosophy and
literature. To recommend this provocative study is not
necessarily to endorse it, and even while assenting to
Cope's demonstration of aspects of Chapman's intention some readers will find the cynicism of the comedy
offensive and its slightness incompatible with so large a
burden of meaning; if Dryden could justly complain of
the Chapman of BUSSY D'AMBOIS that dwarfish
thoughts are dressed in a giant's robes, one might make
the opposite charge here. THE WIDOW'S TEARS is
deficient in that degree of tolerant sympathy that gives
to Mozart's *Cosi Fan Tutte* and Cervantes' "Tale of
Foolish Curiosity," both based on plots that test feminine fidelity, the ability to turn into moving art an
understanding of the limits of human strength. Chapman seems instead to be enraged at a state of affairs
that he sees with the eye of a satirist who appears never
to have expected better of humanity; because he gives
his audience no reason to expect the possibility of
better behavior than they see, the aura of shocking
revelation is inappropriate. But if one regards the play
more as a grim *jeu d'esprit*, it is easy to admire the wit of
plot and language, the cleverness with which the plots
mirror one another, and the recurrent reminders that
the play is a fiction. It is a pity that there is so little
likelihood of performance; the comedy would surely
make a swift and lively entertainment.   N. R.

The Widow's Tears

[DEDICATION]

To the Right Virtuous and Truly Noble Gentleman,
MR. JO. REED,[1]
of Mitton, in the County of Gloucester,
Esquire.

SIR, if any work of this nature be worth the presenting to friends worthy and noble, I presume this will
not want much of that value. Other countrymen have
thought the like worthy of Dukes' and Princes' accepta-
tions; *inguisti sdegni*,[2] *Il pentimento amoroso*,[3] *Calisto*,[4]
Pastor fido,[5] etc., all being but plays, were all dedicate
to Princes of Italy. And therefore I only discourse to
show my love to your right virtuous and noble disposition. This poor comedy, of many desired to see printed,
I thought not utterly unworthy that affectionate 10
design in me, well knowing that your free judgment
weighs nothing by the name, or form, or any vain
estimation of the vulgar; but will accept acceptable
matter as well in plays as in many less materials, masking in more serious titles. And so, till some work more
worthy I can select and perfect out of my other studies,
that may better express me, and more fit the gravity of
your ripe inclination, I rest,
> Yours at all parts most truly affected,
> GEO. CHAPMAN

DRAMATIS PERSONÆ

THARSALIO, *the wooer*
LYSANDER, *his brother*
The Governor *of Cyprus*
LYCUS, *servant to the widow Countess*
ARGUS, *gentleman usher*[1]
REBUS, *suitor to Eudora, the widow Countess*
PSORABEUS⎫
HIARBAS ⎭ *lords, friends of Rebus*
HYLUS, *nephew to Tharsalio and son to Lysander*
CLINIAS, *servant to Eudora*
Captain *of the Watch*

Two Soldiers
Guard
EUDORA, *the widow Countess*
CYNTHIA, *wife to Lysander*
STHENIA⎫
IANTHE ⎭ *gentlewomen attending on Eudora*
ERO, *waiting-woman to Cynthia*
LAODICE, *daughter to Eudora*
ARSACE, *a panderess*
TOMASIN, *a courtesan*

ACT ONE

SCENE ONE

THARSALIO *solus, with a glass in his hand,
making ready.*

Thar. Thou blind imperfect goddess that delights,
Like a deep-reaching statesman, to converse
Only with fools, jealous of knowing spirits,
For fear their piercing judgments might discover
Thy inward weakness and despise thy power,
Contemn thee for a goddess; thou that lad'st
Th' unworthy ass with gold, while worth and merit
Serve thee for nought, weak Fortune, I renounce
Thy vain dependence and convert my duty
And sacrifices of my sweetest thoughts 10
To a more noble deity, sole friend to worth
And patroness of all good spirits, Confidence;[1]

DEDICATION
 [1] *Mr. Jo. Reed:* probably a relative of Sir Fulke Greville.
 [2] *inguisti sdegni: Gli Ingiusti Sdegni*, a play by Bernardino
Pino printed in 1553 and dedicated to Cesare Panfilo.
 [3] *Il pentimento amoroso:* a pastoral play by Luigi Groto
(Cieco di Hadria), printed in 1576 and dedicated to Vin-
cenzo Naldi, Governor of Peschiera for the Signoria of
Venice, and to his wife.
 [4] *Calisto:* Groto dedicated this pastoral play in 1561 to
Alfonso II of Este, Grand Duke of Ferrara.
 [5] *Pastor fido:* Battista Guarini dedicated his famous
pastoral tragicomedy in 1590 to Carlo Emanuele, Duke of
Savoy.

DRAMATIS PERSONÆ
 [1] *gentleman usher:* a gentleman who serves as escort and
attendant in the house of a person (generally a lady) of high
rank.

I.i.
 [1] *Confidence:* Presumption.

She be my guide, and hers the praise of these
My worthy undertakings.

Enter Lysander *with a glass in his hand;*
Cynthia, Hylus, Ero.

Lys. Morrow, brother, not ready yet?

Thar. No; I have somewhat of the brother[2] in me. I dare say your wife is many times ready, and you not up. Save you, sister; how are you enamored of my presence? How like you my aspect?   19

Cyn. Faith, no worse than I did last week; the weather has nothing changed the grain[3] of your complexion.

Thar. A firm proof 'tis in grain,[4] and so are not all complexions. A good soldier's face, sister.

Cyn. Made to be worn under a beaver.[5]

Thar. Ay, and 'twould show well enough under a mask, too.

Lys. So much for the face.

Thar. But is there no object in this suit to whet your tongue upon?   30

Lys. None, but Fortune send you well to wear it, for she best knows how you got it.

Thar. Faith, 'tis the portion she bestows upon younger brothers, valor and good clothes. Marry, if you ask how we come by this new suit, I must take time to answer it, for as the ballad says, "In written books I find it."[6] Brother, these are the blossoms of spirit; and I will have it said for my father's honor that some of his children were truly begotten.

Lys. Not all?   40

Thar. Shall I tell you, brother, that I know will rejoice you? My former suits have been all spenders; this shall be a speeder.[7]

Lys. A thing to be heartily wished; but, brother take heed you be not gulled; be not too forward.

Thar. 'T had been well for me if you had followed that counsel; you were too forward when you stepped into the world before me, and gulled me of the land that my spirits and parts were indeed born to.   49

Cyn. May we not have the blessing to know the aim of your fortunes? What coast, for heaven's love?

Thar. Nay, 'tis a project of state. You may see the preparation, but the design lies hidden in the breasts of the wise.

Lys. May we not know't?

Thar. Not unless you'll promise me to laugh at it, for without your applause, I'll none.

Lys. The quality of it may be such as a laugh will not be ill bestowed upon't; pray heaven I call not Arsace sister.   60

Cyn. What? The panderess?

Thar. Know you—as who knows not?—the exquisite lady of the palace, the late governor's admired widow, the rich and haughty Countess Eudora? Were not she a jewel worth the wearing, if a man knew how to win her?

Lys. How's that? How's that?

Thar. Brother, there is a certain goddess called Confidence, that carries a main stroke in honorable preferments. Fortune waits upon her; Cupid is at her beck; she sends them both of[8] errands. This deity doth promise me much assistance in this business.   71

Lys. But if this deity should draw you up in a basket to your countess's window, and there let you hang for all the wits in the town to shoot at,[9] how then?

Thar. If she do, let them shoot their bolts and spare not. I have a little bird in a cage here that sings me better comfort. What should be the bar? You'll say, I was page to the count her husband. What of that? I have thereby one foot in her favor already. She has taken note of my spirit and surveyed my good   80 parts, and the picture of them lives in her eye, which sleep, I know, cannot close till she have embraced the substance.

Lys. All this savors of the blind goddess you speak of.

Thar. Why should I despair but that Cupid hath one dart in store for her great ladyship, as well as for any other huge lady whom she hath made stoop gallant[10] to kiss their worthy followers? In a word, I am assured of my speed.[11] Such fair attempts led by a brave resolve are evermore seconded by Fortune.   90

Cyn. But, brother, have I not heard you say your own ears have been witness to her vows made solemnly to your late lord, in memory of him to preserve till death the unstained honor of a widow's bed? If nothing else, yet that might cool your confidence.

Thar. Tush, sister. Suppose you should protest with solemn oath, as perhaps you have done, if ever heaven hears your prayers that you may live to see my brother nobly interred, to feed only upon fish, and not endure the touch of flesh during the wretched Lent of your miserable life—would you believe it, brother?   101

Lys. I am therein most confident.

Thar. Indeed, you had better believe it than try it. But pray, sister, tell me—you are a woman—do not you wives nod your heads and smile one upon another when ye meet abroad?

Cyn. Smile? Why so?

Thar. As who should say, "Are not we mad wenches, that can lead our blind husbands thus by the noses?" Do you not brag amongst yourselves how grossly   110 you abuse their honest credulities? How they adore you for saints, and you believe it, while you adhorn[12] their temples, and they believe it not? How you vow widowhood in their lifetime, and they believe you, when even in the sight of their breathless corse,[13] ere they be fully

---

[2] *the brother:* punning on the affliction called "the mother," suffocating hysteria.   [3] *grain:* texture.

[4] *in grain:* fast dyed.

[5] *beaver:* the part of the helmet that covers the face.

[6] *ballad . . . it:* reference to unpaid accounts in tailors' books; the proverbial statement was often printed at the ends of ballads and broadsides to lend them specious credibility.

[7] *speeder:* one that prospers.   [8] *of:* on.

[9] *draw . . . at:* a medieval tale told that Virgil, drawn up to a bedroom window in a basket by a mistress who wants to embarrass him, is stopped halfway and exposed to all Rome; for revenge he extinguishes all the fires in Rome, and they can be relighted only by contact with the mistress's body in the Forum.

[10] *stoop gallant:* lower the flag; i.e., humble herself.

[11] *speed:* success.

[12] *adhorn:* pun on the cuckold's horns.

[13] *corse:* corpse.

cold, you join embraces with his groom, or his physician, and perhaps his poisoner; or at least, by the next moon, if you can expect[14] so long, solemnly plight new hymeneal bonds with a wild, confident, untamed ruffian?

Lys. As for example?   120

Thar. And make him the top of his house and sovereign lord of the palace, as for example. Look you, brother, this glass is mine.

Lys. What of that?

Thar. While I am with it, it takes impression from my face; but can I make it so mine, that it shall be of no use to any other? Will it not do his office to you or you, and as well to my groom as to myself? Brother, monopolies are cried down.[15] Is it not madness for me to believe, when I have conquered that fort of chast-   130 ity the great countess, that if another man of my making and mettle shall assault her, her eyes and ears should lose their function, her other parts their use, as if nature had made her all in vain, unless I only had stumbled into her quarters?

Cyn. Brother, I fear me in your travel you have drunk too much of that Italian air, that hath infected the whole mass of your ingenuous nature, dried up in you all sap of generous disposition, poisoned the very essence of your soul, and so polluted your senses   140 that whatsoever enters there takes from them contagion and is to your fancy represented as foul and tainted which in itself perhaps is spotless.

Thar. No, sister, it hath refined my senses, and made me see with clear eyes, and to judge of objects as they truly are, not as they seem, and through their mask to discern the true face of things. It tells me how short-lived widows' tears are, that their weeping is in truth but laughing under a mask, that they mourn in their gowns and laugh in their sleeves; all which I   150 believe as a Delphian oracle, and am resolved to burn in that faith. And in that resolution do I march to the great lady.

Lys. You lose time, brother, in discourse. By this had you bore up with the lady and clapped her aboard, for I know your confidence will not dwell long in the service.

Thar. No, I will perform it in the conqueror's style. Your way is not to win Penelope by suit but by surprise. The castle's carried by a sudden assault that   160 would perhaps sit out a twelvemonth's siege. It would be a good breeding to my young nephew here if he could procure a stand[16] at the palace to see with what alacrity I'll accost her countess-ship, in what garb I will woo her, with what facility I will win her.

Lys. It shall go hard, but we'll hear your entertainment for your confidence sake.

Thar. And having won her, nephew, this sweet face, Which all the city says is so like me, Like me shall be preferred, for I will wed thee   170 To my great widow's daughter and sole heir, The lovely spark, the bright Laodice.

Lys. A good pleasant dream.

Thar.   In this eye I see That fire that shall in me inflame the mother, And that in this shall set on fire the daughter.

It goes, sir, in a blood; believe me, brother, These destinies go ever in a blood.

Lys. These diseases do, brother; take heed of them. Fare you well; take heed you be not baffled.[17]

Exeunt LYSANDER, CYNTHIA, HYLUS, ERO.

Manet THARSALIO.

Thar. Now, thou that art the third blind deity   180 That governs earth in all her happiness, The life of all endowments, Confidence, Direct and prosper my intention. Command thy servant deities, Love and Fortune, To second my attempts for this great lady Whose page I lately was; that she, whose board I might not sit at, I may board abed And under bring, who bore so high her head.

Exit.

[I.ii]

[Enter] LYSANDER, LYCUS.

Lyc. 'Tis miraculous that you tell me, sir: he come to woo our lady mistress for his wife?

Lys. 'Tis a frenzy he is possessed with, and will not be cured but by some violent remedy. And you shall favor me so much to make me a spectator of the scene. But is she, say you, already accessible for suitors? I thought she would have stood so stiffly on her widow vow that she would not endure the sight of a suitor.

Lyc. Faith, sir, Penelope could not bar her gates against her wooers, but she will still be mistress of   10 herself. It is, as you know, a certain itch in female blood; they love to be sued to; but she'll hearken to no suitors.

Lys. But by your leave, Lycus, Penelope is not so wise as her husband Ulysses, for he, fearing the jaws of the siren, stopped his ears with wax against her voice.[1] They that fear the adder's sting will not come near her hissing. Is any suitor with her now?

Lyc. A Spartan lord, dating[2] himself our great viceroy's kinsman, and two or three other of his country lords, as spots in his train. He comes armed with   20 his altitude's letters in grace of his person, with promise to make her a duchess if she embrace the match. This is no mean attraction to her high thoughts, but yet she disdains him.

Lys. And how then shall my brother presume of acceptance? Yet I hold it much more under her contentment to marry such a nasty braggart than under her honor to wed my brother: a gentleman, though I say't, more honorably descended than that lord, who, perhaps, for all his ancestry, would be much troubled to name you the place where his father was born.   31

---

[14] *expect:* wait.

[15] *monopolies . . . down:* Exclusive control, granted to single parties by the crown, of public services and commodities, was recurrently burdensome; in 1603, James I asked holders of monopolies not to exercise them until the Privy Council could review their social implications.

[16] *stand:* station.   [17] *baffled:* disgraced.

I.ii.

[1] *Ulysses . . . voice:* In *Odyssey,* XII Ulysses stops the ears of his men, but not his own, to protect them from the song he wants to hear.   [2] *dating:* giving himself out as.

Lyc. Nay, I hold no comparison betwixt your brother and him. And the venerean³ disease, to which they say he has been long wedded, shall I hope first rot him ere she endure the savor of his sulfurous breath. Well, her ladyship is at hand; y'are best take you to your stand.

Lys. Thanks, good friend Lycus.

Exit.

Enter ARGUS, *barehead, with whom another usher* LYCUS *joins, going over the stage.* HIARBAS *and* PSORABEUS *next,* REBUS *single before* EUDORA, LAODICE, STHENIA *bearing her train,* IANTHE *following.*

Reb. I admire,⁴ madam, you cannot love whom the viceroy loves.

Hia. And one whose veins swell so with his blood, madam, as they do in his lordship.   41

Psor. A near and dear kinsman his lordship is to his altitude the viceroy; in care of whose good speed here I know his altitude hath not slept a sound sleep since his departure.

Eud. I thank Venus I have, ever since he came.

Reb. You sleep away your honor, madam, if you neglect me.

Hia. Neglect your lordship? That were a negligence no less than disloyalty.   50

Eud. I much doubt that, sir; it were rather a presumption to take him, being of the blood viceroyal.

Reb. Not at all, being offered, madam.

Eud. But offered ware is not so sweet, you know. They are the graces of the viceroy that woo me, not your lordship's, and I conceive it should be neither honor nor pleasure to you to be taken in for another man's favors.

Reb. Taken in, madam? You speak as I had no house to hide my head in.   60

Eud. I have heard so indeed, my lord, unless it be another man's.

Reb. You have heard untruth then. These lords can well witness I can want no houses.

Hia. Nor palaces neither, my lord.

Psor. Nor courts neither.

Eud. Nor temples, I think, neither; I believe we shall have a god of him.

Enter THARSALIO.

Arg. See the bold fellow! Whither will you, sir?

Thar. Away!—All honor to you, madam!   70

Eud. How now, base companion?

Thar. Base, madam? He's not base that fights⁵ as high as your lips.

Eud. And does that beseem my servant?

Thar. Your court-servant,⁶ madam.

Eud. One that waited on my board?

Thar. That was only a preparation to my weight on your bed, madam.

Eud. How dar'st thou come to me with such a thought?   80

Thar. Come to you, madam? I dare come to you at midnight, and bid defiance to the proudest spirit that haunts these your loved shadows, and would any way make terrible the access of my love to you.

Eud. Love me? Love my dog.

Thar. I am bound to that by the proverb, madam.

Eud. Kennel without with him; intrude not here. What is it thou presum'st on?

Thar. On your judgment, madam, to choose a man and not a giant, as these are that come with titles   90 and authority as they would conquer or ravish you. But I come to you with the liberal and ingenuous graces: love, youth, and gentry, which, in no more deformed a person than myself, deserve any princess.

Eud. In your saucy opinion, sir, and sirrah too; get gone, and let this malapert⁷ humor return thee no more, for afore heaven I'll have thee tossed in blankets.

Thar. In blankets, madam? You must add your sheets, and you must be the tosser.

Reb. Nay then, sir, y'are as gross as you are saucy.

Thar. And all one, sir, for I am neither.   101

Reb. [*Drawing*] Thou art both.

Thar. Thou liest; keep up your smiter, Lord Rebus.

Hia. Usest thou thus his altitude's cousin?

Reb. The place, thou know'st, protects thee.

Thar. Tie up your valor then till another place turn me loose to you. You are the lord, I take it, that wooed my great mistress here with letters from his altitude, which while she was reading, your lordship, to entertain time, strodled⁸ and scaled your fingers, as you   110 would show what an itching desire you had to get betwixt her sheets.

Hia. 'Slight, why does your lordship endure him?

Reb. The place, the place, my lord.

Thar. Be you his attorney, sir.

Hia. What would you do, sir?

Thar. Make thee leap out at window at which thou cam'st in. Whoreson bagpipe⁹ lords!

Eud. What rudeness is this?   119

Thar. What tameness is it in you, madam, to stick at the discarding of such a suitor! A lean lord, dubbed¹⁰ with the lard of others; a diseased lord, too, that opening certain magic characters in an unlawful book, up start as many aches in's bones as there are ouches¹¹ in's skin. Send him, mistress, to the widow your tenant, the virtuous panderess Arsace. I perceive he has crowns in's purse that make him proud of a string; let her pluck the goose therefore, and her maids dress him.

Psor. Still, my lord, suffer him?

Reb. The place, sir, believe it, the place.   130

Thar. Oh, good Lord Rebus, the place is never like to be yours that you need respect it so much.

Eud. Thou wrong'st the noble gentleman.

Thar. Noble gentleman? A tumor, an imposthume¹² he is, madam; a very hautboy,¹³ a bagpipe, in whom there is nothing but wind, and that none of the sweetest neither.

---

³ *venerean:* pertaining to sexual desire or intercourse.
⁴ *admire:* wonder.   ⁵ *fights:* strives.
⁶ *court-servant:* i.e., wooing servant.
⁷ *malapert:* impudent.   ⁸ *strodled:* straddled.
⁹ *bagpipe:* James's newly made Scotch lords.
¹⁰ *dubbed:* smeared.   ¹¹ *ouches:* sores.
¹² *imposthume:* abscess.   ¹³ *hautboy:* oboe.

Eud. Quit the house of him by th' head and shoulders.

Thar. Thanks to your honor, madam, and my lord
cousin the viceroy shall thank you.   140

Reb. So shall he indeed, sir.

Lyc, Arg. Will you be gone, sir?

Thar. Away, poor fellows.

Eud. What is he made of? Or what devil sees
Your childish and effeminate spirits in him,
That thus ye shun him?—Free us of thy sight;
Be gone, or I protest thy life shall go.

Thar. Yet shall my ghost stay still, and haunt those
        beauties
And glories that have rendered it immortal.
But since I see your blood runs, for the time,   150
High, in that contradiction that foreruns
Truest agreements, like the elements
Fighting before they generate, and that time
Must be attended most in things most worth,
I leave your honor freely, and commend
That life you threaten, when you please, to be
Adventured in your service, so your honor
Require it likewise.

Eud.   Do not come again.

Thar. I'll come again, believe it, and again.   159
                                        Exit.

Eud. If he shall dare to come again, I charge you
Shut doors upon him.

Arg.   You must shut them, madam,
To all men else then, if it please your honor,
For if that any enter, he'll be one.

Eud. I hope, wise sir, a guard will keep him out.

Arg. Afore heaven, not a guard, an't[14] please your
honor.

Eud. Thou liest, base ass; one man enforce a guard?
I'll turn ye all away, by our isle's goddess,
If he but set a foot within my gates.

Psor. Your honor shall do well to have him poisoned.

Hia. Or begged of your cousin, the viceroy.   170
                                    [Exeunt.]

[I.iii]

LYSANDER *[comes forward] from his stand.*

Lys. This braving wooer hath the success expected;
the favor I obtained made me witness to the sport, and
let his confidence be sure, I'll give it him home. The
news by this is blown through the four quarters of the
city. Alas, good confidence! But the happiness is he has
a forehead of proof[1]; the stain shall never stick there,
whatsoever his reproach be.

Enter THARSALIO.

[Aside] What? In discourse?

Thar. [Aside] Hell and the Furies take this vile
        encounter!
Who would imagine this Saturnian peacock[2]   10
Could be so barbarous to use a spirit
Of my erection with such low respect?
'Fore heaven it cuts my gall; but I'll dissemble it.

Lys. What, my noble lord?

Thar. Well, sir, that may be yet, and means to be.

Lys. What means your lordship then to hang that
head that hath been so erected? It knocks, sir, at your
bosom to come in and hide itself.

Thar. Not a jot.

Lys. I hope by this time it needs fear no horns.   20

Thar. Well, sir, but yet that blessing runs not always
in a blood.

Lys. What, blanketed? O the gods! Spurned out by
grooms, like a base bisogno?[3] Thrust out by th' head
and shoulders?

Thar. You do well, sir, to take your pleasure of me.
[Aside] I may turn tables with you ere long.

Lys. What, has thy wit's fine engine[4] taken cold?
Art stuffed in th' head? Canst answer nothing?

Thar. Truth is, I like my entertainment the better
that 'twas no better.   31

Lys. Now the gods forbid that this opinion should
run in a blood.

Thar. Have not you heard this principle, "All things
by strife engender"?

Lys. Dogs and cats do.

Thar. And men and women, too.

Lys. Well, brother, in earnest; you have now set
your confidence to school, from whence I hope't has
brought home such a lesson as will instruct his   40
master never after to begin such attempts as end in
laughter.

Thar. Well, sir, you lesson[5] my confidence still; I
pray heavens your confidence have not more shallow
ground, for that I know, than mine you reprehend so.

Lys. My confidence? In what?

Thar. May be you trust too much.

Lys. Wherein?

Thar. In human frailty.   49

Lys. Why, brother, know you aught that may im-
peach my confidence as this success may yours? Hath
your observation discovered any such frailty in my wife,
for that is your aim I know, then let me know it.

Thar. [Aside] Good, good.—Nay, brother, I write no
books of observations: let your confidence bear out
itself, as mine shall me.

Lys. That's scarce a brother's speech. If there be
aught wherein your brother's good might any way be
questioned, can you conceal it from his bosom?   59

Thar. [Aside] So, so.—Nay, my saying was but
general. I glanced at no particular.

Lys. Then must I press you further. You spake—as
to yourself, but yet I overheard—as if you knew some
disposition of weakness where I most had fixed my
trust. I challenge you to let me know what 'twas.

Thar. Brother, are you wise?

Lys. Why?

Thar. Be ignorant. Did you never hear of Actaeon?[6]

14 *an't:* if it.
I.iii.
1 *of proof:* impervious.
2 *Saturnian peacock:* one of the birds that drew the
chariot of Saturn's daughter Juno.   3 *bisogno:* needy fellow.
4 *engine:* cunning.   5 *lesson:* teach.
6 *Actaeon:* turned to a stag and killed by his own hunting
dogs as punishment for seeing the goddess Diana naked.

Lys. What then?   69

Thar. Curiosity was his death. He could not be content to adore Diana in her temple, but he must needs dog her to her retired pleasures and see her in her nakedness. Do you enjoy the sole privilege of your wife's bed? Have you no pretty Paris[7] for your page? No mystical[8] Adonis[9] to front you there?

Lys. I think none; I know not.

Thar. Know not still, brother. Ignorance and credulity are your sole means to obtain that blessing. You see your greatest clerks, your wisest politicians, are not that way fortunate; your learned lawyers would lose a   80 dozen poor men's causes to gain a lease on't but for a term. Your physician is jealous his. Your sages in general, by seeing too much, oversee that happiness. Only your blockheadly tradesman, your honest-meaning citizen, your not-headed[10] country gentleman, your unapprehending stinkard is blest with the sole prerogative of his wife's chamber, for which he is yet beholding not to his stars but to his ignorance. For if he be wise, brother, I must tell you, the case alters. How do you relish these things, brother?   90

Lys. Passing ill.

Thar. So do sick men solid meats. Hark you, brother, are you not jealous?

Lys. No; do you know cause to make me?

Thar. Hold you there; did your wife never spice your broth with a dram of sublimate?[11] Hath she not yielded up the fort of her honor to a staring soldado,[12] and, taking courage from her guilt, played open bankrupt[13] of all shame and run the country with him? Then bless your stars, bow your knees to Juno. Look where she appears.   101

Enter CYNTHIA, HYLUS [*and* ERO].

Cyn. We have sought you long, sir; there's a messenger within hath brought you letters from the court and desires your speech.

Lys. [*Aside*] I can discover nothing in her looks.— Go; I'll not be long.

Cyn. Sir, it is of weight, the bearer says; and besides, much hastens his departure. Honorable brother! cry mercy! What, in a conqueror's style? But come and overcome?[14]   110

Thar. A fresh course.

Cyn. Alas, you see of how slight metal widows' vows are made.

Thar. [*Aside*] And that shall you prove too ere long.

Cyn. Yet for the honor of our sex, boast not abroad this your easy conquest; another might perhaps have stayed longer below stairs. It but was your confidence that surprised her love.

Hyl. My uncle hath instructed me how to accost an honorable lady; to win her not by suit but by surprise.

Thar. The whelp and all.   121

Hyl. Good uncle, let not your near honors change your manners; be not forgetful of your promise to me, touching your lady's daughter, Laodice. My fancy runs so upon't that I dream every night of her.

Thar. A good chicken; go thy ways, thou hast done well; eat bread with thy meat.

Cyn. Come, sir, will you in?

Lys. I'll follow you.

Cyn. I'll not stir a foot without you. I cannot satisfy the messenger's impatience.   131

[LYSANDER *takes* THARSALIO *aside*.]

Lys. Will you not resolve me, brother?

Thar. Of what?

LYSANDER *stamps and goes out vexed,*
with CYNTHIA, HYLUS, ERO.

So, there's veney for veney.[15] I have given't him i'th' speeding place[16] for all his confidence. Well, out of this perhaps there may be molded matter of more mirth than my baffling. It shall go hard, but I'll make my constant sister act as famous a scene as Virgil did his mistress, who caused all the fire in Rome to fail so that none could light a torch but at her nose. Now   140 forth! At this house dwells a virtuous dame, sometimes of worthy fame, now like a decayed merchant turned broker, and retails refuse commodities for unthrifty gallants. Her wit I must employ upon this business to prepare my next encounter, but in such a fashion as shall make all split.[17] Ho! Madam Arsace!—pray heaven the oysterwives[18] have not brought the news of my wooing hither amongst their stale pilchards.[19]

Enter ARSACE, TOMASIN.

Ars. What? My lord of the palace?

Thar. Look you—   150

Ars. Why, this was done like a beaten[20] soldier.

Thar. Hark, I must speak with you. I have a share for you in this rich adventure. You must be the ass charged with crowns to make way to the fort, and I the conqueror to follow and seize it. See'st thou this jewel?

Ars. Is't come to that? Why, Tomasin.

Tom. Madam.

Ars. Did not one of the countess's serving men tell us that this gentleman was sped?[21]

Tom. That he did, and how her honor graced and entertained him in very familiar manner.   161

Ars. And brought him downstairs herself.

Tom. Ay, forsooth, and commanded her men to bear him out of doors.

Thar. 'Slight, pelted with rotten eggs?

Ars. Nay more, that he had already possessed her sheets.

Tom. No indeed, mistress, 'twas her blankets.

Thar. Out, you young hedge-sparrow; learn to tread
afore you be fledge.   170

He kicks her out.

Well, have you done now, lady?

Ars. Oh, my sweet kilbuck.²²

Thar. You now, in your shallow pate, think this a
disgrace to me; such a disgrace as is a battered helmet
on a soldier's head, it doubles his resolution. Say, shall
I use thee?

Ars. Use me?

Thar. O holy reformation! How art thou fallen down
from the upper bodies of the church to the skirts of the
city! Honesty is stripped out of his true substance   180
into verbal nicety. Common sinners startle at common
terms, and they that by whole mountains swallow down
the deeds of darkness, a poor mote of a familiar word
makes them turn up the white o'th' eye. Thou art the
lady's tenant.

Ars. For term, sir.

Thar. A good induction; be successful for me, make
me lord of the palace, and thou shalt hold thy tenement
to thee and thine heirs forever, in free smockage,²³ as of
the manner of panderage, provided always—   190

Ars. Nay, if you take me unprovided—

Thar. —Provided, I say, that thou mak'st thy repair
to her presently with a plot I will instruct thee in; and
for thy surer access to her greatness, thou shalt present
her, as from thyself, with this jewel.

Ars. So her old grudge stand not betwixt her and me.

Thar. Fear not that.

Presents are present cures for female grudges,
Make bad seem good, alter the case with judges.

Ex[eunt].

Finis Actus Primi.

ACT TWO

SCENE ONE

[*Enter*] LYSANDER, THARSALIO.

Lys. So, now we are ourselves. Brother, that ill-
relished speech you let slip from your tongue hath
taken so deep hold of my thoughts that they will never
give me rest till I be resolved what 'twas you said you
know touching my wife.

Thar. Tush, I am weary of this subject; I said not so.

Lys. By truth itself you did; I overheard you. Come,
it shall nothing move me, whatsoever it be. Pray thee
unfold briefly what you know.   9

Thar. Why briefly, brother, I know my sister to be
the wonder of the earth and the envy of the heavens,
virtuous, loyal, and what not. Briefly, I know she hath
vowed that till death and after death she'll hold inviolate her bonds to you, and that her black shall take
no other hue, all which I firmly believe. In brief,
brother, I know her to be a woman. But you know,
brother, I have other irons on th'anvil.

*Exiturus.*¹

Lys. You shall not leave me so unsatisfied. Tell me
what 'tis you know.   19

Thar. Why, brother, if you be sure of your wife's
loyalty for term of life, why should you be curious to
search the almanacs for aftertimes, whether some
wand'ring. Aeneas² should enjoy your reversion,³ or
whether your true turtle⁴ would sit mourning on a
withered branch till Atropos⁵ cut her throat? Beware
of curiosity, for who can resolve you? You'll say, perhaps, her vow.

Lys. Perhaps I shall.

Thar. Tush, herself knows not what she shall do
when she is transformed into a widow. You are now   30
a sober and staid gentleman. But if Diana for your
curiosity should translate⁶ you into a monkey, do you
know what gambols you should play? Your only way to
be resolved is to die and make trial of her.

Lys. A dear experiment; then I must rise again to be
resolved.

Thar. You shall not need. I can send you speedier
advertisement of her constancy by the next ripier⁷ that
rides that way with mackerel.⁸ And so I leave you.   39

Exit THARSALIO.

Lys. All the Furies in hell attend thee; h'as given me
A bone to tire on⁹ with a pestilence. 'Slight, know?
What can he know? What can his eye observe
More than mine own, or the most piercing sight
That ever viewed her? By this light, I think
Her privat'st thought may dare the eye of heaven
And challenge th'envious world to witness it.
I know him for a wild, corrupted youth,
Whom profane ruffians, squires to bawds and
    strumpets,
Drunkards spewed out of taverns into th' sinks
Of taphouses and stews, revolts from manhood,   50
Debauched perdus,¹⁰ have by their companies
Turned devil like themselves and stuffed his soul
With damned opinions and unhallowed thoughts
Of womanhood, of all humanity,
Nay, deity itself.

Enter LYCUS.

Welcome, friend Lycus.

Lyc. Have you met with your capricious brother?

Lys. He parted hence but now.

Lyc. And has he yet resolved you of that point you
brake with me about?   59

Lys. Yes, he bids me die for further trial of her
constancy.

---

²² *kilbuck:* fierce-looking fellow.
²³ *smockage:* smock-service, nonce word formed by
analogy with "socage," tenure of land by performance of a
service.
II.i.
   ¹ *Exiturus:* About to go.
   ² *Aeneas:* The Trojan exile had an affair en route with the
widow Dido.
   ³ *reversion:* inheritance of position; i.e., succession of
right to the widow.   ⁴ *turtle:* turtledove.
   ⁵ *Atropos:* one of the Fates.   ⁶ *translate:* transform.
   ⁷ *ripier:* fish-seller.   ⁸ *mackerel:* procurer.
   ⁹ *tire on:* pull, tug (falconry).   ¹⁰ *perdus:* profligates.

Lyc. That were a strange physic for a jealous patient, to cure his thirst with a draught of poison. Faith, sir, discharge your thoughts on't; think 'twas but a buzz[11] devised by him to set your brains a-work and divert your eye from his disgrace. The world hath written your wife in highest lines of honored fame; her virtues so admired in this isle as the report thereof sounds in foreign ears, and strangers oft arriving here as some rare sight desire to view her presence, thereby to compare the picture with the original.   71
Nor think he can turn so far rebel to his blood,
Or to the truth itself, to misconceive
Her spotless love and loyalty; perhaps,
Oft having heard you hold her faith so sacred,
As you being dead, no man might stir a spark
Of virtuous love in way of second bonds,
As if you at your death should carry with you
Both branch and root of all affection;
'T may be, in that point he's an infidel,   80
And thinks your confidence may over ween.
Lys. So think not I.
Lyc. Nor I, if ever any made it good.
I am resolved, of all, she'll prove no changeling.
Lys. Well, I must yet be further satisfied,
And vent this humor by some strain of wit.
Somewhat I'll do; but what, I know not yet.
                                        Exeunt.

[II.ii]

Enter STHENIA, IANTHE.

Sthen. Passion of virginity, Ianthe, how shall we quit ourselves of this panderess that is so importunate to speak with us? Is she known to be a panderess?
Ian. Ay, as well as we are known to be waiting-women.
Sthen. A shrew take your comparison.
Ian. Let's call out Argus, that bold ass that never weighs what he does or says, but walks and talks like one in a sleep, to relate her attendance to my lady and present her.   10
Sthen. Who, an't please your honor? None so fit to set on any dangerous exploit. Ho, Argus!

Enter ARGUS *bare.*

Arg. What's the matter, wenches?
Sthen. You must tell my lady here's a gentlewoman called Arsace, her honor's tenant, attends her to impart important business to her.
Arg. I will presently.
                                        Exit ARGUS.
Ian. Well, she has a welcome present to bear out[1] her unwelcome presence, and I never knew but a good gift would welcome a bad person to the purest.—Arsace!   21

Enter ARSACE.

Ars. Ay, mistress.
Sthen. Give me your present; I'll do all I can to make way both for it and yourself.
Ars. You shall bind me to your service, lady.
Sthen. Stand unseen.

Enter LYCUS, EUDORA, LAODICE; ARGUS *coming to* EUDORA.

Arg. Here's a gentlewoman, an't please your honor, one of your tenants, desires access to you.
Eud. What tenant? What's her name?
Arg. Arsace, she says, madam.   30
Eud. Arsace? What, the bawd?

She strikes [*him*].

Arg. The bawd, madam? That's without my privity.[2]
Eud. Out, ass; know'st not thou the panderess Arsace?
Sthen. She presents your honor with this jewel.
Eud. This jewel! How came she by such a jewel? She has had great customers.
Arg. She had need, madam; she sits at a great rent.
Eud. Alas, for your great rent. I'll keep her jewel, and keep you her out, ye were best. Speak to me for a panderess?   41
Arg. [*Aside*] What shall we do?
Sthen. [*Aside*] Go to; let us alone.—Arsace!
Ars. Ay, lady.
Sthen. You must pardon us; we cannot obtain your access.
Ars. Mistress Sthenia, tell her honor if I get not access to her, and that instantly, she's undone.
Sthen. This is something of importance.—Madam, she swears your honor is undone if she speak not with you instantly.   51
Eud. Undone?
Ars. Pray her, for her honor's sake, to give me instant access to her.
Sthen. She makes her business your honor, madam, and entreats, for the good of that, her instant speech with you.
Eud. How comes my honor in question? Bring her to me.   59

ARSACE *approaches to* EUDORA.

Ars. Our Cyprian goddess save your good honor.
Eud. Stand you off, I pray. How dare you, mistress, importune access to me thus, considering the last warning I gave for your absence?
Ars. Because, madam, I have been moved by your honor's last most chaste admonition to leave the offensive life I led before.
Eud. Ay? Have you left it then?
Ars. Ay, I assure your honor, unless it be for the pleasure of two or three poor ladies that have prodigal knights to their husbands.   70
Eud. Out on thee, impudent.
Ars. Alas, madam, we would all be glad to live in our callings.

---

[11] *buzz:* false rumor.

II.ii.
[1] *bear out:* support.   [2] *privity:* private knowledge.

Eud. Is this the reformed life thou talk'st on?

Ars. I beseech your good honor, mistake me not; I boast of nothing but my charity, that's the worst.

Eud. You get these jewels with charity, no doubt. But what's the point in which my honor stands endangered, I pray?   79

Ars. In care of that, madam, I have presumed to offend your chaste eyes with my presence. Hearing it reported for truth and generally that your honor will take to husband a young gentleman of this city called Tharsalio—

Eud. I take him to husband?

Ars. If your honor does, you are utterly undone, for he's the most incontinent and insatiate man of women that ever Venus blessed with ability to please them.

Eud. Let him be the devil; I abhor his thought, and could I be informed particularly of any of these   90 slanderers of mine honor, he should as dearly dare it as anything wherein his life were endangered.

Ars. Madam, the report of it is so strongly confident that I fear the strong destiny of marriage is at work in it. But if it be, madam, let your honor's known virtue resist and defy it for him, for not a hundred will serve his one turn. I protest to your honor, when—Venus pardon me—I winked at my unmaidenly exercise, I have known nine in a night made mad with his love.   99

Eud. What tell'st thou me of his love? I tell thee I abhor him, and destiny must have another mold for my thoughts than nature or mine honor, and a witchcraft above both, to transform me to another shape, as soon as to another conceit of him.

Ars. Then is your good honor just as I pray for you. And, good madam, even for your virtue's sake and comfort of all your dignities and possessions, fix your whole womanhood against him. He will so enchant you as never man did woman; nay, a goddess, say his light huswives,[3] is not worthy of his sweetness.   110

Eud. Go to, be gone.

Ars. Dear madam, your honor's most perfect admonitions have brought me to such a hate of these imperfections that I could not but attend you with my duty and urge his unreasonable manhood to the fill.

Eud. Manhood, quoth you?

Ars. Nay, beastlihood, I might say indeed, madam, but for saving your honor. Nine in a night, said I?

Eud. Go to, no more.   119

Ars. No more, madam? That's enough, one would think.

Eud. Well, be gone I bid thee.

Ars. Alas, madam, your honor is the chief of our city, and to whom shall I complain of these inchastities, being your ladyship's reformed tenant, but to you that are chastest?

Eud. I pray thee, go thy ways, and let me see this reformation you pretend continued.

Ars. I humbly thank your good honor, that was first cause of it.   130

Eud. Here's a complaint as strange as my suitor.

Ars. I beseech your good honor think upon him, make him an example.

Eud. Yet again?

Ars. All my duty to your excellence.

                                              Exit ARSACE.

Eud. These sorts of licentious persons, when they are once reclaimed, are most vehement against licence. But it is the course of the world to dispraise faults and use them, that so we may use them the safer. What might a wise widow resolve upon this point now?   140 Contentment is the end of all worldly beings. Beshrew her, would she had spared her news.

                                                       Exit.

[*Enter* REBUS, HIARBAS, PSORABEUS.]

Reb. See if she take not a contrary way to free herself of us.

Hia. You must complain to his altitude.

Psor. All this for trial is; you must endure That will have wives, naught else with them is sure.

                                                    [*Exeunt.*]

[II.iii]

[*Enter*] THARSALIO, ARSACE.

Thar. Hast thou been admitted then?

Ars. Admitted? Ay, into her heart, I'll able[1] it. Never was man so praised with a dispraise nor so spoken for in being railed on. I'll give you my word, I have set her heart upon as tickle[2] a pin as the needle of a dial, that will never let it rest till it be in the right position.

Thar. Why dost thou imagine this?

Ars. Because I saw Cupid shoot in my words and open his wounds in her looks. Her blood went and   10 came of errands betwixt her face and her heart; and these changes, I can tell you, are shrewd telltales.

Thar. Thou speak'st like a doctress in thy faculty; but howsoever, for all this foil, I'll retrieve the game once again. He's a shallow gamester that for one displeasing cast gives up so fair a game for lost.

Ars. Well, 'twas a villainous invention of thine, and had a swift operation; it took like sulfur. And yet this virtuous countess hath to my ear spun out many a tedious lecture of pure sister's thread against con-   20 cupiscence; but ever with such an affected zeal as my mind gave me she had a kind of secret titillation[3] to grace my poor house sometimes, but that she feared a spice[4] of the sciatica, which as you know ever runs in the blood.

Thar. And, as you know, soaks into the bones. But to say truth, these angry heats that break out at the lips of these strait-laced ladies are but as symptoms of a lustful fever that boils within them. For wherefore rage wives at their husbands so, when they fly out?[5] For zeal against the sin?   31

Ars. No, but because they did not purge that sin.

---

[3] *light huswives:* loose women.

II.iii.
[1] *able:* warrant.   [2] *tickle:* insecurely poised.
[3] *titillation:* desire.   [4] *spice:* touch.
[5] *fly out:* transgress.

Thar. Th'art a notable siren, and I swear to thee if I prosper, not only to give thee thy manor house gratis, but to marry thee to some one knight or other and bury thy trade in thy ladyship. Go, be gone.

Exit ARSACE.

Enter LYCUS.

Thar. What news, Lycus? Where's the lady?

Lyc. Retired into her orchard.

Thar. A pregnant badge of love, she's melancholy.

Lyc. 'Tis with the sight of her Spartan wooer.   40
But howsoever 'tis with her, you have practiced strangely upon your brother.

Thar. Why so?

Lyc. You had almost lifted his wit off the hinges. That spark jealousy, falling into his dry, melancholy brain, had well near set the whole house on fire.

Thar. No matter, let it work; I did but pay him in's own coin. 'Sfoot, he plied me with such a volley of unseasoned scoffs as would have made Patience itself turn ruffian, attiring itself in wounds and blood. But is his humor better qualified[6] then?   51

Lyc. Yes, but with a medicine ten parts more dangerous than the sickness. You know how strange his dotage ever was on his wife, taking special glory to have her love and loyalty to him so renowned abroad; to whom she oftentimes hath vowed constancy after life till her own death had brought, forsooth, her widow-troth to bed. This he joyed in strangely and was therein of infallible belief, till your surmise began to shake it; which hath loosed it so as now there's nought can settle it but a trial, which he's resolved upon.   61

Thar. As how, man? As how?

Lyc. He is resolved to follow your advice, to die and make trial of her stableness, and you must lend your hand to it.

Thar. What, to cut's throat?

Lyc. To forge a rumor of his death, to uphold it by circumstance, maintain a public face of mourning, and all things appertaining.   69

Thar. Ay, but the means, man? What time, what probability?

Lyc. Nay, I think he has not licked his whelp into full shape yet, but you shall shortly hear on't.

Thar. And when shall this strange conception see light?

Lyc. Forthwith; there's nothing stays him but some odd business of import which he must wind up lest perhaps his absence by occasion of his intended trial be prolonged above his aims.   79

Thar. Thanks for this news, i'faith. This may perhaps prove happy to my nephew. Truth is, I love my sister well and must acknowledge her more than ordinary virtues. But she hath so possessed my brother's heart with vows and disavowings, sealed with oaths of second nuptials, as in that confidence he hath invested her in all his state, the ancient inheritance of our family,

and left my nephew and the rest to hang upon her pure devotion; so as he dead, and she matching—as I am resolved she will—with some young prodigal, what must ensue but her post-issue[7] beggared and our   90 house, already sinking, buried quick in ruin? But this trial may remove it, and since 'tis come to this, mark but the issue, Lycus; for all these solemn vows, if I do not make her prove in the handling as weak as a wafer, say I lost my time in travail. This resolution, then, has set his wits in joint again; he's quiet?

Lyc. Yes, and talks of you again in the fairest manner, listens after your speed—

Thar. Nay, he's passing kind, but I am glad of this trial for all that.   100

Lyc. Which he thinks to be a flight beyond your wing.

Thar. But he will change that thought ere long. My bird you saw even now sings me good news and makes hopeful signs to me.

Lyc. Somewhat can I say, too. Since your messenger's departure, her ladyship hath been something altered, more pensive than before, and took occasion to question of you what your addictions were, of what taste your humor was, of what cut you wore your wit, and all this in a kind of disdainful scorn.   111

Thar. Good calendars,[8] Lycus. Well, I'll pawn this jewel with thee, my next encounter shall quite alter my brother's judgment. Come, let's in; he shall commend it for a discreet and honorable attempt.
Men's judgments sway on that side Fortune leans.
Thy wishes shall assist me.

Lyc.   And my means.

Exeunt.

[II.iv]

[*Enter*] ARGUS, CLINIAS, STHENIA, IANTHE.

Arg. I must confess I was ignorant what 'twas to court a lady till now.

Sthen. And I pray you, what is it now?

Arg. To court her, I perceive, is to woo her with letters from court, for so this Spartan lord's court discipline teacheth.

Sthen. His lordship hath procured a new packet from his altitude.

Clin. If he bring no better ware than letters in's packet, I shall greatly doubt of his good speed.   10

Ian. If his lordship did but know how gracious his aspect is to my lady in this solitary humor.

Clin. Well, these retired walks of hers are not usual, and bode some alteration in her thoughts. What may be the cause, Sthenia?

Sthen. Nay, 'twould trouble Argus with his hundred eyes to descry the cause.

Ian. Venus keep her upright, that she fall not from the state of her honor; my fear is that some of these serpentine suitors will tempt her from her con-   20 stant vow of widowhood. If they do, good night to our good days.

Sthen. 'Twere a sin to suspect her. I have been wit-

---

[6] *qualified:* moderated.

[7] *post-issue:* children by a second marriage.

[8] *calendars:* omens.

ness to so many of her fearful protestations to our late
lord against that course; to her infinite oaths imprinted
on his lips, and sealed in his heart with such imprecations to her bed, if ever it should receive a second impression; to her open and often detestations of that
incestuous life, as she termed it, of widows' marriages
as being but a kind of lawful adultery, like usury,   30
permitted by the law, not approved; that to wed a
second was no better than to cuckold the first; that
women should entertain wedlock as one body, as one
life, beyond which there were no desire, no thought, no
repentance from it, no restitution to it. So as if the
conscience of her vows should not restrain her, yet the
world's shame to break such a constant resolution
should repress any such motion in her.

Arg. Well, for her vows, they are gone to heaven with
her husband; they bind not upon earth. And as for   40
women's resolutions, I must tell you, the planets, and,
as Ptolemy says, the winds have a great stroke in them.
Trust not my learning if her late strangeness and
exorbitant solitude be not hatching some new monster.

Ian. Well applied, Argus. Make you husbands
monsters?

Arg. I spoke of no husbands; but you wenches have
the pregnant wits to turn monsters into husbands, as
you turn husbands into monsters.

Sthen. Well, Ianthe, 'twere high time we made in to
part our lady and her Spartan wooer.   51

Ian. We shall appear to her like the two fortunate
stars[1] in a tempest, to save the shipwreck of her
patience.

Sthen. Ay; and to him too, I believe, for by this time
he hath spent the last dram of his news.

Arg. That is, of his wit.

Sthen. Just, good wittols.[2]

Ian. If not, and that my lady be not too deep in her
new dumps, we shall hear from his lordship what   60
such a lord said of his wife the first night he embraced
her; to what gentleman such a count was beholding for
his fine children; what young lady such an old count
should marry; what revels, what presentments are towards; and who penned the pegmas,[3] and so forth.
And yet for all this, I know her harsh suitor hath tired
her to the uttermost scruple of her forbearance, and
will do more unless we two, like a pair of shears, cut
asunder the thread of his discourse.   69

Sthen. Well then, let's in. But, my masters, wait you
on your charge at your perils; see that you guard her
approach from any more intruders.

Ian. Excepting young Tharsalio.

Sthen. True, excepting him indeed, for a guard of
men is not able to keep him out, an't please your honor.

Arg. O wenches, that's the property of true valor, to
promise like a pigmy and perform like a giant. If he
come, I'll be sworn I'll do my lady's commandment
upon him.

Ian. What, beat him out?   80

Sthen. If he should, Tharsalio would not take it ill at
his hands, for he does but his lady's commandment.

Enter THARSALIO.

Arg. Well, by Hercules, he comes not here.

Sthen. By Venus, but he does, or else she hath heard
my lady's prayers and sent some gracious spirit in his
likeness to fright away that Spartan wooer that haunts
her.

Thar. There stand her sentinels.

Arg. 'Slight, the ghost appears again.   89

Thar. Save ye, my quondam[4] fellows in arms; save
ye, my women.

Sthen. Your women, sir?

Thar. 'Twill be so. What, no courtesies? No preparation of grace? Observe me, I advise you, for your
own sakes.

Ian. For your own sake, I advise you to pack hence,
lest your impudent valor cost you dearer than you think.

Clin. What senseless boldness is this, Tharsalio?

Arg. Well said, Clinias, talk to him.   99

Clin. I wonder that notwithstanding the shame of
your last entertainment and threatenings of worse, you
would yet presume to trouble this place again.

Thar. Come, y'are a widgeon.[5] Off with your hat, sir,
acknowledge! Forecast is better than labor. Are you
squint-eyed? Can you not see afore you? A little foresight, I can tell you, might stead you much, as the stars
shine now.

Clin. 'Tis well, sir, 'tis not for nothing your brother
is ashamed on you. But, sir, you must know we are
charged to bar your entrance.   110

Thar. But, whiffler,[6] know you that whoso shall dare
to execute that charge, I'll be his executioner.

Arg. By Jove, Clinias, methinks the gentleman speaks
very honorably.

Thar. Well, I see this house needs reformation.
Here's a fellow stands behind now, of a forwarder in-
sight than ye all. What place hast thou?

Arg. What place you please, sir.

Thar. Law you, sir, here's a fellow to make a gentleman usher, sir. I discharge you of the place and   120
do here invest thee into his room. Make much of thy
hair, thy wit will suit it rarely. And for the full possession of thine office, come, usher me to thy lady; and to
keep thy hand supple, take this from me.

Arg. No bribes, sir, an't please your worship.

Thar. Go to, thou dost well. But pocket it for all that;
it's no impair to thee, the greatest do't.

Arg. Sir, 'tis your love only that I respect, but since
out of your love you please to bestow it upon me, it were
want of courtship in me to refuse it. I'll acquaint my
lady with your coming.   131

Exit ARGUS.

Thar. How say by this? Have not I made a fit choice,
that hath so soon attained the deepest mystery of his

II.iv.
[1] *fortunate stars:* St. Elmo's fire, electrical phenomenon
seen on shipmasts in storms, identified by ancients with twin
stars Castor and Pollux, protectors of sea travelers.
[2] *wittols:* willing cuckolds, tools.
[3] *pegmas:* inscriptions on a pageant stage.
[4] *quondam:* former.   [5] *widgeon:* duck, fool.
[6] *whiffler:* clearer of the way for a master or procession.

profession? Good sooth, wenches, a few courtesies had
not been cast away upon your new lord.

Sthen. We'll believe that, when our lady has a new
son of your getting.

Enter Argus, Eudora, Rebus, Hiarbas,
Psorabeus.

Eud. What's the matter! Who's that, you say, is
come?

Arg. The bold gentleman, an't please your honor.

Eud. Why, thou fleering ass, thou.　　　　141

Arg. An't please your honor—

Eud. Did not I forbid his approach by all the charge
and duty of thy service?

Thar. Madam, this fellow only is intelligent, for he
truly understood your command according to the style
of the Court of Venus; that is, by contraries: when you
forbid, you bid.

Eud. By heaven, I'll discharge my house of ye all.

Thar. You shall not need, madam, for I have　150
already cashiered your officious usher here and choosed
this for his successor.

Eud. O incredible boldness!

Thar. Madam, I come not to command your love
with enforced letters nor to woo you with tedious
stories of my pedigree, as he who draws the thread of
his descent from Leda's [7] distaff, when 'tis well known
his grandsire cried [8] cony [9] skins in Sparta.

Reb. Who mean you, sir?　　　　159

Thar. Sir, I name none but him who first shall name
himself.

Reb. The place, sir, I tell you still, and this goddess's
fair presence, or else my reply should take a far other
form upon't.

Thar. If it should, sir, I would make your lordship
an answer.

Arg. Anser's Latin for a goose, an't please your
honor.

Eud. Well noted, gander, and what of that?　169

Arg. Nothing, an't please your honor, but that he
said he would make his lordship an answer.

Eud. Thus every fool mocks my poor suitor. Tell me,
thou most frontless [10] of all men, did'st thou, when thou
had'st means to note me best, ever observe so base a
temper in me as to give any glance at stooping to my
vassal—

Thar. Your drudge, madam, to do your drudgery.

Eud. Or am I now so scant of worthy suitors that
may advance mine honor, advance my estate, strengthen my alliance, if I list to wed, that I must stoop to
make my foot my head?　　　　181

---

[7] *Leda:* mother of Helen and Clytemnestra and Castor
and Pollux, who have just been cited on the previous page.
[8] *cried:* peddled.　　　　　[9] *cony:* rabbit.
[10] *frontless:* shameless.　　[11] *Lycurgus:* Spartan lawgiver.
[12] *lamb-skinned:* thrashed.
[13] *Hercules . . . business:* Hercules was made by Apollo to
serve Queen Omphale as a slave and to perform female tasks
for her.
[14] *Sparta-Velvets:* wealthy or effete wearers of velvet.
[15] *Calydonian boar:* inflicted by Diana on kingdom of
Calydon; perhaps with a suggestion of Scotland (Caledonia).

Thar. No, but your side, to keep you warm abed.
But, madam, vouchsafe me your patience to that point's
serious answer. Though I confess, to get higher place in
your graces I could wish my fortunes more honorable,
my person more gracious, my mind more adorned with
noble and heroical virtues; yet, madam, that you think
not your blood disparaged by mixture with mine, deign
to know this: howsoever I once, only for your love,
disguised myself in the service of your late lord　190
and mine, yet my descent is as honorable as the proudest of your Spartan attempters, who, by unknown quills
or conduits underground, draws his pedigree from
Lycurgus [11] his great toe to the viceroy's little finger,
and from thence to his own elbow, where it will never
leave itching.

Reb. 'Tis well, sir, presume still of the place.

Thar. 'Sfoot, madam, am I the first great personage
that hath stooped to disguises for love? What think you
of our countryman Hercules, that for love put on　200
Omphale's apron and sat spinning amongst her wenches
while his mistress wore his lion's skin and lamb-skinned [12] him if he did not his business? [13]

Eud. Most fitly thou resembl'st thyself to that violent outlaw that claimed all other men's possessions as
his own by his mere valor. For what less hast thou
done? Come into my house, beat away these honorable
persons—

Thar. That I will, madam. Hence, ye Sparta-
Velvets. [14]　　　　210

[Beating them.]

Psor. Hold, she did not mean so.

Thar. Away, I say, or leave your lives, I protest, here.

Hia. Well, sir, his altitude shall know you.

Reb. I'll do your errand, sir.

　　　　　　　　　　　　　　　　Exeunt.

Thar. Do, good cousin altitude, and beg the reversion of the next lady, for Dido has betrothed her love to
me. By this fair hand, madam, a fair riddance of this
Calydonian boar. [15]

Eud. O most prodigious audaciousness!　　219

Thar. True, madam. O fie upon 'em, they are intolerable. And I cannot but admire your singular virtue
of patience, not common in your sex, and must therefore carry with it some rare endowment of other masculine and heroical virtues. To hear a rude Spartan court
so ingenuous a lady with dull news from Athens or the
viceroy's court, how many dogs were spoiled at the
last bullbaiting, what ladies dubbed their husbands
knights, and so forth.

Eud. But hast thou no shame? No sense of what disdain I showed thee in my last entertainment,　230
chasing thee from my presence, and charging thy duty
not to attempt the like intrusion for thy life; and dar'st
thou yet approach me in this unmannerly manner? No
question this desperate boldness cannot choose but go
accompanied with other infinite rudenesses.

Thar. Good madam, give not the child an unfit
name; term it not boldness which the sages call true
confidence, founded on the most infallible rock of a
woman's constancy.　　　　239

Eud. If shame cannot restrain thee, tell me yet if any brainless fool would have tempted the danger attending thy approach.

Thar. No, madam, that proves I am no fool. Then had I been here a fool, and a base, low-spirited Spartan, if for a lady's frown, or a lord's threats, or for a guard of grooms, I should have shrunk in the wetting[16] and suffered such a delicious flower to perish in the stalk or to be savagely plucked by a profane finger. No, madam, first let me be made a subject for disgrace; let your remorseless guard seize on my despised body,   250 bind me hand and foot, and hurl me into your ladyship's bed.

Eud. O gods, I protest thou dost more and more make me admire thee.

Thar. Madam, ignorance is the mother of admiration; know me better, and you'll admire me less.

Eud. What would'st thou have me know? What seeks thy coming? Why dost thou haunt me thus?

Thar. Only, madam, that the Aetna[17] of my sighs and Nilus[18] of my tears, poured forth in your   260 presence, might witness to your honor the hot and moist affection of my heart, and work me some measure of favor from your sweet tongue or your sweeter lips or what else your good ladyship shall esteem more conducible to your divine contentment.

Eud. Pen and inkhorn,[19] I thank thee. This you learned when you were a servingman.

Thar. Madam, I am still the same creature, and I will so tie my whole fortunes to that style, as were it my happiness—as I know it will be—to mount into   270 my lord's succession, yet vow I never to assume other title or state than your servant's; not approaching your board, but bidden; not pressing to your bed, but your pleasure shall be first known if you will command me any service.

Eud. Thy vows are as vain as a ruffian's oaths, as common as the air, and as cheap as the dust. How many of the light huswives, thy muses, hath thy love promised this service besides, I pray thee?   279

Thar. Compare shadows to bodies, madam, pictures to the life, and such are they to you, in my valuation.

Eud. I see words will never free me of thy boldness, and will therefore now use blows, and those of the mortalest enforcement. Let it suffice, sir, that all this time, and to this place, you enjoy your safety. Keep back, no one foot follow me further; for I protest to thee, the next threshold passed, lets pass a prepared ambush to thy latest breath.

            Exit EUDORA.

Thar. This for your ambush. [*He draws.*] Dare my love with death?   290
            [*Exit.*]

Clin. 'Slight, follow, an't please your honor.

Arg. Not I, by this light.

Clin. I hope, gentlewomen, you will.

Sthen. Not we, sir; we are no parters of frays.

Clin. Faith, nor I'll be any breaker of customs.

            Exeunt.

Finis Actus Secundi.

ACT THREE

SCENE ONE

Enter LYSANDER *and* LYCUS, *booted.*

Lyc. Would any heart of adamant, for satisfaction of an ungrounded humor, rack a poor lady's innocency as you intend to do? It was a strange curiosity in that emperor that ripped his mother's womb to see the place he lay in.

Lys. Come, do not load me with volumes of persuasion; I am resolved, if she be gold she may abide the tast.[1] Let's away. I wonder where this wild brother is.

Enter CYNTHIA, HYLUS, *and* ERO.

Cyn. Sir—   9

Lys. I pray thee, wife, show but thyself a woman, and be silent. Question no more the reason of my journey, which our great viceroy's charge, urged in this letter, doth enforce me to.

Cyn. Let me but see that letter; there is something
In this presaging blood of mine tells me
This sudden journey can portend no good.
Resolve me, sweet; have not I given you cause
Of discontent by some misprision,[2]
Or want of fit observance? Let me know,
That I may wreak[3] myself upon myself.   20

   Lys. Come, wife, our love is now grown old and
     staid,
And must not wanton it in tricks of court,
Nor interchanged delights of melting lovers,
Hanging on sleeves, sighing, loath to depart.
These toys are past with us; our true love's substance
Hath worn out all the show. Let it suffice
I hold thee dear; and think some cause of weight,
With no excuse to be dispensed withal,
Compels me from thy most desired embraces,
I stay but for my brother; came he not in last night?   30

Hyl. For certain no, sir, which gave us cause of wonder what accident kept him abroad.

Cyn. Pray heaven it prove not some wild resolution bred in him by his second repulse from the countess.

Lys. Trust me, I something fear it. This insatiate spirit of aspiring, being so dangerous and fatal, desire mounted on the wings of it descends not but headlong.

Hyl. Sir, sir, here's my uncle.

Enter THARSALIO [*cloaked*].

Lys. What, wrapped in careless cloak, face hid in hat unbanded? These are the ditches, brother, in   40 which outraging[4] colts plunge both themselves and their riders.

Thar. Well, we must get out as well as we may; if not, there's the making of a grave saved.

---

[16] *shrunk . . . wetting:* failed a test.

[17] *Aetna:* Sicilian volcano.   [18] *Nilus:* the river Nile.

[19] *inkhorn:* i.e., pedantic or bookish language.

III.i.

[1] *tast:* touch, test.

[2] *misprision:* omission, misunderstanding.

[3] *wreak:* revenge.   [4] *outraging:* wild.

Cyn. That's desperately spoken, brother; had it not been happier the colt had been better broken, and his rider not fallen in.

Thar. True, sister, but we must ride colts before we can break them, you know.

Lys. This is your blind goddess Confidence.   50

Thar. Alas, brother, our house is decayed, and my honest ambition to restore it, I hope, be pardonable. My comfort is, the poet that pens the story will write o'er my head *Magnis tamen excidit ausis,*[5] Which, in our native idiom, lets you know, His mind was high, though Fortune was his foe.[6]

Lys. A good resolve, brother, to outjest disgrace. Come, I had been on my journey but for some private speech with you. Let's in.   59

Thar. Good brother, stay a little; help out this ragged colt out of the ditch.

[Uncloaks and reveals a splendid suit.]

Lys. How now?

Thar. Now I confess my oversight; this have I purchased by my confidence.

Lys. I like you, brother; 'tis the true garb, you know; What wants in real worth supply in show.

Thar. In show? Alas, 'twas even the thing itself. I oped my counting house and took away These simple fragments of my treasury, "Husband," my countess cried, "take more, more yet";   70 Yet I, in haste to pay in part my debt And prove myself a husband of her store, Kissed and came off, and this time took no more—

Cyn. But, good brother—

Thar. —Then were our honored spousal rites performed; We made all short, and sweet, and close, and sure—

Lys. He's rapt.

Thar. —Then did my ushers and chief servants stoop; Then made my women curtsies, and envied Their lady's fortune. I was magnified.   80

Lys. Let him alone; this spirit will soon vanish.

Thar. Brother and sister, as I love you and am true servant to Venus, all the premises are serious and true, and the conclusion is, the great countess is mine, the palace is at your service, to which I invite you all to solemnize my honored nuptials.

Lys. Can this be credited?

Thar. Good brother, do not you envy my fortunate achievement?   89

Lys. Nay, I ever said the attempt was commendable—

Thar. Good.

Lys. —If the issue were successful.

---

[5] *L.:* "Though he greatly failed, more greatly dared"; from Phaëthon's epitaph, Ovid, *Metamorphoses,* II. 328.
[6] *Fortune . . . foe:* allusion to a popular song.
[7] *events:* outcomes.   [8] *coyness:* reserve.
[9] *busk points:* tagged laces that secure the bone stiffener of the corset; here signifying bosom.
[10] *occurrents:* occurrences.

Thar. A good state-conclusion; happy events[7] make good the worst attempts. Here are your widow-vows, sister; thus are ye all in your pure naturals. Certain moral disguises of coyness,[8] which the ignorant call modesty, ye borrow of art to cover your busk points,[9] which a blunt and resolute encounter, taken under a fortunate aspect, easily disarms you of; and then,   100 alas, what are you? Poor naked sinners, God wot; weak paper walls thrust down with a finger. This is the way on't: boil their appetites to a full height of lust and then take them down in the nick.

Cyn. Is there probability in this, that a lady so great, so virtuous, standing on so high terms of honor, should so soon stoop?

Thar. You would not wonder, sister, if you knew the lure she stooped at. Greatness? Think you that can curb affection? No, it whets it more. They have   110 the full stream of blood to bear them, the sweet gale of their sublimed spirits to drive them, the calm of ease to prepare them, the sunshine of fortune to allure them, greatness to waft them safe through all rocks of infamy. When youth, wit, and person come aboard once, tell me, sister, can you choose but hoist sail and put forward to the main?

Lys. But let me wonder at this frailty yet. Would she in so short time wear out his memory, So soon wipe from her eyes, nay, from her heart,   120 Whom I myself and this whole isle besides Still remember with grief, the impression of his loss Taking worthily such roots in us? How think you, wife?

Cyn. I am ashamed on't, and abhor to think So great and vowed a pattern of our sex Should take into her thoughts, nay, to her bed— O stain to womanhood—a second love.

Lyc. In so short time.

Cyn.   In any time.

Lys.   No, wife?

Cyn. By Juno no; sooner a loathsome toad.   130

Thar. High words, believe me, and I think she'll keep them. Next turn is yours, nephew; you shall now marry my noblest lady-daughter; the first marriage in Paphos next my nuptials shall be yours. These are strange occurrents,[10] brother, but pretty and pathetical. If you see me in my chair of honor and my countess in mine arms, you will then believe, I hope, I am lord of the palace; then shall you try my great lady's entertainment, see your hands freed of me, and mine taking you to advancement.   140

Lys. Well, all this rids not my business. Wife, you shall be there to partake the unexpected honor of our house. Lycus and I will make it our recreation by the way to think of your revels and nuptial sports. Brother, my stay hath been for you. Wife, pray thee be gone, and soon prepare for the solemnity; a month returns me.

Cyn. Heavens guide your journey.

Lys. Farewell.   149

Thar. Farewell, nephew; prosper in virility, but— do you hear?—keep your hand from your voice. I have a part for you in our hymeneal show.

Hyl. You speak too late for my voice, but I'll discharge the part.

Ex[eunt] CYNTHIA, HYLUS, ERO.

Lys. Occurrents call ye them? Foul shame confound them all! That impregnable fort of chastity and loyalty, that amazement of the world! O ye deities, could nothing restrain her? I took her spirit to be too haughty for such a depression.   159

Thar. But who commonly more short-heeled[11] than they that are high i'th' instep?[12]

Lys. Methinks yet shame should have controlled so sudden an appetite.

Thar. Tush, shame doth extinguish lust as oil doth
    fire;
The blood once het,[13] shame doth enflame the more;
What they before by art dissembled most,
They act more freely; shame once found is lost.
And to say truth, brother, what shame is due to't? Or what congruence doth it carry that a young lady, gallant, vigorous, full of spirit and complexion, her   170 appetite new-whetted with nuptial delights, to be confined to the speculation of a death's head; or for the loss of a husband, the world affording flesh enough, make the noontide of her years, the sunset of her pleasures?

Lyc. And yet there have been such women.

Thar. Of the first stamp, perhaps, when the metal was purer than in these degenerate days; of later years, much of that coin hath been counterfeit and, besides, so cracked and worn with use that they are grown   180 light and indeed fit for nothing but to be turned over in play.

Lys. Not all, brother.

Thar. My matchless sister only excepted; for she, you know, is made of another metal than that she borrowed of her mother. But do you, brother, sadly[14] intend the pursuit of this trial?

Lys. Irrevocably.

Thar. It's a high project. If it be once raised, the earth is too weak to bear so weighty an accident;   190 it cannot be conjured down again without an earthquake. Therefore, believe she will be constant.

Lys. No, I will not.

Thar. Then believe she will not be constant.

Lys. Neither. I will believe nothing but what trial enforces. Will you hold your promise for the governing of this project with skill and secrecy?

Thar. If it must needs be so. But hark you, brother, have you no other capricions in your head to entrap my sister in her frailty but to prove the firmness of her widow-vows after your supposed death?   201

Lys. None in the world.

Thar. Then here's my hand; I'll be as close as my lady's shoe to her foot, that pinches and pleases her, and will bear on with the plot till the vessel split again.

Lys. Forge any death, so you can force belief.
Say I was poisoned, drowned.

Thar.   Hanged.

Lys.   Anything,
So you assist it with likely circumstance; I need not

instruct you. That must be your employment, Lycus.

Lyc. Well, sir.   210

Thar. But, brother, you must set in, too; to countenance truth out, a hearse there must be too. It's strange to think how much the eye prevails in such impressions; I have marked a widow that just before was seen pleasant enough follow an empty hearse and weep devoutly.

Lyc. All those things leave to me.

Lys. But, brother, for the bestowing of this hearse in the monument of our family, and the marshaling of a funeral—   220

Thar. Leave that to my care, and if I do not do the mourner as lively as your heir and weep as lustily as your widow, say there's no virtue in onions. That being done, I'll come to visit the distressed widow, apply old ends of comfort to her grief; but the burden of my song shall be to tell her words are but dead comforts, and therefore counsel her to take a living comfort that might ferret out the thought of her dead husband; and will come prepared with choice of suitors: either my Spartan lord for grace at the viceroy's court, or some   230 great lawyer that may solder up her cracked estate, and so forth. But what would you say, brother, if you should find her married at your arrival?

Lys. By this hand, split her weasand.[15]

Thar. Well, forget not your wager, a stately chariot with four brave horses of the Thracian breed, with all appurtenances. I'll prepare the like for you, if you prove victor. But well remembered, where will you lurk the whiles?

Lys. Mewed[16] up close, some short day's journey
    hence;   240
Lycus shall know the place; write still how all things
    pass.
Brother, adieu; all joy attend you.

Thar. Will you not stay, our nuptial now so near?

Lys. I should be like a man that hears a tale
And heeds it not, one absent from himself.
My wife shall attend the countess, and my son.

Thar. Whom you shall hear at your return call me
Father. Adieu; Jove be your speed.
My nuptials done, your funerals succeed.

Exeunt.

[III.ii]

Enter ARGUS, *barehead.*

Arg. A hall, a hall![1] Who's without there?

[*Enter two or three with cushions.*]

Come on, y'are proper grooms, are ye not? 'Slight,
I think y'are all bridegrooms, ye take your pleasures

---

[11] *short-heeled:* a fashion associated with prostitutes.
[12] *high . . . instep:* proud.   [13] *het:* heated.
[14] *sadly:* seriously.   [15] *weasand:* throat.
[16] *Mewed:* Confined.

III.ii.
[1] *A . . . hall:* Cry used to make room for a masque.

so. A company of dormice. Their honors are upon coming, and the room not ready. Rushes[2] and seats instantly.

[*Enter* THARSALIO.]

Thar. Now alas, fellow Argus, how thou art cumbered with an office!

Arg. Perfume, sirrah, the room's dampish.　　　9

Thar. Nay, you may leave that office to the ladies; they'll perfume it sufficiently.

[ARGUS *perceives* THARSALIO.]

Arg. Cry mercy, sir, here's a whole chorus of Sylvans at hand, cornetting, and tripping o'th' toe, as the ground they trod on were too hot for their feet. The device is rare. And there's your young nephew, too; he hangs in the clouds deified with Hymen's shape.

Thar. Is he perfect in's part? Has not his tongue learned of the Sylvans to trip o' th' toe?

Arg. Sir, believe it, he does it preciously for accent and action, as if he felt the part he played. He　20 ravishes all the young wenches in the palace; pray Venus my young Lady Laodice have not some little prick of Cupid in her, she's so diligent at's rehearsals.

Thar. No force, so my next vows be heard, that if Cupid have pricked her, Hymen may cure her.

Arg. You mean your nephew, sir, that presents Hymen.

Thar. Why so. I can speak nothing but thou art within me.[3] Fie of this wit of thine, 'twill be thy destruction. But howsoever you please to understand,　30 Hymen send thy boy no worse fortune. And where's my lady's honor?

Arg. At hand, sir, with your unparagoned sister. Please you take your chair of honor, sir?

Thar. Most serviceable Argus, the gods reward thy service, for I will not.

Enter EUDORA, *leading* CYNTHIA, LAODICE, STHENIA, IANTHE, ERO, *with others following.*

Eud. Come, sister, now we must exchange that name
For stranger titles,[4] let's dispose ourselves
To entertain these Sylvan revelers
That come to grace our lovèd nuptials.　　　　　40
I fear me we must all turn nymphs tonight,
To side[5] those sprightly wood-gods in their dances;
Can you do't nimbly, sister? 'Slight, what ails you,
Are you not well?

Cyn.　　　　　Yes, madam.

Eud.　　　　　　　　But your looks,
Methinks, are cloudy, suiting ill[6] the sunshine
Of this clear honor to your husband's house.
Is there aught here that sorts not with your liking?

Thar. Blame her not, mistress, if her looks show care.
Excuse the merchant's sadness that hath made

A doubtful venture of his whole estate,　　　　　50
His livelihood, his hopes, in one poor bottom,
To all encounters of the sea and storms.
Had you a husband that you loved as well,
Would you not take his absent plight as ill?
Cavil at every fancy? Not an object
That could present itself, but it would forge
Some vain objection that did doubt his safety;
True love is ever full of jealousy.

Eud. Jealous! Of what? Of every little journey?
Mere fancy then is wanton, and doth cast　　　　60
At those slight dangers there too doting glances;
Misgiving minds ever provoke mischances.
Shines not the sun in his way bright as here?
Is not the air as good? What hazard doubt you?

Arg. His horse may stumble, if it please your honor;
The rain may wet, the wind may blow on him;
Many shrewd hazards watch poor travelers.

Eud. True, and the shrewdest thou hast reckoned us.
Good sister, these cares fit young married wives.

Cyn. Wives should be still young in their husband's
loves;　　　　　　　　　　　　　　　　　70
Time bears no scythe should bear down them before
him;
Our lives he may cut short, but not our loves.

Thar. Sister, be wise, and ship not in one bark
All your ability. If he miscarry,
Your well-tried wisdom should look out for new.

Cyn. I wish them happy winds that run that course;
From me 'tis far. One temple sealed our troth;
One tomb, one hour shall end and shroud us both.

Thar. Well, y'are a Phoenix; there, be that your
cheer;
Love with your husband be, your wisdom here.　80
Hark, our sports challenge it. Sit, dearest mistress.

Eud. Take you place, worthiest servant.

Thar.　　　　　　　　　　　　Serve me
heaven,
　　　　　　　　　　　　　　　　　　Music.
As I my heavenly mistress. Sit, rare sister.

Music. [HYLUS *as*] HYMEN *descends, and six
Sylvans enter beneath, with torches.*

Arg. A hall, a hall! Let no more citizens in there.

Lao. Oh, not my cousin see, by Hymen's self.

Sthen. He does become it most enflamingly.

Hym. Hail, honored bridegroom, and his princely
bride,
With the most famed for virtue, Cynthia;
And this young lady, bright Laodice,
One rich hope of this noblest family.　　　　　90

Sthen. Hark how he courts; he is enamored, too.

Lao. Oh grant it, Venus, and be ever honored.

Hym. In grace and love of you, I Hymen searched
The groves and thickets that embrace this palace,
With this clear-flamed and good-aboding torch,
For summons of these fresh and flowery Sylvans
To this fair presence, with their winding hays,[7]
Active and antic dances, to delight
Your frolic eyes and help to celebrate
These noblest nuptials, which great Destiny　　100

---

[2] *Rushes:* strewn in lieu of a carpet.
[3] *within me:* inside my guard (fencing).
[4] *exchange . . . titles:* call each other that in place of.
[5] *side:* walk beside.　　　　　　[6] *ill:* Q "all."
[7] *hays:* country dances.

Ordained past custom [8] and all vulgar object [9]
To be the readvancement of a house,
Noble and princely, and restore this palace
To that name that six hundred summers since
Was in possession of this bridegroom's ancestors,
The ancient and most virtue-famed Lysandri.
Sylvans! the courtships you make to your Dryads,
Use to this great bride and these other dames,
And heighten with your sports my nuptial flames.   109
    Lao. Oh, would himself descend, and me command.
    Sthen. Dance, and his heart catch in another's hand.

Sylvans *take out the* Bride *and the rest; they dance;
after which, and all set in their places,* HYMEN [*speaks*].

    Hym. Now, what my [10] power and my torch's
    influence
Hath in the blessings of your nuptial joys,
Great bride and bridegroom, you shall amply part
Betwixt your free loves, and forego it never.
    Omnes. Thanks to great Hymen and fair Sylvans
    ever.

                                                Exeunt.

Finis Actus Tertii.

ACT FOUR

SCENE ONE

[*Enter*] THARSALIO, LYCUS, *with his arm in a scarf,
a nightcap on's head.*

    Lyc. I hope, sir, by this time—
    Thar. Put on,[1] man, by ourselves.
    Lyc. The edge of your confidence is well taken off.
Would you not be content to withdraw your wager?
    Thar. Faith, fellow Lycus, if my wager were weakly
built, this unexpected accident might stagger it. For
the truth is, this strain is extraordinary, to follow her
husband's body into the tomb and there for his company to bury herself quick. It's new and stirring; but
for all this, I'll not despair of my wager.   10
    Lyc. Why, sir, can you think such a passion dis-
sembled?
    Thar. All's one for that; what I think, I think. In the
meantime, forget not to write to my brother how the
plot hath succeeded: that the news of his death hath
taken; a funeral solemnity performed; his supposed
corse bestowed in the monument of our family; thou
and I horrible mourners; but above all, that his intolerable virtuous widow, for his love, and, for her love,
Ero, her handmaid, are descended with his corse   20
into the vault; there wipe their eyes time out of mind,
drink nothing but their own tears, and by this time are
almost dead with famine. There's a point will sting it,
for you say 'tis true. Where left you him?
    Lyc. At Dipolis,[2] sir, some twenty miles hence.
    Thar. He keeps close.
    Lyc. Ay, sir, by all means; skulks unknown under
the name of a strange knight.
    Thar. That may carry him without descrying, for

there's a number of strange knights [3] abroad. You left
him well?   31
    Lyc. Well, sir, but for this jealous humor that
haunts him.
    Thar. Well, this news will absolutely purge that
humor. Write all; forget not to describe her passion at
thy discovery of his slaughter. Did she perform it well
for her husband's wager?
    Lyc. Perform it, call you it? You may jest; men
hunt hares to death for their sports, but the poor beasts
die in earnest. You wager of her passions for your   40
pleasure, but she takes little pleasure in those earnest
passions. I never saw such an ecstasy of sorrow since I
knew the name of sorrow. Her hands flew up to her
head like Furies, hid all her beauties in her disheveled
hair, and wept as she would turn fountain. I would you
and her husband had been behind the arras but to have
heard her. I assure you, sir, I was so transported with
the spectacle that, in despite of my discretion, I was
forced to turn woman and bear a part with her. Humanity broke loose from my heart and streamed through
mine eyes.   51
    Thar. In prose, thou wept'st. So have I seen many a
moist auditor do at a play when the story was but a mere
fiction. And didst act the Nuntius [4] well? Would I had
heard it! Could'st thou dress thy looks in a mournful
habit?
    Lyc. Not without preparation, sir, no more than my
speech. 'Twas a plain acting of an interlude to me to
pronounce the part.
    Thar. As how, for heaven's sake?   60
    Lyc. "Phoebus addressed his chariot towards the
        west
To change his wearied coursers," and so forth.
    Thar. Nay on, and thou lov'st me.
    Lyc. "Lysander and myself beguiled the way
With interchanged discourse, but our chief theme
Was of your dearest self, his honored wife,
Your love, your virtue, wondrous constancy."
    Thar. Then was her cue to whimper; on.
    Lyc. "When suddenly appeared as far as sight
A troop of horse, armed, as we might discern,   70
With javelins, spears, and such accouterments.
He doubted naught, as innocency ever
Is free from doubting ill."
    Thar.   There dropped a tear.
    Lyc. "My mind misgave me;
They might be mountaineers. At their approach
They used no other language but their weapons
To tell us what they were. Lysander drew
And bore himself Achilles-like in fight;
And as a mower sweeps off th' heads of bents,[5]

---

[8] *past custom:* above conventions.
[9] *vulgar object:* popular objections.   [10] *my:* Q "the."
IV.i.
    [1] *Put on:* i.e., your hat; treat me as an equal; presumably
Lycus has respectfully removed his nightcap.
    [2] *Dipolis:* There is no such town in Cyprus.
    [3] *strange knights:* James's new knights.
    [4] *Nuntius:* narrating messenger in classical drama.
    [5] *bents:* grasses.

So did Lysander's sword shave off the points   80
Of their assaulting lances.
His horse at last, sore hurt, fell under him;
I, seeing I could not rescue, used my spurs
To fly away."
    Thar.   What, from thy friend?
    Lyc. Ay, in a good quarrel, why not?
    Thar.   Good, I am
     answered.
    Lyc. "A lance pursued me, brought me back again,
And with these wounds left me t'accompany
Dying Lysander. Then they rifled us
And left us.
They gone, my breath not yet gone, 'gan to strive   90
And revive sense. I with my feeble joints
Crawled to Lysander, stirred him, and withal
He gasped, cried 'Cynthia!' and breathed no more."
    Thar. Oh, then she howled outright.
    Lyc. "Passengers came and in a chariot brought us
Straight to a neighbor town, where I forthwith
Coffined my friend in lead, and so conveyed him
To this sad place."   98
    Thar. 'Twas well, and could not show but strangely.
    Lyc. Well, sir, this tale pronounced with terror, suited with action, clothed with such likely circumstance, my wounds in show, her husband's hearse in sight, think what effect it wrought. And if you doubt, let the sad consequence of her retreat to his tomb be your woeful instructor.
    Thar. For all this, I'll not despair of my wager. These griefs that sound so loud, prove always light; True sorrow evermore keeps out of sight. This strain of mourning wi' th' sepulcher, like an over-doing actor, affects grossly, and is indeed so far   110 forced from the life, that it bewrays[6] itself to be altogether artificial. To set open a shop of mourning! 'tis palpable. Truth, the substance, hunts not after the shadow of popular fame. Her officious ostentation of sorrow condemns her sincerity. When did woman ever mourn so unmeasurably but she did dissemble?
    Lyc. O gods! a passion thus borne, thus appareled with tears, sighs, swoonings, and all the badges of true sorrow, to be dissembled! By Venus, I am sorry I ever set foot in't. Could she, if she dissembled, thus   120 dally with hunger, be deaf to the barking of her appetite, not having these four days relieved nature with one dram of sustenance?
    Thar. For this does she look to be deified, to have hymns made of her, nay to her; the tomb where she is to be no more reputed the ancient monument of our family, the Lysandri, but the new-erected altar of Cynthia, to which all the Paphian widows shall after their husbands' funerals offer their wet muckinders[7] for monuments of the danger they have passed,   130 as seamen do their wet garments at Neptune's temple after a shipwrack.
    Lyc. Well, I'll apprehend you at your pleasure. I for

my part will say that if her faith be as constant as her love is hearty and unaffected, her virtues may justly challenge a deity to enshrine them.
    Thar. Ay, there's another point, too. But one of those virtues is enough at once. All natures are not capable of all gifts. If the brain of the West were in the heads of the learned, then might parish clerks be common   140 councilmen, and poets aldermen's deputies. My sister may turn Niobe[8] for love; but till Niobe be turned to a marble, I'll not despair but she may prove a woman. Let the trial run on; if she do not outrun it, I'll say poets are no prophets, prognosticators are but mounte-banks, and none tell true but woodmongers.
                                           Exit.
    Lyc. A sweet gentleman you are! I marvel what man, what woman, what name, what action, doth his tongue glide over, but it leaves a slime upon't! Well, I'll presently to Dipolis, where Lysander stays, and will not say but she may prove frail.   151
But this I'll say, if she should chance to break,
Her tears are true, though women's truths are weak.
                                           Exit.

[IV.ii]

Enter LYSANDER *like a Soldier, disguised at all parts,*
a half pike, gorget, etc. He discovers the tomb, looks in,
and wonders, etc.

    Lys. O miracle of nature! women's glory,
Men's shame, and envy of the deities!
Yet must these matchless creatures be suspected,
Accused, condemned! Now by th'immortal gods,
They rather merit altars, sacrifice,
Than love and courtship.
Yet see, the queen of these lies here interred,
Tearing her hair and drownèd in her tears,
Which Jove should turn to crystal, and a mirror
Make of them, wherein men may see and wonder   10
At women's virtues. Shall she famish then?
Will men, without dissuasions, suffer thus
So bright an ornament to earth, tombed quick
In earth's dark bosom? Ho! who's in the tomb there?
    Ero. [*Within*] Who calls? Whence are you?
    Lys. I am a soldier of the watch and must enter.
    Ero. Amongst the dead?
    Lys. Do the dead speak? Ope, or I'll force it open.

         [ERO *opens the door of the tomb.*]

    Ero. What violence is this? What seek you here,   19
Where naught but Death and her attendants dwell?
    Lys. What wretched souls are you that thus by night
Lurk here amongst the dead?
    Ero.   Good soldier, do not stir
     her.
She's weak and quickly seized with swooning and
     passions,
And with much trouble shall we both recall
Her fainting spirits.
Five days thus hath she wasted, and not once
Seasoned her palate with the taste of meat;
Her powers of life are spent, and what remains

---

    [6] *bewrays:* reveals.   [7] *muckinders:* handkerchiefs.
    [8] *Niobe:* daughter of Tantalus, metamorphosed into stone during her bereavement over the death of her children.

Of her famished spirit serves not to breathe but sigh.
She hath exiled her eyes from sleep or sight,   30
And given them wholly up to ceaseless tears
Over that ruthful hearse of her dear spouse,
Slain by bandittoes, nobly born Lysander.
 Lys. And hopes she with these heavy notes and cries
To call him from the dead? In these five days
Hath she but made him stir a finger or fetch
One gasp of that forsaken life she mourns?
Come, honored mistress, I admire your virtues,
But must reprove this vain excess of moan.
Rouse yourself, lady, and look up from death.   40
Well said, 'tis well; stay by my hand and rise.
This face hath been maintained with better huswifery.[1]

[CYNTHIA *comes to the door of the tomb.*]

 Cyn. What are you?
 Lys.   Lady, I am sentinel,
Set in this hallowed place to watch and guard,
On forfeit of my life, these monuments
From rape and spoil of sacrilegious hands;
And save the bodies, that without you see,
Of crucified offenders, that no friends
May bear them hence to honored burial.
 Cyn. Thou seem'st an honest soldier; pray thee then,
Be as thou seem'st; betake thee to thy charge   51
And leave this place; add not affliction
To the afflicted.
 Lys.   You misname the children.
For what you term affliction now, in you
Is but self-humor, voluntary penance
Imposed upon yourself; and you lament
As did the satyr once that ran affrighted
From that horn's sound that he himself had winded;
Which humor to abate, my counsel tending your
  termed affliction,
What I for physic give, you take for poison.   60
I tell you, honored mistress, these ingredients
Are wholesome, though perhaps they seem
  untoothsome.
 Ero. [*Aside*] This soldier, sure, is some decayed
  pothecary.
 Lys. Dear ghost, be wise and pity your fair self,
Thus by yourself unnaturally afflicted.
Chide back heartbreaking groans, clear up those lamps,
Restore them to their first creation,
Windows for light, not sluices made for tears.
Beat not the senseless air with needless cries,
Baneful to life and bootless to the dead.   70
This is the inn where all Deucalion's race[2]
Sooner or later must take up their lodging;
No privilege can free us from this prison;
No tears, no prayers, can redeem from hence
A captived soul. Make use of what you see;
Let this affrighting spectacle of death
Teach you to nourish life.
 Ero. Good, hear him. This is a rare soldier.
 Lys. Say that with abstinence you should unloose
The knot of life. Suppose that in this tomb   80
For your dear spouse you should entomb yourself
A living corse; say that before your hour,

Without due summons from the Fates, you send
Your hasty soul to hell; can your dear spouse
Take notice of your faith and constancy?
Shall your dear spouse revive to give you thanks?
 Cyn. Idle discourser.
 Lys.   No, your moans are idle.
Go to, I say, be counseled. Raise yourself;
Enjoy the fruits of life; there's viands for you.
Now, live for a better husband. No? Will you none?
 Ero. For love of courtesy, good mistress, eat;   91
Do not reject so kind and sweet an offer.
Who knows but this may be some Mercury
Disguised and sent from Juno to relieve us?
Did ever any lend unwilling ears
To those that came with messages of life?
 Cyn. I pray thee, leave thy rhetoric.
 Ero. By my soul, to speak plain truth, I could rather
wish t'employ my teeth than my tongue, so your
example would be my warrant.   100
 Cyn. Thou hast my warrant.
 Lys.   Well then, eat, my
  wench;
Let obstinacy starve. Fall to.
 Ero.   Persuade
My mistress first.
 Lys.   'Slight, tell me, lady,
Are you resolved to die? If that be so,
Choose not, for shame, a base and beggar's death;
Die not for hunger, like a Spartan lady;
Fall valiantly upon a sword, or drink
Noble death; expel your grief with poison.
There 'tis, seize it.

[*Offers his sword.*]

    Tush, you dare not die.
Come, wench, thou hast not lost a husband;   110
Thou shalt eat. Th'art now within
The place where I command.
 Ero.   I protest, sir—
 Lys. Well said. Eat and protest; or I'll protest,
And do thou eat. Thou eat'st against thy will,
That's it thou would'st say?
 Ero. It is.
 Lys.   And under such a protestation
Thou lost thy maidenhead.
For your own sake, good lady, forget this husband.
Come, you are now become a happy widow,
A blessedness that many would be glad of.   120
That and your husband's inventory together
Will raise you up husbands enow. What think you of
  me?
 Cyn. Trifler, pursue this wanton theme no further,
Lest, which I would be loath, your speech provoke
Uncivil language from me. I must tell you,
One joint of him I lost was much more worth

IV.ii.
 [1] *huswifery*: housekeeping.
 [2] *Deucalion's race*: human race, descended from stones
thrown over their shoulders by Deucalion and his wife, sole
survivors of a universal flood (Ovid, *Metamorphoses*, I. 371
ff).

Than the racked[3] value of thy entire body.

Ero. O know what joint she means.

Lys.   Well, I have done.
And well done, frailty. Proface[4]! How lik'st thou it?

Ero. Very toothsome ingredients surely, sir;   130
Want but some liquor to incorporate them.

Lys. There 'tis; carouse.

Ero.   I humbly thank you, sir.

Lys. Hold, pledge me now!

Ero.   'Tis the poison, sir,
That preserves life, I take it.

Bibit Ancilla.[5]

Lys.   Do so, take it.

Ero. Sighing has made me something short-winded.
I'll pledge y'at twice.

Lys.   'Tis well done; do me right.[6]

Ero. I pray, sir, have you been a pothecary?

Lys. Marry have I, wench; a woman's pothecary.

Ero. Have you good ingredients?
I like your bottle well. Good mistress, taste it.   140
Try but the operation, 'twill fetch up
The roses in your cheeks again.
Doctor Verolles' bottles are not like it;
There's no guaiacum[7] here, I can assure you.

Lys. This will do well anon.

Ero.   Now fie upon't.
Oh, I have lost my tongue in this same limbo.[8]
The spring on't's spoiled, methinks; it goes not off
With the old twang.

Lys. Well said, wench, oil it well; 'twill make it
  slide well.

Ero. Aristotle says, sir, in his *Posterionds*[9]—   150

Lys. This wench is learned.—And what says he?

Ero. —That when a man dies, the last thing that
moves is his heart; in a woman, her tongue.

Lys. Right, and adds further that you women are
A kind of spinners[10]; if their legs be plucked off,
Yet still they'll wag them; so will you your tongues.
[*Aside*] With what an easy change does this same
  weakness
Of women slip from one extreme t'another!
All these attractions take no hold of her,
No, not to take refection[11]; 't must not be thus.—   160
Well said, wench. Tickle that Helicon.[12]
But shall we quit the field with this disgrace
Given to our oratory? Both not gain
So much ground of her as to make her eat?

Ero. Faith, the truth is, sir, you are no fit organ
For this business;
'Tis quite out of your element.
Let us alone, she'll eat, I have no fear;
A woman's tongue best fits a woman's ear.
Jove never did employ Mercury,   170
But Iris, for his messenger to Juno.

Lys. Come, let me kiss thee, wench. Wilt undertake
To make thy mistress eat?

Ero.   It shall go hard, sir,
But I will make her turn flesh and blood,
And learn to live as other mortals do.

Lys. Well said. The morning hastes; next night
  expect me.

Ero. With more provision, good sir.

Lys.   Very good.

Exiturus.

Ero. And bring more wine.

She shuts up the tomb.

Lys.   What else? Shalt have
  enough.
O Cynthia, heir of her bright purity
Whose name thou dost inherit, thou disdain'st,   180
Severed from all concretion,[13] to feed
Upon the base food of gross elements.
Thou all art soul, all immortality.
Thou fasts for nectar and ambrosia,
Which, till thou find'st and eat'st above the stars,
To all food here thou bidd'st celestial wars.

Exit.

[IV.iii]

CYNTHIA, ERO, *the tomb opening.*

Ero. So; let's air our dampish spirits, almost stifled
in this gross, muddy element.

Cyn. How sweet a breath the calmness of the night
Inspires the air withal!

Ero. Well said, now y'are yourself. Did not I tell you
how sweet an operation the soldier's bottle had? And
if there be such virtue in the bottle, what is there in the
soldier? Know and acknowledge his worth when he
comes, in any case, mistress.

Cyn. So maid?   10

Ero. God's my patience! Did you look, forsooth,
that Juno should have sent you meat from her own
trencher in reward of your widow's tears? You might
sit and sigh first till your heartstrings broke, I'll able't.

Cyn. I fear me thy lips have gone so oft to the bottle,
that thy tongue-strings are come broken home.

Ero. Faith, the truth is my tongue hath been so long
tied up that 'tis covered with rust, and I rub it against
my palate as we do suspected coins, to try whether it be
current or no. But now, mistress, for an upshot of[1]   20
this bottle; let's have one carouse to the good speed of
my old master, and the good speed of my new.

Cyn. So, damsel.

Ero. You must pledge it; here's to it. Do me right, I
pray.

Cyn. You say I must.

[*She drinks.*]

---

[3] *racked:* exaggerated.

[4] *L:* May it do you good, a toast.

[5] *L:* The maid drinks.

[6] *do me right:* expression used in pledging healths.

[7] *guaiacum:* drug prepared from resin of the guaiacum
tree.   [8] *limbo:* place of confinement.

[9] *Posterionds:* error for Analytica Posteriora.

[10] *spinners:* spiders.   [11] *refection:* refreshment.

[12] *Helicon:* the Muses' mountain in Boeotia, site of a
fountain inspiring to poets.

[13] *concretion:* material mass.

IV.iii.

[1] *for . . . of:* to finish off.

Ero. Must! What else?

Cyn. How excellent ill this humor suits our habit![2]

Ero. Go to, mistress, do not think but you and I shall have good sport with this jest when we are in 30 private at home. I would to Venus we had some honest shift or other to get off withal, for I'll no more on't; I'll not turn saltpeter in this vault for never a man's company living, much less for a woman's. Sure I am the wonder's over, and 'twas only for that that I endured this; and so, o' my conscience, did you. Never deny it.

Cyn. Nay, pray thee take it[3] to thee.

Enter LYSANDER.

Hark, I hear some footing near us.

Ero. God's me, 'tis the soldier, mistress. By Venus, if you fall to your late black Sanctus[4] again, I'll discover you.   41

Lys. [*Aside*] What's here! The maid hath certainly prevailed with her; methinks those clouds that last night covered her looks are now dispersed. I'll try this further.—Save you, lady.

Ero. Honorable soldier! y'are welcome; please you step in, sir?

Lys. With all my heart, sweetheart; by your patience, lady. Why, this bears some shape of life yet! Damsel, th'ast performed a service of high reckoning, which cannot perish unrewarded.   51

Ero. Faith, sir, you are in the way to do it once, if you have the heart to hold on.

Cyn. Your bottle has poisoned this wench, sir.

Lys. A wholesome poison it is, lady, if I may be judge; of which sort here is one better bottle more.

Wine is ordained to raise such hearts as sink;
Whom woeful stars distemper, let him drink.

I am most glad I have been some mean to this part of your recovery, and will drink to the rest of it.   60

Ero. Go to, mistress, pray simper no more; pledge the man of war here.

Cyn. Come, y'are too rude.

Ero. Good.

Lys. Good sooth, lady, y'are honored in her service; I would have you live, and she would have you live freely, without which life is but death. To live freely is to feast our appetites freely, without which humans are stones; to the satisfaction whereof I drink, lady.

[*She drinks.*]

Cyn. I'll pledge you, sir.   70

Ero. Said like a mistress, and the mistress of yourself. Pledge him in love, too; I see he loves you. She's silent; she consents, sir.

Lys. O happy stars! And now pardon, lady.

[*Kisses her.*]

Methinks these are all of a piece.

Ero. Nay, if you kiss all of a piece,[5] we shall ne'er have done. Well, 'twas well offered, and as well taken.

Cyn. If the world should see this!

Lys. The world! Should one so rare as yourself respect the vulgar world?   80

Cyn. The praise I have had, I would continue.

Lys. What, of the vulgar? Who hates not the vulgar deserves not love of the virtuous. And to affect praise of that we despise, how ridiculous it is!

Ero. Comfortable doctrine, mistress; edify, edify! Methinks even thus it was when Dido and Aeneas met in the cave. And hark, methinks I hear some of the hunters.

She shuts the tomb.

Finis Actus Quarti.

ACT FIVE

SCENE ONE

Enter THARSALIO, LYCUS.

Lyc. 'Tis such an obstinacy in you, sir,
As never was conceited, to run on
With an opinion against all the world
And what your eyes may witness; to adventure
The famishment for grief of such a woman
As all men's merits, met in any one,
Could not deserve.

Thar.   I must confess it, Lycus;
We'll therefore now prevent it if we may.
And that our curious[1] trial hath not dwelt
Too long on this unnecessary haunt,[2]   10
Grief and all want of food not having wrought
Too mortally on her divine disposure[3]—

Lyc. I fear they have, and she is past our cure.

Thar. I must confess with fear and shame as much.

Lyc. And that she will not trust in anything
What you persuade her to.

Thar.   Then thou shalt haste
And call my brother from his secret shroud,
Where he appointed thee to come and tell him
How all things have succeeded.

Lyc.   This is well
If, as I say, the ill be not so grown   20
That all help is denied her. But I fear
The matchless dame is famished.

THARSALIO looks into the tomb.

Thar.   'Slight, who's here?
A soldier with my sister? Wipe, wipe, see,
Kissing, by Jove; she, as I lay,[4] 'tis she.

Lyc. What! Is she well, sir?

Thar.   Oh, no, she is famished;
She's past our comfort; she lies drawing on.[5]

Lyc. The gods forbid!

Thar.   Look thou, she's drawing on.
How say'st thou?

Lyc.   Drawing on? Illustrious witchcrafts!

---

[2] *habit:* dress.   [3] *it:* i.e., the bottle.
[4] *black Sanctus:* parody of the hymn "Sanctus, Sanctus, Sanctus"; lamentation.   [5] *of a piece:* of the same kind.

V.i.
[1] *curious:* exacting.   [2] *haunt:* practice.
[3] *disposure:* disposition.   [4] *lay:* wagered.
[5] *drawing on:* dying; tempting.

Thar. Lies she not drawing on?
Lyc.   She draws on fairly.
Your sister, sir? This she? Can this be she?   30
   Thar. She, she, she, and none but she.

He dances and sings.

She, only queen of love and chastity;
O chastity, this women be.
   Lyc. 'Slight, 'tis prodigious.
   Thar.   Horse, horse, horse,
Four chariot horses of the Thracian breed
Come bring me, brother. Oh, the happiest evening
That ever drew her veil before the sun!
Who is't, canst tell?
   Lyc.   The soldier, sir, that watches
The bodies crucified in this hallowed place
Of which to lose one, it is death to him;   40
And yet the lustful knave is at his venery,
While one might steal one.
   Thar.   What a slave was I
That held not out my mind's strength constantly
That she would prove thus! Oh, incredible!
A poor eightpenny soldier! She that lately
Was at such height of interjection,[6]
Stoop now to such a base conjunction!
By heaven I wonder, now I see't in act,
My brain could ever dream of such a thought.
And yet 'tis true. Rare, peerless, is't not, Lycus?   50
   Lyc. I know not what it is, nor what to say.
   Thar. Oh, had I held out, villain that I was,
My blessed confidence but one minute longer,
I should have been eternized. God's my fortune,
What an unspeakable sweet sight it is!
O eyes, I'll sacrifice to your dear sense
And consecrate a fane[7] to Confidence.
   Lyc. But this you must at no hand tell your brother;
'Twill make him mad; for he that was before
So scourged but only with bare jealousy,   60
What would he be, if he should come to know it?
   Thar. He would be less mad; for your only way
To clear his jealousy is to let him know it.
When knowledge comes, suspicion vanishes.
The sunbeams breaking forth swallow the mists.
But as for you, sir gallant, howsoever
Your banquet seems sweet in your liquorous palate,
It shall be sure to turn gall in your maw.
Thy hand a little, Lycus, here without.
   Lyc. To what?
   Thar.   No booty serve you, sir soldado,   70
But my poor sister? Come, lend me thy shoulder;
I'll climb the cross. It will be such a cooler
To my venerean gentleman's hot liver,
When he shall find one of his crucified bodies
Stol'n down, and he to be forthwith made fast
In place thereof, for the sign

---

    ⁶ *at . . . interjection:* so loud in exclaiming.
    ⁷ *fane:* temple.
V.ii.
    ¹ *complement of:* formality in.

Of the lost sentinel. Come, glorify
Firm Confidence in great inconstancy.
And this believe—for all proved knowledge swears—
He that believes in error, never errs.   80
                                            Exeunt.

[V.ii]

The tomb opens, [*disclosing*] LYSANDER,
                    CYNTHIA, ERO.

   Lys. 'Tis late; I must away.
   Cyn.   Not yet, sweet love.
   Lys. Tempt not my stay, 'tis dangerous. The law is
strict and not to be dispensed with. If any sentinel be
too late in's watch, or that by his neglect one of the
crucified bodies should be stolen from the cross, his
life buys it.
   Cyn. A little stay will not endanger them.
The day's proclaimer has not yet given warning,
The cock yet has not beat his third alarm.   9
   Lys. What! Shall we ever dwell here amongst th'
Antipodes? Shall I not enjoy the honor of my fortune
in public, sit in Lysander's chair, reign in his wealth?
   Cyn. Thou shalt, thou shalt. Though my love to thee
Hath proved thus sudden, and for haste leapt over
The complement of[1] wooing,
Yet only for the world's opinion—
   Lys. Mark that again.
   Cyn. I must maintain a form in parting hence.
   Lys. Out upon't! Opinion, the blind goddess of
fools, foe to the virtuous, and only friend to un-   20
deserving persons, contemn it. Thou know'st thou hast
done virtuously. Thou hast strangely sorrowed for thy
husband, followed him to death; further thou could'st
not; thou hast buried thyself quick—[*Aside*] O that
'twere true—spent more tears over his carcass than
would serve a whole city of saddest widows in a plague
time, besides sighings and swoonings not to be credited.
   Cyn. True, but those compliments might have their
time, for fashion sake.
   Lys. Right, opinion and fashion. 'Sfoot, what call
you time? Th'ast wept these four whole days.   31
   Ero. Nay, by'r Lady, almost five.
   Lys. Look you there, near upon five whole days.
   Cyn. Well, go and see; return, we'll go home.

[*Exeunt* CYNTHIA *and* ERO *into the tomb.*]

   Lys. Hell be thy home! huge monsters damn ye and
your whole creation! O ye gods, in the height of her
mourning, in a tomb, within sight of so many deaths,
her husband's believed body in her eye, he dead a few
days before! This mirror of nuptial chastity, this
votress of widow-constancy, to change her faith,   40
exchange kisses, embraces, with a stranger, and, but my
shame withstood, to give the utmost earnest of her love
to an eightpenny sentinel; in effect, to prostitute
herself upon her husband's coffin! Lust, impiety, hell,
womanhood itself, add, if you can, one step to this!

Enter Captain *with two or three* Soldiers.

Cap. One of the crucified bodies taken down!
Lys. [*Aside*] Enough.

Slinks away.

Cap. And the sentinel not to be heard of?
1 Sol. No, sir.   49
Cap. Make out; haste, search about for him! Does
none of you know him, nor his name?
2 Sol. He's but a stranger here of some four days'
standing, and we never set eye on him, but at setting the watch.
Cap. For whom serves he? You look well to your
watch, masters.
1 Sol. For Seigneur Stratio, and whence he is, 'tis
ignorant to us. We are not correspondent[2] for any but
our own places.   59
Cap. Y'are eloquent. Abroad, I say, let me have him.

Exeunt [Soldiers].

This negligence will by the governor be wholly cast on
me; he hereby will suggest to the viceroy that the city
guards are very carelessly attended.
He loves me not, I know, because of late
I knew him but of mean condition;
But now by Fortune's injudicious hand,
Guided by bribing courtiers, he is raised
To this high seat of honor.
Nor blushes he to see himself advanced
Over the heads of ten time higher worths,   70
But takes it all, forsooth, to his merits,
And looks, as all upstarts do, for most huge observance.
Well, my mind must stoop to his high place,
And learn within itself to sever him from that,
And to adore Authority the Goddess,
However borne by an unworthy beast;
And let the beast's dull apprehension take
The honor done to Isis, done to himself.
I must sit fast and be sure to give no hold
To these fault-hunting enemies.   80

Exit.

[V.iii]

Tomb opens, and LYSANDER *within lies along:*
CYNTHIA *and* ERO.

Lys. Pray thee, disturb me not; put out the lights.
Ero. Faith, I'll take a nap again.
Cyn. Thou shalt not rest before I be resolved
What happy wind hath driven thee back to harbor.
Was it my love?
Lys. No.
Cyn. Yet say so, sweet, that with the thought thereof
I may enjoy all that I wish in earth.
Lys. I am sought for. A crucified body is stol'n while
I loitered here, and I must die for't.   10
Cyn. Die! all the gods forbid! O this affright
Torments me ten parts more than the sad loss
Of my dear husband.
Lys. [*Aside*]   Damnation!—I believe thee.
Cyn. Yet hear a woman's wit;
Take counsel of necessity and it.
I have a body here, which once I loved

And honored above all, but that time's past—
Lys. [*Aside*] It is; revenge it, heaven.
Cyn. That shall supply at so extreme a need   19
The vacant gibbet.
Lys.   *Cancro!*[1] What, thy husband's body!
Cyn. What hurt is't, being dead, it save the living?
Lys. O heart, hold in; check thy rebellious motion!
Cyn. Vex not thyself, dear love, nor use delay.
Tempt not this danger; set thy hands to work.
Lys. I cannot do't; my heart will not permit
My hands to execute a second murder.
The truth is, I am he that slew thy husband.
Cyn. The gods forbid!
Lys. It was this hand that bathed my reeking sword
In his life blood while he cried out for mercy.   30
But I, remorseless, paunched[2] him, cut his throat,
He with his last breath crying, "Cynthia."
Cyn. Oh, thou hast told me news that cleaves my
     heart.
Would I had never seen thee, or heard sooner
This bloody story. Yet see, note my truth;
Yet I must love thee.
Lys.   Out upon thee, monster!
Go, tell the governor. Let me be brought
To die for that most famous villainy,
Not for this miching[3] base transgression
Of truant negligence.
Cyn.   I cannot do't.   40
Love must salve any murder. I'll be judge
Of thee, dear love, and these shall be thy pains,
Instead of iron, to suffer these soft chains.

[*Embracing him.*]

Lys. Oh, I am infinitely obliged.
Cyn. Arise, I say, thou saver of my life.
Do not with vain-affrighting conscience
Betray a life that is not thine, but mine.
Rise and preserve it.
Lys.   Ha! thy husband's body!
Hang't up, you say, instead of that that's stol'n,
Yet I his murderer; is that your meaning?   50
Cyn. It is, my love.
Lys.   Thy love amazes me.
The point is yet how we shall get it thither.
Ha! tie a halter about's neck and drag him to the
     gallows;
Shall I, my love?
Cyn.   So you may do indeed;
Or if your own strength will not serve, we'll aid
Our hands to yours, and bear him to the place.
For heaven's love, come; the night goes off apace.
Lys. [*Aside*] All the infernal plagues dwell in thy
     soul!—
I'll fetch a crow of iron to break the coffin.   59
Cyn. Do, love; be speedy.
Lys. [*Aside*]   As I wish thy damnation!

---

    [2] *correspondent:* answerable.

V.iii.
    [1] *It.:* Cancer take you.   [2] *paunched:* ripped the belly.
    [3] *miching:* sneaking.

Shut the tomb. [LYSANDER *comes forward,*
throwing off his armor.]

Oh, I could tear myself into atoms! off with this antic;[4]
the shirt that Hercules wore for his wife was not more
baneful. Is't possible there should be such a latitude
in the sphere of this sex, to entertain such an extension
of mischief and not turn devil? What is a woman? What
are the worst when the best are so past naming? As
men like this, let them try their wives again. Put women
to the test; discover them; paint them, paint them ten
parts more than they do themselves, rather look on
them as they are; their wits are but painted that dislike
their painting.   71
Thou foolish thirster after idle secrets
And ills abroad, look home, and store and choke thee;
There sticks an Acheloüs'[5] horn of ill,[6]
Copie enough;
As much as Alizon[7] of streams receives,
Or lofty Ida[8] shows of shady leaves.

Enter THARSALIO.

Who's that?

Thar. I wonder Lycus fails me. Nor can I hear what's
become of him. He would not, certain, ride to Dipolis
to call my brother back without my knowledge.   81

Lys. [*Aside*] My brother's voice; what makes he
hereabouts so untimely? I'll slip him.

                                        Exiturus.

Thar. Who goes there?

Lys. A friend.

Thar. Dear friend, let's know you.

[*Recognizes* LYSANDER.]

A friend least looked for but most welcome, and with
many a long look expected here. What sir, unbooted?
Have you been long arrived?

Lys. Not long, some two hours before night.   90

Thar. Well, brother, y'have the most rare, admirable
unmatchable wife that ever suffered for the sin of a
husband. I cannot blame your confidence indeed now,
'tis built on such infallible ground. Lycus, I think, be
gone to call you to the rescue of her life. Why she! Oh,
incomprehensible!

Lys. I have heard all related since my arrival. We'll
meet tomorrow.

                                        [*Going.*]

Thar. What haste, brother? But was it related with
what untolerable pains I and my mistress, her   100
other friends, matrons and magistrates, labored her
diversion from that course?

---

[4] *antic:* disguise.
[5] *Acheloüs:* Q "Achelons"; longest river in Greece.
Hercules fought with its god and tore off one of his horns.
[6] *ill:* Q "all."
[7] *Alizon:* No such river is known. Like the whole passage, *ll.* 72–77, this word is textually corrupt. "Copie," in the
preceding line, may mean "copious."
[8] *Ida:* Q "Ilea"; wooded mountain near Troy.
[9] *collections:* inferences.
[10] *Candian:* from the Cretan town of Candia.
[11] *frubber:* furbisher.

Lys. Yes, yes.

Thar. What streams of tears she poured out, what
tresses of her hair she tore and offered on your supposed hearse!

Lys. I have heard all.

Thar. But above all, how since that time, her eyes
never harbored wink of slumber these six days; no, nor
tasted the least dram of any sustenance!   110

Lys. How, is that assured?

Thar. Not a scruple.

Lys. Are you sure there came no soldier to her, nor
brought her victuals?

Thar. Soldier? What soldier?

Lys. Why some soldier of the watch, that attends
the executed bodies. Well, brother, I am in haste; tomorrow shall supply this night's defect of conference.
Adieu.   119

                                Exit LYSANDER.

Thar. A soldier? Of the watch? Bring her victuals?
Go to, brother, I have you in the wind. He's un-
harnessed of all his traveling accouterments. I came
directly from's house, no word of him there; he knows
the whole relation; he's passionate. All collections[9]
speak he was the soldier. What should be the riddle of
this, that he is stolen hither into a soldier's disguise?
He should have stayed at Dipolis to receive news from
us. Whether he suspected our relation or had not
patience to expect it; or whether that furious, frantic,
capricious devil Jealousy hath tossed him   130
hither on his horns, I cannot conjecture. But the case is
clear: he's the soldier. Sister, look to your fame, your
chastity's uncovered. Are they here still? Here, believe
it, both most woefully weeping over the bottle.

                        He knocks [*on the tomb*].

Ero. Who's there?

Thar. Tharsalio; open.

Ero. Alas, sir, 'tis no boot to vex your sister and
yourself. She is desperate and will not hear persuasion;
she's very weak.   139

Thar. [*Aside*] Here's a truebred chambermaid.—
Alas, I am sorry for't; I have brought her meat and
Candian[10] wine to strengthen her.

Ero. Oh, the very naming on't will drive her into a
swoon. Good sir, forbear.

Thar. Yet open, sweet, that I may bless mine eyes
With sight of her fair shrine,
And of the sweetest self, her famous panderess;
Open, I say! Sister, you hear me well,
Paint not your tomb without; we know too well
What rotten carcasses are lodged within.   150
Open, I say.

            ERO *opens, and he sees* [CYNTHIA'S] *head*
                        laid on the coffin, etc.

Sister, I have brought you tidings to wake you out of
this sleeping mummery.

Ero. Alas, she's faint, and speech is painful to her.

Thar. Well said, frubber![11] was there no soldier here
lately?

Ero. A soldier? When?

Thar. This night, last night, tother night, and I know not how many nights and days.

Cyn. Who's there?   160

Ero. Your brother, mistress, that asks if there were not a soldier here.

Cyn. Here was no soldier.

Ero. Yes, mistress, I think here was such a one, though you took no heed of him.

Thar. Go to, sister! Did not you join kisses, embraces, and plight indeed the utmost pledge of nuptial love with him? Deny't, deny't; but first hear me a short story. The soldier was your disguised husband, dispute it not. That you see yonder is but a   170 shadow, an empty chest containing nothing but air. Stand not to gaze at it, 'tis true. This was a project of his own contriving to put your loyalty and constant vows to the test. Y'are warned, be armed.

Exit.

Ero. O fie o' these perils!

Cyn. O Ero, we are undone!

Ero. Nay, you'd ne'er be warned. I ever wished you to withstand the push of that soldier's pike, and not enter him too deep into your bosom, but to keep sacred your widow's vows made to Lysander.   180

Cyn. Thou did'st, thou did'st.

Ero. Now you may see th'event. Well, our safety lies in our speed; he'll do us mischief if we prevent not his coming. Let's to your mother's and there call out your mightiest friends to guard you from his fury. Let them begin the quarrel with him for practicing this villainy on your sex to entrap your frailties.

Cyn. Nay, I resolve to sit out one brunt more, To try to what aim he'll enforce his project. Were he some other man, unknown to me,   190 His violence might awe me; But knowing him as I do, I fear him not. Do thou but second me, thy strength and mine Shall master his best force, If he should prove outrageous. Despair, they say, makes cowards turn courageous. Shut up the tomb.

Shut the tomb.

[V.iv]

Enter one of the Soldiers *sent out before to seek the sentinel.*

1 Sol. All pains are lost in hunting out this soldier. His fear, adding wings to his heels, outgoes us as far as the fresh hare the tired hounds. Who goes there?

Enter Second Soldier *another way.*

2 Sol. A friend.

1 Sol. Oh, your success and mine touching this sentinel tells, I suppose, one tale; he's far enough, I undertake, by this time.

2 Sol. I blame him not. The law's severe, though just, and cannot be dispensed.   9

1 Sol. Why should the laws of Paphos with more rigor than other city laws pursue offenders, that, not appeased with their lives' forfeit, exact a justice of them

after death? And if a soldier in his watch, forsooth, lose one of the dead bodies, he must die for't. It seems the state needed no soldiers when that was made a law.

2 Sol. So we may chide the fire for burning us, Or say the bee's not good because she stings. 'Tis not the body the law respects, but the soldier's neglect, when the watch, the guard and safety of the city, is left abandoned to all hazards. But let him   20 go, and tell me if your news sort with mine for Lycus, apprehended, they say, about Lysander's murder.

1 Sol. 'Tis true; he's at the captain's lodge under guard, and 'tis my charge in the morning to unclose the leaden coffin and discover the body. The captain will assay an old conclusion, often approved, that at the murderer's sight the blood revives again and boils afresh, and every wound has a condemning voice to cry out guilty 'gainst the murderer.

2 Sol. O world, if this be true! His dearest friend, His bed companion, whom of all his friends   31 He culled out for his bosom!

1 Sol. Tush, man, in this topsy-turvy world, friendship and bosom kindness are but made covers for mischief, means to compass ill. Near-allied trust is but a bridge for treason. The presumptions cry loud against him; his answers found disjointed, cross-legged, tripping up one another. He names a town whither he brought Lysander murdered by mountaineers; that's false; some of the dwellers have been here, and all   40 disclaim it. Besides, the wounds he bears in show are such as shrews closely give their husbands, that never bleed, and find to be counterfeit.

2 Sol. O that jade falsehood is never sound of all, But halts of one leg still. Truth's[1] pace is all upright, sound everywhere, And like a die, sets ever on a square. And how is Lycus his bearing in this condition?

1 Sol. Faith, as the manner of such desperate   49 offenders is till it come to the point, careless and confident, laughing at all that seem to pity him. But leave it to th'event. 'Night, fellow soldier; you'll not meet me in the morning at the tomb and lend me your hand to the unrigging of Lysander's hearse?

2 Sol. I care not if I do, to view heaven's power in this unbottomed cellar. Blood, though it sleep a time, yet never dies; The gods on murderers fix revengeful eyes.

Exeunt.

[V.v]

[Enter] LYSANDER *solus with a crow of iron and a halter, which he lays down, and puts on his disguise again.*

Lys. Come, by borrowed disguise, let me once more Be reconciled to thee, my trustiest friend. Thou that in truest shape hast let me see That which my truer self hath hid from me, Help me to take revenge on a disguise Ten times more false and counterfeit than thou.

V.iv.
[1] *Truth's*: Q "Truth."

Thou, false in show, hast been most true to me;
The seeming true hath proved more false than thee.[1]
Assist me to behold this act of lust;
Note, with a scene of strange impiety,   10
Her husband's murdered corse. O more than horror!
I'll not believe't untried. If she but lift
A hand to act it, by the Fates her brains fly out;
Since she has madded me, let her beware my horns;
For though by goring her no hope be shown
To cure myself, yet I'll not bleed alone.

He knocks.

Ero. Who knocks?
Lys. The soldier; open.

She opens, and he enters.

See, sweet, here are the engines that must do't,
Which, with much fear of my discovery,   20
I have at last procured.
Shall we about this work? I fear the morn
Will overtake's; my stay hath been prolonged
With hunting obscure nooks for these employments.[2]
The night prepares a way. Come, art resolved?
Cyn. Ay, you shall find me constant.
Lys. Ay, so I have; most prodigiously constant.
Here's a rare halter to hug him with.
Ero. Better you and I join our hands and bear him
thither; you take his head.   30
Cyn. Ay, for that was always heavier than's whole
body besides.
Lys. [*Aside*] You can tell best that loaded it.
Ero. I'll be at the feet; I am able to bear against you,
I warrant you.
Lys. Hast thou prepared weak nature to digest
A sight so much distasteful? Hast seared thy heart
It bleed not at the bloody spectacle?
Hast armed thy fearful eyes against th' affront
Of such a direful object,   40
Thy murdered husband ghastly staring on thee,
His wounds gaping to affright thee, his body soiled
    with gore?
'Fore heaven, my heart shrugs at it.
Cyn.   So does not mine!
Love's resolute, and stands not to consult
With petty terror, but in full career
Runs blindfold through an army of misdoubts
And interposing fears; perhaps I'll weep
Or so, make a forced face and laugh again.
Lys. O most valiant love!
I was thinking with myself as I came,   50
How if this break to light; his body known,
As many notes might make it, would it not fix
Upon thy fame an unremovèd brand
Of shame and hate? They that in former times
Adored thy virtue, would they not abhor
Thy loathest memory?
Cyn. All this I know, but yet my love to thee

Swallows all this, or whatsoever doubts
Can come against it.
Shame's but a feather balanced with thy love.   60
Lys. Neither fear nor shame? You are steel to th'
    proof.
[*Aside*] But I shall iron[3] you.—Come then; let's to
    work.
Alas, poor corpse, how many martyrdoms
Must thou endure, mangled by me a villain,
And now exposed to foul shame of the gibbet!
'Fore piety, there is somewhat in me strives
Against the deed; my very arm relents
To strike a stroke so inhuman
To wound a hallowed hearse! suppose 'twere mine:
Would not my ghost start up and fly upon thee?   70
Cyn. No, I'd mall it down again with this!

She snatches up the crow.

Lys. How now?

He catches at her throat.

Cyn. Nay, then I'll assay my strength; a soldier and
afraid of a dead man? A soft-roed[4] milksop! Come, I'll
do't myself.
Lys. And I look on? Give me the iron.
Cyn. No, I'll not lose the glory on't. This hand, etc.
Lys. Pray thee, sweet, let it not be said the savage
act was thine; deliver me the engine.
Cyn. Content yourself, 'tis in a fitter hand.   80
Lys. Wilt thou first? Art not thou the most—
Cyn. Ill-destined wife of a transformed monster,
Who, to assure himself of what he knew,
Hath lost the shape of man!
Lys.   Ha! cross-capers?[5]
Cyn. Poor soldier's case; do not we know you, sir?
But I have given thee what thou cam'st to seek.
Go, satyr, run affrighted with the noise
Of that harsh-sounding horn thyself hast blown.
Farewell; I leave thee there my husband's corpse;
Make much of that.

Exit cum ERO.

Lys.   What have I done?   90
Oh, let me lie and grieve, and speak no more.

[*Tomb closes.*]

[*Enter*] Captain, LYCUS *with a guard of three
or four* Soldiers.

Cap. Bring him away. You must have patience, sir;
if you can say aught to quit you of those presumptions
that lie heavy on you, you shall be heard. If not, 'tis not
your braves[6] nor your affecting looks can carry it. We
must acquit our duties.
Lyc. Y'are captain o'th'watch, sir?
Cap. You take me right.
Lys. So were you best do me. See your presumptions
be strong, or be assured that shall prove a dear   100
presumption, to brand me with the murder of my
friend. But you have been suborned by some close
villain to defame me.
Cap. 'Twill not be so put off, friend Lycus. I could
wish your soul as free from taint of this foul fact as

V.v.
  [1] *thee:* Q "her."   [2] *employments:* implements.
  [3] *iron:* catch, put irons on.
  [4] *soft-roed:* Soft roe is the sperm of a male fish.
  [5] *cross-capers:* unexpected start that crosses another's
plans.   [6] *braves:* threatening behavior.

mine from any such unworthy practice.

Lyc. Conduct me to the governor himself, to confront before him your shallow accusations.

Cap. First, sir, I'll bear you to Lysander's tomb to confront the murdered body and see what evidence the wounds will yield against you.   111

Lyc. Y'are wise, captain. But if the body should chance not to speak; if the wounds should be tongue-tied, captain; where's then your evidence, captain? Will you not be laughed at for an officious captain?

Cap. Y'are gallant, sir.

Lyc. Your captainship commands my service no further.

Cap. Well, sir, perhaps I may, if this conclusion take not; we'll try what operation lies in torture, to pull confession from you.   121

Lyc. Say you so, captain? But hark you, captain, might it not concur with the quality of your office, ere this matter grow to the height of a more threatening danger, to wink a little at a by-slip, or so?

Cap. How's that?

Lyc. To send a man abroad under guard of one of your silliest shack-rags,[7] that he may beat the knave and run's way. I mean this on good terms, captain; I'll be thankful.   130

Cap. I'll think on't hereafter. Meantime, I have other employment for you.

Lyc. Your place is worthily replenished, captain. My duty, sir. Hark, captain, there's a mutiny in your army; I'll go raise the governor.

Exiturus.

Cap. No haste, sir; he'll soon be here without your summons.

Soldiers *thrust up* LYSANDER *from the tomb.*

1 Sol. Bring forth the Knight o'th' Tomb. Have we met with you, sir?   139

Lys. Pray thee, soldier, use thine office with better temper.

2 Sol. Come, convey him to the lord governor.

Lys. First afore the captain, sir. [*Aside*] Have the heavens naught else to do, but to stand still and turn all their malignant aspects upon one man?

2 Sol. Captain, here's the sentinel we sought for; he's some new-pressed soldier, for none of us know him.

Cap. Where found you him?

1 Sol. My truant was miched, sir, into a blind corner of the tomb.   151

Cap. Well said, guard him safe. But for the corpse?

1 Sol. For the corpse, sir? Bare misprision, there's no body, nothing. A mere blandation,[8] a *deceptio visus,* unless this soldier for hunger have eat up Lysander's body.

Lyc. Why, I could have told you this before, captain. The body was borne away piecemeal by devout ladies of Venus' order, for the man died one of Venus' martyrs. And yet I heard since 'twas seen whole   160 o'th' other side the downs upon a colestaff[9] betwixt two huntsmen, to feed their dogs withal; which was a miracle, captain.

Cap. Mischief in this act hath a deep bottom and requires more time to sound it. But you, sir, it seems, are a soldier of the newest stamp. Know you what 'tis to forsake your stand? There's one of the bodies in your charge stol'n away; how answer you that? See, here comes the governor.

Enter a Guard, *bare, after the* Governor ;
THARSALIO, ARGUS, CLINIAS, *before*
EUDORA, CYNTHIA, LAODICE, STHENIA,
IANTHE, ERO, *etc.*

Guard. Stand aside there!   170

Cap. [*Aside*] Room for a strange governor. The perfect draught of a most brainless, imperious upstart. O desert! Where wert thou when this wooden dagger was gilded over with the title of governor?

Guard. Peace, masters, hear my lord.

Thar. [*Aside*] All wisdom be silent; now speaks authority.

Gov. I am come in person to discharge justice.

Thar. [*Aside*] Of his office.   179

Gov. The cause you shall know hereafter, and it is this. A villain, whose very sight I abhor—where is he? Let me see him.

Cap. Is't Lycus you mean, my lord?

Gov. Go to, sirrah, y'are too malapert; I have heard of your sentinel's escape. Look to't.

Cap. My lord, this is the sentinel you speak of.

Gov. How now, sir? What time o'day is't?

Arg. I cannot show you precisely, an't please your honor.   189

Gov. What! Shall we have replications,[10] rejoinders?

Thar. [*Aside*] Such a creature[11] a fool is, when he bestrides the back of authority.

Gov. Sirrah, stand you forth. It is supposed thou hast committed a most inconvenient murder upon the body of Lysander.

Lyc. My good lord, I have not.

Gov. Peace, varlet. Dost chop[12] with me? I say it is imagined thou hast murdered Lysander. How it will be proved, I know not. Thou shalt therefore presently be had to execution, as justice in such cases re-   200 quireth. Soldiers, take him away; bring forth the sentinel.

Lyc. Your lordship will first let my defense be heard.

Gov. Sirrah, I'll[13] no fending[14] nor proving. For my part, I am satisfied it is so; that's enough for thee. I had ever a sympathy in my mind against him. Let him be had away.

Thar. [*Aside*] A most excellent apprehension. He's able, ye see, to judge of a cause at first sight, and hear but two parties. Here's a second Solon.   211

---

[7] *shack-rags:* beggarly, disreputable persons.
[8] *blandation:* illusion—the same as the Latin phrase that follows.
[9] *colestaff:* heavy stick run through handles of tub or basket carried on shoulders of two men.
[10] *replications:* replies.   [11] *creature:* not in Q.
[12] *chop:* bandy words ("chop logic").   [13] *I'll:* I'll have.
[14] *fending:* defending.

Eud. Hear him, my lord. Presumptions oftentimes,
Though likely grounded, reach not to the truth,
And truth is oft abused by likelihood.
Let him be heard, my lord.

Gov. Madam, content yourself. I will do justice; I
will not hear him. Your late lord was my honorable
predecessor, but your ladyship must pardon me. In
matters of justice I am blind.

Thar. [*Aside*] That's true.   220

Gov. I know no persons. If a court favorite write to
me in a case of justice, I will pocket his letter and proceed. If a suitor in a case of justice thrusts a bribe into
my hand, I will pocket his bribe and proceed. Therefore, madam, set your heart at rest. I am seated in the
throne of justice, and I will do justice; I will not hear
him.

Eud. Not hear him, my lord?

Gov. No, my lady, and moreover put you in mind
in whose presence you stand. If you parrot to me long,
go to.   231

Thar. [*Aside*] Nay, the Vice must snap his authority
at all he meets; how shall't else be known what part he
plays?

Gov. Your husband was a noble gentleman, but
alas, he came short; he was no statesman. He has left a
foul city behind him.

Thar. [*Aside*] Ay, and I can tell you 'twill trouble his
lordship and all his honorable assistants of scavengers
to sweep it clean.   240

Gov. It's full of vices, and great ones too.

Thar. [*Aside*] And thou none of the meanest.

Gov. But I'll turn all topsy-turvy, and set up a new
discipline amongst you. I'll cut off all perished members—

Thar. [*Aside*] That's the surgeon's office.

Gov. Cast out these rotten stinking carcasses for
infecting the whole city.

Arg. Rotten they may be, but their wenches use to
pepper them and their surgeons to parboil[15]   250
them, and that preserves them from stinking, an't please
your honor.

Gov. Peace, sirrah, peace; and yet 'tis well said, too.
A good pregnant[16] fellow, i'faith. But to proceed. I will
spew drunkenness out o'th' city.

Thar. [*Aside*] Into th' country.

Gov. Shifters shall cheat and starve, and no man
shall do good but where there is no need. Braggarts
shall live at the head o'[17] the tumult that haunt taverns.
Asses shall bear good qualities and wise men shall   260
use them. I will whip lechery out o'th' city; there shall
be no more cuckolds. They that heretofore were errant

cornutos,[18] shall now be honest shopkeepers, and
justice shall take place. I will hunt jealousy out of my
dominion.

Thar. [*Aside*] Do hear, brother?

Gov. It shall be the only note of love to the husband
to love the wife, and none shall be more kindly welcome
to him than he that cuckolds him.   269

Thar. [*Aside*] Believe it, a wholesome reformation.

Gov. I'll have no more beggars. Fools shall have
wealth, and the learned shall live by their wits. I'll have
no more bankrupts. They that owe money shall pay it at
their best leisure, and the rest shall make a virtue of
imprisonment, and their wives shall help to pay their
debts. I'll have all young widows spaded[19] for marrying
again. For the old and withered, they shall be confiscate
to unthrifty gallants and decayed knights. If they be
poor, they shall be burnt to make soap-ashes, or given
to Surgeon's Hall to be stamped to salve for the   280
French measles.[20] To conclude, I will cart pride out
o'th' town.

Arg. An't please your honor, Pride, an't be ne'er so
beggarly, will look for a coach.

Gov. Well said, o' mine honor. A good significant
fellow, i'faith. What is he? He talks much. Does he
follow your ladyship?

Arg. No, an't please your honor, I go before her.

Gov. A good undertaking presence, a well-promis-
ing forehead. Your gentleman usher, madam?   290

Eud. Yours, if you please, my lord.

Gov. Born i'th' city?

Arg. Ay, an't please your honor, but begot i'th'
court.

Gov. Tressel-legged?[21]

Arg. Ay, an't please your honor.

Gov. The better; it bears a breadth,[22] makes room
o'both sides. Might I not see his pace?[23]

Arg. Yes, an't please your honor.   299

ARGUS *stalks.*

Gov. 'Tis well, 'tis very well. Give me thy hand.
Madam, I will accept this property at your hand,
and will wear it threadbare for your sake. Fall in there,
sirrah. And for the matter of Lycus, madam, I must
tell you, you are shallow. There's a state point in't!
Hark you. The viceroy has given him, and we must
uphold correspondence; he must walk. Say one man
goes wrongfully out o'th' world, there are hundreds to
one come wrongfully into th' world.

Eud. Your lordship will give me but a word in
private?   310

[*Whispers to the* Governor.]

Thar. Come, brother, we know you well. What
means this habit? Why stayed you not at Dipolis as you
resolved, to take advertisement for[24] us of your wife's
bearing?

Lys. O brother, this jealous frenzy has borne me
headlong to ruin.

Thar. Go to, be comforted. Uncase yourself and
discharge your friend.

Gov. Is that Lysander, say you? And is all his story

---

[15] *parboil:* surgeons used a tub to treat venereal diseases.
[16] *pregnant:* resourceful.   [17] *o':* Q "and."
[18] *cornutos:* cuckolds.   [19] *spaded:* spayed.
[20] *French measles:* venereal disease.
[21] *Tressel-legged:* with legs spread, as in supports for
bridges and stools.
[22] *bears a breadth:* carries affairs of importance.
[23] *pace:* proper step for a gentleman usher.
[24] *take . . . for:* learn from.

true? By'r Lady, madam, this jealousy will cost   320
him dear. He under took the person of a soldier, and, as
a soldier, must have justice. Madam, his altitude in this
case cannot dispense. Lycus, this soldier hath acquitted
you.

Thar. And that acquittal I'll for him requite; the
body lost is by this time restored to his place.

1 Sol. It is, my lord.

Thar. These are state points, in which your
    lordship's time
Has not yet trained your lordship; please your
    lordship
To grace a nuptial we have now in hand   330

HYLUS *and* LAODICE *stand together.*

'Twixt this your lady and this gentleman.
Your lordship there shall hear the ample story.
And how the ass wrapped in a lion's skin
Fearfully roared; but his large ears appeared
And made him laughed at that before was feared.

Gov. I'll go with you. For my part, I am at a non-
    plus.[25]

EUDORA *whispers with* CYNTHIA.

Thar. Come, brother, thank the countess. She hath
    sweat
To make your peace. Sister, give me your hand.
So, brother, let your lips compound the strife,
And think you have the only constant wife.   340
                                      Exeunt.

FINIS

---

[25] *at a nonplus:* perplexed.

Thomas Dekker

[*c.* 1572–*c.* 1632]

Thomas Middleton

[*c.* 1580– 1627]

THE ROARING GIRL

THE TITLE page of the 1611 quarto (basis of the present text) announces "*The Roaring Girl.* Or *Moll Cut-Purse*, As it hath lately been Acted on the Fortune-stage by the Prince his Players"; there is no reason to doubt that the play was acted some time during the preceding year. Dekker and Middleton, professionals both, had collaborated with other playwrights, and in fact had already joined their talents, in 1604 and 1605, in a pair of lively plays about London called *The Honest Whore*. Too little is known about how the playwrights of the period actually divided their responsibilities in collaboration to make guessing at who wrote which scenes anything more than a mug's game, but the temptation is almost irresistible at various points to see the distinctive mark of one playwright or the other. Dekker's sentimental view of London low-life, recognizable from THE SHOEMAKER'S HOLIDAY, and his fascination with its argot—which reaches a climax in the "canting" scene of V. i, a veritable course in underworld slang—marks the comedy as personally as his equally characteristic interest in paradoxically virtuous rogues. Much of the play is in effect a dramatization of his prose works about London cheaters, *The Gull's Hornbook*, *English Villainies Discovered by Lantern and Candlelight*, and the like. One suspects Middleton's hand in the multiple intrigue, the would-be adulterer, the sheepish near-cuckold, the interest in "shifts" (a word frequently punned on in the play), or stratagems and tricks. But both writers dealt frequently and vigorously with the London that so vividly comes to life in this play.

The heroine is based on a real London character, and the epilogue seems to indicate that she would shortly make a personal appearance on the stage of the Fortune. Mary Firth, better known as Moll Cutpurse, was born in 1584, and spent her seventy-five years in London, notoriously dressed always in male attire, gaining a reputation for abilities as pickpocket, prostitute, bawd, fortuneteller, fence, thief, ruffian, forger, temporary penitent, and (long after the play) tavern-keeper; she is said to have willed twenty pounds so that the Conduit, the city water system, might run with wine at the restoration of Charles II. London abounded in roaring boys, young rowdies, now as later when Milton would describe the "sons of Belial, flown with insolence and wine," but a roaring girl was something of a rarity, and the inventiveness of Dekker and Middleton can scarcely have surpassed the originality of Moll herself. But the play is not interested in her authentic wickedness: rather it makes her paradoxically virtuous, a more forthright and less pretentious character than the hypocritical Sir Alexander and the scheming young gallants about town. It is striking, in fact, that Sebastian's pretended defense of her as a possible spouse in II. ii (a cover for his intent to marry a perfectly respectable young lady) is utterly just, more so than he seems to realize; only an established and unquestioned class system answers his argument. But that system ultimately dominates the play: Moll's final role is to see to it that everyone keeps his proper place in a comedy that, like THE SHOEMAKER'S HOLIDAY, both morally educates its own characters and reaffirms a sufficiently flexible but enduring hierarchy. For all its fantasy, THE ROARING GIRL is a buzzing re-creation of the London in which Shakespeare and Dekker and Middleton and their audiences lived.

N. R.

The Roaring Girl

TO THE COMIC PLAY-READERS, VENERY AND LAUGHTER.

THE FASHION of play-making I can properly compare to nothing so naturally as the alteration in apparel; for in the time of the great crop-doublet,[1] your huge bombasted[2] plays, quilted with mighty words to lean purpose, was only then in fashion; and as the doublet fell, neater inventions began to set up. Now, in the time of spruceness, our plays follow the niceness[3] of our garments; single plots, quaint[4] conceits,[5] lecherous jests, dressed up in hanging sleeves; and those are fit for the times and the termers.[6] Such a kind of light-color summer stuff, mingled with divers colors,[7] you shall find this published comedy; good to keep you in an afternoon from dice at home in your chambers; and for venery, you shall find enough for sixpence,[8] but well couched and[9] you mark it; for Venus, being a woman, passes through the play in doublet and breeches; a brave disguise and a safe one, if the statute[10] untie not her codpiece point.[11] The book I make no question but is fit for many of your companies, as well as the person itself, and may be allowed both gallery-room at the playhouse, and chamber-room at your lodging. Worse things, I must needs confess, the world has taxed her for than has been written of her; but 'tis the excellency of a writer to leave things better than he finds 'em; though some obscene fellow, that cares not what he writes against others, yet keeps a mystical[12] bawdyhouse himself, and entertains[13] drunkards, to make use of their pockets and vent[14] his private bottle-ale at midnight,— though such a one would have ripped up the most nasty vice that ever hell belched forth, and presented it to a modest assembly, yet we rather wish in such discoveries,[15] where reputation lies bleeding, a slackness of truth than fullness of slander.

THOMAS MIDDLETON.

THE PROLOGUE

A play expected[1] long makes the audience look
For wonders: that each scene should be a book,
Composed to all perfection. Each one comes
And brings a play in's head with him; up he sums
What he would of a roaring girl have writ;
If that he finds not here, he mews[2] at it.
Only we entreat you think our scene
Cannot speak high, the subject being but mean;
A roaring girl, whose notes till now ne'er were,
Shall fill with laughter our vast theater.   10
That's all which I dare promise: tragic passion,
And such grave stuff, is this day out of fashion.
I see Attention sets wide ope her gates
Of hearing, and with covetous listening waits,
To know what girl this roaring girl should be,
For of that tribe are many. One is she
That roars at midnight in deep tavern bowls,
That beats the watch,[3] and constables controls;
Another roars i' th' daytime, swears, stabs, gives braves,[4]
Yet sells her soul to the lust of fools and slaves: 20
Both these are suburb-roarers.[5] Then there's besides
A civil city-roaring girl, whose pride,
Feasting, and riding, shakes her husband's state,
And leaves him roaring through an iron grate.[6]
None of these roaring girls is ours; she flies
With wings more lofty. Thus her character lies—

Yet what need characters,[7] when to give a guess
Is better than the person to express?
But would you know who 'tis? Would you hear her
    name?
She's called mad Moll; her life our acts proclaim.   30

PREFACE
  [1] *crop-doublet:* short jacket.
  [2] *bombasted:* cotton-stuffed.   [3] *niceness:* fastidiousness.
  [4] *quaint:* clever, with a possible bawdy pun.
  [5] *conceits:* fancies.
  [6] *termers:* those who come to London during the law term for business or dishonest purposes.
  [7] *colors:* with pun, rhetorical embellishments.
  [8] *sixpence:* the price of a play.   [9] *and:* if.
  [10] *statute:* sumptuary law, forbidding male attire for women.   [11] *point:* lace.
  [12] *mystical:* secret.   [13] *entertains:* receives.
  [14] *vent:* dispense.   [15] *discoveries:* revelations.

PROLOGUE
  [1] *expected:* awaited.   [2] *mews:* makes catcalls.
  [3] *watch:* watchmen.   [4] *braves:* bravados.
  [5] *suburb-roarers:* the brothels were in the suburbs.
  [6] *iron grate:* i.e., in debtor's prison.
  [7] *characters:* literary form in which a person represents a type.

DRAMATIS PERSONÆ

SIR ALEXANDER WENGRAVE

SEBASTIAN WENGRAVE, *his son*

SIR GUY FITZALLARD

SIR DAVY DAPPER

JACK DAPPER, *his son*

SIR ADAM APPLETON

SIR THOMAS LONG

SIR BEAUTEOUS GANYMEDE

LORD NOLAND

GOSHAWK

LAXTON

GREENWIT

GALLIPOT, *an apothecary*

TILTYARD, *a feather-seller*

OPENWORK, *a sempster*

NEATFOOT, *Sir A. Wengrave's man*

GULL, *page to Jack Dapper*

TRAPDOOR

TEARCAT

Coachman

Porter

Tailor

CURTLEAX, *a sergeant*

HANGER, *his yeoman*

Gentlemen, Cutpurses, etc.

MOLL, *the roaring girl*

MARY FITZALLARD, *daughter to Sir Guy*

MISTRESS GALLIPOT

MISTRESS TILTYARD

MISTRESS OPENWORK

ACT ONE

SCENE ONE

Enter MARY FITZALLARD *disguised like a sempster, with a case for bands,[1] and* NEATFOOT, *a servingman, with her, with a napkin on his shoulder and a trencher[2] in his hand, as from table.*

Neat. The young gentleman, our young master, Sir Alexander's son, is it into his ears, sweet damsel, emblem of fragility, you desire to have a message transported, or to be transcendent?

Mary. A private word or two, sir; nothing else.

Neat. You shall fructify in that which you come for; your pleasure shall be satisfied to your full contentation. I will, fairest tree of generation, watch when our young master is erected, that is to say, up, and deliver him to this your most white hand.   10

Mary. Thanks, sir.

Neat. And withal certify him that I have culled out for him, now his belly is replenished, a daintier bit or modicum than any lay upon his trencher at dinner. Hath he notion of your name, I beseech your chastity?

Mary. One, sir, of whom he bespake[3] falling bands.[4]

Neat. Falling bands? It shall so be given him. If you please to venture your modesty in the hall amongst a curl-pated company of rude serving-men, and take such as they can set before you, you shall be most seriously and ingeniously[5] welcome.   21

Mary. I have dined indeed already, sir.

Neat. Or will you vouchsafe to kiss the lip of a cup of rich orleans[6] in the buttery amongst our waiting-women?

Mary. Not now, in truth, sir.

Neat. Our young master shall then have a feeling of your being here presently; it shall so be given him.

Mary. I humbly thank you, sir.

               [*Exit* NEATFOOT.]

           But that my bosom

Is full of bitter sorrows, I could smile   30

To see this formal ape play antic[7] tricks;

But in my breast a poisoned arrow sticks,

And smiles cannot become me. Love woven slightly,

Such as thy false heart makes, wears out as lightly;

But love being truly bred i' th' soul, like mine,

Bleeds even to death at the least wound it takes;

The more we quench this [fire], the less it slakes.

Oh, me!

Enter SEBASTIAN WENGRAVE *with* NEATFOOT.

Seb. A sempster speak with me, sayest thou?

Neat. Yes sir; she's there, *viva voce*[8] to deliver her auricular confession.   40

Seb. With me, sweetheart? What is't?

Mary. I have brought home your bands, sir.

Seb. Bands?—Neatfoot.

Neat. Sir?

Seb. Prithee, look in, for all the gentlemen are upon rising.

Neat. Yes, sir; a most methodical attendance shall be given.

Seb. And dost hear? If my father call for me, say I am busy with a sempster.   50

Neat. Yes, sir; he shall know it that you are busied with a needle-woman.

Seb. In's ear, good Neatfoot.

Neat. It shall be so given him.

               Exit NEATFOOT.

Seb. Bands? You're mistaken, sweetheart, I bespake none:

I.i.

[1] *bands:* ribbons.   [2] *trencher:* wooden plate.

[3] *bespake:* ordered.

[4] *falling bands:* flat collars, which replaced the ruff.

[5] *ingeniously:* sincerely.

[6] *orleans:* drink made from plums.   [7] *antic:* foolish.

[8] *L.:* in person.

When, where, I prithee? What bands? Let me see them.
  Mary. Yes, sir; a bond fast sealed with solemn oaths,
Subscribed unto, as I thought, with your soul;
Delivered as your deed in sight of heaven:
Is this bond canceled? Have you forgot me?
  Seb.   Ha!   60
Life of my life, Sir Guy Fitzallard's daughter?
What has transformed my love to this strange shape?
Stay; make all sure;
                          [*Shuts the door.*]
             so: now, speak and be brief,
Because the wolf's at door that lies in wait
To prey upon us both. Albeit mine eyes
Are blessed by thine, yet this so strange disguise
Holds me with fear and wonder.
  Mary.   Mine's a loathed sight;
Why from it are you banished else so long?
  Seb. I must cut short my speech. In broken language
Thus much, sweet Moll: I must thy company shun. 70
I court another Moll; my thoughts must run
As a horse runs that's blind round in a mill,
Out every step, yet keeping one path still.
  Mary. Umph! must you shun my company? In one
    knot
Have both our hands by th' hands of heaven been tied,
Now to be broke? I thought me once your bride;
Our fathers did agree on the time when;
And must another bedfellow fill my room?
  Seb. Sweet maid, let's lose no time; 'tis in heaven's
    book
Set down that I must have thee. An oath we took 80
To keep our vows, but when the knight your father
Was from mine parted, storms began to sit
Upon my covetous father's brow, which fell
From them on me. He reckoned up what gold
This marriage would draw from him, at which he
    swore,
To lose so much blood could not grieve him more.
He then dissuades me from thee, called thee not fair,
And asked what is she but a beggar's heir?
He scorned thy dowry of five thousand marks.[9]
If such a sum of money could be found, 90
And I would match with that, he'd not undo it,
Provided his bags might add nothing to it;
But vowed, if I took thee, nay, more, did swear it,
Save birth, from him I nothing should inherit.
  Mary. What follows then? My shipwreck?
  Seb.   Dearest, no:
Though wildly in a labyrinth I go,
My end is to meet thee; with a side-wind
Must I now sail, else I no haven can find,
But both must sink for ever. There's a wench
Called Moll, mad Moll, or merry Moll; a creature 100
So strange in quality, a whole city takes
Note of her name and person. All that affection
I owe to thee, on her in counterfeit passion
I spend, to mad my father. He believes
I dote upon this roaring girl, and grieves
As it becomes a father for a son
That could be so bewitched. Yet I'll go on
This crooked way, sigh still for her, feign dreams

In which I'll talk only of her. These streams
Shall, I hope, force my father to consent 110
That here I anchor, rather than be rent
Upon a rock so dangerous. Art thou pleased,
Because thou seest we're waylaid, that I take
A path that's safe, though it be far about?
  Mary. My prayers with heaven guide thee!
  Seb.   Then I
    will on:
My father is at hand; kiss, and begone!
Hours shall be watched for meetings. I must now,
As men for fear, to a strange idol bow.
  Mary. Farewell.
  Seb.   I'll guide thee forth. When next we
    meet,
A story of Moll shall make our mirth more sweet. 120
                            Exeunt.

[I.ii]

    Enter Sir Wengrave, Sir Davy Dapper,
  Sir Adam Appleton, Goshawk, Laxton,
          and Gentlemen.

  Omnes. Thanks, good Sir Alexander, for our
    bounteous cheer!
  S. Alex. Fie, fie, in giving thanks you pay too dear.
  S. Davy. When bounty spreads the table, faith,
    'twere sin,
At going off, if thanks should not step in.
  S. Alex. No more of thanks, no more. Ay, marry, sir,
Th' inner room was too close; how do you like
This parlor, gentlemen?
  All.   Oh, passing well!
  S. Adam. What a sweet breath the air casts here, so
    cool!
  Gos. I like the prospect best.
  Lax.   See how 'tis furnished!
  S. Davy. A very fair sweet room.
  S. Alex.   Sir Davy Dapper,
The furniture that doth adorn this room   11
Cost many a fair gray groat ere it came here;
But good things are most cheap when they're most dear.
Nay, when you look into my galleries,
How bravely they're trimmed up, you all shall swear
You're highly pleased to see what's set down there:
Stories of men and women, mixed together
Fair ones with foul, like sunshine in wet weather;
Within one square a thousand heads are laid
So close that all of heads the room seems made; 20
As many faces there, filled with blithe looks,
Show like the promising titles of new books
Writ merrily, the readers being their own eyes,
Which seem to move and to give plaudities;[1]
And here and there, whilst with obsequious ears
Thronged heaps do listen, a cutpurse thrusts and leers
With hawk's eyes for his prey. I need not show him;
By a hanging, villainous look yourselves may know him,

---

  [9] *marks:* A mark = 13s. 4d.
I.ii.
  [1] *plaudities:* invitations to applause.

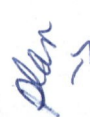

The face is drawn so rarely. Then, sir, below,
The very floor, as 'twere, waves to and fro,   30
And, like a floating island, seems to move
Upon a sea bound in with shores above.

Enter SEBASTIAN WENGRAVE *and* Master
GREENWIT.

All. These sights are excellent!
S. Alex.   I'll show you all:
Since we are met, make our parting comical.
Seb. This gentleman, my friend, will take his leave,
sir.
S. Alex. Ha! take his leave, Sebastian, who?
Seb.   This
gentleman.
S. Alex. Your love, sir, has already given me some
time,
And if you please to trust my age with more,
It shall pay double interest. Good sir, stay.   39
Green. I have been too bold.
S. Alex.   Not so, sir: a merry day
'Mongst friends being spent is better than gold saved—
Some wine, some wine! Where be these knaves I keep?

Enter three or four Servingmen *and* NEATFOOT.

Neat. At your worshipful elbow, sir.
S. Alex. You're kissing my maids, drinking, or fast
asleep.
Neat. Your worship has given it us right.
S. Alex. You varlets, stir!
Chairs, stools, and cushions!—

[Servants *bring in wine, and place chairs, etc.*]

Prithee, Sir Davy Dapper,
Make that chair thine.
S. Davy.   'Tis but an easy gift;
And yet I thank you for it, sir: I'll take it.
S. Alex. A chair for old Sir Adam Appleton!   50
Neat. A back friend[2] to your worship.
S. Adam. Marry, good Neatfoot,
I thank thee for't; back friends sometimes are good.
S. Alex. Pray make that stool your perch, good
Master Goshawk.
Gos. I stoop to your lure, sir.
S. Alex.   Son Sebastian,
Take Master Greenwit to you.
Seb.   Sit, dear friend.
S. Alex. Nay, Master Laxton—furnish Master
Laxton
With what he wants,[3] a stone,[4]—a stool, I would say,
A stool.
Lax. I had rather stand sir.
S. Alex. I know you had, good Master Laxton: so,
so.   60
Exeunt [NEATFOOT *and*] Servants.
Now here's a mess[5] of friends; and gentlemen,

Because time's glass shall not be running long,
I'll quicken it with a pretty tale.
S. Davy.   Good tales do well
In these bad days, where vice does so excel.
S. Adam. Begin, Sir Alexander.
S. Alex.   Last day I met
An agèd man, upon whose head was scored
A debt of just so many years as these
Which I owe to my grave. The man you all know.
Omnes. His name, I pray you, sir.
S. Alex.   Nay, you shall
pardon me.
But when he saw me, with a sigh that brake,   70
Or seemed to break, his heart-strings, thus he spake:
"O my good knight," says he, (and then his eyes
Were richer even by that which made them poor,
They had spent so many tears they had no more),
"O sir," says he, "you know it! for you ha' seen
Blessings to rain upon mine house and me;
Fortune, who slaves men, was my slave; her wheel
Hath spun me golden threads; for, I thank heaven,
I ne'er had but one cause to curse my stars."
I asked him then what that one cause might be.   80
All. So, sir.
S. Alex.   He paused; and as we often see
A sea so much becalmed, there can be found
No wrinkle on his brow, his waves being drowned
In their own rage; but when th' imperious wind[s]
Use strange invisible tyranny to shake
Both heaven's and earth's foundation at their noise,
The seas, swelling with wrath to part that fray,
Rise up, and are more wild, more mad than they;
Even so this good old man was by my question
Stirred up to roughness; you might see his gall   90
Flow even in's eyes; then grew he fantastical.
S. Davy. Fantastical? Ha, ha!
S. Alex.   Yes; and talk[ed]
oddly.
S. Adam. Pray, sir, proceed: how did this old man
end?
S. Alex. Marry, sir, thus:
He left his wild fit to read o'er his cares;[6]
Yet then, though age cast snow on all his hairs,
He joyed, "because," says he, "the god of gold
Has been to me no niggard; that disease,
Of which all old men sicken, avarice,
Never infected me—"   100
Lax. [*Aside*] He means not himself, I'm sure.
S. Alex.   "For, like a lamp
Fed with continual oil, I spend and throw
My light to all that need it, yet have still
Enough to serve myself; Oh, but," quoth he,
"Though heaven's dew fall thus on this aged tree,
I have a son that, like a wedge, doth cleave
My very heart-root!
S. Davy.   Had he such a son?
Seb. [*Aside*] Now I do smell a fox strongly.
S. Alex. Let's see: no, Master Greenwit is not yet
So mellow in years as he; but as like Sebastian,   110
Just like my son Sebastian, such another.
Seb. [*Aside*] How finely, like a fencer, my father

---

fetches his by-blows[7] to hit me, but if I beat you not
at your own weapon of subtlety—.

S. Alex. "This son," saith he, "that should be
The column and main arch unto my house,
The crutch unto my age, becomes a whirlwind
Shaking the firm foundation.

   S. Adam.   'Tis some prodigal.

   Seb. [*Aside*] Well shot, old Adam Bell![8]

   S. Alex. No city-monster neither, no prodigal,   120
But sparing, wary, civil, and, though wifeless,
An excellent husband; and such a traveler,
He has more tongues in his head than some have teeth.

   S. Davy. I have but two in mine.

   Gos.   So sparing and so
   wary?
What, then, could vex his father so?

   S. Alex.   Oh, a woman!

   Seb. A flesh-fly, that can vex any man.

   S. Alex. A scurvy woman,
On whom the passionate old man swore he doted;
"A creature," saith he, "nature hath brought forth
To mock the sex of woman." It is a thing   130
One knows not how to name; her birth began
Ere she was all made; 'tis woman more than man,
Man more than woman; and, which to none can hap,
The sun gives her two shadows to one shape;
Nay, more, let this strange thing walk, stand, or sit,
No blazing star draws more eyes after it.

   S. Davy. A monster! 'tis some monster!

   S. Alex.   She's a varlet.

   Seb. [*Aside*] Now is my cue to bristle.

   S. Alex. A naughty pack.[9]

   Seb.   'Tis false!

   S. Alex.   Ha, boy?

   Seb.   'Tis
   false!

   S. Alex. What's false? I say she's naught.

   Seb.   I say, that
   tongue   140
That dares speak so, but yours, sticks in the throat
Of a rank villain: set yourself aside—

   S. Alex. So, sir, what then?

   Seb.   Any here else had lied.
[*Aside*] I think I shall fit[10] you.

   S. Alex. Lie?

   Seb.   Yes.

   S. Davy.   Doth this concern him?

   S. Alex.   Ah, sirrah-
   boy,
Is your blood heated? Boils it? Are you stung?
I'll pierce you deeper yet.—O my dear friends,
I am that wretched father! this that son,
That sees his ruin, yet headlong on doth run.

   S. Adam. Will you love such a poison?

   S. Davy.   Fie, fie.

   Seb.   You're
   all mad.   150

   S. Alex. Thou'rt sick at heart, yet feel'st it not: of all
   these,
What gentleman but thou, knowing his disease
Mortal, would shun the cure!—O Master Greenwit,

Would you to such an idol bow?

   Green.   Not I, sir.

   S. Alex. Here's Master Laxton; has he mind to a
   woman
As thou hast?

   Lax.   No, not I, sir.

   S. Alex.   Sir, I know it.

   Lax. Their good parts are so rare, their bad so
   common,
I will have nought to do with any woman.

   S. Davy. 'Tis well done, Master Laxton.

   S. Alex.   O thou cruel
   boy,
Thou wouldst with lust an old man's life destroy!   160
Because thou see'st I'm halfway in my grave,
Thou shovel'st dust upon me; would thou might'st have
Thy wish, most wicked, most unnatural!

   S. Davy. Why, sir, 'tis thought Sir Guy Fitzallard's
   daughter
Shall wed your son Sebastian.

   S. Alex.   Sir Davy Dapper,
I have upon my knees wooed this fond[11] boy
To take that virtuous maiden.

   Seb.   Hark you; a word, sir.
You on your knees have cursed that virtuous maiden,
And me for loving her, yet do you now
Thus baffle[12] me to my face. Wear not your knees   170
In such entreats; give me Fitzallard's daughter.

   S. Alex. I'll give thee rats-bane rather.

   Seb.   Well, then,
   you know
What dish I mean to feed upon.

   S. Alex.   Hark, gentlemen!
He swears to have this cut-purse drab, to spite my gall.

   Omnes. Master Sebastian—

   Seb.   I am deaf to you all.
I'm so bewitched, so bound to my desires,
Tears, prayers, threats, nothing can quench out those
   fires
That burn within me.

                      Exit SEBASTIAN.

   S. Alex. [*Aside*] Her blood shall quench it, then.—
Lose him not; Oh, dissuade him, gentlemen!

   S. Davy. He shall be weaned, I warrant you.

   S. Alex.   Before
   his eyes   180
Lay down his shame, my grief, his miseries.

   Omnes. No more, no more; away!

                Exeunt all but SIR ALEX.

   S. Alex.   I wash a negro,
Losing both pains and cost; but take thy flight,
I'll be most near thee when I'm least in sight.
Wild buck, I'll hunt thee breathless; thou shalt run on,
But I will turn thee when I'm not thought upon.—

   Enter RALPH TRAPDOOR[*with a letter*].

---

7 *by-blows:* side-strokes.
8 *Adam Bell:* outlaw famous for his archery.
9 *naughty pack:* woman of bad character.
10 *fit:* punish.   11 *fond:* foolish.
12 *baffle:* treat with contempt.

Now, sirrah, what are you? Leave your ape's tricks, and
speak.

Trap. A letter from my captain to your worship.

S. Alex. Oh, Oh, now I remember; 'tis to prefer[13]
thee into my service.   191

Trap. [*Aside*] To be a shifter under your worship's
nose of a clean trencher, when there's a good bit upon't.

S. Alex. Troth, honest fellow—hum—ha—let me
see—

[*Aside*] This knave shall be the axe to hew that down
At which I stumble; has a face that promiseth
Much of a villain. I will grind his wit,
And, if the edge prove fine, make use of it.—
Come hither, sirrah. Canst thou be secret, ha?

Trap. As two crafty attorneys plotting the undoing of
their clients.   201

S. Alex. Didst never, as thou'st walked about this
town,
Hear of a wench called Moll, mad, merry Moll?

Trap. Moll Cutpurse, sir?

S. Alex. The same; dost thou know her, then?

Trap. As well as I know 'twill rain upon Simon and
Jude's day[14] next. I will sift all the taverns i' th' city,
and drink half pots with all the watermen[15] a' th' Bankside,[16] but, if you will, sir, I'll find her out.

S. Alex. That task is easy; do't then: hold thy hand
up.   210
What's this? Is't burnt?[17]

Trap. No, sir, no; a little singed with making fireworks.

S. Alex. There's money, spend it; that being spent,
fetch[18] more.

[*Gives money.*]

Trap. O sir, that all the poor soldiers in England had
such a leader! For fetching, no water-spaniel is like me.

S. Alex. This wench we speak of strays so from her
kind,
Nature repents she made her; 'tis a mermaid
Has tolled my son to shipwreck.

Trap. I'll cut her comb for you.   220

S. Alex. I'll tell out gold for thee, then. Hunt her
forth,
Cast out a line hung full of silver hooks
To catch her to thy company; deep spendings
May draw her that's most chaste to a man's bosom.

Trap. The jingling of golden bells, and a good fool
with a hobbyhorse,[19] will draw all the whores i' th'
town to dance in a morris.[20]

S. Alex. Or rather, for that's best (they say,
sometimes
She goes in breeches), follow her as her man.

_____

[13] *prefer:* recommend.
[14] *Simon . . . day:* October 28.   [15] *watermen:* boatmen.
[16] *Bankside:* south side of the Thames.
[17] *burnt:* i.e., branded for theft.   [18] *fetch:* come for.
[19] *hobbyhorse:* wicker horse.
[20] *morris:* dance in which participants wore costumes and
bells, often with a hobbyhorse.   [21] *bencher:* magistrate.
[22] *goll:* fist (cant).   [23] *stlll:* always.
II.i.
[1] *what . . . lack:* the hawker's cry.

Trap. And when her breeches are off, she shall follow
me.   231

S. Alex. Beat all thy brains to serve her.

Trap. Zounds, sir, as country wenches beat cream
till butter comes.

S. Alex. Play thou the subtle spider; weave fine nets
To ensure her very life.

Trap.   Her life?

S. Alex.   Yes; suck
Her heart-blood, if thou canst; twist thou but cords
To catch her, I'll find law to hang her up.

Trap. Spoke like a worshipful bencher![21]   239

S. Alex. Trace all her steps. At this she-fox's den
Watch what lambs enter; let me play the shepherd
To save their throats from bleeding, and cut hers.

Trap. This is the goll[22] shall do't.

S. Alex.   Be firm, and gain
me
Ever thine own. This done, I entertain thee.
How is thy name?

Trap. My name, sir, is Ralph Trapdoor, honest
Ralph.

S. Alex. Trapdoor, be like thy name, a dangerous
step
For her to venture on; but unto me—   249

Trap. As fast as your sole to your boot or shoe, sir.

S. Alex. Hence, then; be little seen here as thou
canst;
I'll still[23] be at thine elbow.

Trap.   The trapdoor's set.
Moll, if you budge, you're gone; this me shall crown;
A roaring boy the roaring girl puts down.

S. Alex. God-a-mercy, lose no time.

Exeunt.

ACT TWO

SCENE ONE

*The three shops open in a rank: the first an apothecary's
shop, the next a feather-shop, the third a sempster's
shop;* MISTRESS GALLIPOT *in the first,*
MISTRESS TILTYARD *in the next,* MASTER
OPENWORK *and his wife in the third.*

Enter LAXTON, GOSHAWK, *and* GREENWIT.

Mrs. Open. Gentlemen, what is't you lack?[1] What
is't you buy? See fine bands and ruffs, fine lawns, fine
cambrics. What is't you lack, gentlemen? What is't you
buy?

Lax. Yonder's the shop.

Gos. Is that she?

Lax. Peace.

Green. She that minces tobacco?

Lax. Ay; she's a gentlewoman born, I can tell you,
though it be her hard fortune now to shred Indian pot-
herbs.   11

Gos. O sir, 'tis many a good woman's fortune, when
her husband turns bankrupt, to begin with pipes and
set up again.

Lax. And, indeed, the raising of the woman is the

lifting up of the man's head at all times; if one flourish, t'other will bud as fast, I warrant ye.

Gos. Come, thou'rt familiarly acquainted there, I grope[2] that.   19

Lax. And you grope no better i' th' dark, you may chance lie i' th' ditch when you're drunk.

Gos. Go, thou'rt a mystical lecher!

Lax. I will not deny but my credit may take up an ounce of pure smoke.

Gos. May take up an ell of pure smock! away, go! 'Tis the closest striker![3] life, I think he commits venery forty foot deep; no man's aware on't. I, like a palpable smockster,[4] go to work so openly with the tricks of art that I'm as apparently seen as a naked boy in a vial[5]; and were it not for a gift of treachery that I have in   30 me, to betray my friend when he puts most trust in me —mass, yonder he is too!—and by his injury to make good my access to her, I should appear as defective in courting as a farmer's son the first day of his feather,[6] that doth nothing at court but woo the hangings and glass windows for a month together, and some broken waiting-woman for ever after. I find those imperfections in my venery, that were't not for flattery and falsehood, I should want discourse and impudence; and he that wants impudence among women is worthy to be   40 kicked out at bed's feet. [*Aside*] He shall not see me yet.

Green. Troth, this is finely shred.

Lax. Oh, women are the best mincers.

Mrs. G. 'Thad been a good phrase for a cook's wife, sir.

Lax. But 'twill serve generally, like the front of a new almanac, as thus: calculated for the meridian[7] of cooks' wives, but generally for all Englishwomen.

Mrs. G. Nay, you shall ha't, sir; I have filled it for you.   50

She puts it to the fire.

Lax. The pipe's in a good hand, and I wish mine always so.

Green. But not to be used o' that fashion.

Lax. Oh, pardon me, sir, I understand no French. I pray, be covered.[8] Jack, a pipe of rich smoke!

Gos. Rich smoke? That's sixpence a pipe, is't?

Green. To me, sweet lady,

Mrs. G. Be not forgetful; respect my credit; seem strange: art and wit makes a fool of suspicion; pray, be wary.   60

Lax. Push![9] I warrant you.—Come, how is't, gallants?

Green. Pure and excellent.

Lax. I thought 'twas good, you were grown so silent; you are like those that love not to talk at victuals, though they make a worse noise i' th' nose than a common fiddler's 'prentice, and discourse a whole supper with snuffling.—I must speak a word with you anon.[10]

Mrs. G. Make your way wisely, then.   70

Gos. Oh, what else, sir? He's perfection itself; full of manners, but not an acre of ground belonging to 'em.

Green. Ay, and full of form; has ne'er a good stool in's chamber.

Gos. But above all, religious; he preyeth daily upon elder brothers.

Green. And valiant above measure; has run three streets from a sergeant.

Lax. Puh, puh.

He blows tobacco in their faces.

Green.⎫
Gos. ⎭ Oh, puh, ho, ho.   80

Lax. So, so.

Mrs. G. What's the matter now, sir?

Lax. I protest I'm in extreme want of money; if you can supply me now with any means, you do me the greatest pleasure, next to the bounty of your love, as ever poor gentleman tasted.

Mrs. G. What's the sum would pleasure ye, sir? Though you deserve nothing less at my hands.

Lax. Why, 'tis but for want of opportunity, thou knowest.[*Aside*] I put her off with opportunity still: 90 by this light, I hate her, but for means to keep me in fashion with gallants; for what I take from her, I spend upon other wenches; bear her in hand[11] still: she has wit enough to rob her husband, and I ways enough to consume the money.—Why, how now? What, the chincough?[12]

Gos. Thou hast the cowardliest trick to come before a man's face and strangle him ere he be aware! I could find in my heart to make a quarrel in earnest.   99

Lax. Pox, and thou dost—thou knowest I never use to fight with my friends—thou'll but lose thy labor in't—Jack Dapper!

Enter JACK DAPPER *and his man* GULL.

Green. Monsieur Dapper, I dive down to your ankles.[13]

J. Dap. Save ye, gentlemen, all three in a peculiar salute.

Gos. He were ill to make a lawyer; he dispatches[14] three at once.

Lax. So, well said.—But is this of the same tobacco, Mistress Gallipot?   110

[*She gives him money secretly.*]

Mrs. G. The same you had at first, sir.

Lax. I wish it no better: this will serve to drink[15] at my chamber.

Gos. Shall we taste a pipe on't?[16]

Lax. Not of this, by my troth, gentlemen, I have sworn before you.

---

[2] *grope:* apprehend.   [3] *striker:* wencher.
[4] *smockster:* bawd.   [5] *naked . . . vial:* preserved fetus.
[6] *feather:* honor, prosperity.
[7] *calculated . . . meridian:* designed for the tastes.
[8] *be covered:* put your hat on.
[9] *Push:* Pooh, frequent expletive in Middleton.
[10] *anon:* right away.
[11] *bear . . . hand:* keep her in expectation.
[12] *chincough:* whooping cough.
[13] *dive . . . ankles:* bow to you.
[14] *dispatches:* finishes business and dismisses.
[15] *drink:* smoke.   [16] *on't:* of it.

Gos. What, not Jack Dapper?

Lax. Pardon me, sweet Jack; I'm sorry I made such a rash oath, but foolish oaths must stand. Where art going, Jack?   120

J. Dap. Faith, to buy one feather.

Lax. [*Aside*] One feather? The fool's peculiar still.

J. Dap. Gull.

Gull. Master?

J. Dap. Here's three halfpence for your ordinary,[17] boy; meet me an hour hence in Paul's.[18]

Gull. [*Aside*] How? Three single halfpence? Life, this will scarce serve a man in sauce, a halp'orth[19] of mustard, a halp'orth of oil, and a halp'orth of vinegar,— what's left then for the pickle herring? This   130 shows like small beer i' th' morning after a great surfeit of wine o'ernight; he could spend his three pound last night in a supper amongst girls and brave[20] bawdyhouse boys; I thought his pockets cackled not for nothing; these are the eggs of three pound, I'll go sup 'em up presently.

Exit GULL.

Lax. Eight, nine, ten angels:[21] good wench, i'faith, and one that loves darkness well; she puts out a candle with the best tricks of any drugster's wife in England: but that which mads her, I rail upon opportunity   140 still, and take no notice on't. The other night she would needs lead me into a room with a candle in her hand to show me a naked picture, where no sooner entered, but the candle was sent of[22] an errand. Now, I not intending to understand her, but, like a puny[23] at the inns of venery, called for another light innocently; thus reward I all her cunning with simple mistaking. I know she cozens her husband to keep me, and I'll keep her honest as long as I can, to make the poor man some part of amends. An honest mind of a whore-   150 master! how think you amongst you? What, a fresh pipe? Draw in a third man?

Gos. No, you're a hoarder, you engross[24] by th' ounces.

At the feather-shop now.

J. Dap. Puh, I like it not.

Mrs. T.   What feather is't you'd have, sir?

These are most worn and most in fashion:
Amongst the beaver[25] gallants, the stone riders,

The private stage's audience, the twelvepenny-stool, gentlemen,[26]
I can inform you 'tis the general feather.

J. Dap. And therefore I mislike it: tell me of general! Now, a continual Simon and Jude's rain   161
Beat all your feathers as flat down as pancakes!
Show me—a—spangled feather.

Mrs. T.   Oh, to go a-feasting with;
You'd have it for a hench-boy,[27] you shall.

At the sempster's shop now.

Open. Mass, I had quite forgot!
His Honor's footman was here last night, wife;
Ha' you done with my lord's shirt?

Mrs. O.   What's that to you,
    sir?
I was this morning at his honor's lodging,
Ere such a snake as you crept out of your shell.

Open. Oh, 'twas well done, good wife!

Mrs. O.   I hold it better,
    sir,   170
Than if you had done't yourself.

Open.   Nay, so say I:
But is the countess's smock almost done, mouse?

Mrs. O. Here lies the cambric, sir; but wants, I fear me.

Open. I'll resolve[28] you of that presently.

Mrs. O. Heyday! O audacious groom!
Dare you presume to noble women's linen?
Keep you your yard[29] to measure shepherds' holland;[30]
I must confine you, I see that.

At the tobacco-shop now.

Gos. What say you to this gear?[31]

Lax. I dare the arrant'st critic in tobacco   180
To lay one fault upon't.

Enter MOLL *in a frieze[32] jerkin and
a black safeguard.[33]*

Gos. Life, yonder's Moll!

Lax. Moll! which Moll?

Gos. Honest Moll.

Lax. Prithee, let's call her.—Moll!

Omnes. Moll, Moll, pist, Moll.

Moll. How now? What's the matter?

Gos. A pipe of good tobacco, Moll?

Moll. I cannot stay.

Gos. Nay, Moll, puh, prithee, hark; but one word, i' faith.   191

Moll. Well, what is't?

Green. Prithee, come hither, sirrah.

Lax. [*Aside*] Heart, I would give but too much money to be nibbling with that wench; life, sh'as the spirit of four great parishes, and a voice that will drown all the city. Methinks a brave captain might get[34] all his soldiers upon her, and ne'er be beholding[35] to a company of Mile-end[36] milksops, if he could come on and come off quick enough. Such a Moll were a   200 marrowbone before an Italian; he would cry *bona roba*[37] till his ribs were nothing but bone. I'll lay hard siege to her; money is that aqua fortis[38] that eats into many a

---

17 *ordinary:* tavern.
18 *Paul's:* St. Paul's Cathedral, popular meeting place.
19 *halp'orth:* halfpennyworth.
20 *brave:* splendidly dressed.   21 *angels:* gold coins.
22 *of:* on.
23 *puny:* freshmen at the Inns of Court (law schools).
24 *engross:* buy up wholesale in order to gain a monopoly.
25 *beaver:* hats made of beaver fur.
26 *private . . . gentlemen:* those who paid 12p. to sit on the stage.   27 *hench-boy:* page.   28 *resolve:* satisfy.
29 *yard:* yardstick.   30 *holland:* linen.   31 *gear:* stuff.
32 *frieze:* coarse wool.
33 *safeguard:* large petticoat to protect clothes from soiling.
34 *get:* beget.   35 *beholding:* obligated.
36 *Mile-end:* field where London militia trained.
37 *bona roba:* It. *buona roba,* good stuff, attractive wench, also "prostitute."   38 *aqua fortis:* acid.

maidenhead; where the walls are flesh and blood, I'll ever pierce through with a golden auger.

Gos. Now, thy judgment, Moll? Is't not good?

Moll. Yes, faith, 'tis very good tobacco.—How do you sell an ounce?—Farewell.—God b'i' you, Mistress Gallipot.

Gos. Why, Moll, Moll!   210

Moll. I cannot stay now, i'faith; I am going to buy a shag[39]-ruff; the shop will be shut in presently.

Gos. 'Tis the maddest fantasticalest girl. I never knew so much flesh and so much nimbleness put together.

Lax. She slips from one company to another, like a fat eel between a Dutchman's fingers. [*Aside*] I'll watch my time for her.

Mrs. G. Some will not stick to say she is a man, and some, both man and woman.   220

Lax. That were excellent: she might first cuckold the husband, and then make him do as much for the wife.

The feather-shop again.

Moll. Save you; how does Mistress Tiltyard?

J. Dap. Moll!

Moll. Jack Dapper!

J. Dap. How dost, Moll?

Moll. I'll tell thee by and by; I go but to th' next shop.

J. Dap. Thou shalt find me here this hour about a feather.   231

Moll. Nay, and a feather hold you in play a whole hour, a goose will last you all the days of your life.—Let me see a good shag-ruff.

The sempster's shop.

Open. Mistress Mary, that shalt thou, i'faith, and the best in the shop.

Mrs. O. How now? Greetings! love-terms, with a pox, between you! have I found out one of your haunts? I send you for hollands, and you're i' th' low countries,[40] with a mischief. I'm served with good ware by th'   240 shift; that makes it lie dead so long upon my hands; I were as good shut up shop, for when I open it I take nothing.

Open. Nay, and you fall a-ringing once, the devil cannot stop you.—I'll out of the belfry as fast as I can, Moll.

[Retires.]

Mrs. O. Get you from my shop!

Moll. I come to buy.

Mrs. O. I'll sell ye nothing; I warn[41] ye my house and shop.   250

Moll. You, Goody[42] Openwork, you that prick out a poor living,
And sews many a bawdy skin-coat together;
Thou private pandress between shirt and smock;
I wish thee for a minute but a man,
Thou shouldst ne'er use more shapes; but as thou art,
I pity my revenge. Now my spleen's up,

Enter a Fellow *with a long rapier by his side.*

I would not mock it willingly.—Ha! be thankful; Now I forgive thee.

Mrs. O. Marry, hang thee, I never asked forgiveness in my life.   261

Moll. You, goodman swine's face!

Fel. What, will you murder me?

Moll. You remember, slave, how you abused me t'other night in a tavern.

Fel. Not I, by this light!

Moll. No, but by candlelight you did; you have tricks to save your oaths; reservations have you? And I have reserved somewhat for you.   269

[Strikes him.]

As you like that, call for more; you know the sign again.

Fel. [*Aside*] Pox on't, had I brought any company along with me to have borne witness on't, 'twould ne'er have grieved me; but to be struck and nobody by, 'tis my ill fortune still. Why, tread upon a worm, they say 'twill turn tail; but indeed a gentleman should have more manners.

Exit Fellow.

Lax. Gallantly performed, i'faith, Moll, and manfully! I love thee for ever for't. Base rogue, had he offered but the least counter-buff, by this hand, I was prepared for him!   280

Moll. You prepared for him? Why should you be prepared for him? Was he any more than a man?

Lax. No, nor so much by a yard and a handful, London measure.

Moll. Why do you speak this then? Do you think I cannot ride a stone-horse,[43] unless one lead him by th' snaffle?[44]

Lax. Yes, and sit him bravely; I know thou canst, Moll; 'twas but an honest mistake through love, and I'll make amends for't any way. Prithee, sweet plump Moll, when shall thou and I go out o' town together?   291

Moll. Whither? To Tyburn,[45] prithee?

Lax. Mass, that's out o' town indeed; thou hangest so many jests upon thy friends still. I mean honestly to Brainford, Staines, or Ware.[46]

Moll. What to do there?

Lax. Nothing but be merry and lie together: I'll hire a coach with four horses.

Moll. I thought 'twould be a beastly journey. You may leave out one well; three horses will serve, if I play the jade[47] myself.   301

Lax. Nay, push, thou'rt such another kicking wench! Prithee, be kind, and let's meet.

Moll. 'Tis hard but we shall meet, sir.

---

[39] *shag:* cloth with velvet nap on one side.
[40] *low countries:* bawdy, like much in this scene.
[41] *warn:* i.e., warn you to keep away from.
[42] *Goody:* title for woman of low estate (like Goodman).
[43] *stone-horse:* gelding.   [44] *snaffle:* bridle-bit.
[45] *Tyburn:* the place of public execution, at junction of present Oxford Street, Bayswater Road, and Edgware Road.
[46] *Brainford . . . Ware:* villages near London, visited for amusement; Brainford = Brentford.
[47] *jade:* horse; disreputable woman. "Play the jade" is a stock phrase.

Lax. Nay, but appoint the place then; there's ten angels in fair gold, Moll; you see I do not trifle with you; do but say thou wilt meet me, and I'll have a coach ready for thee.

Moll. Why, here's my hand, I'll meet you, sir.

Lax. [*Aside*] Oh, good gold!—The place, sweet Moll?   311

Moll. It shall be your appointment.

Lax. Somewhat near Holborn, Moll.

Moll. In Gray's Inn⁴⁸ Fields then.

Lax. A match.

Moll. I'll meet you there.

Lax. The hour?

Moll. Three.

Lax. That will be time enough to sup at Brainford.

Fall from them to the other.

Open. I am of such a nature, sir, I cannot en-   320
dure the house when she scolds; sh'as a tongue will be
heard further in a still morning than Saint Antling's⁴⁹
bell. She rails upon me for foreign wenching, that I
being a freeman must needs keep a whore i' th' suburbs,
and seek to impoverish the liberties.⁵⁰ When we fall out,
I trouble you still to make all whole with my wife.

Gos. No trouble at all; 'tis a pleasure to me to join things together.

Open. [*Aside*] Go thy ways, I do this but to try thy honesty, Goshawk.   330

The feather-shop.

J. Dap. How likest thou this, Moll?

Moll. Oh, singularly; you're fitted now for a bunch. [*Aside*] He looks for all the world, with those spangled feathers, like a nobleman's bed-post. The purity of your wench would I fain try; she seems like Kent⁵¹ un-conquered, and, I believe, as many wiles are in her. Oh, the gallants of these times are shallow lechers; they put not their courtship home enough to a wench.'Tis im-possible to know what woman is throughly honest, be-cause she's ne'er thoroughly tried; I am of that   340
certain belief, there are more queans⁵² in this town of their own making than of any man's provoking. Where lies the slackness then? Many a poor soul would down, and there's nobody will push 'em.

Women are courted, but ne'er soundly tried,
As many walk in spurs that never ride.

The sempster's shop.

Mrs. O. Oh, abominable!

Gos. Nay, more, I tell you in private, he keeps a whore i' th' suburbs.   349

Mrs. O. Oh, spital⁵³ dealing! I came to him a gentle-woman born. I'll show you mine arms⁵⁴ when you please, sir.

Gos. [*Aside*] I had rather see your legs, and begin that way.

Mrs. O. 'Tis well known he took me from a lady's service, where I was well beloved of the steward. I had my Latin tongue, and a spice of the French, before I came to him; and now doth he keep a surburbian whore under my nostrils?

Gos. There's ways enough to cry quit with him: hark in thine ear.   361

[Whispers her.]

Mrs. O. There's a friend worth a million!

Moll. [*Aside*] I'll try one spear against your chastity, Mistress Tiltyard, though it prove too short by the burgh.⁵⁵

Enter RALPH TRAPDOOR.

Trap. [*Aside*] Mass, here she is; I'm bound already to serve her, though it be but a sluttish trick.—Bless my hopeful young mistress with long life and great limbs; send her the upper hand of all bailiffs and their hungry adherents!   370

Moll. How now? What art thou?

Trap. A poor ebbing gentleman, that would gladly wait for the young flood of your service.

Moll. My service? What should move you to offer your service to me, sir?

Trap. The love I bear to your historic spirit and masculine womanhood.

Moll. So, sir! put case we should retain you to us, what parts are there in you for a gentlewoman's service?

Trap. Of two kinds, right worshipful; mov-   380
able and immovable—movable to run of errands, and immovable to stand when you have occasion to use me.

Moll. What strength have you?

Trap. Strength, Mistress Moll? I have gone up into a steeple and stayed the great bell as't has been ringing; stopped a windmill going—

Moll. And never struck down yourself?

Trap. Stood as upright as I do at this present.

MOLL *trips up his heels ; he falls.*

Moll. Come, I pardon you for this; it shall be no disgrace to you; I have struck up the heels of the high German's⁵⁶ size ere now. What, not stand?   391

Trap. I am of that nature, where I love, I'll be at my mistress' foot to do her service.

Moll. Why, well said; but say your mistress should receive injury, have you the spirit of fighting in you? Durst you second her?

Trap. Life, I have kept a bridge myself, and drove seven at a time before me!

Moll. Ay?

Trap. [*Aside*] But they were all Lincolnshire bul-locks, by my troth.   401

Moll. Well, meet me in Gray's Inn Fields between three and four this afternoon, and, upon better con-sideration, we'll retain you.

---

⁴⁸ *Gray's Inn:* one of the Inns of Court, law school and social center for lawyers.
⁴⁹ *Saint Antling's:* church frequented by Puritans.
⁵⁰ *liberties:* district around the city subject to municipal jurisdiction.
⁵¹ *Kent:* one of the kingdoms of Anglo-Saxon England, coterminous with the present county.   ⁵² *queans:* whores.
⁵³ *spital:* poorhouse.   ⁵⁴ *arms:* coat of arms.
⁵⁵ *burgh:* iron ring behind the handle of tilting lance.
⁵⁶ *high German's:* perhaps an allusion to a tall German exhibited in London.

Trap. I humbly thank your good mistress-ship.
[*Aside*] I'll crack your neck for this kindness.

Exit TRAPDOOR.

Lax. Remember three.

MOLL *meets* LAXTON,

Moll. Nay, if I fail you, hang me.
Lax. Good wench, i'faith!
Moll. Who's this?   410

then OPENWORK.

Open. 'Tis I, Moll.
Moll. Prithee, tend thy shop and prevent bastards.
Open. We'll have a pint of the same wine,[57] i'faith,
Moll.

[*Exit with* MOLL.]

The bell rings.

Gos. Hark, the bell rings. Come, gentlemen. Jack
Dapper, where shall's all munch?
J. Dap. I am for Parker's ordinary.
Lax. He's a good guest to'm, he deserves his board;
he draws all the gentlemen in a term-time[58] thither.
We'll be your followers, Jack; lead the way.—   420
Look you, by my faith, the fool has feathered his nest
well.

Exeunt JACK DAPPER, LAXTON, GOSHAWK,
and GREENWIT.

Enter MASTER GALLIPOT, MASTER TILTYARD,
and Servants, *with water-spaniels and a duck.*

Tilt. Come, shut up your shops. Where's Master
Openwork?
Mrs. G. Nay, ask not me, Master Tiltyard.
Tilt. Where's his water-dog? Puh—pist—hur—hur
—pist!
Gal. Come, wenches, come; we're going all to Hogs-
don.[59]
Mrs. G. To Hogsdon, husband?   430
Gal. Ay, to Hogsdon, pigsnie.[60]
Mrs. G. I'm not ready, husband.
Gal. Faith, that's well—hum—pist—pist.—

Spits in the dog's mouth.

Come, Mistress Openwork, you are so long!
Mrs. O. I have no joy of my life, Master Gallipot.
Gal. Push, let your boy lead his water-spaniel along,
and we'll show you the bravest sport at Parlous Pond.[61]
—Hey, Trug,[62] hey, Trug, hey, Trug! here's the best
duck in England, except my wife; hey, hey, hey! fetch,
fetch, fetch!—   440
Come, let's away:
Of all the year this is the sportful'st day.

[*Exeunt.*]

[II.ii]

Enter SEBASTIAN WENGRAVE.

Seb. If a man have a free will, where should the use
More perfect shine than in his will to love?
All creatures have their liberty in that,

Enter SIR ALEX. *and listens to him.*

Though else kept under servile yoke and fear;
The very bond-slave has his freedom there.
Amongst a world of creatures voiced and silent,
Must my desires wear fetters—

[SEBASTIAN *sees him.*]

Yea, are you
So near? Then I must break with my heart's truth,
Meet grief at a back way.—Well: why, suppose
The two-leaved[1] tongues of slander or of truth   10
Pronounce Moll loathsome; if before my love
She appear fair, what injury have I?
I have the thing I like: in all things else
Mine own eye guides me, and I find 'em prosper.
Life! what should ail it now? I know that man
Ne'er truly loves,—if he gainsay't he lies,—
That winks[2] and marries with his father's eyes;
I'll keep mine own wide open.

Enter MOLL, *and a* Porter *with a viol on his back.*

S. Alex. [*Aside*] Here's brave wilfullness!   19
A made match! here she comes; they met o' purpose.
Por. Must I carry this great fiddle to your chamber,
Mistress Mary?
Moll. Fiddle, Goodman Hog-rubber? Some of these
porters bear so much for others, they have no time to
carry wit for themselves.
Por. To your own chamber, Mistress Mary?
Moll. Who'll hear an ass speak? Whither else, Good-
man Pageant[3]-bearer? They're people of the worst
memories!

Exit Porter.

Seb. Why, 'twere too great a burden, love, to have
them   30
Carry things in their minds and o' their backs together.
Moll. Pardon me, sir, I thought not you so near.
S. Alex. [*Aside*] So, so, so.
Seb. I would be nearer to thee, and in that fashion
That makes the best part of all creatures honest;
No otherwise I wish it.
Moll. Sir, I am so poor to requite you, you must look
for nothing but thanks of me. I have no humor to
marry; I love to lie o' both sides o' th' bed myself; and
again, o' th' other side, a wife, you know, ought to   40
be obedient, but I fear me I am too headstrong to obey;
therefore I'll ne'er go about it. I love you so well, sir,
for your good will, I'd be loath you should repent your
bargain after; and therefore we'll ne'er come together at

---

[57] *same wine:* i.e., bastard, a sweet wine.
[58] *term-time:* when the courts are in session.
[59] *Hogsdon:* London suburb with popular taverns.
[60] *pigsnie:* little pig, term of endearment.
[61] *Parlous Pond:* springfed pond in London that caused
numerous drownings when it overflowed, enclosed in 1743.
[62] *Trug:* the spaniel's name = "Whore" (cant).

II.ii.
[1] *two-leaved tongues:* hinged, like two-part gates, so that
each part can move its own way.   [2] *winks:* closes his eyes.
[3] *Pageant:* Stage-machinery.

first. I have the head now of myself, and am man enough
for a woman. Marriage is but a chopping and changing,
where a maiden loses one head, and has a worse i' th'
place.

S. Alex. [*Aside*] The most comfortablest answer from
a roaring girl
That ever mine ears drunk in.

Seb.   This were enough   50
Now to affright a fool forever from thee,
When 'tis the music that I love thee for.

S. Alex. [*Aside*] There's a boy spoils all again.

Moll. Believe it, sir, I am not of that disdainful
temper but I could love you faithfully.

S. Alex. [*Aside*] A pox on you for that word! I like
you not now;
You're a cunning roarer, I see that already.

Moll. But sleep upon this once more, sir; you may
chance shift a mind tomorrow. Be not too hasty to wrong
yourself; never while you live, sir, take a wife   60
running; many have run out at heels that have done't.
You see, sir, I speak against myself; and if every woman would deal with their suitor so honestly, poor
younger brothers would not be so often gulled with
old cozening[4] widows, that turn o'er all their wealth in
trust to some kinsman, and make the poor gentleman
work hard for a pension. Fare you well, sir.

Seb. Nay, prithee, one word more.

S. Alex. [*Aside*] How do I wrong this girl! she puts
him off still.   69

Moll. Think upon this in cold blood, sir; you make
as much haste as if you were a-going upon a sturgeon
voyage. Take deliberation, sir; never choose a wife as if
you were going to Virginia.[5]

Seb. And so we parted; my too-cursed fate!

S. Alex. [*Aside*] She is but cunning, gives him longer
time in't.

Enter a Tailor.

Tai. Mistress Moll, Mistress Moll! so ho, ho, so ho!

Moll. There, boy, there, boy! what dost thou go a-
hawking after me with a red clout[6] on thy finger?

Tai. I forgot to take measure on you for your new
breeches.   80

S. Alex. [*Aside*] Hoyda, breeches? What, will he
marry a monster with two trinkets?[7] What age is this?
If the wife go in breeches, the man must wear long coats
like a fool.

Moll. What fiddling's here! would not the old pattern have served your turn?

Tai. You change the fashion: you say you'll have the
great Dutch slop,[8] Mistress Mary.

Moll. Why, sir, I say so still.   89

Tai. Your breeches, then, will take up a yard more.

Moll. Well, pray, look it be put in then.

Tai. It shall stand round and full, I warrant you.

Moll. Pray, make 'em easy enough.

Tai. I know my fault now, t'other was somewhat
stiff between the legs; I'll make these open enough, I
warrant you.

S. Alex. [*Aside*] Here's good gear towards![9] I have
brought up my son to marry a Dutch slop and a French
doublet; a codpiece daughter!

Tai. So, I have gone as far as I can go.   100

Moll. Why, then, farewell.

Tai. If you go presently to your chamber, Mistress
Mary, pray, send me the measure of your thigh by some
honest body.

Moll. Well, sir, I'll send it by a porter presently.

Exit MOLL.

Tai. So you had need, it is a lusty one; both of them
would make any porter's back ache in England.

Exit Tailor.

Seb. I have examined the best part of man,
Reason and judgment; and in love, they tell me,
They leave me uncontrolled. He that is swayed   110
By an unfeeling blood, past heat of love,
His springtime must needs err; his watch ne'er goes
right
That sets his dial by a rusty clock.

[SIR ALEXANDER *comes forward.*]

S. Alex. So; and which is that rusty clock, sir, you?

Seb. The clock at Ludgate,[10] sir; it ne'er goes true.

S. Alex. But thou go'st falser; not thy father's cares
Can keep thee right: when that insensible work
Obeys the workman's art, lets off the hour,
And stops again when time is satisfied;
But thou runn'st on; and judgment, thy main wheel,
Beats by all stops, as if the work would break, 121
Begun with long pains for a minute's ruin;
Much like a suffering man brought up with care,
At last bequeathed to shame and a short prayer.

Seb. I taste you bitterer than I can deserve, sir.

S. Alex. Who has bewitch[ed] thee, son? what devil
or drug
Hath wrought upon the weakness of thy blood,
And betrayed all her hopes to ruinous folly?
Oh, wake from drowsy and enchanted shame.
Wherein thy soul sits, with a golden dream   130
Flattered and poisoned!
I am old, my son; Oh, let me prevail quickly!
For I have weightier business of mine own
Than to chide thee. I must not to my grave
As a drunkard to his bed, whereon he lies
Only to sleep, and never cares to rise.
Let me dispatch in time; come no more near her.

Seb. Not honestly? Not in the way of marriage?

S. Alex. What sayst thou? Marriage? In what place?
the sessions[11]-house?   139
And who shall give the bride, prithee? An indictment?

Seb. Sir, now ye take part with the world to wrong
her.

S. Alex. Why, wouldst thou fain marry to be pointed
at?
Alas, the number's great! do not o'erburden't.
Why, as good marry a beacon on a hill,

---

4 *cozening:* cheating.
5 *sturgeon . . . Virginia:* as if you were going where wives
are scarce.   6 *clout:* cloth.   7 *trinkets:* testicles.
8 *slop:* wide breeches.   9 *towards:* coming.
10 *Ludgate:* old London gate and debtors' prison there.
11 *sessions:* judicial hearings.

Which all the country fix their eyes upon,
As her thy folly dotes on. If thou long'st
To have the story of thy infamous fortunes
Serve for discourse in ordinaries and taverns,
Thou'rt in the way; or to confound thy name,
Keep on, thou canst not miss it, or to strike　　　150
Thy wretched father to untimely coldness,
Keep the left hand still, it will bring thee to't.
Yet, if no tears wrung from thy father's eyes,
Nor sighs that fly in sparkles from his sorrows,
Had power to alter what is willful in thee,
Methinks her very name should fright thee from her,
And never trouble me.
　　Seb. Why, is the name of Moll so fatal, sir?
　　S. Alex. Mary, one,[12] sir, where suspect is entered;
For, seek all London from one end to t'other,　　　160
More whores of that name than of any ten other.
　　Seb. What's that to her? Let those blush for
　　　themselves:
Can any guilt in others condemn her?
I've vowed to love her; let all storms oppose me
That ever beat against the breast of man,
Nothing but death's black tempest shall divide us.
　　S. Alex. Oh, folly that can dote on nought but shame!
　　Seb. Put case a wanton itch runs through one name
More than another; is that name the worse,　　　169
Where honesty sits possessed in't? It should rather
Appear more excellent, and deserve more praise,
When through foul mists a brightness it can raise.
Why, there are of the devils honest gentlemen
And well descended, keep an open house,
And some o' th' good man's[13] that are arrant knaves.
He hates unworthily that by rote contemns,
For the name neither saves nor yet condemns;
And for her honesty, I have made such proof on't
In several forms, so neatly watched her ways,
I will maintain that strict against an army,　　　180
Excepting you, my father. Here's her worst,
Sh'as a bold spirit that mingles with mankind,
But nothing else comes near it; and oftentimes
Through her apparel somewhat shames her birth;
But she is loose in nothing but in mirth.
Would all Molls were no worse!
　　S. Alex. [*Aside*] This way I toil in vain, and give but
　　　aim[14]
To infamy and ruin. He will fall;
My blessing cannot stay him. All my joys
Stand at the brink of a devouring flood,　　　190
And will be willfully swallowed, willfully.
But why so vain let all these tears be lost?
I'll pursue her to shame, and so all's crossed.
　　　　　　　　　　　Exit Sir Alexander.
　　Seb. He's gone with some strange purpose, whose
　　　effect
Will hurt me little if he shoot so wide,
To think I love so blindly: I but feed
His heart to this match, to draw on the other,
Wherein my joy sits with a full wish crowned,
Only his mood excepted, which must change
By opposite policies, courses indirect;　　　200
Plain dealing in this world takes no effect.

This mad girl I'll acquaint with my intent,
Get her assistance, make my fortunes known.
'Twixt lovers' hearts she's a fit instrument,
And has the art to help them to their own.
By her advice, for in that craft she's wise,
My love and I may meet, spite of all spies.
　　　　　　　　　　　Exit Sebastian.

ACT THREE

Scene One

Enter Laxton *in Gray's Inn Fields with the*
Coachman.

　　Lax. Coachman.
　　Coach. Here, sir.
　　Lax. There's a tester[1] more; prithee drive thy coach
to the hither end of Marybone[2] Park, a fit place for
Moll to get in.
　　Coach. Marybone Park, sir?
　　Lax. Ay, it's in our way, thou knowest.
　　Coach. It shall be done, sir.
　　Lax. Coachman.
　　Coach. Anon, sir.　　　10
　　Lax. Are we fitted with good frampold[3] jades?
　　Coach. The best in Smithfield, I warrant you, sir.
　　Lax. May we safely take the upper hand of any
coached velvet cap, or tuftaffety[4] jacket? For they keep
a vile swaggering in coaches nowadays; the highways
are stopped with them.
　　Coach. My life for yours, and baffle 'em too, sir; why,
they are the same jades, believe it, sir, that have drawn
all your famous whores to Ware.
　　Lax. Nay, then, they know their business; they need
no more instructions.　　　21
　　Coach. They're so used to such journeys, sir, I never
use whip to 'em; for if they catch but the scent of a
wench once, they run like devils.
　　　　　　　　　Exit Coachman *with his whip*.
　　Lax. Fine Cerberus![5] that rogue will have the start of
a thousand ones; for whilst others trot a' foot, he'll ride
prancing to hell upon a coach-horse. Stay, 'tis now about
the hour of her appointment, but yet I see her not.

　　　　　　　　　The clock strikes three.

Hark! what's this? One, two, three—three by the clock
at Savoy; this is the hour, and Gray's Inn Fields the　　　30
place, she swore she'd meet me. Ha! yonder's two Inns-
o'-court men with one wench, but that's not she; they
walk toward Islington out of my way. I see none yet
dressed like her; I must look for a shag ruff, a frieze

---

[12] *Mary, one:* Q "Many one."　　[13] *good man's:* i.e., God's.
[14] *give . . . aim:* direct.

III.i.
　[1] *tester:* sixpence.
　[2] *Marybone:* Marylebone, district of London.
　[3] *frampold:* fiery.
　[4] *tuftaffety:* kind of taffeta with pile arranged in tufts.
　[5] *Cerberus:* monstrous guardian of the gate to the Underworld.

jerkin, a short sword, and a safeguard, or I get none.
Why, Moll, prithee, make haste, or the coachman will
curse us anon.

Enter MOLL, *like*[6] *a man.*

Moll. [*Aside*] Oh, here's my gentleman! If they would
keep their days as well with their mercers as their hours
with their harlots, no bankrupt would give seven-   40
score pound for a sergeant's place; for would you know
a catchpoll[7] rightly derived, the corruption of a citizen
is the generation of a sergeant. How his eye hawks for
venery!—Come, are you ready, sir?
Lax. Ready? For what, sir?
Moll. Do you ask that now, sir? Why was this meeting 'pointed?
Lax. I thought you mistook me, sir; you seem to be
some young barrister; I have no suit in law, all my land's
sold; I praise heaven for't, 't has rid me of much
trouble.   51
Moll. Then I must wake you sir; where stands the
coach?
Lax. Who's this? Moll, honest Moll?
Moll. So young, and purblind? You're an old wanton in your eyes, I see that.
Lax. Thou'rt admirably suited for the Three Pigeons[8] at Brainford. I'll swear I knew thee not.
Moll. I'll swear you did not; but you shall know me
now.   60
Lax. No, not here; we shall be spied, i'faith; the
coach is better; come.
Moll. Stay.

She puts off her cloak and draws [*her sword*].

Lax. What, wilt thou untruss a point, Moll?
Moll. Yes; here's the point that I untruss; 't has but
one tag,[9] 't will serve though to tie up a rogue's tongue.
Lax. How!
Moll. There's the gold
With which you hired your hackney, here's her pace;
She racks[10] hard, and perhaps your bones will feel it:
Ten angels of mine own I've put to thine;   71
Win 'em, and wear 'em.
Lax. Hold, Moll! Mistress Mary—
Moll. Draw, or I'll serve an execution on thee
Shall lay thee up till doomsday.
Lax. Draw upon a woman! why, what dost mean,
Moll?
Moll. To teach thy base thoughts manners; thou'rt
one of those
That thinks each woman thy fond flexible whore;
If she but cast a liberal[11] eye upon thee,   79
Turn back her head, she's thine; or amongst company
By chance drink first to thee, then she's quite gone,

There is no means to help her: nay, for a need,
Wilt swear unto thy credulous fellow-lechers,
That thou art more in favor with a lady
At first sight than her monkey all her lifetime.
How many of our sex, by such as thou,
Have their good thoughts paid with a blasted name
That never deserved loosely, or did trip
In path of whoredom beyond cup and lip.
But for the stain of conscience and of soul,   90
Better had women fall into the hands
Of an act silent than a bragging nothing;
There is no mercy in't. What durst move you, sir,
To think me whorish? A name which I'd tear out
From the high German's throat, if it lay ledger[12] there
To dispatch privy slanders against me.
In thee I defy all men, their worst hates
And their best flatteries, all their golden witchcrafts,
With which they entangle the poor spirits of fools,
Distressed needle-women and tradefallen wives;   100
Fish that must needs bite, or themselves be bitten.
Such hungry things as these may soon be took
With a worm fastened on a golden hook.
Those are the lecher's food, his prey; he watches
For quarreling wedlocks[13] and poor shifting sisters;
'Tis the best fish he takes. But why, good fisherman,
Am I thought meat for you, that never yet
Had angling rod cast towards me? 'Cause, you'll say,
I'm given to sport, I'm often merry, jest.
Had mirth no kindred in the world but lust,   110
Oh, shame take all her friends then! but howe'er
Thou and the baser world censure my life,
I'll send 'em word by thee, and write so much
Upon thy breast, 'cause thou shalt bear't in mind,
Tell them 'twere base to yield where I have conquered;
I scorn to prostitute myself to a man,
I that can prostitute a man to me;
And so I greet thee.
Lax. Hear me—
Moll. Would the spirits   120
Of all my sland[er]ers were clasped in thine,
That I might vex an army at one time!

They fight.

Lax. I do repent me; hold!
Moll. You'll die the better Christian then.
Lax. I do confess I have wronged thee, Moll.
Moll. Confession is but poor amends for wrong,
Unless a rope would follow.
Lax. I ask thee pardon.
Moll. I'm your hired whore, sir!
Lax. I yield both purse and body.   130
Moll. Both are mine,
And now at my disposing.
Lax. Spare my life.
Moll. I scorn to strike thee basely.
Lax. Spoke like a noble girl, i'faith! [*Aside*] Heart, I
think I fight with a familiar,[14] or the ghost of a fencer.
Sh'as wounded me gallantly. Call you this a lecherous
voyage? Here's blood would have served me this seven
year in broken heads and cut fingers, and it now runs
all out together. Pox a' the Three Pigeons! I   140

---

⁶ *like:* dressed as.
⁷ *catchpoll:* warrant officer who arrests for debt.
⁸ *Three Pigeons:* low-class inn.
⁹ *tag:* piece of metal, etc., at end of a lace to enable it to
pass through an eyelet.   ¹⁰ *racks:* inflicts pain.
¹¹ *liberal:* wanton.   ¹² *lay ledger:* were lying.
¹³ *wedlocks:* wives.   ¹⁴ *familiar:* demonic spirit.

would the coach were here now to carry me to the
chirurgeon's.

Exit LAXTON.

Moll. If I could meet my enemies one by one thus,
I might make pretty shift with 'em in time,
And make 'em know she that has wit and spirit,
May scorn to live beholding to her body for meat;
Or for apparel, like your common dame,
That makes shame get her clothes to cover shame.
Base is that mind that kneels unto her body,
As if a husband stood in awe on's wife: 150
My spirit shall be mistress of this house
As long as I have time in't.—Oh,

Enter TRAPDOOR.

Here comes my man that would be: 'tis his hour.
Faith, a good well-set fellow, if his spirit
Be answerable to his umbles: [15] he walks stiff,
But whether he'll stand to't stiffly, there's the point.
Has a good calf for't; and ye shall have many a woman
Choose him she means to make her head by his calf;
I do not know their tricks in't. Faith, he seems
A man without; I'll try what he is within.   160
Trap. She told me Gray's Inn Fields, 'twixt three
          and four;
I'll fit her Mistress-ship with a piece of service.
I'm hired to rid the town of one mad girl.

She jostles him.

What a pox ails you, sir?
Moll. He begins like a gentleman.
Trap. Heart, is the field so narrow, or your eyesight—
Life, he comes back again!

She comes towards him.

Moll. Was this spoke to me, sir?
Trap. I cannot tell, sir.
Moll. Go, you're a coxcomb!   170
Trap. Coxcomb?
Moll. You're a slave!
Trap. I hope there's law for you, sir.
Moll. Yea, do you see, sir?

Turns his hat.

Trap. Heart, this is no good dealing! pray, let me
know what house you're of.
Moll. One of the Temple, [16] sir.

Fillips him.

Trap. Mass, so methinks.
Moll. And yet sometime I lie about Chick Lane. 179
Trap. I like you the worse because you shift your
lodging so often; I'll not meddle with you for that
trick, sir.
Moll. A good shift; but it shall not serve your turn.
Trap. You'll give me leave to pass about my busi-
ness, sir?
Moll. Your business? I'll make you wait on me before
I ha' done, and glad to serve me too.
Trap. How, sir? Serve you? Not if there were no
more men in England.   189

Moll. But if there were no more women in England,
I hope you'd wait upon your mistress then?
Trap. Mistress?
Moll. Oh, you're a tried spirit at a push, sir!
Trap. What would your worship have me do?
Moll. You a fighter!
Trap. No, I praise heaven, I had better grace and
more manners.
Moll. As how, I pray, sir?
Trap. Life, 'thad been a beastly part of me to have
drawn my weapons upon my mistress; all the world
would 'a cried shame of me for that.   201
Moll. Why, but you knew me not.
Trap. Do not say so, mistress; I knew you by your
wide straddle, as well as if I had been in your belly.
Moll. Well, we shall try you further; i' th' meantime
we give you entertainment.
Trap. Thank your good mistress-ship.
Moll. How many suits have you?
Trap. No more suits than backs, mistress.   209
Moll. Well, if you deserve, I cast off this, next week,
and you may creep into't.
Trap. Thank your good worship.
Moll. Come, follow me to St. Thomas Apostle's:
I'll put a livery cloak upon your back
The first thing I do.
Trap. I follow, my dear mistress.

Exeunt omnes.

[III.ii]

Enter MISTRESS GALLIPOT *as from supper, her
husband following her.*

Gal. What, Pru! nay, sweet Prudence.
Mrs. G. What a pruing keep you! I think the baby
would have a teat, it kyes[1] so. Pray, be not so fond of
me, leave your city humors; I'm vexed at you, to see
how like a calf you come bleating after me.
Gal. Nay, honey Pru, how does your rising up before
all the table show, and flinging from my friends so uncivilly! fie, Pru, fie! come.
Mrs. G. Then up and ride, i'faith.   9
Gal. Up and ride? Nay, my pretty Pru, that's far
from my thought, duck. Why, mouse, thy mind is
nibbling at something. What is't? What lies upon thy
stomach?
Mrs. G. Such an ass as you: hoyda, you're best turn
midwife, or physician; you're a 'pothecary already, but
I'm none of your drugs.
Gal. Thou art a sweet drug, sweetest Pru, and the
more thou art pounded, the more precious.
Mrs. G. Must you be prying into a woman's secrets,
say ye?   20
Gal. Woman's secrets?
Mrs. G. What! I cannot have a qualm come upon
me, but your teeth waters till your nose hang over it.

---

[15] *umbles:* insides.
[16] *Temple:* district around two of the Inns of Court, the
Inner and Middle Temples.
III.ii.
[1] *kyes:* cries (babytalk).

Gal. It is my love, dear wife.

Mrs. G. Your love? Your love is all words; give me deeds. I cannot abide a man that's too fond over me, so cookish! Thou dost not know how to handle a woman in her kind.

Gal. No, Pru? Why, I hope I have handled—   29

Mrs. G. Handle a fool's head of your own,—fih—fih.

Gal. Ha, ha, 'tis such a wasp. It does me good now to have her s[t]ing me, little rogue.

Mrs. G. Now, fie, how you vex me. I cannot abide these apron husbands; such cotqueans![2] you overdo your things, they become you scurvily.

Gal. [*Aside*] Upon my life she breeds; heaven knows how I have strained myself to please her night and day. I wonder why we citizens should get children so fretful and untoward in the breeding, their fathers being for the most part as gentle as milch kine.—Shall I leave thee, my Pru?   41

Mrs. G. Fie, fie, fie!

Gal. Thou shalt not be vexed no more, pretty, kind rogue; take no cold, sweet Pru.

                        Exit MASTER GALLIPOT.

Mrs. G. As your wit has done. Now, Master Laxton, show your head; what news from you? Would any husband suspect that a woman crying, "Buy any scurvy-grass,"[3] should bring loveletters amongst her herbs to his wife? Pretty trick! Fine conveyance! Had jealousy a thousand eyes, a silly woman with scurvy-grass blinds them all.   51

Laxton, with bays[4]

Crown I thy wit for this, it deserves praise.

This makes me affect thee more, this proves thee wise.

'Lack, what poor shift is love forced to devise!—

To th' point.

                       She reads the letter.

"*O sweet creature*"—a sweet beginning!—"*pardon my long absence, for thou shalt shortly be possessed with my presence: though Demophon was false to Phyllis,[5] I will be to thee as Pan-da-rus was to Cres-sida;[6] though Aeneas* 60 *made an ass of Dido,[7] I will die to thee ere I do so. O sweetest creature, make much of me, for no man beneath the silver moon shall make more of a woman than I do of thee. Furnish me therefore with thirty pounds; you must do it of necessity for me; I languish till I see some comfort come*

---

[2] *cotqueans*: men who act the housewife.

[3] *scurvy-grass*: plant supposed effective against scurvy.

[4] *bays*: wreaths of honor for a poet.

[5] *Demophon . . . Phyllis*: Demophon, returning from the Trojan War, met Phyllis in Thrace and promised to return after settling affairs in Athens, but tired of waiting she hanged herself and was turned into an almond tree, which flowered when Demophon arrived and embraced it.

[6] *Pan-da-rus . . . Cres-sida*: Cressida's uncle Pandarus, in the popular medieval tale about the Trojan War, pandered for her, arranging her affair with Troilus. Mistress Gallipot has some difficulty in pronunciation.

[7] *Aeneas . . . Dido*: On his way to Italy from Troy, Aeneas had an affair with and abandoned the Queen of Carthage, who killed herself.   [8] *adamants*: lodestones.   [9] *beshrew*: curse.

[10] *Bedlam*: Bethlehem Hospital, London institute for the insane.   [11] *factor*: mercantile agent.

[12] *Where*: Whereas.   [13] *wanderer*: planet.

from thee. Protesting not to die in thy debt, but rather to live, so as hitherto I have and will,

                   Thy true Laxton ever."

Alas, poor gentleman! troth, I pity him.

How shall I raise this money? Thirty pound!   70

'Tis thirty sure, a 3 before an o;

I know his threes too well. My childbed linen,

Shall I pawn that for him? Then if my mark

Be known, I am undone; it may be thought

My husband's bankrupt. Which way shall I turn?

Laxton, what with my own fears and thy wants,

I'm like a needle 'twixt two adamants.[8]

         Enter MASTER GALLIPOT *hastily.*

Gal. Nay, nay, wife, the women are all up—Ha! how? Reading o' letters? I smell a goose, a couple of capons, and a gammon of bacon, from her mother out of the country. I hold my life—steal, steal—   81

Mrs. G. Oh, beshrew[9] your heart!

Gal.   What letter's that?

    I'll see't.

                     She tears the letter.

Mrs. G. Oh, would thou hadst no eyes to see the downfall

Of me and thyself! I am forever,

Forever I'm undone!

Gal.   What ails my Pru?

What paper's that thou tear'st?

Mrs. G.   Would I could tear

My very heart in pieces! For my soul

Lies on the rack of shame, that tortures me

Beyond a woman's suffering.

Gal.   What means this?

Mrs. G. Had you no other vengeance to throw down, But even in height of all my joys—

Gal.   Dear woman—   91

Mrs. G. When the full sea of pleasure and content

Seemed to flow over me?

Gal.   As thou desir'st

To keep me out of Bedlam,[10] tell what troubles thee.

Is not thy child at nurse fallen sick, or dead?

Mrs. G. Oh, no!

Gal.   Heavens bless me! are my barns and houses

Yonder at Hockley-hole consumed with fire?

I can build more, sweet Pru.

Mrs. G.   'Tis worse, 'tis worse.

Gal. My factor[11] broke? Or is the Jonas sunk?

Mrs. G. Would all we had were swallowed in the waves,   100

Rather than both should be the scorn of slaves!

Gal. I'm at my wit's end.

Mrs. G.   O my dear husband!

Where[12] once I thought myself a fixèd star,

Placed only in the heaven of thine arms,

I fear now I shall prove a wanderer.[13]

O Laxton, Laxton! Is it then my fate

To be by thee o'erthrown?

Gal.   Defend me, wisdom,

From falling into frenzy! On my knees,
Sweet Pru, speak: what's that Laxton, who so heavy
Lies on thy bosom?
   Mrs. G.   I shall sure run mad!   110
   Gal. I shall run mad for company then. Speak to me;
I'm Gallipot thy husband—Pru—why, Pru!
Art sick in conscience for some villainous deed
Thou wert about to act? Didst mean to rob me?
Tush, I forgive thee. Hast thou on my bed
Thrust my soft pillow under another's head?
I'll wink at all faults, Pru; 'las, that's no more,
Than what some neighbors near thee have done before!
Sweet honey Pru, what's that Laxton?
   Mrs. G.   Oh!   119
   Gal. Out with him!
   Mrs. G.   Oh, he's born to be my undoer!
This hand, which thou call'st thine, to him was given,
To him was I made sure [14] i' th' sight of heaven.
   Gal. I never heard this thunder.
   Mrs. G.   Yes, yes, before
I was to thee contracted, to him I swore.
Since last I saw him, twelve months three times told
The moon hath drawn through her light silver bow;
For o'er the seas he went, and it was said,
But rumor lies, that he in France was dead.
But he's alive, oh he's alive! he sent
That letter to me, which in rage I rent;   130
Swearing with oaths most damnably to have me,
Or tear me from this bosom. O heavens, save me!
   Gal. My heart will break; shamed and undone for
     ever.
   Mrs. G. So black a day, poor wretch, went o'er thee
     never.
   Gal. If thou shouldst wrestle with him at the law,
Thou'rt sure to fall. No odd slight? [15] No prevention?
I'll tell him th'art with child.
   Mrs. G.   Umh!
   Gal.   Or give out
One of my men was ta'en a-bed with thee.
   Mrs. G. Umh, umh!
   Gal.   Before I lose thee, my dear Pru,
I'll drive it to that push.
   Mrs. G.   Worse and worse still;   140
You embrace a mischief to prevent an ill.
   Gal. I'll buy thee of him, stop his mouth with gold;
Think'st thou 'twill do?
   Mrs. G.   Oh, me! heavens grant it would!
Yet now my senses are set more in tune,
He writ, as I remember, in his letter,
That he in riding up and down had spent,
Ere he could find me, thirty pound; send that;
Stand not on thirty with him.
   Gal.   Forty, Pru!
Say thou the word, 'tis done. We venture lives
For wealth, but must do more to keep our wives.   150
Thirty or forty, Pru?
   Mrs. G.   Thirty, good sweet;
Of an ill bargain let's save what we can.
I'll pay it him with my tears. He was a man,
When first I knew him, of a meek spirit,
All goodness is not yet dried up, I hope.

   Gal. He shall have thirty pound, let that stop all.
Love's sweets taste best when we have drunk down gall.

   Enter MASTER TILTYARD *and his* Wife, MASTER
     GOSHAWK, *and* MISTRESS OPENWORK.

God's-so, [16] our friends! come, come, smooth your
   cheek;
After a storm the face of heaven looks sleek.
   Tilt. Did I not tell you these turtles [17] were together?
   Mrs. T. How dost thou, sirrah? [18] Why, sister
     Gallipot—   161
   Mrs. O. Lord, how she's changed!
   Gos. Is your wife ill, sir?
   Gal. Yes, indeed, la, sir, very ill, very ill, never
worse.
   Mrs. T. How her head burns! feel how her pulses
work!
   Mrs. O. Sister, lie down a little; that always does me
good.
   Mrs. T. In good sadness, [19] I find best ease in that
too. Has she laid some hot thing to her stomach?   171
   Mrs. G. No, but I will lay something anon.
   Tilt. Come, come, fools, you trouble her.—Shall's
go, Master Goshawk?
   Gos. Yes, sweet Master Tiltyard.—Sirrah Rosamond,
I hold my life Gallipot hath vexed his wife.
   Mrs. O. She has a horrible high color indeed.
   Gos. We shall have your face painted with the same
red soon at night when your husband comes from his
rubbers [20] in a false alley; thou wilt not believe me that
his bowls run with a wrong bias.   181
   Mrs. O. It cannot sink into me that he feeds upon
stale mutton [21] abroad, having better and fresher at
home.
   Gos. What if I bring thee where thou shalt see him
stand at rack and manger? [22]
   Mrs. O. I'll saddle him in's kind, and spur him till he
kick again.
   Gos. Shall thou and I ride our journey then?
   Mrs. O. Here's my hand.   190
   Gos. No more.—Come, Master Tiltyard, shall we
leap into the stirrups with our women, and amble
home?
   Tilt. Yes, yes.—Come, wife.
   Mrs. T. In troth, sister, I hope you will do well for
all this.
   Mrs. G. I hope I shall. Farewell, good sister. Sweet
Master Goshawk.
   Gal. Welcome, brother, most kindly welcome, sir.
   Omnes. Thanks, sir, for our good cheer.   200
                Exeunt all but GALLIPOT *and his* Wife.
   Gal. It shall be so; because a crafty knave
Shall not outreach me, nor walk by my door
With my wife in arm, as 'twere his whore,
I'll give him a golden coxcomb, thirty pound.

---

[14] *made sure:* affianced.   [15] *slight:* artifice.
[16] *God's-so:* mild oath.   [17] *turtles:* doves.
[18] *sirrah:* used for women as well as for men.
[19] *sadness:* seriousness.   [20] *rubbers:* bowling games.
[21] *stale mutton:* whores.
[22] *at . . . manger:* in the midst of abundance.

Tush, Pru, what's thirty pound? Sweet duck, look
    cheerly.
  Mrs. G. Thou art worthy of my heart, thou buy'st it
    dearly.

          Enter LAXTON *muffled.*

  Lax. [*Aside*] Uds light, the tide's against me; a pox of
your 'pothecaryship! Oh, for some glister [23] to set him
going! 'Tis one of Hercules' labors to tread one of these
city hens, because their cocks are still crowing over
them. There's no turning tail here, I must on.   211
  Mrs. G. O husband, see he comes!
  Gal.   Let me deal with
    him.
  Lax. Bless you, sir.
  Gal. Be you blessed too, sir, if you come in peace.
  Lax. Have you any good pudding tobacco, [24] sir?
  Mrs. G. Oh, pick no quarrels, gentle sir. My husband
Is not a man of weapon, as you are;
He knows all, I have opened all before him,
Concerning you.
  Lax. [*Aside*] Zounds, has she shown my letters?
  Mrs. G. Suppose my case were yours, what would
    you do?   520
At such a pinch, such batteries, such assaults
Of father, mother, kindred, to dissolve
The knot you tied, and to be bound to him;
How could you shift this storm off?
  Lax.   If I know, hang me!
  Mrs. G. Besides a story of your death was read
Each minute to me.
  Lax. [*Aside*]   What a pox means this riddling?
  Gal. Be wise, sir; let not you and I be tossed
On lawyer's pens; they have sharp nibs, and draw
Men's very heart blood from them. What need you, sir,
To beat the drum of my wife's infamy,   230
And call your friends together, sir, to prove
Your precontract, when sh'as confessed it?
  Lax.   Umh, sir,
Has she confessed it?
  Gal.   Sh'as, 'faith, to me, sir,
Upon your letter sending.
  Mrs. G.   I have, I have.
  Lax. [*Aside*] If I let this iron cool, call me slave.
Do you hear, you Dame Prudence? Think'st thou, vile
    woman,
I'll take these blows and wink?

             [MRS. GALLIPOT *kneels.*]

  Mrs. G.   Upon my knees.
  Lax. Out, impudence.
  Gal.   Good sir—
  Lax.   You goatish slaves.
No wild fowl to cut up but mine?
  Gal.   Alas, sir,

You make her flesh to tremble; fright her not.   240
She shall do reason, and what's fit.
  Lax.   I'll have thee,
Wert thou more common than an hospital,
And more diseased.—
  Gal.   But one word, good sir.
  Lax.   So, sir.
  Gal. I married her, have lien with her, and got
Two children on her body; think but on that:
Have you so beggarly an appetite,
When I upon a dainty dish have fed
To dine upon my scraps, my leavings? Ha, sir?
Do I come near you now, sir?
  Lax.   By'r Lady, you touch me!
  Gal. Would not you scorn to wear my clothes, sir?
  Lax. Right, sir.   251
  Gal. Then, pray, sir, wear not her; for she's a
    garment
So fitting for my body, I am loath
Another should put it on; you will undo both.
Your letter, as she said, complained you had spent,
In quest of her, some thirty pound; I'll pay it;
Shall that, sir, stop this gap up 'twixt you two?
  Lax. Well, if I swallow this wrong, let her thank you;
The money being paid, sir, I am gone.
Farewell. O women, happy's he trusts none!   260
  Mrs. G. Dispatch him hence, sweet husband.
  Gal.   Yes,
    dear wife:
Pray, sir, come in: ere Master Laxton part,
Thou shalt in wine drink to him.
  Mrs. G.   With all my heart.—
How dost thou like my wit?
             Exit MASTER GALLIPOT *and his* Wife.
  Lax.   Rarely; that wile,
By which the serpent did the first woman beguile,
Did ever since all women's bosoms fill;
You're apple-eaters all, deceivers still.

                          Exit LAXTON.

[III.iii]

      Enter SIR ALEX. WENGRAVE, SIR DAVY
    DAPPER, SIR ADAM APPLETON *at one door,*
         and TRAPDOOR *at another door.*

  S. Alex. Out with your tale, Sir Davy, to Sir Adam;
A knave is in mine eye deep in my debt.
  S. Davy. Nay, if he be a knave, sir, hold him fast.

            [*Walk aloof with* SIR ADAM.]

  S. Alex. Speak softly; what egg is there hatching
    now?
  Trap. A duck's egg, sir, a duck that has eaten a frog;
I have cracked the shell, and some villainy or other will
peep out presently. The duck that sits is the bouncing
ramp, [1] that roaring girl my mistress; the drake that must
tread is your son Sebastian.
  S. Alex. Be quick.   10
  Trap. As the tongue of an oyster-wench.
  S. Alex. And see thy news be true.
  Trap. As a barber's every Saturday night. Mad
Moll—

S. Alex. Ah—

Trap. Must be let in, without knocking, at your back gate.

S. Alex. So.

Trap. Your chamber will be made bawdy.

S. Alex. Good.   20

Trap. She comes in a shirt of mail.

S. Alex. How? Shirt of mail?

Trap. Yes, sir, or a male shirt; that's to say, in man's apparel.

S. Alex. To my son?

Trap. Close to your son; your son and her moon will be in conjunction, if all almanacs lie not; her black safe-guard[2] is turned into a deep slop, the holes of her upper body to buttonholes, her waistcoat to a doublet, her placket[3] to the ancient seat of a codpiece, and you shall take 'em both with standing[4] collars.   31

S. Alex. Art sure of this?

Trap. As every throng is sure of a pickpocket; as sure as a whore is of the clients all Michaelmas term,[5] and of the pox after the term.[6]

S. Alex. The time of their tilting?

Trap. Three.

S. Alex. The day?

Trap. This.

S. Alex. Away; ply it, watch her.   40

Trap. As the devil doth for the death of a bawd; I'll watch her, do you catch her.

S. Alex. She's fast; here weave thou the nets. Hark.

Trap. They are made.

S. Alex. I told them thou didst owe me money; hold it up; maintain't.

Trap. Stiffly, as a Puritan does contention.—Pox, I owe thee not the value of a halfpenny halter.

                 As in quarrel.

S. Alex. Thou shalt be hanged in it ere thou 'scape so:

Varlet, I'll make thee look through a grate!   50

Trap. I'll do't presently, through a tavern grate. Drawer! pish.

                 Exit TRAPDOOR.

S. Adam. Has the knave vexed you, sir?

S. Alex.   Asked him my money,

He swears my son received it. Oh, that boy

Will ne'er leave heaping sorrows on my heart,

Till he has broke it quite.

S. Adam.   Is he still wild?

S. Alex. As is a Russian bear.

S. Adam.   But he has left

His old haunt with that baggage?

S. Alex.   Worse still and worse;

He lays on me his shame, I on him my curse.

S. Davy. My son, Jack Dapper, then shall run with him   60

All in one pasture.

S. Adam.   Proves your son bad, too, sir?

S. Davy. As villainy can make him; your Sebastian

Dotes but on one drab,[7] mine on a thousand;

A noise[8] of fiddlers, tobacco, wine, and a whore,

A mercer that will let him take up more,[9]

Dice, and a water-spaniel with a duck,—oh,

Bring him abed with these: when his purse jingles,

Roaring boys follow at's tail, fencers and ningles,[10]

Beasts Adam ne'er gave name to; these horse-leeches suck   69

My son; he being drawn dry, they all live on smoke.

S. Alex. Tobacco?

S. Davy.   Right: but I have in my brain

A windmill going that shall grind to dust

The follies of my son, and make him wise,

Or a stark fool. Pray lend me your advice.

S. Alex. } That shall you, good sir Davy.
S. Adam. }

S. Davy.   Here's the springe[11]

I ha' set to catch this woodcock in: an action

In a false name, unknown to him, is entered

I' th' Counter[12] to arrest Jack Dapper.

S. Alex. }
S. Adam. }   Ha, ha, he!

S. Davy. Think you the Counter cannot break him?

S. Adam.   Break him?

Yes, and break's heart too, if he lie there long.   80

S. Davy. I'll make him sing a counter-tenor sure.

S. Adam. No way to tame him like it; there he shall learn

What money is indeed, and how to spend it.

S. Davy. He's bridled there.

S. Alex.   Ay, yet knows not how to mend it.

Bedlam cures not more madmen in a year

Than one of the Counters does; men pay more dear

There for their wit than any where: a Counter,

Why, 'tis an university, who not sees?

As scholars there, so here men take degrees,

And follow the same studies all alike.   90

Scholars learn first logic and rhetoric;

So does a prisoner; with fine honeyed speech

At's first coming in he doth persuade, beseech

He may be lodged with one that is not itchy,

To lie in a clean chamber, in streets not lousy;

But when he has no money, then does he try,

By subtle logic and quaint sophistry,

To make the keepers trust him.

S. Adam.   Say they do.

S. Alex. Then he's a graduate.

S. Davy.   Say they trust him not.

S. Alex. Then is he held a freshman and a sot,   100

And never shall commence; but being still barred,

---

[2] *safeguard:* petticoat worn to protect skirt while riding.

[3] *placket:* opening in petticoat.   [4] *standing:* stiff.

[5] *Michaelmas term:* one of the four annual court sessions, beginning Sept. 29.

[6] *pox . . . term:* plague was generally epidemic in winter.

[7] *drab:* whore.   [8] *noise:* band.

[9] *mercer . . . more:* tradesman who lets him buy more on credit.   [10] *ningles:* homosexual boy-favorites.

[11] *springe:* trap.

[12] *Counter:* court in London and debtor's prison attached to it.

Be expulsed from the Master's side to th' Two-penny
    ward,
Or else i' th' Hole be [13] placed.
S. Adam.   When then, I pray,
Proceeds a prisoner?
S. Alex.   When, money being the theme,
He can dispute with his hard creditors' hearts,
And get out clear, he's then a master of arts.
Sir Davy, send your son to Wood Street college,
A gentleman can nowhere get more knowledge.
S. Davy. There gallants study hard.
S. Alex.   True, to get
    money.
S. Davy. Lies [14] by th' heels, i'faith: thanks, thanks;
    I ha' sent   110
For a couple of bears shall paw him.

     Enter SERGEANT CURTLEAX *and* YEOMAN
               HANGER.

S. Adam.   Who comes yonder?
S. Davy. They look like puttocks; [15] these should be
    they.
S. Alex. I know 'em,
They are officers; sir, we'll leave you.
S. Davy.   My good knights,
Leave me; you see I'm haunted now with spirits.
S. Alex. ⎱
S. Adam. ⎰ Fare you well, sir.

        Exeunt ALEXANDER *and* ADAM.
Cur. This old muzzle-chops should be he by the
fellow's description.—Save you, sir.
S. Davy. Come hither, you mad varlets; did not my
man tell you I watched here for you?   120
Cur. One in a blue coat, [16] sir, told us that in this
place an old gentleman would watch for us; a thing con-
trary to our oath, for we are to watch for every wicked
member in a city.
S. Davy. You'll watch then for ten thousand; what's
thy name, honesty?
Cur. Sergeant Curtleax I, sir.
S. Davy. An excellent name for a sergeant,
    Curtleax: [17]
Sergeants indeed are weapons of the law;
When prodigal ruffians far in debt are grown,   130
Should not you cut them, citizens were o'erthrown.
Thou dwell'st hereby in Holborn, Curtleax?
Cur. That's my circuit, sir; I conjure [18] most in that
circle.
S. Davy. And what young toward whelp is this?

---

[13] *be:* Q "beg."   [14] *Lies:* He lies, shall lie.
[15] *puttocks:* kites, birds of prey.
[16] *blue coat:* servant's livery.
[17] *Curtleax:* Heavy slashing sword, cutlass.
[18] *conjure:* hold, sway.
[19] *Bartholomew Fair:* held every August in West Smithfield.
[20] *counter:* opposite direction to that taken by game in
hunting(?).   [21] *mace:* with pun on the sergeant's weapon.
[22] *caudle:* warm drink of sweetened gruel with wine or ale,
given to the sick.   [23] *ambuscado:* ambush.
[24] *nook:* hide.

Han. Of the same litter; his yeoman, sir; my name's
Hanger.
S. Davy. Yeoman Hanger:
One pair of shears sure cut out both your coats;   139
You have two names most dangerous to men's throats;
You two are villainous loads on gentlemen's backs;
Dear ware this Hanger and this Curtleax!
Cur. We are as other men are, sir; I cannot see but
he who makes a show of honesty and religion, if his
claws can fasten to his liking, he draws blood. All that
live in the world are but great fish and little fish, and
feed upon one another; some eat up whole men, a
sergeant cares but for the shoulder of a man. They call
us knaves and curs, but many times he that sets us on
worries more lambs one year than we do in seven.   150
S. Davy. Spoke like a noble Cerberus! is the action
entered?
Han. His name is entered in the book of unbelievers.
S. Davy. What book's that?
Cur. The book where all prisoners' names stand; and
not one amongst forty, when he comes in, believes to
come out in haste.
S. Davy. Be as dogged to him as your office allows
you to be.
Both. O sir!   160
S. Davy. You know the unthrift, Jack Dapper?
Cur. Ay, ay, sir, that gull, as well as I know my yeo-
man.
S. Davy. And you know his father too, Sir Davy
Dapper?
Cur. As damned a usurer as ever was among Jews; if
he were sure his father's skin would yield him any
money, he would, when he dies, flay it off, and sell it to
cover drums for children at Bartholomew Fair. [19]   169
S. Davy. [*Aside*] What toads are these to spit poison
on a man to his face!—Do you see, my honest rascals?
Yonder Greyhound is the dog he hunts with; out of
that tavern Jack Dapper will sally: sa, sa; give the
counter; [20] on, set upon him!
Both. We'll charge him upo' th' back, sir.
S. Davy. Take no bail; but mace [21] enough into his
caudle [22]; double your files, traverse your ground.
Both. Brave, sir.
S. Davy. Cry arm, arm, arm!
Both. Thus, sir.   180
S. Davy. There, boy, there, boy! away; look to your
prey, my true English wolves; and so I vanish.

                   Exit SIR DAVY.
Cur. Some warden of the sergeants begat this old
fellow, upon my life: stand close.
Han. Shall the ambuscado [23] lie in one place?
Cur. No; nook [24] thou yonder.

                     [*They retire.*]

     Enter MOLL *and* TRAPDOOR.

Moll. Ralph.
Trap. What says my brave captain male and female?
Moll. This Holborn is such a wrangling street!   189
Trap. That's because lawyers walks to and fro in't.
Moll. Here's such jostling, as if every one we met
were drunk and reeled.

Trap. Stand, mistress. Do you not smell carrion?

Moll. Carrion? No; yet I spy ravens.

Trap. Some poor wind-shaken gallant will anon fall into sore labor, and these men-midwives must bring him to bed i' the Counter: there all those that are great with child with debts lie in.

Moll. Stand up.

Trap. Like your new maypole.   200

Han. Whist, whew!

Cur. Hump, no.

Moll. Peeping? It shall go hard, huntsmen, but I'll spoil your game. They look for all the world like two infected malt-men coming muffled up in their cloaks in a frosty morning to London.

Trap. A course, captain; a bear comes to the stake.

Enter JACK DAPPER and GULL.

Moll. It should be so, for the dogs struggle to be let loose.

Han. Whew!   210

Cur. Hemp.

Moll. Hark, Trapdoor, follow your leader.

J. Dap. Gull.

Gull. Master?

J. Dap. Didst ever see such an ass as I am, boy?

Gull. No, by my troth, sir; to lose all your money, yet have false dice of your own; why, 'tis as I saw a great fellow used t'other day: he had a fair sword and buckler, and yet a butcher dry beat[25] him with a cudgel.[26]   220

Both.[26] Honest servant, fly! Fly, Master Dapper! you'll be arrested else.

J. Dap. Run, Gull, and draw.

Gull. Run, master; Gull follows you.

> *Ex[eunt]* DAPPER *and* GULL.

> [MOLL *holds* CURTLEAX.]

Cur. I know you well enough; you're but a whore to hang upon any man!

Moll. Whores, then, are like sergeants; so now hang you.—Draw, rogue, but strike not; for a broken pate they'll keep their beds, and recover twenty marks damages.   230

Cur. You shall pay for this rescue.—Run down Shoe Lane and meet him.

Trap. Shu! is this a rescue, gentlemen, or no?

Moll. Rescue? a pox on 'em! Trapdoor, let's away;

> *Exeunt* CURTLEAX *and* HANGER.

I'm glad I've done perfect one good work today.
If any gentleman be in scrivener's bands,
Send but for Moll, she'll bail him by these hands.

> *Exeunt.*

ACT FOUR

SCENE ONE

Enter SIR ALEX. WENGRAVE.

S. Alex. Unhappy in the follies of a son,
Led against judgment, sense, obedience,
And all the powers of nobleness and wit;

Enter TRAPDOOR.

O wretched father!—Now, Trapdoor, will she come?

Trap. In man's apparel, sir; I'm in her heart now,
And share in all her secrets.

S. Alex.   Peace, peace, peace!
Here, take my German watch,[1] hang't up in sight,
That I may see her hang in English for't.

Trap. I warrant you for that now, next sessions rids her, sir. This watch will bring her in better than a hundred constables.   11

> [*Hangs up the watch.*]

S. Alex. Good Trapdoor, sayst thou so? Thou
          cheer'st my heart
After a storm of sorrow. My gold chain too;
Here, take a hundred marks in yellow links.

Trap. That will do well to bring the watch to light,
          sir;
And worth a thousand of your headborough's[2] lanterns.

S. Alex. Place that o' the court-cupboard;[3] let it lie
Full in the view of her thief-whorish eye.

Trap. She cannot miss it, sir; I see't so plain,
That I could steal't myself.

> [*Places the chain.*]

S. Alex.   Perhaps thou shalt too, 20
That or something as weighty; what she leaves
Thou shalt come closely in and filch away,
And all the weight upon her back I'll lay.

Trap. You cannot assure that, sir.

S. Alex.   No? What lets[4] it?

Trap. Being a stout girl, perhaps she'll desire
          pressing;
Then all the weight must lie upon her belly.

S. Alex. Belly or back I care not, so I've one.

Trap. You're of my mind for that, sir.

S. Alex. Hang up my ruff-band with the diamond at
          it;
It may be she'll like that best.   30

Trap. [*Aside*] It's well for her, that she must have her choice; he thinks nothing too good for her.—If you hold on this mind a little longer, it shall be the first work I do to turn thief myself; ['t]would do a man good to be hanged when he is so well provided for.

> [*Hangs up the ruff-band.*]

S. Alex. So, well said; all hangs well; would she
          hung so too!
The sight would please me more than all their
          glisterings.
Oh, that my mysteries[5] to such straits should run,
That I must rob myself to bless my son!

> *Exeunt.*

---

[25] *dry beat:* beat soundly.
[26] *Both:* i.e., Trapdoor and Moll.

IV.i.

[1] *German watch:* Early clocks and watches came from Germany.   [2] *headborough's:* parish officer's.
[3] *court-cupboard:* movable sideboard for displaying plate.
[4] *lets:* prevents.   [5] *mysteries:* arts.

Enter SEBASTIAN *with* MARY FITZALLARD *like
a Page, and* MOLL [*in man's clothes*].

Seb. Thou hast done me a kind office, without
    touch   40
Either of sin or shame; our loves are honest.
    Moll. I'd scorn to make such shift to bring you
together else.
    Seb. Now have I time and opportunity
Without all fear to bid thee welcome, love.

                                                    Kiss.

    Mary. Never with more desire and harder venture.
    Moll. How strange this shows, one man to kiss
    another!
    Seb. I'd kiss such men to choose, Moll;
Methinks a woman's lip tastes well in a doublet.
    Moll. Many an old madam has the better fortune
    then,   50
Whose breaths grew stale before the fashion came;
If that will help 'em, as you think 'twill do,
They'll learn in time to pluck on the hose[6] too.
    Seb. The older they wax, Moll, troth I speak
    seriously,
As some have a conceit their drink tastes better
In an outlandish cup than in our own,
So methinks every kiss she gives me now
In this strange form is worth a pair o'[7] two,
Here we are safe, and furthest from the eye
Of all suspicion; this is my father's chamber,   60
Upon which floor he never steps till night.
Here he mistrusts me not, nor I his coming;
At mine own chamber he still pries unto me;
My freedom is not there at mine own finding,
Still checked and curbed; here he shall miss his
    purpose.
    Moll. And what's your business, now you have your
    mind, sir?
At your great suit I promised you to come.
I pitied her for name's sake, that a Moll
Should be so crossed in love, when there's so many
That owes nine lays[8] apiece, and not so little.   70
My tailor fitted her; how like you his work?
    Seb. So well, no art can mend it for this purpose;
But to thy wit and help we're chief in debt,
And must live still beholding.
    Moll.   Any honest pity
I'm willing to bestow upon poor ring-doves.[9]
    Seb. I'll offer no worse play.
    Moll.   Nay, and you should, sir,
I should draw first, and prove the quicker man.
    Seb. Hold, there shall need no weapon at this
    meeting;
But 'cause thou shalt not loose thy fury idle,

Here take this viol, run upon the guts,   80
And end thy quarrel singing.

            [*Takes down, and gives her, a viol.*]

    Moll.   Like a swan above bridge;
For look you here's the bridge, and here am I.
    Seb. Hold on, sweet Moll!
    Mary.   I've heard her much
    commended, sir,
For one that was ne'er taught.
    Moll. I'm much beholding to 'em. Well, since you'll
needs put us together, sir, I'll play my part as well as I
can; it shall ne'er be said I came into a gentleman's
chamber, and let his intrument hang by the walls.
    Seb. Why, well said, Moll, i' faith; it had been a
shame for that gentleman then that would have let it
hung still, and ne'er offered thee it.   91
    Moll. There it should have been still then for Moll;
for though the world judge impudently of me, I never
came into that chamber yet where I took down the instrument myself.
    Seb. Pish, let 'em prate abroad; thou'rt here where
thou art known and loved; there be a thousand close[10]
dames that will call the viol an unmannerly instrument
for a woman, and therefore talk broadly of thee, when
you shall have them sit wider to a worse quality.   100
    Moll. Push, I ever fall asleep and think not of 'em,
sir; and thus I dream.
    Seb. Prithee, let's hear thy dream, Moll.

                    THE SONG

Moll. *I dream there is a mistress,*
         And she lays out the money;
         She goes unto her sisters,
         She never comes at any.

        Enter SIR ALEXANDER *behind.*

         She says she went to th' Burse[11] *for patterns;*
         You shall find her at Saint Kathern's,
         And comes home with never a penny.   110

    Seb. That's a free mistress, faith!
    S. Alex. [*Aside*] Ay, ay, ay, like her that sings it; one
of thine own choosing.
    Moll. But shall I dream again?

[*Sings*] *Here comes a wench will brave ye;*
           Her courage was so great,
           She lays with one o' the navy,
           Her husband lying i' the Fleet.[12]
           Yet oft with him she caviled;
           I wonder what she ails: 120
           Her husband's ship lay graveled,[13]
           When hers could hoise up sails:
           Yet she began, like all my foes,
           To call whore first; for so do those—
           A pox of all false tails!

    Seb. Marry, amen, say I!
    S. Alex. [*Aside*]   So say I too.
    Moll. Hang up the viol now, sir. All this while

---

    [6] *hose:* breeches.   [7] *or:* Q "of."
    [8] *lays:* wagers.   [9] *ring-doves:* wood pigeons.
    [10] *close:* rigorous.
    [11] *Burse:* the New Exchange in the Strand, where shops
sold women's clothes.   [12] *the Fleet:* the debtor's prison.
    [13] *graveled:* beached.

I was in a dream; one shall lie rudely then,
But being awake, I keep my legs together.   129
A watch? What's o' clock here?
   S. Alex. [*Aside*]   Now, now she's trapped.
   Moll. Between one and two; nay, then I care not. A
watch and a musician are cousin-germans [14] in one
thing, they must both keep time well, or there's no
goodness in 'em; the one else deserves to be dashed
against a wall, and t'other to have his brains knocked
out with a fiddle-case. What! a loose chain and a dangling diamond? Here were a brave booty for an evening
thief now: There's many a younger brother would be
glad to look twice in at a window for't and wriggle in and
out, like an eel in a sandbag. Oh, if men's secret   140
youthful faults should judge 'em, 'twould be the general'st execution that e'er was seen in England. There
would be but few left to sing the ballads, there would
be so much work; most of our brokers would be chosen
for hangmen ; a good day for them: They might renew
their wardrobes of free cost then.
   Seb. This is the roaring wench must do us good.
   Mary. No poison, sir, but serves us for some use;
Which is confirmed in her.
   Seb. Peace, peace—   150
'Foot, I did hear him sure, where'er he be.
   Moll. Who did you hear?
   Seb. My father;
'Twas like a sight [15] of his; I must be wary.
   S. Alex. [*Aside*] No? Wilt not be? Am I alone so
   wretched
That nothing takes? I'll put him to his plunge [16] for't.
   Seb. Life! here he comes.—Sir, I beseech you take it;
Your way of teaching does so much content me,
I'll make it four pound; here's forty shillings, sir—
I think I name it right—help me, good Moll—   160
Forty in hand.

                         [*Offering money.*]

   Moll.   Sir, you shall pardon me;
I've more of the meanest scholar I can teach;
This pays me more than you have offered yet.
   Seb. At the next quarter,
When I receive the means my father 'lows me,
You shall have t'other forty.
   S. Alex. [*Aside*]   This were well now,
Were't to a man whose sorrows had blind eyes;
But mine behold his follies and untruths
With two clear glasses. [*Aside*] How now?

                         [*Comes forward.*]

   Seb.   Sir?
   S. Alex.   What's
   he there?
   Seb. You're come in good time, sir; I've a suit to you;
I'd crave your present kindness.
   S. Alex.   What's he there?   171
   Seb. A gentleman, a musician, sir; one of excellent
   fingering.
   S. Alex. Ay, I think so; [*Aside*] I wonder how they
   'scaped her.
   Seb. Has the most delicate stroke, sir.

   S. Alex. A stroke indeed! [*Aside*] I feel it at my heart.
   Seb. Puts down all your famous musicians.
   S. Alex. Ay, [*Aside*] a whore may put down a
   hundred of 'em.
   Seb. Forty shillings is the agreement, sir, between us:
Now, sir, my present means mounts but to half on't.
   S. Alex. And he stands upon the whole?   180
   Seb. Ay, indeed, does he, sir.
   S. Alex. And will do still; he'll ne'er be in other tale.
   Seb. Therefore I'd stop his mouth, sir, and I could.
   S. Alex. Hum, true; there is no other way indeed;
[*Aside*] His folly hardens, shame must needs succeed.—
Now, sir, I understand you profess music.
   Moll. I'm a poor servant to that liberal science, sir.
   S. Alex. Where is't you teach?
   Moll.   Right against
   Clifford's Inn.
   S. Alex. Hum, that's a fit place for't; you've many
   scholars?
   Moll. And some of worth, whom I may call my
   masters.   190
   S. Alex. [*Aside*] Ay, true, a company of whore-
   masters.—
You teach to sing too?
   Moll.   Marry, do I, sir.
   S. Alex. I think you'll find an apt scholar of my son,
Especially for prick-song. [17]
   Moll.   I've much hope of him.
   S. Alex. [*Aside*] I'm sorry for't, I have the less for
   that.
You can play any lesson?
   Moll.   At first sight, sir.
   S. Alex. There's a thing call'd "The Witch"; can
   you play that?
   Moll. I would be sorry anyone should mend me in't.
   S. Alex. [*Aside*] Ay, I believe thee; thou'st so
   bewitched my son,
No care will mend the work that thou hast done.   200
I have bethought myself, since my art fails,
I'll make her policy [18] the art to trap her.
Here are four angels [19] marked with holes in them
Fit for his cracked companions; gold he'll give her;
These will I make induction to her ruin,
And rid shame from my house, grief from my heart.—
Here, son, in what you take content and pleasure,
Want shall not curb you; pay the gentleman
His latter half in gold.

                         [*Gives money.*]

   Seb.   I thank you, sir.
   S. Alex. [*Aside*] Oh, may the operation on't end
   three;   210
In her, life, shame in him, and grief in me!
                      Exit ALEXANDER.
   Seb. Faith, thou shalt have 'em; 'tis my father's gift:
Never was man beguiled with better shift.

---

[14] *cousin-germans:* first cousins.   [15] *sight:* sigh.
[16] *plunge:* difficulty.
[17] *prick-song:* written vocal music, with bawdy pun.
[18] *policy:* scheming.   [19] *angels:* coins.

Moll. He that can take me for a male musician, I can't choose but make him my instrument, and play upon him.

Exeunt omnes.

[IV.ii]

Enter Mistress Gallipot *and* Mistress Openwork.

Mrs. G. Is, then, that bird of yours, Master Goshawk, so wild?

Mrs. O. A Goshawk? A puttock, all for prey: he angles for fish, but he loves flesh better.

Mrs. G. Is't possible his smooth face should have wrinkles in't, and we not see them?

Mrs. O. Possible? Why, have not many handsome legs in silk stockings villainous splay feet, for all their great roses?[1]

Mrs. G. Troth, sirrah, thou sayst true.　　　10

Mrs. O. Didst never see an archer, as thou'st walked by Bunhill, look asquint when he drew his bow?

Mrs. G. Yes, when his arrows have fline[2] toward Islington, his eyes have shot clean contrary towards Pimlico.[3]

Mrs. O. For all the world so does Master Goshawk double[4] with me.

Mrs. G. Oh, fie upon him! if he double once, he's not for me.　　　19

Mrs. O. Because Goshawk goes in a shag ruff-band, with a face striking up in't which shows like an agate set in a cramp ring,[5] he thinks I'm in love with him.

Mrs. G. 'Las, I think he takes his mark amiss in thee!

Mrs. O. He has, by often beating into me, made me believe that my husband kept a whore.

Mrs. G. Very good.

Mrs. O. Swore to me that my husband this very morning went in a boat, with a tilt[6] over it, to the Three Pigeons at Brainford, and his punk[7] with him under his tilt.　　　30

Mrs. G. That were wholesome.

Mrs. O. I believed it; fell aswearing at him, cursing of harlots; made me ready to hoise up sail and be there as soon as he.

Mrs. G. So, so.

Mrs. O. And for that voyage Goshawk comes hither incontinently:[8] but, sirrah, this water-spaniel dives after no duck but me; his hope is having me at Brainford to make me cry quack.

Mrs. G. Art sure of it?　　　40

Mrs. O. Sure of it? My poor innocent Openwork came in as I was poking[9] my ruff: presently hit I him i' the teeth with the Three Pigeons; he forswore all, I up and opened all; and now stands he in a shop hard by, like a musket on a rest,[10] to hit Goshawk i' the eye, when he comes to fetch me to the boat.

Mrs. G. Such another lame gelding offered to carry me through thick and thin,—Laxton, sirrah,—but I am rid of him now.　　　49

Mrs. O. Happy is the woman can be rid of 'em all! 'las, what are your whisking gallants to our husbands, weigh 'em rightly, man for man?

Mrs. G. Troth, mere shallow things.

Mrs. O. Idle, simple things, running heads; and yet let 'em run over us never so fast, we shopkeepers, when all's done, are sure to have 'em in our pursenets[11] at length; and when they are in, Lord, what simple animals they are! then they hang the head—

Mrs. G. Then they droop—

Mrs. O. Then they write letters—　　　60

Mrs. G. Then they cog[12]—

Mrs. O. Then deal they underhand with us, and we must ingle[13] with our husbands abed; and we must swear they are our cousins, and able to do us a pleasure at court.

Mrs. G. And yet, when we have done our best, all's but put into a riven[14] dish; we are but frumped[15] at and libeled upon.

Mrs. O. Oh, if it were the good Lord's will there were a law made, no citizen should trust any of 'em all.　70

Enter Goshawk.

Mrs. G. Hush, sirrah! Goshawk flutters.

Gos. How now? Are you ready?

Mrs. O. Nay, are you ready? A little thing, you see, makes us ready.

Gos. Us? Why, must she make one i' the voyage?

Mrs. O. Oh, by any means! do I know how my husband will handle me?

Gos. [*Aside*] 'Foot, how shall I find water to keep these two mills going?—Well, since you'll needs be clapped under hatches, if I sail not with you both　80 till all split,[16] hang me up at the mainyard and duck me. [*Aside*] It's but liquoring them both soundly, and then you shall see their cork heels[17] fly up high, like two swans when their tails are above water, and their long necks under water diving to catch gudgeons.[18]—Come, come, oars stand ready; the tide's with us; on with those false faces; blow winds, and thou shalt take thy husband casting out his net to catch fresh salmon at Brainford.　　　89

Mrs. G. [*Aside*] I believe you'll eat of a cod's head[19] of your own dressing before you reach half way thither.

[*She and* Mistress Openwork *mask themselves.*]

Gos. So, so, follow close; pin as you go.

Enter Laxton *muffled. They speak aloof.*

Lax. Do you hear?

Mrs. G. Yes, I thank my ears.

IV.ii.

[1] *roses*: decorative shoe-ribbons.　　　[2] *fline*: flown.
[3] *Pimlico*: frequented for entertainment.
[4] *double*: act evasively.
[5] *cramp ring*: ring consecrated on Good Friday with power of preventing cramp.　　　[6] *tilt*: awning over a boat.
[7] *punk*: mistress.　　　[8] *incontinently*: immediately.
[9] *poking*: making folds or crimps with a poking-stick.
[10] *rest*: support.
[11] *pursenets*: net bags closed with a drawstring.
[12] *cog*: lie.　　　[13] *ingle*: coax.　　　[14] *riven*: broken.
[15] *frumped*: mocked.　　　[16] *split*: go to pieces.
[17] *cork heels*: fashionable, and worn by whores.
[18] *gudgeons*: bait-fish.　　　[19] *cod's head*: blockhead.

Lax. I must have a bout with your 'pothecaryship.

Mrs. G. At what weapon?

Lax. I must speak with you.

Mrs. G. No.

Lax. No? you shall.

Mrs. G. Shall? away, soused[20] sturgeon! half fish, half flesh.　　　　　　　　　　　　　　　　101

Lax. Faith, gib,[21] are you spitting? I'll cut your tail, puss-cat, for this.

Mrs. G. 'Las, poor Laxton, I think thy tail's cut already; your worst.

Lax. If I do not—

Exit LAXTON.

Enter MASTER OPENWORK.

Gos. Come, ha' you done?
'S foot, Rosamund, your husband!

Open. How now? Sweet master Goshawk! none
　　more welcome;
I've wanted your embracements: when friends meet,
The music of the spheres sounds not more sweet　111
Than does their conference. Who's this? Rosamond?
Wife? How now, sister?

Gos.　　　　　　Silence, if you love me!

Open. Why masked?

Mrs. O.　　　　　Does a mask grieve you, sir?

Open.　　　　　　　　　　　　　　　It
does.

Mrs. O. Then you're best get you a mumming.[22]

Gos.　　　　　　　　　　　　　　　　'S-
foot, you'll spoil all!

Mrs. G. May not we cover our bare faces with masks,
As well as you cover your bald heads with hats?

Open. No masks; why they're thieves to beauty, that
　　rob eyes
Of admiration in which true love lies.
Why are masks worn? Why good? Or why desired?
Unless by their gay covers wits are fired　　121
To read the vilest looks: many bad faces,
Because rich gems are treasured up in cases,
Pass by their privilege current; but as caves
Damn misers' gold, so masks are beauties' graves.
Men ne'er meet women with such muffled eyes,
But they curse her that first did masks devise,
And swear it was some beldam.[23] Come, off with't.

Mrs. O.　　　　　　　　　　　　　　I will
not.

Open. Good faces masked are jewels kept by spirits;[24]
Hide none but bad ones, for they poison men's sights;
Show, then, as shopkeepers do their broidered stuff,
By owl-light;[25] fine wares cannot be open enough.　132
Prithee, sweet Rose, come, strike this sail.

Mrs. O.　　　　　　　　　　　　　Sail?

Open. Ha! yes, wife, strike sail, for storms are in
　　thine eyes.

Mrs. O. They're here, sir, in my brows, if any rise.

Open. Ha, brows?—What says she, friend? pray, tell
　　me why
Your two flags[26] were advanced; the comedy,
Come, what's the comedy?

Mrs. G.　　　　　　Westward Ho.[27]

Open.　　　　　　　　　　　　　　How?

Mrs. O. 'Tis *Westward Ho*, she says.

Gos.　　　　　　　　　　Are you both
mad?　　　　　　　　　　　　　　　　139

Mrs. O. Is't market-day at Brainford, and your ware
Not sent up yet?

Open.　　　　What market-day? What ware?

Mrs. O. A pie with three pigeons in't: 'tis drawn, and
stays
Your cutting up.

Gos.　　　　As you regard my credit—

Open. Art mad?

Mrs. O.　　　　Yes, lecherous goat, baboon!

Open.　　　　　　　　　　　　　Baboon?
Then toss me in a blanket.

Mrs. O.　　　　　　Do I it well?

Mrs. G. Rarely.

Gos. Belike, sir, she's not well; best leave her.

Open.　　　　　　　　　　　　　　No;
I'll stand the storm now, how fierce soe'er it blow.

Mrs. O. Did I for this lose all my friends, refuse
Rich hopes and golden fortunes, to be made　　150
A stale[28] to a common whore?

Open.　　　　　This does amaze me.

Mrs. O. O God, O God! feed at reversion[29] now?
A strumpet's leaving?

Open. Rosamond!

Gos. [*Aside*] I sweat; would I lay in Cold Harbor![30]

Mrs. O. Thou'st struck ten thousand daggers through
　　my heart!

Open. Not I, by heaven, sweet wife!

Mrs. O. Go, devil, go; that which thou swear'st by
　　damns thee!

Gos. 'S heart, will you undo me?

Mrs. O. Why stay you here? The star by which you
　　sail　　　　　　　　　　　　　　　160
Shines yonder above Chelsea; you lose your shore;
If this moon light you, seek out your light whore.

Open. Ha!

Mrs. G.　　Push, your western pug![31]

Gos.　　　　　　　　　　Zounds, now hell
roars!

Mrs. O. With whom you tilted in a pair of oars
This very morning.

Open. Oars?

Mrs. O.　　　　At Brainford, sir.

Open. Rack not my patience.—Master Goshawk,
Some slave has buzzed this into her, has he not?
I run a tilt in Brainford with a woman?
'Tis a lie!

---

[20] *soused:* pickled.　　[21] *gib:* cat, shrewish woman.
[22] *mumming;* masquing.　　[23] *beldam:* witch.
[24] *spirits:* pronounced "sprites."　[25] *owl-light:* dim light.
[26] *flags:* on top of theaters during performance.
[27] *Westward Ho:* 1604 comedy by Dekker and Webster; the title is the cry of boatmen crossing from London toward Brentford.　　　　　[28] *stale:* cover, stalking-horse.
[29] *reversion:* leftovers.
[30] *Cold Harbor:* the grave; literally, old London building, razed in late sixteenth century, used as sanctuary.
[31] *western pug:* man who navigated barges down the Thames to London.

What old bawd tells thee this? 'S death, 'tis a lie!   170
Mrs. O.   'Tis one to thy face shall justify
All that I speak.
 Open.   Ud'soul, do but name that rascal!
Mrs. O. No, sir, I will not.
 Gos. [Aside]   Keep thee there, girl, then!
Open. Sister, know you this varlet?
 Mrs. G.   Yes.
 Open.   Swear true;
Is there a rogue so low damned? A second Judas?—
A common hangman, cutting a man's throat,
Does it to his face,—bite me behind my back?
A cur dog? Swear if you know this hellhound.
 Mrs. G. In truth, I do.
 Open.   His name?
 Mrs. G.   Not for the world;
To have you to stab him.
 Gos. [Aside]   O brave girls, worth gold!   180
Open. A word, honest Master Goshawk.

Draw out his sword.

 Gos.   What do you
 mean, sir?
Open. Keep off, and if the devil can give a name
To this new fury, holla it through my ear,
Or wrap it up in some hid character.
I'll ride to Oxford, and watch out mine eyes,
But I will hear the brazen head [32] speak, or else
Show me but one hair of his head or beard,
That I may sample it. If the fiend I meet
In mine own house, I'll kill him; the street,   189
Or at the church-door,—there, 'cause he seeks t' untie
The knot God fastens, he deserves most to die.
 Mrs. O. My husband titles him!
 Open.   Master Goshawk,
 pray, sir,
Swear to me that you know him, or know him not,
Who makes me at Brainford to take up a petticoat
Besides my wife's.
 Gos.   By heaven, that man I know not!
Mrs. O. Come, come, you lie!
 Gos.   Will you not have all
 out?
By heaven, I know no man beneath the moon
Should do you wrong, but if I had his name,
I'd print it in text letters.
 Mrs. O.   Print thine own then:
Did'st not thou swear to me he kept his whore?   200
 Mrs. G. And that in sinful Brainford they would
 commit
That which our lips did water at, sir,—ha?
 Mrs. O. Thou spider that hast woven thy cunning
 web
In mine own house t' ensnare me! hast not thou
Sucked nourishment even underneath this roof,

And turn'd it all to poison, spitting it
On thy friends' face, my husband, (he as 'twere
 sleeping,)
Only to leave him ugly to mine eyes,
That they might glance on thee?
Mrs. G.   Speak, are these lies?
Gos. Mine own shame me confounds!
 Open.   No more; he's
 stung.   210
Who'd think that in one body there could dwell
Deformity and beauty, heaven and hell?
Goodness I see is but outside; we all set
In rings of gold stones that be counterfeit:
I thought you none.
 Gos.   Pardon me!
 Open.   Truth I do:
This blemish grows in nature, not in you;
For man's creation stick even moles in scorn
On fairest cheeks.—Wife, nothing's perfect born.
 Mrs. O. I thought you had been born perfect.
 Open. What's this whole world but a gilt rotten pill?
For at the heart lies the old core still.   221
I'll tell you, Master Goshawk, in your eye
I have seen wanton fire; and then, to try
The soundness of my judgment, I told you
I kept a whore, made you believe 'twas true,
Only to feel how your pulse beat; but find
The world can hardly yield a perfect friend.
Come, come, a trick of youth, and 'tis forgiven;
This rub [33] put by, our love shall run more even.
 Mrs. O. You'll deal upon men's wives no more?
 Gos.   No;
 you teach me   230
A trick for that.
 Mrs. O. Troth, do not; they'll o'erreach thee.
Open. Make my house yours, sir, still.
 Gos.   No.
 Open.   I say you
 shall:
Seeing thus besieged it holds out, 'twill never fall.

Enter MASTER GALLIPOT, *and* GREENWIT *like*
 a summoner, [34] LAXTON *muffled aloof off.*

Omnes. How now?
Gal. With me, sir?
Green. You, sir. I have gone snaffling [35] up and down
by your door this hour, to watch for you.
 Mrs. G. What's the matter, husband?
 Green. I have caught a cold in my head, sir, by sitting
up late in the Rose tavern; but I hope you understand
my speech.   241
Gal. So, sir.
 Green. I cite you by the name of Hippocrates Galli-
pot, and you by the name of Prudence Gallipot, to
appear upon *Crastino,*—do you see?—*Crastino sancti
Dunstani,* [36] this Easter term, in Bow Church.
 Gal. Where, sir? What says he?
 Green. Bow, Bow Church, to answer to a libel of
precontract on the part and behalf of the said Prudence
and another: you're best, sir, take a copy of the citation,
'tis but twelvepence.   251

---

[32] *brazen head:* the speaking head in *Friar Bacon and Friar
Bungay.*   [33] *rub:* impediment.
[34] *summoner:* messenger who cites persons to appear in
ecclesiastical court.   [35] *snaffling:* snuffling.
[36] *L.:* the day after the feast of St. Dunstan, i.e., May 20.

Omnes. A citation!

Gal. You pocky-nosed rascal, what slave fees you to this?

[LAXTON *comes forward*.]

Lax. Slave? I ha' nothing to do with you; do you hear, sir?

Gos. Laxton, is't not? What fagary[37] is this?

Gal. Trust me, I thought, sir, this storm long ago
Had been full laid, when, if you be remembered,[38]
I paid you the last fifteen pound, besides   260
The thirty you had first; for then you swore—

Lax. Tush, tush, sir, oaths,—
Truth, yet I'm loath to vex you—tell you what,
Make up the money I had an hundred pound,
And take your bellyful of her.

Gal.   An hundred pound?

Mrs. G. What, a hundred pound? He gets none:
what, a hundred pound?

Gal. Sweet Pru, be calm; the gentleman offers thus:
If I will make the moneys that are past
A hundred pound, he will discharge all courts,
And give his bond never to vex us more.   270

Mrs. G. A hundred pound? 'Las, take, sir, but threescore!
Do you seek my undoing?

Lax.   I'll not 'bate one sixpence.—
I'll maul you, puss, for spitting.

Mrs. G.   Do thy worst.—
Will fourscore stop thy mouth?

Lax.   No.

Mrs. G.   You're a slave;
Thou cheat, I'll now tear money from thy throat.—
Husband, lay hold on yonder tawny coat.[39]

Green. Nay, gentlemen, seeing your women are so
hot, I must lose my hair[40] in their company, I see.

[*Takes off his false hair*.]

Mrs. O. His hair sheds off, and yet he speaks not so
much in the nose as he did before.   280

Gos. He has had the better chirurgeon.—Master
Greenwit, is your wit so raw as to play no better a part
than a summoner's?

Gal. I pray, who plays *A Knack to Know an Honest
Man*,[41] in this company?

Mrs. G. Dear husband, pardon me, I did dissemble,
Told thee I was his precontracted wife,
When letters came from him for thirty pound:
I had no shift but that.

Gal.   A very clean shift,[42]   289
But able to make me lousy: on.

Mrs. G.   Husband, I plucked,
When he had tempted me to think well of him,
Gilt feathers from thy wings, to make him fly
More lofty.

Gal.   O' the top of you, wife. On.

Mrs. G. He having wasted them, comes now for
more,
Using me as a ruffian doth his whore,
Whose sin keeps him in breath. By heaven, I vow,
Thy bed he ne'er wronged more than he does now!

Gal. My bed? Ha, ha! like enough; a shopboard will
serve
To have a cuckold's coat cut out upon;
Of that we'll talk hereafter.—You're a villain.   300

Lax. Hear me but speak, sir, you shall find me none.

Omnes. Pray, sir, be patient, and hear him.

Gal. I'm muzzled for biting, sir; use me how you
will.

Lax. The first hour that your wife was in my eye,
Myself with other gentlemen sitting by
In your shop tasting smoke, and speech being used,
That men who've fairest wives are most abused
And hardly scaped the horn, your wife maintained
That only such spots in city dames were stained
Justly but by men's slanders; for her own part,   310
She vowed that you had so much of her heart,
No man, by all his wit, by any wile
Never so finespun, should yourself beguile
Of what in her was yours.

Gal.   Yet, Pru, 'tis well.—
Play out your game at Irish,[43] sir: who wins?

Mrs. O. The trial is when she comes to bearing.[44]

Lax. I scorned one woman thus should brave all men
And, which more vexed me, a she-citizen;
Therefore I laid siege to her; out she held,
Gave many a brave repulse, and me compelled   320
With shame to sound retreat to my hot lust.
Then, seeing all base desires raked up in dust,
And that to tempt her modest ears,[45] I swore
Ne'er to presume again; she said, her eye
Would ever give me welcome honestly;
And, since I was a gentleman, if't run low,
She would my state relieve, not to o'erthrow
Your own and hers; did so; then seeing I wrought
Upon her meekness, me she set at nought;
And yet to try if I could turn that tide,   330
You see what stream I strove with. But, sir, I swear
By heaven, and by those hopes men lay up there,
I neither have nor had a base intent
To wrong your bed. What's done, is merriment;
Your gold I pay back with this interest.
When I had most power to do't, I wronged you least.

Gal. If this no gullery be, sir—

Omnes.   No, no, on my life!

Gal. Then, sir, I am beholden—not to you, wife,—
But, Master Laxton, to your want of doing
Ill, which it seems you have not.—Gentlemen,   340
Tarry and dine here all.

Open.   Brother, we have a jest
As good as yours to furnish out a feast.

Gal. We'll crown our table with't—Wife, brag no
more
Of holding out; who most brags is most whore.

Exeunt omnes.

---

[37] *fagary*: vagary.   [38] *be remembered*: recall.
[39] *tawny coat*: summoner's dress.
[40] *lose . . . hair*: from venereal disease.
[41] *A . . . Man*: anonymous 1594 play.
[42] *shift*: shirt, with pun. [43] *Irish*: game like backgammon.
[44] *bearing*: with pun on a technical term from Irish.
[45] *And . . . ears*: Some text missing(?).

ACT FIVE

SCENE ONE

Enter JACK DAPPER, MOLL, SIR BEAUTEOUS
GANYMEDE, *and* SIR THOMAS LONG.

J. Dap. But, prithee, Master Captain Jack, be plain
and perspicuous with me; was it your Meg of Westminster's[1] courage that rescued me from the Poultry[2]
puttocks indeed?

Moll. The valor of my wit, I ensure you, sir, fetched
you off bravely, when you were i' the forlorn hope
among those desperates. Sir Beauteous Ganymede here
and Sir Thomas Long heard that cuckoo, my man
Trapdoor, sing the note of your ransom from captivity.

S. Beau. Uds so, Moll, where's that Trapdoor?   10

Moll. Hanged, I think, by this time; a justice in this
town, that speaks nothing but "make a mittimus,[3] away
with him to Newgate,"[4] used that rogue like a firework,
to run upon a line betwixt him and me.

Omnes. How, how?

Moll. Marry, to lay trains of villainy to blow up my
life. I smelled the powder, spied what linstock[5] gave
fire to shoot against the poor captain of the galley-foist,[6]
and away slid I my man like a shovel-board shilling.[7] He
struts up and down the suburbs, I think, and eats up
whores, feeds upon a bawd's garbage.   21

S. Tho. Sirrah, Jack Dapper—

J. Dap. What sayst, Tom Long?

S. Tho. Thou hadst a sweet-faced boy, hail-fellow
with thee, to your little gull; how is he spent?

J. Dap. Troth, I whistled the poor little buzzard off
o' my fist, because when he waited upon me at the
ordinaries, the gallants hit me i' the teeth still, and said
I looked like a painted alderman's tomb, and the boy at
my elbow like a death's head.—Sirrah Jack, Moll—

Moll. What says my little Dapper?   31

S. Beau. Come, come; walk and talk, walk and talk.

J. Dap. Moll and I'll be i' the midst.

Moll. These knights shall have squires' places belike
then. Well, Dapper, what say you?

J. Dap. Sirrah Captain, mad Mary, the gull my own
father, Dapper Sir Davy, laid these London boot-
halers,[8] the catchpolls, in ambush to set upon me.

Omnes. Your father? Away, Jack!   39

J. Dap. By the tassels of this handkercher, 'tis true.
And what was his warlike stratagem, think you? He
thought, because a wicker cage tames a nightingale, a
lousy prison could make an ass of me.

Omnes. A nasty plot!

J. Dap. Ay, as though a Counter, which is a park in
which all the wild beasts of the city run head by head,
could tame me!

Moll. Yonder comes my Lord Noland.

Enter LORD NOLAND.

Omnes. Save you, my lord.   49

L. Nol. Well met, gentlemen all.—Good Sir Beauteous Ganymede, Sir Thomas Long,—and how does
Master Dapper?

J. Dap. Thanks, my lord.

Moll. No tobacco, my lord?

L. Nol. No, faith, Jack.

J. Dap. My Lord Noland, will you go to Pimlico
with us? We are making a boon voyage to that nappy[9]
land of spice-cakes.

L. Nol. Here's such a merry ging,[10] I could find in
my heart to sail to the world's end with such company; come, gentlemen, let's on.   61

J. Dap. Here's most amorous weather, my lord.

Omnes. Amorous weather!

They walk.

J. Dap. Is not amorous a good word?

Enter TRAPDOOR *like a poor soldier with a patch
o'er one eye, and* TEARCAT *with him
all tatters.*

Trap. Shall we set upon the infantry, these troops of
foot? Zounds, yonder comes Moll, my whorish master
and mistress. Would I had her kidneys between my
teeth.

Tear. I had rather have a cow-heel.[11]

Trap. Zounds, I am so patched up, she cannot discover me; we'll on.   71

Tear. *Alla corago*[12] then!

Trap. Good your honors and worships, enlarge the
ears of commiseration, and let the sound of a hoarse
military organ-pipe penetrate your pitiful bowels, to
extract out of them so many small drops of silver as may
give a hard straw-bed lodging to a couple of maimed
soldiers.

J. Dap. Where are you maimed?

Tear. In both our nether limbs.   80

Moll. Come, come, Dapper, let's give 'em something.
'Las, poor men, what money have you? By my troth, I
love a soldier with my soul.

S. Beau. Stay, stay; where have you served?

S. Tho. In any part of the Low Countries?

Trap. Not in the Low Countries, if it please your
manhood, but in Hungary against the Turks at the siege
of Belgrade.[13]

L. Nol. Who served there with you, sirrah?

Trap. Many Hungarians, Moldavians, Vallachians,
and Transylvanians, with some Sclavonians;[14]   91
and retiring home, sir, the Venetian galleys took us
prisoners, yet freed us, and suffered us to beg up and
down the country.

J. Dap. You have ambled all over Italy, then?

Trap. O sir, from Venice to Roma, Vecchia, Bononia,[15] Romagna, Bologna, Modena, Piacenza, and Tus-

---

V.i.

[1] *Meg . . . Westminster's:* famous predecessor of Moll Firth.

[2] *Poultry:* street in Cheapside, site of a poultry market.

[3] *mittimus:* warrant.   [4] *Newgate:* London prison.

[5] *linstock:* stick with match at one end, used to fire a
cannon.   [6] *galley-foist:* long barge with oars.

[7] *shovel-board shilling:* slippery coin used in shuffleboard.

[8] *boot-halers:* plundering soldiers.

[9] *nappy:* heady; usually of ale.   [10] *ging:* gang.

[11] *cow-heel:* dish of jelly made from stewing cow's heel.

[12] *corago:* i.e., It. *coragio,* "courage."

[13] *Belgrade:* captured by the Turks in 1521.

[14] *Sclavonians:* Slavs.

[15] *Bononia:* same place as Bologna.

cana, with all her cities, as Pistoia, Volterra, Monte-pulciano, Arezzo; with the Siennois, and divers others.

Moll. Mere rogues! put spurs to 'em once more.

J. Dap. Thou lookest like a strange creature, a fat butterbox,[16] yet speakest English: what art thou?   102

Tear. Ick, mine Here? ick bin den ruffling Tearcat, den brave soldado; ick bin dorick all Dutchlant gereisen; der schellum das meer ine beasa ine woort gaeb, ick slaag um stroakes on tom cop; dastick den hundred touzun divel halle, frollich, mine Here.[17]

S. Beau. Here, here; let's be rid of their jabbering.

[*About to give money.*]

Moll. Not a cross,[18] Sir Beauteous.—You base rogues, I have taken measure of you better than a   110 tailor can; and I'll fit you, as you, monster with one eye, have fitted me.

Trap. Your worship will not abuse a soldier?

Moll. Soldier? Thou deservest to be hanged up by that tongue which dishonors so noble a profession: soldier? You skeldering[19] varlet! hold, stand; there should be a trapdoor hereabouts.

[*Pull off his patch.*]

Trap. The balls of these glasiers[20] of mine, mine eyes, shall be shot up and down in any hot piece of ser-vice for my invincible mistress.   120

J. Dap. I did not think there had been such knavery in black patches as now I see.

Moll. Oh, sir, he hath been brought up in the Isle of Dogs,[21] and can both fawn like a spaniel, and bite like a mastiff, as he finds occasion.

L. Nol. What are you, sirrah? A bird of this feather too?

Tear. A man beaten from the wars, sir.

S. Tho. I think so, for you never stood to fight.

J. Dap. What's thy name, fellow soldier?   130

Tear. I am called, by those that have seen my valor, Tearcat.

All. Tearcat?

Moll. A mere whip-jack,[22] and that is, in the com-monwealth of rogues, a slave that can talk of sea-fight, name all your chief pirates, discover more countries to you than either the Dutch, Spanish, French, or English ever found out; yet indeed all his service is by land, and that is to rob a fair, or some such venturous exploit. Tearcat? 'Foot, sirrah, I have your name, now I   140 remember me, in my book of horners;[23] horns for the thumb,[24] you know how.

Tear. No indeed, Captain Moll, for I know you by sight, I am no such nipping Christian,[25] but a maun-derer[26] upon the pad,[27] I confess; and meeting with honest Trapdoor here, whom you had cashiered from bearing arms, out at elbows, under your colors, I in-structed him in the rudiments of roguery, and by my map made him sail over any country you can name, so that now he can maunder better than myself.   150

J. Dap. So, then, Trapdoor, thou art turned soldier now?

Trap. Alas, sir, now there's no wars, 'tis the safest course of life I could take!

Moll. I hope, then, you can cant, for by your cudgels, you, sirrah, are an upright man.[28]

Trap. As any walks the highway, I assure you.

Moll. And, Tearcat, what are you? A wild rogue,[29] an angler,[30] or a ruffler?[31]   159

Tear. Brother to this upright man, flesh and blood; ruffling Tearcat is my name, and a ruffler is my style, my title, my profession.

Moll. Sirrah, where's your doxy?[32] Halt not with me.

All. Doxy, Moll? What's that?

Moll. His wench.

Trap. My doxy? I have, by the salomon,[33] a doxy that carries a kinchin mort[34] in her slate[35] at her back, besides my dell[36] and my dainty wild dell,[37] with all whom I'll tumble this next darkman's[38] in the strom-mel,[39] and drink ben bouse,[40] and eat a fat gruntling cheat,[41] a cackling cheat,[42] and a quacking cheat.[43]   171

J. Dap. Here's old[44] cheating!

Trap. My doxy stays for me in a bousing ken,[45] brave Captain.

Moll. He says his wench stays for him in an ale-house.—You are no pure rogues!

Tear. Pure rogues? No, we scorn to be pure rogues; but if you come to our lib ken[46] or our stalling ken,[47] you shall find neither him nor me a queer cuffin.[48]

Moll. So, sir, no churl of you.   180

Tear. No, but a ben cove,[49] a brave cove,[50] a gentry cuffin.[51]

L. Nol. Call you this canting?

---

[16] *butterbox:* derogatory term for Dutch.

[17] *Ick . . . Here:* "I, my Lord? I am the ruffling [i.e., vaga-bond] Tearcat, the brave soldier. I have traveled through all Germany (or the land of the Dutch); the rascal who gave me one word, I hit him with blows on the head; thus I beat the hundred thousand devils, happily my Lord(?)." Tearcat's stage Dutch only pretends to meaning.

[18] *cross:* piece of money.

[19] *skeldering:* begging vagabond, often professing to be an ex-soldier.   [20] *glasiers:* eyes.

[21] *Isle of Dogs:* opposite Greenwich, sanctuary for those escaping debt and the law.

[22] *whip-jack:* beggar pretending to be an ex-sailor.

[23] *horners:* makers of cuckolds.

[24] *horns . . . thumb:* horn thimble worn by cutpurse against which he can quickly cut pursestrings.

[25] *nipping Christian:* cutpurse.   [26] *maunderer:* beggar.

[27] *pad:* highway.

[28] *upright man:* as described elsewhere by Dekker, big honest-looking scoundrel.

[29] *wild rogue:* rough member of a gang.

[30] *angler:* thief who uses fishing gear to steal through windows.

[31] *ruffler:* vagabond, like the upright man, carries a cudgel and is a deserting soldier or runaway servant.

[32] *doxy:* thief's mistress.   [33] *salomon:* mass.

[34] *kinchin mort:* beggar's children carried on their mother's back.   [35] *slate:* sheet.   [36] *dell:* wanton girl.

[37] *wild dell:* dell begotten and born under a hedge.

[38] *darkman's:* night.   [39] *strommel:* straw.

[40] *ben bouse:* good drink.   [41] *gruntling cheat:* pig.

[42] *cackling cheat:* fowl.   [43] *quacking cheat:* duck.

[44] *old:* abundant.   [45] *bousing ken:* alehouse.

[46] *lib ken:* lodging.

[47] *stalling ken:* house for the reception of stolen goods.

[48] *queer cuffin:* churl.   [49] *ben cove:* good fellow, friend.

[50] *brave cove:* fine fellow.   [51] *gentry cuffin:* gentleman.

J. Dap. Zounds, I'll give a schoolmaster half-a-crown a week, and teach me this pedlar's French.[52]

Trap. Do but stroll, sir, half a harvest with us, sir, and you shall gabble your bellyful.

Moll. Come, you rogue, cant with me.

S. Tho. Well said, Moll.—Cant with her, sirrah, and you shall have money, else not a penny.   190

Trap. I'll have a bout, if she please.

Moll. Come on, sirrah!

Trap. Ben mort,[53] shall you and I heave a booth,[54] mill a ken,[55] or nip a bung,[56] and then we'll couch a hogshead[57] under the ruffman's,[58] and there you shall wap[59] with me, and I'll niggle[60] with you.

Moll. Out, you damned impudent rascal!

Trap. Cut benar whids,[61] and hold your fambles[62] and your stamps.[63]

L. Noll. Nay, nay, Moll, why art thou angry? what was his gibberish?   201

Moll. Marry, this, my lord, says he: "Ben mort." good wench, "shall you and I heave a booth, mill a ken, or nip a bung?" Shall you and I rob a house, or cut a purse?

Omnes. Very good.

Moll. "And then we'll couch a hogshead under the ruffman's"; and then we'll lie under a hedge.

Trap. That was my desire, captain, as 'tis fit a soldier should lie.   210

Moll. "And there you shall wap with me, and I'll niggle with you,"—and that's all.

S. Beau. Nay, nay, Moll, what's that wap?

J. Dap. Nay, teach me what niggling is; I'd fain be niggling.

Moll. Wapping and niggling is all one, the rogue my man can tell you.

Trap. 'Tis fadoodling,[64] if it please you.

S. Beau. This is excellent! One fit more, good Moll.

Moll. Come, you rogue, sing with me.   220

THE SONG

Moll.   *A gage[65] of ben rum bouse[66]*
            In a bousing ken of Romville,[67]

---

[52] *pedlar's French:* underworld slang.
[53] *Ben mort:* Good wench.   [54] *heave a booth:* rob a house.
[55] *mill a ken:* rob a house.   [56] *nip a bung:* cut a purse.
[57] *couch a hogshead:* lie down and sleep.
[58] *ruffman's:* hedge.   [59] *wap:* copulate.
[60] *niggle:* copulate.
[61] *Cut . . . whids:* Speak better words.   [62] *fambles:* hands.
[63] *stamps:* legs.   [64] *fadoodling:* nothing.
[65] *gage:* quart-pot.   [66] *ben rum bouse:* good wine.
[67] *Romville:* London.   [68] *benar:* better.
[69] *caster:* cloak.
[70] *Peck . . . popler:* Food, bread, buttermilk, or milk-porridge.   [71] *mill:* steal.
[72] *deuse a ville:* daisyville, the country.   [73] *lib:* lie.
[74] *lightman's:* day.   [75] *hartman's:* stocks.
[76] *scour . . . ring:* wear fetters.
[77] *palliard:* beggar who lies on straw.   [78] *docked:* had.
[79] *bousy nab:* drunken head.   [80] *skew:* drink.
[81] *bing:* go.
[82] *stalled . . . rogue:* appointed a member of the underworld.   [83] *trine:* hang.   [84] *cheats:* gallows.
[85] *maundering:* muttering.   [86] *L.:* Go before, I follow.

Tear.   *Is benar[68] than a caster,[69]*
            Peck, pennam, lay, or popler,[70]
            Which we mill[71] in deuse a ville.[72]

Both.   *Oh, I wud lib[73] all the lightman's,[74]*
            Oh, wud lib all the darkman's,
            By the salomon, under the ruffmans,
            By the salomon, in the hartman's,[75]

Tear.   *And scour the queer cramp ring,[76]*   230
            And couch till a palliard[77] docked[78] my dell, .
            So my bousy nab[79] might skew[80] rum bouse
                well.

Both.   *Avast to the pad, let us bing;[81]*
            Avast to the pad, let us bing.

Omnes. Fine knaves, i'faith!

J. Dap. The grating of ten new cartwheels and the gruntling of five hundred hogs coming from Rumford market cannot make a worse noise than this canting language does in my ears. Pray, my Lord Noland, let's give these soldiers their pay.   240

S. Beau. Agreed, and let them march.

L. Nol. Here, Moll.

                                        [*Gives money.*]

Moll. Now I see that you are stalled to the rogue,[82] and are not ashamed of your professions; look you, my Lord Noland here and these gentlemen bestows upon you two two boards and a half, that's two shillings six-pence.

Trap. Thanks to your lordship.

Tear. Thanks, heroical captain.

Moll. Away!   250

Trap. We shall cut ben whids of your masters and mistress-ship wheresoever we come.

Moll. You'll maintain, sirrah, the old justice's plot to his face?

Trap. Else trine[83] me on the cheats,[84]—hang me.

Moll. Be sure you meet me there.

Trap. Without any more maundering,[85] I'll do't.—Follow, brave Tearcat.

Tear. I prae, sequor[86]; let us go, mouse.

                Exeunt they two; manet the rest.

L. Nol. Moll, what was in that canting song?   260

Moll. Troth, my lord, only a praise of good drink, the only milk which these wild beasts love to suck, and thus it was:

>   *A rich cup of wine,*
>   *Oh, it is juice divine!*
>   *More wholesome for the head*
>   *Than meat, drink, or bread:*
>   *To fill my drunken pate*
>   *With that, I'd sit up late;*
>   *By the heels would I lie,*   270
>   *Under a lousy hedge die,*
>   *Let a slave have a pull*
>   *At my whore, so I be full*
>   *Of that precious liquor:*

and a parcel of such stuff, my lord, not worth the opening.

Enter a Cutpurse *very gallant,*[87] *with four or five others, one with a wand.*

L. Nol. What gallant comes yonder?

S. Tho. Mass, I think I know him; 'tis one of Cumberland.

1 Cut. Shall we venture to shuffle in amongst yon heap of gallants, and strike?[88]   281

2 Cut. 'Tis a question whether there be any silver shells[89] amongst them, for all their satin outsides.

All Cut. Let's try.

Moll. Pox on him, a gallant? Shadow me, I know him; 'tis one that cumbers the land indeed; if he swim near to the shore of any of your pockets, look to your purses.

Omnes. Is't possible?

Moll. This brave fellow is no better than a foist.   290

Omnes. Foist! what's that?

Moll. A diver with two fingers, a pickpocket; all his train[90] study the figging law,[91] that's to say, cutting of purses and foisting. One of them is a nip; I took him once i' the two-penny gallery at the Fortune; then there's a cloyer,[92] or snap,[93] that dogs any new brother in that trade, and snaps will have half in any booty. He with the wand is both a stale, whose office is to face a man i' the streets, whilst shells are drawn by another, and then with his black conjuring rod in his hand   300 he, by the nimbleness of his eye and juggling stick, will, in cheaping[94] a piece of plate at a goldsmith's stall, make four or five rings mount from the top of his *caduceus,*[95] and, as if it were at leapfrog, they skip into his hand presently.

2 Cut. Zounds, we are smoked![96]

All Cut. Ha!

2 Cut. We are boiled,[97] pox on her! see, Moll, the roaring drab!

1 Cut. All the diseases of sixteen hospitals boil her!—away!   311

Moll. Bless you, sir.

1 Cut. And you, good sir.

Moll. Dost not ken[98] me, man?

1 Cut. No, trust me, sir.

Moll. Heart, there's a knight to whom I'm bound for many favors, lost his purse at the last new play i' the Swan, seven angels in't; make it good, you're best; do you see? No more.   319

1 Cut. A synagogue[99] shall be called, Mistress Mary; disgrace me not; *pacus palabros,*[100] I will conjure for you: farewell.

                                        Exeunt [Cutpurses].

Moll. Did not I tell you, my lord?

L. Noll. I wonder how thou camest to the knowledge of these nasty villains.

S. Tho. And why do the foul mouths of the world call thee Moll Cutpurse? A name, methinks, damned and odious.

Moll. Dare any step forth to my face and say,
I've ta'en thee doing so, Moll? I must confess,   330
In younger days, when I was apt to stray,
I've sat amongst such adders; seen their stings,

As any here might, and in full playhouses
Watched their quick-diving hands, to bring to shame
Such rogues, and in that stream met an ill name.
When next, my lord, you spy any one of those,
So he be in his art a scholar, question him;
Tempt him with gold to open the large book
Of his close villainies; and you yourself shall cant
Better than poor Moll can, and know more laws   340
Of cheaters, lifters,[101] nips, foists, puggards,[102] curbers,[103]
With all the devil's blackguard,[104] than it's fit
Should be discovered to a noble wit.
I know they have their orders, offices,
Circuits, and circles, unto which they're bound
To raise their own damnation in.

J. Dap. How dost thou know it?

Moll. As you do; I show it you, they to me show it.
Suppose, my lord, you were in Venice—

L. Noll.   Well.

Moll. If some Italian pander there would tell   350
All the close tricks of courtesans, would not you
Hearken to such a fellow?

L. Noll.   Yes.

Moll.   And here,
Being come from Venice, to a friend most dear
That were to travel thither, you would proclaim
Your knowledge in those villainies, to save
Your friend from their quick danger. Must you have
A black ill name, because ill things you know?
Good troth, my lord, I'm made Moll Cutpurse so.
How many are whores in small ruffs and still looks!
How many chaste whose names fill slander's books!
Were all men cuckolds whom gallants in their scorns
Call so, we should not walk for goring horns.   362
Perhaps for my mad going some reprove me;
I please myself, and care not else who loves me.

Omnes. A brave mind, Moll, i'faith!

S. Tho. Come, my lord, shall's to the ordinary?

L. Noll. Ay, 'tis noon sure.

Moll. Good my lord, let not my name condemn me to you, or to the world. A fencer I hope may be called a coward; is he so for that? If all that have ill   370 names in London were to be whipped, and to pay but twelvepence apiece to the beadle, I would rather have his office than a constable's.

J. Dap. So would I, Captain Moll; 'twere a sweet tickling office, i'faith.

                                        Exeunt.

---

[87] *gallant:* well got up.   [88] *strike:* steal.

[89] *shells:* money.   [90] *train:* company.

[91] *figging-law:* pocket-picking.

[92] *cloyer:* thief habitually claiming share of profits of young sharpers.   [93] *snap:* cloyer.

[94] *cheaping:* bargaining for.   [95] *L.:* wand.

[96] *smoked:* ridiculed.   [97] *boiled:* betrayed.

[98] *ken:* know.   [99] *synagogue:* pickpocket's meeting.

[100] *pacus palabros:* Sp. *pocas palabras,* "few words."

[101] *lifters:* shoplifters.   [102] *puggards:* thieves.

[103] *curbers:* thieves who use hooks.

[104] *blackguard:* scoundrels; company of scullions in a great house.

[V.ii]

Enter SIR ALEXANDER WENGRAVE,
GOSHAWK, *and* GREENWIT, *and others.*

S. Alex. My son marry a thief, that impudent girl,
Whom all the world stick their worst eyes upon!
  Green. How will your care prevent it?
  Gos.   'Tis
    impossible;
They marry close, they're gone, but none knows
    whither,
  S. Alex. Oh, gentlemen, when has a father's heart-
    strings

Enter a Servant.

Held out so long from breaking?—Now what news, sir?
  Ser. They were met upo' th' water an hour since, sir,
Putting in towards the Sluice.
  S. Alex.   The Sluice? Come,
    gentlemen,
'Tis Lambeth works against us.
                               [*Exit* Servant.]
  Green.   And that Lambeth
Joins more mad matches than your six wet towns[1]   10
'Twixt that and Windsor Bridge, where fares[2] lie
    soaking.
  S. Alex. Delay no time, sweet gentlemen; to
    Blackfriars!
We'll take a pair of oars, and make after 'em.

Enter TRAPDOOR.

  Trap. Your son and that bold masculine ramp my
    mistress
Are landed now at Tower.
  S. Alex.   Hoyda, at Tower?
  Trap. I heard it now reported.
  S. Alex. Which way gentlemen,
Shall I bestow my care? I'm drawn in pieces
Betwixt deceit and shame.

Enter SIR [GUY] FITZALLARD.

  S. Guy. Sir Alexander,   20
You 're well met, and most rightly servèd;
My daughter was a scorn to you.
  S. Alex.   Say not so, sir.
  S. Guy. A very abject she, poor gentlewoman!
Your house had been dishonored. Give you joy, sir,
Of your son's gaskin[3]-bride. You'll be a grandfather
    shortly
To a fine crew of roaring sons and daughters;
'Twill help to stock the suburbs passing well, sir.
  S. Alex. Oh, play not with the miseries of my heart.
Wounds should be dressed and healed, not vexed, or
    left
Wide open to the anguish of the patient,   30

V.ii.
[1] *towns:* Fulham, Richmond, Kingston, Hampton, Chert-
sey, Staines.   [2] *fares:* passengers.   [3] *gaskin:* breeches.
[4] *culverin's:* cannon's.

And scornful air let in; rather let pity
And advice charitably help refresh 'em.
  S. Guy. Who'd place his charity so unworthily,
Like one that gives alms to a cursing beggar?
Had I but found one spark of goodness in you
Toward my deserving child, which then grew fond
Of your son's virtues, I had eased you now.
But I perceive both fire of youth and goodness
Are raked up in the ashes of your age,
Else no such shame should have come near your house,
Nor such ignoble sorrow touch your heart.   41
  S. Alex. If not for worth, for pity's sake assist me!
  Green. You urge a thing past sense; how can he help
    you?
All his assistance is as frail as ours:
Full as uncertain where's the place that holds 'em;
One brings us water-news; then comes another
With a full-charged mouth, like a culverin's[4] voice,
And he reports the Tower. Whose sounds are truest?
  Gos. In vain you flatter him.—Sir Alexander—
  S. Guy. I flatter him? Gentlemen, you wrong me
    grossly.   50
  Green. He does it well, i'faith.
  S. Guy.   Both news are false,
Of Tower or water; they took no such way yet.
  S. Alex. Oh, strange! hear you this, gentlemen? yet
    more plunges.
  S. Guy. They're nearer than you think for, yet more
    close
Than if they were further off.
  S. Alex.   How am I lost
In these distractions!
  S. Guy.   For your speeches, gentlemen,
In taxing me for rashness, 'fore you all
I will engage my state to half his wealth,
Nay, to his son's revenues, which are less,
And yet nothing at all till they come from him,   60
That I could, if my will stuck to my power,
Prevent this marriage yet, nay, banish her
For ever from his thoughts, much more his arms.
  S. Alex. Slack not this goodness, though you heap
    upon me
Mountains of malice and revenge hereafter!
I'd willingly resign up half my state to him,
So he would marry the meanest drudge I hire.
  Green. He talks impossibilities, and you believe
    'em.
  S. Guy. I talk no more than I know how to finish,
My fortunes else are his that dares stake with me.   70
The poor young gentleman I love and pity;
And to keep shame from him (because the spring
Of his affection was my daughter's first,
Till his frown blasted all), do but estate him
In those possessions which your love and care
Once pointed out for him, that he may have room
To entertain fortunes of noble birth,
Where now his desperate want casts him upon her;
And if I do not, for his own sake chiefly,
Rid him of this disease that now grows on him,   80
I'll forfeit my whole state, before these gentlemen.

Green. Troth, but you shall not undertake such
    matches;
We'll persuade so much with you.
S. Alex.   Here's my ring;

                      [Gives ring.]

He will believe this token. 'Fore these gentlemen
I will confirm it fully: all those lands
My first love 'lotted him, he shall straight possess
In that refusal.
S. Guy.   If I change it not,
Change me into a beggar.
    Green.   Are you mad, sir?
    S. Guy. 'Tis done.
    Gos.   Will you undo yourself by doing,
And show a prodigal trick in your old days?   90
    S. Alex. 'Tis a match, gentlemen.
    S. Guy.   Ay, ay, sir, ay.
I ask no favor, trust to you for none;
My hope rests in the goodness of your son.
              Exit FITZALLARD.
    Green. He holds it up well yet.
    Gos.   Of an old knight, i'
    faith.
    S. Alex. Cursed be the time I laid his first love
    barren,
Wilfully barren, that before this hour
Had sprung forth fruits of comfort and of honor!
He loved a virtuous gentlewoman.

        Enter MOLL *[in man's clothes].*

    Gos.   Life, here's Moll!
    Green. Jack?
    Gos.   How dost thou, Jack?
    Moll.   How dost thou,
    gallant?
    S. Alex. Impudence, where's my son?
    Moll.   Weakness, go
    look him.   100
    S. Alex. Is this your wedding gown?
    Moll.   The man talks
    monthly:[5]
Hot broth and a dark chamber for the knight!
I see he'll be stark mad at our next meeting.
              Exit MOLL.
    Gos. Why, sir, take comfort now, there's no such
    matter;
No priest will marry her, sir, for a woman
Whiles that shape's on; and it was never known
Two men were married and conjoined in one.
Your son hath made some shift to love another.
    S. Alex. Whate'er she be, she has my blessing with
    her:
May they be rich and fruitful, and receive   110
Like comfort to their issue as I take
In them. Has pleased me now. Marrying not this,
Through a whole world he could not choose amiss.
    Green. Glad you're so penitent for your former sin,
    sir.
    Gos. Say he should take a wench with her smock-
    dowry,

No portion with her but her lips and arms?
    S. Alex. Why, who thrive better, sir? They have
    most blessing,
Though other have more wealth, and least repent:
Many that want most know the most content.   119
    Green. Say he should marry a kind youthful sinner?
    S. Alex. Age will quench that; any offense but theft
And drunkenness, nothing but death can wipe away;
Their sins are green even when their heads are gray.
Nay, I despair not now; my heart's cheered, gentlemen;
No face can come unfortunately to me.—

           Enter a Servant.

Now, sir, your news?
    Ser.   Your son, with his fair bride,
Is near at hand.
    S. Alex.   Fair may their fortunes be!
    Green. Now you're resolved, sir, it was never she.
    S. Alex. I find it in the music of my heart.

    Enter MOLL *masked, in* SEBASTIAN'S *hand,*
        and SIR GUY FITZALLARD.

See where they come.
    Gos.   A proper lusty presence, sir.   130
    S. Alex. Now has he pleased me right: I always
    counseled him
To choose a goodly, personable creature.
Just of her pitch was my first wife his mother.
    Seb. Before I dare discover my offense,
I kneel for pardon.
                 [Kneels.]
    S. Alex.   My heart gave it thee
Before thy tongue could ask it:
Rise; thou hast raised my joy to greater height
Than to that seat where grief dejected it.
Both welcome to my love and care for ever!
Hide not my happiness too long; all's pardoned;   140
Here are our friends.—Salute her, gentlemen.

             They unmask her.

    Omnes. Heart, who['s] this? Moll!
    S. Alex. Oh, my reviving shame! is't I must live
To be struck blind? Be it the work of sorrow,
Before age take't in hand!
    S. Guy.   Darkness and death!
Have you deceived me thus? Did I engage
My whole estate for this?
    S. Alex.   You ask'd no favor,
And you shall find as little: since my comforts
Play false with me, I'll be as cruel to thee
As grief to father's hearts.
    Moll.   Why, what's the matter with
    you,   150
'Less too much joy should make your age forgetful?
Are you too well, too happy?
    S. Alex.   With a vengeance.
    Moll. Methinks you should be proud of such a
    daughter,
As good a man as your son.

---

    [5] *monthly:* madly, as if moonstruck.

S. Alex.   O monstrous impudence!

Moll. You had no note before, an unmarked knight;
Now all the town will take regard on you,
And all your enemies fear you for my sake.
You may pass where you list, through crowds most
     thick,
And come off bravely with your purse unpicked.
You do not know the benefits I bring with me;   160
No cheat dares work upon you with thumb or knife,
While you've a roaring girl to your son's wife.

S. Alex. A devil rampant!

S. Guy.   Have you so much charity
Yet to release me of my last rash bargain,
And I'll give in your pledge?

S. Alex.   No, sir, I stand to't;
I'll work upon advantage, as all mischiefs
Do upon me.

S. Guy.   Content. Bear witness all, then,
His are the lands; and so contention ends:
Here comes your son's bride 'twixt two noble friends.

Enter LORD NOLAND *and* SIR BEAUTEOUS
GANYMEDE *with* MARY FITZALLARD *between*
them, the Citizens [GALLIPOT, TILTYARD,
OPENWORK,] *and their* Wives *with them.*

Moll. Now are you gulled as you would be; thank
     me for't,   170
I'd a forefinger in't.

Seb.   Forgive me, father!
Though there before your eyes my sorrow feigned,
This still was she for whom true love complained.

S. Alex. Blessings eternal, and the joys of angels,
Begin your peace here to be signed in heaven!
How short my sleep of sorrow seems now to me,
To this eternity of boundless comforts,
That finds no want but utterance and expression.
My lord, your office here appears so honorably,
So full of ancient goodness, grace, and worthiness,   180
I never took more joy in sight of man
Than in your comfortable presence now.

L. Nol. Nor I more delight in doing grace to virtue
Than in this worthy gentlewoman your son's bride,
Noble Fitzallard's daughter, to whose honor
And modest fame I am a servant vowed;
So is this knight.

S. Alex.   Your loves make my joys proud.
Bring forth those deeds of land my care laid ready,

[*Exit* Servant, *who presently returns*
                              with deeds.]

And which, old knight, thy nobleness may challenge,
Joined with thy daughter's virtues, whom I prize now
As dearly as that flesh I call mine own.   191
Forgive me, worthy gentlewoman; 'twas my blindness:
When I rejected thee, I saw thee not;
Sorrow and willful rashness grew like films
Over the eyes of judgment; now so clear
I see the brightness of thy worth appear.

Mary. Duty and love may I deserve in those,
And all my wishes have a perfect close.

---

⁶ *broached:* opened.

S. Alex. That tongue can never err, the sound's so
     sweet.
Here, honest son, receive into thy hands   200
The keys of wealth, possession of those lands
Which my first care provided; they're thine own;
Heaven give thee a blessing with 'em; the best joys
That can in wordly shapes to man betide
Are fertile lands and a fair fruitful bride,
Of which I hope thou'rt sped.

Seb.   I hope so too, sir.

Moll. Father and son, I ha' done you simple service
     here.

Seb. For which thou shalt not part, Moll, unrequited.

S. Alex. Thou'rt a mad girl, and yet I cannot now
Condemn thee.

Moll.   Condemn me? Troth, and you should,
     sir,   210
I'd make you seek out one to hang in my room:
I'd give you the slip at gallows, and cozen the people.
Heard you this jest, my lord?

L. Noll.   What is it, Jack?

Moll. He was in fear his son would marry me,
But never dreamed that I would ne'er agree.

L. Noll. Why, thou had'st a suitor once, Jack: when
     wilt marry?

Moll. Who, I, my lord? I'll tell you when, i'faith;
          When you shall hear
          Gallants void from sergeants' fear,
          Honesty and truth unslandered,   220
          Woman manned, but never pandered,
          Cheats booted, but not coached,
          Vessels older ere they're broached;⁶
          If my mind be then not varied,
          Next day following I'll be married.

L. Nol. This sounds like doomsday.

Moll.   Then were
     marriage best;
For if I should repent, I were soon at rest.

S. Alex. In troth thou'rt a good wench; I'm sorry
     now
The opinion was so hard I conceived of thee:

Enter TRAPDOOR.

Some wrongs I've done thee.

Trap. [Aside]   Is the wind there now?
'Tis time for me to kneel and confess first,   231
For fear it come too late, and my brains feel it.—

[TRAPDOOR *advances and kneels before* MOLL.]

Upon my paws I ask you pardon, mistress!

Moll. Pardon! for what, sir? What has your
     rogueship done now?

Trap. I have been from time to time hired to
     confound you
By this old gentleman.

Moll.   How?

Trap.   Pray, forgive him;
But may I counsel you, you should never do't.
Many a snare t' entrap your worship's life
Have I laid privily: chains, watches, jewels;
And when he saw nothing could mount you up,   240

Four hollow-hearted angels he then gave you,
By which he meant to trap you, I to save you.
   S. Alex. To all which shame and grief in me cry
    guilty.
Forgive me; now I cast the world's eyes from me,
And look upon thee freely with mine own,
I see the most of many wrongs before me,
Cast from the jaws of envy and her people,
And nothing foul but that. I'll never more
Condemn by common voice, for that's the whore
That deceives man's opinion, mocks his trust,   250
Cozens his love, and makes his heart unjust.
   Moll. Here be the angels, gentlemen; they were given
    me
As a musician. I pursue no pity;

Follow the law, and you can cuck⁷ me, spare not;
Hang up my viol by me, and I care not.
   S. Alex. So far I'm sorry, I'll thrice double 'em,
To make thy wrongs amends.
Come, worthy friends, my honorable lord,
Sir Beauteous Ganymede, and noble Fitzallard,
And you kind gentlewomen, whose sparkling presence
Are glories set in marriage, beams of society,   261
For all your loves give luster to my joys:
The happiness of this day shall be remembered
At the return of every smiling spring;
In my time now 'tis born; and may no sadness
Sit on the brows of men upon that day,
But as I am, so all go pleased away!
                    [*Exeunt omnes.*]

EPILOGUE

A painter having drawn with curious art
The picture of a woman, every part
Limned to the life, hung out the piece to sell.
People who passed along, viewing it well,
Gave several verdicts on it. Some dispraised
The hair; some said the brows too high were raised;
Some hit her o'er the lips, misliked their color;
Some wished her nose were shorter; some, the eyes
    fuller;
Others said roses on her cheeks should grow,
Swearing they looked too pale; others cried no.   10
The workman still, as fault was found, did mend it,
In hope to please all. But this work being ended,
And hung open at stall, it was so vile,
So monstrous, and so ugly, as all men did smile
At the poor painter's folly. Such, we doubt,
Is this our comedy: some perhaps do flout
The plot, saying, 'tis too thin, too weak, too mean;
Some for the person will revile the scene,
And wonder that a creature of her being
Should be the subject of a poet, seeing   20

In the world's eye none weighs so light; others look
For all those base tricks, published in a book
Foul as his brains they flowed from, of cutpurse[s],
Of nips and foists, nasty, obscene discourses,
As full of lies as empty of worth or wit,
For any honest ear or eye unfit.
And thus,
If we to every brain that's humorous¹
Should fashion scenes, we, with the painter, shall,
In striving to please all, please none at all.   30
Yet for such faults as either the writer's wit
Or negligence of the actors do commit,
Both crave your pardons: if what both have done
Cannot full pay your expectation,
The Roaring Girl herself, some few days hence,
Shall on this stage give larger recompense.
Which mirth that you may share in, herself does woo
    you,
And craves this sign, your hands to beckon her to you.

F I N I S

---

   ⁷ *cuck:* submerge in a stinking pond on a stool at the end
of a pole, punishment for scolds.

EPILOGUE
   ¹ *humorous:* whimsical.

Thomas Middleton

[1580–1627]

A CHASTE MAID IN CHEAPSIDE

IKE some other prominent playwrights of his period, Middleton left few footprints outside of his theatrical activities. The son of a London bricklayer, in 1598 he began studies that he never completed at Queen's College, Oxford. He was a precocious poet, publishing when he was a bare seventeen years old. By 1602, still very young, he was writing public plays for Philip Henslowe and private plays for the boys' companies. Some two dozen of his plays survive. He wrote in most of the going genres, though the kind of city satire typified by A CHASTE MAID IN CHEAPSIDE is perhaps his characteristic mode. His most notable success in his lifetime, for which he nearly paid dearly, was *A Game at Chess*, a topical piece written in 1624 to attack Catholics and the Spanish, in which characters in the roles of chess pieces constitute a clever allegory. Critics have habitually lamented their inability to find a formula to encompass the variety of styles and modes in which Middleton composed, but his commitment to the demands of the professional theater and his technical skill are probably the place to begin in coming to terms with his work as a whole. And it should be noted that even before Beaumont and Fletcher he was carrying over to the public theaters the cutting satire and class hostility of the private theaters. In addition to regular employment as a playwright, Middleton was hired regularly to write civic shows for ceremonial occasions in London.

Not printed until 1630, Middleton's comedy was first performed by Lady Elizabeth's Men at the Swan Theater in spring or summer 1613. It has no known sources for its many plots, though Machiavelli's comedy *La Mandragola* may well lie behind the Kix plot. Rather than depending on sources, Middleton fuses together a number of character and plot types familiar to us both from a multitude of English and Italian plays and stories and from his own earlier and later comedies. Some of the action seems to have been inspired by current situations identifiable by topical allusions; thus the normal Lent injunctions against eating meat were enforced with particular rigor in 1613 because of agricultural conditions that caused a fear of shortages, and the dispensations normally made to invalids were not granted this year; *Rider's Dictionary* was in the news because of a lawsuit, and a new waterworks with a windmill caused a stir. Perhaps the most brilliant of Middleton's many multiple-plot plays, A CHASTE MAID is utterly characteristic of his sardonic imagination, his detachment, his deftness in plotting, his extraordinary mimic ability, and his interest in setting against each other plots that reflect one another in a variety of ways.

The text is based on the Huntington copy of the 1630 quarto. Though reliable in most respects, the quarto offers insuperable problems in lineation. Middleton was something of a pioneer in the easy use of prose on the stage, and as a matter of fact much of his verse is itself close to prose. To make the job of distinguishing between different kinds of text more difficult, compositors often compressed verse into prose when they ran out of space on the page assigned to them and expanded prose into apparent verse when they needed to fill empty space. Middleton makes things worse by manuscript habits of not capitalizing the beginnings of verse lines and of running one line over into the next when he needs room. Many modern editors have taken extraordinary liberties in attempting to regularize the verse of the printed text of A CHASTE MAID so that there will be five feet to each line and of "restoring" the verse supposed to lie hidden in much of the prose. Sometimes such tinkering is justified, and modern editors have been able to reconstruct most of THE CHANGELING in accord with what must have been Middleton's original intentions, but in a number of plays, and A CHASTE MAID is one of them, the restoration is more misleading than the quarto itself. The present edition is conservative though not fanatical, turning prose into verse only when the evidence seems overwhelming and leaving the irregular verse of the quarto—which may conceivably have been Middleton's experiment—as it appears there.

N. R.

A Chaste Maid in Cheapside[1]

DRAMATIS PERSONÆ

YELLOWHAMMER, *a goldsmith*
MAUDLIN, *his wife*
TIM, *their son*
MOLL, *their daughter*
Tutor *to Tim*
SIR WALTER WHOREHOUND, *a suitor to Moll*
SIR OLIVER KIX,[1] *kinsman to Sir Walter Whorehound*
LADY KIX
ALLWIT[2]
MISTRESS ALLWIT, *mistress of Sir Walter*
Welsh Gentlewoman, *former mistress of Sir Walter*
WAT *and* NICK, *bastard children of Sir Walter and Mistress Allwit*

DAVY DAHUMMA, *Sir Walter's poor kinsman and attendant*
TOUCHWOOD SENIOR, *a decayed gentleman*
MISTRESS TOUCHWOOD, *his wife*
TOUCHWOOD JUNIOR, *his brother, another suitor to Moll*
Country Wench, *former mistress of Touchwood Senior*
Two Promoters
Servants
Two Watermen
Maid, Parson, Porter, Dry Nurse, Wet Nurse, Midwife, Puritan Women, Gossips, etc.

ACT ONE

SCENE ONE

Enter MAUDLIN *and* MOLL, *a shop being discovered.*

Maud. Have you played over all your old lessons o' the virginals?[1]
Moll. Yes.
Maud. Yes.—You are a dull maid a-late; methinks you had need have somewhat to quicken your green-sickness.[2] Do you weep? A husband. Had not such a piece of flesh been ordained, what had us wives been good for? To make salads, or else cried up and down[3] for samphire.[4] To see the difference of these seasons! When I was of your youth, I was lightsome and 10 quick[5] two years before I was married. You fit for a knight's bed! Drowsy-browed, dull-eyed, drossy-sprited,[6] I hold my life you have forgot your dancing;[7] when was the dancer with you?
Moll. The last week.
Maud. Last week! when I was of your bord,[8] he missed me not a night; I was kept at it; I took delight to learn and he to teach me, pretty brown gentleman; he took pleasure in my company. But you are dull, nothing comes nimbly from you; you dance like a 20 plumber's daughter and deserve two thousand pound in lead to your marriage, and not in goldsmith's ware.

Enter YELLOWHAMMER.

Yell. Now what's the din betwixt mother and daughter, ha?
Maud. Faith, small, telling your daughter Mary of her errors.
Yell. Errors! Nay, the city cannot hold you, wife, but you must needs fetch words from Westminster.[9]

I ha' done, i'faith. Has no attorney's clerk been here a-late and changed his half-crown-piece his 30 mother sent him, or rather cozened you with a gilded twopence,[10] to bring the word in fashion for her faults or cracks in duty and obedience? Term 'em e'en so, sweet wife. As there is no woman made without a flaw, your purest lawns[11] have frays and cambrics[12] bracks.[13]
Maud. But 'tis a husband solders up all cracks.
Moll. What, is he come, sir?
Yell.   Sir Walter's come.
He was met at Holborn bridge,[14] and in his company
A proper fair young gentlewoman, which I guess   40
By her red hair and other rank[15] descriptions
To be his landed niece brought out of Wales,
Which Tim our son, the Cambridge boy, must marry.

THE TITLE
[1] *Cheapside:* London market area frequented by unchaste women.

DRAMATIS PERSONÆ
[1] *Kix:* Dry, hollow plant stem; hence, a sapless man.
[2] *Allwit:* transposition of "Wittol," a willing cuckold.

I.i.
[1] *virginals:* spinet, with sexual innuendo.
[2] *greensickness:* chlorosis, lovesickness.
[3] *cried up and down:* hawked.
[4] *samphire:* edible coastal plant.
[5] *quick:* lively; pregnant.   [6] *sprited:* spirited.
[7] *dancing:* with sexual implication.
[8] *bord:* bore of a gun.
[9] *Westminster:* where courts were conducted in legal language.
[10] *gilded twopence:* silver piece disguised as gold.
[11] *lawns:* fine linens.   [12] *cambrics:* fine white linens.
[13] *bracks:* flaws.
[14] *Holborn bridge:* old London bridge leading through Newgate across Fleetditch to the road to Wales.
[15] *rank:* proud; coarse, lustful.

'Tis a match of Sir Walter's own making,
To bind us to him and our heirs for ever.

Maud. We are honored then, if this baggage would
  be humble
And kiss him with devotion when he enters.
I cannot get her for my life
To instruct her hand [16] thus, before and after,
Which a knight will look for—before and after.   50
I have told her still, 'tis the waving of a woman
Does often move a man and prevails strongly.
But sweet, ha' you sent to Cambridge?
Has Tim word on't?

Yell. H'ad word just the day after, when you sent
him the silver spoon to eat his broth in the hall [17]
amongst the gentlemen commoners. [18]

Maud. Oh, 'twas timely.

Enter Porter.

Yell. How now?

Port. A letter from a gentleman in Cambridge.   60

Yell. Oh, one of Hobson's [19] porters; thou art welcome. I told thee, Maud, we should hear from Tim.
[*Reads.*] *Amantissimis carissimisque ambobus parentibus
patri et matri.* [20]

Maud. What's the matter?

Yell. Nay, by my troth, I know not, ask not me; he's
grown too verbal. This learning is a great witch.

Maud. Pray, let me see it; I was wont to understand
him. [*Reads.*] *Amantissimis carissimis*, he has sent the
carrier's man, he says; *ambobus parentibus*, for a   70
pair of boots; *patri et matri*, pay the porter or it makes
no matter.

Port. Yes, by my faith, mistress, there's no true
construction [21] in that. I have took a great deal of pains
and come from the Bell [22] sweating. Let me come to't,
for I was a scholar forty years ago. 'Tis thus, I warrant
you: [*Reads.*] *Matri*, it makes no matter; *ambobus
parentibus*, for a pair of boots; *patri*, pay the porter;
amantissimis carissimis, he's the carrier's man, and his
name is Sims—and there he says true, forsooth   80

my name is Sims indeed. I have not forgot all my learning. A money matter; I thought I should hit on't.

Yell. Go, thou art an old fox. There's a tester [23] for
thee.

Port. If I see your worship at Goose Fair, [24] I have a
dish of birds for you.

Yell. Why, dost dwell at Bow?

Port. All my lifetime, sir: I could ever say bo to a
goose. [25] Farewell to your worship.

Exit Porter.

Yell. A merry porter.   90

Maud. How can he choose but be so, coming with
Cambridge letters from our son Tim?

Yell. What's here? [*Reads.*] *Maxime* [26] *diligo.* [27]
Faith, I must to my learned counsel with this gear; [28]
'twill never be discerned else.

Maud. Go to my cousin then, at Inns of Court. [29]

Yell. Fie, they are all for French; [30] they speak no
Latin.

Maud. The parson then will do it.   99

Enter a Gentleman *with a chain.*

Yell. Nay, he disclaims it, calls Latin papistry; he
will not deal with it.—What is't you lack, gentleman?

Gent. Pray, weigh this chain.

Enter SIR WALTER WHOREHOUND,
Welsh Gentlewoman, *and* DAVY DAHUMMA.

S. Walt. Now, wench, thou art welcome to the heart
of the city of London.

W. Wom. Dugat a whee. [31]

S. Walt. You can thank me in English, if you list.

W. Wom. I can, sir, simply.

S. Walt. 'Twill serve to pass, wench. 'Twas strange
that I should lie with thee so often to leave thee without
English; that were unnatural. I bring thee up to   110
turn thee into gold, wench, and make thy fortune shine
like your bright trade; a goldsmith's shop sets out a
city maid. Davy Dahumma, not a word.

Davy. Mum, mum, sir.

S. Walt. Here you must pass for a pure virgin.

Davy. [*Aside*] Pure Welsh virgin!
She lost her maidenhead in Brecknockshire. [32]

S. Walt. I hear you mumble, Davy.

Davy. I have teeth, sir; I need not mumble yet this
forty years.   120

S. Walt. [*Aside*] The knave bites plaguily!

Yell. What's your price, sir?

Gent. A hundred pound, sir.

Yell. A hundred marks [33] the utmost; 'tis not for me
else.—What, Sir Walter Whorehound!

[*Exit* Gentleman.]

Moll. Oh, death!

Exit.

Maud. Why, daughter. Faith, the baggage.
[*To* SIR WALTER] A bashful girl, sir; these young
  things are shamefast; [34]
Besides, you have a presence, sweet Sir Walter,
Able to daunt a maid brought up i' the city;   130

Enter MOLL.

---

[16] *instruct . . . hand:* i.e., to make gestures.

[17] *hall:* dining hall.

[18] *gentlemen commoners:* wealthy undergraduates with
special privileges.

[19] *Hobson:* d. 1631, famous Cambridge carrier immortalized by Milton's epitaphs and the phrase "Hobson's choice."

[20] *L.:* To both my most loving and dearest parents, father
and mother.   [21] *construction:* construing.

[22] *Bell:* an inn in Coleman Street used by Cambridge
carriers.   [23] *tester:* sixpence.

[24] *Goose Fair:* annual fair at Stratford le Bow, northeast of
St. Paul's, at which young geese were sold.

[25] *bo . . . goose:* talk (proverbial).

[26] *Maxime:* Q "*Maximus.*"

[27] *L.:* I esteem [you] most highly.   [28] *gear:* stuff.

[29] *Inns of Court:* London law schools.

[30] *French:* Law French, argot of the courts.

[31] *Dugat a whee:* perhaps a phonetic version of "Duw
cadw chi," God preserve you, though the rest of the play's
Welsh is virtually unintelligible.

[32] *Brecknockshire:* county in Wales; "nock" is slang for
female genitals.

[33] *marks:* two-thirds of a pound (13s.4d.).

[34] *shamefast:* bashful.

A brave court spirit makes our virgins quiver
And kiss with trembling thighs. Yet see, she comes, sir.

S. Walt. [*To* MOLL] Why, how now, pretty mistress, now I have caught you. What, can you injure so your time to stray thus from your faithful servant?

Yell. Pish, stop your words, good knight, 'twill make her blush else, which are[35] wound too high for the daughters of the freedom; "honor" and "faithful servant," they are compliments for the worthies of Whitehall or Greenwich;[36] e'en plain, sufficient, 140 subsidy[37] words serves us, sir. And is this gentlewoman your worthy niece?

S. Walt. You may be bold with her on these terms; 'tis she, sir, heir to some nineteen mountains.

Yell. Bless us all, you overwhelm me, sir, with love and riches.

S. Walt. And all as high as Paul's.[38]

Davy. [*Aside*] Here's work, i'faith.

S. Walt. How sayest thou, Davy?   149

Davy. Higher, sir, by far; you cannot see the top of 'em.

Yell. What, man? Maudlin, salute[39] this gentlewoman, our daughter if things hit right.

Enter TOUCHWOOD JUNIOR.

Touch. Jun. [*Aside*] My knight, with a brace of footmen,
Is come, and brought up his ewe mutton[40]
To find a ram at London; I must hasten it
Or else pick[41] a famine. Her blood's[42] mine,
And that's the surest. Well, knight, that choice spoil[43]
Is only kept for me.

[*Speaks to* MOLL *from behind.*]

Moll. Sir?   160

Touch. Jun. Turn not to me till thou mayst lawfully; it but whets my stomach,[44] which is too sharp set[45] already. Read that note carefully.

[*Gives her a letter.*]

Keep me from suspicion still,[46] nor know my zeal but in thy heart. Read and send but thy liking in three words; I'll be at hand to take it.

Yell. [*To* SIR WALTER] Oh, turn, sir, turn.
A poor plain boy, an university man;
Proceeds[47] next Lent to a Bachelor of Art.
He will be called Sir Yellowhammer then   170
Over all Cambridge, and that's half a knight.[48]

Maud. Please you draw near and taste the welcome of the city, sir?

Yell. Come, good Sir Walter, and your virtuous niece here.

S. Walt. 'Tis manners to take[49] kindness.

Yell. Lead 'em in, wife.

S. Walt. Your company, sir?

Yell. I'll give't you instantly.

Touch. Jun. [*Aside*] How strangely busy is the devil and riches.   180
Poor soul, kept in too hard; her mother's eye
Is cruel toward her, being to him.[50]
'Twere a good mirth now to set him awork

To make her wedding ring. I must about it.
Rather than the gain should fall to a stranger,
'Twas honesty in me to enrich my father.

Yell. [*Aside*] The girl is wondrous peevish; I fear nothing
But that she's taken with some other love;
Then all's quite dashed. That must be narrowly looked to;
We cannot be too wary in our children.   190
[*To* TOUCHWOOD JUNIOR] What is't you lack?

Touch. Jun. Oh, nothing now; all that I wish is present.

I would have a wedding ring made for a gentlewoman
With all speed that may be.

Yell.   Of what weight, sir?

Touch. Jun. Of some half ounce; stand fair and comely, with the spark of a diamond. Sir, 'twere pity to lose the least grace.

Yell. Pray, let's see it. Indeed, sir, 'tis a pure one.

Touch. Jun. So is the mistress.

Yell. Have you the wideness of her finger, sir?   200

Touch. Jun. Yes, sure, I think I have her measure about me.
Good faith, 'tis down;[51] I cannot show't you;
I must pull too many things out to be certain.
Let me see—long, and slender, and neatly jointed;
Just such another gentlewoman—that's your daughter, sir?

Yell. And therefore, sir, no gentlewoman.

Touch. Jun. I protest, I never saw two maids handed more alike.
I'll ne'er seek farther, if you'll give me leave, sir.

Yell. If you dare venture by her finger, sir.

Touch. Jun. Aye, and I'll bide all loss, sir.   210

Yell. Say you so, sir? Let's see. Hither, girl.

Touch. Jun. Shall I make bold with your finger, gentlewoman?

Moll. Your pleasure, sir.

Touch. Jun. That fits her to a hair, sir.

Yell. What's your posy[52] now, sir?

Touch. Jun. Mass,[53] that's true. Posy—i'faith, e'en thus, sir:
"Love that's wise blinds parents' eyes."

Yell. How, how? If I may speak without offense, sir, I hold my life—

Touch. Jun. What, sir?   220

Yell. Go to; you'll pardon me?

Touch. Jun. Pardon you? Ay, sir.

---

35 *are:* Not in Q.
36 *Whitehall or Greenwich:* royal palaces.
37 *subsidy:* business.
38 *as . . . Paul's:* the Welsh mountains were proverbially as high as St. Paul's Cathedral.   39 *salute:* kiss.
40 *ewe mutton:* old whore.   41 *pick:* choose.
42 *blood:* sexual passion.   43 *spoil:* Q "spoy."
44 *stomach:* sexual appetite.   45 *sharp set:* eager.
46 *still:* always.   47 *proceeds:* graduates.
48 *half a knight:* entitled to use "sir" (*dominus*) with his last name.   49 *take:* accept.
50 *being to him:* inclining to Whorehound.
51 *down:* in my pocket.   52 *posy:* inscription.
53 *Mass:* By the mass.

Yell. Will you, i'faith?

Touch. Jun. Yes, faith, I will.

Yell. You'll steal away some man's daughter. Am I near you?

Do you turn aside? You gentlemen are mad wags.
I wonder things can be so warily carried
And parents blinded so, but they're served right
That have two eyes and wear [54] so dull a sight.   229

Touch. Jun. [*Aside*] Thy doom take hold of thee.

Yell. Tomorrow noon shall show your ring well done.

Touch. Jun. Being so 'tis soon. Thanks; and your leave, sweet gentlewoman.

                           Exit.

Moll. Sir, you are welcome.

[*Aside*] Oh, were I made of wishes, I went with thee.

Yell. Come, now, we'll see how the rules [55] go within.

Moll. [*Aside*] That robs my joy; there I lose all I win.

                         Exeunt.

[I.ii]

        Enter DAVY *and* ALLWIT *severally.*

Davy. [*Aside*] Honesty wash my eyes! I have spied a wittol.

All. What, Davy Dahumma! welcome from North Wales,
I' faith; and is Sir Walter come?

Davy. New come to town, sir.

All. In to the maids, sweet Davy, and give order his chamber be made ready instantly. My wife's as great as she can wallow,[1] Davy, and longs for nothing but pickled cucumbers and his coming, and now she shall ha't, boy.

Davy. She's sure of them, sir.   10

All. Thy very sight will hold my wife in pleasure
Till the knight come himself. Go in, in, in, Davy.

                    Exit [DAVY].

The founder's come to town. I am like a man
Finding a table furnished to his hand,
As mine is still to me, prays for the founder:
"Bless the right worshipful, the good founder's life."
I thank him, h'as maintained my house this ten years;

Not only keeps my wife, but a[2] keeps me
And all my family;[3] I am at his table;
He gets me all my children and pays the nurse   20
Monthly or weekly, puts me to nothing,
Rent nor church duties, not so much as the scavenger:[4]
The happiest state that ever man was born to.
I walk out in a morning, come to breakfast,
Find excellent cheer, a good fire in winter;
Look in my coalhouse about midsummer eve,
That's full, five or six chaldron[5] new laid up;
Look in my backyard, I shall find a steeple
Made up with Kentish faggots[6] which o'erlooks[7]
The waterhouse[8] and the windmills. I say nothing,   30
But smile and pin[9] the door. When she lies in,
As now she's even upon the point of grunting,
A lady lies not in like her; there's her embossings,
Embroid'rings, spanglings, and I know not what,
As if she lay with all the gaudy shops
In Gresham's Burse[10] about her; then her restoratives,
Able to set up a young pothecary,
And richly stock the foreman of a drugshop,
Her sugar by whole loaves, her wines by rundlets.[11]
I see these things, but like a happy man   40
I pay for none at all, yet fools think's[12] mine.
I have the name, and in his gold I shine.
And where some merchants would in soul kiss hell
To buy a paradise for their wives and dye
Their conscience in the bloods of prodigal heirs
To deck their night-piece,[13] yet all this being done,
Eaten with jealousy to the inmost bone,—
As what affliction nature more constrains
Than feed the wife plump for another's veins?—
These torments stand I freed of: I am as clear   50
From jealousy of a wife as from the charge.
Oh, two miraculous blessings, 'tis the knight
Hath took that labor all out of my hands;
I may sit still and play; he's jealous for me,
Watches her steps, sets spies; I live at ease;
He has both the cost and torment. When the strings
Of his heart frets,[14] I feed, laugh, or sing:

    La dildo,[15] *dildo la dildo, la dildo dildo de dildo.*

           Enter two Servants.

1 Serv. What has he got a singing in his head now?

2 Serv. Now's out of work he falls to making dildoes.

All. Now, sirs, Sir Walter's come.   60

1 Serv. Is our master come?

All. Your master! what am I?

1 Serv. Do not you know, sir?

All. Pray, am not I your master?

1 Serv. Oh, you are but our mistress's husband.

        Enter SIR WALTER *and* DAVY.

All. Ergo,[16] knave, your master.

1 Serv. Negatur argumentum.[17] Here comes Sir Walter. [*Aside to 2* Servant] Now a stands bare as well as we; make the most of him; he's but one pip[18]   69
above a servingman, and so much his horns[19] make him.

S. Walt. How dost, Jack?

All. Proud of your worship's health, sir.

S. Walt. How does your wife?

All. E'en after your own making, sir;
She's a tumbler,[20] i'faith; the nose and belly meets.[21]

S. Walt. They'll part in time again.

All. At the good hour they will, and please your
  worship.

S. Walt. [*To* Servant] Here, sirrah, pull off my
  boots. [*To* ALLWIT] Put on, put on,[22] Jack.   80

All. I thank your kind Worship, sir.

S. Walt. [*To* Servant] Slippers! Heart, you are
sleepy.

All. [*Aside*] The game begins already.

S. Walt. Pish, put on, Jack.

All. [*Aside*] Now I must do it, or he'll be as angry
now as if I had put it on at first bidding.

[*Puts on hat.*]

'Tis but observing, 'tis but observing a man's humor
once, and he may ha' him by the nose all his life.

S. Walt. [*To* Servant] What entertainment has lain
  open here?   90
No strangers in my absence?

1 Serv.   Sure, sir, not any.

All. [*Aside*] His jealousy begins. Am not I happy now
That can laugh inward whilst his marrow melts?

S. Walt. How do you satisfy me?

1 Serv.   Good sir, be
  patient.

S. Walt. For two months absence I'll be satisfied.

1 Serv. No living creature entered—

S. Walt.   Entered? Come,
  swear.

1 Serv. You will not hear me out, sir.

S. Walt.   Yes, I'll hear 't
  out, sir.

1 Serv. Sir, he can tell himself.

S. Walt.   Heart! he can tell?
Do you think I'll trust him? As a usurer
With forfeited lordships.[23] Him! oh, monstrous injury!
Believe him? Can the devil speak ill of darkness?   101
[*To* ALLWIT] What can you say, sir?

All. Of my soul and conscience, sir, she's a wife as
honest of her body to me as any lord's proud lady can be.

S. Walt. Yet, by your leave, I heard you were once
offering to go to bed with her.

All. No, I protest, sir.

S. Walt. Heart, if you do, you shall take all. I'll
marry.

All. Oh, I beseech you, sir.   110

S. Walt. [*Aside*] That wakes the slave and keeps his
flesh in awe.

All. [*Aside*] I'll stop that gap.
Where'er I find it open, I have poisoned
His hopes in marriage already—
Some old rich widows and some landed virgins,

Enter two Children [WAT *and* NICK].

And I'll fall to work still before I'll lose him;
He's yet too sweet to part from.

Wat. [*To* ALLWIT] God-den,[24] father.

All. Ha, villain, peace!   120

Nick. God-den, father.

All. Peace, bastard. [*Aside*] Should he hear 'em!
[*Aloud*] These are two foolish children; they do not
know the gentleman that sits there.

S. Walt. O Wat; how dost, Nick? Go to school?
Ply your books, boys, ha?

All. Where's your legs,[25] whoresons? They should
Kneel indeed if they could say their prayers.

S. Walt. [*Aside*] Let me see; stay;
How shall I dispose of these two brats now   130
When I am married? For they must not mingle
Amongst my children that I get in wedlock;
'Twill make foul work, that, and raise many storms.
I'll bind Wat prentice to a goldsmith, my father
  Yellowhammer,
As fit as can be; Nick with some vintner. Good,
  goldsmith
And vintner; there will be wine in bowls, i'faith.

Enter ALLWIT'S *Wife.*

Mrs. All. Sweet knight,
Welcome. I have all my longings now in town.
Now welcome the good hour.

S. Walt. How cheers my mistress?   140

Mrs. All. Made lightsome e'en by him that made me
  heavy.

S. Walt. Methinks she shows gallantly, like a moon
at full, sir.

All. True, and if she bear a male child, there's the
man in the moon, sir.

S. Walt. 'Tis but the boy in the moon yet, goodman
calf.[26]

All. There was a man; the boy had never been there
else.

S. Walt. It shall be yours, sir.   150

All. No, by my troth, I'll swear it's none of mine;
let him that got it keep it.
[*Aside*] Thus do I rid myself of fear.
Lie soft, sleep hard, drink wine, and eat good cheer.

[*Exeunt.*]

ACT TWO

SCENE ONE

Enter TOUCHWOOD SENIOR *and his* Wife.

Mrs. Touch. 'Twill be so tedious, sir, to live from
  you,
But that necessity must be obeyed.

---

[20] *tumbler:* acrobat, athletic and sexual.

[21] *nose . . . meets:* as a result of pregnancy.

[22] *Put on, put on:* Q "Put on, but on"; put on your hat
(Allwit has removed his hat as a sign of respect; men normally wore hats indoors).

[23] *forfeited lordship:* knighthoods given to a usurer as
security for loans and forfeited when the loan is not repaid
(an imaginary situation).

[24] *God-den:* Good evening, the afternoon greeting.

[25] *legs:* bows.

[26] *calf:* blockhead, with play on "mooncalf," false
pregnancy.

Touch. Sen. I would it might not, wife; the
          tediousness
Will be the most part mine, that understand
The blessings I have in thee; so to part,
That drives the torment to a knowing heart.
But, as thou say'st, we must give way to need
And live awhile asunder. Our desires
Are both too fruitful for our barren fortunes.
How adverse runs the destiny of some creatures: 10
Some only can get riches and no children;
We only can get children and no riches.
Then 'tis the prudent'st part to check our wills[1]
And, till our state rise, make our bloods lie still.
Life,[2] every year a child, and some years two,
Besides drinking abroad,[3] that's never reckoned.
This gear[4] will not hold out.
     Mrs. Touch.   Sir, for a time
I'll take the courtesy of my uncle's house,
If you be pleased to like on 't, till prosperity
Look with a friendly eye upon our states.   20
     Touch. Sen. Honest wife, I thank thee; I ne'er knew
The perfect treasure thou brought'st with thee more
Than at this instant minute. A man's happy
When he's at poorest that has matched his soul
As rightly as his body. Had I married
A sensual fool now, as 'tis hard to 'scape it
'Mongst gentlewomen of our time, she would ha'
          hanged
About my neck and never left her hold
Till she had kissed me into wanton businesses,
Which at the waking of my better judgment   30
I should have cursed most bitterly,
And laid a thicker vengeance on my act
Than misery of the birth, which were enough
If it were born to greatness, whereas mine
Is sure of beggary, though it were got in wine.
Fullness of joy showeth the goodness in thee;
Thou art a matchless wife. Farewell, my joy.
     Mrs. Touch. I shall not want[5] your sight?
     Touch. Sen.   I'll see thee
          often,
Talk in mirth, and play at kisses with thee,
Anything, wench, but what may beget beggars.   40
There I give o'er the set,[6] throw down the cards,

And dare not take them up.
     Mrs. Touch.   Your will be mine, sir.
                                        Exit.
     Touch. Sen. This does not only make her honesty
          perfect,
But her discretion, and approves[7] her judgment.
Had her desires been wanton, they'd been blameless
In being lawful ever, but of all creatures
I hold that wife a most unmatchèd treasure
That can unto her fortunes fix her pleasure
And not unto her blood. This is like wedlock;
The feast of marriage is not lust but love   50
And care of the estate. When I please blood,
Merely I sing[8] and suck out others'; then
'Tis many a wise man's fault, but of all men
I am the most unfortunate in that game
That ever pleased both genders: I ne'er played yet
Under a bastard;[9] the poor wenches curse me
To the pit[10] where'er I come; they were ne'er served
          so,
But used to have more words than one to a bargain.
I have such a fatal finger in such business
I must forth with't, chiefly for country wenches,   60
For every harvest I shall hinder haymaking.

          Enter a [Country] Wench with a child.

I had no less than seven lay in[11] last progress,[12]
Within three weeks of one another's time.
     C. Wen. O snap-hance,[13] have I found you?
     Touch. Sen.   How
          snap-hance?

               [*The* Wench *shows the child.*]

     C. Wen. Do you see your workmanship?
Nay, turn not from it, nor offer to escape, for if you
          do
I'll cry it through the streets and follow you.
Your name may well be called Touchwood. A pox on
          you,
You do but touch and take; thou hast undone me.
I was a maid before; I can bring a certificate for it   70
From both the churchwardens.[14]
     Touch. Sen. I'll have the parson's hand too, or I'll
not yield to't.
     C. Wen. Thou shalt have more, thou villain; nothing
grieves me but Ellen, my poor cousin in Derbyshire;
thou hast cracked her marriage quite. She'll have a
bout[15] with thee.
     Touch. Sen. Faith, when she will, I'll have a bout[16]
          with her.
     C. Wen. A law bout, sir, I mean.
     Touch. Sen. True, lawyers use such bouts as other
          men do,   80
And if that be all thy grief, I'll tender her a husband.
I keep of purpose two or three gulls[17] in pickle[18]
To eat such mutton[19] with, and she shall choose one.
Do but in courtesy, faith, wench, excuse me
Of this half yard of flesh in which I think it wants
A nail[20] or two.
     C. Wen.   No, thou shalt find, villain,
It hath right shape and all the nails it should have.

II.i.
[1] *wills:* sexual desires.   [2] *Life:* By God's life.
[3] *abroad:* away from home.   [4] *gear:* business, genitals.
[5] *want:* lack.   [6] *give . . . set:* abandon the match.
[7] *approves:* proves.
[8] *sing:* have sexual intercourse with.
[9] *under a bastard:* so that I ended with less than a
bastard.
[10] *pit:* hell, with a sexual connotation (like other words in
the speech); the wenches are not accustomed to becoming
pregnant on a first encounter.
[11] *lay in:* were confined for childbirth.
[12] *progress:* royal tour.   [13] *snap-hance:* flintlock.
[14] *churchwardens:* lay parish officials who could issue
certificates of good conduct.   [15] *bout:* law suit.
[16] *bout:* sexual encounter.   [17] *gulls:* fools.
[18] *in pickle:* ready; poxed.   [19] *mutton:* whore.
[20] *nail:* cloth measure; fingernail (lacking in syphilitic
children).

Touch. Sen. Faith, I am poor; do a charitable deed,
   wench;
I am a younger brother and have nothing.   90
   C. Wen. Nothing! thou hast too much, thou lying
      villain,
Unless thou wert more than thankful.
   Touch. Sen.   I have no
      dwelling;
I brake up house but this morning. Pray thee, pity me;
I am a good fellow, faith, have been too kind
To people of your gender; if I ha't
Without my belly,²¹ none of your sex shall want it.
[*Aside*] That word has been of force to move a woman.
[*To her*] There's tricks enough to rid thy hand on't,
      wench:
Some rich man's porch, tomorrow before day
Or else anon²² i'the evening, twenty devices.   100
Here's all I have, i'faith;

                                   [*Gives money.*]

                take purse and all,
[*Aside*] And would I were rid of all the ware i'the shop
      so.
   C. Wen. Where I find manly dealings, I am pitiful;
This shall not trouble you.
   Touch. Sen.   And I protest, wench,
The next I'll keep myself.
   C. Wen.   Soft, let it be got first.
[*Aside*] This is the fifth; if e'er I venture more,
Where now I go for a maid, may I ride for²³ a whore.
                                          Exit.
   Touch. Sen. What shift she'll make now with this
      piece of flesh
In this strict time of Lent, I cannot imagine.
Flesh dare not peep abroad now; I have known   110
This city now above this seven years,
But, I protest, in better state of government
I never knew it yet, nor ever heard of;
There has been more religious, wholesome laws
In the half circle of a year erected
For common good than memory ever knew of,

            Enter SIR OLIVER KIX *and his* LADY.

Setting apart corruption of promoters²⁴
And other poisonous officers that infect
And with a venomous breath taint every goodness. 119
   L. Kix. Oh, that e'er I was begot or bred or born.
   S. Ol. Be content, sweet wife.
   Touch. Sen.[*Aside*]   What's here to do
      now?
I hold my life she's in deep passion
For the imprisonment of veal and mutton
Now kept in garrets, weeps for some calf's-head²⁵
      now;
Methinks her husband's head might serve with bacon.

            Enter TOUCHWOOD JUNIOR.

   L. Kix. Hist.
   S. Ol. Patience, sweet wife.
   Touch. Jun. Brother, I have sought you strangely.
   Touch. Sen. Why, what's the business?

Touch. Jun. With all speed thou canst, procure a
   license for me.   130
   Touch. Sen. How, a license?
   Touch. Jun. Cud's foot,²⁶ she's lost else; I shall miss
      her ever.
   Touch. Sen. Nay, sure thou shalt not miss so fair a
      mark
For thirteen shillings fourpence.

            [TOUCHWOOD SENIOR *listens behind.*]

   Touch. Jun.   Thanks by hundreds.
                                          Exit.
   S. Ol. Nay, pray thee, cease; I'll be at more cost
      yet;
Thou knowst we are rich enough.
   L. Kix.   All but in blessings,
And there the beggar goes beyond us. Oh, oh, oh,
To be seven years a wife and not a child,
Oh, not a child.
   S. Ol.   Sweet wife, have patience.
   L. Kix. Can any woman have a greater cut?   140
   S. Ol. I know 'tis great, but what of that, wife?
I cannot do withal;²⁷ there's things making
By thine own doctor's advice at pothecaries.
I spare for nothing, wife; no, if the price
Were forty marks a spoonful,
I'd give a thousand pound to purchase fruitfulness.
                            [*Exit* TOUCHWOOD SENIOR.]
'Tis but 'bating so many good works
In the erecting of bridewells²⁸ and spittlehouses,²⁹
And fetch it up again; for, having none,
I mean to make good deeds my children.   150
   L. Kix. Give me but those good deeds, and I'll find
      children.
   S. Ol. Hang thee, thou hast had too many.
   L. Kix.   Thou liest,
      brevity.
   S. Ol. Oh, horrible, dar'st thou call me brevity?
Dar'st thou be so short with me?
   L. Kix.   Thou deservest worse.
Think but upon the goodly lands and livings
That's kept back through want on't.
   S. Ol.   Talk not on't, pray
      thee;
Thou'lt make me play the woman and weep too.
   L. Kix. 'Tis our dry barrenness puffs up Sir Walter;
None gets by your not-getting but that knight.   159
He's made by th' means and fats his fortunes shortly
In a great dowry with a goldsmith's daughter.
   S. Ol. They may be all deceived;
Be but you patient, wife.
   L. Kix. I have suffered a long time.

---

²¹ *without my belly:* i.e., not already eaten, with double
entendre.   ²² *anon:* immediately.
²³ *ride for:* be carted in punishment for being.
²⁴ *promoters:* informers.
²⁵ *calf's-head:* with second meaning of fool.
²⁶ *Cud's foot:* By God's foot.
²⁷ *cut . . . withal:* Sir Oliver interprets "cut" with a
sexual connotation.
²⁸ *bridewells:* houses of correction for prostitutes.
²⁹ *spittlehouses:* hospitals for venereal diseases.

S. Ol. Suffer thy heart out; a pox suffer thee.

L. Kix. Nay, thee, thou desertless slave.

S. Ol. Come, come, I ha' done.

You'll to the gossiping [30] of Mr. Allwit's child?

L. Kix. Yes, to my much joy.

Everyone gets before me: there's my sister   170

Was married but at Barthol'mew-Eve last, [31]

And she can have two children at a birth;

Oh, one of them, one of them would ha' served my
    turn.

S. Ol. Sorrow consume thee; thou art still crossing
    me,

And know'st my nature.—

Enter a Maid.

Maid. O mistress! [*Aside*] Weeping or railing,

That's our house harmony.

L. Kix. What say'st, jug?

Maid. The sweetest news.

L. Kix. What is't, wench?   180

Maid. Throw down your doctor's drugs;

They're all but heretics. I bring certain remedy

That has been taught and proved and never failed.

S. Ol. Oh, that, that, that or nothing.

Maid. There's a gentleman—

I haply [32] have his name too—that has got

Nine children by one water [33] that he useth;

It never misses; they come so fast upon him

He was fain to give it over.

L. Kix. His name, sweet jug?   190

Maid. One Master Touchwood, a fine gentleman.

But run behindhand much with getting children.

S. Ol. Is't possible?

Maid. Why, sir, he'll undertake,

Using that water, within fifteen year,

For all your wealth, to make you a poor man,

You shall so swarm with children.

S. Ol. I'll venture that, i'faith.

L. Kix. That shall you, husband.

Maid. But I must tell you first, he's very dear.   200

S. Ol. No matter; what serves wealth for?

L. Kix. True sweet husband,

There's land to come. Put case his water stands me

In some five hundred pound a pint;

'Twill fetch a thousand and a kersten [34] soul,

And that's worth all, sweet husband.

S. Ol. I'll about it. [35]

                                  Exeunt.

---

[30] *gossíping:* christening.

[31] *Barthol'mew's-Eve:* August 23, less than nine months before Lent, so that the marriage was convenient.

[32] *haply:* by chance.   [33] *water:* potion.

[34] *kersten:* Christian.

[35] *I'll about it:* Q prints as next-to-last line of Lady Kix's speech.

II.ii.

[1] *gossips:* godparents, women friends.

[2] *presently:* immediately.   [3] *run ... tailor:* obscure.

[4] *buss:* kiss.

[5] *knocker:* good-looking girl; notable performer of sexual act.   [6] *spoon-meat:* baby food.

[7] *Wipe your mouth:* Make a fool of yourself.

[II.ii]

Enter Allwit.

All. I'll go bid gossips [1] presently [2] myself.

That's all the work I'll do, nor need I stir,

But that it is my pleasure to walk forth

And air myself a little; I am tied to nothing

In this business; what I do is merely recreation,

Not constraint.

Here's running to and fro, nurse upon nurse,

Three charwomen, besides maids and neighbors'
    children.

Fie, what a trouble have I rid my hands on;

It makes me sweat to think on't.   10

Enter Sir Walter Whorehound.

S. Walt. How now, Jack?

All. I am going to bid gossips for your worship's
    child, sir;

A goodly girl, i'faith; give you joy on her;

She looks as if she had two thousand pound

To her portion and run away with a tailor; [3]

A fine plump black-eyed slut;

Under correction, sir,

I take delight to see her. Nurse!

Enter Dry Nurse.

Dry. Do you call, sir?

All. I call not you; I call the wet nurse hither.   20

                            Exit [Dry Nurse].

Give me the wet nurse.

Enter Wet Nurse [*with* Child].

                   Ay, 'tis thou.

Come hither, come hither,

Let's see her once again. I cannot choose

But buss [4] her thrice an hour.

Wet. You may be proud on't, sir;

'Tis the best piece of work that e'er you did.

All. Think'st thou so, nurse? What sayest to Wat
    and Nick?

Wet. They're pretty children both, but here's a
    wench

Will be a knocker. [5]

                [Allwit *plays with the child.*]

All. Pup—say'st thou me so?—Pup, little countess;

Faith, sir, I thank your worship for this girl   31

Ten thousand times and upward.

S. Walt. I am glad I have her for you, sir.

All. Here, take her in, nurse; wipe her, and give her
    spoon-meat. [6]

Wet. [*Aside*] Wipe your mouth, [7] sir.   *Exit.*

All. And now about these gossips.

S. Walt. Get but two; I'll stand for one myself.

All. To your own child, sir?

S. Walt. The better policy; it prevents suspicion;

'Tis good to play with rumor at all weapons.   40

All. Troth, I commend your care, sir; 'tis a thing

That I should ne'er have thought on.

S. Walt. [*Aside*]   The more slave;

When man turns base, out goes his soul's pure flame;
The fat of ease o'erthrows the eyes of shame.
　All. I am studying who to get for godmother
Suitable to your worship. Now I ha' thought on't.
　S. Walt. I'll ease you of that care and please myself
　　in't.
[*Aside*] My love, the goldsmith's daughter; if I send,
Her father will command her.—Davy Dahumma.

Enter DAVY.

　All. I'll fit your worship then with a male partner.
　S. Walt. What is he?   51
　All. A kind proper gentleman, brother to Mr.
　　Touchwood.
　S. Walt. I know Touchwood. Has he a brother
　　living?
　All. A neat[8] bachelor.
　S. Walt. Now we know him, we'll make shift with
　　him.
Dispatch; the time draws near. Come hither, Davy.
　　　　　　　　　　　　　　　　Exit [*with* DAVY].
　All. In troth, I pity him; he ne'er stands still;
Poor knight, what pains he takes: sends this way one,
That way another, has not an hour's leisure;
I would not have thy toil for all thy pleasure.   60

Enter two Promoters.

Ha, how now, what are these that stand so close
At the street corner, pricking up their ears
And snuffing up their noses like rich men's dogs
When the first course goes in? By the mass, promoters.
'Tis so, I hold my life, and planted there
To arrest the dead corpse of poor calves and sheep
Like ravenous creditors that will not suffer
The bodies of their poor departed debtors
To go to th' grave, but e'en in death to vex
And stay the corpse with bills of Middlesex.[9]   70
This Lent will fat the whoresons up with sweetbreads
And lard their whores with lamb-stones;[10] what their
　　golls[11]
Can clutch goes presently to their Molls and Dolls.
The bawds will be so fat with what they earn
Their chins[12] will hang like udders by Easter-eve,
And, being stroked, will give the milk of witches.
How did the mongrels hear my wife lies in?
Well, I may baffle 'em gallantly. [*To them*] By your
　　favor, gentlemen,
I am a stranger both unto the city
And to her carnal strictness.
　1 Prom. 　　　　Good; your will, sir?   80
　All. Pray tell me where one dwells that kills this
　　Lent?
　1 Prom. How, kills? [*Aside to the other*] Come hither,
　　Dick:
A bird, a bird.
　2 Prom. 　　What is't that you would have?
　All. Faith, any flesh,
But I long especially for veal and green sauce.[13]
　1 Prom. Green goose,[14] you shall be sauced.[15]
　All. I have a scornful stomach; no fish will be
　　admitted.

　1 Prom. Not this Lent, sir?
　All. Lent? What cares colon here for Lent?
　1 Prom. You say well, sir;   90
Good reason that the colon of a gentleman,
As you were lately pleased to term your worship, sir,
Should be fulfilled with answerable food
To sharpen blood, delight health, and tickle nature.
Were you directed hither to this street, sir?
　All. That I was, marry.
　2 Prom. 　　　　　And the butcher, belike,
Should kill and sell close[16] in some upper room?
　All. Some apple-loft, as I take it, or a coalhouse,
I know not which, i'faith.
　2 Prom. 　　　　　Either will serve;
This butcher shall kiss Newgate[17] 'less he turn up the
Bottom of the pocket of his apron.[18]   101
You go to seek him?
　All. 　　　　Where you shall not find him;
I'll buy, walk by your noses with my flesh,
Sheep-biting mongrels, hand-basket freebooters.[19]
My wife lies in.—A foutra[20] for promoters.
　　　　　　　　　　　　　　　　　　　　Exit.
　1 Prom. That shall not serve your turn. What a
　　rogue's this.
How cunningly he came over us.

Enter a Man *with meat in a basket.*

　2 Prom. 　　　　　Hush't; stand close.
　Man. I have 'scaped well thus far; they say the
　　knaves
Are wondrous hot and busy.
　1 Prom. 　　　　By your leave, sir,
We must see what you have under your cloak there.
　Man. Have? I have nothing.
　1 Prom. 　　　　　No? Do you tell us
　　that?   111
What makes this lump stick out then? We must see,
　　sir.
　Man. What will you see, sir? A pair of sheets and
　　two
Of my wife's foul smocks going to the washers?
　2 Prom. Oh, we love that sight well; you cannot
　　please us better.

[*Finds meat in basket.*]

What, do you gull us? Call you these shirts and smocks?
　Man. Now a pox choke you.
You have cozened me and five of my wife's kindred

---

　[8] *neat:* elegantly dressed.
　[9] *bills of Middlesex:* arrests on trumped-up charges outside of jurisdiction of London.
　[10] *lamb-stones:* lamb testicles, believed aphrodisiac.
　[11] *golls:* hands.
　[12] *chins:* Bawds were emblematized with double chins;
witches were thought able to give milk to the devil.
　[13] *veal and green sauce:* Both are cant expressions for the
gullible. 　　　　　　　　　　　[14] *green goose:* fool.
　[15] *sauced:* made to pay dearly. 　　[16] *close:* secretly.
　[17] *Newgate:* gLondon ate used as prison.
　[18] *turn . . . apron:* pay a bribe.
　[19] *hand-basket freebooters:* pirates of shopping baskets.
　[20] *foutra:* obscene oath (Fr. *foutre,* "sexual act").

Of a good dinner; we must make it up now
With herrings and milk-pottage.   120
                                                            Exit.

   1 Prom. 'Tis all veal.
   2 Prom. All veal! pox, the worse luck; I promised
faithfully to send this morning a fat quarter of lamb to a
kind gentlewoman in Turnbull Street[21] that longs; and
how I'm crossed.
   1 Prom. Let's share this and see what hap comes
     next, then.

Enter Another *with a basket.*

   2 Prom. Agreed. Stand close again, another booty.
What's he?
   1 Prom. Sir, by your favor.
   Man.   Meaning me, sir?
   1 Prom. Good Master Oliver, cry thee mercy, i'faith.
What hast thou there?   130
   Man. A rack[22] of mutton, sir, and half a lamb;
You know my mistress's diet.
   1 Prom. Go, go, we see thee not; away, keep close.
[*To* Second Promoter] Heart, let him pass. Thou'lt
     never have the wit
To know our benefactors.
   2 Prom.   I have forgot him.
   1 Prom. 'Tis Master Beggarland's man, the wealthy
     merchant
That is in fee[23] with us.
   2 Prom.   Now I have a feeling of him.
   1 Prom. You know he purchased[24] the whole Lent
     together,
Gave us ten groats apiece on Ash Wednesday.
   2 Prom.   True, true.

Enter a [Country] Wench *with a basket and a child
in it under a loin of mutton.*

   1 Prom. A wench.
   2 Prom.   Why, then, stand close indeed.
   C. Wen. [*Aside*] Women had need of wit if they'll
     shift here,   141
And she that hath wit may shift[25] anywhere.
   1 Prom. Look, look; poor fool,
She has left the rump uncovered too,
More to betray her; this is like a murd'rer
That will outface the deed with a bloody band.[26]
   2 Prom. What time of the year is't, sister?
   C. Wen. O sweet gentlemen, I am a poor servant;
Let me go.
   1 Prom. You shall, wench, but this must stay with us.
   C. Wen. Oh, you undo me, sir;   151

---

[21] *Turnbull Street:* notorious for whores and thieves.
[22] *rack:* neck.   [23] *in fee:* in league.
[24] *purchased:* bought protection for.
[25] *shift:* make a living; palm something off on someone.
[26] *band:* collar.   [27] *politic:* scheming.
[28] *L.:* First of all.
[29] *sugar-sops:* bread soaked in sweetened liquid.
[30] *tallow:* suet for candles.   [31] *Checker:* an inn.
[32] *Queenhive:* Queenhithe, busy quay on north bank of
Thames.   [33] *young flood:* rising tide.
[34] *Brainford:* Brentford, eight miles upstream on north
bank of the Thames.

'Tis for a wealthy gentlewoman that takes physic, sir;
The doctor does allow my mistress mutton.
Oh, as you tender the dear life of a gentlewoman;
I'll bring my master to you; he shall show you
A true authority from the higher powers,
And I'll run every foot.
   2 Prom. Well, leave your basket, then,
And run and spare not.
   C. Wen.   Will you swear then to me
To keep it till I come?
   1 Prom.   Now, by this light I will.   160
   C. Wen. What say you, gentleman?
   2 Prom.   What a strange
     wench 'tis.
Would we might perish else.
   C. Wen.   Nay, then, I run, sir.
                                                            Exit.
   1 Prom. And ne'er return, I hope.
   2 Prom.   A politic[27]
     baggage;
She makes us swear to keep it.
I prithee, look what market she hath made.
   1 Prom. Imprimis,[28] sir, a good fat loin of mutton.
What comes next under this cloth?
Now for a quarter of lamb.
   2 Prom. Not for a shoulder of mutton.
   1 Prom. Done.   170
   2 Prom. Why done, sir?
   1 Prom. By the mass, I feel I have lost;
'Tis of more weight, i'faith.
   2 Prom. Some loin of veal?
   1 Prom. No, faith, here's a lamb's head;
I feel that plainly; why, I'll yet win my wager.
   2 Prom. Ha?
   1 Prom. 'Swounds, what's here?
   2 Prom. A child.
   1 Prom. A pox of all dissembling cunning whores.
   2 Prom. Here's an unlucky breakfast.   181
   1 Prom. What shall's do?
   2 Prom. The quean made us swear to keep it, too.
   1 Prom. We might leave it else.
   2 Prom. Villainous strange.
Life, had she none to gull but poor promoters
That watch hard for a living?
   1 Prom. Half our gettings must run in sugar-sops[29]
And nurses' wages now, besides many a pound of soap
And tallow;[30] we have need to get loins of mutton still
To save suet to change for candles.   191
   2 Prom. Nothing mads me but this was a lamb's head
with you; you felt it. She has made calves' heads of us.
   1 Prom. Prithee, no more on't;
There's time to get it up; it is not come
To Mid-Lent Sunday yet.
   2 Prom. I am so angry, I'll watch no more today.
   1 Prom. Faith, nor I neither.
   2 Prom. Why, then, I'll make a motion.
   1 Prom. Well, what is't?   200
   2 Prom. Let's e'en go to the Checker[31] at Queenhive[32] and roast the loin of mutton till young flood;[33]
then send the child to Brainford.[34]
                                                            [*Exeunt.*]

[II.iii]

Enter ALLWIT *in one of* SIR WALTER's *suits and*
DAVY *trussing*[1] *him.*

All. 'Tis a busy day at our house, Davy.
Davy. Always the kurs'ning[2] day, sir.
All. Truss, truss me, Davy.
Davy. [*Aside*] No matter and[3] you were hanged, sir.
All. How does this suit fit me, Davy?
Davy. Excellent neatly; my master's things were
ever fit for you, sir, even to a hair, you know.
All. Thou hast hit it right, Davy.
We ever jumped in one[4] this ten years, Davy,

Enter a Servant *with a box.*

So well said.—What art thou?   10
Serv. Your comfit[5]-maker's man, sir.
All. O sweet youth, into the nurse quick;
Quick, 'tis time, i'faith; your mistress will be here?
Serv. She was setting forth, sir.

Enter two Puritans.

All. Here comes our gossips now. Oh, I shall have
such kissing work today. Sweet Mistress Underman,
welcome, i'faith.
1 Pur. Give you joy of your fine girl, sir;
Grant that her education may be pure
And become one of the faithful.   20
All. Thanks to your sisterly wishes, Mistress
Underman.
2 Pur. Are any of the brethren's wives yet come?
All. There are some wives within, and some at home.
1 Pur. Verily, thanks, sir.
                                    Exeunt [Puritans].
All.   Verily, you are an ass,
forsooth.
I must fit all these times,[6] or else there's no music.

Enter two Gossips.

Here comes a friendly and familiar pair;
Now I like these wenches well.
1 Gos.   How dost, sirrah?
All. Faith, well, I thank you, neighbor, and how
dost thou?
2 Gos. Want nothing but such getting, sir, as thine.
All. My gettings, wench, they are poor.
1 Gos.   Fie, that
thou'lt say so;   30
Th'ast as fine children as a man can get.
Davy. [*Aside*] Aye, as a man can get, and that's my
master.
All. They are pretty, foolish things, put to making
In minutes; I ne'er stand long about 'em.
Will you walk in, wenches?
                                  [*Exeunt* Gossips.]

Enter TOUCHWOOD JUNIOR *and* MOLL.

Touch. Jun. The happiest meeting that our souls
could wish for. Here's the ring ready; I am beholding
unto your father's haste; h'as kept his hour.
Moll. He never kept it better.

Enter SIR WALTER WHOREHOUND.

Touch. Jun. Back; be silent.   40
S. Walt. Mistress and partner, I will put you both
into one cup.
Davy. [*Aside*] Into one cup, most proper:
A fitting compliment for a goldsmith's daughter.
All. Yes, sir, that's he must be your worship's
partner
In this day's business, Master Touchwood's brother.
S. Walt. I embrace your acquaintance, sir.
Touch. Jun. It vows your service, sir.
S. Walt. It's near high time; come, Master Allwit.
All. Ready, sir.   50
S. Walt. Will 't please you walk?
Touch. Jun. Sir, I obey your time.
                                    Ex[*eunt*].

[II.iv]

Enter Midwife *with the child and the* Gossips *to the
kurs'ning* [*with* MAUDLIN *and the two*
Puritans].

1 Gos. [*Offering precedence*] Good Mistress
Yellowhammer.
Maud. In faith, I will not.
1 Gos. Indeed, it shall be yours.
Maud. I have sworn, i'faith.
1 Gos. I'll stand still, then.
Maud. So will you let the child go without
company
And make me forsworn.
1 Gos. You are such another creature.
                    [*Exeunt* MAUDLIN *and* First Gossip.]
2 Gos. Before me? I pray, come down a little.
3 Gos. Not a whit; I hope I know my place.   10
2 Gos. Your place? Great wonder, sure; are you any
better than a comfit-maker's wife?
3 Gos. And that's as good at all times as a pothecary's.
2 Gos. Ye lie. Yet I forbear you too.
                    [*Exeunt* Second *and* Third Gossips.]
1 Pur. Come, sweet sister, we go in unity, and show
the fruits of peace like children of the spirit.
2 Pur. I love lowliness.
                                  [*Exeunt* Puritans.]
4 Gos. True, so say I; though they strive more,
There comes as proud[1] behind as goes before.
5 Gos. Every inch, i'faith.   20
                                    Ex[*eunt*].

II.iii.
  [1] *trussing*: tying the "points" of his breeches to his
doublet.   [2] *kurs'ning*: christening.
  [3] *and*: if.   [4] *jumped in one*: agreed.
  [5] *comfit*: sweet made of fruit preserved with sugar.
  [6] *fit . . . times*: agree with their music, accommodate to
these people.

II.iv.
  [1] *proud*: with second meaning, sexually excited, in next
line.

ACT THREE

SCENE ONE

Enter TOUCHWOOD JUNIOR *and a*
Parson.

Touch. Jun. O sir, if ever you felt the force of love,
pity it in me.

Pars. Yes, though I ne'er was married, sir,
I have felt the force of love from good men's daughters,
And some that will be maids yet three years hence.
Have you got a license?

Touch. Jun. Here, 'tis ready, sir.

Pars. That's well.

Touch. Jun. The ring and all things perfect; she'll
steal hither.

Pars. She shall be welcome, sir. I'll not be long　　10
A-clapping you together.

Enter MOLL *and* TOUCHWOOD SENIOR.

Touch. Jun. Oh, here she's come, sir.

Pars. What's he?

Touch. Jun. My honest brother.

Touch. Sen. Quick, make haste, sirs.

Moll. You must dispatch with all the speed you can,
for I shall be missed straight; I made hard shift for this
small time I have.

Pars. Then I'll not linger;
Place that ring upon her finger;　　　　　　　　　20
This the finger plays the part
Whose master vein shoots from the heart.[1]
Now join hands.

Enter YELLOWHAMMER *and* SIR WALTER.

Yell. Which I will sever;
And so ne'er again meet never.

Moll. Oh, we are betrayed.

Touch. Jun. Hard fate.

S. Walt. I am struck with wonder.

Yell. Was this the politic fetch,[2] thou mystical[3]
baggage,
Thou disobedient strumpet?　　　　　　　　　30
[*To* SIR WALTER] And were you so wise to send for
her to such an end?

S. Walt. Now I disclaim the end; you'll make me
mad.

Yell. And what are you, sir?

Touch. Jun. And you cannot see with those two
glasses, put on a pair more.

Yell. I dreamed of anger still; here, take your ring,
sir.

[*Takes ring from* MOLL's *finger.*]

Ha, this? Life, 'tis the same.
Abominable!
Did not I sell this ring?

Touch. Jun. I think you did; you received money
for 't.　　　　　　　　　　　　　　　　40

Yell. Heart, hark you, knight,
Here's no inconscionable villainy:
Set me a-work to make the wedding ring
And come with an intent to steal my daughter.
Did ever runaway match it?

S. Walt. 'This your brother, sir?

Touch. Sen. He can tell that as well as I.

Yell. The very posy mocks me to my face:
Love that's wise blinds parents' eyes.
I thank your wisdom for blinding of us;　　　50
We have good hope to recover our sight shortly.
In the meantime I will lock up this baggage
As carefully as my gold; she shall see as little sun
If a close room or so can keep her from the light on't.

Moll. O sweet father, for love's sake, pity me.

Yell. Away.

Moll. [*To* TOUCHWOOD JUNIOR] Farewell, sir; all
content bless thee,
And take this for comfort.
Though violence keep me, thou canst lose me never;
I am ever thine although we part forever.　　60

Yell. Ay, we shall part you, minx.

　　　　　　　　　　　　　　Exit [*with* MOLL].

S. Walt. [*To* TOUCHWOOD JUNIOR] Your
acquaintance, sir, came very lately,
Yet it came too soon;
I must hereafter know you for no friend,
But one that I must shun like pestilence
Or the disease of lust.

Touch. Jun. Like enough, sir, you ha' ta'en me at the
worst time for words that e'er ye picked out; faith, do
not wrong me, sir.

　　　　　　　　　　　　　　Exit [*with* Parson].

Touch. Sen. Look after him and spare not; there he
walks　　　　　　　　　　　　　　　　70
That never yet received baffling;[4] you're blest
More than e'er I knew; go, take your rest.

　　　　　　　　　　　　　　　　　　Exit.

S. Walt. I pardon you; you are both losers.

　　　　　　　　　　　　　　　　　　Exit.

[III.ii]

A bed thrust out upon the stage, ALLWIT's *Wife in it.*
Enter all the Gossips [*with* MAUDLIN, LADY KIX,
Dry Nurse *with* Child, *and the* Puritans].

1 Gos. How is't, woman? We have brought you
home
A kersen soul.

Mrs. All. Ay, I thank your pains.

1 Pur. And verily well kursened, i' the right way,
Without idolatry or superstition,
After the pure manner of Amsterdam.[1]

Mrs. All. Sit down, good neighbors.—Nurse.

Dry.　　　　　　　　　　　　　　　　At
hand, forsooth.

III.i.
[1] *Whose . . . heart:* The third finger of the left hand was
supposed to be a direct tributary of the "master vein" of the
heart.　　　[2] *fetch:* trick.　　　[3] *mystical:* secret.
[4] *baffling:* insult.

III.ii.
[1] *Amsterdam:* Puritan center.

Mrs. All. Look, they have all low stools.
Dry.   They have,
    forsooth.
2 Gos. Bring the child hither, nurse. How say you
now, gossip, is't not a chopping[2] girl, so like the father?
3 Gos. As if it had been spit out of his mouth,   10
Eyed, nosed, and browed as like a girl as can be;
Only indeed it has the mother's mouth.
2 Gos. The mother's mouth up and down,[3] up and
    down.
3 Gos. 'Tis a large child; she's but a little woman.
1 Pur. No, believe me, a very spiny[4] creature, but all
    heart,
Well mettled,[5] like the faithful, to endure
Her tribulation here and raise up seed.
2 Gos. She had a sore labor on't, I warrant you;
You can tell, neighbor.
3 Gos.   Oh, she had great speed.[6]
We were afraid once,   20
But she made us all have joyful hearts again.
'Tis a good soul, i'faith;
The midwife found her a most cheerful daughter.
1 Pur. 'Tis the spirit; the sisters are all like her.

> *Enter* SIR WALTER *with two spoons and* [*cup*],[7]
> *and* ALLWIT.

2 Gos. Oh, here comes the chief gossip, neighbors.
                                              [*Exit* Nurse.]
S. Walt. The fatness of your wishes to you all,
    ladies.
3 Gos. Oh, dear sweet gentleman, what fine words
he has:
The fatness of our wishes.
2 Gos.   Calls us all ladies.
4 Gos. I promise you, a fine gentleman and a
    courteous.
2 Gos. Methinks her husband shows like a clown to
    him.   30
3 Gos. I would not care what clown my husband
    were, too,
So I had such fine children.
2 Gos. She's[8] all fine children, gossip.
3 Gos. Ay, and see how fast they come.
1 Pur. Children are blessings if they be got with zeal
By the brethren, as I have five at home.
S. Walt. [*To* MRS. ALLWIT] The worst is past, I
    hope now, gossip.
Mrs. All. So I hope too, good sir.
All. [*Aside*] Why then, so hope I too for company;
I have nothing to do else.   40

> [SIR WALTER *gives the spoons and cup.*]

S. Walt. A poor remembrance, lady,
To the love of the babe; I pray accept of it.
Mrs. All. Oh, you are at too much charge, sir.
2 Gos. Look, look, what has he given her? What is't,
    gossip?
3 Gos. Now, by my faith, a fair high standing cup[9]
and two great 'postle spoons,[10] one of them gilt.
1 Pur. Sure that was Judas[11] then with the red
    beard.

2 Pur. I would not feed my daughter with that spoon
for all the world, for fear of coloring her hair; red hair
the brethren like not; it consumes[12] them much; 'tis
not the sisters' color.   51

> *Enter* Nurse *with comfits and wine.*

All. Well said,[13] nurse;
About, about with them amongst the gossips.
[*Aside*] Now out comes all the tasseled handkerchers;
They are spread abroad between their knees already.
Now in goes the long fingers that are washed
Some thrice a day in urine;[14] my wife uses it.
Now we shall have such pocketing.
See how they lurch[15] at the lower end.
1 Pur. Come hither, nurse.   60
All. [*Aside*] Again—she has taken twice already.

> [1 Puritan *takes the comfits.*]

1 Pur. I had forgot a sister's child that's sick.
All. [*Aside*] A pox! it seems your purity loves sweet
things well that puts in thrice together. Had this been
all my cost now, I had been beggared. These women
have no consciences at sweetmeats, where'er they come;
see and they have not culled out all the long plums,[16]
too; they have left nothing here but short wriggle-tail
comfits, not worth mouthing. No mar'l[17] I heard   70
a citizen complain once that his wife's belly only broke
his back; mine had been all in fitters[18] seven years since
but for this worthy knight, that with a prop upholds my
wife and me, and all my estate buried in Bucklersbury.[19]
Mrs. All. Here, Mistress Yellowhammer and
    neighbors,
To you all that have taken pains with me,
All the good wives at once.

> [*Drinks;* Nurse *takes round the wine.*]

1 Pur. I'll answer for them:
They wish all health and strength
And that you may courageously go forward   80
To perform the like and many such
Like a true sister with motherly bearing.
All. [*Aside*] Now the cups troll[20] about to wet the
    gossips' whistles;
It pours down, i'faith; they never think of payment.
1 Pur.   Fill
    again, nurse.

---

    [2] *chopping:* strapping, vigorous.
    [3] *up and down:* completely.
    [5] *mettled:* courageous.   [4] *spiny:* thin.
    [7] *cup:* Q "plate."   [6] *speed:* fortune.
    [9] *standing cup:* goblet with a base.   [8] *She's:* She has.
    [10] *'postle spoons:* silver spoons with image of an apostle on
    the handle, usual christening gifts; because of the pictorial
    representation, idolatrous from the Puritan point of view.
    [11] *Judas:* traditionally had a red beard.
    [12] *consumes:* burns up, with sexual connotation.
    [13] *well said:* well done.   [14] *urine:* used as a cosmetic.
    [15] *lurch:* cheat, filch.   [16] *plums:* sugar plums.
    [17] *mar'l:* marvel.   [18] *fitters:* little pieces.
    [19] *Bucklersbury:* street running from Cheapside to Wal-
    brook, with many apothecaries and grocers.   [20] *troll:* pass.

All. [*Aside*] Now, bless, thee, two at once. I'll stay no
   longer;
It would kill me and if [21] I paid for't.
[*To* SIR WALTER] Will it please you to walk down and
   leave the women?
S. Walt. With all my heart, Jack.
All. Troth, I cannot blame you.
S. Walt. Sit you all merry, ladies.   90
All Gos. Thank your worship, sir.
I Pur. Thank your worship, sir.
All. [*Aside*] A pox twice tipple [22] ye; you are last and
   lowest.
            Ex[eunt ALLWIT *and* SIR WALTER].
I Pur. Bring hither that same cup, nurse; I would
fain drive away this—hup—antichristian grief.
3 Gos. See, gossip, and she lies not in like a countess;
Would I had such a husband for my daughter.
                                    [*Exit* Nurse.]
4 Gos. Is not she toward marriage?
3 Gos. Oh, no, sweet gossip.
4 Gos. Why, she's nineteen.   100
3 Gos. Aye, that she was last Lammas, [23]
But she has a fault, gossip, a secret fault.
4 Gos. A fault? What is't?
3 Gos. I'll tell you when I have drunk.

                                    [*Drinks.*]

4 Gos. [*Aside*] Wine can do that; I see that friendship
   cannot.
3 Gos. And now I'll tell you: she's too free.
4 Gos. Too free?
3 Gos. Oh, ay, she cannot lie dry in her bed.
4 Gos. What? And nineteen?
3 Gos. 'Tis as I tell you, gossip.   110

      [*Enter* Nurse *and speaks to* MAUDLIN.]

Maud. Speak with me, nurse, who is't?
Nurse. A gentleman from Cambridge;
I think it be your son, forsooth.
Maud. 'Tis my son Tim, i'faith.
Prithee call him up among the women;
                                    [*Exit* Nurse.]
'Twill embolden him well,
For he wants nothing but audacity.
Would the Welsh gentlewoman at home were here
   now.
L. Kix. Is your son come, forsooth?
Maud. Yes, from the university, forsooth.   120
L. Kix. 'Tis great joy on ye.
Maud. There's a great marriage towards for him.
L. Kix. A marriage?

Maud. Yes, sure, a huge heir in Wales,
At least to nineteen mountains,
Besides her goods and cattle. [24]

              Enter [Nurse *and*] TIM.

Tim. Oh, I'm betrayed.
                                              Exit.
Maud. What, gone again? Run after him, good nurse.
                                    [*Exit* Nurse.]
He's so bashful; that's the spoil of youth.
In the university they're kept still to men   130
And ne'er trained up to women's company.
L. Kix. 'Tis a great spoil of youth indeed.

              Enter Nurse *and* TIM.

Nurse. Your mother will have it so.
Maud. Why son, why Tim,
What, must I rise and fetch you? For shame, son.
Tim. Mother, you do entreat like a freshwoman; [25]
'Tis against the laws of the university
For any that has answered under bachelor
To thrust 'mongst married wives.
Maud. Come, we'll excuse you here.   140
Tim. Call up my tutor, mother, and I care not.
Maud. What, is your tutor come? Have you brought
   him up?
Tim. I ha' not brought him up; he stands at door.
Negatur. There's logic to begin with you, mother.
Maud. Run, call the gentleman, nurse; he's my
   son's tutor.
                                    [*Exit* Nurse.]
Here, eat some plums.
Tim. Come I from Cambridge, and offer me six
   plums?
Maud. Why, how now, Tim,
Will not your old tricks yet be left?
Tim. Served like a child,   150
When I have answered under [26] bachelor.
Maud. You'll never lin [27] till I make your tutor whip
you; you know how I served you once at the free school
in Paul's churchyard? [28]
Tim. Oh, monstrous absurdity,
Ne'er was the like in Cambridge since my time;
Life, whip a bachelor, you'd be laughed at soundly.
Let not my tutor hear you;
'Twould be a jest through the whole university.
No more words, mother.   160

              Enter Tutor.

Maud. Is this your tutor, Tim?
Tut. Yes, surely, lady, I am the man that brought
him in league with logic and read the Dunces [29] to him.
Tim. That he did, mother, but now I have 'em all in
my own pate and can as well read 'em to others.
Tut. That can he, mistress, for they flow naturally
from him.
Maud. I'm the more beholding to your pains, sir.
Tut. *Non ideo sane.* [30]
Maud. True, he was an idiot indeed   170
When he went out of London, but now he's well
   mended.

----

[21] *and if:* if.   [22] *tipple:* tumble.
[23] *Lammas:* August 1, Christian harvest festival.
[24] *cattle:* possessions.
[25] *freshwoman:* Tim bases the word on "freshman."
[26] *answered under:* satisfied the requirements of.
[27] *lin:* cease.
[28] *free . . . churchyard:* founded by John Colet in 1512 for
poor students.
[29] *Dunces:* scholastic philosophers (from Duns Scotus).
[30] *L.:* Not for that reason indeed.

Did you receive the two goose pies I sent you?

Tut. And eat them heartily, thanks to your worship.

Maud. [*To* Gossips] 'Tis my son Tim; I pray bid
him welcome, gentlewomen.

Tim. Tim? Hark you, Timotheus, mother, Timotheus.

Maud. How, shall I deny your name? Timotheus,
quoth he? Faith, there's a name; 'tis my son Tim forsooth.   180

L. Kix. You're welcome, Master Tim.

                                             Kiss[*es* TIM.]

Tim. [*Aside*] Oh, this is horrible; she wets as she
kisses. Your handkercher, sweet tutor, to wipe them off
as fast as they come on.

2 Gos. Welcome from Cambridge.

                                             Kiss[*es* TIM.]

Tim. [*Aside*] This is intolerable. This woman has a
villainous sweet breath, did she not stink of comfits.
Help me, sweet tutor, or I shall rub my lips off.

Tut. I'll go kiss the lower end the whilst.   189

Tim. Perhaps that's the sweeter, and we shall dispatch the sooner.

1 Pur. Let me come next. Welcome from the wellspring of discipline that waters all the brethren.[31]

                                             Reels and falls.

Tim. Hoist,[32] I beseech thee.

3 Gos. Oh, bless the woman—Mistress Underman.

1 Pur. 'Tis but the common affliction of the faithful;
We must embrace our falls.

Tim. [*Aside*] I'm glad I 'scaped it; it was some rotten
kiss sure;
It dropped down before it came at me.

                             Enter ALLWIT *and* DAVY.

All. [*Aside*] Here's a noise. Not parted yet?   200
Heyday, a looking-glass.[33] They have drunk so hard in
plate
That some of them had need of other vessels.
[*Aloud*] Yonder's the bravest show.

All Gos. Where? Where, sir?

All. Come along presently by the Pissing Conduit[34]
With two brave drums and a standard-bearer.

Tim. Come, tutor.

                                         Exit [*with* Tutor].

All Gos. Farewell, sweet gossip.

                                         Ex[*eunt* Gossips].

Mrs. All. I thank you all for your pains.

1 Pur. Feed and grow strong.   210

                 [*Exeunt all but* ALLWIT *and* DAVY.]

All. You had more need to sleep than eat.
Go, take a nap with some of the brethren; go
And rise up a well edified, boldified sister.
Oh, here's a day of toil well passed o'er,
Able to make a citizen hare-mad.
How hot they have made the room with their thick
bums.
Dost not feel it, Davy?

Davy. Monstrous strong, sir.

All. What's here under the stools?

Davy. Nothing but wet, sir; some wine spilt here,
belike.   220

All. Is't no worse, think'st thou?
Fair needlework stools cost nothing with them, Davy.

Davy. [*Aside*] Nor you neither, i'faith.

All. Look how they have laid them,
E'en as they lie themselves, with their heels up;
How they have shuffled up the rushes[35] too, Davy,
With their short figging[36] shittlecork[37] heels;
These women can let nothing stand as they find it.
But what's the secret thou'st about to tell me,   229
My honest Davy?

Davy.   If thou shouldst disclose it, sir—

All. Life, rip up my belly to the throat then, Davy.

Davy. My master's upon marriage.

All. Marriage, Davy! send me to hanging rather.

Davy. [*Aside*] I have stung him.

All. When, where, what is she, Davy?

Davy. E'en the same was gossip and gave the spoon.

All. I have no time to stay nor scarce can speak;
I'll stop those wheels, or all the work will break.

                                                     Exit.

Davy. I knew 'twould prick. Thus do I fashion still
All mine own ends by him and his rank toil;   240
'Tis my desire to keep him still from marriage.
Being his poor nearest kinsman, I may fare
The better at his death; there my hopes build
Since my Lady Kix is dry and hath no child.

                                                     Exit.

[III.iii]

                     Enter both the TOUCHWOODS.

Touch. Jun. Y'are in the happiest way to enrich
yourself
And pleasure me, brother, as man's feet can tread in;
For though she be locked up, her vow is fixed
Only to me; then time shall never grieve me,
For by that vow e'en absent I[1] enjoy her,
Assuredly confirmed that none else shall,
Which will make tedious years seem gameful to me.
In the mean space, lose you no time, sweet brother:
You have the mean to strike at this knight's fortunes
And lay him level with his bankrupt[2] merit.   10
Get but his wife with child, perch at tree-top,
And shake the golden fruit into her lap;
About it before she weep herself to a dry ground
And whine out all her goodness.

Touch. Sen.   Prithee cease;

---

[31] *wellspring . . . brethren:* Cambridge was a Puritan
center.   [32] *Hoist:* lift (yourself) up.

[33] *looking-glass:* chamber pot.

[34] *Pissing Conduit:* small conduit at end of Cheapside.

[35] *rushes:* strewn instead of carpets.

[36] *figging:* worthless.

[37] *shittlecork:* shuttlecock, light cork; both the word and
the fashion in shoes were associated with whores.

III.iii.

[1] *I:* not in Q.   [2] *bankrupt:* Q "bankrout."

I find a too much aptness in my blood
For such a business without provocation;
You might well [3] spared this banquet of eringoes, [4]
Artichokes, potatoes, and your buttered crab;
They were fitter kept for your own wedding dinner.
   Touch. Jun. Nay, and you'll follow my suit and save
     my purse too,   20
Fortune dotes on me; he's in happy case
Finds such an honest friend i'the common-place. [5]
   Touch. Sen. Life, what makes thee so merry? Thou
     hast no cause
That I could hear of lately since thy crosses, [6]
Unless there be news come with new additions.
   Touch. Jun. Why there thou hast it right:
I look for her this evening, brother.
   Touch. Sen. How's that? Look for her?
   Touch. Jun. I will deliver you of the wonder straight,
     brother:
By the firm secrecy and kind assistance   30
Of a good wench i'the house, who, made of pity,
Weighing the case her own, she's led through gutters,
Strange hidden ways which none but love could find
Or ha' the heart to venture. I expect her
Where you would little think.
   Touch. Sen.   I care not where,
So she be safe and yours.
   Touch. Jun.   Hope tells me so,
But from your love and time my peace must grow.
                               Exit.
   Touch. Sen. You know the worst then, brother. Now
     to my Kix,
The barren he and she. They're in the next room;
But to say which of their two humors [7] hold them   40
Now at this instant, I cannot say truly.

                 K IX *to his* Lady *within.*

   S. Ol. Thou liest, barrenness.
   Touch. Sen. Oh, is't that time of day? Give you joy
     of your tongue.
There's nothing else good in you; this their life
The whole day from eyes open to eyes shut,
Kissing or scolding, and then must be made friends;
Then rail the second part of the first fit [8] out,
And then be pleased again, no man knows which way;
Fall out like giants and fall in like children;
Their fruit can witness as much.

       Enter S IR O LIVER K IX *and his* Lady.

   S. Ol.   'Tis thy fault.   50
   L. Kix. Mine, drought and coldness?
   S. Ol.   Thine: 'tis
     thou art barren.
   L. Kix. I barren! oh, life, that I durst but speak now
In mine own justice, in mine own right. I barren!

---

    [3] *might well:* Q "might'well" indicates elision of "have."
    [4] *eringoes:* sea-holly fruit, like the foods that follow,
thought aphrodisiac.
    [5] *common-place:* court of common pleas.
    [6] *crosses:* setbacks.   [7] *humors:* moods.
    [8] *fit:* part of a poem.   [9] *outcry:* auction.
    [10] *clap up bills:* put up advertisements.

'Twas otherways with me when I was at court;
I was ne'er called so till I was married.
   S. Ol. I'll be divorced.
   L. Kix.   Be hanged; I need not wish it:
That will come too soon to thee. I may say
"Marriage and hanging goes by destiny"
For all the goodness I can find in't yet.
   S. Ol. I'll give up house and keep some fruitful
     whore,   60
Like an old bachelor, in a tradesman's chamber;
She and her children shall have all.
   L. Kix.   Where be they?
   Touch. Sen. Pray cease.
When there are friendlier courses took for you
To get and multiply within your house
At your own proper costs, in spite of censure,
Methinks an honest peace might be established.
   S. Ol. What, with her? Never.
   Touch. Sen. Sweet sir—
   S. Ol. You work all in vain.   70
   L. Kix. Then he doth all like thee.
   Touch. Sen. Let me entreat, sir—
   S. Ol. Singleness confound her:
I took her with one smock.
   L. Kix. But indeed you came not so single
When you came from shipboard.
   S. Ol. [*Aside*] Heart, she bit sore there.
[*To* T OUCHWOOD S ENIOR] Prithee, make's friends.
   Touch. Sen. [*Aside*] Is't come to that? The peal
     begins to cease.
   S. Ol. I'll sell all at an outcry. [9]   80
   L. Kix. Do thy worst, slave.
[*To* T OUCHWOOD S ENIOR] Good sweet sir, bring us
     into love again.
   Touch. Sen. [*Aside*] Some would think this
     impossible to compass.
[*Aloud*] Pray let this storm fly over.
   S. Ol. Good sir, pardon me; I'm master of this
     house,
Which I'll sell presently; I'll clap up bills [10] this
     evening.
   Touch. Sen. Lady, friends, come!
   L. Kix. If e'er ye loved woman, talk not on't, sir.
What, friends with him? Good faith, do you think I'm
     mad
With one that's scarce the hinder quarter of a man? 90
   S. Ol. Thou art nothing of a woman.
   L. Kix. Would I were less than nothing.

                             Weeps.

   S. Ol. Nay, prithee, what dost mean?
   L. Kix. I cannot please you.
   S. Ol. I'faith, thou art a good soul; he lies that says it.
Buss, buss, pretty rogue.

                       [*Kisses her.*]

   L. Kix. You care not for me.
   Touch. Sen. [*Aside*] Can any man tell now which way
     they came in?
By this light I'll be hanged then.
   S. Ol. Is the drink come?   100

Touch. Sen. [*Aside*] Here's a little vial of almond milk
That stood me in[11] some three pence.
    S. Ol. I hope to see thee, wench, within these few
        years
Circled with children, pranking up a girl
And putting jewels in their little ears;
Fine sport, i'faith.
    L. Kix.   Ay, had you been aught, husband,
It had been done ere this time.
    S. Ol. Had I been aught! hang thee, hadst thou been
        aught;
But a cross thing I ever found thee.
    L. Kix. Thou art a grub to say so.   110
    S. Ol. A pox on thee.
    Touch. Sen. [*Aside*] By this light, they are out again
        at the same door,
And no man can tell which way.
[*To* SIR OLIVER] Come, here's your drink, sir.
    S. Ol.   I will
        not take it now, sir,
And I were sure to get three boys ere midnight.
    L. Kix. Why, there thou show'st now of what breed
        thou comst,
To hinder generation. Oh, thou villain,
That knows how crookedly the world goes with us
For want of heirs, yet put by all good fortune.   119
    S. Ol. Hang, strumpet, I will take it now in spite.
    Touch. Sen. Then you must ride upon't five hours.

                                [*Gives vial.*]

    S. Ol. I mean so. Within there!

                Enter a Servant.

    Serv. Sir?
    S. Ol. Saddle the white mare.
                                [*Exit* Servant.]
I'll take a whore along and ride to Ware.[12]
    L. Kix. Ride to the devil.
    S. Ol.   I'll plague you every way.
Look ye, do you see? 'Tis gone.

                                Drinks.

    L. Kix.   A pox go with it.
    S. Ol. Ay, curse and spare not now.
    Touch. Sen. Stir up and down, sir; you must not
        stand.
    S. Ol. Nay, I'm not given to standing.   130
    Touch. Sen. So much the better, sir, for the . . . .[13]
    S. Ol. I never could stand long in one place yet;
I learned it of my father, ever figient;[14]
How if I crossed[15] this, sir?

                                Capers.

    Touch. Sen. Oh, passing good, sir, and would show
well a-horseback; when you come to your inn, if you
leaped over a joint-stool,[16] 'twere not amiss—[*Aside*]
although you brake your neck, sir.
    S. Ol. What say you to a table thus high, sir?   139
    Touch. Sen. Nothing better, sir, [*Aside*] if it be fur-
nished with good victuals. [*Aloud*] You remember how
the bargain runs about this business?

    S. Ol. Or else I had a bad head: you must receive,
sir, four hundred pounds of me at four several payments; one hundred pound now in hand.
    Touch. Sen. Right, that I have, sir.
    S. Ol. Another hundred when my wife is quick; the
third when she's brought a-bed; and the last hundred
when the child cries, for if it should be stillborn, it doth
no good, sir.   150
    Touch. Sen. All this is even[17] still; a little faster, sir.
    S. Ol. Not a whit, sir;
I'm in an excellent pace for any physic.

                Enter a Servant.

    Serv. Your white mare's ready.
    S. Ol. I shall up presently.

                                [*Exit* Servant.]
                        [*To* LADY KIX] One kiss
        and farewell.
    Lady. Thou shalt have two, love.
    S. Ol. Expect me about three.

                                            Exit.

    L. Kix. With all my heart, sweet.
    Touch. Sen. [*Aside*] By this light they have forgot
        their anger since,
And are as far in again as e'er they were;   160
Which way the devil came they? Heart, I saw 'em not.
Their ways are beyond finding out. [*Aloud*] Come,
        sweet Lady.
    L. Kix. How must I take mine, sir?
    Touch. Sen. Clean contrary; yours must be taken
        lying.
    L. Kix. A-bed, sir?
    Touch. Sen. A-bed or where you will for your own
        ease;
Your coach[18] will serve.
    L. Kix.   The physic must needs please.
                                        Ex[eunt].

                    ACT FOUR

                    SCENE ONE

                Enter TIM *and* Tutor.

    Tim. Negatur argumentum, tutor.[1]
    Tut. Probo tibi, pupil, *stultus non est animal rationale.*[2]
    Tim. Falleris sane.[3]
    Tut. Quaeso ut taceas: probo tibi.[4]

---

    [11] *stood me in:* cost me.
    [12] *Ware:* Hertfordshire town twenty miles from London,
known as a place for lovers' rendezvous and most notable for
a giant square bed at the Saracen's Head Inn.
    [13] *so . . .:* Like other lacunae in Q similarly marked, this
may reflect censorship or whispering.
    [14] *figient:* fidgety.   [15] *crossed:* jumped over.
    [16] *joint-stool:* common piece of furniture about two feet
high.   [17] *even:* just.
    [18] *coach:* often used for sexual trysts.
IV.i.
    [1] *L.:* The argument is denied, tutor.
    [2] *L.:* I prove to you, pupil, a fool is not a rational animal.
    [3] *L.:* Surely you will fail.
    [4] *L.:* I ask you to be silent.

Tim. Quomodo probas, domine?[5]

Tut. Stultus non habet rationem; ergo non est animal rationale.[6]

Tim. Sic argumentaris, domine: stultus non habet rationem; ergo non est animal rationale. Negatur argumentum again, tutor.[7]   10

Tut. Argumentum iterum probo tibi, domine: qui non participat de ratione, nullo modo potest vocari rationalis; but stultus non participat de ratione; ergo stultus nullo modo potest dici rationalis.[8]

Tim. Participat.[9]

Tut. Sic disputas: qui participat, quomodo participat?[10]

Tim. Ut homo, probabo tibi in syllogismo.[11]

Tut. Hunc proba.[12]

Tim. Sic probo, domine: stultus est homo sicut tu et ego sumus; homo est animal rationale, sicut stultus est animal rationale.[13]   21

Enter MAUDLIN.

Maud. Here's nothing but disputing all the day long with 'em.

Tut. Sic disputas: stultus est homo sicut tu et ego sumus; homo est animal rationale, sicut stultus est animal rationale.[14]

Maud. Your reasons are both good, whate'er they be; Pray give them o'er; faith, you'll tire yourselves. What's the matter between you?   29

Tim. Nothing but reasoning about a fool, mother.

Maud. About a fool, son? Alas, what need you trouble your heads about that? None of us all but knows what a fool is.

Tim. Why, what's a fool, mother? I come to you[15] now.

---

[5] *L.:* How do you prove it, master?

[6] *L.:* A fool has no reason; therefore he is not a rational animal.

[7] *L.:* Thus you argue, master: a fool does not have reason; therefore he is not a rational animal. The argument is denied again, tutor.

[8] *L.:* I prove the argument to you again, sir: he who does not participate in the power of reason can in no way be called rational; but a fool does not participate in the power of reason; therefore the fool can in no way be said to be rational.

[9] *L.:* He does participate in it.

[10] *L.:* Thus you argue: he who participates in it, how does he participate in it?

[11] *L.:* As a man; I shall prove it to you in a syllogism.

[12] *L.:* Prove this.

[13] *L.:* Thus I prove it, master: a fool is a man as you and I are; man is a rational animal, so the fool is a rational animal.

[14] *L.:* Thus you argue: the fool is a man as you and I are; man is a rational animal, so the fool is a rational animal.

[15] *Come to you:* Pose a question.

[16] *By . . . will:* Tailors were thought unmanly.

[17] *accidences:* books of the rudiments of Latin grammar.

[18] *haberdins:* salt codfish, probably with sexual connotation.

[19] *as in presenti:* from Lily's *Short Introduction of Latin Grammar*, introducing a section on the conjugation of verbs; the joke that follows involves a pun on "ass."

[20] *L.:* what is grammar?

[21] *L.:* the art of writing and speaking correctly (Maudlin remembers the word *ars*).

[22] *sir-reverence:* saving your reverence, with apologies to.

[23] *kiff:* kith.

Maud. Why, one that's married before he has wit.

Tim. 'Tis pretty, i'faith, and well guessed of a woman never brought up at the university; but bring forth what fool you will, mother, I'll prove him to be as reasonable a creature as myself or my tutor here.   40

Maud. Fie, 'tis impossible.

Tut. Nay, he shall do't forsooth.

Tim. 'Tis the easiest thing to prove a fool by logic. By logic I'll prove anything.

Maud. What, thou wilt not.

Tim. I'll prove a whore to be an honest woman.

Maud. Nay, by my faith, she must prove that herself, or logic will never do't.

Tim. 'Twill do't, I tell you.   49

Maud. Some in this street would give a thousand pounds that you could prove their wives so.

Tim. 'Faith, I can, and all their daughters, too, though they had three bastards. When come your tailor hither?

Maud. Why, what of him?

Tim. By logic I'll prove him to be a man, let him come when he will.[16]

Maud. [*To* Tutor] How hard at first was learning to him. Truly, sir, I thought he would never a' took the Latin tongue. How many accidences[17] do you think he wore out e'er he came to his grammar?   61

Tut. Some three or four.

Maud. Believe me, sir, some four and thirty.

Tim. Pish, I made haberdins[18] of 'em in church porches.

Maud. He was eight years in his grammar and stuck horribly at a foolish place there called *as in presenti.*[19]

Tim. Pox, I have it here now.

Maud. He so shamed me once before an honest gentleman that knew me when I was a maid.   70

Tim. These women must have all out.

Maud. "*Quid est grammatica?*" says the gentleman to him—I shall remember by a sweet token—but nothing could he answer.

Tut. How now, pupil, ha? *Quid est grammatica?*

Tim. *Grammatica?* Ha, ha, ha.

Maud. Nay, do not laugh, son, but let me hear you say it now. There was one word went so prettily off the gentleman's tongue, I shall remember it the longest day of my life.   80

Tut. Come: *quid est grammatica?*[20]

Tim. Are you not ashamed, tutor? *Grammatica?* Why, *recte scribendi atque loquendi ars,*[21] sir-reverence[22] of my mother.

Maud. That was it, i'faith. Why now, son, I see you are a deep scholar. And master tutor, a word, I pray; let us withdraw a little into my husband's chamber. I'll send in the North-Wales gentlewoman to him; she looks for wooing. I'll put together both and lock the door.

Tut. I give great approbation to your conclusion.

Exit [*with* MAUDLIN].

Tim. I mar'l what this gentlewoman should be   91
That I should have in marriage; she's a stranger to me.
I wonder what my parents mean, i'faith,
To match me with a stranger so,
A maid that's neither kiff[23] nor kin to me.

Life, do they think I have no more care of my body
Than to lie with one that I ne'er knew,
A mere stranger,
One that ne'er went to school with me neither,
Nor ever playfellows together?   100
They're mightily o'erseen²⁴ in't, methinks;
They say she has mountains to her marriage;²⁵
She's full of cattle, some two thousand runts;²⁶
Now what the meaning of these runts should be
My tutor cannot tell me.
I have looked in Rider's Dictionary²⁷ for the letter R,
And there I can hear no tidings of these runts neither,
Unless they should be Romford²⁸ hogs;
I know them not.

Enter Welsh Gentlewoman.

And here she comes.   110
If I know what to say to her now
In the way of marriage, I'm no graduate.
Methinks i'faith 'tis boldly done of her
To come into my chamber, being but a stranger.
She shall not say I'm so proud yet but I'll speak to her;
Marry, as I will order it,
She shall take no hold of my words, I'll warrant her;
She looks and makes a cur'sey.—
[*To her*] *Salve tu quoque, puella pulcherrima;*
*Quid vis nescio nec sane curo.*²⁹   120
Tully's³⁰ own phrase to a heart.
    W. Wom. [*Aside*] I know not what he means.
A suitor, quoth a?
I hold my life he understands no English.
    Tim. Fertur me Hercule tu virgo,
*Wallia ut opibus abundis maximis.*³¹
    W. Wom. [*Aside*] What's this *fertur* and *abundundis*?
He mocks me sure and calls me a bundle of farts.
    Tim. [*Aside*] I have no Latin word now for their
runts; I'll make some shift or other. [*To her*]   130
Iterum dico opibus abundat maximis montibus et fontibus
et ut ita dicam rontibus; attamen vero homunculus ego sum
natura simul et arte baccalaureus lecto profecto non
*paratus.*³²
    W. Wom. [*Aside*] This is most strange; maybe he can
speak Welsh: *Avedera whee comrage, der due cog i*
*foginis?*³³
    Tim. [*Aside*] *Cog foggin,* I scorn to cog with her; I'll
tell her so too in a word ne'er her own language: [*Aloud*]
*ego non cogo.*³⁴   140
    W. Wom. Rhegosin a whiggin harle ron corid ambre.
    Tim. [*Aside*] By my faith, she's a good scholar, I see
that already.
She has the tongues plain; I hold my life, she has
    traveled.
What will folks say? There goes the learnèd couple.
Faith, if the truth were known, she hath proceeded.³⁵

Enter MAUDLIN.

    Maud. How now? How speeds your business?
    Tim. I'm glad my mother's come to part us.
    Maud. How do you agree forsooth?
    W. Wom. As well as e'er we did before we met.
    Maud. How's that?   150

    W. Wom. You put me to a man I understand not;
Your son's no Englishman, methinks.
    Maud. No Englishman? Bless my boy, and born
    i'the heart of London?
    W. Wom. I ha' been long enough in the chamber
    with him,
And I find neither Welsh nor English in him.
    Maud. Why, Tim, how have you used the
    gentlewoman?
    Tim. As well as a man might do, mother, in modest
    Latin.
    Maud. Latin, fool?
    Tim. And she recoiled³⁶ in Hebrew.
    Maud. In Hebrew, fool? 'Tis Welsh.   160
    Tim. All comes to one, mother.
    Maud. She can speak English, too.
    Tim. Who told me so much?
Heart, and she can speak English, I'll clap³⁷ to her;
I thought you'd marry me to a stranger.³⁸
    Maud. You must forgive him; he's so inured to
    Latin,
He and his tutor, that he hath quite forgot
To use the Protestant³⁹ tongue.
    W. Wom. 'Tis quickly pardoned forsooth.
    Maud. Tim, make amends and kiss her.   170
[*To* Welsh Gentlewoman] He makes towards you
    forsooth.

[TIM *kisses* Welsh Gentlewoman.]

    Tim. Oh, delicious; one may discover her country by
her kissing. 'Tis a true saying, there's nothing tastes so
sweet as your Welsh mutton.
[*To* Welsh Gentlewoman] It was reported you could
    sing.
    Maud. Oh, rarely, Tim, the sweetest British⁴⁰
    songs.
    Tim. And 'tis my mind, I swear, before I marry
I would see all my wife's good parts⁴¹ at once,
To view how rich I were.
    Maud. Thou shalt hear sweet music, Tim.   180
[*To* Welsh Gentlewoman] Pray, forsooth.

Music and Welsh [Gentlewoman *sings*].

---

²⁴ *o'erseen:* mistaken.   ²⁵ *to . . . marriage:* as dowry.
²⁶ *runts:* small breed of Welsh cattle.
²⁷ *Rider's Dictionary:* English-Latin, Latin-English dictionary published 1589.
²⁸ *Romford:* Essex village twelve miles northeast of London with a famous hog market.
²⁹ *L.:* Hail to you, most beautiful maiden; what you want
I don't know, nor in fact do I care.   ³⁰ *Tully's:* Cicero's.
³¹ *L.:* It is said by Hercules, young lady, that Wales
abounds in the greatest riches.
³² *L.:* Again I say it abounds in the greatest mountains
and fountains and, as I may say, runts, yet I am in truth a
little man by nature and by art a bachelor, not actually ready
for bed.
³³ *Avedera . . . foginis:* obscure and untranslatable stage-
Welsh.   ³⁴ *L.:* I don't gather (with you).
³⁵ *proceeded:* earned a degree.   ³⁶ *recoiled:* responded.
³⁷ *clap:* cling.   ³⁸ *stranger:* foreigner.
³⁹ *Protestant:* English.   ⁴⁰ *British:* Welsh.
⁴¹ *good parts:* accomplishments, with double entendre.

The Song

Cupid is Venus' only joy,
But he is a wanton boy,
A very, very wanton boy;
He shoots at ladies' naked breasts;
He is the cause of most men's crests—
I mean upon the forehead,
Invisible but horrid;
'Twas he first thought upon the way
To keep a lady's lips in play.   190

Why should not Venus chide her son
For the pranks that he hath done,
The wanton pranks that he hath done?
He shoots his fiery darts so thick
They hurt poor ladies to the quick;
Ah me, with cruel wounding;
His darts are so confounding
That life and sense would soon decay
But that he keeps their lips in play.

Can there be any part of bliss   200
In a quickly fleeting kiss,
A quickly fleeting kiss?
To one's pleasure leisures are but waste;
The slowest kiss makes too much haste;
We lose it ere we find it.
The pleasing sport they only know
That close above and close below.

Tim. I would not change my wife for a kingdom;
I can do somewhat too in my own lodging.

Enter YELLOWHAMMER *and* ALLWIT.

Yell. Why, well said, Tim; the bells go merrily;   210
I love such peals alife.[42] Wife, lead them in a while;
Here's a strange gentleman desires private conference.
                [*Exeunt* MAUDLIN, TIM, *and* Welsh
                                    Gentlewoman.]
You're welcome, sir, the more for your name's sake,
Good Master Yellowhammer; I love my name well.
And which o' the Yellowhammers take you descent
    from,
If I may be so bold with you? Which, I pray?
All. The Yellowhammers in Oxfordshire
Near Abingdon.[43]
Yell. And those are the best Yellowhammers and
truest bred. I came from thence myself, though   220
now a citizen. I'll be bold with you: you are most
welcome.
All. I hope the zeal I bring with me shall deserve it.
Yell. I hope no less. What is your will, sir?
All. I understand by rumors you have a daughter,
Which my bold love shall henceforth title cousin.

---

[42] *alife:* extremely.
[43] *Abingdon:* village five miles south of Oxford.
[44] *point, ye:* i.e., point, and ye.
[45] Here, and also at l. 251 below, there are evident lacunae
in the text.   [46] *venting connies:* selling rabbits.
[47] *Cato and Corderius:* common textbooks.

Yell. I thank you for her, sir.
All. I heard of her virtues and other confirmed
    graces.
Yell. A plaguy girl, sir.
All. Fame sets her out with richer ornaments   230
Than you are pleased to boast of. 'Tis done modestly.
I hear she's towards marriage.
Yell. You hear truth, sir.
All. And with a knight in town, Sir Walter
    Whorehound.
Yell. The very same, sir.
All. I am the sorrier for't.
Yell. The sorrier? Why, cousin?
All. 'Tis not too far past, is't? It may be yet
    recalled?
Yell. Recalled? Why, good sir?
All. Resolve me in that point, ye[44] shall hear from
    me.   240
Yell. There's no contract passed.
All. I am very joyful, sir.
Yell. But he's the man must bed her.
All. By no means, coz, she's quite undone then,
And you'll curse the time that e'er you made the match.
He's an arrant whoremaster, consumes his time and
    state
[. . .,][45] whom in my knowledge he hath kept this seven
    years;
Nay, coz, another man's wife too.
Yell. Oh, abominable.
All. Maintains the whole house, apparels the
    husband,   250
Pays servants' wages, not so much, but [. . .]
Yell. Worse and worse. And doth the husband know
    this?
All. Knows? Ay, and glad he may too; 'tis his living,
As other trades thrive, butchers by selling flesh,
Poulters by venting connies,[46] or the like, coz.
Yell. What an incomparable wittol's this!
All. Tush, what cares he for that?
Believe me, coz, no more than I do?
Yell. What a base slave is that!
All. All's one to him: he feeds and takes his ease;
Was ne'er the man that ever broke his sleep   261
To get a child yet, by his own confession,
And yet his wife has seven.
Yell. What, by Sir Walter?
All. Sir Walter's like to keep 'em and maintain 'em
In excellent fashion; he dares do no less, sir.
Yell. Life, has he children too?
All. Children? Boys thus high,
In their Cato and Corderius.[47]
Yell. What, you jest, sir!   270
All. Why, one can make a verse
And is now at Eton College.
Yell. Oh, this news has cut into my heart, coz.
All. It had eaten nearer if it had not been prevented.
One Allwit's wife.
Yell. Allwit? 'Foot, I have heard of him;
He had a girl kursened lately?
All. Ay, that work did cost the knight above a
    hundred mark.

Yell. I'll mark him for a knave and villain for 't.　279
A thousand thanks and blessings; I have done with him.
　All. [*Aside*] Ha, ha, ha, this knight will stick by my
　　ribs [48] still;
I shall not lose him yet; no wife will come;
Where'er he woos, I find him still at home. Ha, ha.
　　　　　　　　　　　　　　　　　　　　　　　　Exit.
　Yell. Well, grant all this; say now his deeds are black;
Pray, what serves marriage but to call him back?
I have kept a whore myself and had a bastard
By Mistress Anne, in *anno* [49]—,
I care not who knows it; he's now a jolly fellow;
H'as been twice warden; so may his fruit [50] be;
They were but base begot, and so was he.　　290
The knight is rich. He shall be my son-in-law.
No matter so the whore he keeps be wholesome;
My daughter takes no hurt then; so let them wed.
I'll have him sweat [51] well e'er they go to bed.

　　　　　　　Enter MAUDLIN.

　Maud. O husband, husband.
　Yell. How now, Maudlin?
　Maud. We are all undone: she's gone, she's gone.
　Yell. Again? Death, which way?
　Maud. Over the houses. [52]
Lay [53] the waterside; she's gone forever else.　　300
　Yell. O vent'rous baggage.
　　　　　　　　　　　　　　　　　　　　　　Exeunt.

[IV.ii]

　　　　　　　Enter TIM *and* Tutor.

　Tim. Thieves, thieves! my sister's stolen;
Some thief hath got her;
Oh, how miraculously did my father's plate 'scape;
'Twas all left out, tutor.
　Tut. Is't possible?
　Tim. Besides three chains of pearl and a box of coral.
My sister's gone; let's look at Trig-stairs [1] for her;
My mother's gone to lay the common-stairs
At Puddle-wharf, [2] and at the dock below
Stands my poor silly father. Run, sweet tutor, run.　10
　　　　　　　　　　　　　　　　　　　　　　Ex[*eunt*].

[IV.iii]

　　　　　Enter both the TOUCHWOODS.

　Touch. Sen. I had been taken, brother, by eight
　　sergeants
But for the honest watermen. [1] I am bound to them;
They are the most requiteful'st [2] people living,
For as they get their means by gentlemen,
They are still the forwardest to help gentlemen.
You heard how one 'scaped out o'the Blackfriars, [3]
But a while since, from two or three varlets
Came into the house with all their rapiers drawn
As if they'd dance the sword-dance on the stage　9
With candles in their hands, like chandlers' [4] ghosts,
Whilst the poor gentleman so pursued and banded [5]
Was by an honest pair of oars safely landed.
　Touch. Jun. I love them with my heart for 't.

　　　　　Enter three or four Watermen.

　1 Wat. Your first man, [6] sir.
　2 Wat. Shall I carry your gentlemen with a pair of
　　oars?
　Touch. Sen. These be the honest fellows.
Take one pair, and leave the rest for her.
　Touch. Jun. Barn Elms. [7]
　Touch. Sen. No more, brother.
　1 Wat. Your first man.　　　　　　　　　　20
　2 Wat. Shall I carry your worship?
　Touch. Jun. Go.
　　　　　　　　　[*Exit* TOUCHWOOD SENIOR *with*
　　　　　　　　　　　　　　　　　　First Waterman.]
　　　　And you honest watermen that stay,
Here's a French crown for you;
There comes a maid with all speed to take water;
Row her lustily to Barn Elms after me.
　2 Wat. To Barn Elms, good sir. Make ready the boat,
　　Sam;
We'll wait below.
　　　　　　　　　　　　　　　　Ex[*eunt* Watermen].

　　　　　　　Enter MOLL.

　Touch. Jun. What made you stay so long?
　Moll. I found the way more dangerous than I looked
　　for.
　Touch. Jun. Away, quick, there's a boat waits for
　　you,　　　　　　　　　　　　　　　　　　30
And I'll take water at Paul's Wharf and overtake you.
　Moll. Good sir, do, we cannot be too safe.
　　　　　　　　　　　　　　　　　　　　[*Exeunt.*]

[IV.iv]

　　　Enter SIR WALTER, YELLOWHAMMER, TIM,
　　　　　　　　　　and Tutor.

　S. Walt. Life, call you this close keeping?
　Yell. She was kept under a double-lock.
　S. Walt. A double devil.
　Tim. That's a buff sergeant, [1] tutor; he'll ne'er wear
　　out.
　Yell. How would you have women locked?

---

[48] *stick . . . ribs:* stay in my clutches.　　[49] *L.:* the year.
[50] *fruit:* pun on warden, "pear" as well as "officer."
[51] *sweat:* treated for venereal disease.
[52] *Over the houses:* Across the roofs.　　[53] *Lay:* Search.

IV.ii.
　[1] *Trig-stairs:* landing place on the Thames.
　[2] *common . . . wharf:* public stairs at a watergate upstream
from Trig-stairs.

IV.iii.
　[1] *watermen:* Thames boatmen.
　[2] *requiteful'st:* readiest to return favors.
　[3] *Blackfriars:* private theater in London.
　[4] *chandlers':* candlemakers'.
　[5] *banded:* bandied, struck to and fro like a tennis ball.
　[6] *Your . . . man:* waterman's cry.
　[7] *Barn Elms:* lovers' retreat up the Thames.

IV.iv.
　[1] *buff sergeant:* sergeants wore light-colored leather
clothing.

Tim. With padlocks, father; the Venetian uses it;
My tutor reads it.[2]

S. Walt. Heart, if she were so locked up, how got
she out?

Yell. There was a little hole looked into the gutter,
But who would have dreamed of that?   10

S. Walt. A wiser man would.

Tim. He says true, father; a wise man for love will
seek every hole; my tutor knows it.

Tut. Verum poeta dicit.[3]

Tim. Dicit Virgilius,[4] father.

Yell. Prithee, talk of thy jills[5] somewhere else; she's
played the jill with me. Where's your wise mother now?

Tim. Run mad, I think; I thought she would have
drowned herself; she would not stay for oars, but took a
smelt-boat. Sure I think she be gone a-fishing for her.

Yell. She'll catch a goodly dish of gudgeons[6] now,
Will serve us all to supper.   22

Enter MAUDLIN *drawing* MOLL *by the hair, and*
Watermen.

Maud. I'll tug thee home by the hair.

Wat. Good mistress, spare her.

Maud. Tend your own business.

Wat. You are a cruel mother.

                              Ex[eunt Watermen.]

Moll. Oh, my heart dies.

Maud. I'll make thee an example for all the neighbors' daughters.

Moll. Farewell, life.   30

Maud. You that have tricks can counterfeit.

Yell. Hold, hold, Maudlin.

Maud. I have brought your jewel by the hair.

Yell. She's here, knight.

S. Walt. Forbear or I'll grow worse.

Tim. Look on her, tutor; she hath brought her from
the water like a mermaid;[7] she's but half my sister now,
as far as the flesh goes; the rest may be sold to fish-
wives.[8]

Maud. Dissembling cunning baggage.   40

Yell. Impudent strumpet.

S. Walt. Either give over both or I'll give over:[9]
Why have you used me thus, unkind mistress?
Wherein have I deserved?

Yell. You talk too fondly, sir. We'll take another
course and prevent all. We might have done't long since.
We'll lose no time now, nor trust to't any longer: tomorrow morn as early as sunrise we'll have you joined.

Moll. O bring me death tonight, love-pitying fates;
Let me not see tomorrow up upon the world.   50

---

[2] *reads it:* has read it.   [3] *L.:* The poet speaks the truth.
[4] *L.:* Virgil says.   [5] *jills:* disreputable women.
[6] *gudgeons:* small bait-fish; like smelt, an emblem of the
fool.   [7] *mermaid:* whore.
[8] *fishwives:* women who sell fish, with play on fishmongers, bawds.
[9] *give . . . over:* stop picking on Moll or I'll give up the
marriage.
[10] *him . . . monuments:* the guide to Westminster Abbey.
[11] *hold . . . play:* make you fight for your life.
[12] *quit:* even.   [13] *of . . . hand:* on equal terms.

Yell. Are you content, sir? Till then she shall be
watched.

Maud. Baggage, you shall.

                              Exit [*with* MOLL.]

Tim. Why, father, my tutor and I will both watch in
armor.

                              [*Exit* YELLOWHAMMER.]

Tut. How shall we do for weapons?

Tim. Take you no care for that. If need be I can send
for conquering metal, tutor, ne'er lost day yet; 'tis but
at Westminster: I am acquainted with him that keeps
the monuments;[10] I can borrow Harry the Fifth's
sword; 'twill serve us both to watch with.   59

                              Exeunt [TIM *and* Tutor].

S. Walt. I ne'er was so near my wish as this chance
Makes me. Ere tomorrow noon
I shall receive two thousand pound in gold
And a sweet maidenhead
Worth forty.

Enter TOUCHWOOD JUNIOR *with a* Waterman.

Touch. Jun. Oh, thy news splits me.

Wat. Half-drowned, she cruelly tugged her by the
hair,
Forced her disgracefully, not like a mother.

Touch. Jun. Enough. Leave me, like my joys.

                              Exit Waterman.
Sir, saw you not a wretched maid pass this way?

S. Walt. Yes, slave, 'tis I.   70

                              Both draw and fight.

Touch. Jun. I must break through thee, then; there
is no stop
That checks my tongue and all my hopeful fortunes,
That breast excepted, and I must have way.

S. Walt. Sir, I believe 'twill hold your life in play.[11]

                              [*Wounds him.*]

Touch. Jun. Sir, you'll gain the heart in my breast at
first.

S. Walt. There is no dealing, then; think on the
dowry for two thousand pounds.

Touch. Jun. Oh, now 'tis quit,[12] sir.

                              [*Wounds* SIR WALTER.]

S. Walt. And, being of even hand,[13] I'll play no
longer.

Touch. Jun. No longer, slave?   80

S. Walt. I have certain things to think on
Before I dare go further.

Touch. Jun.   But one bout?
I'll follow thee to death, but ha't out.

                              Ex[eunt].

ACT FIVE

SCENE ONE

Enter ALLWIT, *his* Wife, *and* DAVY DAHUMMA.

Mrs. All. A misery of a house.

All. What shall become of us?

Davy. I think his wound be mortal.

All. Think'st thou so, Davy?

Then am I mortal too, but a dead man, Davy.

This is no world for me whene'er he goes;

I must e'en truss up all and after him, Davy;

A sheet with two knots,[1] and away.

    Enter SIR WALTER, *led in hurt* [*by two* Servants].

Davy. Oh, see, sir,

How faint he goes; two of my fellows lead him.   10

Mrs. All. Oh, me.

                              [*Faints.*]

All. Heyday, my wife's laid down too; here's like to
    be

A good house kept, when we are all together down.

Take pains with her, good Davy, cheer her up there;

Let me come to his worship, let me come.

S. Walt. Touch me not, villain. My wound aches at
    thee,

Thou poison to my heart.

All.   He raves already,

His senses are quite gone, he knows me not.

Look up, an't like your worship; heave those eyes;

Call me to mind. Is your remembrance lost?   20

Look in my face; who am I, an't like your worship?

S. Walt. If anything be worse than slave or villain,

Thou art the man.

All. Alas, his poor worship's weakness;

He will begin to know me by little and little.

S. Walt. No devil can be like thee.

All.   Ah, poor
    gentleman,

Methinks the pain that thou endurest—

S. Walt. Thou know'st me to be wicked, for thy
    baseness

Kept the eyes open still on all my sins.

None knew the dear account my soul stood charged
    with   30

So well as thou, yet, like hell's flattering angel,

Wouldst never tell me on't, let'st me go on

And join with death in sleep, that if I had not waked

Now by chance, even by a stranger's pity,

I had everlastingly slept out all hope

Of grace and mercy.

All.   Now he is worse and worse.

Wife, to him, wife; thou wast wont to do good on him.

Mrs. All. How is't with you, sir?

S. Walt.   Not as with you,

Thou loathsome strumpet. Some good pitying man

Remove my sins out of my sight a little;   40

I tremble to behold her; she keeps back

All comfort while she stays. Is this a time,

Unconscionable woman, to see thee?

Art thou so cruel to the peace of man

Not to give liberty now? The devil himself

Shows a far fairer reverence and respect

To goodness than thyself; he dares not do this,

But parts in time of penitence, hides his face;

When man withdraws from him he leaves the place.

Hast thou less manners and more impudence   50

Than thy instructor? Prithee show thy modesty,

If the least grain be left, and get thee from me.

Thou shouldst be rather locked many rooms hence

From the poor miserable sight of me,

If either love or grace had part in thee.

Mrs. All. He is lost forever.

All.   Run, sweet Davy,
    quickly,

And fetch the children hither; sight of them

Will make him cheerful straight.

                              [*Exit* DAVY.]

S. Walt. [*To* MRS. ALLWIT] Oh, death! is this

A place for you to weep? What tears are those?   60

Get you away with them; I shall fare the worse.

As long as they are a-weeping, they work against me.

There's nothing but thy appetite in that sorrow;

Thou weep'st for lust; I feel it in the slackness

Of comforts coming towards me.

I was well till thou began'st to undo me.

This shows like the fruitless sorrow of a careless mother

That brings her son with dalliance to the gallows

And then stands by and weeps to see him suffer.

    Enter DAVY *with the* Children.

Davy. There are the children, sir; an't like your
    worship,   70

Your last fine girl; in troth, she smiles;

Look, look, in faith, sir.

S. Walt.   Oh, my vengeance!

Let me forever hide my cursèd face

From sight of those that darkens all my hopes

And stands between me and the sight of heaven;

Who sees me now, he too and those so near me

May rightly say I am o'ergrown with sin.

Oh, how my offenses wrestle with my repentance;

It hath scarce breath.

Still my adulterous guilt hovers aloft   80

And with her black wings beats down all my prayers

Ere they be halfway up. What's he knows now

How long I have to live? Oh, what comes then?

My taste grows bitter, the round world all gall now;

Her pleasing pleasures now hath poisoned me

Which I exchanged my soul for;

Make way a hundred sighs at once for me.

All. Speak to him, Nick.

Nick.   I dare not; I am afraid.

All. Tell him he hurts his wounds, Wat, with
    making moan.

S. Walt. Wretched, death of seven.   90

All. Come, let's be talking somewhat to keep him
    alive.

Ah, sirrah Wat, and did my lord bestow that jewel on
    thee

For an epistle thou mad'st in Latin?

Thou art a good forward boy; there's great joy on thee.

S. Walt. Oh, sorrow.

All.   Heart, will nothing comfort
    him?

V.i.

[1] *A . . . knots:* Shroud.

If he be so far gone, 'tis time to moan.
Here's pen and ink and paper and all things ready.
Will't please your worship to make your will?
    S. Walt. My will? Yes, yes, what else? Who writes
      apace now?
    All. That can your man Davy, an't like your
      worship,   100
A fair, fast, legible hand.
    S. Walt.   Set it down, then:
Imprimis, I bequeath to yonder wittol
Three times his weight in curses.
    All.   How?
    S. Walt. All plagues of body and of mind.
    All. Write them not down, Davy.
    Davy. It is his will; I must.
    S. Walt. Together also
With such a sickness ten days ere his death.
    All. There's a sweet legacy;
I am almost choked with't.   110
    S. Walt. Next I bequeath to that foul whore, his
      wife,
All barrenness of joy, a drought of virtue,
And dearth of all repentance. For her end,
The common misery of an English strumpet,
In French and Dutch[2] beholding, ere she dies,
Confusion of her brats before her eyes,
And never shed a tear for it.

                 Enter a Servant.

    Serv. Where's the knight?
O sir, the gentleman you wounded is newly departed.
    S. Walt. Dead? Lift, lift; who helps me?   120
    All. Let the law lift you now that must have all;
I have done lifting[3] on you, and my wife too.
    Serv. You were best lock yourself close.
    All. Not in my house, sir.
I'll harbor no such persons as men-slayers;
Lock yourself where you will.
    S. Walt. What's this?
    Mrs. All. Why, husband?
    All. I know what I do, wife.
    Mrs. All. You cannot tell yet;   130
For having killed the man in his defense,
Neither his life nor estate will be touched, husband.
    All. Away, wife! hear a fool.[4] His lands will hang
      him.[5]
    S. Walt. Am I denied a chamber?
What say you, forsooth?
    Mrs. All. Alas, sir, I am one that would have all well,
But must obey my husband. Prithee, love,

Let the poor gentleman stay, being so sore wounded.
There's a close chamber at one end of the garret
We never use; let him have that, I prithee.   140
    All. We never use? You forget sickness, then,
And physic times. Is't not a place for easement?[6]

                 Enter a Servant.

    S. Walt. Oh, death. Do I hear this with part
Of former life in me?—What's the news now?
    Serv. Troth, worse and worse; you're like to lose
      your land
If the law save your life, sir, or the surgeon.
    All. [*Aside*] Hark you there, wife.
    S. Walt. Why, how, sir?
    Serv. Sir Oliver Kix's wife is new quickened;
That child undoes you, sir.   150
    S. Walt. All ill at once.
    All. I wonder what he makes here with his consorts.
Cannot our house be private to ourselves
But we must have such guests? I pray, depart, sirs,
And take your murderer along with you;
Good he were apprehended ere he go;
H'as killed some honest gentleman; send for officers.
    S. Walt. I'll soon save you that labor.
    All. I must tell you, sir,
You have been somewhat bolder in my house   160
Than I could well like of; I suffered you
Till it stuck here at my heart. I tell you truly,
I thought you had been familiar with my wife once.
    Mrs. All. With me? I'll see him hanged first; I defy
      him
And all such gentlemen in the like extremity.
    S. Walt. If ever eyes were open, these are they;
Gamesters, farewell; I have nothing left to play.
                            Exit.
    All. And therefore get you gone, sir.
    Davy.   Of all wittols
Be thou the head; [*To* MRS. ALLWIT] thou the grand
      whore of spittles.[7]
                    Exit [*with* Servants].
    All. So, since he's like now to be rid of all,   170
I am right glad I am so well rid of him.
    Mrs. All. I knew he durst not stay when you named
      officers.
    All. That stopped his spirits straight.
What shall we do now, wife?
    Mrs. All. As we were wont to do.
    All. We are richly furnished, wife, with household
      stuff.
    Mrs. All. Let's let out lodgings, then,
And take a house in the Strand.[8]
    All. In troth, a match, wench;
We are simply stocked with cloth-of-tissue[9] cushions
To furnish out bay-windows; push, what not that's
      quaint   181
And costly, from the top to the bottom?
Life, for furniture, we may lodge a countess;
There's a close-stool[10] of tawny velvet too,
Now I think on't, wife.
    Mrs. All. There's that should be, sir;
Your nose must be in everything.

---

    [2] *French and Dutch:* venereal diseases.
    [3] *lifting:* stealing, with double entendre.
    [4] *hear a fool:* listen to a fool talking.
    [5] *His . . . him:* i.e., his property, forfeit to the Crown, will
make his execution more desirable.
    [6] *place for easement:* privy.
    [7] *spittles:* hospitals for venereal diseases.
    [8] *Strand:* fashionable district of London, where courtesans displayed themselves at windows; the Allwits plan to
run a plush brothel.
    [9] *cloth-of-tissue:* cloth with gold and silver threads.
    [10] *close-stool:* commode.

All. I have done, wench;
And let this stand in every gallant's chamber:
There's no gamester like a politic sinner,   190
For whoe'er games, the box[11] is sure a winner.
                                        Ex[eunt].

[V.ii]

              Enter YELLOWHAMMER *and his* Wife.

Maud. O husband, husband, she will die, she will
    die;
There is no sign but death.
Yell.   'Twill be our shame, then.
Maud. Oh, how she's changed in compass of an
    hour.
Yell. Ah, my poor girl! good faith, thou wert too
    cruel
To drag her by the hair.
Maud. You would have done as much, sir,
To curb her of her humor.
Yell. 'Tis curbed sweetly; she catched her bane
    o'th'water.

                     Enter TIM.

Maud. How now, Tim?
Tim. Faith, busy, mother, about an epitaph   10
Upon my sister's death.
Maud. Death! she is not dead, I hope.
Tim. No; but she means to be, and that's as good;
And when a thing's done, 'tis done.
You taught me that, mother.
Yell. What is your tutor doing?
Tim. Making one, too, in principal[1] pure Latin
Culled out of Ovid, *De Tristibus.*[2]
Yell. How does your sister look? Is she not
    changed?
Tim. Changed? Gold into white money[3] was never
    so changed   20
As is my sister's color into paleness.

            Enter MOLL [*led in by* Servants].

Yell. Oh, here she's brought; see how she looks like
    death.
Tim. Looks she like death, and ne'er a word made
    yet?
I must go beat my brains against a bedpost
And get before my tutor.
                                        [*Exit.*]
Yell. Speak, how dost thou?
Moll. I hope I shall be well, for I am as sick at heart
As I can be.
Yell. 'Las, my poor girl,
The doctor's making a most sovereign drink for thee,
The worst ingredients dissolved pearl and amber;   31
We spare no cost, girl.
Moll. Your love comes too late;
Yet timely thanks reward it. What is comfort
When the poor patient's heart is past relief?
It is no doctor's art can cure my grief.

Yell. All is cast away, then;
Prithee look upon me cheerfully.
Maud. Sing but a strain or two; thou wilt not think
How 'twill revive thy spirits; strive with thy fit,[4]   40
Prithee sweet Moll.
Moll. You shall have my good will, mother.
Maud. Why, well said, wench.

                     THE SONG

Moll.   *Weep eyes, break heart,*
          My love and I must part;
          Cruel fates true love do soonest sever;
          Oh, I shall see thee never, never, never.
          Oh, happy is the maid whose life takes end
          Ere it knows parents' frown or loss of friend.
          Weep eyes, break heart,   50
          My love and I must part.

          Enter TOUCHWOOD SENIOR *with a letter.*

Maud. Oh, I could die with music. Well sung, girl.
Moll. If you call it so, it was.
Yell. She plays the swan and sings herself to death.
Touch. Sen. By your leave, sir.
Yell. What are you, sir? Or what's your business,
    pray?
Touch. Sen. I may be now admitted, though the
    brother
Of him your hate pursued. It spreads no further;
Your malice sets[5] in death, does it not, sir?
Yell. In death?   60
Touch. Sen. He's dead. 'Twas a dear love to him;
It cost him but his life; that was all, sir;
He paid enough, poor gentleman, for all his love.
Yell. [*Aside*] There's all our ill removed, if she were
    well now.
[*Aloud*] Impute not, sir, his end to any hate
That sprung from us; he had a fair wound brought
    that.
Touch. Sen. That helped him forward, I must needs
    confess.
But the restraint of love and your unkindness,
Those were the wounds that from his heart drew
    blood.
But, being past help, let words forget it too;   70
Scarcely three minutes ere his eyelids closed
And took eternal leave of this world's light,
He wrote this letter, which by oath he bound me
To give to her own hands. That's all my business.
Yell. You may perform it then; there she sits.
Touch. Sen. Oh, with a following look.
Yell. Ay, trust me, sir, I think she'll follow him
    quickly.
Touch. Sen. Here's some gold

_____

[11] *box:* the "house," with possible connotation of coffin.
V.ii.
   [1] *principal:* excellent.
   [2] Ovid, *De Tristibus:* Ovid's *Tristio,* used as a textbook.
   [3] *white money:* silver.   [4] *fit:* song; attack of sorrow.
   [5] *sets:* abates.

He willed me to distribute faithfully amongst your
     servants.
     Yell. 'Las, what doth he mean, sir?   80
     Touch. Sen. How cheer you, mistress?
     Moll. I must learn of you, sir.
     Touch. Sen. Here's a letter from a friend of yours;

                                        [*Giving letter*]

And where that fails in satisfaction,
I have a sad tongue ready to supply.
     Moll. How does he, ere I look on't?
     Touch. Sen. Seldom better; h'as a contented health
          now.
     Moll. I am most glad on't.
                                              [*Reads.*]
     Maud. Dead, sir?
     Yell. He is. Now, wife, let's but get the girl   90
Upon her legs again, and to church roundly[6] with her.
     Moll. Oh, sick to death, he tells me;
How does he after this?
     Touch. Sen. Faith, feels no pain at all; he's dead,
          sweet mistress.
     Moll. Peace close mine eyes.
                                             [*Faints.*]
     Yell. The girl, look to the girl, wife.
     Maud. Moll! daughter, sweet girl, speak,
Look but once up; thou shalt have all the wishes of thy
     heart
That wealth can purchase.
     Yell. Oh, she's gone forever; that letter broke her
          heart.   100
     Touch. Sen. As good now, then, as let her lie in
          torment
And then break it.

                         Enter SUSAN.

     Maud. O Susan, she thou lovedst so dear is gone.
     Sus. Oh, sweet maid.
     Touch. Sen. This is she that helped her still.
I've a reward here for thee.
     Yell. Take her in;
Remove her from our sight, our shame and sorrow.
     Touch. Sen. Stay, let me help thee; 'tis the last cold
          kindness
I can perform for my sweet brother's sake.   110
          [*Exeunt* TOUCHWOOD SENIOR, SUSAN, *and*
                    Servants, *carrying* MOLL.]
     Yell. All the whole street will hate us, and the world
Point me out cruel. It is our best course, wife,
After we have given order for the funeral,
To absent ourselves till she be laid in ground.
     Maud. Where shall we spend that time?
     Yell. I'll tell thee where, wench: go to some private
          church

---

6 *roundly:* promptly.

V.iii.
     1 *tell:* count.   2 *multipliers:* breeders.
     3 *monopoly:* exclusive right to the sale of commodities,
granted by the Crown.

And marry Tim to the rich Brecknock gentlewoman.
     Maud.   Mass,
          a match!
We'll not lose all at once; somewhat we'll catch.
                                             Ex[*eunt*].

[V.iii]

                 Enter SIR OLIVER *and* Servants.

     S. Ol. Ho, my wife's quickened; I am a man forever.
I think I have bestirred my stumps, i'faith.
Run, get your fellows all together instantly;
Then to the parish church and ring the bells.
     1 Serv. It shall be done, sir.
     S. Ol. Upon my love I charge you, villain, that you
make a bonfire before the door at night.
     2 Serv. A bonfire, sir?
     S. Ol. A thwacking one, I charge you.
     2 Serv. [*Aside*] This is monstrous.   10
                                              [*Exit.*]
     S. Ol. Run, tell[1] a hundred pound out for the
          gentleman
That gave my wife the drink, the first thing you do.
     3 Serv. A hundred pounds, sir?
     S. Ol. A bargain. As our joy grows,
We must remember still from whence it flows,
Or else we prove ungrateful multipliers.[2]
                                  [*Exit* Third Servant.]
The child is coming, and the land comes after.
The news of this will make a poor Sir Walter;
I have struck it home, i'faith.
     4 Serv. That you have, marry, sir.   20
But will not your worship go to the funeral
Of both these lovers?
     S. Ol. Both? Go both together?
     4 Serv. Ay, sir; the gentleman's brother will have it
          so;
'Twill be the pitifulest sight: there's such running,
Such rumors, and such throngs; a pair of lovers
Had never more spectators, more men's pities
Or women's wet eyes.
     S. Ol. My wife helps the number, then?   29
     4 Serv. There's such drawing out of handkerchers;
And those that have no handkerchers lift up aprons.
     S. Ol. Her parents may have joyful hearts at this;
I would not have my cruelty so talked on
To any child of mine for a monopoly.[3]
     4 Serv. I believe you, sir.
'Tis cast so, too, that both their coffins meet,
Which will be lamentable.
     S. Ol.   Come, we'll see't.

[V.iv]

*Recorders dolefully playing. Enter at one door the coffin
of the Gentleman* [TOUCHWOOD JUNIOR], *solemnly
decked, his sword upon it, attended by many in black*
     [*including* SIR OLIVER KIX, ALLWIT, *and a*
Parson], *his brother* [TOUCHWOOD SENIOR] *being
the chief mourner. At the other door, the coffin of the*

virgin [MOLL], *with a garland of flowers, with
epitaphs pinned on't, attended by maids and women
[including* LADY KIX, MISTRESS ALLWIT, *and*
SUSAN]. *Then set them down one right over against the
other, while all the company seem to weep and mourn;
there is a sad song in the music room.*

Touch. Sen. Never could death boast of a richer
  prize
From the first parent;[1] let the world bring forth
A pair of truer hearts. To speak but truth
Of this departed gentleman in a brother
Might, by hard censure, be called flattery,
Which makes me rather silent in his right
Than so to be delivered to the thoughts
Of any envious hearer starved in virtue
And therefore pining to hear others thrive.
But for this maid, whom envy cannot hurt   10
With all her poisons, having left to ages
The true chaste monument of her living name,
Which no time can deface, I say of her
The full truth freely, without fear of censure:
What nature could there shine that might redeem
Perfection home to woman but in her
Was fully glorious? Beauty set in goodness
Speaks what she was, that jewel so infixed
There was no want of anything of life
To make these virtuous precedents[2] man and wife. 20
  All. Great pity of their deaths.
  Omnes.   Ne'er more pity.
  L. Kix. It makes a hundred weeping eyes, sweet
    gossip.
  Touch. Sen. I cannot think there's any one amongst
    you
In this full fair assembly, maid, man, or wife,
Whose heart would not have sprung with joy and
  gladness
To have seen their marriage day.
  All. It would have made a thousand joyful hearts.
  Touch. Sen. [*To* TOUCHWOOD JUNIOR *and* MOLL]
Up then, apace and take your fortunes;
Make these joyful hearts; here's none but friends.

    [MOLL *and* TOUCHWOOD JUNIOR *rise from
    their coffins.*]

  All. Alive, sir? Oh, sweet, dear couple.   30
  Touch. Sen. Nay, do not hinder 'em now; stand from
    about 'em;
If she be caught again, and have this time,
I'll ne'er plot further for 'em, nor this honest
  chambermaid
That helped all at a push.[3]
  Touch. Jun.[4]   Good sir, apace.
  Pars. Hands join now, but hearts forever,
Which no parents' mood shall sever.
You shall forsake all widows, wives, and maids;
You, lords, knights, gentlemen, and men of trades;
And if in haste any article misses,
Go interline it with a brace of kisses.   40
  Touch. Sen. Here's a thing trolled[5] nimbly. Give
    you joy, brother;

Were't not better thou shouldst have her
Than the maid should die?
  Mrs. All. To you, sweet mistress bride.
  Omnes. Joy, joy to you both.
  Touch. Sen. Here be your wedding sheets you
brought along with you; you may both go to bed when
you please to.
  Touch. Jun. My joy wants utterance.
  Touch. Sen. Utter[6] all at night then, brother.   50
  Moll. I am silent with delight.
  Touch. Sen. Sister, delight will silence any woman,
But you'll find your tongue again among maidservants,
Now you keep house, sister.
  Omnes. Never was hour so filled with joy and
    wonder.
  Touch. Sen. To tell you the full story of this
    chambermaid
And of her kindness in this business to us,
'Twould ask an hour's discourse. In brief, 'twas she
That wrought it to this purpose cunningly.
  Omnes. We shall all love her for't.   60

    Enter YELLOWHAMMER *and his* Wife.

See who comes here now.
  Touch. Sen. A storm, a storm, but we are sheltered
    for it.
  Yell. I will prevent[7] you all and mock you thus,
You and your expectations: I stand happy
Both in your lives and your hearts' combination.
  Touch. Sen. Here's a strange day again.
  Yell. The knight's proved villain;
All's come out now, his niece an arrant baggage.
My poor boy Tim is cast away this morning
Even before breakfast, married a whore   70
Next to his heart.
  Omnes.   A whore?
  Yell.   His niece forsooth.
  All. I think we rid our hands in good time of him.
  Mrs. All. I knew he was past the best when I gave
    him over.
What is become of him, pray, sir?
  Yell. Who, the knight? He lies i'th'knight's ward[8]
    now.
[*To* LADY KIX] Your belly, lady, begins to blossom.
    There's no peace for him;
His creditors are so greedy.
  S. Ol. [*To* TOUCHWOOD SENIOR] Master
    Touchwood, hear'st thou this news?
I am so endeared to thee for my wife's fruitfulness
That I charge you both, your wife and thee,   80
To live no more asunder for the world's frowns;
I have purse and bed and board for you;

V.iv.
  [1] *From . . . parent:* Since Adam.
  [2] *precedents:* worthy examples.
  [3] *at a push:* with a determined effort.
  [4] *Touch. Jun.:* Q "Touchwood Senior."
  [5] *trolled:* spoken rapidly.
  [6] *Utter:* with sexual meaning.   [7] *prevent:* anticipate.
  [8] *knight's ward:* one of the four socially segregated sec-
tions of the debtors' prison.

Be not afraid to go to your business roundly;
Get children, and I'll keep them.
> Touch. Sen. Say you so, sir?
> S. Ol. Prove[9] me with three at a birth, and thou
> dar'st now.
> Touch. Sen. Take heed how you dare a man, while
> you live, sir,
That has good skill at his weapon.

Enter TIM *and* Welsh Gentlewoman.

> S. Ol. Foot, I dare you, sir.
> Yell. Look, gentlemen, if ever you saw the picture
Of the unfortunate marriage, yonder 'tis. 90
> W. Wom. Nay, good sweet Tim—
> Tim. Come from the university
To marry a whore in London, with my tutor too!
O tempora! O mores![10]
> Tut. Prithee, Tim, be patient.
> Tim. I bought a jade[11] at Cambridge.
I'll let her out to execution, tutor,
For eighteen pence a day, or Brainford horse-races;
She'll serve to carry seven miles out of town well.
Where be these mountains? I was promised mountains,
But there's such a mist I can see none of 'em. 101
What are become of those two thousand runts?
Let's have a bout with them in the meantime.
A vengeance runt[12] thee!
> Maud. Good sweet Tim, have
> patience.

> Tim. *Flectere si nequeo superos, Acheronta movebo,*[13]
> mother.
> Maud. I think you have married her in logic, Tim:
You told me once by logic you would prove
A whore an honest woman; prove her so, Tim,
And take her for thy labor.
> Tim. Troth, I thank you. 110
I grant you I may prove another man's wife so,
But not mine own.
> Maud. There's no remedy now, Tim;
You must prove her so as well as you may.
> Tim. Why then my tutor and I will about her
As well as we can.
Uxor non est meretrix; ergo falleris.[14]
> W. Wom. Sir, if your logic cannot prove me honest,
There's a thing called marriage, and that makes me
> honest. 118
> Maud. Oh, there's a trick beyond your logic, Tim.
> Tim. I perceive, then, a woman may be honest
according to the English print when she is a whore in
the Latin. So much for marriage and logic. I'll love her
for her wit; I'll pick out my runts there; and for my
mountains, I'll mount upon. . . .
> Yell. So fortune seldom deals two marriages
With one hand, and both lucky. The best is,
One feast will serve them both. Marry, for room
I'll have the dinner kept in Goldsmiths' Hall,[15]
To which, kind gallants, I invite you all.
> *[Exeunt.]*

F I N I S

---

[9] *Prove:* Test. [10] *L.:* famous tag from Cicero.
[11] *jade:* horse; whore. [12] *runt:* reprove.
[13] *L.:* Since I cannot move the gods, I shall move the
lower regions (*Aeneid*, VII. 312).
[14] *L.:* A wife is not a whore; therefore you are wrong.
[15] *Goldsmiths' Hall:* the hall of the Goldsmiths' Company,
near Cheapside.

Thomas Middleton

[*c.* 1580–1627]

William Rowley

[*c.* 1585–*c.* 1625]

THE CHANGELING

FIRST printed only in 1653, THE CHANGELING was licensed for performance by Lady Elizabeth's Company at the Phoenix in 1622, and from the fact that its sources were themselves published in 1621 and 1622 one may infer that it was written just before its first performance. The main plot is based, sometimes virtually verbatim but generally with considerable freedom, on one of thirty lurid and moralistic stories in John Reynolds' *The Triumphs of God's Revenge against the Crying and Execrable Sin of Willful and Premeditated Murder* (1621). An index of the distance the authors of THE CHANGELING moved from their original is the fact that Reynolds' De Flores is a "gallant young gentleman" of conventional appearance and manner. The bedtrick episode involving Diaphanta appears to derive from a 1622 translation by Leonard Digges, *Gerardo, the Unfortunate Spaniard*, though the late date of Digges' work suggests the possibility that the Spanish original was the source; *All's Well That Ends Well* and *Measure for Measure* supply evidence that the trick itself is conventional. The madhouse scenes have no known source. One of the fascinating aspects of the play is the correspondence and careful linking between its two plots, indicating close and thoughtful collaboration (see, for example, the note on the title at the beginning of the text); yet scholars are generally convinced that the subplot and the first and last scenes of the play are Rowley's work and all the rest Middleton's. What actually went on in the process of collaboration remains a mystery. Acknowledged in the order of the authors' names on the title page, Middleton's leadership is evident both in the play's brilliance and in its close connections with others of his plays.

Everything about THE CHANGELING is extraordinary. The great wave of English tragedies that began with GORBODUC and reached its climax in the work of Marlowe, Shakespeare, Webster, and Tourneur had subsided a decade ago, and with Middleton's own *Women Beware Women* and a very few other plays THE CHANGELING stands virtually alone in a period of slick tragicomedy and empty comedy. Equally remarkable is its authorship. Rowley, an actor who seems often to have been type-cast as a fat clown between 1609 and 1624, is credited with a few unimpressive plays and a number of collaborations; the date of his birth is unknown, and that of his death is conjectured at 1625. Middleton was one of the most prolific and skilled of professional playwrights, but his enormous output—over two dozen plays survive—consists primarily of "city comedies," sardonic and clever plays about London life, and the other plays in his canon are competent but usually undistinguished attempts at other fashionable modes—topical satire, romantic tragicomedy, historical drama. Both writers then were professional theater men whose principal objective one may guess to have been to make a living; almost nothing outside of THE CHANGELING suggests its authors' power to create such a play.

If THE CHANGELING shares with other Middleton plays a shrewd gift for theatrical effect, skill in deft and wry characterization, swiftness and economy in language and plot, and a concern with human vice, it differs from all but *Women Beware Women* in its terrifying vision of the easy availability of evil and of the speed with which the most comfortable of lives can turn, through the play of psychic elements that lie below the level at which characters can recognize them, into nightmare. The most dazzling of the lives so ruined is that of Beatrice-Joanna, a spoiled adolescent at the outset whose capacity for destruction is hinted only by her mysterious loathing for the ugly servant who is to become first her agent in murder and then her lover, and whose blackest villainy is disguised, even to herself, by a delicate concern for her "honor." The chasm between her hard, conscious practicality and her hidden motivations, between her sense of her own interest and that interest itself, is a product of the theater that had created Lady Macbeth, and the implications of a metaphysical backdrop (suggested, for example, by the recurrent motif of the game of barley-break with its circle of hell) to this psychologically realistic portrait remind one frequently of Shakespeare. Character, the thematic interrelations between the superficially different plots, language—all contribute to a tragedy of unique and mysterious ambiance, and everything is of a piece. One may note, for example, how much the loneliness of the characters, their isolation from one another as each pursues the obscure goals of his own ego, is supported by the ubiquitous device of the aside:

characters speak to themselves almost as much as they do to each other, as if the chief function of language were to conduct dialogue with oneself.

The basis of the text is the quarto of 1653. Much of the verse in that edition was compressed, perhaps in order to get more text on fewer pages than the manu-script properly required. Our text follows the practice of modern editors in trying to reconstruct the regular versification that seems to have marked the manu-script; largely, this is a matter of turning one line into one and a half or two.

N. R.

The Changeling[1]

DRAMATIS PERSONÆ

VERMANDERO, *father to Beatrice*
TOMAZO DE PIRACQUO, *a noble lord*
ALONZO DE PIRACQUO, *his brother, suitor to Beatrice*
ALSEMERO, *a nobleman, afterwards married to Beatrice*
JASPERINO, *his friend*
ALIBIUS, *a jealous doctor*
LOLLIO, *his man*
PEDRO, *friend to Antonio*
ANTONIO, *the changeling*

FRANCISCUS, *the counterfeit madman*
DE FLORES, *servant to Vermandero*
Madmen
Servants

BEATRICE-JOANNA, *daughter to Vermandero*
DIAPHANTA, *her waiting-woman*
ISABELLA, *wife to Alibus*

The Scene: *Alicant.*[1]

ACT ONE

SCENE ONE

Enter ALSEMERO.

Als. 'Twas in the temple where I first beheld her,
And now again the same; what omen yet
Follows of that? None but imaginary.
Why should my hopes or[1] fate be timorous?
The place is holy, so is my intent;
I love her beauties to the holy purpose,[2]
And that, methinks, admits comparison
With man's first creation, the place blest,[3]
And is his right home back, if he achieve it.
The church hath first begun our interview,   10
And that's the place must join us into one;
So there's beginning and perfection too.

Enter JASPERINO.

Jas. O sir, are you here? Come, the wind's fair with
    you,
Y'are like to have a swift and pleasant passage.
    Als. Sure y'are deceived, friend; 'tis contrary
In my best judgment.
    Jas.   What, for Malta?
If you could buy a gale amongst the witches,[4]
They could not serve you such a lucky pennyworth
As come a' God's name.[5]
    Als.   Even now I observed
The temple's vane[6] to turn full in my face;   20
I know 'tis against me.
    Jas.   Against you?
Then you know not where you are.
    Als.   Not well indeed.
    Jas. Are you not well, sir?
    Als.   Yes, Jasperino.
Unless there be some hidden malady
Within me that I understand not.
    Jas.   And that
I begin to doubt,[7] sir; I never knew
Your inclinations to travels at a pause
With any cause to hinder it, till now.
Ashore you were wont to call your servants up,
And help to trap[8] your horses for the speed;[9]   30
At sea I have seen you weigh the anchor with 'em,
Hoist sails for fear to lose the foremost breath,
Be in continual prayers for fair winds;
And have you changed your orisons?[10]
    Als.   No, friend,
I keep the same church, same devotion.
    Jas. Lover I'm sure y'are none; the stoic was
Found in you long ago; your mother nor
Best friends, who have set snares of beauty (ay,
And choice ones, too), could never trap you that way.
What might be the cause?

THE TITLE
    [1] *Changeling*: (1) one given to change; a fickle or inconstant person; a waverer, turncoat, or renegade; (2) a person or thing (surreptitiously) put in exchange for another; (3) a child (usually stupid or ugly) supposed to have been left by fairies in exchange for one stolen; (4) a half-witted person, idiot, imbecile. Various senses of the word are associated with various characters—(1) with Beatrice-Joanna and initially with Alsemero, (2) with Diaphanta, (4) with Antonio and Franciscus; V. iii. 196–215 suggests that "change" is a significant part of the title.

THE SCENE
    [1] *Alicant*: Mediterranean seaport in the district of Valencia in southeastern Spain.

I.i.
    [1] *or*: perhaps a Q misprint for "of."
    [2] *holy purpose*: marriage.
    [3] *place blest*: Garden of Eden; i.e., marriage can recover the happiness of life before the fall of man.
    [4] *buy . . . witches*: According to a superstition recorded also in *Macbeth*, I. iii. 11ff, witches controlled the winds.
    [5] *a' God's name*: as the gift of God.
    [6] *vane*: weathervane.   [7] *doubt*: fear.   [8] *trap*: harness.
    [9] *for the speed*: to hurry things.   [10] *orisons*: prayers.

Als.   Lord, how violent   40
Thou art! I was but meditating of
Somewhat I heard within the temple.
    Jas. Is this violence? 'Tis but idleness
Compared with your haste yesterday.
    Als. I'm all this while a-going, man.

                    Enter Servants.

    Jas. Backwards, I think, sir. Look, your servants.
    1 Ser. The seamen call; shall we board your trunks?
    Als. No, not today.
    Jas. 'Tis the critical[11] day, it seems, and the sign in
Aquarius.[12]
    2 Ser. [*Aside*] We must not to sea today; this smoke
will bring forth fire.   51
    Als. Keep all on shore; I do not know the end
(Which needs I must do) of an affair in hand
Ere I can go to sea.
    1 Ser. Well, your pleasure.
    2 Ser. [*Aside*] Let him e'en take his leisure too; we
are safer on land.
                        Exeunt Servants.

Enter BEATRICE, DIAPHANTA, *and* Servants.
    [ALSEMERO *greets* BEATRICE *and kisses her.*]

    Jas. [*Aside*] How now! the laws of the Medes[13] are
changed sure. Salute a woman? He kisses too; wonderful! where learnt he this? And does it perfectly   60
too; in my conscience[14] he ne'er rehearsed it before,
Nay, go on, this will be stranger and better news at
Valencia than if he had ransomed half Greece from the
Turk.[15]
    Bea. You are a scholar, sir?
    Als.   A weak one, lady.
    Bea. Which of the sciences is this love you speak of?
    Als. From your tongue I take it to be music.
    Bea. You are skilful in't, can sing at first sight.[16]
    Als. And I have showed you all my skill at once.
I want more words to express me further,   70
And must be forced to repetition:
I love you dearly.
    Bea.   Be better advised, sir.
Our eyes are sentinels unto our judgments
And should give certain judgment what they see;
But they are rash sometimes and tell us wonders
Of common things, which when our judgments find,
They can then check the eyes and call them blind.
    Als. But I am further, lady; yesterday
Was mine eyes' employment, and hither now   79
They brought my judgment, where are both agreed.
Both houses[17] then consenting, 'tis agreed;
Only there wants the confirmation
By the hand royal;[18] that's your part, lady.
    Bea. Oh, there's one[19] above me, sir. [*Aside*] For five
        days past
To be[20] recalled! sure, mine eyes were mistaken,
This was the man was meant me; that he should come
So near his time, and miss it!
    Jas. [*Aside*] We might have come by the carriers[21]
        from Valencia,   88
I see, and saved all our sea-provision: we are at farthest[22]

sure. Methinks I should do something too; I meant to
be a venturer[23] in this voyage. Yonder's another
vessel; I'll board[24] her; If she be lawful prize,[25] down
goes her topsail.[26]

                [*Greets* DIAPHANTA.]

                Enter DE FLORES.

    De F. Lady, your father—
    Bea.   Is in health, I hope.
    De F. Your eye shall instantly instruct you, lady.
He's coming hitherward.
    Bea.   What needed then
Your duteous preface? I had rather
He had come unexpected; you must stall[27]
A good presence with unnecessary blabbing;
And how welcome for your part you are,   100
I'm sure you know.
    De F. [*Aside*]   Will't never mend this scorn,
One side nor other? Must I be enjoined
To follow still[28] whilst she flies from me? Well,
Fates do your worst; I'll please myself with sight
Of her, at all opportunities,
If but to spite her anger; I know she had
Rather see me dead than living, and yet
She knows no cause for't, but a peevish will.
    Als. You seemed displeased, lady, on the sudden.
    Bea. Your pardon, sir, 'tis my infirmity,   110
Nor can I other reason render you
Than his or hers, of[29] some particular thing
They must abandon as a deadly poison,
Which to a thousand other tastes were wholesome.
Such to mine eyes is that same fellow there,
The same that report speaks of the basilisk.[30]
    Als. This is a frequent frailty in our nature;
There's scarce a man amongst a thousand found,[31]
But hath his imperfection: one distastes[32]
The scent of roses, which to infinites[33]   120
Most pleasing is, and odoriferous;
One oil,[34] the enemy of poison;
Another wine, the cheerer of the heart,
And lively refresher of the countenance.

---

[11] *critical:* the day of decision.
[12] *Aquarius:* the sign indicating a favorable time for travel
by water.
[13] *laws of the Medes:* proverbially unalterable laws.
[14] *in my conscience:* upon my word.
[15] *Greece . . . Turk:* Greece was part of the Turkish empire.
[16] *sing . . . sight:* sight-read (music) right off.
[17] *Both houses:* sense perception and reason imagined as
houses of Parliament that have approved a bill.
[18] *Only . . . royal:* Only the Queen's signature is lacking.
[19] *one:* her father; God(?).
[20] *For . . . be:* If only . . . could.
[21] *carriers:* agents of land transportation.
[22] *at farthest:* farthest away from our goal.
[23] *venturer:* commercial partner.
[24] *board:* come up close to, alongside of.
[25] *lawful prize:* a ship that no law forbids him to take.
[26] *down . . . topsail:* in surrender.   [27] *stall:* forestall.
[28] *still:* always.   [29] *of:* concerning (Q reads "or").
[30] *basilisk:* legendary beast whose look was fatal.
[31] *found:* Q "sound."   [32] *distastes:* dislikes.
[33] *infinites:* innumerable people.
[34] *oil:* medicinal extract.

Indeed this fault (if so it be) is general;
There's scarce a thing but is both loved and loathed.
Myself, I must confess, have the same frailty.

    Bea. And what may be your poison, sir? I am bold
with you.

    Als. What³⁵ might be your desire, perhaps, a cherry.

    Bea. I am no enemy to any creature   130
My memory has but yon gentleman.

    Als. He does ill to tempt your sight, if he knew it.

    Bea. He cannot be ignorant of that, sir;
I have not spared to tell him so, and I want
To help myself, since he's a gentleman
In good respect³⁶ with my father and follows him.

    Als. He's out of his place then now.

                                They talk apart.

    Jas. I am a mad wag, wench.

    Dia. So methinks; but for your comfort I can tell
you, we have a doctor³⁷ in the city that undertakes the
cure of such.   141

    Jas. Tush, I know what physic is best for the state
of mine own body.

    Dia. 'Tis scarce a well-governed state, I believe.

    Jas. I could show thee such a thing with an ingre-
dient that we two would compound together, and if it
did not tame the maddest blood i' th' town for two
hours after, I'll ne'er profess physic³⁸ again.

    Dia. A little poppy, sir, were good to cause you sleep.

    Jas. Poppy! I'll give thee a pop i' th' lips for that
first, and begin there: 151

                            [Kisses her.]

poppy³⁹ is one simple⁴⁰ indeed, and cuckoo⁴¹ (what
you call 't) another. I'll discover⁴² no more now; another
time I'll show thee all.

    Bea. My father, sir.

           Enter VERMANDERO *and* Servants.

    Ver. Oh, Joanna, I came to meet thee,
Your devotion's ended?

    Bea.   For this time, sir.
[Aside] I shall change my saint,⁴³ I fear me; I find
A giddy turning in me. [*To* VERMANDERO] Sir, this
    while

---

³⁵ *What:* Q "And what."
³⁶ *respect:* standing; i.e., he has my father's esteem.
³⁷ *doctor:* Alibius.   ³⁸ *physic:* medicine.
³⁹ *poppy:* opium.
⁴⁰ *simple:* plant or herb used for medicinal purposes.
⁴¹ *cuckoo:* wildflower used medicinally.
⁴² *discover:* reveal.   ⁴³ *saint:* the one she prays to.
⁴⁴ *article:* proviso.   ⁴⁵ *use:* customarily do.
⁴⁶ *promonts':* promontories'.
⁴⁷ *native:* pertaining to where one was born.
⁴⁸ *He . . . so:* He used to call me his best love.
⁴⁹ *Iulan down:* the first beard of youth; the trisyllabic
Iulan is made from the name of Aeneas' son, which itself
was said to have been derived from the Greek ἴουλος, first
growth of the beard.
⁵⁰ *Saint Jacques:* Santiago, patron saint of Spain.
⁵¹ *Gibraltar:* the Dutch defeated their Spanish masters in
a sea battle here on April 25, 1607.
⁵² *late league:* Treaty of the Hague, 9 April 1609, which
established a truce.   ⁵³ *toy:* trivial matter.

I am beholding to this gentleman,   160
Who left his own way to keep me company,
And in discourse I find him much desirous
To see your castle. He hath deserved it, sir,
If ye please to grant it.

    Ver.   With all my heart, sir.
Yet there's an article⁴⁴ between; I must know
Your country. We use⁴⁵ not to give survey
Of our chief strengths to strangers; our citadels
Are placed conspicuous to outward view,
On promonts'⁴⁶ tops, but within are secrets.

    Als. A Valencian, sir.

    Ver.   A Valencian?   170
That native,⁴⁷ sir; of what name, I beseech you?

    Als. Alsemero, sir.

    Ver.   Alsemero—not the son
Of John de Alsemero?

    Als.   The same, sir.

    Ver. My best love bids you welcome.

    Bea. [*Aside*]   He was wont
To call me so,⁴⁸ and then he speaks a most
Unfeignèd truth.

    Ver.   Oh, sir, I knew your father;
We two were in acquaintance long ago,
Before our chins were worth Iulan down,⁴⁹
And so continued till the stamp of time
Had coined us into silver. Well, he's gone;   180
A good soldier went with him.

    Als. You went together in that, sir.

    Ver. No, by Saint Jacques,⁵⁰ I came behind him;
Yet I have done somewhat too. An unhappy day
Swallowed him at last at Gibraltar⁵¹
In fight with those rebellious Hollanders,
Was it not so?

    Als.   Whose death I had revenged,
Or followed him in fate, had not the late league⁵²
Prevented me.

    Ver.   Ay, ay, 'twas time to breathe.
Oh, Joanna, I should ha' told thee news: 190
I saw Piracquo lately.

    Bea. [*Aside*]   That's ill news.

    Ver. He's hot preparing for this day of triumph;
Thou must be a bride within this sevennight.

    Als.   Ha!

    Bea. Nay, good sir, be not so violent; with speed
I cannot render satisfaction
Unto the dear companion of my soul,
Virginity, whom I thus long have lived with,
And part with it so rude and suddenly.
Can such friends divide, never to meet again,   199
Without a solemn farewell?

    Ver.   Tush, tush, there's a toy.⁵³

    Als. [*Aside*] I must now part, and never meet again
With any joy on earth. [*To* VERMANDERO] Sir, your
    pardon,
My affairs call on me.

    Ver.   How, sir? By no means;
Not changed so soon, I hope? You must see my castle
And her best entertainment ere we part;
I shall think myself unkindly used else.
Come, come, let's on; I had good hope your stay

Had been a while with us in Alicant;
I might have bid you to my daughter's wedding.

Als. [*Aside*] He means to feast me, and poisons me
    beforehand;   210
[*To* VERMANDERO] I should be dearly glad to be there,
    sir,
Did my occasions suit as I could wish.

Bea. I shall be sorry if you be not there
When it is done, sir;—but not so suddenly.

Ver. I tell you, sir, the gentleman's complete,[54]
A courtier and a gallant, enriched
With many fair and noble ornaments;[55]
I would not change him for a son-in-law
For any he in Spain, the proudest he,
And we have great ones, that you know.

Als.   He's much
Bound to you, sir.

Ver.   He shall be bound to me   221
As fast as this tie can hold him; I'll want
My will[56] else.

Bea. [*Aside*] I shall want mine if you do it.

Ver. But come, by the way I'll tell you more of him.

Als. [*Aside*] How shall I dare to venture in his castle,
When he discharges murderers[57] at the gate?
But I must on, for back I cannot go.

Bea. [*Aside*] Not this serpent gone yet?

                           [*Drops a glove.*]

Ver.   Look, girl,
    thy glove's fall'n;
Stay, stay—De Flores, help a little.
         [*Exeunt* VERMANDERO, ALSEMERO,
            JASPERINO, *and* Servants.]

De F.   Here, lady.

                          [*Offers the glove.*]

Bea. Mischief on your officious forwardness!   230
Who bade you stoop? They touch my hand no more;
There, for t'other's sake I part with this,

    [*Takes off the other glove and throws it down.*]

Take 'em and draw thine own skin off with 'em.
        Exeunt [BEATRICE *and* DIAPHANTA.]

De F. Here's a favor come, with a mischief! Now[58] I
    know
She had rather wear my pelt tanned in a pair,
Of dancing pumps, than I should thrust my fingers
Into her sockets here, I know she hates me,
Yet cannot choose but love her.
No matter, if but to vex her, I'll haunt her still;
Though I get nothing else, I'll have my will.   240
                             Exit.

[I.ii]

          Enter ALIBIUS *and* LOLLIO.

Alib. Lollio, I must trust thee with a secret,
But thou must keep it.

Lol. I was ever close to a secret, sir.

Alib. The diligence that I have found in thee,
The care and industry already past,

Assures me of thy good continuance.
Lollio, I have a wife.

Lol. Fie, sir, 'tis too late to keep her secret, she's
known to be married all the town and country over.

Alib. Thou goest too fast my Lollio; that knowledge
I allow no man can be barred it;   11
But there is a knowledge which is nearer;
Deeper, and sweeter, Lollio.

Lol. Well, sir, let us handle that between you and I.

Alib. 'Tis that I go about, man; Lollio,
My wife is young.

Lol. So much the worse to be kept secret, sir.

Alib. Why, now thou meet'st the substance of the
    point:
I am old, Lollio.

Lol. No, sir, 'tis I am old Lollio.   20

Alib. Yet why may not this concord and sympathize?
Old trees and young plants often grow together,
Well enough agreeing.

Lol. Ay, sir, but the old trees raise themselves higher
and broader than the young plants.

Alib. Shrewd application![1] There's the fear, man;
I would wear my ring on my own finger;[2]
Whilst it is borrowed it is none of mine,
But his that useth it.

Lol. You must keep it on still then; if it but lie by,
one or other will be thrusting into't.   31

Alib. Thou conceiv'st[3] me, Lollio; here thy watchful
    eye
Must have employment; I cannot always be
At home.

Lol. I dare swear you cannot.

Alib. I must look out.

Lol. I know't, you must look out, 'tis every man's
case.

Alib. Here I do say must thy employment be,
To watch her treadings, and in my absence   40
Supply my place.

Lol. I'll do my best, sir, yet surely I cannot see who
you should have cause to be jealous of.

Alib. Thy reason for that, Lollio? 'Tis a comfortable
question.

Lol. We have but two sorts of people in the house,
and both under the whip, that's fools and madmen; the
one has not wit enough to be knaves, and the other not
knavery enough to be fools.

Alib. Ay those are all my patients, Lollio.   50
I do profess the cure of either sort;
My trade, my living 'tis, I thrive by it;
But here's the care that mixes with my thrift:
The daily visitants,[4] that come to see

---

[54] *complete:* perfect.   [55] *ornaments:* distinctions.
[56] *want My will:* fail to achieve what I desire.
[57] *murderers:* small cannon (with an ironic second meaning).
[58] *Now:* Since; perhaps although.

I.ii.
[1] *application:* i.e., the proverb applies in that the cuckold's
horns will make Alibius taller than his wife.
[2] *I . . . finger:* i.e., keep my wife to myself.
[3] *conceiv'st:* understandest.
[4] *visitants:* Madhouses were regularly visited as places of
entertainment.

My brainsick patients I would not have
To see my wife. Gallants I do observe
Of quick enticing eyes, rich in habits,[5]
Of stature and proportion very comely;
These are most shrewd temptations, Lollio.   59

Lol. They may be easily answered, sir; if they come
to see the fools and madmen, you and I may serve the
turn, and let my mistress alone; she's of neither sort.

Alib. 'Tis a good ward;[6] indeed, come they to see
Our madmen or our fools; let 'em see no more
Than what they come for; by that consequent
They must not see her; I'm sure she's no fool.

Lol. And I'm sure she's no madman.

Alib. Hold that buckler[7] fast, Lollio; my trust
Is on thee, and I account it firm and strong.
What hour is't, Lollio?   70

Lol. Towards belly-hour, sir.

Alib. Dinner time? Thou mean'st twelve o'clock.

Lol. Yes, sir, for every part has his hour. We wake at
six and look about us, that's eye-hour; at seven we
should pray, that's knee-hour; at eight walk, that's leg-
hour; at nine gather flowers and pluck a rose,[8] that's
nose-hour; at ten we drink, that's mouth-hour; at
eleven lay about us for victuals, that's hand-hour; at
twelve go to dinner, that's belly-hour.

Alib. Profoundly, Lollio! It will be long   80
Ere all thy scholars learn this lesson, and
I did look to have a new one entered;—stay,
I think my expectation is come home.

Enter PEDRO, *and* ANTONIO *like an idiot.*

Ped. Save you, sir; my business speaks itself,
This sight takes off the labor of my tongue.

Alib. Ay, ay, sir;
'Tis plain enough, you mean him for my patient.

Ped. And if your pains prove but commodious,[9] to
give but some little strength to his sick and weak part
of nature in him,   90

[*Gives him money.*]

these are but patterns to show you of the whole pieces
that will follow to you, beside the charge of diet, washing, and other necessaries fully defrayed.

Alib. Believe it, sir, there shall no care be wanting.

Lol. Sir, an officer in this place may deserve something; the trouble will pass through my hands.

Ped. 'Tis fit something should come to your hands
then, sir.

[*Gives him money.*]

---

[5] *habits:* clothes.
[6] *ward:* defensive position (fencing).   [7] *buckler:* shield.
[8] *pluck a rose:* eliminate (privies were often located in the
garden).   [9] *commodious:* beneficial.   [10] *sweet:* clean.
[11] *laugh . . . beast:* according to long tradition, men were
distinguished from lower creatures by the ability to laugh.
[12] *no cost want:* no expense spared.
[13] *magnifico:* one of high authority.
[14] *constable:* traditionally dimwitted (cf. Dogberry in *Ado*).
[15] *headborough, beadle:* low-ranking parish officers like
constables in authority.
[16] *justice:* also thought of as stupid (cf. Shakespeare's
Shallow and Silence).   [17] *state:* position as keeper.
[18] *try his wit:* test his intelligence.   [19] *form:* class.

Lol. Yes, sir, 'tis I must keep him sweet[10] and read
to him; what is his name?   100

Ped. His name is Antonio; marry, we use but half to
him, only Tony.

Lol. Tony, Tony, 'tis enough, and a very good name
for a fool; what's your name, Tony?

Ant. He, he, he! well, I thank you, cousin; he, he he!

Lol. Good boy! hold up your head. He can laugh; I
perceive by that he is no beast.[11]

Ped. Well, sir,
If you can raise him but to any height,
Any degree of wit, might he attain,   110
As I might say, to creep but on all four
Towards the chair of wit, or walk on crutches,
'Twould add an honor to your worthy pains,
And a great family might pray for you,
To which he should be heir, had he discretion
To claim and guide his own; assure you, sir,
He is a gentleman.

Lol. Nay, there's nobody doubted that. At first sight
I knew him for a gentleman; he looks no other yet.

Ped. Let him have good attendance and sweet
lodging.   121

Lol. As good as my mistress lies in, sir; and as you
allow us time and means, we can raise him to the higher
degree of discretion.

Ped. Nay, there shall no cost want,[12] sir.

Lol. He will hardly be stretched up to the wit of a
magnifico.[13]

Ped. Oh, no, that's not to be expected; far shorter
will be enough.

Lol. I'll warrant you I make him fit to bear office in
five weeks; I'll undertake to wind him up to the wit of
constable.[14]   132

Ped. If it be lower than that it might serve turn.

Lol. No, fie, to level him with a headborough,
beadle,[15] or watchman were but little better than he is;
constable I'll able him. If he do come to be a justice[16]
afterwards, let him thank the keeper. Or I'll go further
with you; say I do bring him up to my own pitch, say I
make him as wise as myself.

Ped. Why, there I would have it.   140

Lol. Well, go to, either I'll be as arrant a fool as he,
or he shall be as wise as I, and then I think 'twill serve
his turn.

Ped. Nay, I do like thy wit passing well.

Lol. Yes, you may; yet if I had not been a fool, I had
had more wit than I have too; remember what state[17]
you find me in.

Ped. I will, and so leave you; your best cares, I
beseech you.

Alib. Take you none with you, leave 'em all with us.

[*Exit* PEDRO.]

Ant. Oh, my cousin's gone, cousin, cousin, oh!   151

Lol. Peace, peace, Tony, you must not cry, child;
you must be whipped if you do; your cousin is here
still, I am your cousin, Tony.

Ant. He, he, then I'll not cry, if thou be'st my
cousin, he, he, he.

Lol. I were best try his wit[18] a little, that I may
know what form[19] to place him in.

Alib. Ay, do, Lollio, do.   159

Lol. I must ask him easy questions at first. Tony, how many true fingers has a tailor on his right hand?[20]

Ant. As many as on his left, cousin.

Lol. Good; and how many on both?

Ant. Two less than a deuce,[21] cousin.

Lol. Very well answered. I come to you again, cousin Tony: how many fools goes to[22] a wise man?

Ant. Forty in a day sometimes, cousin.

Lol. Forty in a day? How prove you that?

Ant. All that fall out amongst themselves, and go to a lawyer to be made friends.   170

Lol. A parlous[23] fool! He must sit in the fourth form at least, I perceive that. I come again, Tony: how many knaves make an honest man?

Ant. I know not that, cousin.

Lol. No, the question is too hard for you. I'll tell you cousin. There's three knaves may make an honest man: a sergeant, a jailor, and a beadle. The sergeant catches him, the jailor holds him, and the beadle lashes him; and if he be not honest then, the hangman must cure him.   180

Ant. Ha, ha, ha, that's fine sport, cousin.

Alib. This was too deep a question for the fool, Lollio.

Lol. Yes, this might have served yourself, though I say't. Once more, and you shall go play, Tony.

Ant. Ay, play at push-pin,[24] cousin, ha, he!

Lol. So thou shalt; say how many fools are here?

Ant. Two, cousin, thou and I.

Lol. Nay, y'are too forward there, Tony; mark my question: how many fools and knaves are here? A fool before a knave, a fool behind a knave, between every two fools a knave; how many fools, how many knaves?

Ant. I never learnt so far, cousin.   192

Alib. Thou putt'st too hard questions to him, Lollio.

Lol. I'll make him understand it easily; cousin, stand there.

Ant. Ay, cousin.

Lol. Master, stand you next the fool.

Alib. Well, Lollio?

Lol. Here's my place: mark now, Tony, there a fool before a knave.   200

Ant. That's I, cousin.

Lol. Here's a fool behind a knave, that's I, and between us two fools there is a knave, that's my master; 'tis but we three, that's all.

Ant. We three,[25] we three, cousin!

Madmen within.

1 [Mad.] Within. Put's head i' th' pillory, the bread's too little.

2 [Mad.] Within. Fly, fly, and he catches the swallow.

3 [Mad.] Within. Give her more onion, or the devil put the rope about her crag.[26]   211

Lol. You may hear what time of day it is, the chimes[27] of Bedlam[28] goes.

Alib. Peace, peace, or the wire[29] comes!

3 [Mad.] Within. Cat-whore,[30] cat-whore, her[31] permasant,[32] her permasant!

Alib. Peace, I say; their hour's come, they must be fed, Lollio.

Lol. There's no hope of recovery of that Welsh madman,[33] was undone by a mouse that spoiled him a permasant; lost his wits for't.   221

Alib. Go to your charge, Lollio; I'll to mine.

Lol. Go you to your madmen's ward; let me alone with your fools.

Alib. And remember my last charge, Lollio.

                                                    Exit.

Lol. Of which your patients do you think I am? Come, Tony, you must amongst your school-fellows now; there's pretty scholars amongst 'em, I can tell you; there's some of 'em at *stultus, stulta, stultum.*[34]

Ant. I would see the madmen, cousin, if they would not bite me.   231

Lol. No, they shall not bite thee, Tony.

Ant. They bite when they are at dinner, do they not, coz?

Lol. They bite at dinner indeed, Tony. Well, I hope to get credit by thee; I like thee the best of all the scholars that ever I brought up, and thou shalt prove a wise man, or I'll prove a fool myself.

                                                  Exeunt.

ACT TWO

SCENE ONE

Enter BEATRICE *and* JASPERINO *severally.*

Bea. Oh, sir, I'm ready now for that fair service
Which makes the name of friend sit glorious on you.
Good angels and this conduct be your guide:

                                        [Gives a paper.]

Fitness of time and place is there set down, sir.

Jas. The joy I shall return rewards my service.

                                                    Exit.

Bea. How wise is Alsemero in his friend!
It is a sign he makes his choice with judgment
Then I appear in nothing more approved[1]
Than making choice of him;

---

[20] *how . . . hand:* tailors were reputed to be dishonest.
[21] *Two . . . deuce:* i.e., None.
[22] *goes to:* make up (Lollio's meaning); visit (Antonio's meaning).   [23] *parlous:* dangerously clever.
[24] *push-pin:* simple game for children; here with sexual connotation.
[25] *We three:* familiar joke in which two fools are pictured above a legend "we three" which thus implicates the spectator.   [26] *crag:* neck.
[27] *chimes:* the inmates' demands for food. ·
[28] *Bedlam:* name for madhouses generalized from the famous Bethlehem Hospital of London.   [29] *wire:* whip.
[30] *Cat-whore:* Abominable cat.
[31] *her:* stage-Welsh for "my."
[32] *permasant:* Parmesan cheese.
[33] *Welsh madman:* Welshmen proverbially loved cheese to point of going mad if a rat deprived them of it.
[34] *L.:* nominative singular declension for "foolish."

II.i.
[1] *approved:* proved (wise).

For 'tis a principle, he that can choose   10
That bosom well, who of his thoughts partakes,
Proves most discreet in every choice he makes.
Methinks I love now with the eyes of judgment
And see the way to merit, clearly see it.
A true deserver like a diamond sparkles;
In darkness you may see him, that's in absence,
Which is the greatest darkness falls on love;
Yet is he best discerned then
With intellectual eyesight. What's Piracquo
My father spends his breath for? And his blessing   20
Is only mine as[2] I regard his name;[3]
Else it goes from me, and turns head against me,
Transformed into a curse. Some speedy way
Must be remembered;[4] he's so forward too,
So urgent that way, scarce allows me breath
To speak to my new comforts.

Enter DE FLORES.

De F. [Aside]   Yonder's she.
Whatever ails me, now a-late especially,
I can as well be hanged as refrain seeing her;
Some twenty times a day, nay, not so little,
Do I force errands, frame ways and excuses   30
To come into her sight, and I have small reason for't,
And less encouragement; for she baits me still
Every time worse than other, does profess herself
The cruellest enemy to my face in town,
At no hand[5] can abide the sight of me,
As if danger or ill luck hung in my looks.
I must confess my face is bad enough,
But I know far worse has better fortune,
And not endured alone, but doted on.
And yet such pick-haired[6] faces, chins like witches',
Here and there five hairs, whispering in a corner,   41
As if they grew in fear one of another,
Wrinkles like troughs, where swine-deformity swills
The tears of perjury that lie there like wash[7]
Fallen from the slimy and dishonest eye,—
Yet such a one plucks[8] sweets[9] without restraint,
And has the grace of beauty to his sweet.[10]
Though my hard fate has thrust me out to servitude,

I tumbled into th'world a gentleman.
She turns her blessèd eye upon me now,   50
And I'll endure all storms before I part with't.
    Bea. [Aside] Again!
This ominous ill-faced fellow more disturbs me
Than all my other passions.
    De F. [Aside]   Now't begins again;
I'll stand this storm of hail though the stones pelt me.
    Bea. Thy business? What's thy business?
    De F. [Aside]   Soft and
    fair,[11]
I cannot part so soon now.
    Bea. [Aside]   The villain's fixed[12]—
[To DE FLORES] Thou standing[13] toad-pool![14]
    De F. [Aside]   The shower
    falls amain[15] now.
    Bea. Who sent thee? What's thy errand? Leave my
    sight.
    De F. My lord your father charged me to deliver   60
A message to you.
    Bea.   What, another since?[16]
Do't and be hanged then; let me be rid of thee.
    De F. True service merits mercy.
    Bea.   What's thy message?
    De F. Let beauty settle but in patience,
You shall hear all.
    Bea.   A dallying, trifling torment!
    De F. Signor Alonzo de Piracquo, lady,
Sole brother to Tomazo de Piracquo—
    Bea. Slave, when wilt make an end?
    De F. [Aside]   Too soon I shall.
    Bea. What all this while of him?
    De F.   The said Alonzo,
With the foresaid Tomazo—
    Bea.   Yet again?   70
    De F. Is new alighted.
    Bea.   Vengence strike the news!
Thou thing most loathed, what cause was there in this
To bring thee to my sight?
    De F.   My lord your father
Charged me to seek you out.
    Bea.   Is there no other
To send his errand by?
    De F.   It seems 'tis my luck
To be i' th'way still.[17]
    Bea.   Get thee from me.
    De F. [Aside]   So;
Why, am not I an ass to devise ways
Thus to be railed at? I must see her still.
I shall have a mad qualm within this hour again,
I know't, and like a common Garden-bull,[18]   80
I do but take breath to be lugged[19] again.
What this may bode I know not; I'll despair the less,
Because there's daily precedents of bad faces
Beloved beyond all reason; these foul chops
May come into favor one day 'mongst his[20] fellows.
Wrangling has proved the mistress of good pastime;
As children cry themselves asleep, I ha' seen
Women have chid themselves abed to men.
                                Exit DE FLORES.

---

[2] *only mine as:* on me only if I.
[3] *regard his name:* honor his reputation.
[4] *remembered:* thought up.
[5] *At no hand:* On no account.
[6] *pick-haired:* with beard and hair as sparse and hard as
picks (?).   [7] *wash:* eyewash.
[8] *plucks:* Q "pluckt."   [9] *sweets:* fragrant flowers.
[10] *grace . . . sweet:* blessing of the fact that his mistress
("sweet") is beautiful; possibly "grace" may pun on the
blessing before a meal, "sweet" on the dessert course.
[11] *Soft and fair:* cf. proverb "Soft and fair goes far."
[12] *villain's fixed:* lowborn, common fellow is immobilized,
staring intently.   [13] *standing:* stagnant.
[14] *toad-pool:* Toads proverbially bred in foul water.
[15] *amain:* with full force.   [16] *since:* yet.
[17] *still:* always.
[18] *Garden-bull:* At the Paris Garden on the Bankside
bears and bulls were baited for entertainment.
[19] *lugged:* teased, worried (of bears and bulls, from the
verb meaning to pull by the hair or ears).   [20] *his:* i.e., their.

Bea. I never see this fellow, but I think
Of some harm towards me; danger's in my mind
    still;   90
I scarce leave trembling of[21] an hour after.
The next good mood I find my father in,
I'll get him quite discarded. Oh, I was
Lost in this small disturbance and forgot
Affliction's fiercer torrent that now comes
To bear down all my comforts.

Enter VERMANDERO, ALONZO, TOMAZO.

Ver.   Y'are both welcome,
But an especial one belongs to you sir,
To whose most noble name our love presents
The addition[22] of a son, our son Alonzo.
Alon. The treasury of honor cannot bring forth   100
A title I should more rejoice in, sir.
Ver. You have improved it well. Daughter, prepare;
The day will steal upon thee suddenly.
Bea. [*Aside*] Howe'er, I will be sure to keep the
    night,[23]
If it should come so near me.

[BEATRICE and VERMANDERO *talk apart.*]

Tom.   Alonzo.
Alon.   Brother?
Tom. In troth I see small welcome in her eye.
Alon. Fie, you are too severe a censurer;
Of love in all points, there's no bringing on you;[24]
If lovers should mark everything a fault,
Affection would be like an ill-set[25] book,   110
Whose faults[26] might prove as big as half the volume.
Bea. That's all I do entreat.
Ver.   It is but reasonable;
I'll see what my son says to't. Son Alonzo,
Here's a motion[27] made but to reprieve
A maidenhead three days longer; the request
Is not far out of reason, for indeed
The former time is pinching.[28]
Alon.   Though my joys
Be set back so much time as I could wish
They had been forward, yet since she desires it,
The time is set as pleasing as before,   120
I find no gladness wanting.
Ver. May I ever meet it in that point still.
Y'are nobly welcome, sirs.

Exeunt VERMANDERO *and* BEATRICE.

Tom. So; did you mark the dullness of her parting
    now?
Alon. What dullness? Thou art so exceptious[29] still.
Tom. Why, let it go then; I am but a fool
To mark[30] your harms so heedfully.
Alon.   Where's the
    oversight?
Tom. Come, your faith's cozened in her, strongly
    cozened;[31]
Unsettle your affection with all speed
Wisdom can bring it to, your peace is ruined else.   130
Think what a torment 'tis to marry one
Whose heart is leaped into another's bosom:
If ever pleasure she receive from thee,

It comes not in thy name or of thy gift;
She lies but with another in thine arms,
He the half-father unto all thy children
In the conception; if he get 'em not,
She helps to get 'em for him; and[32] how dangerous
And shameful her restraint may go in time to,[33]
It is not to be thought on without sufferings.   140
Alon. You speak as if she loved some other, then.
Tom. Do you apprehend so slowly?
Alon.   Nay, and that
Be your fear only, I am safe enough.
Preserve your friendship and your counsel, brother,
For times of more distress. I should depart
An enemy, a dangerous, deadly one
To any but thyself that should but think
She knew the meaning of inconstancy,
Much less the use and practice; yet w'are friends.
Pray let no more be urged; I can endure   150
Much, till I meet an injury to her;
Then I am not myself. Farewell, sweet brother,
How much w'are bound to heaven to depart lovingly.
                                                Exit.
Tom. Why, here is love's tame madness; thus a man
Quickly steals into his vexation.
                                                Exit.

[II.ii]

Enter DIAPHANTA *and* ALSEMERO.

Dia. The place is my charge, you have kept your hour,
And the reward of a just meeting bless you.
I hear my lady coming; complete[1] gentleman,
I dare not be too busy with my praises,
Th'are dangerous things to deal with.
                                                Exit.
Als.   This goes well;
These women are the ladies' cabinets;
Things of most precious trust are locked into 'em.

Enter BEATRICE.

Bea. I have within mine eye all my desires;
Requests that holy prayers ascend heaven for
And brings 'em down to furnish our defects,[2]   10
Come not more sweet to our necessities
Than thou unto my wishes.
Als.   W'are so like

---

[21] *of:* for.   [22] *addition:* title.
[23] *keep the night:* protect myself from Alonzo on the
wedding night.
[24] *there's . . . you:* I cannot make you more reasonable.
[25] *ill-set:* badly typeset.   [26] *faults:* typographical errors.
[27] *motion:* proposal.   [28] *pinching:* scant, constraining.
[29] *exceptious:* cavilling, peevish.   [30] *mark:* note.
[31] *cozened:* deceived.
[32] *him; and:* "him, in his passions, and . . ."
[33] *her . . . to:* it may prove to restrain her.

II.ii.
   [1] *complete:* perfect.
   [2] *And . . . defects:* And bring back from heaven what we
need.

In our expressions, lady, that unless I borrow
The same words, I shall never find their equals.

                    [*Kisses her.*]

   Bea. How happy were this meeting, this embrace,
If it were free from envy![3] This poor kiss,
It has an enemy,[4] a hateful one,
That wishes poison to't. How well were I now
If there were none such name known as Piracquo,
Nor no such tie as the command of parents!   20
I should be but too much blessed.
   Als.   One good service
Would strike off both your fears, and I'll go near it too,
Since you are so distressed. Remove the cause,[5]
The command[6] ceases; so there's two fears blown out
With one and the same blast.[7]
   Bea.   Pray let me find[8] you, sir.
What might that service be so strangely happy?
   Als. The honorablest piece 'bout man, valor.
I'll send a challenge to Piracquo instantly.
   Bea. How? Call you that extinguishing of fear,
When 'tis the only way to keep it flaming?   30
Are not you ventured[9] in the action
That's[10] all my joys and comforts? Pray, no more, sir.
Say you prevailed; y'are danger's and not mine then.
The law would claim you from me, or obscurity
Be made the grave to bury you alive.
I'm glad these thoughts come forth; oh, keep not one
Of this condition, sir; here was a course
Found to bring sorrow on her way to death;
The tears would ne'er ha' dried till dust had choked 'em.
Blood-guiltiness becomes a fouler visage,   40
[*Aside*] And now I think on one. I was to blame,
I ha' marred so good a market with my scorn;[11]
'T had been done questionless. The ugliest creature
Creation framed for some use, yet to see
I could not mark so much where it should be.
   Als. Lady—
   Bea. [*Aside*] Why, men of art[12] make much of
    poison,
Keep one to expel another; where was my art?
   Als. Lady, you hear not me.
   Bea.   I do especially, sir;
The present times are not so sure of our side
As those hereafter may be; we must use 'em then   50
As thrifty folks their wealth, sparingly now,
Till the time opens.[13]
   Als.   You teach wisdom, lady.

   Bea. Within there; Diaphanta!

Enter DIAPHANTA.

   Dia.   Do you call, madam?
   Bea. Perfect your service, and conduct this gentleman
The private way you brought him.
   Dia.   I shall, madam.
   Als. My love's as firm as love e'er built upon.

     Exeunt DIAPHANTA *and* ALSEMERO.

Enter DE FLORES.

   De F. [*Aside*] I have watched this meeting, and do
    wonder much
What shall become of t'other.[14] I'm sure both
Cannot be served unless she transgress; happily
Then I'll put in for one; for if a woman   60
Fly from one point, from him she makes a husband,
She spreads and mounts then like arithmetic,
One, ten, a hundred, a thousand, ten thousand,
Proves in time sutler[15] to an army royal.
Now do I look to be most richly railed at,
Yet I must see her.
   Bea. [*Aside*]   Why, put case I loathed him
As much as youth and beauty hates a sepulchre,
Must I needs show it? Cannot I keep that secret,
And serve my turn upon him?[16] See, he's here.—
[*To him*] De Flores.
   De F. [*Aside*]   Ha, I shall run mad with joy;   70
She called me fairly by my name De Flores,
And neither rogue nor rascal.
   Bea.   What ha' you done
To your face a-late? Y'have met with some good
    physician;
Y'have pruned yourself, methinks; you were not wont
To look so amorously.[17]
   De F. [*Aside*]   Not I;
'Tis the same physnomy,[18] to a hair and pimple,
Which she called scurvy scarce an hour ago.
How is this?
   Bea. Come hither; nearer, man!
   De F. [*Aside*] I'm up to the chin in heaven.
   Bea.   Turn, let
    me see;
Faugh, 'tis but the heat of the liver,[19] I perceiv't.   80
I thought it had been worse.
   De F.   Her fingers touched me!
She smells all amber.[20]
   Bea. I'll make a water[21] for you shall cleanse this
Within a fortnight.
   De F.   With your own hands, lady?
   Bea. Yes, mine own, sir; in a work of cure
I'll trust no other.
   De F. [*Aside*] 'Tis half an act of pleasure
To hear her talk thus to me.
   Bea.   When w'are used
To a hard[22] face 'tis not so unpleasing;
It mends still in opinion, hourly mends,[23]
I see it by experience.
   De F. [*Aside*]   I was blest   90
To light upon this minute; I'll make use on't.[24]
   Bea. Hardness becomes the visage of a man well;

---

    [3] *envy:* malice, hostility.   [4] *enemy:* i.e., Alonzo.
    [5] *cause:* i.e., Alonzo.   [6] *command:* i.e., to marry him.
    [7] *blast:* blowing of air.   [8] *find:* understand, follow.
    [9] *ventured:* risked.   [10] *That's:* Who are.
    [11] *I . . . scorn:* i.e., By scorning De Flores I have spoiled
my chances for a useful bargain, (his) employment.
    [12] *art:* skill.   [13] *opens:* becomes more propitious.
    [14] *t'other:* i.e., Alonzo.
    [15] *sutler:* seller of provisions to soldiers.
    [16] *serve . . . him:* use him for my own purpose.
    [17] *amorously:* like a lover.   [18] *physnomy:* face.
    [19] *liver:* thought to be seat of love and violent passion.
    [20] *amber:* ambergris.   [21] *water:* lotion.
    [22] *hard:* harsh.   [23] *mends:* improves.   [24] *on't:* of it.

It argues service, resolution, manhood,
If cause were of employment.
  De F.   'Twould be soon seen,
If e'er your ladyship had cause to use it.
I would but wish the honor of a service
So happy as that mounts to.
  Bea.   We shall try you—
O my De Flores!
  De F. [*Aside*] How's that?
She calls me hers already, my De Flores!
[*To* BEATRICE] You were about to sigh out somewhat,
  madam,   100
  Bea. No, was I? I forgot,—Oh!
  De F.   There 'tis again,
The very fellow on't.
  Bea.   You are too quick, sir.
  De F. There's no excuse for't now; I heard it twice,
  madam;
That sigh would fain have utterance; take pity on't,
And lend it a free word; 'las, how it labors
For liberty. I hear the murmur yet
Beat at your bosom
  Bea.   Would creation—
  De F. Ay, well said, that's it.
  Bea.   Had formed me man.
  De F. Nay, that's not it.
  Bea.   Oh, 'tis the soul of freedom.
I should not then be forced to marry one 110
I hate beyond all depths; I should have power
Then to oppose my loathings, nay remove 'em
For ever from my sight.
  De F.   O blest occasion!—
Without change to your sex, you have your wishes.
Claim so much man in me.
  Bea.   In thee, De Flores?
There's small cause for that.
  De F.   Put it not from me;
It's a service that I kneel for to you.
            [*Kneels.*]
  Bea. You are too violent to mean faithfully;
There's horror in my service, blood and danger,
Can those be things to sue for?
  De F.   If you knew 120
How sweet it were to me to be employed
In any act of yours, you would say then
I failed and used not reverence enough
When I receive the charge on't.
  Bea. [*Aside*]   This is much, methinks;
Belike his wants are greedy, and to such
Gold tastes like angels' food[25] [*To* DE FLORES] Rise.
  De F. I'll have the work first.
  Bea. [*Aside*]   Possible his need
Is strong upon him;

       [*Gives him money*]

     there's to encourage thee:
As[26] thou art forward and thy service dangerous,
Thy reward shall be precious.
  De F.   That I have thought on;
I have assured myself of that beforehand, 131
And know it will be precious; the thought ravishes.

  Bea. Then take him to thy fury.
  De F.   I thirst for him.
  Bea. Alonzo de Piracquo.
         His end's upon him;
He shall be seen no more.
            [*Rises.*]
  Bea.   How lovely now
Dost thou appear to me! Never was man
Dearlier rewarded.
  De F.   I do think of that.
  Bea. Be wondrous careful in the execution.
  De F. Why, are not both our lives upon the cast?[27]
  Bea. Then I throw all my fears upon thy service.
  De F. They ne'er shall rise to hurt you.
  Bea.   When the
  deed's done,   141
I'll furnish thee with all things for thy flight;
Thou may'st live bravely[28] in another country.
  De F. Ay, ay, we'll talk of that hereafter.
  Bea. [*Aside*]   I shall rid
  myself
Of two inveterate loathings at one time,
Piracquo and his dog-face.
             Exit.

  De F.   Oh, my blood!
Methinks I feel her in mine arms already,
Her wanton fingers combing out this beard,
And, being pleasèd, praising this bad face.
Hunger and pleasure,[29] they'll commend sometimes
Slovenly dishes and feed heartily on 'em; 151
Nay, which is stranger, refuse daintier for 'em.
Some women are odd feeders.—I'm too loud.
Here comes the man goes supperless to bed,
Yet shall not rise tomorrow to his dinner.

     Enter ALONZO.

  Alon. De Flores.
  De F.   My kind, honorable lord.
  Alon. I am glad I ha' met with thee.
  De F.   Sir,
  Alon.   Thou canst
  show me
The full strength of the castle?
  De F.   That I can, sir.
  Alon. I much desire it.
  De F.   And if the ways and straits
Of some of the passages be not too tedious for you, 160
I will assure you, worth your time and sight, my lord.
  Alon. Push,[30] that shall be no hindrance.
  De F.   I'm your
  servant, then.
'Tis now near dinner-time; 'gainst your lordship's rising
I'll have the keys about me.
  Alon.   Thanks, kind De Flores.
  De F. [*Aside*] He's safely thrust upon me beyond
  hopes.
             Exeunt.

---

[25] *angels' food:* manna.   [26] *As:* In proportion as.
[27] *cast:* throw of the dice. [28] *bravely:* in high style.
[29] *pleasure:* sensual gratification, lust. [30] *Push:* Q "Puh."

ACT THREE

SCENE ONE

Enter ALONZO *and* DE FLORES.
(*In the act-time*[1] DE FLORES *hides a naked rapier.*)

De F. Yes, here are all the keys; I was afraid, my
    lord,
I'd wanted[2] for the postern,[3] this is it.
I've all, I've all, my lord: this for the sconce.[4]
    Alon. 'Tis a most spacious and impregnable fort.
    De F. You'll tell me more, my lord. This descent
Is somewhat narrow; we shall never pass
Well with our weapons; they'll but trouble us.
    Alon. Thou say'st true.
    De F.   Pray let me help your
    lordship.
    Alon. 'Tis done. Thanks, kind De Flores.
    De F.   Here are
    hooks, my lord,   9
To hang such things on purpose.

                    [*He hangs up the swords.*]

    Alon.   Lead, I'll follow thee.
    Exeunt at one door and enter at the other.[5]

[III.ii]

De F. All this is nothing; you shall see anon[1]
A place you little dream on.
    Alon.   I am glad
I have this leisure; all your master's house
Imagine I ha' taken a gondola.
    De F. All but myself, sir, [*Aside*] which makes up my
    safety.—
[*To* ALONZO] My lord, I'll place you at a casement
    here
Will show you the full strength of all the castle.
Look, spend your eye awhile upon that object.
    Alon. Here's rich variety, De Flores.
    De F.   Yes, sir.
    Alon. Goodly munition.
    De F.   Ay, there's ordnance, sir,
No bastard metal, will ring you a peal like bells   11
At great men's funerals. Keep your eye straight, my
    lord.

III.i.
    [1] *act-time*: interval between the acts, a feature of Jacobean
performance.
    [2] *wanted*: lacked (the key).
    [3] *postern*: back way, private entrance.
    [4] *sconce*: small fort.
    [5] *Exeunt . . . other*: The action is continuous, the direction
implying only a new location; the conventional scene division
here is only nominal.
III.ii.
    [1] *anon*: shortly.   [2] *approve*: give proof of.
III.iii.
    [1] *pinfold*: pen for animals.
    [2] *pounded*: impounded, with sexual pun.
    [3] *participate*: partake; share in the qualities.

Take special notice of that sconce before you;
There you may dwell awhile.

                    [*Takes up the rapier.*]

    Alon.   I am upon't.
    De F. And so am I.

                    [*Stabs him.*]

    Alon.   De Flores! oh, De Flores,
Whose malice hast thou put on?
    De F.   Do you question
A work of secrecy? I must silence you.

                    [*Stabs him.*]

    Alon. Oh, oh, oh.
    De F.   I must silence you.

                    [*Stabs him.*]

So, here's an undertaking well accomplished.
This vault serves to good use now.—Ha! what's that
Threw sparkles in my eye? Oh, 'tis a diamond   21
He wears upon his finger; it was well found;
This will approve[2] the work. What, so fast on?
Not part in death? I'll take a speedy course then,
Finger, and all shall off.

                    [*Cuts off the finger.*]

                    So, now I'll clear
The passages from all suspect or fear.

                    Exit with body.

[III.iii]

Enter ISABELLA *and* LOLLIO.

    Isa. Why, sirrah? Whence have you commission
To fetter the doors against me?
If you keep me in a cage, pray whistle to me,
Let me be doing something.
    Lol. You shall be doing, if it please you; I'll whistle
to you if you'll pipe after.
    Isa. Is it your master's pleasure or your own
To keep me in this pinfold?[1]
    Lol. 'Tis for my master's pleasure, lest, being taken
in another man's corn, you might be pounded[2] in
another place.   11
    Isa. 'Tis very well, and he'll prove very wise.
    Lol. He says you have company enough in the house,
if you please to be sociable, of all sorts of people.
    Isa. Of all sorts? Why, here's none but fools and
    madmen.
    Lol. Very well; and where will you find any other, if
you should go abroad? There's my master and I to
boot too.
    Isa. Of either sort one, a madman and a fool.   19
    Lol. I would ev'n participate[3] of both then if I were
as you; I know y'are half mad already; be half foolish
too.
    Isa. Y'are a brave saucy rascal. Come on, sir,
Afford me then the pleasure of your bedlam;
You were commending once today to me

Your last come lunatic, what a proper[4]
Body there was without brains to guide it,
And what a pitiful delight appeared
In that defect, as if your wisdom had found
A mirth in madness. Pray, sir, let me partake,   30
If there be such a pleasure.

Lol. If I do not show you the handsomest, discreetest
madman, one that I may call the understanding madman, then say I am a fool.

Isa. Well, a match, I will say so.

Lol. When you have a taste of the madman, you shall
if you please, see Fools' College, o' th' side; I seldom
lock there, 'tis but shooting a bolt[5] or two, and you are
amongst 'em.

                              Exit. Enter presently.[6]

—Come on, sir, let me see how handsomely you'll
behave yourself now.   41

                    Enter FRANCISCUS.

Fran. How sweetly she looks! oh, but there's a
wrinkle in her brow as deep as philosophy. Anacreon,[7]
drink to my mistress' health, I'll pledge it. Stay, stay,
there's a spider[8] in the cup! No, 'tis but a grapestone;
swallow it, fear nothing, poet; so, so, lift higher.

Isa. Alack, alack, 'tis too full of pity
To be laughed at. How fell he mad? Canst thou tell?

Lol. For love, mistress. He was a pretty poet too, and
that set him forwards first; the muses then forsook   50
him, he ran mad for a chambermaid, yet she was but a
dwarf neither.

Fran. Hail, bright Titania!
Why stand'st thou idle on these flow'ry banks?
Oberon is dancing with his Dryades;[9]
I'll gather daisies, primrose, violets,
And bind them in a verse of poesy.

Lol. Not too near; you see your danger.

                         [*Shows the whip.*]

Fran. Oh hold thy hand, great Diomed,[10]
Thou feed'st thy horses well, they shall obey thee.   60
Get up,[11] Bucephalus[12] kneels.

                              [*Kneels.*]

Lol. You see how I awe my flock; a shepherd has not
his dog at more obedience.

Isa. His conscience is unquiet; sure that was
The cause of this. A proper gentleman.

Fran. Come hither, Esculapius;[13] hide the poison.[14]

                              [*Rises.*]

Lol. Well, 'tis hid.

                         [*Conceals the whip.*]

Fran. Didst thou never hear of one Tiresias,[15]
A famous poet?

Lol. Yes, that kept tame wild-geese.   70

Fran. That's he; I am the man.

Lol. No!

Fran. Yes, but make no words on't; I was a man
Seven years ago.

Lol. A stripling I think you might.[16]

Fran. Now I'm a woman, all feminine.

Lol. I would I might see that.

Fran. Juno struck me blind.

Lol. I'll ne'er believe that; for a woman, they say,
has an eye more than a man.   80

Fran. I say she struck me blind.

Lol. And Luna[17] made you mad, you have two
trades[18] to beg with.

Fran. Luna is now big-bellied,[19] and there's room
For both of us to ride with Hecate.[20]
I'll drag thee up into her silver sphere,
And there we'll kick the dog and beat the bush[21]
That barks against the witches of the night;
The swift lycanthropi[22] that walks the round,
We'll tear their wolvish skins, and save the sheep.   90

                    [*Tries to seize* LOLLIO.]

Lol. Is't come to this? Nay, then my poison comes
forth again; mad slave, indeed, abuse your keeper!

                         [*Shows the whip.*]

Isa. I prithee hence with him, now he grows
dangerous.

Fran. [*Sings*]

          Sweet love, pity me;
          Give me leave to lie with thee.

Lol. No, I'll see you wiser first; to your own kennel.

Fran. No noise, she sleeps, draw all the curtains
          round;
Let no soft sound molest the pretty soul
But love, and love creeps in at a mouse-hole.   100

Lol. I would you would get into your hole.

                         [*Exit* FRANCISCUS.]

Now, mistress, I will bring you another sort; you shall

---

[4] *proper*: good-looking.

[5] *shooting a bolt*: pun on proverb, "A fool's bolt is soon
shot."   [6] *presently*: immediately.

[7] *Anacreon*: poet thought to have choked to death on a
grapestone while drinking wine.

[8] *spider*: thought to be poisonous.

[9] *Hail . . . Dryades*: While Oberon, King of the Fairies,
is with the wood nymphs, his wife Titania may take advantage of his absence. The names are from *A Midsummer Night's
Dream.*

[10] *Diomed*: Son of Ares, King of the Bistonians, keeper of
man-eating horses, killed by Hercules and fed to his own
horses.   [11] *Get up*: i.e., Mount.

[12] *Bucephalus*: favorite horse of Alexander the Great.

[13] *Esculapius*: Greek god of medicine.   [14] *poison*: whip.

[15] *Tiresias*: Theban prophet, changed into a woman for
seven years, then back, blinded by Juno (according to Ovid)
for saying that women enjoy love more than men.

[16] *A . . . might*: perhaps a defective line.

[17] *Luna*: moon; cf. "lunatic."

[18] *trades*: i.e., madness and blindness.

[19] *big-bellied*: full.

[20] *Hecate*: Greek goddess associated with supernatural
phenomena and sometimes identified with Artemis, goddess
of the moon.

[21] *dog, bush*: companions of the man in the moon; Franciscus' language free-associates a number of cant and proverbial phrases.

[22] *lycanthropi*: madmen who think they are wolves.

be fooled another while; Tony, come hither, Tony; look
who's yonder, Tony.

Enter ANTONIO.

Ant. Cousin, is it not my aunt[23]?

Lol. Yes, 'tis one of 'em, Tony.

Ant. He, he, how do you, uncle?

Lol. Fear him not, mistress, 'tis a gentle nidget;[24]
you may play with him, as safely with him[25] as with his
bauble.[26]   110

Isa. How long hast thou been a fool?

Ant. Ever since I came hither, cousin.[27]

Isa. Cousin? I'm none of thy cousins, fool.

Lol. Oh mistress, fools have always so much wit as
to claim their kindred.

[*Madman within*] Bounce,[28] bounce, he falls, he falls!

Isa. Hark you, your scholars in the upper room
Are out of order.

Lol. Must I come amongst you there? Keep you the
fool, mistress; I'll go up and play left-handed[29]
Orlando[30] amongst the madmen.   121
                                                            Exit.

Isa. Well, sir.

Ant. 'Tis opportuneful[31] now, sweet lady. Nay,
Cast no amazing[32] eye upon this change.

Isa. Ha!

Ant. This shape[33] of folly shrouds your dearest love,
The truest servant to your powerful beauties,
Whose magic had this force thus to transform me.

Isa. You are a fine fool indeed.

Ant.   Oh, 'tis not strange;
Love has an intellect that runs through all   130
The scrutinous[34] sciences and, like
A cunning poet, catches a quantity
Of every knowledge, yet brings all home
Into one mystery, into one secret
That he proceeds in.

Isa.   Y'are a parlous[35] fool.

Ant. No danger in me; I bring naught but love
And his soft-wounding shafts to strike you with.

---

[23] *aunt:* slang meaning is bawd, prostitute.

[24] *nidget:* idiot.

[25] *with him:* repetition may be a printer's error.

[26] *bauble:* carved stick carried by a fool; here, as often,
phallic association.

[27] *cousin:* Antonio, like lovers in other plays, offers the
pretense of kinship as a ruse to justify amorous meetings.

[28] *Bounce:* Bang.

[29] *left-handed:* second-rate(?), defective(?).

[30] *Orlando:* mad hero of Ariosto's *Orlando Furioso.*

[31] *opportuneful:* convenient.   [32] *amazing:* amazed.

[33] *shape:* appearance.   [34] *scrutinous:* investigative.

[35] *parlous:* cunning, dangerous.

[36] *Galaxia:* Milky Way.   [37] *habit:* apparel.

[38] *discover:* reveal.   [39] *Passing:* Very.

[40] *Catch . . . hell:* In the game of "barley-break," a couple
confined in a circle called "hell" try to capture, as replace-
ments or fellow prisoners, the other players running back
and forth past them.

[41] *wards:* of fools and madmen.

[42] *from:* in a manner inconsistent with.

[43] *orchard . . . Hesperides:* where the golden apples
received by Hera as a wedding gift were guarded by nymphs
and a dragon.

Try but one arrow; if it hurt you,
I'll stand you twenty back in recompense.

                                              [*Kisses her.*]

Isa. A forward fool too.

Ant.   This was love's teaching;
A thousand ways he fashioned out my way,   141
And this I found the safest and the nearest
To tread the Galaxia[36] to my star.

Isa. Profound withal. Certain, you dreamed of this;
Love never taught it waking.

Ant.   Take no acquaintance
Of these outward follies; there is within
A gentleman that loves you.

Isa.   When I see him,
I'll speak with him; so in the meantime keep
Your habit;[37] it becomes you well enough.
As you are a gentleman, I'll not discover[38] you;   150
That's all the favor that you must expect.
When you are weary, you may leave the school,
For all this while you have but played the fool.

Enter LOLLIO.

Ant. And must again.—He, he, I thank you, cousin;
I'll be your valentine tomorrow morning.

Lol. How do you like the fool, mistress?

Isa. Passing[39] well, sir.

Lol. Is he not witty, pretty well for a fool?

Isa. If he hold on as he begins, he is like
To come to something.   160

Lol. Ay, thank a good tutor. You may put him to't;
he begins to answer pretty hard questions. Tony, how
many is five times six?

Ant. Five times six is six times five.

Lol. What arithmetician could have answered better?
How many is one hundred and seven?

Ant. One hundred and seven is seven hundred and
one, cousin.

Lol. This is no wit to speak on. Will you be rid of the
fool now?   170

Isa. By no means, let him stay a little.

[*Madman within*] Catch there, catch the last couple
in hell![40]

Lol. Again? Must I come amongst you? Would my
master were come home! I am not able to govern both
these wards[41] together.

                                                  Exit.

Ant. Why should a minute of love's hour be lost?

Isa. Fie, out again! I had rather you kept
Your other posture; you become not your tongue
When you speak from[42] your clothes.

Ant.   How can he freeze,
Lives near so sweet a warmth? Shall I alone   181
Walk through the orchard of the Hesperides,[43]
And cowardly not dare to pull an apple?
This with the red cheeks I must venture for.

                                         [*Tries to kiss her.*]

Enter LOLLIO *above.*

Isa. Take heed, there's giants keep 'em.

Lol. [*Aside*] How now, fool, are you good at that?

Have you read Lipsius?[44] He's past *Ars Amandi*;[45] I
believe I must put harder questions to him, I perceive
that—   189

Isa. You are bold without fear too.

Ant.   What should I fear,
Having all joys about me? Do you smile,
And love shall play the wanton on your lip,
Meet and retire, retire and meet again;
Look you but cheerfully, and in your eyes
I shall behold mine own deformity
And dress myself up fairer. I know this shape
Becomes me not, but in those bright mirrors
I shall array me handsomely.

Lol. Cuckoo,[46] cuckoo.

                                                                    Exit.

[*Enter*] Madmen *above, some as birds, others as beasts.*

Ant. What are these?

Isa.   Of fear enough to part us;   200
Yet are they but our schools of lunatics
That act their fantasies in any shapes
Suiting their present thoughts; if sad, they cry;
If mirth be their conceit,[47] they laugh again;
Sometimes they imitate the beasts and birds,
Singing, or howling, braying, barking; all
As their wild fancies prompt 'em.

                              [*Exeunt* Madmen *above.*]

Enter LOLLIO.

Ant.   These are no fears.

Isa. But here's a large one, my man.

Ant. Ha, he, that's fine sport indeed, cousin.   209

Lol. I would my master were come home; 'tis too
much for one shepherd to govern two of these flocks,
nor can I believe that one churchman can instruct two
benefices at once; there will be some incurable mad of
the one side and very[48] fools on the other. Come, Tony.

Ant. Prithee, cousin, let me stay here still.

Lol. No, you must to your book now you have
played sufficiently.

Isa. Your fool is grown wondrous witty.

Lol. Well, I'll say nothing, but I do not think but he
will put you down one of these days.   220

                              Exeunt LOLLIO *and* ANTONIO.

Isa. Here the restrainèd current might make breach,
Spite of the watchful bankers.[49] Would a woman stray,
She need not gad abroad to seek her sin;
It would be brought home one ways or other.
The needle's point will to the fixèd north;
Such drawing arctics women's beauties are.

Enter LOLLIO.

Lol. How dost thou, sweet rogue?

Isa. How now?

Lol. Come, there are degrees; one fool may be better
than another.   230

Isa. What's the matter?

Lol. Nay, if thou giv'st thy mind to fool's-flesh, have
at thee!

                              [*Tries to kiss her.*]

Isa. You bold slave, you.

Lol. I could follow now as t'other fool did:
"What should I fear,
Having all joys about me? Do you but smile,
And love shall play the wanton on your lip,
Meet and retire, retire and meet again;
Look you but cheerfully, and in your eyes   240
I shall behold my own deformity
And dress myself up fairer. I know this shape
Becomes me not—" And so as it follows; but is not this
the more foolish way? Come, sweet rogue, kiss me, my
little Lacedemonian.[50] Let me feel how thy pulses beat;
thou hast a thing about thee would do a man pleasure;
I'll lay my hand on't.

Isa. Sirrah, no more. I see you have discovered
This love's knight-errant, who hath made adventure
For purchase of my love; be silent, mute,   250
Mute as a statue, or his injunction
For me enjoying shall be to cut thy throat.
I'll do it, though for no other purpose,
And be sure he'll not refuse it.

Lol. My share, that's all; I'll have my fool's part with
you.

Isa. No more. Your master.

Enter ALIBIUS.

Alib.   Sweet, how dost thou?

Isa. Your bounden servant, sir.

Alib.   Fie, fie, sweetheart,
No more of that.

Isa.   You were best lock me up.

Alib. In my arms and bosom, my sweet Isabella,
I'll lock thee up most nearly. Lollio,   261
We have employment, we have task in hand;
At noble Vermandero's, our castle-captain,
There is a nuptial to be solemnized
Beatrice-Joanna, his fair daughter, bride,
For which the gentleman hath bespoke[51] our pains:
A mixture of our madmen and our fools,
To finish, as it were, and make the fag[52]
Of all the revels the third night from the first.
Only an unexpected passage over   270
To make a frightful pleasure, that is all,
But not the all I aim at; could we so act it,
To teach it in a wild distracted measure,
Though out of form and figure, breaking time's head,
It were no matter; 'twould be healed again
In one age or other, if not in this;
This, this, Lollio, there's a good reward begun
And will beget a bounty, be it known.

Lol. This is easy, sir, I'll warrant you. You have
about you fools and madmen that can dance very   280
well, and 'tis no wonder your best dancers are not the

---

[44] *Lipsius:* humanist scholar (1547–1606) relevant only for
the first syllable of his name.

[45] *Ars Amandi:* Ovid's *Art of Loving* (i.e., he's past the
handbook stage).

[46] *Cuckoo:* i.e., Alibius is going to be cuckolded.

[47] *conceit:* fancy.   [48] *very:* true.

[49] *bankers:* dike-tenders.

[50] *Lacedemonian:* Spartan; i.e., concise and pointed
speaker(?).   [51] *bespoke:* ordered.   [52] *fag:* end.

wisest men; the reason is, with often jumping they jolt
their brains down into their feet, that their wits lie
more in their heels than in their heads.

   Alib. Honest Lollio, thou giv'st me a good reason,
And a comfort in it.

   Isa.   Y'have a fine trade on't;
Madmen and fools are a staple commodity.

   Alib. Oh wife, we must eat, wear clothes, and live;
Just at the lawyer's haven we arrive;
By madmen and by fools we both do thrive.   290
                                  Exeunt.

[III.iv]

   Enter VERMANDERO, ALSEMERO, JASPERINO,
          and BEATRICE.

   Ver. Valencia speaks so nobly of you, sir,
I wish I had a daughter now for you.

   Als. The fellow of this creature were a partner
For a king's love.

   Ver.   I had her fellow once, sir,
But heaven has married her to joys eternal;
'Twere sin to wish her in this vale again.
Come, sir, your friend and you shall see the pleasures
Which my health chiefly joys in.

   Als. I hear the beauty of this seat largely.[1]

   Ver. It falls much short of that.
               Exeunt. Manet BEATRICE.

   Bea.   So, here's one step
Into my father's favor; time will fix him.   11
I have got him now the liberty of the house.
So wisdom by degrees works out her freedom;
And if that eye be darkened that offends me
—I wait but that eclipse—this gentleman
Shall soon shine glorious in my father's liking
Through the refulgent virtue of my love.

          Enter DE FLORES.

   De F. [*Aside*] My thoughts are at a banquet for[2] the
   deed;
I feel no weight in't; 'tis but light and cheap
For the sweet recompense that I set down for't.   20

   Bea. De Flores.

   De F.   Lady?

   Bea.   Thy looks promise cheerfully.

   De F. All things are answerable: time, circumstance,
Your wishes, and my service.

   Bea.   Is it done then?

   De F. Piracquo is no more.

   Bea. My joys start at mine eyes; our sweet'st delights
Are evermore born weeping.

   De F.   I've a token for you.

   Bea. For me?

   De F.   But it was sent somewhat unwillingly,

I could not get the ring without the finger.

              [*Shows her the finger.*]

   Bea. Bless me! What hast thou done?

   De F.   Why, is that
   more
Than killing the whole man? I cut his heart-strings.
A greedy hand thrust in a dish at court   31
In a mistake hath had as much as this.

   Bea. 'Tis the first token my father made me send
   him.

   De F. And I made him send it back again
For his last token; I was loath to leave it,
And I'm sure dead men have no use of jewels.
He was as loath to part with't, for it stuck
As if the flesh and it were both one substance.

   Bea. At the stag's fall the keeper has his fees:
'Tis soon applied; all dead men's fees are yours, sir. 40
I pray, bury the finger, but the stone
You may make use on shortly; the true value,
Take't of my truth, is near three hundred ducats.

   De F. 'Twill hardly buy a capcase[3] for one's
   conscience, though,
To keep it from the worm, as fine as 'tis.
Well, being my fees I'll take it;
Great men have taught me that, or else my merit
Would scorn the way on't.

   Bea.   It might justly, sir.
Why, thou mistak'st, De Flores; 'tis not given
In state of recompense.

   De F.   No, I hope so, lady;   50
You should soon witness my contempt to't then.

   Bea. Prithee, thou look'st as if thou wert offended.

   De F. That were strange, lady; 'tis not possible
My service should draw such a cause from you.
Offended! Could you think so? That were much
For one of my performance and so warm
Yet in my service.

   Bea. 'Twere misery in me to give you cause, sir.

   De F. I know so much; it were so, misery
In her most sharp condition.

   Bea.   'Tis resolved then.   60
Look you, sir, here's three thousand golden florins;
I have not meanly thought upon thy merit.

   De F. What, salary? Now you move me.

   Bea.   How, De
   Flores?

   De F. Do you place me in the rank of verminous
   fellows,
To destroy things for wages? Offer gold?
The life blood of man! Is anything
Valued too precious for my recompense?

   Bea. I understand thee not.

   De F.   I could ha' hired
A journeyman in murder at this rate,
And mine own conscience might have slept at
   ease,[4]   70
And have had the work brought home.[5]

   Bea. [*Aside*]   I'm in a
   labyrinth.
What will content him? I would fain be rid of him.

III.iv.
  [1] *largely:* all over.   [2] *for:* because of.
  [3] *capcase:* traveling bag.   [4] *slept at ease:* not in Q.
  [5] *I ... home:* i.e., I could have hired a professional to
deliver the merchandise.

[*To* DE FLORES] I'll double the sum, sir.

De F.   You take a
course
To double my vexation; that's the good you do.

   Bea. [*Aside*] Bless me! I am now in worse plight than
I was;
I know not what will please him. [*To* DE FLORES]—
   For my fear's sake,
I prithee make away with all speed possible.
And if thou be'st so modest not to name
The sum that will content thee, paper blushes not;
Send thy demand in writing, it shall follow thee,   80
But prithee take thy flight.

De F.   You must fly too then.

Bea. I?

De F. I'll not stir a foot else.

Bea.   What's your meaning?

De F. Why, are not you as guilty, in, I'm sure,
As deep as I? And we should stick together.
Come, your fears counsel you but ill; my absence
Would draw suspect[6] upon you instantly;
There were no rescue for you.

   Bea. [*Aside*]   He speaks home.[7]

De F. Nor is it fit we two, engaged so jointly,
Should part and live asunder.

                      [*Tries to kiss her.*]

Bea.   How now, sir?
This shows not well.

De F.   What makes your lip so strange?[8]
This must not be betwixt us.

   Bea. [*Aside*]   The man talks wildly.   91

De F. Come, kiss me with a zeal now.

   Bea. [*Aside*]   Heaven, I
doubt[9] him!

De F. I will not stand so long to beg 'em shortly.

Bea. Take heed, De Flores, of forgetfulness;
'Twill soon betray us.

De F.   Take you heed first;
Faith, y'are grown much forgetful; y'are to blame in't.

   Bea. [*Aside*] He's bold, and I am blamed for't.

De F.   I have
eased you
Of your trouble, think on't, I'm in pain
And must be eased of you; 'tis a charity.
Justice invites your blood[10] to understand me.   100

Bea. I dare not.

De F.   Quickly.

Bea.   Oh, I never shall.
Speak it yet further off that I may lose
What has been spoken and no sound remain on't.
I would not hear so much offense again
For such another deed.

De F.   Soft, lady, soft;
The last is not yet paid for. Oh, this act
Has put me into spirit; I was as greedy on't
As the parched earth of moisture, when the clouds weep.
Did you not mark, I wrought myself into't,
Nay, sued and kneeled for't. Why was all that pains
took?   110
You see I have thrown contempt upon your gold,

Not that I want it not, for I do piteously;
In order[11] I will come unto't and make use on't,
But 'twas not held so precious to begin with;
For I place wealth after the heels of pleasure,
And were I not resolved in my belief
That thy virginity were perfect in thee,
I should but take my recompense with grudging,
As if I had but half my hopes I agreed for.

   Bea. Why, 'tis impossible thou canst be so wicked,
Or shelter such a cunning cruelty,   121
To make his death the murderer of my honor!
Thy language is so bold and vicious,
I cannot see which way I can forgive it
With any modesty.

De F.   Push, you forget yourself!
A woman dipped in blood, and talk of modesty?

   Bea. Oh, misery of sin! Would I had been bound
Perpetually unto my living hate
In that Piracquo than to hear these words.
Think but upon the distance that creation   130
Set 'twixt thy blood and mine, and keep thee there.

De F. Look but into your conscience, read me there;
'Tis a true book, you'll find me there your equal.
Push, fly not to your birth, but settle you
In what the act has made you; y'are no more now.
You must forget your parentage to[12] me;
Y'are the deed's creature; by that name
You lost your first condition, and I challenge you,
As peace and innocency has turned you out
And made you one with me.

   Bea.   With thee, foul villain?

De F. Yes, my fair murd'ress; do you urge me?   141
Though thou writ'st maid, thou whore in thy affection,
'Twas changed from thy first love, and that's a kind
Of whoredom in thy heart; and he's changed[13] now,
To bring thy second on, thy Alsemero,
Whom by all sweets that ever darkness tasted,
If I enjoy thee not, thou ne'er enjoy'st.
I'll blast the hopes and joys of marriage,
I'll confess all; my life I rate at nothing.

   Bea. De Flores.   150

De F. I shall rest from all lovers' plagues then;
I live in pain now; that shooting eye
Will burn my heart to cinders.

   Bea.   Oh, sir, hear me.

De F. She that in life and love refuses me,
In death and shame my partner she shall be.

   Bea. Stay, hear me once for all;

                           [*Kneels.*]

                     I make thee master
Of all the wealth I have in gold and jewels;
Let me go poor unto my bed with honor,
And I am rich in all things.

De F.   Let this silence thee:

---

[6] *suspect:* suspicion.   [7] *home:* to the point.
[8] *strange:* reserved, unfriendly.   [9] *doubt:* fear, suspect.
[10] *blood:* emotions, sexual appetite.
[11] *order:* due course.   [12] *to:* in favor of.
[13] *changed:* i.e., dead (with a glance at the play's title).

The wealth of all Valencia shall not buy   160
My pleasure from me.
Can you weep fate from its determined purpose?
So soon may you [14] weep me.
   Bea.   Vengeance begins;
Murder I see is followed by more sins.
Was my creation in the womb so cursed
It [15] must engender with a viper first?
   De F. Come, rise, and shroud [16] your blushes in my
     bosom;
                                [Raises her.]
Silence is one of pleasure's best receipts; [17]
Thy peace is wrought for ever in this yielding.
'Las, how the turtle [18] pants! thou'lt love anon   170
What thou so fear'st and faint'st to venture on.
                              Exeunt.

ACT FOUR

SCENE ONE

[Dumb Show.]

Enter Gentlemen, VERMANDERO *meeting them with
action of wonderment at the flight of* PIRACQUO. *Enter*
ALSEMERO, *with* JASPERINO, *and Gallants;*
VERMANDERO *points to him, the* Gentlemen *seeming to
applaud the choice;* [Exeunt in procession] ALSEMERO,
JASPERINO, *and* Gentlemen; BEATRICE *the bride
following in great state, accompanied with* DIAPHANTA,
ISABELLA *and other* Gentlewomen: DE FLORES *after
all, smiling at the accident;* [1] ALONZO'*s ghost appears
to* DE FLORES *in the midst of his smile, startles him,
showing him the hand whose finger he had cut off. They
pass over in great solemnity.*

Enter BEATRICE.

   Bea. This fellow has undone me endlessly.
Never was bride so fearfully distressed.
The more I think upon th'ensuing night,
And whom I am to cope with in embraces,
One who's [2] ennobled both in blood and mind,
So clear in understanding (that's my plague now),
Before whose judgement will my fault appear
Like malefactors' crimes before tribunals—
There is no hiding on't, the more I dive
Into my own distress. How a wise man   10
Stands for [3] a great calamity! There's no venturing
Into his bed, what course soe'er I light upon,

---

[14] *you:* not in Q.   [15] *It:* i.e., I.   [16] *shroud:* hide.
[17] *receipts:* recipes.   [18] *turtle:* turtledove.
IV.i.
  [1] *accident:* incident.   [2] *who's:* Q "both."
  [3] *Stands for:* Constitutes (because he can see a hidden
fault).   [4] *physic:* medicine.
  [5] *folio:* leaf (i.e., p. 89 or 90).   [6] *maid:* virgin.
  [7] *Antonius Mizaldus:* French scholar on these subjects,
1520–1578.   [8] *incontinently:* immediately.
  [9] *Where . . . been:* If I hadn't found this.
  [10] *Cuds:* God's.   [11] *a . . . piece:* a scrupulous girl.
  [12] *pit-hole:* grave.

Without my shame, which may grow up to danger;
He cannot but in justice strangle me
As I lie by him, as a cheater use me.
'Tis a precious craft to play with a false die
Before a cunning gamester. Here's his closet,
The key left in't, and he abroad i' th' park:
Sure 'twas forgot; I'll be so bold as look in't.

                           [Opens closet.]
Bless me! A right physician's closet 'tis,   20
Set round with vials, every one her mark too.
Sure he does practice physic [4] for his own use,
Which may be safely called your great man's wisdom.
What manuscript lies here? "The Book of Experiment,
Call'd Secrets in Nature"; so 'tis, 'tis so;
"How to know whether a woman be with child or no."
I hope I am not yet; if he should try though!
Let me see, folio [5] forty-five. Here 'tis,
The leaf tucked down upon't, the place suspicious.
"If you would know whether a woman be with child or
not, give here two spoonfuls of the white water in glass
C—"   32
Where's that glass C? Oh yonder, I see't now—
"and if she be with child, she sleeps full twelve hours
after; if not, not."
None of that water comes into my belly.
I'll know you from a hundred; I could break you now,
Or turn you into milk, and so beguile
The master of the mystery, but I'll look to you.
Ha! That which is next is ten times worse: 40
"How to know whether a woman be a maid [6] or not";
If that should be applied, what would become of me?
Belike he has a strong faith of my purity
That never yet made proof, but this he calls
"A merry sleight, but true experiment, the author
Antonius Mizaldus. [7] Give the party you suspect the
quantity of a spoonful of the water in the glass M,
which upon her that is a maid makes three several
effects: 'twill make her incontinently [8] gape, then fall
into a sudden sneezing, last into a violent laughing; else
dull, heavy, and lumpish." Where had I been? [9]   51
I fear it, yet 'tis seven hours to bedtime.

Enter DIAPHANTA.

   Dia. Cuds, [10] madam, are you here?
   Bea. [Aside]   Seeing that
     wench now,
A trick comes in my mind; 'tis a nice piece [11]
Gold cannot purchase. *[To* DIAPHANTA*]* I come
     hither, wench,
To look my lord.
   Dia. [Aside] Would I had such a cause to look him
     too!
[To BEATRICE*]* Why, he's i' th' park, madam.
   Bea. There let him be.
   Dia.   Ay, madam, let him compass
Whole parks and forests, as great rangers do;   60
At roosting time a little lodge can hold 'em.
Earth-conquering Alexander, that thought the world
Too narrow for him, in the end had but his pit-hole. [12]
   Bea. I fear thou art not modest, Diaphanta.

Dia. Your thoughts are so unwilling to be known,
madam;
'Tis ever the bride's fashion towards bedtime,
To set light by her joys as if she owed[13] 'em not.
   Bea. Her joys? Her fears, thou would'st say.
   Dia.   Fear of
what?
   Bea. Art thou a maid and talk'st so to a maid?
You leave a blushing business behind,   70
Beshrew your heart for't.
   Dia.   Do you mean good sooth,[14]
madam?
   Bea. Well, if I'd thought upon the fear at first,
Man should have been unknown.
   Dia.   Is't possible?
   Bea. I will give a thousand ducats to that woman
Would try what my fear were and tell me true
Tomorrow when she gets from't; as she likes
I might perhaps be drawn to't.
   Dia.   Are you in earnest?
   Bea. Do you get the woman, then challenge me,
And see if I'll fly from't; but I must tell you
This by the way: she must be a true maid,   80
Else there's no trial, my fears are not hers else.
   Dia. Nay, she that I would put into your hands,
madam,
Shall be a maid.
   Bea.   You know I should be shamed else,
Because she lies for me.
   Dia.   'Tis a strange humor:[15]
But are you serious still? Would you resign
Your first night's pleasure and give money too?
   Bea. As willingly as live. *[Aside]* Alas, the gold
Is but a by-bet[16] to wedge in the honor.
   Dia. I do not know how the world goes abroad
For faith or honesty; there's both required in this.   90
Madam, what say you to me, and stray no further?
I've a good mind, in troth, to earn your money.
   Bea. Y'are too quick,[17] I fear, to be a maid.
   Dia. How? Not a maid? Nay, then you urge me,
madam;
Your honorable self is not a truer
With all your fears upon you—
   Bea. [Aside]   Bad enough then.
   Dia. Than I with all my lightsome joys about me.
   Bea. I'm glad to hear't then; you dare put your
honesty[18]
Upon an easy trial?
   Dia.   Easy? Anything.
   Bea. I'll come to you straight.

                              [Goes to the closet.]

   Dia. [Aside]   She will not search me,
will she,   100
Like the forewoman of a female jury?[19]
   Bea. Glass M, ay, this is it; look Diaphanta,
You take no worse than I do.

                                           [Drinks.]

   Dia.   And in so doing,
I will not question what 'tis, but take it.

                                           [Drinks.]

   Bea. [Aside] Now if the experiment be true, 'twill
praise itself
And give me noble ease:—begins already;

                              [DIAPHANTA gapes.]

There's the first symptom; and what haste it makes
To fall into the second, there by this time.

                              [DIAPHANTA sneezes.]

Most admirable secret! On the contrary,
It stirs not me a whit, which most concerns it.   110
   Dia. Ha, ha, ha.
   Bea. [Aside]   Just in all things and in order
As if 'twere circumscribed; one accident[20]
Gives way unto another.
   Dia.   Ha, ha, ha.
   Bea.   How now, wench?
   Dia. Ha, ha, ha, I am so, so light at heart—ha, ha, ha
—so pleasurable.
But one swig more, sweet madam.
   Bea.   Ay, tomorrow;
We shall have time to sit by't.
   Dia.   Now I'm sad again.
   Bea. [Aside] It lays[21] itself so gently, too! *[To
DIAPHANTA]* Come, wench,
Most honest Diaphanta I dare call thee now.
   Dia. Pray tell me, madam, what trick call you this?
   Bea. I'll tell thee all hereafter; we must study   120
The carriage of this business.
   Dia.   I shall carry't well,
Because I love the burden.
   Bea.   About midnight
You must not fail to steal forth gently
That I may use the place.
   Dia.   Oh, fear not, madam,
I shall be cool by that time;—the bride's place,
And with a thousand ducats! I'm for a justice now;
I bring a portion[22] with me; I scorn small fools.

                                           Exeunt.

[IV.ii]

              Enter VERMANDERO *and* Servant.

   Ver. I tell thee, knave, mine honor is in question,
A thing till now free from suspicion,
Nor ever was there cause; who of my gentlemen
Are absent? Tell me and truly how many and who.
   Ser. Antonio, sir, and Franciscus.
   Ver. When did they leave the castle?
   Ser. Some ten days since, sir, the one intending to
Briamata,[1] th'other for Valencia.

---

[13] *owed:* owned.   [14] *sooth:* truth.   [15] *humor:* whim.
[16] *by-bet:* side-bet, not as important as the proof of her
virginity(?).   [17] *quick:* wanton.   [18] *honesty:* chastity.
[19] *She . . . jury:* perhaps a reference to the divorce trial of
the Countess of Essex in 1613, so examined because she
claimed nonconsummation as her grounds.
[20] *accident:* symptom.   [21] *lays:* allays.   [22] *portion:* dowry.
IV.ii.
   [1] *Briamata:* In source, location of Vermandero's country
house.

Ver. The time accuses 'em. A charge of murder
Is brought within my castle gate, Piracquo's murder;
I dare not answer ² faithfully their absence: 11
A strict command of apprehension
Shall pursue 'em suddenly and either wipe
The stain off clear or openly discover it.
Provide me wingèd warrants for the purpose.

                         Exit Servant.

See, I am set on again.

          Enter TOMAZO.

Tom. I claim a brother of you.
Ver.   Y'are too hot;
Seek him not here.
Tom.   Yes, 'mongst your dearest bloods,
If my peace find no fairer satisfaction.
This is the place must yield account for him,   20
For here I left him, and the hasty tie
Of this snatched marriage gives strong testimony
Of his most certain ruin.
Ver.   Certain falsehood!
This is the place indeed; his breach of faith
Has too much marred both my abusèd love,
The honorable love I reserved for him,
And mocked my daughter's joy: the prepared morning
Blushed at his infidelity; he left
Contempt and scorn to throw upon those friends
Whose belief hurt 'em. Oh, 'twas most ignoble   30
To take his flight so unexpectedly
And throw such public wrongs on those that loved him.
Tom. Then this is all your answer?
Ver.   'Tis too fair
For one of his alliance; and I warn you
That this place no more see you.

                               Exit.

         Enter DE FLORES.

Tom.   The best is,
There is more ground to meet a man's revenge on.
Honest De Flores.
De F.   That's my name indeed.
Saw you the bride? Good sweet sir, which way took
   she?
Tom. I have blessed mine eyes from seeing such a
   false one.
De F. [*Aside*] I'd fain get off; this man's not for my
   company;   40
I smell his brother's blood when I come near him.
Tom. Come hither, kind and true one; I remember
My brother loved thee well.
De F.   Oh, purely, dear sir.
[*Aside*] Methinks I am now again a-killing on him,
He brings it so fresh to me.
Tom.   Thou canst guess, sirrah—

One honest friend has an instinct of jealousy—
At some foul guilty person?
De F. 'Las, sir, I am so charitable, I think none
Worse than myself. You did not see the bride then?
Tom. I prithee name her not. Is she not wicked?   50
De F. No, no, a pretty, easy, round-packed ³
   sinner,
As your most ladies are, else you might think
I flattered her; but, sir, at no hand wicked,
Till th'are so old their chins and noses ⁴ meet,
And they salute witches. I am called, I think, sir:
[*Aside*] His company ev'n o'erlays my conscience.

                               Exit.

Tom. That De Flores has a wondrous honest heart;
He'll bring it out in time, I'm assured on't.
Oh, here's the glorious master of the day's joy.
'Twill ⁵ not be long till he and I do reckon.   60

         Enter ALSEMERO.

Sir.
Als. You are most welcome.
Tom.   You may call that word
   back:
I do not think I am, nor wish to be.
Als. 'Tis strange you found the way to this house
   then.
Tom. Would I'd ne'er known the cause. I'm none of
   those, sir,
That come to give you joy and swill your wine;
'Tis a more precious liquor that must lay
The fiery thirst I bring.
Als.   Your words and you
Appear to me great strangers.
Tom.   Time and our swords
May make us more acquainted. This the business:
I should have a brother in your place;   70
How treachery and malice have disposed of him
I'm bound to enquire of him which holds his right,
Which never could come fairly.
Als.   You must look
To answer for that word, sir.
Tom.   Fear you not,
I'll have it ⁶ ready drawn at our next meeting.
Keep your day solemn. Farewell, I disturb it not;
I'll bear the smart with patience for a time.

                               Exit.

Als. 'Tis somewhat ominous, this, a quarrel entered
Upon this day; my innocence relieves me,

         Enter JASPERINO.

I should be wondrous sad else.—Jasperino,   80
I have news to tell thee, strange news.
Jas.   I ha' some too,
I think as strange as yours; would I might keep
Mine, so my faith and friendship might be kept in't.
Faith, sir, dispense a little with my zeal,
And let it cool in this.⁷
Als.   This puts me on,
And blames thee for thy slowness.
Jas.   All may prove nothing,
Only a friendly fear that leapt from me, sir.

---

   ² *answer:* answer for.
   ³ *round-packed:* plump with sin(?).
   ⁴ *chins and noses:* Q "sins and vices."
   ⁵ *'Twill:* Q "I will."
   ⁶ *it:* his sword ("drawn" puns on the legal sense).
   ⁷ *dispense . . . this:* do without my customary zealous
service and let it be less eager.

Als. No question it may prove nothing; let's partake
it, though.

Jas. 'Twas Diaphanta's chance (for to that wench
I pretend honest love, and she deserves it)   90
To leave me in a back part of the house,
A place we chose for private conference;
She was no sooner gone, but instantly
I heard your bride's voice in the next room to me
And lending more attention, found De Flores
Louder than she.

Als.   De Flores? Thou art out[8] now.

Jas. You'll tell me more anon.

Als.   Still I'll prevent[9] thee;
The very sight of him is poison to her.

Jas. That made me stagger too, but Diaphanta
At her return confirmed it.

Als.   Diaphanta!   100

Jas. Then fell we both to listen, and words passed
Like those that challenge interest in a woman.

Als. Peace, quench thy zeal; 'tis dangerous to thy
bosom.

Jas. Then truth is full of peril.

Als.   Such truths are.
Oh, were she the sole glory of the earth,
Had eyes that could shoot fire into kings' breasts,
And touched,[10] she sleeps not here. Yet I have time,
Though night be near, to be resolved hereof;
And prithee do not weigh me by my passions.

Jas. I never weighed friend so.

Als.   Done charitably.   110
That key will lead thee to a pretty secret

                   [Gives key.]

By a Chaldean[11] taught me, and I've made
My study upon some. Bring from my closet
A glass inscribed there with the letter M,
And question not my purpose.

Jas.   It shall be done, sir.

                        Exit.

Als. How can this hang together? Not an hour
since,
Her woman came pleading her lady's fears,
Delivered her for the most timorous virgin
That ever shrunk at man's name, and so modest
She charged her weep out her request to me   120
That she[12] might come obscurely[13] to my bosom.

         Enter BEATRICE.

Bea. [*Aside*] All things go well; my woman's
preparing yonder
For her sweet voyage, which grieves me to lose;
Necessity compels it; I lose all else.

Als. [*Aside*] Push, modesty's shrine is set in yonder
forehead;
I cannot be too sure though—[*To her*] My Joanna!

Bea. Sir, I was bold to weep a message to you;
Pardon my modest fears.

Als. [*Aside*]   The dove's not meeker,
She's abused, questionless.

     Enter JASPERINO [*with glass*].

     —Oh, are you come, sir?

Bea. [*Aside*] The glass, upon my life! I see the
letter.   130

Jas. Sir, this is M.

Als.   'Tis it.

Bea. [*Aside*]   I am suspected.

Als. How fitly our bride comes to partake with us.

Bea. What is't, my lord?

Als.   No hurt.

Bea.   Sir, pardon me
I seldom taste of any composition.[14]

Als. But this upon my warrant you shall venture
on.

Bea. I fear 'twill make me ill.

Als.   Heaven forbid that.

Bea. [*Aside*] I'm put now to my cunning; th' effects
I know,
If I can now but feign 'em handsomely.

                       [Drinks.]

Als. [*To* JASPERINO] It has that secret virtue, it
ne'er missed, sir,
Upon a virgin.

Jas.   Treble qualified?   140

     *[*BEATRICE *gapes, then sneezes.*]*

Als. By all that's virtuous it takes there, proceeds!

Jas. This is the strangest trick to know a maid by.

Bea. Ha, ha, ha!
You have given me joy of heart to drink, my lord.

Als. No, thou hast given me such joy of heart.
That never can be blasted.

Bea.   What's the matter, sir?

Als. [*To* JASPERINO] See, now 'tis settled in a
melancholy,
Keeps[15] both the time and method; [*To her*] my
Joanna,   148
Chaste as the breath of heaven, or morning's womb,
That brings the day forth, thus my love encloses thee.

            [Embraces her.] Exeunt.

[IV.iii]

     Enter ISABELLA *and* LOLLIO.

Isa. Oh heaven! is this the waiting[1] moon?
Does love turn fool, run mad, and all at once?
Sirrah, here's a madman, akin to the fool too,
A lunatic lover.

Lol. No, no, not he I brought the letter from?

Isa. Compare his inside with his out, and tell me.

           [Gives him the letter.]

---

   [8] *out:* mistaken.
   [9] *prevent:* forestall.   [10] *touched:* tainted.
   [11] *Chaldean:* member of biblical people known as astrologers and magicians.
   [12] *she:* Beatrice.   [13] *obscurely:* in the dark.
   [14] *composition:* medical preparation.
   [15] *Keeps:* Q "Keep."

IV.iii.
   [1] *waiting:* Q; "waning" and "waxing" have been suggested as emendations.

Lol. The out's mad, I'm sure of that; I had a taste
on't.
[*Reads*] "To the bright Andromeda,[2] chief chambermaid to the Knight of the Sun,[3] at the sign of Scorpio,[4]
in the middle region, sent by the bellows mender of
Aeolus.[5] Pay the post." This is stark madness.   11
Isa. Now mark the inside.

[*Takes the letter and reads.*]

"Sweet lady, having now cast off this counterfeit cover
of a madman, I appear to your best judgment a true and
faithful lover of your beauty."
Lol. He is mad still.
Isa. "If any fault you find, chide those perfections
in you which have made me imperfect; 'tis the same
sun that causeth to grow and enforceth to wither—"
Lol. Oh, rogue!   20
Isa. "—Shapes and transshapes, destroys and builds
again; I come in winter to you dismantled of my proper
ornaments; by the sweet splendor of your cheerful
smiles, I spring and live a lover."
Lol. Mad rascal still.
Isa. "Tread him not under foot that shall appear an
honor to your bounties. I remain, mad till I speak with
you, from whom I expect my cure, yours all, or one
beside himself, FRANCISCUS."   29
Lol. You are like to have a fine time on't; my master
and I may give over our professions, I do not think but
you can cure fools and madmen faster than we, with
little pains too.
Isa. Very likely.
Lol. One thing I must tell you, mistress: you perceive
that I am privy to your skill; if I find you minister once
and set up the trade,[6] I put in for my thirds; I shall be
mad or fool else.
Isa. The first place is thine, believe it, Lollio;
If I do fall—   40
Lol. I fall upon you.
Isa. So.
Lol. Well, I stand to my venture.
Isa. But how shall I deal with 'em?
Lol. Why,[7] do you mean to deal with[8] 'em?
Isa. Nay, the fair understanding,[9] how to use 'em.
Lol. Abuse 'em. That's the way to mad the fool, and
make a fool of the madman, and then you use 'em
kindly.[10]
Isa. 'Tis easy, I'll practice; do thou observe it;   50
The key of thy wardrobe.

---

[2] *Andromeda:* rescued by her husband Perseus from a
sea monster.
[3] *Knight . . . Sun:* in a popular romance scorned by the
educated.   [4] *Scorpio:* sign associated with the genitals.
[5] *Aeolus:* god of the wind.
[6] *minister . . . trade:* become a prostitute.
[7] *Why:* Q "We."
[8] *deal with:* pun—have sexual relations with.
[9] *fair understanding:* the more decorous sense which I
intended.   [10] *kindly:* charitably; naturally.
[11] *nice:* fastidious.
[12] *pizzles:* bull penises used as whips.
[13] *morris:* dance performed in costume.
[14] *honor:* bow.

Lol. There; fit yourself for 'em, and I'll fit 'em both
for you.

[*Gives her the key.*]

Isa. Take thou no further notice than the outside.
                                                      Exit.
Lol. Not an inch; I'll put you to the inside.

Enter ALIBIUS.

Alib. Lollio, art there? Will all be perfect, think'st
thou?
Tomorrow night, as if to close up the solemnity,
Vermandero expects us.
Lol. I mistrust the madmen most; the fools will do
well enough; I have taken pains with them.   60
Alib. Tush, they cannot miss; the more absurdity,
The more commends it, so no rough behaviors
Affright the ladies; they are nice[11] things, thou know'st.
Lol. You need not fear, sir; so long as we are there
with our commanding pizzles,[12] they'll be as tame as
the ladies themselves.
Alib. I will see them once more rehearse before they
go.
Lol. I was about it, sir; look you to the madmen's
morris,[13] and let me alone with the other. There is one
or two that I mistrust their fooling; I'll instruct 70
them, and then they shall rehearse the whole measure.
Alib. Do so; I'll see the music prepared. But Lollio,
By the way, how does my wife brook her restraint?
Does she not grudge at it?
Lol. So, so; she takes some pleasure in the house;
she would abroad else. You must allow her a little more
length; she's kept too short.
Alib. She shall along to Vermandero's with us;
That will serve her for a month's liberty.
Lol. What's that on your face, sir?   80
Alib. Where, Lollio? I see nothing.
Lol. Cry you mercy, sir, 'tis your nose; it showed
like the trunk of a young elephant.
Alib. Away, rascal! I'll prepare the music, Lollio.
                                          Exit ALIBIUS.
Lol. Do, sir, and I'll dance the whilst.—Tony, where
art thou, Tony?

Enter ANTONIO.

Ant. Here, cousin; where art thou?
Lol. Come, Tony, the footmanship I taught you.
Ant. I had rather ride, cousin.   89
Lol. Ay, a whip take you, but I'll keep you out.
Vault in; look you, Tony: fa, la la, la la.
                                              [*Dances.*]
Ant. Fa, la la, la la.
                                              [*Dances.*]
Lol. There, an honor.[14]
Ant. Is this an honor, coz?
                                                [*Bows.*]
Lol. Yes, and it please your worship.
Ant. Does honor bend in the hams, coz?
Lol. Marry does it, as low as worship, squireship,
nay, yeomanry itself sometimes, from whence it first
stiffened; there rise, a caper.

Ant. Caper [15] after an honor, coz?   100

Lol. Very proper; for honor is but a caper, rises as fast and high, has a knee or two, and falls to th'ground again. You can remember your figure,[16] Tony?

                                                      Exit.

Ant. Yes, cousin; when I see thy figure,[17] I can remember mine.

        Enter ISABELLA [*like a madwoman*].

Isa. Hey, how he treads the air![18] Shoo,[19] shoo, t'other way!
He burns his wings else; here's wax enough below,
        Icarus,[20]
More than will be canceled[21] these eighteen moons.
He's down, he's down; what a terrible fall he had!
Stand up, thou son of Cretan Dedalus,   110
And let us tread the lower labyrinth;[22]
I'll bring thee to the clue.

Ant. Prithee, coz, let me alone.

Isa. Art thou not drowned?
About thy head I saw a heap of clouds,
Wrapped like a Turkish turban; on thy back
A crooked chameleon-colored rainbow hung
Like a tiara down unto thy hams.
Let me suck out those billows in thy belly;
Hark how they roar and rumble in the straits.[23]   120
Bless thee from the pirates.

Ant. Pox upon you, let me alone.

Isa. Why shouldst thou mount so high as Mercury[24]
Unless thou hadst reversion of his place?[25]
Stay in the moon with me, Endymion,[26]
And we will rule these wild rebellious waves
That would have drowned my love.

Ant. I'll kick thee if again thou touch me,
Thou wild unshapen antic;[27] I am no fool,
You bedlam.

Isa.   But you are, as sure as I am, mad.   130
Have I put on this habit of a frantic,
With love as full of fury to beguile
The nimble eye of watchful jealousy,
And am I thus rewarded?

                                [Reveals herself.]

Ant. Ha! dearest beauty!

Isa.   No, I have no beauty now,
Nor never had, but what was in my garments.
You a quick-sighted lover? Come not near me!
Keep your caparisons;[28] y'are aptly clad;
I came a feigner to return stark mad.

                                                      Exit.

            Enter LOLLIO.

Ant. Stay, or I shall change condition   140
And become as you are.

Lol. Why, Tony, whither now? Why fool?

Ant. Whose fool, usher[29] of idiots? You coxcomb,
I have fooled too much.

Lol. You were best be mad another while then.

Ant. So I am, stark mad; I have cause enough;
And I could throw the full effects on thee
And beat thee like a fury.   148

Lol. Do not, do not; I shall not forbear the gentle-

man under the fool, if you do. Alas, I saw through your fox-skin[30] before now. Come, I can give you comfort: my mistress loves you, and there is as arrant a madman i' th' house as you are a fool, your rival, whom she loves not. If after the masque we can rid her of him, you earn her love, she says, and the fool shall ride her.

Ant. May I believe thee?

Lol. Yes, or you may choose whether you will or no.

Ant. She's eased of him; I have a good quarrel on't.

Lol. Well, keep your old station yet, and be quiet.

Ant. Tell her I will deserve her love.   160

                                                      [Exit.]

Lol. And you are like to have your desire.

            Enter FRANCISCUS.

Fran. [*Sings*] Down, down, down a-down a-down,
        and then with a horse-trick[31]
To kick Latona's[32] forehead and break her bowstring.

Lol. This is t'other counterfeit; I'll put him out of his humor.[33]

                [Takes out letter and reads.]

"Sweet lady, having now cast off[34] this counterfeit cover of a madman, I appear to your best judgment a true and faithful lover of your beauty." This is pretty well for a madman.

Fran. Ha! What's that?   170

Lol. "Chide those perfections in you which have[35] made me imperfect."

Fran. I am discovered to the fool.

Lol. I hope to discover the fool in you ere I have done with you. "Yours all, or one beside himself, FRANCISCUS." This madman will mend sure.

Fran. What do you read, sirrah?

Lol. Your destiny, sir; you'll be hanged for this trick and another that I know.

Fran. Art thou of counsel with thy mistress?   180

---

[15] *Caper:* Upward leap.   [16] *figure:* dance step.
[17] *figure:* face.   [18] *treads the air:* dances, flies.
[19] *shoo:* sound made to scare away birds.
[20] *Icarus:* Isabella imagines the dancing Antonio as Icarus, who flew away from prison on wings of wax and feathers made by Daedalus, his father, came too close to the sun so that the wax melted, plunged into the sea, and drowned.
[21] *canceled:* the wax she thinks of now is that on official documents.
[22] *labyrinth:* Daedalus and Icarus were prisoners of King Minos of Crete, who also imprisoned Theseus in a maze from which Ariadne led him to freedom; Isabella may be seeing herself now as Ariadne and Alibius as the Minotaur, monstrous guardian of the labyrinth.
[23] *straits:* Q "streets"; the allusion is to the sea in which Icarus drowned.   [24] *Mercury:* the gods' messenger.
[25] *hadst . . . place:* were his successor.
[26] *Endymion:* shepherd loved by the moon.
[27] *antic:* clown.   [28] *caparisons:* clothes.
[29] *usher:* attendant; assistant schoolmaster.
[30] *fox-skin:* clever disguise.
[31] *horse-trick:* caper like a horse's.
[32] *Latona:* mother of Apollo and Artemis, here as elsewhere identified with her daughter, goddess of the moon and the hunt.   [33] *humor:* mental state.
[34] *cast off:* Q "cast."   [35] *which have:* Q "which."

Lol. Next her apron strings.

Fran. Give me thy hand.

Lol. Stay, let me put yours[36] in my pocket first;

[Puts away the letter.]

your hand is true, is it not? It will not pick?[37] I partly fear it, because I think it does lie.

Fran. Not in a syllable.

Lol. So; if you love my mistress so well as you have handled the matter here, you are like to be cured of your madness.

Fran. And none but she can cure it.   190

Lol. Well, I'll give you over then, and she shall cast your water[38] next.

Fran. Take for thy pains past.

[Gives him money.]

Lol. I shall deserve more, sir, I hope; my mistress loves you, but must have some proof of your love to her.

Fran. There I meet my wishes.

Lol. That will not serve; you must meet her enemy and yours.

Fran. He's dead already.

Lol. Will you tell me that, and I parted but now with him?   201

Fran. Show me the man.

Lol. Ay, that's a right course now; see him before you kill him in any case; and yet it needs not go so far neither; 'tis but a fool that haunts the house and my mistress in the shape of an idiot; bang but his fool's coat well-favoredly, and 'tis well.

Fran. Soundly, soundly.

Lol. Only reserve him till the masque be past, and if you find him not now in the dance yourself, I'll show you. In, in. My master.   211

Fran. He handles him like a feather. Hey!

[Exit dancing.]

Enter Alibius.

Alib. Well said;[39] in a readiness, Lollio?

Lol. Yes, sir.

Alib. Away then, and guide them in, Lollio; Entreat your mistress to see this sight.

[Exit Lollio.*]*

Hark, is there not one incurable fool
That might be begged?[40] I have friends.

Lol. [*Within*] I have him for you, one that shall deserve it too.   220

Alib. Good boy, Lollio.

---

36 *yours:* your hand (writing), your letter.
37 *pick:* steal.
38 *cast . . . water:* analyze your urine diagnostically.
39 *said:* done.
40 *That . . . begged:* Whose guardianship and estate might be sought.
V.i.
1 *strikes:* Q "strike."   2 *termagants:* shrews.
3 *thanked:* Q "thank."
4 *Phosphorus:* the morning star; Q "Bosphorus."
5 *fall . . . ruin:* devise a catastrophe.
6 *rising:* awakening of the household.
7 *reach:* scheme.

[Enter Isabella, *then* Lollio *with* Madmen *and* Fools.]*

The Madmen *and* Fools *dance.*

'Tis perfect; well, fit but once these strains,
We shall have coin and credit for our pains.

Exeunt.

ACT FIVE

Scene One

Enter Beatrice. *A clock strikes one.*

Bea. One struck, and yet she lies by't!—Oh, my
    fears!
This strumpet serves her own ends, 'tis apparent now,
Devours the pleasure with a greedy appetite
And never minds my honor or my peace,
Makes havoc of my right; but she pays dearly for't:
No trusting of her life with such a secret,
That cannot rule her blood to keep her promise.
Beside, I have some suspicion of her faith to me
Because I was suspected of my lord,
And it must come from her;—hark, by my horrors,   10
Another clock strikes[1] two.

Strikes two.

Enter De Flores.

De F.   Pist, where are you?

Bea. De Flores?

De F.   Ay; is she not come from him yet?

Bea. As I am a living soul, not.

De F.   Sure the devil
Hath sowed his itch within her; who'd trust
A waiting-woman?

Bea.   I must trust somebody.

De F. Push, they are termagants;[2]
Especially when they fall upon their masters
And have their ladies' first-fruits; th'are mad whelps;
You cannot stave 'em off from game royal then.
You are so harsh and hardy, ask no counsel,   20
And I could have helped you to an apothecary's
    daughter
Would have fall'n off before eleven and thanked[3] you
    too.

Bea. Oh me, not yet? This whore forgets herself.

De F. The rascal fares so well; look, y'are undone,
The day-star, by this hand! See Phosphorus[4] plain
    yonder.

Bea. Advise me now to fall upon some ruin;[5]
There is no counsel safe else.

De F.   Peace, I ha't now;
For we must force a rising,[6] there's no remedy.

Bea. How? Take heed of that.

De F.   Tush, be you quiet
Or else give over all.

Bea.   Prithee, I ha' done then.   30

De F. This is my reach:[7] I'll set some part afire
Of Diaphanta's chamber.

Bea.   How? Fire, sir?
That may endanger the whole house.

De F. You talk of danger when your fame's on fire?

Bea. That's true; do what thou wilt now.

De F.   Push, I aim
At a most rich success, strikes all dead sure;
The chimney being afire, and some light parcels
Of the least danger in her chamber only,
If Diaphanta should be met by chance then,
Far from her lodging, which is now suspicious,   40
It would be thought her fears and affrights then
Drove her to seek for succor; if not seen
Or met at all, as that's the likeliest,
For her own shame she'll hasten towards her lodging;
I will be ready with a piece[8] high-charged,
As 'twere to cleanse the chimney; there 'tis proper
    now,
But she shall be the mark.

Bea.   I'm forced to love thee now,
'Cause thou provid'st so carefully for my honor.

De F. 'Slid,[9] it concerns the safety of us both,
Our pleasure and continuance.

Bea.   One word now, prithee:
How for the servants?

De F.   I'll dispatch them   51
Some one way, some another in the hurry,
For buckets, hooks, ladders; fear not you,
The deed shall find its time; and I've thought since
Upon a safe conveyance for the body too.
How this fire purifies wit! Watch you your minute.

Bea. Fear keeps my soul upon't; I cannot stray
    from't.

Enter ALONZO'S GHOST.

De F. Ha! what art thou that tak'st away the light
'Twixt that star and me? I dread thee not;
'Twas but a mist of conscience. All's clear again.   60
                            Exit.

Bea. Who's that, De Flores? Bless me! it slides by;
                     [*Exit* GHOST.]
Some ill thing haunts the house; 't has left behind it
A shivering sweat upon me. I'm afraid now.
This night hath been so tedious. Oh, this strumpet!
Had she a thousand lives, he should not leave her
Till he had destroyed the last. List, oh, my terrors!
Three struck by Saint Sebastian's.
                 Struck three o'clock.

[*Within*] Fire, fire, fire!

Bea. Already? How rare is that man's speed!
How heartily he serves me! His face loathes one,   70
But look upon his care, who would not love him?
The east is not more beauteous than his service.

[*Within*] Fire, fire, fire!

Enter DE FLORES; Servants *pass over, ring a bell.*

De F. Away, dispatch! hooks, buckets, ladders; that's
    well said;
The fire-bell rings, the chimney works; my charge;
The piece is ready.
                         Exit.

Enter DIAPHANTA.

Bea.   Here's a man worth loving—
    [*To* DIAPHANTA] Oh, y'are a jewel.

Dia.   Pardon frailty,
    madam;
In troth I was so well, I ev'n forgot myself.

Bea. Y'have made trim work.

Dia.   What?

Bea.   Hie quickly to
    your chamber;
Your reward follows you.

Dia.   I never made   80
So sweet a bargain.
                         Exit.

Enter ALSEMERO.

Als.   Oh my dear Joanna,
Alas, art thou risen too? I was coming,
My absolute treasure.

Bea.   When I missed you,
I could not choose but follow.

Als.   Th'art all sweetness.
The fire is not so dangerous.

Bea.   Think you so, sir?

Als. I prithee tremble not; believe me, 'tis not.

Enter VERMANDERO, JASPERINO.

Ver. Oh, bless my house and me.

Als.   My lord your
    father.

Enter DE FLORES *with a piece.*

Ver. Knave, whither goes that piece?

De F.   To scour the
    chimney.
                         Exit.

Ver. Oh, well said, well said;
That fellow's good on all occasions.   90

Bea. A wondrous necessary man, my lord.

Ver. He hath a ready wit; he's worth 'em all, sir;
Dog[10] at a house of fire; I ha' seen him singed ere now;
                 The piece goes off.
Ha, there he goes.

Bea.   'Tis done.

Als.   Come, sweet, to bed now;
Alas, thou wilt get cold.

Bea.   Alas, the fear keeps that out;
My heart will find no quiet till I hear
How Diaphanta, my poor woman, fares;
It is her chamber, sir, her lodging chamber.

Ver. How should the fire come there?

Bea. As good a soul as ever lady countenanced,   100
But in her chamber negligent and heavy;[11]
She 'scaped a mine[12] twice.

Ver.   Twice?

Bea.   Strangely, twice, sir.

---

8   *piece:* gun.   9   *'Slid:* By God's eyelid.
10   *Dog:* Skilled.   11   *heavy:* sluggish, clumsy.
12   *mine:* danger.

Ver. Those sleepy sluts are dangerous in a house,
And they be ne'er so good.

Enter DE FLORES.

De F.   Oh, poor virginity!
Thou hast paid dearly for't.
Ver.   Bless us! what's that?
De F. A thing you all knew once—Diaphanta's
   burnt.
Bea. My woman, oh, my woman!
De F.   Now the flames
Are greedy of her; burnt, burnt, burnt to death, sir.
Bea. Oh, my presaging soul!
Als.   Not a tear more,
I charge you by the last embrace I gave you   110
In bed before this raised us.
Bea.   Now you tie me;
Were it my sister, now she gets no more.

Enter Servant.

Ver. How now?
Ser. All danger's past, you may now take your rests,
my lords; the fire is throughly quenched; ah, poor
gentlewoman, how soon was she stifled!
Bea. De Flores, what is left of her inter,
And we as mourners all will follow her.
I will entreat that honor to my servant,
Ev'n of my lord himself.
Als.   Command it, sweetness.   120
Bea. Which of you spied the fire first?
De F.   'Twas I,
   madam.
Bea. And took such pains in't too? A double
   goodness!
'Twere well he were rewarded.
Ver.   He shall be;
De Flores, call upon me.
Als.   And upon me, sir.
                     Exeunt. [*Manet* DE FLORES.]
De F. Rewarded? Precious, here's a trick beyond
   me.
I see in all bouts, both of sport and wit,
Always a woman strives for the last hit.
                                        Exit.

[V.ii]

Enter TOMAZO.

Tom. I cannot taste the benefits of life
With the same relish I was wont to do.
Man I grow weary of, and hold his fellowship
A treacherous bloody friendship; and because
I am ignorant in whom my wrath should settle,

I must think all men villains, and the next
I meet, whoe'er he be, the murderer
Of my most worthy brother. Ha! what's he?

Enter DE FLORES, *passes over the stage.*

Oh, the fellow that some call honest De Flores;
But methinks honesty was hard bested[1]   10
To come there for a lodging, as if a queen
Should make her palace of a pest-house.
I find a contrariety in nature
Betwixt that face and me; the least occasion
Would give me game[2] upon him; yet he's so foul,
One would scarce touch him[3] with a sword he loved
And made account of. So most deadly venomous,
He would go near to poison any weapon
That should draw blood on him; one must resolve
Never to use that sword again in fight,   20
In way of honest manhood, that strikes him;
Some river must devour't, 'twere not fit
That any man should find it. What, again?

Enter DE FLORES.

He walks a' purpose by, sure to choke me up,
To infect my blood.
De F.   My worthy noble lord.
Tom. Dost offer to come near and breathe upon me?

                                   [*Strikes him.*]

De F. A blow.

                                   [*Draws his sword.*]

Tom.   Yea, are you so prepared?
I'll rather like a soldier die by th' sword
Than like a politician[4] by thy poison.

                                        [*Draws.*]

De F. Hold, my lord, as you are honorable.   30
Tom. All slaves that kill by poison are still[5] cowards.
De F. [*Aside*] I cannot strike; I see his brother's
   wounds
Fresh bleeding in his eye as in a crystal.[6]
[*To* TOMAZO] I will not question this, I know y'are
   noble;
I take my injury with thanks given, sir,
Like a wise lawyer; and as a favor,
Will wear it for the worthy hand that gave it.
[*Aside*] Why this from him that yesterday appeared
So strangely loving to me?
Oh, but instinct is of a subtler strain.   40
Guilt must not walk so near his lodge again;
He came near me now.
                                        Exit.
Tom. All league with mankind I renounce for ever
Till I find this murderer; not so much
As common courtesy but I'll lock up:
For in the state of ignorance I live in
A brother may salute his brother's murderer
And wish good speed to th'villain in a greeting.

Enter VERMANDERO, ALIBIUS, *and*
ISABELLA.

Ver. Noble Piracquo.

V.ii.
   [1] *bested:* bestead, put to it.
   [2] *give me game:* provoke me to fight.
   [3] *touch him:* Q "touch."   [4] *politician:* schemer.
   [5] *still:* always.   [6] *crystal:* crystal ball.

Tom.   Pray keep on your way, sir,
I've nothing to say to you.
    Ver.   Comforts bless you sir.   50
    Tom. I have forsworn compliment;[7] in troth I have,
    sir;
As you are merely man, I have not left
A good wish for you, nor any here.
    Ver. Unless you be so far in love with grief
You will not part from't upon any terms,
We bring that news will make a welcome for us.
    Tom. What news can that be?
    Ver.   Throw no scornful
    smile
Upon the zeal I bring you, 'tis worth more, sir.
Two of the chiefest men I kept about me
I hide not from the law, or your just vengeance.   60
    Tom. Ha!
    Ver. To give your peace more ample satisfaction,
Thank these discoverers.
    Tom.   If you bring that calm,
Name but the manner I shall ask forgiveness in
For that contemptuous smile upon you;
I'll perfect it with reverence that belongs
Unto a sacred altar.
                         [*Kneels.*]
    Ver.   Good sir, rise;
                        [*Raises him.*]
Why, now you overdo as much a' this hand,
As you fell short a' t'other. Speak, Alibius.
    Alib. 'Twas my wife's fortune, as she is most lucky
At a discovery, to find out lately   71
Within our hospital of fools and madmen
Two counterfeits slipped into these disguises,
Their names Franciscus and Antonio.
    Ver. Both mine, sir, and I ask no favor for 'em.
    Alib. Now that which draws suspicion to their
    habits,
The time of their disguisings agrees justly
With the day of the murder.
    Tom.   O blest revelation!
    Ver. Nay more, nay more, sir—I'll not spare mine
    own
In way of justice—they both feigned a journey   80
To Briamata, and so wrought out their leaves;
My love was so abused in't.
    Tom.   Time's too precious
To run in waste now; you have brought a peace
The riches of five kingdoms could not purchase.
Be my most happy conduct; I thirst for 'em:
Like subtle lightning will I wind about 'em,
And melt their marrow in 'em.   *Exeunt.*

[V.iii]

        Enter ALSEMERO *and* JASPERINO.

    Jas. Your confidence, I'm sure, is now of proof.[1]
The prospect from the garden has showed
Enough for deep suspicion.
    Als.   The black mask[2]
That so continually was worn upon't

Condemns the face for ugly ere't be seen—
Her despite[3] to him, and so seeming bottomless.[4]
    Jas. Touch it home then: 'tis not a shallow probe
Can search this ulcer soundly; I fear you'll find it
Full of corruption. 'Tis fit I leave you;
She meets you opportunely from that walk.   10
She took the back door at his parting with her.
                    Exit JASPERINO.
    Als. Did my fate wait for this unhappy stroke
At my first sight of woman? She's here.

        Enter BEATRICE.

    Bea. Alsemero!
    Als.   How do you?
    Bea.   How do I?
Alas! how do you? You look not well.
    Als. You read me well enough, I am not well.
    Bea. Not well, sir? Is't in my power to better you?
    Als. Yes.
    Bea. Nay, then y'are cured again.
    Als. Pray resolve me one question, lady.
    Bea.   If I can.
    Als. None can so sure. Are you honest?[5]   20
    Bea. Ha, ha, ha! that's a broad question, my lord.
    Als. But that's not a modest answer, my lady:
Do you laugh? My doubts are strong upon me.
    Bea. 'Tis innocence that smiles, and no rough brew
Can take away the dimple in her cheek.
Say I should strain a tear to fill the vault,[6]
Which would you give the better faith to?
    Als. 'Twere but hypocrisy of a sadder color
But the same stuff; neither your smiles nor tears
Shall move or flatter me from my belief: 30
You are a whore.
    Bea.   What a horrid sound it hath!
It blasts a beauty to deformity;
Upon what face soever that breath falls,
It strikes it ugly; oh, you have ruined
What you can ne'er repair again.
    Als. I'll all demolish, and seek out truth within you,
If there be any left; let your sweet tongue
Prevent your heart's rifling; there I'll ransack
And tear out my suspicion.
    Bea.   You may, sir,
'Tis an easy passage; yet, if you please,   40
Show me the ground whereon you lost your love:
My spotless virtue may but tread on that,
Before I perish.
    Als.   Unanswerable,
A ground you cannot stand on; you fall down
Beneath all grace and goodness when you set
Your ticklish[7] heel on't. There was a visor[8]

---

    [7] *compliment:* courtesy.

V. iii.
    [1] *of proof:* of tested power.
    [2] *black mask:* Beatrice's apparent hostility to De Flores.
    [3] *despite:* contemptuous treatment.
    [4] *Condemns . . . bottomless:* Passage possibly corrupt.
    [5] *honest:* chaste.   [6] *vault:* arched sky.
    [7] *ticklish:* skittish.   [8] *visor:* mask.

O'er that cunning face, and that became you;
Now impudence in triumph rides upon't.
How comes this tender reconcilement else
'Twixt you and your despite, your rancorous loathing,
De Flores? He that your eye was sore at sight of,   51
He's now become your arm's supporter, your
Lips' saint.
    Bea.   Is there the cause?
    Als.   Worse: your lust's devil,
Your adultery.
    Bea.   Would any but yourself say that,
'Twould turn him to a villain.
    Als.   'Twas witnessed
By the counsel of your bosom, Diaphanta.
    Bea.   Is your witness dead then?
    Als.   'Tis to be feared
It was the wages of her knowledge; poor soul,
She lived not long after the discovery.
    Bea.   Then hear a story of not much less horror   60
Than this your false suspicion is beguiled with;
To your bed's scandal I stand up innocence,
Which even the guilt of one black other deed
Will stand for proof of: your love has made me
A cruel murd'ress.
    Als.   Ha!
    Bea.   A bloody one;
I have kissed poison for't, stroked a serpent,
That thing of hate, worthy in my esteem
Of no better employment; and him most worthy
To be so employed, I caused to murder
That innocent Piracquo, having no   70
Better means than that worst to assure
Yourself to me.
    Als.   Oh, the place itself e'er since
Has crying been for vengeance, the temple
Where blood and beauty first unlawfully
Fired their devotion and quenched the right one;
'Twas in my fears at first, 'twill have it now:[9]
Oh, thou art all deformed.
    Bea.   Forget not, sir,
It for your sake was done; shall greater dangers
Make the less welcome?
    Als.   Oh, thou shouldst have gone
A thousand leagues about[10] to have avoided   80
This dangerous bridge of blood; here we are lost.
    Bea.   Remember I am true unto your bed.
    Als.   The bed itself's a charnel, the sheets shrouds
For murdered carcasses; it must ask pause
What I must do in this; meantime you shall
Be my prisoner only: enter my closet;
                           Exit BEATRICE.
I'll be your keeper yet. Oh, in what part
Of this sad story shall I first begin?—Ha!

        Enter DE FLORES.

This same fellow has put me in.[11]—De Flores.
    De F.   Noble Alsemero?
    Als.   I can tell you   90
News, sir; my wife has her commended to you.
    De F.   That's news indeed, my lord; I think she
    would
Commend me to the gallows if she could,
She ever loved me so well, I thank her.
    Als.   What's this blood upon your band,[12] De
    Flores?
    De F.   Blood? No, sure 'twas washed since.
    Als.   Since
when, man?
    De F.   Since t'other day I got a knock
In a sword and dagger school; I think 'tis out.
    Als.   Yes, 'tis almost out, but 'tis perceived, though.
I had forgot my message; this it is: 100
What price goes murder?
    De F.   How, sir?
    Als.   I ask you, sir;
My wife's behindhand with[13] you, she tells me,
For a brave bloody blow you gave for her sake
Upon Piracquo.
    De F.   Upon? 'Twas quite through him,
    sure;
Has she confessed it?
    Als.   As sure as death to both of you,
And much more than that.
    De F.   It could not be much more;
'Twas but one thing, and that—she's a whore.
    Als.   It[14] could not choose but follow; oh cunning
    devils!
How should blind men know you from fair-faced
    saints?
    Bea.   [*Within*] He lies, the villain does belie me.   110
    De F.   Let me go to her, sir.
    Als.   Nay, you shall to her.
Peace, crying crocodile, your sounds are heard.
Take your prey to you; get you in to her, sir.
                         Exit DE FLORES.
I'll be your pander now; rehearse again
Your scene of lust, that you may be perfect
When you shall come to act it to the black audience
Where howls and gnashings shall be music to you.
Clip[15] your adult'ress freely; 'tis the pilot
Will guide you to the Mare Mortuum,[16]
Where you shall sink to fathoms bottomless.   120

    Enter VERMANDERO, ALIBIUS, ISABELLA,
        TOMAZO, FRANCISCUS, *and*
              ANTONIO.

    Ver.   Oh, Alsemero, I have a wonder for you.
    Als.   No, sir, 'tis I, I have a wonder for you.
    Ver.   I have suspicion near as proof itself
For Piracquo's murder.
    Als.   Sir, I have proof
Beyond suspicion for Piracquo's murder.
    Ver.   Beseech you hear me; these two have been
    disguised
E'er since the deed was done.
    Als.   I have two other

---

  9 *'twill . . . now:* the temple will have revenge.
  10 *about:* around in detour.
  11 *put me in:* given me the cue.   12 *band:* neckband.
  13 *behindhand with:* in debt to, in arrears.   14 *It:* Q " I."
  15 *Clip:* Embrace.
  16 *Mare Mortuum:* Dead Sea, thought bottomless.

That were more close disguised than your two could be
E'er since the deed was done.

Ver. You'll hear me: these mine own servants: 130
Als. Hear me: those nearer than your servants
That shall acquit them and prove them guiltless.

Fran. That may be done with easy truth, sir.

Tom. How is my cause bandied[17] through your
delays!
'Tis urgent in blood and calls for haste;
Give me a brother alive or dead:
Alive, a wife with him; if dead, for both
A recompense, for murder and adultery.[18]

Bea. [*Within*] Oh, oh, oh!

Als.   Hark, 'tis coming to you.

De F. [*Within*] Nay, I'll along for company.

Bea.   Oh, oh!

Ver. What horrid sounds are these?   141

Als. Come forth, you twins of mischief.

Enter DE FLORES *bringing in* BEATRICE [*wounded*].

De F. Here we are; if you have any more
To say to us, speak quickly; I shall not
Give you the hearing else; I am so stout yet,
And so, I think, that broken rib[19] of mankind.

Ver. An host of enemies entered my citadel
Could not amaze like this: Joanna! Beatrice-Joanna!

Bea. Oh come not near me, sir; I shall defile you.
I am that of your blood was taken from you   150
For your better health; look no more upon't,
But cast it to the ground regardlessly;
Let the common sewer take it from distinction.
Beneath the stars upon yon meteor
Ever hung my fate, 'mongst things corruptible;
I ne'er could pluck it from him. My loathing
Was prophet to the rest but ne'er believ'd;
Mine honor fell with him and now my life.
Alsemero, I am a stranger to your bed;
Your bed was cozened[20] on the nuptial night,   160
For which your false bride died.

Als.   Diaphanta!

De F. Yes; and the while I coupled with your mate
At barley-brake; now we are left in hell.

Ver. We are all there, it circumscribes[21] here.

De F. I loved this woman in spite of her heart;
Her love I earned out of Piracquo's murder.

Tom. Ha! my brother's murderer.

De F.   Yes, and her
honor's prize
Was my reward. I thank life for nothing
But that pleasure; it was so sweet to me
That I have drunk up all, left none behind   170
For any man to pledge me.

Ver.   Horrid villain!
Keep life in him for further tortures.

De F.   No;
I can prevent you; here's my penknife still.
It is but one thread more,

[*Stabs himself.*]

—and now 'tis cut.
Make haste, Joanna, by that token to thee:

Canst not forget, so lately put in mind—
I would not go to leave thee far behind.

Dies.

Bea. Forgive me, Alsemero, all forgive;
'Tis time to die, when 'tis a shame to live.

Dies.

Ver. Oh, my name is entered now in that record[22]
Where till this fatal hour 'twas never read.   181

Als. Let it be blotted out; let your heart lose it,
And it can never look you in the face
Nor tell a tale behind the back of life
To your dishonor; justice hath so right
The guilty hit that innocence is quit[23]
By proclamation and may joy again.
Sir, you are sensible of what truth hath done;
'Tis the best comfort that your grief can find.

Tom. Sir, I am satisfied; my injuries   190
Lie dead before me. I can exact no more,
Unless my soul were loose and could o'ertake
Those black fugitives[24] that are fled from thence,
To take a second vengeance, but there are wraths
Deeper than mine, 'tis to be feared, about 'em.

Als. What an opacous[25] body had that moon
That last changed on us! here's beauty changed
To ugly whoredom; here, servant obedience
To a master sin, imperious murder;
I, a supposed husband, changed embraces   200
With wantonness,[26] but that was paid before;
Your[27] change is come too, from an ignorant wrath
To knowing friendship. Are there any more on's?

Ant. Yes, sir; I was changed too, from a little ass as
I was to a great fool as I am, and had like to ha' been
changed to the gallows but that you know my innocence[28] always excuses me.

Fran. I was changed from a little wit to be stark
mad,
Almost for the same purpose.

Isa.   Your change is still
behind,[29]
But deserve best your transformation;   210
You are a jealous coxcomb, keep schools of folly,
And teach your scholars how to break your own head.[30]

Alib. I see all apparent, wife, and will change now
Into a better husband, and never keep
Scholars that shall be wiser than myself.

Als. Sir, you have yet a son's duty living;
Please you, accept it; let that your sorrow
As it goes from your eye, go from your heart,
Man and his sorrow at the grave must part.

---

[17] *bandied:* tossed about.   [18] *adultery:* with Alsemero.

[19] *rib:* woman (created from Adam's rib).

[20] *cozened:* cheated.

[21] *circumscribes:* i.e., the circle called "hell" in the game
of barley-break (see III. iii. 172 and note 40).

[22] *record:* divine logbook of sins.   [23] *quit:* acquitted.

[24] *black fugitives:* damned souls in flight.

[25] *opacous:* darkened.   [26] *wantonness:* i.e., Diaphanta.

[27] *Your:* Tomazo's.

[28] *innocence:* guiltlessness, imbecility.

[29] *behind:* to come.

[30] *And . . . head:* i.e., with cuckold's horns.

EPILOGUE

Als. All we can do to comfort one another,
To stay a brother's sorrow for a brother,
To dry a child from the kind father's eyes,
Is to no purpose, it rather multiplies.
Your only [1] smiles have power to cause relive
The dead again, or in their rooms to give
Brother a new brother, father a child;
If these appear, all griefs are reconciled.

Exeunt omnes.

F I N I S

EPILOGUE
[1] *Your only:* Only your.

John Webster

[*c.* 1580–*c.* 1634]

THE WHITE DEVIL

OF JOHN WEBSTER, little is known for certain. Like Bacon, he seems to have been educated as a lawyer; like Jonson, he made his living partly as a tinker of plays for the theatrical entrepreneur Philip Henslowe. The ascertainable facts concerning his career have been assembled by Charles R. Forker in a forthcoming biographical study.

Webster wrote slowly and wrote little. THE WHITE DEVIL, one of the two plays for which he is remembered, is to be dated in the period 1610–12.

Copy text for this edition is the first published edition of the play, a quarto of 1612 emended infrequently and silently by reference to Qq2–4. Numerous copies of Q1 survive but the differences among them are slight. Neither does Q1 differ radically from subsequent editions. Thus Q2 of 1631 is essentially a reprint of its predecessor, Q3 of 1665 reprints Q2 (while adding act divisions for all but one act), and Q4 of 1672 reprints Q3 (while adding scene divisions).

Webster's willingness to utilize the work of other writers has often been remarked. In THE WHITE DEVIL his most conspicuous debt is to Florio's translation of Montaigne. Other sources or quarries include Jonson, Shakespeare (reminiscence of whose tragedies will be apparent to every reader), contemporary emblem books, and travel and courtesy literature (the *Description of Ireland*, 1577, by the Irish Jesuit and poetaster Richard Stanyhurst; *Honours Academie*, 1610, by Nicholas de Montreux).

The lurid story that Webster transmutes into art was notorious in his own time and came to him perhaps in anecdotal form from the newsletter circulated by the German banking house of Fugger. At the heart of the story is the adulterous love of Vittoria Accoramboni, born in 1557, and Paolo Giordano Orsini, Duke of Bracciano, who had most likely strangled his unfaithful wife Isabella in 1576. Five years later, and in order to marry Vittoria, he murdered her husband, Francesco Peretti (Camillo in the play). Unluckily for the newly wedded couple, the Pope elected in 1585 as Sixtus V was Cardinal di Montalto, an uncle of Vittoria's murdered husband. Bracciano's death soon after of an ulcerated leg frustrated the Pope's revenge. Vittoria's more terrible death followed speedily. Under the leadership of Lodovico Orsini, a ruffianly younger kinsman of Bracciano's, she and her brother Flamineo (Webster's Marcello) were surprised and stabbed by assassins. The Republic of Venice took order with Lodovico, who was strangled on December 27, 1585.

It is not a tepid tale Webster inherits. If anything, however, he succeeds in aggrandizing the horror. His success is not necessarily calculated. As opposed to his sanguinary predecessors in the Elizabethan theater—for example, Preston, Kyd, and Peele—he does not revel in brutal incident or in the presentation of perverted character. In fact, he seems to grudge the presentation. Syntactically, his manner is cramped and elliptical, as in much of the poetry of his contemporary John Donne. From his writing, pronouns and prepositions are frequently excised, we might say they are throttled. The utterance that emerges is a concessive utterance and gives the effect of having been wrenched from an unwilling reporter. Webster seems to be saying: "This and no more will I tell you." His violent protagonists are memorable as they are endowed with the same amoral energy with which Barabas and Tamburlaine and Mortimer are endowed. Unlike these Marlovian heroes or hero-villains, they do not speak to us—quoting from Michael Drayton's tribute to Marlowe—of "brave translunary things," rather of the charnel house and the grisly business appurtenant to it. That is as they are deferring to the troubled psychology of their maker.

R. A. F.

The White Devil

TO THE READER

IN publishing this tragedy, I do but challenge to myself that liberty which other men have ta'en before me: not that I affect praise by it, for *nos haec novimus esse nihil;*[1] only, since it was acted in so dull a time of winter, presented in so open and black[2] a theater, that it wanted (that which is the only grace and setting out of a tragedy) a full and understanding auditory; and that, since that time, I have noted most of the people that come to the playhouse resemble those ignorant asses who, visiting stationers' shops, 10 their use[3] is not to inquire for good books, but new books; I present it to the general view with this confidence,—

> *Nec rhonchos metues maligniorum,*
> *Nec scombris tunicas dabis molestas.*[4]

If it be objected this is no true dramatic poem, I shall easily confess it; *non potes in nugas dicere plura meas, ipse ego quam dixi.*[5] Willingly, and not ignorantly, in this kind have I faulted: for, should a man present to such an auditory the most sententious[6] tragedy 20 that ever was written, observing all the critical laws, as height of style, and gravity of person, enrich it with the sententious Chorus, and, as it were, life in death[7] in the passionate and weighty Nuntius;[8] yet, after all this divine rapture, *O dura messorum ilia,*[9] the breath that comes from the uncapable multitude is able to poison it; and, ere it be acted, let the author resolve to fix[10] to every scene this of Horace,

> *—Haec hodie porcis comedenda relinques.*[11]   29

To those who report I was a long time in finishing this tragedy, I confess, I do not write with a goose quill winged with two feathers; and if they will needs make it my fault, I must answer them with that of Euripides to Alcestides,[12] a tragic writer. Alcestides objecting that Euripides had only, in three days, composed three verses, whereas himself had written three hundred, "Thou tellest truth," quoth he, "but here's the difference,—thine shall only be read for three days, whereas mine shall continue three ages."   39

Detraction is the sworn friend to ignorance. For mine own part, I have ever truly cherished my good opinion of other men's worthy labors; especially of that full and heightened style of Master Chapman; the labored and understanding works of Master Jonson; the no less worthy composures[13] of the both worthily excellent Master Beaumont and Master Fletcher; and lastly (without wrong last to be named), the right happy and copious industry of Master Shakespeare, Master Dekker, and Master Heywood; wishing what I write may be read by their light; protesting that, in the 50 strength of mine own judgment, I know them so worthy, that though I rest silent in my own work, yet to most of theirs I dare (without flattery) fix that of Martial,

> *—Non norunt haec monumenta mori.*[14]

TO THE READER
[1] *L.:* "I know this work is worth nothing," Martial, XIII. ii. 8.
[2] *Open and black:* In the public theaters (like the Red Bull where the play was first acted), the pit was open to the sky; hence "black" or "bleak" in winter.   [3] *use:* custom.
[4] *L.:* "You shall not fear the turned-up noses of envious critics, Nor give to mackerel robes of torture": pitch-smeared garments with which criminals about to be burned were clad (Martial, IV. lxxxvi. 7–8).
[5] *L.:* "you are not able to speak worse of my trifles, than I have spoken myself," Martial, XIII. ii. 4–5.
[6] *sententious:* wise or weighty; full of saws and sayings.
[7] *life in death:* make the death of the characters come alive in the language.
[8] *Nuntius:* Messenger, whose function is to report what we do not see enacted.
[9] *L.:* "O strong stomachs of harvesters" who, like the "multitude," can stomach garlic (Horace, *Epodes*, III. iv).
[10] *fix:* attach.
[11] *L.:* "What you leave will only go to feed the pigs today," Horace, *Epistles*, I. vii. 19.
[12] *Alcestides:* The butt of this familiar story, which comes from the Roman writer Valerius Maximus, a compiler of historical anecdotes, is otherwise unknown.
[13] *composures:* compositions.
[14] *L.:* "These memorials do not know how to die" (X. ii. 12).

DRAMATIS PERSONÆ[1]

MONTICELSO, *a Cardinal, afterwards Pope Paul IV*
FRANCISCO DE MEDICIS, *Duke of Florence*
BRACHIANO, *otherwise Paulo Giordano Orsini, Duke of Brachiano, husband of Isabella*
GIOVANNI, *his son*
COUNT LODOVICO, *a profligate*
CAMILLO, *husband of Vittoria*
FLAMINEO, *brother of Vittoria, secretary to Brachiano*
MARCELLO, *brother of Vittoria, attendant of Francisco de Medicis*
HORTENSIO, *officer of Brachiano*
ANTONELLI ⎱ *friends of Lodovico*
GASPARO ⎰
JULIO, *Doctor*

JAQUES, *a Moor, Giovanni's servant (a nonspeaking part)*
CHRISTOPHERO, *Doctor Julio's assistant (a non-speaking part).*
Ambassadors, Cardinals, Courtiers, Lawyers, Physicians, Officers, Conjurer, Armorer, Attendants, *etc.*

ISABELLA, *sister of Francisco de Medicis, wife of Brachiano*
VITTORIA COROMBONA, *married first to Camillo, afterwards to Brachiano.*
CORNELIA, *mother of Vittoria, Flamineo, and Marcello*
ZANCHE, *a Moor, servant of Vittoria*
Matron *of the House of Convertites*

SCENE—Italy

———————

ACT ONE

SCENE ONE

Enter Count LODOVICO, ANTONELLI, *and* GASPARO.

Lod. Banished!
Ant.   It grieved me much to hear the
    sentence.
Lod. Ha, ha! O Democritus,[1] thy gods
That govern the whole world! courtly reward
And punishment. Fortune's a right[2] whore.
If she give aught, she deals it in small parcels,
That she may take away all at one swoop,
This 'tis to have great enemies:—God quite[3] them!
Your wolf no longer seems to be a wolf

Than when she's hungry.[4]
Gasp.   You term those enemies
Are[5] men of princely rank.
Lod.   Oh, I pray for them.   10
The violent thunder is adored by those
Are pashed[6] in pieces by it.
Ant.   Come, my lord,
You are justly doomed: look but a little back
Into your former life; you have in three years
Ruined the noblest earldom.
Gasp.   Your followers
Have swallowed you like mummia[7] and, being sick
With such unnatural and horrid physic,
Vomit you up i' the kennel.[8]
Ant.   All the damnable degrees
Of drinkings have you staggered through: one citizen
Is lord of two fair manors called you master   20
Only for caviare.[9]
Gasp.   Those noblemen
Which were invited to your prodigal feasts,
Wherein the phoenix[10] scarce could scape your throats,
Laugh at your misery; as fore-deeming[11] you
An idle meteor, which, drawn forth the earth,[12]
Would be soon lost i' the air.
Ant.   Jest upon you,
And say you were begotten in an earthquake,
You have ruined such fair lordships.
Lod.   Very good.
This well goes[13] with two buckets: I must tend[14]
The pouring out of either.
Gasp.   Worse than these;   30
You have acted certain murders here in Rome,
Bloody and full of horror.
Lod.   'Las, they were flea-bitings.
Why took they not my head, then?
Gasp.   Oh, my lord,
The law doth sometimes mediate,[15] thinks it good

DRAMATIS PERSONÆ
  [1] The list given here represents editorial addition or amplification of the Dramatis Personae first added in Q3 (1665). Act and scene divisions are also omitted from Q1 and are supplied by subsequent editors.

I.i.
  [1] *Democritus:* In popular acceptance, an "atheistical" philosopher; hence the invocation is sardonic.
  [2] *right:* proper.   [3] *quite:* requite.
  [4] *Your . . . hungry:* i.e., Only the poor man is felt to be a menace to society and hunted by it.
  [5] *Are:* Who are (as also subsequently).
  [6] *pashed:* violently broken.
  [7] *mummia:* medicine or "physic," concocted literally from dead bodies.   [8] *kennel:* gutter.
  [9] *Only . . . caviare:* So that he could dine on caviare at your table(?).
  [10] *phoenix:* eternal; hence the most rare dish conceivable.
  [11] *fore-deeming:* judging (in anticipation).
  [12] *meteor . . . earth:* Meteors were supposed to be terrestrial exhalations sucked up by the sun and ignited in the atmosphere.   [13] *goes:* comes equipped.
  [14] *tend:* wait on.
  [15] *mediate:* take a more temperate course.

Not ever[16] to steep violent sins in blood.
This gentle penance may both end your crimes,
And in the example better these bad times.

Lod. So; but I wonder, then, some great men scape
This banishment: there's Paulo Giordano Orsini,
The Duke of Brachiano, now lives in Rome,   40
And by close[17] panderism seeks to prostitute
The honor of Vittoria Corombona;
Vittoria, she that might have got my pardon
For one kiss to the duke.

Ant. Have a full man within you.[18]
We see that trees bear no such pleasant fruit
There where they grew first as where they are new set.
Perfumes, the more they are chafed,[19] the more they
     render
Their pleasing scents; and so affliction
Expresseth virtue fully, whether true   50
Or else adulterate.

Lod.   Leave your painted comforts.
I'll make Italian cut-works[20] in their guts,
If ever I return.

Gasp.   Oh, sir!

Lod.   I am patient.
I have seen some ready to be executed
Give pleasant looks and money, and grown familiar
With the knave hangman: so do I. I thank them,
And would account them nobly merciful,
Would they dispatch me quickly.

Ant.   Fare you well.
We shall find time, I doubt not, to repeal
Your banishment.

Lod.   I am ever bound to you.[21]   60

[*A sennet*[22] *sounds.*]

This is the world's alms; pray, make use of it.[23]
Great men sell sheep thus to be cut in pieces,
When first they have shorn them bare and sold their
     fleeces.

                                        Exeunt.

[I.ii]

Enter BRACHIANO, CAMILLO, FLAMINEO,
     [and] VITTORIA COROMBONA.

Brach. Your best of rest!

Vit. Cor.   Unto my lord, the duke,
The best of welcome!—More lights! attend the duke.

[*Exeunt* CAMILLO *and* VITTORIA
                                        COROMBONA.]

Brach. Flamineo—

Flam.   My lord?

Brach.   Quite lost, Flamineo.

Flam. Pursue your noble wishes, I am prompt
As lightning to your service. Oh, my lord,

                                        Whisper.

The fair Vittoria, my happy sister,
Shall give you present[1] audience.—Gentlemen,
Let the caroche[2] go on; and 'tis his pleasure
You put out all your torches and depart.

Brach. Are we so happy?

Flam.   Can't be otherwise?   10

Observed you not tonight, my honored lord,
Which way so'eer you went, she threw her eyes?[3]
I have dealt already with her chambermaid,
Zanche the Moor, and she is wondrous proud
To be the agent for so high a spirit.

Brach. We are happy above thought, because 'bove
merit.

Flam. 'Bove merit!—we may now talk freely—'bove
merit! What is't you doubt? Her coyness? That's but
the superficies[4] of lust most women have; yet why   20
should ladies blush to hear that named which they do
not fear to handle? Oh, they are politic:[5] they know
our desire is increased by the difficulty of enjoying,
whereas satiety is a blunt, weary, and drowsy passion.
If the buttery-hatch[6] at court stood continually open,
there would be nothing[7] so passionate crowding, nor
hot suit[8] after the beverage.

Brach. Oh, but her jealous husband.

Flam. Hang him! a gilder[9] that hath his brains
perished with quicksilver[10] is no more cold in the   30
liver;[11] the great barriers[12] molted not more feathers
than he hath shed hairs,[13] by the confession of his
doctor; an Irish gamester that will play himself naked,
and then wage all downwards[14] at hazard, is not more
venturous; so unable to please a woman that, like a
Dutch doublet,[15] all his back[16] is shrunk into his
breeches.
Shroud[17] you within this closet,[18] good my lord:
Some trick now must be thought on to divide
My brother-in-law from his fair bedfellow.   40

Brach. Oh, should she fail to come!

Flam. I must not have your lordship thus unwisely

---

[16] *ever:* always.   [17] *close:* secret.
[18] *Have . . . you:* Keep your courage up.
[19] *chafed:* warmed.
[20] *cut-works:* describing material cut into open patterns,
like eyelets.   [21] *bound to you:* in your debt.
[22] *sennet:* trumpets, which herald the entrance of the
characters who come on in scene ii. As often in Renaissance
drama, the play is best perceived as a seamless whole, with
action flowing continuously across the open stage. Hence
insistence on specific place is mostly gratuitous.
[23] *make . . . it:* learn from the experience.
I.ii.
[1] *present:* immediate.   [2] *caroche:* coach.
[3] *threw her eyes:* looked after you.
[4] *superficies:* covering, outside.
[5] *politic:* cunning, full of policy.
[6] *buttery-hatch:* half-door leading to the store-room
where liquor was kept.   [7] *nothing:* nothing like.
[8] *suit:* pursuit.   [9] *gilder:* gold or silver coin.
[10] *quick-silver:* mercury, used to gild the coin, but
dangerous in that when vaporized it was likely to affect the
brain.   [11] *liver:* thought to be the seat of passion.
[12] *barriers:* jousting entertainments in which opponents
on foot fought—here, with such vigor as to lose the plumes
or feathers from their helmets—across a waist-high barrier.
[13] *hairs:* falling out because he has venereal disease.
[14] *downwards:* private parts; the gambler, having lost
everything else, is now willing to hazard his testicles, etc.
[15] *Dutch doublet:* worn close to the back and featuring
baggy breeches.
[16] *back:* virility; to have a hot back (cf. "hot pants") is to
be lecherous; here, the husband's virility is shrunk.
[17] *Shroud:* Shelter.
[18] *closet:* generically, any sequestered room.

amorous. I myself have loved a lady, and pursued her with a great deal of under-age protestation,[19] whom some three or four gallants that have enjoyed would with all their hearts have been glad to have been rid of. 'Tis just like a summer birdcage in a garden. The birds that are without despair to get in, and the birds that are within despair and are in a consumption for fear they shall never get out: Away, away, my lord!   50

[*Exit* BRACHIANO.]

Enter CAMILLO.

See, here he comes. This fellow by his apparel
Some men would judge a politician;
But call his wit in question, you shall find it
Merely an ass in's foot-cloth.[20]—How now, brother!
What, traveling to bed to your kind wife?

Cam. I assure you, brother, no; my voyage lies
More northerly, in a far colder clime.
I do not well remember, I protest,
When I last lay with her.

Flam. Strange you should lose your count.   60

Cam. We never lay together, but ere morning

There grew a flaw[21] between us.

Flam.   'T had been your part
To have made up that flaw.

Cam.   True, but she loathes
I should be seen in't.

Flam.   Why, sir, what's the matter?

Cam. The duke, your master, visits me, I thank him.
And I perceive how, like an earnest bowler,
He very passionately leans that way[22]
He should have his bowl run.

Flam.   I hope you do not think—

Cam. That noblemen bowl booty?[23] faith, his cheek[24]
Hath a most excellent bias;[25] it would fain[26]   70
Jump[27] with my mistress.[28]

Flam.   Will you be an ass,
Despite your Aristotle?[29] Or a cuckold,
Contrary to your ephemerides,[30]
Which shows you under what a smiling planet
You were first swaddled?

Cam.   Pew-wew,[31] sir, tell not me
Of planets nor of ephemerides.
A man may be made a cuckold in the daytime,
When the stars' eyes are out.

Flam.   Sir, God boy[32] you.
I do commit you to your pitiful pillow
Stuffed with horn-shavings.[33]

Cam.   Brother,—

Flam.   God refuse me,[34]
Might I advise you now, your only course   81
Were to lock up your wife.

Cam.   'Twere very good.

Flam. Bar her the sight of revels.

Cam.   Excellent.

Flam. Let her not go to church, but like a hound
In leon[35] at your heels.

Cam.   'Twere for her honor.

Flam. And so you should be certain in one fortnight
Despite her chastity or innocence,
To be cuckolded, which yet is in suspense:
This is my counsel, and I ask no fee for't.

Cam. Come, you know not where my night-cap wrings[36] me.   90

Flam. Wear it o' the old fashion; let your large ears come through, it will be more easy:—nay, I will be bitter:—bar your wife of her entertainment: women are more willingly and more gloriously chaste when they are least restrained of their liberty. It seems you would be a fine capricious mathematically jealous coxcomb;[37] take the height of your own horns with a Jacob's staff[38] afore they are up. These politic enclosures for paltry mutton[39] makes more rebellion in the flesh than all the provocative electuaries[40] doctors have uttered[41] since last jubilee.[42]   101

Cam. This doth not physic[43] me.

Flam. It seems you are jealous. I'll show you the error of it by a familiar example. I have seen a pair of spectacles fashioned with such perspective art[44] that, lay down but one twelve pence o' the board, 'twill appear as if there were twenty; now, should you wear a

---

[19] *under-age protestation:* callow or adolescent wooing.

[20] *foot-cloth:* which hung low to protect the rider from the mud. The idea is that Camillo, stripped of his apparel, is discovered to be an ass indeed.

[21] *flaw:* quarrel; but, as the next lines make clear, with a sexual pun on "crack" or "opening."

[22] *that way:* i.e., toward Vittoria.

[23] *bowl booty:* play with intent to defraud.

[24] *cheek:* Brachiano's, likened in its roundness to the bowling ball, which is seeking to come against Vittoria's. The terminology of Elizabethan bowling is erotic and hence applicable here.

[25] *bias:* direction, caused by weighting the side of the bowling ball, which then takes a curved path.

[26] *fain:* willingly.

[27] *Jump:* Collide (with sexual *entendre*).

[28] *mistress:* wife; but also the small white ball or "jack" at which the bowling ball is aimed.

[29] *Aristotle:* i.e., learning.

[30] *ephemerides:* astronomical almanac (which denies that Camillo could be betrayed or cuckolded).

[31] *Pew-wew:* Fiddle!   [32] *boy:* be with.

[33] *horn-shavings:* from the horns Camillo wears, as a cuckold.

[34] *God refuse me:* an emphatic oath like "Upon my honor!" and perhaps meaning "God keep me free of sin" (though OED does not cite until late seventeenth century).

[35] *leon:* lyam—"leash."

[36] *wrings:* pinches (with sexual jealousy).

[37] *mathematically jealous coxcomb:* a fool scientifically precise in his jealousy and folly.

[38] *Jacob's staff:* mathematical instrument for gauging height and distance, and shaped like a pilgrim's staff (one of the symbols of St. James; hence "Jacob").

[39] *enclosures . . . mutton:* alluding to the hated practice of penning up common land—hence denying its use to the peasant farmer—as pasturage for sheep; and also punning on the identification of "mutton" and "prostitute."

[40] *electuaries:* aphrodisiacs.   [41] *uttered:* put forth.

[42] *last jubilee:* 1600; alluding to the Catholic practice of designating certain years as periods of grace, when men by performing acts of piety could secure full pardon for their sins.   [43] *physic:* cure.

[44] *spectacles . . . art:* eyeglasses producing as many images or perspectives as the facets or planes into which they were cut.

pair of these spectacles and see your wife tying her
shoe, you would imagine twenty hands were taking up
your wife's clothes, and this would put you into a
horrible causeless fury.   111

   Cam. The fault there, sir, is not in the eyesight.

   Flam. True; but they that have the yellow jaundice
think all objects they look on to be yellow. Jealousy is
worser; her fits present to a man, like so many bubbles
in a basin of water, twenty several[45] crabbed faces;
many times makes his own shadow his cuckold-
maker.

         Enter [VITTORIA] COROMBONA.

See, she comes. What reason have you to be jealous of
this creature? What an ignorant ass or flattering   120
knave might he be counted[46] that should write sonnets
to her eyes, or call her brow the snow of Ida[47] or ivory
of Corinth,[48] or compare her hair to the blackbird's bill
when 'tis liker the blackbird's feather! this is all; be
wise, I will make you friends, and you shall go to bed
together. Marry, look you, it shall not be your seeking;
do you stand upon that[49] by any means: walk you
aloof.[50] I would not have you seen in't.

         [CAMILLO *retires.*]

Sister, my lord attends you in the banqueting-house.
Your husband is wondrous discontented.   130

   Vit. Cor. I did nothing to displease him. I carved[51]
to him at supper-time.

   Flam. You need not have carved[52] him, in faith;
they say he is a capon already. I must now seemingly
fall out with you. Shall a gentleman so well descended
as Camillo—a lousy slave that within this twenty years
rode with the black guard[53] in the duke's carriage,
'mongst spits and dripping-pans—

   Cam.[54] Now he begins to tickle[55] her.   139

   Flam. An excellent scholar—one that hath a head
filled with calves-brains without any sage[56] in them—
come crouching in the hams[57] to you for a night's
lodging?—that hath an itch in's hams, which like the
fire at the glass-house[58] hath not gone out this seven
years.—Is he not a courtly gentleman?—When he
wears white satin, one would take him by his black
muzzle to be no other creature than a maggot.—You
are a goodly foil,[59] I confess, well set out—but covered
with a false stone,[60] yon counterfeit diamond.

   Cam. He will make her know what is in me.   150

   Flam. [*Aside to* VITTORIA] Come, my lord[61] attends you; thou shalt go to bed to my lord—

   Cam. Now he comes to't.

   Flam. With a relish as curious as a vintner going to
taste new wine.— [*To* CAMILLO] I am opening your
case[62] hard.

   Cam. A virtuous brother, o' my credit![63]

   Flam. He will give thee a ring with a philosopher's
stone[64] in it.

   Cam. Indeed, I am studying alchemy.   160

   Flam. Thou shalt lie in a bed stuffed with turtles'[65]
feathers; swoon in perfumed linen, like the fellow was
smothered in roses.[66] So perfect shall be thy happiness,
that, as men at sea think land and trees and ships go

that way they go, so both heaven and earth shall seem
to go your voyage.[67] Shalt meet him? 'Tis fixed with
nails of diamonds[68] to inevitable necessity.

   Vit. Cor. How shall's rid him hence?

   Flam. I will put breese[69] in's tail,—set him gadding
presently.[70]—[*To* CAMILLO] I have almost   170
wrought her to it, I find her coming.[71] But, might I advise you now, for this night I would not lie with her; I
would cross her humor to make her more humble.

   Cam. Shall I, shall I?

   Flam. It will show in you a supremacy of judgment.

   Cam. True, and a mind differing from the tumultuary[72] opinion; for *quae negata, grata.*[73]

   Flam. Right; you are the adamant[74] shall draw her
to you, though you keep distance off.

   Cam. A philosophical reason.   180

   Flam. Walk by her o' the nobleman's fashion, and
tell her you will lie with her at the end of the progress.[75]

   Cam. Vittoria, I cannot be induced, or, as a man
would say, incited—

   Vit. Cor. To do what, sir?

   Cam. To lie with you tonight. Your silkworm[76] useth
to fast every third day, and the next following spins the
better. Tomorrow at night I am for you.

---

[45] *several:* separate.   [46] *counted:* accounted.

[47] *Ida:* mountain in Troy. The comparison here, as to
Corinth below, is hyperbolic; hence ironic.

[48] *Corinth:* Grecian trading city.

[49] *stand upon that:* keep to the course prescribed.

[50] *aloof:* as one "luffs" to windward, away from the lee-
shore.   [51] *carved:* crooked my finger invitingly.

[52] *carved:* castrated, like a capon.

[53] *black guard:* kitchen scullions and coal carriers.

[54] *Camillo:* Concealed, perhaps behind a pillar of the
stage, he does not hear what is being said and assumes he is
being praised.

[55] *tickle:* stir up (in the sense, Camillo imagines, of
"reprove").

[56] *sage:* spice; and with a pun on sagacity.

[57] *hams:* the back of the thigh; and like "back" at n.16,
suggestive of sexual activity.

[58] *glass-house:* constantly burning furnace near the Blackfriars Theater.   [59] *foil:* setting for a precious stone.

[60] *covered . . . stone:* "covered" as in sexual intercourse,
with an allied pun on "stone" and "testicle."

[61] *lord:* Brachiano is meant.

[62] *opening your case:* pleading for you; making your wife
ready for Brachiano.

[63] *o' my credit:* upon my word.

[64] *ring . . . stone:* Alchemists sought the stone that could
convert base metals to gold. But "ring" and "stone" are
again doing double duty for sexual activity.

[65] *turtles':* turtle doves'.

[66] *like . . . roses:* alluding to a contemporary anecdote; but
the primary meaning of exquisite pleasure is clear enough.

[67] *as . . . voyage:* those who are giddy think the earth turns
round.

[68] *fixed . . . diamonds:* i.e., perdurably. Perhaps Webster
is remembering Horace, *Odes,* III. 24.

[69] *breese:* gadflies.   [70] *presently:* immediately.

[71] *coming:* pliable.

[72] *tumultuary:* untested (originally describing the irregular militia called up for an emergency).

[73] *L.:* that which is refused is desired.

[74] *adamant:* magnet.

[75] *progress:* state journey, on which the haughty nobleman
is seen as embarked.

[76] *silkworm:* As editors like to point out, this creature does
not eat at all after it has begun to spin.

Vit. Cor. You'll spin a fair thread, trust to't.

Flam. But, do you hear, I shall have you steal to her chamber about midnight.[77]　　　　　　　191

Cam. Do you think so? Why, look you, brother, because you shall not think I'll gull you, take the key, lock me into the chamber, and say you shall be sure of me.

Flam. In troth, I will; I'll be your jailer once. But have you ne'er a false[78] door?

Cam. A pox on't, as I am a Christian. Tell me tomorrow how scurvily she takes my unkind parting.

Flam. I will.　　　　　　　200

Cam. Didst thou not mark the jest of the silkworm? Good night. In faith, I will use this trick often.

Flam. Do, do, do.

　　　　　　　[*Exit* CAMILLO.]

So now you are safe.—Ha, ha, ha! thou entanglest thyself in thine own work like a silkworm.

　　　　　Enter BRACHIANO.

Come, sister; darkness hides your blush. Women are like curst[79] dogs. Civility[80] keeps them tied all daytime, but they are let loose at midnight; then they do most good, or most mischief.—My lord, my lord!

Brach. Give credit.[81] I could wish time would
　　　stand still　　　　　　　210
And never end this interview, this hour.
But all delight doth itself soon'st devour.

　　　ZANCHE *brings out a carpet, spreads it and lays*
　　　on it two fair cushions. Enter CORNELIA [*listening*].

Let me into your bosom,[82] happy lady.
Pour out, instead of eloquence, my vows:
Loose me not, madam; for if you forego[83] me,
I am lost eternally.

Vit. Cor.　　　　　Sir, in the way of pity,
I wish you heart-whole.

Brach.　　　　　You are a sweet physician.

Vit. Cor. Sure, sir, a loathèd cruelty in ladies
Is as to doctors many funerals;
It takes away their credit.

Brach.　　　　　Excellent creature!　　　220
We call the cruel fair: what name for you
That are so merciful?

Zan.　　　　　See, now they close.

Flam. Most happy union.

Cor. My fears are fallen upon me. Oh, my heart!
My son the pander! now I find our house
Sinking to ruin. Earthquakes leave behind,

---

[77] *I . . . midnight:* Flamineo suggests that Camillo will break his promise to hold off.

[78] *false:* secret—to enable him to get out of the locked room.　　　　　[79] *curst:* vicious.

[80] *Civility:* i.e., in their masters.

[81] *Give credit:* I give you (Flamineo) credit(?).

[82] *bosom:* confidence.　　　　　[83] *forego:* abandon.

[84] *jewel:* a sexual *entendre*, as subsequent lines make clear.

[85] *yew:* a tree ominous of death; with pun subsequently on "You"—Brachiano.

[86] *cross sticks:* wooden crosses(?).

[87] *phlegmatic:* cold (after the watery "humor").

[88] *government:* his own official duties.

Where they have tyrannized, iron, or lead, or stone,
But, woe to ruin, violent lust leaves none!

Brach. What value is this jewel?[84]

Vit. Cor.　　　　　'Tis the ornament
Of a weak fortune.　　　　　230

Brach. In sooth, I'll have it; nay, I will but change
My jewel for your jewel.

Flam.　　　　　Excellent!
His jewel for her jewel.—Well put in, duke.

Brach. Nay, let me see you wear it.

Vit. Cor.　　　　　Here, sir?

Brach. Nay, lower, you shall wear my jewel lower.

Flam. That's better; she must wear his jewel lower.

Vit. Cor. To pass away the time, I'll tell your
　　　grace
A dream I had last night.

Brach.　　　　　Most wishedly.

Vit. Cor. A foolish idle dream.
Methought I walked about the mid of night　　　240
Into a churchyard, where a goodly yew[85] tree
Spread her large root in ground. Under that yew,
As I sate sadly leaning on a grave
Checkered with cross sticks,[86] there came stealing in
Your duchess and my husband. One of them
A pick-axe bore, the other a rusty spade.
And in rough terms they gan to challenge me
About this yew.

Brach.　　　　　That tree?

Vit. Cor.　　　　　This harmless yew.
They told me my intent was to root up
That well-grown yew, and plant i' the stead of it　　　250
A withered blackthorn; and for that they vowed
To bury me alive. My husband straight
With pick-ax, gan to dig, and your fell duchess
With shovel, like a Fury, voided out
The earth and scattered bones. Lord, how, methought,
I trembled! And yet, for all this terror,
I could not pray.

Flam.　　　　　No; the devil was in your dream.

Vit. Cor. When to my rescue there arose,
　　　methought,
A whirlwind, which let fall a massy arm
From that strong plant;　　　　　260
And both were struck dead by that sacred yew,
In that base shallow grave that was their due.

Flam. Excellent devil! She hath taught him in a
　　　dream
To make away his duchess and her husband.

Brach. Sweetly shall I interpret this your dream.
You are lodged within his arms who shall protect
　　　you
From all the fevers of a jealous husband;
From the poor envy of our phlegmatic[87] duchess.
I'll seat you above law and above scandal,
Give to your thoughts the invention of delight,　　　270
And the fruition; nor shall government[88]
Divide me from you longer than a care
To keep you great. You shall to me at once
Be dukedom, health, wife, children, friends, and all.

　　　　　　　[CORNELIA *comes forward.*]

Cor. Woe to light[89] hearts, they still forerun our
    fall!
Flam. What Fury raised thee up?—Away, away!
                                    Exit ZANCHE.
Cor. What make you here, my lord, this dead of
    night?
Never dropped mildew on a flower here
Till now.
Flam. I pray, will you go to bed, then,
Lest you be blasted?
Cor.   Oh, that this fair garden   280
Had with all poisoned herbs of Thessaly[90]
At first been planted; made a nursery[91]
For witchcraft, rather than a burial plot
For both your honors!
    Vit. Cor.   Dearest mother, hear me.
Cor. Oh, thou dost make my brow bend to the earth,
Sooner than nature! See, the curse of children!
In life they keep us frequently[92] in tears,
And in the cold grave leave us in pale fears.
Brach. Come, come I will not hear you.
    Vit. Cor.   Dear, my lord,—
Cor. Where is thy duchess now, adulterous duke?
Thou little dreamd'st this night she is come to Rome.
Flam. How! come to Rome!
    Vit. Cor.   The duchess!
Brach.   She had
    been better—   292
Cor. The lives of princes should like dials[93] move,
Whose regular example is so strong,
They make the times by them go right or wrong.
Flam. So; have you done?
Cor.   Unfortunate Camillo!
Vit. Cor. I do protest, if any chaste denial,
If anything but blood could have allayed
His long suit to me—
Cor.   I will join with thee,
To the most woeful end e'er mother kneeled: 300
If thou dishonor thus thy husband's bed,
Be thy life short as are the funeral tears
In great men's—
Brach.   Fie, fie, the woman's mad.
Cor. Be thy act Judas-like—betray in kissing.
Mayst thou be envied[94] during his short breath,
And pitied like a wretch after his death!
Vit. Cor. O me accursed!
                                    Exit VITTORIA.
Flam. Are you out of your wits, my lord?
I'll fetch her back again.
Brach.   No, I'll to bed.
Send Doctor Julio to me presently.[95]   310
Uncharitable woman! thy rash tongue
Hath raised a fearful and prodigious[96] storm:
Be thou the cause of all ensuing harm.
                                    Exit BRACHIANO.
Flam. Now, you that stand so much upon your
    honor,
Is this a fitting time o' night, think you,
To send a duke home without e'er a man?
I would fain know where lies the mass of wealth
Which you have hoarded for my maintenance,

That I may bear my beard out of the level   319
Of my lord's stirrup.[97]
Cor.   What! because we are poor
Shall we be vicious?[98]
Flam.   Pray, what means have you
To keep me from the galleys the gallows?
My father proved himself a gentleman,
Sold all's land, and, like a fortunate fellow,
Died ere the money was spent. You brought me up
At Padua, I confess, where, I protest,
For want of means, the university judge me,
I have been fain to heel my tutor's stockings,[99]
At least seven years. Conspiring with a beard
Made me a graduate;[100] then to this duke's service.
I visited the court, whence I returned   331
More courteous, more lecherous by far,
But not a suit the richer. And shall I,
Having a path so open and so free
To my preferment, still retain your milk[101]
In my pale forehead? No, this face of mine
I'll arm, and fortify with lusty wine,
'Gainst shame and blushing.
Cor. Oh, that I ne'er had borne thee.
Flam.   So would I;
I would the common'st courtesan in Rome   340
Had been my mother, rather than thyself.
Nature is very pitiful to whores,
To give them but few children, yet those children
Plurality of fathers: they are sure
They shall not want. Go, go,
Complain unto my great lord cardinal;
Yet may be he will justify the act.
Lycurgus[102] wondered much men would provide
Good stallions for their mares, and yet would suffer
Their fair wives to be barren.
Cor.   Misery of miseries!   350
                                    Exit CORNELIA.
Flam. The duchess come to court! I like not that.
We are engaged to mischief, and must on.
As rivers to find out the ocean
Flow with crook[103] bendings beneath forcèd[104] banks;
Or as we see, to aspire[105] some mountain's top,

---

[89] *light:* in sense of "unstable"; hence "wicked."
[90] *Thessaly:* This region in Greece was notorious for its witches and for plants that could "blast" or poison.
[91] *nursery:* seed bed.   [92] *frequently:* constantly.
[93] *dials:* clocks or sundials; like the comparison of princes to mirrors, an Elizabethan commonplace, as familiar from Guevara's *Dial of Princes* (trans. Sir Thomas North, 1557) an exemplary life of the Roman emperor Marcus Aurelius.
[94] *envied:* hated.   [95] *presently:* at once.
[96] *prodigious:* in the modern sense of "huge"; but also "portending disasters" (prodigies).
[97] *bear . . . stirrup:* no longer walk like a footman.
[98] *vicious:* given to vice.
[99] *fain . . . stockings:* compelled to act as servant.
[100] *Conspiring . . . graduate:* He graduated at last by getting older; or else by engaging in crooked business with one of the Masters.
[101] *retain . . . milk:* remain a shame-faced boy.
[102] *Lycurgus:* The lawgiver of ancient Sparta.
[103] *crook:* crooked.
[104] *forcèd:* in the sense of enclosing them.
[105] *aspire:* reach.

The way ascends not straight, but imitates
The subtle foldings of a winter [106] snake;
So who knows policy and her true aspèct [107]
Shall find her ways winding and indirect.

                                              Exit.

ACT TWO

SCENE ONE

Enter FRANCISCO DE MEDICIS, Cardinal
MONTICELSO, MARCELLO, ISABELLA,
young GIOVANNI, *with little* JAQUES *the Moor.* [1]

Fran. Have you not seen your husband since you
        arrived?
Isab. Not yet, sir.
Fran.   Surely he is wondrous kind.
If I had such a dove-house as Camillo's.
I would set fire on't, were't but to destroy
The polecats [2] that haunt to it.—My sweet cousin!
Giov. Lord uncle, you did promise me a horse
And armor.
Fran.   That I did, my pretty cousin.—
Marcello, see it fitted.
Mar. My lord, the duke is here.
Fran.   Sister, away!
You must not be seen.
Isab.   I do beseech you,   10
Entreat him mildly; let not your rough tongue
Set us at louder variance. All my wrongs
Are freely pardoned; and I do not doubt,
As men, to try the precious unicorn's horn, [3]
Make of the powder a preservative circle,

And in it put a spider, so these arms
Shall charm his poison, force it to obeying,
And keep him chaste from an infected straying.
Fran. I wish it may. Be gone.

                                    Exit [ISABELLA].

        Enter BRACHIANO, *and* FLAMINEO.

                        Void the chamber.
    [*Exeunt* FLAMINEO, MARCELLO, GIOVANNI,
                            and JAQUES.]
You are welcome; will you sit?—I pray, my lord   20
Be you my orator, my heart's too full.
I'll second you anon.
Mont.   Ere I begin
Let me entreat your grace forego all passion,
Which may be raisèd by my free discourse.
Brach. As silent as i' the church: you may proceed.
Mont. It is a wonder to your noble friends,
That you, having, as 'twere, entered the world
With a free scepter in your able hand,
And to the use of nature well applied
High gifts of learning, should in your prime age   30
Neglect your awful [4] throne for the soft down
Of an insatiate bed. Oh, my lord,
The drunkard after all his lavish cups
Is dry, and then is sober; so at length,
When you awake from this lascivious dream,
Repentance then will follow, like the sting [5]
Placed in the adder's tail. Wretched are princes
When fortune blasteth but a petty flower
Of their unwieldy crowns, or ravisheth
But one pearl from their scepters. But, alas,   40
When they to willful shipwreck lose good fame,
All princely titles perish with their name!
Brach. You have said, my lord.
Mont.   Enough to give you
            taste
How far I am from flattering your greatness.
Brach. Now you that are his second, what say you?
Do not like young hawks fetch a course about. [6]
Your game flies fair and for you.
Fran.   Do not fear it.
I'll answer you in your own hawking phrase.
Some eagles that should gaze upon the sun [7]
Seldom soar high, but take their lustful ease,   50
Since they from dunghill birds their prey can seize.
You know Vittoria!
Brach.   Yes.
Fran.   You shift your shirt there,
When you retire from tennis? [8]
Brach.   Happily. [9]
Fran. Her husband is lord of a poor fortune;
Yet she wears cloth of tissue. [10]
Brach.   What of this?
Will you urge that, my good lord cardinal,
As part of her confession at next shrift, [11]
And know from whence it sails? [12]
Fran.   She is your strumpet.
Brach. Uncivil sir, there's hemlock [13] in thy breath,
And that black slander. Were she a whore of mine, 60
All thy loud cannons, and thy borrowed Switzers [14]

---

[106] *winter:* alluding perhaps to a mythical serpent, which
alone among its kind remained active in winter; or perhaps
to the more convoluted character of the hibernating, hence
inactive, snake.   [107] *aspèct:* face.

II.i.
    [1] *Jaques the Moor:* to whom, as to several other charac-
ters in the play, no lines are given.
    [2] *polecats:* cant term for prostitutes; hence generically
"lecherous characters."
    [3] *unicorn's horn:* This fabulous beast was supposed to be
an antidote against poison—as attested by the inability of a
spider, placed within a "preservative circle" of powdered
horn, to extricate itself.
    [4] *awful:* full of or making for awe, wonder.
    [5] *sting:* The adder was supposed to poison with its tail as
well as with its bite.
    [6] *young . . . about:* In a Jacobean treatise on falconry,
young hawks are described as fearfully abandoning the chase
of old game.
    [7] *eagles . . . sun:* The ability to look directly at the sun
was the peculiar property attributed to the eagle as the king
of birds.
    [8] *You . . . tennis:* Presumably an innuendo is intended in
the changing of the sweaty shirt after hot "exercise."
    [9] *Happily:* Perhaps.
    [10] *cloth of tissue:* sumptuous attire, often distinguished by
gold or silver thread.   [11] *shrift:* shriving.
    [12] *sails:* comes (i.e., from Brachiano).
    [13] *hemlock:* proverbially poisonous.
    [14] *borrowed Switzers:* mercenary soldiers.

Thy galleys, nor thy sworn confederates,
Durst not supplant her.
    Fran.   Let's not talk on thunder.
Thou hast a wife, our sister: would I had given
Both her white hands to death, bound and locked fast
In her last winding-sheet, when I gave thee
But one!
    Brach. Thou hadst given a soul to God, then.
    Fran.   True.
Thy ghostly father, with all's absolution,
Shall ne'er do so by thee.
    Brach.   Spit thy poison.
    Fran. I shall not need; lust carries her sharp whip
At her own girdle. Look to't, for our anger   71
Is making thunderbolts.
    Brach.   Thunder! in faith,
They are but crackers.[15]
    Fran.   We'll end this with the cannon.
    Brach. Thou'lt get naught by it but iron in thy
    wounds,
And gunpowder in thy nostrils.
    Fran.   Better that,
Than change perfumes for plasters.[16]
    Brach.   Pity on thee:
'Twere good you'd show your slaves or men
    condemned
Your new-ploughed[17] forehead-defiance! and I'll
    meet thee,
Even in a thicket of thy ablest men.
    Mont. My lords, you shall not word it[18] any further
Without a milder limit.
    Fran.   Willingly.   81
    Brach. Have you proclaimed a triumph,[19] that you
    bait
A lion thus!
    Mont. My lord!
    Brach.   I am tame, I am tame, sir.
    Fran. We send unto the duke for conference
'Bout levies 'gainst the pirates; my lord duke
Is not at home. We come ourself in person.
Still my lord duke is busied. But we fear,
When Tiber to each prowling passenger
Discovers flocks of wild ducks;[20] then, my lord,
'Bout molting time[21] I mean, we shall be certain 90
To find you sure enough, and speak with you.
    Brach.   Ha!
    Fran. A mere tale of a tub,[22] my words are idle;
But to express the sonnet by natural reason,[23]

Enter GIOVANNI.

When stags grow melancholic,[24] you'll find the season.
    Mont. No more, my lord; here comes a champion[25]
Shall end the difference between you both.
Your son, the Prince Giovanni. See, my lords,
What hopes you store in him. This is a casket
For both your crowns, and should be held like dear.
Now is he apt for knowledge; therefore know, 100
It is a more direct and even way
To train to virtue those of princely blood
By examples than by precepts. If by examples,
Whom should he rather strive to imitate

Than his own father? Be his pattern, then;
Leave him a stock of virtue that may last,
Should fortune rend his sails and split his mast.
    Brach. Your hand, boy: growing to a soldier?
    Giov. Give me a pike.
    Fran. What, practicing your pike so young, fair
    cuz?[26]   110
    Giov. Suppose me one of Homer's frogs,[27] my lord,
Tossing my bullrush thus. Pray, sir, tell me,
Might not a child of good discretion
Be leader to an army?
    Fran.   Yes, cousin, a young prince
Of good discretion might.
    Giov.   Say you so?
Indeed, I have heard, 'tis fit a general
Should not endanger his own person oft;
So that he make a noise when he's a-horseback,
Like a Dansk[28] drummer,—Oh, 'tis excellent!—
He need not fight—methinks his horse as well 120
Might lead an army for him. If I live,
I'll charge the French foe in the very front
Of all my troops, the foremost man.
    Fran.   What, what!
    Giov. And will not bid my soldiers up and follow,
But bid them follow me.
    Brach.   Forward, lapwing![29]
He flies with the shell on's head.
    Fran.   Pretty cousin!
    Giov. The first year, uncle, that I go to war,
All prisoners that I take I will set free
Without their ransom.
    Fran.   Ha, without their ransom!
How, then, will you reward your soldiers 130
That took those prisoners for you?
    Giov.   Thus, my lord;
I'll marry them to all the wealthy widows
That fall that year.
    Fran.   Why, then, the next year following,
You'll have no men to go with you to war.
    Giov. Why, then, I'll press[30] the women to the
    war,
And then the men will follow.
    Mont.   Witty prince!

---

[15] *crackers:* firecrackers.
[16] *plasters:* dressing for venereal disease, incurred from "perfumes" (sexual indulgence).
[17] *new-ploughed:* wrinkled, as with anger.
[18] *word it:* quarrel.
[19] *triumph:* Roman celebration of victory, accompanied by beast combats ("lion").
[20] *wild ducks:* cant for "prostitutes."
[21] *molting time:* when hair falls out from venereal disease.
[22] *tub:* nonsense; the sweating tub used to cure venereal disease. [23] *express . . . reason:* clarify my words.
[24] *stags grow melancholic:* as during the mating season.
[25] *champion:* Giovanni, wearing his new suit of armor.
[26] *cuz:* term of endearment, not specifically "cousin."
[27] *Homer's frogs:* The burlesque epic, *Batrachomyomachia* (*Battle of Frogs and Mice*), falsely attributed to Homer, had been translated in 1603. [28] *Dansk:* Danish.
[29] *lapwing:* This bird appears often in the literature of the period as a figure of precocity.
[30] *press:* impress, enlist forcibly.

Fran. See, a good habit makes a child a man,
Whereas a bad one makes a man a beast.
Come, you and I are friends.
    Brach.   Most wishedly;
Like bones which, broke in sunder, and well set,   140
Knit the more strongly.
    Fran.   Call Camillo hither.
                      [Exit MARCELLO.]
You have received the rumor, how Count Lodowick
Is turned a pirate?
    Brach.   Yes.
    Fran.   We are now preparing
Some ships to fetch him in.

              [*Enter* ISABELLA.]

              Behold your duchess.
We now will leave you, and expect from you
Nothing but kind entreaty.
    Brach.   You have charmed me.
    Exeunt FRANCISCO, MONTICELSO,
                    GIOVANNI.
You are in health, we see.
    Isab.   And above health,
To see my lord well.
    Brach.   So. I wonder much
What amorous whirlwind hurried you to Rome.
    Isab. Devotion,[31] my lord.
    Brach.   Devotion!   150
Is your soul charged with any grievous sin?
    Isab. 'Tis burdened with too many; and I think,
The oftener that we cast our reckonings up,
Our sleeps will be the sounder.
    Brach.   Take your chamber.
    Isab. Nay, my dear lord, I will not have you angry.
Doth not my absence from you, now two months,
Merit one kiss?
    Brach.   I do not use[32] to kiss.
If that will dispossess your jealousy,
I'll swear it to you.
    Isab.   O my lovèd lord,
I do not come to chide—my jealousy!   160
I am to learn what that Italian[33] means.
You are as welcome to these longing arms
As I to you a virgin.
    Brach.   Oh, your breath!
Out upon sweet-meats and continued physic,[34]

---

  [31] *Devotion:* to her husband, who chooses to interpret Isabella as meaning "religious devotion."
  [32] *I . . . use:* It is not my custom.
  [33] *Italian:* proverbially jealous.   [34] *physic:* medicine.
  [35] *cassia:* cinnamon; hence any rich spice.
  [36] *bandy factions:* form parties.
  [37] *supply our discontinuance:* make up for the cessation of our sexual life together.
  [38] *corpulent:* The historical Brachiano was notoriously corpulent; Webster transfers his condition to Francisco.
  [39] *shaved Polack:* Elizabethan travelers reported of the Poles that their heads, excepting the forehead, were shaved close.   [40] *fly-boat:* small craft, like a pinnace.
  [41] *issue:* progeny.   [42] *latest:* last.
  [43] *doomed:* decreed.   [44] *satisfied:* canceled.
  [45] *present witness:* immediate testimony.

The plague is in them!
    Isab.   You have oft, for these two lips,
Neglected cassia[35] of the natural sweets
Of the spring-violet; they are not yet much withered.
My lord, I should be merry; these your frowns
Show in a helmet lovely; but on me,
In such a peaceful interview, methinks   170
They are too-too roughly knit.
    Brach.   Oh, dissemblance!
Do you bandy factions[36] 'gainst me? Have you learnt
The trick of impudent baseness, to complain
Unto your kindred?
    Isab.   Never, my dear lord.
    Brach. Must I be hunted out? Or was't your trick
To meet some amorous gallant here in Rome,
That must supply our discontinuance?[37]
    Isab. I pray, sir, burst my heart; and in my death
Turn to your ancient pity, though not love.
    Brach. Because your brother is the corpulent[38] duke,
That is, the great duke, 'sdeath, I shall not shortly   181
Racket away five hundred crowns at tennis,
But it shall rest upon record! I scorn him
Like a shaved Polack.[39] All his reverend wit
Lies in his wardrobe; he's a discreet fellow
When he is made up in his robes of state.
Your brother, the great duke, because h'as galleys,
And now and then ransacks a Turkish fly-boat[40]
(Now all the hellish Furies take his soul!)
First made this match: accursèd be the priest   190
That sang the wedding-mass, and even my issue![41]
    Isab. Oh, too-too far you have cursed!
    Brach.   Your hand I'll
  kiss;
This is the latest[42] ceremony of my love.
Henceforth I'll never lie with thee; by this,
This wedding-ring, I'll ne'er more lie with thee:
And this divorce shall be as truly kept
As if the judge had doomed[43] it. Fare you well.
Our sleeps are severed.
    Isab.   Forbid it, the sweet union
Of all things blessèd! why, the saints in heaven
Will knit their brows at that.
    Brach.   Let not thy love   200
Make thee an unbeliever; this my vow
Shall never, on my soul, be satisfied[44]
With my repentance; let thy brother rage
Beyond a horrid tempest or sea-fight,
My vow is fixèd.
    Isab.   O my winding-sheet
Now shall I need thee shortly.—Dear my lord,
Let me hear once more what I would not hear:
Never?
    Brach. Never.
    Isab. O my unkind lord! may your sins find mercy,
As I upon a woeful widowed bed   211
Shall pray for you, if not to turn your eyes
Upon your wretched wife and hopeful son,
Yet that in time you'll fix them upon heaven!
    Brach. No more: go, go complain to the great duke.
    Isab. No, my dear lord; you shall have present
  witness[45]

How I'll work peace between you. I will make
Myself the author of your cursèd vow;
I have some cause to do it, you have none.
Conceal it, I beseech you, for the weal[46] 220
Of both your dukedoms, that you wrought the means
Of such a separation; let the fault
Remain with my supposèd jealousy;
And think with what a piteous and rent heart
I shall perform this sad ensuing part.

Enter FRANCISCO, FLAMINEO, MONTICELSO,
MARCELLO.

Brach. Well, take your course.—My honorable
brother!
Fran. Sister!—This is not well, my lord.—Why,
sister!—
She merits not this welcome.
Brach.   Welcome, say!
She hath given a sharp welcome.
Fran.   Are you foolish?
Come, dry your tears. Is this a modest course, 230
To better what is naught,[47] to rail and weep?
Grow to a reconcilement, or, by heaven,
I'll ne'er more deal between you.
Isab.   Sir, you shall not;
No, though Vittoria, upon that condition,
Would become honest.[48]
Fran.   Was your husband loud
Since we departed?
Isab.   By my life, sir, no;
I swear by that I do not care to lose.
Are all these ruins of my former beauty
Laid out for a whore's triumph?
Fran.   Do you hear?
Look upon other women, with what patience 240
They suffer these slight wrongs, with what justice
They study to requite them; take that course.
Isab. Oh, that I were a man, or that I had power
To execute my apprehended[49] wishes!
I would whip some with scorpions.
Fran.   What! turned Fury!
Isab. To dig the strumpet's eyes out; let her lie
Some twenty months a-dying; to cut off
Her nose and lips, pull out her rotten teeth;
Preserve her flesh like mummia, for trophies
Of my just anger! Hell to my affliction 250
Is mere snow-water. By your favor, sir—
Brother, draw near, and my lord cardinal—
Sir, let me borrow of you but one kiss.
Henceforth I'll never lie with you, by this,
This wedding-ring.
Fran.   How, ne'er more lie with him!
Isab. And this divorce shall be as truly kept
As if in throngèd court a thousand ears
Had heard it, and a thousand lawyers' hands
Sealed to the separation.
Brach.   Ne'er lie with me!
Isab. Let not my former dotage 260
Make thee an unbeliever: this my vow.
Shall never, on my soul, be satisfied
With my repentance; *manet alta mente repostum.*[50]

Fran. Now, by my birth, you are foolish, mad,
And jealous woman.
Brach.   You see 'tis not my seeking.
Fran. Was this your circle of pure unicorn's horn
You said should charm your lord? Now, horns upon
thee,[51]
For jealousy deserves them! Keep your vow
And take your chamber.
Isab. No, sir, I'll presently to Padua; 270
I will not stay a minute.
Mont.   O good madam!
Brach. 'Twere best to let her have her humor:
Some half day's journey will bring down her
stomach,[52]
And then she'll turn in post.[53]
Fran.   To see her come
To my lord cardinal for a dispensation
Of her rash vow will beget excellent laughter.
Isab. Unkindness, do thy office; poor heart, break;
Those are the killing griefs which dare not speak.

Exit.

Enter CAMILLO.

Mar. Camillo's come, my lord.
Fran. Where's the commission? 280
Mar. 'Tis here.
Fran. Give me the signet.
Flam. My lord, do you mark[54] their whispering. I
will compound a medicine out of their two heads,
stronger than garlic, deadlier than stibium:[55] the
cantharides,[56] which are scarce seen to stick upon the
flesh when they work to the heart, shall not do it with
more silence or invisible cunning.

Enter Doctor.

Brach. About the murder. 289
Flam. They are sending him to Naples, but I'll send
him to Candy,[57] her's[58] another property too.
Brach. Oh, the doctor!
Flam. A poor quack-salving[59] knave, my lord; one
that should have been lashed for's lechery, but that he
confessed a judgment, had an execution laid upon him,
and so put the whip to a *non plus.*[60]
Doc. And was cozened, my lord, by an arranter

---

[46] *weal:* good.
[47] *naught:* wrong (perhaps "better" is used here, in sense of "overgo").   [48] *honest:* chaste.
[49] *apprehended:* those that "take" or make me aware of.
[50] *L.:* from Virgil, *Aeneid,* I. 26: "It remains treasured up in my mind."
[51] *horns upon thee:* i.e., let your husband be unfaithful.
[52] *stomach:* pride.
[53] *turn in post:* return hastily, like a courier.
[54] *do you mark:* do mark (injunctively).
[55] *stibium:* arsenic-like poison.
[56] *cantharides:* another poison.
[57] *Candy:* Crete, notorious for pirates; hence, by extension, "death."
[58] *Her's:* alternatively, "Here's," which would refer to the Doctor.
[59] *quack-salving:* acting like a quack.
[60] *L.:* standstill.

knave than myself, and made pay all the colorable[61] execution.[62]   299

Flam He will shoot pills into a man's guts shall make them have more ventages[63] than a cornet[64] or a lamprey;[65] he will poison a kiss; and was once minded for his masterpiece, because Ireland breeds no poison,[66] to have prepared a deadly vapor in a Spaniard's fart[67] that should have poisoned all Dublin.[68]

Brach. Oh, Saint Anthony's fire.[69]

Doc. Your secretary is merry, my lord.

Flam. O thou cursed antipathy to nature!—Look, his eyes' bloodshed, like a needle, a surgeon stitcheth a wound with.—Let me embrace thee, toad,   310 and love thee, O thou abhominable[70] loathsome gargarism,[71] that will fetch up lungs, lights,[72] heart, and liver, by scruples![73]

Brach. No more.—I must employ thee, honest doctor:
You must to Padua, and by the way,
Use some of your skill for us.

Doc.   Sir, I shall.

Brach. But, for Camillo?

Flam. He dies this night, by such a politic strain,[74]
Men shall suppose him by's own engine[75] slain.
But for your duchess' death—

Doc.   I'll make her sure.   320

---

61 *colorable:* specious, plausible.

62 *one . . . execution:* The doctor escaped whipping for lechery by pretending that he had already been sentenced for nonpayment of a debt—which another rascal pretended to be owed to himself, and so had judgment on the doctor for the amount supposedly due.

63 *ventages:* holes for wind.

64 *cornet:* an obsolete wind instrument resembling an oboe.

65 *lamprey:* a fish distinguished by openings, through which water passed, behind the head.

66 *Ireland . . . poison:* alluding to the absence of snakes in that country.

67 *Spaniard's fart:* Contemporary anecdotes are numerous regarding a Spaniard named Don Diego who broke wind in St. Paul's some time before 1598.

68 *Dublin:* apposite here because the Irish were supposed to be ready to kill if wind were broken in their company.

69 *Saint Anthony's fire:* erysipelas, a skin disease; but referring also to the *ignis fatuus* or marsh light, as observable on Irish marshes.

70 *abhominable:* abominable; the Q spelling suggests a false etymology deriving the word from L. *ab homine,* "inhuman."

71 *gargarism:* gargle.   72 *lights:* lungs.

73 *by scruples:* piece by piece.

74 *politic strain:* clever device.   75 *engine:* contrivance.

76 *gallouses:* criminals condemned to die on the gallows.

77 *one . . . shoulders:* When the man on whom the criminal is standing steps aside, the latter is left dangling.

78 *word:* motto, device.

79 *L.:* "Abundance has made me destitute." In the passage from Ovid, *Metamorphoses,* III. 466, Narcissus is complaining to his beautiful reflection in the water: he loves what he sees and cannot possess it. How this connects to the stag is suggested (possibly) by what follows: Camillo, gaining "plenty" of horns, is cuckolded and so made "poor."

80 *tale:* deriving ultimately from Aesop's Fables.

81 *bans:* announcing the impending marriage.

82 *cornucopia:* horn of plenty (referring back to the suggestion of cuckoldry, above).

83 *ranger:* forester, watching over your preserve.

Brach. Small mischiefs are by greater made secure.

Flam. Remember this, you slave; when knaves come to preferment, they rise as gallouses[76] are raised 'i the Low Countries, one upon another's shoulders.[77]

           Exeunt [BRACHIANO, FLAMINEO,
                   and Doctor].

Mont. Here is an emblem, nephew, pray peruse it.
'Twas thrown in at your window.

Cam.   At my window!
Here is a stag, my lord, hath shed his horns,
And, for the loss of them, the poor beast weeps:
The word,[78] *Inopem me copia fecit.*[79]

Mont. That is,   330
Plenty of horns, hath made him poor of horns.

Cam. What should this mean?

Mont.   I'll tell you: 'tis given out
You are a cuckold.

Cam.   Is it given out so?
I had rather such report as that, my lord,
Should keep within doors.

Fran.   Have you any children?

Cam. None, my lord.

Fran.   You are the happier.
I'll tell you a tale.

Cam.   Pray, my lord.

Fran.   An old tale.[80]
Upon a time Phoebus, the god of light,
Or him we call the Sun, would needs be married.
The gods gave their consent, and Mercury   340
Was sent to voice it to the general world.
But what a piteous cry there straight arose
Amongst smiths and felt-makers, brewers and cooks,
Reapers and butterwomen, amongst fishmongers,
And thousand other trades, which are annoyed
By his excessive heat! 'Twas lamentable.
They came to Jupiter all in a sweat,
And do forbid the bans.[81] A great fat cook
Was made their speaker, who entreats of Jove
That Phoebus might be gelded; for, if now,   350
When there was but one sun, so many men
Were like to perish by his violent heat,
What should they do if he were married,
And should beget more, and those children
Make fireworks like their father? So say I.
Only I will apply it to your wife:
Her issue, should not providence prevent it,
Would make both nature, time, and man repent it.

Mont. Look you, cousin,
Go, change the air, for shame; see if your absence   360
Will blast your cornucopia.[82] Marcello
Is chosen with you joint commissioner
For the relieving our Italian coast
From pirates.

Mar.   I am much honored in't.

Cam.   But, sir,
Ere I return, the stag's horns may be sprouted
Greater than these are shed.

Mont.   Do not fear it:
I'll be your ranger.[83]

Cam.   You must watch i' the nights,
Then's the most danger.

Fran.   Farewell, good Marcello.
All the best fortunes of a soldier's wish
Bring you a-ship-board!   370
    Cam. Were I not best, now I am turned soldier
Ere that I leave my wife, sell all she hath,
And then take leave of her?
    Mont.   I expect good from you,
Your parting is so merry.
    Cam. Merry, my lord! o' the captain's humor [84]
   right;
I am resolvèd to be drunk this night.
             Exeunt [CAMILLO *and* MARCELLO].
    Fran. So, 'twas well fitted: now shall we discern
How his wished absence will give violent way
To Duke Brachiano's lust.
    Mont.   Why, that was it;   379
To what scorned purpose else should we make choice
Of him for a sea-captain? And, besides,
Count Lodowick, which was rumored for a pirate,
Is now in Padua.
    Fran.   Is't true?
    Mont.   Most certain.
I have letters from him, which are suppliant [85]
To work his quick repeal from banishment:
He means to address himself for pension
Unto our sister [86] duchess.
    Fran.   Oh, 'twas well.
We shall not want [87] his absence past six days.
I fain would have the Duke Brachiano run
Into notorious scandal; for there's naught   390
In such cursed dotage to repair his name,
Only the deep sense of some deathless shame.
    Mont. It may be objected, I am dishonorable
To play thus with my kinsman; but I answer,
For my revenge I'd stake a brother's life,
That, being wronged, durst not avenge himself.
    Fran. Come, to observe this strumpet.
    Mont.   Curse of
   greatness!
Sure he'll not leave her?
    Fran.   There's small pity in't.
Like mistletoe on sear [88] elms spent by weather,
Let him cleave to her, and both rot together.   400
                     Exeunt.

[II.ii]

    Enter BRACHIANO *with one in the habit of a*
             Conjurer.

    Brach. Now, sir, I claim your promise. 'Tis dead
   midnight,
The time prefixed [1] to show me, by your art,
How the intended murder of Camillo
And our loathed duchess grow to action.
    Conj. You have won by your bounty to a deed
I do not often practice. Some there are
Which by sophistic [2] tricks aspire that name,
Which I would gladly lose, of necromancer;
As some that use to juggle upon cards,
Seeming to conjure, when indeed they cheat;   10

Others that raise up their confederate spirits
'Bout wind-mills, and endanger their own necks
For making of a squib; [3] and some there are
Will keep a curtal [4] to show juggling tricks,
And give out 'tis a spirit; besides these,
Such a whole ream [5] of almanac-makers, figure-
   flingers, [6]
Fellows, indeed, that only live by stealth,
Since they do merely lie about stolen goods,
They'd make men think the devil were fast and loose, [7]
With speaking fustian [8] Latin. Pray, sit down.   20
Put on this night-cap, sir, 'tis charmed; and now
I'll show you, by my strong commanding art,
The circumstance that breaks your duchess' heart.

A DUMB SHOW

Enter suspiciously JULIO *and* CHRISTOPHERO. [9] *They
   draw a curtain* [10] *where* BRACHIANO'S *picture is,
   put on spectacles of glass, which cover their eyes and
   noses, and then burn perfumes afore the picture, and
   wash the lips of the picture; that done, quenching the
   fire, and putting off their spectacles, they depart
   laughing.*

Enter ISABELLA *in her night-gown, as to bed-ward,
   with lights after her,* Count LODOVICO, GIO-
   VANNI, GUIDANTONIO, *and others waiting on
   her; she kneels down as to prayers, then draws the
   curtain of the picture, does three reverences to it,
   and kisses it thrice; she faints, and will not suffer
   them to come near it; dies; sorrow expressed in
  * GIOVANNI *and in* Count LODOVICO; *she is
   conveyed out solemnly.*

    Brach. Excellent! then she's dead.
    Conj.   She's poisonèd
By the fumed picture. 'Twas her custom nightly,
Before she went to bed, to go and visit
Your picture and to feed her eyes and lips
On the dead shadow. Doctor Julio,
Observing this, infects it with an oil
And other poisoned stuff, which presently [11]   30

---

[84] *humor:* disposition: in this case, that of the sailor for
drinking.   [85] *are suppliant:* petition.
   [86] *sister:* denoting relationship in rank rather than blood.
   [87] *want:* lack.   [88] *sear:* dry, withered.

II.ii.
   [1] *prefixed:* appointed.   [2] *sophistic:* speciously clever.
   [3] *squib:* firecracker.
   [4] *curtal:* docked horse, like the famous performing
gelding exhibited around the turn of the century by the
showman Banks.
   [5] *ream:* meaning also "realm."
   [6] *figure-flingers:* horoscope casters, astrologers.
   [7] *fast and loose:* confidence game in which the gull was
asked to wager whether a knotted handkerchief (among
various possibilities) was securely tied or not. Presumably
the confidence man, an equivocator or master of deceiving
appearances like the devil, could have it either way.
   [8] *fustian:* nonsense; "pig Latin."
   [9] *Christophero:* like Guidantonio (below), an "apparition"
or nonspeaking character.
   [10] *curtain:* in lieu of glass, which was not used to cover
pictures until a later date.   [11] *presently:* immediately.

Did suffocate her spirits.
   Brach.   Methought I saw
Count Lodowick there.
   Conj.   He was; and by my art
I find he did most passionately dote
Upon your duchess. Now turn another way,
And view Camillo's far more politic [12] fate.
Strike louder, music, from this charmèd ground,
To yield, as fits the act, a tragic sound

The Second DUMB SHOW

Enter FLAMINEO, MARCELLO, CAMILLO, *with four more as* Captains; *they drink healths, and dance; a vaulting-horse is brought into the room;* MAR-CELLO *and two more whispered out of the room, while* FLAMINEO *and* CAMILLO *strip themselves into*[13] *their shirts, as to vault; compliment who shall begin; as* CAMILLO *is about to vault,* FLAMINEO *pitcheth him upon his neck, and, with the help of the rest, writhes his neck about; seems to see if it be broke, and lays him folded double, as 't were, under the horse; makes shows to call for help:* MARCELLO *comes in, laments; sends for the* Cardinal *and* Duke, *who comes forth with armed men; wonder*[14] *at the act; commands the body to be carried home; apprehends* FLAMINEO, MARCELLO, *and the rest, and go, as 't were, to apprehend* VITTORIA.

   Brach. 'Twas quaintly done; but yet each circumstance
I taste not fully.
   Conj.   Oh, 'twas most apparent:
You saw them enter, charged with their deep healths
To their boon [15] voyage; and, to second that,   40
Flamineo calls to have a vaulting-horse
Maintain their sport; the virtuous Marcello
Is innocently plotted forth the room;
Whilst your eye saw the rest, and can inform you
The engine of all.
   Brach. It seems Marcello and Flamineo
Are both committed.[16]
   Conj.   Yes, you saw them guarded;
And now they are come with purpose to apprehend
Your mistress, fair Vittoria. We are now   50
Beneath her roof.[17] 'Twere fit we instantly

---

[12] *politic:* cleverly contrived.
[13] *into:* to.   [14] *wonder:* perhaps a substantive.
[15] *boon:* bon.   [16] *committed:* imprisoned.
[17] *Beneath her roof:* And so the "scene" is set, perhaps a bit tardily.   [18] *back postern:* back door.
III.i.
   [1] *lieger:* resident.
   [2] *circumstances:* circumstantial evidence.
   [3] *in by the week:* imprisoned (for more than a brief period).   [4] *sit upon:* judge.
   [5] *tickler:* provoker; alternatively, "punisher."
   [6] *tilting:* here, sexual intercourse.
   [7] *private:* sexually intimate.
   [8] *public:* open about their intimacy.
   [9] *ferret:* hunt them, as a polecat hunts rats or rabbits.
   [10] *conies:* rabbits; coney-catching is Elizabethan argot for gulling.   [11] *lighted:* brought on, presumably with torches.

Make out by some back-postern.[18]
   Brach.   Noble friend,
You bind me ever to you. This shall stand
As the firm seal annexèd to my hand;
It shall enforce a payment.
   Conj.   Sir, I thank you.
                   Exit BRACHIANO.
Both flowers and weeds spring when the sun is warm,
And great men do great good or else great harm.
                   Exit Conjurer.

ACT THREE

SCENE ONE

Enter FRANCISCO [DE MEDICIS] *and* MONTICELSO, *their* Chancellor *and* Register.

   Fran. You have dealt discreetly, to obtain the presence
Of all the grave lieger [1] ambassadors,
To hear Vittoria's trial.
   Mont.   'Twas not ill;
For, sir, you know we have naught but circumstances [2]
To charge her with about her husband's death.
Their approbation, therefore, to the proofs
Of her black lust shall make her infamous
To all our neighboring kingdoms. I wonder
If Brachiano will be here.
   Fran.   Oh, fie.
'Twere impudence too palpable.   10
                      [Exeunt.]

Enter FLAMINEO *and* MARCELLO *guarded, and a* Lawyer.

   Law. What, are you in by the week?[3] So, I will try now whether thy wit be close prisoner. Methinks none should sit upon [4] thy sister but old whore-masters.
   Flam. Or cuckolds; for your cuckold is your most terrible tickler [5] of lechery. Whore-masters would serve; for none are judges at tilting [6] but those that have been old tilters.
   Law. My lord duke and she have been very private.[7]
   Flam. You are a dull ass; 'tis threatened they have been very public.[8]   20
   Law. If it can be proved they have but kissed one another—
   Flam. What then?
   Law. My lord cardinal will ferret [9] them.
   Flam. A cardinal, I hope, will not catch conies.[10]
   Law. For to sow kisses (mark what I say), to sow kisses is to reap lechery; and I am sure, a woman that will endure kissing is half won.
   Flam. True, her upper part, by that rule: if you will win her nether part too, you know what follows.   30
   Law. Hark; the ambassadors are lighted.[11]
   Flam [*Aside*] I do put on this feignèd garb of mirth
To gull suspicion.
   Mar. O my unfortunate sister!
I would my dagger-point had cleft her heart
When she first saw Brachiano: you, 'tis said,

Were made his engine and his stalking-horse,
To undo my sister.
 Flam.   I made a kind of path.
To her and mine own preferment.[12]
 Mar.   Your ruin.
 Flam. Hum! thou art a soldier,   50
Follow'st the great duke, feedest his victories,
As witches do their serviceable spirits,
Even with thy prodigal blood: what hast got,
But, like the wealth of captains, a poor handful,
Which in thy palm thou bearest as men hold water?
Seeking to gripe it fast, the frail reward
Steals through thy fingers.
 Mar.   Sir!
 Flam. Thou hast scarce maintenance
To keep thee in fresh chamois.[13]
 Mar.   Brother!
 Flam.   Hear me:—
And thus, when we have even poured ourselves 50
Into great fights, for their ambition
Or idle spleen, how shall we find reward?
But as we seldom find the mistletoe,[14]
Sacred to physic, on[15] the builder[16] oak,
Without a mandrake[17] by it; so in our quest of gain,
Alas, the poorest of their[18] forced[19] dislikes
At a limb proffers,[20] but at heart it strikes!
This is lamented doctrine.
 Mar.   Come, come.
 Flam. When age shall turn thee
White as a blooming hawthorn—
 Mar.   I'll interrupt you.—
For love of virtue bear an honest heart,   61
And stride o'er every politic respect,[21]
Which, where they most advance, they most infect.
Were I your father, as I am your brother,
I should not be ambitious to leave you
A better patrimony.
 Flam.   I'll think on't.—
The lord ambassadors.

  Enter Savoy [Ambassador]. *Here there is a passage of*
   the Lieger Ambassadors *over the stage severally.*[22]
     Enter French Ambassador.

 Law. O my sprightly Frenchman!—Do you know
him? He's an admirable tilter.[23]   69
 Flam. I saw him at last tilting; he showed like a
pewter candlestick, fashioned like a man in armor,
holding a tilting-staff in his hand little bigger than a
candle of twelve i' the pound.[24]
 Law. Oh, but he's an excellent horseman.
 Flam. A lame one in his lofty tricks; he sleeps a-
horseback, like a poulter.[25]

   Enter English *and* Spanish [Ambassadors].

 Law. Lo you, my Spaniard!
 Flam. He carries his face in's ruff,[26] as I have seen a
serving man carry glasses in a cypress[27] hatband,
monstrous steady, for fear of breaking; he looks like
the claw of a blackbird, first salted, and then broiled
in[28] a candle.   82
             Exeunt.

[III.ii]

THE ARRAIGNMENT OF VITTORIA

 Enter FRANCISCO [DE MEDICIS], MONTICELSO,
the six lieger Ambassadors, BRACHIANO, VITTORIA
  [COROMBONA, ZANCHE, FLAMINEO,
  MARCELLO], Lawyer, *and a* Guard.

 Mont. Forbear, my lord, here is no place assigned
  you.
This business by his holiness is left
To our examination.
 Brach.   May it thrive with you!
     Lays a rich gown under him.
 Fran. A chair there for his lordship!
 Brach. Forbear your kindness; an unbidden guest
Should travel as Dutchwomen go to church,
Bear their stools with them.
 Mont.   At your pleasure, sir.
Stand to the table, gentlewoman [*To* VITTORIA]—
 Now, Signior,
Fall to your plea.
 Law. Domine judex, converte oculos in hanc pestem,
mulierum corruptissimam.[1]   11
 Vit. Cor. What's he?
 Fran.   A lawyer that pleads against you.
 Vit. Cor. Pray, my lord, let him speak his usual
  tongue.
I'll make no answer else.
 Fran.   Why, you understand Latin.
 Vit. Cor. I do, sir; but amongst this auditory
Which come to hear my cause, the half or more
May be ignorant in't.
 Mont.   Go on, sir.
 Vit. Cor.   By your favor,
I will not have my accusation clouded

---

 [12] *preferment:* advancement.
 [13] *chamois:* leather vest worn beneath armor.
 [14] *mistletoe:* of great medicinal value, as the appositive
phrase makes clear.
 [15] *on:* emending "or" of Q.
 [16] *builder:* used for building.
 [17] *mandrake:* poisonous plant. The sense of the passage is
that good is generally accompanied by evil.
 [18] *their:* presumably referring to the "great" men for
whose ambition or spleen we spend ourselves.
 [19] *forced:* unnatural; fortified(?).
 [20] *proffers:* offers; tries.
 [21] *politic respect:* crafty consideration.
 [22] *severally:* separately, one by one.
 [23] *tilter:* adept at sexual intercourse (as above).
 [24] *twelve i' the pound:* OED (which first cites 1804) is not
much help: "a thing characterized in some way by the
number twelve." The meaning is clearly "slight" or
"small," like a duodecimo or XII mo.
 [25] *poulter:* one who is bringing fowl to early morning
market and is asleep on his horse.
 [26] *ruff:* swelling collar about the neck, and particularly
associated with Spanish affectation.
 [27] *cypress:* fine lawn.   [28] *in:* by means of.
III.ii.
 [1] *L.:* "My lord judge, turn your eyes on this plague,
most corrupt of women."

In a strange tongue; all this assembly
Shall hear what you can charge me with.
    Fran.   Signior,   20
You need not stand on't much;[2] pray, change your
    language.
    Mont. Oh, for God sake!—Gentlewoman, your
    credit
Shall be more famous by it.
    Law.   Well, then, have at you!
    Vit. Cor. I am at the mark, sir. I'll give aim to
    you,[3]
And tell you how near you shoot.
    Law. Most literated judges, please your lordships
So to connive your judgments[4] to the view
Of this debauched and diversivolent[5] woman;
Who such a black concatenation[6]
Of mischief hath effected, that to extirp[7]   30
The memory of't, must be the consummation
Of her and her projections[8]—
    Vit. Cor.   What's all this?
    Law. Hold your peace:
Exorbitant sins must have exulceration.[9]
    Vit. Cor. Surely, my lords, this lawyer here hath
    swallowed
Some pothecaries' bills,[10] or proclamations;
And now the hard and undigestible words
Come up, like stones we use give hawks for physic.[11]
Why, this is Welsh to Latin.[12]
    Law.   My lords, the woman
Knows not her tropes nor figures, nor is perfect   40
In the academic derivation
Of grammatical elocution.
    Fran.   Sir, your pains
Shall be well spared, and your deep eloquence
Be worthily applauded amongst those
Which understand you.
    Law.   My good lord—

---

   [2] *stand on't much:* insist (on speaking Latin).
   [3] *I'll . . . you:* Vittoria will act as the marker who stands by the archery butts to announce how close the arrow came to the mark.
   [4] *connive your judgments:* The lawyer is a fool who mouths nonsense to impress his auditors.
   [5] *diversivolent:* discord-willing.
   [6] *concatenation:* chain.   [7] *extirp:* extirpate, wipe out.
   [8] *projections:* projects.   [9] *exulceration:* exasperation.
   [10] *bills:* prescriptions (written so as to be incomprehensible to laymen).
   [11] *stones . . . physic:* Sick hawks were dosed with white pebbles.
   [12] *Welsh to Latin:* The lawyer's Latin was bad enough; his jargon in English is still less comprehensible.
   [13] *fustian:* coarse cloth; and in our sense of "bombast."
   [14] *buckram:* stiff linen, of which lawyers' bags were made.
   [15] *effected:* affected(?); alternatively, "made manifest."
   [16] *apples:* Travelers like Mandeville tell of this bitter fruit, which is first reported in Deuteronomy xxxii:32.
   [17] *resolved:* convinced.
   [18] *scarlet:* alluding to the Cardinal's robes.
   [19] *character:* Our sense applies; but allusion is also to prose "Character" descriptions, current in the seventeenth century.
   [20] *tributes . . . paid:* Taxes levied in the Netherlands were said to amount to half the cost of the goods themselves.
   [21] *perdition:* prostitution (also taxed).

    Fran.   Sir,
Put up your papers in your fustian[13] bag—

           FRANCISCO *speaks this as in scorn.*

Cry mercy, sir, 'tis buckram[14]—and accept
My notion of your learned verbosity.
    Law. I most graduatically thank your lordship.
I shall have use for them elsewhere.   50
                                 [*Exit.*]
    Mont. [*To* VITTORIA.] I shall be plainer with you,
    and paint out
Your follies in more natural red and white
That than upon your cheek.
    Vit. Cor.   O you mistake;
You raise a blood as noble in this cheek
As ever was your mother's.
    Mont. I must spare you, till proof cry "whore" to
    that.—
Observe this creature here, my honored lords,
A woman of a most prodigious spirit,
In her effected.[15]
    Vit. Cor.   Honorable my lord,
It doth not suit a reverend cardinal   60
To play the lawyer thus.
    Mont. Oh, your trade instructs your language.—
You see, my lords, what goodly fruit she seems;
Yet, like those apples[16] travelers report
To grow where Sodom and Gomorrah stood,
I will but touch her, and you straight shall see
She'll fall to soot and ashes.
    Vit. Cor.   Your envenomed
Pothecary should do't.
    Mont.   I am resolved,[17]
Were there a second Paradise to lose,
This devil would betray it.
    Vit. Cor.   O poor charity!   70
Thou art seldom found in scarlet.[18]
    Mont. Who knows not how, when several night by
    night
Her gates were choked with coaches, and her rooms
Outbraved the stars with several kind of lights,
When she did counterfeit a prince's court
In music, banquets, and most riotous surfeits?
This whore, forsooth, was holy.
    Vit. Cor.   Ha! whore! what's that!
    Mont. Shall I expound whore to you? Sure, I shall;
I'll give their perfect character.[19] They are first,
Sweetmeats which rot the eater; in man's nostrils   80
Poisoned perfumes; they are cozening alchemy;
Shipwrecks in calmest weather. What are whores!
Cold Russian winters, that appear so barren
As if that nature had forgot the spring.
They are the true material fire of hell,
Worse than those tributes i' the Low Countries paid,[20]
Exactions upon meat, drink, garments, sleep,
Ay, even on man's perdition,[21] his sin.
They are those brittle evidences of law
Which forfeit all a wretched man's estate   90
For leaving out one syllable. What are whores!
They are those flattering bells have all one tune,
At weddings and at funerals. Your rich whores

Are only treasuries by extortion filled,
And emptied by cursed riot. They are worse,
Worse than dead bodies which are begged at gallows,
And wrought upon by surgeons,[22] to teach man
Wherein he is imperfect. What's a whore!
She's like the guilty[23] counterfeited coin
Which, whosoe'er first stamps it, brings in trouble
All that receive it.
　　Vit. Cor.　　　　This character scapes me.　　　　101
　　Mont. You gentlewoman!
Take from all beasts and from all minerals
Their deadly poison—
　　Vit. Cor.　　　　Well, what then?
　　Mont.　　　　　　　　I'll tell thee;
I'll find in thee a pothecary's shop,
To sample[24] them all.
　　Fr. Amb.　　　She hath lived ill.
　　Eng. Amb. True; but the cardinal's too bitter.
　　Mont. You know what whore is. Next the devil
　　　adultery,
Enters the devil murder.
　　Fran.　　　　Your unhappy
Husband is dead.
　　Vit. Cor.　　Oh, he's a happy husband;　　　110
Now he owes nature nothing.
　　Fran. And by a vaulting-engine.
　　Mont.　　　　　　An active plot;
He jumped into his grave.
　　Fran.　　　　What a prodigy[25] was't
That from some two yards' height a slender man
Should break his neck!
　　Mont.　　　　I' the rushes![26]
　　Fran.　　　　　　　And what's more,
Upon the instant lose all use of speech,
All vital motion, like a man had lain
Wound up[27] three days. Now mark each circumstance.
　　Mont. And look upon this creature was his wife.
She comes not like a widow; she comes armed　　　120
With scorn and impudence: is this a mourning habit?
　　Vit. Cor. Had I foreknown his death, as you
　　　suggest,
I would have bespoke my mourning.
　　Mont. Oh, you are cunning.
　　Vit. Cor. You shame your wit and judgment,
To call it so, What! is my just defense
By him that is my judge called impudence?
Let me appeal, then, from this Christian court
To the uncivil Tartar.
　　Mont.　　　　See, my lords,
She scandals[28] our proceedings.
　　Vit. Cor.　　　　Humbly thus,　　　130
Thus low, to the most worthy and respected
Lieger ambassadors, my modesty
And womanhood I tender; but withal,
So entangled in a cursèd accusation,
That my defense, of force,[29] like Perseus,[30]
Must personate masculine virtue to the point.[31]
Find me but guilty, sever head from body,
We'll part good friends. I scorn to hold my life
At yours or any man's entreaty, sir.
　　Eng. Amb. She hath a brave spirit.　　　140

　　Mont. Well, well, such counterfeit jewels
Make true ones oft suspected.
　　Vit. Cor.　　　　　You are deceived.
For know, that all your strict-combinèd[32] heads,
Which strike against this mine of diamonds,
Shall prove but glassen hammers—they shall break.
These are but feignèd shadows of my evils.
Terrify babes, my lord, with painted devils;
I am past such needless palsy. For your names
Of whores and murderers, they proceed from you,
As if a man should spit against the wind;　　　150
The filth returns in's face.
　　Mont. Pray you, mistress, satisfy[33] me one question:
Who lodged beneath your roof that fatal night
Your husband brake his neck?
　　Brach.　　　　That question
Enforceth me break silence: I was there.
　　Mont. Your business?
　　Brach.　　　　Why, I came to comfort her,
And take some course for settling her estate,
Because I heard her husband was in debt
To you, my lord.
　　Mont.　　　He was.
　　Brach.　　　　And 'twas strangely feared
That you would cozen[34] her.
　　Mont.　　　　　Who made you overseer?
　　Brach. Why, my charity, my charity, which should
　　　flow　　　161
From every generous and noble spirit
To orphans and to widows.
　　Mont.　　　　Your lust.
　　Brach. Cowardly dogs bark loudest; sirrah[35] priest,
I'll talk with you hereafter. Do you hear?
The sword you frame[36] of such an excellent temper
I'll sheathe in your own bowels.
There are a number of thy coat[37] resemble
Your common post-boys.
　　Mont.　　　Ha!
　　Brach.　　　　Your mercenary post-boys.
Your letters carry truth, but 'tis your guise[38]　　　170
To fill your mouths with gross and impudent lies.
　　Serv. My lord, your gown.
　　Brach.　　　　Thou liest, 'twas my stool.[39]

---

[22] *dead . . . surgeons:* The Barber-Surgeons were allowed by charter four executed criminals annually—and presumably begged for more on which to practice.
[23] *guilty:* with a pun on "gilt"—speciously colored.
[24] *sample:* ensample; exemplify.　　　[25] *prodigy:* miracle.
[26] *rushes:* matting strewn on the floor in place of carpets.
[27] *Wound up:* In his shroud.　　　[28] *scandals:* demeans.
[29] *of force:* necessarily.
[30] *Perseus:* who did in fact impersonate heroic and masculine virtue in a contemporary masque by Ben Jonson.
[31] *to the point:* in each detail.
[32] *strict-combinèd:* closely allied.
[33] *satisfy:* answer.　　　　　　　[34] *cozen:* cheat.
[35] *sirrah:* a term of contempt, like "boy."
[36] *sword you frame:* i.e., plot you contrive.
[37] *coat:* profession.　　　　[38] *guise:* manner.
[39] *stool:* As Brachiano gets up to go, he is reminded that he has left his cloak on which he has been sitting—since no stool was provided for him. Contemptuously he is waiving claim to the furniture that ought to have been there.

Bestow't upon thy master that will challenge[40]
The rest o' the household-stuff; for Brachiano
Was ne'er so beggarly to take a stool
Out of another's lodging; let him make
Valance[41] for his bed on't, or a demi-foot-cloth[42]
For his most reverendmoil.[43] Monticelso,
Nemo me impune lacessit.[44]

                    Exit BRACHIANO.

   Mont. Your champion's gone.
   Vit. Cor.   The wolf may prey
   the better.   180
   Fran. My lord, there's great suspicion of the
   murder,
But no sound proof who did it. For my part,
I do not think she hath a soul so black
To act a deed so bloody: if she have,
As in cold countries husbandmen plant vines,
And with warm blood manure them, even so
One summer she will bear unsavory fruit,
And ere next spring wither both branch and root.
The act of blood let pass; only descend
To matter of incontinence.
   Vit. Cor.   I discern poison   190
Under your gilded pills.
   Mont. Now the duke's gone, I will produce a letter,
Wherein 'twas plotted he and you should meet
At an apothecary's summer-house,
Down by the river Tiber—view't, my lords—
Where, after wanton bathing and the heat
Of a lascivious banquet—I pray read it,
I shame to speak the rest.
   Vit. Cor.   Grant I was tempted;
Temptation to lust proves not the act:
Casta est quam nemo rogavit.[45]   200
You read his hot love to me, but you want
My frosty answer.
   Mont.   Frost i' the dog-days![46] strange!
   Vit. Cor. Condemn you me for that[47] the duke did
   love me!
So may you blame some fair and crystal river
For that some melancholic distracted man
Hath drowned himself in't.
   Mont.   Truly drowned, indeed.

---

[40] *challenge:* lay claim to.   [41] *Valance:* Canopy.
[42] *demi-foot-cloth:* short covering for a horse, to protect the rider's boots.
[43] *moil:* toil; muddy business, in which the foot-cloth will keep him clean.
[44] *L.:* Motto of the Scottish Order of the Thistle: "No one injures me with impunity."
[45] *L.:* From Ovid, *Amores,* I. viii. 43: "She is chaste whom no one has asked."
[46] *dog-days:* proverbial for heat.   [47] *for that:* because.
[48] *crusadoes:* Portuguese coins of gold or silver.
[49] *use:* interest.
[50] *intelligencing:* as of a spy or "intelligencer."
[51] *loving:* emended generally to "long"; i.e., were your ears long (acute) enough to pick up my thoughts.
[52] *choke-pear:* bitter fruit.   [53] *acquaintance:* knowledge.
[54] *julio:* trivial coin, like a sixpence.
[55] *light:* with a pun on "wanton."
[56] *Rialto talk:* Common gossip.
[57] *ballated:* made the subject of sensational broadside ballads.   [58] *sureties:* bonds.

   Vit. Cor. Sum up my faults, I pray, and you shall
   find,
That beauty, and gay clothes, a merry heart,
And a good stomach to a feast, are all,
All the poor crimes that you can charge me with.   210
In faith, my lord, you might go pistol flies;
The sport would be more noble.
   Mont.   Very good.
   Vit. Cor. But take you your course; it seems you have
   beggared me first,
And now would fain undo me. I have houses,
Jewels, and a poor remnant of crusadoes.[48]
Would those would make you charitable!
   Mont.   If the devil
Did ever take good shape, behold his picture.
   Vit. Cor. You have one virtue left—
You will not flatter me.
   Fran.   Who brought this letter?
   Vit. Cor. I am not compelled to tell you.   220
   Mont. My lord duke sent to you a thousand ducats
The twelfth of August.
   Vit. Cor.   'Twas to keep your cousin
From prison; I paid use[49] for't.
   Mont.   I rather think
'Twas interest for his lust.
   Vit. Cor.   Who says so
But yourself? If you be my accuser,
Pray, cease to be my judge; come from the bench;
Give in your evidence 'gainst me, and let these
Be moderators. My lord cardinal,
Were your intelligencing[50] ears as loving[51]
As to my thoughts, had you an honest tongue,   230
I would not care though you proclaimed them all.
   Mont. Go to, go to.
After your goodly and vainglorious banquet,
I'll give you a choke-pear.[52]
   Vit. Cor.   O' your own grafting?
   Mont. You were born in Venice, honorably
   descended
From the Vitelli: 'twas my cousin's fate—
Ill may I name the hour—to marry you.
He bought you of your father.
   Vit. Cor.   Ha!
   Mont. He spent there in six months   239
Twelve thousand ducats, and to my acquaintance[53]
Received in dowry with you not one julio.[54]
'Twas a hard pennyworth, the ware being so light.[55]
I yet but draw the curtain; now to your picture.
You came from thence a most notorious strumpet,
And so have continued.
   Vit. Cor.   My lord—
   Mont.   Nay, hear me;
You shall have time to prate. My Lord Brachiano—
Alas, I make but repetition
Of what is ordinary and Rialto talk,[56]
And ballated,[57] and would be played o' the stage,
But that vice many times finds such loud friends   250
That preachers are charmed silent.
You gentlemen, Flamineo and Marcello,
The court hath nothing now to charge you with.
Only you must remain upon your sureties[58]

For your appearance.

Fran. I stand for Marcello.

Flam. And my lord duke for me.

Mont. For you, Vittoria, your public fault,
Joined to the condition of the present time,
Takes from you all the fruits of noble pity;
Such a corrupted trial have you made   260
Both of your life and beauty, and been styled
No less an ominous fate than blazing stars
To princes. Here's your sentence; you are confined
Unto a house of convertites, and your bawd—

Flam. [*Aside*] Who, I?

Mont.   The Moor.

Flam. [*Aside*]   Oh, I am a sound [59]
man again.

Vit. Cor. A house of convertites! what's that?

Mont.   A house
Of penitent whores.

Vit. Cor.   Do the noblemen in Rome
Erect it for their wives, that I am sent
To lodge there?

Fran. You must have patience.

Vit. Cor.   I must first have
vengeance.   270
I fain would know if you have your salvation
By patent [60] that you proceed thus.

Mont.   Away with her!
Take her hence.

Vit. Cor. A rape! a rape!

Mont.   How!

Vit. Cor.   Yes, you have ravished
justice,
Forced her to do your pleasure.

Mont.   Fie, she's mad!

Vit. Cor. Die with these pills [61] in your most cursèd
maws [62]
Should bring you health! or while you sit o' the bench
Let your own spittle choke you!

Mont.   She's turned Fury.

Vit. Cor. That the last day of judgment may so find
you,
And leave you the same devil you were before!   280
Instruct me, some good horse-leech, [63] to speak treason;
For since you cannot take my life for deeds,
Take it for words. O woman's poor revenge,
Which dwells but in the tongue! I will not weep;
No, I do scorn to call up one poor tear
To fawn on your injustice; bear me hence
Unto this house of—what's your mitigating title?

Mont. Of convertites.

Vit. Cor. It shall not be a house of convertites;
My mind shall make it honester to me   290
Than the Pope's palace, and more peaceable
Than thy soul, though thou art a cardinal.
Know this, and let it somewhat raise your spite,
Through darkness diamonds spread their richest light.

                    Exit VITTORIA.

                    Enter BRACHIANO.

Brach. Now you and I are friends, sir, we'll shake
hands

In a friend's grave together; a fit place,
Being the emblem of soft peace, to atone [64] our hatred.

Fran. Sir, what's the matter?

Brach. I will not chase more blood from that loved
cheek;
You have lost too much already. Fare you well.   300
                    [*Exit.*]

Fran. How strange these words sound! what's the
interpretation?

Flam. [*Aside*] Good; this is a preface to the discovery
of the duchess' death: he carries it well. Because now I
cannot counterfeit a whining passion for the death of
my lady, I will feign a mad humor for the disgrace of
my sister, and that will keep off idle questions.
Treason's tongue hath a villainous palsy [65] in't. I will
talk to any man, hear no man, and for a time appear a
politic madman.
                    [*Exit.*]

                    Enter GIOVANNI, Count LODOVICO.

Fran. How now, my noble cousin! what, in black!

Giov. Yes, uncle, I was taught to imitate you   311
In virtue, and you must imitate me
In colors of your garments. My sweet mother
Is—

Fran. How! where?

Giov. Is there; no, yonder. [66] Indeed, sir, I'll not tell
you,
For I shall make you weep.

Fran. Is dead?

Giov. Do not blame me now,
I did not tell you so.

Lod.   She's dead, my lord.   320

Fran. Dead!

Mont. Blessed lady, thou are now above thy woes!
Will't please your lordships to withdraw a little?
                    [*Exeunt* Ambassadors.]

Giov. What do the dead do, uncle? Do they eat,
Hear music, go a-hunting, and be merry,
As we that live?

Fran. No, coz; they sleep.

Giov.   Lord, Lord, that I were
dead!
I have not slept these six nights.—When do they wake?

Fran. When God shall please.

Giov.   Good God, let her
sleep ever!
For I have known her wake an hundred nights,   330
When all the pillow where she laid her head
Was brine-wet with her tears. I am to complain to you,
sir.
I'll tell you how they have used her now she's dead.

---

[59] *sound:* whole, healthy.
[60] *by patent:* granted freely, as by royal command.
[61] *pills:* perhaps metaphorically for "hypocritical pieties."
[62] *maws:* mouths.
[63] *horse-leech:* veterinarian; figuratively, "rapacious person."   [64] *atone:* reconcile.
[65] *palsy:* i.e., the wicked tongue blabs.
[66] *yonder:* in heaven.
[67] *fold:* winding sheet.

They wrapped her in a cruel fold [67] of lead,
And would not let me kiss her.

Fran.   Thou didst love her.

Giov. I have often heard her say she gave me suck,
And it should seem by that she dearly loved me,
Since princes seldom do it.

Fran. Oh, all of my poor sister that remains!
Take him away, for God's sake!

                            [Exit GIOVANNI *attended.]*

Mont.   How now, my lord!

Fran. Believe me, I am nothing but her grave,   341
And I shall keep her blessèd memory
Longer than thousand epitaphs.

                                    [Exeunt.]

        Enter FLAMINEO *as distracted.*

Flam. We endure the strokes like anvils or hard steel,
Till pain itself make us pain to feel.
Who shall do me right now? Is this the end of service?
I'd rather go weed garlic; travel through France, and
be mine own ostler; [68] wear sheepskin linings, or shoes
that stink of blacking; [69] be entered into the list of the
forty thousand pedlars in Poland.   350

        Enter SAVOY [*Ambassador*].

Would I had rotted in some surgeon's house at Venice,
built upon the pox as well as on piles, [70] ere I had served
Brachiano!

Savoy Amb. You must have comfort.

Flam. Your comfortable words are like honey; they
relish well in your mouth that's whole, but in mine
that's wounded they go down as if the sting of the bee
were in them. Oh, they have wrought their purpose
cunningly, as if they would not seem to do it of malice!
In this a politician imitates the devil, as the devil   360
imitates a cannon; wheresoever he comes to do mischief,
he comes with his backside towards you. [71]

        Enter the French [*Ambassador*].

---

[67] *ostler:* who cares for the horses.

[69] *blacking:* here, carbon or "lampblack."

[70] *piles:* with a pun on hemorrhoids.

[71] *he . . . you:* The politic devil presents his backside
rather than his face to mask his real purpose; and also(?) to
break wind ("imitates a cannon," which is towed breech
first or backward to the point of action) or(?) to present his
"arse" for kissing.

[72] *diversivolent:* turning wills against each other.

[73] *gudgeons:* little fish: fools.

[74] *victual . . . line:* food at the equator.

[75] *here . . . with:* In England until the eighteenth century,
accused persons who refused to plead were pressed by iron
weights until they spoke, or died.

[76] *pitch:* height—metaphor from falconry rather than
music.   [77] *racked:* tortured.   [78] *commedled:* mingled.

[79] *The first bloodshed:* Cain's murder of Abel.

[80] *benefices:* Clergy at the time held more than one parish
or cure, which they did not serve but from which they
collected money.

[81] *Wolner:* a famous glutton of Elizabeth's reign who
could devour anything, including iron and glass.

[82] *wind:* get the wind of; smell him out.

[83] *purchased:* attained.

[84] *stigmatic:* branded; permanently hideous.

Fr. Amb. The proofs are evident.

Flam. Proof! 'twas corruption. O gold, what a god
art thou! and O man, what a devil art thou to be
tempted by that cursed mineral! You diversivolent [72]
lawyer, mark him: knaves turn informers as maggots
turn to flies; you may catch gudgeons [73] with either. A
cardinal! I would he would hear me; there's nothing so
holy but money will corrupt and putrify it, like victual
under the line. [74]   371

        [*Enter*] *English Ambassador.*

You are happy in England, my lord: here they sell
justice with those weights they press men to death
with. [75] O horrible salary!

Eng. Amb. Fie, fie, Flamineo!

Flam. Bells ne'er ring well, till they are at their full
pitch; [76] and I hope yon cardinal shall never have the
grace to pray well till he come to the scaffold. If they
were racked [77] now to know the confederacy—but your
noblemen are privileged from the rack; and well   380
may, for a little thing would pull some of them a-pieces
afore they came to their arraignment. Religion, oh, how
it is commedled [78] with policy! The first bloodshed [79] in
the world happened about religion. Would I were a Jew!

Mar. Oh, there are too many.

Flam. You are deceived: there are not Jews enough,
priests enough, nor gentlemen enough.

Mar. How?

Flam. I'll prove it; for if there were Jews enough, so
many Christians would not turn usurers; if   390
priests enough, one should not have six benefices; [80]
and if gentlemen enough, so many early mushrooms,
whose best growth sprang from a dunghill, should not
aspire to gentility. Farewell: let others live by begging;
be thou one of them practice the art of Wolner [81] in
England to swallow all's given thee; and yet let one
purgation make thee as hungry again as fellows that
work in a saw-pit. I'll go hear the screech-owl.

                                     Exit.

Lod. [*Aside*] This was Brachiano's pander, and 'tis
    strange
That, in such open and apparent guilt   400
Of his adulterous sister, he dare utter
So scandalous a passion. I must wind [82] him.

             Enter FLAMINEO.

Flam. [*Aside*] How dares this banished count return
    to Rome,
His pardon not yet purchased! [83] I have heard
The deceased duchess gave him pension,
And that he came along from Padua
I' the train of the young prince. There's somewhat in't.
Physicians, that cure poisons, still do work
With counter-poisons.

Mar.   Mark this strange encounter.

Flam. The god of melancholy turn thy gall to
    poison,
And let the stigmatic [84] wrinkles in thy face,   411
Like to the boisterous waves in a rough tide,
One still overtake another.

Lod.   I do thank thee,

And I do wish ingeniously [85] for thy sake
The dog-days [86] all year long.
  Flam.   How croaks the raven?
Is our good duchess dead?
  Lod.   Dead.
  Flam.   O fate!
Misfortune comes, like the crowner's [87] business,
Huddle upon huddle. [88]
  Lod. Shalt thou and I join house-keeping?
  Flam.   Yes, content.
Let's be unsociably sociable.   420
  Lod. Sit some three days together and discourse.
  Flam. Only with making faces; lie in our
    clothes.
  Lod. With faggots [89] for our pillows.
  Flam.   And be lousy.
  Lod. In taffeta [90] linings; that's genteel melancholy.
Sleep all day.
  Flam.   Yes; and, like your melancholic hare, [91]
Feed after midnight.
We are observed; see how yon couple [92] grieve!

    Enter ANTONELLI [*and* GASPARO, *laughing*].

  Lod. What a strange creature is a laughing fool,
As if man were created to no use
But only to show his teeth.
  Flam.   I'll tell thee what,   430
It would do well, instead of looking-glasses,
To set one's face each morning by a saucer
Of a witch's congealèd blood.
  Lod.   Precious grine rouge. [93]
We'll never part.
  Flam. Never, till the beggary of courtiers,
The discontent of churchmen, want of soldiers,
And all the creatures that hang manacled,
Worse than strappadoed, [94] on the lowest felly [95]
Of fortune's wheel, be taught, in our two lives,
To scorn that world which life of means deprives.   440
  Anto. My lord, I bring good news. The Pope, on's
    deathbed,
At the earnest suit of the great Duke of Florence,
Hath signed your pardon, and restored unto you—
  Lod. I thank you for your news.—Look up again,
    Flamineo; see my pardon.
  Flam.   Why do you laugh?
There was no such condition in our covenant. [96]
  Lod. Why!
  Flam. You shall not seem a happier man than I.
You know our vow, sir; if you will be merry,
Do it i' the like posture as if some great man   450
Sate while his enemy were executed;
Though it be very lechery unto thee,
Do't with a crabbèd politician's face.
  Lod. Your sister is a damnable whore.
  Flam.   Ha!
  Lod. Look you, I spake that laughing.
  Flam. Dost ever think to speak again?
  Lod.   Do you hear?
Wilt sell me forty ounces of her blood
To water a mandrake? [97]
  Flam.   Poor lord, you did vow

To live a lousy creature.
  Lod.   Yes.
  Flam.   Like one
That had for ever forfeited the daylight   460
By being in debt.
  Lod.   Ha, ha!
  Flam. I do not greatly wonder you do break; [98]
Your lordship learned 't long since. But I'll tell you—
  Lod. What?
  Flam.   And 't shall stick by you—
  Lod.   I long for it.
  Flam. This laughter scurvily becomes your face.
If you will not be melancholy, be angry.
                        Strikes him.
See, now I laugh too.
  Mar. You are to blame. I'll force you hence.
  Lod.   Unhand
  me.
          Exeunt MARCELLO *and* FLAMINEO.
That e'er I should be forced to right myself
Upon a pander!
  Anto.   My lord—   470
  Lod. H'ad been as good met with his fist a
    thunderbolt.
  Gas. How this shows!
  Lod.   Ud's [99] death, how did my
    sword miss him?
These rogues that are most weary of their lives
Still scape the greatest dangers.
A pox upon him! all his reputation,
Nay, all the goodness of his family,
Is not worth half this earthquake.
I learned it of no fencer to shake thus.
Come, I'll forget him, and go drink some wine.
                        Exeunt.

ACT FOUR

SCENE ONE

Enter FRANCISCO [DE MEDICIS] *and* MONTICELSO.

  Mont. Come, come, my lord, untie your folded
    thoughts,

---

[85] *ingeniously:* ingenuously; frankly.
[86] *dog-days:* hot; a miserable time.
[87] *crowner's:* coroner's.
[88] *Huddle upon huddle:* One upon another.
[89] *faggots:* bundles; also a cant term for a woman.
[90] *taffeta:* silky underclothes, supposedly proof against
lice.   [91] *hare:* proverbially melancholy.
[92] *couple:* presumably Antonelli and Gasparo, though the
1612 quarto does not note their entrance until later in the
scene.
[93] *grine rouge:* girn (grimacing) rogue(?); the Q phrase
seems to be textually corrupt, and has not been definitively
explained.
[94] *strappadoed:* alluding to the torture in which the
victim, with hands crossed and tied behind his back, was
jerked up by a pulley and dropped to the ground, dislo-
cating his bones.   [95] *felly:* piece of the rim of a wheel.
[96] *covenant:* agreement.
[97] *mandrake:* plant supposed to grow under the gallows
and to be nourished by the decomposing bodies left hanging.
[98] *break:* break faith.   [99] *Ud's:* God's.

And let them dangle loose as a bride's hair.[1]
Your sister's poisoned.
   Fran.   Far be it from my thoughts
To seek revenge.
   Mont.   What, are you turned all marble?
   Fran. Shall I defy him, and impose a war
Most burdensome on my poor subjects' necks,
Which at my will I have not power to end?
You know, for all the murders, rapes, and thefts
Committed in the horrid lust of war,
He that unjustly caused it first proceed   10
Shall find it in his grave and in his seed.
   Mont. That's not the course I'd wish you; pray,
     observe me.
We see that undermining more prevails
Than doth the cannon. Bear your wrongs concealed,
And, patient as the tortoise, let this camel
Stalk o'er your back unbruised. Sleep with the lion,
And let this brood of secure foolish mice
Play with your nostrils, till the time be ripe
For the bloody audit and the fatal gripe.
Aim like a cunning fowler,[2] close one eye,   20
That you the better may your game espy.
   Fran. Free me, my innocence, from treacherous
     acts!
I know there's thunder yonder; and I'll stand
Like a safe valley, which low bends the knee
To some aspiring mountain, since I know
Treason, like spiders weaving nets for flies,
By her foul work is found, and in it dies.
To pass away these thoughts, my honored lord,
It is reported you possess a book,
Wherein you have quoted, by intelligence,[3]   30
The names of all notorious offenders
Lurking about the city.
   Mont.   Sir, I do;

IV.i.
  [1] *bride's hair:* alluding to the old convention which required that a bride walk to church with her hair disheveled.
  [2] *fowler:* hunter of birds.
  [3] *quoted, by intelligence:* written down, on the word of informants.
  [4] *black book:* originally, "official register," with the sinister sense already current in the sixteenth century.
  [5] *jealous:* suspicious.
  [6] *taking up commodities:* To avoid the prohibition of usury, the moneylender "sold" the borrower a worthless item at many times its value.
  [7] *politic bankrupts:* cunning swindlers who, pretending to be bankrupt, fled with their gains, leaving their creditors out of pocket.
  [8] *put:* sell; the adulterer purchased silence of the willing cuckold by purchasing "defaced" items from him.
  [9] *reportage:* report; which the scriveners or clerks took care, for a fee, to make favorable in order to gull the potential borrower.
  [10] *antedate their writs:* Crooked lawyers would falsely date a document so that payment fell due before the supposedly agreed-on time.
  [11] *tribute . . . England:* alluding to the device of King Edgar (944–975), who rid the land of wolves by forcing the Welsh to pay tribute, in lieu of money, of 300 wolves' heads each year for three years.
  [12] *Irish rebels:* on whose heads Queen Elizabeth had set a bounty.

And some there are which call it my black book.[4]
Well may the title hold; for though it teach not
The art of conjuring, yet in it lurk
The names of many devils.
   Fran.   Pray, let's see it.
   Mont. I'll fetch it to your lordship.
                Exit MONTICELSO.
   Fran.   Monticelso,
I will not trust thee; but in all my plots
I'll rest as jealous[5] as a town besieged.
Thou canst not reach what I intend to act.   40
Your flax soon kindles, soon is out again;
But gold slow heats, and long will hot remain.

     [*Re-*]*enter* MONTICELSO, *presents* FRANCISCO
     [DE MEDICIS] *with a book.*

   Mont. 'Tis here, my lord.
   Fran. First, your intelligencers, pray, let's see.
   Mont. Their number rises strangely; and some of
     them
You'd take for honest men. Next are panders—
These are your pirates; and these following leaves
For base rogues that undo young gentlemen
By taking up commodities;[6] for politic bankrupts;[7]
For fellows that are bawds to their own wives,   50
Only to put[8] off horses, and slight jewels,
Clocks, defaced plate, and such commodities,
At birth of their first children.
   Fran.   Are there such?
   Mont. These are for impudent bawds
That go in men's apparel; for usurers
That share with scriveners for their good reportage;[9]
For lawyers that will antedate their writs:[10]
And some divines you might find folded there,
But that I slip them o'er for conscience' sake.
Here is a general catalogue of knaves.   60
A man might study all the prison o'er,
Yet never attain this knowledge.
   Fran.   Murderers!
Fold down the leaf, I pray.
Good my lord, let me borrow this strange doctrine.
   Mont. Pray, use't, my lord.
   Fran.   I do assure your lordship,
You are a worthy member of the state,
And have done infinite good in your discovery
Of these offenders.
   Mont.   Somewhat, sir.
   Fran.   O God!
Better than tribute of wolves paid in England.[11]
'Twill hang their skins o' the hedge.
   Mont.   I must make bold
To leave your lordship.
   Fran.   Dearly, sir, I thank you.   71
If any ask for me at court, report
You have left me in the company of knaves.
                  Exit MONTICELSO.
I gather now by this, some cunning fellow
That's my lord's officer, one that lately skipped
From a clerk's desk up to a justice' chair,
Hath made this knavish summons, and intends,
As the Irish rebels[12] wont were to sell heads,

So to make prize of these. And thus it happens,
Your poor rogues pay for't which have not the means
To present bribe in fist. The rest o' the band　　81
Are razed out of the knaves' record; or else
My lord he winks at them with easy will;
His man grows rich, the knaves are the knaves still.
But to the use I'll make of it; it shall serve
To point me out a list of murderers,
Agents for any villainy. Did I want
Ten leash [13] of courtesans, it would furnish me;
Nay, laundress three armies.[14] That in so little paper
Should lie the undoing of so many men!　　　90
'Tis not so big as twenty declarations.
See the corrupted use some make of books.
Divinity, wrested by some factious blood,
Draws swords, swells, battles, and o'erthrows all good.
To fashion my revenge more seriously,
Let me remember my dead sister's face.
Call for her picture? No, I'll close mine eyes,
And in a melancholic thought I'll frame

Enter ISABELLA'S Ghost.

Her figure 'fore me. Now I ha't [15]—how strong
Imagination works! how she can frame　　　100
Things which are not! Methinks she stands afore me,
And by the quick idea of my mind,
Were my skill pregnant,[16] I could draw her picture.
Thought, as a subtle juggler, makes us deem
Things supernatural, which yet have cause
Common as sickness. 'Tis my melancholy.
How cam'st thou by thy death?—How idle am I
To question mine own idleness!—Did ever
Man dream awake till now?—Remove this object;
Out of my brain with't. What have I to do　　110
With tombs, or death-beds, funerals, or tears,
That have to meditate upon revenge?
　　　　　　　　　　　　[*Exit* Ghost.]
So, now 'tis ended, like an old wife's story.
Statesmen think often they see stranger sights
Than madmen. Come, to this weighty business;
My tragedy must have some idle mirth in't,
Else I will never pass. I am in love,
In love with Corombona; and my suit
Thus halts [17] to her in verse.
　　　　　　　　　　　　He writes.
I have done it rarely. O the fate of princes!　　120
I am so used to frequent flattery,
That, being alone, I now flatter myself.
But it will serve; 'tis sealed.

Enter Servant.

Bear this
To the house of convertites, and watch your leisure
To give it to the hands of Corombona,
Or to the matron, when some followers
Of Brachiano may be by. Away!
　　　　　　　　　　　　Exit Servant.
He that deals all by strength, his wit is shallow.
When a man's head goes through, each limb will
　　follow.
The engine for my business, bold Count Lodowick.

'Tis gold must such an instrument procure;　　131
With empty fist [18] no man doth falcons lure.
Brachiano, I am now fit for thy encounter.
Like the wild Irish, I'll ne'er think thee dead
Till I can play at football with thy head.
Flectere si nequeo superos, Acheronta movebo.[19]

　　　　　　　　　　　　　　　　Exit.

[IV.ii]

Enter the Matron *and* FLAMINEO.

Matron. Should it be known the duke hath such
　　recourse
To your imprisoned sister, I were like
To incur much damage by it.
Flam.　　　　　　　　Not a scruple.
The Pope lies on his death-bed, and their heads
Are troubled now with other business
Than guarding of a lady.

Enter Servant.

Serv. [*Aside*] Yonder's Flamineo in conference
With the matrona.—[*To the* Matron] Let me speak
　　with you;
I would entreat you to deliver for me
This letter to the fair Vittoria.　　　　　　10
Matron. I shall, sir.
Serv.　　　　　　With all care and secrecy.
Hereafter you shall know me, and receive
Thanks for this courtesy.
　　　　　　　　　　　　[*Exit* Servant.]
Flam.　　　　　How now! what's that?
Matron. A letter.
Flam.　　　　　To my sister? I'll see't delivered.

Enter BRACHIANO.

Brach. What's that you read, Flamineo?
Flam.　　　　　　　　　　Look.
Brach. Ha! "To the most unfortunate, his best
　　respected Vittoria."
Who was the messenger?
Flam.　　　　　　　I know not.
Brach. No! who sent it?
Flam.　　　　　　　Ud's foot, you speak as if a
　　man
Should know what fowl is coffined [1] in a baked meat
Afore you cut it up.　　　　　　　　　　　20

---

[13] *leash:* technically, "set of three."

[14] *laundress . . . armies:* three armies of laundresses, who
were notoriously unchaste.

[15] *ha't:* have it; Francisco thinks he has succeeded in
imagining his dead sister, who is, however, literally present.

[16] *pregnant:* fertile.

[17] *halts:* Metrically his love poem is halting or imperfect.

[18] *empty fist:* which had to hold a lure; feathers or hide
with meat attached to lure the falcon back to the falconer's
hand.

[19] *L.:* Quoting *Aeneid,* VII. 312: "If I am unable to
prevail on the heavens, I shall move the underworld."

IV.ii.

[1] *coffined:* literally; "enclosed in pie-crust."

Brach. I'll open't, were't her heart.—What's here
    subscribed!
"Florence!" this juggling is gross and palpable.
I have found out the conveyance.[2]—Read it, read it.
    Flam. [*Reads the letter.*] " *Your tears I'll turn to*
        triumphs, be but mine.
    Your prop is fallen. I pity that a vine,
    Which princes heretofore have longed to gather,
    Wanting supporters, now should fade and wither."
Wine, i' faith, my lord, with lees[3] would serve his turn.
    " *Your sad imprisonment I'll soon uncharm,*
    And with a princely uncontrollèd arm   30
    Lead you to Florence, where my love and care
    Shall hang your wishes in my silver hair."
A halter on his strange equivocation![4]
    " *Nor for my years return me the sad willow.*[5]
    Who prefer blossoms before fruit that's mellow?"
Rotten, on my knowledge, with lying too long i' the
    bedstraw.
    "*And all the lines of age this line convinces,*[6]
    The gods never wax old, no more do princes."
A pox on't, tear it; let's have no more atheists, for God's
    sake.
    Brach. Ud's death, I'll cut her into atomies,   40
And let the irregular[7] north wind sweep her up,
And blow her into his nostrils! Where's this whore?
    Flam. That—? What do you call her?
    Brach.   Oh, I could
        be mad,

---

² *conveyance:* trick.   ³ *lees:* dregs.
⁴ *equivocation:* pun; Flamineo associates "hang" in the
preceding line with "halter."
⁵ *willow:* symbol of rejected lovers.
⁶ *And . . . convinces:* This testament of love is proof
against wrinkles (my old age).   ⁷ *irregular:* wild.
⁸ *Prevent:* Anticipate.   ⁹ *disease:* syphilis.
¹⁰ *changeable stuff:* fickle woman (analogy to material or
stuff like shot silk that changes color in different contexts).
¹¹ *O'er . . . water:* In deep trouble.
¹² *wearing:* carrying on the metaphor of "changeable
stuff."   ¹³ *stand:* stand against.   ¹⁴ *run:* as with pus.
¹⁵ *Russia:* proverbial then as now for barbaric customs
like beating delinquent debtors on the shins.
¹⁶ *methodically:* "by the book."
¹⁷ *fig . . . salad:* poison; to give the fig (by inserting the
thumb between the first and second fingers) is also an
ancient and obscene gesture of contempt.
¹⁸ *ply your convoy:* be about your (pandering) business.
¹⁹ *Polyphemus:* the Cyclops or one-eyed giant who (as
Homer relates in *Odyssey,* IX. 369–70) intended the devouring of Ulysses.
²⁰ *turfs:* turf-ants; food. Other editors comment simply
that the cages of birds were supplied with fresh turf or sod.
²¹ *face:* brave; with a pun indicated by the lines that
follow.
²² *characters:* mysterious ciphers, like hieroglyphics.
²³ *comment:* gloss, explanation.   ²⁴ *receiver:* pimp.
²⁵ *precious:* i.e., blood!
²⁶ *reclaimed:* tamed, like a hawk that has been wild.
²⁷ *bells:* which, fastened to the hawk's legs, made it
easier to find her when she had brought her quarry to
ground.
²⁸ *Ware hawk:* proverbial, Beware the bird; by extension,
a cheat.
²⁹ *devil in crystal:* various senses—the White Devil of the
title; a fair-appearing devil; the devil itself conjured up by
necromancers in a crystal glass.

Prevent[8] the cursed disease[9] she'll bring me to,
And tear my hair off! Where's this changeable stuff?[10]
    Flam. O'er head and ears in water,[11] I assure you.
She is not for your wearing.[12]
    Brach.   In, you pander?
    Flam. What, me, my lord, am I your dog?
    Brach. A blood-hound. Do you brave, do you
        stand[13] me?
    Flam. Stand you! let those that have diseases run;[14]
I need no plasters.
    Brach.   Would you be kicked?   51
    Flam. Would you have your neck broke?
I tell you, duke, I am not in Russia;[15]
My shins must be kept whole.
    Brach.   Do you know me?
    Flam. Oh, my lord, methodically.[16]
As in this world there are degrees of evils,
So in this world there are degrees of devils.
You're a great duke, I your poor secretary.
I do look now for a Spanish fig, or an Italian salad,[17]
    daily.
    Brach. Pander, ply your convoy,[18] and leave your
        prating.   60
    Flam. All your kindness to me is like that miserable
courtesy of Polyphemus[19] to Ulysses; you reserve me
to be devoured last; you would dig turfs[20] out of my
grave to feed your larks; that would be music to you.
Come, I'll lead you to her.
    Brach. Do you face[21] me?
    Flam. Oh, sir, I would not go before a politic enemy
with my back towards him, though there were behind
me a whirlpool.

Enter VITTORIA [COROMBONA] *to* BRACHIANO
        and FLAMINEO.

    Brach. Can you read, mistress? Look upon that
        letter.   70
There are no characters[22] nor hieroglyphics;
You need no comment[23]: I am grown your receiver.[24]
God's precious![25] you shall be a brave great lady,
A stately and advancèd whore.
    Vit. Cor.   Say, sir?
    Brach. Come, come, let's see your cabinet, discover
Your treasury of love letters. Death and Furies!
I'll see them all.
    Vit. Cor.   Sir, upon my soul,
I have not any. Whence was this directed?
    Brach. Confusion on your politic ignorance!
You are reclaimed,[26] are you? I'll give you the
    bells,[27]   80
And let you fly to the devil.
    Flam.   Ware hawk,[28] my lord.
    Vit. Cor. "Florence!" This is some treacherous
plot, my lord.
To me he ne'er was lovely, I protest,
So much as in my sleep.
    Brach.   Right! they are plots.
Your beauty! oh, ten thousand curses on't!
How long have I beheld the devil in crystal![29]
Thou hast led me, like an heathen sacrifice,
With music and with fatal yokes of flowers,

To my eternal ruin. Woman to man
Is either a god or a wolf.[30]
   Vit. Cor.   My lord—
   Brach.   Away!   90
We'll be as differing as two adamants;
The one shall shun the other. What, dost weep?
Procure but ten of thy dissembling trade
Ye'd furnish all the Irish funerals
With howling past wild Irish.
   Flam.   Fie, my lord!
   Brach. That hand, that cursèd hand, which I have
     wearied
With doting kisses!—O my sweetest duchess,
How lovely art thou now!—Thy loose thoughts
Scatter like quicksilver.[31] I was bewitched;
For all the world speaks ill of thee.
   Vit. Cor.   No matter;   100
I'll live so now, I'll make that world recant,
And change her speeches. You did name your duchess.
   Brach. Whose death God pardon!
   Vit. Cor.   Whose death God
   revenge
On thee, most godless duke!
   Flam.   Now for two whirlwinds.
   Vit. Cor. What have I gained by thee but infamy?
Thou hast stained the spotless honor of my house,
And frighted thence noble society,
Like those, which, sick o' the palsy, and retain
Ill-scenting foxes[32] 'bout them, are still shunned
By those of choicer[33] nostrils. What do you call this
   house?   110
Is this your palace? Did not the judge style it
A house of penitent whores? Who sent me to it!
Who hath the honor to advance Vittoria
To this incontinent[34] college? Is't not you?
Is't not your high preferment? Go, go brag
How many ladies you have undone like me.
Fare you well, sir; let me hear no more of you.
I had a limb corrupted to an ulcer,
But I have cut it off, and now I'll go
Weeping to heaven on crutches. For your gifts,   120
I will return them all; and I do wish
That I could make you full executor
To all my sins. Oh, that I could toss myself
Into a grave as quickly! for all thou art worth
I'll not shed one tear more—I'll burst first.

              She throws herself upon a bed.

   Brach. I have drunk Lethe.[35]—Vittoria!
My dearest happiness! Vittoria!
What do you ail, my love? Why do you weep?
   Vit. Cor. Yes, I now weep poniards,[36] do you
   see?   129
   Brach. Are not those matchless eyes mine?
   Vit. Cor.   I had rather
They were not matchless.
   Brach.   Is not this lip mine?
   Vit. Cor. Yes; thus to bite it off, rather than give it
   thee.
   Flam. Turn[37] to my lord, good sister.
   Vit. Cor.   Hence, you pander!

   Flam. Pander! am I the author of your sin?
   Vit. Cor. Yes; he's a base thief that a thief lets in.
   Flam. We're blown up,[38] my lord.
   Brach.   Wilt thou hear me?
Once to be jealous of thee, is to express
That I will love thee everlastingly,
And never more be jealous.
   Vit. Cor.   O thou fool,
Whose greatness hath by much o'ergrown thy wit!
What dar'st thou do that I not dare to suffer,   141
Excepting to be still thy whore? For that,
In the sea's bottom sooner thou shalt make
A bonfire.
   Flam. Oh, no oaths, for God's sake!
   Brach. Will you hear me?
   Vit. Cor.   Never.
   Flam. What a damned imposthume[39] is a woman's
   will!
Can nothing break it?—Fie, fie, my lord,
[*Aside to* BRACHIANO] Women are caught as you
   take tortoises,
She must be turned on her back.—[*Aloud*] Sister, by
   this hand,
I am on your side.—Come, come, you have wronged
   her.   150
What a strange credulous man were you, my lord,
To think the Duke of Florence would love her!
[*Aside*] Will any mercer[40] take another's ware
When once 'tis toused and sullied?—[*Aloud*] And yet,
   sister,
How scurvily this frowardness[41] becomes you!
[*Aside*] Young leverets[42] stand[43] not long; and
   women's anger
Should, like their flight, procure a little sport;
A full cry[44] for a quarter of an hour,
And then be put to the dead quat.[45]
   Brach.   Shall these eyes,
Which have so long time dwelt upon your face,   160
Be now put out?
   Flam.   No cruel landlady i' the world,
Which lends forth groats to broom-men,[46] and takes
   use[47] for them,
Would do't.
Hand her, my lord, and kiss her. Be not like

---

[30] *Woman . . . wolf:* Webster redacting a commonplace
familiar from contemporary emblem books and deriving
ultimately from Plautus—"Homo homini lupus" ("Man is
a wolf to man").   [31] *quicksilver:* proverbially unstable.
[32] *Ill-scenting foxes:* whose foul smell was thought to cure
palsy and paralysis.   [33] *choicer:* more fastidious.
[34] *incontinent:* unchaste.
[35] *drunk Lethe:* been forgetful.   [36] *poniards:* daggers.
[37] *Turn:* with a sexual innuendo, appropriate to the
pander.   [38] *blown up:* as by a mine.
[39] *imposthume:* abscess.
[40] *mercer:* dealer in fabrics (resuming the metaphor of
"changeable stuff").   [41] *frowardness:* untoward behavior.
[42] *leverets:* hares; mistresses.
[43] *stand:* technically, "stand up" like a hare; in context,
"hold out."   [44] *cry:* as in hunting.
[45] *quat:* squat, seat of the hare; but also resuming, perhaps
unconsciously, the ugly image of the imposthume—a "quat"
is a "boil."   [46] *broom-men:* street sweepers.
[47] *use:* interest.

A ferret,[48] to let go your hold with blowing.
  Brach. Let us renew right hands.
  Vit. Cor.   Hence!
  Brach. Never shall rage of the forgetful[49] wine
Make me commit like fault.
  Flam. [*Aside*] Now you are i' the way on't, follow't
    hard,
  Brach. Be thou at peace with me, let all the world
Threaten the cannon.
  Flam.   Mark his penitence.   171
Best natures do commit the grossest faults,
When they're given o'er to jealousy, as best wine,
Dying, makes stronger vinegar. I'll tell you,
The sea's more rough and raging than calm rivers,
But not so sweet nor wholesome. A quiet woman
Is a still water under a great bridge;
A man may shoot[50] her safely.
  Vit. Cor. O ye dissembling men!
  Flam.   We sucked that, sister,
From women's breasts, in our first infancy.   180
  Vit. Cor. To add misery to misery!
  Brach.   Sweetest.—
  Vit. Cor. Am I not low enough?
Ay, ay, your good heart gathers like a snowball,
Now your affection's cold.
  Flam.   Ud's foot, it shall melt
To a heart again, or all the wine in Rome
Shall run o' the lees[51] for't.
  Vit. Cor. Your dog or hawk should be rewarded[52]
    better
Than I have been. I'll speak not one word more.
  Flam. Stop her mouth with a sweet kiss, my lord. So,
Now the tide's turned, the vessel's come about.   190
He's a sweet armful. Oh, we curled-haired men
Are still most kind to women! This is well.
  Brach. That you should chide thus!
  Flam.   Oh, sir, your
    little chimneys
Do ever cast most smoke! I sweat for you.
Couple together with as deep a silence
As did the Grecians in their wooden horse.
My lord, supply your promises with deeds;
You know that painted meat no hunger feeds.
  Brach. Stay—ingrateful Rome!
  Flam. Rome! It deserves to be called Barbary   200
For our villainous usage.

Brach. Soft! The same project which the Duke of
    Florence
(Whether in love or gullery I know not)
Laid down for her escape, will I pursue.
  Flam. And no time fitter than this night, my lord:
The Pope being dead, and all the cardinals entered
The conclave for the electing a new Pope;
The city in a great confusion;
We may attire her in a page's suit,
Lay her post-horse,[53] take shipping, and amain   210
For Padua.
  Brach. I'll instantly steal forth the Prince Giovanni,
And make for Padua. You two with your old mother,
And young Marcello that attends on Florence,
If you can work him to it, follow me:
I will advance you all.—For you, Vittoria,
Think of a duchess' title.
  Flam.   Lo you, sister!
Stay, my lord; I'll tell you a tale.[54] The crocodile,
which lives in the river Nilus, hath a worm breeds i' the
teeth of't, which puts it to extreme anguish. A   220
little bird, no bigger than a wren, is barber-surgeon to
this crocodile; flies into the jaws of't, picks out the
worm, and brings present remedy. The fish, glad of
ease, but ingrateful to her that did it, that the bird may
not talk largely of her abroad for nonpayment, closeth
her chaps, intending to swallow her, and so put her to
perpetual silence. But nature, loathing such ingratitude, hath armed this bird with a quill or prick on the
head, the top o' which wounds the crocodile i' the
mouth, forceth her open her bloody prison, and away
flies the pretty tooth-picker from her cruel patient. 231
  Brach. Your application is, I have not rewarded
The service you have done me.
  Flam.   No, my lord.
You, sister, are the crocodile. You are blemished in your
fame, my lord cures it; and though the comparison
hold not in every particle, yet observe, remember what
good the bird with the prick[55] i' the head hath done
you, and scorn ingratitude.
[*Aside*] It may appear to some ridiculous
Thus to talk knave and madman, and sometimes   240
Come in with a dried sentence, stuffed with sage.
But this allows my varying of shapes;
Knaves do grow great by being great men's apes.[56]
                             Exeunt.

---

[48] *ferret:* In popular superstition, the tenacious grip of
the polecat was thought to be loosened by blowing.
[49] *forgetful:* causing forgetfulness.
[50] *shoot:* pass over; with an obvious sexual *entendre.*
[51] *o' the lees:* to the bottom of the cask.
[52] *rewarded:* as with a part of the prey (technical term
from hunting and hawking).
[53] *Lay . . . horse:* Furnish her with a relay of post-horses.
[54] *tale:* familiar from Herodotus and Pliny, and symbo-
lizing in contemporary emblem books the ingratitude of
great men to their servants. Flamineo is the ministering
bird; Brachiano, despite Flamineo's disclaimer, is evidently
the crocodile.
[55] *prick:* punning also on the sexual sense.
[56] *apes:* imitators.

IV.iii.
  [1] *brave:* splendid.   [2] *several:* different.

[IV.iii]

Enter LODOVICO, GASPARO, *and six* Ambassadors.
At another door[FRANCISCO,] *the Duke of Florence.*

  Fran. So, my lord, I commend your diligence.
Guard well the conclave; and, as the order is,
Let none have conference with the cardinals.
  Lod. I shall, my lord.—Room for the ambassadors!
  Gasp. They're wondrous brave[1] today. Why do they
    wear
These several[2] habits?
  Lod.   Oh, sir, they are knights
Of several orders.

That lord i' the black cloak, with the silver cross,
Is Knight of Rhodes; the next, Knight of St. Michael;
That, of the Golden Fleece; the Frenchman there   10
Knight of the Holy Ghost; my lord of Savoy,
Knight of the Annunciation; the Englishman
Is Knight of the honored Garter, dedicated
Unto their saint, St. George. I could describe to you
Their several institutions, with the laws
Annexèd to their orders; but that time
Permits not such discovery.
    Fran.   Where's Count Lodowick?
    Lod. Here, my lord.
    Fran.   'Tis o' the point of dinner time:
Marshal the cardinals' service.
    Lod.   Sir, I shall.

    Enter Servants, *with several dishes covered.*

Stand, let me search your dish. Who's this for?   20
    Serv. For my lord Cardinal Monticelso.
    Lod. Whose this?
    Serv.   For my lord Cardinal of Bourbon.
    Fr. Amb. Why doth he search the dishes? To
    observe
What meat is dressed?
    Eng. Amb.   No, sir, but to prevent
Lest any letters should be cònveyed in,
To bribe or to solicit the advancement
Of any cardinal. When first they enter,
'Tis lawful for the ambassadors of princes
To enter with them, and to make their suit
For any man their prince affecteth best;   30
But after, till a general election,
No man may speak with them.
    Lod. You that attend on the lord cardinals,
Open the window, and receive their viands!

    [*A* Conclavist *appears at the window.*]

A Con. You must return the service. The lord
    cardinals
Are busied 'bout electing of the Pope;
They have given over scrutiny,[3] and are fallen
To admiration.[4]
                         [*Exit.*]
    Lod.   Away, away!
    Fran. I'll lay a thousand ducats you hear news
Of a Pope presently. Hark! sure, he's elected.   40

    A Cardinal [*appears*] *on the terrace.*

Behold, my lord of Arragon appears
On the church-battlements.
    *Arr. Denuntio vobis gaudium magnum. Reverendissi-
mus cardinalis Lorenzo de Monticelso electus est in sedem
apostolicam, et elegit sibi nomen Paulum Quartum.*
    Omnes. Vivat sanctus pater Paulus Quartus![5]

    [*Enter* Servant.]

    Serv. Vittoria, my lord—
    Fran.   Well, what of her?
    Serv. Is fled the city—
    Fran.   Ha!
    Serv.   With Duke Brachiano.

    Fran. Fled! Where's the Prince Giovanni?
    Serv.   Gone
    with his father.
    Fran. Let the matrona of the convertites   50
Be apprehended.—Fled! Oh, damnable!
                         [*Exit* Servant.]
How fortunate are my wishes! why, 'twas this
I only labored; I did send the letter
To instruct him what to do. Thy fame, fond[6] duke,
I first have poisoned, directed thee the way
To marry a whore; what can be worse? This follows—
The hand must act to drown the passionate tongue.
I scorn to wear a sword and prate of wrong.

    Enter MONTICELSO *in state.*

    *Mont. Concedimus vobis apostolicam benedictionem et
remissionem peccatorum.*[7]   60

    [FRANCISCO *whispers to him.*]

My lord reports Vittoria Corombona
Is stolen from forth the house of convertites
By Brachiano, and they're fled the city.
Now, though this be the first day of our state,
We cannot better please the divine power
Than to sequester from the holy church
These cursèd persons. Make it therefore known,
We do denounce excommunication
Against them both. All that are theirs in Rome
We likewise banish. Set on.   70
                            Exeunt.
    Fran. Come, dear Lodovico;
You have ta'en the sacrament to prosecute
The intended murder.
    Lod.   With all constancy.
But, sir, I wonder you'll engage yourself
In person, being a great prince.
    Fran.   Divert me not.
Most of his court are of my faction,
And some are of my council. Noble friend,
Our danger shall be like in this design;
Give leave, part of the glory may be mine.
                        Exit FRANCISCO.

    Enter MONTICELSO.

    Mont. Why did the Duke of Florence with such
    care   80
Labor your pardon? Say.
    Lod. Italian beggars will resolve you that,
Who, begging of an alms, bid those they beg of,
Do good for their own sakes; or it may be,

---

    [3] *scrutiny:* counting secret ballots.
    [4] *admiration:* Webster's error for "adoration," denoting
the making reverence by two-thirds of the cardinals to the
newly elected Pope.
    [5] *L.:* "I announce to you (tidings) of great joy. The
Most Reverend Cardinal Lorenzo de Monticelso has been
elected to the Apostolic Seat, and has chosen for himself the
name of Paul the Fourth." All (say): "Long live the Holy
Father, Paul the Fourth."   [6] *fond:* foolish.
    [7] *L.:* "We grant to you the Apostolic benediction and
remission of sins."

He spreads his bounty with a sowing hand,[8]
Like kings, who many times give out of measure,
Not for desert so much as for their pleasure.
    Mont. I know you're cunning. Come, what devil was
      that
That you were raising?
    Lod.   Devil, my lord!
    Mont.   I ask you
How doth the duke employ you, that this bonnet   90
Fell with such compliment unto his knee,
When he departed from you?
    Lod.   Why, my lord,
He told me of a resty[9] Barbary horse
Which he would fain have brought to the career,
The sault, and the ring-galliard;[10] now, my lord,
I have a rare French[11] rider.
    Mont.   Take you heed
Lest the jade break your neck. Do you put me off
With your wild horse-tricks? Sirrah, you do lie.
Oh, thou'rt a foul black cloud, and thou dost threat
A violent storm!
    Lod.   Storms are i' the air, my lord: 100
I am too low to storm.
    Mont.   Wretched creature!
I know that thou art fashioned for all ill,
Like dogs that once get blood, they'll ever kill.
About some murder? Was't not?
    Lod.   I'll not tell you.
And yet I care not greatly if I do,
Marry,[12] with this preparation. Holy father,
I come not to you as an intelligencer,
But as a penitent sinner. What I utter
Is in confession merely, which you know
Must never be revealed.
    Mont.   You have o'erta'en[13] me.   110
    Lod. Sir, I did love Brachiano's duchess dearly,
Or rather I pursued her with hot lust,
Though she ne'er knew on't. She was poisoned;
Upon my soul, she was; for which I have sworn
To avenge her murder.
    Mont.   To the Duke of Florence?
    Lod. To him I have.
    Mont.   Miserable creature!
If thou persist in this, 'tis damnable.

Dost thou imagine thou canst slide on blood,
And not be tainted with a shameful fall?
Or, like the black and melancholic yew-tree,   120
Dost think to root thyself in dead men's graves,
And yet to prosper? Instruction to thee
Comes like sweet showers to over-hardened ground;
They wet, but pierce not deep. And so I leave thee,
With all the Furies[14] hanging 'bout thy neck,
Till by thy penitence thou remove this evil,
In conjuring from thy breast that cruel devil.
                     Exit MONTICELSO.
    Lod. I'll give it o'er; he says 'tis damnable,
Besides I did expect his suffrage,[15]
By reason of Camillo's death.   130

    Enter Servant *and* FRANCISCO [DE MEDICIS].

    Fran. Do you know that count?
    Serv.   Yes, my lord.
    Fran. Bear him these thousand ducats to his
      lodging;
Tell him the Pope hath sent them. [*Aside*] Happily[16]
That will confirm more than all the rest.
                              [*Exit.*]
    Serv. Sir—
    Lod. To me, sir?
    Serv. His holiness hath sent you a thousand crowns,
And wills you, if you travel, to make him
Your patron for intelligence.
    Lod. His creature ever to be commanded.   140
                          [*Exit* Servant.]
Why, now 'tis come about. He railed upon me;
And yet these crowns were told out[17] and laid ready
Before he knew my voyage. O the art,
The modest form of greatness! that do sit,
Like brides at wedding-dinners, with their looks turned
From the least wanton jest, their puling stomach
Sick of the modesty, when their thoughts are loose,
Even acting of those hot and lustful sports
Are to ensue about midnight: such his cunning.
He sounds my depth thus with a golden plummet.   150
I am doubly armed now. Now to the act of blood.
There's but three Furies found in spacious hell,
But in a great man's breast three thousand dwell.
                             [*Exit.*]

---

   [8] *Italian . . . hand:* Adapted from Montaigne, *Essays,*
III, 5–6.   [9] *resty:* restive.
   [10] *career . . . sault . . . ring-galliard:* technical terms describing the "manage" of horses—to "career" is to run the
horse at full speed and bring it to an abrupt stop; "sault"
denotes leaping or jumping; and the "ring-galliard" a
mixture of bounding forward, curvetting (raising the forelegs together and springing up with the hind legs before the
forelegs touch ground), and yerking (or flinging out the
heels).
   [11] *French:* proverbially excellent in horsemanship.
   [12] *Marry:* To be sure ("By the Virgin Mary").
   [13] *o'erta'en:* got the better of.
   [14] *furies:* Tisiphone, Megaera, and Alecto, the avenging
goddesses.   [15] *suffrage:* approval.
   [16] *Happily:* Perchance.   [17] *told out:* counted.

V.i.
   [1] *closet:* private quarters, "study."

ACT FIVE

SCENE ONE

A passage over the stage of BRACHIANO, FLAMINEO,
MARCELLO, HORTENSIO, [VITTORIA] COROM-
BONA, CORNELIA, ZANCHE, *and others.*
[FLAMINEO *and* HORTENSIO *remain on stage.*]

    Flam. In all the weary minutes of my life,
Day ne'er broke up till now. This marriage
Confirms me happy.
    Hort.   'Tis a good assurance.
Saw you not yet the Moor that's come to court?
    Flam. Yes, and conferred with him i' the duke's
      closet.[1]

I have not seen a goodlier personage,
Nor ever talked with man better experienced
In state affairs or rudiments[2] of war.
He hath, by report, served the Venetian
In Candy these twice seven years, and been chief   10
In many a bold design.
    Hort.   What are those two
That bear him company?
    Flam. Two noblemen of Hungary, that, living in the
emperor's service as commanders, eight years since,
contrary to the expectation of all the court, entered into
religion, into the strict order of Capuchins.[3] But, being
not well settled in their undertaking, they left their
order, and returned to court; for which, being after
troubled in conscience, they vowed their service against
the enemies of Christ, went to Malta, were there   20
knighted, and in their return back, at this great solemnity, they are resolved forever to forsake the world and
settle themselves here in a house of Capuchins in
Padua.
    Hort. 'Tis strange.
    Flam. One thing makes it so: they have vowed for-
ever to wear, next their bare bodies, those coats of mail
they served in.
    Hort. Hard penance! Is the Moor a Christian?
    Flam.   He is.
    Hort. Why proffers he his service to our duke?   30
    Flam. Because he understands there's like to grow
Some wars between us and the Duke of Florence,
In which he hopes employment.
I never saw one in a stern bold look
Wear more command, nor in a lofty phrase
Express more knowing or more deep contempt
Of our slight airy courtiers. He talks
As if he had traveled all the princes' courts
Of Christendom: in all things strives to express,
That all that should dispute with him may know,   40
Glories, like glow-worms,[4] afar off shine bright,
But looked to near, have neither heat nor light.—
The duke!

Enter BRACHIANO, [FRANCISCO DE MEDICIS,
the Duke of] *Florence disguised like* MULINASSAR,
  LODOVICO, ANTONELLI, GASPARO, [*and a*]
    Farnese, *bearing their swords and helmets.*

    Brach. You are nobly welcome. We have heard at
    full
Your honorable service 'gainst the Turk.
To you, brave Mulinassar, we assign
A competent pension, and are inly[5] sorry
The vows of those two worthy gentlemen
Make them incapable of our proffered bounty.
Your wish is, you may leave your warlike swords   50
For monuments in our chapel. I accept it
As a great honor done me, and must crave
Your leave to furnish[6] out our duchess' revels.
Only one thing, as the last vanity.
You e'er shall view, deny me not to stay
To see a barriers prepared tonight.
You shall have private standings.[7] It hath pleased
The great ambassadors of several princes,

In their return from Rome to their own countries,
To grace our marriage, and to honor me   60
With such a kind of sport.
    Fran.   I shall persuade them
To stay, my lord.
    Brach.   Set on there to the presence![8]
                Exeunt BRACHIANO, FLAMINEO,
            [HORTENSIO], *and* MARCELLO.
[*Lod.*] Noble my lord, most fortunately welcome:

        The Conspirators *here embrace.*

You have our vows, sealed with the sacrament,
To second your attempts.
    [*Gasp.*]   And all things ready.
He could not have invented his own ruin,
Had he despaired, with more propriety.
    Lod. You would not take my way.
    Fran.   'Tis better ordered.
    Lod. To have poisoned his prayer-book, or a pair[9]
    of beads,
The pummel of his saddle,[10] his looking-glass,   70
Or the handle of his racket—Oh, that, that!
That while he had been bandying at tennis,
He might have sworn himself to hell, and strook
His soul into the hazard![11] Oh, my lord,
I would have our plot be ingenious,
And have it hereafter recorded for example,
Rather than borrow example.
    Fran.   There's no way
More speeding than this thought on.
    Lod.   On, then.
    Fran. And yet methinks that this revenge is poor,
Because it steals upon him like a thief.   80
To have ta'en him by the casque in a pitched field,[12]
Led him to Florence!
    Lod.   It had been rare—and there
Have crowned him with a wreath of stinking garlic,
To have shown the sharpness[13] of his government
And rankness of his lust.—Flamineo comes.
            Exeunt [*all except* FRANCESCO].

Enter FLAMINEO, MARCELLO, *and* ZANCHE.

    Mar. Why doth this devil[14] haunt you, say?
    Flam.   I know
    not;
For, by this light, I do not conjure for her.

---

    [2] *rudiments:* principles.
    [3] *Capuchins:* sixteenth-century offshoot of the Franciscan
order and dedicated to the old-fashioned austerity.
    [4] *glow-worms:* used commonly in a pejorative or slighting
sense.   [5] *inly:* deeply.   [6] *to furnish:* while I furnish.
    [7] *standings:* accommodations.
    [8] *presence:* royal presence-chamber.
    [9] *pair:* any number; "rosary beads."
    [10] *pummel . . . saddle:* anointed with poison intended for
the Queen in a celebrated case of 1598.
    [11] *hazard:* fatal chance; also alluding to openings in the
wall of the tennis court into which the ball is struck to gain a
point. Here the "gain" is Brachiano's damnation.
    [12] *casque . . . field:* helmet on a field of battle.
    [13] *sharpness:* as of the smell of garlic; also, "severity."
    [14] *devil:* Zanche (since the devil is proverbially black).

'Tis not so great a cunning as men think
To raise the devil; for here's one up already.
The greatest cunning were to lay him down.[15]   90

Mar. She is your shame.

Flam.   I prithee, pardon her.
In faith, you see, women are like to burrs;
Where their affection throws them, there they'll stick.

Zan. That is my countryman, a goodly person.
When he's at leisure, I'll discourse with him
In our own language.

Flam.   I beseech you do.

                         Exit ZANCHE.

How is't, brave soldier? Oh, that I had seen
Some of your iron days! I pray, relate
Some of your service to us.   99

Fran. 'Tis a ridiculous thing for a man to be his own
chronicle! I did never wash my mouth with mine own
praise for fear of getting a stinking breath.

Mar. You're too stoical. The Duke will expect other
discourse from you.

Fran. I shall never flatter him. I have studied man
too much to do that. What difference is between the
duke and I? No more than between two bricks, all
made of one clay; only 't may be one is placed on the
top of a turret, the other in the bottom of a well, by
mere chance. If I were placed as high as the   110
duke, I should stick as fast, make as fair a show, and
bear out weather equally.

Flam. If this soldier had a patent[16] to beg in
churches, then he would tell them stories.[17]

Mar. I have been a soldier too.

Fran. How have you thrived?

Mar. Faith, poorly.

Fran. That's the misery of peace; only outsides are
then respected. As ships seem very great upon the river,
which show very little upon the seas, so some   120
men i' the court seem colossuses in a chamber, who, if
they came into the field, would appear pitiful. Pigmies!

Flam. Give me a fair room yet hung with arras,[18]
and some great cardinal to lug me by the ears as his
endeared minion.

Fran. And thou mayst do the devil knows what
villainy.

Flam. And safely.

Fran. Right! You shall see in the country, in harvest-

time, pigeons,[19] though they destroy never so   130
much corn, the farmer dare not present the fowling-
piece[20] to them. Why? Because they belong to the lord
of the manor; whilst your poor sparrows, that belong
to the Lord of Heaven, they go to the pot for't.

Flam. I will now give you some politic instructions.
The duke says he will give you a pension. That's but
bare promise; get it under his hand.[21] For I have
known men that have come from serving against the
Turk, for three or four months they have had pension
to buy them new wooden legs and fresh   140
plasters; but, after, 'twas not to be had. And this
miserable courtesy shows as if a tormentor should give
hot cordial drinks to one three quarters dead o' the
rack, only to fetch the miserable soul again to endure
more dog-days.

                [*Exit* FRANCISCO DE MEDICIS.]

       Enter HORTENSIO, *a* Young Lord, ZANCHE,
              and two more.

How now, gallants! what, are they ready for the
barriers?

Y. Lord. Yes; the lords are putting on their armor.

Hort. What's he?   149

Flam. A new upstart; one that swears like a falconer,
and will lie in the duke's ear day by day, like a
maker of almanacs.[22] And yet I knew him, since he
came to the court, smell worse of sweat than an under-
tennis-court-keeper.

Hort. Look you, yonder's your sweet mistress.

Flam. Thou art my sworn brother. I'll tell thee, I do
love that Moor, that witch, very constrainedly. She
knows some of my villainy. I do love her just as a man
holds a wolf by the ears;[23] but for fear of turning upon
me and pulling out my throat, I would let her go to the
devil.   161

Hort. I hear she claims marriage of thee.

Flam. Faith, I made to her some such dark promise;
and, in seeking to fly from't, I run on, like a frighted
dog with a bottle at's tail, that fain would bite it off, and
yet dares not look behind him.—Now, my precious
gipsy.[24]

Zan. Ay, your love to me rather cools than heats.

Flam. Marry, I am the sounder lover. We have
many wenches about the town heat too fast.   170

Hort. What do you think of these perfumed gallants,
then?

Flam. Their satin cannot save them. I am confident
They have a certain spice of the disease;
For they that sleep with dogs shall rise with fleas.

Zan. Believe it, a little painting and gay clothes
make you loathe me.[25]

Flam. How! love a lady for painting or gay apparel?
I'll unkennel one example more for thee. Aesop had
a foolish dog that let go the flesh to catch the shadow.[26] I would have courtiers be better diners.   181

Zan. You remember your oaths?

Flam. Lovers' oaths are like mariners' prayers,
uttered in extremity; but when the tempest is o'er, and
that the vessel leaves tumbling,[27] they fall from protesting to drinking. And yet, amongst gentlemen,

---

[15] *To ... down:* punning on tumescence.

[16] *patent:* license, which beggars had to be granted on
pain of whipping.

[17] *tell ... stories:* brag about his exploits.

[18] *arras:* for concealment.

[19] *pigeons:* proverbially a plague, like locusts.

[20] *fowling-piece:* gun for shooting birds.

[21] *under his hand:* in writing.

[22] *maker of almanacs:* lying prognosticator.

[23] *as ... ears:* i.e., unable for fear to let go, as if one had a
tiger by the tail.

[24] *gipsy:* pejorative; and alluding to Zanche's dark skin.

[25] *Believe ... me:* Stuff! You are easily seduced from me
by other women got up with cosmetics and finery.

[26] *Aesop ... shadow:* another commonplace from contemporary emblem books: Flamineo is not going to prefer
shadow to substance.

[27] *tumbling:* with a pun on sexual intercourse.

protesting and drinking go together, and agree as well
as shoemakers and Westphalia bacon.[28] They are both
drawers on; for drink draws on protestation, and protestation draws on more drink. Is not this dis-   190
course better now than the morality[29] of your sunburnt
gentleman?

Enter CORNELIA.

Cor. Is this your perch, you haggard?[30] Fly to the
stews.[31]

[*Striking* ZANCHE.]

Flam. You should be clapped[32] by the heels now:
strike i' the court![33]

[*Exit* CORNELIA.]

Zan. She's good for nothing but to make her maids
Catch cold a-nights: they dare not use a bed-staff[34]
For fear of her light[35] fingers.

Mar.   You're a strumpet,
An impudent one.

[*Kicking* ZANCHE.]

Flam.   Why do you kick her, say?
Do you think that she is like a walnut tree?[36]
Must she be cudgeled ere she bear good fruit?   200
Mar. She brags that you shall marry her.
Flam.   What then?
Mar. I had rather she were pitched upon a stake
In some new-seeded garden, to affright
Her fellow crows thence.
Flam.   You're a boy, a fool.
Be guardian to your hound; I am of age.
Mar. If I take her near you, I'll cut her throat.
Flam. With a fan of feathers?
Mar.   And, for you, I'll whip
This folly from you.
Flam.   Are you choleric?
I'll purge't with rhubarb.[37]
Hort.   Oh, your brother!
Flam.   Hang him,
He wrongs me most that ought to offend me least.   210
I do suspect my mother played foul play
When she conceived thee.
Mar.   Now, by all my hopes,
Like the two slaughtered sons of Oedipus,
The very flames of our affection,
Shall turn two ways.[38] Those words I'll make thee
     answer
With thy heart-blood.
Flam.   Do, like the geese in the
     progress.[39]
You know where you shall find me.
Mar.   Very good.

[*Exit* FLAMINEO.]

And[40] thou be'st a noble friend, bear him my sword,
And bid him fit the length on't.
Y. Lord.   Sir, I shall.

[*Exeunt* Young Lord, MARCELLO,
HORTENSIO, *and the two others.*]

Zan. He comes. Hence petty thought of my
     disgrace!   220

Enter FRANCISCO [DE MEDICIS], *the Duke of
Florence* [disguised].

I ne'er loved my complexion[41] till now,
'Cause I may boldly say, without a blush,
I love you.
Fran. Your love is untimely sown; there's a spring
at Michaelmas,[42] but 'tis but a faint one. I am sunk in
years, and I have vowed never to marry.
Zan. Alas! poor maids get more lovers than hus-
bands; yet you may mistake my wealth. For, as when
ambassadors are sent to congratulate princes, there's
commonly sent along with them a rich present, so   230
that, though the prince like not the ambassador's per-
son nor words, yet he likes well of the presentment; so
I may come to you in the same manner, and be better
loved for my dowry than my virtue.
Fran. I'll think on the motion.
Zan.   Do. I'll now
Detain you no longer. At your better leisure
I'll tell you things shall startle your blood.
Nor blame me that this passion I reveal;
Lovers die inward that their flames conceal.   239
Fran. Of all intelligence this may prove the best.
Sure, I shall draw strange fowl from this foul nest.

Exeunt.

[V.ii]

Enter MARCELLO *and* CORNELIA.

Cor. I hear a whispering all about the court
You are to fight. Who is your opposite?[1]
What is the quarrel?
Mar.   'Tis an idle rumor.
Cor. Will you dissemble? Sure, you do not well
To fright me thus. You never look thus pale

---

[28] *shoemakers . . . bacon:* The former draw shoes onto feet;
the latter, being salty, draws men on to drinking.

[29] *morality:* for Q's "mortality."

[30] *haggard:* wild bird; hence, loose woman.

[31] *stews:* brothels.   [32] *clapped:* fettered.

[33] *strike i' the court:* a heinous offense and severely
punished.

[34] *bed-staff:* laid horizontally across the frame to hold up
the bedding; but punning presumably on "penis."

[35] *light:* quick to strike.

[36] *walnut tree:* supposed to bear the better for being
beaten.   [37] *rhubarb:* prescribed for choler or anger.

[38] *Like . . . ways:* Eteocles and Polynices, the sons of
Oedipus, died fighting each other for their father's throne.
Their bodies were burned but the flames, in token of their
hatred, did not mingle.

[39] *geese in the progress:* presumably a proverbial saying,
the meaning of which has been lost. But cf. Kent's scornful
words to Oswald in *King Lear,* II. ii. 89–90: "Goose, if I
had you upon Sarum plain, I'd drive ye cackling home to
Camelot."   [40] *And:* If.

[41] *complexion:* pronounced as four syllables.

[42] *Michaelmas:* St. Martin's Summer, fair days recurring
briefly as winter prepares.

V.ii.

[1] *opposite:* opponent.

But when you are most angry. I do charge you
Upon my blessing—nay, I'll call the duke,
And he shall school you.
    Mar.   Publish not a fear.
Which would convert to laughter; 'tis not so.
Was not this crucifix² my father's?
    Cor.   Yes.   10
    Mar. I have heard you say, giving my brother suck,
He took the crucifix between his hands,

            Enter FLAMINEO.

And broke a limb off.
    Cor.   Yes; but 'tis mended.
    Flam. I have brought your weapon back.

    FLAMINEO *runs* MARCELLO *through.*

    Cor. Ha! O my horror!
    Mar. You have brought it home, indeed.
    Cor. Help, O, he's murdered!
    Flam. Do you turn your gall up?³ I'll to sanctuary,
And send a surgeon to you.
                         [Exit.]

     Enter [LODOVICO], HORTENSIO,
          [GASPARO].

    Hort.   How! o' the ground!
    Mar. O mother, now remember what I told   20
Of breaking of the crucifix! Farewell.
There are some sins which Heaven doth duly punish
In a whole family. This it is to rise
By all dishonest means! Let all men know,
That tree shall long time keep a steady foot
Whose branches spread no wider⁴ than the root.
                         [Dies.]
    Cor. O my perpetual sorrow!
    Hort.   Virtuous Marcello!
He's dead.—Pray, leave him, lady. Come, you shall.
    Cor. Alas, he is not dead; he's in a trance.
Why, here's nobody shall get any thing by his
    death.   30
Let me call him again, for God's sake!
    [Lod.] I would you were deceived.
    Cor. Oh, you abuse me, you abuse me, you abuse me!
How many have gone away thus, for lack of tendance!
Rear up's head, rear up's head; his bleeding inward
will kill him.
    Hort. You see he is departed.
    Cor. Let me come to him; give me him as he is. If
he be turned to earth, let me but give him one hearty
kiss, and you shall put us both into one coffin.   40
Fetch a looking glass; see if his breath will not stain it;
or pull out some feathers from his pillow, and lay them
to his lips. Will you lose him for a little painstaking?
    Hort. Your kindest office is to pray for him.

---

   ² *crucifix:* which Cornelia wears about her neck.
   ³ *turn . . . up:* figuratively, "die."
   ⁴ *wider:* Q "wilder."
   ⁵ *beaver:* face guard (here worn up) of the helmet.
   ⁶ *grazed:* lost (literally, "fallen in the grass").
   ⁷ *that:* that which.

    Cor. Alas, I would not pray for him yet. He may live
to lay me i' the ground, and pray for me, if you'll let me
come to him.

    Enter BRACHIANO *all armed save the beaver,*⁵ *with*
    FLAMINEO, [FRANCISCO DE MEDICIS *disguised,*
               and Page].

    Brach. Was this your handiwork?
    Flam.   It was my misfortune.
    Cor. He lies, he lies; he did not kill him. These have
killed him that would not let him be better looked to.
    Brach. Have comfort, my grieved mother.
    Cor.   O you
    screech-owl!   51
    Hort. Forbear, good madam.
    Cor.   Let me go, let me go.

    She runs to FLAMINEO *with her knife drawn and,*
                 coming to him, lets it fall.

The God of heaven forgive thee! Dost not wonder
I pray for thee? I'll tell thee what's the reason:
I have scarce breath to number twenty minutes;
I'd not spend that in cursing. Fare thee well.
Half of thyself lies there; and mayst thou live
To fill an hour-glass with his moldered ashes,
To tell how thou shouldst spend the time to come
In blessed repentance!
    Brach.   Mother, pray tell me   60
How came he by his death? What was the quarrel?
    Cor. Indeed, my younger boy presumed too much
Upon his manhood, gave him bitter words,
Drew his sword first; and so, I know not how,
For I was out of my wits, he fell with's head
Just in my bosom.
    Page.   This is not true, madam.
    Cor. I pray thee, peace.
One arrow's grazed⁶ already; it were vain
To lose this for that⁷ will ne'er be found again.
    Brach. Go bear the body to Cornelia's lodging;   70
And we command that none acquaint our duchess
With this sad accident. For you, Flamineo,
Hark you, I will not grant your pardon.
    Flam.   No?
    Brach. Only a lease of your life; and that shall
    last
But for one day. Thou shalt be forced each evening
To renew it, or be hanged.
    Flam.   At your pleasure.

    LODOVICO *sprinkles* BRACHIANO'S *beaver with a*
                  poison.

Your will is law now; I'll not meddle with it.
    Brach. You once did brave me in your sister's
    lodging;
I'll now keep you in awe for't.—Where's our beaver?
    Fran. [*Aside*] He calls for his destruction. Noble
    youth,   80
I pity thy sad fate! Now to the barriers.
This shall his passage to the black lake further;
The last good deed he did, he pardoned murder.
                          Exeunt.

[V.iii]

Charges and shouts. They fight at barriers; first single
pairs, then three to three.
Enter BRACHIANO *and* FLAMINEO, *with others*
[*among them* VITTORIA COROMBONA, GIOVANNI,
FRANCISCO DE MEDICIS *disguised*].

Brach. An armorer! ud's death, an armorer!
Flam. Armorer! where's the armorer?
Brach.   Tear off my
beaver.
Flam. Are you hurt, my lord?
Brach.   Oh, my brain's on fire!

Enter Armorer.

The helmet is poisoned.
Armorer.   My lord, upon my soul—
Brach. Away with him to torture!
                                [*Exit* Armorer, *guarded.*]
There are some great ones that have hand in this,
And near about me.
Vit. Cor.   O my loved lord! poisoned!
Flam. Remove the bar.[1] Here's unfortunate revels!
Call the physicians.

Enter two Physicians.

A plague upon you!
We have too much of your cunning here already: 10
I fear the ambassadors are likewise poisoned.
Brach. Oh, I am gone already! the infection
Flies to the brain and heart. O thou strong heart!
There's such a covenant 'tween the world and it,
They're loath to break.
Giov.   O my most lovèd father!
Brach. Remove the boy away.
Where's this good woman?—Had I infinite worlds,
They were too little for thee. Must I leave thee?—
What say yon screech-owls,[2] is the venom mortal?
1 Phys. Most deadly.
Brach.   Most corrupted politic
hangman,   20
You kill without book;[3] but your art to save
Fails you as oft as great men's needy friends.
I that have given life to offending slaves
And wretched murderers, have I not power
To lengthen mine own a twelvemonth?—
Do not kiss me, for I shall poison thee.
This unction's sent from the great Duke of Florence.
Fran. Sir, be of comfort.
Brach. O thou soft natural death, that art joint-twin
To sweetest slumber! no rough-bearded[4] comet   30
Stares on thy mild departure; the dull owl
Beats not against thy casement; the hoarse wolf
Scents not thy carrion: pity winds thy corse,
Whilst horror waits on princes.
Vit. Cor.   I am lost for ever.
Brach. How miserable a thing it is to die
'Mongst women howling!

[*Enter* LODOVICO *and* GASPARO, *in the habit of*
Capuchins.]

                                What are those?
Flam.   Franciscans.
They have brought the extreme unction.[5]
Brach. On pain of death, let no man name death to
me.
It is a word infinitely terrible.
Withdraw into our cabinet.   40
        Exeunt but FRANCISCO [DE MEDICIS]
                                and FLAMINEO.
Flam. To see what solitariness is about dying
princes! As heretofore they have unpeopled towns,
divorced friends, and made great houses unhospitable,
so now, O justice! Where are their flatterers now?
Flatterers are but the shadows of princes' bodies; the
least thick cloud makes them invisible.
Fran. There's great moan made for him.
Flam. Faith, for some few hours salt-water will run
most plentifully in every office o' the court; but
believe it, most of them do but weep over their step-
mothers' graves.   51
Fran. How mean you?
Flam. Why, they dissemble; as some men do that
live within compass o' the verge.[6]
Fran. Come, you have thrived well under him.
Flam. Faith, like a wolf in a woman's breast;[7] I have
been fed with poultry:[8] but, for money, understand
me, I had as good a will to cozen him as e'er an officer
of them all; but I had not cunning enough to do it.
Fran. What didst thou think of him? Faith, speak
freely.   61
Flam. He was a kind of statesman that would sooner
have reckoned how many cannon-bullets he had discharged against a town, to count his expense that way,
than how many of his valiant and deserving subjects he
lost before it.
Fran. Oh, speak well of the duke.
Flam. I have done. Wilt hear some of my court-
wisdom? To reprehend princes is dangerous; and to
over-commend some of them is palpable lying.   70

Enter LODOVICO.

Fran. How is it with the duke?
Lod.   Most deadly ill.
He's fallen into a strange distraction.
He talks of battles and monopolies,
Levying of taxes; and from that descends
To the most brain-sick language. His mind fastens
On twenty several objects, which confound
Deep sense with folly. Such a fearful end
May teach some men that bear too lofty crest,

V.iii.
    [1] *bar:* the hasp or latch locking the beaver.
    [2] *screech-owls:* to the foreboding physicians.
    [3] *without book:* with no need to study; "naturally."
    [4] *rough-bearded:* alluding to its fiery tail.
    [5] *extreme unction:* administered to the dying.
    [6] *within . . . verge:* inside that privileged area, some
twelve miles in extent, which surrounded the court.
Flamineo is being ironic.
    [7] *wolf . . . breast:* ulcer or cancer consuming the breast.
    [8] *poultry:* medicine, like a pigeon or raw meat, for the
"wolf"; but also cant for women's breasts.

Though they live happiest, yet they die not best.
He hath conferred the whole state of the dukedom   80
Upon your sister, till the prince arrive
At mature age.
    Flam.   There's some good luck in that yet.
    Fran. See, here he comes.

Enter BRACHIANO, *presented in a bed,* VITTORIA
[COROMBONA] *and others.*

                There's death in's face
  already.
    Vit. Cor. O my good lord!
    Brach.   Away! you have abused me.

    These speeches are several kinds of distractions, and
                   in the action should appear so.

You have conveyed coin forth our territories,
Bought and sold offices, oppressed the poor,
And I ne'er dreamt on't. Make up your accounts:
I'll now be mine own steward.
    Flam.   Sir, have patience.
    Brach. Indeed, I am to blame.
For did you ever hear the dusky raven   90
Chide blackness? Or was't ever known the devil
Railed against cloven creatures?
    Vit. Cor.   O my lord!
    Brach. Let me have some quails[9] to supper.
    Flam.   Sir, you
  shall.
    Brach. No, some fried dog-fish; your quails feed on
  poison.
That old dog-fox, that politician, Florence!
I'll forswear hunting, and turn dog-killer.
Rare! I'll be friends with him; for, mark you, sir, one
  dog
Still sets another a-barking. Peace, peace!
Yonder's a fine slave come in now.
    Flam.   Where?
    Brach.   Why, there,
In a blue bonnet, and a pair of breeches   100
With a great cod-piece.[10] Ha, ha, ha!
Look you, his cod-piece is stuck full of pins,

---

    [9] *quails:* punning on the cant term for "prostitutes."
    [10] *cod-piece:* covering the male genitals and emphasizing
them to suggest sexual potency.
    [11] *rose:* decorative rosette.
    [12] *linguist:* i.e., the devil being notably persuasive.
    [13] *whipped:* edged.
    [14] *arras-powder:* violet-scented powder of orris-root.
    [15] *pastry:* i.e., where the pastry is made.
    [16] *L.:* "Listen, Lord Brachiano."
    [17] *L.:* "Lord Brachiano, you were accustomed in battle
to be made safe by your shield; now this shield you shall
oppose against the infernal enemy."
    [18] *L.:* "Once in battle you were victorious with your
spear; now this sacred spear you shall wield against the
enemy of souls."
    [19] *L.:* "Listen, Lord Brachiano, now if also you approve
that which has been done between us, turn (your) head to
the right."
    [20] *L.:* "Be confident, Lord Brachiano; think how many
good deeds you have done; and lastly remember that my
soul is pledged for yours if there should be any danger."

With pearls o' the head of them. Do not you know him?
    Flam. No, my lord.
    Brach.   Why, 'tis the devil;
I know him by a great rose[11] he wears on's shoe
To hide his cloven foot. I'll dispute with him;
He's a rare linguist.[12]
    Vit. Cor.   My lord, here's nothing.
    Brach. Nothing! rare! nothing! when I want
  money,
Our treasury is empty, there is nothing.
I'll not be used thus.
    Vit. Cor.   Oh, lie still, my lord!   110
    Brach. See, see Flamineo, that killed his brother,
Is dancing on the ropes there, and he carries
A money-bag in each hand, to keep him even,
For fear of breaking's neck: and there's a lawyer,
In a gown whipped[13] with velvet, stares and gapes
When the money will fall. How the rogue cuts capers!
It should have been in a halter. 'Tis there. What's
  she?
    Flam. Vittoria, my lord.
    Brach. Ha, ha, ha! her hair is sprinkled with
  arras-powder,[14]
That makes her look as if she had sinned in the
  pastry[15]—   120
What's he?
    Flam. A divine, my lord,

    BRACHIANO *seems here near his end.* LODOVICO
    and GASPARO, *in the habit of* Capuchins, *pre-*
    sent him in his bed with a crucifix and hallowed
                           candle.

    Brach. He will be drunk; avoid him. The argument
Is fearful, when churchmen stagger in't.
Look you, six gray rats that have lost their tails
Crawl up the pillow. Send for a rat-catcher.
I'll do a miracle, I'll free the court
From all foul vermin. Where's Flamineo?
    Flam. I do not like that he names me so often,
Especially on's death-bed; 'tis a sign   130
I shall not live long.—See, he's near his end.
    Lod. Pray, give us leave.—*Attende, domine*
    Brachiane.[16]
    Flam. See, see how firmly he doth fix his eye
Upon the crucifix.
    Vit. Cor.   Oh, hold it constant!
It settles his wild spirits; and so his eyes
Melt into tears.
    Lod. Domine Brachiane, solebas in bello tutus esse tuo
clypeo; nunc hunc clypeum hosti tuo opponas infernali.[17]

                          By the crucifix.

    Gasp. Olim hasta valuisti in bello; nunc hanc sacram
hastam vibrabis contra hostem animarum.[18]   140

                       By the hallowed taper.

    Lod. Attende, domine Brachiane, si nunc quoque probas
ea quae acta sunt inter nos, flecte caput in dextrum.[19]
    Gasp. Esto securus, domine Brachiane; cogita quantum
habeas meritorum; denique memineris means animam pro
tuâ oppignoratam si quid esset periculi.[20]

*Lod. Si nunc quoque probas ea quae acta sunt inter nos,
flecte caput in laevum.*[21]
He is departing. Pray, stand all apart,
And let us only whisper in his ears
Some private meditations, which our order   150
Permits you not to hear.

> *Here, the rest being departed,* LODOVICO *and*
> GASPARO *discover themselves.*

Gasp.   Brachiano—
Lod. Devil Brachiano, thou art damned.
Gasp.   Perpetually.
Lod. A slave condemned and given up to the
    gallows
Is thy great lord and master.
Gasp.   True; for thou
Art given up to the devil.
Lod.   O you slave!
You that were held the famous politician,
Whose art was poison!
Gasp.   And whose conscience, murder!
Lod. That would have broke your wife's neck down
    the stairs,
Ere she was poisoned!
Gasp.   That had your villainous salads!
Lod. And fine embroidered bottles and perfumes,
Equally mortal with a winter-plague!   161
Gasp. Now there's mercury—
Lod.   And copperas[22]—
Gasp.   And
    quicksilver—
Lod. With other devilish pothecary stuff,
A-melting in your politic brains. Dost hear?
Gasp. This is Count Lodovico.
Lod.   This, Gasparo.
And thou shalt die like a poor rogue.
Gasp.   And stink
Like a dead fly-blown dog.
Lod.   And be forgotten
Before thy funeral sermon.
Brach.   Vittoria!
Vittoria!
Lod. Oh, the cursèd devil
Comes to himself again! we are undone.   170
Gasp. Strangle him in private.

> *Enter* VITTORIA [COROMBONA],
> *and the* Attendants.

                          What, will you call
    him again
To live in treble torments? For charity,
For Christian charity, avoid the chamber.
                    [*Exeunt* VITTORIA COROMBONA,
                              and Attendants.]
Lod. You would prate, sir? This is a true-love knot
Sent from the Duke of Florence.

> BRACHIANO *is strangled.*

Gasp.   What, is it done?
Lod. The snuff[23] is out. No woman-keeper[24] i' the
    world,

Though she had practiced seven year at the pest-house,
Could have done't quaintlier.

> [*Re-enter* VITTORIA COROMBONA, FRANCISCO
> DE MEDICIS, FLAMINEO, *and* Attendants.]

                              My lords, he's dead.
Omnes. Rest to his soul!
Vit. Cor.   O me! this place is hell.
                              Exit VITTORIA [COROMBONA].
Fran. How heavily she takes it!
Flam.   Oh, yes, yes;   180
Had women navigable rivers in their eyes,
They would dispend them all. Surely, I wonder
Why we should wish more rivers[25] to the city
When they sell water so good cheap. I'll tell thee,
These are but moonish[26] shades of griefs or fears;
There's nothing sooner dry than women's tears.
Why, here's an end of all my harvest; he has given me
    nothing.
Court promises! Let wise men count them cursed,
For while you live, he that scores best[27] pays worst.
Fran. Sure, this was Florence' doing.
Flam.   Very likely.
Those are found weighty strokes which come from the
    hand,   191
But those are killing strokes which come from the head.
O, the rare tricks of a Machivillian![28]
He doth not come, like a gross plodding slave,
And buffet you to death; no, my quaint knave,
He tickles you to death, makes you die laughing,
As if you had swallowed down a pound of saffron.[29]
You see the feat, 'tis practiced in a trice;
To teach court honesty, it jumps on ice.[30]
Fran. Now have the people liberty to talk,   200
And descant[31] on his vices.
Flam.   Misery of princes,
That must of force be censured by their slaves!
Not only blamed for doing things are ill,
But for not doing all that all men will.
One were better be a thresher.
Ud's death, I would fain speak with this duke yet.
Fran. Now he's dead?

---

[21] *L.:* "If now also you approve that which has been done
between us, turn (your) head to the left."

[22] *mercury . . . copperas:* poisonous.

[23] *snuff:* as of a candle.

[24] *woman-keeper:* female nurse, suspected often of hasten-
ing a patient's demise.

[25] *more rivers:* a topical allusion to the project, completed
in 1613 after many difficulties, to supply London with fresh
water.

[26] *moonish:* changeable.

[27] *scores best:* charges, without paying cash.

[28] *Machivillian:* The eccentric spelling is meant to pun
on "villain."

[29] *saffron:* supposed to make for merriment.

[30] *jumps on ice:* A difficult passage, perhaps to be compared with a similar crux in *Measure for Measure,* II. i. 38–
40 on those sinners who "run from brakes of ice, and
answer none." Whitney, *Emblems,* 1586, p. 22, depicts the
crafty fox on the ice as it breaks, and moralizes: "No subtle
craft will serve, When chance doth throw the dice."

[31] *descant:* sing; discourse at large.

Flam. I cannot conjure; but if prayers or oaths
Will get to the speech of him, though forty devils
Wait on him in his livery of flames,   210
I'll speak to him, and shake him by the hand,
Though I be blasted.

                        Exit FLAMINEO.

Fran.   Excellent Lodovico!
What, did you terrify him at the last gasp?
Lod. Yes, and so idly, that the duke had like
To have terrified us.
Fran.   How?
Lod.   You shall hear that hereafter.

      Enter [ZANCHE] *the* Moor.

See, yon's the infernal that would make up sport.
Now to the revelation of that secret
She promised when she fell in love with you.
Fran. You're passionately met in this sad world.
Zan. I would have you look up, sir; these court-
    tears   220
Claim not your tribute to them. Let those weep
That guiltily partake in the sad cause.
I knew last night, by a sad dream I had,
Some mischief would ensue; yet, to say truth.
My dream most concerned you.
 Lod.   Shall's fall a-dreaming?
Fran. Yes; and for fashion sake I'll dream with her.
Zan. Methought, sir, you came stealing to my bed.
Fran. Wilt thou believe me, sweeting? By this light,
I was a-dreamt on thee too; for methought
I saw thee naked.
Zan.   Fie, sir! As I told you,   230
Methought you lay down by me.
Fran.   So dreamt I;
And lest thou shouldst take cold, I covered thee
With this Irish mantle.[32]
Zan.   Verily, I did dream
You were somewhat bold with me; but to come to't—
Lod. How, how! I hope you will not go to't[33] here.
Fran. Nay, you must hear my dream out.
Zan.   Well, sir,
    forth.
Fran. When I threw the mantle o'er thee, thou
    didst laugh
Exceedingly, methought.
Zan.   Laugh!
Fran.   And cried'st out,
The hair did tickle thee.
Zan.   There was a dream indeed!

---

[32] *Irish mantle:* plaid, covering the naked body.
[33] *go to't:* engage in sexual intercourse.
[34] *collier:* black, from working coal.
[35] *fumed:* perfumed; poisoned.
[36] *bed of snakes:* conspiracy.
[37] *partridge . . . laurel:* This proverbially lascivious bird
cured itself, according to Pliny in his *Natural History*, in
this way. Reference is also to the laurel as emblematic of
fame.
V.iv.
  [1] *favored:* featured.   [2] *minion:* darling, favorite.
[3] *dottrels:* plovers, proverbially stupid birds (and hence,
by transference, stupid people).

Lod. Mark her, I prithee; she simpers like the suds
A collier[34] hath been washed in.   241
Zan. Come, sir, good fortune tends you. I did tell
    you
I would reveal a secret: Isabella,
The Duke of Florence' sister, was impoisoned
By a fumed[35] picture; and Camillo's neck
Was broke by damned Flamineo, the mischance
Laid on a vaulting-horse.
Fran.   Most strange!
Zan.   Most true.
Lod. The bed of snakes[36] is broke.
Zan. I sadly do confess I had a hand
In the black deed.
Fran.   Thou kept'st their counsel?
Zan.   Right;
For which, urged with contrition, I intend   251
This night to rob Vittoria.
Lod.   Excellent penitence!
Usurers dream on't while they sleep out sermons.
Zan. To further our escape, I have entreated
Leave to retire me, till the funeral,
Unto a friend i' the country; that excuse
Will further our escape. In coin and jewels
I shall at least make good unto your use
An hundred thousand crowns.
Fran.   O noble wench!
Lod. Those crowns we'll share.
Zan.   It is a dowry,   260
Methinks, should make that sun-burned proverb false,
And wash the Ethiop white.
Fran.   It shall. Away!
Zan. Be ready for our flight.
Fran.   An hour 'fore day.

          Exit [ZANCHE] *the* Moor.
O strange discovery! why, till now we knew not
The circumstance of either of their deaths.

      Enter [ZANCHE *the*] Moor.

Zan. You'll wait about midnight in the chapel?
                [*Exit* ZANCHE.]
Fran.   There.
Lod. Why, now our action's justified.
Fran.   Tush for justice!
What harms it justice? We now, like the partridge,
Purge the disease with laurel;[37] for the fame
Shall crown the enterprise, and quit the shame.   270
                    Exeunt.

[V.iv]

    Enter FLAMINEO *and* GASPARO *at one door;*
      another way, GIOVANNI, *attended.*

Gasp. The young duke. Did you e'er see a sweeter
prince?
Flam. I have known a poor woman's bastard better
favored;[1] this is behind him; now, to his face, all comparisons were hateful. Wise was the courtly peacock
that, being a great minion,[2] and being compared for
beauty by some dottrels[3] that stood by to the kingly

eagle, said the eagle was a far fairer bird than herself, not in respect of her feathers, but in respect of her long tallants.[4] His will grow out in time.—My gracious lord!

Giov. I pray, leave me, sir.   11

Flam. Your grace must be merry; 'tis I have cause to mourn; for, wot you, what said the little boy that rode behind his father on horseback?

Giov. Why, what said he?

Flam. "When you are dead, father," said he, "I hope then I shall ride in the saddle." Oh, 'tis a brave thing for a man to sit by himself! he may stretch himself in the stirrups, look about, and see the whole compass of the hemisphere. You're now, my lord, i' the saddle.   20

Giov. Study your prayers, sir, and be penitent. 'Twere fit you'd think on what hath former been; I have heard grief named the eldest child of sin.

                                        Exit GIOVANNI.

Flam. Study my prayers! He threatens me divinely. I am falling to pieces already. I care not though, like Anacharsis,[5] I were pounded to death in a mortar; and yet that death were fitter for usurers, gold and themselves to be beaten together, to make a most cordial cullis[6] for the devil.

He hath his uncle's villainous look already,   30
In decimo sexto.[7]

                        Enter Courtier.

                    Now, sir, what are you?

Cour. It is the pleasure, sir, of the young duke, That you forbear the presence, and all rooms That owe him reverence.

Flam.   So, the wolf and the raven Are very pretty fools when they are young. Is it your office, sir, to keep me out?

Cour. So the duke wills.

Flam. Verily, master courtier, extremity is not to be used in all offices. Say that a gentlewoman were taken out of her bed about midnight and committed to   40 Castle Angelo,[8] to the tower[9] yonder, with nothing about her but her smock,[10] would it not show a cruel part in the gentleman-porter to lay claim to her upper garment, pull it o'er her head and ears, and put her in naked?

Cour. Very good. You are merry.

                                        [*Exit.*]

Flam. Doth he make a court-ejectment of me? A flaming fire-brand[11] casts more smoke without a chimney than within't. I'll smoor[12] some of them.

Enter FLORENCE [*i.e.,* FRANCISCO DE MEDICIS, *disguised*].

How now! thou art sad.   50

Fran. I met even now with the most piteous sight.

Flam. Thou meet'st another here, a pitiful Degraded courtier.

Fran.   Your reverend mother Is grown a very old woman in two hours. I found them winding[13] of Marcello's corse; And there is such a solemn melody, 'Tween doleful songs, tears, and sad elegies, Such as old grandams watching by the dead

Were wont to outwear the nights with, that, believe me, I had no eyes to guide me forth the room,   60 They were so o'ercharged with water.

Flam.   I will see them.

Fran. 'Twere much uncharity in you; for your sight Will add unto their tears.

Flam.   I will see them. They are behind the traverse;[14] I'll discover Their superstitious howling.

                                [*Draws the traverse.*]

CORNELIA, [ZANCHE] *the* Moor, *and three other* Ladies *discovered winding* MARCELLO'S *corse.*
                    A Song.

Cor. This rosemary[15] is withered; pray, get fresh. I would have these herbs grow up in his grave When I am dead and rotten. Reach the bays,[16] I'll tie a garland here about his head; 'Twill keep my boy from lightning. This sheet[17]   70 I have kept this twenty year, and every day Hallowed it with my prayers. I did not think He should have wore it.

Zan.   Look you who are yonder.

Cor. Oh, reach me the flowers.

Zan. Her ladyship's foolish.

Lady.   Alas, her grief Hath turned her child again!

                                        To FLAMINEO.

Cor.   You're very welcome. There's rosemary for you—and rue[18] for you— Heart's-ease[19] for you; I pray make much of it. I have left more for myself.

Fran.   Lady, who's this?

Cor. You are, I take it, the grave-maker.

Flam.   So.   80

Zan. 'Tis Flamineo.

Cor. Will you make me such a fool? Here's a white hand. Can blood so soon be washed out? Let me see; When screech-owls croak upon the chimney-tops, And the strange cricket[20] i' the oven sings and hops,

---

[4] *tallants:* talons; with pun on "talents."
[5] *Anacharsis:* As editors point out, it was the Greek philosopher Anaxarchus who suffered this fate.
[6] *cullis:* strong broth, used medicinally.
[7] *L.:* Like a small book or copy.
[8] *Castle Angelo:* across the Tiber in Rome.
[9] *tower:* perhaps, given the indifference of the period to decorum of place, an allusion to the Tower of London.
[10] *smock:* undergarment.
[11] *flaming fire-brand:* Flamineo.   [12] *smoor:* smother.
[13] *winding:* i.e., in funeral cerements or cloths.
[14] *traverse:* presumably a curtain or screen closing off the inner stage.
[15] *rosemary:* associated proverbially with memory, and hence appropriate for funerals.
[16] *bays:* laurel, which the emblem books identified as protecting against lightning.
[17] *sheet:* her own winding sheet.
[18] *rue:* a bitter shrub; hence "rueful."
[19] *Heart's-ease:* Pansies.
[20] *cricket:* ominous of death, like the "yellow spots" below.

When yellow spots do on your hands appear,
Be certain then you of a corse shall hear.
Out upon't, how 'tis speckled! h'as handled a toad,[21]
   sure.
Cowslip-water[22] is good for the memory;
Pray, buy me three ounces of't.   90
   Flam. I would I were from hence.
   Cor.   Do you hear, sir?
I'll give you a saying which my grandmother
Was wont, when she heard the bell toll, to sing o'er
Unto her lute.
   Flam.   Do, an you will, do.

            CORNELIA *doth this in several forms of*
                               distraction.

   Cor. Call for the robin-red-breast and the wren,[23]
Since o'er shady groves they hover,
And with leaves and flowers do cover
The friendless bodies of unburied men.
Call unto his funeral dole
The ant, the field-mouse, and the mole,   100
To rear him hillocks that shall keep him warm,
And (when gay[24] *tombs are robbed) sustain no harm.*
But keep the wolf far thence, that's foe to men,
For with his nails he'll dig them up again.
They would not bury him 'cause he died in a quarrel,
But I have an answer for them:
Let holy church receive him duly,
Since he paid the church-tithes truly.
His wealth is summed, and this is all his store,
This poor men get, and great men get no more.   110
Now the wares are gone, we may shut up shop.
Bless you all, good people.
         Exeunt CORNELIA, [ZANCHE], *and* Ladies.
   Flam. I have a strange thing in me, to the which
I cannot give a name, without[25] it be
Compassion. I pray, leave me.
         Exit FRANCISCO [DE MEDICIS].
This night I'll know the utmost of my fate;
I'll be resolved[26] what my rich sister means
To assign me for my service. I have lived
Riotously ill, like some that live in court,
And sometimes when my face was full of smiles   120
Have felt the maze[27] of conscience in my breast.
Oft gay and honored robes those tortures try.[28]
We think caged birds sing, when indeed they cry.

---

[21] *toad:* proverbially venomous.
[22] *Cowslip-water:* to which contemporary herbals attributed medicinal value.
[23] *robin . . . wren:* The first was thought to care for the dead, the second was in popular mythology made the robin's wife.   [24] *gay:* elaborate.
[25] *without:* unless.   [26] *resolved:* know.
[27] *maze:* i.e., which fills him with amazement or confusion.
[28] *try:* afflict.
[29] *cassock:* great coat.   [30] *stand:* withstand.
[31] *familiars:* spirits.
[32] *melancholy:* hallucination (induced by melancholy).

V.v.
[1] *quit:* requite.   [2] *To:* including.

Enter BRACHIANO'S Ghost, *in his leather cassock*[29]
and breeches, boots, a cowl; [*in his hand*] *a pot of*
lily-flowers, with a skull in it.

Ha! I can stand[30] thee: nearer, nearer yet.
What a mockery hath death made thee! Thou look'st
   sad.
In what place art thou? In yon starry gallery?
Or in the cursèd dungeon?—No? Not speak?
Pray, sir, resolve me, what religion's best
For a man to die in? Or is it in your knowledge
To answer me how long I have to live?   130
That's the most necessary question.
Not answer? Are you still like some great men
That only walk like shadows up and down,
And to no purpose? say—

       The Ghost *throws earth upon him, and shows him the*
                                 skull.

What's that? Oh, fatal! he throws earth upon me!
A dead man's skull beneath the roots of flowers!
I pray, speak, sir: our Italian churchmen
Make us believe dead men hold conference
With their familiars,[31] and many times
Will come to bed to them and eat with them.   140
                         Exit Ghost.
He's gone; and see, the skull and earth are vanished.
This is beyond melancholy.[32] I do dare my fate
To do its worst. Now to my sister's lodging,
And sum up all these horrors: the disgrace
The prince threw on me; next the piteous sight
Of my dead brother; and my mother's dotage;
And last this terrible vision. All these
Shall with Vittoria's bounty turn to good,
Or I will drown this weapon in her blood.

                               Exit.

[V.v]

       Enter FRANCISCO [DE MEDICIS, *disguised*],
        LODOVICO, *and* HORTENSIO [*overhearing them*].

   Lod. My lord, upon my soul, you shall no further;
You have most ridiculously engaged yourself
Too far already. For my part, I have paid
All my debts; so, if I should chance to fall,
My creditors fall not with me; and I vow
To quit[1] all in this bold assembly
To[2] the meanest follower. My lord, leave the city,
Or I'll forswear the murder.
   Fran.   Farewell, Lodovico.
If thou dost perish in this glorious act,
I'll rear unto thy memory that fame   10
Shall in the ashes keep alive thy name.
         [*Exeunt* FRANCISCO *and* LODOVICO
                             severally.]
   Hor. There's some black deed on foot. I'll presently
Down to the citadel, and raise some force.
These strong court-factions that do brook no checks
In the career oft break the riders' necks.

                               [*Exit.*]

[V.vi]

Enter VITTORIA [COROMBONA] *with a book in her hand,* [*and*] ZANCHE; FLAMINEO *following them.*

Flam. What, are you at your prayers? Give o'er.
Vit. Cor.   How, ruffian!
Flam. I come to you 'bout worldly business:
Sit down, sit down—nay, stay, blouze,[1] you may hear it—
The doors are fast enough.
Vit. Cor.   Ha, are you drunk?
Flam. Yes, yes, with wormwood-water. You shall taste
Some of it presently.
Vit. Cor.   What intends the Fury?
Flam. You are my lord's executrix, and I claim
Reward for my long service.
Vit. Cor.   For your service!
Flam. Come, therefore, here is pen and ink; set down
What you will give me.
                                                She writes.
Vit. Cor.   There.
Flam.   Ha! have you done already?
'Tis a most short conveyance.
Vit. Cor.   I will read it.   11
"I give that portion to thee, and no other,
Which Cain groaned under, having slain his brother."
Flam. A most courtly patent to beg[2] by!
Vit. Cor. You are a villain.
Flam. Is't come to this? They say, affrights cure agues.
Thou hast a devil in thee; I will try
If I can scare him from thee. Nay, sit still:
My lord hath left me yet two case[3] of jewels   19
Shall make me scorn your bounty; you shall see them.
                                                [*Exit.*]
Vit. Cor. Sure, he's distracted.
Zan.   Oh, he's desperate.
For your own safety give him gentle language.

He [FLAMINEO] *enters with two cases of pistols.*

Flam. Look, these are better far at a dead lift[4]
Than all your jewel-house.
Vit. Cor.   And yet, methinks,
These stones have no fair luster, they are ill set.
Flam. I'll turn the right side towards you; you shall see
How they will sparkle.
Vit. Cor.   Turn this horror from me!
What do you want? What would you have me do?
Is not all mine yours? Have I any children?
Flam. Pray thee, good woman, do not trouble me   30
With this vain worldly business; say your prayers.
I made a vow to my deceasèd lord,
Neither yourself nor I should outlive him
The numbering of four hours.
Vit. Cor.   Did he enjoin it?
Flam. He did; and 'twas a deadly jealousy,
Lest any should enjoy thee after him,
That urged him vow me to it. For my death,

I did propound it voluntarily, knowing,
If he could not be safe in his own court,
Being a great duke, what hope, then for us?   40
Vit. Cor. This is your melancholy and despair.
Flam.   Away!
Fool thou art to think that politicians
Do use[5] to kill the effects of injuries
And let the cause live. Shall we groan in irons,
Or be a shameful and a weighty burden
To a public scaffold? This is my resolve;
I would not live at any man's entreaty,
Nor die at any's bidding.
Vit. Cor.   Will you hear me?
Flam. My life hath done service to other men;   49
My death shall serve mine own turn. Make you ready.
Vit. Cor. Do you mean to die[6] indeed?
Flam.   With as much pleasure
As e'er my father gat me.
Vit. Cor.   Are the doors locked?
Zan. Yes, madam.
Vit. Cor. Are you grown an atheist? Will you turn your body,
Which is the goodly palace of the soul,
To the soul's slaughter-house? Oh, the cursèd devil,
Which doth present us with all other sins
Thrice-candied o'er; despair with gall and stibium;
Yet we carouse it off[7] [*Aside to* ZANCHE] Cry out for help!—
Makes us forsake that which was made for man,   60
The world, to sink to that was made for devils,
Eternal darkness!
Zan.   Help, help!
Flam.   I'll stop your throat
With winter-plums.[8]
Vit. Cor.   I prithee, yet remember,
Millions are now in graves which at last day
Like mandrakes shall rise shrieking.[9]
Flam.   Leave your prating,
For these are but grammatical[10] laments,
Feminine arguments; and they move me,
As some in pulpits move their auditory,
More with their exclamation than sense
Of reason or sound doctrine.
Zan. [*Aside*]   Gentle madam,   70
Seem to consent, only persuade him teach
The way to death; let him die first.

---

    [1] *blouze:* beggar's trull (though not so cited by OED before the eighteenth century).
    [2] *patent to beg:* alluding as earlier to the requirement that beggars be licensed.
    [3] *case:* pair.   [4] *at a dead lift:* in a tight spot.
    [5] *Do use:* Are accustomed.
    [6] *die:* Flamineo in answering picks up the secondary sense of the word—"to have sexual intercourse."
    [7] *Oh . . . off:* The devil makes every sin except despair attractive, and yet we are able to swallow even the latter.
    [8] *winter-plums:* hard and dry, suggesting bullets(?).
    [9] *shrieking:* which the mandrake was supposed to do when pulled from the ground.
    [10] *grammatical:* academic; to no purpose.

Vit. Cor. 'Tis good. I apprehend it,
To kill one's self is meat that we must take
Like pills, not chew't, but quickly swallow it;
The smart o' the wound, or weakness of the hand,
May else bring treble torments.
Flam.   I have held it
A wretched and most miserable life
Which is not able to die.
Vit. Cor.   Oh, but frailty!
Yet I am now resolved. Farewell, affliction!   80
Behold, Brachiano, I that while you lived
Did make a flaming altar of my heart
To sacrifice unto you, now am ready
To sacrifice heart and all.—Farewell, Zanche!
Zan. How, madam! Do you think that I'll outlive
      you,
Especially when my best self, Flamineo,
Goes the same voyage?
Flam.   Oh, most lovèd Moor!
Zan. Only by all my love let me entreat you—
Since it is most necessary one of us
Do violence on ourselves—let you or I   90
Be her sad taster, teach her how to die.
Flam. Thou dost instruct me nobly. Take these
      pistols,
Because my hand is stained with blood already.
Two of these you shall level at my breast,
The other 'gainst your own, and so we'll die
Most equally contented. But first swear
Not to outlive me.
Vit. Cor. ⎱
Zan.   ⎰   Most religiously.
Flam. Then here's an end of me; farewell, daylight!
And, o contemptible physic, that dost take
So long a study only to preserve   100
So short a life, I take my leave of thee!
These are two cupping-glasses[11] that shall draw

Showing the pistols.

All my infected blood out. Are you ready?
Vit. Cor. and Zan. Ready.
Flam. Whither shall I go now? O Lucian,[12] thy
ridiculous purgatory! To find Alexander the Great
cobbling shoes, Pompey tagging points,[13] and Julius
Caesar making hair-buttons! Hannibal selling blacking,
and Augustus crying[14] garlic! Charlemagne selling
lists[15] by the dozen, and King Pepin[16] crying apples
in a cart drawn with one horse!   111
Whether I resolve to fire, earth, water, air,

Or all the elements by scruples,[17] I know not,
Nor greatly care.—Shoot, shoot.
Of all deaths the violent death is best;
For from ourselves it seals ourselves so fast,
The pain, once apprehended, is quite past.

They shoot and run to him, and tread upon him.

Vit. Cor. What, are you dropped?
Flam. I am mixed with earth already. As you are
      noble,
Perform your vows, and bravely follow me.   120
Vit. Cor. Whither? To hell?
Zan.   To most assured
      damnation?
Vit. Cor. O thou most cursèd devil!
Zan.   Thou art caught—
Vit. Cor. In thine own engine. I tread the fire out
That would have been my ruin.
Flam. Will you be perjured? What a religious oath
was Styx, that the gods never durst swear by, and
violate! Oh, that we had such an oath to minister, and
to be so well kept in our courts of justice!
Vit. Cor. Think whither thou art going.
Zan.   And remember
What villainies thou hast acted.
Vit. Cor.   This thy death   130
Shall make me like a blazing ominous star.
Look up and tremble.
Flam.   Oh, I am caught with a springe![18]
Vit. Cor. You see the fox comes many times short[19]
      home;
'Tis here proved true.
Flam.   Killed with[20] a couple of braches![21]
Vit. Cor. No fitter offering for the infernal Furies
Than one in whom they reigned while he was living.
Flam. Oh, the way's dark and horrid! I cannot see.
Shall I have no company?
Vit. Cor.   Oh, yes, thy sins
Do run before thee to fetch fire from hell,
To light thee thither.
Flam.   Oh, I smell soot,   140
Most stinking soot! the chimney is a-fire;
My liver's parboiled, like Scotch holly-bread;[22]
There's a plumber laying pipes in my guts, it scalds.
Wilt thou outlive me?
Zan.   Yes, and drive a stake[23]
Through thy body; for we'll give it out
Thou didst this violence upon thyself.
Flam. O cunning devils! now I have tried your love,
And doubled all your reaches.[24]—I am not wounded.

FLAMINEO *riseth.*

The pistols held no bullets. 'Twas a plot
To prove your kindness to me, and I live   150
To punish your ingratitude. I knew,
One time or other, you would find a way
To give me a strong potion.—O men
That lie upon your death-beds, and are haunted
With howling wives, ne'er trust them! They'll re-marry
Ere the worm pierce your winding-sheet, ere the spider
Make a thin curtain for your epitaphs.—

---

[11] *cupping-glasses:* for letting blood.
[12] *Lucian:* The satirical *Menippos* of this second-century Greek Sophist ridiculed various penances assigned to the great in Purgatory.
[13] *tagging points:* fixing metal tags on laces.
[14] *crying:* hawking.
[15] *lists:* selvages; strips of cloth; slices of gammon(?).
[16] *Pepin:* with a pun on "pippin" (apple).
[17] *scruples:* little pieces.   [18] *springe:* trap, as for birds.
[19] *short:* lacking(?).   [20] *with:* by.   [21] *braches:* bitches.
[22] *Scotch holly-bread:* a boiled sheep's liver.
[23] *stake:* which was driven through the bodies of suicides.
[24] *doubled . . . reaches:* outwitted your designs.

How cunning you were to discharge! Do you practice
at the Artillery-yard?²⁵—Trust a woman! never, never!
Brachiano be my precedent. We lay our souls   160
to pawn to the devil for a little pleasure, and a woman
makes the bill of sale. That ever man should marry!
For one Hypermnestra²⁶ that saved her lord and
husband, forty-nine of her sisters cut their husbands'
throats all in one night; there was a shoal of virtuous
horse-leeches!—
Here are two other instruments.²⁷

 Vit. Cor.   Help, help!

  Enter LODOVICO [and] GASPARO [*disguised as*
      Capuchins].

 Flam. What noise is that? Ha! false keys i' the court!
 Lod. We have brought you a mask.²⁸
 Flam. A matachin,²⁹ it seems by your drawn swords.
Churchmen turned revelers!   171
 [*Gasp.*] Isabella! Isabella!
 Lod. Do you know us now?
 Flam. Lodovico! and Gasparo!
 Lod. Yes; and that Moor the duke gave pension to
Was the great Duke of Florence.
 Vit. Cor.   Oh, we are lost!
 Flam. You shall not take justice from forth my
  hands—
O, let me kill her!—I'll cut my safety
Through your coats of steel. Fate's a spaniel,³⁰
We cannot beat it from us. What remains now?   180
Let all that do ill, take this precedent—
Man may his fate foresee, but not prevent;
And of all axioms this shall win the prize—
'Tis better to be fortunate than wise.
 Gasp. Bind him to the pillar.³¹
 Vit. Cor.   Oh, your gentle pity!
I have seen a blackbird that would sooner fly
To a man's bosom than to stay the gripe
Of the fierce sparrowhawk.
 Gasp.   Your hope deceives you.
 Vit. Cor. If Florence be i' the court, would he would
  kill me!
 Gasp. Fool! Princes give rewards with their own
  hands,   190
But death or punishment by the hands of others.
 Lod. Sirrah, you once did strike me. I'll strike you
Into the center.³²
 Flam. Thou'lt do it like a hangman, a base hangman,
Not like a noble fellow, for thou see'st
I cannot strike again.
 Lod.   Dost laugh?
 Flam. Would'st have me die, as I was born, in
  whining?
 Gasp. Recommend yourself to heaven.
 Flam. No, I will carry mine own commendations
  thither.
 Lod. Oh, could I kill you forty times a day,   200
And use't four year together, 'twere too little!
Naught grieves but that you are too few to feed
The famine of our vengeance. What dost think on?
 Flam. Nothing; of nothing. Leave thy idle questions.
I am i' the way to study a long silence;

To prate were idle. I remember nothing.
There's nothing of so infinite vexation
As man's own thoughts.
 Lod.   O thou glorious strumpet!
Could I divide thy breath from this pure air
When't leaves thy body, I would suck it up   210
And breathe't upon some dunghill.
 Vit. Cor.   You, my death's-man!
Methinks thou dost not look horrid enough;
Thou hast too good a face to be a hangman.
If thou be, do thy office in right form;
Fall down upon thy knees, and ask forgiveness.
 Lod. Oh, thou hast been a most prodigious
  comet,
But I'll cut off your train³³—kill the Moor first.
 Vit. Cor. You shall not kill her first; behold my
  breast.
I will be waited on in death; my servant
Shall never go before me.
 Gasp.   Are you so brave?   220
 Vit. Cor. Yes, I shall welcome death
As princes do some great ambassadors;
I'll meet thy weapon half way.
 Lod.   Thou dost tremble.
Methinks fear should dissolve thee into air.
 Vit. Cor. Oh, thou art deceived, I am too true a
  woman.
Conceit³⁴ can never kill me. I'll tell thee what,
I will not in my death shed one base tear;
Or if look pale, for want of blood, not fear.
 [*Gasp.*] Thou art my task, black Fury.
 Zan.   I have blood
As red as either of theirs. Wilt drink some?   230
'Tis good for the falling-sickness.³⁵ I am proud
Death cannot alter my complexion,
For I shall ne'er look pale.
 Lod.   Strike, strike,
With a joint motion.

  [*They stab* VITTORIA, ZANCHE, *and* FLAMINEO.]

 Vit. Cor.   'Twas a manly blow.
The next thou giv'st, murder some sucking infant;
And then thou wilt be famous.
 Flam.   Oh, what blade is't?
A Toledo, or an English fox?³⁶

---

²⁵ *Artillery-yard*: in Bishopsgate, where citizens assembled
for military training, a practice revived in 1610.
²⁶ *Hypermnestra*: The fifty daughters of Danaus were
instructed by their father to murder their husbands on their
wedding night. Hypermnestra alone spared her lord.
²⁷ *instruments*: pistols.
²⁸ *mask*: dance of masquers, appropriate to the disguise of
the conspirators.   ²⁹ *matachin*: sword dance.
³⁰ *spaniel*: supposed to remain constant the more it was
beaten.
³¹ *pillar*: which supported the "Heavens" above the
stage.   ³² *center*: of the earth—hell.
³³ *train*: comet's tail.   ³⁴ *Conceit*: Imagination.
³⁵ *falling-sickness*: epilepsy, supposedly cured by sprink-
ling the face with blood.
³⁶ *fox*: sword (English blade makers often counterfeited
the armorers' mark of Solingen—a running fox—to give a
better market to their work).

I ever thought a cutler should distinguish
The cause of my death, rather than a doctor.
Search my wound deeper; tent [37] it with the steel   240
That made it.
    Vit. Cor.   Oh, my greatest sin lay in my blood!
Now my blood pays for't.
    Flam.   Thou'rt a noble sister!
I love thee now. If woman do breed man,
She ought to teach him manhood. Fare thee well.
Know, many glorious women that are famed
For masculine virtue have been vicious,
Only a happier silence did betide them.
She hath no faults who hath the art to hide them.
    Vit. Cor.   My soul, like to a ship in a black storm,
Is driven I know not whither.
    Flam.   Then cast anchor.   250
Prosperity doth bewitch men, seeming clear,
But seas do laugh, show white, when rocks are near.
We cease to grieve, cease to be fortune's slaves,
Nay, cease to die, by dying. Art thou [38] gone?
And thou [39] so near the bottom? False report,
Which says that women vie with the nine Muses
For nine tough durable lives! I do not look
Who went before, nor who shall follow me;
No, at myself I will begin and end.
While we look up to heaven, we confound   260
Knowledge with knowledge. Oh, I am in a mist!
    Vit. Cor.   Oh, happy they that never saw the court,
Nor ever knew great men but by report!
                          VITTORIA *dies.*
Flam. I recover like a spent taper, for a flash,
And instantly go out.
Let all that belong to great men remember the old
wives' tradition, to be like the lions [40] i' the Tower
on Candlemas-day: [41] to mourn if the sun shine, for
fear of the pitiful remainder of winter to come.
'Tis well yet there's some goodness in my death;   270
My life was a black charnel. I have caught
An everlasting cold; I have lost my voice
Most irrecoverably. Farewell, glorious villains!
This busy trade of life appears most vain,
Since rest breeds rest where [42] all seek pain by pain.
Let no harsh flattering bells resound my knell;

Strike, thunder, and strike loud, to my farewell!
                                  Dies.

      Enter Ambassadors *and* GIOVANNI.

    Eng. Amb.   This way, this way! break ope the doors!
    this way!
    Lod.   Ha! are we betrayed?
Why, then let's constantly die all together;   280
And having finished this most noble deed,
Defy the worst of fate, not fear to bleed.
    Eng. Amb.   Keep back the prince. Shoot, shoot.

        [GIOVANNI *shoots* LODOVICO.]

    Lod.   Oh, I
    am wounded!
I fear I shall be ta'en.
    Giov.   You bloody villains,
By what authority have you committed
This massacre?
    Lod.   By thine.
    Giov.   Mine?
    Lod.   Yes; thy uncle,
Which is a part of thee, enjoined us to't.
Thou know'st me, I am sure; I am Count Lodowick;
And thy most noble uncle in disguise
Was last night in thy court.
    Giov.   Ha!
    [*Gasp.*]   Yes, that Moor   290
Thy father chose his pensioner.
    Giov. He turned murderer!—
Away with them to prison and to torture!
All that have hands in this shall taste our justice,
As I hope heaven.
    Lod.   I do glory yet
That I can call this act mine own. For my part,
The rack, the gallows, and the torturing wheel,
Shall be but sound sleeps to me. Here's my rest;
I limned this night-piece, [43] and it was my best.
    Giov. Remove the bodies.—See, my honored lords,
What use you ought make of their punishment.   301
Let guilty men remember, their black deeds
Do lean on crutches made of slender reeds.
                                 [*Exeunt.*]

Instead of an EPILOGUE, only this of Martial supplies me.

    Haec fuerint nobis praemia, si placui. [1]

FOR the action of the play, 'twas generally well, and I
dare affirm, with the joint-testimony of some of their

---

[37] *tent:* search.   [38] *thou:* Zanche.   [39] *thou:* Vittoria.
[40] *lions:* which, with other beasts, were lodged in the
Tower of London.
[41] *Candelmas-day:* February 2, which, if sunny, presaged
a long winter still to come.   [42] *where:* whereas.
[43] *limned this night-piece:* painted this dark picture.
EPILOGUE
   [1] *L.:* "These will be reward to us if I have pleased you,"
Martial, II. 91. 8).

own quality, for the true imitation of life, without striving to make nature a monster, the best that ever became them; whereof as I make a general acknowledgment, so in particular I must remember the well-approved industry of my friend Master Perkins,[2] and confess the worth of his action did crown both the beginning and end.

F I N I S

---

[2] *Perkins:* a well-known actor of the period.

John Webster

THE DUCHESS OF MALFI

Webster's masterpiece, The Duchess of Malfi, was written evidently in 1613–14, and printed for the first time in a quarto of 1623. Presumably the play is later than The White Devil, not only as it is more skillful a performance but also as it appears to levy on two works of 1612: George Chapman's version of *Petrarch's Seven Penitential Psalms* and Donne's *Anatomy of the World* (pt. I, pub. 1611, pt. II, 1612). The Duchess of Malfi was certainly acted before December 16, 1614, on which day William Ostler, who is known to have taken the role of Antonio, died.

The title page of the first quarto ("printed by Nicolas Okes for John Waterson" and bearing Webster's name) advertises the play as having been presented privately by the King's Men, which had been Shakespeare's company, at the Blackfriars, a roofed-in theater, artificially lighted, and hence used for winter performances; and publicly by the same company at the Globe, a theater open to the sky, lit only by daylight, and serving for performances in summer. This initial quarto, on which the present text depends, purports to be "the perfect and exact copy, with diverse things printed, that the length of the play would not bear in the presentment." A Latin epigraph on the title page abridges a passage from Horace's *Epistles*, I. vi. 67–8: "If you know wiser precepts than mine, be kind and tell them to me; if you do not, practice my precepts with me."

As he had done in The White Devil, Webster draws often on Florio's translation of Montaigne and, more heavily than before on Sidney's *Arcadia*, a new edition of which had been published in 1613. Contemporary emblem books continue to furnish incidental material; the debt to Shakespeare in play after play remains insistent. The influence of the new vogue of "character writing," in which Webster probably participated and which is associated chiefly with the name of Sir Thomas Overbury, has been remarked. Webster's story, however it came to him, is rooted in events occurring in Italy in the years 1505–13 and sufficiently current in Renaissance England. The tragedy of the young and widowed Duchess of Amalfi, whose secret marriage to her major-domo, Antonio Bologna, enraged her brothers and precipitated her disappearance and his murder, was most familiar from William Painter's account in his famous collection of sensational tales, *The Palace of Pleasure* (1566–67). Painter's source is François de Belleforest's *Histoires Tragiques* (1565), itself dependent on Matteo Bandello's moralizing *Novelle* of 1554. Other retellings include George Whetstone's *Heptameron of Civil Discourses* (1582), Thomas Beard's *Theatre of God's Judgments* (1597), and Edward Grimestone's translation (1607) of Goulart's *Histoires Admirables* (1600, 1606), whence Webster gathered his gruesome lore on lycanthropy. It is worth noting, finally, that the tragedy of the Duchess and her consort is the inspiration of a play by Webster's great contemporary, Lope de Vega.

The Duchess of Malfi is perhaps the greatest tragedy of the English Renaissance after Shakespeare. It is by no means, however, a continuing or reworking of Shakespeare's kind of play, as exemplified in tragedies like *King Lear* and *Othello*. Lear is a man more sinned against than sinning but he makes love, in Hamlet's phrase, to his employment. Though the Moor of Venice seems the perfect dupe—his pockets, said Bernard Shaw, are picked by the villainous Iago—there is no doubt that he is conceived by the playwright at least partly as a free and responsible agent. Passion collies or blackens his best judgment and attempts to lead the way. As he follows its unholy promptings, he collaborates in his own destruction. There is no suggestion of collaborating or culpability in Webster. The Duchess and her husband are destroyed as they are the natural fools of fortune. The characterization seems to hold for us all. This is a vision of human destiny in which even the unflinching Shakespeare does not readily acquiesce.

R. A. F.

The Duchess of Malfi

[EPISTLE DEDICATORY]

To the Right Honorable
GEORGE HARDING,[1] BARON BERKELEY,
of Berkeley Castle
and Knight of the Order of the Bath
to the illustrious Prince CHARLES.

My noble Lord,

THAT I may present my excuse why, (being a stranger to your lordship), I offer this poem to your patronage, I plead this warrant men who never saw the sea yet desire to behold that regiment[2] of waters, choose some eminent river to guide them thither; and make that, as it were, their conduct or 10 postilion.[3] By the like ingenious means has your fame arrived at my knowledge, receiving it from some of worth, who both in contemplation, and practice, owe to your honor their clearest[4] service. I do not altogether look up at your title, the ancientest nobility being but a relic of time past, and the truest honor indeed being for a man to confer honor on himself, which your learning strives to propagate, and shall make you arrive at the dignity of a great example. I am confident this work is not unworthy your honor's perusal for by such poems as this, poets have kissed the hands of great princes, and drawn their gentle eyes to look down upon their sheets of paper, when the poets themselves were bound up in their winding sheets.[5] The like courtesy from your lordship shall make 20 you live in your grave, and laurel[6] spring out of it; when the ignorant scorners of the muses (that like worms in libraries seem to live only to destroy learning) shall wither, neglected and forgotten. This work and myself I humbly present to your approved censure.[7] It being the utmost of my wishes, to have your honorable self my weighty and perspicuous[8] comment: which grace so done me, shall ever be acknowledged

By your lordship's
in all duty and
observance,
JOHN WEBSTER. 30

DEDICATION

[1] *Harding:* though born in 1601 and hence a youth at the time of the play, a fitting recipient of the dedication in that his father and grandfather, the Lords Hunsdon, had been patrons of the Lord Chamberlain's Men, subsequently the King's Men.

[2] *regiment:* kingdom; more generally, "place" (though not so cited by OED before 1662).

[3] *conduct or postilion:* guide or messenger.

[4] *clearest:* entire.   [5] *bound . . . sheets:* in the grave.

[6] *laurel:* betokening distinction in poetry.

[7] *approved censure:* experienced judgment.

[8] *perspicuous:* lucid.

[COMMENDATORY VERSES]

In the just worth of that well deserver,
MR. JOHN WEBSTER,
and upon this masterpiece of tragedy.

In this thou imitatest one rich, and wise,
That sees his good deeds done before he dies;
As he by works, thou by this work of fame,
Hast well provided for thy living name;
To trust to others' honorings is worth's crime,
Thy monument is raised in thy life time;
And 'tis most just; for every worthy man   10
Is his own marble; and his merit can
Cut him to any figure, and express
More art, than Death's cathedral palaces,
Where royal ashes keep their court: thy note
Be ever plainness, 'tis the richest coat:
Thy epitaph only the title be,
Write, *Duchess,* that will fetch a tear for thee,
For who e'er saw this *Duchess* live, and die,
That could get off under a bleeding eye?

In Tragaediam.   20
Ut lux ex tenebris ictu percussa tonantis,
Illa (ruina malis) claris sit vita poetis.[1]
          Thomas Middletonus,
               Poeta & Chron:
                    Londinensis.[2]

To his friend MR. JOHN WEBSTER
Upon his
DUCHESS OF MALFI.

I never saw thy Duchess, till the day
That she was lively bodied in thy play;
Howe'er she answered[3] her low-rated[4] love,
Her brothers' anger did so fatal prove,
Yet my opinion is, she might speak more;
But never in her life so well before.   9
               WIL: ROWLEY.[5]

To the reader of the author,
and his
DUCHESS OF MALFI.

Crown him a poet, whom nor Rome, nor Greece,
Transcend in all theirs, for a masterpiece:
In which, whiles words and matter change,[6] and men
Act one another; he, from whose clear pen
They all took life, to memory hath lent
A lasting fame, to raise his monument.   9
               JOHN FORD.[7]

DRAMATIS PERSONÆ[1]

FERDINAND, *Duke of Calabria, and twin brother to the Duchess*
The CARDINAL, *their elder brother*
DANIEL DE BOSOLA, *their spy; in the employ of the Duchess*

ANTONIO BOLOGNA, *steward of the Duchess's household*
DELIO, *his friend*
CASTRUCHIO, *an elderly courtier, husband of Julia*
The Marquis of PESCARA, *a soldier*
Count MALATESTE, *a Roman courtier*
SILVIO ⎫
RODERIGO ⎬ *Courtiers at Amalfi*
GRISOLAN ⎭
The Doctor
FOROBOSCO, *a nonspeaking part presenting an official at the Duchess's court*
The DUCHESS OF MALFI, *a widow, afterwards married in secret to Antonio*
CARIOLA, *her waiting woman*
JULIA, *wife of Castruchio, and mistress to the Cardinal*
Old Lady, *a midwife*
Two Pilgrims
Eight Madmen (*an Astrologer, Broker, Doctor, English Tailor, Farmer, Gentleman Usher, Lawyer, and Priest*)
Court Officers; Attendants; Servants; Guards; Executioners; Churchmen
Ladies-in-Waiting

COMMENDATORY VERSES
    [1] *L.:* "To Tragedy. As light from darkness springs from the stroke of the thunderer, So may it (while bringing ruin to the evil) be life to famous poets."
    [2] *Thomas . . . Londinensis:* The playwright and poet Thomas Middleton (1580–1627) had been appointed City Chronologer of London in 1620.   [3] *answered:* justified.
    [4] *low-rated:* not noble in lineage.
    [5] *William Rowley:* A well-known actor, poet, and playwright, who died 1626, and who collaborated with Middleton, Webster, and Ford.
    [6] *whiles . . . change:* so long as plays endure.
    [7] *John Ford:* celebrated dramatist of the earlier seventeenth century, d. 1639.

DRAMATIS PERSONÆ
    [1] In the less descriptive listing of the persons of the play given in the quarto, the names of the chief original actors are included.

ACT ONE

SCENE ONE

[*Enter* ANTONIO *and* DELIO.]

Del. You are welcome to your country, dear Antonio,
You have been long in France, and you return
A very formal Frenchman, in your habit.[1]
How do you like the French court?
Ant.   I admire it.
In seeking to reduce both state and people
To a fixed order, their judicious King
Begins at home. Quits first his royal palace
Of flattering sycophants, of dissolute
And infamous persons, which he sweetly terms
His master's masterpiece, the work of heaven,   10
Considering duly that a prince's court
Is like a common fountain, whence should flow
Pure silver drops in general.[2] But if't chance
Some cursed example poison't near the head,[3]
Death and diseases through the whole land spread.
And what is't makes this blessèd government
But a most provident council, who dare freely
Inform him, the corruption of times?
Though some o'th' court hold it presumption
To instruct princes what they ought to do,   20
It is noble duty to inform them
What they ought to foresee. Here comes Bosola,

[*Enter* BOSOLA.]

The only court-gall:[4] yet I observe his railing
Is not for simple love of piety.
Indeed he rails at those things which he wants,
Would be as lecherous, covetous, or proud,
Bloody, or envious, as any man,
If he had means to do so. Here's the Cardinal.

[*Enter* CARDINAL.]

Bos. I do haunt you still.
Card. So.   30
Bos. I have done you better service than to be
slighted thus. Miserable age, where only the reward[5] of
doing well is the doing of it!
Card. You enforce your merit too much.
Bos. I fell into the galleys in your service, where, for
two years together, I wore two towels instead of a shirt
with a knot on the shoulder, after the fashion of a
Roman mantle. Slighted thus? I will thrive some way:
blackbirds fatten best in hard weather:[6] why not I, in
these dog-days?[7]   40
Card. Would you could become honest—
Bos. With all your divinity, do but direct me the way
to it. I have known many travel far for it, and yet return
as arrant knaves as they went forth; because they carried themselves always along with them.
                              [*Exit* CARDINAL.]
Are you gone? Some fellows, they say, are possessed
with the devil, but this great fellow were able to possess
the greatest devil, and make him worse.
Ant. He hath denied thee some suit?[8]   49
Bos. He and his brother are like plum trees, that

grow crooked over standing[9] pools; they are rich, and
o'erladen with fruit, but none but crows, pies,[10] and
caterpillars feed on them. Could I be one of their
flattering panders, I would hang on their ears like a
horse-leech, till I were full,[11] and then drop off. I pray
leave me. Who would rely upon these miserable dependences,[12] in expectation to be advanced tomorrow?
What creature ever fed worse than hoping Tantalus;[13]
nor ever died any man more fearfully than he that
hoped for a pardon? There are rewards[14] for   60
hawks, and dogs, when they have done us service; but
for a soldier, that hazards his limbs in a battle, nothing
but a kind of geometry[15] is his last supportation.
Del. Geometry?
Bos. Ay, to hang in a fair pair of slings, take his latter
swing in the world, upon an honorable pair of crutches,
from hospital to hospital: fare ye well sir. And yet do
not you scorn us, for places in the court are but like beds
in the hospital, where this man's head lies at the man's
foot, and so lower and lower.   70
                              [*Exit* BOSOLA.]
Del. I knew this fellow seven years in the galleys
For a notorious murder, and 'twas thought
The Cardinal suborned it:[16] he was released
By the French general Gaston de Foix[17]
When he recovered Naples.
Ant.   'Tis great pity
He should be thus neglected. I have heard
He's very valiant. This foul melancholy
Will poison all his goodness, for, I'll tell you,
If too immoderate sleep be truly said
To be an inward rust unto the soul;   80
It then doth follow want of action
Breeds all black malcontents, and their close rearing,
Like moths in cloth, do[18] hurt for want of wearing.

[*Enter* CASTRUCHIO, SILVIO, RODERIGO,
and GRISOLAN.]

I.i.
  [1] *habit:* clothing.   [2] *in general:* everywhere.
  [3] *head:* source.
  [4] *court-gall:* canker or source of venom or soreness in the
court.   [5] *only the reward:* the only reward.
  [6] *blackbirds . . . weather:* whether true or not, a commonplace from medieval times forward.
  [7] *dog-days:* hot; hence, disagreeable.   [8] *suit:* request.
  [9] *standing:* stagnant, the water not moving.
  [10] *pies:* magpies.   [11] *full:* of blood.
  [12] *dependences:* contingencies; deferred promises.
  [13] *Tantalus:* emblematic of the disappointed or "tanta-
lized" man, whose punishment in Hades was to stand up to
the neck in water and be unable to drink or, though fruit
hung near him, to be unable to reach it and eat.
  [14] *rewards:* technical term from hunting, denoting a portion of the prey.
  [15] *geometry:* denoting awkwardness, as of clothing hanging
stiffly on a line; and suggesting also (as the next lines make
clear) crutches, by analogy to a pair of stiff twin compasses.
  [16] *it:* the murder or the punishment.
  [17] *Gaston de Foix:* This famous military figure of the early
sixteenth century died in the moment of his greatest victory,
over the Spanish and Papal armies at Ravenna, but had
nothing to do with the recapturing of Naples.
  [18] *do:* grammatically confused but the sense is clear:
clothing not worn and infested by moths is injured—like
malcontents who are kept idle.

Del. The presence[19] 'gins to fill. You promised me
To make me the partaker of the natures
Of some of your great courtiers.

Ant.   The Lord Cardinal's
And other strangers'[20] that are now in court?
I shall. Here comes the great Calabrian Duke.

[*Enter* FERDINAND.]

Ferd. Who took the ring[21] oftenest?

Sil. Antonio Bologna, my lord.   90

Ferd. Our sister Duchess' great master of her
household? Give him the jewel: when shall we leave
this sportive action, and fall to action indeed?

Cast. Methinks, my lord, you should not desire to
go to war, in person.

Ferd. [*Aside*] Now, for some gravity: why, my lord?

Cast. It is fitting a soldier arise to be a prince, but
not necessary a prince descend to be a captain!

Ferd. No?

Cast. No, my lord, he were far better do it by a
deputy.   101

Ferd. Why should he not as well sleep, or eat, by a
deputy? This might take idle, offensive, and base office
from him, whereas the other deprives him of honor.

Cast. Believe my experience: that realm is never long
in quiet where the ruler is a soldier.

Ferd. Thou told'st me thy wife could not endure
fighting.[22]

Cast. True, my lord.

Ferd. And of a jest she broke,[23] of a captain she met
full of wounds: I have forgot it.   111

Cast She told him, my lord, he was a pitiful fellow,
to lie, like the children of Ismael,[24] all in tents.[25]

Ferd. Why, there's a wit were able to undo all the

chirurgeons o' the city, for although gallants should
quarrel, and had drawn their weapons, and were ready
to go to it; yet her persuasions would make them put
up.[26]

Cast. That she would, my lord.
How do you like my Spanish jennet?[27]   120

Rod. He is all fire.

Ferd. I am of Pliny's opinion,[28] I think he was begot
by the wind; he runs as if he were ballassed[29] with
quicksilver.

Sil. True, my lord, he reels from the tilt[30] often.

Rod. ⎫
Gris. ⎬ Ha, ha, ha!

Ferd. Why do you laugh? Methinks you that are
courtiers should be my touchwood, take fire when I
give fire; that is, laugh when I laugh, were the subject
never so witty—   130

Cast. True, my lord, I myself have heard a very
good jest, and have scorned to seem to have so silly a
wit as to understand it.

Ferd. But I can laugh at your fool, my lord.

Cast. He cannot speak, you know, but he makes
faces; my lady cannot abide him.

Ferd. No?

Cast. Nor endure to be in merry company; for she
says too much laughing, and too much company fills
her too full of the wrinkle.[31]   140

Ferd. I would then have a mathematical instrument
made for her face, that she might not laugh out of
compass.[32] I shall shortly visit you at Milan, Lord
Silvio.

Sil. Your grace shall arrive most welcome.

Ferd. You are a good horseman, Antonio; you have
excellent riders in France,[33] what do you think of good
horsemanship?

Ant. Nobly, my lord: as out of the Grecian horse[34]
issued many famous princes: so out of brave   150
horsemanship, arise the first sparks of growing resolution, that raise the mind to noble action.

Ferd. You have bespoke it worthily.

[*Enter* DUCHESS, CARDINAL, CARIOLA, *and*
JULIA.]

Sil. Your brother, the Lord Cardinal, and sister
Duchess.

Card. Are the galleys come about?[35]

Gris. They are, my lord.

Ferd. Here's the Lord Silvio, is come to take his
leave.   159

Del. [*Aside to* ANTONIO] Now, sir, your promise:
what's that Cardinal? I mean his temper? They say he's
a brave[36] fellow, will play his five thousand crowns at
tennis, dance, court ladies, and one that hath fought
single combats.

Ant. Some such flashes[37] superficially hang on him,
for form. But observe his inward character: he is a
melancholy churchman. The spring[38] in his face is
nothing but the engendering of toads: where he is
jealous of any man, he lays worse plots for them than
ever was imposed on Hercules;[39] for he strews in   170
his way flatterers, panders, intelligencers,[40] atheists

---

[19] *presence:* royal presence or audience chamber.

[20] *strangers':* implying "natures."

[21] *ring:* In running at the ring, the idea was to carry off the
latter suspended in air, on the tip of one's lance.

[22] *fighting:* since Ferdinand is mocking Castruchio, "fighting" has probably a sexual implication, reinforced by what
follows.   [23] *broke:* cracked.

[24] *Ismael:* Ishmael.

[25] *tents:* Since "chirurgeons" or surgeons follow at once,
"tents" must allude also to the rolls of lint used for probing
or "tenting" a wound. In this case the tents, remaining in
the wound like plugs, carry a sexual suggestion.

[26] *put up:* sheathe their swords; also, forbear to "go to it"
sexually.   [27] *Spanish jennet:* valuable sporting horse.

[28] *Pliny's opinion:* gathered from his miscalled *Natural
History*, trans. Philemon Holland, 1601.

[29] *ballassed:* ballasted.

[30] *reels . . . tilt:* declines to run at the ring; but to "tilt" is
also to copulate, and the quicksilver or mercury with which
the horse is ballassed is a remedy for syphilis.

[31] *wrinkle:* with secondary meaning of moral stain or
blemish.

[32] *out of compass:* beyond the scope of that instrument;
"excessively."

[33] *France:* proverbial, as elsewhere, for horsemanship.

[34] *Grecian horse:* the Trojan horse.

[35] *come about:* returned.   [36] *brave:* splendid.

[37] *flashes:* specious or showy displays.

[38] *spring:* pond; but also the springlike promise of his
flashes.

[39] *Hercules:* famous for the labors he was charged to
perform.   [40] *intelligencers:* spies.

and a thousand such political[41] monsters. He should
have been Pope; but instead of coming to it by the
primitive decency[42] of the Church, he did bestow
bribes, so largely, and so impudently, as if he would
have carried it away without heaven's knowledge. Some
good he hath done.

   Del. You have given too much of him. What's his
      brother?

   Ant. The Duke there? A most perverse and
      turbulent nature;

What appears in him mirth is merely outside.   180
If he laugh heartily, it is to laugh
All honesty out of fashion.

   Del.   Twins?

   Ant.   In quality.

He speaks with others' tongues, and hears men's suits
With others' ears: will seem to sleep o'th' bench[43]
Only to entrap offenders in their answers;
Dooms men to death by information.[44]
Rewards, by hearsay.[45]

   Del.   Then the law to him
Is like a foul black cobweb to a spider;
He makes it his dwelling, and a prison
To entangle those shall feed him.

   Ant.   Most true.   190
He never pays debts, unless they be shrewd turns,[46]
And those he will confess that he doth owe.
Last: for his brother, there, the Cardinal,
They that do flatter him most say oracles
Hang at his lips: and verily I believe them,
For the devil speaks in them.
But for their sister, the right noble Duchess,
You never fixed your eye on three fair medals,
Cast in one figure,[47] of so different temper.
For her discourse, it is so full of rapture,   200
You only will begin then to be sorry
When she doth end her speech: and wish, in wonder,
She held it less vainglory to talk much
Than your penance to hear her: whilst she speaks,
She throws upon a man so sweet a look
That it were able to raise one to a galliard[48]
That lay in a dead palsy; and to dote
On that sweet countenance: but in that look
There speaketh so divine a continence[49]
As cut off all lascivious and vain hope.   210
Her days are practiced in such noble virtue
That, sure her nights, nay more, her very sleeps,
Are more in heaven than other ladies' shrifts.[50]
Let all sweet ladies break their flattering glasses,
And dress themselves in her.

   Del.   Fie, Antonio,
You play the wire-drawer[51] with her commendations.

   Ant. I'll case the picture up[52] only thus much:
All her particular worth grows to this sum:
She stains[53] the time past; lights the time to come.

   Car. You must attend my lady, in the gallery,   220
Some half an hour hence.

   Ant.   I shall.
                [*Exeunt* ANTONIO *and* DELIO.]

   Ferd. Sister, I have a suit to you.

   Duch.   To me, sir?

   Ferd. A gentleman here: Daniel de Bosola:
One, that was in the galleys.

   Duch.   Yes, I know him.

   Ferd. A worthy fellow h'is: pray let me entreat for
The provisorship of your horse.

   Duch.   Your knowledge of him
Commends him, and prefers him.

   Ferd.   Call him hither.
                  [*Exit* Attendant.]
We are now upon parting. Good Lord Silvio,
Do us commend to all our noble friends
At the leaguer.[54]

   Sil.   Sir, I shall.   230

   Duch. You are for Milan?

   Sil.   I am.

   Duch. Bring the caroches:[55] we'll bring you down
    to the haven.
        [*Exeunt* DUCHESS, CARIOLA, SILVIO,
        CASTRUCHIO, RODERIGO, GRISOLAN,
                  and JULIA.]

   Card. Be sure you entertain that Bosola
For your intelligence:[56] I would not be seen in't.
And therefore many times I have slighted him,
When he did court our furtherance: as this morning.

   Ferd. Antonio, the great master of her household
Had been far fitter.

   Card.   You are deceived in him,
His nature is too honest for such business.
He comes. I'll leave you.

              [*Enter* BOSOLA.]

   Bos.   I was lured[57] to you.   240
               [*Exit* CARDINAL.]

   Ferd. My brother here, the Cardinal, could never
Abide you.

   Bos.   Never since he was in my debt.

   Ferd. May be some oblique[58] character in your face
Made him suspect you?

   Bos.   Doth he study physiognomy?
There's no more credit to be given to th'face
Than to a sick man's urine, which some call
The physician's whore, because she cozens him.
He did suspect me wrongfully.

   Ferd.   For that
You must give great men leave to take their times.

---

[41] *political:* politic; devious.
[42] *decency:* decorum; fit practice.
[43] *bench:* judge's bench.
[44] *information:* as from "intelligencers" (above).
[45] *hearsay:* on idle or insufficient testimony.
[46] *shrewd turns:* i.e., likely, as he fails to pay them, to
plague him.
[47] *figure:* shape; the two men and their sister are of the
same blood, but there the resemblance ends.
[48] *galliard:* lively dance.
[49] *continence:* modest self-control.
[50] *shrifts:* confessions.
[51] *play the wire-drawer:* spin it out falsely.
[52] *case . . . up:* put the picture away.
[53] *stains:* deprives of light or color.
[54] *leaguer:* military camp.   [55] *caroches:* coaches.
[56] *intelligence:* spy.   [57] *lured:* like a trained hawk.
[58] *oblique:* crooked.

Distrust doth cause us seldom be deceived;   250
You see, the oft shaking of the cedar tree
Fastens it more at root.
    Bos.   Yet take heed,
For to suspect a friend unworthily
Instructs him the next [59] way to suspect you
And prompts him to deceive you.
    Ferd.   There's gold.
    Bos.   So.
What follows? Never rained such showers as these
Without thunderbolts i'th' tail of them; [60]
Whose throat must I cut?
    Ferd. Your inclination to shed blood rides post [61]
Before my occasion to use you. I give you that   260
To live i'th' court, here, and observe the Duchess,
To note all the particulars of her 'havior: [62]
What suitors do solicit her for marriage
And whom she best affects. She's a young widow,
I would not have her marry again.
    Bos.   No, sir?
    Ferd. Do not you ask the reason but be satisfied.
I say I would not.
    Bos.   It seems you would create me
One of your familiars. [63]
    Ferd.   Familiar? What's that?
    Bos. Why, a very quaint invisible devil in flesh:
An intelligencer.
    Ferd.   Such a kind of thriving thing   270
I would wish thee: and ere long, thou mayst arrive
At a higher place by't.
    Bos.   Take your devils
Which hell calls angels: [64] these cursed gifts would make
You a corrupter, me an impudent traitor,
And should I take these they'd take me to hell.
    Ferd. Sir, I'll take nothing from you that I have
    given.
There is a place that I procured for you
This morning, the provisorship o'th' horse,
Have you heard on't?
    Bos.   No.
    Ferd.   'Tis yours, is't not worth
    thanks?
    Bos. I would have you curse yourself now, that your
    bounty,   280
Which makes men truly noble, e'er should make
Me a villain: Oh, that to avoid ingratitude
For the good deed you have done me, I must do

---

[59] *next:* nearest.
[60] *Never . . . them:* alluding to the impregnating of Danaë by Jupiter, who came to her in a shower of gold.
[61] *post:* quickly.   [62] *'havior:* behavior.
[63] *familiars:* evil spirits or minions.
[64] *angels:* gold or silver coins.   [65] *Candies:* Sugars.
[66] *complemental:* accomplished; good.
[67] *luxurious:* lecherous.
[68] *Laban's sheep:* alluding, like Shylock, to Genesis 30: 31–43.   [69] *motion:* intention.
[70] *rank:* luxurious or teeming (here, sexually).
[71] *suck:* proverbially, the office of witches, who were often supplied therefore with an extra nipple.
[72] *Vulcan's engine:* the invisible net in which Vulcan trapped his wife Venus with her lover Mars.

All the ill man can invent. Thus the devil
Candies [65] all sins o'er: and what heaven terms vile,
That names he complemental. [66]
    Ferd.   Be yourself.
Keep your old garb of melancholy: 'twill express
You envy those that stand above your reach,
Yet strive not to come near 'em. This will gain
Access to private lodgings, where yourself   290
May, like a politic dormouse—
    Bos.   As I have seen some
Feed in a lord's dish, half asleep, not seeming
To listen to any talk: and yet these rogues
Have cut his throat in a dream. What's my place?
The provisorship o'th' horse? Say then my corruption
Grew out of horse dung. I am your creature.
    Ferd. Away!
    Bos. Let good men, for good deeds, cover good fame,
Since place and riches oft are bribes of shame;
Sometimes the devil doth preach.   300
                         Exit BOSOLA.

        [*Enter* CARDINAL *and* DUCHESS.]

    Card. We are to part from you: and your own
    discretion
Must now be your director.
    Ferd.   You are a widow.
You know already what man is: and therefore
Let not youth, high promotion, eloquence—
    Card. No, nor anything without the addition,
    Honor,
Sway your high blood.
    Ferd.   Marry? They are most
    luxurious, [67]
Will wed twice.
    Card.   Oh, fie!
    Ferd.   Their livers are more spotted
Than Laban's sheep. [68]
    Duch.   Diamonds are of most value
They say, that have passed through most jewelers'
    hands.
    Ferd. Whores, by that rule, are precious.
    Duch.   Will you
    hear me?   310
I'll never marry—
    Card.   So most widows say.
But commonly that motion [69] lasts no longer
Than the turning of an hourglass; the funeral sermon
And it end both together.
    Ferd.   Now hear me.
You live in a rank [70] pasture here, i'th' court,
There is a kind of honey-dew that's deadly:
'Twill poison your fame; look to't; be not cunning,
For they whose faces do belie their hearts
Are witches ere they arrive at twenty years,   319
Ay, and give the devil suck. [71]
    Duch.   This is terrible good counsel.
    Ferd. Hypocrisy is woven of a fine small thread,
Subtler than Vulcan's engine; [72] yet believe't
Your darkest actions—nay, your privatest thoughts—
Will come to light.
    Card.   You may flatter yourself

And take your own choice: privately be married
Under the eaves of night—
 Ferd.   Think't the best voyage
That e'er you made; like the irregular crab,
Which, though't goes backward, thinks that it goes
 right,
Because it goes its own way; but observe:
Such weddings may more properly be said   330
To be executed[73] than celebrated.
 Card.   The marriage night
Is the entrance into some prison.
 Ferd.   And those joys,
Those lustful pleasures, are like heavy sleeps
Which do forerun man's mischief.
 Card.   Fare you well.
Wisdom begins at[74] the end: remember it.
        [*Exit* CARDINAL.]
 Duch. I think this speech between you both was
 studied,
It came so roundly[75] off.
 Ferd.   You are my sister,
This was my father's poniard:[76] do you see,
I'd be loath to see't look rusty, cause 'twas his. 339
I would have you to give o'er these chargeable[77] revels;
A visor and a mask are whispering-rooms[78]
That were never built for goodness: fare ye well:
And women like that part, which, like the lamprey,[79]
Hath never a bone in't.
 Duch.   Fie, sir!
 Ferd.   Nay,
I mean the tongue: variety of courtship;
What cannot a neat[80] knave with a smooth tale
Make a woman believe? Farewell, lusty widow.
        [*Exit* FERDINAND.]
 Duch. Shall this move me? If all my royal kindred
Lay in my way unto this marriage,   349
I'ld make them my low foot-steps.[81] And even now,
Even in this hate, as men in some great battles
By apprehending[82] danger, have achieved
Almost impossible actions: I have heard soldiers say
 so,—
So I, through frights and threatenings, will assay[83]
This dangerous venture. Let old wives report
I winked,[84] and chose a husband.

    [*Enter* CARIOLA.]

       Cariola,
To thy known secrecy I have given up
More than my life, my fame.
 Car.   Both shall be safe.
For I'll conceal this secret from the world
As warily as those that trade in poison   360
Keep poison from their children.
 Duch.   Thy protestation
Is ingenious[85] and hearty. I believe it.
Is Antonio come?
 Car. He attends you.
 Duch.   Good dear soul,
Leave me; but place thyself behind the arras,
Where thou mayst overhear us. Wish me good speed,
For I am going into a wilderness,

Where I shall find nor path, nor friendly clue[86]
To be my guide.

  [CARIOLA *goes behind the arras; the* DUCHESS
   draws the traverse[87] *to reveal* ANTONIO.]

     I sent for you. Sit down.
Take pen and ink, and write. Are you ready?
 Ant.   Yes.
 Duch. What did I say?
 Ant.   That I should write
 somewhat.   370
 Duch. Oh, I remember.
After these triumphs[88] and this large expense
It's fit, like thrifty husbands,[89] we inquire
What's laid up for tomorrow.
 Ant. So please your beautous excellence.
 Duch.   Beauteous?
Indeed, I thank you: I look young for your sake.
You have tane[90] my cares upon you.
 Ant.   I'll fetch your
 grace
The particulars of your revenue and expense.
 Duch. Oh, you are an upright treasurer: but you
 mistook,
For when I said I meant to make inquiry   380
What's laid up for tomorrow, I did mean
What's laid up yonder for me.
 Ant.   Where?
 Duch.   In heaven.
I am making my will, as 'tis fit princes should
In perfect memory, and I pray, sir, tell me
Were not one better make it smiling, thus?
Than in deep groans, and terrible ghastly looks,
As if the gifts we parted with procured
That violent destruction?
 Ant.   Oh, much better.
 Duch. If I had a husband now, this care were quit.
But I intend to make you overseer;   390
What good deed shall we first remember? Say.
 Ant. Begin with that first good deed, begin i'th'
 world,
After man's creation, the sacrament of marriage.

---

 [73] *executed:* proper liturgical term, like "celebrated," but playing on the more common meaning.
 [74] *begins at:* considers. [75] *roundly:* smoothly.
 [76] *poniard:* dagger.   [77] *chargeable:* costly.
 [78] *whispering-rooms:* occasions for secret and illicit conversation.
 [79] *lamprey:* eel-like fish; the oblique reference, despite the lack of a "bone," is to the penis, as "part" (before) and "tale" (following) make clear. [80] *neat:* well turned out.
 [81] *foot-steps:* rungs, steppingstones.
 [82] *apprehending:* taking hold of; confronting.
 [83] *assay:* try. [84] *winked:* shut my eyes; chose recklessly.
 [85] *ingenious:* modern sense; also, "ingenuous."
 [86] *clue:* thread (to conduct one through the labyrinth or wilderness).
 [87] *traverse:* concealing the inner stage. The direction given here, as mostly in the play, is editorial reconstruction.
 [88] *triumphs:* festivities.
 [89] *husbands:* husbandmen; provident stewards. But the Duchess is using the word with deliberate ambiguity.
 [90] *tane:* taken.

I'd have you first provide for a good husband,
Give him all.
    Duch.   All?
    Ant.   Yes, your excellent self.
    Duch. In a winding sheet?[91]
    Ant.   In a couple.[92]
    Duch. St. Winifred![93] that were a strange will.
    Ant.   'Twere
    strange
If there were no will in you to marry again.
    Duch. What do you think of marriage?
    Ant. I take't, as those that deny purgatory,[94]   400
It locally contains or heaven, or hell;
There's no third place in't.
    Duch.   How do you affect[95] it?
    Ant. My banishment, feeding my melancholy,
Would often reason thus.
    Duch.   Pray let's hear it.
    Ant. Say a man never marry, nor have children,
What takes that from him? Only the bare name
Of being a father, or the weak delight
To see the little wanton ride a-cock-horse
Upon a painted stick, or hear him chatter
Like a taught starling.
    Duch.   Fie, fie, what's all this?   410
One of your eyes is bloodshot. Use my ring to't,
They say 'tis very sovereign;[96] 'twas my wedding
    ring,
And I did vow never to part with it,
But to my second husband.
    Ant. You have parted with it now.
    Duch.   Yes, to help your
    eyesight.
    Ant. You have made me stark blind.
    Duch.   How?
    Ant. There is a saucy and ambitious devil
Is dancing in this circle.[97]
    Duch.   Remove him.
    Ant.   How?
    Duch. There needs small conjuration, when your
    finger
May do it: thus, is it fit?

          [*She puts the ring on his finger.*] *He kneels.*

---

[91] *winding sheet:* grave cloths, since her husband is dead.
[92] *couple:* pair (of sheets); also, coupling, copulating.
[93] *St. Winifred:* Q reads "Winifrid," the name of Boniface, the apostle to the Germans. But Winifred, the Welsh saint who was beheaded for her chastity and restored to life by a miracle, seems more apposite.
[94] *those . . . purgatory:* Protestants.   [95] *affect:* like.
[96] *sovereign:* powerful (in curing).
[97] *circle:* punning on the ring or "circle," which the necromancer drew about the devil he had summoned.
[98] *Conceive:* Imagine.   [99] *aim:* guess.
[100] *darkening:* obscuring; analogy is to the practice of merchants who palmed off shoddy goods by keeping their shops ill lit.
[101] *progress:* make a royal progress or state journey and so discover your own title to rule.   [102] *pays:* requites.
[103] *doubles:* speaks ambiguously.
[104] *fearfully:* inducing fear.
[105] *L.:* Release, as from debt—or life.

    Ant.   What said you?
    Duch.   Sir,   420
This goodly roof of yours is too low built,
I cannot stand upright in't, nor discourse,
Without I raise it higher: raise yourself,
Or if you please, my hand to help you; so.

                      [*Raises him.*]

    Ant. Ambition, madam, is a great man's madness,
That is not kept in chains, and close-pent rooms,
But in fair lightsome lodgings, and is girt
With the wild noise of prattling visitants,
Which makes it lunatic beyond all cure.
Conceive[98] not I am so stupid, but I aim[99]   430
Whereto your favors tend. But he's a fool
That, being a-cold, would thrust his hands i'th' fire
To warm them.
    Duch.   So, now the ground's broke,
You may discover what a wealthy mine
I make you lord of.
    Ant.   Oh, my unworthiness!
    Duch. You were ill to sell yourself;
This darkening[100] of your worth is not like that
Which tradesmen use i'th' city; their false lights
Are to rid bad wares off; and I must tell you,
If you will know where breathes a complete man,   440
I speak it without flattery, turn your eyes,
And progress[101] through yourself.
    Ant.   Were there nor
    heaven nor hell,
I should be honest. I have long served virtue,
And never tane wages of her.
    Duch.   Now she pays[102] it.
The misery of us, that are born great,
We are forced to woo because none dare woo us.
And as a tyrant doubles[103] with his words,
And fearfully[104] equivocates, so we
Are forced to express our violent passions
In riddles and in dreams, and leave the path   450
Of simple virtue, which was never made
To seem the thing it is not. Go, go brag
You have left me heartless, mine is in your bosom,
I hope 'twill multiply love there. You do tremble.
Make not your heart so dead a piece of flesh
To fear, more than to love me. Sir, be confident,
What is't distracts you? This is flesh, and blood, sir,
'Tis not the figure cut in alabaster
Kneels at my husband's tomb. Awake, awake, man,
I do here put off all vain ceremony,   460
And only do appear to you, a young widow
That claims you for her husband, and like a widow,
I use but half a blush in't.
    Ant.   Truth speak for me,
I will remain the constant sanctuary
Of your good name.
    Duch.   I thank you, gentle love,
And 'cause you shall not come to me in debt,
Being now my steward, here upon your lips
I sign your *Quietus est.*[105] This you should have begged
    now.
I have seen children oft eat sweetmeats thus,

As fearful to devour them too soon.   470
   Ant. But for [106] your brothers?
   Duch.   Do not think of them.
All discord, without this circumference, [107]
Is only to be pitied and not feared.
Yet, should they know it, time will easily
Scatter the tempest.
   Ant.   These words should be mine,
And all the parts you have spoke, if some part of it
Would not have savored flattery.
   Duch.   Kneel.

[*Enter* CARIOLA.]

   Ant.   Ha?
   Duch. Be not amazed, this woman's of my counsel.
I have heard lawyers say, a contract in a chamber,
Per verba de presenti, [108] is absolute marriage.   480
Bless, heaven, this sacred Gordian, [109] which let
   violence
Never untwine.
   Ant. And may our sweet affections, like the
   spheres, [110]
Be still in motion.
   Duch.   Quickening, and make
The like soft music.
   Ant. That we may imitate the loving palms, [111]
Best emblem of a peaceful marriage,
That never bore fruit divided.
   Duch. What can the Church force [112] more?
   Ant. That fortune may not know an accident   490
Either of joy or sorrow, to divide
Our fixed wishes.
   Duch.   How can the Church build faster?
We now are man and wife, and 'tis the Church
That must but echo [113] this. Maid, stand apart,
I now am blind.
   Ant.   What's your conceit [114] in this?
   Duch. I would have you lead your fortune [115] by the
   hand,
Unto your marriage bed.
You speak in me this, for we now are one.
We'll only lie, and talk together, and plot   499
T'appease my humorous [116] kindred; and if you please,
Like the old tale, in *Alexander and Lodowick*, [117]
Lay a naked sword between us, keep us chaste.
Oh, let me shroud [118] my blushes in your bosom,
Since 'tis the treasury of all my secrets.
   Car. Whether the spirit of greatness, or of woman
Reigns most in her, I know not, but it shows
A fearful madness. I owe her much of pity.
                      Exeunt.

ACT TWO

SCENE ONE

[*Enter* BOSOLA *and* CASTRUCHIO.]

   Bos. You say you would fain be taken for an eminent
courtier?
   Cast. 'Tis the very main [1] of my ambition.

   Bos. Let me see, you have a reasonable good face
for't already, and your nightcap expresses [2] your ears
sufficient largely; I would have you learn to twirl the
strings of your band [3] with a good grace; and in a set
speech, at th' end of every sentence, to hum, three or
four times, or blow your nose, till it smart again, to
recover your memory. When you come to be a   10
president [4] in criminal causes, if you smile upon a
prisoner, hang him, but if you frown upon him and
threaten him, let him be sure to 'scape the gallows.
   Cast. I would be a very merry president—
   Bos. Do not sup a-nights; 'twill beget you an
admirable wit.
   Cast. Rather it would make me have a good stomach
to quarrel, for they say your roaring boys [5] eat meat
seldom, and that makes them so valiant. But how shall I
know whether the people take me for an eminent
fellow?   21
   Bos. I will teach a trick to know it: give out you lie
a-dying, and if you hear the common people curse you,
be sure you are taken for one of the prime nightcaps. [6]

[*Enter* Old Lady.]

You come from painting now?
   Old. From what?
   Bos. Why, from your scurvy face-physic: to behold
thee not painted inclines somewhat near a miracle.
These in thy face here were deep ruts and foul sloughs, [7]
the last progress. There was a lady in France that,   30
having had the smallpox, flayed the skin off her face to
make it more level; and whereas before she looked like
a nutmeg grater, after she resembled an abortive
hedgehog.
   Old. Do you call this painting?

---

[106] *for*: what of.
[107] *without this circumference*: outside this circle, which is
her ring or her enfolding arms.
[108] *L.*: The consenting words of the participants were
understood in older canon law to constitute a valid marriage.
[109] *Gordian*: knot, which Alexander the Great, being
unable to disentangle, severed with his sword.
[110] *spheres*: in which the planets, in the Ptolemaic universe,
were thought to move continuously ("still"), creating un-
heard music as their peripheries touched.
[111] *palms*: Pliny records that this tree, like the holly, can
bear only if male and female plants grow close together.
[112] *force*: enforce.
[113] *echo*: though the consent of the participants constitu-
ted marriage, a religious service or "echo" had to follow
subsequently.   [114] *conceit*: meaning.
[115] *fortune*: depicted as blind.
[116] *humorous*: full of varying humors or passions.
[117] *Alexander and Lodowick*: who were such fast friends
that the latter, rather than "wrong" the former, placed a
sword between himself and his newly wedded and bedded
wife.   [118] *shroud*: shelter.

II.i.
[1] *main*: objective.
[2] *nightcap expresses*: lawyer's coif presses forth.
[3] *strings ... band*: white tabs worn by Elizabethan
sergeants-at-law.   [4] *president*: chief magistrate.
[5] *roaring boys*: bullies.
[6] *nightcaps*: lawyers (alluding to the coif, above).
[7] *sloughs*: bogs; depressions.

Bos. No, no, but you call it careening[8] of an old morphewed[9] lady, to make her disembogue[10] again. There's rough-cast[11] phrase to your plastic.

Old. It seems you are well acquainted with my closet?[12]   40

Bos. One would suspect it for a shop of witchcraft, to find in it the fat of serpents; spawn of snakes, Jews' spittle, and their young children's ordures,[13] and all these for the face. I would sooner eat a dead pigeon,[14] taken from the soles of the feet of one sick of the plague, than kiss one of you fasting.[15] Here are two of you, whose sin of your youth is the very patrimony of the physician, makes him renew his footcloth[16] with the spring, and change his high-prized courtesan[17] with the fall of the leaf. I do wonder you do not loathe yourselves. Observe my meditation now: 51
What thing is in this outward form of man
To be beloved? We account it ominous,
If nature do produce a colt, or lamb,
A fawn, or goat, in any limb resembling
A man; and fly from't as a prodigy.[18]
Man stands amazed to see his deformity,
In any other creature but himself.
But in our own flesh, though we bear diseases
Which have their true names only tane from beasts,   60
As the most ulcerous wolf,[19] and swinish measle;[20]
Though we are eaten up of lice, and worms,
And though continually we bear about us
A rotten and dead body, we delight
To hide it in rich tissue: all our fear,
Nay, all our terror, is lest our physician
Should put us in the ground, to be made sweet.

---

[8] *careening:* scraping clean, as when a ship is turned over on its side that the paint may be scraped off.

[9] *morphewed:* scurfy.

[10] *disembogue:* empty; in preface, presumably, for new adventures.

[11] *rough-cast:* coarse mixture of lime and gravel for plastering, as opposed to her more expensive "plastic" or modeling. Bosola is speaking harsh truths.

[12] *my closet:* i.e., what I do in private.

[13] *ordures:* excrement, from which, with the other items specified, the lady's face-painting is supposed to be made.

[14] *dead pigeon:* supposed, when applied to the feet or the sore itself, to cure the plague by extracting its poison.

[15] *fasting:* when her breath would be most offensive.

[16] *footcloth:* with which his horse's flanks are covered, to protect the rider's boots from the mud.

[17] *courtesan:* more than a common whore.

[18] *prodigy:* startlingly unnatural thing.

[19] *wolf:* signifying an ulcer or cancer.

[20] *swinish measle:* measles, confused with a skin disease in pigs.   [21] *couple:* copulate.

[22] *Lucca:* famous Italian spa.   [23] *fins:* edges.

[24] *teeming:* denoting pregnancy.   [25] *apricocks:* apricots.

[26] *tetter:* skin disease.

[27] *lord of the ascendant:* from astrology; the ascendant house is that one of the twelve zodiacal constellations that is just appearing above the horizon; its lord is the planet then entering the house.   [28] *cousin-german:* first cousin.

[29] *Pippin:* Pepin the Short, eighth-century King of the Franks; with a contemptuous pun on "apple" or "appleseller."

[30] *tithe-pig:* part of the remuneration (anciently the tenth part of one's income) owed by a parishioner to his clergyman.

Your wife's gone to Rome: you two couple,[21] and get you
To the wells at Lucca,[22] to recover your aches.
                        [*Exeunt* CASTRUCHIO *and* Old Lady.]
I have other work on foot: I observe our Duchess   70
Is sick a-days, she pukes, her stomach seethes,
The fins[23] of her eyelids look most teeming[24] blue,
She wanes i'th' cheek and waxes fat i'th' flank;
And, contrary to our Italian fashion,
Wears a loose-bodied gown: there's somewhat in't.
I have a trick may chance discover it,
A pretty one; I have bought some apricocks,[25]
The first our spring yields.

                [*Enter* ANTONIO *and* DELIO.]

Del.   And so long since married?
You amaze me.
    Ant.   Let me seal your lips forever,
For did I think that anything but th' air   80
Could carry these words from you, I should wish
You had no breath at all. [*To* BOSOLA] Now, sir, in
        your contemplation?
You are studying to become a great wise fellow?
    Bos. O sir, the opinion of wisdom is a foul tetter[26]
that runs all over a man's body: if simplicity direct us
to have no evil, it directs us to a happy being. For the
subtlest folly proceeds from the subtlest wisdom. Let
me be simply honest.
    Ant. I do understand your inside.
    Bos. Do you so?   90
    Ant. Because you would not seem to appear to th'
        world
Puffed up with your preferment, you continue
This out-of-fashion melancholy; leave it, leave it.
    Bos. Give me leave to be honest in any phrase, in any
compliment whatsoever. Shall I confess myself to you?
I look no higher than I can reach; they are the gods that
must ride on winged horses, a lawyer's mule of a slow
pace will both suit my disposition and business. For,
mark me, when a man's mind rides faster than his
horse can gallop they quickly both tire.   100
    Ant. You would look up to heaven, but I think
The devil that rules i'th' air stands in your light.
    Bos. O sir, you are lord of the ascendant,[27] chief man
with the Duchess: a duke was your cousin-german,[28]
removed. Say you were lineally descended from King
Pippin,[29] or he himself, what of this? Search the heads
of the greatest rivers in the world, you shall find them
but bubbles of water. Some would think the souls of
princes were brought forth by some more weighty
cause than those of meaner persons. They are de- 110
ceived, there's the same hand to them; the like passions
sway them; the same reason that makes a vicar go to
law for a tithe-pig[30] and undo his neighbors makes
them spoil a whole province and batter down goodly
cities with the cannon.

            [*Enter* DUCHESS, Old Lady, Ladies.]

Duch. Your arm, Antonio. Do I not grow fat?
I am exceeding short-winded. Bosola,
I would have you, sir, provide for me a litter,

Such a one as the Duchess of Florence rode in.

Bos. The duchess used one when she was great with
    child.   120
Duch. I think she did. Come hither, mend my ruff,
Here; when?[31] Thou art such a tedious lady, and
Thy breath smells of lemon peels; would thou hadst
    done;
Shall I sound[32] under thy fingers? I am
So troubled with the mother.[33]

Bos. [*Aside*]   I fear too much.

Duch. I have heard you say that the French courtiers
Wear their hats on 'fore the King.

Ant.   I have seen it.

Duch. In the presence?[34]

Ant.   Yes.

Duch. Why should not we bring up that fashion?
'Tis ceremony more than duty that consists   130
In the removing of a piece of felt.
Be you the example to the rest o'th' court,
Put on your hat first.

Ant.   You must pardon me.
I have seen, in colder countries than in France,
Nobles stand bare[35] to th' Prince; and the distinction
Methought showed reverently.

Bos. I have a present for your grace.

Duch.   For me, sir?

Bos. Apricocks, madam.

Duch.   O sir, where are they?
I have heard of none to-year.[36]

Bos. [*Aside*]   Good, her color rises.

Duch. Indeed I thank you: they are wondrous fair
    ones.   140
What an unskillful fellow is our gardener!
We shall have none this month.

Bos. Will not your grace pare[37] them?

Duch. No, they taste of musk,[38] methinks; indeed
    they do.

Bos. I know not; yet I wish your grace had pared
    'em.

Duch. Why?

Bos.   I forgot to tell you the knave gardener,
Only to raise his profit by them the sooner,
Did ripen them in horse-dung.

Duch.   Oh, you jest.
[*To* ANTONIO] You shall judge: pray taste one.

Ant.   Indeed,
    madam,
I do not love the fruit.

Duch.   Sir, you are loath   150
To rob us of our dainties: 'tis a delicate fruit,
They say they are restorative?

Bos.   'Tis a pretty art,
This grafting.[39]

Duch.   'Tis so: a bettering of nature.

Bos. To make a pippin grow upon a crab,[40]
A damson[41] on a black-thorn: [*Aside*] How greedily
    she eats them!
A whirlwind strike off these bawd farthingales,[42]
For, but for that, and the loose-bodied gown,
I should have discovered apparently[43]
The young springal[44] cutting a caper in her belly.

Duch. I thank you, Bosola: they were right good
    ones,   160
If they do not make me sick.

Ant.   How now, madam?

Duch. This green fruit and my stomach are not
    friends.
How they swell me!

Bos. [*Aside*] Nay, you are too much swelled already.

Duch. Oh, I am in an extreme cold sweat.

Bos. I am very sorry.

                                      [*Exit.*]

Duch. Lights to my chamber! Oh, good Antonio,
I fear I am undone.

                          Exit [DUCHESS].

Del.   Lights there, lights!

Ant. Oh, my most trusty Delio, we are lost.
I fear she's fallen in labor; and there's left   170
No time for her remove.

Del.   Have you prepared
Those ladies to attend her? And procured
That politic safe conveyance for the midwife
Your Duchess plotted?

Ant.   I have.

Del. Make use then of this forced occasion.
Give out that Bosola hath poisoned her
With these apricocks; that will give some color
For her keeping close.[45]

Ant.   Fie, fie, the physicians
Will then flock to her.

Del.   For that you may pretend
She'll use some prepared antidote of her own,   180
Lest the physicians should repoison her.

Ant. I am lost in amazement: I know not what to
    think on't.

                                     Ex[*eunt*].

II.ii

[*Enter* BOSOLA *and* Old Lady.]

Bos. So, so; there's no question but her tetchiness[1]
and most vulturous eating of the apricocks are apparent[2] signs of breeding,[3] now?

Old. I am in haste, sir.

Bos. There was a young waiting-woman, had a
monstrous desire to see the glass-house[4]—

Old. Nay, pray let me go.

Bos. And it was only to know what strange instru-

---

[31] *when:* how long must I wait on you?
[32] *sound:* swoon.
[33] *mother:* suffocating passion, hysteria; with an obvious
pun on pregnancy.   [34] *presence:* royal presence.
[35] *bare:* bare-headed, as opposed to the French courtiers,
above.   [36] *to-year:* this year.   [37] *pare:* peel.
[38] *musk:* fruit flavor, evidently not to the Duchess' taste.
[39] *grafting:* alluding to horticulture, but also Bosola's
cunning.   [40] *crab:* crabapple.
[41] *damson:* plum.   [42] *farthingales:* hooped petticoats.
[43] *apparently:* clearly enough.   [44] *springal:* stripling.
[45] *close:* hidden.

II.ii
[1] *tetchiness:* irritability.   [2] *apparent:* manifest.
[3] *breeding:* pregnancy.   [4] *glass-house:* factory.

ment it was, should swell up a glass to the fashion of a
woman's belly.   10

Old. I will hear no more of the glass-house, you are
still abusing women!

Bos. Who, I? No, only, by the way now and then,
mention your frailties. The orange tree bears ripe and
green fruit and blossoms altogether. And some of you
give entertainment for pure love: but more, for more
precious reward. The lusty spring smells well: but
drooping autumn tastes well. If we have the same golden
showers that rained in the time of Jupiter the Thunderer, you have the same Danaës[5] still, to hold up   20
their laps to receive them. Didst thou never study the
mathematics?

Old. What's that, sir?

Bos. Why, to know the trick how to make a many
lines meet in one center. Go, go; give your foster-
daughters good counsel: tell them, that the devil takes
delight to hang at a woman's girdle, like a false rusty
watch, that she cannot discern how the time passes.

                                    [*Exit* Old Lady.]

[*Enter* ANTONIO, DELIO, RODERIGO,
            GRISOLAN.]

Ant. Shut up the court gates.
Rod.   Why, sir? What's the
    danger?
Ant. Shut up the posterns presently, and call   30
All the officers o'th' court.
Gris.   I shall instantly.
                                        [*Exit.*]
Ant. Who keeps the key o'th' park-gate?
Rod.   Forobosco.
Ant. Let him bring't presently.
                                [*Exit* RODERIGO.]

[*Enter* Servants, GRISOLAN, RODERIGO.]

1 Serv. Oh, gentlemen o'th' court, the foulest
    treason!
Bos. [*Aside*] If that these apricocks should be
    poisoned now;
Without my knowledge!
1 Serv. There was taken even now a Switzer[6] in the
Duchess' bedchamber.
2 Serv. A Switzer?
1 Serv. With a pistol[7] in his great cod-piece.   40
Bos. Ha, ha, ha.
1 Serv. The codpiece was the case for't.
2 Serv. There was a cunning traitor. Who would
have searched his codpiece?
1 Serv. True, if he had kept out of the ladies' cham-

bers; and all the molds of his buttons were leaden
bullets.
2 Serv. Oh, wicked cannibal:[8] a fire-lock in's
    codpiece?
1 Serv. 'Twas a French plot upon my life.
2 Serv. To see what the devil can do.   50
Ant. All the officers here?
Servs.   We are.
Ant.   Gentlemen,
We have lost much plate, you know; and but this
    evening
Jewels, to the value of four thousand ducats
Are missing in the Duchess' cabinet.[9]
Are the gates shut?
1 Serv.   Yes.
Ant.   'Tis the Duchess' pleasure
Each officer be locked into his chamber
Till the sun-rising; and to send the keys
Of all their chests, and of their outward doors
Into her bedchamber. She is very sick.
Rod. At her pleasure.   60
Ant. She entreats you take't not ill. The innocent
Shall be the more approved[10] by it.
Bos. Gentleman o'th' wood-yard, where's your
    Switzer now?
1 Serv. By this hand 'twas credibly reported by one
    o'th' blackguard.[11]
        [*Exeunt* BOSOLA, RODERIGO, *and* Servants.]
Del. How fares it with the Duchess?
Ant.   She's exposed
Unto the worst of torture, pain, and fear.
Del. Speak to her all happy comfort.
Ant. How I do play the fool with mine own danger!
You are this night, dear friend, to post to Rome,
My life lies in your service.
Del.   Do not doubt me.   70
Ant. Oh, 'tis far from me: and yet fear presents me
Somewhat that looks like danger.
Del.   Believe it,
'Tis but the shadow of your fear, no more.
How superstitiously we mind our evils!
The throwing down salt, or crossing of[12] a hare,
Bleeding at nose, the stumbling of a horse,
Or singing of a cricket, are of power
To daunt whole man in us. Sir, fare you well.
I wish you all the joys of a blessed father;
And, for my faith, lay this unto your breast,   80
Old friends, like old swords, still are trusted best.
                                    [*Exit* DELIO.]

[*Enter* CARIOLA *with a child.*]

Car. Sir, you are the happy father of a son;
Your wife commends him to you.
Ant.   Blessed comfort!
For heaven' sake tend her well. I'll presently
Go set a figure[13] for's nativity.
                                        Exeunt.

[*Enter* BOSOLA *with a dark lantern.*[14]]

Bos. Sure I did hear a woman shriek. List, ha?
And the sound came, if I received it right,

---

[5] *Danaës:* alluding to the woman to whom Jove came in a
shower of gold.   [6] *Switzer:* mercenary soldier.
[7] *pistol:* often, as here, confused deliberately with
'pizzle" ("penis").   [8] *cannibal:* generically, "savage."
[9] *cabinet:* private chamber.
[10] *approved:* applauded for good.
[11] *blackguard:* scullions.   [12] *crossing of:* coming upon.
[13] *set a figure:* cast a horoscope.
[14] *dark lantern:* The shuttered lantern denotes time; it is
night.

From the Duchess' lodgings: there's some stratagem
In the confining all our courtiers
To their several wards.[15] I must have part of it,   90
My intelligence will freeze else. List again,
It may be 'twas the melancholy bird,
Best friend of silence, and of solitariness,
The owl, that screamed so. Ha! Antonio?

[*Enter* ANTONIO *with a candle, his sword drawn.*]

Ant. I heard some noise. Who's there? What art
thou? Speak.
Bos.   Antonio! put not your face nor body
To such a forced expression of fear;
I am Bosola, your friend.
Ant.   Bosola!
[*Aside*] This mole does undermine me—heard you not
A noise even now?
Bos.   From whence?
Ant.   From the Duchess'
lodging.   100
Bos. Not I. Did you?
Ant.   I did; or else I dreamed.
Bos. Let's walk towards it.
Ant.   No. It may be, 'twas
But the rising of the wind.
Bos.   Very likely.
Methinks 'tis very cold, and yet you sweat.
You look wildly.
Ant.   I have been setting a figure
For the Duchess' jewels.
Bos.   Ah! and how falls your
question?
Do you find it radical?[16]
Ant.   What's that to you?
'Tis rather to be questioned what design,
When all men were commanded to their lodgings,
Makes you a night-walker.
Bos.   In sooth I'll tell you: 110
Now all the court's asleep, I thought the devil
Had least to do here; I come to say my prayers,
And if it do offend you[17] I do so,
You are a fine courtier.
Ant. [*Aside*]   This fellow will undo me.
You gave the Duchess apricocks today,
Pray heaven they were not poisoned!
Bos.   Poisoned! a
Spanish fig[18]
For the imputation.
Ant.   Traitors are ever confident
Till they are discovered. There were jewels stolen too.
In my conceit,[19] none are to be suspected
More than yourself.
Bos.   You are a false steward.   120
Ant. Saucy slave! I'll pull thee up by the roots.
Bos. May be the ruin will crush you to pieces.
Ant. You are in an impudent snake, indeed, sir.
Are you scarce warm,[20] and do you show your sting?
[*Bos. . . .*][21]
Ant. You libel well, sir.
Bos.   No, sir, copy it out,
And I will set my hand to't.

Ant.   My nose bleeds.
One that were superstitious would count
This ominous: when it merely comes by chance.
Two letters[22] that are wrought here for my name
Are drowned in blood!   130
Mere accident: for you, sir, I'll take order.
I'th' morn you shall be safe: [*Aside*] 'Tis that must
color
Her lying-in.—Sir, this door you pass not.
I do not hold it fit that you come near
The Duchess' lodgings, till you have quit yourself.
[*Aside*] The great are like the base; nay, they are the
same,
When they seek shameful ways to avoid shame.

                                                    Ex[it].

Bos. Antonio hereabout did drop a paper,
Some of your help, false friend:[23] oh, here it is.
What's here? A child's nativity calculated?   140
[*Reads*] *The Duchess was delivered of a son, 'tween the*
hours twelve and one, in the night: Anno Dom: 1504
(that's this year) decimo nono Decembris (that's this
night), taken according to the meridian of Malfi (that's
our Duchess: happy discovery). The lord of the first house,
being combust[24] in the ascendant, signifies short life: and
Mars being in a human sign,[25] joined to the tail of the
Dragon,[26] in the eight[27] house, doth threaten a violent
death; Caetera non scrutantur.[28]   149
Why now 'tis most apparent.[29] This precise[30] fellow
Is the Duchess' bawd: I have it to my wish.
This is a parcel of intelligency
Our courtiers were cased[31] up for! it needs must follow

---

[15] *wards:* quarters.
[16] *radical:* technical term from astrology—"fit to be
judged."   [17] *you:* you that.
[18] *Spanish fig:* term of contempt accompanied by the
ancient and obscene gesture of thrusting the thumb between
the forefinger and middle finger, or sucking it. The opening
fig resembles the vulva.
[19] *In my conceit:* To my thinking.
[20] *warm:* The frozen snake doesn't sting; Bosola, new to
his appointment, ought not yet to come on so violently.
[21] [*Bos . . .*]: whose reply, presumably countering Antonio,
has dropped out of the quarto. J. R. Brown suggests instead
that ll. 123–24 are Bosola's, and the compositor dropped his
speech heading.
[22] *letters:* initials, wrought or embroidered in his handkerchief.
[23] *false friend:* the dark lantern, "false" as betokening
crooked business.
[24] *combust:* burned up; the lord or planet ascendant in the
first zodiacal house or constellation is so close to the sun that
its "influence" has been destroyed.
[25] *human sign:* like Gemini, Aquarius, Virgo, Sagittarius.
[26] *Dragon:* The Sun in its (supposed) journey around the
earth is crossed in its path or ecliptic by the Moon at two
points, each making for an eclipse. The Dragon, which from
ancient times is thought to "eat" the Sun and Moon in time
of eclipse, denotes the route or territory of the Moon when it
is south of the ecliptic. When the rising Moon crosses the
ecliptic, its ascendancy is called the Dragon's head, a favorable territory; when the Moon, descending, recrosses the
ecliptic, it is known in its downward path as the Dragon's tail,
a territory ominous to those whose nativity takes place within
it.   [27] *eight:* eighth, a house suggestive of death.
[28] *L.:* "The rest is not investigated"; the horoscope is not
complete.   [29] *apparent:* open.
[30] *precise:* puritanical.   [31] *cased:* locked.

That I must be committed, on pretense
Of poisoning her, which I'll endure and laugh at.
If one could find the father now: but that
Time will discover. Old Castruchio
I'th' morning posts to Rome; by him I'll send
A letter that shall make her brothers' galls
O'erflow their livers.[32] This was a thrifty way.   160
Though lust do masque in ne'er so strange disguise
She's oft found witty, but is never wise.

                                                        [*Exit.*]

[II.iii]

        [*Enter* CARDINAL *and* JULIA.]

Card. Sit. Thou art my best of wishes. Prithee tell
        me
What trick didst thou invent to come to Rome[1]
Without thy husband?
    Jul.   Why, my lord, I told him
I came to visit an old anchorite[2]
Here, for devotion.
    Card.   Thou art a witty false one;
I mean to him.
    Jul.   You have prevailed with me
Beyond my strongest thoughts. I would not now
Find you inconstant.
    Card.   Do not put thyself
To such a voluntary torture, which proceeds
Out of your own guilt.
    Jul.   How, my lord?
    Card.   You fear   10
My constancy, because you have approved[3]
Those giddy and wild turnings in yourself.
    Jul. Did you e'er find them?
    Card.   Sooth, generally for
        women.
A man might strive to make glass malleable
Ere he should make them fixed.[4]
    Jul.   So, my lord.
    Card. We had need go borrow that fantastic glass[5]
Invented by Galileo the Florentine
To view another spacious world i'th' moon,
And look to find a constant woman there.
    Jul. This is very well, my lord.
    Card.   Why do you weep?
Are tears your justification? The selfsame tears   21
Will fall into your husband's bosom, lady,

With a loud protestation that you love him
Above the world. Come, I'll love you wisely,
That's jealously,[6] since I am very certain
You cannot me make cuckold.
    Jul.   I'll go home
To my husband.
    Card.   You may thank me, lady,
I have taken you off your melancholy perch,[7]
Bore you upon my fist, and showed you game,
And let you fly at it. I pray thee kiss me.   30
When thou wast with thy husband, thou wast watched
Like a tame elephant. Still you are to thank me.
Thou hadst only kisses from him, and high feeding,
But what delight was that? 'Twas just like one
That hath a little fingering[8] on the lute,
Yet cannot tune it. Still you are to thank me.
    Jul. You told me of a piteous wound i'th' heart,
And sick liver, when you wooed me first,
And spake like one in physic.[9]
    Card.   Who's that?

        [*Enter* Servant.]

Rest firm, for[10] my affection to thee,   40
Lightning moves slow to't.[11]
    Serv.   Madam, a gentleman
That's come post from Malfi desires to see you.
    Card. Let him enter, I'll withdraw.
                                                        Exit.
    Serv.   He says
Your husband, old Castruchio, is come to Rome,
Most pitifully tired with riding post.
                                            [*Exit* Servant.]

        [*Enter* DELIO.]

    Jul. Signior Delio! [*Aside*] 'tis one of my old suitors.
    Del. I was bold to come and see you.
    Jul.   Sir, you are
        welcome.
    Del. Do you lie[12] here?
    Jul.   Sure, your own experience
Will satisfy you no; our Roman prelates
Do not keep lodging for ladies.
    Del.   Very well.   50
I have brought you no commendations from your
        husband,
For I know none by him.
    Jul.   I hear he's come to Rome?
    Del. I never knew man and beast, of a horse and a
        knight,
So weary of each other; if he had had a good back,[13]
He would have undertook to have borne his horse,
His breach was so pitifully sore.
    Jul.   Your laughter
Is my pity.
    Del.   Lady, I know not whether
You want money, but I have brought you some.
    Jul. From my husband?
    Del.   No, from mine own
        allowance.[14]
    Jul. I must hear the condition, ere I be bound to
        take it.   60

---

[32] *livers:* passion's seat.

II.iii.
    [1] *Rome:* In this cursory and customary manner, the scene
is set.   [2] *anchorite:* hermit, holy man.
    [3] *approved:* observed.   [4] *fixed:* constant.
    [5] *glass:* telescope, devised by Galileo in the early
seventeenth century. Note the indifference to anachronistic
reference characteristic of writers of the period.
    [6] *jealously:* suspicious, with a sharp eye.
    [7] *perch:* as if Julia were a falcon.   [8] *fingering:* skill.
    [9] *in physic:* sick, being treated.   [10] *for:* as for.
    [11] *to't:* in comparison with it.
    [12] *lie:* with sexual *entendre.*
    [13] *good back:* with secondary sense of being able to perform
sexually.   [14] *allowance:* income.

Del. Look on't, 'tis gold. Hath it not a fine color?
Jul. I have a bird more beautiful.
Del.   Try the sound on't.
Jul. A lute-string far exceeds it;
It hath no smell, like cassia or civet,[15]
Nor is it physical,[16] though some fond [17] doctors
Persuade us, seethe't in cullises.[18] I'll tell you,
This is a creature bred by—

[*Enter* Servant.]

Serv.   Your husband's come,
Hath delivered a letter to the Duke of Calabria
That, to my thinking, hath put him out of his wits.
                                        [*Exit* Servant.]

Jul. Sir, you hear,   70
Pray let me know your business and your suit,
As briefly as can be.
Del.   With good speed. I would wish you
At such time as you are non-resident
With your husband, my mistress.
Jul. Sir, I'll go ask my husband if I shall,
And straight return your answer.
                                                    Exit.

Del.   Very fine,
Is this her wit, or honesty [19] that speaks thus?
I heard one say the Duke was highly moved
With a letter sent from Malfi. I do fear
Antonio is betrayed: how fearfully   80
Shows his ambition now; unfortunate fortune!
They pass through whirlpools, and deep woes do shun,
Who the event weigh, ere the action's done.
                                                    Exit.

[II.iv]

[*Enter*] CARDINAL, *and* FERDINAND, *with a letter.*

Ferd. I have this night digged up a mandrake.[1]
Card.   Say you?
Ferd. And I am grown mad with't.
Card.   What's the prodigy?[2]
Ferd. Read there, a sister damned; she's loose i'th'
    hilts,[3]
Grown a notorious strumpet.
Card.   Speak lower.
Ferd.   Lower?
Rogues do not whisper't now, but seek to publish't,
As servants do the bounty of their lords,
Aloud; and with a covetous searching eye,
To mark who note them. Oh, confusion seize her,
She hath had most cunning bawds to serve her turn,
And more secure conveyances for lust,   10
Than towns of garrison, for service.[4]
Card.   Is't possible?
Can this be certain?
Ferd.   Rhubarb,[5] oh, for rhubarb
To purge this choler! Here's the cursèd day [6]
To prompt my memory, and here't shall stick
Till of her bleeding heart I make a sponge
To wipe it out.
Card.   Why do you make yourself

So wild a tempest?
Ferd.   Would I could be one,
That I might toss her palace 'bout her ears,
Root up her goodly forests, blast her meads,
And lay her general territory as waste   20
As she hath done her honor's.
Card.   Shall our blood,
The royal blood of Aragon and Castile,
Be thus attainted?
Ferd.   Apply desperate physic,
We must not now use balsamum,[7] but fire,
The smarting cupping-glass,[8] for that's the mean [9]
To purge infected blood, such blood as hers.
There is a kind of pity in mine eye,
I'll give it to my handkercher; and now 'tis here,
I'll bequeath this to her bastard.
Card.   What to do?
Ferd. Why, to make soft lint [10] for his mother's
    wounds,   30
When I have hewed her to pieces.
Card.   Cursed creature!
Unequal [11] nature, to place women's hearts
So far upon the left [12] side.
Ferd.   Foolish men,
That e'er will trust their honor in a bark
Made of so slight, weak bulrush as is woman,
Apt every minute to sink it!
Card. Thus ignorance, when it hath purchased [13]
    honor,
It cannot wield it.
Ferd.   Methinks I see her laughing,
Excellent hyena! Talk to me somewhat, quickly,
Or my imagination will carry me   40
To see her in the shameful act of sin.
Card. With whom?
Ferd. Happily [14] with some strong-thighed barge-
    man;
Or one o'th' wood-yard, that can quoit the sledge [15]
Or toss the bar, or else some lovely squire [16]
That carries coals up to her privy [17] lodgings.
Card. You fly beyond your reason.
Ferd.   Go to,[18] mistress!

---

[15] *cassia . . . civet:* cinnamon . . . perfume.
[16] *physical:* medicinal.   [17] *fond:* foolish.
[18] *cullises:* broths.   [19] *honesty:* chastity.

II.iv.
[1] *mandrake:* portending madness.
[2] *prodigy:* extraordinary event.
[3] *loose i'th' hilts:* sexually promiscuous (metaphor from
screwing the sword hilt into the blade).
[4] *service:* military, also sexual service.
[5] *Rhubarb:* used conventionally for curing an excess of
bile, which made for the choleric or angry "humor."
[6] *day:* presumably the horoscope.
[7] *balsamum:* healing ointment.
[8] *cupping-glass:* for drawing blood.   [9] *mean:* way.
[10] *lint:* a "tent" or probe.   [11] *Unequal:* Partial, unjust.
[12] *left:* by convention, sinister, the worse way.
[13] *purchased:* achieved.   [14] *Happily:* Perhaps.
[15] *quoit the sledge:* throw the hammer.
[16] *squire:* used contemptuously; "low fellow."
[17] *privy:* private.   [18] *Go to:* Carry on (sardonically).

'Tis not your whore's milk that shall quench my
    wildfire,[19]
But your whore's blood.
   Card. How idly shows this rage! which carries you,
As men conveyed by witches, through the air   51
On violent whirlwinds; this intemperate noise
Fitly resembles deaf men's shrill discourse,
Who talk aloud, thinking all other men
To have their imperfection.
   Ferd.   Have not you
My palsy?
   Card.   Yes, I can be angry
Without this rupture; there is not in nature
A thing that makes man so deformed, so beastly
As doth intemperate anger. Chide yourself.
You have divers men, who never yet expressed   60
Their strong desire of rest but by unrest,
By vexing of themselves. Come, put yourself
In tune.
   Ferd. So, I will only study to seem
The thing I am not. I could kill her now,
In you, or in myself, for I do think
It is some sin in us heaven doth revenge
By her.
   Card. Are you stark mad?
   Ferd.   I would have their bodies
Burned in a coal-pit, with the ventage[20] stopped,
That their cursed smoke might not ascend to heaven.
Or dip the sheets they lie in, in pitch or sulfur,   70
Wrap them in't, and then light them like a match.
Or else to boil their bastard to a cullis,
And give't his lecherous father, to renew
The sin of his back.
   Card.   I'll leave you.
   Ferd.   Nay, I have done;
I am confident, had I been damned in hell,
And should have heard of this, it would have put me
Into a cold sweat. In, in, I'll go sleep.
Till I know who leaps my sister, I'll not stir.
That known, I'll find scorpions to string my whips,
And fix her in a general[21] eclipse.   80
                          Exeunt.

ACT THREE

Scene One

[*Enter* Antonio *and* Delio.]

   Ant. Our noble friend, my most beloved Delio,
Oh, you have been a stranger long at court.

---

[19] *wildfire:* skin disease; by transference, "uncontrollable
passion."   [20] *ventage:* passage for air.   [21] *general:* total.
III.i.
  [1] *wink:* shut my eyes.   [2] *insensibly:* without feeling.
  [3] *censure:* judge.   [4] *purchase:* self-aggrandizement.
  [5] *left-hand:* crooked.
  [6] *Pasquil's paper bullets:* printed satires or "pasquinate,"
so called from the practice of affixing lampoons to a Roman
statue excavated at the beginning of the sixteenth century
and supposedly commemorating a sharp-tongued schoolmaster or cobbler celebrated in Rome in the previous century.

Came you along with the Lord Ferdinand?
   Del. I did, sir; and how fares your noble Duchess?
   Ant. Right fortunately well. She's an excellent
Feeder of pedigrees; since you last saw her,
She hath had two children more, a son and daughter.
   Del. Methinks 'twas yesterday. Let me but wink,[1]
And not behold your face, which to mine eye
Is somewhat leaner. Verily I should dream   10
It were within this half hour.
   Ant. You have not been in law, friend Delio,
Nor in prison, nor a suitor at the court,
Nor begged the reversion of some great man's place,
Nor troubled with an old wife, which doth make
Your time so insensibly[2] hasten.
   Del.   Pray, sir, tell me,
Hath not this news arrived yet to the ear
Of the Lord Cardinal?
   Ant.   I fear it hath;
The Lord Ferdinand, that's newly come to court,
Doth bear himself right dangerously.
   Del.   Pray, why?   20
   Ant. He is so quiet, that he seems to sleep
The tempest out, as dormice do in winter;
Those houses that are haunted are most still,
Till the devil be up.
   Del.   What say the common people?
   Ant. The common rabble do directly say
She is a strumpet.
   Del.   And your graver heads,
Which would be politic, what censure[3] they?
   Ant. They do observe I grow to infinite purchase[4]
The left-hand[5] way, and all suppose the Duchess
Would amend it, if she could. For, say they,   30
Great princes, though they grudge their officers
Should have such large and unconfinèd means
To get wealth under them, will not complain
Lest thereby they should make them odious
Unto the people for; other obligation
Of love, or marriage, between her and me,
They never dream of.

[*Enter* Ferdinand, Duchess, *and* Bosola.]

   Del.   The Lord Ferdinand
Is going to bed.
   Ferd.   I'll instantly to bed,
For I am weary: I am to bespeak
A husband for you.
   Duch.   For me, sir! pray, who is't?   40
   Ferd. The great Count Malateste.
   Duch.   Fie upon him,
A count? He's a mere stick of sugar-candy;
You may look quite thorough him. When I choose
A husband, I will marry for your honor.
   Ferd. You shall do well in't. How is't, worthy
    Antonio?
   Duch. But, sir, I am to have private conference with
    you,
About a scandalous report is spread
Touching mine honor.
   Ferd.   Let me be ever deaf to't:
One of Pasquil's paper bullets,[6] court calumny,

A pestilent air, which princes' palaces 50
Are seldom purged of. Yet, say that it were true,
I pour it in your bosom, my fixed love
Would strongly excuse, extenuate, nay, deny
Faults were they apparent in you. Go, be safe
In your own innocency.
 Duch.   Oh, blessed comfort,
This deadly air is purged.
     Exeunt [DUCHESS, ANTONIO, DELIO].
 Ferd.   Her guilt treads on
Hot burning cultures.[7] Now, Bosola,
How thrives our intelligence?
 Bos.   Sir, uncertainly.
'Tis rumored she hath had three bastards, but
By whom, we may go read i'th' stars.
 Ferd.   Why some 60
Hold opinion, all things are written there.
 Bos. Yes, if we could find spectacles to read them;
I do suspect there hath been some sorcery
Used on the Duchess.
 Ferd.   Sorcery, to what purpose?
 Bos. To make her dote on some desertless fellow
She shames to acknowledge.
 Ferd.   Can your faith give way
To think there's power in potions, or in charms,
To make us love, whether we will or no?
 Bos. Most certainly.
 Ferd. Away, these are mere gulleries, horrid
 things 70
Invented by some cheating mountebanks
To abuse us. Do you think that herbs or charms
Can force the will? Some trials have been made
In the foolish practice; but the ingredients
Were lenative[8] poisons, such as are of force
To make the patient mad; and straight the witch
Swears, by equivocation,[9] they are in love.
The witchcraft lies in her rank blood. This night
I will force confession from her. You told me
You had got, within these two days, a false key 80
Into her bed-chamber.
 Bos.   I have.
 Ferd.   As I would wish.
 Bos. What do you intend to do?
 Ferd.   Can you guess?
 Bos.   No.
 Ferd. Do not ask then.
He that can compass me, and know my drifts,
May say he hath put a girdle 'bout the world,
And sounded all her quick-sands.
 Bos.   I do not
Think so.
 Ferd. What do you think then, pray?
 Bos.   That you
Are your own chronicle too much and grossly
Flatter yourself.
 Ferd. Give me thy hand; I thank thee.
I never gave pension but to flatterers, 90
Till I entertained[10] thee. Farewell.
That friend a great man's ruin strongly checks,
Who rails into his belief all his defects.
           Exeunt.

III.ii

[*Enter* DUCHESS, ANTONIO, *and* CARIOLA.]

 Duch. Bring me the casket hither, and the glass;
You get no lodging here tonight, my lord.
 Ant. Indeed, I must persuade one.
 Duch.   Very good.
I hope in time 'twill grow into a custom
That noblemen shall come with cap and knee[1]
To purchase a night's lodging of their wives.
 Ant. I must lie here.
 Duch.   Must? You are a lord of
 mis-rule.[2]
 Ant. Indeed, my rule is only in the night.
 Duch. To what use will you put me?
 Ant.   We'll sleep
 together.
 Duch. Alas, what pleasure can two lovers find in
 sleep? 10
 Car. My lord, I lie with her often: and I know
She'll much disquiet you.
 Ant.   See, you are complained of.
 Car. For she's the sprawling'st bedfellow.
 Ant. I shall like her the better for that.
 Car. Sir, shall I ask you a question?
 Ant. I pray thee, Cariola.
 Car. Wherefore still, when you lie with my lady
Do you rise so early?
 Ant.   Laboring men,
Count the clock oft'nest, Cariola, 19
Are glad when their task's ended.
 Duch.   I'll stop your mouth.

           [*Kisses him.*]

 Ant. Nay, that's but one, Venus had two soft doves
To draw her chariot. I must have another.

           [*Kisses her.*]

When wilt thou marry, Cariola?
 Car.   Never, my lord.
 Ant. Oh, fie upon this single life; forgo it.
We read how Daphne, for her peevish flight
Became a fruitless bay-tree; Syrinx turned
To the pale empty reed; Anaxarete
Was frozen into marble: whereas those
Which married, or proved kind unto their friends
Were, by a gracious influence, transshaped 30
Into the olive, pomegranate, mulberry:

---

 [7] *cultures:* coulters: plowshares which, from ancient times, were heated red hot and over which suspected felons were forced to pass as an "ordeal" to prove their innocence or guilt.
 [8] *lenative:* lenitive(?); soothing (though, as the next word suggest, in a specious sense).
 [9] *equivocation:* quibbling on words.
 [10] *entertained:* took into service.

III.ii.
 [1] *with cap and knee:* humbly; with cap in hand.
 [2] *lord of mis-rule:* Master of the revels (with obvious erotic suggestions).

Became flowers, precious stones, or eminent stars.[3]

Car. This is vain poetry. But I pray you tell me,
If there were proposed me wisdom, riches, and beauty,
In three several[4] young men, which should I choose?

Ant. 'Tis a hard question. This was Paris' case[5]
And he was blind in't, and there was great cause.
For how was't possible he could judge right,
Having three amorous goddesses in view,
And they stark naked? 'Twas a motion[6]
Were able to benight the apprehension
Of the severest counselor of Europe.
Now I look on both your faces, so well formed,
It puts me in mind of a question I would ask.

Car. What is't?

Ant.   I do wonder why hard-favored[7] ladies
For the most part keep worse-favored waiting-women
To attend them, and cannot endure fair ones.

Duch. Oh, that's soon answered.
Did you ever in your life know an ill painter
Desire to have his dwelling next door to the shop   50
Of an excellent picture-maker? 'Twould disgrace
His face-making, and undo him. I prithee
When were we so merry? My hair tangles.

Ant. [*Aside to* CARIOLA] Pray thee, Cariola, let's steal forth the room,
And let her talk to herself. I have divers times
Served her the like, when she hath chafed extremely.
I love to see her angry. Softly, Cariola.
                    Exeunt [ANTONIO *and* CARIOLA].

Duch. Doth not the color of my hair 'gin to change?
When I wax gray, I shall have all the court
Powder their hair with arras,[8] to be like me.   60
You have cause to love me, I entered you into my heart

[*Enter* FERDINAND, *unseen.*]

Before you would vouchsafe to call for the keys.
We shall one day have my brothers take you napping.

---

[3] *We ... stars:* Apollo, because Daphne was perverse ("peevish") in rejecting him, "transshaped" her as indicated; just as Pan converted the reluctant nymph Syrinx to a reed (from which he made his pipes), and Venus the hardhearted Anaxarete (who remained unmoved when her lover Iphis hanged himself) to a stone. The sense of "olive," "pomegranate," "precious stones" is to seek. But "mulberry," as its fruit is red, refers to the sanguinary death of Pyramus, who stabbed himself, supposing Thisbe dead before him; "flowers" to Clytie, who loved Apollo and was transformed to a sunflower; and "stars" (to take one example only) to the nymph Callisto, beloved of Jupiter, and changed by the jealous Juno into the constellation called the Great Bear. Most of these stories were familiar from Ovid's *Metamorphoses.*   [4] *several:* separate.
[5] *Paris' case:* Having to pass judgment on the comparative beauty of Juno, Venus, and Athena, Paris, the son of King Priam of Troy, chose the second (being promised as his reward Helen, the most beautiful of earthly women)—and so brought on the Trojan War.   [6] *motion:* spectacle.
[7] *favored:* featured.
[8] *arras:* sweet-smelling white powder made from the iris root.   [9] *get:* beget.   [10] *gossips:* godparents.
[11] *basilisk:* to gaze on which was fatal.
[12] *to:* compared to.   [13] *vile:* Q "vild."
[14] *Such a room:* i.e., a hermit's cell.
[15] *use:* capacity.   [16] *bewray:* reveal.

Methinks his presence, being now in court,
Should make you keep your own bed. But you'll say
Love mixed with fear is sweetness. I'll assure you
You shall get[9] no more children till my brothers
Consent to be your gossips.[10] Have you lost your tongue?

[*She sees* FERDINAND *holding a poniard.*]

'Tis welcome.
For know, whether I am doomed to live, or die,   70
I can do both like a prince.

FERDINAND *gives her a poniard.*

Ferd.   Die then, quickly.
Virtue, where art thou hid? What hideous thing
Is it, that doth eclipse thee?

Duch.   Pray, sir, hear me—

Ferd. Or is it true, thou art but a bare name,
And no essential thing?

Duch.   Sir—

Ferd.   Do not speak.

Duch. No, sir.
I will plant my soul in mine ears, to hear you.

Ferd. O most imperfect light of human reason,
That mak'st so unhappy, to foresee
What we can least prevent. Pursue thy wishes   80
And glory in them; there's in shame no comfort,
But to be past all bounds and sense of shame.

Duch. I pray, sir, hear me. I am married—

Ferd.   So.

Duch. Happily, not to your liking: but for that
Alas, your shears do come untimely now
To clip the bird's wings, that's already flown.
Will you see my husband?

Ferd.   Yes, if I could change
Eyes with a basilisk.[11]

Duch.   Sure, you came hither
By his confederacy.

Ferd.   The howling of a wolf
Is music to[12] thee, screech-owl; prithee, peace.   90
What'eer thou art, that hast enjoyed my sister
(For I am sure thou hear'st me), for thine own sake
Let me not know thee. I came hither prepared
To work thy discovery; yet am now persuaded
It would beget such violent effects
As would damn us both. I would not for ten millions
I had beheld thee; therefore use all means
I never may have knowledge of thy name;
Enjoy thy lust still, and a wretched life,
On that condition. And for thee, vile[13] woman,   100
If thou do wish thy lecher may grow old
In thy embracements, I would have thee build
Such a room[14] for him, as our anchorites
To holier use inhabit. Let not the sun
Shine on him till he's dead. Let dogs and monkeys
Only converse with him, and such dumb things
To whom nature denies use[15] to sound his name.
Do not keep a paraquito, lest she learn it;
If thou do love him, cut out thine own tongue
Lest it bewray[16] him.

Duch.   Why might not I marry?   110

I have not gone about, in this, to create
Any new world, or custom.
   Ferd.   Thou art undone;
And thou hast tane that massy sheet of lead
That hid thy husband's bones, and folded it
About my heart.
   Duch.   Mine bleeds for't.
   Ferd.   Thine? Thy heart?
What should I name't, unless a hollow bullet
Filled with unquenchable wildfire?
   Duch.   You are in this
Too strict, and were you not my princely brother,
I would say too willful. My reputation
Is safe.
   Ferd. Dost thou know what reputation is?   120
I'll tell thee, to small purpose, since th'instruction
Comes now too late:
Upon a time Reputation, Love, and Death
Would travel o'er the world; and it was concluded
That they should part, and take three several ways.
Death told them, they should find him in great battles,
Or cities plagued with plagues. Love gives them counsel
To inquire for him 'mongst unambitious shepherds,
Where dowries were not talked of, and sometimes
'Mongst quiet kindred, that had nothing left   130
By their dead parents. "Stay," quoth Reputation,
"Do not forsake me; for it is my nature
If once I part from any man I meet
I am never found again." And so, for you:
You have shook hands with Reputation,
And made him invisible. So fare you well.
I will never see you more.
   Duch.   Why should only I,
Of all the other princes of the world
Be cased up, like a holy relic? I have youth,
And a little beauty.
   Ferd.   So you have some virgins   140
That are witches. I will never see thee more.
                           Exit.

   Enter [CARIOLA *and*] ANTONIO *with a pistol.*

   Duch. You saw this apparation?
   Ant.   Yes; we are
Betrayed. How came he hither? I should turn
This to thee, for that.

   [*He points the pistol at* CARIOLA.]

   Car.   Pray, sir, do; and when
That you have cleft my heart, you shall read there
Mine innocence.
   Duch.   That gallery gave him entrance.
   Ant. I would this terrible thing would come again,
That, standing on my guard, I might relate
My warrantable love. Ha! what means this?
   Duch. He left this with me.

               She shows the poniard.

   Ant.   And it seems, did wish
You would use it on yourself?
   Duch.   His action seemed   151
To intend so much.

   Ant.   This hath a handle to't,
As well as a point. Turn it towards him, and
So fasten the keen edge in his rank gall.

              [*Knocking within.*]

How now? Who knocks? More earthquakes?
   Duch.   I stand
As if a mine, beneath my feet, were ready
To be blown up.
   Car.   'Tis Bosola.
   Duch.   Away!
Oh, misery, methinks unjust actions
Should wear these masks and curtains, and not we.
You must instantly part hence. I have fashioned it
already.   160
                Ex[*it*] ANT[ONIO].

         [*Enter* BOSOLA.]

   Bos. The Duke your brother is tane up in a
     whirlwind;
Hath took horse, and's rid post to Rome.
   Duch.   So late?
   Bos. He told me, as he mounted into th' saddle,
You were undone.
   Duch.   Indeed, I am very near it.
   Bos. What's the matter?
   Duch. Antonio, the master of our household
Hath dealt so falsely with me, in's accounts:
My brother stood engaged with me for money
Tane up of certain Neapolitan Jews,
And Antonio lets the bonds be forfeit.   170
   Bos. Strange; [*Aside*] this is cunning.
   Duch.   And hereupon
My brother's bills at Naples are protested
Against. Call up our officers.
   Bos.   I shall.
                           Exit.

         [*Enter* ANTONIO.]

   Duch. The place that you must fly to is Ancona.
Hire a house there. I'll send after you
My treasure, and my jewels. Our weak safety
Runs upon enginous [17] wheels; short syllables
Must stand for periods. I must now accuse you
Of such a feignèd crime, as Tasso [18] calls
Magnanima menzogna: a noble lie,   180
'Cause it must shield our honors—hark, they are
     coming.

      [*Enter* BOSOLA *and* Officers.]

   Ant. Will your grace hear me?
   Duch. I have got well by you: you have yielded me

---

[17] *enginous:* ingenious; intricate (with collateral sense of "swift").
[18] *Tasso:* In his epic poem, *Gerusalemme Liberata* (II. 22), this sixteenth-century Italian poet tells of the persecution by the pagan ruler of Jerusalem of Christians, occasioned by the disappearance of a statue of the Virgin that had been erected, sacrilegiously, in a mosque. The Christian maiden Soprina, to save her coreligionists, tells the generous lie alluded to, by taking the blame on herself.

A million of loss; I am like to inherit
The people's curses for your stewardship.
You had the trick, in audit time to be sick,
Till I had signed your *Quietus;*[19] and that cured you
Without help of a doctor. Gentlemen,
I would have this man be an example to you all:
So shall you hold my favor. I pray let[20] him;   190
For h'as done that, alas! you would not think of,
And, because I intend to be rid of him,
I mean not to publish. Use your fortune elsewhere.

Ant. I am strongly armed to brook my overthrow,
As commonly men bear with a hard year.
I will not blame the cause on't; but do think
The necessity of my malevolent star
Procures this, not her humor. Oh, the inconstant
And rotten ground of service, you may see;
'Tis even like him that, in a winter night,   200
Takes a long slumber o'er a dying fire,
As loath to part from't; yet parts thence as cold
As when he first sat down.

Duch.   We do confiscate,
Towards the satisfying of your accounts,
All that you have.

Ant.   I am all yours; and 'tis very fit
All mine should be so.

Duch.   So, sir; you have your pass.

Ant. You may see, gentlemen, what 'tis to serve
A prince with body and soul.

                                        Exit.

Bos. Here's an example for extortion; what moisture
is drawn out of the sea, when foul weather comes, pours
down, and runs into the sea again.   211

Duch. I would know what are your opinions
Of this Antonio.

2 Off. He could not abide to see a pig's head gaping; I thought your grace would find him a Jew.

3 Off. I would you had been his officer, for your
own sake.

4 Off. You would have had more money.

1 Off. He stopped his ears with black wool,[21] and

to those came to him for money said he was thick of
hearing.   221

2 Off. Some said he was an hermaphrodite, for he
could not abide a woman.

4 Off. How scurvy proud he would look, when the
treasury was full. Well, let him go.

1 Off. Yes, and the chippings[22] of the buttery[23]
fly after him, to scour his gold chain.[24]

Duch. Leave us. What do you think of these?

                              Exeunt [Officers].

Bos. That these are rogues, that in's prosperity,
But to have waited on his fortune, could have wished
His dirty stirrup riveted through their noses;   231
And followed after's mule, like a bear in a ring.[25]
Would have prostituted their daughters to his lust;
Made their first-born intelligencers; thought none
   happy
But such as were born under his blessed planet;
And wore his livery. And do these lice drop off now?
Well, never look to have the like again;
He hath left a sort[26] of flattering rogues behind him;
Their doom must follow. Princes pay flatterers
In their own money. Flatterers dissemble their[27] vices,
And they dissemble their lies;[28] that's justice.   241
Alas, poor gentleman!

Duch. Poor! He hath amply filled his coffers.

Bos. Sure, he was too honest. Pluto,[29] the god of
   riches,
When he's sent, by Jupiter, to any man,
He goes limping, to signify that wealth
That comes on God's name,[30] comes slowly; but when
   he's sent
On the devil's errand, he rides post, and comes in by
   scuttles.[31]
Let me show you what a most unvalued[32] jewel
You have, in a wanton humor, thrown away,   250
To bless the man shall find him. He was an excellent
Courtier, and most faithful; a soldier, that thought it
As beastly to know his own value too little,
As devilish to acknowledge it too much;
Both his virtue and form deserved a far better
   fortune.
His discourse rather delighted to judge itself, than show
   itself.
His breast was filled with all perfection,
And yet it seemed a private whispering room;
It made so little noise of't.

Duch.   But he was basely
   descended.

Bos. Will you make yourself a mercenary herald,
Rather to examine men's pedigrees than virtues?   261
You shall want[33] him;
For know an honest statesman to a prince
Is like a cedar, planted by a spring;
The spring bathes the tree's root, the grateful tree
Rewards it with his shadow. You have not done so.
I would sooner swim to the Bermudas[34] on
Two politicians' rotten bladders, tied
Together with an intelligencer's heartstring,
Than depend on so changeable a prince's favor.   270
Fare thee well, Antonio, since the malice of the world

---

[19] *L.:* Release.

[20] *let:* hinder; but, also, "let him go" or "let him be made
an example of." The Duchess in these lines speaks with
deliberate ambiguity.

[21] *black wool:* evidently possessed of healing power; compare, as possibly analogous, the talismanic power still
attributed in American lore to black kinky hair.

[22] *chippings:* bread crumbs.   [23] *buttery:* pantry.

[24] *gold chain:* denoting the steward, like Malvolio in
Twelfth Night.

[25] *in a ring:* probably "with a ring in his nose" rather than
"in an enclosure."   [26] *sort:* group, set.

[27] *their:* i.e., princes'.

[28] *they . . . lies:* princes pretend that the flatterers are not
telling lies.

[29] *Pluto:* properly, Plutus; the confusion occurring because of the former's association with the underworld, whence
precious metal is dug.   [30] *on God's name:* i.e., honestly.

[31] *by scuttles:* scuttling; quickly, like a crab.

[32] *unvalued:* invaluable.   [33] *want:* miss.

[34] *Bermudas:* famous, or infamous, because of reports
attendant on the shipwreck there of Sir George Somers in
1609.

Would needs down with thee, it cannot be said yet
That any ill happened unto thee,
Considering thy fall was accompanied with virtue.
   Duch. Oh, you render me excellent music.
   Bos.   Say you?
   Duch. This good one that you speak of is my
    husband.
   Bos. Do I not dream? Can this ambitious age
Have so much goodness in't as to prefer
A man merely for worth, without these shadows
Of wealth, and painted honors? Possible?   280
   Duch. I have had three children by him.
   Bos.   Fortunate
    lady,
For you have made your private nuptial bed
The humble and fair seminary[35] of peace.
No question but many an unbeneficed scholar
Shall pray for you, for this deed, and rejoice
That some preferment in the world can yet
Arise from merit. The virgins of your land,
That have no dowries, shall hope your example
Will raise them to rich husbands. Should you want
Soldiers, 'twould make the very Turks and Moors   290
Turn Christians, and serve you for this act.
Last, the neglected poets of your time,
In honor of this trophy of a man,
Raised by that curious[36] engine, your white hand,
Shall thank you in your grave for't; and make that
More reverend than all the cabinets
Of living princes. For Antonio,
His fame shall likewise flow from many a pen,
When heralds shall want coats,[37] to sell to men.
   Duch. As I taste comfort in this friendly speech,
So would I find concealment—
   Bos.   Oh, the secret of my
    prince,   301
Which I will wear on th'inside of my heart.
   Duch. You shall take charge of all my coin, and
    jewels,
And follow him, for he retires himself
To Ancona.
   Bos. So.
   Duch.   Whither, within few days,
I mean to follow thee.
   Bos.   Let me think:
I would wish your grace to feign a pilgrimage
To Our Lady of Loreto,[38] scarce seven leagues
From fair Ancona, so may you depart
Your country with more honor, and your flight   310
Will seem a princely progress, retaining
Your usual train about you.
   Duch.   Sir, your direction
Shall lead me, by the hand.
   Car.   In my opinion,
She were better progress to the baths at Lucca,
Or go visit the Spa
In Germany;[39] for, if you will believe me,
I do not like this jesting with religion,
This feigned pilgrimage.
   Duch.   Thou art a superstitious fool.
Prepare us instantly for our departure.

Past sorrows, let us moderately lament them,   320
For those to come, seek wisely to prevent them.
                   Exit [DUCHESS *with* CARIOLA].
   Bos. A politician is the devil's quilted anvil,
He fashions all sins on him, and the blows
Are never heard; he may work in a lady's chamber,
As here for proof. What rests,[40] but I reveal
All to my lord? Oh, this base quality
Of intelligencer! Why, every quality i'th' world
Prefers but gain, or commendation.
Now for this act, I am certain to be raised,
And men that paint weeds, to the life, are praised.   330
                                   Exit.

III.iii

[Enter] CARDINAL, FERDINAND, MALATESTE,
PESCARA, SILVIO, DELIO.

   Card. Must we turn soldier then?
   Mal.   The Emperor,[1]
Hearing your worth that way, ere you attained
This reverend garment, joins you in commission
With the right fortunate soldier, the Marquis of Pescara
And the famous Lannoy.[2]
   Card.   He that had the honor
Of taking the French King prisoner?
   Mal.   The same.
Here's a plot[3] drawn for a new fortification
At Naples.
   Ferd.   This great Count Malateste, I perceive,
Hath got employment.
   Del.   No employment, my lord,
A marginal note in the muster book, that he is   10
A voluntary lord.
   Ferd.   He's no soldier?
   Del. He has worn gunpowder, in's hollow tooth,
For the tooth-ache.
   Sil. He comes to the leaguer with a full intent
To eat fresh beef, and garlic; means to stay
Till the scent[4] be gone, and straight return to court.
   Del. He hath read all the late service,[5]
As the City chronicle[6] relates it,

---

   [35] *seminary:* seed-plot.   [36] *curious:* excelling.
   [37] *coats:* of arms; whose sale was notorious under King
James I.
   [38] *Loreto:* still famous as a place of pilgrimage, because of
the miraculous transporting there of the Holy House inhabited by Mary at Nazareth.
   [39] *Spa in Germany:* celebrated watering place in Belgium
(the Low Countries being lumped together by the Elizabethans as "Dutch" or "German").   [40] *rests:* remains.

III.iii.
   [1] *Emperor:* Charles V.
   [2] *Pescara . . . Lannoy:* Respectively, Duke Ferdinand's
brother-in-law, a celebrated soldier who died young (despite
Webster, who makes him an old man); and the Viceroy of
Naples, a favorite of the Emperor Charles, and the man to
whom François I surrendered his sword at the battle of Pavia.
   [3] *plot:* plan.   [4] *scent:* of garlic.
   [5] *service:* account of military operations.
   [6] *chronicle:* chronologer; historian.

And keeps two painters going, only to express
Battles in model.[7]

Sil.   Then he'll fight by the book.[8]   20

Del. By the almanac, I think,
To choose good days, and shun the critical.
That's his mistress' scarf.

Sil.   Yes, he protests
He would do much for that taffeta—

Del. I think he would run away from a battle
To save it from taking[9] prisoner.

Sil.   He is horribly afraid
Gunpowder will spoil the perfume on't—

Del. I saw a Dutchman break his pate once
For calling him pot-gun;[10] he made his head
Have a bore in't, like a musket.   30

Sil. I would he had made a touch-hole[11] to't.
He is indeed a guarded sumpter-cloth[12]
Only for the remove[13] of the court.

[*Enter* BOSOLA.]

Pes. Bosola arrived? What should be the business?
Some falling out amongst the cardinals.
These factions amongst great men, they are like
Foxes[14] when their heads are divided:
They carry fire in their tails, and all the country   38
About them goes to wrack for't.

Sil.   What's that Bosola?

Del. I knew him in Padua, a fantastical scholar, like
such who study to know how many knots was in Hercules' club; of what color Achilles' beard was, or whether
Hector were not troubled with the toothache. He hath
studied himself half blear-eyed, to know the true sym-
metry of Caesar's nose by a shoeing-horn: and this he
did to gain the name of a speculative man.

Pes. Mark Prince Ferdinand,
A very salamander[15] lives in's eye,
To mock the eager violence of fire.   49

Sil. That cardinal hath made more bad faces with his
oppression[16] than ever Michael Angelo made good ones:
he lifts up's nose, like a foul porpoise[17] before a storm—

Pes. The Lord Ferdinand laughs.

Del. Like a deadly cannon, that lightens ere it smokes.

Pes. These are your true pangs of death,
The pangs of life, that struggle with great statesmen—

Del. In such a deformed silence, witches whisper
Their charms.

---

[7] *model:* plan.
[8] *by the book:* theoretically, like a pedant who knows
nothing of real fighting.   [9] *taking:* being taken.
[10] *pot-gun:* popgun, braggart.
[11] *touch-hole:* for igniting the charge; hence, "blowing
him up."
[12] *guarded sumpter-cloth:* trimmed or ornamented saddle
covering.   [13] *remove:* royal progress or journeying.
[14] *Foxes:* properly, Jackals, whose tails Samson tied together and set on fire to destroy the crops of the Philistines
(Judges 15:4–5).
[15] *salamander:* able proverbially to live in the fire.
[16] *oppression:* turbulent emotion.
[17] *porpoise:* the harbinger of tempests.
[18] *state:* ruler.
[19] *counters:* "chips" for tallying accounts.

Card. Doth she make religion her riding hood
To keep her from the sun and tempest?

Ferd.   That—   60
That damns her. Methinks her fault and beauty
Blended together show like leprosy,
The whiter, the fouler. I make it a question
Whether her beggarly brats were ever christened.

Card. I will instantly solicit the state[18] of Ancona
To have them banished.

Ferd.   You are for Loreto?
I shall not be at your ceremony. Fare you well.
Write to the Duke of Malfi, my young nephew
She had by her first husband, and acquaint him
With's mother's honesty.

Bos.   I will.

Ferd.   Antonio!   70
A slave, that only smelled of ink and counters,[19]
And never in's life looked like a gentleman,
But in the audit time. Go, go presently,
Draw me out an hundred and fifty of our horse,
And meet me at the fort-bridge.

                    Exeunt.

III.iv

[*Enter*] Two Pilgrims *to the Shrine of Our Lady of
Loreto.*

1 Pilg. I have not seen a goodlier shrine than this,
Yet I have visited many.

2 Pilg.   The Cardinal of Aragon
Is this day to resign his cardinal's hat;
His sister duchess likewise is arrived
To pay her vow of pilgrimage. I expect
A noble ceremony.

1 Pilg.   No question. They come.

*Here the ceremony of the Cardinal's instalment in
the habit of a soldier: performed in delivering up his
cross, hat, robes, and ring at the shrine; and investing
him with sword, helmet, shield, and spurs. Then*
ANTONIO, *the* DUCHESS *and their children, having
presented themselves at the shrine, are (by a form of
banishment in dumb-show expressed towards them by
the* CARDINAL, *and the state of* ANCONA) *banished.
During all which ceremony this ditty is sung to
very solemn music, by divers churchmen; and then*
                    exeunt.

Arms and honors deck thy story,   The Author
To thy fame's eternal glory,   disclaims
Adverse fortune ever fly thee,   this Ditty
No disastrous fate come nigh thee.   to be his.   10

I alone will sing thy praises,
Whom to honor virtue raises;
And thy study that divine is,
Bent to martial discipline is.
Lay aside all those robes lie by thee,
Crown thy arts with arms; they'll beautify thee.

O worthy of worthiest name, adorned in this manner,
Lead bravely thy forces on, under war's warlike
*   banner.*
Oh, mayst thou prove fortunate in all martial courses,
Guide thou still by skill, in arts and forces.   20
Victory attend thee nigh, whilst fame sings loud thy
*   powers,*
Triumphant conquest crown thy head, and blessings
*   pour down showers.*

1 Pilg. Here's a strange turn of state: who would
    have thought
So great a lady would have matched herself
Unto so mean a person? Yet the Cardinal
Bears himself much too cruel.
2 Pilg.   They are banished.
1 Pilg. But I would ask what power hath this state
Of Ancona, to determine of¹ a free prince?
2 Pilg. They are a free state, sir, and her brother
    showed
How that the Pope, forehearing of her looseness,   30
Hath seized into th' protection of the Church
The dukedom which she held as dowager.
1 Pilg. But by what justice?
2 Pilg.   Sure I think by none,
Only her brother's instigation.
1 Pilg. What was it, with such violence he took
Off from her finger?
2 Pilg.   'Twas her wedding-ring,
Which he vowed shortly he would sacrifice
To his revenge.
1 Pilg.   Alas, Antonio!
If that a man be thrust into a well,
No matter who sets hand to't, his own weight   40
Will bring him sooner to th' bottom. Come, let's
    hence
Fortune makes this conclusion general,²
All things do help th'unhappy man to fall.

                                              Exeunt.

III.v

         [*Enter* ANTONIO, DUCHESS, Children,
              CARIOLA, Servants.]

Duch. Banished Ancona?
Ant.   Yes, you see what power
Lightens in great men's breath.
Duch.   Is all our train
Shrunk to this poor remainder?
Ant.   These poor men,
Which have got little in your service, vow
To take your fortune. But your wiser buntings¹
Now they are fledged are gone.
Duch.   They have done wisely;
This puts me in mind of death; physicians thus,
With their hands full of money, use² to give o'er
Their patients.
Ant.   Right³ the fashion of the world.
From decayed fortunes every flatterer shrinks,   10
Men cease to build where the foundation sinks.

Duch. I had a very strange dream tonight.
Ant.   What
    was't?
Duch. Methought I wore my coronet of state,
And on a sudden all the diamonds
Were changed to pearls.
Ant.   My interpretation
Is, you'll weep shortly; for, to me the pearls
Do signify your tears.
Duch.   The birds, that live i'th' field
On the wild benefit⁴ of nature, live
Happier than we; for they may choose their mates,
And carol their sweet pleasures to the spring.   20

              [*Enter* BOSOLA *with a letter.*]

Bos. You are happily o'ertane.
Duch.   From my brother?
Bos. Yes, from the Lord Ferdinand; your brother,
All love, and safety—
Duch.   Thou dost blanch mischief;
Wouldst make it white. See, see; like to calm weather
At sea before a tempest, false hearts speak fair
To those they intend most mischief.

                              [*She reads*] *a letter.*

Send Antonio *to me; I want his head in a business—*
A politic equivocation⁵—
He doth not want your counsel, but your head;
That is, he cannot sleep till you be dead.   30
And here's another pitfall, that's strewed o'er
With roses. Mark it, 'tis a cunning one:
I stand engaged for your husband for several debts at
Naples: let not that trouble him, I had rather have his
heart than his money.
And I believe so, too.
Bos.   What do you believe?
Duch. That he so much distrusts my husband's love,
He will by no means believe his heart is with him
Until he see it. The devil is not cunning enough
To circumvent us in riddles.   40
Bos. Will you reject that noble and free league
Of amity and love which I present you?
Duch. Their league is like that of some politic kings
Only to make themselves of strength and power
To be our after-ruin; tell them so.
Bos. And what from you?
Ant.   Thus tell him: I will not
    come.
Bos. And what of this?⁶
Ant.   My brothers have dispersed

III.iv.
¹ *determine of:* pass judgment on.
² *general:* applicable to all.

III.v.
¹ *buntings:* small birds, like larks.
² *use:* are accustomed.   ³ *Right:* Precisely.
⁴ *benefit:* allowance, provision.
⁵ *equivocation:* phrase used in a double sense; and
especially meaningful to Webster's audience because associated with the Jesuits, who were understood to countenance
politic lies.   ⁶ *this:* the letter.

Bloodhounds abroad; which till I hear are muzzled
No truce, though hatched with ne'er such politic skill,
Is safe, that hangs upon our enemies' will.   50
I'll not come at them.
    Bos.   This proclaims your breeding.
Every small thing draws a base mind to fear,
As the adamant[7] draws iron. Fare you well, sir,
You shall shortly hear from's.
                                Exit.
    Duch.   I suspect some ambush.
Therefore by all my love, I do conjure you
To take your eldest son, and fly towards Milan;
Let us not venture all this poor remainder
In one unlucky bottom.[8]
    Ant.   You counsel safely.
Best of my life, farewell. Since we must part,
Heaven hath a hand in't; but no otherwise   60
Than as some curious artist takes in sunder
A clock, or watch, when it is out of frame
To bring't in better order.
    Duch.   I know not which is best,
To see you dead, or part with you. Farewell, boy,
Thou art happy, that thou hast no understanding
To know thy misery. For all our wit
And reading brings us to a truer sense
Of sorrow. In the eternal Church, sir,
I do hope we shall not part thus.
    Ant.   Oh, be of comfort,
Make patience a noble fortitude.   70
And think not how unkindly we are used.
Man, like to cassia,[9] is proved best being bruised.
    Duch. Must I like to a slave-born Russian
Account it praise to suffer tyranny?
And yet, O heaven, thy heavy hand is in't.
I have seen my little boy oft scourge[10] his top,
And compared myself to't: nought made me e'er go
    right,
But heaven's scourge-stick.[11]
    Ant.   Do not weep.
Heaven fashioned us of nothing; and we strive
To bring ourselves to nothing. Farewell, Cariola,   80
And thy sweet armful. [*To the* DUCHESS] If I do never
    see thee more,
Be a good mother to your little ones,
And save them from the tiger. Fare you well.
    Duch. Let me look upon you once more, for that
    speech
Came from a dying father. Your kiss is colder
Than I have seen an holy anchorite
Give to a dead man's skull.
    Ant. My heart is turned to a heavy lump of lead,
With which I sound[12] my danger. Fare you well.
                       Exit [*with elder* Son].

---

    [7] *adamant:* lodestone.   [8] *bottom:* hold; hence, "ship."
    [9] *cassia:* cinnamon.   [10] *scourge:* whip.
    [11] *scourge-stick:* with which the top is whipped.
    [12] *sound:* nautical image; the lead sounds or determines
the depth of the water.   [13] *adventure:* quarry.
    [14] *Charon's:* alluding to the ferryman who carried the
bodies of the dead across the river Styx into Hades.
    [15] *counterfeit:* the vizard or mask that Bosola wears.

    Duch. My laurel is all withered.   90
    Car. Look, madam, what a troop of armèd men
Make toward us.

        Enter BOSOLA *with a* Guard [*vizarded*].

    Duch.   Oh, they are very welcome.
When Fortune's wheel is over-charged with princes,
The weight makes it move swift. I would have my ruin
Be sudden. I am your adventure,[13] am I not?
    Bos. You are. You must see your husband no more—
    Duch. What devil art thou, that counterfeits heaven's
    thunder?
    Bos. Is that terrible? I would have you tell me
    whether
Is that note worse that frights the silly birds
Out of the corn; or that which doth allure them   100
To the nets? You have hearkened to the last too much.
    Duch. Oh, misery! like to a rusty o'ercharged
    cannon,
Shall I never fly in pieces? Come: to what prison?
    Bos. To none.
    Duch.   Whither then?
    Bos.   To your palace.
    Duch. I have heard that Charon's[14] boat serves to
    convey
All o'er the dismal lake, but brings none back again.
    Bos. Your brothers mean you safety and pity.
    Duch. Pity!
With such a pity men preserve alive
Pheasants and quails, when they are not fat enough
To be eaten.   111
    Bos. These are your children?
    Duch.   Yes.
    Bos.   Can they prattle?
    Duch. No.
But I intend, since they were born accursed,
Curses shall be their first language.
    Bos.   Fie, madam!
Forget this base, low fellow.
    Duch.   Were I a man,
I'd beat that counterfeit[15] face into thy other—
    Bos. One of no birth.
    Duch.   Say that he was born mean,
Man is most happy, when's own actions
Be arguments and examples of his virtue.   120
    Bos. A barren, beggarly virtue.
    Duch. I prithee, who is greatest, can you tell?
Sad tales befit my woe: I'll tell you one.
A salmon, as she swam unto the sea,
Met with a dog-fish; who encounters her
With this rough language: "Why art thou so bold
To mix thyself with our high state of floods
Being no eminent courtier, but one
That for the calmest and fresh time o'th' year
Dost live in shallow rivers, rankest thyself   130
With silly smelts and shrimps? and darest thou
Pass by our dog-ship without reverence?"
"Oh," quoth the salmon, "sister, be at peace:
Thank Jupiter, we both have passed the net,
Our value never can be truly known,
Till in the fisher's basket we be shown;

I'th' market then my price may be the higher
Even when I am nearest to the cook, and fire."
So, to great men, the moral may be stretchèd.
Men oft are valued high, when th'are most wretched.
But come: whither you please. I am armed 'gainst
    misery: 141
Bent to all sways of the oppressor's will.
There's no deep valley, but near some great hill.
                                  Ex[eunt].

ACT FOUR

SCENE ONE

[*Enter* FERDINAND *and* BOSOLA.]

   Ferd. How doth our sister Duchess bear herself
In her imprisonment?
   Bos.   Nobly; I'll describe her.
She's sad, as one long used to't: and she seems
Rather to welcome the end of misery
Than shun it: a behavior so noble
As gives a majesty to adversity:
You may discern the shape of loveliness
More perfect in her tears, than in her smiles;
She will muse four hours together; and her silence,
Methinks, expresseth more than if she spake.   10
   Ferd. Her melancholy seems to be fortified
With a strange disdain.
   Bos.   'Tis so; and this restraint
(Like English mastiffs, that grow fierce with tying)
Makes her too passionately apprehend
Those pleasures she's kept from.
   Ferd.   Curse upon her!
I will no longer study in the book
Of another's heart; Inform her what I told you.
                                  Exit.

[BOSOLA *draws the traverse*[1] *to reveal the*
DUCHESS, CARIOLA, *and* Servants.]

   Bos. All comfort to your grace—
   Duch.   I will have none.
Pray thee, why dost thou wrap thy poisoned pills
In gold and sugar?   20
   Bos. Your elder brother the Lord Ferdinand
Is come to visit you, and sends you word
'Cause once he rashly made a solemn vow
Never to see you more, he comes i'th' night;
And prays you, gently, neither torch nor taper
Shine in your chamber. He will kiss your hand
And reconcile himself; but, for his vow,
He dares not see you.
   Duch.   At his pleasure.
Take hence the lights: he's come.
                 [*Exeunt* Servants *with lights.*]

[*Enter* FERDINAND.]

   Ferd.   Where are you?
   Duch.   Here, sir.
   Ferd. This darkness suits you well.
   Duch.   I would ask your
    pardon.   30

   Ferd. You have it;
For I account it the honorablest revenge
Where I may kill, to pardon. Where are your cubs?
   Duch. Whom?
   Ferd. Call them your children;
For though our national law distinguish bastards,
From true legitimate issue, compassionate nature
Makes them all equal.
   Duch.   Do you visit me for this?
You violate a sacrament[2] o'th' Church
Shall make you howl in hell for't.
   Ferd.   It had been well,   40
Could you have lived thus always; for indeed
You were too much i'th' light.[3] But no more;
I come to seal my peace with you: here's a hand

             [*He*] *gives her a dead man's hand.*

To which you have vowed much love: the ring
    upon't
You gave.
   Duch. I affectionately kiss it.
   Ferd. Pray do; and bury the print of it in your
    heart.
I will leave this ring with you, for a love-token;
And the hand, as sure as the ring; and do not doubt
But you shall have the heart, too. When you need a
    friend
Send it to him that owed[4] it; you shall see   50
Whether he can aid you.
   Duch.   You are very cold.
I fear you are not well after your travel:
Ha! lights! Oh, horrible!
   Ferd.   Let her have lights enough.
                                  Exit.

[*Enter* Servants *with lights.*]

   Duch. What witchcraft doth he practice, that he hath
    left
A dead man's hand here?

   *Here is discovered, behind a traverse, the artificial
   figures of* ANTONIO *and his children, appearing as
                           if they were dead.*

   Bos. Look you; here's the piece from which 'twas
    tane.
He doth present you this sad spectacle,
That now you know directly they are dead.
Hereafter you may, wisely, cease to grieve
For that which cannot be recoverèd.   60
   Duch. There is not between heaven and earth one
    wish
I stay for after this. It wastes me more,
Than were't my picture, fashioned out of wax,
Struck with a magical needle, and then buried

IV.i.
   [1] *traverse:* curtain concealing the inner stage, from which
the Duchess presumably comes forward.
   [2] *sacrament:* marriage.
   [3] *too much i' th' light:* conspicuous; with allied sense of
"promiscuous."   [4] *owed:* owned.

In some foul dunghill;[5] and yond's an excellent
    property
For a tyrant, which I would account mercy—
   Bos. What's that?
   Duch. If they would bind me to that lifeless
    trunk,
And let me freeze to death.
   Bos.   Come, you must live.
   Duch. That's the greatest torture souls feel in
    hell: 70
In hell that they must live, and cannot die.
Portia,[6] I'll new kindle thy coals again,
And revive the rare and almost dead example
Of a loving wife.
   Bos.   Oh, fie! despair? Remember
You are a Christian.
   Duch.   The Church enjoins fasting;
I'll starve myself to death.
   Bos.   Leave this vain sorrow;
Things being at the worst, begin to mend:
The bee when he hath shot his sting into your hand
May then play with your eyelid.
   Duch.   Good comfortable
    fellow,
Persuade a wretch that's broke upon the wheel   80
To have all his bones new set: entreat him live,
To be executed again. Who must dispatch me?
I account this world a tedious theater,
For I do play a part in't 'gainst my will.
   Bos. Come, be of comfort, I will save your life.
   Duch. Indeed I have not leisure to tend so small a
business.
   Bos. Now by my life, I pity you.
   Duch. Thou art a fool then,
To waste thy pity on a thing so wretched   90
As cannot pity itself. I am full of daggers.
Puff! let me blow these vipers from me.

          [*Enter* Servant.]

What are you?
   Serv.   One that wishes you long life.
   Duch. I would thou wert hanged for the horrible
    curse
Thou hast given me; I shall shortly grow one
Of the miracles of pity. I'll go pray. No,
I'll go curse.
   Bos.   Oh, fie!
   Duch.   I could curse the stars.
   Bos.   Oh, fearful!
   Duch. And those three smiling seasons of the year
Into a Russian winter; nay the world
To its first chaos.   100

   Bos. Look you, the stars shine still.
   Duch.   Oh, but you must
Remember, my curse hath a great way to go:
Plagues, that make lanes through largest families,
Consume them.
   Bos.   Fie, lady!
   Duch.   Let them like tyrants
Never be remembered, but for the ill they have done;
Let all the zealous prayers of mortified[7]
Churchmen forget them—
   Bos.   O uncharitable!
   Duch. Let Heaven, a little while, cease crowning
    martyrs
To punish them.
Go, howl them this: and say I long to bleed.   110
It is some mercy when men kill with speed.
                      Exit [*with* Servants].

        [*Enter* FERDINAND.]

   Ferd. Excellent; as I would wish; she's plagued in
    art.
These presentations are but framed in wax
By the curious master in that quality,
Vincentio Lauriola,[8] and she takes them
For true substantial bodies.
   Bos.   Why do you do this?
   Ferd. To bring her to despair.
   Bos.   'Faith, end here;
And go no farther in your cruelty,
Send her a penitential garment, to put on
Next to her delicate skin, and furnish her   120
With beads and prayerbooks.
   Ferd.   Damn her! that body of
    hers,
While that my blood ran pure in't, was more worth
Than that which thou wouldst comfort, called a soul.
I will send her masques of common courtesans,
Have her meat served up by bawds and ruffians,
And, 'cause she'll needs be mad, I am resolved
To remove forth the common hospital[9]
All the mad folk, and place them near her lodging:
There let them practice together, sing, and dance,
And act their gambols to the full o'th' moon.[10]   130
If she can sleep the better for it, let her.
Your work is almost ended.
   Bos.   Must I see her again?
   Ferd. Yes.
   Bos.   Never.
   Ferd.   You must.
   Bos.   Never in mine own
    shape;
That's forfeited by my intelligence,[11]
And this last cruel lie; when you send me next,
The business shall be comfort.
   Ferd.   Very likely;
Thy pity is nothing of kin to thee. Antonio
Lurks about Milan; thou shalt shortly thither,
To feed a fire as great as my revenge,
Which never will slack, till it have spent his fuel;   140
Intemperate agues make physicians cruel.
                         Exeunt.

---

   [5] *dunghill:* which, as it decomposes, gives off heat and
melts the waxen image.
   [6] *Portia:* Brutus's wife, who killed herself by swallowing
hot coals.
   [7] *mortified:* i.e., who mortify or deny the flesh.
   [8] *Lauriola:* unknown to history.
   [9] *remove . . . hospital:* take from the insane asylum.
   [10] *full o' th' moon:* when madness is at its height.
   [11] *intelligence:* role as spy.

IV.ii

[*Enter* DUCHESS *and* CARIOLA.]

Duch. What hideous noise was that?
Car.   'Tis the wild
  consort[1]
Of madmen, lady, which your tyrant brother
Hath placed about your lodging. This tyranny,
I think, was never practiced till this hour.
  Duch. Indeed, I thank him: nothing but noise, and
    folly
Can keep me in my right wits, whereas reason
And silence make me stark mad. Sit down,
Discourse to me some dismal tragedy.
  Car. Oh, 'twill increase your melancholy.
  Duch.   Thou art
    deceived;
To hear of greater grief would lessen mine.   10
This is a prison?
  Car.   Yes, but you shall live
To shake this durance off.
  Duch.   Thou art a fool;
The robin red-breast and the nightingale
Never live long in cages.
  Car.   Pray dry your eyes.
What think you of, madam?
  Duch.   Of nothing;
When I muse thus, I sleep.
  Car. Like a madman, with your eyes open?
  Duch. Dost thou think we shall know one another
In th'other world?
  Car.   Yes, out of question.
  Duch. Oh, that it were possible we might   20
But hold some two days' conference with the dead,
From them I should learn somewhat I am sure
I never shall know here. I'll tell thee a miracle,
I am not mad yet, to my cause of sorrow.
Th'heaven o'er my head seems made of molten brass,
The earth of flaming sulfur, yet I am not mad.
I am acquainted with sad misery,
As the tanned galley-slave is with his oar.
Necessity makes me suffer constantly,
And custom makes it easy. Who do I look like now?
  Car. Like to your picture in the gallery,   31
A deal of life in show, but none in practice;
Or rather like some reverend monument
Whose ruins are even pitied.
  Duch.   Very proper;
And Fortune seems only to have her eyesight,
To behold my tragedy.
How now! what noise is that?

[*Enter* Servant.]

  Serv.   I am come to tell you,
Your brother hath intended you some sport.
A great physician when the Pope was sick
Of a deep melancholy, presented him   40
With several sorts of madmen, which wild object,
Being full of change and sport, forced him to laugh,
And so th'imposthume[2] broke; the selfsame cure
The Duke intends on you.

Duch.   Let them come in.
  Serv. There's a mad lawyer, and a secular priest,[3]
A doctor that hath forfeited his wits
By jealousy; an astrologian,
That in his works said such a day o'th' month
Should be the day of doom;[4] and, failing of't,
Ran mad; an English tailor, crazed i'th' brain   50
With the study of new fashion; a gentleman usher
Quite beside himself with care to keep in mind
The number of his lady's salutations,
Or "How do you?" she employed him in each morning;
A farmer too, an excellent knave in grain,[5]
Mad, 'cause he was hindered transportation;[6]
And let one broker,[7] that's mad, loose to these,
You'ld think the devil were amongst them.
  Duch. Sit, Cariola: let them loose when you please,
For I am chained to endure all your tyranny.   60

[*Enter* Madmen.]

Here, by a madman, this song is sung to a dismal kind
                                   of music.

> *Oh, let us howl, some heavy note,*
>   *Some deadly-doggèd howl,*
> *Sounding, as from the threatening throat,*
>   *Of beasts, and fatal fowl.*
> *As ravens, screech-owls, bulls, and bears,*
>   *We'll bell,[8] and bawl our parts,*
> *Till yerksome[9] noise have cloyed your ears,*
>   *And corrosived[10] your hearts.*
> *At last when as our choir wants breath,*
>   *Our bodies being blessed,*   70
> *We'll sing like swans, to welcome death,*
>   *And die in love and rest.*

  1 Mad. Doomsday not come yet? I'll draw it nearer
by a perspective,[11] or make a glass that shall set all the
world on fire upon an instant. I cannot sleep; my pillow
is stuffed with a litter of porcupines.
  2 Mad. Hell is a mere glass-house,[12] where the
devils are continually blowing up women's souls on
hollow irons, and the fire never goes out.   79
  3 Mad. I will lie with every woman in my parish the
tenth night; I will tithe them over[13] like haycocks.
  4 Mad. Shall my pothecary outgo me, because I am
a cuckold? I have found out his roguery: he makes alum
of his wife's urine, and sells it to Puritans, that have
sore throats with over-straining.[14]
  1 Mad. I have skill in heraldry.

IV.ii.
  [1] *consort:* company, as of musicians.
  [2] *imposthume:* abscess.
  [3] *secular priest:* who lived in the world, as opposed to a
member of a monastic order.   [4] *doom:* judgment.
  [5] *in grain:* fast-dyed, through and through; with pun on
"grain" as appropriate to a farmer.
  [6] *transportation:* export.
  [7] *broker:* pawnbroker; pimp.   [8] *bell:* bellow.
  [9] *yerksome:* irksome.   [10] *corrosived:* corroded.
  [11] *perspective:* telescope.   [12] *glass-house:* glass factory.
  [13] *tithe them over:* exact of them my due (tenth part) as
priest; but also "decimate" (sexually), "knock them over."
  [14] *over-straining:* in preaching.

2 Mad. Hast?

1 Mad. You do give for your crest a woodcock's[15] head, with the brains picked out on't. You are a very ancient gentleman.   90

3 Mad. Greek is turned Turk; we are only to be saved by the Helvetian[16] translation.

1 Mad. Come on, sir, I will lay[17] the law to you.

2 Mad. Oh, rather lay[18] a corrosive; the law will eat to the bone.

3 Mad. He that drinks but to satisfy nature is damned.

4 Mad. If I had my glass[19] here, I would show a sight should make all the women here call me mad doctor.   100

1 Mad. What's he, a rope-maker?[20]

2 Mad. No, no, no, a snuffling[21] knave, that while he shows the tombs will have his hand in a wench's placket.[22]

3 Mad. Woe to the caroche that brought home my wife from the masque, at three o'clock in the morning; it had a large feather bed in it.

4 Mad. I have pared the devil's nails forty times, roasted them in raven's eggs, and cured agues with them.

3 Mad. Get me three hundred milch[23] bats, to make possets[24] to procure sleep.   111

4 Mad. All the college may throw their caps[25] at me; I have made a soap-boiler costive;[26] it was my masterpiece.

> *Here the dance consisting of eight* Madmen, *with music answerable thereunto, after which* BOSOLA, *like an old man, enters.*

Duch. Is he mad, too?

Serv.   Pray, question him; I'll leave you.
                    [*Exeunt* Servant *and* Madmen.]

Bos. I am come to make thy tomb.

Duch.   Ha! my tomb?
Thou speakest as if I lay upon my death-bed,
Gasping for breath. Dost thou perceive me sick?

Bos. Yes, and the more dangerously, since thy sickness is insensible.[27]   120

Duch. Thou art not mad, sure; dost know me?

Bos. Yes.

Duch. Who am I?

Bos. Thou art a box of worm seed, at best, but a salvatory of green mummy.[28] What's this flesh? A little crudded[29] milk, fantastical puff-paste.[30] Our bodies are weaker than those paper prisons boys use to keep flies in—more contemptible, since ours is to preserve earthworms. Didst thou ever see a lark in a cage? Such is the soul in the body: this world is like her little turf[31] 130 of grass; and the heaven o'er our heads, like her looking-glass, only gives us a miserable knowledge of the small compass of our prison.

Duch. Am not I thy Duchess?

Bos. Thou art some great woman sure; for riot begins to sit on thy forehead (clad in gray hairs) twenty years sooner than on a merry milkmaid's. Thou sleepest worse than if a mouse should be forced to take up her lodging in a cat's ear. A little infant, that breeds its teeth, should it lie with thee, would cry out, as if thou wert the more unquiet bedfellow.   141

Duch. I am Duchess of Malfi still.

Bos. That makes thy sleeps so broken:
Glories, like glow-worms, afar off shine bright,
But looked to near, have neither heat nor light.

Duch. Thou art very plain.

Bos. My trade is to flatter the dead, not the living;
I am a tomb-maker.

Duch. And thou comest to make my tomb?

Bos. Yes.   150

Duch. Let me be a little merry;
Of what stuff wilt thou make it?

Bos. Nay, resolve[32] me first, of what fashion?

Duch. Why, do we grow fantastical in our
death-bed?
Do we affect fashion in the grave?

Bos. Most ambitiously. Princes' images on their
    tombs
Do not lie as they were wont, seeming to pray
Up to heaven, but with their hands under their
    cheeks,
As if they died of the tooth-ache. They are not carved
With their eyes fixed upon the stars, but as   160
Their minds were wholly bent upon the world,
The self-same way they seem to turn their faces.

Duch. Let me know fully therefore the effect
Of this thy dismal preparation,
This talk, fit for a charnel.

Bos.   Now I shall;

[*Enter* Executioners *with] a coffin, cords,
                    and a bell.*

Here is a present from your princely brothers,
And may it arrive welcome, for it brings
Last benefit, last sorrow.

Duch.   Let me see it.
I have so much obedience, in my blood,
I wish it in their veins, to do them good.   170

Bos. This is your last presence chamber.

Car. O my sweet lady!

Duch.   Peace; it affrights not me.

---

[15] *woodcock's:* alluding to the brainlessness associated with this fowl.

[16] *Helvetian:* Genevan text ("Breeches" Bible) of 1560; the sneer is at the expense of the Puritan or precisian who, as he abandons the canonical Greek text, turns infidel.

[17] *lay:* expound.   [18] *lay:* apply.

[19] *glass:* telescope(?); natural perspective(?), which revealed different images when looked at from different points of view.

[20] *rope-maker:* hangman's confederate.

[21] *snuffling:* nasal-sounding, like a Puritan.

[22] *placket:* opening in a dress.

[23] *milch:* milk-producing.

[24] *possets:* preparations of hot milk, curdled with wine or ale, and with spice and sugar added.

[25] *throw their caps:* scorn(?); emulate(?).

[26] *soap-boiler costive:* soap is an emetic; to use it to induce constipation ("costive") is a masterpiece.

[27] *insensible:* not felt.

[28] *salvatory of green mummy:* ointment box containing medicine made from corpses.   [29] *crudded:* curdled.

[30] *puff-paste:* pastry; hence "light," nothing.

[31] *turf:* with which the lark's cage was supplied.

[32] *resolve:* satisfy.

Bos. I am the common bellman,[33]
That usually is sent to condemned persons,
The night before they suffer.
　　Duch.　　　　　　　　Even now thou said'st
Thou wast a tomb-maker?
　　Bos.　　　　　　　　'Twas to bring you
By degrees to mortification.[34] Listen:

　　　　　　　　　　　　[He rings the bell.]

> *Hark, now every thing is still,*
> *The screech-owl and the whistler*[35] *shrill*
> *Call upon our dame, aloud,*　　　　　180
> *And bid her quickly don her shroud.*
> *Much you had of land and rent;*
> *Your length in clay's now competent.*[36]
> *A long war disturbed your mind;*
> *Here your perfect peace*[37] *is signed.*
> *Of what is't fools make such vain keeping?*
> *Sin their conception, their birth, weeping;*
> *Their life, a general mist of error,*
> *Their death, a hideous storm of terror.*
> *Strew your hair with powders sweet;*　　190
> *Don clean linen, bathe your feet,*
> *And, the foul fiend more to check,*
> *A crucifix let bless your neck.*
> *'Tis now full tide 'tween night and day,*
> *End your groan, and come away.*

　　　　　　　　　　　[Executioners *approach.*]

Car. Hence, villains, tyrants, murderers. Alas!
What will you do with my lady? Call for help.
　　Duch. To whom, to our next neighbors? They are
　　mad-folks.
　　Bos. Remove that noise.

　　　　　[Executioners *seize* CARIOLA, *who struggles.*]

　　Duch.　　　　　　　Farewell, Cariola,
In my last will I have not much to give.　　200
A many hungry guests have fed upon me;
Thine will be a poor reversion.[38]
　　Car.　　　　　　　I will die with her.
　　Duch. I pray thee look thou givest my little boy
Some syrup for his cold, and let the girl
Say her prayers ere she sleep.

　　　　　　　　　　[CARIOLA *is forced off.*]
　　　　　　　　　　Now what you please,
What death?
　　Bos. Strangling: here are your executioners.
　　Duch. I forgive them.
The apoplexy, catarrh,[39] or cough o'th' lungs
Would do as much as they do.　　210
　　Bos. Doth not death fright you?
　　Duch.　　　　　　　Who would be
　　afraid on't?
Knowing to meet such excellent company
In th'other world.
　　Bos.　　　　　　　Yet, methinks,
The manner of your death should much afflict you,
This cord should terrify you?
　　Duch.　　　　　　　Not a whit.

What would it pleasure me, to have my throat cut
With diamonds? Or to be smothered
With cassia? Or to be shot to death, with pearls?
I know death hath ten thousand several doors
For men to take their exits; and 'tis found　　220
They go on such strange geometrical hinges,
You may open them both ways:[40]—any way, for
　　heaven sake,
So I were out of your whispering. Tell my brothers
That I perceive death, now I am well awake,
Best gift is, they can give, or I can take.
I would fain put off my last woman's fault,
I'd not be tedious to you.
　　Exec.　　　　　　　We are ready.
　　Duch. Dispose my breath how please you, but my
　　body
Bestow upon my women, will you?
　　Exec.　　　　　　　Yes.
　　Duch. Pull, and pull strongly, for your able
　　strength　　230
Must pull down heaven upon me;
Yet stay, heaven gates are not so highly arched
As princes' palaces; they that enter there
Must go upon their knees. Come, violent death,
Serve for mandragora[41] to make me sleep;
Go tell my brothers, when I am laid out,
They then may feed in quiet.

　　　　　　　　　　　　They strangle her.

　　Bos.　　　　　　　Where's the waiting-
　　woman?
Fetch her. Some other strangle the children.
　　　　　　　　　　　[*Exeunt* Executioners.]

　　　　　　　　　[*Enter one with* CARIOLA.]

Look you, there sleeps your mistress.
　　Car.　　　　　　　Oh, you are
　　damned
Perpetually for this. My turn is next,　　240
Is't not so ordered?
　　Bos.　　　　　　　Yes, and I am glad
You are so well prepared for't.
　　Car.　　　　　　　You are deceived, sir,
I am not prepared for't. I will not die,
I will first come to my answer; and know
How I have offended.
　　Bos.　　　　　　　Come, dispatch her.

---

　　[33] *common bellman:* whose office, initially, was to ban evil
spirits and invite prayers for the dying by tolling the bell;
from the beginning of the seventeenth century, this office was
extended to include an exhortation to condemned criminals.
　　[34] *mortification:* denying of the flesh; death itself.
　　[35] *whistler:* This immemorial harbinger of death has been
associated with various birds, as also with the "Seven
Whistlers" or souls of Jews who participated in the Crucifixion.　　　　　　　　　　　　　　[36] *competent:* enough.
　　[37] *peace:* as of a treaty; hence "signed."
　　[38] *reversion:* legacy.
　　[39] *catarrh:* cerebral hemorrhage; original reads "cathar,"
which signifies also Puritan or spirit-intoxicated man.
Whether there is an etymological connection is moot.
　　[40] *both ways:* i.e., our exit is easy enough.
　　[41] *mandragora:* a narcotic.

You kept her counsel, now you shall keep ours.
   Car. I will not die, I must not, I am contracted
To a young gentleman.
   Exec.   Here's your wedding-ring.[42]
   Car. Let me but speak with the Duke. I'll discover
Treason to his person.
   Bos.   Delays; throttle her.   250
   Exec. She bites and scratches.
   Car.   If you kill me now
I am damned. I have not been at confession
This two years.
   Bos.   When![43]
   Car.   I am quick with child.
   Bos.   Why then,
Your credit's saved;—

                [CARIOLA *is strangled.*]

         bear her into th' next room.
Let this lie still.
     [*Exeunt* Executioners *with* CARIOLA'S *body.*]

         [*Enter* FERDINAND.]

   Ferd.   Is she dead?
   Bos   She is what
You'd have her. But here begin your pity.

       Shows[44] *the children strangled.*

Alas, how have these offended?
   Ferd.   The death
Of young wolves is never to be pitied.
   Bos. Fix your eye here.
   Ferd.   Constantly.
   Bos.   Do you not
  weep?
Other sins only speak; murder shrieks out.   260
The element of water moistens the earth,
But blood flies upwards, and bedews the heavens.
   Ferd. Cover her face. Mine eyes dazzle. She died
  young.
   Bos. I think not so; her infelicity
Seemed to have years too many.
   Ferd.   She and I were twins;
And should I die this instant, I had lived
Her time to a minute.
   Bos.   It seems she was born first.
You have bloodily approved[45] the ancient truth,
That kindred commonly do worse agree
Than remote strangers.
   Ferd.   Let me see her face again;   270
Why didst not thou pity her? What an excellent
Honest man mightest thou have been
If thou hadst borne her to some sanctuary!
Or, bold in a good cause, opposed thyself
With thy advancèd sword above thy head,
Between her innocence and my revenge!

I bade thee, when I was distracted of my wits,
Go kill my dearest friend, and thou hast done 't.
For let me but examine well the cause;
What was the meanness of her match to me?   280
Only I must confess, I had a hope,
Had she continued widow, to have gained
An infinite mass of treasure by her death;
And that was the main cause. Her marriage,
That drew a stream of gall quite through my heart;
For thee (as we observe in tragedies
That a good actor many times is cursed
For playing a villain's part), I hate thee for 't;
And, for my sake, say thou hast done much ill, well.
   Bos. Let me quicken your memory, for I perceive
You are falling into ingratitude. I challenge   291
The reward due to my service.
   Ferd.   I'll tell thee,
What I'll give thee—
   Bos.   Do.
   Ferd.   I'll give thee a pardon
For this murder.
   Bos.   Ha?
   Ferd.   Yes; and 'tis
The largest bounty I can study to do thee.
By what authority didst thou execute
This bloody sentence?
   Bos.   By yours.
   Ferd.   Mine? Was I her
  judge?
Did any ceremonial form of law
Doom her to not-being? Did a complete jury
Deliver her conviction up i'th' court?   300
Where shalt thou find this judgment registered
Unless in hell? See: like a bloody fool
Th' hast forfeited thy life, and thou shalt die for 't.
   Bos. The office of justice is perverted quite
When one thief hangs another. Who shall dare
To reveal this?
   Ferd.   Oh, I'll tell thee:
The wolf shall find her grave, and scrape it up;
Not to devour the corpse, but to discover
The horrid murder.
   Bos.   You, not I, shall quake for 't.
   Ferd. Leave me.
   Bos.   I will first receive my pension.   310
   Ferd. You are a villain.
   Bos.   When your ingratitude
Is judge, I am so—
   Ferd.   O horror!
That not the fear of him which binds the devils
Can prescribe man obedience.
Never look upon me more.
   Bos.   Why, fare thee well.
Your brother and yourself are worthy men;
You have a pair of hearts are hollow graves,
Rotten, and rotting others; and your vengeance,
Like two chained bullets, still goes arm in arm.
You may be brothers; for treason, like the plague,   320
Doth take much in a blood.[46] I stand like one
That long hath tane a sweet and golden dream.
I am angry with myself, now that I wake.

---

[42] *wedding-ring:* a noose.
[43] *When:* Bosola wishes to get on with it.
[44] *Shows:* As by drawing the curtain which concealed the
inner stage.   [45] *approved:* confirmed.
[46] *take . . . blood:* go by families.

Ferd. Get thee into some unknown part o'th'
      world
That I may never see thee.
      Bos.   Let me know
Wherefore I should be thus neglected? Sir,
I served your tyranny: and rather strove
To satisfy yourself, than all the world;
And, though I loathed the evil, yet I loved
You that did counsel it, and rather sought   330
To appear a true servant than an honest man.
      Ferd. I'll go hunt the badger by owl-light;[47]
'Tis a deed of darkness.

                                        Exit.

      Bos. He's much distracted. Off my painted[48]
      honor!
While with vain hopes our faculties we tire,
We seem to sweat in ice and freeze in fire;
What would I do, were this to do again?
I would not change my peace of conscience
For all the wealth of Europe. She stirs; here's life.
Return, fair soul, from darkness, and lead mine   340
Out of this sensible[49] hell. She's warm, she breathes:
Upon thy pale lips I will melt my heart
To store[50] them with fresh color. Who's there?
Some cordial[51] drink! Alas! I dare not call:
So pity would destroy pity.[52] Her eye opes,
And heaven in it seems to ope, that late[53] was shut,
To take me up to mercy.
      Duch.   Antonio!
      Bos. Yes, madam, he is living.
The dead bodies you saw were but feigned statues;
He's reconciled to your brothers; the Pope hath
      wrought   350
The atonement.[54]
      Duch.   Mercy.

                                She dies.

      Bos. Oh, she's gone again. There the cords of life
      broke.
O sacred innocence, that sweetly sleeps
On turtles'[55] feathers; whilst a guilty conscience
Is a black register, wherein is writ
All our good deeds and bad; a perspective
That shows us hell! That we cannot be suffered
To do good when we have a mind to it!
This is manly sorrow.
These tears, I am very certain, never grew   360
In my mother's milk. My estate is sunk
Below the degree of fear. Where were
These penitent fountains while she was living?
Oh, they were frozen up! Here is a sight
As direful to my soul as is the sword
Unto a wretch hath slain his father. Come,
I'll bear thee hence,
And execute thy will; that's deliver
Thy body to the reverend dispose[56]
Of some good women. That the cruel tyrant   370
Shall not deny me. Then I'll post to Milan,
Where somewhat I will speedily enact
Worth my dejection.
                    Exit [*with the body of the* DUCHESS].

ACT FIVE

SCENE ONE

[*Enter* ANTONIO *and* DELIO.]

      Ant. What think you of my hope of reconcilement
To the Aragonian brethren?
      Del.   I misdoubt it.
For though they have sent their letters of safe conduct
For your repair[1] to Milan, they appear
But nets to entrap you. The Marquis of Pescara,
Under whom you hold certain land in cheat,[2]
Much 'gainst his noble nature, hath been moved
To seize those lands, and some of his dependants
Are at this instant making it their suit
To be invested in your revenues.   10
I cannot think they mean well to your life,
That do deprive you of your means of life,
Your living.
      Ant.   You are still an heretic
To any safety I can shape myself.
      Del. Here comes the Marquis. I will make myself
Petitioner for some part of your land,
To know whither it is flying.
      Ant.   I pray do.

[*Enter* PESCARA.]

      Del. Sir, I have a suit to you.
      Pes.   To me?
      Del.   An easy one:
This is the citadel of St. Bennet,[3]
With some demesnes,[4] of late in the possession   20
Of Antonio Bologna; please you bestow them on me?
      Pes. You are my friend. But this is such a suit
Nor fit for me to give, nor you to take.
      Del. No, sir?
      Pes.   I will give you ample reason for't
Soon, in private. Here's the Cardinal's mistress.

[*Enter* JULIA.]

      Jul. My lord, I am grown your poor petitioner,
And should be an ill beggar, had I not
A great man's letter here, the Cardinal's,
To court you in my favor.

                    [*She gives him a letter.*]

      Pes.   He entreats for you
The citadel of St. Bennet, that belonged   30

---

[47] *by owl-light:* moonlight; the accepted time for hunting
the badger, which sleeps by day.
[48] *painted:* specious; Bosola knows himself a scoundrel.
[49] *sensible:* felt.   [50] *store:* provision.
[51] *cordial:* restorative.
[52] *pity . . . pity:* as by bringing back Ferdinand.
[53] *late:* recently.   [54] *atonement:* reconciliation.
[55] *turtles':* doves'.   [56] *dispose:* disposing.
V.i.
  [1] *repair:* return.
  [2] *hold . . . cheat:* Land held "in escheat" reverted to the
lord (here, Pescara) if the holder died without a will or heirs
or had committed a felony.   [3] *Bennet:* Benedict.
  [4] *demesnes:* lands.

To the banished Bologna.

Jul.   Yes.

Pes. I could not have thought of a friend I could
Rather pleasure with it; 'tis yours.

Jul.   Sir, I thank you.
And he shall know how doubly I am engaged
Both in your gift, and speediness of giving,
Which makes your grant the greater.

                                      Exit.

Ant. [*Aside*]   How they fortify
Themselves with my ruin!

Del.   Sir, I am
Little bound to you.

Pes.   Why?

Del. Because you denied this suit to me, and gave't
To such a creature.

Pes.   Do you know what it was?   40
It was Antonio's land, not forfeited
By course of law, but ravished from his throat
By the Cardinal's entreaty; it were not fit
I should bestow so main a piece of wrong
Upon my friend. 'Tis a gratification
Only due to a strumpet; for it is injustice.
Shall I sprinkle the pure blood of innocents
To make those followers I call my friends
Look ruddier upon me? I am glad
This land, tane from the owner by such wrong,   50
Returns again unto so foul an use,
As salary for his lust. Learn, good Delio,
To ask noble things of me, and you shall find
I'll be a noble giver.

Del.   You instruct me well.

Ant. [*Aside*] Why, here's a man, now, would fright
      impudence
From sauciest beggars.

Pes.   Prince Ferdinand's come to
      Milan
Sick, as they give out, of an apoplexy.
But some say 'tis a frenzy; I am going
To visit him.

                                      Exit.

Ant.   'Tis a noble old fellow.[5]

Del. What course do you mean to take, Antonio?   60

Ant. This night I mean to venture all my fortune,
Which is no more than a poor lingering life,
To the Cardinal's worst of malice. I have got
Private access to his chamber: and intend
To visit him, about the mid of night,
As once his brother did our noble Duchess.
It may be that the sudden apprehension
Of danger (for I'll go in mine own shape)
When he shall see it fraught with love and duty,
May draw the poison out of him, and work   70

---

⁵ *'Tis . . . fellow:* Pescara.
V.ii.
   ¹ *lycanthropia:* as the doctor explains, denoting one's
belief that he had been changed to a wolf.
   ² *nearer:* more direct or rigorous.
   ³ *Paracelsus:* sixteenth-century German-Swiss physician
and magician.

A friendly reconcilement. If it fail,
Yet it shall rid me of this infamous calling,
For better fall once, than be ever falling.

Del. I'll second you in all danger; and, howe'er,
My life keeps rank with yours.

Ant. You are still my loved and best friend.

                                    Exeunt.

V.ii

                [*Enter* PESCARA *and* Doctor.]

Pes. Now, Doctor, may I visit your patient?

Doc. If't please your lordship: but he's instantly
To take the air here in the gallery,
By my direction.

Pes.   Pray thee, what's his disease?

Doc. A very pestilent disease, my lord,
They call lycanthropia.[1]

Pes.   What's that?
I need a dictionary to't.

Doc.   I'll tell you:
In those that are possessed with't there o'erflows
Such melancholy humor, they imagine
Themselves to be transformed into wolves,   10
Steal forth to churchyards in the dead of night,
And dig dead bodies up; as two nights since
One met the Duke, 'bout midnight in a lane
Behind St. Mark's church, with the leg of a man
Upon his shoulder; and he howled fearfully,
Said he was a wolf; only the difference
Was, a wolf's skin was hairy on the outside,
His on the inside; bade them take their swords,
Rip up his flesh, and try. Straight I was sent for,
And having ministered to him, found his grace   20
Very well recovered.

Pes.   I am glad on't.

Doc. Yet not without some fear
Of a relapse. If he grow to his fit again
I'll go a nearer[2] way to work with him
Than ever Paracelsus[3] dreamed of. If
They'll give me leave, I'll buffet this madness out of
      him.
Stand aside; he comes.

     [*Enter* CARDINAL, FERDINAND, MALATESTE,
       and BOSOLA, *who remains in the background.*]

Ferd. Leave me.

Mal. Why doth your lordship love this solitariness?

Ferd. Eagles commonly fly alone. They are   30
crows, daws, and starlings that flock together. Look,
what's that follows me?

Mal. Nothing, my lord.

Ferd. Yes.

Mal. 'Tis your shadow.

Ferd. Stay it; let it not haunt me.

Mal. Impossible, if you move, and the sun shine.

Ferd. I will throttle it.

          [*Throws himself upon his shadow.*]

Mal. Oh, my lord: you are angry with nothing.   39

Ferd. You are a fool. How is't possible I should catch my shadow unless I fall upon't? When I go to hell, I mean to carry a bribe; for, look you, good gifts evermore make way for the worst persons.

Pes. Rise, good my lord.

Ferd. I am studying the art of patience.

Pes. 'Tis a noble virtue.

Ferd. To drive six snails before me, from this town to Moscow; neither use goad nor whip to them, but let them take their own time (the patientest man i'th' world match me for an experiment!) and I'll crawl after like a sheep-biter.[4]　　　　　　　　　　　　　　　　　51

Card. Force him up.

[*They raise* FERDINAND *to his feet.*]

Ferd. Use me well, you were best.
What I have done, I have done; I'll confess nothing.

Doc. Now let me come to him. Are you mad, my lord?
Are you out of your princely wits?

Ferd.　　　　　　　　　　　What's he?

Pes. Your doctor.

Ferd. Let me have his beard sawed off, and his eyebrows
Filed more civil.[5]

Doc.　　　　I must do mad tricks with him,
For that's the only way on't. I have brought　　60
Your grace a salamander's skin, to keep you
From sun-burning.

Ferd.　　　　　I have cruel sore eyes.

Doc. The white of a cocatrice's egg is present remedy.

Ferd. Let it be a new-laid one, you were best.
Hide me from him. Physicians are like kings,
They brook no contradiction.

Doc.　　　　　　　　Now he begins
To fear me; now let me alone with him.[6]

[FERDINAND *tries to take off his gown; the* CARDINAL *prevents him.*]

Card. How now, put off your gown?

Doc. Let me have some forty urinals filled with rose-water: he and I'll go pelt one another with them;　70
now he begins to fear me. Can you fetch a frisk,[7] sir?
[*Aside to* CARDINAL] Let him go, let him go upon my peril. I find by his eye, he stands in awe of me. I'll make him as tame as a dormouse.

[CARDINAL *releases* FERDINAND.]

Ferd. Can you fetch your frisks, sir! I will stamp him into a cullis;[8] flay off his skin, to cover one of the anatomies[9] this rogue hath set i'th' cold yonder, in Barber-Chirurgeons'[10] Hall. Hence, hence! you are all of you like beasts for sacrifice,

[*Throws the* Doctor *down and beats him.*]

there's nothing left of you, but tongue and belly,[11] flattery and lechery.　　　　　　　　　　　81
　　　　　　　　　　　　　　　　　　　[*Exit.*]

Pes. Doctor, he did not fear you throughly.[12]

Doc. True, I was somewhat too forward.

Bos. [*Aside*] Mercy upon me, what a fatal judgment
Hath fallen upon this Ferdinand!

Pes.　　　　　　　　　　Knows your grace
What accident hath brought unto the prince
This strange distraction?

Card. [*Aside*] I must feign somewhat. Thus they say
　it grew:
You have heard it rumored for these many years,
None of our family dies, but there is seen　　90
The shape of an old woman, which is given
By tradition, to us, to have been murdered
By her nephews, for her riches. Such a figure
One night, as the prince sat up late at's book,
Appeared to him; when crying out for help,
The gentlemen of's chamber found his grace
All on a cold sweat, altered much in face
And language. Since which apparition
He hath grown worse and worse, and I much fear
He cannot live.　　　　　　　　　　　100

Bos. Sir, I would speak with you.

Pes.　　　　　　　We'll leave your grace,
Wishing to the sick prince, our noble lord,
All health of mind and body.

Card.　　　　　　You are most welcome.

[*Exeunt* PESCARA, MALATESTE, *and* Doctor.]

[*Aside*] Are you come? So: this fellow must not know
By any means I had intelligence
In[13] our Duchess' death. For, though I counseled it,
The full of all th' engagement[14] seemed to grow
From Ferdinand. Now, sir, how fares our sister?
I do not think but sorrow make her look
Like to an oft-dyed garment. She shall now　　110
Taste comfort from me—why do you look so wildly?
Oh, the fortune of your master here, the prince,
Dejects you—but be you of happy comfort:
If you'll do one thing for me I'll entreat,
Though he had a cold tombstone o'er his bones,
I'ld make you what you would be.

Bos.　　　　　　　　Anything;
Give it me in a breath, and let me fly to't:
They that think long, small expedition[15] win,
For musing much o'th'end, cannot begin.

[*Enter* JULIA.]

Jul. Sir, will you come in to supper?

Card.　　　　　　　I am busy, leave
　me.　　　　　　　　　　　　　　　120

Jul. [*Aside*] What an excellent shape hath that fellow!
　　　　　　　　　　　　　　　　　　　Exit.

---

[4] *sheep-biter:* dog that worries sheep; hence a sheep-stealer or thief.　　[5] *civil:* decorous; also, "less haughty."

[6] *let . . . him:* leave him to me.

[7] *fetch a frisk:* cut a caper.

[8] *cullis:* This broth was made partly by bruising the flesh and bones of a fowl.　　[9] *anatomies:* skeletons.

[10] *Barber-Chirurgeons':* The Barber-Surgeons were allowed yearly by charter the bodies of four executed criminals for dissection.

[11] *belly:* entrails which, with the tongue, were left to the gods when the body had been sacrificed.

[12] *throughly:* thoroughly.　　[13] *In:* Of.

[14] *full . . . engagement:* whole business; alternatively, the engaging of Bosola.　　[15] *expedition:* success.

Card. 'Tis thus: Antonio lurks here in Milan;
Inquire him out, and kill him: while he lives
Our sister cannot marry, and I have thought
Of an excellent match for her: do this, and style me
Thy advancement.
    Bos.   But by what means shall I find him
    out?
    Card. There is a gentleman, called Delio
Here in the camp, that hath been long approved
His loyal friend. Set eye upon that fellow,
Follow him to mass; may be Antonio,   130
Although he do account religion
But a school-name, for fashion of the world,
May accompany him; or else go inquire out
Delio's confessor, and see if you can bribe
Him to reveal it. There are a thousand ways
A man might find to trace him: as, to know
What fellows haunt the Jews for taking up
Great sums of money, for sure he's in want;
Or else go to th' picture-makers, and learn
Who brought[16] her picture lately: some of these   140
Happily may take[17]—
    Bos.   Well, I'll not freeze i'th' business;
I would see that wretched thing, Antonio,
Above all sights i'th' world.
    Card.   Do, and be happy.

                                Exit.

    Bos. This fellow doth breed basilisks in's eyes,
He's nothing else but murder: yet he seems
Not to have notice of the Duchess' death.
'Tis his cunning: I must follow his example;
There cannot be a surer way to trace,
Than that of an old fox.

            [*Enter* JULIA *with a pistol.*]

    Jul.   So, sir, you are well met.
    Bos. How now?
    Jul.   Nay, the doors are fast enough.   150
Now, sir, I will make you confess your treachery.
    Bos. Treachery?
    Jul.   Yes, confess to me
Which of my women 'twas you hired to put
Love-powder into my drink?
    Bos.   Love-powder?
    Jul. Yes, when I was at Malfi;
Why should I fall in love with such a face else?
I have already suffered for thee so much pain,
The only remedy to do me good
Is to kill my longing.
    Bos.   Sure, your pistol holds
Nothing but perfumes or kissing-comfits;[18] excellent
    lady,   160
You have a pretty way on't to discover
Your longing. Come, come, I'll disarm you
And arm[19] you thus: yet this is wondrous strange.

---

[16] *brought:* Most editors emend to "bought."
[17] *take:* work.   [18] *kissing-comfits:* breath sweeteners.
[19] *arm:* embrace.   [20] *nice:* overly fastidious.
[21] *familiar:* spirit.   [22] *want:* lack.
[23] *presently:* now.

    Jul. Compare thy form and my eyes together,
You'll find my love no such great miracle.
[*Kisses him.*] Now you'll say
I am a wanton. This nice[20] modesty in ladies
Is but a troublesome familiar[21]
That haunts them.   169
    Bos. Know you me, I am a blunt soldier.
    Jul.   The better;
Sure, there wants fire where there are no lively sparks
Of roughness.
    Bos.   And I want[22] compliment.
    Jul.   Why, ignorance
In courtship cannot make you do amiss,
If you have a heart to do well.
    Bos.   You are very fair.
    Jul. Nay, if you lay beauty to my charge,
I must plead unguilty.
    Bos.   Your bright eyes
Carry a quiver of darts in them, sharper
Than sunbeams.
    Jul.   You will mar me with commendation;
Put yourself to the charge of courting me,
Whereas now I woo you.   180
    Bos. [*Aside*] I have it, I will work upon this creature,
Let us grow most amorously familiar.—
If the great Cardinal now should see me thus,
Would he not count me a villain?
    Jul. No, he might count me a wanton,
Not lay a scruple of offense on you;
For if I see, and steal a diamond,
The fault is not i'th' stone, but in me the thief
That purloins it. I am sudden with you;
We that are great women of pleasure, use to cut off
These uncertain wishes and unquiet longings,   191
And in an instant join the sweet delight
And the pretty excuse together. Had you been i'th'
    street,
Under my chamber window, even there
I should have courted you.
    Bos.   Oh, you are an excellent
    lady.
    Jul. Bid me do somewhat for you presently[23]
To express I love you.
    Bos.   I will, and if you love me,
Fail not to effect it.
The Cardinal is grown wondrous melancholy,
Demand the cause, let him not put you off   200
With feigned excuse; discover the main ground on't.
    Jul. Why would you know this?
    Bos.   I have depended on
    him,
And I hear that he is fallen in some disgrace
With the Emperor: if he be, like the mice
That forsake falling houses, I would shift
To other dependence.
    Jul. You shall not need follow the wars:
I'll be your maintenance.
    Bos. And I, your loyal servant;
But I cannot leave my calling.
    Jul.   Not leave   210
An ungrateful general for the love of a sweet lady?

You are like some, cannot sleep in feather-beds,
But must have blocks for their pillows.
 Bos.   Will you do this?
 Jul. Cunningly.
 Bos.   Tomorrow I'll expect th'intelligence.
 Jul. Tomorrow? Get you into my cabinet,
You shall have it with you. Do not delay me,
No more than I do you. I am like one
That is condemned: I have my pardon promised,
But I would see it sealed. Go, get you in;
You shall see me wind my tongue about his heart 220
Like a skein of silk.

        [BOSOLA *withdraws.*]

    [*Enter* CARDINAL.]

 Card. Where are you?

    [*Enter* Servants.]

 Servs.   Here.
 Card.   Let none upon your lives
Have conference with the Prince Ferdinand,
Unless I know it. [*Aside*] In this distraction
He may reveal the murder.

        [*Exeunt* Servants.]

Yond's my lingering consumption:
I am weary of her; and by any means
Would be quit of—
 Jul.   How now, my lord?
What ails you?
 Card. Nothing.
 Jul.   Oh, you are much altered.
Come, I must be your secretary,[24] and remove 230
This lead from off your bosom; what's the matter?
 Card. I may not tell you.
 Jul. Are you so far in love with sorrow,
You cannot part with part of it? Or think you
I cannot love your grace when you are sad,
As well as merry? Or do you suspect
I, that have been a secret to your heart
These many winters, cannot be the same
Unto your tongue?
 Card.   Satisfy thy longing.
The only way to make thee keep my counsel 240
Is not to tell thee.
 Jul.   Tell your echo this,
Or flatterers, that, like echoes, still report
What they hear, though most imperfect, and not me:
For, if that you be true unto yourself,
I'll know.
 Card. Will you rack[25] me?
 Jul.   No, judgment shall
Draw it from you. It is an equal fault,
To tell one's secrets unto all, or none.
 Card. The first argues folly.
 Jul.   But the last tyranny.
 Card. Very well; why, imagine I have committed
Some secret deed which I desire the world 250
May never hear of!
 Jul.   Therefore may not I know it?
You have concealed for me as great a sin
As adultery. Sir, never was occasion

For perfect trial of my constancy
Till now. Sir, I beseech you.
 Card.   You'll repent it.
 Jul.   Never.
 Card. It hurries thee to ruin. I'll not tell thee.
Be well advised, and think what danger 'tis
To receive a prince's secrets. They that do,
Had need have their breasts hooped with adamant
To contain them. I pray thee yet be satisfied, 260
Examine thine own frailty; 'tis more easy
To tie knots, than unloose them; 'tis a secret
That, like a lingering poison, may chance lie
Spread in thy veins, and kill thee seven year hence.
 Jul. Now you dally with me.
 Card.   No more; thou shalt
  know it.
By my appointment the great Duchess of Malfi
And two of her young children four nights since
Were strangled.
 Jul.   O heaven! Sir, what have you done?
 Card. How now? How settles[26] this? Think you
  your bosom
Will be a grave dark and obscure enough 270
For such a secret?
 Jul.   You have undone yourself, sir.
 Card. Why?
 Jul.   It lies not in me to conceal it.
 Card.   No?
Come, I will swear you to't upon this book.
 Jul. Most religiously.
 Card.   Kiss it.

       [*She kisses the book.*]

Now you shall never utter it; thy curiosity
Hath undone thee; thou'rt poisoned with that book.
Because I knew thou couldst not keep my counsel,
I have bound thee to't by death.

    [*Enter* BOSOLA.]

 Bos. For pity sake, hold.
 Card.   Ha, Bosola!
 Jul.   I forgive you
This equal piece of justice you have done; 280
For I betrayed your counsel to that fellow;
He overheard it; that was the cause I said
It lay not in me to conceal it.
 Bos.   O foolish woman,
Couldst not thou have poisoned him?
 Jul.   'Tis weakness,
Too much to think what should have been done. I go,
I know not whither.

        [*Dies.*]

 Card.   Wherefore com'st thou hither?
 Bos. That I might find a great man, like yourself,
Not out of his wits, as the Lord Ferdinand,
To remember my service.
 Card.   I'll have thee hewed in pieces.

---

[24] *secretary:* confidant.
[25] *rack:* torture.   [26] *settles:* sits (in your mind).

Bos. Make not yourself such a promise of that life
Which is not yours to dispose of.
　Card. 　　　　　　　　Who placed thee here?
　Bos. Her lust, as she intended.
　Card. 　　　　　　　　Very well; 　　　292
Now you know me for your fellow murderer.
　Bos. And wherefore should you lay fair marble
　　colors
Upon your rotten purposes to me?[27]
Unless you imitate some that do plot great treasons,
And when they have done, go hide themselves i'th'
　　graves
Of those were actors in't.
　Card. No more; there is a fortune attends thee.
　Bos. Shall I go sue to fortune any longer? 　300
'Tis the fool's pilgrimage.
　Card. 　　　　　　I have honors in store for thee.
　Bos. There are a-many ways that conduct to seeming
Honor, and some of them very dirty ones.
　Card. 　　Throw to the devil
Thy melancholy; the fire burns well,
What need we keep a-stirring of't, and make
A greater smother? Thou wilt kill Antonio?
　Bos. Yes.
　Card 　　Take up that body.
　Bos. 　　　　　　　I think I shall
Shortly grow the common bier for churchyards!
　Card. I will allow thee some dozen of attendants,
To aid thee in the murder. 　　　　　311
　Bos. Oh, by no means: physicians that apply horse-
leeches to any rank swelling, use to cut off their tails,
that the blood may run through them the faster. Let me
have no train, when I go to shed blood, lest it make me
have a greater, when I ride to the gallows.
　Card. Come to me after midnight, to help to remove
　　that body
To her own lodging. I'll give out she died o'th' plague;
'Twill breed the less inquiry after her death.
　Bos. Where's Castruchio, her husband? 　320
　Card. He's rode to Naples to take possession
Of Antonio's citadel.
　Bos. Believe me, you have done a very happy turn.
　Card. Fail not to come. There is the master-key
Of our lodgings: and by that you may conceive
What trust I plant in you.
　　　　　　　　　　　　　　　Exit.
　Bos. 　　　　　　You shall find me ready.
Oh, poor Antonio, though nothing be so needful
To thy estate, as pity, yet I find
Nothing so dangerous. I must look to my footing;
In such slippery ice-pavements men had need 　330
To be frost-nailed well: they may break their necks else.
The precedent's here afore me: how this man
Bears up in blood![28] seems fearless! Why, 'tis well;
Security[29] some men call the suburbs of hell,
Only a dead wall between. Well, good Antonio,

---

[27] *And . . . me?:* Why paint rotten wood (your crooked
purposes) to give it the appearance of marble?
[28] *Bears up in blood!:* Plays the man!
[29] *Security:* Overconfidence. 　　[30] *biters:* deceivers.

I'll seek thee out; and all my care shall be
To put thee into safety from the reach
Of these most cruel biters,[30] that have got
Some of thy blood already. It may be,
I'll join with thee in a most just revenge. 　340
The weakest arm is strong enough, that strikes
With the sword of justice. Still methinks the Duchess
Haunts me. There, there— 'tis nothing but my
　　melancholy.
O penitence, let me truly taste thy cup,
That throws men down, only to raise them up.
　　　　　　　　　　　　　　　Exit.

V.iii

[*Enter* ANTONIO *and* DELIO. *There is an*] Echo
(*from the* Duchess' *grave*).

　Del. Yond's the Cardinal's window. This fortification
Grew from the ruins of an ancient abbey:
And to yond side o'th' river lies a wall,
Piece of a cloister, which in my opinion
Gives the best echo that you ever heard;
So hollow, and so dismal, and withal
So plain in the distinction of our words,
That many have supposed it is a spirit
That answers.
　Ant. 　　I do love these ancient ruins.
We never tread upon them, but we set 　　10
Our foot upon some reverend history.
And, questionless, here in this open court,
Which now lies naked to the injuries
Of stormy weather, some men lie interred
Loved the church so well, and gave so largely to't,
They thought it should have canopied their bones
Till doomsday. But all things have their end:
Churches and cities, which have diseases like to men,
Must have like death that we have.
　Echo. 　　　　　　*Like death that we*
have.
　Del. Now the echo hath caught you.
　Ant. 　　　　　　　　It groaned,
　　methought, and gave 　　　　20
A very deadly accent!
　Echo. 　　　*Deadly accent.*
　Del. I told you 'twas a pretty one. You may make it
A huntsman, or a falconer, a musician
Or a thing of sorrow.
　Echo. 　　　*A thing of sorrow.*
　Ant. Ay, sure; that suits it best.
　Echo. 　　　　　　*That suits it best.*
　Ant. 'Tis very like my wife's voice.
　Echo. 　　　　　　*Ay, wife's voice.*
　Del. Come; lets' walk farther from't.
I would not have you go to th' Cardinal's tonight:
Do not.
　Echo. Do not.
　Del. Wisdom doth not more moderate wasting
　　sorrow 　　　　　30
Than time: take time for't: be mindful of thy safety.
　Echo. Be mindful of thy safety.
　Ant. 　　　　　Necessity compels me:

Make scrutiny throughout the passes
Of your own life; you'll find it impossible
To fly your fate.
   Echo.   *Oh, fly your fate.*
   Del. Hark: the dead stones seem to have pity on you
And give you good counsel.
   Ant. Echo, I will not talk with thee,
For thou art a dead thing.
   Echo.   *Thou art a dead thing.*
   Ant. My Duchess is asleep now,   40
And her little ones, I hope, sweetly. O heaven,
Shall I never see her more?
   Echo.   *Never see her more.*
   Ant. I marked[1] not one repetition of the echo
But that, and on the sudden, a clear light
Presented me a face folded in sorrow.
   Del. Your fancy, merely.
   Ant.   Come. I'll be out of this
   ague;
For to live thus is not indeed to live:
It is a mockery and abuse of life.
I will not henceforth save myself by halves;
Lose all, or nothing.
   Del.   Your own virtue save you.   50
I'll fetch your eldest son; and second you.
It may be that the sight of his[2] own blood
Spread in so sweet a figure, may beget
The more compassion.
   Ant.   However,[3] fare you well.
Though in our miseries fortunes have a part
Yet in our noble sufferings she hath none:
Contempt of pain, that we may call our own.
                            Exe[unt].

V.iv

   [Enter] CARDINAL, PESCARA, MALATESTE,
           RODERIGO, GRISOLAN.

   Card. You shall not watch tonight by the sick
   Prince;
His grace is very well recovered.
   Mal. Good my lord, suffer[1] us.
   Card.   Oh, by no means.
The noise and change of object in his eye
Doth more distract him. I pray, all to bed,
And though you hear him in his violent fit,
Do not rise, I entreat you.
   Pes.   So, sir, we shall not—
   Card. Nay, I must have you promise
Upon your honors, for I was enjoined to't
By himself; and he seemed to urge it sensibly.[2]   10
   Pes. Let our honors bind this trifle.
   Card. Nor any of your followers.
   Pes.   Neither.
   Card. It may be, to make trial of your promise
When he's asleep, myself will rise, and feign
Some of his mad tricks, and cry out for help,
And feign myself in danger.
   Mal.   If your throat were cutting,
I'ld not come at you, now I have protested against it.

   Card. Why, I thank you.
                           [Withdraws.]
   Gris.   'Twas a foul storm tonight.
   Rod. The Lord Ferdinand's chamber shook like an
   osier.[3]
   Mal. 'Twas nothing but pure kindness in the devil
To rock his own child.   21
    Exeunt [RODERIGO, MALATESTE, PESCARA,
                    GRISOLAN].
   Card. The reason why I would not suffer these
About my brother is because at midnight
I may with better privacy convey
Julia's body to her own lodging. Oh, my conscience!
I would pray now; but the devil takes away my heart
For having any confidence in prayer.
About this hour I appointed Bosola
To fetch the body. When he hath served my turn,
He dies.   30
                              Exit.

            [Enter BOSOLA.]

   Bos. Ha! 'twas the Cardinal's voice. I heard him
   name
Bosola, and my death. Listen, I hear one's footing.

            [Enter FERDINAND.]

   Ferd. Strangling is a very quiet death.
   Bos. Nay, then, I see I must stand upon my guard.
   Ferd. What say' to that? Whisper, softly. Do you
   agree to't?
So it must be done i'th' dark: the Cardinal
Would not for a thousand pounds the doctor should see
   it.
                              Exit.
   Bos. My death is plotted; here's the consequence of
   murder.
We value not desert, nor Christian breath,
When we know black deeds must be cured with death.
                           [Withdraws.]

       [Enter ANTONIO *and a* Servant.]

   Serv. Here stay, sir, and be confident, I pray.   41
I'll fetch you a dark[4] lantern.
                              Exit.
   Ant.   Could I take him
At his prayers, there were hope of pardon.
   Bos. Fall right, my sword.

       [Strikes ANTONIO *down.]*

I'll not give thee so much leisure as to pray.
   Ant. Oh, I am gone. Thou hast ended a long suit,[5]
In a minute.
   Bos.   What art thou?
   Ant.   A most wretched thing

V.iii.
   [1] *marked:* paid attention to.   [2] *his:* the Cardinal's.
   [3] *However:* Whatever happens.
V.iv.
   [1] *suffer:* allow.   [2] *sensibly:* feelingly.
   [3] *osier:* willow.   [4] *dark:* shuttered.
   [5] *suit:* petition, endeavoring.

That only have thy[6] benefit in death,
To appear myself.

[*Enter* Servant *with a dark lantern.*]

Serv.   Where are you, sir?
Ant. Very near my home. Bosola?
Serv.   O misfortune! 50
Bos. [*to* Servant] Smother thy pity, thou art dead
   else. Antonio!
The man I would have saved 'bove mine own life!
We are merely the stars' tennis balls, struck and
   banded[7]
Which way please them. O good Antonio,
I'll whisper one thing in thy dying ear,
Shall make thy heart break quickly. Thy fair Duchess
And two sweet children—
Ant.   Their very names
Kindle a little life in me.
Bos.   Are murdered!
Ant. Some men have wished to die
At the hearing of sad tidings: I am glad   60
That I shall do't in sadness.[8] I would not now
Wish my wounds balmed nor healed, for I have no use
To put my life to. In all our quest of greatness,
Like wanton boys whose pastime is their care,
We follow after bubbles, blown in th' air.
Pleasure of life, what is't? Only the good hours
Of an ague; merely a preparative to rest,
To endure vexation. I do not ask
The process[9] of my death. Only, commend me
To Delio.
Bos.   Break, heart!   70
Ant. And let my son fly the courts of princes.
                                        [*Dies.*]
Bos. Thou seemest to have loved Antonio?
Serv.   I brought
   him hither,
To have reconciled him to the Cardinal.
Bos. I do not ask[10] thee that.
Take him up, if thou tender[11] thine own life,
And bear him where the Lady Julia
Was wont to lodge. Oh, my fate moves swift.
I have this Cardinal in the forge already,
Now I'll bring him to th' hammer. (O direful
   misprision![12])
I will not imitate things glorious,   80
No more than base; I'll be mine own example.
On, on: and look thou represent, for silence,
The thing thou bearest.

                                        Exeunt.

---

[6] *thy:* misprint for "the"(?); which would allow the
reading, "death is good only in this, that it permits me to
put off my disguise."   [7] *banded:* bandied.
   [8] *in sadness:* seriously, in earnest; which seems tautol-
ogous unless "sad" in the previous line is a misprint for
"glad."   [9] *process:* account.
   [10] *ask:* require (reconciliation is too late).
   [11] *tender:* value.   [12] *misprision:* mistake.
V.v.
   [1] *He:* The author of the book, presumably on theology,
the Cardinal has been reading.   [2] *lightens:* quickens.
   [3] *howsoever:* come what may.   [4] *aloof:* afar.

V.v

[*Enter*] CARDINAL (*with a book*).

Card. I am puzzled in a question about hell.
He[1] says, in hell there's one material fire,
And yet it shall not burn all men alike.
Lay him by. How tedious is a guilty conscience!
When I look into the fishponds in my garden,
Methinks I see a thing, armed with a rake
That seems to strike at me. Now? Art thou come?

[*Enter* BOSOLA *and* Servant *with* ANTONIO'S
body.]

Thou lookest ghastly.
There sits in thy face some great determination,
Mixed with some fear.
Bos.   Thus it lightens[2] into action: 10
I am come to kill thee.
Card.   Ha? Help! our guard!
Bos. Thou art deceived:
They are out of thy howling.
Card. Hold, and I will faithfully divide
Revènues with thee.
Bos.   Thy prayers and proffers
Are both unseasonable.
Card.   Raise the watch.
We are betrayed!
Bos.   I have confined your flight;
I'll suffer your retreat to Julia's chamber,
But no further.
Card.   Help. We are betrayed!

[*Enter* PESCARA, MALATESTE, RODERIGO, *and*
GRISOLAN, *above.*]

Mal.   Listen.
Card. My dukedom for rescue!
Rod.   Fie upon his
   counterfeiting.   20
Mal. Why, 'tis not the Cardinal.
Rod.   Yes, yes, 'tis he.
But I'll see him hanged, ere I'll go down to him.
Card. Here's a plot upon me; I am assaulted. I am
   lost,
Unless some rescue!
Gris.   He doth this pretty well,
But it will not serve to laugh me out of mine honor.
Card. The sword's at my throat!
Rod.   You would not bawl
   so loud then.
Mal. Come, come,
Let's go to bed; he told us thus much aforehand.
Pes. He wished you should not come at him; but
   believe't,
The accent of the voice sounds not in jest.   30
I'll down to him, howsoever,[3] and with engines
Force ope the doors.
                                        [*Exit.*]
Rod.   Let's follow him aloof.[4]
And note how the Cardinal will laugh at him.
                                  [*Exeunt above.*]
Bos. There's for you first;

'Cause you shall not unbarricade the door
To let in rescue.

He kills the Servant.

Card. What cause hast thou to pursue my life?
Bos.   Look
there.
Card. Antonio!
Bos.   Slain by my hand unwittingly.
Pray, and be sudden. When thou killed'st thy sister,
Thou tookest from justice her most equal balance,[5]   40
And left her naught but her sword.
Card.   O mercy!
Bos. Now it seems thy greatness was only outward,
For thou fallest faster of thyself than calamity
Can drive thee. I'll not waste longer time. There.

[Stabs the CARDINAL.*]*

Card. Thou hast hurt me.
Bos.   Again.

[Stabs him again.]

Card.   Shall I die like a
leveret[6]
Without any resistance? Help, help, help!
I am slain.

[Enter FERDINAND.*]*

Ferd.   Th'alarum? Give me a fresh horse.
Rally the vaunt-guard;[7] or the day is lost.
Yield, yield! I give you the honor of arms,[8]
Shake my sword over you, will you yield?   50
Card. Help me, I am your brother.
Ferd.   The devil?
My brother fight upon the adverse party?

He wounds the CARDINAL *and, in the scuffle,*
gives BOSOLA *his death wound.*

There flies your ransom.[9]
Card.   O Justice:
I suffer now for what hath former been.
Sorrow is held the eldest child of sin.
Ferd. Now you're brave fellows. Caesar's fortune
was harder than Pompey's: Caesar died in the arms of
prosperity, Pompey at the feet of disgrace. You both
died in the field, the pain's nothing. Pain many times
is taken away with the apprehension of greater, as   60
the toothache with the sight of a barber[10] that comes to
pull it out. There's philosophy for you.
Bos. Now my revenge is perfect. Sink, thou main
cause
Of my undoing. The last part of my life
Hath done me best service.

He kills FERDINAND.

Ferd. Give me some wet hay, I am broken winded.[11]
I do account this world but a dog-kennel.
I will vault credit,[12] and affect high pleasures
Beyond death.
Bos.   He seems to come to himself,
Now he's so near the bottom.   70

Ferd. My sister. Oh! my sister, there's the cause on't.
Whether we fall by ambition, blood, or lust,
Like diamonds we are cut with our own dust.

[Dies.]

Card. Thou hast thy payment too.
Bos. Yes, I hold my weary soul in my teeth;
'Tis ready to part from me, I do glory
That thou, which stoodest like a huge pyramid
Begun upon a large and ample base,
Shalt end in a little point, a kind of nothing.

[Enter PESCARA, MALATESTE, RODERIGO, *and*
GRISOLAN.*]*

Pes. How now, my lord?
Mal.   O sad disaster!
Rod.   How comes
this?   80
Bos. Revenge, for the Duchess of Malfi, murdered
By th' Aragonian brethren; for Antonio,
Slain by this hand; for lustful Julia,
Poisoned by this man; and lastly, for myself,
That was an actor in the main of all,
Much 'gainst mine own good nature, yet i'th' end
Neglected.
Pes.   How now, my lord?
Card.   Look to my brother:
He gave us these large wounds, as we were struggling
Here i'th' rushes.[13] And now, I pray, let me
Be laid by, and never thought of.   90
[Dies.]

Pes. How fatally, it seems, he did withstand
His owu rescue!
Mal.   Thou wretched thing of blood,
How came Antonio by his death?
Bos. In a mist; I know not how;
Such a mistake as I have often seen
In a play. Oh, I am gone.
We are only like dead walls, or vaulted graves
That ruined, yields no echo. Fare you well;
It may be pain, but no harm to me to die
In so good a quarrel. Oh, this gloomy world,   100
In what a shadow, or deep pit of darkness
Doth womanish and fearful mankind live?
Let worthy minds ne'er stagger in distrust
To suffer death or shame for what is just.
Mine is another voyage.

[Dies.]

Pes. The noble Delio, as I came to th' palace,
Told me of Antonio's being here, and showed me
A pretty gentleman, his son and heir.

[Enter DELIO *with* ANTONIO'*s son.]*

---

5 *equal balance:* impartial scales.   6 *leveret:* hare.
7 *vaunt-guard:* vanguard (Ferdinand in his madness
imagines himself doing battle).
8 *honor of arms:* right to retain arms on surrendering.
9 *There . . . ransom:* because the potential prisoner is dead
and hence worthless.   10 *barber:* who served as dentist.
11 *Give . . . winded:* the appropriate diet for a horse out of
breath.   12 *vault credit:* transcend belief.
13 *rushes:* which acted as carpeting for the floor.

Mal. O sir, you come too late.

Del.   I heard so, and   109
Was armed for't ere I came. Let us make noble use
Of this great ruin; and join all our forces
To establish this young hopeful gentleman
In's mother's right. These wretched eminent things
Leave no more fame behind 'em than should one
Fall in a frost, and leave his print in snow;
As soon as the sun shines, it ever melts
Both form and matter. I have ever thought
Nature doth nothing so great for great men,
As when she's pleased to make them lords of truth.
Integrity of life is fame's best friend,   120
Which nobly, beyond death, shall crown the end.

                                         Exeunt.

FINIS

Francis Beaumont

[*c.* 1584–1616]

THE KNIGHT OF THE BURNING PESTLE

UNLIKE Marlowe, Greene, Kyd, and others, Beaumont has left little of biographical record to interest readers of his plays; that his name figures so largely in our awareness of the drama of his period, in fact, is to some degree accidental, since the "Beaumont and Fletcher" sobriquet is only the convenient cover attached, by those who put together two folio collections in 1647 and 1679, to work in which the dominant share was Fletcher's and the second Massinger's, while Beaumont's considerable contribution was abetted by the participation of a number of other collaborators and revisers including Middleton, Shirley, Rowley, Jonson, Field, Tourneur, and Daborne (or so, at least, scholars have found at various times). Born of a gentle Leicestershire family, brother of the poet Sir John Beaumont, he was educated at Oxford and at the Inner Temple, where he began his studies in 1600. The latter fact is one of the two most significant bits of information to be reported about his life, for it sets Beaumont in the intellectually and socially sophisticated ambiance of the law schools, matrix of a sardonic satirical spirit, of frequent theatrical performance, and of a close-knit society that traded in wit and skepticism. Philip J. Finkelpearl has written brilliantly about that world in *John Marston of the Middle Temple*, a study of a playwright who, like Beaumont and Fletcher, learned his craft in the private theaters; it is probably impossible to exaggerate the effect on their plays of these men's membership in the social class that centered around the Temples. Beaumont's first plays seem to have been written *c.* 1606. By 1608 he had begun collaborating with Fletcher. Aubrey's *Brief Lives*, appropriately offering a single biographical sketch of Beaumont and Fletcher, tells us that "they lived together on the Bankside, not far from the playhouse, both bachelors; lay together; had one wench in the house between them which they did so admire; the same clothes and cloak, etc. between them." But by 1613 Beaumont had found a rich heiress to marry, and the collaboration ended: they ceased to share not only the wench but also the writing of plays. And this fact is the second most eloquent in the record. For though money figures unmistakably in the lives of Shakespeare and Jonson, one cannot easily imagine them giving up play writing because they had found another source of income; but in the work of Beaumont and Fletcher one often senses an art directly calculated to achieve commercial success. The unabashed desire to please an audience that demanded and applauded the plays of Shakespeare and Webster and Jonson and the rest is no more pernicious than the identical motivation in the majority of movie-makers in our period, but a purely commercial intent may be the limiting factor in many of the often brilliant but just as often empty plays in the Beaumont and Fletcher canon. Beaumont died forty-five days before Shakespeare. In addition to his share in the plays he left a number of nondramatic poems.

Whatever cavils one wants to make against "Beaumont and Fletcher" are misapplied to THE KNIGHT OF THE BURNING PESTLE, a comedy unique not only in its Pirandellesque exploration of the nature of theatrical illusion but also, for a playwright of the private theaters, for its sympathetic portrayal of the merchant class it mocks. If at the outset one guesses that Beaumont's target is to be the naïve audience that fostered the romantic plays he parodies, one learns quickly that the play aims more directly and interestingly at the necessary confusions of all audiences between actors and roles, fictions and imagined reality, and at the conventions of expository technique, storytelling, and style on which all drama of the period was built. It has often been suggested, in fact, that the failure of this brilliant play—pithily described in the publisher's preface—might be explained by the unwillingness of its coterie audience, whose characteristics are authoritatively described in Alfred Harbage's *Shakespeare and the Rival Traditions*, to share Beaumont's charitable if patronizing picture of the citizens.

THE KNIGHT OF THE BURNING PESTLE was published by Walter Burre in 1613 with no authorial ascription, and republished in two quarto editions in 1635 as "written by Francis Beaumont and John Fletcher, Gent."; it appeared again in the second folio of 1679. All the later editions derive from the first quarto, which itself seems to have been based on the original manuscript, and the present edition is therefore based on Q1, here called Q. The standard collation of the extant copies of that quarto is provided in the old-spelling *Dramatic Works in the Beaumont and Fletcher Canon* under the general editorship of Fredson Bowers.

Burre's dedication to the Master of the Queen's Revels and the references to boy actors for all parts establish THE KNIGHT OF THE BURNING PESTLE as a Queen's Revels play. About both the date of composition and the sources there is considerable difficulty. The play obviously owes something, in conception and detail, to *Don Quixote*, though Beaumont could have written it on the basis of no more than he had heard about the novel. The first part of Cervantes' masterpiece appeared in Spanish in 1605, was reprinted in

Brussels, translated by Thomas Shelton *c.* 1608, and published in his English version only in 1612. Burre's allusion to the play's priority by a year to *Don Quixote* perhaps intends Shelton's translation, which was entered on the Stationers' Register in 1611, but may point rather to the Brussels edition. But an allusion to Day's *Travels of Three English Brothers*, played at the Red Bull in 1607, provides a fixed date for the earliest possible composition, and 1607—before Beaumont had joined forces with Fletcher—is a plausible possibility.

Apart from Cervantes, the "sources" are a multitude of popular plays by Day, Heywood, Dekker, and others, cited in the footnotes, and of popular romances and ballads. Peele's *The Old Wives' Tale* had similarly used a parody of popular romance, set in a relatively realistic framework, as a device to explore the idea of a play. It is tempting to see Old Master Merrythought as a parody of Simon Eyre in THE SHOEMAKER'S HOLIDAY, but that is only speculation.

N. R.

The Knight of the Burning Pestle

[EPISTLE DEDICATORY]

TO HIS MANY WAYS ENDEARED FRIEND MASTER ROBERT KEYSAR[1]

SIR, this unfortunate child, who in eight days (as lately I have learned) was begot and born, soon after was by his parents (perhaps because he was so unlike his brethren) exposed to the wide world, who, for want of judgment, or not understanding the privy mark of irony about it (which showed it was no offspring of any vulgar brain) utterly rejected it; so that for want of acceptance it was even ready to give up the ghost, and was in danger to have been smothered in perpetual oblivion, if you (out of your direct antipathy to ingratitude) had not been moved both to relieve and cherish it; wherein I must needs commend both your judgment, understanding, and singular love to good wits. You afterwards sent it to me; yet, being an infant and somewhat ragged, I have fostered it privately in my bosom these two years, and now to show my love return it to you, clad in good lasting clothes, which scarce memory will wear out, and able to speak for itself; and withal, as it telleth me, desirous to try his fortune in the world, where, if yet it be welcome, father, foster-father, nurse, and child all have their desired end. If it be slighted or traduced, it hopes his father will beget him a younger brother, who shall revenge his quarrel and challenge the world either of fond and merely literal interpretation or illiterate misprision.[2] Perhaps it will be thought to be of the race of *Don Quixote*: we both may confidently swear, it is his elder above a year; and therefore may (by virtue of his birth-right) challenge the wall of him.[3] I doubt not but they will meet in their adventures, and I hope the breaking of one staff will make them friends; and perhaps they will combine themselves and travel through the world to seek their adventures. So I commit him to his good fortune and myself to your love.

Your assured friend
W. B.[4]

TO THE READERS OF THIS COMEDY[1]

GENTLEMEN, the world is so nice[2] in these our times that for apparel there is no fashion; for music, which is a rare art (though now slighted), no instrument; for diet, none but the French kickshaws[3] that are delicate; and for plays, no invention but that which now runneth an invective way, touching some particular person, or else it is contemned before it is throughly understood. This is all I have to say, that the author had no intent to wrong anyone in this comedy, but as a merry passage here and there interlaced it with delight, which he hopes will please all and be hurtful to none.

DRAMATIS PERSONÆ

The Prologue
Then a Citizen
The Citizen's Wife
RAFE, *her man, sitting below amidst the spectators*
[VENTUREWELL,] *a rich merchant*
JASPER, *his apprentice* [*son of Merrythought*]

LUCE, *the merchant's daughter*
MISTRESS MERRYTHOUGHT
MICHAEL, *a second son of Mistress Merrythought*
OLD MASTER MERRYTHOUGHT
[TIM,] *a squire*
[GEORGE,] *a dwarf* } [*Apprentices*]
A Tapster[1]
A Boy that danceth and singeth
An Host
A Barber
[Three Captive] Knights
[Captive Women]
A Sergeant
Soldiers
Boys
WILLIAM HAMMERTON, *pewterer*
GEORGE GREENGOOSE, *poulterer*
POMPIONA, *daughter to the King of Moldavia*
MASTER HUMPHREY, *a friend to the merchant*

EPISTLE DEDICATORY
  [1] *Master . . . Keysar:* manager of the Children of the Queen's Revels, 1607–1610.
  [2] *misprision:* misunderstanding.
  [3] *challenge . . . him:* take the position of greater honor.
  [4] *W.B.:* Walter Burre, the publisher.

TO THE READERS OF THIS COMEDY
  [1] This replaced the dedication in the 1635 quartos and the 1679 folio.
  [2] *nice:* fastidious.
  [3] *kickshaws:* worthless trifles, from Fr. *quelques choses.*

DRAMATIS PERSONÆ
  [1] *Tapster:* Beer-drawer.

[INDUCTION]

[Gentlemen *sitting on stage*.]

Enter Prologue.

Prol. From all that's near the court, from all that's great,
Within the compass of the city-walls,
We now have brought our scene——

Enter Citizen [*from audience below*].

Cit. Hold your peace, goodman boy.

Prol. What do you mean, sir?

Cit. That you have no good meaning: this seven years there hath been plays at this house, I have observed it, you have still girds[1] at citizens; and now you call your play *The London Merchant*. Down with your title,[2] boy; down with your title.   10

Prol. Are you a member of the noble city?[3]

Cit. I am.

Prol. And a freeman?[4]

Cit. Yea, and a grocer.

Prol. So, grocer, then, by your sweet favor, we intend no abuse to the city.

Cit. No, sir? Yes, sir; if you were not resolved to play the Jacks,[5] what need you study for new subjects, purposely to abuse your betters? Why could not you be contented, as well as others, with *The Legend of*   20 *Whittington*,[6] or *The Life and Death of Sir Thomas Gresham, with the Building of the Royal Exchange*,[7] or *The Story of Queen Eleanor, with the Rearing of London Bridge upon Woolsacks*?[8]

Prol. You seem to be an understanding[9] man; what would you have us do, sir?

Cit. Why, present something notably in honor of the commons[10] of the city.

Prol. Why, what do you say to *The Life and Death of Fat Drake*,[11] or the *Repairing of Fleet-privies*?[12]   30

Cit. I do not like that; but I will have a citizen, and he shall be of my own trade.

Prol. Oh, you should have told us your mind a month since; our play is ready to begin now.

Cit. 'Tis all one for that; I will have a grocer, and he shall do admirable things.

Prol. What will you have him do?

Cit. Marry, I will have him——

Wife. Husband, husband!   Wife *below.*

Rafe. Peace, mistress.   RAFE *below.*

Wife. [*Below*] Hold thy peace, Rafe; I know what I do, I warrant ye.—Husband, husband!   42

Cit. What sayst thou, cony?[13]

Wife. [*Below*] Let him kill a lion with a pestle, husband; let him kill a lion with a pestle.[14]

Cit. So he shall; I'll have him kill a lion with a pestle.

Wife. [*Below*] Husband, shall I come up, husband?

Cit. Ay, cony,—Rafe, help your mistress this way.—Pray, gentlemen, make her a little room.—I pray you, sir, lend me your hand to help up my wife; I thank you, sir.—So.   52

[Wife *comes on the stage*.]

Wife. By your leave, gentlemen all, I'm something troublesome;[15] I'm a stranger here; I was ne'er at one of these plays, as they say, before; but I should have seen[16] *Jane Shore*[17] once; and my husband hath promised me, any time this twelvemonth, to carry me to *The Bold Beauchamps*,[18] but in truth he did not. I pray you, bear with me.   59

Cit. Boy, let my wife and I have a couple of stools, and then begin, and let the grocer do rare things.

[*Stools are brought.*]

Prol. But, sir, we have never a boy to play him; everyone hath a part already.

Wife. Husband, husband, for God's sake, let Rafe play him; beshrew me if I do not think he will go beyond them all.

Cit. Well remembered, wife.—Come up, Rafe.—I'll tell you, gentlemen; let them but lend him a suit of reparel[19] and necessaries, and, by gad, if any of   69 them all blow wind in the tail on[20] him, I'll be hanged.

[RAFE *comes on the stage.*]

Wife. I pray you, youth, let him have a suit of reparel.—I'll be sworn, gentlemen, my husband tells you true: he will act you sometimes at our house, that all the neighbors cry out on him; he will fetch you up a couraging[21] part so in the garret, that we are all as feared,[22] I warrant you, that we quake again. We'll fear our children with him; if they be never so unruly, do but cry, "Rafe comes, Rafe comes!" to them, and they'll be as quiet as lambs.—Hold up thy head, Rafe; show the gentlemen what thou canst do; speak a   80

INDUCTION

[1] *girds:* jeers.   [2] *title:* title-board, presented on stage.

[3] *member . . . city:* citizen with certain class privileges.

[4] *freeman:* one who possesses the class privileges comprised in "the freedom of the city."

[5] *play . . . Jacks:* play a mean trick.

[6] *The . . . Whittington:* lost play about the legendary poor boy who became Lord Mayor of London.

[7] *The . . . Exchange:* Part II of Thomas Heywood's *If You Know Not Me, You Know Nobody*, printed 1606, about another London hero.

[8] *The . . . Woolsacks:* perhaps George Peele's *Edward I*, printed 1593.

[9] *understanding:* with pun, "standing below" in the pit among the less affluent patrons.

[10] *commons:* the body of free citizens, common in rights and duties.

[11] *Fat Drake:* perhaps a local tradesman or scavenger.

[12] *Fleet-privies:* Fleet Ditch, the terminus of Fleet Lane, was a common sewer.   [13] *cony:* rabbit.

[14] *lion . . . pestle:* perhaps a mocking allusion to Thomas Heywood's *The Four Prentices of London, c.* 1592, about Godfrey of Boulogne, Jerusalem, and some adventurous apprentices.   [15] *something troublesome:* a bit of a nuisance.

[16] *should . . . seen:* was going to see.

[17] *Jane Shore:* bourgeois mistress of Edward IV, subject of a 1594 play by Heywood.

[18] *The . . . Beauchamps:* perhaps a lost Heywood play about a legendary hero.

[19] *reparel:* apparel.   [20] *blow . . . on:* keep up with.

[21] *couraging:* encouraging, although she seems to think it means brave.   [22] *feared:* frightened.

huffing [23] part; I warrant you, the gentlemen will accept of it.

Cit. Do, Rafe, do.

Rafe. "By heavens, methinks, it were an easy leap
To pluck bright honor from the pale-faced moon,
Or dive into the bottom of the sea,
Where never fathom-line touched any ground,
And pluck up drownèd honor from the lake of hell." [24]

Cit. How say you, gentlemen, is it not as I told you? 90

Wife. Nay, gentlemen, he hath played before, my husband says, *Mucedorus,* [25] before the wardens [26] of our company.

Cit. Ay, and he should have played Jeronimo [27] with a shoemaker for a wager.

Prol. He shall have a suit of apparel, if he will go in. [28]

Cit. In, Rafe, in, Rafe; and set out the grocery in their kind, if thou lovest me.

[*Exit* RAFE.]

Wife. I warrant, our Rafe will look finely when he's dressed. 100

Prol. But what will you have it called?

Cit. The Grocer's Honor.

Prol. Methinks *The Knight of the Burning Pestle* [29] were better.

Wife. I'll be sworn, husband, that's as good a name as can be.

Cit. Let it be so.—Begin, begin; my wife and I will sit down.

Prol. I pray you, do. 109

Cit. What stately music have you? You have shawms? [30]

Prol. Shawms? No.

Cit. No? I'm a thief if my mind did not give me [31] so. Rafe plays a stately part, and he must needs have shawms: I'll be at the charge of them myself, rather than we'll be without them.

Prol. So you are like to be.

Cit. Why, and so I will be: there's two shillings.—

[*Gives money.*]

Let's have the waits [32] of Southwark; [33] they are as rare fellows as any are in England; and that will fetch 120 them all o'er the water [34] with a vengeance, as if they were mad.

Prol. You shall have them. Will you sit down, then?

Cit. Ay.—Come, wife.

Wife. Sit you merry all, gentlemen; I'm bold to sit amongst you for my ease.

[Citizen *and* Wife *sit down.*]

Prol. From all that's near the court, from all that's great
Within the compass of the city-walls
We now have brought our scene. Fly far from hence
All private taxes, [35] immodest phrases, 130
Whatever may but show like [36] vicious.
For wicked mirth never true pleasure brings,
But honest minds are pleased with honest things.—
Thus much for that [37] we do; but for Rafe's part you must answer for yourself.

[*Exit.*]

Cit. Take you no care for Rafe; he'll discharge himself, I warrant you.

Wife. I' faith, gentlemen, I'll give my word for Rafe.

ACT ONE

Enter Merchant [VENTUREWELL] *and* JASPER, *his Prentice.*

Vent. Sirrah, I'll make you know you are my prentice,
And whom my charitable love redeemed
Even from the fall of fortune; gave thee heat
And growth, to be what now thou art; new-cast thee;

Adding the trust of all I have at home
In foreign staples, [1] or upon the sea,
To thy direction; tied the good opinions
Both of myself and friends to thy endeavors;
So fair were thy beginnings. But with these,
As I remember, you had never charge 10
To love your master's daughter, and even then
When I had found a wealthy husband for her;
I take it, sir, you had not; but, however,
I'll break the neck of that commission,
And make you know you are but a merchant's factor. [2]

Jas. Sir, I do liberally confess I am yours,
Bound both by love and duty to your service,
In which my labor hath been all my profit:
I have not lost in bargain, nor delighted
To wear your honest gains upon my back; [3] 20
Nor have I given a pension to my blood, [4]
Or lavishly in play [5] consumed your stock;
These, and the miseries that do attend them,
I dare with innocence proclaim are strangers
To all my temperate actions. For your daughter,
If there be any love to my deservings
Borne by her virtuous self, I cannot stop it;
Nor am I able to refrain her wishes.
She's private to herself, and best of knowledge [6]
Whom she will make so happy as to sigh for. 30

[23] *huffing:* ranting.
[24] *"By . . . hell":* slightly misquoted from Hotspur's lines, *I Henry IV,* I, iii, 199*ff.*
[25] *Mucedorus:* the 1598 comedy printed here, Vol. I, pp.463–80.   [26] *wardens:* officers of a livery guild.
[27] *Jeronimo:* Hieronimo of *The Spanish Tragedy.*
[28] *go in:* i.e., to the tiring house to be costumed.
[29] *Pestle:* probably with a pun on "pizzle," bull's penis.
[30] *shawms:* oboe-like instruments making a fierce and rude noise.   [31] *my . . . me:* I did not think.
[32] *waits:* town band.
[33] *Southwark:* district on south side of Thames across from London.   [34] *water:* i.e., the Thames.
[35] *private taxes:* attacks on individuals.
[36] *show like:* appear.   [37] *that:* what.
I.
[1] *staples:* market towns.   [2] *factor:* agent.
[3] *wear . . . back:* buy clothes with what I pilfer from your earnings.   [4] *blood:* lust.   [5] *play:* gambling.
[6] *best . . . knowledge:* knows best.

Besides, I cannot think you mean to match her
Unto a fellow of so lame a presence,
One that hath little left of nature in him.
 Vent. 'Tis very well, sir; I can tell your wisdom
How all this shall be cured.
 Jas.   Your care becomes you.
 Vent. And thus it shall be, sir: I here discharge you
My house and service; take your liberty;
And when I want a son, I'll send for you.
              [Exit.]
 Jas. These be the fair rewards of them that love.
O you that live in freedom, never prove   40
The travail of a mind led by desire.

Enter LUCE.

 Luce. Why, how now, friend? Struck with my
  father's thunder?
 Jas. Struck, and struck dead, unless the remedy
Be full of speed and virtue; I am now,
What I expected long, no more your father's.
 Luce. But mine.
 Jas.   But yours, and only yours, I am;
That's all I have to keep me from the statute.[7]
You dare be constant still?
 Luce.   Oh, fear me not.
In this I dare be better than a woman.
Nor shall his anger nor his offers move me, 50
Were they both equal to a prince's power.
 Jas. You know my rival?
 Luce.   Yes, and love him
  dearly—
Even as I love an ague or foul weather;
I prithee, Jasper, fear him not.
 Jas.   Oh, no,
I do not mean to do him so much kindness.
But to our own desires: you know the plot
We both agreed on?
 Luce.   Yes, and will perform
My part exactly.
 Jas.   I desire no more.
Farewell, and keep my heart; 'tis yours.
 Luce.   I take it;
He must do miracles makes me forsake it. 60
              Exeunt.
 Cit. Fie upon 'em, little infidels! what a matter's
here now! Well, I'll be hanged for a halfpenny if there
be not some abomination knavery in this play. Well;
let 'em look to't; Rafe must come, and if there be any
tricks a-brewing—

[Enter Boy.]

 Wife. Let 'em brew and bake too, husband, a' God's
name; Rafe will find all out, I warrant you, and[8] they
were older than they are.—I pray, my pretty youth,
is Rafe ready?
 Boy. He will be presently.   70
 Wife. Now, I pray you, make my commendations
unto him, and withal carry him this stick of licorice:
tell him his mistress sent it him, and bid him bite a
piece; 'twill open his pipes the better, say.
              [Exit Boy.]

Enter Merchant [VENTUREWELL] *and*
Master HUMPHREY.

 Vent. Come, sir, she's yours; upon my faith, she's
  yours;
You have my hand; for other idle lets[9]
Between your hopes and her, thus with a wind
They are scattered and no more. My wanton prentice,
That like a bladder blew himself with love,
I have let out, and sent him to discover   80
New masters yet unknown.
 Hump.   I thank you, sir,
Indeed, I thank you, sir; and, ere I stir,
It shall be known, however you do deem,
I am of gentle blood, and gentle seem.[10]
 Vent. Oh, sir, I know it certain.
 Hump.   Sir, my friend,
Although, as writers say, all things have end,
And that we call a pudding[11] hath his two,
Oh, let it not seem strange, I pray, to you,
If in this bloody simile I put
My love, more endless than frail things or gut. 90
 Wife. Husband, I prithee, sweet lamb, tell me one
thing; but tell me truly.—Stay, youths, I beseech you
till I question my husband.
 Cit. What is it, mouse?
 Wife. Sirrah, didst thou ever see a prettier child?
How it behaves itself, I warrant ye, and speaks and
looks, and perts[12] up the head!—I pray you, brother,
with your favor, were you never none of Master
Moncaster's[13] scholars?   99
 Cit. Chicken, I prithee heartily, contain thyself; the
childer[14] are pretty childer, but when Rafe comes,
lamb—
 Wife. Ay, when Rafe comes, cony.—Well, my youth,
you may proceed.
 Vent. Well, sir, you know my love, and rest, I hope,
Assured of my consent; get but my daughter's,
And wed her when you please. You must be bold,
And clap in close unto her; come, I know
You have language good enough to win a wench.
 Wife. A whoreson tyrant! h' as been an old stringer[15]
in 's days, I warrant him.   111
 Hump. I take your gentle offer, and withal
Yield love again for love reciprocal.
 Vent. What, Luce! within there!

Enter LUCE.

 Luce.   Called you, sir?
 Vent.   I did:
Give entertainment to this gentleman;
And see you be not froward.[16]—To her, sir;
My presence will but be an eye-sore to you.
              [Exit.]

---

[7] *statute:* concerning apprentices.   [8] *and:* if.
[9] *lets:* obstacles.
[10] *gentle seem:* have the appearance of one well-born.
[11] *pudding:* sausage.   [12] *perts:* perks.
[13] *Master Moncaster:* Richard Mulcaster, Master of St.
Paul's School (whence "Paul's boys") 1598–1608.
[14] *childer:* children.   [15] *stringer:* fornicator.
[16] *froward:* difficult.

Hump. Fair Mistress Luce, how do you? Are you
well?
Give me your hand, and then I pray you tell
How doth your little sister, and your brother,   120
And whether you love me or any other.
　Luce. Sir, these are quickly answered.
　Hump.   So they are,
Where women are not cruel. But how far
Is it now distant from the place we are in,
Unto that blessèd place, your father's warren?
　Luce. What makes you think of that, sir?
　Hump.   Even that
face.
For, stealing rabbits whilom[17] in that place,
God Cupid, or the keeper, I know not whether,[18]
Unto my cost and charges brought you thither,
And there began—
　Luce.   Your game, sir.
　Hump.   Let no game,   130
Or any thing that tendeth to the same,
Be ever more remembered, thou fair killer,
For whom I sat me down, and brake my tiller.[19]
　Wife. There's a kind gentleman, I warrant you;
when will you do as much for me, George?
　Luce. Beshrew me, sir, I am sorry for your losses,
But, as the proverb says, I cannot cry;
I would you had not seen me.
　Hump.   So would I,
Unless you had more maw[20] to do me good.
　Luce. Why, cannot this strange passion be
withstood?   140
Send for a constable, and raise the town.
　Hump. Oh, no! my valiant love will batter down
Millions of constables, and put to flight
Even that great watch[21] of Midsummer-day at night.
　Luce. Beshrew me, sir, 'twere good I yielded, then;
Weak women cannot hope, where valiant men
Have no resistance.
　Hump.   Yield, then; I am full
Of pity, though I say it, and can pull
Out of my pocket thus a pair of gloves.
Look, Lucy, look; the dog's tooth nor the dove's   150
Are not so white as these; and sweet they be,
And whipped about with silk, as you may see.
If you desire the price, shoot from your eye
A beam to this place, and you shall espy
FS,[22] which is to say, my sweetest honey,
They cost me three and twopence, or no money.
　Luce. Well, sir, I take them kindly, and I thank you.
What would you more?
　Hump.   Nothing.
　Luce.   Why, then, farewell.
　Hump. Nor so, nor so; for, lady, I must tell,

Before we part, for what we met together: 160
God grant me time and patience and fair weather.
　Luce. Speak, and declare your mind in terms so
brief.
　Hump. I shall: then, first and foremost, for relief
I call to you, if that you can afford it;
I care not at what price, for, on my word, it
Shall be repaid again, although it cost me
More than I'll speak of now, for love hath tossed me
In furious blanket like a tennis-ball,
And now I rise aloft, and now I fall.
　Luce. Alas, good gentleman, alas the day.   170
　Hump. I thank you heartily; and, as I say,
Thus do I still continue without rest,
I' the morning like a man, at night a beast,
Roaring and bellowing mine own disquiet,
That much I fear, forsaking of my diet
Will bring me presently to that quandary,
I shall bid all adieu.
　Luce.   Now, by St. Mary,
That were great pity.
　Hump.   So it were, beshrew me;
Then, ease me, lusty[23] Luce, and pity show me.
　Luce. Why, sir, you know my will is nothing worth
Without my father's grant; get his consent,   181
And then you may with assurance try me.
　Hump. The worshipful your sire will not deny me,
For I have asked him, and he hath replied,
"Sweet Master Humphrey, Luce shall be thy bride."
　Luce. Sweet Master Humphrey, then I am content.
　Hump. And so am I, in truth.
　Luce.   Yet take me with you;[24]
There is another clause must be annexed,
And this it is: I swore, and will perform it,
No man shall ever joy me as his wife   190
But he that stole me hence. If you dare venture,
I am yours; you need not fear; my father loves you;
If not, farewell forever.
　Hump.   Stay, nymph, stay:
I have a double[25] gelding, colored bay,
Sprung by his father from Barbarian[26] kind;
Another for myself, though somewhat blind,
Yet true as trusty tree.
　Luce.   I am satisfied;
And so I give my hand. Our course must lie
Through Waltham Forest,[27] where I have a friend
Will entertain us. So, farewell, Sir Humphrey,   200
And think upon your business.
                                Exit LUCE.
　Hump.   Though I die,
I am resolved to venture life and limb
For one so young, so fair, so kind, so trim.
                                Exit HUMPHREY.
　Wife. By my faith and troth, George, and as I am
virtuous, it is e'en the kindest young man that ever
trod on shoe-leather.—Well, go thy ways; if thou hast
her not, 'tis not thy fault, 'faith.
　Cit. I prithee, mouse, be patient; 'a shall have her,
or I'll make some of 'em smoke[28] for 't.   209
　Wife. That's my good lamb, George.—Fie, this
stinking tobacco kills me! would there were none in

---

[17] *whilom:* once.
[18] *whether:* which.
[19] *tiller:* crossbow handle.
[20] *maw:* stomach, desire.
[21] *watch:* annual assembly of London militia.
[22] *FS:* a shopkeeper's mark.
[23] *lusty:* lively.
[24] *take . . . you:* understand me.
[25] *double:* large.
[26] *Barbarian:* Barbary.
[27] *Waltham Forest:* reached almost to northern boundary
of London.
[28] *smoke:* suffer.

England.—Now, I pray, gentlemen, what good does this stinking tobacco do you? Nothing, I warrant you: make chimneys o' your faces! Oh, husband, now, now! there's Rafe, there's Rafe.

Enter RAFE, *like a grocer in's shop,*
with two Prentices [TIM *and* GEORGE],
reading Palmerin of England.[39]

Cit. Peace, fool! let Rafe alone.—Hark you Rafe, do not strain yourself too much at the first.—Peace!—Begin, Rafe.

Rafe. [*Reads*] "Then Palmerin and Trineus, snatch-ing their lances from their dwarfs, and clasping 220 their helmets, galloped amain after the giant; and Palmerin having gotten a sight of him, came posting amain, saying, 'Stay, traitorous thief, for thou mayst not so carry away her that is worth the greatest lord in the world;' and, with these words, gave him a blow on the shoulder, that he struck him besides his elephant. And Trineus, coming to the knight that had Agricola behind him, set him soon besides his horse, with his neck broken in the fall; so that the princess, getting out of the throng, between joy and grief, said, 230 'All happy knight, the mirror of all such as follow arms, now may I be well assured of the love thou bearest me.'"—I wonder why the kings do not raise an army of fourteen or fifteen hundred thousand men, as big as the army that the Prince of Portigo[30] brought against Rosicleer,[31] and destroy these giants; they do much hurt to wandering damsels, that go in quest of their knights.

Wife. Faith, husband, and Rafe says true; for they say the King of Portugal cannot sit at his meat, but 240 the giants and the ettins[32] will come and snatch it from him.

Cit. Hold thy tongue.—On, Rafe!

Rafe. And certainly those knights are much to be commended, who, neglecting their possessions, wander with a squire and a dwarf through the deserts[33] to relieve poor ladies.

Wife. Ay, by my faith, are they, Rafe; let 'em say what they will, they are indeed. Our knights neglect their possessions well enough, but they do not the rest. 250

Rafe. There are no such courteous and fair well-spoken knights in this age; they will call one "the son of a whore" that Palmerin of England would have called "fair sir"; and one that Rosicleer would have called "right beauteous damsel" they will call "damned bitch."

Wife. I'll be sworn will they, Rafe; they have called me so an hundred times about a scurvy pipe of tobacco.

Rafe. But what brave spirit could be content to sit in his shop, with a flappet[34] of wood, and a blue[35] 260 apron before him, selling mithridatum and dragon's-water[36] to visited[37] houses that might pursue feats of arms, and, through his noble achievements, procure such a famous history to be written of his heroic prowess?

Cit. Well said, Rafe; some more of those words, Rafe!

Wife. They go finely, by my troth.

Rafe. Why should not I, then, pursue this course,

both for the credit of myself and our company? For amongst all the worthy books of achievements, I 270 do not call to mind that I yet read of a grocer-errant: I will be the said knight. Have you heard of any that hath wandered unfurnished of his squire and dwarf? My elder prentice Tim shall be my trusty squire, and little George my dwarf. Hence, my blue apron! yet, in remembrance of my former trade, upon my shield shall be portrayed a burning pestle, and I will be called the Knight of the Burning Pestle.

Wife. Nay, I dare swear thou wilt not forget thy old trade; thou wert ever meek. 280

Rafe. Tim.

Tim. Anon.

Rafe. My beloved squire, and George my dwarf, I charge you that from henceforth you never call me by any other name but "the right courteous and valiant Knight of the Burning Pestle;" and that you never call any female by the name of a woman or wench, but "fair lady," if she have her desires, if not, "distressed damsel;" that you call all forests and heaths "deserts," and all horses "palfreys." 290

Wife. This is very fine, faith. Do the gentlemen like Rafe, think you, husband?

Cit. Ay, I warrant thee; the players would give all the shoes in their shop for him.

Rafe. My beloved squire Tim, stand out. Admit this were a desert, and over it a knight-errant pricking,[38] and I should bid you inquire of his intents, what would you say?

Tim. Sir, my master sent me to know whither you are riding? 300

Rafe. No, thus: "Fair sir, the right courteous and valiant Knight of the Burning Pestle commanded me to inquire upon what adventure you are bound, whether to relieve some distressed damsel, or otherwise."

Cit. Whoreson blockhead, cannot remember!

Wife. I' faith, and Rafe told him on't before: all the gentlemen heard him.—Did he not, gentlemen? Did not Rafe tell him on't?

Geo. Right courteous and valiant Knight of the Burning Pestle, here is a distressed damsel to have a halfpenny-worth of pepper. 311

Wife. That 's a good boy! see, the little boy can hit it; by my troth, it's a fine child.

Rafe. Relieve her, with all courteous language. Now shut up shop; no more my prentice, but my trusty squire and dwarf. I must bespeak my shield and arming[39] pestle.

[*Exeunt* TIM *and* GEORGE.]

Cit. Go thy ways, Rafe! as I'm a true man, thou art the best on[40] 'em all.

Wife. Rafe, Rafe! 320

---

[29] *Palmerin of England:* Spanish romance popular in England, but Rafe quotes from another, *Palmerin de Oliva.*
[30] *Portigo:* Portugal.
[31] *Rosicleer:* Spanish romance hero.   [32] *ettins:* giants.
[33] *deserts:* wild regions.   [34] *flappet:* small flap.
[35] *blue:* color of tradesmen's outfit.
[36] *mithridatum ... water:* antidotes for plague.
[37] *visited:* i.e., by plague.   [38] *prickling:* riding.
[39] *arming:* heraldic.   [40] *on:* of.

Rafe. What say you, mistress?

Wife. I prithee, come again quickly, sweet Rafe.

Rafe. By and by.

Exit RAFE.

Enter JASPER *and his mother,* MISTRESS
MERRYTHOUGHT.

Mist. Give thee my blessing? No, I'll ne'er give thee
my blessing; I'll see thee hanged first; it shall ne'er be
said I gave thee my blessing. Thou art thy father's own
son, of the right blood of the Merrythoughts. I may
curse the time that e'er I knew thy father; he hath
spent all his own and mine too; and when I tell him of
it, he laughs, and dances, and sings, and cries, "A   330
merry heart lives long-a." And thou art a wastethrift,
and art run away from thy master that loved thee well,
and art come to me; and I have laid up a little for
my younger son Michael, and thou thinkest to bezzle[41]
that, but thou shalt never be able to do it.—Come
hither, Michael!

Enter MICHAEL.

Come, Michael, down on thy knees; thou shalt have
my blessing.

[MICHAEL *kneels.*]

Mich. I pray you, mother, pray to God to bless
me.   340

Mist. God bless thee; but Jasper shall never have
my blessing; he shall be hanged first; shall he not,
Michael? How sayst thou?

Mich. Yes, forsooth, mother, and grace of God.

Mist. That's a good boy!

Wife. I' faith, it's a fine-spoken child.

Jas. Mother, though you forget a parent's love
I must preserve the duty of a child.
I ran not from my master, nor return
To have your stock maintain my idleness.   350

Wife. Ungracious child, I warrant him; hark, how
he chops logic with his mother!—Thou hadst best tell
her she lies; do, tell her she lies.

Cit. If he were my son, I would hang him up by the
heels, and flay him, and salt him, whoreson haltersack![42]

Jas. My coming only is to beg your love,
Which I must ever, though I never gain it;
And, howsoever you esteem of me,
There is no drop of blood hid in these veins   360
But, I remember well belongs to you
That brought me forth, and would be glad for you
To rip them all again, and let it out.

Mist. I' faith, I had sorrow enough for thee, God
knows; but I'll hamper thee well enough. Get thee in,
thou vagabond; get thee in, and learn of thy brother
Michael.

[*Exeunt* JASPER *and* MICHAEL.]

Merry. within. [*Sings*]

Nose, nose, jolly red nose,
    And who gave thee this jolly red nose?   369

Mist. Hark, my husband! he's singing and hoiting,[43]
and I'm fain to cark[44] and care, and all little enough.—
Husband. Charles. Charles Merrythought.

Enter old MERRYTHOUGHT.

Merry. [*Sings*]

Nutmegs and ginger, cinnamon and cloves;
    And they gave me this jolly red nose.

Mist. If you would consider your state, you would
have little list[45] to sing, i-wis.[46]

Merry. It should never be considered, while it were
an estate, if I thought it would spoil my singing.

Mist. But how wilt thou do, Charles? Thou art an
old man, and thou canst not work, and thou hast   380
not forty shillings left, and thou eatest good meat, and
drinkest good drink, and laughest.

Merry. And will do.

Mist. But how wilt thou come by it, Charles?

Merry. How! why, how have I done hitherto this
forty years? I never came into my dining room, but, at
eleven and six o'clock, I found excellent meat and
drink o' the table; my clothes were never worn out, but
next morning a tailor brought me a new suit; and without question it will be so ever; use makes perfect-   390
ness. If all should fail, it is but a little straining myself
extraordinary, and laugh myself to death.

Wife. It's a foolish old man this; is not he, George?

Cit. Yes, cony.

Wife. Give me a penny i' the purse while I live,
George.

Cit. Ay, by lady, cony, hold thee there.

Mist. Well, Charles, you promised to provide for
Jasper, and I have laid up for Michael. I pray you, pay
Jasper his portion: he's come home, and he shall   400
not consume Michael's stock; he says his master turned
him away, but, I promise you truly, I think he ran
away.

Wife. No, indeed, Mistress Merrythought; though
he be a notable gallows,[47] yet I'll assure you his master
did turn him away, even in this place; 'twas i' faith,
within this half-hour, about his daughter; my husband
was by.

Cit. Hang him, rogue; he served him well enough—
love his master's daughter! By my troth, cony, if   410
there were a thousand boys, thou wouldst spoil them all
with taking their parts; let his mother alone with him.

Wife. Ay, George; but yet truth is truth.

Merry. Where is Jasper? He's welcome, however.
Call him in; he shall have his portion. Is he merry?

Mist. Ah, foul chive[48] him, he is too merry.—Jasper.
Michael.

Enter JASPER *and* MICHAEL.

Merry. Welcome, Jasper. Though thou runnest
away, welcome. God bless thee. 'Tis thy mother's mind
thou shouldst receive thy portion; thou hast been   420
abroad, and I hope hast learned experience enough

---

[41] *bezzle:* embezzle.   [42] *haltersack:* gallows-bird.
[43] *hoiting:* indulging in loud mirth.
[44] *cark:* be anxious.   [45] *list:* inclination.
[46] *i-wis:* indeed.   [47] *gallows:* gallows-bird.
[48] *foul chive:* may bad luck afflict.

to govern it; thou art of sufficient years; hold thy
hand—one, two, three, four, five, six, seven, eight,
nine, there is ten shillings for thee.

[Gives money.]

Thrust thyself into the world with that, and take some
settled course. If fortune cross thee, thou hast a retiring
place; come home to me; I have twenty shillings left. Be
a good husband; that is, wear ordinary clothes, eat the
best meat, and drink the best drink; be merry, and give
to the poor, and, believe me, thou hast no end of thy
goods.   431

Jas. Long may you live free from all thought of ill,
And long have cause to be thus merry still.
But, father—

Merry. No more words, Jasper; get thee gone. Thou
hast my blessing; thy father's spirit upon thee. Farewell, Jasper.

[Sings] But yet, or ere you part (oh, cruel)
    Kiss me, kiss me, sweeting, mine own dear jewel!

So, now begone; no words.   440

Exit JASPER.

Mist. So, Michael, now get thee gone, too.

Mich. Yes, forsooth, mother; but I'll have my
father's blessing first.

Mist. No, Michael. 'Tis no matter for his blessing;
thou hast my blessing; begone. I'll fetch my money and
jewels, and follow thee. I'll stay no longer with him, I
warrant thee.—Truly, Charles, I'll be gone too.

[Exit MICHAEL.*]*

Merry. What! you will not?

Mist. Yes, indeed will I.

Merry. *[Sings]*

    Hey-ho, farewell, Nan.   450
    I'll never trust wench more again, if I can.

Mist. You shall not think, when all your own is gone,
to spend that I have been scraping up for Michael.

Merry. Farewell, good wife; I expect it not. All I
have to do in this world is to be merry, which I shall, if
the ground be not taken from me, and if it be,

[Sings] When earth and seas from me are reft,
    The skies aloft for me are left.

Exeunt.

Boy *danceth. Music.*   *Finis Actus primi.*

Wife. I'll be sworn he's a merry old gentleman for
all that. Hark, hark, husband, hark, fiddles,   460
fiddles; now surely they go finely. They say 'tis present
death for these fiddlers, to tune their rebecks[49] before
the great Turk's grace; is't not, George? But, look,
look! here's a youth dances.—Now, good youth, do a
turn o' the toe.—Sweetheart, i' faith, I'll have Rafe
come and do some of his gambols. He'll ride the wild
mare,[50] gentlemen, 'twould do your hearts good to see
him.—I thank you, kind youth; pray, bid Rafe come.

Cit. Peace, cony.—Sirrah, you scurvy boy, bid the
players send Rafe; or, by God's —— an they do   470
not, I'll tear some of their periwigs beside their heads;
this is all riff-raff.

[Exit Boy.*]*

ACT TWO

Enter Merchant [VENTUREWELL] *and* HUMPHREY.

Vent. And how, 'faith, how goes it now, son
    Humphrey?

Hump. Right worshipful, and my belovèd friend
And father dear, this matter's at an end.

Vent. 'Tis well; it should be so; I'm glad the girl.
Is found so tractable.

Hump.   Nay, she must whirl
From hence (and you must wink;[1] for so, I say,
The story tells) to-morrow before day.

Wife. George, dost thou think in thy conscience
now 'twill be a match? Tell me but what thou think'st,
sweet rogue. Thou seest the poor gentleman, dear   10
heart, how it labors and throbs, I warrant you, to be at
rest. I'll go move the father for't.

Cit. No, no; I prithee, sit still, honeysuckle; thou'lt
spoil all. If he deny him, I'll bring half a dozen good
fellows myself, and in the shutting of an evening knock
't up,[2] and there's an end.

Wife. I'll buss[3] thee for that, i' faith, boy. Well,
George, well, you have been a wag in your days, I
warrant you; but God forgive you, and I do with all
my heart.   20

Vent. How was it son? You told me that to-morrow
Before daybreak you must convey her hence.

Hump. I must, I must, and thus it is agreed:
Your daughter rides upon a brown-bay steed,
I on a sorrel, which I bought of Brian,
The honest host of the Red Roaring Lion,
In Waltham situate. Then, if you may,
Consent in seemly sort, lest, by delay,
The fatal sisters[4] come, and do the office,
And then you'll sing another song.

Vent.   Alas,   30
Why should you be thus full of grief to me,
That do as willing as yourself agree
To anything, so it be good and fair?
Then, steal her when you will, if such a pleasure
Content you both; I'll sleep and never see it,
To make your joys more full. But tell me why
You may not here perform your marriage.

Wife. God's blessing o' thy soul, old man. I' faith,
thou art loath to part true hearts. I see 'a has her,
George; and I'm as glad on 't.—Well, go thy ways,   40
Humphrey, for a fair-spoken man; I believe thou hast
not thy fellow within the walls of London; and I should
say the suburbs too, I should not lie.—Why dost not
rejoice with me, George?

Cit. If I could but see Rafe again, I were as merry
as mine host, i' faith.

Hump. The cause you seem to ask, I thus declare—
Help me, O muses nine. Your daughter sware
A foolish oath, the more it was the pity;

---

[49] *rebecks:* three-stringed violins.

[50] *ride . . . mare:* seesaw, with unintentional but proverbial
sexual connotation.

II.

[1] *wink:* close your eyes.   [2] *knock't up:* conclude it.

[3] *buss:* kiss.   [4] *sisters:* the fates of classical mythology.

Yet none but myself within this city   50
Shall dare to say so, but a bold defiance
Shall meet him, were he of the noble science.[5]
And yet she sware, and yet why did she swear?
Truly, I cannot tell, unless it were
For her own ease; for, sure sometimes an oath,
Being sworn, thereafter is like cordial[6] broth.
And this it was she swore: never to marry
But such a one whose mighty arm could carry
(As meaning me, for I am such a one)
Her bodily away, through stick and stone,   60
Till both of us arrive, at her request,
Some ten miles off, in the wild Waltham Forest.

Vent. If this be all, you shall not need to fear
Any denial in your love. Proceed;
I'll neither follow, nor repent the deed.

Hump. Good night, twenty good nights, and twenty
more,
And twenty more good nights,—that makes threescore!

Exeunt.

Enter MISTRESS MERRYTHOUGHT [*with jewel
casket and purse*] *and her son* MICHAEL.

Mist. Come, Michael; art thou not weary, boy?
Mich. No, forsooth, mother, not I.
Mist. Where be we now, child?   70
Mich. Indeed, forsooth, mother, I cannot tell, unless
we be at Mile End.[7] Is not all the world Mile End,
mother?
Mist. No, Michael, not all the world, boy; but I can
assure thee, Michael, Mile End is a goodly matter:
there has been a pitchfield,[8] my child, between the
naughty Spaniels[9] and the Englishmen; and the
Spaniels ran away, Michael, and the Englishmen
followed. My neighbor Coxstone was there, boy, and
killed them all with a birding-piece.[10]   80
Mich. Mother, forsooth—
Mist. What says my white boy?[11]
Mich. Shall not my father go with us, too?
Mist. No, Michael, let thy father go snick-up;[12] he
shall never come between a pair of sheets with me again
while he lives; let him stay at home, and sing for his
supper, boy. Come, child, sit down, and I'll show
my boy fine knacks,[13] indeed. Look here, Michael;
here's a ring, and here's a brooch, and here's a bracelet,
and here's two rings more, and here's money and gold
by th' eye,[14] my boy.   91
Mich. Shall I have all this, mother?
Mist. Ay, Michael, thou shalt have all, Michael.
Cit. How lik'st thou this, wench?
Wife. I cannot tell; I would have Rafe, George. I'll

see no more else, indeed, la; and I pray you, let the
youths understand so much by word of mouth, for,
I tell you truly, I'm afraid o' my boy. Come, come,
George, let's be merry and wise; the child's a fatherless
child; and say they should put him into a strait   100
pair of gaskins,[15] 'twere worse than knot-grass[16]; he
would never grow after it.

Enter RAFE, [TIM *as*] Squire, *and* [GEORGE *as*] Dwarf.

Cit. Here's Rafe, here's Rafe.
Wife. How do you, Rafe? You are welcome, Rafe,
as I may say; it's a good boy, hold up thy head, and be
not afraid; we are thy friends, Rafe; the gentlemen will
praise thee, Rafe, if thou playest thy part with audacity.
Begin, Rafe, a' God's name.
Rafe. My trusty squire, unlace my helm; give me
my hat.
Where are we, or what desert may this be?   110
Geo. Mirror of knighthood, this is, as I take it, the
perilous Waltham Down; in whose bottom stands the
enchanted valley.
Mist. Oh, Michael, we are betrayed, we are betrayed. Here be giants. Fly, boy; fly, boy; fly.

Exeunt Mother *and* MICHAEL [*dropping purse
and casket*].

Rafe. Lace on my helm again. What noise is this?
A gentle lady flying the embrace
Of some uncourteous knight! I will relieve her.
Go, squire, and say, the Knight, that wears this Pestle
In honor of all ladies, swears revenge   120
Upon that recreant[17] coward that pursues her.
Go, comfort her, and that same gentle squire
That bears her company.
Tim.   I go, brave knight.

[*Exit.*]

Rafe. My trusty dwarf and friend, reach me my
shield,
And hold it while I swear. First, by my knighthood;
Then by the soul of Amadis de Gaul,[18]
My famous ancestor; then by my sword
The beauteous Brionella[19] girt about me;
By this bright burning Pestle, of mine honor
The living trophy; and by all respect   130
Due to distressèd damsels; here I vow
Never to end the quest of this fair lady
And that forsaken squire till by my valor
I gain their liberty.
Geo.   Heaven bless the knight
That thus relieves poor errant gentlewomen.

Exeunt.

Wife. Ay, marry, Rafe, this has some savor in't. I
would see the proudest of them all offer to carry his
books after him. But, George, I will not have him go
away so soon; I shall be sick if he go away, that I
shall. Call Rafe again, George, call Rafe again; I   140
prithee, sweetheart, let him come fight before me, and
let 's ha' some drums and some trumpets, and let him
kill all that comes near him, an thou lov'st me,
George.
Cit. Peace a little, bird: he shall kill them all, and
they were twenty more on 'em than there are.

---

[5] *noble science:* fencing.   [6] *cordial:* medicinal.
[7] *Mile End:* a mile from Aldgate, where militia trained.
[8] *pitchfield:* pitched battle.   [9] *Spaniels:* Spaniards.
[10] *birding-piece:* gun.   [11] *white boy:* favorite.
[12] *snick-up:* hang.   [13] *knacks:* trinkets.
[14] *by . . . eye:* in great quantity. [15] *gaskins:* breeches.
[16] *knot-grass:* weed held to stunt growth.
[17] *recreant:* craven.
[18] *Amadis de Gaul:* hero of Spanish romance.
[19] *Brionella:* woman in Palmerin de Oliva.

Enter JASPER.

Jas. Now, fortune, if thou beest not only ill,
Show me thy better face, and bring about
Thy desperate wheel, that I may climb at length,
And stand. This is our place of meeting,   150
If love have any constancy. Oh, age,
Where only wealthy men are counted happy!
How shall I please thee, how deserve thy smiles,
When I am only rich in misery?
My father's blessing and this little coin
Is my inheritance, a strong revenue.
From earth thou art, and to the earth I give thee:

[*Throws away the money.*]

There grow and multiply, whilst fresher air
Breeds me a fresher fortune.—How, illusion!

Spies the casket.

What, hath the devil coined himself before me?   160
'Tis metal good, it rings well. I am waking,
And taking[20] too, I hope. Now, God's dear blessing
Upon his heart that left it here. 'Tis mine;
These pearls, I take it, were not left for swine.

Exit [*with the casket*].

Wife. I do not like that this unthrifty youth should
embezzle away the money; the poor gentlewoman his
mother will have a heavy heart for it, God knows.
Cit. And reason good, sweetheart.   168
Wife. But let him go; I'll tell Rafe a tale in 's ear
shall fetch him again with a wanion,[21] I warrant him,
if he be above ground; and besides, George, here be a
number of sufficient gentlemen can witness, and myself,
and yourself, and the musicians, if we be called in
question.

Enter RAFE *and* [GEORGE *as*] Dwarf.

But here comes Rafe, George; thou shalt hear him
speak, an he were an emperal.[22]
Rafe. Comes not sir squire again?
Geo.   Right courteous
          knight,
Your squire doth come, and with him comes the lady,
For and[23] the squire of damsels, as I take it.

Enter MISTRESS MERRYTHOUGHT, *and*
MICHAEL, *and* Squire [TIM].

Rafe. Madam, if any service or devoir[24]   180
Of a poor errant knight may right you wrongs,
Command it; I am prest[25] to give your succor;
For to that holy end I bear my armor.
Mist. Alas, sir, I am a poor gentlewoman, and I have
lost my money in this forest.
Rafe. Desert, you would say, lady; and not lost
Whilst I have sword and lance. Dry up your tears,
Which ill befit the beauty of that face,
And tell the story, if I may request it,
Of your disastrous fortune.   190
Mist. Out, alas! I left a thousand pound, a thousand
pound, e'en all the money I had laid up for this youth,
upon the sight of your mastership, you looked so grim,

and, as I may say it, saving your presence, more like a
giant than a mortal man.
Rafe. I am as you are, lady; so are they;
All mortal. But why weeps this gentle squire?
Mist. Has he not cause to weep, do you think, when
he hath lost his inheritance?
Rafe. Young hope of valor, weep not; I am here   200
That will confound thy foe, and pay it dear
Upon his coward head, that dares deny
Distressèd squires and ladies equity.
I have but one horse, on which shall ride
This fair lady behind me, and before
This courteous squire: fortune will give us more
Upon our next adventure. Fairly speed
Besides us, squire and dwarf, to do us need.[26]

Exeunt.

Cit. Did not I tell you, Nell, what your man would
do? By the faith of my body, wench, for clean   210
action and good delivery, they may all cast their caps[27]
at him.
Wife. And so they may, i' faith, for I dare speak it
boldly, the twelve companies[28] of London cannot match
him, timber for timber. Well, George, and he be
not inveigled by some of these paltry players, I ha'
much marvel. But, George, we ha' done our parts, if
the boy have any grace to be thankful.
Cit. Yes, I warrant you, duckling.   219

Enter HUMPHREY *and* LUCE.

Hump. Good Mistress Luce, however I in fault am
For your lame horse, you're welcome unto Waltham;
But which way now to go, or what to say,
I know not truly, till it be broad day.
Luce. Oh, fear not, Master Humphrey; I am guide
For this place good enough.
Hump.   Then, up and ride;
Or, if it please you, walk for your repose;
Or sit, or, if you will, go pluck a rose;[29]
Either of which shall be indifferent
To your good friend and Humphrey, whose consent
Is so entangled ever to your will,   230
As the poor harmless horse is to the mill.
Luce. Faith, and you say the word, we'll e'en sit
          down
And take a nap.
Hump.   'Tis better in the town,
Where we may nap together; for, believe me,
To sleep without a snatch[30] would mickle[31] grieve me.
Luce. You're merry, Master Humphrey.
Hump.   So I am,
And have been ever merry from my dam.[32]
Luce. Your nurse had the less labor.
Hump.   Faith, it may be,
Unless it were by chance I did beray[33] me.

---

[20] *taking:* seizing.   [21] *wanion:* vengeance.
[22] *an emperal:* as if he were an imperial soldier.
[23] *For and:* As well as.   [24] *devoir:* effort.   [25] *prest:* ready.
[26] *need:* service.   [27] *cast . . . caps:* salute.
[28] *twelve companies:* the incorporated guilds.
[29] *pluck a rose:* urinate, defecate.
[30] *snatch:* snack; with unintended pun, a hasty copulation.
[31] *mickle:* much.   [32] *dam:* mother.   [33] *beray:* befoul.

Enter JASPER.

Jas. Luce. Dear friend Luce.
Luce.   Here, Jasper.
Jas.   You are
     mine.   240
Hump. If it be so, my friend, you use me fine.
What do you think I am?
Jas.   An arrant noddy.[34]
Hump. A word of obloquy! Now, by God's body,
I'll tell thy master, for I know thee well.
Jas. Nay, and you be so forward for to tell,
Take that, and that, and tell him, sir, I gave it,
And say, I paid you well.

                              [*Beats him.*]

Hump.   Oh, sir, I have it
And do confess the payment. Pray, be quiet.
Jas. Go, get you to your nightcap and the diet,
To cure your beaten bones.
Luce.   Alas, poor Humphrey;   250
Get thee some wholesome broth, with sage and
     comfrey;[35]
A little oil of roses and a feather
To 'noint thy back withal.
Hump.   When I came hither,
Would I had gone to Paris with John Dory![36]
Luce. Farewell, my pretty nump;[37] I am very sorry
I cannot bear thee company.
Hump.   Farewell:
The devil's dam was ne'er so banged in hell.
               Exeunt [LUCE *and* JASPER].
                    Manet HUMPHREY.
Wife. This young Jasper will prove me another
thing, o' my conscience, and he may be suffered.
George, dost not see, George, how 'a swaggers,   260
and flies at the very heads o' folks, as he were a dragon?
Well, if I do not do his lesson for wronging the poor
gentleman, I am no true woman. His friends that
brought him up might have been better occupied, i-wis,
than have taught him these fegaries:[38] he's e'en in the
high way to the gallows, God bless him.
Cit. You're too bitter, cony; the young man may do
well enough for all this.
Wife. Come hither, Master Humphrey. Has he hurt
you? Now, beshrew his fingers for't. Here, sweet-   270
heart, here's some green ginger for thee. Now, beshrew
my heart, but 'a has peppernel[39] in's head, as big as a
pullet's egg! Alas, sweet lamb, how thy temples beat.
Take the peace[40] on him, sweetheart, take the peace
on him.

Enter a Boy.

Cit. No, no, you talk like a foolish woman. I'll ha'
Rafe fight with him, and swinge[41] him up well-

---

favoredly.—Sirrah boy, come hither. Let Rafe come in
and fight with Jasper.   279
Wife. Ay, and beat him well; he's an unhappy[42] boy.
Boy. Sir, you must pardon us; the plot of our play
lies contrary, and 'twill hazard the spoiling of our play.
Cit. Plot me no plots. I'll ha' Rafe come out; I'll
make your house too hot for you else.
Boy. Why, sir, he shall; but if any thing fall out of
order, the gentlemen must pardon us.
Cit. Go your ways, Goodman Boy.

                              [*Exit* Boy.]
—I'll hold him a penny, he shall have his bellyful of
fighting now. Ho, here comes Rafe; no more.

Enter RAFE, MISTRESS MERRYTHOUGHT, MICHAEL, [TIM *as*] Squire *and* [GEORGE *as*] Dwarf.

Rafe. What knight is that, squire? ask him if he
     keep   290
The passage, bound by love of lady fair,
Or else but prickant.[43]
Hump.   Sir, I am no knight,
But a poor gentleman, that this same night
Had stolen from me, on yonder green,
My lovely wife, and suffered (to be seen
Yet extant on my shoulders) such a greeting,
That whilst I live I shall think of that meeting.
Wife. Ay, Rafe, he beat him unmercifully Rafe; and
thou sparest him, Rafe, I would thou wert hanged.
Cit. No more, wife, no more.   300
Rafe. Where is the caitiff[44] wretch hath done this
     deed?
Lady, your pardon; that I may proceed
Upon the quest of this injurious knight.—
And thou, fair squire, repute me not the worse,
In leaving the great venture of the purse
And the rich casket till some better leisure.

Enter JASPER *and* LUCE.

Hump. Here comes the broker[45] hath purloined my
     treasure.
Rafe. Go, squire, and tell him I am here,
An errant knight-at-arms, to crave delivery
Of that fair lady to her own knight's arms.   310
If he deny, bid him take choice of ground,
And so defy him.
Tim.   From the knight that bears
The golden pestle, I defy thee, knight,
Unless thou make fair restitution
Of that bright lady.
Jas.   Tell the knight that sent thee
He is an ass, and I will keep the wench
And knock his head-piece.
Rafe.   Knight, thou art but dead
If thou recall not thy uncourteous terms.
Wife. Break 's pate, Rafe; break 's pate, Rafe,
soundly!   320
Jas. Come, knight, I am ready for you.
Now your pestle

                    Snatches away his pestle.

Shall try what temper, sir, your mortar's of.

With that he stood upright in his stirrups,
And gave the Knight of the Calf-skin such a knock,

[*Knocks* RAFE *down.*]

That he forsook his horse, and down he fell;
And then he leaped upon him, and plucking off
His helmet—
Hump. Nay, and my noble knight be down so soon,
Though I can scarcely go,[46] I needs must run.   330
                        Exeunt HUMPHREY *and* RAFE.
Wife. Run, Rafe, run Rafe; run for thy life, boy;
Jasper comes, Jasper comes.
Jas. Come, Luce, we must have other arms for you.
Humphrey and Golden Pestle, both adieu!
                                        Exeunt.
Wife. Sure the devil, God bless us, is in this sprin-
gald.[47] Why, George, didst ever see such a fire-drake?[48]
I am afraid my boy's miscarried. If he be, though he
were Master Merrythought's son a thousand times, if
there be any law in England, I'll make some of them
smart for't.   340
Cit. No, no; I have found out the matter, sweetheart. Jasper is enchanted. As sure as we are here, he is
enchanted. He could no more have stood in Rafe's
hands than I can stand in my lord mayor's. I'll have a
ring to discover all enchantments, and Rafe shall beat
him yet. Be no more vexed, for it shall be so.

Enter RAFE, [TIM, *as*] Squire, [GEORGE *as*] Dwarf,
  MISTRESS MERRYTHOUGHT, *and* MICHAEL.

Wife. Oh, husband, here's Rafe again.—Stay, Rafe,
again, let me speak with thee. How dost thou, Rafe?
Art thou not shrewdly hurt? The foul great lungies[49]
laid unmercifully on thee. There's some sugar-   350
candy for thee. Proceed; thou shalt have another bout
with him.
Cit. If Rafe had him at the fencing-school, if he did
not make a puppy of him and drive him up and down
the school, he should ne'er come in my shop more.
Mist. Truly, Master Knight of the Burning Pestle,
I am weary.
Mich. Indeed, la, mother, and I am very hungry.
Rafe. Take comfort, gentle dame, and you, fair
  squire,
For in this desert there must needs be placed   360
Many strong castles, held by courteous knights;
And till I bring you safe to one of those,
I swear by this my order ne'er to leave you.
Wife. Well said, Rafe.—George, Rafe was ever
comfortable, was he not?
Cit. Yes, duck.
Wife. I shall ne'er forget him. When he had lost our
child (you know it was strayed almost alone to Puddle
Wharf,[50] and the criers were abroad for it, and there it
had drowned itself but for a sculler), Rafe was the   370
most comfortablest to me: "Peace, mistress," says he,
"let it go; I'll get you another as good." Did he not,
George, did he not say so?
Cit. Yes, indeed did he, mouse.
Geo. I would we had a mess of pottage and a pot of
drink, squire, and were going to bed.

Tim. Why, we are at Waltham town's end, and that's
the Bell Inn.
Geo. Take courage, valiant knight, damsel, and
  squire.
I have discovered, not a stone's cast off,   380
An ancient castle, held by the old knight
Of the most holy order of the Bell,
Who gives to all knights-errant entertain.[51]
There plenty is of food, and all prepared
By the white hands of his own lady dear.
He hath three squires that welcome all his guests:
The first, hight[52] Chamberlino, who will see
Our beds prepared, and bring us snowy sheets,
Where never footman stretched his buttered hams;[53]
The second, hight Tapstero, who will see   390
Our pots full fillèd, and no froth therein;
The third, a gentle squire, Ostlero hight,
Who will our palfreys slick with wisps of straw,
And in the manger put them oats enough.
And never grease their teeth with candle-snuff.[54]
Wife. That same dwarf's a pretty boy, but the
squire's a groutnol.[55]
Rafe. Knock at the gates, my squire, with stately
  lance.

[TIM *knocks at the door.*]

Enter Tapster.

Tap. Who's there?—You're welcome, gentlemen.
Will you see a room?   400
Geo. Right courteous and valiant Knight of the
Burning Pestle, this is the Squire Tapstero.
Rafe. Fair Squire Tapstero, I a wandering knight,
Hight of the Burning Pestle, in the quest
Of this fair lady's casket and wrought purse,
Losing myself in this vast wilderness,
Am to this castle well by fortune brought,
Where, hearing of the goodly entertain
Your Knight of Holy Order of the Bell
Gives to all damsels and all errant knights,   410
I thought to knock, and now am bold to enter.
Tap. An't please you see a chamber, you are very
welcome.
                                        Exeunt.
Wife. George, I would have something done, and I
cannot tell what it is.
Cit. What is it, Nell?
Wife. Why, George, shall Rafe beat nobody again?
Prithee, sweetheart, let him.
Cit. So he shall, Nell; and if I join with him, we'll
knock them all.   420

Enter HUMPHREY *and* Merchant [VENTUREWELL].

Wife. Oh, George, here's Master Humphrey, again,

---

[46] *go:* walk.   [47] *springald:* youngster.
[48] *fire-drake:* firework.   [49] *lungies:* tall thin lout.
[50] *Puddle Wharf:* landing place on the Thames.
[51] *entertain:* entertainment.   [52] *hight:* named, called.
[53] *footman . . . hams:* Running couriers greased their
calves to prevent cramps.
[54] *grease . . . snuff:* ostler's trick to prevent horses from
eating.   [55] *groutnol:* blockhead.

now, that lost Mistress Luce, and Mistress Luce's
father. Master Humphrey will do somebody's errand,
I warrant him.

   Hump. Father, it's true in arms I ne'er shall clasp
      her;
For she is stolen away by your man Jasper.

   Wife. I thought he would tell him.

   Vent. Unhappy that I am, to lose my child!
Now I begin to think on Jasper's words,
Who oft hath urged to me thy foolishness.   430
Why didst thou let her go? Thou lov'st her not,
That wouldst bring home thy life, and not bring her.

   Hump. Father, forgive me. Shall I tell you true?
Look on my shoulders; they are black and blue:
Whilst to and fro fair Luce and I were winding,
He came and basted[56] me with a hedge-binding.

   Vent. Get men and horses straight: we will be there
Within this hour. You know the place again?

   Hump. I know the place where he my loins did
      swaddle.[57]
I'll get six horses, and to each a saddle.   440

   Vent. Meantime I will go talk with Jasper's father.
                            Exeunt.

   Wife. George, what wilt thou lay with me now, that
Master Humphrey has not Mistress Luce yet? Speak,
George, what wilt thou lay with me?

   Cit. No, Nell, I warrant thee, Jasper is at Puckeridge[58] with her by this.

   Wife. Nay, George, you must consider Mistress
Luce's feet are tender, and besides 'tis dark, and, I
promise you truly, I do not see how he should get out
of Waltham Forest with her yet.   450

   Cit. Nay, cony, what wilt thou lay with me that Rafe
has her not yet?

   Wife. I will not lay against Rafe, honey, because I
have not spoken with him.

            Enter old MERRYTHOUGHT.

But look, George, peace; here comes the merry old
gentleman again.

   Merry. [*Sings*]

>   *When it was grown to dark midnight,*
>   *And all were fast asleep,*
>   *In came Margaret's grimly ghost,*
>   *And stood at William's feet.*   460

I have money, and meat and drink beforehand till
to-morrow at noon. Why should I be sad? Methinks I
have half a dozen jovial spirits within me.

   [*Sings*] *I am three merry men, and three merry men.*

To what end should any man be sad in this world?
Give me a man that when he goes to hanging cries,

   [*Sings*]   *Troll*[59] *the black bowl to me!*

and a woman that will sing a catch in her travail. I have
seen a man come by my door with a serious face, in a
black cloak, without a hatband, carrying his head   470
as if he looked for pins in the street. I have looked out
of my window half a year after, and have spied that
man's head upon London Bridge.[60] 'Tis vile. Never
trust a tailor that does not sing at his work; his mind
is of nothing but filching.

   Wife. Mark this, George; 'tis worth noting. Godfrey
my tailor, you know, never sings, and he had fourteen
yards to make this gown; and I'll be sworn, Mistress
Pennystone, the draper's wife, had one made with
twelve.   480

   Merry. [*Sings*]

>   *'Tis mirth that fills the veins with blood,*
>   *More than wine, or sleep, or food;*
>   *Let each man keep his heart at ease*
>   *No man dies of that disease.*
>   *He that would his body keep*
>   *From diseases must not weep;*
>   *But whoever laughs and sings,*
>   *Never he his body brings*
>   *Into fevers, gouts, or rheums,*
>   *Or lingeringly his lungs consumes,*   490
>   *Or meets with aches in the bone,*
>   *Or catarrhs or griping stone,*[61]
>   *But contented lives for ay;*
>   *The more he laughs, the more he may.*

   Wife. Look, George; how sayst thou by this,
George? Is't not a fine old man?—Now God's blessing
o' thy sweet lips.—When wilt thou be so merry,
George? Faith, thou art the frowningest little thing,
when thou art angry, in a country.

   Cit. Peace, cony; thou shalt see him taken down,
too, I warrant thee.—   501

          Enter Merchant [VENTUREWELL].

Here's Luce's father come now.

   Merry. [*Sings*]

>   *As you came from Walsingham,*[62]
>   *From that holy land,*
>   *There met you not with my true love*
>   *By the way as you came?*

   Vent. Oh, Master Merrythought, my daughter's
gone.

   Merry. [*Sings*]

>   *Why, an if she be, what care I?*
>   *Or let her come, or go, or tarry.*

   Vent. Mock not my misery; it is your son,   510
Whom I have made my own, when all forsook him,
Has stolen my only joy, my child, away.

   Merry. [*Sings*]

>   *He set her on a milk-white steed,*
>   *And himself upon a grey;*
>   *He never turned his face again,*
>   *But he bore her quite away.*

   Vent. Unworthy of the kindness I have shown

---

   [56] *basted:* beat.   [57] *swaddle:* beat.
   [58] *Puckeridge:* Hertfordshire village twenty-five miles
north of London.   [59] *Troll:* Pass.
   [60] *man's . . . Bridge:* heads of executed traitors were displayed there.   [61] *griping stone:* painful gallstone.
   [62] *Walsingham:* Norfolk village with a shrine to the Virgin.

To thee and thine! too late I well perceive
Thou art consenting to my daughter's loss.   519
   Merry. Your daughter! what a stir's here wi' your
daughter? Let her go, think no more on her, but sing
loud. If both my sons were on the gallows, I would sing,

> [*Sings*] *Down, down, down they fall,*
>   *Down, and arise they never shall.*

   Vent. Oh, might I behold her once again,
And she once more embrace her agèd sire.
   Merry. Fie, how scurvily this goes. "And she once
more embrace her agèd sire?" You'll make a dog on
her, will ye? She cares much for her agèd sire, I
warrant you.   530

> [*Sings*]   *She cares not for her daddy, nor*
>   *She cares not for her mammy,*
>   *For she is, she is, she is, she is*
>   *My Lord of Lowgave's lassy.*

   Vent. For this thy scorn I will pursue that son
Of thine to death.
   Merry. Do; and when you ha' killed him,

> [*Sings*] *Give him flowers enow,*[63] *palmer; give him*
>   *flowers enow;*
>   *Give him red, and white, and blue, green,*
>   *and yellow.*

   Vent. I'll fetch my daughter.   540
   Merry. I'll hear no more o' your daughter; it spoils
my mirth.
   Vent. I say, I'll fetch my daughter.
   Merry. [*Sings*]

>   *Was never man for lady's sake,*
>   *Down, down,*
>   *Tormented as I poor Sir Guy,*[64]
>   *De derry down,*
>   *For Lucy's sake, that lady bright,*
>   *Down, down,*
>   *As ever men beheld with eye,*   550
>   *De derry down.*

   Vent. I'll be revenged, by heaven!

                            Exeunt.

      Music.   *Finis Actus secundi.*

   Wife. How dost thou like this, George?
   Cit. Why, this is well, cony; but if Rafe were hot
once, thou shouldst see more.
   Wife. The fiddlers go again, husband.
   Cit. Ay, Nell, but this is scurvy music. I gave the
whoreson gallows-money, and I think he has not got
me the waits of Southwark. If I hear 'em not anon, I'll
twinge[65] him by the ears.—You musicians, play
"Baloo.[66]"   561
   Wife. No, good George, let's ha' "Lachrymae."[67]
   Cit. Why, this is it, cony.
   Wife. It's all the better, George. Now, sweet lamb,
what story is that painted upon the cloth? the Confuta-
tion[68] of St. Paul?
   Cit. No, lamb; that's Rafe and Lucrece.[69]
   Wife. Rafe and Lucrece! which Rafe? our Rafe?

   Cit. No, mouse, that was a Tartarian.[70]
   Wife. A Tartarian? Well, I would the fiddlers had
done, that we might see our Rafe again!   571

ACT THREE

Enter JASPER *and* LUCE.

   Jas. Come, my dear dear; though we have lost our
     way,
We have not lost ourselves. Are you not weary
With this night's wandering, broken from your rest,
And frighted with the terror that attends
The darkness of this wild unpeopled place?
   Luce. No, my best friend; I cannot either fear,
Or entertain a weary thought, whilst you,
The end of all my full desires, stand by me.
Let them that lose their hopes, and live to languish
Amongst the number of forsaken lovers,   10
Tell[1] the long weary steps, and number time,
Start at a shadow, and shrink up their blood,
Whilst I, possessed with all content and quiet,
Thus take my pretty love, and thus embrace him.
   Jas. You have caught me, Luce, so fast, that, whilst
     I live,
I shall become your faithful prisoner,
And wear these chains forever. Come, sit down,
And rest your body, too, too delicate
For these disturbances.
                             [*They sit down.*]
              So: will you sleep?
Come, do not be more able than you are;   20
I know you are not skilful in these watches,
For women are no soldiers. Be not nice,
But take it; sleep, I say.
   Luce.   I cannot sleep;
Indeed, I cannot, friend.
   Jas.   Why, then, we'll sing,
And try how that will work upon our senses.
   Luce. I'll sing, or say, or anything but sleep.
   Jas. Come, little mermaid, rob me of my heart
With that enchanting voice.
   Luce. You mock me, Jasper.
                             [*They sing.*]
   Jas.   *Tell me, dearest, what is love?*   30
   Luce.   *'Tis a lightning from above;*
             'Tis an arrow, 'tis a fire,
             'Tis a boy they call Desire;
               'Tis a smile
               Doth beguile
   Jas.   *The poor hearts of men that prove.*[2]

---

[63] *enow:* enough.
[64] *Sir Guy:* Guy of Warwick, legendary romance hero.
[65] *twinge:* tweak.   [66] *Baloo:* a ballad.
[67] *Lachrymae:* famous lute-song by John Dowland (1563?
–1626?).   [68] *Confutation:* She means "Conversion."
[69] *Rafe and Lucrece:* error for "the rape of Lucrece" by a
Tarquin prince.   [70] *Tartarian:* thief; error for Tarquin.
III.
[1] *Tell:* Count.   [2] *prove:* experience.

Tell me more, are women true?

Luce. *Some love change, and so do you.*

Jas. *Are they fair and never kind?*

Luce. *Yes, when men turn with the wind.*   40

Jas.   *Are they froward?*

Luce.   *Ever toward*

       Those that love, to love anew.

Jas. Dissemble it no more; I see the god
Of heavy sleep lay on his heavy mace
Upon your eyelids.

Luce.   I am very heavy.

                                     [*Sleeps.*]

Jas. Sleep, sleep; and quiet rest crown thy sweet
       thoughts.
Keep from her fair blood distempers, startings,
Horrors, and fearful shapes. Let all her dreams
Be joys and chaste delights, embraces, wishes,   50
And such new pleasures as the ravished soul
Gives to the senses. So; my charms have took.
Keep her, you powers divine, whilst I contemplate
Upon the wealth and beauty of her mind.
She is only fair and constant, only kind,
And only to thee, Jasper. O my joys,
Whither will you transport me? Let not fullness
Of my poor buried hopes come up together
And overcharge my spirits. I am weak.
Some say (however ill) the sea and women   60
Are governed by the moon: both ebb and flow,
Both full of changes; yet to them that know,
And truly judge, these but opinions are,
And heresies, to bring on pleasing war
Between our tempers, that wihout these were
Both void of after-love and present fear,
Which are the best of Cupid. O thou child
Bred from despair, I dare not entertain thee,
Having a love without the faults of women,
And greater in her perfect goods than men;   70
Which to make good, and please myself the stronger,
Though certainly I am certain of her love,
I'll try her, that the world and memory
May sing to aftertimes her constancy.—

                              [*Draws his sword.*]

Luce, Luce, awake.

Luce.   Why do you fright me, friend,
With those distempered looks? What makes your
       sword
Drawn in your hand? Who hath offended you?
I prithee, Jasper, sleep; thou art wild with watching.

Jas. Come, make your way to heaven, and bid the
       world,
With all the villainies that stick upon it,   80
Farewell; you're for another life.

Luce.   Oh, Jasper,
How have my tender years committed evil,
Especially against the man I love,
Thus to be cropped untimely?

Jas.   Foolish girl,

---

³ *mittimus:* warrant.
⁴ *Sir Bevis:* Bevis of Hampton, popular romance hero.

Canst thou imagine I could love his daughter
That flung me from my fortune into nothing?
Dischargèd me his service, shut the doors
Upon my poverty, and scorned my prayers,   90
Sending me, like a boat without a mast,
To sink or swim? Come, by this hand you die.
I must have life and blood, to satisfy
Your father's wrongs.

Wife. Away, George, away; raise the watch at Ludgate, and bring a mittimus³ from the justice for this
desperate villain.—Now, I charge you, gentlemen, see
the King's peace kept.—O my heart, what a varlet's
this to offer manslaughter upon the harmless gentlewoman.

Cit. I warrant thee, sweetheart, we'll have him
hampered.   100

Luce. Oh, Jasper, be not cruel.
If thou wilt kill me, smile, and do it quickly,
And let not many deaths appear before me.
I am a woman, made of fear and love,
A weak, weak woman. Kill not with thy eyes,
They shoot me through and through. Strike, I am
       ready;
And, dying, still I love thee.

Enter Merchant [VENTUREWELL], HUMPHREY,
                and his men.

Vent.   Whereabouts?

Jas. [*Aside*] No more of this; now to myself again.

Hump. There, there he stands, with sword, like
       martial knight,
Drawn in his hand; therefore beware the fight,   110
You that be wise, for, were I good Sir Bevis,⁴
I would not stay his coming, by your leavès.

Vent. Sirrah, restore my daughter.

Jas.   Sirrah, no.

Vent. Upon him, then.

              [*They attack* JASPER, *and force* LUCE *from him.*]

Wife. So; down with him, down with him, down
with him; cut him i' the leg, boys, cut him i' the leg.

Vent. Come your ways, minion. I'll provide a cage
For you, you're grown so tame.—Horse her away.

Hump. Truly, I'm glad your forces have the day.

                    Exeunt. Manet JASPER.

Jas. They are gone, and I am hurt; my love is lost,
Never to get again. O me unhappy!   121
Bleed, bleed and die, I cannot. O my folly,
Thou hast betrayed me. Hope, where art thou fled?
Tell me, if thou beest anywhere remaining,
Shall I but see my love again? Oh, no!
She will not deign to look upon her butcher,
Nor is it fit she should; yet I must venture.
O Chance, or Fortune, or whate'er thou art
That men adore for powerful, hear my cry,
And let me loving live, or losing die.   130

                                     Exit.

Wife. Is 'a gone, George?

Cit. Ay, cony.

Wife. Marry, and let him go, sweetheart. By the
faith o' my body, 'a has put me into such a fright, that

I tremble as they say, as 'twere an aspen leaf. Look o'
my little finger, George, how it shakes. Now, i' truth,
every member of my body is the worse for 't.

Cit. Come, hug in mine arms, sweet mouse; he shall
not fright thee any more. Alas, mine own dear heart,
how it quivers.　　　　　　　　　　　　　　140

Enter MISTRESS MERRYTHOUGHT, RAFE,
MICHAEL, [TIM *as*] Squire, [GEORGE *as*] Dwarf,
Host *and a* Tapster.

Wife. O, Rafe, how dost thou, Rafe? How hast thou
slept to-night?[5] Has the knight used thee well?

Cit. Peace, Nell; let Rafe alone.[6]

Tap. Master, the reckoning is not paid.

Rafe. Right courteous knight, who, for the order's
sake
Which thou hast ta'en hang'st out the holy Bell,
As I this flaming Pestle bear about,
We render thanks to your puissant self,
Your beauteous lady, and your gentle squires,
For thus refreshing of our wearied limbs,　　　150
Stiffened with hard achievements in wild desert.

Tap. Sir, there is twelve shillings to pay.

Rafe. Thou, merry Squire Tapstero, thanks to thee
For comforting our souls with double jug:
And if adventurous fortune prick[7] thee forth,
Thou jovial squire, to follow feats of arms,
Take heed thou tender[8] every lady's cause,
Every true knight, and every damsel fair;
But spill the blood of treacherous Saracens,
And false enchanters that with magic spells　　160
Have done to death full many a noble knight.

Host. Thou valiant Knight of the Burning Pestle,
give ear to me; there is twelve shillings to pay, and, as
I am a true knight, I will not bate[9] a penny.

Wife. George, I prithee, tell me, must Rafe pay
twelve shillings now?

Cit. No, Nell, no; nothing but the old knight is
merry with Rafe.

Wife. Oh, is 't nothing else? Rafe will be as merry as
he.　　　　　　　　　　　　　　　　　170

Rafe. Sir knight, this mirth of yours becomes you
well;
But, to requite this liberal courtesy,
If any of your squires will follow arms,
He shall receive from my heroic hand
A knighthood, by the virtue of this Pestle.

Host. Fair knight, I thank you for your noble offer:
Therefore, gentle knight,
Twelve shillings you must pay, or I must cap[10] you.

Wife. Look George, did not I tell thee as much?
The Knight of the Bell is in earnest. Rafe shall not　180
be beholding to him. Give him his money, George, and
let him go snick-up.

Cit. Cap Rafe. No.—Hold your hand, Sir Knight of
the Bell; there's your money.

[*Gives money*].

Have you any thing to say to Rafe now? Cap Rafe!

Wife. I would you should know it, Rafe has friends
that will not suffer him to be capped for ten times so

much, and ten times to the end of that.—Now take thy
course, Rafe.　　　　　　　　　　　　　189

Mist. Come, Michael, thou and I will go home to
thy father; he hath enough left to keep us a day or two,
and we'll set fellows abroad to cry[11] our purse and
casket. Shall we, Michael?

Mich. Ay, I pray, mother; in truth, my feet are full
of chilblains with traveling.

Wife. Faith, and those chilblains are a foul trouble.
Mistress Merrythought, when your youth comes home,
let him rub all the soles of his feet, and the heels and
his ankles with a mouse-skin; or, if none of your people
can catch a mouse, when he goes to bed, let him　200
roll his feet in the warm embers, and I warrant you he
shall be well; and you may make him put his fingers
between his toes and smell to them; it's very sovereign
for his head, if he be costive.[12]

Mist. Master Knight of the Burning Pestle, my son
Michael and I bid you farewell. I thank your worship
heartily for your kindness.

Rafe. Farewell, fair lady, and your tender squire.
If pricking through these deserts I do hear
Of any traitorous knight who through his guile　210
Hath light upon your casket and your purse,
I will despoil him of them and restore them.

Mist. I thank your worship.

Exit with MICHAEL.

Rafe. Dwarf, bear my shield; squire, elevate my
lance.—
And now farewell, you Knight of Holy Bell.

Cit. Ay, ay, Rafe, all is paid.

Rafe. But yet, before I go, speak, worthy knight,
If aught you do of sad adventures know,
Where errant knight may through his prowess win
Eternal fame and free some gentle souls　　220
From endless bonds of steel and lingering pain.

Host. [*To* Tapster] Sirrah, go to Nick the barber, and
bid him prepare himself, as I told you before, quickly.

Tap. I am gone, sir.

Exit Tapster.

Host. Sir knight, this wilderness affordeth none
But the great venture, where full many a knight
Hath tried his prowess and come off with shame,
And where I would not have you lose your life
Against no man, but furious fiend of hell.

Rafe. Speak on, sir knight; tell what he is and
where:　　　　　　　　　　　　　　　230
For here I vow, upon my blazing badge,
Never to blaze[13] a day in quietness,
But bread and water will I only eat,
And the green herb and rock shall be my couch,
Till I have quelled[14] that man, or beast, or fiend,
That works such damage to all errant knights.

Host. Not far from hence, near to a craggy cliff,
At the north end of this distressèd town,

---

[5] *tonight:* last night.
[6] *let . . . alone:* leave it to him.　　　　　　[7] *prick:* goad.
[8] *tender:* treat graciously.　　　　　　　　[9] *bate:* forgo.
[10] *cap:* arrest.　　　　[11] *cry:* raise hue and cry.
[12] *costive:* constipated, slow in action.
[13] *blaze:* allow to shine.　　　　[14] *quelled:* killed.

There doth stand a lowly house,
Ruggedly builded, and in it a cave   240
In which an ugly giant now doth won,[15]
Yclepèd[16] Barbaroso. In his hand
He shakes a naked lance of purest steel,
With sleeves turned up; and him before he wears
A motley[17] garment, to preserve his clothes
From blood of those knights which he massacres
And ladies gent.[18] Without his door doth hang
A copper basin on a prickant[19] spear,[20]
At which no sooner gentle knights can knock
But the shrill sound fierce Barbaroso hears,   250
And, rushing forth, brings in the errant knight
And sets him down in an enchanted chair.
Then with an engine which he hath prepared
With forty teeth, he claws his courtly crown;
Next makes him wink, and underneath his chin
He plants a brazen piece[21] of mighty bord,[22]
And knocks his bullets[23] round about his cheeks,
Whilst with his fingers and an instrument
With which he snaps his hair off he doth fill
The wretch's ears with a most hideous noise.   260
Thus every knight-adventurer he doth trim,
And now no creature dares encounter him.
   Rafe. In God's name, I will fight with him; kind sir,
Go but before me to this dismal cave,
Where this huge giant Barbaroso dwells,
And, by that virtue that brave Rosicleer
That damnèd brood of ugly giants slew,
And Palmerin Frannarco[24] overthrew,
I doubt not but to curb this traitor foul,
And to the devil send his guilty soul.   270
   Host. Brave-sprighted knight, thus far I will perform
This your request; I'll bring you within sight
Of this most loathsome place, inhabited
By a more loathsome man; but dare not stay,
For his main force swoops all he sees away.
   Rafe. Saint George, set on before. March, squire and
    page.
                                            Exeunt.
   Wife. George, dost think Rafe will confound the
giant?
   Cit. I hold my cap to a farthing he does: why, Nell,
I saw him wrestle with the great Dutchman and hurl
him.   281
   Wife. Faith, and that Dutchman was a goodly man,
if all things were answerable to his bigness. And yet
they say there was a Scotchman higher than he, and

that they two and a knight met, and saw one another
for nothing. But of all the sights that ever were in
London, since I was married, methinks the little child
that was so fair grown about the members[25] was the
prettiest, that and the hermaphrodite.   289
   Cit. Nay, by your leave, Nell, Ninivie[26] was better.
   Wife. Ninivie? Oh, that was the story of Joan and
the wall,[27] was it not, George?
   Cit. Yes, lamb.

                Enter MISTRESS MERRYTHOUGHT.

   Wife. Look, George, here comes Mistress Merrythought again, and I would have Rafe come and fight
with the giant. I tell you true, I long to see 't.
   Cit. Good Mistress Merrythought, begone, I pray
you, for my sake. I pray you, forbear a little. You shall
have audience presently; I have a little business.   299
   Wife. Mistress Merrythought, if it please you to
refrain your passion a little, till Rafe have dispatched
the giant out of the way, we shall think ourselves much
bound to you.

                Exit MISTRESS MERRYTHOUGHT.
I thank you, good Mistress Merrythought.

                        Enter a Boy.

   Cit. Boy, come hither. Send away Rafe and this
whoreson giant quickly.
   Boy. In good faith, sir, we cannot. You'll utterly
spoil our play, and make it to be hissed, and it cost
money. You will not suffer us to go on with our plot.—
I pray, gentlemen, rule him.   310
   Cit. Let him come now and dispatch this, and I'll
trouble you no more.
   Boy. Will you give me your hand of that?
   Wife. Give him thy hand, George, do, and I'll kiss
him. I warrant thee, the youth means plainly.
   Boy. I'll send him to you presently.

                            [Wife *kisses the* Boy.]

   Wife. I thank you, little youth.
                                            Exit Boy.
Faith, the child hath a sweet breath, George, but I
think it be troubled with the worms; *carduus bene-
dictus*[28] and mare's milk were the only thing in the
world for 't.   321

   Enter RAFE, Host, [TIM *as*] Squire *and* [GEORGE
                    as] Dwarf.

Oh, Rafe's here, George.—God send thee good luck,
Rafe.
   Host. Puissant knight, yonder his mansion is.
Lo, where the spear and copper basin are.
Behold that string, on which hangs many a tooth,[29]
Drawn from the gentle jaw of wandering knights.
I dare not stay to sound; he will appear.
                                            Exit Host.
   Rafe. Oh, faint not, heart. Susan, my lady dear,
The cobbler's maid in Milk Street,[30] for whose sake
I take these arms, oh, let the thought of thee   331
Carry thy knight through all adventurous deeds;
And, in the honor of thy beauteous self,

---

[15] *won:* dwell.   [16] *yclepèd:* named.
[17] *motley:* variegated, the fool's costume.
[18] *gent:* gentle.
[19] *prickant:* mock-heraldic for "*pricking*" (with pun—
"riding," "sharp."). [20] *copper . . . spear:* barber's sign.
[21] *piece:* bowl.   [22] *bord:* rim.   [23] *bullets:* soap pellets.
[24] *Frannarco:* the giant of the passage Rafe read from
Palmerin de Oliva, I, ll. 223–33.   [25] *members:* legs, genitals.
[26] *Ninivie:* Niniveh, subject of a puppet show.
[27] *Joan . . . wall:* Jonah and the whale.
[28] *L.:* "blessed thistle," a medicinal extract.
[29] *tooth:* Barbers drew teeth.
[30] *Milk Street:* market street where dairy products were
sold.

May I destroy this monster Barbaroso.—
Knock, squire, upon the basin, till it break
With the shrill strokes, or till the giant speak.

[TIM *knocks upon the basin.*]
Enter Barber.

Wife. Oh, George, the giant, the giant.—Now,
Rafe, for thy life.
Barb. What fond unknowing wight is this, that dares
So rudely knock at Barbaroso's cell,   340
Where no man comes but leaves his fleece [31] behind?
Rafe. I, traitorous caitiff, who am sent by fate
To punish all the sad enormities
Thou hast committed against ladies gent
And errant knights. Traitor to God and men,
Prepare thyself. This is the dismal hour
Appointed for thee to give strict account
Of all thy beastly treacherous villainies.
Barb. Foolhardy knight, full soon thou shalt aby [32]
This fond reproach. Thy body will I bang;   350

He takes down his pole.

And, lo, upon that string thy teeth shall hang.
Prepare thyself, for dead soon shalt thou be.

They fight.

Rafe. Saint George for me!
Barb.   Gargantua [33] for me!
Wife. To him, Rafe, to him. Hold up the giant; set
out thy leg before, Rafe!
Cit. Falsify [34] a blow, Rafe, falsify a blow. The giant
lies open on the left side.
Wife. Bear [35] 't off, bear 't off still. There, boy.—
Oh, Rafe's almost down, Rafe's almost down.
Rafe. Susan, inspire me. Now have up again.   360
Wife. Up, up, up, up, up! so, Rafe! down with him,
down with him, Rafe!
Cit. Fetch him o'er the hip, boy!

[RAFE *knocks down the* Barber.]

Wife. There, boy! kill, kill, kill, kill, kill, Rafe.
Cit. No, Rafe; get all out of him first.
Rafe. Presumptuous man, see to what desperate end
Thy treachery hath brought thee. The just gods,
Who never prosper those that do despise them,
For all the villainies which thou hast done
To knights and ladies, now have paid thee home   370
By my stiff arm, a knight adventurous.
But say, vile wretch, before I send thy soul
To sad Avernus, [36] whither it must go,
What captives holdst thou in thy sable cave?
Barb. Go in, and free them all; thou hast the day.
Rafe. Go, squire and dwarf, search in this dreadful
cave,
And free the wretched prisoners from their bonds.

Exeunt [TIM *as*] Squire *and* [GEORGE
as] Dwarf.

Barb. I crave for mercy, as thou art a knight,
And scornest to spill the blood of those that beg.
Rafe. Thou showed'st no mercy, nor shalt thou have
any;   380
Prepare thyself, for thou shalt surely die.

Enter [TIM *as*] Squire *leading one winking, with a
basin* [37] *under his chin.*

Tim. Behold, brave knight, here is one prisoner,
Whom this wild man hath usèd as you see.
Wife. This is the first wise word I heard the squire
speak.
Rafe. Speak what thou art and how thou hast been
used,
That I may give him condign [38] punishment.
1 Kni. I am a knight that took my journey post [39]
Northward from London, and in courteous wise
This giant trained [40] me to his loathsome den,   390
Under pretense of killing of the itch,
And all my body with a powder strewed,
That smarts and stings; and cut away my beard,
And my curlèd locks wherein were ribands [41] tied;
And with a water washed my tender eyes,
(Whilst up and down about me still he skipped,)
Whose virtue is, that, till my eyes be wiped
With a dry cloth, for this my foul disgrace,
I shall not dare to look a dog i' the face.
Wife. Alas, poor knight.—Relieve him, Rafe, relieve
poor knights, whilst you live.   401
Rafe. My trusty squire, convey him to the town,
Where he may find relief.—Adieu, fair knight.

Exit Knight [*with* TIM, *who presently re-enters*].

Enter [GEORGE *as*] Dwarf *leading one with a patch
o'er his nose.* [42]

Geo. Puissant Knight, of the Burning Pestle hight,
See here another wretch, whom this foul beast
Hath scorched [43] and scored in this inhuman wise.
Rafe. Speak me thy name and eke thy place of birth,
And what hath been thy usage in this cave.
2 Kni. I am a knight, Sir Pockhole is my name,
And by my birth I am a Londoner,   410
Free by my copy, [44] but my ancestors
Were Frenchmen [45] all; and riding hard this way
Upon a trotting horse, my bones did ache;
And I, faint knight, to ease my weary limbs,
Light at this cave; when straight this furious fiend,
With sharpest instrument of purest steel,
Did cut the gristle of my nose away,
And in the place this velvet plaster stands.
Relieve me, gentle knight, out of his hands.
Wife. Good Rafe, relieve Sir Pockhole, and send him
away; for in truth his breath stinks.   421
Rafe. Convey him straight after the other knight.—
Sir Pockhole, fare you well.
2 Kni.   Kind sir, good night.

Exit.
Cries within.

---

[31] *fleece:* beard.   [32] *aby:* pay for.
[33] *Gargantua:* Rabelais' giant.   [34] *Falsify:* Feint.
[35] *Bear:* Ward.
[36] *Avernus:* lake near Naples, the classical gate to hell.
[37] *basin:* barber's implement for shaving and bloodletting.
[38] *condign:* fitting.   [39] *post:* posthaste.   [40] *trained:* lured.
[41] *ribands:* ribbons.   [42] *with ... nose:* syphilitic.
[43] *scorched:* cut.   [44] *Free ... copy:* Enrolled as freeman.
[45] *Frenchmen:* i.e., had syphilis, the French disease.

3 Kni. [*Within*] Deliver us.

Woman. [*Within*] Deliver us.

Wife. Hark, George, what a woeful cry there is. I think some woman lies in there.

3 Kni. [*Within*] Deliver us.

Woman. [*Within*] Deliver us.

Rafe. What ghastly noise is this? Speak, Barbaroso, Or, by this blazing steel, thy head goes off.   431

Barb. Prisoners of mine, whom I in diet keep.
Send lower down into the cave,
And in a tub that's heated smoking hot,[46]
There may they find them, and deliver them.

Rafe. Run, squire and dwarf; deliver them with
    speed.

Exeunt Squire [TIM] *and* Dwarf [GEORGE.]

Wife. But will not Rafe kill this giant? Surely I am afeared if he let him go, he will do as much hurt as ever he did.

Cit. Not so, mouse, neither, if he could convert him.   441

Wife. Ay, George, if he could convert him; but a giant is not so soon converted as one of us ordinary people. There's a pretty tale of a witch, that had the devil's mark[47] about her, God bless us, that had a giant to her son, that was called Lob-lie-by-the-Fire; didst never hear it, George?

Enter [TIM *as*] Squire *leading a Man with a glass of lotion in his hand, and* [GEORGE *as*] *the* Dwarf *leading a* Woman *with diet bread and drink.*

Cit. Peace, Nell, here comes the prisoners.

Geo. Here be these pinèd[48] wretches, manful knight, That for this six weeks have not seen a wight.[49]   450

Rafe. Deliver[50] what you are, and how you came
To this sad cave, and what your usage was.

3 Kni. I am an errant[51] knight that followed arms
With spear and shield, and in my tender years
I stricken was with Cupid's fiery shaft,
And fell in love with this, my lady dear,
And stole her from her friends in Turnbull Street,[52]
And bore her up and down from town to town,
Where we did eat and drink, and music hear,
Till at the length at this unhappy town   460
We did arrive, and coming to this cave,
This beast us caught, and put us in a tub,
Where we this two months sweat, and should have done
Another month, if you had not relieved us.

Woman. This bread and water hath our diet been,
Together with a rib cut from a neck
Of burnèd mutton; hard hath been our fare.
Release us from this ugly giant's snare.

3 Kni. This hath been all the food we have received;
But only twice a day, for novelty,   470
He gave a spoonful of this hearty broth
To each of us, through this same slender quill.

---

[46] *tub . . . hot:* cure for syphilis.
[47] *mark:* identifying birthmark set on witches by devil.
[48] *pinèd:* wasted by suffering.   [49] *wight:* man.
[50] *Deliver:* Recount.   [51] *errant:* wandering.
[52] *Turnbull Street:* disreputable street, haunt of prostitutes.
[53] *conductor:* military officer.

Pulls out a syringe.

Rafe. From this infernal monster you shall go,
That useth knights and gentle ladies so.—
Convey them hence.

Exeunt Man *and* Woman.

Cit. Cony, I can tell thee, the gentlemen like Rafe.

Wife. Ay, George, I see it well enough.—Gentlemen, I thank you all heartily for gracing my man Rafe; and I promise you, you shall see him oftener.

Barb. Mercy, great knight. I do recant my ill,   480
And henceforth never gentle blood will spill.

Rafe. I give thee mercy, but yet shalt thou swear
Upon my Burning Pestle, to perform
Thy promise uttered.

Barb. I swear and kiss.

[*Kisses the pestle.*]

Rafe. Depart, then, and amend.—

[*Exit* Barber.]

Come, squire and dwarf; the sun grows towards his set,
And we have many more adventures yet.

Exeunt.

Cit. Now Rafe is in this humor, I know he would ha' beaten all the boys in the house, if they had been set on him.   491

Wife. Ay, George, but it is well as it is: I warrant you, the gentlemen do consider what it is to overthrow a giant. But, look, George; here comes Mistress Merrythought, and her son Michael.—Now you are welcome, Mistress Merrythought. Now Rafe has done, you may go on.

Enter MISTRESS MERRYTHOUGHT *and* MICHAEL.

Mist. Mick, my boy.

Mich. Ay, forsooth, mother.   499

Mist. Be merry, Mick; we are at home now, where, I warrant you, you shall find the house flung out of the windows.

[*Music within.*]

Hark! hey, dogs, hey! this is the old world, i' faith with my husband. If I get in among them, I'll play them such a lesson that they shall have little list to come scraping hither again.— Why, Master Merrythought, husband, Charles Merrythought.

Merry. within. [*Sings*]

If you will sing, and dance, and laugh,
    And hollo and laugh again,
And then cry "There, boy, there," why, then,
    One, two, three, and four,   511
We shall be merry within this hour.

Mist. Why, Charles, do you not know your own natural wife? I say, open the door, and turn me out those mangy companions; 'tis more than time that they were fellow and fellow-like with you. You are a gentleman, Charles, and an old man, and father of two children; and I myself (though I say it) by my mother's side niece to a worshipful gentleman and a conductor;[53] he has been three times in his Majesty's service   520 at Chester, and is now the fourth time, God bless him and his charge, upon his journey.

Merry. [Sings within]

> *Go from my window, love, go;*
> *Go from my window, my dear.*
> *The wind and the rain*
> *Will drive you back again;*
> *You cannot be lodgèd here.*

Hark you, Mistress Merrythought, you that walk upon
adventures and forsake your husband because he sings
with never a penny in his purse. What, shall I   530
think myself the worse? Faith, no, I'll be merry. You
come not here; here's none but lads of mettle, lives of a
hundred years and upwards; care never drunk their
bloods, nor want made them warble "Heigh-ho, my
heart is heavy."

Mist. Why, Master Merrythought, what am I, that
you should laugh me to scorn thus abruptly? Am I not
your fellow-feeler, as we may say in all our miseries?
Your comforter in health and sickness? Have I not
brought you children? Are they not like you,   540
Charles? Look upon thine own image, hard-hearted
man. And yet for all this—

Merry. within. [Sings]

> *Begone, begone, my juggy, my puggy,*
> *Begone, my love, my dear.*
> *The weather is warm,*
> *'Twill do thee no harm;*
> *Thou canst not be lodgèd here.—*

Be merry, boys; some light music, and more wine.

Wife. He's not in earnest, I hope, George, is he?

Cit. What if he be, sweetheart?   550

Wife. Marry, if he be, George, I'll make bold to tell
him he's an ingrant[54] old man to use his bedfellow so
scurvily.

Cit. What, how does he use her, honey?

Wife. Marry, come up, Sir Saucebox, I think you'll
take his part, will you not? Lord, how hot you are
grown. You are a fine man, and you had a fine dog; it
becomes you sweetly.

Cit. Nay, prithee, Nell, chide not; for, as I am an
honest man and a true Christian grocer, I do not like
his doings.   561

Wife. I cry you mercy, then, George. You know we
are all frail and full of infirmities.—D'ee hear, Master
Merrythought? May I crave a word with you?

Merry. within. Strike up lively, lads.

Wife. I had not thought, in truth, Master Merrythought, that a man of your age and discretion, as I
may say, being a gentleman, and therefore known by
your gentle conditions,[55] could have used so little respect to the weakness of his wife. For your wife is   570
your own flesh, the staff of your age, your yokefellow,
with whose help you draw through the mire of this
transitory world; nay, she's your own rib; and again.—

Merry. [Sings within]

> *I come not hither for thee to teach;*
> *I have no pulpit for thee to preach;*
> *I would thou hadst kissed me under the breech,*
> *As thou art a lady gay.*

Wife. Marry, with a vengeance. I am heartily sorry
for the poor gentlewoman, but if I were thy wife, i'
faith, greybeard, i' faith—   580

Cit. I prithee, sweet honeysuckle, be content.

Wife. Give me such words, that am a gentlewoman
born! hang him, hoary rascal! get me some drink,
George; I am almost molten with fretting; now, beshrew his knave's heart for it.

[Exit Citizen.]

Merry. [within] Play me a light lavolta.[56] Come, be
frolic.[57] Fill the good fellows wine.

Mist. Why, Master Merrythought, are you disposed
to make me wait here? You'll open, I hope. I'll fetch
them that shall open else.   590

Merry. [within] Good woman, if you will sing, I'll
give you something; if not—

> *[Sings] You are no love for me, Marg'ret,*
> *I am no love for you.—*

Come aloft, boys, aloft!

Mist. Now a churl's fart in your teeth, sir!—come,
Mick, we'll not trouble him; 'a shall not ding[58] us i' the
teeth with his bread and his broth, that he shall not.
Come, boy, I'll provide for thee, I warrant thee. We'll go
to Master Venturewell's, the merchant. I'll get his   600
letter to mine host of the Bell in Waltham; there I'll
place thee with the tapster. Will not that do well for
thee, Mick? And let me alone for that old cuckoldly
knave your father; I'll use him in his kind, I warrant ye.

[Exeunt.]

Finis Actus tertii.   *Music.*

[Re-enter Citizen with beer.]

Wife. Come, George, where's the beer?

Cit. Here, love.

Wife. This old fornicating fellow will not out of my
mind yet.—Gentlemen, I'll begin to you all, and I
desire more of your acquaintance with all my heart.

[Drinks.]

Fill the gentlemen some beer, George.   610

Boy danceth.

Look, George, the little boy's come again: methinks
he looks something like the Prince of Orange[59] in
his long stocking, if he had a little harness about
his neck. George, I will have him dance Fading.[60]
Fading is a fine jig, I'll assure you, gentlemen.—Begin,
brother. Now 'a capers, sweetheart.—Now a turn o'
the toe, and then tumble.[61] Cannot you tumble, youth?

Boy. No, indeed, forsooth.

Wife. Nor eat fire?

Boy. Neither.   620

Wife. Why, then, I thank you heartily: there's twopence to buy you points[62] withal.

---

54 *ingrant:* ignorant.   55 *conditions:* social rank.
56 *lavolta:* high-stepping dance.   57 *frolic:* merry.
58 *ding:* hit.   59 *Orange:* principality in the Netherlands.
60 *Fading:* Irish dance; sexual orgasm.
61 *tumble:* do acrobatics.   62 *points:* laces for hose.

ACT FOUR

Enter JASPER *and* Boy.

Jas. There, boy, deliver this; but do it well.

[*Gives a letter.*]

Hast thou provided me four lusty fellows,
Able to carry me? And art thou perfect
In all thy business?
    Boy.   Sir, you need not fear;
I have my lesson here and cannot miss it;
The men are ready for you, and what else
Pertains to this employment.
    Jas.   There, my boy;

[*Gives money.*]

Take it, but buy no land.
    Boy.   Faith, sir, 'twere rare
To see so young a purchaser. I fly,
And on my wings carry your destiny.   10
    Jas. Go, and be happy.

                         Exit [Boy].
           Now, my latest hope,
Forsake me not, but fling thy anchor out,
And let it hold. Stand fixed, thou rolling stone,
Till I enjoy my dearest. Hear me all,
You powers that rule in men celestial.

                             Exit.

Wife. Go thy ways; thou art as crooked a sprig
as ever grew in London. I warrant him, he'll come to
some naughty end or other; for his looks say no less.
Besides, his father (you know, George) is none of the
best; you heard him take me up like a flirt-gill,[1]   20
and sing bawdy songs upon me; but, i' faith, if I
live, George—
    Cit. Let me alone, sweetheart. I have a trick in my
head shall lodge him in the Arches[2] for one year, and
make him sing *peccavi*[3] ere I leave him, and yet he
shall never know who hurt him, neither.
    Wife. Do, my good George, do.
    Cit. What shall we have Rafe do now, boy?
    Boy. You shall have what you will, sir.   29
    Cit. Why, so, sir; go and fetch me him, then, and
let the Sophy of Persia come and christen him a child.[4]
    Boy. Believe me, sir, that will not do so well; 'tis
stale; it has been had before at the Red Bull.[5]
    Wife. George, let Rafe travel over great hills, and
let him be very weary, and come to the King of
Cracovia's[6] house, covered with [black][7] velvet; and
there let the King's daughter stand in her window, all

IV.
    [1] *flirt-gill:* coquette.
    [2] *Arches:* London ecclesiastical court and prison.
    [3] *L.:* I have sinned.
    [4] *Sophy . . . child:* scene in *The Travels of the Three
English Brothers,* by Day, Rowley, and Wilkins (1607).
    [5] *Red Bull:* low-class theater in London.
    [6] *Cracovia:* Polish capital.   [7] *black:* not in Q.
    [8] *Dagonet:* fool at King Arthur's court.
    [9] *The . . . London:* by Thomas Heywood.
    [10] *Moldavia:* province in Rumania.   [11] *sad:* serious.
    [12] *Strand:* London business street.   [13] *nipitato:* good ale.
    [14] *powdered:* salted.

---

in beaten gold, combing her golden locks with a comb
of ivory; and let her spy Rafe, and fall in love with
him, and come down to him, and carry him into her
father's house; and then let Rafe talk with her.   41
    Cit. Well said, Nell; it shall be so.—Boy, let's ha't
done quickly.
    Boy. Sir, if you will imagine all this to be done
already, you shall hear them talk together; but we
cannot present a house covered with black velvet and
a lady in beaten gold.
    Cit. Sir Boy, let's ha't as you can, then.
    Boy. Besides, it will show ill-favoredly to have a
grocer's prentice to court a king's daughter.   50
    Cit. Will it so, sir? You are well read in histories!
I pray you, what was Sir Dagonet?[8] was not he
prentice to a grocer in London? Read the play of *The
Four Prentices of London,*[9] where they toss their pikes
so. I pray you fetch him in, sir, fetch him in.
    Boy. It shall be done.—It is not our fault, gentle-
men.

                             Exit.

    Wife. Now we shall see fine doings, I warrant 'ee,
George.

Enter RAFE *and the* Lady [POMPIONA], [TIM *as*]
        Squire *and* [GEORGE *as*] Dwarf.

Oh, here they come. How prettily the King of Cracovia's
daughter is dressed.   61
    Cit. Ay, Nell, it is the fashion of that country, I
warrant 'ee.
    Pomp. Welcome, sir knight, unto my father's court,
King of Moldavia;[10] unto me Pompiona,
His daughter dear. But, sure, you do not like
Your entertainment, that will stay with us
No longer but a night.
    Rafe.   Damsel right fair,
I am on many sad[11] adventures bound,
That call me forth into the wilderness;   70
Besides, my horse's back is something galled,
Which will enforce me ride a sober pace.
But many thanks, fair lady, be to you
For using errant knight with courtesy.
    Pomp. But say, brave knight, what is your name and
        birth?
    Rafe. My name is Rafe; I am an Englishman,
As true as steel, a hearty Englishman,
And prentice to a grocer in the Strand[12]
By deed indent, of which I have one part;
But, fortune calling me to follow arms,   80
On me this holy order I did take
Of Burning Pestle, which in all men's eyes
I bear, confounding ladies' enemies.
    Pomp. Oft have I heard of your brave countrymen,
And fertile soil and store of wholesome food;
My father oft will tell me of a drink
In England found, and nipitato[13] called,
Which driveth all the sorrow from your hearts.
    Rafe. Lady, 'tis true; you need not lay your lips
To better nipitato than there is.   90
    Pomp. And of a wild fowl he will often speak,
Which powdered[14] beef and mustard callèd is;

For there have been great wars 'twixt us and you;
But truly, Rafe, it was not 'long [15] of me.
Tell me then, Rafe, could you contented be
To wear a lady's favor in your shield?
  Rafe. I am a knight of religious order,
And will not wear a favor of a lady
That trusts in Antichrist and false traditions.
  Cit. Well said, Rafe; convert her, if thou canst.   100
  Rafe. Besides, I have a lady of my own
In merry England, for whose virtuous sake
I took these arms; and Susan is her name,
A cobbler's maid in Milk Street, whom I vow
Ne'er to forsake whilst life and Pestle last.
  Pomp. Happy that cobbling dame, whoe'er she be,
That for her own, dear Rafe, hath gotten thee.
Unhappy I, that ne'er shall see the day
To see thee more, that bear'st my heart away.   109
  Rafe. Lady, farewell; I needs must take my leave.
  Pomp. Hard-hearted Rafe, that ladies dost deceive.
  Cit. Hark thee, Rafe, there's money for thee; give
something in the King of Cracovia's house; be not
beholding to him.

[Gives money]

  Rafe. Lady, before I go, I must remember
Your father's officers, who, truth to tell,
Have been about me very diligent.
Hold up thy snowy hand, thou princely maid.
There's twelve-pence for your father's chamberlain;
And another shilling for his cook,   120
For, by my troth, the goose was roasted well;
And twelve-pence for your father's horsekeeper,
For 'nointing my horse-back, and for his butter
There is another shilling; to the maid
That washed my boot-hose, there's an English groat
And twopence to the boy that wiped my boots;
And last, fair lady, there is for yourself
Threepence to buy you pins at Bumbo [16] Fair.
  Pomp. Full many thanks, and I will keep them safe
Till all the heads be off,[17] for thy sake, Rafe.   130
  Rafe. Advance, my squire and dwarf; I cannot stay.
  Pomp. Thou kill'st my heart in parting thus away.
Exeunt.
  Wife. I commend Rafe yet, that he will not stoop to
a Cracovian; there's properer women in London than
any are there, i-wis. But here comes Master Humphrey
and his love again now, George.
  Cit. Ay, cony; peace.

Enter Merchant [VENTUREWELL], HUMPHREY,
LUCE, and a Boy.

  Vent. Go, get you up. I will not be entreated.
And, gossip mine, I'll keep you sure hereafter   139
From gadding out again with boys and unthrifts.[18]
Come, they are women's tears; I know your fashion.—
Go, sirrah, lock her in, and keep the key
Safe as you love your life.
Exeunt LUCE and Boy.
Now, my son Humphrey,
You may both rest assurèd of my love
In this, and reap your own desire.

  Hump. I see this love you speak of, through your
    daughter,
Although the hole be little; and hereafter
Will yield the like in all I may or can,
Fitting a Christian and a gentleman.
  Vent. I do believe you, my good son, and thank you;
For 'twere an impudence to think you flattered.   151
  Hump. It were, indeed; but shall I tell you why?
I have been beaten twice about the lie.
  Vent. Well, son, no more of compliment. My
    daughter
Is yours again. Appoint the time and take her;
We'll have no stealing for it. I myself
And some few of our friends will see you married.
  Hump. I would you would, i' faith, for be it known,
I ever was afraid to lie alone.
  Vent. Some three days hence, then.
  Hump.   Three days; let
    me see;   160
'Tis somewhat of the most; yet I agree,
Because I mean against the appointed day
To visit all my friends in new array.

Enter Servant.

  Serv. Sir, there's a gentlewoman without would
speak with your worship.
  Vent. What is she?
  Serv. Sir, I asked her not.
  Vent. Bid her come in.

[Exit Servant.]

Enter MISTRESS MERRYTHOUGHT and MICHAEL.

  Mist. Peace be to your worship. I come as a poor
suitor to you, sir, in the behalf of this child.   170
  Vent. Are you not wife to Merrythought?
  Mist. Yes, truly. Would I had ne'er seen his eyes.
He has undone me and himself and his children,
and there he lives at home, and sings and hoits and
revels among his drunken companions; but, I warrant
you, where to get a penny to put bread in his mouth he
knows not: and therefore, if it like your worship, I
would entreat your letter to the honest host of the Bell
in Waltham, that I may place my child under the
protection of his tapster in some settled course of life.
  Vent. I'm glad the heavens have heard my prayers.
    Thy husband,   181
When I was ripe in sorrows, laughed at me;
Thy son, like an unthankful wretch, I having
Redeemed him from his fall, and made him mine,
To show his love again, first stole my daughter,
Then wronged this gentleman, and, last of all,
Gave me that grief had almost brought me down
Unto my grave, had not a stronger hand
Relieved my sorrows. Go, and weep as I did,
And be unpitied; for I here profess   190
An everlasting hate to all thy name.
  Mist. Will you so, sir? How say you by that?—

---

15 *'long:* because.
16 *Bumbo:* drink of rum, sugar, water, and nutmeg.
17 *heads . . . off:* faces are worn off.
18 *unthrifts:* shiftless lads.

Come, Mick; let him keep his wind to cool his porridge.
We'll go to thy nurse's, Mick; she knits silk stockings,
boy; and we'll knit too, boy, and be beholding to none
of them all.

Exeunt MICHAEL *and* Mother.

Enter a Boy *with a letter.*

Boy. Sir, I take it you are the master of this house.
Vent. How then, boy?
Boy.   Then to yourself, sir, comes
this letter.
Vent. From whom, my pretty boy?
Boy. From him that was your servant; but no more
Shall that name ever be, for he is dead.   201
Grief of your purchased[19] anger broke his heart.
I saw him die, and from his hand received
This paper, with a charge to bring it hither;
Read it, and satisfy yourself in all.

LETTER.

Vent. [*Reads*] "Sir, that I have wronged your love I
must confess, in which I have purchased to myself, besides mine own undoing, the ill opinion of my friends.
Let not your anger, good sir, outlive me, but suffer me
to rest in peace with your forgiveness; let my   210
body (if a dying man may so much prevail with you) be
brought to your daughter, that she may truly know my
hot flames are now buried, and withal receive a testimony of the zeal I bore her virtue. Farewell for ever,
and be ever happy.

JASPER."

God's hand is great in this: I do forgive him;
Yet I am glad he's quiet, where I hope
He will not bite again.—Boy, bring the body,
And let him have his will, if that be all.   220
Boy. 'Tis here without, sir.
Vent.   So, sir; if you please,
You may conduct it in; I do not fear it.
Hump. I'll be your usher, boy; for, though I say it,
He owed me something once, and well did pay it.
Exeunt.

Enter LUCE *alone.*

Luce. If there be any punishment inflicted
Upon the miserable, more than yet I feel,
Let it together seize me, and at once
Press down my soul. I cannot bear the pain
Of these delaying tortures. Thou that art
The end of all and the sweet rest of all,   230
Come, come, O death; bring me to thy peace,
And blot out all the memory I nourish
Both of my father and my cruel friend.
Oh, wretched maid, still living to be wretched,
To be a say[20] to fortune in her changes,
And grow to number times and woes together!
How happy had I been, if, being born,
My grave had been my cradle.

Enter Servant.

Serv.   By your leave,
Young mistress, here's a boy hath brought a coffin:
What 'a would say, I know not, but your father   240
Charged me to give you notice. Here they come.
[*Exit.*]

Enter [Boy *and*] *two bearing a coffin,* JASPER *in it.*

Luce. For me I hope 'tis come, and 'tis most
welcome.
Boy. Fair mistress, let me not add greater grief
To that great store you have already. Jasper,
That whilst he lived was yours, now dead
And here enclosed, commanded me to bring
His body hither, and to crave a tear
From those fair eyes, though he deserved not pity,
To deck his funeral, for so he bid me
Tell her for whom he died.
Luce.   He shall have many.—
Good friends, depart a little, whilst I take   251
My leave of this dead man, that once I loved.—
Exeunt Coffin-Carrier[s] *and* Boy.
Hold yet a little, life, and then I give thee
To thy first heavenly being. O, my friend,
Hast thou deceived me thus, and got before me?
I shall not long be after. But, believe me,
Thou wert too cruel, Jasper, 'gainst thyself,
In punishing the fault I could have pardoned,
With so untimely death; thou didst not wrong me,
But ever wert most kind, most true, most loving;   260
And I the most unkind, most false, most cruel!
Didst thou but ask a tear? I'll give thee all,
Even all my eyes can pour down, all my sighs,
And all myself, before thou goest from me.
These[21] are but sparing[22] rites; but if thy soul
Be yet about this place, and can behold
And see what I prepare to deck thee with,
It shall go up, borne on the wings of peace,
And satisfied. First will I sing thy dirge,
Then kiss thy pale lips, and then die myself,   270
And fill one coffin and one grave together.

SONG.

Come, you whose loves are dead,
And, whiles I sing,
Weep, and wring
Every hand, and every head
Bind with cypress and sad yew,
Ribands black and candles blue
For him that was of men most true.

Come with heavy moaning,[23]
And on his grave   280
Let him have
Sacrifice of sighs and groaning;
Let him have fair flowers enow,
White and purple, green and yellow,
For him that was of men most true.

Thou sable cloth, sad cover of my joys,

---

[19] *purchased:* incited.
[20] *say:* test.
[22] *sparing:* mean, stingy.
[21] *These:* Q "There."
[23] *moaning:* Q "mourning."

I lift thee up, and thus I meet with death.

[*Removes the cloth, and* JASPER *rises out of the coffin.*]

Jas. And thus you meet the living.
Luce.   Save me, heaven!
Jas. Nay, do not fly me, fair; I am no spirit:
Look better on me; do you know me yet?   290
  Luce. O thou dear shadow of my friend.
  Jas.   Dear
    substance,
I swear I am no shadow; feel my hand;
It is the same it was. I am your Jasper,
Your Jasper that's yet living, and yet loving.
Pardon my rash attempt, my foolish proof
I put in practice of your constancy;
For sooner should my sword have drunk my blood,
And set my soul at liberty, than drawn
The least drop from that body: for which boldness
Doom me to anything; if death, I take it,   300
And willingly.
  Luce.   This death I'll give you for it;
                                          [*Kisses him.*]
So; now I am satisfied: you are no spirit,
But my own truest, truest, truest friend,
Why do you come thus to me?
  Jas.   First, to see you;
Then to convey you hence.
  Luce.   It cannot be;
For I am locked up here, and watched at all hours,
That 'tis impossible for me to 'scape.
  Jas. Nothing more possible. Within this coffin
Do you convey yourself. Let me alone;
I have the wits of twenty men about me;   310
Only I crave the shelter of your closet
A little, and then fear me not.²⁴ Creep in,
That they may presently convey you hence.
Fear nothing, dearest love; I'll be your second.

[LUCE *lies down in the coffin, and* JASPER *covers her
                                  with the cloth.*]

Lie close. So; all goes well yet.—Boy.

[*Enter* Coffin-Carriers *and* Boy.]

Boy.   At hand, sir.
Jas. Convey away the coffin, and be wary.
Boy. 'Tis done already.
Jas.   Now must I go conjure.
                                          Exit.

Enter Merchant [VENTUREWELL].

Vent. Boy, boy.
Boy. Your servant, sir.   319
Vent. Do me this kindness, boy (hold, here's a
crown): before thou bury the body of this fellow, carry
it to his old merry father and salute him from me and
bid him sing; he hath cause.
  Boy. I will, sir.
Vent. And then bring me word what tune he is in,
and have another crown; but do it truly. I have fitted
him a bargain now will vex him.
  Boy. God bless your worship's health, sir.

Vent. Farewell, boy.   329
        Exeunt [VENTUREWELL, Boy, *and the*
                    Coffin-Carriers *with the coffin*].

Enter MASTER MERRYTHOUGHT.

Wife. Ah, old Merrythought, art thou there again?
Let's hear some of thy songs.
  Merry. [*Sings*]

        Who can sing a merrier note
        Than he that cannot change a groat?

Not a denier²⁵ left, and yet my heart leaps. I do
wonder yet, as old as I am, that any man will follow a
trade, or serve, that may sing and laugh and walk the
streets. My wife and both my sons are I know not
where; I have nothing left, nor know I how to come
by meat to supper; yet am I merry still, for I know
I shall find it upon the table at six o'clock. Therefore,
hang thought.   341

[*Sings*] *I would not be a serving-man*
        To carry the cloak-bag still,
        Nor would I be a falconer
        The greedy hawks to fill;
        But I would be in a good house,
        And have a good master too;
        But I would eat and drink of the best,
        And no work would I do.

This is it that keeps life and soul together, mirth; this
is the philosopher's stone that they write so much on,
that keeps a man ever young.   352

Enter a Boy.

Boy. Sir, they say they know all your money is gone,
and they will trust you for no more drink.
  Merry. Will they not? Let 'em choose. The best is,
I have mirth at home, and need not send abroad for
that; let them keep their drink to themselves.
[*Sings*]
        For Jillian of Berry, she dwells on a hill,
        And she hath good beer and ale to sell,
        And of good fellows she thinks no ill;   360
        And thither will we go now, now, now, now,
        And thither will we go now.

        And when you have made a little stay,
        You need not ask what is to pay.
        But kiss your hostess, and go your way;
        And thither will we go now, now, now, now,
        And thither will we go now.

Enter another Boy.

2 Boy. Sir, I can get no bread for supper.
  Merry. Hang bread and supper. Let's preserve our
mirth, and we shall never feel hunger, I'll warrant you.
Let's have a catch,²⁶ boy; follow me, come.   371

------

²⁴ *fear . . . not:* have no fear for me.
²⁵ *denier:* French coin of minimal value.
²⁶ *catch:* round. The following stage direction was printed
in roman in Q1 at the end of the text line and may have been
intended as part of the text.

Sing this catch
    Ho, ho, nobody at home!
    Meat, nor drink, nor money ha' we none.
    Fill the pot, Eedy,
    Never more need I.

Merry. So, boys; enough; follow me. Let's change our place, and we shall laugh afresh.

                                    Exeunt.

Finis Act. 4.

Wife. Let him go, George; 'a shall not have any countenance from us, nor a good word from any i' the company, if I may strike stroke in't.[27]   380

Cit. No more 'a sha' not, love. But, Nell, I will have Rafe do a very notable matter now, to the eternal honor and glory of all grocers.—Sirrah, you there, boy. Can none of you hear?

                  [*Enter* Boy.]

Boy. Sir, your pleasure?

Cit. Let Rafe come out on May-day in the morning and speak upon a conduit[28] with all his scarfs about him, and his feathers, and his rings, and his knacks.

Boy. Why, sir, you do not think of our plot; what will become of that, then?   390

Cit. Why, sir, I care not what become on't. I'll have him come out, or I'll fetch him out myself. I'll have something done in honor of the city. Besides, he hath been long enough upon adventures. Bring him out quickly, or, if I come in amongst you—

Boy. Well, sir, he shall come out; but if our play miscarry, sir, you are like to pay for't.

Cit. Bring him away, then.

                            Exit Boy.

Wife. This will be brave, i' faith. George, shall not he dance the morris[29] too, for the credit of the Strand?

Cit. No, sweetheart, it will be too much for the boy. Oh, there he is, Nell. He's reasonable well in reparel: but he has not rings enough.   403

    Enter RAFE [*dressed as a May-lord*].

Rafe. London, to thee I do present the merry month of May.
Let each true subject be content to hear me what I say:

---

[27] *may . . . in't:* have anything to do with it.
[28] *conduit:* public water supply station, a fountain or hydrant.
[29] *morris:* festive dance of moorish origin, in which bells are worn and a wicker hobbyhorse is employed.
[30] *birchen . . . cry:* because switches are made of birch.
[31] *feateously:* nimbly.   [32] *phlebotomy:* bloodletting.
[33] *cast . . . bellies:* spawn.
[34] *mute:* snails could "speak" on May Day, making predictions about love affairs; they spelled out lovers' initials in hearth ashes.   [35] *rascal:* young lean dear.
[36] *pricket:* buck in second year.
[37] *velvet heads:* deer with new horns, alluding to the cuckold-horns and the velvet caps of citizens.
[38] *Hogsdon:* district north of London popular for recreation.   [39] *Newington:* suburb south of London.
[40] *thrumming:* affixing tufts or thrums of wool.

For from the top of conduit-head, as plainly may
    appear,
I will both tell my name to you, and wherefore I came
    here.
My name is Rafe, by due descent, though not ignoble I,
Yet far inferior to the flock of gracious grocery;
And by the common counsel of my fellows in the
    Strand,   410
With gilded staff and crossèd scarf, the May-lord here I
    stand.
Rejoice, o English hearts, rejoice; rejoice, o lovers
    dear;
Rejoice, o city, town, and country; rejoice, eke every
    shire.
For now the fragrant flowers do spring and sprout in
    seemly sort;
The little birds do sit and sing, the lambs do make fine
    sport;
And now the birchen-tree doth bud, that makes the
    schoolboy cry;[30]
The morris rings, while hobby-horse doth foot it
    feateously;[31]
The lords and ladies now abroad, for their disport and
    play,
Do kiss sometimes upon the grass, and sometimes in
    the hay.
Now butter with a leaf of sage is good to purge the
    blood.   420
Fly Venus and phlebotomy,[32] for they are neither good.
Now little fish on tender stone begin to cast their
    bellies,[33]
And sluggish snails, that erst were mute,[34] do creep out
    of their shellies;
The rumbling rivers now do warm, for little boys to
    paddle;
The sturdy steed now goes to grass, and up they hang
    his saddle;
The heavy hart, the bellowing buck, the rascal,[35] and
    the pricket,[36]
Are now among the yeoman's peas, and leave the
    fearful thicket.
And be like them, o you, I say, of this same noble
    town,
And lift aloft your velvet heads,[37] and slipping off your
    gown,
With bells on legs, and napkins clean unto your
    shoulders tied,   430
With scarfs and garters as you please, and "Hey for our
    town" cried,
March out, and show your willing minds, by twenty
    and by twenty,
To Hogsdon[38] or to Newington,[39] where ale and cakes
    are plenty.
And let it ne'er be said for shame, that we the youths of
    London
Lay thrumming[40] of our caps at home, and left our
    custom undone.
Up, then, I say, both young and old, both man and
    maid a-maying,
With drums, and guns that bounce aloud, and merry
    tabor playing.

Which to prolong, God save our King, and send his
     country peace,
And root out treason from the land; and so, my friends,
     I cease.

                         [Exit.]

ACT FIVE

Enter Merchant [VENTUREWELL], *solus*

Vent. I will have no great store of company at the
wedding, a couple of neighbors and their wives, and
we will have a capon in stewed broth, with marrow,
and a good piece of beef stuck with rosemary.

Enter JASPER, *his face mealed.*[1]

Jas. Forbear thy pains, fond man; it is too late.
Vent. Heaven bless me! Jasper?
Jas.   Ay, I am his ghost,
Whom thou hast injured for his constant love.
Fond worldly wretch, who dost not understand
In death that true hearts cannot parted be.
First know, thy daughter is quite borne away   10
On wings of angels, through the liquid air,
To far out of thy reach, and nevermore
Shalt thou behold her face; but she and I
Will in another world enjoy our loves,
Where neither father's anger, poverty,
Nor any cross that troubles earthly men,
Shall make us sever our united hearts.
And never shalt thou sit or be alone
In any place, but I will visit thee
With ghastly looks, and put into thy mind   20
The great offenses which thou didst to me.
When thou art at thy table with thy friends,
Merry in heart, and filled with swelling[2] wine,
I'll come in midst of all thy pride and mirth,
Invisible to all men but thyself,
And whisper such a sad tale in thine ear
Shall make thee let the cup fall from thy hand,
And stand as mute and pale as death itself.
Vent. Forgive me, Jasper. Oh, what might I do,
Tell me, to satisfy thy troubled ghost?   30
Jas. There is no means; too late thou think'st on this.
Vent. But tell me what were best for me to do?
Jas. Repent thy deed, and satisfy my father,
And beat fond Humphrey out of thy doors.

                    Exit JASPER.

Enter HUMPHREY.

Wife. Look, George; his very ghost would have folks
beaten.
Hump. Father, my bride is gone, fair Mistress Luce.
My soul's the fount of vengeance, mischief's sluice.
Vent. Hence, fool, out of my sight with thy fond
     passion.[3]
Thou hast undone me.

                    [Beats him.]

Hump.   Hold, my father dear,   40
For Luce thy daughter's sake, that had no peer.
Vent. Thy father, fool? There's some blows more;
     begone.—

                    [Beats him.]

Jasper, I hope thy ghost be well appeased
To see thy will performed. Now will I go
To satisfy thy father for thy wrongs.

                         Exit.

Hump. What shall I do? I have been beaten twice,
And Mistress Luce is gone. Help me, device!
Since my true love is gone, I never more,
Whilst I do live, upon the sky will pore;
But in the dark will wear out my shoe-soles   50
In passion in Saint Faith's church under Paul's.[4]

                         Exit.

Wife. George, call Rafe hither; if you love me, call
Rafe hither: I have the bravest thing for him to do,
George; prithee, call him quickly.
Cit. Rafe, why, Rafe, boy!

Enter RAFE.

Rafe. Here, sir.
Cit. Come hither, Rafe; come to thy mistress, boy.
Wife. Rafe, I would have thee call all the youths
together in battle-ray, with drums, and guns, and flags,
and march to Mile End in pompous fashion, and   60
there exhort your soldiers to be merry and wise, and to
keep their beards from burning, Rafe; and then skirmish, and let your flags fly, and cry, "Kill, kill, kill!"
My husband shall lend you his jerkin, Rafe, and there's
a scarf; for the rest, the house shall furnish you, and
we'll pay for't. Do it bravely, Rafe; and think before
whom you perform, and what person you represent.
Rafe. I warrant you, mistress; if I do it not, for the
honor of the city and the credit of my master, let me
never hope for freedom.[5]   70
Wife. 'Tis well spoken, i' faith. Go thy ways; thou
art a spark[6] indeed.
Cit. Rafe, Rafe, double your files[7] bravely, Rafe.
Rafe. I warrant you, sir.

                     Exit RAFE.

Cit. Let him look narrowly to his service; I shall
take him else. I was there myself a pikeman once, in the
hottest of the day, wench; had my feather shot sheer
away, the fringe of my pike burnt off with powder, my
pate broken with a scouring-stick,[8] and yet, I thank
God, I am here.   80

                    Drum within.

Wife. Hark, George, the drums.
Cit. Ran, tan, tan, tan; ran, tan. O wench, an thou
hadst but seen little Ned of Aldgate,[9] Drum-Ned, how
he made it roar again, and laid on like a tyrant, and then
struck softly till the ward came up, and then thundered

V.

   [1] *mealed:* floured.
   [2] *swelling:* provocative of arrogance.
   [3] *fond passion:* foolish grief.
   [4] *Saint . . . Paul's:* a church in the crypt of old St. Paul's
Cathedral under the choir.
   [5] *freedom:* freeman's rank in the grocers' guild.
   [6] *spark:* fine young man, with deprecatory implication of
which Wife seems unaware.
   [7] *double . . . files:* march your men two by two.
   [8] *scouring stick:* cleaning rod for guns.
   [9] *Aldgate:* gate in old walls of London and adjoining
district.

again, and together we go. "Sa, sa, sa, bounce," quoth the guns; "Courage, my hearts," quoth the captains; "Saint George," quoth the pikemen; and withal, here they lay, and there they lay; and yet for all this I am here, wench. 90

Wife. Be thankful for it, George; for indeed 'tis wonderful.

Enter Rafe *and his Company, with drums and colors.*

Rafe. March fair, my hearts. Lieutenant, beat the rear up.—Ancient,[10] let your colors fly; but have a great care of the butchers' hooks at Whitechapel;[11] they have been the death of many a fair ancient.—Open your files that I may take a view both of your persons and munition.—Sergeant, call a muster.

Ser. A stand![12]—William Hammerton, pewterer!

Ham. Here, captain! 100

Rafe. A corselet and a Spanish pike; 'tis well; can you shake it with a terror?

Ham. I hope so, captain.

Rafe. Charge upon me.

[*He charges on* Rafe.]

'Tis with the weakest: put more strength, William Hammerton, more strength. As you were again.—Proceed seargeant.

Ser. George Greengoose, poulterer!

Gre. Here.

Rafe. Let me see your piece, neighbor Greengoose. When was she shot in?[13] 111

Gre. An like you, master captain, I made a shot even now, partly to scour her, and partly for audacity.

Rafe. It should seem so certainly, for her breath is yet inflamed; besides, there is a main fault in the touchhole; it runs and stinketh; and I tell you, moreover, and believe it, ten such touchholes would breed the pox in the army. Get you a feather, neighbor, get you a feather, sweet oil, and paper, and your piece may do well enough yet. Where's your powder? 120

Gre. Here.

Rafe. What, in a paper? As I am a soldier and a gentleman, it craves a martial court. You ought to die for't. Where's your horn[14]? Answer me to that.

Gre. An't like you, sir, I was oblivious.

Rafe. It likes me not you should be so; 'tis a shame for you, and a scandal to all our neighbors, being a man of worth and estimation, to leave your horn behind you; I am afraid 'twill breed example. But let me tell you no more on't.—Stand, till I view you all.—What's become o' the nose of your flask? 131

1 Sol. Indeed, la, captain, 'twas blown away with powder.

Rafe. Put on a new one at the city's charge.—Where's the stone[15] of this piece?

2 Sol. The drummer took it out to light tobacco.

Rafe. 'Tis a fault, my friend; put it in again.—You want a nose,—and you a stone.—Sergeant, take a note on't, for I mean to stop it in the pay.—Remove, and march. 140

[*They march.*]

Soft and fair, gentlemen, soft and fair! double your files! as you were! faces about! Now, you with the sodden face, keep in there. Look to your match,[16] sirrah, it will be in your fellow's flask anon. So; make a crescent now; advance your pikes; stand and give ear.—Gentlemen, countrymen, friends, and my fellow-soldiers, I have brought you this day, from the shops of security and the counters of content, to measure out in these furious fields honor by the ell,[17] and prowess by the pound. Let it not, oh, let it 150 not, I say, be told hereafter, the noble issue of this city fainted, but bear yourselves in this fair action like men, valiant men, and free men. Fear not the face of the enemy, nor the noise of the guns, for, believe me, brethren, the rude rumbling of a brewer's car is far more terrible, of which you have a daily experience; neither let the stink of powder offend you, since a more valiant stink is nightly with you. To a resolved mind his home is everywhere: I speak not this to take away the hope of your return; for you shall see, I do not 160 doubt it, and that very shortly, your loving wives again and your sweet children, whose care doth bear you company in baskets.[18] Remember, then, whose cause you have in hand, and, like a sort[19] of true-born scavengers, scour me this famous realm of enemies. I have no more to say but this: stand to[20] your tacklings,[21] lads, and show to the world you can as well brandish a sword as shake an apron. Saint George, and on, my hearts! 169

Omnes. Saint George, Saint George!

Exeunt.

Wife. 'Twas well done, Rafe! I'll send thee a cold capon a-field and a bottle of March beer[22] and, it may be, come myself to see thee.

Cit. Nell, the boy hath deceived me much; I did not think it had been in him. He has performed such a matter, wench, that, if I live, next year I'll have him captain of the galley-foist,[23] or I'll want my will.[24]

Enter old Merrythought.

Merry. Yet, I thank God, I break not a wrinkle more than I had. Not a stoup,[25] boys? Care, live with cats; I defy thee. My heart is as sound as an oak; and though I want drink to wet my whistle, I can sing; 181 [*Sings.*]
Come no more there, boys, come no more there;
For we shall never whilst we live come any more there.

Enter a Boy [*and* Coffin-Carriers] *with a Coffin.*

Boy. God save you, sir.

Merry. It's a brave boy. Canst thou sing?

---

[10] *Ancient:* Ensign-bearer.
[11] *Whitechapel:* London road with a number of butcher's shops. [12] *A stand:* halt. [13] *in:* i.e., with.
[14] *horn:* powderhorn. [15] *stone:* flint.
[16] *match:* wick for igniting gunpowder.
[17] *ell:* 45-inch measure.
[18] *baskets:* i.e., box lunches. [19] *sort:* group.
[20] *stand to:* stick to. [21] *tacklings:* weapons.
[22] *March beer:* strong first brew.
[23] *galley-foist:* barge used in Lord Mayor's Day celebrations. [24] *want . . . will:* be disappointed.
[25] *stoup:* tankard.

Boy. Yes, sir, I can sing, but 'tis not so necessary at this time.

Merry. [*Sings*]

> Sing we, and chant it,
> Whilst love doth grant it.

Boy. Sir, sir, if you knew what I have brought you, you would have little list to sing.   191

Merry. [*Sings*]

> Oh, the minion[26] round,
> Full long I have thee sought,
> And now I have thee found,
> And what hast thou here brought?

Boy. A coffin, sir, and your dead son Jasper in it.
                    [*Exeunt* Boy *and* Coffin-Carriers.]

Merry. Dead?

[*Sings*]   Why, farewell he!
> Thou wast a bonny boy,
> And I did love thee.   200

Enter JASPER.

Jas. Then, I pray you, sir, do so still.

Merry. Jasper's ghost?

[*Sings*]
Thou art welcome from Stygian lake[27] so soon;
Declare to me what wondrous things in Pluto's court are done.

Jas. By my troth, sir, I ne'er came there; 'tis too hot for me, sir.

Merry. A merry ghost, a very merry ghost.

[*Sings*]
> And where is your true love? Oh, where is yours?

Jas. Marry, look you, sir.

Heaves up the coffin. [LUCE *steps out.*]

Merry. Ah, ha! art thou good at that, i' faith?   210

[*Sings*]   With hey, trixy, terlery-whiskin,
> The world it runs on wheels:
> When the young man's ——
> Up goes the maiden's heels.

MISTRESS MERRYTHOUGHT *and* MICHAEL
within.

Mist. [*Within*] What, Master Merrythought, will you not let's in? what do you think shall become of us?

Merry. [*Sings*]

> What voice is that that calleth at our door?

Mist. [*Within*] You know me well enough; I am sure I have not been such a stranger to you.

Merry. [*Sings*]

> And some they whistled, and some they sung,   220
> Hey, down, down!
> And some did loudly say,
> Ever as the Lord Barnet's horn blew,
> "Away, Musgrave, away!"

Mist. [*Within*] You will not have us starve here, will you, Master Merrythought?

Jas. Nay, good sir, be persuaded; she is my mother;
If her offenses have been great against you,
Let your own love remember she is yours,
And so forgive her.

Luce.   Good Master Merrythought,   230
Let me entreat you; I will not be denied.

Mist. [*Within*] Why, Master Merrythought, will you be a vexed thing still?

Merry. Woman, I take you to my love again, but you shall sing before you enter; therefore dispatch your song and so come in.

Mist. [*Within*] Well, you must have your will, when all's done.—Mick, what song canst thou sing, boy?

Mich. [*Within*] I can sing none, forsooth, but "A Lady's Daughter, of Paris properly,"   240

Mist. Song.

> It was a lady's daughter, etc.

[MERRYTHOUGHT *admits* MISTRESS
MERRYTHOUGHT *and* MICHAEL.]

Merry. Come, you're welcome home again.

[*Sings*]   If such danger be in playing,
> And jest must to earnest turn,
> You shall go no more a-maying—

Vent. within. Are you within, sir? Master Merrythought!

Jas. It is my master's voice; good sir, go hold him
In talk, whilst we convey ourselves into
Some inward room.   250
                    [*Exit with* LUCE.]

Merry. What are you? Are you merry?
You must be very merry, if you enter.

Vent. [*Within*] I am, sir.

Merry. Sing, then.

Vent. [*Within*] Nay, good sir, open to me.

Merry.   Sing, I say,
Or, by the merry heart, you come not in.

Vent. [*Within*] Well, sir, I'll sing.

[*Sings*]   Fortune my foe, etc.

[MERRYTHOUGHT *admits* VENTUREWELL.]

Merry. You are welcome, sir, you are welcome: you see your entertainment; pray you, be merry.   260

Vent. O Master Merrythought, I am come to ask you
Forgiveness for the wrongs I offered you
And your most virtuous son. They're infinite;
Yet my contrition shall be more than they.
I do confess my hardness broke his heart,
For which just heaven hath given me punishment
More than my age can carry; his wandering spirit,
Not yet at rest, pursues me everywhere,
Crying, "I'll haunt thee for thy cruelty."
My daughter, she is gone, I know not how,   270
Taken invisible, and whether living

---

26 *minion:* sweetheart; mimon Q.
27 *Stygian lake:* the River Styx in classical Underworld.

Or in grave, 'tis yet uncertain to me.
O Master Merrythought, these are the weights
Will sink me to my grave; forgive me, sir.

Merry. Why, sir, I do forgive you; and be merry:
And if the wag in's lifetime played the knave,
Can you forgive him too?

Vent.   With all my heart, sir.

Merry. Speak it again, and heartily.

Vent.   I do, sir;
Now, by my soul, I do.

Enter LUCE *and* JASPER.

Merry. [*Sings*]

> With that came out his paramour;   280
> She was as white as the lily flower.
> Hey, troll, trolly, lolly!
> With that came out her own dear knight;
> He was as true as ever did fight, etc.

Sir, if you will forgive 'em, clap their hands together;
there's no more to be said i' the matter.

Vent. I do, I do.

Cit. I do not like this. Peace, boys! hear me, one of
you: everybody's part is come to an end but Rafe's,
and he's left out.   290

Boy. 'Tis 'long of yourself, sir; we have nothing to
do with his part.

Cit. Rafe, come away!—make on him, as you have
done of the rest, boys; come.

Wife. Now, good husband, let him come out and die.

Cit. He shall, Nell.—Rafe, come away quickly, and
die, boy.

Boy. 'Twill be very unfit he should die, sir, upon no
occasion—and in a comedy, too.   299

Cit. Take you no care of that, sir boy; is not his
part at an end, think you, when he's dead?—Come
away, Rafe!

Enter RAFE, *with a forked* [28] *arrow through
his head.*

Rafe. When I was mortal, [29] this my costive corpse
Did lap up figs and raisins in the Strand,
Where sitting, I espied a lovely dame,
Whose master wrought with lingel [30] and with awl,
And underground he vampied [31] many a boot.
Straight did her love prick forth me, tender sprig,
To follow feats of arms in warlike wise
Through Waltham Desert, where I did perform   310
Many achievements, and did lay on ground
Huge Barbaroso, that insulting giant,
And all his captives soon set at liberty.
Then honor pricked me from my native soil

Into Moldavia, where I gained the love
Of Pompiona, his belovèd daughter,
But yet proved constant to the black-thumbed maid
Susan, and scornèd Pompiona's love.
Yet liberal I was, and gave her pins,
And money for her father's officers.   320
I then returnèd home, and thrust myself
In action, and by all men chosen was
Lord of the May, where I did flourish it,
With scarfs and rings, and posy in my hand.
After this action I preferrèd was,
And chosen city captain at Mile End,
With hat and feather, and with leading-staff,
And trained my men, and brought them all off clear,
Save one man that berayed him with the noise.
But all these things I, Rafe, did undertake   330
Only for my belovèd Susan's sake.
Then coming home, and sitting in my shop
With apron blue, death came into my stall
To cheapen [32] aqua vitae; [33] but ere I
Could take the bottle down and fill a taste,
Death caught a pound of pepper in his hand,
And sprinkled all my face and body o'er,
And in an instant vanishèd away.

Cit. 'Tis a pretty fiction, i' faith.

Rafe. Then took I up my bow and shaft in hand,
And walked into Moorfields [34] to cool myself: 341
But there grim cruel death met me again,
And shot this forkèd arrow through my head,
And now I faint. Therefore be warned by me,
My fellows every one, of forkèd heads. [35]
Farewell, all you good boys in merry London!
Ne'er shall we more upon Shrove Tuesday [36] meet,
And pluck down houses of iniquity;—
My pain increaseth;—I shall never more
Hold open, whilst another pumps, both legs,   350
Nor daub a satin gown with rotten eggs;
Set up a stake, Oh, nevermore I shall.
I die; fly, fly, my soul, to Grocers' Hall.
Oh, Oh, Oh, etc.

                                          [*Dies.*]

Wife. Well said, Rafe; do your obeisance to the
gentlemen, and go your ways: well said, Rafe.

                                    Exit RAFE.

Merry. Methinks all we, thus kindly and unexpectedly reconciled, should not depart without a song.

Vent. A good motion.

Merry. Strike up, then.   360

SONG

> Better music ne'er was known
> Than a choir of hearts in one,
> Let each other, that hath been
> Troubled with the gall or spleen,
> Learn of us to keep his brow
> Smooth and plain, as ours are now.
> Sing, though before the hour of dying;
> He shall rise, and then be crying,
> "Hey, ho, 'tis nought but mirth
> That keeps the body from the earth."   370

                                    Exeunt omnes.

---

[28] *forked:* barbed.

[29] *mortal:* a parody of the Ghost's speech in *Richard III*,
V.iii. 125; the whole speech also parodies that of Don
Andrea's ghost at the beginning of *The Spanish Tragedy.*

[30] *lingel:* cobbler's thread.   [31] *vampied:* patched.

[32] *cheapen:* bargain for.   [33] *aqua vitae:* alcoholic drinks.

[34] *Moorfields:* recreation area north of London.

[35] *forked heads:* cuckolds' horned heads.

[36] *Shrove Tuesday:* apprentices' holiday, on which it was
sport to attack brothels.

EPILOGUS

Cit. Come, Nell, shall we go? The play's done.

Wife. Nay, by my faith, George, I have more manners than so; I'll speak to these gentlemen first.— I thank you all gentlemen, for your patience and countenance to Rafe, a poor fatherless child; and if I might see you at my house, it should go hard but I would have a pottle of wine and a pipe of tobacco for you; for truly I hope you do like the youth, but I would be glad to know the truth. I refer it to your own discretions, whether you will applaud him or no, 10 for I will wink, and whilst you shall do what you will, I thank you with all my heart. God give you good night.—Come, George.

[*Exeunt.*]

F I N I S

Francis Beaumont

[c. 1584–1616]

John Fletcher

[1579–1625]

A KING AND NO KING

THE PARTNERSHIP between Beaumont and Fletcher is one of the marvels of the age, and it was so regarded in its own time. The bare facts about their collaboration are given in this volume in the introduction to THE KNIGHT OF THE BURNING PESTLE, along with biographical information about Beaumont. Fletcher's father, a churchman, was to become Bishop of London in 1594, and two of his cousins, Giles and Phineas, earned fame as the modish writers of huge Spenserian poems read now chiefly by scholars. About the playwright's life little is known. He began his theatrical career with an undated comedy called *The Woman's Prize* and *The Faithful Shepherdess*, a pastoral written in 1608–1609 for the children's company at Blackfriars and prefaced with an explanation of the ground rules of the new form tragicomedy that he claimed to be introducing to England. By this time his collaboration with Beaumont had already begun. After the latter's retirement in 1613 Fletcher found other collaborators. When the lease of the Blackfriars Theater expired in 1608, the King's Men, which owned it, took over the profitable operation of its subsidiary; thus Fletcher found himself writing for the public as well as the private theater, and after Shakespeare's retirement and death he became principal playwright to the company until his own death in 1625. That succession says as much about changing taste as it does about his own merits.

Late in the century the gossip Aubrey would claim that he "heard Dr. John Earles, since Bishop of Sarum, who knew them, say that Mr. Beaumont's main business was to lop the overflowings of Mr. Fletcher's luxuriant fancy and flowing wit," and William Cartwright makes the same suggestion in a prefatory poem to the 1647 folio. A long line of scholars have worked at the problem of disentangling the contributions of the two men from the thirteen plays in which they worked together, and there is something like a consensus on some matters. Since Fletcher's orthographical mannerisms—the use of "'em," for example, frequent in THE WILD-GOOSE CHASE as in other plays exclusively his—appear less in his collaborations than in his independent work, Beaumont is presumed to have made the final manuscripts. But one cannot deduce from this, as some have done, that Fletcher supplied the plots and Beaumont worked them up. We simply do not know

enough about the methods of collaboration in the period. No less a poet than Robert Herrick claims, in another commendatory verse to the first folio, that "that high design" and "the rare plot" of A KING AND NO KING are Fletcher's, but one need only look at the profusion of loose statements by a remarkable number of writers printed with Herrick's little poem to realize how little credibility it has.

Much more important than the question of who did exactly what, which is really only a matter of curiosity, is the phenomenal consistency of the great bulk of the fifty-two plays in the folios. The real achievement of "Beaumont and Fletcher" is the creation of a characteristic dramatic style that triumphed in the theater and kept its preeminence for many years after the playwrights had died and their theaters had ceased to exist, and that was capable of creating authentic "Beaumont and Fletcher" plays in which only one, or neither, of them had any part. If the mode they invented suppresses the personalities of individual playwrights in an age of enormous individuality in the theater, if it suggests the turning out of anonymous products from a workshop rather than the creation of personal art, it bears much similarity to the production of movies in the days of their largest audiences, when not an *auteur* but an industry stood behind a successful film.

In one of the truly indispensable books on the drama of this period, *The Pattern of Tragicomedy in Beaumont and Fletcher*, Eugene M. Waith notes a number of similarities among the tragicomedies. Many of these mark the comedies and tragedies in the canon as well; all of them apply to A KING AND NO KING, which, like the earlier *Philaster*, is virtually an archetype of the form. Some characteristics Professor Waith isolates are imitation of the manners of the familiar world; remoteness from the familiar world; intricacy of plot, involving the use of surprise and of symmetrical constrasts and parallels between elements; an improbable hypothesis as the basis of a plot (e.g., a king and his sister fall in love); an atmosphere of threatening evil; protean characters, changing their nature to suit the requirements of the plot; what Dryden called "lively touches of passion"; and the language of emotion. In the tragedies evil achieves its ends and the improbable hypothesis eventuates in catastrophe; in the tragicomedies the atmosphere is suddenly dissipated and the problem posed by the improbable hypothesis solved by an often outrageous cutting of the Gordian knot (e.g., the king turns out not to be king or his mistress' brother after all). In A KING AND NO KING Beaumont and Fletcher play with the theme of incest, which surfaces in some of the most intense tragedies of the period (e.g., *Hamlet*, THE DUCHESS OF MALFI, and 'TIS PITY SHE'S A WHORE) and which Robert Ornstein has demonstrated in *The Moral Vision of Jacobean Tragedy* is often, as in 'TIS PITY and *The Atheist's Tragedy* and a good deal of nondramatic literature, a test case for "naturalism," the Renaissance version of atheism in which man sees himself as licensed to violate theological injunctions. But "play with" is the operative term: characteristically Beaumont and Fletcher and their audience do not have to solve the moral problem of the play, for circumstances make it moot. The ability to touch on troublesome issues and thus to spirit them away may account in some part for the unprecedented success of Beaumont and Fletcher. But it would be unfair to deny that the sheer mastery of their technique had a great deal to do with it as well.

A KING AND NO KING was first performed in 1611; its first known performance was at court in December of that year, during a period in which the playwrights were writing for the King's Men at the Globe and the Children of the Revels at the Blackfriars. The play has no single source but draws on a variety of materials. The device of saving the protagonists from feared incest by the discovery that they are not related occurs in Spanish, French, and Italian tales; characters' names derive from the work of ancient historians; the braggart Bessus is in the tradition of the *miles gloriosus* that had already produced Shakespeare's Nym, Bardolph, and Pistol and Jonson's Bobadill. The text was registered in the Stationers' Register on 7 August 1618, and published in quarto (Q1) by Thomas Walkley in 1619. A second quarto (Q2) was published under the same auspices in 1625; whereas the first claimed performance at the Globe, the second says it had been performed at Blackfriars. There were seven more editions during the century, indicating enduring popularity. The first quarto is the basic text, but the second may derive from a playhouse promptbook, an annotated copy of the first, and in some instances its corrections of errors in the first seem authoritative enough to be adopted here as in other editions.   N. R.

A King and No King

[EPISTLE DEDICATORY]

To the Right Worshipful and Worthy Knight,
SIR HENRY NEVILL

WORTHY SIR,

I present, or rather return, unto your view that which formerly hath been received from you, hereby effecting what you did desire. To commend the work in my unlearned method were rather to detract from it than to give it any luster. It sufficeth it hath your worship's approbation and patronage, to the commendation of the authors and encouragement of their further labors. And thus wholly committing myself and it to your worship's dispose, I rest ever ready to do you service not only in the like but in what I may.

THOMAS WALKLEY.

DRAMATIS PERSONÆ

ARBACES, *King of Iberia*
TIGRANES, *King of Armenia*
GOBRIUS, *Lord Protector of Iberia, father of Arbaces*
BACURIUS, *an Iberian lord*
MARDONIUS ⎱ *captains in the Iberian army*
BESSUS ⎰
LIGONES, *an Armenian statesman, father of Spaconia*
PHILIP, *servant of a Citizen's Wife*

Two Swordmen
A Boy, *servant of Bessus*
ARANE, *the Iberian Queen Mother*
PANTHEA, *her daughter*
SPACONIA, *an Armenian lady, daughter of Ligones*
Two Citizens' Wives
Gentlemen, Attendants, Servants, Messengers, Citizens, Waiting-women

SCENE

In the first act, Armenia; afterwards, the Iberian court.

ACT ONE

SCENE ONE

Enter MARDONIUS *and* BESSUS.

Mard. Bessus, the King has made a fair hand on't; h'as ended the wars at a blow. Would my sword had a close basket hilt to hold wine, and the blade would make knives, for we shall have nothing but eating and drinking.

Bess. We that are commanders shall do well enough.

Mard. Faith, Bessus, such commanders as thou may; I had as lief set thee *perdu*[1] for a pudding i'th' dark as Alexander the Great.

Bess. I love these jests exceedingly.   10

Mard. I think thou lov'st them better than quarreling, Bessus; I'll say so much i'thy behalf. And yet thou art valiant enough upon a retreat; I think thou would'st kill any man that stopped thee, an thou couldst.

Bess. But was not this a brave[2] combat, Mardonius?

Mard. Why, didst thou see't?

Bess. You stood with me.

Mard. I did so, but methought thou wink'st[3] every blow they strake.[4]   19

Bess. Well, I believe there are better soldiers than I that never saw two princes fight in lists.[5]

Mard. By my troth, I think so too, Bessus, many a thousand; but certainly all that are worse than thou have seen as much.

Bess. 'Twas bravely[6] done of our King.

Mard. Yes, if he had not ended the wars. I am glad thou dar'st talk of such dangerous businesses.

I.i.
[1] *set . . . perdu:* I would just as soon put you in a dangerous post—against nothing more than a pudding—as I would Alexander the Great.   [2] *brave:* fine.
[3] *winkst:* closed your eyes at.   [4] *strake:* struck.
[5] *lists:* place of single combat, fought within barriers.
[6] *bravely:* well.

Bess. To take a prince prisoner in the heart of his own country in single combat!   29

Mard. See how thy blood cruddles[7] at this. I think thou wouldst be contented to be beaten in this passion.

Bess. Shall I tell you truly?

Mard. Ay.

Bess. I could willingly venture for it.

Mard. Um, no venture neither, good Bessus.

Bess. Let me not live if I do not think it is a braver piece of service than that I'm so famed for.

Mard. Why, art thou famed for any valor?

Bess. I famed? Ay, I warrant you.   39

Mard. I am very heartily glad on't. I have been with thee ever since thou cam'st o'th' wars, and this is the first word that ever I heard on't. Prithee, who fames thee?

Bess. The Christian world.

Mard. 'Tis heathenishly done of them; in my conscience thou deserv'st it not.

Bess. Yes, I ha' done good service.

Mard. I do not know how thou may'st wait of[8] a man in's chamber or thy agility in shifting a trencher,[9] but otherwise no service, good Bessus.   50

Bess. You saw me do the service yourself.

Mard. Not so hasty, sweet Bessus. Where was it? Is the place vanished?

Bess. At Bessus' Desperate Redemption.

Mard. Bessus' Desperate Redemption? Where's that?

Bess. There where I redeemed the day; the place bears my name.

Mard. Prithee, who christened it?

Bess. The soldier.   60

Mard. If I were not a very merrily disposed man, what would become of thee? One that had but a grain of choler[10] in the whole composition of his body would send thee of an errand to the worms for putting thy name upon that field. Did not I beat thee there i'th' head o'th' troops with a truncheon because thou wouldst needs run away with thy company when we should charge the enemy?

Bess. True, but I did not run.

Mard. Right, Bessus; I beat thee out on't.   70

Bess. But came not I up when the day was gone and redeemed all?

Mard. Thou know'st, and so do I, thou meant'st to fly, and, thy fear making thee mistake, thou ran'st upon the enemy; and a hot charge thou gav'st, as, I'll do thee right, thou art furious in running away, and I think we owe thy fear for our victory. If I were the King, and were sure thou wouldst mistake always, and run away upon the enemy, thou shouldst be general, by this light.

Bess. You'll never leave this till I fall foul.[11]   80

Mard. No more such words, dear Bessus. For though I have ever known thee a coward and therefore durst never strike thee, yet if thou proceed'st, I will allow thee valiant and beat thee.

Bess. Come, come—our King's a brave fellow.

Mard. He is so, Bessus: I wonder how thou com'st to know it. But if thou wert a man of understanding, I would tell thee he is vainglorious and humble, and

angry and patient, and merry and dull, and joyful and sorrowful, in extremities,[12] in an hour. Do not   90 think me thy friend for this, for if I cared who knew it, thou shouldst not hear it, Bessus. Here he is, with the prey in his foot.

Enter ARBACES *and* TIGRANES, *with* [*two* Gentlemen *and*] attendants.

Arb. Thy sadness, brave Tigranes, takes away
From my full victory; am I become
Of so small fame that any man should grieve
When I o'ercome him? They that placed me here
Intended it an honor large enough
For the most valiant living but to dare
Oppose me single, though he lost the day.   100
What should afflict you? You are free as I.
To be my prisoner is to be more free
Than you were formerly, and never think
The man I held worthy to combat me
Shall be used servilely. Thy ransom is
To take my only sister to thy wife—
A heavy one, Tigranes, for she is
A lady that the neighbor princes send
Blanks[13] to fetch home. I have been too unkind
To her, Tigranes. She but nine year old,   110
I left her, and ne'er saw her since; your wars
Have held me long, and taught me, though a youth,
The way to victory. She was a pretty child
Then; I was little better. But now fame
Cries loudly on her, and my messengers
Make me believe she is a miracle.
She'll make you shrink, as I did, with a stroke
But of her eye, Tigranes.

Tig.   Is it the course of
Iberia to use their prisoners thus?
Had fortune thrown my name above Arbaces',   120
I should not thus have talked, for in Armenia
We hold it base. You should have kept your temper
Till you saw home again, where 'tis the fashion
Perhaps to brag.

Arb.   Be you my witness, Earth:
Need I to brag? Doth not this captive prince
Speak me[14] sufficiently, and all the acts
That I have wrought upon his suffering land?
Should I then boast? Where lies that foot of ground
Within his whole realm that I have not passed
Fighting and conquering? Far then from me   130
Be ostentation. I could tell the world
How I have laid his kingdom desolate
With this sole arm propped by divinity,[15]
Stripped him out of his glories, and have sent
The pride of all his youth to people graves,

---

   [7] *cruddles:* curdles.   [8] *of:* on.
   [9] *trencher:* dinner plate.
   [10] *choler:* one of the four humors, or fluids, that governed the body and mind; this one caused anger.
   [11] *fall foul:* quarrel.
   [12] *in extremities:* at the extremes of emotion's range.
   [13] *Blanks:* Documents with space to be filled in according to Arbaces' wishes.   [14] *Speak me:* Testify.
   [15] *propped by divinity:* aided by God.

And made his virgins languish for their loves,
If I would brag. Should I, that have the power
To teach the neighbor world humility,
Mix with vainglory?

   Mard. [*Aside*]   Indeed, this is none?

   Arb. Tigranes, no; did I but take delight   140
To stretch my deeds, as others do, on words,
I could amaze my hearers.

   Mard. [*Aside*]   So you do.

   Arb. But he shall wrong his and my modesty
That thinks me apt to boast. After an act
Fit for a god to do upon his foe,
A little glory in a soldier's mouth
Is well becoming; be it far from vain.

   Mard. [*Aside*] It's pity that valor should be thus
drunk.

   Arb. I offer you my sister, and you answer
I do insult, a lady that no suit   150
Nor treasure nor thy crown could purchase thee,
But that thou fought'st with me.

   Tig.   Though this be worse
Than that you spoke before, it strikes [16] not me;
But that you think to overgrace me with
The marriage of your sister troubles me;
I would give worlds for ransoms, were they mine,
Rather than have her.

   Arb.   See if I insult
That am the conqueror and for a ransom
Offer rich treasure to the conquered
Which he refuses, and I bear his scorn!   160
It cannot be self-flattery to say,
The daughters of your country, set by her,
Would see their shame, run home, and blush to death
At their own foulness. Yet she is not fair
Nor beautiful; those words express her not.
They say her looks are something excellent
That wants a name. Yet were she odious,
Her birth deserves the empire of the world,
Sister to such a brother, that hath ta'en
Victory prisoner and throughout the earth   170
Carries her bound; and should he let her loose,
She durst not leave him. Nature did her wrong
To print continual conquest on her cheeks
And make no man worthy for her to take
But me that am too near her, and as strangely
She did for me. But you will think I brag.

   Mard. [*Aside*] I do, I'll be sworn. Thy valor and thy
passions severed would have made two excellent fellows
in their kinds. I know not whether I should be sorry
thou art so valiant or so passionate. Would one of 'em
were away.   181

   Tig. Do I refuse her that [17] I doubt her worth?
Were she as virtuous as she would be thought,
So perfect that no one of her own sex
Would find a want, had she so tempting fair [18]

---

[16] *strikes:* impresses.
[17] *that:* because.
[18] *fair:* a beauty.
[19] *for damning:* lest it damn.
[20] *await:* attend.
[21] *lay too high:* encamped in too high a position.
[22] *wake:* festival.
[23] *occasion:* opportunity.
[24] *falsified a blow:* feinted.

That she could wish it off for damning [19] souls,
I would pay any ransom twenty times
Rather than meet her married in my bed.
Perhaps I have a love where I have fixed
Mine eyes, not to be moved, and she on me.   190
I am not fickle.

   Arb.   Is that all the cause?
Think you, you can so knit yourself in love
To any other that her searching sight
Cannot dissolve it? So, before you tried,
You thought yourself a match for me in fight.
Trust me, Tigranes, she can do as much
In peace as I in war; she'll conquer too.
You shall see, if you have the power to stand
The force of her swift looks. If you dislike,
I'll send you home with love, and name your ransom
Some other way; but if she be your choice,   201
She frees you. To Iberia you must.

   Tig. Sir, I have learnt a prisoner's sufferance
And will obey, but give me leave to talk
In private with some friends before I go.

   Arb. Some two await [20] him forth and see him safe,
But let him freely send for whom he please,
And none dare to disturb his conference.
I will not have him know what bondage is
Till he be free from me.

        Exeunt TIGRANES [*and two* Attendants].
                This prince, Mardonius,   210
Is full of wisdom, valor, all the graces
Man can receive.

   Mard.   And yet you conquered him?

   Arb. And yet I conquered him, and could have done
Hadst thou joined with him, though thy name in arms
Be great. Must all men that are virtuous
Think suddenly to match themselves with me?
I conquered him and bravely, did I not?

   Bess. And please your majesty, I was afraid at first—

   Mard. When wert thou other?

   Arb. Of what?   220

   Bess. That you would not have spied your best
advantages, for your majesty, in my opinion, lay too
high; [21] methinks, under favor, you should have lain
thus.

   Mard. Like a tailor at a wake. [22]

   Bess. And then, if't please your majesty to remember, at one time, by my troth, I wished myself with you.

   Mard. By my troth, thou wouldst have stunk 'em
both out o'th lists.

   Arb. What to do?   230

   Bess. To put your majesty in mind of an occasion: [23]
you lay thus, and Tigranes falsified a blow [24] at your
leg, which you by doing thus avoided; but if you had
whipped up your leg thus and reached him on the'ear
you had made the blood royal run about's head.

   Mard. What country fence-school didst thou learn
that at?

   Arb. Puft! did I not take him nobly?

   Mard.   Why, you did,
And you have talked enough on't.

   Arb.   Talked enough!
While you confine my words? By heaven and earth,

I were much better be a king of beasts   240
Than such a people. If I had not patience
Above a god, I should be called a tyrant
Thoughout the world. They will offend to death
Each minute. Let me hear thee speak again,
And thou art earth again. Why, this is like
Tigranes' speech, that needs would say I bragged.
Bessus, he said I bragged.
    Bess. Ha, ha, ha.
    Arb.   Why dost thou laugh?
By all the world, I'm grown ridiculous
To my own subjects. Tie me to a chair   250
And jest at me; but I shall make a start
And punish some, that other will take heed
How they are haughty. Who will answer me?
He said I boasted.—Speak, Mardonius;
Did I?—He will not answer. Oh, my temper!
I give you thanks above that taught my heart
Patience; I can endure his silence.—What, will none
Vouchsafe to give me audience? Am I grown
To such a poor respect? Or do you mean   259
To break my wind?[25] Speak; speak soon, one of you,
Or else, by heaven—
    1 Gent.   So please your—
    Arb.   Monstrous!
I cannot be heard out; they cut me off
As if I were too saucy. I will live
In woods and talk to trees: they will allow me
To end what I begin. The meanest subject
Can find a freedom to discharge his soul,
And not I.—Now it is a time to speak;
I harken.
    1 Gent. May it please—
    Arb.   I mean not you;
Did not I stop you once? But I am grown
To talk but idly;[26] let another speak.   270
    2 Gent. I hope your majesty—
    Arb.   Thou drawest[27] thy words
That I must wait an hour where other men
Can hear in instants. Throw your words away
Quick and to purpose; I have told you this.
    Bess. An't please your majesty—
    Arb. Wilt thou devour me? This is such a rudeness
As yet you never showed me, and I want
Power to command too, else Mardonius
Would speak at my request.—Were you my king,
I would have answered at your word, Mardonius.   280
I pray you speak, and truly: did I boast?
    Mard. Truth will offend you.
    Arb.   You take all great care
What will offend me, when you dare to utter
Such things as these.
    Mard. You told Tigranes you had won his land
With that sole arm propped by divinity.
Was not that bragging and a wrong to us
That daily ventured lives?
    Arb.   Oh, that thy name
Were great as mine; would I had paid my wealth[28]
It were as great, that I might combat thee.   290
I would through all the regions habitable
Search thee, and, having found thee, with my sword

Drive thee about the world till I had met
Some place that yet man's curiosity
Hath missed of; there, there would I strike thee dead.
Forgotten of mankind, such funeral rites
As beasts would give thee thou shouldst have.
    Bess. [*Apart*]   The King
Rages extremely; shall we slink away?
He'll strike us.
    2 Gent. [*Apart*] Content.   300
    Arb. There I would make you know 'twas this sole
    arm.
I grant you were my instruments and did
As I commanded you, but 'twas this arm
Moved you like wheels; it moved you as it pleased—
Whither slip you now? What, are you too good
To wait on me?—Puff! I had need have temper,
That rule such people; I have nothing left
At my own choice. I would I might be private:[29]
Mean men enjoy themselves, but 'tis our curse
To have a tumult[30] that, out of their loves,   310
Will wait on us whether we will or no.—
Will you be gone?—Why, here they stand like death;
My word moves nothing.
    1 Gent.   Must we go?
    Bess.   I know not.
    Arb. I pray you leave me, sirs.—I'm proud of this,
That they will be entreated from my sight.
        Exeunt all but ARBACES *and* MARDONIUS.

        [MARDONIUS *starts to go.*]

Why, now they leave me all.—Mardonius!
    Mard. Sir?
    Arb. Will you leave me quite alone? Methinks
Civility should teach you more than this,
If I were but your friend. Stay here and wait.   320
    Mard. Sir, shall I speak?
    Arb.   Why, you would now think
    much
To be denied, but I can scarce entreat
What I would have. Do, speak.
    Mard. But will you hear me out?
    Arb. With me you article[31] to talk thus. Well,
I will hear you out.
    Mard.   Sir, that I have ever loved you

        [*Kneels.*]

My sword hath spoken for me; that I do,
If it be doubted, I dare call an oath,
A great one, to my witness. And were you
Not my King, from amongst men I should   330
Have chose you out to love above the rest.
Nor can this challenge[32] thanks. For my own sake,
I should have doted, because I would have loved
The most deserving man, for so you are.

---

[25] *break my wind:* use up my breath.
[26] *talk but idly:* Q1 "balke, but I desire"; Q2 "balke,
but I defie."   [27] *drawest:* draw out.
[28] *paid my wealth:* given away all that I had that we might
equal.   [29] *private:* alone; a private citizen.
[30] *tumult:* noisy crowd.   [31] *article:* stipulate.
[32] *challenge:* demand.

Arb. Alas, Mardonius, rise; you shall not kneel.

[*Raises him.*]

We all are soldiers and all venture lives,
And where there is no difference in men's worths
Titles are jests. Who can outvalue thee?
Mardonius, thou hast loved me and hast wrong;
Thy love is not rewarded; but believe   340
It shall be better, more than friends in arms,
My father and my tutor, good Mardonius.
Mard. Sir, you did promise you would hear me out.
Arb. And so I will; speak freely, for from thee
Nothing can come but worthy things and true.
Mard. Though you have all this worth, you hold some qualities
That do eclipse your virtues.
Arb.   Eclipse my virtues?
Mard. Yes, your passions, which are so manifold
that they appear even in this: when I commend you,
you hug me for that truth; when I speak of your faults,
you make a start and fly the hearing. But—   351
Arb. When you commend me? Oh, that I should live
To need such commendations. If my deeds
Blew not my praise themselves above the earth,
I were most wretched. Spare your idle praise.
If thou didst mean to flatter, and shouldst utter
Words in my praise that thou thought'st impudence,
My deeds should make 'em modest. When you praise,
I hug you. 'Tis so false that wert thou worthy
Thou shouldst receive a death, a glorious death,   360
From me. But thou shalt understand thy lies,
For shouldst thou praise me into heaven and there
Leave me enthroned, I would despise thee then[33]
As much as now, which is as much as dust,
Because I see thy envy.
Mard. However you will use me after, yet
For your own promise' sake hear me the rest.
Arb. I will, and after call unto the winds,
For they shall lend as large an ear as I
To what you utter. Speak.
Mard.   Would you but leave   370
These hasty tempers, which I do not say
Take from you all your worth, but darken 'em,
Then you would shine indeed.
Arb. Well.
Mard. Yet I would have you keep some passions, lest
men should take you for a god, your virtues are such.
Arb. Why, now you flatter.
Mard. I never understood the word. Were you no
king and free from these wild moods, should I choose

---

a companion for wit and pleasure, it should be   380
you; or for honesty[34] to interchange my bosom[35] with,
it would be you; or wisdom to give me counsel, I would
pick out you; or valor to defend my reputation, still I
would find out you; for you are fit to fight for all the
world, if it could come in question. Now I have spoke,
consider to yourself, find out a use,[36] if so, then what
shall fall to me is not material.
Arb. Is not material? More than ten such lives
As mine, Mardonius. It was nobly said;
Thou hast spoke truth, and boldly, such a truth   390
As might offend another. I have been
Too passionate and idle; thou shalt see
A swift amendment. But I want[37] those parts[38]
You praise me for. I fight for all the world?
Give thee a sword, and thou wilt go as far
Beyond me as thou art beyond in years;
I know thou dar'st and wilt. It troubles me
That I should use so rough a phrase to thee;
Impute it to my folly, what thou wilt,
So thou wilt pardon me. That thou and I   400
Should differ thus!
Mard.   Why, 'tis no matter, sir.
Arb. Faith, but 'tis; but thou dost ever take
All things I do thus patiently, for which
I never can requite thee but with love,
And that thou shalt be sure of. Thou and I
Have not been merry lately. Pray thee, tell me
Where hadst thou that same jewel in thine ear?
Mard. Why, at the taking of a town.
Arb.   A wench,
Upon my life, a wench, Mardonius,
Gave thee that jewel.   410
Mard. Wench! they respect not me; I'm old and
rough, and every limb about me, but that which should,
grows stiffer. I'those businesses I may swear I am truly
honest,[39] for I pay justly for what I take, and would be
glad to be at a certainty.[40]
Arb. Why, do the wenches encroach upon[41] thee?
Mard. Ay, by this light, do they.
Arb. Didst thou sit at an old rent[42] with 'em?
Mard. Yes, 'faith.
Arb. And do they improve themselves?[43]   420
Mard. Ay, ten shillings to me[44] every new young
fellow they come acquainted with.
Arb. How canst live on't?[45]
Mard. Why, I think I must petition to you.
Arb. Thou shalt take 'em up at my price.[46]

Enter two Gentlemen *and* BESSUS.

Mard. Your price?
Arb. Ay, at the King's price.
Mard. That may be more than I am worth.
1 Gent. Is he not merry now?
2 Gent. I think not.   430
Bess. He is, he is; we'll show ourselves.
Arb. Bessus, I thought you had been in Iberia by
this; I bade you haste. Gobrius will want entertainment[47] for me.
Bess. An't please your majesty, I have a suit.
Arb. Is't not lousy, Bessus? What is't?

---

[33] *then:* Q1, 2 "though."
[34] *honesty:* Q2; Q1 "honest."
[35] *interchange my bosom:* exchange confidences.
[36] *use:* serviceable activity.   [37] *want:* lack.
[38] *parts:* qualities.   [39] *honest:* chaste; honorable.
[40] *at a certainty:* sure (of what I get).
[41] *encroach upon:* (law) ask more than they should.
[42] *sit . . . rent:* hold out for the old price.
[43] *improve themselves:* with pun—raise prices.
[44] *ten . . . me:* it costs me ten shillings more.
[45] *live on't:* i.e., at the expense.   [46] *price:* expense.
[47] *entertainment:* accommodations.

Bess. I am to carry a lady with me—

Arb. Then thou hast two suits.[48]

Bess. And if I can prefer[49] her to the Lady Panthea, your majesty's sister, to learn fashions, as her friends term it, it will be worth something to me.   441

Arb. So many nights' lodgings as 'tis thither, will't not?

Bess. I know not that, sir, but gold I shall be sure of.

Arb. Why, thou shalt bid her entertain her from me so thou wilt resolve me one thing.

Bess. If I can.

Arb. 'Faith, 'tis a very disputable question, and yet I think thou canst decide it.

Bess. Your majesty has a good opinion of my understanding.   451

Arb. I have so good an opinion of it: 'tis whether thou be valiant.

Bess. Somebody has traduced me to you. Do you see this sword, sir?

                                        [*Draws.*]

Arb. Yes.

Bess. If I do not make my backbiters eat it to a knife within this week, say I am not valiant.

                Enter Messenger *with a packet.*

Mess. Health to your majesty!

Arb.   From Gobrius?

Mess.   Yes, sir.

Arb. How does he? Is he well?

Mess.   In perfect health.

Arb. Thank thee for thy good news.   461
A trustier servant to his prince there lives not
Than is good Gobrius.

                                        [*Reads.*]

1 Gent. The King starts back.

Mard.   His blood goes back as
    fast.

2 Gent. And now it comes again.

Mard.   He alters strangely.

Arb. The hand of heaven is on me; be it far
From me to struggle. If my secret sins
Have pulled this curse upon me, lend me tears
Enough to wash me white, that I may feel
A childlike innocence within my breast,   470
Which once performed, oh, give me leave to stand
As fixed as constancy herself, my eyes
Set here unmoved, regardless of the world,
Though thousand miseries encompass me.

Mard. [*Aside*] This is strange.—Sir, how do you?

Arb. Mardonius, my mother—

Mard.   Is she dead?

Arb. Alas, she's not so happy. Thou dost know
How she hath labored since my father died
To take by treason hence this loathèd life
That would but be to serve her. I have pardoned   480
And pardoned, and by that have made her fit
To practice new sins, not repent the old.
She now has hired a slave to come from thence
And strike me here, whom Gobrius, sifting out,[50]
Took and condemned and executed there,
The careful'st servant. Heaven let me but live

To pay that man; nature is poor to me,
That will not let me have as many deaths
As are the times that he hath saved my life,
That I might die 'em over, all for him.   490

Mard. Sir, let her bear her sins on her own head;
Vex not yourself.

Arb.   What will the world
Conceive of me? With what unnatural sins
Will they suppose me laden, when my life
Is sought by her that gave it to the world?
But yet he writes me comfort here: my sister,
He says, is grown in beauty and in grace,
In all the innocent virtues that become
A tender, spotless maid. She stains her cheeks
With mourning tears to purge her mother's ill,   500
And 'mongst that sacred dew she mingles prayers,
Her pure oblations for my safe return.
If I have lost the duty of a son;
If any pomp or vanity of state
Made me forget my natural offices;
Nay, farther, if I have not every night
Expostulated with my wandering thoughts,
If aught unto my parent they have erred,
And called 'em back; do you direct her arm
Unto this foul dissembling heart of mine.   510
But if I have been just to her, send out
Your power to compass me, and hold me safe
From searching treason. I will use no means
But prayers, for rather suffer me to see
From mine own veins issue a deadly flood
Than wash my dangers off with mother's blood.

Mard. I ne'er saw such sudden extremities.

                                        Exeunt.

[I.ii]

                Enter TIGRANES *and* SPACONIA.

Tig. Why, wilt thou have me die, Spaconia?
What should I do?

Spac.   Nay, let me stay alone,
And when you see Armenia again,
You shall behold a tomb more worth than I.
Some friend that either loves me or my cause
Will build me something to distinguish me
From other women. Many a weeping verse
He will lay on and much lament those maids
That place their loves unfortunately too high,[1]
As I have done, where they can never reach.   10
But why should you go to Iberia?

Tig. Alas, that thou wilt ask me. Ask the man
That rages in a fever why he lies
Distempered there when all the other youths
Are coursing[2] o'er the meadows with their loves!
Can I resist? Am I not a slave
To him that conquered me?

---

48 *suits:* i.e., one to her and the other to me.
49 *prefer:* recommend.   50 *sifting out:* discovering.
I.ii.
1 *high:* Q2; Q1 "light."   2 *coursing:* hunting.

Spac.   That conquered thee?
Tigranes, he has won but half of thee,
Thy body; but thy mind may be as free
As his; his will did never combat thine   20
And take it prisoner.
    Tig.   But if he by force   *
Convey my body hence, what helps it me
Or thee to be unwilling?
    Spac.   O Tigranes,
I know you are to see a lady there,
To see and like, I fear; perhaps the hope
Of her makes you forget me ere we part.
Be happier than you know to wish. Farewell.
    Tig. Spaconia, stay and hear me what I say.
In short, destruction meet me, that I may
See it and not avoid it when I leave   30
To be³ thy faithful lover. Part with me
Thou shalt not. There are none that know our love,
And I have given gold to a captain
That goes unto Iberia from the King,
That he would place a lady of our land
With the King's sister that is offered me;
Thither shall you and, being once got in,
Persuade her by what subtle means you can
To be as backward in her love as I.
    Spac. Can you imagine that a longing maid,   40
When she beholds you, can be pulled away
With words from loving you?
    Tig.   Dispraise my health,
My honesty, and tell her I am jealous.
    Spac. Why, I had rather lose you. Can my heart
Consent to let my tongue throw out such words?
And I, that ever yet spoke what I thought,
Shall find it such a thing at first to lie.
    Tig. Yet do thy best.

Enter BESSUS.

Bess. What, is your majesty ready?
    Tig. There is the lady, captain.   50
    Bess. Sweet lady, by your leave.

                              [*Kisses her.*]

I could wish myself more full of courtship⁴ for your
fair sake.
    Spac. Sir, I shall find no want of that.
    Bess. Lady, you must haste; I have received new
letters from the King that requires more speed than I
expected.—He will follow me suddenly himself, and
begins to call for your majesty already.
    Tig. He shall not do so long.
    Bess. Sweet lady, shall I call you my charge here-
after?   61
    Spac. I will not take upon me to govern your tongue,
sir; you shall call me what you please.

                              [*Exeunt.*]

Finis Actus Primi.

---

³ *leave . . . be:* stop being.   ⁴ *courtship:* courtliness.
II.i.
¹ *close:* confined.   ² *paid down:* immediately paid for.

ACT TWO
SCENE ONE

Enter GOBRIUS, BACURIUS, ARANE, PANTHEA, *and*
                Waiting-women, *with attendance.*

Gob. My Lord Bacurius, you must have regard
Unto the Queen. She is your prisoner;
'Tis at your peril if she make escape.
    Bac. My lord, I know't; she is my prisoner
From you committed. Yet she is a woman.
And, so I keep her safe, you will not urge me
To keep her close.¹ I shall not shame to say
I sorrow for her.
    Gob.   So do I, my lord.
I sorrow for her that so little grace
Doth govern her that she should stretch her arm   10
Against her King, so little womanhood
And natural goodness as to think the death
Of her own son.
    Ara.   Thou know'st the reason why,
Dissembling as thou art, and wilt not speak.
    Gob. There is a lady takes not after you;
Her father is within her, that good man
Whose tears paid down² his sins. Mark how she weeps,
How well it does become her. And if you
Can find no disposition in yourself
To sorrow, yet by gracefulness in her   20
Find out the way, and by your reason weep.
All this she does for you, and more she needs,
When for yourself you will not lose a tear.
Think how this want of grief discredits you,
And you will weep because you cannot weep.
    Ara. You talk to me as having got a time
Fit for your purpose, but you know I know
You speak not what you think.
    Pan.   I would my heart
Were stone before my softness should be urged
Against my mother. A more troubled thought   30
No virgin bears about her: should I excuse
My mother's fault, I should set light a life
In losing which a brother and a King
Were taken from me. If I seek to save
That life so loved, I lose another life
That gave me being. I shall lose a mother,
A word of such a sound in a child's ear
That it strikes reverence through it. May the will
Of Heaven be done, and if one needs must fall,
Take a poor virgin's life to answer all.   40
    Ara. But, Gobrius, let us talk.

                              [*They walk apart.*]

                    You know this fault
Is not in me as in another woman.
    Gob. I know it is not.
    Ara.   Yet you make it so.
    Gob. Why, is not all that's past beyond your help?
    Ara. I know it is.
    Gob.   Nay, should you publish it
Before the world, think you 'twill be believed?
    Ara. I know it would not.
    Gob.   Nay, should I join with you,

Should we not both be torn?[3] And yet both die
Uncredited?

Ara.   I think we should.

Gob.   Why then
Take you such violent courses? As for me,   50
I do but right in saving of the King
From all your plots.

Ara.   The King?

Gob.   I bade you rest
With patience, and a time would come for me
To reconcile all to your content.
But by this way you take away my power,
And what was done unknown was not by me
But you. Your urging being done,
I must preserve mine own; but time may bring
All this to light and happily for all.

Ara. Accursèd be this over-curious[4] brain   60
That gave that plot a birth; accurst this womb
That after did conceive to my disgrace.

Bac. My lord protector, they say there are divers
letters come from Armenia that Bessus has done good
service and brought again[5] a day by his particular
valor. Received you any to that effect?

Gob. Yes, 'tis most certain.

Bac. I'm sorry for't, not that the day was won but
that 'twas won by him. We held him here a coward; he
did me wrong once, at which I laughed, and so did   70
all the world, for nor I nor any other held him worth
my sword.

Enter BESSUS and SPACONIA.

Bess. Health to my lord protector. From the King
these letters, and to your grace, madam, these.

Gob. How does his majesty?

Bess. As well as conquest by his own means, and his
valiant commanders', can make him. Your letters will
tell you all.

Pan. I will not open mine till I do know
My brother's health; good captain, is he well?   80

Bess. As the rest of us that fought are.

Pan. But how's that? Is he hurt?

Bess. He's a strange soldier that gets not a knock.

Pan. I do not ask how strange that soldier is
That gets no hurt, but whether he have one.

Bess. He had divers.[6]

Pan. And is he well again?

Bess. Well again, an't please your grace? Why, I was
run twice through the body and shot i'th' head with a
cross arrow[7] and yet am well again.   90

Pan. I do not care how thou dost. Is he well?

Bess. Not care how I do! Let a man out of the
mightiness of his spirit fructify[8] foreign countries with
his blood for the good of his own, and thus he shall be
answered. Why, I may live to relieve with spear and
shield such a lady as you distressed.

Pan. Why, I will care; I am glad that thou art well.
I prithee, is he so?   98

Gob. The King is well and will be here tomorrow.

Pan. My prayers are heard; now I will open mine.

[*Reads.*]

Gob. Bacurius, I must ease you of your charge.—
Madam, the wonted mercy of the King,
That overtakes[9] your faults, has met with this
And struck it out; he has forgiven you freely.
Your own will is your law; be where you please.

Ara. I thank him.

Gob.   You will be ready to wait
Upon his majesty tomorrow?

Ara.   I will.

Bac. Madam, be wise hereafter. I am glad
I have lost this office.   109

Exit ARANE.

Gob. Good Captain Bessus, tell us the discourse[10]
Between Tigranes and our King, and how
We got the victory.

Pan.   I prithee do.
And if my brother were in any danger,
Let not thy tale make him abide there long
Before thou bring him off, for all that while
My heart will beat.

Bess. Madam, let what will beat, I must tell the
truth, and thus it was. They fought single in lists but
one to one. As for my own part, I was dangerously hurt
but three days before, else perhaps we had been   120
two to two; I cannot tell; some thought we had. And
the occasion of my hurt was this: the enemy had made
trenches—

Gob. Captain, without[11] the manner of your hurt
Be much material to this business,
We'll hear it some other time.

Pan.   Ay, I prithee
Leave it, and go on with my brother.

Bess. I will, but 'twould be worth your hearing. To
the lists they came, and single sword[12] and gauntlet[13]
was their fight.   130

Pan. Alas!

Bess. Without the lists there stood some dozen
captains of either side mingled, all which were sworn,[14]
and one of those was I. And 'twas my chance to stand
near a captain of the enemy's side called Tiribasus;
valiant they said he was. Whilst these two kings were
stretching themselves, this Tiribasus cast something
a scornful look on me and asked me whom I thought
would overcome. I smiled and told him if he would
fight with me he should perceive by the event of   140
that whose king would win. Something he answered,
and a scuffle was like to grow, when one Zipetus offered
to help him. I—

Pan. All this is of thyself; I prithee, Bessus,
Tell something of my brother. Did he nothing?

---

[3] *torn:* torn to death.   [4] *over-curious:* too subtle, clever.
[5] *brought again:* recovered.   [6] *divers:* several.
[7] *cross arrow:* arrow shot from a crossbow.
[8] *fructify:* i.e., fertilize.   [9] *overtakes:* exceeds.
[10] *discourse:* course of arms, combat.
[11] *without:* outside.
[12] *single sword:* sword without other weapons.
[13] *gauntlet:* mailed glove worn to protect the other hand
when fighting thus armed.
[14] *sworn:* i.e., to abide the issue of single combat and
refrain from fighting themselves.

Bess. Why, yes; I'll tell your grace. They were not to fight till the word given, which, for my own part, by my troth, I confess I was not to give.

Pan. See, for his own part.

Bac. I fear yet this fellow's abused[15] with a good report. 151

Bess. Ay, but I—

Pan. Still of himself.

Bess. Cried, "Give the word," whenas, some of them said Tigranes was stooping, but the word was not given then; yet one Cosroes, of the enemy's part, held up his finger to me, which is as much with us martialists as "I will fight with you." I said not a word nor made sign during the combat, but that once done—

Pan. He slips o'er all the fight. 160

Bess. I called him to me. "Cosroes," said I—

Pan. I will hear no more.

Bess. No, no, I lie—

Bac. I dare be sworn thou dost.

Bess. "Captain," said I; 'twas so.

Pan. I tell thee, I will hear no further.

Bess. No? Your grace will wish you had.

Pan. I will not wish it. What, is this the lady My brother writes to me to take?

Bess. An't please your grace, this is she.—Charge, will you come nearer the princess? 171

Pan. Y'are welcome from your country, and this land Shall show unto you all the kindnesses That I can make it. What's your name?

Spac. Thalestris.

Pan. Y'are very welcome; you have got a letter To put you to me that has power enough To place mine enemy here; then much more you, That are so far from being so to me That you ne'er saw me.

Bess. Madam, I dare pass my word for her truth.[16]

Spac. My truth! 181

Pan. Why, captain, do you think I am afraid she'll steal?[17]

Bess. I cannot tell; servants are slippery; but I dare give my word for her and for her honesty.[18] She came along with me, and many favors she did me by the way, but, by this light, none but what she might do with modesty to a man of my rank.

Pan. Why, captain, here's nobody thinks otherwise.

Bess. Nay, if you should, your grace may think 190 your pleasure. But I am sure I brought her from Armenia, and in all that way, if ever I touched any bare[19] on her above her knee, I pray God I may sink where I stand.

Spac. Above my knee!

Bess. No, you know I did not, and if any man will say I did, this sword shall answer. Nay, I'll defend the reputation of my charge whilst I live.—Your grace shall understand I am secret in these businesses, and know how to defend a lady's honor. 200

Spac. I hope your grace know him so well already, I shall not need to tell you he's vain and foolish.

Bess. Ay, you may call me what you please, but I'll defend your good name against the world.—And so I take my leave of your grace—and of you, my lord protector. I am likewise glad to see your lordship well.

Bac. Oh, Captain Bessus, I thank you; I would speak with you anon.[20]

Bess. When you please, I will attend your lordship.

Exit.

Bac. Madam, I'll take my leave too.

Pan.   Good Bacurius.

Exit [BACURIUS].

Gob. Madam, what writes his majesty to you? 211

Pan. Oh, my lord,
The kindest words; I'll keep 'em whilst I live
Here in my bosom. There's no art in 'em;
They lie disordered in this paper just
As hearty nature speaks 'em.

Gob.   And to me
He writes what tears of joy he shed to hear
How you were grown in every virtuous way,
And yields all thanks to me for that dear care
Which I was bound to have in training you. 220
There is no princess living that enjoys
A brother of that worth.

Pan.   My lord, no maid
Longs more for anything or feels more heat
And cold within her breast than I do now
In hope to see him.

Gob.   Yet I wonder much
At this: he writes he brings along with him
A husband for you, that same captive prince.
And if he love you as he makes a show,
He will allow you freedom in your choice.

Pan. And so he will, my lord; I warrant you 230
He will but offer and give me the power
To take or leave.

Gob.   Trust me, were I a lady,
I could not like that man were bargained with
Before I choose him.

Pan.   But I am not built
On such wild humors; if I find him worthy,
He is not less because he's offered.

Spac. [*Aside*] 'Tis true, he is not; would he would
seem less.

Gob. I think there is no lady can affect[21]
Another prince, your brother standing by;
He does eclipse men's virtues so with his. 240

Spac. [*Aside*] I know a lady may; and more I fear
Another lady will.

Pan.   Would I might see him.

Gob. Why, so you shall. My businesses are great;
I will attend you when it is his pleasure
To see you, madam.

Pan.   I thank you, good my lord.

Gob. You will be ready, madam?

Pan. Yes.

Exit GOBRIUS [*with* Attendants].

Spac. I do beseech you, madam, send away
Your other women, and receive from me

---

15 *abused:* wronged.
16 *truth:* chastity.
17 *steal:* Panthea interprets "truth" as honesty, integrity.
18 *honesty:* chastity.
19 *bare:* bare skin.
20 *anon:* right away.
21 *affect:* like.

A few sad [22] words, which set against your joys   250
May make 'em shine the more.
    Pan.   Sirs,[23] leave me all.
                                Exeunt Women.
    Spac. I kneel a stranger here to beg a thing
Unfit for me to ask and you to grant;
'Tis such another strange, ill-laid request
As if a beggar should intreat a king
To leave his scepter and his throne to him
And take his rags to wander o'er the world
Hungry and cold.
    Pan.   That were a strange request.
    Spac. As ill is mine.
    Pan.   Then do not utter it.
    Spac. Alas, 'tis of that nature that it must   260
Be uttered—ay, and granted—or I die.
I am ashamed to speak it; but where life
Lies at the stake, I cannot think her woman
That will not talk something unreasonably
To hazard saving of it. I shall seem
A strange petitioner, that wish all ill
To them I beg of ere they give me aught,
Yet so I must. I would you were not fair
Nor wise, for in your ill consists my good.
If you were foolish, you would hear my prayer;   270
If foul, you had not power to hinder me;
He would not love you.
    Pan.   What's the meaning of it?
    Spac. Nay, my request is more without the bounds
Of reason yet, for 'tis not in the power
Of you to do what I would have you grant.
    Pan. Why, then, 'tis idle. Prithee speak it out.
    Spac. Your brother brings a prince into this land
Of such a noble shape, so sweet a grace,
So full of worth withal, that every maid
That looks upon him gives away herself   280
To him forever, and for you to have
He brings him. And so mad is my demand
That I desire you not to have this man,
This excellent man, for whom you needs must die
If you should miss him. I do now expect
You should laugh at me.
    Pan.   Trust me, I could weep
Rather, for I have found in all thy words
A strange, disjointed sorrow.
    Spac.   'Tis by me
His own desire too that you would not love him.
    Pan. His own desire! Why, credit me, Thalestris,
I am no common wooer. If he shall woo me,   291
His worth may be such that I dare not swear
I will not love him, but if he will stay
To have me woo him, I will promise thee
He may keep all his graces to himself
And fear no ravishing from me.
    Spac.   'Tis yet
His own desire, but when he sees your face,
I fear it will not be. Therefore, I charge you
As you have pity, stop those tender ears
From his enchanting voice, close up those eyes   300
That you may neither catch a dart from him
Nor he from you. I charge you as you hope

To live in quiet, for when I am dead
For certain I shall walk to visit him
If he break promise with me, for as fast
As oaths, without a formal ceremony,
Can make me, I am to him.
    Pan.   Then be fearless,
For if he were a thing 'twixt god and man
I could gaze on him, if I knew it sin
To love him, without passion. Dry your eyes.   310
I swear you shall enjoy him still [24] for me; [25]
I will not hinder you. But I perceive
You are not what you seem; rise, rise, Thalestris,
If your right name be so.
    Spac.   Indeed, it is not.
Spaconia is my name, but I desire
Not to be known to others.
    Pan.   Why, by me
You shall not. I will never do you wrong;
What good I can, I will. Think not my birth
Or education such that I should injure
A stranger [26] virgin. You are welcome hither.   320
In company you wish to be commanded,
But when we are alone, I shall be ready
To be your servant.
                          Exeunt.

[II.ii]

           Enter three Men *and a* Woman.

    1 Man. Come, come, run, run, run.
    2 Man. We shall outgo her.
    3 Man. One were better be hanged than carry women
out fiddling,[1] to these shows.
    Woman. Is the King hard by?
    1 Man. You heard he with the bottles say he thought
we should come too late. What abundance of people
here is.
    Woman. But what had he in those bottles?
    3 Man. I know not.   10
    2 Man. Why, ink, goodman fool.
    3 Man. Ink? What to do?
    1 Man. Why, the King, look you, will many times
call for those bottles and break his mind to his friends.
    Woman. Let's take our places quickly; we shall have
no room else.
    2 Man. The man told us he would walk afoot
through the people.
    3 Man. Ay, marry, did he.
    1 Man. Our shops are well looked to now.   20
    2 Man. 'Slife,[2] yonder's my master, I think.
    1 Man. No, 'tis not he.

          Enter two Citizens' Wives *and* PHILIP.

    1 Wife. Lord, how fine the fields be. What sweet
living 'tis in the country.

---

22 *sad:* serious.   23 *Sirs:* Includes ladies.
24 *still:* always.   25 *for me:* as far as I'm concerned.
26 *stranger:* foreigner.

II.ii.
    1 *fiddling:* fooling around.   2 *'Slife:* God's life.

2 Wife. Ay, poor souls, God help 'em; they live as contentedly as one of us.

1 Wife. My husband's cousin would have had me gone into the country last year. Wert thou ever there?

2 Wife. Ay, poor souls, I was amongst 'em once. 29

1 Wife. And what kind of creatures are they, for love of God?

2 Wife. Very good people, God help 'em.

1 Wife. Wilt thou go with me down this summer, when³ I am brought abed?

2 Wife. Alas, 'tis no place for us.

1 Wife. Why, prithee?

2 Wife. Why, you can have nothing there; there's nobody cries⁴ brooms.

1 Wife. No!

2 Wife. No, truly, nor milk. 40

1 Wife. Nor milk? How do they?

2 Wife. They are fain⁵ to milk themselves i'th' country.

1 Wife. Good Lord! but the people there, I think, will be very dutiful to one of us?

2 Wife. Ay, God knows, will they, and yet they do not greatly care for our husbands.

1 Wife. Do they not, alas? In good faith, I cannot blame them, for we do not greatly care for them ourselves.—Philip, I pray choose us a place. 50

Phil. There's the best, forsooth.

1 Wife. By your leave, good people, a little.

3 Man. What's the matter?

Phil. I pray you, my friend, do not thrust my mistress so; she's with child.

2 Man. Let her look to herself then; has she not had shroving⁶ enough yet? If she stay shouldering here, she may hap to go home with a cake in her belly.

3 Man. How now, goodman squitter-breech;⁷ why do you lean so on me? 60

Phil. Because I will.

3 Man. Will you, sir sauce-box?

[*Strikes him.*]

1 Wife. Look if one have not struck Philip—Come hither, Philip; why did he strike thee?

Phil. For leaning on him.

1 Wife. Why didst thou lean on him?

Phil. I did not think he would have struck me.

1 Wife. As God save me, law, thou art as wild as a buck; there is no quarrel but thou art at one end or other of it. 70

3 Man. It's at the first end then, for he will never stay the last.

1 Wife. Well, Slipstring,⁸ I shall meet with you.

3 Man. When you will.

1 Wife. I'll give a crown to meet⁹ with you.

3 Man. At a bawdy house.

1 Wife. Ay, you are full of your roguery [*Aside*] but if I do meet you, it shall cost me a fall.

*3 Man.*¹⁰ The King, the King, the King, the King! Now, now, now, now! 80

Enter ARBACES, TIGRANES, MARDONIUS, *and others.*

All. God preserve your majesty.

Arb. I thank you all. Now are my joys at full, When I behold you safe, my loving subjects. By you I grow, 'tis your united love That lifts me to this height. All the account that I can render you For all the love you have bestowed on me, All your expenses to maintain my war, Is but a little word. You will imagine 'Tis slender payment, yet 'tis such a word 90 As is not to be bought without our bloods: 'Tis peace.

All.   God preserve your majesty.

Arb. Now you may live securely in your towns, Your children 'round about you; you may sit Under your vines and make the miseries Of other kingdoms a discourse for you And lend them sorrows. For yourselves, you may Safely forget there are such things as tears, And may you all whose good thoughts I have gained Hold me unworthy when I think my life 100 A sacrifice too great to keep you thus In such a calm estate.

All.   God bless your majesty.

Arb. See, all good people, I have brought the man Whose very name you feared a captive home. Behold him; 'tis Tigranes. In your hearts Sing songs of gladness and deliverance.

1 Wife. Out upon him.

2 Wife. How he looks.

Woman. Hang, him, hang him, hang him.

Mard. These are sweet people.

Tig.   Sir, you do me wrong To render me a scornèd spectacle 111 To common people.

Arb.   It was far from me To mean it so.—If I have aught deserved, My loving subjects, let me beg of you Not to revile this prince, in whom there dwells All worth of which the nature of a man Is capable, valor beyond compare. The terror of his name has stretched itself Wherever there is sun. And yet for you I fought with him single and won¹¹ him too; 120 I made his valor stoop and brought that name, Soared to so unbelieved¹² a height, to fall Beneath mine. This, inspired with all your loves, I did perform, and will, for your content, Be ever ready for a greater work.

All. The Lord bless your majesty.

Tig. [*Aside*]   So, he has made me Amends now with a speech in commendations Of himself. I would not be so vainglorious.

Arb. If there be anything in which I may

---

³ *when:* after.   ⁴ *cries:* hawks.   ⁵ *fain:* obliged.
⁶ *shroving:* merrymaking; Q1 "thrusting"; Q2 "showing".   ⁷ *squitter-breech:* one who has diarrhea.
⁸ *Slipstring:* Rogue.   ⁹ *meet:* get even.
¹⁰ *3* MAN: Q1; Q2 "Flourish, Enter one running, *4*
MAN."   ¹¹ *won:* beat.   ¹² *unbelieved:* unbelievable.

Do good to any creature, here speak out;   130
For I must leave you, and it troubles me
Thus my occasions for the good of you
Are such as calls me from you; else my joy
Would be to spend my days amongst you all.
You show your loves in these large multitudes
That come to meet me. I will pray for you;
Heaven prosper you that you may know old years,
And live to see your children's children
Eat at your boards, with plenty. When there is
A want of anything, let it be known   140
To me, and I will be a father to you.
God keep you all.

   All. God bless your majesty. God bless your majesty.

                         Exeunt Kings *and their* train.

   1 Man Come, shall we go? All's done.

   Woman. Ay, for God's sake; I have not made a fire yet.

   2 Man. Away, away, all's done.

   3 Man. Content.—Farewell, Philip.

   1 Wife. Away, you haltersack,[13] you.   150

   2 Man. Philip will not fight; he's afraid on's[14] face.

   Phil. Ay, marry am I, afraid of my face.

   3 Man. Thou wouldst be, Philip, if thou saw'st it in a glass; it looks so like a visor.[15]

   1 Wife. You'll be hanged, sirrah.

               [*Exeunt the three* Men *and the* Woman.]
Come, Philip, walk afore us homeward.—Did not his majesty say he had brought us home peas for all our money?

   2 Wife. Yes, marry, did he.   159

   1 Wife. They are the first I heard on this year, by my troth. I longed for some of 'em; did he not say we should have some?

   2 Wife. Yes, and so we shall anon, I warrant you, have every one a peck brought home to our houses.

                              [*Exeunt.*]

   Finis Actus Secundi.

ACT THREE

SCENE ONE

Enter ARBACES *and* GOBRIUS.

   Arb. My sister take it ill?

   Gob.   Not very ill;
Something unkindly she doth take it, sir,
To have her husband chosen to her hands.[1]

   Arb. Why, Gobrius, let her; I must have her know
My will, and not her own, must govern her.
What, will she marry with some slave at home?

   Gob. Oh, she is far from any stubbornness—
You much mistake her—and no doubt will like
Where you will have her; but when you behold her,
You will be loath to part with such a jewel.   10

   Arb. To part with her! Why, Gobrius, art thou mad?
She is my sister.

   Gob.   Sir, I know she is,

But it were pity to make poor our land
With such a beauty to enrich another.

   Arb. Pish! will she have him?

   Gob. [*Aside*]   I do hope she will not.—
I think she will, sir.

   Arb. Were she my father and my mother too,
And all the names for which we think folks friends,
She should be forced to have him when I know
'Tis fit. I will not hear her say she's loath.   20

   Gob. [*Aside*] Heaven bring my purpose luckily to pass;
You know 'tis just.—Sir, she'll not need constraint,
She loves you so.

   Arb.   How does she love me? Speak.

   Gob. She loves you more than people love their health
That live by labor, more than I could love
A man that died for me if he could live
Again.

   Arb.   She is not like her mother then?

   Gob. Oh, no; when you were in Armenia,
I durst not let her know when you were hurt,
For at the first on every little scratch,   30
She kept her chamber, wept, and would not eat,
Till you were well. And many times the news
Was so long coming that before we heard
She was as near her death as you your health.

   Arb. Alas, poor soul; but yet she must be ruled.
I know not how I shall requite her well.
I long to see her; have you sent for her
To tell her I am ready?

   Gob.   Sir, I have.

Enter 1 Gentleman *and* TIGRANES.

   1 Gent. Sir, here's the Armenian king.

   Arb.   He's welcome.

   1 Gent. And the Queen Mother and the princess wait without.   40

   Arb. Good Gobrius, bring them in.

                    [*Exit* GOBRIUS.]
                    Tigranes, you
Will think you are arrived in a strange land,
Where mothers cast[2] to poison their only sons;
Think you, you shall be safe?

   Tig.   Too safe[3] I am, sir.

Enter GOBRIUS, ARANE, PANTHEA, SPACONIA,
BACURIUS, MARDONIUS, Gentleman, *and* BESSUS.

   Ara. As low as this I bow to you, and would
As low as is my grave, to show a mind
Thankful for all your mercies.

   Arb.   Oh, stand up
And let me kneel; the light will be ashamed
To see observance[4] done to me by you.

   Ara. You are my king.

---

  [13] *haltersack:* gallows-bird.   [14] *on's:* for his.
  [15] *visor:* mask.

III.i.
  [1] *to . . . hands:* for her.   [2] *cast:* plot.
  [3] *safe:* confined.   [4] *observance:* obeisance.

Arb.   You are my mother; rise.   50
As far be all your faults from your own soul
As from my memory; then you shall be
As white as innocence herself.
    Ara.   I came
Only to show my duty and acknowledge
My sorrow for my sins; longer to stay
Were but to draw eyes more attentively
Upon my shame. That power that kept you safe
From me preserve you still.
    Arb.   Your own desires
Shall be your guard.

                              Exit ARANE.

    Pan.   Now let me die;
Since I have seen my lord the King return   60
In safety, I have seen all good that life
Can show me. I have ne'er another wish
For heaven to grant, nor were it fit I should,
For I am bound to spend my age to come
In giving thanks that this was granted me.
    Gob. Why does not your majesty speak?
    Arb. To whom?
    Gob. To the princess.
    Pan. Alas, sir, I am fearful; you do look
On me as if I were some loathèd thing   70
That you were finding out a way to shun.
    Gob. Sir, you should speak to her.
    Arb. Ha?
    Pan. I know I am unworthy, yet not ill
Armed, with which innocence here I will kneel
Till I am one with earth, but I will gain
Some words and kindness from you.
    Tig. Will you speak, sir?
    Arb. [*Aside*]   Speak! Am I what I was?
What art thou that dost creep into my breast
And dar'st not see my face? Show forth thyself.   80
I feel a pair of fiery wings displayed
Hither, from thence. You shall not tarry there;
Up and begone. If thou beest love, begone,
Or I will tear thee from my wounded flesh,
Pull thy loved down away, and with a quill,
By this right arm drawn from thy wanton wing,
Write to thy laughing mother in thy blood
That you are powers belied and all your darts
Are to be blown away by men resolved
Like dust. I know thou fear'st my words; away.   90
    Tig. [*Aside*] Oh, misery, why should he be so slow?
There can no falsehood come of loving her,
Though I have given my faith; she is a thing
Both to be loved and served beyond my faith.
I would he would present me to her quickly.
    Pan. Will you not speak at all? Are you so far
From kind words? Yet to save my modesty,
That must talk till you answer, do not stand
As you were dumb; say something, though it be
Poisoned with anger that may strike me dead.   100
    Mard. Have you no life at all? For manhood' sake,
Let her not kneel and talk neglected thus.

A tree would find a tongue to answer her,
Did she but give it such a loved respect.
    Arb. You mean this lady? Lift her from the earth;
Why do you let her kneel so long?—Alas,
Madam, your beauty uses to command
And not to beg; what is your suit to me?
It shall be granted; yet the time is short
And my affairs are great.—But where's my sister?   110
I bade she should be brought.
    Mard. [*Aside*]   What, is he mad?
    Arb. Gobrius, where is she?
    Gob. Sir?
    Arb. Where is she, man?
    Gob. Who, sir?
    Arb. Who? Hast thou forgot? My sister.
    Gob. Your sister, sir?
    Arb. Your sister, sir? Someone that has a wit
Answer, where is she?
    Gob.   Do you not see her there?
    Arb. Where?   120
    Gob. There.
    Arb. There? Where?
    Mard. 'Slight,[5] there; are you blind?
    Arb. Which do you mean? That little one?

                    [*Indicates* SPACONIA.]

    Gob.   No, sir.
    Arb. No, sir! Why do you mock me? I can see
No other here but that petitioning lady.
    Gob. That's she.
    Arb.   Away.
    Gob.   Sir, it is she.
    Arb.   'Tis false—
    Gob. Is it?
    Arb.   As hell; by heaven, as false as hell!
My sister—is she dead? If it be so,
Speak boldly to me, for I am a man   130
And dare not quarrel with divinity,
But do not think to cozen[6] me with this.
I see you all are mute and stand amazed,
Fearful to answer me; it is too true
A decreed instant cuts off every life,
For which to mourn is to repine. She died
A virgin, though, more innocent than sleep,
As clear as her own eyes, and blessedness
Eternal waits upon her where she is.
I know she could not make a wish to change   140
Her state for new, and you shall see me bear
My crosses like a man. We all must die,
And she hath taught us how.
    Gob.   Do not mistake
And vex yourself for nothing, for her death
Is a long life off yet, I hope. 'Tis she;
And if my speech deserve not faith, lay death
Upon me, and my latest words shall force
A credit from you.
    Arb.   Which, good Gobrius?
That lady dost thou mean?
    Gob.   That lady, sir.
She is your sister, and she is your sister   150
That loves you so; 'tis she for whom I weep

---

[5] *'Slight:* By God's light.   [6] *cozen:* cheat.

To see you use her thus.

Arb.   It cannot be.

Tig. [*Aside*] Pish, this is tedious.
I cannot hold; I must present myself.
And yet the sight of my Spaconia
Touches me as a sudden thunderclap
Does one that is about to sin.

Arb.   Away;
No more of this. Here I pronounce him traitor,
The direct plotter of my death, that names
Or thinks her for my sister. 'Tis a lie,   160
The most malicious of the world, invented
To mad your King; he that will say so next,
Let him draw out his sword and sheath it here.
It is a sin fully as pardonable.
She is no kin to me, nor shall she be;
If she were any, I create her none,
And which of you can question this? My power
Is like the sea, that is to be obeyed
And not disputed with. I have decreed her
As far from having part of⁷ blood with me   170
As the naked Indians. Come and answer me,
He that is boldest now; is that my sister?

Mard. [*Aside*] Oh, this is fine.

Bess. No, marry, is she not, an't please your majesty.
I never thought she was; she's nothing like you.

Arb. No; 'tis true, she is not.

Mard. [*To* BESSUS]   Thou shouldst be hanged.

Pan. Sir, I will speak but once. By the same power
You make my blood a stranger unto yours,
You may command me dead, and, so much love
A stranger may importune, pray you, do.   180
If this request appears too much to grant,
Adopt me of⁸ some other family
By your unquestioned word, else I shall live
Like sinful issues that are left in streets
By their regardless⁹ mothers, and no name
Will be found for me.

Arb.   I will hear no more.
[*Aside*] Why should there be such music in a voice
And sin for me to hear it? All the world
May take delight in this, and 'tis damnation
For me to do so.—You are fair and wise   190
And virtuous, I think, and he is blest
That is so near you as your brother is;
But you are naught to me but a disease,
Continual torment without hope of ease.
Such an ungodly sickness I have got,
That he that undertakes my cure must first
O'erthrow divinity, all moral laws,
And leave mankind as unconfined as beasts,
Allowing them to do all actions
As freely as they drink when they desire.   200
Let me not hear you speak again; yet so
I shall but languish for the want of that,
The having which would kill me.—No man here
Offer to speak for her, for I consider
As much as you can say.—I will not toil
My body and my mind too. Rest thou there;

                    [*Sits.*]

Here's one within will labor for you both.

Pan. I would I were past speaking.

Gob.   Fear not, madam;
The King will alter. 'Tis some sudden change,
And you shall see it end some other way.   210

Pan. Pray God it do.

Tig. [*Aside*] Though she to whom I swore be here, I
    cannot
Stifle my passion longer. If my father
Should raise again, disquieted with this,
And charge me to forbear, yet it would out.—
[*To* PANTHEA] Madam, a stranger and a prisoner begs
To be bid welcome.

Pan.   You are welcome, sir,
I think; but if you be not, 'tis past me
To make you so, for I am here a stranger
Greater than you. We know from whence you come,
But I appear a lost thing, and by whom   221
Is yet uncertain, found here in the court,
And only suffered to walk up and down
As one not worth the owning.

Spac. [*Aside*]   Oh, I fear
Tigranes will be caught; he looks, methinks,
As he would change¹⁰ his eyes with her. Some help
There is above for me, I hope.

Tig. Why do you turn away and weep so fast,
And utter things that misbecome your looks?
Can you want owning?

Spac. [*Aside*]   Oh, 'tis certain so.   230

Tig. Acknowledge yourself mine—

Arb.   How now!

Tig.   —And then
See if you want an owner.

Arb.   They are talking.

Tig. Nations shall own you for their queen.

Arb. Tigranes, art not thou my prisoner?

Tig. I am.

Arb.   And who is this?

Tig.   She is your sister.

Arb. She is so—

Mard. [*Aside*] Is she so again? That's well.

Arb. And how dare you then offer to change
Words with her?

Tig. Dare do it! Why, you brought me hither, sir,
To that intent.

Arb.   Perhaps I told you so.   240
If I had sworn it, had you so much folly
To credit it? The least word that she speaks
Is worth a life. Rule your disordered tongue,
Or I will temper it.

Spac. [*Aside*]   Blest be that breath.

Tig. Temper my tongue! Such incivilities
As these no barbarous people ever knew.
You break the law of nature and of nations.
You talk to me as if I were a prisoner
For theft. My tongue be tempered? I must speak
If thunder check me, and I will.

Arb.   You will?   250

---

⁷ *having part of:* sharing.   ⁸ *of:* into.
⁹ *regardless:* uncaring.   ¹⁰ *change:* exchange.

Spac. [*Aside*] Alas, my fortune!
Tig.   Do not fear his frown;
Dear madam, hear me.
    Arb. Fear not my frown! But that 'twere base in me
To fight with one I know I can o'ercome,
Again thou shouldst be conquerèd by me.
    Mard. [*Aside*] He has one ransom with him [11] already; methinks 'twere good to fight double or quit. [12]
    Arb. Away with him to prison.—Now, sir, see
If my frown be regardless. [13]—Why delay you?
Seize him, Bacurius.—You shall know my word   260
Sweeps like a wind, and all it grapples with
Are as the chaff before it.
    Tig.   Touch me not.
    Arb. Help there.
    Tig.   Away.
    1 Gent.   It is in vain to struggle.
    2 Gent. You must be forced.
    Bac.   Sir, you must pardon us;
We must obey.

                          [*They seize him.*]

    Arb.   Why do you dally there?
Drag him away by anything.
    Bac.   Come, sir.
    Tig. Justice, thou ought'st to give me strength enough
To shake all these off.—This is tyranny,
Arbaces, subtler than the burning bull's [14]
Or that famed tyrant's bed. [15] Thou might'st as well
Search in the depth of winter through the snow   271
For half-starved people to bring home with thee
To show 'em fire and send 'em back again
As use me thus.
    Arb.   Let him be close, Bacurius.
    Exeunt Tigranes [*led by the two* Gentlemen] *and*
                                  Bacurius.
    Spac. [*Aside*] I ne'er rejoiced at any ill to him
But this imprisonment; what shall become
Of me forsaken?
    Gob.   You will not let your sister
Depart thus discontented from you, sir?
    Arb. By no means, Gobrius; I have done her wrong,
And made myself believe much of myself   280
That is not in me. [*To* Panthea] You did kneel to me
Whilst I stood stubborn and regardless [16] by
And, like a god incensèd, gave no ear
To all your prayers. Behold, I kneel to you.
Show a contempt as large as was my own,
And I will suffer it; yet at the last
Forgive me.

    Pan.   Oh, you wrong me more in this

                                 [*Kneels.*]

Than in your rage you did; you mock me now.
    Arb. Never forgive me, then, which is the worst
Can happen to me.
    Pan.   If you be in earnest,   290
Stand up and give me but a gentle look
And two kind words, and I shall be in heaven.
    Arb. Rise you then, too.

                [*Rises and raises* Panthea.]

                       Here I acknowledge thee
My hope, the only jewel of my life,
The best of sisters, dearer than my breath,
A happiness as high as I could think;
And when my actions call thee otherwise,
Perdition light upon me.
    Pan.   This is better
Than if you had not frowned. It comes to me
Like mercy at the block, and when I leave   300
To serve you with my life, your curse be with me.
    Arb. Then thus do I salute thee—and again.

                                [*Kisses her.*]

To make this knot the stronger. [*Aside*] Paradise
Is there.—It may be you are still in doubt;
This, this third kiss, blots it out. [*Aside*] I wade in sin,
And foolishly entice myself along.—
Take her away; see her a prisoner
In her own chamber, closely, Gobrius.
    Pan. Alas, sir, why?
    Arb.   I must not stay the answer—
Do it.
    Gob. Good sir—
    Arb.   No more—do it, I say.   310
    Mard. [*Aside*] This is better and better.
    Pan. Yet hear me speak.
    Arb.   I will not hear you speak.—
Away with her; let no man think to speak
For such a creature, for she is a witch,
A poisoner, and a traitor.
    Gob. Madam, this office grieves me.
    Pan.   Nay, 'tis well;
The King is pleased with it.
    Arb. Bessus, go you along too with her.—I will prove
All this that I have said, if I may live
So long. But I am desperately sick,   320
For she has given me poison in a kiss—
She had it 'twixt her lips, and with her eyes
She witches people. Go without a word.—
    Exeunt omnes praeter [17] Arbaces, Mardonius.
Why should you that have made me stand in war
Like fate itself, cutting what threads [18] I pleased,
Decree such an unworthy end of me
And all my glories? What am I, alas,
That you oppose me? If my secret thoughts
Have ever harbored swellings [19] against you,
They could not hurt you, and it is in you   330
To give me sorrow that will render me
Apt to receive your mercy. Rather so—

---

[11] *has . . . him:* must pay one ransom.   [12] *quit:* nothing.
[13] *regardless:* unworthy of respect.
[14] *burning bull's:* Phalaris, tyrant of Acragas, roasted victims in a brazen bull.
[15] *bed:* Procrustes, Attic highwayman, stretched and cut his victims to fit his iron bed.
[16] *regardless:* heedless.   [17] *L.:* except.
[18] *threads:* i.e., of life; the classical Fates were imagined so to end lives.
[19] *swellings:* feelings of arrogance, pride, anger.

Let it be rather so—than punish me
With such unmanly sins. Incest is in me
Dwelling already, and it must be holy
That pulls it thence.—Where art, Mardonius?
 Mard. Here, sir.
 Arb.   I prithee, bear me, if thou canst.
Am I not grown a strange weight?
 Mard.   As you were.
 Arb. No heavier?
 Mard.   No sir.
 Arb.   Why, my legs
Refuse to bear my body. Oh, Mardonius,   340
Thou hast in field beheld me, when thou know'st
I could have gone,[20] though I could never run.
 Mard. And so I shall again.
 Arb.   Oh, no, 'tis past.
 Mard. Pray ye go; rest yourself.
 Arb.   Wilt thou hereafter
When they talk of me, as thou shalt hear
Nothing but infamy, remember some
Of those things?
 Mard.   Yes, I will.
 Arb.   I prithee, do;
For thou shalt never see me so again.
 Mard. I warrant ye.
             Exeunt.

[III.ii]

Enter BESSUS.

Bess. They talk of fame; I have gotten it in the wars and will afford[1] any man a reasonable pennyworth. Some will say they could be content to have it but that it is to be achieved with danger; but my opinion is otherwise, for if I might stand still in cannon-proof[2] and have fame fall upon me, I would refuse it. My reputation came principally by thinking to run away, which nobody knows but Mardonius, and I think he conceals it to anger me. Before I went to the wars, I came to the town a young fellow without means or 10 parts to deserve friends; and my empty guts persuaded me to lie and abuse people for my meat,[3] which I did, and they beat me. Then would I fast two days, till my hunger cried out on me, "Rail still"; then, methought, I had a monstrous stomach[4] to abuse them again, and did it. In this state I continued till they hung me up by th'heels and beat me with hazel sticks, as if they would have baked me and have cozened[5] somebody with me for venison. After this I railed and eat quietly; for the whole kingdom took notice of me for a baffled,[6] 20 whipped fellow, and what I said was remembered in mirth but never in anger, of which I was glad. I would it were at that pass again. After this, God called an aunt of mine that left two hundred pounds in a cousin's hand for me, who, taking me to be a gallant young spirit, raised a company for me with the money and sent me into Armenia with 'em. Away I would have run from them but that I could get no company, and alone I durst not run. I was never at battle but once, and there I was running, but Mardonius cudgeled 30

me; yet I got loose at last, but was so afraid that I saw no more than my shoulders do, but fled with my whole company amongst my enemies, and overthrew 'em. Now the report of my valor is come over before me, and they say I was a raw young fellow but now I am improved. A plague of their eloquence; 'twill cost me many a beating. And Mardonius might help this too if he would; for now they think to get honor of me, and all the men I have abused call me freshly to account, worthily, as they call it, by the way of challenge. 40

Enter a Gentleman.

 Gent. Good morrow, Captain Bessus.
 Bess. Good morrow, sir.
 Gent. I come to speak with you—
 Bess. You are very welcome.
 Gent. From one that holds himself wronged by you some three years since. Your worth, he says, is famed, and he nothing doubts but you will do him right, as beseems a soldier.
 Bess. [*Aside*] A pox on 'em; so they cry all. 49
 Gent. And a slight note I have about me for you, for the delivery of which you must excuse me; it is an office that friendship calls upon me to do and no way offensive to you, since I desire but right on both sides.

       [*Gives him a letter.*]

 Bess. 'Tis a challenge, sir, is it not?
 Gent. 'Tis an inviting to the field.
 Bess. An inviting? Oh, cry you mercy. [*Aside*] What a compliment he delivers it with! He might as agreeably to my nature present me poison with such a speech. [*Reads aside*] Um, um, um—reputation; um, um, um—call you to an account; um, um, um—forced to this; 60 um, um, um—with my sword; um, um, um—like a gentleman; um, um, um—dear to me; um, um, um—satisfaction.—'Tis very well, sir; I do accept it, but he must await an answer this thirteen weeks.
 Gent. Why, sir, he would be glad to wipe off his stain as soon as he can.
 Bess. Sir, upon my credit, I am already engaged to two hundred and twelve, all which must have their stains wiped off, if that be the word, before him. 69
 Gent. Sir, if you be truly engaged but to one, he shall stay a competent[7] time.
 Bess. Upon my faith, sir, to two hundred and twelve; and I have a spent body, too much bruised in battle, so that I cannot fight, I must be plain with you, above three combats a day. All the kindness I can do him is to set him resolutely in my roll the two hundred and thirteenth man, which is something, for I tell you I think there will be more after him than before him. I think so. Pray ye commend me to him and tell him this. 80

---

[20] *gone:* walked.
III.ii.
 [1] *I will afford:* can spare.   [2] *cannon-proof:* armor.
 [3] *abuse . . . meat:* earn dinner by slanderous gossip.
 [4] *stomach:* appetite; will.   [5] *cozened:* deceived.
 [6] *baffled:* disgraced.   [7] *competent:* sufficient.

Gent. I will, sir; good morrow to you.

Bess. Good morrow, good sir.

[*Exit* Gentleman.]

Certainly my safest way were to print myself a coward, with a discovery[8] how I came by my credit, and clap it upon every post. I have received above thirty challenges within this two hours. Marry, all but the first I put off with engagement, and, by good fortune, the first is no madder of fighting than I, so that that's reserved.[9] The place where it must be ended is four days' journey off, and our arbitrators are these: he has chosen a   90 gentleman in travel, and I have a special friend with a quartan ague[10] likely to hold him this five year for mine, and when his man comes home, we are to expect[11] my friend's health. If they would send me challenges thus thick, as long as I lived I would have no other living; I can make seven shillings a day o'th' paper to the grocers.[12] Yet I learn nothing by all these but a little skill in comparing of styles. I do find evidently that there is some one scrivener in this town that has a great hand in writing of challenges, for they are   100 all of a cut[13] and six of 'em in a hand; and they all end "My reputation is dear to me, and I must require satisfaction."—Who's there? More paper, I hope. No, 'tis my lord Bacurius; I fear all is not well betwixt us.

Enter BACURIUS.

Bac. Now, Captain Bessus, I come about a frivolous matter caused by as idle a report. You know you were a coward.

Bess. Very right.

Bac. And wronged me.

Bess. True, my lord.   110

Bac. But now people will call you valiant—desertlessly, I think; yet, for their satisfaction, I will have you fight with me.

Bess. Oh, my good lord, my deep engagements—

Bac. Tell not me of your engagements, Captain Bessus; it is not to be put off with an excuse. For my own part, I am none of the multitude that believe your conversion from coward.

Bess. My lord, I seek not quarrels, and this belongs not to me; I am not to maintain it.   120

Bac. Who then, pray?

Bess. Bessus the coward wronged you.

Bac. Right.

Bess. And shall Bessus the valiant maintain what Bessus the coward did?

Bac. I prithee, leave these cheating tricks. I swear thou shalt fight with me, or thou shalt be beat extremely and kicked.

Bess. Since you provoke me thus far, my lord, I will fight with you, and, by my sword, it shall cost me   130 twenty pounds but I will have my leg well a week sooner purposely.

Bac. Your leg! Why, what ails your leg? I'll do a cure on you; stand up.

Bess. My lord, this is not noble in you.

Bac. What dost thou with such a phrase in thy mouth? I will kick thee out of all good words before I leave thee.

[*Kicks him.*]

Bess. My lord, I take this as a punishment for the offense I did when I was a coward.   140

Bac. When thou wert! Confess thyself a coward still, or, by this light, I'll beat thee into sponge.

Bess. Why, I am one.

Bac. Are you so, sir? And why do you wear a sword then? Come, unbuckle, quick!

Bess. My lord—

Bac. Unbuckle, I say, and give it me; as I live, thy head will ache extremely.

Bess. It is a pretty hilt, and if your lordship take an affection to it, with all my heart I present it to you for a New Year's gift.[14]   151

[*Gives him his sword, with a knife attached.*]

Bac. I thank you very heartily. Sweet captain, farewell.

Bess. One word more. I beseech your lordship to render me my knife again.

Bac. Marry, by all means, captain.

[*Gives back the knife.*]

Cherish yourself with it, and eat hard, good Captain; we cannot tell whether we shall have any more such. Adieu, dear captain.   159

Exit.

Bess. I will make better use of this than of my sword. A base spirit has this vantage of a brave one; it keeps always at a stay;[15] nothing brings it down, not beating. I remember I promised the King in a great audience that I would make my backbiters eat my sword to a knife. How to get another sword I know not, nor know any means left for me to maintain my credit but impudence; therefore, will I outswear him and all his followers that this is all is left uneaten of my sword.

Exit.

[III.iii]

Enter MARDONIUS.

Mard. I'll move[1] the King. He is most strangely altered; I guess the cause, I fear, too right. Heaven has some secret end in't, and 'tis a scourge, no question, justly laid upon him. He has followed me through twenty rooms, and ever when I stay to await his command, he blushes like a girl and looks upon me as if modesty kept in his business; so turns away from me, but if I go on, he follows me again.

---

[8] *discovery:* revelation.   [9] *reserved:* deferred.
[10] *quartan ague:* fever with recurrent chills.
[11] *expect:* await.
[12] *o' . . . grocers:* i.e., selling it to them for wrapping.
[13] *cut:* style.
[14] *New Year's gift:* the equivalent of modern Christmas gifts.   [15] *keeps . . . stay:* stays the same.

III.iii.
[1] *move:* i.e., prompt.

[*Enter* ARBACES.]

See, here he is. I do not use² this, yet, I know not how,
I cannot choose but weep to see him. His very   10
enemies, I think, whose wounds have bred his fame,
if they should see him now, would find tears in their
eyes.
    Arb. [*Aside*] I cannot utter it. Why should I keep
A breast to harbor thoughts I dare not speak?
Darkness is in my bosom, and there lies
A thousand thoughts that cannot brook the light.
How wilt thou vex me when this deed is done,
Conscience, that art afraid to let me name it?
    Mard. How do you, sir?
    Arb.   Why, very well, Mardonius;
How dost thou do?
    Mard.   Better than you, I fear.   21
    Arb. I hope thou art, for, to be plain with thee,
Thou art in hell else. Secret scorching flames,
That far transcend earthly material fires,
Are crept into me, and there is no cure.
Is not that strange, Mardonius, there's no cure?
    Mard. Sir, either I mistake or there is something hid
That you would utter to me.
    Arb. So there is, but yet I cannot do it.   29
    Mard. Out with it, sir. If it be dangerous, I shall not
shrink to do you service. I shall not esteem my life a
weightier matter than indeed it is. I know 'tis subject
to more chances than it hath hours, and I were better
lose it in my King's cause than with an ague, or a fall,
or, sleeping, to a thief, as all these are probable enough.
Let me but know what I shall do for you.
    Arb. [*Aside*] It will not out.—Were you with
        Gobrius,
And bade him give my sister all content
The place affords, and give her leave to send
And speak to whom she please?
    Mard.   Yes, sir, I was.   40
    Arb. And did you to Bacurius say as much
About Tigranes?
    Mard.   Yes.
    Arb.   That's all my business.
    Mard. Oh, say not so.
You had an answer of³ all this before.
Besides, I think this business might be uttered
More carelessly.
    Arb. Come, thou shalt have it out; I do beseech thee,
By all the love thou hast professed to me,
To see my sister from me.⁴
    Mard.   Well, and what?
    Arb. That's all.
    Mard.   That's strange. Shall I say nothing to
        her?   50
    Arb. Not a word;
But if thou lovest me, find some subtle way
To make her understand by signs.
    Mard.   But what?
What should I make her understand?
    Arb. O Mardonius, for that I must be pardoned.
    Mard. You may, but I can only see her then.
    Arb. 'Tis true.

Bear her this ring, then, and, on more advice,⁵
Thou shalt speak to her. Tell her I do love
My kindred all, wilt thou?   60
    Mard. Is there no more?
    Arb.   Oh, yes. And her the best,
Better than any brother loves his sister.
That's all.
    Mard. Methinks this need not have been
Delivered with such a caution; I'll do it.
    Arb. There is more yet—wilt thou be faithful to me?
    Mard. Sir, if I take upon me to deliver it
After I hear it, I'll pass through fire to do it.
    Arb. I love her better than a brother ought.
Dost thou conceive me?
    Mard. I hope I do not, sir.
    Arb.   No? Thou art dull.   70
Kneel down before her, and ne'er rise again
Till she will love me.
    Mard.   Why, I think she does.
    Arb. But better than she does—another way—
As wives loves husbands.
    Mard.   Why, I think there are
Few wives that love their husbands better than
She does you.
    Arb. Thou wilt not understand me. Is it fit
This should be uttered plainly? Take it, then,
Naked as it is. I would desire her love
Lasciviously, lewdly, incestuously,   80
To do a sin that needs must damn us both
And thee, too. Dost thou understand me now?
    Mard. Yes. There's your ring again. What have I
        done
Dishonestly in my whole life, name it,
That you should put so base a business to me?
    Arb. Didst thou not tell me thou wouldst do it?
    Mard. Yes, if I undertook it; but if all
My hairs were lives, I would not be engaged
In such a cause to save my last life.
    Arb. O, guilt, how poor and weak a thing art thou!
This man that is my servant, whom my breath   91
Might blow about the world, might beat me here,
Having his cause, whilst I, pressed down with sin,
Could not resist him.—Dear Mardonius,
It was a motion misbeseeming man,
And I am sorry for it.
    Mard. Pray God you may be so. You must under-
stand, nothing that you can utter can remove my love
and service from my Prince. But otherwise, I think I
shall not love you more; for you are sinful, and,   100
if you do this crime, you ought to have no laws, for after
this it will be great injustice in you to punish any
offender for any crime. For myself, I find my heart too
big; I feel I have not patience to look on whilst you run
these forbidden courses. Means I have none but your
favor, and I am rather glad that I shall lose 'em both
together than keep 'em with such conditions. I shall
find a dwelling amongst some people where, though
our garments perhaps be coarser, we shall be richer far

---

² *do . . . use:* am not accustomed.   ³ *of:* to.
⁴ *from me:* on my behalf.   ⁵ *advice:* reflection.

within and harbor no such vices in 'em. God preserve
you, and mend you.   111
   Arb. Mardonius! stay, Mardonius! for though
My present state require nothing but knaves
To be about me, such as are prepared
For every wicked act, yet who does know
But that my loathèd fate may turn about,
And I have use of honest men again?
I hope I may. I prithee, leave me not.

Enter BESSUS *to them.*

   Bess. Where is the King?
   Mard. There.   120
   Bess. An't please your majesty, there's the knife.
   Arb. What knife?
   Bess. The sword is eaten.
   Mard. Away, you fool. The King is serious,
And cannot now admit your vanities.
   Bess. Vanities! I am no honest man if my enemies
have not brought it to this. What, do you think I lie?
   Arb. No, no; 'tis well, Bessus, 'tis very well. I am
glad on't.
   Mard. If your enemies brought it to that, your
enemies are cutlers. Come, leave the King.   131
   Bess. Why, may not valor approach him?
   Mard. Yes, but he has affairs. Depart, or I shall be
something unmannerly with you.
   Arb. No, let him stay, Mardonius, let him stay.
I have occasion with him very weighty,
And I can spare you now.
   Mard. Sir?
   Arb. Why, I can spare you now.
   Bess. Mardonius, give way to the state affairs.   140
   Mard. Indeed, you are fitter for his present purpose.
Exit.
   Arb. Bessus, I should[6] employ thee; wilt thou do't?
   Bess. Do't for you? By this air, I will do anything
without exception, be it a good, bad, or indifferent
thing.
   Arb. Do not swear.
   Bess. By this light, but I will; anything whatsoever.
   Arb. But I shall name a thing
Thy conscience will not suffer thee to do.
   Bess. I would fain hear that thing.   150
   Arb. Why, I would have thee get my sister for me;
Thou understand'st me—in a wicked manner.
   Bess. Oh, you would have a bout[7] with her? I'll do't;
I'll do't, i'faith.
   Arb. Wilt thou? Dost make no more on't?
   Bess. More? No. Why, is there anything else? If
there be, tell me; it shall be done, too.
   Arb. Hast thou no greater sense of such a sin?
Thou art too wicked for my company,
Though I have hell within me, and mayst yet   160
Corrupt me further. Pray thee, answer me,
How do I show to thee after this motion?

---

   6 *should:* would.   7 *bout:* sexual encounter.
   8 *set it hard:* work actively on that.
   9 *lust:* desire; i.e., his only motivation is the impulse to
break a law.

   Bess. Why, your majesty looks as well, in my
opinion, as ever you did since you were born.
   Arb. But thou appearest to me after thy grant
The ugliest, loathed, detestable thing
That I have ever met with. Thou hast eyes
Like flames of sulphur, which, methinks, do dart
Infection on me, and thou hast a mouth
Enough to take me in, where there do stand   170
Four rows of iron teeth.
   Bess. I feel no such thing. But 'tis no matter how I
look; I'll do your business as well as they that look
better. And when this is dispatched, if you have a mind
to your mother, tell me, and you shall see I'll set it
hard.[8]
   Arb. My mother!—heaven forgive me to hear this;
I am inspired with horror.—I hate thee
Worse than my sin, which, if I could come by,
Should suffer death eternal, ne'er to rise   180
In any breast again. Know I will die
Languishing mad, as I resolve I shall,
Ere I will deal by such an instrument.
Thou art too sinful to employ in this.
Out of the world; away!

[*Beats him.*]

   Bess.   What do you mean, sir?
   Arb. Hung 'round with curses, take thy fearful flight
Into the deserts, where, 'mongst all the monsters,
If thou find'st one so beastly as thyself,
Thou shalt be held as innocent.
   Bess.   Good sir—
   Arb. If there were no such instruments as thou,   190
We kings could never act such wicked deeds.
Seek out a man that mocks divinity,
That breaks each precept both of God's and man's
And nature's too, and does it without lust,[9]
Merely because it is a law and good,
And live with him, for him thou canst not spoil.
Away, I say.

Exit BESSUS.
I will not do this sin.
I'll press it here till it do break my breast.
It heaves to get out; but thou art a sin,
And, spite of torture, I will keep thee in.   200
[*Exit.*]

Finis Actus Tertii.

ACT FOUR

SCENE ONE

Enter GOBRIUS, PANTHEA, SPACONIA.

   Gob. Have you written, madam?
   Pan.   Yes, good Gobrius.
   Gob. And with a kindness and such winning words
As may provoke him at one instant feel
His double fault, your wrong and his own rashness?
   Pan. I have sent words enough, if words may win
     him
From his displeasure, and such words, I hope,

As shall gain much upon his goodness, Gobrius.
Yet fearing, since th'are many and a woman's,
A poor belief may follow, I have woven
As many truths within 'em to speak for me   10
That, if he be but gracious and receive 'em—
  Gob. Good lady, be not fearful. Though he should
    not
Give you your present end [1] in this, believe it,
You shall feel, if your virtue can induce you
To labor out [2] this tempest, which I know
Is but a poor proof [3] against your patience,
All those contents [4] your spirit will arrive at
Newer and sweeter to you. Your royal brother,
When he shall once collect himself and see
How far he has been asunder from himself,   20
What a mere [5] stranger to his golden temper,
Must from those roots of virtue, never dying
Though somewhat stopped with humor,[6] shoot again
Into a thousand glories, bearing his fair branches
High as our hopes can look at, straight as justice,
Loaden with ripe contents. He loves you dearly—
I know it—and I hope I need not further
Win you to understand it.
  Pan.   I believe it.
But howsoever, I am sure I love him dearly.
So dearly that if anything I write   30
For my enlarging [7] should beget his anger—
Heaven be a witness with me, and my faith—
I had rather live entombèd here.
  Gob. You shall not feel a worse stroke than your grief;
I am sorry 'tis so sharp. I kiss your hand
And this night will deliver this true story
With this hand to your brother.
  Pan.   Peace go with you;
You are a good man.
                              [*Exit* GOBRIUS.]
              My Spaconia,
Why are you ever sad thus?
  Spac.   Oh, dear lady.
  Pan. Prithee, discover not a way to sadness   40
Nearer than I have in me. Our two sorrows
Work like two eager [8] hawks, who shall get highest.
How shall I lessen thine? For mine, I fear,
Is easier known than cured.
  Spac.   Heaven comfort both
And give yours happy ends, however I
Fall in my stubborn fortunes.
  Pan.   This but teaches
How to be more familiar with our sorrows,
That are too much our masters. Good Spaconia,
How shall I do you service?
  Spac.   Noblest lady,
You make me more a slave still to your goodness   50
And only live to purchase [9] thanks to pay you,
For that is all the business of my life now.
I will be bold, since you will have it so,
To ask a noble favor of you.
  Pan. Speak it; 'tis yours, for from so sweet a virtue
No ill demand has issue.
  Spac. Then, ever virtuous, let me beg your will
In helping me to see the Prince Tigranes,

With whom I am equal prisoner, if not more.
  Pan. Reserve me to a greater end, Spaconia;   60
Bacurius cannot want so much good manners
As to deny your gentle visitation,
Though you came only with your own command.
  Spac. I know they will deny me, gracious madam,
Being a stranger and so little famed,
So utter [10] empty of those excellencies
That tame authority. But in you, sweet lady,
All these are natural, beside a power
Derived immediate from your royal brother,   69
Whose least word in you may command the kingdom.
  Pan. More than my word, Spaconia, you shall carry,
For fear it fail you.
  Spac.   Dare you trust a token?
Madam, I fear I'm grown too bold a beggar.
  Pan. You are a pretty one, and trust me, lady,
It joys me I shall do a good to you
Though to myself I never shall be happy.
Here, take this ring, and from me as a token
Deliver it; I think they will not stay you.
So all your own desires go with you, lady.   79
  Spac. And sweet peace to your grace.
  Pan.   Pray God I find it.
                                        Exeunt.

[IV.ii]

              Enter TIGRANES.

  Tig. Fool that I am, I have undone myself,
And with mine own hand turned my fortune 'round,
That was a fair one. I have childishly
Played with my hope so long till I have broke it,
And now too late I mourn for't. Oh, Spaconia,
Thou hast found an even [1] way to thy revenge now.
Why didst thou follow me, like a faint shadow,
To wither my desires? But, wretched fool,
Why did I plant thee 'twixt the sun and me
To make me freeze thus? Why did I prefer her   10
To the fair princess?—Oh, thou fool, thou fool,
Thou family of fools, live like a slave still
And in thee bear thine own hell and thy torment;
Thou hast deserved it. Couldst thou find no lady
But she that has thy hopes [2] to put her to [3]
And hazard [4] all thy peace? None to abuse
But she that loved thee ever, poor Spaconia,
And so much loved thee that in honesty
And honor thou art bound to meet [5] her virtues?
She that forgot the greatness of her griefs   20

IV.i.
  [1] *present end:* immediate goal.   [2] *labor out:* endure.
  [3] *proof:* resistance.   [4] *contents:* contentments.
  [5] *mere:* absolute.   [6] *humor:* sap.
  [7] *enlarging:* setting free.   [8] *eager:* hungry.
  [9] *purchase:* get.   [10] *utter:* utterly.

IV.ii.
  [1] *even:* appropriate.
  [2] *she . . . hopes:* the one you are devoted to.
  [3] *put her to:* put her in the service of.
  [4] *hazard:* endanger.   [5] *meet:* equal.

And miseries that must follow such mad passions,
Endless and wild as woman's; she that for thee
And with thee lost her liberty, her name,
And country. You have paid me equal,[6] heavens,
And sent my own rod to correct me with,
A woman. For inconstancy I'll suffer;
Lay it on, justice, till my soul melt in me
For my unmanly, beastly, sudden doting
Upon a new face, after all my oaths,
Many and strange ones.   30
I feel my old fire flame again and burn
So strong and violent that should I see her
Again, the grief and that would kill me.

Enter BACURIUS *and* SPACONIA.

Bac.   Lady,
Your token I acknowledge; you may pass.
There is the King.

Spac.   I thank your lordship for it.
                    Exit BACURIUS.

Tig. [*Aside*] She comes, she comes. Shame hide me
ever from her.
Would I were buried or so far removed
Light might not find me out. I dare not see her.

Spac. Nay, never hide yourself, for were you hid
Where earth hides all her riches, near her center,   40
My wrongs, without more day, would light me to you.
I must speak ere I die. Were all your greatness
Doubled upon you, y'are a perjured man
And only mighty in the wickedness
Of wronging women. Thou art false, false prince;
I live to see it. Poor Spaconia lives
To tell thee thou art false, and then no more.
She lives to tell thee thou art more unconstant
Than all ill women ever were together,
Thy faith as firm as raging overflows   50
That no bank can command, and as lasting
As boy's gay bubbles blown in the air and broken.
The wind is fixed, to[7] thee; and sooner shall
The beaten mariner with his shrill whistle[8]
Calm the loud murmurs of the troubled main
And strike it smooth again, than thy soul fall
To have peace in love with any. Thou art all
That all good men must hate, and if thy story
Shall tell succeeding ages what thou wert,
Oh, let it spare me in it,[9] lest true lovers   60
In pity of my wrongs burn thy black legend[10]
And with their curses shake thy sleeping ashes.

Tig. Oh, oh.

Spac. The destinies, I hope, have pointed out
Our ends alike, that thou mayst die for love,
Though not for me; for, this assure thyself,

The princess hates thee deadly, and will sooner
Be won to marry with a bull, and safer,
Than such a beast as thou art. [*Aside*] I have struck,
I fear, too deep; beshrow[11] me for't.—Sir,   70
This sorrow works[12] me, like a cunning friendship,
Into the same piece with it. [*Aside*] He's ashamed;
Alas, I have been too rugged.—Dear my lord,
I am sorry I have spoken anything,
Indeed I am, that may add more restraint
To that too much you have. Good sir, be pleased
To think it was a fault of love, not malice,
And do as I will do—forgive it, prince;
I do, and can, forgive the greatest sins
To me you can repent of. Pray believe me.   80

Tig. O, my Spaconia. O, thou virtuous woman.

Spac. No more; the King, sir.

Enter ARBACES, BACURIUS, *and* MARDONIUS.

Arb. Have you been careful of our noble prisoner,
That he want nothing fitting for his greatness?

Bac. I hope his grace will quit[13] me for my care, sir.

Arb. 'Tis well.—Royal Tigranes, health.

Tig. More than the strictness[14] of this place can give
sir,
I offer back again to great Arbaces.

Arb. We thank you, worthy prince, and pray excuse
us;
We have not seen you since your being here.   90
I hope your noble usage has been equal
With your own person. Your imprisonment,
If it be any, I dare say is easy,
And shall not outlast two days.

Tig.   I thank you.
My usage here has been the same it was,
Worthy a royal conqueror. For my restraint,
It came unkindly because much unlooked for,
But I must bear it.

Arb. What lady is that, Bacurius?

Bac. One of the princess' women, sir.   100

Arb. I feared it. Why comes she hither?

Bac. To speak with the Prince Tigranes.

Arb. From whom, Bacurius?

Bac. From the princess, sir.

Arb. I know I had seen her.

Mard. [*Aside*] His fit begins to take him now again;
'tis a strange fever, and 'twill shake us all anon, I fear.
Would he were well cured of this raging folly. Give me
the wars, where men are mad and may talk what they
list[15] and held[16] the bravest fellows. This pelt-   110
ing,[17] prattling peace is good for nothing. Drinking's a
virtue to it.

Arb. I see there's truth in no man, nor obedience
But for his own ends. Why did you let her in?

Bac. It was your own command to bar none from
him;
Besides, the princess sent her ring, sir, for my warrant.

Arb. A token to Tigranes, did she not?
Sirrah, tell truth.

Bac.   I do not use to lie, sir;
'Tis no way I eat or live by. And I think
This is no token, sir.   120

---

[6] *equal:* fairly.   [7] *to:* compared to.
[8] *whistle:* proverbially said to raise the wind.
[9] *spare . . . it:* leave me out of it.
[10] *legend:* tombstone inscription.   [11] *beshrow:* curse.
[12] *works:* with "piece," the metaphor is of embroidering.
[13] *quit:* reward.
[14] *strictness:* constriction; rigor, severity.
[15] *list:* like.   [16] *held:* accounted.
[17] *pelting:* worthless.

Mard. [*Aside*] This combat has undone him. If he had been well beaten, he had been temperate. I shall never see him handsome [18] again till he have a horseman's staff poked through his shoulders or an arm broke with a bullet.

Arb. I am trifled with.

Bac. Sir?

Arb. I know it, as I know thee to be false.

Mard. [*Aside*] Now the clap [19] comes.

Bac. You never knew me so, sir. I dare speak it　130
And durst [20] a worse man tell me though my better.

Mard. [*Aside*] 'Tis well said, by my soul.

Arb. Sirrah, you answer as [21] you had no life.

Bac. That I fear, sir, to lose nobly.

Arb. I say, sir, once again—

Bac. You may say, sir, what you please.

Mard. [*Aside*] Would I might do so.

Arb. 　　　　　　　　　　I will, sir, and
　　say openly
This woman carries letters. By my life,
I know she carries letters; this woman does it.　139

Mard. Would Bessus were here to take her aside and search her; he would quickly tell you what she carried, sir.

Arb. I have found it out; this woman carries letters.

Mard. [*Aside*] If this hold, 'twill be an ill world for bawds, chambermaids, and post-boys.[22] I thank God I have none but his letters-patents,[23] things of his own inditing.[24]

Arb. Prince, this cunning cannot do it.

Tig. Do what, sir? I reach [25] you not.

Arb. It shall not serve your turn, prince.　150

Tig. Serve my turn, sir?

Arb. Ay, sir, it shall not serve your turn.

Tig. Be plainer, good sir.

Arb. This woman shall carry no more letters back to your love, Panthea. By heaven, she shall not; I say she shall not.

Mard. [*Aside*] This would make a saint swear like a soldier and a soldier like Termagant.[26]

Tig. This beats me more, King, than the blows you gave me.　160

Arb. Take 'em away both and together let 'em be prisoners strictly and closely kept, or, sirrah, your life shall answer it; and let nobody speak with 'em hereafter.

Bac. Well, I am subject to you and must endure these passions.

Spac. [*Aside*] This is the imprisonment I have looked for always
And the dear place I would choose.

　　　　　　　Exit BACURIUS *with* TIGRANES *and*
　　　　　　　　　　　　　　　SPACONIA.

Mard. Sir, have you done well now?

Arb. Dare you reprove it?

Mard. 　　　　No.

Arb. 　　　　　　　You must be crossing
　　me.

Mard. I have no letters, sir, to anger you　170
But a dry [27] sonnet of my corporal's
To an old saddler's wife, and that I'll burn, sir.

'Tis like to prove a fine age for the ignorant.

Arb. How darest thou so often forfeit thy life?
Thou knowest 'tis in my power to take it.

Mard. Yes, and I know you wonnot,[28] or, if you do,
You'll miss it quickly.

Arb. Why?

Mard. Who shall then tell you of these childish follies
When I am dead? Who shall put to his power　180
To draw those virtues out of a flood of humors
Where they are drowned and make 'em shine again?
No, cut my head off. Do, kill me.
Then you may talk, and be believed, and grow,
And have your too self-glorious temper rocked [29]
Into a dead sleep, and the kingdom with you,
Till foreign swords be in your throats and slaughter
Be everywhere about you, like your flatterers.
Do, kill me.

Arb. Prithee, be tamer, good Mardonius.　190
Thou know'st I love thee; nay, I honor thee.
Believe it, good old soldier, I am all thine,
But I am racked clean from myself. Bear with me;
Wo't thou bear with me, my Mardonius?

　　　　　　　　Enter GOBRIUS.

Mard. There comes a good man. Love him, too; he's
　　temperate.
You may live to have need of such a virtue;
Rage is not still in fashion.

Arb. 　　　　　Welcome, good Gobrius.

Gob. My service and this letter to your grace.

Arb. From whom?

Gob. From the rich mine of virtue and all beauty,
Your mournful sister.　200

Arb. She is in prison, Gobrius, is she not?

Gob. She is, sir, till your pleasure do enlarge her,
Which on my knees I beg. Oh, 'tis not fit
That all the sweetness of the world in one,
The youth and virtue that would tame wild tigers
And wilder people that have known no manners,
Should live thus cloistered up. For your love's sake,
If there be any in that noble heart
To her, a wretched lady and forlorn,　210
Or for her love to you, which is as much
As nature and obedience ever gave,
Have pity on her beauties.

Arb. Prithee stand up. 'Tis true she is too fair
And all these commendations but her own.
Would thou hadst never so commended her,
Or I ne'er lived to have heard it, Gobrius.
If thou but knew of the wrong her beauty does her,
Thou wouldst in pity of her be a liar.
Thy ignorance has drawn me, wretched man,　220

---

[18] *handsome:* easy to deal with.
[19] *clap:* thunderclap.　　　　　[20] *durst:* dare.
[21] *as:* as if.　　　[22] *post-boys:* letter-carriers.
[23] *letters patents:* official documents.
[24] *inditing:* writing.　　　[25] *reach:* understand.
[26] *Termagant:* Moslem deity imagined by medieval Christians and portrayed in plays as violent blusterer.
[27] *dry:* unadorned.　　　　[28] *wonnot:* will not.
[29] *rocked:* Q1, 2 "rott."

Whither myself nor thou canst well tell. Oh, my fate,
I think she loves me, but I fear another
Is deeper in her heart. How think'st thou, Gobrius?

Gob. I do beseech your grace, believe it not,
For let me perish if it be not false.
Good sir, read her letter.

Mard. [*Aside*] This love, or what a devil is it, I know
not, begets more mischief than a wake. I had rather be
well beaten, starved, or lousy than live within the air
on't. He that had seen this brave fellow charge   230
through a grove of pikes but t'other day, and look upon
him now, will ne'er believe his eyes again. If he continue thus but two days more, a tailor[30] may beat him
with one hand tied behind him.

Arb. Alas, she would be at liberty,
And there be thousand reasons, Gobrius,
Thousands that will deny it,
Which if she knew, she would contentedly
Be where she is and bless her virtue for it
And me, though she were closer.[31] She would,
    Gobrius;   240
Good man, indeed she would.

Gob.   Then, good sir, for
Her satisfaction send for her and with
Reason make her know why she must live
Thus from you.

Arb.   I will; go bring her to me.

                                              Exeunt.

[IV.iii]

    Enter Bessus, *and two* Swordmen,[1] *and a* Boy.

Bess. Y'are very welcome both.—Some stools there,
    boy,
And reach a table.—Gentlemen o'th' sword,
Pray, sit without more compliment.—Begone, child.

                                    [*Boy withdraws.*]

I have been curious[2] in the searching of you,
Because I understood you wise and valiant persons.

1 Sword. We understand[3] ourselves, sir.

Bess. Nay, gentlemen and my dear friends o'th'
    sword,
No compliment, I pray; but to the cause
I hang upon, which, in few,[4] is my honor.

2 Sword. You cannot hang too much, sir, for your
    honor   10
But to your cause—be wise and speak truth.

Bess. My first doubt[5] is my beating by my prince.

1 Sword. Stay there a little, sir. Do you doubt[6] a
    beating,
Or have you had a beating by your prince?

Bess. Gentlemen o'th' sword, my prince has beaten
    me.

2 Sword. Brother, what think you of this case?

1 Sword. If he have beaten him, the case is clear.

2 Sword. If he have beaten him, I grant the case.
But how? We cannot be too subtle in this business.
I say, but how?

Bess.   Even with his royal hand.   20

1 Sword. Was it a blow of love or indignation?

Bess. 'Twas twenty blows of indignation, gentlemen,
Besides two blows o'th' face.

2 Sword. Those blows o'th' face have made a new
    case on't;
The rest were but an honorable rudeness.

1 Sword. Two blows o'th' face and given by a worse
man, I must confess, as we swordsmen say, had turned
the business.[7] Mark me, brother—by a worse man.
But being, by his prince, had they been ten and
those ten drawn[8] ten teeth beside the hazard of his   30
nose forever; all these had been but favors. This is my
flat[9] opinion, which I'll die in.

2 Sword. The King may do much, captain, believe it,
for had he cracked your skull through like a bottle, or
broke a rib or two with crossing[10] of you, yet you had
lost no honor. This is strange, you may imagine, but
this is truth now, captain.

Bess. I will be glad to embrace it, gentlemen.
But how far may he strike me?

1 Sword.   There's another,
A new cause rising from the time and distance,   40
In which I will deliver my opinion.
He may strike, beat, or cause to be beaten, for these
are natural to man. Your prince, I say, may beat you so
far forth as his dominion reacheth—that's for the
distance. The time—ten mile a day, I take it.

2 Sword. Brother, you err; 'tis fifteen mile a day.
His stage[11] is ten; his beatings are fifteen.

Bess. 'Tis o'the longest, but we subjects must—

1 Sword. Be subject to it. You are wise and virtuous.

Bess. Obedience ever makes that noble use on't,   50
To which I dedicate my beaten body.
I must trouble you a little further, gentlemen o'th
    sword.

2 Sword. No trouble at all to us, sir, if we may
Profit your understanding; we are bound
By virtue of our calling to utter
Our opinions shortly and discreetly.

Bess. My sorest business is I have been kicked.

2 Sword. How far, sir?

Bess. Not to flatter myself in it, all over—
My sword lost[12] but not forced,[13] for discreetly   60
I rendered[14] it to save that imputation.

1 Sword. It showed discretion, the best part of valor.

2 Sword. Brother, this is a pretty[15] case; pray ponder
    on't.
Our friend here has been kicked.

1 Sword.   He has so, brother.

2 Sword. Sorely, he says. Now had he sit down here
Upon the mere kick, it had been cowardly.

 1 Sword. I think it had been cowardly indeed.

 2 Sword. But our friend has redeemed it in delivering
His sword without compulsion, and that man
That took it of him I pronounce a weak one 70
And his kicks nullities.
He should have kicked him after the delivery.
Which is the confirmation of a coward.

 1 Sword. Brother, I take it you mistake the question.
For say that I were kicked—

 2 Sword.   I must not say so,
Nor I must not hear it spoke by th' tongue of man.
You kicked, dear brother! you are merry.

 1 Sword. But put the case I were kicked.

 2 Sword.   Let them put it
That are things weary of their lives and know
Not honor. Put the case you were kicked! 80

 1 Sword. I do not say I was kicked.

 2 Sword.   Nor no silly
Creature that wears his head without a case,[16]
His soul in a skin coat. You kicked, dear brother!

 Bess. Nay, gentlemen, let us do what we shall do
Truly and honestly.—Good sir, to th' question.

 1 Sword. Why, then, I say, suppose your boy kicked,
captain.

 2 Sword. The boy may be supposed; he's liable.[17]
But kick my brother?

 1 Sword [*To* BESSUS] A foolish, forward zeal, sir, in
my friend.—
But to the boy; suppose the boy were kicked. 90

 Bess. I do suppose it.

 1 Sword.   Has your boy a sword?

 Bess. Surely, no; I pray suppose a sword too.

 1 Sword. I do suppose it. You grant your boy was
kicked, then?

 2 Sword. By no means, captain; let it be supposed
still.
This word "grant" makes not for us.

 1 Sword. I say this must be granted.

 2 Sword. This must be granted, brother?

 1 Sword. Ay, this must be granted.

 2 Sword.   Still the "must."

 1 Sword. I say this must be granted.

 2 Sword. Give me the "must" again. Again. Brother,
you palter.[18] 100

 1 Sword. I will not hear you, wasp.

 2 Sword. Brother,
I say you palter. The "must" three times together!
I wear as sharp steel as another man,
And my fox[19] bites as deep. "Musted," my dear
brother!
But to the cause again.

 Bess.   Nay, look you, gentlemen—

 2 Sword. In a word, I ha' done.

 1 Sword. [*To* BESSUS] A tall[20] man but untemperate;
'tis great pity.—
Once more, suppose the boy kicked—

 2 Sword. Forward. 110

 1 Sword. And, being thoroughly kicked, laughs at
the kicker.

2 Sword. So much for us; proceed.

 1 Sword. And in this beaten scorn, as I may call it,
Delivers up his weapon. Where lies the error?

 Bess. It lies i'th' beating, sir; I found it
Four days since.

 2 Sword. The error, and a sore one, as I take it,
Lies in the thing kicking.

 Bess. I understand that well; 'tis sore indeed, sir.

 1 Sword. That is, according to the man that did it.

 2 Sword. There springs a new branch. Whose was
the foot?

 Bess. A lord's. 121

 1 Sword. The cause is mighty; but had it been two
lords
And both had kicked you, if you laughed, 'tis clear.

 Bess. I did laugh, but how will that help me,
gentlemen?

 2 Sword. Yes, it shall help you, if you laughed aloud.

 Bess. As loud as a kicked man could laugh, I laughed,
sir.

 1 Sword. My reason now; the valiant man is known
By suffering and contemning. You have
Enough of both, and you are valiant.

 2 Sword. If he be sure he has been kicked enough.
For that brave sufferance you speak of, brother, 131
Consists not in a beating and away[21]
But in a cudgeled body from eighteen
To eight and thirty, in a head rebuked[22]
With pots of all size, daggers, stools, and bedstaffs.[23]
This shows a valiant man.

 Bess. Then I am valiant, as valiant as the proudest,
For these are all familiar things to me,
Familiar as my sleep or want of money.
All my whole body's but one bruise with beating; 140
I think I have been cudgeled with all nations
And almost all religions.

 2 Sword. Embrace him, brother; this man is valiant!
I know it by myself, he's valiant.

 1 Sword. Captain, thou art a valiant gentleman
To abide upon't,[24] a very valiant man.

 Bess. My equal friends o'th' sword, I must request
Your hands to this.

 2 Sword. 'Tis fit it should be.
Boy, get some wine and pen and ink within.

             [*Exit* Boy.]
Am I clear, gentlemen? 150

 1 Sword. Sir, when the world has taken notice what
We have done, make much of your body, for,
I'll pawn my steel, men will be coyer[25] of
Their legs hereafter.

 Bess.   I must request you go
Along and testify to the Lord Bacurius,
Whose foot has struck me, how you find my cause.

---

[16] *case:* unhelmeted.   [17] *liable:* suitable; subject.
[18] *palter:* equivocate. [19] *fox:* sword. [20] *tall:* brave.
[21] *away:* i.e., get up and run away.
[22] *rebuked:* punished.
[23] *bedstaffs:* stout sticks used to support a mattress, a
ready and familiar weapon.
[24] *abide upon't:* insist on the point.
[25] *coyer:* i.e., they'll be more chary of kicking you.

2 Sword. We will and tell that lord he must be
    ruled,
Or there be those abroad will rule his lordship.
                      Exeunt.

[IV.iv]

    Enter ARBACES *at one door,* GOBRIUS *and*
        PANTHEA *at another.*

Gob. Sir, here's the princess.
Arb.   Leave us then alone.
For the main cause of her imprisonment
Must not be heard by any but herself.—
                   Exit GOBRIUS.
You are welcome, sister, and I would to God
I could so bid you by another name.—
[*Aside*] If you above love not such sins as these,
Circle my heart with thoughts as cold as snow
To quench these rising flames that harbor here.
    Pan. Sir, does it please you I should speak?
    Arb.   Please me?
Ay, more than all the art of music can,   10
Thy speech does please me, for it ever sounds
As thou brought'st joyful, unexpected news.
And yet it is not fit thou shouldst be heard:
I prithee, think so.
    Pan.   Be it so; I will.
I am the first that ever had a wrong
So far from being fit to have redress
That 'twas unfit to hear it; I will back
To prison rather than disquiet you
And wait till it be fit.
    Arb.   No, do not go,
For I will hear thee with a serious thought.   20
I have collected all that's man about me
Together strongly, and I am resolved
To hear thee largely,[1] but, I do beseech thee,
Do not come nearer to me, for there is
Something in that that will undo us both.
    Pan. Alas, sir, am I venom?
    Arb.   Yes, to me.
Though of thyself I think thee to be in
As equal a degree of heat or cold
As nature can make, yet as unsound men
Convert the sweetest and the nourishing'st meats 30
Into diseases, so shall I, distempered,[2]
Do thee. I prithee, draw no nearer to me.
    Pan. Sir, this is that I would:[3] I am of late
Shut from the world, and why it should be thus
Is all I wish to know.
    Arb.   Why, credit me,
Panthea, credit me that am thy brother,
Thy loving brother, that there is a cause
Sufficient, yet unfit for thee to know,
That might undo thee everlastingly

IV.iv.
  [1] *largely:* at length.   [2] *distempered:* diseased; disturbed.
  [3] *that I would:* what I want.   [4] *in:* nearer.
  [5] *make a proof:* test.   [6] *bound:* restraint.
  [7] *start:* sudden move.

Only to hear. Wilt thou but credit this?   40
By heaven, 'tis true; believe it if thou canst.
    Pan. Children and fools are ever credulous,
And I am both, I think, for I believe.
If you dissemble, be it on your head.
I'll back unto my prison; yet, methinks,
I might be kept in some place where you are,
For in myself I find—I know not what
To call it, but it is a great desire
To see you often.   49
    Arb. Fie, you come in[4] a step; what do you mean,
Dear sister? Do not so. Alas, Panthea,
Where I am would you be? Why, that's the cause
You are imprisoned, that you may not be
Where I am.
    Pan.   Then I must endure it, sir;
God keep you.
    Arb. Nay, you shall hear the cause in short, Panthea,
And when thou hear'st it, thou wilt blush for me
And hang thy head down like a violet
Full of the morning's dew. There is a way
To gain thy freedom, but 'tis such a one   60
As puts thee in worse bondage, and I know
Thou wouldst encounter fire and make a proof[5]
Whether the gods have care of innocents
Rather than follow it. Know I have lost
The only difference betwixt man and beast,
My reason.
    Pan.   Heaven forbid.
    Arb.   Nay, it is gone,
And I am left as far without a bound[6]
As the wild ocean that obeys the winds;
Each sudden passion throws me as it lists,
And overwhelms all that oppose my will.   70
I have beheld thee with a lustful eye.
My heart is set on wickedness, to act
Such sins with thee as I have been afraid
To think of. If thou dar'st consent to this,
Which, I beseech thee, do not, thou mayst gain
Thy liberty and yield me a content.
If not, thy dwelling must be dark and close
Where I may never see thee; for God knows,
That laid this punishment upon my pride,
Thy sight at some time will enforce my madness 80
To make a start[7] e'en to thy ravishing.
Now spit upon me and call all reproaches
Thou canst devise together, and at once
Hurl 'em against me, for I am a sickness
As killing as the plague ready to seize thee.
    Pan. Far be it from me to revile the King.
But it is true that I should rather choose
To search out death, that else would search out me,
And in a grave sleep with my innocence
Than welcome such a sin. It is my fate;   90
To these cross accidents I was ordained
And must have patience, and, but that my eyes
Have more of woman in 'em than my heart,
I would not weep. Peace enter you again.
    Arb. Farewell, and, good Panthea, pray for me—
Thy prayers are pure—that I may find a death,
However soon, before my passions grow

That they forget what I desire is sin,
For thither they are tending, If that happen,
Then I shall force thee, though thou wert a virgin   100
By vow to heaven, and shall pull a heap
Of strange,[8] yet uninvented sins upon me.

   Pan. Sir, I will pray for you, yet you shall know
It is a sullen fate that governs us.
For I could wish as heartily as you
I were no sister to you; I should then
Embrace your lawful love sooner than health.

   Arb. Could'st thou affect me then?

   Pan.   So perfectly
That, as it is, I ne'er shall sway my heart
To like another.

   Arb.   Then I curse my birth.   110
Must this be added to my miseries,
That thou art willing too? Is there no stop
To our full happiness but these mere sounds,
"Brother" and "sister"?

   Pan.   There is nothing else,
But these, alas, will separate us more
Than twenty worlds betwixt us.

   Arb.   I have lived
To conquer men, and now am overthrown
Only by words, "brother" and "sister." Where
Have those words dwelling? I will find 'em out
And utterly destroy them, but they are   120
Not to be grasped. Let 'em be men or beasts,
And I will cut 'em from the earth, or towns
And I will raze 'em and then blow 'em up.
Let 'em be seas, and I will drink them off
And yet have unquenched fire left in my breast.
Let 'em be anything but merely voice.

   Pan. But 'tis not in the power of any force
Or policy[9] to conquer them.

   Arb.   Panthea,
What shall we do? Shall we stand firmly here
And gaze our eyes out?

   Pan.   Would I could do so,   130
But I shall weep out mine.

   Arb.   Accursèd man,
Thou bought'st thy reason at too dear a rate,
For thou hast all thy actions bounded in
With curious rules when every beast is free.
What is there that acknowledges a kindred
But wretched man? Whoever saw the bull
Fearfully leave the heifer that he liked
Because they had one dam?

   Pan.   Sir, I disturb you
And myself, too; 'twere better I were gone.
I will not be so foolish as I was.   140

   Arb. Stay, we will love just as becomes our births,
No otherwise. Brothers and sisters may
Walk hand in hand together; so will we.
Come nearer. Is there any hurt in this?

   Pan. I hope not.

   Arb.   Faith, there's none at all.
And tell me truly now, is there not one
You love above me?

   Pan.   No, by heaven.

   Arb.   Why yet,

You sent unto Tigranes, sister.

   Pan.   True,
But for another. For the truth—

   Arb.   No more;
I'll credit thee. I know thou canst not lie;   150
Thou art all truth.

   Pan.   But is there nothing else
That we may do but only walk? Methinks
Brothers and sisters lawfully may kiss.

   Arb. And so they may, Panthea; so will we
And kiss again, too. We were scrupulous
And foolish, but we will be so no more.

                   [*They kiss.*]

   Pan. If you have any mercy, let me go
To prison, to my death, to anything.
I feel a sin growing upon my blood
Worse than all these, hotter, I fear, than yours.   160

   Arb. That is impossible. What should we do?

   Pan. Fly, sir, for God's sake.

   Arb.   So we must; away.
Sin grows upon us more by this delay.

                   Exeunt.

        Finis Actus Quarti.

ACT FIVE

SCENE ONE

Enter MARDONIUS *and* LIGONES.

   Mard. Sir, the King has seen your commission, and
     believes it,
And freely by this warrant gives you leave
To visit Prince Tigranes, your noble master.

   Lig. I thank his grace and kiss his hands.

   Mard.   But is
The main of all your business ended in this?

   Lig. I have another, but a worse. I am ashamed.
It is a business—

   Mard.   You seem[1] a worthy person,
And a stranger I am sure you are; you may employ me,
If you please, without your purse. Such offices
Should ever be their own rewards.   10

   Lig. I am bound to your nobleness.

   Mard. I may have need of you, and then this
     courtesy,
If it be any, is not ill bestowed.
But may I civilly desire the rest?
I shall not be a hurter, if no helper.

   Lig. Sir, you shall know I have lost a foolish daughter
And with her all my patience, pilfered away
By a mean captain of your King's.

   Mard.   Stay there, sir.
If he have reached the noble worth of captain,
He may well claim a worthy gentlewoman,   20
Though she were yours and noble.

   Lig. I grant all that, too. But this wretched fellow
Reaches no further than the empty name

---

      [8] *strange:* rare.   [9] *policy:* scheme.
V.i.
    [1] *seem:* Q1, 2 "serve."

That serves to feed him; were he valiant
Or had but in him any noble nature
That might hereafter promise him a good man,
My cares were something lighter and my grave
A span yet from me.
  Mard.   I confess such fellows
Be in all royal camps, and have and must be,
To make the sin of coward more detested   30
In the mean soldier, that with such a foil²
Sets off much valor. By the description
I should now guess him to you. It was Bessus;
I dare almost with confidence pronounce it.
  Lig. 'Tis such a scurvy name as Bessus; and now
I think, 'tis he.
  Mard.   "Captain" do you call him?
Believe me, sir, you have a misery
Too mighty for your age. A pox upon him,
For that must be the end of all his service.   39
Your daughter was not mad, sir?
  Lig.   No, would she had been:
The fault had had more credit. I would do something.
  Mard. I would fain counsel you, but to what I know
    not.
He's so below a beating that the women
Find him not worthy of their distaffs³ and
To hang him were to cast away a rope;
He's such an airy, thin, unbodied coward
That no revenge can catch him.
I'll tell you sir, and tell you truth; this rascal
Fears neither God nor man, h'as been so beaten.
Sufferance has made him wainscot.⁴ He has had   50
Since he was first a slave
At least three hundred daggers set in his head,
As little boys do new knives in hot meat.
There's not a rib in's body, o' my conscience,
That has not been thrice broken with dry⁵ beating,
And now his sides look like to wicker targets,⁶
Every way bended.
Children will shortly take him for a wall
And set their stone-bows in his forehead.⁷ He
Is of so low a sense, I cannot in   60
A week imagine what should be done to him.
  Lig. Sure, I have committed some great sin,
That this strange fellow should be made my rod.⁸
I would see him, but I shall have no patience.
  Mard. 'Tis no great matter if you have not. If a
laming of him, or such a toy,⁹ may do you pleasure, sir,
he has it for you, and I'll help you to him. 'Tis no news
to him to have a leg broke or a shoulder out with being
turn'd o'th' stones¹⁰ like a tansy.¹¹ Draw not your

sword, if you love it, for, of my conscience, his   70
head will break it. We use him i'th' wars like a ram to
shake a wall withal. Here comes the very person of
him; do as you shall find your temper. I must leave
you, but if you do not break him like a biscuit, you are
much to blame, sir.

                                              Exit.

        Enter BESSUS *and* Swordmen.

  Lig. Is your name Bessus?
  Bess. Men call me Captain Bessus.
  Lig. Then, Captain Bessus, you are a rank rascal,
without more exordiums, a dirty, frozen slave; and,
with the favor of your friends here, I will beat you.   80
  2 Sword. Pray use your pleasure, sir; you seem to be
A gentleman.
  Lig.   Thus, Captain Bessus, thus;

                                        [*Beats him.*]

Thus twinge your nose, thus kick you, and thus tread
    you.
  Bess. I do beseech you, yield¹² your cause, sir,
    quickly.
  Lig. Indeed, I should have told you that first.
  Bess. I take it so.
  1 Sword. Captain, 'a should indeed; he is mistaken.
  Lig. Sir, you shall have it quickly and more beating.
You have stol'n away a lady, Captain Coward,
And such a one—

                                    [*Beats him again.*]

  Bess.   Hold! I beseech you, hold, sir!   90
I never yet stole any living thing
That had a tooth about it.¹³
  Lig. Sir, I know you dare lie—
  Bess. With none but summer whores,¹⁴ upon my
    life, sir.
My means and manners never could attempt
Above a hedge or haycock.¹⁵
  Lig. Sirrah, that quits¹⁶ not me. Where is this lady?
Do that you do not use to do, tell truth,
Or, by my hand, I'll beat your captain's brains out,
Wash 'em, and put 'em in again, that will I.   100
  Bess. There was a lady, sir, I must confess,
Once in my charge; the Prince Tigranes gave her
To my guard for her safety. How I used her
She may herself report; she's with the prince now.
I did but wait upon her like a groom,
Which she will testify, I am sure. If not,
My brains are at your service when you please, sir,
And glad I have 'em for you.
  Lig. This is most likely; sir, I ask your pardon
And am sorry I was so intemperate.   110
  Bess. Well, I can ask no more. You would think it
    strange
Now to have me beat you at first sight.
  Lig. Indeed I would, but I know your goodness can
Forget twenty beatings. You must forgive me.
  Bess. Yes, there's my hand. Go where you will; I
    shall
Think you a valiant fellow for all this.

---

² *foil:* contrast.
³ *distaffs:* cleft poles on which women wound wool in
making thread.
⁴ *wainscot:* fine foreign oak used for furniture and paneling.
⁵ *dry:* bloodless.   ⁶ *targets:* shields.
⁷ *set . . . forehead:* shoot stones from toy crossbows at him
(passage obscure and perhaps corrupt).
⁸ *my rod:* punishment.   ⁹ *toy:* trifle.
¹⁰ *stones:* hearthstones.   ¹¹ *tansy:* herb-flavored cake.
¹² *yield:* reveal.   ¹³ *that . . . it:* young.
¹⁴ *summer whores:* who plied their trade outdoors.
¹⁵ *haycock:* conical haystack.   ¹⁶ *quits:* requites.

Lig. [*Aside*] My daughter is a whore;
I feel it now too sensible.[17] Yet I will see her,
Discharge myself of being father to her,
And then back to my country and there die—   120
Farewell, captain.
    Bess.   Farewell, sir, farewell.
Commend me to the gentlewoman, I pray'ee.

                         Exit LIGONES.

    1 Sword. How now, captain; bear up, man.
    Bess. Gentlemen o'th' sword, your hands once more.
I have been kicked again, but the foolish fellow is
    penitent;
H'as asked me mercy, and my honor's safe.
    2 Sword. We knew that, or the foolish fellow had
    better
A' kicked his grandsire.
    Bess.   Confirm, confirm, I pray.
    1 Sword. There be our hands again.
    2 Sword.   Now let him come
And say he was not sorry, and he sleeps[18] for it.   130
    Bess. Alas, good, ignorant old man. Let him go.
Let him go; these courses will undo him.

                         Exeunt.

[V.ii]

        Enter LIGONES *and* BACURIUS.

    Bac. My lord, your authority is good, and I am glad
it is so, for my consent would never hinder you from
seeing your own King. I am a minister, but not a
governer, of this state. Yonder is your King; I'll leave
you.

                         Exit.

        Enter TIGRANES *and* SPACONIA.

    Lig. [*Aside*] There he is, indeed, and with him my
Disloyal child.
    Tig. [*To* SPACONIA] I do perceive my fault
So much that yet, methinks, thou shouldst not have
Forgiven me.
    Lig.   Health to your majesty.   10
    Tig. What? Good Ligones, welcome; what business
Brought thee hither?
    Lig.   Several businesses.
My public business will appear by this.

                [*Gives him a paper.*]

I have a message to deliver, which,
If it please you so to authorize, is
An embassage from the Armenian state
Unto Arbaces for your liberty.
The offer's there set down; please you to read it.
    Tig. There is no alteration happened since
I came thence?
    Lig.   None, sir; all is as it was.   20
    Tig. And all our friends are well?
    Lig.   All very well.

               [TIGRANES *reads.*]

    Spac. [*Aside*] Though I have done nothing but what
    was good,

I dare not see my father; it was fault
Enough not to acquaint him with that good.
    Lig. Madam, I should have seen you.
    Spac.   O good sir,
    forgive me.
    Lig. Forgive you! Why, I am no kin to you, am I?
    Spac. Should it be measured by my mean deserts,
Indeed you are not.
    Lig.   Thou couldst prate unhappily
Ere thou couldst go;[1] would thou couldst do as well.
And how does your custom[2] hold out here?
    Spac.   Sir?
    Lig.   Are you
In private still, or how?
    Spac.   What do you mean?   31
    Lig. Do you take money? Are you come to sell sin
yet? Perhaps I can help you to liberal clients, or has not
the King cast you off yet? Oh, thou vile creature, whose
best commendation is that thou art a young whore! I
would thy mother had lived to see this, or, rather,
would I had died ere I had seen it. Why didst not make
me acquainted when thou wert first resolved to be a
whore? I would have seen thy hot lust satisfied more
privately. I would have kept a dancer and a whole   40
consort[3] of musicians in mine own house only to fiddle
thee.
    Spac. Sir, I was never whore.
    Lig.   If thou couldst not
Say so much for thyself, thou shouldst be carted.[4]
    Tig. Ligones, I have read it and like it;
You shall deliver it.
    Lig.   Well, sir, I will.
But I have private business with you.
    Tig.   Speak; what is't?
    Lig. How has my age deserved so ill of you,
That you can pick no strumpets in the land
But out of my breed?
    Tig.   Strumpets, good Ligones?   50
    Lig. Yes, and I wish to have you know I scorn
To get a whore for any prince alive,
And yet scorn will not help, methinks. My daughter
Might have been spared; there were enough beside.
    Tig. May I not prosper but she's innocent
As morning light for me, and, I dare swear,
For all the world.
    Lig.   Why is she with you then?
Can she wait on you better than your men?
Has she a gift in plucking off your stockings?
Can she make caudles[5] well or cut your corns?   60
Why do you keep her with you? For your queen
I know you do contemn her; so should I,
And every subject else think much at it.
    Tig. Let 'em think much, but 'tis more firm than
    earth
Thou seest thy queen there.

---

[17] *sensible:* sensibly.   [18] *sleeps:* dies.
V.ii.
    [1] *go:* walk.   [2] *custom:* business.   [3] *consort:* group.
    [4] *carted:* Whores and pimps were punished by public
exposure in carts.   [5] *caudles:* sweetened gruel, a medicine.

Lig. Then have I made a fair hand;[6] I called her
"whore." If I shall speak now as her father, I cannot
choose, but greatly rejoice that she shall be a queen.
But if I should speak to you as a statesman, she were
more fit to be your whore.   70

Tig. Get you about your business to Arbaces;
Now you talk idly.

Lig.   Yes, sir, I will go.
And shall she be a queen? She had more wit
Than her old father when she ran away.
Shall she be a queen? Now, by my troth, 'tis fine.
I'll dance out of all measure[7] at her wedding.
Shall I not, sir?

Tig.   Yes, marry, shalt thou.

Lig. I'll make these withered kexes[8] bear my body
Two hours together above ground.

Tig.   Nay, go;   79
My business requires haste.

Lig.   Good God preserve you;
You are an excellent king.

Spac.   Farewell, good father.

Lig. Farewell, sweet, virtuous daughter.
I never was so joyful in my life,
That I remember. Shall she be a queen?
Now I perceive a man may weep for joy;
I had thought they had lied that said so.

                                              Exit.

Tig. Come, my dear love.

Spac.   But you may see another
May alter that again.

Tig.   Urge it no more;
I have made up a new strong constancy
Not to be shook with eyes.[9] I know I have   90
The passions of a man, but if I meet
With any subject that shall hold my eyes
More firmly than is fit, I'll think of thee
And run away from it. Let that suffice.

                                              Exeunt.

[V.iii]

                Enter BACURIUS *and a* Servant.

Bac. Three gentlemen without[1] to speak with me?

Ser. Yes, sir.

Bac. Let them come in.

Ser. They are entered, sir, already.

                Enter BESSUS *and* Swordmen.

Bac. Now, fellows, your business. [*To* Servant] Are
these the gentlemen?

---

    [6] *made . . . hand:* done well.
    [7] *out . . . measure:* immoderately.
    [8] *kexes:* dry hollow stems.   [9] *with eyes:* by sight.
V.iii.
    [1] *without:* outside.
    [2] *surfeits:* overeating; indigestion.
    [3] *Stockfish:* dried fish beaten to make it tender.
    [4] *billets:* logs.   [5] *book:* Bible, for swearing on.
    [6] *draws wide:* misses the point.
    [7] *motion:* puppet show.   [8] *tilting:* joust.
    [9] *bilbo-men:* swordmen, bullies.   [10] *rent:* debt.
    [11] *apple-squires:* pimps.

Bess. My lord, I have made bold to bring these
gentlemen, my friends o'th' sword, along with me.

Bac. I am afraid you'll fight then.   9

Bess. My good lord, I will not; your lordship is
mistaken. Fear not, lord.

Bac. Sir, I am sorry for't.

Bess. I can ask no more in honor.—Gentlemen, you
hear my lord is sorry.

Bac. Not that I have beaten you, but beaten one that
will be beaten, one whose dull body will require a
lancing, as surfeits[2] do the diet, spring and fall. Now
to your swordmen: what come they for, good Captain
Stockfish?[3]   19

Bess. It seems your lordship has forgot my name.

Bac. No, nor your nature neither, though they are
things fitter, I confess, for anything than my remembrance or any honest man's. What shall these billets[4]
do, be piled up in my woodyard?

Bess. Your lordship holds your mirth still; God
continue it. But, for these gentlemen, they come—

Bac. To swear you are a coward. Spare your book;[5]
I do believe it.

Bess. Your lordship still draws wide;[6] they come to
vouch under their valiant hands I am no coward.   30

Bac. That would be a show indeed worth seeing.
Sirrah, be wise and take money for this motion;[7] travel
with it, and where the name of Bessus has been known
or a good coward stirring 'twill yield more than a
tilting.[8] This will prove more beneficial to you, if you
be thrifty, than your captainship and more natural.—
Men of most valiant hands, is this true?

2 Sword. It is so, most renowned.

Bac. 'Tis somewhat strange.   39

1 Sword. Lord, it is strange, yet true. We have examined, from your lordship's foot there to this man's
head, the nature of the beatings, and we do find his
honor is come off clean and sufficient. This as our
swords shall help us.

Bac. You are much bound to your bilbo-men;[9] I am
glad you are straight again, captain. 'Twere good you
would think some way to gratify them. They have
undergone a labor for you, Bessus, would have puzzled
Hercules with all his valor.   49

2 Sword. Your lordship must understand we are no
men o'th' law, that take pay for our opinions. It is
sufficient we have cleared our friend.

Bac. Yet here is something due which I, as touched
in conscience, will discharge, captain. I'll pay this
rent[10] for you.

Bess. Spare yourself, my good lord.
My brave friends aim at nothing but the virtue.

Bac. That's but a cold discharge, sir, for their pains.

2 Sword. O lord, my good lord!   59

Bac. Be not so modest; I will give you something.

Bess. They shall dine with your lordship; that's
sufficient.

Bac. Something in hand the while.—Ye rogues! ye
apple-squires![11] Do you come hither with your bottled
valor, your windy froth, to limit out my beatings?

                                              [*Kicks them.*]

1 Sword. I do beseech your lordship—

2 Sword. Oh, good lord—

Bac. 'Sfoot, what a many[12] of beaten slaves are here!—Get me a cudgel, sirrah, and a tough one.

[*Exit* Servant.]

2 Sword. More of your foot, I do beseech your lordship. 71

Bac. You shall, you shall, dog, and your fellow beagle.

1 Sword. O' this side, good my lord.

Bac. Off with your swords, for if you hurt my foot, I'll have you flayed, you rascals.

1 Sword. Mine's off, my lord.

2 Sword. I beseech your lordship stay a little; my strap's tied to my codpiece point.[13] Now, when you please. 80

Bac. Captain, these are your valiant friends. You long for a little too?

Bess. I am very well, I humbly thank your lordship.

Bac. What's that in your pocket, slave? My key, you mongrel? Thy buttocks cannot be so hard; out with't quickly.

2 Sword. Here 'tis, sir; a small piece of artillery

[*Hands him a pistol.*]

That a gentleman, a dear friend of your lordship's, sent me with to get it mended, sir; for if you mark, the nose[14] is somewhat loose. 90

Bac. A friend of mine, you rascal!—I was never wearier of doing nothing than kicking these two footballs.

Enter Servant.

Ser. Here's a good cudgel, sir.

Bac. It comes too late.
I am weary; prithee do thou beat 'em.

2 Sword. My lord, this is foul play, i'faith, to put a fresh man upon us; men are but men.

Bac. That jest shall save your bones. [*To* BESSUS] Up with your rotten regiment and be gone.—I 100 had rather thresh than be bound to kick these rascals till they cried hold.—Bessus, you may put your hand to them now, and then you are quit.—Farewell; as you like this, pray visit me again. 'Twill keep me in good breath.

Exit BACURIUS.

2 Sword. H'as a devilish hard foot; I never felt the like.

1 Sword. Nor I, and yet I'm sure I ha' felt a hundred.

2 Sword. If he kick thus i'th' dog days,[15] he will be dry-foundered.[16]—What cure now, Captain, besides oil of bays?[17] 111

Bess. Why, well enough, I warrant you. You can go?

2 Sword. Yes, God be thanked. But I feel a shrewd[18] ache; sure, he has sprang my huckle[19] bone.

1 Sword. I ha' lost a haunch.

Bess. A little butter, friend, a little butter; butter and parsley is a sovereign matter. *Probatum est.*[20]

2 Sword. Captain, we must request your hands now to our honors. 119

Bess. Yes, marry, shall ye, and then let all the world come; we are valiant to ourselves, and there's an end.

1 Sword. Nay, then we must be valiant.—Oh, my ribs!

2 Sword. Oh, my small guts! A plague upon these sharp-toed shoes; they are murderers.

Exeunt.

[V.iv]

Enter ARBACES *with his sword drawn.*

Arb. It is resolved. I bore it whilst I could;
I can no more. Hell, open all thy gates,
And I will through them; if they be shut,
I'll batter 'em, but I will find the place
Where the most damned have dwelling. Ere I end,
Amongst them all they shall not have a sin
But I may call it mine. I must begin
With murder of my friend, and so go on
To an incestuous ravishing, and end
My life and sins with a forbidden blow   10
Upon myself.

Enter MARDONIUS.

Mard.   What tragedy is near?
That hand was never wont to draw a sword
But it cried dead to something.

Arb.   Mardonius,
Have you bid Gobrius come?

Mard.   How do you, sir?

Arb. Well. Is he coming?

Mard.   Why, sir, are you thus?
Why does your hand proclaim a lawless war
Against yourself?

Arb. Thou answerest me one question with another.
Is Gobrius coming?

Mard.   Sir, he is.

Arb.   'Tis well;
I can forbear[1] your questions then. Begone.   20

Mard. Sir, I have marked—

Arb. Mark less; it troubles you and me.

Mard.   You are
More variable than you were.

Arb.   It may be so.

Mard. Today no hermit could be humblier
Than you were to us all.

Arb.   And what of this?

Mard. And now you take new rage into your eyes,
As you would look us all out of the land.

Arb. I do confess it; will that satisfy?
I prithee, get thee gone.

---

[12] *many:* multitude.
[13] *point:* lace for attaching codpiece to hose.
[14] *nose:* muzzle.
[15] *dog days:* the hot days of midsummer when Sirius is above the horizon.   [16] *dry-foundered:* lame.
[17] *oil of bays:* bayberry liniment.   [18] *shrewd:* sharp.
[19] *huckle:* hipbone.   [20] *L.:* It has been proved.

V.iv.
[1] *forbear:* do without.

Mard. Sir, I will speak.

Arb.   Will ye?

Mard.   It is my duty;   30
I fear you will kill yourself. I am a subject,
And you shall do me wrong in't. 'Tis my cause,
And I may speak.

Arb.   Thou art not trained in sin,
It seems, Mardonius. Kill myself? By heaven,
I will not do it yet, and, when I will,
I'll tell thee. Then I shall be such a creature
That thou wilt give me leave without a word.
There is a method in man's wickedness;
It grows up by degrees. I am not come
So high as killing of myself; there are   40
A hundred thousand sins 'twixt me and it
Which I must do. I shall come to't at last,
But, take my oath, not now. Be satisfied,
And get thee hence.

Mard. I am sorry 'tis so ill.

Arb.   Be sorry then.
True sorrow is alone; grieve by thyself.

Mard. I pray you, let me see your sword put up
Before I go. I'll leave you then.

Arb.   Why, so!

[*Puts up his sword.*]

What folly is this in thee! Is it not
As apt to mischief as it was before?   50
Can I not reach it, thinkest thou? These are toys
For children to be pleased with, and not men.
Now I am safe, you think. I would the book
Of fate were here. My sword is not so sure
But I should get it out and mangle that,
That all the destinies should quite forget
Their fixed decrees and haste to make us new,
Far-other fortunes. Mine could not be worse.
Wilt thou now leave me?   59

Mard. God put into your bosom temperate thoughts.
I'll leave you though I fear.

Arb.   Go; thou art honest.

Exit MARDONIUS.

Why should the hasty errors of my youth
Be so unpardonable, to draw a sin
Helpless upon me?

Enter GOBRIUS.

Gob. [*Aside*]   There is the King.
Now it is ripe.

Arb.   Draw near, thou guilty man,
That art the author of the loathèd'st crime
Five ages have brought forth, and hear me speak.
Curses incurable and all the evils
Man's body or his spirit can receive
Be with thee.

Gob.   Why, sir, do you curse me thus?   70

Arb. Why do I curse thee? If there be a man
Subtle in curses, that exceeds the rest,
His worst wish on thee. Thou hast broke my heart.

Gob. How, sir! Have I preserved you from a child
From all the arrows malice or ambition
Could shoot at you, and have I this for pay?

Arb. 'Tis true thou didst preserve me and in that
Wert crueler than hardened murderers
Of infants and their mothers; thou didst save me
Only till thou hadst studied out a way   80
How to destroy me cunningly thyself.
This was a curious way of torturing.

Gob. What do you mean?

Arb. Thou know'st the evils thou hast done to me.
Dost thou remember all those witching letters
Thou sent'st unto me to Armenia
Filled with the praise of my beloved sister,
Where thou extol'st her beauty? What had I
To do with that? What could her beauty be
To me? And thou didst write how well she loved me—
Dost thou remember this?—So that I doted   91
Something before I saw her.

Gob.   This is true.

Arb. Is it? And when I was returned, thou know'st
Thou didst pursue it till thou wound'st me in
To such a strange and unbelieved affection
As good men cannot think on.

Gob.   This I grant;
I think I was the cause.

Arb.   Wert thou? Nay, more,
I think thou meant'st it.

Gob.   Sir, I hate a lie
As I love God and honesty; I did.
It was my meaning.

Arb.   Be thine own sad judge;   100
A further condemnation will not need.
Prepare thyself to die.

Gob.   Why, sir, to die?

Arb. Why wouldst thou live? Was ever yet offender
So impudent that had a thought of mercy
After confession of a crime like this?
Get out I cannot where thou hurl'st me in,
But I can take revenge; that's all the sweetness
Left for me.

Gob. [*Aside*] Now is the time.—Hear me but speak.

Arb. No. Yet I will be far more merciful
Than thou wert to me. Thou didst steal into me   110
And never gavest me warning; so much time
As I give thee now had prevented thee
Forever. Notwithstanding all thy sins,
If thou hast hope that there is yet a prayer
To save thee, turn and speak it to yourself.

Gob. Sir, you shall know your sins before you do 'em.
If you kill me—

Arb.   I will not stay then.

Gob.   Know
You kill your father.

Arb.   How?

Gob.   You kill your father.

Arb. My father! Though I know it for a lie
Made out of fear to save thy stainèd life,   120
The very reverence of the word comes cross me
And ties mine arm down.

Gob.   I will tell you that
Shall heighten you again. I am thy father;
I charge thee hear me.

Arb.   If it should be so,

As 'tis most false, and that I should be found
A bastard issue, the despisèd fruit
Of lawless lust, I should no more admire[2]
All my wild passions. But another truth
Shall be wrung from thee. If I could come by
The spirit of pain, it should be poured on thee   130
Till thou allowest thyself more full of lies
Than he[3] that teaches thee.

            Enter ARANE.

   Ara.   Turn thee about.
I come to speak to thee, thou wicked man;
Hear me, thou tyrant.
   Arb.   I will turn to thee.
Hear me, thou strumpet. I have blotted out
The name of mother as thou hast thy shame.
   Ara. My shame! Thou hast less shame than anything.
Why dost thou keep my daughter in a prison?
Why dost thou call her sister and do this?
   Arb. Cease, thou strange impudence, and answer
      quickly.   140
If thou contemnst me, this will ask an answer.

                        [*Draws his sword.*]

And have it.
   Ara.   Help me, gentle Gobrius.
   Arb. Guilt dare not help guilt; though they grow
      together
In doing ill, yet at the punishment
They sever and each flies the noise of other.
Think not of help—answer.
   Ara.   I will; to what?
   Arb. To such a thing as, if it be a truth,
Think what a creature thou hast made thyself
That didst not shame to do what I must blush
Only to ask thee. Tell me who I am,   150
Whose son I am, without all circumstance.[4]
Be thou as hasty as my sword will be
If thou refusest.
   Ara.   Why, you are his son.
   Arb. His son? Swear; swear, thou worse than
      woman damned.
   Ara. By all that's good, you are.
   Arb.   Then art thou all
That ever was known bad. Now is the cause
Of all my strange misfortunes come to light.
What reverence expect'st thou from a child
To bring forth which thou hast offended heaven,
Thy husband, and the land? Adulterous witch,   160
I know now why thou wouldst have poisoned me;
I was thy lust which thou wouldst have forgot.
Thou wicked mother of my sins and me,
Show me the way to the inheritance
I have by thee, which is a spacious world
Of impious acts, that I may soon possess it.
Plagues rot thee as thou liv'st, and such diseases
As use to pay lust recompense thy deed.
   Gob. You do not know why you curse thus.
   Arb.   Too well.
You are a pair of vipers, and behold   170
The serpent you have got.[5] There is no beast,

But, if he knew it, has a pedigree
As brave as mine, for they have more descents,[6]
And I am every way as beastly got,
As far without the compass of a law,
As they.
   Ara. You spend your rage and words in vain
And rail upon a guess. Hear us a little.
   Arb. No, I will never hear, but talk away
My breath and die.
   Gob.   Why, but you are no bastard.
   Arb. How's that?
   Ara.   Nor child of mine.
   Arb.   Still you go on
In wonders to me.
   Gob.   Pray you be more patient;   181
I may bring comfort to you.
   Arb.   I will kneel
And hear with the obedience of a child.
Good father, speak; I do acknowledge you,
So you bring comfort.
   Gob. First know, our last King, your supposèd father,
Was old and feeble when he married her,
And almost all the land, as she, past hope
Of issue from him.
   Arb.   Therefore, she took leave
To play the whore because the King was old.   190
Is this the comfort?
   Ara.   What will you find out
To give me satisfaction when you find
How you have injured me? Let fire consume me,
If ever I were whore.
   Gob.   Forbear these starts,
Or I will leave you wedded to despair
As you are now. If you can find a temper,
My breath shall be a pleasant western wind
That cools and blasts not.
   Arb.   Bring it out, good father,
I'll lie and listen here as reverently
As to an angel. If I breathe too loud,   200
Tell me, for I would be as still as night.
   Gob. Our King, I say, was old, and this our Queen
Desired to bring an heir, but yet her husband,
She thought, was past it, and to be dishonest[7]
I think she would not; if she would have been,
The truth is she was watched so narrowly,
And had so slender opportunity,
She hardly could have been. But yet her cunning
Found out this way; she feigned herself with child;
And posts were sent in haste throughout the land,   210
And God was humbly thanked in every church,
That so had blessed the Queen, and prayers were made
For her safe going[8] and delivery.
She feigned now to grow bigger; and perceived
This hope of issue made her feared[9] and brought
A far more large respect from every man,
And saw her power increase and was resolved,

---

[2] *admire:* wonder at.   [3] *he:* i.e., the devil.
[4] *all circumstance:* any detail.   [5] *got:* begotten.
[6] *descents:* descendants.   [7] *dishonest:* unchaste.
[8] *going:* pregnancy.   [9] *feared:* respected.

Since she believed she could not hav't indeed,
At least she would be thought to have a child.
   Arb. Do I not hear it well? Nay, I will make   220
No noise at all, but pray you to the point
Quick as you can.
   Gob.   Now when the time was full
She should be brought abed, I had a son
Born, which was you. This the Queen hearing of
Moved me to let her have you, and such reasons
She showed me as she knew would tie
My secrecy—she swore you should be King.
And, to be short, I did deliver you
Unto her and pretended you were dead,
And in mine own house kept a funeral,   230
And had an empty coffin put in earth.
That night the Queen feigned hastily to labor,
And, by a pair of women of her own
Which she had charmed,[10] she made the world believe
She was delivered of you. You grew up
As the King's son till you were six year old.
Then did the King die, and did leave to me
Protection of the realm and, contrary
To his own expectation, left this Queen
Truly with child indeed of the fair princess   240
Panthea. Then she could have torn her hair
And did alone to me, yet durst not speak
In public, for she knew she would be found
A traitor, and her talk would have been thought
Madness or anything rather than truth.
This was the only cause why she did seek
To poison you, and I to keep you safe,
And this the reason why I sought to kindle
Some spark of love in you to fair Panthea,
That she might get part of her right again.   250
   Arb. And have you made an end now; is this all?
If not, I will be still till I am agèd,
Till all my hairs are silver.
   Gob.   This is all.
   Arb. And is it true, say you too, madam?
                            [Rises.]
   Ara.   Yes,
God knows it is most true.
   Arb. Panthea, then, is not my sister?
   Gob.   No.
   Arb. But can you prove this?
   Gob.   If you will give consent,
Else who dare go about it?
   Arb.   Give consent!
Why, I will have them all that know it racked
To get this from 'em.—All that waits without,   260
Come in; whate'er you be, come in and be
Partakers of my joy!

   Enter MARDONIUS, BESSUS, *[the two* Gentlemen,]
                and others.

           Oh, you are welcome.
Mardonius, the best news—nay, draw no nearer;

---

[10] *charmed:* exercised influence over.
[11] *fury:* frenzy.   [12] *bare:* bore.

They all shall hear it—I am found no king!
   Mard. Is that so good news?
   Arb.   Yes, the happiest news
That e'er was heard.
   Mard.   Indeed, 'twere well for you
If you might be a little less obeyed.
   Arb. One call the Queen.
   Mard.   Why, she is there.
   Arb.   The Queen,
Mardonius. Panthea is the Queen,
And I am plain Arbaces.—Go some one;   270
She is in Gobrius' house.
                   Exit 1 Gentleman.
             Since I saw you
There are a thousand things delivered to me
You little dream of.
   Mard.   So it should seem.—My lord,
What fury's this?
   Gob.   Believe me, 'tis no fury;[11]
All that he says is truth.
   Mard.   'Tis very strange.
   Arb. Why do you keep your hats off, gentlemen?
Is it to me? I swear it must not be.
Nay, trust me; in good faith, it must not be.
I cannot now command you, but I pray you,
For the respect you bare[12] me when you took   280
Me for your King, each man clap on his hat
At my desire.
   Mard.   We will, but you are not found
So mean a man but that you may be covered
As well as we, may you not?
   Arb.   Oh, not here;
You may but not I, for here is my father
In presence.
   Mard.   Where?
   Arb.   Why, there. Oh, the whole story
Would be a wilderness to lose thyself
Forever.—Oh, pardon me, dear father,
For all the idle and unreverent words
That I have spoke in idle moods to you.—   290
I am Arbaces; we all fellow-subjects;
Nor is the Queen, Panthea, now my sister.
   Bess. Why, if you remember, fellow-subject Arbaces,
I told you once she was not your sister. I said she looked
nothing like you.
   Arb. I think you did, good Captain Bessus.
   Bess. [*Aside*] Here will arise another question now
amongst the swordmen, whether I be to call him to
account for beating me now he's proved no king.

                Enter LIGONES.

   Mard. Sir, here's Ligones, the agent for the
     Armenian state.   300
   Arb. Where is he?—I know your business, good
     Ligones.
   Lig. We must have our King again, and will.
   Arb. I knew that was your business. You shall have
Your King again and have him so again
As never King was had.—Go, one of you,
And bid Bacurius bring Tigranes hither
And bring the lady with him that Panthea—

The Queen, Panthea—sent me word this morning
Was brave Tigranes' mistress.

Exit 2 Gentleman.

Lig. 'Tis Spaconia.
Arb. Ay, ay, Spaconia.
Lig. She is my daughter. 310
Arb. She is so; I could now tell anything
I never heard. Your King shall go so home
As never man went.
Mard. Shall he go on's head?
Arb. He shall have chariots easier than air
That I will have invented, and ne'er think
He shall pay any ransom; and thyself,
That art the messenger, shall ride before him
On a horse cut out of an entire diamond
That shall be made to go with golden wheels,
I know not how yet.
Lig. [*Aside*] Why, I shall be made 320
Forever; they belied this King with us
And said he was unkind.
Arb. And then thy daughter—
She shall have some strange thing; we'll have the
   kingdom
Sold utterly and put into a toy
Which she shall wear about her carelessly
Somewhere or other.

Enter PANTHEA *and* Gentleman.

See the virtuous Queen!—
Behold the humblest subject that you have
Kneel here before you.
Pan. Why kneel you to me
That am your vassal?
Arb. Grant me one request.
Pan. Alas, what can I grant you? What I can,
   I will. 330

Arb. That you will please to marry me,
If I can prove it lawful.
Pan. Is that all?
More willingly than I would draw this air.
Arb. I'll kiss this hand in earnest.[13]

Enter Second Gentleman.[14]

2 Gent. Sir, Tigranes
Is coming, though he made it strange[15] at first
To see the princess any more.
Arb. The Queen,
Thou meanest.

Enter [BACURIUS, *with*] TIGRANES *and* SPACONIA.

Oh, my Tigranes, pardon me.
Tread on my neck; I freely offer it,
And if[16] thou beest so given. Take revenge,
For I have injured thee.
Tig. No, I forgive 340
And rejoice more that you have found repentance
Than I my liberty.
Arb. Mayst thou be happy
In thy fair choice, for thou art temperate.
You owe no ransom to the state, know that.
I have a thousand joys to tell you of
Which yet I dare not utter till I pay
My thanks to heaven for 'em. Will you go
With me and help me? Pray you do.
Tig. I will.
Arb. Take then your fair one with you.—And you,
   Queen
Of goodness and of us, oh, give me leave 350
To take your arm in mine.—Come everyone
That takes delight in goodness; help to sing
Loud thanks for me, that I am proved no King.

[*Exeunt.*]

F I N I S

---

[13] *in earnest:* as a pledge.
[14] *Enter . . . Gentleman:* Q2; Q1 gives the speech implausibly to Mardonius.
[15] *made . . . strange:* was unwilling.   [16] *And if:* If.

John Fletcher

[1579–1625]

THE WILD-GOOSE CHASE

W HEN in 1646 Humphrey Mosely and Humphrey Robinson announced, through an entry in the Stationers' Register, their intention to publish a multitude of plays by Beaumont and Fletcher, their list was headed by "Wild goose chase . . . by mr Beaumont & mr Fflesher." But in the following year the first folio appeared minus this comedy alone. In his prefatory remarks Mosely explained its absence:

> One only play I must except (for I mean to deal openly); 'tis a comedy called the *Wild-Goose Chase*, which hath been long lost, and I fear irrecoverable; for a person of quality borrowed it from the actors many years since, and, by the negligence of a servant, it was never returned. Therefore I now put up this *Si quis* [if anyone], that whosoever hereafter happily meets with it shall be thankfully satisfied if he please to send it home.

The person of quality seems to have been moved, for in April 1652 Mosely entered the play in the Stationers' Register, and that year it appeared in a splendid folio edition with commendatory verses and a particularly elaborate *Dramatis Personae* including actors' names— presumably from a 1632 revival—as well as characterizations of the principal roles. The title page announces

> *The Wild-Goose Chase.* A Comedy. As it hath been acted with singular applause at the Blackfriars: being the noble, last, and only remains of those incomparable dramatists Francis Beaumont and John Fletcher, Gent. Retrieved for the public delight of all the ingenious, and private benefit of John Lowin and Joseph Taylor [the leading members of the King's Men until the theaters were closed], servants to his late majesty, by a person of honor.

The play was included in the second Beaumont and Fletcher folio in 1679; the present text is based on the first edition (F1).

The first recorded performance was at court in the Christmas season 1621–2. It is not impossible that the play had been in the company's repertory for some time, even years, before, and more likely that it had been performed publicly earlier in the same season, but there is no reason to assume that its composition antedated the court production by very much time. Beaumont's collaboration with Fletcher, which had extended to sharing a house on the Bankside, a cloak, and a wench, had come to an end in 1613 when he married an heiress. It is almost a certainty, therefore, that Fletcher wrote THE WILD-GOOSE CHASE without the assistance of his old friend, and no other collaborator has been seriously claimed. There is no known source.

The profitable revival in 1632 supports other evidence of the play's popularity during the remaining years of the pre-civil war theater, and it was revived again when the theaters reopened after the demise of the Commonwealth, but it lost ground quickly, being performed less frequently in Restoration days than many other plays in the Beaumont and Fletcher canon. That invaluable barometer Samuel Pepys records that on January 11, 1667/8 he went "to the King's house, there to see *The Wild-Goose Chase*, which I never saw, but have longed to see it, being a famous play, but as it was yesterday I do find that where I expect most I find least satisfaction, for in this play I met with nothing extraordinary at all, but very dull inventions and designs." In 1702 Farquhar published an adaptation called *The Inconstant, or The Way to Win Him.*

The relative failure of THE WILD-GOOSE CHASE in the Restoration is a curious phenomenon, since the play bears such marked resemblance to the comedy of the later period. Like Shirley's HYDE PARK, which Pepys thought only a "moderate" entertainment, it may well have struck the new audience as a primitive version of a kind of play only now coming into its own and being written with more focus, and it may have seemed wanting in the period charms of less prophetic antebellum plays. For the modern reader it is a fine achievement in comedy. If it manifests the familiar limitations of Fletcherian comedy—episodic plot development dependent on surprise rather than on the satisfaction of watching the inevitable occur, simplistic characterization, verse so irregular and flaccid that lineation is often difficult to determine, language seldom rich in implication or colloquial illusion—it makes a virtue of those limitations by creating a series of vivid scenes in which a variety of amusing characters plot and counterplot to a rhythm of ploy, exposure, and comeuppance, and by juggling a number of intriguingly similar plot elements. The essential artificiality of the Fletcherian ambiance works more congenially in comedy than in the tragedies and tragicomedies in which he and his associates take often irritating pains to suggest that both their fake toads and their imaginary gardens significantly resemble the world of reality; and development by surprise, though eschewed by Shakespeare, has an honorable place in the history of comedy. The war between the sexes relates THE WILD-GOOSE CHASE to *Much Ado About Nothing* before it and to HYDE PARK and *The Way of the World* afterward, and a social historian might well note in Fletcher's comedy an emerging consciousness of the impropriety—as well as the blunt impossibility—of continuing to regard women exclusively as marketable commodities. But, as its ambiguous title suggests, the real place of THE WILD-GOOSE CHASE is in the company of comedies, headed by *The Importance of Being Earnest*, which earns our laughter by their consistent commitment to sheer nonsense. If *Much Ado* leads us to ponder the conflict between love and belief on the one hand and reason and empiricism as a feckless defense against them on the other, if *The Way of the World* suggests a new commercial basis for value, morality, and relationship, THE WILD-GOOSE CHASE promulgates nothing: it plays with the materials for such considerations only in order to achieve a structure that is its own end. What keeps it alive, then, is not its "Elizabethan" or "Restoration" qualities, though their juxtaposition is fascinating, but its essential and almost abstract comedy.   N. R.

The Wild-Goose Chase

THE DEDICATION

To the Honored Few Lovers of
Dramatic Poesy

Noble Spirits!

IT will seem strange to you that we should beg a pardon from you before you know a crime committed; but such is our harsh fate that we shall want as much of your mercy to the forgiving of this sad presumption of offering to your view these few poor sheets, the rich remains of our too-long-since lost friend Mr. Fletcher, as we shall your favorable acceptance and encouragement in it. The play was of so general a received acceptance that (he himself a spectator) we have known him unconcerned, and to have wished it had been none of his; he, as well as the thronged theater (in spite of his innate modesty) applauding this rare issue of his brain. His complacency in his own work may be perhaps no argument   10 to you of the goodness of the play, any more than our confidence of it; and we do not expect our encomium can do anything with you when the play itself is so near: that will commend itself unto you. And now, farewell, our glory![1] Farewell, your choice delight, most noble gentlemen! farewell, th' grand wheel that set us smaller motions in action![2] farewell, the pride of life o' th' stage! nor can we (though to our ruin) much repine that we are so little, since he that gave us being is no more.

Generous Souls!

'Tis not unknown unto you all how by a cruel destiny we have a long time been mutes and bound,[3] although our miseries have been sufficiently clamorous   20 and expanded, yet, till this happy opportunity, never durst vex your open ears and hands. But this we're confident will be the surest argument for you noblesses. What an ingenious person of quality once spake of his amours we apply to our necessities:

> Silence in love betrays more woe
>   Than words, though ne'er so witty:
> The beggar that is dumb, you know,
>   Deserves a double pity.

But be the comedy at your mercy as we are. Only we wish that you may have the same kind of joy in perusing of it as we had in acting.   30

So *exeunt.*
Your grateful servants
JOHN LOWIN[4]
JOSEPH TAYLOR[5]

DEDICATION
   [1] *farewell . . . glory:* This passage may parody *Othello*, III. iii. 347–357.
   [2] *wheel . . . action:* The image is of a clockwork.
   [3] *how . . . bound:* i.e., by the closing of the theaters.
   [4] *Lowin: c.* 1576–1669, a leading actor in Shakespeare's company.
   [5] *Taylor: d.* 1652, another leading member; after the deaths of Heminge and Condell, Taylor and Lowin managed the company together and held shares in its theaters, the Globe and the Blackfriars.

DRAMATIS PERSONÆ

DE GARD, *a noble staid gentleman that, being newly lighted from his travels, assists his Sister Oriana, in her chase of Mirabel the Wild-Goose, acted by Mr. Robert Benfield*

LA CASTRE, *the indulgent father to Mirabel, acted by Mr. Richard Robinson*

MIRABEL, THE WILD-GOOSE, *a traveled monsieur, and a great defier of all ladies in the way of Marriage, otherwise their much loose servant,[1] at last caught by the despised Oriana, incomparably acted by Mr. Joseph Taylor*

PINAC, *his fellow-traveler, of a lively spirit, and servant to the no less sprightly Lillia-Bianca, admirably well acted by Mr. Thomas Pollard*

BELLEUR, *companion to both, of a stout blunt humor, in love with Rosalura, most naturally acted by Mr. John Lowin*

NANTOLET, *father to Rosalura and Lillia Bianca, acted by Mr. William Penn*

LUGIER, *the rough and confident tutor to the ladies, and chief engine to entrap the Wild Goose, acted by Mr. Hilliard Swanston*

ORIANA, *the fair betrothed of Mirabel, and witty follower of the chase, acted by Mr. Steph. Hammerton*

ROSALURA,   ⎱ *the airy daughters* ⎰ William Trigg
LILLIA-BIANCA ⎰ *of Nantolet*   ⎱ Sander Gough

PETELLA, *their waiting woman, Mr. Shanck*

MARIANA, *an English courtesan, by Mr. John Hongman*

A Young [Man *disguised as a*] Factor.[2]

Page, Servants, Singing-Boy, Two Merchants, Priest, Four Women.

The Scene: Paris.

ACT ONE

SCENE ONE

Enter MONSIEUR DE GARD, *and a* Footboy.

De Ga. Sirrah, you know I have rid hard; stir my horse well,
And let him want no litter.

Boy. I am sure I have run hard;
Would somebody would walk me, and see me littered,
For I think my fellow horse cannot in reason
Desire more rest nor take up his chamber before me;
But we are the beasts now, and the beasts are our masters.

De Ga. When you have done, step to the ten-crown ordinary[1]—

Boy. With all my heart, sir; for I have a twenty-crown stomach.   9

De Ga. And there bespeak a dinner.

Boy.   Yes, sir, presently.[2]

De Ga. For whom, I beseech you, sir?

Boy.   For myself, I take it, sir.

De Ga. In truth, ye shall not take it; 'tis not meant for you.
There's for your provender.[3]

[*Gives money.*]

                              Bespeak a dinner
For Monsieur Mirabel, and his companions;
They'll be in town within this hour. When you have done, sirrah,
Make ready all things at my lodgings for me
And wait me there.

Boy.   The ten-crown ordinary?

De Ga. Yes, sir, if you have not forgot it.

Boy. I'll forget my feet first:
'Tis the best part of a footman's faith.

Exit Boy.

De Ga.   These youths, 20
For all they have been in Italy to learn thrift
And seem to wonder at men's lavish ways,
Yet they cannot rub off old friends, their French itches;[4]
They must meet sometimes to disport their bodies
With good wine, and good women, and good store, too.
Let 'em be what they will, they are armed at all points,
And then hang saving, let the sea grow high!
This ordinary can fit 'em of all sizes.

Enter LA CASTRE *and* ORIANA.

They must salute their country with old customs.

Ori. Brother.

De Ga.   My dearest sister.

Ori.   Welcome, welcome.
Indeed, ye are welcome home, most welcome.

De Ga.   Thank ye.
You are grown a handsome woman, Oriana;   32
Blush at your faults. I am wondrous glad to see ye.
Monsieur La Castre, let not my affection
To my fair sister make me held unmannerly;
I am glad to see ye well, to see ye lusty,[5]
Good health about ye, and in fair company.
Believe me, I am proud—

La Ca.   Fair sir, I thank ye.
Monsieur De Gard, you are welcome from your journey;
Good men have still[6] good welcome: Give me your hand, sir.   40
Once more, you are welcome home. You look still younger.

DRAMATIS PERSONÆ
  [1] *servant:* lover.   [2] *factor:* mercantile agent.
I.i.
  [1] *ordinary:* inn.   [2] *presently:* immediately.
  [3] *provender:* fodder.   [4] *itches:* cravings.
  [5] *lusty:* merry.   [6] *still:* always.

De Ga. Time has no leisure to look after us;
We wander everywhere; age cannot find us.
    La Ca. And how does all?
    De Ga.   All well, sir, and all lusty.
    La Ca. I hope my son be so. I doubt not, sir,
But you have often seen him in your journeys,
And bring me some fair news.
    De Ga.   Your son is well, sir,
And grown a proper gentleman; he is well and lusty.
Within this eight hours I took leave of him,
And over-hied[7] him, having some slight business   50
That forced me out o' th' way. I can assure you
He will be here tonight.
    La Ca.   Ye make me glad, sir,
For, o' my faith, I almost long to see him.
Methinks he has been away—
    De Ga.   'Tis but your tenderness;
What are three years? A lovesick wench will allow it,
His friends, that went out with him, are come back, too,
Belleur and young Pinac. He bid me say little,
Because he means to be his own glad messenger.
    La Ca. I thank ye for this news, sir. He shall be
    welcome,
And his friends too. Indeed, I thank you heartily.   60
And how—for I dare say you will not flatter him—
Has Italy wrought on him? Has he mewed[8] yet
His wild fantastic toys?[9] They say that climate
Is a great purger of those humorous fluxes.[10]
How is he improved, I pray ye?
    De Ga.   No doubt, sir, well;
He has borne himself a full and noble gentleman;
To speak him further is beyond my charter.
    La Ca. I am glad to hear so much good. Come, I see
You long to enjoy your sister; yet I must entreat ye,
Before I go, to sup with me tonight,   70
And must not be denied.
    De Ga.   I am your servant.
    La Ca. Where you shall meet fair, merry, and noble
    company,
My neighbor Nantolet and his two fair daughters.
    De Ga. Your supper's seasoned well, sir; I shall wait
    upon ye.
    La Ca. Till then I'll leave ye: And y' are once more
    welcome.
                            Exit.

    De Ga. I thank you, noble sir.—Now, Oriana,

---

    [7] *over-hied:* left him behind by hastening on; F "over-eyed."
    [8] *mewed:* shed, molted.   [9] *toys:* whims.
    [10] *humorous fluxes:* outflows of the bodily fluids that make up personality.   [11] *bated:* abated, dwindled.
    [12] *doubt:* fear.   [13] *provoked:* instigated.
    [14] *close:* secret.   [15] *censure's:* judgment's.
    [16] *sack:* dry white wine.
    [17] *Amadis . . . England:* romances.   [18] *to:* compared to.
    [19] *honest:* chaste.
    [20] *Lucretia . . . Tarquin:* The Roman matron was raped by the Etruscan prince.
    [21] *Portia:* daughter of Cato, wife of Brutus, paragon of Roman wives, who, like Lucretia, committed suicide.
    [22] *pox:* syphilis.

How have ye done since I went? Have ye had your
    health well?
And your mind free?
    Ori.   You see I am not bated;[11]
Merry, and eat my meat.
    De Ga.   A good preservative.
And how have you been used? You know, Oriana,   80
Upon my going out, at your request,
I left your portion in La Castre's hands,
The main means you must stick to. For that reason,
And 'tis no little one, I ask ye, sister,
With what humanity he entertains ye,
And how ye find his courtesy?
    Ori.   Most ready;
I can assure you, sir, I am used most nobly.
    De Ga. I am glad to hear it. But, I prithee, tell me,
And tell me true, what end had you, Oriana,
In trusting your money here? He is no kinsman,   90
Nor any tie upon him of a guardian;
Nor dare I think ye doubt[12] my prodigality.
    Ori. No, certain, sir; none of all this provoked[13] me;
Another private reason.
    De Ga.   'Tis not private,
Nor carried so; 'tis common, my fair sister,
Your love to Mirabel; your blushes tell it.
'Tis too much known, and spoken of too largely;
And with no little shame I wonder at it.
    Ori. Is it a shame to love?
    De Ga.   To love undiscreetly:
A virgin should be tender of her honor,   100
Close,[14] and secure.
    Ori.   I am as close as can be,
And stand upon as strong and honest guards too;
Unless this warlike age needs a portcullis.
Yet, I confess, I love him.
    De Ga.   Hear the people.
    Ori. Now, I say, hang the people. He that dares
Believe what they say dares be mad and give
His mother, nay, his own wife, up to rumor.
All grounds of truth they build on is a tavern;
And their best censure's[15] sack,[16] sack in abundance;
For as they drink, they think. They ne'er speak
    modestly,   110
Unless the wine be poor or they want money.
Believe them? Believe *Amadis de Gaul,*
The Knight o' th' Sun, or *Palmerin of England,*[17]
For these, to[18] them, are modest and true stories.
Pray understand me; if their tongues be truth,
As if *in vino veritas* be an oracle,
What woman is or has been ever honest?[19]
Give 'em but ten round cups, they'll swear Lucretia
Died not for want of power to resist Tarquin,[20]
But want of pleasure that he stayed no longer: 120
And Portia,[21] that was famous for her piety
To her loved lord, they'll face ye out, died o' th' pox.[22]
    De Ga. Well, there is something, sister.
    Ori.   If there be,
    brother,
'Tis none of their things; 'tis not yet so monstrous.
My thing is marriage; and at his return
I hope to put their squint eyes right again.

De Ga. Marriage? 'Tis true, his father is a rich man,
Rich both in land and money; he his heir,
A young and handsome man, I must confess too;
But of such qualities, and such wild flings,   130
Such admirable[23] imperfections, sister,
For all his travel, and bought experience,
I should be loath to own him for my brother.
Methinks, a rich mind in a state indifferent[24]
Would prove the better fortune.
    Ori.   If he be wild.
The reclaiming him to good and honest, brother,
Will make much for my honor; which, if I prosper,
Shall be the study of my love, and life, too.
    De Ga. Ye say well; would he thought as well, and
        loved, too.   139
He marry? He'll be hanged first. He knows no more
What the conditions and the ties of love are,
The honest purposes and grounds of marriage,
Nor will know, nor be ever brought to endeavor,
Than I do how to build a church. He was ever
A loose and strong defier of all order.
His loves are wanderers; they knock at each door
And taste each dish, but are no residents.
Or say he may be brought to think of marriage—
As 'twill be no small labor—thy hopes are strangers.
I know there is a labored match now followed,   150
Now at this time, for which he was sent for home, too.
Be not abused:[25] Nantolet has two fair daughters,
And he must take his choice.
    Ori.   Let him take freely.
For all this I despair not; my mind tells me
That I, and only I, must make him perfect;
And in that hope I rest.
    De Ga.   Since you're so confident,
Prosper your hope. I'll be no adversary;
Keep[26] yourself fair and right, he shall not wrong ye.
    Ori. When I forget my virtue, no man know me.
                                        Exeunt.

I.ii

Enter MIRABEL, PINAC, BELLEUR, *and* Servants.

    Mir. Welcome to Paris once more, gentlemen.
We have had a merry and a lusty ordinary,
And wine, and good meat, and a bouncing[1] reckoning.[2]
And let it go for once; 'tis a good physic.
Only the wenches are not for my diet;
They are too lean and thin, their embraces
        brawnfallen.[3]
Give me the plump Venetian, fat, and lusty,
That meets me soft and supple, smiles upon me
As if a cup of full wine leaped to kiss me.
These slight things I affect[4] not.
    Pinac.   They are ill-built;   10
Pin-buttocked,[5] like your dainty Barbaries,[6]
And weak i' th' pasterns; they'll endure no hardness.
    Mir. There's nothing good or handsome bred
        amongst us;
Till we are traveled, and live abroad, we are coxcombs.
Ye talk of France; a slight unseasoned country,
Abundance of gross food, which makes us blockheads.

We are fair set out indeed, and so are forehorses:[7]
Men say we are great courtiers; men abuse us.
We are wise and valiant, too; *non credo, signor.*[8]
Our women the best linguists; they are parrots;   20
O' this side the Alps they're nothing but mere
        drolleries.[9]
Ha! *Roma la Santa,*[10] Italy for my money.
Their policies, their customs, their frugalities,
Their courtesies so open, yet so reserved, too,
As, when ye think ye are known best, ye are a stranger;
Their very pickteeth[11] speak more man than we do,
And season of more salt.
    Pinac.   'Tis a brave[12] country;
Not pestered with your stubborn precise[13] puppies
That turn all useful and allowed contentments
To[14] scabs[15] and scruples: hang 'em, capon-
        worshippers.[16]   30
    Bel. I like that freedom well, and like their women,
        too,
And would fain do as others do; but I am so bashful,
So naturally an ass—Look ye, I can look upon 'em,
And very willingly I go to see 'em—
There's no man willinger—and I can kiss 'em,
And make a shift—
    Mir.   But if they chance to flout ye,
Or say, "Ye are too bold! fie, sir, remember!
I pray, sit further off—"
    Bel.   'Tis true; I am humbled,
I am gone; I confess ingenuously I am silenced;
The spirit of amber[17] cannot force me answer.   40
    Pinac. Then would I sing and dance—
    Bel.   You have
        wherewithal, sir.
    Pinac. And charge her up again.
    Bel.   I can be hanged first;
Yet, where I fasten well, I am a tyrant.
    Mir. Why, thou dar'st fight?
    Bel.   Yes, certainly I dare
        fight,
And fight with any man at any weapon;
'Would th' other were no more! but a pox on't!
When I am sometimes in my height of hope,
And reasonable valiant that way, my heart hardened,
Some scornful jest or other chops between me
And my desire. What would ye have me to do then,
        gentlemen?   50

---

[23] *admirable:* noteworthy.
[24] *state indifferent:* ordinary rank.   [25] *abused:* deceived.
[26] *Keep:* i.e., If you keep.

I.ii.
[1] *bouncing:* whopping.   [2] *reckoning:* bill.
[3] *brawnfallen:* unmuscular.   [4] *affect:* like.
[5] *pin-buttocked:* sharp-buttocked.
[6] *Barbaries:* African horses.
[7] *forehorses:* leading horses in a team.
[8] *It.:* I don't believe it, sir.   [9] *drolleries:* puppets.
[10] *It.:* Holy Rome.   [11] *pickteeth:* toothpicks.
[12] *brave:* fine.   [13] *precise:* puritanical.
[14] *turn . . . . To:* make a question of.
[15] *scabs:* from venereal disease.
[16] *capon-worshippers:* i.e., enemies of sexual pleasure
(capon = eunuch).   [17] *amber:* an aphrodisiac.

Mir. Belleur, ye must be bolder. Travel three years,
And bring home such a baby to betray ye
As bashfulness? A great fellow, and a soldier?
Bel. You have the gift of impudence; be thankful;
Every man has not the like talent. I will study,
And if it may be revealed to me—
    Mir.   Learn of me.
And of Pinac. No doubt, you'll find employment;
Ladies will look for courtship.
    Pinac.   'Tis but fleshing,[18]
But standing one good brunt or two. Hast thou any
mind to marriage?
We'll provide thee some soft-natured wench, that's
  dumb, too.   60
    Mir. Or an old woman that cannot refuse thee in
  charity.
    Bel. A dumb woman, or an old woman, that were
  eager,
And cared not for discourse, I were excellent at.
    Mir. You must now put on boldness—there's no
  avoiding it—
And stand all hazards, fly at all games bravely;
They'll say, you went out like an ox and returned like
  an ass else.
    Bel. I shall make danger,[19] sure.
    Mir.   I am sent for home
  now;
I know it is to marry; but my father shall pardon me.
Although it be a witty ceremony,
And may concern me hereafter in my gravity,   70
I will not lose the freedom of a traveler;
A new strong lusty bark cannot ride at one anchor.
Shall I make divers suits to show to the same eyes?
'Tis dull and home-spun. Study several pleasures,
And want employments for 'em? I'll be hanged first!
Tie me to one smock? Make my travels fruitless?
I'll none of that; for every fresh behavior,
By your leave, father, I must have a fresh mistress,
And a fresh favor[20] too.
    Bel.   I like that passingly;[21]
As many as you will, so they be willing,   80
Willing, and gentle,[22] gentle.
    Pinac.   There's no reason
A gentleman and a traveler should be clapped up,
(For 'tis a kind of bilboes[23] to be married)
Before he manifest to the world his good parts.[24]
Tug ever, like a rascal,[25] at one oar?
Give me the Italian liberty.
    Mir.   That I study,
And that I will enjoy. Come, go in, gentlemen;
There mark how I behave myself, and follow.
                              Exeunt.

---

[18] *fleshing:* becoming inured, battle-hardened.
[19] *make danger:* risk it.
[20] *favor:* ribbon, emblem of a romance; face.
[21] *passingly:* surpassingly.   [22] *gentle:* well-born.
[23] *bilboes:* shackles; F "baeboes."   [24] *parts:* qualities.
[25] *rascal:* lowborn fellow; here, galley slave.

I.iii.
  [1] *curious:* particular.

I.iii

Enter LA CASTRE, NANTOLET, LUGIER,
    ROSALURA, [*and*] LILLIA-BIANCA.

    La Ca. You and your beauteous daughters are most
  welcome.
Beshrew my blood they are fair ones.—Welcome,
  beauties,
Welcome, sweet birds.
    Nant.   They are bound much to your
  courtesies.
    La Ca. I hope we shall be nearer acquainted.
    Nant.   That's
  my hope, too;
For, certain, sir, I much desire your alliance.
You see 'em; they are no gypsies; for their breeding,
It has not been so coarse but they are able
To rank themselves with women of fair fashion.
Indeed, they have been trainèd well.
    Lug.   Thank me.
    Nant. Fit for the heirs of that state I shall leave 'em;
To say more is to sell 'em. They say your son,   11
Now he has traveled, must be wondrous curious[1]
And choice in what he takes; these are no coarse ones.
Sir, here's a merry wench; let him look to himself;
All heart, i'faith—may chance to startle him;
For all his care and traveled caution,
May creep into his eye. If he love gravity,
Affect a solemn face, there's one will fit him.
    La Ca. So young and so demure?
    Nant.   She is my
  daughter,
Else I would tell you, sir, she is a mistress   20
Both of those manners and that modesty
You would wonder at. She is no often-speaker,
But, when she does, she speaks well; nor no reveler,
Yet she can dance, and has studied the court elements,
And sings, as some say, handsomely; if a woman,
With the decency of her sex, may be a scholar,
I can assure ye, sir, she understands, too.
    La Ca. These are fit garments, sir.
    Lug.   Thank them that
  cut 'em.
Yes, they are handsome women; they have handsome
  parts too,
Pretty becoming parts.
    La Ca.   'Tis like they have, sir.   30
    Lug. Yes, yes, and handsome education they have
  had, too,
Had it abundantly; they need not blush at it;
I taught it, I'll avouch it.
    La Ca.   Ye say well, sir.
    Lug. I know what I say, sir, and I say but right, sir:
I am no trumpet of their commendations
Before their father; else I should say farther.
    La Ca. Pray you, what's this gentleman?
    Nant.   One that
  lives with me, sir;
A man well bred and learned, but blunt and bitter;
Yet it offends no wise man; I take pleasure in't.
Many fair gifts he has, in some of which,   40

That lie most easy to their understandings,
He has handsomely bred up my girls, I thank him.
   Lug. I have put it to 'em, that's my part, I have
     urged it;
It seems, they are of years now to take hold on't.
   Nant. He's wondrous blunt.
   La Ca.   By my faith, I was afraid
     of him.
Does he not fall out with the gentlewomen sometimes?
   Nant. No, no; he's that way moderate and discreet,
     sir.
   Ros. If he did, we should be too hard for him.
   Lug. Well said, sulfur![2]
Too hard for thy husband's head, if he wear not
     armor.[3]   50

     Enter MIRABEL, PINAC, [BELLEUR,] DE GARD,
         and ORIANA.

   Nant. Many of these bickerings, sir.
   La Ca. I am glad they are no oracles.
Sure as I live, he beats them, he's so puissant.
   Ori. Well, if ye do forget—
   Mir.   Prithee, hold thy peace.
I know thou art a pretty wench; I know thou lov'st me.
Preserve it till we have a fit time to discourse on't,
And a fit place; I'll ease my heart, I warrant thee,
Thou seest, I have much to do now.
   Ori.   I am answered, sir:
With me you shall have nothing on these conditions.
   De Ga. Your father and your friends.
   La Ca.   You are
     welcome home, sir.   60
Bless ye, ye are very welcome. Pray know this
     gentleman
And these fair ladies.
   Nant.   Monsieur Mirabel,
I am much affected with your fair return, sir;
You bring a general joy.
   Mir.   I bring you service,
And these bright beauties, sir.
   Nant.   Welcome home,
     gentlemen.
Welcome with all my heart.
   Bel. ⎫
               We thank ye, sir.
   Pinac.⎭
   La Ca. Your friends will have their share, too.
   Bel.   Sir, we
     hope
They'll look upon us, though we show like strangers.
   Nant. Monsieur De Gard, I must salute you also,
And this fair gentlewoman. You are welcome from your
     travel, too.   70
All welcome, all.

     [LA CASTRE *and* MIRABEL *speak apart.*]

   De Ga.   We render ye our loves, sir,
The best wealth we bring home. By your favors,
     beauties,
One of these two. You know my meaning.
   Ori.   Well, sir;
They are fair and handsome, I must needs confess it,

And, let it prove the worst, I shall live after it:
Whilst I have meat and drink, love cannot starve me;
For, if I die o' th' first fit, I am unhappy,
And worthy to be buried with my heels upward.
   Mir. To marry, sir?
   La Ca.   You know I am an old man,
And every hour declining to my grave,   80
One foot already in; more sons I have not,
Nor more I dare not seek whilst you are worthy.
In you lies all my hope and all my name,
The making good or wretched of my memory;
The safety of my state.
   Mir.   And you have provided,
Out of this tenderness, these handsome gentlewomen,[4]
Daughters to this rich man, to take my choice of?
   La Ca. I have, dear son.
   Mir.   'Tis true, ye are old and
     feebled;
Would you were young again and in full vigor!
I love a bounteous father's life, a long one;   90
I am none of those that, when they shoot to ripeness,
Do what they can to break the boughs they grew on;
I wish ye many years and many riches,
And pleasures to enjoy 'em. But for marriage,
I neither yet believe in't nor affect[5] it,
Nor think it fit.
   La Ca.   You will render me your reasons?
   Mir. Yes, sir, both short and pithy, and these they
     are:
You would have me marry a maid?
   La Ca.   A maid? What else?
   Mir. Yes, there be things called widows, dead men's
     wills,[6]
I never loved to prove those; nor never longed yet   100
To be buried alive in another man's cold monument.
And there be maids appearing and maids being:
The appearing are fantastic things, mere shadows;
And, if you mark 'em well, they want their heads[7] too;
Only the world, to cozen misty eyes,
Has clapped 'em on new faces. The maids being
A man may venture on, if he be so mad to marry,
If he have neither fear before his eyes nor fortune;
And let him take heed how he gathers these, too.
For look ye, father, they are just like melons;   110
Muskmelons are the emblems of these maids:
Now they are ripe; now cut 'em they taste pleasantly,
And are a dainty fruit, digested easily;
Neglect this present time, and come tomorrow,
They are so ripe, they are rotten gone, their sweetness
Run into humor,[8] and their taste to surfeit.
   La Ca. Why, these are now ripe, son.
   Mir.   I'll try them
     presently,
And, if I like their taste—
   La Ca.   Pray ye please yourself, sir.

---

2 *sulfur:* i.e., hellfire.
3 *Too . . . armor:* The line has bawdy implications.
4 *these gentlewomen:* F "this gentlewoman."
5 *affect:* like.   6 *wills:* testamentary gifts; sexual desires.
7 *heads:* maidenheads.   8 *humor:* moisture.

Mir. That liberty is my due, and I'll maintain it.—
Lady, what think you of a handsome man now?   120
Ros. A wholesome[9] too, sir?
Mir.   That's as ye make your
   bargain.
A handsome, wholesome man then, and a kind man,
To cheer your heart up, to rejoice ye, lady?
Ros. Yes, sir, I love rejoicing.
Mir.   To lie close to ye?
Close as a cockle? Keep the cold nights from ye?
Ros. That will be looked for, too; our bodies ask it.
Mir. And get two boys at every birth?
Ros.   That's
   nothing;
I have known a cobbler do it, a poor thin cobbler
A cobbler out of moldy cheese perform it,
Cabbage, and coarse black bread; methinks, a
   gentleman   130
Should take foul scorn to have an awl outname[10] him.
Two at a birth? Why, every house-dove has it.
That man that feeds well promises as well, too,
I should expect indeed something of worth from.
Ye talk of two?
Mir. [*Aside*] She would have me get two dozen,
Like buttons, at a birth.
Ros.   You love to brag, sir;
If you proclaim these offers at your marriage,
Ye are a pretty-timbered man; take heed.
They may be taken hold of, and expected,
Yes, if not hoped for at a higher rate, too.   140
Mir. I will take heed, and thank ye for your
   counsel.—
Father, what think ye?
La Ca.   'Tis a merry gentlewoman;
Will make, no doubt, a good wife.
Mir.   Not for me.
I marry her, and happily[11] get[12] nothing;
In what a state am I then, father? I shall suffer,
For anything I hear to th' contrary, *more majorum*;[13]
I were as sure to be a cuckold, father,
A gentleman of antler—
La Ca.   Away, away, fool.
Mir. As I am sure to fail her expectation.
I had rather get the pox than get her babies.   150
La Ca. Ye are much to blame! If this do not affect[14]
   ye,
Pray, try the other; she's of a more demure way.
Bel. [*Aside*] That I had but the audacity to talk thus!
I love that plainspoken gentlewoman admirably;
And, certain, I could go as near to please her,
If downright doing—she has a perilous countenance—

If I could meet one that would believe me,
And take my honest meaning without circumstance[15]—
Mir. You shall have your will, sir; I will try the
   other;
But 'twill be to small use.—I hope, fair lady   160
(For, methinks, in your eyes, I see more mercy),
You will enjoin your lover a less penance;
And though I'll promise much, as men are liberal,
And vow an ample sacrifice of service,
Yet your discretion, and your tenderness,
And thriftness in love, good housewife's carefulness
To keep the stock entire—
Lil.   Good sir, speak, louder,
That these may witness too, ye talk of nothing;
I should be loath to bear the burden
Of so much indiscretion.
Mir.   Hark ye, hark ye!   170
Ods-bobs, you are angry, lady.
Lil.   Angry? No, sir;
I never owned an anger to lose poorly.
Mir. But you can love, for all this; and delight, too,
For all your set austerity, to hear
Of a good husband, lady?
Lil.   You say true, sir;
For, by my troth, I have heard of none these ten years,
They are so rare; and there are so many, sir,
So many longing women on their knees, too,
That pray the dropping-down of these good husbands—
The dropping-down from heaven; for they are not bred
   here—   180
That you may guess at all my hope, but hearing—
Mir. Why may not I be one?
Lil.   You were near 'em
   once, sir,
When ye came o'er the Alps; those are near heaven:
But since ye missed that happiness, there's no hope of
   ye.
Mir. Can ye love a man?
Lil.   Yes, if the man be lovely;
That is, be honest, modest. I would have him valiant,
His anger slow, but certain for his honor;
Traveled he should be, but through himself exactly,
For 'tis fairer to know manners well than countries;
He must be no vain talker, nor no lover   190
To hear himself talk; they are brags of a wanderer,
Of one[16] finds no retreat[17] for fair behavior.
Would ye learn more?
Mir.   Yes.
Lil.   Learn to hold your peace,
   then:
Fond[18] girls are got with tongues, women with tempers
Mir. Women, with I know what; but let that vanish.
Go thy way, Goodwife Bias.[19] Sure thy husband
Must have a strong philosopher's stone,[20] he will ne'er
   please thee else.
Here's a starched piece of austerity.—Do you hear,
   father?
Do you hear this moral lecture?
La Ca.   Yes, and like it.
Mir. Why, there's your judgment now; there's an
   old bolt shot.   200

---

9 *wholesome:* free from venereal disease.
10 *outname:* outdo.   11 *happily:* haply, perhaps.
12 *get:* beget.   13 *L.:* in the manner of our ancestors.
14 *affect:* please.   15 *circumstance:* ceremony.
16 *one:* i.e., one who.   17 *retreat:* return.
18 *Fond:* Foolish.
19 *Bias:* of Priene, in Ionia, sixth century B.C.; one of the seven sages of Greece.
20 *philosopher's stone:* with which alchemists might make gold of base metals.

This thing must have the strangest observation[21]—
Do you mark me, father?—when she is married once,
The strangest custom, too, of admiration
On all she does and speaks; 'twill be past sufferance.
I must not lie with her in common language,
Nor cry, "Have at thee, Kate!" I shall be hissed then;
Nor eat my meat without the sauce of sentences,[22]
Your powdered[23] beef and problems, a rare diet.
My first son, Monsieur Aristotle, I know it,
Great master of the metaphysics, or so;   210
The second, Solon,[24] and the best lawsetter;
And I must look[25] Egyptian godfathers,
Which will be no small trouble. My eldest daughter,
Sappho,[26] or such a fiddling kind of poetess,
And brought up, *invita Minerva*,[27] at her needle;
My dogs must look their names, too, and all Spartan,
Lelaps,[28] Melampus[29]; no more Fox and Bawdyface,[30]
I married to a sullen set of sentences?
To one that weighs her words and her behaviors   219
In the gold weights of discretion! I'll be hanged first.
    La Ca. Prithee reclaim thyself.
    Mir.   Pray ye, give me time
        then:
If they can set me anything to play at,
That seems fit for a gamester, have at the fairest.
Till then, see more and try more.
    La Ca.   Take your time then:
I'll bar ye no fair liberty.—Come, gentlemen;
And, ladies, come; to all, once more, a welcome.
And now let's in to supper.
    Mir.   How dost like 'em?
    Pinac. They are fair enough, but of so strange
        behaviors—
    Mir. Too strange for me; I must have those have
        mettle,
And mettle to my mind. Come, let's be merry.   230
    Bel. Bless me from this woman. I would stand the
        cannon
Before ten words of hers.
    De Ga.   Do you find him now?
Do you think he will be ever firm?
    Ori.   I fear not.
                                                Exeunt.

ACT TWO

SCENE ONE

Enter MIRABEL, PINAC, [*and*] BELLEUR.

    Mir. Ne'er tell me of this happiness; 'tis nothing.
The state they bring with being sought-to,[1] scurvy.
I had rather make mine own play, and I will do.
My happiness is in mine own content
And the despising of such glorious[2] trifles,
As I have done a thousand more. For my humor,[3]
Give me a good free fellow that sticks to me,
A jovial fair companion; there's a beauty.
For[4] women, I can have too many of them;
Good women, too, as the age reckons 'em,   10
More than I have employment for.
    Pinac.   You are happy.

    Mir. My only fear is that I must be forced,
Against my nature, to conceal myself.
Health and an able body are two jewels.
    Pinac. If either of these two women were offered to
        me now,
I would think otherwise and do accordingly,
Yes, and recant my heresies; I would, sir,
And be more tender of opinion,[5]
And put a little of my traveled liberty
Out of the way, and look upon 'em seriously.   20
Methinks, this grave-carried wench—
    Bel.   Methinks, the
        other,
The home-spoken gentlewoman that desires to be
        fruitful,
That treats of the full manage of the matter,
For there lies all my aim, that wench, methinks,
If I were but well set on, for she is affable,
If I were but hounded[6] right, and one to teach me—
She speaks to th' matter, and comes home to th' point—
Now do I know I have such a body to please her
As all the kingdom cannot fit her with, I am sure on't
If I could but talk myself into her favor.   30
    Mir. That's easily done.
    Bel.   That's easily said; would
        'twere done.
You should see then how I would lay about me.
If I were virtuous, it would never grieve me,
Or anything that might justify my modesty;
But when my nature is prone to do a charity,
And my calf's tongue will not help me—
    Mir.   Will ye go to
        'em?
They cannot but take it courteously.
    Pinac.   I'll do my part,
Though I am sure 'twill be the hardest I e'er played
        yet,
A way I never tried, too, which will stagger me;
And, if it do not shame me, I am happy.   40
    Mir. Win 'em and wear 'em; I give up my interest.
    Pinac. What say ye, Monsieur Belleur?
    Bel.   Would I
        could say,
Or sing, or anything that were but handsome.
I would be with her presently.
    Pinac.   Yours is no venture;
A merry, ready wench.

---

[21] *observation*: attention.
[22] *sentences*: moral apothegms.   [23] *powdered*: salted.
[24] *Solon*: c. 640–560 B.C.; Athenian statesman, constitutional reformer.   [25] *look*: look for.
[26] *Sappho*: Greek poetess from Lesbos, b. 612 B.C.
[27] *L.*: the goddess of wisdom unwilling.
[28] *Lelaps*: the hound given by Procris to her husband Cephalus (Ovid, *Metamorphoses*, VII).
[29] *Melampus*: prophet, missionary of Dionysus.
[30] *Bawdyface*: Dirtyface.

II.i.
[1] *sought-to*: sought after.
[2] *glorious*: vainglorious, worthless.
[3] *humor*: disposition, taste.   [4] *For*: As for.
[5] *opinion*: reputation.   [6] *hounded*: urged on.

Bel.   A vengeance[7] squibber![8]
She'll fleer[9] me out of faith, too.
   Mir.   I'll be near thee;
Pluck up thy heart; I'll second thee at all brunts.[10]
Be angry if she abuse thee, and beat her a little;
Some women are won that way.
   Bel.   Pray be quiet.
And let me think. I am resolved to go on;   50
But how I shall get off again—
   Mir.   I am persuaded
Thou wilt so please her, she'll go near to ravish thee.
   Bel. I would 'twere come to that once. Let me pray a
      little.
   Mir. Now for thine honor, Pinac! Board[11] me this
      modesty,
Warm but this frozen snowball, 'twill be a conquest
(Although I know thou art a fortunate wencher
And hast done rarely in thy days) above all thy ventures.
   Bel. You will be ever near?
   Mir.   At all necessities;
And take thee off, and set thee on again, boy,   59
And cherish thee, and stroke thee.
   Bel.   Help me out, too;
For I know I shall stick i' th' mire. If ye see us close
      once,
Begone, and leave me to my fortune, suddenly,
For I am then determined to do wonders.
Farewell, and fling an old shoe.[12] How my heart throbs!
Would I were drunk! farewell, Pinac! heaven send us
A joyful and a merry meeting, man.
   Pinac.   Farewell,
And cheer thy heart up; and remember, Belleur,
They are but women.
   Bel.   I had rather they were lions.
   Mir. About it; I'll be with you instantly.—

              Exeunt [BELLEUR *and* PINAC].

           Enter ORIANA.

Shall I ne'er be at rest? No peace of conscience?   70
No quiet for these creatures? Am I ordained
To be devoured quick[13] by these she-cannibals?
Here's another they call handsome; I care not for her;
I ne'er look after her. When I am half tippled,
It may be I should turn her, and peruse her;
Or, in my want of women, I might call for her;
But to be haunted when I have no fancy,
No maw[14] to th' matter—Now, why do you follow me?
   Ori. I hope, sir, 'tis no blemish to my virtue;
Nor need you, out of scruple, ask that question,   80
If you remember you, before you travel,
The contract you tied to me. 'Tis my love, sir,

That makes me seek ye, to confirm your memory;
And that being fair and good, I cannot suffer.
I come to give you thanks too.
   Mir.   For what, prithee?
   Ori. For that fair piece of honesty ye showed, sir,
That constant nobleness.
   Mir.   How? For I am short-
      headed.[15]
   Ori. I'll tell ye then; for refusing that free offer
Of Monsieur Nantolet's, those handsome beauties,
Those two prime ladies, that might well have pressed
      ye   90
If not to have broken, yet to have bowed your promise.
I know it was for my sake, for your faith' sake,
You slipped 'em off; your honesty compelled ye;
And let me tell ye, sir, it showed most handsomely.
   Mir. And let me tell thee, there was no such matter;
Nothing intended that way, of that nature.
I have more to do with my honesty than to fool it,
Or venture it in such leak barks[16] as women.
I put 'em off because I loved 'em not,
Because they are too queasy[17] for my temper,   100
And not for thy sake, nor the contract sake,
Nor vows nor oaths. I have made a thousand of 'em;
They are things indifferent, whether kept or broken;
Mere venial slips, that grow not near the conscience.
Nothing concerns those tender parts; they are trifles,
For, as I think, there was never man yet hoped for
Either constancy or secrecy for a woman,
Unless it were an ass ordained for sufferance;
Nor to contract with such can be a tie-all.
So let them know again; for 'tis a justice,   110
And a main point of civil policy,
Whate'er we say or swear, they being reprobates,
Out of the state of faith, we are clear of[18] all sides,
And 'tis a curious blindness to believe us.
   Ori. You do not mean this, sure?
   Mir.   Yes, sure, and
      certain;
And hold it positively, as a principle,
As ye are strange things, and made of strange fires and
      fluxes,
So we are allowed as strange ways to obtain ye,
But not to hold; we are all created errant.
   Ori. You told me other tales.
   Mir.   I not deny it;   120
I have tales of all sorts for all sorts of women,
And protestations likewise of all sizes,
As they have vanities to make us coxcombs.
If I obtain a good turn, so it is,
I am thankful for it; if I be made an ass,
The mends are in mine own hands, or the surgeon's,[19]
And there's an end on't.
   Ori.   Do not you love me then?
   Mir. As I love others; heartily I love thee;
When I am high and lusty, I love thee cruelly.
After I have made a plenteous meal, and satisfied   130
My senses with all delicates, come to me,
And thou shalt see how I love thee.
   Ori.   Will not you marry
      me?

---

[7] *vengeance:* terrific.   [8] *squibber:* mocker.
[9] *fleer:* jeer.   [10] *brunts:* attacks.
[11] *Board:* Accost; make advances to.
[12] *fling ... shoe:* i.e., after me, for good luck, as at a
wedding.   [13] *quick:* alive.
[14] *maw:* appetite.   [15] *short-headed:* short-memoried.
[16] *leak barks:* leaky ships.
[17] *queasy:* delicate, fastidious.   [18] *of:* on.
[19] *surgeon's:* i.e., if he contracts a venereal disease.

Mir. No, certain, no, for anything I know yet.
I must not lose my liberty, dear lady,
And, like a wanton slave, cry for more shackles.
What should I marry for? Do I want[20] anything?
Am I an inch the farther from my pleasure?
Why should I be at charge[21] to keep a wife of mine
    own,
When other honest married men's will ease me,
And thank me, too, and be beholding[22] to me?   140
Thou think'st I am mad for a maidenhead; thou art
    cozened;
Or, if I were addicted to that diet,
Can you tell me where I should have one? Thou art
    eighteen now,
And if thou hast thy maidenhead yet extant,
Sure, 'tis as big as cod's-head;[23] and those grave dishes
I never love to deal withal. Dost thou see this book here?
Look over all these ranks. All these are women,
Maids, and pretenders to maidenheads; these are my
    conquests;
All these I swore to marry, as I swore to thee,
With the same reservation, and most righteously;   150
Which I need not have done neither, for, alas, they made
    no scruple,
And I enjoyed 'em at my will and left 'em.
Some of 'em are married since, and were as pure maids
    again,
Nay, o' my conscience, better than they were bred for;
The rest, fine sober women.
    Ori.   Are you not ashamed, sir?
    Mir. No, by my troth, sir; there's no shame belongs
    to it;
I hold it as commendable to be wealthy in pleasure
As others do in rotten sheep and pasture.

            Enter DE GARD.

    Ori. Are all my hopes come to this? Is there no faith,
No troth nor modesty in men?

                                [*Weeps.*]

    De Ga.   How now, sister?   160
Why weeping thus? Did I not prophesy?
Come, tell me why—
    Ori.   I am not well; pray ye, pardon me.
                                 Exit.
    De Ga. Now, Monsieur Mirabel, what ails my sister?
You have been playing the wag with her.
    Mir.   As I take it,
She is crying for a codpiece.[24] Is she gone?
Lord, what an age is this! I was calling for ye;
For, as I live, I thought she would have ravished me.
    De Ga. Ye are merry, sir.
    Mir. Thou know'st this book, De Gard, this
    inventory?
    De Ga. The debt-book of your mistresses; I
    remember it.   170
    Mir. Why, this was it that angered her. She was
    stark mad
She found not her name here, and cried downright
Because I would not pity her immediately
And put her in my list.

    De Ga.   Sure she had more modesty.
    Mir. Their modesty is anger to be overdone;[25]
They'll quarrel sooner for precedence here,
And take it in more dudgeon to be slighted
Than they will in public meetings; 'tis their natures;
And, alas, I have so many to dispatch yet,
And to provide myself for my affairs, too,   180
That, in good faith—
    De Ga.   Be not too glorious[26] foolish;
Sum not your travels up with vanities;
It ill becomes your expectation.[27]
Temper your speech, sir. Whether your loose story
Be true or false (for you are so free,[28] I fear it)
Name not my sister in't, I must not hear it;
Upon your danger, name her not. I hold her
A gentlewoman of those happy parts and carriage
A good man's tongue may be right proud to speak her.
    Mir. Your sister, sir? D' ye blench at that? D' ye
    cavil?   190
Do ye hold her such a piece she may not be played
    withal?
I have had an hundred handsomer and nobler,
Have sued to me, too, for such a courtesy;
Your sister comes i' th' rear. Since ye are so angry,
And hold your sister such a strong recusant,[29]
I tell ye I may do it; and it may be, will, too;
It may be, have too. There's my free confession;
Work upon that now.
    De Ga.   If I thought ye had, I would work,
And work such stubborn work should make your heart
    ache;
But I believe ye, as I ever knew ye,   200
A glorious talker, and a legendmaker
Of idle tales and trifles; a depraver
Of your own truth; their honors fly about ye!
And so I take my leave; but with this caution:
Your sword be surer than your tongue; you'll smart
    else.
    Mir. I laugh at thee, so little I respect[30] thee;
And I'll talk louder, and despise thy sister;.
Set up a chambermaid that shall outshine her,
And carry her in my coach, too, and that will kill her.
Go, get thy rents up,[31] go.
    De Ga.   Ye are a fine gentleman.   210
                                 Exit.
    Mir. Now, have at my two youths. I'll see how they
    do,
How they behave themselves, and then I'll study
What wench shall love me next, and when I'll loose[32]
    her.

                                 Exit.

---

[20] *want:* lack.   [21] *charge:* expense.
[22] *beholding:* obligated.
[23] *cod's-head:* in addition to the literal sense, fool.
[24] *codpiece:* ornamental appendage to male breeches worn
over genitals.   [25] *overdone:* outdone.
[26] *glorious:* boastfully.
[27] *your expectation:* what is expected of you.
[28] *free:* licentious.   [29] *recusant:* dissenter.
[30] *respect:* take into account.   [31] *get . . . up:* collect.
[32] *loose:* get rid of.

II.ii

Enter PINAC *and a* Servant.

Pinac. Art thou her servant, say'st thou?
Serv.   Her poor
    creature;
But servant to her horse, sir.
Pinac.   Canst thou show me
The way to her chamber, or where I may conveniently
See her, or come to talk to her?
Serv.   That I can, sir;
But the question is whether I will or no.
Pinac.   Why, I'll
    content thee.
Serv. Why, I'll content thee then; now ye come to
    me.
Pinac. There's for your diligence.

[*Gives money.*]

Serv.   There's her
    chamber, sir,
And this way she comes out; stand ye but here, sir,
You have her at your prospect or your pleasure.
Pinac. Is she not very angry?
Serv.   You'll find that quickly
Maybe she'll call ye saucy, scurvy fellow,   11
Or some such familiar name; maybe she knows ye,
And will fling a pisspot at ye, or a pantofle,[1]
According as you are in acquaintance. If she like ye,
Maybe she'll look upon ye, maybe no;
And two months hence call for ye.
Pinac.   This is fine.
She is monstrous proud then?
Serv.   She is a little haughty;
Of a small body, she has a mind well mounted.
Can you speak Greek?
Pinac.   No, certain.
Serv.   Get ye gone then.—
And talk of stars, and firmaments, and firedrakes?[2]   20
Do you remember who was Adam's schoolmaster,
And who taught Eve to spin? She knows all these,
And will run you over the beginning o' th' world
As familiar as a fiddler.
Can you sit seven hours together and say nothing?
Which she will do, and when she speaks speak oracles,
Speak things that no man understands, nor herself,
    neither.
Pinac. Thou mak'st me wonder.
Serv.   Can you smile?
Pinac.   Yes,
    willingly,
For naturally I bear a mirth about me.
Serv. She'll ne'er endure ye then; she's never merry;

If she see one laugh, she'll swoon past *aqua vitae*.[3]   31
Never come near her, sir; if ye chance to venture,
And talk not like a doctor,[4] you are damned, too.
I have told ye enough for your crown,[5] and so good
    speed ye.

Exit.

Pinac. I have a pretty task if she be thus curious,[6]
As, sure, it seems she is. If I fall off now,
I shall be laughed at fearfully; if I go forward,
I can but be abused, and that I look for;
And yet I may hit right, but 'tis unlikely.
Stay! in what mood and figure shall I attempt her?   40
A careless way? No, no, that will not waken her;
Besides, her gravity will give me line[7] still,
And let me lose myself; yet this way often
Has hit, and handsomely. A wanton method?
Ay, if she give it leave to sink into her consideration.
But there's the doubt. If it but stir her blood once,
And creep into the crannies of her fancy,
Set her agog; but if she chance to slight it,
And by the power of her modesty fling it back,
I shall appear the arrant'st rascal to her,   50
The most licentious knave—for I shall talk lewdly.
To bear myself austerely? Rate[8] my words?
And fling a general gravity about me,
As if I meant to give laws? But this I cannot do;
This is a way above my understanding:
Or, if I could, 'tis odds she'll think I mock her;
For serious and sad[9] things are ever still
Suspicious. Well, I'll say something;
But learning I have none, and less good manners,

Enter LILLIA [-BIANCA *and*] PETELLA.

Especially for ladies. Well, I'll set my best face.   60
I hear some coming. This is the first woman
I ever feared yet, the first face that shakes me.

[*Stands apart.*]

Lit. Give me my hat, Petella; take this veil off,
This sullen cloud; it darkens my delights.
Come, wench, be free, and let the music warble;
Play me some lusty measure.

[*Music.*]

Pinac. [*Aside*]   This is she, sure,
The very same I saw, the very woman,
The gravity I wondered at. Stay, stay;
Let me be sure. Ne'er trust me, but she danceth.
Summer is in her face now, and she skippeth.   70
I'll go a little nearer.

Enter MIRABEL.

Lil.   Quicker time, fellows!
I cannot find my legs yet. Now, Petella!
Pinac. [*Aside*] I am amazed. I am foundered[10] in my
    fancy.
Mir. [*Aside*] Ha! say[11] you so? Is this your gravity?
This the austerity ye put upon ye?
I'll see more o' this sport.
Lil.   A song now;
Call in for a merry and a light song,
And sing it with a liberal spirit.

II.ii.
[1] *pantofle:* slipper.   [2] *firedrakes:* meteors.
[3] *aqua vitae:* alcoholic spirits.   [4] *doctor:* scholar.
[5] *crown:* the tip given the servant.
[6] *curious:* particular.
[7] *give . . . line:* allow me full play.   [8] *Rate:* Weigh.
[9] *sad:* sober.   [10] *foundered:* bowled over, wrecked.
[11] *say:* do; is this the way it is?

Enter a [Singing Boy[12]].

Boy.   Yes, madam.
Lil. And be not amazed, sirrah, but take us for your
   own company.

[Boy *sings a song, and exit.*]

Let's walk ourselves. Come, wench. Would we had a
   man or two.   80
Pinac. Sure, she has spied me, and will abuse me
   dreadfully;
She has put on this for the purpose; yet I will try her.—
Madam, I would be loth my rude intrusion,
Which I must crave a pardon for—
Lil.   Oh, ye are welcome,
Ye are very welcome, sir. We want such a one.—
Strike up again.—I dare presume ye dance well.
Quick, quick, sir, quick! the time steals on.
Pinac.   I would talk
   with ye.
Lil. Talk as ye dance.

[*They dance.*]

Mir.   She'll beat him off his legs first.
This is the finest masque.
Lil.   Now, how do ye, sir?
Pinac. You have given me a shrewd[13] heat.
Lil.   I'll give
   ye a hundred.   90
Come, sing now, sing; for I know ye sing well;
I see ye have a singing face.
Pinac.   A fine modesty!
If I could, she'd never give me breath.—Madam, would
I might sit and recover.
Lil.   Sit here, and sing now;
Let's do things quickly, sir, and handsomely.—
Sit close, wench, close.—Begin, begin.
Pinac.   I am lessoned.

Song [*by* PINAC].

Lil. 'Tis very pretty, i'faith. Give me some wine now.
Pinac. I would fain speak to ye.
Lil.   You shall drink first,
   believe me.
Here's to you a lusty health.

[*They drink.*]

Pinac.   I thank ye, lady.—
Would I were off again. I smell my misery;   100
I was never put to this rack, I shall be drunk too.
Mir. If thou beest not a right one,[14] I have lost mine
   aim much;
I thank heaven that I have 'scaped thee. To her, Pinac;
For thou art as sure to have her, and to groan for her—
I'll see how my other youth does; this speeds trimly.
A fine grave gentlewoman, and worth much honor!

Exit.

Lil. How do ye like me, sir?
Pinac.   I like ye rarely.
Lil. Ye see, sir, though sometimes we are grave and
   silent,
And put on sadder dispositions,

Yet we are compounded of free parts, and sometimes
   too   110
Our lighter, airy, and our fiery metals
Break out and show themselves; and what think you of
   that, sir?
Pinac. Good lady, sit, for I am very weary,
And then I'll tell ye.
Lil.   Fie! a young man idle?
Up, and walk; be still in action;
The motions of the body are fair beauties:
Besides, 'tis cold. Odds me,[15] sir, let's walk faster.
What think ye now of the lady Felicia?
And Bellafronte, the duke's fair daughter? Ha?
Are they not handsome things? There is Duarta,   120
And brown Olivia—
Pinac.   I know none of 'em.
Lil. But brown must not be cast away,[16] sir. If young
   Lelia
Had kept herself till this day from a husband,
Why, what a beauty, sir! Ye know Ismena,
The fair gem of Saint Germains?[17]
Pinac.   By my troth, I do not.
Lil. And then, I know, you must hear of Brisac,
How unlike a gentleman—
Pinac.   As I live, I heard nothing.
Lil. Strike me another galliard.[18]
Pinac.   By this light, I cannot.
In troth, I have sprained my leg, madam.
Lil.   Now sit ye
   down, sir,
And tell me why ye came hither? why ye chose me out?
What is you business? Your errand? Dispatch,
   dispatch.   131
May be ye are some gentleman's man, and I mistook ye,
That have brought me a letter or a haunch of venison
Sent me from some friend of mine.
Pinac.   Do I look like a
   carrier?
You might allow me what I am, a gentleman.
Lil. Cry ye mercy, sir! I saw ye yesterday.
You are new come out of travel; I mistook ye.
And how does all our impudent friends in Italy?
Pinac. Madam, I came with duty, and fair courtesy,
Service, and honor to ye.
Lil.   Ye came to jeer me.   140
Ye see I am merry, sir; I have changed my copy:
None of the sages now, and pray ye proclaim it.
Fling on me what aspersion you shall please, sir,
Of wantonness or wildness; I look for it;
And tell the world I am an hypocrite,
Mask in a forced and borrowed shape; I expect it;
But not to have you believed: For, mark ye, sir,
I have won a nobler estimation,
A stronger tie by my discretion

---

12 *Singing Boy:* F "Man."   13 *shrewd:* intense.
14 *right one:* i.e., a real devil.
15 *Odds me:* a mild expletive derived from "Odd," a genteel circumlocution for "God."
16 *brown . . . away:* proverbial.
17 *Saint Germains:* St. Germain-en-laye, village near
Paris.   18 *galliard:* lively dance in triple time.

Upon opinion, howe'er you think I forced it,   150
Than either tongue or art of yours can slubber;[19]
And, when I please, I will be what I please, sir,
So I exceed not mean;[20] and none shall brand it
Either with scorn or shame, but shall be slighted.
   Pinac. Lady, I come to love ye.
   Lil.   Love yourself, sir;
And when I want observers [I]'ll send for ye.
Heigh-ho! my fit's almost off; for we do all by fits, sir.
If you be weary, sit till I come again to ye.
                    Exit [*with* PETELLA].
   Pinac. This is a wench of a dainty spirit; but
Hang me if I know yet either what to think   160
Or make of her. She had her will of me,
And baited me abundantly, I thank her;
And, I confess, I never was so blurted[21]
Nor ever so abused. I must bear mine own sins.
Ye talk of travels; here's a curious country.
Yet I will find her out, or forswear my faculty.[22]
                       Exit.

II.iii

       Enter ROSALURA *and* ORIANA.

   Ros. Ne'er vex yourself, nor grieve; ye are a fool
then.
   Ori. I am sure I am made so. Yet, before I suffer
Thus like a girl and give him leave to triumph—
   Ros. You say right; for as long as he perceives ye
Sink under his proud scornings, he'll laugh at ye.
For me, secure yourself;[1] and for my sister,
I partly know her mind, too. Howsoever,
To obey my father we have made a tender
Of our poor beauties to the traveled monsieur,
Yet two words to a bargain. He slights us   10
As skittish things, and we shun him as curious.
May be my free behavior turns his stomach
And makes him seem to doubt a loose opinion:[2]
I must be so sometimes, though all the world saw it.
   Ori. Why should not ye? Are not minds only
measured?[3]
As long as here ye stand secure—
   Ros.   Ye say true;
As long as mine own conscience makes no question,
What care I for report? That woman's miserable
That's good or bad for their tongue's sake. Come, let's
retire,
And get my veil, wench. By my troth, your sorrow   20
And the consideration of men's humorous maddings
Have put me into a serious contemplation.

       Enter MIRABEL *and* BELLEUR.

---

   [19] *slubber:* sully.   [20] *mean:* moderation.
   [21] *blurted:* treated contemptuously.   [22] *faculty:* ability.
II.iii.
   [1] *secure yourself:* don't worry.
   [2] *doubt . . . opinion:* suspect I have a reputation for wantonness.
   [3] *minds . . . measured:* obscure; perhaps "moderation is a
mark of minds alone, whereas behavior is naturally impul-
sive."   [4] *as:* as if.   [5] *thrumming of:* fiddling with.
   [6] *hum:* strong ale.   [7] *i' th' suds:* in difficulties.

   Ori. Come, 'faith, let's sit and think.
   Ros.   That's all my
business.

                       [*They retire.*]

   Mir. Why stand'st thou peeping here? Thou great
slug, forward!
   Bel. She is there; peace!
   Mir.   Why stand'st thou here then,
Sneaking and peeking as[4] thou wouldst steal linen?
Hast thou not place and time?
   Bel.   I had a rare speech
Studied and almost ready, and your violence
Has beat it out of my brains.
   Mir.   Hang your rare speeches;
Go me on like a man.
   Bel.   Let me set my beard up.   30
How has Pinac performed?
   Mir.   He has won already:
He stands not thrumming of[5] caps thus.
   Bel.   Lord, what
should I ail!
What a cold I have over my stomach; would I had some
hum.[6]
Certain I have a great mind to be at her,
A mighty mind.
   Mir.   On, fool.
   Bel.   Good words, I beseech ye;
For I will not be abused by both.
   Mir.   Adieu, then;
I will not trouble you; I see you are valiant,
And work your own way.
   Bel.   Hist, hist! I will be ruled;
I will, i' faith; I will go presently.
Will ye forsake me now, and leave me i' th' suds?[7]   40
You know, I am false-hearted this way. I beseech ye,
Good sweet Mirabel—I'll cut your throat if you leave
me,
Indeed I will!—sweet-heart.
   Mir.   I will be ready,
Still at thine elbow. Take a man's heart to thee
And speak thy mind, the plainer still the better.
She is a woman of that free behavior,
Indeed, that common courtesy, she cannot deny thee.
Go bravely on.
   Bel.   Madam—keep close about me,
Still at my back.—Madam, sweet madam—
   Ros.   Ha!
What noise is that? What saucy sound to trouble me?
   Mir. What said she?
   Bel.   I am saucy.
   Mir.   'Tis the better.   51
   Bel. She comes; must I be saucy still?
   Mir.   More saucy.

     [ROSALURA, *in a veil, and* ORIANA
                      come forward.]

   Ros. Still troubled with these vanities? Heaven bless
us!
What are we born to?—Would ye speak with any of
my people?

Go in, sir; I am busy.
   Bel.   This is not she, sure:
Is this two children at a birth? I'll be hanged, then.
Mine was a merry gentlewoman, talked daintily,
Talked of those matters that befitted women;
This is a parcel[8] prayer-book; I'm served sweetly!
And now I am to look to;[9] I was prepared for th' other
   way.   60
   Ros. Do you know that man?
   Ori.   Sure, I have seen him,
   lady.
   Ros. Methinks 'tis pity such a lusty fellow
Should wander up and down and want employment.
   Bel. She takes me for a rogue.[10]—You may do well,
   madam,
To stay this wanderer and set him awork, forsooth,
He can do something that may please your ladyship;
I have heard of women that desire good breedings,
Two at a birth, or so.
   Ros. The fellow's impudent.
   Ori.   Sure, he is crazed.
   Ros. I have heard of men too that have had good
   manners;   70
Sure, this is want of grace. Indeed, 'tis great pity
The young man has been bred so ill, but this lewd age
Is full of such examples.
   Bel.   I am foundered,
And some shall rue the setting of me on.
   Mir. Ha! so bookish, lady? Is it possible?
Turned holy at the heart, too? I'll be hanged then.
Why, this is such a feat, such an activity.
Such fast and loose—A veil, too, for your knavery?
O Dio,[11] Dio!
   Ros.   What do you take me for, sir?
   Mir. An hypocrite, a wanton, a dissembler,   80
Howe'er you seem; and thus ye are to be handled;
Mark me, Belleur

                  [Attempts to remove the veil.]

            and this you love, I know it;
   Ros. Stand off, bold sir!
   Mir.   You wear good clothes to
   this end,
Jewels; love feasts and masques.
   Ros.   Ye are monstrous saucy.
   Mir. All this to draw on fools; and thus, thus, lady,

                      [Tries again.]

Ye are to be lulled.
   Bel.   Let her alone, I'll swinge[12] ye else,
I will, i' faith! for though I cannot skill o'[13] this matter
Myself, I will not see another do it before me,
And do it worse.
   Ros.   Away! ye are a vain thing.
You have traveled far, sir, to return again   90
A windy and poor bladder. You talk of women,
That are not worth the favor of a common one,
The grace of her grew[14] in an hospital.[15]
Against a thousand such blown fooleries,
I am able to maintain good women's honors,
Their freedoms, and their fames, and I will do it—

   Mir. She has almost struck me dumb, too.
   Ros.   And
   declaim
Against your base malicious tongues, your noises,
For they are nothing else. You teach behaviors?
Or touch us for our freedoms? Teach yourselves
   manners,   100
Truth, and sobriety, and live so clearly
That our lives may shine in ye, and then task[16] us.
It seems ye are hot; the suburbs[17] will supply ye.
Good women scorn such gamesters; so I'll leave ye.
I am sorry to see this. Faith, sir, live fairly.
                      Exit [with ORIANA].
   Mir. This woman, if she hold on, may be virtuous;
'Tis almost possible. We'll have a new day.
   Bel. Ye brought me on, ye forced me to this foolery.
I am shamed, I am scorned, I am flirted.[18] Yes, I am so.
Though I cannot talk to a woman like your worship,
And use my phrases and my learnèd figures,   111
Yet I can fight with any man.
   Mir.   Fie!
   Bel.   I can, sir;
And I will fight.
   Mir.   With whom?
   Bel.   With you; with any man;
For all men now will laugh at me.
   Mir.   Prithee be moderate.
   Bel. And I['ll] beat all men. Come.
   Mir.   I love thee dearly.
   Bel. I will beat all that love; love has undone me.
Never tell me; I will not be a history.
   Mir. Thou art not.
   Bel.   'Sfoot, I will not. Give me room,
And let me see the proudest of ye jeer me;
And I'll begin with you first.
   Mir.   Prithee, Belleur!   120
If I do not satisfy thee—
   Bel.   Well, look ye do.
But, now I think on't better, 'tis impossible!
I must beat somebody; I am mauled myself,
And I ought in justice—
   Mir.   No, no, no, ye are cozened:
But walk, and let me talk to thee.
   Bel.   Talk wisely,
And see that no man laugh, upon no occasion;
For I shall think then 'tis at me.
   Mir.   I warrant thee.
   Bel. Nor no more talk of this.
   Mir.   Dost think I am
   maddish?
   Bel. I must needs fight yet; for I find it concerns me;
A pox on't! I must fight.
   Mir.   I' faith, thou shalt not.   130
                         Exeunt.

---

8 *parcel:* little bit of a.
9 *I . . . look to:* I'm the one to be watched over.
10 *rogue:* vagabond.   11 *It.:* God.
12 *swinge:* beat.   13 *skill o':* have competence in.
14 *her grew:* her who was raised.   15 *hospital:* orphanage.
16 *task:* accuse.   17 *suburbs:* where the brothels were.
18 *flirted:* sneered at.

ACT THREE

SCENE ONE

Enter DE GARD *and* LEVERDURE, *alias* LUGIER.

De Ga. I know ye are a scholar and can do wonders.
Lug. There's no great scholarship belongs to this,
 sir;
What I am I am: I pity your poor sister,
And heartily I hate these travelers,
These gimcracks, made of mops[1] and motions.[2]
There's nothing in their houses here but hummings;
A bee has more brains. I grieve and vex, too,
The insolent licentious carriage
Of this outfacing[3] fellow Mirabel,
And I am mad to see him prick his plumes up. 10
 De Ga. His wrongs you partly know.
 Lug.   Do not you stir,
 sir;
Since he has begun with wit, let wit revenge it.
Keep your sword close;[4] we'll cut his throat a new
 way.
I am ashamed the gentlewoman should suffer
Such base, lewd wrongs.
 De Ga.   I will be ruled; he shall live,
And left to your revenge.
 Lug.   Ay, ay, I'll fit him.
He makes a common scorn of handsome women;
Modesty and good manners are his May games;
He takes up maidenheads with a new commission;
The church-warrant's[5] out of date. Follow my counsel,
For I am zealous in the cause.
 De Ga.   I will, sir, 21
And will be still directed; for the truth is,
My sword will make my sister seem more monstrous:
Besides, there is no honor won on reprobates.
 Lug. You are i' th' right. The slight he has showed
 my pupils
Sets me afire too. Go; I'll prepare your sister,
And, as I told ye—
 De Ga.   Yes; all shall be fit, sir.
 Lug. And seriously and handsomely.
 De Ga.   I warrant ye.
 Lug. A little counsel more.
            [Whispers.]
 De Ga.   'Tis well.
 Lug.   Most stately.
See that observed; and then—
 De Ga.   I have you every way. 30
 Lug. Away then, and be ready.
 De Ga.   With all speed, sir.
             Exit.

III.i.
[1] *mops:* grimaces.   [2] *motions:* gestures.
[3] *outfacing:* insolent.   [4] *close:* sheathed.
[5] *church-warrant's:* permit to marry.
[6] *documents:* lessons.
[7] *coy:* forbidding.
[8] *Jack . . . Straw:* Straw man, scarecrow.
[9] *fast . . . loose:* a cheating game played with a stick and a
piece of leather the victim erroneously thinks fastened down.

Enter LILLIA[-BIANCA], ROSALURA, [*and*]
   ORIANA.

 Lug. We'll learn to travel too, maybe beyond him.
Good day, fair beauties.
 Lil.   You have beautified us,
We thank you, sir; you have set us off most gallantly
With your grave precepts.
 Ros.   We expected husbands
Out of your documents[6] and taught behaviors,
Excellent husbands; thought men would run stark mad
 on us,
Men of all ages and all states; we expected
An inundation of desires and offers,
A torrent of trim suitors; all we did 40
Or said or purposed to be spells about us,
Spells to provoke.
 Lil.   Ye have provoked us finely.
We followed your directions, we did rarely,
We were stately, coy,[7] demure, careless, light, giddy,
And played at all points. This you swore would carry.
 Ros. We made love and contemned love; now seemed
 holy,
With such a reverend put-on reservation
Which could not miss according to your principles;
Now gave more hope again; now close, now public,
Still up and down we beat it like a billow; 50
And ever those behaviors you read to us,
Subtle and new; but all this will not help us.
 Lil. They help to hinder us of all acquaintance;
They have frighted off all friends. What am I better
For all my learning if I love a dunce,
A handsome dunce? To what use serves my reading?
You should have taught me what belongs to horses,
Dogs, dice, hawks, banquets, masques, free and fair
 meetings,
To have studied gowns and dressings.
 Lug.   Ye are not mad,
 sure.
 Ros. We shall be, if we follow your encouragements:
I'll take mine own way now.
 Lil.   And I my fortune; 61
We may live maids else till the moon drops millstones.
I see your modest women are taken for monsters;
A dowry of good breeding is worth nothing.
 Lug. Since ye take it so to th' heart, pray ye, give me
 leave yet,
And ye shall see how I'll convert this heretic.
Mark how this Mirabel—
 Lil.   Name him no more;
For, though I long for a husband, I hate him,
And would be married sooner to a monkey
Or to a Jack of Straw,[8] than such a juggler. 70
 Ros. I am of that mind too; he is too nimble.
And plays at fast and loose[9] too learnedly
For a plain-meaning woman; that's the truth on't.
Here's one, too, that we love well, would be angry;

       [Pointing to ORIANA.]

And reason why. No, no, we will not trouble you
Nor him at this time: May he make you happy.

We'll turn ourselves loose now to our fair fortunes;
And the downright way—
 Lil.   The winning way we'll
 follow;
We'll bait that men may bite fair and not be frighted;
Yet we'll not be carried so cheap neither; we'll have
 some sport,   80
Some mad morris[10] or other for our money, tutor.
 Lug. 'Tis like enough. Prosper your own devices.
Ye are old enough to choose: But, for this gentlewoman,
So please her give me leave—
 Ori.   I shall be glad, sir,
To find a friend whose pity may direct me.
 Lug. I'll do my best, and faithfully deal for ye,
But then ye must be ruled.
 Ori.   In all, I vow to ye.
 Ros. Do, do. He has a lucky hand sometimes, I'll
 assure ye,
And hunts the recovery of a lost lover deadly.
 Lug. You must away straight.
 Ori.   Yes.
 Lug.   And I'll instruct
 ye;   90
Here ye can know no more.
 Ori.   By your leave, sweet
 ladies;
And all our fortunes arrive at our own wishes.
 Lil. Amen, amen.
 Lug.   I must borrow your man.
 Lil.   Pray take
 him;
He is within; to do her good, take anything,
Take us and all.
 Lug. No doubt ye may find takers;
And so we'll leave ye to your own disposes.
       Exit [LUGIER *with* ORIANA].
 Lil. Now, which way, wench?
 Ros.   We'll go a brave way,
 fear not;
A safe and sure way, too; and yet a byway.
I must confess I have a great mind to be married.
 Lil. So have I too a grudging[11] of good will that way;
And would as fain be dispatched. But this Monsieur
 Quicksilver—   101
 Ros. No, no; we'll bar him, by and main.[12] Let him
 trample;
There is no safety in his surquedry.[13]
An army-royal of women are too few for him.
He keeps a journal of his gentleness,
And will go near to print his fair dispatches
And call it his triumph over time and women.
Let him pass out of memory. What think ye
Of his two companions?
 Lil.   Pinac, methinks, is reasonable;
A little modesty he has brought home with him, 110
And might be taught in time some handsome duty.
 Ros. They say he is a wencher, too.
 Lil.   I like him better;
A free light touch or two becomes a gentleman
And sets him seemly off. So[14] he exceed not,
But keep his compass[15] clear, he may be looked at.

I would not marry a man that must be taught,
And conjured up with kisses; the best game
Is played still by the best gamesters.
 Ros.   Fie upon thee.
What talk hast thou!
 Lil.   Are not we alone, and merry?
Why should we be ashamed to speak what we think?
 Thy gentleman,   120
The tall fat fellow, he that came to see thee—
 Ros. Is't not a goodly man?
 Lil.   A wondrous goodly.
He has weight enough, I warrant thee. Mercy upon me,
What a serpent wilt thou seem under such a St.
 George![16]
 Ros. Thou art a fool. Give me a man brings mettle,
Brings substance with him, needs no broths to lard[17]
 him.
These little fellows show like fleas in boxes,
Hop up and down, and keep a stir to vex us.
Give me the puissant pike;[18] take you the small shot.
 Lil. Of a great thing, I have not seen a duller: 130
Therefore methinks, sweet sister—
 Ros.   Peace, he's modest;
A bashfulness; which is a point of grace, wench:
But, when these fellows come to molding, sister,
To heat, and handling.—as I live, I like him;

      Enter MIRABEL.

And, methinks, I could form him.
 Lil.   Peace; the fire-
 drake.[19]
 Mir. Bless ye, sweet beauties, sweet incomparable
 ladies,
Sweet wits, sweet humors. Bless you, learnèd lady.
And you, most holy nun, bless your devotions.
 Lil. And bless your brains, sir, your most pregnant
 brains, sir.
They are in travail; may they be delivered 140
Of a most hopeful Wild-Goose.
 Ros.   Bless your manhood.
They say ye are a gentleman of action,
A fair accomplished man, and a rare engineer;[20]
You have a trick to blow up maidenheads,
A subtle trick, they say abroad.
 Mir.   I have, lady.
 Ros. And often glory in their ruins.
 Mir.   Yes, forsooth;
I have a speedy trick, please you to try it:
My engine will dispatch ye instantly.
 Ros. I would I were a woman, sir, fit for ye,
As there be such, no doubt, may engine you too; 150

---

[10] *morris:* morris-dance, performed on festive occasions
with costumes and a wicker horse. [11] *grudging:* touch.
[12] *by and main:* entirely. [13] *surquedry:* arrogance.
[14] *So:* If. [15] *compass:* limits.
[16] *St. George:* dragon-slayer, patron saint of England.
[17] *lard:* F "lare."
[18] *puissant pike:* with bawdy suggestions; there are other
such implications in this dialogue.
[19] *fire-drake:* fiery dragon.
[20] *engineer:* constructor of military works, mine-layer.

May, with a countermine, blow up your valor.
But, in good faith, sir, we are both too honest;
And, the plague is we cannot be persuaded:
For, look ye, if we thought it were a glory
To be the last of all your lovely ladies—
    Mir. Come, come; leave prating; this has spoiled
      your market.
This pride and puffed-up heart will make ye fast, ladies,
Fast, when ye are hungry too.
    Ros.   The more our pain, sir.
    Lil. The more our health, I hope, too.
    Mir.   Your behaviors
Have made men stand amazed; those men that loved ye;
Men of fair states [21] and parts. Your strange
    conversions [22]   161
Into I know not what nor how nor wherefore;
Your scorns of those that came to visit ye;
Your studied whim-whams, [23] and your fine set faces—
What have these got ye ? Proud and harsh opinions.
A traveled monsieur was the strangest creature,
The wildest monster to be wondered at;
His person made a public scoff, his knowledge,   168
As if he had been bred 'mongst bears or bandogs, [24]
Shunned and avoided; his conversation snuffed at: [25]
What harvest brings all this ?
    Ros.   I pray ye proceed, sir.
    Mir. Now ye shall see in what esteem a traveler,
An understanding gentleman, and a monsieur,
Is to be held, and to your griefs confess it,
Both to your griefs and galls.
    Lil.   In what, I pray ye, sir ?
We would be glad to understand your excellence.
    Mir. Go on, sweet ladies; it becomes ye rarely.
For me, I have blessed me from ye; scoff on seriously.
And note the man ye mocked. You, Lady Learning,
Note the poor traveler that came to visit ye,   180
That flat unfurnished fellow; note him throughly.
You may chance to see him anon.
    Lil.   'Tis very likely.
    Mir. And see him courted by a traveled lady,
Held dear and honored by a virtuous virgin,
May be a beauty not far short of yours, neither;
It may be, clearer.
    Lil.   Not unlikely.
    Mir.   Younger;
As killing eyes as yours, a wit as poignant;
May be a state, too, that may top your fortune.
Inquire how she thinks of him, how she holds him;
His good parts, in what precious price already;   190
Being a stranger to him, how she courts him;
A stranger to his nation too, how she dotes on him.
Inquire of this; be sick to know. Curse, lady,
And keep your chamber; cry and curse. A sweet one,
A thousand in yearly land, well bred, well friended,
Traveled, and highly followed for her fashions.

---

[21] *states:* estates.   [22] *conversions:* F "conventions."
[23] *whim-whams:* fantastic notions.
[24] *bandogs:* fierce dogs kept chained.
[25] *snuffed at:* scorned.   [26] *scab:* scoundrel.
[27] *set-off:* ornament.
[28] *stale:* cover for other designs; low woman.

    Lil. Bless his good fortune, sir.
    Mir.   This scurvy fellow,
I think they call his name Pinac, this servingman
That brought you venison, as I take it, madam,
Note but this scab. [26] 'Tis strange that this coarse
    creature,   200
That has no more set-off [27] but his jugglings,
His traveled tricks—
    Lil.   Good sir, I grieve not at him,
Nor envy not his fortune; yet I wonder.
He's handsome, yet I see no such perfection.
    Mir. Would I had his fortune. For 't is a woman
Of that sweet-tempered nature and that judgment,
Besides her state, that care, clear understanding,
And such a wife to bless him—
    Ros.   Pray you whence is she ?
    Mir. Of England, and a most accomplished lady;
So modest that men's eyes are frighted at her,   210
And such a noble carriage—

Enter a Boy.

                        How now, sirrah ?
    Boy. Sir, the great English lady—
    Mir.   What of her, sir ?
    Boy. Has newly left her coach, and coming this way,
Where you may see her plain; Monsieur Pinac
The only man that leads her.

Enter PINAC, MARIANA, *and* Attendants.

    Mir.   He is much honored;
Would I had such a favor.—Now vex, ladies,
Envy and vex and rail.
    Ros.   Ye are short of us, sir.
    Mir. Bless your fair fortune, sir.
    Pinac.   I nobly thank ye.
    Mir. Is she married, friend ?
    Pinac.   No, no.
    Mir.   A goodly lady;
A sweet and delicate aspect!—Mark, mark, and wonder.
Hast thou any hope of her ?
    Pinac.   A little.
    Mir.   Follow close then;
Lose not that hope.

                   [MARIANA *curtsies to* MIRABEL.]

    Pinac.   To you, sir.
    Mir.   Gentle lady.   222
    Ros. She is fair, indeed.
    Lil.   I have seen a fairer; yet
She is well.
    Ros. Her clothes sit handsome, too.
    Lil.   She dresses
    prettily.
    Ros. And, by my faith, she is rich; she looks still
    sweeter.
A well-bred woman, I warrant her.
    Lil.   Do you hear, sir ?
May I crave this gentlewoman's name ?
    Pinac.   Mariana, lady.
    Lil. I will not say I owe ye a quarrel, monsieur,
For making me your stale. [28] A noble gentleman

Would have had more courtesy, at least more faith,   230
Than to turn off his mistress at first trial.
You know not what respect I might have showed ye;
I find ye have worth.
   Pinac.   I cannot stay to answer ye;
Ye see my charge. I am beholding to ye
For all your merry tricks you put upon me,
Your bobs[29] and base accounts. I came to love ye,
To woo ye, and to serve ye; I am much indebted to ye
For dancing me off my legs and then for walking me,
For telling me strange tales I never heard of,
More to abuse me: for mistaking me,   240
When ye both knew I was a gentleman,
And one deserved as rich a match as you are.
   Lil. Be not so bitter, sir.
   Pinac.   You see this lady;
She is young enough and fair enough to please me;
A woman of a loving mind, a quiet,[30]
And one that weighs the worth of him that loves her.
I am content with this, and bless my fortune:
Your curious wits and beauties—
   Lil.   'Faith, see me once
   more.
   Pinac. I dare not trouble ye.
   Lil.   May I speak to your lady?
   Pinac. I pray ye content yourself: I know ye are
   bitter,   250
And in your bitterness you may abuse her;
Which, if she comes to know, for she understands ye
   not,
It may breed such a quarrel to your kindred,
And such an indiscretion fling on you too,
For she is nobly friended—
   Lil. [*Aside*]   I could eat her.
   Pinac. Rest as ye are, a modest noble gentlewoman,
And afford your honest neighbors some of your prayers
          Exit [PINAC, MARIANA, *and* Attendants].
   Mir. What think you now?
   Lil.   'Faith, she's a pretty
   whiting;[31]
She has got a pretty catch, too.
   Mir.   You are angry,
Monstrous angry now, grievously angry;   260
And the pretty heart does swell now.
   Lil.   No, in troth, sir.
   Mir. And it will cry anon, "A pox upon it!"
And it will curse itself, and eat no meat, lady;
And it will sigh.[32]
   Lil.   Indeed you are mistaken;
It will be very merry.
   Ros.   Why, sir, do you think
There are no more men living, nor no handsomer,
Than he or you? By this light, there be ten thousand,
Ten thousand thousand. Comfort yourself, dear
   monsieur.
Faces, and bodies, wits, and all abiliments[33]—
There are so many we regard 'em not.   270

      Enter BELLEUR *and two* Gentlemen.

   Mir. That such a noble lady [*Aside*] I could burst
   now—

So far above such trifles—
   Bel.   You did laugh at me;
And I know why ye laughed.
   1 Gent.   I pray ye be satisfied
If we did laugh, we had some private reason,
And not at you.
   2 Gent.   Alas, we know you not, sir.
   Bel. I'll make you know me. Set your faces soberly;
Stand this way, and look sad; I'll be no May game.
Sadder, demurer yet.
   Ros.   What is the matter?
What ails this gentleman?
   Bel. Go off now backward, that I may behold ye;
And not a simper, on your lives.
          [*Exeunt* Gentlemen, *going backward.*]
   Lil.   He's mad, sure.   281
   Bel. Do you observe me too?
   Mir.   I may look on ye.
   Bel. Why do you grin? I know your mind.
   Mir.   You do
   not.
You are strangely humorous.[34] Is there no mirth nor
   pleasure
But you must be the object?
   Bel. Mark, and observe me: Wherever I am named,
The very word shall raise a general sadness,
For the disgrace this scurvy woman did me,
This proud pert thing. Take heed ye laugh not at me;
Provoke me not; take heed.
   Ros.   I would fain please ye;   290
Do anything to keep ye quiet.
   Bel.   Hear me:
Till I receive a satisfaction
Equal to the disgrace and scorn ye gave me,
Ye are a wretched woman; till thou woo'st me,
And I scorn thee as much, as seriously
Jeer and abuse thee; ask, what jill[35] thou art,
Or any baser name; I will proclaim thee,
I will so sing thy virtue, so bepaint thee—
   Ros. Nay, good sir, be more modest.
   Bel.   Do you laugh
   again?
Because ye are a woman, ye are lawless,[36]   300
And out of compass of an honest anger.
   Ros. Good sir, have a better belief of me.
   Lil.   Away, dear
   sister.
          Exit [*with* ROSALURA].
   Mir. Is not this better now, this seeming madness,
Than falling out with your friends?
   Bel.   Have I not frighted
   her?
   Mir. Into her right wits, I warrant thee: Follow this
   humor,
And thou shalt see how prosperously 'twill guide thee.

---

[29] *bobs:* mockeries.   [30] *quit:* F "quiet."
[31] *whiting:* dear, from the small fish with pearly white
flesh.   [32] *sigh:* F "fight."
[33] *abiliments:* mental capacities. [34] *humorous:* whimsical.
[35] *jill:* wench (abbreviation of "gillian").
[36] *lawless:* licentious.

Bel. I am glad I have found a way to woo yet; I was
 afraid once
I never should have made a civil suitor.
Well, I'll about it still.

               Exit.

 Mir.   Do, do, and prosper.— 309
What sport do I make with these fools! what pleasure
Feeds me, and fats my sides at their poor innocence!

    Enter LUGIER [*as* LEVERDURE].

Wooing and wiving—hang it! give me mirth,
Witty and dainty mirth. I shall grow in love, sure,
With mine own happy head. Who's this?—To me,
 sir?—
[*Aside*] What youth is this?
 Lug.   Yes, sir, I would speak with
 you,
If your name be Monsieur Mirabel.
 Mir.   Ye have hit it:
Your business, I beseech ye?
 Lug.   This it is, sir:
There is a gentlewoman hath long time affected ye,
And loved ye dearly.
 Mir.   Turn over, and end that story;
'Tis long enough; I have no faith in women, sir. 320
 Lug. It seems so. I do not come to woo for her,
Or sing her praises, though she well deserve 'em;
I come to tell ye, ye have been cruel to her,
Unkind and cruel, false of faith, and careless;
Taking more pleasure in abusing her,
Wresting her honor to your wild disposes,
Than noble in requiting her affection:
Which, as ye are a man, I must desire ye,
A gentleman of rank, not to persist in,
No more to load her fair name with your injuries. 330
 Mir. Why, I beseech you, sir?
 Lug.   Good sir, I'll tell ye,
And I'll be short; I'll tell ye, because I love ye,
Because I would have you shun the shame may follow.
There is a nobleman, new come to town, sir,
A noble and a great man, that affects her,
A countryman of mine, a brave Savoyan,
Nephew to th' duke, and so much honors her
That 'twill be dangerous to pursue your old way,
To touch at anything concerns her honor,
Believe, most dangerous: Her name is Oriana, 340
And this great man will marry her. Take heed, sir;
For howsoe'er her brother, a staid gentleman,
Lets things pass upon better hopes, this lord, sir,
Is of that fiery and that poignant metal,
Especially provoked on by affection,
That 'twill be hard—but you are wise.
 Mir.   A lord, sir?
 Lug. Yes, and a noble lord.
 Mir.   Send her good fortune.

---

37 *brave:* splendid.
38 *topgallant:* most elevated, from the name of the plat-
form at the head of the topmast, loftier than the topcastle.
39 *servant:* lover.   40 *jovy:* merry.
41 *It.:* enough.
42 *hanging:* piece of drapery (i.e., his clothes).

This will not stir her lord? A baroness?
Say ye so? Say ye so? By Lady, a brave 37 title.
Top and topgallant 38 now. Save her great ladyship.
I was a poor servant 39 of hers, I must confess, sir, 351
And in those days I thought I might be jovy,40
And make a little bold to call in to her,
But *basta*,41 now; I know my rules and distance;
Yet, if she want an usher, such an implement,
One that is throughly paced, a clean-made gentleman,
Can hold a hanging 42 up with approbation,
Plant his hat formally, and wait with patience,
I do beseech you, sir—
 Lug.   Sir, leave your scoffing,
And, as ye are a gentleman, deal fairly: 360
I have given ye a friend's counsel; so I'll leave ye.
 Mir. But, hark ye, hark ye, sir! Is't possible
I may believe what you say?
 Lug.   You may choose, sir.
 Mir. No baits? No fishhooks, sir? No gins? No
 nooses?
No pitfalls to catch puppies?
 Lug.   I tell you certain:
You may believe; if not, stand to the danger.

               Exit.

 Mir. A lord of Savoy, say he? The duke's nephew?
A man so mighty? By Lady, a fair marriage!
By my faith, a handsome fortune! I must leave prating,
For, to confess the truth, I have abusèd her, 370
For which I should be sorry, but that will seem scurvy.
I must confess she was, ever since I knew her,
As modest as she was fair; I am sure she loved me;
Her means good and her breeding excellent;
And for my sake she has refused fair matches:
I may play the fool finely.—

    Enter DE GARD [*disguised*], ORIANA, *and*
        Attendants.

       Stay. Who are these?
'Tis she, I am sure; and that the lord, it should seem;
He carries a fair port, is a handsome man, too.
I do begin to feel I am a coxcomb.
 Ori. Good my lord, choose a nobler; for I know
I am so far below your rank and honor 381
That what ye can say this way I must credit
But spoken to beget yourself sport. Alas, sir,
I am so far off from deserving you,
My beauty so unfit for your affection,
That I am grown the scorn of common railers,
Of such injurious things, that, when they cannot
Reach at my person, lie with my reputation.
I am poor, besides.
 De Ga.   Ye are all wealth and goodness;
And none but such as are the scum of men, 390
The ulcers of an honest state, spite-weavers,
That live on poison only, like swol'n spiders,
Dare once profane such excellence, such sweetness.
 Mir. This man speaks loud indeed.
 De Ga.   Name but the
 men, lady;
Let me but know these poor and base depravers,
Lay but to my revenge their persons open,

And you shall see how suddenly, how fully,
For your most beauteous sake, how direfully,
I'll handle their despites. Is this thing one?
Be what he will—
 Mir.   Sir!
 De Ga.   Dare your malicious tongue, sir—
 Mir. I know you not, nor what ye mean.
 Ori.   Good my
  lord.—   401
 De Ga. If he, or any he—
 Ori.   I beseech your honor.
This gentleman's a stranger to my knowledge,
And, no doubt, sir, a worthy man.
 De Ga.   Your mercy.
But, had he been a tainter [43] of your honor,
A blaster of those beauties reign within ye—
But we shall find a fitter time. Dear lady,
As soon as I have freed ye from your guardian,
And done some honored offices unto ye,
I'll take ye, with those faults the world flings on ye,
And dearer than the whole world I'll esteem ye. 411
   [*Exeunt* DE GARD, ORIANA, *and* Attendants.]
 Mir. This is a thundering lord; I am glad I 'scaped
  him.
How lovingly the wench disclaimed my villainy.
I am vexed now heartily that he shall have her;
Not that I care to marry or to lose her,
But that this bilbo-lord [44] shall reap that maidenhead
That was my due; that he shall rig [45] and top [46] her!
I'd give a thousand crowns now, he might miss her.

     Enter a Servant.

 Serv. [*Aside*] Nay, if I bear your blows, and keep
  your counsel,   419
You have good luck, sir: I'll teach you to strike lighter.
 Mir. Come hither, honest fellow; can'st thou tell me
Where this great lord lies, this Savoy lord? Thou met'st
  him;
He now went by thee, certain.
 Serv.   Yes, he did, sir;
I know him, and I know you are fooled.
 Mir.   Come hither;
Here's all this, give me truth.

     [*Gives money.*]

 Serv.   Not for your money,
And yet that may do much, but I have been beaten,
And by the worshipful contrivers beaten, and I'll tell
  ye.
This is no lord, no Savoy lord.
 Mir.   Go forward.
 Serv. This is a trick, and put upon ye grossly
By one Lugier. The lord is Monsieur De Gard, sir, 430
An honest gentleman, and a neighbor here:
Their ends you understand better than I, sure.
 Mir. Now I know him, know him now plain.
 Serv. I have discharged my cholers; [47] so God by ye,
  sir.
              Exit.
 Mir. What a purblind puppy was I. Now I remember
  him;

All the whole cast on's face, though it were umbered
And masked with patches. What a dunderwhelp, [48]
To let him domineer thus! How he strutted,
And what a load of lord he clapped upon him!
Would I had him here again. I would so bounce [49] him,
I would so thank his lordship for his lewd plot. 441
Do they think to carry it away, [50] with a great band [51]
  made of birdpots, [52]
And a pair of pin-buttocked breeches?—Ha!

   Enter DE GARD [*disguised*], ORIANA,
     and [Attendants].

'Tis he again; he comes, he comes, he comes, have at
  him. *Sings.*—

  My Savoy lord, why dost thou frown on me?
  And will that favor never sweeter be?
  Wilt thou, I say, forever play the fool? [53]
  De Gard, be wise, and, Savoy, go to school.
  My Lord De Gard, I thank ye for your antic; [54]
  My lady bright, that will be sometime frantic; 450
  You worthy train that wait upon this pair,
  Send you more wit, and them a bouncing bair. [55]

And so I take my humble leave of your honors!
              Exit.

 De Ga. We are discovered; there's no remedy.
Lillia-Bianca's man, upon my life,
In stubborness because Lugier corrected him—
A shameless slave! plague on him for a rascal!
 Ori. I was in perfect hope. The bane on't is now,
He will make mirth on mirth to persecute us.
 De Ga. We must be patient; I am vexed to th' proof,
  too.   460
I'll try once more; then if I fail, here's one speaks.

     [*Puts his hand on his sword.*]

 Ori. Let me be lost and scorned first!
 De Ga.   Well, we'll
  consider.
Away, and let me shift; [56] I shall be hooted else.
              Exeunt.

ACT FOUR

SCENE ONE

Enter LUGIER, LILLIA[-BIANCA], [*and*] Servant,
   [*with a willow garland*].

 Lug. Faint not, but do as I direct ye; trust me.
Believe me, too, for what I have told you, lady,
As true as you are Lillia, is authentic;

---

[43] *a tainter:* F "attaint."   [44] *bilbo-lord:* swashbuckler.
[45] *rig:* fit out with tackle, make ready to sail; with pun.
[46] *top:* (nautical) tip up a yard by tilting the arm; with pun.
[47] *cholers:* F "colours."   [48] *dunderwhelp:* blockhead.
[49] *bounce:* bang.   [50] *carry . . . away:* get away with it.
[51] *band:* collar, ruff.
[52] *made . . . birdpots:* shaped like birdpots(?).
[53] *My . . . fool:* parody of a popular song.
[54] *antic:* act.   [55] *bair:* bairn, child.
[56] *shift:* change clothes.

I know it, I have found it; 'tis a poor courage
Flies off for one repulse. These travelers
Shall find, before we have done, a homespun wit,
A plain French understanding, may cope with 'em.
They have had the better yet, thank your sweet squire
　　here.
And let 'em brag. You would be revenged?
　　Lil.　　　　　　　　　　　　　　Yes, surely.
　　Lug.　And married too?
　　Lil.　　　　　　　　I think so.
　　Lug.　　　　　　　　　　　Then be counseled;
You know how to proceed. I have other irons　　11
Heating as well as yours, and I will strike
Three blows with one stone home. Be ruled, and happy;
And so I leave you. Now is the time.
　　　　　　　　　　　　　　　　[*Exit* LUGIER.]
　　Lil.　　　　　　　　　I am ready,
If he do come to do [1] me.
　　Serv.　　　　　　　Will ye stand here,
And let the people think you are God knows what,
　　mistress?
Let boys and prentices presume upon you?
　　Lil.　　　　　　　　　　Prithee hold
　　thy peace.
　　Serv.　Stand at his door that hates ye?
　　Lil.　　　　　　　　　　Prithee leave
　　prating.
　　Serv.　Pray ye, go to th' tavern: I'll give ye a pint of
　　wine there.
If any of the madcap gentlemen should come by　　20
That take up [2] women upon special warrant,
You were in a wise case now.

　　Enter MIRABEL, PINAC, MARIANA, Priest,
　　　　　[*and*] Attendants.

　　Lil. [*To* Servant.]　　　　Give me the garland;
And wait you here.
　　　　　　　　　　　　　　　[*Servant retires.*]
　　Mir.　　　　　She is here to seek thee, sirrah.
I told thee what would follow; she is mad for thee.
Show, and advance.—So early stirring, lady?
It shows a busy mind, a fancy troubled.
A willow garland, too? Is't possible?
'Tis pity so much beauty should lie musty;
But 'tis not to be helped now.
　　Lil.　　　　　　　The more's my misery.
Good fortune to ye, lady, you deserve it;　　30
To me, too-late repentance, I have sought it.
I do not envy, though I grieve a little,
You are mistress of that happiness, those joys,
That might have been had I been wise.—But fortune—
　　Pinac.　She understands ye not; pray ye do not
　　trouble her.
And do not cross me like a hare [3] thus; 'tis as ominous.
　　Lil.　I come not to upbraid your levity,
Though you made show of love, and though I liked you,
To claim an interest (we are yet both strangers;

―――――――――――――
IV.i.
　[1] *do:* "dor," = "mock," has been suggested as an emendation.　　　　　　　　　　[2] *take up:* arrest.
　[3] *cross . . . hare:* bad luck; cf. black cats.

But what we might have been, had you persevered, sir!)
To be an eyesore to your loving lady.　　41
This garland shows, I give myself forsaken,
(Yet, she must pardon me, 'tis most unwillingly!)
And all the power and interest I had in you
(As I persuade myself, somewhat ye loved me!)
Thus patiently I render up, I offer
To her that must enjoy ye, and so bless ye.
Only, I heartily desire this courtesy,
And would not be denied, to wait upon ye
This day, to see you tied, then no more trouble ye.　　50
　　Pinac.　It need[s] not, lady.
　　Lil.　　　　　　　Good sir, grant me so
　　much.
　　Pinac.　'Tis private, and we make no invitation.
　　Lil.　My presence, sir, shall not proclaim it public.
　　Pinac.　Maybe 'tis not in town.
　　Lil.　　　　　　　　　I have a coach, sir,
And a most ready will to do you service.
　　Mir. [*Aside to* PINAC.] Strike, now or never. Make
　　it sure. I tell thee,
She will hang herself if she have thee not.
　　Pinac.　　　　　　　　　Pray ye, sir,
Entertain my noble mistress. Only a word or two
With this importunate woman and I'll relieve ye—
Now ye see what your flings are, and your fancies,　　60
Your states, and your wild stubbornness; now ye find
What 'tis to gird and kick at men's fair services,
To raise your pride to such a pitch and glory,
That goodness shows like gnats, scorned under ye,
'Tis ugly, naught; a self-will in a woman,
Chained to an overweening thought, is pestilent,
Murders fair fortune first, then fair opinion.
There stands a pattern, a true patient pattern,
Humble, and sweet.
　　Lil.　　　　　I can but grieve my ignorance.
Repentance, some say too, is the best sacrifice;　　70
For sure, sir, if my chance had been so happy—
As I confess I was mine own destroyer—
As to have arrived at you, I will not prophesy,
But certain, as I think, I should have pleased ye;
Have made ye as much wonder at my courtesy,
My love, and duty, as I have disheartened ye.
Some hours we have of youth, and some of folly;
And being freeborn maids, we take a liberty,
And to maintain that sometimes we strain highly.
　　Pinac.　Now ye talk reason.
　　Lil.　　　　　　　But being yoked and
　　governed,　　80
Married, and those light vanities purged from us,
How fair we grow, how gentle; and how tender
We twine about those loves that shoot up with us.
A sullen woman fear, that talks not to ye;
She has a sad and darkened soul, loves dully:
A merry and a free wench, give her liberty,
Believe her, in the lightest form she appears to ye,
Believe her excellent, though she despise ye;
Let but these fits and flashes pass, she'll show to you
As jewels rubbed from dust or gold new burnished:　　90
Such had I been, had you believed.
　　Pinac.　　　　　　　　Is't possible?

Lil. And to your happiness I dare assure ye,
If true love be accounted so. Your pleasure,
Your will, and your command, had tied my motions.
But that hope's gone. I know you are young and
   giddy,
And, till you have a wife can govern with ye,
You sail upon this world's sea, light and empty;
Your bark in danger daily. 'Tis not the name neither
Of wife can steer ye, but the noble nature,
The diligence, the care, the love, the patience;   100
She makes the pilot, and preserves the husband,
That knows and reckons every rib he is built on.
But this I tell you to my shame.
   Pinac.   I admire you;
And now am sorry that I aim beyond you.—
   Mir. [*Aside to* PINAC] So, so, so, fair and softly.
      She is thine own, boy;
She comes now without lure.[4]
   Pinac.   But that it must needs
Be reckoned to me as a wantonness,
Or worse, a madness, to forsake a blessing,
A blessing of that hope—
   Lil.   I dare not urge ye:
And yet, dear sir—
   Pinac.   'Tis most certain, I had rather,   110
If 'twere in my own choice—for you are my
      countrywoman,
A neighbor, here born by me; she a stranger,
And who knows how her friends—
   Lil.   Do as you please, sir;
If you be fast, not all the world—I love ye.
It is most true, and clear, I would persuade ye;
And I shall love ye still.
   Pinac.   Go, get before me:
So much ye have won upon me—do it presently:
Here's a priest ready—I'll have you.
   Lil.   Not now, sir;
No, you shall pardon me!—Advance your lady;
I dare not hinder your most high preferment: 120
'Tis honor enough for me I have unmasked ye.
   Pinac. How's that?
   Lil. I have caught ye, sir. Alas, I am no stateswoman,
Nor no great traveler, yet I have found ye;
I have found your lady, too, your beauteous lady;
I have found her birth and breeding too, her discipline,
Who brought her over, and who kept your lady,
And, when he laid her by, what virtuous nunnery
Received her in; I have found all these. Are ye blank
      now?   129
Methinks, such traveled wisdoms should not fool thus,
Such excellent indiscretions—
   Mir. [*Aside*]   How could she know
      this?
   Lil. 'Tis true she is English born, but most part
      French[5] now,
And so I hope you will find her to your comfort.
Alas, I am ignorant of what she cost ye!
The price of these hired clothes I do not know,
      gentlemen.
Those jewels are the broker's; how ye stand bound for
      'em.

Pinac. Will you make this good?
Lil.   Yes, yes; and to her
      face, sir,
That she's an English whore, a kind of fling-dust,[6]
One of your London light o' loves,[7] a right one.
Came over in thin pumps and half a petticoat,   140
One faith and one smock, with a broken haberdasher;
I know all this without a conjurer.
Her name is Jumping Joan, an ancient sin-weaver.
She was first a lady's chambermaid, there slipped
And broke her leg above the knee;[8] departed
And set up shop herself; stood the fierce conflicts
Of many a furious term;[9] there lost her colors,
And last shipped over hither.
   Mir. [*Aside*]   We are betrayed.
   Lil. Do you come to fright me with this mystery?
To stir me with a stink none can endure, sir?   150
I pray ye proceed; the wedding will become ye!
Who gives the lady? You? An excellent father;
A careful man, and one that knows a beauty.
Send you fair shipping, sir; and so I'll leave ye.
Be wise and manly; then I may chance to love ye.
                                    Exit [*with* Servant].
   Mir. As I live, I am ashamed this wench has
      reached[10] me,
Monstrous ashamed; but there's no remedy.
This skewed-eyed carrion—
   Pinac.   This I suspected ever.
Come, come, uncase;[11] we have no more use for you;
Your clothes must back again.   160
   Mar. Sir, you shall pardon me;
'Tis not our English use to be degraded.
If you will visit me, and take your venture,
You shall have pleasure for your properties;
And so, sweetheart—
                                          [*Exit.*]
   Mir. Let her go, and the devil go with her.
We have never better luck with these preludiums.[12]
Come, be not daunted; think she is but a woman,
And let her have the devil's wit, we'll reach her.
                                    Ex[*eunt*].

IV.ii

Enter ROSALURA *and* LUGIER.

Ros. Ye have now redeemed my good opinion, tutor,
And ye stand fair again.
   Lug.   I can but labor
And sweat in your affairs. I am sure Belleur
Will be here instantly and use his anger,
His wonted harshness.
   Ros.   I hope he will not beat me.

---

   [4] *come . . . lure:* metaphor from falconry.
   [5] *French:* having contracted the French or venereal disease.   [6] *fling-dust:* whore.
   [7] *light o' loves:* inconstant women, whores.
   [8] *leg . . . knee:* i.e., her maidenhead.
   [9] *term:* period during which courts were in session and
London attracted visitors.   [10] *reached:* hit.
   [11] *uncase:* undress.   [12] *preludiums:* preliminaries.

Lug. No, sure, he has more manners. Be you ready.

Ros. Yes, yes, I am; and am resolved to fit him,
With patience to outdo all he can offer.
But how does Oriana?

Lug.   Worse, and worse still;
There is a sad house for her; she is now,   10
Poor lady, utterly distracted.

Ros.   Pity,
Infinite pity. 'Tis a handsome lady.
That Mirabel's a beast, worse than a monster,
If this affliction work not.

Enter LILLIA-BIANCA.

Lil.   Are ye ready?
Belleur is coming on here hard behind me.
I have no leisure to relate my fortune;
Only I wish you may come off as handsomely.
Upon the sign you know what.

                    Exit [*with* LUGIER].

Ros.   Well, well; leave me.

Enter BELLEUR.

Bel. How now?

Ros.   Ye are welcome, sir.

Bel.   'Tis well ye have
manner[s].
That curtsey again, and hold your countenance staidly.
That look's too light; take heed! so, sit ye down now;
And to confirm me that your gall is gone,   22
Your bitterness dispersed (for so I'll have it)
Look on me steadfastly, and, whatsoe'er I say to ye,
Move not, nor alter in your face; ye are gone then.
For if you do express the least distaste,
Or show an angry wrinkle—mark me, woman!
We are now alone—I will so conjure[1] thee,
The third part of my execution
Cannot be spoke.

Ros.   I am at your dispose, sir.   30

Bel. Now rise, and woo me a little; let me hear that
faculty;
But touch me not; nor do not lie, I charge ye.
Begin now.

Ros.   If so mean and poor a beauty
May ever hope the grace—

Bel.   Ye cog, ye flatter
Like a lewd thing, ye lie. "May hope that grace?"
Why, what grace canst thou hope for? Answer not;
For if thou dost, and liest again, I'll swinge thee.
Do not I know thee for a pestilent woman?
A proud at both ends? Be not angry,
Nor stir not o' your life.

Ros.   I am counsel[ed], sir.   40

Bel. Art thou not now (confess, for I'll have the truth
out)
As much unworthy of a man of merit,
Or any of ye all, nay, of mere man,
Though he were crooked, cold, all wants upon him,

IV.ii.
[1] *conjure:* affect as if by magic.   [2] *culled:* picked out.
[3] *greased:* gulled.

Nay, of any dishonest thing that bears that figure,
As devils are of mercy?

Ros.   We are unworthy.

Bel. Stick to that truth, and it may chance to save
thee.
And is it not our bounty that we take ye?
That we are troubled, vexed, or tortured with ye,
Our mere and special bounty?

Ros.   Yes.

Bel.   Our pity,   50
That for your wickedness we swinge ye soundly;
Your stubbornness, and your stout hearts, we belabor
ye?
Answer to that.

Ros.   I do confess your pity.

Bel. And dost not thou deserve in thine own person,
Thou impudent, thou pert—do not change
countenance.

Ros. I dare not, sir.

Bel.   For if ye do—

Ros.   I am settled.

Bel. Thou wagtail, peacock, puppy, look on me:
I am a gentleman.

Ros.   It seems no less, sir.

Bel. And darest thou in thy surquedry—

Ros.   I beseech ye.
It was my weakness, sir, I did not view ye,   60
I took not notice of your noble parts,
Nor culled[2] your person, nor your proper fashion.

Bel. This is some amends yet.

Ros.   I shall mend, sir, daily,
And study to deserve.

Bel.   Come a little nearer!
Canst thou repent thy villainy?

Ros.   Most seriously.

Bel. And be ashamed?

Ros.   I am ashamed.

Bel.   Cry.

Ros. It will be hard to do, sir.

Bel.   Cry now instantly;
Cry monstrously, that all the town may hear thee;
Cry seriously, as if thou hadst lost thy monkey;
And, as I like thy tears—

Enter LILLIA [-BIANCA] *and four* Women, *laughing.*

Ros.   Now!

Bel.   How! how! do ye jeer
me?   70
Have ye broke your bounds again, dame?

Ros.   Yes, and
laugh at ye,
And laugh most heartily.

Bel.   What are these? Whirlwinds?
Is hell broke loose, and all the furies fluttered?
Am I greased[3] once again?

Ros.   Yes, indeed are ye;
And once again ye shall be, if ye quarrel.
Do you come to vent your fury on a virgin?
Is this your manhood, sir?

1 Wom.   Let him do his best;
Let's see the utmost of his indignation;

I long to see him angry. Come; proceed, sir.
Hang him, he dares not stir; a man of timber!   80

[*The* Women *display knives.*]

2 Wom. Come hither to fright maids with thy bull-
    faces?
To threaten gentlewomen! Thou a man? A maypole,
A great dry pudding![4]
    3 Wom.   Come, come, do your worst, sir;
Be angry if thou darest.
    Bel.   The Lord deliver me!
    4 Wom. Do but look scurvily upon this lady,
Or give us one foul word—we are all mistaken;
This is some mighty dairymaid in man's clothes.
    Lil. I am of that mind, too.
    Bel.   What will they do to me?
    Lil. And hired to come and abuse us. A man has
    manners;
A gentleman, civility and breeding.   90
Some tinker's trull, with a beard glued on.
    1 Wom.   Let's search
    him,
And as we find him—
    Bel.   Let me but depart from ye,
Sweet Christian women.
    Lil.   Hear the thing speak,
    neighbors.
    Bel. 'Tis but a small request: if e'er I trouble ye,
If e'er I talk again of beating women,
Or beating anything that can but turn to me,
Of ever thinking of a handsome lady
But virtuously and well, of ever speaking
But to her honor—this I'll promise ye
I will take rhubarb and purge choler[5] mainly,[6]   100
Abundantly I'll purge.
    Lil.   I'll send ye broths, sir.
    Bel. I will be laughed at and endure it patiently;
I will do anything!
    Ros.   I'll be your bail then.
When ye come next to woo, pray ye come not
    boisterously,
And furnished like a bear ward.[7]
    Bel.   No, in truth, forsooth.
    Ros. I scented ye long since.
    Bel.   I was to blame, sure;
I will appear a gentleman.
    Ros.   'Tis the best for you,
For a true noble gentleman's a brave[8] thing.
Upon that hope we quit you. You fear seriously?
    Bel. Yes, truly do I; I confess I fear ye,   110
And honor ye, and anything.
    Ros.   Farewell then.
    Wom. And when ye come to woo next, bring more
    mercy!

Exeunt [ROSALURA *and* Women].

Enter two Gentlemen.

    Bel. A dairymaid! a tinker's trull! Heaven bless me!
Sure, if I had provoked 'em, they had quartered[9] me.
I am a most ridiculous ass, now I perceive it;
A coward, and a knave, too.

---

    1 Gent.   'Tis the mad gentleman;
Let's set our faces right.
    Bel.   No, no; laugh at me,
And laugh aloud.
    2 Gent.   We are better mannered, sir.
    Bel. I do deserve it; call me patch[10] and puppy,
And beat me, if you please.
    1 Gent.   No, indeed; we know ye.
    Bel. Death, do as I would have ye.
    2 Gent.   You are an ass
    then,   121
A coxcomb, and a calf.
    Bel.   I am a great calf.
Kick me a little now: Why, when? Sufficient.

[*They kick him.*]

Now laugh aloud, and scorn me; so God by ye!
And ever when ye meet me, laugh.
    1 Gent.   We will, sir.

Exeunt.

IV.iii

Enter NANTOLET, LA CASTRE, DE GARD,
    LUGIER, [*and*] MIRABEL.

    Mir. Your patience, gentlemen. Why do ye bait me?
    Nant. Is't not a shame you are so stubborn-hearted,
So stony and so dull, to such a lady,
Of her perfections and her misery?
    Lug. Does she not love ye? Does not her distraction
For your sake only, her most pitied lunacy
Of all but you, show ye? Does it not compel ye?
    Mir. Soft and fair, gentlemen; pray ye proceed
    temperately.
    Lug. If ye have any feeling, any sense in ye,
The least touch of a noble heart—
    La Ca.   Let him alone: 10
It is his glory that he can kill beauty.—
Ye bear my stamp but not my tenderness;
Your wild unsavory courses set that in ye.
For shame, be sorry, though ye cannot cure her;
Show something of a man, of a fair nature.
    Mir. Ye make me mad.
    De Ga.   Let me pronounce this to ye;
You take a strange felicity in slighting
And wronging women, which my poor sister feels now;
Heaven's hand be gentle on her. Mark me, sir,
That very hour she dies—there's small hope
    otherwise—   20
That minute, you and I must grapple for it;
Either your life or mine.
    Mir.   Be not so hot, sir;
I am not to be wrought on by these policies,
In truth, I am not; nor do I fear the tricks
Or the high-sounding threats of a Savoyan.
I glory not in cruelty—ye wrong me—

---

    [4] *pudding:* sausage.
    [5] *choler:* the humor that causes anger.
    [6] *mainly:* forcefully.   [7] *ward:* keeper.
    [8] *brave:* splendid.   [9] *quartered:* cut into quarters.
    [10] *patch:* fool.

Nor grow up watered with the tears of women.
This let me tell ye, howso'er I show to ye,
Wild, as ye please to call it, or self-willed,

Enter ROSALURA *and* LILLIA[-BIANCA].

When I see cause I can both do and suffer,   30
Freely, and feelingly, as a true gentleman.
    Ros. Oh, pity, pity! thousand, thousand pities!
    Lil. Alas, poor soul, she will die. She is grown
        senseless;
She will not know, nor speak now.
    Ros.   Die for love?
And love of such a youth? I would die for a dog first.
He that kills me, I'll give him leave to eat me.
I'll know men better ere I sigh for any of 'em.
    Lil. Ye have done a worthy act, sir, a most famous;
You have killed a maid the wrong way; ye are a
        conqueror.
    Ros. A conqueror? A cobbler. Hang him, souter.[1]
Go hide thyself, for shame. Go lose thy memory.   41
Live not 'mongst men; thou art a beast, a monster,
A blatant beast.
    Lil.   If ye have yet any honesty,
Or ever heard of any, take my counsel;
Off with your garters, and seek out a bough,
A handsome bough, for I would have you hang like a
        gentleman;
And write some doleful matter to the world.
A warning to hard-hearted men.
    Mir.   Out, kitlings![2]
What caterwauling's here! what gibbing![3]
Do you think my heart is softened with a black santis?[4]
Show me some reason.

Enter ORIANA *on a bed.*

    Ros.   Here then, here is a reason.   51
    Nant. Now, if ye be a man, let this sight shake ye.
    La Ca. Alas, poor gentlewoman!—do you know me,
        lady?
    Lug. How she looks up and stares.
    Ori.   I know you very
        well;
Ye are my godfather; and that's the monsieur.
    De Ga. And who am I?
    Ori.   You are Amadis de Gaul,
        sir.—
Oh, oh, my heart! Were you never in love, sweet lady?
And do you never dream of flowers and gardens?
I dream of walking fires. Take heed; it comes now.
Who's that? Pray stand away. I have seen that face
        sure.   60
How light my head is!
    Ros.   Take some rest.
    Ori.   I cannot;
For I must be up tomorrow to go to church,
And I must dress me, put my new gown on,

And be as fine to meet my love. Heigh-ho!
Will not you tell we where my love lies buried?
    Mir. He is not dead. [*Aside*] Beshrew my heart, she
        stirs me.
    Ori. He is dead to me.
    Mir. [*Aside*]   Is't possible my nature
Should be so damnable to let her suffer?—
Give me your hand.
    Ori.   How soft you feel, how gentle!
I'll tell ye your fortune, friend.
    Mir.   How she stares on me!
    Ori. You have a flattering face, but 'tis a fine one;
I warrant you may have a hundred sweethearts.   72
Will ye pray for me? I shall die tomorrow;
And will ye ring the bells?
    Mir.   I am most unworthy,
I do confess, unhappy. Do you know me?
    Ori. I would I did.
    Mir.   Oh, fair tears, how ye take me!
    Ori. Do ye weep, too? You have not lost your lover?
You mock me; I'll go home and pray.
    Mir.   Pray ye pardon
        me;
Or, if it please you to consider justly,
Scorn me, for I deserve it; scorn and shame me,   80
Sweet Oriana.
    Lil.   Let her alone; she trembles:
Her fits will grow more strong if ye provoke her.
    La Ca. Certain she knows ye not, yet loves to see ye.
How she smiles now!

Enter BELLEUR.

    Bel. Where are ye? Oh, why do not ye laugh? Come,
        laugh at me!
Why a devil art thou sad, and such a subject,
Such a ridiculous subject as I am,
Before thy face?
    Mir.   Prithee put off this lightness;
This is no time for mirth, nor place; I have used too
        much on't:
I have undone myself and a sweet lady   90
By being too indulgent to my foolery,
Which truly I repent. Look here.
    Bel.   What ails she?
    Mir. Alas, she is mad.
    Bel.   Mad?
    Mir.   Yes, too sure; for me too
    Bel. Dost thou wonder at that? By this good light,
        they are all so;
They are cozening mad, they are brawling mad, they
        are proud mad;
They are all, all mad. I came from a world of
        madwomen,
Mad as March hares. Get 'em in chains, then deal with
        'em.
There's one that's mad; she seems well, but she is dog
        mad.
Is she dead, dost think?
    Mir.   Dead? Heaven forbid!
    Bel.   Heaven
        further it!

IV.iii.
    [1] *souter:* cobbler.   [2] *kitlings:* kittens.
    [3] *gibbing:* acting like a cat.
    [4] *black santis:* burlesque hymn.

For, till they be key-cold dead, there's no trusting of
    'em.   100
Whate'er they seem, or howsoe'er they carry it,
Till they be chapfallen, and their tongues at peace,
Nailed in their coffins sure, I'll ne'er believe 'em.
Shall I talk with her?
    Mir.   No, dear friend, be quiet,
And be at peace awhile.
    Bel.   I'll walk aside,
And come again anon. But take heed to her.
You say she is a woman?
    Mir.   Yes.
    Bel.   Take great heed;
For if she do not cozen thee, then hang me.
Let her be mad, or what she will, she'll cheat thee.
                              Exit.
    Mir. Away, wild fool.—How vile this shows in him
    now.   110
Now take my faith—before ye all I speak it—
And with it my repentant love.
    La Ca.   This seems well.
    Mir. Were but this lady clear again, whose sorrows
My very heart melts for, were she but perfect
(For thus to marry her would be two miseries)
Before the richest and the noblest beauty
France, or the world could show me, I would take
    her.
As she now is, my tears and prayers shall wed her.
    De Ga. This makes some small amends.
    Ros.   She beckons
    to ye;
To us too, to go off.
    Nant.   Let's draw aside all.   120
          [*Exeunt all but* ORIANA *and* MIRABEL.]
    Ori. Oh, my best friend! I would fain—
    Mir.   What! she
    speaks well,
And with another voice.
    Ori.   But I am fearful,
And shame a little stops my tongue—
    Mir.   Speak boldly.
    Ori. Tell ye, I am well, I am perfect well (pray ye
    mock not);
And that I did this to provoke your nature;
Out of my infinite and restless love,
To win your pity. Pardon me.
    Mir.   Go forward;
Who set ye on?
    Ori.   None, as I live, no creature;
Not any knew, or ever dreamed what I meant.
Will ye be mine?
    Mir.   'Tis true, I pity ye;   130
But when I marry ye, ye must be wiser.
Nothing but tricks? Devices?
    Ori.   Will ye shame me?
    Mir. Yes, marry, will I.—Come near, come near! a
    miracle!
The woman's well; she was only mad for marriage,
Stark mad to be stoned[5] to death; give her good
    counsel.—
Will this world never mend?—Are ye caught, damsel?

Enter BELLEUR, LA CASTRE, LUGIER,
NANTOLET, DE GARD, ROSALURA, *and*
LILLIA[-BIANCA].

    Bel. How goes it now?
    Mir.   Thou art a kind of prophet;
The woman's well again, and would have gulled me;
Well, excellent well, and not a taint upon her.
    Bel. Did not I tell you? Let 'em be what can be, 140
Saints, devils, anything, they will abuse us.
Thou wert an ass to believe her so long, a coxcomb;
Give 'em a minute, they'll abuse whole millions.
    Mir. And am not I a rare physician, gentlemen,
That can cure desperate mad minds?
    De Ga.   Be not insolent.
    Mir. Well, go thy ways: From this hour I disclaim
    thee,
Unless thou hast a trick above this; then I'll love thee.
You owe me for your cure.—Pray, have a care of her,
For fear she fall into a relapse.—Come, Belleur;
We'll set up bills[6] to cure diseasèd virgins.   150
    Bel. Shall we be merry?
    Mir.   Yes.
    Bel.   But I'll no more
    projects;
If we could make 'em mad, it were some mastery.
            Exeunt [MIRABEL *and* BELLEUR].
    Lil. I am glad she is well again.
    Ros.   So am I, certain.—
Be not ashamed.
    Ori.   I shall never see a man more.
    De Ga. Come ye're a fool! had ye but told me this
    trick,
He should not have gloried thus.
    Lug.   He shall not long,
    neither.
    La Ca. Be ruled, and be at peace. Ye have my
    consent,
And what power I can work with.
    Nant.   Come, leave blushing;
We are your friends; an honest way compelled ye.
Heaven will not see so true a love unrecompensed. 160
Come in, and slight him too.
    Lug.   The next shall hit him.
                                Exeunt.

ACT FIVE

SCENE ONE

Enter DE GARD *and* LUGIER.

    De Ga. 'Twill be discovered.
    Lug.   That's the worst can
    happen.
If there be any way to reach and work upon him,
Upon his nature suddenly, and catch him—that he
    loves,

---

    [5] *stoned:* with pun on stone, testicle.
    [6] *bills:* advertisements.

Though he dissemble it and would show contrary,
And will at length relent, I'll lay [1] my fortune;
Nay, more, my life.
    De Ga.   Is she won? [2]
    Lug.   Yes, and ready,
And my designments set.
    De Ga.   They are now for travel;
All for that game again; they have forgot wooing.
    Lug. Let 'em; we'll travel with 'em.
    De Ga.   Where's his
    father?
    Lug. Within; he knows my mind, too, and allows it,
Pities your sister's fortune most sincerely;   11
And has appointed, for our more assistance,
Some of his secret friends.
    De Ga.   Speed the plow! [3]
    Lug.   Well said;
And be you serious, too.
    De Ga.   I shall be diligent.
    Lug. Let's break the ice for one, the rest will drink,
    too,
Believe me, sir, of the same cup. My young gentle-
    women
Wait but who sets the game afoot; though they seem
    stubborn,
Reserved, and proud now, yet I know their hearts,
Their pulses how they beat, and for what cause, sir,
And how they long to venture their abilities   20
In a true quarrel. Husbands they must and will have,
Or nunneries and thin collations
To cool their bloods. Let's all about our business;
And, if this fail, let nature work!
    De Ga.   You have armed me.
                             Exeunt.

V.ii

Enter MIRABEL, NANTOLET, [*and*] LA CASTRE.

    La Ca. Will ye be willful then?
    Mir.   Pray, sir, your
    pardon;
For I must travel. Lie lazy here,
Bound to a wife? Chained to her subtleties,
Her humors, and her wills, which are mere fetters?
To have her today pleased, tomorrow peevish,
The third day mad, the fourth rebellious?
You see, before they are married, what moriscoes, [1]
What masques and mummeries they put upon us:
To be tied here, and suffer their lavoltas! [2]

    Nant. 'Tis your own seeking.
    Mir.   Yes, to get my freedom.
Were they as I could wish 'em—
    La Ca.   Fools and meacocks, [3]
To endure what you think fit to put upon 'em.   12
Come, change your mind.
    Mir.   Not before I have changed
    air, father.
When I know women worthy of my company,
I will return again and wait upon 'em;
Till then, dear sir, I'll amble all the world over,
And run all hazards, misery, and poverty,
So I escape the dangerous bay of matrimony.

Enter BELLEUR *and* PINAC.

    Pinac. Are ye resolved?
    Mir.   Yes, certain; I will out again.
    Pinac. We are for you, sir; we are your servants once
    more: 20
Once more we'll seek our fortune in strange countries:
Ours is too scornful for us.
    Bel.   Is there ne'er a land
That ye have read, or heard of for I care not how far it
    be,
Nor under what pestiferous star it lies—
A happy kingdom, where there are no women?
Nor have been ever? Nor no mention
Of any such lewd [4] things with lewder qualities?
For thither would I travel; where 'tis felony
To confess he had a mother; a mistress, treason.
    La Ca. Are you for travel, too?
    Bel.   For anything,   30
For living in the moon and stopping hedges, [5]
Ere I stay here to be abused and baffled. [6]
    Nant. Why did ye not break your minds to me? They
    are my daughters,
And sure I think I should have that command over 'em
To see 'em well bestowed. I know ye are gentlemen,
Men of fair parts and states; I know your parents;
And had ye told me of your fair affections—
Make but one trial more, and let me second ye.
    Bel. No; I'll make hobnails first, and mend old
    kettles.
Can ye lend me an armor of high proof to appear in,   40
And two or three fieldpieces to defend me?
The king's guard are mere pigmies.
    Nant.   They'll not eat you.
    Bel. Yes, and you, too, and twenty fatter monsieurs,
In their high stomachs [7] hold. They came with
    chopping-knives,
To cut me into rands [8] and sirloins, and so powder [9]
    me.—
Come, shall we go?
    Nant.   You cannot be so discourteous,
If ye intend to go, as not to visit 'em,
And take your leaves.
    Mir.   That we dare do, and civilly,
And thank 'em, too.
    Pinac.   Yes, sir, we know that honesty. [10]
    Bel. I'll come i' th' rear, forty foot off, I'll assure you,
With a good gun in my hand; I'll no more Amazons;

V.i.
    [1] *lay:* wager.   [2] *won:* persuaded.
    [3] *Speed the plow:* May God prosper it; proverbial.
V.ii.
    [1] *moriscoes:* morris-dances.
    [2] *lavoltas:* high-stepping lively dances.
    [3] *meacocks:* weaklings.   [4] *lewd:* good-for-nothing.
    [5] *living . . . hedges:* The man in the moon carried a bundle
of sticks.   [6] *baffled:* disgraced.
    [7] *stomachs:* appetites, spirits.   [8] *rands:* strips.
    [9] *powder:* salt.   [10] *honesty:* decorum.

I mean no more of their frights. I'll make my three
    legs,[11]   52
Kiss my hand twice, and, if I smell no danger,
If the interview be clear, may be I'll speak to her;
I'll wear a privy[12] coat,[13] too, and behind me,
To make those parts secure, a bandog.[14]
    La Ca. You are a merry gentleman.
    Bel. A wary gentleman, I do assure ye;
I have been warned, and must be armed.
    La Ca.   Well, son,
These are your hasty thoughts; when I see you are bent
    to it,   60
Then I'll believe, and join with ye; so we'll leave ye.
[Aside] There is a trick will make ye stay.
    Nant.   I hope so.
                 Exeunt [LA CASTRE *and* NANTOLET].
    Mir. We have won immortal fame now, if we leave
    'em.
    Pinac. You have, but we have lost.
    Mir.   Pinac, thou art
    cozened;
I know they love ye; and to gain ye handsomely,
Not to be thought to yield, they would give millions.
Their father's willingness, that must needs show ye.
    Pinac. If I thought so—
    Mir.   Ye shall be hanged, ye
    recreant!
Would ye turn renegado now?
    Bel.   No; let's away, boys,
Out of the air and tumults of their villainies.   70
Though I were married to that grasshopper,
And had her fast by th' legs, I should think she would
    cozen me.

        Enter a young [Man, *disguised as a*] Factor.

    Fac. Monsieur Mirabel, I take it?
    Mir.   You are i' th'
    right, sir.
    Fac. I am come to seek ye, sir; I have been at your
    father's,
And understanding you were here—
    Mir. Ye are welcome.
                 May I crave your name?
    Fac. Fosse, sir, and your servant.
That you may know me better, I am factor
To your old merchant Leverdure.
    Mir.   How does he?
    Fac. Well, sir, I hope; he is now at Orleans,   80
About some business.
    Mir.   You are once more welcome.
Your master's a right honest man, and one
I am much beholding to, and must very shortly
Trouble his love again.
    Fac.   You may be bold, sir.
    Mir. Your business, if you please now?
    Fac.   This it is, sir.
I know you well remember, in your travel,
A Genoa merchant—
    Mir.   I remember many.
    Fac. But this man, sir, particularly; your own
    benefit

Must needs imprint him in ye; one Alberto,
A gentleman you saved from being murdered   90
A little from Bologna: I was then myself
In Italy, and supplied ye; though happily you have
Forgot me now.
    Mir.   No, I remember ye,
And that Alberto, too; a noble gentleman.
More to remember were to thank myself, sir.
What of that gentleman?
    Fac.   He's dead.
    Mir.   I am sorry.
    Fac. But on his deathbed, leaving to his sister
All that he had, beside some certain jewels,
Which, with a ceremony, he bequeathed to you,
In grateful memory, he commanded strictly   100
His sister, as she loved him and his peace,
To see those jewels safe and true delivered,
And with them his last love. She, as tender
To observe this will, not trusting friend nor servant
With such a weight, is come herself to Paris,
And at my master's house.
    Mir.   You tell me a wonder.
    Fac. I tell you a truth, sir. She is young and
    handsome,
And well attended; of much state and riches;
So loving and obedient to her brother,
That, on my conscience, if he had given her also,   110
She would most willingly have made her tender.
    Mir. May not I see her?
    Fac.   She desires it heartily.
    Mir. And presently?
    Fac.   She is now about some business,
Passing accounts of some few debts here owing,
And buying jewels of a merchant.
    Mir.   Is she wealthy?
    Fac. I would ye had her, sir, at all adventure:
Her brother had a main state.[15]
    Mir.   And fair, too?
    Fac. The prime of all those parts of Italy,
For beauty and for courtesy.
    Mir.   I must needs see her.
    Fac. 'Tis all her business, sir. Ye may now see her;
But tomorrow will be fitter for your visitation,   121
For she's not yet prepared.
    Mir.   Only her sight, sir;
And, when you shall think fit, for further visit.
    Fac. Sir, you may see her, and I'll wait your coming.
    Mir. And I'll be with ye instantly. I know the house;
Meantime, my love, and thanks, sir.
    Fac.   Your poor servant.
                         Exit.
    Pinac. Thou hast the strangest luck. What was that
    Alberto?
    Mir. An honest noble merchant, 'twas my chance
To rescue from some rogues had almost slain him;
And he in kindness to remember this.   130
    Bel. Now we shall have you,

---

[11] *legs:* bows.   [12] *privy:* secret.
[13] *coat:* of mail.   [14] *bandog:* watchdog.
[15] *main state:* large estate.

For all your protestations and your forwardness,
Find out strange fortunes in this lady's eyes,
And new enticements to put off your journey;
And who shall have honor then?
    Mir.   No, no, never fear it;
I must needs see her to receive my legacy.
    Bel. If it be tied up in her smock, heaven help thee!
May not we see, too?
    Mir.   Yes, afore we go;
I must be known myself ere I be able   139
To make thee welcome. Wouldst thou see more women?
I thought you had been out of love with all.
    Bel.   I may be,
(I find that) with the least encouragement;
Yet I desire to see whether all countries
Are naturally possessed with the same spirits,
For if they be, I'll take a monastery,
And never travel; for I had rather be a friar,
And live mewed up than be a fool and flouted.
    Mir. Well, well, I'll meet you anon, then tell you
      more, boys;
However, stand prepared, prest [16] for our journey;
For certain, we shall go, I think, when I have seen her,
And viewed her well.
    Pinac.   Go, go, and we'll wait for ye;   151
Your fortune directs ours.
    Bel.   You shall find us i' th' tavern,
Lamenting in sack and sugar for our losses.
If she be right Italian and want servants,[17]
You may prefer [18] the properest man. How I could
Worry [19] a woman now!
    Pinac.   Come, come, leave prating;
You may have enough to do, without this boasting.
                               Exeunt.

V.iii

Enter LUGIER, DE GARD, ROSALURA, *and*
LILLIA[-BIANCA].

    Lug. This is the last adventure.
    De Ga.   And the happiest,
As we hope, too.
    Ros.   We should be glad to find it.
    Lil. Who shall conduct us thither?
    Lug.   Your man is ready,
For I must not be seen; no, nor this gentleman;
That may beget suspicion; all the rest
Are people of no doubt. I would have ye, ladies,
Keep your old liberties and do as we instruct ye.
Come, look not pale; ye shall not lose your wishes,
Nor beg 'em neither, but be yourselves and happy.
    Ros. I tell ye true, I cannot hold off longer,   10
Nor give no more hard language.
    De Ga.   You shall not need.
    Ros. I love the gentleman, and must now show it:

---

[16] *prest:* ready.   [17] *servants:* lovers.
[18] *prefer:* recommend.   [19] *Worry:* Harass.
V.iii.
[1] *scant:* leave in need.

Shall I beat a proper man out of heart?
    Lug.   There's none
    advises ye.
    Lil. Faith, I repent me, too.
    Lug.   Repent and spoil all;
Tell what ye know, ye had best.
    Lil.   I'll tell what I think;
For if he ask me now, if I can love him,
I'll tell him yes, I can. The man's a kind man,
And out of his true honesty affect[s] me.
Although he played the fool, which I requited,
Must I still hold him at the staff's end?
    Lug.   You are two
    strange women.   20
    Ros. We may be, if we fool still.
    Lug.   Dare ye believe me?
Follow but this advice I have set you in now,
And if ye lose—would ye yield now so basely?
Give up without your honors saved?
    De Ga.   Fie, ladies!
Preserve your freedom still.
    Lil.   Well, well, for this time.
    Lug. And carry that full state—
    Ros.   That's as the wind
    stands;
If it begin to chop about and scant [1] us,
Hang me, but I know what I'll do. Come, direct us;
I make no doubt we shall do handsomely.
    De Ga. Some part o' th' way we'll wait upon ye,
    ladies;   30
The rest your man supplies.
    Lug.   Do well, I'll honor ye.
                              Exeunt.

V.iv

Enter [*the* young Man *disguised as a*] Factor *and*
MIRABEL *above;* ORIANA [*disguised*], *and two*
[*disguised as*] Merchants.

    Fac. Look ye, sir, there she is; you see how busy.
Methinks you are infinitely bound to her for her journey.
    Mir. How gloriously she shows! She's a tall woman.
    Fac. Of a fair size, sir. My master not being at home,
I have been so out of my wits to get her company.
I mean, sir, of her own fair sex and fashion—
    Mir. Afar off, she is most fair too.
    Fac.   Near, most
    excellent.—
At length, I have entreated two fair ladies
(And happily you know 'em), the young daughters
Of Monsieur Nantolet—
    Mir.   I know 'em well, sir.   10
What are those? Jewels?
    Fac.   All.
    Mir.   They make a rich show.
    Fac. There is a matter of ten thousand pounds, too,
Was owing here: You see those merchants with her:
They have brought it in now.
    Mir.   How handsomely her shape
    shows!

Fac. Those are still neat;[1] your Italians are most
  curious.[2]
Now she looks this way.
  Mir.   She has a goodly presence.
How full of courtesy! Well, sir, I'll leave ye;
And if I may be bold to bring a friend or two,
Good noble gentlemen—
  Fac.   No doubt, ye may, sir;   19
For you have most command.
  Mir.   I have seen a wonder.
                                              Exit.

  Ori. Is he gone?
  Fac.   Yes.
  Ori.   How?
  Fac.   Taken to the utmost:
A wonder dwells about him.
  Ori.   He did not guess at me?
  Fac. No; be secure, ye show another woman.
He is gone to fetch his friends.
  Ori.   Where are the
  gentlewomen?

     Enter ROSALURA, LILLIA[-BIANCA], [*and*]
                     Servant.

  Fac. Here, here; now they are come,
Sit still, and let them see ye.
  Ros.   Pray ye, where's my friend,
  sir?
  Fac. She is within, ladies; but here's another
  gentlewoman,
A stranger to this town; so please you visit her,   28
'Twill be well taken.
  Lil.   Where is she?
  Fac.   There, above, ladies.
  Serv. Bless me, what thing is this? Two pinnacles[3]
Upon her pate! Is't not a glode[4] to catch woodcocks?
  Ros. Peace, ye rude knave.
  Serv.   What a bouncing bum she
  has too.
There's sail enough for a carrack.[5]
  Ros.   What is this lady?
For, as I live, she is a goodly woman.
  Fac. Guess, guess.
  Lil.   I have not seen a nobler presence.
  Serv. 'Tis a lusty wench! Now could I spend my
  forty pence,
With all my heart, to have but one fling at her,
To give her but a washing[6] blow.
  Lil.   Ye rascal.
  Serv. Ay, that's all a man has for's good will. 'Twill
  be long enough
Before ye cry, "Come, Anthony, and kiss me."   40
  Lil. I'll have ye whipped.
  Ros.   Has my friend seen this
  lady?
  Fac. Yes, yes, and is well known to her.
  Ros. I much admire her presence.
  Lil.   So do I, too;
For, I protest, she is the handsomest,
The rarest, and the newest to mine eye,
That ever I saw yet.

  Ros.   I long to know her;
My friend shall do that kindness.
  Ori.   So she shall, ladies;
Come, pray ye come up.
  Ros.   Oh, me!
  Lil.   Hang me, if I knew her.
Were I a man myself, I should now love ye;
Nay, I should dote.
  Ros.   I dare not trust mine eyes;   50
For, as I live, ye are the strangest altered.
I must come up to know the truth.
  Serv.   So must I, lady;
For I'm a kind of unbeliever too.
  Lil.   Get ye gone, sirrah;
And what ye have seen be secret in; you are paid, else.
No more of your long tongue.
  Fac.   Will ye go in, ladies,
And talk with her? These venturers will come straight.
Away with this fellow.
  Lil.   There, sirrah; go, disport ye.
  Serv. I would the trunk-hosed[7] woman would go
  with me.
                                              [*Exeunt.*]

V.v

     Enter MIRABEL, PINAC, [*and*] BELLEUR.

  Pinac. Is she so glorious handsome?
  Mir.   You would
  wonder;
Our women look like gypsies, like jills to her;
Their clothes and fashions beggarly and bankrupt,
Base, old, and scurvy.
  Bel.   How looks her face?
  Mir.   Most
  heavenly;
And the becoming motion of her body
So sets her off.
  Bel.   Why then, we shall stay.
  Mir.   Pardon me,
That's more than I know. If she be that woman
She appears to be—
  Bel.   As 'tis impossible.
  Mir. I shall then tell ye more.
  Pinac.   Did ye speak to her?
  Mir. No, no, I only saw her, she was busy.   10
Now I go for that end; and mark her, gentlemen,
If she appear not to ye one of the sweetest,
The handsomest, the fairest, in behavior—
We shall meet the two wenches there, too; they come
  to visit her,
To wonder, as we do.
  Pinac.   Then we shall meet 'em.
  Bel. I had rather meet two bears.

V.iv.
  [1] *still neat:* always elegant.   [2] *curious:* fastidious.
  [3] *pinnacles:* i.e., her elaborate headdress, with suggestion
of her future husband's cuckold horns.   [4] *glode:* glade.
  [5] *carrack:* galleon.   [6] *washing:* swashing, slashing.
  [7] *trunk-hosed:* wearing full, baglike breeches, sometimes
stuffed with wool.

Mir. There you may take your leaves, dispatch that
  business,
And, as ye find their humors—
  Pinac.   Is your love there, too?
  Mir. No, certain; she has no great heart to set out
  again.
This is the house; I'll usher ye.
  Bel.   I'll bless me   20
And take a good heart, if I can.
  Mir.   Come, nobly.
                              Exeunt.

V.vi

    Enter [the young Man *disguised as a]* Factor,
    ROSALURA, LILLIA[-BIANCA], [*and*] ORIANA
              [*disguised as before*].

Fac. They are come in. Sit you two off, as strangers.

              Enter Boy.

There, lady.—Where's the boy?—Be ready, sirrah,
And clear your pipes; the music now; they enter.
                              Music.

    Enter MIRABEL, PINAC, *and* BELLEUR.

Pinac. What a state she keeps! How far off they sit
  from her!
How rich she is! Ay, marry, this shows bravely.
  Bel. She is a lusty wench, and may allure a good man;
But if she have a tongue, I'll not give twopence for her.
There sits my fury; how I shake to see her!
  Fac. Madam, this is the gentleman.

          [MIRABEL *kisses* ORIANA.]

Mir.   How sweet she
  kisses!
She has a spring dwells on her lips, a paradise.   10
This is the legacy?
  [*Boy. Sings.*]

              SONG
    From the honored dead I bring
    Thus his love and last off'ring.
    Take it nobly; 'tis your due,
    From a friendship ever true.
    From a faith, etc.

Ori. Most noble sir,
This from my now-dead brother, as his love,
And grateful memory of your great benefit;
From me my thanks, my wishes, and my service.   20
Till I am more acquainted, I am silent;
Only I dare say this, you are truly noble.
  Mir. What should I think?
  Pinac.   Think ye have a
  handsome fortune:
Would I had such another.
  Ros.   Ye are well met, gentlemen;
We hear ye are for travel?

  Pinac.   Ye hear true, lady;
And come to take our leaves.
  Lil.   We'll along with ye:
We see you are grown so witty by your journey,
We cannot choose but step out, too. This lady
We mean to wait upon as far as Italy.   29
  Bel. I'll travel into Wales, amongst the mountains,
[*Aside*] In hope they cannot find me.
  Ros.   If you go further,
So good and free society we hold ye,
We'll jog along, too.
  Pinac.   Are ye so valiant, lady?
  Lil. And we'll be merry, sir, and laugh.
  Pinac.   It may be
We'll go by sea.
  Lil.   Why, 'tis the only voyage;
I love a sea-voyage, and a blustering tempest;
And let all split!
  Pinac.   This is a dainty damosel.
I think 'twill tame ye.—Can ye ride post?[1]
  Lil. Oh, excellently. I am never weary that way;
A hundred mile a day is nothing with me.   40
  Bel. [*Aside*] I'll travel underground.—Do you hear,
  sweet lady?
I find it will be dangerous for a woman.
  Ros. No danger, sir; I warrant; I love to be under.
  Bel. I see she will abuse me all the world over.—
But say we pass through Germany, and drink hard?
  Ros. We'll learn to drink and swagger, too.
  Bel. [*Aside*]   She'll
  beat me.—
Lady, I'll live at home.
  Ros.   And I'll live with thee;
And we'll keep house together.
  Bel. [*Aside*]   I'll keep hounds first;
And those I hate right heartily.
  Pinac.   I go for Turkey;
And so it may be up into Persia.   50
  Lil. We cannot know too much; I'll travel with ye.
  Pinac. And you'll abuse me?
  Lil.   Like enough.
  Pinac.   'Tis
  dainty.
  Bel. I will live in a bawdyhouse.
  Ros.   I dare come to ye.
  Bel. Say I'm disposed to hang myself?
  Ros.   There I'll
  leave ye.
  Bel. I am glad I know how to avoid ye—
  Mir.   May I speak
  yet?
  Fac. She beckons to ye.
  Mir. Lady, I could wish I knew to recompense,
Even with the service of my life, those pains,
And those high favors you have thrown upon me:
Till I be more desertful in your eye,   60
And till my duty shall make known I honor ye,
Noblest of women, do me but this favor,
To accept this back again, as a poor testimony.

                    [*Offers the casket.*]

[1] *post:* by post-horse, the fastest mode of travel.

Ori. I must have you, too, with 'em; else the will.
That says they must rest with ye, is infringed, sir;
Which, pardon me, I dare not do.
    Mir.   Take me then,
And take me with the truest love.
    Ori.   'Tis certain
My brother loved ye dearly, and I ought
As dearly to preserve that love: But, sir,
Though I were willing, these are but your ceremonies.[2]
    Mir. As I have life, I speak my soul.
    Ori.   I like ye: 71
But how you can like me, without I have testimony,
A stranger to ye—
    Mir.   I'll marry ye immediately;
A fair state I dare promise ye.
    Bel.   Yet she'll cozen thee.
    Ori. 'Would some fair gentlemen durst promise for
    you.
    Mir. By all that's good—

    Enter LA CASTRE, NANTOLET, LUGIER,
           and DE GARD.

    All.   And we'll make up the rest,
    lady.
    Ori. Then, Oriana takes you. Nay, she has caught
    ye.
If ye start now, let all the world cry shame on ye!
I have out-traveled ye.
    Bel.   Did not I say she would cheat
    thee?
    Mir. I thank ye. I am pleased you have deceived me,
And willingly I swallow it, and joy in't: 81
And yet, perhaps, I knew[3] you. Whose plot was this?
    Lug. He's not ashamed that cast[4] it; he that
    executed,
Followed your father's will.
    Mir.   What a world's this!
Nothing but craft and cozenage?
    Ori.   Who begun, sir?
    Mir. Well; I do take thee upon mere compassion;
And I do think I shall love thee. As a testimony,

I'll burn my book and turn a new leaf over.
But these fine clothes you shall wear still.
    Ori.   I obey you, sir,
    in all.
    Nant. And how, how, daughters? What say you to
    these gentlemen?   90
What say ye, gentlemen, to the girls?
    Pinac. By my troth—if she can love me—
    Lil. How long?
    Pinac.   Nay, if once ye love—
    Lil.   Then take me,
And take your chance.
    Pinac.   Most willingly! Ye are mine,
    lady;
And if I use ye not, that ye may love me—
    Lil. A match, i' faith.
    Pinac.   Why, now ye travel with me.
    Ros. How that thing stands!
    Bel.   It will, if ye urge it.
Bless your five wits!
    Ros.   Nay, prithee, stay; I'll have thee.
    Bel. You must ask me leave first.
    Ros.   Wilt thou use me
    kindly,
And beat me but once a week?
    Bel.   If ye deserve no more.
    Ros. And wilt thou get me with child?   101
    Bel. Dost thou ask me seriously?
    Ros. Yes, indeed do I.
    Bel. Yes, I will get thee with child. Come presently,
An't be but in revenge, I'll do thee that courtesy.
Well, if thou wilt fear God, and me, have at thee!
    Ros. I'll love ye, and I'll honor ye.
    Bel.   I am pleased then.
    Mir. This Wild-Goose Chase is done; we have won
    o' both sides.
Brother, your love, and now to church of all hands;
Let's lose no time.
    Pinac.   Our traveling lay by.   110
    Bel. No more for Italy; for the Low Countries,[5] [I].
                              Exeunt.

F I N I S

---

   [2] *ceremonies:* empty formalities, meaningless protestations.   [3] *knew:* F "know."
   [4] *cast:* planned.
   [5] *Low Countries:* with bawdy implications.

John Ford

[c. 1586–c. 1639]

PERKIN WARBECK

BIOGRAPHICAL information about Ford is so slight as to be almost useless. He was born to a Devonshire family related on his mother's side to the Lord Chief Justice; as a younger son apparently not on good terms with his father he inherited very little; he was resident for many years in the Middle Temple and may be presumed to have been a lawyer. Between 1606 and 1616 he published occasional poems and pamphlets of no particular distinction. A number of lost plays attributed to Ford may have been written before the first extant plays that can be confidently dated, but only in 1621 does his known career as a dramatist begin in a series of collaborations with Thomas Dekker. Some of those plays are effective treatments of subjects that had recently been in the news, most notably *The Witch of Edmonton* (1621), which turns a pamphlet about the conviction and execution of a witch into a supernaturalistic tragedy featuring the devil and adds another plot in which similar evil takes the shape of a relatively realistic story bearing some resemblance to *An American Tragedy*. Apart from 'TIS PITY SHE'S A WHORE and PERKIN WARBECK, Ford's most notable extant work is *The Broken Heart* (c. 1627–31), a powerful tragedy characterized by the sense of life as hopeless suffering that in one way or another underlies all of his serious work; one critic has called the play "Ford's *Wasteland*." Ford is a determinist who tends to see the passions as inevitably and destructively dominant and society as repressive and insufficient to satisfy men's needs. In *The Lover's Melancholy* (1628) Ford presents his typical world through the device of characters operated by the mechanistic psychology Burton had described in his famous *Anatomy of Melancholy* (1621). Ford's career as a playwright, writing seventeen known plays first for the King's Men and then for the Queen's Men, Christopher Beeston's company at the Phoenix, began after Shakespeare's death and Jonson's prime, and spanned the last decades of the theaters' duration.

PERKIN WARBECK was entered in the Stationers' Register in 1624 and published, for the only time in the century, later that year, its title page—which gave it the subtitle *A Strange Truth*—claiming it had been "Acted (Sometimes) by the Queen's Majesty's Servants at the Phoenix in Drury Lane." The quarto publication is the basis of the present text. The date of the first performance is less certain, indeed something of a mystery. A curious phrase in the Stationers' Register entry— "observing the caution of the license"—and the "Some-times" of the title page have suggested to a number of scholars the likelihood that the play met with political censorship and may have been delayed in publication. Its principal source, Bacon's *History of the Reign of King Henry the Seventh*, was published in 1622, and the play may have been written and performed shortly thereafter. Though his suggestion has not been widely accepted, Alfred Harbage has argued the possibility that the play is the product of collaboration between Ford and Dekker, and has pointed to 1625, just after the writing of *The Witch of Edmonton*, as the most plausible date for the continuation of their work together.

In addition to Bacon's *History*, Ford drew heavily on Thomas Gansford's *The True and Wonderful History of Perkin Warbeck* (1618); scholars disagree as to whether he consulted other historical works. For all his fidelity to the known sources in matters large and small, his deviations from them are more interesting. Most significant is his translation of historical materials into an atavistic chronicle play—the genre had been out of fashion virtually since Shakespeare—with frequent allusion to *Richard II*, *Richard III*, and other history plays that his audience might remember. Ford changed the story, bringing Perkin Warbeck and Henry VII together for an imaginary confrontation, suppressing the pretender's escape from the Tower, and altering details and characterizations. Most importantly, he created as his protagonist a character very different from the one he met in his reading. The historical Perkin Warbeck was a knowing charlatan, pooling his resources with those of others in the Yorkist faction and pretending to be Richard, Duke of York, Edward IV's second son, one of the two princes Richard III was thought to have murdered in the Tower in order to ensure his own accession to the throne. In thus trying to revive the War of the Roses and replace Henry VII, who had ended it, on the throne of England, the real Perkin Warbeck schemed opportunistically for power based on a lie about his identity. But Ford's hero is no charlatan. Though the play does not allow a shred of possibility that Perkin's claim corresponds to the facts of the case, Ford's Perkin nevertheless believes that he is the true heir to the throne, and his belief in the truth of his cause radically changes the way in which one must respond to him. Like other Ford heroes, Perkin Warbeck is an attractive rebel caught in a delusion that the audience does not share.   N. R.

Perkin Warbeck

[EPISTLE DEDICATORY]

To the rightly honorable
WILLIAM CAVENDISH,[1]
Earl of Newcastle, Viscount Mansfield, Lord Bolsover and Ogle.

My Lord,

Out of the darkness of a former age (enlightened by a late both learned and an honorable pen[2]) I have endeavored to personate[3] a great attempt, and in it a greater danger. In other labors you may read actions of antiquity discoursed; in this abridgement, find the actors themselves discoursing: in some kind, practiced as well what to speak, as speaking why to do.[4] Your lordship is a most competent judge in expressions[5] of such credit,[6] commissioned[7] by your known ability in examining and enabled by your knowledge in determining[8] the monuments of time. Eminent titles may indeed inform who their owners are, not often what. To yours the addition of that information in both cannot in any application   10 be observed flattery, the authority being established by truth. I can only acknowledge the errors in writing mine own, the worthiness of the subject written being a perfection in the story, and of it. The custom of your lordship's entertainments,[9] even to strangers, is rather an example than a fashion: in which consideration I dare not profess a curiosity, but am only studious that your lordship will please, amongst such as best honor your goodness, to admit into your noble construction.[10]

JOHN FORD

DRAMATIS PERSONÆ

HENRY VII, *King of England*
GILES, *Lord Daubeney* (DAUBENEY)
SIR WILLIAM STANLEY, *King's Chamberlain*
JOHN DE VERE, *Earl of Oxford* (OXFORD)
THOMAS HOWARD, *Earl of Surrey* (SURREY)
CHRISTOPHER URSWICK, *chaplain to Henry VII*
SIR ROBERT CLIFFORD
DON PEDRO DE AYALA, *ambassador from Ferdinand and Isabella of Spain* (HIALAS)
LAMBERT SIMNEL
Constable, Officers, [Post[1]], Servingmen, and Soldiers

JAMES IV, *King of Scotland*
GEORGE[2] GORDON, *second Earl of Huntly* (HUNTLY)
EARL OF CRAWFORD
LORD DALYELL
MARCHMOUNT, *a herald*

PERKIN WARBECK
STEPHEN FRION, *his secretary*
JOHN A-WATER, *Mayor of Cork*
JOHN HERON, *a merchant*
RICHARD[3] SKELTON,[4] *a tailor*
NICHOLAS ASTLEY, *a scrivener*

Women
LADY KATHERINE GORDON, *daughter to Huntly, later wife to Perkin* (KATHERINE)
COUNTESS OF CRAWFORD
JANE DOUGLAS, *maid-in-waiting to Lady Katherine* (JANE)

EPISTLE DEDICATORY
  [1] *Cavendish:* first earl of Cavendish, 1592–1676, poet, patron of Ben Jonson, later a royalist military leader.
  [2] *pen:* i.e., that of Bacon, who died in 1626.
  [3] *personate:* represent dramatically.
  [4] *why to do:* why something is done.
  [5] *expressions:* accounts.
  [6] *of such credit:* of matters of reputation.
  [7] *commissioned:* authorized.
  [8] *determining:* identifying.
  [9] *entertainments:* support.
  [10] *construction:* charitable interpretation of behavior.

DRAMATIS PERSONÆ
  [1] *Post:* Courier.
  [2] *George:* Ford erroneously calls him Alexander.
  [3] *Richard:* Edward in some sources.
  [4] *Skelton:* Q "Sketon."

PROLOGUE

Studies have of this nature been of late
So out of fashion, so unfollowed, that
It is become more justice[1] to revive
The antic[2] follies of the times than strive
To countenance wise industry. No want
Of art doth render wit or[3] lame or scant[4]
Or slothful in the purchase of fresh bays,
But want of truth in them who give the praise
To their self-love, presuming to outdo
The writer, or, for need,[5] the actors too.   10
But such this author's silence best befits,
Who bids them be in love with their own wits.
From him to clearer judgments we can say
He shows a history couchèd in a play,

A history of noble mention, known,
Famous, and true—most noble, 'cause our own;
Not forged[6] from Italy, from France, from Spain,
But chronicled at home; as rich in strain[7]
Of brave attempts as ever fertile rage
In action could beget to grace the stage.   20
We cannot limit scenes, for the whole land
Itself appeared too narrow to withstand
Competitors for kingdoms; nor is here
Unnecessary mirth forced, to endear
A multitude. On these two rests the fate
Of worthy expectation: Truth and State.

ACT ONE

SCENE ONE

Enter King HENRY, DURHAM, OXFORD, SURREY,
Sir WILLIAM STANLEY (Lord Chamberlain),
Lord DAUBENEY. *The* King *supported*[1] *to his throne
by* STANLEY *and* DURHAM. *A* Guard.

Hen. Still[2] to be haunted, still to be pursued,
Still to be frightened with false apparitions
Of pageant majesty and new-coined greatness,
As if we were a mockery[3] king in state,
Only ordained to lavish sweat and blood
In scorn and laughter to the ghosts of York,[4]
Is all below our merits; yet, my lords,
My friends and counselors, yet we sit fast
In our own royal birthright. The rent face
And bleeding wounds of England's slaughtered
        people   10
Have been by us, by the best physician,
At last both throughly cured and set in safety;
And yet for all this glorious work of peace
Ourself is scarce secure.
Dur.   The rage of malice

Conjures fresh spirits with the spells of York.
For ninety years ten English kings and princes,
Threescore great dukes and earls, a thousand lords
And valiant knights, two hundred fifty thousand
Of English subjects have in civil wars
Been sacrificed to an uncivil thirst   20
Of discord and ambition. This hot vengeance
Of the just powers above to utter ruin
And desolation had rained on, but that
Mercy did gently sheathe the sword of Justice
In lending to this blood-shrunk commonwealth
A new soul, new birth, in your sacred person.
Dau. Edward the Fourth, after a doubtful fortune,
Yielded to nature, leaving to his sons,
Edward and Richard, the inheritance
Of a most bloody purchase.[5] These young princes   30
Richard the tyrant,[6] their unnatural uncle,
Forced to a violent grave. So just is heaven,
Him hath your majesty by your own arm,
Divinely strengthened, pulled from his boar's sty[7]
And struck the black usurper to a carcass.
Nor doth the house of York decay in honors,
Though Lancaster doth repossess his right.
For Edward's daughter is King Henry's queen,
A blessèd union, and a lasting blessing
For this poor panting island, if some shreds,   40
Some useless remnant of the house of York,
Grudge not at this content.
Oxf.   Margaret of Burgundy[8]
Blows fresh coals of division.
Sur.   Painted fires,
Without or heat to[9] scorch or light to cherish.
Dau. York's headless trunk, her father; Edward's
        fate,
Her brother king; the smothering of her nephews
By tyrant Gloucester,[10] brother to her nature;
Nor Gloucester's own confusion[11]—all decrees
Sacred in heaven—can move this woman-monster
But that she still from the unbottomed mine   50
Of devilish policies doth vent the ore
Of troubles and sedition.

PROLOGUE
[1] *justice:* judiciousness.   [2] *antic:* grotesque.
[3] *or:* either.   [4] *scant:* insufficient.
[5] *for need:* if need be.   [6] *forged:* made.
[7] *strain:* stock.

I.i.
[1] *supported:* escorted.   [2] *Still:* Always.
[3] *mockery:* imitation.
[4] *ghosts of York:* pretenders from the dead rivalry between the houses of Lancaster and York, ended by Henry's accession in 1485.
[5] *purchase:* acquisition.
[6] *Richard . . . tyrant:* Richard III.
[7] *boar's sty:* alluding to the heraldic arms of Richard III.
[8] *Margaret of Burgundy:* daughter of Richard, Duke of York, sister of Edward IV, widow of Charles the Bold of Burgundy.   [9] *or . . . to:* Q "to . . . or."
[10] *Gloucester:* Richard III.   [11] *confusion:* destruction.

Oxf.   In her age—
Great sir, observe the wonder—she grows fruitful,
Who in her strength of youth was always barren,
Nor are her births as other mothers' are,
At nine or ten months' end—she has been with child
Eight or seven years at least; whose twins[12] being born
—A prodigy in nature—even the youngest
Is fifteen years of age at his first entrance,
As soon as known i' th' world, tall striplings, strong,
And able to give battle unto kings.   61
Idols of Yorkish malice.
    Dau.[13]   And but idols;
A steely hammer crushes 'em to pieces.
    Hen. Lambert the eldest, lords, is in our service,
Preferred[14] by an officious[15] care of duty
From the scullery to a falc'ner—strange example—
Which shows the difference between noble natures
And the base born. But for the upstart duke,
The new-revivèd York, Edward's second son,
Murdered long since i' th' Tower[16]—he lives again   70
And vows to be your king.
    Stan.   The throne is filled, sir.
    Hen. True, Stanley, and the lawful heir sits on it;
A guard of angels and the holy prayers
Of loyal subjects are a sure defense
Against all force and counsel of intrusion.
But now, my lords, put case[17] some of our nobles,
Our "great ones,"[18] should give countenance and
        courage
To trim duke Perkin, you will all confess
Our bounties have unthriftily been scattered
Amongst unthankful men.
    Dau.   Unthankful beasts,   80
Dogs, villains, traitors!
    Hen.   Daubeney, let the guilty
Keep silence. I accuse none, though I know
Foreign attempts against a state and kingdom
Are seldom without some great friends at home.
    Stan. Sir, if no other abler reasons else
Of duty or allegiance could divert
A headstrong resolution, yet the dangers
So lately passed by men of blood and fortunes
In Lambert Simnel's party must command
More than a fear, a terror to conspiracy.   90
The high-born Lincoln, son to De la Pole,
The earl of Kildare, Lord Geraldine,
Francis, Lord Lovell, and the German baron,
Bold Martin Swart, with Broughton and the rest—
Most spectacles of ruin, some of mercy—
Are precedents sufficient to forewarn
The present times, or any that live in them,
What folly, nay, what madness 'twere to lift
A finger up in all defense but yours,
Which can be but impostorous in a title.   100
    Hen. Stanley, we know thou lovest us, and thy heart
Is figured[19] on thy tongue; nor think we less
Of any's here. How closely we have hunted
This cub, since he unlodged, from hole to hole,
Your knowledge is our chronicle. First Ireland,
The common stage of novelty, presented
This gewgaw to oppose us; there the Geraldines

And Butlers once again stood in support
Of this colossic[20] statue. Charles of France
Thence called him into his protection,   110
Dissembled him the lawful heir of England.
Yet this was all but French dissimulation,
Aiming at peace with us, which being granted
On honorable terms on our part, suddenly
This smoke of straw was packed from France again
T' infect some grosser air. And now we learn,
Maugre[21] the malice of the bastard Neville,
Sir Taylor, and a hundred English rebels,
They're all retired to Flanders, to the dam
That nursed this eager whelp, Margaret of Burgundy.
But we will hunt him there too, we will hunt him,   121
Hunt him to death even in the beldam's[22] closet,[23]
Though the archduke[24] were his buckler.
    Sur. She has styled him "the fair white rose[25] of
        England."
    Dau. Jolly gentleman, more fit to be a swabber
To the Flemish after a drunken surfeit.

                    Enter URSWICK.

    Urs. Gracious sovereign, please you peruse this
        paper.
    Dur. The king's countenance gathers a sprightly
        blood.
    Dau. Good news, believe it.
    Hen.   Urswick, thine ear.
Tha'st[26] lodged him?
    Urs.   Strongly safe, sir.   130
    Hen. Enough. Is Barley come too?
    Urs.   No, my lord.
    Hen. No matter—phew, he's but a running weed,
At pleasure to be plucked up by the roots.
But more of this anon.—I have bethought me.
My lords, for reasons which you shall partake,
It is our pleasure to remove our court
From Westminster to th' Tower. We will lodge
This very night there; give, Lord Chamberlain,
A present order for it.
    Stan. [*Aside*]   The Tower! I shall, sir.
    Hen. Come, my true, best, fast friends. These clouds
        will vanish;   140
The sun will shine at full; the heavens are clearing.
                               Flourish. Exeunt.

---

[12] *twins:* i.e., Lambert Simnel and Perkin Warbeck, impostors whom she claimed to be her nephews and the nephew and son of Edward IV.   [13] DAU.: Q "OXFORD."
[14] *Preferred:* Promoted.   [15] *officious:* dutiful.
[16] *York . . . Tower:* i.e., Perkin Warbeck, who claimed to be Richard, Duke of York, Edward IV's second son, supposed murdered by Richard III in the Tower to prevent his becoming king.   [17] *put case:* suppose.
[18] *"great ones":* Q "GREAT ONES," so printed to underscore its sardonic contempt.   [19] *figured:* portrayed.
[20] *colossic:* implying a statue larger than its subject warrants.   [21] *Maugre:* In spite of.
[22] *beldam:* witch.   [23] *closet:* private room.
[24] *archduke:* Maximilian I, Hapsburg emperor who supported Perkin Warbeck.
[25] *white rose:* Yorkist emblem in War of the Roses (the Lancastrian emblem was a red rose).
[26] *Th'ast:* Thou hast.

[I.ii]

Enter HUNTLY *and* DALYELL.

Hunt. You trifle time, sir.
Dal.   O my noble lord,
You construe my griefs to so hard a sense
That where the text is argument[1] of pity,
Matter of earnest love, your gloss corrupts it
With too much ill-placed mirth.
Hunt.   Much mirth, Lord Dalyell?
Not so, I vow. Observe me, sprightly gallant.
I know thou art a noble lad, a handsome,
Descended from an honorable ancestry,
Forward and active, dost resolve to wrestle
And ruffle[2] in the world by noble actions   10
For a brave mention to posterity.
I scorn not thy affection to my daughter,
Not I, by good St. Andrew; but this bugbear,
This whoreson tale of honor—honor, Dalyell—
So hourly chats and tattles in mine ear
The piece of royalty that is stitched up
In my Kate's blood,[3] that 'tis as dangerous
For thee, young lord, to perch so near an eagle
As foolish for my gravity to admit[4] it.
I have spoke all at once.
Dal.   Sir, with this truth   20
You mix such wormwood that you leave no hope
For my disordered palate e'er to relish
A wholesome taste again; alas, I know, sir,
What an unequal distance lies between
Great Huntly's daughter's birth and Dalyell's fortunes.
She's the King's kinswoman, placed near the crown,
A princess of the blood, and I a subject.
Hunt. Right; but a noble subject—put in that too.
Dal. I could add more; and in the rightest line
Derive my pedigree from Adam Mure,   30
A Scottish knight, whose daughter was the mother
To him that first begot the race of Jameses
That sway the sceptre to this very day.
But kindreds are not ours when once the date
Of many years have swallowed up the memory
Of their originals; so pasture fields,
Neighboring too near the ocean, are soopèd[5] up
And known no more; for, stood I in my first
And native greatness, if my princely mistress
Vouchsafed me not her servant,[6] 'twere as good   40
I were reduced to clownery, to nothing,
As to a throne of wonder.
Hunt. [*Aside*]   Now, by St. Andrew,
A spark of mettle, a'[7] has a brave fire in him,
I would a' had my daughters so I knew 't not.
But 't must not be so, must not.—Well, young lord,
This will not do yet. If the girl be headstrong

And will not hearken to good counsel, steal her
And run away with her; dance galliards,[8] do,
And frisk about the world to learn the languages.
'Twill be a thriving trade; you may set up by't.   50
Dal. With pardon, noble Gordon, this disdain
Suits not your daughter's virtue or my constancy.
Hunt. You are angry.—[*Aside*] Would a' would beat
me, I deserve it.
—Dalyell, thy hand; we're friends. Follow thy
courtship;
Take thine own time and speak; if thou prevail'st
With passion more than I can with my counsel,
She's thine. Nay, she is thine; 'tis a fair match,
Free and allowed. I'll only use my tongue
Without a father's power; use thou thine.
Self do, self have; no more words; win and wear her.
Dal. You bless me; I am now too poor in thanks   61
To pay the debt I owe you.
Hunt.   Nay, tha'rt poor
Enough. [*Aside*] I love his spirit infinitely.—
Look ye, she comes; to her now, to her, to her.

Enter KATHERINE *and* JANE.

Kath. The king commands your presence, sir.
Hunt.   The
gallant—
This, this, this lord, this servant, Kate, of yours
Desires to be your master.
Kath.   I acknowledge him
A worthy friend of mine.
Dal.   Your humblest creature.
Hunt. [*Aside*] So, so, the game's afoot. I'm in cold
hunting;
The hare and hounds are parties.[9]
Dal.   Princely lady,   70
How most unworthy I am to employ
My services in honor of your virtues,
How hopeless my desires are to enjoy
Your fair opinion, and much more your love,
Are only matter of despair, unless
Your goodness give large warrant to my boldness,
My feeble-winged ambition.
Hunt. [*Aside*]   This is scurvy.
Kath. My lord, I interrupt you not.
Hunt. [*Aside*]   Indeed?
Now, on my life, she'll court him.—Nay, nay, on, sir.
Dal. Oft have I tuned the lesson[10] of my sorrows
To sweeten discord and enrich your pity,   81
But all in vain. Here had my comforts sunk
And never ris'n again to tell a story
Of the despairing lover, had not now,
Even now, the earl your father—
Hunt. [*Aside*]   A' means me, sure.
Dal. After some fit disputes of your condition,
Your highness and my lowness, giv'n a license
Which did not more embolden than encourage
My faulting tongue.
Hunt.   How, how? How's that? Embolden
Encourage? I encourage ye? D'ye hear, sir?   90
A subtle trick, a quaint[11] one—will you hear, man?
What did I say to you? Come, come, to th' point.

I.ii.
    [1] *argument:* proof.   [2] *ruffle:* battle.
    [3] *blood:* Huntly's wife was daughter of James I of Scot-
land.   [4] *admit:* permit.   [5] *soopèd:* swept.
    [6] *servant:* suitor.   [7] *a':* he.
    [8] *galliards:* lively dances.   [9] *parties:* partners.
    [10] *tuned the lesson:* modulated the performance.
    [11] *quaint:* clever.

Kath. It shall not need, my lord.
Hunt.   Then hear me,
    Kate.—
Keep you on that hand of her; I on this.—
Thou stand'st between a father and a suitor,
Both striving for an interest in thy heart.
He courts thee for affection, I for duty;
He as a servant pleads; but by the privilege
Of nature though I might command, my care
Shall only counsel what it shall not force.   100
Thou canst but make one choice; the ties of marriage
Are tenures not at will [12] but during life.
Consider whose thou art, and who: a princess,
A princess of the royal blood of Scotland,
In the full spring of youth and fresh in beauty.
The King that sits upon the throne is young
And yet unmarried, forward in attempts
On any least occasion to endanger
His person. Wherefore, Kate, as I am confident
Thou dar'st not wrong thy birth and education   110
By yielding to a common servile rage
Of female wantonness, so I am confident
Thou wilt proportion all thy thoughts to side [13]
Thy equals, if not equal thy superiors.
My lord of Dalyell, young in years, is old
In honors, but nor eminent in titles
Or in estate, that may support or add to
The expectation of thy fortunes. Settle
Thy will and reason by a strength of judgment;
For, in a word, I give thee freedom; take it.   120
If equal fates have not ordained to pitch
Thy hopes above my height, let not thy passion
Lead thee to shrink mine honor in oblivion.
Thou art thine own; I have done.
    Dal.   Oh, y'are all oracle,
The living stock and root of truth and wisdom!
    Kath. My worthiest lord and father, the
        indulgence
Of your sweet composition [14] thus commands
The lowest of obedience. You have granted
A liberty so large that I want skill
To choose without direction of example,   130
From which I daily learn by how much more
You take off from the roughness of a father,
By so much more I am engaged to tender
The duty of a daughter. For respects
Of birth, degrees of title, and advancement,
I nor admire nor slight them; all my studies
Shall ever aim at this perfection only,
To live and die so that you may not blush
In any course of mine to own me yours.
    Hunt. Kate, Kate, thou grow'st upon my heart like
        peace,   140
Creating every other hour a jubilee.
    Kath. To you, my lord of Dalyell, I address
Some few remaining words: the general fame
That speaks your merit, even in vulgar tongues
Proclaims it clear; but in the best, a precedent. [15]
    Hunt. Good wench, good girl, i'faith!
    Kath.   For my part,
    trust me,

I value mine own worth at higher rate
'Cause you are pleased to prize it. If the stream
Of your protested [16] service, as you term it,
Run in a constancy more than a compliment,   150
It shall be my delight that worthy love
Leads you to worthy actions, and these guide ye
Richly to wed an honorable name. [17]
So every virtuous praise in after-ages
Shall be your heir, and I in your brave mention
Be chronicled the mother of that issue, [18]
That glorious issue.
    Hunt.   Oh, that I were young again!
She'd make me court proud danger and suck spirit
From reputation.
    Kath.   To the present motion [19]
Here's all that I dare answer: when a ripeness   160
Of more experience and some use of time
Resolves to treat [20] the freedom of my youth
Upon exchange of troths, I shall desire
No surer credit of a match with virtue
Than such as lives in you. Meantime my hopes are
Preserved secure in having you a friend.
    Dal. You are a blessed lady, and instruct
Ambition not to soar a farther flight
Than in the perfumed air of your soft voice.—
My noble lord of Huntly, you have lent   170
A full extent of bounty to this parley,
And for it shall command your humblest servant.
    Hunt. Enough. We are still friends and will
        continue
A hearty love. O Kate, thou art mine own—
No more—my lord of Crawford.

                    Enter CRAWFORD.

    Craw.   From the King
I come, my lord of Huntly, who in council
Requires your present aid.
    Hunt.   Some weighty business?
    Craw. A secretary from a Duke of York,
The second son to the late English Edward,
Concealed I know not where these fourteen years,   180
Craves audience from our master; and 'tis said
The duke himself is following to the court.
    Hunt. Duke upon duke; 'tis well, 'tis well; here's
        bustling
For majesty. My lord, I will along with ye.
    Craw. My service, noble lady.
    Kath.   Please ye walk, sir?
    Dal. [*Aside*] Times have their changes; sorrow makes
        men wise;
The sun itself must set as well as rise;
Then why not I?— Fair madam, I wait on ye.
                                   Exeunt omnes.

---

[12] *at will:* i.e., to be terminated when one wants them
ended.   [13] *side:* rival.   [14] *composition:* nature.
[15] *in . . . precedent:* spoken by the best tongues, your merit
is proclaimed an example.
[16] *protested:* affirmed.   [17] *name:* reputation.
[18] *issue:* i.e., his fame, achieved by her inspiration.
[19] *motion:* proposal.   [20] *treat:* bargain away.

[I.iii]

Enter DURHAM, Sir ROBERT CLIFFORD, *and*
URSWICK. *Lights.*

Dur. You find, Sir Robert Clifford, how securely [1]
King Henry our great master doth commit
His person to your loyalty; you taste
His bounty and his mercy even in this,
That at a time of night so late, a place
So private as his closet, he is pleased
To admit you to his favor. Do not falter
In your discovery, [2] but as you covet
A liberal grace and pardon for your follies,
So labor to deserve it by laying open   10
All plots, all persons, that contrive against it.
Urs. Remember not the witchcraft or the music,
The charms and incantations, which the sorceress
Of Burgundy hath cast upon your reason.
Sir Robert, be your own friend now, discharge
Your conscience freely. All of such as love you
Stand sureties for your honesty and truth.
Take heed you do not dally with the King;
He is wise as he is gentle.
Cliff.   I am miserable
If Henry be not merciful.
Urs.   The King comes.   20

Enter King HENRY.

Hen. Clifford!
Cliff.   Let my weak knees rot on the earth

[CLIFFORD *kneels.*]

If I appear as leprous in my treacheries
Before your royal eyes, as to mine own
I seem a monster by my breach of truth.
Hen. Clifford, stand up; for instance [3] of thy safety,
I offer thee my hand.
Cliff.   A sovereign balm
For my bruised soul, I kiss it with greediness.
[*He rises.*]
Sir, you are a just master, but I—
Hen.   Tell me,
Is every circumstance thou hast set down
With thine own hand within this paper true?   30
Is it a sure intelligence of all
The progress of our enemies' intents
Without corruption?
Cliff.   True, as I wish heaven,
Or my infected honor white again.
Hen. We know all, Clifford, fully, since this meteor,
This airy apparition, first discradled [4]
From Tournay into Portugal, and thence
Advanced his fiery blaze for adoration
To th' superstitious Irish; since the beard
Of this wild comet, conjured into France,   40

I.iii.
[1] *securely:* confidently.   [2] *discovery:* disclosure.
[3] *for instance:* as a mark.
[4] *discradled:* left its cradle.   [5] *sometimes:* formerly.
[6] *mercer:* dealer in textile fabrics.   [7] *list:* please.

Sparkled in antic flames in Charles his court,
But shrunk again from thence, and, hid in darkness,
Stole into Flanders, flourishing the rags
Of painted power on the shore of Kent,
Whence he was beaten back with shame and scorn,
Contempt, and slaughter of some naked outlaws.
But tell me, what new course now shapes Duke Perkin?
Cliff. For Ireland, mighty Henry; so instructed
By Stephen Frion, sometimes [5] secretary.
In the French tongue unto your sacred excellence, 50
But Perkin's tutor now.
Hen.   A subtle villain,
That Frion, Frion—you, my lord of Durham,
Knew well the man.
Dur.   French both in heart and actions.
Hen. Some Irish heads work in this mine of treason;
Speak 'em.
Cliff.   Not any of the best; your fortune
Hath dulled their spleens. Never had counterfeit
Such a confused rabble of lost bankrupts
For counselors: first Heron, a broken mercer, [6]
Then John a-Water sometimes mayor of Cork,
Skelton a tailor, and a scrivener   60
Called Astley; and whate'er these list [7] to treat of,
Perkin must hearken to. But Frion, cunning
Above these dull capacities, still prompts him
To fly to Scotland to young James the Fourth,
And sue for aid to him; this is the latest
Of all their resolutions.
Hen.   Still more Frion!
Pestilent adder, he will hiss out poison
As dang'rous as infectious. We must match him.
Clifford, thou hast spoke home; we give thee life.
But Clifford, there are people of our own   70
Remain behind untold; who are they, Clifford?
Name those and we are friends, and will to rest;
'Tis thy last task.
Cliff.   O sir, here I must break
A most unlawful oath to keep a just one.
Hen. Well, well, be brief, be brief.
Cliff.   The first in rank
Shall be John Ratcliffe, Lord Fitzwater, then
Sir Simon Mountford and Sir Thomas Thwaites,
With William Daubeney, Cressoner, Astwood,
Worsley the dean of Paul's, two other friars,
And Robert Ratcliffe.
Hen.   Churchmen are turned devils. 80
These are the principal?
Cliff.   One more remains
Unnamed, whom I could willingly forget.
Hen. Ha, Clifford! one more?
Cliff.   Great sir, do not hear him:
For when Sir William Stanley your lord chamberlain
Shall come into the list, as he is chief,
I shall lose credit with ye; yet this lord,
Last named, is first against you.
Hen.   Urswick, the light!
View well my face, sirs; is there blood left in it?
Dur. You alter strangely, sir.
Hen.   Alter, Lord Bishop?
Why, Clifford stabbed me, or I dreamed a' stabbed me.

Sirrah, it is a custom with the guilty 91
To think they set their own stains off by laying
Aspersions on some nobler than themselves.
Lies wait on treasons, as I find it here.
Thy life again is forfeit; I recall
My word of mercy, for I know thou darest
Repeat the name no more.
    Cliff.   I dare, and once more
Upon my knowledge name Sir William Stanley
Both in his counsel and his purse the chief
Assistant to the feignèd Duke of York.   100
    Dur. Most strange!
    Urs.   Most wicked!
    Hen.   Yet again, once
    more.
    Cliff. Sir William Stanley is your secret enemy,
And if time fit will openly profess it.
    Hen. Sir William Stanley! Who? Sir William
    Stanley,
My chamberlain, my counselor, the love,
The pleasure of my court, my bosom friend,
The charge and the controlment of my person,
The keys and secrets of my treasury,
The all of all I am! I am unhappy.
Misery of confidence—let me turn traitor   110
To mine own person, yield my scepter up
To Edward's sister and her bastard duke!
    Dur. You lose your constant temper.
    Hen.   Sir William
    Stanley!
Oh, do not blame me; he, 'twas only he
Who, having rescued me in Bosworth field
From Richard's bloody sword, snatched from his head
The kingly crown, and placed it first on mine.
He never failed me. What have I deserved
To lose this good man's heart, or he his own?
    Urs. The night doth waste; this passion ill becomes
    ye;   120
Provide against your danger.
    Hen.   Let it be so.
Urswick, command straight Stanley to his chamber.
'Tis well we are i' th' Tower; set a guard on him;
Clifford, to bed; you must lodge here tonight,
We'll talk with you tomorrow. My sad soul
Divines strange troubles.
    Dau. [*Within*]   Ho, the King, the King!
I must have entrance.
    Hen.   Daubeney's voice; admit him.
What new combustions huddle next to keep
Our eyes from rest?

    Enter DAUBENEY.

              The news?
    Dau.   Ten thousand Cornish,
Grudging to pay your subsidies, have gathered   130
A head;[8] led by a blacksmith and a lawyer,
They make for London, and to them is joined
Lord Audley; as they march, their number daily
Increases; they are—
    Hen.   Rascals! Talk no more;
Such are not worthy of my thoughts tonight.

To bed; and if I cannot sleep, I'll wake.
When counsels fail, and there's in man no trust,
Even then an arm from heaven fights for the just.
                        Exeunt.

ACT TWO

SCENE ONE

Enter above Countess of CRAWFORD, KATHERINE,
JANE, *with other* Ladies.

    Countess. Come, ladies, here's a solemn preparation
For entertainment of this English prince.
The King intends grace more than ordinary;
'Twere pity now if a' should prove a counterfeit.
    Kath. Bless the young man, our nation would be
    laughed at
For honest[1] souls through Christendom. My father
Hath a weak stomach to the business, madam,
But that the King must not be crossed.
    Countess.   A' brings
A goodly troop, they say, of gallants with him,
But very modest people, for they strive not   10
To fame their names too much; their godfathers
May be beholding to them, but their fathers
Scarce owe them thanks. They are disguisèd princes,
Brought up, it seems, to honest trades. No matter,
They will break forth in season.
    Jane.   Or break out,
For most of 'em are broken by report.
                        Flourish.
The King.
    Kath. Let us observe 'em and be silent.

    Enter King JAMES, HUNTLY, CRAWFORD, *and*
DALYELL.

    King Ja. The right of Kings, my lords, extends not
    only
To the safe conservation of their own,
But also to the aid of such allies   20
As change of time and state hath oftentimes
Hurled down from careful[2] crowns to undergo
An exercise of sufferance in both fortunes.
So English Richard, surnamed Coeur-de-Lion,
So Robert Bruce, our royal ancestor,
Forced by the trial of the wrongs they felt,
Both sought and found supplies from foreign kings
To repossess their own. Then grudge[3] not, lords,
A much distressèd prince. King Charles of France
And Maximilian of Bohemia both   30
Have ratified his credit by their letters.
Shall we then be distrustful? No; compassion
Is one rich jewel that shines in our crown,
And we will have it shine there.
    Hunt.   Do your will, sir.

---

8 *head:* armed force.

II.i.
1 *honest:* gullible.   2 *careful:* full of care.
3 *grudge:* begrudge support to.

King Ja. The young Duke is at hand. Dalyell, from
    us
First greet him, and conduct him on; then Crawford
Shall meet him next, and Huntly last of all
Present him to our arms. Sound sprightly music,
Whilst majesty encounters majesty.
                              Hautboys.

DALYELL *goes out, brings in* PERKIN [WARBECK]
at the door where CRAWFORD *entertains[4] him, and
from* CRAWFORD, HUNTLY *salutes him and presents him to the* King. *They embrace.* PERKIN *in
state retires some few paces back, during which
ceremony the* Noblemen *slightly salute* FRION,
HERON, *a mercer,* SKELTON, *a tailor,* ASTLEY,
a scrivener, with JOHN A-WATER, *all* PERKIN'S
followers. Salutations ended, cease music.

War. Most high, most mighty King! that now there
    stands   40
Before your eyes, in presence of your peers,
A subject of the rarest kind of pity
That hath in any age touched noble hearts,
The vulgar[5] story of a prince's ruin
Hath made it too apparent. Europe knows,
And all the western world, what persecution
Hath raged in malice against us, sole heir
To the great throne of old Plantagenets.
How from our nursery we have been hurried
Unto the sanctuary, from the sanctuary   50
Forced to the prison, from the prison haled
By cruel hands to the tormentor's fury,
Is registered already in the volume
Of all men's tongues, whose true relation draws
Compassion, melted into weeping eyes
And bleeding souls. But our misfortunes since
Have ranged a larger progress through strange lands,
Protected in our innocence by heaven.
Edward the Fifth, our brother, in his tragedy
Quenched their hot thirst of blood, whose hire[6] to
    murder   60
Paid them their wages of despair and horror;
The softness of my childhood smiled upon
The roughness of their task, and robbed them farther
Of hearts to dare or hands to execute.
Great King, they spared my life, the butchers spared
    it;
Returned[7] the tyrant, my unnatural uncle,
A truth[8] of my dispatch; I was conveyed
With secrecy and speed to Tournay, fostered
By obscure means, taught to unlearn myself.
But as I grew in years I grew in sense   70
Of fear and of disdain: fear of the tyrant
Whose power swayed the throne then; when disdain
Of living so unknown, in such a servile
And abject lowness, prompted me to thoughts

Of recollecting who I was, I shook off
My bondage, and made haste to let my aunt
Of Burgundy acknowledge me her kinsman,
Heir to the crown of England snatched by Henry
From Richard's head, a thing scarce known i'th' world.
    King Ja. My lord, it stands not with your counsel
        now   80
To fly upon[9] invectives. If you can
Make this apparent what you have discoursed
In every circumstance, we will not study
An answer, but are ready in your cause.
    War. You are a wise and just king, by the powers
Above reserved beyond all other aids
To plant me in mine own inheritance;
To marry these two kingdoms in a love
Never to be divorced while time is time.
As for the manner, first of my escape,   90
Of my conveyance next, of my life since,
The means and persons who were instruments,
Great sir, 'tis fit I overpass in silence;
Reserving the relation to the secrecy
Of your own princely ear, since it concerns
Some great ones living yet, and others dead,
Whose issue[10] might be questioned. For your bounty,
Royal magnificence, to him that seeks it,
We vow hereafter to demean ourself
As if we were your own and natural brother,   100
Omitting no occasion in our person
To express a gratitude beyond example.
    King Ja. He must be more than subject who can
        utter
The language of a king, and such is thine.
Take this for answer: be whate'er thou art,
Thou never shalt repent that thou hast put
Thy cause and person into my protection.
Cousin of York, thus once more we embrace thee;
Welcome to James of Scotland! For thy safety,
Know, such as love thee not shall never wrong thee.
Come, we will taste a while our court delights,   111
Dream hence afflictions past, and then proceed
To high attempts of honor. On, lead on;
Both thou and thine are ours, and we will guard ye.
Lead on.
                   Exeunt. Manent[11] the Ladies *above.*
    Countess. I have not seen a gentleman
Of a more brave aspect or goodlier carriage;
His fortunes move not him—madam, y'are passionate.[12]
    Kath. Beshrew me, but his words have touched me
        home
As if his cause concerned me; I should pity him
If a' should prove another than he seems.   120

                    Enter CRAWFORD.

    Craw. Ladies, the King commands your presence
        instantly
For entertainment of the duke.
    Kath.   The duke
Must then be entertained, the King obeyed.
It is our duty.
    Countess. We will all wait on him.
                                     Exeunt.

---

    [4] *entertains:* receives.   [5] *vulgar:* commonly known.
    [6] *hire:* being hired to.   [7] *Returned:* Reported to.
    [8] *truth:* a supposedly true account.
    [9] *fly upon:* burst into.   [10] *issue:* offspring.
    [11] *Manent:* Remain.   [12] *passionate:* moved.

[II.ii]

Flourish. Enter King HENRY, OXFORD, DURHAM,
SURREY.

Hen. Have ye condemned my chamberlain?
Dur.   His
     treasons
Condemned him, sir, which were as clear and manifest
As foul and dangerous. Besides, the guilt
Of his conspiracy pressed him so nearly [1]
That it drew from him free confession
Without an importunity.
     Hen.   O Lord Bishop,
This argued shame and sorrow for his folly,
And must not stand in evidence against
Our mercy and the softness of our nature;
The rigor and extremity of law   10
Is sometimes too, too bitter, but we carry
A chancery [2] of pity in our bosom.
I hope we may reprieve him from the sentence
Of death; I hope we may.
     Dur.   You may, you may,
And so persuade your subjects that the title
Of York is better, nay, more just and lawful
Than yours of Lancaster. So Stanley holds, [3]
Which if it be not treason in the highest,
Then we are traitors all, perjured and false,
Who have took oath to Henry and the justice   20
Of Henry's title—Oxford, Surrey, Daubeney,
With all your other peers of state and church,
Forsworn, and Stanley true alone to heaven
And England's lawful heir.
     Oxf.   By Vere's [4] old honors,
I'll cut his throat dares speak it.
     Sur.   'Tis a quarrel
T' engage a soul in.
     Hen.   What a coil [5] is here
To keep my gratitude sincere and perfect!
Stanley was once my friend and came in time
To save my life; yet to say truth, my lords,
The man stayed long enough t' endanger it.   30
But I could see no more into his heart
Than what his outward actions did present,
And for 'em have rewarded him so fully
As that there wanted [6] nothing in our gift
To gratify his merit, as I thought,
Unless I should divide my crown with him
And give him half; though now I well perceive
'Twould scarce have served his turn without the whole.
But I am charitable, lords; let justice
Proceed in execution, whiles I mourn   40
The loss of one whom I esteemed a friend.
     Dur. Sir, he is coming this way.
     Hen.   If a' speak to me
I could deny him nothing; to prevent it,
I must withdraw. Pray, lords, commend my favors [7]
To his last peace, which I with him will pray for.
That done, it doth concern us to consult
Of other following troubles.
     Oxf.   I am glad

He's gone; upon my life, he would have pardoned
The traitor, had a' seen him.
     Sur.   'Tis a king
Composed of gentleness.
     Dur.   Rare and unheard of;   50
But every man is nearest to [8] himself,
And that the King observes; 'tis fit a' should.

     Enter STANLEY, Executioner, [Confessor,]
          URSWICK *and* DAUBENEY.

     Stan. May I not speak with Clifford ere I shake
This piece of frailty off?
     Dau.   You shall, he's sent for.
     Stan. I must not see the King?
     Dur.   From him, Sir William,
These lords and I am sent; he bade us say
That he commends his mercy to your thoughts,
Wishing the laws of England could remit
The forfeit of your life as willingly
As he would in the sweetness of his nature   60
Forget your trespass. But howe'er your body
Fall into dust, he vows, the King himself
Doth vow to keep a requiem for your soul,
As for a friend close treasured in his bosom.
     Oxf. Without remembrance of your errors past,
I come to take my leave and wish you heaven,
     Sur. And I; good angels guard ye.
     Stan.   Oh, the King,
Next to my soul, shall be the nearest subject
Of my last prayers. My grave lord of Durham,
My lords of Oxford, Surrey, Daubeney, all,   70
Accept from a poor dying man a farewell.
I was as you are once—great, and stood hopeful
Of many flourishing years; but fate and time
Have wheeled about, to turn me into nothing.

          Enter CLIFFORD.

     Dau. Sir Robert Clifford comes—the man, Sir
          William,
You so desire to speak with.
     Dur.   Mark their meeting.
     Cliff. Sir William Stanley, I am glad your conscience
Before your end hath emptied every burden
Which charged it, as [9] that you can clearly witness
How far I have proceeded in a duty   80
That both concerned my truth and the state's safety.
     Stan. Mercy, how dear is life to such as hug it!
Come hither; by this token think on me—

     Makes a cross on CLIFFORD'S *face with his finger.*

     Cliff. This token! What! I am abused?
     Stan.   You are not.
I wet upon your cheeks a holy sign,
The cross, the Christian's badge, the traitor's infamy.

II.ii.
  [1] *nearly:* closely.   [2] *chancery:* court of appeal.
  [3] *holds:* argues.   [4] *Vere's:* i.e., the Oxford family's.
  [5] *coil:* tumult.   [6] *wanted:* lacked.
  [7] *commend . . . favors:* convey my good wishes.
  [8] *nearest to:* most concerned for.   [9] *as:* so.

Wear, Clifford, to thy grave this painted emblem.
'Water shall never wash it off; all eyes
That gaze upon thy face shall read there written
A state-informer's character, more ugly   90
Stamped on a noble name than on a base.
The heavens forgive thee. Pray, my lords, no change [10]
Of words; this man and I have used too many.
    Cliff. Shall I be disgraced
Without reply?
    Dur.   Give losers leave to talk;
His loss is irrecoverable.
    Stan.   Once more
To all a long farewell; the best of greatness
Preserve the King. My next suit is, my lords,
To be remembered to my noble brother,   99
Derby, my much grievèd brother. O, persuade him
That I shall stand no blemish to his house
In chronicles writ in another age.
My heart doth bleed for him and for his sighs;
Tell him he must not think the style [11] of Derby,
Nor being husband to King Henry's mother,
The league with peers, the smiles of fortune, can
Secure his peace above the state of man.
I take my leave, to travel to my dust:
Subjects deserve their deaths whose kings are just.—
Come, confessor. On with thy axe, friend, on.   110
                                        Exeunt.

    Cliff. Was I called hither by a traitor's breath
To be upbraided? Lords, the King shall know it.

         Enter King HENRY *with a white staff.*

    Hen. The King doth know it, sir; the King hath
         heard
What he or you could say. We have given credit
To every point of Clifford's information,
The only evidence 'gainst Stanley's head.
A' dies for t'; are you pleased?
    Cliff.   I pleased, my lord!
    Hen. No echoes. For your service, we dismiss
Your more attendance on the court; take ease
And live at home; but, as you love your life,   120
Stir not from London without leave from us.
We'll think on your reward; away!
    Cliff.   I go, sir.
                                        Exit.
    Hen. Die all our griefs with Stanley! Take this staff
Of office, Daubeney; henceforth be our chamberlain.
    Dau. I am your humblest servant.
    Hen.   We are followed
By enemies at home that will not cease
To seek their own confusion; 'tis most true
The Cornish under Audley are marched on
As far as Winchester. But let them come;
Our forces are in readiness; we'll catch 'em   130
In their own toils. [12]

    Dau.   Your army, being mustered,
Consist in all, of horse and foot, at least
In number six and twenty thousand, men
Daring and able, resolute to fight,
And loyal in their truths.
    Hen.   We know it, Daubeney.
For them we order thus: Oxford in chief,
Assisted by bold Essex and the Earl
Of Suffolk, shall lead on the first battalia. [13]—
Be that your charge.
    Oxf.   I humbly thank your majesty.
    Hen. The next division we assign to Daubeney.   140
These must be men of action, for on those
The fortune of our fortunes must rely.
The last and main ourself commands in person,
As ready to restore the fight at all times
As to consummate an assurèd victory.
    Dau. The king is still oraculous. [14]
    Hen.   But, Surrey,
We have employment of more toil for thee;
For our intelligence comes swiftly to us
That James of Scotland late hath entertained
Perkin the counterfeit with more than common   150
Grace and respect, nay, courts him with rare favors.
The Scot is young and forward; we must look for
A sudden storm to England from the North;
Which to withstand, Durham shall post to Norham
To fortify the castle and secure
The frontiers against an invasion there.
Surrey shall follow soon, with such an army
As may relieve the bishop and encounter
On all occasions the death-daring Scots.
You know your charges all; 'tis now a time   160
To execute, not talk. Heaven is our guard still.
War must breed peace; such is the fate of kings.
                                        Exeunt.

[II.iii]

         Enter CRAWFORD *and* DALYELL.

    Craw. 'Tis more than strange; my reason cannot
         answer
Such argument of fine imposture, couched
In witchcraft of persuasion, that it fashions
Impossibilities, as if appearance
Could cozen truth itself; this dukeling mushroom
Hath doubtless charmed the King.
    Dal.   A' courts the ladies,
As if his strength of language chained attention
By power of prerogative.
    Craw.   It madded
My very soul to hear our master's motion. [1]
What surety both of amity and honor   10
Must of necessity ensue upon
A match betwixt some noble of our nation
And this brave prince, forsooth.
    Dal.   'Twill prove too fatal;
Wise Huntley fears the threat'ning. Bless the lady
From such a ruin.
    Craw.   How the council privy

---

[10] *change:* exchange.   [11] *style:* title.   [12] *toils:* traps.
[13] *battalia:* division.   [14] *oraculous:* oracular.
II.iii.
   [1] *motion:* proposal.

Of this young Phaëthon[2] do screw their faces
Into a gravity their trades, good people,
Were never guilty of! the meanest of 'em
Dreams of at least an office in the state.
    Dal. Sure, not the hangman's—'tis bespoke already
For service to their rogueships. Silence!   21

    Enter King JAMES *and* HUNTLY.

    King Ja.   Do not
Argue against our will; we have descended
Somewhat, as we may term it, too familiarly
From justice of our birthright, to examine
The force of your allegiance—sir, we have;
But find it short of duty.
    Hunt.   Break my heart,
Do, do, king. Have my services, my loyalty.—
Heaven knows, untainted ever—drawn upon me
Contempt now in mine age, when I but wanted
A minute of a peace not to be troubled?   30
My last, my long one? Let me be a dotard,
A bedlam,[3] a poor sot, or what you please
To have me, so you will not stain your blood,
Your own blood, royal sir, though mixed with mine,
By marriage of this girl[4] to a straggler![5]
Take, take my head, sir; whilst my tongue can wag
It cannot name him other.
    King Ja.   Kings are counterfeits
In your repute,[6] grave oracle, not presently[7]
Set on their thrones with scepters in their fists.
But use your detraction.[8] 'Tis our pleasure   40
To give our cousin York for wife our kinswoman,
The lady Katherine. Instinct of sovereignty[9]
Designs the honor, though her peevish father
Usurps our resolution.[10]
    Hunt.   Oh, 'tis well,
Exceeding well. I never was ambitious
Of using congees[11] to my daughter-queen:
A queen? Perhaps a quean![12] Forgive me, Dalyell,
Thou honorable gentleman; none here
Dare speak one word of comfort?
    Dal.   Cruel misery!
    Craw. The lady, gracious prince, maybe hath settled
Affection on some former choice.
    Dal.   Enforcement   51
Would prove but tyranny.
    Hunt.   I thank 'ee heartily.
Let any yeoman of our nation challenge[13]
An interest in the girl, then the King
May add a jointure[14] of ascent in titles,
Worthy a free consent; now a' pulls down
What old desert hath builded.
    King Ja.   Cease persuasions.
I violate no pawns of faiths,[15] intrude not
On private loves; that I have played the orator
For kingly York to virtuous Kate, her grant   60
Can justify, referring her contents
To our provision.[16] The Welsh Harry[17] henceforth
Shall therefore know, and tremble to acknowledge,
That not the painted idol of his policy
Shall fright the lawful owner from a kingdom.

We are resolved.
    Hunt.   Some of thy subjects' hearts,
King James, will bleed for this!
    King Ja.   Then shall their bloods
Be nobly spent. No more disputes; he is not
Our friend who contradicts us.
    Hunt.   Farewell, daughter!
My care by one is lessened; thank the King for't,   70
I and my griefs will dance now.

    Enter [PERKIN] WARBECK *leading* KATHERINE,
    complimenting; Countess *of* CRAWFORD, JANE,
    FRION, [JOHN A-WATER] Mayor *of* Cork,
    ASTLEY, HERON *and* SKELTON.

                        Look, lords, look,
Here's hand in hand already!
    King Ja.   Peace, old frenzy.
How like a king a' looks! Lords, but observe
The confidence of his aspect! Dross cannot
Cleave to so pure a metal; royal youth!
Plantagenet undoubted!
    Hunt [*Aside*]   Ho, brave! Youth,[18]
But no Plantagenet, by'r lady, yet,
By red rose or by white.
    War.   An union this way
Settles possession in a monarchy
Established rightly, as in my inheritance.   80
Acknowledge me but sovereign of this kingdom,
Your heart, fair princess, and the hand of providence
Shall crown you queen of me and my best fortunes.
    Kath. Where my obedience is, my lord, a duty,
Love owes true service.
    War.   Shall I?—
    King Ja.   Cousin, yes,
Enjoy her; from my hand accept your bride;
And may they live at enmity with comfort
Who grieve at such an equal pledge of troths.
Y'are the prince's wife now.
    Kath.   By your gift, sir.
    War. Thus I take seizure of mine own.
    Kath.   I miss yet 90
A father's blessing. Let me find it. Humbly
Upon my knees I seek it.
                        [*She kneels.*]
    Hunt.   I am Huntly,
Old Alexander Gordon, a plain subject,
Nor more nor less; and lady, if you wish for

---

    [2] *Phaëthon:* son of the sun-god, who drove his father's chariot too close to earth and was killed by Zeus.
    [3] *bedlam:* madman.   [4] *girl:* disyllabic.
    [5] *straggler:* vagabond.   [6] *repute:* opinion.
    [7] *not presently:* if not actually.
    [8] *use . . . detraction:* defame as you see fit.
    [9] *sovereignty:* i.e., my own royal nature.
    [10] *resolution:* power of decision.
    [11] *congees:* obeisances.   [12] *quean:* whore.
    [13] *challenge:* claim.   [14] *jointure:* dowry.
    [15] *pawns . . . faiths:* exchange of pledges.
    [16] *provision:* providing.
    [17] *Welsh Harry:* Henry VII was of Welsh descent.
    [18] *Ho . . . youth:* Q "Ho . . . lady."

A blessing, you must bend your knees to heaven,
For heaven did give me you. Alas, alas,
What would you have me say? May all the happiness
My prayers ever sued to fall upon you
Preserve you in your virtues! Prithee, Dalyell,
Come with me; for I feel thy grief as full   100
As mine; let's steal away and cry together.

Dal. My hopes are in their ruins.

      Exeunt HUNTLY *and* DALYELL.

King Ja.   Good kind Huntly
Is overjoyed; a fit solemnity
Shall perfect these delights. Crawford, attend
Our order for the preparation.

    Exeunt. Manent FRION, JOHN A-WATER,
    ASTLEY, HERON, *and* SKELTON.

Fri. Now, worthy gentlemen, have I not followed
My undertakings with success? Here's entrance
Into a certainty above a hope.

Her. Hopes are but hopes; I was ever confident,
when I traded but in remnants,[19] that my stars   110
had reserved me to the title of a viscount at least.
Honor is honor, though cut out of any stuffs.

Skel. My brother Heron hath right wisely delivered
his opinion; for he that threads his needle with the
sharp eyes of industry shall in time go through-stitch
with[20] the new suit of preferment.

Ast. Spoken to the purpose, my fine-witted brother
Skelton; for as no indenture but has its counterpawn,[21]
no noverint[22] but his condition or defeasance,[23] so no
right but may have claim, no claim but may   120
have possession, any act of parliament to the contrary
notwithstanding.

Fri. You are all read in mysteries of state,
And quick of apprehension, deep in judgment,
Active in resolution; and 'tis pity
Such counsel should lie buried in obscurity.
But why in such a time and cause of triumph
Stands the judicious mayor of Cork so silent?
Believe it, sir, as English Richard[24] prospers
You must not miss employment of high nature.   130

A-Wat. If men may be credited in their mortality,
which I dare not peremptorily aver but they may or
not be, presumptions by this marriage are then, in
sooth, of fruitful expectation. Or else I must not justify
other men's belief more than other should rely on
mine.

Fri. Pith of experience! Those that have borne office
Weigh every word before it can drop from them.
But, noble counselors, since now the present
Requires in point of honor—pray mistake not—   140
Some service to our lord, 'tis fit the Scots
Should not engross all glory to themselves
At this so grand and eminent solemnity.

Skel. The Scots! the motion is defied. I had rather,
for my part, without trial of my country,[25] suffer persecution under the pressing-iron of reproach; or let my
skin be punched[26] full of eyelet-holes with the bodkin
of derision.

Ast. I will sooner lose both my ears on the pillory of
forgery.   150

Her. Let me first live a bankrupt, and die in the
lousy Hole[27] of hunger, without compounding for sixpence in the pound.

A-Wat. If men fail not in their expectations, there
may be spirits also that digest no rude affronts, master
secretary Frion, or I am cozened; which is possible, I
grant.

Fri. Resolved like men of knowledge; at this feast,
 then,
In honor of the bride, the Scots, I know,
Will in some show, some masque, or some device,   160
Prefer their duties. Now it were uncomely
That we be found less forward for our prince
Than they are for their lady; and by how much
We outshine them in person of account,
By so much more will our endeavors meet with
A livelier applause. Great emperors
Have for their recreations undertook
Such kind of pastimes; as for the conceit,[28]
Refer it to my study. The performance   169
You all shall share a thanks in. 'Twill be grateful.[29]

Her. The motion is allowed. I have stole to a dancing
school when I was a prentice.

Ast. There have been Irish hubbubs,[30] when I have
made one too.

Skel. For fashioning of shapes[31] and cutting a cross-
caper,[32] turn me off to my trade again.

A-Wat. Surely there is, if I be not deceived, a kind
of gravity in merriment, as there is, or perhaps ought to
be, respect of persons in the quality of carriage, which
is, as it is construed, either so, or so.[33]   180

Fri. Still you come home to me; upon occasion
I find you relish courtship[34] with discretion;
And such are fit for statesmen of your merits.
Pray 'ee wait the prince, and in his ear acquaint him
With this design; I'll follow and direct 'ee.

     Exeunt; mane[t] FRION.

Oh, the toil
Of humoring this abject scum of mankind!
Muddy-brained peasants! princes feel a misery
Beyond impartial sufferance, whose extremes
Must yield to such abettors; yet[35] our tide   190
Runs smoothly without adverse winds. Run on!
Flow to a full sea! Time alone debates[36]
Quarrels forewritten in the book of fates.

          Exit.

---

[19] *remnants:* i.e., of cloth.
[20] *go . . . with:* finish completely.
[21] *counterpawn:* counterpart, matching part torn from the
original.   [22] *noverint:* bond.
[23] *defeasance:* stipulations which void the bond if not
fulfilled.   [24] *English Richard:* i.e., Warbeck.
[25] *trial . . . country:* jury trial.
[26] *punched:* Q "pincht."
[27] *Hole:* one of the worst parts of the Counter Prison in
London.   [28] *conceit:* idea.
[29] *grateful:* pleasing, welcome.
[30] *hubbubs:* noisy entertainments.
[31] *shapes:* stage costumes. [32] *cross-caper:* dance step.
[33] *so, or so:* thus or thus. [34] *courtship:* court behavior.
[35] *yet:* so far.   [36] *debates:* abates.

ACT THREE

SCENE ONE

Enter King HENRY, *his gorget* [1] *on, his sword,
plume of feathers, leading staff,* [2] *and* URSWICK.

Hen. How runs the time of day?
Urs.   Past ten, my lord.
Hen. A bloody hour will it prove to some,
Whose disobedience, like the sons o' th' earth, [3]
Throw a defiance 'gainst the face of heaven.
Oxford, with Essex and stout De la Pole,
Have quieted the Londoners, I hope,
And set them safe from fear?
Urs.   They are all silent.
Hen. From their own battlements they may behold
Saint George's Fields [4] o'erspread with armèd men,
Amongst whom our own royal standard threatens   10
Confusion to opposers. We must learn
To practice war again in time of peace,
Or lay our crown before our subjects' feet;
Ha, Urswick, must we not?
Urs.   The powers who seated
King Henry on his lawful throne will ever
Rise up in his defense.
Hen.   Rage shall not fright
The bosom of our confidence. In Kent
Our Cornish rebels, cozened [5] of their hopes,
Met brave resistance by that country's [6] earl,
George Aberg'enny, [7] Cobham, Poynings, Guildford,
And other loyal hearts; now, if Blackheath [8]   21
Must be reserved the fatal tomb to swallow
Such stiff-necked abjects [9] as with weary marches
Have traveled from their homes, their wives and
    children,
To pay instead of subsidies their lives,
We may continue sovereign. Yet, Urswick,
We'll not abate one penny what in parliament
Hath freely been contributed; we must not;
Money gives soul to action. Our competitor,
The Flemish counterfeit, with James of Scotland,   30
Will prove [10] what courage, need, and want can nourish
Without the food of fit supplies. But, Urswick,
I have a charm in secret that shall loose
The witchcraft wherein young King James is bound,
And free it at my pleasure without bloodshed.
Urs. Your majesty's a wise king, sent from heaven
Protector of the just.
Hen.   Let dinner cheerfully
Be servèd in. This day of the week is ours,
Our day of providence, for Saturday
Yet never failed in all my undertakings   40
To yield me rest at night.

                                    A flourish.

                          What means this warning?
Good fate, speak peace to Henry!

Enter DAUBENEY, OXFORD, *and* Attendants.

Dau.   Live the King,
Triumphant in the ruin of his enemies!

Oxf. The head of strong rebellion is cut off,
The body hewed in pieces.
Hen.   Daubeney, Oxford,
Minions [11] to noblest fortunes, how yet stands
The comfort of your wishes?
Dau.   Briefly thus:
The Cornish under Audley, disappointed
Of flattered expectation from the Kentish,
Your majesty's right-trusty liegemen, flew,   50
Feathered [12] by rage and heartened by presumption,
To take the field even at your palace gates,
And face you in your chamber royal. Arrogance
Improved their ignorance; for they, supposing,
Misled by rumor, that the day of battle
Should fall on Monday, rather braved your forces
Than doubted [13] any onset; yet this morning,
When in the dawning I by your direction
Strove to get Dartford [14] Strand Bridge, there I found
Such a resistance as might show what strength   60
Could make. Here arrows hailed in showers upon us
A full yard long at least, but we prevailed.
My lord of Oxford, with his fellow peers
Environing the hill, fell fiercely on them
On the one side, I on the other, till,—great sir,
Pardon the oversight—eager of doing
Some memorable act, I was engaged
Almost a prisoner, but was freed as soon
As sensible of danger. Now the fight
Began in heat, which quenchèd in the blood of   70
Two thousand rebels, and as many more
Reserved to try your mercy, have returned
A victory with safety.
Hen.   Have we lost
An equal number with them?
Oxf.   In the total
Scarcely four hundred. Audley, Flammock, Joseph,
The ringleaders of this commotion,
Railed [15] in ropes, fit ornaments for traitors,
Wait your determinations.
Hen.   We must pay
Our thanks where they are only due. O lords,
Here is no victory, nor shall our people   80
Conceive that we can triumph in their falls.
Alas, poor souls! Let such as are escaped
Steal to the country back without pursuit.
There's not a drop of blood spilt but hath drawn
As much of mine. Their swords could have wrought
    wonders

III.i.
    [1] *gorget:* piece of armor for the throat, a sign of rank when
worn without other armor.   [2] *leading staff:* baton.
    [3] *sons . . . earth:* Titans.
    [4] *Saint George's Fields:* southeast of London.
    [5] *cozened:* cheated.   [6] *country's:* county's.
    [7] *Aberg'enny:* Abergavenny.
    [8] *Blackheath:* five miles from London.
    [9] *abjects:* outcasts.   [10] *prove:* test.
    [11] *Minions:* Favorites.   [12] *Feathered:* Winged.
    [13] *doubted:* feared.
    [14] *Dartford:* Q "Dertford," a village seventeen miles
from London; actually the battle was fought at Deptford.
    [15] *Railed:* Bound in a row.

On their king's part, who faintly were unsheathed
Against their prince, but wounded their own breasts.
Lords, we are debtors to your care; our payment
Shall be both sure and fitting your deserts.

  Dau. Sir, will you please to see those rebels, heads
Of this wild monster-multitude?

  Hen.   Dear friend,   91
My faithful Daubeney, no; on them our justice
Must frown in terror; I will not vouchsafe
An eye of pity to them. Let false Audley
Be drawn upon an hurdle [16] from the Newgate
To Tower Hill in his own coat of arms
Painted on paper, with the arms reversed,
Defaced and torn; there let him lose his head.
The lawyer and the blacksmith shall be hanged,
Quartered, their quarters into Cornwall sent,   100
Examples to the rest, whom we are pleased
To pardon and dismiss from further quest. [17]
My Lord of Oxford, see it done.

  Oxf.   I shall, sir.
  Hen. Urswick.
  Urs.   My lord?
  Hen.   To Dinham, our high-treasurer,
Say we command commissions be new granted
For the collection of our subsidies
Through all the west, and that speedily.
Lords, we acknowledge our engagements due
For your most constant services.

  Dau.   Your soldiers
Have manfully and faithfully acquitted   110
Their several duties.

  Hen.   For it we will throw
A largesse free amongst them, which shall hearten
And cherish [18] up their loyalties. More yet
Remains of like employment; not a man
Can be dismissed till enemies abroad,
More dangerous than these at home, have felt
The puissance of our arms. O happy kings,
Whose thrones are raisèd in their subjects' hearts!

                                      Exeunt omnes.

[III.ii]

              Enter HUNTLY *and* DALYELL.

  Hunt. Now, sir, a modest word with you, sad
gentleman:

---

[16] *hurdle:* frame or sled on which traitors were drawn
through the streets to execution.
  [17] *quest:* inquest.   [18] *cherish:* cheer.
III.ii.
  [1] *I trow:* indeed.   [2] *rare:* fine.
  [3] *twingle-twangles:* sound of the Gaelic harp.
  [4] *quiristers:* choristers.
  [5] *Bedlam:* Bethlehem Hospital for the insane, in London.
  [6] *Trolling:* Singing.   [7] *catch:* round.
  [8] *stomachs:* appetites.   [9] *usquebaugh:* whiskey.
  [10] *bonny-clabber:* soured and clotted milk.
  [11] *knacks:* delicacies.
  [12] *King . . . Mab:* king and queen of fairies.
  [13] *by'r:* by our.
  [14] *quartan:* ague with paroxysms recurring every fourth
day.

Is not this fine, I trow, [1] to see the gambols,
To hear the jigs, observe the frisks, b' enchanted
With the rare [2] discord of bells, pipes and tabors,
Hotch-potch of Scotch and Irish twingle-twangles, [3]
Like to so many quiristers [4] of Bedlam [5]
Trolling [6] a catch? [7] The feasts, the manly stomachs, [8]
The healths in usquebaugh [9] and bonny-clabber, [10]
The ale in dishes never fetched from China,   9
The hundred thousand knacks [11] not to be spoken of,
And all this for King Oberon and Queen Mab, [12]
Should put a soul int' ee. Look 'ee, good man,
How youthful I am grown; but, by your leave,
This new queen-bride must henceforth be no more
My daughter; no, by'r [13] lady, 'tis unfit.
And yet you see how I do bear this change,
Methinks courageously; then shake off care
In such a time of jollity.

  Dal.   Alas, sir,
How can you cast a mist upon your griefs?
Which, howsoe'er you shadow, but present   20
To any judging eye the perfect substance
Of which mine are but counterfeits.

  Hunt.   Foh, Dalyell,
Thou interrupts the part I bear in music
To this rare bridal feast. Let us be merry,
Whilst flattering calms secure us against storms.
Tempests, when they begin to roar, put out
The light of peace and cloud the sun's bright eye
In darkness of despair; yet we are safe.

  Dal. I wish you could as easily forget
The justice of your sorrow as my hopes   30
Can yield to destiny.

  Hunt.   Pish, then I see
Thou dost not know the flexible condition
Of my apt nature. I can laugh, laugh heartily
When the gout cramps my joints; let but the stone
Stop in my bladder, I am straight a-singing;
The quartan [14] fever, shrinking every limb,
Sets me a-cap'ring straight; do but betray me,
And bind me a friend ever. What! I trust
The losing of a daughter, though I doted
On every hair that grew to trim her head,   40
Admits not any pain like one of these.
Come, th'rt deceived in me: give me a blow,
A sound blow on the face, I'll thank thee for't.
I love my wrongs; still th'rt deceived in me.

  Dal. Deceived? O noble Huntly, my few years
Have learned experience of too ripe an age
To forfeit fit credulity. Forgive
My rudeness, I am bold.

  Hunt.   Forgive me first
A madness of ambition; by example
Teach me humility, for patience scorns   50
Lectures which schoolmen use to read to boys
Uncapable of injuries. Though old,
I could grow tough in fury, and disclaim
Allegiance to my King; could fall at odds
With all my fellow peers that durst not stand
Defendants 'gainst the rape done on mine honor.
But kings are earthly gods, there is no meddling
With their anointed bodies; for their actions,

They only are accountable to heaven.
Yet in the puzzle of my troubled brain   60
One antidote's reserved against the poison
Of my distractions; 'tis in thee t'apply it.
    Dal. Name it; oh, name it quickly, sir!
    Hunt.   A pardon
For my most foolish slighting thy deserts;
I have culled out this time to beg it. Prithee
Be gentle; had I been so, thou hadst owned
A happy bride, but now a castaway,
And never child of mine more.
    Dal.   Say not so, sir;
It is not fault in her.
    Hunt.   The world would prate
How she was handsome; young I know she was,   70
Tender, and sweet in her obedience;
But lost now; what a bankrupt am I made
Of[15] a full stock of blessings! Must I hope
A mercy from thy heart?
    Dal.   A love, a service,
A friendship to[16] posterity.
    Hunt.   Good angels
Reward thy charity; I have no more
But prayers left me now.
    Dal.   I'll lend you mirth, sir,
If you will be in consort.[17]
    Hunt.   Thank ye truly.
I must, yes, yes, I must; here's yet some ease,
A partner in affliction; look not angry.   80
    Dal. Good noble sir.

                                  Flourish.

    Hunt.   Oh, hark! we may be quiet,
The King and all the others come, a meeting
Of gaudy sights. This day's the last of revels;
Tomorrow sounds of war; then new exchange:
Fiddles must turn to swords. Unhappy marriage!

Enter King JAMES, [PERKIN] WARBECK *leading*
KATHERINE, CRAWFORD, Countess [*of* CRAWFORD],
and JANE; HUNTLY *and* DALYELL *fall among them.*

    King Ja. Cousin of York, you and your princely
      bride
Have liberally enjoyed such soft delights
As a new-married couple could forethink.
Nor has our bounty shortened expectation;
But after all those pleasures of repose,   90
Or amorous safety, we must rouse the ease
Of dalliance with achievements of more glory
Than sloth and sleep can furnish. Yet, for farewell,
Gladly we entertain a truce with time
To grace the joint endeavors of our servants.
    War. My royal cousin, in your princely favor
The extent of bounty hath been so unlimited
As only an acknowledgement in words
Would breed suspicion in[18] our state and quality.
When we shall in the fullness of our fate—   100
Whose minister, necessity, will perfect[19]—
Sit on our own throne, then our arms, laid open
To gratitude, in sacred memory
Of these large benefits, shall twine them close

Even to our thoughts and heart without distinction.
Then James and Richard, being in effect
One person, shall unite and rule one people,
Divisible in titles only.
    King Ja.   Seat ye.
Are the presenters ready?
    Craw.   All are ent'ring.
    Hunt. Dainty sport toward, Dalyell; sit; come, sit,
Sit and be quiet; here are kingly bug's-words.[20]   111

Enter at one door four Scotch Antics,[21] *accordingly*
    habited; enter at another four wild Irish *in trowses,*[22]
    long-haired, and accordingly habited. Music. The
                  Maskers *dance.*

    King Ja. To all a general thanks.
    War.   In the next room
Take your own shapes again; you shall receive
Particular acknowledgment.
                        [*Exeunt* Maskers.]
    King Ja.   Enough
Of merriments. Crawford, how far's our army
Upon the march?
    Craw.   At Heydonhall, great King;
Twelve thousand well prepared.
    King Ja.   Crawford, tonight
Post thither. We in person, with the prince,
By four o'clock tomorrow after dinner
Will be wi' ye; speed away!
    Craw.   I fly, my lord.   120
                                    [*Exit.*]
    King Ja. Our business grows to head now; where's
      your secretary,
That he attends 'ee not to serve?
    War.   With Marchmount,
Your herald.
    King Ja. Good: the proclamation's ready;
By that it will appear how the English stand
Affected to your title. Huntly, comfort
Your daughter in her husband's absence; fight
With prayers at home for us, who for your honors
Must toil in fight abroad.
    Hunt.   Prayers are the weapons
Which men so near their graves as I do use;
I've little else to do.
    King Ja.   To rest, young beauties!   130
We must be early stirring; quickly part;
A kingdom's rescue craves both speed and art.
Cousins, goodnight.
                                  Flourish.
    War.   Rest to our cousin King.
    Kath. Your blessing, sir.
    Hunt. Fair blessings on your highness; sure, you
      need 'em.
    Exeunt. Manent [PERKIN] WARBECK,
                      KATHERINE [*and* JANE].
    War. Jane, set the lights down, and from us return

---

15 *of:* from.   16 *to:* lasting into.   17 *consort:* accord.
18 *in:* regarding.   19 *perfect:* i.e., our fate.
20 *bug's-words:* swaggering language.
21 *Antics:* grotesque performers.
22 *trowses:* close-fitting trousers.

To those in the next room this little purse;
Say we'll deserve their loves.

Jane.   It shall be done, sir.
                                        [*Exit.*]

War. Now, dearest, ere sweet sleep shall seal those
    eyes,
Love's precious tapers, give me leave to use   140
A parting ceremony, for tomorrow
It would be sacrilege to intrude upon
The temple of thy peace. Swift as the morning
Must I break from the down of thy embraces
To put on steel, and trace the paths which lead
Through various hazards to a careful throne.

Kath. My lord, I would fain go wi' ye; there's small
    fortune
In staying here behind.

War.   The churlish brow
Of war, fair dearest, is a sight of horror
For ladies' entertainment. If thou hear'st   150
A truth of my sad ending by the hand
Of some unnatural subject, thou withal
Shalt hear how I died worthy of my right
By falling like a king; and in the close
Which my last breath shall sound, thy name, thou
    fairest,
Shall sing a requiem to my soul, unwilling
Only of greater glory 'cause divided
From such a heaven on earth as life with thee.
But these are chimes for funerals; my business
Attends on fortune of a sprightlier triumph,   160
For love and majesty are reconciled,
And vow to crown thee empress of the west.

Kath. You have a noble language, sir; your right
In me is without question, and however
Events of time may shorten my deserts
In others' pity, yet it shall not stagger [23]
Or constancy or duty in a wife.
You must be king of me, and my poor heart
Is all I can call mine.

War.   But we will live,
Live, beauteous virtue, by the lively test   170
Of our own blood, to let the counterfeit
Be known the world's contempt.

Kath.   Pray do not use
That word; it carries fate in't. The first suit
I ever made I trust your love will grant.

War. Without denial, dearest.

Kath.   That hereafter,
If you return with safety, no adventure
May sever us in tasting any fortune:
I ne'er can stay behind again.

War.   You're lady
Of your desires, and shall command your will;
Yet 'tis too hard a promise.

Kath.   What our destinies   180

---

[23] *stagger:* unsettle.   [24] *ruled:* marked.   [25] *search:* query.
III.iii.
  [1] *providence:* foresight.   [2] *partage:* share.
  [3] *treaty:* treaty-making.
  [4] *by:* with.   [5] *beadsman:* humble servant.

Have ruled [24] out in their books we must not search, [25]
But kneel to.

War.   Then to fear when hope is fruitless
Were to be desperately miserable,
Which poverty our greatness dares not dream of,
And much more scorns to stoop to. Some few minutes
Remain yet; let's be thrifty in our hopes.

                                        Exeunt.

[III.iii]

Enter King HENRY, HIALAS, *and* URSWICK.

Hen. Your name is Pedro Hialas, a Spaniard?

Hial. Sir, a Castilian born.

Hen.   King Ferdinand,
With wise queen Isabel his royal consort,
Writes 'ee a man of worthy trust and candor.
Princes are dear to heaven who meet with subjects
Sincere in their employments; such I find
Your commendation, sir. Let me deliver
How joyful I repute the amity
With your most fortunate master, who almost
Comes near a miracle in his success   10
Against the Moors, who had devoured his country,
Entire now to his scepter. We, for our part,
Will imitate his providence [1] in hope
Of partage [2] in the use on't. We repute
The privacy of his advisement to us
By you, intended an ambassador
To Scotland for a peace between our kingdoms,
A policy of love, which well becomes
His wisdom and our care.

Hial.   Your majesty
Doth understand him rightly.

Hen.   Else,   20
Your knowledge can instruct me; wherein, sir,
To fall on ceremony would seem useless,
Which shall not need, for I will be as studious
Of your concealment in our conference
As any counsel shall advise.

Hial.   Then, sir,
My chief request is that on notice given
At my dispatch in Scotland you will send
Some learned man of power and experience
To join in treaty [3] with me.

Hen.   I shall do it,
Being that way well provided by [4] a servant   30
Which may attend 'ee ever.

Hial.   If King James
By any indirection should perceive
My coming near your court, I doubt the issue
Of my employment.

Hen.   Be not your own herald;
I learn sometimes without a teacher.

Hial.   Good days
Guard all your princely thoughts.

Hen.   Urswick, no further
Than the next open gallery attend him.
A hearty love go with you.

Hial.   Your vowed beadsman. [5]

                    Exeunt URSWICK *and* HIALAS.

Hen. King Ferdinand is not so much a fox
But that a cunning huntsman may in time   40
Fall on the scent. In honorable actions
Safe imitation best deserves a praise.

Enter URSWICK.

What, the Castilian's passed away?
    Urs.   He is,
And undiscovered; the two hundred marks
Your majesty conveyed a' gently pursed
With a right modest gravity.
    Hen.   What was't
A' muttered in the earnest[6] of his wisdom?
A' spoke not to be heard; 'twas about—
    Urs.   Warbeck:
How if King Henry were but sure of subjects,
Such a wild runagate[7] might soon be caged,   50
No great ado withstanding.
    Hen.   Nay, nay; something
About my son Prince Arthur's match.
    Urs.   Right, right, sir.
A' hummed it out, how that King Ferdinand
Swore that the marriage 'twixt the lady Katherine
His daughter and the Prince of Wales your son
Should never be consummated as long
As any Earl of Warwick lived in England,
Except by new creation.[8]
    Hen.   I remember,
'Twas so indeed; the King his master swore it?
    Urs. Directly,[9] as he said.
    Hen.   An Earl of Warwick!   60
Provide a messenger for letters instantly
To Bishop Fox. Our news from Scotland creeps,
It comes so slow; we must have airy spirits;
Our time requires dispatch. The Earl of Warwick!
Let him be son to Clarence, younger brother
To Edward! Edward's daughter is, I think,
Mother to our Prince Arthur. Get a messenger.
                                                    Exeunt.

[III.iv]

Enter King JAMES, [PERKIN] WARBECK,
CRAWFORD, DALYELL, HERON, ASTLEY, JOHN
A-WATER, SKELTON, *and* Soldiers.

King Ja. We trifle time against these castle walls;
The English prelate will not yield; once more
Give him a summons.

          [*A trumpet is sounded for a*] *parley.*

Enter above DURHAM *armed, a truncheon*[1] *in his
hand, and* Soldiers.

War.   See, the jolly clerk[2]
Appears, trimmed[3] like a ruffian.[4]
    King Ja.   Bishop, yet
Set ope the ports, and to your lawful sovereign,
Richard of York, surrender up this castle,
And he will take thee to his grace; else Tweed
Shall overflow his banks with English blood,
And wash the sand that cements those hard stones

From their foundation.
    Dur.   Warlike King of Scotland.   10
Vouchsafe a few words from a man enforced
To lay his book aside and clap on arms
Unsuitable to my age or my profession.
Courageous prince, consider on what grounds
You rend the face of peace, and break a league
With a confederate king that courts your amity;
For whom too? For a vagabond, a straggler,
Not noted in the world by birth or name,
An obscure peasant, by the rage of hell
Loosed from his chains to set great kings at strife.   20
What nobleman, what common man of note,
What ordinary subject hath come in,
Since first you footed on our territories,
To only feign a welcome? Children laugh at
Your proclamations, and the wiser pity
So great a potentate's abuse by one
Who juggles merely with the fawns[5] and youth
Of an instructed compliment;[6] such spoils,
Such slaughters as the rapine of your soldiers
Already have committed, is enough   30
To show your zeal in a conceited justice.[7]
Yet, great King, wake not yet my master's vengeance,
But shake that viper off which gnaws your entrails.
I and my fellow subjects are resolved,
If you persist, to stand your utmost fury
Till our last blood drop from us.
    War.   O sir, lend
No[8] ear to this traducer[9] of my honor!
What shall I call thee, thou gray-bearded scandal,
That kick'st against the sovereignty to which
Thou owest allegiance? Treason is bold-faced   40
And eloquent in mischief; sacred King,
Be deaf to his known malice!
    Dur.   Rather yield
Unto those holy motions which inspire
The sacred heart of an anointed body.
It is the surest policy in princes
To govern well their own than seek encroachment
Upon another's right.
    Craw.   The King is serious,
Deep in his meditation[s].
    Dal.   Lift them up
To heaven, his better genius!
    War.   Can you study
While such a devil raves? O Sir!
    King Ja.   Well, Bishop   50
You'll not be drawn to mercy?
    Dur.   Construe me
In like case by a subject of your own;

---

6 *earnest:* seriousness.   7 *runagate:* vagabond.
    8 *new creation:* conferring title on new family after
destruction of the old one.   9 *Directly:* Absolutely.

III.iv.
    1 *truncheon:* baton.   2 *clerk:* churchman.
    3 *trimmed:* accoutered.   4 *ruffian:* bully.
    5 *fawns:* fawnings.
    6 *instructed compliment:* taught ceremoniousness.
    7 *conceited justice:* imagined act of justice.
    8 *No:* Q "Me."   9 *traducer:* Q "seducer."

My resolution's fixed. King James, be counseled.
A greater fate waits on thee.

                          Exit with his Soldiers.

   King Ja.   Forage through
The country; spare no prey of life or goods.
   War. O sir, then give me leave to yield to nature;
I am most miserable. Had I been
Born what this clergyman would by defame [10]
Baffle belief with, I had never sought
The truth of mine inheritance with rapes   60
Of women, or of infants murdered, virgins
Deflowered, old men butchered, dwellings fired,
My land depopulated, and my people
Afflicted with a kingdom's devastation.
Show more remorse, [11] great King, or I shall never
Endure to see such havoc with dry eyes.
Spare, spare, my dear, dear England.
   King Ja.   You fool [12] your piety
Ridiculously, careful of an interest
Another man possesseth. Where's your faction?
Shrewdly the bishop guessed of your adherents,   70
When not a petty burgess of some town,
No, not a villager hath yet appeared
In your assistance; that should make 'ee whine,
And not your country's sufferance, [13] as you term it.
   Dal. The King is angry.
   Craw.   And the passionate duke
Effeminately dolent. [14]
   War.   The experience
In former trials, sir, both of mine own
Or other princes cast out of their thrones
Have so acquainted me how misery
Is destitute of friends or of relief   80
That I can easily submit to taste
Lowest reproof, without contempt or words.
   King Ja. An humble-minded man!

                 Enter FRION.

                  —Now, what intelligence
Speaks master secretary Frion?
   Fri.   Henry
Of England hath in open field o'erthrown
The armies who oppose him in the right
Of this young prince.
   King Ja.   His subsidies, [15] you mean.
More, if you have it?
   Fri.   Howard, Earl of Surrey,
Backed by twelve earls and barons of the north,
An hundred knights and gentlemen of name,   90
And twenty thousand soldiers, is at hand
To raise your siege. Brooke, with a goodly navy,

Is admiral at sea; and Daubeney follows
With an unbroken army for a second.
   War. 'Tis false! they come to side with us.
   King Ja.   Retreat;
We shall not find them stones and walls to cope with.
Yet, Duke of York, for such thou sayest thou art,
I'll try thy fortune to the height. To Surrey
By Marchmount I will send a brave defiance
For single combat; once [16] a king will venture   100
His person to an earl, with condition
Of spilling lesser blood. [17] Surrey is bold,
And James resolved.
   War.   Oh, rather, gracious sir,
Create [18] me to this glory, since my cause
Doth interest [19] this fair quarrel; valued least,
I am his equal.
   King Ja.   I will be the man.
March softly off; where victory can reap
A harvest crowned with triumph, toil is cheap.

                             Exeunt omnes.

ACT FOUR

SCENE ONE

Enter SURREY, DURHAM, Soldiers, *with drums
and colors.*

   Sur. Are all our braving enemies shrunk back,
Hid in the fogs of their distempered climate,
Not daring to behold our colors wave
In spite of this infected air? Can they
Look on the strength of Cundrestine defaced,
The glory of Heydonhall devasted, [1] that
Of Edington cast down, the pile of Foulden
O'erthrown? And this the strongest of their forts,
Old Ayton Castle, yielded and demolished,
And yet not peep abroad? The Scots are bold,   10
Hardy in battle; but it seems the cause
They undertake, considerèd, appears
Unjointed in the frame on't.
   Dur.   Noble Surrey,
Our royal master's wisdom is at all times
His fortune's harbinger; for when he draws
His sword to threaten war, his providence
Settles on peace, the crowning of an empire.

                             Trumpet.

   Sur. Rank all in order; 'tis a herald's sound,
Some message from King James; keep a fixed station.

   Enter MARCHMOUNT *and another* Herald *in
their coats.*

   March. From Scotland's awful majesty we come
Unto the English general.
   Sur.   To me?   21
Say on.
   March. Thus, then: the waste and prodigal
Effusion of so much guiltless blood
As in two potent armies of necessity
Must glut the earth's dry womb, his sweet compassion
Hath studied to prevent; for which to thee,

---

[10] *defame:* defamation.   [11] *remorse:* pity.
[12] *fool:* make foolish.   [13] *sufferance:* suffering.
[14] *dolent:* sorrowful.
[15] *subsidies:* taxes (as opposed to Warbeck's right).
[16] *once:* for once.
[17] *with . . . blood:* on the condition that less blood will be
spilled.   [18] *Create:* Advance.
[19] *Doth interest:* Is concerned in.
IV.i.
   [1] *devasted:* devastated.

Great Earl of Surrey, in a single fight
He offers his own royal person; fairly
Proposing these conditions only, that
If victory conclude our master's right,   30
The earl shall deliver for his ransom
The town of Berwick to him, with the fishgarths.[2]
If Surrey shall prevail, the King will pay
A thousand pounds down present[3] for his freedom,
And silence further arms. So speaks King James.
    Sur. So speaks King James; so like a king a' speaks.
Heralds, the English general returns
A sensible devotion from his heart,
His very soul, to this unfellowed[4] grace.
For let the king know, gentle heralds, truly,   40
How his descent from his great throne to honor
A stranger subject with so high a title
As his compeer in arms, hath conquered more
Than any sword could do. For which—my loyalty
Respected—I will serve his virtues ever
In all humility. But Berwick, say,
Is none of mine to part with. In affairs
Of princes, subjects cannot traffic rights
Inherent to the crown. My life is mine;
That I dare freely hazard; and—with pardon   50
To some unbribed vainglory[5]—if his majesty
Shall taste a change of fate, his liberty
Shall meet no articles.[6] If I fall, falling
So bravely, I refer me to his pleasure
Without condition; and for this dear favor,
Say, if not countermanded, I will cease
Hostility, unless provoked.
    March.   This answer
We shall relate unpartially.
    Dur.   With favor,
Pray have a little patience. [*To* SURREY] Sir, you find
By these gay flourishes how wearied travail   60
Inclines to willing rest; here's but a prologue,
However confidently uttered, meant
For some ensuing acts of peace. Consider
The time of year, unseasonableness of weather,
Charge, barrenness of profit; and occasion
Presents itself for honorable treaty,
Which we may make good use of. I will back,
As sent from you in point of noble gratitude
Unto King James, with these his heralds; you
Shall shortly hear from me, my lord, for order   70
Of breathing[7] or proceeding; and King Henry,
Doubt not, will thank the service.
    Sur.   To your wisdom,
Lord Bishop, I refer it.
    Dur.   Be it so then.
    Sur. Heralds, accept this chain and these few crowns.
    March. Our duty, noble General.
    Dur.   In part
Of retribution[8] for such princely love,
My lord the general is pleased to show
The King your master his sincerest zeal
By further treaty, by no common man:
I will myself return with you.
    Sur.   Y' oblige   80
My faithfullest affections t'ee, Lord Bishop.

March. All happiness attend your lordship.
                        [*Exeunt* DURHAM *and* Heralds.]
    Sur.   Come, friends
And fellow soldiers. We I doubt shall meet
No enemies but woods and hills to fight with.
Then 'twere as good to feed and sleep at home;
We may be free from danger, not secure.[9]
                                    Exeunt omnes.

[IV.ii]

                Enter [PERKIN] WARBECK *and* FRION.

    War. Frion, O Frion, all my hopes of glory
Are at a stand! The Scottish king grows dull,
Frosty, and wayward, since this Spanish agent
Hath mixed discourses with him; they are private,
I am not called to council now. Confusion
On all his crafty shrugs! I feel the fabric
Of my designs are tottering.
    Fri.   Henry's policies
Stir with too many engines.[1]
    War.   Let his mines,[2]
Shaped in the bowels of the earth, blow up
Works raised for my defense, yet can they never   10
Toss into air the freedom of my birth,
Or disavow my blood Plantagenet's.
I am my father's son still. But, O Frion,
When I bring into count with my disasters
My wife's compartnership, my Kate's, my life's,
Then, then my frailty feels an earthquake. Mischief
Damn Henry's plots! I will be England's King,
Or let my aunt of Burgundy report
My fall in the attempt deserved[3] our ancestors!
    Fri. You grow too wild in passion. If you will   20
Appear a prince indeed, confine your will[4]
To moderation.
    War.   What a saucy rudeness
Prompts this distrust! If? If I will appear?
Appear a prince? Death throttle such deceits
Even in their birth of utterance! cursed cozenage
Of trust! ye make me mad. 'Twere best, it seems,
That I should turn impostor to myself,
Be mine own counterfeit, belie the truth
Of my dear mother's womb, the sacred bed
Of a prince murdered and a living baffled.   30
    Fri. Nay, if you have no ears to hear, I have
No breath to spend in vain.
    War.   Sir, sir, take heed!
Gold and the promise of promotion rarely
Fail in temptation.

---

    [2] *fishgarths:* riverside or seashore enclosures for catching
or preserving fish.   [3] *present:* immediately.
    [4] *unfellowed:* unique.
    [5] *unbribed vainglory:* pride, unchecked by the honor the
King does him, in his ability to win.
    [6] *meet . . . articles:* be subject to no conditions.
    [7] *breathing:* pausing.
    [8] *retribution:* recompense.   [9] *secure:* overconfident.
IV.ii.
    [1] *engines:* contrivances.
    [2] *mines:* underground ammunition depots.
    [3] *deserved:* was worthy of.   [4] *will:* passion.

Fri.   Why to me this?
War.   Nothing.
Speak what you will; we are not sunk so low
But your advice may piece⁵ again the heart
Which many cares have broken. You were wont
In all extremities to talk of comfort;
Have ye none left now? I'll not interrupt ye.
Good, bear with my distractions! If King James   40
Denied us dwelling here, next whither must I?
I prithee be not angry.
Fri.   Sir, I told ye
Of letters come from Ireland, how the Cornish
Stomach their last defeat, and humbly sue
That with such forces as you could partake⁶
You would in person land in Cornwall, where
Thousands will entertain your title gladly.
War. Let me embrace thee, hug thee! th'ast revived
My comforts; if my cousin King will fail,
Our cause will never.

    Enter JOHN A-WATER, HERON, ASTLEY, [*and*]
           SKELTON.

          Welcome, my tried friends.   50
You keep your brains awake in our defense.
Frion, advise with them of these affairs,
In which be wondrous secret; I will listen
What else concerns us here; be quick and wary.
                                     Exit.
Ast. Ah, sweet young prince! secretary, my fellow
counselors and I have consulted, and jump⁷ all in one
opinion directly, that if these⁸ Scotch garboils⁹ do not
fadge¹⁰ to our minds, we will pell-mell run amongst
the Cornish choughs¹¹ presently and in a trice.   59
Skel. 'Tis but going to sea and leaping ashore, cut
ten or twelve thousand unnecessary throats, fire seven
or eight towns, take half a dozen cities, get into the
market-place, crown him Richard the Fourth, and the
business is finished.
A-Wat. I grant ye, quoth I, so far forth as men
may do, no more than men may do; for it is good to
consider, when consideration may be to the purpose;
otherwise—still you shall pardon me—little said is soon
amended.   69
Fri. Then you conclude the Cornish action surest?
Her. We do so, and doubt not but to thrive abundantly. Ho, my masters, had we known of the commotion
when we set sail out of Ireland, the land had been ours
ere this time.
Skel. Pish, pish, 'tis but forbearing being an earl or a
duke a month or two longer; I say, and I say it again, if
the work go not on apace, let me never see new fashion
more. I warrant ye, I warrant ye; we will have it so, and
so it shall be.   79

---

⁵ *piece:* repair.   ⁶ *partake:* bring together.
⁷ *jump:* agree.   ⁸ *these:* Q "this."
⁹ *garboils:* tumults.   ¹⁰ *fadge:* succeed.
¹¹ *Cornish choughs:* crowlike birds.   ¹² *batten:* fatten.
¹³ *muscadine:* a sweet wine.
IV.iii.
¹ *combination:* treaty.   ² *motion:* propose.
³ *weal:* benefit.

Ast. This is but a cold phlegmatic country, not
stirring enough for men of spirit; give me the heart of
England for my money.
Skel. A man may batten¹² there in a week only with
hot loaves and butter and a lusty cup of muscadine¹³
and sugar at breakfast, though he make never a meal all
the month after.
A-Wat. Surely, when I bore office I found by
experience that to be much troublesome was to be much
wise and busy. I have observed how filching and bragging has been the best service in these last wars,   90
and therefore conclude peremptorily on the design in
England. If things and things may fall out, as who can
tell what or how; but the end will show it.
Fri. Resolved like men of judgment! here to linger
More time is but to lose it. Cheer the prince
And haste him on to this; on this depends
Fame in success, or glory in our ends.
                        Exeunt omnes.

[IV.iii]

    Enter King JAMES; DURHAM *and* HIALAS *on*
               either side.

Hial. France, Spain, and Germany combine a league
Of amity with England; nothing wants
For settling peace through Christendom but love
Between the British monarchs, James and Henry.
Dur. The English merchants, sir, have been received
With general procession into Antwerp;
The emperor confirms the combination.¹
Hial. The King of Spain resolves a marriage
For Katherine his daughter with Prince Arthur.
Dur. France courts this holy contract.
Hial.   What can hinder
A quietness in England?—
Dur.   But your suffrage   11
To such a silly creature, mighty sir,
As is but in effect an apparition,
A shadow, a mere trifle?
Hial.   To this union
The good of both the church and commonwealth
Invite 'ee.
Dur.   To this unity, a mystery
Of providence points out a greater blessing
For both these nations than our human reason
Can search into. King Henry hath a daughter,
The Princess Margaret; I need not urge   20
What honor, what felicity can follow
On such affinity 'tixt two Christian Kings
Inleagued by ties of blood; but sure I am,
If you, sir, ratify the peace proposed,
I dare both motion² and effect this marriage
For weal³ of both the kingdoms.
King Ja.   Darest thou, Lord Bishop?
Dur. Put it to trial, royal James, by sending
Some noble personage to the English court
By way of embassy.
Hial.   Part of the business
Shall suit my mediation.
King Ja.   Well, what heaven   30

Hath pointed out to be, must be; you two
Are ministers, I hope, of blessèd fate.
But herein only I will stand acquitted:
No blood of innocents shall buy my peace.
For Warbeck, as you nick [4] him, came to me
Commended by the states of Christendom,
A prince, though in distress; his fair demeanor,
Lovely behavior, unappallèd spirit,
Spoke him not base in blood, however clouded.   39
The brute beasts have both rocks and caves to fly to,
And men the altars of the church; to us
He came for refuge. Kings come near in nature
Unto the gods in being touched with pity.
Yet, noble friends, his mixture with our blood,
Even with our own, shall no way interrupt
A general peace; only I will dismiss him
From my protection, throughout my dominions
In safety, but not ever to return.
   Hial. You are a just king.
   Dur.   Wise, and herein happy.
   King Ja. Nor will we dally in affairs of weight: 50
Huntly, lord bishop, shall with you to England,
Ambassador from us; we will throw down
Our weapons; peace on all sides now! repair
Unto our council; we will soon be with you.
   Hial. Delay shall question [5] no dispatch; [6] heaven
    crown it.
            Exeunt DURHAM *and* HIALAS.
   King Ja. A league with Ferdinand, a marriage
With English Margaret, a free release
From restitution for the late affronts,
Cessation from hostility! and all
For Warbeck not delivered, but dismissed!   60
We could not wish it better.—Dalyell!

           Enter DALYELL.

   Dal.   Here, sir.
   King Ja. Are Huntly and his daughter sent for?
   Dal.   Sent
    for
And come, my lord.
   King Ja.   Say to the English prince,
We want his company.
   Dal.   He is at hand, sir.

Enter [PERKIN] WARBECK, KATHERINE, JANE,
  FRION, HERON, SKELTON, JOHN A-WATER,
            ASTLEY.

   King Ja. Cousin, our bounty, favors, gentleness,
Our benefits, the hazard of our person,
Our people's lives, our land, hath evidenced
How much we have engaged on your behalf.
How trivial and how dangerous our hopes
Appear, how fruitless our attempts in war,   70
How windy, rather smoky, your assurance
Of party [7] shows, we might in vain repeat.
But now obedience to the mother church,
A father's care upon his country's weal,
The dignity of state, directs our wisdom
To seal an oath of peace through Christendom,
To which we are sworn already. 'Tis you

Must only seek new fortunes in the world.
And find an harbor elsewhere. As I promised
On your arrival, you have met no usage   80
Deserves repentance in your being here;
But yet I must live master of mine own.
However, what is necessary for you
At your depart I am well content
You be accommodated with, provided
Delay prove not my enemy.
   War.   It shall not,
Most glorious prince. The fame of my designs
Soars higher than report of ease and sloth
Can aim at; I acknowledge all your favors
Boundless and singular, am only wretched   90
In words as well as means to thank the grace
That flowed so liberally. Two empires firmly
You're lord of—Scotland and Duke Richard's heart.
My claim to mine inheritance shall sooner
Fail than my life to serve you, best of kings.
And witness Edward's blood in me, I am
More loath to part with such a great example
Of virtue than all other mere respects.
But, sir, my last suit is, you will not force
From me what you have given: this chaste lady,   100
Resolved on all extremes. [8]
   Kath.   I am your wife;
No human power can or shall divorce
My faith from duty.
   War.   Such another treasure
The earth is bankrupt of.
   King Ja.   I gave her, cousin,
And must avow the gift; will add withal
A furniture [9] becoming her high birth
And unsuspected [10] constancy; provide
For your attendance. We will part good friends.
           Ex[eunt] King *and* DALYELL.
   War. The Tudor hath been cunning in his plots:
His Fox of Durham would not fail at last.   110
But what! our cause and courage are our own.
Be men, my friends, and let our cousin king
See how we follow fate as willingly
As malice follows us. You're all resolved
For the west parts of England?
   Omnes.   Cornwall, Cornwall!
   Fri. The inhabitants expect you daily.
   War.   Cheerfully,
Draw all our ships out of the harbor, friends;
Our time of stay doth seem too long, we must
Prevent [11] intelligence; [12] about it suddenly.
   Omnes. A prince, a prince, a prince!   120
        Exeunt HERON, SKELTON, ASTLEY *and*
                    JOHN A-WATER.
   War. Dearest, admit not into thy pure thoughts
The least of scruples, which may charge their softness

---

   [4] *nick:* nickname.   [5] *question:* call into question.
   [6] *dispatch:* speedy conclusion.
   [7] *party:* supporters.   [8] *extremes:* extremities.
   [9] *furniture:* provision of clothing, etc.
   [10] *unsuspected:* undoubted.   [11] *Prevent:* Forestall.
   [12] *intelligence:* reports.

With burden of distrust. Should I prove wanting
To noblest courage now, here were the trial;
But I am perfect, sweet; I fear no change,
More than thy being partner in my sufferance.

Kath. My fortunes, sir, have armed me to encounter
What chance soe'er they meet with.—Jane, 'tis fit
Thou stay behind, for whither wilt thou wander?

Jane. Never till death will I forsake my mistress,
Nor then, in wishing to die with 'ee gladly.   131

Kath. Alas, good soul!

Fri.   Sir, to your aunt of Burgundy
I will relate your present undertakings;
From her expect on all occasions welcome.
You cannot find me idle in your services.

War. Go, Frion, go! Wise men know how to soothe
Adversity, not serve it. Thou hast waited
Too long on expectation; never yet
Was any nation read of so besotted
In reason as to adore the setting sun.   140
Fly to the Archduke's court; say to the duchess,
Her nephew with fair Katherine his wife
Are on their expectation to begin
The raising of an empire. If they fail,
Yet the report [13] will never. Farewell, Frion.—

                              Exit FRION.
This man, Kate, has been true, though now of late
I fear too much familiar with the Fox.

                Enter HUNTLY *and* DALYELL.

Hunt. I come to take my leave. You need not doubt
My interest in this sometime child of mine;
She's all yours now, good sir. O poor lost creature,   150
Heaven guard thee with much patience! If thou canst
Forget thy title to old Huntly's family,
As much of peace will settle in thy mind
As thou canst wish to taste, but in thy grave.
Accept my tears yet, prithee; they are tokens
Of charity, as true as of affection.

Kath. This is the cruell'st farewell!

Hunt.   Love, young
    gentleman,
This model of my griefs. She calls you husband;
Then be not jealous of a parting kiss;
It is a father's, not a lover's off'ring;   160
Take it, my last.

            [HUNTLY *kisses* KATHERINE.]

    —I am too much a child.
Exchange of passion is to little use;
So [14] I should grow too foolish. Goodness guide thee!
                                        Exit.

Kath. Most miserable daughter! Have you aught
To add, sir, to our sorrows?

Dal.   I resolve,
Fair lady, with your leave, to wait on all
Your fortunes in my person, if your lord

Vouchsafe me entertainment.

War. We will be bosom-friends, most noble Dalyell,
For I accept this tender of your love   170
Beyond ability of thanks to speak it.
Clear thy drowned eyes, my fairest: time and industry
Will show us better days, or end the worst.

                              Exeunt omnes.

[IV.iv]

                Enter OXFORD *and* DAUBENEY.

Oxf. No news from Scotland yet, my lord?

Dau.   Not any
But what King Henry knows himself. I thought
Our armies should have marched that way; his mind,
It seems, is altered.

Oxf.   Victory attends
His standard everywhere.

Dau.   Wise princes, Oxford,
Fight not alone with forces. Providence
Directs and tutors strength; else elephants
And barbèd [1] horses might as well prevail
As the most subtle stratagems of war.

Oxf. The Scottish King showed more than common
    bravery   10
In proffer of a combat hand to hand
With Surrey.

Dau.   And but showed it; northern bloods
Are gallant being fired, but the cold climate,
Without good store of fuel, quickly freezeth
The glowing flames.

Oxf.   Surrey, upon my life,
Would not have shrunk an hair's breadth.

Dau.   May a' forfeit.
The honor of an English name and nature
Who would not have embraced it with a greediness
As violent as hunger runs to food.
'Twas an addition [2] any worthy spirit   20
Would covet next to immortality,
Above all joys of life. We all missed shares
In that great opportunity.

            Enter King HENRY *and* URSWICK, *whispering.*

Oxf.   The King!
See, a' comes smiling.

Dau.   Oh, the game runs smooth
On his side, then believe it; cards well shuffled
And dealt with cunning bring some gamester thrift, [3]
But others must rise losers.

Hen.   The train [4] takes?

Urs. Most prosperously.

Hen.   I knew it should not miss.
He fondly [5] angles who will hurl his bait
Into the water 'cause the fish at first   30
Plays round about the line and dares not bite.
Lords, we may reign your king yet; Daubeney, Oxford,
Urswick, must Perkin wear the crown?

Dau.   A slave!

Oxf. A vagabond!

Urs.   A glow-worm!

Hen.   Now, if Frion,

---

[13] *report*: fame.   [14] *So*: Thus.
IV.iv.
    [1] *barbèd*: caparisoned.   [2] *addition*: honor.
    [3] *thrift*: success.   [4] *train*: bait.   [5] *fondly*: foolishly.

His practiced politician, wear a brain
Of proof, King Perkin will in progress ride
Through all his large dominions. Let us meet him
And tender homage; ha, sirs? Liegemen ought
To pay their fealty.
  Dau.   Would the rascal were,
With all his rabble, within twenty miles   40
Of London.
  Hen. Farther off is near enough
To lodge[6] him in his home; I'll wager odds
Surrey and all his men are either idle
Or hasting back; they have not work, I doubt,
To keep them busy.
  Dau.   'Tis a strange conceit, sir.
  Hen. Such voluntary favors as our people
In duty aid us with, we never scattered
On cobweb parasites, or lavished out
In riot or a needless hospitality.
No undeserving favorite doth boast   50
His issues[7] from our treasury; our charge
Flows through all Europe, proving us but steward
Of every contribution which provides
Against the creeping canker of disturbance.
Is it not rare then, in this toil of state
Wherein we are embarked, with breach of sleep,
Cares, and the noise of trouble, that our mercy
Returns nor thanks nor comfort? Still the West
Murmur and threaten innovation,[8]
Whisper our government tyrannical,   60
Deny us what is ours, nay, spurn their lives,
Of which they are but owners by our gift.
It must not be.
  Oxf.   It must not, should not.

      Enter a Post.

  Hen.   So then.—
To whom?
  Post. This packet to your sacred majesty.
  Hen. Sirrah, attend without.
            [Exit Post.]
  Oxf. News from the north, upon my life.
  Dau.   Wise Henry
Divines aforehand of events; with him
Attempts and execution are one act.
  Hen. Urswick, thine ear: Frion is caught; the man
Of cunning is outreached. We must be safe. 70
Should reverend Morton our archbishop move
To a translation[9] higher yet, I tell thee,
My Durham owns a brain deserves that see.[10]
He's nimble in his industry, and mounting.[11]
Thou hear'st me?
  Urs.   And conceive[12] your highness fitly.
  Hen. Daubeney and Oxford, since our army stands
Entire, it were a weakness to admit
The rust of laziness to eat amongst them.
Set forward toward Salisbury; the plains
Are most commodious for their exercise. 80
Ourself will take a muster of them there,
And or disband them with reward or else
Dispose as best concerns us.
  Dau.   Salisbury?

Sir, all is peace at Salisbury.
  Hen.   Dear friend,
The charge must be our own; we would a little
Partake the pleasure with our subjects' ease.
Shall I entreat your loves?
  Oxf.   Command our lives.
  Hen. You're men know how to do, not to forethink.
My bishop is a jewel tried and perfect;
A jewel, lords. The post who brought these letters 90
Must speed another to the mayor of Exeter;
Urswick, dismiss him not.
  Urs.   He waits your pleasure.
  Hen. Perkin a king? A king!
  Urs.   My gracious lord?
  Hen. Thoughts busied in the sphere of royalty
Fix not on creeping worms[13] without their stings,
Mere excrements of earth. The use of time
Is thriving safety, and a wise prevention
Of ills expected. We're resolved for Salisbury.
          Exeunt omnes.

[IV.v.]

  A general shout within. Enter [PERKIN]
  WARBECK, DALYELL, KATHERINE,
    and JANE.

  War. After so many storms as wind and seas
Have threatened to our weather-beaten ships,
At last, sweet fairest, we are safe arrived
On our dear mother earth, ingrateful only
To heaven and us in yielding sustenance
To sly usurpers of our throne and right.
These general acclamations are an omen
Of happy process[1] to their welcome lord;
They flock in troops, and from all parts with wings
Of duty fly to lay their hearts before us. 10
Unequalled pattern of a matchless wife,
How fares my dearest yet?
  Kath.   Confirmed in health:
By which I may the better undergo
The roughest face of change; but I shall learn
Patience to hope, since silence courts affliction
For comforts, to this truly noble gentleman,
Rare unexampled pattern of a friend,
And my beloved Jane, the willing follower
Of all misfortunes.
  Dal.   Lady, I return
But barren crops of early protestations, 20
Frost-bitten in the spring of fruitless hopes.
  Jane. I wait but as the shadow to the body;

---

  [6] *lodge:* discover.   [7] *issues:* disbursements.
  [8] *innovation:* revolution.
  [9] *translation:* change of status, by death or ecclesiastical
promotion.
  [10] *see:* position of Archbishop of Canterbury.
  [11] *mounting:* ambitious.   [12] *conceive:* understand.
  [13] *worms:* snakes.

IV.v.
  [1] *process:* progress.

For, madam, without you let me be nothing.
War. None talk of sadness, we are on the way
Which leads to victory. Keep cowards thoughts
With[2] desperate sullenness! The lion faints not
Locked in a grate;[3] but, loose, disdains all force
Which bars his prey; and we are lion-hearted,
Or else no king of beasts.

                     [*Another shout.*]

            Hark, how they shout,
Triumphant in our cause! bold confidence   30
Marches on bravely, cannot quake at danger.

Enter SKELTON.

Skel. Save King Richard the Fourth, save thee, king
of hearts! The Cornish blades are men of mettle; have
proclaimed through Bodmin[4] and the whole county
my sweet prince monarch of England; four thousand
tall yeoman, with bow and sword, already vow to live
and die at the foot of King Richard.

Enter ASTLEY.

Ast. The mayor our fellow-counselor is servant for
an emperor. Exeter is appointed for the rendezvous,
and nothing wants to victory but courage and   40
resolution. *Sigillatum et datum decimo Septembris, anno
regni regis primo, et cetera; confirmatum est.*[5] All's cock-
sure.[6]
War. To Exeter! to Exeter, march on!
Commend us to our people; we in person
Will lend them double spirits; tell them so.
Skel. & Ast. King Richard, King Richard!
            [*Exeunt* SKELTON *and* ASTLEY.]
War. A thousand blessings guard our lawful arms!
A thousand horrors pierce our enemies' souls!
Pale fear unedge their weapons' sharpest points,   50
And when they draw their arrows to the head,
Numbness shall strike their sinews; such advantage
Hath majesty in its pursuit of justice
That on the proppers-up of truth's old throne
It both enlightens counsel and gives heart
To execution, whiles the throats of traitors
Lie bare before our mercy. O divinity
Of royal birth! how it strikes dumb the tongues
Whose prodigality of breath is bribed
By trains[7] to greatness! Princes are but men   60
Distinguished by the fineness of their frailty,
Yet not so gross in beauty of the mind,
For there's a fire more sacred purifies
The dross of mixture. Herein stands the odds:
Subjects are men on earth, kings men and gods.
                     Exeunt omnes.

---

[2] *Keep ... with:* let cowards have thoughts of.
[3] *grate:* cage.   [4] *Bodmin:* Q "Bodnam."
[5] *L.:* sealed and dated on September 10 in the first year of
the King's reign, etc; confirmed.
[6] *cocksure:* absolutely certain.   [7] *trains:* stratagems.

V.i.
[1] *his:* my husband's.   [2] *after:* for.

ACT FIVE

SCENE ONE

Enter KATHERINE *and* JANE *in riding suits,
with one* Servant.

Kath. It is decreed; and we must yield to fate,
Whose angry justice, though it threaten ruin,
Contempt, and poverty, is all but trial
Of a weak woman's constancy in suffering.
Here in a stranger's and an enemy's land,
Forsaken and unfurnished of all hopes
But such as wait on misery, I range
To meet affliction wheresoe'er I tread.
My train and pomp of servants is reduced
To one kind gentlewoman and this groom.   10
Sweet Jane, now whither must we?
Jane.   To your ships,
Dear lady, and turn home.
Kath.   Home! I have none.
Fly thou to Scotland; thou hast friends will weep
For joy to bid thee welcome; but, O Jane,
My Jane, my friends are desperate of comfort,
As I must be of them; the common charity,
Good people's alms and prayers of the gentle,
Is the revenue must support my state.
As for my native country, since it once
Saw me a princess in the height of greatness   20
My birth allowed me, here I make a vow
Scotland shall never see me being fallen
Or lessened in my fortunes. Never, Jane,
Never to Scotland more will I return.
Could I be England's Queen—a glory, Jane,
I never fawned on—yet the King who gave me
Hath sent me with my husband from his presence,
Delivered us suspected to his[1] nation,
Rendered us spectacles to time and pity.
And is it fit I should return to such   30
As only listen after[2] our descent
From happiness enjoyed to misery
Expected, though uncertain? Never, never!
Alas, why dost thou weep, and that poor creature
Wipe his wet cheeks too? Let me feel alone
Extremities, who know to give them harbor;
Nor thou nor he has cause. You may live safely.
Jane. There is no safety whiles your dangers, madam,
Are every way apparent.
Serv.   Pardon, lady;
I cannot choose but show my honest heart;   40
You were ever my good lady.
Kath.   O dear souls,
Your shares in grief are too, too much!

Enter DALYELL.

Dal.   I bring,
Fair Princess, news of further sadness yet
Than your sweet youth hath been acquainted with.
Kath. Not more, my lord, than I can welcome;
    speak it;
The worst, the worst I look for.
Dal.   All the Cornish

At Exeter were by the citizens
Repulsed, encountered by the Earl of Devonshire
And other worthy gentlemen of the country.
Your husband marched to Taunton, and was there   50
Affronted[3] by King Henry's chamberlain,
The King himself in person, with his army,
Advancing nearer to renew the fight
On all occasions. But the night before
The battles were to join, your husband privately,
Accompanied with some few horse, departed
From out the camp, and posted none knows whither.

    Kath. Fled without battle given?

    Dal.   Fled, but followed
By Daubeney, all his parties[4] left to taste
King Henry's mercy—for to that they yielded—   60
Victorious without bloodshed.

    Kath.   Oh, my sorrows!
If both our lives had proved the sacrifice
To Henry's tyranny, we had fallen like princes,
And robbed him of the glory of his pride.

    Dal. Impute it not to faintness or to weakness
Of noble courage, lady, but foresight;
For by some secret friend he had intelligence
Of being bought and sold by his base followers.
Worse yet remains untold.

    Kath.   No, no, it cannot.

    Dal. I fear y'are betrayed. The Earl of Oxford   70
Runs hot in your pursuit.

    Kath.   A' shall not need;
We'll run as hot in resolution gladly
To make the earl our jailor.

    Jane.   Madam, madam,
They come, they come!

Enter OXFORD *with followers.*

    Dal.   Keep back, or he who dares
Rudely to violate the law of honor
Runs on my sword.

    Kath.   Most noble sir, forbear.
What reason draws you hither, gentlemen?
Whom seek 'ee?

    Oxf.   All stand off. With favor, lady,
From Henry, England's King, I would present
Unto the beauteous princess, Katherine Gordon,   80
The tender of a gracious entertainment.

    Kath. We are that princess, whom your master King
Pursues with reaching arms to draw into
His power. Let him use his tyranny;
We shall not be his subjects.

    Oxf.   My commission
Extends no further, excellentest lady,
Than to a service; 'tis King Henry's pleasure
That you, and all that have relation t' ee,
Be guarded as becomes your birth and greatness.
For rest assured, sweet princess, that not aught   90
Of what you do call yours shall find disturbance,
Or any welcome other than what suits
Your high condition.

    Kath.   By what title, sir,
May I acknowledge you?

    Oxf.   Your servant, lady,
Descended from the line of Oxford's earls,
Inherits what his ancestors before him
Were owners of.

    Kath.   Your king is herein royal,
That by a peer so ancient in desert
As well as blood commands us to his presence.   99

    Oxf. Invites 'ee, princess, not commands.

    Kath.   Pray use
Your own phrase as you list; to your protection
Both I and mine submit.

    Oxf.   There's in your number
A nobleman whom fame hath bravely[5] spoken.
To him the King my master bade me say
How willingly he courts his friendship; far
From an enforcement more than what in terms
Of courtesy so great a prince may hope for.

    Dal. My name is Dalyell.

    Oxf.   'Tis a name hath won
Both thanks and wonder from report; my lord,
The court of England emulates your merit,   110
And covets to embrace 'ee.

    Dal.   I must wait on
The princess in her fortunes.

    Oxf.   Will you please,
Great lady, to set forward?

    Kath.   Being driven
By fate, it were in vain to strive with heaven.

                      Exeunt omnes.

[V.ii]

Enter King HENRY, SURREY, URSWICK, *and a*
guard of Soldiers.

    Hen. The counterfeit, King Perkin, is escaped;
Escape, so let him; he is hedged too fast
Within the circuit of our English pale
To steal out of our ports or leap the walls
Which guard our land; the seas are rough and wider
Than his weak arms can tug with.—Surrey, henceforth
Your King may reign in quiet. Turmoils past,
Like some unquiet dream, have rather busied
Our fancy than affrighted rest of state.
But, Surrey, why, in articling a peace   10
With James of Scotland, was not restitution
Of losses which our subjects did sustain
By the Scotch inroads questioned?

    Sur.   Both demanded
And urged, my lord; to which the King replied,
In modest merriment but smiling earnest,
How that our master Henry was much abler
To bear the detriments than he repay them.

    Hen. The young man, I believe, spake honest truth;
A' studies to be wise betimes.[1] Has, Urswick,
Sir Rhys ap Thomas and Lord Brooke our steward   20

---

    [3] *Affronted:* Confronted.
    [4] *parties:* supporters, troops.   [5] *bravely:* splendidly.
V.ii.
    [1] *betimes:* early.

Returned the western gentlemen full thanks
From us for their tried loyalties?
Urs.[2]   They have;
Which, as if health and life had reigned amongst 'em,
With open hearts they joyfully received.
Hen. Young Buckingham is a fair-natured prince,
Lovely in hopes and worthy of his father:
Attended by an hundred knights and squires
Of special name, he tendered humble service,
Which we must ne'er forget. And Devonshire's wounds,
Though slight, shall find sound cure in our respect.[3]   30

Enter DAUBENEY, *with* [PERKIN] WARBECK,
HERON, JOHN A-WATER, ASTLEY, SKELTON.

Dau. Life to the King, and safety fix his throne!
I here present you, royal sir, a shadow
Of majesty, but in effect a substance
Of pity; a young man, in nothing grown
To ripeness but th' ambition of your mercy:
Perkin, the Christian world's strange wonder.
Hen.   Daubeney,
We observe no wonder; I behold, 'tis true,
An ornament of nature, fine and polished,
A handsome youth indeed, but not admire[4] him.
How came he to thy hands?
Dau.   From sanctuary   40
At Beaulieu, near Southampton, registered,
With these few followers, for[5] persons privileged.
Hen. I must not thank you, sir! you were to blame
To infringe the liberty of houses sacred;
Dare we be irreligious?
Dau.   Gracious lord,
They voluntarily resigned themselves
Without compulsion.
Hen.   So? 'Twas very well;
'Twas very, very well. Turn now thine eyes,
Young man, upon thyself, and thy past actions.
What revels in combustion[6] through our kingdom   50
A frenzy of aspiring youth hath danced,
Till, wanting breath, thy feet of pride have slipped
To break thy neck.
War.   But not my heart; my heart
Will mount till every drop of blood be frozen
By death's perpetual winter. If the sun
Of majesty be darkened, let the sun
Of life be hid from me in an eclipse
Lasting and universal. Sir, remember
There was a shooting in of light when Richmond,
Not aiming at a crown, retired, and gladly,   60
For comfort to the duke of Bretagne's[7] court.
Richard, who swayed the scepter, was reputed
A tyrant then; yet then a dawning glimmered

To some few wand'ring remnants, promising day
When first they ventured on a frightful shore
At Milford Haven—
Dau.   Whither speeds his boldness?
Check his rude tongue, great sir!
Hen.   Oh, let him range:
The player's on the stage still; 'tis his part;
A'does but act. What followed?
War.   Bosworth Field,[8]
Where, at an instant, to the world's amazement,   70
A morn to Richmond and a night to Richard
Appeared at once. The tale is soon applied:
Fate, which crowned these attempts when least assured
Might have befriended others like resolved.
Hen. A pretty gallant! thus your aunt of Burgundy,
Your Duchess aunt, informed her nephew; so,
The lesson, prompted and well conned, was molded
Into familiar dialogue, oft rehearsed,
Till, learnt by heart, 'tis now received for truth.
War. Truth in her pure simplicity wants art   80
To put a feignèd blush on. Scorn wears only
Such fashion as commends to gazers' eyes
Sad ulcerated novelty, far beneath
The sphere of majesty. In such a court,
Wisdom and gravity are proper robes
By which the sovereign is best distinguished
From zanies[9] to[10] his greatness.
Hen.   Sirrah, shift[11]
Your antic pageantry, and now appear
In your own nature, or you'll taste the danger
Of fooling out of season.
War.   I expect   90
No less than what severity calls justice,
And politicians safety; let such beg
As feed on alms. But if there can be mercy
In a protested[12] enemy, then may it
Descend to these poor creatures, whose engagements
To th' bettering of their fortunes have incurred
A loss of all; to them, if any charity
Flow from some noble orator, in death
I owe the fee of thankfulness.
Hen.   So brave!
What a bold knave is this! Which of these rebels   100
Has been the mayor of Cork?
Dau.   This wise formality.
Kneel to the King, ye rascals

                                        [*They kneel.*]

Hen.   Canst thou hope
A pardon where thy guilt is so apparent?
A-Wat. Under your good favors, as men are men,
they may err. For I confess, respectively,[13] in taking
great parts, the one side prevailing, the other side must
go down. Herein the point is clear, if the proverb hold
that hanging goes by destiny, that it is to little purpose
to say, this thing or that shall be thus or thus; for as the
fates will have it, so it must be, and who can help it?
Dau. O blockhead! thou a privy counselor?   111
Beg life, and cry aloud, "Heaven save King Henry!"
A-Wat. Every man knows what is best, as it happens.
For my own part, I believe it is true, if I be not

---

[2] *Urs.* Q "Sur."   [3] *respect:* admiration.
[4] *admire:* wonder at.   [5] *for:* as.
[6] *combustion:* disorder, hubbub.
[7] *Bretagne's:* Q "Britaine's."
[8] *Bosworth Field:* where Richmond defeated Richard III
in 1485 and became Henry VII.
[9] *zanies:* comic mimics.   [10] *to:* of.
[11] *shift:* change.   [12] *protested:* proclaimed.
[13] *respectively:* respectfully.

deceived, that kings must be kings and subjects subjects. But which is which—you shall pardon me for
that; whether we speak or hold our peace, all are
mortal; no man knows his end.

    Hen. We trifle time with follies.

    Omnes.   Mercy, mercy!

    Hen. Urswick, command the dukeling and these
       fellows   120
To Digby, the lieutenant of the Tower:
With safety let them be conveyed to London.
It is our pleasure no uncivil outrage,
Taunts or abuse be suffered to their persons;
They shall meet fairer law than they deserve.
Time may restore their wits, whom vain ambition
Hath many years distracted.

    War.   Noble thoughts
Meet freedom in captivity. The Tower—
Our childhood's dreadful nursery!

    Hen.   No more.

    Urs. Come, come, you shall have leisure to bethink
       'ee.   130

        Exit URSWICK *with* PERKIN[WARBECK]
                     and his[followers].

    Hen. Was ever so much impudence in forgery?[14]
The custom, sure, of being styled a king
Hath fastened in his thought that he is such;
But we shall teach the lad another language.
'Tis good we have him fast.

    Dau.   The hangman's physic
Will purge this saucy humor.

    Hen.   Very likely;
Yet we could temper mercy with extremity,
Being not too far provoked.

    Enter OXFORD, KATHERINE *in her richest attire,*
       [DALYELL], JANE, *and* Attendants.

    Oxf.   Great sir, be pleased
With your accustomed grace to entertain
The Princess Katherine Gordon.

    Hen.   Oxford, herein   140
We must beshrew[15] thy knowledge of our nature.
A lady of her birth and virtues could not
Have found us so unfurnished of good manners
As not, on notice given, to have met her
Halfway in point of love. Excuse, fair cousin,
The oversight. O fie, you may not kneel;
'Tis most unfitting; first, vouchsafe this welcome,
A welcome to your own, for you shall find us
But guardian to your fortune and your honors.

    Kath. My fortunes and mine honor are weak
       champions,   150
As both are now befriended, sir; however,
Both bow before your clemency.

    Hen.   Our arms
Shall circle them from malice.—A sweet lady!
Beauty incomparable! Here lives majesty
At league with love.

    Kath.   O sir, I have a husband.

    Hen. We'll prove your father, husband, friend, and
       servant;
Prove what you wish to grant us. Lords, be careful

A patent presently be drawn for issuing
A thousand pounds from our exchequer yearly
During our cousin's life. Our Queen shall be   160
Your chief companion, our own court your home,
Our subjects all your servants.

    Kath.   But my husband?

    Hen. By all descriptions, you are noble Dalyell,
Whose generous truth hath famed a rare observance.
We thank 'ee; 'tis a goodness gives addition
To every title boasted from your ancestry,
In all most worthy.

    Dal.   Worthier than your praises,
Right princely sir, I need not glory in.

    Hen. Embrace him, lords. [*To* KATHERINE]
       Whoever calls you mistress
Is lifted in our charge: a goodlier beauty   170
Mine eyes yet ne'er encountered.

    Kath.   Cruel misery
Of fate, what rests[16] to hope for?

    Hen.   Forward, lords,
To London.—Fair, ere long I shall present 'ee
With a glad object, peace, and Huntly's blessing.

                          Exeunt omnes.

[V.iii]

    Enter Constable *and* Officers, [PERKIN] WARBECK,
    URSWICK, *and* LAMBERT SIMNEL *like a falconer.*
              A pair of stocks.

    Const. Make room there! keep off, I require 'ee, and
none come within twelve foot of his majesty's new
stocks, upon pain of displeasure. Bring forward the
malefactor.[1] Friend, you must to this gear,[2] no remedy.
Open the hole, and in with his legs, just in the middle
hole; there, that hole.

           [WARBECK *is put in the stocks.*]

Keep off, or I'll commit you all. Shall not a man in
authority be obeyed? So, so there, 'tis as it should be.
Put on the padlock, and give me the key; off, I say,
keep off!   10

    Urs. Yet, Warbeck, clear thy conscience; thou hast
       tasted
King Henry's mercy liberally; the law
Has forfeited thy life; an equal[3] jury
Have doomed thee to the gallows; twice, most wickedly,
Most desperately, hast thou escaped the Tower,
Inveigling to thy party with thy witchcraft
Young Edward, Earl of Warwick, son to Clarence,
Whose head must pay the price of that attempt.
Poor gentleman, unhappy in his fate,
And ruined by thy cunning; so a mongrel   20
May pluck the true stag down. Yet, yet, confess
Thy parentage; for yet the King has mercy.

    Lamb. You would be Dick the Fourth; very likely!

---

[14] *forgery:* deceit.   [15] *beshrew:* blame greatly.
[16] *rests:* is left.
V.iii.
  [1] *malefactor:* Q "malefactors."   [2] *gear:* business.
  [3] *equal:* impartial.

Your pedigree is published; you are known
For Osbeck's son of Tournay, a loose runagate,
A landloper.[4] Your father was a Jew,
Turned Christian merely to repair his miseries.
Where's now your kingship?
    War.   Baited to my death?
Intolerable cruelty! I laugh at
The Duke of Richmond's practice[5] on my fortunes.   30
Possession of a crown ne'er wanted heralds.
    Lamb. You will not know who I am?
    Urs.   Lambert Simnel,
Your predecessor in a dangerous uproar;
But, on submission, not alone received
To grace, but by the King vouchsafed his service.
    Lamb. I would be Earl of Warwick, toiled and ruffled
Against my master, leapt to catch the moon,
Vaunted my name Plantagenet, as you do.
An earl, forsooth! whenas in truth I was,
As you are, a mere rascal. Yet his majesty,   40
A prince composed of sweetness—heaven protect
    him!—
Forgave me all my villainies, reprieved
The sentence of a shameful end, admitted
My surety[6] of obedience to his service;
And I am now his falconer, live plenteously,
Eat from the king's purse, and enjoy the sweetness
Of liberty and favor, sleep securely;
And is not this now better than to buffet[7]
The hangman's clutches, or to brave the cordage
Of a tough halter, which will break your neck?   50
So then the gallant totters.[8] Prithee, Perkin,
Let my example lead thee; be no longer
A counterfeit; confess, and hope for pardon!
    War. For pardon! Hold, my heart-strings, whiles
    contempt
Of injuries,[9] in scorn, may bid defiance
To this base man's foul language. Thou poor vermin,
How darest thou creep so near me? Thou an earl?
Why, thou enjoy'st as much of happiness
As all the swinge[10] of slight ambition flew at.
A dunghill was thy cradle. So a puddle,   60
By virtue of the sunbeams, breathes a vapor
To infect the purer air, which drops again
Into the muddy womb that first exhaled it.
Bread and a slavish case, with some assurance
From the base beadle's whip, crowned all thy hopes.
But, sirrah, ran there in thy vains one drop
Of such a royal blood as flows in mine,
Thou wouldst not change condition to be second
In England's state without the crown itself.
Coarse creatures are incapable of excellence.   70
But let the world, as all to whom I am
This day a spectacle, to time deliver,
And by tradition fix[11] posterity,

Without another chronicle than truth,
How constantly my resolution suffered
A mardyrdom of majesty.
    Lamb.   He's past
Recovery; a Bedlam cannot cure him.
    Urs. Away, inform the king of his behavior.
    Lamb. Perkin, beware the rope; the hangman's
    coming.
                    Exit [LAMBERT] SIMNEL.
    Urs. If yet thou hast no pity of thy body,   80
Pity thy soul!

Enter KATHERINE, JANE, DALYELL, *and* OXFORD.

    Jane.   Dear lady!
    Oxf.   Whither will 'ee,
Without respect of shame?
    Kath.   Forbear me,[12] sir,
And trouble not the current of my duty.—
O my loved lord! Can any scorn be yours
In which I have no interest? Some kind hand
Lend me assistance, that I may partake
Th' infliction of this penance. My life's dearest,—
Forgive me; I have stayed too long from tend'ring
Attendance on reproach; yet bid me welcome.
    War. Great miracle of constancy! My miseries   90
Were never bankrupt of their confidence,
In worst afflictions, till this; now I feel them.
Report and thy deserts, thou best of creatures,
Might to eternity have stood a pattern
For every virtuous wife without this conquest.
Thou hast outdone belief; yet may their ruin
If after-marriages be never pitied
To whom thy story shall appear a fable.
Why wouldst thou prove so much unkind to greatness
To glorify thy vows by such a servitude?   100
I cannot weep, but trust me, dear, my heart
Is liberal of passion. Harry Richmond,
A woman's faith hath robbed thy fame of triumph.
    Oxf. Sirrah, leave off your juggling, and tie up
The devil that ranges in your tongue.
    Urs.   Thus witches,
Possessed, even [to][13] their deaths deluded, say
They have been wolves and dogs and sailed in egg-
    shells
Over the sea and rid on fiery dragons,
Passed in the air more than a thousand miles
All in a night. The enemy of mankind   110
Is powerful but false, and falsehood confident.
    Oxf. Remember, lady, who you are; come from
That impudent impostor.
    Kath.   You abuse us,
For when the holy churchman joined our hands,
Our vows were real then; the ceremony
Was not in apparition, but in act.
Be what these people term thee, I am certain
Thou art my husband; no divorce in heaven
Has been sued out[14] between us; 'tis injustice
For an earthly power to divide us;   120
Or we will live or let us die together.
There is a cruel mercy.
    War.   Spite of tyranny,

---

[4] *landloper*: vagabond.   [5] *practice*: scheme.
[6] *admitted . . . surety*: accepted my pledge.
[7] *buffet*: beat back.
[8] *totters*: swings from a rope.   [9] *injuries*: insults.
[10] *swinge*: inclination, impetus.   [11] *fix*: convince.
[12] *Forbear me*: Let me alone.   [13] *to*: not in Q.
[14] *sued out*: entered in court.

We reign in our affections, blessèd woman!
Read in my destiny the wrack of honor;
Point out, in my contempt of death, to memory
Some miserable happiness, since herein,
Even when I fell, I stood enthroned a monarch
Of one chaste wife's troth pure and uncorrupted.
Fair angel of perfection, immortality
Shall raise thy name up to an adoration,   130
Court every rich opinion of true merit,
And saint it in the calendar of virtue,
When I am turned into the self-same dust
Of which I was first formed.

    Oxf.   The lord ambassador,
Huntly your father, madam, should a'look on
Your strange subjection in a gaze so public,
Would blush on your behalf, and wish his country
Unleft for entertainment to such sorrow.

    Kath. Why art thou angry, Oxford? I must be
More peremptory in my duty. Sir,   140
Impute it not unto immodesty
That I presume to press you to[15] a legacy
Before we part for ever.

    War.   Let it be, then,
My heart, the rich remains of all my fortunes.

    Kath. Confirm it with a kiss, pray.

    War.   Oh, with that
I wish to breathe my last! Upon thy lips,
Those equal twins of comeliness, I seal
The testament of honorable vows.

                              [*Kisses her.*]
Whoever be that man that shall unkiss
This sacred pι int next, may he prove more thrifty   150
In this world's just applause, not more desertful.

    Kath. By this sweet pledge of both our souls, I swear
To die a faithful widow to thy bed,
Not to be forced or won. Oh, never, never!

          Enter SURREY, DAUBENEY, HUNTLY, *and*
                  CRAWFORD.

    Dau. Free the condemnèd person, quickly free him.
What has a' yet confessed?

    Urs.   Nothing to purpose;
But still a' will be king.

    Sur.   Prepare your journey
To a new kingdom, then. Unhappy madam,
Willfully foolish!—see, my lord ambassador,
Your lady daughter will not leave the counterfeit   160
In this disgrace of fate.

    Hunt.   I never pointed[16]
Thy marriage, girl, but yet, being marrièd,
Enjoy thy duty to a husband freely.
The griefs are mine. I glory in thy constancy;
And must not say I wish that I had missed
Some partage in these trials of a patience.

    Kath. You will forgive me, noble sir?

    Hunt.   Yes, yes;
In every duty of a wife and daughter
I dare not disavow thee. To your husband—
For such you are, sir,—I impart a farewell   170
Of manly pity; what your life has passed through,
The dangers of your end will make apparent.

And I can add, for comfort to your sufferance,
No cordial but the wonder of your frailty,
Which keeps so firm a station. We are parted.

    War. We are. A crown of peace renew thy age,
Most honorable Huntly. Worthy Crawford,
We may embrace; I never thought thee injury.

    Craw. Nor was I ever guilty of neglect   179
Which might procure such thought. I take my leave, sir.

    War. To you, Lord Dalyell—what? Accept a sigh,
'Tis hearty and in earnest.

    Dal.   I want utterance:
My silence is my farewell.

    Kath.   Oh—oh—

    Jane.   Sweet madam,
What do you mean? My lord, your hand.

    Dal.   Dear lady,
Be pleased that I may wait[17] 'ee to your lodging.

          Exit KATHERINE, DALYELL, JANE.

    Enter Sheriff *and* Officers; SKELTON, ASTLEY,
    HERON *and* JOHN A-WATER, *with halters about*
               their necks.

    Oxf. Look 'ee; behold your followers, appointed
To wait on 'ee in death.

    War.   Why, peers of England,
We'll lead 'em on courageously. I read
A triumph over tyranny upon
Their several foreheads. Faint not in the moment   190
Of victory! Our ends, and Warwick's head,
Innocent Warwick's head—for we are prologue
But to his tragedy—conclude the wonder
Of Henry's fears; and then the glorious race
Of fourteen kings, Plantagenets, determines[18]
In this last issue male; heaven be obeyed.
Impoverish time of its amazement, friends,
And we will prove as trusty in our payments
As prodigal to nature in our debts.
Death? Pish, 'tis but a sound, a name of air,   200
A minute's storm, or not so much. To tumble
From bed to bed, be massacred[19] alive
By some physicians for a month or two,
In hope of freedom from a fever's torments,
Might stagger manhood; here, the pain is passed
Ere sensibly 'tis felt. Be men of spirit;
Spurn coward passion! So illustrious mention
Shall blaze[20] our names, and style us kings o'er death.

    Dau. Away, impostor beyond precedent!
No chronicle records his fellow.

              Exeunt [Sheriff], *all* Officers *and* Prisoners.

    Hunt.   I have   210
Not thoughts left; 'tis sufficient in such cases
Just laws ought to proceed.

    Enter King HENRY, DURHAM, *and* HIALAS.

    Hen.   We are resolved.
Your business, noble lords, shall find success[21]
Such as your King importunes.

---

15 *to:* for.   16 *pointed:* appointed.   17 *wait:* attend.
18 *determines:* terminates.   19 *massacred:* mutilated.
20 *blaze:* proclaim.   21 *success:* outcome.

Hunt.　　　　　　　You are gracious.

Hen. Perkin, we are informed, is armed [22] to die;
In that we'll honor him. Our lords shall follow
To see the execution; and from hence

We gather this fit use: [23] that public states,
As our particular bodies, taste most good
In health when purgèd of corrupted blood.　　　220

Exeunt omnes.

EPILOGUE

Here has appeared, though in a several fashion,
The threats of majesty, the strength of passion,
Hopes of an empire, change of fortunes; all
What can to theaters of greatness fall,
Proving their weak foundations. Who will please,
Amongst such several sights, to censure [1] these
No births abortive, nor a bastard brood—
Shame to a parentage or fosterhood—
May warrant [2] by their loves all just excuses,
And often find a welcome to the Muses.　　　10

F I N I S

---

[22] *armed:* prepared.　　　　[23] *use:* moral application.

EPILOGUE
　[1] *censure:* judge.　　　　　　[2] *warrant:* justify.

John Ford

'TIS PITY SHE'S A WHORE

'TIS PITY SHE'S A WHORE was first published in 1633, and its title page declares that it was "Acted by the Queen's Majesty's Servants at the Phoenix in Drury Lane." There is no firm evidence for the date of its composition and first performance, but the Queen's company did not begin performing until 1626, and the best guess is that the earliest performance was sometime between 1629 and the date of publication. There is no known source, though there are a number of analogues; Ford alludes frequently and dramatically to *Romeo and Juliet*, TAMBURLAINE, and DOCTOR FAUSTUS. The text printed here is modernized from the quarto (Q); only those quarto variants are listed which are more significant than simple printer's errors. There was no second edition in the century.

For all the apparent complexity and busyness added by the subplot, Ford's scheme is simple and stark: the play's protagonists rebel against a society presented from first to last as hopelessly depraved by attempting to create their own morality; in doing so they abandon not only the sanctions of traditional morality but also the limits of their humanity, and they are punished as retributively as if the universe were as moral as the corrupt spokesmen of political and ecclesiastical establishment claim it to be. Giovanni is thus a late version of the familiar villain-hero, the superman who is destroyed in trying to find adequate scope for his ego. But in the patent self-deception of his incestuous ambitions and in his rhetoric he embodies a heroism as unattractive as the world against which he rebels. Compared, as the play asks to be compared, to *Romeo and Juliet*, romantic escape is now no less vicious than what it flees; compared to TAMBURLAINE, and again allusions demand that we make the comparison, both the hero and the world he wants to conquer are significantly shrunken. In this sense 'TIS PITY continues in the direction established by Shakespeare and Webster; after it, tragedy would seem to be without a subject. It is probably the success with which Ford conveys the sense of a world in its evening, as much as the luridness of the action and the attractiveness to actors of the principal roles, that has made 'TIS PITY one of the most frequently produced of Renaissance plays in the twentieth century.   N. R.

'Tis Pity She's a Whore

[EPISTLE DEDICATORY]

To the Truly Noble JOHN, EARL OF PETERBOROUGH,
LORD MORDAUNT, BARON OF TURVEY

MY LORD,

WHERE a truth of merit hath a general warrant, there love is but a debt, acknowledgment a justice. Greatness cannot often claim virtue by inheritance; yet in this, yours appears most eminent, for that you are not more rightly heir to your fortunes than glory shall be to your memory. Sweetness of disposition ennobles a freedom of birth; in both, your lawful interest adds honor to your own name and mercy to my presumption. Your noble allowance [1] of these first fruits of my leisure in the action [2] emboldens my confidence of your as noble construction [3] in this presentment [4]; especially since my service must ever owe particular duty to your favors by a particular engagement. The gravity of the subject may easily excuse the lightness of the title, otherwise I had been a 10 severe judge against mine own guilt. Princes have vouchsafed grace to trifles offered from a purity of devotion; your lordship may likewise please to admit into your good opinion, with these weak endeavors, the constancy of affection from the sincere lover of your deserts in honor,

JOHN FORD

[COMMENDATORY VERSE]

TO MY FRIEND THE AUTHOR

With admiration I beheld this Whore
Adorned with beauty such as might restore
(If ever being as thy muse hath famed)
Her Giovanni, in his love unblamed;
The ready Graces lent their willing aid,
Pallas herself now played the chambermaid,
And helped to put her dressings on. Secure
Rest thou that thy name herein shall endure
To th' end of age; and Annabella be
Gloriously fair, even in her infamy.   10
THOMAS ELLICE [1]

DRAMATIS PERSONÆ

BONAVENTURA, *a friar*
A Cardinal, *nuncio to the Pope*
SORANZO, *a nobleman*
FLORIO, *a citizen of Parma*
DONADO, *another citizen*
GRIMALDI, *a Roman gentleman*
GIOVANNI, *son to Florio*
BERGETTO, *nephew to Donado.*
RICHARDETTO, *a supposed physician*
VASQUES, *servant to Soranzo*
POGGIO, *servant to Bergetto*
Banditti, [Officers, Servants, etc.]

Women

ANNABELLA, *daughter to Florio.*

HIPPOLITA, *wife to Richardetto*
PHILOTIS, *his niece*
PUTANA, [1] *tut'ress to Annabella.*

The Scene: PARMA.

EPISTLE DEDICATORY
  [1] *allowance:* approval.   [2] *action:* stage performance.
  [3] *construction:* interpretation.   [4] *presentment:* print.

COMMENDATORY VERSE
  [1] *Thomas Ellice:* Ford's admirer has not been identified.

DRAMATIS PERSONÆ
  [1] *Putana:* The name means "whore."

ACT ONE

SCENE ONE

Enter Friar [BONAVENTURA] *and* GIOVANNI.

Fri. Dispute no more in this, for know, young man,
These are no school-points;[1] nice[2] philosophy
May tolerate unlikely arguments,
But heaven admits no jest: wits that presumed
On wit too much, by striving how to prove
There was no God, with foolish grounds of art,[3]
Discovered first the nearest way to hell,
And filled the world with devilish atheism.
Such questions, youth, are fond;[4] for better 'tis
To bless the sun than reason why it shines;   10
Yet he thou talk'st of is above the sun.
No more; I may not hear it.
Giov.   Gentle father,
To you I have unclasped my burdened soul,
Emptied the storehouse of my thoughts and heart,
Made myself poor of secrets; have not left
Another word untold, which hath not spoke
All what I ever durst, or think, or know;
And yet is here the comfort I shall have,
Must I not do what all men else may, love?
Fri. Yes, you may love, fair son.
Giov.   Must I not praise
That beauty which, if framed anew, the gods   21
Would make a god of, if they had it there,
And kneel to it, as I do kneel to them?
Fri. Why, foolish madman.
Giov.   Shall a peevish sound,
A customary form,[5] from man to man,
Of brother and of sister, be a bar
'Twixt my perpetual happiness and me?
Say that we had one father, say one womb
(Curse to my joys) gave both us life and birth;
Are we not therefore each to other bound   30
So much the more by nature by the links
Of blood, of reason—nay, if you will have't,
Even of religion—to be ever one:
One soul, one flesh, one love, one heart, one all?
Fri. Have done, unhappy youth, for thou art lost.
Giov. Shall, then, for that I am her brother born,
My joys be ever banished from her bed?
No, father; in your eyes I see the change
Of pity and compassion; from your age,
As from a sacred oracle, distils   40
The life of counsel. Tell me, holy man,

What cure shall give me ease in these extremes.
Fri. Repentance, son, and sorrow for this sin;
For thou hast moved a majesty above
With thy unrangèd[6]—almost—blasphemy.
Giov. Oh, do not speak of that, dear confessor.
Fri. Art thou, my son, that miracle of wit
Who once, within these three months, wert esteemed
A wonder of thine age throughout Bononia?[7]
How did the University applaud   50
Thy government,[8] behavior, learning, speech,
Sweetness, and all that could make up a man!
I was proud of my tutelage, and chose
Rather to leave my books than part with thee.
I did so; but the fruits of all my hopes
Are lost in thee, as thou art in thyself.
O Giovanni,[9] hast thou left the schools
Of knowledge to converse with lust and death?
For death waits on thy lust. Look through the world,
And thou shalt see a thousand faces shine   60
More glorious than this idol thou ador'st.
Leave her, and take thy choice; 'tis much less sin,
Though in such games as those they lose that win.
Giov. It were more ease to stop the ocean
From floats[10] and ebbs than to dissuade my vows.[11]
Fri. Then I have done, and in thy willful flames
Already see thy ruin; heaven is just.
Yet hear my counsel.
Giov.   As a voice of life.
Fri. Hie to thy father's house, there lock thee fast
Alone within thy chamber, then fall down   70
On both thy knees, and grovel on the ground:
Cry to thy heart, wash every word thou utter'st
In tears—and—if't be possible—of blood;
Beg heaven to cleanse the leprosy of lust
That rots thy soul; acknowledge what thou art,
A wretch, a worm, a nothing; weep, sigh, pray
Three times a day, and three times every night.
For seven day's space do this; then if thou findst
No change in thy desires, return to me:
I'll think on remedy. Pray for thyself   80
At home, whilst I pray for thee here.—Away,
My blessing with thee, we have need to pray.
Giov. All this I'll do, to free me from the rod
Of vengeance; else I'll swear my fate's my god.

Exeunt.

[I.ii]

Enter GRIMALDI *and* VASQUES *ready to fight.*

Vasq. Come, sir, stand to your tackling;[1] if you prove
craven, I'll make you run quickly.
Grim. Thou art no equal match for me.
Vasq. Indeed, I never went to the wars to bring home
news, nor cannot play the mountebank for a meal's
meat, and swear I got my wounds in the field. See you
these grey hairs? They'll not flinch for a bloody nose.
Wilt thou to this gear?[2]
Grim. Why, slave, think'st thou I'll balance my reputation with a cast-suit?[3] Call thy master, he shall
know that I dare—   11

Vasq. Scold like a cot-quean,[4] that's your profession. Thou poor shadow of a soldier, I will make thee know my master keeps servants thy betters in quality and performance. Com'st thou to fight or prate?

Grim. Neither, with thee. I am a Roman and a gentleman, one that have got mine honor with expense of blood.

Vasq. You are a lying coward and a fool. Fight, or by these hilts I'll kill thee. Brave my lord! you'll fight?   20

Grim. Provoke me not, for if thou dost—

Vasq. Have at you!

They fight; GRIMALDI *hath the worst.*

Enter FLORIO, DONADO, SORANZO.

Flo. What mean these sudden broils so near my
    doors?
Have you not other places but my house
To vent the spleen of your disordered bloods?
Must I be haunted still with such unrest
As not to eat or sleep in peace at home?
Is this your love, Grimaldi? Fie, 'tis naught.

Don. And, Vasques, I may tell thee, 'tis not well
To broach these quarrels; you are ever forward   30
In seconding contentions.

Enter above ANNABELLA *and* PUTANA.

Flo.   What's the ground?

Sor. That, with your patience, signors, I'll resolve:
This gentleman, whom fame reports a soldier,
(For else I know not) rivals me in love
To Signor Florio's daughter, to whose ears
He still prefers his suit, to my disgrace,
Thinking the way to recommend himself
Is to disparage me in his report.
But know, Grimaldi, though, may be, thou art
My equal in thy blood, yet this bewrays[5]   40
A lowness in thy mind which, wert thou noble,
Thou wouldst as much disdain as I do thee
For this unworthiness; and on this ground
I willed my servant to correct his tongue,
Holding a man so base no match for me.

Vasq. And had not[6] your sudden coming prevented
us, I had let my gentleman blood under the gills;[7] I
should have wormed[8] you, sir, for running mad.

Grim. I'll be revenged, Soranzo.   49

Vasq. On a dish of warm broth to stay your stomach
—do, honest innocence,[9] do; spoon-meat is a whole-
somer diet than a Spanish blade.

Grim. Remember this.

Sor. I fear thee not, Grimaldi.

Exit GRIMALDI.

Flo. My Lord Soranzo, this is strange to me;
Why you should storm, having my word engaged?
Owing[10] her heart, what need you doubt her ear?
Losers may talk by law[11] of any game.

Vasq. Yet the villainy of words, Signor Florio, may
be such as would make any unspleened[12] dove choleric.
Blame not my lord in this.   61

Flo. Be you more silent.
I would not for my wealth my daughter's love
Should cause the spilling of one drop of blood.

Vasques, put up,[13] let's end this fray in wine.

Exeunt [FLORIO, DONADO, SORANZO, *and*
VASQUES].

Put. How like you this, child? Here's threatening, challenging, quarreling, and fighting, on every side, and all is for your sake; you had need look to yourself, charge, you'll be stolen away sleeping else shortly.

Ann. But, tut'ress, such a life gives no content   70
To me, my thoughts are fixed on other ends;
Would you would leave me.

Put. Leave you? No marvel else.[14] Leave me no leaving, charge; this is love outright. Indeed, I blame you not, you have choice fit for the best lady in Italy.

Ann. Pray do not talk so much.

Put. Take the worst with the best; there's Grimaldi the soldier, a very well-timbered fellow. They say he is a Roman, nephew to the Duke Montferrato; they say he did good service in the wars against the Milanese,   80
but faith, charge, I do not like him, an[15] 't be for nothing but for being a soldier; not one[16] amongst twenty of your skirmishing captains but have some privy maim or other that mars their standing upright.[17] I like him the worse, he crinkles[18] so much in the hams; though he might serve if there were no more men, yet he's not the man I would choose.

Ann. Fie, how thou prat'st.

Put. As I am a very woman, I like Signor Soranzo well; he is wise, and what is more, rich; and what is   90
more than that, kind, and what is more than all this, a nobleman; such a one, were I the fair Annabella myself, I would wish and pray for. Then he is bountiful; besides, he is handsome, and by my troth, I think wholesome[19] (and that's news in a gallant of three and twenty); liberal, that I know; loving, that you know; and a man sure, else he could never ha' purchased such a good name with Hippolita, the lusty widow, in her husband's lifetime: and 'twere but for that report, sweetheart, would 'a were thine. Commend a man   100
for his qualities, but take a husband as he is a plain-sufficient, naked man; such a one is for your bed, and such a one is Signor Soranzo, my life for't.

Ann. Sure the woman took her morning's draught too soon.

Enter BERGETTO *and* POGGIO.

Put. But look, sweetheart, look what thing comes now: here's another of your ciphers to fill up the number. Oh, brave old ape in a silken coat. Observe.

Berg. Didst thou think, Poggio, that I would spoil my new clothes and leave my dinner, to fight?   110

---

4 *cot-quean:* shrew.   5 *bewrays:* betrays.
6 *had not:* Q "had."   7 *let . . . gills:* cut his throat.
8 *wormed:* operated on your tongue, as was done to
prevent worms in dogs.   9 *innocence:* fool.
10 *Owing:* Owning.   11 *by law:* legally.
12 *unspleened:* immune to anger.
13 *put up:* i.e., your sword.
14 *No . . . else:* If that were so, nothing else would be a
wonder.   15 *an:* if.   16 *not one:* Q "one."
17 *mars . . . upright:* i.e., makes them impotent.
18 *crinkles:* bends.   19 *wholesome:* healthy.

Pog. No, sir, I did not take you for so arrant a baby.

Berg. I am wiser than so; for, I hope, Poggio, thou never heardst of an elder brother that was a coxcomb. Didst, Poggio?

Pog. Never indeed, sir, as long as they had either land or money left them to inherit.

Berg. Is it possible, Poggio? Oh, monstrous! Why, I'll undertake with a handful of silver to buy a headful of wit at any time; but, sirrah, I have another purchase in hand; I shall have the wench, mine uncle says.   120
I will but wash my face, and shift [20] socks, and then have at her i' faith. Mark my pace, Poggio.

                              [*Walks.*]

Pog. Sir—[*Aside*] I have seen an ass and a mule trot the Spanish pavin [21] with a better grace, I know not how often.

                    Exeunt [BERGETTO *and* POGGIO].

Ann. This idiot haunts me, too.

Put. Ay, ay, he needs no description; the rich magnifico [22] that is below with your father, charge, Signor Donado his uncle, for that he means to make this his cousin [23] a golden calf, thinks that you will be   130
a right Israelite and fall down to him presently; but I hope I have tutored you better. They say a fool's bauble [24] is a lady's playfellow, yet you having wealth enough, you need not cast [25] upon the dearth of flesh [26] at any rate. Hang him, innocent.

              Enter GIOVANNI.

Ann. But see, Putana, see: what blessèd shape
Of some celestial creature now appears?
What man is he, that with such sad aspect
Walks careless of himself?

Put.   Where?

Ann.   Look below.

Put. Oh, 'tis your brother, sweet.

Ann.   Ha!

Put.   'Tis your
brother.   140

Ann. Sure 'tis not he; this is some woful thing
Wrapped up in grief, some shadow of a man.
Alas, he beats his breast, and wipes his eyes
Drowned all in tears; methinks I hear him sigh.
Let's down, Putana, and partake the cause;
I know my brother, in the love he bears me,
Will not deny me partage [27] in his sadness.
[*Aside*] My soul is full of heaviness and fear.

                    Exit [*with* PUTANA].

Giov. Lost, I am lost. My fates have doomed my
     death.

---

[20] *shift:* change.   [21] *pavin:* pavane, a stately dance.
[22] *magnifico:* important person.   [23] *cousin:* kinsman.
[24] *bauble:* stick, with obscene implication.
[25] *cast:* wager.
[26] *dearth of flesh:* i.e., Bergetto is slight and unmasculine.
[27] *partage:* a share.   [28] *throughly:* thoroughly.
[29] *Keep:* Let remain.
[30] *of . . . credit:* deserving payment.
[31] *Juno:* wife and sister of Jupiter.
[32] *Promethean fire:* In Greek mythology, Prometheus stole fire from heaven and gave it to men.

The more I strive, I love; the more I love,   150
The less I hope. I see my ruin certain.
What judgment or endeavors could apply
To my incurable and restless wounds
I throughly [28] have examined, but in vain.
Oh, that it were not in religion sin
To make our love a god, and worship it.
I have even wearied heaven with prayers, dried up
The spring of my continual tears, even starved
My veins with daily fasts; what wit or art
Could counsel, I have practiced; but alas,   160
I find all these but dreams and old men's tales
To fright unsteady youth; I'm still the same.
Or I must speak, or burst. 'Tis not, I know,
My lust, but 'tis my fate that leads me on.
Keep [29] fear and low faint-hearted shame with slaves;
I'll tell her that I love her, though my heart
Were rated at the price of that attempt.
Oh, me! she comes.

          Enter ANNABELLA *and* PUTANA.

Ann.   Brother.

Giov. [*Aside*]   If such a thing
As courage dwell in men, ye heavenly powers,
Now double all that virtue in my tongue.   170

Ann. Why, brother, will you not speak to me?

Giov. Yes; how d'ee, sister?

Ann. Howsoever I am, methinks you are not well.

Put. Bless us, why are you so sad, sir?

Giov. Let me entreat you, leave us a while, Putana.
     Sister,
I would be private with you.

Ann. Withdraw, Putana.

Put. I will. [*Aside*] If this were any other company
for her, I should think my absence an office of some
credit; [30] but I will leave them together.   180

                              Exit PUTANA.

Giov. Come, sister, lend your hand, let's walk
     together.
I hope you need not blush to walk with me;
Here's none but you and I.

Ann. How's this?

Giov. Faith, I mean no harm.

Ann. Harm?

Giov. No, good faith; how is't with 'ee?

Ann. [*Aside*] I trust he be not frantic.—I am very
     well, brother.

Giov. Trust me, but I am sick, I fear so sick
'Twill cost my life.   190

Ann. Mercy forbid it. 'Tis not so, I hope.

Giov. I think you love me, sister.

Ann. Yes, you know I do.

Giov. I know't indeed.—Y'are very fair.

Ann. Nay, then, I see you have a merry sickness.

Giov. That's as it proves. The poets feign, I read,
That Juno [31] for her forehead did exceed
All other goddesses; but I durst swear
Your forehead exceeds hers, as hers did theirs.

Ann. Troth, this is pretty.

Giov.   Such a pair of stars   200
As are thine eyes would, like Promethean fire, [32]

If gently glanced, give life to senseless stones.
    Ann. Fie upon 'ee.
    Giov. The lily and the rose, most sweetly strange,
Upon your dimpled cheeks do strive for change.
Such lips would tempt a saint; such hands as those
Would make an anchorite lascivious.
    Ann. D'ee mock me, or flatter me?
    Giov. If you would see a beauty more exact
Than art can counterfeit or nature frame,   210
Look in your glass and there behold your own.
    Ann. Oh, you are a trim [33] youth.
    Giov. Here.

                          Offers his dagger to her.

    Ann. What to do?
    Giov. And here's my breast, strike home.
Rip up my bosom, there thou shalt behold
A heart in which is writ the truth I speak.
Why stand 'ee?
    Ann.   Are you earnest?
    Giov.   Yes, most earnest.
You cannot love?
    Ann.   Whom?
    Giov.   Me. My tortured soul
Hath felt affliction in the heat of death.   220
O Annabella, I am quite undone.
The love of thee, my sister, and the view
Of thy immortal beauty hath untuned
All harmony both of my rest and life.
Why d'ee not strike?
    Ann.   Forbid it, my just fears.
If this be true, 'twere fitter I were dead.
    Giov. True, Annabella; 'tis no time to jest.
I have too long suppressed the hidden flames
That almost have consumed me; I have spent
Many a silent night in sighs and groans,   230
Ran over all my thoughts, despised my fate,
Reasoned against the reasons of my love,
Done all that smooth-cheeked [34] virtue could advise,
But found all bootless: [35] 'tis my destiny
That you must either love, or I must die.
    Ann. Comes this in sadness [36] from you?
    Giov.   Let some
    mischief
Befall me soon, if I dissemble aught.
    Ann. You are my brother Giovanni.
    Giov.   You
My sister Annabella; I know this,
And could afford you instance why to love   240
So much the more for this; to which intent
Wise nature first in your creation meant
To make you mine; else't had been sin and foul
To share one beauty to a double soul. [37]
Nearness in birth or blood doth but persuade
A nearer nearness in affection.
I have asked counsel of the holy church,
Who tells me I may love you, and 'tis just
That since I may, I should; and will, yes, will.
Must I now live, or die?
    Ann.   Live. Thou hast won   250
The field, and never fought; what thou hast urged
My captive heart had long ago resolved.

I blush to tell thee—but I'll tell thee now—
For every sigh that thou hast spent for me
I have sighed ten; for every tear shed twenty;
And not so much for that [38] I loved, as that
I durst not say I loved, nor scarcely think it.
    Giov. Let not this music be a dream, ye gods,
For pity's sake, I beg 'ee.
    Ann.   On my knees,

                            She kneels.

Brother, even by our mother's dust, I charge you,   260
Do not betray me to your mirth or hate,
Love me, or kill me, brother.
    Giov.   On my knees,

                            He kneels.

Sister, even by my mother's dust, I charge you,
Do not betray me to your mirth or hate,
Love me, or kill me, sister.
    Ann. You mean good sooth [39] then?
    Giov.   In good troth I
    do,
And so do you, I hope: say, I'm in earnest.
    Ann. I'll swear't, I.
    Giov.   And I, and by this kiss,

                            Kisses her.

(Once more, yet once more; now let's rise by this)

                            [They rise.]

I would not change this minute for Elysium.   270
What must we now do?
    Ann.   What you will.
    Giov.   Come then,
After so many tears as we have wept,
Let's learn to court in smiles, to kiss, and sleep.

                            Exeunt.

[I.iii]

                Enter FLORIO *and* DONADO.

    Flo. Signor Donado, you have said enough,
I understand you; but would have you know
I will not force my daughter 'gainst her will.
You see I have but two, a son and her;
And he is so devoted to his book,
As I must tell you true, I doubt [1] his health.
Should he miscarry, all my hopes rely
Upon my girl; as for worldly fortune,
I am, I thank my stars, blessed with enough.
My care is how to match her to her liking.   10
I would not have her marry wealth, but love,
And if she like your nephew, let him have her.
Here's all that I can say.
    Don.   Sir, you say well,

---

[33] *trim:* fine.   [34] *smooth-cheeked:* Q "smooth'd-cheek."
[35] *bootless:* useless.   [36] *in sadness:* seriously.
[37] *share . . . soul:* to parcel out one beauty to two souls.
[38] *for that:* because.   [39] *sooth:* truth.
I.iii.
    [1] *doubt:* am apprehensive about.

Like a true father, and for my part I,
If the young folks can like ('twixt you and me),
Will promise to assure my nephew presently
Three thousand florins yearly during life,
And, after I am dead, my whole estate.

Flo. 'Tis a fair proffer, sir; meantime your nephew
Shall have free passage to commence his suit.　　20
If he can thrive, he shall have my consent.
So for this time I'll leave you, signor.

　　　　　　　　　　　　　　　　　　Exit.

Don.　　　　　　　　Well,
Here's hope yet, if my nephew would have wit;
But he is such another dunce, I fear
He'll never win the wench. When I was young
I could have done't, i'faith, and so shall he
If he will learn of me; and in good time
He comes himself.

　　　　Enter BERGETTO *and* POGGIO.

How now, Bergetto, whither away so fast?

Berg. O uncle, I have heard the strangest news that
ever came out of the mint,[2] have I not, Poggio?　　31

Pog. Yes, indeed, sir.

Don. What news, Bergetto?

Berg. Why, look ye, uncle, my barber told me just
now that there is a fellow come to town who undertakes
to make a mill go without the mortal help of any water
or wind, only with sand bags; and this fellow hath a
strange horse, a most excellent beast, I'll assure you,
uncle (my barber says), whose head, to the wonder of
all Christian people, stands just behind where his tail is.
Is't not true, Poggio?　　41

Pog. So the barber swore, forsooth.

Don. And you are running thither?

Berg. Ay, forsooth, uncle.

Don. Wilt thou be a fool still?[3] Come, sir, you shall
not go: you have more mind of a puppet-play than on
the business I told ye; why, thou great baby, wilt never
have wit, wilt make thyself a may-game[4] to all the
world?

Pog. Answer for yourself, master.　　50

Berg. Why, uncle, should I sit at home still, and not
go abroad to see fashions like other gallants?

Don. To see hobbyhorses! What wise talk, I pray,
had you with Annabella, when you were at Signor
Florio's house?

Berg. Oh, the wench! Uds sa' me,[5] uncle, I tickled
her with a rare speech, that I made her almost burst
her belly with laughing.

Don. Nay, I think so; and what speech was't?

Berg. What did I say, Poggio?　　60

Pog. Forsooth, my master said that he loved her
almost as well as he loved parmasent,[6] and swore (I'll

be sworn for him) that she wanted but such a nose as
his was to be as pretty a young woman as any was in
Parma.

Don. Oh, gross.

Berg. Nay, uncle, then she asked me whether my
father had any more children than myself: and I said
"No, 'twere better he should have had his brains
knocked our first."　　70

Don. This is intolerable.

Berg. Then said she "Will Signor Donado your
uncle leave you all his wealth?"

Don. Ha! that was good; did she harp upon that
string?

Berg. Did she harp upon that string? Ay, that she
did. I answered "Leave me all his wealth? Why, woman, he hath no other wit; if he had, he should hear
on't to his everlasting glory and confusion: I know,"
quoth I, "I am his white boy,[7] and will not be　　80
gulled"; and with that she fell into a great smile and
went away. Nay, I did fit[8] her.

Don. Ah, sirrah, then I see there is no changing of
nature. Well, Bergetto, I fear thou wilt be a very ass
still.

Berg. I should be sorry for that, uncle.

Don. Come, come you home with me. Since you are
no better a speaker, I'll have you write to her after some
courtly manner, and enclose some rich jewel in the
letter.　　90

Berg. Ay, marry, that will be excellent.

Don. Peace, innocent.
Once in my time I'll set my wits to school,
If all fail, 'tis but the fortune of a fool.

Berg. Poggio, 'twill do, Poggio.

　　　　　　　　　　　　　　　　　　Exeunt.

ACT TWO

SCENE ONE

Enter GIOVANNI *and* ANNABELLA, *as from
their chamber.*

Giov. Come, Annabella: no more sister now,
But love, a name more gracious; do not blush,
Beauty's sweet wonder, but be proud to know
That yielding thou hast conquered, and inflamed
A heart whose tribute is thy brother's life.

Ann. And mine is his. Oh, how these stol'n contents
Would print a modest crimson on my cheeks,
Had any but my heart's delight prevailed.

Giov. I marvel why the chaster of your sex
Should think this pretty toy called maidenhead　　10
So strange a loss, when, being lost, 'tis nothing,
And you are still the same.

Ann.　　　　　　　　'Tis well for you;
Now you can talk.

Giov.　　　　　　　Music as well consists
In th'ear as in the playing.

Ann.　　　　　　　　Oh, y'are wanton.
Tell on't, y'are best; do.

Giov.　　　　　　　Thou wilt chide me then.
Kiss me:—so. Thus hung Jove on Leda's neck,[1]

---

[2] *came . . . mint:* was minted.　　　[3] *still:* always.
[4] *may-game:* laughingstock.
[5] *Uds sa' me:* God save me.
[6] *parmasent:* parmesan cheese.
[7] *white boy:* favorite.　　　[8] *fit:* answer appropriately.

II.i.
[1] *hung . . . neck:* Jupiter transformed himself into a swan
to rape the wife of Tyndareus.

And sucked divine ambrosia from her lips.
I envy not the mightiest man alive,
But hold myself, in being king of thee,
More great than were I king of all the world.   20
But I shall lose you, sweetheart.
    Ann.   But you shall not.
    Giov. You must be married, mistress.
    Ann.   Yes? To
    whom?
    Giov. Someone must have you.
    Ann.   You must.
    Giov.   Nay, some
    other.
    Ann. Now, prithee, do not speak so; without jesting,
You'll make me weep in earnest.
    Giov.   What, you will not?
But tell me, sweet, canst thou be dared to swear
That thou wilt live to me, and to no other?
    Ann. By both our loves I dare, for didst thou know,
My Giovanni, how all suitors seem
To my eyes hateful, thou wouldst trust me then.   30
    Giov. Enough, I take thy word. Sweet, we must part.
Remember what thou vowst; keep well my heart.
    Ann. Will you be gone?
    Giov.   I must.
    Ann.   When to return?
    Giov. Soon.
    Ann.   Look you do.
    Giov.   Farewell.
                                    Exit.
    Ann. Go where thou wilt, in mind I'll keep thee here,
And where thou art, I know I shall be there.
Guardian!

                Enter PUTANA.

    Put. Child, how is't, child? Well, thank heaven, ha?
    Ann. O guardian, what a paradise of joy
Have I passed over!   40
    Put. Nay, what a paradise of joy have you passed
under! why, now I commend thee, charge; fear
nothing, sweetheart; what though he be your brother?
Your brother's a man, I hope, and I say still, if a young
wench feel the fit upon her, let her take anybody,
father or brother, all is one.
    Ann. I would not have it known for all the world.
    Put. Nor I, indeed, for the speech of the people; else
'twere nothing.
    Flo. [*Within*] Daughter Annabella.   50
    Ann. Oh, me, my father!—here, sir!—Reach[2] my
    work.
    Flo. [*Within*] What are you doing?
    Ann.   So: let him come now.

    Enter FLORIO, RICHARDETTO *like a doctor of*
    physic, and PHILOTIS *with a lute in her hand.*

    Flo. So hard at work? That's well; you lose no time.
Look, I have brought you company. Here's one,
A learned doctor lately come from Padua,[3]
Much skilled in physic, and for that I see
You have of late been sickly, I entreated
This reverend man to visit you some time.

    Ann. Y'are very welcome, sir.
    Rich.   I thank you, mistress.
Loud fame in large report hath spoke your praise   60
As well for virtue as perfection;
For which I have been bold to bring with me
A kinswoman of mine, a maid, for song
And music one perhaps will give content;
Please you to know her.
    Ann.   They are parts[4] I love,
And she for them most welcome.
    Phil.   Thank you, lady.
    Flo. Sir, now you know my house, pray make not
    strange,[5]
And if you find my daughter need your art,
I'll be your paymaster.
    Rich.   Sir, what I am
She shall command.
    Flo.   You shall bind me to you.   70
Daughter, I must have conference with you
About some matters that concerns us both.
Good Master Doctor, please you but walk in,
We'll crave a little of your cousin's cunning.[6]
I think my girl hath not quite forgot
To touch an instrument; she could have done't.
We'll hear them both
    Rich.   I'll wait upon you, sir.
                                    Exeunt.

[II.ii]

    Enter SORANZO *in his study reading a book.*

    Sor. "Love's measure is extreme, the comfort, pain,
The life unrest, and the reward disdain."
What's here? Look't o'er again. 'Tis so, so writes
This smooth licentious poet in his rhymes.
But, Sannazar,[1] thou liest, for had thy bosom
Felt such oppression as is laid on mine,
Thou wouldst have kissed the rod that made thee
    smart.
To work then, happy muse, and contradict
What Sannazar hath in his envy writ.
"Love's measure is the mean, sweet his annoys,   10
His pleasure's life, and his reward all joys."
Had Annabella lived when Sannazar
Did in his brief encomium[2] celebrate
Venice, that queen of cities, he had left
That verse which gained him such a sum of gold,
And for one only look from Annabel
Had writ of her and her diviner cheeks.
Oh, how my thoughts are—
    Vasq. [*Within*] Pray forbear; in rules of civility, let

---

    [2] *Reach:* Hand me.
    [3] *Padua:* site of famous medical school.
    [4] *parts:* abilities.
    [5] *make . . . strange:* do not stand on ceremony.
    [6] *cunning:* skill.

II.ii.
    [1] *Sannazar:* Iacopo Sannazaro (?), 1456–1530, Italian pastoral poet.
    [2] *encomium:* Latin poem about Venice, which rewarded the poet for it.

me give notice on't: I shall be taxed of[3] my neglect of
duty and service.   21

Sor. What rude intrusion interrupts my peace?
Can I be nowhere private?

Vasq. [*Within*] Troth, you wrong your modesty.

Sor. What's the matter, Vasques? Who is't?

Enter HIPPOLITA *and* VASQUES.

Hip.   'Tis I.
Do you know me now? Look, perjured man, on her
Whom thou and thy distracted lust have wronged.
Thy sensual rage of blood hath made my youth
A scorn to men and angels, and shall I
Be now a foil[4] to thy unsated change?   30
Thou knowst, false wanton, when my modest fame
Stood free from stain or scandal, all the charms
Of hell or sorcery could not prevail
Against the honor of my chaster bosom.
Thine eyes did plead in tears, thy tongue in oaths
Such and so many, that a heart of steel
Would have been wrought to pity, as was mine;
And shall the conquest of my lawful bed,
My husband's death urged on by his disgrace,
My loss of womanhood, be ill rewarded   40
With hatred and contempt? No; know, Soranzo,
I have a spirit doth as much distaste
The slavery of fearing thee as thou
Dost loathe the memory of what hath passed.

Sor. Nay, dear Hippolita—

Hip.   Call me not dear,
Nor think with supple words to smooth the grossness
Of my abuses; 'tis not your new mistress,
Your goodly Madam Merchant, shall triumph
On my dejection; tell her thus from me,
My birth was nobler and by much more free.   50

Sor. You are too violent.

Hip.   You are too double
In your dissimulation. Seest thou this,
This habit, these black mourning weeds of care?
'Tis thou art cause of this, and hast divorced
My husband from his life and me from him,
And made me widow in my widowhood.

Sor. Will you yet hear?

Hip.   More of thy perjuries?
Thy soul is drowned too deeply in those sins;
Thou need'st not add to th' number.

Sor.   Then I'll leave you;
You are past all rules of sense.

Hip.   And thou of grace.   60

Vasq. Fie, mistress, you are not near the limits of
reason; if my lord had a resolution as noble as virtue
itself, you take the course to unedge[5] it all. Sir, I
beseech you, do not perplex[6] her; griefs, alas, will have
a vent. I dare undertake Madam Hippolita will now
freely hear you.

Sor. Talk to a woman frantic! are these the fruits of
your love?

Hip. They are the fruits of thy untruth, false man.
Didst thou not swear, whilst yet my husband lived,   70
That thou wouldst wish no happiness on earth
More than to call me wife? Didst thou not vow,
When he should die, to marry me? For which
The devil in my blood and thy protests
Caused me to counsel him to undertake
A voyage to Ligorn,[7] for that we heard
His brother there was dead, and left a daughter
Young and unfriended, who, with much ado,
I wished him to bring hither: he did so,
And went; and as thou know'st died on the way.   80
Unhappy man, to buy his death so dear
With my advice. Yet thou for whom I did it
Forget'st thy vows, and leav'st me to my shame.

Sor. Who could help this?

Hip.   Who? Perjured man, thou
      couldst,
If thou hadst faith or love.

Sor.   You are deceived.
The vows I made, if you remember well,
Were wicked and unlawful; 'twere more sin
To keep them than to break them. As for me,
I cannot mask my penitence. Think thou
How much thou hast digressed from honest shame   90
In bringing of a gentleman to death
Who was thy husband; such a one as he,
So noble in his quality, condition,
Learning, behavior, entertainment, love,
As Parma could not show a braver man.

Vasq. You do not well; this was not your promise.

Sor. I care not; let her know her monstrous life.
Ere I'll be servile to so black a sin,
I'll be accursed.[8] Woman, come here no more.
Learn to repent and die, for by my honor   100
I hate thee and thy lust; you have been too foul.
                                           [*Exit.*]

Vasq. [*Aside*] This part has been scurvily played.[9]

Hip. How foolishly this beast contemns his fate,
And shuns the use of that which I more scorn
Than I once loved, his love. But let him go;
My vengeance shall give comfort to this woe.

                               She offers to go away.

Vasq. Mistress, mistress, Madam Hippolita, pray, a
word or two.

Hip. With me, sir?

Vasq. With you, if you please.   110

Hip. What is't?

Vasq. I know you are infinitely moved now, and you
think you have cause; some I confess you have, but sure
not so much as you imagine.

Hip. Indeed.

Vasq. Oh, you were miserably bitter, which you
followed even to the last syllable. Faith, you were somewhat too shrewd;[10] by my life you could not have took
my lord in a worse time, since I first knew him;
tomorrow you shall find him a new man.   120

Hip. Well, I shall wait his leisure.

---

   [3] *taxed of:* rebuked for.   [4] *foil:* background.
   [5] *unedge:* dull.   [6] *perplex:* torment.
   [7] *Ligorn:* Leghorn (Livorno).
   [8] *accursed:* Q "a Curse."
   [9] *scurvily played:* badly acted.
  [10] *shrewd:* outspoken.

Vasq. Fie, this is not a hearty patience, it comes sourly from you; troth, let me persuade you for once.

Hip. [*Aside*] I have it, and it shall be so; thanks, opportunity!—Persuade me to what?

Vasq. Visit him in some milder temper. Oh, if you could but master a little your female spleen, how might you win him.

Hip. He will never love me. Vasques, thou hast been a too trusty servant to such a master, and I believe thy reward in the end will fall out like mine.   131

Vasq. So, perhaps, too.

Hip. Resolve thyself it will. Had I one so true, so truly honest, so secret to my counsels, as thou hast been to him and his, I should think it a slight acquittance,[11] not only to make him master of all I have, but even of myself.

Vasq. Oh, you are a noble gentlewoman.

Hip. Wilt thou feed always upon hopes? Well, I know thou art wise, and seest the reward of an old servant daily, what it is.   141

Vasq. Beggary and neglect.

Hip. True. But, Vasques, wert thou mine, and wouldst be private to me and my designs, I here protest myself and all what I can else call mine should be at thy dispose.

Vasq. [*Aside*] Work you that way, old mole? Then I have the wind[12] of you.—I were not worthy of it by any desert that could lie within my compass; if I could—

Hip. What then?   150

Vasq. I should then hope to live in these my old years with rest and security.

Hip. Give me thy hand: now promise but thy silence, And help to bring to pass a plot I have, And here in sight of heaven, that being done, I make thee lord of me and mine estate.

Vasq. Come, you are merry; this is such a happiness that I can neither think or believe.

Hip. Promise thy secrecy, and 'tis confirmed.   159

Vasq. Then here I call our good genii for witnesses, whatsoever your designs are, or against whomsoever, I will not only be a special actor therein, but never disclose it till it be effected.

Hip. I take thy word, and with that, thee for mine; Come, then, let's more confer of this anon. On this delicious bane my thoughts shall banquet. Revenge shall sweeten what my griefs have tasted.

Exeunt.

[II.iii]

Enter RICHARDETTO *and* PHILOTIS.

Rich. Thou seest, my lovely niece, these strange mishaps, How all my fortunes turn to my disgrace, Wherein I am but as a looker-on, Whiles others act my shame, and I am silent.

Phil. But, uncle, wherein can this borrowed shape[1] Give you content?

Rich.   I'll tell thee, gentle niece: Thy wanton aunt in her lascivious riots Lives now secure, thinks I am surely dead

In my late journey to Ligorn for you, As I have caused it to be rumored out.   10 Now would I see with what an impudence She gives scope to her loose adultery, And how the common voice allows hereof.[2] Thus far I have prevailed.

Phil.   Alas, I fear You mean some strange revenge.

Rich.   Oh, be not troubled; Your ignorance shall plead for you in all.[3] But to our business: what, you learned for certain How Signor Florio means to give his daughter In marriage to Soranzo?

Phil.   Yes, for certain.

Rich. But how find you young Annabella's love   20 Inclined to him?

Phil.   For aught I could perceive, She neither fancies him or any else.

Rich. There's mystery in that which time must show. She used you kindly?

Phil.   Yes.

Rich.   And craved your company?

Phil. Often.

Rich.   'Tis well; it goes as I could wish. I am the doctor now, and as for you, None knows you; if all fail not, we shall thrive. But who comes here?

Enter GRIMALDI.

       I know him: 'tis Grimaldi, A Roman and a soldier, near allied Unto the Duke of Montferrato, one   30 Attending on the nuncio of the Pope That now resides in Parma, by which means He hopes to get the love of Annabella.

Grim. Save you, sir.

Rich.   And you, sir.

Grim.   I have heard Of your approvèd[4] skill, which through the city Is freely talked of, and would crave your aid.

Rich. For what, sir?

Grim.   Marry, sir, for this— But I would speak in private.

Rich.   Leave us, cousin.

Exit PHILOTIS.

Grim. I love fair Annabella, and would know Whether in art there may not be receipts[5]   40 To move affection.

Rich.   Sir, perhaps there may, But these will nothing profit you.

Grim.   Not me?

Rich. Unless I be mistook, you are a man Greatly in favor with the Cardinal.

---

[11] *acquittance:* discharge of debt.
[12] *have the wind:* smell your intention.

II.iii.
   [1] *borrowed shape:* disguise.
   [2] *how . . . hereof:* what is being said about it.
   [3] *ignorance . . . all:* you'll be exonerated because you know nothing.   [4] *approvèd:* proven.
   [5] *receipts:* recipes (for potions).

Grim. What of that?

Rich.   In duty to his grace,
I will be bold to tell you, if you seek
To marry Florio's daughter, you must first
Remove a bar 'twixt you and her.

Grim.   Who's that?

Rich. Soranzo is the man that hath her heart;
And while he lives, be sure you cannot speed.[6]   50

Grim. Soranzo! what, mine enemy! is't he?

Rich. Is he your enemy?

Grim.   The man I hate
Worse than confusion;
I'll kill him straight.

Rich.   Nay, then, take mine advice,
Even for his grace's sake, the Cardinal.
I'll find a time when he and she do meet,
Of which I'll give you notice, and, to be sure
He shall not 'scape you, I'll provide a poison
To dip your rapier's point in; if he had
As many heads as Hydra[7] had, he dies.   60

Grim. But shall I trust thee, doctor?

Rich.   As yourself;
Doubt not in aught. [*Aside*] Thus shall the fates decree:
By me Soranzo falls, that ruined me.

                                            Exeunt.

[II.iv]

Enter DONADO, BERGETTO, *and* POGGIO.

Don. Well, sir, I must be content to be both your
secretary and your messenger myself. I cannot tell what
this letter may work, but as sure as I am alive, if thou
come once to talk with her, I fear thou wilt mar whatsoever I make.

Berg. You make, uncle? Why, am not I big enough
to carry mine own letter, I pray?

Don. Ay, ay, carry a fool's head o' thy own. Why, thou
dunce, wouldst thou write a letter and carry it thyself?

Berg. Yes, that I would, and read it to her with   10
my own mouth; for you must think, if she will not
believe me myself when she hears me speak, she will
not believe another's handwriting. Oh, you think I am
a blockhead, uncle. No, sir, Poggio knows I have indited
a letter myself, so I have.

Pog. Yes, truly, sir; I have it in my pocket.

Don. A sweet one, no doubt; pray let's see't.

Berg. I cannot read my own hand very well, Poggio;
read it, Poggio.

Don. Begin.   20

Pog. [*Reads*] "Most dainty and honey-sweet mistress, I could call you fair, and lie as fast as any that
loves you, but my uncle being the elder man, I leave it
to him, as more fit for his age and the color of his

---

beard. I am wise enough to tell you I can bourd[1] where
I see occasion; or if you like my uncle's wit better than
mine, you shall marry me; if you like mine better than
his, I will marry you in spite of your teeth. So commending my best parts to you, I rest—Yours upwards
and downwards, or you may choose, Bergetto."   30

Berg. Aha, here's stuff, uncle.

Don. Here's stuff indeed to shame us all. Pray whose
advice did you take in this learned letter?

Pog. None, upon my word, but mine own.

Berg. And mine, uncle, believe it, nobody's else;
'twas mine own brain, I thank a good wit for't.

Don. Get you home, sir, and look you keep within
doors till I return.

Berg. How! that were a jest indeed; I scorn it, i'faith.

Don. What! you do not?   40

Berg. Judge me, but I do now.

Pog. Indeed, sir, 'tis very unhealthy.

Don. Well, sir, if I hear any of your apish running to
motions[2] and fopperies, till I come back, you were as
good not:[3] look to't.

                                    Exit DONADO.

Berg. Poggio, shall's steal to see this horse with the
head in's tail?

Pog. Ay, but you must take heed of whipping.

Berg. Dost take me for a child, Poggio? Come,
honest Poggio.   50

                                            Exeunt.

[II.v]

Enter Friar [BONAVENTURA] *and* GIOVANNI.

Fri. Peace. Thou hast told a tale, whose every word
Threatens eternal slaughter to the soul.
I'm sorry I have heard it; would mine ears
Had been one minute deaf, before the hour
That thou cam'st to me. O young man castaway,
By the religious number[1] of mine order,
I day and night have waked my aged eyes,
Above my strength, to weep on thy behalf:
But heaven is angry, and be thou resolved,
Thou art a man remarked[2] to taste a mischief.[3]   10
Look for't; though it come late, it will come sure.

Giov. Father, in this you are uncharitable;
What I have done I'll prove both fit and good.
It is a principle, which you have taught
When I was yet your scholar, that the frame[4]
And composition of the mind doth follow
The frame and composition of the body;
So where the body's furniture is beauty,
The mind's must needs be virtue; which allowed,
Virtue itself is reason but refined,   20
And love the quintessence of that. This proves
My sister's beauty being rarely fair
Is rarely virtuous; chiefly in her love,
And chiefly in that love, her love to me.
If hers to me, then so is mine to her;
Since in like causes are effects alike.

Fri. Oh, ignorance in knowledge. Long ago,
How often have I warned thee this before?
Indeed, if we were sure there were no deity,

Nor heaven nor hell, then to be led alone   30
By nature's light, as were philosophers
Of elder times, might instance some defense.
But 'tis not so; then, madman, thou wilt find
That nature is in heaven's positions [5] blind.
   Giov. Your age o'errules you; had you youth like
     mine,
You'd make her love your heaven, and her divine.
   Fri. Nay then, I see th'art too far sold to hell;
It lies not in the compass of my prayers
To call thee back. Yet let me counsel thee:
Persuade thy sister to some marriage.   40
   Giov. Marriage? Why, that's to damn her. That's to
     prove
Her greedy of variety of lust.
   Fri. Oh, fearful! if thou wilt not, give me leave
To shrive her, lest she should die unabsolved.
   Giov. At your best leisure, father; then she'll tell you
How dearly she doth prize my matchless love.
Then you will know what pity 'twere we two
Should have been sundered from each other's arms.
View well her face, and in that little round
You may observe a world of variety: 50
For color, lips; for sweet perfumes, her breath;
For jewels, eyes; for threads of purest gold,
Hair; for delicious choice of flowers, cheeks;
Wonder in every portion of that throne.
Hear her but speak, and you will swear the spheres
Make music to the citizens in heaven.[6]
But, father, what is else for pleasure framed,
Lest I offend your ears, shall go unnamed.
   Fri. The more I hear, I pity thee the more,
That one so excellent should give those parts   60
All to a second death;[7] what I can do
Is but to pray: and yet I could advise thee,
Wouldst thou be ruled.
   Giov.   In what?
   Fri.   Why, leave her yet;
The throne of mercy is above your trespass;
Yet time is left you both—
   Giov.   To embrace each other,
Else let all time be struck quite out of number.
She is like me, and I like her, resolved.
   Fri. No more! I'll visit her. This grieves me most:
Things being thus, a pair of souls are lost.
                             Exeunt.

[II.vi]

   Enter FLORIO, DONADO, ANNABELLA, PUTANA.

   Flo. Where's Giovanni?
   Ann.   Newly walked abroad,
And, as I heard him say, gone to the friar,
His reverend tutor.
   Flo.   That's a blessed man,
A man made up of holiness; I hope
He'll teach him how to gain another world.
   Don. Fair gentlewoman, here's a letter sent
To you from my young cousin; I dare swear
He loves you in his soul; would you could hear
Sometimes what I see daily, sighs and tears,
As if his breast were prison to his heart.   10

   Flo. Receive it, Annabella.
   Ann. Alas, good man.
   Don. What's that she said?
   Put. An't[1] please you, sir, she said, "Alas, good
man." Truly I do commend him to her every night
before her first sleep, because I would have her dream
of him, and she hearkens to that most religiously.
   Don. Say'st so? God-a-mercy, Putana, there's something for thee, and prithee do what thou canst on his
behalf; sha' not be lost labor, take my word for't.   20

                           [*Gives money.*]

   Put. Thank you most heartily, sir; now I have a
feeling of your mind, let me alone to work.
   Ann. Guardian.
   Put. Did you call?
   Ann. Keep this letter.
   Don. Signor Florio, in any case bid her read it
instantly.
   Flo. Keep it for what? Pray read it me hereright.[2]
   Ann. I shall, sir.
                              She reads.
   Don. How d'ee find her inclined, signor?   30
   Flo. Troth, sir, I know not how; not all so well
As I could wish.
   Ann. Sir, I am bound to rest your cousin's debtor.
The jewel I'll return; for if he love,
I'll count that love a jewel.
   Don.   Mark you that?
Nay, keep them both, sweet maid.
   Ann.   You must excuse me,
Indeed, I will not keep it.
   Flo.   Where's the ring,
That which your mother in her will bequeathed,
And charged you on her blessing not to give't
To any but your husband? Send back that.   40
   Ann. I have it not.
   Flo.   Ha, have it not! Where is't?
   Ann. My brother in the morning took it from me,
Said he would wear't today.
   Flo.   Well, what do you say
To young Bergetto's love? Are you content
To match with him? Speak.
   Don.   There's the point, indeed.
   Ann. [*Aside*] What shall I do? I must say something
     now.
   Flo. What say? Why d'ee not speak?
   Ann.   Sir, with your
     leave,
Please you to give me freedom?
   Flo.   Yes, you have it.[3]
   Ann. Signor Donado, if your nephew mean
To raise his better fortunes in his match,   50
The hope of me will hinder such a hope.

---

   [5] *positions:* doctrines.
   [6] *spheres . . . heaven:* The music made by the heavenly
spheres in their motion was an ancient belief.
   [7] *second death:* damnation.
II.vi.
   [1] *An't:* If it.   [2] *hereright:* immediately.
   [3] *have it:* Q "have."

Sir, if you love him, as I know you do,
Find one more worthy of his choice than me.
In short, I'm sure I sha' not be his wife.

Don. Why, here's plain dealing; I commend thee
for't,
And all the worst I wish thee is, heaven bless thee.
Your father yet and I will still be friends,
Shall we not, Signor Florio?

Flo.   Yes, why not?
Look, here your cousin comes.   59

     Enter BERGETTO *and* POGGIO.

Don. [*Aside*] Oh, coxcomb, what doth he make here?

Berg. Where's my uncle, sirs?

Don. What's the news now?

Berg. Save you, uncle, save you. You must not think
I come for nothing, masters; and how, and how is't?
What, you have read my letter? Ah, there I—tickled
you, i'faith.

Pog. But 'twere better you had tickled her in another
place.

Berg. Sirrah Sweetheart, I'll tell thee a good jest;
and riddle what 'tis.   70

Ann. You say you'd tell me.

Berg. As I was walking just now in the street, I met
a swaggering fellow would needs take the wall of me,[4]
and because he did thrust me, I very valiantly called
him rogue. He hereupon bade me draw; I told him I
had more wit than so, but when he saw that I would
not, he did so maul me with the hilts of his rapier that
my head sung whilst my feet capered in the kennel.[5]

Don. [*Aside*] Was ever the like ass seen?

Ann. And what did you all this while?   80

Berg. Laugh at him for a gull, till I see the blood run
about mine ears, and then I could not choose but find in
my heart to cry; till a fellow with a broad beard—they
say he is a new-come doctor—called me into his house,
and gave me a plaster—look you, here 'tis—and, sir,
there was a young wench washed my face and hands
most excellently, i'faith, I shall love her as long as I live
for't, did she not, Poggio?

Pog. Yes, and kissed him too.   89

Berg. Why, la now, you think I tell a lie, uncle, I
warrant.

Don. Would he that beat thy blood out of thy head
had beaten some wit into it; for I fear thou never wilt
have any.

Berg. Oh, uncle, but there was a wench would have
done a man's heart good to have looked on her—by this
light she had a face methinks worthy twenty of you,
Mistress Annabella.

Don. Was ever such a fool born?

Ann. I am glad she liked[6] you, sir.   100

Berg. Are you so? By my troth, I thank you, forsooth.

---

    [4] *take . . . me:* push me to the dirtier side of the street.
    [5] *kennel:* gutter.   [6] *liked:* pleased.
    [7] *dry:* without bloodshed.   [8] *recourse:* passage.
    [9] *'gainst:* in preparation for.   [10] *only:* supremely.
III.i.
    [1] *sconce:* head.

Flo. Sure 'twas the doctor's niece, that was last day
with us here.

Berg. 'Twas she, 'twas she.

Don. How do you know that, simplicity?

Berg. Why, does not he say so? If I should have said
no, I should have given him the lie, uncle, and so have
deserved a dry[7] beating again; I'll none of that.

Flo. A very modest well-behaved young maid   110
As I have seen.

Don.   Is she indeed?

Flo.   Indeed
She is, if I have any judgment.

Don. Well, sir, now you are free, you need not care
for sending letters; now you are dismissed, your mistress here will none of you.

Berg. No. Why, what care I for that? I can have
wenches enough in Parma for half-a-crown apiece,
cannot I, Poggio?

Pog. I'll warrant you, sir.

Don. Signor Florio,   120
I thank you for your free recourse[8] you gave
For my admittance; and to you, fair maid,
That jewel I will give you 'gainst[9] your marriage.
Come, will you go, sir?

Berg. Ay, marry, will I. Mistress, farewell, mistress. I'll come again tomorrow. Farewell, mistress.

    Exit DONADO, BERGETTO, *and* POGGIO.

     Enter GIOVANNI.

Flo. Son, where have you been? What, alone, alone
still?
I would not have it so, you must forsake
This over-bookish humor. Well, your sister
Hath shook the fool off.

Giov.   'Twas no match for her.   130

Flo. 'Twas not indeed, I meant it nothing less:
Soranzo is the man I only[10] like—
Look on him, Annabella. Come, 'tis supper-time,
And it grows late.

               Exit FLORIO.

Giov. Whose jewel's that?

Ann.   Some sweetheart's.

Giov.   So I
think.

Ann. A lusty youth,
Signor Donado, gave it me to wear
Against my marriage.

Giov.   But you shall not wear it.
Send it him back again.

Ann.   What, you are jealous?   139

Giov. That you shall know anon, at better leisure.
Welcome, sweet night. The evening crowns the day.

                  Exeunt.

ACT THREE

SCENE ONE

     Enter BERGETTO *and* POGGIO.

Berg. Does my uncle think to make me a baby still?
No, Poggio, he shall know I have a sconce[1] now.

Pog. Ay, let him not bob[2] you off like an ape with an apple.

Berg. 'Sfoot, I will have the wench if he were ten uncles, in despite of his nose, Poggio.

Pog. Hold him to the grindstone and give not a jot of ground. She hath in a manner promised you already.

Berg. True, Poggio, and her uncle the doctor swore I should marry her.   10

Pog. He swore, I remember.

Berg. And I will have her, that's more. Didst see the codpiece-point[3] she gave me and the box of marmalade?

Pog. Very well; and kissed you, that my chops watered at the sight on't. There's no way but to clap up a marriage in hugger-mugger.[4]

Berg. I will do't; for I tell thee, Poggio, I begin to grow valiant, methinks, and my courage begins to rise.

Pog. Should you be afraid of your uncle?   19

Berg. Hang him, old doting rascal. No, I say I will have her.

Pog. Lose no time then.

Berg. I will beget a race of wise men and constables, that shall cart[5] whores at their own charges, and break the duke's peace ere I have done myself.—Come away.

                                                      Exeunt.

[III.ii]

Enter FLORIO, GIOVANNI, SORANZO,
ANNABELLA, PUTANA, *and* VASQUES.

Flo. My Lord Soranzo, though I must confess
The proffers that are made me have been great
In marriage of my daughter, yet the hope
Of your still rising honors have prevailed
Above all other jointures. Here she is;
She knows my mind; speak for yourself to her;
And hear you, daughter, see you use him nobly;
For any private speech I'll give you time.
Come, son, and you the rest, let them alone;
Agree they[1] as they may.

Sor.   I thank you, sir.   10

Giov.[*Aside*] Sister, be not all woman, think on me.

Sor. Vasques.

Vasq. My lord?

Sor. Attend me without.

                    Exeunt omnes, manet SORANZO *and*
                                        ANNABELLA.

Ann. Sir, what's your will with me?

Sor.   Do you not know
What I should tell you?

Ann.   Yes, you'll say you love me.

Sor. And I'll swear it too; will you believe it?

Ann. 'Tis no point of faith.[2]

Enter GIOVANNI *above.*

Sor.   Have you not will to
    love?

Ann. Not you.

Sor.   Whom then?

Ann.   That's as the fates infer.[3]

Giov.[*Aside*] Of those I'm regent now.

Sor.   What mean
    you, sweet?   20

Ann. To live and die a maid.

Sor.   Oh, that's unfit.

Giov.[*Aside*] Here's one can say that's but a woman's
    note.

Sor. Did you but see my heart, then would you
    swear—

Ann. That you were dead.

Giov.[*Aside*]   That's true, or somewhat
    near it.

Sor. See you these true love's tears?

Ann.   No.

Giov.[*Aside*]   Now she
    winks.

Sor. They plead to you for grace.

Ann.   Yet nothing speak.

Sor. Oh, grant my suit.

Ann.   What is't?

Sor.   To let me live—

Ann. Take it.

Sor.   —Still yours.

Ann.   That is not mine to give.

Giov.[*Aside*] One such another word would kill his
    hopes.

Sor. Mistress, to leave those fruitless strifes of wit,
Know I have loved you long and loved you truly;   31
Not hope of what you have, but what you are,
Have drawn me on; then let me not in vain
Still feel the rigor of your chaste disdain.
I'm sick, and sick to th' heart.

Ann.   Help, aqua vitae.[4]

Sor. What mean you?

Ann.   Why, I thought you had been
    sick.

Sor. Do you mock my love?

Giov.[*Aside*]   There, sir, she was too
    nimble.

Sor.[*Aside*] 'Tis plain, she laughs at me.—These
    scornful taunts
Neither become your modesty or years.

Ann. You are no looking glass; or if you were,   40
I'd dress my language by you.

Giov.[*Aside*]   I'm confirmed.

Ann. To put you out of doubt, my lord, methinks
Your common sense should make you understand
That if I loved you, or desired your love,
Some way I should have given you better taste;[5]
But since you are a nobleman, and one
I would not wish should spend his youth in hopes,
Let me advise you here to forbear your suit,
And think I wish you well, I tell you this.

Sor. Is't you speak this?

Ann.   Yes, I myself; yet know—

---

² *bob:* fob.   ³ *point:* lace.
⁴ *hugger-mugger:* secret.
⁵ *cart:* Whores were punished by public exposure in carts.

III.ii.
¹ *Agree they:* Q "Agree."
² *point . . . faith:* part of the creed.
³ *infer:* bring about.   ⁴ *aqua vitae:* alcoholic spirits.
⁵ *taste:* pleasure.

Thus far I give you comfort—if mine eyes   51
Could have picked out a man, amongst all those
That sued to me, to make a husband of,
You should have been that man. Let this suffice;
Be noble in your secrecy and wise.
  Giov. [*Aside*] Why, now I see she loves me.
  Ann.   One word
    more:
As ever virtue lived within your mind,
As ever noble courses were your guide,
As ever you would have me know you loved me,
Let not my father know hereof by you;   60
If I hereafter find that I must marry,
It shall be you or none.
  Sor.   I take that promise.
  Ann. Oh, oh, my head.
  Sor. What's the matter? Not well?
  Ann. Oh, I begin to sicken.
  Giov. [*Aside*] Heaven forbid.

Exit from above.

  Sor. Help, help within there, ho!

Enter FLORIO, GIOVANNI, PUTANA.

Look to your daughter, Signor Florio.
  Flo. Hold her up, she swoons.
  Giov. Sister, how d'ee?   70
  Ann. Sick—brother, are you there?
  Flo. Convey her to her bed instantly, whilst I send
for a physician; quickly, I say.
  Put. Alas, poor child.

Exeunt, manet SORANZO.

Enter VASQUES.

  Vasq. My lord.
  Sor. O Vasques, now I doubly am undone
Both in my present and my future hopes.
She plainly told me that she could not love,
And thereupon soon sickened, and I fear
Her life's in danger.   80
  Vasq. [*Aside*] By'r lady, sir, and so is yours, if you
knew all.—'Las, sir, I am sorry for that; may be 'tis but
the maid's-sickness,[6] an over-flux[7] of youth, and then,
sir, there is no such present remedy as present[8]
marriage. But hath she given you an absolute denial?
  Sor. She hath and she hath not; I'm full of grief,
But what she said I'll tell thee as we go.

Exeunt.

[III.iii]

Enter GIOVANNI *and* PUTANA.

  Put. Oh, sir, we are all undone, quite undone, utterly
undone, and shamed forever; your sister, oh, your
sister.

  Giov. What of her? For heaven's sake, speak; how
does she?
  Put. Oh, that ever I was born to see this day.
  Giov. She is not dead, ha? Is she?
  Put. Dead? No, she is quick;[1] 'tis worse, she is with
child. You know what you have done; heaven forgive
'ee. 'Tis too late to repent now, heaven help us.   10
  Giov. With child? How dost thou know't?
  Put. How do I know't? Am I at these years ignorant
what the meanings of qualms and water-pangs be? Of
changing of colours, queasiness of stomachs, pukings,
and another thing that I could name? Do not, for
her and your credit's sake, spend the time in asking
how, and which way, 'tis so; she is quick, upon my
word; if you let a physician see her water, y'are undone.
  Giov. But in what case[2] is she?   19
  Put. Prettily amended; 'twas but a fit which I soon
espied, and she must look for often henceforward.
  Giov. Commend me to her, bid her take no care;[3]
Let not the doctor visit her, I charge you,
Make some excuse, till I return.—Oh, me!
I have a world of business in my head.—
Do not discomfort her.—
How does this news perplex me!—If my father
Come to her, tell him she's recovered well,
Say 'twas but some ill diet; d'ee hear, woman?
Look you to't.   30
  Put. I will, sir.

Exeunt.

[III.iv]

Enter FLORIO *and* RICHARDETTO.

  Flo. And how d'ee find her, sir?
  Rich.   Indifferent well;
I see no danger, scarce perceive she's sick,
But that she told me she had lately eaten
Melons, and, as she thought, those disagreed
With her young stomach.
  Flo.   Did you give her aught?
  Rich. An easy surfeit-water,[1] nothing else.
You need not doubt her health; I rather think
Her sickness is a fullness of her blood—
You understand me?
  Flo.   I do; you counsel well,
And once, within these few days, will so order't   10
She shall be married ere she know the time.
  Rich. Yet let not haste, sir, make unworthy choice;
That were dishonor.
  Flo.   Master Doctor, no;
I will not do so neither; in plain words,
My Lord Soranzo is the man I mean.
  Rich. A noble and a virtuous gentleman.
  Flo. As any is in Parma. Not far hence
Dwells Father Bonaventure, a grave friar,
Once tutor to my son; now at his cell
I'll have 'em married.
  Rich.   You have plotted wisely.   20
  Flo. I'll send one straight to speak with him tonight.
  Rich. Soranzo's wise; he will delay no time.
  Flo. It shall be so.

---

  [6] *maid's-sickness:* greensickness, anemia.
  [7] *over-flux:* over-flow.   [8] *present:* immediate.
III.iii.
  [1] *quick:* alive; pregnant.   [2] *case:* condition.
  [3] *take no care:* not worry.
III.iv.
  [1] *easy surfeit-water:* gentle cure for indigestion.

Enter Friar [BONAVENTURA] *and* GIOVANNI.

Fri.   Good peace be here and love.
Flo. Welcome, religious friar; you are one
That still bring blessing to the place you come to.
  Giov. Sir, with what speed I could, I did my best
To draw this holy man from forth his cell
To visit my sick sister, that with words
Of ghostly[2] comfort, in this time of need,
He might absolve her, whether she live or die.   30
  Flo. 'Twas well done, Giovanni; thou herein
Hast showed a Christian's care, a brother's love.
Come, father, I'll conduct you to her chamber,
And one thing would entreat you.
  Fri.   Say on, sir.
  Flo. I have a father's dear impression,
And wish, before I fall into my grave,
That I might see her married, as 'tis fit;
A word from you, grave man, will win her more
Than all our best persuasions.
  Fri.   Gentle sir,
All this I'll say, that heaven may prosper her.   40
                                        Exeunt.

[III.v]

Enter GRIMALDI.

  Grim. Now if the doctor keep his word, Soranzo,
Twenty to one you miss your bride; I know
'Tis an unnoble act, and not becomes
A soldier's valor, but in terms of love,
Where merit cannot sway, policy[1] must.
I am resolved; if this physician
Play not on both hands, then Soranzo falls.

Enter RICHARDETTO.

  Rich. You are come as I could wish; this very night
Soranzo, 'tis ordained, must be affied[2]
To Annabella, and, for aught I know,   10
Married.
  Grim. How!
  Rich.   Yet your patience:—
The place, 'tis Friar Bonaventure's cell.
Now I would wish you to bestow this night
In watching thereabouts; 'tis but a night;
If you miss now, tomorrow I'll know all.
  Grim. Have you the poison?
  Rich.   Here 'tis in this box.
Doubt nothing, this will do't; in any case,
As you respect your life, be quick and sure.
  Grim. I'll speed him.
  Rich.   Do. Away; for 'tis not safe
You should be seen much here.—Ever my love!   20
  Grim. And mine to you.
                                        Exit GRIMALDI.
  Rich. So. If this hit,[3] I'll laugh and hug revenge;
And they that now dream of a wedding-feast
May chance to mourn the lusty bridegroom's ruin.
But to my other business.—Niece Philotis.

Enter PHILOTIS.

Phil. Uncle?
Rich. My lovely niece,
You have bethought 'ee?
Phil.   Yes, and, as you counseled,
Fashioned my heart to love him; but he swears
He will tonight be married, for he fears   30
His uncle else, if he should know the drift,
Will hinder all, and call his coz[4] to shrift.[5]
  Rich. Tonight? Why, best of all;—but let me see,
I—ha—yes—so it shall be; in disguise
We'll early to the friar's, I have thought on't.

Enter BERGETTO *and* POGGIO.

Phil. Uncle, he comes.
Rich.   Welcome, my worthy coz.
Berg. Lass, pretty lass, come buss,[6] lass!—Aha,
Poggio!
                                  [*Kisses her.*]
Pog.[7] There's hope of this yet.
Rich. You shall have time enough; withdraw a little,
We must confer at large.[8]   41
Berg. Have you not sweetmeats or dainty devices for
me?
Phil. You shall have[9] enough, sweetheart.
Berg. Sweetheart! mark that, Poggio. By my troth, I
cannot choose but kiss thee once more for that word
"sweetheart."—Poggio, I have a monstrous swelling
about my stomach, whatsoever the matter be.
Pog. You shall have physic for't, sir.
Rich. Time runs apace.   50
Berg. Time's a blockhead.
Rich. Be ruled; when we have done what's fit to do,
Then you may kiss your fill, and bed her too.
                                        Exeunt.

[III.vi]

Enter the Friar *sitting in a chair,* ANNABELLA
kneeling and whispering to him; a table before
them and wax-lights; she weeps and
wrings her hands.

Fri. I am glad to see this penance; for, believe me,
You have unripped[1] a soul so foul and guilty
As I must tell you true, I marvel how
The earth hath borne you up; but weep, weep on,
These tears may do you good; weep faster yet,
Whiles I do read a lecture.[2]
Ann.   Wretched creature!
Fri. Ay, you are wretched, miserably wretched,
Almost condemned alive. There is a place—
List, daughter—in a black and hollow vault,

---

[2] *ghostly:* spiritual.

III.v.
  [1] *policy:* scheming.   [2] *affied:* affianced.
  [3] *hit:* works.   [4] *coz:* nephew.   [5] *shrift:* confession.
  [6] *buss:* kiss.   [7] *Pog.:* Q "Philotis."
  [8] *at large:* at length.   [9] *shall have:* Q "shall."

III.vi.
  [1] *unripped:* exposed.
  [2] *read a lecture:* deliver a reprimand.

Where day is never seen; there shines no sun,   10
But flaming horror of consuming fires,
A lightless sulfur, choked with smoky fogs
Of an infected darkness. In this place
Dwell many thousand thousand sundry sorts
Of never-dying deaths; there damnèd souls
Roar without pity; there are gluttons fed
With toads and adders; there is burning oil
Poured down the drunkard's throat; the usurer
Is forced to sup whole draughts of molten gold;
There is the murderer forever stabbed,   20
Yet can he never die; there lies the wanton
On racks of burning steel, whiles in his soul
He feels the torment of his raging lust.
    Ann. Mercy, oh, mercy!
    Fri.   There stands these wretched
        things
Who have dreamed out whole years in lawless sheets
And secret incests, cursing one another.
Then you will wish each kiss your brother gave
Had been a dagger's point; then you shall hear
How he will cry, "Oh, would my wicked sister
Had first been damned, when she did yield to lust!"—
But, soft, methinks I see repentance work   31
New motions in your heart; say, how is't with you?
    Ann. Is there no way left to redeem my miseries?
    Fri. There is, despair not; heaven is merciful,
And offers grace even now. 'Tis thus agreed,
First, for your honor's safety, that you marry
The lord Soranzo; next, to save your soul,
Leave off this life, and henceforth live to him.
    Ann. Ay, me!
    Fri.   Sigh not; I know the baits of sin
Are hard to leave. Oh, 'tis a death to do't.   40
Remember what must come. Are you content?
    Ann. I am.
    Fri.   I like it well; we'll take the time.³
Who's near us there?

            Enter FLORIO *and* GIOVANNI.

    Flo.   Did you call, father?
    Fri. Is Lord Soranzo come?
    Flo.   He stays below.
    Fri. Have you acquainted him at full?
    Flo.   I have,
And he is overjoyed.
    Fri.   And so are we.
Bid him come near.
    Giov. [*Aside*]   My sister weeping, ha?
I fear this friar's falsehood.—I will call him.
                                                Exit.

    Flo. Daughter, are you resolved?
    Ann.   Father, I am.

        Enter GIOVANNI, SORANZO, *and* VASQUES.

    Flo. My Lord Soranzo, here   50
Give me your hand; for that I give you this.
                            [*Joins their hands.*]
    Sor. Lady, say you so too?

---

³ *take . . . time:* seize the opportunity.

    Ann.   I do, and vow
To live with you and yours.
    Fri.   Timely resolved:
My blessing rest on both; more to be done,
You may perform it on the morning sun.
                                            Exeunt.

[III.vii]

        Enter GRIMALDI *with his rapier drawn and a dark
                        lantern.*

    Grim. 'Tis early night as yet, and yet too soon
To finish such a work; here I will lie
To listen who comes next.
                                        He lies down.

    Enter BERGETTO *and* PHILOTIS *disguised, and after*
            RICHARDETTO *and* POGGIO.

    Berg. We are almost at the place, I hope, sweetheart.
    Grim. [*Aside*] I hear them near, and heard one say
        "sweetheart."
'Tis he; now guide my hand, some angry justice,
Home to his bosom.—Now have at you, sir!
                        Strikes BERGETTO *and exit.*

    Berg. Oh, help, help! here's a stitch fallen in my guts.
Oh, for a flesh-tailor quickly!—Poggio!
    Phil. What ails my love?   10
    Berg. I am sure I cannot piss forward and backward,
and yet I am wet before and behind.—Lights, lights!
ho, lights!
    Phil. Alas, some villain here has slain my love.
    Rich. Oh, heaven forbid it.—Raise up the next
        neighbors
Instantly, Poggio, and bring lights.
                                        Exit POGGIO.
How is't, Bergetto? Slain? It cannot be;
Are you sure y'are hurt?
    Berg. Oh, my belly seethes like a porridge-pot; some
cold water, I shall boil over else; my whole body is   20
in a sweat, that you may wring my shirt; feel here—
why, Poggio!

    Enter POGGIO *with* Officers *and lights and halberts.*

    Pog. Here. Alas, how do you?
    Rich. Give me a light. What's here? All blood! oh,
        sirs,
Signor Donado's nephew now is slain.
Follow the murderer with all the haste
Up to the city, he cannot be far hence;
Follow, I beseech you.
    Offs. Follow, follow, follow.
                                        Exeunt Officers.
    Rich. Tear off thy linen, coz, to stop his wounds.—
Be of good comfort, man.   31
    Berg. Is all this mine own blood? Nay then, good
night with me. Poggio, commend me to my uncle, dost
hear? Bid him for my sake make much of this wench.
Oh!—I am going the wrong way sure, my belly aches
so.—Oh, farewell, Poggio!—oh!—oh!—
                                            Dies.

Phil. Oh, he is dead.
Pog.   How! dead!
Rich.   He's dead indeed.
'Tis now too late to weep; let's have him home,
And, with what speed we may, find out the murderer.
    Pog. Oh, my master, my master, my master!   40
                                              Exeunt.

[III.viii]

                Enter VASQUES *and* HIPPOLITA.

Hip. Betrothed?
Vasq. I saw it.
Hip. And when's the marriage-day?
Vasq. Some two days hence.
Hip. Two days? Why, man, I would but wish two
    hours
To send him to his last and lasting sleep.
And, Vasques, thou shalt see I'll do it bravely.
Vasq. I do not doubt your wisdom, nor, I trust, you
my secrecy; I am infinitely yours.
Hip. I will be thine in spite of my disgrace.   10
So soon? Oh, wicked man, I durst be sworn,
He'd laugh to see me weep.
Vasq. And that's a villainous fault in him.
Hip. No, let him laugh, I'm armed in my resolves;
Be thou still true.
Vasq. I should get little by treachery against so
hopeful a preferment as I am like to climb to.
Hip. Even to my bosom, Vasques. Let my youth[1]
Revel in these new pleasures; if we thrive,
He now hath but a pair of days to live.   20
                                              Exeunt.

[III.ix]

        Enter FLORIO, DONADO, RICHARDETTO,
                POGGIO, *and* Officers.

Flo. 'Tis bootless now to show yourself a child,
Signor Donado; what is done is done.
Spend not the time in tears, but seek for justice.
Rich. I must confess, somewhat I was in fault
That had not first acquainted you what love
Passed 'twixt him and my niece; but, as I live,
His fortune grieves me as it were mine own.
Don. Alas, poor creature, he meant no man harm,
That I am sure of.
Flo.   I believe that, too.
But stay, my masters, are you sure you saw   10
The murderer pass here?
Off. And it please you, sir, we are sure we saw a
ruffian, with a naked weapon in his hand all bloody, get
into my lord Cardinal's grace's gate, that we are sure
of; but for fear of his grace, bless us, we durst go no
further.
Don. Know you what manner of man he was?
Off. Yes, sure, I know the man; they say 'a is a
soldier; he that loved your daughter, sir, an't please ye;
'twas he for certain.   20
Flo. Grimaldi, on my life.

Off.   Ay, ay, the same.
Rich. The Cardinal is noble; he no doubt
Will give true justice.
Don. Knock someone at the gate.
Pog. I'll knock, sir.
                                        POGGIO *knocks.*
Serv. [*Within*] What would 'ee?
Flo. We require speech with the lord Cardinal
About some present business; pray inform
His grace that we are here.

                Enter Cardinal *and* GRIMALDI.

Card. Why, how now, friends! what saucy mates are
    you   30
That know nor duty nor civility?
Are we a person fit to be your host,
Or is our house become your common inn,
To beat our doors at pleasure? What such haste
Is yours as that it cannot wait fit times?
Are you the masters of this commonwealth,
And know no more discretion? Oh, your news
Is here before you; you have lost a nephew,
Donado, last night by Grimaldi slain:
Is that your business? Well, sir, we have knowledge
    on't.   40
Let that suffice.
Grim.   In presence of your grace,
In thought I never meant Bergetto harm.
But, Florio, you can tell, with how much scorn
Soranzo, backed with his confederates,
Hath often wronged me; I, to be revenged,
For that I could not win[1] him else to fight,
Had thought by way of ambush to have killed him,
But was unluckily therein mistook;
Else he had felt what late Bergetto did;
And though my fault to him were merely chance,   50
Yet humbly I submit me to your grace,
To do with me as you please.
Card.   Rise up, Grimaldi.
You citizens of Parma, if you seek
For justice, know, as nuncio from the Pope,
For this offense I here receive Grimaldi
Into his holiness' protection.
He is no common man, but nobly born;
Of princes' blood, though you, Sir Florio,
Thought him too mean a husband for your daughter.
If more you seek for, you must go to Rome,   60
For he shall thither; learn more wit, for shame.
Bury your dead.—Away, Grimaldi; leave 'em.
                        Exeunt Cardinal *and* GRIMALDI.
Don. Is this a churchman's voice? Dwells justice
    here?
Flo. Justice is fled to heaven[2] and comes no nearer.

III.viii.
    [1] *my youth:* i.e., Soranzo.
III.ix.
    [1] *win:* persuade.
    [2] *Justice ... heaven:* At the end of the golden age,
Astraea, goddess of justice, fled to heaven.

Soranzo. Was't for him? Oh, impudence.
Had he the face to speak it, and not blush?
Come, come, Donado, there's no help in this,
When cardinals think murder's not amiss.
Great men may do their wills, we must obey;
But heaven will judge them for't another day.   70
                                              Exeunt.

ACT FOUR

SCENE ONE

A Banquet. Hautboys.[1] *Enter the* Friar, GIOVANNI,
ANNABELLA, PHILOTIS, SORANZO, DONADO,
FLORIO, RICHARDETTO, PUTANA,
and VASQUES.

Fri. These holy rites performed, now take your
        times
To spend the remnant of the day in feast;
Such fit repasts are pleasing to the saints,
Who are your guests, though not with mortal eyes
To be beheld.—Long prosper in this day,
You happy couple, to each other's joy.
   Sor. Father, your prayer is heard; the hand of
        goodness
Hath been a shield for me against my death;
And, more to bless me, hath enriched my life
With this most precious jewel; such a prize   10
As earth hath not another like to this.
Cheer up, my love, and, gentlemen, my friends,
Rejoice with me in mirth; this day we'll crown
With lusty cups to Annabella's health.
   Giov. [*Aside*] O torture. Were the marriage yet
        undone,
Ere I'd endure this sight, to see my love
Clipped[2] by another, I would dare confusion,
And stand the horror of ten thousand deaths.
   Vasq. Are you not well, sir?
   Giov.   Prithee, fellow, wait;[3]   20
I need not thy officious diligence.
   Flo. Signor Donado, come, you must forget
Your late mishaps, and drown your cares in wine.
   Sor. Vasques.
   Vasq.   My lord?
   Sor.   Reach me that weighty bowl.
Here, brother Giovanni, here's to you;
Your turn comes next, though now a bachelor.
Here's to your sister's happiness and mine.
   Giov. I cannot drink.
   Sor.   What?
   Giov.   'Twill indeed offend me.
   Ann. Pray, do not urge him, if he be not willing.

                                            Hautboys.

IV.i.
[1] *Hautboys:* the French name for oboes.
[2] *clipped:* embraced.   [3] *wait:* i.e., on the guests.
[4] *noise:* music.   [5] *bound:* obliged.
[6] *willows:* emblem of disappointed love.
[7] *engaged:* put under obligation.   [8] *single:* absolute.

   Flo. How now, what noise[4] is this?   29
   Vasq. O sir, I had forgot to tell you; certain young
maidens of Parma, in honor to Madam Annabella's
marriage, have sent their loves to her in a masque, for
which they humbly crave your patience and silence.
   Sor. We are much bound[5] to them, so much the
        more
As it comes unexpected; guide them in.

Enter HIPPOLITA *and* Ladies *in* [*masks and*] *white
robes, with garlands of willows.*[6] *Music and
a dance.*

Thanks, lovely virgins; now might we but know
To whom we have been beholding for this love,
We shall acknowledge it.
   Hip.   Yes, you shall know;
                                            [*Unmasks.*]
What think you now?
   Omnes.   Hippolita!
   Hip.   'Tis she,
Be not amazed; nor blush, young lovely bride,   40
I come not to defraud you of your man.
'Tis now no time to reckon up the talk
What Parma long hath rumored of us both:
Let rash report run on; the breath that vents it
Will, like a bubble, break itself at last.
But now to you, sweet creature. Lend's your hand;
Perhaps it hath been said that I would claim
Some interest in Soranzo, now your lord.
What I have right to do, his soul knows best;
But in my duty to your noble worth,   50
Sweet Annabella, and my care of you,
Here take, Soranzo, take this hand from me:
I'll once more join what by the holy church
Is finished and allowed. Have I done well?
   Sor. You have too much engaged[7] us.
   Hip.   One thing
        more.
That you may know my single[8] charity,
Freely I here remit all interest
I e'er could claim, and give you back your vows;
And to confirm't—reach me a cup of wine—
My Lord Soranzo, in this draught I drink   60
Long rest t'ee.—Look to it, Vasques.
   Vasq. Fear nothing.

                He gives her a poisoned cup; she drinks.

   Sor. Hippolita, I thank you, and will pledge
This happy union as another life;
Wine, there!
   Vasq. You shall have none, neither shall you pledge
her.
   Hip. How!
   Vasq. Know now, Mistress She-Devil, your own
mischievous treachery hath killed you; I must not
marry you.   71
   Hip. Villain.
   Omnes. What's the matter?
   Vasq. Foolish woman, thou art now like a firebrand
that hath kindled others and burnt thyself; *troppo sperar,*

inganna,[9] thy vain hope hath deceived thee, thou art but
dead; if thou hast any grace, pray.

   Hip. Monster.

   Vasq. Die in charity, for shame.—This thing of
malice, this woman, had privately corrupted me 80
with promise of marriage, under this politic[10] reconciliation, to poison my lord, whiles she might laugh at
his confusion on his marriage[11] day. I promised her
fair, but I knew what my reward should have been; and
would willingly have spared her life, but that I was
acquainted with the danger of her disposition, and now
have fitted her a just payment in her own coin. There
she is, she hath yet—and[12] end thy days in peace, vile
woman; as for life there's no hope, think not on't.

   Omnes. Wonderful justice!

   Rich.   Heaven, thou art
   righteous.   90

   Hip. Oh, 'tis true;
I feel my minute coming. Had that slave
Kept promise—oh, my torment—thou this hour
Hadst died, Soranzo—heat above hell fire—
Yet ere I pass away—cruel, cruel flames—
Take here my curse amongst you: may thy bed
Of marriage be a rack unto thy heart,
Burn blood and boil in vengeance—oh, my heart,
My flame's intolerable—mayst thou live
To father bastards, may her womb bring forth 100
Monsters, and die together in your sins,
Hated, scorned, and unpitied—oh!—oh!—

                                Dies.

   Flo. Was e'er so vile a creature?

   Rich.   Here's the end
Of lust and pride.

   Ann.   It is a fearful sight.

   Sor. Vasques, I know thee now a trusty servant,
And never will forget thee.—Come, my love,
We'll home, and thank the heavens for this escape.
Father and friends, we must break up this mirth;
It is too sad a feast.

   Don.   Bear hence the body.

   Fri. Here's an ominous change;   110
Mark this, my Giovanni, and take heed.
I fear the event;[13] that marriage seldom's good,
Where the bride-banquet so begins in blood.

                           Exeunt.

[IV.ii]

Enter RICHARDETTO *and* PHILOTIS.

   Rich. My wretched wife, more wretched in her
   shame
Than in her wrongs to me, hath paid too soon
The forfeit of her modesty and life;
And I am sure, my niece, though vengeance hover,
Keeping aloof yet from Soranzo's fall,
Yet he will fall, and sink with his own weight.
I need not now—my heart persuades me so—
To further his confusion; there is One
Above begins to work, for, as I hear,

Debates already 'twixt his wife and him   10
Thicken and run to head; she, as 'tis said,
Slightens[1] his love, and he abandons hers.
Much talk I hear. Since things go thus, my niece,
In tender love and pity of your youth,
My counsel is, that you should free your years
From hazard of these woes by flying hence
To fair Cremona, there to vow your soul
In holiness a holy votaress.
Leave me to see the end of these extremes.
All human worldly courses are uneven;   20
No life is blessed but the way to heaven.

   Phil. Uncle, shall I resolve to be a nun?

   Rich. Ay, gentle niece, and in your hourly prayers
Remember me, your poor unhappy uncle.
Hie to Cremona now, as fortune leads,
Your home your cloister, your best friends your beads.
Your chaste and single life shall crown your birth;
Who dies a virgin lives a saint on earth.

   Phil. Then farewell, world, and worldly thoughts,
   adieu.
Welcome, chaste vows; myself I yield to you.   30

                             Exeunt.

IV.iii]

Enter SORANZO *unbraced*,[1] *and* ANNABELLA
dragged in.

   Sor. Come, strumpet, famous whore! Were every
   drop
Of blood that runs in thy adulterous veins
A life, this sword—dost see't?—should in one blow
Confound them all. Harlot, rare, notable harlot,
That with thy brazen face maintainst thy sin,
Was there no man in Parma to be bawd
To your loose cunning whoredom else but[2] I?
Must your hot itch and pleurisy[3] of lust,
The heyday of your luxury,[4] be fed
Up to a surfeit, and could none but I   10
Be picked out to be cloak to your close[5] tricks,
Your belly-sports? Now I must be the dad
To all that gallimaufry[6] that's stuffed
In thy corrupted bastard-bearing womb,
Say, must I?

   Ann.   Beastly man! why, 'tis thy fate.
I sued not to thee; for, but that I thought
Your over-loving lordship would have run
Mad on denial, had ye lent me time,
I would have told 'ee in what case I was.
But you would needs be doing.

---

     9 *It.*: too much hope deceives.   10 *politic*: deceptive.
    11 *marriage*: Q "malice."
    12 *yet—and*: Text may be corrupt.   13 *event*: outcome.

IV.ii.
    1 *Slightens*: Disdains.

IV.iii.
    1 *unbraced*: with clothing untied.
    2 *else but*: other than.   3 *pleurisy*: excess.
    4 *luxury*: lust.   5 *close*: secret.
    6 *gallimaufry*: mixture.

Sor.   Whore of whores!   20
Dar'st thou tell me this?
    Ann.   Oh, yes, why not?
You were deceived in me; 'twas not for love
I chose you, but for honor; yet know this,
Would you be patient yet, and hide your shame,
I'd see whether I could love you.
    Sor.   Excellent quean!⁷
Why, art thou not with child?
    Ann.   What needs all this
When 'tis superfluous? I confess I am.
    Sor. Tell me by whom.
    Ann.   Soft, sir, 'twas not in my
        bargain.
Yet, somewhat, sir, to stay your longing stomach,
I am content t'acquaint you with; the man,   30
The more than man, that got this sprightly boy—
For 'tis a boy, and therefore glory, sir,
Your heir shall be a son—
    Sor.   Damnable monster!
    Ann. Nay, and you will not hear, I'll speak no more.
    Sor. Yes, speak, and speak thy last.
    Ann.   A match, a
        match!⁸
This noble creature was in every part
So angel-like, so glorious, that a woman
Who had not been but human, as was I,
Would have kneeled to him, and have begged for love.
You! why, you are not worthy once to name   40
His name without true worship, or, indeed,
Unless you kneeled, to hear another name him.
    Sor. What was he called?
    Ann.   We are not come to that.
Let it suffice that you shall have the glory
To father what so brave a father got.
In brief, had not this chance fallen out as't doth,
I never had been troubled with a thought
That you had been a creature; but for marriage,
I scarce dream yet of that.
    Sor. Tell me his name.
    Ann.   Alas, alas, there's all.   50
Will you believe?
    Sor.   What?
    Ann.   You shall never know.
    Sor. How!
    Ann.   Never; if you do, let me be cursed.
    Sor. Not know it, strumpet? I'll rip up thy heart,
And find it there.
    Ann.   Do, do.
    Sor.   And with my teeth
Tear the prodigious lecher joint by joint.
    Ann. Ha, ha, ha, the man's merry!
    Sor.   Dost thou laugh?
Come, whore, tell me your lover, or, by truth,
I'll hew thy flesh to shreds; who is't?
    Ann. [*Sings*] *Che morte piu dolce che morire per*
        *amore!*⁹

Sor. Thus will I pull thy hair, and thus I'll drag   60
Thy lust-be-lepered body through the dust.
Yet tell his name.
    Ann. [*Sings*] *Morendo in gratia Dei, morirei senza*
        *dolore.*¹⁰
    Sor. Dost thou triumph? The treasure of the earth
Shall not redeem thee; were there kneeling kings
Did beg thy life, or angels did come down
To plead in tears, yet should not all prevail
Against my rage. Dost thou not tremble yet?
    Ann. At what? To die? No, be a gallant hangman.
I dare thee to the worst: strike, and strike home;   70
I leave revenge behind, and thou shalt feel't.
    Sor. Yet tell me ere thou diest, and tell me truly,
Knows thy old father this?
    Ann.   No, by my life.
    Sor. Wilt thou confess, and I will spare thy life?
    Ann. My life? I will not buy my life so dear.
    Sor. I will not slack my vengeance.

Enter VASQUES.

    Vasq. What d'ee mean, sir?
    Sor. Forbear, Vasques; such a damnèd whore
Deserves no pity.   79
    Vasq. Now the gods forfend! And would you be
her executioner, and kill her in your rage too? Oh,
'twere most unmanlike. She is your wife: what faults
hath been done by her before she married you, were not
against you; alas, poor lady, what hath she committed
which any lady in Italy in the like case would not? Sir,
you must be ruled by your reason and not by your fury;
that were unhuman and beastly.
    Sor. She shall not live.
    Vasq. Come, she must. You would have her confess
the author of her present misfortunes, I warrant   90
'ee; 'tis an unconscionable demand, and she should lose
the estimation that I, for my part, hold of her worth, if
she had done it. Why, sir, you ought not of all men
living to know it. Good sir, be reconciled; alas, good
gentlewoman.
    Ann. Pish, do not beg for me; I prize my life
As nothing; if the man will needs be mad,
Why, let him take it.
    Sor.   Vasques, hear'st thou this?
    Vasq. Yes, and commend her for it; in this she shows
the nobleness of a gallant spirit, and beshrew my   100
heart, but it becomes her rarely. [*Aside*] Sir, in any
case, smother your revenge; leave the scenting-out
your wrongs to me; be ruled, as you respect your honor,
or you mar all. [*Aloud*] Sir, if ever my service were of
any credit with you, be not so violent in your distractions. You are married now; what a triumph might the
report of this give to other neglected suitors. 'Tis as
manlike to bear extremities as godlike to forgive.
    Sor. O Vasques, Vasques, in this piece of flesh,
This faithless face of hers, had I laid up   110
The treasure of my heart.—Hadst thou been virtuous,
Fair, wicked woman, not the matchless joys
Of life itself had made me wish to live
With any saint but thee; deceitful creature,
How hast thou mocked my hopes, and in the shame

---

⁷ *quean:* whore.   ⁸ *a match:* agreed.
⁹ *It.:* What sweeter death than to die for love?
¹⁰ *It.:* Dying in God's grace, I should die without grief.

Of thy lewd womb even buried me alive.
I did too dearly love thee.

Vasq. [*Aside*] This is well; follow this temper with
some passion. Be brief and moving; 'tis for the purpose.

Sor. Be witness to my words thy soul and thoughts,
And tell me, didst not think that in my heart   121
I did too superstitiously[11] adore thee?

Ann. I must confess I know you loved me well.

Sor. And wouldst thou use me thus? O Annabella,
Be thou assured, whatsoe'er the villain was
That thus hath tempted thee to this disgrace,
Well he might lust, but never loved like me.
He doted on the picture that hung out
Upon thy cheeks, to please his humorous[12] eye;
Not on the part I loved, which was thy heart,   130
And, as I thought, thy virtues.

Ann.   O my lord!
These words wound deeper than your sword could do.

Vasq. Let me not ever take comfort, but I begin to
weep myself, so much I pity him; why, madam, I knew
when his rage was over-past, what it would come to.

Sor. Forgive me, Annabella. Though thy youth
Hath tempted thee above thy strength to folly,
Yet will not I forget what I should be,
And what I am, a husband; in that name
Is hid divinity; if I do find   140
That thou wilt yet be true, here I remit
All former faults, and take thee to my bosom.

Vasq. By my troth, and that's a point of noble charity.

Ann. Sir, on my knees—

Sor.   Rise up, you shall not kneel.
Get you to your chamber, see you make no show
Of alteration;[13] I'll be with you straight.
My reason tells me now that 'tis as common
To err in frailty as to be a woman.
Go to your chamber.   150

Exit ANNABELLA.

Vasq. So, this was somewhat to the matter; what do
you think of your heaven of happiness now, sir?

Sor. I carry hell about me; all my blood
Is fired in swift revenge.

Vasq. That may be, but know you how, or on whom?
Alas, to marry a great[14] woman, being made great in
the stock[15] to your hand,[16] is a usual sport in these days;
but to know what ferret[17] it was that haunted your
cony-berry,[18] there's the cunning.

Sor. I'll make her tell herself, or—   160

Vasq. Or what? You must not do so. Let me yet
persuade your sufferance a little while; go to her, use
her mildly, win her if it be possible to a voluntary,[19]
to a weeping tune; for the rest, if all hit, I will not miss
my mark. Pray, sir, go in; the next news I tell you shall
be wonders.

Sor. Delay in vengeance gives a heavier blow.

Exit.

Vasq. Ah, sirrah, here's work for the nonce. I had a
suspicion of a bad matter in my head a pretty whiles[20]
ago; but after my madam's scurvy looks here at   170
home, her waspish perverseness and loud fault-finding,
then I remembered the proverb, that where hens crow

and cocks hold their peace there are sorry houses.
'Sfoot, if the lower parts of a she-tailor's cunning can
cover such a swelling in the stomach, I'll never blame a
false stitch in a shoe[21] whiles I live again. Up[22] and up
so quick? And so quickly, too? 'Twere a fine policy to
learn by whom; this must be known; and I have thought
on't—   179

Enter PUTANA.

Here's the way, or none—What, crying, old mistress!
Alas, alas, I cannot blame 'ee, we have a lord, heaven
help us, is so mad as the devil himself, the more shame
for him.

Put. Oh, Vasques, that ever I was born to see this
day. Doth he use thee so too, sometimes, Vasques?

Vasq. Me? Why, he makes a dog of me. But if some
were of my mind, I know what we would do; as sure as
I am an honest man, he will go near to kill my lady
with unkindness. Say she be with child, is that such a
matter for a young woman of her years to be blamed for?

Put. Alas, good heart, it is against her will full sore.

Vasq. I durst be sworn, all his madness is for   192
that she will not confess whose 'tis, which he will know,
and when he doth know it, I am so well acquainted with
his humor, that he will forget all straight. Well, I could
wish she would in plain terms tell all, for that's the way
indeed.

Put. Do you think so?

Vasq. Foh, I know't; provided that he did not win
her to't by force. He was once in a mind that you   200
could tell, and meant to have wrung it out of you, but I
somewhat pacified him for that; yet sure you know
a great deal.

Put. Heaven forgive us all! I know a little, Vasques.

Vasq. Why should you not? Who else should? Upon
my conscience, she loves you dearly, and you would not
betray her to any affliction for the world.

Put. Not for all the world, by my faith and troth,
Vasques.   209

Vasq. 'Twere pity of your life if you should; but in
this you should both relieve her present discomforts,
pacify my lord, and gain yourself everlasting love and
preferment.

Put. Dost think so, Vasques?

Vasq. Nay, I know't; sure 'twas some near and entire
friend.

Put. 'Twas a dear friend indeed; but—

Vasq. But what? Fear not to name him; my life
between you and danger. Faith, I think 'twas no base
fellow.   220

---

[11] *superstitiously:* with too much care.
[12] *humorous:* capricious.
[13] *alteration:* our changed relations.
[14] *great:* pregnant.   [15] *stock:* body.
[16] *to . . . hand:* ready for you.   [17] *ferret:* Q "secret."
[18] *cony-berry:* rabbit warren.
[19] *voluntary:* extemporary music; spontaneous confession.
[20] *a . . . whiles:* some time.
[21] *I'll . . . shoe:* The cobbler's work is even lower down and
hence must be even more cunning.
[22] *up:* swollen(?), pregnant.

Put. Thou wilt stand between me and harm?

Vasq. 'Ud's pity, what else? You shall be rewarded, too, trust me.

Put. 'Twas even no worse than her own brother.

Vasq. Her brother Giovanni, I warrant 'ee!

Put. Even he, Vasques; as brave a gentleman as ever kissed fair lady. Oh, they love most perpetually.

Vasq. A brave gentleman indeed; why, therein I commend her choice.—Better and better!—You are sure 'twas he?   230

Put. Sure; and you shall see he will not be long from her, too.

Vasq. He were to blame if he would: but may I believe thee?

Put. Believe me! Why, dost think I am a Turk or a Jew? No, Vasques, I have known their dealings too long to belie them now.

Vasq. Where are you? There within, sirs.

Enter Banditti.

Put. How now, what are these?   239

Vasq. You shall know presently. Come, sirs, take me this old damnable hag, gag her instantly, and put out her eyes. Quickly, quickly!

Put. Vasques, Vasques!

Vasq. Gag her, I say. 'Sfoot, d'ee suffer her to prate? What d'ee fumble about? Let me come to her; I'll help your old gums, you toad-bellied bitch. Sirs, carry her closely[23] into the coalhouse, and put out her eyes instantly; if she roars, slit her nose. D'ee hear, be speedy and sure. Why, this is excellent and above expectation.

Exeunt [Banditti] *with* PUTANA.

Her own brother! oh, horrible! To what a height 250 of liberty in damnation hath the devil trained[24] our age. Her brother! Well, there's yet but a beginning: I must to my lord, and tutor him better in his points of vengeance; now I see how a smooth tale goes beyond a smooth tail.[25] But soft—What thing comes next?

Enter GIOVANNI.

Giovanni! as I would wish; my belief is strengthened, 'tis as firm as winter and summer.

Giov. Where's my sister?

Vasq. Troubled with a new sickness, my lord; she's somewhat ill.   260

Giov. Took too much of the flesh,[26] I believe.

Vasq. Troth, sir, and you, I think, have e'en hit it. But my virtuous lady—

Giov. Where's she?

---

[23] *closely:* secretly.   [24] *trained:* lured.
[25] *smooth tail:* wanton woman.
[26] *took . . . flesh:* ate too much meat; indulged in too much sexual activity.
[27] *liberality:* generosity; sexual license.
[28] *am . . . man:* have been successful.
[29] *plied . . . cue:* worked my part.   [30] *them:* others.

V.i.
[1] *against:* in preparation for.
[2] *depositions:* Q "dispositions."
[3] *turtle:* turtledove.

Vasq. In her chamber; please you visit her; she is alone.

[GIOVANNI *gives him money.*]

Your liberality[27] hath doubly made me your servant, and ever shall, ever.

Exit GIOVANNI.

Enter SORANZO.

Sir, I am made a man,[28] I have plied my cue[29] with cunning and success; I beseech you let's be private. 270

Sor. My lady's brother's come; now he'll know all.

Vasq. Let him know't; I have made some of them[30] fast enough. How have you dealt with my lady?

Sor. Gently, as thou hast counseled. Oh, my soul Runs circular in sorrow for revenge. But, Vasques, thou shalt know—

Vasq. Nay, I will know no more, for now comes your turn to know; I would not talk so openly with you. Let my young master take time enough, and go at pleasure; he is sold to death, and the devil shall not ransom him. Sir, I beseech you, your privacy. 281

Sor. No conquest can gain glory of my fear.

Exeunt.

ACT FIVE

SCENE ONE

Enter ANNABELLA above.

Ann. Pleasures, farewell, and all ye thriftless minutes Wherein false joys have spun a weary life. To these my fortunes now I take my leave. Thou, precious Time, that swiftly rid'st in post Over the world, to finish up the race Of my last fate, here stay thy restless course, And bear to ages that are yet unborn A wretched, woeful woman's tragedy. My conscience now stands up against[1] my lust With depositions[2] charactered in guilt,   10

Enter Friar [BONAVENTURA, *below*].

And tells me I am lost; now I confess Beauty that clothes the outside of the face Is cursèd if it be not clothed with grace. Here like a turtle,[3] mewed up in a cage, Unmated, I converse with air and walls, And descant on my vile unhappiness. O Giovanni, that hast had the spoil Of thine own virtues and my modest fame, Would thou hadst been less subject to those stars That luckless reigned at my nativity;   20 Oh, would the scourge due to my black offense Might pass from thee, that I alone might feel The torment of an uncontrollèd flame.

Fri. [*Aside*] What's this I hear?

Ann.   That man, that blessèd friar, Who joined in ceremonial knot my hand To him whose wife I now am, told me oft

I trod the path to death, and showed me how.
But they who sleep in lethargies of lust
Hug their confusion, making heaven unjust,
And so did I.
    Fri. [*Aside*] Here's music to the soul.   30
    Ann. Forgive me, my good genius, and this once
Be helpful to my ends. Let some good man
Pass this way, to whose trust I may commit
This paper double-lined with tears and blood:
Which being granted, here I sadly[4] vow
Repentance, and a leaving of that life
I long have died in.
    Fri.   Lady, heaven hath heard you,
And hath by providence ordained that I
Should be his minister for your behoof.
    Ann. Ha, what are you?
    Fri.   Your brother's friend, the
    friar;   40
Glad in my soul that I have lived to hear
This free confession 'twixt your peace and you.
What would you, or to whom? Fear not to speak.
    Ann. Is heaven so bountiful? Then I have found
More favor than I hoped. Here, holy man—

                                Throws a letter.

Commend me to my brother; give him that,
That letter; bid him read it and repent.
Tell him that I, imprisoned in my chamber,
Barred of all company, even of my guardian,
Who gives me cause of much suspect,[5] have time   50
To blush at what hath passed; bid him be wise,
And not believe the friendship of my lord.
I fear much more than I can speak: good father,
The place is dangerous, and spies are busy;
I must break off—you'll do't?
    Fri.   Be sure I will;
And fly with speed—my blessing ever rest
With thee, my daughter; live, to die more blessed.
                             Exit Friar.
    Ann. Thanks to the heavens, who have prolonged
    my breath
To this good use: now I can welcome death.
                                Exit.

[V.ii]

              Enter SORANZO *and* VASQUES.

    Vasq. Am I to be believed now? First marry a
strumpet that cast herself away upon you but to laugh
at your horns, to feast on your disgrace, riot in your
vexations, cuckold you in your bride-bed, waste your
estate upon panders and bawds!
    Sor. No more, I say, no more.
    Vasq. A cuckold is a goodly tame beast, my lord.
    Sor. I am resolved; urge not another word.
My thoughts are great, and all as resolute
As thunder; in mean time I'll cause our lady   10
To deck herself in all her bridal robes,
Kiss her, and fold her gently in my arms.
Begone—yet, hear you, are the banditti ready
To wait in ambush?

    Vasq. Good sir, trouble not yourself about other
business than your own resolution; remember that
time lost cannot be recalled.
    Sor. With all the cunning words thou canst, invite
The states[1] of Parma to my birthday's feast;
Haste to my brother-rival and his father,   20
Entreat them gently, bid them not to fail.
Be speedy, and return.
    Vasq. Let not your pity betray you till my coming
back; think upon incest and cuckoldry.
    Sor. Revenge is all the ambition I aspire:
To that I'll climb or fall; my blood's on fire.
                              Exeunt.

[V.iii]

                 Enter GIOVANNI.

    Giov. Busy opinion is an idle fool,
That, as a school-rod keeps a child in awe,
Frights the unexperienced temper of the mind:
So did it me; who, ere my precious sister
Was married, thought all taste of love would die
In such a contract; but I find no change
Of pleasure in this formal law of sports.[1]
She is still one to me, and every kiss
As sweet and as delicious as the first
I reaped, when yet the privilege of youth   10
Entitled her a virgin. Oh, the glory
Of two united hearts like hers and mine!
Let poring book-men dream of other worlds;
My world, and all of happiness, is here,
And I'd not change it for the best to come.
A life of pleasure is Elysium.

            Enter Friar [BONAVENTURA].

Father, you enter on the jubilee[2]
Of my retired delights; now I can tell you,
The hell you oft have prompted[3] is naught else
But slavish and fond superstitious fear;   20
And I could prove it, too—
    Fri.   Thy blindness slays thee.
Look there, 'tis writ to thee.
                          Gives the letter.
    Giov. From whom?
    Fri. Unrip the seals and see;
The blood's yet seething hot, that will anon
Be frozen harder than congealèd coral.
Why d'ee change color, son?
    Giov.   'Fore heaven, you make
Some petty devil factor 'twixt my love
And your religion-maskèd sorceries.
Where had you this?
    Fri.   Thy conscience, youth, is seared,[4]

Else thou wouldst stoop to warning.

Giov.   'Tis her hand,   31
I know't; and 'tis all written in her blood.
She writes I know not what. Death? I'll not fear
An armèd thunderbolt aimed at my heart.
She writes, we are discovered—pox on dreams
Of low faint-hearted cowardice! discovered?
The devil we are; which way is't possible?
Are we grown traitors to our own delights?
Confusion take such dotage, 'tis but forged;
This is your peevish chattering, weak old man.   40

Enter VASQUES.

Now, sir, what news bring you?

Vasq. My lord, according to his yearly custom
keeping this day a feast in honor of his birthday, by me
invites you thither. Your worthy father, with the Pope's
reverend nuncio, and other magnificoes of Parma, have
promised their presence; will't please you to be of the
number?

Giov. Yes, tell him I dare come.
Vasq. Dare come?
Giov. So I said; and tell him more, I will come.   50
Vasq. These words are strange to me.
Giov. Say I will come.
Vasq. You will not miss?
Giov. Yet more? I'll come! sir, are you answered?
Vasq. So I'll say.—My service to you.

                                   Exit VASQUES.

Fri. You will not go, I trust.
Giov.   Not go? For what?
Fri. Oh, do not go. This feast, I'll gage[5] my life,
Is but a plot to train you to your ruin.
Be ruled, you sha' not go.
Giov.   Not go? Stood Death
Threatening his armies of confounding plagues,   60
With hosts of dangers hot as blazing stars,
I would be there. Not go? Yes, and resolve
To strike as deep in slaughter as they all.
For I will go.
Fri.   Go where thou wilt; I see
The wildness of thy fate draws to an end,
To a bad fearful end. I must not stay
To know thy fall; back to Bononia I
With speed will haste, and shun this coming blow.
Parma, farewell; would I had never known thee,
Or aught of thine. Well, young man, since no prayer
Can make thee safe, I leave thee to despair.   71

                                   Exit Friar.

Giov. Despair, or tortures of a thousand hells,
All's one to me; I have set up my rest.[6]
Now, now, work serious thoughts on baneful plots.
Be all a man, my soul; let not the curse

---

[5] *gage*: pledge.
[6] *set . . . rest*: from card game primero; "made my stand."
[7] *curse . . . prescription*: biblical injunction.
[8] *splits*: splinters.

V.iv.
[1] *sharp . . . bit*: eager to pursue his old course.
[2] *law*: a "start" before the hunt.   [3] *expect*: await.

Of old prescription[7] rend from me the gall
Of courage, which enrolls a glorious death.
If I must totter like a well-grown oak,
Some under-shrubs shall in my weighty fall
Be crushed to splits:[8] with me they all shall perish.   80

                                   Exit.

[V.iv]

Enter SORANZO, VASQUES, *and* Banditti.

Sor. You will not fail, or shrink in the attempt?
Vasq. I will undertake for their parts. Be sure, my
masters, to be bloody enough, and as unmerciful as if
you were preying upon a rich booty on the very moun-
tains of Liguria; for your pardons, trust to my lord, but
for reward you shall trust none but your own pockets.
Band. Omnes. We'll make a murder.
Sor. Here's gold, here's more; want nothing; what
    you do
Is noble, and an act of brave revenge.
I'll make ye rich banditti, and all free.   10
Omnes. Liberty, liberty!
Vasq. Hold, take every man a vizard; when ye are
withdrawn, keep as much silence as you can possibly.
You know the watchword; till which be spoken, move
not, but, when you hear that, rush in like a stormy
flood; I need not instruct ye in your own profession.
Omnes. No, no, no.
Vasq. In, then; your ends are profit and preferment.
—Away!

                                   Exeunt Banditti.

Sor. The guests will all come, Vasques?   20
Vasq. Yes, sir. And now let me a little edge your
resolution. You see nothing is unready to this great
work, but a great mind in you; call to your remembrance your disgraces, your loss of honor, Hippolita's
blood, and arm your courage in your own wrongs; so
shall you best right those wrongs in vengeance, which
you may truly call your own.
Sor. 'Tis well; the less I speak, the more I burn,
And blood shall quench that flame.   29
Vasq. Now you begin to turn Italian. This beside—
when my young incest-monger comes, he will be sharp
set on his old bit:[1] give him time enough, let him have
your chamber and bed at liberty; let my hot hare have
law[2] ere he be hunted to his death, that if it be possible,
he may post to hell in the very act of his damnation.

Enter GIOVANNI.

Sor. It shall be so; and see, as we would wish,
He comes himself first. Welcome, my much-loved
    brother,
Now I perceive you honor me; y'are welcome.
But where's my father?
Giov.   With the other states,
Attending on the nuncio of the Pope,   40
To wait upon him hither. How's my sister?
Sor. Like a good housewife, scarcely ready yet;
Y'are best walk to her chamber.
Giov.   If you will.
Sor. I must expect[3] my honorable friends;

Good brother, get her forth.

Giov.   You are busy, sir.

                                Exit GIOVANNI.

Vasq. Even as the great devil himself would have
it; let him go and glut himself in his own destruction.

                                      [Flourish.]

Hark, the nuncio is at hand; good sir, be ready to
receive him.

       Enter Cardinal, FLORIO, DONADO,
          RICHARDETTO, *and* Attendants.

Sor. Most reverend lord, this grace hath made me
    proud,   50
That you vouchsafe⁴ my house; I ever rest
Your humble servant for this noble favor.

Card. You are our friend, my lord; his holiness
Shall understand how zealously you honor
Saint Peter's vicar in his substitute:
Our special love to you.

Sor.   Signors, to you
My welcome, and my ever best of thanks
For this so memorable courtesy.
Pleaseth your grace to walk near?

Card.   My lord, we come
To celebrate your feast with civil mirth,   60
As ancient custom teacheth: we will go.

Sor. Attend his grace there!—signors, keep your
    way.

                                Exeunt.

[V.v]

   Enter GIOVANNI *and* ANNABELLA *lying on a bed.*

Giov. What, changed so soon? Hath your new
    sprightly lord
Found out a trick in night-games more than we
Could know in our simplicity? Ha! is't so?
Or does the fit come on you, to prove treacherous
To your past vows and oaths?

Ann.   Why should you jest
At my calamity, without all sense
Of the approaching dangers you are in?

Giov. What danger's half so great as thy revolt?
Thou art a faithless sister, else thou knowst
Malice, or any treachery beside,   10
Would stoop¹ to my bent brows; why, I hold fate
Clasped in my fist, and could command the course
Of time's eternal motion, hadst thou been
One thought more steady than an ebbing sea.
And what? You'll now be honest, that's resolved?

Ann. Brother, dear brother, know what I have been,
And know that now there's but a dining-time²
'Twixt us and our confusion: let's not waste
These precious hours in vain and useless speech.
Alas, these gay attires were not put on   20
But to some end; this sudden solemn feast
Was not ordained to riot in expense;
I, that have now been chambered here alone,
Barred of my guardian, or of any else,
Am not for nothing at an instant freed

To fresh access. Be not deceived, my brother,
This banquet is an harbinger of death
To you and me; resolve yourself it is,
And be prepared to welcome it.

Giov.   Well, then;
The schoolmen³ teach that all this globe of earth   30
Shall be consumed to ashes in a minute.

Ann. So I have read, too.

Giov.   But 'twere somewhat
    strange
To see the waters burn; could I believe
This might be true, I could believe as well
There might be hell or heaven.

Ann.   That's most certain.

Giov. A dream, a dream! else in this other world
We should know one another.

Ann.   So we shall.

Giov. Have you heard so?

Ann.   For certain.

Giov.   But d'ee think
That I shall see you there?—You look on me?
May we kiss one another, prate or laugh,   40
Or do as we do here?

Ann.   I know not that.
But good, for the present, what d'ee mean
To free yourself from danger? Some way think
How to escape; I'm sure the guests are come.

Giov. Look up, look here; what see you in my face?

Ann. Distraction and a troubled countenance.

Giov. Death, and a swift repining wrath—yet, look,
What see you in mine eyes?

Ann.   Methinks you weep.

Giov. I do, indeed; these are the funeral tears
Shed on your grave; these furrowed up my cheeks   50
When first I loved and knew not how to woo.
Fair Annabella, should I here repeat
The story of my life, we might lose time.
Be record all the spirits of the air,
And all things else that are, that day and night,
Early and late, the tribute which my heart
Hath paid to Annabella's sacred love
Hath been these tears, which are her mourners now.
Never till now did Nature do her best
To show a matchless beauty to the world,   60
Which in an instant, ere it scarce was seen,
The jealous destinies required again.
Pray, Annabella, pray; since we must part,
Go thou, white in thy soul, to fill a throne
Of innocence and sanctity in heaven.
Pray, pray, my sister.

Ann.   Then I see your drift—
Ye blessèd angels, guard me.

Giov.   So say I.
Kiss me. If ever after-times should hear
Of our fast-knit affections, though perhaps

----

⁴ *vouchsafe:* deign (to visit).

V.v.
  ¹ *stoop:* bow down.   ² *dining-time:* a meal's time.
  ³ *schoolmen:* scholastic theologians.

The laws of conscience and of civil use   70
May justly blame us, yet when they but know
Our loves, that love will wipe away that rigor
Which would in other incests be abhorred.
Give me your hand; how sweetly life doth run
In these well-colored veins. How constantly
These palms do promise health. But I could chide
With Nature for this cunning flattery.
Kiss me again—forgive me.
    Ann.   With my heart.
    Giov. Farewell.
    Ann.   Will you be gone?
    Giov.   Be dark, bright sun,
And make this midday night, that thy gilt rays   80
May not behold a deed will turn their splendor
More sooty than the poets feign their Styx.[4]
One other kiss, my sister.
    Ann.   What means this?
    Giov. To save thy fame, and kill thee in a kiss.

                                Stabs her.

Thus die, and die by me, and by my hand.
Revenge is mine; honor doth love command.
    Ann. O brother, by your hand?
    Giov.   When thou art dead
I'll give my reasons for't; for to dispute
With thy (even in thy death) most lovely beauty,
Would make me stagger to perform this act,   90
Which I most glory in.
    Ann. Forgive him, heaven—and me my sins;
      farewell.
Brother unkind,[5] unkind!—mercy, great heaven—Oh!
    —oh!—

                                  Dies.

    Giov. She's dead, alas, good soul. The hapless fruit
That in her womb received its life from me
Hath had from me a cradle and a grave.
I must not dally. This sad marriage-bed,
In all her best, bore her alive and dead.
Soranzo, thou hast missed thy aim in this;
I have prevented[6] now thy reaching[7] plots,   100
And killed a love, for whose each drop of blood
I would have pawned my heart. Fair Annabella,
How over-glorious art thou in thy wounds,
Triumphing over infamy and hate!
Shrink not, courageous hand, stand up, my heart,
And boldly act my last and greater part.

                            Exit with the body.

[V.vi]

A Banquet. Enter Cardinal, FLORIO, DONADO,
    SORANZO, RICHARDETTO, VASQUES, *and*
    Attendants; *they take their places.*

    Vasq. Remember, sir, what you have to do; be wise
and resolute.

---

[4] *Styx:* river of hell.   [5] *unkind:* cruel; unnatural.
[6] *prevented:* anticipated.
[7] *reaching:* far-reaching, cunning.

    Sor. Enough—my heart is fixed.—Pleaseth your
      grace
To taste these coarse confections; though the use
Of such set entertainments more consists
In custom than in cause, yet, reverend sir,
I am still made your servant by your presence.
    Card. And we your friend.
    Sor. But where's my brother Giovanni?

    Enter GIOVANNI *with a heart upon his dagger.*

    Giov. Here, here, Soranzo; trimmed in reeking
      blood,   10
That triumphs over death; proud in the spoil
Of love and vengeance! fate or all the powers
That guide the motions of immortal souls
Could not prevent me.
    Card. What means this?
    Flo. Son Giovanni!
    Sor. Shall I be forestalled?
    Giov. Be not amazed; if your misgiving hearts
Shrink at an idle sight, what bloodless fear
Of coward passion would have seized your senses,   20
Had you beheld the rape of life and beauty
Which I have acted? My sister, oh, my sister.
    Flo. Ha! what of her?
    Giov.   The glory of my deed
Darkened the midday sun, made noon as night.
You came to feast, my lords, with dainty fare;
I came to feast, too, but I digged for food
In a much richer mine than gold or stone
Of any value balanced; 'tis a heart,
A heart, my lords, in which is mine entombed.
Look well upon't; d'ee know't?   30
    Vasq. What strange riddle's this?
    Giov. 'Tis Annabella's heart, 'tis; why d'ee startle?
I vow 'tis hers; this dagger's point plowed up
Her fruitful womb, and left to me the fame
Of a most glorious executioner.
    Flo. Why, madman, art thyself?
    Giov. Yes, father; and that times to come may know
How as my fate I honored my revenge,
List, father, to your ears I will yield up
How much I have deserved to be your son.   40
    Flo. What is't thou say'st?
    Giov.   Nine moons have had
      their changes
Since I first throughly viewed and truly loved
Your daughter and my sister.
    Flo.   How!—alas,
My lords, he's a frantic madman!
    Giov.   Father, no.
For nine months' space in secret I enjoyed
Sweet Annabella's sheets; nine months I lived
A happy monarch of her heart and her.
Soranzo, thou know'st this; thy paler cheek
Bears the confounding print of thy disgrace,
For her too fruitful womb too soon bewrayed   50
The happy passage of our stolen delights,
And made her mother to a child unborn.
    Card. Incestuous villain!
    Flo.   Oh, his rage belies him.

Giov. It does not, 'tis the oracle of truth;
I vow it is so.
    Sor.   I shall burst with fury.
Bring the strumpet forth.
    Vasq. I shall, sir.

Exit VASQUES.

    Giov.   Do, sir.—Have you all no faith
To credit yet my triumphs? Here I swear
By all that you call sacred, by the love
I bore my Annabella whilst she lived,   60
These hands have from her bosom ripped this heart.

Enter VASQUES.

Is't true or no, sir?
    Vasq.   'Tis most strangely[1] true.
    Flo. Cursed man!—have I lived to—

Dies.

    Card.   Hold up, Florio.—
Monster of children, see what thou hast done,
Broke thy old father's heart. Is none of you
Dares venture on him?
    Giov.   Let 'em.—Oh, my father,
How well his death becomes him in his griefs.
Why, this was done with courage; now survives
None of our house but I, gilt in the blood
Of a fair sister and a hapless father.   70
    Sor. Inhuman scorn of men, hast thou a thought
T'outlive thy murders?
    Giov.   Yes, I tell thee, yes;
For in my fists I bear the twists[2] of life.
Soranzo, see this heart, which was thy wife's;
Thus I exchange it royally for thine,

[*Stabs him.*]

And thus and thus. Now brave revenge is mine.
    Vasq. I cannot hold any longer.—You, sir, are you
grown insolent in your butcheries? Have at you!

[*They*] *fight.*

    Giov. Come, I am armed to meet thee.
    Vasq. No, will it not be yet? If this will not, another
shall. Not yet? I shall fit you anon.—Vengeance![3] 81

Enter Banditti [*and fight* GIOVANNI].

    Giov. Welcome, come more of you whate'er you be,
I dare your worst—
Oh, I can stand no longer! Feeble arms,
Have you so soon lost strength?
    Vasq. Now you are welcome, sir!—away, my mas-
ters, all is done, shift for yourselves. Your reward is
your own; shift for yourselves.
    Band. Away, away!

Exeunt Banditti.

    Vasq. How d'ee, my lord; see you this? How is't?
    Sor. Dead; but in death well pleased that I have
        lived   91
To see my wrongs revenged on that black devil.
O Vasques, to thy bosom let me give
My last of breath; let not that lecher live—oh!—

Dies.

    Vasq. The reward of peace and rest be with him, my
ever dearest lord and master.
    Giov. Whose hand gave me this wound?
    Vasq. Mine, sir, I was your first man; have you
enough?
    Giov. I thank thee; thou hast done for me but what
I would have else done on myself. Art sure   101
Thy lord is dead?
    Vasq. Oh, impudent slave! As sure as I am sure to
see thee die.
    Card. Think on thy life and end, and call for mercy.
    Giov. Mercy? Why, I have found it in this justice.
    Card. Strive yet to cry to heaven.
    Giov.   Oh, I bleed fast.
Death, thou art a guest long looked for; I embrace
Thee and thy wounds. Oh, my last minute comes.
Where'er I go, let me enjoy this grace,   110
Freely to view my Annabella's face.

Dies.

    Don. Strange miracle of justice!
    Card. Raise up the city; we shall be murdered all.
    Vasq. You need not fear, you shall not; this strange
task being ended, I have paid the duty to the son
which I have vowed to the father.
    Card. Speak, wretched villain, what incarnate fiend
Hath led thee on to this?
    Vasq. Honesty, and pity of my master's wrongs; for
know, my lord, I am by birth a Spaniard, brought 120
forth my country in my youth by Lord Soranzo's
father, whom whilst he lived I served faithfully; since
whose death I have been to this man as I was to him.
What I have done was duty, and I repent nothing but
that the loss of my life had not ransomed his.
    Card. Say, fellow, know'st thou any yet unnamed
Of counsel in this incest?
    Vasq. Yes, an old woman, sometimes[4] guardian to
this murdered lady.
    Card. And what's become of her?   130
    Vasq. Within this room she is; whose eyes, after her
confession, I caused to be put out, but kept alive, to
confirm what from Giovanni's own mouth you have
heard. Now, my lord, what I have done you may
judge of, and let your own wisdom be a judge in
your own reason.
    Card. Peace!—first this woman,[5] chief in these
        effects:
My sentence is, that forthwith she be ta'en
Out of the city, for example's sake,
There to be burnt to ashes.
    Don.   'Tis most just.   140
    Card. Be it your charge, Donado, see it done.
    Don. I shall.
    Vasq. What for me? If death, 'tis welcome; I have
been honest to the son as I was to the father.

V.vi.
   [1] *strangely:* extremely.
   [2] *twists:* threads twisted by the fates.
   [3] *Vengeance:* the watchword of V. iv. 14.
   [4] *sometimes:* formerly.
   [5] *this woman:* either Putana or Annabella.

Card. Fellow, for thee, since what thou didst was
    done
Not for thyself, being no Italian,
We banish thee forever, to depart
Within three days; in this we do dispense
With grounds of reason, not of thine offense.[6]
    Vasq. 'Tis well; this conquest is mine, and I rejoice
that a Spaniard outwent an Italian in revenge.   151
                          Exit VASQUES.
    Card. Take up these slaughtered bodies, see them
    buried;
And all the gold and jewels, or whatsoever,
Confiscate by the canons of the church,
We seize upon to the Pope's proper use.

            [RICHARDETTO *discovers himself.*]

    Rich. Your grace's pardon: thus long I lived
    disguised
To see the effect of pride and lust at once
Brought both to shameful ends.
    Card. What, Richardetto whom we thought for
    dead?
    Don. Sir, was it you—
    Rich.   Your friend.
    Card.   We shall have
    time   160
To talk at large of all. But never yet
Incest and murder have so strangely met.
Of one so young, so rich in nature's store,
Who could not say, 'tis pity she's a whore?
                                Exeunt.

                    F I N I S

---

[6] *With . . . offense:* i.e., Because it is politic, not because it punishes your crime.

Philip Massinger

[1583–1640]

A NEW WAY TO PAY OLD DEBTS

PHILIP MASSINGER is among the most prolific of Renaissance dramatists. During a career that spanned approximately thirty years, he wrote himself or had a hand in the writing of more than fifty plays. His output is not only vast but varied. In *The Fatal Dowry* (with Nathaniel Field) and *The Duke of Milan*, he shows what he can do as a writer of tragedy. The achievement is considerable. His most impressive venture in that kind is, however, THE ROMAN ACTOR, worked up from the histories of Suetonius and Dio Cassius. In *The Maid of Honor*, notable for the creation of Camiola, Massinger's finest portrait of a woman, this opportunistic playwright tries his hand at the popular and equivocal genre of romance or tragicomedy. *The City Madam* is, as comedy, inferior only to A NEW WAY TO PAY OLD DEBTS. Tragicomedy is evidently the form most congenial to Massinger's taste and temper, as witness his success in *The Great Duke of Florence*, and *The Bondman*, in which he exploits the current animus against the Duke of Buckingham, the reigning favorite at Court.

Massinger's first plays were written for the King's Men at the Globe and Blackfriars. In the decade 1613–23 he was collaborating with John Fletcher, whom he succeeded in 1626 as the company's chief playwright and whom he took as his model in the writing of tragicomedy. The years 1623–25 represent a brief hiatus, during which Massinger left the King's Men temporarily to write for the Queen's Men at the Cockpit, subsequently renamed the Phoenix, a private theater in which A NEW WAY TO PAY OLD DEBTS was played for the first time. Other playwrights with whom Massinger collaborated include Dekker and Nathaniel Field and—it is sometimes argued—Shakespeare in his final plays (*Henry VIII, The Two Noble Kinsmen*).

Probably the best of Massinger's plays, certainly the play that is best remembered, is A NEW WAY TO PAY OLD DEBTS. The only early edition of this comedy is a quarto of 1633, printed by E. P. for Henry Seyle. Because the printer corrected his sheets as he worked, the quarto survives in different states. But the differences are minor and the text presents few problems. Minor misprints are corrected silently in this edition; more substantial emendations are cited in the footnotes.

Date of composition is generally assigned to the 1620s but is largely conjectural. Evidently the play was acted about 1625–26, certainly not much later than that. The title page of the 1633 quarto reads: "A Comedy as it hath been often acted at the Phoenix in Drury Lane by the Queen's Majesty's Servants." A reference in I.ii to the celebrated siege of Breda suggests composition anterior to 1 July, 1625, on which date that city finally capitulated. Of course, the reference may represent an interpolation at some subsequent time, though this seems a finicking supposition. A further but rather tenous clue is provided by the trial in 1621 of Sir Giles Mompesson, on whom the character of Overreach is modeled at a remove. Mompesson, who held the monopoly of tavern licenses—which he dispensed on payment of bribes—remained to the age a type of infamy for many years after his fall.

The plot of the play or the treatment of the plot is basically Massinger's, a statement that holds despite the fact that Massinger went for his governing idea to Middleton's earlier comedy, *A Trick to Catch the Old One*, printed in 1608. Comparison of the two plays will show how much they differ in sensibility and in the emphasis on romantic incident. There is, for example, nothing in Middleton that corresponds to the Allworth–Margaret subplot, a sentimental story that seems to anticipate the easy emotionalism of the early eighteenth century or to hark back to the disingenuous comedy of Thomas Dekker, a generation before. And in fact sentimentality is the single blemish that mars this admirable play. Lady Allworth's long first speech is illustrative, so is the sudden—too sudden—recollecting by the servants of Wellborn's previous good deeds. Wellborn himself, though Massinger affects to think highly of him, should be grateful for having escaped hanging. Though Margaret scorns to be a titled lady ("Kind hearts are more than coronets"), Lord Lovell scorns her exactly as she is untitled. Massinger's heart is with Margaret, his head knows better. A just critique of the play will focus, however, not on its faults but its virtues. The denouement, in which Overreach swells in prelude to disaster, is tremendous.

Philip Massinger was born in Salisbury, the son of a steward to Henry Herbert, Earl of Pembroke. To the Herbert family, Massinger in later years addressed minor poems and dedications. It is supposed that, like Shakespeare, he attended his local grammar school. Thereafter he enrolled in St. Alban Hall, Oxford, but left for London without taking a degree, probably about 1606. By 1613 he had joined the stable of indigent writers presided over by Philip Henslowe, who perhaps was instrumental in freeing him from debtors' prison. Massinger's death was almost coeval with the suspension of the drama and the outbreak of the Civil War. He was buried in Southwark Cathedral, close to the site of the old Globe Theater.

R. A. F.

A New Way to Pay Old Debts

[EPISTLE DEDICATORY]

To the Right Honorable
ROBERT
EARL OF CARNARVON,[1]
MASTER FALCONER OF ENGLAND

MY GOOD LORD,

PARDON, I beeseech you, my boldness, in presuming to shelter this comedy under the wings of your lordship's favor and protection. I am not ignorant (having never yet deserved you in my service) that it cannot but meet with a severe construction if, in the clemency of your noble disposition, you fashion not a better defense for me than I can fancy for myself. All I can allege is that   10 divers Italian princes and lords of eminent rank in England have not disdained to receive and read poems of this nature, nor am I wholly lost in my hopes but that your honor (who have ever expressed yourself a favorer and friend to the Muses) may vouchsafe, in your gracious acceptance of this trifle, to give me encouragement to present you with some labored work and of a higher strain hereafter. I was born a devoted servant to the thrice noble family of your incomparable lady,[2] and am most ambitious, but with a becoming distance, to be known to your lordship, which if you please to admit, I shall embrace it as a bounty, that while I live shall oblige me to acknowledge you for my noble patron, and profess myself to be   20

Your honor's true servant,
PHILIP MASSINGER.

[COMMENDATORY POEMS]

TO THE INGENIOUS
AUTHOR Master
PHILIP MASSINGER
On His Comedy
called *A New Way to Pay Old Debts*

'Tis a rare charity, and thou couldst not
So proper to the time have found a plot:
Yet whilst you teach to pay, you lend:[1] the age
We wretches live in, that to come, the stage,
The throngèd audience that was thither brought
Invited by your fame, and to be taught
This lesson. All are grown indebted more,
And when they look for freedom run in score.[2]
It was a cruel courtesy to call
In hope of liberty, and then, enthrall.[3]   10
The nobles are your bondmen, gentry, and
All besides[4] those that did not understand.
They were no men of credit, bankrupts born,
Fit to be trusted with no stock[5] but scorn.
You have more wisely credited to such
That, though they cannot pay, can value much.
I am your debtor, too, but to my shame
Repay you nothing back, but your own fame.

Henry Moody, *miles.*[6]

To his friend the Author

You may remember how you chid me when
I ranked you equal with those glorious men,
Beaumont, and Fletcher: if you love not praise
You must forbear the publishing of plays.
The crafty mazes of the cunning plot,
The polished phrase, the sweet expressions got
Neither by theft nor violence, the conceit[7]
Fresh and unsullied; all is of weight,
Able to make the captive reader know
I did but justice when I placed you so.   10
A shamefast[8] blushing would become the brow
Of some weak virgin writer; we allow
To you a kind of pride; and there where most
Should blush at commendations, you should boast.
If any think I flatter, let him look
Off[9] from my idle trifles on the book.

Thomas Jay, *miles.*[10]

DRAMATIS PERSONÆ

LOVELL, *an English lord*
SIR GILES OVERREACH, *a cruel extortioner*
FRANK WELLBORN, *a prodigal*
TOM ALLWORTH, *a young gentleman, page to Lord Lovell*
GREEDY, *a hungry justice of peace*
MARALL, *a term driver [1]; a creature of Sir Giles Overreach*
ORDER, *a steward* ⎫
AMBLE, *an usher* ⎬ *servants to the Lady Allworth*
FURNACE, *a cook* ⎪
WATCHALL, *a porter* ⎭

WILLDO, *a parson*
TAPWELL, *an alehouse keeper*
Three Creditors

THE LADY ALLWORTH, *a rich widow*
MARGARET, *Overreach his daughter*
Waiting Woman
Chambermaid
FROTH, *Tapwell's wife*
Servants

ACT ONE

SCENE ONE

[*Enter*] WELLBORN, TAPWELL, [*and*] FROTH.

Well. No booze? Nor no tobacco?
Tap.   Not a suck, sir,
Nor the remainder of a single can
Left by a drunken porter, all night palled [1] too.
Froth. Not the dropping of the tap for your
     morning's draught, sir.
'Tis verity, I assure you.

Well.   Verity, you brach! [2]
The devil turned precisian? [3] Rogue, what am I?
Tap. Troth, durst I trust you with a looking-glass
To let you see your trim shape, [4] you would quit [5] me
And take the name yourself.
Well.   How, dog?
Tap.   Even so, sir.
And I must tell you, if you but advance   10
Your Plimworth cloak [6] you shall be soon instructed
There dwells, and within call, if it please your worship,
A potent monarch called the constable,
That does command a citadel called the stocks,
Whose guards are certain files of rusty billmen [7]
Such as with great dexterity will hale
Your tattered, lousy—
Well.   Rascal! Slave!
Froth.   No rage, sir.
Tap. At his own peril. Do not put yourself
In too much heat, there being no water
To quench your thirst; and sure, for other liquor,   20
As mighty ale or beer, they are things, I take it,
You must no more remember—not in a dream, sir.
Well. Why, thou unthankful villain, darest thou talk
     thus?
Is not thy house, and all thou hast, my gift?
Tap. I find it not in chalk; [8] and Timothy Tapwell
Does keep no other register.
Well.   Am not I he
Whose riots fed and clothed thee? Wert thou not
Born on my father's land, and proud to be
A drudge in his house?
Tap.   What I was, sir, it skills [9] not;
What you are, is apparent. Now, for a farewell,   30
Since you talk of father, in my hope it will torment you,
I'll briefly tell your story. Your dead father,
My quondam [10] master, was a man of worship,
Old Sir John Wellborn, justice of peace and quorum, [11]
And stood fair to be *custos rotulorum ;* [12]
Bare the whole sway of the shire, kept a great house,
Relieved the poor, and so forth; but, he dying,
And the twelve hundred a year coming to you,
Late Master Francis, but now forlorn Wellborn—
Well. Slave, stop, or I shall lose myself!

EPISTLE DEDICATORY
   [1] *Carnarvon:* Robert Dormer (*d.* 1643), subsequently a celebrated Royalist soldier, was first Earl of Carnarvon and, as befitting an eminent sportsman, master of the hawks.
   [2] *lady:* Anne Sophia Herbert, daughter of Philip Herbert, Earl of Montgomery, whose father, the Earl of Pembroke, Massinger's own father had served.

COMMENDATORY POEMS
   [1] *you lend:* i.e., as by putting the present age, the future, the theater, and the audience that first saw the play, in your debt.   [2] *score:* debt.
   [3] *enthrall:* in our sense, but also "to imprison," "dash the hope of liberty."   [4] *besides:* except.
   [5] *stock:* revenue, portion.
   [6] Sir Henry Moody of Garesdon, Wiltshire, second baronet, *d.* 1661 or 1662 in Virginia as a bankrupt. *Miles* (*L.*) = soldier.   [7] *conceit:* happy or witty idea.
   [8] *shamefast:* abashed.
   [9] *Off:* Away (emending Q's "of").
   [10] Sir Thomas Jay of Wiltshire, graduated 1613 from Queen's College, Oxford, member of Lincoln's Inn.

DRAMATIS PERSONÆ
   [1] *term driver:* one who comes to the law courts or court during sessions: obviously pejorative.

I.i.
   [1] *palled:* staled, made flat.   [2] *brach:* bitch.
   [3] *precisian:* Puritan.
   [4] *shape:* costume (Wellborn's is the reverse of "trim").
   [5] *quit:* acquit.
   [6] *Plimworth cloak:* A Plymouth cloak is a cudgel.
   [7] *files . . . billmen:* troops of watchmen armed with rusty pikes.
   [8] *in chalk:* in the tally the barman keeps to mark the "score" or debt of the drinker; hence, "in the record."
   [9] *skills:* matters.   [10] *quondam:* sometimes.
   [11] *quorum:* a principal justice, whose presence was required to make up a quorum.
   [12] *L.:* keeper of the records: the chief justice.

Froth.   Very hardly;
You cannot out of your way.[13]
    Tap.   But to my story.   41
You were then a lord of acres, the prime gallant,
And I your underbutler. Note the change now.
You had a merry time of 't—hawks and hounds,
With choice of running horses; mistresses
Of all sorts and all sizes, yet so hot
As their embraces made your lordships[14] melt,
Which your uncle, Sir Giles Overreach, observing,
Resolving not to lose a drop of 'em
On foolish mortgages, statutes,[15] and bonds,   50
For a while supplied your looseness, and then left you.
    Well. Some curate hath penned this invective,
      mongrel,
And you have studied it.
    Tap.   I have not done yet.
Your land gone, and your credit not worth a token,[16]
You grew the common borrower; no man scaped
Your paper pellets,[17] from the gentleman
To the beggars on highways, that sold you switches
In your gallantry.
    Well.   I shall switch your brains out!
    Tap. Where poor Tim Tapwell, with a little stock,
Some forty pounds or so, bought a small cottage,   60
Humbled myself to marriage with my Froth here,
Gave entertainment—
    Well.   Yes, to whores and canters,[18]
Clubbers[19] by night.
    Tap.   True, but they brought in profit,
And had a gift to pay for what they called for,
And stuck[20] not like your mastership. The poor
      income
I gleaned from them hath made me in my parish
Thought worthy to be scavenger,[21] and in time
May rise to be overseer of the poor,[22]
Which if I do, on your petition, Wellborn,
I may allow you thirteenpence a quarter,   70
And you shall thank my worship.
    Well.   Thus, you dogbolt,[23]
And thus—

                Beats and kicks him.

    Tap. [*To* FROTH] Cry out for help!
    Well.   Stir, and thou
      diest.
Your potent prince, the constable, shall not save you.
Hear me, ungrateful hellhound! Did not I
Make purses[24] for you? Then you licked my boots,
And thought your holy day[25] cloak too coarse to clean
      'em.
'Twas I that, when I heard thee swear if ever
Thou couldst arrive at forty pounds thou wouldst
Live like an emperor, 'twas I that gave it
In ready gold. Deny this, wretch!
    Tap.   I must, sir,   80
For, from the tavern to the taphouse, all,
On forfeiture of their licenses, stand bound
Never to remember who their best guests were,
If they grew poor like you.
    Well.   They are well rewarded

That beggar themselves to make such cuckolds rich.
Thou viper, thankless viper! impudent bawd!
But, since you are grown forgetful, I will help
You memory, and tread thee into mortar,
Not leave one bone unbroken.

                [*Beats him again.*]
    Tap.   Oh!
    Froth.   Ask mercy.

           Enter ALLWORTH.

    Well. 'Twill not be granted.
    All.   Hold—for my sake,
      hold!   90
Deny me, Frank? They are not worth your anger.
    Well. For once thou hast redeemed them from this
      scepter.

                [*Shows*] *His cudgel.*

But let 'em vanish, creeping on their knees,
And, if they grumble, I revoke my pardon.
    Froth. This comes of your prating, husband; you
      presumed
On your ambling wit, and must use your glib tongue,
Though you are beaten lame for 't.
    Tap.   Patience, Froth;
There's law to cure our bruises.

        They go off on their hands and knees.

    Well.   Sent to your mother?
    All. My lady, Frank, my patroness, my all!
She's such a mourner for my father's death,   100
And, in her love to him, so favors me
That I cannot pay too much observance to her.
There are few such stepdames.
    Well.   'Tis a noble widow,
And keeps her reputation pure and clear
From the least taint of infamy; her life,
With the splendor of her actions, leaves no tongue
To envy or detraction. Prithee, tell me,
Has she no suitors?
    All.   Even the best of the shire, Frank,
My lord excepted, such as sue and send,
And send and sue again, but to no purpose.   110
Their frequent visits have not gained her presence.
Yet she's so far from sullenness and pride
That I dare undertake you shall meet from her
A liberal entertainment. I can give you

---

    [13] *You ... way:* i.e., You cannot lose yourself being
already lost.   [14] *lordships:* estates.
    [15] *statutes:* promissory notes that, if taken up, meant the
forfeiting of the estates.
    [16] *token:* a piece of metal resembling a coin and used by
merchants as a medium of exchange.
    [17] *paper pellets:* IOUs.
    [18] *canters:* thieves or rascals who spoke their peculiar cant
or argot.   [19] *Clubbers:* Companions.
    [20] *stuck:* without payment.
    [21] *scavenger:* paid street cleaner: garbage man.
    [22] *overseer of the poor:* another paid officer, functioning
under the Poor Law.
    [23] *dogbolt:* blunted arrow, and hence "worthless."
    [24] *make purses:* get trade (money).   [25] *holy day:* holiday.

A catalogue of her suitors' names.
Well.   Forbear it,
While I give you good counsel. I am bound to it;
Thy father was my friend, and that affection
I bore to him, in right descends to thee.
Thou art a handsome and a hopeful youth,
Nor will I have the least affront stick on thee,   120
If I with any danger can prevent it.
All. I thank your noble care; but, pray you, in what
Do I run the hazard?
Well.   Art thou not in love?
Put it not off with wonder.[26]
All.   In love, at my years?
Well. You think you walk in clouds, but are
        trans[pa]rent.
I have heard all, and the choice that you have made,
And with my finger can point out the north star
By which the loadstone[27] of your folly's guided.
And, to confirm this true, what think you of
Fair Margaret, the only child and heir   130
Of cormorant[28] Overreach? Does it[29] blush and start,
To hear her only named? Blush at your want
Of wit and reason.
All.   You are too bitter, sir.
Well. Wounds of this nature are not to be cured
With balms, but corrosives. I must be plain:
Art thou scarce manumized[30] from the porter's lodge[31]
And yet sworn servant to the pantofle,[32]
And dar'st thou dream of marriage? I fear
'Twill be concluded for impossible
That there is now, nor e'er shall be hereafter,   140
A handsome page or player's boy[33] of fourteen
But either loves a wench, or drabs[34] love him—
Court-waiters[35] not exempted.
All.   This is madness.
Howe'er you have discovered my intents,
You know my aims are lawful; and, if ever
The queen of flowers, the glory of the spring,
The sweetest comfort to our smell, the rose,
Sprang from an envious brier, I may infer
There's such disparity in their conditions
Between the goddess of my soul, the daughter,   150
And the base churl of her father.

Well.   Grant this true,
As I believe it, canst thou ever hope
To enjoy a quiet bed with her whose father
Ruined thy state?
All.   And yours too.
Well.   I confess it.
True, I must tell you as a friend, and freely,
That, where impossibilities are apparent,
'Tis indiscretion to nourish hopes.
Canst thou imagine (let not self-love blind thee)
That Sir Giles Overreach, that, to make her great
In swelling titles, without touch of conscience   160
Will cut his neighbor's throat, and I hope his own too,
Will e'er consent to make her thine? Give o'er,
And think of some course suitable to thy rank,
And prosper in it.
All.   You have well advised me.
But in the meantime you that are so studious
Of my affairs wholly neglect your own.
Remember yourself, and in what plight you are.
Well. No matter, no matter.
All.   Yes, 'tis much material.[36]
You know my fortune and my means; yet something
I can spare from myself to help your wants.
Well.   How's this?
All. Nay, be not angry; there's eight pieces[37]   171
To put you in better fashion.
Well.   Money from thee?
From a boy? A stipendary?[38] One that lives
At the devotion of a stepmother
And the uncertain favor of a lord?
I'll eat my arms first. Howsoe'er blind Fortune
Hath spent the utmost of her malice on me—
Though I am vomited out of an alehouse,
And, thus accoutered,[39] know not where to eat,
Or drink, or sleep, but underneath this canopy[40]—   180
Although I thank thee, I despise thy offer,
And, as I in my madness broke my state[41]
Without th' assistance of another's brain,
In my right wits I'll piece it;[42] at the worst,
Die thus and be forgotten.
All.   A strange humor![43]
                                        Exeunt.

---

[26] *Put . . . wonder:* Don't try to turn the question aside by
pretending astonishment.

[27] *loadstone:* magnet; by inference, "compass."

[28] *cormorant:* a rapacious bird; hence defining Overreach's
greedy character.   [29] *it:* i.e., you (baby talk).

[30] *manumized:* manumitted, enfranchised.

[31] *porter's lodge:* suggesting the most menial employment
possible for a page.

[32] *pantofle:* slipper (which he is charged with fetching; his
duties are still base enough).

[33] *player's boy:* actor's apprentice.   [34] *drabs:* sluts.

[35] *Court-waiters:* Pages at Court.

[36] *'tis much material:* i.e., it does matter.

[37] *pieces:* of gold or silver.   [38] *stipendary:* dependent.

[39] *accoutered:* habited.   [40] *this canopy:* the heavens.

[41] *broke my state:* bankrupted my estate.

[42] *piece it:* put it right again, mend it.

[43] *humor:* disposition.

I.ii.
[1] *places:* i.e., in the hot kitchen, suggesting choler.

I.ii

[Enter] ORDER, AMBLE, FURNACE,
        [*and*] WATCHALL.

Ord. Set all things right, or, as my name is Order,
And by this staff of office that commands you,
This chain and double ruff, symbols of power,
Whoever misses in his function,
For one whole week makes forfeiture of his breakfast
And privilege in the wine cellar.
Amb.   You are merry,
Good Master Steward.
Furn.   Let him; I'll be angry.
Amb. Why, fellow Furnace, 'tis not twelve a-clock
        yet,
Nor dinner taking up; then, 'tis allowed,
Cooks by their places[1] may be choleric.   10

Furn. You think you have spoke wisely, Goodman
    Amble,
My lady's go-before![2]
    Ord.   Nay, nay, no wrangling.
    Furn. Twit me with the authority of the kitchen?
At all hours and all places, I'll be angry;
And, thus provoked, when I am at my prayers,
I will be angry.
    Amb.   There was no hurt meant.
    Furn. I am friends with thee; and yet I will be angry.
    Ord. With whom?
    Furn.   No matter whom—yet, now I
    think on 't,
I am angry with my lady.
    Watch.   Heaven forbid, man!
    Ord. What cause has she given thee?
    Furn.   Cause enough,
    Master Steward.   20
I was entertained[3] by her to please her palate.
And, till she forswore eating, I performed it.
Now since our master, noble Allworth, died,
Though I crack my brains to find out tempting sauces,
And raise fortifications in the pastry
Such as might serve for models in the Low Countries,
Which, if they had been practiced at Breda,[4]
Spinola might have thrown his cap at it,[5] and ne'er took
    it—
    Amb. But you had wanted matter there to work on.
    Furn. Matter? With six eggs and a strike[6] of rye
    meal   30
I had kept the town till doomsday, perhaps longer.
    Ord. But what's this to your pet[7] against my lady?
    Furn. What's this? Marry, this: when I am three
    parts roasted
And the fourth part parboiled[8] to prepare her viands,
She keeps her chamber, dines with a panada[9]
Or water gruel my sweat never thought on.
    Ord. But your art is seen in the dining room.
    Furn.   By
    whom?
By such as pretend love to her, but come
To feed upon her. Yet, of all the harpies
That do devour her, I am out of charity   40
With none so much as the thin-gutted squire
That's stolen into commission.
    Ord.   Justice Greedy?
    Furn. The same, the same. Meat's cast away upon
    him;
It never thrives. He holds this paradox:
Who eats not well, can ne'er do justice well.
His stomach's as insatiate as the grave,
Or strumpets' ravenous appetites.
    Watch.   One knocks.

         ALLWORTH *knocks, and enters.*

    Ord. Our late[10] young master!
    Amb.   Welcome, sir.
    Furn.   Your
    hand.
If you have a stomach, a cold bakemeat's ready.
    Ord. His father's picture in little.[11]

    Furn.   We are all your
    servants.   50
    Amb. In you he lives.
    All.   At once, my thanks to all;
This is yet some comfort. Is my lady stirring?

   Enter the LADY ALLWORTH, Waiting Woman,
         [*and*] Chambermaid.

    Ord. Her presence answer for us.
    Lady All.   Sort those silks well.
I'll take the air alone.
         Exeunt Waiting Woman *and* Chambermaid.
    Furn.   You air and air;
But will you never taste but spoonmeat[12] more?
To what use serve I?
    Lady All.   Prithee, be not angry;
I shall, ere long. I' the meantime, there is gold
To buy thee aprons and a summer suit.[13]
    Furn. I am appeased, and Furnace now grows cook.
    Lady All. And, as I gave directions, if this morning
I am visited by any, entertain 'em[14]   61
As heretofore; but say, in my excuse,
I am indisposed.
    Ord.   I shall, madam.
    Lady All.   Do, and leave me.—
Nay, stay you, Allworth.
         Exeunt ORDER, AMBLE, FURNACE,
             [*and*] WATCHALL.
    All.   I shall gladly grow here,
To wait on your commands.
    Lady All.   So soon turned courtier!
    All. Style not that courtship, madam, which is duty
Purchased on your part.
    Lady All.   Well, you shall o'ercome;
I'll not contend in words. How is it with
Your noble master?
    All.   Ever like himself,
No scruple[15] lessened in the full weight of honor.   70
He did command me, pardon my presumption,
As his unworthy deputy to kiss
Your ladyship's fair hands.
    Lady All.   I am honored in
His favor to me. Does he hold his purpose
For the Low Countries?
    All.   Constantly, good madam;
But he will in person first present his service.
    Lady All. And how approve you of his course? You
    are yet

---

    [2] *go-before:* usher.   [3] *entertained:* employed.
    [4] *Breda:* which surrendered from starvation to the
Spanish general, the Marquis of Spinola, in 1625—thus
establishing a terminal date for the writing of the play, unless
the reference is a later interpolation.
    [5] *thrown . . . it:* given up trying.
    [6] *strike:* measure—"bushel."   [7] *pet:* peeve.
    [8] *parboiled:* boiled altogether.
    [9] *panada:* bread pudding.
    [10] *late:* i.e., when his father was still living.
    [11] *little:* miniature.   [12] *spoonmeat:* pap, babyfood.
    [13] *summer suit:* to cool his anger.
    [14] *entertain 'em:* give them welcome.
    [15] *scruple:* slightest particle.

Like virgin parchment, capable of any
Inscription, vicious, or honorable.
I will not force your will, but leave you free   80
To your own election.[16]
 All.   Any form you please
I will put on; but, might I make my choice,
With humble emulation I would follow
The path my lord marks to me.
 Lady All.   'Tis well answered,
And I commend your spirit. You had a father—
Blessèd be his memory!—that some few hours
Before the will of heaven took him from me,
Who did commend you, by the dearest ties
Of perfect love between us, to my charge;
And therefore what I speak you are bound to hear   90
With such respect as if he lived in me.
He was my husband, and, howe'er you are not
Son of my womb, you may be of my love,
Provided you deserve it.
 All.   I have found you,
Most honored madam, the best mother to me,
And, with my utmost strength of care and service,
Will labor that you never may repent
Your bounties showered upon me.
 Lady All.   I much hope it.
These were your father's words: "If e'er my son
Follow the war, tell him it is a school   100
Where all the principles tending to honor
Are taught, if truly followed. But for such
As repair thither as a place in which
They do presume they may with license practice
Their lusts and riots, they shall never merit
The noble name of soldiers. To dare boldly
In a fair cause, and for the country's safety
To run upon the cannon's mouth undaunted;
To obey their leaders, and shun mutinies;
To bear with patience the winter's cold   110
And summer's scorching heat, and not to faint,
When plenty of provision[17] fails, with hunger—
Are the essential parts make up a soldier,
Not swearing, dice, or drinking."
 All.   There's no syllable
You speak but is to me an oracle,
Which but to doubt were impious.
 Lady All.   To conclude:
Beware ill company, for often men
Are like to those with whom they do converse;
And from one man I warned[18] you, and that's
 Wellborn,
Not cause he's poor—that rather claims your pity—

But that he's in his manners so debauched,   121
And hath to vicious courses sold himself.
'Tis true, your father loved him while he was
Worthy the loving; but if he had lived
To have seen him as he is, he had cast him off,
As you must do.
 All.   I shall obey in all things.
 Lady All. You follow me[19] to my chamber; you shall
 have gold
To furnish you like my son, and still supplied
As I hear from you.[20]
 All.   I am still your creature.
           Exeunt.

I.iii

 [*Enter*] OVERREACH, GREEDY, ORDER, AMBLE,
  FURNACE, WATCHALL, [*and*] MARALL.

 Greedy. Not to be seen?
 Over.   Still cloistered up? Her
 reason,
I hope, assures her, though she make herself
Close prisoner ever for her husband's loss,
'Twill not recover him.
 Ord.   Sir, it is her will,
Which we that are her servants ought to serve it
And not dispute. Howe'er, you are nobly welcome;
And, if you please to stay, that you may think so,
There came not six days since from Hull a pipe[1]
Of rich Canary, which shall spend itself
For my lady's honor.
 Greedy.   Is it of the right race?[2]   10
 Ord. Yes, Master Greedy.
 Amb. [*Aside*]   How his mouth runs o'er!
 Furn. [*Aside*] I'll make it run, and run.—Save your
 good worship!
 Greedy. Honest Master Cook, thy hand again! how I
 love thee!
Are the good dishes still in being? Speak, boy.
 Furn. If you have a mind to feed, there is a chine
Of beef, well seasoned.
 Greedy.   Good!
 Furn.   A pheasant, larded.[3]
 Greedy. That I might now give thanks for't!
 Furn.   Other
 kickshaws.[4]
Besides, there came last night from the forest of
 Sherwood
The fattest stag I ever cooked.
 Greedy.   A stag, man?
 Furn. A stag, sir—part of it prepared for dinner,   20
And baked in puff paste.
 Greedy.   Puff paste too, Sir Giles!
A ponderous chine of beef! a pheasant larded!
And red deer too, Sir Giles, and baked in puff paste!
All business set aside, let us give thanks here.
 Furn. How the lean skeleton's raped![5]
 Over.   You know we
 cannot.
 Mar. Your worships are to sit on a commission,
And, if you fail to come, you lose the cause.

---

[16] *election:* choosing.

[17] *plenty of provision:* supplies (food) to be provided.

[18] *warned:* the present tense, "warn," makes better sense.

[19] *You follow me:* Omission of either subject or object pronoun would make line scan.

[20] *still . . . you:* i.e., gold will be forthcoming continually to the degree that I hear good report of you.

I.iii.

[1] *pipe:* large cask used for wine (here, Canary wine).

[2] *race:* flavor.   [3] *larded:* dressed with bacon.

[4] *kickshaws:* delicate trifles. [5] *raped:* rapt, ecstatic.

Greedy. Cause me no causes. I'll prove 't, for such a dinner
We may put off a commission: you shall find it
Henrici decimo quarto[6]—
    Over.   Fie, Master Greedy!   30
Will you lose me a thousand pounds for a dinner?
No more, for shame! We must forget the belly
When we think of profit.
    Greedy.   Well, you shall o'errule me.
I could even cry now.—Do you hear, Master Cook?
Send but a corner of that immortal pasty,
And I in thankfulness will by your boy
Send you—a brace[7] of threepences.
    Furn.   Will you be so
    prodigal?

        Enter WELLBORN.

    Over. Remember me to your lady.—Who have we
    here?
    Well. You know me.
    Over.   I did once, but now I will not;
Thou art no blood of mine. Avaunt, thou beggar!   40
If ever thou presume to own[8] me more,
I'll have thee caged and whipped.
    Greedy.   I'll grant the warrant.
Think of Pie Corner,[9] Furnace!
        Exeunt OVERREACH, GREEDY, MARALL.
    Watch.   Will you out,[10] sir?
I wonder how you durst creep in.
    Ord.   This is rudeness
And saucy impudence.
    Amb.   Cannot you stay
To be served, among your fellows, from the basket,[11]
But you must press into the hall?
    Furn.   Prithee, vanish
Into some outhouse, though it be the pigsty;
My scullion shall come to thee.

        Enter ALLWORTH.

    Well.   This is rare.
O, here's Tom Allworth.—Tom!
    All.   We must be strangers;
Nor would I have you seen here for a million.   51
        Exit ALLWORTH.
    Well. Better and better. He contemns[12] me too!

    Enter [Waiting] Woman *and* Chambermaid.

    Woman. Foh, what a smell's here! What thing's this?
    Cham.   A
    creature
Made out of the privy; let us hence, for love's sake,
Or I shall sown.[13]
    Woman.   I begin to feel faint already.
        Exeunt [Waiting] Woman *and* Chambermaid.
    Watch. Will you know your way?
    Amb.   Or shall we teach
    it you
By the head and shoulders?
    Well.   No; I will not stir.
Do you mark, I will not. Let me see the wretch
That dares attempt to force me. Why, you slaves,

Created only to make legs[14] and cringe,   60
To carry in a dish and shift a trencher,
That have not souls only to hope a blessing
Beyond blackjacks[15] or flagons—you that were born
Only to consume meat and drink, and batten
Upon reversions![16]—who advances? Who
Shows me the way?
    Ord.   My lady!

      Enter LADY [ALLWORTH, Waiting] Woman,
          [*and*] Chambermaid.

    Cham.   Here's the monster.
    Woman. Sweet madam, keep your glove to your
    nose.
    Cham. Or let me
Fetch some perfumes may be predominant;
You wrong yourself else.
    Well.   Madam, my designs   69
Bear me to you.
    Lady All. To me?
    Well.   And, though I have met with
But ragged entertainment from your grooms here,
I hope from you to receive that noble usage
As may become the true friend of your husband,
And then I shall forget these.
    Lady All.   I am amazed
To see and hear this rudeness. Darest thou think,
Though sworn, that it can ever find belief
That I, who to the best men of this country
Denied my presence since my husband's death,
Can fall so low as to change words with thee?   80
Thou son of infamy, forbear my house,
And know and keep the distance that's between us,
Or, though it be against my gentler temper,
I shall take order you no more shall be
An eyesore to me.
    Well.   Scorn me not, good lady;
But, as in form you are angelical;
Imitate the heavenly natures and vouchsafe
At the least awhile to hear me. You will grant
The blood that runs in this arm is as noble
As that which fills your veins; those costly jewels,   90
And those rich clothes you wear, your men's
    observance
And women's flattery are in you no virtues,
Nor these rags, with my poverty, in me vices.
You have a fair fame,[17] and, I know, deserve it;
Yet, lady, I must say, in nothing more
Than in the pious sorrow you have shown
For your late noble husband.
    Ord. [*Aside*]   How she starts!
    Furn. [*Aside*] And hardly can keep finger from the eye
To hear him named.

---

  6 *L.:* (In a law of) the fourteenth year of Henry.
  7 *brace:* pair.   8 *own:* recognize, greet.
  9 *Pie Corner:* London street populated by cooks' stalls.
  10 *out:* leave.
  11 *basket:* of scraps and broken meats reserved for the poor.
  12 *contemns:* shuns.   13 *sown:* swoon.
  14 *make legs:* bow.   15 *blackjacks:* leather jugs of beer.
  16 *batten . . . reversions:* grow fat on what's left over.
  17 *fame:* reputation.

Lady All.   Have you aught else to say?
Well. That husband, madam, was once in his
     fortune   100
Almost as low as I; want, debts, and quarrels
Lay heavy on him. Let it not be thought
A boast in me, though I say I relieved him.
'Twas I that gave him fashion; [18] mine the sword
That did on all occasions second his;
I brought him on and off with honor, lady;
And, when in all men's judgments he was sunk
And in his own hopes not to be bunged [19] up,
I stepped unto him, took him by the hand,
And set him upright.
     Furn. [*Aside*]   Are not we base rogues,   110
That could forget this?
     Well.   I confess, you made him
Master of your estate; nor could your friends,
Though he brought no wealth with him, blame you
     for 't,
For he had a shape, and to that shape a mind,
Made up of all parts either great or noble—
So winning a behavior not to be
Resisted, madam.
     Lady All.   'Tis most true, he had.
     Well. For his sake, then, in that I was his friend,
Do not contemn me.
     Lady All.   For what's past, excuse me;
I will redeem it.—Order, give the gentleman   120
A hundred pounds.
     Well.   No, madam, on no terms.
I will nor beg nor borrow sixpence of you,
But be supplied elsewhere, or want thus ever.
Only one suit I make, which you deny not
To strangers; and 'tis this.

                              Whispers to her.

Lady All.   Fie! nothing else?
Well. Nothing, unless you please to charge your
     servants
To throw away a little respect upon me.
Lady All. What you demand is yours.
Well.   I thank you,
     lady.
Now what can be wrought out of such a suit
Is yet in supposition. I have said all;   130
When you please, you may retire.
                              [*Exit* LADY ALLWORTH.]
                         —Nay, all's forgotten;

---

[18] *gave him fashion:* brought him up in the world.
[19] *bunged:* stopped, staunched.

II.i.
     [1] *out:* emended generally, although perhaps not neces-
sarily, to "on't": "You know the way." *Worship* is sometimes
emended to "worships," i.e., "you justices."
     [2] *unthrifts:* spendthrifts.
     [3] *chapfallen:* slackjawed and hence "accommodating."
     [4] *Where:* Whereas.   [5] *or:* either.
     [6] *L.:* legal writ (which would expose him to prosecution).
     [7] *at my devotion:* attending on my business.
     [8] *for:* as for.   [9] *hedge in:* enclose.
     [10] *it:* i.e., the thought or scheme.

And for a lucky omen to my project
Shake hands and end all quarrels in the cellar.
     Ord. Agreed, agreed.
     Furn.   Still merry Master Wellborn!
                                   Exeunt.

ACT TWO

SCENE ONE

[Enter] OVERREACH, [*and*] MARALL.

Over. He's gone, I warrant thee; this commission
     crushed him.
Mar. Your worship have the way out,[1] and ne'er
     miss
To squeeze these unthrifts[2] into air; and yet
The chapfallen[3] justice did his part, returning
For your advantage the certificate,
Against his conscience and his knowledge too
(With your good favor), to the utter ruin
Of the poor farmer.
     Over.   'Twas for these good ends
I made him a justice; he that bribes his belly
Is certain to command his soul.
     Mar.   I wonder,   10
Still with your license, why your worship, having
The power to put this thin-gut in commission,
You are not in 't yourself?
     Over.   Thou art a fool.
In being out of office I am out of danger;
Where,[4] if I were a justice, besides the trouble,
I might or[5] out of wilfulness or error
Run myself finely into a *praemunire*,[6]
And so become a prey to the informer.
No, I'll have none of 't. 'Tis enough I keep
Greedy at my devotion;[7] so he serve   20
My purposes, let him hang or damn, I care not.
Friendship is but a word.
     Mar.   You are all wisdom.
     Over. I would be worldly wise; for[8] the other
     wisdom,
That does prescribe us a well-governed life,
And to do right to others as ourselves,
I value not an atom.
     Mar.   What course take you,
With your good patience, to hedge in[9] the manor
Of your neighbor, Master Frugal, as 'tis said
He will nor sell nor borrow nor exchange?   29
And his land, lying in the midst of your many lordships,
Is a foul blemish.
     Over.   I have thought on 't, Marall,
And it[10] shall take. I must have all men sellers,
And I the only purchaser.
     Mar.   'Tis most fit, sir.
     Over. I'll therefore buy some cottage near his manor,
Which done, I'll make my men break ope his fences,
Ride o'er his standing corn, and in the night
Set fire on his barns, or break his cattle's legs.
These trespasses draw on suits and suits, expenses,
Which I can spare, but will soon beggar him.

When I have harried him thus two or three year,　40
Though he sue *in forma pauperis*,[11] in spite
Of all his thrift and care he'll grow behindhand.
　　Mar. The best I ever heard! I could adore you.
　　Over. Then, with the favor of my man of law,
I will pretend some title.[12] Want will force him
To put it to arbitrament;[13] then, if he sell
For half the value, he shall have ready money,
And I possess his land.
　　Mar.　　　　　　'Tis above wonder!
Wellborn was apt[14] to sell, and needed not
These fine arts, sir, to hook him in.
　　Over.　　　　　　Well thought on.　50
This varlet, Marall, lives too long to upbraid me
With my close cheat[15] put upon him. Will nor cold
Nor hunger kill him?
　　Mar.　　　　I know not what to think on 't.
I have used all means, and the last night I caused
His host, the tapster, to turn him out of doors,
And have been since with all your friends and tenants
And on the forfeit of your favor charged him,[16]
Though a crust of moldy bread would keep him from
　　starving,
Yet they should not relieve him. This is done sir.
　　Over. That was something, Marall; but thou must
　　go further,　　　　　　　　　　　　　60
And suddenly, Marall.
　　Mar.　　　　Where and when you please, sir.
　　Over. I would have thee seek him out and, if thou
　　canst,
Persuade him that 'tis better steal than beg;
Then, if I prove he has but robbed a henroost,
Not all the world shall save him from the gallows.
Do anything to work him to despair,
And 'tis thy masterpiece.
　　Mar.　　　　I will do my best, sir.
　　Over. I am now on my main work with the Lord
　　Lovell,
The gallant-minded, popular Lord Lovell,
The minion[17] of the people's love. I hear　70
He's come into the country,[18] and my aims are
To insinuate myself into his knowledge,
And then invite him to my house.
　　Mar.　　　　I have[19] you;
This points at my young mistress.
　　Over.　　　　　　She must part with
That humble title, and write "honorable,"
"Right honorable," Marall, my "right honorable"
　　daughter,
If all I have, or e'er shall get, will do it.
I will have her well attended; there are ladies
Of errant[20] knights decayed and brought so low
That for cast[21] clothes and meat will gladly serve her.
And 'tis my glory, though I come from the city,　81
To have their issue[22] whom I have undone,
To kneel to mine as bondslaves.
　　Mar.　　　　　　'Tis fit state, sir.
　　Over. And therefore I'll not have a chambermaid
That ties her shoes, or any meaner office,
But such whose fathers were worshipful.
'Tis a rich man's pride, there having ever been

More than a feud, a strange antipathy,
Between us and true gentry.

　　　　　　　Enter WELLBORN.

　　Mar.　　　　　　See who's here, sir.
　　Over. Hence, monster! prodigy![23]
　　Well.　　　　　　Sir, your wife's
　　nephew;　　　　　　　　　　　　　90
She and my father tumbled in one belly.
　　Over. Avoid my sight! thy breath's infectious,
　　rogue!
I shun thee as a leprosy or the plague.—
Come hither, Marall. [*Aside*] This is the time to work
　　him.
　　Mar. I warrant you, sir.
　　　　　　　　　　　　Exit OVERREACH.
　　Well.　　　　By this light, I think he's
　　mad.
　　Mar. Mad? Had you took compassion on yourself,
You long since had been mad.
　　Well.　　　　You have took a course,
Between you and my venerable uncle,
To make me so.
　　Mar.　　　　The more pale-spirited you,
That would not be instructed. I swear deeply—　100
　　Well. By what?
　　Mar.　　　　By my religion.
　　Well.　　　　　　Thy religion!
The devil's creed!—But what would you have done?
　　Mar. Had there been but one tree in all the shire,
Nor any hope to compass[24] a penny halter,
Before, like you, I had outlived my fortunes,
A withe[25] had served my turn to hang myself.
I am zealous in your cause; pray you, hang yourself,
And presently,[26] as you love your credit.
　　Well.　　　　　　I thank you.
　　Mar. Will you stay till you die in a ditch, or lice
　　devour you?
Or, if you dare not do the feat yourself,　110
But that you'll put the state to charge and trouble,
Is there no purse to be cut,[27] house to be broken,
Or market women with eggs, that you may murder,
And so dispatch the business?
　　Well.　　　　　　Here's variety,
I must confess; but I'll accept of none
Of all your gentle offers, I assure you.
　　Mar. Why, have you hope ever to eat again,
Or drink, or to be the master of three farthings?

---

[11] *L.:* as a pauper (and hence not obligated to pay legal
fees).　　　[12] *pretend some title:* affect a (trumped-up) claim.
[13] *arbitrament:* judgment, settlement.　　　[14] *apt:* ready.
[15] *close cheat:* secret fraud.
[16] *charged him:* laid his burden on him ("him" is frequently emended to "them").　　　[17] *minion:* darling.
[18] *country:* neighborhood.　　　[19] *have:* understood.
[20] *errant:* traveling, as on a quest; but with a pun on
"arrant," suggested by "decayed."　　　[21] *cast:* discarded.
[22] *issue:* progeny.　　　[23] *prodigy:* monster.
[24] *compass:* achieve.
[25] *withe:* twig or branch of willow or osier.
[26] *presently:* immediately.　　　[27] *cut:* stolen.

If you like not hanging, drown yourself! Take some
    course
For your reputation.
  Well.   'Twill not do, dear tempter,   120
With all the rhetoric the fiend hath taught you.
I am as far as thou art from despair;
Nay, I have confidence, which is more than hope,
To live, and suddenly, better than ever.
  Mar. Ha, ha! these castles you build in the air
Will not persuade me or to give or lend
A token to you.
  Well.   I'll be more kind to thee.
Come, thou shalt dine with me.
  Mar.   With you?
  Well.   Nay, more,
    dine gratis.
  Mar. Under what hedge, I pray you? Or at whose
    cost?
Are they padders or Abram-men[28] that are your
    consorts?[29]   130
  Well. Thou art incredulous; but thou shalt dine
Not alone[30] at her house, but with a gallant lady—
With me and with a lady.
  Mar.   Lady? What lady?
With the Lady of the Lake,[31] or Queen of Fairies?
For I know it must be an enchanted dinner.
  Well. With the Lady Allworth, knave.
  Mar.   Nay, now
there's hope
Thy brain is cracked.
  Well.   Mark there, with what respect
I am entertained.
  Mar.   With choice, no doubt, of dog whips.
Why, dost thou ever hope to pass her porter?
  Well. 'Tis not far off; go with me. Trust thine own
    eyes.   140
  Mar. Troth, in my hope, or my assurance rather,
To see thee curvet[32] and mount like a dog in a blanket,

---

[28] *padders . . . Abram-men:* footpads . . . beggars feigning
madness.   [29] *consorts:* companions.
[30] *alone:* only.
[31] *Lady of the Lake:* the enchantress in Malory's *Morte
d'Arthur.*
[32] *curvet:* leap (more precisely, like a horse); be tossed in a
blanket.

II.ii.
[1] *still before:* always anticipating.
[2] *severally:* separately.   [3] *chamberers:* waiting women.
[4] *tits:* hussies.   [5] *ravish:* rape.
[6] *are:* Editors suggest an error for "hear."
[7] *elixir:* the quintessence or sovereign potion sought by
the alchemists.
[8] *quintessence:* absolute distillation.
[9] *potato roots:* sweet potatoes.
[10] *Coral:* Q "Curral," because precious; also, "lobster roe"
(although OED does not record before late eighteenth
century).
[11] *ambergris:* odoriferous secretion in the intestines of the
sperm whale; perfume.   [12] *bait:* eat.
[13] *ride:* with sexual *entendre,* since Furnace's elixir is an
aphrodisiac.
[14] *within:* presumably in the "alcove" whence they are
admitted to the main stage by Watchall.

If ever thou presume to pass her threshold,
I will endure thy company.
  Well.   Come along then.
                           Exeunt.

II.ii

[*Enter*] ALLWORTH, [Waiting] Woman, Chambermaid,
  ORDER, AMBLE, FURNACE, [*and*] WATCHALL.

  Woman. Could you not command your leisure one
    hour longer?
  Cham. Or half an hour?
  All.   I have told you what my
    haste is.
Besides, being now another's, not mine own,
Howe'er I much desire to enjoy you longer,
My duty suffers, if, to please myself,
I should neglect my lord.
  Woman.   Pray you, do me the favor
To put these few quince cakes into your pocket;
They are of mine own preserving.
  Cham.   And this marmalade;
'Tis comfortable for your stomach.
  Woman.   And, at parting,
Excuse me if I beg a farewell from you.   10
  Cham. You are still before[1] me. I move the same
    suit, sir.

           [ALLWORTH] *Kisses 'em severally.*[2]

  Furn. How greedy these chamberers[3] are of a
    beardless chin!
I think the tits[4] will ravish[5] him.
  All.   My service
To both.
  Woman. Ours waits on you.
  Cham.   And shall do ever.
  Ord. You are[6] my lady's charge; be therefore careful
That you sustain your parts.
  Woman.   We can bear, I warrant you.
            Exeunt [Waiting] Woman *and*
                     Chambermaid.
  Furn. Here, drink it off. The ingredients are cordial,
And this the true elixir;[7] it hath boiled
Since midnight for you. 'Tis the quintessence[8]
Of five cocks of the game, ten dozen of sparrows,   20
Knuckles of veal, potato roots[9] and marrow,
Coral[10] and ambergris.[11] Were you two years elder,
And I had a wife or gamesome mistress,
I durst trust you with neither. You need not bait[12]
After this, I warrant you, though your journey's long;
You may ride[13] on the strength of this till tomorrow
    morning.
  All. Your courtesies overwhelm me. I much grieve
To part from such true friends, and yet find comfort—
My attendance on my honorable lord,
Whose resolution holds to visit my lady,   30
Will speedily bring me back.

        Knocking at the gate; MARALL *and*
             WELLBORN *within.*[14]

Mar.   Darest thou venture
   further?
Well. Yes, yes, and knock again.
Ord.   'Tis he; disperse!
Amb. Perform it bravely.[15]
Furn.   I know my cue; ne'er doubt
   me.
                    They go off several ways.
Watch. Beast that I was, to make you stay![16] Most
   welcome;
You were long since expected.
Well.   Say so much
To my friend, I pray you.
Watch.   For your sake, I will, sir.
Mar. For his sake!
Well.   Mum; this is nothing.
Mar.   More than
   ever
I would have believed, though I had found it in my
   primer.[17]
All. When I have given you reasons for my late
   harshness,
You'll pardon and excuse me, for, believe me,   40
Though now I part abruptly, in my service
I will deserve it.[18]
Mar.   Service! with a vengeance!
Well. I am satisfied. Farewell, Tom.
All.   All joy stay with
   you!

                    Exit ALLWORTH.

                    Enter AMBLE.

Amb. You are happily encountered; I yet never
Presented one so welcome as I know
You will be to my lady.
Mar.   This is some vision,
Or, sure, these men are mad, to worship a dunghill;
It cannot be a truth.
Well.   Be still a pagan,
An unbelieving infidel; be so, miscreant,[19]
And meditate on blankets and on dog whips!   50

                    Enter FURNACE.

Furn. I am glad you are come; until I know your
   pleasure
I knew not how to serve up my lady's dinner.
Mar. His pleasure! is it possible?
Well.   What's thy will?
Furn. Marry, sir, I have some grouse, and turkey
   chickens,[20]
Some rails[21] and quails, and my lady willed me ask you
What kind of sauces best affect[22] your palate
That I may use my utmost skill to please it.
Mar. The devil's entered this cook. Sauce for his
   palate,
That, on my knowledge, for almost this twelvemonth
Durst wish but cheese parings, and brown bread on
   Sundays.[23]   60
Well. That way I like 'em best.
Furn.   It shall be done, sir.
                    Exit FURNACE.

Well. What think you of "the hedge we shall dine
   under"?
Shall we feed gratis?
Mar.   I know not what to think.
Pray you, make me not mad.

                    Enter ORDER.

Ord.   This place becomes you
   not;
Pray you, walk, sir, to the dining room.
Well.   I am well here,
Till her ladyship quits her chamber.
Mar.   Well here, say
   you?
'Tis a rare change! But yesterday you thought
Yourself well in a barn, wrapped up on peas-straw.[24]

       Enter [Waiting] Woman *and* Chambermaid.

Woman. O sir, you are wished[25] for.
Cham.   My lady dreamt,
   sir, of you.
Woman. And the first command she gave after she
   rose,   70
Was, her devotions done, to give her notice
When you approached here.
Cham.   Which is done, on my
   virtue.
Mar. I shall be converted; I begin to grow
Into a new belief, which saints nor angels
Could have won me to have faith in.
Woman.   Sir, my lady!

              Enter LADY [ALLWORTH].

Lady All. I come to meet you, and languished till I
   saw you.
This first kiss is for form;[26] I allow a second
To such a friend.

                    [*Kisses* WELLBORN.]

Mar. [*Aside*]   To such a friend! heaven bless me!
Well. I am wholly yours; yet, madam, if you please
To grace this gentleman with a salute—   80
Mar. [*Aside*] Salute me at his bidding!
Well.   I shall receive it
As a most high favor.
Lady All.   Sir, you may command me.

                    [MARALL *draws back.*]

Well. Run backward from a lady? And such a lady?
Mar. To kiss her foot is to poor me a favor
I am unworthy of—

                    Offers to kiss her foot.

---

[15] *bravely:* with spirit; make a good show.
[16] *stay:* wait.   [17] *primer:* prayer book.
[18] *it:* i.e., pardon.   [19] *miscreant:* heretic.
[20] *turkey chicken:* young turkeys.   [21] *rails:* game birds.
[22] *affect:* like.
[23] *Sundays:* when the "best" meal of the week was
served.
[24] *peas-straw:* from the leguminous plant and suggesting
worthless chaff.   [25] *wished:* asked.   [26] *form:* convention.

Lady All.   Nay, pray you, rise,
And, since you are so humble, I'll exalt you.
You shall dine with me today at mine own table.

Mar. Your ladyship's table? I am not good enough
To sit at your steward's board.

Lady All.   You are too modest;
I will not be denied.

Enter FURNACE.

Furn.   Will you still be babbling   90
Till your meat freeze on the table? The old trick still;
My art ne'er thought on!

Lady All.   Your arm, Master Wellborn.—
[*To* MARALL] Nay, keep us company.

Mar.   I was never so
graced.

          Exeunt WELLBORN, LADY [ALLWORTH],
          AMBLE, MARALL, [Waiting] Woman, [*and*
                              Chambermaid].

Ord. So we have played our parts, and are come off
well;
But, if I know the mystery, why my lady
Consented to it, or why Master Wellborn
Desired it, may I perish!

Furn.   Would I had
The roasting of his heart that cheated him,
And forces the poor gentleman to these shifts!
By fire (for cooks are Persians, and swear by it),   100
Of all the griping and extorting tyrants
I ever heard or read of, I ne'er met
A match to Sir Giles Overreach.

Watch.   What will you take
To tell him so, fellow Furnace?

Furn.   Just as much
As my throat is worth, for that would be the price on't.
To have a usurer that starves himself
And wears a cloak of one-and-twenty years
On a suit of fourteen groats, bought of the hangman,[27]
To grow rich, and then purchase, is too common;
But this Sir Giles feeds high, keeps many servants,   110
Who must at his command do any outrage.
Rich in his habit, vast in his expenses,
Yet he to admiration[28] still increases
In wealth and lordships.

Ord.   He frights men out of their
estates,
And breaks through all law nets, made to curb ill men,
As they were cobwebs. No man dares reprove him.

Such a spirit to dare and power to do were never
Lodged so unluckily.

Enter AMBLE.

Amb.   Ha, ha! I shall burst.

Ord. Contain thyself, man.

Furn.   Or make us partakers
Of your sudden mirth.

Amb.   Ha, ha! My lady has got   120
Such a guest at her table—this term driver, Marall,
This snip of an attorney!

Furn.   What of him, man?

Amb. The knave thinks still he's at the cook's shop
in Ram Alley,[29]
Where the clerks divide,[30] and the elder is to choose;[31]
And feeds so slovenly!

Furn.   Is this all?

Amb.   My lady
Drank to him for fashion sake, or to please Master
Wellborn.
As I live, he rises, and takes up a dish
In which there were some remnants of a boiled capon,
And pledges her in white broth![32]

Furn.   Nay, 'tis like
The rest of his tribe.

Amb.   And, when I brought him wine,
He leaves his stool and after a leg[33] or two   131
Most humbly thanks my worship.

Ord.   Rose already!

Amb. I shall be chid.[34]

          #### Enter LADY [ALLWORTH], WELLBORN,
                    [*and*] MARALL.

Furn.   My lady frowns.

Lady All.   You wait[35]
well!
Let me have no more of this; I observed your jeering.
Sirrah, I'll have you know, whom I think worthy
To sit at my table, be he ne'er so mean,[36]
When I am present, is not your companion.[37]

Ord. Nay, she'll preserve what's due to her.

Furn.   This
refreshing[38]
Follows your flux of laughter.

Lady All. [*To* WELLBORN] You are master
Of your own will. I know so much of manners   140
As not to inquire your purposes; in a word,
To me you are ever welcome, as to a house
That is your own.

Well.   Mark that.

Mar.   With reverence, sir,
And it like[39] your worship.

Well.   Trouble yourself no farther,
Dear madam; my heart's full of zeal and service,
However in my language I am sparing.—
Come, Master Marall.

Mar.   I attend your worship.
                    Exeunt WELLBORN, MARALL.

Lady All. I see in your looks you are sorry, and you
know me
An easy mistress. Be merry; I have forgot all.—

---

²⁷ *hangman:* who inherited the garments of his victims.
²⁸ *to admiration:* for a wonder.
²⁹ *Ram Alley:* like Pie Corner, famous for food shops.
³⁰ *divide:* share the cost of a meal.
³¹ *to choose:* have first choice.
³² *white broth:* chicken sauces.
³³ *leg:* bow.   ³⁴ *chid:* criticized.
³⁵ *wait:* attend.   ³⁶ *mean:* i.e., in station.
³⁷ *companion:* sort (i.e., not for your jeering).
³⁸ *refreshing:* rebuke; with allied sense of "sustenance,"
picking up "preserve" in the previous line and "flux"
(diarrhea) in the line that follows.
³⁹ *And it like:* If it please.

Order and Furnace, come with me; I must give you
Further directions.
   Ord.   What you please.
   Furn.   We are ready. 151
                                            [Exeunt.]

II.iii

[Enter] WELLBORN, *[and]* MARALL.

   Well. I think I am in a good way.
   Mar.   Good sir, the best
     way,
The certain best way.
   Well.   There are casualties
That men are subject to.
   Mar.   You are above 'em;
And, as you are already worshipful,
I hope ere long you will increase in worship,
And be right worshipful.
   Well.   Prithee, do not flout[1] me.
What I shall be, I shall be. Is't for your ease
You keep your hat off?
   Mar.   Ease, and it like your worship?
I hope Jack Marall shall not live so long,
To prove himself such an unmannerly beast, 10
Though it hail hazelnuts, as to be covered
When your worship's present.
   Well. Aside   Is not this a true rogue
That, out of mere hope of a future cozenage,[2]
Can turn thus suddenly? 'Tis rank[3] already.
   Mar. I know your worship's wise, and needs no
     counsel;
Yet, if in my desire to do you service
I humbly offer my advice (but still
Under correction[4]), I hope I shall not
Incur your high displeasure.
   Well.   No; speak freely.
   Mar. Then, in my judgment, sir, my simple
     judgment   20
(Still with your worship's favor), I could wish you
A better habit, for this cannot be
But much distasteful to the noble lady
(I say no more) that loves you, for, this morning
To me (and I am but a swine to[5] her),
Before th' assurance of her wealth perfumed you,
You savored not of amber.[6]
   Well.   I do now then?

*[*MARALL*] Kisses the end of his [*WELLBORN'S*]*
cudgel.

   Mar. This your batoon[7] hath got a touch of it.
Yet, if you please, for change[8] I have twenty pounds
   here
Which out of my true love I presently   30
Lay down at your worship's feet; 'twill serve to buy you
A riding suit.
   Well.   But where's the horse?
   Mar.   My gelding
Is at your service; nay, you shall ride me
Before your worship shall be put to the trouble

To walk afoot. Alas, when you are lord
Of this lady's manor, as I know you will be,
You may with the lease of glebe[9] land, called Knave's
   Acre,
A place I would manure,[10] requite your vassal.
   Well. I thank thy love, but must make no use of it.
What's twenty pounds?
   Mar.   'Tis all that I can make,[11] sir.
   Well. Dost thou think, though I want clothes, I
     could not have 'em   41
For one word to my lady?
   Mar.   As[12] I know not that!
   Well. Come, I tell thee a secret, and so leave thee.
I'll not give her the advantage, though she be
A gallant-minded lady, after we are married
(There being no woman but is sometimes froward[13]),
To hit me in the teeth,[14] and say she was forced
To buy my wedding clothes, and took me on
With a plain riding suit and an ambling nag.
No, I'll be furnished something like myself,   50
And so farewell. For thy suit[15] touching Knave's Acre,
When it is mine, 'tis thine.
   Mar.   I thank your worship.—
                               Exit WELLBORN.
How [I] was cozened in the calculation
Of this man's fortune! my master cozened too,
Whose pupil I am in the art of undoing men,
For that is our profession! well, well, Master Wellborn,
You are of a sweet nature and fit again to be cheated,
Which, if the fates please, when you are possessed
Of the land and lady, you, sans[16] question, shall be,
I'll presently think of the means.
                          Walk by, musing.[17]

Enter OVERREACH.

   Over. *[To a* Servant *offstage]* Sirrah, take my horse.
I'll walk to get me an appetite; 'tis but a mile,   61
And exercise will keep me from being pursy.[18]
Ha! Marall! is he conjuring? Perhaps
The knave has wrought the prodigal to do
Some outrage on himself, and now he feels
Compunction in his conscience for 't. No matter,
So it be done.—Marall!
   Mar.   Sir.
   Over.   How succeed we
In our plot on Wellborn?
   Mar.   Never better, sir.
   Over. Has he hanged or drowned himself?
   Mar.   No, sir,
     he lives—

II.iii.
  [1] *flout:* mock.   [2] *cozenage:* cheating.   [3] *rank:* stinking.
  [4] *Under correction:* Speaking under correction (i.e., "I
don't mean to presume").   [5] *to:* compared to.
  [6] *amber:* ambergris, perfume.   [7] *batoon:* cudgel.
  [8] *change:* i.e., of habit or attire.   [9] *glebe:* farm.
  [10] *manure:* operate (as lease holder).   [11] *make:* make up.
  [12] *As:* As if.   [13] *froward:* forthputting, headstrong.
  [14] *hit . . . teeth:* i.e., throw it in my face.
  [15] *suit:* application.   [16] *sans:* without.
  [17] *musing:* Q reads "masing."
  [18] *pursy:* short-winded, fat.

Lives once more to be made a prey to you,   70
A greater prey than ever.
    Over.   Art thou in thy wits?
If thou art, reveal this miracle, and briefly.
    Mar. A lady, sir, is fallen in love with him.
    Over. With him? What lady?
    Mar.   The rich Lady
    Allworth.
    Over. Thou dolt! how darest thou speak this?
    Mar.   I speak
    truth;
And I do so but once a year, unless
It be to you, sir. We dined with her ladyship,
I thank his worship.
    Over.   His worship!
    Mar.   As I live, sir,
I dined with him at the great lady's table,
Simple as I stand here, and saw when she kissed him,
And would at his request have kissed me too;   81
But I was not so audacious as some youths are,
And dare do anything, be it ne'er so absurd,
And sad after performance.[19]
    Over.   Why, thou rascal,
To tell me these impossibilities!
Dine at her table? And kiss him? Or thee?
Impudent varlet, have not I myself,
To whom great countesses' doors have oft flew open,
Ten times attempted, since her husband's death,
In vain to see her, though I came —a suitor?   90
And yet your good solicitorship and rogue Wellborn
Were brought into her presence, feasted with her!
But that I know thee a dog that cannot blush,[20]
This most incredible lie would call up one
On thy buttermilk[21] cheeks.
    Mar.   Shall I not trust my eyes,
    sir,
Or taste? I feel her good cheer in my belly.
    Over. You shall feel me, if you give not over,[22]
    sirrah.
Recover your brains again, and be no more gulled
With a beggar's plot, assisted by the aids
Of serving-men and chambermaids, for beyond these
Thou never sawest a woman, or I'll quit[23] you   101
From my employments.
    Mar.   Will you credit this yet?
On my confidence of their marriage, I offered
    Wellborn—
Aside I would give a crown now I durst say "his
    worship"—

My nag and twenty pounds.
    Over.   Did you so, idiot?[24]

                  Strikes him down.

Was this the way to work him to despair,
Or rather to cross[25] me?
    Mar.   Will your worship kill me?
    Over. No, no; but drive the lying spirit out of you.
    Mar. He's gone.
    Over.   I have done then. Now, forgetting
Your late imaginary feast and lady,   110
Know my Lord Lovell dines with me tomorrow.
Be careful naught be wanting to receive him;
And bid my daughter's women trim her up;
Though they paint her, so she catch the lord I'll thank
    'em.
There's a piece[26] for my late blows.
    Mar. Aside   I must yet suffer.
But there may be a time—
    Over.   Do you grumble?
    Mar.   No, sir.
                  [Exeunt.]

ACT THREE

Scene One

[Enter] Lovell, Allworth, *[and]* Servants.

    Lov. Walk the horses down the hill. Something in
    private
I must impart to Allworth.
                  Exeunt servi.[1]
    All.   Oh, my lord,
What sacrifice of reverence, duty, watching,
Although I could put off the use of sleep,
And ever wait on your commands [to] serve 'em,
What dangers, though in ne'er so horrid shapes,
Nay, death itself, though I should run to meet it,
Can I, and with a thankful willingness, suffer!
But still the retribution will fall short
Of your bounties showered upon me.
    Lov.   Loving youth,   10
Till what I purpose be put into act,
Do not o'erprize it. Since you have trusted me
With your soul's nearest, nay, her dearest secret,
Rest confident 'tis in a cabinet locked
Treachery shall never open. I have found you
(For so much to your face I must profess,
Howe'er you guard[2] your modesty with a blush for 't)
More zealous in your love and service to me
Than I have been in my rewards.
    All.   Still great ones,
Above my merit.
    Lov.   Such your gratitude calls 'em;   20
Nor am I of that harsh and rugged temper
As some great men are taxed with, who imagine
They part from the respect due to their honors
If they use not all such as follow 'em,
Without distinction of their births, like slaves.

---

[19] *sad after performance:* with sexual *entendre;* coitus ("performance") is supposed to be followed by melancholy.
[20] *dog . . . blush:* i.e., a black dog; both rascally and incapable of changing color.
[21] *buttermilk:* white (with fear).
[22] *give not over:* stop this nonsense.   [23] *quit:* discharge.
[24] *idiot:* Q reads "I doe."   [25] *cross:* thwart.
[26] *piece:* i.e., of money.

III.i.
[1] *L.:* servants.
[2] *guard:* "adorn" has been suggested ("guards" are adornments, as on Elizabethan hose), but the conventional sense seems adequate.

I am not so conditioned;[3] I can make
A fitting difference between my footboy
And a gentleman by want compelled to serve me.
   All. 'Tis thankfully acknowledged. You have been
More like a father to me than a master.   30
Pray you, pardon the comparison.
   Lov.   I allow it;
And, to give you assurance I am pleased in't,
My carriage and demeanor[4] to your mistress,
Fair Margaret, shall truly witness for me
I can command my passions.
   All.   'Tis a conquest
Few lords can boast of when they are tempted.—Oh!
   Lov. Why do you sigh? Can you be doubtful of me?
By that fair name I in the wars have purchased
And all my actions hitherto untainted,
I will not be more true to mine own honor   40
Than to my Allworth!
   All.   As you are the brave Lord Lovell,
Your bare word only given is an assurance
Of more validity and weight to me
Than all the oaths bound up with imprecations,
Which, when they would deceive, most courtiers
    practice;
Yet, being a man (for, sure, to style you more
Would relish of gross flattery), I am forced
Against my confidence of your worth and virtues
To doubt, nay, more, to fear.
   Lov.   So young, and jealous?
   All. Were you to encounter with a single foe,   50
The victory were certain; but to stand
The charge of two such potent enemies,
At once assaulting you, as wealth and beauty,
And those too seconded with power, is odds
Too great for Hercules.
   Lov.   Speak your doubts and fears,
Since you will nourish 'em, in plainer language
That I may understand 'em.
   All.   What's your will,
Though I lend arms against myself (provided
They may advantage[5] you), must be obeyed.
My much-loved lord, were Margaret only fair,   60
The cannon of her more than earthly form,
Though mounted high, commanding all beneath it,
And rammed with bullets of her sparkling eyes,
Of all the bulwarks that defend your senses
Could batter none[6] but that which guards your sight.
But, when the well-tuned accents of her tongue
Make music to you, and with numerous[7] sounds
Assault your hearing (such as[8] if Ulysses
Now lived again, howe'er he stood[9] the Sirens,
Could not resist), the combat must grow doubtful   70
Between your reason and rebellious passions.
Add this too: when you feel her touch, and breath
Like a soft western wind when it glides o'er
Arabia, creating gums and spices,
And, in the van,[10] the nectar of her lips,
Which you must taste, bring the battalia[11] on,
Well armed, and strongly lined[12] with her discourse
And knowing manners, to give entertainment—
Hippolytus[13] himself would leave Diana

To follow such a Venus.
   Lov.   Love hath made you   80
Poetical, Allworth.
   All.   Grant all these beat[14] off
(Which, if it be in man to do, you'll do it),
Mammon, in Sir Giles Overreach, steps in
With heaps of ill-got gold, and so much land,
To make her more remarkable, as would tire
A falcon's wings in one day to fly over.
Oh, my good lord! these powerful aids, which would
Make a misshapen negro beautiful
(Yet are but ornaments to give her luster,
That in herself is all perfection), must   90
Prevail for her. I here release your trust;
'Tis happiness enough for me to serve you
And sometimes with chaste eyes to look upon her.
   Lov. Why, shall I swear?
   All.   Oh, by no means, my lord;
And wrong not so your judgment to the world
As from your fond indulgence to a boy,
Your page, your servant, to refuse a blessing
Divers[15] great men are rivals for.
   Lov.   Suspend
Your judgement till the trial. How far is it
To Overreach' house?
   All.   At the most, some half hour's
    riding;   100
You'll soon be there.
   Lov.   And you the sooner freed
From your jealous fears.
   All.   Oh, that I durst but hope it!
                                   Exeunt.

III.ii

[*Enter*] OVERREACH, GREEDY, [*and*] MARALL.

   Over. Spare for no cost; let my dressers crack with
    the weight
Of curious[1] viands.
   Greedy.   Store indeed's no sore,[2] sir.
   Over. That proverb fits your stomach, Master
    Greedy.
And let no plate be seen but what's pure gold,
Or such whose workmanship exceeds the matter

---

   [3] *so conditioned:* of such character.
   [4] *carriage and demeanor:* behavior (which will be circum-
spect).   [5] *advantage:* help.
   [6] *none:* Q "more."
   [7] *numerous:* numbered, as in musical notation.
   [8] *such as:* i.e., sounds such that.
   [9] *howe'er he stood:* notwithstanding that he was able to
resist.   [10] *van:* forefront of battle.
   [11] *battalia:* army.   [12] *lined:* reinforced.
   [13] *Hippolytus:* the victim of the incestuous passion of
Phaedra, who persuaded his father, Theseus, to bring about
his death. He is associated with Diana, goddess of chastity,
as he was himself chaste.   [14] *beat:* be beaten.
   [15] *Divers:* Sundry.

III.ii.
   [1] *curious:* exotic.
   [2] *Store . . . sore:* It doesn't hurt to have plenty.

That it is made of; let my choicest linen
Perfume the room, and, when we wash, the³ water,
With precious powders mixed, so please my lord
That he may with envy wish to bathe so ever.
Mar. 'Twill be very chargeable.⁴
Over.   Avaunt, you drudge!
Now all my labored ends are at the stake,   11
Is't a time to think of thrift? Call in my daughter.—
                    [*Exit* MARALL.]
And, Master Justice, since you love choice dishes,
And plenty of 'em—
Greedy.   As I do, indeed, sir,
Almost as much as to give thanks for 'em.⁵
Over. I do confer that providence,⁶ with my power
Of absolute command to have abundance,
To your best care.
Greedy.   I'll punctually discharge it
And give the best directions. Now am I
In mine own conceit⁷ a monarch—at the least,   20
Archpresident of the boiled, the roast, the baked,
For which I will eat often and give thanks
When my belly's braced⁸ up like a drum—and that's
          pure justice.
Over. I[t] must be so. Should the foolish girl prove
          modest,⁹
                                        Exit GREEDY.
She may spoil all. She had it not from me,
But from her mother; I was ever forward,
As she must be, and therefore I'll prepare her.

                    [*Enter*] MARGARET.

Alone—and let your women wait without.
Marg. Your pleasure, sir?
Over.   Ha, this is a neat dressing!
These orient¹⁰ pearls and diamonds well placed too!
The gown affects¹¹ me not; it should have been   31
Embroidered o'er and o'er with flowers of gold;
But these rich jewels and quaint fashion help it.
And how below, since oft the wanton eye,
The face observed,¹² descends unto the foot,
Which, being well proportioned, as yours is,
Invites as much as perfect white and red,¹³
Though without art. How like you your new woman,
The Lady Downfallen?
Marg.   Well, for a companion;
Not as a servant.
Over.   Is she humble, Meg,   40
And careful¹⁴ too, her ladyship forgotten?
Marg. I pity her fortune.

Over.   Pity her? Trample on her!
I took her up in an old tamine¹⁵ gown
(Even starved for want of twopenny chops) to serve
          thee;
And if I understand she but repines
To do thee any duty, though ne'er so servile,
I'll pack her to her knight, where I have lodged him,
Into the Counter¹⁶ and there let 'em howl together.
Marg. You know your own ways; but, for me, I
Blush when I command her that was once attended   50
With persons not inferior to myself
In birth.
Over. In birth? Why, art thou not my daughter,
The blessed child of my industry and wealth?
Why, foolish girl, was't not to make thee great
That I have ran, and still pursue, those ways
That hale down curses on me, which I mind not?
Part with these humble thoughts, and apt thyself¹⁷
To the noble state I labor to advance thee,
Or, by my hopes to see thee honorable,
I will adopt a stranger to my heir,   60
And throw thee from my care. Do not provoke me.
Marg. I will not, sir; mold me which way you please.

                    Enter GREEDY.

Over. How! Interrupted?
Greedy.   'Tis matter of importance.
The cook, sir, is self-willed, and will not learn
From my experience, There's a fawn brought in, sir,
And, for my life, I cannot make him roast it
With a Norfolk dumpling in the belly of it;
And, sir, we wise men know, without the dumpling
'Tis not worth threepence.
Over.   Would it were whole in thy
          belly,
To stuff it out! Cook it any way; prithee, leave me.   70
Greedy. Without order for the dumpling?
Over.   Let it be
          dumpled
Which way thou wilt, or tell him I will scald him
In his own caldron.
Greedy.   I had lost my stomach
Had I lost my Mistress Dumpling I'll¹⁸ give thanks for.
Over. But to our business, Meg. You have heard who
          dines here?
                                        Exit GREEDY.
Marg. I have, sir.
Over.   'Tis an honorable man;
A lord, Meg, and commands a regiment
Of soldiers, and, what's rare, is one himself,
A bold and understanding one; and to be
A lord and a good leader, in one volume,   80
Is granted unto few but such as rise¹⁹ up
The kingdom's glory.

                    Enter GREEDY.

Greedy.   I'll resign my office,
If I be not better obeyed.
Over.   'Slight,²⁰ art thou frantic?
Greedy. Frantic? 'Twould make me a frantic²¹ and
          stark mad,

---

³ *the:* i.e., let the.   ⁴ *chargeable:* expensive.
⁵ *Almost ... 'em:* i.e., I love best to give thanks after
eating.   ⁶ *providence:* office of providing.
⁷ *conceit:* fancy.   ⁸ *braced:* tightened.
⁹ *modest:* retiring.   ¹⁰ *orient:* eastern, lustrous.
¹¹ *affects:* pleases.   ¹² *observed:* having been observed.
¹³ *perfect...red:* i.e., colors of the face.
¹⁴ *careful:* diligent.   ¹⁵ *tamine:* thin woolen.
¹⁶ *Counter:* London debtor's prison.
¹⁷ *apt thyself:* make thyself apt.   ¹⁸ *I'll:* i.e., that I'll.
¹⁹ *rise:* raise.   ²⁰ *'Slight:* by God's light.
²¹ *frantic:* lunatic.

Were I not a justice of peace and coram[22] too,
Which this rebellious cook cares not a straw for.
There are a dozen of woodcocks—
    Over.   Make thyself
Thirteen,[23] the baker's dozen.
    Greedy.   I am contented,
So they may be dressed to my mind. He has found out
A new device for sauce, and will not dish 'em   90
With toasts and butter. My father was a tailor,
And my name, though a justice, Greedy Woodcock;
And, ere I'll see my lineage so abused,
I'll give up my commission.
    Over. [*To* Cook *within*]   Cook? rogue, obey him!
I have given the word; pray you, now remove yourself
To a collar of brawn,[24] and trouble me no farther.
    Greedy. I will, and meditate what to eat at dinner.
                          Exit GREEDY.
    Over. And, as I said, Meg, when this gull disturbed
    us,
This honorable lord, this colonel,[25]
I would have thy husband.
    Marg.   There's too much disparity
Between his quality[26] and mine to hope it.   101
    Over. I more than hope 't, and doubt not to effect it.
Be thou no enemy to thyself; my wealth
Shall weigh his titles down, and make you equals.
Now for the means to assure him thine, observe me:
Remember he's a courtier and a soldier,
And not to be trifled with; and, therefore, when
He comes to woo you, see[27] you do not coy it.[28]
This mincing modesty hath spoiled many a match
By a first refusal, in vain after hoped for.   110
    Marg. You'll have me, sir, preserve the distance that
Confines a virgin?
    Over.   Virgin me no virgins!
I must have you lose that name, or you lose me.
I will have you private[29]—start not—I say, private.
If thou art my true daughter, not a bastard,
Thou wilt venture alone with one man, though he came
Like Jupiter to Semele,[30] and come off, too;
And therefore, when he kisses you, kiss close.
    Marg. I have heard this is the strumpet's fashion, sir,
Which I must never learn.
    Over.   Learn anything,   120
And from any creature that may make thee great—
From the devil himself.
    Marg. [*Aside*]   This is but devilish doctrine!
    Over. Or, if his blood grow hot, suppose he offer
Beyond this, do not you stay till it cool,
But meet his ardor; if a couch be near,
Sit down on 't, and invite him.
    Marg.   In your house,
Your own house, sir? For heaven's sake, what are you
    then?
Or what shall I be, sir?
    Over.   Stand not on form;
Words are no substances.
    Marg.   Though you could dispense
With your own honor, cast aside religion,   130
The hopes of heaven or fear of hell, excuse me.
In worldly policy[31] this is not the way

To make me his wife; his whore, I grant it may do.
My maiden honor so soon yielded up,
Nay, prostituted, cannot but assure him
I, that am light[32] to him, will not hold weight
When he is[33] tempted by others; so, in judgment,
When to his lust I have given up my honor,
He must and will forsake me.
    Over.   How? Forsake thee?
Do I wear a sword for fashion? Or is this arm   140
Shrunk up or withered? Does there live a man
Of that large list I have encountered with
Can truly say I e'er gave inch of ground
Not purchased with his blood that did oppose me?
Forsake thee when the thing is done? He dares not.
Give me but proof he has enjoyed thy person,
Though all his captains, echoes to his will,
Stood armed by his side to justify the wrong,
And he himself in the head of his bold troop,
Spite of his lordship and his colonelship,   150
Or the judge's favor, I will make him render
A bloody and a strict accompt,[34] and force him,
By marrying thee, to cure thy wounded honor!
I have said it.

                Enter MARALL.

    Mar.   Sir, the man of honor's come,
Newly alighted.
    Over.   In, without reply.
And do as I command, or thou art lost.
                        Exit MARGARET.
Is the loud music I gave order for
Ready to receive him?
    Mar.   'Tis, sir.
    Over.   Let 'em sound
A princely welcome.—
                   [*Exit* MARALL.]
                Roughness, awhile leave me,
For fawning now, a stranger to my nature,   160
Must make way for me.

    Loud music. Enter LOVELL, GREEDY, ALLWORTH,
              [*and*] MARALL.

    Lov.   Sir, you meet your trouble.
    Over. What you are pleased to style so is an honor
Above my worth and fortunes.
    All. [*Aside*]   Strange, so humble.
    Over. A justice of peace, my lord.

                Presents GREEDY *to him.*

    Lov.   Your hand, good sir.

---

[22] *coram:* quorum.
[23] *Thirteen:* One extra was added by the baker lest he give fewer than a dozen and so be liable for punishment.
[24] *brawn:* fattened boar or swine.   [25] *colonel:* trisyllabic.
[26] *quality:* rank.   [27] *see:* look.
[28] *coy it:* hang back, be coy.   [29] *private:* intimate.
[30] *Semele:* to whom Jupiter appeared as lover in his full majesty and so consumed her with fire.   [31] *policy:* craft.
[32] *light:* loose.
[33] *When he is:* Perhaps to be emended to "Whene'er" or "When his," followed by a comma.   [34] *accompt:* account.

Greedy. [*Aside*] This is a lord, and some think this a
favor;
But I had rather have my hand in my dumpling.
Over. Room for my lord.
Lov.   I miss, sir, your fair daughter
To crown my welcome.
Over.   May it please my lord
To taste a glass of Greek wine first, and suddenly
She shall attend my lord.
Lov.   You'll be obeyed, sir.   170
                    Exeunt omnes praeter [35] OVERREACH.
Over. 'Tis to my wish. As soon as come, ask for
her!—
Why, Meg! Meg Overreach!—

                    [*Enter* MARGARET.]

                    How! tears in your eyes!
Ha! dry 'em quickly, or I'll dig 'em out.
Is this a time to whimper? Meet that greatness
That flies into thy bosom; think what 'tis
For me to say, "My honorable daughter,"
And thou, when I stand bare,[36] to say, "Put on,"[37]
Or, "Father, you forgot yourself." No more.
But be instructed, or expect—He comes.—   179

            Enter LOVELL, GREEDY, ALLWORTH,
                    [*and*] MARALL.

A black-browed[38] girl, my lord.
Lov.   As I live a rare one.

                    They salute.[39]

All. [*Aside*] He's took already. I am lost.
Over. [*Aside*]   That kiss
Came twanging off; I like it—Quit the room.—
                    The Rest off.
A little bashful, my good lord, but you,
I hope, will teach her boldness.
Lov.   I am happy
In such a scholar, but—
Over   I am past learning,
And therefore leave you to yourselves.—*To his
    Daughter* Remember!
                    Exit OVERREACH.
Lov. You see, fair lady, your father is solicitous
To have you change the barren name of virgin
Into a hopeful wife.
Marg.   His[40] haste, my lord,

---

[35] L.: except.
[36] *bare:* bareheaded.   [37] *Put on:* i.e., your hat.
[38] *black-browed:* Overreach is depreciating his daughter,
blonde being considered more comely than brunette.
[39] *They salute:* i.e., Lovell kisses Margaret.
[40] *His:* Q "He."
[41] *tissues . . . scarlet:* fabric stitched with gold or silver . . .
heavier material denoting the dignity of the wearer.
[42] *run out:* i.e., through the pie crust.
[43] *barathrum . . . shambles:* glutton (gulf of the meat market, a reminiscence of Horace, *Epistles,* I. xv. 31).
[44] L.: According to the statute of the fifth year of King
Edward.   [45] *mainprize:* security.
[46] *Thrust . . . off:* Overreach also must exit at this point,
at least retire to the rear of the stage, in view of his subsequent entrance.

Holds no power o'er my will.
Lov.   But o'er your duty.   190
Marg. Which, forced too much, may break.
Lov.   Bend
rather, sweetest.
Think of your years.
Marg.   Too few to match with yours—
And choicest fruits, too soon plucked, rot and wither.
Lov. Do you think I am old?
Marg.   I am sure I am too
young.
Lov. I can advance you.
Marg.   To a hill of sorrow,
Where every hour I may expect to fall,
But never hope firm footing. You are noble,
I of a low descent, however rich;
And tissues matched with scarlet[41] suit but ill.
Oh, my good lord, I could say more, but that   200
I dare not trust these walls.
Lov.   Pray you, trust my ear then.

                    Enter OVERREACH, *listening.*

Over. Close at it! whispering! this is excellent!
And, by their postures, a consent on both parts.

                    Enter GREEDY.

Greedy. Sir Giles, Sir Giles!
Over.   The great fiend stop that
clapper!
Greedy. It must ring out, sir, when my belly rings
noon.
The baked-meats are run out,[42] the roast turned
powder.
Over. I shall powder you.
Greedy.   Beat me to dust, I care not;
In such a cause as this, I'll die a martyr.
Over. Marry, and shall, you barathrum of the
shambles![43]

                    Strikes him.

Greedy. How! strike a justice of peace? 'Tis petty
treason,   210
Edwardi quinto.[44] But that you are my friend,
I could commit you without bail or mainprize.[45]
Over. Leave your bawling, sir, or I shall commit you
Where you shall not dine today. Disturb my lord
When he is in discourse?
Greedy.   Is 't a time to talk
When we should be munching?
Lov.   Ha! I heard some noise.
Over. Mum, villain; vanish! Shall we break a
bargain
Almost made up?

                    Thrust GREEDY *off.*[46]

Lov.   Lady, I understand you,
And rest most happy in your choice, believe it:
I'll be a careful pilot to direct   220
Your yet uncertain bark to a port of safety.
Marg. So shall your honor save two lives and bind us
Your slaves forever.

Lov.   I am in the act rewarded,
Since it is good; howe'er, you must put on
An amorous carriage towards me to delude
Your subtle father.
   Marg.   I am prone to that.
   Lov. Now break we off our conference.—Sir Giles!
Where is Sir Giles?

             Enter OVERREACH *and the* Rest.

   Over.   My noble lord! And how
Does your lordship find her?
   Lov.   Apt, Sir Giles, and
      coming;[47]
And I like her the better.
   Over.   So do I too.   230
   Lov. Yet we take forts at the first assault,
'Twere poor in the defendant; I must confirm her
With a love letter or two, which I must have
Delivered by my page, and[48] you give way to 't.
   Over. With all my soul—a towardly[49] gentleman!—
Your hand, good Master Allworth. Know my house
Is ever open to you.
   All. Aside   'Twas shut till now.
   Over. Well done, well done, my honorable daughter!
Th' art so already. Know this gentle youth,
And cherish him, my honorable daughter.   240
   Marg. I shall, with my best care.

                  Noise within, as of a coach.

Over.   A coach!
Greedy.   More stops
Before we go to dinner! O my guts!

      Enter LADY [ALLWORTH] *and* WELLBORN.

   Lady All.   If I find welcome,
You share in it; if not, I'll back again,
Now I know your ends, for I come armed for all
Can be objected.
   Lov.   How! the Lady Allworth!
   Over. And thus attended![50]

     LOVELL *salutes the* LADY; *the* LADY *salutes*
                                 MARGARET.

   Mar.   No, I am a dolt!
The spirit of lies had entered me!
   Over.   Peace, patch![51]
'Tis more than wonder! An astonishment
That does possess me wholly!
   Lov.   Noble lady,
This is a favor, to prevent[52] my visit,   250
The service of my life can never equal.
   Lady All. My lord, I laid wait for you, and much
      hoped
You would have made my poor house your first inn;
And therefore, doubting[53] that you might forget me
Or too long dwell here, having such ample cause
In this unequaled beauty for your stay,
And fearing to trust but myself
With the relation of my service to you,
I borrowed so much from my long restraint[54]
And took the air in person to invite you.   260

Lov. Your bounties are so great they rob me,
      madam,
Of words to give you thanks.
   Lady All.   Good Sir Giles
      Overreach!—

                                Salutes him.

How doest thou, Marall? Liked you my meat so ill
You'll dine no more with me?
   Greedy.   I will, when you please,
And it like your ladyship.
   Lady All.   When you please, Master
      Greedy;
If meat can do it, you shall be satisfied.—
And now, my lord, pray take into your knowledge
This gentleman; howe'er his outside's coarse,

                          Presents WELLBORN.

His inward linings are as fine and fair
As any man's. Wonder not I speak at large.[55]   270
And howsoe'er his humor carries him
To be thus accoutered, or what taint soever
For his wild life hath stuck upon his fame,[56]
He may ere long with boldness rank himself
With some that have contemned him—Sir Giles
      Overreach,
If I am welcome, bid him so.
   Over.   My nephew!
He has been too long a stranger. Faith, you have;
Pray, let it be mended.

            LOVELL *conferring with* WELLBORN.

   Mar.   Why, sir, what do you mean?
This is "rogue Wellborn, monster, prodigy,
That should hang or drown himself," no man of
      worship,   280
Much less your nephew.
   Over.   Well, sirrah, we shall reckon
For this hereafter.
   Mar. [*Aside*]   I'll not lose my jeer,
Though I be beaten dead for 't.
   Well.   Let my silence plead
In my excuse, my lord, till better leisure
Offer itself to hear a full relation
Of my poor fortunes.
   Lov.   I would hear, and help 'em.
   Over. Your dinner waits you.
   Lov.   Pray you, lead; we
      follow.
   Lady All. Nay, you are my guest.—Come, dear
      Master Wellborn.

                    Exeunt. Manet[57] GREEDY.

-----

47 *coming:* forthcoming.
48 *and:* meaning either "if," or "and have."
49 *towardly:* promising.
50 *thus attended:* i.e., with the ragged Wellborn.
51 *patch:* fool.   52 *prevent:* anticipate.
53 *doubting:* fearing.
54 *long restraint:* mourning; hence, confinement, which
she has now intermitted.   55 *at large:* freely.
56 *fame:* reputation.   57 *L.:* Remains.

Greedy. "Dear Master Wellborn!" so she said.
Heaven! heaven!
If my belly would give me leave, I could ruminate   290
All day on this. I have granted twenty warrants
To have him committed, from all prisons in the shire,
To Nottingham jail. And now "Dear Master
Wellborn!"
And "My good nephew!"—but I play the fool
To stand here prating, and forget my dinner.

Enter MARALL.

Are they set,[58] Marall?
  Mar.   Long since. Pray you, a word,
    sir.
  Greedy. No wording now.
  Mar.   In troth, I must. My
    master,
Knowing you are his good friend, makes bold with you
And does entreat you, more guests being come in
Than he expected, especially his nephew,   300
The table being full too, you would excuse him
And sup with him on the cold meat.
  Greedy.   How! No dinner
After all my care?
  Mar.   'Tis but a penance for
A meal; besides, you broke your fast.
  Greedy.   That was
But a bit to stay my stomach. A man in commission
Give place to a tatterdemalion![59]
  Mar.   No bug[60] words, sir;
Should his worship hear you—
  Greedy.   Lose my dumpling too,
And buttered toasts, and woodcocks?
  Mar.   Come, have
    patience.
If you will dispense a little with your worship,[61]   309
And sit with the waiting women, you[62] have dumpling,
Woodcock, and buttered toasts too.
  Greedy.   This revives me;
I will gorge there sufficiently.
  Mar.   This is the way, sir.
                  Exeunt.

III.iii

[Enter] OVERREACH, *as from dinner.*

Over. She's caught! O women! She neglects my
    lord,
And all her compliments applied to Wellborn!

---

[58] *set:* seated at table.   [59] *tatterdemalion:* ragged beggar.
[60] *bug:* high.   [61] *worship:* dignity.
[62] *you:* you shall.

III.iii.
[1] *work:* manipulate.
[2] *Pasiphaë:* Daughter of the Sun and wife of Minos,
whose refusal to sacrifice a bull to Poseidon caused the god
to make Pasiphaë fall in love with the bull, which begot on
her the Minotaur.
[3] *Excuse my manners:* i.e., in rising from the board.

The garments of her widowhood laid by,
She now appears as glorious as the spring.
Her eyes fixed on him, in the wine she drinks,
He being her pledge, she sends him burning kisses,
And sits on thorns till she be private with him.
She leaves my meat to feed upon his looks,
And, if in our discourse he be but named,
From her a deep sigh follows. But why grieve I   10
At this? It makes for me; if she prove his,
All that is hers is mine, as I will work[1] him.

Enter MARALL.

  Mar. Sir, the whole board is troubled at your
    rising.
  Over. No matter, I'll excuse it. Prithee, Marall,
Watch an occasion to invite my nephew
To speak with me in private.
  Mar.   Who? "The rogue
The lady scorned to look on"?
  Over.   You are a wag.

Enter LADY [ALLWORTH] *and* WELLBORN.

  Mar. See, sir, she's come, and cannot be without
    him.
  Lady All. With your favor, sir, after a plenteous
    dinner,
I shall make bold to walk a turn or two   20
In your rare garden.
  Over.   There's an arbor too,
If you ladyship please to use it.
  Lady All.   Come, Master Wellborn.
          Exeunt LADY [ALLWORTH] *and*
                  WELLBORN.
  Over. Grosser and grosser! now I believe the
    poet
Feigned not, but was historical, when he wrote
Pasiphaë[2] was enamored of a bull.
This lady's lust's more monstrous.—My good lord,

Enter LOVELL, MARGARET, *and the* Rest.

Excuse my manners.[3]
  Lov.   There needs none, Sir Giles—
I may ere long say father, when it pleases
My dearest mistress to give warrant to it.
  Over. She shall seal to it, my lord, and make me
    happy.   30

Enter WELLBORN *and the* LADY [ALLWORTH].

  Marg. My lady is returned.
  Lady All.   Provide my coach;
I'll instantly away. My thanks, Sir Giles,
For my entertainment.
  Over.   'Tis your nobleness
To think it such.
  Lady All.   I must do you a further wrong
In taking away your honorable guest.
  Lov. I wait on you, madam; farewell, good Sir
    Giles.
  Lady All. Good Mistress Margaret!—Nay, come,
    Master Wellborn,
I must not leave you behind; in sooth, I must not.

Over. Rob me not, madam, of all joys at once;
Let my nephew stay behind. He shall have my
    coach,   40
And, after some small conference between us,
Soon overtake your ladyship.
    Lady All.   Stay not long, sir.
    Lov. This parting kiss!

                [*Kisses* MARGARET.]

            You shall every day hear
from me
By my faithful page.
    All.   'Tis a service I am proud of.

        Exeunt LOVELL, LADY [ALLWORTH],
      ALLWORTH, MARGARET, [*and*] MARALL.
    Over. Daughter, to your chamber.—You may
    wonder, nephew,
After so long an enmity between us,
I should desire your friendship.
    Well.   So I do, sir;
'Tis strange to me.
    Over.   But I'll make it no wonder;
And, what is more, unfold my nature to you.
We worldly men, when we see friends and kinsmen   50
Past hopes sunk in their fortunes, lend no hand
To lift 'em up, but rather set our feet
Upon their heads to press 'em to the bottom,
As, I must yield,⁴ with you I practiced it.
But, now I see you in a way to rise,
I can and will assist you. This rich lady
(And I am glad of 't) is enamored of you;
'Tis too apparent, nephew.
    Well.   No such thing—
Compassion rather, sir.
    Over.   Well, in a word,
Because your stay is short, I'll have you seen   60
No more in this base shape;⁵ nor shall she say
She married you like a beggar, or in debt.
    Well. Aside He'll run into the noose and save my
    labor.
    Over. You have a trunk of rich clothes not far
    hence
In pawn; I will redeem 'em. And, that no clamour
May taint your credit for your petty debts,
You shall have a thousand pounds to cut 'em off,
And go a free man to the wealthy lady.
    Well. This done, sir, out of love, and no ends else—
    Over. As it is, nephew.
    Well.   Binds me still your servant.
    Over. No compliments; you are stayed⁶ for. Ere
    y'ave supped,   71
You shall hear from me.—My coach, knaves, for my
    nephew!—
Tomorrow I will visit you.
    Well.   Here's an uncle
In a man's extremes!⁷ how much they do belie you,
That say you are hard-hearted!
    Over.   My deeds, nephew,
Shall speak my love; what men report, I weigh not.
                     Exeunt.

    FINIS ACTUS TERTII.

ACT FOUR

SCENE ONE

    [*Enter*] LOVELL, [*and*] ALLWORTH.

    Lov. 'Tis well; give me my cloak; I now discharge
    you
From further service. Mind your own affairs;
I hope they will prove successful.
    All.   What is blessed
With your good wish, my lord, cannot but prosper.
Let aftertimes report, and to your honor,
How much I stand engaged,¹ for I want language
To speak my debt. Yet, if a tear or two
Of joy for your much goodness can supply
My tongue's defects, I could—
    Lov.   Nay, do not melt;
This ceremonial thanks to me 's superfluous.   10
    Over. Within Is my lord stirring?
    Lov. 'Tis he! Oh, here's your letter. Let him in.

    Enter OVERREACH, GREEDY, [*and*] MARALL.

    Over. A good day to my lord!
    Lov.   You are an early riser,
    Sir Giles.
    Over. And reason,² to attend your lordship.
    Lov. And you too, Master Greedy, up so soon?
    Greedy. In troth, my lord, after the sun is up.
I cannot sleep, for I have a foolish stomach
That croaks for breakfast. With your lordship's favor,
I have a serious question to demand
Of my worthy friend Sir Giles.
    Lov.   Pray you, use your
    pleasure.   20
    Greedy. How far, Sir Giles, and, pray you, answer
    me
Upon your credit, hold you it to be
From your manor house to this of my Lady Allworth's?
    Over. Why some four mile.
    Greedy.   How! four mile? Good
    Sir Giles,
Upon your reputation think better,
For, if you do abate but one half-quarter
Of five, you do yourself the greatest wrong
That can be in the world: for four miles' riding
Could not have raised so huge an appetite
As I feel gnawing on me.
    Mar.   Whether you ride   30
Or go afoot, you are that way still³ provided,
And it please your worship.
    Over.   How now, sirrah? Prating
Before my lord! No difference?⁴ Go to my nephew,
See all his debts discharged, and help his worship
To fit on his rich suit.

---

    ⁴ *yield:* confess.   ⁵ *shape:* attire.
    ⁶ *stayed:* waited.   ⁷ *extremes:* extremities.
IV.i.
    ¹ *engaged:* indebted.   ² *reason:* with reason.
    ³ *still:* continually.
    ⁴ *difference:* perception of difference in rank.

Mar. [*Aside*]   I may fit you too.
Tossed like a dog still!

                              Exit Marall.

Lov.   I have writ this morning
A few lines to my mistress, your fair daughter.

Over. 'Twill fire her, for she's wholly yours
    already.—

Sweet Master Allworth, take my ring. 'Twill carry you
To her presence, I dare warrant you; and there plead
For my good lord, if you shall find occasion.   41
That done, pray ride to Nottingham; get a license,
Still by this token. I'll have it dispatched,
And suddenly, my lord, that I may say
My "honorable," nay, "right honorable" daughter.

Greedy. Take my advice, young gentleman; get your
    breakfast.
'Tis unwholesome to ride fasting. I'll eat with you
And eat to purpose.

Over.   Some fury's in that gut!
Hungry again! Did you not devour this morning
A shield of brawn[5] and a barrel of Colchester oysters?

Greedy. Why, that was, sir, only to scour my
    stomach,[6]   51
A kind of a preparative. Come, gentleman,
I will not have you feed like the hangman of Vlushing[7]
Alone, while I am here.

Lov.   Haste your return.

All. I will not fail, my lord.

Greedy.   Nor I, to line
My Christmas coffer.[8]

                    Exeunt Greedy *and* Allworth.

Over.   To my wish, we are private.
I come not to make offer with my daughter
A certain portion[9]—that were poor and trivial.
In one word, I pronounce all that is mine,
In lands or leases, ready coin or goods,   60
With her, my lord, comes to you; nor shall you have
One motive to induce you to believe
I live too long, since every year I'll add
Something unto the heap, which shall be yours too.

Lov. You are a right kind father.

Over.   You shall have
    reason
To think me such. How do you like this seat?[10]
It is well wooded, and well watered, the acres
Fertile and rich. Would it not serve for change,
To entertain your friends in a summer progress?[11]
What thinks my noble lord?

Lov.   'Tis a wholesome air,   70

_____

[5] *shield of brawn:* the swine or boar cooked in its own skin.
[6] *scour my stomach:* whet my appetite.
[7] *hangman of Vlushing:* i.e., Flushing, with whom no
one would like to dine.
[8] *coffer:* stomach (a receptacle for rich provisions).
[9] *certain portion:* stipulated dowry.
[10] *seat:* location (estate).   [11] *progress:* tour.
[12] *engines:* contrivances.   [13] *candor:* literally, whiteness.
[14] *L.:* nothing beyond.
[15] *Equivalent:* Of sufficient worth.
[16] *port:* manner of living.
[17] *sinister:* crooked (because "lefthanded").
[18] *common:* i.e., to all.

And well-built pile; and she that's mistress of it
Worthy the large revenue.

Over.   She the mistress?
It may be so for a time, but, let my lord
Say only that he likes it, and would have it,
I say, ere long 'tis his.

Lov.   Impossible.

Over. You do conclude too fast, not knowing me,
Nor the engines[12] that I work by. 'Tis not alone
The Lady Allworth's lands, for those once Wellborn's
(As by her dotage on him I know they will be)
Shall soon be mine; but point out any man's   80
In all the shire, and say they lie convenient
And useful for your lordship, and once more
I say aloud, they are yours.

Lov.   I dare not own
What's by unjust and cruel means extorted;
My fame and credit are more dear to me
Than so to expose 'em to be censured by
The public voice.

Over.   You run, my lord, no hazard.
Your reputation shall stand as fair
In all good men's opinions as now;
Nor can my actions, though condemned for ill,   90
Cast any foul aspersion upon yours,
For, though I do contemn report myself
As a mere sound, I still will be so tender
Of what concerns you, in all points of honor,
That the immaculate whiteness of your fame
Nor your unquestioned integrity
Shall e'er be sullied with one taint or spot
That may take from your innocence and candor.[13]
All my ambition is to have my daughter
Right honorable, which my lord can make her.   100
And, might I live to dance upon my knee
A young Lord Lovell, borne by her unto you,
I write *nil ultra*[14] to my proudest hopes.
As for possessions and annual rents,
Equivalent[15] to maintain you in the port[16]
Your noble birth and present state requires,
I do remove that burden from your shoulders
And take it on mine own, for, though I ruin
The country to supply your riotous waste,   109
The scourge of prodigals, want, shall never find you.

Lov. Are you not frighted with the imprecations
And curses of whole families, made wretched
By your sinister[17] practices?

Over.   Yes, as rocks are,
When foamy billows split themselves against
Their flinty ribs, or as the moon is moved
When wolves, with hunger pined, howl at her
    brightness.
I am of a solid temper and like these
Steer on a constant course. With mine own sword,
If called into the field, I can make that right
Which fearful enemies murmured at as wrong.   120
Now, for these other piddling complaints
Breathed out in bitterness, as when they call me
Extortioner, tyrant, cormorant, or intruder
On my poor neighbor's right, or grand encloser
Of what was common,[18] to my private use,

Nay, when my ears are pierced with widow's cries,
And undone orphans wash with tears my threshold,
I only think what 'tis to have my daughter
Right honorable; and 'tis a powerful charm
Makes me insensible of remorse or pity   130
Or the least sting of conscience.
    Lov.   I admire [19]
The toughness of your nature.
    Over.   'Tis for you,
My lord, and for my daughter, I am marble;
Nay, more, if you will have my character
In little, I enjoy more true delight
In my arrival to my wealth these dark
And crooked ways than you shall e'er take pleasure
In spending what my industry hath compassed.
My haste commands me hence. In one word, therefore,
Is it a match?
    Lov.   I hope that is past doubt now.   140
    Over. Then rest secure; not the hate of all mankind
    here,
Nor fear of what can fall on me hereafter
Shall make me study aught but your advancement
One story higher. An earl, if gold can do it!
Dispute not [20] my religion nor my faith.
Though I am borne thus headlong by thy will,
You may make choice of what belief you please;
To me they are equal. So, my lord, good morrow.
                                Exit.

    Lov. He's gone—I wonder how the earth can bear
Such a portent! [21] I, that have lived a soldier,   150
And stood the enemy's violent charge undaunted,
To hear this blasphemous beast am bathed all over
In a cold sweat. Yet, like a mountain, he,
Confirmed in atheistical assertions,
Is no more shaken than Olympus is
When angry Boreas [22] loads his double [23] head
With sudden drifts of snow.

    Enter AMBLE, LADY [ALLWORTH], [*and* Waiting]
                  Woman.

    Lady All.   Save you, my lord!
Disturb I not your privacy?
    Lov.   No, good madam;
For your own sake I am glad you came no sooner,
Since this bold, bad man, Sir Giles Overreach,   160
Made such a plain discovery of himself,
And read this morning such a devilish matins [24]
That I should think it a sin next to his
But to repeat it.
    Lady All.   I ne'er pressed, my lord,
On others' privacies; yet, against my will,
Walking, for health' sake, in the gallery
Adjoining to your lodgings, I was made
(So vehement and loud he was) partaker
Of his tempting offers.
    Lov.   Please you to command
Your servants hence, and I shall gladly hear   170
Your wiser counsel.
    Lady All.   'Tis, my lord, a woman's
But true and hearty.—[*To* AMBLE] Wait in the next
    room,

But be within call; yet not so near to force me
To whisper my intents.
    Amb.   We are taught better
By you, good madam.
    Woman.   And well know our distance.
    Lady All. Do so, and talk not; 'twill become your
    breeding.
               Exeunt AMBLE *and* [Waiting] Woman.
Now, my good lord, if I may use my freedom,
As to an honored friend—
    Lov.   You lessen else
Your favor to me.
    Lady All.   I dare then say thus:
As you are noble (howe'er common men   180
Make sordid wealth the object and sole end
Of their industrious aims), 'twill not agree
With those of eminent blood, who are engaged
More to prefer [25] their honors than to increase
The state [26] left to 'em by their ancestors,
To study large additions to their fortunes
And quite neglect their births—though I must grant
Riches, well got, to be a useful servant,
But a bad master.
    Lov.   Madam, 'tis confessed.
But what infer you from it?
    Lady All.   This, my lord: 190
That as all wrongs, though thrust into one scale,
Slide of themselves off when right fills the other
And cannot bide the trial, so all wealth,
I mean if ill-acquired, cemented to honor
By virtuous ways achieved and bravely purchased,
Is but as rubbage [27] poured into a river
(Howe'er intended to make good the bank),
Rendering the water, that was pure before,
Polluted and unwholesome. I allow [28]
The heir of Sir Giles Overreach, Margaret,   200
A maid well qualified and the richest match
Our north part can make boast of; yet she cannot,
With all that she brings with her, fill [29] their mouths,
That never will forget who was her father,
Or that my husband Allworth's lands and Wellborn's
(How wrung from both needs now no repetition)
Were real motive that more worked [30] your lordship
To join your families than her form and virtues.
You may conceive [31] the rest.
    Lov.   I do, sweet madam,
And long since have considered it. I know,   210
The sum of all that makes a just man happy
Consists in the well choosing of his wife;
And there, well to discharge it, does require
Equality of years, of birth, of fortune,
For beauty, being poor and not cried [32] up

---

[19] *admire:* wonder at.   [20] *Dispute not:* Don't inquire into.
[21] *portent:* prodigy.   [22] *Boreas:* North Wind.
[23] *double:* twin peaked (actually descriptive of Parnassus rather than Olympus).
[24] *matins:* morning service in the church.
[25] *prefer:* advance.   [26] *state:* estate.
[27] *rubbage:* rubbish. [28] *allow:* concede. [29] *fill:* shut.
[30] *worked:* moved.   [31] *conceive:* imagine.
[32] *cried:* raised.

By birth or wealth, can truly mix with neither.
And wealth, where there's such difference in years
And fair descent, must make the yoke uneasy.
But I come nearer.[33]
   Lady All.   Pray you, do, my lord.
   Lov. Were Overreach' states thrice centupled, his
     daughter   220
Millions of degrees much fairer than she is,
Howe'er I might urge precedents to excuse me,
I would not so adulterate my blood
By marrying Margaret, and so leave my issue
Made up of several pieces, one part scarlet
And the other London blue.[34] In my own tomb
I will inter my name first.
   Lady All. Aside   I am glad to hear this.—
Why then, my lord, pretend you marriage to her?
Dissimulation but ties false knots
On that straight line by which you hitherto   230
Have measured all your actions.
   Lov.   I make answer,
And aptly, with a question. Wherefore have you
That, since your husband's death, have lived a strict
And chaste nun's life, on the sudden given yourself
To visit and entertainments? Think you, madam,
'Tis not grown public conference?[35] Or the favors
Which you too prodigally have thrown on Wellborn,
Being too reserved before, incur not censure?
   Lady All. I am innocent here; and, on my life, I
     swear
My ends are good.
   Lov.   On my soul, so are mine   240
To Margaret; but leave both to the event.[36]
And, since this friendly privacy does serve
But as an offered means[37] unto ourselves
To search each other farther, you having shown
Your care of me, I my respect to you,
Deny me not, but still in chaste words, madam,
An afternoon's discourse.
   Lady All.   So I shall hear you.
                           [Exeunt.]

IV.ii

[*Enter*] Tapwell, [*and*] Froth.

   Tap. Undone, undone! this was your counsel,
     Froth.
   Froth. Mine! I defy thee. Did not Master Marall
(He has marred all, I am sure) strictly command us,

---

[33] *come nearer:* speak more particularly now.
[34] *London blue:* cloth denoting the servant class.
[35] *conference:* talk
[36] *event:* issue—"Let time try."
[37] *offered means:* chance opportunity.

IV.ii.
[1] *passages:* transactions.   [2] *close:* secret.
[3] *R:* Denoting "Receiver of Stolen Goods."
[4] *nine days' wonder:* proverbial for a passing sensation.
[5] *credit:* reputation.   [6] *custom:* business.
[7] *chronicled:* celebrated in history.
[8] *pageants:* public processions.
[9] *admittance:* i.e., to your service.

On pain of Sir Giles Overreach' displeasure,
To turn the gentleman out of doors?
   Tap.   'Tis true;
But now he's his uncle's darling, and has got
Master Justice Greedy, since he filled his belly,
At his commandment, to do anything.
Woe, woe to us!
   Froth.   He may prove merciful.
   Tap. Troth, we do not deserve it at his hands.   10
Though he knew all the passages[1] of our house,
As the receiving of stolen goods, and bawdry,
When he was rogue Wellborn no man would believe
     him,
And then his information could not hurt us;
But now he is "right worshipful" again,
Who dares but doubt his testimony? Methinks,
I see thee, Froth, already in a cart,
For a close[2] bawd, thine eyes even pelted out
With dirt and rotten eggs, and my hand hissing
If I scape the halter, with the letter R[3]   20
Printed upon it.
   Froth.   Would that were the worst!
That were but nine days' wonder.[4] As for credit,[5]
We have none to lose, but we shall lose the money
He owes us, and his custom[6]—there's the hell on't.
   Tap. He has summoned all his creditors by the drum,
And they swarm about him like so many soldiers
On the pay day, and has found out such a new way
To pay his old debts as 'tis very likely
He shall be chronicled[7] for it!
   Froth.   He deserves it
More than ten pageants.[8] But are you sure his worship
Comes this way, to my lady's?

        A cry within: "Brave Master Wellborn!"

   Tap.   Yes. I hear him.   31
   Froth. Be ready with your petition and present it
To his good grace.

     Enter Wellborn *in a rich habit,* [Marall,]
     Greedy, Order, Furnace, *three* Creditors;
     Tapwell, *kneeling, delivers his bill of debt.*

   Well.   How's this? Petitioned, too?
But note what miracles the payment of
A little trash, and a rich suit of clothes,
Can work upon these rascals! I shall be,
I think, Prince Wellborn.
   Mar.   When your worship's married,
You may be—I know what I hope to see you.
   Well. Then look thou for advancement.
   Mar.   To be known
Your worship's bailiff is the mark I shoot at.   40
   Well. And thou shalt hit it.
   Mar.   Pray you, sir, dispatch
These needy followers, and for my admittance,[9]
Provided you'll defend me from Sir Giles,

     This interim, Tapwell *and* Froth *flattering*
             and bribing Justice Greedy.

Whose service I am weary of, I'll say something
You shall give thanks for.

Well.   Fear me not [10] Sir Giles.

Greedy. Who? Tapwell? I remember thy wife brought me

Last New Year's tide a couple of fat turkeys.

Tap. And shall do every Christmas, let your worship
But stand my friend now.

Greedy.   How? With Master Wellborn?
I can do anything with him on such terms.—   50

[*To* WELLBORN] See you this honest couple? They are good souls

As ever drew out faucet. [11] Have they not

A pair of honest faces?

Well.   I o'erheard you,
And the bribe he promised. You are cozened in 'em,
For of all the scum that grew rich by my riots
This, for a most unthankful knave, and this,
For a base bawd and whore, have worst deserved me, [12]
And therefore speak not for 'em. By your place
You are rather to do me justice. Lend me your ear.—

[*Aside*] Forget his turkeys, and call in his license,   60
And at the next fair I'll give you a yoke of oxen
Worth all his poultry.

Greedy.   I am changed on the sudden
In my opinion!—Come near; nearer, rascal.
And, now I view him better, did you e'er see
One look so like an archknave? His very countenance,
Should an understanding judge but look upon him,
Would hang him, though he were innocent.

Tap. and Froth.   Worshipful sir!

Greedy. No, though the great Turk came, instead of turkeys,

To beg any favor, I am inexorable.

Thou hast an ill name; besides thy musty ale,   70
That hath destroyed many of the King's liege [13] people,
Thou never hadst in thy house, to stay men's stomachs,
A piece of Suffolk cheese or gammon of bacon,
Or any esculent, [14] as the learned call it,
For their emolument, [15] but sheer drink only,
For which gross fault I here do damn thy license,
Forbidding thee ever to tap or draw;
For instantly I will in mine own person
Command the constable to pull down thy sign,
And do it before I eat.

Froth.   No mercy?

Greedy.   Vanish!   80
If I show any, may my promised oxen gore me!

Tap. Unthankful knaves are ever so rewarded.

                    Exeunt GREEDY, TAPWELL, [*and*]
                                        FROTH.

Well. Speak, what are you?

1 Cred.   A decayed vintner, [16] sir,
That might have thrived, but that your worship broke me
With trusting you with muscadine [17] and eggs,
And five-pound suppers, with your afterdrinkings,
When you lodged upon the Bankside. [18]

Well.   [I] remember.

1 Cred. I have not been hasty, nor e'er laid [19] to arrest you;

And therefore, sir—

Well.   Thou art an honest fellow.

I'll set thee up again; see his bill paid.—   90
What are you?

2 Cred.   A tailor once, but now mere botcher. [20]
I gave you credit for a suit of clothes,
Which was all my stock, but, you failing in payment,
I was removed from the shopboard, [21] and confined
Under a stall. [22]

Well.   See him paid—and botch no more.

2 Cred. I ask no interest, sir.

Well.   Such tailors need not;
If their bills are paid in one-and-twenty year,
They are seldom losers.—[*To* 3 Creditor] Oh, I know thy face;

Thou wert my surgeon. You must tell no tales;
Those days are done. I will pay you in private. [23]   100

Ord. A royal gentleman!

Furn.   Royal as an emperor!
He'll prove a brave master; my good lady knew
To choose a man.

Well.   See all men else discharged;
And, since *old debts are cleared by a new way*,
A little bounty will not misbecome me.
There's something, honest cook, for thy good breakfasts.—

[*To* ORDER] And this, for your respect. Take 't; tis' good gold,

And I able to spare it.

Ord.   You are too munificent.

Furn. He was ever so.

Well.   Pray you, on before.

3 Cred.   Heaven bless you!

Mar. At four o'-clock the rest know where to meet me.   110

                    Exeunt ORDER, FURNACE, [*and*]
                                        Creditors.

Well. Now, Master Marall, what's the weighty secret
You promised to impart?

Mar.   Sir, time nor place
Allow me to relate each circumstance.
This only, in a word: I know Sir Giles
Will come upon you for security
For his thousand pounds, which you must not consent to.

As he grows in heat, as I am sure he will,
Be you but rough, and say he's in your debt
Ten times the sum, upon sale of your land.

---

[10] *Fear me not:* Don't fear.
[11] *drew out faucet:* tapped a barrel.
[12] *worst deserved me:* deserved worst at my hands.
[13] *liege:* loyal.   [14] *any esculent:* anything edible.
[15] *emolument:* reward.   [16] *vintner:* wine merchant.
[17] *muscadine:* sweet wine.
[18] *Bankside:* south bank of the Thames.
[19] *laid:* enjoined the constable.   [20] *botcher:* patcher.
[21] *shopboard:* tailor's bench in his own shop.
[22] *stall:* i.e., in the public market (he has come down in the world).
[23] *private:* punning on "private parts"; the third creditor has cured Wellborn of venereal disease.

I had a hand in 't (I speak it to my shame)   120
When you were defeated [24] of it.
 Well.   That's forgiven.
 Mar. I shall deserve 't then. Urge him to produce
The deed in which you passed it over to him,
Which I know he'll have about him, to deliver
To the Lord Lovell with many other writings
And present monies. I'll instruct you further,
As I wait on your worship. If I play not my price [25]
To your full content and your uncle's much vexation,
Hang up Jack Marall.
 Well.   I rely upon thee.
              Exeunt.

IV.iii

[*Enter*] ALLWORTH, [*and*] MARGARET.

 All. Whether to yield the first praise to my lord's
Unequaled temperance or your constant sweetness
That I yet live, my weak hands fastened on
Hope's anchor, spite of all storms of despair,
I yet rest doubtful.
 Marg.   Give it to Lord Lovell,
For what in him was bounty, in me's duty.
I make but payment of a debt to which
My vows, in that high office [1] registered,
Are faithful witnesses.
 All.   'Tis true, my dearest;
Yet, when I call to mind how many fair ones   10
Make willful shipwreck of their faiths, and oaths
To God and man, to fill the arms of greatness,
And you rise up [no] less than a glorious star,
To the amazement of the world, that hold out
Against the stern authority of a father,
And spurn at honor when it comes to court you,
I am so tender of your good that, faintly, [2]
With your wrong I can wish myself that right
You yet are pleased to do me.
 Marg.   Yet and ever.
To me what's title, when content is wanting?   20
Or wealth, raked up together with much care
And to be kept with more, when the heart pines
In being dispossessed of what it longs for
Beyond the Indian [3] mines? Or the smooth brow
Of a pleased sire, that slaves me to his will,
And, so his ravenous humor may be feasted
By my obedience, and he see me great,
Leaves to my soul nor faculties nor power
To make her own election?

 All.   But the dangers
That follow the repulse—
 Marg.   To me they are nothing.   30
Let Allworth love, I cannot be unhappy.
Suppose the worst, that in his rage he kill me.
A tear or two, by you dropped on my hearse
In sorrow for my fate, will call back life
So far as but to say that I die yours;
I then shall rest in peace. Or should he prove
So cruel, as one death would not suffice
His thirst of vengeance, but with lingering torments
In mind and body I must waste to air,
In poverty joined with banishment, so you share   40
In my afflictions, which I dare not wish you,
So high I prize you, I could undergo 'em
With such a patience as should look down
With scorn on his worst malice.
 All.   Heaven avert
Such trials of your true affection to me!
Nor will it unto you, that are all mercy,
Show so much rigor. But, since we must run
Such desperate hazards, let us do our best
To steer between 'em.
 Marg.   Your lord's ours, and sure;
And, though but a young actor, [4] second [5] me   50
In doing to the life what he has plotted,

Enter OVERREACH [*behind*].

The end may yet prove happy. Now, my Allworth—

[*Sees her father.*]

 All. [*Aside*] To your letter, [6] and put on a seeming
  anger.
 Marg. I'll pay my lord all debts due to his title;
And when, with terms not taking from his honor,
He does solicit me, I shall gladly hear him.
But in this peremptory, nay, commanding way,
To appoint a meeting and, without my knowledge,
A priest to tie the knot can ne'er be undone
Till death unloose it, is a confidence [7]   60
In his lordship will deceive him.
 All.   I hope better,
Good lady.
 Marg. Hope, sir, what you please. For me
I must take a safe and secure course; I have
A father, and without his full consent,
Though all lords of the land kneeled for my favor,
I can grant nothing.

[OVERREACH *comes forward.*]

 Over.   I like this obedience.—
But whatsoever my lord writes must and shall be
Accepted and embraced. Sweet Master Allworth,
You show yourself a true and faithful servant
To your good lord; he has a jewel of [8] you.   70
How? Frowning, Meg? Are these looks to receive
A messenger from my lord? What's this? Give me it.
 Marg. A piece of arrogant paper, like th'
  inscriptions.

OVERREACH *read*[*s*] *the letter.*

---

[24] *defeated:* defrauded.   [25] *price:* value, worth.

IV.iii.
 [1] *high office:* heaven.   [2] *faintly:* only halfheartedly.
 [3] *Indian:* East and West Indian, each proverbial for precious metals. [4] *young actor:* referring to Allworth(?).
 [5] *second:* if you second; alternatively, imperative voice: "support me."
 [6] *letter:* which Allworth bears in his role as page.
 [7] *confidence:* presumption.   [8] *of:* in.

Over. "Fair mistress, from your servant learn, all
    joys
That we can hope for, if deferred, prove toys;[9]
Therefore this instant, and in private, meet
A husband, that will gladly at your feet
Lay down his honors, tendering them to you
With all content, the church being paid her due."—
Is this the arrogant piece of paper? Fool,   80
Will you still be one? In the name of madness what
Could his good honor write more to content you?
Is there aught else to be wished, after these two,
That are already offered: marriage first,
And lawful pleasure after? What would you more?
   Marg. Why, sir, I would be married like your
    daughter,
Not hurried away i' th' night I know not whither,
Without all ceremony—no friends invited
To honor the solemnity.
   All.   An 't please your honor,
For so before tomorrow I must style you,   90
My lord desires this privacy, in respect[10]
His honorable kinsmen are far off,
And his desires to have it done brook not
So long delay as to expect[11] their coming;
And yet he stands resolved, with all due pomp,
As running at the ring,[12] plays, masques, and tilting,
To have his marriage at court celebrated
When he has brought your honor up to London.
   Over. He tells you true; 'tis the fashion, on my
    knowledge.
Yet the good lord, to please your peevishness,   100
Must put it off, forsooth, and lose a night,
In which perhaps he might get[13] two boys on thee.
Tempt me no farther; if you do, this goad.[14]
Shall prick you to him.
   Marg.   I could be contented,
Were you but by to do a father's part
And give me in the church.
   Over.   So my lord have you,
What do I care who gives you? Since my lord
Does purpose to be private, I'll not cross him.
I know not, Master Allworth, how my lord
May be provided, and therefore there's a purse   110
Of gold—'twill serve this night's expense; tomorrow
I'll furnish him with any sums. In the meantime,
Use my ring to my chaplain; he is beneficed
At my manor of Gotam,[15] and called Parson Willdo.
'Tis no matter for a license; I'll bear him out in 't.
   Marg. With your favor, sir, what warrant is your
    ring?
He may suppose I got that twenty ways,
Without your knowledge; and then to be refused
Were such a stain upon me! if you pleased, sir,
Your presence would do better.
   Over.   Still perverse?   120
I say again, I will not cross my lord;
Yet I'll prevent you[16] too.—Paper and ink there!
   All. I can furnish you.
   Over.   I thank you; I can write then.

                Writes on his book.[17]

   All. You may, if you please, put out[18] the name of
    my lord,
In respect he comes disguised, and only write,
"Marry her to this gentleman."
   Over.   Well advised.—

                 MARGARET *kneels.*

'Tis done; away!—My blessing, girl? Thou hast it.
Nay, no reply; begone.—Good Master Allworth,
This shall be the best night's work you ever made.   129
   All. I hope so, sir.
           Exeunt ALLWORTH *and* MARGARET.
   Over.   Farewell!—Now all's cocksure.[19]
Methinks I hear already knights and ladies
Say, "Sir Giles Overreach, how is it with
Your honorable daughter? Has her honor
Slept well tonight?" or, "Will her honor please
To accept this monkey? Dog? Or paraquit?"[20]
(This is state[21] in ladies) "or my eldest son
To be her page, and wait upon her trencher?"[22]
My ends, my ends are compassed! then for Wellborn
And the lands. Were he once married to the widow,
I have him here.[23] I can scarce contain myself,   140
I am so full of joy, nay, joy all over.

                        Exit.

      THE END OF THE FOURTH ACT

ACT FIVE

SCENE ONE

[Enter] LOVELL, LADY [ALLWORTH],
      [and] AMBLE.[1]

   Lady All. By this you know how strong the motives
    were
That did, my lord, induce me to dispense
A little with my gravity to advance,
In personating[2] some few favors to him,
The plots and projects of the downtrod Wellborn.
Nor shall I e'er repent, although I suffer
In some few men's opinions for 't, the action,
For he that ventured all for my dear husband
Might justly claim an obligation from me
To pay him such a courtesy, which had I   10
Coyly or overcuriously[3] denied,

---

   [9] *toys:* trifles.   [10] *in respect:* because.
   [11] *expect:* wait on.
   [12] *running . . . ring:* hooking a ring with a lance while
riding at full tilt.   [13] *get:* beget.
   [14] *goad:* i.e., his sword. Q "good."
   [15] *Gotam:* Gotham, near Nottingham.
   [16] *prevent you:* anticipate your objection.
   [17] *his book:* the "tables" or paper Allworth keeps ready at
hand.   [18] *put out:* omit.   [19] *cocksure:* safe.
   [20] *paraquit:* parakeet.   [21] *is state:* denotes dignity.
   [22] *wait . . . trencher:* serve her at table.
   [23] *here:* between my thumb and forefinger.
V.i.
   [1] *Amble:* who, in his capacity of usher, presumably
stands apart throughout the scene, once having led on Lady
Allworth.   [2] *personating:* pretending.
   [3] *overcuriously:* too nicely, fastidiously.

It might have argued me of little love
To the deceased.
    Lov.   What you intended, madam,
For the poor gentleman hath found good success,
For, as I understand, his debts are paid,
And he once more furnished for fair employment.
But all the arts that I have used to raise
The fortunes of your joy and mine, young Allworth,
Stand yet in supposition, though I hope well,
For the young lovers are in wit more pregnant   20
Than their years can promise; and for their desires,
On my knowledge, they are equal.
    Lady All.   —As my wishes
Are with yours,⁴ my lord. Yet give me leave to fear
The building, though well grounded. To deceive
Sir Giles, that's both a lion and a fox
In his proceedings, were a work beyond
The strongest undertakers—not the trial
Of two weak innocents.
    Lov.   Despair not, madam.
Hard things are compassed oft by easy means;
And judgment, being a gift derived from heaven,   30
Though sometimes lodged i' th' hearts of worldly men,
That ne'er consider from whom they receive it,
Forsakes such as abuse the giver of it—
Which is the reason that the politic
And cunning statesman, that believes he fathoms
The counsels of all kingdoms on the earth,
Is by simplicity oft overreached.
    Lady All. May he be so! Yet in his name to express
    it
Is a good omen.
    Lov.   May it to myself
Prove so, good lady, in my suit to you!   40
What think you of the motion?⁵
    Lady All.   Troth, my lord,
My own unworthiness may answer for me,
For had you, when that I was in my prime
(My virgin flower uncropped), presented me
With this great favor, looking on my lowness
Not in a glass of self-love, but of truth,
I could not but have thought it as a blessing
Far, far beyond my merit.
    Lov.   You are too modest,
And undervalue that which is above
My title, or whatever I call mine.   50
I grant, were I a Spaniard, to marry
A widow might disparage me; but, being
A true-born Englishman, I cannot find
How it can taint my honor. Nay, what's more,
That which you think a blemish is to me
The fairest luster. You already, madam,
Have given sure proofs how dearly you can cherish
A husband that deserves you, which confirms me
That, if I am not wanting in my care

To do you service, you'll be still the same   60
That you were to your Allworth. In a word,
Our years, our states, our births are not unequal,
You being descended nobly, and allied so;
If then you may be won to make me happy,
But join your lips to mine, and that shall be
A solemn contract.
    Lady All.   I were blind to my own good
Should I refuse it.
                          [*Kisses him.*]
              Yet, my lord, receive me
As such a one, the study of whose whole life
Shall know no other object but to please you.
    Lov. If I return not with all tenderness   70
Equal respect to you, may I die wretched!
    Lady All. There needs no protestation, my lord,
To her that cannot doubt.

            Enter WELLBORN.

                  You are welcome, sir.
Now you look like yourself.⁶
    Well.   And will continue
Such in my free acknowledgement that I am
Your creature, madam, and will never hold
My life mine own, when you please to command it.
    Lov. It is a thankfulness that well becomes you.
You could not make choice of a better shape
To dress your mind in.
    Lady All.   For me, I am happy   80
That my endeavors prospered. Saw you of late
Sir Giles, your uncle?
    Well.   I heard of him, madam,
By his minister,⁷ Marall; he's grown into strange
    passions
About his daughter. This last night he looked for
Your lordship at his house, but, missing you,
And she not yet appearing, his wisehead⁸
Is much perplexed and troubled.
    Lov.   It may be,
Sweetheart, my project took.

    Enter OVERREACH, *with distracted looks,*
    driving in MARALL *before him* [*with a box*].

    Lady All.   I strongly hope.
    Over. Ha! find her, booby, thou huge lump of
    nothing;
I'll bore thine eyes out else.
    Well.   May it please your lordship,
For some ends of mine own but to withdraw   91
A little out of sight, though not of hearing,
You may perhaps have sport.
    Lov.   You shall direct me.
                            Steps aside.
    Over. I shall *sol fa*⁹ you, rogue!
    Mar.   Sir, for what cause
Do you use me thus?
    Over.   Cause, slave? Why, I am angry,
And thou a subject only fit for beating,
And so to cool my choler. Look to the writing;
Let but the seal be broke upon the box

---

⁴ *As ... yours:* i.e., equal (like the desires Lovell has just
alluded to).   ⁵ *motion:* proposal.
    ⁶ *Now ... yourself:* i.e., because of his new apparel.
    ⁷ *minister:* instrument, tool.
    ⁸ *wisehead:* wisdomship (satirically).
    ⁹ *sol fa:* play a tune on.

That has slept in my cabinet these three years,
I'll rack thy soul for 't.
    Mar. [*Aside*]   I may yet cry quittance,[10]   100
Though now I suffer, and dare not resist.
    Over. Lady, by your leave, did you see my daughter,
    lady?
And the lord her husband? Are they in your house?
If they are, discover, that I may bid 'em joy;
And, as an entrance to her place of honor,
See your ladyship on her left hand, and make curtseys
When she nods on you, which you must receive
As a special favor.
    Lady All.   When I know, Sir Giles,
Her state[11] requires such ceremony, I shall pay it;
But in the meantime, as I am myself,   110
I give you to understand I neither know
Nor care where her honor is.
    Over.   When you once see her
Supported and led by the lord her husband,
You'll be taught better.—Nephew!
    Well.   Sir.
    Over.   No more?[12]
    Well. 'Tis all I owe you.
    Over.   Have your redeemed rags
Made you thus insolent?
    Well. In scorn   Insolent to you?
Why, what are you, sir, unless in your years,
At the best more than myself?
    Over.   His fortune swells him.
'Tis rank[13] he's married.
    Lady All.   This is excellent!
    Over. Sir, in calm language, though I seldom use it,
I am familiar with the cause that makes you   121
Bear up thus bravely.[14] There's a certain buzz[15]
Of a stolen marriage—do you hear?—of a stolen
    marriage,
In which, 'tis said, there's somebody hath been cozened.
I name no parties.
    Well.   Well, sir, and what follows?
    Over. Marry, this, since you are peremptory:
    remember.
Upon mere hope of your great match, I lent you
A thousand pounds. Put me in good security,
And suddenly, by[16] mortgage or by statute,
Of some of your possessions, or I'll have you   130
Dragged in your lavender[17] robes to the jail. You know
    me,
And therefore do not trifle.
    Well.   Can you be
So cruel to your nephew, now he's in
The way to rise? Was this the courtesy
You did me "in pure love, and no ends else"?
    Over. End me no ends! Engage the whole estate,
And force your spouse to sign it, you shall have
Three or four thousand more, to roar and swagger
And revel in bawdy taverns.
    Well.   And beg after—
Mean you not so?
    Over.   My thoughts are mine, and free.   140
Shall I have security?
    Well.   No, indeed, you shall not,

Nor bond, nor bill, nor bare acknowledgment;
Your great looks fright not me.
    Over.   But my deeds shall.
Outbraved?
                     They both draw.

        The Servants *enter.*

    Lady All. Help, murder! Murder!
    Well.   Let him come on,
With all his wrongs and injuries about him,
Armed with his cutthroat practices to guard him;
The right that I bring with me will defend me,
And punish his extortion.
    Over.   That I had thee
But single in the field!
    Lady All.   You may; but make not
My house your quarreling scene.
    Over.   Were 't in a church,
By heaven and hell, I'll do 't!
    Mar. [*Aside to* WELLBORN] Now put him to   151
The showing of the deed.
    Well.   This rage is vain, sir.
For fighting, fear not, you shall have your hands full
Upon the least incitement; and whereas
You charge me with a debt of a thousand pounds,
If there be law (howe'er you have no conscience),
Either restore my land or I'll recover
A debt that's truly due to me from you,
In value ten times more than what you challenge.[18]
    Over. I in thy debt! O impudence! Did I not
    purchase   160
The land left by thy father, that rich land
That had continuèd in Wellborn's name
Twenty descents, which, like a riotous fool,
Thou didst make sale of? Is not here inclosed
The deed that does confirm it mine?
    Mar. [*Aside*]   Now, now!
    Well. I do acknowledge none; I ne'er passed o'er
Any such land. I grant for a year or two
You had it in trust, which if you do discharge,
Surrendering the possession, you shall ease
Yourself and me of chargeable suits in law,   170
Which, if you prove not honest, as I doubt, it
Must of necessity follow.
    Lady All.   In my judgment
He does advise you well.
    Over.   Good! good! conspire
With your new husband, lady; second him
In his dishonest practices; but, when
This manor is extended[19] to my use,
You'll speak in an humbler key, and sue for favor.
    Lady All. Never; do not hope it.
    Well.   Let despair first
    seize me.

---

[10] *cry quittance:* be revenged.   [11] *state:* social position.
[12] *No more:* i.e., "No more than a curt 'Sir' in responding
to me?"   [13] *rank:* plain ("I smell it").
[14] *bravely:* haughtily.   [15] *buzz:* rumor.   [16] *by:* Q "my."
[17] *lavender:* pawned (because only recently laid away in
lavender by the pawnbroker).
[18] *challenge:* claim as your due.   [19] *extended:* seized.

Over. Yet, to shut up thy mouth, and make thee give
Thyself the lie, the loud lie, I draw out   180
The precious evidence; if thou canst forswear
Thy hand and seal, and make a forfeit of

Opens the box.

Thy ears to the pillory—see, here's that will make
My interest [20] clear.—Ha!
     Lady All.   A fair skin of parchment.
Well.   Indented,[21] I confess, and labels [22] too;
But neither wax nor words. How! Thunderstruck?
Not a syllable to insult with? My wise uncle,
Is this your precious evidence? Is this that makes
Your interest clear?
     Over.   I am o'erwhelmed with wonder!
What prodigy is this? What subtle devil   190
Hath razed out the inscription, the wax
Turned into dust? The rest of my deeds whole
As when they were delivered, and this only
Made nothing! Do you deal with witches, rascal?
There is a statute for you, which will bring
Your neck in a hempen circle; [23] yes, there is.
And now 'tis better thought,[24] for, cheater, know
This juggling shall not save you.
     Well.   To save thee
Would beggar the stock of mercy.
     Over.   Marall!
     Mar.   Sir.
Over. Flattering him Though the witnesses are dead,
     your testimony—   200
Help with an oath or two; and for thy master,
Thy liberal master, my good honest servant,
I know you will swear anything to dash
This cunning sleight.[25] Besides, I know thou art
A public notary, and such stand in law
For a dozen witnesses. The deed, being drawn too
By thee, my careful Marall, and delivered
When thou wert present, will make good my title.
Wilt thou not swear this?
     Mar.   I? No, I assure you.
I have a conscience not seared up like yours;   210
I know no deeds.
     Over.   Wilt thou betray me?
     Mar.   Keep him
From using of his hands, I'll use my tongue
To his no little torment.

---

[20] *interest:* legal title.
[21] *Indented:* To guard against forgery, documents were drawn up in duplicate on a single sheet, which was then torn in half—the point being that the ragged edges had to match.
[22] *labels:* ribbons, to which the seals of the signatories were attached.   [23] *hempen circle:* hangman's noose.
[24] *thought:* considered.   [25] *sleight:* trick.
[26] *uncase:* unmask.
[27] *anatomize:* dissect (an "anatomy" is a skeleton.)
[28] *gabions:* fortifications made by filling baskets with earth.
[29] *discovered:* revealed.
[30] *With:* The preposition seems gratuitous and should perhaps be omitted.   [31] *but:* if (they were).
[32] *take in:* capture.   [33] *here:* i.e., in my breast.
[34] *they:* i.e., the swords protecting Marall.
[35] *bandog:* fierce watchdog.   [36] *bearing:* substantial.

Over.   Mine own varlet
Rebel against me?
     Mar.   Yes, and uncase [26] you too.
The "idiot," the "patch," the "slave," the "booby,"
The property fit only to be beaten
For your morning exercise, your "football," or
"Th' unprofitable lump of flesh," your "drudge,"
Can now anatomize [27] you, and lay open
All your black plots, and level with the earth   220
Your hill of pride, and, with these gabions [28] guarded,
Unload my great artillery and shake,
Nay, pulverize the walls you think defend you.
     Lady All.   How he foams at the mouth with rage!
     Well.   To
     him again.
     Over. Oh, that I had thee in my gripe; I would tear
     thee
Joint after joint!
     Mar.   I know you are a tearer,
But I'll have first your fangs pared off, and then
Come nearer to you, when I have discovered,[29]
And made it good before the judge, what ways
And devilish practices you used to cozen   230
With [30] an army of whole families, who yet live,
And, but [31] enrolled for soldiers, were able
To take in [32] Dunkirk.
     Well.   All will come out.
     Lady All.   The better.
     Over. But that I will live, rogue, to torture thee,
And make thee wish, and kneel in vain, to die,
These swords that keep thee from me should fix here,[33]
Although they [34] made my body but one wound,
But I would reach thee.
     Lov. [Aside]   Heaven's hand is in this;
One bandog [35] worry the other!
     Over.   I play the fool,
And make my anger but ridiculous;   240
There will be a time and place, there will be, cowards,
When you shall feel what I dare do.
     Well.   I think so.
You dare do any ill, yet want true valor
To be honest and repent.
     Over.   They are words I know not,
Nor e'er will learn. Patience, the beggar's virtue,

Enter GREEDY *and* PARSON WILLDO.

Shall find no harbor here.—After these storms
At length a calm appears. Welcome, most welcome!
There's comfort in thy looks. Is the deed done?
Is my daughter married? Say but so, my chaplain,
And I am tame.
     Willdo.   Married? Yes, I assure you.   250
     Over. Then vanish, all sad thoughts! There's more
     gold for thee.
My doubts and fears are in the titles drowned
Of my "right honorable," my "right honorable"
     daughter.
     Greedy. Here will I be feasting! At least for a month
I am provided. Empty guts, croak no more.
You shall be stuffed like bagpipes, not with wind,
But bearing [36] dishes.

Over. Whispering to WILLDO Instantly be here?
To my wish! to my wish! Now you that plot against me,
And hope to trip my heels up, that contemned me,
Think on 't and tremble.—

                                        Loud music.

                              They come! I hear the music.
A lane there for my lord!
    Well.   This sudden heat   261
May yet be cooled, sir.
    Over.   Make way there for my lord!

          Enter ALLWORTH *and* MARGARET.

    Marg. Sir, first your pardon, then your blessing, with
Your full allowance of the choice I have made.
As ever you could make use of your reason,

                                        Kneeling.

Grow not in passion, since you may as well
Call back the day that's past, as untie the knot
Which is too strongly fastened. Not to dwell
Too long on words, this is my husband.
    Over.   How!
    All. So I assure you; all the rites of marriage,   270
With every circumstance, are past. Alas, sir,
Although I am no lord, but a lord's page,
Your daughter and my loved wife mourns not for it;
And, for "right honorable" son-in-law, you may say,
Your "dutiful" daughter.
    Over.   Devil! Are they married?
    Willdo. Do a father's part, and say, "Heaven give
        'em joy!"
    Over. Confusion and ruin! Speak, and speak
        quickly,
Or thou art dead.
    Willdo.   They are married.
    Over.   Thou hadst better
Have made a contract with the king of fiends
Than these. My brain turns!
    Willdo.   Why this rage to me?   280
Is not this your letter, sir, and these the words?
"Marry her to this gentleman."
    Over.   It cannot—
Nor will I e'er believe it—'sdeath, I will not!—
That I, that in all passages I touched
At wordly profit have not left a print
Where I have trod for the most curious search
To trace my footsteps, should be gulled by children,
Baffled and fooled, and all my hopes and labors
Defeated and made void.
    Well.   As it appears,
You are so, my grave uncle.
    Over.   Village nurses   290
Revenge their wrongs with curses; I'll not waste
A syllable, but thus I take the life
Which, wretched, I gave to thee.

                    Offers to kill MARGARET.

    Lov.   Hold, for your own
        sake!
Though charity to your daughter hath quite left you,
Will you do an act, though in your hopes lost here,[37]

Can leave no hope for peace or rest hereafter?[38]
Consider; at the best you are but a man,
And cannot so create your aims but that
Thy may be crossed.
    Over.   Lord, thus I spit at thee
And at thy counsel, and again desire thee,   300
And as thou art a soldier, if thy valor
Dares show itself where multitude and example
Lead not the way, let's quit the house, and change
Six words in private.
    Lov.   I am ready.
    Lady All.   Stay, sir.
Contest with one distracted?
    Well.   You'll grow like him
Should you answer his vain challenge.
    Over.   Are you pale?[39]
Borrow his help; though Hercules call it odds,
I'll stand against both, as I am hemmed in thus.
Since, like Libyan lion in the toil,
My fury cannot reach the coward hunters,   310
And only spends itself, I'll quit the place.
Alone I can do nothing; but I have servants
And friends to second me; and, if I make not
This house a heap of ashes (by my wrongs,
What I have spoke I will make good!) or leave[40]
One throat uncut—if it be possible,
Hell add to my afflictions!

                              Exit OVERREACH.

    Mar.   Is 't not brave sport?
    Greedy. Brave sport? I am sure it has ta'en away my
        stomach;
I do not like the sauce.
    All.   Nay, weep not, dearest,
Though it express your pity; what's decreed   320
Above, we cannot alter.
    Lady All.   His threats move me
No scruple, madam.
    Mar.   Was it not a rare trick,
And it please your worship, to make the deed nothing?
I can do twenty neater, if you please
To purchase and grow rich, for I will be
Such a solicitor and steward for you
As never worshipful had.
    Well.   I do believe thee.
But first discover the quaint[41] means you used
To raze out the conveyance?[42]
    Mar.   They are mysteries
Not to be spoke in public: certain minerals   330
Incorporated in the ink and wax.
Besides, he gave me nothing, but still fed me
With hopes and blows; and that was the inducement
To this conundrum. If it please your worship
To call to memory, this mad beast once caused me
To urge you or to drown or hang yourself;
I'll do the like to him, if you command me.
    Well. You are a rascal! He that dares be false

---

37 *lost here:* you are disappointed on earth.
38 *hereafter:* after death.
39 *pale:* i.e., with fear.
40 *leave:* Q "leav'd."
41 *quaint:* subtle.
42 *conveyance:* deed.

To a master, though unjust, will ne'er be true
To any other. Look not for reward   340
Or favor from me; I will shun thy sight
As I would do a basilisk's.[43] Thank my pity
If thou keep thy ears; howe'er, I will take order
Your practice shall be silenced.
  Greedy.   I'll commit him,
If you'll have me, sir.
  Well.   That were to little purpose;
His conscience be his prison. Not a word,
But instantly begone!
  Ord.   Take this kick with you.
  Amb. And this.
  Furn.   If that I had my cleaver here,
I would divide your knave's head.
  Mar.   This is the heaven
False servants still arrive at.

                     Exit MARALL.

         Enter OVER[REACH].

Lady All.   Come again!   350
Lov. Fear not, I am your guard.
Well.   His looks are ghastly.
Willdo. Some little time I have spent, under your
     favors,
In physical[44] studies, and, if my judgment err not,
He's mad beyond recovery. But observe him,
And look to yourselves.
  Over.   Why, is not the whole world
Included in myself? To what use then
Are friends and servants? Say there were a squadron
Of pikes, lined through with shot,[45] when I am mounted
Upon my injuries, shall I fear to charge 'em?
No; I'll through the battalia, and, that routed,   360

     Flourishing his sword sheathed.[46]

I'll fall to execution. Ha! I am feeble;
Some undone widow sits upon mine arm,
And takes away the use of 't; and my sword,
Glued to my scabbard with wronged orphans' tears,
Will not be drawn. Ha! What are these? Sure,
     hangmen
That come to bind my hands, and then to drag me
Before the judgment seat. Now they are new shapes,
And do appear like Furies, with steel whips
To scourge my ulcerous soul. Shall I then fall

Ingloriously, and yield? No; spite of fate,   370
I will be forced to hell like to myself.
Though you were legions of accursèd spirits,
Thus would I fly among you.
  Well.   There's no help;
Disarm him first, then bind him.
  Greedy.   Take a *mittimus*,[47]
And carry him to Bedlam.[48]
  Lov.   How he foams!
  Well. And bites the earth!
  Willdo.   Carry him to some dark
     room;
There try what art can do for his recovery.
  Marg. O my dear father!

          They force OVERREACH *off.*

  All.   You must be patient,
     mistress.
  Lov. Here is a precedent to teach wicked men
That when they leave religion, and turn atheists,   380
Their own abilities leave 'em. Pray you, take comfort;
I will endeavor you shall be his guardians
In his distractions. And for your land, Master
     Wellborn,
Be it good or ill in law, I'll be an umpire
Between you and this,[49] th' undoubted heir
Of Sir Giles Overreach. For me, here's[50] the anchor
That I must fix on.
  All.   What you shall determine,
My lord, I will allow of.[51]
  Well.   'Tis the language
That I speak too; but there is something else
Beside the repossession of my land   390
And payment of my debts that I must practice.
I had a reputation, but 'twas lost
In my loose course, and, till I redeem it
Some noble way, I am but half made up.
It is a time of action; if your lordship
Will please to confer a company upon me
In your command, I doubt not in my service
To my king and country but I shall do something
That may make me right again.
  Lov.   Your suit is granted
And you loved for the motion.
  Well. [*To the audience*]   Nothing wants then   400
But your allowance—

THE EPILOGUE

But your allowance, and in that our all
Is comprehended, it being known nor we
Nor he that wrote the comedy can be free
Without your manumission,[1] which if you
Grant willingly, as a fair favor due

To the poet's and our labors (as you may,
For we despair not, gentlemen, of the play),
We jointly shall profess your grace[2] hath might
To teach us action,[3] and him how to write.

                     [*Exeunt.*]

F I N I S

---

[43] *basilisk's:* alluding to the fabulous creature whose look was fatal.   [44] *physical:* medical.
[45] *lined . . . shot:* reinforced with musketeers.
[46] *sheathed:* Q "unsheathed".
[47] *L.:* writ for confinement.
[48] *Bedlam:* the London lunatic asylum.

[49] *this:* Allworth.   [50] *here's:* i.e., the Lady Allworth.
[51] *allow of:* agree with.

EPILOGUE

[1] *manumission:* setting (us) free by applauding.
[2] *grace:* tendering of good fortune.   [3] *action:* how to act.

Philip Massinger

THE ROMAN ACTOR

THE ROMAN ACTOR was licensed for production by the King's Men in 1626 and printed in 1629 with a title page that proclaimed it "hath divers times been with good allowance acted at the private playhouse in the Blackfriars." The Dramatis Personæ, which lists the principal players, is something of a rarity and appropriate to a play in which actors enact the roles of actors. There is no evidence of frequent performance, although the tragedy was revived after the Restoration with the great Betterton as Paris and although it later attracted such actors as Kemble and Kean in England and others in America.

The plot is based on Suetonius' *Lives of the Twelve Caesars* and Dio Cassius' *Roman History*. Though no source has been found for Paris' third play, *The False Servant*, Massinger drew the first, *The Cure of Avarice*, from Horace's *Satires* and the second, *Iphis and Anaxarete*, from Ovid's *Metamorphoses*.

THE ROMAN ACTOR is a curiously schematic play, unrelievedly melodramatic in its simplistic characterization and exaggerated good and evil. What gives it its powerful life is Massinger's constant ingenuity in playing with the idea of the play. Like many other dramatists of the period, he alludes implicitly and explicitly to the notion that all the world is a stage and life itself a kind of play. Domitian is undone on one level by his hubristic assumption that he is a god, and just as literally on another by his assumption that he is playwright of the part he acts. The audience watches as actors play the parts of actors in three plays within the play. In one of them, as in the plays Paris cites in defending the theater, the audience is morally instructed; in the second, as in *Hamlet*, the action provokes a revelation of secret knowledge from an auditor; in the third, as in THE SPANISH TRAGEDY, play turns into reality as an actual murder occurs on stage and we are brought to realize that one actor is only pretending to play the part of an actor. Apart from such entertaining complexities, the plot has the stark sequentiality and simplicity of Ben Jonson's two Roman tragedies, and one wonders whether Massinger is trying to suggest an authentically Roman atmosphere by imitating the form of other plays about Rome that, whether derived from Seneca's tragedies or like Jonson's from respectable historiography, share a kind of plot seldom found elsewhere in Renaissance English tragedy. The Roman ambiance is reinforced by a style that manages consistently to suggest Latin through its use of suspended periods, absolute phrases, and occasionally Latinate diction, without ever ceasing to be a smooth and efficient stage English; the Latinism, that is, is rather a patina than an essential quality.

Paris' apology for theater in I.iii is orthodox, the kind of thing one said to Puritans who decried the iniquity of the stage. Thomas Heywood had advanced similar arguments in his *Apology for Actors* in 1612, but the attacks persisted, and it has been suggested that Paris's address is Massinger's rebuttal of *A Short Treatise Against Stage Players*, presented to Parliament in May 1625 not long before the licensing of THE ROMAN ACTOR. If so, however, the defense must be rather tongue in cheek, since the play refutes Paris's arguments one by one, demonstrating that plays can traduce their actors' superiors and can indeed reveal the secret crimes of "Such / That are above us," that drama does not necessarily improve its auditors, that it can in fact use real violence, and that adultresses and corrupt men are not always punished. What is lacking in complexity of dramaturgy is to some extent made up for by the essential wit of Massinger's conception.

If the tricks of presenting a play about plays and of betraying an elaborately announced theme suggest a certain emptiness, there are other marks of the same sort. The sexualization of politics, in which Domitian's ultimate villainy is not his violation of the ideals and self-interest of Rome but his mistreatment of a marriage, is characteristic of Fletcher's frequent collaborator. THE ROMAN ACTOR is a play that pretends to deal with serious political issues but invokes them only to treat them frivolously. Thus Domitian's invocation of divine right is a hollow parody of the serious questions raised by earlier stage monarchs like Richard II; by claiming that he is the god who confers the right he dissolves the issue. And the final repudiation of regicide similarly parodies the agonized recognition of earlier tragedies that there is no solution to criminal government within the system of absolute monarchy; the First Tribune's formulaic peroration merely states the classic argument against regicide in order to bring the play to a close, and perhaps to reassure court censors that Massinger has no antimonarchical ax to grind. The invocation of this atavistic formula resembles other characteristically nostalgic Massinger touches: Domitian's passionate remorse and punishment in the last act, for example, which like Overreach's possession by devils at the close of A NEW WAY TO PAY OLD DEBTS recalls the retributive justice of moralistic plays of an earlier generation such as A LOOKING GLASS FOR LONDON AND ENGLAND; the formula in which a villain of tragic heroic proportion is given an access of brute courage at the last. In its superficial sophistication THE ROMAN ACTOR bears the marks of its lateness in the period; in its essential simplicity it suggests that the period and its dramatic genres are growing old.   N. R.

The Roman Actor

[EPISTLE DEDICATORY]

To my much honored and most true friends,
SIR PHILIP KNYVET,[1] KNIGHT AND BARONET,
AND TO SIR THOMAS JAY,[2] KNIGHT,
AND THOMAS BELLINGHAM,[3]
of Newtimber in Sussex ESQUIRE.

How much I acknowledge myself bound for your so many and extraordinary favors conferred upon me (as far as it is in my power,) posterity shall take notice; I were most unworthy of such noble friends, if I should not, with all thankfulness, profess and own them. In the composition of this tragedy you were my only supporters, and it being now by your principal encouragement to be 10 turned into the world, it cannot walk safer than under your protection. It hath been happy in the suffrage of some learned and judicious gentlemen when it was presented, nor shall they find cause, I hope, in the perusal, to repent them of their good opinion of it. If the gravity and height of the subject distaste[4] such as are only affected[5] with jigs and ribaldry, as I presume it will, their condemnation of me and my poem can no way offend me: my reason teaching me such malicious and ignorant detractors deserve rather contempt than satisfaction. I ever held it the most perfect birth of my Minerva,[6] and therefore in justice offer it to those that have best deserved of me, who I hope in their courteous acceptance will render it worth their receiving, and ever, in their 20 gentle construction of my imperfections, believe they may at their pleasure dispose of him that is wholly and sincerely

Devoted to their service,
PHILIP MASSINGER.

DRAMATIS PERSONÆ

The persons presented.	The principal Actors.
DOMITIANUS CAESAR	John Lowin
PARIS *the tragedian*	Joseph Taylor
PARTHENIUS *a freeman of Caesar's*	Richard Sharpe
AELIUS LAMIA, *and* STEPHANOS	Thomas Pollard
JUNIUS RUSTICUS	Robert Benfield
ARETINUS CLEMENS, *Caesar's spy*	Eyllardt Swanstone
AESOPUS *a player*	Richard Robinson
PHILARGUS *a rich miser*	Anthony Smith
PALPHURIUS SURA *a senator*	William Pattricke
[FULCINIUS *a senator*]	
LATINUS *a player*	Curtise Grevill
3 Tribunes	George Vernon
2 Lictors	James Horne
[ASCLETARIO *an Astrologer*]	
SEJEIUS ⎱ *Conspirators*	
ENTELLUS ⎰	
DOMITIA *the wife of Aelius Lamia*	John Tompson
DOMITILLA *cousin-german*[1] *to Caesar*	John Hunnieman
JULIA, *Titus' Daughter*	William Trigge
CAENIS, *Vespasian's Concubine*	Alexander Gough
[A Lady]	

[Centurions, Soldiers, Hangmen, Servants, Captives.]

ACT ONE

SCENE ONE

Enter PARIS, LATINUS, *and* AESOPUS.

Aesop. What do we act today?

Lat.   Agave's frenzy,
With Pentheus' bloody end.[1]

Par.   It skills[2] not what;
The times are dull, and all that we receive
Will hardly satisfy the day's expense.
The Greeks, to whom we owe the first invention
Both of the buskined[3] scene[4] and humble sock,[5]
That reign in every noble family,
Declaim against us; and our amphitheater,
Great Pompey's work,[6] that hath giv'n full delight
Both to the eye and ear of fifty thousand   10
Spectators in one day, as if it were
Some unknown desert[7] or great Rome unpeopled,
Is quite forsaken.

Lat.   Pleasures of worse natures
Are gladly entertained, and they that shun us
Practice in private sports the stews[8] would blush at.
A litter borne by eight Liburnian slaves,
To buy diseases from a glorious[9] strumpet,
The most censorious of our Roman gentry,
Nay, of the guarded[10] robe, the senators,
Esteem an easy purchase.

Par.   Yet grudge us   20
That with delight join profit and endeavor
To build their minds up fair and on the stage
Decipher to the life what honors wait
On good and glorious actions, and the shame
That treads upon the heels of vice, the salary
Of six sestertii.[11]

Aesop.   For the profit, Paris,
And mercenary gain, they are things beneath us,
Since while you hold your grace and power with
    Caesar
We from your bounty find a large supply,
Nor can one thought of want ever approach us.   30

Par. Our aim is glory and to leave our names
To aftertimes.

Lat.   And, would they give us leave,
There ends all our ambition.

Aesop.   We have enemies,
And great ones too, I fear. 'Tis given out lately
The consul Aretinus, Caesar's spy,
Said at his table ere a month expired,
For being galled[12] in our last comedy,
He would silence us for ever.

Par.   I expect
No favor from him; my strong Aventine[13] is
That great Domitian, whom we oft have cheered   40
In his most sullen moods, will once return,
Who can repair with ease the consul's ruins.

Lat. 'Tis frequent in the city he hath subdued
The Catti and the Daci, and ere long
The second time will enter Rome in triumph.

Enter two Lictors.

Par. Jove hasten it! With us? I now believe
The consul's threats, Aesopus.

1 Lict.   You are summoned
T'appear today in senate.

2 Lict.   And there to answer
What shall be urged against you.

Par.   We obey you.
Nay, droop not, fellows; innocence should be
    bold.   50
We that have personated in the scene
The ancient heroes and the falls of princes
With loud applause, being to act ourselves,
Must do it with undaunted confidence.
Whate'er our sentence be, think 'tis in sport;
And, though condemned, let's hear it without sorrow,
As if we were to live again tomorrow.

1 Lict. 'Tis spoken like yourself.

Enter AELIUS LAMIA, JUNIUS RUSTICUS, *and*
    PALPHURIUS SURA.

Lam.   Whither goes Paris?

1 Lict. He's cited to the senate.

Lat.   I am glad the state is
So free from matters of more weight and trouble   60
That it has vacant time to look on us.

Par. That reverend place, in which the affairs of
    kings
And provinces were determined, to descend
To the censure[14] of a bitter word, or jest
Dropped from a poet's pen! peace to your lordships.
We are glad that you are safe.

Exeunt Lictors, PARIS, LATINUS,
    [*and*] AESOPUS.

Lam.   What times are these?
To what is Rome fall'n? May we being alone

EPISTLE DEDICATORY
   [1] *Knyvet:* 1583–1655, one of Massinger's numerous
patrons.
   [2] *Jay:* 1585–1636, Keeper of the King's Armory at
Greenwich, author of commendatory verses published with
the play.   [3] *Bellingham:* died *c.* 1648, another patron.
   [4] *distaste:* displease.   [5] *affected:* pleased.
   [6] *Minerva:* Roman goddess of wisdom.

DRAMATIS PERSONÆ
   [1] *cousin-german:* first cousin.

I.i.
   [1] *Agave's . . . end:* Agave, daughter of Cadmus, led a
group of women who tore her son Pentheus to pieces for
denying the divinity of Dionysus and spying on them.
   [2] *skills:* matters.
   [3] *buskined:* wearing the high, thicksoled boot of Athenian
tragic actors, emblem of tragedy.
   [4] *scene:* stage of the Greek and Roman theater.
   [5] *sock:* low shoe worn by Athenian comic actors, emblem
of comedy; Q "stocke."
   [6] *amphitheater . . . work:* theater in the Campus Martius
in Rome, dedicated 55 B.C. by Caeser's great rival.
   [7] *desert:* wilderness.   [8] *stews:* brothels.
   [9] *glorious:* vainglorious, boastful.
   [10] *guarded:* bordered.
   [11] *sestertii:* small silver coins of low value.
   [12] *galled:* mocked.
   [13] *Aventine:* stronghold; one of the seven hills of Rome.
   [14] *censure:* judgment.

Speak our thoughts freely of the prince and state,
And not fear the informer?
   Rust.   Noble Lamia,
So dangerous the age is, and such bad acts   70
Are practised everywhere, we hardly sleep,
Nay, cannot dream with safety. All our actions
Are called in question; to be nobly born
Is now a crime, and to deserve too well
Held capital treason. Sons accuse their fathers,
Fathers their sons; and but to win a smile
From one in grace at court our chastest matrons
Make shipwreck of their honors. To be virtuous
Is to be guilty. They are only safe
That know to soothe the prince's appetite   80
And serve his lusts.
   Sura.   'Tis true; and 'tis my wonder
That two sons of so different a nature
Should spring from good Vespasian. We had a Titus,
Styled justly the delight of all mankind,
Who did esteem that day lost in his life
In which some one or other tasted not
Of his magnificent bounties; one that had
A ready tear when he was forced to sign
The death of an offender; and so far
From pride that he disdained not the converse   90
Even of the poorest Roman.
   Lam.   Yet his brother,
Domitian, that now sways the power of things,
Is so inclined to blood that no day passes
In which some are not fastened to the hook
Or thrown down from the Gemonies.[15] His freemen
Scorn the nobility, and he himself,
As if he were not made of flesh and blood,
Forgets he is a man.
   Rust.   In his young years,
He showed what he would be when grown to ripeness;
His greatest pleasure was, being a child,   100
With a sharp-pointed bodkin[16] to kill flies,
Whose rooms[17] now men supply. For his escape
In the Vitellian war,[18] he raised a temple
To Jupiter, and proudly placed his figure
In the bosom of the god; and in his edicts
He does not blush or start to style himself,
As if the name of Emperor were base,
Great Lord and God Domitian.
   Sura.   I have letters
He's on his way to Rome, and purposes
To enter with all glory. The flattering senate   110
Decrees him divine honors, and to cross[19] it
Were death with studied torments; for my part,
I will obey the time; it is in vain
To strive against the torrent.
   Rust.   Let's to the curia,[20]
And, though unwillingly, give our suffrages,
Before we are compelled.
   Lam.   And since we cannot
With safety use the active, let's make use of
The passive fortitude, with this assurance:
That the state, sick in him, the gods to friend,[21]
Though at the worst, will now begin to mend.   120
                   Exeunt.

I.ii

Enter DOMITIA *and* PARTHENIUS, *with a letter.*

   Dom.   To me this reverence!
   Parth.   I pay it, lady,
As a debt due to her that's Caesar's[1] mistress.
For understand with joy, he that commands
All that the sun gives warmth to is your servant.
Be not amazed, but fit you to your fortunes,
Think upon state and greatness and the honors
That wait upon Augusta, for that name
Ere long comes to you. Still you doubt your vassal,
But, when you've read this letter, writ and signed
With his imperial hand, you will be freed   10
From fear and jealousy, and I beseech you
When all the beauties of the earth bow to you
And senators shall take it for an honor,
As I do now, to kiss these happy feet,
When every smile you give is a preferment[2]
And you dispose of provinces to your creatures,
Think on Parthenius.
   Dom.   Rise, I am transported,
And hardly dare believe what is assured here.
The means, my good Parthenius, that wrought Caesar,
Our god on earth, to cast an eye of favor   20
Upon his humble handmaid?
   Parth.   What but your beauty?
When Nature framed you for her masterpiece,
As the pure abstract of all rare in woman,
She had no other ends but to design you
To the most eminent place. I will not say,
For it would smell of arrogance to insinuate
The service I have done you, with what zeal
I oft have made relation of your virtues,
Or how I have sung your goodness; or how Caesar
Was fired with the relation of your story;   30
I am rewarded in the act, and happy
In that my project prospered.
   Dom.   You are modest;
And were it in my power I would be thankful.
If that, when I was mistress of myself
And, in my way of youth, pure and untainted,
The Emperor had vouchsafed to seek my favors,
I had with joy given up my virgin fort
At the first summons to his soft embraces;
But I am now another's, not mine own.
You know I have a husband. For my honor,   40

---

[15] *Gemonies:* steps on the Aventine hill leading to the Tiber, on which bodies of executed criminals were dragged to be thrown into the river.
  [16] *bodkin:* dagger.   [17] *rooms:* place.
  [18] *Vitellian war:* A.D. 69 against Aulus Vitellius, incompetent proclaimed emperor by his troops in January of that year and defeated and killed in December in Rome, succeeded by the exemplary Titus Vespasian, father of Domitian.
  [19] *cross:* thwart.
  [20] *curia:* senate-house, restored by Domitian, who dedicated part of it to his patron goddess Minerva.
  [21] *to friend:* befriending.
  I.ii.
  [1] *Caesar's:* the emperor's.   [2] *preferment:* promotion.

I would not be his strumpet; and how law
Can be dispensed with to become his wife
To me's a riddle.
    Parth.   I can soon resolve it:
When power puts in its plea the laws are silenced.
The world confesses one Rome and one Caesar,
And, as his rule is infinite, his pleasures
Are unconfined; this syllable, his will,
Stands for a thousand reasons.
    Dom.   But with safety,
Suppose I should consent, how can I do it?
My husband is a senator of a temper   50
Not to be jested with.

               Enter LAMIA.

    Parth.   As if he durst
Be Caesar's rival! Here he comes; with ease
I will remove this scruple.
    Lam.   How! so private!
My own house made a brothel! Sir, how durst you,
Though guarded with your power in court and
    greatness,
Hold conference with my wife? As for your minion,[3]
I shall hereafter treat—
    Parth.   You are rude and saucy
Nor know to whom you speak.
    Lam.   This is fine, i' faith!
    Parth. Your wife? But touch her, that respect
    forgotten
That's due to her whom mightiest Caesar favors,   60
And think what 'tis to die. Not to lose time,
She's Caesar's choice. It is sufficient honor
You were his taster in this heavenly nectar,
But now must quit the office.
    Lam.   This is rare!
Cannot a man be master of his wife,
Because she's young and fair, without a patent?[4]
I in mine own house am an emperor,
And will defend what's mine. Where are my knaves?
If such an insolence escape unpunished—
    Parth. In yourself, Lamia. Caesar hath forgot   70
To use his power, and I, his instrument,
In whom, though absent, his authority speaks,
Have lost my faculties.[5]

                        Stamps.

     Enter a Centurion *with* Soldiers.

    Lam.   The guard! why, am I
Designed for death?
    Dom.   As you desire my favor,
Take not so rough a course.
    Parth.   All your desires
Are absolute commands. Yet give me leave
To put the will of Caesar into act.

Here's a bill of divorce between your lordship
And this great lady. If you refuse to sign it,
And so as if you did it uncompelled,   80
Won to it by reasons that concern yourself,
Her honor too untainted, here are clerks
Shall in your best blood write it new till torture
Compel you to perform it.
    Lam.   Is this legal?
    Parth. Monarchs that dare not do unlawful things,
Yet bear them out, are constables, not kings.
Will you dispute?
    Lam.   I know not what to urge
Against myself but too much dotage on her,
Love, and observance.[6]
    Parth.   Set it under your hand
That you are impotent and cannot pay   90
The duties of a husband, or that you are mad;
Rather than want just cause, we'll make you so.
Dispatch, you know the danger else; deliver it,
Nay, on your knee. Madam, you are now free,
And mistress of yourself.
    Lam.   Can you, Domitia,
Consent to this?
    Dom.   'Twould argue a base mind
To live a servant when I may command.
I now am Caesar's, and yet, in respect
I once was yours, when you come to the palace,
Provided you deserve it in your service,   100
You shall find me your good mistress. Wait me,
    Parthenius;
And now farewell, poor Lamia!
                   Exeunt all but LAMIA.
    Lam.   To the gods
I bend my knees, for tyranny hath banished
Justice from men, and as they would deserve
Their altars and our vows, humbly invoke 'em
That this my ravished wife may prove as fatal
To proud Domitian, and her embraces
Afford him in the end as little joy
As wanton Helen brought to him of Troy.

                               Exit.

I.iii

    Enter Lictors, ARETINUS, FULCINIUS,
   RUSTICUS, SURA, PARIS, LATINUS, [*and*]
                AESOPUS.

    Aret. Fathers conscript,[1] may this our meeting be
Happy to Caesar and the commonwealth.
    Lict. Silence.
    Aret.   The purpose of this frequent[2] senate
Is first to give thanks to the gods of Rome
That for the propagation of the empire
Vouchsafe us one to govern it like themselves.
In height of courage, depth of understanding,
And all those virtues and remarkable graces,
Which make a prince most eminent, our Domitian
Transcends the ancient Romans. I can never   10
Bring his praise to a period. What good man
That is a friend to truth dares make it doubtful

That he hath Fabius'[3] staidness, and the courage
Of bold Marcellus,[4] to whom Hannibal[5] gave
The style[6] of Target, and the Sword of Rome?
But he has more, and every touch more Roman,
As Pompey's dignity, Augustus'[7] state,
Antony's[8] bounty, and great Julius'[9] fortune,
With Cato's[10] resolution. I am lost
In th' ocean of his virtues. In a word,   20
All excellencies of good men in him meet,
But no part of their vices.
     Rust.   This is no flattery.
     Sura. Take heed, you'll be observed.
     Aret.   'Tis then most fit
That we, as to the father of our country,
Like thankful sons, stand bound to pay true service
For all those blessings that he show'rs upon us,
Should not connive and see his government
Depraved and scandalized by meaner men
That to his favor and indulgence owe
Themselves and being.
     Par.   Now he points at us   30
     Aret. Cite Paris, the tragedian.
     Par.   Here.
     Aret.   Stand forth.
In thee, as being the chief of thy profession,
I do accuse the quality[11] of treason,
As libelers against the state and Caesar.
     Par. Mere accusations are not proofs, my lord.
In what are we delinquents?
     Aret.   You are they
That search into the secrets of the time
And, under feigned names, on the stage present
Actions not to be touched at; and traduce
Persons of rank and quality of both sexes,   40
And, with satirical and bitter jests,
Make even the senators ridiculous
To the plebeians.
     Par.   If I free not myself,
And in myself the rest of my profession,
From these false imputations and prove
That they make that a libel which the poet
Writ for a comedy, so acted too,
It is but justice that we undergo
The heaviest censure.
     Aret.   Are you on the stage,
You talk so boldly?
     Par.   The whole world being one,   50
This place is not exempted: and I am
So confident in the justice of our cause
That I could wish Caesar, in whose great name
All kings are comprehended, sat as judge,
To hear our plea and then determine of[12] us.
If to express a man sold to his lusts,
Wasting the treasure of his time and fortunes
In wanton dalliance, and to what sad end
A wretch that's so given over does arrive at;
Deterring careless youth, by his example,   60
From such licentious courses; laying open
The snares of bawds and the consuming arts
Of prodigal strumpets, can deserve reproof;
Why are not all your golden principles,

Writ down by grave philosophers to instruct us
To choose fair virtue for our guide, not pleasure,
Condemned unto the fire?
     Sura.   There's spirit in this.
     Par. Or if desire of honor was the base
On which the building of the Roman empire
Was raised up to this height; if to inflame   70
The noble youth with an ambitious heat
T' endure the frosts of danger, nay, of death,
To be thought worthy the triumphal wreath
By glorious undertakings, may deserve
Reward or favor from the commonwealth,
Actors may put in for as large a share
As all the sects of the philosophers;
They with cold precepts, perhaps seldom read
Deliver[13] what an honorable thing
The active virtue is. But does that fire   80
The blood or swell the veins with emulation
To be both good and great equal to that
Which is presented on our theaters?
Let a good actor in a lofty scene
Show great Alcides[14] honored in the sweat
Of his twelve labors; or a bold Camillus[15]
Forbidding Rome to be redeemed with gold
From the insulting Gauls; or Scipio[16]
After his victories imposing tribute
On conquered Carthage. If done to the life,   90
As if they saw their dangers and their glories
And did partake with them in their rewards,
All that have any spark of Roman in them,
The slothful arts laid by, contend to be
Like those they see presented.
     Rust.   He has put
The consuls to their whisper.
     Par.   But 'tis urged
That we corrupt youth and traduce superiors
When do we bring a vice upon the stage,
That does go off unpunished? Do we teach,
By the success of wicked undertakings,   100
Others to tread in their forbidden steps?
We show no arts of Lydian panderism,
Corinthian poisons, Persian flatteries,
But mulcted so in the conclusion that
Even those spectators that were so inclined

---

     [3] *Fabius:* Fabius Cunctator, patrician leader from his consulship in 233 B.C. to his death in 203, unimaginative but brave in wars against Hannibal, called the Shield of Rome.
     [4] *Marcellus:* great general against Hannibal, killed in action 208 B.C., called the Sword of Rome.
     [5] *Hannibal:* Carthaginian general and enemy of Rome, 247–183 B.C., defeated by Scipio Africanus.
     [6] *style:* title.
     [7] *Augustus:* first Roman emperor, 63 B.C.–A.D. 14.
     [8] *Antony:* Mark Antony's bounty is cited by Shakespeare's Cleopatra.   [9] *Julius:* Julius Cæsar.
     [10] *Cato:* 234–149 B.C., stern and upright conservative leader, writer, enemy of Carthage.
     [11] *quality:* acting profession.
     [12] *determine of:* judge.   [13] *deliver:* expound.
     [14] *Alcides:* Hercules.
     [15] *Camillus:* savior and second founder of Rome after the Gallic invasion, 387 B.C.
     [16] *Scipio:* Africanus, 236–184 B.C., victor over Carthage.

Go home changed men. And, for [17] traducing such
That are above us, publishing to the world
Their secret crimes, we are as innocent
As such as are born dumb. When we present
An heir that does conspire against the life   110
Of his dear parent, numb'ring every hour
He lives as tedious to him, if there be
Among the auditors one whose conscience tells him
He is of the same mold, we cannot help it.
Or, bringing on the stage a loose adult'ress,
That does maintain the riotous expense
Of him that feeds her greedy lust, yet suffers
The lawful pledges of a former bed
To starve the while for hunger; if a matron,
However great in fortune, birth, or titles,   120
Guilty of such a foul unnatural sin,
Cry out, "'Tis writ by [18] me," we cannot help it.
Or, when a covetous man's expressed, whose wealth
Arithmetic cannot number and whose lordships [19]
A falcon in one day cannot fly over,
Yet he so sordid in his mind, so griping, [20]
As not to afford himself the necessaries
To maintain life; if a patrician,
Though honored with a consulship, find himself
Touched to the quick in this, we cannot help it.   130
Or, when we show a judge that is corrupt,
And will give up his sentence as he favors
The person, not the cause; saving the guilty
If of his faction, and as oft condemning
The innocent out of particular [21] spleen;
If any in this reverend assembly,
Nay, e'en yourself, my lord, that are the image
Of absent Caesar, feel something in your bosom
That puts you in remembrance of things past,
Or things intended, 'tis not in us to help it.   140
I have said, my lord; and now, as you find cause,
Or censure us or free us with applause.
    Lat. Well pleaded, on my life. I never saw him
Act an orator's part before.
    Aesop.   We might have given
Ten double fees to Regulus, [22] and yet
Our cause delivered worse.

                            A shout within.

          Enter PARTHENIUS.

    Aret.   What shout is that?
    Parth. Caesar, our lord, married to conquest, is
Returned in triumph.
    Ful.   Let's all haste to meet him.

---

[17] *for*: as for.   [18] *by*: i.e., about.
[19] *lordships*: estates.   [20] *griping*: avaricious.
[21] *particular*: partisan.
[22] *Regulus*: contemporary informer and scoundrel admired
for his oratorical successes, which led to many convictions.

I.iv.
[1] *minion*: low creature, mistress.
[2] *prove*: experience.   [3] *conduct*: leadership.
[4] *Plautus*: comic playwright, d. 184 B.C.
[5] *braggart*: the boastful soldier of the eponymous *Miles Gloriosus*.

    Aret. Break up the court; we will reserve to him
The censure of this cause.
    All.   Long life to Caesar.   150
                            Exeunt omnes.

I.iv

          Enter JULIA, CAENIS, DOMITILLA,
                    [*and*] DOMITIA.

    Caenis. Stand back—the place is mine.
    Jul.   Yours! Am I not
Great Titus' daughter and Domitian's niece?
Dares any claim precedence?
    Caenis.   I was more,
The mistress of your father, and in his right
Claim duty from you.
    Jul.   I confess you were useful
To please his appetite—
    Dom.   To end the controversy,
For I'll have no contending, I'll be bold
To lead the way myself.
    Domit.   You, minion? [1]
    Dom.   Yes;
And all ere long shall kneel to catch my favors.
    Jul. Whence springs this flood of greatness?
    Dom.   You shall know
Too soon for your vexation, and perhaps   11
Repent too late and pine with envy when
You see whom Caesar favors.
    Jul.   Observe the sequel.

    Enter Captains *with laurels*, DOMITIAN *in his
triumphant chariot*, PARTHENIUS, PARIS, LATINUS,
[*and*] AESOPUS, *met by* ARETINUS, SURA, LAMIA,
RUSTICUS, FULCINIUS, *and* Prisoners *led by him.*

    Caes. As we now touch the height of human glory,
Riding in triumph to the Capitol,
Let these whom this victorious arm hath made
The scorn of fortune and the slaves of Rome
Taste the extremes of misery. Bear them off
To the common prisons, and there let them prove [2]
How sharp our axes are.

                        Exeunt with Prisoners.
    Rust.   A bloody entrance!   20
    Caes. To tell you you are happy in your prince
Were to distrust your love or my desert,
And either were distasteful. Or to boast
How much, not by my deputies but myself,
I have enlarged the empire, or what horrors
The soldier in our conduct [3] hath broke through,
Would better suit the mouth of Plautus' [4] braggart [5]
Than the adorèd monarch of the world.
    Sura. This is no boast.
    Caes.   When I but name the Daci
And gray-eyed Germans whom I have subdued,   30
The ghost of Julius will look pale with envy,
And great Vespasian's and Titus' triumph,—
Truth must take place of father and of brother,—
Will be no more rememb'rèd. I am above
All honors you can give me; and the style

Of lord and god, which thankful subjects give me,
Not my ambition, is deserved.
　　Aret.　　　　　　　　　At all parts
Celestial sacrifice is fit for Caesar,
In our acknowledgment.
　　Caes.　　　　　　　　Thanks, Aretinus;
Still [6] hold our favor. Now the god of war,　　　40
And famine, blood, and death, Bellona's [7] pages,
Banished from Rome to Thrace, in our good fortune,
With justice he may taste the fruits of peace
Whose sword hath ploughed the ground and reaped
　　the harvest
Of your prosperity. Nor can I think
That there is one among you so ungrateful,
Or such an enemy to thriving virtue
That can esteem the jewel he holds dearest
Too good for Caesar's use.
　　Sura.　　　　　　　　All we possess—
　　Lam. Our liberties—
　　Ful.　　　　　Our children—
　　Parth.　　　　　　　Wealth—
　　Aret.　　　　　　　　　And throats
Fall willingly beneath his feet.
　　Rust. [Aside]　　　　　Base flattery.　　　51
What Roman can endure this!
　　Caes.　　　　　　　This calls on
My love to all, which spreads itself among you,
The beauties of the time. Receive the honor
[*To the ladies*] To kiss the hand which reared up thus
　　holds thunder;
To you 'tis an assurance of a calm.
Julia, my niece, and Caenis, the delight
Of old Vespasian; Domitilla, too,
A princess of our blood.
　　Rust. [Aside]　　　　'Tis strange his pride
Affords no greater courtesy to ladies　　　60
Of such high birth and rank.
　　Sura.　　　　　Your wife's forgotten.
　　Lam. No, she will be rememb'red, fear it not;
She will be graced and greased. [8]
　　Caes.　　　　　　　But, when I look on
Divine Domitia, methinks we should meet
The lesser gods applauding the encounter,
As Jupiter, the Giants lying dead
On the Phlegraean plain, embraced his Juno. [9]
Lamia, 'tis your honor that she's mine.
　　Lam. You are too great to be gainsaid.
　　Caes.　　　　　　　Let all
That fear our frown or do affect [10] our favor　　70
Without examining the reason why,
Salute her—by this kiss I make it good
With the title of Augusta.
　　Dom.　　　　　　Still your servant.
　　All. Long live Augusta, great Domitian's Empress.
　　Caes. Paris, my hand.
　　Par.　　　　　The gods still honor Caesar.
　　Caes. The wars are ended, and, our arms laid by,
We are for soft delights. Command the poets
To use their choicest and most rare invention
To entertain the time, and be you careful
To give it action. We'll provide the people　　80

Pleasures of all kinds.—My Domitia, think not
I flatter, though thus fond.—On to the Capitol;
'Tis death to him that wears a sullen brow.
This 'tis to be a monarch, when alone
He can command all but is awed by none.

　　　　　　　　　　　　　　　　　Exeunt.

ACT TWO

SCENE ONE

Enter PHILARGUS [*and*] PARTHENIUS.

　　Phil. My son to tutor me! know your obedience,
And question not my will.
　　Parth.　　　　　Sir, were I one
Whom want compelled to wish a full possession
Of what is yours, or had I ever numbered
Your years, or thought you lived too long, with reason
You then might nourish ill opinions of me;
Or did the suit that I prefer to you
Concern myself and aimed not at your good,
You might deny and I sit down [1] with patience,
And after never press you.
　　Phil.　　　　I' the name of Pluto, [2]　　10
What wouldst thou have me do?
　　Parth.　　　　　　　Right to yourself;
Or suffer me to do it. Can you imagine
This nasty hat, this tattered cloak, rent shoe,
This sordid linen, can become the master
Of your fair fortunes? Whose superfluous means,
Though I were burdensome, could clothe you in
The costliest Persian silks, studded with jewels,
The spoils of provinces, and every day
Fresh change of Tyrian purple.
　　Phil.　　　　　　Out upon thee!
My moneys in my coffers melt to hear thee.　　20
Purple! hence, prodigal! Shall I make my mercer
Or tailor my heir? Or see my jeweller purchase? [3]
No, I hate pride.
　　Parth.　　Yet decency would do well.
Though for your outside you will not be altered,
Let me prevail so far yet as to win you
Not to deny your belly nourishment;
Neither to think you have feasted when 'tis crammed
With moldy barleybread, onions and leeks,
And the drink of bondmen, water.
　　Phil.　　　　　　Wouldst thou have me
Be an Apicius [4] or a Lucullus, [5]　　30
And riot out my state in curious [6] sauces?

---

　　[6] *Still:* Always.　　　　　[7] *Bellona:* goddess of war.
　　[8] *greased:* bribed.
　　[9] *Jupiter . . . Juno:* The Giants, sons of Earth, attacked
the gods, one of them attempting to rape Juno, and were
destroyed by Jupiter with the aid of Hercules.
　　[10] *affect:* value.

II.i.
　　[1] *sit down:* acquiesce, put up.
　　[2] *Pluto:* god of the Underworld.
　　[3] *purchase:* acquire property, get rich.
　　[4] *Apicius:* proverbial gourmet under Augustus and
Tiberius.
　　[5] *Lucullus:* 117–56 B.C., general and consul devoted to
elegant living.　　　　　　　　　[6] *curious:* elaborate.

Wise nature with a little is contented;
And following her, my guide, I cannot err.
 Parth. But you destroy her in your want of care—
I blush to see, and speak it—to maintain her
In perfect health and vigor when you suffer—
Frighted with the charge of physic—rheums, catarrhs,
The scurf,[7] ache in your bones, to grow upon you
And hasten on your fate with too much sparing,
When a cheap purge, a vomit, and good diet,   40
May lengthen it. Give me but leave to send
The Emperor's doctor to you.
 Phil.   I'll be borne first
Half-rotten to the fire that must consume me.
His pills, his cordials, his electuaries,[8]
His syrups, juleps, bezoar stone,[9] nor his
Imagined unicorn's horn, comes in my belly;
My mouth shall be a draught first. 'Tis resolved.
No, I'll not lessen my dear golden heap,
Which every hour increasing does renew
My youth and vigor; but, if lessened, then,   50
Then my poor heartstrings crack. Let me enjoy it
And brood o'er while I live, it being my life,
My soul, my all. But when I turn to dust,
And part from what is more esteemed by me
Than all the gods Rome's thousand altars smoke to,
Inherit thou my adoration of it,
And, like me, serve my idol.
              Exit.

 Parth.   What a strange torture
Is avarice to itself! What man that looks on
Such a penurious spectacle but must
Know what the fable meant of Tantalus,[10]   60
Or the ass whose back is cracked with curious viands,
Yet feeds on thistles? Some course I must take,
To make my father know what cruelty
He uses on himself.

       Enter PARIS.

 Par.   Sir, with your pardon,
I make bold to inquire the Emperor's pleasure;
For, being by him commanded to attend,
Your favor may instruct us what's his will
Shall be this night presented.
 Parth.   My loved Paris,
Without my intercession you well know,
You may make your own approaches, since his ear 70
To you is ever open.
 Par.   I acknowledge
His clemency to my weakness, and if ever
I do abuse it, lightning strike me dead.
The grace he pleases to confer upon me,—
Without boast I may say so much,—was never
Employed to wrong the innocent or to incense
His fury.

 Parth. 'Tis confessed many men owe you
For provinces they ne'er hoped for; and their lives,
Forfeited to his anger, you being absent,
I could say more.
 Par.   You still are my good patron;   80
And lay it in my fortune to deserve it,
You should perceive the poorest of your clients
To his best abilities thankful.
 Parth.   I believe so.
Met you my father?
 Par.   Yes, sir, with much grief,
To see him as he is. Can nothing work him
To be himself?
 Parth.   Oh, Paris, 'tis a weight
Sits heavy here; and could this right hand's loss
Remove it, it should off; but he is deaf
To all persuasion.
 Par.   Sir, with your pardon,
I'll offer my advice. I once observed   90
In a tragedy of ours in which a murder
Was acted to the life a guilty hearer
Forced by the terror of a wounded conscience
To make discovery of that which torture
Could not wring from him. Nor can it appear
Like an impossibility but that
Your father, looking on a covetous man
Presented on the stage, as in a mirror,
May see his own deformity and loathe it.
Now, could you but persuade the Emperor   100
To see a comedy we have, that's styled
The Cure of Avarice, and to command
Your father to be a spectator of it,
He shall be so anatomized in the scene
And see himself so personated, the baseness
Of a self-torturing miserable wretch
Truly described, that I much hope the object
Will work compunction in him.
 Parth.   There's your fee;
I ne'er bought better counsel. Be you in readiness;
I will effect the rest.
 Par.   Sir, when you please,   110
We'll be prepared to enter.—Sir, the Emperor.
             Exit PARIS.

   Enter CAESAR, ARETINUS, [*and*] Guard.

 Caes. Repine[11] at us!
 Aret.   'Tis more, or my informers
That keep strict watch upon him are deceived
In their intelligence. There is a list
Of malcontents, as Junius Rusticus,
Palphurius Sura, and this Aelius Lamia,
That murmur at your triumphs as mere pageants,
And at their midnight meetings tax your justice,
For so I style what they call tyranny,
For Paetus Thrasea's death, as if in him   120
Virtue herself were murdered; nor forget they
Agricola, who for his service done
In the reducing Britain to obedience
They dare affirm to be removed with poison;
And he compelled to write you a coheir
With his daughter, that his testament might stand

---

 [7] *scurf:* scaly skin affliction.
 [8] *electuaries:* medicines mixed with honey or syrup.
 [9] *bezoar stone:* antidote to poison.
 [10] *Tantalus:* punished perpetually by being forced to hunger and thirst for nearby but unattainable food and drink.
 [11] *Repine:* manifest discontent.

Which else you had made void. Then your much love
To Julia your niece, censured as incest,
And done in scorn of Titus, your dead brother;
But the divorce Lamia was forced to sign   130
To her you honor with Augusta's title
Being only named, they do conclude there was
A Lucrece once, a Collatine, and a Brutus;[12]
But nothing Roman left now but in you
The lust of Tarquin.
 Caes.   Yes. His fire, and scorn
Of such as think that our unlimited power
Can be confined. Dares Lamia pretend
An interest to that which I call mine?
Or but remember she was ever his,
That's now in our possession? Fetch him hither.   140
        The Guard *go off.*
I'll give him cause to wish he rather had
Forgot his own name than e'er mentioned hers.
Shall we be circumscribed? Let such as cannot
By force make good their actions, though wicked,
Conceal, excuse, or qualify their crimes.
What our desires grant leave and privilege to,
Though contradicting all divine decrees,
Or laws confirmed by Romulus[13] and Numa,[14]
Shall be held sacred.
 Aret.   You should else take from
The dignity of Caesar.
 Caes.   Am I master   150
Of two and thirty legions that awe
All nations of the triumphed world,
Yet tremble at our frown, yield an account
Of what's our pleasure to a private man?
Rome perish first, and Atlas'[15] shoulders shrink,
Heav'n's fabric fall; the sun, the moon, the stars
Losing their light and comfortable heat;
Ere I confess that any fault of mine
May be disputed.
 Aret.   So you preserve your power
As you should, equal and omnipotent here   160
With Jupiter's above.

     PARTHENIUS *kneeling, whispers to*
           CAESAR.

 Caes.   Thy suit is granted,
Whate'er it be, Parthenius, for thy service
Done to Augusta. Only so? A trifle:
Command him hither. If the comedy fail
To cure him, I will minister something to him
That shall instruct him to forget his gold
And think upon himself.
 Parth.   May it succeed well,
Since my intents are pious.

        Exit PARTHENIUS.

 Caes.   We are resolved
What course to take, and therefore, Aretinus,
Inquire no farther. Go you to my Empress,   170
And say I do entreat—for she rules him
Whom all men else obey—she would vouchsafe
The music of her voice at yonder window,
When I advance my hand thus. I will blend

        Exit ARETINUS.

My cruelty with some scorn, or else 'tis lost;
Revenge, when it is unexpected, falling
With greater violence; and hate clothed in smiles,
Strikes, and with horror, dead the wretch that comes
 not
Prepared to meet it.—

    Enter LAMIA *with the* Guard.

       Our good Lamia, welcome.
So much we owe you for a benefit,   180
With willingness on your part conferred upon us,
That 'tis our study, we that would not live
Engaged to any for a courtesy,
How to return it.
 Lam.   'Tis beneath your fate
To be obliged that in your own hand grasp
The means to be magnificent.[16]
 Caes.   Well put off;
But yet it must not do. The empire, Lamia,
Divided equally, can hold no weight
If balanced with your gift in fair Domitia—
You, that could part with all delights at once,   190
The magazine of rich pleasures being contained
In her perfections, uncompelled, delivered
As a present fit for Caesar. In your eyes,
With tears of joy, not sorrow, 'tis confirmed
You glory in your act.
 Lam.   Derided too!
Sir, this is more—
 Caes.   More than I can requite:
It is acknowledged, Lamia. There's no drop
Of melting nectar I taste from her lip
But yields a touch of immortality
To the blessed receiver; every grace and feature,   200
Prized to the worth, bought at an easy rate
If purchased for a consulship. Her discourse
So ravishing and her action so attractive
That I would part with all my other senses
Provided I might ever see and hear her.
The pleasures of her bed I dare not trust
The winds or air with, for that would draw down,
In envy of my happiness, a war
From all the gods, upon me.
 Lam.   Your compassion
To me in your forbearing to insult   210
On my calamity, which you make your sport,
Would more appease those gods you have provoked
Than all the blasphemous comparisons
You sing unto her praise.
 Caes.   I sing her praise?
'Tis far from my ambition to hope it,

---

 [12] *Lucrece . . . Brutus:* The rape of Lucretia, wife of
Tarquinius Collatinus, by Sextus, son of Tarquinius Super-
bus, led to the expulsion of the Tarquin kings by a popular
revolt led by Lucius Junius Brutus, and to the founding of the
republic.
 [13] *Romulus:* one of the mythical founders of Rome.
 [14] *Numa:* Numa Pompilius, 715–673 B.C., second king of
Rome, legendary for reforms.
 [15] *Atlas:* Titan who held up the sky.
 [16] *magnificent:* munificent.

It being a debt she only can lay down,
And no tongue else discharge.

Music above and a song.

                                    Hark, I think, prompted
With my consent that you once more should hear her,
She does begin. An universal silence
Dwell on this place. 'Tis death with ling'ring
        torments   220
To all that dare disturb her.

The song ended, CAESAR *go[es] on.*

                                    Who can hear this,
And falls not down and worships? In my fancy,
Apollo being judge, on Latmos' hill
Fair-haired Calliope [17] on her ivory lute
(But something short of this) sung Ceres' [18] praises
And grisly Pluto's rape on Proserpine. [19]
The motion of the spheres are out of time,
Her musical notes but heard. Say, Lamia, say,
Is not her voice angelical?
    Lam.   To your ear:
But I, alas, am silent.
    Caes.   Be so ever,   230
That without admiration canst hear her.
Malice to my felicity strikes thee dumb,
And in thy hope or wish to repossess
What I love more than empire, I pronounce thee
Guilty of treason.—Off with his head! Do you stare?
By her that is my patroness, Minerva,
Whose statue I adore of all the gods,
If he but live to make reply, thy life
Shall answer it!
    The Guard *lead off* LAMIA, *stopping his mouth.*
                                    My fears of him are freed now;
And he that lived to upbraid me with my wrong   240
For an offense he never could imagine
In wantonness removed.—Descend, my dearest.
Plurality of husbands shall no more
Breed doubts or jealousies in you. 'Tis dispatched,
And with as little trouble here as if
I had killed a fly.

Enter DOMITIA, *ushered in by* ARETINUS, *her
train with all state borne up by* JULIA, CAENIS,
and DOMITILLA.

                                    Now you appear, and in
That glory you deserve and these that stoop
To do you service, in the act much honored!
Julia, forget that Titus was thy father;
Caenis, and Domitilla, ne'er remember   250
Sabinus, or Vespasian. To be slaves
To her is more true liberty than to live

---

[17] *Calliope:* muse of heroic poetry.
[18] *Ceres:* goddess of grain.
[19] *Pluto's . . . Proserpine:* Ceres' daughter was carried off
to the Underworld by Pluto.
[20] *Phoebe:* name for Diana, goddess of the moon.
[21] *interlude:* play.   [22] *in . . . scene:* on the stage.
[23] *Priam:* king of Troy, father of Hector.
[24] *get:* beget.

Parthian or Asian queens. As lesser stars
That wait on Phoebe [20] in her full of brightness
Compared to her you are. Thus I seat you
By Caesar's side, commanding these, that once
Were the adorèd glories of the time,
To witness to the world they are your vassals,
At your feet to attend you.
    Dom.   'Tis your pleasure
And not my pride. And yet, when I consider   260
That I am yours, all duties they can pay
I do receive as circumstances due
To her you please to honor.

Enter PARTHENIUS *and* PHILARGUS.

    Parth.   Caesar's will
Commands you hither, nor must you gainsay it.
    Phil. Lose time to see an interlude? [21] must I pay too
For my vexation?
    Parth.   Not in the court;
It is the Emperor's charge.
    Phil.   I shall endure
My torment then the better.
    Caes.   Can it be
This sordid thing, Parthenius, is thy father?
No actor can express him. I had held   270
The fiction for impossible in the scene, [22]
Had I not seen the substance.—Sirrah, sit still
And give attention; if you but nod,
You sleep for ever. Let them spare the prologue,
And all the ceremonies proper to ourself,
And come to the last act, there where the cure
By the doctor is made perfect. The swift minutes
Seem years to me, Domitia, that divorce thee
From my embraces; my desires increasing
As they are satisfied, all pleasures else   280
Are tedious as dull sorrows. Kiss me;—again;
If I now wanted heat of youth, these fires
In Priam's [23] veins would draw his frozen blood,
Enabling him to get [24] a second Hector
For the defense of Troy.
    Dom.   You are wanton, sir.
Pray you, forbear. Let me see the play.
    Caes.   Begin there.

Enter PARIS *like a doctor of physic,* AESOPUS, [*and*]
    LATINUS *brought forth asleep in a chair, a key in
    his mouth.*

    Aesop. O master doctor, he is past recovery;
A lethargy hath seized him; and, however
His sleep resemble death, his watchful care
To guard that treasure he dares make no use of   290
Works strongly in his soul.
    Par.   What's that he holds
So fast between his teeth?
    Aesop.   The key that opens
His iron chests, crammed with accursèd gold,
Rusty with long imprisonment. There's no duty
In me, his son, nor confidence in friends
That can persuade him to deliver up
That to the trust of any.
    Phil.   He is the wiser.

We were fashioned in one mold.—
   Aesop.   He eats with it;
And when devotion calls him to the temple
Of Mammon,[25] whom of all the gods he kneels to,   300
That held thus still, his orisons are paid;
Nor will he, though the wealth of Rome were pawned
For the restoring of it, for one short hour
Be won to part with it.
   Phil.   Still, still myself!
And if like me he love his gold, no pawn
Is good security.
   Par.   I'll try if I can force it.
It will not be. His avaricious mind,
Like men in rivers drowned, makes him gripe fast
To his last gasp what he in life held dearest;
And, if that it were possible in nature,   310
Would carry it with him to the other world.
   Phil. As I would do to hell rather than leave it.—
   Aesop. Is he not dead?
   Par.   Long since to all good actions,
Or to himself or others, for which wise men
Desire to live. You may with safety pinch him,
Or under his nails stick needles, yet he stirs not.
Anxious fear to lose what his soul dotes on
Renders his flesh insensible. We must use
Some means to rouse the sleeping faculties
Of his mind; there lies the lethargy. Take a trumpet,
And blow it into his ears; 'tis to no purpose;   321
The roaring noise of thunder cannot wake him;
And yet despair not, I have one trick left yet.
   Aesop. What is it?
   Par.   I will cause a fearful dream
To steal into his fancy and disturb it
With the horror it brings with it, and so free
His body's organs.
   Dom.   'Tis a cunning fellow;
If he were indeed a doctor, as the play says,
He should be sworn my servant, govern my slumbers,
And minister to me waking.

                 A chest brought in.

   Par.   If this fail,   330
I'll give him o'er. So; with all violence
Rend ope this iron chest. For here his life lies
Bound up in fetters, and in the defense
Of what he values higher 'twill return
And fill each vein and artery.—Louder yet.
'Tis open, and already he begins
To stir; mark with what trouble.

         LATINUS *stretches himself.*

   Phil.   As you are Caesar,
Defend this honest, thrifty man. They are thieves
And come to rob him.
   Parth.   Peace! the Emperor frowns.
   Par. So; now pour out the bags upon the table;   340
Remove his jewels, and his bonds. Again,
Ring a second golden peal. His eyes are open;
He stares as he had seen Medusa's[26] head,
And were turned marble.—Once more.
   Lat.   Murder! murder!

They us murder. My son in the plot?
Thou worse than parricide! if it be death
To strike thy father's body, can all tortures
The Furies in hell practice be sufficient
For thee that dost assassinate my soul?—
My gold! my bonds! my jewels! dost thou envy   350
My glad possession of them for a day?
Extinguishing the taper of my life
Consumed unto the snuff?
   Par.   Seem not to mind him.
   Lat. Have I to leave thee rich denied myself
The joys of human being; scraped and hoarded
A mass of treasure which, had Solon[27] seen,
The Lydian Croesus[28] had appeared to him
Poor as the beggar Irus?[29] And yet I,
Solicitous to increase it, when my entrails
Were clemmed[30] with keeping a perpetual fast,   360
Was deaf to their loud windy cries, as fearing,
Should I disburse one penny to their use,
My heir might curse me. And to save expense
In outward ornaments, I did expose
My naked body to the winter's cold,
And summer's scorching heat. Nay, when diseases
Grew thick upon me, and a little cost
Had purchased my recovery, I chose rather
To have my ashes closed up in my urn
By hasting on my fate than to diminish   370
The gold my prodigal son while I am living
Carelessly scatters.
   Aesop.   Would you would dispatch and die
   once.
Your ghost should feel in hell, that is my slave
Which was your master.
   Phil.   Out upon thee, varlet!
   Par. And what then follows all your cark[31] and
   caring
And self-affliction, when your starved trunk is
Turned to forgotten dust? This hopeful youth
Urines upon your monument, ne'er rememb'ring
How much for him you suffered; and then tells
To the companions of his lusts and riots   380
The hell you did endure on earth, to leave him
Large means to be an epicure and to feast
His senses all at once, a happiness
You never granted to yourself. Your gold, then,
Got with vexation and preserved with trouble,
Maintains the public stews, panders, and ruffians,
That quaff damnations to your memory
For living so long here.
   Lat.   'Twill be so; I see it.
Oh, that I could redeem the time that's past.

---

[25] *Mammon:* as a New Testament personification of riches, a curious god for a pagan to cite.
[26] *Medusa:* monster whose ugly face transformed viewers to stone.
[27] *Solon:* 640/635–561/560 B.C., Athenian statesman, poet, and constitutional reformer, legendary for his wisdom.
[28] *Croesus:* last king of Lydia, 560–546 B.C., proverbial for his wealth.
[29] *Irus:* beggar who mocks Odysseus on his return to Ithaca.   [30] *clemmed:* pinched with hunger.
[31] *cark:* distress.

I would live and die like myself, and make true use 390
Of what my industry purchased.

Par.   Covetous men,
Having one foot in the grave, lament so ever.
But grant that I by art could yet recover
Your desperate sickness, lengthen out your life
A dozen of years as I restore your body
To perfect health, will you with care endeavor
To rectify your mind?

Lat.   I should so live then
As neither my heir should have just cause to think
I lived too long for being close-handed to him
Or cruel to myself.

Par.   Have your desires.   400
Phoebus assisting me, I will repair
The ruined building of your health; and think not
You have a son that hates you; the truth is,
This means with his consent I practiced on you
To this good end, it being a device,
In you to show the *Cure of Avarice.*

             Exeunt PARIS, LATINUS, AESOPUS.

Phil. An old fool, to be gulled thus! had he died
As I resolve to do, not to be altered,
It had gone off twanging.

Caes.   How approve you, sweetest,
Of the matter, and the actors?

Dom.   For the subject,   410
I like it not; it was filched out of Horace.
—Nay, I have read the poets;—but the fellow
That played the doctor did it well, by Venus.
He had a tuneable tongue and neat delivery;
And yet in my opinion he would perform
A lover's part much better. Prithee, Caesar,
For I grow weary, let us see tomorrow
Iphis and Anaxarete.[32]

Caes.   Anything
For thy delight, Domitia. To your rest,
Till I come to disquiet you. Wait upon her.   420
There is a business that I must dispatch,
And I will straight be with you.

         Exeunt ARETINUS, DOMITIA, JULIA, CAENIS,
                           DOMITILLA.

Parth.   Now, my dread sir,
Endeavor to prevail.

Caes.   One way or other
We'll cure him, never doubt it. Now, Philargus,
Thou wretched thing, hast thou seen thy sordid baseness
And but observed what a contemptible creature
A covetous miser is? Dost thou in thyself
Feel true compunction, with a resolution
To be a new man?

Phil.   This crazed body's Caesar's,
But for my mind—

Caes.   Trifle not with my anger.   430
Canst thou make good use of what was now presented?
And imitate in thy sudden change of life
The miserable rich man that expressed
What thou art to the life?

Phil.   Pray you, give me leave
To die as I have lived. I must not part with
My gold; it is my life; I am past cure.

Caes. No; by Minerva, thou shalt never more
Feel the least touch of avarice. Take him hence,
And hang him instantly. If there be gold in hell,
Enjoy it; thine here and thy life together   440
Is forfeited.

Phil.   Was I sent for to this purpose?

Parth. Mercy for all my service, Caesar, mercy!

Caes. Should Jove plead for him, 'tis resolved he dies,
And he that speaks one syllable to dissuade me;
And therefore tempt me not. It is but justice:
Since such as willfully will hourly die
Must tax themselves, and not my cruelty.

                         Exeunt omnes.

ACT THREE

SCENE ONE

Enter JULIA, DOMITILLA, [*and*] STEPHANOS.

Jul. No, Domitilla; if you but compare
What I have suffered with your injuries,
Though great ones, I confess, they will appear
Like molehills to Olympus.

Domit.   You are tender
Of your own wounds, which makes you lose the feeling
And sense of mine. The incest he committed
With you and publicly professed in scorn
Of what the world durst censure may admit
Some weak defense, as being borne headlong to it,
But in a manly way, to enjoy your beauties.   10
Besides, won by his perjuries that he would
Salute you with the title of Augusta,
Your faint denial showed a full consent
And grant to his temptations. But poor I,
That would not yield, but was with violence forced
To serve his lusts, and in a kind Tiberius
At Capreae[1] never practiced, have not here
One conscious touch to rise up my accuser,
I in my will being innocent.

Steph.   Pardon me,
Great princesses, though I presume to tell you,   20
Wasting your time in childish lamentations
You do degenerate from the blood you spring from:
For there is something more in Rome expected
From Titus' daughter and his uncle's heir
Than womanish complaints after such wrongs
Which mercy cannot pardon. But you'll say
Your hands are weak, and should you but attempt
A just revenge on this inhuman monster,
This prodigy[2] of mankind, bloody Domitian,
Hath ready swords at his command as well   30
As islands to confine you, to remove

---

[32] *Iphis . . . Anaxarete:* legend about a Cyprian man who, rejected by the noblewoman he loved, hanged himself at her door; for her indifference she was turned into stone.

III.i.

[1] *Tiberius . . . Capreae:* The Emperor spent his last ten years in notorious debauchery at what is now Capri.

[2] *prodigy:* monster.

His doubts and fears did he but entertain
The least suspicion you contrived or plotted
Against his person.
 Jul.   'Tis true, Stephanos;
The legions that sacked Jerusalem
Under my father Titus are sworn his,
And I no more rememb'rèd'
 Domit.   And to lose
Ourselves by building on impossible hopes
Were desperate madness.
 Steph.   You conclude too fast.
One single arm, whose master does contemn   40
His own life, holds a full command o'er his,
Spite of his guards. I was your bondman, lady,
And you my gracious patroness; my wealth
And liberty your gift; and, though no soldier,
To whom or custom or example makes
Grim death appear less terrible, I dare die
To do you service in a fair revenge;
And it will better suit your births and honors
To fall at once than to live ever slaves
To his proud Empress that insults upon   50
Your patient sufferings. Say but you, "Go on!"
And I will reach his heart or perish in
The noble undertaking.
 Domit.   Your free offer
Confirms your thankfulness, which I acknowledge
A satisfaction for a greater debt
Than what you stand engaged for; but I must not
Upon uncertain grounds hazard so grateful
And good a servant. The immortal powers
Protect a prince, though sold to impious acts,
And seem to slumber till his roaring crimes 60
Awake their justice; but then, looking down,
And with impartial eyes, on his contempt
Of all religion and moral goodness,
They in their secret judgments do determine
To leave him to his wickedness, which sinks him
When he is most secure.
 Jul.   His cruelty
Increasing daily of necessity
Must render him as odious to his soldiers,
Familiar friends, and freemen, as it hath done
Already to the senate; then forsaken   70
Of his supporters and grown terrible
Ev'n to himself and her he now so dotes on,
We may put into act what now with safety
We cannot whisper.
 Steph.   I am still prepared
To execute when you please to command me;
Since I am confident he deserves much more
That vindicates[3] his country from a tyran[4]
Than he that saves a citizen.

     Enter CAENIS.

 Jul.   Oh, here's Caenis.
 Domit. Whence come you?
 Caenis.   From the Empress, who
  seems moved
In that you wait[5] no better. Her pride's grown 80
To such a height that she disdains the service

Of her own women and esteems herself
Neglected when the princesses of the blood
On every coarse employment are not ready
To stoop to her commands.
 Domit.   Where is her greatness?
 Caenis. Where you would little think she could
  descend
To grace the room or persons.
 Jul.   Speak; where is she?
 Caenis. Among the players; where, all state laid by,
She does inquire who plays this part, who that,
And in what habits;[6] blames the tire-women[7] 90
For want of curious dressings; and so taken
She is with Paris the tragedian's shape
That is to act a lover, I thought once
She would have courted him.
 Domit.   In the mean time
How spends the Emperor his hours?
 Caenis.   As ever
He hath done heretofore, in being cruel
To innocent men whose virtues he calls crimes.
And, but this morning, if't be possible,
He hath outgone himself, having condemned,
At Aretinus his informer's suit,   100
Palphurius Sura and good Junius Rusticus,
Men of the best repute in Rome for their
Integrity of life; no fault objected[8]
But that they did lament his cruel sentence
On Paetus Thrasea, the philosopher,
Their patron and instructor.
 Steph.   Can Jove see this
And hold his thunder?
 Domit.   Nero and Caligula
Commanded only mischiefs; but our Caesar
Delights to see 'em.
 Jul.   What we cannot help,
We may deplore with silence.
 Caenis.   We are called for 110
By our proud mistress.
 Domit.   We a while must suffer.
 Steph. It is true fortitude to stand firm against
All shocks of fate when cowards faint and die
In fear to suffer more calamity.

             Exeunt.

III.ii

   Enter CAESAR [*and*] PARTHENIUS.

 Caes. They are then in fetters?
 Parth.   Yes, sir, but—
 Caes.   But? What?
I'll have thy thoughts. Deliver them.
 Parth.   I shall, sir:
But still submitting to your godlike pleasure,
Which cannot be instructed—

---

 ³ *vindicates:* frees.
 ⁴ *tyran:* tyrant; Q "tyrannie," evident misprint for
"tyranne," Q's frequent spelling.   ⁵ *wait:* serve.
 ⁶ *habits:* dress. ⁷ *tire-women:* wardrobe-mistresses.
 ⁸ *objected:* charged.

Caes.   To the point.
Parth. Nor let your sacred majesty believe
Your vassal, that with dry eyes looked upon
His father dragged to death by your command,
Can pity these that durst presume to censure
What you decreed.
Caes.   Well. Forward.
Parth.   'Tis my zeal
Still to preserve your clemency admired,   10
Tempered with justice, that emboldens me
To offer my advice. Alas! I know, sir,
These bookmen, Rusticus and Palphurius Sura,
Deserve all tortures; yet, in my opinion,
They being popular senators and cried up
With loud applauses of the multitude
For foolish honesty and beggarly virtue,
'Twould relish more of policy to have them
Made away in private, with what exquisite torments
You please—it skills not—than to have them drawn   20
To the degrees[1] in public; for 'tis doubted[2]
That the sad object may beget compassion
In the giddy rout and cause some sudden uproar
That may disturb you.
Caes.   Hence, pale-spirited coward!
Can we descend so far beneath ourself
As or to court the people's love or fear
Their worst of hate? Can they that are as dust
Before the whirlwind of our will and power
Add any moment[3] to us? Or thou think
If there are gods above or goddesses,   30
But wise Minerva, that's mine own, and sure,
That they have vacant hours to take into
Their serious protection or care,
This many-headed monster? Mankind lives
In few as potent monarchs and their peers;
And all those glorious constellations
That do adorn the firmament, appointed
Like grooms with their bright influence to attend
The actions of kings and emperors,
They being the greater wheels that move the less.   40
Bring forth those condemned wretches; let me see
One man so lost as but to pity 'em,
And though there lay a million of souls
Imprisoned in his flesh my hangmen's hooks
Should rend it off and give 'em liberty.
Caesar hath said it.

                              Exit PARTHENIUS.

Enter PARTHENIUS, ARETINUS, *and the* Guard;
Hangmen *dragging in* JUNIUS RUSTICUS, *and*
PALPHURIUS SURA, *bound back to back.*

Aret.   'Tis great Caesar's pleasure
That with fixed eyes you carefully observe
The people's looks. Charge upon any man
That with a sigh or murmur does express
A seeming sorrow for these traitors' deaths.   50
You know his will; perform it.
Caes.   A good bloodhound,
And fit for my employments.
Sura.   Give us leave
To die, fell tyrant.
Rust.   For, beyond our bodies,
Thou hast no power.
Caes.   Yes; I'll afflict your souls,
And force them groaning to the Stygian[4] lake,
Prepared for such to howl in that blaspheme
The power of princes that are gods on earth.
Tremble to think how terrible the dream is
After this sleep of death.
Rust.   To guilty men
It may bring terror, not to us that know   60
What 'tis to die, well taught by his example
For whom we suffer. In my thought I see
The substance of that pure untainted soul
Of Thrasea,[5] our master, made a star,
That with melodious harmony invites us,
Leaving this dunghill Rome, made hell by thee,
To trace his heavenly steps and fill a sphere
Above yon crystal canopy.
Caes.   Do, invoke him
With all the aids his sanctity of life
Have won on the rewarders of his virtue;   70
They shall not save you.—Dogs, do you grin?
     Torment 'em.

          The Hangmen *torment 'em, they still smiling.*

So, take a leaf of Seneca[6] now and prove
If it can render you insensible
Of that which but begins here. Now an oil,
Drawn from the Stoics' frozen principles,
Predominant over fire, were useful for you.
Again, again. You trifle. Not a groan!—
Is my rage lost? What cursèd charms defend 'em!
Search deeper, villains. Who looks pale? Or thinks
That I am cruel?
Aret.   Over-merciful: 80
'Tis all your weakness, sir.
Parth. [*Aside*]   I dare not show
A sign of sorrow; yet my sinews shrink,
The spectacle is so horrid.
Caes.   I was never
O'ercome till now. For my sake roar a little,
And show you are corporeal, and not turned
Aerial spirits.—Will it not do? By Pallas,[7]
It is unkindly done to mock his fury
Whom the world styles omnipotent. I am tortured
In their want of feeling torments. Marius'[8] story,
That does report him to have sat unmoved   90
When cunning chirurgeons[9] ripped his arteries
And veins to cure his gout, compared to this
Deserves not to be named. Are they not dead?
If so, we wash an Aethiop.

III.ii.
  [1] *degrees:* the Gemonies.   [2] *doubted:* feared.
  [3] *moment:* importance.   [4] *Stygian:* in the Underworld.
  [5] *Thrasea:* Thrasea Paetus, Stoic noted for uprightness
and republican sympathies, condemned to death by Nero,
A.D. 66.
  [6] *Seneca:* Lucius Annaeus Seneca, 5/4 B.C.–A.D. 65,
leading Stoic philosopher and courtier to Nero.
  [7] *Pallas:* Athena = Minerva.
  [8] *Marius:* Gaius Marius, 157–86 B.C., soldier and consul.
  [9] *chirurgeons:* surgeons.

Sura.   No, we live.
Rust. Live to deride thee, our calm patience
        treading
Upon the neck of tyranny. That securely,[10]
As 'twere a gentle slumber, we endure
Thy hangmen's studied tortures is a debt
We owe to grave philosophy, that instructs us
The flesh is but the clothing of the soul,   100
Which growing out of fashion, though it be
Cast off or rent or torn like ours, 'tis then,
Being itself divine, in her best luster.
But unto such as thou, that have no hopes
Beyond the present, every little scar,
The want of rest, excess of heat or cold,
That does inform them only they are mortal,
Pierce through and through them.
    Caes.   We will hear no more.
    Rust. This only, and I give thee warning of it.
Though it is in thy will to grind this earth[11]   110
As small as atoms, they thrown in the sea too,
They shall seem recollected to thy sense,
And when the sandy building of thy greatness
Shall with its own weight totter, look to see me
As I was yesterday, in my perfect shape;[12]
For I'll appear in horror.
    Caes. [*Aside*]   By my shaking
I am the guilty man and not the judge.—
Drag from my sight these cursèd ominous wizards,
That, as they are now, like to double-faced Janus,[13]
Which way soe'er I look, are Furies to me.   120
Away with 'em! first show them death, then leave
No memory of their ashes. I'll mock fate.
        Exeunt Hangmen *with* RUSTICUS *and* SURA.
Shall words fright him, victorious armies circle?
No, no, the fever doth begin to leave me.

    Enter DOMITIA, JULIA, [*and*] CAENIS;
            STEPHANOS *following.*

Or, were it deadly, from this living fountain
I could renew the vigor of my youth,
And be a second Virbius.[14] O my glory!
My life! command! my all!
    Dom.   As you to me are.

        Embracing and kissing mutually.

I heard you were sad; I have prepared you sport
Will banish melancholy. Sirrah, Caesar,   130
(I hug myself for't), I have been instructing
The players how to act and to cut off
All tedious impertinency have contracted
The tragedy into one continued scene.
I have the art of't, and am taken more
With my ability that way than all knowledge
I have but of thy love.
    Caes.   Thou art still thyself,
The sweetest, wittiest—
    Dom.   When we are a-bed
I'll thank your good opinion. Thou shalt see
Such an Iphis of thy Paris! and, to humble   140
The pride of Domitilla, that neglects me
(Howe'er she is your cousin), I have forced her

To play the part of Anaxarete.
You are not offended with it?
    Caes.   Anything
That does content thee yields delight to me.
My faculties and powers are thine.
    Dom.   I thank you.
Prithee let's take our places. Bid 'em enter
Without more circumstance.

    After a short flourish enter PARIS *as* IPHIS.

                        How do you like
That shape? Methinks it is most suitable
To the aspect of a despairing lover.   150
The seeming late-fallen, counterfeited tears
That hang upon his cheeks, was my device.
    Caes. And all was excellent.
    Dom.   Now hear him speak.
    Par. That she is fair, and that an epithet
Too foul to express her, or descended nobly,
Or rich, or fortunate, are certain truths
In which poor Iphis glories. But that these
Perfections, in no other virgin found,
Abused, should nourish cruelty and pride
In the divinest Anaxarete,   160
Is to my love-sick, languishing soul a riddle,
And with more difficulty to be dissolved
Than that the monster Sphinx[15] from the steep rock
Offered to Oedipus. Imperious Love,
As at thy ever-flaming altars Iphis,
Thy never-tired votary, hath presented
With scalding tears whole hecatombs of sighs,
Preferring thy power and thy Paphian mother's,[16]
Before the Thunderer's,[17] Neptune's, or Pluto's
(That after Saturn did divide the world,   170
And had the sway of things, yet were compelled
By thy unevitable shafts to yield,
And fight under thy ensigns), be auspicious
To this last trial of my sacrifice
Of love and service.
    Dom.   Does he not act it rarely?
Observe with what a feeling he delivers
His orisons to Cupid; I am rapt with't.—
    Par. And from thy never-emptied quiver take
A golden arrow to transfix her heart
And force her love like me, or cure my wound   180
With a leaden one that may beget in me
Hate and forgetfulness of what's now my idol—
But I call back my prayer; I have blasphemed
In my rash wish. 'Tis I that am unworthy,
But she all merit, and may in justice challenge,

---

[10] *securely:* confidently.
[11] *earth:* flesh.   [12] *shape:* appearance.
[13] *Janus:* god of beginnings, symbolized by a two-faced
head.
[14] *Virbius:* obscure god conflated with Hippolytus, who
was killed by his rejected lover Phaedra and resurrected by
Asclepius.
[15] *Sphinx:* mythological monster who plagued Thebes by
asking a riddle and devouring those who could not solve it.
Oedipus freed the country by answering the riddle.
[16] *Paphian mother:* Venus.   [17] *Thunderer:* Jupiter.

From the assurance of her excellencies,
Not love but adoration. Yet bear witness
All-knowing powers, I bring along with me,
As faithful advocates to make intercession,
A loyal heart with pure and holy flames,   190
With the foul fires of lust never polluted.
And, as I touch her threshold, which with tears,
My limbs benumbed with cold, I oft have washed,
With my glad lips I kiss this earth grown proud
With frequent favors from her delicate feet.
 Dom. By Caesar's life he weeps. And I forbear
Hardly to keep him company.—
 Par. Blessed ground, thy pardon,
If I profane it with forbidden steps.
I must presume to knock, and yet attempt it 200
With such a trembling reverence as if
My hands held up for expiation
To the incensèd gods to spare a kingdom.
Within there, ho! something divine come forth
To a distressèd mortal.

    Enter LATINUS *as a Porter.*

 Lat.   Ha! who knocks there?
 Dom. What a churlish look this knave has!
 Lat.   Is't you,
 sirrah?
Are you come to pule and whine? Avaunt, and quickly;
Dogwhips shall drive you hence else.
 Dom.   Churlish devil!
But that I should disturb the scene, as I live
I would tear his eyes out.
 Caes.   'Tis in jest, Domitia. 210
 Dom. I do not like such jesting; if he were not
A flinty-hearted slave, he could not use
One of his form so harshly. How the toad swells
At the other's sweet humility!
 Caes.   'Tis his part:
Let 'em proceed.
 Dom.   A rogue's part, will ne'er leave him.
 Par. As you have, gentle sir, the happiness,
When you please, to behold the figure of
The masterpiece of nature, limned to the life,
In more than human Anaxarete,
Scorn not your servant that with suppliant hands 220
Takes hold upon your knees, conjuring you,
As you are a man and did not suck the milk
Of wolves and tigers or a mother of
A tougher temper, use some means these eyes,
Before they are wept out, may see your lady.
Will you be gracious, sir?
 Lat.   Though I lose my place for't,
I can hold out no longer.
 Dom.   Now he melts,
There is some little hope he may die honest.
 Lat. Madam!

    Enter DOMITILLA *for* ANAXARETE.

---

 [18] *Niobe:* boasted that her children outnumbered Latona's two, Diana and Apollo, for which Latona killed all six, and the grief-stricken nymph turned to stone.
 [19] *Resolve:* Decide. [20] *Hymen:* god of marriage.

 Domit. Who calls? What object have we here?
 Dom. Your cousin keeps her proud state still; I
 think   230
I have fitted her for a part.
 Domit.   Did I not charge thee
I ne'er might see this thing more?
 Par.   I am indeed
What things you please; a worm that you may tread on;
Lower I cannot fall to show my duty
Till your disdain hath digged a grave to cover
This body with forgotten dust; and, when
I know your sentence, cruelest of women,
I'll by a willing death remove the object
That is an eyesore to you.
 Domit.   Wretch, thou dar'st not.
That were the last and greatest service to me 240
Thy doting love could boast of. What dull fool
But thou could nourish any flattering hope,
One of my height in youth, in birth, and fortune,
Could e'er descend to look upon thy lowness?
Much less consent to make me lord of one
I'd not accept, though offered for my slave.
My thoughts stoop not so low.
 Dom.   There's her true nature,
No personated scorn.
 Domit.   I wrong my worth,
Or to exchange a syllable or look
With one so far beneath me.
 Par.   Yet take heed, 250
Take heed of pride, and curiously consider
How brittle the foundation is, on which
You labor to advance it. Niobe,[18]
Proud of her numerous issue, durst contemn
Latona's double burden; but what followed?
She was left a childless mother and mourned to marble.
The beauty you o'erprize so time or sickness
Can change to loathed deformity; your wealth
The prey of thieves; queen Hecuba, Troy fired,
Ulysses' bondwoman: but the love I bring you 260
Nor time nor sickness, violent thieves nor fate,
Can ravish from you.
 Dom.   Could the oracle
Give better counsel!
 Par.   Say will you relent yet
Revoking your decree that I should die?
Or shall I do what you command? Resolve;[19]
I am impatient of delay.
 Domit.   Dispatch then:
I shall look on your tragedy unmoved,
Peradventure laugh at it, for it will prove
A comedy to me.
 Dom.   Oh devil! devil!
 Par. Then thus I take my last leave. All the curses
Of lovers fall upon you; and hereafter 271
When any man, like me contemned, shall study
In the anguish of his soul to give a name
To a scornful cruel mistress, let him only
Say, "This most bloody woman is to me
As Anaxarete was to wretched Iphis!"—
Now feast your tyrannous mind, and glory in
The ruins you have made: for Hymen's[20] bands

That should have made us one this fatal halter
For ever shall divorce us; at your gate,   280
As a trophy of your pride and my affliction,
I'll presently²¹ hang myself.
    Dom.   Not for the world.
Restrain him, as you love your lives.
    Caes.   Why are you
Transported thus, Domitia? 'Tis a play;
Or, grant it serious, it at no part merits
This passion in you.
    Par.   I ne'er purposed, madam,
To do the deed in earnest, though I bow
To your care and tenderness of me.
    Dom.   Let me, sir,
Entreat your pardon; what I saw presented,
Carried me beyond myself.
    Caes.   To your place again,   290
And see what follows.
    Dom.   No, I am familiar
With the conclusion; besides, upon the sudden
I feel myself much indisposed.
    Caes.   To bed then;
I'll be thy doctor.
    Aret.   There is something more
In this than passion, which I must find out
Or my intelligence freezes.
    Dom.   Come to me, Paris,
Tomorrow, for your reward.
    Steph.   Patroness, hear me;
Will you not call for your share?²² Sit down with this,
And, the next action,²³ like a Gaditan²⁴ strumpet,
I shall look to see you tumble!
    Domit.   Prithee be patient.   300
I, that have suffered greater wrongs, bear this;
And that, till my revenge, my comfort is.
                            Exeunt.

ACT FOUR

SCENE ONE

Enter PARTHENIUS, JULIA, DOMITILLA,
    [*and*] CAENIS.

    Parth. Why, 'tis impossible! Paris?
    Jul.   You observed not,
As it appears, the violence of her passion
When, personating Iphis, he pretended,
For your contempt, fair Anaxarete,
To hang himself.
    Parth.   Yes, yes, I noted that;
But never could imagine it could work her
To such a strange intemperance of affection
As to dote on him.
    Domit.   By my hopes, I think
That she respects¹ not, though all here saw and marked
    it,
Presuming she can mold the Emperor's will   10
Into what form she likes, though we and all
Th' informers of the world conspired to cross it.
    Caenis. Then with what eagerness this morning,
    urging

The want of health and rest, she did entreat
Caesar to leave her.
    Domit.   Who no sooner absent,
But she calls, "Dwarf!"—so in her scorn she styles
    me—
"Put on my pantofles;² fetch pen and paper,
I am to write"; and with distracted looks,
In her smock, impatient of so short delay
As but to have a mantle thrown upon her,   20
She sealed I know not what, but 'twas endorsed,
"To my loved Paris."
    Jul.   Add to this, I heard her
Say, when a page received it, "Let him wait me,
And carefully, in the walk called our retreat,"
Where Caesar, in his fear to give offense,
Unsent for never enters.
    Parth.   This being certain,
For these are more than jealous suppositions,
Why do not you that are so near in blood
Discover³ it?
    Domit.   Alas! you know we dare not.
'Twill be received for a malicious practice⁴   30
To free us from that slavery which her pride
Imposes on us. But if you would please
To break the ice, on pain to be sunk ever,
We would aver it.
    Parth.   I would second you,
But that I am commanded with all speed
To fetch in Ascletario the Chaldaean,
Who in his absence is condemned of treason
For calculating the nativity
Of Caesar, with all confidence foretelling
In every circumstance when he shall die   40
A violent death. Yet if you could approve
Of my directions I would have you speak
As much to Aretinus as you have
To me delivered. He in his own nature
Being a spy, on weaker grounds, no doubt,
Will undertake it, not for goodness' sake,
With which he never yet held correspondence,
But to endear his vigilant observings
Of what concerns the Emperor, and a little
To triumph in the ruins of this Paris,   50
That crossed him in the senate-house. Here he comes,

               Enter ARETINUS.

His nose held up; he hath something in the wind,
Or I much err, already. My designs
Command me hence, great ladies; but I leave
My wishes with you.
                      Exit PARTHENIUS.
    Aret.   Have I caught your greatness
In the trap, my proud Augusta!

Domit.   What is't raps [5] him?

Aret. And my fine Roman actor! Is't even so?
No coarser dish to take your wanton palate,
Save that which but the Emperor none durst taste of!
'Tis very well. I needs must glory in   60
This rare discovery, but the rewards
Of my intelligence bid me think, even now,
By an edict from Caesar I have power
To tread upon the neck of slavish Rome,
Disposing offices and provinces
To my kinsmen, friends, and clients.

Domit.   This is more
Than usual with him.

Jul.   Aretinus!

Aret.   How!
No more respect and reverence tendered to me,
But "Aretinus"! 'Tis confessed that title,
When you were princesses and commanded all,   70
Had been a favor; but being as you are
Vassals to a proud woman, the worst bondage,
You stand obliged with as much adoration
To entertain him that comes armed with strength
To break your fetters as tanned galley-slaves
Pay such as do redeem them from the oar.
I come not to entrap you, but aloud
Pronounce that you are manumized; [6] and to make
Your liberty sweeter, you shall see her fall,
This Empress, this Domitia, what you will,   80
That triumphed in your miseries.

Domit.   Were you serious,
To prove your accusation I could lend
Some help.

Caenis.   And I.

Jul.   And I.

Aret.   No atom to me.
My eyes and ears are everywhere; I know all,
To the line and action in the play that took her;
Her quick dissimulation to excuse
Her being transported, with her morning passion.
I bribed the boy that did convey the letter,
And having perused it made it up again:
Your griefs and angers are to me familiar;   90
That Paris is brought to her, and how far
He shall be tempted.

Domit.   This is above wonder.

Aret. My gold can work much stranger miracles
Than to corrupt poor waiters. Here, join with me.

                          [*Offers a paper.*]

'Tis a complaint to Caesar. This is that
Shall ruin her and raise you. Have you set your hands
To the accusation?

Jul.   And will justify
What we have subscribed to.

Caenis.   And with vehemency.

Domit. I will deliver it.

Aret.   Leave the rest to me then.

---

[5] *raps:* transports.
[6] *manumized:* manumitted, released from bondage.
[7] *fond:* foolish.   [8] *doubted:* suspected.

Enter CAESAR *with his* Guard.

Caes. Let our lieutenants bring us victory,   100
While we enjoy the fruits of peace at home,
And, being secured from our intestine foes,
Far worse than foreign enemies, doubts and fears,
Though all the sky were hung with blazing meteors,
Which fond [7] astrologers give out to be
Assured presages of the change of empires
And deaths of monarchs, we, undaunted yet,
Guarded with our own thunder, bid defiance
To them and fate, we being too strongly armed
For them to wound us.

Aret.   Caesar.

Jul.   As thou art   110
More than a man—

Caenis.   Let not thy passions be
Rebellious to thy reason—

                          The petition delivered.

Domit.   But receive
This trial of your constancy, as unmoved
As you go to or from the Capitol,
Thanks given to Jove for triumphs.

Caes.   Ha!

Domit.   Vouchsafe
A while to stay the lightning of your eyes,
Poor mortals dare not look on.

Aret.   There's no vein
Of yours that rises high with rage but is
An earthquake to us.

Domit.   And, if not kept closed
With more than human patience, in a moment   120
Will swallow us to the center.

Caenis.   Not that we
Repine to serve her are we her accusers.

Jul. But that she's fall'n so low.

Aret.   Which on sure proofs
We can make good.

Domit.   And show she is unworthy
Of the least spark of that diviner fire
You have conferred upon her.

Caes.   I stand doubtful,
And resolved what to determine of you.
In this malicious violence you have offered
To the altar of her truth and pureness to me,
You have but fruitlessly labored to sully   130
A white robe of perfection black-mouthed envy
Could belch no spot on. But I will put off
The deity you labor to take from me,
And argue out of probabilities with you
As if I were a man. Can I believe
That she that borrows all her light from me
And knows to use it would betray her darkness
To your intelligence; and make that apparent
Which, by her perturbations in a play,
Was yesterday but doubted, [8] and find none   140
But you that are her slaves, and therefore hate her,
Whose aids she might employ to make way for her?
Or Aretinus, whom long since she knew
To be the cabinet counselor, nay, the key

Of Caesar's secrets? Could her beauty raise her
To this unequaled height, to make her fall
The more remarkable? Or must my desires
To her and wrongs to Lamia be revenged
By her and on herself that drew on both?
Or she leave our imperial bed to court   150
A public actor?
    Aret.   Who dares contradict
These more than human reasons that have power
To clothe base guilt in the most glorious shape
Of innocence?
    Domit.   Too well she knew the strength
And eloquence of her patron to defend her,
And thereupon presuming fell securely,
Not fearing an accuser nor the truth
Produced against her which your love and favor
Will ne'er discern from falsehood.
    Caes.   I'll not hear
A syllable more that may invite a change   160
In my opinion of her. You have raised
A fiercer war within me by this fable,
Though with your lives you vow to make it story,[9]
Than if, and at one instant, all my legions
Revolted from me and came armed against me.
Here in this paper are the swords predestined
For my destruction; here the fatal stars,
That threaten more than ruin; this the death's head
That does assure me, if she can prove false,
That I am mortal, which a sudden fever   170
Would prompt me to believe and faintly yield to.
But now in my full confidence what she suffers
In that from any witness but myself
I nourish a suspicion she's untrue,
My toughness returns to me. Lead on, monsters,
And, by the forfeit of your lives, confirm
She is all excellence, as you all baseness;
Or let mankind for her fall boldly swear
There are no chaste wives now, nor ever were.
                     Exeunt omnes.

IV.ii

       Enter DOMITIA, PARIS, [*and*] Servants.

    Dom. Say we command that none presume to dare
On forfeit of our favor, that is life,
Out of a saucy curiousness, to stand
Within the distance of their eyes or ears,
Till we please to be waited on. And, sirrah,
                  Exeunt Servants.
Howe'er you are excepted, let it not
Beget in you an arrogant opinion
'Tis done to grace you.
    Par.   With my humblest service
I but obey your summons, and should blush else
To be so near you.
    Dom.   'Twould become you rather   10
To fear the greatness of the grace vouchsafed you
May overwhelm you, and 'twill do no less,
If, when you are rewarded, in your cups
You boast this privacy.

    Par.   That were, mightiest Empress,
To play with lightning.
    Dom.   You conceive it right.
The means to kill or save is not alone
In Caesar circumscribed, for, if incensed,
We have our thunder too that strikes as deadly.
    Par. 'Twould ill become the lowness of my fortune
To question what you can do, but with all   20
Humility to attend what is your will,
And then to serve it.
    Dom.   And would not a secret,
Suppose we should commit it to your trust,
Scald you to keep it?
    Par.   Though it raged within me
Till I turned cinders, it should ne'er have vent.
To be an age a-dying, and with torture
Only to be thought worthy of your counsel,
Or actuate whatever you command me,
A wretched obscure thing, not worth your knowledge,
Were a perpetual happiness.
    Dom.   We could wish   30
That we could credit thee, and cannot find
In reason but that thou, whom oft I have seen
To personate a gentleman, noble, wise,
Faithful, and gamesome[1] and what virtues else
The poet pleases to adorn you with,
But that, as vessels still partake the odor
Of the sweet precious liquors they contained
Thou must be really, in some degree,
The thing thou dost present. Nay, do not tremble;
We seriously believe it, and presume   40
Our Paris is the volume in which all
Those excellent gifts the stage hath seen him graced
    with
Are curiously bound up.
    Par.   The argument
Is the same, great Augusta, that I acting
A fool, a coward, a traitor, or cold cynic,
Or any other weak and vicious person,
Of force[2] I must be such. O gracious madam,
How glorious soever or deformed,
I do appear in the scene, my part being ended
And all my borrowed ornaments put off,   50
I am no more nor less than what I was
Before I entered.
    Dom.   Come, you would put on
A willful ignorance and not understand
What 'tis we point at. Must we in plain language,
Against the decent modesty of our sex,
Say that we love thee, love thee to enjoy thee,
Or that in our desires thou art preferred,
And Caesar but thy second? Thou in justice,
If from the height of majesty we can
Look down upon thy lowness and embrace it,   60
Art bound with fervor to look up to me.

---

[9] *story:* history.

IV.ii.
   [1] *gamesome:* spirited; Q "gainsome."
   [2] *Of force:* Perforce.

Par. O madam, hear me with a patient ear,
And be but pleased to understand the reasons
That do deter me from a happiness
Kings would be rivals for. Can I, that owe
My life and all that's mine to Caesar's bounties,
Beyond my hopes or merits show'red upon me,
Make payment for them with ingratitude,
Falsehood and treason? Though you have a shape
Might tempt Hippolytus, and larger power   70
To help or hurt than wanton Phaedra had,
Let loyalty and duty plead my pardon,
Though I refuse to satisfy—
Dom.   You are coy,
Expecting I should court you. Let mean ladies
Use prayers and entreaties to their creatures
To rise up instruments to serve their pleasures;
But for Augusta so to lose herself,
That holds command o'er Caesar and the world,
Were poverty of spirit. Thou must, thou shalt.
The violence of my passions knows no mean,   80
And in my punishments and my rewards
I'll use no moderation. Take this only,
As a caution from me: threadbare chastity
Is poor in the advancement of her servants,
But wantonness magnificent; and 'tis frequent
To have the salary of vice weigh down
The pay of virtue. So, without more trifling,
Thy sudden answer.
Par.   In what a strait am I brought in!
Alas, I know that the denial's death;
Nor can my grant discovered, threaten more.   90
Yet to die innocent, and have the glory
For all posterity to report that I
Refused an empress to preserve my faith
To my great master, in true judgment must
Show fairer than to buy a guilty life
With wealth and honors. 'Tis the base I build on.
I dare not, must not, will not.
Dom.   How! contemned?
Since hopes, nor fears, in the extremes, prevail not,
I must use a mean. Think who 'tis sues to thee.
Deny not that yet which a brother may   100
Grant to a sister; as a testimony

[*Enter*] CAESAR, ARETINUS, JULIA, DOMITILLA,
       CAENIS *and* Guard, *above.*

I am not scorned, kiss me. Kiss me again.
Kiss closer. Thou art now my Trojan Paris,
And I thy Helen.
Par.   Since it is your will.
Caes. And I am Menelaus, But I shall be

                    CAESAR *descends.*

Something I know not yet.
Dom.   Why lose we time

---

³ *Alcmena:* mother, by Jupiter, of Hercules.
⁴ *Amphitrio:* Alcmena's husband.
⁵ *taken . . . filing:* as the smith-god took his wife Venus
in the embrace of Mars.

And opportunity? These are but salads
To sharpen appetite. Let us to the feast,

              Courting PARIS *wantonly.*

Where I shall wish that thou wert Jupiter,
And I Alcmena,³ and that I had power   110
To lengthen out one short night into three,
And so beget a Hercules.
Caes.   While Amphitrio⁴
Stands by and draws the curtains.
Par.   Oh!—

                    Falls on his face.

Dom.   Betrayed!
Caes. No, taken in a net of Vulcan's filing,⁵
Where, in myself, the theater of the gods
Are sad spectators, not one of them daring
To witness, with a smile, he does desire
To be so shamed for all the pleasure that
You have sold your being for! What shall I name thee?
Ingrateful, treacherous, insatiate, all   120
Invectives which, in bitterness of spirit,
Wronged men have breathed out against wicked
        women,
Cannot express thee! Have I raised thee from
Thy low condition to the height of greatness,
Command, and majesty, in one base act
To render me, that was, before I hugged thee,
An adder in my bosom more than man,
A thing beneath a beast! Did I force these
Of mine own blood as handmaids to kneel to
Thy pomp and pride, have myself no thought   130
But how with benefits to bind thee mine;
And am I thus rewarded? Not a knee?
Nor tear? Nor sign of sorrow for thy fault?
Break, stubborn silence; what canst thou allege
To stay my vengeance?
Dom.   This. Thy lust compelled me
To be a strumpet, and mine hath returned it
In my intent and will, though not in act,
To cuckold thee.
Caes.   O impudence! take her hence,
And let her make her entrance into hell
By leaving life with all the tortures that   140
Flesh can be sensible of. Yet stay. What power
Her beauty still holds o'er my soul, that wrongs
Of this unpardonable nature cannot teach me
To right myself and hate her!—Kill her.—Hold!
Oh that my dotage should increase from that
Which should breed detestation! By Minerva,
If I look on her longer, I shall melt,
And sue to her, my injuries forgot,
Again to be received into her favor;
Could honor yield to it! Carry her to her chamber;
Be that her prison, till in cooler blood   151
I shall determine of her.
                    Exit [Guard] *with* DOMITIA.
Aret.   Now step I in,
While he's in this calm mood, for my reward.—
Sir, if my service hath deserved—
Caes.   Yes, yes:

And I'll reward thee. Thou hast robbed me of
All rest and peace and been the principal means
To make me know that of which if again

Enter Guard.

I could be ignorant of, I would purchase it
With the loss of empire. Strangle him; take these
    hence too,
And lodge them in the dungeon. Could your reason,
Dull wretches, flatter you with hope to think   161
That this discovery that hath showered upon me
Perpetual vexation should not fall
Heavy on you? Away with 'em—stop their mouths;
I will hear no reply. Oh, Paris, Paris,
     Exit Guard, ARETINUS, JULIA, CAENIS,
        [*and*] DOMITILLA.
How shall I argue with thee? How begin
To make thee understand, before I kill thee,
With what grief and unwillingness 'tis forced from me?
Yet, in respect I have favored thee, I will hear
What thou canst speak to qualify or excuse   170
Thy readiness to serve this woman's lust,
And wish thou couldst give me such satisfaction,
As I might bury the remembrance of it.
Look up; we stand attentive.
   Par.   O dread Caesar,
To hope for life or plead in the defense
Of my ingratitude were again to wrong you.
I know I have deserved death, and my suit is,
That you would hasten it; yet, that your highness,
When I am dead, as sure I will not live,
May pardon me, I'll only urge my frailty,   180
Her will, and the temptation of that beauty
Which you could not resist. How could poor I, then,
Fly that which followed me and Caesar sued for?
This is all. And now your sentence.
   Caes.   Which I know not
How to pronounce. Oh that thy fault had been
But such as I might pardon! If thou hadst
In wantonness, like Nero, fired proud Rome,
Betrayed an army, butchered the whole senate,
Committed sacrilege or any crime
The justice of our Roman laws calls death,   190
I had prevented[6] any intercession
And freely signed thy pardon.
   Par.   But for this
Alas you cannot, nay, you must not, sir.
Nor let it to posterity be recorded,
That Caesar, unrevenged, suffered a wrong
Which, if a private man should sit down with it,
Cowards would baffle[7] him.
   Caes.   With such true feeling
Thou arguest against thyself that it
Works more upon me than if my Minerva,
The grand protectress of my life and empire,   200
On forfeit of her favor, cried aloud,
"Caesar, show mercy!" and, I know not how,
I am inclined to it. Rise. I'll promise nothing;
Yet clear thy cloudy fears, and cherish hopes.
What we must do, we shall do; we remember
A tragedy we oft have seen with pleasure,

Called *The False Servant.*
   Par.   Such a one we have, sir.
   Caes. In which a great lord takes to his protection
A man forlorn, giving him ample power
To order and dispose of his estate   210
In his absence, he pretending then a journey,
But yet with this restraint, that on no terms
This lord suspecting his wife's constancy,
She having played false to a former husband
The servant, though solicited, should consent,
Though she commanded him, to quench her flames.
   Par. That was, indeed, the argument.
   Caes.   And what
Didst thou play in it?
   Par.   The false servant, sir.
   Caes. Thou didst indeed. Do the players wait
    without?
   Par. They do, sir, and prepared to act the story   220
Your majesty mentioned.
   Caes.   Call them in. Who presents
The injured lord?

      Enter AESOPUS, LATINUS, [*and*]
        a Boy *dressed for a lady.*

   Aesop.   'Tis my part, sir.
   Caes.   Thou didst not
Do it to the life. We can perform it better.
Off with my robe and wreath; since Nero scorned not
The public theater, we in private may
Disport ourselves. This cloak and hat, without
Wearing a beard or other property
Will fit the person.
   Aesop.   Only, sir, a foil,
The point and edge rebutted,[8] when you are
To do the murder. If you please to use this,   230
And lay aside your own sword.
   Caes.   By no means:
In jest or earnest this parts never from me.
We'll have but one short scene, that where the lady
In an imperious way commands the servant
To be unthankful to his patron. When
My cue's to enter, prompt me. Nay, begin,
And do it sprightly; though but a new actor,
When I come to execution, you shall find
No cause to laugh at me.
   Lat.   In the name of wonder,
What's Caesar's purpose?
   Aesop.   There is no contending.   240
   Caes. Why, when?[9]—
   Par.   I am armed:[10]
And, stood Death now within my view, and his
Unevitable dart aimed at my breast,
His cold embraces should not bring an ague
To any of my faculties till his pleasures
Were served and satisfied; which done, Nestor's[11] years
To me would be unwelcome.

---

   [6] *prevented:* anticipated.   [7] *baffle:* mock.
   [8] *rebutted:* blunted.
   [9] *Why, when:* exclamation of impatience.
   [10] *armed:* prepared.
   [11] *Nestor:* oldest of the Greek princes at Troy.

Boy.   Must we entreat,
That were born to command? Or court a servant,
That owes his food and clothing to our bounty,
For that which thou ambitiously shouldst kneel for?
Urge not, in thy excuse, the favors of   251
Thy absent lord or that thou stand'st engaged
For thy life to this charity; nor thy fears
Of what may follow, it being in my power
To mold him any way.
    Par.   As you may me,
In what his reputation is not wounded,
Nor I, his creature, in my thankfulness suffer.
I know you're young and fair; be virtuous too,
And loyal to his bed, that hath advanced you
To the height of happiness.
    Boy.   Can my lovesick heart   260
Be cured with counsel? Or durst reason ever
Offer to put in an exploded plea
In the court of Venus? My desires admit not
The least delay, and therefore instantly
Give me to understand what I shall trust to.
For if I am refused and not enjoy
Those ravishing pleasures from thee I run mad for,
I'll swear unto my lord at his return,
Making what I deliver good with tears,
That brutishly thou wouldst have forced from me   270
What I make suit for. And then but imagine
What 'tis to die, with these words "slave" and
    "traitor,"
With burning corrosives writ upon thy forehead,
And live preparèd for't.
    Par.   This he will believe
Upon her information, 'tis apparent;
And then I am nothing; and of two extremes,
Wisdom says, choose the less.—Rather than fall
Under your indignation, I will yield.
This kiss, and this, confirms it.
    Aesop.   Now, sir, now.
    Caes. I must take them at it?
    Aesop.   Yes, sir; be but perfect.
    Caes. O villain! thankless villain!—I should talk
    now,   281
But I have forgot my part. But I can do—
Thus, thus, and thus.

                   Kills PARIS.

    Par.   Oh! I am slain in earnest.
    Caes. 'Tis true; and 'twas my purpose, my good
    Paris.
And yet, before life leave thee, let the honor
I have done thee in thy death bring comfort to thee.
If it had been within the power of Caesar,
His dignity preserved, he had pardoned thee,
But cruelty of honor did deny it.
Yet, to confirm I loved thee, 'twas my study   290
To make thy end more glorious, to distinguish
My Paris from all others, and in that

Have shown my pity. Nor would I let thee fall
By a centurion's sword or have thy limbs
Rent piecemeal by the hangman's hook, however
Thy crime deserved it; but, as thou didst live
Rome's bravest actor, 'twas my plot that thou
Shouldst die in action, and to crown it die
With an applause enduring to all times,
By our imperial hand.
                        [PARIS *dies.*]
              His soul is freed   300
From the prison of his flesh; let it mount upward.
And for this trunk, when that the funeral pile
Hath made it ashes, we'll see it enclosed
In a golden urn. Poets adorn his hearse
With their most ravishing sorrows, and the stage
For ever mourn him, and all such as were
His glad spectators weep his sudden death,
The cause forgotten in his epitaph.
    Exeunt. A sad music, the Players *bearing off* PARIS'
          body, CAESAR *and the rest following.*

ACT FIVE

SCENE ONE

Enter PARTHENIUS, STEPHANOS, [*and*] Guard.

    Parth. Keep a strong guard upon him, and admit
    not
Access to any to exchange a word
Or syllable with him till the Emperor pleases
To call him to his presence. The relation
That you have made me, Stephanos, of these late
Strange passions in Caesar much amaze me.
The informer Aretinus put to death
For yielding him a true discovery
Of the Empress' wantonness; poor Paris killed first,
And now lamented; and the princesses   10
Confined to several islands; yet Augusta,
The machine on which all this mischief moved,
Received again to grace!
    Steph.   Nay, courted to it:
Such is the impotence [1] of his affection. [2]
Yet to conceal his weakness he gives out
The people made suit for her whom they hate more
Than civil war or famine. But take heed,
My lord, that nor in your consent nor wishes
You lent or [3] furtherance or favor to
The plot contrived against her; should she prove it,   20
Nay, doubt it only, you are a lost man,
Her power o'er doting Caesar being now
Greater than ever.
    Parth.   'Tis a truth I shake at,
And, when there's opportunity—
    Steph.   Say but "Do";
I am yours, and sure.
    Parth.   I will stand one trial more,
And then you shall hear from me.
    Steph.   Now observe
The fondness of this tyran, and her pride.

V.i.
   [1] *impotence:* lack of self-restraint.
   [2] *affection:* passion.   [3] *or:* either.

Enter CAESAR *and* DOMITIA.

Caes. Nay, all's forgotten.
Dom.   It may be, on your part.
Caes. Forgiven too, Domitia; 'tis a favor
That you should welcome with more cheerful looks. 30
Can Caesar pardon what you durst not hope for,
That did the injury, and yet must sue
To her whose guilt is washed off by his mercy
Only to entertain it?
Dom.   I asked none:
And I should be more wretched to receive
Remission for what I hold no crime,
But by a bare acknowledgement than if,
By slighting and contemning it, as now,
I dared thy utmost fury. Though thy flatterers
Persuade thee that thy murders, lusts, and rapes, 40
Are virtues in thee, and what pleases Caesar
Though never so unjust is right and lawful;
Or work in thee a false belief that thou
Art more than mortal, yet I to thy teeth
When circled with thy guards, thy rods, thy axes,
And all the ensigns of thy boasted power,
Will say, Domitian, nay, add to it Caesar,
Is a weak, feeble man, a bondman to
His violent passions, and in that my slave,
Nay, more my slave than my affections made me 50
To my loved Paris.
Caes.   Can I live and hear this?
Or hear and not revenge it? Come, you know
The strength that you hold on me; do not use it
With too much cruelty; for, though 'tis granted
That Lydian Omphale[4] had less command
O'er Hercules than you usurp o'er me,
Reason may teach me to shake off the yoke
Of my fond dotage.
Dom.   Never; do not hope it;
It cannot be. Thou being my beauty's captive,
And not to be redeemed, my empire's larger 60
Than thine, Domitian, which I'll exercise
With rigor on thee for my Paris' death.
And, when I have forced those eyes, now red with
     fury,
To drop down tears, in vain spent to appease me,
I know thy fervor such to my embraces,
Which shall be, though still kneeled for, still denied
     thee,
That thou with languishment shalt wish my actor
Did live again, so thou mightst be his second
To feed upon those delicates, when he's sated.
Caes. O my Minerva!
Dom.   There she is, invoke her: 70

[*Points to image of* MINERVA.]

She cannot arm thee with ability
To draw thy sword on me, my power being greater;
Or only say to thy centurions,
"Dare none of you do what I shake to think on?
And, in this woman's death, remove the Furies
That every hour afflict me?" Lamia's wrongs,
When thy lust forced me from him, are in me

At the height revenged, nor would I outlive Paris,
But that thy love, increasing with my hate,
May add unto thy torments; so, with all 80
Contempt I can, I leave thee.

Exit DOMITIA.

Caes.   I am lost,
Nor am I Caesar. When I first betrayed
The freedom of my faculties and will
To this imperious siren, I laid down
The empire of the world and of myself
At her proud feet. Sleep all my ireful powers?
Or is the magic of my dotage such
That I must still make suit to hear those charms
That do increase my thralldom? Wake, my anger.
For shame break through this lethargy, and appear 90
With usual terror and enable me,
Since I wear not a sword to pierce her heart,
Nor have a tongue to say this, "Let her die,"
Though 'tis done with a fever-shaken hand,

Pulls out a table-book.[5]

To sign her death. Assist me, great Minerva,
And vindicate thy votary.—So; she's now
Among the list of those I have proscribed,
And are, to free me of my doubts and fears,
To die tomorrow.

Writes.

Steph.   That same fatal book
Was never drawn yet, but some men of rank 100
Were marked out for destruction.

[*Exit.*]

Parth.   I begin
To doubt myself.
Caes.   Who waits there?
Parth.   Caesar.
Caes.   So.
These that command armed troops quake at my
     frowns,
And yet a woman slights 'em. Where's the wizard
We charged you to fetch in?
Parth.   Ready to suffer
What death you please to appoint him.
Caes.   Bring him in.

Enter ASCLETARIO, Tribunes, [*and*] Guard.

We'll question him ourself. Now, you, that hold
Intelligence with the stars, and dare prefix[6]
The day and hour in which we are to part
With life and empire, punctually foretelling 110
The means and manner of our violent end,
As you would purchase credit to your art,
Resolve me, since you are assured of us,
What fate attends yourself?
Ascle.   I have had long since
A certain knowledge, and as sure as thou
Shalt die tomorrow, being the fourteenth of

---

[4] *Omphale:* Lydian queen who held Hercules slave and
had him perform labors so that he could be purified of a
crime he had committed.   [5] *table-book:* notebook.
[6] *prefix:* ascertain in advance.

The kalends of October, the hour five,
Spite of prevention, this carcass shall be
Torn and devoured by dogs; and let that stand
For a firm prediction.
    Caes.   May our body, wretch,   120
Find never nobler sepulcher if this
Fall ever on thee. Are we the great disposer
Of life and death, yet cannot mock the stars
In such a trifle? Hence with the impostor,
And having cut his throat erect a pile
Guarded with soldiers till his cursèd trunk
Be turned to ashes. Upon forfeit of
Your life and theirs perform it.
    Ascle.   'Tis in vain.
When what I have foretold is made apparent,
Tremble to think what follows.
    Caes.   Drag him hence,   130
    The Guard [*and* Tribunes] *bear off*
                 ASCLETARIO.
And do as I command you. I was never
Fuller of confidence; for having got
The victory of my passions in my freedom
From proud Domitia, who shall cease to live
Since she disdains to love, I rest unmoved,
And in defiance of prodigious meteors,
Chaldaeans' vain predictions, jealous fears
Of my near friends and freemen, certain hate
Of kindred and alliance, or all terrors
The soldier's doubted faith or people's rage   140
Can bring to shake my constancy, I am armed.
That scrupulous thing styled conscience is seared up,
And I insensible of all my actions,
For which by moral and religious fools
I stand condemned as they had never been.
And since I have subdued triumphant love,
I will not deify pale captive fear,
Nor in a thought receive it. For till thou,
Wisest Minerva, that from my first youth
Hast been my sole protectress, dost forsake me,   150
Not Junius Rusticus' threat'nèd apparition,
Nor what this soothsayer but ev'n now foretold,
Being things impossible to human reason,
Shall in a dream disturb me. Bring my couch there;
A sudden but a secure drowsiness
Invites me to repose myself. Let music

    Enter [Servants] *with couch* [*and exit*].

With some choice ditty second it.
                 I' the mean time,
Rest there, dear book, which opened when I wake

    Lays the book under his pillow.

Shall make some sleep for ever.

    The music and a song. CAESAR *sleeps.*
    Enter PARTHENIUS *and* DOMITIA.

    Dom.   Write my name
In his bloody scroll, Parthenius? The fear's idle;   160

---

[7] *discourse:* reason.

He durst not, could not.
    Parth.   I can assure nothing;
But I observed, when you departed from him,
After some little passion, but much fury,
He drew it out; whose death he signed, I know not,
But in his looks appeared a resolution
Of what before he staggered at. What he hath
Determined of is uncertain, but too soon
Will fall on you, or me, or both, or any,
His pleasure known to the tribunes and centurions,
Who never use to inquire his will but serve it.   170
Now if out of the confidence of your power,
The bloody catalogue being still about him,
As he sleeps you dare peruse it or remove it,
You may instruct yourself or what to suffer,
Or how to cross it.
    Dom.   I would not be caught
With too much confidence. By your leave, sir. Ha!
No motion! You lie uneasy, sir,
Let me mend your pillow.
    Parth.   Have you it?
    Dom.   'Tis here.
    Caes. Oh!
    Parth.   You have waked him; softly, gracious
    madam,   179
While we are unknown, and then consult at leisure.
        Exeunt PARTHENIUS *and* DOMITIA.

A dreadful music sounding, enter JUNIUS RUSTICUS
    and PALPHURIUS SURA, *with bloody swords; they*
    wave them over his head. CAESAR *in his sleep troubled,*
    seems to pray to the image; they scornfully take it away.

    Caes. Defend me, goddess, or this horrid dream
Will force me to distraction. Whither have
These Furies borne thee? Let me rise and follow.
I am bathed o'er with the cold sweat of death,
And am deprived of organs to pursue
These sacrilegious spirits. Am I at once
Robbed of my hopes and being? No, I live,

                 Rises distractedly.

Yes, live, and have discourse,[7] to know myself
Of gods and men forsaken. What accuser
Within me cries aloud, I have deserved it   190
In being just to neither? Who dares speak this?
Am I not Caesar? How! again repeat it?
Presumptuous traitor, thou shalt die.—What traitor?
He that hath been a traitor to himself,
And stands convicted here. Yet who can sit
A competent judge o'er Caesar? Caesar. Yes,
Caesar by Caesar's sentenced, and must suffer.
Minerva cannot save him. Ha! where is she?
Where is my goddess? Vanished! I am lost then.
No, 'twas no dream but a most real truth,   200
That Junius Rusticus and Palphurius Sura,
Although their ashes were cast in the sea,
Were by their innocence made up again,
And in corporeal forms but now appeared,
Waving their bloody swords above my head,
As at their deaths they threat'nèd. And methought
Minerva, ravished hence, whispered that she

Was for my blasphemies disarmed by Jove,
And could no more protect me. Yes, 'twas so.

Thunder and lightning.

His thunder does confirm it, against which,   210
Howe'er it spare the laurel, this proud wreath
Is no assurance.—Ha! come you resolved

Enter three Tribunes.

To be my executioners?
   1 Trib.   Allegiance
And faith forbid that we should lift an arm
Against your sacred head.
   2 Trib.   We rather sue
For mercy.
   3 Trib. And acknowledge that in justice
Our lives are forfeited for not performing
What Caesar charged us.
   1 Trib.   Nor did we transgress it
In our want of will or care; for, being but men,
It could not be in us to make resistance,   220
The gods fighting against us.
   Caes.   Speak, in what
Did they express their anger? We will hear it,
But dare not say undaunted.
   1 Trib.   In brief, thus, sir:
The sentence given by your imperial tongue
For the astrologer Ascletario's death
With speed was put in execution.
   Caes.   Well.
   1 Trib. For, his throat cut, his legs bound, and his
      arms
Pinioned behind his back, the breathless trunk
Was with all scorn dragged to the Field of Mars,[8]
And there, a pile being raised of old dry wood,   230
Smeared o'er with oil and brimstone, or what else
Could help to feed or to increase the fire,
The carcass was thrown on it; but no sooner
The stuff, that was most apt, began to flame,
But suddenly, to the amazement of
The fearless soldier, a sudden flash
Of lightning, breaking through the scattered clouds,
With such a horrid violence forced its passage,
And as disdaining all heat but itself,
In a moment quenched the artificial fire.   240
And before we could kindle it again
A clap of thunder followed, with such noise
As if then Jove, incensed against mankind,
Had in his secret purpose determined
An universal ruin to the world.
This horror past, not at Deucalion's[9] flood
Such a stormy shower of rain, and yet that word is
Too narrow to express it, was e'er seen.
Imagine rather, sir, with less fury
The waves rush down the cataracts of Nile;   250
Or that the sea, spouted into the air
By the angry Orc,[10] endangering tall ships
But sailing near it, so falls down again.
Yet here the wonder ends not, but begins;
For as in vain we labored to consume
The witch's body, all the dogs of Rome,

Howling and yelling like to famished wolves,
Brake in upon us; and though thousands were
Killed in th' attempt, some did ascend the pile,
And with their eager fangs seized on the carcass.   260
   Caes. But have they torn it?
   1 Trib.   Torn it, and devoured it.
   Caes. I then am a dead man, since all predictions
Assure me I am lost. O my loved soldiers,
Your Emperor must leave you! yet, however
I cannot grant myself a short reprieve,
I freely pardon you. The fatal hour
Steals fast upon me. I must die this morning
By five, my soldiers; that's the latest hour
You e'er must see me living.
   1 Trib.   Jove avert it!
In our swords lies your fate, and we will guard it.   270
   Caes. Oh no, it cannot be; it is decreed
Above, and by no strengths here to be altered.
Let proud mortality but look on Caesar,
Compassed of late with armies, in his eyes
Carrying both life and death, and in his arms
Fathoming the earth; that would be styled a god,
And is for that presumption cast beneath
The low condition of a common man,
Sinking with mine own weight.—
   1 Trib.   Do not forsake
Yourself, we'll never leave you.
   2 Trib.   We'll draw up   280
More cohorts of your guard, if you doubt treason.
   Caes. They cannot save me. The offended gods,
That now sit judges on me from their envy
Of my power and greatness here conspire against me.
   1 Trib. Endeavor to appease them.
   Caes.   'Twill be fruitless:
I am past hope of remission. Yet could I
Decline[11] this dreadful hour of five, these terrors
That drive me to despair would soon fly from me;
And could you but till then assure me—
   1 Trib.   Yes, sir;
Or we'll fall with you, and make Rome the urn   290
In which we'll mix our ashes.
   Caes.   'Tis said nobly;
I am something comforted. Howe'er, to die
Is the full period of calamity.

Exeunt.

V.ii

Enter PARTHENIUS, DOMITIA, JULIA, CAENIS,
   DOMITILLA, STEPHANOS, SEJEIUS,
      [*and*] ENTELLUS.

   Parth. You see we are all condemned; there's no
      evasion;
We must do, or suffer.
   Steph.   But it must be sudden;

---

   [8] *Field of Mars:* Campus Martius, site of many imperial
buildings and monuments.
   [9] *Deucalion:* the classical Noah.
   [10] *Orc:* fabulous sea-monster.   [11] *Decline:* Escape.

The least delay is mortal.
Dom.   Would I were
A man, to give it action.
   Domit. Could I make my approaches, though my
    stature
Does promise little, I have a spirit as daring
As hers that can reach higher.
   Steph.   I will take
That burden from you, madam. All the art is
To draw him from the tribunes that attend him;
For could you bring him but within my sword's
    reach,   10
The world should owe her freedom from a tyran
To Stephanos.
   Sej.   You shall not share alone
The glory of a deed that will endure
To all posterity.
   Ent.   I will put in
For a part myself.
   Parth.   Be resolute and stand close.[1]
I have conceived a way, and with the hazard
Of my life I'll practice it to fetch him hither.
But then no trifling.
   Steph.   We'll dispatch him, fear not;
A dead dog never bites.
   Parth.   Thus then at all—

     PARTHENIUS *goes off; the rest stand aside.*

    Enter CAESAR *and* Tribunes.

   Caes. How slow-paced are these minutes! in
    extremes,   20
How miserable is the least delay!
Could I imp[2] feathers to the wings of time,
Or with as little ease command the sun
To scourge his coursers up heaven's eastern hill,
Making the hour I tremble at past recalling,
As I can move this dial's tongue[3] to six,
My veins and arteries, emptied with fear,
Would fill and swell again. How do I look?
Do you yet see Death about me?
   1 Trib.   Think not of him;
There is no danger; all these prodigies   30
That do affright you rise from natural causes,
And though you do ascribe them to yourself,
Had you ne'er been, had happened.
   Caes.   'Tis well said,
Exceeding well, brave soldier. Can it be,
That I that feel myself in health and strength
Should still believe I am so near my end,
And have my guards about me? Perish all
Predictions! I grow constant[4] they are false,
And built upon uncertainties.
   1 Trib.   This is right;
Now Caesar's hard[5] like Caesar.
   Caes.   We will to   40

The camp, and having there confirmed the soldier
With a large donative and increase of pay,
Some shall—I say no more.

    Enter PARTHENIUS.

   Parth.   All happiness,
Security, long life, attend upon
The monarch of the world.
   Caes.   Thy looks are cheerful.
   Parth. And my relation full of joy and wonder.
Why is the care of your imperial body,
My lord, neglected, the feared hour being past,
In which your life was threatened?
   Caes.   Is't past five?
   Parth. Past six, upon my knowledge; and in
    justice   50
Your clock-master should die that hath deferred
Your peace so long. There is a post new lighted,
That brings assured intelligence that your legions
In Syria have won a glorious day,
And much enlarged your empire. I have kept him
Concealed, that you might first partake the pleasure
In private and the senate from yourself
Be taught to understand how much they owe
To you and to your fortune.
   Caes.   Hence, pale fear, then.
Lead me, Parthenius.
   1 Trib.   Shall we wait you?
   Caes.   No.   60
After losses guards are useful. Know your distance.
    Exeunt CAESAR *and* PARTHENIUS.
   2 Trib. How strangely hopes delude men. As I
    live,
The hour is not yet come.
   1 Trib.   Howe'er, we are
To pay our duties and observe the sequel.
           Exeunt Tribunes.
   Dom. I hear him coming. Be constant.

    Enter CAESAR *and* PARTHENIUS.

   Caes.   Where, Parthenius,
Is this glad messenger?
   Steph.   Make the door fast.—Here;
A messenger of horror.
   Caes.   How! betrayed?
   Dom. No; taken, tyran.
   Caes.   My Domitia
In the conspiracy!
   Parth.   Behold this book.
   Caes. Nay, then I am lost. Yet, though I am
    unarmed,   70
I'll not fall poorly.
        Overthrows STEPHANOS.
   Steph.   Help me.
   Ent.   Thus, and thus!
   Sej. Are you so long a-falling?
   Caes.   'Tis done basely.

           Falls and dies.

   Parth. This for my father's death.
   Dom.   This for my Paris.

V.ii.
[1] *close:* hidden.   [2] *imp:* graft.
[3] *dial's tongue:* anachronism.   [4] *constant:* confident.
[5] *hard:* sometimes emended, unnecessarily, to "heard."

Jul. This for thy incest.

Domit.   This for thy abuse
Of Domitilla.

                              These severally stab him.

                    Enter Tribunes.

1 Trib.   Force the doors. O Mars,
What have you done?

Parth.   What Rome shall give us thanks
for.

Steph. Dispatched a monster.

1 Trib.   Yet he was our prince,
However wicked; and, in you, 'tis murder,
Which whosoe'er succeeds him will revenge;
Nor will we that served under his command   80

Consent that such a monster as thyself,
For in thy wickedness Augusta's title
Hath quite forsook thee, thou that wert the ground
Of all these mischiefs shall go hence unpunished.
Lay hands on her and drag her to her sentence.
We will refer the hearing to the senate,
Who may at their best leisure censure you.
Take up his body. He in death hath paid
For all his cruelties. Here's the difference:
Good kings are mourned for after life; but ill,   90
And such as governed only by their will
And not their reason, unlamented fall;
No good man's tear shed at their funeral.

                                        Exeunt omnes.

                    Flourish

F I N I S

James Shirley

[1596–1666]

HYDE PARK

BY THE time of Shirley's birth, in London, Marlowe, Greene, and Kyd were already dead, Shakespeare had presented some of his finest plays, and Jonson, Chapman, Dekker, and Heywood had emerged as a new generation of playwrights. By the time his plays began to appear, in 1624/5, Shakespeare, Webster, and Fletcher were dead, Massinger was about to replace the last as Shakespeare's heir to the position of principal writer for the King's Men, and Jonson was writing his last major play, *The Staple of News*, a steep decline from BARTHOLOMEW FAIR a decade earlier. Shirley thus represents a new theatrical world, one that like the England he grew up in must have seemed far less rich in promise than that of a generation earlier. But the theater none the less claimed much of his energy. He wrote at least twenty-five plays, for a number of companies, and on Massinger's death in 1640 he became the last principal dramatist of the King's Men. When the theaters were closed for plague during several seasons in the 1630s, Shirley went to Dublin where they were still open; and neither his position as an ordained clergyman early in life nor that as a teacher after the civil war closed the theaters for good in 1642 seems to have satisfied his primary interests, though late in life he did produce works on grammar. He died in the year of the great fire of London and the eve of the publication of *Paradise Lost*, having lived into an age that is in some ways as remote from Elizabeth's as our own is.

HYDE PARK, along with *The Lady of Pleasure* one of Shirley's two best comedies—his numerous tragedies and tragicomedies are less original and less admirable—was licensed on April 20, 1632, and was probably performed at about that date, its opening perhaps timed to coincide with the annual opening of the Park for the spring and summer months. Hyde Park, on property that Henry VIII had taken from the Abbey of Westminster when he dissolved the monasteries, had been turned into a public park by James I, under the jurisdiction of the earl to whom the comedy is dedicated, and its life is convincingly imitated here. Though the world that the play pictures is unmistakably that of Cavalier London, the picturing itself is reminiscent of the genre-painting of Dekker and other earlier playwrights; as in THE SHOEMAKER'S HOLIDAY and

THE ROARING GIRL, the portrayal of London as subject to itself as audience is much of the play's *raison d'être*. Other qualities too are Elizabethan: the old-fashioned defense of chastity, the skillful manipulation of three parallel plots, each with its smug lover who to his surprise is done out of the amorous triumph he confidently expects, each with its woman who knows her own mind; the Beatrice-and-Benedick relationship of Fairfield and Mistress Carol. But in equally significant ways this comedy looks forward more than Shirley could possibly have known to the comedy that would be produced less than a generation later in a new kind of theater. Like Restoration comedies, HYDE PARK is concerned with the fitness of lovers for marriage and with the establishment of a complex and explicit social code. Fairfield and Mistress Carol anticipate the sparring and contract-making of Mirabel and Millamant in Congreve's *The Way of the World* as much as they look back to Shakespeare's witty lovers; the action concerns the amusements of the upper classes without much of Dekker's or Middleton's interest in the lower life of the city. And Shirley seems to find the blank verse he has inherited as a dominant convention for the imitation of speech as much an impediment as would those Restoration comedians who dropped it for prose; his verse is almost self-consciously prosaic except in such purple passages as Julietta's inflamed defense of chastity. Uncharitably one might suggest that Shirley uses the old conventions rather tiredly—even the multiple plot, with its thematic parallels made all too obvious and explicit—while lacking the imagination to invent the conventions of the new comedy it anticipates; but such a judgment ignores the bright comedy of manners and the vivid portrayal of life in London that Shirley achieves, as well as the significance of theater that so resembles what is too often thought to be the entirely new creation of the Restoration. Pepys would enjoy the comedy a generation later as "a very moderate play," and his pleasure seems primarily derived from the fact that the King's Men brought real horses on stage for the race scenes.

There are no known sources for HYDE PARK. The play was first printed in 1637, and the Bancroft Library copy of that quarto edition is the basis of the present text.

N. R.

743

Hyde Park

[EPISTLE DEDICATORY]

To the Right Honorable

HENRY EARL OF HOLLAND,[1]

Knight of the most noble Order of the Garter, one of his Majesty's most Honorable Privy Council, Chancellor of the University of Cambridge. etc.

MY LORD,

THE comedy, in the title, is a part of your lordship's command, which heretofore graced and made happy by your smile, when it was presented, after a long silence, upon first opening of the Park,[2] is come abroad to kiss your lordship's hand. The applause it once received in the action, is not considerable with that honor your lordship may give it in your acceptance; that was too large, and might with some narrow and stoical judgment render it suspected; but this, depending upon your censure[3] (to me above many theaters) is able to impart a merit to the poem and prescribe opinion. If your lordship, retired from business into a calm, and at truce with those high affairs wherein your counsel and   10 spirit is fortunately active, vouchsafe to peruse these unworthy papers, you not only give a life to the otherwise languishing numbers,[4] but quicken and exalt the genius of the author, whose heart pointeth at no greater ambition than to be known,

My lord,
to your name and honor,
the most humbly devoted,
JAMES SHIRLEY.

DRAMATIS PERSONÆ

LORD BONVILE
FAIRFIELD ⎫
RIDER   ⎬ *amorous servants to Mistress Carol*
VENTURE   ⎭
LACY, *suitor to Mistress Bonavent*
TRIER, *suitor to Julietta*
BONAVENT, *a merchant, supposed to have been lost at sea*
JARVIS, *servant to Mistress Bonavent*
Page to *Lord Bonvile*
Gentlemen
Jockey

Officers
Runners
Bagpiper
Park-keepers, Servants, *etc.*

MISTRESS CAROL
MISTRESS BONAVENT, *supposed to be a widow*
JULIETTA, *Sister to Fairfield*
Waiting-woman
Milkmaid, *etc.*

ACT ONE

SCENE ONE

Enter TRIER *and* LACY.

Tri. And how, and how?
Lacy.   The cause depends—
Tri.   No
  mistress?
Lacy. Yes, but no wife.
Tri.   For now she is a widow.

DEDICATION
   [1] *Henry . . . Holland:* Henry Rich, first Earl of Holland, given his title, Keeper of the Crown Land of Hyde Park, by James I.
   [2] *opening . . . Park:* the annual opening for the spring and summer months.   [3] *censure:* judgment.
   [4] *numbers:* meter, verses.

Lacy. But I resolve—

Tri.   What does she say to thee?

Lacy. She says—I know not what she says—but I
Must take another course; and yet she is—

Tri. A creature of much sweetness, if all tongues
Be just in her report; and yet 'tis strange,
Having seven years expected,[1] and so much
Remonstrance[2] of her husband's loss at sea,
She should continue thus.

Lacy.   What if she should   10
Renew the bond of her devotion
For seven years more?

Tri.   You will have time enough
To pay in your affection

Lacy.   I would make
A voyage to Cassandra's[3] temple first
And marry a deformed maid; yet I must
Confess, she gives me a fair respect.

Tri.   Has she
A hope her husband may be living yet?

Lacy. I cannot tell; she may have a conceit[4]
Some dolphin has preserved him in the storm,
Or that he may be tenant to some whale,   20
Within whose belly he may practice Lent,
And feed on fish till he be vomited
Upon some coast; or, having 'scaped the seas,
And bills of exchange[5] failing, he might purpose
To foot it o'er the Alps in his return,
And by mischance is fallen among the mice
With whom, perhaps, he battens upon sleep,
Beneath the snow.

Tri.   This was a vagary.

Lacy. I know not what to think; or, is she not
The worse for the coy[6] lady that lives with her?   30

Tri. Her kinswoman?

Lacy.   Such a malicious piece,
(I mean to love,) 'tis pity any place
But a cold nunnery should be troubled with her.
If all maids[7] were but her disciples, we
Should have no generation, and the world,
For want of children, in few years undone by't:
Here's one can tell you more. Is not that Jarvis,
The widow's servant?

Enter VENTURE *and* Servant [JARVIS] [*separately*].

Vent.   Whither in such haste, man?

Jar. I am commanded, sir, to fetch a gentleman.

Vent. To thy mistress? To give her a heat[8] this
morning?   40

I.i.
   [1] *expected:* waited.   [2] *Remonstrance:* Proof.
   [3] *Cassandra:* Priam's daughter, raped by Ajax at Athena's
altar, given both the gift of prophecy and the curse of not
being believed when as a girl she was visited by Apollo at
the temple.   [4] *conceit:* fancy.
   [5] *bills . . . exchange:* IOUs.   [6] *coy:* reluctant to love.
   [7] *maids:* virgins.   [8] *a heat:* a fever.
   [9] *touched:* magnetized.   [10] *toy:* trifle.
   [11] *spark:* diamond; dandy.   [12] *napery:* linen.
   [13] *lady of pleasure:* courtesan. Shirley's play of this title
was first performed in 1635.
   [14] *running-horse:* racehorse.

Jar. I have spied him—With your pardon—

                     The Servant *goes to* LACY.

Tri. Good morrow, Master Venture.

Vent.   Frank Trier?

Tri.   You
Look high and jocund; Venus has been propitious.
I dreamt last night thou wert a bridegroom.

Vent. Such a thing may be; the wind blows now
From a more happy coast.

Lacy.   I must leave you;
I am sent for.

Tri.   To thy mistress?

Lacy.   Without
More ceremony, gentlemen, my service.
Farewell.

                                Exit [*with* JARVIS].

Vent. I'll tell thee, I have a mistress.

Tri. I believe it.

Vent.   And yet I have her not.   50

Tri. But you have hope.

Vent.   Or rather certainty.

Tri. Why, I hear she is
A very tyrant over men.

Vent.   Worse, worse,
The needle of a dial never had
So many waverings; but she is touched,[9]
And she points only this way now, true north;
I am her pole.

Tri.   And she your *Ursa minor.*

Vent. I laugh to think how other of her rivals
Will look when I enjoy her.

Tri. You are not yet contracted?

Vent.   No, she changed   60
Some amorous tokens; do you see this diamond?
A toy[10] she gave me.

Tri.   'Cause she saw you a spark.[11]

Vent. Her flame of love is here; and in exchange
She took a chain of pearl.

Tri.   You'll see it hanged.

Vent. These to the wise are arguments of love,
And mutual promises.

Enter LORD [BONVILE] *and* Page.

Tri. Your lordship's welcome to town.
I am blessed to see your honor in good health.

Lord. B. Prithee visit my lodgings.

Tri. I shall presume to tender my humble service.

                     Exeunt LORD [BONVILE] *and* Page.

Vent. What's he?

Tri.   A sprig of the nobility.   71
That has a spirit equal to his fortunes;
A gentleman that loves clean napery.[12]

Vent. I guess your meaning.

Tri. A lady of pleasure;[13] 'tis no shame for men
Of his high birth to love a wench; his honor
May privilege more sins. Next to a woman,
He loves a running-horse.[14]
Setting aside these recreations,
He has a noble nature, valiant, bountiful.   80

Vent. I was of his humor till I fell in love,

I mean for wenching; you may guess a little
By my legs; but I will now be very honest,
And when I am married—
    Tri.   Then you are confident
To carry away your mistress from them all?
    Vent. From Jove himself, though he should practice all
His shapes to court her; 'tis impossible
She should put any trick upon me; I
Have won her very soul.
    Tri.   Her body must
Needs be your own then.
    Vent.   I have a brace of rivals;   90
Would they were here, that I might jeer them!
And see how opportunely one is come!

Enter MASTER RIDER.

I'll make you a little sport.
    Tri.   I ha' been
Melancholy; you will express a favor in't.
    Rid. Master Venture! the first man in my wish;
What gentleman is that?
    Vent.   A friend of mine.
    Rid. I am his servant; look ye, we are friends,
And't shall appear, however things succeed,
That I have loved you; and you cannot take
My counsel in ill part.
    Vent.   What's the business.   100
    Rid. For my part, I have
Used no enchantment, philter, no devices[15]
That are unlawful, to direct the stream
Of her affection; it flows naturally.
    Vent. How's this? [*Aside to* TRIER] Prithee observe.
    Tri. I do, and shall laugh presently.
    Rid.   For your anger,
I wear a sword, though I have no desire
It should be guilty of defacing any
Part of your body; yet upon a just
And noble provocation, wherein   110
My mistress' love and honor is engaged,
I dare draw blood.
    Tri. Ha, ha, ha!
    Vent. A mistress' love and honor! this is pretty.
    Rid. I know you cannot but understand me;
Yet, I say I love you, and with a
Generous breast, and in the confidence you
Will take it kindly, I return to that
I promised you, good counsel; come, leave off
The prosecution.
    Vent.   Of what, I prithee?   120
    Rid. There will be less affront than to expect
Till the last minute, and behold the victory
Another's. You may guess why I declare this:
I am studious to preserve an honest friendship;
For though it be my glory to be adorned
With trophies of her vanquished love—
    Vent. Whose love?
    Tri. [*Aside to* VENTURE] This sounds as if he jeered you.
    Vent.   Mushroom!

[*Draws.*]

    Tri. What d'ee mean, gentlemen? Friends, and fall out
About good counsel!
    Vent.   I'll put up again,
Now I think better on't.
    Tri.   'Tis done discreetly.   130
Cover the nakedness of your tool, I pray.
    Vent. Why, look you, sir; if you bestow this counsel
Out of your love, I thank you; yet there is
No great necessity why you should be at
The cost of so much breath, things well considered.
A lady's love is mortal, I know that,
And if a thousand men should love a woman,
The dice must carry her; but one of all
Can wear the garland.
    Tri.   Now you come to him.
    Vent. For my own part, I loved the lady well,   140
But you must pardon me, if I demonstrate
There's no such thing as you pretend, and therefor
In quittance[16] of your loving, honest counsel,
I would not have you build an airy castle.
Her stars have pointed her another way;
This instrument will take her height.

Shows the ring.

    Rid.   Ha!
    Vent. And you may guess what cause you have to triumph;
I would not tell you this, but that I love you
And hope you will not run yourself into
The cure of Bedlam.[17] He that wears this favor   150
Hath sense to apprehend.
    Rid.   That diamond?
    Vent. Observe it perfectly, there are no trophies
Of vanquished love, I take it, coming toward you;
"It will be less affront, than to expect
Till the last minute, and behold the victory
Another's."
    Rid.   That ring I gave her.
    Tri.   Ha, ha, ha!
    Vent. This was his gift to her; ha, ha, ha!
Have patience, spleen, ha, ha!
    Tri.   The scene is changed!
    Rid. She wo' not use me thus; she did receive it
With all the circumstances of love.   160
    Vent. I pity him; my eyes run o'er. Dost hear?—
I cannot choose but laugh, and yet I pity thee.
She has a jeering wit, and I shall love her
More heartily for this. What dost think?
Poor gentleman, how he has fooled himself!
    Rid. I'll to her again.
    Vent.   Nay, be not passionate!
I' faith, thou wert too confident, I knew
It could not hold; dost think I'd say so much else?
I can tell thee more; but lose her memory.[18]
    Rid. Were it more rich than that   170

He shows a chain of pearl.

---

[15] *devices:* stratagems.   [16] *quittance:* repayment.
[17] *Bedlam:* Bethlehem Hospital, London insane asylum.
[18] *lose ... memory:* forget her.

Which Cleopatra gave to Antony,
With scorn I would return it.
   Tri.   She give you this chain?
   Rid. She shall be hanged in chains ere I will keep it.
   Vent. Stay, stay; let my eye examine that—this
     chain?—
   Rid. Who would trust woman after this?
   Vent.   The very
     same
She took of me, when I received this diamond!
   Rid. Ha, ha! you do but jest; she will not fool
You o' this fashion; look a little better,
One may be like another.
   Vent.   'Tis the same.
   Rid. Ha, ha! I would it were, that we might laugh
At one another; by this hand I will   181
Forgive her; prithee tell me—ha, ha, ha!
   Tri. You will "carry her
From jove himself, though he should practice all
His shapes to court her."
   Rid.   By this pearl,—O rogue,
How I do love her for't!—be not dejected;
"A lady's love is mortal, one of all
Must wear the garland; do not fool yourself
Beyond the cure of Bedlam."
   Tri.   She has fitted you
With a pair of fools' coats, as handsomely   190
As any tailor, that had taken measure.
   Vent. Give me thy hand.
   Tri.   Nay, lay your heads
     together
How to revenge it; and so, gentlemen,
I take my leave.
                            [Exit.]
   Vent.   She has abused us.
   Rid. Let us take his counsel; we can be but
What we are.
   Vent.   A pair of credulous fools.
   Rid. This other fellow, Fairfield, has prevailed.
   Vent. Which if he have—
   Rid.   What shall we do?
   Vent. I think we were best let him alone.[19]
   Rid. Do you hear? We'll to her again; you will   200
Be ruled by me; and tell her what we think of her.
   Vent. She may come to herself and be ashamed
     on't.[20]
   Rid. If she would affect one of us, for my part
I am indifferent.
   Vent. So say I too, but to give us both the
     canvas![21]
Let's walk, and think how to behave ourselves.
                            Exeunt.

---

[19] *let . . . alone:* leave her to him.   [20] *on't:* of it.
[21] *give . . . canvas:* dismiss, fire.

I.ii.
[1] *intelligence:* news.
[2] *overseen:* betrayed into blunders.
[3] *burn blue:* Candles thus portend death or indicate
presence of the devil or an evil spirit.
[4] *Amazonian ladies:* Amazons.

[I.ii]

     Enter MISTRESS BONAVENT *and* MISTRESS
                       CAROL.

   Mist. Car. What d'ee mean to do with him?
   Mist. Bon.   Thou art
Too much a tyrant; the seven years are past
That did oblige me to expect my husband,
Engaged to sea; and though within those limits
Frequent intelligence[1] hath reported him
Lost, both to me and his own life, I have
Been careful of my vow; and were there hope
Yet to embrace him, I would think another
Seven years no penance; but I should thus
Be held a cruel woman, in his certain   10
Loss, to despise the love of all mankind.
And therefore I resolve, upon so large
A trial of his constancy, at last
To give him the reward of his respects
To me, and—
   Mist. Car. Marry him.
   Mist. Bon.   You have apprehended.
   Mist. Car. No marvel if men rail upon you then,
And doubt whether a widow may be saved.
We maids are thought the worse on, for your easiness.
How are poor women overseen?[2] We must
Cast away ourselves upon a whining lover,   20
In charity: I hope my cousin's ghost
Will meet you as you go to church, or if
You 'scape it then, upon the wedding night—
   Mist. Bon. Fie! fie!
   Mist. Car.   When you are both abed, and
Candles out.
   Mist. Bon. Nay, put not out the candles.
   Mist. Car. May they burn blue[3] then, at his second
     kiss,
And fright him from—well, I could say something;
But take your course—He's come already.

              Enter LACY.

Put him off but another twelvemonth.

      [MISTRESS BONAVENT *walks aside*
                     with LACY.]
                    —So, so.
Oh love, into what foolish labyrinths   30
Dost thou lead us! I would all women were
But of my mind, we would have a new world
Quickly. I will go study poetry
On purpose to write verses in the praise
Of th' Amazonian ladies,[4] in whom only
Appears true valor (for the instruction
Of all posterity), to beat their husbands.
   Lacy. How you endear your servant!
   Mist. Car.   I will not
Be guilty of more stay.

         Enter MR. FAIRFIELD.

   Fair.   Sweet lady!   39
   Mist. Car. You're come in time, sir, to redeem me.
   Fair. Why, lady?

Mist. Car. You will be as comfortable[5] as strong
  waters;[6]
There's a gentleman—
Fair.   So uncivil to affront you?
Mist. Car. I had no patience to hear him longer;
Take his offense, before you question him.
Fair. And be most happy if, by any service,
You teach me to deserve your fair opinion.
Mist. Car. It is not civil to eavesdrop him, but
I'm sure he talks on't now.
Fair.   Of what?
Mist. Car.   Of love;
Is any thing more ridiculous?   50
You know I never cherish that condition.
In you 'tis the most harsh, unpleasing discord;
But I hope you will be instructed better,
Knowing how much my fancy goes against it.
Talk not of that, and welcome.
Fair.   You retain,
I see, your unkind temper; will no thought
Soften your beauty? Disdain agrees but ill
With so much beauty. If you would persuade
Me not to love you, strive to be less fair;
Undo that face, and so become a rebel   60
To heaven and nature.
Mist. Car.   You do love my face then?
Fair. As heavenly prologue to your mind; I do not
Dote, like Pygmalion, on the colors.[7]
Mist. Car. No, you cannot; his was a painted
  mistress.
Or, if it be the mind you so pretend
To affect my wonder of your folly,
For I have told you that so often.
Fair.   What?
Mist. Car. My mind, so opposite to all your
  courtship
That I had rather hear the tedious tales
Of Holinshed[8] than any thing that trenches[9]   70
On love. If you come fraught with any o'
Cupid's devices, keep them for his whirligigs;[10]
Or load the next edition of his messenger,
Or post, with a mad packet, I shall but laugh
At them and pity you.
Fair.   That pity—
Mist. Car. Do not mistake me, it shall be a very
Miserable pity, without love!
Were I a man, and had but half that handsomeness,
(For though I have not love, I hate detraction),
Ere I would put my invention to the sweat   80
Of compliment, to court my mistress' hand,
And call her smile blessing beyond a sunbeam,
Entreat to wait upon her, give her rings
With wanton or most lamentable poesies,
I would turn thresher.
Fair.   This is a new doctrine,
From women.
Mist. Car. 'Twill concern your peace, to have
Some faith in it.
Fair.   You would not be neglected?
Mist. Car. You neglect
Your selves, the nobleness of your birth and nature,

By servile flattery of this jigging,   90
And that coy mistress; keep your privilege,
Your masculine property.
Fair.   Is there so great
A happiness in nature?
Mist. Car.   There is one

[*Points to* LACY.]

Just o' your mind; can there be such happiness
In nature? Fie upon't, if it were possible
That ever I should be so mad to love,
To which, I thank my stars, I am not inclined,
I should not hold such servants worth my garters,
Though they would put me in security
To hang themselves, and ease me of their visits.   100
Fair. You are a strange gentlewoman; why, look
  you lady:
I am not so enchanted with your virtues,
But I do know myself, and at what distance
To look upon such mistresses; I can
Be scurvily conditioned; you are—
Mist. Car. As thou dost hope for any good, rail now
But a little.
Fair.   I could provoke you.
Mist. Car. To laugh, but not to lie down. Why,
  prithee do.
Fair. Go, you are a foolish creature, and not worth
My services.
Mist. Car. Aloud, that they may hear;   110
The more the merrier, I'll take't as kindly
As if thou hadst given me the Exchange.[11] What, all
  this cloud
Without a shower?
Fair.   Y' are most ingrateful.
Mist. Car. Good! abominable peevish, and a wench
That would be beaten, beaten black and blue,
And then, perhaps, she may have color[12] for't.
Come, come, you cannot scold with confidence,
Nor with grace; you should look big, and swear
You are no gamester; practice dice
And cards a little better, you will get   120
Many confusions and fine curses by't.
Fair. Is not she mad?
Mist. Car.   To show I have my reason,
I'll give you some good counsel, and be plain wi' ye;
None that have eyes will follow the direction
Of a blind guide, and what d'ee think of Cupid?
Women are either fools or very wise,
Take that from me; the foolish women are
Not worth your love, and if a woman know
How to be wise, she wo' not care for you.

---

  [5] *comfortable:* comforting.
  [6] *strong waters: aqua fortis,* alcoholic spirits.
  [7] *Pygmalion . . . colors:* Pygmalion, King of Cyprus, fell
in love with an ivory statue he had made of a woman; the
speakers seem to think it was a painting he loved.
  [8] *Holinshed:* Raphael Holinshed, *d.* 1580, author of a
famous *History of England.*   [9] *trenches:* bears.
  [10] *whirligigs:* playthings.
  [11] *Exchange:* the New Exchange, in the Strand, frequented
by fashionable people.   [12] *color:* an excuse.

Fair. Do you give all this counsel without a fee? 130
Come, be less wild. I know you cannot be
So hard of soul.

                 [Offers to take her hand.]

Mist. Car.   Prithee let my body alone!
Fair. Why are you thus peremptory? Had
Your mother been so cruel to mankind,
This heresy to love with you had been
Unborn.
    Mist. Car. My mother was no maid.
    Fair.   How, lady?
    Mist. Car. She was married long ere I was born, I
    take it,
Which I shall never be, that rule's infallible;
I would not have you fooled in the expectation,
A favor all my suitors cannot boast of.   140
Go home, and say your prayers, I wo' not look
For thanks till seven year hence.
    Fair.   I know not what
To say; yes I will home, and think a satire.—
Was ever man jeered thus for his good will?

                             Exit.

    Mist. Bon. The license will be soon dispatched
    Lacy.   Leave
    that
To my care, lady, and let him presume,
Whom you intend to bless with such a gift,
Seal on your lips the assurance of his heart.

                           [Kisses her.]

I have more wings than Mercury; expect
Your servant in three minutes.
    Mist. Car.   Take more time.   150
You'll overheat yourself and catch a surfeit.[13]
    Lacy. My nimble lady, I have business; we
Will have a dialogue another time.

                             Exit.

    Mist. Car. You do intend to marry him, then?
    Mist. Bon.   I have
    promised
To be his wife; and, for his more security,
This morning—
    Mist. Car. How! this morning?
    Mist. Bon.   What should one
That has resolved lose time? I do not love
Much ceremony; suits in love should not,
Like suits in law, be racked[14] from term[15] to term.
    Mist. Car. You will join issue presently, without
    your council,   160
You may be o'erthrown; take heed, I have known wives
That have been o'erthrown in their own case, and after.
Nonsuited[16] too, that's twice to be undone.

---

[13] *surfeit:* fever.
[15] *term:* court session.
[14] *racked:* stretched out.
[16] *nonsuited:* with pun on legal term for ending of a suit when plaintiff withdraws or is declared by the judge not to have adequate grounds.
[17] *mortified:* been made dead to pleasure.
[18] *wagtail:* whore.
[19] *islands:* Iceland-dogs.
[20] *without control:* freely.
[21] *still:* always.

But take your course; some widows have been
    mortified.[17]
    Mist. Bon. And maids do now and then meet with
    their match.
    Mist. Car. What is in your condition makes you
    weary?
You are sick of plenty and command; you have
Too, too much liberty, too many servants;
Your jewels are your own, and you would see
How they will show upon your husband's wagtail.[18]
You have a coach now, and a Christian livery   171
To wait on you to church, and are not catechized
When you come home; you have a waiting-woman,
A monkey, squirrel, and a brace of islands,[19]
Which may be thought superfluous in your family
When husbands come to rule. A pretty wardrobe,
A tailor of your own, a doctor too,
That knows your body, and can make you sick
I' the spring, or fall, or when you have a mind to't,
Without control;[20] you have the benefit   180
Of talking loud and idle at your table,
May sing a wanton ditty and not be chid,
Dance, and go late to bed, say your own prayers,
Or go to heaven by your chaplain.
    Mist. Bon.   Very fine.
    Mist. Car. And will you lose all this, for "I, Cicely,
    take thee, John
To be my husband"? Keep him still[21] to be your
    servant;
Imitate me; a hundred suitors cannot
Be half the trouble of one husband. I
Dispose my frowns and favors like a princess;
Deject, advance, undo, create again;   190
It keeps the subjects in obedience,
And teaches 'em to look at me with distance.

            Enter VENTURE *and* RIDER.

    Mist. Bon. But you encourage some.
    Mist. Car. 'Tis when I have nothing else to do for
    sport,
As, for example—
    Mist. Bon. But I am not now in tune to hear 'em;
    prithee
Let's withdraw.

                        [Exeunt Ladies.]
    Vent.   Nay, nay, lady, we must follow ye.
                [Exeunt VENTURE *and* RIDER.]

ACT TWO

SCENE ONE

[Enter] BONAVENT *[in disguise] listening.*

    Bona. Music and revels? they are very merry.

                Enter a Servant.

By your favor, sir.
    Serv.   You are welcome.
    Bona. Pray, is this a dancing school?
    Serv.   No dancing
    school.

Bona. And yet some voices sound like women.

Serv.   Wilt
please you
To taste a cup of wine? 'Tis this day free
As at a coronation; you seem
A gentleman.

Bona.   Prithee, who dwells here?

Serv. The house this morning was a widow's, sir,
But now her husband's; without circumstance,
She is married.

Bona.   Prithee, her name?

Serv.   Her name
Was Mistress Bonavent.   10

Bona. How long is't since her husband died?

Serv. 'Tis two years since she had intelligence
He was cast away; at his departure, he
Engaged her to a seven years expectation,
Which full expired, this morning she became
A bride.

Bona. What's the gentleman she has married?

Serv. A man of pretty fortune, that has been
Her servant many years.

Bona.   How do you mean?
Wantonly? Or does he serve for wages?

Serv. Neither, I mean a suitor.

Bona.   Cry mercy;   20
May I be acquainted with his name?

Serv. And his person too, if you have a mind to't;
Master Lacy; I'll bring you to him.

Bona. Master Lacy, maybe 'tis he; would thou
Couldst help me to a sight of this gentleman!
I have business with one of his name,
And cannot meet with him.

Serv.   Please you walk in.

Bona. I would not be intruder in such a day;
If I might only see him.—

Serv. Follow me, and I'll do you that favor.   30
                                          Exeunt.

[II.ii]

Enter LACY, *and his Bride*, RIDER, *and* [MISTRESS]
CAROL, [*and*] VENTURE, *dancing;* BONAVENT
aloof.

Vent. Who's that peeps?

Lacy.   Peeps!—Who's that?

[LACY *brings forward* BONAVENT.]

                                          —Faith,
you shall dance.

Bona. Good sir, you must excuse me, I am a stranger.

Lacy. Your tongue does walk our language, and
your feet
Shall do as we do: take away his cloak
And sword.—By this hand, you shall dance, Monsieur,
No *pardonnez moi.*

Mist. Car.   Well said, master bridegroom,
The gentleman may perhaps want exercise.

Mist. Bon. He will not take it well.

Vent. The bridegroom's merry.

Lacy.   Take me no takes;

Come, choose your firk,[1] for dance you shall.

Bona.   I cannot;
You'll not compel me?

Lacy.   I ha' sworn.   11

Bona. 'Tis an affront; as I am a gentleman,
I know not how to foot your chamber[2] jigs.

Lacy. No remedy;
Here's a lady longs for one vagary[3]—
Fill a bowl of sack, and then to the Canaries.[4]

Bona. You are circled with your friends, and do not
well
To use this privilege to a gentleman's
Dishonor.

Lacy. You shall shake your heels.

Bona.   I shall?
Ladies, it is this gentleman's desire   20
That I should make you mirth; I cannot dance,
I tell you that afore.

Mist. Bon. He seems to be a gentleman and a soldier.

Mist. Car. Good Mars, be not so sullen; you'll do
more
With Venus privately.

Bona. Because this gentleman is engaged, I'll try.

                                          Dance.

Will you excuse me yet?

Lacy. Pray excuse me; yes, any thing you'll call for.

Mist. Car. This motion every morning will be
wholesome
And beneficial to your body, sir.   30

Bona. So, so.

Mist. Car.   Your pretty lump[5] requires it.

Bona. Where's my sword, sir? I have been your
hobbyhorse.[6]

Mist. Car. You danced something like one.

Bona. Jeer on, my whimsy lady.

Mist. Bon.   Pray impute it
No trespass studied to affront you, sir,
But to the merry passion of a bridegroom.

Lacy. Prithee stay: we'll to Hyde Park together.

Bona. There you may meet with morris-dancers:[7]
for
You, lady, I wish you more joy, so farewell.   39
                                          [*Exit.*]

Lacy. Come, let's have t'other whirl, lustily, boys!
                                They dance in. Exeunt.

[II.iii]

Enter [MASTER] FAIRFIELD *and his sister*
JULIETTA[, *and* Waiting-woman].

Jul. You are resolved then?

Fair.   I have no other cure left,

II.ii.
   [1] *firk:* dance-partner(?); dance-step, motion(?) cf. IV. iii.
64.   [2] *chamber:* parlor.   [3] *vagary:* frolic.
   [4] *Canaries:* Canary Islands, source of light sweet wine.
   [5] *lump:* heaviness.   [6] *hobbyhorse:* buffoon.
   [7] *morris-dancers:* performers of a lively costumed folk
dance, often with a wicker hobbyhorse.

And if I do it not quickly, my affection
May be too far spent, and all physic ¹ will
Be cast away.
 Jul.   You will show a manly fortitude.
 Fair. When saw you Master Trier?
 Jul.   Not since
 yesterday.
 Fair. Are not his visits frequent?
 Jul.   He does see me
 sometimes.
 Fair. Come, I know thou lov'st him, and he will
Deserve it; he's a pretty gentleman.
 Jul. It was your character that first commended
Him to my thoughts.
 Fair.   If he be slow to answer it, 10
He loses me again; his mind, more than
His fortune, gained me to his praise; but I
Trifle my precious time.

Enter TRIER.

Farewell! all my good wishes stay with thee.
Exit.

 Jul. And mine attend you!—Master Trier!
 Tri. I come to kiss your hand.
 Jul. And take your leave?
 Tri.   Only to kiss't again!
 Jul. You begin to be a stranger; in two mornings
Not one visit where you profess affection!
 Tri. I should be surfeited with happiness 20
If I should dwell here.
 Jul.   Surfeits in the spring
Are dangerous, and yet I never heard,
A lover would absent him from his mistress
Through fear to be more happy; but I allow
That for a compliment, and dispute not with you
A reason of your actions. Y' are now welcome,
And though you should be guilty of neglect,
My love would overcome any suspicion.
 Tri. You are all goodness.—

Enter Servant *and* Page. [Servant *whispers*
to TRIER.]

With me? Prithee admit him.
[*Exit* Servant.]
 Page.   Sir, my lord 30
Saw you enter, and desires to speak with you.
 Tri. His lordship shall command; where is he?
 Page. Below, sir.
 Tri.   Say, I instantly wait on him.—
[*Exit* Page.]
Shall I presume upon your favor, lady?
 Jul. In what?
 Tri.   That I may entreat him hither?
You will honor me to bid him welcome;
He is a gentleman to whom I owe
All services, and in himself is worthy

---

 ¹ *physic:* medicine.
 ² *want:* lack.   ³ *you:* Q "your."

Of your entertainment.
 Jul. If he be yours command me.

Enter [LORD] BONVILE [*and* Page].

 Tri.   My lord, excuse—
 Lord B. Nay, I prevent your trouble.—Lady,
 I am   41
Your humble servant.—Pardon my intrusion.
I ha' no business, only I saw you enter.
 Tri. Your lordship honors me.
 Lord B.   What gentlewoman's
 this?
[TRIER *whispers to him.*]
 Tri. Why—
 Lord B. A lady of pleasure! I like her eye, it has
A pretty twirl with't; will she bid one welcome?
 Tri. Be confident, my lord.—Sweet lady, pray
Assure his lordship he is welcome.
 Jul.   I want ² words.
 Lord B. O sweet lady, your lip in silence 50
Speaks the best language.
 Jul. Your lordship's welcome to this humble roof.
 Lord B. [*Aside*] I am confirmed.
 Tri.   If you ³ knew, lady,
 what
Perfection of honor dwells in him,
You would be studious with all ceremony
To entertain him! beside, to me
His lordship's goodness hath so flowed, you cannot
Study what will oblige me more than in
His welcome.
 Lord B. Come, you compliment.
 Jul. Though I want both ability and language, 60
My wishes shall be zealous to express me
Your humble servant.
 Lord B.   Come, that "humble" was
But compliment in you, too.
 Jul.   I would not
Be guilty of dissembling with your lordship;
I know words that have more proportion
With my distance to your noble birth and fortune
Than humble servant.
 Lord B. I do not love these distances.
 Tri. You would have her be more humble.—[*Aside*]
 This will try her;
If she resist his siege, she is a brave one; 70
I know he'll put her to't. He that doth love
Wisely will see the trial of his mistress
And what I want in impudence myself
Another may supply for my advantage;
I'll frame excuse.
 Lord B.   Frank, thou art melancholy.
 Tri. My lord, I now reflected on a business
Concerns me equal with my fortune, and
It is the more unhappy that I must
So rudely take my leave.
 Lord B.   What! not so soon?
 Tri. Your honor's pardon.
 Jul.   Are you, sir, in earnest?
 Tri. Love will instruct you to interpret fairly; 81
They are affairs that cannot be dispensed with.

I leave this noble gentleman.

   Jul.   He's a stranger;
You wo' not use me well, and show no care
Of me, nor of my honor; I pray stay.

   Tri. Thou hast virtue to secure all; I am confident
Temptations will shake thy innocence
No more than waves that climb a rock, which soon
Betray their weakness, and discover [4] thee
More clear and more impregnable.   90

   Jul. How is this?

   Tri.   Farewell.
I will not sin against your honor's clemency,
To doubt your pardon.

   Lord B. Well, and [5] there be no remedy, I shall see
    you
Anon in the Park; the match holds.

                       [*Exit* TRIER.]
                 I am not willing
To leave you alone, lady.

   Jul.   I have a servant.

   Lord B. You have many; in their number pray write
    me;
I shall be very dutiful.

   Jul.   Oh, my lord.

   Lord B. And when I have done a fault, I shall be
    instructed,
But with a smile, to mend it.

   Jul.   Done what fault?   100

   Lord B. Faith, none at all, if you but think so.

   Jul. I think your lordship would not willingly
Offend a woman.

   Lord B.   I would never hurt 'em;
It has been my study still to please those women
That fell within my conversation.
I am very tenderhearted to a lady,
I can deny them nothing.

   Jul.   The whole sex
Is bound to you.

   Lord B.   If they well considered things,
And what a stickler I am in their cause,
The common cause, but most especially   110
How zealous I am in a virgin's honor,
As all true knights should be, no woman could
Deny me hospitality, and let down,
When I desire access, the rude portcullis.
I have a natural sympathy with fair ones;
As they do, I do; there's no handsome woman
Complains that she has lost her maidenhead,
But I wish mine had been lost with it.

   Jul. Your lordship's merry.

   Lord B.   'Tis because you look
    pleasant.—
A very handsome lodging. Is there any   120
Accommodations that way?

   Jul.   There's a garden,
Will't please your lordship taste the air on't.

   Lord B. I meant other conveniency; but if
You please, I'll wait upon you thither.

         Exeunt [LORD BONVILE *and* JULIETTA].

   Page. You and I had better stay, and in their absence

Exercise one another.

   Wait. Wo.   How mean you, page?

   Page. I'll teach you a way that we may follow 'em,
And not remove from hence.

   Wait. Wo.   How, prithee?

   Page. Shall I beg your lip?

   Wait. Wo.   I cannot spare it.

   Page. I'll give you both mine.

   Wait. Wo.   What means the
    child?   130

   Page. Because I have no upper lip, [6] d'ee scorn me?
I have kissed ladies before now, and have
Been sent for to their chambers.

   Wait. Wo.   You sent for!

   Page. Yes, and been trusted with their closets too!
We are such pretty things, we can play at
"All hid under a farthingale"; how long
Have you been a waiting creature?

   Wait. Wo.   Not a month yet.

   Page. Nay then, I cannot blame your ignorance;
You have perhaps your maidenhead.

   Wait. Wo.   I hope so.

   Page. Oh, lamentable! away with it, for shame;   140
Chaffer [7] it with the coachman, for the credit
Of your profession; do not keep it long,
'Tis fineable in court.

   Wait. Wo.   Good master page,
How long have you been skilled in those affairs?

   Page. E'er since I was in breeches; and you'll find
Your honesty so troublesome.

   Wait. Wo.   How so?

   Page. When you have trucked [8] away your maiden-
    head,
You have excuse lawful to put off gamesters,
For you may swear, and give 'em satisfaction,
You have not what they looked for; beside the benefit
Of being impudent as occasion serves,   151
A thing much in request with waiting creatures;
We pages can instruct you in that quality,
So you be tractable.

   Wait. Wo.   The boy is wild.

   Page. An you will lead me a chase, I'll follow you.

                         Exeunt.

[II.iv]

   Enter [MISTRESS] CAROL, RIDER, *and* VENTURE.

   Mist. Car. Why, did you ever think I could affect, [1]
Of all men living, such a thing as you are?
What hope or what encouragement did I give you?
Because I took your diamond, must you presently
Bound like a stoned [2] horse?

   Rid.   She's a very colt.

   Mist. Car. 'Cause you can put your hat off like a
    dancer,

---

   [4] *discover:* reveal.   [5] *and:* if.   [6] *upper lip:* moustache.
   [7] *Chaffer:* Barter.   [8] *trucked:* bartered.
II.iv.
   [1] *affect:* like.   [2] *stoned:* castrated.

And make a better leg[3] than you were born to,
For, to say truth, your calf is well amended,[4]
Must this so overtake me, that I must
Straight fall in love with you? One step to church.   10
Another into the streets? More[5] to a bargain:
You are wide a bow,[6] and something overshot.
    Vent. Then this is all that I must trust to, you
Will never have me?
    Mist. Car.   In my right mind, I think so.
Why, prithee tell me, what I should do with thee?
    Vent. Can you find nothing to do with me?
    Mist. Car. To find any monkey spiders[7] were an
        office,
Perhaps, you would not execute?
    Vent.   Y' are a gipsy,
And none of the twelve sibyls[8] in a tavern
Have such a tanned complexion; there be dogs   20
And horses in the world.
    Mist. Car. They'll keep you company.
    Vent.   Tell me of
        spiders?
I'll wring your monkey's neck off.
    Mist. Car.   And then puzzle
Your brain to make an elegy, which shall be sung
To the tune of "The Devil and the Baker"; good!
You have a pretty ambling wit in summer;
Do you let it out, or keep't for your own
Riding? who holds your stirrup while you jump
Into a jest, to the endangering
Of your ingenious quodlibets?[9]   30
    Rid. Come, th'ast said enough.
    Mist. Car.   To him; you would
        have some?
    Rid. Some testimony of your love, if it please you.
    Mist. Car. Indeed, I have heard you are a precious
        gentleman,
And in your younger days could play at trap[10] well.
    Rid. Fare you well, gentlewoman! by this light a
        devil;
I'll follow my old game of horseracing.
    Vent. I could tear her ruff! I would thou wert
A whore; then I'd be revenged, and bring the
'Prentices to arraign thee on Shrove Tuesday;[11]
A pox upon you!   40

                    Enter FAIRFIELD.

    Mist. Car. A third man, a third man! two fair
        gamesters;
    Rid. For shame! let's go.

---

    [3] *leg:* bow.   [4] *amended:* stuffed out.
    [5] *more:* i.e., more steps.   [6] *a bow:* a bow's length.
    [7] *monkey spiders:* spider monkeys.
    [8] *sibyls:* gipsy fortune tellers.
    [9] *quodlibets:* philosophical disputations.
    [10] *trap:* trap-ball, a children's game.
    [11] *Shrove Tuesday:* holiday on which apprentices tradi-
tionally raided whorehouses.
    [12] *brazen . . . speak:* In *Friar Bacon and Friar Bungay,*
Bacon's laboratory assistant must stay awake to hear the
magic head speak.   [13] *Fr.:* very good; Q "forboone."

    Mist. Car. Will you stay, gentlemen? You have no
        more wit

                    Ex[eunt VENTURE *and* RIDER].

To venter; keep your heads warm in any case,
There may be dregs in the bottom o' the brain pan
Which may turn to somewhat in seven years, and set
You up again.—Now, sir.
    Fair. Lady, I am come to you.
    Mist. Car.   It does appear so.
    Fair. To take my leave.
    Mist. Car.   'Tis granted, sir; goodbye.
    Fair. But you must stay and hear a little more.   50
I promise not to trouble you with courtship,
I am as weary as you can be displeased wi't.
    Mist. Car. On these conditions, I would have the
        patience
To hear the brazen head speak.[12]
    Fair. Whether or how I purpose to dispose
Myself hereafter, as I know you have
No purpose to enquire, I have no great
Ambition to discourse; but how I have
Studied your fair opinion, I remit
To time, and come now only to request   60
That you would grant, in lieu of my true service,
One boon at parting.
    Mist. Car.   Fort bon![13] proceed.
    Fair. But you must swear to perform truly what
I shall desire; and that you may not think
I come with any cunning to deceive you,
You shall except whate'er you would deny me;
And after all, I'll make request.
    Mist. Car.   How's this?
    Fair. But it concerns my life, or what can else
Be nearer to me, that you swear.
    Mist. Car.   To what?
    Fair. When you have made exceptions, and thought
What things in all the world you will exempt   71
From my petition, I'll be confident
To tell you my desire.
    Mist. Car.   This is fair play.
    Fair. I would not, for an empire, by a trick
Oblige you to perform what should displease you.
    Mist. Car. 'Tis a very strange request; are you in
        earnest?
Ere you begin, shall I except? 'Tis odds
But I may include what you have a mind to; then
Where's your petition?
    Fair.   I will run that hazard.
    Mist. Car. You will? Why, look you; for a little
        mirth's sake,   80
And since you come so honestly, because
You shall not say, "I am composed of marble,"
I do consent.
    Fair. Swear.
    Mist. Car.   I am not come to that;
I'll first set bounds to your request, and when
I have left nothing for you worth my grant,
I'll take a zealous oath to grant you any thing.
    Fair. You have me at your mercy.
    Mist. Car.   First, you shall not

Desire that I should love you.

   Fair.   That's first; proceed.

   Mist. Car.   No more but "proceed"? D'ee know
       what I say?

   Fair.   Your first exception forbids to ask   90
That you should love me.

   Mist. Car.   And you are contented?

   Fair.   I must be so.

   Mist. Car.   [*Aside*] What, in the name of wonder, will
       he ask me?
You shall not desire me to marry you.

   Fair.   That's the second.

   Mist. Car.   You shall neither directly
Nor indirectly wish me to lie with you.
Have I not clipped the wings of your conceit? [14]

   Fair.   That's the third.

   Mist. Car.   "That's the third!" is there
       any thing
A young man would desire of his mistress,
When he must neither love, marry, nor lie with her?

   Fair.   My suit is still untouched.   101

   Mist. Car.   Suit! if you have another 'tis out of
       fashion,
You cannot beg my state, yet I would willingly
Give part of that to be rid of thee.

   Fair.   Not one jewel.

   Mist. Car.   You would not have me spoil my face,
       drink poison,
Or kill anybody?

   Fair.   Goodness forbid that I should wish you
       danger!

   Mist. Car.   Then you would not have me ride through
       the city naked,
As once a princess of England did through Coventry? [15]

   Fair.   All my desires are modest.   110

   Mist. Car.   You shall not beg my parrot, nor entreat
       me
To fast, or wear a hair smock.

   Fair.   None of these.

   Mist. Car.   I will not be confined to make me ready
At ten, and pray till dinner; I will play
At gleek [16] as often as I please, and see
Plays when I have a mind to't, and the races,
Though men should run Adamites [17] before me.

   Fair.   None of these trench on what I have to ask.

   Mist. Car.   Why, then I swear—stay,
You sha' not ask me before company   120
How old I am, a question most untoothsome.
I know not what to say more; I'll not be
Bound from Spring-garden, [18] and the 'Sparagus. [19]
I will not have my tongue tied up, when I've
A mind to jeer my suitors, among which
Your worship shall not doubt to be remembered,
For I must have my humor, I am sick else;
I will not be compelled to hear your sonnets,
A thing before I thought to advise you of;
Your words of hard concoction, rude poetry,   130
Have much impaired my health. Try sense another
       while,
And calculate some prose according to
The elevation of our pole at London,

As says the learnèd almanac—but, come on,
And speak your mind, I have done; I know not what
More to except; if it be none of these,
And, as you say, feasible on my part,
I swear.

   Fair.   By what?

   Mist. Car.   For once, a kiss, it may be a parting blow.
By that I will perform what you desire.   141

                           [*Kisses him.*]

   Fair.   In few words thus receive it: by that oath
I bind you never to desire my company
Hereafter; for no reason to affect me;
This, I am sure, was none of your exceptions.

   Mist. Car.   What has the man said?

   Fair.   'Tis clear, I am
       confident,
To your understanding.

   Mist. Car.   You have made me swear
That I must never love you, nor desire
Your company.

   Fair.   I know you will not violate   149
What you have sworn, so all good thoughts possess you.
                                Exit.

   Mist. Car.   Was all this circumstance for this? I never
Found any inclination to trouble him
With too much love; why should he bind me from it,
And make me swear? An oath that for the present
I had no affection to him had been reasonable;
But for the time to come, never to love
For any cause or reason that may move me
Hereafter, very strange! I know not what to think on't,
Although I never meant to think well on him,
Yet to be limited, and be prescribed,   160
I must not do it,—'twas a poor trick in him;
But I'll go practice something to forget it.

                                [*Exit.*]

ACT THREE

SCENE ONE

Enter LORD BONVILE, [*and*] MISTRESS JULIETTA.[1]

   Lord B.   Lady, you are welcome to the spring; the
       Park
Looks fresher to salute you; how the birds
On every tree sing with more cheerfulness

---

[14] *conceit:* fancy.

[15] *As ... Coventry:* Lady Godiva, wife of Leofric, Earl of
Mercia, rode naked through the streets of Coventry in order
to win for the people of the town relief from burdensome
taxes.   [16] *gleek:* card game.

[17] *Adamites:* members of a sect who imitated Adam's
nakedness.

[18] *Spring-garden:* near Charing Cross, noted for its bowling alley, tavern, and outdoor drinking.

[19] *'Sparagus:* place of amusement in Lambeth Marsh
(London), later frequented by Pepys.

III.i.

[1] S.D.: In Q the s.d. adds "Fairfield, with their attendants.", an evident error, as Fairfield only enters at l. 130, also
a s.d. in Q.

At your access, as if they prophesied
Nature would die and resign her providence
To you, fit only to succeed her!
Jul.   You express
A master of all compliment; I have
Nothing but plain humility, my lord,
To answer you.
  Lord B.   But I'll speak our own English;
Hang these affected strains which we sometimes   10
Practice to please the curiosity
Of talking ladies; by this lip thou'rt welcome;

                                           [*Kisses her.*]

I'll swear a hundred oaths upon that book,
An't please you.

             Enter TRIER[*, behind*].

  Tri.   They are at it.
  Jul. You shall not need, my lord, I'm not
    incredulous,
I do believe your honor, and dare trust
For more than this.
  Lord B.   I will not break my credit
With any lady that dares trust me.
  Jul. She had a cruel heart that would not venture
Upon the engagement of your honor.
  Lord B.   What?   20
What durst thou venture now, and be plain wi' me?
  Jul. There's nothing in the verge of my command,
That should not serve your lordship.
  Lord B.   Speak, speak truth,
And flatter not, upon what security?
  Jul. On that which you propounded, sir, your
    honor:
It is above all other obligation,
And he that's truly noble will not stain it.
  Lord B. Upon my honor will you lend me then
But a night's lodging?
  Jul.   How, sir?
  Lord B. [*Aside*]   She is angry;
I shall obtain, I know the trick on't; had   30
She yielded at the first, it had been fatal.
  Jul. It seems your lordship speaks to one you know
    not.
  Lord B. But I desire to know you better, lady.
  Jul. Better I should desire, my lord.
  Lord B. Better or worse, if you dare venture one,
I'll hazard t'other.
  Jul.   'Tis your lordship's mirth.
  Lord B. You're in the right, 'tis the best mirth of all.
  Jul. I'll not believe, my lord, you mean so wantonly
As you profess.
  Lord B.   Refuse me,[2] if I do not.
Not mean? I hope you have more charity   40
Than to suspect I'll not perform as much
And more than I have said; I know my fault:

---

  [2] *Refuse me:* a mild oath.
  [3] *let . . . alone:* leave it to me.
  [4] *rook:* normally cheat, but not here; OED suggests
meaning lost.   [5] *lay:* bet.

I am too modest when I undertake,
But when I am to act, let me alone.[3]
  Tri. You shall be alone no longer.
                              [*Comes forward.*]
My good lord.
  Lord B.   Frank Trier.
  Tri.   Which side holds your honor?
  Lord B. I am o' thy side, Frank.
  Tri.   I think so, for
All the Park's against me; but six to four
Is odds enough.
  Jul.   Is it so much against you?
  Tri. Lady, I think 'tis two to one.   50
  Lord B. We were on even terms till you came
    hither.—
I find her yielding.—And when do they run?
  Tri. They say presently.
  Lord B. Will you venture anything, lady?
  Tri. Perhaps she reserves herself for the horserace.
  Jul. There I may venture somewhat with his
    lordship.
  Lord B. [*Aside*] That was a witty one.
  Tri.   You will be
    doing.
  Lord B. You are for the footmen.
  Tri. I run with the company.

      Enter RIDER *and* VENTURE.

  Vent.   I'll go your half.
  Rid. No, thank you, Jack; would I had ten pieces   60
More on't.
  Lord B. Which side?
  Rid.   On the Irishman.
  Lord B. Done; I'll maintain the English.
As many more with you; I love to cherish
Our own countrymen.
  Vent.   'Tis done, my lord.
  Tri. I'll rook[4] for once; my lord, I'll hold you
    twenty more.
  Lord B. Done with you, too.
  Jul.   Your lordship is very
    confident.
  Lord B. I'll lay[5] with you, too.
  Tri. [*Aside*]   Lie with her, he
    means.
  Lord B. Come; you shall venture something.
What gold against a kiss? But if you lose,
You shall pay it formally down upon my lip.   70
  Tri. Though she should win, it would be held
    extortion
To take your money.
  Jul.   Rather want of modesty,
A great sin, if you observe the circumstance.
I see his lordship has a disposition
To be merry, but proclaim not this free lay
To every one; some women in the world
Would hold you all day.
  Lord B.   But not all night, sweet lady.
  Vent. Will you not see 'em, my lord?
  Lord B. Frank Trier, you'll wait upon this gentle-
    woman;

I must among the gamesters; I shall quickly   80
Return to kiss your hand.

[*Exit.*]

Tri.   How d'ee like this gallant?
Jul. He's one it becomes not me to censure.
Tri. D'ee not find him coming?⁶ A wild
  gentleman;
You may in time convert him.
  Jul. You made me acquainted with him to that
    purpose;
It was your confidence; I'll do what I can,
Because he is your noble friend, and one
In whom was hid so much perfection
Of honor, for at first 'twas most invisible,
But it begins to appear, and I do perceive   90
A glimmering, it may break out a flame;
I shall know all his thoughts at our next conference.
He has a secret to impart, he says,
Only to me.
  Tri.   And will you hear it?
  Jul.   Yes, sir;
If it be honorable, there is no harm in't;
If otherwise, you do not doubt my innocence.
  Tri. But do not tempt a danger.
  Jul.   From his lordship?
  Tri. I do not say from him.
  Jul.   From mine own
    frailty?
  Tri. I dare not conclude that, but from the matter
Of his discourse, on which there may depend   100
A circumstance that may not prove so happy.
  Jul. Now I must tell you, sir, I see your heart
Is not so just as I deserve; you have
Engaged me to this conversation,
Provoked by jealous thoughts, and now your fear
Betrays your want of goodness, for he never
Was right at home that dare suspect his mistress.
Can love degenerate in noble breasts?
Collect the arguments that could invite you
To this unworthy trial; bring them to   110
My forehead, where you shall inscribe their names
For virgins to blush at me if I do not
Fairly acquit myself.
  Tri.   Nay, be not passionate.
  Jul. I am not, sir, so guilty to be angry;
But you shall give me leave, unless you will
Declare you dare not trust me any further,
Not to break off so rudely with his lordship.
I will hear what he means to say to me,
And if my counsel may prevail with you,
You sha' not interrupt us; have but patience,   120
I'll keep the story for you, and assure
My ends have no base mixture; not my love
To you could bribe me to the least dishonor,
Much less a stranger; since I have gone so far
By your commission, I will proceed
A little further at my peril, sir.
  Tri. I know thou art proof against a thousand
    engines.⁷
Pursue what ways you please.

They walk aside.

Enter LACY, MISTRESS BONAVENT, MISTRESS
                CAROL[, *and* Servant].

Jul.   This morning married?
Tri. That's your brother's mistress.
Jul.   She that jeers
All within gunshot?
  Tri.   In the way of suitors,   130
She is reported such a tyrant.
  Jul. My brother.

Enter MASTER FAIRFIELD.

Fair.   Frank Trier.
Jul. Brother, do you know that gentlewoman?
Fair. 'Tis she; then you and I must seem more
  familiar,
[*To* LACY] And you sha' not be angry,
  Lacy. What gentlewoman's that?
  Tri.   She does not know
    thee.

[MISTRESS CAROL *sees* FAIRFIELD
              and JULIETTA.]

Mist. Car. [*Aside*] Was this his reason?—Pray, if you
  love me, let's
Walk by that gentleman.
  Lacy.   Master Fairfield.
Mist. Car. Is that well-trussed gentleman one of
  them that run?
Mist. Bon. Your sweetheart.
Mist. Car.   Ha, ha! I'd laugh at that.
If you allow a bushel of salt⁸ to acquaintance,   141
Pray vouchsafe two words to a bargain while you live.
I scarce remember him. [*Aside*] Keep in, great heart.

Enter MASTER BONAVENT.

Lacy. O sir, you are very well met here.
Bona. We are met indeed, sir; thank you for your
  music.
Lacy. It is not so much worth.
Bona. I made you merry, Master Bridegroom.
Lacy. I could not choose but laugh.
Bona. Be there any races here?
Lacy. Yes, sir, horse and foot.   150
Bona. You'll give me leave to take my course, then.
Mist. Car. This is the captain that did dance.
Bona. Not so nimbly as your wit.

[*Takes* MISTRESS CAROL *aside.*]

                              Pray let me
Ask you a question:
I hear that gentlewoman's married.
  Mist. Car. Married! without question, sir.
Bona. Do you think he has been aforehand?
Mist. Car. How do you mean?
Bona. In English, has he played the forward
  gamester,
And turned up trump?

---

⁶ *coming:* forward.   ⁷ *engines:* stratagems.
⁸ *allow . . . salt:* are generous.

Mist. Car.   Before the cards be shuffled?—
I lay my life you mean a coat⁹ card.   161
Deal again; you gave one too many
In the last trick, yet I'll tell you what I think.
  Bona. What?
  Mist. Car. I think she and you might have shown
    more wit.
  Bona. Why she and I?
  Mist. Car. She to have kept herself a widow, and
You not to have asked me such a foolish question;
But if she had been half so wise as in
My conscience she is honest, you had missed   170
That excellent occasion to show
Your notable skill in dancing; but it pleased
The learned destinies to put things together,
And so we separate.

                [They rejoin the others.]

  Bona.   Fare you well, mistress.
  Mist. Car. [*To* RIDER]—Come hither; go to that
    gentleman, Master Fairfield—
                  [Whispers to him.]
  Mist. Bon. Prithee, sweetheart, who runs?
  Lacy. An Irish and an English footman.
  Mist. Bon. Will they run this way?
  Lacy. Just before you; I must have a bet.
                        Exit.
  Mist. Bon. Nay, nay, you sha' not leave me.   180
  Mist. Car. Do it discreetly;
                    [Exit RIDER.]
          I must speak to him,
To ease my heart; I shall burst else,
We'll expect 'em here. [*Aside*] Cousin, do they run
    naked?
  Mist. Bon. That were a most immodest sight.
  Mist. Car. Here have been such fellows, cousin.
  Mist. Bon. It would fright the women.
  Mist. Car. Some are of opinion it brings us hither.

                    [Noise within.]

Hark, what a confusion of tongues there is!
Let you and I venture a pair of gloves
Upon their feet; I'll take the Irish.   190
  Mist. Bon. 'Tis done; but you shall pay if you lose.
  Mist. Car. Here's my hand, you shall have the
    gloves, if you win.
  Mist. Bon. I think they are started.

    The Runners, *after them the* Gentlemen.

  Omnes. A¹⁰ Teague!¹¹ a Teague! make way, for
    shame!
      [The Runners *cross the stage and exeunt.]*
  Lord B. I hold any man forty pieces, yet.
  Vent. A hundred pounds to ten! a hundred pieces
To ten! will no man take me?
  Bona.   I hold you, sir.
  Vent. Well, you shall see.—

---

⁹ *coat:* habited (i.e., jack, queen, king).
¹⁰ *A:* introducing a cheer.   ¹¹ *Teague:* Irishman (slang).
¹² *leers:* looks askance.   ¹³ *switch:* strike.
¹⁴ *the Rose:* famous tavern in Covent Garden.

  [*Omnes.*]   —A Teague! a Teague! hey!
  Tri. Ha! well run Irish!
    Exeunt [all but MISTRESS CAROL *and* MISTRESS
                  BONAVENT].
  Mist. Bon. He may be in a bog anon.   200
  Mist. Car. Can they tell what they do in this noise?
Pray heaven it do not break into the tombs
At Westminster and wake the dead.

    Enter FAIRFIELD *and his* Sister [JULIETTA].

  Fair. She's yonder still; she thinks thee a new
    mistress.
  Jul. I observe her.

              Enter TRIER.

  Fair.   How go things, Frank?
Prithee, observe that creature.
  Tri.   She leers¹² this way.
  Fair. I have done such a strange cure upon her!
Sh'as sent for me, and I will entreat thee, Frank,
To be a witness of my triumph; 'tis
Now in my power to punish all her jeers;   210
But I'll go to her; thou shalt keep at distance,
Only to hear how miraculously
I have brought things about.
  Tri.   The cry returns.
          [Exeunt FAIRFIELD *and* TRIER.]
  [*Omnes. Within*] Make way there! a Teague! a
    Teague! a Teague!

    Enter Runners *and* Gentlemen.

  Vent. Forty, fifty, a hundred pieces to ten!
      [The Runners *cross the stage and exeunt.]*
  Bona. I hold you.
  Vent.   Well, you shall see, you shall see.
  Bona. This gentleman does nothing but talk;
He makes good no bet.
  Vent. Talk? You prate; I'll make good what I please,
    sir.
  Bona. Make the best you can of that.   220
      *They switch,*¹³ *and draw and exeunt.*

    Enter LORD [BONVILE].

  Mist. Bon. For heaven's sake, let's remove.
  Mist. Car. What! for a naked weapon?
    *Exeunt [*MISTRESS BONAVENT *and*
              MISTRESS CAROL].
  Lord B.   Fight,
    gentlemen,
You are fine fellows, 'tis a noble cause.—
Come, lady, I'll discharge your fears.
A cup of sack, and Anthony at the Rose¹⁴
Will reconcile their furies.
      *Exeunt [*LORD BONVILE *and* JULIETTA].

[III.ii]

    Enter FAIRFIELD *and* TRIER.

  Fair. I make a doubt whether I should go to her
Upon a single summons.
  Tri.   By any means.

Fair. What women are forbidden
They're mad to execute. She's here: be you
I' the reach of her voice, and see how
I will humble her.

    Enter [MISTRESS] CAROL *and* RIDER.

Mist. Car. But keep at some fit distance.
Rid. You honor me, and shall
Command me any service.
                Exit.
Mist. Car. [*Aside*] He has gone a strange way to
  work with me.   10
Fair. Well advised; observe and laugh without a
  noise.

        [TRIER *goes behind.*]

Mist. Car. [*Aside*] I am ashamed to think what I
  must say now.
Fair. By your leave, lady! I take it you sent for me?
Mist. Car. You will not be so impudent? I send for
  you!
By whom, or when?
  Fair. Your servant [1]—
  Mist. Car.   Was a villain, if he mentioned
I had any such desire; he told me, indeed,
You courted him to entreat me, that I would
Be pleased to give you another audience,
And that you swore I know not what, confound you,
You would not trouble me above six words. 21
  Fair. You are prettily disposed.
  Mist. Car. With much ado, you see, I have
  consented.
What is it you would say?
  Fair. Nay, what is't you would say?
  Mist. Car. Have you no prompter, to insinuate
The first word of your studied oration?—
He's out on's part.—Come, come, I'll imagine it,
Was it not something to this purpose—"Lady,"
Or "Mistress," or what you will, "although 30
I must confess you may with justice laugh at
My most ridiculous suit, and you will say
I am a fool—"
  Fair.   You may say any thing.
  Mist. Car. "To come again, whom you have so
  tormented;
For ne'er was simple camomile [2] so trod on,
Yet still I grow in love; but since there is
No hope to thaw your heart, I now am desperate;
Oh give me, lend me but the silken tie
About your leg, which some do call a garter,
To hang myself, and I am satisfied." 40
Am not I a witch?
  Fair.   I think thou art past it.
Which of the Furies art thou made already?
I shall depart the world, ne'er fear it, lady.
Without a necklace. Did not you send for me?
  Tri. I shall laugh aloud sure.
  Mist. Car. What madness has possessed you? Have
  I not sworn,
You know by what, never to think well of you,
Of all men living, not to desire your company?

And will you still intrude? Shall I be haunted
Forever? No place give me privilege? 50
O man, what art thou come to?
  Fair.   O woman!
How far thy tongue and heart do live asunder!
Come, I ha' found you out; off with this veil,
It hides not your complexion; I do tell thee,
I see thy heart, and every thought within it;
A little peevishness to save your credit
Had not been much amiss, but this over-
Over-doing the business,—it appears
Ridiculous, like my suit, as you inferred;
But I forgive thee and forget thy tricks 60
And trillibubs,[3] and will swear to love thee heartily;
Wenches must ha' their ways.
  Mist. Car. Pardon me, sir, if I have seemed too
  light;
It was not rudeness from my heart, but a
Disguise to save my honor if I found
You still incredulous.
  Fair.   I love thee better
For thy vagaries.
  Mist. Car. In vain, I see, I should dissemble w'ee,
I must confess you have caught me; had you still
Pursued the common path, I had fled from you; 70
You found the constitution of women
In me, whose will, not reason, is their law;
Most apt to do what most they are forbidden,
Impatient of curbs in their desires.
  Fair. Thou say'st right.
  Mist. Car. O love, I am thy captive;—but I am
  forsworn,
Am I not, sir?
  Fair. Ne'er think of that.
  Mist. Car.   Ne'er think on't!
  Fair. 'Twas a vain oath, and well may be dispensed
  with.
  Mist. Car. Oh, sir, be more religious; I never
Did violate an oath in all my life; 80
Though I have been wild, I had a care of that.
An oath's a holy obligation,
And never dreaming of this chance, I took it
With true intention to perform your wishes.
  Fair. 'Twas but a kiss, I'll give it thee again.
  Mist. Car. But 'tis enrolled in that high court
  already.
I must confess, I could look on you now
With other eyes, for my rebellious heart
Is soft and capable of love's impression;
Which may prove dangerous, if I cherish it, 90
Having forsworn your love.
  Fair.   Now I am fitted!
I have made twigs to jerk [4] myself. [*Aside*]—Well
  thought on!

III.ii.
 [1] *servant:* lover (i.e., Rider).
 [2] *camomile:* creeping herb known proverbially, and
claimed by Lyly (in a passage imitated by Falstaff in *I Henry
IV* II. iv. 393–95) to grow faster for being trod upon.
 [3] *trillibubs:* literally, entrails; by analogy to "tripes and
trillibubs" frequently used thus.   [4] *jerk:* whip.

You shall absolve yourself; your oath does not
Oblige you to perform what you excepted,
And among them, if you remember, you
Said you must have your humor, you'd be sick else;
Now, if your humor be to break your oath,
Your obligation's void.

    Mist. Car.   You have relieved me!
But do not triumph in your conquest, sir,
Be modest in your victory.

    Fair.   Will not you   100
Fly off again, now you're at large?

    Mist. Car.   If you
Suspect it, call some witness of my vows,
I will contract myself.

    Fair.   And I am provided.—
Frank Trier, appear, and show thy physnomy.[5]—
He is a friend of mine, and you may trust him.

                         [TRIER *comes forward.*]

    Mist. Car. What sum of money is it you would
         borrow?

    Tri. I borrow?

    Mist. Car.   This gentleman, your friend, has fully
Possessed me with your wants; nay, do not blush,
Debt is no sin: though my own monies, sir,
Are all abroad, yet, upon good security,   110
Which he answers you can put in, I will speak
To a friend of mine.

    Fair.   What security?

    Mist. Car. Yourselves, and two sufficient aldermen,
For men are mortal and may break.

    Fair.   What mean you?

    Mist. Car. You shall have fifty pounds for forty
         weeks,
To do you a pleasure.

    Fair.   You'll not use me thus?

    Tri. Fare you well;
You have miraculously brought things about.

                             Exit.

    Mist. Car. You work by stratagem and ambuscado.[6]
Do you not think yourself a proper gentleman,   120
Whom by your want of hair some hold a wit too?
You know my heart and every thought within it!
How I am caught! do I not melt like honey
I' the dog-days?[7] Why do you look so staring?

    Fair. Do not you love me for all this?

    Mist. Car. Would I had art enough to draw your
         picture,
It would show rarely at the Exchange; you have
A medley in your face of many nations:
Your nose is Roman, which your next debauchment
At tavern, with the help of pot or candlestick,   130
May turn to Indian, flat; your lip is Austrian,
And you do well to bite it; for your chin,
It does incline to the Bavarian poke,[8]

But seven years may disguise it with a beard,
And make it more ill favored; you have eyes,
Especially when you goggle thus, not much
Unlike a Jew's, and yet some men might take 'em
For Turk's by the two half moons that rise about
     'em.—

    [*Aside*] I am an infidel to use him thus.

    Fair. Till now, I never was myself; farewell   140
For ever, woman, not worth love or anger.

    Mist. Car. Do you hear? One word. [*Aside*] I'd fain
         speak kindly to him.
Why dost not rail at me?

    Fair. No, I will laugh at thee and at myself,
To have been so much a fool; y' are a fine may game.

    Mist. Car. [*Aside*] I shall fool too much.—But one
         word more;
By all the faith and love of womankind,
Believe me now—[*Aside*] it will not out.

    Fair.   Farewell;
When next I dote upon thee, be a monster.

    Mist. Car. Hark, sir, the nightingale; there is better
         luck   150
Coming towards us.

    Fair.   When you are out of breath,
You will give over; and for better luck,
I do believe the bird, for I can leave thee,
And not be in love with my own torment.

    Mist. Car. How, sir?

    Fair. I have said; stay you and practice with the
         bird;
'Twas Philomel,[9] they say; and thou wert one,
I should new ravish thee.

                             Exit.

    Mist. Car. I must to the coach and weep; my heart
         will break else.
I'm glad he does not see me.   160
                             Exit.

ACT FOUR

SCENE ONE

[*Enter* LORD] BONVILE, [*and*] MISTRESS
FAIRFIELD [i.e., JULIETTA].

    Jul. Whither will you walk, my lord? you may
         engage
Yourself too far and lose your sport.

    Lord B.   I would
Go farther for a little sport. You mean
The horserace; they're not come into the Park yet;
I might do something else, and return time
Enough to win five hundred pieces.

    Jul. Your lordship had no fortune in the last match;
I wished your confidence a happier success.

    Lord B. We must lose sometimes.—Hark the
         nightingale!

    Jul. You win, my lord, I dare engage myself.   10

    Lord B. You make the omen fortunate; this bird
Doth prophesy good luck.

    Jul. 'Tis the first time I heard it.

    Lord B. And I, this spring; let's walk a little further.

---

    [5] *physnomy:* face.   [6] *ambuscado:* ambush.
    [7] *dog-days:* hot summer days.   [8] *Bavarian poke:* goiter.
    [9] *Philomel:* princess changed into a nightingale to pro-
tect her from further violence after she had been raped and
had her tongue cut out by her brother-in-law.

Jul. I am not weary, but—

Lord B. You may trust your person, lady.

Jul. I were too much wicked to suspect your honor,
And in this place.

Lord B.   This place! the place were good
    enough,
If you were bad enough, and as prepared
As I. There have been stories, that some have   20
Struck many deer within the Park.

Jul.   Foul play.
If I did think your honor had a thought
To venture at unlawful game, I should
Ha' brought less confidence.

Enter TRIER[, *at a distance*].

Lord B.   Ha! Trier?
What, does he follow us?

Jul.   To show I dare
Be bold upon your virtue, take no notice;
I'll waft him back again; my lord, walk forward.

> [*Waves her hand, and*] *Exit* [*with* LORD
> BONVILE].

Tri. Thus far alone? Yet why do I suspect?
Hang jealousy, 'tis naught, it breeds too many
Worms in our brains; and yet she might have suffered
    me—   30

Enter LACY *and* MISTRESS BONAVENT.

Master Lacy, and his bride!

Mist. Bon. I was wont to have one always in my
    chamber.

Lacy. Thou shalt have a whole choir of nightingales.

Mist. Bon. I heard it yesterday warble so prettily!

Lacy. They say 'tis lucky when it is the first
Bird that salutes our ear.

Mist. Bon.   Do you believe it?

Tri. I am of his mind, and love a happy augury.

Lacy. Observe the first note always—

[*Cuckoo. Within*]   Cuckoo!

Lacy. Is this the nightingale?

Mist. Bon.   Why do you look so?

Lacy. Are not we married?   40
I would not have been a bachelor to have heard it.

Mist. Bon. To them they say 'tis fatal.

Tri.   And to married men
Cuckoo[1] is no delightful note; I shall
Be superstitious.

Mist. Bon.   Let's walk a little further.

Lacy. I wait upon thee.

[*Cuckoo. Within* Cuckoo!]

[*Lacy.*]   Hark, still, ha, ha, ha!

> *Ex*[*eunt* MISTRESS BONAVENT *and*
> LACY].

Tri. I am much in love with the broad[2] ditty.[3]

Enter FAIRFIELD.

Fair. Frank Trier, I have been seeking thee
About the Park.

Tri.   What to do?

Fair. To be merry for half an hour; I find
A scurvy melancholy creep upon me,   50

I'll try what sack will do; I have sent my footman
To the Maurice[4] for a bottle; we shall meet him.
I'll tell thee t'other story of my lady.

Tri. I'll wait on you.

Fair.   But that she is my sister,
I'd have thee forswear women; but let's walk.

> [*Exeunt.*]

[IV.ii]

Enter BONAVENT.

Bona. This way they marched; I hope they will not
    leap
The pale; I do not know the disposition
Of my capering gentleman, and therefore 'twill not
Be indiscretion to observe him; things
Must be a little better reconciled.—

> [*Nightingale* sings within.]

The nightingale!—this can presage no hurt,
But I shall lose my pigeons;[1]—they are in view,
Fair and far off.

> *Exit.*

[IV.iii]

Enter VENTURE *and* RIDER.

Vent. He must be a Pegasus[1] that beats me.

Rid. Yet your confidence may deceive you; you will
    ride
Against a jockey that has horsemanship.

Vent. A jockey! a jackanapes a-horseback rather;
A monkey or a masty[2] dog would show
A giant to him; and I were Alexander,
I would lay the world upon my mare; she shall
Run with the devil for a hundred pieces,
Make the match who will.

Rid.   Not I, you shall excuse me,
Nor would I win his money.

Vent.   Whose?

Rid.   The devil's;   10
My gold has burnt this twelve months in my pocket;
A little of his amongst, would scorch my thighs,
And make such tinder of my linings, that
My breeches never after would hold money.
But let this pass; where's Lacy and his bride?

Vent. They are walked to hear the nightingale.

Rid. The nightingale! I ha' not heard one this year.

Vent. Listen, and we shall hear one presently.—

[*Cuckoo. Within*] Cuckoo!

Vent.   The bird speaks to you.

IV.i.
  [1] *Cuckoo:* i.e., Cuckold.
  [2] *broad:* common, indecent.   [3] *ditty:* birdsong.
  [4] *Maurice:* tavern, its sign the head of the sixteenth-
century elector of Saxony.

IV.ii.
  [1] *pigeons:* victims of deception.

IV.iii.
  [1] *Pegasus:* legendary winged horse of antiquity.
  [2] *masty:* mastiff.

Rid.   No, 'tis
   to you.
Vent. Now do I suspect   20
I shall lose the race.
   Rid.   Despair for a cuckoo!
   Vent. A cuckoo will not flatter;
His word will go before a gentleman's
In the city; 'tis an understanding bird,
And seldom fails; a cuckoo! I'll hedge in[3]
My money presently.
   Rid.   For shame, be confident.
   Vent. Will you go half?
   Rid.   I'll go it all, or any thing.
   Vent. Hang cuckoos then.

   Enter LORD BONVILE, LACY, MISTRESS
   FAIRFIELD [*i.e.*, JULIETTA], *and* MISTRESS
                   BONAVENT.

   Lord B.   How now, gentlemen?
   Vent. Your honor's servants.
   Rid.   Ladies, I kiss your hands.
   Lord. B. You are the man will run away with all   30
The gold anon.
   Vent.   Your jockey must fly else.
   Rid. I'll hold your honor thirty pieces more.
   Lord B. 'Tis done.
   Jul.   Do you ride yourself?
   Vent. I shall have the reins in my own hand, lady.
   Mist. Bon. Master Rider, saw you not my cousin?

            Enter [MISTRESS] CAROL.

Cry mercy, she is here.—I thought you'd followed us.
   Lord B. Your kinswoman?—
I shall be honored to be your servant, lady.
   Mist. Car. Alas, my lord, you'll lose by't!
   Lord B.   What?
   Mist. Car. Honor, by being my servant; here's a
      brace   40
Of gentlemen will tell you as much.
   Vent.   But will
Say nothing, for our credits.
   Mist. Bon. You look as you had wept.
   Mist. Car.   I weep! for
      what?
Come towards the lodge, and drink a sillabub.[4]
   Mist. Bon. A match!
   Lacy. And as we walk, Jack Venture, thou shalt sing
The song thou mad'st o' the horses.
   Vent. You shall pardon me.
   Rid. What, among friends? My lord, if you'd speak
      to him.
   Lord B. A song by all means, prithee let me   50
Entreat it; what's the subject?
   Lacy. Of all the running horses.
   Vent. Horses and mares, put them together.

---

   [3] *hedge in:* get better security for.
   [4] *sillabub:* sweetened drink made of milk curdled with
wine or cider.   [5] *Curiosity:* Sophistication.
   [6] *crotchets:* quarter-notes.   [7] *firked:* pressed hard.
   [8] *Newmarket:* town famous for horseracing.
   [9] *rarely:* Q "early."

   Lord B. Let's have it; come, I heard you can sing
      rarely.
   Rid. An excellent voice.
   Lacy.   A ravishing tone.
   Vent. 'Tis a very ballad, my lord, and a coarse tune.
   Lord B. The better; why, does any tune become
A gentleman so well as a ballad? Hang
Curiosity[5] in music; leave those crotchets[6]
To men that get their living with a song.—   60
Come, come, begin.

                              [VENTURE *sings.*]

                    THE SONG.

   Come, Muses all, that dwell nigh the fountain,
   Made by the wingèd horse's heel,
   Which firked[7] *with his rider over each mountain,*
   Let me your galloping raptures feel.
      I do not sing of fleas, or frogs,
      Nor of the well-mouthed hunting dogs.
   Let me be just, all praises must
   Be given to well-breathed Jilian Thrust.

   Young Constable and Kill Deer's famous,   70
   The Cat, the Mouse, and Noddy Gray;
   With nimble Peggybrig, you cannot shame us
   With Spaniard nor with Spinola.
      Hill-climbing White Rose praise doth not lack,
      Handsome Dunbar, and Yellow Jack;
   But if I be just, all praises must
   Be given to well-breathed Jilian Thrust.

   Sure-spurred Sloven, true-running Robin,
   Of Young Shaver I do not say less,
   Strawberry Soam, and let Spider pop in,   80
   Fine Brackly, and brave Lurching Bess.
      Victorious too was Herring Shotten,
      And Spit-in's-arse is not forgotten;
   But if I be just, all honor must
   Be given to well-breathed Jilian Thrust.

   Lusty George, and, gentlemen, hark yet,
   To winning Mackerel, fine-mouthed Freak,
   Bay Tarrall, that won the cup at Newmarket,[8]
   Thundering Tempest, Black Dragon eke.
      Precious Sweet Lips, I do not lose,   90
      Nor Toby with his golden shoes;
   But if I be just, all honor must
   Be given to well-breathed Jilian Thrust.

   Lord B. Excellent! how think you, lady?
   Jul. I like it very well.
   Mist. Car. I never thought you were a poet, sir.
   Vent. No, no, I do but dabble.
   Mist. Car. You can sing rarely[9] too; how were these
      parts
Unobserved, invisible?   99
   Vent. You may see, lady.
   Jul.   Good sir, your pardon.
   Vent. Do you love singing? [*Sings*] Hum; la, la.
   Mist. Car. Who would have thought these qualities
      were in you?

Vent. Now or never.

Mist. Car.   Why, I was cozened.

Vent. You are not the first I have cozened; shall I
wash

Your faces with the drops of Helicon? [10]

I ha' fancies in my head.

Mist. Car. Like Jupiter, you want a Vulcan but

To cleave your skull, and out peeps bright Minerva.

Jul. When you return I'll tell you more, my lord.

Vent. Give me a subject.

Mist. Bon.   Prithee coz, do.   110

Mist. Car. Let it be how much you dare suffer
for me.

Vent. Enough—[*Sings*] hum, fa, la, la.

Enter Page.

Page. Master Venture, you are expected.

Lord B. Are they come?

Page.   This half hour, my lord.

Lord B. I must see the mare; you will excuse this
rudeness.—

Sirrah, stay you and wait upon these ladies.

                     Ex[it LORD BONVILE].

Vent. 'Tis time to make me ready.

Ladies, I take this leave in prose,

You shall see me next in other feet.

                                   [*Exit.*]

Rid. I wish your sillabub were nectar, lady.   120

Mist. Bon. We thank you, sir, and here it comes
already.

Enter Milkmaid [*with a bowl*].

Jul. So, so; is it good milk?

Mist. Bon.   Of a red cow?

Mist. Car. You talk as you inclined to a consumption;

Is the wine good?

Milkmaid.   It comes from his Excellence' head. [11]

Mist. Car. My service to you, lady, and to him

Your thoughts prefer.

Mist. Bon.   A health!

Mist. Car. No deep one; [12] 'tis lawful for gentlewomen

To wish well to their friends.

Jul. You have obliged me—the wishes of all
happiness

To him your heart hath chosen!

Mist. Bon.   Duty now   130

Requires I should be willing to receive it;

As many joys to you both when you are married!

Mist. Car. Married?

Jul.   You have not vowed to die a
virgin?

I know an humble servant of yours, lady—

Mist. Car. Mine!

Jul.   Would be sorry you should be a
nun.

Mist. Car. D'ee think he loves me, then?

Jul.   I do not
think

He can dissemble where he does profess

Affection; I know his heart by mine:

Fairfield is my brother!

Mist. Car. Your brother? Then the danger's not so
great; but   140

Let us change our argument. With your pardon,

Come hither, pretty one; how old are you?

Page. I am young, lady; I hope you do not

Take me for a dwarf.

Mist. Bon.   How young, I pray then?

Page. Four summers since my life was questioned,

And then a jury of years did pass upon me. [13]

Mist. Car. He is upon the matter, then, fifteen.

Page. A game at noddy. [14]

Mist. Car. You can play your cards already, it seems:

Come, drink o' this sillabub.   150

Page. I shall spoil your game, ladies;

For if there be sack in't, it may make

You flush a three. [15]

Jul.   The boy would seem witty.

Page. I hope, ladies, you will pardon me; my lord
commanded me to wait upon you, and I can do you no
better service than to make you laugh.

Enter FAIRFIELD *and* TRIER.

Fair. They're here, bless you!

Mist. Bon. Master Fairfield, you are welcome.

Fair. I presume so, but howsoever it skills [16] not.

Tri. I do not come to borrow money.   160

Mist. Car. And yet all they that do so are no fools;

Money or lands make not a man the wiser;

I know handsome gentlemen have pawned their
clothes.

Tri. I'll pawn my skin too with a woman.

Mist. Car. Wipe your mouth; here's to you, sir!

Tri. I'll pledge ye, quicksilver. Where is your lord?

Page. He has left Virgo, [17] sir, to go to Libra, [18]

To see the horsemen weighed.

                                   [*Exit* Page.]

Tri.   Lady, my service!

Jul. Brother, you interpose too far; my lord

Has used me honorably, and I must tell you,   170

Somebody has made a fault.

Mist. Bon.   Master Fairfield!

Fair. I kiss your hand.

Tri.   My lord and you have walked.

Jul. Yes, sir.

Fair.   My sister shall excuse; here's to

Thee and thy cream bowl.

Milkmaid.   I thank your worship.

Fair. There is more honesty in thy petticoat

Than twenty satin ones.

Mist. Bon.   Do you know that?

Fair. I know by her pail; and she were otherwise,

---

[10] *Helicon:* mountain site of Muses' sanctuary and of a
spring that inspired poets.

[11] *his . . . head:* the Maurice.   [12] *deep one:* great toast.

[13] *questioned . . . me:* called to account, and then I was 12
(nonsensical circumlocution).

[14] *noddy:* card game, alternatively called noddy-fifteen.

[15] *flush a three:* hold a flush of three; faces redden.

[16] *skills:* matters.   [17] *Virgo:* the sign of the Virgin.

[18] *Libra:* the sign of the Scales.

T'would turn her milk.—Come hither, let me kiss thee.

> [*Kisses the* Milkmaid.]

Now I am confirmed, he that shall marry thee
Shall take thee a virgin at my peril.   180
  Mist. Bon. Have you such skill in maidenheads?
  Fair. I'll know't by a kiss,
Better than any doctor by her urine.—
Be merry with thy cow, farewell!—

> [*Exit* Milkmaid.]
> Come, Frank:

That wit and good clothes should infect a woman!
  Jul. I'll tell you more hereafter; pray let's hear
Who wins.
  Tri.   Your servant, ladies.

> [*Exeunt* FAIRFIELD *and* TRIER.]

Enter Jockey *and* Gentlemen.

  1 Gent. What dost think, Jockey?
  2 Gent. The crack o' th' field's against you.
  Jock. Let 'em crack nuts.   190
  1 Gent. What weight?
  2 Gent. I think he has the heels.
  3 Gent. Get but the start.
  Jock. However, if I get within his quarters, let me
alone.
  3 Gent. Montez à cheval.[19]

> *Exeunt.*

Confused noise of betting within, after that a shout.

Mist. Car. They are started.

Enter [LORD] BONVILE, RIDER, TRIER, *and* FAIRFIELD.

  Rid.   Twenty pounds to
fifteen!
  Lord B. 'Tis done wi' ye!
  Fair.   Forty pounds to thirty!
  Lord B. Done! done! I'll take all odds.
  Tri.   My lord,
  I hold as much.
  Lord B. Not so.
  Tri.   Forty pounds to twenty.
  Lord B.   Done, done!

[*Enter* LACY.]

  Lacy. You have lost all, my lord, and it were a
million.   201
  Lord B. In your imagination; who can help it?
  Lacy. Venture had the start, and keeps it.
  Lord B. Gentlemen, you have a fine time to
triumph,
'Tis not your odds that makes you win.
  [*Omnes.*] *Within* Venture! Venture!

> *Exeunt* Men.

  Jul. Shall we venture nothing o' th' horses?

---

[19] *Fr.:* Mount your horse.   [20] *lay:* bet.
[21] *sped:* prospered.
[22] *mortified:* bruised; Gifford proposed amending to
"mortarified."
[23] *Bucephalus:* Alexander the Great's favorite horse.

What odds against my lord?
  Mist. Car.   Silk stockings.
  Jul. To a pair of perfumed gloves—I take it.   209
  Mist. Car. Done!
  Mist. Bon.   And I as much.
  Jul.   Done, with you both!
  Mist. Car. I'll have 'em Spanish scent.
  Jul. The stockings shall be scarlet; if you choose
Your scent, I'll choose my color.
  Mist. Car.   'Tis done, if Venture
Knew but my lay,[20] it would half break his neck now.

> *A shout within. And crying* [:]

  [*Omnes. Within*] A jockey! Hey!
  Jul. Is the wind in that coast? Hark! the noise
Is jockey now.
  Mist. Car. 'Tis but a pair of gloves.
  [*Omnes.*] *Within* A jockey!
  Jul.   Still it holds.—

Enter my LORD [BONVILE].

How have you sped,[21] my lord?
  Lord B. Won, won! I knew by instinct
The mare would put some trick upon him.   220
  Mist. Bon. Then we have lost; but, good my lord,
the circumstance.
  Lord B. Great John-at-all-adventure and grave
Jockey
Mounted their several mares—I sha' not tell
The story out for laughing, ha, ha, ha!—
But this in brief: Jockey was left behind,
The pity and the scorn of all; the odds
Played 'bout my ears like cannon, but less dangerous.
I took all still, the acclamations was
For Venture, whose disdainful mare threw dirt
In my old Jockey's face, all hopes forsaking us,   230
Two hundred pieces desperate, and two thousand
Oaths sent after them. Upon the sudden,
When we expected no such trick, we saw
My rider, that was domineering ripe,
Vault o'er his mare into a tender slough,
Where he was much beholding to one shoulder
For saving of his neck; his beast recovered,
And he by this time somewhat mortified,

> [*Points to his shoulder.*]

Besides mortified,[22] hath left the triumph
To his Olympic adversary, who shall   240
Ride hither in full pomp on his Bucephalus,[23]
With his victorious bagpipe.
  Mist. Car.   I would fain see
How Venture looks.
  Lord B. He's here; ha, ha!

Enter VENTURE *and* RIDER.

  Vent.   I told you as much before;
You would not believe the cuckoo.
  Mist. Car.   Why, how now, sir?
  Vent. And I had broke my neck in a clean way,
'Twould ne'er have grieved me.—Lady, I am yours;
Thus Caesar fell.

Lord B.   Not in a slough, dear Jack.
Vent. You shall hear further from me.
Rid.   Come to
     Knightsbridge.
Vent. That cuckoo was a witch, I'll take my death
     on't.   250
                                              Exit.

Lord B. Here comes the conqueror.

                    In triumph.
     [*Enter*] *A* Bagpiper *playing, and* Jockey,
     BONAVENT, TRIER, *and* FAIRFIELD.

"Lo, from the conquest of Jerusalem
Returns Vespasian!"[24]—Ha, ha! mer—mercy, Jockey.
     Jock. I told you, if I came within his quarters.
     All. A jockey, a jockey!
          Exeunt all but LACY, *his* Bride, *and* MISTRESS
                                        [CAROL].

     Enter BONAVENT *and the* Bagpiper.

Bona. This shall be but[25] your earnest;[26]

                    [*Gives* Bagpiper *money.*]

                                        —follow me
At pretty distance, and when I say "Draw,"
Play me a galliard.[27]—[*To* LACY] By your favor, sir,
Shall I speak a cool word with you?
     Lacy.   With all my heart.
     Bona. You do owe me a dance, if you remember,
And I will have it now; no dispute.—Draw!   261

          [Bagpiper *plays.* LACY *draws his sword.*]

That will not serve your turn; come, shake your heels,
You hear a tune; I will not change my tool
For a case[28] of rapiers; keep off, at your perils,
I have sworn.
     Mist. Bon. For heaven's sake some to part 'em.
     Lacy. Dost hear?
     Bona. And you may hear the bagpipe is not dumb:
Will you to this gear? Or do you mean to try

                    [*Draws his sword.*]

How this will scour[29] you? Come, come, I will have it.
     Lacy. Hold! I will.   270

     He dances, meantime comes in my LORD [BONVILE]
                              and TRIER.

Bona. So; now we are on equal terms, and if
You like it not, I'll use my t'other instrument.
     Lacy. Thou art a brave fellow; come your ways.
     Lord B.   Hold!
You sha' not fight, I'll understand your quarrel.[30]
     Lacy. Good my lord.
Let's have one pass.
     Mist. Bon.   Your weapons shall run
     through me;
And I must tell you, sir, you have been injurious—
     Bona. Good lady, why? In doing myself right?
     Mist. Bon. In wronging me.
     Bona.   I am not sensible of
     that.

Mist. Bon. Could any shame be fastened upon him,
Wherein I have no share?
     Bona.   I was provoked   281
By him, if you remember, and was not
Born so unequal to him, I should suffer
His poor affront.
     Mist. Bon.   This was a day of peace,
The day wherein the holy priest hath tied
Our hearts together; Hymen's[31] tapers yet
Are burning, and it cannot be a sin
Less than a sacrilege to extinguish them
With blood, and in contempt of heaven's proceeding,
Thus to conspire our separation.
No Christian would profane the marriage day: 290
And when all other wish us joys, could you
Intrude yourself to poison all our mirth,
Blast in the very budding all our happiness
Our hopes had laid up for us?
     Bona.   I was a stranger.
     Mist. Bon. That makes you more uncivil; we were
     merry,
Which could not offend you.
     Bona.   I had no thought
To violate your mirth.
     Mist. Bon.   What came you for?
With whom had you acquaintance? Or what favor
Gave you access at so unfit a time
To interrupt our calm and free delights?   300
You cannot plead any abuse where you
Were never known that should incite you to
Revenge it there: I take it you were never
His rival.
     Bona. 'Tis confessed.
     Mist. Bon.   What malice then
Prevailed above your reason to pursue us
With this injustice?
     Bona.   Lady, give me leave.
I were a villain to be guilty of
The baseness you accuse me; your servant
Shall quit me from intrusion, and my soul
Is my best witness that I brought no malice   310
But unstained thoughts into your roof; but when
I was made the common laughter, I had been
Less than a man to think of no return,
And had he been the only of my blood,
I would not be so much the shame of soldier
To have been tamed and suffered; and you are
Too hasty in your judgment; I could say more,
But 'tis dishonor to expostulate
These causes with a woman. I had reason
To call him to account; you know not all   320
My provocation; things are not with me
As with another man.
     Mist. Bon.   How is that? The matter

---

[24] *Vespasian:* Titus Vespasian, Roman emperor A.D. 70–79, conqueror of Jerusalem and Judaea.
[25] *but:* Q "by."   [26] *earnest:* token of more to come.
[27] *galliard:* lively dance tune in triple time.
[28] *case:* couple.   [29] *scour:* thrust.
[30] *understand . . . quarrel:* get between you.
[31] *Hymen:* god of marriage.

May spread too far; some former quarrel,—'tis
My best to reconcile 'em. [*Aside*] Sir, I may
Be ignorant; if anything have passed
Before this morning, I pray pardon me;
But as you are a gentleman, let me
Prevail, your differences may here conclude;
'Las, I am part of him now, and between
A widow and his wife, if I be thus   330
Divorced—
   Bona.   I'll be his servant.
   Mist. Bon.   Sir, you show
A noble disposition.—Good my lord,
Compose their differences.—Prithee meet his friend-
    ship.
   Bona.   I have satisfaction, and desire his love.
   Lacy.   Th'ast done but like a gentleman; thy hand,
I'll love thee while I live.
   Lord B.   Why, so; all friends.
   Bona.   I meet it with a heart; and for disturbing
Your mirth today—
   Lacy.   No, no disturbance.
   Bona.   Then give me but the favor
To show I wish no sorrow to the bride,   340
I have a small oblation, which she must
Accept, or I shall doubt[32] we are not friends;
'Tis all I have to offer at your wedding.

       [*Gives* MISTRESS BONAVENT *a paper.*]

   Mist. Bon.   Ha!
   Bona.   There's my hand to justify it at fit time.—
Peruse it, my lord; I shall be studious
How to deserve your favor.
   Lord B.   I am yours.
   Lacy.   My lord, let me obtain you'll honor me
Tonight.   349
   Mist. Bon. Reads [*aside*] "I was taken by a Turkish
pirate, and detained many years a prisoner in an island,
where I had died his captive, had not a worthy
merchant thence redeemed and furnished me."—
Blessed delivery!

   Enter one with another letter [*to* MISTRESS CAROL].

   Mist. Car.   To me? From Venture? He is very
    mindful;
                         [*Reads.*]
Good, I shall make use of this.
   Mist. Bon. [*Reading*]   —"Till then conceal me."
   Mist. Car.   Excellent stuff, but I must have another
Name subscribed.
   Lord B.   Will you walk, ladies?

       [*Gives money to the* Park-keepers.]

   Mist. Car.   Your servants wait upon you.   360
   Keepers.   We humbly thank your honor.
   2 Keep.   A brave spark.
   1 Keep.   Spark! he's the very bonfire of nobility.
                          Exeunt.

---

[32] *doubt:* fear.
V.i.
  [1] *affect:* seek.

ACT FIVE

SCENE ONE

Enter LACY, MISTRESS BONAVENT, [LORD]
BONVILE, MISTRESS FAIRFIELD, [JULIETTA],
MISTRESS CAROL, *and* TRIER.

   Lacy.   My lord, you honor us.
   Mist. Bon.   And what we want
In honorable entertainment, we beseech
Our duties may supply in your construction.
   Lord B.   What needs this ceremony?
   Lacy.   Thou art welcome, too, Frank Trier.
   Tri.   I give you thanks, and wish you still more joy,
    sir.
   Mist. Bon.   We'll show your lordship a poor gallery.
   Lacy.   But where's my new acquaintance?
   Mist. Bon.   His nag outstripped the coaches;
He'll be your guest anon, fear not!
        Ex[*eunt all but* MISTRESS CAROL *and*
                            JULIETTA].
   Mist Car.   While they   10
Compliment with my lord, let you and I
Change a few words.
   Jul.   As many as you please.
   Mist. Car.   Then to the purpose.
Touching your brother, lady,
'Twere tedious to repeat he has been pleased
To think well of me; and to trouble you
With the discourse how I have answered it,
'Twere vain; but thus—howe'er he seem to carry it
While you were present, I do find him desperate.
   Jul.   How!   20
   Mist. Car.   Nay, I speak no conjecture; I have more
Intelligence than you imagine. You are his sister,
And nature binds you to affect[1] his safety.
By some convenient messenger send for him;
But, as you love his life, do not delay it:
Alas, I shall be sorry any gentleman
Should for my sake take any desperate course.
   Jul.   But are you serious?
   Mist. Car.   Perhaps good counsel
Applied while his despair is green may cure him,
If not—
   Jul.   You make me wonder.   30
   Mist. Car.   I know the inconsiderate will blame
Me for his death; I shall be railed upon
And have a thousand cruelties thrown on me;
But would you have me promise love and flatter him?
I would do much to save his life. I could
Show you a paper that would make you bleed
To see his resolution, and what
Strange and unimitable ways he has
Vowed to pursue; I tremble to think on 'em.
There's not a punishment in fiction,   40
(And poets write enough of hell, if you
Have read their story,) but he'll try the worst.
Were it not that I fear him every minute,
And that all haste were requisite to save him,
You should peruse his letter.
   Jul.   Letter! Since we saw him?

Mist. Car. Since; I must confess I wondered,
But you in this shall see I have no malice.
I pray send for him, as I am a gentlewoman,
I have pure intention to preserve his life;
And 'cause I see the truth of his affliction,   50
Which may be yours, or mine, or anybody's,
Whose passions are neglected, I will try
My best skill to reduce[2] him. Here's Master Trier.

Enter TRIER.

He now depends upon your charity;
Send for him, by the love you bear a brother.
    Tri. Will you not chide my want of manners,
        gentlewomen,
To interrupt your dialogue?
    Jul.   We have done, sir.
    Mist. Car. I shall be still your servant.
    Jul.   Here's a riddle
But I will do't.—
Shall I presume upon you for a favor?   60

Enter LORD [BONVILE].

    Tri. You shall impose on me a greater trouble.
My lord!
    Jul.   Your ear.
                        [*Whispers to* TRIER.]
    Lord B.   We miss you above, lady.
    Jul. My lord, I wait upon you; I beseech
Your pardon but a minute.—Will you do this?
It is an office he may thank you for,
Beside my acknowledgment.
    Tri.   Yes, I'll go,
[*Aside*] And yet I do not like to be sent off;
This is the second time.
                            [*Exit.*]
    Jul. Now I am for your lordship. What's your
        pleasure?
    Lord B. I would be your echo, lady, and return   70
Your last word—pleasure.
    Jul.   May you never want it!
    Lord B. This will not serve my turn.
    Jul.   What, my lord?
    Lord B. This is the charity of some rich men,
That, passing by some monument that stoops
With age, whose ruins plead for a repair,
Pity the fall of such a goodly pile,
But will not spare from their superfluous wealth
To be the benefactor.
    Jul.   I acknowledge
That empty wishes are their shame that have
Ability to do a noble work   80
And fly the action.
    Lord B.   Come, you may apply it.
I would not have you a gentlewoman of your word
Alone; they're deeds that crown all; what you wish me,
Is in your own ability to give;
You understand me: will you at length consent
To multiply? We'll 'point a place and time,
And all the world shall envy us.
    Jul.   My lord!
    Lord B. Lord me no lords; shall we join lips upon't?

Why do you look as you still wondered at me?
Do I not make a reasonable motion?[3]   90
Is't only in myself? Shall not you share
I' the delight? Or do I appear a monster
'Bove all mankind, you shun my embraces thus?
There be some ladies in the world have drawn
Cuts[4] for me; I have been talked on and commended,
Howe'er you please to value me.
    Jul.   Did they
See you thus perfectly?
    Lord B.   Not always; 'twas
Sometimes a little darker, when they praised me.
I have the same activity.
    Jul.   You are
Something—I would not name, my lord.   100
    Lord B. And yet you do; you call me lord, that's
        something,
And you consider all men are not born to't.
    Jul. 'Twere better not to have been born to honors,
Than forfeit them so poorly; he is truly
Noble, and then best justifies his blood,
When he can number the descents of virtue.
    Lord B. You'll not degrade me?
    Jul.   'Tis not in my power
Or will, my lord, and yet you press me strangely.
As you are a person, separate and distinct,
By your high blood, above me and my fortunes,   110
Thus low I bend; you have no noble title
Which I not bow to; they are characters
Which we should read at distance, and there is
Not one that shall with more devotion
And honor of your birth express her service:
It is my duty, where the king has sealed
His favors, I should show humility,
My best obedience, to his act.
    Lord B.   So should
All handsome women that will be good subjects.
    Jul. But if to all those honorable names,   120
That marked you for the people's reverence,
In such a vicious age, you dare rise up
Example too of goodness, they which teach
Their knees a compliment will give their heart;
And, I among the number of the humblest,
Most proud to serve your lordship, and would refuse
No office or command that should engage me
To any noble trial; this addition
Of virtue is above all shine of state,
And will draw more admirers: but I must   130
Be bold to tell you, sir, unless you prove
A friend to virtue, were your honor centupled,
Could you pile titles till you reach the clouds,
Were every petty manor you possess
A kingdom, and the blood of many princes
United in your veins, with these had you
A person that had more attraction
Than poesy can furnish, love withal,
Yet I, I in such infinite distance, am
As much above you in my innocence.   140

---

² *reduce:* recover.   ³ *motion:* proposal.
⁴ *Cuts:* Lots.

Lord B. This becomes not.

Jul.   'Tis the first liberty
I ever took to speak myself; I have
Been bold in the comparison, but find not
Wherein I have wronged virtue, pleading for it.

Lord B. How long will you continue thus?

Jul.   I wish
To have my last hour witness of these thoughts;
And I will hope before that time to hear
Your lordship of another mind.

Lord B.   I know not,
'Tis time enough to think o' that hereafter:
I'll be a convertite within these two days,   150
Upon condition you and I may have
One bout tonight; nobody hears.

Jul.   Alas!
You plunge too far, and are within this minute,
Further from heaven than ever.

Lord B.   I may live
To requite the courtesy.

Jul.   Live, my lord, to be
Your country's honor and support, and think not
Of these poor dreams.

Lord B.   I find not
Desire to sleep;—an I were abed w'ee—

Jul. 'Tis not improbable, my lord, but you
May live to be an old man and fill up   160
A seat among the grave nobility;
When your cold blood shall starve your wanton
    thoughts,
And your slow pulse beat like your body's knell,
When time hath snowed upon your hair, oh then
Will it be any comfort to remember
The sins of your wild youth? How many wives
Or virgins you have dishonored? In their number,
Would any memory of me (should I
Be sinful to consent) not fetch a tear
From you, perhaps a sigh, to break your heart?   170
Will you not wish then you had never mixed
With atheists, and those men whose wits are vented
In oaths and blasphemy, now the pride of gentlemen,
That strike at heaven and make a game of thunder?

Lord B. [*Aside*] If this be true, what a wretched thing
    should I
Appear now, if I were anything but a lord?
I do not like myself.—
Give me thy hand; since there's no remedy,
Be honest!—there's no harm I' this, I hope.
I wi' not tell thee all my mind at once;   180
If I do turn Carthusian,[5] and renounce
Flesh upon this, the devil is like to
Have the worst on't. But I am expected.

                               Exit.

---

[5] *Carthusian:* member of a rigorous monastic order.

[6] *long:* because.

[7] *Charon:* ferryman who carried souls of the dead across the River Styx.

[8] *Tantalus:* punished in the Underworld by standing thirstily in water up to his chin that disappears when he tries to drink.

[9] *Ixion:* punished for the attempted rape of Hera by being bound to a revolving wheel.

Jul. My lord, I'll follow you.—

            Enter FAIRFIELD *and* TRIER.

                       Brother, welcome!—
Sir, we are both obliged to you. A friend
Of yours desires some private conference.

Fair. With me?

Jul. [*Aside*]   He does not look so desperate.—
How d'ee, brother?

Fair.   Well:—dost not see me?—

Jul. I'll come to thee presently.

                                    Exit.

Fair.   What's the meaning?

Tri. Nay, I know not;   190
She is full of mysteries o' late.

   Enter [JULIETTA] *again with* [MISTRESS]
              CAROL.

She's here again; there is some trick in it.

Jul. Brother, I sent for you, and I think 'twas time.
Pray hearken to this gentlewoman, she will
Give you good counsel.—You and I withdraw, sir.

Tri. Whither you please.

               Exeunt JULIETTA *and* TRIER.

Mist. Car.   Y' are a strange
    gentleman;
Alas! what do you mean? Is it because
I have dealt justly with you, without flattery
Told you my heart, you'll take these wicked courses?
But I am loath to chide, yet I must tell you,   200
Y' are to blame; alas! you know affection
Is not to be compelled; I have been as kind
To you as other men; nay, I still thought
A little better of you, and will you
Give such example to the rest?
Because, forsooth, I do not love you, will you
Be desperate?

Fair.   I will be desperate?

Mist. Car. 'Twere a fine credit for you, but perhaps
You'll go to hell to be revenged o' me,
And teach the other gentlemen to follow ye,   210
That men may say, 'twas long[6] of me, and rail at
My unkindness; is this all your Christianity?
Or could you not prosecute your impious purpose,
But you must send me word on't, and perplex
My conscience with your devilish devices?
Is this a letter to be sent a mistress?

Fair. I send a letter?

                     [*Gives him the letter.*]

Mist. Car.   You were best deny
Your hand.

Fair.   My name's subscribed! who has done this?

                            Reads.

"Rivers of hell, I come; Charon,[7] thy oar
Is needless, I will swim unto the shore,   220
And beg of Pluto, and of Proserpine,
That all the damnèd torments may be mine;
With Tantalus[8] I'll stand up to the chin
In waves; upon Ixion's[9] wheel I'll spin

The sisters' thread;[10] quail Cerberus[11] with my groan,
And take no physic for the rolling stone:[12]
I'll drown myself a hundred times a day—"
   Mist. Car. There be short days in hell.
   Fair. "And burn myself as often, if you say
The word—"
   Mist. Car. Alas! not I.   230
   Fair. "And if I ever chance to come
Within the confines of Elysium,
The amazèd ghosts shall be aghast to see
How I will hang myself on every tree,
          Yours, till his neck be broke, Fairfield."
Here's a strange resolution!
   Mist. Car.   Is it not?
Whither is fled your piety? But, sir,
I have no meaning to exasperate
Thoughts that oppose your safety, and to show
I have compassion and delight in no   240
Man's ruin, I will frame myself to love you.
   Fair. Will you? Why, thank you.
   Mist. Car.   Here's my hand, I will;
Be comforted; I have a stronger faith.
   Fair. I see then you have charity for a need.
   Mist. Car. I'll lose my humor to preserve a life.
You might have met with some hardhearted mistress
That would have suffered you to hang or drown
Yourself.
   Fair. I might indeed.
   Mist. Car.   And carried news
To the distressèd ghosts; but I am merciful:
But do not you mistake me, for I do not   250
This out of any extraordinary
Former good will, only to save your life.
There be so many beams convenient,
And you may slip out of the world before
We are aware; beside, you dwell too near
The river; if you should be melancholy,
After some tides, you would come in, and be
More talked off than the pilchards;[13] but I ha' done.
You sha' not go to hell for me: I now
Am very serious, and if you please   260
To think well of me, instantly we'll marry;
I'll see how I can love you afterward.
Shall we to the priest?
   Fair.   By your good favor, no;
I am in no such tune.
   Mist. Car.   You do suspect
I jeer still? By my troth, I am in earnest.
   Fair. To save my life, you are content to marry me?
   Mist. Car. Yes.
   Fair. To save thy life, I'll not be troubled with thee.
   Mist. Car. How?
   Fair. No, madam jeer-all, I am now resolved: 270
Talk, and talk out thy heart, I wi' not lose
Myself a scruple; have you no more letters?
They're pretty mirth; would I knew who subscribed
My name! I am so far from hanging of myself
That I will live yet to be thy tormentor.
Virtue, I thank thee for't! and for the more
Security, I'll never dote again;
Nor marry nor endure the imagination

Of your frail sex: this very night I will
Be fitted for you all. I'll geld myself;   280
'Tis something less than hanging; and when I
Have carved away all my concupiscence,
Observe but how I'll triumph; nay, I'll do it,
And there were no more men in the world.
   Mist. Car. Sir, sir! as you love goodness,—
I'll tell you all; first hear me, and then execute;
You will not be so foolish; I do love you.
   Fair. I hope so, that I may revenge thy peevishness.
   Mist. Car. My heart is full, and modesty forbids
I should use many words; I see my folly;   290
You may be just, and use me with like cruelty,
But if you do, I can instruct myself,
And be as miserable in deed as I
Made you in supposition: my thoughts
Point on[14] no sensuality; remit
What's past, and I will meet your best affection.
I know you love me still; do not refuse me.
If I go once more back, you ne'er recover me.
   Fair. I am as ticklish.[15]
   Mist. Car.   Then, let's clap 't up wisely,
While we are both i' the humor; I do find   300
A grudging, and your last words stick in my stomach.
Say, is 't a match? Speak quickly, or for ever
Hereafter hold your peace.
   Fair.   Done!
   Mist. Car.   Why, done!
   Fair. Seal and deliver.
   Mist. Car. My hand and heart; this shall suffice till
   morning.
   Fair. Each other's now by conquest, come let's to
   'em.
If you should false now!—
   Mist. Car.   Hold me not worth the
   hanging.
                    Exeunt.

[V.ii]

Enter MISTRESS FAIRFIELD [JULIETTA], TRIER,
and LORD [BONVILE].

   Lord B. I knew not
She was thy mistress, which encouraged
All my discourses.
   Tri. My lord, you have richly satisfied me, and
Now I dare write myself the happiest lover
In all the world. Know, lady, I have tried you.
   Jul. You have, it seems!
   Tri.   And I have found thee right
And perfect gold, nor will I change thee for
A crown imperial.
   Jul.   And I have tried you,

---

[10] *sisters' thread:* in Greek mythology, the three Fates, who
spun the threads of human destiny, which one of them cut
as she pleased.
[11] *Cerberus:* monstrous dog guarding entrance to the
underworld.
[12] *rolling stone:* Sisyphus was punished by having to roll a
stone incessantly to the top of a hill from which it repeatedly
fell; perhaps with play on "stone" = "gallstones."
[13] *pilchards:* herringlike fish.
[14] *Point on:* Tend toward.   [15] *ticklish:* unstable.

And found you dross; nor do I love my heart   10
So ill, to change it with you.
   Tri.   How's this?
   Jul. Unworthily you have suspected me,
And cherished that bad humor, for which know
You never must have hope to gain my love.
He that shall doubt my virtue, out of fancy,
Merits my just suspicion and disdain.
   Lord B. Oh fie, Frank, practice jealousy so soon!
Distrust the truth of her thou lov'st! suspect
Thy own heart sooner.—What I have said I have
Thy pardon for; thou wert a wife for him   20
Whose thoughts were ne'er corrupted.
   Tri. 'Twas but a trial, and may plead for pardon.
   Jul. I pray deny me not that liberty:
I will have proof, too, of the man I choose
My husband; and believe me, if men be
At such a loss of goodness, I will value
Myself, and think no honor equal to
Remain a virgin.
   Tri.   I have made a trespass,
Which if I cannot expiate, yet let me
Dwell in your charity.
   Jul.   You shall not doubt that.—   30

   Enter FAIRFIELD, MISTRESS CAROL, LACY,
        [*and*] MISTRESS BONAVENT.

Pray, my lord, know him for your servant.
   Fair. I am much honored.
   Lord B.   You cannot but
Deserve more by the title of her brother.
   Lacy. Another couple!
   Mist. Bon. Master Fairfield and my cousin are
   contracted.
   Mist. Car. 'Tis time, I think; sister I'll shortly call
   you.
   Jul. I ever wished it.
   Fair. Frank Trier is melancholy.—How hast thou
   sped?
   Tri. No, no, I am very merry.   39
   Jul. Our banns, sir, are forbidden.
   Fair.   On what terms?
   Lacy. My lord, you meet but a coarse entertainment.
How chance the music speaks not? Shall us dance?

       Enter VENTURE *and* RIDER.

   Vent. "Rivers of hell, I come!"
   Rid. "Charon, thy oar is needless."—Save you,
   gallants!
   Vent. "I will swim unto thy shore." Art not thou
   Hero?
   Mist. Car. But you are not Leander,[1] if you be not
   drowned
In the Hellespont.

   Vent.   I told thee I would
Drown myself a hundred times a day.
   Mist. Car. Your letter did.
   Vent.   Ah ha!
   Mist. Car. It was a devilish good one.
   Vent.   Then I am
   come   50
To tickle the "confines of Elysium."—
My lord, I invite you to my wedding,
And all this good company.
   Lord B.   I am glad your
Shoulder is recovered; when is the day?
   Vent. Do thou set the time.
   Mist. Car.   After tomorrow,
Name it. This gentleman and I shall be
Married in the morning, and you know we
Must have a time to dine, and dance to bed.
   Vent. Married?
   Fair. Yes, you may be a guest, sir, and be welcome.
   Vent. I am bobbed[2] again!   61
I'll bob for no more eels; let her take her course.
   Lacy. Oh for some willow garlands![3]

             Recorders [*within*].

   Enter Page *and* MASTER BONAVENT *disguised*[, *with*
      willow garlands in his hand].

   Lord B. This is my boy; how now, sirrah?
   Page. My lord, I am employed in a device.[4]

     Room for the melancholy wight,[5]
     Some do call him willow knight,
     Who this pains hath undertaken,
     To find out lovers are forsaken,
     Whose heads, because but little witted,   70
     Shall with garlands straight be fitted.
     Speak, who are tossed on Cupid's billows,
     And receive the crown of willows,
     This way, that way, round about,
     Keep your heads from breaking out.

   Lacy. This is excellent! nay, nay, gentlemen,
You must obey the ceremony.

   [BONAVENT *puts garlands on* VENTURE'S *and*
            RIDER'S *heads*.]

   Vent. He took measure of my head.
   Rid.   And mine.
   Tri. It must be my fate too.

   [BONAVENT *puts a garland on* TRIER'S *head*.]

   Vent.   Now we be three.
   Bona. And if you please to try, I do not think   80
But this would fit you excellently.
   Lacy.   Mine!
What does he mean?
   Mist. Bon. I prithee, Master Lacy, try for once;
Nay, he has some conceit.
   Lacy. For thy sake, I'll do anything; what now?

   [BONAVENT *puts a garland on* LACY'S *head*.]

   Bona. You are now a mess[6] of willow—gentlemen—
And now, my lord,—I'll presume to bid you welcome.

V.ii.
  [1] *Leander:* lover drowned on one of his nightly swims
across the Hellespont to visit his mistress Hero.
  [2] *bobbed:* tricked.
  [3] *willow garlands:* worn as a sign of grief in love.
  [4] *device:* emblem.   [5] *wight:* man.   [6] *mess:* company.

[BONAVENT *throws off his disguise*; MISTRESS
BONAVENT *takes* LORD BONVILE *aside*.]

Fair. Is not this the gentleman you made dance?

Lacy. My new acquaintance! where's thy beard?

Bona. I left it at the barber's; it grew rank,   90
And he has reaped it.

Lacy. Here, take thy toy again.

[*Takes off the garland.*]

Bona.   It sha' not need.

Lord B. You tell me wonders, lady; is this gentleman
Your husband?

Lacy ⎫
Mist. Car. ⎭ How! her husband, my lord?

Bona. Yes, indeed, lady; if you please you may
Call me your kinsman; seven year and misfortune,
I confess, had much disguised me, but I was,
And by degrees may prove again, her husband.

Mist. Bon. After a tedious absence, supposed death,
Arrived to make me happy.

Vent.   This is rare!   100

Bona. My lord, and gentlemen, you are no less
Welcome than before.—Master Lacy, droop not.

Lord B. This turn was above all expectation,
And full of wonder; I congratulate
Your mutual happiness.

Vent.   All of a brotherhood!

Lacy. Master Bonavent! on my conscience it is he!
Did fortune owe me this?

Mist. Car.   A thousand welcomes.

Mist. Bon. Equal joys to thee and Master Fairfield.

Lord B. Nay, then, you but obey the ceremony.

Lacy. I was not ripe for such a blessing; take her,
And with an honest heart I wish you joys.   111
Welcome to life again! I see a providence
In this, and I obey it.

Vent. In such good company 'twould never grieve
A man to wear the willow.

Bona.   You have but changed
Your host, whose heart proclaims a general welcome.

Mist. Bon. He was discovered to me in the Park,
Though I concealed it.

Bona.   Every circumstance
Of my absence, after supper we'll discourse of.
I will not doubt your lordship means to honor us.   120

Lord B. I'll be your guest, and drink a jovial
    health
To your new marriage, and the joys of your
Expected bride; hereafter you may do
As much for me.—Fair lady, will you write
Me in your thoughts? If I desire to be
A servant to your virtue, will you not
Frown on me then?

Jul.   Never in noble ways;
No virgin shall more honor you.

Lord B.   By thy cure
I am now myself, yet dare call nothing mine,
Till I be perfect blessed in being thine.   130

Exeunt.

F I N I S